COMPETITION LAW

COMPETITION LAW

Ioannis Lianos
Professor in Competition Law and Public Policy,
Faculty of Laws, University College London
Academic Director, BRICS Competition Law Centre, HSE

Valentine Korah
Emeritus Professor of Competition Law, Faculty of Laws,
University College London

with Paolo Siciliani
Senior Technical Specialist—Policy Strategy & Implementation Division,
Bank of England

OXFORD
UNIVERSITY PRESS

Great Clarendon Street, Oxford, OX2 6DP,
United Kingdom

Oxford University Press is a department of the University of Oxford.
It furthers the University's objective of excellence in research, scholarship,
and education by publishing worldwide. Oxford is a registered trade mark of
Oxford University Press in the UK and in certain other countries

First Edition published in 2019
Impression: 1

Published in the United States of America by Oxford University Press
198 Madison Avenue, New York, NY 10016, United States of America

British Library Cataloguing in Publication Data
Data available

Library of Congress Control Number: 2018951261

ISBN 978–0–19–882654–5

Printed in Italy by
L.E.G.O S.p.A.

PREFACE AND ACKNOWLEDGEMENTS

The book aims to serve as a source of critical analysis and comment for advanced undergraduate and graduate courses in competition law in the EU and the UK, and as a source of materials for practitioners (lawyers, economic consultants, competition law officials, and judges) in competition law. It is profoundly interdisciplinary, combining legal and economic analysis. Many courses in competition law include economic analysis and courses on the economics of antitrust are now offered in most graduate programmes in Europe in the area of law as well as in public policy. We thought that it would make sense to offer with this casebook a 'one-stop shop', or an integrated method of teaching that aims to introduce graduate students to the legal, economic, and public policy aspects of competition law, offering them an unparalleled in-depth understanding of this area. The book aims to provide the latest developments in the economics of competition law in an approachable and non-technical way. The book also offers extensive coverage of the interaction between EU and national competition law (mainly UK competition law). The UK referendum in favour of Brexit and the subsequent initiation by the UK government of the withdrawal of the UK from the European Union will bring important changes in the enforcement of competition law in Europe. Should Brexit happen in the 'hard' way it will become essential, not just for students based in the UK, but also for those on the Continent, to engage with two of the most important, for practical reasons, competition law regimes in Europe.

More than just offering an educational environment (including extensive digital material), we conceived this book as a vehicle for changing the way competition law is understood and practised in Europe, but also beyond.

The political and economic context that form the 'superstructure' of competition law have been changing drastically over the last decade. The 'roaring 2000s' were followed by the global financial crisis of 2008 and various quarters of economic recession. Topics that have not been explored for many years, such as economic concentration, inequality, populist antitrust, and the link between markets and democracy, came back to fashion attracting the attention first of the public opinion, then of competition law experts. There is an important movement to question the narrow perception of economic efficiency of the Chicago School and to abandon some of the principles that have regulated the action of competition authorities and courts in the last three to four decades. Although in pre-crisis years economists were on their way to become the 'kings' of the competition law enterprise in Europe, their failure to predict the economic crisis and the way out of it, led to mistrust towards them in the largest part of the population, and to virulent criticism, even from inside the profession, of some of the fundamentals of the mainstream economic paradigm that has been followed since the 1970s. The Internet revolution, the advent of artificial intelligence, and other important technological developments, also set important challenges to competition authorities and courts that attempt to navigate the troubled waters of global markets. We have taken account of these changes and tried to offer a perspective of EU and UK competition law, looking not only to the past, but also offering a vision for the future.

Ioannis Lianos is the main author of this book, having the overall responsibility for all chapters and having authored a little more than 90 per cent of it.

Valentine Korah has contributed to Chapter 1 and has read through the various drafts of the book providing comments. It has been a great pleasure to work with Val, not only as she is a cherished colleague at University College London (UCL) Faculty of Laws, but also because she is a pioneer of both EU and UK competition law, having been one of the first full-time academics to write and teach in this area since the mid-1950s. Val is not just one of the 'sacred animals' of competition law in Europe. During her distinguished academic career she put forward what were considered at that time iconoclastic views, directly contesting the received orthodoxies of EU competition law. She has been a precursor to the neo-liberal tide that shifted the focus of competition law in Europe from a 'formalistic' perspective to focusing on economic efficiency and 'consumer welfare'. But, in contrast to many authors of the Chicago School, Val was not an ideologue, but a pragmatist, someone striving to understand the reason entrepreneurs have adopted a specific practice, and what they have aimed to achieve, before condemning it. What may appear now as a simple exercise of common sense was not, according to Val, common practice 'in the old days' at the Commission. We believe that this book fits well into Val's spirit of innovation and unconventional thinking, although it is clear that the tide may now be shifting away from the consensus her work contributed to elaborate.

We have been joined in this venture by Dr Paolo Siciliani, who completed his PhD at UCL Faculty of Laws, but who is also a trained economist with important experience in economic consultancies, competition authorities and, more recently, as an adviser at the Bank of England. Paolo Siciliani has contributed to the co-drafting, with Ioannis Lianos, of Chapters 3, 11, and some sections of Chapter 12, the last with the active research assistance of Marianna Filippakopoulou, on the basis of ground research work by Dr. Andriani Kalintiri. He has also read through Chapter 9.

The authors would like to thank Marianna Filippakopoulou who has been a tireless research assistant throughout the whole drafting period, working with incredible efficiency, good humour, and creativity, to such an extent that none of us has ever been lucky to witness before with a research assistant. Marianna is a talented competition lawyer, graduating top of her class at the LLM at UCL, and is now working at the UK Competition and Markets Authority.

We have also benefitted from excellent research assistance by Peter O'Loughlin, Riccardo Savona-Siemens, and Dr Andriani Kalintiri.

All authors would like to thank their families for their support and their students for their questions, comments, and interesting term papers that have throughout all these years kept alive the flame of competition law, a decidedly inexhaustible resource of intellectual excitement and wonder.

Ioannis would like to dedicate this book to the memory of his beloved father, Konstantinos Lianos, who passed away in 2016.

He would also like to acknowledge the financial assistance of the Leverhulme Trust for a period of research leave that enabled him to complete this project, as well as UCL Faculty of Laws and HSE Skolkovo Institute for Law and Development for their support. We would like to thank the colleagues and publishing houses that authorized use of some limited excerpts of published work.

We have included the most recent developments until 15 January 2019.

London, Paris, and Athens, 15 January 2019
Ioannis Lianos, Valentine Korah, and Paolo Siciliani

TABLE OF CONTENTS

Supplementary material is available at
oxcat.ouplaw.com/page/lianoscomplaw

ABBREVIATIONS

AAC	average avoidable cost(s)
ACM	Authority for Consumers and Markets (the Netherlands)
AEA	Agricultural Engineers Association (UK)
AEC	adverse effect to competition
AEC test	as-efficient-competitor test
AFA	anti-fragmentation agreements
AFC	average fixed cost(s)
AG	Advocate General
AGCM	Autorità Garante della Concorrenza e del Mercato (Italian competition authority)
AI	artificial intelligence
AIC	average incremental cost(s)
AKKA	Consulting Agency on Copyright and Communications (Latvia)
AMA	Association of Model Agents
AMC	Antitrust Modernization Commission (US, 2004–7)
AMD	Advanced Micro Devices
AML	anti-money laundering
APO	association of producer organizations
APPA	across platform parity agreement
ASCAP	American Society of Composers, Authors and Publishers (US)
ATC	average total cost(s)
AVC	average variable cost(s)
B2B	business-to-business
B2C	business-to-business
BAR	backend aggregate rebates
BATNA	best alternative to a negotiated agreement
BE	behavioural economics
BER	Block Exemption Regulation
BEREC	Body of European Regulators for Electronic Communications
BIS	Department for Business, Innovation and Skills
BMI	Broadcast Music, Inc (US)
BoT	Board of Trade
CA98	Competition Act 1998
CAA	Civil Aviation Authority
CAP	Common Agricultural Policy

CARE	clear, accurate, responsible, and easy
CAT	Competition Appeal Tribunal (UK)
CBA	cost benefit analysis
CCE	Chief Competition Economist
CCMSA	Caisse Centrale de la Mutualité Sociale Agricole
CETA	Comprehensive Economic and Trade Agreement
CFI	Court of First Instance
CISAC	International Confederation of Societies of Authors and Composers
CJEU	Court of Justice of the European Union
CMA	Competition and Markets Authority (UK, successor to OFT)
CNF	Consiglio Nazionale Forense (National Council of the Bar) (Italy)
CNSD	Consiglio Nazionale degli Spedizioneri Doganali (National Council of Customs Agents) (Italy)
CoCo	Competition Commission (UK, 1999–2014, succeeded by CMA)
COREPER	Committee of Permanent Representatives
CPU	central processing unit
CQS	Conveyancing Quality Scheme
CRM	customer relationship management
CRS	computer reservation system
CSD	carbonated soft drinks
CV	contingent valuation
DCB	drug-coated balloons
DCF	discounted cash flow
DCFR	Draft Common Frame of Reference
DCT	digital comparison tool
DG Comp	Directorate General for Competition
DGFT	Director General of Fair Trading
DOB	distributor's own brand
DOJ	Department of Justice (US)
Domco	dominant company
EA 2002	Enterprise Act 2002 (UK)
EAEPC	European Association of Euro-Pharmaceutical Companies
EAGCP	Economic Advisory Group on Competition Policy
EBU	European Broadcasting Union
ECEC	European Cement Export Committee
ECHR	European Convention on Human Rights
ECMR	Council Regulation (EEC) No 4064/89 ('Merger Regulation')
ECN	European Competition Network

ECPR	efficient component pricing rule
ECSC Treaty	European Coal and Steel Community Treaty, 1951
EDI	electronic data interchanges
EEA	European Economic Area
EEC	European Economic Community
EFIM	European Federation of Ink and Ink Cartridge Manufacturers
EFTA	European Free Trade Association
EMC	Entreprise minière et chimique
EPC	European Export Policy Committee
EPC	European Payment Council
EphMRA	European Pharmaceutical Marketing Research Association
ERRA 2013	Enterprise and Regulatory Reform Act, 2013
EU	European Union
EUI	European University Institute
EUMR	European Union Merger Regulation 139/2004
Eurocontrol	European Organisation for the Safety of Air Navigation
FAO	Food and Agriculture Organization (UN)
FAPL	Football Association Premier League
FCA	Financial Conduct Authority (UK)
FSA	Financial Services Authority (UK, predecessor of FCA)
FERM	full equilibrium relevant market
FIFA	Fédération Internationale de Football Association
f.o.r.	freight on road
FRAND	fair, reasonable, and non-discriminatory
FSBR	Financial Services (Banking Reform)
FSMA	Financial Services and Markets Act
FTC	Federal Trade Commission (US)
FTP	file transfer protocol
GBER	General Block Exemption Regulation
GC	General Court (formerly Court of First Instance)
GCV	global value chain
GDF	Gaz de France
GDPR	General Data Protection Regulation
GE	General Electric
GE	general equilibrium
GECAS	GE Capital Aviation Services
GISC	General Insurance Standards Council
GM	genetically modified

GMS	Google Mobile Services
GPD	geographic price discrimination
GRI	general rate increase
GSCOP	Groceries Supply Code of Practice
GSK	GlaxoSmithKline
GUPPI	gross upward pricing pressure index
GVC	global value chain
GWB	Gesetz gegen Wettbewerbsbeschränkungen (German Act Against Restraints of Competition)
H&SP	hub and spoke practice
HCC	Hellenic Competition Commission
HHI	the Herfindahl–Hirschman index
HMT	hypothetical monopolist test
HP	Hewlett-Packard
HRS	Hotel Reservation Service
HSR Act	Hart–Scott–Rodino Act (US)
IBER	Insurance Block Exemption Regulation
ICA	Italian Competition Authority
ICN	International Competition Network
IHG	InterContinental Hotels Group
INAIL	insurance against accidents at work and occupational diseases
INET	Institute of New Economic Thinking
IP	intellectual property
IP	Internet protocol
IPO	Initial Public Offering
IPR	illustrative price rise
JBA	joint business arrangement
JV	joint venture
LAA	Latvian Authors' Association
LBO	leveraged buyout
LCC	Latvian Competition Council
LCC	low-cost carrier
LRAIC	long-run average incremental cost
LTE	long-term evolution
M&A	mergers and acquisitions
MA	market authorization
MADA	mobile application distribution agreements
MAP	minimum advertised price/pricing

MC	marginal cost(s)
MEO	market economy operator
MFC	most favoured customer
MFN	most favoured nation
MIF	multilateral interchange fees
MIT	merchant indifference test
MLP	master limited partnerships
MMC	Monopolies and Mergers Commission (UK)
MNO	mobile network operator
MR	marginal revenue
MRS	marginal rate of substitution
MSC	merchant service charges
MVNO	mobile virtual network operator
NAAT	no appreciable affectation of trade
NBA	Net Book Agreement (UK)
NCA	national competition authority
NHS	National Health Service (UK)
NIAUR	Northern Ireland Authority for Utility Regulation
NPT	neoclassical price theory
NPV	net present value
NRA	national regulatory authority
O&D	origin and destination
OECD	Organisation for Economic Co-operation and Development
OEM	original equipment manufacturer
OFCOM	Office for Communications
OFGEM	Gas and Electricity Markets Authority
OFT	Office of Fair Trading (UK, predecessor of CMA)
OFWAT	Water Services Regulation Authority
ORR	Office of Rail and Road (UK, formerly Office of Rail Regulation)
OS	Operating System
OTA	online travel agency
OTC	over the counter
P&I	protection and indemnity
PC	personal computer
PCA	personal current account
PCW	price comparison website
PE	partial equilibrium
PET	polyethylene terephthalate

PFDC	Pierre Fabré Dermo-Cosmétique
PGM	platinum group metal
PMI	private motor insurance
PND	portable navigation devices
PO	producer organization
PPI	payment protection insurance
PSR	payments systems regulator
quango	quasi-non-governmental organization
R&D	research and development
RAN	radio access network
RLAH	roam-like-at-home
RNC	radio network controller
ROS	return on sales
RPM	resale price maintenance
RRA	reciprocal representation agreement
RRC	raising rivals' costs
RRP	recommended retail price
RSA	revenue share agreement
RTL	Radio and Television Luxembourg
RTPA	Restrictive Trade Practices Act, 1956 (UK)
RTPC	Restrictive Trade Practices Court
RVM	reverse vending machines
SANI	State Aid Notification Interactive
SBM	stretch blow moulding
SCA	Swedish Competition Authority
SCC	Standard Commercial Corporation
SCLP	Supreme Council of the Legal Profession (Bulgaria)
SCOP	société cooperative et participative (workers' cooperative)
SCP	structure–conduct–performance
SCPA	Société commerciale des potasses et de l'azote
SCTC	Standard Commercial Tobacco Company
SEP	standard essential patent
SERP	search engine results page
SEU	subjective expected utility
SGEI	services of general economic interest
SIEC	significant impediment of effective competition
SIII	significant impediment to industry innovation
SIL	Systematics International Group of Companies Limited

SLC	substantial lessening of competition
SMEs	small- and medium-sized businesses
SMP	substantial market power
SNS	Spanish national health system
SOE	State-owned enterprise
S of S	Secretary of State
SPC	supplementary protection certificate
SSNDQ	small but significant, non-transitory decrease in quality
SSNIP	small but significant non transitory increase in price
STIM	Svedska Tonsättares Internationella Musikbyrå (Swedish Copyright Management Organization)
SWF	social welfare function
TCE	transaction costs economics
TCLT	Trans-Continental Leaf Tobacco Corporation
TEC	Treaty Establishing the European Community
TEU	Treaty on the European Union
TFEU	Treaty on the Functioning of the European Union
TTBER	Technology Transfer Block Exemption Regulation
UKCN	UK Competition Network
UKEAT	UK Employment Appeal Tribunal
ULL	unbundled local loops
UPP	upward pricing pressure
URD	upfront route-specific discount
VBER	Vertical Block Exemption Regulation
VCSE	voluntary, community, and social enterprise
VMS	vertical market share
WHO	World Health Organization
WIB	War Industries Board (US, 1917–19)
WMP	Windows Media Player
WTO	World Trade Organization
WWTE	World Wide Tobacco España

LIST OF FIGURES

TABLE OF CASES

Please note that page references to Online Supplements will be followed by the letter 's'

COMMISSION OF THE EUROPEAN COMMUNITIES

EFTA COURT

EUROPEAN COURT OF HUMAN RIGHTS

EUROPEAN COURT OF JUSTICE

NATIONAL CASES

Belgium

France

Germany

Greece

Ireland

Italy

Lithuania

Netherlands

United Kingdom

Competition Appeal Tribunal (UK)

Competition Commission (UK)

Competition and Markets Authority (UK)

Office of Fair Trading (UK)

United States

Federal Trade Commission (US)

TABLE OF LEGISLATION

Council Regulation EC No 1/ 2013
Art 27(4) . . . 736
Regulation (EU) No 1308/ 2013 of the European Parliament and of the Council of 17 December 2013 establishing a Common Organisation of the Markets in agricultural products and repealing Council Regulations (EEC) No 922/ 72, (EEC) No 234/ 79, (EC) No 1037/ 2001 and (EC) No 1234/ 2007 [2013] OJ L 347/ 671 (CMO Regulation)
Art 169 . . . 322
Art 170 . . . 322
Art 171 . . . 322
Articles 169, 170 and 171
Commission Regulation (EU) No 1407/2013 of 18 December 2013 on the application of Articles 107 and108 of the Treaty on the Functioning of the European Union to de minimis aid [2013] OJ L 352/1 (De Minimis Regulation) . . . 13–14
Commission Regulation (EU) No 316/2014 of 21 March 2014 on the application of Article 101(3) of the Treaty on the Functioning of the European Union to categories of technology transfer agreements [2014] OJ L93/17 . . . 32, 247, 643, 780, 786, 1278, 1372–3
Art 7 . . . 645
Commission Regulation (EU) No 651/ 2014 of 17 June 2014 declaring certain categories of aid compatible with the internal market in application of Articles 107 and 108 of the Treaty [2014] OJ L 187/ 1 (General Block Exemption Regulation (GBER)) . . . 13–14
Commission Regulation (EU) No 697/2014 [2014] OJ L 184/3.160 Commission Regulation (EC) No 773/2004 of 7 April 2004 relating to the conduct of proceedings by the Commission pursuant to Articles 81 and 82 of the EC Treaty [2004] OJ L 123/18 . . . 32, 644
Regulation (EU) 2015/ 751 of the European Parliament and of the Council of 29 April 2015 on interchange fees for card-based payment transactions [2015] OJ L 123/ 1
Arts 3–4 . . . 172, 607
Council Regulation (EC) 2015/ 1589 of 13 July 2015 laying down detailed rules for the application of Article 108 of the Treaty on the Functioning of the European Union [2015] OJ L 248/ 99 . . . 14
General Data Protection Regulation (EU) 2016/ 679 the protection of natural persons with regard to the processing of personal data and on the free movement of such data [2016] OJ L 119/ 1 . . . 190, 192, 1234, 1237, 1474, 1652
Art 5(1) . . . 1234
Art 5(1)(b) . . . 1652
Art 9(1) . . . 1234
Regulation (EU) 2017/ 1128 of the European Parliament and of the Council of 14 June 2017 on cross-border portability of online content services in the Internal Market [2017] OJ L 168/ 1
Recital 1 . . . 175
Regulation (EU) 2018/302 of the European Parliament and of the Council of 28 February 2018 on addressing unjustified geo-blocking and other forms of discrimination based on customers' nationality, place of residence or place of establishment within the internal market and amending Regulations (EC) No 2006/2004 and (EU) 2017/2394 and Directive 2009/22/EC (Geo-blocking Regulation) . . . 167, 169–72, 134s
Art 1(3) . . . 169
Art 1(6) . . . 170
Art 3(1) . . . 170
Art 3(2) . . . 170
Article 3(3)–(4) . . . 171
Art 4(1) . . . 170, 176
Art 5 . . . 171
Art 5(1)(a) . . . 171
Art 5(2) . . . 171
Art 6 . . . 171
Art 9 . . . 176
Recital 5 . . . 170
Recital 6 . . . 176
Recital 12 . . . 170
Recital 14 . . . 170
Recital 23 . . . 170
Recital 26 . . . 171

FRANCE

Commercial Code
Art L 420–1 . . . 574
Art L 420–2 . . . 830
Art L 464–2–1 . . . 574

GERMANY

Commercial Code . . . 1269
Gesetz gegen Wettbewerbsbeschränkungen (GWB) [German Act against restraints of competition (GWB)] . . . 100, 832, 897, 1490
s 1 . . . 474, 1237
s 19 . . . 1237
s 22(2) . . . 474
s 25(1) . . . 474

UNITED KINGDOM

Agriculture Act 1993
c 37 . . . 323
Civil Aviation Act 1982 . . . 129
Civil Aviation Act 2012 . . . 129
Company Act 2006 . . . 331

UNITED STATES

TABLE OF TREATIES AND INSTRUMENTS

1

INSTITUTIONAL ACTORS, DESIGN, AND HISTORY OF THE EU AND UK COMPETITION LAW SYSTEMS

1.1. THE LEGAL FRAMEWORK

1.1.1. OVERVIEW OF THE MAIN COMPETITION LAW PROVISIONS IN THE EU AND UK

This Section will focus on a brief presentation of the main provisions of competition law in the EU and UK. The institutional structure of their enforcement will be presented in more detail at the companion volume on Enforcement and Procedure.[1]

1.1.1.1. EU competition law provisions and their role within the EU treaties

The European Union (EU) Treaty, originally comprised the European Coal and Steel Community Treaty of 1951 (ECSC now expired) and the European Economic Community (EEC) established by the Treaty of Rome 1957. The provisions on competition law are now included in the Treaty on the Functioning of the European Union (TFEU). They have remained largely unchanged, since the Constitutive Treaties, despite various minor modifications and the expiry of the European Community due to the expiry of the ECSC. The numbering of the articles has changed three times, the latest one being at the Treaty of Lisbon in 2009. At the time of the Treaty of Rome, Germany was the only Member State of the Union with a

[1] I Lianos, *Competition Law Enforcement and Procedure* (OUP, forthcoming 2019).

competition law enforced by an independent administrative authority, the *Bundeskartellamt*, established in 1958. The provisions on competition in the other five original Member States related only to unfair or disloyal competition although some countries also regulated prices in large sectors of their economies.[2]

Despite the relative minor modifications brought in the substantive provisions of EU competition law, the negotiation and the conclusion of the Treaty of Lisbon marked the first time in the chronicles of European integration that the role of competition law in the structure of the Treaties has been questioned, in particular because of proposal to abolish Article 3(1)(g) of the Treaty of European Communities (TEC). This provision recognized the vital importance of establishing 'a system ensuring that competition in the internal market is not distorted'. Based on a teleological interpretation of this provision, the Court of Justice of the EU (CJEU) was able to extend the application of certain competition law provisions, such as Article 102 TFEU on abuse of a dominant position to exclusionary conduct that harms the effective competition structure and prejudices consumers in an indirect way.[3] The first merger regulation in 1989,[4] as well as the new one in 2004, also make reference to Article 3(1)(g) in their first recitals.[5] The Court of Justice relied on this provision to apply the principle of free competition to State measures in a number of cases,[6] as well as to put in place EU remedies for the effective enforcement of competition law.[7] Furthermore, the Court has placed particular emphasis on Article 3(1)(g) when confronted with a conflict between competition rules and other policies and objectives[8] and has pronounced, on the basis of this provision, that competition law constitutes a 'fundamental objective of the Community'.[9] Finally, the Court referred to this provision when it granted to national competition authorities the power to set aside provisions of domestic legislation that jeopardize the '*effet utile*' of Article 101 TFEU.[10]

The existence of a specific provision emphasizing the role of competition law in the text of the so-called 'Principles' part of the founding treaty, led to specific implications as to the interpretation of this provision and its relation with other Community/EU activities. This was reinforced by Article 4 TEC, introduced by the Maastricht Treaty in 1992, enabling

[2] For an historical overview of the evolution of the competition law idea in Europe, see D Gerber, *Law and Competition in Twentieth Century Europe: Protecting Prometheus* (OUP, 1998); KK Patel and H Schweitzer, *The Historical Foundations of EU Competition Law* (OUP, 2013).

[3] Case 6/72, *Europemballage Corporation and Continental Can Company Inc v Commission* [1973] ECR 215, paras 23–6; Joined Cases 6 & 7/73, *Instituto Chemiotherapico Italiano SpA & Commercial Solvents Corp v Commission* [1974] ECR 223, para 32; Case 85/76 *Hoffmann-La Roche & Co AG v Commission* [1979] ECR 461, paras 38 and 125; Case 27/76, *United Brands Company and United Brands Continentaal BV v Commission* [1978] ECR 207, paras 63 and 183.

[4] Council Regulation (EEC) No 4064/89 of 21 December 1989 on the control of concentrations between undertakings [1989] OJ L 395/1, Recital 1.

[5] Council Regulation (EC) No 139/2004 on the control of concentrations between undertakings [2004] OJ L 24/1, Recital 2.

[6] See eg Case 13/77, *SA GB-Inno BM v Association des détaillants en tabac (ATAB)* [1977] ECR 2115, para 29; C-260/89, *Elliniki Radiophonia Tileorasi AE & Panellinia Omospondia Syllogon Prossopikou v Dimotiki Etairia Pliroforissis et al* [1991] ECR I–2925, para 27; Case 229/83, *Association des Centres distributeurs Edouard Leclerc v SARL 'Au blé vert'* [1985] ECR 1, para 9.

[7] Case 453/99, *Courage Ltd v Bernard Crehan* [2001] ECR I–6297, para 20.

[8] Case C-67/96, *Albany International BV v Stichting Bedrijfspensioenfonds Textielindustrie* [1999] ECR I–5751; Case C-309/99 *JCJ Wouters et al v Algemene Raad can de Nederlandse Orde van Advocaten* [2002] ECR I–1577.

[9] Case C-289/04 P, *Showa Denko KK v Commission* [2006] ECR I–5859, para 55; Joined Cases T-259–64 & 271/02, *Raiffeisen Zentralbank Österreich AG & Others v Commission* [2006] ECR II–5169, para 255.

[10] Case C-198/01, *Consorzio Industrie Fiammiferi* [2003] ECR I–8055, paras 54–5.

joint action of the Community and the Member States in the 'adoption of an economic policy, which is based on the close coordination of Member States' economic policies, on the Internal Market and on the definition of common objectives, and conducted in accordance with the principle of an open market economy with free competition'. The scope of the principle of 'free competition' was thus extended beyond the narrow confines of the competences of the Community (although these were already broadly defined). The Member States should be inspired by this principle in conducting their economic policies. In a similar vein, 'competitiveness' was also added as an aim of the Community by the Treaty of Amsterdam in 1997. The distinction between 'aims' and 'activities' did not adequately represent the role of competition law in the legal framework put in place by the successive European treaties. In reality, competition was conceived as an important intermediate objective, the aims of Article 2 being more difficult to assess and representing long term goals. Progressively, the role of competition law evolved from an instrument for the completion of broader aims to an important objective of the Community. Indeed, as the Court of Justice recognized in *Continental Can*, the objectives pursued by Article 3(1)(g) were 'indispensable' for the achievement of the Community's tasks.[11]

The new Article 3 introduced by the Treaty on the European Union (TEU) merges the old Articles 2 and 3 TEC into an integrated framework that includes the broad economic and non-economic objectives and tasks of the Union. There is no reference to the principle of 'undistorted competition' or 'free competition'. Article 3(3) TEU provides that the Union shall establish an internal market with the goal of achieving 'a highly competitive social market economy', aiming at full employment and social progress. The concept of 'social market economy' replaced the expression 'open market economy with free competition' in former Article 4(1) TEC. Competition law in the EU is thus inexorably linked to the objectives of the Internal Market and the establishment of a 'social market economy'. We will explore the implications of these changes in Chapter 2. For the time being, we introduce the main EU competition law provisions.

There are provisions applying to all 'undertakings', private, public, non-profit, etc,[12] and provisions applying only to State activities and public undertakings or private undertakings granted special or exclusive rights by Member States.

1.1.1.1.1. Provisions applying to all undertakings

One may distinguish between antitrust law and merger control.

Antitrust

Article 101 TFEU

Article 101(1) TFEU prohibits agreements, concerted practices, and decisions of associations of undertakings which may affect trade between Member States and have as their object or effect the prevention, restriction, or distortion of competition within the Internal Market. The different elements of Article 101(1) have been defined by the case law of the European courts. There follows a list of examples of conduct that may be anti-competitive, without any express distinction being drawn between agreements between competitors and those between firms operating at different levels of trade or between restrictions that are necessary to make some legitimate transaction viable and those that are not.

11 Case 6/72, *Continental Can v Commission* [1973] ECR 215, para 23. See further Chapter 2.

12 For a definition of the concept of 'undertaking', see Section 4.4.2.

Article 101(3) provides that Article 101(1) may be inapplicable to collusion that contributes to *improving the production or distribution of goods or to promoting technical or economic progress*, while allowing *consumers a fair share of the resulting benefit* and which does *not impose on the undertakings concerned restrictions which are not indispensable* to the attainment of these objectives or *afford such undertakings the possibility of eliminating competition in respect of a substantial part of the products* in question. This provides a limited exception to the prohibition. The conditions are very strict and difficult to establish. The burden of proof under Article 101(3) falls on the person wanting the exemption. The Commission initiated a reform of the EU enforcement system proposing a fundamentally different system based on the direct applicability of Article 101(3), enabling national competition authorities and courts to apply Article 101(3). The Council adopted the Commission's proposal in Regulation 1/2003 after making some changes.

Article 101(2) TFEU deals with some of the civil law effects of the prohibition of Article 101(1). It provides that agreements that infringe the article are void. The CJEU ruled that the nullity applies only to the provisions having the object or effect of restricting competition: it is for national law to decide whether what remains can be enforced. In deciding whether trade between Member States may be affected, however, the agreement as a whole is appraised, and not only the provision in issue. National courts will not be able to order parties to fulfil their contracts if the provisions in question infringe Article 101. This can have far-reaching consequences. When enforcing an exclusive agreement, one may be met by a Euro-defence that, in its legal and economic context, parts of the agreement infringe Article 101 and are void. It is also possible to claim compensation for damages suffered following an infringement of EU (and national) competition law.

Article 102 TFEU

Article 102 prohibits the abuse by one or more undertakings of a dominant position within the Internal Market, or in a substantial portion of the market, in so far as it affects trade between Member States. Both Articles 101 and 102 TFEU provide examples of prohibited or abusive conduct. These lists, however, are not exhaustive, and the case law of the European courts as well as the decisional practice of the Commission show an extensive interpretation of them, leading, for example, to the expansion of the application of Article 102 to situations where the dominant position is detained by more than one undertaking (collective dominant position)[13] or to situations where the abuse and the dominant position are not at the same relevant market.[14]

'Abuse' is a poor authentic translation of the double concept of 'abusive exploitation' used in most EU languages. It was thought that this provision forbids the exploitation of market power to harm customers or suppliers, providing for regulation of prices and conditions imposed by firms with market power. In *Continental Can v Commission*,[15] the CJEU held that the acquisition by a dominant firm of a potential competitor might infringe Article 102 TFEU, because buyers may be harmed indirectly by the reduction of competition. Hence, the CJEU construed the words 'abusive exploitation of a dominant position' to include conduct that affects the *structure* of a concentrated market by absorbing a potential competitor, and not only conduct that exploits the lack of competition. The increased concentration of the market

[13] See Joined Cases C-395 & 396/96 P, *Compagnie Maritime Belge Transports SA et al v Commission* [2000] ECR I-1365.

[14] See Case C-333/94, *Tetra Pak II* [1996] ECR II-5951.

[15] Case 6/72, *Continental Can v Commission* [1973] ECR 215, paras 26–7.

might lead to higher prices to the detriment of consumers later. This has been extended in many later cases to conduct of a dominant firm that makes it more difficult for other undertakings to compete.

It is difficult to advise firms on the application of Article 102, as markets are often defined very narrowly, thus leading to the finding of a dominant position, and it is not clear what conduct is forbidden. The EU Courts have had difficulty distinguishing conduct that excludes others through efficiency, by giving better value for money, from methods of exclusion not based on competition on the merits. They have used a formula suggesting that competition on the basis of performance is lawful, but it is not clear what is included in this category. Consequently, kinds of conduct that would not infringe US antitrust law, for instance, may well infringe that of the EU. Moreover, until fairly recently, the EU Courts and Commission seem to have been concerned about the interest of a trader entering a market of his choice and, more generally, the competitive process. Recently, there have been some signs that the Commission and, to a lesser extent, the courts, are more concerned with the interests of consumers, although these are not unambiguous (see our analysis in Chapters 8 and 9).

Combination of Articles 101 TFEU and 102 TFEU

Conduct may infringe both Articles, when the conditions of both provisions are satisfied. In *Hoffmann-La Roche* (*Vitamins*), the Court of Justice of the EU (CJEU) confirmed the Commission's decision that Hoffmann-La Roche had infringed Article 102 TFEU by granting discounts to large buyers who had bought, or who agreed to buy, a large proportion of their requirements from it, making it difficult for its smaller suppliers to compete.[16] Such a contract might also be forbidden by Article 101 TFEU. In *Tetra Pak I*, the General Court (GC) of the EU upheld a decision condemning under Article 102 the acquisition by a dominant firm of a potential competitor that had an exclusive licence to the main alternative technology although the licence had been exempted from the prohibition of Article 101(1).[17]

Merger control

There was no effective system of merger control by the European Communities[18] at least until the first EU (then European Communities) Merger Regulation (EUMR) came into force in 1990.[19] Prior to the Regulation, in *Continental Can*, the CJEU gave the Commission power under Article 102 TFEU to forbid an acquisition by a firm already dominant of an actual or potential competitor when this would virtually eliminate competition. The Commission,

16 Case 85/76, *Hoffmann-La Roche & Co AG v Commission (Vitamins)* [1979] ECR 461.

17 Case T-51/89, *Tetra Pak I* [1990] ECR II–309, paras 23–5 and 37. See also Joined Cases C-395 & 396/96, *Compagnie Maritime Belge Transports SA et al v Commission* [2000] ECR I–1365, para 33 ('It is clear from the very wording of Articles [101(1)(a), (b), (d), and (e) and 102(a)–(d) TFEU] that the same practice may give rise to an infringement of both provisions. Simultaneous application of Articles [101 and 102 TFEU] cannot therefore be ruled out a priori.').

18 Neither the Treaty of Rome nor the German Competition Act (Gesetz gegen Wettbewerbsbeschränkungen) provided any specific provision for controlling mergers, with the exception of Article 66(1)–(6) of the ECSC Treaty, which established an exclusive competence for the High Authority of the ECSC without any residual competence to Member States for establishing national merger control and without the requirement of an effect on trade between Member States. The ECSC has, now expired and with it, Article 66. Mergers of coal and steel producers are now handled under Regulation 139/2004 of 20 January 2004 on the control of concentrations between undertakings [2004] OJ L 24/1.

19 Council Regulation (EEC) No 4064/89 of 21 December 1989 on the control of concentrations between undertakings [1989] OJ L 395/1 (ECMR). The case law of the European Court of Justice has, however, extended the scope of application of Article 101 of the Treaty on the Functioning of the EU [2008] OJ C 115/47 (hereinafter TFEU) (Joined Cases 142 and 156/84, *BAT and Reynolds v Commission* [1987] ECR) and 101 TFEU to

however, wanted to be able to monitor mergers before they were consummated and was concerned by mergers that might lead to a dominant position. In 1973, it proposed that the Council should adopt a regulation requiring the parties to a merger between companies with large turnovers to notify it in advance and giving the Commission power to restrain mergers likely to lead to a significant reduction of competition. Eventually, in 1989, the Council adopted Regulation 4064/89, giving the Commission such powers.[20] The Council of Ministers has revised the merger regulation in 2004.[21]

The regulation established a centralized and one-stop-shop system of merger control. The competence to examine and forbid a merger with a Community dimension lies exclusively with the European Commission. Member States are free to develop their own merger control systems for mergers without a Community dimension, or when the investigation of a merger has been referred to the national authority from the Commission (Chapter 12). The concept of 'Community dimension' is defined by Article 1 of the ECMR, which refers to specific quantitative thresholds of turnover of the undertakings concerned and the probable influence of the transaction[22] on trade between Member States.

The regulation requires the merging parties or one of them to notify a qualifying merger to the Commission before implementing it. A substantial fine may be imposed if the merger is implemented before being authorized.

The inquisitorial administrative procedure of the Merger Regulation differs from the adversarial procedure for controlling mergers developed by some national systems, where decisions to prohibit can be adopted only by courts or court-like institutions.[23] It differs also from the procedure in some Member States, where the decisions to prohibit are adopted by a specialized competition agency.[24] The merger regulation in the EU is enforced by the college of the European Commissioners, which is the 'executive power' or 'government' of the EU.[25] The revised Merger Regulation 139/2004 defines the substantive criterion as mergers that create a significant impediment to effective competition, and not only mergers that create or reinforce a dominant position, as was the situation under the previous merger regulation.[26] All mergers with a Community dimension have to be notified. The new framework also explicitly recognizes the role of efficiency gains in the competition assessment of mergers

the acquisition of shares. See V Korah and P Lasok, 'Philip Morris and its Aftermath—Merger Control' (1988) 25 *Common Market L Rev* 333, 353. Nevertheless, after *BAT v Reynolds* and before the merger regulation was operative, the Commission managed to prevent some large mergers by threatening to open proceedings under Article 101 or 102. V Korah & P Lasok, 'Philip Morris and its Aftermath—Merger Control' (1988) 25 *Common Market L Rev* 333.

20 Council Regulation (EEC) No 4064/89 of 21 December 1989 on the control of concentrations between undertakings [1989] OJ L 395/1.

21 Regulation 139/2004 of 20 January 2004 on the control of concentrations between undertakings [2004] OJ L 24/1.

22 Article 1 (ECMR) contains a general cap which is relevant to most of concentrations reviewed by the Commission (Article 1(2) and a lower cap which applies if the quantitative caps in Article 1(2) are not met (Article 1(3).

23 See eg in Austria.

24 See eg in Germany or France.

25 Because of the large number of merger cases, the European Commission has empowered one of its Members to take management or administrative measures if these are not of fundamental importance: see Article 13 of the Commission's Rules of Procedures [2000] OJ L 308. This task is often delegated to the Director General of DG Competition who also communicates with the other Directorates-General of the European Commission. However, other Members of the Commission have the right to involve the President of the Commission, for politically sensitive cases.

26 Council Regulation (EC) No 139/2004 of 20 January 2004 on the control of concentrations between undertakings [2004] OJ L 24/1, Recital 24 and Article 2(2).

under Regulation 139/2004,[27] thus increasing the discretion of the European Commission in implementing its merger control policy to various types of mergers.

1.1.1.1.2. Provisions applying to State activity and public undertakings

Although these provisions will not be examined in detail in this book, we briefly introduce Articles 106–9 and the possibility for Articles 4(3), 101 and/or 102 to apply to State activity. Some distortions of trade between Member States caused by the buying practices of State monopolies can also be controlled under Article 37 TFEU.

Article 106 TFEU

Article 106(1)[28] prohibits State measures[29] that provide undertakings (this concept will be explained below), which are public[30] or to which Member States grant special[31] or exclusive rights[32] that are contrary to the EU Treaties and could contravene not just the competition rules (Articles 101, 102 TFEU), or Article 28 (non-discrimination), which are explicitly mentioned, but also other provisions of the EU Internal Market (including free movement of goods, free movement of workers, freedom of establishment, free movement of services, free movement of capital). We will assume here that the State-owned monopoly will be an undertaking, and that it exercises an economic activity.[33] In *Klaus Höfner and Fritz Elser v Macrotron*, the Court of Justice found that although conferring a legal monopoly did not in itself entail a breach of Article 106(1) (and Article 102 TFEU),[34] the fact that this legal

27 Council Regulation (EC) No 139/2004 of 20 January 2004 on the control of concentrations between undertakings [2004] OJ L 24/1, Recital 29 and Article 2(1)b. See also Guidelines on the assessment of horizontal mergers under the Council Regulation on the control of concentrations between undertakings [2004] OJ C 31/5, Part VII.

28 There is a considerable literature on Article 106 TFEU. For some recent commentary, see J Burke, *A Critical Account of Article 106(2) TFEU—Government Failure in Public Service Provision* (Hart, 2018); JL Buendía Sierra, 'Enforcement of Article 106(1) TFEU by the European Commission and the EU Courts' in P Lowe, M Marquis, and G Monti (eds) *Effective and Legitimate Enforcement of Competition Law* (Hart, 2016), ch 9; JL Buendía Sierra, 'Article 106—Exclusive Rights and Other Anti-competitive State Measures' in J Faull and A Nikpay (eds) *The EC Law of Competition* (OUP, 3rd ed, 2014); M Marquis, 'The State of State Action in EU Competition Law (post-*Greek Lignite*) and a National Competition Strategy for China' in M Philipsen et al (eds) *Market Integration: The EU Experience and Implications for Regulatory Reform in China* (Springer, 2016), 41.

29 The case law provides a wide definition of this term, as it is the case in the interpretation of Article 34 TFEU, so it could be laws, regulations, administrative provisions, and all instruments issues from a public authority, including recommendations.

30 Which means undertakings over which the public authorities may exercise, directly, or indirectly, a dominant influence by virtue of their ownership, financial participation, or rules which govern it: Article 2(1)(b) of the Transparency Directive 2006/111/EC, OJ [2006] L 318/17.

31 These are generally rights granted by a Member State to a limited number of undertakings (two to three), the operators being designed otherwise than according to objective, proportional, and non-discriminatory criteria.

32 According to the case law exclusive rights may also be granted to more than one undertakings (Case C-209/98), and the conferral of a dominant position is not sufficient as such to qualify for the characterization of exclusive right, a competitive advantage must also be conferred.

33 In *Klaus Höfner and Fritz Elser v Macrotron*, the CJEU explained that any entity 'engaged in an economic activity, irrespective of the legal status in which it is financed' may be qualified as an undertaking for the purposes of competition law: Case C-41/90, *Klaus Höfner and Fritz Elser v Macrotron* [1991] ECR I–1979, para 21. See also Case C-244/94, *Fédération Française des Sociétés d'Assurance (FFSA) and Others v Ministère de l'Agriculture et de la Pêche* [1995] ECR I–4013, para 14; Case C-55/96, *Job Centre coop arl* [1997] ECR I–7119, para 21; Case C-138/11, *Compass Datenbank v Republik Östereich*, ECLI:EU:C:2012:449, para 35; Case C-440/11 P, *Commission v Stichting Administrattiekantoor Portielje*, ECLI:EU:C:2013:514, para 36.

34 Case C-41/90, *Klaus Höfner and Fritz Elser v Macrotron* [1991] ECR I–1979, para 29.

monopoly is exercised by an undertaking unable to satisfy demand, and the fact that this legal monopoly could prevent a competitor from trying to satisfy that demand,[35] constituted an infringement of Article 106(1).[36]

It results from this case law, that the existence of a legal State monopoly or the conferral to a public undertaking of a dominant position does not constitute by itself an infringement of Article 106(1),[37] but only if this creates a situation in which the legal monopoly would lead to an infringement of another competition law provision, such as Articles 102 TFEU (or Article 101 TFEU). This may be, for instance, the case if the public undertaking in question (the undertaking with exclusive or special rights) adopts a discriminatory policy,[38] reserves to itself an ancillary activity in neighbouring but related market and in a sector open to competition where the activity might be carried out by another undertaking (prohibition of leveraging of a dominant position from one relevant market to another),[39] applies excessive pricing,[40] the State measure establishes an inequality of opportunity between economic operators,[41] adopts predatory pricing and loyalty rebates,[42] selectively low prices,[43] or commits other forms of abuse.

Some case law has found that the State may also be found to have infringed Article 106(1) jointly with Article 102 TFEU when granting exclusive or special rights to a privileged undertaking may lead this undertaking, by the mere exercise of the exclusive or special rights conferred upon it, to exploit its dominant position in an abusive manner, or where those rights are capable of creating a situation in which that undertaking is led to commit such abuses.[44] The State may be found to infringe these two provisions, even if this does not involve any *actual* abusive conduct by the privileged undertaking.[45] The risk of a *potential* abuse may be sufficient to infringe Articles 106(1) and 102 TFEU if this may be imputed to State conduct (eg the conferral of exclusive rights).

35 Ibid, paras 30–131.

36 See also, for a similar finding, Case C-55/96, *Job Centre coop arl* [1997] ECR I–7119; Case C-258/98, *Criminal proceedings against Giovanni Carra and Others* [2000] ECR I–4217.

37 See also Case C-260/89, *ERT v Dimotiki* [1991] ECR I–2925, para 12; Case C-179/90, *Merci Convenzionali Port di Genova v Siderurgica Gabrielli* [1991] ECR I–5889, para 16.

38 Case C-260/89, *ERT v Dimotiki* [1991] ECR I–2925.

39 Case C-18/88, *RTT v GB-Inno BM* [1991] ECR I–5941. In the postal sector, see *Spanish International Courier Services* [1990] OJ L 233/19; *Dutch Express Delivery Services* [1990] OJ L 10/47; *Slovakian postal legislation*, Case COMP/39.652, upheld by Case T-556/08, *Slovenská pošta a.s. v European Commission*, ECLI:EU:T:2015:189.

40 Case C-351/12, *OSA—Ochranný svaz autorský pro práva k dílům hudebním o.s.*, ECLI:EU:C:2014:110.

41 Case C-553/12, *Commission v DEI*, ECLI:EU:C:2014:2083, paras 43–4; Case T-169/08 RENV, *DEI v Commission*, ECLI:EU:T:2016:733, para 114.

42 *Deutsche Post AG I* [2001] OJ L 125/57 and *Deutsche Post AG II*, [2001] OJ L 331/40 (finding that using revenues from Deutsche Post's profitable letter-mail monopoly to finance a strategy of below-cost selling in business parcel services, which are open to competition, could constitute a violation of Article 102 TFEU. Note that what was found illegal under Article 102 TFEU was not cross-subsidization as such, but the fact that this cross-subsidization facilitated below-cost selling—predatory pricing—that could foreclose competitors in the open to competition market).

43 Case C-209/10, *Post Danmark A/S v Konkurrencerådet*, ECLI:EU:C:2012:172.

44 See eg C-163/96, *Criminal proceedings against Silvano Raso and Others* [1998] ECR I–533; Case C-179/90, *Merci convenzionali porto di Genova SpA v Siderurgica Gabrielli SpA* [1991] ECR I–5889.

45 Starting with Case C-18/88, *RTT v GB-Inno BM* [1991] ECR I–5941; Case C-260/89, *Elliniki Radiophonia Tiléorassi AE and Panellinia Omospondia Syllogon Prossopikou v Dimotiki Etairia Pliroforissis et al* [1991] ECR I–2925 (the case concerned the grant of transmission rights to a TV station already benefiting from exclusive broadcasting rights) [hereinafter *ERT*]. See also Case C-393/92, *Municipality of Almelo and others v NV Energiebedrijf Ijsselmij* [1994] ECR I–1477; Case C-203/96, *Chemische Afvalstoffen Dusseldorp BV and Others v Minister* [1998] ECR I–4075, para 63 (restricting the possibility of an undertaking to process dangerous waste while providing this possibility to a national undertaking, thus putting the latter in a favourable situation).

This 'automatic abuse' doctrine[46] has been scaled back in *La Crespelle*,[47] but the recent *Greek Lignite* case seems to have given this doctrine some new life. The case concerned the conferral by the Hellenic government to the Greek public power corporation DEI the exploration and exploitation rights for lignite mines situated in Greece, lignite constituting the primary fuel for the purposes of generating electricity in Greece. The Commission found that the grant and maintenance of those rights was contrary to Article 106(1) TFEU, read together with Article 102 TFEU, as it created a 'situation of inequality of opportunity' between economic operators with regard to access to resources of the most economically attractive primary fuel, thus allowing DEI to maintain or reinforce its dominant position on the Greek wholesale electricity market by excluding or hindering any new entrants, even following the liberalization of the electricity sector in 2005.[48] The General Court annulled the Commission's decision.[49] First, the GC held that the fact that it was impossible, for other economic operators, to gain access to the lignite deposits still available could not be imputed to DEI since the granting of lignite exploitation licences depended exclusively from the Greek State. Second, there was no evidence that DEI had abused its dominant position, by for instance 'having, without objective justification, extended its dominant position on the market for the supply of lignite to the wholesale electricity market',[50] thus concluding that the Commission 'has neither identified nor established to a sufficient legal standard' the existence of an abuse.[51] Rejecting the 'automatic abuse' doctrine, the GC refused to hold that 'the mere fact that the undertaking in question finds itself in an advantageous situation in comparison with its competitors, by reason of a State measure, in itself constitutes an abuse of a dominant position', thus requiring at least evidence of an actual abuse.[52] The CJEU nevertheless set aside the judgment of the GC, finding that 'it is not necessary that any abuse should actually occur', the State being in breach of Articles 106(1) and 102 TFEU 'where a measure imputable to a Member State gives rise to a risk of an abuse of a dominant position'.[53] Hence, the risk of a *potential* abuse by the privileged undertaking may be sufficient to lead to a joint infringement of Articles 106(1) and 102 TFEU by the State if it can be imputed to the State conduct in question (here the grant of lignite exploitation licences without any other being offered to competing undertakings and although there were significant unallocated deposits of lignite). The case was sent back to the GC, which implemented the CJEU's judgment and examined, among other things, if the State conduct (the granting of lignite exploitation licences only to DEI) created an inequality of opportunity to the disadvantage of new competitors, accepting that this was indeed the case.[54]

There is also some case law which may be interpreted as challenging the exclusive rights and the public monopoly itself, if the breadth of the legal monopoly given to it is greater than what was necessary to enable it to carry out the task of general economic interest entrusted to it (*Corbeau*).[55] Hence, the interpretation of what would constitute a restriction infringing

46 This qualification was made in French competition law doctrine ('*la doctrine de l'abus automatique*'). See also JL Buendía Sierra, *Exclusive Rights and State Monopolies Under EC Law* (OUP, 1999), 173.

47 Case C-323/93, *Société Civile Agricole du Centre d'Insémination de la Crespelle v Coopérative d'Elevage et d'Insémination Artificielle du Département de la Mayenne* [1994] ECR I–5077.

48 *Public Power Corporation SA* (Case COMP/B-1/38.700) Commission Decision C(2008) 824 final.

49 Case T-169/08, *Dimosia Epicheirisi Ilektrismou AE (DEI) v European Commission*, ECLI:EU:T:2012:448.

50 Ibid, para 92. 51 Ibid, para 93. 52 Ibid, paras 104–18.

53 Case C-553/12, *Commission v DEI*, ECLI:EU:C:2014:2083, paras 41–2.

54 Case T-169/08 RENV, *DEI v Commission*, ECLI:EU:T:2016:733.

55 Case C-320/91, *Criminal proceedings against Paul Corbeau*, ECLI:EU:C:1993:198.

Article 106(1) in this case would depend on the necessity test performed under Article 106(2) TFEU,[56] thus effectively shifting the burden to the undertaking to justify its conduct under Article 106(2) TFEU.[57]

There is also case law accepting that 'the mere fact that an exclusive right is granted to an undertaking in order to guarantee that it provides a service of general economic interest does not preclude that undertaking from earning profits from the activities reserved to it or from extending its activities into non-reserved area'.[58] In principle, it is possible, at least under primary EU law, for an undertaking to use profits derived from an exclusive right, which was granted solely in order to guarantee the performance of a service of general economic interest, in order to acquire control of undertakings active in neighbouring markets, without this being found an infringement of Article 102 TFEU, and consequently Article 106 TFEU. What may be found to constitute an infringement of Article 102 TFEU is the fact that these profits were 'derived from excessive or discriminatory prices or from other unfair practices in [the undertaking's] reserved market'.[59] As the Court accepted in *UPS*, the use of income from activities in the reserved market to finance the acquisition of an undertaking in a liberalized market, do not infringe, as such, Article 102 TFEU. It is therefore necessary 'to examine the source of the funds used' in order to determine if these result from an abuse of a dominant position.[60] This judgment leaves open the question of the compatibility with Article 102 TFEU of the subsidization by an undertaking benefiting from a reserved market of its activities in a liberalized market, in the absence of predatory pricing or other abuse in the open to competition sector.[61]

These restrictions may be justified under Article 106(2) TFEU 'in so far as the application of such rules does not obstruct the performance, in law or in fact, of the particular tasks assigned to them' and does not affect inter-State EU trade 'to an extent that is contrary to the interests of the [EU]'.[62] This article is interpreted strictly and subjects the measures

[56] In this case the Court found that postal monopolies may be consistent with EU competition law, subject to some conditions and tests set out in the judgment. See, in particular, ibid, para 19.

[57] See M Marquis, 'The State of State Action in EU Competition Law (post-*Greek Lignite*) and a National Competition Strategy for China' in M Philipsen et al (eds) *Market Integration: The EU Experience and Implications for Regulatory Reform in China* (Springer, 2016), 41, 57 (noting that this 'burden-shifting terminology' of Corbeau 'occasionally resurfaces, but it has not been adopted as a blanket standard', extending beyond services of general economic interest to cover exclusive rights at large, also citing W Sauter and H Schepel, *State and Market in European Union Law* (CUP, 2009) who support this statement).

[58] Case T-175/99, *UPS Europe SA v Commission*, ECLI:EU:T:2002:78, para 51.

[59] Ibid, para 55.

[60] Ibid, paras 61–2.

[61] Ibid, para 64. See nevertheless on this issue Communication from the Commission—Guidance on the Commission's enforcement priorities in applying Article 82 of the EC Treaty to abusive exclusionary conduct by dominant undertakings [2009] OJ C 45/02, para 63 (noting that '[t]he Commission may also pursue predatory practices by dominant undertakings on secondary markets on which they are not yet dominant. In particular, the Commission will be more likely to find such an abuse in sectors where activities are protected by a legal monopoly. While the dominant undertaking does not need to engage in predatory conduct to protect its dominant position in the market protected by legal monopoly, it may use the profits gained in the monopoly market to cross-subsidize its activities in another market and thereby threaten to eliminate effective competition in that other market'). For a similar approach, see Opinion of Advocate General Mengozzi in Case C-209/10, *Post Danmark AS v Konkurrencerådet*, ECLI:EU:C:2011:342, para 123, explaining that in order to establish the existence of unlawful cross-subsidization of the dominant undertaking, it is necessary to determine whether the earnings generated by the undertaking's services in the market on which it carries out universal service obligations exceed the 'stand-alone' cost of those services. In any case, it seems that the EU case law does not find cross-subsidization, as such, to infringe Article 102 TFEU, but only if this relates to another abuse, such as predatory pricing, selective price-cutting, tying, etc. For an example of the latter, see Case T-83/91, *Tetra Pak II* [1994] ECR II–762.

[62] Case C-157/94, *Commission of the European Communities v Kingdom of the Netherlands*, ECLI:EU:C:1997:499, paras 65–8.

to a proportionality test, but this restrictive interpretation does not go as far as requiring evidence that the State-owned company with exclusive or special rights' survival would be threatened, if it were to be subject to competition.[63] Although, in most cases, Article 106(2) has been unsuccessful, there here have been instances where Article 106(2) has been used with success.[64] In particular, the restriction of competition may be justified if it enables the undertaking in question (eg State-owned monopoly) to maintain the universal service and guarantee, for instance, the permanent provision of a public service (eg postal service) of specified quality at all points in their territory at affordable prices for all users, as this is also recognized by the liberalization directives. More broadly, the undertaking in question may argue that it is entrusted with services of general economic interest (SGEI) or it has the character of a revenue-producing monopoly[65] and is subject to certain obligations (eg universal service[66]). Member States enjoy a wide discretion to determine what constitutes a SGEI[67] and SGEI are recognized by Article 14 TFEU and Protocol 26 on services of general economic interest. Article 106(2) and the concept of SGEI may thus be relied upon for justifying a restriction of Article 106(1) for purposes of general interest, and this possibility has been codified in the liberalization directives as well (with regard to universal service or security of supply).

Articles 107–9 TFEU

State aids are prohibited by virtue of Article 107 of the TFEU.[68] It has been a unique characteristic of the European system of protecting competition to include control of State subsidies to undertakings. The main reason is to curtail the development of protectionist industrial policies that could compromise the objectives of the Internal Market. For the prohibition of Article 107(1) to apply, the specific State assistance scheme should be considered as State aid.

63 Ibid.

64 See Case C-266/96, *Corsica Ferries France SA v Gruppo Antichi Ormeggiatori del porto di Genova Coop arl, Gruppo Ormeggiatori del Golfo di La Spezia Coop arl and Ministero dei Trasporti e della Navigazione*, ECLI:EU:C:1998:306 (justifying under Article 106(2) the inclusion in the price of a component designed to cover the cost of maintaining universal service); Joined Cases C-147 & 148/97, *Deutsche Post AG v Gesellschaft für Zahlungssysteme mbH GZS) & Citicorp Kartenservice GmbH*, ECLI:EU:C:2000:74 (justifying under Article 106(2) the grant by a State to its postal services of the statutory right to charge internal postage on items of re-mail in large quantities with the postal services of another Member State); Case C-209/98, *Entreprenørforeningens Affalds/Miljøsektion (FFAD) v Københavns Kommune*, ECLI:EU:C:2000:279 (justifying under Article 106(2) the grant of an exclusive right to an undertaking, limited in time to the period over which the investments could foreseeably be written off, for environmental reasons as it was impossible owing to the lack of undertakings capable of processing the waste for an undertaking without exclusive rights to make the necessary investments); Case C-475/99, *Firma Ambulanz Glöckner v Landkreis Südwestpfalz*, ECLI:EU:C:2001:577 (justifying under Article 106(2) the protection by the State of providers of emergency ambulance services against competition from independent operators, even extending this to a related non-emergency transport market, if the existing private operators were manifestly unable to satisfy demand in the area of emergency ambulance and patient transport services).

65 Which means that this is a monopoly whose purpose is to raise revenue for the State and contribute its profits to the State.

66 See Case T-289/03, *BUPA v Commission* [2008] ECR II-81, paras 186–7, 203.

67 Case T-17/02, *Fred Olsen SA v Commission* [2005] ECR II-2031, paras 215–28.

68 There is a considerable literature on State aids law. For some recent book-length commentary, see JJ Piernas López, *The Concept of State Aid under EU Law: From Internal Market to Competition and Beyond* (OUP, 2015); F-J Säcker and F Montag (eds) *European State Aid Law: A Commentary* (Hart/Nomos/Beck, 2016); H Hofmann and C Micheau (eds) *State Aid Law of the European Union* (OUP, 2016); C Quigley, *European State Aid Law and Policy* (Hart, 2015).

There are four criteria, all of which should be satisfied for State assistance to be considered a State aid:[69]

(i) the assistance should be granted by State, that is any public or private body controlled by the State (including local government), or through State resources, that is any measure with an impact on the State budget or where the State has significant control, for example, tax exemptions;

(ii) the assistance provides an advantage to one or more 'undertakings'[70] over others. It should be 'selective', by affecting the balance between the beneficiary firm and its competitors. The advantage can take many forms. It may be a grant, a loan, or a tax break, but it may also include the use of a State asset for free or below market price. In any case, it is something an undertaking could not get in the normal course of events by a private investor applying ordinary commercial criteria (the 'market economy operator' or 'MEO' principle);

(iii) the assistance should not distort or have the potential to distort competition. Even small amounts of financial support to firms with modest market share may fall under the prohibition of State aids;

(iv) the assistance affects trade between Member States.

Note, however, that aid does not arise where Member States invest in companies to make a return. Member States can also pay a subsidy to companies to conduct activities where no one can make a return. What is potentially problematic is where a Member State pays a subsidy to keep a company operating on market where it cannot make a return, but where other private companies could do so.

Nevertheless, it is possible for State assistance justified by the common interest, to escape the qualification of 'State aid', as long as the restrictions do not distort competition in such a way as to operate against the public interest. In *Altmark*, the European Court of Justice held that compensation paid by the State to an utility company for reasons of public service may not constitute State aid when four cumulative conditions are met: (i) the recipient undertaking must have public service obligations and the obligations must be clearly defined; (ii) the parameters for calculating the compensation must be objective, transparent, and established in advance; (iii) the compensation cannot exceed what is necessary to cover all or part of the costs incurred in the discharge of the public service obligations, taking into account the relevant receipts and a reasonable profit; (iv) where the undertaking, which is to discharge public service obligations, is not chosen pursuant to a public procurement procedure which would allow for the selection of the tenderer capable of providing those services at the least cost to the community, as this would be the case should the public undertaking in question be the result of nationalization, the level of compensation needed must be determined on the basis of an analysis of the costs of a typical well-run company.[71] Investments necessary for the provision of a service of general economic interest, or other public service obligations, such as investments to ensure security of electricity supply, do not constitute an illegal State aid and therefore do not fall under the prohibition of Article 107(1) TFEU if *Altmark* criteria are satisfied. Where at least one of the *Altmark* criteria is not satisfied, the public service compensation

[69] Commission Notice on the notion of State aid as referred to in Article 107(1) of the Treaty on the Functioning of the European Union [2016] OJ C 262/1.

[70] On this concept, see Chapter 4. This may include non-profit organizations, charities, and public bodies.

[71] Case C-280/00, *Altmark* [2003] ECR I–7747.

will be examined under State aid rules. Hence, construction of infrastructure that is linked to public service obligations and is, therefore, necessary for their provision does not also constitute an illegal State aid.[72]

There are various reasons a State aid may be declared lawful. Article 107(2)(a)–(c) provides an automatic justification, although the measures need to be notified to the Commission who will assess if they fall under the scope of Article 107(2).[73] Article 107(3)(a)–(d) provides further possibilities when an aid may be permitted, the Commission disposing of a considerable discretion in evaluating the compatible of the aid scheme with that provision.[74] The Commission has adopted block exemptions covering various categories of aid measures and has published various guidelines setting out the criteria that it will apply when assessing the compatibility of particular categories of aid measures with Article 107(3) TFEU. If an aid scheme falls outside one of the block exemptions or the relevant guidelines, or where no guidelines exist, the Commission will apply Article 107(3) TFEU directly to assess the compatibility of the State aid scheme on an individual basis, balancing the positive effect of the measure against its potentially negative effects. Essentially, a State aid may be found necessary, justified, and compatible with EU rules, in particular if it remedies a genuine market failure. It should be in this case proportionate, produce an incentive effect, changing the behaviour of the organization that receives it, be the most appropriate way to address the market failure, and be beneficial enough to outweigh any negative effects on competition.[75]

First, the Commission has adopted some block exemptions for certain categories of 'horizontal' State aid, that is, aid that is not specific to particular industry sectors). The Commission has taken the view that small amounts of aid are unlikely to distort competition. The *De Minimis* Regulation allows small amounts of aid (less than €200 000 over three rolling years) to be given to an undertaking for a wide range of purposes, without that aid being notified to the Commission if all the rules of the *de minimis* regulation are satisfied.[76] The General Block Exemption Regulation (GBER) also authorizes aid in favour of a number of activities, but still requires notification of the aid to the Commission using the online system (State Aid Notification Interactive, or SANI) within twenty working days of giving the aid.[77] The

72 Article 5(3)d of Commission Decision of 20 December 2011 on the application of Article 106(2) of the Treaty on the Functioning of the European Union to State aid in the form of public service compensation granted to certain undertakings entrusted with the operation of services of general economic interest [2012] OJ L 7/3.

73 This provision exempts an (i) aid having a social character, granted to individual consumers, provided it is granted in a way which does not discriminate according to the origin of the products concerned; (ii) aid to make good the damage caused by natural disasters or other exceptional occurrences; and (iii) aid to the economy of certain areas of the Federal Republic of Germany affected by the division of Germany, in so far as such aid is required to compensate for the economic disadvantage caused by that division.

74 This includes (i) an aid to promote the economic development of underdeveloped areas of the EU (with abnormally poor living standards or high levels of unemployment); (ii) an aid to promote the execution of an important project of common European interest or to remedy a serious disturbance in the economy of a Member State; (iii) an aid to facilitate the development of certain economic activities or areas (provided it does not adversely affect trading conditions to an extent contrary to the common interest); and (iv) an aid to promote culture and heritage conservation (again provided it does not affect trading conditions and competition in the EU to an extent contrary to the common interest).

75 Commission Staff Working Document, Common methodology for State aid evaluation, SWD(2014) 179 final.

76 Commission Regulation (EU) No 1407/2013 of 18 December 2013 on the application of Articles 107 and 108 of the Treaty on the Functioning of the European Union to *de minimis* aid [2013] OJ L 352/1.

77 Commission Regulation (EU) No 651/2014 of 17 June 2014 declaring certain categories of aid compatible with the internal market in application of Articles 107 and 108 of the Treaty [2014] OJ L 187/1.

Commission has also published guidelines for other 'horizontal' aids for which it takes a favourable view under Article 107(3) TFEU.[78]

Second, there are special rules and guidance for particular industries (sector-specific rules), such as broadcasting,[79] film and audio-visual works,[80] broadband,[81] financial services,[82] airports and airlines,[83] and postal services.[84]

Public service compensation may also be justified under Article 106(2) and/or Article 107(2)-(3) TFEU.[85]

Where there is an aid, and this cannot benefit from the *de minimis* regulation, or the GBER (in which case the notification will be done using the online system), the acceptability of aid should be subject to a lengthy notification and assessment process, as the aid should be approved by the Commission before it can be given.[86] The Commission has exclusive competence to decide whether the State aid is permitted in accordance with State aid policy.[87]

Article 108(3) TFEU requires plans to grant a State aid to be notified to the Commission in sufficient time to enable it to submit comments. A standard notification takes at least 9–12 months to be approved, but more contentious matters may take longer. The applicant has to show that: (i) it is aimed at making a material improvement that the market alone will not deliver; (ii) there is a logical connection between the provision of aid and a change in the behaviour of the undertaking that receives the aid that will bring about the outcome the aid is intended to achieve; (iii) the aid is limited to the minimum necessary to achieve the outcome; and (iv) the benefits of the aid outweigh any costs in terms of damage to trade; and (v) the grant is transparent. There is no need to notify State measures that may infringe Article 106(1) as the benefit of the exception provided by Article 106(2) may be assessed by a national court without this being previously notified.[88] The monitoring and control of State

78 Guidelines on regional State aid for 2014–2020 [2013] OJ C 209/1; Guidelines on State aid for rescuing and restructuring non-financial undertakings in difficulty [2014] OJ C 249/1; Guidelines on State aid for environmental protection and energy 2014–2020 [2014] OJ C 200/1.

79 Communication from the Commission on the application of State aid rules to public service broadcasting [2009] OJ 257/1.

80 Communication from the Commission on State aid for films and other audiovisual works [2013] OJ C332/1.

81 EU Guidelines for the application of State aid rules in relation to the rapid deployment of broadband networks [2013] OJ 25/1.

82 Commission Communication on the application, from 1 August 2013, of State aid rules to support measures in favour of banks in the context of the financial crisis [2013] OJ C 216/1.

83 Guidelines on State aid to airports and airlines, 4 April 2014, [2014] OJ C 99.

84 Notice from the Commission on the application of the competition rules to the postal sector and on the assessment of certain State measures relating to postal services [1998] OJ C 39/2.

85 Commission Decision 2012/21/EU of 20 December 2011 on the application of Article 106(2) of the Treaty on the Functioning of the European Union to State aid in the form of public service compensation granted to certain undertakings entrusted with the operation of services of general economic interest [2011] OJ L 7/3; Communication from the Commission on the application of the European Union State aid rules to compensation granted for the provision of services of general economic interest [2012] OJ C 8/4.

86 Procedures for the notification and assessment are detailed in the Procedural Regulation: Council Regulation (EC) 2015/1589 of 13 July 2015 laying down detailed rules for the application of Article 108 of the Treaty on the Functioning of the European Union [2015] OJ L 248/99.

87 Although Article 108(2) TFEU, third paragraph, exceptionally provides the Council (acting unanimously) similar discretion.

88 See also Commission Decision of 20 December 2011 on the application of Article 106(2) of the Treaty on the Functioning of the European Union to State aid in the form of public service compensation granted to certain undertakings entrusted with the operation of services of general economic interest [2012] OJ L 7/3, setting conditions under which certain compensation arrangements are compatible with Article 106(2) and Article 93 TFEU, respectively, and are not subject to the prior notification requirement of Article 108(3) TFEU.

aid is carried out by the European Commission. The Commission may act against unlawfully granted aid either of its own motion or following a complaint. If the aid is found to be unlawful, the Commission is usually required to take a recovery decision requiring repayment of the aid with interest.[89] National courts are responsible for enforcing the standstill obligation, which prevents Member States from putting proposed State aids into effect until authorized by the Commission. They may rule on whether a measure amounts to aid,[90] they may use all appropriate measures and provisions of national law to implement the direct effect of the Article 108(3) prohibition on implementation of unauthorized State aid, also involving the implementation of decisions over the recovery of an illegal State aid.

Application of Articles 101–2 TFEU to State conduct
Usually, Articles 101, 102 (and Article 106) TFEU apply to autonomous conduct by 'undertakings'. The concept of 'undertaking' is discussed in detail in Chapter 4. However, the case law of the EU Courts has explored the possibility that State conduct may also infringe Articles 101 and/or 102 TFEU (and/or Article 106 TFEU) in conjunction with Article 4(3) TEU, thus expanding the scope of these competition law provisions to apply to State conduct.

Undertakings infringe only by autonomous conduct
Undertakings could infringe Articles 101, 102 (and/or 106) TFEU only if their conduct is autonomous. Government encouragement or persuasion is no defence to the finding of a competition law infringement unless when the State conduct precludes any possibility for the undertaking to adopt its conduct on the marketplace (the State compulsion defence).[91] In *Commission and France v Ladbroke Racing*, the CJEU, following considerable case law, stated:

> Articles [101] and [102] of the Treaty apply only to anti-competitive conduct engaged in by undertakings on their own initiative [. . .]. If anti-competitive conduct is required of undertakings by national legislation or if the latter creates a legal framework which itself eliminates any possibility of competitive activity on their part, Articles [101] and [102] do not apply. In such a situation, the restriction of competition is not attributable, as those provisions implicitly require, the autonomous conduct of the undertaking.
>
> Articles [101] and [102] may apply however, if it is found that the national legislation does not preclude undertakings from engaging in autonomous conduct which prevents, restricts or distorts competition.
>
> When the Commission is considering the applicability of Articles [101] and [102] of the Treaty to the conduct of undertakings, a prior evaluation of national legislation affecting such conduct should therefore be directed solely to ascertaining whether that legislation prevents undertakings from engaging in autonomous conduct which prevents, restricts or distorts competition.[92]

In *Deutsche Telekom*, the CJEU confirmed that Articles 101 and/or 102 TFEU do not apply if the national measure precludes any possibility for the undertaking to adopt its conduct on

[89] See Commission Notice—Towards an effective implementation of Commission decisions ordering Member States to recover unlawful and incompatible State aid [2007] OJ C 272/4.

[90] They cannot, however, declare a State aid compatible with Article 107 TFEU, in view of the exclusivity from which enjoys the Commission to decide whether or not State aid is permitted.

[91] More on the State compulsion defence at Section 5.2.1.3.2.

[92] Joined Cases C-359 & 379/95P, *Commission and France v Ladbroke Racing* [1997] ECR I-6265, paras 33–5. National competition authorities as well as courts may declare national legislation incompatible with Article 101 or 102 in combination with Article 4(3) TEU.

the marketplace (the State compulsion defence).[93] If the State compulsion defence does not succeed, and the conduct of the undertaking(s) is found to be autonomous, then Article 101 and/or 102 apply. However, the fact that the conduct of the undertaking was induced by the national legal framework is taken into account as a mitigating factor when determining the fines to the undertaking(s) for infringing Articles 101 and/or 102 TFEU.[94]

The Commission may initiate proceedings against both the undertakings, in case their conduct is autonomous, and the Member State which adopted legislation facilitating the infringement of Articles 101 and/or 102 by the undertaking(s). In *CNSD*, the CJEU found that 'even though the Italian legislation imposed major limitations on competition and made it difficult in practice for there to be real competition in terms of prices between customs agents, it did not as such preclude the continued existence of a certain amount of competition capable of being prevented, restricted or distorted by the autonomous activity of customs agents'. This gave the Consiglio Nazionale degli Spedizionieri Doganali (National Council of Customs Agents, CNSD) room for manoeuvre in performing the obligations imposed on it by the legislation within which it could 'and ought to have acted in such a way as not to restrict the existing level of competition'. The Commission found that there was a decision by an association of undertakings entailing restrictive effects on competition and adopted by the CNSD on its own initiative.[95] It is worth noting that in *Commission v Italy*, the CJEU found, with regard to the same regulation, after the Commission had initiated proceedings against Italy for failure to fulfil its obligations under Article 4(3) TEU in combination with Article 101 TFEU, that by requiring the CNSD to adopt a decision by an association of undertakings contrary to Article 101 TFEU the Italian Republic had infringed these provisions.[96]

Non-binding action, such as mere persuasion or encouragement by a government to enter into an anti-competitive agreement, is no defence—hardly even mitigation—under the competition rules.

In *BNIC v Clair*,[97] the CJEU stated that the recommendation by a private trade association of minimum prices for cognac and the '*eau de vie*' from which it is distilled infringed Article 101 TFEU, although the association was set up by ministerial order. The minister appointed the members of the board and sent a nominee to its meetings. The CJEU added that the recommendation was not excused by a subsequent ministerial order that made the prices binding on non-members. The minister initiated and supervised the cartel and ensured its success by making it illegal for outsiders to undercut it. The CJEU has limited the effect of this judgment by subsequently finding in other industries that traders consulted by the minister were operating on his behalf and not that of the industry. Consequently, there was no agreement between undertakings, as it is required by Article 101 TFEU.[98]

In the French bovine cartel,[99] after the scare about mad cow disease, the French farmers complained to the minister about imports from England and went as far as vandalizing the equipment of the slaughterers. The minister did not arrange for legislation, but told the

93 Case C-280/08 P, *Deutsche Telekom AG v European Commission* [2010] ECR I–9555.

94 Case C-198/01, *Consorzio Industrie Fiammiferi (CIF) v Autorità Garante della Concorrenza e del Mercato* [2003] ECR I–8055, paras 52–8.

95 Case T-513/93, *CNSD v Commission* [2000] ECR II–1807.

96 Case C-35/96, *Commission v Italy* [1998] ECR I–3851.

97 Case 123/83, *BNIC v Clair* [1985] ECR 391, paras 22–3.

98 See Section 5.3.

99 *Federation Nationale des Syndicats Exploitants Agricoles and others* [2003] OJ L 209/12. See also Joined Cases T-217 & 245/03, *Fédération nationale de la coopération bétail et viande (FNCBV)*, ECLI:EU:T:2006:391; Joined Cases C-101 & 110/07 P, *Coop de France bétail and viande v Commission* [2008] ECR I–10193.

farmers to go ahead and arrange a cartel. They agreed on minimum prices and suspending imports into France. The agreement was against the interest of the slaughterers, who joined only after the minister encouraged the cartel. These facts were no justification for the farmers, but 30 per cent of the fine the slaughterers would have been charged was forgiven.

Combined application of Articles 4(3) TEU, 101, 102 TFEU to State conduct

Article 4(3) TEU provides that '[p]ursuant to the principle of sincere cooperation, the Union and the Member States shall, in full mutual respect, assist each other in carrying out tasks which flow from the Treaties.'[100] According to the same provision, '[t]he Member States shall take any appropriate measure, general or particular, to ensure fulfilment of the obligations arising out of the Treaties or resulting from the acts of the institutions of the Union' and '[t]he Member States shall facilitate the achievement of the Union's tasks and refrain from any measure which could jeopardise the attainment of the Union's objectives'. This provision imposes both positive and negative duties on Member States. Together with the principle of supremacy, it requires States to abstain from any action or enact any rule conflicting with EU norms, including the EU competition law provisions of the Treaty, or any measure that could jeopardise the attainment of the Treaty objectives. Hence, a Member State has the obligation to disapply national legislation that contravenes EU competition law. This rule applies to all State authorities, including national courts and administrative authorities, such as a competition authority. In *Consorzio Industries Fiammiferi (CIF) Autorità Garante della Concorrenza e del Mercato* the CJEU ruled that the direct effect and primacy of EU law obliges a national administrative authority which is authorized to apply Articles 101 and 102 to disapply national legislation that requires undertakings to act so as to restrict competition when this may affect trade between Member States.[101]

Consequently, national competition authorities (NCAs) may disapply the illegal national law for the future. If the legislation required firms to enter into an agreement that infringed Article 101 TFEU, it would be a defence for the past. If the law merely encouraged an infringement, it would be no defence. If the State breaches its obligations under Article 4(3) TEU, it would also be possible for the Commission to initiate an infringement procedure under Article 258 TFEU.

From this very general provision of Article 4(3) TEU, the CJEU has ruled in a series of cases that effect should not be given by national courts to measures that encourage, require, or reinforce the effects of an agreement that infringes Article 101(1) and/or Article 102 TFEU.

The INNO *doctrine*

In *INNO v ATAB*, the CJEU pronounced in a preliminary ruling regarding a Belgian taxation scheme for tobacco prohibiting the sale of cigarettes to consumers at a price lower

100 For a more detailed analysis, see P Pescatore, 'Public and Private Aspects of European Community Competition Law' (1986) 10 *Fordham Int'l LJ* 373, 411; R Joliet, 'National Anti-Competitive Legislation and Community Law' (1988) 12 *Fordham Int'l LJ* 163, 187; JT Lang, 'European Community Competition Law and Member State Action' (1989) 10 *Northwestern J Int'l L & Bus* 114, 123; G Marenco, 'Government Action and Antitrust In the United States: What Lessons for Community Law?' (1987) 14(1) *Legal Issues of Economic Integration* 1; N Reich, 'The "November Revolution" of the European Court of Justice: Keck, Meng and Audi Revisited' (1994) 31 *Common Market L Rev* 459; H Schepel, 'Delegation of Regulatory Powers to Private Parties under EC Competition Law: Towards a Procedural Public Interest Test' (2002) 39(1) *Common Market L Rev* 31; E Fox, 'State Action in Comparative Context: What if *Parker v. Brown* were Italian?' in B Hawk (ed) *International Antitrust Law & Policy: Fordham Corporate Law Institute* (Juris, 2003), ch 19; W Sauter & H Schepel, *State and Market in European Union Law* (CUP, 2009); D Gerard, 'EU Competition Policy After Lisbon: Time to Review the "State Action" Doctrine?' (2010) 1(3) *J Eur Competition L & Practice* 202.

101 Case C-198/01, *Consorzio Industrie Fiammiferi (CIF) v Autorità Garante della Concorrenza e del Mercato* [2003] ECR I–8055.

than that stated on the tax label affixed to the packet. This provision was applicable to both the imported and domestically manufactured products, had the effect of imposing on all persons, including traders not bound by contractually agreed prices, the selling price fixed by the manufacturers or the importers. The legislation therefore gave private traders the means to implement unilaterally a policy of imposing minimum resale prices. The CJEU held that 'while it is true that Article [102 TFEU] is directed at undertakings, none the less it is also true that the Treaty imposes a duty on Member States not to adopt or maintain in force any measure which could deprive that provision of its effectiveness' (the so-called '*effet utile* doctrine').[102] The *INNO v ATAB* principle would have made it possible to make any national measure having a restrictive effect on competition subject to competition law.

However, as AG Maduro explained in his Opinion in *Cipolla*, the Court subsequently adopted a more restrictive approach with regard to the joint application of what are now Articles 4(3) TEU and 101 TFEU.[103] Those articles are regarded as having been infringed only in two cases:[104]

(i) where a Member State requires or favours the adoption of agreements, decisions or concerted practices contrary to Article [101 TFEU] or reinforces their effects,[105] or
(ii) where that State divests its own rules of the character of legislation by delegating to private economic operators responsibility for taking decisions affecting the economic sphere.[106] The application of the '*effet utile* doctrine' requires that the undertakings in question have engaged in anti-competitive behaviour.[107]

According to Maduro,

> 32. There is a clear difference between the two cases. In the first case an agreement between undertakings is in existence before the State measure which validates or reinforces it. The State's liability arises from the fact that it aggravates by its action conduct that is already anti-competitive. In the second case, in which the State delegates its authority to private entities, undertakings adopt a decision which is then codified in a legislative measure. Application of Articles [Article 4(3) TEU] and [101 TFEU] is therefore designed to prevent a measure's form alone making it subject to competition law. In my view, that means that the concept of delegation must be interpreted in a substantive way by requiring an assessment of the decision-making process leading to the adoption of the State legislation. [. . .]
>
> 33. This is why the case-law cited above must certainly be construed as meaning that it is necessary to be aware what aims the State is pursuing in order to determine when its action may be made subject to competition law. It is necessary to establish whether legislative action by the State is dominated by a concern to protect the public interest or, on the other hand, whether the degree to which private interests are being taken into account is likely to alter the overriding objective of the State measure, which is

102 Case 13/77, *INNO v ATAB* [1977] ECR 2115, para 31.

103 Opinion of AG Maduro in Case C-94/04, *Federico Cipolla v Rosaria Fazari (née Portolese)* [2006] ECR I-11421 [hereinafter *Cipolla*].

104 Case 267/86, *Pascal Van Eycke v ASPA NV* [1988] ECR 4769, paras 16, 19–20.

105 Case C-198/01, *Consorzio Industrie Fiammiferi (CIF) v Autorità Garante della Concorrenza e del Mercato* [2003] ECR I-8055, para 46.

106 Case 136/86, *Aubert* [1987] ECR 4789, para 23; Case C-35/96, *Commission v Italy* [1998] ECR I-3851; Case C-35/99, *Arduino* [2002] ECR I-1529.

107 Case 267/86, *Pascal Van Eycke v ASPA NV* [1988] ECR 4769, para 18.

> therefore to protect those interests. Involvement of private operators in the legislative process, at the stage at which a rule is proposed, or by their presence within a body responsible for drafting that rule, is likely to have a determining influence on the content of the rule. The danger is that a legislative provision might have the sole purpose of protecting certain private interests from the elements of competition, to the detriment of the public interest.

State measures reinforcing the effects of anti-competitive agreements/concerted practices (or more broadly anti-competitive conduct)

In *BNIC v Aubert*,[108] the CJEU ruled that the ministerial order extending the effect of the same anti-competitive agreement to bind all traders in '*eau de vie*' was itself subject to now Articles 4(3) TEU and 101 TFEU in combination. Similar principles applied in other cases, the crucial thing being that private parties participate in the decision-making process leading up to the adoption of the anti-competitive State regulation.[109]

In *Cipolla*,[110] the CJEU focused on the decision-making process leading to the adoption of the State measure. Old Italian legislation dating from 1933 set the scale of lawyers' fees on the basis of criteria laid down by decision of the National Lawyers' Council and approved by the Minister of Justice following an opinion of the Interministerial Committee on Prices (and the Council of State). Any agreement derogating from the minimum fees set by the scale for lawyers' services was considered void. Two Italian courts sent preliminary references to the CJEU in the context of proceedings between lawyers and their respective clients with regard to fees paid, the courts asking the CJEU to examine the compatibility with competition law of the Italian legislation. The CJEU proceeded to a detailed examination of the procedure leading to the adoption of the scale and concluded that it was the Italian State (and not the professional body) that exercised the power to take decisions on lawyers' minimum fees. The Italian State retained its power to make decisions of last resort or to review implementation of that scale. Furthermore, the draft scale was not binding and was subject to the Minister of Justice's approval. National courts were also able to depart in certain exceptional circumstances from the maximum and minimum limits fixed in the scale.[111] Consequently, the Italian State could not be criticized for requiring or encouraging the adoption of agreements, decisions, or concerted practices contrary to the rules of free competition or of reinforcing their effects, or requiring or encouraging abuses of a dominant position or reinforcing the effects of such abuses.

State measures that delegate the fixing of prices to undertakings

One may envisage different possibilities. In *Leclerc v Au Blé Vert*,[112] Leclerc operated a supermarket chain with a policy of price-cutting. The French Lang Act, however, required publishers or importers of books to fix minimum retail prices for the books they published or imported, and it was made a criminal offence for retail sales to be made at a discount of more than 5 per cent. Provision was made for competitors and various kinds of trade associations to seek an injunction or damages, as well as for criminal prosecutions to be brought. Leclerc sold various titles below the permitted price level, and following suits filed by several competing booksellers, was

108 Case 136/86, *BNIC v Aubert* [1987] ECR 4789.

109 Case C-311/85, *Vlaamse Reisbureaus* [1987] ECR 3801, where the government had not encouraged and supervised the restrictive agreement as the minister had done in *BNIC*, but merely reinforced the agreement that had been freely made.

110 Joined Cases C-94/04 & C-202/04, *Cipolla* [2006] ECR I-11421.

111 Ibid, paras 48–51.

112 Case 229/83, *Leclerc v Au Blé Vert* [1985] ECR 32.

ordered to comply with the law. The Court of Appeal at Poitiers, however, asked the CJEU for a preliminary ruling whether the French law infringed the EU rules of competition in the light of what was then Article 3(1)(g) and the principle of sincere cooperation (Article 4(3) TEU). Leclerc argued that the law did not simply consist in price control by the State, since the prices could be fixed freely by publishers and importers. In effect, Leclerc argued that the Lang Act set up a resale price maintenance system, which would be illegal for the undertakings to arrange. The Commission, however, asked the Court to distinguish State measures from agreements between undertakings, since Article 101 applies only to the conduct of undertakings. The CJEU referred to the *INNO* doctrine, which underlies its later judgments:

> 15. Whilst it is true that the rules on competition are concerned with the conduct of undertakings and not with national legislation, Member States are none the less obliged [. . .] [Article 4(3) TEU] not to detract, by means of national legislation, from the full and uniform application of [EU] law or from the effectiveness of its implementing measures; nor may they introduce or maintain in force measures, even of a legislative nature, which may render ineffective the competition rules applicable to undertakings (cf. judgment in *Wilhelm v Bundeskartellamt*, and judgment in *Inno v ATAB*).

The CJEU observed that the French law did not restrain the conclusion of agreements, but only unilateral conduct. It then went on to consider whether the Lang Act deprived the competition rules of their effectiveness by making collusion unnecessary. It mentioned that the French measure protected book prices on cultural grounds, that the resale prices of books are maintained in many Member States, and that the Commission had, so far, attacked only one system of resale price maintenance for Dutch-language books embracing two Member States, and never a national system. The CJEU concluded that, as the duty of sincere cooperation then stood (what is now Article 4(3) TEU), combined with then Articles 3(1)(g) (now Article 3(3) in combination with Protocol no 27) and 101 TFEU, was not sufficiently well defined to prevent Member States from enacting legislation such as that in issue.[113]

Another possibility that may be covered by the above combination of Articles 4(3) TEU and 101 TFEU would consist in situations where the State delegates to a professional association the power to regulate prices (rates), that is, a form of self-regulation by the profession of the prices that may be charged. In the *Italian Customs Agents* case, the CJEU found that by adopting a national legislation that wholly relinquished to private economic operators, and in particular the CNSD, a professional body governed by public law, the powers of the public authorities as regards the setting of tariffs for the profession of custom agents, Italy had clearly not only required the conclusion of an agreement contrary to Article 101 TFEU and declined to influence its terms, but also assisted in ensuring compliance with that agreement, thus infringing Articles 4(3) TEU and 101 TFEU.[114] Setting maximum and/or minimum rates often form part of occupational licensing, which is quite prevalent in

113 Ibid, para 20.

114 See Case C-35/96, *Commission of the European Communities v Italian Republic* [1998] ECR I-3851. In this case the customs agents contravening the tariff are liable to face disciplinary measures, ranging from a reprimand to temporary suspension from the professional register where the offence is repeated, or removal from the register if suspended twice in five years, thus excluding them from the exercise of the profession. The Commission had previously found that the mandatory tariffs for services provided by custom agents which were adopted by their professional association constituted an infringement of Article 101 TFEU: Commission Decision 93/438/EC, *Italian Customs Agents* [1993] OJ L 203/27.

the regulation of professions in Europe.[115] We will discuss self-regulation by professional bodies and other conditions of occupational licensing that may restrict competition in the subsequent section.

If a State delegates the power to fix prices to a monopoly, public undertaking and undertaking to which the Member State in question has granted special or exclusive rights, Article 106 TFEU will apply to this undertaking, although it may also be possible to also find the State liable for jointly infringing Articles 106(1) and 102 TFEU, should the undertaking in question exploit, or is led, by the mere exercise of the exclusive or special rights conferred upon it, to exploit its dominant position in an abusive manner or where the exclusive rights conferred are capable of creating a situation in which that undertaking is led to commit such abuses,[116] without being necessary that any abuse actually occurred.[117] According to the case law, 'a Member State will be in breach of those provisions where a measure imputable to a Member State gives rise to a risk of an abuse of a dominant position.'[118] Indeed, '[a]ll that is necessary is for the Commission to identify a potential or actual anti-competitive consequence liable to result from the State measure at issue.'[119] Delegating the power to fix prices to a State monopoly or a privileged undertaking may therefore constitute an 'automatic abuse' of both Articles 106(1) and 102 TFEU, to the extent that State conduct leads to effects similar to those of an abuse, even if there has not been any actual abusive behaviour (just evidence of potential abuse is sufficient). Of course, it should be possible to justify the conduct under Article 106(2) TFEU and find no infringement. It seems, however, that the theory of automatic abuse does not apply in the context of the joint application of Articles 4(3) TEU and 101 TFEU, where it is necessary to at least have some actual conduct/behaviour, such as the existence of an agreement/concerted practice between undertakings or decision of association of undertakings that restricts competition (by object or effect), the conduct (agreement/concerted practice/decision of association of undertakings) that may restrict competition cannot just be potential. Hence, a risk to competition may not be sufficient to lead to the joint application of Articles 4(3) TEU and 101 TFEU to State conduct.

Developing the INNO *doctrine*

The scope of the *INNO* doctrine was narrowed down by subsequent jurisprudence of the EU Courts. These have developed an approach that focuses on the decision-making process that has led to the development of State conduct, in order to determine whether the State action has been in essence mainly driven by private interests, rather than an expression of public interest.

Narrowing INNO*: The 'November Revolution'*

The jurisprudence of the CJEU seems to have shifted more recently in favour of States' rights, requiring the prior finding that the agreement entered into infringes Article 101 TFEU. In a

115 For an economic analysis, see M Koumenta & M Pagliero, 'Measuring Prevalence and Labour Market Impacts of Occupational Regulation in the EU', European Commission (16 January 2017) (finding that occupational licensing affects about 22 per cent of workers in the EU).

116 See Case C-462/99, *Connect Austria Gesellschaft für Telekommunikation GmbH v Telekom-Control-Kommission, and Mobilkom Austria AG* [2003] ECR I–5197, para 80; Case C-49/07, *Motosykletistiki Omospondia Ellados NPID (MOTOE) v Elliniko Dimosio* [2008] ECR I–4863, para 49; Case C-553/12 P, *European Commission v Dimosia Epicheirisi Ilektrismou AE (DEI)*, ECLI:EU:C:2014:2083, para 41 [hereinafter *Greek Lignite*].

117 Case C-553/12 P, *Greek Lignite*, para 41.

118 Case C-49/07, *Motosykletistiki Omospondia Ellados NPID (MOTOE) v Elliniko Dimosio* [2008] ECR I–4863, para 50; Case C-553/12 P, *Greek Lignite*, para 42.

119 Case C-553/12 P, *Greek Lignite*, para 46. According to the CJEU, 'it is not necessary to identify an abuse other than that which results from the situation brought about by the State measure at issue' (ibid, para 47).

series of cases in favour of a less aggressive stance towards State intervention in the economy (the so-called 'November Revolution'[120]) the CJEU held that national measures that make it unnecessary for undertakings to agree, such as a national legislative prohibition on an agent sharing his commission with his customer, do not infringe what was then Article 3(1)g (now replaced by Protocol 27), Article 4(3) TEU and 101 TFEU even though a horizontal agreement between the agents would certainly restrict competition and might well affect trade between Member States.

In *Meng*, the CJEU examined some German State rules which prohibited insurance intermediaries from transferring to their clients all or part of the commission paid by insurance companies.[121] The insurance companies challenged these measures for being incompatible to what was prior to the Lisbon Treaty Article 3(1)g (now replaced by Protocol 27), combined with Articles 4(3) TEU and 101 TFEU. Nonetheless, the CJEU highlighted that these rules neither required nor favoured the conclusion of any unlawful agreement, decision, or concerted practice by insurance intermediaries, since the prohibition they laid down was a self-contained one. The Court noted that 'the rules themselves prohibit the grant of special advantages to policyholders and do not delegate to private traders responsibility for taking decisions affecting the economic sphere.'[122] Consequently, it was held that these rules do not fall within the categories of State rules that, according to the case law of the Court of Justice, undermine the effectiveness of EU competition law.[123]

In *Reiff*, the Court considered the mandatory approval procedure laid down by the German law for road transport tariffs.[124] The question was raised in proceedings between the Federal Office for Long-Distance Carriage of Goods by Road ('Federal Office'), and Reiff, which had carried out a transport operation for a price lower than that prescribed by the tariff. The Federal Office commenced proceedings against it to recover the difference between the price paid to the carrier and the tariff. The German court stayed proceedings and sent a preliminary question to the CJEU regarding the compatibility of the German law on road transport tariffs with Article 3(1)(g) as it was prior to the Lisbon Treaty and Article 101 TFEU. The law granted competence to fix the tariffs to Tariff Boards, which consisted of tariff experts in the relevant branches of the industry, chosen by the Federal Minister of Transport from among the persons suggested to him by the undertakings or associations in this sector. The Court first delved into whether the legislation in question was indicative of the existence of an agreement, decision, or concerted practice within the meaning of Article 101 TFEU. The fact that the public authority appoints as members of a body responsible for fixing prices persons proposed by trade organizations which are directly concerned does not exclude the existence of an agreement under Article 101 TFEU if those persons have negotiated and concluded an agreement on prices as representatives of the organizations which proposed them. The Court found, however, that the Tariff Boards were made up of tariff experts from the relevant sectors of the road haulage industry who were not bound by orders or instructions from the undertakings or associations that had recommended them to the Federal Minister of Transport for

120 This expression was first used by N Reich, 'The "November Revolution" of the European Court of Justice: Keck, Meng and Audit Revisited' (2004) 31 *Common Market L Rev* 459 noting the series of cases of the CJEU titling the balance in favour of States' right to regulate their economy.

121 Case C-2/91, *Criminal proceedings against Wolf W Meng* [1993] ECR I–5751.

122 Ibid, para 20.

123 See also, for a similar position, Case C-245/91, *Criminal proceedings against Ohra Schadeverzekeringen NV* [1993] ECR I–5851.

124 Case C-185/91, *Bundesanstalt für den Güterfernverkehr v Gebrüder Reiff GmbH & Co KG* [1993] ECR I–5801.

appointment. In addition, the Tariff Boards were not allowed to fix the tariffs solely by reference to the interests of undertakings or associations of undertakings engaged in transport but were also required to take account of the interests of the agricultural sector and of medium-sized undertakings or regions which are economically weak or have inadequate transport facilities. Consequently, the Court considered the industry members of the Boards as not strictly representing the interests of their industry. Furthermore, the State had not delegated powers regarding the fixing of tariffs to private economic agents in view of the important role of the Federal Minister of Transport in the decision-making process of Tariff Boards. There were various elements in favour of not applying Article 101 TFEU: the Tariff Boards and advisory committees were established by the Minister who had competence to decide on their composition and structure but also to personally attend their meetings or to be represented at them and eventually to reverse the tariffs fixed by the Tariff Boards, had these be inimical to the public interest.

In *Arduino*,[125] a case concerning the setting of tariff of fees for members of the legal profession in Italy (*avvocati* and *procuratori*), delegated by the State to the National Council of the Bar (CNF), and then approved by Ministerial decree, AG Léger argued that what was then Article 3(1)g (now replaced by Protocol 27) and Articles 4(3) TEU and 101 TFEU would not apply if the public authority exercises effective control, follows a legitimate aim in the public interest and the measure is proportionate to the need. The CJEU found that 'the fact that a Member State requires a professional organization to produce a draft tariff for services does not automatically divest the tariff finally adopted of the character of legislation'.[126] Examining the facts in this case, the CJEU held that the national legislation at issue did not contain 'either procedural arrangements or substantive requirements capable of ensuring, with reasonable probability, that, when producing the draft tariff, the CNF conducts itself like an arm of the State working in the public interest'.[127] However, the Italian State, and in particular the Minister, had not waived his power to make decisions of last resort or to review implementation of the tariff, and was also assisted by two public bodies whose opinions he had to obtain before approving the tariff. In certain exceptional circumstances, the Courts could also depart from the maximum and minimum limits fixed. All these factors led the CJEU to conclude that the Italian State had not delegated in this case to private economic operators responsibility for taking the tariff decisions.[128]

An objective functional process approach?

In their recent case law, the EU Courts seem to have embraced what may be characterized as an 'objective functional process approach', focusing on 'the nature and incentive structures of the decision making processes producing the [anti-competitive conduct] and not on the substance of those restraints',[129] or a 'procedural public interest'[130] analysis, focusing on the existence of State oversight over the measures adopted, in order to distinguish between measures that are adopted by financially disinterested decision-makers, with the sole aim to promote

125 Case C-35/99, *Criminal proceedings against Manuele Arduino* [2002] ECR I-1529.

126 Ibid, para 36. 127 Ibid, para 39.

128 Similar conclusions may also be reached for other forms of occupational licensing conditions, such as rules prohibiting the practice of the profession of lawyer concurrently with employment as a part-time public employee: see Case C-225/09, *Edyta Joanna Jakubowska v Alessandro Maneggia* [2010] ECR I-12329, paras 49–53.

129 E Elhauge, 'Making Sense of Antitrust Petitioning Immunity' (1992) 80(5) *California L Rev* 1177, 1180

130 H Schepel, 'Delegation of Regulatory Powers To Private Parties Under EC Competition Law: Towards a Procedural Public Interest Test' (2002) 39 *Common Market L Rev* 31.

the public interest, which may escape prohibition under Article 4(3) TEU and Articles 101 or 102 TFEU altogether, and measures that result from the capture of public decision-makers from private sector financially interested decision-makers.

In *Centro Servizi Spediporto*, the CJEU found relevant the fact that the committee, whose recommendations the legislation providing for road-haulage tariffs put into effect, was composed by a majority of representatives of the public authorities and a minority of representatives of the economic operators concerned, and that the proposals had to observe certain public interest criteria, therefore concluding that the tariffs were not incompatible with EU competition law rules.[131]

In *CNSD*, the General Court confirmed the decision of the Commission finding that the CNSD, a body governed by public law and whose members were elected by secret ballot by the customs agents, that drew up the compulsory tariff for customs services provided by independent customs agents completing customs clearance formalities, had infringed Article 101 TFEU, because the State had delegated its authority in this case.[132] The tariff was adopted by the CNSD and subsequently approved by decree of the Minister for Financial Affairs in 1988. It set minimum and maximum charges for each customs transaction and professional service concerning monetary, commercial, or fiscal matters. According to the Italian legislation, the CNSD was empowered to grant derogations from that tariff. In 1993, following a complaint against the tariff, the Commission adopted a decision declaring that Italian customs agents were 'undertakings' engaged in an economic activity and that the CNSD was 'an association of undertakings', thus indicating that the State had delegated its authority to the private actors in this case.[133] A reminder also that the CJEU had already declared (in 1998) that the Italian legislation, in requiring the CNSD to set a tariff compulsory for all customs agents, conflicted with EU competition law (the *CNSD* judgment examined in the previous section).[134] The CNSD applied to the General Court for annulment of the Commission decision alleging, among other things, that the restrictive effects on competition were attributed solely to the operation of the national legislation. The General Court closely examined CNSD's decision-making process. It found that Italian Law required the CNSD to adopt a tariff, but was silent as to the level of charges, did not specify maximum levels or criteria for setting charges, nor did it determine the way in which charges were to be applied providing that a separate charge must be made for each operation.

The Court distinguished the case from the facts in *Reiff*, finding that the members of the CNSD could not be characterized as independent experts as they were not required, under the law, to set tariffs taking into account the general interest and the interests of undertakings in other sectors or users of the services in question, as well as the interests of the undertakings or associations of undertakings in the sector which had appointed them.[135] The Court also found that, in practice, the CNSD had applied substantial increases to the minimum charges previously in force and had established how the charges were to be applied. Furthermore, the CNSD also availed itself of the options legally available to it of according derogations in certain cases from the minimum charges, of authorizing customs agents acting on behalf of a principal or agent to charge reduced fees, and of exempting from the tariff certain categories of customs services. These showed, according to the General Court, that the CNSD enjoyed broad discretion in the implementation of national legislation capable, in principle,

131 Case C-96/94, *Centro Servizi Spediporto Srl v Spedizioni Marittima del Golfo Srl*, ECLI:EU:C:1995:308.

132 Case T-513/93, *CNSD v Commission* [2000] ECR II–1807.

133 *CNSD* (Case IV/33.407) 93/438/EEC Commission Decision [1993] OJ L 203/27.

134 Case C-35/96, *Commission v Italy* [1998] ECR I–3851.

135 Case T-513/93, *CNSD v Commission* [2000] ECR II–1807, para 55.

of accommodating a different approach—one that would not have restricted competition in the sector. The Court concluded that the nature and scope of competition in the sector was shaped by decisions taken by the CNSD itself and therefore, the tariff constituted a restriction of competition attributable to the CNSD.

More recently, in *API*, the CJEU was seized by an Italian court with regard to the compatibility with, among other provisions, Article 4(3) TEU and Article 101 TFEU of an Italian legislation that had introduced a regulated system for the liberalization of road transport, which although it was based on free bargaining for setting the prices for road transport services, it also entrusted an entity, the Consulta, whose membership was mostly drawn from industry associations or road transport operators, albeit with some limited representation of State authorities and customers, with the task to ensure that prices for road transport were not lower than the minimum operating costs fixed by a specific body of the Consulta, allegedly for the purpose of ensuring compliance with safety standards.[136] The CJEU, first, explored the internal process of decision-making of the entity deciding these minimum operating costs, noting that the majority of its members were representatives of the undertakings concerned and that the State representatives had no right of veto or a casting vote, and therefore unable to 'rebalance power between the public authorities and the private sector', distinguishing the case from the facts in *Reiff*.[137] Interestingly, the CJEU did not find that this denied any legislative character to the measure, noting that the members of the entity could have acted in their capacity as experts and be independent from the economic operators concerned, taking into account the broader public interest and the interests of other undertakings and users of the services in question. However, this was not the case here, as the national legislation establishing this entity did not indicate 'the guiding principles which those bodies must observe and [did] not contain any provision such as to prevent the representatives of the professional organizations from acting in the exclusive interest of the profession'.[138] The reference to the public interest of road safety was found to be relatively vague and to provide a 'very large margin of discretion and independence' to the members of the entity, 'in the interest of the professional organizations which appointed them'.[139] The CJEU concluded that the national legislation in questions did not contain 'either procedural arrangements or substantive requirements' capable of ensuring, that, when establishing minimum operating costs, the entity conducted itself 'like an arm of the State working in the public interest'.[140] With regard to the delegation of the power of public authorities to the mostly private entity, the CJEU found relevant the fact that the public authorities did not seem to exercise a review over the assessments of the entity and that they were not consulted prior to the costs being set, and reached the conclusion that the entity could be qualified as an association of undertakings within the meaning of Article 101 TFEU. The CJEU found that the fixing of minimum operating costs, made mandatory by national legislation, prevented undertakings from setting the tariffs lower than those costs and therefore amounted to a horizontal restriction to competition, applying Article 101(1) TFEU, read in conjunction with Article 4(3) TEU. However, it explored if that restriction of competition was justified by the pursuance of public interest objectives, such as road safety, concluding that the measures in question went beyond what was necessary and that there were other less restrictive measures to reach this legitimate objective.[141] Occupational licensing conditions may certainly

136 Joined Cases C-184–7, 194–5 & 208/13, *API v Ministero delle Infrastrutture e dei Transporti*, ECLI:EU:C:2014:2147.

137 Ibid, paras 32–3. 138 Ibid, para 35. 139 Ibid, para 37. 140 Ibid, para 38.

141 Ibid, para 55.

restrict price competition, restrict entry into the profession, and limit intra-EU mobility of professionals;[142] however, they may also be justified from a welfare perspective,[143] or because of professional ethics considerations and other public interest objectives. These aims may be taken into account in the context of applying Article 101(1) TFEU (or Article 102 TFEU) and should they be found proportional,[144] the State conduct in question may be found not to infringe EU competition law.

The Court took a similar stance in *CHEZ Elektro Bulgaria v Yordan Kotsev*,[145] concerning the setting of minimum fee amounts by a lawyers' professional organization (the Supreme Council of the Legal Profession—SCLP in Bulgaria), the Court considering that Article 4(3) TEU and Article 101 TFEU could not apply 'where the tariffs are fixed with due regard for the public-interest criteria defined by law and the public authorities do not delegate their rights and powers to private economic operators' and this 'even if representatives of the economic operators are not in the minority on the committee proposing those tariffs'.[146] The CJEU also noted that these experts should be 'independent of the economic operators' concerned and 'required, under the law, to set tariffs taking into account not only the interests of the undertakings or associations of undertakings in the sector which has appointed them but also the public interest and the interests of undertakings in other sectors or users of the services in question'.[147] In this case, the SCLP was composed exclusively of lawyers elected by their peers, the legislation did not provide any specific criterion ensuring that the minimum amounts of lawyers' remuneration, as this was determined by the SCLP, was fair and justified in accordance with the general interest, and it was subject to a limited constitutionality review. Hence, the CJEU concluded that the SCLP was not an arm of the State working in the public interest subject to actual review, but an association of undertakings. By making mandatory a decision of an association of undertakings which has the object or effect of restricting competition or restricting the freedom of action of the parties or of one of them could be subject to the joint application of Article 101(1) TFEU with Article 4(3) TEU. The CJEU nevertheless raised the possibility that this restriction of competition may be justified if it is necessary to ensure the implementation of legitimate objectives of public interest.[148]

The jurisprudence of EU Courts remains nevertheless ambiguous concerning the exercise of a substantive review of State legislation with regard to its compatibility with EU competition law. In *Consorzio Industrie Fiammiferi (CIF)*,[149] Italian legislation conferred a fiscal and

142 MM Kleiner, 'Occupational Licensing' (2000) 14(4) *J Economic Perspectives* 189; MM Kleiner and E Vorotnikov, 'Analyzing Occupational Licensing Among the States' (2017) 52(2) *J Regulatory Economics* 132; M Koumenta and M Pagliero, 'Occupational Licensing in the European Union: Coverage and Wage Effects', CEPR Discussion Paper No DP12577 (2018).

143 HE Leland, 'Quacks, Lemons and Licensing: A Theory of Minimum Quality Standards' (1979) 87 *J Political Economy* 1328 (the main narrative is to regulate market failures that result from the informational asymmetry between the professionals and the consumers).

144 See our analysis in Chapter 6 in particular of the following cases: Case C-309/99 *Wouters, Savelbergh and Price Waterhouse v Algemene Raad Van de Nederlandse Orde van Advocaten* [2002] ECR I–15; Case C-519/04 P, *David Meca-Medina and Igor Majcen v Commission* [2006] ECR I–699; Case C-1/12 *Ordem dos Técnicos Oficiais de Contas*, ECLI:EU:C:2013:127; Case C-136/12, *Consiglio nazionale dei geologi v Autorità garante della concorrenza e del mercato*, ECLI:EU:C:2013:489.

145 Joined Cases C-427/16 & C-428/16, *CHEZ Elektro Bulgaria v Yordan Kotsev*, ECLI:EU:C:2017:890.

146 Ibid, para 43.

147 Ibid, paras 44–5.

148 See our analysis in Section 6.3.4.2.2, question/note 6.

149 Case C-198/01 *Consorzio Industrie Fiammiferi (CIF) v Autorità Garante della Concorrenza e del Mercato* [2003] ECR I–8055.

commercial monopoly on CIF to manufacture and sell matches for consumption in Italy. CIF was a consortium of match manufacturers whose operations were governed by agreements between CIF and the Italian State. The legislation was amended several times. At first membership was limited and compulsory. As required by this legislation a quota allocation committee of CIF allocated production and sales quotas. The Committee consisted of an official of the State Monopolies Board, who acted as chairman, a representative of the CIF, and three representatives of the member undertakings. Its decisions were taken by simple majority, so the chairman could be outvoted. This committee was representing the interests of the members rather than the State. This agreement was held unconstitutional by the Italian Constitutional Court as new manufacturers were excluded and subsequent changes to the legislation was brought, including the abolition of the commercial monopoly and compulsory membership by match manufacturers.

Nevertheless, a match manufacturer in Germany complained to the Italian competition authority that it was still having difficulty distributing its products on the Italian market. The Italian competition authority distinguished three kinds of conduct among the CIF's activities: conduct required by legislation, conduct facilitated by legislation when a legislative change abolished the CIF's monopoly but made the participation in the CIF voluntary, and conduct attributable to CIF's own initiatives. It found that legislation shielded the first category of conduct, but that this legislation should be disapplied for the future by any court or public administrative body because of the direct effect and priority of EU competition law. Once CIF's fiscal and commercial monopoly was terminated, Article 101 clearly applied. An appeal was brought against this decision, and the national court made a reference to the CJEU, asking whether Article 101 TFEU requires or permits a national competition authority to disapply a State measure and to penalize anti-competitive conduct of undertakings, and, if so, with what legal consequences. It also asked whether compulsory membership of a body with power to allocate production and fix retail prices precluded undertakings from engaging in autonomous conduct that may affect trade between Member States and prevent, restrict, or distort competition.

The CJEU cited many of the cases considered above and others, noting that since the Treaty of Maastricht entered into force, 'the EC Treaty has expressly provided that in the context of their economic policy the activities of the Member States must observe the principle of an open market economy with free competition' (now Article 119(1) TFEU and Article 120 TFEU).[150] It also noted that the principle of primacy of EU law requires any provision of national law that contravenes an EU rule to be disapplied, regardless of whether it was adopted before or after that rule:

> 49. The duty to disapply national legislation which contravenes Community law applies not only to national courts but also to all organs of the state including administrative authorities [. . .], which entails, if the circumstance so require, the obligation to take all appropriate measures to enable Community law to be fully applied [. . .] [Citations omitted.]
>
> 50. Since a national authority such as the Authority is responsible for ensuring, *inter alia* that Article [101 TFEU] is observed and that provision, in conjunction with Article [4(3) TEU] imposes a duty on Member States to refrain from introducing measures contrary to the [EU] competition rules, those rules would be rendered less effective, if in the course of an investigation

150 Ibid, para 47.

> under Article [101 TFEU] into the conduct of undertakings, the authority were not able to declare a national measure contrary to the combined provisions of Art. [4(3) TEU] and [101 TFEU] and if, consequently, it failed to disapply it.

Since May 2004, all Member States have been required to empower their competition authorities to apply Articles 101 and 102 (Article 35 of Regulation 1/2003), thus enabling paragraph 50 of *CIF* to have a wide application.

The CJEU also found of 'little significance' that the undertakings would not be held accountable, under competition law, for anti-competitive conduct required by national legislation, holding that 'Member States' obligations under [what are now, Protocol No 27, Article 4(3) TEU, and Articles 101 and 102 TFEU], [. . .] are distinct from those to which undertakings are subject under Articles [101 and 102 TFEU], none the less continue to exist and therefore the national competition authority remains duty-bound to disapply the national measure at issue'.[151] The CJEU explained that where the undertakings had no autonomy under national law, they should not be penalized for activities before the national legislation was disapplied because of the general principle of legal certainty.[152] If conduct after the disapplication of the legislation becomes definitive, however, penalties may be imposed. Where the legislation merely encourages or facilitates anti-competitive conduct, penalties may be imposed to undertakings for conduct preceding the decision of disapplication, although the conflict of legislation may mitigate the penalty. In this case, the State's legislation or regulation encouraging or facilitating anti-competitive conduct could also enter into the scope of the joint application of Article 4(3) TEU and Articles 101 and/or 102 TFEU. The CJEU made it clear that it is for the national court to find the facts, but it suggested that the freedom of the members of the CIF to buy and sell quotas might be autonomous conduct of the members contrary to Article 101 TFEU.

When examining the facts of the case, the CJEU held that price competition is not 'the only effective form of competition or that to which absolute priority must in all circumstances be given', and consequently, 'pre-determination of the sales price of matches by the Italian State does not, on its own, rule out all scope for competitive conduct', as '[e]ven if limited, competition may operate through other factors'.[153] The CJEU noted that the legislation in question did not set out either the rules or the criteria by reference to which allocation of the production of matches was to be carried out, and that following the abolition of the commercial monopoly 'the remaining competition between the member undertakings [was] liable to distortion going beyond that already brought about by the legal obligation itself'.[154] The CJEU also invited the referring court to examine the composition and procedure of decision-making of the committee entrusted with the task of allocating production between the undertakings members of CIF (the alleged restriction of competition) so as to explore if these are capable of engaging in 'autonomous' conduct (read financially interested conduct), or if autonomous action is precluded by the effective control of public authorities.

In conclusion, State regulation that interferes with 'undistorted competition' may fall under the joint application of Article 4(3) TEU and Articles 101/102 TFEU. The case law of the EU Courts has condemned as contrary to a combination of, what was prior to the Treaty of Lisbon, Article 3(1)g (now Protocol No 27), in conjunction with Articles 4(3) TEU and 101 TFEU, government measures that require, favour, or reinforce agreements that infringe Article 101. It has gone further and condemned national measures that delegate to a private firm or trade

[151] Ibid, para 51. [152] Ibid, paras 52–4. [153] Ibid, para 69. [154] Ibid, para 71.

association the fixing of terms on which outsiders may trade. It has, however, drawn back from ruling that a government measure might be invalid when there had never been any agreement between undertakings restricting competition in the common market. Where prices are fixed by government based on advice from industry, the CJEU no longer states that that amounts to collusion between undertakings. It examines whether the advisors were looking to criteria set by the State rather than to their own interest, thus in practice applying an objective functional process approach. Further action against anti-competitive regulation must probably be left to measures of harmonization under Article 114 TFEU, and to Article 106 TFEU, which empowers the Commission to take action against State monopolies.

1.1.1.2. Main UK competition law provisions

Two key statutes which apply today in the UK regarding substantive competition law are

- the Competition Act 1998
- the Enterprise Act 2002

These Acts apply competition law to most sectors of the economy, and even where some sectors, such as utilities operate under special regimes, the competition rules of these Acts are generally applicable to them, although the body applying the law may vary.

In addition, the Common Law of Restraints of Trade doctrine sits alongside competition law. The earlier UK legislation on restrictive trade practices has been repealed, but some of the reports of the Monopolies and Merger Commission may possibly be helpful for their analysis of the economic issues.

1.1.1.2.1. Competition Act 1998

The Competition Act 1998 (CA98) includes provisions on the control of agreements, horizontal or vertical between two or more undertakings, for which provision is made in the prohibition of Chapter I: The Act covers also abuses committed by dominant firms (Chapter II prohibition). Both provisions are modelled to Articles 101 and 102 TFEU and are intended to operate in much the same way as the application of EU Competition law and, to this end, section 60 of the Act contains provisions regarding the necessary consistency between the application of EU and UK competition law, although this is also subject to some limitations. The relations between the EU and the UK competition law will certainly be affected by Brexit.[155]

Some amendments to the Act were made by the Enterprise Act 2002 and the Competition Act 1998 and Other Enactments (Amendment) Regulation 2004 that was adopted in order to bring the UK competition system in line with EU Regulation 1/2003.[156]

1.1.1.2.2. Enterprise Act 2002

The Act contains provisions for merger control and market investigation references, which enabled the UK competition authorities to conduct sector enquiries and impose industry-wide remedies. Furthermore, the Act has introduced a new and separate 'competition law offence'

[155] See our analysis in Section 1.3.3.3. For a more detailed discussion with regard to aspects of enforcement see the companion volume: I Lianos, *Competition Law Enforcement and Procedure* (OUP, forthcoming 2019).

[156] SI 2004/1261. See OFT442, Modernisation (December 2004), available at www.gov.uk/government/uploads/system/uploads/attachment_data/file/284432/oft442.pdf.

(section 188 of the Act), thus adding criminal enforcement to the competition law toolbox. As a result of this Act, upon indictment, an individual may be imprisoned for up to five years and/or a fine may be imposed. The director of a company found guilty of a 'cartel offence' may also face disqualification, upon certain conditions. The institutional changes to the enforcement of competition law in the UK by the Enterprise Act are examined in Section 1.2.2.

1.1.1.2.3. Enterprise and Regulatory Reform Act 2013

The recent Enterprise and Regulatory Reform Act 2013 (ERRA 2013) entered into force on 1 April 2014. In addition to the quite important institutional changes it brought with the constitution of the Competition and Markets Authority (CMA), it also streamlined and strengthened the competition law tools at the disposal of the CMA by enhancing its powers. It authorized the CMA to investigate practices across markets, provided it with expanded powers with regard to merger remedies, made decision-making in the enforcement of the antitrust prohibitions in the Competition Act 1998 more robust, and introduced important changes to the design of the 'criminal offence' with the aim to make it easier to prosecute the offence and thus increase its deterrence. The Act also enabled the Secretary of State to request the CMA to investigate public interest issues alongside competition issues in a market investigation and included new statutory timescales for market investigations.

1.1.1.2.4. Consumer Rights Act 2015

The Consumer Rights Act entered into force on 1 October 2015 and aims to facilitate private enforcement of competition law in the UK, in particular in particular by consumers and small- and medium-sized businesses (SMEs). As these changes are of institutional dimension, they will be examined in Section 1.2.2.

1.1.2. OVERVIEW OF THE MAIN ACTORS IN THE PROCESS

1.1.2.1. The EU competition law process

1.1.2.1.1. The European Commission

The European Commission has the primary responsibility for enforcing Articles 101 TFEU (on anti-competitive collusive practices), 102 TFEU (on abuse of dominant position), 106 TFEU (on anti-competitive activities adopted by public undertakings or undertakings with exclusive rights conferred by law), and the Merger Regulation (Regulation 139/2004) on mergers above the threshold of turnover. The Commission has competence also to apply the provisions of the Treaty on the monitoring and prohibition of illegal State aids (contained in Articles 107–9 TFEU).

The Commission is composed of twenty-seven members, appointed for a renewable period of five years by the Council of the European Union, after being nominated by their Member States and approved by the European Parliament. They should be independent in the performance of their duties and should not receive instructions from their respective governments. The Commission promotes the general interest of the Union and adopts decisions on a majority basis. Each member of the Commission has responsibility over one or more specific policy areas. The Commission is organized into a number of Directorates General, including the Directorate General for Competition (DG Comp) responsible for the enforcement of competition law. Other DGs, such as the Directorate

General for the Internal Market, or for Enterprise and Industry, may also be involved in the broader issues of competition policy.

DG Comp is headed by a Director General, working under the authority of the Commissioner responsible for competition policy. The Commissioner also has his own cabinet. The Director General is assisted by three deputy Directors General (one on antitrust and mergers, one on operations, and one on State aids) and a number of directorates dealing with specific industries or general operational issues (policy and strategy, registry, and resources). Since September 2003, there has also been a Chief Competition Economist's (CCE) office, comprising over thirty specialized economists, all of whom hold a PhD in Industrial Organization and headed by a Chief Economist who is appointed by the European Commission for no more than three years, although on one occasion the mission was extended. The CCE's office fulfils a 'support function', being involved in competition investigations and providing economic guidance and 'methodological assistance', but also exercises a 'checks-and-balances' function, giving the Commissioner an 'independent opinion' before any proposal for a final decision to the College of Commissioners.[157] The Chief Economist also coordinates the work of the Economic Advisory Group on Competition Policy (EAGCP), which consists of a number of academic economists who have a recognized reputation in the field of industrial organization, proposed by the Chief Economist and nominated by the Commissioner. The EAGCP prepares opinions on the projected reviews of EU competition law policies and regulations.

Of particular interest is the function of 'hearing officer', established in 1982, in order to enhance impartiality and objectivity in competition proceedings before the Commission. Hearing officers (at the moment two, assisted by their team) are independent from DG Comp and are attached directly to the Commissioner responsible for competition, to whom they report. The hearing officers have a mandate to ensure due process and the fairness of competition proceedings before the Commission for any proceedings under Articles 101, 102, 106 TFEU or merger control. They are concerned only with procedural fairness, not with substantive matters.

The Commission has an important array of powers in the area of competition law. It performs a 'supervisory task', which includes 'the duty to investigate and punish individual infringements as well as the duty to pursue a general policy designed to apply, in competition matters, the principles laid down by the Treaty'.[158]

The Commission benefits from broad regulatory competence in adopting measures of general application. Article 105(3) TFEU, introduced by the Treaty of Lisbon, entrusts the Commission with an explicit legal basis for the adoption of regulations and directives on certain categories of agreements. This merely codifies previous practice of ad hoc delegation by Council regulations. The Commission has, indeed, adopted block exemption regulations that disapply the prohibition of Article 101(1) TFEU to certain categories of agreements, under specific circumstances,[159] or on the implementation of the competition law

157 L-H Röller and P Buigues, 'The Office of the Chief Competition Economist at the European Commission' (May 2005), 6, available at http://ec.europa.eu/dgs/competition/economist/officechiefecon_ec.pdf.

158 Joined Cases C-189, 202, 208 & 213/02, *Dansk Rørindustri A/S & others v Commission* [2005] ECR I-5425, para 170.

159 Commission Regulation (EU) 330/2010 of 20 April 2010 on the application of Article 101(3) of the Treaty on the Functioning of the European Union to categories of vertical agreements and concerted practices [2010] OJ L 102/1; Commission Regulation (EU) 461/2010 on the application of Article 101(3) of the Treaty on the Functioning of the European Union to categories of vertical agreements and concerted practices in the motor vehicle sector [2010] OJ L 129/52; Commission Regulation (EU) No 1217/2010 of 14 December 2010 on the

provisions of the Treaty.[160] Most of these provisions are completed by a series of guidelines, Communications, notices, priority guidance, best practices, annual reports, oral statements, press releases, guidance letters, expert reports, and third-party studies, which provide invaluable information about the enforcement of competition law. They are not binding but constitute very important soft law.

The procedure for the application of Articles 101 and 102 TFEU before the Commission is set out in Regulation 1/2003, Regulation 774/2003, and various tertiary legislative instruments, such as the Notice on Access to the File.[161]

Regulation 1/2003, adopted by the Council and the European Parliament, is the most important text indicating the tasks and powers of the Commission. The Commission may investigate competition law infringements on its own initiative or after complaint.[162] It may obtain information from companies,[163] it can take statements and conduct interviews with natural or legal persons,[164] and it may carry out inspections at the undertaking's premises,[165] including private as well as business premises.[166] The Commission can adopt a decision finding an infringement and order the undertaking to bring the infringement to an end, if it has not been terminated already,[167] it may take decisions ordering interim measures,[168] or may adopt a decision, which renders commitments given by the parties binding upon them.[169]

If an infringement of competition law is found, the Commission has extensive powers to impose sanctions (fines and periodic penalties),[170] including penalties of up to 10 per cent of the annual worldwide turnover of an undertaking.[171] The case law of the European Court of Justice recognizes that the Commission has discretion to increase the level of fines for reasons

application of Article 101(3) of the Treaty on the Functioning of the European Union to certain categories of research and development agreements [2010] OJ L 335/36; Commission Regulation (EU) No 1218/2010 of 14 December 2010 on the application of Article 101(3) of the Treaty on the Functioning of the European Union to certain categories of specialisation agreements [2010] OJ L 335/43; Commission Regulation (EU) No 316/2014 of 21 March 2014 on the application of Article 101(3) of the Treaty on the Functioning of the European Union to categories of technology transfer agreements [2014] OJ L 93/17; Commission Regulation (EC) of 24 March 2010 on the application of Article 101(3) of the Treaty to certain categories of agreements, decisions and concerted practices in the insurance [2010] OJ L 83/1; Commission Regulation (EC) No 906/2009 of 28 September 2009 on the application of Article 81(3) of the Treaty to certain categories of agreements, decisions and concerted practices between liner shipping companies (consortia) [2009] OJ L 256/31, modified by Commission Regulation (EU) No 697/2014 [2014] OJ L 184/3.

160 Commission Regulation (EC) No 773/2004 of 7 April 2004 relating to the conduct of proceedings by the Commission pursuant to Articles 81 and 82 of the EC Treaty [2004] OJ L 123/18, amended by Commission Regulation (EC) No 622/2008 as regards the conduct of settlement procedures in cartel cases [2008] OJ L 171/3. On merger control, see Commission Regulation (EC) 802/2004 implementing Council Regulation (EC) No 139/2004 (The 'Implementing Regulation') and its annexes (Form CO, Short Form CO, and Form RS) [2004] OJ L 133/1, as amended by Commission Regulation (EC) No 1033/2008 of 20 October 2008 amending Regulation (EC) No 802/2004 implementing Council Regulation (EC) No 139/2004 on the control of concentrations between undertakings [2008] OJ L 279/3 and Commission Implementing Regulation (EU) No 1269/2013 [2013] OJ L 336/1.

161 Commission Notice on the rules for access to the Commission file in cases pursuant to Articles 81 and 82 of the EC Treaty, Articles 53, 54, and 57 of the EEA Agreement and Council Regulation (EC) No 139/2004 [2005] OJ C 325/7, amended in 2015 [2015] OJ C 256/3 [hereinafter Access to File Notice].

162 Council Regulation (EC) No 1/2003 of 16 December 2002 on the implementation of the rules on competition laid down in Articles 81 and 82 of the Treaty, Article 7 [hereinafter Regulation 1/2003].

163 Ibid, Article 18. 164 Ibid, Article 19. 165 Ibid, Article 20. 166 Ibid, Article 21.

167 Ibid, Article 7. 168 Ibid, Article 8. 169 Ibid.

170 Ibid, Articles 23 (fines) and 24 (periodic penalty payments).

171 The fines have been steadily increasing, with the largest single penalty being that of €1.06 billion imposed on Intel in 2009 for having abused its dominant position.

Table 1.1. The highest fines to individual undertakings imposed by the Commission.

Name of the company	Fine (amount)	Infringement
Google (2018)	€4.3. billion	102 TFEU
Google (2017)	€2.4 billion	102 TFEU
Intel (2009)	€1.06 billion	102 TFEU
Qualcomm (2018)	€997.4 million	102 TFEU
Microsoft (2004)	€497 million Added: €860 million	102 TFEU
Microsoft (2013)	€561 million	102 TFEU
Servier (2014)	€330.9 million	102 & 101 TFEU
Telefonica (2007)	€151 million	102 TFEU
Facebook (2017)	€110 million	Procedural

of deterrence.[172] The Commission enjoys an important discretion in imposing fines.[173] The amount of fines has been increased considerably since 2004 (see Table 1.1).

The Commission can also impose conduct or structural remedies (including a break-up of the undertaking).[174] Furthermore, the Commission can initiate general inquiries into a sector of the economy, which can give rise to fines and penalties (but not remedies).[175]

Following the modernization of EU competition law enforcement under Regulation 1/2003, the previous system of notification of illegal agreements to the Commission was abrogated in favour of a legal exception regime. Regulation 1/2003, however, allows the Commission to adopt decisions to the effect that Article 101 or 102[176] is inapplicable, or to issue 'guidance letters' for novel questions concerning Articles 101 and 102 TFEU[177] that arise in individual cases.[178] In the past, the Commission adopted informal settlements for some minor cases, although the possibility of commitment decisions is now used systematically.[179] The Commission has also adopted a regulation establishing a settlement procedure for cartel cases to enable the Commission to encourage cooperation with it by reducing a fine by up to 10 per cent if the infringer accepts that it participated in a cartel. It hopes that it will be able to handle the cases faster and more efficiently.[180] Moreover, appeals will be less likely.

172 Joined Cases 100–3/80, *Musique Diffusion française v Commission* [1983] ECR 1825, para 109, confirmed by the Court in many more recent judgments.

173 See, however, Guidelines on the method of setting fines imposed pursuant to Article 23(2)(a) of Regulation No 1/2003 [2006] OJ C 210/2.

174 Regulation 1/2003, Article 7(1). 175 Ibid, Article 17. 176 Ibid, Article 10.

177 Ibid, Recital 38 specifically contemplates the possibility that parties should be able to seek and obtain informal guidance from the Commission in cases giving rise to genuine uncertainty because they present novel or unresolved questions (see also the subsequent Notice on informal guidance in which the Commission outlined the policy it intended to adopt in granting such guidance: Notice on informal guidance relating to novel questions concerning Articles 81 and 82 of the EC Treaty that arise in individual cases (guidance letters [2004] OJ C 101/78) [hereinafter Notice on informal guidance].

178 These options have not been used so far.

179 For a more detailed discussion see the companion volume on enforcement: I Lianos, *Competition Law Enforcement and Procedure* (OUP, forthcoming 2019).

180 Commission Regulation (EC) No 622/2008 of 30 June 2008 amending Regulation (EC) No 773/2004, as regards the conduct of settlement procedures in cartel cases [2008] OJ L 171/3; Commission Notice on the conduct of settlement procedures in view of the adoption of Decisions pursuant to Article 7 and Article 23 of Council Regulation (EC) No 1/2003 in cartel cases [2008] OJ C 167/1.

The Commission had earlier established a procedure rewarding voluntary production of evidence to trigger or advance the Commission's investigations (leniency policy).[181] The reduction of a fine under the leniency notice can be cumulated with reduction under the settlement procedure, at the discretion of the Commission.

In addition to Regulation 1/2003, there are specific provisions for the enforcement of EU Merger control in Regulation 139/2004.[182]

Concerning the interpretation of the substantive provisions of the Treaty and the merger regulation, the Commission has issued a significant number of Regulations, including block exemption regulations, Guidelines, Communications, and Notices. These are published at the Official Journal of the EU, C series, and thus have some normative effect. The main purpose is to assist firms, national competition authorities, and courts in the interpretation of the various Treaty provisions and block exemption regulations, provide transparency as to the enforcement priorities of the European Commission, and encourage compliance efforts by firms. The guidelines have also been instrumental in importing some degree of economic analysis into EU competition law, following the pattern initiated in US antitrust law with the issuance of the first merger guidelines in 1968.[183] The Commission has been publishing annual reports on competition policy since 1972 with an overview of the main developments over the past year and priorities for the upcoming year.[184] The Annual report is adopted by the College of Commissioners. Important information on the Commission's mission, challenges, objectives, and impact is also provided at the DG Comp Annual Management Plan, published at the website of the European Commission. The Management Plan attempts to quantify the impact of the Commission's action in a number of areas of activity, by employing a number of indicators on consumer savings resulting from the application of competition policy tools, surveys of citizens, consumers, businesses etc.

Individual speeches by the Commissioner or senior officials of DG Comp also aim to provide information on the Commission's activity and to explain current and future policy action and priorities.[185] Discussion papers or non-papers provide a detailed analysis by Commission officials or contractors of their current thinking in the interpretation of the various provisions of the Treaty.[186] In addition, the Commission publishes a monthly Competition Policy Newsletter, accessible on the Commission's website, which includes articles from members of DG Comp staff clarifying the Commission's reasoning in recent investigations or decisions,[187] competition weekly news summaries,[188] press releases.[189] DG Comp often commissions

181 Commission Notice on Immunity from fines and reduction of fines in cartel cases [2006] OJ C 298/17.

182 Council Regulation (EC) No 139/2004 on the control of concentrations between undertakings [2004] OJ L 24/1 [hereinafter Merger Regulation].

183 H Greene, 'Guideline Institutionalization: The Role of Merger Guidelines in Antitrust Discourse' (2006) 48(3) *William & Mary L Rev* 771.

184 See European Commission, Publications on EU competition policy, available at ec.europa.eu/competition/publications/index.html.

185 See European Commission, Competition publication: Articles and speeches, available at ec.europa.eu/competition/speeches/.

186 See eg the DG Competition discussion paper on the application of Article 82 of the Treaty to exclusionary abuses by dominant undertakings (December 2005), available at ec.europa.eu/competition/antitrust/art82/discpaper2005.pdf, published only on the Commission's website.

187 See European Commission, Competition publications, available at ec.europa.eu/competition/publications/cpn/.

188 See European Commission Newsroom, http://ec.europa.eu/newsroom/index.cfm.

189 See the European Commission's Press Release database, at europa.eu/rapid/searchResultAction.do?search=OK&query=comp&username=PROF&advanced=0&guiLanguage=en.

external reports and expert studies from experts,[190] or organizes workshops with the aim of gathering data on a specific policy area and to promote discussion on a projected reform programme.[191] DG Comp has also recently conducted and published a survey of how professional stakeholders and EU citizens more generally perceive the quality of the DG Comp's actions.[192]

1.1.2.1.2. National competition authorities

Since the enactment of Regulation 1/2003, national competition authorities have been more directly involved in the enforcement of EU competition law than they were under Regulation 17/62, in particular with regard to the application of Article 101(3) TFEU, which now has direct effect and in consequence can be enforced by national competition authorities and courts. The new legal exception regime adopted by Regulation 1/2003 establishes a system where the burden of competition law enforcement is shared between the Commission and national competition authorities.

National competition authorities act on their own initiative or following a complaint and have the power to require that the infringement be brought to an end, order interim measures, accept commitments, impose fines, periodic penalty payments, or any other penalty provided for in their national law.[193] However, the legal exception regime and the competences set forth by Article 5 of Regulation 1/2003 prevent the NCAs from adopting 'positive decisions' in the sense of clearance or exemption decisions, although some NCAs have taken the view that when deciding that there are no grounds for action on their part, they should declare the reasons for such decision—in the relevant cases—why the conditions of Article 101(3) met, such action have a declaratory rather than a constitutive function.[194]

Regulation 1/2003 requires NCAs to apply Articles 101 and 102 when they apply national competition law to collusive or unilateral practices.[195] The Member States are free to determine which body will enforce the EU competition law provisions and the procedure and mechanisms for investigations and for the enforcement of the decisions reached.[196] The Commission can, however, initiate proceedings, and this removes the competence of the Member States. The Member States may allocate different powers and functions to those different national authorities, whether administrative or judicial. The Commission's Notice on the cooperation within the network of competition authorities explains:

> The structure of the NCAs varies between Member States. In some Member States, one body investigates cases and takes all types of decisions. In other Member States, the functions are divided between two bodies, one which is in charge of the investigation of the case and another, often a college, which is responsible for deciding the case. Finally, in certain Member States, prohibition decisions and/or decisions imposing a fine can be taken only by a court: another competition authority acts as a prosecutor bringing the case before that court. Subject to the general principle of effectiveness, Article 35 of the Council Regulation

190 See eg European Commission, Merger control publications, available at ec.europa.eu/competition/mergers/studies_reports/studies_reports.html.

191 See, most recently, the workshop organized by the Commission on 26 January 2010, available at ec.europa.eu/competition/antitrust/actionsdamages/documents.html.

192 See European Commission, Eurobarometer—DG Competition Stakeholder Survey 2014, available at ec.europa.eu/competition/publications/reports/surveys_en.html.

193 Regulation 1/2003, Article 5.

194 See *MasterCard UK Members Forum Ltd and others v the Office of Fair Trading* [2006] CAT 14.

195 Regulation 1/2003, Article 3(1). 196 Ibid, Article 35.

> 1/2003 allows Member States to choose the body or bodies which will be designated as national competition authorities and to allocate functions between them. Under general principles of Community law, Member States are under an obligation to set up a system providing for sanctions which are effective, proportionate and dissuasive for infringements of [EU] law.[197]

The NCAs' role in the enforcement of EU competition law has been steadily rising,[198] following the Commission's relative disinvestment from active competition law enforcement in certain specific areas, such as vertical restraints, in order to focus on international cartel investigations,[199] State aids, and mergers following the decentralization of competition law enforcement in 2004. Many NCAs have also acquired the ability to adopt commitment decisions, as has the Commission since Regulation 1/2003, and have used this possibility actively in recent years.[200]

NCAs contribute also to the investigative capabilities of the European Commission. For example, Article 22 of Regulation 1/2003, enables national competition authorities to carry out inspections or other fact-finding measures on their territory on behalf and for the account of another competition authority (paragraph 1) and inspections upon request by the Commission (paragraph 2). In both cases, inspections under Article 22 are carried out in accordance with the national law of the Member State where the inspection or fact-finding measure takes place. The assisting authority may use all investigative tools at its disposal independently of the fact that they may differ from the investigative tools at the disposal of the requesting authority.

The European Competition Network (ECN) was established with the aim of promoting cooperation between the NCAs and in order to guarantee that as coordinator of the network the Commission would keep, a close eye on the enforcement of Articles 101 and 102 TFEU by the NCAs. The network is 'a forum for discussion and cooperation' between the NCAs and the Commission in the application and enforcement of EU competition policy, 'provides a framework for the cooperation of European competition authorities' in cases where Articles 101 and 102 TFEU are applied and 'is the basis for the creation and maintenance of a common competition culture in Europe'.[201]

Most recently, the Commission has been thinking about the reform of Regulation 1/2003 and has put forward proposals in March 2017 for a Directive 'empowering the national competition authorities to be more effective enforcers', noting that 'NCAs should, like the Commission, act in the general interest of the EU' (the so-called 'ECN+' initiative).[202] Directive (EU) 2019/1 of the European Parliament and of the Council of 11 December 2018

197 Commission Notice on cooperation within the Network of Competition Authorities [2004] OJ C 101/43, para 2.

198 See also Commission Staff Working Paper, Report on the Functioning of Regulation 1/2003, COM(2009) 206 final, documenting more than 1000 cases initiated between 2004 and 2009 by NCAs on the enforcement of EU competition law.

199 The re-centralization of the Commission's activity on cartel investigations constituted one of the principal aims of the reform: see 'Report on the functioning of Regulation 1/2003', Communication from the Commission to the European Parliament and the Council, COM(2009) 206 of 29 April 2009; Commission Staff Working Paper, SEC(2009) 574.

200 See Commission Staff Working Paper, Report on the Functioning of Regulation 1/2003, COM(2009) 206 final, para 190 and n 238; Commission Staff Working Document, Enhancing competition enforcement by the Member States' competition authorities: institutional and procedural issues, SWD(2014) 231/2, para 59 (noting 'the increasingly significant role played by commitment decisions in the ECN' and indicating that around 25 per cent of envisaged decisions by NCAs consisted in commitment decisions.

201 Commission Notice on cooperation within the Network of Competition Authorities [2004] OJ C 101/43, para 1.

202 Communication from the Commission to the European Parliament and the Council—Report on the functioning of Regulation 1/2003 {SEC(2009)574}, COM(2009) 206 final; Commission Staff Working Paper,

to empower the competition authorities of the Member States to be more effective enforcers and to ensure the proper functioning of the internal market, [2019] OJ L 11/3.

The ECN+ 2019/1 Directive was published in January 2019.[203] It goes beyond in harmonizing the enforcement tools at the disposal of NCAs, Regulation 1/2003 Regulation 1/2003 not including any provisions on procedure and sanctions for cases brought before the NCAs (with the limited exception of Article 5 Regulation 1/2003) and the procedural autonomy of Member States being only circumscribed by the general principles of equivalence and effectiveness. Directive 2019/1 covers the application of Articles 101 and 102 TFEU and the parallel application of domestic competition law by NCAs (Article 1(2) of the Directive). Article 4 of the Directive aims to guarantee the independence of NCAs, prohibiting, among other things, political or other external interference with the NCAs' decision making, or the fact that enforcers seek to take any instructions from government or any other public or private entity when carrying out their duties and exercising their powers for the application of Articles 101 and 102 TFEU, guaranteeing that national competition law enforcers will not be inappropriately dismissed, and including provisions for the prevention of conflicts of interests. Article 5 also aims to ensure that NCAs will be given 'a sufficient number of qualified staff and sufficient financial, technical and technological resources'. Articles 6 to 16 of the Directive grant the NCAs similar investigatory and decision-making powers as those enjoyed by the Commission under Regulation 1/2003. Articles 17–23 of the Directive contain provisions concerning leniency programmes. Of particular interest is Article 23 of the Directive on the interaction between individual sanctions and leniency programmes. Article 23(1) of the Directive provides that 'current and former directors, managers and other members of staff of applicants for immunity from fines to competition authorities are fully protected from sanctions imposed in administrative and non-criminal judicial proceedings, in relation to their involvement in the secret cartel covered by the application for immunity from fines, for violations of national laws that pursue predominantly the same objectives to those pursued by Article 101 TFEU' if certain conditions are satisfied. Article 23(2) of the Directive also provides criminal immunity to the same, under the same conditions, provided they cooperate with the prosecuting authority. However, Article 23(5) of the Directive provides that any immunity under Article 23 is without prejudice to a right to damages of those harmed by a competition infringement. Chapter VII (Articles 24–28) of the Directive includes rules on mutual legal assistance among NCAs and organize the process of such assistance in various circumstances. Article 29 of the Directive includes common rules for limitation periods for the imposition of fines and periodic penalty payments. Article 30 of the Directive reinforces the possibilities of NCAs to bring actions to the national courts and 'to

'Enhancing competition enforcement by the Member States' competition authorities: institutional and procedural issues' accompanying the Communication from the Commission (SWD(2014 231 final); Communication from the Commission, Ten Years of Antitrust Enforcement under Regulation 1/2003: Achievements and Future Perspectives (COM(2014) 453); DG Competition, Inception Impact Assessment 'Enhancing Competition in the EU for the benefit of businesses and consumers: reinforcement of the Application of EU Competition Law by National Competition Authorities' (2015); Proposal for a Directive to empower the competition authorities of the Member States to be more effective enforcers and to ensure the proper functioning of the Internal Market. Documentation is available here: http://ec.europa.eu/competition/antitrust/nca.html. On 30 May 2018, political agreement was reached by European Parliament and Council on the proposal put forward by the Commission. For a more detailed analysis of the functioning of the ECN, see the companion volume on enforcement and procedure: I Lianos, *Competition Law Enforcement and Procedure* (OUP, forthcoming 2019).

203 Directive (EU) 2019/1 of the European Parliament and of the Council of 11 December 2018 to empower the competition authorities of the Member States to be more effective enforcers and to ensure the proper functioning of the internal market, [2019] OJ L 11/3.

participate as appropriate as a prosecutor, defendant or respondent in [judicial] proceedings and to enjoy the same rights as such public parties to these proceedings'. Article 31 deals with access to the NCAs file by parties and limitations on the use of information, these provisions applying, not only as for the rest of the Directive when the NCAs enforce EU competition law, but they only apply national law (as the matter, for instance, does not affect trade between Member States). Article 32 of the Directive concerns the admissibility of evidence (in particular electronic) before NCAs. Finally, Article 33 of the Directive puts forward the development of the central information system of the ECN whose expenses will be borne by the general budget of the Union and provides the ECN the possibility to publish best practices on issues covered by the Directive. The Directive certainly constitutes an important step in the process of Europeanization of national competition law systems in Europe.

1.1.2.1.3. The European judiciary

The Court of Justice of the EU

The Court of Justice is composed of twenty-seven Judges and eight Advocates General. The Judges and Advocates General are appointed by common accord of the governments of the Member States after consultation of a panel responsible for giving an opinion on prospective candidates' suitability to perform the duties concerned. They are appointed for a term of office of six years or, when they take over on the retirement of a former judge, the remainder of his or her term, which is renewable. They are chosen from among individuals whose independence is beyond doubt and who possess the qualifications required for appointment, in their respective countries, to the highest judicial offices, or who are of recognized competence. The Judges of the Court of Justice elect one of themselves as President for a renewable term of three years. The President directs the work of the Court and presides at hearings and deliberations of the full Court or the Grand Chamber. The Advocates General assist the Court. They are responsible for presenting, with complete impartiality and independence, an 'opinion' in the cases assigned to them. The Registrar is the institution's secretary general and manages its departments under the authority of the President of the Court.

The Court may sit as a full court, in a Grand Chamber of thirteen Judges or in Chambers of three or five Judges. The Court sits as a full court in the particular cases prescribed by the Statute of the Court (including proceedings to dismiss the European Ombudsman or a Member of the European Commission who has failed to fulfil his or her obligations) and where the Court considers that a case is of exceptional importance. It sits in a Grand Chamber when a Member State or an institution that is a party to the proceedings so requests, and in particularly complex or important cases. Other cases are heard by Chambers of three or five Judges. The Presidents of the Chambers of five Judges are elected for three years, and those of the Chambers of three Judges for one year.

The Court of Justice interprets EU law to make sure it is applied in the same way in all EU countries. It also settles legal disputes between EU governments and EU institutions. Individuals, companies, or organizations can also bring cases before the Court if they feel their rights have been infringed by an EU institution. The Court of Justice has one judge per EU country. The Court is helped by eight 'advocates-general' whose job is to present opinions on the cases brought before the Court. They must do so publicly and impartially. Each judge and advocate general is appointed for a term of six years or for the remainder of the term of his predecessor, which can be renewed.[204] The governments of EU countries agree on whom

204 The smaller Member States share Advocates General. Their mandate cannot normally be renewed.

they want to appoint. To enable it properly to fulfil its task, the Court has been given clearly defined jurisdiction, which it exercises on references for preliminary rulings and in various other categories of proceedings.

From the various types of proceedings the following are of relevance to competition law:

- *References for preliminary rulings*: To ensure the effective and uniform application of European Union legislation and to prevent divergent interpretations, the national courts may, and sometimes must, refer to the Court of Justice and ask it to clarify a point concerning the interpretation of EU law, so that they may ascertain, for example, whether their national legislation complies with that law (Article 267 TFEU). A reference for a preliminary ruling may also seek the review of the validity of an act of EU law. The Court of Justice's reply is not merely an opinion, but takes the form of a judgment or reasoned order. The national court to which it is addressed, in deciding the dispute before it is, bound by the interpretation given. The Court's judgment likewise binds other national courts before which the same problem is raised.
- *Appeals*: Appeals on points of law may be brought only before the Court of Justice against judgments and orders of the General Court. If the appeal is admissible and well founded, the Court of Justice sets aside the judgment of the General Court. Where the state of the proceedings so permits, the Court of Justice may itself decide the case. Otherwise, it refers the case back to the General Court, which is bound by the decision given by the Court of Justice on the appeal. New points not raised in the pleadings or in the court below cannot be raised. They are said to be 'ultra petitio'.
- *Applications for interim measures*: Applications for interim measures seek suspension of the operation of measures which an institution has adopted and which form the subject-matter of an action, or any other interim order necessary to prevent serious and irreparable damage to a party.

The General Court

The General Court is made up of at least one Judge from each Member State (forty-six judges as of 4 October 2017). The Judges are appointed by common accord of the governments of the Member States after consultation of a panel responsible for giving an opinion on the candidates' suitability. They are appointed for a term of office of six years renewable or for the remainder of their predecessor's term. They appoint their President, for a period of three years, from amongst themselves. They appoint a Registrar for a term of office of six years. Unlike the Court of Justice, the General Court does not have permanent Advocates General and judges have operated as Advocates General only in the first few cases after the institution of the Court of First Instance (now General Court of the EU). The General Court sits in Chambers of five or three judges or, in some cases, as a single judge. It may also sit as a Grand Chamber (fifteen judges) or as a full court when this is justified by the legal complexity or importance of the case. More than 80 per cent of the cases brought before the General Court are heard by a Chamber of three judges. The Presidents of the Chambers of five judges are elected from amongst the judges for a period of three years.

The General Court has its own Registry, but uses the services of the Court of Justice for its other administrative and linguistic requirements. Among the different grounds of jurisdiction of the General Court that are relevant for competition law, are included:

- direct actions brought by natural or legal persons against acts of the institutions, bodies, offices, or agencies of the European Union (which are addressed to them or are of direct and individual concern to them) and against regulatory acts (which concern them directly and which do not entail implementing measures) or against a failure to act on the part of those institutions, bodies, offices, or agencies; for example, a case brought by a company against a Commission decision imposing a fine on that company;

- actions brought by the Member States against the Commission.

There are provisions for penalties (Article 261 TFEU) different from those for actions for annulment of Commission's decisions (Article 263 TFEU) or failures to act (Article 265 TFEU). The rulings made by the General Court may be subject, within two months, to an appeal, limited to points of law, to the Court of Justice. The General Court has its own Rules of Procedure. In general, the proceedings include a written phase and an oral phase. An application, drawn up by a lawyer or agent and sent to the Registry, opens the proceedings. The main causes of the action are published in a notice, in all official languages, in the Official Journal of the European Union. The Registrar sends the application to the other party to the case, which then has a period within which to file a defence. Within a certain time limit, the applicant may file a reply, to which the defendant may respond with a rejoinder.

Any person, and any body, office, or agency of the European Union, who/which can prove an interest in the outcome of a case before the General Court, as well as the Member States and the institutions of the European Union, may intervene in the proceedings. The intervener submits a statement in intervention, supporting or opposing the claims of one of the parties, to which the parties may then respond. In some cases, the intervener may also submit its observations at the oral phase.

Before the hearing, the Juge-Rapporteur summarizes, in a report for the hearing, the facts relied on and the arguments of each party and, if applicable, of the interveners. This document is available to the public in the language of the case, but in no other, not even French which is the language of the court.

During the *oral phase* a public hearing is held. When the parties have been heard, usually through their lawyers, the Judges can put questions to the parties' representatives. The standard of the judges' questions is very high. The Judges then deliberate on the basis of a draft judgment prepared by the Juge-Rapporteur and the final order is delivered at a public hearing. The reasons are made available to the public when the judgment is given.

Interim measures: An action brought before the General Court does not suspend the operation of the contested act. The Court may, however, order suspension or another interim measure. The President of the General Court or, if necessary, another Judge rules on the application for interim measures in a reasoned order.

Interim measures are granted only if three conditions are met: (i) the action in the main proceedings must appear, at first sight, to be well founded; (ii) the applicant must show that the measures are urgent and that it would suffer serious and irreparable harm without them; (iii) the interim measures must take account of the balance of the parties' interests and of public interest. The order is provisional in nature and in no way prejudges the decision of the General Court in the main proceedings. In addition, an appeal against it may be brought before the Court of Justice.

Expedited procedure: This procedure allows the General Court to rule quickly on the substance of the dispute in cases considered to be particularly urgent. The expedited procedure may be requested by the applicant or by the defendant. The language used for the application, which may be any one of the twenty-four official languages of the European Union, will be the language of the case (without prejudice to the application of specific provisions). The proceedings in the oral phase of the procedure are simultaneously interpreted, as necessary, into different official languages of the European Union. The Judges deliberate, without interpreters, in a common language which, traditionally, is French.

National courts as EU judges

The competition rules, like many others in the Treaty, were incorporated into the law of the six original Member States—Belgium, France, Germany, Italy, Luxembourg, and the Netherlands—on the establishment of the Common Market, although the first implementing regulation was adopted only in 1962. The rules became part of the law of the first three new Member States (the United Kingdom, Denmark, and the Republic of Ireland) by dint of their accession to the Community at the beginning of 1973. They applied to Greece on its accession at the end of 1980, to Spain and Portugal from 1986, and to Austria, Finland, and Sweden from the beginning of 1995. Similar rules also apply throughout the European Economic Area (EEA)—Norway, Iceland and Liechtenstein—as well as the members of the European Union. The new Member States from Eastern Europe and the Mediterranean had already introduced laws based on Article 101 and 102 TFEU, and became subject to those Articles when they acceded to the EU Treaty. National courts therefore are brought to implement EU law acting as an organ of EU law, and not only in their role as national judge.[205]

The prohibitions in Articles 101 and 102 have direct effect in the law of Member States and give rise to actions in tort in national courts.[206] It is for national law to establish procedural rules, such as which court has jurisdiction, but the remedy must be efficacious, and no worse than that available for infringement of national law. In the UK, the House of Lords held in *Garden Cottage Foods v Milk Marketing Board* that the appropriate action would be for breach of statutory duty.[207]

In *Peterbroeck*,[208] the CJEU ruled that a national court could not be prevented by domestic rules of procedure from considering of its own motion whether a measure of domestic law is compatible with a provision of EU law.

In *Leclerc v Commission*,[209] the General Court stated that, according to consistent case law, national courts could apply Article 101(1) as a result of its direct effect. Consequently, a dealer wrongly excluded from a selective distribution system can bring an action before national courts or before national authorities

Contractual provisions with the object or effect of restricting competition are void and national courts should not enforce them.[210] This gives rise to considerable difficulty, as it may be necessary to analyse the market in order to assess the effect on competition of an agreement or the conduct of a dominant firm. Frequently, it may not be simple to tell whether a provision infringes Article 101 TFEU or may be enforced.

A Directive on antitrust damages actions was adopted in November 2014 with the aim of promoting actions for damages against infringements of EU competition law in front of national courts, in order to ensure a more effective compensation of the victims of antitrust violations and to increase deterrence for would-be violators.[211]

There is considerable concern about the ability of many national judges to appraise matters of economic law.

Under Article 267 TFEU, a national court may request the CJEU for a preliminary ruling on the interpretation of EU law or the validity of subordinate legislation. Judgments given under

205 According to the well-known theory of 'role splitting' or '*dédoublement fonctionnel*'.

206 Case C-453/99, *Courage v Crehan* [2001] ECR I–62976.

207 *Garden Cottage Foods v Milk Marketing Board* [1984] AC 130. For more information, see the analysis in the companion volume: I Lianos, *Competition Law Enforcement and Procedure* (OUP, forthcoming 2019).

208 Case C-312/93, *Peterbroeck, Van Campenhout & Cie v Belgian State* [1995] ECR I–4599; Joined Cases C-430 & 431/93, *Van Schijndel* [1995] ECR I–4705.

209 Case T-19/92, *Yves Saint Lauren* [1996] ECR II–995; Case T-88/92, *Givenchy* [1996] ECR II–1961, para 122.

210 Case 55/65, *Société la Technique Minière v Machinenbau Ulm* [1966] ECR 235, at 250.

211 Directive 2014/104/EU of the European Parliament and of the Council of 26 November 2014 on certain rules governing actions for damages under national law for infringements of the competition law provisions of the Member States and of the European Union, [2014] OJ L 349/1.

Article 267 TFEU are, by and large, less helpful than those given on an appeal from a decision of the Commission. The CJEU is required to give an abstract ruling rather than apply it to the facts, although, on occasion, it has applied the law.

1.1.2.1.4. Other actors involved in the EU competition law process

The European Commission is subject to an external mechanism of administrative control, ensuring its political accountability and its compliance with principles of good administration.

First, advisory committees ensure the involvement of Member States in the development of EU competition law. An Advisory Committee on Restrictive Practices and Dominant Positions, composed by representatives of national competition authorities, is consulted on all draft decisions of the European Commission and prepares an opinion on the draft decision, which is not, however, binding on the Commission but which is disclosed to the parties concerned by the Commission's investigation. The Committee attends oral hearings and is consulted on legislative proposals in the area of antitrust law and merger control (in the last case the advice is issued by the Advisory Committee on Concentrations).

Second, the Economic and Social Committee, an advisory body representing various societal groups, such as employers, trade unions, consumers, small and medium undertakings comprises a specific section dealing with 'Single Market, Production and Consumption', which addresses competition policy.[212] The Committee may be consulted on legislative proposals by the Commission, the Council, and the European Parliament, or it may issue an opinion on its own initiative. The Committee also issues an opinion every year on the Commission's Annual Report on Competition Policy.

Article 228 TFEU empowers the European Ombudsman also to receive complaints on alleged instances of maladministration and to open an inquiry if the complainant has put forward sufficient evidence on facts that, in addition, have not been or are not the subject of legal proceedings.[213] The concept of maladministration has a broader scope than the principle of legality. Recently, in *Intel*, the Ombudsman examined the scope of the European Commission's discretion in not taking minutes of meetings with third parties where inculpatory or exculpatory evidence might have been collected. It found that the Commission's failure to take notes of a meeting with a senior Dell representative (the complainant) was an act of 'maladministration' and could also be considered to be a breach of Intel's rights of defence, in case that evidence was not previously at the disposal of the Commission and the Commission made use of it in its eventual decision.[214]

Finally, the Council of the European Union and of the European Parliament in the design of EU competition policy and indirectly the activity of the European Commission in this area. Both have adopted legislation of paramount importance for the enforcement of EU competition law (eg Regulation 1/2003, block exemption regulations, the Merger regulation).

The Committee of Permanent Representatives (COREPER) at the Council follows up the activity of the European Commission.

212 See European Economic and Social Committee, Single Market, Production and Consumption (INT) http://www.eesc.europa.eu/?i=portal.en.int-section.

213 For an analysis, see PN Diamandouros, 'Improving EU Competition Law Procedures by Applying Principles of Good Administration: The Role of the Ombudsman' (2010) 1(5) *J European Competition L & Practice* 379.

214 Decision of the European Ombudsman, Case 1935/2008/FOR, available at www.ombudsman.europa.eu/cases/summary.faces/en/4399/html.bookmark. See also, for examples of other decisions of the Ombudsman in competition cases, Case 2953/2008/FOR, available at www.ombudsman.europa.eu/cases/summary.faces/en/5416/html.bookmark; Case 3699/2006/ELB, available at www.ombudsman.europa.eu/cases/decision.faces/en/4752/html.bookmark.

The 'Competitiveness Council', established in 2002 is a formation of the Council of the EU. Depending on the items on the agenda, this Council is composed of European Affairs Ministers, Industry Ministers, Research Ministers, etc. It meets about five or six times a year. The Competitiveness Council assumes a horizontal role in ensuring an integrated approach to the enhancement of competitiveness and growth in Europe, by reviewing horizontal and sectoral competitiveness issues, ensuring that competitiveness is integrated in all actions and legislative proposals.

Two Committees at the European Parliament oversee the Commission's activities in the area of competition policy: the Committee on Internal Market and Consumer Protection and the Committee on Economic and Monetary Affairs.

The Commission reports to the European Parliament every year as to the outcomes of its competition policy and enforcement activities. The Report allows a review of whether the objectives identified in the Plan have been attained.[215]

The European Parliament also adopts each year a resolution on the Commission's Annual Report on Competition Policy and comments on all proposals of the European Commission.

1.1.2.2. The UK competition law process

The UK competition law regime was overhauled with the enactment of the Competition Act in 1998, a few years later by the Enterprise Act 2002 and more recently by the Enterprise and Regulatory Reform Act 2013, which proceeded to the merger of the two administrative authorities previously in charge of competition law enforcement, the Office of Fair Trading (OFT) and the Competition Commission (CoCo) into the unitary Competition and Markets Authority, and by the Consumer Rights Act 2015.

The new framework establishes an administrative structure of competition law enforcement with the addition of regulators each responsible for a particular product, such as energy or telecommunications and a specialized tribunal, the Competition Appeal Tribunal (CAT). It is interesting to note that although the UK competition law system is close to the integrated agency model, as is the case with EU competition law, with a unitary competition enforcement authority, the CMA, in practice the UK competition law regime functions as a quasi-prosecutorial model, in view of the extensive judicial scrutiny of the competition law decisions of the CMA by a specialized tribunal, the CAT. Although the choice of the term 'quasi-prosecutorial' may appear excessive, in view of the fact that the CMA takes full and final decisions, including the imposition of a penalty and if there is an appeal, the CAT considers the CMA decision only as regards those aspects challenged in the appeal—most often not every aspect of the decision, in practice the strict scrutiny of the CMA's decisions by the CAT may have deterred a more aggressive competition law enforcement agenda by the CMA and its predecessor, the OFT. In the context of the ERRA 2013 reform, the government's initial proposals included the option to move to a more prosecutorial model with the CMA initiating the case and with the Competition Appeal Tribunal adjudicating the case at first instance. This proposal was ultimately rejected in the process of reform leading to enactment of the ERRA 2013, the government opting instead for the creation of an internal tribunal within the CMA (the CMA panel) to act as a decision maker in investigations into breaches of the civil prohibitions of anti-competitive agreements and abuse of dominance. Following a request for proposals for legislative and institutional reforms to protect consumer rights and improve market confidence by the Secretary of State for Business, Energy and Industrial Strategy, Lord Tyrie, chairman of

215 See Report on competition policy 2009, published on 3 June 2010, available at ec.europa.eu/competition/publications/annual_report/2009/en.pdf.

the CMA, suggested a number of radical reforms of the UK competition law system.[216] Among them is the proposal to amend the standard of review of the CMA's Competition Act decisions, reverting to a judicial review standard or to another standard of review as opposed to 'full-merits' review by the CAT in order to reduce the duration of the appeal process and improve the effectiveness of the CMA to bring cases in particular in digital markets.

1.1.2.2.1. *The Secretary of State*

Among his various duties, the Secretary of State (S of S) for Business, Enterprise and Industrial Strategy (BEIS) (previously Business, Innovation and Skills) makes most of the senior appointments in competition law (the members of the Board of the CMA, the ordinary members of the CAT) and designates bodies which represent consumers to make 'super-complaints' under section 11 of the Enterprise Act 2002. The S of S has the power to make a market investigation reference on public interest grounds, alongside competition issues. The S of S intervenes also in merger control, having the power to amend the time limits for making merger references, but also for making and completing market investigation references. Under sections 3(2)–(5) and 19(2)–(4) of the CA98, the S of S may amend Schedules 1 and 3 of the Competition Act and adopt exclusions for agreements from either or both prohibitions (Chapters I and II) on grounds of compliance with international obligations or exceptional and compelling reasons of public policy. Furthermore, since the ERRA Act 2013, the S of S is able to make a sectoral regulator order removing the concurrent powers given to a regulator to enforce the CA98. The S of S is also charged with conducting a review of the operation of the Competition Act post-ERRA 2013 reform, and publish a report on the outcome of that review within five years of the transfer of the relevant functions of the OFT to the CMA.

The Consumer and Competition Policy Directorate at the BEIS is in charge of all aspects of competition law and policy. In the exercise of his functions, he is assisted by a Parliamentary Under-Secretary of State for Employment Relations, Consumer and Postal Affairs.

While ERRA 2013 enhanced the independence of the Competition and Markets Authority, which may fulfil its tasks within the context of its primary duty to seek to promote competition, both within and outside the United Kingdom, for the benefit of consumers,[217] the Department for Business, Innovation and Skills (now BEIS) also published a ministerial statement of strategic priorities for the CMA (the so-called 'Strategic steer'), initially intended to provide guidance for a period of three years (2014–17) and requesting the CMA to focus its work on some high level priorities. However, the 'Strategic steer' document also stressed that 'there will be a presumption that all recommendations [of the CMA] will be accepted unless there are strong policy reasons not to do so'.[218]

There have been some limited instances of political influence or interference by the government on the work of the UK competition authorities in the past, since the adoption of the Competition Act 1998 (OFT, Competition Commission). An example is the acquisition by the banking group Lloyds of competing banking group HBOS. Normally, a merger of this size and scale should have been referred by the Office of Fair Trading, to the Competition

216 Letter of Lord Tyrie to the Secretary of State for Business, Energy and Industrial Strategy (February 21, 2019), available at https://assets.publishing.service.gov.uk/government/uploads/system/uploads/attachment_data/file/781151/Letter_from_Andrew_Tyrie_to_the_Secretary_of_State_BEIS.pdf, p. 2 (noting that 'businesses [...] [may] "game the system", resulting in unduly long and costly proceedings') & 36.

217 Enterprise and Regulatory Reform Act, 2013 c 14, section 25(3).

218 Department for Business, Innovation & Skills (now BEIS), Competition Regime: Response to Consultation on Statement of Strategic Priorities for the CMA (1 October 2013), Annex 1, available at www.gov.uk/government/uploads/system/uploads/attachment_data/file/245607/bis-13-1210-competition-regime-response-to-consultation-on-statement-of-strategic-priorities-for-the-cma.pdf.

Commission for a full inquiry into the effects on competition before it could be cleared. The OFT had found that the merger situation would be expected to result in a 'substantial lessening of competition within a market or markets in the United Kingdom for goods or services, including personal current accounts, banking services to small- and medium-sized enterprises, and mortgages and that further inquiry by the Competition Commission was necessary. However, in this case, the Secretary of State for Business and Enterprise opposed this referral, stating that the public interest of ensuring the stability of the UK financial system outweighed competition concerns raised by the OFT and as such, the merger did not need to be referred.[219]

1.1.2.2.2. The Lord Chancellor

The Lord Chancellor is responsible for appointing the President of the CAT and the panel of chairmen, pursuant to a recommendation from the Judicial Appointments Commission. By virtue of section 16(1)–(4) of the Enterprise Act 2002, the Lord Chancellor may make provision enabling the civil courts in England and Wales to transfer to the CAT for its determination cases based on an infringement decision of the European Commission, of the CMA, or sectoral regulators under Articles 101 and/or 102 TFEU or the Chapter I and II prohibitions.

1.1.2.2.3. The Competition and Markets Authority

The central institution for the enforcement of competition law in the UK is the Competition and Markets Authority, which was formally established on 1 April 2014. ERRA 2013 had abolished the two previous competition authorities in the UK, the Office of Fair Trading and the Competition Commission, and transferred their powers to the CMA. The merger of the two authorities was considered necessary in view of the need to eliminate the duplication and inefficiencies caused by the division of responsibility for competition enforcement between two competition authorities. It formed part of a major government initiative for abolishing or merging a large number of quasi-non-governmental organizations (quangos). According to the government's policy paper on the reform, the Competition and Markets Authority will ensure greater coherence in competition enforcement and a more streamlined approach to decision-making, but also a single strong centre of competition expertise which will provide national and international leadership.

The CMA consists in an independent regulatory agency (a non-ministerial department, in the UK jargon) led by a board consisting of a (non-executive) chairman and no fewer than four other members, appointed by the Secretary of State. The S of S also appoints a Chief executive of the CMA, who may not be the same person as the chairman or another member of the Board. The Board ensures that the CMA fulfils its statutory duties and functions and establishes the overall strategic direction of the CMA, putting forward proposals for the CMA annual plan. An innovation introduced by ERRA 2013 is the constitution of the CMA panel, comprising senior, independent members, who are appointed by the Department for BIS and whose function is to conduct a Phase 2 merger and market inquiries and regulatory appeals. The S of S designates a chair of the CMA panel and inquiry chairs who chair Phase 2 merger and market inquiries and regulatory appeals in relation to price controls, terms of licences, or other regulatory arrangements. Each panel group has at least three members. CMA panel groups can act independently of the CMA board.

The CMA has a duty to seek to promote competition, both within and outside the UK, for the benefit of the consumer. The CMA is responsible for enforcing the provisions against

[219] An action against the S of S's decision not to refer the merger examined by the Competition Appeal Tribunal failed: *Merger Action Group v Secretary of State for Business, Enterprise and Regulatory Reform* [2008] CAT 36.

anti-competitive agreements and abuses of dominant position, merger control, for conducting market studies, and for investigating and prosecuting cartels under the criminal law.

The CMA may take decisions to open a formal investigation if there are reasonable grounds for suspecting that one or more of the relevant prohibitions of the Competition Act 1998 has been infringed. When exercising its powers to enforce the provisions against anti-competitive agreements and abuses of dominant position, the CMA can investigate, hear the evidence, and make a decision imposing a sanction or a remedy. The CMA's decisions can be challenged before a specialized judicial body, the Competition Appeal Tribunal. Under section 36 of the CA98, the CMA has discretion to impose hefty financial penalties on an undertaking that has intentionally or negligently infringed the provisions of the CA98 or Articles 101 and 102 TFEU. Sections 38(1) and 38(1A) of the Competition Act require the CMA to prepare and publish guidance as to the appropriate amount of a penalty, including guidance as to the circumstances in which, in determining a penalty, the CMA may take into account the effects of an infringement in another Member State. This may of course change as a result of Brexit. Section 38(2) of the Act provides that the CMA may alter the guidance on penalties at any time. Section 38(3) of the Act provides that, if altered, the CMA must publish the guidance as altered. Under section 38(4), the Secretary of State must approve any guidance on penalties before it can be published. The CMA is required to have regard to the guidance for the time being in force when setting the amount of any penalty to be imposed. Although there is no equivalent statutory obligation on the Regulators to publish guidance as to the appropriate amount of a penalty, the Regulators are required to have regard to the guidance for the time being in force when setting the amount of any penalty to be imposed. The CMA has adopted guidance as to appropriate amounts of penalty.[220] The amount of fines is limited to 10 per cent of the undertaking's worldwide turnover. The method of calculating fines is clearly explained by CMA Guidance. The Guidance also sets a leniency policy, which is further explained in specific detailed guidelines published by the CMA.

Since the enactment of the Enterprise Act 2002, the CMA has also been empowered to investigate the existence of the cartel offence, provided by section 188 of the Enterprise Act. Indeed, the CMA has the primary responsibility for investigating breaches of the cartel offence although in the investigation and prosecution of such offences it will act in partnership with the Serious Fraud Office in England and Wales, or with the Lord Advocate in Scotland. The CMA has been granted power to apply to the court for disqualification of company directors when their company breaches competition law and their behaviour makes them unfit to be directors.

The CMA may decide to investigate a suspected infringement of the CA98 and/or Articles 101–2 TFEU, as well as a suspected commission of the cartel offence (parallel proceedings), which raises a number of complexities.[221]

The review of the mergers under the Enterprise Act 2002 regime is divided in two phases. During Phase 1, a CMA case team examines if a completed or anticipated merger has to be referred for a Phase 2 review. The CMA has a duty to refer, with some limited exceptions, whether the merger situation (existing or in the making) results or may be expected to result in a substantial lessening of competition (SLC) on any market(s) in the UK. If the merger is referred for Phase 2 review, a CMA Inquiry group has to decide on the balance

220 CMA73, Appropriate CA98 penalty calculation (18 April 2018), available at https://www.gov.uk/government/publications/appropriate-ca98-penalty-calculation.

221 These will be examined in more detail in the companion volume on enforcement: I Lianos, *Competition Law Enforcement and Procedure* (OUP, forthcoming 2019).

of probabilities if there actually is a SLC and eventually the necessary remedies in order to prevent or mitigate that risk. Prior to the changes introduced by ERRA 2013, Phase 2 of the merger review was performed by a separate authority, the Competition Commission, which was institutionally independent of the authority in charge of the investigation during Phase 1, the Office of Fair Trading.

Introduced by the Enterprise Act 2002, the Market Investigations regime enables the UK competition authorities to examine whether competition is in fact prevented, restricted, or distorted by 'features' of markets, rather than by specific market conduct, as the case for the Chapter I and II CA98 prohibitions, and to adopt wide-ranging structural or behavioural remedies. Prior to ERRA 2013, the OFT (and sectoral regulators) were granted the power to conduct, at a first stage, reviews of markets and to refer them, at a second stage, for a more detailed investigation by the Competition Commission. Since ERRA 2013, the two stages are conducted within the same authority, the CMA, the decision to initiate the first stage of the investigation being made by the CMA board, while the detailed review at the second stage is conducted by a CMA Inquiry Group appointed by the CMA panel chair.

The CMA also exercises competition law powers under a number of specific regimes.[222]

In addition to being a competition authority, the CMA has also major responsibilities in the field of consumer protection,[223] under the Consumer Rights Act 2015 (unfair contract terms),[224] the Consumer Protection from Unfair Trading Regulations Act 2008,[225] Part 8 of the Enterprise Act 2002,[226] or the Consumer Protection Cooperation Regulation.[227]

The CMA is accountable to the public through Parliamentary scrutiny in the House of Commons and its select committees,[228] and its annual accounts are audited by the National Audit Office, which also reports on its activity.[229] According to its Performance Management Framework,[230] the CMA is obliged 'to achieving direct financial benefit to consumers of at least ten times the cost

222 The CMA may conduct regulatory appeals and references in relation to price controls, terms of licences, or other regulatory arrangements under sector specific legislation (gas, electricity, water, post, communications, aviation, rail, and health).

223 On CMA's consumer protection powers, see CMA58, Consumer protection: enforcement guidance, available at www.gov.uk/government/uploads/system/uploads/attachment_data/file/546521/cma58-consumer-protection-enforcement-guidance.pdf.

224 See Consumer Rights Act 2015, c 15, available at www.legislation.gov.uk/ukpga/2015/15/contents/enacted (giving consumers rights and remedies when traders supply goods, digital content or services and also protects consumers against unfair terms in consumer contracts and unfair notices).

225 See The Consumer Protection from Unfair Trading Regulations 2008, No 1277, available at www.legislation.gov.uk/uksi/2008/1277/contents/made (implementing the Unfair Commercial Practices Directive in the UK and including a general duty not to trade unfairly and seek to ensure that traders act honestly and fairly towards consumers. The Act applies primarily to business to consumer practices (but elements of business to business practices are also covered where they affect, or are likely to affect, consumers).

226 Providing the CMA powers to seek court orders against businesses that breach a range of specific laws protecting consumers: see Enterprise Act 2002, c 40, Part 8, available at www.legislation.gov.uk/ukpga/2002/40/part/8.

227 Regulation (EC) No 2006/ 2004 of the European Parliament and of the Council of 27 October 2004 on cooperation between national authorities responsible for the enforcement of consumer protection laws [2004] OJ L 364/1.

228 See, for instance, the report of the Committee of Public Accounts, Enforcing Competition in Markets, HC (2005–6).

229 See National Audit Office, The Office of Fair Trading: Enforcing competition in markets, HC (2005–6).

230 See Department for Business, Innovation & Skills (now BEIS), Competition and Markets Authority: Performance Management Framework (January 2014), available at www.gov.uk/government/uploads/system/uploads/attachment_data/file/274146/bis-14-559-competition-and-markets-authority-performance-management-framework.pdf.

to the taxpayer' (measured over a rolling three-year period), this calculation being regularly performed in the context of the Impact Assessment, annexed to the CMA's annual report.[231]

Reports of the National Audit Office had criticized the CMA's predecessor, OFT, for the way it decided priorities, its lack of operational transparency, and poor communication with the parties. In response to these criticisms, the OFT published 'Prioritisation Principles' in October 2008 and launched a transparency review in 2009, which led to a statement on the OFT's approach in May 2010, providing for additional OFT's commitments to transparency and a clear explanation of how the OFT interacts with the media. The CMA continued this trend by adopting its prioritization principles in April 2014.[232] The CMA also publishes a Strategic assessment setting out its medium term priorities and exploring the main risks to consumers and to the efficient functioning of markets across the UK economy.

In its effort to promote a clear understanding of the law and increase legal certainty with positive decisions, the CMA's predecessor, the OFT, had initiated the 'short-form opinion process', under which it provided guidance, within a prompt timetable, to businesses seeking clarity on how the law applies to prospective collaboration agreements, having a material link with the UK, or between competitors which raise novel or unresolved competition issues. This process has been used in response to feedback from business that some potentially beneficial collaboration between companies is not proceeding owing to concerns about infringing competition law, which carries civil and in some circumstances criminal sanctions. The process involved parties submitting a mutually agreed statement of facts. The CMA continues this trend and has adopted specific guidance on its approach to short-form opinions.[233]

1.1.2.2.4. The sector-specific regulators

In addition to the CMA, the UK legislator has chosen a regime of concurrent jurisdiction with regard to the application of EU and national competition law by sector-specific regulators in their area of competence. The Civil Aviation Authority (CAA),[234] the Office for Communications (OFCOM),[235] Monitor (now part of the National Health Service (NHS) Improvement),[236] the Gas and Electricity Markets Authority (OFGEM),[237] the Water Services Regulation Authority (OFWAT),[238] the Office of Rail and Road (ORR),[239] the Northern Ireland Authority for Utility Regulation (NIAUR),[240] the Financial Conduct Authority (FCA), and the Payment Systems Regulator, which was incorporated as a subsidiary of the FCA on 1 April 2014, have concurrent

231 For the latest one, see CMA's annual report and impact assessment 2016 to 2017, available at https://www.gov.uk/government/publications/cma-impact-assessment-2016-to-2017.

232 CMA16, Prioritisation Principles for the CMA, available at www.gov.uk/government/uploads/system/uploads/attachment_data/file/299784/CMA16.pdf.

233 CMA27, Guidance on the CMA's approach to Short-form Opinions, available at www.gov.uk/government/uploads/system/uploads/attachment_data/file/301112/CMA_s_approach_to_Short-form_opinions.pdf.

234 Concerning agreements or conduct relating to the provision of airport operation services and the supply of air traffic services.

235 Concerning agreements or conduct relating to activities connected to electronic communications, broadcasting, and postal services matters.

236 Concerning agreements or conduct relating to the provision of health care services in England.

237 Concerning agreements or conduct relating to shipping, conveyance or supply of gas, and activities ancillary thereto or connected with the generation, transmission, or supply of electricity.

238 Concerning agreements or conduct relating to commercial activities connected with the supply of water or securing a supply of water or with the provision or securing of sewerage services.

239 Concerning agreements or conduct relating to the supply of services relating to railways.

240 Concerning agreements or conduct relating to commercial activities connected with the generation, transmission, or supply of electricity in Northern Ireland, the supply of water or securing a supply of water, or with the provision or securing of sewerage services in Northern Ireland and the conveyance, storage, or supply of gas in Northern Ireland.

powers for the enforcement of EU and UK competition law. The Regulators have all the powers of the CMA to apply and enforce Articles 101 and 102 TFEU and the CA98 in order to deal with anti-competitive agreements or abuses of a dominant position which relate to activities in relation to their respective sectors, including the possibility to consider complaints about possible infringements of any of Article 101 of the TFEU, Article 102 of the TFEU, the Chapter I and/or Chapter II CA98 prohibitions, carry out investigations both on the Regulator's own initiative and in response to complaints, impose financial penalties, taking account of the statutory guidance on penalties issued by the CMA, accept commitments that are binding on an undertaking, agree to settle a case, to carry out market studies, and make market investigation references in their respective sectors under Part 4 of the EA 2002.

The concurrent jurisdiction is exercised according to a process set by the Competition Act (Concurrency) Regulations 2014,[241] which determines which body is well placed to act in a particular case of an alleged breach of competition law. The CMA has published Guidelines on concurrency,[242] setting the general framework about the affected regulated sectors by the concurrency provisions and the scope of the concurrent powers, the sector regulators have adopted more specific guidance on their competition enforcement powers in a number of regulated sectors, and a number of memoranda of understanding between the CMA and the sector regulators were set out in order to coordinate work, avoid duplication of effort, and enable the best practice sharing.[243] ERRA 2013 also introduced a number of measures to improve the use of general competition powers in the regulated sectors and to improve coordination between the authorities which have those powers. According to the S of S strategic steer to the CMA, 'the CMA should engage in a broad strategic dialogue with the Regulators and look for opportunities to promote effective competition'.[244] ERRA 2013 also allowed the S of S to make an order to remove the competition functions from a sector regulator if it is considered that it is appropriate to do so for the purpose of promoting competition, within any market or markets in the UK, for the benefit of consumers. This power applies to all sectoral regulators with concurrent competition powers except Monitor, which does not have a duty to promote competition but acts to prevent anti-competitive behaviour where this is against patients' interests.

The UK Competition Network (UKCN) is a forum of the CMA and all the sector specific regulators in the area of competition law. The Monitor is not a member of the UKCN but has the status of observer. The network aims to encourage stronger competition for the benefit of consumers and to prevent anti-competitive behaviour in the regulated industries.[245]

1.1.2.2.5. The Competition Appeal Tribunal

By virtue of the Enterprise Act 2002, an independent specialized judicial body, the Competition Appeal Tribunal, with cross-disciplinary expertise in law, economics, business

[241] See SI 2014/536 made on 6 March 2014 and came into force on 1 April 2014, available at http://www.legislation.gov.uk/uksi/2014/536/contents/made.

[242] CMA10, Guidance on concurrent application of competition law to regulated industries (March 2014), available at www.gov.uk/government/uploads/system/uploads/attachment_data/file/288958/CMA10_Guidance_on_concurrent_application_of_competition_law_to_regulated_industries.pdf.

[243] See UK Competition Network Statement of Intent (3 December 2013), available at https://www.gov.uk/government/publications/uk-competition-network-statement-of-intent.

[244] Department for Business, Innovation & Skills (now BEIS), Strategic steer for the Competition and Markets Authority 2014–17, in Annex 1 to its Response to consultation on statement of specific priorities for the CMA, 1 October 2013, paras 6 and 9.

[245] For more information on the UKCN, see www.gov.uk/government/groups/uk-competition-network.

and accountancy has been established, in order to hear appeals against appealable decisions of now the CMA and of the sector-specific regulators that have concurrent powers, under the CA98 and Articles 101 and 102 TFEU.[246] The CAT can also hear actions for damages and monetary claims arising from infringement decisions made by the UK competition authorities or the European Commission. Schedule 8 of the Consumer Rights Act 2015 allows parties to bring a claim in respect of an infringement or alleged infringement of EU and/or UK competition law for stand-alone claims for damages, any other sum of money, and/or injunctions to be brought before the CAT. This considerably expanded the CAT's role from an appellate body with limited jurisdiction to that of a judicial body with full jurisdiction to determine issues of liability and quantum in the field of competition law.[247] Of course, stand-alone claims may be brought also in front of ordinary civil courts (see Section 1.1.2.2.6). The CAT has exclusive jurisdiction to hear collective proceedings for damages enabling defined classes of claimants, such as consumers or small and medium-sized enterprises, to seek damages from undertakings found to have infringed EU and/or UK competition law. This 'opt out' collective actions regime was introduced by the Consumer Rights Act 2015. The CAT can also hear and decide applications against decisions made by the Secretary of State and the CMA in respect of merger and market investigations under the Enterprise Act 2002. It can also hear appeals against certain decisions made by OFCOM and/or the Secretary of State for infringements of the Communications Act 2003 or under the Mobile EU Roaming Regulations 2007.

A further appeal on a point of law or as to the amount of a penalty lies from decisions of the Tribunal either on a point of law or in penalty cases as to the imposition or the amount of any penalty lies to the Court of Appeal in relation to proceedings in England and Wales, to the Court of Session for Scotland and the Court of Appeal in Northern Ireland for proceedings in Northern Ireland. Such a further appeal may only be made with the permission of the Tribunal or the relevant appellate court. From the Court of Appeal, a further appeal may be brought, with permission, to the UK Supreme Court. The CAT may also refer a preliminary ruling question to the Court of Justice of the EU.

The CAT consists of a President, who is appointed by the Lord Chancellor (upon the recommendation of the Judicial Appointments Commission) and must appear to the Lord Chancellor to have appropriate experience and knowledge of competition law and practice, and two panels: a panel of chairmen appointed by the Lord Chancellor following a recommendation from the Judicial Appointments Commission and a panel of ordinary members appointed by the Secretary of State. Cases commenced on or after 1 October 2015 are governed by the Competition Appeal Tribunal Rules 2015.[248]

The intensity of judicial assessment varies according to the decisions brought to the attention of the CAT. If these decisions relate to the enforcement of Articles 101 and 102 TFEU or of their national equivalent (such as Chapters I and II CA98), or concern the cancelling or withdrawal of

246 By virtue of the Competition Act 1998, the CAT formed part of the Competition Commission but became an independent judicial body by virtue of the Enterprise Act 2002.

247 As a result of this change, the CAT expects to see a continued caseload growth. CAT President Peter Roth noted in CAT's 2016/17 annual report, that more consumers are expected to take advantage of the enhanced private enforcement procedures introduced by the Consumer Rights Act 2015. The number of hearings against CMA decisions has also increased in line with the CMA taking more cases. The report also notes that the CAT will work closely with BEIS to assess the implications of Brexit on its workload: see http://www.catribunal.org.uk/files/Annual_Report_16_17.pdf.

248 See Competition Appeal Tribunal Rules 2015, available at www.catribunal.org.uk/files/The_Competition_Appeal_Tribunal_Rules_2015.pdf.

a block exemption regulation, the imposition of a penalty or the acceptance, interim measures, direction to bring the infringement to an end, the release, non-release, or variation of commitments taken under CA98, the CAT may confirm, set aside, revoke, or vary the CMA's/sector-specific regulator's decision or penalty, or remit the matter to the CMA/sector-specific regulator, or make any other decision that the CMA/sector-specific regulator could have made (appeal on the merits).[249] The CAT may also set aside any finding of fact on which the decision is based.

According to the Tribunal itself, the existence of this jurisdiction 'on the merits' allows the overall framework for the application of the CA98 to comply with Article 6 of the European Convention, in accordance with section 2(1) of the Human Rights Act 1998. It was held in the *NAPP* judgment[250] that the enforcement of the competition rules, despite being primarily entrusted to an administrative agency, is of a 'criminal nature'.[251] Accordingly, conferring the power to scrutinize the CMA decisions in respect to 'all matters' of fact and of law conforms with the principles established by the European Court of Human Rights in respect to the conformity of like proceedings with Article 6 of the Convention, ie the right to a fair trial.[252]

The intensity of CAT's judicial control for the review of mergers and market investigations (judicial review) is more limited. According to the Enterprise Act 2002, any person aggrieved by a decision of the CMA or the Secretary of State in connection with a reference or possible reference (of a merger or a market investigation), may apply to the CAT for a review of that decision.[253] This involves a lower level of scrutiny than an appeal[254] and could, it is submitted, be justified in light of the 'civil' nature of merger proceedings, as opposed to the 'penal' essence of antitrust investigations.[255] Furthermore, in reviewing the relevant decision, the CAT may either confirm the decision or quash it in whole or part. In this case, the CAT refers back to the original decision maker with a direction to reconsider and make a new decision in accordance with its ruling.

1.1.2.2.6. Ordinary civil and criminal courts

Private enforcement of competition law is also encouraged. Direct or indirect consumers, competitors or parties to an unlawful agreement may bring an action for damages on the basis of a competition law infringement found by the CAT (follow-on actions), either under Section 47A or under Section 47B of the Competition Act (for consumer claims brought by a 'specified body' appointed by the Secretary of State). Stand-alone actions, where the alleged breach of competition law is not already the subject of an infringement decision by the European Commission or CMA may be brought to the High Court, as well as, since the Consumer Rights Act 2015, to the CAT. Civil courts are also involved when a warrant is required to enter premises in relation to investigations under the UK and EU competition rules.

249 Competition Act 1998, sections 46–7.

250 *NAPP Pharmaceuticals v Director General of Fair Trading* [2002] ECC 13.

251 Ibid, para 97; see also ibid, para 113.

252 Ibid, para 118; see also Appl Nos 7299/75 and 7496/76, *Albert & LeCompte v Belgium* [1983] 5 EHRR 533, para 29.

253 Enterprise Act 2002, section 120.

254 Although in subsequent case law the CAT has adopted a broad view of its jurisdiction in scrutinizing mergers. See *Unichem v OFT* [2005] CAT 8, where the CAT took the view that it had jurisdiction to determine whether the OFT's conclusions were adequately supported by evidence, the facts had been properly found, all material factual considerations had been taken into account and that material facts had not been omitted, as well as that a fair procedure has been followed.

255 See eg, mutatis mutandis, Appl No 7598/76, *Kaplan v United Kingdom* [1982] 4 EHRR 64, para 159; see also Appl No 18064/91, *Ortenberg v Austria* [1995] 19 EHRR 524, para 70.

Criminal courts are also involved, in the cartel offence,[256] as well as in criminal offences committed where investigations have been obstructed, documents destroyed or falsified, or misleading information provided.

1.2. HISTORY OF COMPETITION LAW

1.2.1. COMMON LAW ANTECEDENTS OF COMPETITION LAW

The common law has been a significant inspiration to the substance and methodologies adopted by competition law. There are three doctrines of the common law that have exercised significant influence in competition law. These developed and changed direction during the eighteenth and nineteenth centuries depending upon the economic policies being espoused at a particular time.

- The common law against monopolies
- The common law of contracts in restraint of trade
- The common law doctrine of conspiracy to injure

Initially, common law supported an economic order in which the individual's getting and spending were closely controlled by kings, parliament, and customs, and their opportunities limited by the exclusive powers of the guilds, chartered companies, and patentees. The common law began to oppose this system of regulation and privilege from the end of the sixteenth century until the eighteenth century. The battle against monopolies (in the sense that it referred to an exclusive right conferred generally by the king on a specific trade) was carried out by Parliament and culminated with the adoption of the *Statute of Monopolies* in 1624. Though it was certainly directed against monopolies, it was based not on a preference for competition, but on constitutional objections to the power which the Crown presumed in granting monopolies and to the arbitrary reasons for which it had granted them. Parliament did not, at the time, oppose monopolies as such.

The Statute of Monopolies declared void all monopolies. Patents that were conferred to the first inventor or inventors of a new manufacture were, however, exempted from this prohibition, as well as monopolies and privileges granted to corporations, cities, boroughs, guilds, and chartered trading companies. These had still the power to exclude strangers from various trades. The objective was therefore to limit the royal power, which had led to abuse.

The excesses of unjustified grants of privilege by the King led to an increasing unrest of the courts and the legislature, which sought to create boundaries for these exercises of 'royal prerogative'. In the case *Darcy v Allein*, decided in 1602,[257] the King's Bench, applying the common law against monopolies, considered that the grant of an exclusive privilege damages everyone who wants to use the product because the monopolist will raise the price and reduce the quality of the goods and 'deprive other workmen of a living'. The Court added, 'or we read in Justinian that monopolies are not to be meddled with, because they do not conduce to the benefit of the common weal but to its ruin and damage. The civil Laws forbid monopolies [. . .]. The Emperor Zeno ordained that those practising monopolies should be deprived of all their goods. Zeno added that even imperial rescripts were not to be accepted if they granted monopolies to anyone.'

256 See the companion volume on enforcement, I Lianos, *Competition Law Enforcement and Procedure* (OUP, forthcoming 2019).

257 *Darcy v Allen* (The Case of Monopolies) (1602), Moore (KB) 671; 77 Eng Rep 1260.

The Court, however, exempted from the prohibition patents granted for a limited term in order to reward creativity. In *East India Company v Sandys* (1684), the Court also found that exclusive rights (monopolies) to trade only outside the realm were legitimate.[258]

The common law against monopolies is only one aspect of the common law tradition that inspired competition law. The common law doctrine of contracts in restraint of trade, which include agreements restricting a party from engaging in a particular trade or occupation or restricting the time, place, or manner in which that trade or occupation could be engaged is the second tradition. The earliest reported case was decided in 1414 (Case of *John Dyer*, according to which the defendant was restricted from engaging in the trade if dyeing. The restriction was declared void).

The most famous judgment was *Mitchel v Reynolds* (1711).[259] The plaintiff had entered a contract to lease a bakehouse for a period of years on the condition that the lessor, also a baker, would refrain from engaging in the bakery business for the term of the lease. The court held that a contract not to compete in a particular trade or occupation was valid and enforceable, as long as certain conditions were met. The first requirement was that the covenant not to compete was supported by valid consideration. Second, the covenant not to compete had to be voluntary. Third, a determination was to be made whether the contract was reasonable in limitations of time and place. Finally, the restraint could only be lawful if it were ancillary, that is, secondary to an otherwise lawful main purpose.

Mitchel v Reynolds thus established the ancillary restraints doctrine at common law: a contract not to compete which is ancillary to an otherwise lawful main purpose, such as the sale of a business or employment contract, is lawful when specifically limited in scope, time, and geographic area. Indeed, the purpose served by this doctrine is clear. If an employer could not to a certain extent restrain the activities of an employee once he or she leaves the employment there might be less incentive to employ the worker in the first place. The same may be true for someone buying a business, who would be less attracted if the vendor were able to immediately set up competition to the new purchaser. To the extent that the court in *Mitchel v Reynolds* required an inquiry into the purpose behind the restraint and the effects of the restraint, it established a reasonableness test, which later came to be known as the rule of reason standard.

Consequently, in subsequent cases, the English courts also considered whether the lawful purpose of the restraint could be obtained through less restrictive means. The test was perfected in *Maxim Nordenfelt Guns and Ammunition Co Ltd* (1894).[260] The case concerned a restriction that had been accepted by a manufacturer of guns who had sold his business and all the patents associated with it, and who had accepted a worldwide restriction in order to protect the commercial interests of the purchaser of the business. According to Lord Macnaghten,

> The public have an interest in every person's carrying on his trade freely: so has the individual. All interference with individual liberty of action in trading, and all restraints of trade of themselves, if there is nothing more, are contrary to public policy, and therefore void. That is the general rule. But there are exceptions: restraints of trade and interference with individual liberty of action may be justified by the special circumstances of a particular case. It is a sufficient justification, and indeed it is the only justification, if the restriction is reasonable—reasonable, that is, in reference to the interests of the parties concerned and reasonable in reference to the interests of the public, so framed and so guarded as to afford adequate protection to the party in whose favour it is imposed, while at the same time it is in no way injurious to the public.

258 *East India Company v Sandys*, Howell's St Tr 371 (KB) 1684.
259 *Mitchel v Reynolds* (1711) 1 P Wms.
260 *Maxim Nordenfelt Guns and Ammunition Co Ltd* (1894) Ac 535.

The doctrine of restraints to trade brings two principles in conflict: first, the principle of the freedom of contract, which requires that the parties are free to define their obligations, the government (courts) intervening only in exceptional circumstances, and second, the classical economic theory of the free market, according to which the individual pursuit of self-interest serves the best interests of society as a whole. According to Adam Smith

> Every individual is constantly exerting himself to find out the most advantageous employment for whatever capital he can command. It is his own advantage indeed, and not that of society, which he has in view. But the study of his own advantage naturally, or rather necessarily, leads him to prefer that employment which is most advantageous to the society.[261]

As has been rightly noted by some commentators: 'The doctrine of restraint of trade is a strange beast. Its role in contract law is traditionally understood to be that of denying validity to contracts that unduly restrain the freedom of one or both of the contracting parties. The doctrine appears to place non-procedural limitations on freedom of contract and, moreover, to place these limitations because of a concern for the contracting parties freedom. A concern for freedom is being used, it appears, to limit freedom.'[262]

There are three requirements for the doctrine to apply:

- the restraint must protect a legitimate interest of the party in whose favour it operates,
- the restraint must be no wider than is necessary to protect this interest, and
- the restraint must be reasonable in relation to the public interest.

The current presumption is, therefore, that contracts or provisions within a contract that are in restraint of trade are unenforceable. That presumption can, however, be rebutted by proving that the restraint is 'reasonable', both as between the parties and in relation to the public interest. Much of the case law in this area is concerned with deciding what is 'reasonable' in this context. It is for the party claiming the benefit of the restraint to show that it is reasonable. It is the defendant that bears the burden of proof for the reasonableness between the parties, while for reasonableness from a public policy perspective the burden of proof is on the plaintiff. If, however, as happens in most cases, the question turns on the reasonableness of the restriction to the public interest, then the onus of proof will be on the party challenging the restraint.

The reasonableness of the restraint is assessed in relation to a number of factors: the length of time for which it operates (eg in *Esso Petroleum Co Ltd v Harpers*, the House of Lords held that a five-year exclusive dealing restraint was reasonable but a twenty-one years one was found unreasonable), the geographical area covered or the range of activities covered by the restraint.[263]

Contracts in restraints of trade are void. The court has, however, the power to remove a void provision and enforce the remainder of the contract (severance). Severance would not be possible if it would eliminate the whole or substantially the whole of the consideration given by a party to the contract. The courts apply the Blue Pencil Test, which means that severance must be possible simply by cutting out the offending words. The restrictions should not be given their literal meaning, but must be interpreted within the factual context in which they had been put forward.

Despite the existence of the restraints of trade doctrine during the laissez-faire period, it has been scarcely applied in such a way as to avoid cartels and other anti-competitive

261 Adam Smith [1776] IV, ii.4.

262 SA Smith, 'Reconstructing Restraint of Trade' (1995) 15(4) *Oxford J Legal Studies* 565.

263 *Esso Petroleum Co Ltd v Harper's Garage (Stourport) Ltd* [1967] UKHL 1, [1968] AC 269.

activity.[264] The anti-competitive conduct was more often sanctioned by the common law doctrine of conspiracy to injure.

The *doctrine of conspiracy to injure* merely outlawed agreements between two or more competitors to injure a third. However, the courts took the view that a conspiracy was lawful if the primary object of the conspirators was to further their own interests. For example, in *Mogul Steamship Co Ltd v McGregor Gow & Co*, a group of ship owners formed an association to raise their profits and hence tariffs. The Court found that the agreement had the lawful object of protecting and increasing the association's profits; hence, it did not provide any cause of action under the doctrine of conspiracy to injure.[265] As a result, there were important cartels in the British manufacturing industry, either in the form of powerful trade associations operating price fixing and collective boycotts, the existence of which was encouraged by the government.

The practical interest of the restraints of trade doctrine nowadays is limited, as the courts have interpreted it in conformity with the statutory provisions protecting competition (competition law) adopted in the UK and in the EU.[266] The following case constitutes the reference concerning this point.

1.2.2. THE RISE OF STATUTORY COMPETITION LAW

1.2.2.1. The United States

Competition law (called antitrust law in the United States) has developed as a separate area of law in the late nineteenth century, when the US Congress enacted the Sherman Act, 1890, with the aim of prohibiting certain business activities deemed to be anti-competitive, in particular cartels (section 1 of the Sherman Act) and monopolization (section 2 of the Sherman Act). Although the Sherman Act today still forms the basis for most antitrust litigation, US Congress enacted the Clayton Act, 1915 (which specifically prohibited exclusive dealing agreements, particularly tying agreements and interlocking directorates, and mergers achieved by purchasing stock) and the Federal Trade Commission (FTC) Act, 1914 (establishing the Federal Trade Commission and providing it with the power to investigate and prevent deceptive trade practices (section 5 FTC Act). US antitrust law is enforced by the generalist courts (at the federal and state level), the Federal Trade Commission and the Department of Justice—Antitrust Division.

1.2.2.2. The United Kingdom

The process of adopting specific legislation on competition law dates from 1948. Legislation still in force includes the Competition Act 1998 and the Enterprise Act 2002, as amended.

1.2.2.3. The European Union

The European Coal and Steel Treaty of 1951 (ECSC now expired) and the European Economic Community established by the Treaty of Rome 1957 are the historic antecedents of the modern

264 See eg *English Hop Growers v Dering* (1928) 2 KB 174, where the Court uphold an agreement between manufacturers to restrict output and fix prices, finding that it was reasonable in order to avoid a glut on the market.

265 *Mogul Steamship Co Ltd v McGregor Gow & Co* [1892] AC 25.

266 *Days Medical Aids Limited v Pihsiang machinery Manufacturing Co. Ltd* [2004] EWHC 44, [2004] ECC 21. The Court considered (paras 265–6) that the common restraints of trade doctrine did not pursue an objective different from Articles 101 and 102 and therefore because of Article 3 of Regulation 1/2003 and the general principles governing the relation between EU law and national law (principle of supremacy) the Court was precluded from applying the doctrine in situations in which Article 101 TFEU was applicable.

EU competition law regime, as now set in the Treaty on the Functioning of the European Union, it is only after the adoption of the first enforcement regulation in 1962, however, that EU competition law developed as an effective legal instrument.

1.2.2.3.1. The institutional 'modernization' of EU competition law

Regulation 17 of 1962[267] governed the enforcement of the EC Treaty's provisions on anti-competitive agreements and abuses of dominant position until the 'modernization' of the EU competition policy[268] with the implementation of Regulation 1/2003.[269]

In the early days, the Commission obtained exclusive power to grant individual exemptions so that it could keep control over the key, difficult decisions. Otherwise, the courts or authorities in the different Member States might have come to very different decisions. By creating the precedent that any restrictions on conduct of importance on the market restricted competition, the Commission increased this control. It could be argued that it had virtually unfettered discretion whether to grant an exemption. None was quashed by either Community court until *Métropole I* in 1996.[270]

The enforcement of Articles 101 and 102 TFEU has been radically altered by Regulation 1/2003. This came into force in May 2004. Until recently, the articles have been enforced mainly by the Commission. Its exclusive power under Regulation 17 (now repealed) to grant individual exemptions discouraged national courts and authorities from using Community law.

The Commission wanted to devote its scarce resources to controlling international cartels, since national institutions might have problems obtaining evidence from abroad and enforcing their orders. Moreover, only the Commission had exclusive powers to control the conduct of undertakings granted special or exclusive rights by government licensing requirements. It wanted national courts and authorities to play a larger role under Articles 101 and 102 TFEU.

Regulation 1/2003 transformed the previous legal authorization system, whereby practices were judged illegal unless they were authorized by the European Commission after notification, to a legal exception regime, to a process whereby practices that infringed article 101(1) are found illegal only after a thorough analysis of their possible negative and positive effects on competition by the competition authorities or courts. It provides that Articles 101 and 102 TFEU have direct effect. National courts are required to give effect to them, and national authorities and the Commission may do so. The notification system and the Commission's

267 Council Regulation No 17 (EEC): First Regulation implementing Articles 85 and 86 of the Treaty [1962] OJ P 13/204.

268 On the process of modernization, see White Paper on the Modernisation of the Rules implementing Articles 85 and 86 of the EC Treaty (1999) OJ C 132/1. For an analysis, see CD Ehlermann, 'The Modernization of EC Antitrust Policy. A Legal and Cultural Revolution, Robert Schuman Centre for Advanced Studies', RSC No 2000/17; JS Venit, 'Brave New World: The Modernization and Decentralization of Enforcement under Articles 81 and 82 of the EC Treaty' (2003) 40 *Common Market L Rev* 545; R Wesseling, *The Modernisation of EC Antitrust Law* (Hart, 2010).

269 Council Regulation (EC) No 1/2003 of 16 December 2002 on the implementation of the rules on competition laid down in Articles 81 and 82 of the Treaty (2003) OJ L 1/1, as amended by Council Regulation (EC) No 411/2004 of 26 February 2004 repealing Regulation (EEC) No 3975/87 and amending Regulations (EEC) No 3976/87 and (EC) No 1/2003, in connection with air transport between the Community and third countries (2004) OJ L 68/1 and Council Regulation (EC) No 1419/2006 of 25 September 2006 repealing Regulation (EEC) No 4056/86 laying down detailed rules for the application of Articles 85 and 86 of the Treaty to maritime transport, and amending Regulation (EC) No 1/2003 as regards the extension of its scope to include cabotage and international tramp services (2006) OJ L 269/1.

270 Joined Cases T-528, 542, 543 & 546/93, *Métropole Télévision SA and Others v Commission* [1996] ECR II–649.

exclusive power to apply Article 101(3) to individual agreements have been ended. National courts and competition authorities were empowered to apply fully the competition law provisions of the Treaty, for instance by being able to decide whether an agreement infringes Article 101 as a whole and will no longer have to adjourn if one of the parties requests an exemption from the Commission as they did under Regulation 17 (now repealed) when only the Commission was empowered to grant an individual exemption.

D Gerber, 'Two Forms of Modernization in European Competition Law' (2008) 31(5) *Fordham Int'l LJ* 1235, 1235–41

In European competition law, the term 'modernization' has been a catchword and focus of attention since the late 1990s. Usually, the reference is to 'procedural' or 'institutional' modernization. The European Commission used the term 'modernization' when referring to the important set of changes in the institutional structure and procedures of competition law that it introduced in 2004, and it called the new regulation and its accompanying materials its 'modernization package'. This procedural modernization has fundamentally changed the procedures for developing and applying competition law in Europe.

During the same period in which this form of modernization was proceeding, another form of 'modernization' also took shape. It represents a fundamental reorientation of much of the thinking about substantive competition law in Europe. Given that the term 'modernization' was already occupied by the procedural programme noted above, it is generally not used to refer to these substantive law changes. Nevertheless, these changes have also been fundamental and very much represent a program of 'modernization'. They are often referred to as a new and more 'modern' form of competition law.

The seeds of modernization were sown in the 1990s by the fall of the Soviet Union. With that event, perceptive officials in the European Commission realized that the new independence of eastern European States was likely to lead to major changes in the process of European integration. It became clear that many of these States were likely to become members of the European Union (EU). Given that membership was already been expanded by the addition of new members in 1995, this would represent a significant expansion in the workload of many director generals (DGs), including the competition directorate. [. . .] A central concern was that the competition DG would not be able to effectively deal with a significantly expanded workload. [. . .]

Pressure for change came from several sources. Large European business firms and their legal advisors voiced particular concerns about the costs and uncertainties of Commission procedures. Representatives of this group complained, for example, about the need to notify agreements, claiming that this imposed undue compliance costs and served little purpose. They also pushed for a streamlining of Commission procedures, particularly those regarding mergers.

There was also significant pressure for change from outside Europe. One source was U.S. government officials, especially from the U.S. Department of Justice, who showed much interest in this process and complained that Commission procedures were unwieldy, costly and potentially discriminatory towards non-EU (i.e., U.S.) firms. A second form of outside pressure began to emerge that was specifically transnational. It came from what I will dub the 'transatlantic competition law group ('TCL group'). This rather loose group includes competition lawyers heavily involved in EU competition law and mainly from large international law firms, top competition law officials from the United States and Europe, and occasionally a few academics. The group began to take shape and develop continuity from about the time that the two modernization processes started—i.e. in the mid-1990s. One factor in its formation was the increasing frequency and intensity of contacts among members of the group, including a dramatic increase in the number and perceived importance of international conferences on international competition law issues. Another was the rapidly growing importance of transnational cooperation in competition law enforcement. A small number of these competition law experts became 'regulars' at the most influential conferences—such as the Fordham International Antitrust Law and Policy Conference and the European University Institute ('EUI') competition law conference in Florence. This group does not represent 'an interest group' in the traditional sense, and its membership is not fixed or formalized. Nevertheless, the regularity of contact among members of the group, a growing calescence of views on relevant issues, and a perception of shared interests began to give the group identifiable contours in the mid-1990s, and this process has continued since then. Meetings of this group have provided the main international forum for modernization and a source of impetus and support for that process.

The European Commission responded to these challenges by proceeding to encourage decentralization of administrative authorities to the EU Member States and private competition litigation (institutional modernization process). These changes were, however, motivated by the more profoundly felt need to proceed to a substantive 'modernization' of EU Competition law.

1.2.2.3.2. The substantive 'modernization' of EU competition law

According to Gerber, the substantive modernization of EU competition law included the narrowing of the objectives of competition law to ensure 'consumer welfare' and, consequently, the use of neoclassical price theory that would provide the standards, methods and measurement tools to implement this narrow perspective, this package being known in Europe as 'the more economic approach'.[271] According to Gerber, procedural/institutional modernization supported and encouraged substantive modernization by operating as an 'icebreaker' decreasing initial resistance to change.

The Commission has taken various steps to adopt a 'more economic approach'. The EU competition law 'model' that has since emerged may be characterized as 'economics-based', or more accurately as 'neoclassical price theory economics based' or 'NPT-based' model, as the economic knowledge inspiring this model emanates from the neoclassical price theory approach and ignores to a great extent other traditions in economics. As its name indicates, the NPT-based model of competition law largely relies on economic concepts, methods, and overall narratives. State intervention in markets should be limited in the confined, by neoclassical price theory, situations of 'market failure'.[272] In these cases, the technology of economic efficiency, developed by economists, will provide the necessary direction and, if performed well, will produce similar results to those expected by free markets. These two principles,

[271] D Gerber, 'Two Forms of Modernization in European Competition Law' (2008) 31(5) *Fordham Int'l LJ* 1235

[272] A market failure is a general term describing situations in which market outcomes are not Pareto efficient. Pareto efficiency, also referred to as allocative efficiency, occurs when resources are so allocated that it is not possible to make anyone better off without making someone else worse off, or stated otherwise, where (scarce) resources are used to produce the mix of good and services which is most valued by society. This is a very abstract concept, which is grounded on the theoretical construct of general equilibrium, which looks at the economy in its entirety, that is, where all markets are considered together. In practice, though, the case against monopoly (as the archetypal example of market failure due to market power) is based on partial equilibrium analysis, which looks at only one market at a time, characterized by its demand and supply curves. To focus on a single market rests on the assumption that the levels of income and the prices of both substitute and complement products are fixed.

free markets and economic efficiency, are interchangeable, the core of economic theory being based on the idea that free markets are efficient.[273] To the extent that competition law adheres to the goal of economic efficiency, its intervention will be considered adequate when artificial barriers, either public or private, impede free markets to produce their full potential. This approach led the Commission to introduce some important changes in the implementation of EU competition law.

First, the distortions to commercial transactions caused by the narrow ambit of group exemptions for the different ways of bringing goods to market have been greatly reduced by the new, broader-based regulations, relying on some abridged form of market analysis before determining if the specific contractual clause or agreement constitutes an infringement to Article 101 TFEU. Regulation 2790/99[274] for vertical distribution agreements was the first one to fully follow this new approach,[275] by including market share thresholds providing 'safe harbour' to agreements concluded by parties disposing of market shares below these thresholds, and by only black-listing some hardcore restrictions of competition, leaving for the rest the parties free to express their contractual creativity. Subsequent group exemptions have followed a similar pattern.

Second, in 2003, the Commission established the position of the Chief competition economist with a team of twenty PhD economists with the aim to provide the necessary economic input to the decisions of the European Commission and other legislative proposals, thus going far to meet the criticism of its decisions for not stating cogent reasons.[276] The institution of chief economist has expanded to national competition authorities. The surge in recruiting economists in competition authorities was partly the consequence and partly the reason of the introduction of economic analysis in EU competition law. The European Courts, however, have usually been reluctant to re-assess the economic analysis of the European Commission, although the situation has recently evolved towards a more intensive judicial review, in particular in the area of EU merger control. The chief economist has the right to speak directly to the Member of the Commission responsible for competition and his Director General. All stage-two merger decisions, most decisions under Article 102 and some other cases (not cartels) will be considered by a second team of officials from DG Comp to see whether they come to the same decision (peer review). A member of the Chief Economist's team will join the review team. If the review team has little success in persuading senior officials to change their mind, the Chief Economist can put in a word at the top.

DG Comp has been re-organized with a heavy influx of staff trained as economists.[277] Officials have been redistributed among the sectoral directorates, which will now also

[273] Economics relies on free markets, real or fictitious, in order to develop evaluation criteria: see the seminal works of A Cournot, *Recherches sur les principes mathématiques de la théorie des richesses* (1838) translated into English as A Cournot, *Researches on the Mathematical Principles of the Theory of Wealth* (Macmillan & Co, 1897) and A Marshall, *Principles of Economics* (Macmillan & Co, 8th ed, 1890).

[274] [1999] OJ L336/21 modified by Commission Regulation (EU) 330/2010 of 20 April 2010 on the application of Article 101(3) of the Treaty on the Functioning of the European Union to categories of vertical agreements and concerted practices [2010] OJ L 102/1.

[275] The Commission's approach towards vertical restraints was subject to intense criticism during the 1980s and 1990s. See, in particular, B Hawk, 'System Failure: Vertical Restraints and EC Competition Law' (1995) 32(4) *Common Market L Rev* 973 & V Korah, 'EEC Competition Policy—Legal Form or Economic Efficiency' (1986) 39(1) *Current Legal Problems* 85.

[276] See DG Competition, Chief Competition Economist, ec.europa.eu/dgs/competition/economist/role_en.html.

[277] D Neven, 'Competition Economics an Antitrust in Europe' (2006) 21(48) *Economic Policy* 741 noted that there are eighty-three professional economists out of 267 professional staff at the Directorate General of Competition at the European Commission that have a background in economics.

handle mergers. Consequently, there will usually be some members of the case team familiar with the relevant market. Whereas almost all case handlers used to be lawyers, many of them straight from university, now many have degrees in economics and even more have had practical experience in the field of competition.

Third, the European Commission also introduced reforms with regard to a more economic analysis in the context of Article 102 TFEU. Its staff published in 2005 a discussion paper on exclusionary abuses for consultation, where it was stated that:

> With regard to exclusionary abuses the objective of Article [102 TFEU] is the protection of competition on the market as a means of enhancing consumer welfare and of ensuring an efficient allocation of resources. Effective competition brings benefits to consumers, such as low prices, high quality products, a wide selection of goods and services and innovation. Competition and market integration serve these ends since the creation and preservation of an open single market promotes an efficient allocation of resources throughout the Community for the benefit of consumers. In applying Article [102 TFEU], the Commission will adopt an approach which is based on likely effects on the market.[278]

The central concern of Article 102 with regard to exclusionary abuses is thus foreclosure that hinders competition and thereby harms consumers. Many academics and consultants to business welcomed these words, which depart from the more 'formalistic' approach used by the General Court and the CJEU on rebates that are capable of foreclosing markets, which insists on the specific form of the rebate without systematically examining its effects on consumer welfare. The Commission published guidance on its enforcement priorities in applying Article 102 to exclusionary abuses in 2009, taking aboard the economic approach suggested in the 2005 Discussion paper.[279] However, the introduction of a more economic approach in the context of exclusionary abuses has collided to the indifference or even, some cases, outright opposition of the EU Courts,[280] which in some important judgments set clear limits to the expansion of economic methodology in the context of Article 102, in particular rejecting standards of enforcement that rely exclusively on efficiency considerations and that do not seriously engage with the idea of competition as a process.[281] Some more recent case law of the EU Courts nevertheless seems to indicate some change of direction and a higher receptivity to some of the precepts of the economic approach.[282]

The advent of the economic approach is also visible in the development of enforcement tools modelled to the optimal enforcement theory put forward by some Chicago School economists.[283] This economic approach to sanction is based on the same assumption underlying the economic model of competition law, that firms are rational profit maximizers and they will engage in an illegal practice if their expected benefits of such practices are sufficiently large compared to their

[278] See DG Competition Discussion paper on the application of Article 82 of the Treaty to exclusionary abuses (December 2005), para 4, available at ec.europa.eu/competition/antitrust/art82/discpaper2005.pdf.

[279] Communication from the Commission—Guidance on the Commission's enforcement priorities in applying Article 82 of the EC Treaty to abusive exclusionary conduct by dominant undertakings [2009] OJ C 45/7.

[280] But also it seems some Commission's officials as well: see W Wils, 'The Judgment of the EU General Court in Intel and the So-Called "More Economic Approach" to Abuse of Dominance' (2014) 37(4) *World Competition* 405.

[281] See eg Case T-203/01, *Manufacture française des pneumatiques Michelin v Commission* [2003] ECR II-4071 [hereinafter *Michelin II*); Case T-219/99, *British Airways plc v Commission* [2003] ECR II-5917. See also the ruling in the latter on appeal: Case C-95/04 P, *British Airways plc v Commission* [2007] ECR I-2331; Case T-286/09, *Intel Corp v European Commission*, ECLI:EU:T:2014:547.

[282] This is particularly the case for pricing abuses. See our analysis in Chapter 9.

[283] GS Becker, 'Crime and Punishment: An Economic Approach' (1968) 76(2) *J Political Economy* 169.

expected costs. As the goal of law enforcement is to reduce the number of violations of the law, this is achieved by catching at least some violators and punishing them, thus increasing the *ex post* cost of the violation for these violators and reducing the expected profitability of such violations for would-be violators. This will of course decrease the *ex ante* profitability of the violations for would-be violators and will, in principle, reduce the number of violations by discouraging at least some would-be violators (deterrence). This is generally achieved by imposing sanctions that will amount to a multiple of the offender's benefits from crime and which are negatively related to the probability of detection (the lower the probability of detection, the higher the fines).[284]

The Commission used to have great difficulty in establishing the existence of a cartel. It adopted few decisions, and most of those were appealed to the General Court. Considerable resources were thus consumed by the Commission, the General Court, and the parties. It was difficult to persuade industry that cartels were not worthwhile. Over time, the Commission increased the level of fines and, even if they were suspended during an appeal, interest had to be paid and a bank bond tendered guaranteeing payment. Although the level of fines has been increased, it was still insufficient to deter infringements. The Commission's Leniency Notice for cartels transformed the position.[285] Cartels became unstable, as each party fears that one of the others will tell the Commission first and gain total immunity from fines. Many investigations have started with one of the parties claiming leniency, although some involving international cartels have resulted from the leniency programme in the US. The Commission now gets good evidence of many cartels and, when it adopts a decision to fine the participants, any appeal is usually limited to procedural points, such as a failure to observe fundamental rights. Participants rarely contest the existence of the cartel. DG Comp attaches great importance and devotes substantial resources to the Leniency Programme. Since the introduction of criminal sanctions, such as imprisonment for individuals, is unthinkable in many Member States, the equivalent leniency programme in the US is even more effective, but this is an area where the Commission has been very successful.

The modernization process has benefitted many actors. Although modernization seemed at first to enhance the Commission's power by enabling it to control competition law enforcement activity across Member States, through the works of the European Competition Network, the ECN has empowered NCAs to feed in the EU competition law process their own priorities, by the constitution of a number of working groups,[286] to coordinate their activity, not always through the intermediary of the European Commission, for instance by taking joint action in cases of EU-wide interest[287] or undertaking preparatory work for future

284 WM Landes, 'Optimal Sanctions for Antitrust Violations' (1983) 50 *U Chicago L Rev* 652.

285 Commission notice on immunity from fines and reduction of fines in cartel cases [2006] OJ C 298/17.

286 There is an EU working group on mergers, established in Brussels in 2010, which consists of representatives of the European Commission and the national authorities of the European Union who have responsibility for merger review (NCAs) together with observers from the NCAs of the European Economic Area and whose objective is to foster increased consistency, convergence and cooperation among EU merger jurisdictions. In addition, groups of experts in specific sectors (banking, securities, energy, insurance, food, pharmaceuticals, professional services, healthcare, environment, motor vehicles, telecommunications, media, IT, information & communication, abuse of dominant positions, Competition Chief Economists, and railways) discuss competition problems and promote a common approach.

287 In their investigations on price parity' clauses contained in agreements between online travel agencies (OTAs) and hotels, the French Competition Authority (French CA), the Italian Competition Authority (ICA), and the Swedish Competition Authority (SCA) coordinated their investigations and, on 21 April 2015, adopted parallel decisions accepting identical commitments from the market-leading OTA, Booking.com, and making them binding in their respective jurisdictions. The European Commission assisted the authorities in coordinating their work. See 'The French, Italian and Swedish Competition Authorities Accept the Commitments Offered by Booking.com', available at https://webgate.ec.europa.eu/multisite/ecn-brief/en/content/french-italian-and-swedish-competition-authorities-accept-commitments-offered-bookingcom.

competition law enforcement,[288] and to ultimately evolve as significant independent actors on the own right in the EU competition law process. The Commission recognizes that NCAs play a key role in the enforcement of EU antitrust rules alongside the Commission and has been promoting a more active role for NCAs in the European competition law system.[289] The changes introduced by the 'modernization' of EU competition law have also benefitted some other actors, in particular transnational law firms and economic consultancies, based in the US with experience in a more economics-oriented competition law.

1.3. EU COMPETITION LAW AND NATIONAL COMPETITION LAW: SCOPE OF APPLICATION, INTERACTION

The multi-level governance of competition law in Europe leads to the frequent interaction of EU competition law and national competition law. This is of course a topic on its own,[290] but we will focus here on the concept of effect on trade, which constitutes the main legal operational criterion in determining the respective scopes of application of EU and national competition law in the EU.

1.3.1. APPLICABILITY OF EU COMPETITION LAW: THE CONCEPT OF EFFECT ON TRADE

Articles 101, 102, and 106 TFEU apply only to conduct which may affect trade between Member States. EU Member States are free to apply their own national competition law to conduct that does not appreciably affect trade between Member States.

The condition that trade between Member States be affected is easily satisfied. Even an agreement confined to activities in a single Member State may infringe Article 101(1). The concept of trade is very broad, and covers all economic activities relating to goods or services, even the right of a trader in one Member State to set up business in another. Since May 2004, the condition has been more important, as national competition authorities are not allowed to apply national competition law without also applying EU law where trade between Member States may be affected, according to Article 3(1) Regulation 1/2003. Note that where Article 101 TFEU applies (in particular if the conduct in question is capable of affecting trade between Member States, the same rules apply across the EU, but if the agreement is not capable of affecting inter-State trade, EU law does not apply, and Member States are free to apply their own rules, regardless whether they are stricter or more lenient than Article 101 TFEU.[291]

[288] See the recent joint paper by the French Autorité de la concurrence and the German Bundeskartellamt on data and its implications for Competition Law, published in 2016: https://www.bundeskartellamt.de/SharedDocs/Publikation/DE/Berichte/Big%20Data%20Papier.html.

[289] See Commission Communication—Ten Years of Antitrust Enforcement under Regulation 1/2003: Achievements and Future Perspectives, COM(2014) 453 and the recent 'ECN+' initiative.

[290] For some excellent comparative and inter-disciplinary analysis on EU competition law federalism, see F Cenzig, *Antitrust Federalism in the EU and the US* (Routledge, 2013).

[291] This does not apply to unilateral conduct for which undertakings still need to comply with Article 102 TFEU, as well as the various Member State rules even if these are stricter than Article 102 TFEU (the double burden): Article 3(2), second sentence, of Regulation 1/2003.

Historically, two criteria have been used by the CJEU: (i) a change in the pattern of trade, and (ii) a change in the competitive structure of the market.

The condition that trade between Member States may be affected has been construed in the light of the need to establish and maintain a single market. In its first judgment on appeal from the Commission, *Consten and Grundig v Commission*, the CJEU stated that the concept of an agreement 'which may affect trade between Member States' 'is intended to define, in the law governing cartels, the boundary between the areas respectively covered by [EU] law and national law'.[292] According to the CJEU,

> [W]hat is particularly important is whether the agreement is capable of constituting a threat, either direct or indirect, actual or potential, to freedom of trade between Member States in a manner which might harm the attainment of the objectives of a single market between states. Thus the fact that an agreement encourages an increase, even a large one, in the volume of trade between states is not sufficient to exclude the possibility that the agreement may 'affect' such trade in the above-mentioned manner.[293]

This broad concept results in few agreements that significantly restrict competition escaping the prohibition of Article 101 TFEU.

In *Groupement des Fabricants de Papiers Peints de Belgique v Commission*, Advocate General Trabucchi suggested a third possible meaning for the condition about trade between Member States as the Single Market matured:

> Moreover, as has been brought out in legal writings, [. . .] in a unified multinational market, within which there are no longer any national frontiers impeding the movement of goods, the [. . .] criterion ['may affect trade between Member States'] must assume a significance to match the new situation which has come into being; it must be interpreted in such a way as to bring within the prohibitions of Article [101 TFEU] agreements in restraint of competition *which affect the attainment of the objectives for which the [Internal] Market was established.* In this sense, the criterion relating to the effect of the restriction of competition on trade between Member States serves to define that restriction itself by requiring that, in order to come within the purview of [EU] law, it must be of importance within the ambit of the [EU] system *in respect of the objectives pursued.*[294]

The CJEU, however, did not take up the idea invoked by its Advocate General.

There is no need to prove an actual effect on trade between States: a potential effect is enough. The goods immediately subject to an agreement may not move between Member States. Nor is it necessary to show that there is an adverse effect to commerce.

Some kinds of agreement are particularly likely to affect trade between Member States. Export bans and functional equivalents obviously affect trade. The same goes for international cartels, which may lead to inflated prices and thus may affect, directly or indirectly, patterns of trade. Single branding clauses preventing a dealer from importing rival brands, or exclusive distribution clauses and other territorial restrictions also affect market access and prevent competition within the territory from other distributors.

292 Joined Cases 56 & 58/64, *Consten and Grundig v Commission* [1966] ECR 299, at 341.
293 Ibid.
294 Case 73/74, *Groupement des Fabricants de Papiers Peints de Belgique and Others v Commission* [1975] ECR 1491, 1522–3 (emphasis added).

An agreement confined to activities in a single Member State may infringe Article 101(1). As the CJEU held in *Vereeniging van Cementhandelaren v Commission*:

> 29. An agreement extending over the whole of the territory of a Member State by its very nature has the effect of reinforcing the compartmentalization of markets on a national basis, thereby holding up the economic inter-penetration which the treaty is designed to bring about and protecting domestic production.
>
> 30. In particular, the provisions of the agreement which are mutually binding on the members of the applicant association and the prohibition by the association on all sales to resellers who are not authorized by it make it more difficult for producers or sellers from other Member States to be active in or penetrate the Netherlands market.

In *Belasco v Commission*, Advocate General Mischo and the CJEU observed that cartels confined to a single Member State have to take measures to restrict imports, and that is why national agreements may normally be prohibited. Hence, where the barriers to cross-frontier trade are not created by the parties, it could be argued that a national agreement does not affect inter-State trade.[295] There is also an effect on trade where the parties accept direct restrictions on imports or exports between Member States.

In other cases where only one Member State is directly affected, the final conclusion reached depended on the facts of the case. Although in some cases the CJEU asked the Commission to put forward the mechanism restraining imports or exports, in most recent cases, the EU Court just observed that patterns of trade were appreciably affected even if no specific mechanism restraining trade across frontiers was indicated. In *Bagnasco*, the CJEU also required some market analysis.[296]

In *Austrian banks*, the General Court, confirmed by the CJEU, held that a banking cartel (the Lombard club agreements) which involved only Austrian credit establishments and which was concerned only with the provision of services on the Austrian national market, or indeed regional or local markets in Austria produced a cumulative effect on inter-State trade, as the cartel affected the entire country, even if the cartel resulted from a series of regional committees which, viewed in isolation, may not have been considered as affecting inter-State trade.[297] The GC also held that '[i]t follows from [the] case-law that there is, at least, a strong presumption that a practice restrictive of competition applied throughout the territory of a Member State is liable to contribute to compartmentalization of the markets and to affect intra-Community trade', adding that '[t]hat presumption can only be rebutted if an analysis of the characteristics of the agreement and its economic context demonstrates the contrary'.[298]

For the EU competition law provisions to apply the effect on trade should be appreciable. The Commission adopted guidelines in order to set out the principles developed by the EU

295 Case 246/86, *SC Belasco and Others v Commission* [1989] ECR I-2117, 2174 (opinion of Mischo AG) and paras 33–5 (judgment).

296 Joined Cases C-215 & 216/96, *Carlo Bagnasco and Others v Banca Popolare di Novara soc coop arl* [1999] ECR I-135.

297 Case T-259/02, *Raiffeisen Zentralbank Österreich v Commission* [2006] ECR II-5169, paras 162–86 [the GC noting in para 170 that '[a] link justifying and necessitating an overall examination of the capability of affecting trade between Member States exists in particular between agreements or other types of conduct amounting to a single infringement' and finding that 'the Commission was legally entitled to conclude that the concerted practices within the various Lombard Club committees were part of a single infringement in that they were elements of an overall plan designed to distort competition']; confirmed by Case C-125/07 P, *Erste Bank der Österreichischen Sparkassen AG v Commission* [2009] ECR I-8681, paras 36–70.

298 Case T-259/02, *Raiffeisen Zentralbank Österreich v Commission* [2006] ECR II-5169, para 181 (for an example of a rebuttal of that presumption, see Joined Cases C-215 & 216/96, *Carlo Bagnasco and Others v Banca Popolare di Novara soc coop arl* [1999] ECR I-135).

Courts in relation to the interpretation of the concept of effect on trade of Articles 101 and 102 TFEU and determine what constitutes an 'appreciable' effect. The concept of effect on trade is considered an 'autonomous [EU] law criterion, which must be assessed separately in each case' and a 'jurisdictional criterion defining the scope of application of EU competition law.[299] The Guidelines also indicate when conduct is in general unlikely to be capable of appreciably affecting trade between Member States (the absence of an appreciable effect on trade rule or NAAT-rule).

Commission Notice—Guidelines on the effect on trade concept contained in Articles [101] and [102] of the Treaty [2004] OJ C 101/81 (excerpts)

According to the Commission, there are three elements that should be addressed in the application of the effect on trade criterion.

(a) *The concept of 'trade between Member States'*

The Commission adopts a wide interpretation of the concept of 'trade between member States', which is conceived as a concept, covering all cross-border economic activity involving at least two Member States and cases where agreements or practices affect the competitive structure of the market. If an undertaking is or risks being eliminated, the competitive structure within the Community is affected and so are the economic activities in which the undertaking is engaged. It is not required that the agreement or practice affect trade between the whole of one Member State and the whole of another Member State. Articles 101 and 102 may be applicable also in cases involving part of a Member State, provided that the effect on trade is appreciable.

(b) *The notion of 'may affect'*

According to the Commission, the notion 'may affect' implies that it must be possible to foresee with a sufficient degree of probability on the basis of a set of objective factors of law or fact that the agreement or practice may have an influence, direct or indirect, actual or potential, on the pattern of trade between Member States.

The 'pattern of trade' test developed by the CJEU contains the following main elements:

(i) *'a sufficient degree of probability on the basis of a set of objective factors of law or fact' (the subjective intent on the part of the undertakings concerned is not required) that the agreement will or 'is capable' of having such an effect. Relevant factors considered by the Commission include the nature of the agreement and practice (e.g. cross border cartels are thought 'by their very nature' capable of having an effect on trade), the nature of the products covered by the agreement or practice and the position and importance of the undertakings concerned. In addition, the market position of the undertakings concerned and their sales volumes are indicative from a quantitative point of view of the ability of the agreement or practice concerned to affect trade between Member States;*

(ii) *an influence on the 'pattern of trade between Member States';*

(iii) *'a direct or indirect, actual or potential influence' on the pattern of trade. According to the Commission, potential effects are those that may occur in the future with a sufficient degree of probability. In other words, foreseeable market developments must be taken into account.*

299 Commission Notice—Guidelines on the effect on trade concept contained in Articles [101] and [102] of the Treaty [2004] OJ C 101/81.

Even if trade is not capable of being affected at the time the agreement is concluded or the practice is implemented, Articles [101] and [102] remain applicable if the factors which led to that conclusion are likely to change in the foreseeable future.

The Commission also noted that the Court of Justice has in addition developed a test based on whether or not the agreement or practice affects the competitive structure. In cases where the agreement or practice is liable to affect the competitive structure inside the EU, EU law jurisdiction is established. The Commission follows the same approach.

(c) *The concept of 'appreciability'*

The effect on trade criterion incorporates a quantitative element, limiting EU law jurisdiction to agreements and practices that are capable of having effects of a certain magnitude. The assessment of appreciability depends on the circumstances of each individual case, in particular the nature of the agreement and practice, the nature of the products covered, and the market position of the undertakings concerned. When by its very nature the agreement or practice is capable of affecting trade between Member States, the appreciability threshold is lower than in the case of agreements and practices that are not by their very nature capable of affecting trade between Member States. The stronger the market position of the undertakings concerned, the more likely it is that an agreement or practice capable of affecting trade between Member States can be held to do so appreciably. Market share and the turnover of the undertakings in the products concerned are among the factors to take into account (para 45). The application of the appreciability test does not necessarily require that relevant markets be defined and market shares calculated: in particular, for agreements and practices that by their very nature are liable to affect trade between Member States, such as cross-border cartels, the turnover is sufficient information. Agreements and practices must always be considered in the economic and legal context in which they occur. In the case of vertical agreements, it may be necessary to have regard to any cumulative effects of parallel networks of similar agreements. Hence, even if a single agreement or network of agreements is not capable of appreciably affecting trade between Member States, the effect of parallel networks of agreements, taken as a whole, may be capable of doing so. In this case, it is necessary that the individual agreement or network of agreements make a significant contribution to the overall effect on trade. With regard to the quantification of the appreciability, the Commission notes the following.

Absence of an appreciable effect on trade rule (NAAT rule)

50. It is not possible to establish general quantitative rules covering all categories of agreements indicating when trade between Member States is capable of being appreciably affected. It is possible, however, to indicate when trade is normally not capable of being appreciably affected. Firstly, in its notice on agreements of minor importance which do not appreciably restrict competition in the meaning of Article [101] (1) of the Treaty (the de minimis rule) the Commission has stated that agreements between [micro,] small and medium-sized undertakings (SMEs) [which are defined by the Commission in Recommendation 2003/361/EC concerning the definition of micro, small and medium-sized enterprises as made up of enterprises which employ fewer than 250 persons and which have an annual turnover not exceeding EUR 50 million, and/or an annual balance sheet total not exceeding EUR 43 million[300]] are normally not capable of affecting trade between Member States. The reason for this presumption is the fact that the activities of SMEs are normally local or at most regional in nature.

300 [2003] OJ L 124/36.

However, SMEs may be subject to Community law jurisdiction in particular where they engage in cross-border economic activity. Secondly, the Commission considers it appropriate to set out general principles indicating when trade is normally not capable of being appreciably affected, i.e. a standard defining the absence of an appreciable effect on trade between Member States (the NAAT rule). When applying Article [101], the Commission will consider this standard as a negative rebuttable presumption applying to all agreements within the meaning of Article [101(1)] irrespective of the nature of the restrictions contained in the agreement, including restrictions that have been identified as hardcore restrictions in Commission block exemption regulations and guidelines. In cases where this presumption applies the Commission will normally not institute proceedings either upon application or on its own initiative. Where the undertakings assume in good faith that an agreement is covered by this negative presumption, the Commission will not impose fines.

51. Without prejudice to paragraph below, this negative definition of appreciability does not imply that agreements, which do not fall within the criteria set out below, are automatically capable of appreciably affecting trade between Member States. A case by case analysis is necessary.

The negative rebuttable presumption of appreciability

52. The Commission holds the view that in principle agreements are not capable of appreciably affecting trade between Member States when the following cumulative conditions are met:

(a) The aggregate market share of the parties on any relevant market within the Community affected by the agreement does not exceed 5%, and

(b) In the case of horizontal agreements, the aggregate annual Community turnover of the undertakings concerned in the products covered by the agreement does not exceed 40 million euro. In the case of agreements concerning the joint buying of products, the relevant turnover shall be the parties' combined purchases of the products covered by the agreement.

In the case of vertical agreements, the aggregate annual Community turnover of the supplier in the products covered by the agreement does not exceed 40 million euro. In the case of licence agreements the relevant turnover shall be the aggregate turnover of the licensees in the products incorporating the licensed technology and the licensor's own turnover in such products. In cases involving agreements concluded between a buyer and several suppliers, the relevant turnover shall be the buyer's combined purchases of the products covered by the agreements.

[The same presumption applies] where during two successive calendar years the above turnover threshold is not exceeded by more than 10 per cent and the above market threshold is not exceeded by more than 2 percentage points. The presumption will not apply to an emerging not yet existing market, in which case appreciability may have to be assessed on the basis of the position of the parties on related product markets or their strength in technologies relating to the agreement.

The positive rebuttable presumption of appreciability

53. The Commission will also hold the view that where an agreement by its very nature is capable of affecting trade between Member States, for example, because it

concerns imports and exports or covers several Member States, there is a rebuttable positive presumption that such effects on trade are appreciable when the turnover of the parties in the products covered by the agreement calculated as indicated in paragraphs 52 and 54 exceeds 40 million euro. In the case of agreements that by their very nature are capable of affecting trade between Member States it can also often be presumed that such effects are appreciable when the market share of the parties exceeds the 5% threshold set out in the previous paragraph. However, this presumption does not apply where the agreement covers only part of a Member State [. . .].

54. With regard to the threshold of 40 million euro (cf. paragraph 52 above), the turnover is calculated on the basis of total Community sales excluding tax during the previous financial year by the undertakings concerned, of the products covered by the agreement (the contract products). Sales between entities that form part of the same undertaking are excluded.

55. In order to apply the market share threshold, it is necessary to determine the relevant market. This consists of the relevant product market and the relevant geographic market. The market shares are to be calculated on the basis of sales value data or, where appropriate, purchase value data. If value data are not available, estimates based on other reliable market information, including volume data, may be used.

56. In the case of networks of agreements entered into by the same supplier with different distributors, sales made through the entire network are taken into account.

57. Contracts that form part of the same overall business arrangement constitute a single agreement for the purposes of the NAAT-rule. Undertakings cannot bring themselves inside these thresholds by dividing up an agreement that forms a whole from an economic perspective.

[. . .]

The Commission further notes that agreements that are local in nature are 'in themselves not capable of appreciably affecting trade between Member States', even if the local market is located in a border region.

With regard to abuse of a dominant position and the concept of effect on trade, the Commission notes that exclusionary abuses that affect the competitive market structure inside a Member State, for instance by eliminating or threatening to eliminate a competitor, may also be capable of affecting trade between Member States. However, where the undertaking that risks being eliminated only operates in a single Member State, 'the abuse will normally not affect trade between Member States', but inter-State trade may be affected where the targeted undertaking exports to or imports from other Member States and where it also operates in other Member States. The Commission goes as far as accept that the effect on trade may arise from the dissuasive impact of the abuse on other competitors, in particular if, through repeated conduct the dominant undertaking has acquired a reputation for adopting exclusionary practices towards competitors that attempt to engage in direct competition, thus dissuading competitors from other Member States to compete aggressively. Furthermore, 'as long as an undertaking has a dominant position which covers the whole of a Member State it is normally immaterial whether the specific abuse engaged in by the dominant undertaking only covers part of its territory or affects certain buyers within the national territory', the Commission considering 'any abuse which makes it more difficult to enter the national market' as likely to appreciably affect trade.

1.3.2. APPLICABILITY OF UK COMPETITION LAW

The conditions for the application of Chapter I, section 2(1) of the CA98 are similar to those of Article 101(1) TFEU (except the condition of the existence of an appreciable effect on trade) and Chapter I of the CA98 applies to agreements between undertakings, decisions by associations of undertakings or concerted practices which 'may affect trade within the United Kingdom'. According to Chapter I, section 2(3) of the CA98, 'Subsection (1) applies only if the agreement, decision or practice is, or is intended to be, implemented in the United Kingdom'. The effect of trade in the UK does not need to be appreciable, although this is still a controversial issue.[301] Chapter I also applies even if the agreement is intended to operate 'only in part of the UK', according to Chapter I, section 2(7) of the CA98. No exemption is possible under section 8 or 9 of the Act, if the agreement falls within the scope of Article 101 TFEU because it affects inter-State trade. Indeed, according to Article 3(2) of Regulation 1/2003, '[t]he application of national competition law may not lead to the prohibition of agreements, decisions by associations of undertakings or concerted practices which may affect trade between Member States but which do not restrict competition within the meaning of Article [101(1) TFEU], or which fulfil the conditions of Article [101(3) TFEU] or which are covered by a Regulation for the application of Article [101(3) TFEU]'. Under section 60 of the CA98, the CMA, other authorities (sector-specific regulators that can also enforce the Competition Act), and the courts (including the CAT) are under an obligation to deal with questions arising under Part I of the UK Competition Act 1998 *in relation to competition within the UK* in such a way as to ensure consistency with the treatment of corresponding questions arising in EU law in so far as this is possible, having regard to any relevant differences between any of the provisions concerned. Therefore, this provision will be of no practical use if there is an effect on trade and the restrictive practice is also caught by Article 101(1) as in this case Article 3(2) of Regulation 1/2003 will be applicable. Section 60 may (and will most times) apply if there is no effect on intra-Community trade and the agreement is only assessed under the CA98.

Chapter II, section 18(1) of the CA98 (the Chapter II prohibition principle) applies to any conduct on the part of one or more undertakings which amounts to the abuse of a dominant position in a market is prohibited if it may affect trade within the United Kingdom. According to Chapter II, section 18(3) of the CA98, 'dominant position means a dominant position within the United Kingdom; and the United Kingdom' means the United Kingdom or any part of it'.

D Bailey, 'Appreciable effect on trade within the United Kingdom' (2009) 30(8) *European Competition L Rev* 353, 353–4

> As with arts [101] and [102] [TFEU], there is a requirement that agreements or conduct should be capable of having an effect on trade in order for the equivalent prohibitions in the 1998 Act to apply. The effect on trade clause is purely jurisdictional in both cases, so that it is of little importance that the influence of an agreement is unfavourable, neutral or favourable. However, the Ch. I and II prohibitions naturally adapt the [EU] law effect on trade criterion to the domestic context, i.e. that agreements or conduct 'may affect trade *within* the United Kingdom' (as opposed to inter-state trade).

301 See *Aberdeen Journals Ltd v OFT* [2003] CAT 11, paras 459–62 (Chapter II); *North Midland Construction plc v OFT* [2011] CAT 14, para 49 (Chapter I) (noting that the essential purpose of the rule on appreciability in EU competition law is to demarcate the fields of EU law and domestic law respectively and that in terms of section 60(1) of the CA98, that seems to us to be a 'relevant difference' between the 1998 Act and the provisions of EU law). However, this position was criticized by Morritt C in *P&S Amusements v Valley House Leisure* [2006] EWHC 1510, para 22, and by Briggs J in *Pirtek v Jinplace* [2010] EWHC 1461 (Ch), para 62.

Another difference between the [EU] and domestic concepts of effect on trade, and one that is not apparent on the face of the legislation, derives from the fact that [EU] law has long been concerned with the integration of national markets. [. . .]

The concept of effect on trade between Member States has been construed widely in light of this concern. A sufficient effect on inter-state trade was identified in cases that ranged from withholding discounts from exports of Martell cognac to charging higher prices for maritime pilotage services on international routes than on domestic routes [. . .]. The 1998 Act, on the other hand, has (understandably) not been applied with this issue in mind. In its Opinion on *Newspaper and magazine distribution*, the OFT [now replaced by the CMA] stated that '[i]t would appear likely that a national court would not import the single market objective into [. . .] national law'.

1.3.3. THE INTERACTION BETWEEN EU COMPETITION LAW AND UK COMPETITION LAW

1.3.3.1. Concerning conduct that affects trade between Member States

In *Walt Wilhelm*, the CJEU held that conflicts between EU competition law and national law (in this case rules on cartels) must be resolved by applying the principle that EU law takes precedence (primacy of EU law).[302] The operation of this principle leads, among other effects, to the exclusion of national legislation when this is in conflict with EU legislation.[303]

The interaction between national and EU competition law is now dealt in detail by Regulation 1/2003.

Recital 8 of Regulation 1/2003 provides:

Regulation 1/2003, [2003] OJ L 1/1

Recital 8

In order to ensure the effective enforcement of the [EU] competition rules and the proper functioning of the cooperation mechanisms contained in this Regulation, it is necessary to oblige the competition authorities and courts of the Member States to also apply Articles [101] and [102] of the Treaty where they apply national competition law to agreements and practices which may affect trade between Member States. In order to create a level playing field for agreements, decisions by associations of undertakings and concerted practices within the internal market, it is also necessary to determine [. . .] the relationship between national laws and [EU] competition law. To that effect it is necessary to provide that the application of national competition laws to agreements, decisions or concerted practices within the meaning of Article [101(1)] of the Treaty may not lead to the prohibition of such agreements, decisions and concerted practices if they are not also prohibited under [EU] competition law. The notions of agreements, decisions and concerted practices are autonomous concepts of Community competition law covering the coordination of behaviour of undertakings on the market as interpreted by the [EU] Courts. Member States should not under this Regulation be precluded

302 Case 14/68, *Walt Wilhelm v Bundeskartellamt* [1969] ECR 1.

303 For an introduction to this principle, see R Schütze, *European Union Law* (CUP, 2015), ch 4; A Dashwood, M Dougan, B Rodger, E Spaventa, and D Wyatt, *Wyatt and Dashwood's EU Law* (Hart, 6th ed, 2011), ch 8.

from adopting and applying on their territory stricter national competition laws which prohibit or impose sanctions on unilateral conduct engaged in by undertakings. These stricter national laws may include provisions which prohibit or impose sanctions on abusive behaviour toward economically dependent undertakings. Furthermore, this Regulation does not apply to national laws which impose criminal sanctions on natural persons except to the extent that such sanctions are the means whereby competition rules applying to undertakings are enforced.

According to Article 3(1) of Regulation 1/2003, which implements these principles, where NCAs or national courts apply national competition law to agreements, decisions by associations of undertakings, or concerted practices that may affect trade between Member States, they shall also apply Article 101. Similarly, when they apply national competition law to any abuse prohibited by Article 102 TFEU, they shall also apply Article 102.

When both national and EU competition law are applied, Article 3(2) of Regulation 1/2003 sets some conflict rules. When national competition law is being applied to agreements that are caught by Article 101 TFEU, it may not be used to prohibit agreements which do not restrict competition or which benefit from Article 101(3) TFEU. All Member States have adopted competition law statutes that are heavily inspired by the EU competition law, although they do not pursue the objective of the Internal Market. In particular, Regulation 1/2003 has initiated a process of convergence across Europe of the substantive competition law provisions of several Member States, with subsequent revisions of national competition legislation towards a system of legal exception and with a specific provision mandating convergence in the context of the application of national provisions equivalent to Article 101 TFEU, ensuring a level playing field ('the convergence rule'[304]) with regard to the scope of competition law in Europe.[305] However, according to the last sentence of Article 3(2), Member States are not precluded from adopting and applying stricter national laws which prohibit or sanction unilateral conduct. Unilateral behaviour capable of affecting trade between Member States can thus be prohibited by national law, even if it occurs below the level of dominance or is not considered abusive within the meaning of Article 102. Article 3(2), last sentence, thus contains an exception from the level playing field and implies that undertakings doing cross-border business in the Internal Market may be subjected to a variety of standards as to their unilateral behaviour. As an example of stricter national rules concerning unilateral conduct, Recital 8 of Regulation 1/2003 explicitly mentions national provisions which prohibit or impose sanctions on abusive behaviour toward economically dependent undertakings. Some national provisions also regulate behaviour known as 'abuse of superior bargaining power' or 'abuse of significant influence', including where neither the supplier nor the distributor holds a dominant position on a specific market.[306]

National competition authorities are therefore required to apply Articles 101 and 102 TFEU when they enforce national competition law. They are acting in this case as an EU institution, rather than as a national body. Regulation 1/2003 does not, however, require a specific institutional setting for the enforcement of EU competition law, the choice being left to each Member State. Article 5 of Regulation 1/2003 sets only some minimal standards with regard

304 R Whish and D Bailey, *Competition Law* (OUP, 8th ed, 2015), 80.

305 Regulation 1/2003, Article 3(2).

306 Countries with statutes on the abuse of economic dependence or equivalent provisions include Germany, France, Portugal, Greece, Italy, Spain, Ireland, Latvia, Hungary, and Slovakia.

to the powers that Member States should confer to the national competition authorities, such as the power to take decisions requiring that the infringement be brought to an end, ordering interim measures, accepting commitments, imposing fines, periodic penalty payments, or deciding on the basis of the information in their possession that the conditions for prohibition are not met and that there are no grounds for action on their part.

In *Toshiba*,[307] the CJEU examined the allocation of respective competences of the Commission and national competition authorities in the context of an international cartel for gas insulated switchgear that was implemented both in the EU and the Czech Republic before its accession to the EU. The Czech competition authority initiated proceedings after the Commission had done so, and its decision was adopted later than the Commission's decision. Both those sets of proceedings and the imposition of fines took place after 1 May 2004, the day of the accession of the Czech Republic to the European Union. The Commission examined the anti-competitive effects of the cartel on the EU market and applied EU competition rules, while the Czech competition authority examined the effects of the cartel in Czech territory, applying Czech competition law, focusing on the effects produced by the cartel in the Czech Republic before 1 May 2004 and confining the penalty to the cartel's effects in the territory of the Czech Republic during a period prior to 1 May 2004. Toshiba and other companies involved in the cartel initiated an action against the decision of the Czech competition authority before the Czech courts, alleging that by virtue of Regulation 1/2003, competition authorities of the Member States automatically lose their jurisdiction when the Commission commences a proceeding for infringement of the EU competition rules. As the cartel had ended after the accession of the Czech Republic to the Union, the Commission's decision also concerned the effects of the cartel in Czech territory and therefore they argued that they were doubly penalized (the *ne bis in idem* principle). Indeed, the Czech competition authority imposed a fine on them for an infringement that had already formed the subject-matter of a decision by the European Commission.

The Regional Court of Brno referred preliminary questions to the CJEU asking in essence if the Czech competition authority has lost all jurisdiction to examine the cartel and penalize the effects which were produced before that accession, in view of the fact that, following the Czech's Republic accession, the Commission had already opened an investigation, prior to the one initiated by the Czech authority concerning that same conduct, and that it had already adopted a decision before the Czech authority adopted its own penalty decision. The CJEU found that neither the Treaties nor the Act of Accession of the Czech Republic contained any indication that EU competition laws should be applied retroactively to anti-competitive effects that were produced in that country prior to its accession. The EU competition rules were therefore not applicable to the anti-competitive effects that were produced by the cartel in the territory of the Czech Republic before its accession to the Union.

The CJEU then explored the delimitation of the jurisdiction of the national authorities and of the Union in cartel proceedings in order to determine whether proceedings for the imposition of a fine which were initiated by the European Commission after the Czech's Republic accession permanently prevented the Czech competition authority from prosecuting under domestic competition law a cartel the effects of which were produced in the territory of the Czech Republic before its accession to the Union. After examination of Articles 11(6)[308] and 3(1) Regulation 1/2003 taken together, the CJEU concluded that the

[307] Case C-17/10, *Toshiba Corporation and Others v Úřad pro ochranu hospodářské soutěže*, ECLI:EU:C:2012:72.

[308] According to Regulation 1/2003, Article 11(6), '[t]he initiation by the Commission of proceedings for the adoption of a decision under Chapter III shall relieve the competition authorities of the Member States

national competition authorities can no longer apply EU competition law as well as their domestic competition law once the Commission initiates proceedings for the adoption of an infringement decision under Regulation No 1/2003. The CJEU nevertheless held that the opening of a proceeding by the Commission does not permanently and definitively remove the NCA's power to apply national legislation on competition matters, their power being restored once the proceeding initiated by the Commission is concluded.[309] EU law and national competition law may apply in parallel. After the Commission has taken its decision, NCAs may rule on the cartel on the basis of EU competition law. Regulation 1/2003, however, prohibits the NCAs from contradicting a previous decision of the Commission. The Czech authority could therefore rule on the anti-competitive effects produced by the cartel in the Czech Republic before its accession.

The CJEU also found that the *ne bis in idem* principle was not infringed by the parallel national proceedings, as the Commission's decision did not penalize the possible anti-competitive effects produced by the cartel in the territory of the Czech Republic during the period prior to its accession and the Czech competition authority had only taken into account, when determining the penalty, the consequences of the cartel produced in the Czech territory before the Czech's Republic accession.

According to Recital 8 of Regulation 1/2003, the Regulation does not apply to national laws that impose criminal sanctions on natural persons, except to the extent that such sanctions are the means whereby competition rules applying to undertakings are enforced. The issue may be raised with regard to the cartel offence of section 188 of the Enterprise Act 2002, which enables the CMA to prosecute *individuals* (not undertakings) entering into certain forms of an illegal cartel under certain conditions. In *IB v The Queen*, the Court of Appeal held that, although the cartel offence constituted 'one arrow in the UK legislative quiver designed to prevent anti-competitive practices', it could not be considered as 'national competition law', in the sense of Recital 8 of Regulation 1/2003, the test for this characterization being not 'as broad as whether the law in question pursues the objective of preventing anti-competitive practices'.[310] The defendant in question had argued at first instance that the Crown Court had no jurisdiction to try the case or impose punishment in a case such as this where the agreements in question had an effect on trade between EU Member States and that only the national competition authority designated by the UK under EU Regulation 1/2003 (the Modernisation Regulation) had any powers of enforcement in such circumstances. The Crown Court has not been designated by the UK under the Modernisation Regulation. The Crown Court did not accept this argument, and the defendant brought the case to the Court of appeal. The Court of appeal held that the concern manifested by Regulation 1/2003 was, 'plainly and understandably', 'with avoiding the risk of 'limping' agreements, which are enforceable in one jurisdiction and not in another, and with ensuring that the same standards are applied throughout Member States to the question whether there has or has not been an infringement'.[311] However, '[t]he risk of any inconsistency arising between a prosecution under section 188 and a decision on the validity of an agreement (etc) under Article [101/102 TFEU] is likely to be small. First, in

of their competence to apply Articles [101 and 102 TFEU]. If a competition authority of a Member State is already acting on a case, the Commission shall only initiate proceedings after consulting with that national competition authority.'

309 Case C-17/10, *Toshiba Corporation and Others v Úřad pro ochranu hospodářské soutěže*, ECLI:EU:C:2012:72, paras 91–2.

310 *IB v The Queen* [2009] EWCA Crim 2575, para 35.

311 Ibid, para 34.

practice a prosecution under section 188 is unlikely without there being parallel regulatory proceedings against the undertaking(s), as there are in the present case. Second, it is very probable that an arrangement within section 188(2) would be regarded in European terms as an 'object-based' infringement, that is (broadly speaking) to say that the agreement is *per se* contrary to Article [101] [. . .]. Third, and vitally, Articles [101] and [102] are directly effective in English law, independently of the Modernisation Regulation, under decisions of the Court of Justice.'[312]

It follows, that if the enforcement of the cartel offence by the CMA does not trigger the obligation to apply Article 101 TFEU, although in practice, it is highly likely that when the CMA introduces proceedings under section 188 of the Enterprise Act 2002, it will also conduct an investigation under Chapter I of the CA98 and/or Article 101 TFEU.

EU competition law's interaction with national legislation that protects 'legitimate interests', other than competition on the market, is explained by Recital 9 of Regulation 1/2003 and Article 3(3) of Regulation 1/2003.

Regulation 1/2003 [2003] OJ L 1/1

Recital 9

Articles [101] and [102] [TFEU] have as their objective the protection of competition on the market. This Regulation, which is adopted for the implementation of these Treaty provisions, does not preclude Member States from implementing on their territory national legislation, which protects other legitimate interests provided that such legislation is compatible with general principles and other provisions of [EU] law. In so far as such national legislation pursues predominantly an objective different from that of protecting competition on the market, the competition authorities and courts of the Member States may apply such legislation on their territory. Accordingly, Member States may under this Regulation implement on their territory national legislation that prohibits or imposes sanctions on acts of unfair trading practice, be they unilateral or contractual. Such legislation pursues a specific objective, irrespective of the actual or presumed effects of such acts on competition on the market. This is particularly the case of legislation which prohibits undertakings from imposing on their trading partners, obtaining or attempting to obtain from them terms and conditions that are unjustified, disproportionate or without consideration.

Article 3(3) of Regulation 1/2003 therefore provides that '[w]ithout prejudice to general principles and other provisions of [EU] law, paragraphs 1 and 2 do not apply when the competition authorities and the courts of the Member States apply national merger control laws nor do they preclude the application of provisions of national law that predominantly pursue an objective different from that pursued by Articles [101] and [102] [TFEU].'

Some examples are provided in Recital 9. As we have previously noted, however, the common law of restraint of trade does not form part of national law protecting 'other legitimate interests' as it does not pursue an objective that is different from that pursued by

312 Ibid, para 36.

Article 101 TFEU and therefore could not apply in order to invalidate an agreement that was found compatible with Article 101 TFEU.[313]

1.3.3.2. Concerning conduct that does not affect trade between Member States

In principle, if the alleged anti-competitive conduct does not affect trade between Member States, EU competition law is not applicable and consequently there is no problem with regard to the interaction between EU and UK competition law. However, the Competition Act 1998 includes provisions linking UK competition law to EU competition law standards, even if the specific conduct does not affect trade between Member States.

Section 10 of the CA98 provides for a system of 'parallel exemptions' and provides that an agreement that is covered by an EU Block Exemption Regulation will be exempted also under UK competition law (see section 10(2) of the CA98 for agreements that to not affect trade between Member States).

Competition Act 1998

Section 10. Parallel exemptions

(1) An agreement is exempt from the Chapter I prohibition if it is exempt from the [EU Competition Law] prohibition—

(a) by virtue of a Regulation,

(b) because it has been given exemption by the Commission, or

(c) because it has been notified to the Commission under the appropriate opposition or objection procedure and—

(i) the time for opposing, or objecting to, the agreement has expired and the Commission has not opposed it; or

(ii) the Commission has opposed, or objected to, the agreement but has withdrawn its opposition or objection.

(2) An agreement is exempt from the Chapter I prohibition if it does not affect trade between Member States but otherwise falls within a category of agreement which is exempt from the [EU Competition Law] prohibition by virtue of a Regulation.

(3) An exemption from the Chapter I prohibition under this section is referred to in this Part as a parallel exemption.

[. . .]

(11) This section has effect in relation to the prohibition contained in paragraph 1 of Article 53 of the EEA Agreement (and the EFTA Surveillance Authority) as it has effect in relation to the [EU Competition Law] prohibition (and the Commission) subject to any modifications which the Secretary of State may by order prescribe.

Furthermore, section 60 of the CA98, containing 'governing principles' to be applied in determining questions which arise in relation to competition within the UK, ensures that the

313 *Days Medical Aids Ltd v Pihsiang* [2004] EWHC 44 (Comm), paras 254–66; *Jones v Ricoh Uk Ltd* [2010] EWHC 1743 (Ch), para 49.

UK prohibitions remain in line with the Articles 101 and 102 prohibitions in EU law, even if EU competition law does not apply for lack of an effect on intra-EU trade.

Competition Act 1998

Section 60. Principles to be applied in determining questions

(1) The purpose of this section is to ensure that so far as is possible (having regard to any relevant differences between the provisions concerned), questions arising under this Part in relation to competition within the United Kingdom are dealt with in a manner which is consistent with the treatment of corresponding questions arising in Community law in relation to competition within the Community.

(2) At any time when the court determines a question arising under this Part, it must act (so far as is compatible with the provisions of this Part and whether or not it would otherwise be required to do so) with a view to securing that there is no inconsistency between—

(a) the principles applied, and decision reached, by the court in determining that question; and

(b) the principles laid down by the Treaty and the European Court, and any relevant decision of that Court, as applicable at that time in determining any corresponding question arising in [EU] law.

(3) The court must, in addition, have regard to any relevant decision or statement of the Commission.

[. . .]

(6) In subsections (2)(b) and (3), 'decision' includes a decision as to—

(a) the interpretation of any provision of [EU] law;

(b) the civil liability of an undertaking for harm caused by its infringement of [EU] law.

Section 60(1) sets out the purpose of the section, which is to ensure, so far as possible, that questions relating to competition within the United Kingdom *are dealt with in a manner* which is consistent with the treatment of corresponding questions in EU law. Hence, if the factual background of a case differs, this does not raise obligations of consistency. Section 60(2) then sets out the specific *duty* which is expressly imposed on the courts of the United Kingdom, including the CAT, as well as the UK competition authorities (the CMA and the sector-specific regulators when exercising their competition law powers). In *BetterCare*, the CAT held that so far its activity is concerned, 'that duty is to ensure that there is *no inconsistency* between the principles we apply, and the decisions we reach, and the principles laid down by the Treaty or the European Court, and any relevant decisions of that Court, in determining 'any corresponding question arising in [EU] law' (in this context the European Court meaning the Court of Justice and the General Court of the EU).[314]

Hence, in *BetterCare* the CAT found that 'the question whether a particular body is or is not an 'undertaking' for the purpose of the Chapter II prohibition (or indeed the Chapter I prohibition) is a question which, in a broad sense, 'corresponds' to the question of whether a particular body is or is not an undertaking for the purpose of Articles [101] and [102] [TFEU]' and

314 *BetterCare Group v Director General of Fair Trading* [2002] CAT 7, para 30.

attempted to deduce certain broad principles from the jurisprudence of the CJEU, even if it recognized that the factual circumstances of those decisions are rather far from those of the specific case at hand.[315] The CAT held that it conceived its duty under section 60(1) 'to approach the 'undertaking' issue in the manner in which [. . .] the European Court would approach it, as regards the principles and reasoning likely to be followed by that Court' and that, by virtue of section 60(2), it should seek to arrive at a result 'which is not inconsistent with [EU] law'.[316] The CAT added that '[s]ubject to the overriding requirements of [EU] law, in our view the result reached should, so far as possible, also be in harmony with the overall structure and purpose of the Act in the particular economic circumstances of the United Kingdom'.[317] One of the possible 'relevant differences' to be taken into account consists in the fact that the UK competition law does not follow as EU competition law the aim of market integration and consequently, a court would be unlikely to import such a concern into its UK competition law assessment. Although it is mentioned in section 60 of the CA98 that the duty of consistent interpretation applies 'in relation to competition', it is now accepted that 'high level principles' relating to enforcement and procedure, such as the principle of equality, legitimate expectations, legal certainty, proportionality, privilege against self-incrimination, and general principles of law recognized by the EU Courts should also be imported into domestic competition analysis.[318]

In *Skyscanner v Competition and Markets Authority*,[319] a case concerning a challenge to a decision of the Office of Fair Trading, now the CMA, to accept commitments regarding a restrictive practice between hotels and online travel agents, the CAT referred to section 60 of the CA98, in order to draw on the principles in the *Alrosa* judgment of the CJEU considering the approach to judicial review of acceptance of commitments by the European Commission.[320] The CAT held:

> We are required by section 60 of the Act to ensure that so far as possible (having regard to any relevant differences between the provisions concerned) questions relating to competition within the United Kingdom are dealt with in a manner which is consistent with the treatment of corresponding questions arising in EU law. Although the power to accept binding commitments may be regarded as a matter of enforcement and procedure rather than the substance of the law, there are broad similarities between the commitments regimes of the EU and the UK and any judicial authority at EU level is likely to be useful and relevant in interpreting the UK commitment powers. The Court of Justice's decision in the *Alrosa* case is the only significant judicial assessment of the EU commitments regime and we have considered it closely. It is not 'on all fours' with the case we have to decide, and some of its more important observations relate to matters not pleaded in our case. Thus the lengthy consideration given by both the Advocate General and the Court to comparing the principle of proportionality in commitments and infringement cases is not applicable here, as Skyscanner is not claiming the OFT's decision breached that principle. Also the discussion of the position of Alrosa as a third party is specific to the EU procedural regime.[321]

Despite these differences, the CAT deduced a number of propositions from *Alrosa*, in particular, from the Advocate General's opinion, which it found useful and relevant for its own decision.[322]

315 Ibid, para 31. 316 Ibid, para 32. 317 Ibid, para 33.
318 *Napp Pharmaceutical Holdings Ltd v DGFT* [2001] CAT 3.
319 *Skyscanner v Competition and Markets Authority* [2014] CAT 16.
320 Case C-441/07 P, *European Commission v Alrosa Co Ltd* [2010] ECR I–5949.
321 *Skyscanner v Competition and Markets Authority* [2014] CAT 16, para 38.
322 Ibid, para 40.

In addition to the governing principle that UK law should not diverge in its substantive application from EU law and the obligation on national courts, tribunals and the NCAs to ensure consistency of interpretation between the CA98, TFEU, and established jurisprudence of the European Courts, section 60(3) provides that UK courts and NCAs are required to have regard to any relevant decision or statement of the Commission. This imposes a lower intensity obligation than section 60(2), as there is no obligation of avoiding any inconsistency as such, but simply 'to have regard' to any relevant decision or statement of the Commission (persuasive authority). In *MasterCard*, the OFT considered that, according to 'an ordinary interpretation' of the terms of section 60(3) of the CA98, 'this means that while the OFT or a court must consider any relevant decision or statement of the Commission and accord it due weight, they are nevertheless free to depart from it in a proper case',[323] noting that 'there is a clear distinction between the "weak" wording of section 60(3) and the "strong" wording of section 60(2)'.[324] The category of Commission's statements includes the Commission's Notices and Guidelines, guidance on its enforcement priorities, as well as clear statements of its approach published in its annual Report on Competition Policy.[325] The provision is silent as to the statements by European institutions other than the Commission. The general rule is that 'the weight that it is appropriate for the [CMA] to attach to them will vary depending on the nature of the Commission decision or statement (eg whether it is of specific or general application) and the degree of reasoning it contains'.[326] It is expected that this discussion may take a different direction following Brexit.

1.3.3.3. Competition law in the UK after Brexit

Following the 23 June 2016 referendum vote, the UK government has announced that it will be leaving the EU (Brexit). The possibility for the government to exit the EU, the process of Brexit, as such, and the exact relationship that will exist between the EU and the UK, if and when the decision to exit is implemented, are topics on which there is great uncertainty at the time of writing this book. For this reason, we will explore some of the available options for a relationship between the EU and the UK, and the implications for competition law, under the assumption that the government will decide to enter in exit negotiations with the EU. According to Article 50 of the Lisbon Treaty, a Member State that decides to withdraw from the Union in accordance with its own constitutional requirements shall notify the European Council of its intention. In the light of the guidelines provided by the European Council, the EU will then negotiate and conclude an agreement with that State, setting out the arrangements for its withdrawal, taking account of the framework for its future relationship with the EU.[327] According to the same provision '[t]he Treaties shall cease to apply to the State in question from the date of entry into force of the withdrawal agreement or, failing that, two years after the notification [. . .] unless the European Council, in agreement with the Member State concerned, unanimously decides to extend this period.'

Following some initial uncertainty with regard to the involvement of the UK Parliament in the decision to trigger Article 50, the UK Supreme Court finally held that an Act of Parliament

323 OFT Decision CA98/05/05, *Mastercard UK Members Forum Limited* (8 September 2005).

324 Ibid, para 113.

325 R Whish and D Bailey, *Competition Law* (OUP, 8th ed, 2015), 396.

326 OFT Decision CA98/05/05, *Mastercard*, para 115.

327 According to the CJEU in Case C-621/18, *Wightman v Secretary of State* ECLI:EU:C:2018:999, a Member State can unilaterally withdraw from Article 50 up until the point that a withdrawal agreement enters into force, or the expiry of the two-year Article 50 period (or any extension of it).

is required to authorize ministers to give Notice of the decision of the UK to withdraw from the European Union.[328] Following this judgment, the Government's European Union (Notification of Withdrawal) Act was voted by both Houses of the Parliament on 16 March 2017 conferring power on the Prime Minister to notify, under Article 50(2) TEU, the United Kingdom's intention to withdraw from the EU. UK Prime Minister Theresa May has officially triggered Article 50 with a letter informing the European Council of Britain's intention to leave the European Union sent on 30 March 2017. The UK Government outlined its plans for Brexit in the Brexit White Paper, published in February 2017.[329] The UK has now entered into withdrawal negotiations with the EU. The European Union (Notification of Withdrawal) Act 2017 stipulates that the 'Prime Minister may notify, under Article 50(2) of the Treaty on European Union, the United Kingdom's intention to withdraw from the EU' and that 'this section has effect despite any provision made by or under the European Communities Act 1972 or any other enactment'.[330] The European Union (Withdrawal) Act 2018 (formerly referred to as the Great Repeal Bill, before its introduction to Parliament) received Royal Assent on 26 June 2018. The European Union (Withdrawal) Act 2018 has four main functions: to repeal the European Communities Act 1972, ending the supremacy of EU law after Brexit, to preserve and convert EU law (by way of savings provisions for EU law and EU-derived law that will be retained in domestic legislation), to create powers to make secondary legislation, where the government considers it appropriate and to amend to the devolution statutes to remove restrictions on the devolved authorities acting incompatibly with EU law.[331] On 26 November 2018 the Withdrawal Agreement for the exit of the UK from the EU has been endorsed by the EU.

The government has taken specific initiatives in the event that no agreement is reached after 29 March 2019.[332]

With regard to State aid, the government confirmed in Guidance published in August 2018 that existing EU State aid rules will also be fully transposed into UK law after Brexit through the EU Withdrawal Bill. The bill will transfer any state aid legislation applicable in the UK through EU law at the point that the UK leaves the EU directly onto the UK statute book.[333]

328 *R (on the application of Miller and another) v Secretary of State for Exiting the European Union* [2017] UKSC 5; on appeal from *Miller & Anor, R (On the Application of) v The Secretary of State for Exiting the European Union* (Rev 1) [2016] EWHC 2768 (Admin).

329 HM Government, The United Kingdom's exit from and new partnership with the European Union, Cm 9417 (February 2017).

330 See European Union (Notification of Withdrawal) Act 2017, available at https://services.parliament.uk/bills/2017-19/europeanunionwithdrawal.html.

331 European Union (Withdrawal) Act 2018, available at http://www.legislation.gov.uk/ukpga/2018/16/contents/enacted.

332 The government has developed a 'no deal' competition statutory instrument (SI) which was laid before Parliament on 29 October 2018. See, The Competition (Amendment etc.) (EU Exit) Regulations 2019 SI 2019/93 http://www.legislation.gov.uk/uksi/2019/93/pdfs/uksi_20190093_en.pdf. The CMA has also published guidance in the event of no Brexit deal: See, CMA, Merger cases if there's no Brexit deal, https://www.gov.uk/government/publications/cmas-role-in-mergers-if-theres-no-brexit-deal; Role of the CMA in antitrust cases if there's 'no deal': overview for businesses https://www.gov.uk/government/publications/cmas-role-in-antitrust-if-theres-no-brexit-deal.

333 BEIS—Guidance—*State Aid if There's no Brexit Deal* (23 August 2018), available at https://www.gov.uk/government/publications/state-aid-if-theres-no-brexit-deal/state-aid-if-theres-no-brexit-deal. The government's formal response to a House of Lords sub-committee report on the impact of Brexit on competition and State aid rules also expresses the government's commitment to a rigorously enforced competition law regime with regard to state aids post-Brexit, independently regulated by the CMA. See Letter from Andrew Griffiths MP to Rt Hon The Lord Witty (29 March 2018), available at https://www.parliament.uk/documents/lords-committees/eu-internal-market-subcommittee/brexit-competition/290318-Government-Response-to-HoL-EU-Internal-Market-Sub-Committee-competition.pdf. The government has also laid draft State Aid (EU) Exit Regulations

With regard to mergers and conduct regulation, the government published in September 2018 a technical notice on the provisions for merger review and competition enforcement if there is no Brexit deal.[334] The UK government sets out that all UK merger control and domestic competition law will remain the same, and that in a no deal scenario the UK would transpose EU block exemption regulation into UK law. The notice also proposes that European Commission decisions made before exit will continue to have the same legal status in UK law as now, but the Competition and Markets Authority and UK courts will no longer be bound to follow future ECJ case law. On transition, the technical notice observes that the EU merger regime continues to apply as normal until the point of Brexit, but in a 'no deal' scenario there may be no agreement on jurisdiction over 'live' EU merger and antitrust cases to the extent that they produce effects on UK markets.

There are still various options on the negotiation table. Some of these options entail some degree of participation of the UK in the European Single Market, or to the Customs Union ('soft Brexit'), while others involve the UK leaving the European Single market and possibly Customs Union, entering into some form of bilateral trade deal/association agreement with the EU, or resorting to World Trade Organization (WTO) rules ('hard Brexit'). We will explore the implications of each option for substantive competition law.[335]

A possible option would be for the UK to join the European Economic Area regime from which benefit Iceland, Lichtenstein and Norway, and be bound by the EEA provisions on competition (the so-called 'Norway Model').[336] These provisions, included in Articles 53 to 60, Annex XIV and Protocols 21–4 of the EEA Agreement, are modelled on their EU equivalent provisions. EEA Members are also subject to the same State Aid rules.[337] EU Regulations and Directives are also transposed in the EEA legal order through decisions of the EEA Joint Committee. EU Notices, Communications, Guidelines are also usually re-adopted by the European Free Trade Association (EFTA) Surveillance Authority. Joining the EEA will be the least disruptive option from the status quo.

There will be no serious substantive change to be brought to the Enterprise Act 1998, with the exception perhaps of section 10 of the CA98 providing that an agreement that is covered by an EU Block Exemption Regulation (BER) will be exempted under UK competition law (the 'parallel exemptions' system), although in practice is seems unlikely that the UK competition law will diverge from the approach followed in the various EU BER and Guidelines. Following the enactment of the European Union (Withdrawal) Act in the relevant part, the current EU BER will be incorporated into domestic law. In order to avoid regulatory divergence, it would be desirable to give the CMA the power to recommend to the Secretary of State adoption of future versions of the EU BER through Statutory Instruments, where necessary

2019, available at http://www.legislation.gov.uk/ukdsi/2019/9780111178768 to ensure a domestic state aid regime would be in place by 29 March 2019, in the event the UK leaves the EU without a deal. See also, CMA, The CMA's state aid role if there's no Brexit deal Published 23 January 2019 https://www.gov.uk/government/publications/the-cmas-state-aid-role-if-theres-no-brexit-deal/uk-state-aid-if-theres-no-brexit-deal.

334 BEIS—Guidance—*Merger Review and Anti-competitive Activity if There's no Brexit Deal* (13 September 2018), available at https://www.gov.uk/government/publications/merger-review-and-anti-competitive-activity-if-theres-no-brexit-deal/merger-review-and-anti-competitive-activity-if-theres-no-brexit-deal.

335 Issues relating to enforcement and procedure are examined in depth in the companion volume: I Lianos, *Competition Law: Enforcement and Procedure* (OUP, forthcoming 2019). We will not also examine State aids law, as this area is not covered in this book. On this, see House of Lords—European Union Committee, 12th Report of Session 2017–19, Brexit: competition and State aid (2 February 2018), ch 6.

336 EEA Agreement [1994] OJ L1/1 [hereinafter EEA Agreement].

337 Ibid, Articles 61–4.

with the required modifications. Similarly, it may make sense to amend the 'convergence clause' of section 60 of the CA98 with regard to general principle of dealing with the questions relating to competition within the United Kingdom in a manner that is consistent with the treatment of corresponding questions in EU law. The government may decide that it does not make sense to impose on UK courts and competition enforcers the duty to avoid any inconsistency between the enforcement of UK competition law and the principles laid down by the jurisprudence of the EU Courts. However, it appears desirable to continue requiring the courts and competition enforcers to 'have regard' to the decisions of, principles established by, and interpretations of the law found by the Court of Justice of the European Union, decisions by the European Commission, Commission's Notices and Guidelines, and to avoid inconsistency with the decisions of, principles established by and interpretations of the law found by the EFTA Court and the EFTA Surveillance Authority. The EEA/EFTA option will not alter the current dynamics in merger control, as the European Commission has exclusive jurisdiction in the EEA to deal with all cases that have an EU dimension (Article 57 of the EEA Agreement). Similarly, the UK will still be subject to State aid rules under the EEA option.

From an institutional perspective, the CMA will have no competence to apply EU competition law, although it may apply EEA law, which is practically the same. It will also cease to be a national competition authority within the EU competition law system and cease to participate in the ECN. A vibrant and effective European Competition Network exists, of which the UK's Competition and Markets Authority is a prominent member. The ECN facilitates coordination and cooperation in the development and enforcement of competition policy with, among other things, detailed notifications of enforcement activities among ECN members, exchange of non-confidential and confidential information, and intensive investigative assistance including joint inspections.

Another route would be for the UK to negotiate a bilateral deal providing some access to the EU Internal Market. This may result in anything ranging from the 'Swiss Model' or pure EFTA Model with tailor-made bilateral agreements to the 'Turkish Model' of a Customs Union-style Association Agreement with the EU, or a simple free trade deal ('the Canada or CETA Model'[338]). If any of these options is chosen, the bilateral agreement between the EU and the UK, which will have to be negotiated, may cover some but not all areas of trade and, in any case, is unlikely to impose a general duty to apply EU laws. Competition law may be covered by such an agreement, with varying degrees of convergence and cooperation envisaged between the EU and UK competition law regimes. For instance, the recent EU–Switzerland competition cooperation agreement, which entered into force on 1 December 2014, provides for extensive cooperation and coordination between the EU and the Swiss competition authorities, including the exchange of and transmission of confidential information.[339]

If any of these options is chosen, this may have some implications with regard to the substantive provisions of antitrust law (in addition to the ones indicated above for the 'Norway Model'), although both Swiss, and to a certain extent Turkish, competition laws resemble EU competition law in many respects. However, the EU Merger Regulation will cease to apply and, as a result, there will be no longer a one-stop-shop principle for notification of mergers, as transactions in the UK will need to be notified to the European Commission, as well as to the UK competition authorities, which may decide to opt for a mandatory, and not voluntary

338 See Comprehensive Economic and Trade Agreement (CETA), will enter into force provisionally from 21 September 2017.

339 Agreement between the European Union and the Swiss Confederation concerning cooperation on the application of their competition laws [2014] OJ L 347/3. See also below on Question 5.

as it is now, merger notification system. State aid rules will no longer apply. Of course, the parties in the negotiations are free to decide otherwise.

Choosing this option will also have significant implications with regard to enforcement and procedure. In addition to the implications hinted at above with regard to the 'Norway Model', in any of the models of the second route, the CMA will only apply UK competition law. Regulation 1/2003 will no longer apply, and consequently the CMA will be able to initiate proceedings even if the European Commission has started investigations on the same case and irrespective of whether there is already an investigation by another NCA. Among the various other procedural issues one may refer to the legal professional privilege, as lawyers solely qualified in England & Wales, Scotland, and Northern Ireland would no longer be enrolled in an EU Member State Bar or Law Society with the result that their advice would not be privileged in investigations conducted by the European Commission or NCAs from the EU27, and would not be entitled to plead before the European Courts, the case law of the CJEU reserving this benefit solely to EU-qualified lawyers.[340]

Although Brexit will not affect the jurisdiction of UK courts to apply EU competition law as an integral part of the law of an EU Member State, if this is the law applicable to the dispute pending before the UK courts (foreign applicable law), Rome II and Brussels I Regulations, with regard to applicable law and jurisdiction in cross-border disputes, would no longer apply.[341] This may affect London's standing as an EU-wide competition litigation hotspot, with implications for law firms and economic consultancies based in the UK. However, it is possible that the arrangements negotiated with the EU will include some provisions re-establishing the effect of Rome II and Brussels I, or some equivalent regime, for the UK.

Another option that may be chosen is the WTO only (default) option, without any bilateral agreement between the EU and the UK being concluded ('The WTO Model'). Such option will have similar effects as those described in the previous (bilateral agreement) option, without any possibility for the parties to devise a regime that may carry some of the characteristics of the current relation between the EU and the UK competition law systems. In this option, the WTO rules on subsidies will continue to apply, thus constraining somewhat the possibility of the UK government to hand out subsidies and State aid.

There would also be some implications of Brexit on the jurisdiction of UK competition authorities and courts to apply competition law. Jurisdiction can be defined as the government's general power to exercise authority over all persons and entities within its territory. We generally distinguish three forms of jurisdiction: prescriptive jurisdiction (which refers to the ability of a State to create, amend or repeal legislation, in our case applicable substantive competition law), adjudicative jurisdiction (which consists of the power of a court to hear and resolve legal and factual issues under substantive legal rules and to provide the adjudicative and remedial forum to resolve disputes over rights), and enforcement jurisdiction (the State's right to enforce this legislation by investigating an infringement of its laws and punishing the infringers, or the possibility of implementing a judgment). We focus here on prescriptive jurisdiction.

With regard to extraterritorial enforcement (prescriptive jurisdiction), in the event of Brexit, UK-based conduct may still fall within the scope of EU competition law, should this

340 Case 155/79, *AM & S Europe Limited v Commission* [1982] ECR 1575; Case C-550/07 P, *Akzo and Akcros v Commission*, ECLI:EU:C:2010:512.

341 Regulation (EC) No 864/2007 of the European Parliament and of the Council of 11 July 2007 on the law applicable to non-contractual obligations (Rome II) [2007] OJ L 199/40; Regulation (EU) No 1215/2012 of the European Parliament and of the Council on jurisdiction and the recognition and enforcement of judgments in civil and commercial matters [2012] OJ L 351/2. See further A Dickinson, 'Back to the Future: The UK's EU Exit and the Conflict of Laws' (2016) 12(2) *J Private Int'l L* 195.

produce 'qualified' effects in the EU.[342] The Commission would have in this case prescriptive jurisdiction to implement the provisions of EU competition law. EU-based conduct may also fall within the prescriptive jurisdiction of UK-based authorities, including courts. UK competition law has traditionally taken a cautious approach with regard to the possibility of extraterritorial enforcement of competition law, being traditionally hostile to the effects doctrine.[343] The implementation of ERRA 2013 may alter this trend, as in its section 25(3) provides that the CMA 'must seek to promote competition, both within *and outside the United Kingdom*, for the benefit of consumers'.[344]

With regard to Chapter I, section 2(3) of the CA98 provides that the prohibition principle for anti-competitive agreements between undertakings, decisions by associations of undertakings, or concerted practices contained in section 2(1) of the CA98, 'applies only if the agreement, decision or practice is, or is intended to be, implemented in the United Kingdom'. Hence, it seems that the UK competition law adopts the *Wood Pulp* implementation doctrine.[345] Things are less clear with regard to the application of the 'qualified effects' doctrine. The principle of consistent treatment under UK competition law of corresponding questions arising in EU law, according to section 60 of the CA98, would indicate that the UK competition authorities and courts should apply the 'qualified effects' doctrine. However, section 60 of the CA98 provides that consistency should be achieved, 'having regard to any relevant differences between the provisions concerned', and it has been alleged that section 2(3) of the CA98 with its explicit wording on the implementation doctrine qualifies as a 'relevant difference'.[346]

With regard to Chapter II of the CA98, there is no equivalent to section 2(3), although section 18(3) requires that the dominant position being (wholly or partly) within the UK. By virtue of the same section 60 of the CA98 and the *Intel* judgment of the Court of Justice, one may expect that the 'qualified effects' doctrine would apply and bring within the scope of Chapter II conduct occurring in a related market outside the UK if it has immediate, substantial and foreseeable effects within the UK. That said, much will depend on whether section 60 of the CA98 will be repealed at the end of the transition period, for instance.

There is a long history of opposition of the UK to the extraterritorial enforcement of the competition laws of other jurisdictions, in particular the United States, following the implementation of the effects test in *Alcoa*.[347] The UK Protection of Trading Interests Act 1980 was specifically passed by the UK Parliament in order to counteract the extraterritorial enforcement of US antitrust law and applies where there is harm to UK commercial interests.[348] The Statute aims to block the extraterritorial application of the foreign law, by enabling the Secretary of State to make orders requiring UK firms to give notice to the S of S of any requirement or prohibition imposed or threatened to be imposed on them as a result of measures taken under the law of a foreign country affecting international trade and threatening to damage the commercial interests of the UK and to give them directions for prohibiting compliance with any

342 Case C-413/14 P, *Intel Corporation v European Commission*, ECLI:EU:C:2016:788, para 45.

343 See R Whish and D Bailey, *Competition Law* (OUP, 8th ed, 2015), 533.

344 Emphasis added.

345 Joined Cases C-89, 104, 114, 116, 117 & 125–9/85, *A Ahlström Osakeyhtiö and others v Commission*, ECLI:EU:C:1988:447.

346 R Whish and D Bailey, *Competition Law* (OUP, 8th ed, 2015), 534.

347 *United States v Aluminum Co of America*, 148 F.2d 416 (2d Cir 1945), in which Judge Hand held that sections 1 and 2 of the Sherman Act attached liability to wholly foreign activities that were intended to, and did, affect imports and exports of the United States.

348 On the passage of this Act, see eg TJ Kahn, 'The Protection of Trading Interests Act of 1980: Britain's Response to U.S. Extraterritorial Antitrust Enforcement' (1980) 2(2) *Northwestern J Int'l L & Business* 476.

such requirement or prohibition.[349] Similarly, the S of S has the power to prohibit compliance with the request of a foreign authority to provide commercial information to it in case that foreign authority does not have territorial jurisdiction. The S of S is also authorized to forbid a UK court to comply with a foreign court's letter of request if the information sought infringes on British sovereignty or would prejudice national security or foreign trade relations. Foreign multiple damages awards, such as the US treble damages, cannot be enforced in the UK. Defendants are even entitled to recover multiple-damages awards paid in a foreign court as the UK Protection of Trading Interests Act 1980 enables the UK defendants to bring an action in the UK to 'claw back' the non-compensatory part of damages award. Although most of these restrictions relate to enforcement jurisdiction, they have an impact on prescriptive jurisdiction by foreign antitrust law, as the limits placed on enforcement jurisdiction may influence the exercise of prescriptive jurisdiction. One may expect that such legislation could also be used with regard to the application of EU competition law in the event of Brexit.

SELECTIVE BIBLIOGRAPHY

BOOKS

Cenzig, F, *Antitrust Federalism in the EU and the US* (Routledge, 2012).

Gerber, D, *Law and Competition in Twentieth Century Europe: Protecting Prometheus* (OUP, 1998).

Korah, V, *Monopolies and Restrictive Practices* (Foundations of Law, Penguin Education, 1968), 2nd ed. under the title *Competition of Britain and the Common Market* (Kluwer, 1975), (Martinus Nijhoff, 3rd ed., 1982).

Lever, J, *The Law of Restrictive Trade Practices and Resale Price Maintenance* (Sweet and Maxwell, 1964).

Lianos, I, and Geradin, D, *Handbook on European Competition Law: Enforcement and Procedure* (Edward Elgar, 2013).

Mercer, H, *Constructing a Competitive Order—The Hidden History of British Antitrust Policies* (CUP, 1995).

Patel, KK, and Schweitzer, H, *The Historical Foundations of EU Competition Law* (OUP, 2013).

Sauter, W, *Coherence in EU Competition Law* (OUP, 2016).

Stevens, RB, and Yamey, B, *The Restrictive Practices Court—A Study of the Judicial Process and Economic Policy* (Weidenfeld and Nicolson, 1965).

Trebilcock, M, *The Common Law of Restraints of Trade: A Legal and Economic Analysis* (Carswell, 1986).

Van Cleynenbreugel, P, *Market Supervision in the European Union* (Brill Nijhoff, 2015).

Wesseling, R, *The Modernisation of EC Antitrust Law* (Hart, 2010).

Whish, R, & Bailey, D, *Competition Law* (OUP, 8th ed, 2015).

Wilks, S, *In the Public Interest: Competition Policy and the Monopolies and Mergers Commission* (Manchester University Press, 1999).

349 Three orders have been made under this section, the most relevant one for antitrust purposes being the Protection of Trading Interests (US Antitrust Measures) Order 1983, SI 1983/900, which gave rise to the *Laker Airways* litigation in UK Courts: *British Airways Board v Laker Airways Ltd* [1985] AC 58.

CHAPTERS IN BOOKS

Lianos, I, and Andreangeli, A, 'The Competition Law System and the Union's Norms' in Fox, E, and Trebilcock, M (eds) *The Design of Competition Law Institutions—Global Norms, Local Choices* (OUP, 2012), 384.

Monti, G, 'Legislative and Executive Competences in Competition Law' in Azoulai, L (ed) *The Question of Competence in the European Union* (OUP, 2014), 101.

JOURNAL ARTICLES

Budzinski, O, and Christiansen, A, 'Competence Allocation in the EU Competition Policy System as an Interest-Driven Process', (2005) 3 *J Public Policy* 313.

Hawk, B, 'System Failure: Vertical Restraints and EC Competition Law' (1995) 32(4) *Common Market L Rev* 973.

Korah, V, 'EEC Competition Policy – Legal Form or Economic Efficiency' (1986) 39(1) *Current Legal Problems* 85.

Neven, D, 'Competition Economics an Antitrust in Europe' (2006) 21(48) *Economic Policy* 741.

Scott, S, 'The Evolution of Competition Law and Policy in the United Kingdom', LSE Law, Society and Economy Working Papers 9/2009.

Smith, SA, 'Reconstructing Restraint of Trade' (1995) 15(4) *Oxford J Legal Studies* 565.

Venit, JS, 'Brave New World: The Modernization and Decentralization of Enforcement under Articles 81 and 82 of the EC Treaty' (2003) 40(3) *Common Market L Rev* 545.

Wils, W, 'Ten Years of Regulation 1/2003—A Retrospective' (2013) 4(4) *J European Competition Law and Practice* 1.

2

THE GOALS OF EU AND UK COMPETITION LAW

2.1. THE OBJECTIVES/AIMS OF COMPETITION LAW: A NORMATIVE PERSPECTIVE

Although the EU Treaties do not provide for specific aims/objectives with regard to the EU competition law provisions, section 25(3) of the Enterprise and Regulatory Reform Act (ERRA 2013) stipulates that the 'CMA must seek to promote competition, both within and outside the United Kingdom, for the benefit of consumers'. While the Act elevates the interest of consumers as the important factor in the evaluation of conduct restricting competition, it does not provide a precise definition of what is meant by 'benefit of consumers', how this relates to the aim of promoting 'competition', and how these aims will be integrated in the decision procedure adopted when assessing conduct that may allegedly restrict competition. Nevertheless, it is explicitly recognized that the Competition and Markets Authority (CMA) should seek to promote competition for the benefit of consumers, which contrasts with the more general public interest approach that formed the core of the UK competition law approach since the Monopolies and Restrictive Trade Practices Act 1948 and the Restrictive Trade Practices Act of 1956.

The institutional setting exercises an important influence on the issue of the goals of competition law, rather than the opposite.[1] The issue of goals of EU competition law still remains an open question. The EU Courts have occasionally listed a number of goals allegedly pursued by EU competition law. Since the modernization of EU competition law in early 2000s, the Commission has put forward a 'more economics approach' that accepts as relevant goals economic efficiency and the protection of the interests of consumers, while accepting the specific attachment of EU competition law to the goal of market integration. In any case, the starting

[1] I Lianos, 'Some Reflections on the Question of the Goals of EU Competition Law' in I Lianos & D Geradin (eds) *Handbook on European Competition Law: Substantive Aspects* (Edward Elgar, 2013), 1–84.

point of an economics-oriented competition law is that promoting competition is good for growth and economic development, to which we now turn.

2.1.1. COMPETITION LAW, COMPETITION POLICY, AND GROWTH/ECONOMIC DEVELOPMENT

Competition policies give the framework for markets and thus largely influence resource allocation required for economic development. In fact, a discussion of competition policies and other policies that are related to the functioning of the market should precede any discussion of competition law regimes. They are the context in which competition law and enforcement takes place.

The policies that are more directly related to the functioning of the market, and that can promote more competitive outcomes, are market infrastructure policies, external trade policies, entry and exit of firms' policies, intellectual property (IP), privatization, investment policies, procurement, regulation, and innovation policies.

There are a number of other important policies required for the efficient functioning of competitive markets, which go beyond the scope of this book. Policies related to entry and exit of firms and market mobility in general are also very important. When there are costly regulations to set up business or to operate it, the phenomena of informality takes large chunks of the economy, with clear inefficiency.[2] Moreover, even fiscal and monetary policies can have important competitive market implications. When the law stipulates fiscal loopholes and tax evasion is tolerated, firms in dominant positions may acquire an unfair advantage vis-à-vis their smaller competitors. Furthermore, there can be competition distortions when firms in a dominant position have access to credit or capital markets beyond what a proper risk analysis would dictate.

These are all policies that have to be taken into account when defining a competition law regime. They constitute the foundation in which a competition law regime operates. They should also be used in defining, on a case-by-case analysis, the different thresholds for defining the above regimes, together with other institutional elements.

There are important links between competition policy and economic development/growth. First, there are indications that more competition enhances the development potential of an economy. Second, it is also widely accepted that competition promotes institutional innovation and the emergence of efficient institutions that support economic growth. Competition law is an important dimension of competition policy and should be conceived in a much broader perspective than simply antitrust rules, merger control, or a system of competition law enforcement.

OFT 1390, *Competition and Growth* (November 2011)

> The central role of competition as a driver for economic growth and innovation is supported by a wide body of macroeconomic and sectoral evidence. We have long known that effective competition provides significant benefits for consumers through greater choice, lower prices, and better

[2] De Sotto has contributed to this analysis. See H De Sotto, *The Other Path: The Economic Answer to Terrorism* (Basic Books, 2002).

quality goods and services. Competition also drives growth because it provides strong incentives for firms to be more efficient than their rivals and to reduce their costs, and rewards innovation.

The role of competition in driving economic growth is especially important at times of moderate economic growth and fiscal constraints. With macroeconomic tools likely to prove insufficient and their use restricted by the need for fiscal consolidation, microeconomic instruments (such as the removal of unnecessary regulatory burdens and the protection and promotion of competition) become all the more important.

[. . .] There are effectively two important arms of competition policy: that which is pursued by government itself, and that undertaken by the (usually independent) competition agencies.

Government can directly support and drive competition in a variety of ways. It can choose proactively to open up markets to competition, as has been done successfully with telecommunications and airlines. It can ensure that government regulation generally fosters competition, for example by maintaining consistency and stability of regulation, and taking care that it does not create barriers to entry for new business and innovative business models. More generally, the objective of promoting competition should also influence government's behaviour in public procurement, in subsidisation and industrial policy actions, and in ensuring competitive neutrality in taxation and other areas.

A strong consumer and competition regime is a key complement to this, ensuring that competition thrives in those markets already open to it, focusing on ensuring markets work well, and driving compliance through enforcement and other tools. [. . .]

Competition is well understood to be a key factor in driving growth. It does this in a variety of ways. Firstly, within firms, competition acts as a disciplining device, placing pressure on the managers of firms to become more efficient, hence decreasing 'x-inefficiency' (that is, the difference between the most efficient behaviour that the firm is capable of and its observed behaviour in practice). This is sometimes called the 'within firm' effect.

Secondly, competition ensures that higher productivity firms increase their market share at the expense of the less productive. These low productivity firms may then exit the market, and are replaced by higher productivity firms, with the subsequent positive cross-firm impact on productivity. This is sometimes called the 'across-firm' effect. The relative importance of entry and exit in driving productivity can vary according to where a market sits on the product life cycle: entry and exit are more prominent, and have greater productivity-enhancing potential, at early stages of a product's life cycle. Entry and exit tend to have relatively lower effects on productivity in mature industries, and of the two it is exit that seems to have the more significant effect.

In any case, competition as a driver of 'across-firm' productivity improvements is especially important in periods of prolonged macroeconomic accommodating policies (typically following a severe financial crisis) when the issue of 'zombie' firms, comparatively inefficient firms that manage to survive thanks to exceptionally accommodating financial conditions, is particularly relevant. It is important to notice that this long tail of comparatively inefficient firms that drag down overall productivity levels can co-exist with 'superstar' firms that adopt state of the art managerial practices and enjoy comparatively higher levels of profitability.[3]

Thirdly, and crucially, competition drives firms to innovate. Innovation often increases dynamic efficiency through technological improvements of production processes, or the creation of new products and services. Innovation is traditionally seen as an engine for growth and productivity as, in the presence of competition, firms will aim to innovate to gain a cost advantage, to differentiate their products and/or to bring new products to the market place.

[3] See A Haldane, 'The UK's Productivity Problem: Hub No Spokes', Speech at the Academy of Social Sciences Annual Lecture, London (28 June 2018), available at https://www.bankofengland.co.uk/-/media/boe/files/speech/2018/the-uks-productivity-problem-hub-no-spokes-speech-by-andy-haldane.pdf.

Competition can also contribute to growth in other ways. By bringing down costs through 'within firm' and 'across firm' effects and by driving innovation, competition also reduces inflation rates, both at the sectoral and aggregate level, creating a more stable macroeconomic environment. Crucially, competition is also a defence against the entrenchment of vested interests and protectionism, contributing to the opening up of markets to new entrants, and increasing the attractiveness of a country as a recipient of foreign direct investment (with potential associated spillover in the form of novel techniques and management systems).

The positive impact of competition on economic growth can be furthered by empowered consumers, with clear synergies here between competition and consumer policy. When consumers trust firms and markets (because of consumer protection) and when consumers actively choose and buy what is best for them (with the aid of consumer protection), then firms will compete fairly to deliver what consumers want, in order to gain business from each other.

There is now important empirical evidence that competition law enforcement is linked to economic growth in developed countries.[4] More generally, there is evidence that competition promotes productivity. Disney et al[5] conclude that competition increases productivity levels and the rate of growth of productivity. Recently, Bloom and van Reenen[6] show that good management practices are strongly associated with productivity, and those are better when product market competition is higher. Finally, an efficient market for corporate control with open rules for takeovers reinforces the impact of competition on productivity.[7] Other studies by Blundell et al[8] and Aghion and Griffith[9] also confirm the above results. A study for Australia shows that competition-enhancing reforms in the 1990s contributed to an increase in GDP.[10] However, it has also been alleged that the appropriate level of competition may differ for different stages of economic development.[11] Some recent empirical research has also examined the negative macro-economic implications of market power, in particular a decline in the labour and capital shares, with an increase in the share of monopolistic rents, as well as the decrease in labour market dynamism.[12]

[4] For overviews of the empirical evidence, see TC Ma, 'The Effect of Competition Law Enforcement on Economic Growth', (2011) 7(2) *J Competition L & Economics* 301; P Buccirossi, L Ciari, T Duso, G Spagnolo, and C Vitale, 'Competition Policy and Productivity Growth: An Empirical Assessment' (2013) 95(4) *Rev of Economics & Statistics* 1324.

[5] R Disney, J Haskel, and Y Heden, 'Restructuring and Productivity Growth in UK Manufacturing' [2003] 113 *Economic J* 666.

[6] N Bloom and J van Reenen, 'Measuring and Explaining Management Practices Across Firms and Across Countries' CEP Discussion Paper 716 (2006).

[7] S Nickel, D Nickolitsas, and N Dryden, 'What Makes Firms Perform Well? [1997] 41 *European Economic Rev* 783; S Januszewski, J Koke, and J Winter, 'Product Market Competition, Corporate Governance and Firm Performance: An Empirical Analysis for Germany' (2001) (on file with author).

[8] R Blundell, R Griffith, and J van Reenen, 'Market Share, Market Value and Innovation in a Panel of British Manufacturing Sector' (1999) 66(3) *Rev Economic Studies* 529.

[9] P Aghion & R Griffith, 'Competition and Growth: Reconciling Theory and Evidence' (MIT Press, 2005) (noting that the greatest rate of innovation is observed in industries where the two main firms are technologically neck-and-neck. In these instances the incentive to innovate and thus to escape competition is the greatest).

[10] Organisation for Economic Co-operation and Development (OECD), *Sources of Economic Growth in OECD Countries* (OECD, Paris, 2003).

[11] See eg A Singh, 'Competition and Competition Policy in Emerging Markets: International and Developmental Dimensions', ESRC Center for Business Research, University of Cambridge Working Paper No 246 (2002).For a discussion, see D Sokol, T Cheng, and I Lianos (eds) *Competition Law and Development* (Stanford University Press, 2013).

[12] See, J de Loecker and Jan Eeckhout, The Rise of Market Power and the Macroeconomic Implications, NBER Working Paper No. 23687 (August 2017), available at https://www.nber.org/papers/w23687.

2.1.2. COMPETITION LAW AND ECONOMIC WELFARE/EFFICIENCY

The current paradigm of competition law in the EU, the UK, but also globally, is based on the double tradition of classical and neoclassical economics.[13]

Classical economics make the assumption that competitive markets in which privately owned companies seek to make profits for their shareholders, compete with each other to supply products to other businesses and consumers enjoying unconstrained choice, are essential in order to achieve 'material progress' or 'economic progress'. Adam Smith was the first widely recognized economist to refer to the role of markets for economic development and growth. Smith's ingredients for a theory of growth were that growth depends on productivity, labour, and capital. Smith characterized the increase in productivity as the interaction of the division of labour and market expansion. The process of development is characterized by specialization and productivity increases associated with the division of labour, which is only possible with market expansion and multiplication. Growth is generated by the interaction of the division of labour and market building.

This emphasis on the dynamic element was lost in the effort of neoclassical economists, on which competition law economics is currently largely based, to address, primarily, issues of static allocation of given resources at a given period of time. Starting with Stanley Jevons and the marginal revolution, neoclassical price theory took as a given the level of population, the various needs and capacities of production, land, and other resources, to concentrate on the mode of employing labour that would maximize utility. Economic analysis concentrated 'on the conditions that would make possible various optima rather than on the conditions that would allow an economy to achieve ever-changing optima of ever-increasing range'.[14] Their concern was how consumer choice could be maximized (allocative efficiency) or producers' costs minimized (productive efficiency). In their standard model, interactions between producers and consumers are mediated through the price system, thus leading to a unique Pareto efficient equilibrium.[15] In these individual markets, neoclassical theory holds that competition between the various producers drives economic efficiency, which in turn maximizes welfare. Markets are assumed to tend towards equilibrium, the firms active in these markets being constrained to act by the external pressures of the market. Inter-firm competition is also believed to promote innovation and lead to higher growth.

Neoclassical price theorists do not assume that markets always work well. They pin down instances of 'market failure', where suboptimal results occur. One of the examples of market failure is when firms have monopolistic power, which restricts competition and thus harms buyers, who pay higher prices for the product. The theory of 'market failure' provides the main rationale for government intervention in markets, in the context of neoclassical economic theory. The government may address market failures resulting from monopolistic power by

[13] The term 'classical economics' was coined by Karl Marx in his description of Ricardo's formal economics in contrast to 'romantic economics' (ie economics close to the people). It usually covers a period between 1776 and 1870. D Colander, 'The Death of Neoclassical Economics' (2002) 22 *J History of Economic Thought* 127, 130. Neoclassical economics constitutes the mainstream economic tradition now days and covers the period since 1870s, and in particular since the mid-1880s, when economics progressively evolved to a separate scientific field; Alfred Marshall, one of the founders of neoclassical economics being appointed professor of political economy at the University of Cambridge and publishing in 1890 his highly influential *Principles of Economics*.

[14] G Meier, *Biography of a Subject: Evolution of Development Economics* (OUP, 2004), 38.

[15] See eg R Solow, 'A Contribution to the Theory of Economic Growth' (1956) 70(1) *Q J Economics* 64 (presenting a neoclassical growth model). On Pareto efficiency see our analysis in Section 2.1.3.

promoting competition. However, neoclassical economists also accept that it is not only markets that fail, but also governments may fail as well, because, for instance, public institutions may be captured by special interests with the result that government action does not reflect the general welfare of society. Hence, according to the mainstream neoclassical economics view, before intervening in markets one needs to balance the benefits of government intervention (correcting market failures) versus the costs of such intervention (competition law failure). We will come back to this 'balancing act' later in this chapter.[16] Note how in this efficiency-oriented competition law paradigm neoclassical price theory assists decision-makers to develop prescriptive standards for State action on the basis of the 'balancing act' performed through the means of neoclassical economics and, more generally, economic efficiency analysis. This is a major difference between the classical economics' approach and the neoclassical one.

In the following sections, we will explore the fundamental assumptions of the efficiency paradigm of competition law, its different variants, and competing paradigms.

2.1.3. THE CONCEPT OF ECONOMIC WELFARE/ECONOMIC EFFICIENCY

The proponents of an economic efficiency approach distinguish between Pareto efficiency and Kaldor–Hicks efficiency. If one focuses on efficiency in consumption,[17] Pareto efficiency requires allocating goods between consumers so that it would not be possible by any reallocation to make people better off without making anybody else worse off. The Potential Pareto Improvement Criterion (or Kaldor–Hicks efficiency) advances that if the magnitude of the gains from moving from one state of the economy to another is greater than the magnitude of the losses, then social welfare is increased by making the move even, if no actual compensation is made.[18] According to Kaldor–Hicks efficiency, an outcome is efficient if those who are made better off can, *potentially*, compensate those that were made worse off, with the resulting outcome still being Pareto optimal. The winners should, in theory, be able to compensate the losers, but there is no requirement that compensation should be effectively paid.

The Kaldor–Hicks efficiency is based on the following two fundamental theorems of welfare economics:[19]

The First Fundamental Theorem of Welfare Economics: Assume that all individuals and firms are selfish price takers. Then a competitive equilibrium is Pareto optimal.

The Second Fundamental Theorem of Welfare Economics: Assume that all individuals and producers are selfish price takers. Then almost any Pareto optimal equilibrium can be supported via the competitive mechanism, provided appropriate lump sum taxes and transfers are imposed on individuals and firms.

[16] On the 'antitrust's balancing act', see A Ayal, *Fairness in Antitrust* (Hart, 2014), 8–10.

[17] One could advance a growth-related theory of competition law emphasizing the supply side, instead of the demand side (consumers). On the relation of competition law and economic growth, see Section 2.1.1.

[18] JR Hicks, 'The Foundations of Welfare Economics' (1939) 49(196) *Economic J* 696; N Kaldor, 'Welfare Propositions in Economics and Interpersonal Comparisons of Utility' (1939) 49(145) *Economic J* 549.

[19] See M Blaug, 'The Fundamental Theorems of Modern Welfare Economics, Historically Contemplated' (2007) 39(2) *History of Political Economy* 185.

Contemporary economists do not rely on the First Fundamental Theorem as externalities, market failures, and imperfect competition are almost universally recognized, yet, the Second Fundamental Theorem implies that if a particular state of the economy is judged to be desirable, it may be achieved through lump-sum transfers, hence separating efficiency from distributive justice. Following the Kaldor–Hicks criterion of efficiency, economic policy recommendations should be determined by efficiency, distribution remaining a problem for the political realm (the separability thesis).[20]

2.1.4. ECONOMIC EFFICIENCY AND CONSUMER WELFARE

According to the welfare approach to competition law, the goal of competition law enforcement should be to enable the agents/households to satisfy these (revealed) preferences at the lower cost for them. Assuming that households are consumers (final and intermediary) and producers/suppliers/shareholders, the objective should be to ensure the maximum level of efficiency for all these categories. This includes allocative efficiency, for example, the possibility for consumers to pay a price that corresponds to their willingness to pay or in some cases less than their willingness to pay (leading to consumer surplus). It should also include the possibility for producers to use production processes that yield the highest output levels for a given set of inputs or for consumers the possibility to enjoy innovative products and services, what is usually referred to as dynamic efficiency. Finally, one should take into account the scale efficiencies producers may enjoy, enabling them to reduce the production costs of a specific good (productive efficiency) and thus to raise their surplus in the sense that if a producer has a willingness to sell, and the market price for a product is above that price, then they would be able gain a surplus equal to the gap (producer surplus).

The application of the Kaldor–Hicks standard in judging the efficiency of a change from one competitive situation to another in competition law, takes the form of a 'total welfare standard'. The latter is a measure that aggregates the surplus of different groups in the economy (eg producers, consumers) and measures the welfare consequences of the change. It is important that total (consumer and producer) surplus increases, even if the surplus of one of the groups (consumers or producers) diminishes. In conformity to the second fundamental theorem of welfare economics, only the size of the economic pie matters, not its distribution among each group.

As we indicated above, the primary duty of the CMA in UK competition law is to promote competition for the benefit of consumers, thus indicating a preference for promoting or prioritizing consumer surplus. EU competition law also seems to emphasize consumer surplus rather than producer surplus, and goes as far as accepting that wealth transfers from final consumers to producers might be a matter of concern for competition law enforcement. Article 101(3) of the Treaty on the Functioning of the European Union (TFEU) provides that consumers/users should be awarded a fair share of the possible efficiency gains that are claimed

20 The separability between questions of economic efficiency and issues of distribution has been criticized by L Robbins who advanced the view that there is a distinction between normative and positive economics but that economists should avoid value-laden policy recommendations, without making explicit their normative predispositions: see L Robbins, 'Economics and Political Economy (1981) 71 *American Economic Rev* 1. For a position justifying Kaldor–Hicks hypothetical compensation, and thus the separability thesis, from an ethical and political perspective, see RA Posner, 'The Ethical and Political Basis of the Efficiency Norm in Common Law Adjudication' (1980]) 8(3) *Hofstra L Rev* 487; RA Posner, 'Utilitarianism, Economics, and Legal Theory' (1979) 8(1) *J Legal Studies* 103.

by a producer and resulting from an anti-competitive agreement. For instance, it would be impossible to justify under Article 101(3) an agreement that affects consumers because it leads to higher prices, lower output, less innovation or lower quality, even if on aggregate that agreement provides important efficiency gains to the producers enabling them to theoretically compensate the consumers for their losses.[21] This indicates that neither UK nor EU competition law may adopt a purely economic efficiency-based approach (Kaldor–Hicks), but must take into account consumer-welfare standards or the interests of the consumer, and that issues of distribution play an important role in both UK and EU competition law.

2.1.5. CRITICISM OF THE NARROW ECONOMIC WELFARE PERSPECTIVE IN COMPETITION LAW AND THE SEPARABILITY THESIS

In addition to the point previously made that EU and UK competition law does not adhere to an economic efficiency/total welfare standard view, one may claim that there are strong normative arguments for opposing the implementation of such a standard in EU competition law.

The Kaldor–Hicks compensation approach suffers from various fundamental problems that may preclude its practical application. The separability thesis may be criticized for not taking into account the inevitable distributive effects of an economic efficiency criterion. The second welfare theorem of economics denotes a *status quo* bias for the existing allocation of resources, deemed efficient. Yet, the existing resource allocation may be the product of an unjust initial distribution of income that may contravene principles of social justice, as these are defined by non-utilitarian theories of justice.[22] The proponents of the economic efficiency approach often advance that inequalities in the initial distribution may be addressed by the political system, which might decide to impose a lump sum tax compensating the losers and ensuring an equality of opportunity. The implicit assumption is that the tax system is a more efficient way of engaging in redistribution than the regulatory system.[23] However, one may reverse the order of these arguments and suggest instead that it is *only* if the question of fair and equitable income distribution is adequately addressed by the political system that it may be legitimate for competition law to focus exclusively on economic efficiency.

One needs also to factor in the inability of the EU to employ fiscal instruments to redistribute wealth across the Union. EU Member States differ greatly in their levels of wealth, a disparity that is currently increasing as a result of the expansion of the EU to the east and the important economic crisis affecting southern Europe.[24] It has been noted that powerful firms are not randomly distributed across Europe, and hence 'producer surplus is likely to accrue

21 The trade-off between dynamic efficiency gains and static allocative efficiency gains in a total welfare context might be complicated. See our analysis later in this Section.

22 See, for instance, the perspective of J Rawls, *A Theory of Justice* (Harvard University Press, 1971), introducing the idea that society should be conceived as a system of cooperation designed to advance the mutual advantage of each members and of each of its members. Individuals should be recognized primary social goods, as rights and liberties, powers and opportunities, income and wealth, chosen by the parties to the social contract from an original position behind a veil of ignorance that prevents them from knowing anything about their future position.

23 This is related to the discussion over the comparison between taxation by regulation and direct taxation, the latter being considered more efficient, under very specific conditions, see A Atkinson and J Stiglitz, 'The Design of Tax Structure: Direct versus Indirect Taxation' (1976) 6(1–2) *J Public Economics* 55.

24 B McDonnel and DA Farber, 'Are Efficient Antitrust Rules Always Optimal?' [2003] *Fall Antitrust Bulletin* 807, 825.

primarily to the most powerful and wealthy EU members, increasing existing wealth disparities at the margins'.[25] Efficient rules that would focus only on total surplus with no attention to the allocation of that surplus between producers and consumers (which is excluded by efficiency analysis as a distributive justice issue) will tend to pump wealth in the 'wrong' direction.[26] In the absence of adequate resources and a competence for the EU to mitigate these distributional consequences across the Union (in view of the absence of an EU corporate income tax and the low transfer of wealth from rich to poor Member States, assuming that the qualification of 'rich' and 'poor' States represents average disposable income for consumers), there may be a less strong argument for the separability thesis in the EU than in jurisdictions, such as the United States, which dispose the adequate fiscal instruments to pursue redistribution at the federal level.

In addition to these practical difficulties for the application of a total welfare standard in EU competition law there are also a number of theoretical objections that raise doubts about the desirability of the Kaldor–Hicks or the economic efficiency total welfare standard, in general.[27]

An important one is that the Kaldor–Hicks efficiency criterion relates to the preferences of each agent for different outcomes or states of affairs. However, the test takes account only of the preferences of the specific set of agents to which it is applied, by exploring their revealed preferences, without paying any attention to other agents that may be affected. This is accentuated by the fact that competition analysis is limited to the participants of a relevant market (as a result of the partial equilibrium analysis performed) and does not include all the other markets or sectors of the economy that may be affected by the restriction of competition and/or the remedial action adopted by the competition authority. If neoclassical price theory examines interrelationships between different sectors of the economy, the analysis focuses on a particularly short time horizon and the impersonal setting of a market for all goods and all periods. History and institutions do not matter and cannot influence the choice of the equilibrium. The possibility that there can be multiple equilibria, inferior or superior, at a given point in time, which could be chosen because of historical, cultural, or institutional reasons or the existing distribution of wealth, have not been seriously contemplated.

The extreme version of this argument may take the form of the theory of second best,[28] suggesting that government interventions to make a market more competitive, may not make consumers better off, as if the first best solution is not realized (eg perfect competition), then there is nothing enabling us to choose between the second or the third best. This is contrary to the belief in welfare economics that if first best is unattainable, then second best may be attained, even if some Pareto optimality conditions are not satisfied (such as Kaldor–Hicks efficiency). In view of the fact that the competition law assessment is partial and refers to a specific market, ignoring all other effects to non-relevant markets, the criticism of the theory of the second best may have a devastating effect in competition law. This may be particularly important if the change in the competitive conditions that has to be assessed may bring new parties into existence (consumers or firms), or exclude others in other relevant markets or economic sectors, for which there is no account of their preferences.

One may also note that the Potential Pareto Improvement criterion has been used to argue that increases in output (shifts in the frontier of production possibilities) are an improvement

[25] Ibid. [26] Ibid.

[27] For analysis, see I Lianos, 'Some Reflections on the Question of the Goals of EU Competition Law' in I Lianos and D Geradin (eds) *Handbook on European Competition Law—Substantive Aspects* (Edward Elgar, 2013), 1–84.

[28] RG Lipsey & KK Lancaster, 'The General Theory of Second Best' (1956–7) 24(1) *Rev Economic Studies* 11.

because they are potentially welfare enhancing, assuming that the production (or consumption) of more commodities is welfare enhancing. Indeed, by definition, more production of something leads to more units of that something to be distributed (with the result that allocative efficiency is improved). However, one may argue that this does not increase the 'right' output mix. The decision over the proper mix of goods and productive inputs involves some normative judgments over what constitutes 'good' or 'bad consumption'. For example, producing more industrial waste might not be a 'good' commodity from a welfare perspective, in view of the possible lasting effects of such waste on the standards for the environment and quality of life.

Further difficulties emerge from the assumption made that the consumer preferences to be satisfied are always exogenous, and hence they should be the starting point of the analysis. However, research on behavioural economics has provided evidence of biases,[29] indicating that the context of choice may have an important role to play in the way consumers develop their preferences (framing effects). Preferences are formed within a specific social context and may be endogenous, in the sense that they depend on the individual's personal history and the social and cultural context in which this individual is integrated.[30] One may also criticize the linkage between consumer preferences and welfare (see our analysis in Section 3.2.2.4).

Inter-generation effects should also been taken into account in cases involving some lasting effects (eg environmental or sustainable development objectives as opposed to lower prices for actual consumers), thus increasing the complexity and difficulty of analysing cost and benefit in this context.[31]

Preferences may not relate to outcomes (eg the quantity and quality of the products exchanged) but to the process of achieving these outcomes (eg fairness, competition). There is no doubt that sport fans would enjoy more a fair competition with no record performances than a sporting competition profoundly distorted by doping, even if this will lead to record performances. Welfare economics are indifferent on the content of preferences: 'by taking preferences to be total comparative evaluations (as they must if preferences are to determine choices), economists allow preferences to be influenced by everything agents regard as relevant to their choices, whether these be moral or aesthetic considerations, ideals, whims, fantasies, or passions of all sorts'.[32] However, this ignores all instances in which preferences relate to a process rather than an outcome.

There is also an inherent problem in inferring preferences by choice, as it is the case in revealed preference theory, which limits preferences to those alternatives among which the agents choose in fact: when there is no choice, there is no preference.[33] This inference may prove far-fetched. Indeed, 'preferences cannot be defined by choice, because the same choice reflects different preferences when beliefs differ'.[34] Preferences can be inferred from choices *only given premises regarding beliefs*.[35] Inferences concerning preferences depend on

[29] OFT1224, 'What does Behavioral Economics Mean for Competition Policy?' (March 2010), available at http://webarchive.nationalarchives.gov.uk/20140402182927/http:/www.oft.gov.uk/shared_oft/economic_research/oft1224.pdf.

[30] For an interesting critique, based on the role of culture, see VH Storr, *Understanding the Culture of Markets* (London & New York: Routledge, 2013).

[31] T Cowen, 'The Scope and Limits of Preference Sovereignty' (1993) 9 *Economics and Philosophy* 253, 258–60.

[32] DM Hausman, *Preference, Value, Choice, and Welfare* (CUP, 2012). [33] Ibid, 27.

[34] Ibid, 27–8. Hausman gives the example of Romeo choosing death to life under the mistaken belief that Juliet was dead. But of course, he does not prefer death to life with Juliet: '[h]is choice does not reveal his preference, because he is mistaken about what the alternatives are among which he is choosing'.

[35] Ibid, 28 (emphasis added).

assumptions about the constraints faced by the particular agents and the way they would be able to individualize the alternatives. However, the idea that *one* preference ordering may reflect the person's interests, represent her welfare, and describe her actual choice and behaviour has been criticized for not accounting for situations when choice of alternatives can be explained by other reasons (eg a person may be motivated by altruism or moved by malevolent purposes).[36]

It is wrong to assume that the satisfaction of revealed preferences will necessarily promote welfare as people often prefer what is worse for their welfare in the long run because 'their preferences are evil, ignorant, adaptive, or otherwise misshapen.'[37] Responding to this criticism, some authors advance the need for a laundered set of preferences, removing the lack of information, cognitive biases, or anti-social preferences (*non-ideal* preferences) from the welfare calculus.[38] However, if this route is followed, actual preferences cannot be a proxy for informed and laundered self-interested preferences.

Some recent studies have also advanced the view that although welfare cannot be defined as the satisfaction of revealed preferences, preferences may be considered at least as *evidence* of well-being among other types of evidence.[39] This view still recognizes that relying on people's revealed preferences, as expressed in the marketplace, might be more informative on their well-being than relying on the judgment of government officials, judges, legislators, or moral philosophers.

An alternative approach to that of actual or laundered revealed preferences is to construct an objective list of preferences (or capabilities) that might reasonably be expected to promote an agent's well-being.[40] Some recent work of the Organisation for Economic Co-operation and Development (OECD) has taken a multi-dimensional view of well-being, adopting an objective-list approach identifying a number of dimensions of well-being, including material living standards (income, consumption, and wealth), health, education, personal activities including work, political voice and governance, social connections and relationships, environment (present and future conditions), and insecurity of an economic or physical nature.[41] Although it is clear that wealth is only one factor among the many determining well-being, it is difficult to imagine how such an approach could be incorporated in competition law adjudication and how information on all these factors could be collected and assessed by competition authorities or courts on a case-by-case basis.

Other approaches to welfare question the insistence on preferences, supporting instead a hedonic approach, close to that of the old utilitarianism of Jeremy Bentham, that would measure the happiness of agents by evaluating the way that person feels throughout her life (subjective experience of life).[42] However, the application of happiness studies in the

[36] A Sen, *Choice, Welfare and Measurement* (Harvard University Press, 1982).

[37] MD Adler and EA Posner, *New Foundations of Cost Benefit Analysis* (Harvard University Press, 2006), 33.

[38] Ibid, 34. [39] DM Hausman, *Preference, Value, Choice, and Welfare* (CUP, 2012), 93–102.

[40] See eg A Sen, *Commodities and Capabilities* (North-Holland, 1985) advancing the moral significance of individuals' capability of achieving the kind of lives they have reason to value. For a different objective list approach, see M Nussbaum, *Creating Capabilities: The Human Development Approach* (Harvard University Press, 2011). For Sen, well-being depends on the agent using these capabilities, while for Nussbaum this is not essential.

[41] See OECD, *Better Life Initiative*, available at www.oecdbetterlifeindex.org/. The OECD's work follows the work of the Commission on the Measurement of Economic Performance and Social Progress (J Stiglitz, A Sen, and JP Fitoussi), Report by the Commission on the Measurement of Economic Performance and Social Progress, available at https://ec.europa.eu/eurostat/documents/118025/118123/Fitoussi+Commission+report.

[42] R Layard, *Happiness: Lessons from a New Science* (Allen Lane, 2005). On the measurement of happiness, see D Kahneman, 'Objective Happiness' in D Kahneman et al (eds) *Well Being: The Foundations of Hedonic Psychology* (Russel Sage Foundation, 1999), 3–25.

competition law context also runs into the same practical difficulties as the objective list or multi-factored analysis, with the additional limitation that measuring the change in happiness following a specific anti-competitive conduct would prove an extremely difficult or almost impossible task, under the current circumstances, unless subjective well-being is determined by contingent valuation surveys, as is the case in some procedures of cost–benefit analysis. One might also raise important objections to happiness surveys, including measurement problems in the multi-cultural environment of the EU, as the concept of 'happiness' may not have the same meaning in all Member States. Additional concerns include the ethical problems raised by the 'hedonic engineering' of the State required in this case, or because of the assumption of the 'aggregative understanding of happiness' (the assumption that happiness of a whole life is 'the sum of the happiness of its individual moments'), which is not a view shared by all cultures.[43] In any case, even if measuring happiness was practically possible and ethically acceptable, the decision-maker should also incorporate in the analysis the risk of forecasting errors, cognitive heuristics and the possible discrepancy between predicted happiness and experienced happiness or well-being.

2.1.6. PROMOTING INNOVATION

As innovation is considered a major engine of growth,[44] public authorities play a direct role in fostering innovation,[45] but also in supporting the emergence of an innovation-friendly market environment.

The role of the competitive process in the promotion of innovation is well recognized and widely accepted. Certainly, research and development requires up front investments for uncertain rewards. Intellectual property rights were initially conceived as an exception to the rule of competitive markets. By providing some economic rents, intellectual property rights ensure that the inventor has adequate incentives to innovate at the first place.[46] Although IP may provide some certainty over the ability of an undertaking to retain the benefits from the innovation it put in place (and internalize the positive externalities thus produced), the social return to innovation largely exceeds its private return.[47] In reality, imperfect IP

43 See eg the criticisms of R Skidelsky and E Skidelsky, *How Much in Enough?* (Allen Lane-Penguin Books, 2012), 96–123.

44 This objective of competition law is thoroughly analysed in the companion volume I Lianos, *Competition Law and the Intangible Economy* (OUP, forthcoming 2019).

45 This is either done through public investment in science and basic research, which can play an important role in developing general-purpose technologies and, hence, in enabling further innovation, as well as public support to innovative activity in the private sector, which is usually taking the form of a mix of direct and indirect instruments such as tax credits, soft loans, direct support etc. On the important role of the State in supporting innovation, see M Mazucatto, *The Entrepreneurial State: Debunking Public vs. Private Sector Myths* (Anthem, 2013).

46 This simple trade-off was already recognized by the UK Statute of Monopolies (1623) which declared 'all monopolies [. . .] for the sole buying, selling, making, working or using of anything within this realm, or of any other monopolies, or of power to give license or toleration to do, use or exercise anything against any law [. . .] are contrary to the laws of this realm, and so are and shall be utterly void [. . .]' but also recognized an exception from this prohibition for '[. . .] any letters patents and grants of privilege for the term of fourteen years or under, hereafter to be made, of the sole working or making of any manner of new manufactures within this realm, to the true and first inventor or inventors of such manufactures [. . .]'.

47 This was highlighted by K Arrow, 'Economic Welfare and the Allocation of Resources for Invention in The Rate and Direction of Inventive Activity: Economic and Social Factors' in *The Rate and Direction of Inventive Activity: Economic and Social Factors* (NBER, 1962), 609.

protection may lead the competitors to gain some of the rewards from the rival's innovation (the problem of limited appropriability).[48] Technological spillovers and imitation across the industry or cross-industries may boost growth to a considerable extent, without it being possible that these indirect benefits are appropriated by the IP holder, thus illustrating the inadequacy of a policy relying on intellectual property rights only to spur innovation and the importance of public funding of research. It has been argued that disruptive innovation may also challenge monopoly positions that become temporary (the process of 'creative destruction').[49] Determining what is the appropriate market structure for innovation remains, however, an open and hotly debated issue.[50] For example, it has been argued that there is an inverted U-shaped relation between market competition and innovation. Whilst initially the 'escape competition' incentive dominates and innovation increases with competition, at higher levels of market competition, however, innovation decreases, as firms lack both the internal funds to finance their R&D efforts and the confidence that success in innovation will result in a lasting competitive advantage.[51]

2.1.7. COMPETITION LAW AND NON-ECONOMIC EFFICIENCY RELATED CONSIDERATIONS

Analysing in detail all the possible aims of EU competition law, other than economic welfare, considered by the competition authorities, courts, and academic commentators is beyond the aims of this study.[52] Among these objectives, one may include economic democracy, fairness, completing the Internal Market, the principle of freedom of competition, the protection of a group of market actors, such as final consumers or small and medium undertakings.

2.1.7.1. Economic democracy

Antitrust law and its antecedents in common law were not initially perceived as having merely an economic rationale. Their role was political. It consisted, for the restraints of trade doctrine and the Statute of Monopolies, to ensure that the King would not bypass the Parliament in order to raise revenue by conceding privileges and monopolies as well as to protect the

48 Ibid, 619.

49 J Schumpeter, *Capitalism, Socialism and Democracy* (1942; Harper & Bros, 1950), 83, noting that 'The opening up of new markets, foreign or domestic, and the organizational development from the craft shop and factory to such concerns as U.S. Steel illustrate the same process of industrial mutation—if I may use that biological term—that incessantly revolutionizes the economic structure *from within*, incessantly destroying the old one, incessantly creating a new one. This process of Creative Destruction is the essential fact about capitalism. It is what capitalism consists in and what every capitalist concern has got to live in.'

50 For a critical analysis, see the companion volume. See also J Baker, 'Beyond *Schumpeter vs. Arrow*: How Antitrust Fosters Innovation' [2007] 74 *Antitrust LJ* 575; RJ Gilbert, 'Competition and Innovation' in WD Collins (ed) *Issues in Competition Law and Policy* (American Bar Association, 2008), 573.

51 See P Aghion, N Bloom, R Blundell, R Griffith, and P Howitt, 'Competition and Innovation: an Inverted-U Relation' (2005) 120 *Q J Economics* 701. For recent evidence corroborating this theory, see FJ Díez, D Leigh, and S Tambunlertchai, 'Global Market Power and its Macroeconomic Implications' IMF WP/18/137 (2018), available at https://www.imf.org/en/Publications/WP/Issues/2018/06/15/Global-Market-Power-and-its-Macroeconomic-Implications-45975.

52 On the most popular objectives of competition law, see the survey of competition authorities prepared by the International Competition Network (ICN), 'Competition Enforcement and Consumer Welfare—Setting the Agenda', 10th Annual Conference, The Hague, 10–11 May 2011, available at http://internationalcompetitionnetwork.org/uploads/library/doc857.pdf.

entrepreneurial freedom of the tradesmen, the ascending bourgeoisie, to invest in new markets without incurring barriers to entry and the risk of free riding. Similarly, the role of the Granger movement (the coalition of US farmers, principally in the Midwest) and their revolt against the monopolistic grain transport practices of railways in the passage of the US Sherman Act has long being highlighted.[53] The rising consolidation of the US industry at the turn of the century with the development of large conglomerates (trusts) in various key industries, such as steel, copper, oil, iron, sugar, tin, coal, paper bags, and salt was a major concern for the US public and played an important role in the adoption of the US Sherman Act. In the seminal *Standard Oil Co of New Jersey v United States*, the Supreme Court broke the monopoly in oil business formed by John Rockefeller in more than thirty separate companies that competed with each other.[54] The general public's hostility to big business was prevalent during the social reforms of the so-called Progressive Era (1890–1920) and led to the adoption of specific legislation against merger activity and certain practices that were found to be anticompetitive (the Clayton Act and the Federal Trade Commission Acts of 1914), or against price discrimination practices harming small retail shops and favouring big retail chains (the Robinson Patman Act 1936). Some agricultural cooperatives were excluded from the scope of the Sherman Act by section 6 of the Clayton Act 1914, which also provided an exemption for labour unions, with the aim to enhance their collective bargaining power vis-à-vis big business and the trusts that were dominating the US economy at the time.

The period between 1940s and 1970s was characterized by the emergence of 'populist' antitrust law, where the fight against bigness and economic concentration became consistent features of the antitrust law enterprise, at least in the US. Summarizing this trend, some commentators at the time noted that '[t]he grounds for the laws against collusion and monopoly include not only a dislike of restriction of output and of one-sided bargaining power, but also a desire to prevent excessive concentration of wealth and power and a desire to keep open the channels of opportunity'.[55] The quest for more 'economic democracy' became a major ingredient of the antitrust populist movement at the time. A group of conservative economists, based at the University of Chicago criticized the emphasis put by US antitrust on economic concentration and bigness in the 1960s and 1970s, alleging that much of this was the result of superior efficiency that led certain businesses to grow exponentially, while others declined or stayed stagnant.[56] The group became influential in the 1980s, following the Republican administration of Ronald Reagan came to power, with the result that in a few years, US antitrust shifted its attention away from economic democracy and concentration, and focused on the objective of economic efficiency. Following the financial and economic crisis of 2008, a different trend is emerging, as the general public, but also the government, are concerned by 'too big to fail' banks and more generally by the rising levels of economic concentration in many industries.[57] Social movements around the world are calling for the 'democratization' of the

[53] H Thorelli, *The Federal Antitrust Policy* (John Hopkins, 1955), 143. See, however, the criticism on the influence of the agrarian movement in the passage of the Sherman Act by G Stigler, 'The Origins of the Sherman Act' Working Paper No 27 (August 1983), available at http://www.chicagobooth.edu/assests/stigler/27.pdf

[54] *Standard Oil Co of New Jersey v United States*, 221 US 1 (1911).

[55] CD Edwards, 'An Appraisal of the Antitrust Laws' (1946) 36(2) *American Economic Rev* 172, 172.

[56] RA Posner, 'The Chicago School of Antitrust Analysis' (1978–9) 127 *U Pennsylvania L Rev* 926.

[57] See the concerns over increasing consolidation of a number of industrial and economic sectors expressed by the Council of Economic Advisers to the US President, Benefits of Competition and Indicators of Market Power (April 2016), available at https://obamawhitehouse.archives.gov/sites/default/files/page/files/20160414_cea_competition_issue_brief.pdf.

market system and, more generally, a reform of capitalism towards a markets-based system subject to democratic control.[58] It remains to be seen if such calls will influence the political mainstream in the US and will lead to a more active enforcement of antitrust law against economic concentration.

A similar focus on 'economic power' occurred in EU competition law.[59] A feature of the ordoliberal approach to competition law, which has exercised quite an important intellectual influence on the development of EU competition law is the emphasis put on the links between competition law and the democratic ideal, in view of the realization that a specific economic order is intrinsically related to the social and political spheres and thus there is an important inter-dependence between them.[60] The 'negative dimension' of this interdependence is the belief that the elimination of competition could undermine democracy in the political sphere and thus facilitate the rise of totalitarianism.[61] It is the same belief that pushed the Allied Powers, post-Second World War, to adopt measures for the immediate decentralization of the German and Japanese economies, including the adoption of a competition law regime.[62] Indeed, competition law may prevent that big firm's economic power may translate in political influence and power, democratic rule of law depending on the State being stronger than any of the parties that it regulates.[63] The positive dimension of these interlinkages between the economic and the political/social spheres is the promotion of economic freedom as an essential feature of a good functioning democracy, to the same extent as other fundamental and political rights, such as the right to vote, freedom of speech, and freedom of assembly.[64] We will examine the economic freedom rationale for competition law in the following sections, as well as the input of the ordoliberal school in EU competition law. It is possible that restrictions of market competition may be traded for political support (power) and thus limit electoral competition. Governments also frequently act through private actors. This democracy–antitrust interaction seems also to be recognized to a certain extent by the proponents of the Chicago School of antitrust, albeit in a different form, as they consider the economic and the political as distinct spheres, and not as interdependent, as the ordoliberals seem to believe. For instance, in the absence of a proper 'democratic process,' they consider that antitrust always apply in order to preserve some form of market competition, the assumption being that in the absence of electoral competition, market or 'quasi-market' (in the case of an administered economy)

58 T Malleson, *After Occupy—Economic Democracy for the 21st Century* (OUP, 2014).

59 G Amato, *Antitrust and the Bounds of Power* (Hart, 1997).

60 See E Deutscher and S Makris, 'Exploring the Ordoliberal Paradigm: The Competition–Democracy Nexus' (2016) 11(2) *Competition L Rev* 181, 183.

61 Ibid, 186.

62 Article III(B)(12) of the Final Declaration of the Potsdam Conference, which was issued on 2 August 1945, provided for the immediate decentralization of the German economy in order to put an end to the excessive concentration of economic power of cartels, trusts, and other monopolies. 'Report on the Tripartite Conference of Berlin' (1945) 13 *Department of State Bulletin* 153, 156. In order to comply with this article, American, British, and French military governments within the zone of occupation adopted regulations prohibiting excessive economic concentration. See also the adoption of the Law Relating to the Prohibition of Private Monopoly and Methods of Preserving Fair Trade, adopted in Japan on 12 April 1947. In Germany, the Gesetz gegen Wettbewerbsbeschränkungen (GWB) was adopted in 1958. This text replaced the anti-cartel laws adopted by the occupation powers (the United States, England, and France) in 1945.

63 A Ayal, *Fairness in Antitrust* (Hart, 2014), 67–72 who nevertheless stresses that, from this perspective, '[l]arge conglomerates, with interests ranging over diverse and unconnected industries might be argued to be more problematic than large firms as such' (ibid, 69).

64 E Deutscher & S Makris, 'Exploring the Ordoliberal Paradigm: The Competition-Democracy Nexus' (2016) 11(2) *Competition L Rev* 181, 189.

competition is the only option left to promote efficiency, the latter concept conceived as policies corresponding to citizens' (for the purpose of political competition) preferences?[65]

A related issue on the linkage between competition law and democracy consists in the de-politicization of competition law, with the rise in importance of independent, from the executive but also legislative power, competition authorities, and the role of courts in the enforcement of competition law. Competition law relies on the work of a pro-active technocracy, assuming tasks of forecast, knowledge gathering/sharing, and communication with the public.[66] Technocracy pre-supposes the systematic integration of scientific expertise in policy-making, not only at the level of the policy conception but also at the implementation level. The assumption is that the realm of politics and that of scientific expertise have convergent logics and that politics and policy-making are driven by scientific consensus, thus inversing the primacy of politics approach that characterizes the bureaucratic form of organization. Some authors have expressed concern over the apparent dissociation of competition law technocracy, relying on neoclassical price theory economics, from the political sphere, under the guise of the opposition to the misfits of 'antitrust populism'.[67]

However, not everyone is convinced on the positive contribution of competition law to democracy. If one adopts a public choice perspective, it is possible to argue that any form of State intervention in the marketplace, including competition law, carries the risk of capture and inefficiency: there is a wealth of empirical literature on the inefficiency of sector-specific regulations, but similar claims have also been made with regard to competition law.[68] As with any other field of law, firms may behave strategically by using competition law in order to harm their competitors, raise their costs and protect weak firms, vis-à-vis more efficient competitors.[69]

2.1.7.2. The integration of the Internal Market

The objective of market integration has of course affected considerably the history of EU competition law, and still does to this day. We will explore the role of this objective in EU competition law in another section in this Chapter.

2.1.7.3. The protection of consumers

According to the case law of the European Courts, one of the principal functions of EU competition law is to prevent 'consumer harm'.[70] The European Commission has inferred from the role of 'consumer harm' in the case law of the European Courts with regard to identifying the existence of a restriction of competition, that the principal goal of EU competition law is the protection of final or intermediary consumers.[71] The terminology employed is not

65 See M Friedman, *Capitalism and Freedom* (University of Chicago Press, 1962), 10 (noting that 'it is therefore clearly possible to have economic arrangements that are fundamentally capitalist [preserving economic freedom] and political arrangements that are not free').

66 DA Crane, 'Technocracy and Antitrust' [2009] 86 *Texas L Rev* 1159.

67 H First and S Weber Waller, 'Antitrust's Democracy Deficit' (2013) 81(5) *Fordham L Rev* 2543.

68 FS McChesney and WF Shughart II, *The Causes and Consequences of Antitrust: The Public Choice Perspective* (University of Chicago Press, 1995).

69 WJ Baumol and JA Ordover, 'The Use of Antitrust to Subvert Competition' (1985) 28(2) *J L & Economics* 247; LA Graglia, 'Is Antitrust Obsolete?' (1999) 23 *Harvard J L & Public Policy* 11.

70 See eg Case C-209/10, Post *Danmark A/S v Konkurrencerådet*, ECLI:EU:C:2012:172, para 20.

71 Commission Guidelines on the application of Article 81(3) of the Treaty [2004] OJ C 101/97, para 13 (noting that '[t]he objective of Article [101 TFEU] is to protect competition on the market as a means of

always clear-cut. For example, in the Commission's Guidance on its Enforcement Priorities in Applying Article [102 TFEU] to Abusive Exclusionary Conduct by Dominant Undertakings, the concept of 'consumer harm' is defined broadly as covering all practices restricting competition in the form of higher prices, lower innovation, and/or narrower consumer choice.[72] The Commission's approach remains impressionistic: sometimes the guidance refers to 'consumer harm' or 'detriment to consumers', other times to 'consumer welfare':[73] no definition is provided. The concept of consumer welfare has never been explicitly endorsed by the Court of Justice of the European Union (CJEU), and the distinction between consumer welfare, consumer surplus, and consumer choice has been a matter of theoretical speculation.[74] Some authors argue that although the concept of consumer harm is used as a proxy for anti-competitive effects, it does not follow that the protection of the final consumer becomes the principal goal of competition law, as the consumer harm standard would be also compatible with a total (social) welfare approach.[75]

The concept of 'consumer harm' may include multiple dimensions, when one tries to extrapolate from it information on the goals of EU competition law:

(i) In the economic jargon, the protection of consumer surplus constitutes an important part of the total welfare standard test. In this context, consumer surplus denotes the consumer part of the deadweight loss suffered as a result of the restriction of competition. For example, a price increase might lead to a volume effect that would be suffered by a certain category of consumers: because of the price increase some consumers will not be able to buy the product any more, although past consumption patterns (revealed preferences) indicate that they would have preferred to do so, if the price had not increased. Under this narrow definition of consumer surplus, the overcharge paid by the consumers as a result of the price increase should not be of concern for competition law enforcement, as it constitutes a wealth transfer from the buyers to the sellers. The suppliers may be in a position to compensate (hypothetically, not actually) the loss that consumers have suffered while still being able to compensate with this wealth transfer their own losses following the volume effect (producer surplus). In this configuration, the situation will be Kaldor–Hicks efficient. We will call this view of consumer harm: the 'consumer surplus standard'.

enhancing consumer welfare and of ensuring an efficient allocation of resources. Competition and market integration serve these ends since the creation and preservation of an open single market promotes an efficient allocation of resources throughout the Community for the benefit of consumers') and para 84 (observing that the concept of consumer encompasses both direct and indirect consumers).

[72] Communication from the Commission—Guidance on the Commission's enforcement priorities in applying Article 102 of the EC Treaty to abusive exclusionary conduct by dominant undertakings [2009] OJ C 45/7, para 19 ('The aim of the Commission's enforcement activity in relation to exclusionary conduct is to ensure that dominant undertakings do not impair effective competition by foreclosing their competitors in an anti-competitive way, thus having an adverse impact on consumer welfare, whether in the form of higher price levels than would have otherwise prevailed or in some other form such as limiting quality or reducing consumer choice.'). The Commission also employs in this text the concepts of 'consumer detriment' and 'consumer harm'.

[73] Ibid, paras 19, 30, 86 (referring to 'consumer welfare').

[74] See, for instance, the discussion in B Orbach, 'The Antitrust Consumer Welfare Paradox' (2011) 7(1) *J Competition L & Economics* 133; K Cseres, 'The Controversies of the Consumer Welfare Standard' (2007) 3(2) *Competition L Rev* 121.

[75] R Nazzini, *The Foundations of European Union Competition Law—The Objective and Principles of Article 102* (OUP, 2011), 49.

(ii) It is possible to decide that consumer surplus should be preserved at any cost and thus reject any compensation by the supplier that does not compensate actually and effectively the losses incurred by these consumers as a result of the volume effect. For clarity purposes, we will refer to this view as the 'narrow consumer welfare standard'.

(iii) There is also an argument to move beyond consumer surplus and include in the analysis the wealth transfer that consumers have incurred because of the overcharges following the restriction of competition. These may relate not only to higher prices but could cover any other parameter of competition, such as quality, variety, and innovation. In this case, both the loss of consumer surplus and wealth transfers will be compared to the total efficiency gains pertaining to the supplier(s), thus enabling a cost–benefit analysis of the effect of the conduct on the welfare of a specific group of market actors, direct and indirect consumers (not all market actors). The idea is that following the change from an equilibrium situation to another, the consumers of the specific product will benefit from a surplus and/or wealth transfer, in the sense that their ability to satisfy their preferences will increase. Again, for clarity, this standard will be referred to as the 'extended consumer welfare standard'.

(iv) Some authors argue also that competition authorities should aim to preserve an optimal level of 'consumer choice', defined as 'the state of affairs where the consumer has the power to define his or her own wants and the ability to satisfy these wants at competitive prices'.[76] This concept seems broader than the concepts of 'consumer surplus' and 'consumer welfare' (the latter including consumer surplus + the wealth transfer because of the overcharge) as it may include other parameters than price, in particular 'variety'. The same authors have used interchangeably the term of 'consumer sovereignty', which is defined as 'the set of societal arrangements that causes that economy to act primarily in response to the aggregate signals of consumer demand, rather than in response to government directives or the preferences of individual businesses'.[77] Defining the 'optimal degree' of consumer choice or consumer sovereignty and measuring it using some operational parameters seems, however, a daunting task. Consumer sovereignty may be conceptually appealing but may prove empirically weak to implement in competition law enforcement.[78]

One might be obliged to go a step further and claim that consumer sovereignty can be preserved by the ability of consumers to influence the characteristics of the product bundle according to their own hypothetical revealed preferences. Hypothetical revealed preference theory defines an agent's preferences in terms of what she would choose if she were able to choose, thus switching from actual to hypothetical choice.[79] The way this theory will work in

[76] RH Lande, 'Consumer Choice as the Ultimate Goal of Antitrust' (2001) 62(3) *U Pittsburgh L Rev* 503, 503. For an import of this concept in EU competition law, see P Nihoul, N Charbit, and E Ramundo (eds) *Choice—A New Standard for Competition Law Analysis?* (Concurrences, 2016).

[77] NW Averitt & RH Lande, 'Consumer Sovereignty: A Unified Theory of Antitrust and Consumer Protection Law' (1997) 65 *Antitrust LJ* 713, 715.

[78] See also R Nazzini, *The Foundations of European Union Competition Law—The Objective and Principles of Article 102* (OUP, 2011), 30–2 (noting that 'when consumer choice is seen as an objective in its own right, it may become a disguised form of competitor protection: a competitor deserves to be protected solely on the basis that it offers a differentiated product').

[79] For a critical analysis, see DM Hausman, *Preference, Value, Choice, and Welfare* (CUP, 2012), 31–3, citing as the main proponent of this theory; K Binmore, *Playing Fair: Game Theory and the Social Contract* (MIT Press, 1994).

practice is still a matter of speculation. It is clear that consumers are influenced in their decisions by 'the context of choice, defined by the set of options under consideration. In particular, the addition and removal of options from the offered set can influence people's preferences among options that were available all along.'[80] The firms with their marketing activities may, for example, shape endogenously consumer preferences by establishing an artificial selection process, 'preferences are actually constructed—not merely revealed.'[81] A greater focus on consumer sovereignty may thus, in some cases, lead to more intensive competition law intervention to establish the parameters of independent consumer choice and specific presumptions against commercial practices that deny the sovereignty of consumer choice. Open and contestable markets are a prerequisite for the empowerment of consumers. The consumer choice or consumer sovereignty standard may also accommodate the psychological aspect of the formation of these preferences, which is usually ignored in neoclassical price theory. The integration of behavioural economics and neuro-economics evidence in order to understand consumers' behaviour and build counterfactuals of hypothetical choice, based on predictions about what someone would choose in a specific choice context may also be one of the implications of this theory.

It is also important to acknowledge the difficulty of engaging in the analysis of the long-term interest of the consumers for innovation and dynamic efficiency, as opposed to their short-term interest on lower prices and allocative efficiency. A report on *Innovation and Dynamic Efficiencies*, commissioned by the Canadian Bureau of Competition explains:

> To sustain innovative efforts, and thus support dynamic efficiency, firms do not expect to price at short-run marginal cost at every point in time and as a result some degree of allocative inefficiency may be inevitable. Motivating firms to make costly investments in R&D requires some prospect of 'profit,' which as noted above is in the form of quasi-rents. In the absence of this positive return per unit of output sold, a firm would never be able to recoup its up-front investment in R&D, and would therefore have no incentive to undertake this investment. In other words, innovating firms anticipate a period of 'incumbency' during which they are able to sell a product at a price exceeding not only the short-run marginal cost of production, but potentially also the price of existing products (if any) that do not incorporate the innovation. Consumers are willing to pay the higher price because they value the additional attributes embodied in the new or improved product sufficiently to pay a premium for it over other firms' products.[82]

Hence, firms engaged in considerable research and development and other innovative activity should price significantly above their marginal costs (the costs of producing an additional unit of output) in order to earn a competitive return in the long run. This might at first seem in contradiction with the static allocative efficiency concern for lower prices and will certainly deviate from the model of perfect competition. From a dynamic *total welfare* (Kaldor–Hicks) perspective, this sacrifice in static allocative efficiency may be compensated by the benefits flowing from dynamic efficiency: higher profitability for the undertakings and new or better quality products for the consumers in the long run. However, increasing R&D does not necessarily lead to socially optimal innovation, as firms might have an excessive incentive

80 E Shafir, I Simonson, and A Tversky, 'Reason-Based Choice' (1993) 49(1–2) *Cognition* 11, 21.
81 Ibid, 34.
82 A Tepperman and M Sanderson, 'Innovation and Dynamic Efficiencies in Merger Review' (Canadian Competition Bureau, 2007), 6–7, available at http://www.competitionbureau.gc.ca/eic/site/cb-bc.nsf/eng/02376.html.

(relative to that which is socially optimal) to seek to replace other firms ('the business stealing effect').[83] As it is noted by the same report, 'consumers do not derive benefits from an additional dollar of R&D spending unless that dollar results in an increased likelihood of either a new product being developed or an existing product being made available for a lower price'.[84] In other words, from a non-total welfare (Kaldor–Hicks perspective) what is important is not to focus on R&D but on the innovation process and its outcomes. If only the welfare (short and long term) of consumers matters, then it is important to engage in a difficult exercise of distinguishing between R&D investment from which consumer will ultimately benefit from R&D investment which will cost consumers more (in terms of allocative efficiency) than what it will provide them in terms of dynamic efficiency. In contrast, from a total welfare perspective, the cost to consumers of the increase of innovative activity is only one component of the analysis, the other being the profits that undertakings derive from the R&D activity long run. A change will thus be deemed Kaldor–Hicks efficient, even if there is over-investment on R&D, with regard to what is socially optimal, should the firms' profitability increase as a result of this R&D effort, enabling it to potentially compensate the consumers' loss. A Kaldor–Hicks total welfare approach could also look to the possible effects of innovation across markets, so not only the effects on consumers present in the specific relevant market, but also the effects on suppliers and consumers in other markets that will be affected by the innovative process, hence performing some form of general equilibrium analysis. General equilibrium analysis focuses on the economy as a whole and studies economic changes in *all* the markets of an economy simultaneously.

Consumer harm: In competition law, the aim of protecting consumers implies that the outcome/consequences of a specific practice on consumers matters, before any decision on the lawfulness or unlawfulness of this practice has been reached. A reduction of competitive rivalry, following the exclusion of a competitor or an agreement between two competitors to cooperate with each other, will not be found unlawful, if they do not also lead to a likely consumer harm or consumer detriment. A different approach would take a deontological perspective emphasizing competitive rivalry, irrespective of any actual or potential consequences of the specific practice/conduct on consumers. Effects may indicate empirical observable findings on the worsening, in terms of price or quality, of the situation of specific groups of consumers, following the adoption of the anti-competitive practice (actual effects). It may also refer to situations where there are no observable findings of effects on these groups of consumers but there is 'a consistent theory of consumer harm' which is empirically validated: that is, 'the theory of harm should be consistent with factual observations' (*ex ante* validation) and 'that the market outcomes should be consistent with the predictions of the theory' (*ex post* validation).[85] The *theory of (consumer) harm* has the objective to establish a relation of causality between the specific practice and the consumer detriment.

It should be by now clear that some of the dimensions of consumer harm that we have previously examined are concerned only with efficiency or wealth maximization and adopt a Kaldor–Hicks total welfare standard [dimension (i) and (ii)], while others seem to go beyond efficiency and wealth maximization and integrate concerns about distributive justice.

Distributive justice: The concept of distributive justice has multiple dimensions and its meaning has evolved through time,[86] but it is possible to define it as referring to the

83 Ibid, 8. 84 Ibid, 9.

85 P Papandropoulos, 'Implementing an Effects-Based Approach under Article 82' (2008) 1 *Concurrences* 1, 3.

86 S Fleischacker, *A Short History of Distributive Justice* (Harvard University Press, 2005).

morally required distribution of shares of resources among members of a given group, either because of their membership in that group or in accordance with some measure of entitlement which applies to them in virtue of their membership. This is understood dynamically, that is across various situations in the specific jurisdiction. Rights and duties in distributive justice are thus 'agent-general',[87] as they relate to a specific category of actors or group.

As previously explained, the problem of distribution was relegated from the realm of economics because of the Kaldor–Hicks' thesis of separability.[88] Hence, it may not constitute an objective for EU competition law for those advocating as its sole aim total welfare. The concept of 'consumer harm' breaks with this tradition as it advances a view of competition law that would promote the interest of a group of consumers, to the detriment of other groups of actors (eg managers, shareholders, employees). According to the second condition of Article 101(3), 'consumers', a concept encompassing all direct and indirect users of the product, should receive a 'fair share' of the efficiencies generated by the restrictive agreements in order for the agreement to benefit from the exception provided by Article 101(3) TFEU. According to the Commission's Guidelines on the application of Article 101(3),

> The concept of '*fair share*' implies that the pass-on of benefits must at least compensate consumers for any actual or likely negative impact caused to them by the restriction of competition found under Article [101(1)]. In line with the overall objective of Article [101] to prevent anti-competitive agreements, the net effect of the agreement must *at least be neutral from the point of view of those consumers directly or likely to be affected by the agreement*. If such consumers are worse off following the agreement, the second condition of Article 101(3) is not fulfilled. The positive effects of an agreement must be balanced against and *compensate* for its negative effects on consumers. When that is the case consumers are not harmed by the agreement [. . .]. [Emphasis added]

It is not required that the same consumers benefit from each and every efficiency gain identified under the first condition. It suffices that sufficient benefits are passed on to the broader sociological category of consumers so as to compensate, overall, for the negative effects of the restrictive agreement. In that case, consumers obtain a fair share of the overall benefits. If a restrictive agreement is likely to lead to higher prices, *consumers must be fully compensated* through increased quality or other benefits. If not, the second condition of Article [101(3)] is not fulfilled.[89]

Although the Commission accepts that consumer harm assessed under Article 101(1) TFEU (eg higher prices) might be compensated by some benefits provided by the anti-competitive agreement assessed under Article 101(3) ('efficiency gains'), they require that these benefits *effectively* (and not only hypothetically) and *fully* compensate the consumer

87 S Perry, 'On the Relationship between Corrective and Distributive Justice' in J Horder (ed) *Oxford Essays in Jurisprudence* (OUP, 2000), 237, 238

88 AM Okun, *Equality and Efficiency: The Big Tradeoff* (Brookings Institution Press, 1975). See however, L Kaplow and S Shavell, *Fairness versus Welfare* (Harvard University Press, 2002), arguing for an incorporation of distributive justice concerns in defining individual well-being, although advancing that no independent weight should be accorded to notions of fairness that are not concerned exclusively with individuals' well-being.

89 Commission Guidelines on the application of Article 81(3) of the Treaty [2004] OJ C 101/97, paras 85 and 86.

harm in a way or another.[90] This does not amount to a Kaldor–Hicks efficiency standard but to a distributive justice standard.[91]

2.1.7.4. Freedom to compete/freedom to trade

The 'freedom to compete' (*Wettbewerbsfreiheit*) view is often credited to the ideas of the ordoliberal school of thought, founded in the 1930s at the University of Freiburg (Germany).[92] It is frequently alleged that the importance given to the concept of 'economic freedom' in subsequent cases of the European Courts illustrates the influence of ordoliberal thought.[93] In essence, according to this view, the principal aim of competition law is to protect the economic freedom of undertakings to compete on the market.

This is often interpreted as a deontological standpoint: the competitive process and the economic freedom of undertakings to participate in this competitive process must be preserved, irrespective of the effects of such competition on social welfare.[94] According to this view, the ordoliberals value individual economic freedom as part of political freedom and autonomy. Their objective is to achieve an economic order, based on the principle of competition, a task that requires a positive agenda by the State to protect the competitive process from private economic power and political power. For these authors, the main concern for ordoliberals is 'complete competition', 'that is competition in which no firm in a market has power to coerce other firms in that market'.[95] The model of 'complete competition' provides 'the substantive standards for competition law, requiring that law be used to prevent the creation of monopolistic power, abolish existing monopoly positions where possible, and where this was not possible, control the conduct of monopolies'.[96] State interventions in the market would aim to remove market disruptions by breaking up 'avoidable monopolies' and regulating 'unavoidable monopolies' (natural monopoles).[97] Competition law has thus to provide a standard of conduct for dominant firms. The 'as if' competition standard applies to all kinds of

[90] The compensation must take a form that is axiomatically valued by consumers, such as innovation or higher quality. The last condition of Article 101(3) preserves consumer choice and enables the consumers to indicate their preferences, as competition should not be substantially eliminated. Hence, it is always possible for consumers to indicate that they value lower prices than higher quality or innovation.

[91] For a more detailed analysis on distributive justice and competition law, see I Lianos, 'The Poverty of Competition Law', CLES Research Paper 2/2018, available at https://ssrn.com/abstract=3160054.

[92] For a discussion, see DJ Gerber, 'Constitutionalizing the Economy: German Neo-liberalism, Competition Law and the "New" Europe' (1994) 42 *American J Comparative L* 25; H Rieter & M Schmolz, 'The Ideas of German Ordoliberalism 1938–45: Pointing the Way to a New Economic Order' (1993) 1(1) *European J History of Economic Thought* 87; W Möschel, 'Competition Policy from an Ordo Point of View' in A Peacock and H Willgerodt (eds) *German Neo-Liberals and the Social Market Economy* (Macmillan, 1989), 142–59. For a translation in English of the views of one of the principal authors of the ordoliberal group, see W Eucken, *The Foundations of Economics—History and Theory in the Analysis of Economic Reality* (Springer, 1939; repr. 1992).

[93] D Gerber, *Law and Competition in Twentieth Century Europe: Protecting Prometheus* (Clarendon Press, 1998); L Lovdahl Gormsen, 'The Concept between Economic freedom and consumer welfare in the modernisation of Article 82 EC' (2007) 3(2) *European Competition J* 32.

[94] O Andriychuk, 'Rediscovering the Spirit of Competition: On the Normative Value of the Competitive Process' (2010) 6(3) *European Competition J* 575.

[95] P Akman, *The Concept of Abuse in EU Competition Law: Law and Economic Approaches* (Hart, 2012), 58.

[96] D Gerber, Constitutionalizing the Economy: German Neo-liberalism, Competition Law and the "New" Europe' (1994) 42 *American J Comparative L* 25, 50–1.

[97] P Akman, *The Concept of Abuse in EU Competition Law: Law and Economic Approaches* (Hart, 2012), 59. See also C Ahlborn and A J Padilla, 'From Fairness to Welfare: Implications for the Assessment of Unilateral Conduct under EC Competition Law' in CD Ehlermann and M Marquis (eds) *European Competition Law Annual 2007* (Hart, 2008), 55–101.

exclusionary practices and requires dominant firms to behave as if they are subject to competition.[98] It is conceived 'as an objectively applicable measure that in most cases would provide clear guidance' to dominant firms.[99]

The concept embodied in this standard is based on the distinction between 'performance competition' and 'impediment competition': dominant firms are entitled to do the former but not the latter. The categorization of a specific business practice as being performance or impediment competition depends on the ability of an undertaking to perform them in the absence of market power. Several categories of conduct, such as predatory pricing, boycotts, and loyalty rebates, are considered as inconsistent with the 'as if' standard, 'because a firm would not be able to engage in such practices unless it had monopolistic power'.[100] One could thus classify certain commercial practices as falling a priori within the category of impediment competition, and thus suspect if adopted by dominant firms, without any ad hoc analysis of their specific effects on the relevant market.

Others have criticized this interpretation of the ordoliberal approach to competition law as being historically contingent to the first phase of the development of this doctrine, in pre-war Germany, but in no way representative of the latest versions of this 'doctrine', in the 1950s, and of the heterogeneous theoretical approaches followed by the various authors inspired by ordoliberal ideas.[101] According to this view, post-war versions of ordoliberalism have abandoned the idea that monopolies are harmful per se, considering that this is not the case when 'they have emerged from competition on the merits, i.e. due to their success on the market'. Consequently, the concepts of 'complete competition' and that of 'as if' competition were not any more used as operational criteria for the intervention of competition authorities in the market.[102] According to this interpretation of the ordoliberal point of view, 'a restraint of competition may be found wherever (1) the number of freely competing producers is artificially reduced in ways that do not result from the normal process of competition itself, and (2) where this reduces the scope of alternatives among which consumers may freely chose'.[103]

The link between freedom to trade and the competitive process has also been highlighted by other commentators, drawing on the tradition of the common law's restraints of trade doctrine.[104] Defining the competitive process as 'the process of sellers and buyers forming improving coalitions', they argue that

> [competition law] protects the *potential beneficial trades between* competitors and consumers. Since both consumers and competitors gain from such trade, this view can explain why both consumers and thwarted competitors have antitrust rights, even though

[98] D Gerber, 'Constitutionalizing the Economy: German Neo-liberalism, Competition Law and the "New" Europe' (1994) 42 *American J Comparative L* 25, 52.

[99] Ibid, 53. [100] Ibid.

[101] See, most recently, P Behrens, 'The Ordoliberal Concept of "Abuse" of a Dominant Position and its Impact on Article 102 TFEU' in P Nihoul and I Takahashi (eds) *Abuse Regulation in Competition Law* (Proceedings of the 10th ASCOLA Conference, Tokyo, 2015), available at https://ssrn.com/abstract=2658045.

[102] Ibid. See also E-J Mestmäcker, 'The Development of German and European Competition Law with Special Reference to the EU Commission's Article 82 Guidelines of 2008' in LF Pace (ed) *European Competition Law: The Impact of the Commission's Guidance on Article 102* (Edward Elgar, 2011), 43.

[103] P Behrens, 'The Ordoliberal Concept of "Abuse" of a Dominant Position and its Impact on Article 102 TFEU' in P Nihoul and I Takahashi (eds) *Abuse Regulation in Competition Law* (Proceedings of the 10th ASCOLA Conference, Tokyo, 2015), available at https://ssrn.com/abstract=2658045.

[104] See A Edlin and J Farrell, 'Freedom to Trade and the Competitive Process' in R Blair & DD Sokol (eds) *The Oxford Handbook of International Antitrust Economics*, vol 1 (OUP, 2014), ch 13.

antitrust protects 'competition and not competitors'. Consumers are not protected from all high prices, but only from those that a competitor would be happy to beat but for some thwarting action; this explains why a pure monopoly does not violate the law simply, but only from tactics such as moving he goalposts that block them from giving customers a better deal than a monopoly does.[105]

Such an approach may dispense, to a certain extent, with focusing on all practices that reduce consumer welfare in equilibrium and may provide a useful starting point for the competition assessment.

2.1.7.5. Fairness, equality of opportunity

The post-Second World War consensus among economic growth theorists was that income inequality is a driving force behind income growth, both within and between nations. This led to the perception that there is an efficiency–equality trade-off. This consensus has been more recently subject to increased criticism. There is empirical evidence from several cross-country studies that shows how inequality has slowed down national growth rates and may be an impediment to growth.[106] More importantly, sharp inequalities of income or wealth may produce negative consequences by establishing some form of path dependence affecting growth, but also personal development, starting with the 'unequal prenatal development of the foetus', 'unequal early childhood development', and investments by parents, including educational opportunities, but also 'unequal returns to human capital because of discrimination at one end and use of parental connections in the job market at the other end'.[107] This 'inter-generational transmission of inequality' may lead to 'genetic inequalities'.[108] The growing levels of inequality may also lead to political capture, thus creating a vicious cycle where elites influence policy making and regulations to the benefit of their interests, often resulting in policies that are detrimental to the interests of the many, which in turn makes inequality worse and reinforces the power of elites still further. This may be cause for major distrust in government and a surge in populism.

But are inequality and poverty the result of market distortions and of the exercise of market power? There are certainly many causes that could explain the recent rise in poverty and inequality: the globalization of production, 'labour-saving' technological development, the erosion of collective bargaining systems all resulting in the continued drop in real wage values,[109]

105 Ibid.

106 See eg A Berg and JD Ostry, 'Inequality and Unsustainable Growth: Two Sides of the Same Coin?', IMF Staff Discussion Note SDN/11/08 (8 April 2011), available at www.imf.org/external/pubs/ft/sdn/2011/sdn1108.pdf (finding that countries with high inequality experience shortened growth spells); E Dabla-Norris, K Kochharm, N Suphaphiphat, F Ricka, and E Tsounta, 'Causes and Consequences of Income Inequality: A Global Perspective', IMF Staff Discussion Note SDN/15/13 (15 June 2015), available at www.imf.org/external/pubs/cat/longres.aspx?sk=42986.0 (finding that income distribution matters for growth).

107 R Kanbur and J Stiglitz, 'Wealth and Income Distribution: New Theories Needed for a New Era', VOX CEPR Policy Portal (18 August 2015), available at www.voxeu.org/article/wealth-and-income-distribution-new-theories-needed-new-era.

108 See PL Menchick, 'Inter-generational Transmission of Inequality: An Empirical Study of Wealth Mobility' [1979] 46(184) *Economica* new series (Special Issue on the Economics of Inheritance) 349.

109 In this respect, it is worth emphasizing that the persistent sluggishness of real wages, notwithstanding the presence of tight labour markets due to a robust overall level of economic activity, is a puzzle that is central to the current macroeconomic debate, as witnessed by the fact that this was the theme of the 2018 gathering of central bankers in Jackson Hole, WY: 'Changing Market Structures and Implications for Monetary Policy'.

tax evasion or unfair tax systems. However, it is increasingly accepted that market power may be a significant source of both inefficiency *and* inequality. For example, Alan Krueger observes that the erosion of employee bargaining power is also the result of collusive non-compete and no-poaching practices among rivals firms.[110] Joseph Stiglitz notes that 'today's markets are characterised by the persistence of high monopoly profits',[111] rejecting Joseph Schumpeter's view that monopolists would only be temporary.[112] He also argues that 'policies aimed at reducing market power can accordingly play some role in the reduction of inequality', although he remains careful of setting this as an explicit aim of competition law.[113] Other economists have been equally vocal on the need for a robust competition law and policy against inequality. Tony Atkinson has argued for public policy to aim at a proper balance of power among stakeholders, and in particular suggested the integration of explicitly distributional dimension into competition policy, among some of his proposals for limiting the growing inequality.[114] A recent report of the Council of Economic Advisers to the White House published in April 2016, tracks the rise of the concentration of various industries in the US, and notes that the 'majority of industries have seen increases in the revenue share enjoyed by the 50 largest firms between 1997 and 2012'.[115] Is increasing economic concentration leading to higher degrees of inequality of wealth? This may be a difficult question to answer in view of the overall tendency of wealth concentration that has been observed during the twentieth century and at least part of the nineteenth century,[116] and according to more recent studies, apparently since the

See Federal Reserve Bank of Kansas City Annual Economic Policy Symposium, Jackson Hole, 23–5 August 2018, available at https://www.kansascityfed.org/publications/research/escp/symposiums/escp-2018.

110 See A Krueger, 'Reflections on Dwindling Worker Bargaining Power and Monetary Policy', Remarks at 2018 Luncheon Address at the Jackson Hole Economic Symposium (24 August 2018), available at https://www.kansascityfed.org/~/media/files/publicat/sympos/2018/papersandhandouts/kc%20fed%20lunch%20remarks%20-%20as%20prepared%20for%20delivery%20v2.pdf?la=en. See also RM Stutz, 'The Evolving Antitrust Treatment of Labor-Market Restraints: From Theory to Practice', AAI White Paper (31 July 2018), available at https://www.antitrustinstitute.org/wp-content/uploads/2018/09/AAI-Labor-Antitrust-White-Paper_0-1.pdf. Similarly, there are proposals aimed at improving workers bargaining power by increasing transparency on wages, as employers hold a better understanding on the distribution of wages: see B Harris, 'Information Is Power—Fostering Labor Market Competition through Transparent Wages', The Hamilton Project (Brookings, February 2018), available at https://www.brookings.edu/wp-content/uploads/2018/02/es_2272018_information_is_power_harris_pp.pdf.

111 J Stiglitz, 'Monopoly's New Era', Project Syndicate (13 May 2016), available at www.project-syndicate.org/commentary/high-monopoly-profits-persist-in-markets-by-joseph-e--stiglitz-2016-05.

112 In this respect, there is growing evidence that the observed secular increase in concentration and market power, and the resulting boost in firms' profitability, were also accompanied by a reduction in firms' investment (ie, presumably due to weaker 'escape competition' incentives), which would tend over time to depress overall productivity and thus economic growth: see T Philippon, 'A Primer On Concentration, Investment and Growth', Remarks at 2018 Jackson Hole Economic Symposium (24 August 2018), available at https://www.kansascityfed.org/~/media/files/publicat/sympos/2018/papersandhandouts/824180819philipponhandout.pdf?la=en.

113 J Stiglitz, 'Towards a Broader View of Competition Policy' in T Bonakele, E Fox, and L McNube (eds) *Competition Policy for the New Era—Insights from the BRICS Countries* (OUP, 2017), 4, 15; J Stiglitz, N Abernathy, A Hersh, S Holmberg, and M Konczal, *Rewriting the Rules of the American Economy: An Agenda for Growth and Shared Prosperity* (WW Norton, 2015), http://www.rewritetherules.org.)

114 T Atkinson, *Inequality: What can be done?* (Harvard University Press, 2015).

115 White House CEA, 'Benefits of Competition and Indicators of Market Power' (April 2016), available at https://obamawhitehouse.archives.gov/sites/default/files/page/files/20160414_cea_competition_issue_brief.pdf. See also G Grullon, Y Larkin, and R Michaely, 'Are U.S. Industries Becoming More Concentrated?' (31 August 2017), available at https://ssrn.com/abstract=2612047.

116 See eg F Alvaredo, AB Atkinson, T Piketty, and E Saez, 'The Top 1 Percent in International and Historical Perspective' (2013) 27(3) *J Economic Perspectives* 3; A Atkinson, T Piketty, and E Saez, 'Top Incomes in the Long Run of History, (2011) 49(1) *J Economic Literature* 3; T Piketty, G Postel-Vinay, and J-L Rosenthal, 'Wealth Concentration in a Developing Economy: Paris and France, 1807–1994' (2006) 96(1) *American Economic Rev*

fourteenth century,[117] although one should note that there are various measurement and data related difficulties for such research endeavours.

A recent paper of the OECD on Market Power and Wealth Distribution has attracted attention, as it shows a substantial impact of market power on wealth inequality.[118] This relies in terms of methodology on some work previously completed by Comanor and Smiley in 1975[119] and explains that market power may account for a substantial amount of wealth inequality. The increased margins charged to customers as a result of market power will disproportionately harm the poor who will pay more for goods without receiving a counter-balancing share of increased profits as they are not usually shareholders, while the wealthy benefit more from higher profits, due to their generally higher ownership of the stream of corporate profits and capital gains.

In the UK, the CMA is actively researching the challenges faced by 'vulnerable consumers' (not necessarily poorer consumers but those with limited access to the Internet) in actively pursuing the best option in digital markets, and it envisages possible solutions to this disengagement.[120]

Is there a case for equality beyond a possible negative effect of inequality on growth and efficiency? Can competition law integrate 'equality' concerns, without necessarily these being related to economic efficiency? And if this is done, how could this be integrated in competition law assessment and what would be its limiting principles, as competition law may not have the means, or it may not be desirable, to go after any form of inequality, in particular if this results from 'business acumen' and 'competition on the merits'. One may argue that competition authorities should intervene in situations of 'pervasive inequality',[121] which do not only affect wealth, income, and social status, but more generally the equality of moral status of individuals and their equal participation in the political realm. This intervention is all the more necessary that it is questionable whether redistributive policies implemented through the taxation system could be considered as a superior option to integrating redistributive concerns in competition law.[122]

In his book on *Inequality: What Can Be Done?*, British economist Tony Atkinson suggests that '[p]ublic policy should aim at a proper balance of power among stakeholders, and to this end should a) introduce an explicitly distributional dimension into competition policy; [. . .].'[123] This proposal raises a number of questions with regard to the way competition law may square with inequality concerns. Some other authors have also argued that '[m]arket power also contributes to growing inequality', and providing the examples of network effects and the role of IP rights, which may entrench positions of economic power, a number of authors are ready to contemplate the possibility of a competition policy response.[124] There is also convincing econometric evidence that the increase of market power the last three decades globally,

236; J Roine and D Waldenström, 'Long Run Trends in the Distribution of Income and Wealth' in A Atkinson and F Bourguignon (eds) *Handbook of Income Distribution*, vol 2A (North-Holland, 2015), 469.

117 G Alfani, 'Economic Inequality in Northwestern Italy: A Long-Term View (Fourteenth to Eighteenth Centuries)' (2015) 75(4) *J Economic History* 1058; G Alfani, 'The Rich in Historical Perspective: Evidence for Preindustrial Europe (ca. 1300–1800)' (2017) 11(3) *Cliometrica* 321.

118 OECD, *Market Power and Wealth Distribution*, DAF/COMP(2015)10 (27–28 October 2015), available at www.oecd.org/officialdocuments/publicdisplaydocumentpdf/?cote=DAF/COMP(2015)10&docLanguage=En.

119 WS Comanor and RH Smiley, 'Monopoly and the Distribution of Wealth' (1975) 89(2) *Q J Economics* 177.

120 CMA, Research and Analysis—Markets that Work for All—Helping Vulnerable Consumers: CMA Symposium Summary (12 September 2018), available at https://www.gov.uk/government/publications/vulnerable-consumers/consumer-vulnerability-in-digital-markets-summary-of-stakeholder-roundtable.

121 M Walzer, *Spheres of Justice: In Defense of Pluralism and Equality* (Basic Books, 1984).

122 For a detailed analysis, see I Lianos, 'The Poverty of Competition Law', CLES Research Paper 2/2018, available at https://ssrn.com/abstract=3160054.

123 T Atkinson, *Inequality: What Can Be Done?* (Harvard University Press, 2015).

124 JB Baker and SC Salop, 'Antitrust, Competition Policy, and Inequality' (2015) 104 *Georgetown LJ* 1, 11. See also L Khan and S Vaheesan, 'Market Power and Inequality: The Antitrust Counterrevolution and Its

with the average global markup going up from close to 1.1 in 1980 to around 1.6 in 2016, has important distributional implications: it has led to a decline of both the labour and the capital shares, without the increasing profits going for investments, but mostly being monopolistic rents that are distributed to the owners of the corporations.[125] This may call for a more aggressive competition law enforcement against the abuse of market power,[126] with a continued reliance on the consumer welfare standard,[127] calibrated so as to prioritize antitrust action that takes into account the distribution of income and wealth and benefits the middle class and the less well advantaged,[128] eventually leading to the possibility that 'anticompetitive conduct by the less well-off that extracts wealth from the rich might not be condemned',[129] as well as to antitrust remedies that primarily benefit less advantaged consumers.[130] There are various ways this concern may be operationalized: economic and social equality can be recognized as one of the goals of competition law, along with consumer welfare and efficiency,[131] for instance by forming part of a broader and explicit 'public interest' standard, which would consider distributional considerations as explicit and higher priority public interest goals than consumer welfare and efficiency, such standard being applied also in non-merger cases.[132] These authors are also open to the possibility of enforcing competition law provisions against excessive prices.[133] Others put forward the importance of simplifying antitrust rules, away from the complicated and expensive to implement rule of reason approaches, which are perceived as defendant-biased, also adopting structural remedies, instead of 'complicated conduct remedies', rendering antitrust agencies more accountable and transparent, presumably in setting their priorities in a way that is understandable to citizens, ultimately adopting a 'citizen interest standard'.[134] The goals of antitrust should be to tame economic concentration and distribute economic ownership and control, to prevent unjust wealth transfers from consumers to firms with market power, and to preserve open markets so that independent entrepreneurs have an opportunity to enter.[135]

It also seems that the growing financialization of the economy has played some role in exacerbating inequalities. As a Center for Economic Policy and Research (CEPR) blog report recently noted, '[t]he financial sector has seen a moderate increase in its share of the workforce and a dramatic increase in pay per worker'. These two factors have allowed finance to capture a growing share of wages and made it so 'most Americans are unable to share in the economy's gains'.[136] There is currently research exploring how the existing competition law tools may take into account the growing importance of overlapping financial investor ownership and what can be done to remedy this problem, providing of course this is something one considers to be a priority.[137]

Discontents' (2017) 11 *Harvard L & Policy Rev* 235, 245 noting that '[g]iven managerial norms that prize the interests of the generally affluent shareholder class, the inability of workers to demand a share of market power rents, and the higher fraction of income devoted to consumption by working and middle class Americans, market power in most sectors can be expected to redistribute wealth upwards.'

125 See, J de Loecker & J Eeckhout, Global Market Power (May 18, 2018), available at http://www.janeeckhout.com/wp-content/uploads/Global.pdf.

126 JB Baker and SC Salop, 'Antitrust, Competition Policy, and Inequality' (2015) 104 *Georgetown LJ* 1, 22–3.

127 Ibid, 15–17. 128 Ibid, 18–20. 129 Ibid, 17 n 61. 130 Ibid, 20.

131 Ibid, 25. 132 Ibid. 133 Ibid, 23.

134 L Khan and S Vaheesan, 'Market Power and Inequality: The Antitrust Counterrevolution and Its Discontents' (2017) 11 *Harvard L & Policy Rev* 235, 276.

135 Ibid, 279.

136 N Buffie, 'The Growth of Finance, In Graphs', CEPR blog (12 April 2016), available at http://cepr.net/blogs/cepr-blog/the-growth-of-finance-in-graphs.

137 Starting with J Azar, *A New Look at Oligopoly: Implicit Collusion through Portfolio Diversification* (PhD thesis, Princeton University, 2012). See, more recently, J Azar, MC Schmalz, and I Tecu, 'Anti-Competitive Effects of Common Ownership, Ross School of Business Paper No 1235 (23 March 2017), available at https://ssrn.com/abstract=2427345.

Although most of this literature has been generated in the US, where for the last three decades competition law enforcement has embraced the economic efficiency rationale, this movement has expanded in Europe.[138] The emphasis on 'populist' antitrust is understood as a counterpoint to the technocratic consensus built the last three decades, first in the US, and then in the EU and some other jurisdictions, which is that competition law should build on the learnings of neoclassical price theory and should rely, although to an extent that varies from jurisdiction to jurisdiction, on economic efficiency considerations.[139] Technocracy pre-supposes the systematic integration of scientific (here exclusively economic) expertise in policy-making and expertise at the implementation level. In addition to the criticisms, mostly coming from academics and activists outside the community of 'mainstream' antitrust experts, a growing number of competition law scholars have also expressed concern over the apparent dissociation of competition law technocracy, relying on neoclassical price theory economics, with the political sphere, and the resulting 'democratic deficit' that has probably ignited the 'populist' backlash we have observed in recent years.[140]

Fairness may not only concern equality of social outcomes (resources), but equality of opportunity. That is, equality in the choice sets of all the outcomes an individual agent can reach given her/his will, the latter concept being defined as encompassing all factors for which the individual agent can be deemed morally responsible as they are under her/his control).[141] Equality of opportunity makes a distinction between legitimate inequalities and illegitimate inequalities. Authors adopting the principle of equality of opportunity accept that inequalities of social outcome (eg welfare) may sometimes be justified and that individual agents (eg undertakings), should be held responsible for their failings.[142] The reason is that curing these failings, for instance through State curative action against inequality, will impose burdens to society (eg by harming efficient undertakings), leading to worsen everybody's prospects. One may for instance distinguish between large undertakings and small medium sized firms, as different types/categories of individual agents. Should the outcomes in terms of market power and profits (for the undertakings) be judged unequal, one should aim, according to this theory, not to reward/cure the inequalities between the individuals of the same category/group, but only those resulting for the unfavourable objective circumstances which led to this different performance, to the extent that the differential of outcomes may not here be justified by the level of effort, the merit or desert of the individual agent (undertaking) in question. For instance, prohibiting a dominant undertaking enjoying a large installed base of consumers to adopt a specific business practice, while not doing the same thing for a small and medium undertaking makes sense, if the aim of the law is to enhance the equality of opportunity of the small undertaking, in view of the fact that these undertakings are facing a significantly higher

138 See M Vestager, 'EU Competition Commissioner, Competition for a Fairer Society', Speech at the 2016 Global Antitrust Enforcement Symposium, Georgetown (20 September 2016), available at https://ec.europa.eu/commission/commissioners/2014-2019/vestager/announcements/competition-fairer-society_en.

139 This could be considered as the essence of the 'economic approach' in competition law. For a discussion of the view of antitrust as technocracy, see DA Crane, 'Technocracy and Antitrust' (2009) 86 *Texas L Rev* 1159.

140 H First & S Weber Waller, 'Antitrust's Democracy Deficit' (2013) 81(5) *Fordham L Rev* 2543.

141 'Will' is therefore distinguished from 'talent', the latter concept including all factors that are outside the individual agent's control: M Fleurbaye, 'Equal Opportunity or Equal Social Outcome?' (1995) 11 *Economics & Philosophy* 25, 26.

142 JE Roemer, *Equality of Opportunity* (Harvard University Press, 1998).

burden, because of their different objective circumstances (here market shares and a large installed base of consumers), and whatever the intensity of their competitive efforts, or their efficiency and merit, they will not be able to compete effectively for the benefit of consumers and the public at large. One may therefore understand competition on the merits as a way to promote equality of opportunity.[143]

2.1.7.6. Conflict of goals or is it possible for the efficiency perspective to take into account these multiple objectives?

The opposition to the mainstream view is the development of a different approach that argues for a pluralistic competition law, which will integrate the preferences not taken into account by the classic analysis of economic efficiency. Most authors include in this list economic democracy, fairness, the political objective of the completion of the Internal Market, and the protection of the principle of freedom of competition. How far competition law is capable of furthering all these goals without a considerable loss in efficiency is controversial. Small firms that are efficient need no special treatment. Help required for those that are not reduces efficiency as it consumes resources and encourages the creation and growth of firms that are less efficient.

The ability to trade across national frontiers has strengthened competition within the EU and increased efficiency immensely, but when Member States have different laws, for instance those relating to patents or maximum prices, it may not be possible to sell at all in some Member States and still less to sell at the same price and subject to the same conditions throughout the Internal Market. Many of these different measures have been harmonized under the 1992 programme for market integration, but some differences remain, especially for pharmaceutical products, the maximum price of which is fixed, directly or indirectly, at a different level in each Member State. Export bans and geographic price discrimination have been prohibited without any analysis of the reasons for imposing them.

A careful analysis of these objectives will show, however, that some of them may be related and taken into account by the principle of economic efficiency and welfare standards, if welfare is interpreted more broadly than is usually the case by neoclassical price theory. For example, the Internal Market objective might have various interpretations: it might be that

143 As explained in Chapter 1, Articles 106(1) and 102 TFEU may apply to State measures distorting competition by creating a situation of inequality of opportunity between economic operators, the case law recognizing that 'a system of undistorted competition [cannot] be guaranteed unless equality of opportunity between the various economic operators [is] assured': see Case C-49/07, *Motosykletistiki Omospondia Ellados NPID (MOTOE) v Elliniko Dimosio* [2008] ECR I–4863, para 51; Case C-553/12 P, *European Commission v Dimosia Epicheirisi Ilektrismou AE (DEI)*, ECLI:EU:C:2014:2083, para 57 [hereinafter *Greek Lignite*]. This approach may also explain the recent focus of competition authorities in Europe on leveraging practices by super-dominant digital platforms, with the aim to ensure the 'equality of opportunity' of economic operators (see European Commission, Case AT 39.740—Google Search, paras 332 and 334), as well as recent ideas to regulate from a fairness perspective platform to business relations (see Inception Impact Assessment, Fairness in Platform to Business Relation, Ares(2017)5222469, available at https://ec.europa.eu/info/law/better-regulation/initiatives/ares-2017-5222469_en. The extension of the principle of equality of opportunity beyond the strict confines of the case law on State action is a remarkable development and could perhaps be justified by the considerable economic power of certain digital platforms that act as gatekeepers in the digital economy: See EU Communication on digital platforms of 25 May 2016 (COM(2016)288 fin) (noting that 'online platforms play an increasing role in the economy' and that 'the terms of access to online platforms can be an important factor for online and offline companies [. . .] some online platforms constitute important, sometimes the main, entry points to certain markets and data').

we value volumes of trade even if this is not efficient (from the point of view of the welfare of the citizens/consumers—eg volume of trade in drugs and other dangerous products affecting health) or we can take the aim to promote efficient trade. The Treaty actually favours the efficient trade thesis as it incorporates these public interest objectives as an exception to the principle of free trade. Hence, it is possible to take a welfare-oriented perspective on the Internal Market objective in EU competition law.

The same approach may be followed to a certain extent by the principle of fairness. Fairness might mean different things (equality of opportunity, a fair distribution of outputs, capabilities . . .) but someone may also consider it as a facet of distributive justice, which may be taken into account by welfare analysis incorporating these fairness concerns. A different tradition of new welfare economics, starting with Bergson and Samuelson defined a broader social welfare function, as a value depending on *all* the variables that might affect welfare.[144] The social welfare function (SWF) approach does not take the strong moral/value judgment of Kaldor–Hicks, in that compensation is only hypothetical and does not provide a complete social ordering. It offers a more complete analysis, which is devised as the means to weigh the utilities of different households. The SWF framework is sensitive to considerations of fairness. Economists who use the SWF approach are comfortable with comparisons of interpersonal utility between categories of consumers (eg 'rich' and 'poor'). Under normal conditions, they can estimate individuals' 'extended preferences' by looking to the ordinary preference data and use behaviour or surveys to infer individuals' preferences over bundles of attributes such as health, income, leisure, or environmental goods—and thereby also to make inferences about their extended preferences. From then on, a particular social welfare function will be used to compare different arrangements of individual utility. One may adopt a '*prioritarian*' SWF: one that gives greater weight to utility changes affecting individuals at lower utility levels, as compared to individuals at higher utility levels. This method has already been used in cost benefit analysis (CBA)/impact assessment, although distributionally weighted CBA is controversial—in part because no clear basis has yet been furnished for the calculation of weights.

Ordoliberal authors and the principle of free (complete) competition they advocate often lend themselves to misunderstanding. Certainly, for ordoliberal writers, the objective of competition law, as well as of all State regulation, is to promote the competitive process, perceived as an institution, and not to protect individuals or specific groups, such as consumers or the competitors of the dominant firm. However, some ordoliberal authors adopt a perspective that is compatible with a welfare approach.[145] Finally, potentially all aspects of human happiness or capabilities (Amartya Sen) may be included in a welfare economics framework. One might note the report of the Commission on the Measurement of Economic Performance and Social Progress[146] which adopts a wide perspective on the measurement of welfare and well-being (quality of life depends on people's objective conditions and capabilities—people's health, education, personal activities and environmental conditions, social connections, political voice, insecurity, and life satisfaction.)

144 A Bergson, 'A Reformulation of Certain Aspects of Welfare Economics' (1938) 52(2) *Q J Economics* 310; P Samuelson, *Foundations of Economic Analysis* (Harvard University Press, 1947).

145 See our discussion in Chapter 8.

146 J Stiglitz, A Sen, and JP Fitoussi, Report by the Commission on the Measurement of Economic Performance and Social Progress, available at https://ec.europa.eu/eurostat/documents/118025/118123/Fitoussi+Commission+report.

2.2. A POSITIVE LAW ACCOUNT OF COMPETITION LAW AIMS

2.2.1. THE AIMS OF EU COMPETITION LAW

2.2.1.1. The objectives of competition law according to the EU Courts

The current state of the case law of the European Courts (General Court and the Court of Justice of the EU) may cast doubt on the appeal of the theory of a unitary objective (welfare or the protection of the competitive process) and may indicate that EU competition law adheres to multiple goals. This may be contrasted to the rule-making activity of the European Commission, which has been moving in recent years towards an 'economic approach' that would value, probably higher than other objectives, the goal of 'consumer welfare' or the protection of consumers.[147]

If we focus for illustration purposes at some jurisprudence of the European Courts,[148] it would be difficult to find a clear trend towards one objective.[149] One might argue that there is a

[147] See J Gual et al, 'Report by the EAGCP on an Economic Approach to Article 82 EC' (July 2005), available at ec.europa.eu/dgs/competition/economist/eagcp_july_21_05.pdf; European Commission, Vertical Restraints Guidelines [2010] OJ C 130/1, para 7 ('The objective of Article 101 is to ensure that undertakings do not use agreements—in this context, vertical agreements—to restrict competition on the market to the detriment of consumers. Assessing vertical restraints is also important in the context of the wider objective of achieving an integrated internal market.'); European Commission, Guidance on the Commission's enforcement priorities in applying Article 82 of the EC Treaty to abusive exclusionary conduct by dominant undertakings [2009] OJ C 45/7, para 5 ('In applying Article [102] to exclusionary conduct by dominant undertakings, the Commission will focus on those types of conduct that are most harmful to consumers. Consumers benefit from competition through lower prices, better quality and a wider choice of new or improved goods and services.'); European Commission, Guidelines on the application of Article 81(3) of the Treaty [2004] OJ C 101/7, para 13, ('The objective of Article 81 is to protect competition on the market as a means of enhancing consumer welfare and of ensuring an efficient allocation of resources. Competition and market integration serve these ends since the creation and preservation of an open single market promotes an efficient allocation of resources throughout the Community for the benefit of consumers.').

[148] For an excellent analysis of the objectives of EU Competition Law in the context of Article 101 TFEU, see B Van Rompuy, *Economic Efficiency: The sole Concern of Modern Antitrust Policy?—Non-efficiency Considerations under Article 101 TFEU* (Wolters Kluwer, 2012). On Article 102 TFEU, see P Akman, 'The Reform of the Application of Article 102 TFEU: Mission Accomplished' (2016) 81(1) *Antitrust L J* 145; P Behrens, 'The "Consumer Choice" Paradigm in German Ordoliberalism and its Impact Upon EU Competition Law', Europa-Kolleg Hamburg, Discussion Paper No 1/14 (22 July 2014), available at ssrn.com/abstract=2568304; R Nazzini, *The Foundations of European Union Competition Law—The Objective and Principles of Article 102* (OUP, 2011). More generally, on the objectives of EU competition law, see I Lianos, 'Some Reflections on the Question of the Goals of EU Competition Law' in I Lianos and D Geradin (eds) *Handbook on European Competition Law: Substantive Aspects* (Edward Elgar, 2013), 1–84; D Zimmer (ed) *The Goals of Competition Law* (Edward Elgar, 2012).

[149] This is not only the case in Europe but characterizes most jurisdictions. See the recent survey by the International Competition Network of thirty-three competition authorities: ICN, Unilateral Conduct Working Group, Report on the Objectives of Unilateral Conduct Laws, Assessment of Dominance/Substantial Market Power, and State-Created Monopolies, Doc No 353 (2007), available at www.internationalcompetitionnetwork.org/uploads/library/doc353.pdf, noting that '[r]espondents identified ten different objectives of unilateral conduct laws, regulations, and policies, with all but one member agency identifying more than one objective as relevant to their unilateral conduct regimes. [...] [T]hese objectives (listed in order of the number of times cited by respondents) include: ensuring an effective competitive process; promoting consumer welfare; maximizing efficiency; ensuring economic freedom; ensuring a level playing field for small and medium size enterprises; promoting fairness and equality; promoting consumer choice; achieving market integration; facilitating privatization and market liberalization; and promoting competitiveness in international markets.'

tendency for the aim of the protection of consumers to become the 'apple of discord' between those advancing the view that the aim of EU competition law, in particular Article 102 TFEU, is the protection of the competitive process, the institution of competition, and others arguing for a 'more economic approach' that would interpret the same provision in conformity with neoclassical price theory and the overall objective of 'consumer welfare'. This concept has again to be distinguished from that of 'the interest of the consumers', which might refer to the different paradigm of 'consumer choice' (see Section 2.1.7.3). Both groups, however, recognize the importance of the objective of market integration in the interpretation and application of Article 102 TFEU.[150]

EU Courts, in particular the General Court, have emphasized many times that the aim of EU competition law is to protect the interest of consumers, in particular final consumers. In *GlaxoSmithKline Services Unlimited v Commission*, the General Court held that 'the objective assigned to Article 101(1) TFEU, which constitutes a fundamental provision indispensable for the achievement of the missions entrusted to the [EU], in particular for the functioning of the internal market [. . .] is to prevent undertakings, by restricting competition between themselves or with third parties, from reducing the welfare of the final consumer of the products in question'.[151] The CJEU did not agree with this interpretation of Article 101(1) TFEU by the GC.[152] Some Advocates General of the CJEU linked, however, the protection of the interest of consumers with the Internal Market objective.[153] In *Austrian Banks*, the GC also held the following

> [. . .] the ultimate purpose of the rules that seek to ensure that competition is not distorted in the internal market is to increase the well-being of consumers [. . .]. Competition law and competition policy therefore have an undeniable impact on the specific economic interests of final customers who purchase goods or services'.[154]

In *Astra/Zenecca*, the GC noted the importance of preserving competition on the merits, which benefits consumers.[155]

150 For a discussion, see H Schweitzer, 'The History, Interpretation and Underlying Principles of Section 2 Sherman Act and Article 82 EC' in CD Ehlermann and M Marquis (eds) *European Competition Annual 2007: A Reformed Approach to Article 82 EC* (Hart, 2008), 120–64, esp 128–38.

151 Case T-168/01, *GlaxoSmithKline Services Unlimited v Commission* [2006] ECR II–2969, para 118. The GC referred to the following case law for this proposition: Joined Cases T-213/01 and T-214/01, *Österreichische Postsparkasse and Bank für Arbeit und Wirtschaft* v *Commission* [2006] ECR II–1601, para 115; Joined Cases 56 & 58/64, *Consten & Grundig v Commission* [1966] ECR 299; and Case 28/77, *Tepea v Commission* [1978] ECR 1391, para 56.

152 Joined Cases C-501, 513, 515 & 519/06, *GlaxoSmithKline Services Unlimited v Commission* [2009] ECR I–9291, paras 62–4 (noting that for a finding that an agreement has an anti-competitive object under Article 101(1) TFEU, it is not necessary that final consumers be deprived of the advantages of effective competition in terms of supply or price).

153 See Opinion of AG Trstenjak in Case C-209/07, *Competition Authority v Beef Industry Development Society Ltd, Barry Brothers (Carrigmore) Meats Ltd* [2008] ECR I–8637, para 42, 'Article [101 TFEU] protects competition in particular in regard to its function of forming a single market with conditions akin to an internal market and its function of supplying consumers as well as possible'.

154 Joined Cases T-213/01 and T-214/01, *Österreichische Postsparkasse AG and Bank für Arbeit und Wirtschaft AG v Commission* [2006] ECR II–1601, para 115.

155 Case T-321/05, *AstraZeneca AB and AstraZeneca plc v European Commission* [2010] ECR II–2805, para 804.

Moving beyond consumers, in *Konkurrenverket v TeliaSonera Sverige AB*, an abuse of dominance case concerning the practice of margin squeeze, the CJEU held that:

> The function of [competition] rules is precisely to prevent competition from being distorted to the *detriment of the public interest, individual undertakings and consumers, thereby ensuring the well-being of the European Union*. [. . .]
>
> Accordingly, Article 102 TFEU must be interpreted as referring not only to practices which may cause damage to consumers directly, but also to those which are detrimental *to them* through their impact on competition.[156]

An adept of the economic efficiency approach can of course find satisfaction in the reference to the concept of public interest (consumers and undertakings), thus indicating that the Court adopts a total welfare standard approach. The Court does not refer only to the structure of competition but also to impact on competition, thus indicating that this term might be interpreted as the appropriate degree of competition for the achievement of the objectives of a total welfare standard. It is also clear that harm to consumers is a crucial element of a competition law case, although consumers are not the primary focus of the Court (which also refers to individual undertakings, unless this concept is to be interpreted as intermediate consumers), thus implicitly rejecting a consumer welfare standard (widely or narrowly defined).

EU Courts and their Advocates General stressed in many instances the importance of preserving the process of competition or more generally an 'effective competitive structure'. In her Opinion in *British Airways*, Advocate General Kokott provides a succinct summary of this trend with regard to the interpretation of Article 102 TFEU:

> [Article 102] forms part of a system designed to protect competition within the internal market from distortions [Article 3(1)g TEC]. Accordingly, Article [102 TFEU], like the other competition rules of the Treaty, is not designed only or primarily to protect the immediate interests of individual competitors or consumers, but to protect the *structure of the market* and thus *competition as such (as an institution)*, which has already been weakened by the presence of the dominant undertaking on the market. In this way, consumers are also indirectly protected. Because where competition as such is damaged, disadvantages for consumers are also to be feared.[157]

Recent case law has confirmed the importance of the protection of the structure of competition or competition as such, in the context of Article 102 and Article 101 TFEU.[158]

156 Case C-52/09, *Konkurrenverket v TeliaSonera Sverige AB* [2011] ECR 527, paras 21–4 (emphasis added).

157 Opinion AG J Kokott, in Case C-95/04, *British Airways plc v Commission* [2007] ECR I–2331, para 68 (emphasis added). See also, in the context of Article 101 TFEU for a similar formulation, Opinion AG J Kokott in Case C-8/08, *T-Mobile Netherlands BV and Others* [2009] ECR I–4529, para 71.

158 See eg Joined Cases C-501, 513, 515 & 519/06 P, *GlaxoSmithKline Services Unlimited v Commission* [2009] ECR I–9291, para 63 ('Secondly, it must be borne in mind that the Court has held that, like other competition rules laid down in the Treaty, Article 81 EC aims to protect not only the interests of competitors or of consumers, but also the structure of the market and, in so doing, competition as such.'); Joined Cases C-501, 513, 515 & 519/06 P, *GlaxoSmithKline Services Unlimited v Commission* [2009] ECR I–9291, para 63 ('like other competition rules laid down in the Treaty, Article [101 TFEU] aims to protect not only the interests of competitors or of consumers, but also the structure of the market and, in so doing, competition as such'); Case C-8/08, *T-Mobile Netherlands BV v Raad van bestuur van de Nederlandse Mededingingsautoriteit* [2009] ECR I–4529, para 38 ('Article [101 TFEU], like the other competition rules of the Treaty, is designed to protect not only the immediate interests of individual competitors or consumers but also to protect the structure of the market and

The EU Courts have also referred to other objectives. In *MOTOE*, the Court and Advocate General identified 'equality of opportunity' as an aim pursued by EU competition law.[159] In *Deutsche Telekom*, the General Court asserted that a margin squeeze by a dominant telecoms operator was abusive because it unfairly limited access by downstream competitors to the market, violating Article 102(a) TFEU.[160] In *British Airways* and *Michelin II*, confirmed by the European Courts, the European Commission's decisions both found that rebate schemes (as well as being exclusionary and discriminatory) were 'unfair' to the affected travel agents and dealers.[161]

In the recent *Intel* case, Advocate General Niels Wahl argued in his Opinion that the main aim pursued by EU competition law is economic efficiency. According to the AG,

> From the outset, EU competition rules have aimed to put in place a system of undistorted competition, as part of the internal market established by the EU. In that regard, it cannot be overemphasised that protection under EU competition rules is afforded to the competitive process as such, and not, for example, to competitors. In the same vein, competitors that are forced to exit the market due to fierce competition, rather than anticompetitive behaviour, are not protected. Therefore, not every exit from the market is necessarily a sign of abusive conduct, but rather a sign of aggressive, yet healthy and permissible, competition. *This is because, given its economic character, competition law aims, in the final analysis, to enhance efficiency.* The importance placed on efficiency is also in my view clearly reflected in the case-law of the EU Courts.[162]

The CJEU's judgment contains some ambiguous language on this issue but seems to accept that efficiency constitutes an important aim of EU competition law, at least with regard to Article 102 TFEU, although it also mentions that efficiency should 'also benefit the consumer':

> The analysis of the capacity to foreclose is also relevant in assessing whether a system of rebates which, in principle, falls within the scope of the prohibition laid down in Article 102 TFEU, may be objectively justified. It has to be determined whether the exclusionary effect arising from such a system, which is disadvantageous for competition, may be counterbalanced, or outweighed, by advantages *in terms of efficiency which also benefit the consumer.* That balancing of the favourable and unfavourable effects of the practice in question

thus competition as such'); Case T-201/04, *Microsoft Corp v Commission* [2007] ECR II–3601, para 664 (noting that 'Article [102 TFEU] covers not only practices which may prejudice consumers directly but also those which indirectly prejudice them by impairing an effective competitive structure').

159 Case C-49/07, *Motosykletistiki Omospondia Ellados NPID (MOTOE) v Elliniko Dimosio* [2008] ECR I–4863, para 51 ('A system of undistorted competition, such as that provided for by the Treaty, can be guaranteed only if equality of opportunity is secured as between the various economic operators'); Opinion of AG J Kokott in Case C-49/07, para 100.

160 C-280/08, *Deutsche Telekom v European Commission* [2010] ECR I–9555.

161 Case C-95/04 P, *British Airways plc v Commission* [2007] ECR I–2331; See also Opinion of AG Kokott in Case C–95/04 P, *British Airways plc v Commission* [2007] ECR I–2331; Case T-203/01, *Manufacture française des pneumatiques Michelin v Commission (Michelin II)* [2003] ECR II–4071, paras 110 and 240 (noting that as a result of its loyalty-inducing character, the quantity rebate scheme 'limited the dealers' choice of supplier and made access to the market more difficult for competitors').

162 Opinion of AG N Wahl in Case C-413/14 P, *Intel v Commission*, ECLI:EU:C:2016:788, paras 41–2 (emphasis added).

on competition can be carried out in the Commission's decision only after an analysis of the intrinsic capacity of that practice to foreclose competitors which are at least as efficient as the dominant undertaking.[163]

The fact that the Court uses the term 'the consumer' instead of 'consumers' may indicate that this analysis could be abstract and that the efficiencies put forward by the dominant undertaking should not necessarily benefit the consumers of the specific relevant market(s) that were affected by the alleged abuse, but, that they may more generally benefit future consumers or consumers in other (related?) markets, which could be of interest in a multi-sided markets context. If such an interpretation is confirmed, the approach followed by the Court will move closer to the concept of Kaldor–Hicks efficiency, where the losers (consumers of the relevant market), following the adoption of the specific abuse, will not necessarily be effectively compensated by the winners (the dominant undertaking) in lower prices, higher quality, or other parameters of competition they may value, compensation remaining purely hypothetical and assessed at an abstract level, that of 'the consumer'.

Notwithstanding a possible evolution of the jurisprudence of the CJEU towards an economic efficiency approach, following the *Intel* judgment, positive law still supports the view that EU competition law pursues multiple goals. To this case law, one might add the drafting of the Treaty of Lisbon, which sets the broader framework of competition law and policy in the EU and advances the idea of a more holistic competition law.

2.2.1.2. EU competition law's interaction with other EU and national public policies

The Founding Treaties : Article 3(1)g of the earlier Treaty of European Communities (TEC) recognized the vital importance of establishing 'a system ensuring that competition in the internal market is not distorted'. Based on a teleological interpretation of this provision, the Court of Justice of the EU was able to extend the application of Article 102 TFEU to exclusionary conduct that harms the effective structure of competition and prejudices consumers indirectly.[164] The first merger regulation in 1989,[165] as well as the new one in 2004, also refer to Article 3(1)g in their first recitals.[166] The Court of Justice relied on this provision to apply the principle of free competition to State measures in a number of cases,[167] as well as to put in place EU remedies for the effective enforcement of competition law.[168] Furthermore, the Court has placed particular emphasis on Article 3(1)g when confronted with a conflict between

[163] Case C-413/14 P, *Intel v Commission*, ECLI:EU:C:2017:632, para 140 (emphasis added).

[164] Case 6/72, *Europemballage Corporation and Continental Can Company Inc v Commission* [1973] ECR 215, paras 23–6; Joined Cases 6 & 7/73, *Instituto Chemiotherapico Italiano SpA & Commercial Solvents Corp v Commission* [1974] ECR 223, para 32; Case 85/76, *Hoffmann-La Roche & Co AG v Commission* [1979] ECR 461, paras 38 and 125; Case 27/76, *United Brands Company and United Brands Continentaal BV v Commission* [1978] ECR 207, paras 63 and 183.

[165] Council Regulation (EEC) No 4064/89 of 21 December 1989 on the control of concentrations between undertakings [1989] OJ L 395/1, Recital 1.

[166] Council Regulation (EC) No 139/2004 of 20 January 2004 on the control of concentrations between undertakings [2004] OJ L 24/1, Recital 2.

[167] See eg Case 13/77, *SA GB-Inno BM v Association des détaillants en tabac* (ATAB) [1977] ECR 2115, para 29; Case C-260/89, *Elliniki Radiophonia Tileorasi AE & Panellinia Omospondia Syllogon Prossopikou v Dimotiki Etairia Pliroforissis et al* [1991] ECR I–2925, para 27; Case 229/83, *Association des Centres distributeurs Edouard Leclerc v SARL 'Au blé vert'* [1985] ECR 1, para 9.

[168] Case 453/99, *Courage Ltd v Bernard Crehan* [2001] ECR I–6297, para 20.

competition rules and other policies and objectives[169] and has pronounced, on the basis of this provision, that competition law constitutes a 'fundamental objective of the Community'.[170] Finally, the Court referred to this article when it granted to national competition authorities the power to set aside provisions of domestic legislation that jeopardize the '*effet utile*' of Article 101 TFEU.[171]

The existence of a specific provision emphasizing the role of competition law in the text of the so-called 'principles' part of the European Economic Community (EEC) Treaty, led to specific implications for the interpretation of this provision and its relation with other Community activities. This was reinforced by Article 4 TEC, introduced by the Maastricht Treaty in 1992, adding a new joint action of the Community and the Member States in the 'adoption of an economic policy, which is based on the close coordination of Member States' economic policies, on the Internal Market, and on the definition of common objectives, and conducted in accordance with the principle of an open market economy with free competition'. The scope of the principle of 'free competition' was thus extended beyond the narrow confines of the competences of the Community (although these were already broadly defined). The Member States should be inspired by this principle in conducting their economic policies. 'Competitiveness' was also added as an aim of the Community by the Treaty of Amsterdam in 1997. The distinction between 'aims' and 'activities' did not adequately represent the role of competition law in the legal framework put in place by the successive European treaties. In reality, competition was conceived as an important intermediate objective, the aims of Article 2 being more difficult to assess and representing long term aims. Progressively, the role of competition law evolved from an instrument for the completion of broader aims to an important objective of the Community. Indeed, as the Court of Justice recognized in *Continental Can*, the objectives pursued by Article 3(1)g were 'indispensable' for the achievement of the Community's tasks.

The Constitutional Treaty of 2004 :This upgraded role was reflected in the ill-fated Treaty Establishing a Constitution for Europe in 2004 (Constitutional Treaty), which listed competition not only as one of the guiding principles, but also as one of the 'objectives' of the EU. According to Article I-3(2) of the Constitutional Treaty, 'the Union shall offer its citizens an area of freedom, security and justice without internal frontiers, and an internal market where competition is free and undistorted'. Competition policy was portrayed as the 'fifth freedom' and included in the chapter on the Internal Market, thus linking competition to the aim of market integration and raising the rank of competition law to that of the fundamental freedoms of movement (free movement of goods, services, persons, and capital). These were interpreted by the jurisprudence of the CJEU at the time as equivalent to fundamental rights, at the core of the European constitutional project.[172] Note that, during almost

[169] Case C-67/96, *Albany International BV v Stichting Bedrijfspensioenfonds Textielindustrie* [1999] ECR I–5751; Case C-309/99, *JCJ Wouters et al v Algemene Raad can de Nederlandse Orde van Advocaten* [2002] ECR I–1577.

[170] Case C-289/04 P, *Showa Denko KK v Commission* [2006] ECR I–5859, para 55; Joined Cases T-259–64 & 271/02, *Raiffeisen Zentralbank Österreich AG & Others v Commission* [2006] ECR II–5169, para 255.

[171] Case C-198/01, *Consorzio Industrie Fiammiferi* [2003] ECR I–8055, paras 54–5.

[172] Case C-112/00, *Schmidberger (Eugen), Internationale Transporte und Planzüge v Republic of Austria* [2003] ECR I–5659; Case C-36/02, *Omega Spielhallen- und Automatenaufstellungs-GmbH v Oberbürgermeisterin der Bundesstadt Bonn* [2004] ECR I–9609; Case C-438/05, *International Transport Workers' Federation & Finish Seamen's Union v Viking Line ABP and OÜ Viking Line Eesti* [2007] ECR I–1077; Case C-341/05, *Laval un Partneri Ltd v Svenska Byggnadsarbetareförbundet* [2007] ECR I–11767; Case C-346/06 *Rüffert* [2008] ECR I–1989.

the same period, the jurisprudence of the Court recognized that the principle of free movement constitutes a source of individual rights that may be granted against public powers.[173] This constitutionalization process aimed to bestow to the provisions on free movement and consequently the 'fifth freedom' of competition law a normative status equivalent to that of fundamental rights.

The Lisbon Treaty of 2009 : Following the rejection of the Constitutional Treaty by French and Dutch voters in May and June 2005, the ratification process was abandoned and negotiations for a new Treaty started. Despite the relative minor modifications brought in the substantive provisions of EU competition law, the negotiation and conclusion of the Treaty of Lisbon marked the first time in the chronicles of European integration that the role of competition law in the structure of the Treaties has been questioned. The debate was ignited by the attempt of the president of France, Nicolas Sarkozy, to abolish any reference to competition law as an objective of the Union, competition law being considered rather as a means to accomplish the broader tasks of the Union.[174] The Treaty of Lisbon of 2009 introduced a new Article 3 in the Treaty on the European Union (TEU) merging the old Articles 2 and 3 TEC into an integrated framework that includes the broad economic and non-economic objectives and tasks of the Union. There is no reference to the principle of 'undistorted competition' or 'free competition'. Article 3(3) TEU provides that the Union shall establish an internal market with the goal of achieving 'a highly competitive social market economy', aiming at full employment and social progress. As previously mentioned in Chapter 1, the concept of 'social market economy' replaces the expression 'open market economy with free competition' in former Article 4(1) TEC. Competition law in the EU is thus inexorably linked to the objectives of the Internal Market and the establishment of a 'social market economy'. It gets transformed from an objective (as it was suggested under the ill-fated draft Constitutional Treaty[175]) into a means of completion of other objectives. These are much more precise than the ones mentioned in former Article 2 TEC and consist of the Internal Market and the 'Social Market Economy'. Furthermore, contrary to the Constitutional Treaty, competition law is not considered as a 'fifth freedom', nor has it been moved to the Internal Market chapter of the TFEU. Article 3(c) TFEU indicates that competition law is, as before, one of the EU's exclusive competences confined to the establishment of competition rules 'necessary for the functioning of the Internal Market'. The link to the Internal Market objective becomes even more explicit in Protocol No 27 on 'the Internal Market and Competition', annexed to the TEU and TFEU with the aim of neutralizing the repeal of former Article 3(1)g. The Protocol provides that 'the Internal Market as set out in Article 3 TEU includes a system ensuring that competition is not

[173] See Case C-265/95, *Commission v France* [1997] ECR I–6959, para 24; Case C-320/03, *Commission v Austria* [2005] ECR I–7929, para 63; Opinion AG Trstenjak in Case C-445/06, *Danske Slagterier* [2009] ECR I–2119, para 83.

[174] The tension between the conception of competition law as an end in itself and as a means for the completion of other objectives has been noted by French competition literature: see P Bonassies, 'Les fondements du droit communautaire de la concurrence: La théorie de la concurrence-moyen' in *Études dédiées à Alex Weill*, (Dalloz-Litec, 1983), 51–68.

[175] According to Article I-3(2) of the Constitutional Treaty, 'the Union shall offer its citizens an area of freedom, security and justice without internal frontiers, and an internal market where competition is free and undistorted'. Competition policy was portrayed as the 'fifth freedom' and included in the chapter on the Internal Market, thus linking competition to the aim of market integration and raising the rank of competition law to that of the fundamental freedoms of movement (free movement of goods, services, persons and capital). These were interpreted by the jurisprudence of the Court of Justice at the time as equivalent to fundamental rights, at the core of the European constitutional project.

distorted'. Interestingly, the Protocol does not include any reference to the concept of 'social market economy' and merely reproduces the text of the old Article 3(1)g.

Interaction with other EU policies and objectives : Conceiving competition law as a means to achieve the Internal Market *as well as* the other objectives of the Treaty, offer discrete interpretative choices to courts, eventually that of broadening the aims of EU competition law when protecting an 'effective competitive structure'. We will explore this angle in Section 2.3 on Market integration. The protection of consumers figures is also an important objective of the Union in the wake of the Treaty of Lisbon. Article 12 TFEU provides that 'consumer protection requirements shall be taken into account in defining and implementing other Union policies and activities'. This article may be interpreted as requiring that the protection of the interest of the consumer should be an integral part of EU competition law and policy,[176] as it should be for any other policy of the Union. The interpretation would therefore depend on the balance between allocative efficiency (the price of pharmaceuticals is lower with parallel imports) and dynamic efficiency (there is more innovation by the pharmaceutical industry if restrictions on parallel trade are allowed). Protocol No 27 stresses that the 'system' of competition law is part of the broader Internal Market objective. By doing so, it clarifies that market integration constitutes the *specific* aim of competition law, meaning that in case of conflict between this aim and other more general aims followed by the Treaty, such as the protection of the interest of consumers, the objective of the Internal Market should take priority. Certainly, the repeal of Article 3(1)g raises the issue of the rank of competition law and its relation to other provisions of the Treaty, in case of conflict. In terms of legal effect, pursuant to Article 51 TEU, Protocol No 27 has, however, clearly the same legal status as the TEU and the TFEU. The Courts retain their ability to ensure the '*effet utile*' of this provision, as was previously the case with Article 3(1)g.

Social Market Economy : The inclusion in Article 3(3) TEU of the concept of 'a highly competitive social market economy' constitutes a highlight of the Treaty of Lisbon. The concept rests undefined in the Lisbon Treaty. It first made its appearance in the context of EU primary law in the Constitutional Treaty.[177] The concept certainly has German origins.[178] One could also argue that it might refer to a specific variety of capitalism linked to the 'coordinated market economies' model of Continental Europe, as opposed to the 'liberal market economy' model.[179] Hence, although the EU Treaties contain language that recognizes 'the principle of an open market economy with free competition',[180] and include provisions limiting the discretion of Member States, or undertakings, to impose distortions of competition,[181] they also accept that the EU aims to develop a 'highly competitive *social* market economy',[182] and recognize the importance of services of general interest.[183]

176 For a strong correlation between competition law and consumer policy, see J Stuyck, 'EC Competition Policy after Modernisation: More Than Ever in the Interest of Consumers' (2005) 28(1) *J Consumer Policy* 1.

177 For a commentary, see C Joerges and F Rödl, 'Social Market Economy' as Europe's Social Model?', EUI Working Paper LAW No 2004/8.

178 AT Peacock and H Willgerodt (eds) *German Neo-liberals and the Social Market Economy* (Macmillan, 1989); V Vanberg, 'Freiburg School of Law and Economics' in P Newman (ed) *The New Palgrave Dictionary of Economics and the Law*, vol 2 (MacMillan, 1998), 172–79.

179 See, on this opposition, PA Hall and D Soskice, 'An Introduction to Varieties of Capitalism' in PA Hall & D Soskice (eds) *Varieties of Capitalism: The Institutional Foundations of Comparative Advantage* (OUP, 2001), ch 1.

180 TFEU, Articles 119, 120, and 127.

181 Ibid, Articles 32(c), 101–9, 113, 116, and 348.

182 TEU, Article 3(3).

183 Services of general interest are recognised by Protocol No 26, while the concept of Services of General Economic Interest appears in Articles 14 and 106(2) TFEU and in Protocol No 26 to the TFEU. See also Article 36 of the Charter of Fundamental Rights, according to which '[t]he Union recognises and respects access to

Alternatively, it is possible to infer from this juxtaposition of the concept of 'social market economy' with that of free competition, the opposition between the 'two organizing principles in society': from one side, economic liberalism with the establishment and institutionalization of markets, and, from the other side, the principle of social protection,[184] might influence the Courts when deciding on the interaction of competition law with other policies pursued by the Treaty.[185] This situation should be distinguished from that relating to the existence of a specific objective of EU competition law, the Internal Market, following Protocol No 27. One could analyse the inclusion of the concept of 'social market economy' in the text of the Treaties as profoundly interlinked with the addition of broad horizontal integration provisions with the aim of managing the interaction between the different policies pursued by the Treaty, included in Title II of the TFEU entitled 'Provisions having general application'.[186]

The concept of 'social market economy' operates more as an interpretative principle or ideal, rather than as an objective of EU competition law.[187] The idea is to transform the Union to some form of holistic polity with competence to act, or at least to consider, all aspects of the welfare of its citizens. Article 9 of the TFEU states that '[i]n defining and implementing its policies and activities, the Union shall take into account requirements linked to the promotion of a high level of employment, the guarantee of adequate social protection, the fight against social exclusion, and a high level of education, training and protection of human health'.[188] As discussed above, one could also add Article 12 on consumer protection. Such broad policy integration provisions did not exist in the part of the previous Treaties devoted to general principles, albeit in some specific areas, such as the protection of the environment.[189] The inclusion of these provisions will inevitably lead the Commission, and arguably the Courts, to grant more importance to broader public interest concerns in some circumstances.

Would this bring any change to current practice? The Commission has a clear stance against aggregating effects across markets[190] and balancing competition with other public interests, to the extent that these public interest objectives cannot be taken, at least directly, into account in the assessment of the existence of a restriction of competition.[191] The Commission takes into

services of general economic interest as provided for in national laws and practices, in accordance with the Treaty establishing the European Community, in order to promote the social and territorial cohesion of the Union'.

184 K Polanyi, *The Great Transformation* (Beacon Press, 2nd ed, 2001 [1st ed, 1957]), 138.

185 It is interesting to note that Europe is not the only major competition law jurisdiction attempting to reconcile the concept of 'market' with the 'social' dimension, perceived, at least if one follows Polanyi (ibid, n 16) as two opposing organizing principles of the society. Article 1 of the Chinese Anti-Monopoly Law, enacted in 2007, provides that the law is enacted with the purpose of 'enhancing economic efficiency, safeguarding the interests of consumers and social public interest', as well as 'promoting the healthy development of the socialist market economy'. Of course, the exact meaning and degree of difference between what is conceived as the 'social' and the 'socialist' dimension of a 'market economy' is a matter for speculation. . .

186 See, for instance, the new general integration clause at Article 7 TFEU: 'The Union shall ensure consistency between its policies and activities, taking all of its objectives into account and in accordance with the principle of conferral of powers'.

187 For a discussion, see L Azoulai, 'The Court of Justice and the Social Market Economy: The Emergence of an Idea and the Conditions for its Realization' (2008) 45(5) *Common Market L Rev* 1335.

188 TFEU, Article 9.

189 TEC, Article 6, now TFEU, Article 11. One could note the difference between the terms employed in Article 11 TFEU and those in Articles 9 and 12: 'Environmental protection requirements must be integrated into the definition and implementation of the Union's policies and activities', while 'a high level of employment', 'the guarantee of adequate social protection', 'consumer protection requirements' 'shall be taken into account'. It is not clear if this different formulation suggests a difference in the degree of legal effect of these provisions.

190 See Commission, Notice—Guidelines on the application of article 81(3) [2004] OJ C 101/7, para 43.

191 See our analysis in Chapter 6.

account the positive welfare effects of an agreement as long as 'the group of consumers affected by the restriction and benefiting from the efficiency gains are substantially the same'.[192] However, in a number of cases on the application of Article 101(3) TFEU the CJEU had regard to advantages arising from the agreement, not only for the specific relevant market but also for 'every other market on which the agreement in question might have beneficial effects'.[193] Public interest objectives have occasionally outweighed the finding of a restriction of competition in the context of Article 101(1), when an activity is (self-regulated) and the restraints are ancillary for its organization and operation.[194] To this, might be added the interpretation of the concept of 'undertaking' by the Commission and the courts with the aim of excluding from the scope of the competition law provisions of the Treaty certain activities, when applying competition law might jeopardize the public interest pursued.[195] The Court has also recognized the discretion of the Commission in balancing public interest objectives with the restriction to competition in a small number of cases regarding the enforcement of Article 101(3).[196]

Implications : The drafting of the Treaty of Lisbon might accentuate that trend and lead to a more explicit consideration of public policy concerns, thus aligning the competition assessment under Article 101 TFEU (and eventually Article 102 TFEU) with the European Union Merger Regulation (EUMR), which allows for the consideration of public interest objectives, although under quite limited circumstances.[197]

192 Commission, Notice—Guidelines on the application of article 81(3) [2004] OJ C 101/7, para 43.

193 Case T-86/95, *Compagnie Générale Maritime and others v Commission* [2002] ECR II-2011, para 130. It should be noted, however, that the Court also mentions Article 5 of Regulation 1017/68, specifying that any benefit or economic advantage should be assessed with regard to 'the interest of the transport users', thus restricting the type of consumers/users considered. See Case T-213/00, *CMA GCM & Others v Commission* [2003] ECR II-913, para 227, where the Court notes that '*both* Article [Article 101(3) TFEU] and Article 5 of Regulation No 1017/68 envisage the possibility of exemption for, amongst others, agreements which contribute to promoting technical or economic progress, without requiring a specific link with the relevant market' (emphasis added).

194 Case C-309/99, *Wouters and Others* [2002] ECR I-1557; Case C-519/04, *Meca-Medina and Majcen* [2006] ECR I-6991.

195 For instance, solidarity between generations and the social security system: Joined Cases C-159 & 160/91, *Poucet v Assurances Générales de France* [1993] ECR I-637; Joined Cases C-264, 306, 354 & 355, *AOK Bundesverband* [2004] ECR I-2493.

196 Case C-26/76, *Metro v Commission* [1977] ECR 1875, para 21 [hereinafter *Metro I*]: 'The powers conferred upon the Commission under [Article 101(3) TFEU] show that the requirements for the maintenance of workable competition may be reconciled with the safeguarding of objectives of different nature and to this end certain restrictions of competition are permissible, provided they are essential to the attainment of those objectives and they do not result in the elimination of competition for a substantial part of the common market.'; Joined Cases T-538, 542, 543 & 546/93, *Métropole Télévision v Commission* [1996] ECR II-649, para 118: 'in the context of an overall assessment, the Commission is entitled to base itself on considerations connected with the pursuit of the public interest in order to grant exemption under Article [101(3) TFEU].' See our analysis in Chapter 6.

197 Council Regulation (EC) No 139/2004 of 20 January 2004 on the control of concentrations between undertakings [2004] OJ L 24/1, Recital 23 (requiring the Commission to place its appraisal within the general framework of the fundamental objectives of the Treaties, thus allowing broader public interest concerns to be taken into account in the appraisal process) & Article 21(4) EUMR, which includes a legitimate interest clause providing that Member States may take appropriate measures to protect three specified legitimate interests: public security, plurality of the media and prudential rules, and other unspecified public interests that are recognised by the Commission after notification by the Member State). See also Case T-12/93, *Comité Central d'Entreprise de la Société Anonyme Vittel v Commission* [1995] ECR II-1247, paras 38–40 (taking into account the collective interest of employees—social protection).

The Commission and the courts dispose of some instruments to integrate public interest concerns, in order to manage conflicts between the application of competition law and the completion of the wider objectives of the EU: they can exclude its application, finding that there is no economic activity and consequently 'undertaking'; they can perform some form of intuitive balancing, based on the proportionality test;[198] they might resort to a sort of quantitative cost–benefit analysis, similar to the instrument of assessing impact (or cost–benefit analysis) employed for other governmental policies,[199] when benefits brought for the public interests are quantifiable.[200] Based on the horizontal integration clauses of the Treaty, perceived as indicating the preferences of EU citizens, they may also adopt an approach that would rely on a social welfare function taking into account additional dimensions of welfare than price and quality (a more 'holistic' or 'polycentric' approach).[201]

Moving to a holistic approach that would rely on a social welfare function faces, nevertheless, two important obstacles. First, contrary to Articles 101 and 102 TFEU, the horizontal integration clauses do not produce any direct effect.[202] Their formulation is vague and inconclusive as to the legal effects produced. The clauses seem to be addressed to the EU Institutions. Nevertheless, it is possible, as with the EU Directives, that integration clauses may produce indirect effects, including the duty of conform interpretation for the authorities in charge of their enforcement.[203] Facing a choice between two possible interpretations of Articles 101 or 102 TFEU, the Commission and the courts should make efforts to select the option that maximizes the policy aim stated in the integration clause, while preserving the competitive process.[204] This form of legal pluralism enables the EU Institutions to connect the different spheres of their action and to ensure policy coherence between them. Second, a further difficulty for adopting a social welfare function model is the increasing involvement of national courts in the interpretation and application of Articles 101 and 102 TFEU. The decentralization of the decision-making process and the inevitable focus of national courts on local costs and benefits, as opposed to effects on trade between Member States, makes any effort to

198 See eg Case C-309/99, *Wouters and Others* [2002] ECR I–1557, with regard to Article 101(1) TFEU.

199 OFT, Article 101(3)—A Discussion of Narrow versus Broad Definition of Benefits (2010), 21–2 (on file with author) (noting that 'aligning the competition assessment under Article 101(3) with the standard cost–benefit analysis used in government policy would reduce the likelihood of competition analysis being out of step with wider government analysis or being seen as a block to desirable government policy'.

200 The *CECED* case constitutes an illustration of this approach: *CECED* (Case IV.F.1/36.718) Commission Decision 2000/475/EC, [2000] OJ L 187/47.

201 On the concept of 'social welfare function' and modern cost–benefit analysis, see KJ Arrow, *Social Choice and Individual Values* (John Willey & Sons, 2nd ed, 1963), ch 3; MD Adler and CW Sanchirico, 'Inequality and Uncertainty: Theory and Legal Applications' (2006) 155 *U Pennsylvania L Rev* 279; M D Adler, 'Future Generations: A Prioritarian View' (2009) 77 *George Washington L Rev* 1478. On 'polycentric competition law', see I Lianos, 'Polycentric Competition Law', (2018) Current Legal Problems 1.

202 See, for instance, concerning Article 6 TEC (now Article 11 TFEU), the Opinion of AG Jacobs in Case C-379/98, *PreussenElektra* [2001] ECR I–2099, para 231: 'Article 6 is not merely programmatic; it imposes legal obligations' and the Opinion of AG Gelhoed in Case C-161/04, *Austria v Parliament and Council* [2006] ECR I–7183, paras 59–60, noting that Article 6 TEC 'cannot be regarded as laying down a standard according to which in defining Community policies environmental protection must always be taken to be the prevalent interest', but '[a]t most (this provision) is to be regarded as an obligation on the part of the Community institutions to take due account of ecological interests in policy areas outside that of environmental protection stricto sensu'. Compare with the position of AG Cosmas in Case C-321/95 *Greenpeace* [1998] ECR I–1651, suggesting that the integration principle should have some form of direct effect.

203 Case C-106/89, *Marleasing* [1990] ECR I–4135.

204 For the proposition that the environmental integration clauses result in the priority of environmental protection when balanced against other Treaty objectives, see T Schumacher, 'The Environmental Integration Clause in Article 6 of the EU Treaty: Prioritising Environmental Protection' (2001) 3 *Environmental L R* 29.

broaden the competition assessment under Articles 101 and 102 problematic. Another obstacle may be the complexity of performing the sophisticated quantitative analysis required by CBA for non-specialized courts. The Commission and national competition authorities (NCAs) are better equipped for this task, although one could object that they lack adequate resources to perform this holistic analysis systematically.

The increasing role of the public interest in the enforcement of EU competition law is also recognized in the context of Article 106 TFEU. Moreover, Protocol No 26 on Services of General Interest, has been annexed to the Treaty with the aim of emphasizing the importance of services of general interest. Already Article 14 TFEU (former Article 16 TEC) recognized the role of services of general economic interest (SGEI) in the 'shared values of the Union' and provided that Member States should 'take care that such services operate on the basis of principles and conditions, particularly economic and financial conditions, which enable them to fulfil their missions'. Nevertheless, Protocol No 26 includes some important interpretative provisions, such as the need to take into account the diversity between various services of general economic interest because of the 'differences in the needs and preferences of users that may result from different geographical, social or cultural situations, which also implies that national, regional, and local authorities have a wide discretion in providing, commissioning and organizing SGEI closer to the needs of their citizens, as well as the need to ensure 'a high level of quality, safety and affordability, equal treatment and the promotion of universal access and of user rights'. The Protocol affirms that 'the provisions of the Treaties do not affect in any way the competence of Member States to provide, commission and organize non-economic services of general interest'.[205] To a large extent, these provisions reaffirm the principles that have been progressively developed by the jurisprudence of the Court and the decisional practice of the European Commission.[206]

Furthermore, Article 36 of the Charter of Fundamental Rights, which has a legal value similar to the Treaties, states that 'the Union recognizes and respects access to services of general economic interest as provided for in national laws and practices', 'in order to promote the social and territorial cohesion of the Union'. Would the reinforced legal effect of the Charter in conjunction to the interpretative principle of 'social market economy' provide more discretion to Member States with regard to the organization of public service obligations? Would the scope of Article 106(1) be narrowed, or that of Article 106(2) extended, as a consequence of

205 It should thus be possible for a Member State to exclude certain services not presenting any economic, commercial and industrial character from the scope of competition law, with the exception of course of cases where the activity is pursued in a competitive environment, which implies that it possesses economic (commercial) characteristics. See Joined Cases C-223 & 260/99, *Agorà Srl and Excelsior Snc di Pedrotti Bruna & C v Ente Autonomo Fiera Internazionale di Milano* [2001] ECR I–3605.

206 For example, in order to ensure the adequate operation of services of general economic interest with regard to quality, safety, affordability, equal treatment, and the promotion of universal access, the financing of services of general economic interest is permitted, under certain circumstances, under the State aids regime of Article 107 TFEU. The issue is not addressed under Article 106 TFEU. One should, however, remark that even in this case, there is a need for a competitive benchmark, linked to the adoption of a specific procedure for the selection of the operators to receive compensation based on a public tender (public procurement). For a commentary on the relation between services of general interest and competition, see E Szyszczak, 'Services of General Economic Interest and State Measures Affecting Competition' (2013) 4(6) *J European Competition L & Practice* 514; L Gyselen, 'Services of General Economic Interest and Competition under European Law: A Delicate Balance' (2010) 1(6) *J European Competition L & Practice* 491; J-L Buendia Sierra, 'Article 86—Exclusive Rights and other Anti-Competitive State Measures' in N Faull and A Nikpay, *The EC Law of Competition* (OUP, 2007), 593–657; C Bovis, 'Financing Services of General Interest in the EU: How do Public Procurement and State Aids Interact to Demarcate between Market Forces and Protection?' (2005) 11(1) *European L J* 79.

these Treaty modifications? One cannot exclude these potential outcomes, should the Court be receptive to this interpretative option.

With regard to public interest objectives pursued by national law, the CJEU has been unwilling in *Metro* to override the protection of smaller retailers conferred by national law, where it considered the separation of functions between wholesalers and retailers that is protected by German law and it approved restraints on wholesalers selling to the public and earning a double margin.[207] In *Wouters*, the CJEU held that rules in the ethical code of the Dutch Bar did not infringe Article 101 TFEU, although they restricted competition and might affect trade between Member States.[208]

2.2.2. THE AIMS OF UK COMPETITION LAW

As indicated above, by virtue of section 25(3) ERRA 2013, the CMA's primary duty is to seek to promote competition, both within and outside the UK, for the benefit of consumers.[209] Many of the sector-specific regulators who were also given the power to enforce the Chapter I and Chapter II prohibitions of the Competition Act 1998 and Articles 101 and 102 TFEU also have a general duty to promote competition under their statutory role, in addition to other duties in the public interest relevant to their individual sectors. The sector specific regulators are subject to the 'primacy obligation' to consider before taking enforcement action whether the use of their concurrent competition powers is more appropriate.[210]

For instance, according to section 3(1) of the Communications Act 2003, Office for Communication (OFCOM) has the principal duty to '(a) further the interests of citizens in relation to communications matters, and (b) to further the interests of consumers in relevant markets, where appropriate by promoting competition'. In addition, under section 29(1) of the Postal Services Act, OFCOM 'must carry out their functions in relation to postal services in a way that they consider will secure the provision of a universal postal service'.

Gas and Electricity Markets Authority's (OFGEM) principal objective, as set by the relevant legislation,[211] is 'to protect the interests of existing and future consumers in relation to gas conveyed through pipes and electricity conveyed by distribution or transmission systems', these interest being 'taken as a whole, including their interests in the reduction of greenhouse gases in the security of the supply of gas and electricity to them'.[212] According to the same

207 Case 26/76, *Metro SB-Großmärkte GmbH & Co KG v Commission* [1977] ECR 1875, paras 28–30.

208 Case C-309/99, *JCJ Wouters, JW Savelbergh και Price Waterhouse Belastingadviseurs BV v Algemene Raad van de Nederlandse Orde van Advocaten* [2002] ECR I–1577.

209 On the legislative history of Chapter I of the Competition Act 1998 and the aims of this provision, see C Townley, 'The Goals of Chapter I of the UK's Competition Act 1998' (25 May 2010), available at SSRN: ssrn.com/abstract=1615592. In a letter sent to the Secretary of State for Business, Energy and Industrial Strategy, Lord Tyrie, chairman of the CMA, suggested the introduction of a new statutory duty, binding on the courts (including the CAT), as well as on the CMA, to ensure that the economic interests of consumers, and their protection from detriment, become central in the competition law assessment, the CMA having 'a primary duty directly to protect consumers'. As Lord Tyrie observes, '(t)he current duty can leave the CMA constrained from acting to protect consumers' interests unless doing so through purely competition-based remedies'. See, Letter to the Secretary of State for Business, Energy and Industrial Strategy from the Rt Hon Lord Tyrie (February 21, 2019), available at https://assets.publishing.service.gov.uk/government/uploads/system/uploads/attachment_data/file/781151/Letter_from_Andrew_Tyrie_to_the_Secretary_of_State_BEIS.pdf, p. 9.

210 For the Financial Conduct Authority (FCA), this obligation is set out in section 234K of the Financial Services and Markets Act, 2000 [hereinafter FSMA].

211 Part I of the Gas Act 1986 and the Electricity Act 1989; the Utilities Act 2000; the Energy Acts of 2004, 2008, 2010, and 2011.

212 OFGEM, Powers and Duties of GEMA, 19 July 2013, para 1.4, available at www.ofgem.gov.uk/publications-and-updates/powers-and-duties-gema.

guidance, '[t]he Authority is generally required to carry out its functions in the manner it considers is best calculated to further the principal objective, wherever appropriate by promoting effective competition', by considering, prior to exercising its duties, 'the extent to which the interests of consumers would be protected by that manner of carrying out those functions and whether there is any other manner (whether or not it would promote competition) in which the Authority could carry out those functions which would better protect those interests'.[213]

Water Services Regulation Authority (OFWAT) is also subject to a variety of statutory duties by the Water Industry Act 1991 and the Water Act 2003, as well as to the requirement to exercise its powers in the manner it considers is best fit to further the consumer objective, wherever appropriate by promoting and facilitating effective competition.

Office of Rail and Road (ORR) duties are laid out in section 4 of the Railways Act 1993 and subsequent regulations implementing the EU liberalization legislation, including, among its economic duties, that of promoting competition in the provision of railway services for the benefit of users of railway services.[214]

The Civil Aviation Authority's functions and duties, as they result from the Civil Aviation Act 1982, the Civil Aviation Act 2012, and the Transport Act 2000, include that consumers have choice and value for money.

Since April 2016, Monitor is part of National Health Service (NHS) Improvement, which is responsible for overseeing foundation trusts and NHS trusts, as well as independent providers that provide NHS-funded care. Earlier versions of the Health and Social Care Act included the promotion of competition as one of the primary functions of Monitor. However, this was met with widespread opposition and the Bill was amended to make it clear that competition is not an end in itself to be promoted by Monitor in carrying out its main duty 'to protect and promote the interests of people who use health care services by promoting provision of healthcare services which is economic, efficient and effective and maintains or improves the quality of the services'.[215] However, Monitor 'must exercise its function with a view to preventing anti-competitive behaviour in the provision of healthcare services for the purposes of the NHS which is against the interests of people who use such services'.[216]

The Financial Conduct Authority has a single strategic objective of ensuring that the markets for financial services function well. This is achieved through three operational objectives: (i) securing an appropriate degree of protection for consumers; (ii) protecting and enhancing he integrity of the UK financial system; and last but not least, promoting effective competition in the interests of consumers in the markets for financial services and services provided by recognized investment exchanges.[217] The competition objective was introduced by the Financial Services Act 2012 (FSA). The Financial Services (Banking Reform) (FSBR) Act 2013 introduced new concurrent competition powers in relation to the provision of financial services in order to support FCA's competition objective.

The FSBR Act also provided for the establishment of a payments systems regulator (PSR), which has been fully operational since April 2015 for the regulation of a number of payment systems.[218] According to this legislation, the PSR has three objectives:[219] (i) to promote effective competition in the markets for payment systems and the services provided by payment

213 Ibid, paras 1.5 and 1.6.

214 See ORR, About: The Law and Our Duties, available at orr.gov.uk/about-orr/what-we-do/the-law/our-railway-duties.

215 Health and Social Care Act 2012, section 62(1).

216 Ibid, section 62(3).

217 FSMA, section 1, as amended by the Financial Services Act 2012, which came into force on 1 April 2013.

218 These are Bacs, CHAPS, Faster Payments, Cheque & Credit, LINK, Northern Ireland Clearing, Visa, and MasterCard.

219 Financial Services (Banking Reform) Act 2013, sections 50–2.

systems, between operators, payment service providers, and infrastructure providers; (ii) to promote the development of and innovation in payment systems; and (iii) to ensure payment systems are operated and developed in a way that takes account of and promotes the interests of service-users. Furthermore, the PSR is required to have regard to, among other things, the importance of maintaining the stability of and confidence in the UK financial system and the regulatory principles set out in the FSBR Act.[220]

Finally, the Northern Ireland Authority for Utility Regulation (NIAUR), which is responsible for regulating the gas, electricity, and water and sewerage industries in Northern Ireland has also the primary duty to safeguard the interests of consumers of these services, wherever appropriate by promoting and facilitating effective competition between commercial operators of these services.

It follows from the above that the protection of consumers and effective competition are the objectives followed by the CMA and all other UK competition authorities. The protection of consumers may take various forms, going from embracing the concept of consumer welfare to ensuring there is consumer choice.[221] The role of these competition-related objectives in the overall activity and priorities of sector-specific regulators depends on their interaction with the more general public interest duties they also pursue.

2.3. MARKET INTEGRATION AS A PRIMARY OBJECTIVE OF EU COMPETITION LAW

Many economic advantages were expected to flow from the establishment of the European Internal Market embracing an area that had been divided by national customs duties and quotas for over a century. Goods and services should be produced in the areas most suited to each and sold in the areas where they were wanted. Opportunities for specialization leading to automatic production lines and substantial cost savings would be possible in larger geographic markets. In many industries, firms might be able to grow to a size at which they enjoyed economies of scale and scope in production and distribution, while leaving room for other producers to compete with them.

In the EU Internal Market, all economic resources should be free to move throughout, unimpeded by national boundaries. Consequently, the TFEU provides for the free movement of goods, services, workers, and capital, as well as the right to establish a business in other Member States. It would, however, be of little use to abolish government restrictions, such as customs barriers and quotas between Member States, if traders in different countries were allowed to replace them by cartels, under which they agreed reciprocally to keep out of each other's home market. Agreements having the object or effect of restricting competition are, therefore, controlled under the competition rules in the Treaty. Von der Gröben, the first Member of the Commission responsible for competition policy, believed that these rules also had a longer-term function—to encourage the expansion of efficient firms and sectors of the economy at the expense of those less good at supplying what people want to pay for. This view is receiving greater acceptance, although some concern remains that the rules have been applied in order to protect parallel trade as such, irrespective of efficiency and/or the interest of final consumers at the end of the value chain.

220 Ibid, section 53.

221 See eg *Genzyme v OFT* [2004] CAT 4, paras 255, 468, and 585.

2.3.1. THE SEMINAL *CONSTEN & GRUNDIG* CASE

As explained above, Article 101(1) prohibits collusion that may affect trade between Member States and has the object or effect of restricting competition. Article 101(2) renders such agreements void but they may be exempted by virtue of Article 101(3) if it is established that that the collusion produces sufficient countervailing advantages.

Joined Cases 56 & 58/64, *Consten & Grundig v Commission*
[1966] ECR 299

Grundig, a manufacturer operating in Germany, decided to sell the dictating machines, radio and television sets it made in Germany in other countries too. In 1957, shortly before the EEC Treaty came into operation, it appointed Consten as its sole and exclusive distributor for France. Consten, like Grundig's other exclusive distributors and its wholesalers in Germany, agreed not to sell the contract products outside its territory and not to handle competing products. Consten also agreed to promote Grundig's products, organize repair facilities, provide continuing after sales services, guarantees, etc. Consten agreed not to sell any products competing with the contract items.

The restraints on cross-border trade were reinforced by Grundig's practice of marking its products not only with the trademark 'GRUNDIG', which indicated their origin, but also with the mark 'GINT' (Grundig International). It permitted its local exclusive distributor in each country to register the trademark 'GINT' in its territory to enable each distributor to sue under its national law on trademarks for infringing the mark 'GINT' if parallel trade should develop. Grundig retained the mark 'GINT' for Germany and, as long as a distributor enjoyed a sole and exclusive territory, it was licensed to use the mark, 'GRUNDIG', within its exclusive territory, but there were provisions to prevent it from using it if the buyer should cease to be an exclusive distributor for Grundig in the buyer's territory.

When, pursuant to the EEC Treaty, customs restrictions for the various contract products were abrogated in 1960 and 1961, UNEF and other merchants, began to buy Grundig products more cheaply from German wholesalers and to sell them to retailers in France at prices below those charged by Consten. The differences in the catalogue prices on products selected by the parties as typical were 44 per cent but, if discounts were taken into account, the real price difference was 23 per cent and still falling in 1966 when the Court gave judgment. The differences in margins were due not to double taxes or customs duties but to the difference in margins at the wholesale level.

In 1962, Consten sued UNEF for unfair competition in a French civil court. The French tort of unfair competition consisted of undermining a widely known exclusive distribution agreement, for instance, by selling products in the distributor's exclusive sales territory. Consten sued UNEF also for infringing its 'GINT' mark in France, and Grundig sued UNEF for infringing the 'GRUNDIG' mark. The court of first instance in Paris granted relief because Grundig's agreement with Consten was not a horizontal cartel.

In 1963, Grundig notified the exclusive distribution agreement to the Commission EU with a request for exemption under Article 101(3) TFEU and Regulation 17/62, then the main implementing regulation for competition.

On appeal from the actions against UNEF, the French appeal court ruled that since the Commission had initiated proceedings on UNEF's complaint, a French court was required to adjourn its proceedings pursuant to Article 9(3) of Regulation 17/62 and wait for the Commission's decision.

In 1964, the Commission adopted the decision and found that the distribution agreement between Grundig and Consten plus the arrangements for registration in France by Consten of the ancillary mark 'GINT' infringed Article 101(1) and refused to exempt them under Article 101(3).[222] *The Commission treated the arrangement for the 'GINT' mark as an ancillary agreement subject to Article 101(1). The Commission noted that the export bans insulated France from other Member States. It considered that even if the mark 'GINT' had a function in identifying the origin of products, its registration of the 'GINT' mark was not indispensable to obtaining the benefits of the exclusive dealership agreement since the identification of the products as being made by Grundig was accomplished by the 'GRUNDIG' mark. It added that the exclusive distribution contract plus the ancillary agreement relating to the 'GINT' mark had the object of protecting Consten from intra-brand competition. Consequently, it restricted competition contrary to Article 101(1) TFEU.*

The agreement was also capable of affecting trade between Member States because it caused trade to develop differently from the way it would otherwise have done. The Commission did not assess all the various benefits to consumers raised by Consten and Grundig because they had not established that the benefits of an exclusive distribution agreement would be passed on to consumers or that it was indispensable to achieving the improvements in production and distribution as was required under Article 101(3) TFEU. For similar reasons, the Commission did not examine whether the contract enabled competition to be eliminated in respect of a substantial part of the goods concerned.

The Commission concluded that the agreement was capable of affecting trade between member states. Its main reason being the isolation of France from other Member States attempted by the agreement. The Commission went on to conclude that absolute territorial protection appears as particularly noxious to the realisation of the Internal Market in making more difficult or in preventing the alignment of the market conditions of the products covered by the contract in the Internal Market. It has led to lawsuits between Consten and UNEF following the parallel imports made by UNEF and led to the submission of a request under Article 3 of Regulation 17/62. The problem of the admission of parallel imports was consequently of a particular importance in this case. The Commission found it expedient to require Grundig and Consten to refrain from obstructing or impeding, by any means whatsoever including the use to this end of the 'GINT' trademark, to obstruct the parallel import of Grundig products into France. According to the Commission, this obligation did not prevent Consten from exercising its rights over the 'GINT' mark against third parties, in so far as it did not act to obstruct or impede the parallel imports of Grundig products into the contract territory. Hence, the Commission concluded that the exclusive distribution agreement and use of the 'GINT' mark infringed Article 101(1) TFEU and refused to grant an exemption under Article 101(3) TFEU.

The CJEU pronounced itself on appeal to the Commission's decision. The Opinion of AG Roemer is quite important and should be read before the CJEU judgment.

The Judgment of the CJEU

The complaints concerning the applicability of Article 101(1) TFEU to sole distributorship contracts

14. The applicants submit that the prohibition in Article [101(1)] applies only to so-called horizontal agreements. The Italian Government submits furthermore that sole distributorship contracts do not constitute 'agreements between undertakings' within the meaning of that provision, since the parties are not on a footing of equality. With

[222] *Consten & Grundig* (Case IV-A/00004-03344) Commission Decision [1964] OJ 2545/64.

regard to these contracts, freedom of competition may only be protected by virtue of Article [102 TFEU].

15. Neither the wording of Article [101] nor that of Article [102] gives any ground for holding that distinct areas of application are to be assigned to each of the two Articles according to the level in the economy at which the contracting parties operate. Article [101] refers in a general way to all agreements which distort competition within the [Internal] Market and does not lay down any distinction between those agreements based on whether they are made between competitors operating at the same level in the economic process or between non-competing persons operating at different levels. In principle, no distinction can be made where the Treaty does not make any distinction.

16. Furthermore, the possible application of Article [101] to a sole distributorship contract cannot be excluded merely because the grantor and the concessionaire are not competitors *inter se* and not on a footing of equality. Competition may be distorted within the meaning of Article [101(1)] not only by agreements which limit it as between the parties, but also by agreements which prevent or restrict the competition which might take place between one of them and third parties. For this purpose, it is irrelevant whether the parties to the agreement are or not on a footing of equality as regards their position and function in the economy. This applies all the more, since, by such an agreement, the parties might seek, by preventing or limiting the competition of third parties in respect of the products, to create or guarantee for their benefit an unjustified advantage at the expense of the consumer or user, contrary to the general aims of Article [101].

17. It is thus possible that, without involving an abuse of a dominant position, an agreement between economic operators at different levels may affect trade between Member States and at the same time have as its object or effect the prevention, restriction or distortion of competition, thus falling under the prohibition of Article [101(1)] [. . .]

20. The submissions set out above are consequently unfounded [. . .]

The complaints relating to the concept of 'agreements [. . .] which may affect trade between Member States'

25. The applicants and the German Government maintain that the Commission has relied on a mistaken interpretation of the concept of an agreement which may affect trade between Member States and has not shown that such trade would have been greater without the agreement in dispute.

26. The defendant replies that this requirement in Article [101(1)] is fulfilled once trade between Member States develops, as a result of the agreement, differently from the way in which it would have done without the restriction resulting from the agreement, and once the influence of the agreement on market conditions reaches a certain degree. Such is the case here, according to the defendant, particularly in view of the impediments resulting within the [Internal] Market from the disputed agreement as regards the exporting and importing of Grundig products to and from France.

27. The concept of an agreement 'which may affect trade between Member States' is intended to define, in the law governing cartels, the boundary between the areas respectively covered by Community law and national law. It is only to the extent to which the agreement may affect trade between Member States that the deterioration in competition caused by the agreement falls under the prohibition of Community law contained in Article [101]; otherwise it escapes the prohibition.

28. In this connexion, what is particularly important is whether the agreement is capable of constituting a threat, either direct or indirect, actual or potential, to freedom of trade between Member States in a manner which might harm the attainment of the objectives of a single market between States. Thus the fact that an agreement encourages an increase, even a large one, in the volume of trade between States is not sufficient to exclude the possibility that the agreement may 'affect' such trade in the above-mentioned manner. In the present case, the contract between Grundig and Consten, on the one hand by preventing undertakings other than Consten from importing Grundig products into France, and on the other hand by prohibiting Consten from re-exporting those products to other Member States of the Common Market, indisputably affects trade between Member States. These limitations on the freedom of trade, as well as those which might ensue for third parties from the registration in France by Consten of the GINT trade mark, which Grundig places on all its products, are enough to satisfy the requirement in question.

29. Consequently, the complaints raised in this respect must be dismissed.

The complaints concerning the criterion of restriction on competition

30. The applicants and the German Government maintain that since the Commission restricted its examination solely to Grundig products the decision was based upon a false concept of competition and of the rules on prohibition contained in Article [101(1)], since this concept applies particularly to competition between similar products of different makes; the Commission, before declaring Article [101(1)] to be applicable, should, by basing itself upon the 'rule of reason', have considered the economic effects of the disputed contrast [*sic*] upon competition between the different makes. There is a presumption that vertical sole distributorship agreements are not harmful to competition and in the present case there is nothing to invalidate that presumption. On the contrary, the contract in question has increased the competition between similar products of different makes.

31. The principle of freedom of competition concerns the various stages and manifestations of competition. Although competition between producers is generally more noticeable than that between distributors of products of the same make, it does not thereby follow that an agreement tending to restrict the latter kind of competition should escape the prohibition of Article [101(1)] merely because it might increase the former.

32. Besides, for the purpose of applying Article 81(1), there is no need to take account of the concrete effects of an agreement once it appears that it has as its object the prevention, restriction or distortion of competition.

33. Therefore the absence in the contested decision of any analysis of the effects of the agreement on competition between similar products of different makes does not, of itself, constitute a defect in the decision.

34. It thus remains to consider whether the contested decision was right in founding the prohibition of the disputed agreement under Article [101(1)] on the restriction on competition created by the agreement in the sphere of the distribution of Grundig products alone. The infringement which was found to exist by the contested decision results from the absolute territorial protection created the said contract in favour of Consten on the basis of French law. The applicants thus wished to eliminate any possibility of competition at the wholesale level in Grundig products in the territory specified in the contrast [*sic*] essentially by two methods.

35. First, Grundig undertook not to deliver even indirectly to third parties products intended for the area covered by the contract. The restrictive nature of that undertaking is obvious if it is considered in the light of the prohibition on exporting which was imposed not only on Consten but also on all the other sole concessionaires of Grundig, as well as the German wholesalers. Secondly, the registration in France by Consten of the GINT trade mark, which Grundig affixes to all its products, is intended to increase the protection inherent in the disputed agreement, against the risk of parallel imports into France of Grundig products, by adding the protection deriving from the law on industrial property rights. Thus no third party could import Grundig products from other Member States of the Community for resale in France without running serious risks.

36. The defendant properly took into account the whole distribution system thus set up by Grundig. In order to arrive at a true representation of the contractual position the contract must be placed in the economic and legal context in the light of which it was concluded by the parties. Such a procedure is not to be regarded as an unwarrantable interference in legal transactions or circumstances which were not the subject of the proceedings before the Commission.

37. The situation as ascertained above results in the isolation of the French market and makes it possible to charge for the products in question prices which are sheltered from all effective competition. In addition, the more producers succeed in their efforts to render their own makes of product individually distinct in the eyes of the consumer, the more the effectiveness of competition between producers tends to diminish. Because of the considerable impact of distribution costs on the aggregate cost price, it seems important that competition between dealers should also be stimulated. The efforts of the dealer are stimulated by competition between distributors of products of the same make. Since the agreement thus aims at isolating the French market for Grundig products and maintaining artificially, for products of a very well-known brand, separate national markets within the Community, it is therefore such as to distort competition in the Common Market.

38. It was therefore proper for the contested decision to hold that the agreement constitutes an infringement of Article [101(1)]. No further considerations, whether of economic data (price difference between France and Germany, representative character of the type of appliance considered, level of overheads borne by Consten) or of the corrections of the criteria upon which the Commission relied in its comparisons between the situations of the French and German markets, and no possible favourable effects of the agreement in other respects, can in any way lead, in the face of abovementioned restrictions, to a different solution under Article [101(1)]

The complaints relating to the extent of the prohibition

39. The applicant Grundig and the German Government complain that the Commission did not exclude from the prohibition, in the operative part of the contested decision, those clauses of the contract in respect of which there was found no effect capable of restricting competition, and that it thereby failed to define the infringement.

40. It is apparent [. . .] that the infringement declared to exist by Article 1 of the operative part is not to be found in the undertaking by Grundig not to make direct deliveries in France except to Consten. That infringement arises from the clauses which, added to this grant of exclusive rights, are intended to impede, relying upon national law, parallel imports of Grundig products into France by establishing absolute territorial protection in favour of sole concessionaire.

41. The provision in Article [101(2)] that agreements prohibited pursuant to Article [101] shall be automatically void applies only to those parts of the agreement which are subject to the prohibition, or to the agreement as a whole if those parts do not appear to be severable from the agreement itself. The Commission should, therefore, either have confined itself in the operative part of the contested decision to declaring that an infringement lay in those parts only of the agreement which came within the prohibition, or else it should have set out in the preamble to the decision the reasons why those parts did not appear to it to be severable from the whole agreement.

42. It follows, however, from Article 1 of the decision that the infringement was found to lie in the agreement as a whole, although the Commission did not adequately state the reasons why it was necessary to render the whole of the agreement void when it is not established that all the clauses infringed the provisions of Article [101(1)]. The state of affairs found to be incompatible with Article [101(1)] stems from certain specific clauses of the contract [. . .] concerning absolute territorial protection and from the additional agreement on the GINT trade mark rather than from the combined operation of all the clauses of the agreement, that is to say, from the aggregate of its effects.

43. Article 1 of the contested decision must therefore be annulled in so far as it renders void, without any valid reason, all the clauses of the agreement by virtue of Article [101(2)].

The submissions concerning the finding of an infringement in respect of the agreement on the GINT trade mark

44. The applicants complain that the Commission infringed Articles [36 TFEU], [345 TFEU] [. . .] and furthermore exceeded the limits of its powers by declaring that the agreement on the registration in France of the GINT trade-mark served to ensure absolute territorial protection in favour of Consten and by excluding thereby, in [. . .] the operative part of the contested decision, any possibility of Consten's asserting its rights under national trade-mark law, in order to oppose parallel imports.

45. The applicants maintain more particularly that the criticized effect on competition is due not to the agreement but to the registration of the trade mark in accordance with French law, which gives rise to an original inherent right of the holder of the trade-mark from which the absolute territorial protection derives under national law.

46. Consten's right under the contract to the exclusive user in France of the GINT trade mark, which may be used in a similar manner in other countries, is intended to make it possible to keep under surveillance and to place an obstacle in the way of parallel imports. Thus, the agreement by which Grundig, as the holder of the trade-mark by virtue of an international registration, authorized Consten to register it in France in its own name tends to restrict competition.

47. Although Consten is, by virtue of the registration of the GINT trade-mark, regarded under French law as the original holder of the rights relating to that trade-mark, the fact nevertheless remains that it was by virtue of an agreement with Grundig that it was able to effect the registration.

48. That agreement therefore is one which may be caught by the prohibition in Article [101(1)]. The prohibition would be ineffective if Consten could continue to use the trade-mark to achieve the same object as that pursued by the agreement which has been held to be unlawful.

49. Articles [36 TFEU], [345 TFEU] [. . .] relied upon by the applicants do not exclude any influence whatever of [EU] law on the exercise of national industrial property rights.

50. Article [36 TFEU], which limits the scope of the rules on the liberalization of trade contained [. . .] cannot limit the field of application of Article [101]. Article [345 TFEU] confines itself to stating that the 'Treaty shall in no way prejudice the rules in Member States governing the system of property ownership'. The injunction contained in [. . .] the operative part of the contested decision to refrain from using rights under national trade-mark law in order to set an obstacle in the way of parallel imports does not affect the grant of those rights but only limits their exercise to the extent necessary to give effect to the prohibition under Article [101(1)]. The power of the Commission to issue such an injunction [. . .] is in harmony with the nature of the [EU] rules on competition which have immediate effect and are directly binding on individuals.

51. Such a body of rules by reason of its nature described above and its function does not allow the improper use of rights under any national trade-mark law in order to frustrate the [EU]'s law on cartels. [. . .]

53. The above mentioned submissions are therefore unfounded.

The complaints concerning the application of Article 101(3) TFEU

54. The applicants, supported on several points by the German Government, allege *inter alia* that all the conditions for application of the exemption, the existence of which is denied in the contested decision, are met in the present case. The defendant starts from the premise that it is for the undertakings concerned to prove that the conditions required for exemption are satisfied. [. . .]

59. The undertakings are entitled to an appropriate examination by the Commission of their requests for Article [101(3) TFEU] to be applied. For this purpose the Commission may not confine itself to requiring from the undertakings proof of the fulfilment of the requirements for the grant of the exemption but must, as a matter of good administration, play its part, using the means available to it, in ascertaining the relevant facts and circumstances.

60. Furthermore, the exercise of the Commission's powers necessarily implies complex evaluations on economic matters. A judicial review of these evaluations must take account of their nature by confining itself to an examination of the relevance of the facts and of the legal consequences which the Commission deduces therefrom. This review must in the first place be carried out in respect of the reasons given for the decisions which must set out the facts and considerations on which the said evaluations are based.

61. The contested decision states that the principal reason for the refusal of exemption lies in the fact that the requirement contained in Article [101(3)] is not satisfied.

62. The German Government complains that the said decision does not answer the questions whether certain factors, especially the advance orders and the guarantee and after-sales services, the favourable effects of which were recognised by the Commission, could be maintained intact in the absence of absolute territorial protection.

63. The contested decision admits only by way of assumption that the sole distributorship contract in question contributes to an improvement in production and distribution.

Then the contested decision examines the question 'whether an improvement in the distribution of goods by virtue of the sole distribution agreement could no longer be achieved if parallel imports were admitted'. After examining the arguments concerning advance orders, the observation of the market and the guarantee and after-sales services, the decision concluded that 'no other reason which militates in favour of the necessity for absolute territorial protection has been put forward to hinted at'.

64. The question whether there is an improvement in the production of [*sic*] distribution of the goods in question, which is required for the grant of exemption, is to be answered in accordance with the spirit of Article 81. First, this improvement cannot be identified with all the advantages which the parties to the agreement obtain from it in their production or distribution activities. These advantages are generally indisputable and show the agreement as in all respects indispensable to an improvement as understood in this sense. This subjective method, which makes the content of the concept of 'improvement' depend upon the special features of the contractual relationships in question, is not consistent with the aims of Article [101]. Furthermore, the very fact that the Treaty provides that the restriction of competition must be 'indispensable' to the improvement in question clearly indicates the importance which the latter must have. This improvement must in particular show appreciable objective advantages of such a character as to compensate for the disadvantages which they cause in the field of competition.

65. The argument of the German Government, based on the premise that all those features of the agreement which favour the improvement as conceived by the parties to the agreement must be maintained intact, presupposes that the question whether all these features are not only favourable but also indispensable to the improvement of the production or distribution of the goods in question has already been settled affirmatively. Because of this the argument not only tends to weaken the requirement of indispensability but also among other consequences to confuse solicitude for the specific interests of the parties with the objective improvements contemplated by the Treaty.

66. In its evaluation of the relative importance of the various factors submitted for its consideration, the Commission on the other hand had to judge their effectiveness by reference to an objectively ascertainable improvement in the production and distribution of the goods, and to decide whether the resulting benefit would suffice to support the conclusion that the consequent restrictions upon competition were indispensable. The argument based on the necessity to maintain intact all arrangements of the parties in so far as they are capable of contributing to the improvement sought cannot be reconciled with the view propounded in the last sentence. Therefore, the complaint of the Federal Government, based on faulty premises, is not such as can invalidate the Commission's assessment.

67. The applicants maintain that the admission of parallel imports would mean that the sole representative would no longer be in a position to engage in advance planning.

68. A certain degree of uncertainty is inherent in all forecasts of future sales possibilities.

Such forecasting must in fact be based on a series of variable and uncertain factors. The admission of parallel imports may indeed involve increased risks for the concessionaire who gives firm orders in advance for the quantities of goods which he considers he will be able to sell. However, such a risk is inherent in all commercial activity and thus cannot justify special protection on this point.

69. The applicants complain that the Commission did not consider on the basis of concrete facts whether it is possible to provide guarantee and after-sales services without absolute territorial protection. They emphasize in particular the importance for the reputation of the Grundig name of the proper provision of these services for all the Grundig machines put on the market. The freeing of parallel imports would compel Consten to refuse these services for machines imported by its competitors who did not themselves carry out these services satisfactorily. Such a refusal would also be contrary to the interests of consumers.

70. As regards the free guarantee service, the decision states that a purchaser can normally enforce his right to such a guarantee only against his supplier and subject to conditions agreed with him. The applicant parties do not seriously dispute that statement.

71. The fears concerning the damage which might result for the reputation of Grundig products from an inadequate service do not, in the circumstances, appear justified.

72. In fact, UNEF, the main competitor of Consten, although it began selling Grundig products in France later than Consten and while having had to bear not inconsiderable risks, nevertheless supplies a free guarantee and after-sales services against remuneration upon conditions which, taken as a whole, do not seem to have harmed the reputation of the Grundig name. Moreover, nothing prevents the applicants from informing consumers, through adequate publicity, of the nature of the services and any other advantages which may be offered by the official distribution network for Grundig products. It is thus not correct that the publicity carried out by Consten must benefit parallel importers to the same extent.

73. Consequently, the complaints raised by the applicants are unfounded.

74. The applicants complain that the Commission did not consider whether absolute territorial protection was still indispensable to enable the high costs borne by Consten in launching the Grundig products on the French market to be amortized.

75. The defendant objects that before the adoption of the contested decision it had at no time become aware of any market introduction costs which had not been amortized.

76. This statement by the defendant has not been disputed. The Commission cannot be expected of its own motion to make inquiries on this point. Further, the argument of the applicants amounts in substance to saying that the concessionaire would not have accepted the agreed conditions without absolute territorial protection. However, that fact has no connexion with the improvements in distribution referred to in Article [101(3)].

77. Consequently this complaint cannot be upheld.

78. The applicant Grundig maintains, further, that without absolute territorial protection the sole distributor would not be inclined to bear the costs necessary for market observation since the result of his efforts might benefit parallel importers.

79. The defendant objects that such market observation, which in particular allows the application to the products intended for export to France of technical improvements desired by the French consumer, can be of benefit only to Consten.

80. In fact, Consten, in its capacity as sole concessionaire which is not threatened by the contested decision, would be the only one to receive the machines equipped with the features adapted especially to the French market.

81. Consequently this complaint is unfounded.

NOTES AND QUESTIONS ON CONSTEN & GRUNDIG

1. In *Consten & Grundig*, it may have been not only the effects of the absolute territorial protection on the allocation of markets that had the object of restricting competition and so fell within the prohibition, but, possibly, also the exclusivity provisions whereby Consten agreed not to handle competing equipment and Grundig agreed not to supply anyone in France other than Consten, although these do not figure in the list of anti-competitive practices given in Article [101(1)]. However, as will be explained

elsewhere in this volume, such restrictions have frequently been exempted and do not always infringe Article 101(1). Moreover, the CJEU quashed the Commission's decision in part for failing to give reasons for condemning the exclusivity. The CJEU held in *Consten & Grundig* that there is no need to examine the effects of an agreement if its object is to restrict competition. Consten and Grundig asked the CJEU to quash the Commission's decision for not having made a sufficient analysis of the market for the kinds of equipment affected by the agreement. The CJEU stated that the brand was important, but perceived the issue *ex post* from 1964, when the Commission adopted a decision, and not *ex ante* when the agreement was made and Consten had still to establish the brand in France. In 1957, before the Common Market had removed quotas, Consten incurred significant risks when it undertook to incur costs promoting the product. It might not be able to obtain import licences for many or even any items of equipment. Even if Consten managed to obtain a licence, the expenditure would have to be spread over a limited number of items and would be wasted unless Consten was able to sell enough of the Grundig product. The costs were sunk: the investment had no value save for promoting the Grundig brand. Consequently, Consten would need to expect unusually high profits if it were to be successful. A high margin would attract imports from Germany, where there is no need for an import licence, and average costs and risk would be lower. Traders from Germany could take a free ride on Consten's investment in making the product acceptable. Unless Consten were sufficiently protected from these parallel imports, it might well have found the risk unacceptable. If Grundig could not have found someone to promote its product in the early days, Grundig products might have been less attractive to the parallel importers. The Commission never investigated how much protection was necessary to induce the optimal amount of investment in promotion by Consten. Nor was the question raised whether Grundig, which backed its judgment as to the amount of protection needed with its expectation of profit, was better able to judge than officials in the Commission. On appeal from the Commission, the CJEU said that the Commission had found that the object of this agreement was to restrict competition between Consten and Grundig's other dealers. The Commission had properly taken into account not just the agreement in issue but the whole network of Grundig distribution agreements, which clearly attempted to insulate the national markets from competition from other distributors of the same brand. It confirmed the Commission's condemnation of the agreement.

2. What difficulties would Grundig expect in 1957 in penetrating the French market? Would it have been better, for the parties to the agreement, to argue that in 1957 sunk costs would have been riskier since the investment in the network had to be made before it was clear that Consten would obtain an import licence from the French authorities or whether the French would have been prepared to buy a German product only twelve years after the German occupation during the second world war?
3. How did the arrangement about the 'GINT' mark help to isolate the French market?
4. Do you think the exclusive distribution agreement made the French market less competitive?
5. Should agreements between competitors be treated with greater hostility than vertical agreements between supplier and dealer? Give reasons. The Commission now accepts

that vertical agreements are less likely to restrict competition than horizontal ones. See our analysis in Chapter 10.

6. It is interesting to compare this case with the approach followed at the time of the CJEU's judgment in US antitrust law. In *White Motor*, the US Supreme Court held that obligations not to poach in the territory of another exclusive dealer imposed by one of the smaller makers of large trucks was not necessarily an unreasonable restraint of trade contrary to section 1 of the Sherman Act (the equivalent provision to Article 101 TFEU).[223] The Supreme Court had had too little experience of such obligations to come to a conclusion as a matter of law without more information about the commercial reasons and effects of imposing them. Since then, it has come to treat favourably restraints ancillary to distribution agreements and which may assist competition between brands. In the US, hostility towards vertical restraints was reduced from the mid-1970s as a result of the insight of economists connected to the University of Chicago. They argued that whereas parties to an agreement between competitors want the other parties to sell less at higher prices, the reverse is true of agreements between parties at a different level of trade or production. Each wants the others to produce more at lower prices. Relationships in a vertical chain were thought to be complementary, not competitive. If territorial restraints or quotas are placed on dealers by their suppliers, it is probably to encourage other dealers to invest in supplying services that promote the brand as a whole. Why may this sometimes be necessary? This argument has been limited since. The supplier may be encouraging dealers to provide services wanted only by marginal consumers, and thereby increasing the prices paid by other consumers who do not need the services.
7. In his Opinion, AG Roemer compared the position after the agreement with what would have happened without it, now usually called 'the counterfactual' test. Did the CJEU proceed to such an analysis?
8. Do you think the question should be whether inter-brand is more important than intra-band competition, or whether there would have been any intra-brand competition without the exclusive territory?
9. In his opinion in relation to Article 101(3), AG Roemer criticized several aspects of the Commission's decision: the Commission had taken information two years old, based on notes prepared in a hurry by national cartel authorities, relating to a recorder that was not shown to be representative of Grundig's products; the Commission had looked to retail prices, although Consten sold to wholesalers.
10. Do you think that the object of the parties in 1957 was to restrict competition or to enable Grundig to penetrate the French market? In what conditions may territorial protection increase or decrease competition? Is the amount of territorial protection needed to encourage Consten to make the optimal amount of investment a question of fact into which the Commission should enquire? Would an official be likely to come to a better conclusion in 1964 or Grundig in 1957? Give reasons.
11. Did the Court perceive the issues as of 1957 when the agreement was made, in 1961 when the parallel imports started, 1964 when the Commission adopted its decision or

223 *White Motor Co v United States*, 372 US 253 (1963).

in 1966 when the Court gave judgment? Which do you think is the appropriate date? Should that matter in the Court's judgment?

12. How did the trade mark GINT help to exclude parallel imports? What is the difference between the grant and exercise of a right? Can the distinction be drawn by logical analysis? Note that in later cases, the Court speaks of 'existence' rather than 'grant'.
13. The most important constitutional event of 1966 was the French boycott of the Council of Ministers leading to the break down in important legislation in the EEC (the empty chair crisis). The Treaty mainly provided a framework for future legislation and few actual rules. Can this have influenced the Court's use of the distinction? How might the distinction between the grant of and exercise of a right enable the Court to fill the legislative gap?
14. After the judgment, Grundig bought Consten. Why might it have done so? Would the acquisition provide protection from parallel imports? Should the competition rules encourage firms to integrate forward?
15. Grundig told the case handler that it was happy not to have to protect its dealers. It was glad that the price in France had declined. Of course it was happy. It had benefited from the sunk costs incurred by Consten. Do you think that brand owners may now find it more difficult to persuade exclusive dealers to invest initially?
16. Why do you think the Court and Advocate General came to different conclusions?[224]

2.3.2. TOWARDS A MORE PRAGMATIC APPROACH?

Following *Consten & Grundig*, in relation to the application of Article 101 TFEU, the EU Court's case law has held that an agreement between a producer and a distributor which might tend or aim to restore the national divisions in trade between Member States might be such as to frustrate the objective of the Treaty to achieve the establishment of a single market. At the aftermaths of Grundig, the Commission fined BMW Belgium NV and almost fifty Belgian BMW dealers for having implemented measures to hinder parallel imports.[225] In *BMW Belgium v Commission* the Court has confirmed the condemnation of export bans and the imposition of fines even where there was governmental price control leading to artificially low prices in the country of export.[226] The Commission took active steps to facilitate price comparisons for cars between Member States by publishing between 1993 and 2011 an annual report on the prices of cars within the EU.[227] Subsequent enforcement action from the Commission in the motor vehicle industry focused on practices impeding parallel trade.[228]

224 The best criticism of this case published within a year of the judgment is by R Joliet, *The Rule of Reason in Antitrust Law* (Nijhoff, 1967).

225 *BMW Belgium NV and Belgian BMW Dealers* (Case IV/29.146) Commission Decision [1977] OJ L 46/33.

226 Joined Cases 32 & 36–82/78, *BMW Belgium SA and others v Commission* [1979] ECR 2435.

227 See European Commission, Competition: Car Price Reports, available at ec.europa.eu/competition/sectors/motor_vehicles/prices/report.html.

228 *VW* (Case IV/35.733) Commission Decision [1998] OJ L 124/60; *Opel* (Case COMP/36.653) Commission Decision [2001] OJ L 59/42; *Mercedes-Benz* (Case COMP/36.624) Commission Decision [2002] OJ L 257/1; *Automobiles Peugeot SA* (Case COMP/36.623) Commission Decision [2005] OJ L 173/20, confirmed by Case

In *Zanussi*, the Commission objected to a system of after-sales guarantees that did not apply to washing machines used in a different Member State from that where they had been bought.[229] This view was accepted by the Court in *Hasselblad v Commission*.[230]

On a number of occasions, the Court has held that agreements either aimed at partitioning national markets according to national borders or making the interpenetration of national markets more difficult, in particular those aimed at preventing or restricting parallel exports, and more generally parallel trade, restricted competition within the meaning of that Treaty article.[231] This, even when the products in question incorporated an intellectual property (IP) right. Of course, only parallel imports from the EU are offered competition law protection. This choice is intrinsically related to that of the EU exhaustion regime as the IP holders, for those of these products that are protected by IP rights, such as patents, trademarks, copyright, cannot use their IP rights to oppose the sale of the products in an EU Member Stare after a so-called authorized sale in another EU Member State (see our analysis of the EU exhaustion doctrine in Chapter 13). However, the IP holder can control the individual product incorporating the IP right, and thus oppose import, if there has not been an authorized sale in another EU Member State, even if there was an authorized sale in a third non-EU member country. In other words, there is no international exhaustion of IP rights in the EU. Consequently, an undertaking may establish barriers, through the conclusion of agreements prohibiting exports, with its third non-EU country distributors, safeguarding its domestic (EU) market from re-imports of its own goods released in international markets at lower prices without infringing EU competition law.

In *Javico*,[232] before the accessions of 2004, there were contractual restrictions forbidding a distributor in Eastern Europe to sell trademarked products in the EU Internal Market. The CJEU held that such a ban did not necessarily have the object or effect of restricting competition within the Internal Market.[233] The legal and economic context was important. Such a restraint might have an effect in the Internal Market when the market was oligopolistic or where there was a significant difference in price between products inside and outside the Internal Market. It was for the national court to decide the facts.[234]

In *Micro Leader*,[235] the issue related to Microsoft's attempts to prevent the import into France of French-language software sold in Canada, because it was cheaper in Canada than in France. The Commission dismissed a complaint by Micro Leader Business that Microsoft had reached agreements with French and Canadian distributors introducing a number of measures intended to reinforce the ban on the sale of Canadian products outside Canada, thus creating obstacles to the freedom to set prices within the EU. The General Court confirmed

T-450/05, *Automobiles Peugeot SA and Peugeot Nederland NV v Commission* [2009] ECR II-2533. For a list of competition cases in the car sector concluded by the Commission, see ec.europa.eu/competition/sectors/motor_vehicles/cases/decisions.html.

229 *Zanussi* (Case IV/1.576) Commission Decision [1978] OJ L 322/26.

230 Case 86/82, *Hasselblad (GB) Limited v Commission* [1984] ECR 883, paras 32–5.

231 See eg Case 19/77, *Miller International Schallplaten v Commission* [1978] ECR 131; Joined Cases 100–3/80, *SA Musique Diffusion française and others v Commission* [1983] ECR 1825; Joined Cases 96–102, 104–5, 108 & 110/82, *IAZ International Belgium and Others v Commission* [1983] ECR 3369, paras 23–7; Joined Cases 25 & 26/84, *Ford-Werke AG and Ford of Europe Inc v Commission* [1985] ECR 2725; Case C-277/87, *Sandoz prodotti farmaceutici SpA v Commission* [1989] ECR I-045; Case T-77/92, *Parker Pen Ltd v Commission* [1994] ECR II-549; Case C-306/96, *Javico* [1998] ECR I-1983, paras 13–14; Case T-13/03, *Nintendo Co, Ltd and Nintendo of Europe GmbH v Commission* [2009] ECR II-975 [hereinafter *Nintendo*]; Case C-551/03 P, *General Motors v Commission* [2006] ECR I-3173, paras 67–9.

232 Case C-306/96, *Javico* [1998] ECR I-1983. 233 Ibid, paras 20–1. 234 Ibid, para 22.

235 Case T-198/98, *Micro Leader Business v Commission* [1999] ECR II-3989.

that the sale into Canada did not exhaust the copyright, as this is exhausted only when the products have been put on the market in the EU by the owner of that right or with his consent, and that there was no evidence that the holder had discouraged its Canadian distributor from exporting to France. It added, at paragraph 34, that even if the holder had discouraged such trade into the Internal Market, any agreement or concerted practice would have done no more than enforce the holder's copyright which was not exhausted, the conduct being therefore a lawful enforcement by Microsoft of its copyright. The complaint also alleged that the higher price in France amounted to the abuse of a dominant position. The Commission dismissed this complaint on the grounds that the complainant had neither brought sufficient evidence nor proposed a remedy. The GC observed that the higher price seemed to show discrimination contrary to Article 102(c). The holder had issued bulletins to its dealers in France that suggested that the imported products were in direct competition with those sold in France. The GC noted that whilst, as a rule, the enforcement of copyright by its holder, as in the case of the prohibition on importing certain products from outside the EU in to a Member State of the EU, is not in itself a breach of Article 102 of the Treaty, such enforcement may, in exceptional circumstances, involve abusive conduct and that, consequently, the Commission was wrong to dismiss the complaint under Article 102 without further investigation.

Conditions outside the Internal Market may be very different from those within. A firm that has spent large sums on R&D may want to sell the results at lower prices in some countries and this makes sense as long as it covers its incremental costs. The pharmaceutical companies were persuaded to make cures or palliatives for AIDS available in Africa at prices which, if applied to total sales, would not enable them to recover much of their investment in R&D.

One may also note that in some cases relating to IP rights, the *Consten & Grundig* rule regarding the prohibitions of restrictions to parallel trade was not always followed so that such restrictions were not found to be a restriction of competition by object.

For instance, in *Coditel I*, the CJEU had held that the IP holder was entitled to rely on its copyright to restrain Coditel from relaying the film transmitted with consent in another Member State,[236] and that consequently, broadcast diffusion rights were not exhausted by a performance in another Member State, in view of the fact that a copyright holder and its assigns have a legitimate interest in calculating royalties on the basis of the number of performances by the licensee and that exploitation of copyright involves various methods, including television, thus demonstrating the symmetry between the interpretation of the exhaustion doctrine by the CJEU and its subsequent enforcement of Article 101(1) TFEU against an absolute territorial protection.[237] In *Coditel II*, the CJEU ruled that exclusive licences of performing rights, even if these led to absolute territorial protection, would not infringe Article 101(1) in light of the commercial practice in the particular industry and the need for a film producer to obtain an adequate return.[238] In *Erauw-Jacquery*, with regard to licensing agreements related to IP rights, the CJEU held that the holder of the plant breeder's rights

> [. . .] must be allowed to protect himself against improper handling of those varieties of seeds. To that end the breeder must have the right to reserve propagation for the propagating

[236] Case 62/79, *SA Compagnie générale pour la diffusion de la télévision, Coditel, and Others v Ciné Vog Films and Others* [1980] ECR 881, para 18 [hereinafter *Coditel I*].

[237] Ibid.

[238] Case 262/81, *Coditel SA, Compagnie générale pour la diffusion de la télévision, and Others v Ciné-Vog Films SA and Others* [1982] ECR 3381 [hereinafter *Coditel II*].

establishments chosen by him as licensees. To that extent, the clause prohibiting the licensee from selling and exporting basic seeds does not come within the prohibition laid down by Article [101(1) TFEU.[239]

The ability to trade across national frontiers has strengthened competition within the EU and increased efficiency immensely, but when Member States have different laws, for instance those relating to patents or maximum prices, it may not be possible to sell at all in some Member States and still less to sell at the same price and subject to the same conditions throughout the Internal Market. Many of these different measures have been harmonized under the 1992 programme for market integration, but some differences in law remain, especially for pharmaceutical products, the maximum price of which is fixed, directly or indirectly, at a different level in each Member State. Export bans and geographic price discrimination have been prohibited without any analysis of the reasons for imposing them.

The British firm Distillers[240] charged some £5 a case of twelve bottles more for whisky that was to be exported from the UK at a time when, contrary to Community law, France was discriminating against the kinds of alcohol that were not produced in France. It prohibited the advertising of whisky but not of alcohol distilled from fruit that was produced in France. Moreover, like several other Member States, it taxed whisky more heavily than the locally produced liquor.

Distillers claimed that differential prices were necessary because on the Continent, owing to high and discriminatory taxes, demand had to be increased through the promotional efforts of its exclusive dealers. These would not be able to afford to keep three months' stock and perform other promotional activities if at popular times, such as Christmas, local supermarkets, which did not bear these expenses, were able to import large quantities from the UK and undercut them. Yet, in the United Kingdom, because demand was very sensitive to price differences, Distillers would lose sales to other brands if it were to charge the extra £5.

The Commission did not address this argument but adopted a decision condemning the extra charge for exports. Consequently, Distillers divided its brands, ceasing to supply 'red label' in the United Kingdom and raising the prices of two other brands. These brands continued to be promoted on the Continent but virtually ceased to be bought in the UK, whereas distributors on the Continent ceased to invest in promoting the other brands, which would be bought cheaply by parallel importers from the United Kingdom.

It seems that Distillers' sales of the three brands, which could not be bought cheaply in the UK, increased on the Continent more than did those of its other brands, presumably because they continued to be worth promoting on the Continent.

Demand in the United Kingdom was very responsive to price: that on the Continent to promotion. There was no way in which the same brands could be sold at the same prices in the two markets. This was recognized by Advocate General Warner when the case was appealed, but for procedural reasons the CJEU did not address the issue.

In this case, the Commission's simple view that an extra charge for the whisky exported to other Member States divided the Common Market must have delayed its integration. When the illegal discrimination on the Continent against whisky ended, Distillers had different brands known in the two areas. The Commission objected to the symptom of differential prices before the cause, the illegal discrimination in taxes, was removed.

239 Case 27/87, *Erauw-Jacquéry (Louis) v La Hesbignonne* [1988] ECR 1919.
240 Case 30/78, *Distillers Co Ltd v Commission* [1980] ECR 2229.

Moreover, it is more difficult to introduce a foreign product than to continue to sell that to which the local population is accustomed. The Commission failed to analyse the transaction *ex ante*, from the time when Distillers was trying to persuade its distributors to spend money promoting its brands, but looked only *ex post*, to competition at the time the decision was adopted from the firms that wanted to take a free ride on that promotion and undercut the distributors without having to make the same investments. It did not consider whether, without the investment induced by the territorial protection, parallel importers would have wanted to stock Distillers' products.

On appeal, AG Warner strongly rejected the Commission's view. He accepted that the markets in the UK and on the Continent were very different, and that promotion was needed on the Continent if whisky was to be sold there. He added that Distillers could not afford to raise its prices in the UK to cover the overseas promotional costs in view of the evidence given of the extreme elasticity of price there. The dual pricing system had not eliminated parallel exports as had the *Grundig* agreements. Three hundred and forty thousand cases had been sold at the higher price for export to the Continent. He would, therefore, have recommended that the decision not to exempt should be quashed had Distillers notified its agreement.

The Court did not deal with the points of substance, but merely confirmed that an exemption could not be granted as the agreement had not been properly notified. It had not been pleaded that the agreement did not infringe Article 101(1) and this would probably not have been accepted by the judges in those days. AG Warner's opinion on the substance was cogent. Distillers reacted to the decision by raising the price of some brands in the UK, and those almost ceased to sell there. It also ceased to sell Johnny Walker Red Label Whisky in the UK. The other brands ceased to be promoted on the Continent. The result was that the Distillers' brands sold in the UK differed from those sold on the Continent. This splitting of the brands and the Commission's decision that led to it must have retarded the integration of the Internal Market once the discriminatory taxes and other disadvantages imposed on the sale of whisky on the Continent were abrogated.

2.3.3. THE PARALLEL IMPORTS OF PHARMACEUTICALS SAGA

Restrictions of parallel imports of pharmaceutical products, either through contractual obligations or through unilateral action of brand pharmaceutical products manufacturers, are an area where EU competition law has been actively and frequently implemented. Parallel trade in pharmaceutical products is prevalent in Europe, essentially as a result of the price differential between Member States because of differences in price regulation. Consequently, parallel traders operate as arbitrageurs, taking advantage of these price differences.

G Tsouloufas, 'Limiting Pharmaceutical Parallel Trade in the European Union: Regulatory and Economic Justifications' (2011) *European L Rev* 385, 387–9

Pharmaceutical price regulation within the European Union

Parallel trade of pharmaceuticals within the European Union is primarily explained by the variations in prices of these products between the Member States of the Union. Member States apply regulatory policies culminating in the adoption of diverging pricing schemes.

An initial observation that can be made is that Member States can be divided into two distinct groups: high-price countries and low-price countries. In the *Glaxo Wellcome* decision the

Commission made this distinction, accepting that Germany, the United Kingdom, Denmark, Sweden, Finland, Ireland, and Austria belong to the first group while the second one comprises Belgium, Portugal, Italy, France, Greece, and Spain. The divergence in medicine prices between these two groups can be explained by the fact that, through pharmaceutical regulation, Member States aim at achieving non-identical goals. Specifically, it can be argued that the incentive of national governments that introduce high medicine prices is to foster pharmaceutical innovation and to secure the pharmaceutical companies' recoupment of R & D expenditure. In contrast, the ambition of Member States that apply low-pricing regulatory policies is presumably to attain allocative efficiency goals. [. . .]

[P]rice control of pharmaceutical products within the European Union is decentralised. There are only few examples of the Union's activity which pertain to pharmaceutical regulation [. . .]. Substantive regulation, thus, falls within the authority and scope of Member States.

Regulation of the pharmaceutical sector can be achieved through direct price controls, which result in the setting of reasonable price ceilings. However, there exists no unequivocal definition of what is a reasonable maximum price, as it depends on several factors, namely prescribing behaviour, budget limits, patterns of utilisation, as well as whether the pharmaceutical industry is salient for the national economy

Member States do not exercise their direct regulatory power concerning the adoption of a pricing scheme in a uniform manner. Several Member States employ the method of external reference pricing, by virtue of which prices in other EU countries are taken into account in domestic price setting of medicines, without, however, using the same criteria of international comparison. In Bulgaria, for example, the prices for a given medicine in eight countries (Greece, Slovakia, Estonia, Romania, France, Lithuania, Portugal and Spain) are used as reference and the lowest one is adopted. [. . .] In Greece, under the current regulatory regime, reference is made to the three lowest prices across the EU Member States, and the average is adopted. Furthermore, the system in Spain takes into account the prices of medicines in the Member States of the European Union, alongside with an assessment of other qualitative factors: the severity, duration and consequences of the disease for which it is prescribed; the specific needs of certain groups; the therapeutic and social utility of the medicine; a rationalisation of public expenditure on pharmaceutical benefits; the presence of drugs or other alternatives for the same conditions; and the degree of innovation associated with the medicine.

In other EU Member States where reference schemes are not adopted agencies exercise their control by using specific formulas to set medicine prices. In Latvia, for example, the maximum allowed wholesaler's price for non-reimbursable pharmaceuticals is calculated by multiplying manufacturer's price by the correction index and adding correction sum and value added tax in the domestic currency.

Notwithstanding the preponderance of direct price fixing, other means of regulating the price of pharmaceutical products do exist. Medicine prices can also be fixed following a negotiation process between pharmaceutical companies and public agencies. In Italy, for instance, the prices of all reimbursable medicines are the result of negotiations between the manufacturers and the Pricing and Reimbursement Committee. Further, the method of negotiation is central in the system adopted in the United Kingdom. The result of negotiations between the Association of the British Pharmaceutical Industry and the Department of Health is the Pharmaceutical Price Regulation Scheme, which was first adopted in 1957 and is periodically reviewed. Importantly, the 2009 Pharmaceutical Price Regulation Scheme introduced medicine price cuts, but it also provided for flexible, value-based pricing for initially launched medicines.

Free-pricing systems are introduced by national legislation in some EU Member States. [. . .]

Regulation of medicine prices can by itself undermine innovation. As already analysed, the method of international comparison is not unusual between EU Member States. However, it has negative effects on pharmaceutical R & D, as it enables the diffusion of low prices that exist in one country to another.

The corollary of this process is that pricing based on marginal cost can lead to low average prices that cannot sufficiently cover the joint costs of innovation. It can generally be argued that the method of reference pricing has an impact on R & D, as it tends to drive prices at low levels.

These dynamic inefficiencies are directly attributed to national regulation. However, national regulation has an indirect yet significant impact on pharmaceutical R & D investments. Specifically, it exacerbates innovation in this sector by providing fertile ground for parallel trade.

As investment in R&D is central in pharmaceutical industry,[241] it is feared that parallel trade will lead to a considerable reduction in manufacturer's revenues, and this will inevitably affect R&D, first by rendering funding insufficient, reducing prospective innovation and interfering with government's ability to promote/support the R&D efforts of the domestic pharma industry by fixing higher prices for pharmaceutical products.[242] It is also often alleged that the primary beneficiaries of parallel trade are, in particular, arbitrageurs/parallel traders, since the parallel trade market is not competitive and, consequently, prices in destination countries are not driven down by parallel trade in the long run.[243] Some economists remarked that the approach should be consistent with that followed with regard to price discrimination, which may be positive for the consumers.

P Rey and T Vergé, 'Vertical Restraints in European Competition Policy' (2014) 4 Concurrences 44, 50 (references omitted)

Analyzing the effects of practices that are implemented to enforce territorial restrictions (such as export bans), it is thus important to evaluate the welfare-effect of price discrimination. However, the legal framework for price discrimination (at least between national markets) in the EU is at odds with such economic evaluation.

The economic literature on price discrimination is now well-established and suggests that price discrimination has ambiguous effects on welfare. [. . .]

Looking at competition between firms does not provide stronger arguments against price discrimination.

Suppose, for instance, that two 'spatially' differentiated firms compete against each other and that firms are able to determine (and thus possibly take advantage of) the consumers' locations.

When firms can price-discriminate (i.e., set different prices for different locations), consumers located close to one of the firms constitute that firm's strong market and the competitor's weak market, as consumers will be willing to pay more for the local firm's product in order to avoid

241 A recent report published by the Tufts Centre for the Study of Drug Development in 2016 indicates that the cost of developing a prescription drug that gains market approval amounts to $2.6 billion, more than doubling the last decade: see JA DiMasi, H Grabowski, and RW Hansen, 'Innovation in the Pharmaceutical Industry: New Estimates of R & D Costs' [2016] 47 *J Health Economics* 20.

242 G Tsouloufas, 'Limiting Pharmaceutical Parallel Trade in the European Union: Regulatory and Economic Justification' (2011) *European L Rev* 385, 389.

243 See P Kanavos et al, 'The Economic Impact of Pharmaceutical Parallel Trade in European Union Member States: A Stakeholder Analysis, Special Research Paper', LSE Health and Social Care Discussion Paper (January 2004), available at www.lse.ac.uk/LSEHealthAndSocialCare/pdf/Workingpapers/Paper.pdf.

travelling too far to get a product at a lower price. Firms, thus, essentially compete fiercely for those consumers that are not in either firm's local market. Those consumers who are more or less indifferent are *a priori* between the two firms, and thus will get the best deals, whereas more captive consumers will pay higher prices. However, the price in a firm's strong market is still constrained by the ability of the competitor to set a specific low price for that market (for instance, selling at cost). In its local market, a firm can thus only charge a price that is close to its cost plus the transport cost that a consumer can avoid by buying locally. When price discrimination is forbidden, firms compete by setting a uniform price. This means that each firm's market power is now much higher in its local market. Indeed, a firm can no longer set low prices in its weak market and keep high prices in its strong market. Therefore, the competitive pressure will be reduced in the firms' strong markets, which is likely to lead to uniform prices that are higher than all prices set under price discrimination. In this setting, *all* consumers benefit from price discrimination.

This is not to say that price discrimination is necessarily good for consumers under competition, as it can also be shown that price discrimination will be harmful for consumers, but also for total welfare in some situations, but simply that there are no good economic argument to justify an outright ban on price discrimination. Given that banning of the practices that are used to prevent arbitrage is equivalent to banning price discrimination, the same can be said about the fight against absolute territorial restrictions. More specifically, even though the incentives (and the ability) to price discriminate will exist for a firm with little market power (i.e., small market share), the effect that price discrimination by such a firm will have on consumer surplus (or total welfare)—and remember that it may well be positive—is small. It is therefore even harder to justify an outright ban on absolute territorial restrictions for such a firm.

Some economic studies have nevertheless noted that parallel trade may lead to important direct public savings in the pharmaceutical sector, in view of the fact that, following the entry into the market of parallel imports, brand manufacturers and their official distributors reduce the prices of the pharmaceutical products. According to empirical research, these price cutbacks were significant and ranged between 12 and 19 per cent.[244] There is even evidence that this effect increases with multiple parallel importations of brand-named pharmaceuticals. The effect is thus quite similar to the one observed once after the introduction of generics competition, once the patent covering the specific drug expired, although in the case of generics this is more inter-brand competition, while parallel imports lead to more intra-brand competition. In any case, there is inter-dependence between the consumption patterns of generics and parallel imports of branded pharmaceuticals as patients switch from the original products to the parallel imports but also some patients who would consume generics in the absence of parallel imports may switch to parallel imports (which are usually more expensive than generics) when they come to the market.[245] Another empirical study exploring the welfare effects of parallel trade found that parallel imports of anti-diabetic drugs sold in Germany between 2004 and 2010 reduced the prices for patented drugs by 11 per cent.[246] The study found that the variable profits for the manufacturers of original drugs from the German market suffered

244 M Ganslandt and K Maskus, 'Parallel Imports and the Pricing of Pharmaceutical Products: Evidence from the European Union' [2005] 23 *J Health Economics* 1035.

245 T Duso, A Herr, and M Suppliet, 'The Welfare Impact of Parallel Imports: A Structural Approach Applied to the German Market for Oral Anti-diabetics', Deutsches Institut für Wirtschaftsforschung, Discussion Paper No 1373 (2014), 18.

246 Ibid.

a reduction of 37 per cent per year when parallel trade was allowed; however, they also noted that only one-third of this difference was appropriated by the parallel importers. The same study noted that parallel imports might well have positive effects on the innovation intensity due to the different incentives firms and regulators face when IP rights are internationally, rather than nationally, exhausted,[247] and concluded that the assessment of the welfare effects of parallel trade is essentially an empirical issue. The welfare effects of parallel trade are therefore ambiguous and depend on various factors, such as the differences in the national price regulations, the patients' preferences, the vertical integration of the trade firms,[248] as well as the extent of the participation of the specific traders in global value chains. One may also take with a grain of salt the argument made by pharma companies that the reduction of their profits, immediately and to a similar extent, affects their incentives to fund R&D for new drugs. Indeed, recent studies show that pharma companies do not invest the majority of their profits in R&D, but prefer instead to buy their own shares so as to provide higher revenues to their management and shareholders.[249] Other studies have shown that a lot of R&D in this sector is publicly funded, State resources funding the riskier parts of the pharma R&D effort, and that the rate of innovation has fallen with few new drugs being brought into the market, as a result of reduction of the part of profits spent on R&D and the prevalence of the share-buybacks practice.[250]

2.3.3.1. Article 101 TFEU cases

Pharmaceutical companies made important efforts to halve or substantially reduce parallel trade, by experimenting with various strategies.

For instance, Bayer had refused to supply dealers in the countries where its drug Adalat was cheap with as much as they wanted. Although the dealers did everything they could to obtain additional Adalat and export it, the Commission found a concerted practice in view of the long-term relationship with each distributor and to Bayer's system for identifying wholesalers which exported and progressively reducing the volume supplied to them.[251] On appeal, the General Court,[252] confirmed by the CJEU,[253] annulled the decision of the Commission, taking into account the unilateral nature of Bayer's rationing, which did not constitute, according to them, an agreement and/or concerted practice under Article 101 TFEU. Bayer's success may be difficult to copy. It is not easy to ensure that no salesman discourages customers from engaging in parallel trade. Moreover, the wholesalers had not implemented any discouragement by Bayer: they had circumvented the quotas in every way they could.

GlaxoSmithKline tried a variety of strategies, including the following dual pricing approach.

247 Ibid, at 19 (noting that while original drugs manufacturers lose some profits in markets with parallel trade due to increased competition, they most likely increase their profits in other markets by selling their drugs to parallel importers and, more generally, gain profits by the expansion of overall demand resulting from the decreased overall price level of brand pharmaceuticals). See also AR Bennato and T Valletti, 'Pharmaceutical Innovation and Parallel Trade' (2014) 33 *Int'l J Industrial Organization* 83; G Grossman and E Lai, 'Parallel Imports and Price Controls' (2008) 39(2) *RAND J Economics* 378.

248 T Duso, A Herr, and M Suppliet, 'The Welfare Impact of Parallel Imports: A Structural Approach Applied to the German Market for Oral Anti-diabetics', Deutsches Institut für Wirtschaftsforschung, Discussion Paper No. 1373 (2014), 2 and the economic studies cited there.

249 W Lazonick, 'Profits Without Prosperity' (2014) 92(9) *Harvard Business Rev* 46.

250 M Mazzucato, *The Entrepreneurial State: Debunking Public vs. Private Sector Myths* (Anthem Press, 2013).

251 *Adalat* (Case IV/34.279/F3) Commission Decision [1996] OJ L 201/1.

252 Case T-41/96, *Bayer AG v Commission* [2000] ECR II–3383.

253 Joined Cases C-2 & 3/01 P, *Bundesverband der Arzneimittel-Importeure eV and Commission v Bayer AG* [2004] ECR I–23.

Case T-168/01, *GlaxoSmithKline Services Unlimited v Commission*
[2006] ECR II–2969 (some references omitted)

Glaxo Welcome, a subsidiary of GlaxoSmithKline (GSK) supplied medicines to wholesalers in Spain. Maximum prices for medicines were controlled by national legislation in virtually all Member States, and prices in Spain were amongst the lowest. Consequently, wholesalers in Spain ordered as much of eight specific medicines as possible in order to export them to other countries, especially the UK, Denmark, and the Netherlands, where much higher prices could be charged. Not only did this prevent GSK being able to charge higher prices where this was legal, reducing the profits available to fund R&D and to induce such investment, it also made it difficult to ensure that sufficient quantities were available in Spain as they were immediately bought for export. Distribution of medicines was also controlled in most Member States, making it illegal to stop supplying a particular medicine once supply had started.

GSK, therefore, wanted to limit parallel trade. First, it limited the amount of the medicine it would supply to each wholesaler to a level only a little above that supplied previously, hoping that this was more than enough to satisfy local needs.[254] *Then it introduced a clause into its General Sales Conditions to wholesalers, providing that the price for eighty-two medicines, of which eight were supplied to be reimbursed by the national health service and were prime candidates for parallel trade, would be charged at the maximum price permitted by Spanish law, but those for use elsewhere would be supplied at prices based on real, objective and non-discriminatory economic criteria. It notified this agreement to the Commission with a request for clearance or exemption under Regulation 17/62 (now replaced by Regulation 1/2003). The notification protected it from fines for infringing Article 101 or 102 TFEU.*

The Commission condemned the agreement, which operated like an export ban, as having the object and effect of restricting competition contrary to Article 101 TFEU and as not meriting exemption. It was not alleged that GSK was dominant over any of the medicines.

The General Court examined if the clause inserted in the General Sales Conditions was by its object (nature) restrictive of competition, simply from the fact that it aimed to limit the parallel trade between Spain and other Member States, in particular the United Kingdom in the eighty-two medicines sold by GSK.[255] *Put succinctly the main difference relates to the need, or not, to perform a thorough analysis of the (economic) effects of the agreement, this not being deemed necessary for restrictions of competition by object. The CJEU held the following.*

Characterization as a restriction of competition by object

115. It follows from the case-law that agreements which ultimately seek to prohibit parallel trade must in principle be regarded as having as their object the prevention of competition [. . .]

116. It also follows from the case-law that agreements that clearly intend to treat parallel trade unfavourably must in principle be regarded as having as their object the restriction of competition [. . .]

117. However, GSK is correct to maintain that, having regard to the legal and economic context, the Commission could not rely on the mere fact that Clause 4 of the

254 This practice led to complaints by Greek wholesalers against GSK that came to the CJEU through a preliminary ruling proceeding in Joined Cases C-468–78/06, *Sot Lelos kai Sia EE and Others v GlaxoSmithKline AEVE* [2008] ECR I–7139 (see Section 2.3.3.2).

255 On the distinction between restrictions of competition by object and restrictions of competition by effect, see our analysis Chapter 5.

General Sales Conditions established a system of differentiated price intended to limit parallel trade as the basis for its conclusion that that provision had as its object the restriction of competition.

118. In effect, the objective assigned to Article [101(1) TFEU], which constitutes a fundamental provision indispensable for the achievement of the missions entrusted to the Community, in particular for the functioning of the internal market [. . .], is to prevent undertakings, by restricting competition between themselves or with third parties, from reducing the welfare of the final consumer of the products in question [. . .]. At the hearing, in fact, the Commission emphasised on a number of occasions that it was from that perspective that it had carried out its examination in the present case, initially concluding that the General Sales Conditions clearly restricted the welfare of consumers, then considering whether that restriction would be offset by increased efficiency which would itself benefit consumers.

119. Consequently, the application of Article [101(1) TFEU] to the present case cannot depend solely on the fact that the agreement in question is intended to limit parallel trade in medicines or to partition the common market, which leads to the conclusion that it affects trade between Member States, but also requires an analysis designed to determine whether it has as its object or effect the prevention, restriction or distortion of competition on the relevant market, to the detriment of the final consumer. As may be seen from the case-law, that analysis, which may be abridged when the clauses of the agreement reveal in themselves the existence of an alteration of competition, as the Commission observed at the hearing, must, on the other hand, be supplemented, depending on the requirements of the case, where that is not so.

120. In particular, in *Consten & Grundig v Commission* [. . .] which gave rise to the case-law [. . .], the Court of Justice, contrary to the Commission's contention in its written submissions, did not hold that an agreement intended to limit parallel trade must be considered by its nature, that is to say, independently of any competitive analysis, to have as its object the restriction of competition. On the contrary, the Court of Justice merely held, first, that an agreement between a producer and a distributor which might tend to restore the national divisions in trade between Member States might be of such a kind as to frustrate the most fundamental objectives of the Community, a consideration which led it to reject a plea alleging that Article [101(1) TFEU] was not applicable to vertical agreements. The Court of Justice then carried out a competitive analysis, abridged but real, during the course of which it held, in particular, that the agreement in question sought to eliminate any possibility of competition at the wholesale level in order to charge prices which were sheltered from all effective competition, considerations which led it to reject a plea alleging that there was no restriction of competition.

121. While it has been accepted since then that parallel trade must be given a certain protection, it is therefore not as such but, as the Court of Justice held, in so far as it favours the development of trade, on the one hand, and the strengthening of competition, on the other hand, that is to say, in this second respect, in so far as it gives final consumers the advantages of effective competition in terms of supply or price Consequently, while it is accepted that an agreement intended to limit parallel trade must in principle be considered to have as its object the restriction of competition, that applies in so far as the agreement may be presumed to deprive final consumers of those advantages.

122. However, if account is taken of the legal and economic context in which GSK's General Sales Conditions are applied, it cannot be presumed that those conditions deprive the final consumers of medicines of such advantages. In effect, the wholesalers, whose function, as the Court of Justice has held, is to ensure that the retail trade

receives supplies with the benefit of competition between producers (*Metro I* [. . .], paragraph 40), are economic agents operating at an intermediate stage of the value chain and may keep the advantage in terms of price which parallel trade may entail, in which case that advantage will not be passed on to the final consumers.

(Paragraphs 124–32). The General Court explored the main characteristics of the legal and economic context. First, the price of medicines reimbursed by the national health insurance schemes was not determined as a result of a competitive process throughout the EU but was directly fixed following an administrative procedure in most Member States and indirectly controlled by the other Member States. Second, at this stage the EU harmonization of the applicable national provisions was limited, as national law could provide that various criteria to be taken into account, depending on the policy pursued by the Member State concerned as regards public health and the financing of the national sickness insurance scheme. Spanish law provided for the direct fixing of a maximum wholesale price and the indirect fixing of a maximum retail price, while the United Kingdom law did not provide for the fixing of prices but for control of pharmaceutical companies' profits. Third, the differences between the applicable national provisions were a structural cause of the existence of significant price differentials between Member States. Fourth, fluctuations in exchange rates were a cyclical cause of those price differentials. Fifth, those price differentials were themselves the cause of parallel trade in medicines in the EU, the main Member States of destination of that parallel trade being Denmark, the Netherlands, and the United Kingdom. Sixth, certain Member States had adopted provisions which had the effect to encourage parallel trade. Seventh, the patient generally bore only a limited part, although this varied from Member State to Member State, of the price of the medicines reimbursed by the national sickness insurance scheme which he consumed, the essential part being covered by the national sickness insurance schemes.

133. At no point, however, does the Commission examine the specific and essential characteristic of the sector, which relates to the fact that the prices of the products in question, which are subject to control by the Member States, which fix them directly or indirectly at what they deem to be the appropriate level, are determined at structurally different levels in the Community and, unlike the prices of other consumer goods to which the Commission referred in its written submissions and at the hearing, such as sports items or motor cycles, are in any event to a significant extent shielded from the free play of supply and demand.

134. That circumstance means that it cannot be presumed that parallel trade has an impact on the prices charged to the final consumers of medicines reimbursed by the national sickness insurance scheme and thus confers on them an appreciable advantage analogous to that which it would confer if those prices were determined by the play of supply and demand.

135. Incidentally, the Commission itself agrees with what is at first sight the ambiguous impact of parallel trade in medicines on the welfare of final consumers, since it states in Communication COM(1998) 588 final of 25 November 1999 on the single market in pharmaceuticals [. . .] that unless parallel trade can operate dynamically on prices, it creates inefficiencies because most, although not all, of the financial benefit accrues to the parallel trader rather than to the health care system or the patient [. . .]

136. Accordingly, it cannot be considered that examination of Clause 4 of the General Sales Conditions, which according to GSK is designed to ensure that the wholesale price set by the Kingdom of Spain is actually charged only for the medicines to which it was intended by law to apply, reveals in itself that competition is prevented, restricted or distorted.

The GC concluded that the Commission was not entitled to draw parallels with the agreements which it has had occasion to examine in its previous practice in taking decisions and take the view that Clause 4 of the General Sales Conditions resembles those agreements or can be treated in the same way as them. According to the GC, '[s]uch an approach ultimately ignores the elements of legal and economic context described above, which are not present in the decisions adopted pursuant to Article 101(1) TFEU to which the Commission referred'.[256]

147. Consequently, the principal conclusion reached by the Commission, namely that Clause 4 of the General Sales Conditions must be considered to be prohibited by Article [101(1) TFEU] in so far it has as its object the restriction of parallel trade, cannot be upheld. As the prices of the medicines concerned are to a large extent shielded from the free play of supply and demand owing to the applicable regulations and are set or controlled by the public authorities, it cannot be taken for granted at the outset that parallel trade tends to reduce those prices and thus to increase the welfare of final consumers. An analysis of the terms of Clause 4 of the General Sales Conditions, carried out in that context, therefore does not permit the presumption that that provision, which seeks to limit parallel trade, thus tends to diminish the welfare of final consumers. In this largely unprecedented situation, it cannot be inferred merely from a reading of the terms of that agreement, in its context, that the agreement is restrictive of competition, and it is therefore necessary to consider the effects of the agreement, if only to ascertain what the regulatory authority was able to apprehend on the basis of such a reading.

The GC then examined if the practices in question had an anti-competitive effect. With regard to the relevant market, the GC examined demand side substitutability[257] *and concluded:*

Characterization as a restriction of competition by effect

159. It does not appear to be manifestly incorrect to consider that the buyer, that is to say, the Spanish wholesaler who might engage in parallel trade, is less interested, for that purpose, in the therapeutic indication and the pharmacological products of each of the medicines which he buys from GW than in the fact that all of those medicines are reimbursed by the Spanish sickness insurance scheme and that their price is therefore set by the Spanish authorities. Likewise, it does not appear to be manifestly incorrect to consider that the buyer is less interested in the price of each of the medicines as such than in the fact that there is a sufficient price differential to render parallel trade lucrative, for all of those medicines, between Spain and the Member State of destination. In those circumstances, it is not manifestly incorrect to accept that all the medicines reimbursed by the Spanish sickness insurance scheme which are capable of being sold at a profit owing to the price differential between Spain and the Member State of destination constitute a product market.

Counterfactual

The GC went on to confirm[258] *that the counterfactual was the situation without the agreement and that the burden of establishing an anti-competitive effect to the detriment of consumers was on the Commission: consumer harm was not mentioned in* Consten & Grundig.

[256] Case T-168/01, *GlaxoSmithKline Services Unlimited v Commission* [2006] ECR II–2969, para 138.
[257] Ibid, para 159. [258] Ibid, para 162.

168. [. . .] [T]fact that in the absence of Clause 4 of the General Sales Conditions the Spanish wholesalers would be able to buy medicines at the wholesale price set by the Spanish authorities, independently of the Member State in which those medicines are intended to be resold and of the national sickness insurance scheme by which they are intended to be reimbursed, and then to resell them in any Member State in which the price is sufficiently higher than the Spanish price to allow them to make a profit, taking into account the transaction costs, does not, independently of any examination of the extent to which parallel trade contributes to price competition, regard being had to the role played by the Member States in that regard, permit the conclusion that there is an effect restrictive of competition.

169. In consequence, GSK is correct to maintain that, after referring to the effect which Clause 4 of the General Sales Conditions has on parallel trade, the Commission was still required to demonstrate the effect on competition.

170. [. . .] [I]t is not disputed that [. . .] Clause 4 of the General Sales Conditions has the effect of restricting the freedom of action of the Spanish wholesalers, in particular their freedom to choose their customers.

171. However, not every agreement which restricts the freedom of action of the participating undertakings, or of one of them, necessarily falls within the prohibition in Article 101(1) TFEU (Case C-309/99 *Wouters and Others* [2002] ECR I–1577, paragraph 97, and Case T-112/99 *M6 and Others v Commission* [2001] ECR II–2459, paragraph 76). In particular, any contract concluded between economic agents operating at different stages of the production and distribution chain has the consequence of binding them and, consequently, of restricting them, according to the stipulated terms, in their freedom of action. In the present case, whatever the price at which the Spanish wholesalers agree to buy a medicine from GW on the Spanish market (the Clause 4A price or the Clause 4B price), they are limited in their freedom of action since, from an economic point of view, they are not capable in the long term of reselling them at a lower price on the other national markets of the [EU]. However, as the objective of the [EU] competition rules is to prevent undertakings, by restricting competition between themselves or with third parties, from reducing the welfare of the final consumer of the products in question (paragraph 118 above), it is still necessary to demonstrate that the limitation in question restricts competition, to the detriment of the final consumer. Incidentally, the Commission itself explained, at the hearing, that the limitation of the freedom of action of the Spanish wholesalers was difficult to envisage in isolation and constituted only the starting-point of its examination.

172. Consequently, GSK is correct to maintain that, after relying on the effect of Clause 4 of the General Sales Conditions on the freedom of action of the Spanish wholesalers, the Commission was still required to demonstrate how that provision had the effect of restricting competition to the detriment of the final consumer.

Price differentiation may not amount to illegal discrimination. The GC observed that GSK imposed different prices on the wholesalers depending on where the goods were resold.

176. In the present case, it is not open to doubt that the Spanish wholesalers are GSK's trading partners and that GSK imposes unequal conditions on them according to whether they resell those medicines in Spain or in other Member States of the Community. On the other hand, it is not demonstrated that those sales constitute equivalent transactions and that the constituent elements of Article 101(1)(d) TFEU are therefore satisfied.

177. It follows from the case-law to which the Commission refers that Article 102(c) TFEU does not preclude an undertaking in a dominant position from setting different prices in the various Member States, in particular where the price differences are justified by variations in the conditions of marketing and the intensity of competition, but prohibits it from applying artificial price differences in the various Member States such as to place its customers at a disadvantage and to distort competition in the context of an artificial partitioning of national markets [. . .]. More generally, it follows from that case-law that, while the fact that an undertaking in a dominant position applies different prices may, in the absence of objective explanation, constitute an indicium of discrimination where those prices are applied on a particular geographic market, characterised by sufficiently homogeneous conditions of competition, that is not the case where they are applied on separate geographic markets, characterised by insufficiently homogeneous conditions of competition, regard being had in particular to the relevant regulatory framework.

178. Those considerations may be transposed to the present case, where a producer and its wholesalers agree to apply different prices according to the Member State in which the products in question are intended to be resold and reimbursed. It is common ground that each of those Member States constitutes a distinct market, in so far as the relevant geographic market is national owing, in particular, to the differences in the national regulations on the prices and the reimbursement of the medicines in question. The Commission itself therefore found in the Decision that where it supplied one or other of those national markets, a Spanish wholesaler operated, having regard in particular to the relevant regulatory framework, in conditions of competition which, as regards price, the parameter specifically concerned by Clause 4 of the General Sales Conditions, were heterogeneous.

179. Consequently, GSK is correct to maintain that the finding of a difference in price is not sufficient to support the conclusion that there is discrimination. It is possible that GSK applies different prices because different markets exist and not so that different markets will exist [. . .]

Increased prices paid by consumers abroad

183. [. . .] [T]he Commission found [. . .] that Clause 4 of the General Sales Conditions required the Spanish wholesalers who bought the medicines sold in Spain by GW to pay a higher price [. . .] than the price set by the Spanish authorities, which they would have paid in the absence of the General Sales Conditions [. . .]. Clause 4 thus has the effect of reducing or cancelling, in numerous cases, the differential hitherto existing between the prices applicable in Spain and those applicable in other Member States of the [EU] [. . .].

184. Next, the Commission found [. . .] that in some Member States an admittedly small part of the price of medicines covered by the General Sales Conditions was borne by the patient, who in that sense constituted a final consumer, within the economic sense of that term, of the products in question. The Commission also found [. . .] that the remainder of the price of those medicines was reimbursed by the national sickness insurance scheme, which also constituted a final consumer of the products in question, in that it spread the economic risks borne for their health by those covered by the insurance schemes. The Court of Justice has already referred to the special nature, in that respect, of the trade in pharmaceutical products, namely the fact that social security institutions are substituted for consumers as regards responsibility for the payment of medical expenses [. . .]. GSK does not dispute those findings of fact, the

importance of which the Commission recalled to mind in the context of the reasoning which it had applied in the Decision.

185. Even accepting that competition between the Spanish wholesalers who engage in parallel trade, or between those wholesalers and the distributors established on the market of the Member State of destination of the parallel trade, is limited to the point of allowing them to apply resale prices which are lower than the prices applied by those distributors only to the extent strictly necessary to attract retailers, as convincingly explained in some of the documents produced by GSK, the Commission was entitled to infer [. . .] from the findings of fact set out in the preceding paragraphs that Clause 4 of the General Sales Conditions impeded that competition and, in substance, the pressure which in its absence would have existed on the unit price of the medicines in question, to the detriment of the final consumer, taken to mean both the patient and the national sickness insurance scheme acting on behalf of claimants.

186. It is true that, as the Commission observed [. . .] that pressure, considered at the individual level of one of the national markets affected by Clause 4 of the General Sales Conditions, such as the United Kingdom market, may be marginal. However, the Commission also observed [. . .] that the fact of impeding this pressure, by means of an agreement concluded with a significant number of Spanish wholesalers and affecting a significant number of products and national markets in the Community, contributed or could contribute, by a network effect, to reinforcing the pre-existing price rigidity on the market. Such reinforcement infringes Article 101(1) TFEU [. . .].

187. GSK has not adduced evidence of an error on that point. On the contrary, it acknowledged at the hearing that Clause 4 of the General Sales Conditions, although mainly intended to prevent the transfer of surplus to the wholesalers, might have the effect of reducing the admittedly restricted benefit which their participation in competition provides for the final consumer on the markets of destination of the parallel trade.

188. Last, the Commission found [. . .] that some national sickness insurance schemes took advantage, to various degrees and according to different procedures, of parallel trade in order to reduce the cost of the medicines which they reimburse. Although GSK denies that the national measures to which the Commission refers have as their object to encourage parallel trade, it does not deny that they may have such an effect, as the Commission observed at the hearing, without being contradicted. Some of the documents which GSK produced, on the contrary, emphasise convincingly that that may be the case. GSK also acknowledges, most recently in its answers to the written questions and at the hearing, that some Member States have adopted measures in order to recover a proportion of the savings which pharmacists have made by means of parallel trade.

189. By focusing on the example of the United Kingdom, which in GSK's submission was the main target market for parallel trade in medicines sold in Spain by GW, the Commission was able to infer [. . .] that Clause 4 of the General Sales Conditions had the effect of depriving the national sickness insurance schemes of the advantage which they would have derived, in the form of a reduction in costs and even independently of any reduction in the retail price, from the participation of the Spanish wholesalers in intrabrand competition. Although it emphasised that that effect is minor, GSK also acknowledged its existence at the hearing. It also acknowledged that such an effect might be produced in Member States other than the United Kingdom.

190. Accordingly, it must be concluded that the Commission was entitled to find, in the light of elements whose relevance has not been validly called in question by GSK, that Clause 4 of the General Sales Conditions had the effect of reducing the welfare of final consumers by preventing them from taking advantage, in the form of a reduction

in prices and costs, of the participation of the Spanish wholesalers in intrabrand competition on the national markets of destination of the parallel trade originating in Spain.

191. None of GSK's arguments appears to be capable of upsetting that conclusion.

The GC concluded by confirming the Commission's conclusion that the General Sales Conditions constituted an agreement within the meaning of Article 101(1) TFEU and although it held that the Commission's principal conclusion that Clause 4 of the General Sales Conditions has as its object the restriction of competition was incorrect, it also concluded that GSK had not succeeded in calling in question the Commission's subsidiary conclusion that that provision had the effect of depriving final consumers of the advantage which they would have derived, in terms of price and costs, from the participation of the Spanish wholesalers in intra-brand competition on the national markets of destination of the parallel trade originating in Spain.

The GC went on to dismiss three arguments, one based on misuse of powers,[259] *the second on the doctrine of subsidiarity,*[260] *and the third on Article 43.*[261] *It also rejected arguments based on the adequacy of the Commission's reasoning.*[262] *It then examined if the agreement in question could benefit from Article 101(3) TFEU, by exploring how the four conditions of Article 101(3) TFEU could be satisfied in this case. The GC arrived at the conclusion that the Commission had wrongly dismissed the possibility that the agreement in question benefits from the exemption of Article 101(3) TFEU in this case and annulled Article 2 of the Commission's decision in so far as it rejected GSK's request for an exemption.*

NOTES AND QUESTIONS ON GSK AND THE AIMS OF EU COMPETITION LAW

1. (Paragraph 117) Note that the *Consten & Grundig* rule that clauses intended to limit parallel trade have as their object to restrict competition under Article 101(1) TFEU has been reduced to a rebuttable presumption. Do you think this presumption is strong?
2. (Paragraphs 120–2) Do you think that in Grundig, the CJEU carried out a competitive analysis, abridged but real? What was the view at the time? Is the view of the GC in *GSK* compatible with *Consten & Grundig*? Is this an important re-interpretation of a forty-year-old case?
3. (Paragraphs 118–22) Reference to consumer harm was unusual before the modernisation project of the 1990s. Was consumer harm mentioned in *Consten & Grundig*?
4. (Paragraphs 124–34) What were the circumstances to be considered in the economic and legal context of the agreement? Is this assessment introducing some economic analysis? How is this different from the analysis of the economic and legal context performed by the GC when examining the existence of a restriction of competition by effect?
5. (Paragraph 150) If a firm with large sunk costs, that is costs that have already been incurred and cannot be recovered, may not recover more than its marginal cost (marginal cost being the cost of producing an extra unit of output), is it likely to incur those costs, otherwise than by mistake?

[259] Ibid, paras 198–9. [260] Ibid, paras 200–3. [261] Ibid, paras 204–7.
[262] Ibid, paras 210–13.

6. (Paragraphs 170–2) Is every restriction of conduct restrictive of competition?
7. (Paragraphs 183–90) Was the loss of the benefit of parallel trade borne by consumers or by Spanish wholesalers? Was any loss to consumers appreciable? If not was the notice on minor agreements relevant?
8. Did the General Court accept that dual pricing did not infringe Article 101(1) TFEU?
9. The minor loss to consumers outweighed the efficiencies due to Clause 4: the additional funds available for R&D and the distortion of competition due to medicines being routed through those countries with a lower maximal price permitted by law. Was the GC divided and compromising, or was it insisting that any balancing must take place under Article 101(3) TFEU? On the application of Article 101(3) TFEU by the GC in this case, see our analysis in Chapter 5.
10. The interpretation of Article 101(1) TFEU by the GC was rejected by the Court of Justice pronouncing itself on appeal.

Joined Cases C-501, 513, 515 & 519/06 P, *GlaxoSmithKline Services Unlimited v Commission*

[2009] ECR I–9291 (some references omitted)

The CJEU dismissed the appeal (by GSK and the Commission among others) against the GC's decision. Even though the CJEU found that the GC erred in its assessment of the agreement as an effects-based restriction, rather than an object-based restriction, it considered that the operative part of the GC's judgment in which it confirms the Commission's finding that the pricing system breached Article 101(1) TFEU need not be set aside. The CJEU has also confirmed the GC's findings in relation to its assessment of the Article 101(3) TFEU criteria, although it added some important elements regarding the evidential burden of proof for undertakings. We include here the relevant parts of the judgment with regard to Article 101(1) TFEU. Those relevant to Article 101(3) are included in Chapter 5.

57. [. .] [I]t is appropriate to ascertain whether the [General Court's] assessment as to whether the agreement has an anti-competitive object [. . .] is in accordance with the principles extracted from the relevant case-law.

58. According to settled case-law, in order to assess the anti-competitive nature of an agreement, regard must be had inter alia to the content of its provisions, the objectives it seeks to attain and the economic and legal context of which it forms a part [. . .]. In addition, although the parties' intention is not a necessary factor in determining whether an agreement is restrictive, there is nothing prohibiting the Commission or the Community judicature from taking that aspect into account [. . .].

59. With respect to parallel trade, the Court has already held that, in principle, agreements aimed at prohibiting or limiting parallel trade have as their object the prevention of competition (see, to that effect, Case 19/77 *Miller International Schallplaten v Commission* [1978] ECR 131, paragraphs 7 and 18, and Joined Cases 32/78, 36/78 to 82/78 *BMW Belgium and Others v Commission* [1979] ECR 2435, paragraphs 20 to 28 and 31).

60. As observed by the Advocate General [. . .] that principle, according to which an agreement aimed at limiting parallel trade is a 'restriction of competition by object', applies to the pharmaceuticals sector.

61. The Court has, moreover, held in that regard, in relation to the application of Article [101 TFEU] and in a case involving the pharmaceuticals sector, that an agreement between producer and distributor which might tend to restore the national divisions in trade between Member States might be such as to frustrate the Treaty's objective of achieving the integration of national markets through the establishment of a single market. Thus on a number of occasions the Court has held agreements aimed at partitioning national markets according to national borders or making the interpenetration of national markets more difficult, in particular those aimed at preventing or restricting parallel exports, to be agreements whose object is to restrict competition within the meaning of that article of the Treaty (Joined Cases C-468/06 to C-478/06 *Sot. Lélos kai Sia and Others* [2008] ECR I–7139, paragraph 65 and case-law cited).

62. With respect to the [GC's] statement that, while it is accepted that an agreement intended to limit parallel trade must in principle be considered to have as its object the restriction of competition, that applies in so far as it may be presumed to deprive final consumers of the advantages of effective competition in terms of supply or price, the Court notes that neither the wording of Article [101(1) TFEU] nor the case-law lend support to such a position.

63. First of all, there is nothing in that provision to indicate that only those agreements which deprive consumers of certain advantages may have an anti-competitive object. Secondly, it must be borne in mind that the Court has held that, like other competition rules laid down in the Treaty, Article [101 TFEU] aims to protect not only the interests of competitors or of consumers, but also the structure of the market and, in so doing, competition as such. Consequently, for a finding that an agreement has an anti-competitive object, it is not necessary that final consumers be deprived of the advantages of effective competition in terms of supply or price [. . .]

64. It follows that, by requiring proof that the agreement entails disadvantages for final consumers as a prerequisite for a finding of anti-competitive object and by not finding that that agreement had such an object, the [GC] committed an error of law.

65. However, where the grounds of a judgment of the [GC] are contrary to [EU] law, that judgment need not be set aside if the operative part of the judgment appears to be well founded on other legal grounds [. . .].

66. That is the case here [. . .].

The CJEU dismissed GSK's appeal as unfounded in so far as it seeks to establish that the agreement was compatible with Article 101(1) TFEU.

2.3.3.2. Article 102 TFEU cases

In the wake of the General Court's judgment in *Bayer*, Commissioner Mario Monti, the competition commissioner at the time, was concerned and indicated that unless he won the appeal (which the Commission ultimately lost) he would use Article 102 against dominant firms that bar parallel trade. The Commission treats each group of medicines with a particular function as a separate market, so patentees of breakthrough medicines may be treated as dominant. In *GlaxoSmithKline v Commission*, however, the General Court suggested that the relevant product market might be medicines attractive to parallel traders.[263] On this basis, few pharmaceutical companies would enjoy a dominant position.

[263] Case T-168/01, *GlaxoSmithKline Services Unlimited v Commission* [2006] ECR II–2969, para 159.

In *Syfait*, the Greek competition authority (Hellenic Competition Commission—HCC) asked the CJEU for a preliminary ruling whether it was contrary to Article 102 for a dominant firm to refuse to supply wholesalers in order to limit parallel trade. Greek wholesalers had complained that GlaxoSmithKline (GSK) had ceased in November 2000 to meet in full their orders for three medicines over which it held a dominant position and that GSK had stated that it would supply hospitals and pharmacies directly. GSK alleged that parallel exports by the wholesalers had led to significant shortages on the Greek market. The HCC accepted that GSK enjoyed a dominant position over the three medicines and observed that all the Member States fix the maximum prices of pharmaceutical products within their territories. Prices in Greece were consistently the lowest in any Member States. Consequently, Greek wholesalers bought large quantities of important drugs in order to export them to Member States where prices were higher.

Eventually, the CJEU declined jurisdiction on the ground that the HCC was subject to ministerial influence and as such was not an independent court or tribunal entitled to a preliminary ruling. AG Jacobs had, however, perceptively analysed the case law and the economic context of the pharmaceutical industry. In paragraphs 89–91 of his Opinion, the Advocate General analysed the economics of the innovative pharmaceutical industry, with substantial investment in high fixed costs, which were mostly sunk (of little use save for developing the particular drug), and relatively low variable costs. This made it rational for the pharmaceutical companies to sell wherever they could cover their variable cost. The mere fact that this might be possible does not ensure that a producer could recover its total costs if that price were generalized throughout the EU. This statement impliedly accepts that unilateral discriminatory pricing does not necessarily infringe Article 102. Usually parallel trade leads to consumers in the lower-priced countries paying less, but that is not the position for medicines, where the government normally bears the cost. In some Member States, the government reimburses as much for medicines subject to parallel trade as for those bought by wholesalers directly from the producer at a higher price.

He concluded, therefore, that for a pharmaceutical producer to restrict supplies

> 100. [. . .] to limit parallel trade is capable of justification as a reasonable and proportional measure in defence of that undertaking's commercial interests. Such a restriction does not protect price disparities, which are of the undertaking's own making, not does it directly impede trade, which is rather blocked by public service obligations imposed by the Member States. To require the undertaking to supply all export orders placed with it would in many cases impose a disproportionate burden given the moral and legal obligations on it to maintain supplies in all Member States. Given the specific economic characteristics of the pharmaceutical industry a requirement to supply would not necessarily promote either free movement or competition, and might harm the incentive for pharmaceutical undertakings to innovate. Moreover, it cannot be assumed that parallel trade would in fact benefit either the ultimate consumers of pharmaceutical products or the Member States as primary purchasers of such products.

The opinion is clearly limited to markets subject to specific controls such as those exercised by Member States over the pharmaceutical industry. Competition is distorted by the control over prices and distribution. The HCC decided that there was no abuse contrary to Article 102 but that the conduct infringed Greek competition law.

Actions were also brought in parallel proceedings by the wholesalers before the Greek Civil Courts.

Joined Cases C-468 to 478/06, *Sot Lelos kai Sia v GlaxoSmithKline*
[2008] ECR I–7139

A Greek subsidiary of GSK has imported the group's pharmaceutical products in Greece and held the marketing authorization in Greece for a number of prescription only medicinal products. A number of wholesalers had for a number of years bought those medicinal products from GSK's Greek subsidiary in order both to distribute them on the Greek market and in other Member States. In November 2000, GSK restructured its distribution strategy, by starting distributing itself these products to Greek hospitals and pharmacies through a vertically integrated to GSK company, F AE. It also stopped meeting the orders placed by the wholesalers for those products. In February 2001, GSK started supplying limited quantities of drugs to the wholesalers, who issued proceedings before the Greek courts, alleging that GSK's conduct in interrupting supplies of medicinal products which had been ordered and distributing them through its own subsidiary F AE amounted to abuse of a dominant position, contrary to Article 102 TFEU and the domestic Greek competition rules. Those claims were dismissed at first instance but on appeal, the domestic court stayed the proceedings and referred the matter to the CJEU for a preliminary ruling.

AG Colomer took a hawkish position with regard to the application of Article 102 TFEU to conduct barring parallel trade. He did not agree with the considerations of AG Jacobs regarding the impact of pharmaceutical price regulation on the industry and examined the argument put forward by GSK concerning reduced income due to loss of market share in favour of the wholesalers and its effect on recouping investment in research and development. GSK was citing the enormous cost of investing in the R&D for the launch of a medicinal product, adding that the average time between obtaining the patent for the active ingredient and the product becoming available for therapeutic purposes is twelve or thirteen years, and consequently the period during which the marketing of the product produces returns is only seven or eight years. In these circumstances, they argued that parallel trade and the manufacture of generic drugs once the patent protection has expired reduced their ability to recoup R&D costs. AG Colomer was not impressed by these arguments.

Opinion of AG Colomer

109. I cannot see that there is necessarily any causal link between any possible negative impact on R&D investment and parallel trade, since, in the first place, GSK and the writers in question have not provided any information relating to the reasons for the period during which the patent is not revenue producing. However, this long delay is a result of the internal cost structures of pharmaceutical undertakings. In any event, as they consider the period during which the patent is profitable to be very short, they are experiencing how it feels to enjoy rights for a limited period only. I would even hazard a guess that there are other sectors in which something similar occurs in relation to this type of intangible property.

110. Secondly, although it would be logical to suppose that only the economic success of a patent ensures that more funding is obtained to keep up the research, R&D policy in the pharmaceutical sector has become central to the entire business. In this branch of the economy, it is only the constant search for innovatory medicines which helps companies to survive in a very competitive, globalised and lucrative market. But without a well-thought-out commercial policy, the most brilliant inventions run the risk of going unnoticed. That is why any research company must seek out the best ways of appealing to and reaching the consumer.

111. GSK was free to design its own distribution system in Europe. It decided on a strategy which incorporated the Greek wholesalers because it considered it more economically efficient and advantageous. It could have opted instead for a vertically integrated system for the distribution of its medicines, as it did in November 2000. Even though it was at liberty to restructure its distribution networks, as long as it respected normal commercial practice, in the present case GSK is being criticised for punishing the wholesalers for having taken better advantage of market conditions and preventing them from carrying out their export business.

112. Thirdly, looking at the figures provided in the literature referred to in point 107 of this Opinion, which show that the market share of the parallel importers increased from 1.8% to 6.8% between 1998 and 2003, one has the impression that the real battle is about winning back these profit margins which the rivals of the big pharmaceutical companies have appropriated.

113. Against this background, I find the argument that the loss of income resulting from parallel imports of patented medicines acts as a disincentive misleading, since it is aimed only at seducing public opinion, which is sensitised to the vital importance of R&D for competitiveness, by shifting the focus from business rivalry to research policy, an area which the European Union has taken on [. . .] into the [TFEU].

114. The European Union offers undertakings a favourable environment in this respect by encouraging them, through the granting of a block exemption for horizontal agreements of this type, to minimise R&D costs because it realises that cooperation in this area and in the exploitation of the results promotes technical and economic progress by increasing the dissemination of know-how; it also avoids duplication of R&D work, stimulates advances through the exchange of complementary discoveries and encourages greater rationalisation of the manufacture of the products or application of the methods arising out of the R&D.

115. Consequently, even if it were possible to justify the conduct, it would have to be considered disproportionate, since it eliminates competition in distribution within Europe by smothering parallel imports from Greece.

The CJEU's Judgment

The CJEU noted that parallel exports of medicinal products from a Member State where the prices are low to other Member States in which the prices are higher 'open up in principle an alternative source of supply to buyers of the medicinal products in those latter States, which necessarily brings some benefits to the final consumer of those products'.[264] *Indeed, 'the attraction of the other source of supply which arises from parallel trade in the importing Member State lies precisely in the fact that that trade is capable of offering the same products on the market of that Member State at lower prices than those applied on the same market by the pharmaceuticals companies' and '[a]t the same time [. . .] parallel trade in medicines from one Member State to another is likely to increase the choice available to entities in the latter Member State'.*[265] *The CJEU also implicitly recognized in this case that restrictions of parallel trade lead to a presumption of negative effects on consumers and hence shift the burden of proof to the defendant, in the context of Article 102 TFEU, without it being necessary for the*

264 Joined Cases C-468–78/06, *Sot Lelos kai Sia EE and Others v GlaxoSmithKline AEVE* [2008] ECR I-7139, para 54.

265 Ibid, paras 55–6.

claimant to bring additional evidence as to the causal link between the specific conduct and consumer harm.

54. It is true, as GSK AEVE has pointed out, that, for medicines subject to parallel exports, the existence of price differences between the exporting and the importing Member States does not necessarily imply that the final consumer in the importing Member State will benefit from a price corresponding to the one prevailing in the exporting Member State, inasmuch as the wholesalers carrying out the exports will themselves make a profit from that parallel trade.

55. Nevertheless, the attraction of the other source of supply which arises from parallel trade in the importing Member State lies precisely in the fact that that trade is capable of offering the same products on the market of that Member State at lower prices than those applied on the same market by the pharmaceuticals companies.

56. As a result, even in the Member States where the prices of medicines are subject to State regulation, parallel trade is liable to exert pressure on prices and, consequently, to create financial benefits not only for the social health insurance funds, but equally for the patients concerned, for whom the proportion of the price of medicines for which they are responsible will be lower. At the same time, as the Commission notes, parallel trade in medicines from one Member State to another is likely to increase the choice available to entities in the latter Member State which obtain supplies of medicines by means of a public procurement procedure, in which the parallel importers can offer medicines at lower prices.

57. Accordingly, without it being necessary for the Court to rule on the question whether it is for an undertaking in a dominant position to assess whether its conduct vis-à-vis a trading party constitutes abuse in the light of the degree to which that party's activities offer advantages to the final consumers, it is clear that, in the circumstances of the main proceedings, such an undertaking cannot base its arguments on the premise that the parallel exports which it seeks to limit are of only minimal benefit to the final consumers.

The CJEU then examined the impact of State price and supply regulation in the pharmaceuticals sector.

58. Turning, next, to the argument based on the degree of regulation of the pharmaceuticals markets in the [EU], it must first be examined whether State regulation of the prices of medicinal products has an impact on the assessment of whether a refusal to supply those products constitutes abuse.

59. It is clear that, in the majority of Member States, medicines, in particular those available only on prescription, are subject to regulation aimed at setting, at the request of the manufacturers concerned and on the basis of information provided by them, selling prices for those medicines and/or the scales of reimbursement of the cost of prescription medicines by the relevant social health insurance systems. The price differences between Member States for certain medicines are thus the result of the different levels at which the prices and/or the scales to be applied to those medicines are fixed.

60. The main proceedings relate to a non-harmonised area in which the [EU] legislature has limited itself, in adopting Directive 89/105, to placing Member States under a duty to guarantee that decisions in respect of the regulation of prices and reimbursement are taken with complete transparency, without discrimination and within certain specific time-limits.

61. In that respect, it should be noted, on one hand, that the control exercised by Member States over the selling prices or the reimbursement of medicinal products

does not entirely remove the prices of those products from the law of supply and demand.

62. Thus, in some Member States, the public authorities do not intervene in the process of setting prices or limit themselves to setting the scale of reimbursement of the cost of prescription medicines by the national health insurance systems, thereby leaving to the pharmaceuticals companies the task of deciding their selling prices. Furthermore, even though the public authorities in other Member States set the selling prices of medicines as well, that does not in itself mean that the manufacturers of the medicines concerned have no influence upon the level at which the selling prices are set or the proportion of those prices which is reimbursed.

63. As the Commission has pointed out, even in the Member States where the selling prices or the amounts of reimbursement of medicines are set by the public authorities, the producers of the medicines concerned take part in the negotiations which are initiated by those producers and take their price proposals as a starting point and end with the setting of the prices and the amounts of reimbursement to be applied. As the second and third recitals to Directive 89/105 state, the task of the authorities when setting prices of medicines is not only to control expenditure connected with public health systems and to ensure the availability of adequate supplies of medicinal products at a reasonable cost, but also to promote efficiency in the production of medicinal products and to encourage research and development into new medicinal products. As the Advocate General indicated in points 90 to 93 of his Opinion, the level at which the selling price or the amount of reimbursement of a given medicinal product is fixed reflects the relative strength of both the public authorities of the relevant Member State and the pharmaceuticals companies at the time of the price negotiations for that product.

64. On the other hand, it should be recalled that, where a medicine is protected by a patent which confers a temporary monopoly on its holder, the price competition which may exist between a producer and its distributors, or between parallel traders and national distributors, is, until the expiry of that patent, the only form of competition which can be envisaged. [. . .]

66. In the light of the abovementioned Treaty objective as well as that of ensuring that competition in the internal market is not distorted, there can be no escape from the prohibition laid down in Article [102 TFEU] for the practices of an undertaking in a dominant position which are aimed at avoiding all parallel exports from a Member State to other Member States, practices which, by partitioning the national markets, neutralise the benefits of effective competition in terms of the supply and the prices that those exports would obtain for final consumers in the other Member States.

67. Although the degree of price regulation in the pharmaceuticals sector cannot therefore preclude the Community rules on competition from applying, the fact none the less remains that, when assessing, in the case of Member States with a system of price regulation, whether the refusal of a pharmaceuticals company to supply medicines to wholesalers involved in parallel exports constitutes abuse, it cannot be ignored that such State intervention is one of the factors liable to create opportunities for parallel trade.

Consequently, the CJEU accepted that a restriction to parallel trade does not amount to an absolute presumption of consumer harm or a per se prohibition rule. The presumption of anti-competitive effects may still be rebutted by the defendant in limited circumstances: a company must be 'in a position to take steps that are reasonable and in proportion to the need to protect its own commercial interests'.[266] *The CJEU accepts a reasonable and*

266 Ibid, para 69.

proportionate protection of the commercial interests of the dominant undertaking. Hence, dominant firms may justify restrictions on parallel trade in some specific circumstances: (a) State intervention is one of the factors liable to create the opportunities for parallel trade in the first place[267] *and (b) where a different interpretation of Article 102, rejecting any possibility of justification, would have left dominant firms only the choice 'not to place its medicines on the market at all in a Member State where the prices of those products are set at a relatively low level'.*[268]

NOTES AND QUESTIONS ON SOT LELOS KAI SIA V GLAXOSMITHKLINE

1. Are you more convinced by AG Colomer's perspective on the effect of parallel trade on the incentives of pharma companies to invest on R&D and develop new drugs, or that of AG Jacobs?
2. Should competition law care about the incentives of market actors to invest in R&D and innovate, or should it focus on allocative efficiency only, that is, lower prices for consumers?
3. How does the objective of market integration relate to that of the protection of consumers? Do you think that the CJEU in *Sot Lelos* attempted to establish a connection between the two? Explain your conclusions.
4. Were you the CEO of a pharmaceutical company, would you choose to restrict parallel imports through an export contractual ban, a dual pricing system, or a unilateral refusal to deliver more drugs than what can cover normal domestic demand?

2.3.3.3. Digital single market and EU competition law: Geo-blocking and geo-filtering

In his 2014 Political Guidelines for the next European Commission, Jean-Claude Juncker, the President of the Commission, put forward the need to create a connected digital single market as one of the new Commission's priorities.[269] Indeed, Europe is lagging behind the US and China with regard to the development of large digital companies, as this is illustrated by the very few unicorns (start-up companies valued more than $1 billion) established in Europe, in comparison to those based in the United States or Asia.[270] The follow-up process has been rather quick. In 2015, the European Commission adopted a Communication setting a Digital

[267] Ibid, para 67. [268] Ibid, para 68.

[269] Political Guidelines for the next European Commission—A New Start for Europe: My Agenda for Jobs, Growth, Fairness and Democratic Change (15 July 2014). The establishment of a Connected Digital Single Market was listed as priority number two.

[270] Attracta Mooney, 'European Unicorns Remain Elusive', *Financial Times* (16 June 2016), available at www.ft.com/cms/s/2/10a73408-2e37-11e6-bf8d-26294ad519fc.html. Most of the unicorns in Europe are UK-based, which is also the Member State that enjoys the highest levels of e-commerce in Europe: European Union Committee, Online Platforms and the Digital Single Market, 10th Report of Session 2015–16, HL Paper 129 (April 2016), ch 8.

Single Market Strategy for Europe.[271] This will be built on three pillars, one of which includes better access for consumers and businesses to online goods and services across Europe.

The recent efforts to promote a 'digital single market' testify to the continuing relevance of the idea of economic integration and of the need to break down 'national silos in telecoms regulation, in copyright and data protection legislation, in the management of radio waves and in the application of competition law', all of which reduce the 'great opportunities offered by digital technologies, which know no borders'.[272] The digital single market aims to allow seamless access for consumers and businesses to online goods and services across Europe. Among the various tools, the Commission has adopted specific rules prohibiting geo-blocking and geo-filtering that may raise barriers to cross-border online activity.[273]

The European Commission has expressed concerns about geo-blocking and geo-filtering practices, as firms may have the incentive to take advantage of technology to block the free flow of intra-EU commerce.[274] Geo-blocking 'refers to practices used for commercial reasons by online sellers that result in the denial of access to websites based in other Member States'.[275] Geo-filtering consists of offering different terms and/or conditions depending on the location of the user, when situated in a different Member State than that of the online provider.[276] Geo-blocking may occur even if consumers are able to access the website, when they are not able to purchase products or services from it, particularly when they are re-routed to a local website of the same company with different prices or a different product or service. Geo-filtering occurs when 'geo-localising practices are used as a result of which different prices are automatically applied on the basis of geographic location, for example when online car rental customers in one Member State pay more for the identical car rental in a given destination than online customers in another Member State'.[277] More generally, geo-filtering also may occur when 'online providers allow users to access and purchase consumer goods/digital content services cross-border, but offer different terms and/or conditions depending on the location of the user in a Member State different from that of the provider'.[278] According to the Commission, '[g]eo-blocking is one of several tools used by companies to segment markets along national borders (territorial restrictions)'; it is further explained that '[b]y limiting

[271] Communication from the Commission to the European Parliament, the Council, the European Economic and Social Committee and the Committee of the Regions, COM(2015) 192 final 6; Commission Staff Working Document, Digital Single Market Strategy for Europe—Analysis and Evidence, COM(2015) 192 final.

[272] J-C Juncker, 'A New Start For Europe: My Agenda for Growth, Fairness and Democratic Change. Political Guidelines for the Next European Commission' (15 July 2014), available at https://ec.europa.eu/commission/sites/beta-political/files/juncker-political-guidelines-speech_en.pdf.

[273] Regulation (EU) 2018/302 of the European Parliament and of the Council of 28 February 2018 on addressing unjustified geo-blocking and other forms of discrimination based on customers' nationality, place of residence or place of establishment within the internal market and amending Regulations (EC) No 2006/2004 and (EU) 2017/2394 and Directive 2009/22/EC, [2018] OJ L 601/1 [hereinafter Geo-blocking Regulation].

[274] For a detailed analysis of the various legal frameworks in the EU that may apply to 'geo-blocking', see DG Internal Policies, 'The Geo-Blocking Proposal: Internal Market, Competition Law and Regulatory Aspects' (January 2017).

[275] Commission Staff Working Document, 'Geo-blocking Practices in e-Commerce: Issues paper presenting initial findings of the e-commerce sector inquiry conducted by the Directorate-General for Competition' SWD(2016) 70 final, para 32.

[276] Ibid, para 33.

[277] Communication from the Commission to the European Parliament, the Council, the European Economic and Social Committee and the Committee of the Regions, COM(2015) 192 final, 6.

[278] Commission Staff Working Document, 'Geo-blocking Practices in e-Commerce: Issues paper presenting initial findings of the e-commerce sector inquiry conducted by the Directorate-General for Competition', SWD(2016) 70 final, para 33.

consumer opportunities and choice, geo-blocking is a significant cause of consumer dissatisfaction and of fragmentation of the Internal Market'.[279] Geo-blocking or geo-filtering may be applied by various operators: retailers operating an online store, online marketplaces and price comparison websites.[280]

In the context of the Digital Single Market strategy, the Commission launched a sector inquiry into e-commerce in the EU, on the basis of Article 17 of Regulation 1/2013.[281] This provision enables the Commission to open investigations into sectors of the economy and into types of agreements, if there are some indications that competition may be restricted. Although the Commission cannot adopt remedies, it publishes a report, which informs its subsequent enforcement action under Article 101 and/or 102 TFEU. The aim of the e-sector inquiry was to allow the Commission to gather data on the functioning of e-commerce markets so as to identify possible restrictions of competition, in particular with regard to cross-border online trade, the Commission's findings being merely based on surveys of companies present in the sector.

The Commission published its initial findings in March 2016 in relation to geo-blocking, finding that geo-blocking is applied by the majority of online digital content providers and is largely based on contractual restrictions, although it may also be adopted through unilateral conduct. The Commission also acknowledged the existence of 'technical geo-blocking', which aims to restrict a user's ability to access and use content in a given Member State from outside that Member State's territory (access and portability restrictions), which is often used for digital content services.[282] Technical geo-blocking may limit the user's ability to play previously downloaded content in certain territories, restrict the catalogue of content and/or services available to a given user in different territories, and inhibit the ability of an existing user to access the service in different territories.[283] The Commission's Staff Discussion paper makes it clear that limiting the ability of European users to shop online cross borders, 'may run counter to the objective of establishing a *single* market'.[284]

Although the European Commission considered in the Final Report that online price transparency and price competition had a significant impact on companies' distribution strategies and consumer behaviour, it castigated the increased use of contractual restrictions that could hinder the development of inter-State e-commerce in the EU.[285] Indeed, according to the report, certain licensing practices may make it more difficult for new online business models and services to develop across the EU, and consumers in all EU Member States may not benefit from a similar level of services and choice. One of the key findings of the sector inquiry was that almost 60 per cent of digital content providers who participated in the inquiry have contractually agreed with right holders to 'geo-block', as online rights are to a large extent licensed on a national basis or for the territory of a limited number of Member States which

279 Communication from the Commission to the European Parliament, the Council, the European Economic and Social Committee and the Committee of the Regions, COM(2015) 192 final, at 6.

280 Commission Staff Working Document, 'Geo-blocking Practices in e-Commerce: Issues paper presenting initial findings of the e-commerce sector inquiry conducted by the Directorate-General for Competition', SWD(2016) 70 final, para 67.

281 See European Commission, Antitrust: Sector Inquiry into e-Commerce, available at ec.europa.eu/competition/antitrust/sector_inquiries_e_commerce.html.

282 Commission Staff Working Document, 'Geo-blocking Practices in e-Commerce: Issues paper presenting initial findings of the e-commerce sector inquiry conducted by the Directorate-General for Competition', SWD(2016) 70 final, para 174.

283 Ibid, para 176. 284 Ibid, para 41.

285 See European Commission, 'Final Report on the e-Commerce Sector Inquiry', COM(2017) 229 final (10 May 2017), available at http://ec.europa.eu/competition/antitrust/sector_inquiry_final_report_en.pdf.

share a common language. According to the Commission, '[g]eo-blocking is most prevalent in agreements for TV series (74 %), films (66 %) and sport events (63 %). It is less prevalent in agreements for other digital content categories such as music (57 %), children's TV (55 %), non-fiction TV (51 %) and news (24 %)'.[286] The Commission stressed that any competition enforcement in relation to geo-blocking would have to be based on a case-by-case analysis of potential justifications for the restrictions imposed. Another point stressed was the need 'to avoid diverging interpretations of the EU competition rules regarding business practices in e-commerce markets which may, in turn, create serious obstacles for companies actively competing, in a compliant manner, in multiple Member States, to the detriment of a Digital Single Market'.[287]

In February 2018, the EU adopted a Geo-blocking Regulation, on the legal basis of Article 114 TFEU, to end unjustified geo-blocking for consumers wishing to buy products or services online within the EU, and which will enter into force by the end of 2018. The main drive for adopting the Regulation is the realization that the implementation of the non-discrimination principle in Article 20(2) of Directive 2006/123/EC has proven insufficient to guarantee that customers will not confront refusals to sell and various other limiting conditions, when buying goods or services across borders.[288] The material scope of the Geo-blocking Regulation was aligned with that of the Services Directive.[289] Non-economic services of general interest, transport services, audio-visual services, gambling activities, retail financial services, healthcare and some other social services are excluded from the latter's scope.[290] The Regulation applies to traders when selling to consumers (B2C) and also businesses (B2B) in their capacity as end users. It does not apply to purely internal transactions within a country.

The Regulation prohibits discrimination against customers based, directly or indirectly, on the nationality, place of residence, or place of establishment of the customer in three specific cases: where a customer seeks to (a) 'buy goods from a trader and either those goods are delivered to a location in a Member State to which the trader offers delivery in the general conditions of access or those goods are collected at a location agreed upon between the trader and the customer in a Member State in which the trader offers such an option in the general

286 Ibid, para 66. 287 Ibid, para 73.

288 Directive 2006/123/EC of the European Parliament and of the Council of 12 December 2006 on Services in the Internal Market [2006] OJ L 376/36 providing that 'Member States shall ensure that the general conditions of access to a service, which are made available to the public at large by the provider, do not contain discriminatory provisions relating to the nationality or place of residence of the recipient, but without precluding the possibility of providing for differences in the conditions of access where those differences are directly justified by objective criteria'. Article 20(1) of the Services Directive may apply to the unilateral conduct of service providers even if they do not dispose of a dominant position. This provision targets general conditions of access to a service that is made available to the public at large, and that relates to rules on prices, payment and delivery conditions, rather than rules on terms and conditions that are individually negotiated between the trader and the customer. The provision enables the imposition by the service provider of different conditions of access if these are directly justified by objective criteria, such as 'additional costs incurred because of the distance involved or the technical characteristics of the provision of the service, or different market conditions, such as higher or lower demand influenced by seasonality, different vacation periods in the Member States and pricing by different competitors, or extra risks linked to rules differing from those of the Member State of establishment'. A Commission Staff Work Document noted that few complaints of different treatment have led to enforcement decisions by competent authorities in the Member States, and concluded that 'Article 20 does not sufficiently address discrimination of customers and has not reduced legal uncertainty': Commission Staff Working Document with a view to establishing guidance on the application of Article 20(2) of Directive 2006/123/EC on services in the internal market, SWD(2012) 146 final, 27 [hereinafter Services Directive].

289 Directive 123/2006/EC of the European Parliament and of the Council of 12 December 2006 on services in the internal market, [2006] OJ L 376/36.

290 Geo-blocking Regulation, Article 1(3).

conditions of access';[291] (b) 'receive electronically supplied services from the trader', such as cloud services, data warehousing services, website hosting and the provision of firewalls, use of search engines, and Internet directories, other than services the main feature of which is the provision of access to and use of copyright protected works or other protected subject matter;[292] and (c) 'receive services from a trader, other than electronically supplied services, in a physical location within the territory of a Member State where the trader operates' (for instance, hotel accommodation, sports events, car rental, and entrance tickets for music festivals or leisure parks).[293] To the extent that there could be conflict between the rules of the Geo-blocking Regulation and the Services Directive in these situations, the text of the former will prevail.[294]

The Geo-blocking Regulation also covers indirect forms of discrimination that could lead to similar results as the application of the forbidden criteria of nationality, residence and place of establishment, including, for instance, criteria that rely on information indicating the physical location of customers (IP address when assessing an online interface, the address submitted for the delivery of the goods, the choice of language made or the Member State where the customer's payment instrument has been issued).[295] The protection of customers from discrimination does not extend to customers purchasing a good or a service for resale, and therefore does not apply in a B2B (business-to-business) context, unless a consumer or business receives a service or purchases a good for the sole purpose of end use. Geo-blocking in a B2B context and without the sole purpose of end use is, however, subject to Article 101 TFEU, in particular for selective and exclusive distribution agreements, and eventually Article 102 TFEU (in case there is a dominant position).[296]

The Geo-blocking Regulation also establishes an obligation on 'traders' not to block or limit customers' access to their online interface, such as websites and apps, for instance through the use of technological means, when this is done on the basis of the prohibited criteria of nationality, place of residence, or place of establishment of the customer.[297] These technological measures include any technologies used to determine the physical location of customers, including tracking their IP address, coordinates obtained through a global navigation satellite system, or data related to a payment transaction.[298] A similar prohibition applies to the re-routing of the customer to another online interface, unless the customer has provided consent. In any case, the trader should keep easily accessible the version of the online interfaces that the customer sought to access before having been rerouted.[299] It is nevertheless made clear that the prohibition of discrimination with regard to access to online services 'should not be understood as creating an obligation for the trader to engage in commercial transactions with customers', as such an interpretation would have seemed disproportional and could have infringed rights protected by the Charter of Fundamental Rights (in particular the 'freedom to conduct a business' under Article 16 and the 'right to

291 According to Recital 23 of the Geo-blocking Regulation, 'the customer should be able to purchase goods, under exactly the same conditions, including price and conditions relating to the delivery of the goods, as similar customers who are residents of or are established in the Member State in which the goods are delivered or in which the goods are collected'. However, foreign customers 'will have to pick up the goods in that Member State, or in a different Member State to which the trader delivers, or arrange, by their own private means, the cross- border delivery of the goods'.

292 Hence, the Regulation does not include online television, films, e-books, music, online games, and streamed sports.

293 Geo-blocking Regulation, Article 4(1). 294 Ibid, Article 1(6). 295 Ibid, Recital 5.

296 Ibid, Recital 12. See also our analysis in Section S.10.8.1.2.5.

297 Geo-blocking Regulation, Article 3(1). 298 Ibid, Recital 14. 299 Ibid, Article 3(2).

property' under Article 17). Consequently, the Geo-blocking Regulation provides to traders an exemption from these obligations where the access restrictions or the rerouting are necessary, they constitute a mandatory requirement of the EU and/or national legislation, and where the trader provides a clear justification.[300]

Specific rules prevent traders from applying different payment conditions on the basis of nationality, place of residence, or place of establishment of the customer, the location of the payment account, the place of establishment of the payment service provider, or the place of issue of the payment instrument within the Union.[301] This rule provides that in certain cases traders cannot reject or othewise discriminate with regard to payment instruments (such as credit or debit cards), although it is also stipulated that traders may request charges for the use of a card-based instrument, to the extent the interchanges fees are not regulated. In this case the charge should not exceed the costs borne by the trader in using the payment instrument.[302]

Finally, circumventing such a ban on discrimination in passive sales agreements is not allowed.[303] Hence, the prohibition of passive sales becomes absolute, notwithstanding the trader's market position. The Geo-blocking Regulation offers an interesting example of the intersection and congruent implementation of the single market rules and those of competition law with the aim to promote market integration, as it is explicitly stipulated that the projected Regulation will not affect the application of the rules on competition. The Vertical Block Exemption Regulation provides that restrictions on passive sales to certain customers or to customers in certain territories are generally restrictive of competition and cannot normally be exempted.[304] The Geo-blocking Regulation moves nevertheless beyond competition law as it recognizes that this prohibition on discrimination may apply to agreements that may not be caught by Article 101 TFEU, but could still disrupt 'the proper functioning of the Internal Market' and could be used to 'circumvent' the provisions of the Geo-blocking Regulation. If this proves to be the case, the Geo-blocking Regulation deems 'automatically void' the relevant provisions of such agreements and of other agreements in respect of passive sales requiring the trader to act in violation of this Regulation.[305] However, the Geo-blocking Regulation does not affect agreements restricting active sales.

In conclusion, the Regulation does not impose an obligation to sell and does not harmonize prices. It focuses on discrimination, access to online interfaces, and non-differential access to goods and services where the undertaking cannot objectively justify such actions.

This is not the first time that the EU legislator has intervened to promote market integration by establishing an EU-wide space for competition between undertakings and protecting EU consumers from geographic price discrimination.

Regulation 717/2007 (Roaming Regulation), adopted in 2007, capped and reduced prices for mobile phone consumers who used their devices abroad in other Member States of the EU.[306] The Regulation was thought as a complement to the electronic communications EU regulatory framework adopted in 2002, which had not provided national regulatory authorities

300 Ibid, Article 3(3)–(4). 301 Ibid, Article 5. 302 Ibid, Articles 5(1)(a) and 5(2).

303 Ibid, Article 6. This provision relating to passive sales will apply twenty-four months from the Regulation's entry into force.

304 Commission Regulation No 330/2010 of 20 April 2010 on the application of Article 101(3) of the Treaty on the Functioning of the European Union to categories of vertical agreements and concerted practices [2010] OJ L 102/1. See our analysis in Chapter 10.

305 Geo-blocking Regulation, Recital 26.

306 Regulation (EC) No 717/2007 of the European Parliament and of the Council of 27 June 2007 on roaming on public mobile telephone networks within the Community and amending Directive 2002/21/EC, [2007] OJ L 171/32 [hereinafter Roaming Regulation].

'with sufficient tools to take effective and decisive action with regard to the pricing of roaming services within the [EU]', thus failing 'to ensure the smooth functioning of the internal market for roaming services'.[307] Although it initially covered only voice calls, it was later extended to text messages (SMS)[308] and Internet data.[309] The abolition of all retail roaming surcharges was finally implemented in June 2017 so that European consumers now can 'roam-like-at-home' (RLAH),[310] with an EU-wide regulation of wholesale roaming charges ensuring only that operators can recover their costs, including joint and common costs.[311]

Regulation 2015/751, adopted in 2015 by the European Parliament and the European Council, following a proposal by the Commission, introduced a cap on the level of interchange fees for card-based payment transactions at 0.2 per cent for debit card payments and 0.3 per cent for credit card payments (cross-border or national).[312] Although market integration was not the only rationale for adopting such EU-price regulation, since fairness considerations as to preserving consumer welfare were important considerations, it was recognized at Recitals 10 and 14 of this Regulation that '[i]n addition to a consistent application of the competition rules to interchange fees, regulating such fees would improve the functioning of the internal market and contribute to reducing transaction costs for consumers'. It is noteworthy that both these Regulations were also adopted on the basis of Article 114 TFEU.

This intensive legislative activity is complemented by competition law enforcement activity aiming geo-blocking and geo-filtering practices integrated in licensing agreements, which are, for the moment, excluded from the scope of the Geo-blocking Regulation, as they involve the complex balancing between the EU interest for cross-border trade and the ability of the IP holder to benefit from the territorially limited scope of its IP right, which is also a principle recognized by EU law.[313]

With regard to geo-blocking affecting copyrighted works, one may refer to the CJEU judgment in *FAPL and Karen Murphy v Media Protection Services Ltd*, which concerned territorial restrictions in media rights licensing and imported satellite decoder cards. In order to protect such territorial exclusivity and to prevent the public from receiving broadcasts outside the relevant Member State, each broadcaster undertakes, in the licence agreement concluded with the FAPL, to encrypt its satellite signal and to transmit the signal, so encrypted, by satellite solely to subscribers in the territory which it has been awarded. The licence agreement therefore prohibited the broadcasters from supplying decoder cards to persons who wished to watch their broadcasts outside the Member State for which the licence was granted. Certain

[307] Ibid, Recital 4.

[308] Regulation (EC) No 544/2009 of the European Parliament and of the Council of 18 June 2009 amending Regulation (EC) No 717/2007 on roaming on public mobile telephone networks within the Community and Directive 2002/21/EC on a common regulatory framework for electronic communications networks and services [2009] OJ L 167/12.

[309] Regulation (EC) No 531/2012 of the European Parliament and of the Council of 13 June 2012 on roaming on public mobile communications networks within the Union (recast) [2012] OJ L 172/10.

[310] See Regulation (EU) 2015/2120 of the European Parliament and of the Council of 25 November 2015 laying down measures concerning open internet access and amending Directive 2002/22/EC on universal service and users' rights relating to electronic communications networks and services and Regulation (EU) No 531/2012 on roaming on public mobile communications networks within the Union [2015] OJ L 310/1.

[311] Regulation (EU) 2017/920 of the European Parliament and of the Council of 17 May 2017 amending Regulation (EU) No 531/2012 as regards rules for wholesale roaming markets [2017] OJ L 147/1.

[312] Regulation (EU) 2015/751 of the European Parliament and of the Council of 29 April 2015 on interchange fees for card-based payment transactions [2015] OJ L 123/1, Articles 3–4.

[313] Joined Cases C-403 & 429/08, *Football Association Premier League Ltd and Others v QC Leisure and Others and Karen Murphy v Media Protection Services Ltd* [2011] ECR I–9083.

publicans in the United Kingdom have begun to use foreign decoder cards, issued by a Greek broadcaster to subscribers resident in Greece, in order to access Premier League matches. The publicans bought a card and a decoder box from a dealer at prices lower than those of Sky, the holder of the broadcasting rights in the United Kingdom. The FAPL took the view that such activities undermined the exclusivity of the television broadcasting rights and the value of those rights, and sought to bring them to an end by means of legal proceedings, the national court seized, the High Court of Justice of England and Wales, referring to the CJEU a number of preliminary questions. The first case (C-403/08) concerned a civil action brought by the FAPL against pubs that have screened Premier League matches by using Greek decoder cards and against the suppliers of such decoder cards to those pubs. The second case (C-429/08) had arisen from criminal proceedings against Karen Murphy, the landlady of a pub that screened Premier League matches using a Greek decoder card.

The CJEU applied Article 56 TFEU (on the free movement of services) and competition law. With regard to the first set of EU law rules, it held that national legislation which prohibits the import, sale, or use of foreign decoder cards is contrary to the freedom to provide services and cannot be justified either in light of the objective of protecting intellectual property rights or by the objective of encouraging the public to attend football stadiums. The Court found that payment by the television stations of a premium in order to ensure themselves absolute territorial exclusivity goes beyond what is necessary to ensure the right holders appropriate remuneration, because such a practice may result in artificial price differences between the partitioned national markets. Such partitioning and such an artificial price difference are irreconcilable with the fundamental aim of the Treaty, which is completion of the Internal Market.

The Court also applied the competition law provisions of the Treaty, exploring whether licence agreements pursue an anti-competitive object where a programme content provider enters into a series of exclusive licences, each for the territory of one or more Member States, under which the broadcaster is licensed to broadcast the programme content only within that territory (including by satellite), and a contractual obligation is included in each licence requiring the broadcaster to prevent its satellite decoder cards which enable reception of the licensed programme content from being used outside the licensed territory.[314] The Court held that '[a]n agreement between a producer and a distributor which might tend to restore the national divisions in trade between Member States might be such as to frustrate the Treaty's objective of achieving the integration of national markets through the establishment of a single market', and that the agreement in question 'had the same effect as agreements to prevent or restrict parallel exports', to the extent that they led to absolute territorial protection and to 'a reciprocal compartmentalisation of licensed territories'.[315] It is noteworthy that the CJEU did not condemn the exclusive licences granted by the FAPL, but only what it regarded as the additional obligations on broadcasters not to supply decoding devices with a view to their use outside the territory covered by the licence agreement. This was done on the basis that these provisions '*prohibit broadcasters from effecting any cross-border provision of services*', '*granted absolute territorial exclusivity*', and eliminated '*all competition between broadcasters*'.[316]

Noting that 'conflicting assessments of the fundamental freedoms and competition law are to be avoided in principle', the CJEU examined the possibility for these restrictions to be justified under Article 101(3) TFEU.[317] In particular, the CJEU referred to the proportionality test which it applied for the free movement provisions part of the judgment. The Court did

[314] Ibid, para 245. [315] Ibid, paras 247–8. [316] Ibid, para 142 (emphases added).
[317] Ibid, para 249.

not accept the objective justifications put forward: that the restrictions had the objective of encouraging the public to attend football stadiums (in connection with the prohibition on broadcasting football matches in the UK during the Saturday afternoon 'close period'); and the objective of protecting intellectual property (or similar) rights, by ensuring that rights-holders are appropriately remunerated, remarking that these restrictions were not necessary in order to ensure appropriate remuneration for the rights-holders, as the rights-holder in this case was remunerated for the broadcasting of the protected subject-matter (in the country of origin). The 'premium' paid by rights-holders for absolute territorial protection was thus not necessary to ensure appropriate remuneration for exploitation of the rights, in particular as such absolute territorial exclusivity results in the partitioning of national markets and artificial price differences between markets, which is irreconcilable with the fundamental aims of the TFEU and the remuneration agreed between a rights-holder and broadcaster could be set so as take account of the potential audience in other Member States. It remains an open question as to how the CJEU's reasoning in respect of the broadcasting of football matches will be applied to other markets where digital rights are often licensed on a territorial basis (eg computer software, music, e-books, or films made available via the Internet, as envisaged by Advocate General Kokott in her Opinion in this judgment). It is also noteworthy that in its vertical restraints guidelines, the Commission acknowledges that in exceptional circumstances hardcore restrictions may be objectively necessary for an agreement of a particular type or nature and therefore fall outside Article 101(1) TFEU.[318]

In the specific case, the CJEU held, however, that the publican was still in breach of Article 3(1) of the Copyright Directive,[319] to the extent that the activity in question was profit-making and that the re-transmission in the UK amounted to a transmission to a new public, and therefore could not, on this basis, escape a finding of copyright infringement.[320] Hence, broadcasters can rely on their copyright to restrict cross border sales when this is done for profit to a new public of potential viewers, which could not have been considered by the authors when they authorised the broadcasting of their works,[321] and they can, in theory, impede consumers from having access to online content services when travelling outside their country of residence and want to continue to have access to services they have subscribed to (portability of online content services).[322] This issue has, however, been dealt with the recent regulation on cross-border portability of online content services, which although it does not challenge the territoriality of the licences, it assumes (*fictio iuris*) that the consumption of the online service

[318] EU Vertical Restraints Guidelines, para 60.

[319] Directive 2001/29/EC of the European Parliament and of the Council of 22 May 2001 on the harmonisation of certain aspects of copyright and related rights in the information society [2001] L 167/10 [hereinafter Copyright Directive].

[320] Joined Cases C-403 & 429/08 *Football Association Premier League Ltd and Others v QC Leisure and Others and Karen Murphy v Media Protection Services Ltd* [2011] ECR I–9083, paras 204–6. Hence, the copyright holder had a right to authorize and to require payment for the screenings by Ms Murphy and other publicans. On the follow-ups of this case in UK courts, see Craig Giles, 'Broadcasting: Post-*Murphy*: The Territorial TV Sports Licensing Landscape', Bird & Bird (15 July 2014), available at https://www.twobirds.com/en/news/articles/2014/global/broadcasting-post-murphy-the-territorial-tv-sports-licensing-landscape.

[321] Joined Cases C-403 & 429/08 *Football Association Premier League Ltd and Others v QC Leisure and Others and Karen Murphy v Media Protection Services Ltd* [2011] ECR I–9083, paras 198–9.

[322] See G Monti and G Coelho, 'Geo-Blocking: Between Competition Law and Regulation', CPI Antitrust Chronicle (17 January 2017), 1, 4, available at https://www.competitionpolicyinternational.com/geo-blocking-between-competition-law-and-regulation/ (noting that FAPL includes certain FAPL copyright logos on the broadcast image, thus bundling 'copyright-free' image with copyright-protected elements, so that anyone showing such a video is breaching that copyright).

is taking place in the country of residence of the subscriber (thus applying a country of origin principle in this context), with the aim to provide a '[s]eamless access throughout the Union to online content services that are lawfully provided to consumers in their Member State of residence.'[323]

The Commission has also recently taken enforcement action with regard to copyrighted work by opening an investigation of licensing arrangements between Sky UK and six major Hollywood film studios which contained restrictions affecting cross-border provision of pay-TV services.[324] A statement of objections was sent to Paramount, Sony, Twentieth Century Fox, Disney, NBC Universal, and Warner Bros, as well as Sky UK, alleging that certain of the content licensing agreements contained geo-blocking clauses that required Sky UK to block access to films to consumers outside the UK and Ireland through its online and satellite pay-TV services, and that granted absolute territorial exclusivity to Sky UK and eliminated competition between broadcasters, which infringed Article 101 TFEU. The Commission viewed the clauses requiring Sky UK to block access to films to consumers outside its licensed territory of the UK and Ireland, as restricting Sky UK's ability to accept unsolicited requests for its pay-TV services from consumers located in other Member States (passive sales). Furthermore, certain other contractual obligations in these film studios' agreements with Sky required them to prohibit or limit other broadcasters than Sky UK from responding to unsolicited requests from consumers residing and located inside Sky UK's licensed territory, thus preventing them from making their pay-TV services available in the UK and Ireland, which eliminated cross-border competition between pay-TV broadcasters and partitioned the Internal Market. The Commission found that such restrictions would constitute a restriction of competition by object. In April 2016, Paramount offered commitments to address the Commission's concerns, and the Commission adopted a commitment decision under Article 9 of Regulation 1/2003, making them binding.[325] These essentially removed the absolute territorial protection and the prohibitions of active and passive sales that had benefitted Sky UK. Interestingly, one of the commitments requires Sky UK to abstain from bringing an action before a court or tribunal for the violation of the obligation preventing or limiting passive and/or active sales in an existing licensing agreement.

323 Regulation (EU) 2017/1128 of the European Parliament and of the Council of 14 June 2017 on cross-border portability of online content services in the Internal Market [2017] OJ L 168/1, Recital 1. The Directive includes in its Article 3 an obligation of a provider of an online content service provided against payment of money to enable cross-border portability of online content services by providing to 'a subscriber who is temporarily present in a Member State to access and use the online content service in the same manner as in the Member State of residence, including by providing access to the same content, on the same range and number of devices, for the same number of users and with the same range of functionalities', without any additional charges, but with no similar quality requirements, unless otherwise agreed between the provider and the subscriber. According to Article 4 of the Directive, the provision of an online content service to a subscriber who is temporarily present in a Member State, as well as the access to and the use of that service by the subscriber, is deemed to occur solely in the subscriber's Member State of residence. Article 6 makes explicit the duty of cross-border portability of an online content service. According to Article 7 of the Directive, any contractual provision contrary to EU portability shall be unenforceable.

324 This competition enforcement action complemented the Commission's legislative actions modernizing EU copyright rules and reviewing the EU Satellite and Cable Directive so as to reduce the differences between national copyright regimes and allow for wider access to online content across the EU. See Council Directive 93/83/EEC of 27 September 1993 on the coordination of certain rules concerning copyright and rights related to copyright applicable to satellite broadcasting and cable retransmission [1993] OJ L 248/15 [hereinafter Cable and Satellite Directive].

325 *Cross border access to Pay TV Content* (Case AT 40.023) Commission Decision of 26 July 2016, press release available at europa.eu/rapid/press-release_IP-16-2645_en.htm.

These recent developments show that competition law enforcement activity complements the new legislative framework against geo-blocking and other forms of prohibited nationality or geographic discrimination, in particular as audio-visual services, including services the main feature of which is the provision of access to broadcasts of sports events provided on the basis of exclusive territorial licences, have been excluded from the scope of the Regulation on geo-blocking.[326]

2.4. THE POLITICAL AND IDEOLOGICAL CONTENT OF COMPETITION LAW

2.4.1. IS THERE SOMETHING LIKE A VALUE-FREE COMPETITION LAW?

The influence of the objective of market integration in EU competition law[327] shows the importance of normative principles and values in the enforcement of competition law rules in the EU. This mostly political goal may contrast with the more 'economics-based' model of competition law according to which 'economics should be the basis for competition law norms'.[328] The role of economics in enhancing policy convergence in this area among EU Member States, but also beyond has been duly highlighted.[329] Many competition law regimes make use of economic methodologies and policy frameworks put in place by the 'global profession' of economics.[330] Various soft law texts, guidelines, and best practices published by competition authorities aim to elevate economics' driven evidence-based decision-making at the rank of best practice at the global scale.[331]

Because economics exercises an important influence on the implementation (and also the design) of competition law, the latter has been transformed to some form of technocratic discipline.[332] The use of the term technocracy (which means the rule of the experts) in this context means that competition law relies on 'technologies of government', such as economics (but potentially also other 'policy sciences'[333]), which set limitations on governmental reason by separating the sphere of intervention of public authorities (the public order) from that of individual independence or autonomy in which government does not intervene (the civic order). In contrast to classic bureaucracies, which are structures performing merely tasks of execution of decisions made in the realm of politics, technocracies assume tasks of forecast, knowledge gathering/sharing, and communication with the public, and to a certain degree

326 Geo-blocking Regulation, Recital 6. According to Article 9 of the Regulation, the application of the prohibition of Article 4(1) to electronically supplied services the main feature of which is the provision of access to and use of copyright protected works or other protected subject matter will, however, be assessed in the first evaluation of the Regulation two years after its entry into force.

327 The title is partly inspired by R Pitofsky, 'The Political Content of Antitrust' (1979) 127 *U Pennsylvania L Rev* 1074.

328 DJ Gerber, 'Global Competition Law Convergence: Potential Roles for Economics' in T Eisenberg and DM Ramello (eds) *Comparative Law and Economics* (Edward Elgar, 2016), 213.

329 Ibid, 206–35.

330 M Fourcade, 'The Construction of a Global Profession: The Transnationalization of Economics' (2006) 112(1) *American J Sociology* 145.

331 See our discussion on the economics of competition law in Chapter 3.

332 DA Crane, 'Technocracy and Antitrust' (2008) 86 *Texas L Rev* 1159.

333 On the emergence of 'policy sciences', see HD Laswell, *A Pre-View of Policy Sciences* (Elsevier, 1971). These could be social, technical, or natural sciences.

substitute politics, or more generally the conflictual political process, with experts' consensus and an 'evidence-based' decision-making process.

The above distinction between politics (or policy), which is assumed to be value-oriented and therefore conflictual, and expertise based on science, which is alleged to be value-neutral, does not, however, stand critical scrutiny for various reasons. First, it is true that the philosophical movement of positivism perceives facts as the manifestation of the external world: 'facts in the concrete', which should be distinguished from abstract reasoning, the latter involving opinion. However, describing facts involves to a certain degree some selection and interpretation process. After all, we do not work on facts but on observations of facts (data) and inferences from these observations of facts. The values of the observant will inevitably introduce a certain degree of subjective judgment and abstract reasoning in this context, hence they will be influenced by the values of the observant. Second, more recent studies on the process of scientific discovery insist on the role of scientific practice instead of philosophical principles in understanding the domain of science, with the development of 'scientific paradigms', 'schools of thought', and intellectual 'networks'.[334] Scientific knowledge, as any other knowledge is being shaped in a complex social process:[335] even empirical findings are not valueless, but their meaning is not given and has to be negotiated among competent scientists (persons who are regarded competent by their peers) who may hold different interpretations of the same 'facts'.[336] Third, it is clear that economics is not unidimensional but that there is a methodological or assumptions-related pluralism in economic thought. The 2008 financial and economic crisis led many to challenge the assumptions of 'mainstream' economics and to put forward alternative 'heterodox' theoretical frameworks.[337]

334 For instance, starting with TS Kuhn, *The Structure of Scientific Revolutions* (University of Chicago Press, 2nd ed, 1970), some sociologists of science argue that it is possible that different 'paradigms' emerge and succeed in gradually shifting the current scientific consensus to another one. These 'revolutionary' theories may rely on a contested, from the current scientific consensus perspective, theoretical assumption, or methodology. Their success depends on the capacity of the new paradigm to provide satisfactory explanations for the anomalies the previously dominant paradigm was unable to explain. See also LE Johnson, 'Economic Paradigms: A Missing Dimension' [1983] 17 (4) *J Economic Issues* 1097. Others argue that it is important to understand scientists as being involved in 'trials of strength', at which their claims about the validity of their findings and the usefulness of their research has to withstand challenges made by competing colleagues. A successful trial means that the contribution 'was incorporated into an institutional set of practices', transforming their work to an obligatory passage point, that is, something that cannot be dispensed with (also called 'black box'). See B Latour, *Science in Action* (Harvard University Press, 1987); YP Yonay, *The Struggle over the Soul of Economics* (Princeton University Press, 1998). Of course, these views form part of a larger, richer literature spanning in the philosophy and sociology of social sciences and of scientific methodology in general.

335 See A Pickering (ed) *Science as Practice and Culture* (University of Chicago Press, 1992).

336 YP Yonay, *The Struggle over the Soul of Economics* (Princeton University Press, 1998), 15. Hence, it is not excluded that individual experts, a whole discipline, a sub-discipline, or a research group may be biased, for instance because of 'the exclusion or underrepresentation of certain viewpoints or standpoints within a discipline or expert community, or the economics or politics of the research community and the constant need of 'experts' to 'exaggerate the probativeness' of evidence that supports their findings, especially to outsiders': AI Goldman, 'Experts: Which Ones Should you Trust?' (2001) 63 *Philosophy and Phenomenological Research* 85, 104–5.

337 The economic crisis of 2008 led a number of people to question the usefulness of economic science, at least when it comes to its ability to make accurate predictions, not least, as it was reported, Queen Elisabeth II!: see Chris Giles, 'The Economic Forecasters' Failing Vision', *Financial Times* (15 December 2008), www.ft.com/content/50007754-ca35-11dd-93e5-000077b07658. This perceived failure of economics sparked initiatives like the Institute of New Economic Thinking (INET), www.ineteconomics.org/ or the recent manifesto of economics students to change their syllabus and criticizing the fact that economics ignore evidence from other disciplines: see eg Phillip Inman, 'Economics Students Call for Shakeup of the Way Their Subject is Taught', *The Guardian* (4 May 2014), available at www.theguardian.com/education/2014/may/04/

It is neither the first nor certainly the last time the fundamentals of economics have been questioned.

An illustration of this plurality is the different conceptions in economics on the concept of 'competition'. The concept of competition was the central ordering mechanism in Adam Smith,[338] as it tends to the equalization of wages rates and profits rates, thus leading the 'market price' to oscillate around the production price (also called 'natural price'), although remaining different from it. Among the reasons explaining the deviation of 'market prices' from 'natural prices' is the existence of artificial conditions in this market, such as monopoly power. The price is 'natural' in the sense that it is a price that would be set if competition were truly free. Competition thus helps to regulate actual profits over the long run. In the classical school of economics, founded by Adam Smith,[339] competition was thus perceived as a continuous struggle or antagonistic process between aggressive cost-cutting firms that invest in order to create techniques with lower production costs than their rivals and thus being able to set market prices, competition leading to the equalization of profits rates, that is the regulation of market prices by prices of production.

As we will explain in Chapter 3, this conception of competition was transformed by economists of the neoclassical school, which, attempting to measure the degree of competition, defined it by reference to an abstract ideal, that of the 'perfect competition' where all traders are assumed to be price-takers if certain ideal conditions in this 'perfect market' are satisfied, such as the number of rivals approaches infinity or that all traders have perfect knowledge of the conditions of demand and supply.[340] At the opposite of 'perfect competition' lies the model of 'perfect monopoly', relying on completely the opposite assumptions, and where firms are assumed to be price-setters. In contrast to the classical school, for which competition was denoting a dynamic process of rivalry between traders, the authors of the neoclassical school assumed that such disorder was temporary, part of an adjustment process by economic agents, and that at this end of this process there would be a state of rest (equilibrium) in which the particular market (partial equilibrium), or all markets (general equilibrium or Walrasian equilibrium), will be simultaneously in balance.[341] Anonymous market forces, or a super-agent, an exogenous benevolent auctioneer, provide the mechanism for altering price when demands and supplies do not balance. This approach assumes that individuals make optimal choices, to produce or to consume, on the basis of their marginal utilities, a concept we will explain in Chapter 3.

A different approach emerged in the 1930s, when economists departed from the model of perfect competition and that of perfect monopoly, which they thought did not adequately represent reality, for an approach that would relax the assumptions of the theory of perfect competition. These theories of 'imperfect competition' or 'monopolistic competition' showed that firms may benefit from some partial monopoly in a particular market, leading these

economics-students-overhaul-subject-teaching. There is a long literature on 'heterodox' economics and of their demarcation criterion from 'mainstream' economics. One view is that that 'mainstream' economics is 'axiomatized' and heavily 'mathematized', which often explains the narrowness or simplicity of its assumptions: BP Stigum, *Towards a Formal Science of Economics: the Axiomatic Method in Economics and Econometrics* (CUP, 1990); G Debreu, 'Theoretic Models: Mathematical Form and Economic Content' (1986) 54(6) *Econometrica* 1259; G Debreu, 'The Mathematization of Economic Theory' (1991) 81(1) *American Economic Rev* 1; T Lawson, 'The Nature of Heterodox Economics' (2006) 30(4) *Cambridge J Economics* 483.

338 A Smith, *An Inquiry into the Nature and Causes of the Wealth of Nations* (1776), bk I, ch 7.

339 Other members of the school include David Ricardo and Karl Marx.

340 The neoclassical school of economics relies on the mathematical analysis of competition by Augustin Cournot, in particular as developed further by S Jevons, L Walras, FY Edgeworth, and A Marshall. See our analysis in Chapter 3.

341 Partial equilibrium analysis was put forward by A Marshall and general equilibrium by L Walras.

economists to conclude that firms do not operate as price-takers but as price-setters, while also competing with other firms.[342] For the proponents of the 'imperfect competition' school, State intervention may be needed for instance in situations of market power which enable individual firms to set discriminatory prices, the market being managed back (or engineered) towards the conditions of the ideal of perfect competition.[343]

In the perfect competition model, all agents make decisions without considering any costs other than their own. Perfect competition may fail to account for these external costs of the transactions, these costs being incurred by other agents (externalities). These externalities may be considered as 'market failures', as the pursuit of private interest does not lead to an efficient use of society's resources, leading to the need for some form of collective action, such as State intervention in the market through regulation. According to another view, however, the problem is not the market, but the lack of a market for externalities that would enable the price system to clear these external costs. Ronald Coase has famously put forward the idea that if property rights are completely defined and if there are zero transaction costs in using the market system, then, the market outcome will efficiently internalize all externalities.[344] The Coase theorem, as it is known, may set limits to State intervention, markets being considered in certain circumstances, as a more efficient institution to take care of these externalities. This transaction costs approach has been used in order to explain the constitution of varieties of organizational structure, such as firms, or the use of long-term contracts for certain transactions, while for others making use of markets (the make or buy decision).[345]

The static approach of the perfect competition paradigm was criticized by Joseph Schumpeter fir not taking into account the market perturbations brought in by disruptive innovation.[346] Schumpeter did not question the essence of the perfect competition paradigm, as he simply argued that it might be temporarily suspended during these periods of change, before a new state of equilibrium emerges. Other authors, such as Hayek and the so-called Austrian school, rejected the concept of perfect competition, as well as that of equilibrium, as fictions based on invalid assumptions and put forward the idea that competition is a dynamic process where the entrepreneurs seek to exploit opportunities afforded by the disequilibrium of fast moving markets.[347] This view of competition was embedded in specific values or politics, as the development of neoclassical price theory, in particular the 'imperfect competition' tradition, and the concept of Walrasian equilibrium, had led to the perceived risk of intrusive State intervention in markets, or even the substitution of markets by a social planner (administered economy). Hayek developed his theories in opposition to the views of some neoclassical economists arguing for the superior efficiency of the administered economy in the so-called 'socialist calculation debate'.[348] Other authors took a more pragmatic perspective. While still adopting the analysis and tools of the neoclassical price theory, they substituted the benchmark of perfect competition with the more realistic one of 'workable competition'.[349]

342 See J Robinson, *The Economics of Imperfect Competition* (Macmillan, 1933); J Robinson, *The Economics of Imperfect Competition* (Macmillan, 1933).

343 See Chapter 3.

344 RH Coase, 'The Nature of the Firm' (1937) 16(4) *Economica* 386; RH Coase, 'The Problem of Social Cost' (1960) 3 *J L & Economics* 1.

345 O Williamson, *The Economic Institutions of Capitalism* (Free Press, 1985).

346 JA Schumpeter, *Capitalism, Socialism, and Democracy* (1942; Harper and Row, 3d ed, 1950), 1104–5.

347 See eg FA Hayek, *Individualism and Economic Order* (Routledge & Kegan, 1948), ch V.

348 For a discussion, see LH White, *The Clash of Economic Ideas* (CUP, 2012), ch 2.

349 JM Clark, 'Toward a Concept of Workable Competition' (1940) 30(2) *American Economic Rev* 241. This approach provides policy makers the discretion to determine through the use of economic theory and tools whether a market is workably competitive.

Beyond the value-oriented or value-colourful fundamentals of the economic inquiry, one may also put forward different conceptions of the relation between State intervention (also through competition law) and markets in modern capitalist economies. Classical liberalism conceived the role of the State as supportive of the principle of individual autonomy; its only precept was for the State not to intervene, with the exception of rules guaranteeing some minimum standards for an equitable exchange (eg absence of fraud and coercion in contracts). The Great Depression in the 1930s led to an expansion of the role of government and to some intense governmental intervention in the market so as to preserve society from perceived 'market failures', the idea being that markets may fail to perform in ways that best promote the larger interests of society.[350] During the same period, Keynesian economics legitimized more intrusive State intervention in markets, in particular during times of economic turmoil. This period of State intervention in markets was based on the ideal of 'democratic capitalism', that is, the view that the process of capitalistic accumulation through the operation of markets, should be governed by the democratic process, which can occasionally override market outcomes when these are not 'fair' or efficient in a wider sense, because they do not correspond to the preferences of citizens/voters (not just market actors).[351]

This consensus has been under attack by a number of neoliberal movements, in both Europe and the United States in the 1960s and after.[352] In the US, this has taken various forms. A number of authors based at the University of Chicago put forward the view that the legal system should mimic efficient markets, State action being subject to an economic efficiency filter before any intervention in markets. This view has been particularly influential in competition law, starting in the late 1970s, mostly in the US, although also to a lesser extent more recently in Europe (the so-called Chicago school of antitrust law and economics).[353] Others have put forward the view that diffused and large group interests (eg citizens) suffer from collective action problems, while smaller groups with common interests are more likely to capture policymakers, thus showing that State intervention in markets carries the risk of not promoting the public interest but the goals of powerful interest groups in what can be characterized as a theory of government failure (the public choice school).[354] Finally, one may note the ordoliberal version of neo-liberalism, which has been particularly influential in Europe, in particular in the area of competition law.[355] Born in Germany in the 1930s, ordoliberalism was opposed to any variant of planned State interventionism. Ordoliberal authors emphasized the risks of State management of the economy, thus adhering partly to the government failure theory but also to the idea that the distinction between the 'market' and the 'State' is intellectually sterile. They advanced instead market economy as the principle and model for the State, which should be organized on the basis of the principle of competition, perceived as a constitutional imperative.[356] Some members of the ordoliberal movement have taken

350 On the origins of the concept of market failure and its evolution, see the excellent special issue on Market Failure in Context 47 (Suppl No 1) *History of Political Economy* (2015).

351 On democratic capitalism, see eg M Novak, *The Spirit of Democratic Capitalism* (Madison Books, 1991); W Streeck, 'The Crises of Democratic Capitalism' (2011) 71 *New Left Rev* 5.

352 On neoliberalism, see eg DS Grewal and J Purdy, 'Law and Neoliberalism' (2015) 77 *L & Contemporary Problems* 1.

353 Prominent representatives of this school in antitrust are Judges Richard Posner and Frank Easterbrook.

354 On the public choice school, see DC Mueller, *Public Choice III* (CUP, 2003); FS McChesney and WF Shughart, *The Causes and Consequences of Antitrust: the Public Choice Perspective* (University of Chicago Press, 1995).

355 See W Möschel, 'Competition Policy from an Ordo Point of View' in A Peacock and H Willgerodt (eds) *German Neo-Liberals and the Social Market Economy*, vol 1 (MacMillan, 1989), 142; P Behrens, 'The "Consumer Choice" Paradigm in German Ordoliberalism and its Impact Upon EU Competition Law', Europa-Kolleg Hamburg, Discussion Paper No 1/14 (22 July 2014), available at ssrn.com/abstract=2568304

356 See W Eucken, *The Foundations of Economics: History and Theory in the Analysis of Economic Reality* (1950; Springer, 1992); A Peacock and H Willgerodt (eds) *German Neo-Liberals and the Social Market Economy*,

positions that would appear closer to the democratic capitalism perspective than to the other variants of neoliberalism, and have promoted a more 'holistic' perspective on the competitive process, beyond purely economic aims.[357]

This short bestiary of economic doctrines of relevance to competition law indicates the plurality of theoretical approaches and the importance of values or prior-beliefs on State intervention in economic inquiry.

2.4.2. THE CHANGING FACE OF COMPETITION IN THE DIGITAL AGE—A BUSINESS STRATEGY PERSPECTIVE

New technologies require important investments and fixed costs for their developments. This may lead to increasing returns to scale, the average cost of producing output being smaller at larger levels of output. From the demand side, consuming such technologies which often leads to network effects, as use of a product or service by any user increases the product's value for other users (sometimes even all users). In other words, the value of the product to one user is positively affected when another user joins and enlarges the network (positive network externalities or network effects).[358] Furthermore, an additional user of a search engine may increase the quality of search provided by this search engine, therefore benefitting all users, in view of the additional queries that this may direct to the search engine and consequently the increase in the stock of data/information the specific search engine disposes about users and their preferences which can help search engines to offer better search services to all consumers (learning by doing effects). These positive feedback loop mechanisms explain why these markets are tippy and are characterized by 'winner takes it all' competition. For instance, there might be fierce competition to conquer a market share advantage over rivals, with regard to the specific technology or standard applying in the industry, as the market may switch almost completely to the winner (competition for the market).[359]

Quite often, these products or services constitute a package of complementary products and technologies, which form a system competing with other systems ('systems competition').[360] The value of the product does not always depend directly on the number of adopters, but on the adoption of some complementary products that are bundled/packaged with the first product (think about a book reader and the content of the book). Network effects lead to collective switching costs and lock-in effects, which reduce competition and may entrench the dominant position of the winner for a significant period of time. Firms are quite imaginative in their business models, sometimes distributing the product for free in one side of the market, thus inducing more users to join the network and therefore increasing the value of the product for other users situated at the paying side of the market, the platform facilitating

vol 1 (MacMillan 1989); V J Vanberg, 'Freiburg School of Law and Economics' in P Newman (ed) *The New Palgrave: Dictionary of Economics and the Law* (Macmillan, 1998), 172.

357 See A Müller-Armack, 'The Social Market Economy as an Economic and Social Order' (1978) 36 *Rev Social Economy* 325.

358 This positive feedback loop may work in reverse and in case the technology/product fails to reach a critical mass of users, it may fall into a 'death spiral' and ultimately disappear: see H Varian, Use and Abuse of Network Effects (September 17, 2017). Available at SSRN: https://ssrn.com/abstract=3215488.

359 Usual examples include the videotape format war between VHS and Sony's BETAMAX, or the competition between Windows and Intel from one side and Apple from the other for the microcomputer market. For an analysis of competition in open and closed systems, see CMA and Autorité de la Concurrence, 'The Economics of Open and Closed Systems' (16 December 2014), available at http://www.autoritedelaconcurrence.fr/doc/economics_open_closed_systems.pdf.

360 ML Katz and C Shapiro, 'Systems Competition and Network Effects' (1994) 8(2) *J Economic Perspectives* 93.

the interaction between two different groups of customers (multi or two-sided market platforms).[361] They may also use various business practices, such as penetration pricing where they charge low prices (even below their costs) to gain market share, or strategically bundling their products so as to take hold of another market and then expand. In these markets, it is possible that firms may incur losses for a significant period of time in order to invest in acquiring market share (either through natural growth or by buying out actual or potential competitors through mergers and acquisitions) in order to constitute one stop shop solutions or essential platforms for various groups of customers.[362] Competition between firms takes unexpected forms, such as competing for consumers' attention (or eyeballs), eventually profiling them and using algorithms in order to predict and possibly manipulate their behaviour.[363] It has been alleged that now that the harvesting of a variety of personal data has enabled the digital platforms to dispose of the 'digital replicas' of our personalities, that is the 'digital representation of an individual, object, or asset' 'constructed based on an individual, object, or asset's interactions with its environment', they have access to various facets of their users' personality, for instance 'how they interact with a whole host of appliances and other objects in their homes', information that 'industrial-age firms' specializing in a specific industry might not be able, or even interested, in using in their marketing or for the design of their products.[364] Other authors have put forward the predictable evolution of the competitive struggle from the harvesting of data from users 'during earlier, consumer-oriented stages of development' in order to build artificial intelligence (AI) capacity; 'once built, this AI capacity can be lucratively rented out to governments and companies', competition thus moving to provision of AI services.[365] These developments thus require a renewal of the theoretical frameworks so far used by economics for traditional markets, as well as a clear understanding of business strategy, thus widening the sources of wisdom for competition law beyond neoclassical price theory economics.[366]

Similarly, one may criticize the relatively narrow perspective of the mainstream neoclassical price theory economics, which is based on methodological individualism, the idea that social action and the ensuing order are perceived as generated by objective economic interests of the individual actor, the latter behaving in an instrumental (rational) way in order to maximize his welfare. What is absent from such analysis is the role that social relations and social institutions play in the economy, the latter being considered as distinct configurations of interests and social relations. Work in political economy and economic sociology may provide the bigger picture we need in order to understand the full dimension of competitive interactions.

361 See our analysis in Chapter 3.

362 For an example of this strategy, see LM Khan, 'Amazon's Antitrust Paradox' (2017) 126(3) *Yale LJ* 564.

363 F Pasquale, *The Black Box Society: The Secret Algorithms That Control Money and Information* (Harvard University Press, 2015).

364 B Iyer, M Subramanian, and U Srinivasa Rangan, 'The Next Battle in Antitrust Will be About Whether One Company Knows Everything About You', *Harvard Business Rev* (6 July 2017). The authors note that access to the digital replicas of consumers will lead to 'new-age' monopolies. They explain that '[s]uch new-age monopolies may not be visible through traditional industry concentration measures, but they will wield tremendous influence over consumers. Their allure will be their ability to provide unprecedented personalization based on the information they hold. Yet with such personalization customers may be restricted to see only what the provider wants them to see.'

365 See E Morozov, 'Will Tech Giants Move on from the Internet, Now We've All Been Harvested?', *The Guardian* (28 January 2018).

366 On the importance, for instance, of other fields than economics see, among others, the special issues of the *Antitrust Bulletin* on 'Entrepreneurship and Antitrust' [2016, 61(4)] and on 'Antitrust as a Multi-disciplinary Field' [2014, 59(4)].

To give an example, the last two decades we have witnessed a profound shift in the global economy, as a result of the globalization of economic activity, from markets to global value chains, where 'the research, design, production, and retail of most products take place through coordinated chain components that stretch systemically across multiple—from a few to a few thousand—firms'.[367] These global value chains (GVCs) are characterized by their 'systemic, coordination-driven nature', as they rely on various systems of transnational governance and different sorts of linkages, some traditional such as contract law, others novel and relying on corporate law, property law, or some more informal mechanisms. GVCs are prevalent in the global economy, and cover according to some calculations two-thirds of global trade.[368]

Visualizing economic organization through the perspective of value chains is further justified by the fact that competition does not only take place in *product* markets (competition between products), as mainstream competition law assumes,[369] but also in *capital* markets ('competition between capitals'). Competition becomes a struggle to lower costs per unit of output with the aim to gain more profit and market share and thus raise the rate of return of the capital invested.[370] Some have also distinguished between *competition within an industry*, which forces individual producers to set prices that keep them in the game and compels them to lower costs so that they can compete effectively, thus leading to a turbulent equalization of selling prices but a dis-equalization of profit margin and profit rates, and *competition between industries*, the capital moving from one industry to another in search of higher profits, thus bringing about the equalization of profit rates between industries.[371] Financial markets play a crucial role in determining the market value of corporations, and consequently the compensation of their management, market valuation relying on the expectation of future profits, rather than on actual profits being made by the firm. This may explain a number of competitive strategies that would often not make sense if one only takes into account product competition. This dimension of competition may have significant effects on productivity, innovation and the share of labour.

If one is to fully understand the various competitive interactions between undertakings that lead them to develop specific strategies, there is need to take into account of both product competition and competition between capitals. The latter puts emphasis on the allocation of value between the various segments of the specific value chain. Focusing on GVCs re-emphasizes issues relating to the distribution of the total surplus value produced by the value chain, as well as on the competitive interactions between the various economic actors situated in different segments of the supply chain, for instance on who will have the higher rate of return and thus be able to attract new capital, what some authors called 'vertical competition', opposing it to 'horizontal competition' between firms situated in the same segment of the chain.[372] Economic sociologists have developed the GVC approach in order to provide

367 KB Sobel-Read, 'Global Value Chains: A Framework for Analysis' (2014) 5(3) *Transnat'l Legal Theory* 364.

368 OECD, WTO, and World Bank Group, 'Global Value Chains; Challenges, Opportunities and Implications for Policy' (19 July 2014), 13, available at www.oecd.org/tad/gvc_report_g20_july_2014.pdf. See also UNCTAD, *Global Value Chains: Investment and Trade for Development: World Investment Report 2013* (United Nations, 2013), available at unctad.org/en/PublicationsLibrary/wir2013_en.pdf.

369 Assessing competitive interactions in the context of enforcing Articles 101, 102 TFEU, or the merger regulation, requires the definition of the relevant product or service market, which 'includes products or services which are substitutable or sufficiently interchangeable with the product or service in question, not only in terms of their objective characteristics, by virtue of which they are particularly suitable for satisfying the constant needs of consumers, but also in terms of the conditions of competition and the structure of supply and demand on the market in question': see eg Case C-62/86, *AKZO v Commission* [1991] ECR I–3359, para 51.

370 A Shaikh, *Capitalism: Competition, Conflict, Crises* (OUP, 2016).

371 Ibid, 34.

372 RL Steiner, 'Intrabrand Competition—Stepchild of Antitrust' [1991] 36 *Antitrust Bulletin* 155 I Lianos, The Vertical Horizontal Dichotomy in Competition Law: Some Reflections with Regard to Dual Distribution

a theoretical framework enabling us to understand how the global division and integration of labour in the world economy has evolved over time and, more importantly, how the distribution of awards, from the total surplus value, is allocated between the various segments of the chain.[373]

The financialization movement, the increasing influence of global financial markets in the real economy, started in the early to mid-1970s and has since taken unprecedented proportions.[374] It has led to phenomenal leveraging, which has allegedly reduced the rate of return of working capital in relation to other forms of capital investment, such as lobbying, rent-seeking activities, or short-term investments in financial assets.[375] One should also take into account the level of development of capital markets as part of the overall economic context, when examining competitive strategies, for instance exploring if firms have multiple source of finance beyond traditional bank lending. Competition law may benefit from works in political economy and finance that could provide a more complete picture of competitive interactions in the global economy. We will explore in Chapter 3 the various forms of competitive advantage in the digital economy.

2.4.3. COMPETITION LAW AND GOVERNMENT INTERVENTION

Competition law is one among various tools for State intervention in markets, and its contours must be defined with regard to other forms of State intervention, such as regulation.[376] Governments intervene widely in markets to achieve various policy goals. Sometimes these policy goals align with one another and sometimes they conflict and require various trade-offs in policy responses, such as to pursue efficiency, to correct market failures, or to ensure equity and distributive justice.

The importance of the principle of competition in the EU Treaty explains why the current EU framework may impose some limits to drastic distortions of competition, such as government intervention through price controls, which have been considered by some Advocates General of the Court of Justice, as 'one of the most intrusive forms of intervention in the

and Private Labels, in A Ezrachi & U Bernitz, (eds.), Private Labels, Brands and Competition Policy (OUP, 2009) 161. See also, I Lianos, Global Food Value Chains and Competition Law - BRICS Draft Report (January 1, 2018). Available at SSRN: https://ssrn.com/abstract=3076160 (extending the concept of 'vertical competition' to situations beyond vertically related adjacent transactions to competition for the surplus value produced by the whole value chain). For a more detailed analysis of the way preserving vertical competition may become an important concern in the era of digitalization, see our discussion in Chapter 3.

373 See eg G Gereffi and M Korzeniewicz (eds) *Commodity Chains and Global Capitalism* (Praeger, 1994); G Gereffi, J Humphrey, and T Sturgeon, 'The Governance of Global Value Chains' (2005) 12(1) *Rev Int'l Political Economy* 78.

374 J Montgomerie and K Williams, 'Financialised Capitalism: After the Crisis and Beyond Neoliberalism' (2009) 13(2) *Competition & Change* 99. For a historical and explanatory analysis of the concept financialization, with regards to profitability, shareholder value and shifted incentives on innovation, see N van der Zwan, 'State of the Art: Making Sense of Financialisation' (2014) 12 *Socio-Economic Rev* 99.

375 J Bessen, 'Accounting for Rising Corporate Profits: Intangibles or Regulatory Rents?', Boston University School of Law, Law and Economics Research Paper No 16-18 (2016), available at ssrn.com/abstract=2778641; O Orhangazi, *Financialisation and the US Economy* (Edward Elgar, 2008) (showing that investment in financial assets crowds out investment in real assets, companies preferring to make investor pay outs through dividends or stock buybacks, rather than investing in R&D or in promoting productivity).

376 There is a massive literature on this distinction between competition and regulation, perceived as separate spheres but still in constant interaction with each other. We note some recent contributions in Europe: N Dunne, *Competition Law and Economic Regulation: Making and Managing Markets* (CUP, 2015); J Drexl and F DiPorto (eds) *Competition Law as Regulation* (Edward Elgar, 2015).

market' (or an 'extreme' form of intervention),[377] or, even more, the replacement of the market by a (State) monopoly. Even if, in recent decades, the pendulum has swung too far in favour of 'open markets' and 'free competition', the text of the Treaty remains flexible to accommodate well-reasoned concerns and well-defined policies pursuing other values and economic and social rights included in the EU Treaties and/or the Charter of Fundamental Rights. Other public interests may be taken into account in the EU Treaties: some of them may eventually override, under strict conditions, the rule of thumb in favour of open markets and free competition, such as national security,[378] while others may be taken into account in order to justify distortions of competition, although competition should not be entirely sacrificed.[379] Finally, one needs to keep in mind that the EU competition law provisions apply to 'undertakings', that is, entities exercising an 'economic activity' (see Chapter 4). Consequently, what does not constitute an 'economic activity' is not covered by the Internal Market and competition rules of the Treaty, thus providing further flexibility for government intervention. Article 345 TFEU also accepts that 'the Treaty shall in no way prejudice the rules in Member States governing the system of property ownership'.

Liberalization directives have been adopted in the case of electronic communications, post, rail, and energy markets to open up markets and encourage the emergence of competition.[380] Note, however, that liberalization, in the EU jargon, does not mean privatization or even for instance the break-up of national operators.[381] The main purpose of these provisions is not to privatize public utilities, but to ensure that there will be a single European market for these utility services, without denying the possibility to State-owned undertakings to perform public service obligations, the level of which will be defined by the Member State in question. In addition to the provisions opening the market and limiting the extent of the permissible monopoly/reserved sector, or in some limited cases abolishing a monopoly or reserved sector altogether,[382] the liberalization directives also include an EU regulatory framework which is to be applied by national regulatory authorities, in particular with the aim to impose regulatory obligations on undertakings that have significant market power. There are no liberalization directives with regard to water, which nevertheless remains, as all liberalized sectors, subject to the procurement[383] and transparency

377 Opinion of Advocate General Poiares Maduro in Case C-58/08 *Vodafone* EU:C:2009:596, paras 38 and 42.

378 Article 346 TFEU accepting that 'Member State may take such measures as it considers necessary for the protection of the essential interests of its security which are connected with the production of or trade in arms, munitions and war material'.

379 See, for instance, environmental protection: Commission Decision, *CECED* OJ [2000] L 187/47 (but this is a unique case so far).

380 For a complete list, see European Commission, Liberalisation, available at http://ec.europa.eu/competition/general/liberalisation_en.html.

381 For instance, the fourth rail package does not require that rail infrastructure and services are split into separate organizations and does not require that these are not State-owned. See European Commission, Fourth railway package of 2016, available at https://ec.europa.eu/transport/modes/rail/packages/2013_en. Although there have been proposals to include some ownership unbundling in the initial proposal, this was finally dropped. The ownership and the infrastructure can be under the same company, the only things that is required is that there is an independent infrastructure manager.

382 See Directive 2008/6/EC of the European Parliament and of the Council of 20 February 2008 amending Directive 97/67/EC with regard to the full accomplishment of the internal market of Community postal services [2008] OJ L 52/3.

383 See, in particular, Directive 2014/25/EU of the European Parliament and of the Council of 26 February 2014 on procurement by entities operating in the water, energy, transport and postal services sectors and repealing Directive 2004/17/EC [2014] OJ L 94/243; but see also Directive 2014/24 EU of the European Parliament and of the Council of 26 February 2014 on public procurement [2014] OJ L 94/65; Directive 2014/

directives.[384] Note that the liberalization directives should also be interpreted in conformity with primary EU competition law. However, as telecommunications and the postal and energy sectors have been harmonized at Union level, and objectives of general interest have already been taken into account in the liberalization directives,[385] the Member States' policy discretion is limited, and can be reviewed under a control of manifest error standard by the EU Courts.

The broader competition policy (which includes not only competition law but also other measures to address issues of competition in the economy) interfaces with State activity across many different levels of how government organizes economic behaviour. Government organizes economic activity in part through the shape and nature of regulation and overall State involvement. Understanding the distinction between competition law and policy clarifies competition authorities' capabilities and limitations when it comes to promoting competition in situations of a broader regulatory overlay. When considering the question of institutional design, how countries design optimal competition policy involves three choices: what to leave to the jurisdiction of competition law (and competition agencies and judges), what to assign to noncompetition authorities (such as sector regulators) exclusively as part of their jurisdiction, and how to establish concurrent jurisdiction among the competition authority and two or more regulatory authorities.

Government intervention may take different forms, depending on the policy area and the dimension of government action with the preservation of some form of market competition.[386] For example, governments may intervene as market makers: they might decide to use competitive tendering to introduce competition for goods and services that were previously supplied solely by the public sector; they might introduce more choice in the provision of public services by opening access to private or voluntary sector providers; or they might make tradable permits accessible in such a way as to most efficiently allocate among private providers the costs of engaging in an activity that is harmful to society. The State may operate to create or facilitate markets, or in some cases to act as a market participant. Governments can affect markets through direct participation as a supplier to provide public goods and services that free markets are unlikely to supply at an adequate level. Governments also act as significant buyers of goods and services from the private sector to deliver public services and perform their normal functions. In dispensing public services, the government may establish a State-owned enterprise (SOE) or a public–private partnership (a relatively recent phenomenon), or it may decide to procure services through a competitive tendering process. Alternatively, the State may act as a deregulator in which it removes regulation to unleash market forces within various parts of the economy. A possible way of intervention in the economy by the State is through State Owned Enterprises. These are generally subject to Article 106 TFEU (succinctly examined in Chapter 1).

Governments may intervene indirectly by influencing private markets when they create either negative or positive impacts on consumer or total welfare. In this case, command and

23/EU of the European Parliament and of the Council of 26 February 2014 on the award of concession contracts [2014] OJ L 94/1.

384 Commission Directive 2006/111/EC of 16 November 2006 on the transparency of financial relations between Member States and public undertakings as well as on financial transparency within certain undertakings [2006] OJ L 318/17.

385 Case C-206/98, *Commission of the European Communities v Kingdom of Belgium*, ECLI:EU:C:2000:256, para 45.

386 For an introduction to the interaction between competition and government action, see T Cheng, I Lianos, and D Sokol, *Competition and the State* (Stanford University Press, 2014).

control regulation or more market-based incentive forms of regulation might be other venues for taxes and subsidies to influence the incentives and behaviours of private firms. Sometimes, governments deliberately try to influence consumer behaviours in a variety of ways—for example, by providing information on hidden costs associated with certain types of consumption (eg advertising campaigns against tobacco or alcohol), or by nudging consumers to adopt a behaviour that will protect their self-interest. They might also attempt to indirectly influence businesses by coordinating private-sector activities to generate the appropriate amount of information for the adoption of public policies or by promoting self-regulation by business, as this generally saves implementation costs. In some situations, government intervention may be the by-product of corruption, may be captured by special interests, or it may be following the right objectives but be badly designed—what is called 'government failure'. In this case, it will be, in general, welfare reducing. In other instances, however, government intervention is justified by legitimate public interest objectives. Of course, it is not the aim of competition law to correct any form of government failure if that failure does not impact the competitive process. Competition law may supplement other areas of law in an effort to improve government action and increase efficiency. Yet, the role of competition law is also relevant in the context of legitimate State action, depending on the forms that the latter may take, some of which may affect the competitive process more than others.

Conflicts between competition law and regulation may be direct, if regulation affects the core parameters of competitive markets by restricting competition on price, entry and quantity, as it is often the case for economic regulation, or lateral, in case these core dimensions of competition are not directly targeted, but regulation may nevertheless indirectly affect them, as it may be the case in situations of social or technical regulation. Economic regulation denotes the government intervention in a sector to correct a market failure arising from, for example, a natural monopoly (telecom, energy) or asymmetric information. It acts *a priori*, requires continuous monitoring and is intrusive in management. In contrast, competition law consists in a set of rules for market operation that prevents and sanctions abuses of market power, across all sectors. It acts *a posteriori*, once behaviour has been observed and relies mostly on the dissuasive power of sanctions. From this perspective, it is a less intrusive tool for market management in comparison to regulation.

Economic regulation's role is complementary to competition law since regulation controls monopolies that would never function efficiently under competition, its main function being to adopt measures that can control monopoly pricing. By ensuring non-discriminatory access to necessary inputs, for example network infrastructure, economic regulation may also facilitate competition in markets, thus enabling a greater scope of intervention for competition law. The less the regulatory regime interferes with the workings of the market, the more room for competition law. Expanded confidence in competition and markets may lead some previously regulated sectors to towards a specific competition law regime, taking into account the specificities of the economic sector, and even leading to the application of general competition law rules. This movement across the regulation/competition continuum may be observed in various sectors, such as airlines, maritime transports, telecoms.

However, regulation may also be substitutable to competition law, as experience has shown that when markets or segments of network industries become competitive then sector-specific regulation is often substituted by competition law. Indeed, this may happen when the interaction of competition law and regulation could prove problematic, in particular if the regulatory regime aims to control prices, restrict entry, give incumbents a competitive advantage, or requires or permits some practice that competition law prohibits. Note that price or entry regulation by Member States may be subject to EU competition law, under a joint application of Articles 4(3) TEU and 101/102 TFEU (see Chapter 1).[387] Risks of substantive conflict may be exacerbated if different institutions are in charge of competition law enforcement from those in charge of regulating the specific economic sector.[388] The rules regulating the interaction between competition law and regulation are briefly examined in the companion volume on Enforcement and Procedure.[389] In a nutshell, EU Competition law accepts the cumulative application of competition law and economic regulation. *Ex ante* regulation by a National Regulatory Authority does not prevent the *ex post* intervention on the basis of EU competition rules.[390]

In conclusion, the balance between State intervention (either in the form of competition law enforcement or regulation) and markets will depend on the dominant perception of the moment with regard to the likelihood of market failure vis-à-vis governmental failure and on the policy space that is left by EU law (primary and secondary) to Member States for government intervention.

Periods favouring government intervention in markets may be followed by periods limiting government intervention. For instance, the British experience on the interaction of government with the competition principle in socially sensitive sectors, such as healthcare, has changed through time. The monolithic welfare State that emerged from the Beveridge plan in the 1950s and 1960s was subject to the neoliberal cure of liberalization and privatization during the Thatcher era in the 1980s and to 'third way' management in the 1990s and 2000s. A key objective of New Public Management was to achieve a 'post-bureaucratic' government, where the introduction of purchaser/provider separation, the creation of quasi-markets, outsourcing and user control would allow multiple forms of provision to be developed in order to create more competition amongst potential providers.[391] The UK Government's White book *Open Public Services* published in 2011, and subsequent legislation adopted or in preparation also aim to introduce consumer choice and competition in the provision of services by opening public services to a range of providers, not only from the public sector, but also coming from the voluntary and private sector.[392] The White Book went as far as to declare that '[a] part from those public services where the Government has a special reason to operate a monopoly (e.g. the military) every public service should be open so that, in line with people's demands, services can be delivered by a diverse range of providers'. This was to be achieved by having suppliers from the private and voluntary sectors entering the public procurement process, providers competing with one

387 On price regulation and EU competition law in general, see AD Macculloch, 'State Intervention in Pricing: An Intersection of EU Free Movement and Competition Law' (2017) 42(2) *European L Rev* 190; A Andreangelli, 'Making Markets Work in the Public Interest: Combating Hazardous Alcohol Consumption through Minimum Pricing Rules in Scotland' (2017) 36(1) *Yearbook of European L* 522; N Dunne, 'Price Regulation in the Social Market Economy' LSE Legal Studies Working Paper No 3/2017 (21 February 2017), repr as N Dunne, 'Regulating Prices in the European Union' Yearbook of European Law (forthcoming), available at https://doi.org/10.1093/yel/yey002.

388 This may be the case in the EU, as the Commission and a network of national competition authorities are in charge of competition law enforcement but national regulatory authorities (NRAs) are in charge of regulation. In the UK, the risk of conflict is mitigated by the fact that sector-specific regulators have concurrent enforcement powers with regard to competition law enforcement in their respective economic sector of responsibility.

389 I Lianos, *Competition Law Enforcement and Procedure* (OUP, forthcoming 2019).

390 See Case C-280/08, *Deutsche Telekom AG v Commission* [2010] ECR I–9555; Case C-295/12, *Telefónica SA and Telefónica de España SAU v Commission*, ECLI:EU:C:2014:2062. For a more detailed analysis, see G Monti, 'Managing the Intersection of Utilities Regulation and EC Competition Law' (2008) 4(2) *Competition L Rev* 123; J Tapia and D Mantzari, 'The Regulation/Competition Interaction' in I Lianos and D Geradin (eds) *Handbook on European Competition Law: Substantive Aspects* (Edward-Elgar, 2013), 588. Concerning UK competition law, see G Monti, 'Utilities Regulators and the Competition Act 1998' in B Rodger (ed) *Ten Years of UK Competition Law Reform* (Dundee University Press, 2010), 139.

391 K Kernaghan, 'The Post-bureaucratic Organization and Public Service Values' (2000) 66(1) *Int'l Rev Administrative Sciences* 91.

392 HM Government, Open Public Services—White Paper, July 2011.

another to deliver services directly to individuals armed with personal budgets and entitlements or the power of choice and the full development of a voluntary, community, and social enterprise (VCSE) sector, accountable to local communities and thus to democratic electoral competition.[393] These reforms indicate that the provision of most government services in the UK would be organized according to the principle of free competition, thus opening space for the intervention of competition law, albeit a different kind of competition law, as competition on price is limited, or there is only competition on non-price dimensions, and is mostly taking place in 'quasi-markets', rather than conventional markets.[394] These 'quasi-markets' replace monopolistic State providers with competitive independents ones, and to the difference of conventional markets, on the supply side, the providers competing with each other do not necessarily aim to maximize profits, nor are they privately owned and on the demand side, purchasing decisions are not made by the consumers, but by a third party, in some cases a State authority, acting as an intermediary.[395] Calls for government's 'competitive neutrality',[396] that is that there is no discrimination between public and private providers of these services, constitute another dimension of the integration of the principle of competition in the provision of 'public' services. A political change may nevertheless change the tide in favour of greater government intervention in the economy, through a more active competition law enforcement, regulation, or State ownership.

The situation is more complex with regard to social and technical regulation, which for instance sets and monitors standards to ensure compatibility between various products, to address privacy, or safety and environmental concerns. One may distinguish between situations of lateral conflict which may occur because competition law enforcement can jeopardize the aims followed by these various regulatory tools, from what we can call situations of regulatory osmosis, that is, the absorption of regulatory aims in the enforcement of competition law. This process may occur as a result of the pressure to interpret and enforce competition law principles in congruence to the aims and the structure of the entire legal system to which competition law is integrated. It is we think uncontroversial to argue that a competition authority or a judge enforcing competition law should strive to interpret the law in accordance to the broader moral and legal principles undergirding the legal system.

One may distinguish two broad situations here. First, it is possible that competition law includes among its own objectives the consideration of public policy (as this is for instance the case with the public interest test in UK merger control or with the possibility for national governments to intervene in mergers that would otherwise be considered by the European Commission, specifically under Article 21(4) of the ECMR), or that sector-specific regulators that have concurrent jurisdiction to apply competition law may have more than one aims in their mission statement and they often need to take into account and satisfy all these objectives. In the EU context, the interaction between competition law and public policies pursued by mostly national regulation is particularly complex.[397] Second, even if one does not integrate these concerns as 'objectives' to be followed by the competition authority, one needs to 'take into account' the broader principles of the legal system when interpreting the law, focusing on the way these are transcribed in its legal and institutional context, in particular for areas like competition law, where the legal rules do not provide much detail

393 Ibid, 39–49. 394 J Le Grand, 'Quasi-Markets and Social Policy' (1991) 101 *Economic J* 1256.

395 The application of competition law to the healthcare sector, as well as in higher education, has led to numerous official publications and legislative developments, which it is not of course possible to explore in this book in detail. See Health and Social Care Act 2012; National Health Service (Procurement, Patient Choice and Competition) (No 2) Regulations 2013; Monitor, Substantive guidance on the Procurement, Patient Choice and Competition Regulations (December 2013); OFT1529, Higher Education in England (March 2014).

396 See OFT1242, Competition in mixed markets: Ensuring competitive neutrality (July 2010).

397 See our analysis in Section 2.2.1.2.

on the way one should interpret them, and statutory interpretation plays an important role. For instance, one may argue that interpreting the concept of undertaking and agreement in Article 101 TFEU as prohibiting trade unions, because these will be setting wages and operate as a cartel, is certainly not compatible within the context of the EU treaty, in view of other provisions of the EU treaty emphasising the importance of collective bargaining and consequently the role of trade unions in this context.[398] Hence, one may distinguish between various degrees of the 'duty' to take into account public interest concerns followed by social and technical regulation. A strong and extensive in scope duty if these are listed among the objectives of competition law or in the mission statement of regulators enforcing competition law, which means that the decision-maker should maximize all the objectives or to the extent there is some hierarchy between them prioritize some objectives. A weaker one, in all other circumstances, when these objectives must be taken to a certain degree into account so that the legal system does not create conflicting demands from economic actors, and, more broadly, the integrity of the legal system does not suffer.

2.4.4. CASE STUDY: COMPETITION LAW, BIG DATA/ ALGORITHMS, AND DATA PROTECTION/PRIVACY

The recent controversy on the intersection of competition law with the protection of privacy, following the emergence of big data and social media, may provide an interesting case study. The concept of 'big data' is usually employed to refer to gigantic digital datasets, which are often held by corporations, governments and other large organizations, and which are extensively analysed using computer algorithms.[399] Breaches of privacy or data protection may affect millions of people and, depending on the purpose, even compromise the democratic process.[400] The EU, as well as EU Member States, value privacy[401] and have established an elaborate system of data protection.[402]

398 See our analysis of Case C-67/96, *Albany International BV v Stichting Bedrijfspensioenfonds Textielindustrie* [1999] ECR I–5751 in Chapter 4.

399 'Aspects of "big data" that are often mentioned are large amounts of different types of data, produced at high speed from multiple sources, whose handling and analysis require new and more powerful processors and algorithms': Autorité de la Concurrence & Bundeskartellamt, Competition Law and Data (16 May 2016), 4. 'Big data' is often characterized by the various 'V's, which go from four, according to certain descriptions, *velocity, variety, volume*, and *value* (to be extracted) to six, according to others, adding *veracity* and *validation*.

400 See the recent controversy concerning the use of Facebook generated data from Cambridge Analytica, a political strategy firm, for uses for which Facebook's clients had not provided their consent, in particular in order to design algorithms that enabled Cambridge Analytical to build a system that could profile individual voters in the 2016 Brexit referendum, as well as the 2016 US Presidential election, in order to target them with personalised political advertisements and influence their votes. See C Cadwalladr and E Graham-Harrison, 'Revealed: 50 Million Facebook Profiles Harvested for Cambridge Analytica in Major Data Breach', *The Guardian* (17 March 2018), available at https://www.theguardian.com/news/2018/mar/17/cambridge-analytica-facebook-influence-us-election; M Scott, 'Cambridge Analytica Helped "Cheat" Brexit Vote and US Election, Claims Whistleblower', Politico (27 March 2018), available at https://www.politico.eu/article/cambridge-analytica-chris-wylie-brexit-trump-britain-data-protection-privacy-facebook/.

401 Article 7 of the Charter of Fundamental Rights lays down the right to respect for private and family life, home and communications, protecting the individual primarily against interference by the State.

402 Article 8 of the Charter of Fundamental Rights recognizes the protection of personal data as a separate right, which goes beyond simply protecting against interference by the State, but entitles the individual to expect that his or her information will only be processed, by anyone, if this processing is fair and lawful and for specified purposes, that it is transparent to the individual who is entitled to access and rectification of his/her information. The rights must also be subject to control by an independent authority. Article 16 TFEU requires rules to be laid down relating to data protection and to the free movement of such data in the internal market. The EU has adopted General Data Protection Regulation (EU) 2016/679 on the protection of natural persons

In recent years, the digital sector has attracted the attention of competition authorities and regulators involved in data protection.[403] Competition authorities have also looked to these questions when exploring the changes brought by platform competition.[404] Competition authorities have commissioned reports exploring the necessary changes to be brought to competition law enforcement in order to take into account the emergence of digital platforms and competition in the digital era.[405] Various issues have been identified.

First, was the need for merger control to take into account the fact that access to personal data may constitute an important source of market power.[406] In its decision in the *Google/DoubleClick* merger, the Commission examined if mere combination of DoubleClick's assets with Google's assets, and in particular the combination of customer data (generated by the use of Internet) obtained by both of them, would allow the merged entity to achieve an important competitive advantage 'that could not be replicated by its integrated competitors (mainly Yahoo! and Microsoft)' or competitors in the various segments of the product markets affected.[407] The Commission found that such combination of data 'using information about users' IP addresses, cookie IDs and connection times to correctly match records from both databases, could result in individual users' search histories being linked to the same users' past surfing behaviour on the internet', and would provide the new entity the possibility to better target ads to users.[408] The Commission held that 'data about users' web surfing behaviour was already available to a number of Google's competitors and that, in any case, DoubleClick did not have the ability or the incentive to stop being a neutral service provider, as its consumers would have switched to other providers. In conclusion, it was found that this combination of data would not have conferred on the merged entity a competitive advantage that could not be matched by its competitors.[409]

In *Facebook/WhatsApp*, a possible theory of harm explored by the Commission was that 'the merged entity could start collecting data from WhatsApp users with a view to improving the accuracy of the targeted ads served on Facebook's social networking platform to WhatsApp users that are also Facebook users,[410] thus strengthening Facebook's position in the provision of online advertising services as a result of the increased amount of data which

with regard to the processing of personal data and on the free movement of such data [2016] OJ L 119/1, which applies from 25 May 2018. Its scope is significant and wide-ranging. For a commentary, see O Lysnkey, 'The "Europeanisation" of Data Protection Law' (2017) 17 *Cambridge Yearbook of European Legal Studies* 252.

403 See European Data Protection Supervisor, Privacy and competitiveness in the age of big data: The interplay between data protection, competition law and consumer protection in the Digital Economy (March 2014); Autorité de la Concurrence & Bundeskartellamt, Competition Law and Data (16 May 2016); US FTC, Big Data—A Tool for Inclusion or Exclusion? (January 2016) and the references included.

404 European Commission, Online Platforms and the Digital Single Market Opportunities and Challenges for Europe, COM/2016/0288 final; House of Lords, Online Platforms and the Digital Single Market, HL Paper 129 (2016); OECD, Big Data: Bringing Competition Policy to the Digital Era, DAF/COMP(2016)14.

405 In the EU, the European Commissioner for Competition Margrethe Vestager appointed in March 2018 three special advisers, professors Heike Schweitzer, Jacques Crémer and Assistant Professor Yves-Alexandre de Montjoye to prepare a report on future challenges of digitisation for competition policy. The report was published in April 2019: see, Jacques Crémer Yves-Alexandre de Montjoye Heike Schweitzer, Competition Policy for the Digital Era (Directorate General for Competition, April 2019), available at http://ec.europa.eu/competition/publications/reports/kd0419345enn.pdf. In the UK, the Chancellor of the Exchequer established in August 2018 an expert panel chaired by former US President Barack Obama's chief economic advisor, Professor Jason Furman, which issued a report, published in March 2019, on the state of competition in digital markets with suggestions on competition law reform see, Digital Competition Expert Panel (Jason Furman review), Unlocking Digital Competition (March 2019), available at https://assets.publishing.service.gov.uk/government/uploads/system/uploads/attachment_data/file/785547/unlocking_digital_competition_furman_review_web.pdf.

406 See M Stucke and A Grunes, Big Data and Competition Policy (OUP, 2016), chs 6–8.

407 *Google/DoubleClick* (Case No COMP/M.473) C(2008) 927 final, para 359.

408 Ibid, para 360.

409 Ibid, para 366.

410 *Facebook/Whatsapp* (Case No COMP/M.7217) C(2014) 7239 final, para 180.

will come under Facebook's control.[411] However, the Commission found no concern with regard to the strengthening of Google's position in the online advertising service market, as there was a sufficient number of alternative providers of online advertising services and a significant number of market participants that collected user data alongside Facebook, not least Google. This left a large amount of Internet user data that are valuable for advertising purposes outside Facebook's exclusive control.[412]

In *Microsoft/LinkedIn*, the Commission raised two types of concerns relating to data combination.[413] One of the theories of harm was that the merged entity could integrate LinkedIn into Microsoft Office and thus combine, to the extent allowed by contract and applicable privacy laws, LinkedIn's and Microsoft's user databases, giving Microsoft's the possibility to shut out its competitors in the customer relationship management market. In particular, Microsoft could deny its competitors access to the full LinkedIn database, and thus prevent them from developing advanced customer relationship management functionalities also through machine learning. The Commission was not, however, convinced that access to the full LinkedIn database was essential to compete on the market, and held that LinkedIn's product was not a 'must-have' solution.[414]

The second theory of harm was more directly concerned with data concentration and its effects on online advertising services. The Commission explored how the regulatory framework in the EU relating to data protection could mitigate some of the competition law concerns:

> [177] As a preliminary remark, it should be noted that any such data combination could only be implemented by the merged entity to the extent it is allowed by applicable data protection rules. In this respect, the Commission notes that, today, Microsoft and LinkedIn are subject to relevant national data protection rules with respect to the collection, processing, storage and usage of personal data, which, subject to certain exceptions, limit their ability to process the dataset they maintain. Currently, the data protection rules of the EU Member State(s) where Microsoft and LinkedIn have their registered seat and/or where they have subsidiaries processing data apply. [. . .]
>
> [178] Moreover, the Commission notes that the newly adopted General Data Protection Regulation ('GDPR')[415] [. . .] provides for a harmonised and high level of protection of personal data and fully regulates the processing of personal data in the EU, including inter alia the collection, use of, access to and portability of personal data as well as the possibilities to transmit or to transfer personal data. This may further limit Microsoft's ability to have access and to process its users' personal data in the future since the new rules will strengthen the existing rights and empowering individuals with more control over their personal data (i.e. easier access to personal data; right to data portability; etc.).[416]

In view of the GDPR, the Commission found that it was not likely that LinkedIn data could become in the next two to three years an important input in this market and that in any case, LinkedIn's privacy policy allowed it to share the personal data it collects, processes, stores and uses with third parties.[417] Higher concentration of data could nevertheless

[411] Ibid, para 184. [412] Ibid, para 189. [413] Ibid, para 400. [414] Ibid, para 277.

[415] General Data Protection Regulation (EU) 2016/679 the protection of natural persons with regard to the processing of personal data and on the free movement of such data [2016] OJ L 119/1.

[416] *Facebook/Whatsapp* (Case COMP/M.7217) Competition Decision C(2014) 7239 final, paras 177–8.

[417] Ibid, para 255.

have a potential impact to competition. The Commission found that the merger could lead to the marginalization of XING, a competitor of LinkedIn which offered a greater degree of privacy protection to users than LinkedIn (or making the entry of any such competitor more difficult), therefore restricting 'consumer choice in relation to this important parameter of competition'.[418] To address the competition concerns identified by the Commission in the professional social network services market, Microsoft offered a series of commitments, which the Commission found to address the competition concerns identified and therefore conditionally cleared the merger. This case offers the possibility to conceptualize privacy as a parameter of competition that may eventually be subject to measurement.[419]

Second, beyond merger control, there are various competition law issues that may arise out of the control of an essential bottleneck for competition without this being adequately mapped by the traditional approaches followed in competition law, for instance market definition.[420] Big data may also constitute a barrier to entry, which can be used strategically in order to exclude competitors and competition in various markets for which data constitutes an essential input.[421] Although there have not been any exclusionary antitrust cases with regard to the exclusionary potential of big data related conduct by competition authorities in Europe, this eventuality should not be excluded.[422]

Third, big data and algorithms may facilitate collusion, firms delegating pricing decisions to 'intelligent' computer algorithms that may facilitate the conclusion of 'digital cartels' to the detriment of consumers, both in terms of price and privacy protection (should algorithms facilitate the monitoring of a cartel by identifying if some consumers have benefited from discounts).[423]

Furthermore, it is possible that privacy breaches, discrimination and exploitative contracts may be facilitated by control of big data, companies interchanging individualized offers on the basis of the information they acquire on individuals' willingness to pay through their past browsing history or other personalising factors, thus leading to different prices charged to various customers for homogeneous products (online personalized pricing).[424]

418 Ibid, para 350. Indeed, the Commission had found that privacy was an important parameter of competition and driver of customer choice in the market for professional social networking services.

419 K Bania, 'The Role of Consumer Data in the Enforcement of EU Competition Law' (2018) 1 *European Competition J* 38; E Deutscher, 'How to Measure Privacy-Related Consumer Harm in Merger Analysis? A Critical Reassessment of the EU Commission's Merger Control in Data-Driven Markets', Faculty of Law, Stockholm University Research Paper No 40 (2017), available at https://ssrn.com/abstract=3075200.

420 I Graef, 'Market Definition and Market Power in Data: The Case of Online Platforms' (2015) 38(4) *World Competition* 473.

421 DL Rubinfeld and M Gal, 'Access Barriers to Big Data' (2017) 59 *Arizona L Rev* 339.

422 Autorité de la Concurrence and Bundeskartellamt, 'Competition Law and Data' (16 May 2016), 17–20.

423 See A Ezrachi and ME Stucke, 'Artificial Intelligence and Collusion: When Computers Inhibit Competition', Oxford Legal Studies Research Paper No 18/2015, University of Tennessee Legal Studies Research Paper No 267 (2015); SK Mehra, 'Antitrust and the Robo-Seller: Competition in the Time of Algorithms' (2016) 100 *Minnesota L Rev* 1323. This topic is explored in more detail in Chapters 5 and 12.

424 Autorité de la Concurrence & Bundeskartellamt, Competition Law and Data (16 May 2016), 21–2. See also A Acquisti and HR Varian, 'Conditioning Prices on Purchase History' (2005) 24(3) *Marketing Science* 367; OFT1489, *Personalised Pricing* (May 2013), finding also evidence of search discrimination, targeted discounting and dynamic pricing (use fluctuations in demand to change the prices of products depending on availability); A Ezrachi and M Stucke, 'The Rise of Behavioural Discrimination' (2016) 37 *European Competition L Rev* 484; A Ezrachi and M Stucke, *Virtual Competition* (Harvard University Press, 2016), ch 12; M Bourreau et al, 'Big Data and Competition Policy: Market Power, Personalised Pricing and Advertising', CERRE Project Report (February 2017).

Certain competition authorities have also opened investigations exploring the possibility that these practices may represent an abusive imposition of unfair conditions on users.[425]

These practices raise the question of the interaction between competition law and other social and technical regulatory regimes protecting consumers or personal data.[426] In *Asnef-Equifax*, the CJEU stated that 'any possible issues relating to the sensitivity of personal data are not, as such, a matter for competition law, they may be resolved on the basis of the relevant provisions governing data protection'.[427] However, in *Allianz Hungária*, the CJEU also held that frustrating the objectives pursued by another set of national rules may be taken into account in the consideration of the economic and legal context when assessing a restriction of competition.[428] In *Astra Zenecca*, the CJEU found that misleading representations to the patent office, a possible regulatory offence, could constitute abusive conduct if it was part of an overall strategy of a dominant undertaking seeking to unlawfully exclude rivals.[429] One may indeed argue that the existence of strict regulatory rules limiting the use of personal data in the context of consumer protection or privacy regulation, indicates that personal data should be seen as a scarce resource as there are clear limits set by the regulatory environment on the collection, aggregation and use of these data. Consequently, companies having access to high quality personal data may be found to control a bottleneck. It is also possible to argue that because of this regulatory environment the protection of privacy should be considered, from a normative perspective, as forming part of the welfare function of consumers, even if their revealed preferences do not provide a solid evidence for this finding, on the basis of an objective list approach,[430] or on behavioural economics' grounds.[431] This may open up the possibilities of intervention of competition authorities, should they prove deception or manipulation by a dominant undertaking controlling access to essential data, for instance the fact that consumers have not provided their explicit concern for the specific use of their personal data. Taking a social contract perspective, it is also possible to consider that the consumer is also a citizen that values plurality of views and information in a democratic society built on the principle of democratic capitalism, that is, a pluralistic social system based on a differentiation of society into various non-overlapping and autonomous 'power centres', 'spheres of justice', or 'orders of worth'.[432]

425 The German Bundeskartellamt opened in March 2016 proceedings against Facebook on suspicion of having abused its market power by infringing data protection rules: see www.bundeskartellamt.de/SharedDocs/Meldung/EN/Pressemitteilungen/2016/02_03_2016_Facebook.html.

426 European Data Protection Supervisor, Privacy and competitiveness in the age of big data: The interplay between data protection, competition law and consumer protection in the Digital Economy (March 2014); F Costa-Cabral and O Lynskey, 'Family Ties: The Intersection Between Data Protection and Competition in EU Law' (2017) 54(1) *Common Market L Rev* 11; H Kalimo and C Majcher, 'The Concept of Fairness: Linking EU Competition and Data Protection Law in the Digital Marketplace' (2017) 42(2) *European L Rev* 210.

427 Case C-238/05, *Asnef-Equifax et al v Ausbanc* [2006] ECR I–11125, para 63. This was followed by the Commission in *Facebook/Whatsapp* (Case COMP/M.7217) Commission Decision C(2014) 7239 final, para 164.

428 Case C-32/11, *Allianz Hungária Biztosító Zrt and Others v Gazdasági Versenyhivatal*, ECLI:EU:C:2013:160, paras 46–7.

429 Case C-457/10, *AstraZeneca v Commission*, ECLI:EU:C:2012:770, paras 105–12.

430 See our analysis in Section 2.1.5.

431 See our analysis in Chapter 3.

432 See M Novak, *The Spirit of Democratic Capitalism* (Simon & Schuster, 1982) (differentiating society into three power centres: a political sector, an economic sector, and a moral-cultural sector); M Walzer, *Spheres of Justice: A Defense of Pluralism and Equality* (Basic Books, 1983) (arguing that '[t]he principles of justice are themselves pluralistic in form', as different 'social goods' ought to be distributed for different reasons, in accordance to different distributive procedures, by different agents and criteria); L Boltansky and L Thévenot, *On Justification: The Economies of Worth* (Princeton University Press, 2006) (arguing that society is marked by the interplay of various 'orders of worth' functioning according to different tests of justification).

Competition law should intervene whenever there is a restriction of the competitive process, and the decision to intervene, or not to intervene, needs to be justified, as scarce enforcement resources are used and chilling effects may be created for welfare-enhancing conduct.[433] The process of justification may involve arguments in favour of such restriction of competition and thus of the decision not to intervene on the basis of economic efficiency gains considerations, but also arguments relating to the need to intervene against this restriction of competition, these taking into account all the social costs engendered by such restriction, including the social costs of the increase of prices on the market, less consumer choice, but also restrictions on privacy, these being important parameters of competition. It is possible that regulation will offer a superior institutional alternative than competition law in order to alleviate these concerns. This requires a careful comparative institutional analysis, the final choice to act through a specific tool (competition or, eg, some form of transparency regulation) being at the end between imperfect institutional alternatives. It is possible that the extent of remedial action and possibly the continuous supervision of data markets this may entail could be considered as outside the traditional remit of competition law and the technical competences of competition authorities and may require the intervention of regulation, in particular in view of the reticence of competition authorities to intervene in this sector. Designing appropriate institutions for algorithmic accountability still remains an open question.

SELECTIVE BIBLIOGRAPHY

BOOKS

Amato, G, *Antitrust and the Bounds of Power* (Hart, 1997).

Andriychuk, O, *The Normative Foundations of European Competition Law* (Edward Elgar, 2017).

Ayal, A, *Fairness in Antitrust* (Hart, 2014).

Cheng, T, Lianos, I, and Sokol, D, *Competition and the State* (Stanford University Press, 2014).

Diplock, WJK, *The Role of the Judicial process in the Regulation of Competition* (OUP, 1967).

Drex, J, and DiPorto, F (eds) *Competition Law as Regulation* (Edward Elgar, 2015).

Drexl, J, Kerber, W, and Posdzun, R (eds) *Competition Policy and the Economic Approach: Foundations and Limitations* (Edward Elgar, 2011)

Dowdle, MW, Gillespie, J, and Maher, I (eds) *Asian Capitalism and the Regulation of Competition: Towards a Regulatory Geography of Global Competition Law* (CUP, 2013).

Dunne, N, *Competition law and Economic Regulation—Making and Managing Markets* (CUP, 2015).

Ezrachi, A, and Stucke, M, *Virtual Competition* (Harvard University Press, 2016).

Gerber, D, *Law and Competition in Twentieth Century Europe: Protecting Prometheus* (Clarendon Press, 1998).

Heide-Jørgensen, C, Bergqvist, C, and Neergard U (eds) *Aims and Values in Competition Law* (Djøf, 2013).

433 See our analysis in Chapter 6.

Kingston, S, *Greening EU Competition Law and Policy* (CUP, 2012).

Lianos, I, *La Transformation du droit de la concurrence par le recours à l'analyse économique* (Bruylant, 2007).

McChesney, FS, and Shughart, WF, *The Causes and Consequences of Antitrust: The Public Choice Perspective* (University of Chicago Press, 1995).

Monti, G, *EC Competition Law* (CUP, 2007).

Nowag, J, *Environmental Integration in Competition and Free-Movement Laws* (OUP, 2016).

Pasquale, F, *The Black Box Society—The Secret Algorithms That Control Money and Information* (Harvard University Press, 2015).

Peacock, AT, and Willgerodt, H (eds) *German Neo-liberals and the Social Market Economy* (Macmillan, 1989).

Shaikh, A, *Capitalism: Competition, Conflict, Crises* (Oxford University Press, 2016).

Stucke, M, and Grunes, A, *Big Data and Competition Policy* (OUP, 2016).

Townley, C, *Article 81 EC and Public Policy* (Hart, 2009).

Thorelli, H, *The Federal Antitrust Policy* (John Hopkins, 1955).

Van Rompuy, B, *Economic Efficiency: The Sole Concern of Modern Antitrust Policy?—Non-efficiency Considerations under Article 101 TFEU* (Wolters Kluwer, 2012).

Williamson, O, *The Economic Institutions of Capitalism* (Free Press, 1985).

Zimmer, D (ed) *The Goals of Competition Law* (Edward Elgar, 2012).

CHAPTERS IN BOOKS

Gerber, DJ, 'Global Competition Law Convergence: Potential Roles for Economics' in Eisenberg, T, and Ramello, D (eds) *Comparative Law and Economics* (Edward Elgar, 2016).

Lianos, I, 'Some Reflections on the Question of the Goals of EU Competition Law' in Lianos, I, and Geradin, D (eds) *Handbook on European Competition Law: Substantive Aspects* (Edward Elgar, 2013).

Maier-Rigaux, F, 'On the Normative Foundations of Competition Law: Efficiency, Political Freedom and the Freedom to Compete' in Zimmer, D (ed) *The Goals of Competition Law* (Edward Elgar, 2012).

Möschel, W, 'Competition Policy from an Ordo Point of View' in Peacock, A, and Willgerodt, H (eds) *German Neo-Liberals and the Social Market Economy* (Macmillan, 1989).

Schweitzer, H, 'The History, Interpretation and Underlying Principles of Section 2 Sherman Act and Article 82 EC' in Ehlermann, CD, and Marquis, M (eds) *European Competition Annual 2007: A Reformed Approach to Article 82 EC* (Hart, 2008).

Vanberg, V, 'Freiburg School of Law and Economics' in Newman, P (ed) *The New Palgrave Dictionary of Economics and the Law*, vol 2 (MacMillan, 1998).

JOURNAL ARTICLES

Akman, P, 'Searching for the Long-Lost Soul of Article 82E' (2009) 29(2) *Oxford J Legal Studies* 267.

Andriychuk, O, 'Rediscovering the Spirit of Competition: On the Normative Value of the Competitive Process' (2010) 6(3) *European Competition J* 575.

Baker, J, and Salop, S, 'Antitrust, Competition Policy and Inequality' (2015) 104(1) *Georgetown L J* 1.

Behrens, P, 'The "Consumer Choice" Paradigm in German Ordoliberalism and its Impact Upon EU Competition Law' Europa-Kolleg Hamburg, Discussion Paper No. 1/14 (22 July 2014), available at ssrn.com/abstract=2568304.

Buch-Hansen, H, and Wigger, A, 'Revisiting 50 Years of Market Making: The Neoliberal Transformation of European Competition Policy' (2010) 17(1) *Rev Int'l Political Economy* 20.

Costa-Cabral, F, and Lynskey, O, 'Family Ties: The Intersection between Data Protection and Competition in EU Law' (2017) 54(1) *Common Market L Rev* 11.

Chirita, A, 'A Legal-Historical Overview of the EU Competition Rules' (2014) 63 *Int'l and Comparative L Q* 281.

Clark, JM, 'Toward a Concept of Workable Competition' (1940) 30(2) *American Economic Rev* 241.

Coase, RH, 'The Problem of Social Cost' (1960) 3 *J L and Economics* 1.

Comanor, WS, and Smiley, RH, 'Monopoly and the Distribution of Wealth' (1975) 89(2) *Q J Economics* 177.

Crane, DA, 'Technocracy and Antitrust' (2008) 86 *Texas L Rev* 1159.

Cseres, K, 'The Controversies of the Consumer Welfare Standard' (2007) 3 *Competition L Rev* 121.

Deutscher, E, and Makris, S, 'Exploring the Ordoliberal Paradigm: The Competition-Democracy Nexus' (2016) 11(2) *Competition L Rev* 181.

Ezrachi, A, and Stucke, M, 'The Rise of Behavioural Discrimination' (2016) 37 *European Competition L Rev* 484.

Farell, J, and Katz, M, 'The Economics of Welfare Standards in Antitrust' (2006) 2(2) *Competition Policy Int'l*, available at https://www.competitionpolicyinternational.com/the-economics-of-welfare-standards-in-antitrust/.

First, H, and Weber Waller, S, 'Antitrust's Democracy Deficit' (2013) 81(5) *Fordham L Rev* 2543.

Fox, E, 'We Protect Competition, You Protect Competitors' (2003) 26(2) *World Competition* 149.

Gerber, DJ, 'Constitutionalizing the Economy: German Neo-liberalism, Competition Law and the "New" Europe' (1994) 42 *American J Comparative L* 25.

Kovacic, W, and Shapiro, C, 'Antitrust Policy: A Century of Economic and Legal Thinking' (2000) 14(1) *J Economic Perspectives* 43.

Lande, RH, 'Consumer Choice as the Ultimate Goal of Antitrust' [2001] 62(3) *University of Pittsburgh L R* 503.

Lianos, I, 'Lost in Translation?' Towards a Theory of Economic Transplants' (2009) 62(1) *Current Legal Problems* 346.

Neven, D, and Röller, L-H, 'Consumer Surplus vs. Welfare Standard in a Political Economy Model of Merger Control' (2005) 23 *Int'l J Industrial Organization* 829.

Odudu, O, 'The Wider Concerns of Competition Law' (2010) 30(3) *Oxford J Legal Studies* 599.

Orbach, B, 'The Antitrust Consumer Welfare Paradox' (2011) 7 *J Competition L & Economics* 133.

Pitofsky, R, 'The Political Content of Antitrust' (1979) 127 *University of Pennsylvania L Rev* 1074.

Posner, RA, 'The Chicago School of Antitrust Analysis' (1978–9) 127 *University of Pennsylvania L Rev* 926.

Townley, C, 'The Goals of Chapter I of the UK's Competition Act 1998' (25 May 2010), available at ssrn.com/abstract=1615592.

3

THE ECONOMICS OF COMPETITION LAW: RELEVANT MARKET AND MARKET POWER

3.1. COMPETITION: AN ECONOMIC PERSPECTIVE

3.1.1. THE MEANING OF COMPETITION: HORIZONTAL AND VERTICAL COMPETITION

The use of economics permeates all areas of competition law enforcement, from the control of mergers on an *ex-ante* basis to the *ex-post* assessment of alleged infringements under Articles 101 and 102 of the Treaty on the Functioning of the European Union (TFEU).[1] The ultimate goal of competition law is to protect the process of competitive rivalry, which in practice entails preventing the creation of positions of significant market power through external growth and cooperation agreements, whilst stamping on attempts to buttress existing position of substantial market power through market foreclosure. Hence, in interpreting the competition law provisions of the Treaty, the Commission, the Competition and Markets Authority (CMA), and the courts refer, to variable degree, to external sources of expertise, in most cases, economics, and integrate within the interpretation and enforcement of competition law the concepts, tools, and methodology of economics. It becomes therefore important to explore the way economics define competition.

[1] Arguably, under the self-assessment regime (introduced with the Modernisation Regulation in May 2004) firms should rely on economic insights themselves to comply with Articles 101 and 102 TFEU on an *ex-ante* basis.

The meaning of 'competition' in economics changed at some point during the nineteenth century. One may compare its conceptualization by classical economists, in particular Adam Smith, as a process of rivalry and the approach later followed by the mathematical economists of the neoclassical paradigm, in particular Augustin Cournot, who focused instead on an outcome/situation.

Paul J McNulty, 'A Note on the History of Perfect Competition' (1967) 75(4) *J Political Economy* 395, 398

Not only did Smith fail to see competition as a 'situation in which P [Price] does not vary with Q [Quantity]—in which the demand curve facing the firm is horizontal' (Stigler); he did not conceive of competition as a 'situation' at all but, rather, as an active process leading to a certain predicted result. The Smithian concept of competition is essentially one of business behavior which might reasonably be associated with the verb 'to compete.' The essence of that behavior was the active effort to undersell one's rival in the market, although, to be sure, Smith was not unaware of the organizational and technological elements in competition, as when he wrote that lowered prices and increased demand 'encourages production, and thereby, increases the competition of producers who, in order to undersell one another, have recourse to new divisions of labour and new improvements of art, which might never otherwise have been thought of' (Smith). The concept of competition originating with Cournot, on the other hand, is totally devoid of behavioral content. This is because Cournot's focus was entirely on the effects, rather than the actual workings, of competition [. . .]. For Smith, [. . .] competition was a process through which a predicted result, the equation of price and cost, was achieved. With Cournot, it became the realized result itself. The two concepts are not only different; they are fundamentally incompatible. Competition came to mean, with the mathematical economists, a hypothetically realized situation in which business rivalry, or competition in the Smithian sense, was ruled out by definition.

NOTES AND QUESTIONS

1. The above excerpt emphasizes the distinction between competition perceived as a market outcome/structure and competition perceived as behavioural activity.
2. Some may argue that the problem with that interpretation (focussed on the process of rivalry) is that it is very hard to pin down prescriptively the situations where State intervention in the marketplace is justified, from the point of view of economic efficiency, so as to be useful from a regulatory perspective. All that Cournot and all the other one-shot equilibrium analyses do is to provide something one could work on to guide regulatory intervention. Do you agree with this statement?

The concept of 'competitive advantage' in strategy analysis could also become a source of inspiration for competition law. Strategy analysis focuses on competition, taking into account the corporate strategy to maximize firm's performance, in terms of surplus value and economic profit.[2] Corporations seek a competitive advantage, either by imitating successful

[2] Economic profit is 'the surplus available after all inputs (including capital) have been paid for': RM Grant, *Contemporary Strategy Analysis* (Wiley, 2013), 38. To the extent that financial markets look to the actual but also expected stream of economic profit (or cash flows), the net present value (NPV) (or stock market value) of

competitors while lowering their costs, or by differentiating themselves from their competitors, by developing internal resources and capabilities and designing strategies to exploit these differences. The business environment in which competitive advantage strategies are integrated is formed by the relationship the corporation has with three sets of players: customers, suppliers, and competitors.[3] Firms make profits but they must also provide value to their customers. 'Value is created when the price the customer is willing to pay for a product exceeds the costs incurred by the firm'.[4] This surplus is distributed between the customers and the producers by the forces of competition. If competition is strong, consumers will receive the higher percentage of the surplus value (the so-called consumer surplus, which measures the difference between the price they paid and the price they were willing to pay). The rest of the surplus value will be received by producers (the so-called producer surplus, which measures the difference between the amount a producer receives and the minimum amount the producer is willing to accept for the product). The profitability of industries varies, some earning high rates of profit, while others can cover a little more than their cost of capital.[5] This largely depends on the degree of competition that prevails in each industry, as intense price competition generally leads to weak margins. Profitability within a specific industry may also be quite different, some firms earning significant profits, while others struggling to maintain themselves on the market.[6]

The most widely used competition framework in business strategy is that put forward by Michael Porter, the 'five forces of competition framework' (see Figure 3.1).[7] According to this framework, the profitability of an industry is determined by five sources of competitive pressure: competition from substitutes, competition from new entrants in the industry, competition from established rivals, which can be characterized as sources of 'horizontal' competition, and competition from the bargaining power of suppliers and the power of buyers, which can be characterized as sources of 'vertical competition'.[8]

Competition economics has largely focused on horizontal competition from established competitors (producing substitute products), or on the threat of entry of potential competitors. Rivalry between established competitors is often measured by reference to the level of market concentration, often measured by a concentration ratio, the market share of the largest producers in a specific market. However, it is still unclear how the level of market concentration impacts on profitability, and consequently the allocation of the surplus between consumers and producers.[9] The likelihood of a new entry (potential competition) largely depends

a firm provides a forward-looking performance measure, which has become extremely important, in view of the financialization of the economy and the intense competition between capitals. Enterprise value depends on three drivers: rate of return on capital, cost of capital, and profit growth: ibid, 42.

3 Ibid, 61. 4 Ibid, 62. 5 Ibid.

6 The advent of the digital economy has led to the development of what has been characterized as the rise of 'superstar firms' which are able to take advantage of technology, including Big Data and artificial intelligence, in understanding better than 'standard' firms the competitive game. See D Autor, D Dorn, LF Katz, Ch Patterson, J Van Reenen, 'The Fall of the Labor Share and the Rise of Superstar Firms', NBER Working Paper No 23396 (May 2017).

7 ME Porter, 'The Five Competitive Forces that Shape Strategy' (January 2008) *Harvard Business Rev* 25.

8 RM Grant, *Contemporary Strategy Analysis* (Wiley, 2013) 65.

9 See the different positions of the so-called 'Harvard' or Structure–Conduct–Performance school, which found a causal link between a concentrated market structure and profitability (see JS Bain, 'Relation of Profit Rate to Industry Concentration: American Manufacturing, 1936–1940' (1951) 65 *Q J Economics* 293, who showed that the after-tax returns on shareholder equity across forty-two US manufacturing industries were higher when the eight-firm concentration ratio (sum of the shares of the eight leading firms) was above 70 per cent; HM Mann, 'Seller Concentration, Barriers to Entry and Rates of Return in Thirty Industries' (1966) 48 *Rev Economics & Statistics* 296), and that of the so-called Chicago School, which found that this effect was weak

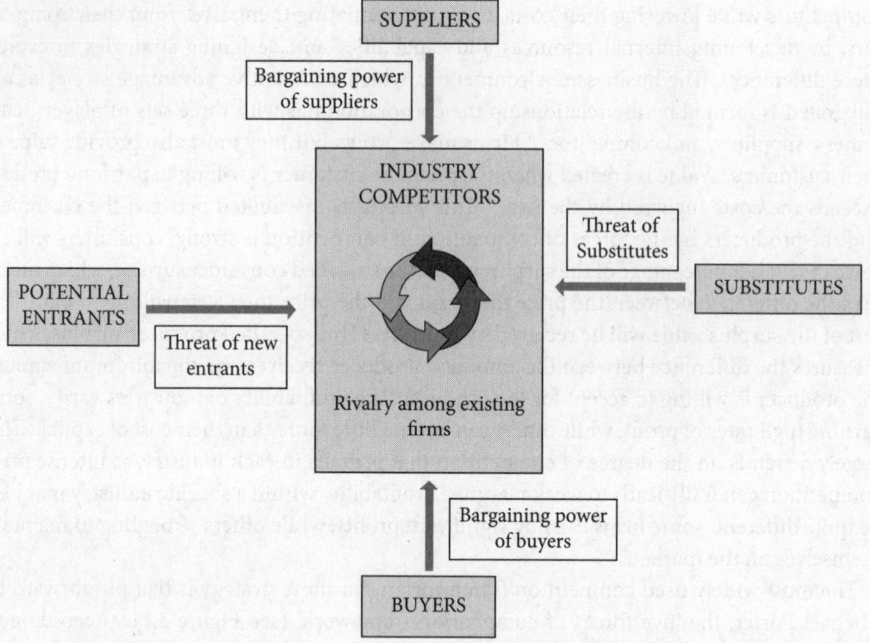

Figure 3.1. Porter's five forces.
Source: RM Grant, *Contemporary Strategy Analysis* (Wiley, 2013) 65 fig. 3.2.

on barriers to entry, that is, an advantage that an established firm enjoys vis-à-vis its rivals, which may include economies of scale (to the extent that large, indivisible investments in production facilities, research & technology, or marketing may be more easily amortized over a large volume of output), absolute cost advantages (which may come from an easy access to an indispensable input), capital requirements (because of the large fixed costs required in order to kick start economic activity in an industry), product differentiation (as it might be quite difficult to enter a market where consumers have strong loyalty ties to existing brands), access to channels of efficient distribution, strategic barriers to entry because of competitive strategies that aim to increase the potential rivals' costs if they enter the market, legal and regulatory barriers, etc. Competition law aims to limit the effectiveness of barriers to entry, so as to increase the 'contestability' of the market.[10]

In contrast, vertical competition has not been the focus of competition economics, even if it may play a significant role with regard to the allocation of the total surplus value that is generated by a value chain. The relative bargaining power of a supplier upstream, or of a customer downstream, has been considered as playing a less important role than 'horizontal competition', in particular because it is assumed that, in most cases, it plays a quite limited role on the overall economic efficiency of the transactions. To the extent that economic efficiency, rather

statistically and usually quite small (see Y Brozen, 'Bain's Concentration and Rates of Returns, Revisited' (1971) 14 *J L & Economics* 351; H Demsetz, 'Two Systems of Belief about Monopoly' in HJ Goldschmidt and H Michael Mann (eds) *Industrial Concentration: The New Learning* (Little, Brown, 1974), 164).

10 WJ Baumol, JC Panzar, and RD Willig, *Contestable Markets and the Theory of Industry Structure* (Harcourt Brace Jovanovic, 1982).

than fairness in the distribution of the total surplus value, still constitutes one of the main goals of competition law, the exercise of relative bargaining power or vertical economic power is not considered as being a primary concern for competition law, with the exception of course of the situation where its exercise may harm economic efficiency (eg the rather confined case of monopsony or buyer power).[11] Vertical competition may, however, become an important concern, if one wants to focus on productivity and on the ability of 'superstar' large digital platforms to pull away from both horizontal and vertical competition and enjoy tremendous levels of profitability, without these accumulated profits being used for productive investments.

In the digital economy, important network effects lead to 'winner-takes-most' competition, with only one platform controlling a market, or being the significant player on a relevant market (thus restricting horizontal competition), or more broadly dominating a value chain (thus restricting vertical competition). Markets marked by platform competition are thus horizontally concentrated, sometimes to such an extent that the second or third player in the market may not offer a viable competitive alternative to the established platform. Inter-platform competition remains weak, and there is significant *inequality in the distribution of market shares* among horizontal competitors.

At the same time, the centralized platform forms a bottleneck, with the power to determine the allocation of the surplus generated by the value chain between the various contributors, and in particular to keep the overwhelming part of this surplus, thus accumulating significant profits (exercising vertical economic power). In view of the anchoring of users and the low levels of switching to competing platforms, the platform operators can be confident that the reduction of vertical competition, between the different segments of the value chain, with regard to the allocation of the total surplus value generated by the value chain, will not lead to the desertion of their platform from a significant number of applications developers. Hence, value chains dominated by digital platforms are also marked by a very *unequal distribution of profits* between the established platforms and the participants to their ecosystem.

The digital economy gives rise to a variety of strategies to acquire competitive advantage and convert this to surplus value to be later collected in product and financial markets. In this fast-moving environment, innovation competition provides the main constraint to 'winner-takes-most' competition, as new economic actors rely on cost-cutting technology to break into markets, disrupt the existing competitive structure, and eventually acquire a position of economic power, before they give way to new actors making a more efficient use of the technology or relying on a better technological alternative.

Competition does not only take place within a product or a technology market, or even an industry, but also within broader competition 'ecosystems',[12] which may include various industries, as inter-industrial investment flows focus on the lowest-cost techniques that provide higher rates of return for the capital invested, with capital moving from one industry to another in search of higher profits.[13]

The strategy of the various firms is to capture a disproportionate amount of the surplus value created by innovation resulting from the emergence of a new industry thanks to some new technological developments. In some situations, the most effective strategy will be to opt for an 'open architecture' that nurtures complementarity through an open eco-system, should a system of 'open innovation' be the most effective way to generate higher value in

[11] See our analysis in Section 3.2.2.4.

[12] MG Jacobides, Industry Architecture, in M Augier and DJ Teece, *The Palgrave Encyclopedia of Strategic Management* (Palgrave Macmillan, 2016).

[13] A Shaikh, *Capitalism: Competition, Conflict, Crises* (OUP, 2016).

this industry.[14] In other situations, firms may go for a 'walled garden approach', opting for a closed architecture with regard to firms with competing assets and capabilities entering the value chain while keeping it open for firms with complementary assets. Finally, in other circumstances, firms may opt for vertical integration; taking full control over the rents generated by the complementarities brought by the innovation whilst maintaining the possibility to exclude or marginalize any new entrant, for instance, by denying interoperability with regard to some indispensable technological interfaces.

As the focus of competition authorities switches to innovation competition, it becomes important to ensure that the players contributing to this effort are properly incentivized with regard to their returns on their investment on innovation, in particular if this takes place in an open innovation ecosystem.[15] Hence, the focus of competition authorities should also shift on the way the value brought by innovation is captured, shared, and generated, the three processes being intrinsically linked with each other. It is also important to keep in mind the role of vertical innovation competition in challenging competitive bottlenecks resulting from the control of essential inputs by dominant players in an industry. In a digital economy marked by network effects, it is quite frequent that the position of incumbents can only be challenged by vertically situated firms in complementary markets that may also benefit from network effects, rather than competitors situated on the same relevant market.[16]

In the digital economy, what constitutes an established or a potential competitor also becomes blurred, as the companies are actively pursuing strategies to alter industry structure in order to alleviate competitive pressures, by positioning the company where competition, horizontal and vertical, is the weakest.[17] A way to achieve durable competitive advantage is by being in a position to reshape the industry in their own advantage and acquire, what has been referred to as 'architectural advantage',[18] which plays an important role in periods of profound technological transformation, with the development of new General Purpose Technologies, like the one that we are now witnessing.[19] This approach focuses on the position of the undertaking at the industry and value chain levels, rather than on the market level. It challenges the idea that there are cycles in the life of an industry, an industry being marked by a dominant design, with an established hierarchy and stable market shares, that slowly erodes as the industry matures and product innovation mainly occurs through new entry. According to the architectural advantage view, the boundaries of an industry should not be considered as a given, as firms with superior performance (due to superior resources and capabilities[20]) aim

14 See, for instance, the discussion in A Gawer, 'Bridging Differing Perspectives on Technological Platforms: Toward an Integrative Framework' (2014) 43 *Research Policy* 1239.

15 See M Bogers et al, 'The Open Innovation Research Landscape: Established Perspectives and Emerging Themes across Different Levels of Analysis' (2017) 24(1) *Industry and Innovation* 8.

16 For instance, the dominant position of IBM on the computer industry until the early 1980s was not challenged by another hardware company, but by Microsoft, which was present in the complementary segment of software, and controlled the market of the operating system, an essential input for personal computers (PCs). Microsoft, with time, benefitted from important network effects, which provided it with the power to commoditize hardware and thus change computer industry architecture, thus becoming able to acquire the largest percentage of the surplus value generated by the industry, the centre of power moving from hardware to software in the mid-1980s–90s. See TF Bresnahan and S Greenstein, 'Technological Competition and the Structure of the Computer Industry' (14 December 1997), available at https://pdfs.semanticscholar.org/0675/051e52dc04ec384951242a82f95022abe71f.pdf.

17 RM Grant, *Contemporary Strategy Analysis* (Wiley, 2013), 74–6.

18 MG Jacobides, T Knudsen, and M Augier, 'Benefiting From Innovation: Value Creation, Value Appropriation and the Role of Industry Architectures' (2006) 35(8) *Research Policy* 1200.

19 CH Ferguson and CR Morris, 'How Architecture Wins Technology Wars' (1993) 71(2) *Harvard Business Rev* 86.

20 B Wernerfelt, 'A Resource-based View of the Firm' (1984) 5(2) *Strategic Management J* 171; KC Prahalad and G Hamel, 'The Core Competence of the Corporation' (May–June 1990) *Harvard Business Rev* 79.

to develop 'industry architectures', that are 'sector-wide templates that circumscribe the terms of the division of labor', which help those firms to constitute a 'bottleneck', enabling them to leverage their position of strength over all other companies that collaborate with them in the creation of surplus value.[21] Hence, according to this view, 'the competition of capabilities takes place not only at market/segment level (eg among mobile handset manufacturers) but also at the value-chain level (eg among mobile handset manufacturers, network providers, content providers and so on)'.[22] Contrary to (industrial) economics, which assumes that '[f]irms compete only within a market, and it is their performance within that market, relative to other firms, that determines their profitability',[23] the architectural advantage perspective focuses on the role of vertical competition and the way this affects the relative proportion of value (ie, the NPV of future profits) that each segment captures, thus leading to important value shifts from one part of the value chain to another. The firms acquiring architectural advantage (the 'kingpins') take a central role in the overall industry architecture, influencing not only the segment they belong, but multiple segments within a single industry.[24]

Business strategy-inspired approaches also put forward the idea that one cannot appropriately conceptualize competition law, unless one takes into account the strategies of the firms participating in the industry environment. This may call for the development of new conceptual tools that may go beyond assessing competition in the context of a narrowly defined product market. The concept of 'strategic group', that is, 'the group of firms in an industry following the same or a similar strategy along the strategic dimensions',[25] such as product range, geographical scope, level of product quality, choice of technology, etc, may offer a broader canvass to assess the wide variety of competitive interactions between firms, at least with regard to horizontal competition.

There should also be additional conceptual tools developed in order to assess restrictions on vertical competition.[26] The conceptual tool of value chain (or global value chain or GVC) may offer an excellent mapping tool for this purpose. Although the tool was initially framed so as to help policy-makers to design industrial strategies geared towards a greater participation of firms, active in their jurisdiction, in the global economy, we think that its descriptive potential is wider than that. By exploring the sequences of tangible and intangible value adding activities, 'from conception and production to end use', GVC analysis offers a picture of global industries both 'from the top-down', by examining for instance 'how lead firms govern their global-scale affiliate and supplier networks', but also from 'the bottom-up', asking 'how these business decisions affect the trajectory of economic and social "upgrading" or 'downgrading' in specific countries'.[27]

21 MG Jacobides and CJ Tae, 'Kingpins, Bottlenecks, and Value Dynamics Along a Sector' (2015) 26(3) *Organization Science* 889, 889.
22 Ibid, 889. 23 Ibid. 24 Ibid.
25 ME Porter, *Competitive Strategy: Techniques for Analysing Industries and Competitors* (Free Press, 1980), 129, defines 'strategic groups' as a 'group of firms in an industry following the same or similar strategy along the strategic dimensions', the firms within a 'strategic group' competing more intensely with each other than with firms outside this core group.
26 On this issue, see also our analysis in Chapter 10.
27 RM Grant, *Contemporary Strategy Analysis* (Wiley, 2013), 105. One of the authors of this volume has been particularly vocal in promoting the GVC approach in competition law: see I Lianos, Global Governance of Antitrust and the Need for a BRICS Joint Research Platform in Competition Law and Policy, in T Bonakele, E Fox, and L Mncube (eds), Competition Policy for the New Era: Insights from the BRICS Countries (OUP, 2017), 51; I Lianos, Global Food Value Chains and Competition Law - BRICS Draft Report (January 1, 2018). Available at SSRN: https://ssrn.com/abstract=3076160.

This mapping approach examines various dimensions: (i) the input–output structure of a GVC, by focusing on the process of transformation of raw materials and factors of inputs of production to final products; (ii) the geographic scope of GVCs which explains the degree of global dispersion of the chain; (iii) the governance structure of the GVC, which delves into the issue of control of the chain; (iv) the upgrading, which describes 'the dynamic movement within the value chain' and 'how producers shift between different stages of the chain'; (v) the local (or global) institutional context in which the value chain is embedded, including regulation and self-regulation; (vi) industry stakeholders that may be various local (but also global) actors of the value chain that interact to achieve industry upgrading. These may not only be companies, but also industry associations, workers, educational or research institutions, government agencies, and ministerial departments. All these actors are involved to a certain degree in the operation of the global value chains and influence their development.

The framework shares Michael Porter's emphasis on '*value systems*'; a concept that has been used in order to describe a set of inter-firm linkages through which different economic actors (and their value chains) are interconnected.[28] GVC's 'holistic view' of global industries focuses on the governance of the value chain, that is, how some actors can shape the distribution of profits and risks in the chain. Taking a political economy perspective, the GVC approach explores the way economic actors may maintain or improve ('upgrade') their position in the global value chain, 'economic upgrading' being defined as 'the process by which economic actors—firms and workers— move from low-value to relatively high-value activities in GVC'.[29] There are different types of upgrading: some relate to the entry in the value chain, where firms participate for the first time in national, regional, or global value chains; others relate to 'end-market upgrading', where firms move into more sophisticated markets that require compliance with new, more rigorous quality standards, or into larger markets that call for investments in production scale.[30] The GVC also proceeds to some analysis of the governance structures of an industry, by identifying 'the lead firms in the sector, their location, how they interact with their supply chain and their sources of influence and power over them'.[31]

3.1.1. THE CENTRAL ROLE OF THE CONCEPT OF MARKET POWER

Neoclassical economics is based on resource scarcity. Scarcity entails that any choice as to how resources get allocated—as a result of decisions made by individuals, firms and/or the State—must reckon with the idea that there are alternative uses that would yield valuable outcomes—for example, a dismissed warehouse in a trendy location could be reconfigured for either residential or commercial purposes, subject to the constraints posed by planning policies. In economic jargon, the best alternative use corresponds to an 'opportunity cost', which the decision maker would want to factor in when choosing how best to allocate what he is endowed with.

28 ME Porter, *Competitive Advantage: Creating and Sustaining Superior Performance* (Free Press, 1985).

29 G Gereffi, 'Global Value Chains in a Post-Washington Consensus World' (2014) 21(1) *Rev Int'l Political Economy* 9, 18.

30 G Gereffi and K Fernandez-Stark, *Global Value Chain Analysis: A Primer* (CGGC, 2nd ed, 2016), 12.

31 Ibid, 10.

Ultimately, society would want to adopt an allocation mechanism that is capable of maximizing the benefits from consumption of scarce resources over the long term. It turns out that markets where producers compete for customers' business is superior to an antithetical system where producers and consumers are told what to do by a 'benevolent central planner'.

Markets, though, are not faultless; they can sometimes fail to pursue consumer welfare. One particular source of market failure is market power, whereby competitive rivalry is lessened so that consumers are left with little choice but to buy from a dominant firm. Under these circumstances, consumer detriment might arise due to higher prices (leading to lower quantity sold), lower quality and variety on offer.

Adam Smith was very much aware of this risk:

> Consumption is the sole end and purpose of all production; and the interest of the producer ought to be attended to only so far as it may be necessary for promoting that of the consumer. The maxim is so perfectly self-evident that it would be absurd to attempt to prove it. But in the mercantile system the interest of the consumer is almost constantly sacrificed to that of the producer; and it seems to consider production, and not consumption, as the ultimate end and object of all industry and commerce.[32]

Competition law, with its various provisions, is meant to address such market failures in order to preserve well-functioning markets by either protecting (through *ex-ante* intervention and indirect deterrence), or reinstituting (through *ex-post* intervention and direct deterrence) competitive rivalry.

Market power, though, is not always detrimental to consumers. More often than not, where a firm comes to detain a position of substantial market power through organic, internal growth—as opposed to acquisition of rivals, for example—it is because the majority of consumers have valued its offer more than rivals'. Hence, under these circumstances, intervention on an *ex-post* basis would be unwarranted, even if the dominant firm was earning high profits. In other words, one would have to infer that high prices reflect consumer preferences in terms of superior quality and/or strong brand loyalty.

Doing otherwise would reduce the incentives to compete on anything other than price, which would prove clearly detrimental in terms of reduced firms' incentives to improve quality and variety in order to gain a competitive advantage and be able to sustain a price mark-up. This is not to say, though, that low prices are to be sniffed at. Quite the contrary: where consumer prefer low prices for what can be thought as a commoditized product, market power can result from superior efficiency which allows the dominant firm to price below rivals (whilst still making a profit overall) and hence conquer a large share of the market. Ideally, one would want to see both competitive modes thriving in a market; that is, whereby the entire product range, from basic and cheap to niche at a premium, is well presided.

The inherent ambiguity in what underpins a position of substantial market power means that intervention under competition law is triggered primarily where market power is likely to be significantly increased through external growth, such as via mergers, joint ventures, or other forms of coordination among firms. Moreover, enforcement can also be triggered where an alleged conduct undertaken by an already dominant firm is likely to entrench its position of substantial market power by cutting out rivals from a large chunk of the addressable

32 A Smith, *The Wealth of Nations* (1776), bk IV, ch 8, para 49.

market. The idea is that, absent the alleged conduct, the large portion of demand served by the dominant firm would have been more 'contestable'; that is, the alleged conduct has made it more difficult for customers to be able to switch to a rival's product if they so preferred.[33]

By and large, these two types of trigger for enforcement correspond to the partition between exploitative and exclusionary infringements, where the latter is about protecting or enhancing market power by disadvantaging rivals, and the former is about directly exploiting market power to the detriment of customer because of higher prices and/or lower quality. Usually, the term exploitative is used, narrowly, with reference specifically to abuses of dominance; whereas here a broader meaning is adopted in order to encompass mergers and any form of coordination leading to a reduction of competitive rivalry (ie, even in the absence of anti-competitive foreclosure) and, hence, to exploitation of market power.

The term 'quality' is also used in a broad sense, including both what in economic jargon is called vertical and horizontal differentiation. With vertical differentiation, consumers have the same opinion regarding what constitutes higher quality, such as with respect to the number of years old a bottle of whisky is; whereas with horizontal differentiation, consumers' preferences regarding quality attributes can differ, such as with music genres. So, in the latter case, lower quality means lower variety of choice.[34] Finally, innovation is encompassed too, to the extent that it would ultimately translate into higher quality (or same quality at lower costs), more variety, or a combination of both.

Competition law infringement can also be partitioned depending on whether it takes place within a single market or cuts across more than one market. In the latter case, it could be about either a (vertical) supply relationship (such as between an input supplier and a manufacturer, or a manufacturer and a retail distributor), or a situation where two complementary products can be sold together (such as the classic printer/ink-cartridges case).[35]

In summary, competition law infringements (ie, including prohibited mergers) can be categorized alongside three dichotomies:

- exploitative as opposed to exclusionary;
- internal/single-firm as opposed to external/multi-firm; and
- multi-market/product as opposed to single-market/product.

Table 3.1 maps examples of competition law infringements accordingly.

The integration of the concept of market power in competition law is an illustration of the growing importance of neoclassical economics and price theory in competition law analysis. The neoclassical definition of market power focuses on the ability of a firm to raise prices profitably and reduce output, which essentially fits to the competition as an efficient outcome approach.

[33] See European Commission, Guidance on the Commission's enforcement priorities in applying Article 82 of the EC Treaty to abusive exclusionary conduct by dominant undertakings [2009] OJ C 45/02, para 19 ('the term "anti-competitive foreclosure" is used to describe a situation where effective access of actual or potential competitors to supplies or markets is hampered or eliminated as a result of the conduct of the dominant undertaking whereby the dominant undertaking is likely to be in a position to profitably increase prices to the detriment of consumers.').

[34] This is not to say, however, that more choice is always to be preferred in terms of consumer welfare. Variety is beneficial insofar as consumers seek out different versions of the same product; although it is impracticable to tell where this is not the case.

[35] In this respect, it is often hotly debated whether the two products do actually constitute separate markets for antitrust purposes, or whether there is only one market for the combination of the two products, as discussed later on in this chapter.

Table 3.1. Competition law infringements.

	Internal/single-firm	External/multi-firm
Exploitative	**Single-market:** Excessive prices **Multi-market:** n.a.	**Single-market:** Mergers and cartels; MFN and price-matching clauses **Multi-market:** Vertical restraints such as RPM
Exclusionary	**Single-market:** Predatory prices Loyalty discounts **Multi-market:** Bundled discounts Tying & bundling Refusal to supply & margin-squeeze	**Single-market:** Coordinated predatory practices (ie instrumental to cartels' stability) **Multi-market:** Vertical restraints such as exclusive agreements and quantity forcing

Market power, or substantial market power, operates as a unifying concept for the application of Articles 101 and 102 TFEU and the introduction of a more economics-oriented approach in justifying antitrust intervention on the marketplace. In a similar formulation for the purposes of Articles 101, 102 TFEU and EU merger control, the Commission defines market power as 'the ability of one or more firms profitably to increase prices, reduce output, choice or quality of goods and services, diminish innovation, or otherwise negatively influence parameters of competition.'[36] This broad definition accommodates the emphasis of EU competition law on the protection of various dimensions of the competitive process, not just price and output. Although the ability to increase price remains the primary concern of competition law, in conformity with the approach of neoclassical price theory, the emphasis on other parameters of competition than price, in particular consumer choice, epitomizes the broad definition of what constitutes a restriction of competition under EU competition law and the recognition of the importance of quality and variety investment competition instead of just price competition.

3.1.2. COMPETITION AND THE NATURE OF STRATEGIC INTERACTION

Another useful way of analysing competition law infringements is by looking at the type of strategic interaction underpinning them. Firms normally take decisions (such as setting the price, quality, or advertising expenditure) by also considering how rivals will react. In this

[36] Guidelines on the assessment of non-horizontal mergers under the Council Regulation on the control of concentrations between undertakings [2008] OJ C 265/6, para 10; Guidelines on the application of Article 81(3) [2004] OJ C 101/97, para 25; Communication from the Commission, Guidance on the Commission's enforcement priorities in applying Article 82 of the EC Treaty to abusive exclusionary conduct by dominant undertakings, C(2009) 864 final, para 11.

respect, a firm can choose to be either aggressive or accommodative, whereby the selected conduct is meant, respectively, to reduce or increase rivals' profitability. By and large, this dichotomy coincides with the distinction between exclusionary and exploitative infringements discussed above.

Having decided which competitive stance to adopt, 'soft' as opposed to 'tough', its execution varies depending on the variable of choice (eg price or quantity). There are two possibilities:[37]

- firms' decisions are *strategic complements* in that they tend to reinforce each other (ie, firms move in the same direction). Setting prices among rivals is such a case, in that a decision to raise (reduce) prices will incentivize (force) rivals to do likewise;
- firms' decisions are *strategic substitutes* in that they tend to offset each other (ie, firms move in opposite direction). Setting capacity is such a case, in that a decision to expand (reduce) capacity will force (incentivize) rivals to reduce (expand) theirs.

Accordingly, to be 'tough' under strategic complements requires a reduction in the choice variable (eg lower prices under predatory pricing and single-product loyalty discounts), whereas an accommodative stance would require the opposite (eg price increase post-merger). Vice versa, an aggressive stance under strategic substitutes requires an increase in the choice variable (eg capacity expansion/quantity forcing), whereas to be 'soft' firms should opt for a reduction in order to create more room for rivals (eg production quotas in a cartel).

There is a difference, though, between the two strategic settings: since under strategic complements firms' moves reinforce each other—ie there is a positive feedback loop—this competitive mode tends to produce more extreme outcomes than under strategic substitutes. For example, where firms set prices (and then produce whatever quantities are demanded at the posted price) competitive rivalry due to an aggressive stance is harsher than when firms set quantities (and then let prices adjust to absorb their inventories).[38] By the same token, the potential for consumer detriment due to a 'soft' stance under strategic complements tends to be higher than under strategic substitutes. For example, in a merger under quantity competition, in the absence of significant cost synergies the joint profitability of the merging firms is normally lower than before the merger, whereas rivals' profits increase.[39]

That prices are strategic complements and that quantities and capacities are strategic substitutes rests on the assumption that the two products concerned are substitutes (not to be confounded with strategic substitutes), that is, products are perceived by consumers as fungible. The reverse holds where prices are set for complementary products (not to be confused with strategic complements), that is, product that are consumed together. A classic example is demands for cars and petrol. Here, an increase in the price of petrol tends to depress the demand for cars. Under these circumstances decisions on prices of complementary products

37 This terminology was introduced by J Bulow, J Geanakoplos, and P. Klemperer, 'Multimarket Oligopoly: Strategic Substitutes and Strategic Complements' (1985) 93 *J Political Economy* 488. This framework was further developed to analyse incumbent's incentives to deter or accommodate entry in D Funderberg and J Tirole, 'The Fat-Cat Effect, the Puppy-Dog Ploy, and the Lean and Hungry Look' (1984) 74 *American Economic Rev* 361.

38 This theoretical result was first established by N Singh and X Vives, 'Price and Quantity Competition in a Differentiated Duopoly' (1984) 15 *RAND J Economics* 546.

39 This odd theoretical result, called the Cournot paradox, was first formalized by S Salant, S Switzer, and R Reynolds, 'Losses from Horizontal Merger: The Effects of an Exogenous Change in Industry Structure on Cournot–Nash Equilibrium' (1983) 98 *Q J Economics* 185. For a critical discussion of this result, see S Huck, KA Konrad, and W Müller, 'Mergers Without Cost Advantages' in WD Collins (ed) *Issues in Competition Law and Policy*, vol. 2 (ABA Section of Antitrust Law, 2008), 1575.

are strategic substitutes, and vice versa for decision on quantities and installed capacities. Let's take, for example, bundled discounts. Here the alleged firm sells two products together at a price cheaper than the sum of its individual prices, so that a rival who only sells one or some of the two products (called, the bundled product) is forced to lower its price in order to maintain competitiveness. The bundled discount is therefore tantamount to an increase in the individual price of the product not sold by the rival (called, the bundling product), hence is an aggressive move under strategic complements.

This reversed strategic interaction applies also to (vertical) supply relationship, since an input can be thought of as a complement in the final product. Similarly, if all producers of a consumer product were to raise their prices, the volume of activity of retail distributors (and hence their profits) would suffer.

Let's take the example of margin squeeze, where the alleged vertically integrated firm set the wholesale price for the essential input sold to downstream rivals at such a level that the latter is not able to compete with the downstream division of the former. Similarly to the case of bundled discounts, the increase of the wholesale price is an aggressive move against the rival who cannot purchase the essential input elsewhere.

By the same token, exclusivity distribution agreements (eg I buy a product only from you or you sell only to me) can be anti-competitive where they prevent the rival producer of a consumer product from being able to sell in the corresponding local market. In principle, the retail distributor must be compensated for the exclusivity, since by renouncing it right to stock other brands its assortment will suffer. Therefore, this implicit premium for exclusivity can be thought of as an increase in the price of a complement under strategic substitutes, since the foreclosed rival has to either offer a higher premium or rely on worse retailers (eg located in a less convenient location). In the latter case, the price for the consumer good will have to be lowered in order to attract consumers (ie, compensate them for the lower quality of the complementary service, the retail distributor).[40]

3.2. MARKET POWER AND WELFARE ECONOMICS

Although market power is not the direct trigger of competition law enforcement, it has a pivotal role in this enforcement regime. This makes it important to explore the conceptual foundations of the concept of market power in the broader discipline of welfare economics, before looking more closely at its social costs, which essentially builds the case for competition law intervention in modern competition law.[41]

The economic welfare perspective taken by modern competition law is based on a theoretical framework that is approximately one hundred and fifty years old and derives from Bentham's utilitarian theory. Much effort was spent by economists during these one hundred

[40] One vertical restraints where pricing decision are strategic complements is the case of retail price maintenance. Here the upstream firm removes price competition among retailers for its products (ie intra-brand pricing rivalry is muted), thus sending a signal to rival upstream firms of an accommodative pricing stance. This way also inter-brand pricing rivalry is potentially softened.

[41] Note, however, the view that competition law should expand its scope and intervene, not just in situations of market power, but when the exercise of economic power may harm consumers or the process of competition. See A Ayal, 'The Market for Bigness: Economic Power and Competition Agencies' Duty to Curtail It' (2013) 1(2) *J Antitrust Enforcement* 221; I Lianos and C Lombardi, 'Superior Bargaining Power and the Global Food Value Chain: The Wuthering Heights of Holistic Competition Law?' (2016) 1 *Concurrences* 22.

and fifty odd years on issues relating to the definition and measurement of welfare. This was considered important as it built the claim for relevance of economics in the policy-making process. The neoclassical paradigm that emerged from the mid-nineteenth century onwards and is still considered the mainstream economic theoretical framework turned to the individual, rather than collective entities, such as the nation, which were traditionally the focus of classical economists, as the main unit of analysis, adhering to what is called methodological individualism, which attempts to explain social phenomena by assessing the motivations and actions of *individual* actors (agents). Starting from the level of individual agents, and making the way up to collective organizations, with a process that we will briefly sketch, neoclassical economists relied on marginal analysis, or marginalism. Assuming that an individual operates according to the principle of utility maximization, which following Jeremy Bentham is the appropriate unifying principle of human motivation, an individual will stop acting when the rate of change in utility that may be enjoyed, for instance by buying an ice cream (if one focuses on the demand side) or working an additional hour (if one focuses on the supply side) equals the rate of change in disutility. In our examples, the disutility represents the cost of an additional ice cream—either monetary or, for instance, in terms of health effect—or that of the opportunity cost of spending this additional hour of work with friends, watching a movie, relaxing at home, etc. Hence, what counts is marginal utility (the rate of change in utility), rather than the total utility enjoyed.

According to this theory, neoclassical economists were able to develop a framework that is based on the idea that the measure of welfare is the extent to which the preferences of the *individual* agents are satisfied. An individual agent will be assumed to act in order to satisfy her (or his) preferences in the most efficient way (the principle of rationality). From this perspective, rationality is purely instrumental and is linked to the satisfaction of preferences, whatever these may be. Inspired by Newtonian physics, neoclassical economics examined the action of individual agents, by using the metaphor of equilibrium, that is, the state of rest, from which the individual actor(s) do not have an incentive to move. By using the concept of equilibrium, economists purport to make predictions about the way instrumentally rational individual agents will choose to act in order to satisfy their preferences.

These concepts are particularly important if one wants to understand consumer choice. In the first section, we will succinctly explore the conceptual foundations of welfare economics and their link to the theory of consumer choice, the bread and butter of competition economics. In the second section, we will study the implications of this marginalist model of thinking for the study of firms, products and markets. Our hope is that by understanding the theoretical foundations of competition economics, students of competition law will be able to engage critically with the input of economists and understand the theoretical underpinnings of the concepts of 'market power' and 'market definition' that have been the first transplants from economics in the competition law jargon and methodology.

3.2.1. THE CONCEPTUAL FOUNDATIONS OF WELFARE ECONOMICS: ORDINAL UTILITY, REVEALED PREFERENCES, AND BEHAVIOURISM

Modern welfare theory profoundly transformed Bentham's concept of utility. First, the concept was redefined from a measure of the wealth of a nation into a measurement of the mental state (pain and pleasure) of an economic subject, which, as it is not amenable to direct measurement and observation, is measured through indirect, but observable effects on markets, notably through prices, which represent the exchange value (relative price) of the commodity (the marginalist revolution).[42] The marginal utility that an individual enjoys from the consumption of a product can thus be measured by the money the individual agent is willing to pay to purchase an additional unit of that product, assuming that the utility of money is constant. It is important to repeat here that economists assume that decisions are always reached by comparing additional benefits to additional costs at each instance of decision-making, what is called marginal analysis or marginalism. Utility is marginal, as the choice over this or other alternative of consumption is marginal. Second, welfare theory abandoned the hedonic concept of utility for its representation as a preference ordering (the ordinal revolution). The concept of preference was itself interpreted in terms of choice, preferences representing comparative evaluations (choice). Behavioural economics has challenged this equation of choice to preference and ultimately to welfare. By emphasizing the possibility of a 'market failure' this time not due to 'externalities', which identify imperfections of the price system because of a divergence between private (to the parties of a transaction) and public benefits and costs, but due to 'internalities', that is situations in which people do not internalize all consequences of their actions on themselves because of bounded rationality and limits in their cognitive capacity, behavioural economics seems to take a more pro-State-intervention stance than mainstream neoclassical price theory economics, as it relies on asymmetric paternalism (also called libertarian paternalism[43]), that is, the idea of framing options in a way as to promote the individual's freedom of choice, by 'creating large benefits for those who make errors, while imposing little or no harm on those who are fully rational' may satisfy the 'true', 'cold' preferences of consumers.[44] These approaches do not challenge the normative value of the rationality assumption, but acknowledge that this may not describe well the interactions between the different actors in real world situations.

3.2.2. FIRMS, PRODUCTION, AND MARKETS

3.2.2.1. The factors of production and commodification

While consumers buy commodities (inputs) in order to produce utility (output) that will satisfy their consumption preferences, firms buy commodities (inputs) in order to produce other commodities (outputs). The commodities that are used as inputs may also be described as factors of production, as they form an intrinsic part of the production process. Economists usually list as factors of production land, labour, capital, and entrepreneurship. The process of commodification of these factors of production, that is, that they are perceived as commodities, basically an 'object produced for sale on the market', has been long, some of them not considered as commodities prior to the first industrial revolution in the late eighteenth century and the development of modern capitalism. Political economist Karl Polanyi has explained in his *magnum opus, The Great Transformation*, how land, labour and money were 'fictitious commodities' developed as a result of a process of marketization, where these

42 Marginalists focused on the *marginal utility*, that is, the additions and subtractions to the enjoyment of an agent, which are observable and measurable, rather than on the *total utility* enjoyed by that person, which would be more difficult to measure.

43 RH Thaler and CR Sunstein, 'Libertarian Paternalism' (2003) 93(2) *American Economic Rev* 175.

44 C Camerer, S Issacharoff, G Loewenstein, T O'Donoghue, and M. Rabin, 'Regulation for Conservatives: Behavioral Economics and the Case for "Asymmetric Paternalism"' (2003) 151(3) *University of Pennsylvania L Rev* 1211.

various elements that were not previously sold on a market, became part of a process of exchange which could be (self-)regulated by the invisible hand of the market.[45] According to Polanyi, 'the extension of the market mechanism to the elements of industry—land, labour, and money—was the inevitable consequence of the introduction of the factory system in a commercial society'.[46]

The development of large corporations was the result of the second industrial revolution that took place from the last half of the nineteenth century until the First World War in the twentieth century, with the development of railways, electricity, and mass production. This led to the separation of ownership and control and to the development of a new managerial class of experts and the bureaucratization of corporations.[47] Although for some economists, like Joseph Schumpeter, this managerial class was to be distinguished to that of entrepreneurs,[48] entrepreneurship was soon commoditized with the development of a market of professional managers/experts/engineers selling their entrepreneurial talent and technical/organizational skills to shareholders eager to maximize their shares' value.[49] Hence, entered entrepreneurship as a new factor of production, now becoming a commodity. The third industrial revolution with the development of information technology led to the expansion of new spaces of commodification, exemplified by the expansion of intellectual property rights. The emergent or already occurring fourth industrial revolution will certainly add a new process of commodification, digital identities and personal information.[50]

3.2.2.2. Firms as hierarchies: Applying marginalism to the question of economic organization

Firms may decide to purchase these commodities (inputs) at a market, or to substitute the market by producing these inputs on their own (integration). The decision to use the market mechanism or to integrate the activities within the firm, the 'make or buy problem', has been explained by economist Ronald Coase in his seminal contribution on The Nature of the Firm in 1937.[51] Applying marginalism essentially to a question of economic organization, Coase explained that a firm will expand (integrate) an activity until the cost of organizing an additional transaction within the firm becomes equal to the cost of carrying out the same transaction by means of an open market exchange. The emphasis on transactions as the unit of analysis for issues of economic organization was not Coase's idea but that of John Commons, who reformulated the problem of economic organization as follows: 'the ultimate unit of activity [. . .] must contain in itself the three principles of conflict, mutuality, and order[;] [t]his unit is a transaction'.[52] Ronald Coase's major insight in 'The Nature of the Firm' that the price mechanism is not the only way of coordinating the economic system, through a series of exchange transactions on a market, but that the firm, in which the coordinating function is the entrepreneur, constitutes an alternative method of coordination. Coase indicated that using

45 K Polanyi, *The Great Transformation* (1944; Beacon Press, 2001). 46 Ibid, 78.

47 FW Taylor, *The Principles of Scientific Management* (1911; Harper & Brothers, 1919); A Berle and G Means, *The Modern Corporation and Private Property* (Transaction Publishers, 1932).

48 J Schumpeter, *Capitalism, Socialism and Democracy* (Harper and Brothers, 1942; Harper Colophon, 1976).

49 T Veblen, *The Engineers and the Price System* (1921; Viking Press, 1934).

50 Boston Consulting Group, *The Value of Our Digital Identity* (Liberty Global Series, 2012), available at https://www.libertyglobal.com/wp-content/uploads/2017/06/The-Value-of-Our-Digital-Identity.pdf.

51 R Coase, 'The Nature of the Firm' (1937) 4 *Economica* 387.

52 J Commons, 'The Problem of Correlating Law, Economics and Ethics' (1932) 8 *Wisconsin L Rev* 3.

the market system (or price mechanism) involves costs (the so-called transaction costs) and that these are comparable to the organizational costs (the cost of setting a hierarchy controlling the transaction). According to Coase, 'the main reason why it is profitable to establish a firm would seem to be that there is a cost of using the price mechanism'.[53] Organization within a firm also involves costs. The choice between the firm or the market depends on a trade-off between the costs of using the market mechanism and the costs of carrying out the same transaction within the firm.

Coase's work radically changed the way the concept of firm was perceived by economics. Although, previously, economic analysis relied on the concept of firm as having essentially a production function and insisted on the economies of scale in production as the principal motivation in creating firms (productive efficiencies), it became apparent that in some circumstances there were important transactional efficiencies in organizing a transaction within a firm. Firms were therefore considered as governance structures that were alternative forms of organization with respect to the price mechanism in a market.

The theory has been developed further by Oliver Williamson, who contrasted hierarchies and markets, as different methods of organizing production. The choice between these two forms of organization is made according to the 'discrete alignment principle'.[54] In view of the attributes of each transaction: 'agents operating in a competitive environment will adopt the mode of organization that fits better with the attributes of the transactions at stake'.[55] The attributes of the transactions that explain variations are of three sorts: (1) the specificity of assets involved, which are defined as 'the value of investments that would be lost in any alternative use';[56] (2) uncertainty that may surround the organization of the transaction; and (3) the frequency of the transaction. Indeed, if a transaction takes place often, this spreads the fixed costs necessary to establish a non-market governance mechanism,[57] which explains the emergence of hierarchies. The more these variables are present, the more it makes sense to move from the residual situation of the market to that of hierarchy. Williamson puts forward a comparative institutional approach, analysing the make-or-buy problem as the efficient choice from a discrete set of alternative governance mechanisms (namely, integration and non-integration). We will return to transactions costs economics in Chapter 9 on distribution agreements, but for the time being it is important to keep in mind that the marginalist approach followed with regard to firms is similar than the one we previously explained about consumers.

3.2.2.3. The distinction between firms and consumers

There are, however, important differences. First, firms do not consume inputs or a combination of inputs by purchasing them, in order to satisfy their 'preferences', under the limitation of their budget constraints, as consumers do, but use an input or a combination of inputs so long as this will generate the maximum profits. Firms may decide to increase the use of one

53 R Coase, 'The Nature of the Firm' (1937) 4 *Economica* 387, 388.

54 O Williamson, *Markets and Hierarchies: Analysis and Antitrust Implications* (Free Press, 1st edn, 1975); O Williamson, *The Mechanisms of Governance* (OUP, 1st edn, 1996).

55 O Williamson, 'Comparative Economic Organization: The Analysis of Discrete Structural Alternatives' (1991) 36 *Administrative Science Q* 269, 277; C Ménard, 'The Economics of Hybrid Organizations' (2004) 160 *J Institutional and Theoretical Economics* 345, 354.

56 C Ménard, 'A New Institutional Approach to Organization' in C Ménard and M Shirley (eds) *Handbook of New Institutional Economics* (Springer, 1st edn, 2005), 281, 286.

57 Ibid, 285.

factor of production (machines or capital) to compensate for the loss of another factor of production (labour), what is called the marginal rate of technical substitution. This is because these commodities/factors of production are indifferent to the firm as long as they give rise to the same quantity of output (these are represented by isoquants, which is the equivalent of indifference curves for consumers). The production costs incurred should be within the firm's budget line (or constraint). Neoclassical economists assume that the objective of the firm is profit maximization, which is equivalent to the concept of utility maximization that we employed previously for consumers. Profit is the difference between revenue and economic cost. Economic cost should not be confused with accounting cost, as it also includes opportunity costs. For instance, in order to assess the economic cost of a PhD degree, an economist will not only focus on tuition fees, subsistence expenses, etc, but will also include the opportunity costs of the salary or wage that otherwise could be earned during the period of study for the PhD.

For a firm, it makes sense to increase output as long as this leads the firm to increase its revenue sufficiently. When deciding if it will increase its output, the firm will carefully assess if an additional unit of output will bring more revenue (marginal revenue) that it will cost (marginal cost). The profit maximizing level of production is thus the one at which marginal cost equals marginal revenue. The revenue curve of the firm is affected by the extent of competition it faces at the market. A firm may decide to raise its price for a product and decrease output as long as it does not expect or predict that a competing firm will not cut down its prices, and therefore eat away its market share and revenue. A competitive market thus breeds an inherent uncertainty about a firm's revenue at different prices and output levels.

In a monopolized market things are simpler, as one would expect that the monopolist will produce as long as the marginal revenue is higher than the marginal cost. Uncertainty in this case will be limited, as the monopolist will set the supply according to the demand. Take note that by referring to monopoly, we mean a firm that has a 100 per cent share of a market, well defined in terms of substitutes, and does not face any risk of entry by a new competitor, or a powerful buyer. One may derive easily the monopolist's revenue curve by looking to the consumer's demand curve. The monopolist does not have to take into account the supply curve of its competitors, as in competitive markets. That means that if a monopolist decides to decrease output, the total market output will decline as the monopolist is the only producer in this market. The monopolist charges the price that yields the highest profits, which is higher than the price it would charge if the market was a competitive one. However, a monopolist will not charge the higher prices he can get (an infinite price for his product), if this will have as a possible effect of reducing demand for his product leading only to consumers that have the highest willingness to pay to continue buying it. For instance, assuming that there is a State monopoly for selling beer with a high alcoholic content, and the monopoly decides to triple the price of beer, one may expect that many consumers will stop purchasing high alcoholic beer and switch to low alcoholic beer or another type of drink. There is a point where pricing above will lead to a loss of customers that will be so large that it will outweigh the gain in profit from this specific transaction. So the sky is not the limit for monopoly price rises. A monopolist's power to charge a high price is ultimately function of the elasticity of demand for its product, that is, the possibility that his product may be substituted by another one (cross-price elasticity). What is clear is that in a monopoly the total profit is maximized. Monopoly markets can be described by three structural and functional factors: (i) one seller occupies the market; (ii) there are no close substitutes for the consumers; and (iii) there are substantial barriers to entry, and exit is difficult.

3.2.2.4. Monopsony

Monopsony refers to the converse situation of a monopoly buyer. In the standard model of monopsony, the supply side of a market is perfectly competitive and is represented by an upward-sloping supply curve. As a mirror image of a monopolist's behaviour, a monopsonist can take advantage of his power by reducing his demand so as to force suppliers to sell to it at a lower price than what would have prevailed in a competitive market. The monopsonist buyer's purchasing volume will influence the market price for the whole product, reducing the overall market price that is paid. The lower price obtained by the buyer will reflect the lower marginal cost of supply, with the result that the least efficient or marginal suppliers who have the higher average total costs will reduce output to the level that equals their marginal costs, in order to reduce their average total costs. These firms will assign their production capacities to other products that would have been the supplier's second choice in a competitive market. Assuming that the monosponist uses the product bought as an input in a production process for an output which he then sells to consumers, one may want to assess the impact of monopsony on the price paid by final consumers. This will depend on the position of the monopsonist at the downstream market for the output. If the monopsonist in the input market is also a monopolist in the downstream output market, a reduction of the supply of the input, following the reduction of the price paid for it by the monopolist, will lead to a reduction in the supply of the products that incorporate the input at the downstream market. This drop in output could lead to an increase of the price paid by the final consumers, making them worse-off, if the monosponist in the input market, which is also a monopolist in the output market decides to charge higher prices, keeping the additional profits for himself instead of passing through to the final consumers the profits he made from the reduction in the price of the input he purchased. However, if competition in the downstream output market is intense, then the buyer may have an incentive to lower prices and increase output to the benefit of the final consumers.

3.2.2.5. *Monopoly versus perfect competition*

Economists tend to contrast the situation of monopoly to that of perfect competition. This usually denotes a situation where no individual supplier can influence the market price and all suppliers are price-takers. Such a market situation is rarely met in reality (except, perhaps, in foreign exchange or commodity markets), but constitutes an ideal type—'perfect' meaning that the competitive situation cannot be done better. As it was demonstrated by Augustin Cournot, the excess of price over marginal cost approached zero as the number of like producers became large and the difference approached zero as the number of rivals approached infinity (a situation of 'unlimited competition'). In a situation of perfect competition, production takes place at the lowest level of cost. This indicates productive efficiency. Consumers who are willing to pay the price that covers this production cost are served at the lowest possible price, which indicates allocative efficiency. This also leads to a great number of transactions occurring as more consumers are able to benefit from the fact that the price of the good is at or below the level of the price they are willing to pay and more producers benefit from the fact that the price is at or below their cost of supply, thus enabling them to earn a 'normal profit' or reasonable rate of return, that is it covers the entrepreneur's opportunity costs and/or compensates the capital owner for the risk incurred. Perfect competition may also serve as a yardstick in order to assess the social costs of monopoly, essentially by comparing the level of output under perfect competition and that under monopoly.

A perfectly competitive market is deemed to present certain characteristics, which are looked favourably at, from the point of view of productive and allocative efficiency, but also welfare. These are the following.

A firm in a perfectly competitive market has little discretion over the price it may charge, but may decide the level of output to produce, even if this will be sold at the perfectly competitive market established single market price. Each competitor will decide whether to produce an additional unit of output taking into account the marginal costs (MC) of that unit, which are the costs incurred for the production of an additional unit of output. A firm's costs may be either fixed or variable. Fixed costs do not vary with the level of output over the short-run, for instance the lifetime of an industrial plant. They may encompass costs, such as the costs of land, the machinery, any other form of durable equipment, the salaries of the management. These are the expenses that a firm incurs whatever the level of output it produces. As their name indicates, variable costs vary with the level of output. This will usually include the costs of inputs, the cost of hourly wages for employees, the costs of transportation. These costs vary because, for instance a firm that decides to increase its production may need to buy more raw materials required for the production of the output. One should, however, take into account that the classification of a cost as being fixed or variable depends on the time-frame one takes into account. In the long run, some fixed costs, such as the costs of land or equipment, will become variable if for instance, the industry decides to expand production or replace its plant equipment with more technically advanced machines.

Fixed and variable costs are represented as costs per unit of output. Average variable costs (AVC) indicate the total of variable costs divided by the output the firm produces. Average fixed costs (AFC) indicate the total of fixed costs divided by the output the firm produces. The AVC curve usually takes a U shape, as AVC declines as output increases up to a point where the plant produces the optimal output it was designed to produce. After this point, AVC increases. Average total costs (ATC) include all costs (variable and fixed) divided by output and, as its name indicates, represent the total costs a firm incurs. The ATC curve has the same shape as the AVC curve, but tends to be higher than AVC at lower levels of output. However, as output grows, the two curves converge. When output increases, AFC decrease up to a point approaching zero. Marginal costs are function of variable costs essentially, as the firm does not incur any fixed costs by expanding its output by an additional unit in the short run. The MC curve may, however, vary considerably. For instance, if one considers an airline company that serves the route between London and Paris with an Airbus A-320 aircraft that can carry up to 180 passengers, the marginal cost of the 181st passenger will rise dramatically, in comparison to the marginal cost of the 180th passenger, as in this case the airline will need to put in place a second plane. We will explore in more detail the various measures of costs in Chapter 9 on abuse of a dominant position.

For the time being, however, we need only the concepts of MC, AVC, and ATC in order to understand how a firm in a perfectly competitive market will decide of the output it will produce. If all firms are profit maximizing, they will produce one additional unit of output up to the level that its marginal cost equals the market price. If this level is reached, the firm may increase profits only by decreasing its output. In a perfectly competitive market, firms will all have similar marginal cost curves at current output levels. If there are any differences in efficiency, these transcribe only at the rate of output the firm will produce at the same marginal cost level. The efficiency differential between each firm will also show in its profitability. For a firm to be profitable, it is essential that the point on the firm's marginal cost curve regarding the additional unit of output is at or above the firm's average total cost curve. If this is not the case, the firm will be producing in order to minimize losses, rather than maximize profits.

One should bear in mind that the firm will have an incentive to produce even if the market price does not cover its average total cost, as long as the market price is above its average variable costs. Indeed, the firm may suffer 'sunk' fixed costs, in case it decided to stop production and go out of the market. The 'sunk' costs are those that the firm cannot recover, such as the costs of some old plant equipment that it would be impossible to sell if a firm decides to go out of business. In any case, fixed costs are incurred, and must be paid, whether the firm produces, or not.

In order to characterize a market as perfectly competitive, a large number of restrictive assumptions are made which, as we highlighted, are seldom satisfied in real markets: (i) there should be an infinite number of buyers and sellers in this market; (ii) the quantity of the market's products sought by any buyer or sold by any seller is so small relative to the total quantity traded that changes in these quantities leave market prices unaffected; (iii) all sellers make a homogeneous product so that consumers are really indifferent as to which producer they purchase from, as long as the price is the same; (iv) buyers and sellers dispose of perfect information about market prices and the nature of the product; (v) there is complete freedom of entry and exit out of the market.

A number of authors have criticized the concept of 'perfect competition' as being unrealistic and therefore a poor approximation of the way 'real' markets work. They suggested instead that economics' reasoning should be based on more realistic standard models of analysis, such as that of 'monopolistic competition'[58] or 'imperfect competition'.[59] In most of the real-world markets, firms have some control over their price and face a downward sloping demand curve for their output (not a horizontal one as in situations of perfect competition). It is very easy to see the reason why. Large firms may benefit from economies of scale and produce at lower costs than smaller firms, thus destroying the conditions for perfect competition as a few firms can produce the industry's output most efficiently. In the perfect competition model, it is assumed that the unit of production remains constant as the scale of production increases (there are no returns to scale). One may also add various barriers to entry that characterize some markets, such as intellectual property rights, legal regulations, product differentiation, advertising, etc, which result in high entry costs, thus limiting the number of new competitors that can enter the market when price increases. Hence, most industries are characterized by market structures that present the features of oligopoly (an industry with few producers recognizing that their price depends on their own actions and those of their rivals), monopolistic competition (where there are many sellers producing products that are differentiated but which are also close substitutes to each other, each firm having a limited ability to influence its output price), or that of a dominant firm with a competitive fringe of smaller competitors (a monopolist facing a certain amount of competition). Despite these unrealistic assumptions, some economists responded to these criticisms by providing a different function to the concept of perfect competition:

> [W]e should notice the most common and the most important criticism of the concept of perfect competition-that it is unrealistic. This criticism has been widespread since the concept was completely formulated and underlies the warm reception which the profession gave to the doctrines of imperfect and monopolistic competition in the 1930's. One could reply to this criticism that all concepts sufficiently general and sufficiently precise to be useful in scientific

58 EH Chamberlin, *The Theory of Monopolistic Competition* (Harvard University Press, 1933).
59 J Robinson, *The Economics of Imperfect Competition* (Macmillan, 1933).

> analysis must be abstract: that, if a science is to deal with a large class of phenomena, clearly it cannot work with concepts that are faithfully descriptive of even one phenomenon, for then they will be grotesquely undescriptive of others.[60]

The rise of behavioural economics does not have an impact only on the demand side through the analysis of consumer biases but may also have influence on the way the supply side of the market is analysed.

OFT1224, 'What does Behavioural Economics Mean for Competition Policy?' (March 2010) (references omitted)

> Such consumer biases are not simply relevant to understanding how consumers act in a market; they also have a bearing on firms' [suppliers'] behaviour. Where such biases exist, firms can act to exacerbate and exploit them, at every stage in the decision-making process. Indeed, [. . .] a number of common practices by firms can have significant impacts on the extent of the biases exhibited by consumers. This is not a new finding. Arguably, marketing experts have long known it. Moreover, the standard economic literature already indicates that firms may have an incentive to increase search or switching costs in order to increase the barriers. Introducing intuitions from behavioural economics, however, suggests that such behaviour may be more prevalent and longer-lasting than initially thought:
>
> *Accessing information.* Firms can make it more difficult for consumers to perform optimal search. For example, behavioural economics shows that consumers do not tend to look at pricing terms that are not provided upfront. Firms may exploit this by putting more of the price into add-on services; restructuring their tariffs, adding clauses within the terms and conditions; or making price searching harder (for example, by drip pricing—only revealing the true price after the customer has spent some time choosing).
>
> *Assessing offers.* Firms can make it more difficult for consumers to assess the best deal. Because behavioural economics indicates that consumers have difficulties comparing across differently structured offers, firms may exploit this by obfuscating their prices or increasing choice or complexity. They may also use price promotions and framing to distract and distort decision-making.
>
> *Acting on information and analysis.* Firms can make it more difficult for consumers to act to get the best deals. Behavioural economics indicates that consumers may display more inertia than traditionally suggested, perhaps due to overconfidence in their capacity to improve things at a later time. Firms, knowing that consumers display this inertia, can increase switching costs (for example, making consumers use registered post to cancel). They can also use defaults and automatic enrolments, or use time limited offers to inhibit switching.

Of course, in many circumstances, firms' ability to exploit such biases in this way will be limited, for example, by the potential for new firms to enter and provide products which make a virtue out of not exploiting biases. Such market solutions to problems arising from behavioural biases are discussed in the last section. However, some of the recent behavioural literature suggests that there may be equilibriums in which all firms exploit consumer biases and none of them has a unilateral incentive to correct this situation.

60 G Stigler, 'Perfect Competition, Historically Contemplated' (1957) 65(1) *J Political Economy* 1, 17. Stigler also added a further argument for perfect competition to be the standard model of analysis in economics, its frequent use by economists.

The nature, prevalence, and self-awareness of consumer biases can also differ across markets, and this too can have an impact on how firms react. For example, in some markets there will be a proportion of consumers that know about their biases and correct for them (termed 'sophisticated' in the literature) and a proportion who do not (termed 'myopes'). In such markets, firms may have an incentive to exploit the myopes, but competition will force them to compete away some of the resulting rents on low upfront prices in order to entice them in the first place. This is competition from which the sophisticated gain. Effectively, the sophisticated get a better price than they would absent the exploitation of the myopes.

In such a situation, any firm that tried to stop exploiting the myopes would have to raise its initial price, which would, in turn, cause both types of customer to switch away. The myopes switch because they no longer see a cheap upfront price, and the sophisticated switch because they are no longer subsidized by myopes. The result is that under certain conditions no firm can profit from moving to a non-exploitative outcome unilaterally.

Behavioural economics may thus alert competition authorities on instances of exploitation of consumers by firms that the neoclassical price theory framework may not have picked up.[61] One may nevertheless argue that consumers are not always natural persons and that in many cases suppliers sell to intermediary consumers, which are also firms, and presumably less prone to the challenge of 'bounded rationality', the standard approach to firm behaviour assuming that this is always instrumentally rational to profit maximization. In practice, however, behavioural economics insights have also been applied to analyse firm behaviour, and there is ample empirical evidence that the literature on heuristics and biases may also apply in the context of natural as well as moral persons.[62]

3.2.3. THE SOCIAL COSTS OF MARKET POWER: STATIC VERSUS DYNAMIC COMPETITION

3.2.3.1. Implications for economic efficiency

At its simplest, the case for intervention against market power, albeit not directly, is based on an understanding that a substantial position of market power is a classic case of market failure. Market failure is a general term describing situations in which market outcomes are not Pareto efficient. Pareto efficiency, also referred to as allocative efficiency, occurs when resources are so allocated that it is not possible to make anyone better off without making someone else worse off, or stated otherwise, where (scarce) resources are used to produce the mix of good and services which is most valued by society.

This is an abstract concept, which is grounded on the theoretical construct of general equilibrium, which looks at the economy in its entirety, that is, where all markets are considered together. In practice, though, the case against monopoly (as the archetypal example of market failure due to market power) is based on partial equilibrium analysis, which looks at only one market at a time, characterized by its demand and supply curves, as sketched in Figure 3.2.[63]

61 For analysis, see GA Akerlof and RJ Shiller, *Phishing for Phools, The Economics of Manipulation & Deception* (Princeton University Press, 2015).

62 M Armstrong and S Huck, 'Behavioral Economics as Applied to Firms: A Primer' (2010) 6(1) *Competition Policy Int'l* 3.

63 See, for a discussion, GJ Werden, 'Antitrust's Rule of Reason: Only Competition Matters' (1 March 2013), available at https://ssrn.com/abstract=2227097. In a nutshell, to focus on a single market rests on the assumption that the levels of income and the prices of both substitute and complement products are fixed. Otherwise, an increase in income levels would shift the demand schedule outwards. The same holds for a reduction in the

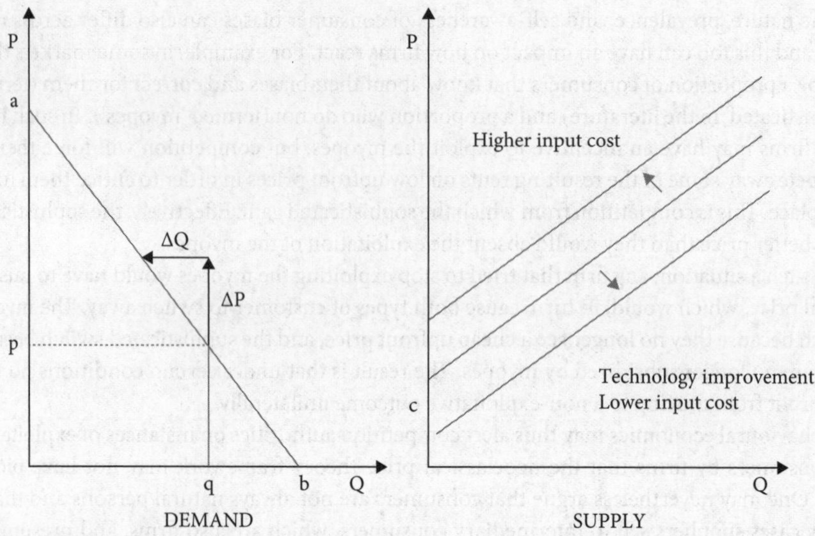

Figure 3.2. Partial equilibrium analysis

On the left side, the (inverse)[64] demand schedule is downward sloping to the right. There are two main explanations for this: (a) at an individual level, consumers value (and therefore are willing to pay for) the consumption of an additional unit of the product sold decreases as the overall quantity consumed (purchased) increases; (b) at an aggregate level, under the assumption that consumers differ in how much they are willing to pay for the first unit of product purchased, as prices fall more consumers are willing to buy the product sold.

Consumer sensitivity to prices is measured by the (own-price) elasticity of demand,[65] which gives the per cent (percentage) decline in quantity sold that results from a 1 per cent increase in price (ie, a unit-free measure).[66] For very small variation in prices, the demand elasticity can be expressed as the inverse of the slope of the demand schedule times the ratio of current price to quantity. For example, in the case of the linear demand depicted in Figure 3.2, $b/a\ p/q$.

price of complement products (which correspond to a discount in the price for the combination of products); whereas a reduction in the price of substitute products would shift the demand schedule inwards (since consumer would demand a similar price reduction to keep purchasing the product sold).

64 People normally decide how much to buy depending on prices, whereas Figure 3.2 shows the price charged depending on the quantity purchased.

65 A distinction needs to be made between the concept of market demand (price) elasticity and firm demand (price) elasticity. Whilst the former depends on whether there are substitutes for the product/service sold in the market; the latter depends on how substitutable (homogeneous) are the products/services sold by rivals (ie in the same market). For example, utility services such as electricity are likely to exhibit an inelastic market demand, since there is no concrete replacement for a service than every household requires. Nevertheless, to the extent that the retail offers of competing energy firms are perceived as fungible by consumers, firm price elasticity is likely to be pretty high—ie pricing rivalry is intense. That is to say, demand for substitutes raises in response to an increase in price for the product in question. This effect is captured by the cross-price elasticity, which is the ratio between the percentage increase is volume sold for the substitute product that results from a 1 per cent increase in price for the product concerned. The closer the substitute the higher is the corresponding cross-price elasticity.

66 Although the own-price demand elasticity is negative in value by definition, the absolute (positive) value is conventionally used.

The linear demand is based on the assumption that consumers' marginal valuation of the product sold keeps decreasing at a constant rate, which yields the counter-intuitive result that even if the price is zero, consumers would only want to consume a finite quantity, *b* in the picture above. This means that demand elasticity grows as we move upwards along the demand schedule.[67] Conversely, a demand specification with constant elasticity of demand (also known as iso-elastic or log-linear demand) doesn't have intercepts, ie quantity demanded is infinite for prices approaching zero, and vice versa. Conventionally, for elasticity values below one the demand is called inelastic, since volumes sold decrease less than proportionally to prices. For values above one the demand is described as elastic.

On the right side, the supply curve is typically upward sloping to the right, showing that sellers are willing to sell higher quantities if prices are higher. This pattern is a reflection of the fact that the cost of producing an additional unit of output increases as output rises. For example, to increase production, a firm might have to pay higher salaries to existing workers for longer hours or hire less skilled workers who would be less productive and require more training.[68] Similarly, commodity producers would typically face higher incremental (in economic jargon, marginal) costs to expand output (eg due to the utilization of quarries less easy to reach or less productive crop fields). There are primarily two factors which would cause a shift in the supply schedule (as depicted in Figure 3.2): (a) an increase (reduction) in the price on an input would shift the supply curve inward to the left (outward to the right), thus reducing (increasing) the quantity offered at the same price; (b) technological improvement in the production process normally shift the supply curve outward to the right.[69]

As depicted in Figure 3.3, the trigger for competition law enforcement is (likely) changes to consumer surplus, which is basically treated as a proxy for consumer welfare, caused by an increase in price/restriction in output due to the exploitation of market power (or, more concretely, the likelihood that an increase in market power will lead to its exploitation).

Consumer surplus can be graphically depicted as the area under the downward sloping demand curve but above the price charged (ie, the residual consumer willingness to pay). Total surplus is the sum of consumer and producer surplus, the latter roughly corresponding to the accounting concept of operating profit margin, so that changes in producer surplus should equate to changes in profits.

Usually, looking at changes in total or consumer surplus makes no difference in practice, since both tend to move in the same direction, as graphically captured by the deadweight loss, which is the loss of consumer and producer surplus due to a restriction in output caused by an increase in price, and stands to signify how allocative efficiency has worsened due to the exploitation of market power. As put by Werden '[a]nything enlarging the metaphorical pie offers a potential Pareto improvement because it is possible to make at least one individual better off while no one is worse off.'[70]

67 Specifically, at price zero demand elasticity is equally zero. Conversely, at the intercept *a* (where quantity is zero), demand elasticity is infinite.

68 Alternatively, skilled staff would have to be poached (by offering higher salaries) from rivals. This would be particularly the case for professional service firms, whose main asset is normally reckoned to be their 'human capital'.

69 A classic example is the observation that computing processing power doubles every 18 months under the so-called Moore's law, which nowadays has broader application to other technological areas such as energy efficiency: see eg DL Chandler, 'How to Predict the Progress of Technology', *MIT News* (6 March 2013), available at http://web.mit.edu/newsoffice/2013/how-to-predict-the-progress-of-technology-0306.html.

70 GJ Werden, 'Antitrust's Rule of Reason: Only Competition Matters' (1 March 2013), 28, available at https://ssrn.com/abstract=2227097.

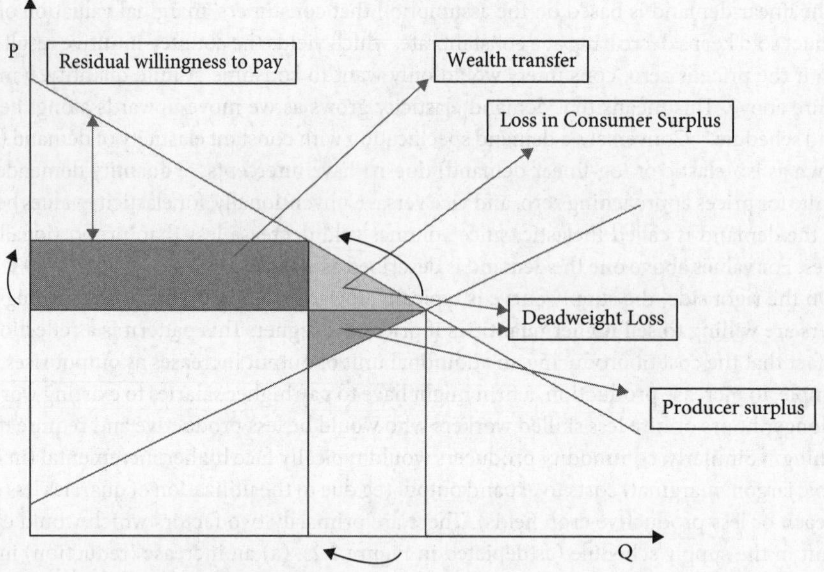

Figure 3.3. Market power and efficiency

In this sense, the case against the exploitation of substantial market power is not linked to the transfer of wealth from consumer to producers over those (infra-marginal) units of output still sold (ie, the light blue rectangle in Figure 3.3), but merely on the lost transactions which could have taken place under a more competitive scenario.[71] In any case, for operational purposes the focus is on consumer harm, as captured by the (likelihood of) higher prices and lower quantity; bearing in mind that in practice hardly anyone in the field of enforcement ever actually attempts to measure/estimate actual changes in either total or consumer welfare.[72]

It is worth noting that in Figure 3.3, the equilibrium price before the price increase corresponds to the competitive equilibrium, where the supply-curve (reflective of the industry's marginal costs) intersects with the demand curve (reflective of consumers' aggregate willingness to pay), which entails that allocative efficiency is maximized. The idea, therefore, is that the preservation of competitive rivalry (the protection of the competitive process) is essential to prevent a prolonged departure from that optimal outcome.

Beside allocative efficiency, it is often argued that a competitive equilibrium will also maximize productive efficiency, where output is produced with the least amount of resources, given the current set of production technologies—ie demand is served by the most efficient firms. This is not always the case, though, in the sense that there are market configurations

[71] The irrelevance of distributional concerns is normally justified with reference to the 'compensation principle' (also known as Kaldor–Hicks efficiency criterion, or Potential Pareto Improvement) which posits that, if gainers can compensate losers and still be better off, the change observed in the partial equilibrium analysis is desirable. That is to say, even if the compensation never actually takes place, it is down to the political system to take care of the redistribution of the 'pie' (the separability thesis).

[72] There are some examples of competition authorities commissioning studies into the effects of their past decision, thus basically assessing whether their intervention (or lack thereof) has increased consumer surplus. For an overview, see OECD, 'Impact Evaluation of Merger Decisions', DAF/COMP(2011)24 (2011), available at http://www.oecd.org/daf/competition/Impactevaluationofmergerdecisions2011.pdf.

where a trade-off between allocative and productive efficiencies triggered by an increase in a position of substantial market power might emerge.[73]

Let's imagine that thanks to the exclusion of a less (productively) efficient rival (ie, as a result of a merger or foreclosure) a larger share of demand is now allocated to a dominant firm with lower costs, so that the supply curve shifts outward to the right. At the same time, though, the exclusion of a less efficient rival will reduce competitive constraints in the market making it possible for the dominant firm to increase prices. As shown in Figure 3.3, the reduction in costs may not be large enough to offset the increase in price, so that whilst consumer surplus is reduced the net impact on total surplus is ambivalent (ie, the difference between the areas of the light green quadrilateral shape and the light blue triangle).

This trade-off between productive and allocative efficiency takes place within a static framework, that is, holding technology and the product space fixed. In reality, though, firms compete also through innovation, which could either be process oriented (ie, increasing productive efficiency) or product oriented (improving the variety and/or quality of their offer).

The latter case can be subsumed in the static trade-off presented above, in particular, since an aggressive stance following process innovation is virtually indistinguishable from a scenario where a more efficient firm excludes rivals in order to then exploit its enhanced market power (as depicted in Figure 3.4 with the black arrow).

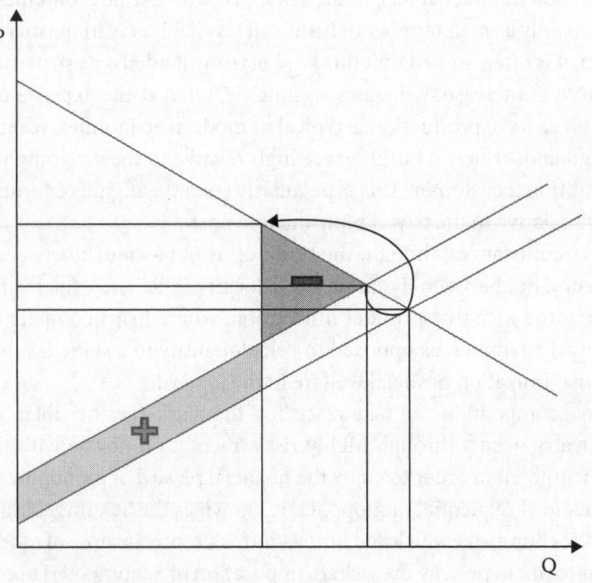

Figure 3.4. The allocative/productive efficiency trade-off (Schumpeterian trade-off) from a dynamic perspective

[73] The discovery of this efficiency trade-off is due to Oliver Williamson, who came to the conclusion that small cost savings can offset relatively larger price increases, thus entailing a more permissive standard for antitrust enforcement: see OE Williamson, 'Economies as an Antitrust Defense: Welfare Tradeoffs' (1968) 58 *American Economic Rev* 18. However, his conclusions were reliant on strong assumptions such as that the market configuration before the increase in market power was competitive; whereas if firms had already some degree of market power (so that prices were already above costs) total welfare would most likely be reduced, ie, alongside consumer welfare: see MD Whinston, 'Antitrust Policy Towards Horizontal Mergers' in M Armstrong and RH Porter (eds) *Handbook of Industrial Organization*, vol 3 (2007), 2371, 2374.

A classic example of such a sequence of exclusion and exploitation is predatory pricing. As discussed in detail in Chapter 8, predatory pricing, however, is mainly about temporarily pricing below unit incremental costs in order to exclude equally efficient rivals. Nevertheless, defendants often argue that through the alleged predatory phase their productive efficiency improved thanks to 'learning by doing' and scale economies. The former is about finding better (ie, more efficient) ways to produce an existing product over time as output accumulates (ie, by cutting waste); whereas the latter is about lowering unit costs as volumes increase. In other words, 'learning by doing' can be thought of as dynamic scale economies.

There are mainly two broad categories of sources of scale economies:

- technical specialization: a larger output makes it convenient for a firm to specialize both in human and physical capital (eg expensive specialist robotic machinery, specialist workforce)[74] whose higher costs can be spread across higher volumes of production; and
- input indivisibilities: a larger scale is needed to allow the firm to absorb large quantities of input procured in bulk deals. For example, the purchase of a large aircraft, or an expensive TV advertising campaign. By the same token, scale advantages can also result from volume discounts awarded by input suppliers. One peculiar example, here, is the ability to secure financing at cheaper prices (eg a lower interest rate over larger loans or easier access to equity finance for firms with a large market capitalization).

The controversial aspect of scale economies is that they can raise barriers to entry (as discussed in more detail later on in this chapter), in the sense that where scale economies are large relative to overall demand only a small number of firms can profitably stay in the market.[75]

In this respect, it is often argued that this kind of front-loaded cost structure, whereby firms are under pressure to increase their sales volume (ie, often at the expense of rivals) in order to lower their unit costs of production is typical of modern economies, where the initial costs of product design and/or brand building are high relative to the on-going incremental costs of serving an additional customer. This is peculiarly so in the digital economy where the 'first copy' cost is high relative to the trivial reproduction cost.

Under these circumstances, though, the trade-off is not as much between productive and allocative efficiency, but between dynamic and allocative efficiency, the former, more elusive, concept capturing the idea that product innovation, where firms compete on quality (horizontal and vertical) attributes, as opposed to price/quantity in a static fashion, is equally important for the maximization of social welfare in the long run.

At the extreme, competition can take place 'for' the market, rather than 'in' the market, in the sense that rivalry occurs through highly risky 'races' to innovate with the aim of utterly displacing the incumbent in order to enjoy the financial reward of monopoly power. This competitive mode, made of sequential monopolies, is known as the Schumpeterian mode, after the economist Joseph Schumpeter who listed innovation as a central feature of modern economies.[76] Figure 3.4 is an attempt to portray the welfare implication of Schumpeterian competition.

74 The latter source of specialization can be 'learning by doing' where workers specialize on-the-job over time, rather than been hired already specialized with an aim to increase output.

75 At the extreme, where scale economies are so large that only one firm can profitably serve the entire demand, economists talk about a 'natural monopoly', in the sense that the monopolistic market structure is unavoidable, ie, it is not the fault of the incumbent. Under such circumstances, however, competition law has little to no role to play, whereas regulatory intervention (for example, in the form of mandatory access to the essential infrastructure of the incumbent) is often required to allow other firms to profitably operate in the market.

76 J Schumpeter, *Capitalism, Socialism and Democracy* (Harper and Brothers, 1942; Harper Colophon, 1976), 84 ('[C]ompetition from the new commodity, the new technology, the new source of supply, the new

Here, it is the demand schedule that is shifted outward to the right as a result of product innovation. This demand shift reflects the fact that consumers have higher willingness to pay for the new generation of products which, therefore, supplants the current generation. Let's assume first that the latter, however, was produced under competitive conditions (ie, the product life-cycle reached the maturity stage of commoditization). Similarly to the previous trade-off between productive and allocative efficiency, the assessment of the net impact in terms of total welfare requires the balancing between the anti-competitive deadweight-loss triangle and the pro-competitive quadrilateral shaped area.

In this case, however, rather than being entirely appropriated by the dominant firm in the form of higher producer surplus, the pro-competitive effect is mostly beneficial to consumer, thanks to higher consumer surplus. This is even more the case where the sellers of the displaced product had market power (ie, as in the sequence of monopolist), so that allocative efficiency was already not being maximized. Under these circumstances, the disruption due to dynamic competition would be unambiguously beneficial for consumers.

This sketchy analysis suggests that, at least in principle, a more permissive standard of enforcement under a consumer surplus standard is more justifiable with respect to dynamic innovation than to a (static) trade-off between productive and allocative efficiency, since in the latter case the improvement in terms of total welfare would be appropriated entirely by producers (that is, unless the reduction in costs is large enough to totally offset likely increase in price due to the increase in market power).

Therefore, the observation than an incumbent is being displaced by a new entrant in a Schumpeterian fashion shall hardly be a matter of concern for a competition authority. Paradoxically, though, arguments about dynamic efficiency, and how wrong-headed enforcement action might chill out incentives for innovation, are usually deployed by incumbents alleged of foreclosing the adoption of a new product that poses a threat to their position of substantial market power. That is to say, the incumbent should be allowed to defend its turf with the aim of paying back the initial risky investment. Hence, the essential question is for how long an incumbent should be allowed to defend its dominance in order to preserve the incentives to innovate; keeping in mind that the alleged foreclosure would deter (potential) competitors from investing themselves in disrupting innovation.[77]

Suffice to say that this line of inquiry is very difficult to implement in practice, which is why competition law enforcers tend to stick to the assessment of anti-competitive foreclosure, whilst leaving it open to the defendant to prove that the alleged conduct is justified by the need to preserve their incentives to innovate to the benefit of consumers.

In this respect, it has been argued that to balance static with dynamic considerations, the analysis should focus on five sources of competitive restraints, known as 'forces',[78] specifically: (i) threat of entry; (ii) threat of substitute products or services; (iii) bargaining power of buyers; (iv) bargaining power of suppliers; and (v) rivalry among current competitors. Reassuringly, this approach is basically the same adopted in practice in the definition of relevant markets, not merely aimed at the calculation of market shares, but seen as a fundamental

organization [. . .] competition which commands a decisive cost or quality advantage and which strikes not at the margins of the profits and outputs of the existing firms but at their very foundations and their very lives.').

[77] Not surprisingly, the trade-off between incumbent and potential competitors in terms of incentives to innovate is at the core of the debate around the optimal length of the legal (monopoly) protection that should be awarded to the firm owning a patented innovation under an intellectual property (IP) right regime.

[78] See ME Porter, 'Competition and Antitrust: Toward a Productivity-based Approach to Evaluating Mergers and Joint Ventures' (2001) 46 *Antitrust Bulletin* 919.

step to the assessment of market power through the identification of barriers to entry and expansion, the main dimension of differentiation among substitutable products, and the countervailing bargaining power of suppliers and buyers.

The next section presents the analytical framework used to define relevant markets for antitrust purposes, and how to adapt it to take account of the presence of bundles and complement products, feedback loops between the buyer and the seller sides in the operation of platforms (two-sided markets), and lumpy winner-takes-all rivalry in bidding markets. The following section briefly explores the use of market shares and indices of concentration, and various indices of pricing pressure. First, however, we briefly discuss what the hotly contested debate around the issue of growing economic inequality entails, if any, for the role of policies aimed at promoting competitive outcomes.

3.2.3.2. Implications for economic inequality

Traditionally, the analysis of market power, and the corresponding trade-offs outlined above, does not explicitly deal with distributional issues. The case against monopoly is motivated by the desire to correct for the inefficiency caused by lost (marginal) transactions—the deadweight loss—rather than the implicit wealth transfer from consumers to producers over (infra-marginal) transactions. Moreover, reliance on firms' profitability as a guide for enforcement is problematic in light of the difficulty to tell whether high profits are the results of superior efficiency/quality, or the outcome of anti-competitive entry and expansion barriers.

Nevertheless, tackling market power in order to improve consumer surplus is good for inequality given that lower prices (or, better still, higher quality/price ratios) improve the purchasing power of disposable income. Moreover, where high profits are siphoned off by corporate elites (ie, rather than returned to dispersed shareholders), the concern might be that the resulting concentration of income (and, over time, accumulated wealth) is deployed to lobby against redistributive fiscal policies aimed at addressing economic inequality. From a macro-economic perspective, the concern may be that high profits induced by anti-competitive entry and expansion barriers are not re-invested. The resulting low levels of corporate investments would not only reduce aggregate demand, but also suppress productivity growth, which would ultimately constraints wage growth.[79] Hence, under these circumstances, tough antitrust enforcement ought to be welcome from a distributional perspective as well.

There are circumstances, though, where the relationship between policies aimed at promoting competition and economic inequality is not as straightforward. Low levels of corporate investments may be the result of excessive capacity spurring cut-throat price competition. This can be particularly the case where competition takes place on a global scale and the bargaining power of the local workforce is greatly undermined (eg, steel production). Similar dynamics can take place where the mobile factor of production is not capital (ie, with employers threatening to relocate where the cost of labour is lower) but labour itself, thanks to immigration at all skill levels, from seasonal or construction workers to knowledge-economy professionals. Under these circumstances, the popular (or, better still, populist) belief is that

[79] 'Too Much of a Good thing—Profits are too High. America Needs a Giant Dose of Competition', *The Economist* (26 May 2016), available at http://www.economist.com/news/briefing/21695385-profits-are-too-high-america-needs-giant-dose-competition-too-much-good-thing.

only firms' top executives can emerge as winners from these ultra-competitive labour markets, whereas the rest of us (ie, the 99.9 per cent) feel the pressure to keep up with the Joneses. These concerns may prompt protectionist calls for State intervention aimed at restricting competition, with the result that both productive and allocative efficiency would suffer. That is to say, policies that may cause economic inefficiencies are called upon to address economic inequality.

This topsy-turvy political outcome may also lead to dynamic inefficiency. It is often argued that hyper-competitive rivalry is the norm in digital industries subject to 'winners-take-all' competitive dynamics, where a position of super-dominance is the market outcome of strategies based on very aggressive pricing and/or relentless product and process innovation. On the one hand, competition 'for' (rather than 'in') the market means that consumers benefit greatly from lower prices, more convenient mode of consumption and strong innovation. On the other hand, 'winner-takes-all' dynamics raise concerns about excessive economic (and, thus, political) power concentrated in very few massive corporations, to the benefit of a new breed of corporate elites consisting of technical (rather than finance) experts. The picture is made doomier by the concern that these high-tech giants are the driving force behind automation, which threatens to further weaken the employment prospects of future generations. In summary, this would be a world where economic scarcity is no longer the foundation of the market-driven allocation mechanisms underpinning modern capitalistic societies, and where policies aimed at promoting competition in the pursuit of (allocative, productive, and dynamic) efficiency could be seen as self-defeating. In contrast, an ordoliberal approach may become more appealing, in particular where the emphasis is on the principle of freedom of economic enterprise, interpreted as the freedom of small local entrepreneur to prosper protected by global unrestricted competition; that is, despite the resulting economic inefficiencies.

3.3. MARKET DEFINITION: ACTUAL COMPETITION

A market is the actual or virtual space where competition operates. A supplier competes not only with suppliers of identical products, but also with suppliers of products to which its customers might turn if it were to raise its price. It also competes, although usually less immediately, with suppliers who might start to supply the same or substitute goods if it were to raise its price.

The relevant market has two dimensions: the product or service and the geographic area affected. Markets do not always have clear limits, and the insistence on definition rather than analysis may be misleading. There may be substitutes that are not perfect; in which case, selecting a narrow definition will overstate the market power of a firm supplying a large proportion of the defined product. It may not be able to raise prices substantially above the competitive level without losing too many sales for it to be profitable. A wide definition will usually indicate a smaller market share which understates the firm's market power.

Competition from close substitutes may constrain the firm's conduct closely and in the short term, while that from more remote substitutes only in the longer term when customers have time to adapt to the new product. Both, however, may be expected to affect its conduct. It is important that remote substitutes be considered when appraising dominance within the market defined. Market definitions are often arbitrary and should not determine whether the firm has market power, but they help to focus attention on the factors relevant to appraising market power.

3.3.1. THE HISTORY AND MANY DIMENSIONS OF MARKET DEFINITION

Writing on the concept of market power in 1934, American economist Abba Lerner noted that market shares and concentration were not necessarily good indicators of market power.[80] Lerner developed instead an index (the Lerner index), describing a firm's market power on the basis of its price and marginal costs.[81] However, computing the necessary information on marginal costs was an impossible task, hence the index had no practical use in competition law enforcement. The index's focus on the relationship between elasticity of demand and price margins for profit maximizing firms, indicated that for economists the level of market concentration or a high market share were not the only relevant factors. During the same time, US economist Edward Mason explained the different conceptions of monopoly power in law and in economics, by opposing the neoclassical price theory view of market power as the ability to raise prices profitably and reduce output, to the legal conception of monopoly power as the ability to exclude competitors and to affect the competitive process.[82] As Gregory Werden notes 'hostility to market delineation was particularly intense from the early 1930s to the mid-1950s, in view of the perception shared by economists at the time that product differentiation enabled each firm to a certain extent to behave as a monopolist on a particular market, at least to a certain extent'.[83] However, it was clear that the concept of industry was not useful, as '[q]uestions relating to competition, monopoly and oligopoly must be considered in terms of markets'.[84]

Economists of the neoclassical paradigm defined the market by reference to a single seller or buyer, including in it all considerations they took into account in determining his business policies and practices. The market was therefore seen as a group of firms that are significant competitors to the single firm in question. This specified even more the classical economic notion of market as an 'area within which price tends to uniformity, allowance being made for transportation costs'.[85] US economist Jo Bain developed the concept by setting the boundaries of the market as relating to the group of products that are not only 'identical or perfect substitutes' to each other, but also alternatively 'close substitute products', close substitutability therefore becoming the general criterion for inclusion in the market.[86] This concept is based on cross-price elasticity of demand. US economist Fritz Machlup added cross price elasticity of supply dimension as a factor for determining market boundaries, noting the importance of significant interdependence between the firms included within the boundary of the market.[87] The concept of market definition was then gradually adopted by US courts, incorporating the cross-price elasticity of demand test. The courts developed various tests in order to determine

80 AP Lerner, 'The Concept and Measurement of Monopoly Power' (1934) 1 *Rev Economic Studies* 157.

81 The Lerner index L = P – MC/P.

82 E Mason, 'Monopoly in Law and Economics' (1937) 47 *Yale L J* 34.

83 GJ Werden, 'The History of Antitrust Market Delineation' (1992) 76(1) *Marquette L Rev* 123, 125.

84 J Robinson, 'The Industry and the Market' (1956) 66(262) *Economic J* 360, 361. See also E Chamberlin, 'Product Heterogeneity and Public Policy' (1950) 40 *American Economic Rev (Papers & Proceedings)* 85, 86–87, noting that '"industry" or "commodity" boundaries are a snare and a delusion—in the highest degree arbitrarily drawn, and wherever drawn, establishing at once wholly false implications both as to competition of substitutes within their limits, which supposedly stops at their borders, and as to the possibility of ruling on the presence or absence of oligopolistic forces by the simple device of counting the number of producers included'.

85 G Stigler, *The Theory of Competitive Price* (Macmillan, 1942; revised ed, *The Theory of Price*), 92, cited by GJ Werden, 'The History of Antitrust Market Delineation' (1992) 76(1) *Marquette L Rev* 123, 125.

86 JS Bain, Price Theory (1952), 24–25.

87 F Machlup, *The Economics of Sellers' Competition* (Johns Hopkins University Press, 1952), 213–4.

the reasonable substitutability between products, some of which focused on the peculiar characteristics and uses of the products, their distinct prices, actual and potential competition, as well as cross-elasticity of demand between the product itself and substitutes for it. In 1959, US economist Morris Adelman developed the small but significant non-transitory increase in price (SSNIP) test in an article published in a legal journal, measuring cross-price elasticity between two products through a speculative experiment postulating a hypothetical small but lasting change in relative prices (5–10 per cent) and evaluating the likely reactions of customers to that increase.[88] The test was reformulated by US economist FM Scherer in an expert deposition he presented at the Federal District Court for the Eastern District of Michigan during April 1972, who then included this test in the 1980s edition of his famous industrial organization textbook.[89] The test found its way in official antitrust legal discourse when economist Lawrence White used it in the 1982 Department of Justice (DOJ) Merger Guidelines, in his capacity of chief economist of the DOJ Antitrust Division.[90] Since 1982, cross-price elasticity and the SSNIP test has gradually acquired prominence in US merger control discourse before migrating to Europe.

It is important to pause a little here in order to understand that demand substitutability and cross-price elasticity of demand and supply are not the only ways to delineate markets, other routes than neoclassical price theory being also open. The point we want to make is that market definition is as much a legal construct as an economic one. What is clear is that there is no clear-cut boundary of the market, so long as this identifies an arena/field for competition. Some have considered that the market can be 'the smallest area within which it is possible to be a viable competitor'.[91] One may take a strategic approach, starting from the perspective of the firm, which either focuses on its potential consumers whose needs and functions it tries to satisfy (demand side), or ignores demand by focusing on comparable (and competing) firms (supply side). If one focuses on the supply side, it may be possible to consider as competitors and thus forming part of the 'relevant market' for the purposes of competition law analysis, firms with resources similar to the firm under investigation, which in all likelihood may pose a competitive threat to its competitive position. These resources may include physical capital, such as an industrial plant, equipment, technology, geographical location, but also human capital resources (managerial skills, innovation capabilities), organizational resources as well as important assets for production (eg crucially important for the competitive process personal data) that may sustain the competitive advantage of the firm.[92] Firms following similar strategies, thus constituting a 'strategic group',[93] disposing of similar resources, and serving the same customers' needs,[94]

88 MA Adelman, 'Economic Aspects of the Bethlehem Opinion' (1959) 45 *Virginia L Rev* 684, 688.

89 FM Scherer, 'On the Paternity of a Market Delineation Approach' (12 January 2009), available at http://ssrn.com/abstract=1337079.

90 L White, 'Present at the Beginning of a new Era for Antitrust: Reflections on 1982–1983', New York University, Center for Law and Business, Working Paper No 99-005 (March 1999).

91 PA Geroski, 'Thinking Creatively about Markets' (1998) 16(6) *Int'l J Industrial Organization* 677.

92 JB Barney, 'Firm Resources and Sustained Competitive Advantage' (1991) 17(1) *J Management* 99B; B Wernerfelt, 'A Resource-based View of the Firm' (1984) 5(2) *Strategic Management J* 171.

93 See KG Smith, CM Grimm, S Wally, and G Young, 'Strategic Groups and Rivalrous Firm Behaviour: Towards a Reconciliation' (1997) 18(2) *Strategic Management J* 149; RK Reger and AS Huff, Strategic Groups: A Cognitive Perspective' (1993) 14(2) *Strategic Management J* 103 (emphasizing the need to take into account psycho-sociological factors influencing manager's cognitive perception about their competitors).

94 M Bergen and MA Peteraf, 'Competitor Identification and Competitor Analysis: A Broad-based Managerial Approach' (2002) 23(4/5) *Managerial and Decision Economics* 157.

may thus, under such an approach, be considered as competitors, constraining the action of each other, even if their products do not overlap in the same relevant market. In a period of convergence of physical, biological, and digital worlds, as a result of the recent transformations of industrial production, and the dislocation of boundaries between markets, one may find that such an approach fits better the economics of the fourth industrial revolution than the narrower market definition based on the principle of cross-price elasticity between products, from the point of view of the consumer. How could one proceed to market delineation in a world in which personalization of production means that consumers become the designers of the individually customized products they will consume, the products being produced by 3-D printing and robots, firms competing mainly on the market for personal information, which will serve as the raw material on which personalized production will take place? Which of the various approaches is chosen depends greatly on the type of competition/tournament taking place in the specific 'field'.[95] Competition can be for the market, as well as taking place in the market.[96] Platform or system competition characterizes a lot of competitive interactions in the network economy.

3.3.2. THE CONCEPT AND FUNCTION OF MARKET DEFINITION IN EU AND UK COMPETITION LAW

For economists, a market is defined in terms of substitutes on both the demand and the supply side. The EU Courts in Luxembourg first used concrete tests based on demand-side substitution, as had the Commission in some of its non-merger cases. The Courts defined the relevant market by exploring substitutes on both the demand and supply sides of the market.

In *Continental Can v Commission*,[97] the Commission condemned, as an abuse of its dominant position in northwest Germany, the acquisition of a potential competitor in the Netherlands in the production of cans for packing meat and fish and of metal closures. The CJEU required the Commission to define the relevant market and give reasons for its definition. It quashed the Commission's finding that Continental Can was dominant over the supply of cans used for meat and fish products and for metal closures other than crown corks. The Commission had to some extent considered substitutes on the demand side of the market, the possibility for meat and fish suppliers to use plastic and glass containers. It had not considered substitutes on the supply side: how easily the makers of cylindrical cans could start making the more complex shapes traditionally used for meat and fish. If it were easy to switch production in this way, Continental Can would have had little discretion. If it were to raise prices significantly above costs (including a normal return on capital), it would pay off for one of the other canmakers to enter a profitable market by making cans for meat and fish. Continental Can would foresee the likelihood of such entry, so would be constrained from initiating a price rise which

95 On the concept of 'field' and its possible contribution to address complex competitive interactions, see P Bourdieu, 'Principles of an Economic Anthropology' in P Bourdieu, *The Social Structures of the Economy* (Polity Press, 2005), 193; N Fligstein and D McAdam, 'Toward a General Theory of Strategic Action Fields' (2011) 29 *Sociological Theory* 1.

96 PA Geroski, 'Competition in Markets and Competition for Markets' (2003) 3(3) *J Industry, Competition and Trade* 151.

97 Case 6/72, *Europemballage Corporation and Continental Can Company Inc v Commission* [1973] ECR 215.

would not pay except in the very short term. Hence, it would be constrained even in the short term by potential competition.

The CJEU, however, did not consider the possibility of a completely new entrant obtaining a technology licence from another can maker, but only of the makers of cylindrical cans making the irregular shaped ones traditionally used for meat and fish, or of a canner starting to make its own cans. The subsequent case law of the CJEU has since been referring to substitutes on both sides of the market.[98]

Where there are competitive pressures from outside the market as defined, the definition may not be very helpful to an assessment of power over price. The difficult questions are then postponed until a second stage and, if there are such pressures, the firm accused can bring them to the attention of the competition authority or court to show that it is not dominant even within the narrow market. The bifurcation of the analysis can be avoided under the newer hypothetical monopolist test. Markets have been very narrowly defined, mainly from the demand side.

In *United Brands*, the CJEU upheld the Commission's choice of bananas as the relevant market:

> 22. For the banana to be regarded as forming a market which is sufficiently differentiated from the other fruit markets it must be possible for it to be singled out by special factors distinguishing it from other fruits that it is only to a limited extent interchangeable with them and is only exposed to their competition in a way that is hardly perceptible.[99]

The CJEU confirmed that oranges were not interchangeable with bananas, and apples only to a limited extent, despite evidence of the easing of banana prices and a reduction in the quantities sold during the seasons for summer fruit and oranges, perhaps because of a finding in a report by the Food and Agriculture Organization (FAO) in 1975 that 'the price of oranges in all cases had no significant impact on banana consumption'.

In its decision, the Commission was concerned about the need of the young, the old, and the infirm, who may have difficulty eating other fruit. The interests of the toothless, however, are sufficiently protected by the inability of the dominant firm to discriminate against them. They rarely do their own shopping, and United Brands would lose so much market share from the rest of the population that it would not be worth raising prices to exploit the weak.

Few economists would define a market so narrowly and if the hypothetical monopolist test described below is used, the Commission would not do so these days. The European Commission referred to cross-price elasticity in its *Eurofix-Bauco v Hilti* decision in 1987, later reviewed by the General Court.[100] The Commission argued that its emphasis of cross-price elasticity was a 'synthesis of all the factors that determine whether or not two different products can properly be said to be in the same relevant market, according to the previous case law of the Court'.[101] The CJEU repeated its previous case law emphasizing product characteristics and interchangeability (a functional approach based on its *Continental Can* case

98 See our analysis in Chapter 8.

99 Case 22/76, *United Brands Company and United Brands Continental BV v Commission* [1978] ECR 207, para 22.

100 Decision 88/138/EEC, *Eurofix Bauco v Hilti* [1988] OJ L 65/19, para 73; Case T-30/89, *Hilti AG v Commission* [1991] ECR II–1439.

101 Case T-30/89, *Hilti AG v Commission* [1991] ECR II–1439, para 55.

law) but found the Commission's decision 'sufficiently clear and convincing' to carry its belief. In its group exemptions, the Commission has taken the view that the relevant product market comprises all those products and/or services which are regarded as interchangeable or substitutable by the consumer, by reason of the products' characteristics, their prices or intended use. The SSNIP test has been employed in other occasions by the Court.[102] Following the implementation of the first EU merger regulation in 1990, the Commission has expressed the test more abstractly by publishing in 1997 a Commission's Notice on the definition of relevant market,[103] formally incorporating the SSNIP test (or hypothetical monopolist test in EU jargon) as the first step of the 'modernization' effort of EU competition law, in other words, the attempt to put EU competition law in conformity with neoclassical price theory and economics. The Commission's notice states that the SSNIP test will in the future be used also under Articles 101 and 102 TFEU.[104] In subsequent cases the Court has explicitly and systematically cited the Commission's Notice, in particular in the merger area, but also beyond.

The Commission will consider what would happen if the alleged monopolist were to raise the price of the products affected by 5 or 10 per cent and this were perceived to be a permanent relative change. If so many customers would then switch to other products that the original price rise would be unprofitable, those substitutes would constrain the monopolist's power over price and they should be included in the market.

Notice on market definition [1997] OJ C 372/5 replacing a series of notices since 1970 (some headings have been added, footnotes omitted)

[. . .]

Concept of relevant market and objectives of Community Competition policy

Market share indicates market power—e.g. mergers

10. The concept of relevant market is closely related to the objectives pursued under Community competition policy. For example under the Community's merger control, the objective in controlling structural changes in the supply of a product/service is to prevent the creation or reinforcement of a dominant position as a result of which effective competition would be significantly impeded in a substantial part of the common market. Under the Community's competition rules, a dominant position is such that a firm or group of firms would be in a position to behave to an appreciable extent independently of its competitors, customers and ultimately of its consumers. Such a position would usually arise when a firm or group of firms accounted for a large share of the supply in any given market, provided that other factors analysed in the assessment (such as entry barriers, capacity of reaction of customers, etc.) point in the same direction.

102 See eg Case T-83/91, *Tetra Pak International SA v Commission* [1994] ECR II–755, paras 67–8; Case C-333/94, *Tetra Pak International SA v Commission* [1996] ECR I–5951, para 16.

103 Commission Notice on the definition of relevant market for the purposes of Community competition law [1997] OJ C 372/5, para 17.

104 Ibid, para 11.

Articles 101 and 102 TFEU

11. The same approach is followed by the Commission in its application of Article [102 TFEU] of the Treaty to firms that enjoy a single or collective dominant position. Under Regulation No [1/2003] the Commission has the power to investigate and bring to an end abuses of such a dominant position, which must also be defined by reference to the relevant market.

Markets may also need to be defined in the application of Article [101 TFEU], in particular, in determining whether an appreciable restriction of competition exists or in establishing if the condition under Article [101(3)(b) TFEU] for an exemption from the application of Article [101(1) TFEU] is met.

Merger analysis prospective

12. The criteria for defining the relevant market are applied generally for the analysis of certain types and behaviour in the market and for the analysis of structural changes in the supply of products. This methodology, though, might lead to different results depending on the nature of the competition issue being examined. For instance, the scope of the geographic market might be different when analysing a concentration, where the analysis is essentially prospective, from an analysis of past behaviour. The different time horizon considered in each case might lead to the result that different geographic markets are defined for the same products depending on whether the Commission is examining a change in the structure of supply, such as a concentration or a cooperative joint venture, or issues relating to certain past behaviour.

Basic principles for market definition

Competitive constraints

13. Firms are subject to three main sources of competitive constraints: demand substitutability, supply substitutability and potential competition. From an economic point of view, for the definition of the relevant market, demand substitution constitutes the most immediate and effective disciplinary force on the suppliers of a given product, in particular in relation to their pricing decisions. A firm or a group of firms cannot have a significant impact on the prevailing conditions of sale, such as prices, if its customers are in a position to switch easily to available substitute products or to suppliers located elsewhere. Basically, the exercise of market definition consists in identifying the effective alternative sources of supply for the customers of the undertakings involved, both in terms of products/services and geographic location of suppliers.

14. The competitive constraints arising from supply side substitutability other then those described in paragraphs 20 to 23 and from potential competition are in general less immediate and in any case require an analysis of additional factors. As a result such constraints are taken into account at the assessment stage of competition analysis.

Demand substitution

SSNIP Test

15. The assessment of demand substitution entails a determination of the range of products which are viewed as substitutes by the consumer. One way of making this

determination can be viewed, as a speculative experiment, postulating a hypothetical small, lasting change in relative prices and evaluating the likely reactions of customers to that increase. The exercise of market definition focuses on prices for operational and practical purposes, and more precisely on demand substitution arising from small, permanent changes in relative prices. This concept can provide clear indications as to the evidence that is relevant to define markets.

Chain of substitution

16. Conceptually, this approach means that, starting from the type of products that the undertakings involved sell and the area in which they sell them, additional products and areas will be included in, or excluded from, the market definition depending on whether competition from these other products and areas affect or restrain sufficiently the pricing of the parties' products in the short term.

Buying or selling power

17. The question to be answered is whether the parties' customers would switch to readily available substitutes or to suppliers located elsewhere in response to an hypothetical small (in the range 5% to 10%) but permanent relative price increase in the products and areas being considered. If substitution were enough to make the price increase unprofitable because of the resulting loss of sales, additional substitutes and areas are included in the relevant market. This would be done until the set of products and geographic areas is such that small, permanent increases in relative prices would be profitable. The equivalent analysis is applicable in cases concerning the concentration of buying power, where the starting point would then be the supplier and the price test allows to identify the alternative distribution channels or outlets for the supplier's products.

[. . .]

The test, sometimes called 'the hypothetical monopolist test', was developed by the enforcement agencies in the US and was adopted even before the Commission's Notice in practice also by the merger task force in the competition department of the Commission in charge at the time of the implementation the first EU merger regulation.

The Commission also integrates the supply side.

Supply substitution

If as effective and immediate as demand substitution

20. Supply-side substitutability may also be taken into account when defining markets in those situations in which its effects are equivalent to those of demand substitution in terms of effectiveness and immediacy. This requires that suppliers are able to switch production to the relevant products and market them in the short term4 without incurring significant additional costs or risks in response to small and permanent changes in relative prices. When these conditions are met, the additional production that is put on the market will have a disciplinary effect on the competitive behaviour of the companies involved. Such an impact in terms of effectiveness and immediacy is equivalent to the demand substitution effect.

21. These situations typically arise when companies market a wide range of qualities or grades of one product; even if for a given final customer or group of consumers, the different qualities are not substitutable, the different qualities will be grouped into one

product market provided that most of the suppliers are able to offer and sell the various qualities under the conditions of immediacy and without the significant increases in costs described above. In such cases, the relevant product market will encompass all products that are substitutable in demand and supply, and the current sales of those products will be aggregated so as to give the total value or volume of the market. The same reasoning may lead to group different geographic areas.

The Commission, however, considers substitutes on the supply side only if entry would be as fast and effective as substitutes on the demand side.[105] *Where supply side substitution entails adjusting existing tangible and intangible assets significantly, new investment, strategic decision or delay, it will be considered only at a second stage when appraising dominance within the narrower market.*

The Notice then goes on to describe some of the factors that have been taken into account when defining relevant markets, for instance what happened in response to market shocks when a substitute product ceased to be available for a time, a shortage developed or a new brand was introduced. The Commission is sceptical of market surveys prepared ad hoc. These days, however, one can obtain a great deal of objective information from the barcoding techniques widely used in large retail chains, and surveys based on them should be reliable.

The rest of the guidelines is available at the Commission's website. Please read it and then try to answer the following questions.

NOTES AND QUESTIONS ON THE NOTICE ON THE DEFINITION OF RELEVANT MARKET

1. Is this notice binding on Commission, NCAs, or national courts?
2. (Paragraph 1) The criteria were developed under the Merger Regulation, but are to be applied also to Articles 101 and 102 TFEU. For problems see paragraph 19 of the Notice (not replicated in this Book).
3. (Paragraph 2) It might be less confusing to look directly to the competitive constraints on firms. How would this do as a test of market power when imposing thresholds for the application of block exemption regulations?
4. (Paragraph 4) Is a definition that is often decisive satisfactory? Should close substitutes be seen as more important than remote ones? Does the SSNIP test (paragraph 15) allow for this? Why should markets be defined? Should they be analysed rather than defined?
5. (Paragraph 5) The guidelines and precedents under the Merger Regulation help firms, often aided by economic advisers, to decide on the relevant market. Often, however, frequently, there are various markets that might be treated as relevant under its criteria.
6. (Paragraph 7) Note the concrete test taken from Judgments of the CJEU. Contrast the SSNIP test at paragraphs 15–19 of the Notice.

[105] Commission Notice on the definition of relevant market for the purposes of Community competition law [1997] OJ C 372/3, paras 20 and 23.

7. (Paragraph 12) In appraising the likely effect of mergers, the Commission has to consider the probable future. In deciding whether past conduct has infringed Article 101 or 102, it focuses on past or existing markets.
8. (Paragraph 13) Does the only supplier of a product have any market power in the absence of entry barriers? In *Continental Can*, the Court looked to firms that might enter the market with little change to their existing business, but did not consider remoter possibilities, such as a light engineering firm taking a technology licence from American Can and starting to compete. Such a possibility might constrain the conduct of the dominant firm.
9. (Paragraphs 15–18) The hypothetical monopolist test is sometimes referred to by the acronym, small but significant increase in price or SSNIP.
10. (Paragraph 19) When the SSNIP test is extended from mergers to the application of Articles 101 and 102 TFEU it does not work, because a firm with market power may well already have raised its price above the competitive level. At the level of prices it charges, demand substitution may be high. This is called the 'cellophane fallacy'.[106] How would you determine what prices would prevail if the market were more competitive?
11. Note that findings about the relevant market in previous cases are not binding if markets have changed.[107]
12. (Paragraph 40) Should the Commission place much faith in the views of competitors? If they make adverse comments is that likely to show that the conduct is pro-competitive? The Commission can assess the reasons given for their views.
13. (Paragraph 41) Do you think that the Commission should ever look to evidence prepared ad hoc? How about the results of barcoding which are commercially collected and sold to business by firms like AC Nielsen?
14. In *Atlantic Container Line*, the General Court held that:

    834. Although potential competition and supply-side substitution are conceptually different issues [. . .] those issues overlap in part, as the distinction lies primarily in whether the restriction of competition is immediate or not.[108]

    Discuss.
15. On occasion, complementary products have been held to be in the same market: for instance, in *Tiercé Ladbroke v Commission*, the General Court treated the supply of live film of horse races by satellite as part of the market for supplying betting services.[109] This is not consistent with either the Commission's notice or the earlier case law. Admittedly, some complements may be treated as a single product, for instance a left and right shoe, since most customers want their shoes to match, but

[106] See Section 3.3.3.2.

[107] See Joined Cases T-125 & 127/97, *The Coca-Cola Company and Coca-Cola Enterprises Inc v Commission* [2000] ECR II–1733, [2000] 5 CMLR 467.

[108] Joined Cases T-191 & 212–14/98, *Atlantic Container Line AB and Others v Commission* [2003] ECR II–3275.

[109] Case T-471/93, *Tiercé Ladbroke v Commission* [1995] ECR II–2537.

there must be uses of live film of horse races other than as a supplement to betting shops—for instance, television news or sports programmes.

16. In *Atlantic Container Line*, the General Court confirmed that, when demand substitution is only minimal, it can be ignored in defining the market, because demand substitutes constrain conduct only if the demand is fairly stable.[110]
17. In *Coca-Cola Company and Coca-Cola Enterprises Inc v Commission*,[111] the General Court held that the Commission could not automatically apply market definitions from earlier decisions under Article 102. Markets may have changed meanwhile, and a fresh analysis should be made each time an infringement is alleged. Moreover, a national court is not bound by previous definitions of the Commission relating to the same product.[112] An actual decision finding an infringement may, however, serve as a basis for an action for damages by a third party, even when the Commission's decision did not impose a fine.
18. *The time dimension of defining a relevant market:* In *Michelin I*, the CJEU accepted that the Commission should assess the cross elasticities of supply and demand, but it assessed the alleged barriers to entry on a shorter time scale than would usually be used by economists[113] The CJEU observed that it takes time to build or modify a factory, or for customers to assess the quality of a new brand of heavy tyres. So the creation of new capacity could be ignored. However, Michelin could not have exploited its position for long, if at all, if Goodyear could profitably have built a factory in the Netherlands. The desire to discourage it from doing so would constrain Michelin's conduct meanwhile. On the shorter time scale, which is used in many decisions of the Commission and judgments of the CJEU, entry barriers are pervasive. They include the need to invest in plant, an established reputation, a good commercial network, access to technology, and many other assets of existing firms which do not give them power to maintain high prices for any length of time without the risk, or even the certainty, of losing market share. The Commission's notice on market definition does not indicate over what period switching by customers to other products is relevant. It is also mentioned that supply side substitutability which is 'less immediate' (paragraph 14) will not be taken into account in defining the market. The US merger guidelines speak of one or two years.

3.3.3. PRODUCT MARKET DEFINITION

At its simplest, market definition is about finding a market that is worth monopolizing, in the sense that the relevant market is the smallest set of products which can profitably be monopolized. Accordingly, a hypothetical monopolist would not be constrained by firms/products outside the relevant market.

110 Joined Cases T-191 & 212–14/98, *Atlantic Container Line AB and Others v Commission* [2003] ECR II-3275, paras 797–800.

111 Case T-125/97, *The Coca-Cola Company and Coca-Cola Enterprises Inc v Commission* [2000] ECR II-1733.

112 Ibid, para 85.

113 Case 322/81, *NV Nederlandsche Banden Industrie Michelin v Commission* [1983] ECR 3461.

3.3.3.1. Determining substitutability: The hypothetical monopolist test

This framework corresponds, of course, to the *hypothetical monopolist test* (HMT). The most common implementation of the HMT test is the SSNIP test, where the acronym stands for *small but significant non-transitory increase in price*, above the price that would prevail under competitive market conditions. Conventionally, the SSNIP is considered to be an increase of 5 to 10 per cent, lasting for at least a year,[114] whilst all prices for the products outside the relevant market are held constant. It is important to keep in mind, however, that in some industries the key dimension of strategic interaction is not price, but quality or the level of advertising, hence the SSNIP price would not capture accurately how competitive constraints work under these circumstances.[115]

The starting point in the implementation of the HMT/SSNIP test is to identify the first candidate market, which naturally includes the core set of products that triggered the investigation: for example, the products sold by the merging parties, or by the dominant firm alleged of anti-competitive foreclosure. This entails that the product dimension is normally the first to be analysed, to be followed by the geographic scope of the market, which starts with the locations of the corresponding firms.

The candidate market is then enlarged in an iterative way alongside both product and geographic dimensions. To this end, the key legal test set out by the CJEU in *Continental Can* is to look at the extent to which products are *interchangeable* by virtue of their characteristics.[116] According to the EU Commission's Notice on the Definition of the Relevant Market there are three sources of interchange, specifically: demand-side substitution, supply-side substitution, and potential competition.[117]

Demand-side substitutability is by far the most important element to consider.[118] According to the Commission, '[t]he goal of the assessment of demand side substitutability is to identify the group of products or services that are alternatives in satisfying the needs normally served by the product in question in the eye of the relevant customers. The respective product characteristics, product use and prices are usually important factors in such an assessment.'[119]

The first step of any product market definition, therefore, is a quality assessment aimed at identifying potential substitutes on the basis of product characteristics and intended use (eg it is obvious to rule out a motorcycle as a substitute for a white wan, less so perhaps with a large SUV). These fungible products are sometimes referred to as 'functional' substitutes.[120] This is not enough, however, since a substitute product must be able to constraint the hypothetical monopolist's pricing decision. Therefore, it is important to also check that the 'functional' substitute is a convenient alternative price-wise relative to the products in the candidate market

114 For markets where volumes are high but unit profit margin thin, though, it is advisable to use a lower percentage figure. For example, when the unit profit margin is 1 per cent, a 5 per cent price increase would correspond to a 500 per cent increase in profitability. See P Davis and E Garcés, *Quantitative Techniques for Competition and Antitrust Analysis* (Princeton University Press, 2010), 202.

115 Nevertheless, in what follows we simply refer to a SSNIP for the sake of simplicity.

116 Case 6/72 *Continental Can Company v Commission* [1973] ECR 215; [1973] CMLR 199, para 32.

117 Commission Notice on the definition of relevant market for the purposes of Community competition law [1997] OJ C 372/5, para 13.

118 Ibid.

119 OECD, 'Market Definition—Policy Roundtables', DAF/COMP(2012)19 (2012), 334, available at http://www.oecd.org/daf/competition/Marketdefinition2012.pdf.

120 See P Davis and E Garcés, *Quantitative Techniques for Competition and Antitrust Analysis* (Princeton University Press, 2010), 166.

(eg large SUVs might be too expensive to constitute a realistic alternative when compared to prevailing prices for white wans).[121]

In *Unilever/Sarah Lee*, the Commission proceeded in applying a SSNIP test of the gender segments (male/non-male) deodorants in order to find if these could be separate relevant markets for competition law purposes.[122] The Commission employed a merger simulation model showing that the profits of a hypothetical monopolist of the male (or non-male) segment would increase if the prices of all male (or non-male) deodorants increased by 5 per cent. These results supported the conclusions of the market investigation and confirmed that a hypothetical monopolist in the non-male market would not be constrained by the male deodorant products, indicating that those products belonged to a distinct relevant market.

In *Google/Doubleclick*, the Commission declared the merger between Google, an Internet search engine providing online advertising space, and DoubleClick, a firm selling ad serving, management and reporting technology, to be in accordance with EU law. The relevant product market for Google could in its widest interpretation be seen as the overall market for advertising. The Commission rejected such a broad definition, preferring to consider the offline and the online advertising as separate relevant markets, in view of their perception as separate markets by the majority of respondents to the Commission's survey, but also in view of the fact that they are used for specific purposes:

> As opposed to offline advertising, online advertising is considered to be capable of reaching a more targeted audience in a more effective way. Advertisers can precisely target their audience by combining information regarding geographical location, time of day, areas of interest, previous purchasing record of the user and search preferences. This option is not available in the case of offline advertising, for which the amount of 'wasted circulation' is undoubtedly higher. In addition to this specific targeting, [. . .] online advertising has a unique reporting system that enables the advertiser to check exactly how many users have viewed the ad or clicked on it, moreover allowing a rapid 'retargeting' of the ad. Hence the measurement of the effectiveness of online ads can also be more precise compared with the traditional measurement systems used in offline advertising.[123]

The Commission then assessed whether this market may have to be subdivided further on the basis of different forms of advertisements (text versus non-text (display) ads and/or search ads versus non-search ads) or on the basis of different sales channels (direct sales versus intermediated sales through ad networks and ad exchanges). In the end, it stated that the exact definition of relevant product market does not need to be defined in this case. DoubleClick's relevant market showed that display ad serving technology constituted a separate market from ad serving technology for text ads. Therefore, a further subdivision had to be made between the provision of such services to advertisers and the provision of such services to publishers.

121 Similarly, see ibid, 167, makes the more glamorous example of smoked salmon and caviar.

122 *Unilever/Sara Lee Body Care* (Case COMP/M.5658) Commission Decision (17 November 2010), para 94, available at http://ec.europa.eu/competition/mergers/cases/decisions/m5658_20101117_20600_2193231_EN.pdf.

123 *Google/DoubleClick* (Case COMP/M.4731) Commission Decision (11 March 2008), para 45, available at http://ec.europa.eu/competition/elojade/isef/case_details.cfm?proc_code=2_M_4731.

The Commission also explored the distinction between online and offline advertising when it approved the acquisition of the Internet search and search advertising business of Yahoo! by Microsoft.[124] In line with the Google/DoubleClick decision the Commission found that online advertising constituted a relevant market. Whether segments of that market constituted relevant markets in their own right was, however, left open, in view of the fact that Google constituted such a formidable competitor in relation to Microsoft's and Yahoo's market shares and abilities to pose any threat to competition in the near future.

In the *Facebook/WhatsApp* merger, the Commission found that Facebook Messenger and WhatsApp were not close competitors and that consumers would continue to dispose of a wide choice of alternative consumer communication apps following the transaction.[125] Although consumer communication apps are characterized by network effects, the investigation showed that the merged entity would continue to face sufficient competition after the merger. The relevant product market was analysed from three different angles: (i) consumer communication services, (ii) social networking services, and (iii) online advertising services.

With regard to the first angle, the Commission explored 'messaging' markets and identified separate markets for consumer communication services and enterprise communication services. The Commission further explored whether the markets should also be subdivided into functionality, by platform or Operating System (OS). The market definition was nevertheless left open, as for the specific case the market could be assessed on the basis of a relevant product market including only consumer communications apps for smartphones. The Commission noted that consumer communications services can be offered as a stand-alone app (eg WhatsApp, Viber, Facebook Messenger, and Skype), or as functionality that is part of a broader offering such as a social networking platform (eg Facebook or LinkedIn). The Commission found that the relevant product market should encompass consumer communication apps offered for all OS's and should include all communication functionalities. Initially, the Commission also wanted to include in the relevant product market definition regular voice calls, SMS, MMS, e-mails, as substitutes, but decided in the end to opt for a narrower definition (among other reasons, due to the fact that there is a difference in the pricing conditions, since consumer communications apps are mainly offered free of charge and in any event not priced per messages, while users are still usually charged separately when they send MMS, messages to other countries or messages from abroad).

With regard to the second angle, the Notifying Party explained that Facebook's social network service consisted of users' profile, newsfeed and timeline, and continued by stating that WhatsApp is in no way competing in this market. The Commission noted in its assessment that there might be some overlap in functionality, but that social networks normally provide a richer experience, and that consumer communication apps are normally more personal and targeted. The Commission maintained that social networking services should not be further segmented according to platform or OS's. However, they could be differentiated depending on their intended use (eg between Facebook and LinkedIn)—but this was still left open. Concluding, the Commission observed that the exact boundaries of the market for social networking services, in particular whether consumer communications apps such as Facebook Messenger and

[124] *Microsoft/Yahoo! Search Business* (Case COMP/M.5727) Commission Decision (18 February 2010), available at http://ec.europa.eu/competition/elojade/isef/case_details.cfm?proc_code=2_M_5727.

[125] *Facebook/Whatsapp* (Case COMP/M.7217) Commission Decision (3 October 2014), section 4.2.2, available at http://ec.europa.eu/competition/elojade/isef/case_details.cfm?proc_code=2_M_7217.

WhatsApp fall within the scope of such a potential market, can be left open since the merger would not give rise to serious doubts as to its compatibility under any market definition.

Lastly, with regard to the third angle, the Commission's conclusion was in line with its decisions in *Google/DoubleClick* and *Microsoft/Yahoo! Search Business*, the Commission arriving at the conclusion that online ads constituted a separate relevant market from offline ads. Whether segments of that market could constitute relevant markets in their own right, however, was left open for the purposes of the decision, because the merger would not give rise to serious doubts as to its compatibility with EU merger law under any such narrower product market definition.

Demand-side substitutability does not constitute the only dimension taken into account in delineating a relevant market. According to the Commission, *supply-side substitutability* and, to a larger extent, the threat of *potential competition* rarely change a conclusion based on demand-side substitutability.[126] The idea is that a firm producing a different product could promptly switch production to start supplying the relevant product attracted by the profit opportunity created by the SSNIP within a year. Therefore, the firm in question must be able to repurpose its production facilities within a year without incurring significant additional costs or risks (eg production capacity should not be tied up under long-term contracts). Regarding the costs, besides being technically feasible, the firm must also have access to the necessary distribution channels and marketing levers (eg a trained sales force).

In terms of risk, on the one hand, to the extent that the firm is operating at capacity switching production would entail an 'opportunity cost' given by the profit margins earned on the existing production, which would have to be at least scaled back to make room for the production of the substitutable product. On the other hand, the firm in question faces the prospect of deterrence whereby the SSNIP might be reversed in case of entry. In this respect, the credibility of supply-side substitution and further potential competition might rely on the belief that the incumbent's prices are hard to adjust in the relevant timeframe (from two to three years for potential competitors) so that current prices can safely be interpreted as the likely post-entry prices.[127]

According to the European Commission's Notice on market definition, supply side substitutability is an equally important concern as demand side substitutability when delineating a relevant market. The UK Merger Assessment Guidelines takes a slightly different perspective providing that supply side substitutability may be taken into account as a complement to demand side substitution:

> The boundaries of the relevant product market are generally determined by reference to demand-side substitution alone. However, there are circumstances where the Authorities may aggregate several narrow relevant markets into one broader one on the basis of considerations about the response of suppliers to changes in prices. They may do so when:
>
> - production assets can be used by firms to supply a range of different products that are not demand-side substitutes, and the firms have the ability and incentive quickly (generally within a year) to shift capacity between these different products depending on demand for each; and

126 OECD, 'Market Definition—Policy Roundtables', DAF/COMP(2012)19 (2012), 335, available at http://www.oecd.org/daf/competition/Marketdefinition2012.pdf.

127 P Davis and E Garcés, *Quantitative Techniques for Competition and Antitrust Analysis* (Princeton University Press, 2010), 165.

- the same firms compete to supply these different products and the conditions of competition between the firms are the same for each product; in this case aggregating the supply of these products and analysing them as one market does not affect the Authorities' decision on the competitive effect of the merger.[128]

With regard to UK decision practice, in *ABF/Elephant Atta* (ME/5374/2012), the OFT (now replaced by the CMA) considered the supply of chappati flour. Chapatti flour is particularly suited to producing certain types of flat bread, and there is limited demand-side substitution since other flour types are not functionally suited to baking flat breads. It appeared that chapatti flour and other types of flour can be considered as supply side substitutes, because (i) there were no special facilities or machinery required to manufacture chapatti flour and (ii), the parties' information indicated that it was costless for millers to switch between producing different flour types. However, as the OFT did not receive sufficient evidence from third parties to conclude on this point, it assessed the merger with the frame of reference being the supply of chappati flour.[129]

One may wonder whether such analysis should be performed at the level of defining the relevant market, or whether it should form part of the next step of competition assessment.[130]

3.3.3.2. The 'cellophane fallacy' and the 'reverse-cellophane fallacy'

The implementation of the SSNIP test requires, first, the identification of the proper price benchmark. In the assessment of a merger, actual prices prevailing before the merger are normally used, since the assessment is about the likely increase in market power due the merger. Whereas in the investigation of an abuse of a position of substantial market power or a cartel, the correct implementation of the SSNIP test requires the identification of a competitive price benchmark, since the assessment is about the absolute (as opposed to the incremental) degree of market power.

Alas, in these cases, current prices may be unsuitable since they already reflect the exploitation of market power (ie, either enjoyed by the dominant firm or due to the formation of a cartel). Hence, to use current prices would lead to drawing the boundaries of the relevant market too narrowly. This is because current prices have presumably already been raised as much as possible, so that to add a SSNIP on top of them would, by definition, be unprofitable, due to customers either switching to inferior substitutes which would have not been taken into consideration had the candidate product been priced at competitive levels, or stop purchasing altogether.

[128] OFT/CC, Merger Assessment Guidelines (CC2/OFT1254 also adopted by the CMA) (September 2010), para 5.2.17, available at http://www.oft.gov.uk/shared_oft/mergers/642749/OFT1254.pdf.

[129] See *ABF/Elephant Atta* (ME/5374/2012) OFT Decision (6 September 2012). Other examples where supply-side substitution was considered include *Akzo Nobel/Metlac* (ME/5319/12) Competition Commission Decision (1 June 2012); *DCC (GB Oil)/Brogan* (ME/4406/10) OFT Decision (20 April 2010); *Jewson (St Gobain)/Build Center* (ME/5252/11) OFT Decision (8 February 2012); *Ericsson/Red Bee* (ME/6110/13) OFT Decision (30 September 2013).

[130] In favour of such a position, see A Fletcher and B Lyons, Geographic Market Definition in European Commission Merger Control, A Study for DG Competition (January 2016), 17, available at http://ec.europa.eu/competition/publications/reports/study_gmd.pdf (finding that there is duplication of evidence between market definition and competitive assessment in merger control).

This problem is known as 'cellophane fallacy' after a 1957 case where the US Supreme Court relied on current prices prevailing in the candidate market for plastic wrap where the largest incumbent alleged of monopolization, DuPont, had a 75 per cent share. This way the Court erroneously endorsed the defendant's claim that the market ought to be enlarged in order to include what, at current price levels, looked as substitutes (flexible packaging material), thus lowering DuPont's market share to a mere 20 per cent.[131]

In contrast there may be circumstances where this fallacy is reversed, that is, where current prices are alleged to be below the competitive benchmark.[132] Predatory pricing is, by definition, such a case, since the allegation is that prices have been artificially set below average variable/incremental costs for a prolonged period of time in such a way that an equally efficient competitor could not last. Here the risk is that the product concerned is seen as too good a bargain to trigger any material substitution away from it as a result of a SSNIP. The boundaries of the relevant market might, therefore, be drawn too narrowly, thus leading to a (circular) finding of dominance (and, abuse thereof) since the firm alleged of predatory pricing is assigned a market share that is too large.[133]

3.3.3.3. Relevant market definition and quality competition

Price is not the only, or even sometimes the most important, parameter of competition. Quality competition, which may be determined as relating to all the other than price variables that matter to consumers, plays an important role and may explain consumers' choice in many circumstances. There has recently been a discussion over the role of quality competition in determining the boundaries of the relevant market and in particular its measurement and its use in defining markets.

OECD, The Role and Measurement of Quality in Competition Analysis, DAF/COMP (2013)17, 14–15

Can quality be used to define markets? For example, could the well-known SSNIP test be replaced with a SSNDQ (small but significant, non-transitory decrease in quality) test? Even if it could, would we ever want to do that in the first place? In other words, are there situations in which the SSNIP test would yield an incomplete or inaccurate result because it focuses on price, and in which the SSNDQ test would yield a more accurate result? Hartman, Teece, Mitchell, and Jorde have argued that a SSNDQ test is not only feasible, but necessary, for defining markets and assessing market power in sectors subject to rapid technological change.[134] Starting from Schumpeter's premise that antitrust analysis focuses too often

131 For a recognition of the problem in UK competition law, see CMA Decision, Case CE/9742-13, Unfair pricing in respect of the supply of Phenytoin sodium capsules in the UK (7 December 2016), para 4.34, also confirmed by the CAT in *Pfizer & Flynn v CMA* [2018] CAT 11 n 24.

132 This issue was first raised by LM Froeb and GJ Werden, 'The Reverse Cellophane Fallacy in Market Delineation' (1991) 7 *Rev Industrial Organization* 241.

133 Presumably, though, the candidate market would also include the products of the targeted firms, whose prices ought to be at or above competitive levels, so perhaps this problem is less of an issue in practice.

134 R Hartman, D Teece, W Mitchell, and T Jorde, 'Assessing Market Power in Regimes of Rapid Technological Change' (1993) 2 *Industrial and Corporate Change* 317.

on existing market structures rather than how those structures are created and destroyed, Hartman, et al. lay out a case for complementing the static SSNIP test with a dynamic SSNDQ test. Firms do not compete only on price, they emphasize, but on innovation and quality. That is especially true in markets featuring swift technological progress. Customers in such markets may care far more about product features than about price. To assume that two products in those markets can be in competition with each other only if customers are so price-sensitive that a hypothetical five percent increase in the price of one induces a switch to the other leads to overly narrow market definitions, the authors argue. Therefore, some markets should not be defined with a method that relies on price alone. Hartman, et al. do have a good point about competition not always taking place on the basis of price alone. Google did not topple Yahoo in the internet search market and Facebook did not crush MySpace in social networking, for example, because of price competition. That was quality competition. [. . .]

Hartman, et al. roughly delineate what [a SSDQ test] would look like. The primary question, they say, is whether 'a change in the performance attributes of one commodity would induce substitution to or from another. If the answer is affirmative, then the differentiated products, even if based on alternative technologies, ought to be included in the relevant product market'.[135] Rather than the five percent price increase that is typically used in the SSNIP test, the authors propose a 25 percent decrease in a major performance attribute for their SSNDQ test. So the idea is that if an existing manufacturer were to reduce quality to that extent, holding all else equal, and no substitution to other products occurs, then the first type of product is a relevant market. If substitution takes place, then the other products are in the relevant market, too.

But this is the type of exercise on which differences in the nature of price and quality have a substantial impact – one that makes implementing the authors' proposal quite challenging. As they acknowledge, performance changes are more difficult to quantify than price changes because performance is multi-dimensional. As a result, quantification requires measuring both the change in an individual attribute and the relative importance of that attribute. Unlike price changes that involve altering the value of a common base unit [currency], performance changes often involve changing the units by which performance is measured.[136] Hartman, et al.'s idea is therefore probably more useful as a loose conceptual guide than as a precise tool that courts and competition authorities should actually attempt to apply.

3.3.3.4. Technology markets

It is possible that the market affected by the anti-competitive conduct is not a product market, but a technology market. This is particularly the case if the conduct in question concerns the licensing of IP rights. The Commission and NCAs should in this case assess the actual and/or potential effect of the conduct on each of the technology or product markets or on both markets. The Commission explains in its Guidelines on the Technology Transfer Block Exemption Regulation (TTBER) that '[t]echnology is an input, which is integrated either into a product or a production process' and technology right licensing may therefore affect competition 'both upstream in input markets and downstream in output markets'.[137] The relevant product market

135 Ibid, 334. 136 Ibid, 339.

137 European Commission, Guidelines on the application of Article 101 of the Treaty on the Functioning of the European Union to technology transfer agreements [2014] OJ C 89/3, para 20 [hereinafter TTBER Guidelines].

comprises the contract products (incorporating the licensed technology) and products regarded by the buyers as interchangeable with or substitutable for the contract products, by reason of the products' characteristics, their prices and their intended use. As to the relevant technology market, the Commission notes that '[it] consist[s] of the licensed technology rights and its substitutes, that is to say, other technologies which are regarded by the licensees as interchangeable with or substitutable for the licensed technology rights, by reason of the technologies' characteristics, their royalties and their intended use'.[138] Indeed, '[s]tarting from the technology which is marketed by the licensor, it is necessary to identify those other technologies to which licensees could switch in response to a small but permanent increase in relative prices, that is to say, to the royalties.' An alternative approach is to look at the technology's 'footprint' on the product market, that is the market for products incorporating the licensed technology rights,[139] this figure being calculated on the basis of both the licensor's and the licensee's sales.[140]

3.3.3.5. Market definition and innovation

The recent focus of competition law on innovation raises important challenges for the competition assessment in rapidly developed industries.[141] Indeed, it may not be possible to determine an existing product or technology market, which may be affected by the allegedly anti-competitive conduct, although the competition authority could hold the view that the conduct may affect future prospects for new products and technologies to emerge and for innovation to develop. Some competition authorities have made use of the concept of 'innovation market' in order to assess the effect on future effects on innovation competition. For instance, the US Department of Justice and the Federal Trade Commission Guidelines for the licensing of IP note that an arrangement can affect price or output in three types of markets: a market for existing goods and services, a technology market consisting of intellectual property that is licensed and its close substitutes, and an innovation market consisting of the research and development directed to particular new or improved goods or processes and the close substitutes for that research and development, 'tomorrow's products'.[142] The concept of innovation markets enables competition authorities to assess the effects of an anti-competitive practice on research and development efforts and eventually future product markets.[143] An alternative to the innovation markets approach would be to use potential competition theory

138 Ibid, para 22.

139 Ibid, paras 25, 87–8. See also Regulation 316/2014 of 21 March 2014 on the application of Article 101(3) TFEU to categories of technology transfer agreements [2014] OJ L 93/17, Article 8(d).

140 TTBER Guidelines, para 86.

141 This focus on innovation or dynamic competition assumes that innovation is the first order preference of consumers and that dynamic competition is the process that enables consumers to maximize their utility.

142 The distinction between these three markets was first noted by WF Baxter, 'The Definition and Measurement of Market Power in Industries Characterized by Rapidly Developing and Changing Technologies' (1984) 53 *Antitrust LJ* 717.

143 Gilbert and Sunshine have suggested a five steps process for identifying innovation markets: first, identify the overlapping R&D activities of the merging firms; second, locate any alternative sources of R&D; third, evaluate actual and potential competition from downstream products that could make it unprofitable for a hypothetical R&D monopolist to raise price or reduce output; fourth, assess potential competitive effects on investment and R&D that could result from the increased concentration brought about by the practice; fifth, assess any efficiencies arising from the practice that would likely increase output and lower the post practice price of R&D in the innovation market under review, in order to determine whether such efficiencies would be sufficient to outweigh any likely anti-competitive effects. See RJ Gilbert and SC Sunshine, 'Incorporating Dynamic Efficiency Concerns in Merger Analysis: The Use of Innovation Markets' (1995) 63 *Antitrust LJ* 569.

and in particular consider the possibility of limit pricing, the strategy of constraining price in order to reduce the risk of future entry.[144] Applying potential competition analysis would, however, require that one of the firms is already an established supplier of the relevant good and service, which is not always the case, and some effects, for example possible delays in introducing a new drug in the market, cannot be captured by the tool of potential competition. The concept of innovation market thus extends the ability of competition law to assess effects on research tools or the competitive process.

The concept has nevertheless been subject to a number of criticisms: first, R&D is only an input to the production of goods and services and competition law analysis should focus on outputs, the actual supply of future goods and services; second, economic theory does not provide a solid empirical basis on the assumption that the decrease in the number of firms engaged in R&D will affect negatively innovation (the link between market structure and innovation), as the elimination of redundant expenditure, the reduction of costs and the possibility for the firm to fully capture the results of the R&D programme might accelerate the process of innovation; third, the sources of R&D may be difficult to identify as discoveries may come from unexpected places. An 'innovation market' approach may not provide an appropriate framework to the extent that it does not take into account the possibility of drastic innovation and the possible entry of undertakings that are not presently active in the specific industry or market, but may have some technological capabilities that could enable it to constitute a possible competitive constraint in innovation competition.[145]

In some recent merger cases concerning the seed/agrochem sector, the European Commission took a broader perspective and employed the concept of 'innovation space' and the 'industry' when assessing the possible effect of the merger transaction on innovation.[146] According to the Commission, when analysing the effects on innovation it becomes important to assess the impact of the transaction 'at the level of innovation efforts by the Parties and its competitors'.[147] The assessment of innovation competition follows three steps:

> [349] First, the assessment of innovation competition requires the identification of those companies which, at an industry level, do have the assets and capabilities to discover and develop new products which, as a result of the R&D effort, can be brought to the market.
>
> [350] Secondly, it is also relevant to identify and analyse those spaces in which innovation competition occurs in the crop protection industry. The R&D players do not innovate for all the product markets composing the entire crop protection industry at the same time. They also do not innovate randomly without targeting specific spaces within that industry. When setting up their innovation capabilities and conducting their research R&D players have specific discovery targets [. . .].
>
> [351] A given discovery target is based on lead crops and lead pests and may thus comprise AIs that can be used in several downstream formulated product markets (for example chewing Lepidopteran insecticides, broadleaf herbicides). The spaces where innovation competition takes place are thus broader than an individual downstream crop protection market, but are nonetheless small. In fact, in light of increasing regulatory hurdles, which require crop

144 RJ Hoerner, 'Innovation Markets: New Wine in Old Bottles?' (1995) 64 *Antitrust LJ* 49.

145 RJ Gilbert, 'Competition and Innovation' in WD Collins (ed) *Issues in Competition Law and Policy*, vol 1 (ABA Section of Antitrust Law, 2008), 577, 583.

146 *Dow/Dupont* (Case COMP/M.7932) Commission Decision (27 March 2017), paras 348–52, available at http://ec.europa.eu/competition/elojade/isef/case_details.cfm?proc_code=2_M_7932.

147 Ibid, para 348.

> protection products to be ever more selective, the innovation spaces in the crop protection industry are getting ever smaller: the innovation output tends to be confined to ever narrower spaces from which it is more difficult to adapt the innovation to other purposes.
>
> [352] In conclusion, in order to assess innovation competition, the Commission will both consider metrics of innovation taking place at industry level, as well as innovation taking place in spaces consisting of groupings of crop/pest combinations [. . .] [areas where the parties' activities overlapped].[148]

The concept of 'innovation space' may also affect the way we proceed to the definition of the geographic boundaries in which competitive interactions take place (on this see the following Section).[149] In its assessment of the *Dow/Dupont* merger, the Commission focused both on innovation competition 'at the level of innovation spaces within the crop protection industry and on innovation competition at the industry level'.[150] More specifically, the Commission focused on the line of research the merging companies were active, the latter concept comprising 'the set of scientists, patents, assets, equipment and chemical class(es) which are dedicated to a given discovery target whose final output are successive pipeline [products] targeting a given innovation space'.[151]

3.3.4. GEOGRAPHIC MARKET DEFINITION

The geographic market must be wide enough to include 'a substantial part of the Common Market'. Moreover, it is an abuse of the dominant position only within the Common Market that infringes Article 102 TFEU. For some products, economists might say that the relevant market is worldwide, as the sole producer of a substance in the Common Market would have no monopolistic discretion were the market liable to be swamped by imports. In the first judgment in *Wood Pulp*, the CJEU treated the relevant market under Article 101 TFEU as global.[152] In *United Brands*, the CJEU excluded from the relevant market three Member States where tariff preference was given to bananas from their former colonies because the applicants argued that the relevant geographic market 'should comprise only areas where the conditions of competition are homogenous'.[153] Although this phrase has frequently been repeated by the CJEU, competition from areas where the conditions of competition are not homogeneous may constrain the conduct of a firm that might otherwise enjoy market power. Paragraph 8 of the Commission's Notice on Market Definition also refers to conditions being homogeneous. The idea is, however, ignored thereafter. The focus on 'conditions of competition' may indicate that function of geographic market definition is to identify various alternative sources of supply that may be chosen by the consumers. The Commission's Notice indicates that the Commission

> [. . .] will take a preliminary view of the scope of the geographic market on the basis of broad indications as to the distribution of market shares between the parties and their competitors, as well as a preliminary analysis of pricing and price differences at national and

148 Ibid, paras 349–52. 149 Ibid, para 361. 150 Ibid, para 1956. 151 Ibid, para 1958.

152 Joined Cases 89, 104, 114, 116, 117 & 125–9/85, *A Ahlström Osakeyhtiö and others v Commission* [1988] ECR 5193.

153 Case 27/76, *United Brands Company and United Brands Continentaal BV v Commission* [1978] ECR 207, para 11.

Community or EEA level. The initial view is used basically as a working hypothesis to focus the Commission's enquiries for the purposes of arriving at a precise geographic market definition.[154]

The Commission insists that the 'reasons behind any particular configuration of prices and market shares need to be explored', in particular if there are alternative explanations for similarities and differences, other than the existence of separate geographic markets. This 'working hypothesis' has to be confirmed by looking to a number of demand characteristics which may impede cross-price substitutability, focusing on 'whether the customers of the parties would switch their orders to companies located elsewhere in the short term and at a negligible cost'.[155] Factors to be considered include national and local preferences, current patterns of purchases by customers, product differentiation, brands, etc. Supply factors will also form part of the analysis performed by the Commission, in particular the existence of a distribution system, possible barriers to trade resulting from regulation, the costs of establishing a distribution system. The 'process of market integration' in the EU is also to lead the Commission to widen the geographic market definition when appropriate.[156] The Notice provides detailed guidelines on the type of evidence the Commission may collect in order to define the relevant geographic market.[157]

Substitution on the supply side should also be carefully considered when defining a product relevant market. According to the Commission's Notice, '[t]his means that suppliers are able to switch production to the relevant products and market them in the short term without incurring significant additional costs or risks in response to small and permanent changes in relative prices'.[158]

It is also common practice among many national competition authorities in Europe, but also more recently the European Commission, to focus on the local effects of market power by defining geographic markets on the basis of isochrones, which measures distance or travel time, drawing a boundary around a firm's location, enclosing a significant part of it customers (eg 80 per cent) and then considering competition between firms with overlapping markets.[159] Both the European Commission and the CMA have defined catchment areas

154 Commission Notice on the definition of relevant market for the purposes of Community competition law [1997] OJ C 372/5, para 28.

155 Ibid, para 29. 156 Ibid, para 32.

157 Ibid, paras 45–50. These constitute six broad types of evidence: (i) past evidence of diversion of orders to other areas; (ii) basic demand characteristics, including language, culture and life style, national brands, etc; (iii) views of consumers and competitors; (iv) current geographic patterns of purchases; (v) trade flows; (vi) barriers and switching costs, such as transport costs or transport restrictions, that may affect the diversion of orders to companies located in other areas.

158 Ibid, para 20.

159 A Fletcher and B Lyons, 'Geographic Market Definition in European Commission Merger Control, A Study for DG Competition' (January 2016), 17–18, available at http://ec.europa.eu/competition/publications/reports/study_gmd.pdf (noting that this is particularly the case when examining anti-competitive conduct in retail markets and where there is potential for firms to price discriminate across large customers). Isochrones are usually drawn by specialist software such as Microsoft's MapPoint®, the various software taking into account how fast one can travel, the type of road being used, whether the road is in a non-urban, urban, or large urban area, the peak or non-peak time of the travel. In its decisional practice, the UK competition authorities have used isochrones in relation to mergers concerning betting shops, cinemas, book shops, and supermarkets: CMA62, OFT/CC Commentary on Retail Mergers (10 April 2017), para 2.14, available at https://www.gov.uk/government/publications/retail-mergers-commentary-cma62.

based on isochrones of multiple sizes, namely 15 and 20 minute walking times and 15 and 20 minute drive times in various recent cases.[160]

In *Michelin I*, the Commission fined the Dutch subsidiary of a French company for abusing its dominant position over the supply of tyres for heavy vehicles to dealers in the Netherlands without enquiring whether the dealers' customers could easily have bought Michelin tyres outside that country.[161] If they could have done so, Michelin's Dutch subsidiary, Michelin NV, could not have earned a monopoly profit from dealers without driving them out of business to its own disadvantage. The CJEU confirmed the Commission's selection of the Netherlands as the relevant market on the ground that the decision was addressed to the Dutch subsidiary, since (i) its activities were concentrated in the Netherlands; (ii) its main competitors also carried on activities there through local subsidiaries; (iii) the alleged abuse related to discounts given to dealers there; and (iv) dealers there obtained their supplies only from suppliers operating there. The CJEU held that the Commission was right to take the view that the competition facing Michelin NV was mainly on the Dutch market and that was the 'level at which the objective conditions of competition are alike for traders'. It added, however, that this did not exclude the position of the Michelin group and its competitors as a whole, or a much wider market being relevant to the existence of a dominant position on the relevant product market. The Michelin group may have been equally dominant in the areas outside the Netherlands, but this was not established. In *European Night Services v Commission*, the General Court quashed a Commission decision under Article 101(1) TFEU for failure to give reasons for its definition of the product market and for its appraisal of the appropriate geographic market.[162]

Where a narrow market is taken as relevant, the firm alleged to be dominant should take the initiative to defend itself and establish that competitive pressures from outside the market defined as relevant are so strong that it is futile to concentrate only on it. As in the case of product markets, it does not greatly matter whether this is done at the stage of defining the relevant market or when the dominant position is being assessed, as long as it is done. Both CJEU and Commission have, however, selected narrow markets where they fear that a firm granted a special or exclusive right by the government of a Member State controls an essential facility. The port of Genoa, for instance, was considered a substantial part of the Common Market in view of its importance to trade into and out of Italy.[163] The Commission has been accepting even narrower markets, such as rather less important ports in Denmark.

In some cases, the criteria for defining the market have been based on the nature of the complaint. As there is no complainant in merger investigations, control of concentrations

160 See eg *Virgin/Esporta* (ME/4994/11) OFT Decision (11 July 2011); *Virgin Active/Holmes Place* (ME/2628/06) OFT Decision (19 October 2006); *Pure Gym/The Gym* CMA Decision (11 September 2014). With regard to the European Commission, see the recent mergers in the cement industry, *Holcim/Cemex West* (Case COMP/M.7009) Commission Decision (5 June 2014), available at http://ec.europa.eu/competition/elojade/isef/case_details.cfm?proc_code=2_M_7009; *Crh/Holcim Lafarge* (Case COMP/M.7550) Commission Decision (24 April 2015), available at http://ec.europa.eu/competition/elojade/isef/case_details.cfm?proc_code=2_M_7550; *Cemex/Holcim Assets* (Case COMP/M.7054) Commission Decision (9 September 2014), available at http://ec.europa.eu/competition/elojade/isef/case_details.cfm?proc_code=2_M_7054.

161 Case 322/81, *NV Nederlandsche Banden Industrie Michelin v Commission* [1983] ECR 3461.

162 Joined Cases T-374–5, 384 & 388/94, *European Night Services Ltd et al v Commission* [1998] ECR II–3141.

163 Case C-179/90, *Merci Convenzionali Porto di Genova SpA v Siderurgica Gabrielli SpA* [1990] ECR I–5889.

has been based on the future structure of the market. Will the dominant position persist? Consequently, rather broader markets have often been the starting point for the analysis of mergers under the regulation. The Commission takes into account the continuing process of market integration. As barriers to cross-border trade have been abolished under the Internal Market programme, many markets have become geographically wider. Many, however, remain national or regional, especially at the retail level.

3.3.5. MARKET DEFINITION *SUI GENERIS*

Before presenting an overview of the quantitative techniques (old and new) used to define markets, this Section looks at peculiar cases of market definition where the orthodox framework presented in the in the previous sections needs to be adjusted.

3.3.5.1. Aftermarkets

The term 'aftermarket' refers to a situation where consumers buy a durable (called primary) product first, in the knowledge that they will also have to buy a consumable (called secondary) product over the life-time of the durable product (hence, the expression aftermarkets). Usually, the quantity of secondary product purchased depends on the intensity of use of the primary product. Familiar examples are ink cartridges for printers, and specifically designed spare parts for cars, where in the latter case although it is not certain that spare parts will be needed, the chances increase with the intensity of usage of the primary product.

Typically, the manufacturer of the primary product can act as a gatekeeper for the secondary product, ie, thanks to the *de facto* control of the technical specifications that allow compatibility and/or legal IP rights protection.[164] Therefore, the risk is that the primary product is subsidized thanks to the ability to charge locked-in customers high prices for the secondary products. Accordingly, the key question is whether the secondary product can constitute a separate market.

According to established case law,[165] the answer depends on whether customers can and do consider the overall cost of the combination of primary and (proprietary) secondary products over the life-cycle of the former (presumably, based on their expected intensity of usage). If so, the idea is to see whether enough customers would switch to another combination of primary/secondary products within a reasonable period of time in order to make unprofitable any attempt to raise prices for the secondary product. In that case, what counts is that there is rivalry in the primary product, regardless of whether the secondary product

164 In contrast, there is no gatekeeping issue where the universal compatibility of the secondary product with all primary products is essential to the viability of the primary product market itself. For example, although petrol is a consumable product purchased by car users it would be impossible for car manufacturers to act as gatekeepers, since they would not be able to guarantee the same coverage through their own network of (incompatible) petrol stations. A perhaps fanciful question to ponder is whether the transition to a different fuelling source might change the balance in favour of car manufacturers (eg similarly to, say, the ability of mobile device manufacturers to require that consumers buy their own (incompatible) peripheral accessories).

165 The CJEU has recently endorsed this approach in Case C-56/12 P, *EFIM v Commission*, ECLI:EU:C:2013:575, paras 36–7, in dismissing a challenge against the European Commission who refused to open an investigation for abuse of dominant position because of lack of evidence that customers did not exert a disciplining constraint in the primary market (ie, the burden of proof was on the complainant).

is effectively monopolized. Under these circumstances, the primary and secondary product form a single product market (so-called 'systems markets').[166]

3.3.5.2. Bundles

Whilst in the case of aftermarkets joint consumption of the primary and the secondary products is necessary for the fruition of the former, with bundles it is in principle possible to buy and use just one product without the need to purchase also the other complementary products. For example, bundles of broadband, telephony, and pay-TV services are increasingly popular (so-called 'triple-play'), although each of them could in principle be purchased and used in isolation.

In theory, there are two types of bundles, pure and mixed, depending on whether the individual elements are sold on a standalone basis. Nevertheless, it could be argued that a mixed bundle is a *de facto* pure bundle, when the price for the bundle is far cheaper than the sum of the individual prices.[167]

Under these circumstances, the imposition of a SSNIP over the price for the bundle might not induce enough customers to unpick the bundle and start purchasing its elements individually, so that the price rise would be unprofitable. Accordingly, the bundle may constitute a separate market, that is, alongside the standalone markets for the individual elements.

The risk, though, is that the prevailing price for the bundle is below competitive levels (as, eg, the result of predatory pricing by the seller of the bundle against sellers of the individual components). Hence, the 'reverse-cellophane fallacy' would loom. In contrast, where the ability to offer a cheaper price for the bundle was due to superior efficiencies—for example, lower cost for customer acquisition, billing, and customer care—the finding of a separate market for the bundle would be justified.[168]

Fixed/mobile bundles cases in telecoms provide some interesting insights. In its recent decisional practice, the European Commission has left open the question of a separate market for multi-play services, whereas it acknowledges the likely increase in demand of these type of services in the coming years.[169] The Commission has also added that due to the different services included in various bundles, instead of one possible market, there could be also several markets for different multi-play products.[170] The Commission also notes that even dual-play

166 For some examples in the UK competition law cases on aftermarkets, see *Macquarie Bank Ltd/Utility Metering Services Ltd* (ME/5260/2011) OFT Decision (9 January 2012) (MAP-Meter asset provision and MAM-meter asset management services); *Chargemaster/Elektromotive UK* (ME/5897/2013) OFT Decision (25 March 2013) (Electric vehicle supply equipment (EVSE) and EVSE installation and maintenance); *Ratcliff/Ross & Bonnyman* (ME/4811/2010) OFT Decision (18 February 2011) (commercial vehicles tail lifts-spare parts).

167 This would, of course, only be the case where no consumer would ever consider buying only a subset of the bundle—ie, consumer would in any case still want to buy all the elements albeit from different firms (mix-and-match).

168 For a discussion with respect to the assessment of 'triple-play', see Body of European Regulators for Electronic Communications (BEREC), 'Report on Impact of Bundled Offers in Retail and Wholesale Market Definition', BoR (10) 64 (2010), available at https://berec.europa.eu/eng/document_register/subject_matter/berec/reports/209-berec-report-on-impact-of-bundled-offers-in-retail-and-wholesale-market-definition.

169 *Telefonica Deutschland/E-plus* (Case COMP/M.7018) Commission Decision (2013), available at http://ec.europa.eu/competition/elojade/isef/case_details.cfm?proc_code=2_M_7018.

170 *Orange/Jazztel* (Case COMP/M.7421) Commission Decision (2014), para 51, available at http://ec.europa.eu/competition/elojade/isef/case_details.cfm?proc_code=2_M_7421.

services can constitute a separate market while grouping triple and quadruple-play services together. Therefore, it concludes that the ultimate question will be if there are five separate markets for multi-play services: (a) a general one for all; (b) a separate market for dual-play services; (c) one of triple-play services; (d) one of quadruple-play services; and (e) a market combining triple and quadruple services.[171] The Commission also makes one interesting observation in relation to the market for fixed Internet access services: if multi-play services were not to form a separate market, the market for fixed Internet access services would include all fixed Internet services either sold in a stand-alone basis or as part of a bundle. On the other hand, if multi-play services were to form a separate market, the market for fixed Internet access services would include only stand-alone services and services offered as part of a dual-play bundle.[172]

In its recent merger inquiry in the anticipated *BT/EE* merger, the UK CMA rejected the suggestion that the market should be defined as a bundle consisting of fixed and mobile services.[173] To reach this conclusion, the CMA has taken into account the low uptake of fixed–mobile bundles in the UK, evidenced by survey evidence on consumer interest in fixed–mobile bundles, and forecast uptake of fixed–mobile bundles in the UK. In order to reach its decision, the CMA also assessed the supply-side and demand-side reasons for fixed–mobile bundling and took into account the European Commission's decisional practice and OFCOM's recent findings.

In *Deutsche Börse/London Stock Exchange Group*, the Commission held that '[w]here a concrete product inevitably implies the purchase of at least two complementary services [. . .] and customers are limited in their choices of these complementary services, the Commission considers that exchanges compete in offering bundles of services (or integrated services)'.[174] According to the Commission, '[a]ssessing the competitive implications of a merger requires in such a case evaluating the impact of a transaction on the bundle (and not merely on a component-by-component basis)'.[175] In *DBAG/NYSE Euronext*, the Commission had taken the view that with regard to exchange-traded derivatives, although in theory, trading and clearing could potentially be provided as separate services, many exchanges were providing users with an integrated service including the trading and clearing of derivative contracts and for which they may charge a single fee and considered that competition was bundle-to-bundle.[176] The important elements considered in these cases, relate to the existence of an obligation or practice or a market structure inherently linking the bundled products together.

[171] Ibid. [172] Ibid, paras 83–4.

[173] *BT/EE* merger (CMA 2016), in particular Appendix H of the Final report, paras 89–90.

[174] *Deutsche Börse/London Stock Exchange Group* (Case COMP/M.7995) Commission Decision (29 March 2017), para 40, available at http://ec.europa.eu/competition/elojade/isef/case_details.cfm?proc_code=2_M_7995.

[175] Ibid, para 41.

[176] *DBAG/NYSE Euronext* (Case COMP/M.6166) Commission Decision (2012), para 240, available at http://ec.europa.eu/competition/elojade/isef/case_details.cfm?proc_code=2_M_6166. The Commission took nevertheless a different perspective for over the counter (OTC) traded derivatives and bonds, where it considered it more appropriate 'to assess competition on each service layer separately', as there is 'neither an obligation to clear, nor a market structure or practice that entails that clearing is inherently linked to trading': *Deutsche Börse/London Stock Exchange Group* (Case COMP/M.7995) Commission Decision (29 March 2017), para 43, available at http://ec.europa.eu/competition/elojade/isef/case_details.cfm?proc_code=2_M_7995.

3.3.5.3. Bidding markets

Bidding processes can be used either to sell (eg a public authority auctioning off spectrum for wireless applications) or to buy (eg a procurement tender to outsource complex IT systems). For the sake of simplicity, however, we focus on the latter. Typically, the reason why a product (or service) is tendered for is that it is bespoke in terms of product specifications, so that it cannot be suitably standardized. Hence, there is a distinct lack of 'functional' substitutes, which suggest that demand-side substitutability might not be much of a constraint. Moreover, prices may hardly be comparable across bids for similar albeit not fungible products or services (eg bids for large infrastructure building projects). The risk is, therefore, that markets could be delineated very narrowly, where each bespoke auction could be considered as a separate relevant market.

However, supply-side substitutability, to the extent that there is a significant overlap in terms of actual or potential bidders competing across separate auctions, is the key competitive constraint. Accordingly, the boundaries of the relevant market should be based on the intensity of competition—ie, the closeness of supply-side substitution—among bidders.[177]

In this respect, an analysis of bidding participation (known as 'win–loss' analysis) could prove extremely informative, covering information such as the identity of bidders (including location) and their ranking (in particular, the identity of the incumbent, the winner, and the runner-up).[178] The idea is that if two bidders are close substitutes, so that their joint presence could spur each other to bid aggressively, each bidder would tend to be the runner-up when the other wins.

Market shares might not be very informative. This is particularly the case where bids occur infrequently (say, once in a year) and are relatively large in scale. Under these circumstances, market shares could prove very volatile, in that the winner of a large bid during the current year would show a large market share, only potentially to lose it the year after if a close competitor wins the next large bid.

3.3.5.4. Two-sided markets and platform competition

Platforms that operate in two-sided markets facilitate the interaction between two groups of customers, where members on each side are more willing to 'be on board' if they expect the other side to be equally popular.[179] Classic examples are:

- credit cards, where users want a card that is accepted ubiquitously, and merchants do not want to lose business by not offering to their client the convenience of being able to pay with their credit card;

177 See eg OFT/CC, 'Merger Assessment Guidelines' (CC2/OFT1254 also adopted by the CMA) (September 2010), para 5.2.18, available at http://www.oft.gov.uk/shared_oft/mergers/642749/OFT1254.pdf ('An example of where the Authorities may aggregate products which are not demand-side substitutes is in markets characterised by bidding and tendering processes where firms bid on the basis of the service they can offer to supply customers with bespoke products. The competitive constraint on firms in this case comes from a customer's willingness to award the contract to a rival rather than to switch to a different bespoke product. Aggregating a range of contracts where the same set of firms would have been credible bidders can provide more useful information about the competitive constraints on each firm than is available from focusing on just one bespoke product.').

178 For a detailed discussion of the application of these methodologies applied to the assessment of horizontal mergers in the EU, see D Gore, S Lewis, F Dethmers, and A Lofaro, *The Economic Assessment of Mergers Under European Competition Law* (CUP, 2013), 231.

179 For a useful and more detailed analysis of two-sided markets in competition law, see DS Evans and R Schmalensee, 'The Antitrust Analysis of *Multi-Sided Platform Businesses*' in R Blair and D Sokol (eds) *Oxford Handbook on International Antitrust Economics*, vol 1 (OUP, 2014), 404.

- online marketplaces (eg auction sites): where both sellers and buyers are keen to trade in a tick market with plenty of choice;
- game consoles (and App [application] stores): where users wants a variety of compatible games (Apps) and game (Apps) developers do not want to waste their energies developing a game (App) for a proprietary platform unless it is expected to attract many potential clients.

What these examples share is the fact that members from each side join the platform to execute an interaction (often carry out a transaction) with a member from the other side—ie, the platform is a match-maker. Hence, a decision of a member to join the platform on side *A* will benefit members on the other side *B*; and vice versa, in the sense that to the extent that side *B* becomes more attractive (thanks to the new affiliation on side *A*) this will in return increase the utility of joining side *A* in the first place.

In economic jargon these cross-sided dynamics are called 'indirect network externalities', as opposed to 'direct network externalities' where there is only one side and users benefit if other users join the network—for example, mobile telephony. The term 'externality' refers to the idea that, when an individual user decides to join in, he/she will normally fail to appreciate that his/her decision will benefit others (either on the same side under direct network externalities, or on the other side as with multi-sided platforms).

Hence, the theory goes, individual adaptions should be encouraged through some form of subsidization in order to achieve the optimal critical mass on the network. Accordingly, the role of the two-sided platform is to 'internalize' these externalities, by solving the 'chicken-and-egg' problem that typically besets such platforms thus managing to get 'both sides on board'. This is typically done by subsidizing the side that at first brings the strongest benefits to the other side, for example, users' access to a property website (whilst estate agents are charged to list their properties). Therefore, the fees charged on both sides may not reflect the underlying costs incurred for each side.[180] Indeed, one side might not be charged at all, or even there could be negative prices on one side to bring them on board—for example, a free voucher.[181]

These peculiarities make it tricky to implement the SSNIP test. To impose a SSNIP only on one side, would ignore the fact that a reduction in membership (ie, following an increase in the membership fee) or intensity of usage (ie, due to an increase in the transaction fee) on one side will cause a similar knock-on effect on the other side, and so on. That is to say, indirect network externalities provide a constraint on the ability to impose a SSNIP on one side only.[182] Therefore, it has been argued that the hypothetical monopolist should be required to increase the overall *level* of prices, whilst allowing the platform to adjust the *structure* of prices across each side in order to minimize the negative feedback loop thereof.[183]

180 There can two types of fees: (a) membership fee to just become an affiliate; and (b) transaction fee, levied each time an interaction with a member of the other side is executed.

181 This is typically the case where the members of one side are promiscuous, in the sense that they can use multiple platforms, often at the same time (so-called 'multi-homing').

182 Hence, in its decision on Google Search, the Commission did not apply the SSNIP test: *Google Search (Shopping)* (Case AT.39740) Commission Decision C(2017) 4444 final, para 245 (noting that 'the SSNIP test would not have been appropriate in the present case because Google provides its search services for free to users').

183 For a discussion on this topic, see L Filistrucchi, D Geradin, E van Damme, and P Affeldt, 'Market Definition in Two-Sided Markets: Theory and Practice' (2014) 10(2) *J Competition L & Economics* 293.

The analysis of two-sided markets/platforms presented so far is uncontroversial, in the sense that there is little doubt that the examples presented above fit the concept. However, there is a tendency to stretch the definition of two-sided markets, as by doing so it is possible to argue that antitrust intervention is unwarranted since the ability to exercise market power is naturally constrained by the kind of negative feedback loops (fuelled by indirect network externalities) described above.[184]

In particular, media markets are regularly considered to be two-sided markets *sui generis*, where on one side there is the audience (readers/listeners/viewers) and on the other side there are advertisers seeking to reach that audience. However, media markets definitely constitute an outlier in terms of their presupposed two-sidedness for at least three reasons:[185]

- indirect network externalities are only one directional, rather than reciprocal: advertisers benefit from larger audiences, but not vice versa. Indeed, ads normally constitute a nuisance for the audience;[186]
- the two sides do not interact on the platform. It is true that the aim of advertisers is to ultimately trigger a transaction, but none of this is hosted by the platform—ie, the primary purpose for the audience to affiliate the media outfit is to access content, whilst tolerating advertisers' attempt to build brand awareness;
- for media firms two-sidedness is an optional business model, not a necessity—ie, their core business is not about match-making in nature. For example, a TV operator can either adopt a free-to-air business model—where content is free for the audience whilst advertisers pay to have their ads aired—or a pay-TV business model—where the audience has to pay to view content of their choice, often without the nuisance of advertising.[187]

By the same token, it is debatable whether social networks, such as Facebook and Twitter, and search engines, such as Google search, are truly two-sided platforms. In both cases usage is driven by the desire to interact, respectively, with other users (ie, direct network externalities), or find the right content on the web for free, whilst tolerating the fact that their data are used by the host operator to allow advertisers to target them with their impressions (ie, the externality is one-directional rather than reciprocal).

Accordingly, in all these (*sui generis*) cases, to impose a SSNIP on advertisers would hardly set off the kind of negative feedback loop described above. The ability to exercise market power on one side is not restrained by the need to keep both sides on board, since the audience would not be bothered by the fact that there is less advertising on the platform (ie, as a consequence of an increase in price).[188] It is true that the ability to offer, potentially for free,

184 In contrast, though, two-sided markets may be subject to 'winners-take-all' dynamics, where the incumbent platform becomes the *de facto* place to be for users on both sides. Therefore, the chances of rival platforms being able to build their own critical mass are low due to an insurmountable 'chicken-and-egg' problem. The role of network externalities as potential barrier to entry and expansion is discussed in the next section.

185 For a detailed discussion, see G Luchetta, 'Is the Google Platform a Two-Sided Market?' (2013) 10(1) *J Competition L & Economics* 185.

186 There are exceptions, of course, as with readers of fashion/glamour magazines and with classified ads. In the latter case, though, advertisers have radically deserted media outfits and, nowadays, normally prefer to reach the other side by posting their ads on dedicated two-sided platforms such as Gumtree, eBay, and many others.

187 It is true, of course, that a pay-TV business model would not be viable without premium content such as sports and recent blockbusters, but the choice of what type of content to broadcast is endogenous, in the sense that an FTA TV operator could over time decide to switch to a pay-TV business model.

188 See I Lianos & E Motchenkova, 'Market Dominance and Search Quality in the Search Engine Market' (2013) 9(2) *J Competition L and Economics* 419.

good quality content and online services, such as search and social networking, relies on the monetization of audience's attention, but the audience decision as to of which services to use is not affected by an expectation in terms of adoption numbers on the other side.

That is to say, there is no 'chicken-and-egg' problem, in that it is the quality of the content provided (for free) that determines audience's affiliation, and advertisers do not determine the quality, they only exploit it (at a price) in order to reach their target audience.[189] As a final example, let's consider price comparison sites, which are free to consult for user whereas sellers are charged, typically, a commission on a per-click basis. On the one hand, users look for a comparison that is both accurate and covers the entire market (eg car insurance quotes); on the other hand, sellers are in two minds, as they want to be listed on popular websites but are aware that accurate comparison spurs pricing rivalry.

Usually, though, sellers have no choice as they know that the website may list their offer in any case. This is the key intuition as to why price comparison sites are not two-sided platform in a strict sense: users' decision to consult is based on the expectation of a comprehensive and accurate comparison, regardless of whether sellers accept to be charged for sponsored links or on a click-through basis. Indeed, the fact that price comparison websites are financially reliant on sellers' commission fees makes users uneasy, if not suspicious; and this is notwithstanding the fact that users would hardly pay for a comparison that is financially independent.[190]

In conclusion, whilst it is important to be aware of the type of unidirectional externality that characterizes these types of (*sui generis*) platforms, a one-sided approach to market definition may nevertheless still be appropriate.[191]

This is still the approach followed by the EU Courts, which usually address the issue of multi-sidedness not when they determine the competitive constraints directly faced by the undertaking in question in defining the appropriate antitrust relevant market that will serve as the starting point for competition assessment, but when determining the existence of a restriction on competition, since the two-sidedness is part and parcel of the overall economic context that needs to be taken into account by the competition decision-maker before concluding on the existence of a restriction of competition by object or by effect.[192] In contrast, in a five to four judgment in *Ohio v American Express Co*, drafted by Justice Thomas, the majority of the US Supreme Court highlighted the fact that some two-sided platforms, such as credit card operators like American Express, facilitate a single, simultaneous transaction between merchants and cardholders and thus supply 'only one product', namely transactions, which are jointly consumed by the card-holder and the merchant.[193] The Supreme Court stressed the importance of evaluating *both* sides of a two-sided transaction platform in order to accurately assess competition and thus analyzed the two-sided

189 One peculiar feature that distinguishes media business from social networking and web searching is that in the latter case the quality of the content is determined in a positive way by the number of users (ie, positive direct network externalities). For example, Goggle's search engine gets better and better thanks to the cumulated intelligence gathered as to what constitutes a good search result. Hence the importance to maintain high volume of traffic.

190 For a detailed discussion, see HC Gamper, 'How Can Internet Comparison Sites Work Optimally for Consumers?' (2012) 35 *J Consumer Policy* 333.

191 See L Filistrucchi, D Geradin, E van Damme, and P Affeldt, 'Market Definition in Two-Sided Markets: Theory and Practice' (2014) 10(2) *J Competition L & Economics* 293. For some examples of cases in the UK where multi-sided markets were considered, see *Global Radio/GMG* (CC, 2013); OFT, *WRI/Hostelbookers.com* (ME/6062/13); OFT, *BSkyB/Virgin Media* (ME/4568/10); OFT, *Capital Shopping Centres/Trafford* (ME/4903/11).

192 See the analysis in Chapter 6 of the CJEU's approach in Case C-67/13 P, *Groupement des cartes bancaires (CB) v Commission*, ECLI:EU:C:2014:2204, paras 76-81 [hereinafter *Cartes bancaires*].

193 *Ohio v American Express Co*, 585 US ___ (2018),

market for credit-card transactions as a whole, at least for 'transaction platforms'.[194] In its recent judgment in *Sainsbury's v Mastercard*, the CAT in the UK also addressed the issue of two-sided 'transaction platforms':

> 70. It is uncontroversial that the MasterCard Scheme is – like all payment systems—what is commonly referred to by economists as a 'two-sided platform'. The essence of a two-sided platform, as its name implies, is that 'the platform brings together two types of user. In payment card schemes, these are the consumers who carry the card in their wallet (cardholders), and the retailers and other types of merchant who accept the card for payment (merchants).
>
> 71. There is an essential relationship between the two types of user: 'the more users there are on one side, the more attractive the platform is to the other side. The more consumers with a MasterCard in their wallet, the more attractive it is for retailers to accept MasterCard, and vice versa.
>
> 72. In an article published in 1983 in the Journal of Law and Economics, Professor William Baxter noted that payment systems—which he defined as including card systems like the MasterCard Scheme—involved a degree of co-operation between cardholder and merchant not necessarily found in other two-sided markets.
>
> 73. The point is an obvious, but important, one: '*without co-operation between Cardholder and Merchant, there can be no purchase. And that co-operation implies a co-operation between the Issuing Bank (with whom the Cardholder has contracted) and the Acquiring Bank (with whom the Merchant has contracted). Unless there is such co-operation between the Issuing and Acquiring Banks—by which we mean a form of legal agreement along the lines described above—the transaction will not go ahead*'.
>
> 74. It is important to note that this is not a feature of all two-sided platforms [. . .].[195]

Do you think that the concept of 'transaction platforms' is useful for competition law analysis? What are the broader implications for antitrust plaintiffs? Should they evaluate net harm to competition on *all* sides of the platform? What are the broader societal implications in substituting the concept of 'platform' to that of 'relevant market' as the starting point for competition law assessment? To the extent that competition law is based on the idea that markets reward undertakings according to their individual economic productivity, how does the intervention of a 'platform' that is controlled by an intermediary, and the assessment of competition at the 'transaction platform', rather than relevant market, level change the original calculus of competition law?

[194] According to the majority Opinion, the key feature of transaction platforms is that they cannot make a sale to one side of the platform without simultaneously making a sale to the other. This approach was criticized by the minority of the Supreme Court in an Opinion drafted by Justice Breyer, who considered that the relationship between merchant-related card services and shopper-related card services is primarily that of complements, not substitutes, and thus the two could not form part of the same product market. Justice Breyer rejected the concept of 'transaction platform', *inter alia*, because of the difficulty to determine its limiting principles and to distinguish clearly these platforms from other platforms in which the two sides should be considered separately. The approach of the minority of the US Supreme Court seems close to that adopted by the CJEU in *Cartes Bancaires*. According to the approach followed in the EU, the fact that the two sides are complements and that the level of pricing at one side may affect demand on the other side does not make them a single relevant market for competition law purposes. As an example, lets transpose the situation of the Amex case in EU competition law. One would need to distinguish at least two markets in a three-part payment system, such as Amex: market 1 (between payment networks and merchants) and market 2 (between payment networks and cardholders). As these provide complementary, not substitute, services, markets 1 and 2 are considered as separate markets for competition law purposes. Platforms engage in a variety of activities, e.g. advertising and rewarding cardholders, that are complementary to market 1. Advertising and rewards to cardholders are not 'sold' in market 1; they just shift upwards demand in market 1. This interdependence between markets 1 and 2 is not taken into account in defining the relevant market but when assessing the existence of a restriction of competition and its possible justification by out-of-market efficiency gains. See our analysis in Chapter 6.

[195] *Sainsbury's v Mastercard* [2016] CAT 1 (emphasis added).

3.3.5.5. Brands and product differentiation

Product differentiation became the focus of an economic inquiry in the 1930s.[196] Two positions emerged in the literature. Relying on the paradigm of welfare economics and having as a starting point for the analysis the concept of 'industries' producing a single/homogeneous commodity, Robinson's *Economics of Imperfect Competition* viewed product differentiation as a departure from the ideal of perfect competition, hence the use of the term 'imperfect' to qualify the situation of product heterogeneity, the term 'imperfect' indicating the direction to go (that of 'perfect' competition).[197] In his *Theory of Monopolistic Competition*, Chamberlin took a different perspective, focusing on the concept of firm, rather than that of industry and viewing product differentiation as a normal fact of economic life, the concept of monopolistic competition describing the process of many sellers who produce heterogeneous products in response to divergent demands and preferences of consumers.[198] Chamberlin noted that:

> the consequences of product heterogeneity for welfare economics have been either ignored or seriously misunderstood. Monopoly elements are built into the economic system and the ideal necessarily involves them. Thus, wherever there is a demand for diversity of product, pure competition turns out to be not the ideal but a departure from it.[199]

According to Chamberlin, 'if heterogeneity is part of the welfare ideal, there is no prima facie case for doing anything at all', the choice to be made being ultimately that of a 'less heterogeneous output as against a smaller, more heterogeneous one'.[200] This brings to the fore the idea that price is not the only, or the most important, parameter of competition and that quality and variety may also constitute important parameters one should take into account.

These contrasting views over product differentiation reflect the difficulties of 'brands' and 'brand theory' to gain acceptance as a useful operational concept in competition law, as economic models do not engage systematically with the psychological aspect of consumer behaviour and the formation of consumer preferences, for instance the emotional and cognitive appeal of brands. As it has been highlighted by some authors, brands, advertising, or other past experiences and social milieu, such as childhood, lead to 'preference capital', which may be a valuable asset for incumbent firms and a source of long-term economic rents for them.[201] This explains, according to these authors, why consumers have high willingness to pay for particular brands, even when the alternatives are objectively similar.[202] This raises

196 Part of this chapter draws on I Lianos, 'Brands, Product Differentiation and EU Competition Law' in D Desai, I Lianos, and S Weber Waller (eds) *Brands, Competition Law and IP* (CUP, 2015), 146.

197 J Robinson, *The Economics of Imperfect Competition* (Macmillan, 1933).

198 EH Chamberlin, *The Theory of Monopolistic Competition* (Harvard University Press, 1933).

199 EH Chamberlin, 'Product Heterogeneity and Public Policy' (1950) 40(2) *American Economic Rev* 85, 92.

200 Ibid, 89–90. Two basic formalizations of product heterogeneity emerged in economics. The spatial model, which treats competition as a localized phenomenon, the assumption being that 'consumers purchase a limited number of brands (often one) from a small subset that are most preferred' and the representative consumer model, according to which 'a representative consumer purchases many brands, varying the proportions of each according to their prices and exogenously given utility weights': JM Perloff and SC Salop, 'Equilibrium with Product Differentiation'(1985) 52(1) *Rev Economic Studies* 107.

201 BJ Bronnenberg, J-PH Dubé, and M Grentzkow, 'The Evolution of Brand Preferences: Evidence from Consumer Migration' (2012) 102(6) *American Economic Rev* 2472.

202 Ibid. See also BJ Bronnenberg, SK Dhar, J-PH Dubé, 'Brand History, Geography, and the Persistence of Brand Shares' (2009) 117(1) *J Political Economy* 87. Yet, these preferences are shaped during a considerable period of time.

the possibility that brands and product differentiation may limit the competitive constraints an undertaking faces. This evidence also indicates that brand loyalty may not always be a natural outgrowth of consumer preferences and that there is value for firms to use advertising, branding, or other forms of product differentiation in order to establish some form of 'preference capital'. This strategy may generate high willingness to pay for consumers and presumably steady economic rents for the incumbents in the future. In other words, incumbent firms may have the incentives and the ability to alter the utility function of consumers in order to increase their profits. Should that lead us to define relevant markets narrowly, eventually even defining a specific brand as a relevant market, thus enabling competition authorities to intervene?

Such an approach would not take into account the positive effects of branding to competition. Indeed, some authors advance an informative view by distinguishing between search goods (whose quality can be determined prior to purchase, even if at high cost) and experience goods (whose quality can only be determined after consumption) and observing the benefits of enhanced product differentiation for experience goods (through the provision of indirect information about the product).[203] Product differentiation and branding stimulate price comparisons and therefore price competition. Finally, brands in general assist the consumer to draw positive associations between specific products and quality, reminding them of their previous experience with the product ('the repeat-business effect').[204]

Some authors also consider that 'consumers possess stable preferences, and advertising (and branding) directly enters these preferences in a manner that is complementary to the consumption of the advertised product', as consumer values 'social prestige' and 'advertising by a firm may be an input that contributed toward the prestige that is enjoyed when the firm's products is consumed'.[205] This view takes for granted the preferences of consumers for 'social prestige' and argues that consumer utility in this case derives from the consumption of various commodities, brand image being one of them. Branding does not alter consumer preferences but 'instead enters as an argument in a stable utility function'.[206] Hence, it is possible that 'firms may compete in the same commodity (eg prestige) market even though they produce different market goods (eg jewelry and fashion) and advertise at different levels)'.[207] Hence, branding may be beneficial to consumers, as consumers value directly the 'social prestige' image that this generates, which is part of their utility function.

One could here refer to the issues raised by Veblen goods. Veblen, among others, has emphasized the phenomenon of 'conspicuous consumption',[208] which brings attention to the role interpersonal effects have on utility functions or the need to focus on the inner motivations of consumers.[209] Leibenstein proceeded to a classification of consumer demand for goods and services according to the motivation behind consumer's demand. He distinguished between 'functional demand', which refers to the 'part of the demand for a commodity which is due to the qualities inherent in the commodity', and 'non-functional demand', which is 'the portion of the demand for a consumers' good which is due to factors other than the qualities inherent

203 P Nelson, 'Advertising as Information' (1974) 82 *J Political Economy* 729, 732–4.

204 Ibid.

205 K Bagwell, *The Economic Analysis of Advertising*, Columbia University, Department of Economics, Discussion Paper No 0506-01 (August 2005), 20–1.

206 Ibid, 143.

207 Ibid, 21.

208 T Veblen, *The Theory of the Leisure Class* (Macmillan, 1899).

209 H Leibenstein, 'Bandwagon, Snob, and Veblen Effects in the Theory of Consumers Demand' (1950) 64 *Q J Economics* 183.

in the commodity'.[210] This relates to 'utility derived from the commodity is enhanced or decreased owing to the fact that others are purchasing and consuming the same commodity, or owing to the fact that the commodity bears a higher rather than a lower price tag'.[211] This non-functional demand may take different forms: (i) the 'bandwagon effect', which refers to 'the extent to which the demand for a commodity is increased due to the fact that others are also consuming the same commodity'; (ii) the 'snob effect', which refers to the 'extent to which the demand for a consumers' good is decreased owing to the fact that others are also consuming the same commodity (or that others are increasing their consumption of that commodity)'; and, finally, (iii) the 'Veblen effect' which refers to 'the phenomenon of conspicuous consumption, to the extent to which the demand for a consumers' good is increased because it bears a higher rather than a lower price', which is different from the 'snob effect' in the sense that it is a function of price, and not of the consumption of others.[212] Typical Veblen goods are luxury products for which brand differentiation constitutes an important asset. According to some authors, if 'the Veblen effect is the predominant one, the demand curve is less elastic than otherwise, and some portions of it may even be positively inclined',[213] hence showing that higher prices may in some instances correspond to the preferences of consumers.

The decision to intervene in this context, by defining narrowly the market and finding the existence of market power, will therefore depend on the view one takes of product differentiation and its relation with the *real* preferences of the consumers. Some would emphasize the value of product differentiation as an instrument to promote consumer welfare and consumer choice and would consider that product differentiation often responds to the heterogeneity of consumer demand[214] and to the need to reward 'pioneering brands' for risk bearing innovation.[215] Others would be more reticent to define the relevant market narrowly. Behavioural economics or neuro-economics research has also highlighted how 'affective/hot-mode' decision-making, encompassing emotions and motivational drives may alter consumers' tastes and create brand loyalty, in comparison to a counterfactual where decision-making would have been entirely based on the deliberative effort of consumers to maximize their objective function, as this derives from their 'cold-state' preferences.[216] A regulator inspired by paternalistic objectives would strive in this case to ensure that brand differentiation responds to the 'cold-state' preferences of the consumers rather than instigated by 'hot-mode' decision-making. However, it remains difficult to distinguish, outside the laboratory, what constitutes a 'hot-state' or a 'cold-state' preference.

The emergence of 'social branding' promotes the idea that brands communicate vital consumer meaning and that consumers and brand owners are interdependent to the extent that brands are connected, networked and socialized. The result is that people and communities identify with the brands they use and become co-creators to a certain extent of the brand meaning, along with the brand owner. This perception of branding breaks with the 'broadcast' or 'one-way information transmission model' of the persuasive/informative/complementary views and perceives branding as a 'dialogic and iterative' interaction between active consumers and brand owners.[217] Iconic brands resonate with the identity of large groups of

[210] Ibid, 189. [211] Ibid. [212] Ibid. [213] Ibid, 207.

[214] KJ Lancaster, 'Socially Optimal Product Differentiation' (1975) 65(4) *American Economic Rev* 567.

[215] R Schmalensee, 'Product Differentiation Advantages of Pioneering Brands' (1982) 72(3) *American Economic Rev* 349.

[216] K Bagwell, 'The Economic Analysis of Advertising', Columbia University, Department of Economics, Discussion paper No 0506-01 (August 2005), 143–6.

[217] See eg DR Desai, 'From Trademarks to Brands' (2012) 64(4) *Florida L Rev* 981 (noting the 'noncorporate dimension of branding' which 'involves consumers and communities as stakeholders in brands'); DS Ganjee, 'Property in Brands' in H Howe and J Griffiths (eds) *Property Concepts in Intellectual Property Law* (CUP, 2013) 35.

consumers and lead to the formation of 'brand communities' that display brand loyalty but which also expect that this loyalty will not be betrayed by the brand-owner, whose discretion as brand manager is restricted by the broader values and reference points of the specific brand community.[218] The perception that brands are co-created by consumers and manufacturers or retailers renders more complex the discussion over the correspondence of product differentiation to consumer preferences and the complex interaction between consumer preferences and brand management by the brand owner.

By driving the demand curve of branded product or service to become more inelastic, brands, and more generally product differentiation, may, in theory, be considered as a source of market power, in the economic sense of the word: the ability to raise prices profitably and reduce output. The vertical restraints guidelines summarize this tradition of hostility of EU competition law towards branding power by stipulating that:

> Vertical restraints agreed for non-branded goods and services are in general less harmful than restraints affecting the distribution of branded goods and services. Branding tends to increase product differentiation and reduce substitutability of the product, leading to a reduced elasticity of demand and an increased possibility to raise price.[219]

Brands are considered in several parts of the guidelines as indicating the existence of market power of the brand-owner and as barriers to entry.[220]

This does not, however, mean that branding will always drive the demand curve to become more inelastic. It may also increase demand. The development of low-cost brands in different economic sectors (eg air transport, clothing, food, retail services) may raise doubts as to the validity of this correlation. Firms may combine a strategy of product differentiation and low cost leadership, which explains the successful emergence of low-cost brands.[221] Indeed, major traditional 'quality-focused' brands are also launching low-cost 'no-frills' brands as a way to compete with mono 'low-cost' brands.[222] This increased product or service differentiation augments the elasticity of the demand curve and increases consumer choice.

The complex interrelation between low-cost and 'quality-focused' brands has not yet been thoroughly considered in EU competition law, which adheres to the assumption that brands and product differentiation lead to a more inelastic demand curve.[223] The objective of the firm may indeed be to use product differentiation (in variety or quality) to create a firm-specific demand curve that is more inelastic than the industry-wide demand curve. The Commission and the EU Courts have relied occasionally on the inelastic demand curve of after-sales services or replacement equipment markets to define the brand as the relevant market, with the aim of protecting from exploitation consumers that were 'locked in' the specific brand. Although these cases concern aftermarkets, with the presence of information imperfections and asymmetries

218 AM Munir, Jr and TC O'Guinn, 'Brand Community' (2001) 27 *J Consumer Research* 412; D Holt, *How Brands Become Icons* (Harvard University Press, 2004).

219 Commission Guidelines on Vertical Restraints [2010] C 130/1, para 104.

220 See eg ibid, paras 114, 117, 180.

221 CWL Hill, 'Differentiation versus Low Cost or Differentiation and Low Cost: A Contingency Framework' (1988) 13(3) *Academy of Management Rev* 401.

222 In the air transport sector, see, for instance, the plans of German carrier Lufthansa to launch in collaboration with Turkish Airlines a low-cost long haul carrier: see R Weiss, 'Lufthansa Plans Long-Haul Discount Carrier With Turkish Airlines', Bloomberg (9 July 2014), available at www.bloomberg.com/news/2014-07-09/lufthansa-to-expand-low-cost-push-as-spohr-mulls-long-haul-model.html.

223 See, for instance, the classic CJEU judgment in Case C-27/76, *United Brands v Commission (Chiquita)* [1978] ECR I–207 (where the brand was considered as enhancing United Brands' dominant position).

between sellers and purchasers, and the brands involved are not household names, they illustrate that in certain circumstances, competition authorities and courts may define brands as a relevant market in order to protect consumers 'locked in' a specific brand in certain contexts.[224]

Product differentiation has played a more active role in EU merger control, in view of the recent emphasis put on unilateral (non-coordinated) effects theory and a significant impediment of effective competition below the levels of dominance.[225] In all these cases the merging firms may find it profitable to alter their behaviour unilaterally, following the acquisition, by elevating the price and suppressing output and by acting independently of the remaining firms. Econometric techniques used in the context of differentiated products in order to assess these effects take also into account the multiple dimensions of consumer choice, as the parameters of the choice increase with the number of products considered.[226]

3.3.5.6. Pharmaceuticals

In its merger and antitrust decisions in the pharmaceutical sector, the European Commission has been strongly relying on the anatomical therapeutic chemical classification (ATC) devised by the European Pharmaceutical Marketing Research Association (EphMRA) and the World Health Organization (WHO), as a relevant criterion for product market definition. The ATC classifies pharmaceutical products into different groups, according to the organs or systems on which they act and their chemical, pharmacological, and therapeutic properties, and divides them into five different levels. The third-level ATC groups pharmaceutical products according to their therapeutic indications, the fourth normally takes into consideration the mode of action, and the fifth level defines the narrowest classes, including active substances taken individually. The third level of the anatomic therapeutic chemical classification, ATC3, has been generally, taken as the starting point for product market definition, especially in merger investigations.

In its recent decision in *Perindopril Servier*,[227] the Commission has emphasized, citing its merger decision in *Abbott/Solvay*[228] that it might be appropriate to carry out analyses also at other levels, for example at ATC4, or molecule, level or even across classes. In that decision, it has adopted the same approach, taking the ATC3 level as relevant for its inter-class analysis but relying also in case-specific evidence relating to the relative strength of the intra-class constraints faced by perindopril from other inhibitors. The General Court however annulled the Commission's decision with regard to its market definition, noting that, even if defining a market at level ATC5 could not be criticized as such (para 1428), it nevertheless should be dully justified in view of the overall economic and legal context, and in particular non-price related competitive pressures, something that, according to the GC, the Commission has not appropriately done in this case.[229] Also, in *Glaxo Wellcome*, the Commission has stated that in specific cases, the market definition may be narrower or wider than the ATC3.[230]

224 Case 22/78, *Hugin Kassaregister AB and Hugin Cash Registers Ltd v Commission* [1979] ECR 1869. For analysis, see Chapter 8.

225 Council Regulation (EC) No 139/2004 of 20 January 2004 on the *control* of concentrations between undertakings [2004] OJ L 24/1. For a recent account, see T Mäger, 'Unilateral Effects in European Merger Analysis' in BE Hawk (ed) *Annual Proceedings of the Fordham Corporate Law Institute 2010*, vol 37 (Juris, 2011), 123; I Kokkoris and H Shelanski, *EU Merger Control: A Legal and Economic Analysis* (OUP, 2014), 221.

226 See eg *Unilever/Sara Lee* (Case COMP/M.5658) Commission Decision (17 November 2010), para 182, available at http://ec.europa.eu/competition/elojade/isef/case_details.cfm?proc_code=2_M_5658.

227 *Perindopril (Servier)* (Case AT.39612) Commission Decision [2016] OJ C 393/7 n 3215.

228 *Abbott/Solvay Pharmaceuticals* (Case COMP/M.5661), Commission Decision C (5 October 2010) 950, available at http://ec.europa.eu/competition/mergers/cases/decisions/m5661_1030_2.pdf.

229 Case T-691/14, *Servier SAS and Others v European Commission*, ECLI:EU:T:2018:922, paras 1418-1565.

230 *Glaxo Wellcome et al* (Case IV/36.957/F3) Commission Decision [2001] OJ L 302/1, para 111.

In the *Generics/Astra Zeneca* case, the Commission held that it is appropriate to carry out analyses at other ATC levels if the circumstances of a case show that sufficiently strong competitive constraints faced by the undertakings involved are situated at another level.[231] In this decision, the Commission reached a conclusion that corresponded to the fourth ATC level.[232] In its *AstraZeneca* judgment, the General Court recognized that 'the taking into account of the ATC level in which the medicines are placed constituted only a preliminary step in the Commission's analysis'.[233] The Commission's early decisional practice on mergers cases has also been in favour of the fourth level of the ATC system for market definition purposes.[234] More recently in *Mylan/Perrigo*,[235] the Commission defined the relevant product market at a narrower level, including at the ATC4 level or at level of the 'molecule' (active ingredient) or group of molecules (that is, ATC5 level) that were considered as interchangeable from a therapeutic perspective and between them there are proven economic substitution patterns so as to exercise competitive pressure on one another.[236]

The case law of the General Court also emphasizes the need to look to other factors of competition, beyond price, and for a careful analysis of the economic and legal context, to the extent that demand for prescription medicines is determined for the most part not by the ultimate consumers, but by the doctors prescribing those medicines, who are primarily guided by therapeutic use when choosing what to prescribe, rather than by the cost of treatment, but also by some other competitive forces, such as the promotional strategies of the pharmaceutical companies aiming to promote the 'loyalty' of the doctors to the specific drug, as once the doctors have chosen the relevant pharmaceutical among others that can be substitutable from a therapeutic perspective, they may show some 'inertia' in switching to a competing drug, in particular if this is new and not widely used.[237]

The Commission also considers pipeline products in its competition assessment (market-to-pipeline and pipeline-to-pipeline), which are assessed by reference to the products' characteristics, intended therapeutic use, and expected therapeutic and economic substitutability.[238]

231 *AstraZeneca* (Case COMP/A.37.507/F3) Commission Decision [2015] OJ C 332/24, para 371.

232 Ibid, para 504.

233 Case T-321/05, *AstraZeneca v Commission*, ECLI:EU:T:2010:266, paras 154–5.

234 See *Sanofi/Sterling Drug* (Case No IV/M.072) Commision Decision [1991] OJ C 156/10; *Procordia/Erbamont* (Case No IV/M.323) Commission Decision [1993] OJ C 128/5; *La Roche/Syntex* (Case No IV/M.457) Commission Decision [1994] OJ C 178/15.

235 See *Mylan/Perrigo* (Case COMP/M.7645) Commission Decision (29 July 2015), para 11, available at http://ec.europa.eu/competition/mergers/cases/decisions/m7645_20150729_20310_4436524_EN.pdf.

236 See also the recent merger cases: *Watson/Actacis* (Case COMP/M.6613) Commission Decision (5 October 2012), available at http://ec.europa.eu/competition/mergers/cases/decisions/m6613_1147_2.pdf (at the molecule level); *Teva/Ratiopharm* (Case COMP/M.5865) Commission Decision (3 August 2010), available at http://ec.europa.eu/competition/mergers/cases/decisions/m5865_20100803_20212_1565851_EN.pdf (narrower market definition, only drugs that are based on the same molecule or active pharmaceutical ingredient).

237 In *Medtronic/Covidien* (medical device) (Case COMP/M.7326) Commission Decision (28 November 2014), available at http://ec.europa.eu/competition/elojade/isef/case_details.cfm?proc_code=2_M_7326, the Commission assessed the closeness of competition of parties' advanced pipeline/existing drug-coated balloons (DCB), considering their potential for elimination of future competition using the Horizontal Merger Guidelines criteria for actual competition (ibid, para 178). Covidien's Phase III device was viewed by the market as the future closest competitor to Medtronic's existing device (ibid, para 242). Medtronic's internal documents showed that it intended to cease developing Covidien's pipeline device (ibid, para 247). A similar approach was adopted in *Novartis/Glaxosmithkline* (oncology business) (COMP/M.7275) Commission Decision (2014), available at http://ec.europa.eu/competition/elojade/isef/case_details.cfm?proc_code=2_M_7275. With regard to the UK case law on pharmaceuticals and market definition, see *GlaxoSmithKline/Pfize* (ME/4136/2009) OFT Decision (9 July 2009) and *Reckitt Benckiser* (CA98/02/2011) OFT Decision (April 2011).

238 The analysis of these non-price related competitive pressures needs however to be done thoroughly as the recent GC's judgment in *Servier* instructs us: see, Case T-691/14, *Servier SAS and Others v European Commission*, ECLI:EU:T:2018:922.

3.4. BARRIERS TO ENTRY AND/OR EXPANSION: POTENTIAL COMPETITION

Entry and expansion barriers are possibly the most important element in the definition of market and in the assessment of market power. Regarding the former, they might not only forestall supply-side substitutability, but also hamper demand-side substitutability: for example, where consumers are 'locked-in' due to switching costs (so that they might not be able to react to the imposition of a SSNIP). By the same token, barriers to entry and expansion are also relevant to the assessment of whether the exploitation of market power could be prevented by the threat of potential competitors and/or the exercise of bargaining power.[239]

In a nutshell, if barriers to entry and expansion are low, one should not care about a lasting large market share (and high profitability), since unless it is the result of superior efficiency and/or quality, entry would have already occurred to take advantage of the implied profit opportunity. This narrative is strongly reminiscent of the debate about the trade-off between allocative and productive/dynamic efficiency presented in Section 3.2.3.

There is no consensus on what constitute a barrier to entry.[240] By and large, though, an entry barrier is supposed to put an incumbent at a comparative advantage vis-à-vis a potential entrant, so that the former is able to exercise market power to the detriment of consumers (ie, although superior quality could be, in absolute term, an entry barrier, it should not be a concern for competition law's enforcers).

Entry barriers can either be a contextual element in an investigation (ie, whether or not the exercise of market power is likely), or be themselves at the focus of the investigation (ie, when the entry barrier is the result of anti-competitive foreclosure). The latter broadly corresponds to the category called 'strategic' entry barrier, as opposed to 'natural', 'structural', or 'intrinsic' ones, which the incumbent should not be held liable for.[241] What follows is by no means a comprehensive overview of entry barriers.[242]

One prominent entry barrier that is a hybrid between strategic and structural ones is that of sunk cost. Sunk costs are cost that have already been incurred and that cannot be recovered in case of exit, meaning that there isn't an alternative use to the current economic activity. For example, the purchase of specialized machinery that could not even be resold, save as scrap metal, at liquidation. Other examples of activities whose costs can be largely sunk are: customer acquisition, brand building campaign for brands that could not be diversified, recruitment and training, R&D that did not lead to patents and had no value on the resale of the product.

Although sunk costs are often fixed (ie, they do not vary over a range of output), the two categories are distinct, since there are fixed costs which could be recovered on exit: for example, versatile machinery with resale value. Whilst the extent to which industry costs are sunk is

[239] For the sake of simplicity, in what follows reference is made only to entry barrier.

[240] See eg RP McAfee, H Mialon, and M Williams, 'What Is a Barrier to Entry?' (2004) 94 *American Economic Rev* 461.

[241] It is often argued that the use of the term 'barrier' bears a negative connotation in terms of implications for consumer welfare, which not always help the debate as to why we should actually care about them. See, in this respect, OECD, 'Barriers to Entry', Policy Roundtables, DAF/COMP(2005)42, 24–6, available at http://www.oecd.org/regreform/sectors/36344429.pdf.

[242] See ibid, for more.

largely 'structural' in nature (ie, it cannot be avoided), the reason why they can constitute a barrier to entry is more 'strategic' in nature.

This is because sunk costs can make the incumbent less likely to accommodate entry, since the incumbent would rather keep selling at a lower price in order to earn even little incremental revenue than exit the market in the knowledge that none of the sunk costs would be recovered. That is to say, sunk costs constitute a loss in case of exit and thus act as an exit barrier from the incumbent's perspective.

This in turn tends to add credibility to the prospect that the incumbent might respond fiercely upon entry. The incumbent could, however, still avoid exit (and the corresponding loss) by accommodating entry, instead of reacting aggressively. Therefore, the credibility of an aggressive response depends on a guess as to whether the incumbent is better off with an accommodative strategy instead.[243]

In this respect, from an entrant's perspective, sunk costs represent instead an option, in the sense that the entrant can still decide not to enter and thus save the sunk costs. This flexibility tends to deter and/or delay entry when the entrant is uncertain as to whether the incumbent is aggressive or accommodative.

The committal nature of sunk costs is, of course, key to the assessment of scale economies. An incumbent can signal its commitment to be aggressive post-entry by investing in large capacity (ie, relative to current market demand) that is largely sunk. Thus, the incumbent is committing to be 'tough' strategically by increasing its scale of production beyond what would be optimal absent the threat of entry (ie, strategic over-investment).

Scale economies can also be a barrier to entry, regardless of whether fixed capacity costs are sunk, when customers exhibit brand loyalty towards the incumbent. From an entrant's perspective, brand loyalty towards the incumbent increases the former customer acquisition costs (ie, poaching customers will be costlier). Hence, even if the entrant has the same level of capacity, the incumbent will know that the newcomer will find it more difficult to achieve similar scale, thus making it less likely that the latter will accommodate entry.[244]

Under these circumstances, brand loyalty can give the incumbent a first mover advantage, to the extent that it would be costlier for the entrant to gain similar brand awareness where the product space is already occupied (ie, an absolute cost advantage). In this respect, the incumbent could strategically increase this entry barrier by further investing in brand building advertising campaign and brand proliferation, which, incidentally, are likely to be largely sunk in nature. By the same token, the incumbent could further (strategically) increase the entrant's customer acquisition costs by introducing loyalty rebates.

Another potential source of first mover advantage can be the presence of network effects, where consumers value a product more as the overall customer base increases. It is often argued that markets with strong network effects can 'tip' in favour of the incumbent firm, making it more difficult for an entrant to build the critical mass needed to become an attractive alternative. Nevertheless, whilst network effects can constitute a formidable entry barrier for rivals offering a similar (ie, imitative) product, there are plenty of examples that show that innovative products can quickly overcome this barrier and displace the incumbent's

243 See RP McAfee, H Mialon, and M Williams, 'What Is a Barrier to Entry?' (2004) 94 *American Economic Rev* 461, 463. Of course, the incumbent may try to skew this guess in his favour by developing a reputation for aggressiveness built upon, for example, past episodes of alleged predatory pricing.

244 Ibid, 464.

product altogether (eg MySpace versus Facebook).[245] That is to say, consumers exhibit also a taste for variety and an appetitive for innovative products.

3.5. THE USE OF QUANTITATIVE EVIDENCE

As explained in Section 2.2, market shares can be used as proxy for market power to the extent that competitors sell homogeneous goods.[246] Specifically, under the assumption that firms compete by setting quantities for homogeneous products (so-called competition à la Cournot), the Herfindahl–Hirschman index (HHI) is proportional to industry profitability.[247] The HHI is a concept developed by economists and used by many competition authorities as a screen to assess likely market power of two or more merging firms. It is derived by adding the square of the market share of every firm in the market. This emphasizes the importance for competition by the larger firms. The higher the square of the share of the firms wanting to merge the more likely is the merged firm to have market power after the merger. Economists have suggested levels of the firm's squared percentage market share where a merger should be investigated. The HHI is higher if the market structure is more asymmetric.[248]

To calculate market shares, though, it is first necessary to draw the boundaries of the relevant market in terms of both the product and geographic dimension. To this end, besides the reliance on qualitative insights in terms of product attributes and intended use, the analysis can be based on a number of quantitative techniques. What follows is just a brief overview.[249]

The simplest approach is *price correlation analysis* which looks at how the prices of two substitute products differ and to what extent they vary together; the idea being that if the products are indeed close substitutes their prices should move together and should only differ because of higher transportation costs (the law of one price).[250]

The observation that two prices are correlated, though, may give the mistaken impression that the two products are substitutes, whereas the co-movement could be due to a change in the price of a common input (eg common feed used in livestock farming for two distinct product categories), or thanks to a general increase in disposable income that has lifted all

[245] For a detailed discussion, see H Koski and T Kretschmer, 'Survey on Competing in Network Industries: Firm Strategies, Market Outcomes, and Policy Implications' (2004) 4 *J Industry, Competition and Trade* 5.

[246] For a more extensive analysis of the use of quantitative evidence in EU competition law, see I Lianos and C Genakos, 'Econometric Evidence in EU Competition Law: An Empirical and Theoretical Analysis' in I Lianos and D Geradin, *Handbook on European Competition Law: Enforcement and Procedure* (Edward Elgar, 2013), 1.

[247] In detail, in can be shown that the sum of firms' unit margins of profit, weighted by their respective market shares, is equal to the HHI divided by the market demand elasticity; and the individual firm's unit margin of profit is given by its market share divided by the market demand elasticity.

[248] For example, in a market with five symmetric firm (each having a 20 per cent market share) the HHI is 2 000; whereas in a market with six firms, but where one leading firm has half the market, a second has a market share of 20 per cent and the remaining four have each 5 per cent, the HHI is 2 950.

[249] For a thorough discussion, see P Davis and E Garcés, *Quantitative Techniques for Competition and Antitrust Analysis* (Princeton University Press, 2010), ch 4.

[250] See eg *Ryanair/Aer Lingus* (Case COMP/M.4439) Commission Decision (27 June 2007), available at http://ec.europa.eu/competition/elojade/isef/case_details.cfm?proc_code=2_M_4439 (where the Commission performed an extensive price-correlation analysis to determine whether two or more airports in the vicinity were substitutable, although the quantitative evidence had an auxiliary character in the conclusions reached by the Commission, as there was ample qualitative evidence originating from a customer survey and research into travel costs and time for each of the particular airports).

prices. In contrast to the risk of false positives due to common supply and demand 'shocks', two substitute products might fail the correlation test because only one of them is subject to short-term changes in the price on an input not used in the production of the other, even if in the medium-long term the two products are indeed restricting each other prices (ie, false negatives).

The risk of false positives or negatives is greatly reduced where it is possible to identify a contextual change that is not linked to a demand or supply shift. For example, the firm under investigation may run a marketing experiment by lowering the price in a local area in order to gauge price sensibility. Such a *natural experiment* would, therefore, be exogenous by design; that is, certainly not caused by an unobserved movement in demand or supply shift that might affects other substitute products as well.[251]

The two methodologies presented so far are used to gather indirect evidence of substitution patterns, that is, without the need directly to estimate consumer price sensitivity and diversion ratios. There are two ways of gathering direct evidence regarding pattern of substitution. First of all, one would ideally rely on the observation of consumers' actual choices (ie, *revealed preferences*) based on products prices, characteristics and locations, as well as those consumers' characteristics that could explain their preferences such as age, income and location. Suffice to say, this kind of fact finding is demanding, alas. Alternatively, the analysis could rely on survey evidence, where a representative sample of consumers is first profiled and then asked about how they would choose among alternative products in a hypothetical scenario where prices for their current choice were increased by a specified amount (ie, *stated preferences*).[252]

Evidence regarding the patterns of substitution would be needed to identify the next best substitutes in order to enlarge the candidate product/geographic market, as signalled by the failure to implement a SSNIP profitably. The data needed to implement the SSNIP test are: (i) firms' profit margin under competitive conditions; and (ii) the product's own-price elasticity of demand (for the candidate market) over the range of a 5–10 per cent increase above the competitive price benchmark.[253]

An alternative way of implementing the SSNIP test is the *critical loss analysis*, which looks at how much sales of the candidate product need to drop in order to make a SSNIP unprofitable. If this critical loss in sales is lower than the actual loss than would be observed on the basis of the estimated own-price demand elasticity, the SSNIP would be unprofitable and the candidate market needs to be enlarged to the next best substitute. It is worth noting that the same data on own-price elasticity and profit margins are required.

Somewhat less demanding data requirements are needed for the use of pricing pressure indices, to be applied as a first screen in the assessment of mergers. These instruments are considered particularly useful in the assessment of mergers between differentiated products, where it is more important to focus on the closeness of competition in the product space,

251 Other examples of exogenous source of natural experiments can be a new entry in a local market or a regulatory change imposed only on the product in question.

252 For a detailed discussion on the use of consumer survey evidence, see OFT/CC, 'Good Practice in the Design and Presentation of Consumer Survey Evidence in Merger Inquiries' (revised May 2018), available at http://www.oft.gov.uk/shared_oft/consultations/merger-inquiries/Good-practice-guide.pdf.

253 In this respect, the use of the own-price demand elasticity also rests on the assumption that the SSNIP does not induce a squeeze in disposable incomes, so that the reduction in sales of the product in question is entirely attributable to consumers switching to substitute products, rather than renouncing to buy altogether (in economic jargon, income effect, or substitution to the 'outside good').

rather than trying precisely to draw market boundaries by including all substitute products (ie, even those that are not close substitutes in terms of quality attributes).[254]

The most basic version, the *gross upward pricing pressure* index (GUPPI), requires data about merging firms' profit margins and the diversion ratios between their products (ie, considered to be substitutable). The idea is that the merged entity will want to raise prices if it is expected that part of the lost sales will be captured (in economic jargon, internalized) by the other substitute products in its portfolio.

Other indices such as the UPP and the UPP* are even more demanding in that they require the analyst to make a conjecture as to the expected cost synergies resulting from the proposed merger. Here the idea is to allow for merger-specific efficiency improvements which would tend to offset the upward pricing pressure identified under the GUPPI. The UPP* takes into account also how the increase in revenue diverted to other products within the merged entity's portfolio will trigger similar price increases, which in turn will reinforce the initial price rise (ie, pricing decisions as strategic complements). The *illustrative price rise* (IPR) attempts to measure the likely price increase post-merger (rather than merely whether there will be any), but it requires the assumption of a specific curvature of the demand schedule (ie, linear or iso-elastic).

Data requirements are even more demanding for the *full equilibrium relevant market* (FERM) test, which can be thought of as a augmented version of the previous tests, in that whilst the SSNIP, and the various pricing pressure indices described above, assume that prices for products outside the candidate market, or the merged entity's portfolio, are held constant, the former allows for pricing reactions of firms outside it. Accordingly, when firms compete by setting prices, the application of the FERM test would lead to narrower markets since the profitability of a SSNIP would be reinforced by similar price increases by firms outside the candidate market.

Finally, there are full-fledged simulations models,[255] which require the analyst to define how rival firms compete (ie, by setting prices or quantities), besides estimating both demand and cost functions. The aim is to calculate the equilibrium post-merger and to compare it with the pre-merger situation. Therefore, they are normally deployed only if phase II in a merger investigation has been reached.

A careful analysis of the decisional practice shows that these quantitative methods are merely employed at the stage of market definition and that various techniques are sometimes combined.[256] In some recent merger cases the Commission has relied on quantitative economic techniques in the competitive assessment of horizontal mergers. These techniques have

254 For a detailed overview, see OECD, 'Market Definition—Policy Roundtables', DAF/COMP(2012)19 (2012), 59–68, available at http://www.oecd.org/daf/competition/Marketdefinition2012.pdf.

255 For a detailed discussion, see P Davis and E Garcés, *Quantitative Techniques for Competition and Antitrust Analysis* (Princeton University Press, 2010), ch.

256 For a detailed discussion, see I Lianos and C Genakos, 'Econometric Evidence in EU Competition law: An Empirical and Theoretical Analysis' in I Lianos and D Geradin, *Handbook on European Competition Law: Enforcement and Procedure* (Edward Elgar, 2013), 1. In 2014–15, the Commission used standard UPP/GUPPI in *Telefonica Deutschland/E-plus* (Case COMP/M.7018) Competition Decision (2013), available at http://ec.europa.eu/competition/elojade/isef/case_details.cfm?proc_code=2_M_7018, as well as a full merger simulation. Price correlation analysis was used in *Huntsman Corporation/Equity Interests* (Case COMP/M.7061) Commission Decision (2014), available at http://ec.europa.eu/competition/elojade/isef/case_details.cfm?proc_code=2_M_7061, for the product market definition, although the final decision did not rely much on the quantitative analysis. Price correlation was also used in *SSAB/Rautaruukki* (Case COMP/M.7155) Commission Decision (2014), available at http://ec.europa.eu/competition/elojade/isef/case_details.cfm?proc_code=2_M_7155, for the geographic market definition to assess divergence/co-movement of prices between the Nordic countries and the rest of Europe.

ranged from the use of merger simulation models to the deployment of direct estimation methods to study the effects of relevant events in the past. An article by members of the Chief Economist Team in the Commission describes the appropriate use of these techniques and explains the rationale for reliance on these methods.[257]

3.6. THE FUTURE OF MARKET DEFINITION

According to the European Commission, '[m]arket power is the ability to profitably maintain prices above competitive levels for a period of time or to profitably maintain output in terms of product quantities, product quality and variety or innovation below competitive levels for a period of time'.[258] This definition may lead to the mistaken impression that the assessment of market power (or, more precisely, of whether there is substantial market power) hinges on a benchmarking exercise where the observed market outcome (ie, in terms of price and quality) is compared to what would be considered to be a competitive outcome, whereby prices are reflective of average costs plus a reasonable profit margin to compensate for the capital invested into the business (ie, the 'opportunity cost' of capital).

This rarely happens, though. No competition law enforcer would rely heavily on a study of the alleged firm's profitability and/or its price mark-ups over time to reach a finding of substantial market power. Apart from issues around measurability,[259] there is the fundamental ambiguity in being able to tell whether profits are the result of a superior offer or lack of competition.[260] Indeed, the European Commission is well aware of this conundrum.[261] Therefore, at most profitability analysis may be one among several factors taken into consideration by competition authorities in assessing market power.[262]

Instead, rather than focussing on market outcomes, the assessment of market power is usually based on a contextual analysis that looks, in the round, at various indicators,

257 T Buettner, G Federico, and S Lorincz, 'The Use of Quantitative Economic Techniques in EU Merger Control' (2016) 31(1) *Antitrust Magazine* 68.

258 Guidelines on the applicability of Article 101 of the Treaty on the Functioning of the European Union to horizontal co-operation agreements [2011] OJ C 11/01, para 39.

259 For a methodological review, see OFT, *Assessing Profitability in Competition Policy Analysis*, Economic Discussion Paper No 6, Report prepared by OXERA (July 2003), available at http://webarchive.nationalarchives.gov.uk/20140402182826/http://www.oft.gov.uk/shared_oft/reports/comp_policy/oft657.pdf.

260 For a critique of the use of profitability measures, see Charles River Associates, 'The (Mis)use of Profitability Analysis in Competition Law Cases (2003), available at https://pdfs.semanticscholar.org/f34b/12a49ae81e33b6238bcd54aab8eac40aeedf.pdf.

261 Guidelines on the applicability of Article 101 of the Treaty on the Functioning of the European Union to horizontal co-operation agreements [2011] OJ C 11/01, para 40 ('In markets with fixed costs undertakings must price above their variable costs of production in order to ensure a competitive return on their investment. The fact that undertakings price above their variable costs is therefore not in itself a sign that competition in the market is not functioning well and that undertakings have market power that allows them to price above the competitive level. It is when competitive constraints are insufficient to maintain prices, output, product quality, product variety and innovation at competitive levels that undertakings have market power [. . .].').

262 A notable exception may be found in the UK Market Investigation Reference regime, where the Competition Commission (to be merged into the new Competition Market Authority from April 2014) has relied on profitability measures in the context of market investigations. For example, in August 2012, the CC found that the profitability of the dominant pay-TV retail provider, BSkyB, had consistently been above its cost of capital for such a long period of time that it could no longer be explained in terms of payoff from risky investments: see CC (2012), *Movies on pay TV market investigation*, paras 5.92–5.116, available at https://www.gov.uk/cma-cases/movies-on-pay-tv-market-investigation-cc.

typically: market shares and concentration, entry and expansion barriers, and countervailing buyer power. Market definition is, therefore, propaedeutic to the use of market shares and indices of market concentration.

This mainstream approach has, however, come under some pressure of late, in particular, following the 2010 US Horizontal Merger Guidelines, which stated that market definition is no longer mandatory in every merger analysis.[263] Professor Louis Kaplow called into question the practice of market definition at all, arguing that it would be preferable to dispense with it altogether, and instead try to measure firms' price–cost mark-ups directly.[264] In contrast, Gregory Werden maintained that the process of market delineation still provides an analytical framework that helps practitioners to focus on those factors more likely to be determinative for the analysis of anti-competitive effects, in particular barrier to entry, expansion, and exit.[265]

The main criticism is that the use of market shares is only going to be accurate where the product concerned is homogeneous (ie, alternative products are perceived as fungible), so that market shares are a good reflection of competitive constraints; that is, provided that the relevant market is not perfectly contestable because of no barriers to entry/expansion and exit, otherwise even firms with very large market shares would be constrained by the threat posed by potential entrants. By the same token, only under these specific conditions the use of concentration indices provides a proxy for the extent of market power.

Whereas, when products are differentiated (ie, both in terms of horizontal and vertical quality) the degree to which consumers perceive two products as close substitutes varies across the market, which means that the picture presented by market shares could be misleading (eg a product with a large market share might be a basic product which is not perceived by consumers as a close substitute for niche up-market versions).

Accordingly, different methodologies have been advanced to try to better capture the varying pattern of substitution in a differentiated product market. There are two distinct approaches depending on the nature of the alleged infringement: exploitative as opposed to exclusionary. In the former category, the idea is to try to directly estimate the substitution effect following a hypothetical increase in price by the firm under investigation. That is to say, an approach based on market outcomes. It is not surprising, therefore, that this approach has been advocated specifically for the assessment of mergers, where the risk of false positives is low, given that the increase in market power would be the result of external (as opposed to internal) growth.[266]

In this respect, pricing pressure indices rely on the calculation of diversion ratios between the products of the merging firms and the corresponding unit profit margins.[267] These recent methodologies are less demanding in terms of data requirements than the use of full-fledged simulation models, which compute the change in the equilibrium outcome post-merger.

263 FTC/DoJ, US Horizontal Merger Guidelines (2010), 7, available at http://ftc.gov/os/2010/08/100819hmg.pdf.

264 L Kaplow, 'On the Relevance of Market Power' (2017) 130(5) *Harvard L Rev* 1303. See also L Kaplow, 'Market Definition, Market Power', Harvard Law School, Discussion Paper No 826 (May 2015); L Kaplow, 'Why (Ever) Define Markets?' (2010) 124 *Harvard L Rev* 437.

265 GJ Werden, 'Why (Ever) Define Markets? An Answer to Professor Kaplow' (2013) 78(3) *Antitrust LJ* 729.

266 Moreover, the assessment of the likelihood and magnitude of a price increase post-merger is benchmarked against current prices—ie, does not require the identification of a competitive benchmark, since what is of concern is merely the merger-dependent increase in market power, rather than the absolute level of market power of the merged entity.

267 Diversion ratios represent the proportion of lost sales (ie, due to a price increase) which are captured by a substitute product (ie, as a result of consumers' switching).

However, the trade-off is that pricing pressure indices ignore the reaction of non-merging firms, which could vary from a mere price increase in response to the post-merger price increase (ie, prices as strategic complement), an expansion of output (ie, quantity choices as strategic substitutes), to product repositioning (ie, in terms of both horizontal and/or vertical quality dimension). Therefore, these techniques should only be used as a first screening device, rather than substitute for a thorough analysis of competitive restraints faced by the merging firms.

Regarding the category of exclusionary infringements, the idea is that rather than looking at market shares and concentration indices, the investigation should focus on the evidence of substantial foreclosure straightaway, since the ability to foreclose in a substantive way must entail a position of substantial market power.[268] However, evidence of actual foreclosure—ie, competitors loosing market shares or exiting the market—will only be available if the alleged conduct has been in place for a sufficiently long period of time.[269] Whereas, where the assessment of foreclosure is forward looking, thus focussed on the potential for substantial foreclosure, the same circumstantial evidence used to assess market power will have to be relied upon.[270]

In exercising their judicial scrutiny/review function, courts are generally vigilant on issues of market definition, and often set limits to the creativity of competition authorities. This is particularly the case in the UK where the decisions of the CMA are subject to strict and intensive scrutiny in law, facts, and policy by the Competition Appeal Tribunal (CAT), the CAT having the authority to substitute its assessment to that of the CMA. For instance, in the leased lines appeal,[271] the CAT considered in detail how the Office for Communications (OFCOM) defined the relevant product and geographical markets and, as such, took a detailed look at its economic assessment. A central issue in the appeal concerned OFCOM's finding that there was no break in the chain of substitution between 1G and 10G (bandwidth) services and, in reaching that conclusion, its application of the SSNIP test and the HMT. The CAT ultimately found that OFCOM erred in both its product and geographical market definitions.[272] The CAT remitted the matter to OFCOM for reconsideration.

In conclusion, whilst market definition is not an end in itself, it is still a valuable exercise, not only because it allows the computation of market shares and concentration indices, but

268 Daniel Crane pointed out, however, that where a position of substantial market power is based on the existence of high (structural) entry barriers it is increasingly unlikely that the dominant firm would have to recur to exclusionary practices to buttress its position. By the same token, it is decreasingly unlikely that the counterfactual absent the alleged conduct would be competitive. Therefore, enforcement against exclusionary abuses should target cases where entry barriers are surmountable absent the alleged anti-competitive conduct: C Daniel, 'Market Power Without Market Definition' (2014) 90(1) *Notre Dame L Rev* 31. Similarly, Louis Kaplow observed that where an alleged anti-competitive practice is carried out by a firm with great market power, the anti-competitive effect can be small compared to a counterfactual absent the anti-competitive conduct. Therefore, Kaplow argues that it is wrong to treat the inquiries into the existence of market power and anti-competitive effects as separate: see L Kaplow, 'On the Relevance of Market Power' (2017) 130(5) *Harvard L Rev* 1303.

269 European Commission, Guidance on the Commission's enforcement priorities in applying Article 82 of the EC Treaty to abusive exclusionary conduct by dominant undertakings [2009] OJ 2009/C 45/02, para 20.

270 Ibid.

271 *BT v Ofcom, Virgin Media and others* [2017] CAT 25.

272 The ruling is likely to be especially of interest in relation to product market definition: see ibid, paras 112–22 for a discussion of the general principles; and section F (particularly ibid, paras 150–73, which discuss the principles, in general terms, in relation to product definition) for the application of these principles to the detailed facts of the case.

most of all because it provides a robust framework for identifying the key contextual elements needed to assess market power, such as barriers to entry and expansion, the main dimension of differentiation among substitutable products, and the countervailing bargaining power of suppliers and buyers.

SELECTIVE BIBLIOGRAPHY

Books

Bishop, S, and Walker, M, *Economics of EC Competition Law* (Sweet & Maxwell, 3rd ed, 2010).

Chamberlin, EH, *The Theory of Monopolistic Competition* (Harvard University Press, 1933).

Davis, P, and Garcés, E, *Quantitative Techniques for Competition and Antitrust Analysis* (Princeton University Press, 2010).

Niels G, Jenkins H, and Kavanagh J, *Economics for Competition Lawyers* (OUP, 2016).

Hausman, D, *Preference, Value, Choice and Welfare* (CUP, 2012).

Heukelom, F, *Behavioral Economics: A History* (CUP, 2014).

Kahneman, D, *Thinking, Fast and Slow* (Allen Lane, 2011).

Lichtenstein, S, and Slovic, P (eds) *The Construction of Preference* (CUP, 2006).

Moscatti, I, *From Classical Political Economy to Behavioral Economics* (Egea, 2012).

Motta, M, *Competition Policy* (CUP, 2004).

Robinson, J, *The Economics of Imperfect Competition* (Macmillan, 1933).

Schumpeter, J, *Capitalism, Socialism and Democracy* (Harper and Brothers, 1942; repr. Harper Colophon, 1976).

Tirole, J, *The Theory of Industrial Organization* (MIT, 1988).

Williamson, O, *Markets and Hierarchies: Analysis and Antitrust Implications* (Free Press, 1st edn, 1975).

Chapters in books

Evans, DS, and Schmalensee R, 'The Antitrust Analysis of Multi-Sided Platform Businesses' in Blair, R, and Sokol, D (eds) *Oxford Handbook on International Antitrust Economics*, vol. 1 (OUP, 2014), 404.

Lianos, I, and Genakos, C, 'Econometric Evidence in EU Competition law: An Empirical and Theoretical Analysis' in Lianos, I and Geradin, D (eds) *Handbook on European Competition Law: Enforcement and Procedure* (Edward Elgar, 2013) 1–128.

Journal articles

Armstrong, M, and Huck, S, 'Behavioral Economics as Applied to Firms: A Primer' (2010) 6 *Competition Policy Int'l* 3.

Coase, R, 'The Nature of the Firm' (1937) 4 *Economica* 386.

Cooter, R, and Rappoport, P, 'Were the Ordinalists Wrong About Welfare Economics?' (1984) 22 *J Economic Literature* 507.

Filistrucchi, L, Geradin, D, Van Damme, E, and Affeldt, P, 'Market Definition in Two-Sided Markets: Theory and Practice' (2014) 10 *J Competition L & Economics* 293.

Geroski, PA, 'Competition in Markets and Competition for Markets' (2003) 3 *J Industry, Competition and Trade* 151.

Geroski, PA, 'Thinking Creatively about Markets' (1998) 16 *Int'l J Industrial Organization* 677.

Lerner, A, 'The Economics and Politics of Consumer Sovereignty' (1972) 62 *American Economic Rev* 258.

Lianos, I, 'Lost in Translation: Towards a Theory of Economic Transplants' (2009) *Current Legal Problems* 346.

Mason, E, 'Monopoly in Law and Economics' (1937) 47 *Yale LJ* 34.

McNulty, PJ, 'A Note on the History of Perfect Competition, Part 1' (1967) 75 *J Political Economy* 395.

Porter, ME, 'Competition and Antitrust: Toward a Productivity-based Approach to Evaluating Mergers and Joint Ventures' (2001) 46 *Antitrust Bulletin* 919.

McAfee, RP, Mialon, H, and Williams, M, 'What Is a Barrier to Entry?' (2004) 94 *American Economic Rev* 461

Tor, A, 'Understanding Behavioral Antitrust' (2014) 92 *Texas L Rev* 573.

Werden, GJ, 'The History of Antitrust Market Delineation' (1992) 76 *Marquette L Rev* 123.

Williamson, O, 'Economies as an Antitrust Defense: Welfare Tradeoffs' (1968) 58 *American Economic Rev* 18.

Other papers

Fletcher, A, and Lyons, B, 'Geographic Market Definition in European Commission Merger Control', A Study for DG Competition (January 2016).

OFT1228, 'What does Behavioural Economics Mean for Competition Policy?' (March 2010).

OECD, Barriers to Entry, Policy Roundtables, DAF/COMP(2005) 42 (2005).

OECD '*Market Definition – Policy Roundtables*', DAF/COMP(2012) 19 (2012).

OECD, The Role and Measurement of Quality in Competition Analysis, DAF/COMP(2013) 17 (2013).

Werden, GJ, 'Antitrust's Rule of Reason: Only Competition Matters' (1 March 2013), available at https://ssrn.com/abstract=2227097.

4

THE PERSONAL SCOPE OF THE EU AND UK COMPETITION LAW

4.1. FOUNDATIONS

The various provisions of EU and UK competition law apply to 'undertakings'. Article 101 of the Treaty on the Functioning of the European Union (TFEU) and Chapter 1 of the Competition Act 1998 (CA98) apply to agreements between undertakings, decisions by associations of undertakings or concerted practices between undertakings. Article 102 TFEU and Chapter 2 CA98 apply to the abuse of a dominant position by an undertaking. EU Merger Regulation 139/2004 applies also to a concentration between undertakings or part of undertakings; either this takes the form of a merger or through 'the acquisition, by one or more persons already controlling at least one undertaking, or by one or more undertakings, whether by purchase of securities or assets, by contract or by any other means, of direct or indirect control of the whole or parts of one or more other undertakings'.[1]

The UK merger control system resulting from the Enterprise Act 2002 applies to mergers between two or more 'enterprises'. The concept is defined by section 129(1) of the Enterprise Act 2002 as 'the activities, or part of the activities, of a business'. The term 'business' is itself defined as including a 'professional practice' and 'any other undertaking which is carried on for gain or reward or which is an undertaking in the course of which goods or services are supplied otherwise than free of charge'.

The concept of 'undertaking' is therefore the main unit of analysis used in both EU and UK competition law. EU and UK competition law take a functional approach on the concept of undertaking, as they do not rely on the form or corporate structure of the entity, but define instead the concept of 'undertaking' as closely linked to the existence of an 'entity' exercising an

[1] Council Regulation 139/2004 of 20 January 2004 on the control of concentrations between undertakings [2004] OJ L24/1, Article 3(1).

'economic activity'. The second section of this Chapter will focus on this functional definition of the concept of undertaking and what is usually meant by the concept of 'economic activity'. The third section will focus on what is meant by the concept of 'entity' and its implications on the attribution of responsibility for competition law infringements.

4.2. SETTING THE BOUNDARIES OF THE SCOPE OF COMPETITION LAW: THE CONCEPTS OF 'UNDERTAKING, 'ECONOMIC ACTIVITY', AND BEYOND

4.2.1. WHAT IS MEANT BY 'ECONOMIC ACTIVITY'?

The concept of economic activity is multi-dimensional as the functions it exercises are multiple. The concept provides a first attempt to distinguish between the EU and the national (local) level, as this is practised in various federal systems which regulate commerce between the various entities but stay short of regulating activity that does not relate to commerce. For instance, the Supreme Court of the United States, in trying to distinguish the 'truly national' from the 'truly local' in the context of the Commerce Clause of the US Constitution, differentiated in *United States v Morrison*, 'economic' activity, which Congress may regulate, from 'non-economic' activity, which Congress may not regulate.[2] The distinction between economic and non-economic activity has been criticized by some US scholars as mostly irrelevant in order to answer the question of what is the most appropriate level of governance to deal with collective action problems. They contend that this issue should be the focus of analysis in a federalist regime that aims to allocate responsibility for decision-making efficiently, as economic activity does not generally cause collective action problems among the states, nor is non-economic activity generally free from collective action problems.[3]

In the EU, however, the differentiation between economic activity and non-economic activity may have deeper intellectual roots in the way the project of European integration progressed. One may consider that it emanates from the 'separation thesis' of the economic and the social spheres, resulting from the neo-functionalist perspective that has been quite influential in the conceptualization of the project of European integration after the Second World War. Its foundation is not a comparative efficiency analysis exploring which level of governance is better fit to address a collective action problem, but is based on the understanding that it was impossible for a piece-meal project of transnational integration to work, unless progress was made first in carefully selected economic areas, on which supra-national expert bodies could exercise control, without being subject to the political tensions that are inevitable in all areas of 'social' policy. From that perspective, the distinction between 'economic'/'commercial' and 'non-economic' or social/'non-commercial' was crucial in the development of a competition law and policy that appeared 'neutral' from a political perspective, in the somewhat polarized political environment of the post-World War II era in Europe and

2 *United States v Morrison*, 529 US 598, 617–18 (2000).

3 RD Cooter and NS Siegel, 'Collective Action Federalism: A General Theory of Article I, Section 8' (2010) 63 *Stanford L Rev* 115, noting that the distinction between individual and collective action by states relates to the relative advantages of the federal and state governments and that the economic/non-economic distinction does not provide any information on their respective comparative efficiency.

enabled each Member State to maintain without any major external pressure its version of the Social State: *Sozialstaat*, the Welfare State, *service public/état-providence*, etc. Things, however, changed with the ascendancy of 'neo-liberalism' in the 1980s and 1990s, with the liberalization of services previously entrusted to State-owned monopolies or undertakings with exclusive rights and the privatization of public services. The distinction between economic activity and non-economic activity gained importance in the case law of the EU Courts, as is attested by the number of cases involving the application of competition law to actors involved in what was previously considered as part of the 'social sphere'. The EU Courts were called to define what constituted an 'economic activity' and thus to determine the scope of competition law in a period of important political tensions and disagreements. The approach followed was thus piece-meal and consisted in reaching acceptable (political) compromises while being open to creative legal interpretation when circumstances changed.

Differences appeared between Member States advancing actively a neo-liberal agenda and others attempting to tame the neo-liberal wave by maintaining the essentials of the structure of the 'Social State' and requesting the market to be embedded with social values. Supporters of neo-liberal reform called for an extensive scope of application of competition law, calling for the 'opening' of public services to competition, while its opponents resisted the application of competition law to the social sphere and argued for a counter-movement of expanding the role of the EU to facilitating transnational social protection. These divergent perspectives led to important tensions, which are reflected by the revision of the constitutive treaties in the 1990s and early 2000, with the inclusion of a number of provisions providing competence to EU institutions on social policy matters and with the adoption of a Charter of Fundamental Rights containing a number of 'social' rights. Although the provisions of the constitutive treaties on competition law have not been altered, these changes of the broader legal context may have lasting effects on competition law and policy.[4]

The 'neo-liberal' effort of breaking the boundaries between the economic and the social spheres was particularly driven by the increasing importance given to the value of economic efficiency, not only with regard to the way markets should operate, but also with regard to how public services should be organized. According to this view, governments should also aim to increase their efficiency, either through their organization according to market principles, or through the evaluation of State activities, as if they were market activities, for instance with a systematic cost-benefit analysis and impact assessment. From this perspective, the development of what is economic and what remains in the non-economic sphere does not only depend on the existence of a political consensus over which activities should be open to competition and which should be organized under a different order, for instance that of co-operation or of a hierarchy, but also on the availability of tools that would enable 'experts' to determine what is economically efficient and what is not. While the definition of the concept of 'economic activity' is not the same as that of 'economic analysis', as the tools of economic analysis can also apply to what has traditionally been considered as a non-economic activity, that is, an activity not open to competition, the possibility for economic experts to measure the efficiency of a broader range of activities, undeniably put pressure for the expansion of the economic sphere. There may be some correlation between the development of evaluation techniques and the expansion of the economic sphere. We will first explore the way the EU (and UK) courts and competition authorities have defined the concept of 'undertaking' and

[4] I Lianos, 'Competition Law in the European Union After the Treaty of Lisbon' in D Ashiagbor, N Countouris, and I Lianos (eds) *The European Union After the Treaty of Lisbon* (CUP, 2012), 252.

'economic activity' and hence the scope of EU and UK competition law before looking to legislative exceptions and limits set to the scope of competition law in both the EU and the UK.

In *Hydrotherm*, the Court of Justice of the European Union (CJEU) held that 'the term "undertaking" must be understood as designating an economic unit for the purpose of the subject-matter of the agreement in question even if in law that economic unit consists of several persons, natural or legal'.[5] The case involved a preliminary reference concerning an exclusive dealing agreement concluded between a legal person and a physical person, which also controlled the legal person. The Court considered that 'if one of the parties to the agreement is made up of undertakings having identical interests and controlled by the same natural person, who also participates in the agreement, for in those circumstances competition between the persons participating together, as a single party, in the agreement in question is impossible'.[6] The CJEU put emphasis on three elements of the concept of 'undertaking':

- It is a functional concept and designates an economic unit 'for the purpose of the subject-matter' of the specific anti-competitive conduct in question. This means that, in theory, the same entity may be considered as an undertaking for a specific conduct or context but not an undertaking for another conduct or context.
- It may consist of several 'persons', natural or legal. Hence, it applies without any regard as to the qualification of an entity by national company law. It may apply to entities that are not incorporated under company law or even to entities that do not take any other legally recognized form, from the perspective of company law or any other area of national law. A physical person may also constitute an 'undertaking' for the purposes of competition law. It is a purely an EU law concept.
- With regard to relations between different entities, the qualification of 'undertaking' is closely related to the question of the possibility of 'competition' between them. If the various entities have 'identical interests' or are 'controlled' by the same person, then they form a single 'economic unit' because competition between them is 'impossible'. The concept of undertaking is therefore linked to a relation of competition (actual or potential) among the various entities whose conduct is assessed. In other words, it is only if the relation may be analysed through the lens of the possible emergence of a competitive order that these entities may be subject to the disciplines of competition law.

Subsequent case law of the EU courts examined the various elements of the concept of undertaking. In *Klaus Höfner and Fritz Elser v Macrotron*, the CJEU explained that any entity 'engaged in an economic activity, irrespective of the legal status in which it is financed' may be qualified as an undertaking for the purposes of competition law.[7] In *Commission v Italy*, the CJEU explained that the concept of 'economic activity' should be interpreted as 'any activity consisting in offering goods and services on a given market', an often repeated definition of the concept of economic activity.[8] The following sub-sections will engage with the definition of

5 Case 170/83, *Hydrotherm Gerätebau GmbH v Compact del Dott Ing Mario Andreoli & C Sas* [1984] ECR 2999, para 11.

6 Ibid, para 11.

7 Case C-41/90, Klaus *Höfner and Fritz Elser v Macrotron* [1991] ECR I–1979, para 21. See also Case C-244/94, *Fédération Française des Sociétés d'Assurance (FFSA) and Others v Ministère de l'Agriculture et de la Pêche* [1995] ECR I–4013, para 14; Case C-55/96, *Job Centre coop arl* [1997] ECR I–7119, para 21; Case C-138/11, *Compass Datenbank v Republik Östereich*, para 35; Case C-440/11 P, *Commission v Stichting Administrattiekantoor Portielje and Gosselin Group NV*, ECLI:EU:C:2013:514, para 36.

8 Case C-118/85, *Commission v Italy* [1987] ECR 2599, para 7. See also Case C-82/01 P, *Aéroports de Paris v Commission* [2002] ECR I–9297, para 79; Case C-49/07, *Motosykletistiki Omospondia Ellados NPID (MOTOE)*

the concept of 'economic activity' and will attempt to determine the intellectual foundations of the distinction between economic and non-economic activities in competition law.

4.2.2. OFFERING PRODUCTS ON A MARKET: THE SCOPE OF THE COMPETITIVE ORDER

The functional approach followed the CJEU focuses on the concept of 'activity', rather than that of 'entity', hence the important question to ask, at least with regard to the definition of the material scope of the competition law, is not 'who is an undertaking but what is economic activity'.[9] Advocate General F Jacobs provided in *AOK Bundesverband*, some insights on the rationale of the emphasis on activities. The case involved anti-competitive conduct by a German sickness fund which was also providing health insurance services. Advocate General Jacobs notes that:

> 25. [. . .] the Court's general approach to whether a given entity is an undertaking within the meaning of the Community competition rules can be described as functional, in that it focuses on the type of activity performed rather than on the characteristics of the actors which perform it, the social objectives associated with it, or the regulatory or funding arrangements to which it is subject in a particular Member State. Provided that an activity is of an economic character, those engaged in it will be subject to [EU] competition law.
>
> 26. The status of actors in national law is not therefore relevant when assessing whether they amount to undertakings in [EU] law. Hence, no weight can be attached to the fact that in German law sickness funds are classified as bodies subject to public law or as part of the administration of the State. Likewise, the regulatory or funding arrangements applied by a Member State to a given field of activity will not determine the applicability of the [EU] competition rules. Such choices may themselves fall to be assessed under those rules. Nor will the existence of social or general interest objectives associated with a given field of activity deprive it of its economic character. Such objectives may, however, supply a justification under Article [106(2) TFEU] for arrangements which would otherwise infringe [EU] competition law.
>
> 27. In assessing whether an activity is economic in character, the basic test appears to me to be whether it could, at least in principle, be carried on by a private undertaking in order to make profits. If there were no possibility of a private undertaking carrying on a given activity, there would be no purpose in applying the competition rules to it.
>
> 28. However, the application of that test in relation to certain fields of activity is by no means straightforward, and the Court has developed a more elaborate set of criteria to assist in the assessment. [. . .][10]

The test suggested by AG Jacobs in order to distinguish economic activities from non-economic activities relies on a hypothetical analysis of the possibility for an activity to be 'at least in principle' exercised by a 'private undertaking in order to make profits'. An important element in the test is the possibility of competition between the public entities in question

v Elliniko Dimosio [2008] ECR I–4863, para 22; Case C-138/11, *Compass Datenbank v Republik Österreich*, ECLI:EU:C:2012:449, para 35.

[9] O Odudu, 'The Meaning of Undertaking within 81 EC' (2004–5) 7 *Cambridge Yearbook of European Legal Studies* 211, 212–13.

[10] Opinion of AG F Jacobs in Joined Cases C-264, 306, 354 & 355/01, *AOK Bundesverband and Others* [2004] ECR I-2493, paras 25–8.

with private entities with regard to the specific activity, otherwise 'there is no purpose in applying competition rules'. But how this criterion fits to the definition by the CJEU of economic activity in *Commission v Italy* as an activity 'consisting in offering goods and services on a given *market*'? The definition of the CJEU puts emphasis on the existence of a 'market', as an essential step in the definition of the economic nature of an activity. While AG Jacobs does not refer to the concept of 'market' in his definition of 'economic activity', at the core of his argument lays the assumption that, should a 'degree of competition' be possible between various entities, presumably acting on a 'given market', then the activity may be considered as being of 'economic' nature. This, however, leaves open the question of what is meant by 'degree of competition'. The Advocate general explains that this refers either to 'price competition', or to competition on parameters other than price, for instance the quality of services offered.[11] Hence, the concept of economic activity is closely related to the possibility for an activity to be organized as a competitive order. The possibility of competition between the various entities involved also defines the boundaries of the 'market'.

It is important to examine the concept of 'market'. Markets presuppose a capitalist order in which products are produced not with the sole aim of being consumed in the household but also in order to constitute *commodities*, that is, products whose sole/main reason for being produced is that they can be sold to 'strangers' and thus be the object of an exchange (on some market) for profit purposes. The separation between the private sphere of the household (what the Greeks called *oikos*) and the public sphere of the marketplace, conceived as an institution (*nomos*) constitutes the stepping stone on which classical economics was built upon.

If one takes this perspective, cooking a meal for one's family or friends will not be considered as production but as consumption, and consequently it will not fall within the public sphere of the marketplace. One cannot expect a competitive order to develop within a household, and if there is one, it is not a matter for the legal system to interfere with. The division of labour between the members of the family or the small closed group is a matter that may be decided by tradition, the members of the group and/or the leader of the family or tribe. However, once we expand our productive capacities by including people outside the immediate circle of family and non-relatives in the closed group, we are facing the problem of devising ways to manage the more extensive division of labour and the need to adopt institutions/tools that would enable exchange of products between the various members of this wider group. In this configuration, more activities are taking place within the public sphere of the marketplace where goods are exchanged for money, a commodity whose primary usefulness is that it can be traded for purchasing other goods. Markets constitute the places where the interconnections between the various individuals (strangers) are taking place and where trust, which is not personal and linked to familiarity and friendship, but institutions-based (and in this case market-based), can be 'purchased'.[12] Hence, *markets can be considered as the public sphere enabling exchange following the production of a product for profit purposes*.

Neoclassical economists attempted to provide a common metric for the theories of consumption and production by putting emphasis on 'utility'. Production is the activity of generating utility by incurring some cost. Although consumption is considered as a distinct concept, it still relies on the idea that rational consumers choose bundles of products in order to maximize their lifetime utility function, which itself depends on current and future

[11] Ibid, paras 38–40.

[12] P Seabright, *In the Company of Strangers: A Natural History of Economic Life* (Princeton University Press, 2004).

consumption. From this perspective, it is easy to imagine a situation where an activity that was once completed within the household and thus considered as consumption, in the classical economics perspective, may become an activity of production followed by exchange in a specific market, if its completion carries some cost. For example, providing domestic services (eg cooking, cleaning, ironing) for one's own family was an activity that was until recently exercised within the household and usually perceived in traditional societies as a woman's *duty*. It was not perceived as *work* and constituted, from this perspective, an activity of consumption. However, the development of various alternatives (substitutes) in the marketplace (eg restaurants, various domestic services companies) led us to think of this activity in terms of work and thus classify it as a form of production if the activity generates utility at some cost. The cost here refers to the labour someone will put into the production of the good as the hours he/she will spend working will involve some opportunity cost in view of the fact the same amount of time could not be spent on leisure or activities that would maximize the person's lifetime utility function. This exchange, of labour for money, is voluntary in the sense that the person working today, for instance cooking meals in a delivery restaurant, accepts to incur this opportunity cost (of work) now, in order to be able to satisfy its future utility function, for instance to buy a ticket for a U2 concert she/he has always dreamt of attending.

It is true that from the point of view of this definition, activities of entertainment could also be considered as production in case the entertainment services are sold on a market for money, enabling the entertainer to satisfy his wants by buying other products. The assumption is that people are rational and egoistic maximizers of their own utility and that the only reason one would cook for strangers would be to maximize the profits they can earn from this activity, which will enable them to satisfy their own wants. One may remark that the existence of a market for domestic services enables us to evaluate in money terms what has been considered until then in traditional societies as a duty. Hence, one of the functions of a market is to enable the evaluation of the worth of an activity. This does not necessarily mean that the activity in question will automatically be considered as work. After all, providing domestic services may still be considered a duty in some traditional families (which should be equally shared between men and women!). However, the existence of a market may provide an estimate of the cost of that activity, should this be analysed as work. This of course depends on the person's perception of that activity. It is nevertheless assumed that if such activity aims strangers, it will be considered as work, while if it is performed in the context of a family, it consists in a duty and henceforth should be analysed as consumption.

Consequently, one may argue that the definition by AG Jacobs of the test of economic activity in *AOK Bundesverband* confuses the issue of the distinction between the public and private *spheres* with that of public and private *ownership* of the entities engaging in a specific activity. The fact that an activity is exercised by a private entity does not provide us with any conclusive evidence on the existence of a market and thus of an economic activity, if one follows the definition of the CJEU in *Commission v Italy*.[13] The important test is whether an activity takes place within the public sphere of the *market*, in which case it constitutes an economic activity, or within the private sphere of the *household*, in which case it may not be qualified as such.

Such definition may, however, be criticised, in that it suffices that an activity may be exercised within the marketplace to conclude on its economic nature, even if the same activity is

[13] Case C-118/85, *Commission v Italy* [1987] ECR 2599, para 7.

exercised predominately within the household. For instance, domestic cleaning services will be considered an economic activity as long as there are entities offering domestic cleaning services at the marketplace in exchange for money. Had the CJEU adopted such a definition of the concept of economic activity, the scope of application of EU competition law would have been quite wide. Certainly, Member States would have been able to ban a specific activity from the public sphere of the market because of health or other considerations (eg producing absinthe, growing marihuana or other recreational drugs), even if one would have been able to exercise the same activity on his own in the household. If one Member State decides, however, to authorize the activity of producing this product and selling it in the market, this should be enough for it to be considered an economic activity and thus be subject to EU competition law rules. Indeed, the CJEU noted, the fact that an activity leads to offering goods and services in the marketplace is sufficient for it to be considered as an activity of production, that is, an economic activity.

Neoclassical economics does not offer a clear separation between activities of production and consumption. These are analysed through the common prism of utility theory. With the exception of activities that are exercised only within the household, all other activities may be considered as potentially of economic nature. The political consequences of such a wide conception of economic activity being quite significant, one needs to temper this definition by noting the reference of the CJEU in *Hydrotherm* on the fact that competition between the entities should be 'possible'. Although this reference may be understood in the context of the issue raised by this case, we believe that the Court hinted at the existence of an additional element in the definition of economic activity than just the possibility of offering goods and services on the market: that of a *value judgement* that the activity in question may be subject to a competitive order and thus competition law. The question one may ask is who should make this value judgement: is it the Member States, the CJEU, other EU Institutions? One may argue that the recent inclusion of 'the principle of open economy with free competition' in the EU Treaties indicates a preference for activities to be open to competition and consequently for a broad scope of the activities that may considered as 'economic' and thus subject to competition law.[14]

However, this does not mean that there are no activities which may, by their essence, not be qualified as 'economic'. It is possible that certain activities may not be subject to the 'market order' in view of their 'market inalienability'.[15] A thing is 'market-inalienable', if it 'is not to be sold, which in our economic system means it is not to be traded in the market', mostly for ethical reasons.[16] One may also imagine activities that may be economic (ie, subject to commodification), as potentially they can lead to the offering for goods and services on a market, but which, for different reasons, one may think that they should not be organized according to the precepts of a competitive order. This may, for instance, be for reasons relating to neoclassical price theory instructing us that a competitive market order will not be the most efficient solution in the specific market or that, from an economic perspective, it will not be possible for a competitive order to emerge (think of natural monopolies). One

[14] The 'principle of an open market economy with free competition' is duly recognized in Articles 119, 120, and 127 TFEU.

[15] MJ Radin, 'Market-Inalienability' (1987) 100 *Harvard L Rev* 1849. This category may include inalienable personal rights, identified '*with a person, with her self-constitution and self-development in the context of her environment*' (emphasis added).

[16] Ibid, 1937. Non-saleable things may, however, be transferred in other ways than a market transaction, such as, for instance, a gift.

could also give the example of public goods, such as collective security or clean air, whose characteristics of non-excludability and non-rivalrous consumption makes them resistant to market pricing.

It is also possible to think of situations, for which a competitive order is theoretically possible, but still not desirable, as a matter of politics, by which we mean the decision of the sovereign. William Davies explains that there are additional logics to the one linked to the lessons of neoclassical price theory, justifying the limitation and suspension of market principles, and more specifically of the competitive market order. '[T]here are market exemptions, which are those areas of social interaction where market principles could be applied, but conventionally are not, for instance the pricing of friendship or access to a religious ceremony [. . .]. There are market exceptions, which are moments of such emergency, that market norms and laws must be suspended and special sovereign powers mobilized to establish order in whatever way is deemed necessary by those using them.'[17]

Hence, while the first type of logic excluding an activity from the domain of activities organized according to the principles of a competitive market order is explained by neoclassical economics and their concepts of 'externalities', 'public goods', and 'natural monopoly', other reasons may refer to politics and social conventions.

These different logics limiting the playground of the principle of a competitive market order may lead to various institutional arrangements. A comparison with US law may provide useful insights on the method used in EU competition law to confine the scope of economic versus non-economic activities.

The scope of US antitrust law: Comparative insights

US antitrust law applies in principle to 'persons', the concept being broad enough to cover entities having various forms, without being necessary to define *ex ante* if the specific entity exercises an economic activity. Indeed, Section 1 of the Sherman Act prohibits '[e]very contract, combination in the form of trust or otherwise, or conspiracy, in restraint of trade [. . .]. Every person who shall make any contract or engage in any combination or conspiracy hereby declared to be illegal shall be deemed guilty of a felony'. The term 'person' is defined in section 7 of the Sherman Act as including '[. . .] corporations and associations existing under or authorized by the laws of either the United States, the laws of any of the Territories, the laws of any State, or the laws of any foreign country', hence a purely organic definition of the concept, which contrasts with the functional definition of the concept of 'undertaking' in EU law. However, this does not mean that US antitrust law applies to activities that would be considered as of non-economic nature in EU law as US law recognizes exceptions to the principle of free competition.

These are of the following three sorts: '(1) statutory immunities or exemptions from some or all of the antitrust laws; (2) limitations on the full application of antitrust law as a consequence of continued economic regulation of certain industries; and (3) an overly broad interpretation of the state action doctrine that permits private anticompetitive conduct not authorized or supervised by state regulatory programs.'[18]

17 W Davies, 'When is a Market Not a Market? "Exemption", "Externality" and "Exception" in the Case of European State Aid Rules' (2012) 30(2) *Theory, Culture & Society* 1, 3.

18 Antitrust Modernization Commission, Report and Recommendations (April 2007), 333.

With regard to the first category, a wide variety of antitrust exemptions, both partial and whole, currently exist in US federal law, as 'in response to concerns about particular societal values, Congress has at times exempted certain groups or activities from the full or partial application of the antitrust laws'.[19] The scope of these exemptions and statutory immunities is interpreted by the US courts, but the decision to exempt an area results from a legislative act, adopted by the US Congress.

Turning now to EU competition law, the EU Treaty does not exclude any activity from the scope of competition law, although there are Treaty provisions establishing a specific competition law regime for the agricultural sector.[20] Potentially, any activity qualified by the courts as 'economic' falls within the scope of the EU competition law provisions. This provides a considerable leeway to the EU courts.

The EU legislative power is nevertheless empowered to intervene and adopt specific derogations in various economic areas. For instance, according to Article 42 TFEU, the extent of the application of the rules on competition to agricultural products is determined by the European Parliament and the Council.[21] Articles 101 and 102 TFEU may also apply in theory to a specific economic sector, without, however, the Commission having enforcement power to implement them. For instance, although transport was subject to Articles 101 and 102 TFEU, the Commission did not have the necessary powers, for period of time, to implement competition rules in this sector.[22]

In the UK, the approach followed is mixed: Chapters I and II of the Competition Act 1998 apply to 'undertakings', the concept being interpreted to include any natural or legal person capable of carrying on commercial or economic activities. However, section 3 of the Act provides for a number of exclusions from the prohibition of Chapter I. These are included in Schedules 1 (on mergers and concentrations), 2 (competition scrutiny under other enactments), and 3 of the Act (planning obligations and general exclusions). Schedule 4 excluded from the Competition Act 1998 the regulatory rules of various professions, but it was repealed by section 207 of the Enterprise Act 2002. Schedule 3 exclusions also apply in the case of the Chapter II prohibition (section 19(1) of the CA98). According to section 3(2)–(5) CA98, the Secretary of State may amend Schedules 1 and 3 in certain circumstances, either by adding further exclusions or removing existing ones. Schedule 3 also gives the Secretary of State power to exclude agreements from the Chapter I prohibition in certain circumstances. The power to establish the scope of UK competition law is thus divided between the judiciary, when interpreting the concept of 'undertaking', and the political power, when the Secretary of State decides to amend the list of excluded agreements in Schedule 3.

In interpreting the concept of 'undertaking' the EU courts exercise an important choice between the following three options:

(i) One may adopt the first logic of excluding activities and delegate the task of defining which activities should be subject to a competitive market order only to

19 Ibid, 348. 20 TFEU, Articles 38–44.

21 See Council Regulation (EC) No 1184/2006 of 24 July 2006 applying certain rules of competition to the production of, and trade in, agricultural products [2006] OJ L 214/7; Council Regulation (EC) No 1234/2007 establishing a Common Organization of Agricultural Markets and on specific provisions for certain agricultural products [2007] OJ L 299/1 [hereinafter Single CMO Regulation].

22 The transport sector was subject to special competition law procedural rules, which are now referred to in Regulation 1/2003.

neoclassical economics, neoclassical price theory determining when competition is efficient and when competition may lead to inefficiency (eg public goods, natural monopoly, etc);

(ii) One may consider that the competitive order is a process that always leads to fair distribution and, from that perspective, subjects all activities to the discipline of the competitive market order without any exception or exemption;

(iii) One may take the second logic and consider that it is the State (read here politics) that should decide which activity is better organized under a competitive market order and which should be subject to a different form of governance.

Option (ii) will subject to the competitive order, and hence to competition law, any activity if that leads, in one way or another, to offer goods and services on a market. This naturalist perspective on markets assumes that markets pre-exist any decision of the State to constitute them[23] and that markets constitute a site of 'veridiction–falsification' for governmental practice, based on the assumption that '[. . .] inasmuch as prices are determined in accordance with the natural mechanisms of the market they constitute a standard of truth which enables us to discern which governmental practices are correct and which are erroneous'.[24]

Option (iii) provides a wide discretion to the State to constitute, or suppress, markets. However, the Member States' practice may diverge, which makes it necessary for the EU courts to determine the scope of the concept of 'undertaking' on an ad hoc basis. But, determining the existence of one, or more, undertaking(s) may not always be the end of the story with regard to the application of competition law. As the General Court (GC) explained in *E.On Ruhrgas*, the sector should also be 'open to competition'. This implies that 'there are real concrete possibilities for the undertakings concerned to compete among themselves or for a new competitor to enter the relevant market and compete with established undertakings', this finding not being based 'on a mere hypothesis',[25] but 'supported by evidence or an analysis of the structures of the relevant market'.[26] This is, however, an element that is taken into account when examining the existence of a restriction of (actual or potential) competition, and not that of the concept of undertaking, for which it seems that a 'mere hypothesis' of a competitive order may be sufficient.[27]

Option (i) recognizes that markets are constructed by the State but at the same time limits the State's discretion in creating or suppressing them by subjecting the State's decision to neoclassical economics as a site of 'veridiction–falsification'. Although such an option would provide a clear direction to the EU courts, as long as these could accept only economic justifications for considering an activity as 'non-economic', it has not prevailed so far. The EU courts avoid any reliance on economics when defining the scope of the concept of 'undertaking', as a brief analysis of the case law will illustrate.

23 See, however, BE Harcourt, *The Illusion of Free Markets—Punishment and the need of Natural Order* (Harvard University Press, 2012) criticizing 'the "illusion" of "free markets" perceived as a natural order that pre-exists regulation'.

24 M Foucault, *The Birth of Biopolitics—Lectures at the Collège de France 1978–1979* (Picador, repr. ed, 2010), 32.

25 Case T-360/09, *E.ON Ruhrgas and E.ON v Commission*, EU:T:2012:332, paras 84–5.

26 Ibid, para 86.

27 See our analysis in Chapter 6.

4.2.3. 'UNDERTAKING' AND NON-ECONOMIC ACTIVITY: THE LIMITS OF THE COMPETITIVE ORDER

It follows from the above that the decision to consider an activity as 'economic', and thus the entity engaged with it as an 'undertaking' for the purpose of applying competition law, is a purely normative issue that largely depends on the interpretation of the EU courts as to (i) which of the activities it may be justifiable from an economic theory perspective not to subject to the market discipline and hence to a competitive order (e.g. public goods, externalities, etc) and (ii) which of the activities it might not be (politically) desirable to subject to market/competitive order principles of justification.[28]

4.2.3.1. Production and consumption markets

The EU courts are careful not to presume the existence of an economic activity from the fact that an entity offers goods and services on a market, thus avoiding a mechanical application of EU competition law. Instead, they consider the overall purpose of the activity in question.

In *FENIN v Commission*, the issue raised concerned the possible application of EU competition law to the purchase of medical instruments by a public body responsible for the management of the Spanish national health system (SNS). The Commission had rejected the complaint introduced by FENIN, an association of the majority of undertakings marketing medical goods and equipment used in Spanish hospitals. The Commission found that the organizations managing the SNS were in a dominant position on the Spanish market for medical goods and equipment and that they had abused that position by delaying payment of their debts. However, it held that competition law did not apply to the body in question, on the basis that it was not an undertaking.

The General Court confirmed the approach followed by the Commission.[29] It first distinguished between purchasing and supplying activities, stating that 'it is the activity consisting in offering goods and services on a given market that is the characteristic feature of an economic activity [. . .], not the business of purchasing, as such'.[30] It then went on to hold that 'it would be incorrect, when determining the nature of that subsequent activity, to dissociate the activity of purchasing goods from the subsequent use to which they are put'.[31] According to the General Court, it is necessary to consider whether or not the use of the purchased goods amounts to an economic activity. In this case, 'the SNS, managed by the ministries and other organisations cited in the applicant's complaint, operates according to the principle of solidarity in that it is funded from social security contributions and other State funding and in that it provides services free of charge to its members on the basis of universal cover'.[32] Consequently, the purchasing activities linked to an activity which was not of an economic nature were classified in the same way and the organisations covered by FENIN's complaint were not undertakings for the purposes of Article 102 TFEU.

28 This is of course our interpretation of the case law, the jurisprudence of the EU courts never explicitly acknowledging the political dimension of this choice.

29 Case T-319/99, *Federación Nacional de Empresas de Instrumentación Científica, Médica, Técnica y Dental (FENIN) v Commission* [2003] ECR II–357.

30 Ibid, para 36. 31 Ibid, para 36. 32 Ibid, para 39.

FENIN appealed to the CJEU, which confirmed the judgment of the General Court, reaffirming the definition of economic activity as the 'activity consisting in offering goods and services on a given market' but also holding that:

> The Court of First Instance rightly deduced [. . .] that there is no need to dissociate the activity of purchasing goods from the subsequent use to which they are put in order to determine the nature of that purchasing activity, and that the nature of the purchasing activity must be determined according to whether or not the subsequent use of the purchased goods amounts to an economic activity.[33]

It is remarkable that in a judgment adopted a few years before FENIN (2002), in a case known as *Bettercare II*, the UK Competition Appeal Tribunal (CAT) (then Competition Commission Appeal Tribunal) took a different approach. The case involved the conduct of a local authority in Northern Ireland (North & West Belfast Health and Social Services Trust) in procuring nursing home places from private companies whilst also providing some places itself. The CAT disagreed with the decision of the Director General of the Office of Fair Trading (OFT) (the predecessor of the Competition and Markets Authority, CMA) according to whom, as a matter of principle, the purchase from the private sector by a local authority, National Health Service (NHS) trusts or Health and Social Services (HSS) trusts, of residential and nursing care for those in need, was not an activity to which the Competition Act is capable of applying, on the grounds that those entities are not, in that context, acting as 'undertakings'. The CAT noted that the local authority in question exercised an activity of 'contracting out' to independent providers, which could properly be described as engaging in commercial transactions in services. The CAT observed that '[i]n effect, the essence of many, if not most, "economic" activities is the making of commercial contracts' and that 'the independent providers in question are providing services for which (the local authority in question) has a demand', resulting from the fact that it has decided to fulfil its functions on the basis of commercial transactions.[34] In conclusion, the CAT found that the local authority in question was an active economic actor on various markets.

First, it was present as a contracting out purchaser on the market for the supply of residential and nursing care services in Northern Ireland, the public authority having withdrawn from the provision of these services through its own means (statutory homes), and choosing instead to contract out to independent providers. The CAT noted that '[t]he fact that that market or sub-market has been created or expanded by the decision of the public authority to rely on independent providers, does not alter the fact that there is such a market', thus adopting a naturalist perspective that markets pre-existed State intervention in this area.[35] The presence of various operators in this market, such as the private (for profit) operators, the voluntary (not for profit) organizations, and the statutory homes, constituted for the CAT evidence of the existence of such market, a 'very substantial proportion of the residents in the private (for profit) sector (being) provided with beds on the basis of commercial transactions entered into between private homes, on the one hand, and NHS trusts and local authorities, on the other'.[36]

Second, the local authority was active in running residential homes, and thus being part of 'the offer' in the market for residential care services in Northern Ireland, the residents having

[33] Case C-205/03 P, *Federación Española de Empresas de Tecnología Sanitaria (FENIN) v Commission* [2006] ECR I-2695, para 26.

[34] *Bettercare Group Limited & DGFT* [2002] CAT 7, paras 191–2.

[35] Ibid, para 197.

[36] Ibid, para 198.

a choice of home, and thus able to choose between a private, voluntary or statutory home. The CAT found that this activity also constituted an economic activity, merely on the basis of a normative argument that the activities in question could be organized on the basis of a competitive order, the CAT observing that '[w]hile competition between the various homes may perhaps be imperfect in practice, because of the special features of this particular market, we can see no reason to exclude in principle the possibility that all three kinds of home in Northern Ireland are in fact competing for the custom of the potential resident, whether that potential resident is "self-funded" or not, at least as regards the services and facilities offered and probably, at least to some extent, on price.'[37] The CAT further noted that the local authority did not supply its services gratuitously but sought to recover as much as possible of the cost for the services it provided from the resident in question, whether in respect of its purchasing activities, or in respect of its own residential homes. Although it may not be able to recover the full cost, it was 'undoubtedly' remunerated for the activities that it carried on, this constituting additional evidence of an economic activity.

The CAT also objected to the argument that the local authority in question was simply entering an act of purchasing without resale, which could not be considered as 'economic' activity. The CAT noted that this is not similar to the case of a simple purchase for household needs by a consumer, or with the purchase of a new computer by a Government Department.

> In the first place, we are concerned here with the widespread making of commercial contracts in the context of a policy of contracting out pursued by North & West. In that context it seems to us that North & West can fairly be said to be 'trading' in a competitive market for the purposes of the application of the Act. In the second place, the legal analysis in this case is that North & West, having purchased the 'bed' in question, then 're-supplies' that bed by means of a further contract with the resident who is liable to pay North & West the cost of his accommodation, up to his available means. Here again, it seems to us that that is activity of an 'economic' character, albeit in a social context. Thirdly, North & West is not simply engaging in the activity of purchasing and re-supplying beds, but it is also running its own statutory homes as one of the offerors in the market for residential care services in Northern Ireland, and seeking remuneration from the residents.[38]

Following the FENIN judgment of the CJEU, the OFT (now CMA) issued a policy note on 'Public bodies and competition' (OFT 1389), which replaced the initial note published in 2004 (OFT 443). This notice has also been adopted by the board of the CMA. The OFT explains that the 'fact that a public body's conduct was capable of having anti-competitive effects in the market has been taken by the UK Competition Appeal Tribunal as evidence that that conduct was economic' in *BetterCare II* but 'to the extent that that judgment focused on purchasing conduct, it must now be considered in the light of the principles subsequently endorsed by the (Court of Justice) in *FENIN* and *SELEX*'.[39] Notwithstanding these differences between *FENIN* and *BetterCare II*, it may be possible to distinguish the two cases as relying on compatible principles. In *BetterCare*, the trust purchasing services from the private provider also provided care services and was thus in competition with the provider in the market for care services, not just for purchasing. As the aim of the purchasing was to sell services on a market, the activity could be considered as an economic one.

[37] *Bettercare Group Limited & DGFT* [2002] CAT 7, para 200. [38] Ibid, para 264.
[39] OFT 1389, Public bodies and competition law (December 2011), n 34.

It is also possible that the same entity might be found an 'undertaking' for some activities, while not qualified as an undertaking for other activities. The following cases illustrate the flexibility of the approach followed by the EU courts.

4.2.3.2. Regulatory function and acts in the exercise of official authority

Regulation or when the State 'acts in the exercise of official authority' does not constitute in principle an economic activity and thus might be exempt from the application of Article 101 and 102 TFEU, as such. Nevertheless, EU law also provides for the possibility for these provisions to create obligations to States to preserve the competitive process, in some circumstances (see Chapter 1).

Case C-343/95, *Diego Cali & Figli SrL v Servizi Ecologici Porto di Genova Spa*
[1997] ECR I–1547

The case concerned the Genoa port authority (Consorzio Autonomo del Porto, CAP), a body with administrative and economic functions conferred by legislation, which adopted a decree entrusting surveillance and other preventative anti-pollution services at the port to a company, SEPG, in the form of an exclusive concession. The tariffs charged to port users were approved by decree by the President of the Genoa CAP. Charges were paid by all the port users, whether or not they had actually caused any pollution. A port user challenged a court order requiring payment of invoices in respect of the services provided by SEPG on the grounds that SEPG was abusing a dominant position contrary to Article 102 TFEU. The CJEU found that a public body is not acting as an undertaking when it performs a task in the public interest which forms part of the essential functions of the State. The CJEU concluded that:

> 22. The anti-pollution surveillance for which SEPG was responsible in the oil port of Genoa is a task in the public interest which forms part of the essential functions of the State as regards the protection of the environment in maritime areas.
>
> 23. Such surveillance is connected by its nature, its aim and the rules to which it is subject with the exercise of powers relating to the protection of the environment which are typically those of a public authority. It is not of an economic nature justifying the application of the treaty rules on competition [. . .].
>
> 24. The levying of a charge by SEPG for preventive anti-pollution surveillance is an integral part of its surveillance activity in the maritime area of the port and cannot affect the legal status of that activity [. . .]. Moreover [. . .] the tariffs applied by SEPG have been approved by the public authorities.
>
> 25. In the light of the foregoing considerations, the answer [. . .] must be that Article [102 TFEU] is to be interpreted as not being applicable to anti-pollution surveillance with which a body governed by private law has been entrusted by the public authorities in an oil port of a Member State, even where port users must pay dues to finance that activity.

The judgment of the CJEU relied on the approach followed in *SAT Fluggesellschaft v Eurocontrol*, regarding an international organization for the safety of air navigation.

Case C-364/92, *SAT Fluggesellschaft mbH v Eurocontrol*
[1994] ECR I–43

Eurocontrol (European Organisation for the Safety of Air Navigation) was an international organization established by a convention concluded between fourteen European States and was entrusted with the establishment and collection of charges levied on the users of air navigation services. Eurocontrol sued in Belgian courts the airline SAT Fluggesellschaft mbH which had refused to pay the route charges for some flights. The defendant argued that the procedure followed by Eurocontrol in fixing the route charges amounted to an abuse of a dominant position prohibited by Article 102 TFEU. The Belgian Cour de Cassation asked the Court for a preliminary ruling on the question whether Eurocontrol could be considered as an undertaking in the sense of Articles 102 and 106 TFEU. SAT claimed that research and coordination activities carried on by that organization and the collection of route charges do not fall within the 'jus imperii', but constituted economic activities that could be carried on by bodies governed by private law. SAT also noted that air navigation control was an economic activity, in view of the fact that in some Member States it is private undertakings that exercise such control. The French, German, and Greek Governments and the United Kingdom argued against by finding that air navigation control is a supervisory activity intended to ensure public safety and the same for the collection of route charges, the charges merely constituting the consideration for the air navigation services provided by those States. The Commission also found that air navigation control was not of an economic nature, since that activity constitutes a service in the public interest which is intended to protect both the users of air transport and the populations affected by aircraft flying over them. The CJEU examined the 'nature of those activities'. It noted that Eurocontrol's main task involved research, planning, coordination of national policies and staff training, that it was competent to establish and collect the route charges levied on users of air space and that its activities were activities financed by the contributions of the Contracting States. The CJEU concluded:

> 27. Eurocontrol thus carries out, on behalf of the Contracting States, tasks in the public interest aimed at contributing to the maintenance and improvement of air navigation safety.
>
> 28. Contrary to SAT's contention, Eurocontrol's collection of route charges, which gave rise to the dispute in the main proceedings, cannot be separated from the organization's other activities. Those charges are merely the consideration, payable by users, for the obligatory and exclusive use of air navigation control facilities and services. [. . .]
>
> 30. Taken as a whole, Eurocontrol's activities, by their nature, their aim and the rules to which they are subject, are connected with the exercise of powers relating to the control and supervision of air space which are typically those of a public authority. They are not of an economic nature justifying the application of the Treaty rules of competition.
>
> 31. Accordingly, an international organization such as Eurocontrol does not constitute an undertaking subject to the provisions of Articles [102] and [106 TFEU].

In a subsequent judgment, the General Court, found, however, that some activities exercised by Eurocontrol were of 'economic' nature and that consequently it constituted an 'undertaking' for these activities.

Case T-155/04, *SELEX Sistemi Integrati SpA v Commission*
[2006] ECR II–4797

SELEX Sistemi Integrati SpA, a company present in the sector of air traffic management systems lodged a complaint with the Commission in which it drew the Commission s attention to certain alleged infringements of the competition rules by Eurocontrol in carrying out its standardization tasks in relation to air traffic management equipment and systems. SELEX argued that Eurocontrol's activities on standardization, research and development, and assistance to the national administrations, were economic activities and that Eurocontrol had therefore to be regarded as an undertaking within the meaning of Article 102 TFEU. The Commission rejected the complaint, taking the view that the activities of Eurocontrol which are the subject of the complaint were not of an economic nature, and, consequently, Eurocontrol could not be considered to be an undertaking within the meaning of Article 102 TFEU; and, in any event, even if those activities were considered to be activities of an undertaking, they would not be contrary to Article 102 TFEU. The Commission considered that Eurocontrol was not an undertaking, referring to the CJEU's conclusion in Case C-364/92, SAT Fluggesellschaft v Eurocontrol *[1994] ECR I–43, and that, excluded the possibility of regarding Eurocontrol, in all circumstances and in respect of all of its activities, as an undertaking for the purposes of Community competition law. The General Court rejected this reading of the case law of the CJEU noting that:*

> 54. [. . .] [I]n arriving at this finding, the Court based its reasoning exclusively on a review, in the light of the concept of an economic activity, of Eurocontrol's activities at issue in the case between SAT Fluggesellschaft mbH and Eurocontrol, namely the creation and collection of route charges on behalf of the Contracting States from users of air navigation services. While the Court referred [. . .] to some of the activities at issue in the present case, it did not, however, consider whether they were economic activities within the meaning of the case-law. However, since the Treaty provisions on competition are applicable to the activities of an entity which can be severed from those in which it engages as a public authority (Case 107/84 *Commission* v *Germany* [1985] ECR 2655, paragraphs 14 and 15, and Case T-128/98 *Aéroports de Paris* v *Commission* [2000] ECR II–3929, paragraph 108), the various activities of an entity must be considered individually and the treatment of some of them as powers of a public authority does not mean that it must be concluded that the other activities are not economic (see, to that effect, *Aéroports de Paris* v *Commission*, paragraph 109). In light of the limited scope of the Courts examination, it is thus apparent that, despite the general nature of the wording in paragraph 31 and its operative part, the judgment in *SAT Fluggesellschaft*, does not preclude Eurocontrol from being regarded as an undertaking within the meaning of Article [102 TFEU] in relation to its other activities.

The General Court then assessed whether, in relation to each of Eurocontrol's activities, they were separable from its activities falling within its public remit and if they were economic activities within the meaning of the case law.

With regard to Eurocontrol's activity of technical standardization, that is the preparation or production of technical standards and their adoption by the Council of Eurocontrol, the General Court noted that this constituted a 'legislative activity' and therefore not an economic activity, the GC noting that 'Eurocontrol's role is thus akin to that of a minister who, at national level, prepares legislative or regulatory measures which are then adopted by the government', this activity therefore falling 'within the public tasks of

Eurocontrol'.[40] *The preparation or production of technical standards by Eurocontrol, could indeed be separated from its tasks of managing air space and developing air safety, the GC observing that 'the need to adopt standards at an international level does not necessarily mean that the body which sets those standards must also be the same as that which subsequently adopts them'.*[41] *The GC further noted:*

> 61. However, Eurocontrol's activity of producing standards cannot be deemed to be an economic activity. It is clear from established case-law that any activity consisting in offering goods and services on a given market is an economic activity (see *Aéroports de Paris* v *Commission*, paragraph 107 [. . .]). In this case, the applicant has not shown that there is a market for 'technical standardisation services in the sector of ATM equipment'. The only purchasers of such services can be States in their capacity as air traffic control authorities. However, they chose to develop those standards themselves in the context of international cooperation through Eurocontrol. Since the standards developed are subsequently adopted by the Council of Eurocontrol, the results of the development activity stay within the organisation itself and are not offered on a given market. In the field of standardisation, Eurocontrol, for its Member States, is therefore only a forum for concerted action which those States established in order to coordinate the technical standards of their ATM systems. It cannot therefore be considered that, in this area, Eurocontrol 'offers them goods and services'.
>
> 62. In the present case, the applicant has thus still failed to show that the activity at issue consisted of offering goods or services on a given market, as is required by the case law referred to in the previous paragraph.
>
> 63. As regards the applicants' argument that the activity of standardisation should be assessed separately from that of acquiring prototypes necessary for producing technical standards and then it can be inferred from the economic nature of the activity of acquiring prototypes that the activity of standardisation is also economic, clearly that argument cannot be upheld.
>
> 64. The applicant does not give reasons as to why the classification of the activity of acquiring prototypes as an economic activity, supposing this is the case, would necessarily lead to the same classification for the activity of standardisation. While it is not disputed by the parties that Eurocontrol acquires goods and services on the market, this does not mean that the activities for which those goods and services are acquired are economic activities.
>
> 65. In addition, it must be stated that an approach consisting of inferring from the nature of the upstream activity (the acquisition of prototypes) the nature of the downstream activity (standardisation), as proposed by the applicant, is at odds with the case-law of the Court of First Instance. According to the criteria laid down in the settled case-law of the Community judicature, cited above, economic activity consists of the offer of goods and services on a given market and not the acquisition of such goods and services. In that regard, it has been held that it is not the business of purchasing, as such, which is the characteristic feature of an economic activity and that it would be incorrect, when determining whether or not a given activity is economic, to dissociate the activity of purchasing goods from the subsequent use to which they are put. The nature of the purchasing activity must therefore be determined according to whether

40 Case T-155/04, *SELEX Sistemi Integrati SpA v Commission* [2006] ECR II-4797, para 59.

41 Ibid, para 60.

or not the subsequent use of the purchased goods amounts to an economic activity (Case T-319/99 *FENIN* v *Commission* [2003] ECR II–357, paragraph 36). In the context of the present case, this means that the fact that the standardisation activity is not an economic activity implies that the acquisition of prototypes in the context of that standardisation is also not an economic activity, despite the fact that Eurocontrol is acting in the capacity of a buyer on the market for ATM equipment.

66. In that regard, the Court rejects the applicants argument that reasoning of the Court of First Instance in the case of *FENIN* v *Commission*, cannot be transposed to the present case or that its application cannot be absolute.

67. To the extent that the applicant submits, first, that the situation in the case of *FENIN* v *Commission* is very different from that in the present case, it must be pointed out that the Court of First instance considered in that case, generally, that an organisation which purchases goods not for the purpose of offering goods and services as part of an economic activity but in order to use them in the context of a different activity, such as one of a purely social nature, does not act as an undertaking simply because it is a purchaser in a given market (*FENIN* v *Commission*, paragraph 37). The general wording of that sentence, and in particular the fact that it expressly refers to a social activity only as an example, permits the approach adopted in that judgment to be transposed to any organisation purchasing goods for non-economic activities. As set out above, this is precisely the case with Eurocontrol. [. . .]

69. Accordingly, it must be held that the Commission has not committed a manifest error of assessment in taking the view that Eurocontrol's technical standardization activities were not economic activities within the meaning of Community case-law and that the competition rules of the Treaty therefore did not apply to them.

The General Court arrived at a similar conclusion with regard to the research and development activity of Eurocontrol, in particular the acquisition of prototypes and the intellectual property rights resulting from the research funded by Eurocontrol. The acquisition of prototypes is only an activity which is subsidiary to their development, the latter being carried out not by Eurocontrol itself, but by undertakings in the relevant sector to which the organization granted public subsidy incentives with a view to promoting research and development. The intellectual property rights resulting from the research and development activities, owned by Eurocontrol, were made available to interested undertakings at no cost. This was not found to be an economic activity, the absence of remuneration being one indication among several others excluding the possibility that the activity in question is economic in nature.

The General Court, however, reached a different conclusion for the activity of Eurocontrol to provide technical assistance to national administrations.

86. [. . .] [I]t should be pointed out that the activity of assisting the national administrations is separable from Eurocontrol's tasks of air space management and development of air safety. Although the assistance may serve the public interest by maintaining and improving the safety of air navigation, that relationship is only a very indirect one, since the assistance provided by Eurocontrol only covers technical specifications in the implementation of tendering procedures for ATM equipment and therefore only impacts on the safety of air navigation by means of those tendering procedures. Such an indirect relationship does not imply that there is a necessary link between the two activities. In that respect, the Court recalls that Eurocontrol only offers assistance in that field on the request of the national administrations. The activity of assistance is therefore in no way an activity which is essential or even indispensable to ensuring the safety of air navigation.

87. Next, it should be recalled that any activity consisting in offering goods and services on a given market is an economic activity [. . .]. In relation to the assistance to the national administrations in the form of advice given at the time of drafting the contract documents for calls for tender or during the selection procedure of undertakings participating in those calls for tender, this is precisely a case of an offer of services on the market for advice, a market on which private undertakings specialised in this area could also very well offer their services.

88. In that regard, the Court of First Instance has held that the fact that an activity may be exercised by a private undertaking is a further indication that the activity in question may be described as a business activity (*Aéroports de Paris* v *Commission*, paragraph 124, upheld in Case C-82/01 P *Aéroports de Paris* v *Commission* [2002] ECR I–9297, paragraph 82).

89. In addition, it should be pointed out that the Court has held, on several occasions, that the fact that activities are normally entrusted to public offices cannot affect the economic nature of such activities, since they have not always been, and are not necessarily, carried out by public entities [. . .]. In the circumstances under consideration in this case, this means that the fact that the services in question are not at the current time offered by private undertakings does not prevent their being described as an economic activity, since it is possible for them to be carried out by private entities.

90. Since the Commission contends that the assistance which Eurocontrol provides to the national administrations is not remunerated as such, it should be stated that that fact may be a pointer, but is not in itself decisive [. . .].

91. Similarly, the fact that the assistance is given in pursuit of a public service objective may be an indication that it is a non-economic activity, but this does not prevent an activity consisting, as is the case here, in offering services on a given market from being considered to be an economic activity. [. . .]

92. It follows from the foregoing that the activity whereby Eurocontrol provides assistance to the national administrations is an economic activity and that, consequently, Eurocontrol, in the exercise of that activity, is an undertaking within the meaning of Article [102 TFEU].

NOTES AND QUESTIONS ON EUROCONTROL

1. Subsequent case law of the CJEU confirmed that the same entity may be characterized an undertaking for some activities but not for others. In *MOTOE*, the CJEU found that a body vested with public powers to grant applications to organize motorcycling events was not an undertaking when making such authorization decisions, but was considered to act as an undertaking when carrying out economic advertising and sponsorship activities relating to such events.[42] However, to the extent that the body also participates in the market, such participation may constitute an economic activity.
2. In *Compass v Austria* (*Compass Datenbank*) the Supreme court of Austria sent a preliminary reference to the Court on the question whether the Austrian State is acting as an 'undertaking' in the sense of Article 102 TFEU when prohibiting both the re-use of data contained on its public register of businesses and the commercialization of this data to create a more comprehensive business information service.[43] According

[42] Case C-49/07, *MOTOE v Elliniko Dimosio* [2008] ECR I–4863, para 25.

[43] Case C-138/11, *Compass v Austria* (*Compass Datenbank*), ECLI:EU:C:2012:449.

to the Austrian legislation, businesses were required to place certain information on the corporations' register to be made available to the public via the Internet. Access to this database on which the Austrian State held a *sui generis* right was provided subject to the payment of court fees and of a separate remuneration, levied by five billing agencies which were transmitting the documents, thus establishing the connection between the final customer and the corporations register. The court fee was forwarded to the State and the remuneration to the billing agencies had to be approved by the Ministry of Justice. Compass Datenbank GmbH was operating a more extensive trade and industry database, accessible via the Internet, which relied partly on information provided by the State computer centre with no restriction as to its re-use. It also included information additional to that appearing in the corporations register.

In 2001, the Austrian State initiated proceedings seeking an injunction against Compass Datenbank to prohibit it from using data from the undertakings register, in particular by storage, reproduction or transmission to third parties. An Austrian court ordered Datenbank to refrain from using this data in so far as it had not received it for reasonable remuneration transferred to the Austrian State. In the meantime, Compass Datenbank introduced proceedings requesting the Austrian State to provide to it access to the data of the registry, subject to payment of an appropriate fee, its arguments being grounded in competition law, in particular an alleged abuse by the Republic of Austria (considered as an undertaking in this case) of its dominant position on the market, with the argument that it refused Compass Datenbank access to an essential facility. The Austrian courts rejected this request, the status of 'undertaking' being ruled out where State bodies are concerned, where and in so far as they act as public authorities.

Following its well-established case law, the CJEU repeated that a public entity may be considered as an undertaking when exercising an economic activity which can be separated from the exercise of its public powers. According to the CJEU, '[. . .] a data collection activity in relation to undertakings, on the basis of a statutory obligation on those undertakings to disclose the data and powers of enforcement related [. . .] falls within the exercise of public powers' and '[a]s a result, such activity is not an economic activity'.[44] The fact that access to the public database (the registry) was provided in return for remuneration was not considered by the CJEU as sufficient on its own right for the activity carried out to be classified as an economic activity, as its payment was laid down by law and not determined, directly or indirectly by that entity.[45] The CJEU found that the activity of maintaining and making available to the public this data could not be separated from the activity of collecting such data, concluding that they did not also constitute an economic activity.[46] Relying on IP rights was not also constitutive of an economic activity, 'by reason of that fact alone', as '[s]uch entity is not obliged to authorize free use of the data which it collects and make available to the public'.[47]

3. In *Institute of Independent Insurance Brokers v Director General of Fair Trading*, the CAT examined the distinction between 'public powers' or 'official authority' on the one hand and 'economic activity' on the other hand.[48] The CAT found that the General

[44] Ibid, para 40. [45] Ibid, paras 39 and 42. [46] Ibid, para 41. [47] Ibid, para 47.

[48] *Institute of Independent Insurance Brokers v Director General of Fair Trading* [2001] CAT 4, paras 254–8.

Insurance Standards Council (GISC) was a private company that has been set up by the industry itself without any statutory basis and that it existed solely by contract. The CAT also noted that GISC was 'not accountable to Parliament, nor to Ministers, nor indeed to anyone other than those in the industry who belong to GISC' and as far as the constitution of GISC is concerned, GISC was run by a Board of Directors 'most of whom are, or have been, active in the industry'. The CAT also observed that the 'public interest' directors that formed approximately a third of the board were recruited through head-hunters and not appointed by a public authority, thus leaving the 'outside' directors in a substantial minority vis-à-vis the ten 'industry' directors. The CAT added that there was no independent chairman ('without industry connections'). The CAT concluded that the GISC presented 'features normally to be found in a private sector organisation or company accountable to its members, rather than a publicly constituted body exercising "public powers"'.[49] It also noted that the activity in question was not exercised on the basis of a statutory foundation, but on the basis of statements by Government ministers, which is not a legal basis founded in public law. Furthermore, it was observed that 'the setting up of a framework for promoting professional standards and consumer protection in general insurance is not an activity which, by reason of its intrinsic nature, can *necessarily* only be carried out by public authorities, as the case law appears to require'.[50] Indeed, these self-regulatory professional bodies are acting 'not solely in the public interest but also in the commercial interests of their members in promoting the various schemes in question' with the aim to avoid 'the threat of statutory intervention'.[51]

4.2.3.3. The solidarity function

In a series of cases, the EU courts considered that a public body is not acting as an undertaking when it performs an exclusively social function based on the principle of 'solidarity'. Solidarity entails the redistribution of income between those who are better off and those who, in view of their resources and state of health, would otherwise be deprived of the necessary social cover. Essentially, the exclusion of activities based on the principle of 'solidarity' may be considered as a normative decision that a competitive order may not be desirable for activities of such nature.

Joined Cases C-159 & 160/91, *Poucet and Pistre v AGF and Cancava*
[1993] ECR I–637

French law required artisans to make payments to two organizations which managed social security schemes. One such scheme was a compulsory old-age insurance scheme for artisans, while the other was a compulsory sickness and maternity insurance scheme for self-employed persons in non-agricultural occupations. Both the level of contributions and benefits were subject to the control of the public authorities. The applicants challenged the orders that required them to make contributions to those schemes on the basis that they were

[49] Ibid, para 255. [50] Ibid, para 257. [51] Ibid.

contrary to the competition rules of the Treaty. The French Court referred to the European Court under Article 234 TFEU the question whether the bodies managing those schemes should be regarded as undertakings for the purposes of Articles 101 and 102 TFEU. The CJEU responded as follows.

8. Those schemes pursue a social objective and embody the principle of solidarity.

9. They are intended to provide cover for all the persons to whom they apply, against the risks of sickness, old age, death and invalidity, regardless of their financial status and their state of health at the time of affiliation.

10. The principle of solidarity is, in the sickness and maternity scheme, embodied in the fact that the scheme is financed by contributions proportional to the income from the occupation and to the retirement pensions of the persons making them; only recipients of an invalidity pension and retired insured members with very modest resources are exempted from the payment of contributions, whereas the benefits are identical for all those who receive them. Furthermore, persons no longer covered by the scheme retain their entitlement to benefits for a year, free of charge. Solidarity entails the redistribution of income between those who are better off and those who, in view of their resources and state of health, would be deprived of the necessary social cover.

11. In the old-age insurance scheme, solidarity is embodied in the fact that the contributions paid by active workers serve to finance pensions of retired workers. It is also reflected by the grant of pension rights where no contributions have been made and of pension rights that are not proportional to the contributions paid.

12. Finally, there is solidarity between the various social security schemes, in that those in surplus contribute to the financing of those with structural financial difficulties.

13. It follows that the social security schemes, as described, are based on a system of compulsory contribution, which is indispensable for application of the principle of solidarity and the financial equilibrium of those schemes.

14. It is apparent from the documents that the management of the schemes at issue in the main proceedings were entrusted by statute to social security funds whose activities are subject to control by the State, acting through, in particular, the Minister for Social Security, the Minister for the Budget and public bodies such as the Inspectorate General of Finance and the Inspectorate General for Social Security.

15. In the discharge of their duties, the funds apply the law and thus cannot influence the amount of the contributions, the use of assets and the fixing of the level of benefits. For management of the sickness and maternity scheme, the regional sickness funds may entrust to certain organizations, such as those that are governed in France by the Code de la Mutualité (Code governing mutual societies) or the Code des Assurances (Insurance Code), the task of collecting contributions and paying out benefits. However, it does not appear that those organizations, which, in the performance of that task, act only as agents of the sickness funds, are referred to by judgments of the national court.

16. The foregoing considerations must be taken into account in examining whether the term 'undertaking', within the meaning of Articles [101 and 102 TFEU], includes organisations charged with managing a social security scheme of the kind referred to by national court.

17. The Court has held (in particular in Case C-41/90 *Höfner* v *Elser* [1991] ECR I–1979, paragraph 21) that in the context of competition law the concept of an undertaking encompasses every entity engaged in an economic activity, regardless of the legal status of the entity and the way in which it is financed.

18. Sickness funds, and the organisations involved in the management of the public social security system, fulfil an exclusively social function. That activity is based on the

principle of national solidarity and is entirely non profit-making. The benefits paid are statutory benefits bearing no relation to the amount of the contributions.

19. Accordingly, that activity is not an economic activity and, therefore, the organisations to which it is entrusted are not undertakings within the meaning of Articles [101 and 102 TFEU].

NOTES AND QUESTIONS ON POUCET AND PISTRE

1. The French social security system in question was funded by a compulsory contribution which, according to the CJEU, was 'indispensable for application of the principle of solidarity and the financial equilibrium of those schemes'.[52] Can one draw a parallel with situations in which funding by the tax payer is considered indispensable for the financial equilibrium of the scheme?
2. The CJEU took a different approach from the one followed with regard to the insurance regimes that were optional and did not operate according to the redistributive principle of the social security scheme in *Poucet and Pistre*. In *FFSA*,[53] a number of private insurance companies challenged a French law establishing an optional supplementary old-age insurance scheme for self-employed farmers financed by voluntary contributions known as the *Coreva* scheme. The scheme was managed by a non-profit organization, the Caisse Centrale de la Mutualité Sociale Agricole (CCMSA) which also operated a compulsory scheme. The voluntary scheme operated according to the principle of capitalization, that is to say the benefits payable under the scheme depended solely on the amount of contributions paid by the members of the scheme and the results of the investments made by the managing organization, rather than on a redistributive principle. The French Administrative Supreme Court (Conseil d'État) asked for a preliminary ruling from the CJEU. The Court distinguished this case from *Poucet and Pistre* for the following reasons:

   > '[. . .] Under the sickness and maternity insurance scheme there in question, the benefits were identical for all recipients, but contributions were proportionate to income. Under the old-age insurance scheme, retirement pensions were financed by active workers. Further, the pension rights, laid down by legislation, were not proportionate to the contributions paid under the old-age insurance scheme. Finally, schemes which were in surplus helped finance those which had financial difficulties of a structural nature. Such solidarity necessarily required the various schemes to be managed by a single body and membership of those schemes to be compulsory.[54]

   In the *FFSA* context, membership of the Coreva scheme was optional and the scheme operated in accordance with the principle of capitalization, as the benefits to which the scheme conferred entitlement depended solely on the amount of contributions paid by the recipients and the financial results of the investments made by the managing organization. From this perspective, the CCMSA carried on an economic activity in

52 Joined Cases C-159 & 160/91, *Poucet and Pistre v AGF and Cancava* [1993] ECR I–637, para 13.

53 Case C-244/94, *Fédération Française des Sociétés d'Assurance (FFSA) v Ministère de l'Agriculture et de la Pêche* [1995] ECR I–4013.

54 Ibid, para 15.

competition with life assurance companies, as a farmer wishing to supplement his basic pension should have opted either for the CCMSA or for an insurance company for a solution that would have guaranteed better investment, and hence more benefits. Although the CJEU found 'elements of solidarity' in the scheme under review, it highlighted the optional nature of the scheme, the fact that the principle of solidarity was extremely limited in scope and that the scheme was managed by a non-profit-making body to conclude on the economic character of activity in question.

3. In another interesting case the Italian national regime of compulsory insurance against accidents at work and occupational diseases (INAIL) claimed the payment from Cisal of a compulsory insurance contribution, even though Cisal's managing partner was insured under a private insurance policy. The Tribunale di Vicenza referred to the European Court the question of whether or not INAIL constituted an undertaking, and whether the compulsory payment of premiums, even where there was a private insurance policy in force, amounted to a competition law infringement. Advocate General Jacobs suggested in his Opinion that INAIL was not an undertaking, essentially because (i) the statutory framework was closer to 'a social security scheme which guarantees basic social protection' rather than to private insurance; and (ii) the level of both benefits and contributions were ultimately determined by the State. The CJEU found that a number of elements in this case tended to demonstrate that the insurance scheme applied the principle of solidarity, such as the fact that the insurance scheme was financed by contributions the rate of which was not systematically proportionate to the risk insured, or the fact that the amount of benefits paid was not necessarily proportionate to the insured persons' earnings. The absence of any direct link between the contributions paid and the benefits granted entailed solidarity between better paid workers and those who, given their low earnings, would be deprived of proper social cover if such a link existed. The activity of the INAIL, which was entrusted by law to the management of the scheme in question, was also subject to supervision by the State, as the amount of benefits and of contributions was, in the last resort, fixed by the State. The compulsory affiliation was also essential for the financial balance of the scheme. INAIL was found to fulfil an exclusively social function and hence not an economic activity.

Joined Cases C-264/01, 306 & 355/01, *AOK Bundesverband and Others* [2004] ECR I–2493 (some references are omitted)

The great majority of employees in Germany are required to belong to the statutory health insurance system. Employees are subject to statutory health insurance unless their income exceeds a certain level or unless they receive sufficient cover from another statutory source, as in the case of civil servants. The system is funded by compulsory contributions from insured persons and their employers, the levels of which are fixed according to the insured person's income. The system is managed by sickness funds, which are independently managed bodies governed by public law possessing legal personality. The sickness funds compete with each other with regard to contribution rates in order to attract people for whom insurance under the scheme is obligatory and those for whom it is voluntary. Insured persons may freely choose their sickness fund as well as their doctor or the hospital in which they have treatment. Yet, the sickness funds also operate in accordance with a solidarity mechanism under which an equalization is effected between sickness funds in order to remedy the financial disparities resulting from differences in the degree of risk insured. Thus, the sickness funds insuring the least costly risks contribute to the financing of those insuring more onerous risks. The inability of sickness funds to influence the choice made between medicinal products whose cost is borne under the scheme was considered as increasing the costs. With the aim of reducing the costs of the health insurance system the sickness funds have been offered by the legislator means of influencing doctors' and patients' choice of medicines and by developing awareness of the cost of medicines on the part of insured persons. One of these is the determination of fixed maximum amounts payable by sickness funds towards the cost of medicinal products and treatment materials. With regard to medicinal products, the prescription fees are borne by the patient, but it is the sickness fund which pays the pharmacy for the medicinal products supplied by it, within the limits of the fixed maximum amounts determined in accordance with the law. If the price of the medicinal product is lower than or equal to the fixed maximum amount, the fund pays the price in full. On the other hand, if the price exceeds the fixed maximum amount, the insured person pays the difference between that amount and the sale price for the product. An independent body composed of doctors' representatives and representatives of the sickness funds determine the groups of medicinal products for which fixed maximum amounts must be laid down. Then, the fund associations jointly determine the uniform fixed maximum amounts applicable to the medicinal products falling within the categories as defined. The fixed maximum amounts are generally determined taking account of the products offered by a number of manufacturers and are based on the lowest pharmacy sale prices. If the fund associations do not succeed in determining fixed maximum amounts, the decision is taken at ministerial level.

Manufacturers of medicinal products challenged these measures requesting the sickness funds to refrain from applying the fixed maximum amounts concerning them and for compensation in respect of the loss suffered. A preliminary reference was sent by the appeal courts to the CJEU asking, among others, if statutory sickness funds of a Member State are to be regarded as associations of undertakings or as undertakings within the meaning of Article 101(1) TFEU when they jointly determine the applicable level of uniform fixed amounts for medicinal products in the Member State. On one side, the fund associations submitted that the activities of the sickness funds did not constitute economic activities, as well as the activities of the fund associations. According to them, the sickness funds fulfil a function which is exclusively social and entirely non-profit-making, as their operation is founded on a principle of solidarity and the State exercises control over the activity of the fund associations. The Commission expressed similar views. On the other side, the pharmaceutical companies challenging these measures submitted that the sickness funds compete strongly with one another in the following three areas: the amount of the contributions, the benefits offered, and the management and organization of their services. The amount of the contributions is determined by each fund, all striving to offer the lowest possible contribution rate, particularly by restricting their management costs. The sickness funds also retained some freedom of action in the field of optional additional benefits, in particular with regard to rehabilitation, alternative and natural methods of treatment, or preventive measures for certain chronic illnesses, such as diabetes or asthma. The sickness funds also competed with one another with regard to the management and organization of their operations and engaged in intense promotional and marketing activity. The CJEU responded:

> 46. The concept of an undertaking in competition law covers any entity engaged in economic activity, regardless of the legal status of the entity or the way in which it is financed.
>
> 47. In the field of social security, the Court has held that certain bodies entrusted with the management of statutory health insurance and old-age insurance schemes pursue an exclusively social objective and do not engage in economic activity. The Court has found that to be so in the case of sickness funds which merely apply the law

and cannot influence the amount of the contributions, the use of assets and the fixing of the level of benefits. Their activity, based on the principle of national solidarity, is entirely non-profit-making and the benefits paid are statutory benefits bearing no relation to the amount of the contributions (Joined Cases C-159/91 and C-160/91 *Poucet and Pistre* [1993] ECR I–637, paragraphs 15 and 18). [. . .]

51. Sickness funds in the German statutory health insurance scheme, like the bodies at issue in *Poucet and Pistre* [. . .] are involved in the management of the social security system. In this regard they fulfil an exclusively social function, which is founded on the principle of national solidarity and is entirely non-profitmaking.

52. It is to be noted in particular that the sickness funds are compelled by law to offer to their members essentially identical obligatory benefits which do not depend on the amount of the contributions. The funds therefore have no possibility of influence over those benefits.

53. [. . .] [T]he sickness funds are joined together in a type of community founded on the basis of solidarity [. . .] which enables an equalisation of costs and risks between them. [. . .] [A]n equalisation is thus effected between the sickness funds whose health expenditure is lowest and those which insure costly risks and whose expenditure connected with those risks is highest.

54. The sickness funds are therefore not in competition with one another or with private institutions as regards grant of the obligatory statutory benefits in respect of treatment or medicinal products which constitutes their main function.

55. It follows from those characteristics that the sickness funds are similar to the bodies at issue in *Poucet and Pistre* and *Cisal* and that their activity must be regarded as being non-economic in nature.

56. The latitude available to the sickness funds when setting the contribution rate and their freedom to engage in some competition with one another in order to attract members does not call this analysis into question. As is apparent from the observations submitted to the Court, the legislature introduced an element of competition with regard to contributions in order to encourage the sickness funds to operate in accordance with principles of sound management, that is to say in the most effective and least costly manner possible, in the interests of the proper functioning of the German social security system. Pursuit of that objective does not in any way change the nature of the sickness funds' activity.

57. Since the activities of bodies such as the sickness funds are not economic in nature, those bodies do not constitute undertakings within the meaning of Articles [101 TFEU] and [102 TFEU].

58. However, the possibility remains that, besides their functions of an exclusively social nature within the framework of management of the German social security system, the sickness funds and the entities that represent them, namely the fund associations, engage in operations which have a purpose that is not social and is economic in nature. In that case the decisions which they would be led to adopt could perhaps be regarded as decisions of undertakings or of associations of undertakings.

59. It must therefore be examined whether determination of the fixed maximum amounts by the fund associations is linked to the sickness funds' functions of an exclusively social nature or whether it falls outside that framework and constitutes an activity of an economic nature. [. . .]

61. However, as is apparent from the documents before the Court, when the fund associations determine the fixed maximum amounts they merely perform an obligation which is imposed upon them [. . .] in order to ensure continuance of operation of the German social security system. That paragraph also lays down in detail the applicable

procedure for determining the amounts and specifies that the fund associations must observe certain requirements as to quality and profitability. [. . .] [I]f the fund associations do not succeed in determining fixed maximum amounts, the competent minister must then decide them.

62. Thus, only the precise level of the fixed maximum amounts is not dictated by legislation, but decided by the fund associations having regard to the criteria laid down by the legislature. Furthermore, while the fund associations have a certain discretion in this regard, the discretion relates to the maximum amount paid by the sickness funds in respect of medicinal products which is an area where the latter do not compete.

63. It follows that, in determining those fixed maximum amounts, the fund associations do not pursue a specific interest separable from the exclusively social objective of the sickness funds. On the contrary, in making such a determination, the fund associations perform an obligation which is integrally connected with the activity of the sickness funds within the framework of the German statutory health insurance scheme.

64. It must accordingly be found that, in determining the fixed maximum amounts, the fund associations merely perform a task for management of the German social security system which is imposed upon them by legislation and that they do not act as undertakings engaging in economic activity.

NOTES AND QUESTIONS ON AOK BUNDESVERBAND

1. In paragraphs 53–4, 56, the CJEU notes that the system is based on the principle of solidarity, in view of the equalization effected between the sickness funds and concluded that they are 'therefore' not in competition with one another or with private institutions in particular with regards to the grant of the obligatory statutory benefits in respect of treatment or medicinal products which constitutes their main function. According to the Court, the fact that the sickness funds enjoy some discretion when setting the contribution rate and they engage in some competition with one another in order to attract members does not call this analysis into question. If there is some competition between the funds (with regard to contribution rates), this was done with the aim of reducing costs and promoting sound management. The CJEU finds that this aim is not in conflict with the principle of solidarity and does not alter the 'nature' of the sickness funds' activity. Do you find the CJEU reasoning convincing? Does this mean that some degree of residual competition may still be compatible with the characterization of an activity as being non-economic? Is it a matter of degree?

   For instance, if there was more intensive competition between the sickness funds, not just on contribution rates or the existence of optional additional benefits (which indicate competition on some parameter of quality), would the solidarity function played a more limited role? Is it a matter relating to the degree of competition possible between the various entities (public or private), for instance if the degree of competition is significant, then the principle of solidarity will not operate? Or does it relate to a political decision not to subject activities based on the solidarity principle to competition law? If it is the latter, should there be a limiting principle to circumscribe the operation of the solidarity principle?

2. In paragraphs 58–9, 61–2, the CJEU notes that if the purpose of the activity is not of a social nature, it may be characterized as economic. It also examined if the anti-competitive conduct in question concerned an area of the activity of the sickness funds for which there was some degree of competition and it found that the funds enjoyed

some discretion with regard to the maximum amount paid by the funds in respect of medicinal products but that this was an area where the latter did not compete.

3. Do you think that the approach followed by the EU courts limits Member States' discretion to close their social security systems, or more generally social public services, such as healthcare, to competition? Is this case law creating some constraints on the policy space of the Member States? Would a State that has opened the market for the provision of healthcare services to 'any qualified provider' (as it is the case in the UK where profit-making hospitals are able to provide NHS care), made such activities economic in nature and thus subject to competition law? What about a State that has opted for a monopoly provider of healthcare services? What about a State that has organized the provision of healthcare services by public only providers according to a competitive order setting, by introducing quasi-markets? The following excerpt may provide some food for thought.

T Prosser, 'EU competition law and public Services' in E Mossialos, G Permanand, R Baeten, and TK Hervey (eds) *Health Systems Governance in Europe: The Role of European Union Law and Policy* (CUP, 2010), 315, 317 (footnotes omitted)

The [principle] of social solidarity [. . .] is based on a commitment to equality, notably to equal access to services irrespective of ability to pay. In this sense, the principle is based on an ideal of citizenship: that all public services are based on our inclusion in a community, not on our financial resources. It is not difficult to see that this principle may come into conflict with market-based principles.

Thus, a government may wish to coordinate a health service in order to guarantee equal treatment for all, rather than enhancing consumer choice, which may further promote inequalities. It may wish to ensure that services are provided free or at prices that do not reflect underlying costs; again, this will be incompatible with the free play of markets, one of the aims of which is to distribute goods and services on the basis of willingness (and ability) to pay for the costs involved. As we shall see later, there is nothing in European law that prevents national governments from organizing health care systems on a basis of solidarity. However, where governments attempt to mix markets and solidarity-based provision, difficulties may arise with competition law.

The highly political nature of these different principles complicates matters further, not only in the obvious sense that they represent fundamental choices about social organization, but also because they have been associated with the approaches of different Member States of the Union. Thus (to simplify a complex picture), the markets-based approach is often characterized as 'Anglo-Saxon' and associated with the United Kingdom, which is seen as almost a Trojan horse, bringing to the Union support for the unfettered market principles of the United States. By contrast, the solidarity approach is associated in particular with France, and can be seen both as reflecting its strong republican values of equal citizenship rights and as protecting a large and influential public sector. The main point is that both market-based principles and those of solidarity appear in Community law and the balance between them is highly contested and potentially politically incendiary.

In *Albany*, organizations representing employers and employees had collectively agreed to set up a single pension fund responsible for managing a supplementary pension scheme and had made requests to the public authorities to make affiliation to the fund compulsory.[55] One of

[55] Case C-67/96, *Albany International BV v Stichting Bedrijfspensioenfonds Textielindustrie* [1999] ECR I-5751.

the questions referred to the CJEU by the national court related to the concept of undertaking (the other one related to the possible justification of the collective agreement on the basis of the Treaty provisions for collective bargaining), the national court asking if a pension fund responsible for managing a supplementary pension scheme set up by a collective agreement concluded between organizations representing employers and workers in a given sector and to which affiliation has been made compulsory by the public authorities for all workers in that sector was an undertaking. The pension fund argued that it pursued an essential social function within the pension system applicable in the Netherlands. It noted the extremely limited amount of the statutory pension calculated on the basis of the minimum statutory wage, that it was not profit-making and that it was based on the principle of solidarity, in view of the absence of equivalence between the contributions paid and the pension rights and the need for adherence to the system to be compulsory so as to guarantee its financial equilibrium.

The CJEU rejected these arguments, concluding that the pension fund was an undertaking. It noted that the sectoral pension fund itself determined the amount of the contributions and benefits and that the Fund operated in accordance with the principle of capitalization, as the amount of the benefits provided depended on the financial results of the investments made by the fund. The CJEU considered that a sectoral pension fund of the kind at issue engaged in an economic activity in competition with insurance companies and consequently the fact that the fund was non-profit-making and that it manifested some degree of solidarity were not sufficient to deprive it of its status as an undertaking within the meaning of the competition rules of the Treaty. According to the CJEU, '[u]ndoubtedly, the pursuit of a social objective [. . .] may render the service provided by the fund less competitive than comparable services rendered by insurance companies' but 'such constraints do not prevent the activity engaged in by the fund from being regarded as an economic activity' although 'they might justify the exclusive right of such a body to manage a supplementary pension scheme'.[56] Although the CJEU subjected the fund to the EU competition law provisions, it also opened the door for a possible justification of a restriction of competition, with a possible application of Article 106(2) TFEU.

The CJEU arrived at a similar conclusion in *AG2R Prévoyance v Beaudout Père et Fils SARL*.[57] In France, reimbursement of the costs incurred in the event of illness or accident is covered in part by the basic social security scheme and the portion of the costs which remains payable by the insured party may be reimbursed in part by a supplementary health insurance scheme. Persons employed within a given occupational sector may join such a supplementary scheme pursuant to a sectoral agreement or a collective agreement signed by the employers' and employees' respective representatives. The case was initiated by a bakery which had refused to join the compulsory scheme for supplementary reimbursement of healthcare costs offered by AG2R in respect of the traditional bakery sector in France. The question was raised whether AG2R was exercising an economic activity and thus an undertaking subject to EU competition law provisions.

The CJEU noted that AG2R was a non-profit-making legal person which was governed by private law and had as its object to insure all employees of the sector, irrespective of the risk to be covered, in consideration of a single rate of contribution borne equally by the employer and the employee, irrespective of the size of the undertaking or the remuneration of the employee insured, thus finding that AG2R followed a social objective. However, the CJEU also held that '[. . .] the social aim of an insurance scheme is not in itself sufficient to preclude the activity

56 Case C-67/96, *Albany International BV v Stichting Bedrijfspensioenfonds Textielindustrie* [1999] ECR I-5751, para 86.

57 Case C-437/09, *AG2R Prévoyance v Beaudout Père et Fils SARL* [2011] ECR I-973.

in question from being classified as an economic activity' and that it is 'further necessary to examine, in particular, whether that scheme can be regarded as applying the principle of solidarity and to what extent it is subject to supervision by the State which instituted it, given that these are factors that are liable to preclude a given activity from being regarded as economic'.[58] The CJEU acknowledged that the scheme was characterized by a high degree of solidarity. However, it was also found to benefit from some autonomy from the State. An important element that influenced the Court's approach was the existence of other provident societies and insurance companies which, prior to the appointment of AG2R, offered services which were substantially identical to those provided by that body. The CJEU concluded that AG2R, although being non-profit-making and acting on the basis of the principle of solidarity, was an undertaking engaged in an economic activity. It was chosen by the social partners, on the basis of financial and economic considerations, from among other undertakings with which it was in competition on the market of the provided services.

4.2.4. SOME FURTHER ILLUSTRATIONS OF THE FUNCTIONAL APPROACH WITH REGARD TO THE CONCEPT OF UNDERTAKING AND THE QUESTION OF THE SCOPE OF COMPETITION LAW VIS-À-VIS COLLECTIVE AGREEMENTS

4.2.4.1. The employment exception and liberal professions

An employee cannot be an undertaking, as it does not exercise an autonomous economic activity, in the sense of offering goods or services on a market and bearing the financial risk attached to the performance of such activity. Hence, a labour agreement between an employer and an employee will not fall under the scope of Article 101(1) TFEU, as it will not be an agreement between 'undertakings'.[59] Could it fall under the scope of Article 102 TFEU in case the employer holds a dominant position in the relevant market?

In *Jean Claude Becu* the CJEU examined a collective labour agreement relating to dock work at the Port of Ghent, made mandatory by Royal Decree, which allowed only duly recognized dockers to perform dock work, and also made the outcome of collective bargaining between employers' and employees' representatives negotiations binding *erga omnes*. The preliminary question sent to the CJEU by the national court involved the possible application of both Articles 102 and 106(1) TFEU to the Belgian Royal Decree. The CJEU assessed if these dock workers could be considered an 'undertaking'. The CJEU held that

> [. . .] the employment relationship which recognised dockers have with the undertakings for which they perform dock work is characterised by the fact that they perform the work in question for and under the direction of each of those undertakings, so they must be regarded as 'workers' within the meaning of [Article 45 TFEU], as interpreted in the case law [. . .].

[58] Ibid, paras 45–6.

[59] See Joined Cases 40–8/73 etc, *Coöperatieve Vereniging 'Suiker Unie' UA and others v Commission* [1975] ECR 1663, para 539 (referring to the situation of an agent forming integral part of the undertaking of a principal). For a discussion, see P Nihoul, 'Do Workers Constitute Undertakings for the Purpose of the Competition Rules?' (2000) 25(4) *European L Rev* 408; C Townley, 'The Concept of "Undertaking": The Boundaries of the Corporation—A Discussion of Agency, Employees and Subdidiaries' in G Amato and C-D Ehlermann (eds) *EC Competition Law: A Critical Assessment* (Hart, 2007), 3.

> Since they are, for the duration of that relationship, incorporated into the undertakings concerned and thus form an economic unit with each of them, dockers do not therefore in themselves constitute undertakings.[60]

Note that the CJEU linked the concept of employee with that of the 'worker' under Article 45 TFEU.[61] It follows that they could not be considered as an undertaking if they were taken collectively. Often the contract of employment was for only a day or less to a particular shipowner. Of course other dockers' employment schemes may be different. The CJEU focused on the *nature* of the employment contract in this instance, but it may have reached a different characterization in a different factual context.[62]

4.2.4.1.1. Collective labour agreements between employers and employees: The Albany *exception*

The possible application of Article 101 TFEU to collective agreements concluded between trade unions and associations of employers has led to the development of an exception to the application of EU competition law, for reasons of social policy. EU competition law provides immunity from competition law to collective labour agreements concluded between associations of workers (labour unions) and employers, when two cumulative conditions

60 Case C-22/98, *Criminal proceedings against Jean Claude Becu, Annie Verweire, Smeg NV and Adia Interim NV* [1999] ECR I–5665. It is noteworthy that the situation of employees is dealt differently in the EU than in the US. In US law, all 'persons' are subject to the Sherman Act, unless they benefit from an exemption. Labour benefits from a statutory and a non-statutory exemption. The statutory labour exemption (Clayton Antitrust Act, 15 USC §§ 12–27; Norris–La Guardia Act, 29 USC §§ 101–15) enables workers to organize to eliminate competition among themselves, and to pursue their legitimate labour interests, so long as they act in their self-interest and do not combine with a non-labour group. Yet, the statutory labour exemption did not immunize the collective bargaining process or collective bargaining agreements themselves from potential antitrust liability, but covered only labour's organizations unilateral actions. The US courts thus developed the non-statutory basis of the labour exemption in order to remove from antitrust scrutiny restraints in trade that are the product of a collective bargaining agreement between labour and management (see *Local Union No 189, Amalgamated Meat Cutters & Butcher Workmen of N Am v Jewel Tea Co Inc*, 381 US 676 (1965)). These more typically apply to agreements between employees or their unions and employers when the agreements are intimately related to a mandatory subject of bargaining, and do not have 'a potential for restraining competition in the business market in ways that would not follow naturally from elimination of competition over wages and working conditions': *Connell Constr Co v Plumbers & Steamfitters Local Union No 100*, 421 US 616, 635 (1975). According to the US Supreme Court (ibid, 622),

> The non statutory exemption has its source in the strong labor policy favoring the association of employees to eliminate competition over wages and working conditions. Union success in organizing workers and standardizing wages ultimately will affect price competition among employers, but the goals of federal labour law never could be achieved if this effect on business competition were held a violation of the antitrust laws. The Court therefore has acknowledged that labour policy requires tolerance for the lessening of business competition based on differences in wages and working conditions.

Courts have even extended this immunity beyond the expiration of a collective bargaining agreement: see *Brown v NFL*, 518 US 231 (1996).The non-statutory labour exemption has been frequently applied in the field of professional sports, for instance exempting a labour agreement between the US National Football League (NFL) or the National Basketball Association (NBA) and a national union of student-athletes. For a discussion, see G Feldman, 'Antitrust versus Labor Law in Professional Sports: Balancing the Scales after *Brady v. NFL* and *Anthony v. NBA*' (2012) 45 *University of California Davis L Rev* 1221.

61 See also AG N Wahl Opinion in Case C-413/13 *FNV Kunsten Informatie en Media v Staat der Nederlanden* [2014] ECLI:EU:C:2014:2215, n 4 (using the terms 'employee' and 'worker' interchangeably).

62 C Townley, 'The Concept of "Undertaking": The Boundaries of the Corporation—A Discussion of Agency, Employees and Subdidiaries' in G Amato and C-D Ehlermann (eds) *EC Competition Law: A Critical Assessment* (Hart, 2007), 5.

are met: (i) they are entered into in the framework of collective bargaining between employers and employees and (ii) they contribute directly to improving the employment and working conditions of workers. This case law does not, however, relate to the concept of 'undertaking' as such, but mostly to that of the restriction of competition and is known as the *Albany* exception.

This exception results from the *Albany* case,[63] where the CJEU explored whether a decision taken by the organizations representing employers and workers, in the context of a collective agreement, to set up in that sector a single pension fund responsible for managing a supplementary pension scheme and to request the public authorities to make affiliation to that fund compulsory for all workers in that sector infringed Article 101(1) TFEU. Having previously concluded that the pension fund was an undertaking (see our analysis in Section 4.2.3.3), the CJEU considered if the collective agreement could nevertheless escape the scope of Article 101(1) TFEU. The case raised the important issue of how possible conflicts between competition law and the social policy provisions of the Treaties could be dealt with. Indeed, the CJEU noted that the provisions of the EU Treaties on 'employment' (now Articles 145–50 TFEU) and 'social policy' (now Articles 151–61 TFEU) promoted a close cooperation between Member States in the social field, particularly in matters relating to the right of association and collective bargaining between employers and workers, and in particular the dialogue between management and labour at European level.[64] The CJEU also noted the broader aims pursued by the EU and its Member States regarding 'improved living and working conditions, proper social protection, dialogue between management and labour, the development of human resources with a view to lasting high employment and the combatting of exclusion'.[65] On the basis of these theoretical foundations, the CJEU held the following:

> 59. It is beyond question that certain restrictions of competition are inherent in collective agreements between organisations representing employers and workers. However, the social policy objectives pursued by such agreements would be seriously undermined if management and labour were subject to Article [101(1) TFEU] when seeking jointly to adopt measures to improve conditions of work and employment.
>
> 60. It therefore follows from an interpretation of the provisions of the Treaty as a whole which is both effective and consistent that agreements concluded in the context of collective negotiations between management and labour in pursuit of such objectives must, by virtue of their nature and purpose, be regarded as falling outside the scope of Article [101(1) TFEU].

The CJEU found that, first, the collective agreement at issue was concluded in the form of a collective agreement and was the outcome of collective negotiations between organizations representing employers and workers, and second, its purpose, the establishment of a supplementary pension scheme aiming to guarantee a certain level of pension for all workers in the sector 'contributed directly to improving one of their working conditions, namely their remuneration',[66] consequently excluding this agreement from the scope of Article 101(1) TFEU.

63 Case C-67/96, *Albany International BV v Stichting Bedrijfspensioenfonds Textielindustrie* [1999] ECR I–5751.

64 Ibid, paras 55–6. 65 Ibid, para 57. 66 Ibid, paras 62–3.

4.2.4.1.1. Collective labour agreements between self-employed and employers to which they provide their services

Exercising a liberal professions has usually being found to constitute an economic activity falling under the scope of competition law if there is no relation of employment.[67] But would the *Albany* exception apply to exclude from the scope of Article 101(1) TFEU collective agreements concluded between the members of liberal professions with regard to the fixing of minimum rates or other agreements restricting competition between them, to the extent that self-employed are considered to be undertakings?[68] The CJEU has examined the categorization of an association acting on behalf of self-employed persons, and has also explored the extension of the *Albany* exception to collective agreements concluded by unions representing both employees and self-employed persons.

An association acting on behalf of self-employed persons is to be regarded as an association of undertakings

An association acting on behalf of self-employed persons is to be regarded as an association of undertakings under Article 101(1) TFEU.

Case C-309/99, *JCJ Wouters, JW Savelbergh and Price Waterhouse Belastingadviseurs BV v Algemene Raad van de Nederlandse Orde van Advocaten*, intervener: *Raad van de Balies van de Europese Gemeenschap*
[2002] ECR I–1577

In Wouters, *the CJEU examined the compatibility with Article 101 TFEU of a regulation adopted by the Netherlands Bar Association prohibiting lawyers practising in the Netherlands from entering into multi-disciplinary partnerships with members of the professional category of accountants. The CJEU examined whether the activities undertaken by self-employed lawyers could be considered to be an economic activity with the consequence that the regulation of the Netherlands Bar Association could be qualified as an association of undertakings.*

48. Members of the Bar offer, for a fee, services in the form of legal assistance consisting in the drafting of opinions, contracts and other documents and representation of clients in legal proceedings. In addition, they bear the financial risks attaching to the performance of those activities since, if there should be an imbalance between expenditure and receipts, they must bear the deficit themselves.

49. That being so, registered members of the Bar in the Netherlands carry on an economic activity and are, therefore, undertakings for the purposes of Articles [101, 102 and 106 TFEU]. The complexity and technical nature of the services they provide and the fact that the practice of their profession is regulated cannot alter that conclusion [. . .].

The CJEU then examined the extent to which a professional body such as the Bar of the Netherlands is to be regarded as an association of undertakings, within the meaning of

67 See, for instance, self-employed accountants (Case C-1/12, *Ordem dos Técnicos Oficiais de Contas*, ECLI:EU:C:2013:127), pharmacists (Case T-23/09, *CNOP & CCG v Commission* [2010] ECR II–5291), medical doctors (Joined Cases C-180–4/98, *Pavel Pavlov and Others v Stichting Pensioenfonds Medische Specialisten* [2000] ECR I–6451), and musicians (Case C-413/13, *FNV Kunsten Informatie en Media*, ECLI:EU:C:2014:2411).

68 See Joined Cases C-180–4/98, *Pavel Pavlov and Others v Stichting Pensioenfonds Medische Specialisten* [2000] ECR I–6451; *Belgian Architects Association* (Case 2005/8/CE) Commission Decision [2005] OJ L 4/10.

Article 101(1) TFEU where it exercises some regulatory function, as in this case, the Bar of the Netherlands being a body governed by public law and given by it regulatory powers in order to perform a task in the public interest. The CJEU noted:

> 57. According to the case-law of the Court, the Treaty rules on competition do not apply to activity which, by its nature, its aim and the rules to which it is subject does not belong to the sphere of economic activity [. . .], or which is connected with the exercise of the powers of a public authority [. . .].
>
> 58. When it adopts a regulation such as the 1993 Regulation, a professional body such as the Bar of the Netherlands is neither fulfilling a social function based on the principle of solidarity, unlike certain social security bodies [. . .], nor exercising powers which are typically those of a public authority [. . .]. It acts as the regulatory body of a profession, the practice of which constitutes an economic activity.
>
> 59. In that respect, the fact that Article 26 of the Advocatenwet also entrusts the General Council with the task of protecting the rights and interests of members of the Bar cannot *a priori* exclude that professional organisation from the scope of application of Article [101 TFEU], even where it performs its role of regulating the practice of the profession of the Bar.

The CJEU also noted other indications supporting the conclusion that a professional organization with regulatory powers, such as the Bar of the Netherlands, cannot escape the application of Article 101 TFEU.

> 61. First, it is clear from the Advocatenwet that the governing bodies of the Bar are composed exclusively of members of the Bar elected solely by members of the profession. The national authorities may not intervene in the appointment of the members of the Supervisory Boards, College of Delegates or the General Council [. . .].
>
> 62. Second, when it adopts measures such as the 1993 Regulation, the Bar of the Netherlands is not required to do so by reference to specified public-interest criteria. Article 28 of the Advocatenwet, which authorises it to adopt regulations, does no more than require that they should be in the interest of the proper practice of the profession [. . .].
>
> 63. Lastly, having regard to its influence on the conduct of the members of the Bar of the Netherlands on the market in legal services, as a result of its prohibition of certain multi-disciplinary partnerships, the 1993 Regulation does not fall outside the sphere of economic activity.

The CJEU concluded that such a regulation constitutes the expression of the intention of the delegates of the members of a profession that they should act in a particular manner in carrying on their economic activity and found 'immaterial' that the constitution of the Bar of the Netherlands was regulated by public law, the classification given by the various national legal systems, being irrelevant as far as the applicability of the EU rules on competition is concerned. The Court stated that for professionals to be members of both professions would have benefits for some consumers, who want tax certificates as well as legal advice, so the bar rule did restrict competition, but was justified because the control of lawyers was a matter for national law.

Collective agreements concluded by trade unions also representing self-employed

In its most recent case law, the CJEU has taken a more circumspect view of the implications for the scope of EU competition law of the distinction between workers and self-employed persons, suggesting that the effective scope of EU competition law with regard to the self-regulation by the social partners of labour relations may be less based on categorical distinctions between workers and self-employed than on their conceptualization as a *continuum* going from situations of complete dependence (in which case the relation will be considered as akin to employment) to a situation of complete independence (in which case the entity in question will be considered as an independent undertaking).

The case raised the crucial question of the scope of competition law in view of the changing nature of labour relationships in today's 'gig' or 'collaborative' economy and the collapse of the traditional binary divide between employment and self-employment.[69] It also raised important questions as to the optimal boundaries between competition law and labour law, and the possible extension of the workers' protection to the 'new jobs', a politically sensitive issue.[70]

Case C-413/13, *FNV Kunsten Informatie en Media*, ECLI:EU:C:2014:2411

In 2006 and 2007, the Dutch musician's union (FNV) representing contractual and self-employed workers in the performing arts sector (Dutch law allowing trade unions to represent both workers and self-employed persons) and an association representing orchestras in the Netherlands (employers' association) concluded a collective labour agreement relating to musicians substituting for members of an orchestra which included a minimum fees not only for substitutes hired under an employment contract ('the employed substitutes'), but also for substitutes having a freelance status and therefore not regarded as 'employees' ('self-employed substitutes'). The Dutch NCA objected to this arrangement, considering that a collective labour agreement laying down minimum fees for self-employed substitutes was not excluded from the scope of Dutch and EU competition law and was essentially a price-fixing scheme. As a result, the employer's and the employees' associations terminated the collective labour agreement and refused to conclude a fresh agreement containing a provision on minimum fees for self-employed substitutes. The FNV brought the case to the Dutch courts, seeking a declaration that a provision of a collective labour agreement to require the employer to adhere to minimum fees for employed and self-employed substitutes was not contrary to Netherlands or EU competition law, the Hague Court of appeal eventually deciding to send preliminary questions to the CJEU.

In his Opinion, Advocate General Wahl noted that in Albany and subsequent cases, the CJEU has limited the scope of Article 101(1) TFEU for collective agreements 'only if two cumulative *conditions are met: (i) they are entered into in the framework of collective bargaining between employers and employees and (ii) they contribute directly to improving the employment and working conditions of workers'.*[71] *The AG further noted that self-employed are not covered by the TFEU provisions relating to employment or social policy and that self-employed may fall within the competences of the EU under 'industrial policy' under Article 173 TFEU, which does not encourage the self-employed to conclude collective agreements with a view*

69 For a useful discussion, from a labour law but also an economic perspective, see MR Freedland and N Kountouris, *The Legal Construction of Personal Work Relations* (OUP, 2011); N Kountouris, 'The Concept of "Worker" in European Labour Law: Fragmentation, Autonomy and Scope' (2017) 47(2) *Industrial LJ* 192; A Stewart and J Stanford, 'Regulating Work in the Gig Economy: What are the Options?' (2017) 28(3) *Economic and Labour Relations Rev* 420.

70 See, most recently, European Parliament, The Social Protection of Workers in the Platform Economy: Study for the EMPL Committee (November 2017), 11, available at www.europarl.europa.eu/RegData/etudes/STUD/2017/614184/IPOL_STU(2017)614184_EN.pdf (finding that 'the greater the level of financial dependence [of the labourer] on platform work, the lower the access that workers have to social protections').

71 Opinion of AG Wahl in Case C-413/13, *FNV Kunsten Informatie en Media v Staat der Nederlanden*, ECLI:EU:C:2014:2215, para 24 (emphasis in the original).

to improving their working conditions.[72] *The AG then went on to emphasize the binary divide between workers and self-employed that had served as the foundation of delimiting the scope of competition law in labour relations:*

> 44. One of the key features of any employment relationship is the *subordination* of the worker to his employer. The employer is not only empowered to give instructions and direct the activities of his employees, but he may also exercise certain powers of authority and control over them. A self-employed person follows the instructions of his customers but, generally speaking, they do not wield extensive powers of supervision over him. Because of the absence of a subordinate relationship, the self-employed person has more independence when choosing the type of work and tasks to be executed, the manner in which that work or those tasks are to be performed, his working hours and place of work, as well as the members of his staff.
>
> 45. Furthermore, a self-employed person must assume the commercial and financial risks of the business, whereas a worker normally does not bear any such risk, being entitled to remuneration for the work provided irrespective of the performance of the business. It is the employer who, in principle, is responsible towards the outer world for the activities carried out by his employees within the framework of their work relationship. The higher risks and responsibilities borne by the self-employed are, on the other hand, meant to be compensated by the possibility of retaining all profit generated by the business.
>
> 46. Lastly, it is barely necessary to point out that, while self-employed persons offer goods or services on the market, workers merely offer their labour to one (or, on rare occasions, more) particular employer(s).
>
> 47. Thus, it is inherent in the status of being self-employed that, at least if compared with workers, self-employed persons enjoy more independence and flexibility. In return, however, they inevitably have to bear more economic risks and will often find themselves in more unstable and uncertain working relationships. All these aspects seem to be closely interrelated.
>
> 48. Therefore, the legal and economic reasons which justify the Albany exception are not valid in the case of self-employed persons. This is why a complete and *a priori* exclusion from the scope of Article 101 TFEU for collective agreements negotiated on behalf of and in the interests of the self-employed is inconceivable to me.

That said, the AG, recognized that 'in today's economy, the distinction between the traditional categories of worker and self-employed person is at times somewhat blurred' and that 'there are some self-employed persons who, in terms of their professional relationship with actual or potential customers, are in a position rather similar to that typically existing between a worker and his employer', noting in particular the lack of independence, their 'weak position at the negotiating table' and the situation of 'false self-employed', that is employees disguised as self-employed to avoid the full implementation of the relevant labour regulation.[73] *Noting that self-employed are a notoriously vast and heterogeneous group, some welcoming minimum tariffs, others not, and that trade unions represent only a limited number of the self-employed, he concluded against 'a complete and a priori assimilation of the two categories of economic actors' and therefore against the outright exclusion of collective agreements concluded by self-employed from the scope of EU competition law.*[74]

The AG then went on to examine the second condition for the application of the Albany exception, stating that collective agreements contribute directly to improving the employment and working conditions of workers. Although he noted that the collective agreement in

[72] Ibid, para 40. [73] Ibid, paras 51–2. [74] Ibid, paras 58 and 65.

question did not deal with remuneration, working hours, annual leave, pensions, insurance, or health-care, which are 'at the very heart of collective negotiations', he accepted that 'preventing social dumping is an objective that can be legitimately pursued by a collective agreement containing rules affecting self-employed persons and that it may also constitute one of the core subjects of negotiation'.[75] *The AG highlighted the complexity of the issue as the national courts need each time to examine, not abstractly, but* in concreto *whether a collective agreement has been entered into for the benefit of the labourers and aims to improve employment or working conditions directly, or whether alternatively 'it is primarily intended to restrict competition between self-employed persons and should consequently fall outside the scope of the Albany exception'. He suggested the national courts to assess: (i) 'if there exists a real and serious risk of social dumping, and, if so, whether the provisions in question are necessary to prevent such dumping', and (ii) 'to investigate the scope and thrust of the provisions in question, that is to say, whether they go beyond what would seem to be necessary to achieve the objective of preventing social dumping',*[76] *insisting that 'the notion of direct improvement of the employment and working conditions of employees must not be too narrowly construed'.*[77]

The CJEU examined whether the nature and purpose of the collective agreement in question enable it to be included in collective negotiations between employers and employees and justify its exclusion, as regards minimum fees for self-employed substitutes, from the scope of Article 101(1) TFEU. The Court first noted that 'although they perform the same activities as employees', service providers such as the substitutes at issue in the main proceedings, should, in principle, be considered as 'undertakings' within the meaning of Article 101(1) TFEU and that an association representing these self-employed in collective negotiations 'does not act as a trade union association and therefore as a social partner, but, in reality, acts as an association of undertakings'.[78] *It also noted that the TFEU does not promote an open dialogue between self-employed and employers to which they provide services.*

> 30. In those circumstances, it follows that a provision of a collective labour agreement, such as that at issue in the main proceedings, in so far as it was concluded by an employees' organisation in the name, and on behalf, of the self-employed services providers who are its members, does not constitute the result of a collective negotiation between employers and employees, and cannot be excluded, by reason of its nature, from the scope of Article 101(1) TFEU.
>
> 31. That finding cannot, however, prevent such a provision of a collective labour agreement from being regarded also as the result of dialogue between management and labour if the service providers, in the name and on behalf of whom the trade union negotiated, are in fact 'false self-employed', that is to say, service providers in a situation comparable to that of employees.
>
> 32. [. . .] [I]n today's economy it is not always easy to establish the status of some self-employed contractors as 'undertakings', such as the substitutes at issue in the main proceedings.
>
> 33. As far as concerns the case in the main proceedings, it must be recalled that, according to settled case-law, on the one hand, a service provider can lose his status of an independent trader, and hence of an undertaking, if he does not determine independently his own conduct on the market, but is entirely dependent on his principal, because he does not bear any of the financial or commercial risks arising out of the latter's activity and operates as an auxiliary within the principal's undertaking (see, to that effect, judgment in *Confederación Española de Empresarios de Estaciones de Servicio*, EU:C:2006:784, paragraphs 43 and 44).

75 Ibid, paras 72–9. 76 Ibid, paras 89 and 92. 77 Ibid, para 99.

78 Case C-413/13, *FNV Kunsten Informatie en Media v Staat der Nederlanden*, ECLI:EU:C:2014:2411, paras 27–8.

34. On the other hand, the term 'employee' for the purpose of EU law must itself be defined according to objective criteria that characterise the employment relationship, taking into consideration the rights and responsibilities of the persons concerned. In that connection, it is settled case-law that the essential feature of that relationship is that for a certain period of time one person performs services for and under the direction of another person in return for which he receives remuneration [. . .].

35. From that point of view, the Court has previously held that the classification of a 'self-employed person' under national law does not prevent that person being classified as an employee within the meaning of EU law if his independence is merely notional, thereby disguising an employment relationship [. . .].

36. It follows that the status of 'worker' within the meaning of EU law is not affected by the fact that a person has been hired as a self-employed person under national law, for tax, administrative or organisational reasons, as long as that persons acts under the direction of his employer as regards, in particular, his freedom to choose the time, place and content of his work [. . .] does not share in the employer's commercial risks [. . .] and, for the duration of that relationship, forms an integral part of that employer's undertaking, so forming an economic unit with that undertaking [. . .].

37. In the light of those principles, in order that the self-employed substitutes concerned in the main proceedings may be classified, not as 'workers' within the meaning of EU law, but as genuine 'undertakings' within the meaning of that law, it is for the national court to ascertain that, apart from the legal nature of their works or service contract, those substitutes do not find themselves in the circumstances set out in paragraphs 33 to 36 above and, in particular, that their relationship with the orchestra concerned is not one of subordination during the contractual relationship, so that they enjoy more independence and flexibility than employees who perform the same activity, as regards the determination of the working hours, the place and manner of performing the tasks assigned, in other words, the rehearsals and concerts.

38. As regards, second, the purpose of the collective labour agreement at issue in the main proceedings, it must be held that the analysis [. . .] would be justified, on that point, only if the referring court were to classify the substitutes involved in the main proceedings not as 'undertakings' but as 'false self-employed'.

39. That being said, it must be held that the minimum fees scheme put in place by the provision in Annex 5 to the collective labour agreement directly contributes to the improvement of the employment and working conditions of those substitutes, classified as 'false self-employed'.

40. Such a scheme not only guarantees those service providers basic pay higher than they would have received were it not for that provision but also, as found by the referring court, enables contributions to be made to pension insurance corresponding to participation in the pension scheme for workers, thereby guaranteeing them the means necessary to be eligible in future for a certain level of pension.

41. Accordingly, a provision of a collective labour agreement, in so far as it sets minimum fees for service providers who are 'false self-employed', cannot, by reason of its nature and purpose, be subject to the scope of Article 101(1) TFEU.

NOTES AND QUESTIONS ON FNV

1. Are you convinced by the approach put forward by the Advocate General? From an interpretive perspective, should he have insisted that much on the differences between self-employed and workers, or should he have also explored if there are functional similarities between the two categories, for instance in situations when these hold weak bargaining position vis-à-vis employers (or principal business partners)?

2. Note that the CJEU has maintained the distinction between self-employed and employees, but has at the same time indicated that these broader categories are quite complex and should not necessarily lead to the implications with regard to the scope of Article 101(1) TFEU before at least some *in concreto* analysis. The CJEU provides definitions for the situations of 'genuine' undertaking and 'workers' but also holds that the classification of a 'self-employed person' under national law does not prevent that person being classified as an employee within the meaning of EU law if his independence is merely notional, thereby disguising an employment relationship.
3. The CJEU seems therefore to establish an intermediary category, that of 'false self-employed', in which case collective agreements setting minimum fees may, by reason 'of their nature and purpose', benefit from an immunity from Article 101(1) TFEU. The Court is open to the possibility that Article 101(1) TFEU will not apply to collective agreements involving 'false self-employed' on the basis that its established jurisprudence accepts that 'a service provider can lose his status of an independent trader, and hence of an undertaking, if he does not determine independently his own conduct on the market, but is entirely dependent on his principal, because he does not bear any of the financial or commercial risks arising out of the latter's activity and operates as an auxiliary within the principal's undertaking' (para 33 of *FNV Kunsten*). Note the similarity of language used in this context and that for the immunity under Article 101(1) TFEU of genuine commercial agency agreements (see Section 10.4.1.2.). Such flexible approach on the distinction between employed and self-employed can also be found in the context of the case law on Free Movement of Workers: see Case C-256/01, *Debra Allonby v Accrington & Rossendale College*, ECLI:EU:C:2004:18, para 71, where the CJEU held that the formal classification of a 'self-employed person' under national law 'does not exclude the possibility that a person must be classified as a worker [...] if his independence is merely notional, thereby disguising an employment relationship'.
4. Does the CJEU follow a similar approach as that in *Albany*? Although the CJEU noted that the Treaty provisions do not promote dialogue between management and self-employed, it has not made any effort to integrate in implementing Article 101(1) TFEU public policy concerns in the same way the CJEU has done in *Albany*. The CJEU could have made reference to the economic and social rights proclaimed by the EU Charter, in particular those referred to in Chapter IV on solidarity (including Article 28 on collective bargaining), applied by analogy to situations of self-employed that have a weak bargaining position, functionally similar to that of workers. The CJEU could have also referred to Article 9 TFEU, according to which '[i]n defining and implementing its policies and activities, the Union shall take into account requirements linked to the promotion of a high level of employment, the guarantee of adequate social protection, the fight against social exclusion [. . .]', by ensuring that Article 101(1) TFEU is interpreted (shown) in its 'best light',[79] in coherence with the principles and values uncovered and articulated in the broader EU's norms, practices, and means of action.
5. Note that the EU Charter of Fundamental Rights (and its binding effect) was adopted after the CJEU's judgment in *Albany* and the horizontal social clause of Article 9 TFEU was included with the Lisbon Treaty in 2009 with no direct predecessor in the EC Treaties, this inclusion being understood in the context of the model of 'social market

[79] This standard requires that the judge proceeds to the most desirable interpretation of the legal text according to the fundamental principles of morality inherent in the law so that the law is congruent to morality and the legal interpretation is morally justified. See R Dworkin, *Law's Empire* (Belknap Press of Harvard University Press, 1986).

economy' enshrined in Article 3(3) TEU. Note that the case law of the CJEU has already accepted that both Article 9 TFEU and Article 3(3) TEU can play a fundamental role in expanding the Court's understanding of the social policy justification: see, Case C-201/15, *Anonymi Geniki Etairia Tsimenton Iraklis (AGET Iraklis) v Ypourgos Ergasias*, ECLI:EU:C:2016:972, paras 76 and 78.

6. A different explanation of the CJEU's approach is that the Court thought that the all or nothing approach of the antitrust immunity, had it chosen the same interpretive approach as in *Albany*, was inferior to a balancing approach that would have engaged with these public interest concerns about social precariat and the economic dependence of the freelancers when assessing the existence of a restriction of competition and an infringement of Article 101(1) TFEU.[80] Assess the advantages and disadvantages of each approach.
7. A recent judgment of the UK Employment Appeal Tribunal (UKEAT) regarding the employment status of Uber drivers presents an interesting example of a functional approach that could have also been adopted in the *FNV* case.[81] The UKEAT rejected the label of agency used in the written contract between Uber and the drivers and qualified them as employees, although the drivers incurred commercial risks as they were responsible for all costs incidental to owning and running the vehicle, and were also able to work for or through other organizations, including direct competitors with Uber operating through digital platforms. The UKEAT arrived at this conclusion by adopting a purposive interpretation, taking into account the relative bargaining power of the parties, the integration of Uber drivers into Uber's business, in particular as, among other things, they were prevented from building up a business relationship with the end user of the service, they were in practice obliged to accept all trip requests if they wanted to keep their account status, and Uber held a significant market share in London, which left them no other equally effective competitive alternative.

4.2.4.2. Public bodies

Public law entities may be considered as 'undertakings' and thus subject to the competition law provisions of the Treaty (Articles 101, 102, 106, and 107 TFEU). This is certainly the case if the public services provided by these public bodies are open to the private and voluntary sector. In some cases, public services that were not open to the private and voluntary sector were, however, found to constitute economic activities and thus subject to competition law. In the UK, the aspiration currently is that public services are open to the private and voluntary, community and social enterprise sector and thus to competition. The White Paper *Open Public Services* adopted by the previous coalition government noted that '[a]part from those public services where the Government has a special reason to operate a monopoly (e.g. the military) every public service should be open so that, in line with peoples demands, services can be delivered by a diverse range of providers'.[82] In such context, it is possible that public bodies may be found to exercise an economic activity and thus subject to the competition law

80 See our discussion in Chapter 6 about *Wouters, Meca Medina*, and subsequent case law.

81 *Uber BV and Others v Mr Y Aslam and Others*, UKEAT/0056/17/DA, Employment Appeal Tribunal judgment of Judge Eady, 10 November 2017.

82 Government, *Open Public Services*—White Paper, Cm8145, July 2011, available at <https://www.gov.uk/government/publications/open-public-services-white-paper>.

provisions of the Treaty. Indeed, the simple fact that the activity is also exercised by private entities, or could be exercised by private entities, with whom the public body will be in competition is sufficient to characterize the activity as economic.[83] However, activities that 'could not conceivably be carried out for profit by a private sector body may be wholly social' and thus not constitute an economic activity.[84] Furthermore, even if 'public bodies do act as undertakings, there may be certain limited circumstances in which their conduct may fall within the scope of a specific exclusion from competition law provided for in the relevant UK and/or EU legislation'.[85] We will discuss the implications of the competitive architecture of the UK system for the provision of public services for the enforcement of competition law in the healthcare sector in the following section.

In case a government has opted for the provision of public services through the sole intervention of a State monopoly, thus not opting to open the provision of public services to the private or the voluntary sector, the question would arise if such public body could be considered as exercising an economic activity and thus falling within the scope of the competition law provisions of the Treaty. The crucial element here would be to examine if the public body in question exercises an activity that may fall under the two categories of non-economic activity, that is, the regulatory function and the solidarity function. If this is the case, the activity will not be considered as economic and the public body will not be qualified as an undertaking. If the public body does not fall within these two categories, then it is considered as an undertaking and competition law may apply, eventually compromising the Member State's choice for a regime of the provision of such public service by a State monopoly and the closed public service model. The following case provides a useful illustration.

Case C-41/90, *Höfner and Elser v Macrotron*
[1991] ECR I–1979

*The German Federal Office of Employment (*Bundesanstalt für Arbeit*), a public body, possessed a statutory monopoly on placing employees with employers. However, German law also allowed the* Bundesanstalt *after consulting with workers and employers associations to entrust other institutions or people with employment procurement services under its supervision. As a result of this practice, a number of business executive private recruitment businesses developed, such as the one operated by Mr Höfner and Mr Elser. Their private recruitment agency had placed a candidate as a sales director with a company called Macrotron GmbH. In the context of a contractual dispute between Mr Höfner and Mr Elser and Macrotron GmbH, Macrotron argued that the contract was void under German law, because it breached the statutory monopoly of the Bundesanstalt in Germany. Mr Höfner and Mr Elser challenged the statutory provision declaring the contract void arguing that this was incompatible with EU competition law. The German court found that as the contract infringed a statutory provision it should be considered void but sent a preliminary question to the CJEU with regard to the possibility that the* Bundesanstalt *had committed an abuse of a dominant position incompatible with what is now Articles 102 and 106 TFEU. The CJEU examined if the* Bundesanstalt *could be considered as an undertaking.*

---

83 See OFT 1389, *Public Bodies and Competition Law* (December 2011), paras 2.17–2.18.

84 See ibid, paras 2.23–2.24. This category of 'social' and thus non-economic activity is extended to redistributive activities 'carried out according to principles of "solidarity"', which in some cases may be wholly social. See ibid, paras 2.25–2.27.

85 See ibid, para 3.1.

20. Having regard to the foregoing considerations, it is necessary to establish whether a public employment agency such as the Bundesanstalt may be regarded as an undertaking within the meaning of Articles [101] and [102 TFEU].

21. It must be observed, in the context of competition law, first that the concept of an undertaking encompasses every entity engaged in an economic activity, regardless of the legal status of the entity and the way in which it is financed and, secondly, that employment procurement is an economic activity.

22. The fact that employment procurement activities are normally entrusted to public agencies cannot affect the economic nature of such activities. Employment procurement has not always been, and is not necessarily, carried out by public entities. That finding applies in particular to executive recruitment.

23. It follows that an entity such as a public employment agency engaged in the business of employment procurement may be classified as an undertaking for the purpose of applying the Community competition rules.

24. It must be pointed out that a public employment agency which is entrusted, under the legislation of a Member State, with the operation of services of general economic interest [. . .] remains subject to the competition rules pursuant to Article [106(2) TFEU] unless and to the extent to which it is shown that their application is incompatible with the discharge of its duties (see judgment in Case 155/73 *Sacchi* [1974] ECR 409).

NOTES AND QUESTIONS ON HÖFNER

1. (Paragraph 22) Does the CJEU refer to the fact that in Germany private recruitment agents were offering the same services in order to infer the 'economic nature' of such activities? Do you think that the CJEU would have arrived at the same conclusion in case the *Bundesanstalt* had effectively implemented the statutory monopoly from which it benefitted, by taking action to prohibit other entities to provide such services? Or, does the CJEU refer to the situation in other Member States in order to conclude that employment procurement is an economic activity? The second approach would have limited the discretion of each Member State to opt for the constitution of a public monopoly.
2. The CJEU found that Macrotron, which was considered as an undertaking, had abused its dominant position by the simple fact that the German State had granted it an exclusive right extending to executive recruitment activities, while manifestly not being in a position to satisfy the demand prevailing on the market for activities of that kind, the CJEU finding that this automatically limited the provision of a service, to the prejudice of those seeking to avail themselves of it.[86] Do you think the CJEU's judgment as to the existence of an economic activity may have been influenced by the fact that the public body in question was not able to satisfy demand? What is the legitimacy of the EU intervention through competition law to 'correct' a failure of the government of the Member State to design an efficient regime for the provision of public services (efficient being here defined as one that corresponds to the demand for such public services)?

   The Lisbon Treaty, which entered into force in December 2009, includes a Protocol No 26 on Services of General Interest, at its Annex, in order to emphasize the importance of services of general interest. The Protocol affirms that 'the provisions of the Treaties do not affect in any way the competence of Member States to provide,

[86] Case C-41/90, *Höfner and Elser v Macrotron* [1991] ECR I–1979, para 31.

commission and organize non-economic services of general interest'. It should thus be possible for a Member State to exclude certain services not contributing any economic, commercial and industrial character from the scope of competition law, with the exception of cases in which the activity is pursued in a competitive environment, which implies that it possesses economic (commercial) characteristics.[87]

The Protocol also includes some important interpretative provisions with regard to services of general economic interest (SGEI), that is, services that are considered as forming an economic activity, which are subject to the scope of EU competition law provisions. Article 14 TFEU already recognized the role of SGEI in the 'shared values of the Union' and provided that Member States 'shall take care that such services operate on the basis of principles and conditions, particularly economic and financial conditions, which enable them to fulfill their missions'. Nevertheless, Protocol No 26 also adds the need to take into account diversity among various services of general economic interest because of the 'differences in the needs and preferences of users that may result from different geographical, social or cultural situations'. This also implies that national, regional and local authorities have a wide discretion in providing, commissioning and organizing SGEI closer to the needs of their citizens, as well as the need to ensure 'a high level of quality, safety and affordability, equal treatment and the promotion of universal access and of user rights'. Hence, services of general interest are immune from competition law, as long as they are not service of general *economic* interest. Member States are free, from a competition law perspective, to opt for a public monopoly. If they constitute a service of general economic interest, then they may be subject to competition law, although Member States are recognized some discretion. Do you think that if the facts of the *Höfner* case occurred after Protocol No 26 entered in force, would the approach followed by the CJEU have been different?

3. In a recent decision in the State aid sector, the Commission explored the distinction between services of general interest and services of general economic interest, although it did not cite Protocol No 26.[88] The case concerned a complaint concerning alleged aid granted by the Dutch authorities for the creation and introduction of the electronic procurement ('e-procurement') platform TenderNed by competing e-procurement platforms in The Netherlands. The market for e-procurement platforms gradually took shape within the Union, with commercial offers developed in the Netherlands by eight companies which provided some e-procurement services for free, while charging for others. Following the revision of the EU public procurement regulatory framework in 2014, which pushed for the organization of e-procurement services, the Dutch Ministry of Economic Affairs, Agriculture, and Innovation established the TenderNed platform which aimed at supporting the public procurement process from the publication of the notice to the award of the contract. Exclusive publication rights were granted to TenderNed, the Dutch government promoted all of TenderNed's activities and also provided funding for it.

   The complainants alleged that the financing of TenderNed constituted unlawful and incompatible State aid and that the exclusive publication rights constituted an abuse of a dominant position. The complainants alleged that TenderNed was an undertaking

87 See Joined Cases C-223 & 260/99, *Agorà Srl and Excelsior Snc di Pedrotti Bruna & C v EnteAutonomo Fiera Internazionale di Milano and Ciftat Soc coop arl* [2001] ECR I–3605.

88 *The Netherlands E-procurement platform TenderNed*, State aid SA.34646 (2014/NN) (ex 2012/CP)—C(2014) 9548 final.

within the meaning of Article 107(1) TFEU as it offered services on the market in competition with services of third parties such as those offered by them, while TenderNed advanced that it was an SGEI not subject to the competition law provisions of the Treaty.

Remarkably, the Commission agreed with TenderNed and found that this did not constitute an undertaking. The Commission rejected the complainants' argument that the market already provided for the services TenderNed offered and thus it should be considered an undertaking, following closely the CJEU approach in *Höfner*. The Commission disagreed, observing that such approach 'does not adequately take into consideration the progressive evolution and availability of e-Procurement' and, more importantly that 'the State does not forego the right to carry out an activity that it deems necessary to ensure its public bodies comply with their statutory obligations by acting at a point in time when private operators—perhaps due to lack of prior action by the State—have already taken the initiative to offer services to the same end'.[89] Indeed, for the Commission, 'ensuring public authorities comply with their statutory obligations by channelling public procurement may be an economic activity for the complainants' yet, '[i]t is not, however, an inherent economic activity, but rather a service of general interest, which can be commercially exploited only so long as the State fails to offer that service itself'.[90] The Commission concluded that TenderNed was exercising a service of general interest, not an economic activity, and thus did not constitute an undertaking, finding that there was no State aid[91].

With which approach do you agree the most: that followed by the CJEU in *Höfner* or that adopted by the Commission in its TenderNed decision? What could be the implications of the Commission's approach to the discretion of Member States to organize the provision of public services?

4.2.4.3. Non-profit entities

The absence of a profit-motive does not mean that the entity does not exercise an economic activity. Sports associations have been found to exercise an economic activity and thus to be an undertaking. In *Distribution of Package Tours during the 1990 World Cup*, the Commission held that FIFA, the international governing body of football/soccer and the Italian Football Association were undertakings.[92] The CJEU recognized in *Albany* that the fact that a body is intended to be non-profit making will not, of itself, be sufficient to deprive it of its status as an undertaking.[93] Charities can thus be subject to competition law, when they exercise an economic activity. Agricultural cooperatives are also falling within the scope of EU competition law.[94] A similar situation prevails in the UK, where Chapter I CA98 has been notoriously applied to fifty fee-paying independent schools which had engaged in the exchange of specific

89 Ibid, para 68. 90 Ibid.

91 The decision was confirmed by the GC in Case T-138/15, *Aanbestedingskalender BV and Others v Commission*, ECLI:EU:T:2017:675, paras 57–8. The GC found relevant the fact that 'when contracting authorities initiate a procurement procedure and comply with the procurement rules, they are acting as public authorities' and the fact that these were non-profit-making, although it also noted that the last factor is 'not sufficient' for the purpose of determining whether or not an activity is of an economic nature.

92 *Distribution of Package Tours during the 1990 World Cup*, [1992] OJ L 326/31.

93 Case C-67/96, *Albany International BV v Stichting Bedrijfspensioenfonds Textielindustrie* [1999] ECR I-5751, para 79

94 Case 61/80, *Coöperatieve Stremsel- en Kleurselfabriek v Commission* [1981] ECR 851.

information regarding future pricing intentions on the intended fees and fee increases for both boarding and day pupils on a regular and systematic basis. The schools were all non-profit making charitable bodies.[95] Both EU and UK competition law thus do not make any distinction between altruistic entities and entities motivated by profits, as in both cases it is possible that the specific conduct reduces competition and/or welfare regardless of the motives and preferences of the producers.[96]

4.2.5. EXCLUSIONS—SPECIFIC REGIMES

Even if an entity is considered as an undertaking, there are limited circumstances in which its conduct may fall within the scope of a specific exclusion from competition law.

Although there is no proper 'exclusion' to the application of EU competition law for entities engaging in economic activities, Article 346(1)(b) TFEU allows Member States to take measures they consider necessary for the protection of their essential security interests in connection with the production of/trade in arms, munitions, and war material. Measures taken under Article 346(1)(b) may nevertheless not adversely affect competition on the common market for products not specifically intended for military purposes. The Council has drawn up a list of the products to which Article 346(1) applies.

Certain sectors are subject to a specific regime. Article 42 provides that the 'rules on competition shall apply to production of and trade in agricultural products only to the extent determined by the European Parliament and the Council', thus enabling the political power to override through the adoption of a specific regulation the normal application of competition law in this sector. Subsequent legislation excluded certain types of practices from the scope of specific provisions of EU competition law. Regulation 1184/2006 provides that Articles 101 and 102 TFEU apply to the production of or trade in the products listed in Annex I of the TFEU, subject to certain specific derogations.[97] For instance, Article 2 of Regulation 1184/2006 provides that Article 101(1) TFEU shall not apply to agreements that form an integral part of a national market organization or which are necessary for the attainment of the objectives set out in Article 39 TFEU. These are to increase agricultural productivity, to ensure a fair share standard of living for the agricultural community, to stabilize markets, to ensure the availability of supplies and to ensure supplies to consumers at reasonable prices. In implementing these objectives, account should be taken, according to Article 39(2) TFEU, 'the particular nature of agricultural activity, which results from the social structure of agriculture and from structural and natural disparities between the various agricultural regions'. Similarly, Regulation 1234/2007 establishes a common organization for many agricultural markets and provides that Article 101 TFEU shall not apply to agreements involving a common organization of agricultural markets (these replaced the various national marketing organizations. However, products that are not included in Annex I of the TFEU are considered as industrial products (not agricultural products) and they cannot benefit from the derogations provided for by Article 2 of Regulation 1184/2006. Practices involving such products are fully subject to competition law.[98] Furthermore, EU competition law also includes derogations for producer

95 OFT, *Exchange of information on future fees by certain independent fee-paying schools*, No CA98/05/2006.

96 See the analysis of TJ Philipson and RA Posner, 'Antitrust in the Not-for-profit Sector', National Bureau of Economic Research (2006).

97 Council Regulation (EC) No 1184/2006 applying certain rules of competition to the production of, and trade in, agricultural products [2006] OJ L 214/7.

98 See, for instance, regarding Armagnac, *Pabst and Richarz/BNIA* (Case IV/28.980) Commission Decision [1976] OJ L 231/24.

organizations, on the basis of the Common Agricultural Policy (CAP) provisions of the EU Treaties and related secondary legislation.[99] It is worthy of note that the extent of such specific regimes of immunity for agricultural cooperatives have been expanding in the EU. These exemptions aim to protect farmers from the superior bargaining power of the distributors downstream.[100]

Changes to agricultural provisions, which simplify the CAP, have recently been published in a wide-ranging 'Omnibus' EU budget reform, extending the exemptions from competition law, with the aim to strengthening the position of farmers in the supply chain, by allowing all recognized farmers' organizations to plan production and negotiate supply contracts on behalf of their members without clashing with EU competition rules.[101]

It is noteworthy that in *Président de l'Autorité de la concurrence v APVE*, the CJEU found that a number of producer organizations (POs) and associations of POs (APOs) were liable for agreements, decisions, or concerted practices contrary to EU law, although it also noted that the objectives of the CAP take precedence, under the TFEU, over the objectives of competition.[102] Therefore, certain actions taken by POs and APOs, which were strictly necessary for the fulfilment of their tasks, could escape the application of competition law.[103] The CJEU noted that for the practices to escape the application of competition law it must also be established that they were adopted within a PO/APO, which must be recognized by the Member State concerned, and charged with managing the production and marketing of the relevant product.

Important litigation has also occurred in the UK with regard to the monopoly powers of the Milk Marketing Board.[104] The Milk Marketing Board was a government agency established in 1933 to control milk production and distribution in the United Kingdom. Functioning as a buyer of last resort in the British milk market, it guaranteed a minimum price for milk

99 See Regulation (EU) No 1308/2013 of the European Parliament and of the Council of 17 December 2013 establishing a Common Organisation of the Markets in agricultural products and repealing Council Regulations (EEC) No 922/72, (EEC) No 234/79, (EC) No 1037/2001 and (EC) No 1234/2007 [2013] OJ L 347/671, Articles 169, 170 and 171 [hereinafter CMO Regulation], and the Commission Notice, Guidelines on the Application of the Specific Rules Set out in Articles 169, 170 and 181 of the CMO Regulation for the Olive Oil, beef and veal and arable crops sectors [2015] OJ C 431/1.

100 See I Lianos & C Lombardi, 'Superior Bargaining Power and the Global Food Value Chain: The Wuthering Heights of Holistic Competition Law?' (2016) 1 *Concurrences* 22.

101 These changes were introduced by the Council of the European Union in Regulation (EU) 2017/2393 of the European Parliament and of the Council [2017] OJ L 350/15 [hereinafter Omnibus Regulation]. It is noteworthy that the Commission added a statement in the Regulation regretting 'the very limited role for both the Commission and the National Competition authorities to act to preserve effective competition' as a consequence of these reforms.

102 Case C-671/15, *Président de l'Autorité de la concurrence v Association des producteurs vendeurs d'endives (APVE) and Others*, ECLI:EU:C:2017:860, paras 37–8.

103 Ibid, para 49. For instance, the CJEU considered that 'exchanges of strategic information between producers within the same PO or APO are liable to be proportionate if they are in fact made for the purposes of one or more of the objectives assigned to that PO or APO and are limited only to the information that is strictly necessary for those purposes': ibid, para 53. However, 'the collective fixing of minimum sale prices within a PO or an APO may not be considered, under the practices necessary in order to fulfil the responsibilities that have been assigned to them under the common organisation of the market concerned, to be proportionate to the objectives of stabilising prices and concentrating supply where it does not allow producers selling their own products themselves [. . .] to sell at a price below those minimum prices, since it has the effect of reducing the already low level of competition in the markets for agricultural products as a result, in particular, of the possibility given to producers to form POs and APOs in order to concentrate their supply': ibid, para 66.

104 Mainly private actions for the enforcement of Article 102 TFEU, see *Garden Cottage Foods v Milk Marketing Board* [1984] AC 130.

producers. The Milk Marketing Board was dissolved following the deregulation of the British Milk Market under the Agriculture Act 1993.[105]

Section 3 of the Competition Act 1998 provides for a number of exclusions from the Chapter I prohibition, some of which apply also to the Chapter II prohibition.

Chapter I of the Enterprise Act

Excluded agreements

3. Excluded agreements

(1) The Chapter I prohibition does not apply in any of the cases in which it is excluded by or as a result of—

(a) Schedule 1 (mergers and concentrations);[106]

(b) Schedule 2 (competition scrutiny under other enactments);[107]

(c) Schedule 3 (planning obligations and other general exclusions);[108] or

[. . .]

(2) The Secretary of State may at any time by order amend Schedule 1, with respect to the Chapter I prohibition,[109] by—

(a) providing for one or more additional exclusions; or

(b) amending or removing any provision (whether or not it has been added by an order under this subsection).

(3) The Secretary of State may at any time by order amend Schedule 3, with respect to the Chapter I prohibition, by—

(a) providing for one or more additional exclusions; or

(b) amending or removing any provision—

(i) added by an order under this subsection; or

(ii) included in paragraph 1, 2, 8 or 9 of Schedule 3.

(4) The power under subsection (3) to provide for an additional exclusion may be exercised only if it appears to the Secretary of State that agreements which fall within the additional exclusion—

(a) do not in general have an adverse effect on competition, or

(b) are, in general, best considered under Chapter II [. . .].

105 Agriculture Act 1993, c 37.

106 This does not constitute a proper exclusion from the application of competition law, but simply provides that the prohibition of Chapter I will not apply to mergers under the Enterprise Act or to concentrations for which the European Commission has exclusive jurisdiction under the EUMR. Schedule 1 will be examined in detail in Chapter 9.

107 This exclusion refers to agreements subject to 'competition scrutiny' under a sector-specific legislation, such as the Communications Act 2003 (section 293 imposing a duty on the Office for Communications (OFCOM) to carry out general competition reviews of the networking arrangements between Independent Television Ltd and the regional Channel 3 licensees), the Financial Services and Markets Act 2000 (section 164 providing for exclusion from both Chapters I and II of the conduct or practices of an authorized person(s) or any person(s) otherwise subject to the regulating provisions to the extent to which the practices are encouraged by any of the Authority's regulating provisions; see also sections 95, 159–63, 302–6, 311–12), and the Legal Services Act 2007).

108 A summary of Schedule 3 of the Competition Act 1998 is provided subsequently in this Section.

109 This power is subject under section 71 of the Competition Act 1998 to an affirmative resolution of each House of Parliament.

(5) An order under subsection (2)(a) or (3)(a) may include provision (similar to that made with respect to any other exclusion provided by the relevant Schedule) for the exclusion concerned to cease to apply to a particular agreement.

(6) Schedule 3 also gives the Secretary of State power to exclude agreements from the Chapter I prohibition in certain circumstances.

Schedule 3 includes a series of general exclusions of the application of Chapter I and II of the Competition Act 1998 for certain types of agreements:

- Agreements involving planning obligations (Schedule 3, paragraph 1);
- Agreements for the constitution of an EEA regulated market to the extent to which the agreement relates to any of the rules made, or guidance issued, by that market (Schedule 3, paragraph 3);
- Conduct involving (an) undertaking(s) entrusted with providing 'services of general economic interest' or that are 'revenue-producing monopolies', insofar as those prohibitions would obstruct, in law or in fact, the performance of the particular tasks assigned to the undertaking(s) (this being the UK equivalent of Article 106(2) TFEU) (Schedule 3, paragraph 4). The OFT has published a Guidance on the Exclusion for Services of General Economic Interest (OFT 421, adopted by the CMA), which notes that 'although not identical' the substance of this exclusion is closely modelled on Article 106(2) TFEU. The Guidance also noted that the exclusion will be interpreted strictly and that undertakings seeking to benefit from the exclusion will have to demonstrate that all the requirements are met, thus bearing the burden of proof for the exclusion from the application of Chapters I and II of the Competition Act;
- Agreements or conduct that are/is made or engaged in with the aim to comply with a 'legal requirement' (Schedule 3, paragraph 5). 'Legal requirement' is defined as imposed by or under any enactment in force in the United Kingdom, for example, a requirement imposed by primary or secondary UK legislation or also by any directly effective EU legislation. As it is explained in the OFT Guidance on Public Bodies and Competition Law (OFT 1389, now adopted by the CMA),

  [. . .] this exclusion will be applicable in only a very limited number of circumstances. These might include, for example:

  - agreements that are entered into as a result of formal directions issued by a sector regulator,
  - or where a party is specifically required by legislation to disclose publicly certain information that would otherwise be considered competitively sensitive. Thus, the Chapter I prohibition has previously been found not to apply to a regulated undertaking's publication of its prices, insofar as such publication was mandated by the terms of its statutory licence.

  The legislation or other legal instrument must **require** (explicitly or in practice) undertakings to engage in the agreement or conduct in question. If that agreement or conduct is only encouraged or facilitated by the relevant legal instrument and the undertaking therefore retains some freedom of action, competition law will still apply.

- The Secretary of State has also the power to issue orders excluding certain categories of agreement between undertakings from the scope of the CA98, if such exclusion is necessary either to avoid conflict with international obligations or for compelling reasons of public policy. To date, only three such orders have been made, each excluding on public policy grounds narrow categories of agreement in the defence sector from the application of the CA98. Furthermore, such orders do not serve to disapply EU competition law where the agreement affects trade between EU Member States. (Schedule 3, paragraph 6).

- The Secretary of State has also the power to exclude from the application of Chapters I and II of the CA98 a particular agreement, or any agreement of a particular description, or to conduct in case there are 'exceptional and compelling reasons of public policy', either concluding that these provisions deemed never to have applied to such agreement(s)/conduct or in specific circumstances only (Schedule 3, paragraph 7).
- According to Schedule 3, paragraph 9, the Chapter I prohibition does not apply to an agreement to the extent to which it relates to production of or trade in an agricultural product and (a) forms an integral part of a national market organization and (b) is necessary for the attainment of the objectives of the Common Agricultural Policy or (c) is an agreement of farmers or farmers' associations (or associations of such associations) belonging to a single Member State which concerns the production or sale of agricultural products, or the use of joint facilities for the storage, treatment, or processing of agricultural products, and under which there is no obligation to charge identical prices. The agriculture exclusion does not apply to a particular agreement if the Director gives a direction to that effect.

4.2.6. ABSENCE OF A POSSIBILITY OF ACTUAL OR POTENTIAL COMPETITION

Even if the activity in question is economic, and the entity in question would be considered as an undertaking, thus leading to the application of the competition law provisions of the Treaty, it is still possible to avoid a finding of infringement if the alleged distortion of competition did not effectively restrict any actual or potential competition that would have existed in its absence. As the General Court explained in *E.On Ruhrgas*, for Articles 101 (and consequently, Articles 102 and 106 TFEU) to apply the sector should already be 'open to competition'. This implies, before examining the existence of a restriction of competition, the consideration of the conditions of competition in the relevant market, not only with regard to existing competition between undertakings already present, but also with regard to potential competition, in order to ascertain whether, in the light of the structure of the market and the economic and legal contexts within which it functions, there are real concrete possibilities for the specific undertakings to compete among themselves, or for a new competitor to enter the relevant market and compete with established undertakings. This finding should not be based 'on a mere hypothesis',[110] but 'supported by evidence or an analysis of the structures of the relevant market'.[111] According to the GC, '[t]he essential factor on which such a description must be based is whether [another undertaking] has the ability to enter that

[110] Case T-360/09, *E.ON Ruhrgas and E.ON v Commission*, EU:T:2012:332, paras 84–5.
[111] Ibid, para 86.

market'.[112] Hence, according to the CG, 'an undertaking cannot be described as a potential competitor if its entry into a market is not an economically viable strategy'.[113]

In this case, which involved the recently liberalized market for gas in the EU, prior to the liberalization directive, the GC distinguished between the German and the French markets for gas. With regard to the French market, it noted that the legal monopoly on the import and supply of gas which Gaz de France (GDF) had enjoyed since 1946 was abolished in 2003, although the deadline for the transposition, into national law, of the first gas directive expired on 10 August 2000. Consequently, at least until 2000, the Court found that there was no competition, even potential, on the French market for gas, leading it to the conclusion that the conduct in question 'could not, as regards that market, be covered by Article [101 TFEU]'.[114] A similar argument could be made with regard to the application of Article 102 TFEU and/or Article 106 TFEU. Following the implementation of the liberalization directive in France and the possibility of gas suppliers to penetrate the French market for eligible customers gas suppliers the GC considered that potential competition could be restricted as the market was open to competition, customers being able to change suppliers.

With regard the German market for gas, the GC noted that at least until 1998 (and the intervention of the liberalization directive), the German legislator had established a *de facto* system of areas of exclusive supply within which a single gas undertaking could supply customers with gas, although there was no legal prohibition against other companies supplying gas. The German market for gas was therefore characterised by the existence of *de facto* territorial monopolies. The GC took a similar position as in *EDP*[115] and found that 'it is clear that that situation [. . .] was likely to result in the absence of any competition, not only actual, but also potential, on that market', as 'a geographical monopoly which local gas distribution undertakings enjoyed precluded any competition between them'.[116] The fact that there was in Germany no legal monopoly was found irrelevant.[117] According to the GC, the analysis of the possibility for potential competition 'must be made on the objective basis of those possibilities, with the result that the fact that they are precluded on account of a monopoly which derives directly from national legislation or, indirectly, from the factual situation arising from the implementation of that legislation is irrelevant'.[118] The 'purely theoretical possibility' of a new competitor's entry into the market 'is not sufficient to establish the existence of such competition', as this is based 'on a mere hypothesis and does not constitute a demonstration supported by factual evidence or an analysis of the structures of the relevant market'.[119] That would be also the case even if there are neighbouring and closely connected markets (here France and Germany) or foreign companies have the 'necessary strength, resources and infrastructure to enable them to enter the market', which would have increased the chances of success of penetrating the market. According to the GC, '[s]uch general and abstract information does not serve to show that, despite the competitive situation existing in the German market for gas, GDF would have been in a position, [in the absence of the specific distortion of competition], to enter that market'.[120] The Court thus applies a counterfactual test, assessing the possibilities of competition, in the absence of the alleged restriction in question. It is only if it finds that, in the absence of the restriction in question, there would be possibilities of actual or potential competition, that it may find a competition law infringement. Furthermore, in order to be considered credible, the possibility of new entry should be done 'sufficiently quickly for the

112 Ibid, para 87. 113 Ibid. 114 Ibid, 89.

115 Case T-87/05, *EDP v Commission* [2005] ECR II–3745, para 117.

116 Case T-360/09, *E.ON Ruhrgas and E.ON v Commission*, ECLI:EU:T:2012:332, para 103.

117 Ibid, para 105. 118 Ibid. 119 Ibid, para 106. 120 Ibid, paras 107–8.

threat of a potential entry to influence the conduct of the participants in the market', or on the basis of costs which would have been economically viable, thus constituting an 'economically viable strategy'.[121]

The above case law concerns situations where there is not even a possibility of potential competition. The situations, where there might be a possibility of potential competition and this could be restricted by the specific conduct under examination, are examined, with regard to the application of Article 101 TFEU, in Chapter 6 on the concept of restriction of competition.

4.3. INSIDE THE BOUNDARIES OF THE UNDERTAKING: THE SINGLE ENTITY CONCEPT

Both Articles 101 and 102 TFEU (and their UK equivalents) apply to undertakings. For the purposes of Article 101(1), at least two undertakings should participate in the illegal conduct. As we have explained above, EU competition law adopts a functional approach of the concept of undertaking, the legal status of that 'entity' being irrelevant for its qualification as an 'undertaking' under competition law.

4.3.1. THE BOUNDARIES OF THE 'UNDERTAKING' AND THE LIMITS OF ENTERPRISE/FIRM LIABILITY: AN ECONOMIC PERSPECTIVE

As previously explained in Section 4.2.3, the concept of 'undertaking' in EU and UK competition law has been interpreted as covering an entity that exercises an economic activity. We focused in the earlier section on the concept of 'economic activity'. This Section will explore the meaning of 'entity'.

In economics there are various theories about why firms exist and what determines their scale/scope or in other words their boundaries. Breaking with the neoclassical theory's perspective on the firm as mainly exercising a productive function, the question of its size and boundaries being left unresolved, Ronald Coase has emphasized the role of transaction costs in determining the size and boundaries of the firm and has established a distinction between the market and the firm, regarding them as alternative methods of coordinating production.[122] In the presence of transaction costs, the direction of resources by an authority (the firm) may constitute a substitute to the decentralized price mechanism operating in the context of a market. Firms emerge when hierarchy is more efficient than market transactions. Diminishing returns to management may thus determine the firm's size and its boundaries.

Taking a different perspective, Armen Alchian and Harold Demsetz expanded Coase's transaction costs framework in order to explain the role of firms in managing cooperative teams in the presence of information costs. There is a demand for economic organizations which facilitate cooperation, since monitoring of each team member's performance is costly and market competition cannot exercise sufficient control. The specialized monitors will be granted residual claimant status on the residual created by the teams under their direction. Contrary to Coase, who emphasized the relative importance of hierarchy over markets and

121 Ibid, para 114.

122 RH Coase, 'The Nature of the Firm' (1937) 4 *Economica* 386.

thus perceived differences between firms and markets and viewed the firm as a 'centralized contractual agent in a team productive process—not some superior authoritarian directive or disciplinary power'.[123] Its essence is a 'contractual structure with: 1) joint input production; 2) several input owners; 3) one party who is common to all the contracts of the joint inputs; 4) who has rights to renegotiate any input's contract independently of con-tracts with other input owners; 5) who holds the residual claim; and 6) who has the right to sell his central contractual residual status', not involving any authoritarian control but being simply a 'contractual structure subject to continuous renegotiation with the central agent'.[124]

According to the contractual structure framework, a firm, or in more lawyerly language, an entity holding a legal personality may be perceived as a set of contracts between various business participants that interact within a certain economic and legal context.[125] The approach of firms as contracts does not, however, support that the set of contracts from which a firm is composed should be subject to scrutiny, for instance on the basis of competition law. These voluntary arrangements between participants to a venture are perceived as promoting efficiency because they enhance party autonomy. Transaction costs theory can also arrive at the conclusion that firms may be the most efficient organizational structures when the costs of market exchange are greater than the costs of procurement within the firm. However, in this case, the firm is perceived as an alternative mechanism of governance.[126] These theories were completed by the property rights theory of the firm which identifies the allocation of residual decision rights with the ownership of the assets of the firm (tangible and intangible).[127]

A different approach considers firms as 'a nexus of agency relationships including managerial lines of authority, employment and structures of governance', thus emphasizing the single economic dimension of the firm.[128] According to this view, managers will not be considered as the agents of shareholders but the agents of the firm, conceived as an entity in its own right.[129] This may have implications as to the assumption of the shareholder primacy principle in the theory of the firm as a nexus of contracts, the primary duty of the management and the officers of the corporation being to maximize the shareholder's value. If the firm is perceived as the principal, other objectives, such as the long-term viability of the corporation, its reputation and broader social objectives other than just profits, which may be followed by the specific entity. This approach may also alter the consideration of the business participants who matter most.

123 A Alchian and H Demsetz, 'Production, Information Costs, and Economic Organization' (1972) 66 *American Economic Rev* 777, 778.

124 Ibid, 794.

125 See eg E Fama, 'Agency Problems and the Theory of the Firm' (1980) 88(2) *J Political Economy* 288 (viewing firms as a 'set of contracts among factors of production, with each factor motivated by its self interest'; MC Jensen and WH Meckling, 'Theory of the Firm: Managerial Behavior, Agency Costs and Ownership Structure' (1976) 3(4) *J Financial Economics* 305, 310 '[i]t is important to recognize that most organizations are simply legal fictions which serve as a nexus for a set of contracting relationships among individuals. This includes firms [. . .]'; F Easterbrook and D Fischel, *The Economic Structure of Corporate Law* (Harvard University Press, 1996).

126 OE Williamson, *The Economic Institutions of Capitalism* (The Free Press, 1985). The question of the boundaries of firms has been interestingly addressed as an issue relating to the limits of integration, thus illustrating the links between the two questions. See eg BR Holmstrom and J Tirole, 'The Theory of the Firm' in R Schmalensee and RD Willig (eds) *Handbook of Industrial Organization*, vol 1 (North Holland, 1989), 62, 65, noting that the need to consider the trade-off between the costs and benefits of integration, instead of organizing a specific activity within the context of a market.

127 SJ Grossman and OD Hart, 'The Costs and Benefits of Ownership: A Theory of Vertical and Lateral Integration' [1986] 94(4) *J Political Economy* 691.

128 EW Orts, *Business Persons—A Legal Theory of the Firm* (OUP, 2013), 60.

129 Ibid, 82.

In the traditional theory of firms as a set of contracts, these are equity investors/shareholders and managers. However, as EW Orts rightly observes, '[. . .] other business participants are considered important in different societies [. . .] including non-owner managers and employees as well as other capital providers and financial owners.'[130]

These other capital providers may be creditors or participants employing mixed debt-equity instruments, such as hybrid securities (eg convertible loans, preference shares, derivatives and other innovative financial instruments), which are along the 'debt to equity continuum.'[131] The 'financial revolution' and the 'knowledge economy' has also reduced the importance of alienable assets such as the plant and equipment, personnel/managers having specific skills constituting, according to some authors, the most important asset of a corporation, as 'they can break away, raise finance directly in the market, and replicate the assets.'[132] Hence,

> [. . .] as a result of the financial revolution, links within the firm may be much weaker than in the past, and conversely, links between firms, tied together for instance by complementary technologies, may be stronger. This matters.
>
> For example, one of the concerns about monopoly is that the monopolist may lose the incentive to innovate. But when financing is easy and the ownership of growth options is up for grabs, the fear of employees leaving with crucial technology and appropriating a share of the rents forces a monopolist to maintain its technological lead. Potential internal competition may be more of a threat than external competition!
>
> As another example, horizontal mergers in some industries may not be attempts by firms to gain some market power over customers, but to regain some power over the employees and key suppliers they used to have when alienable assets were a bigger source of rents.[133]

Should these considerations be taken into account, one may finish by adopting a quite broad conception on the appropriate scope of competition law, allegedly also intervening within the boundaries of the corporate entity, regulating the interaction between the business participants within the entity and with those outside the entity.

The concept of 'control' plays an important role in the process of defining the scope of the competition law intervention against an 'economic entity' as it determines the tangible or intangible assets that constitute the core of the 'undertaking', define its boundaries and are thus presumed to be under the authority of the undertaking's agents, which may engage through anti-competitive strategies the undertaking's liability.

Following the financial revolution and in view of the possible systemic risks of cascade corporate bankruptcies one may, for instance, focus not only on 'managerial operational control' but also on 'financial structural control', as it is explained by EW Orts:

> Control of the firm in an everyday operational sense refers to the internal relationships of agency authority and power [. . .]. This kind of control is conferred mostly to executive managers. However, debt financing can also create highly powered incentives (via severe consequences imposed for default) on top managers to meet strict schedules for interest payments.

130 Ibid, 26.

131 The terminology 'debt to equity continuum' results from a publication by Moody's of its Tool Kit for Assessing Hybrid Securities in December 199.

132 RG Rajan and L Zingales, 'The Influence of the Financial Revolution on the Nature of Firms' (2001) 91 *American Economic Rev* 206.

133 Ibid.

> [. . .] Enterprise-level debt carries a contingent ownership interest in the firm [. . .]. Although managerial operational control remains usually with the managers who owe their positions to the equity ownership authority structures of an enterprise, the effective financial structural control of large firms is now very often shared between equity owners and creditors.[134]

Firms are held strictly liable as principals for the actions (or material omissions) of their agents (vicarious liability) when these are found to constitute a restriction of competition under the competition law provisions. One may distinguish here between different liability regimes for harm:[135]

(1) Enterprise (corporate) liability

(2) Business participant liability (ie, liability of an individual business participant or group of participants)

(3) Both enterprise liability and business participant liability

(4) Neither enterprise liability nor liability of any business participant.

The term 'business participant' refers to the actors operating within the specific corporation:

(i) *Management and other agents of the corporation*: this may include the company's directors, these terms being defined, in the context of competition law, quite broadly,[136] as well as any other company's agent who qualify as an 'employee' (the requirement of an employment relation excludes independent contractors from this category).

(ii) *Equity owners and shareholders*: this category comprises all those holding shares in the company's capital (common stock) or its retained earnings. The distinction between management and equity owners/shareholders has been one of the features of the emergence of the modern corporation and the separation of ownership and control in public corporations.

(iii) *Creditors*: this category includes those holding debt (bank loans, supply/distribution credit agreements, corporate bonds or other legal rights to future payment of debt) against the company. Company financing may occur either through equity or through debt. These are considered financially equivalent, according to some economic theory (Modigliani–Miller theorem).[137] Debt can be held by private

[134] EW Orts, *Business Persons—A Legal Theory of the Firm* (OUP, 2013), 86 and 88.

[135] Ibid, 134.

[136] OFT 1340, *Company Director's and Competition Law* (2011), para 2.2, available at https://www.gov.uk/government/uploads/system/uploads/attachment_data/file/284410/oft1340.pdf:

> 'Company' includes unregistered companies and limited liability partnerships. For these purposes, a 'director' includes any person occupying the position of director, by whatever name called. This includes a person formally appointed to a company board, as well as any person who assumes to act as a director (a de facto director). It also includes a 'shadow director', defined as any person in accordance with whose directions or instructions the directors of a company are accustomed to act (other than advice given purely in a professional capacity). The rules do not extend to other company officers who hold the title 'director' but who do not fall within this definition.

[137] According to this theorem, '[. . .] with well-functioning markets (and neutral taxes) and rational investors, who can "undo" the corporate financial structure by holding positive or negative amounts of debt, the market value of the firm—debt plus equity—depends *only* on the income stream generated by its assets. It follows, in particular, that the value of the firm should not be affected by the share of debt in its financial structure or by what will be done with the returns – paid out as dividends or reinvested (profitably)':

individuals, institutional investors, public investors (eg sovereign wealth funds), trade-creditors.[138]

(iv) *Subsidiaries*: In complex business structures it is possible that several assets are allocated to a distinct entity, a subsidiary or a daughter company, that is owned or controlled by another company, the parent or holding company. Subsidiaries are defined as following by the UK Company Act 2006, section 1159(1): 'A company is a "subsidiary" of another company, its "holding company", if that other company (a) holds a majority of the voting rights in it, or (b) is a member of it and has the right to appoint or remove a majority of its board of directors, or (c) is a member of it and controls alone, pursuant to an agreement with other members, a majority of the voting rights in it—or if it is a subsidiary of a company that is itself a subsidiary of that other company'. A company is a 'wholly owned subsidiary' of another company if it has no members except that other and that other's wholly owned subsidiaries or persons acting on behalf of that other or its wholly owned subsidiaries (section 1159(2)).

One may also list, among affected business participants, separate legal entities that operate the strict confines of the corporation, but which are quasi-integrated in its operations, because of the existence of economic/business or personal links on a long-term basis. Indeed, in *Shell v Commission*, the General Court provided the following definition of a single economic entity: 'economic units which consist of a unitary organization of personal, tangible and intangible elements which pursues a specific economic aim on a long-term basis and can contribute to the commission of an infringement [. . .].'[139]

(v) *Commercial agents, franchisees, quasi-integrated vertical distributors*: As we will examine in Chapter 10, the governance structure of a franchise network, perceived as a distinct organizational entity, relies on a complex interaction between residual decision and ownership rights allocated among the franchisor and the franchisee in a way that eventually may have the appearance, although not form one, single economic entity. Similarly, the position of commercial agents, that is in principle entities having a distinct legal personality, that are acting on behalf of the principal who assumes the most significant part of the commercial risks, has been a subject of controversy, as we will also examine in Chapter 10.

(vi) *Sister companies/siblings*: sister companies or siblings are companies that are owned by the same person or company. For instance, subsidiaries of the same company are considered as siblings, sister companies to each other.

F Modigliani, 'Introduction' in A Abel and S Johnson (eds) *The Collected Papers of Franco Modigliani*, vol 3 (MIT Press,1980), xi, xiii. The theorem was first presented in F Modigliani and MH Miller, 'The Cost of Capital, Corporate Finance and the Theory of Investment' (1958) 48 *American Economic Rev* 261. The general acceptance of the Modigliani–Miller theorem led to the great expansion of debt financing and to the development of highly leveraged corporations (leverage denoting the prevalence of debt financing to equity financing). It has been widely criticized for underestimating economic systemic risks resulting from leveraging. It has also been argued that investment in stock markets (equity) has outperformed in the long run debt financing in most developed countries, that is, that there is an 'equity premium': See JJ Siegel and RH Thaler, 'Anomalies: The Equity premium Puzzle' (1997) 11 *J Economic Perspectives* 191.

138 EM Iacobucci and GG Triantis, 'The Economic and Legal Boundaries of Firms' (2007) 93 *Virginia L Rev* 515.

139 Case T-11/89, *Shell International Chemical Company Ltd v Commission of the European Communities* [1992] ECR II–757, para 311. According to a well-established jurisprudence of the CJEU, an entity could consist of 'several persons, natural or legal': Case 170/83, *Hydrotherm Gerätebau GmbH v Compact del Dott Ing Mario Andreoli & C Sas* [1984] ECR 2999, para 11.

The allocation of the entrepreneurial risk through the separation of ownership and control in modern corporations and the need to incentivize investment through a reasonable calculation of enterprise risk led to the development of the legal technology of limited enterprise (corporate) liability. If a corporation is held liable this only concerns the assets of the legal person of the corporation, the personal assets of its business participants being normally exonerated unless the creditor negotiated a guarantee from the business participants.[140] Hence, equity owners'/shareholders' assets cannot normally be used in order to compensate for the wrong committed by the corporation's agents holding the corporation sole liable.

The legal person of the corporation thus interrupts the causation chain between the wrong and the various business participants within the boundaries of the corporation, at least in principle. Although such an approach may have the result that potential victims may not be eventually compensated if the corporations' assets and financial resources do not suffice to cover the payment for the wrongful harms suffered, there are economic efficiency considerations that may justify this restriction of liability. As it is well explained by Orts: 'Economic policy judgments involve the extent to which taking business risks should be promoted (or not). Limited liability in particular instances may promote business values of risk-taking, investment, and economic growth—which should be balanced (in a general welfare calculation) against values of economic compensation required for any resulting wrongful harm (or the deterrence of any prospective and foreseeable wrongful harm).'[141]

Indeed, one may envision various possible liability regimes in view of the balancing of the above considerations for a specific type of harm. For instance, if one accords much weight to the value of deterrence in competition law, it is possible to opt for a legal regime that engages the liability of both the corporation and some key business participants (individual employees). This, for instance, might be the situation in the case of illegal cartels in US antitrust law, for which the legal person of the corporation may be found liable and required to pay (treble) damages, but also cartels are prosecuted as criminal offences, and both pecuniary and non-pecuniary penalties may be imposed: fines to the corporations, but also to implicated individuals, as well as imprisonment of the individuals involved in the cartel. Business participant liability is limited to managers and other agents of the corporation who conspired for the commission of the cartel infringement. The ultimate costs of unlawful cartel activity resulting from the important fines and damages imposed on the corporation may certainly fall on its shareholders (thus amounting to an indirect business participant liability regime), although it was noted that this indirect effect on shareholders may be limited as 'large antitrust fines barely affect each shareholder of public companies because the economic burden of the fine is so broadly dispersed.'[142]

In contrast, in the EU, liability for cartels is limited to 'undertakings', with no possibility of imposing sanctions, pecuniary or otherwise, on any business participant, with the exception of certain EU Member States that have established a criminal liability regime for competition

[140] For instance, London Stock Exchange is a corporation limited by guarantee and there are also unlimited companies.

[141] WE Orts, *Business Persons—A Legal Theory of the Firm* (OUP, 2013), 135.

[142] JW Markham, 'The Failure of Corporate Governance Standards and Antitrust Compliance' (2013) 58 *South Dakota L Rev* 499, 500 (also noting that '[o]ften, when antitrust investigations are closed, share prices often respond favorably to the resolution and certainty rather than adversely in response to the fine itself').

law infringements that apply to management and agents of the corporation.[143] Responsibility for committing an infringement is also personal in EU competition law, according to a well-established case law.[144] In the words of AG Kokott, the principle of personal responsibility is 'founded in the rule of law and the principle of fault' and in principle the competition law infringement 'is to be attributed to the natural or legal person who operates the undertaking which participates in (the competition law infringement); in other words the principal of the undertaking is liable'.[145]

The situation is similar in UK competition law. In *Safeway Stores Limited & Others & Twigger*, the Court of Appeal (Civil Division) held in an unanimous judgment that undertakings found to infringe competition law provisions have a personal responsibility, and not a vicarious one. In the words of Longmore LJ, '[t]hey are not liable for the illegal acts of their agents or employees because [Section] 36 of the [UK] Competition Act [1998] only imposes liability on an undertaking which is a party to an agreement which infringes the prohibition in Chapter I of the Act and that liability can only be imposed if the infringement has been committed intentionally or negligently by the undertaking.'[146] The case involved an action for damages and/or equitable compensation brought by Safeway against some of its former employees, including directors, who had engaged in a repeated direct and indirect exchange of commercially sensitive retail pricing information with other large supermarkets and dairy processors leading to an increase of the price of milk and other dairy products for consumers, part of which were passed back to the farmers. The OFT (now CMA) launched an investigation against the undertakings participating in this concerted conduct, as a result of which Safeway, along with several of the other undertakings involved, concluded an early resolution agreement with the OFT admitting a breach of Chapter I prohibition. A fine was also imposed by the OFT, which was later reduced as a result of Safeway's cooperation in the investigation. Safeway argued that its employees and directors had conspired by participating in, facilitating, and failing to report the initiatives to their superiors or the Board of Directors, thus committing a breach of their contract, a breach of fiduciary duties, and negligence. As a consequence of this conduct, Safeway argued that it had suffered a loss and damage. The former employees applied to have Safeway's claim struck down, claiming that it was against the principle of *ex turpi causa non oritur actio*, according to which a claimant may not recover for damage which is the consequence of his own criminal act, as 'it would be inconsistent for a claimant to be criminally and personally liable (or liable to pay penalties to a regulator such as the OFT) but for the same claimant to say to a civil court that he is not personally answerable for that conduct'.[147]

The High Court declined to strike out the action. It held in favour of the defendants to engage the maxim explaining that the claimants' liability was not a personal one and determination

143 See our analysis of the cartel offence in the companion volume I Lianos, *Competition Law Enforcement and Procedure* (OUP, forthcoming 2019).

144 Case C-49/92 P, *Commission v Anic Partecipazioni* [1999] ECR I–4125, para 145; Case C-279/98 P, *Cascades v Commission* [2000] ECR I–9693, para 78; Case C-280/06, *ETI and Others* [2007] ECR I–10893, para 39.

145 Opinion of AG J Kokott in Case C-280/06, *Autorità Garante della Concorrenza e del Mercato v Ente tabacchi italiani—ETI SpA and Others* [2007] ECR I–10893, para 71, also noting with regard to the foundations of this principle that 'the consequence of the sanctionative nature of measures imposed by competition authorities for punishing cartel offences—in particular fines—that the area is at least akin to criminal law'.

146 *Safeway Stores limited & Others & Twigger & Others* [2010] EWCA Civ 1472, para 20 (see also para 23) (Longmore LJ).

147 Ibid, para 16 (Longmore LJ).

of this question depended on whether it could be said that each of the defendant employees was the 'directing mind or will of the claimant companies', thus making it more difficult for lower level employees to claim the benefit of the maxim. The Court of Appeal unanimously disagreed, holding that the maxim of *ex turpi causa* applied, and prevented Safeway from recovering loss and damages suffered because of the competition law infringement, as a result of the personal responsibility of the undertaking, in this case Safeway. Indeed, the purpose of competition law and its deterrent effect could be jeopardized if an undertaking found liable for a breach of competition law and fined could recover the fine (and other losses) from employees. EU and UK Competition law attributes liability to the undertaking as a whole (following the enterprise liability principle), not to its business participants.[148] The UK Supreme Court refused the application to appeal against the Court of appeal's ruling.[149]

The situation becomes more complex, however, once one considers the relation between parent companies and subsidiaries. Assuming that a subsidiary was found liable for its participation in a competition law infringement, one may be tempted, in order to ensure the effective enforcement of competition law and in particular deterrence, to pierce the corporate veil and find the parent company of the subsidiary also liable; although in reality the parent is just an equity owner/shareholder, albeit a special one. Indeed, unlike normal equity owners/shareholders, parent companies are in principle able to supervise the conduct of their subsidiaries, to the extent they exercise 'control', in the sense of corporate law. Restricting the liability of subsidiaries to the amount of capital invested would have also limited the effectiveness of competition law enforcement, since managers could have set subsidiaries with low capitalization in order artificially partition their conduct and thus to escape significant liability for the commission of competition law infringements. This approach may challenge the traditional conceptualization of enterprise liability in company law but competition law pursues different values and purposes from corporate law, hence the balance between enterprise liability and business participant liability may be different in this context.[150]

The concept of control rights becomes therefore extremely important in order to ascertain the extension of the liability of the parent company for the anti-competitive behaviour of its subsidiary. Control rights are in principle linked to the economic integration of two entities, the latter concept being quite broad to cover various situations. Nada Ina Pauer remarks various manifestations of control in the context of corporate law, '[g]iven the objective of general corporate law to protect the interests of creditors':

- personal interrelations on the level of the companies' management board;
- the use of the same commercial name by the parent company and the subsidiary;
- a subsidiary's financial, administrative, or operational dependence;
- a manipulation of corporate assets;

148 Ibid, para 44 (Pill LJ).

149 See, however, the recent judgment of the Supreme Court in *Jetivia SA and another v Bilta Ltd (in liquidation) and others* [2015] UKSC 23.

150 As it is rightly noted by NI Pauer, *The Single Economic Entity Doctrine and Corporate Group Responsibility in European Antitrust Law* (Kluwer Law International, 2014), 207, '[. . .] the aims pursued by the specific area in which an intragroup attribution of conduct or responsibility is to be carried out must necessarily be taken into account. While in company law this is regularly deemed essential in cases of "qualified undercapitalization" or an illicit transfer of assets between a legal entity and the respective shareholders, the previous analysis has shown that European competition law pursues the objective of "deterrence".'

- a subsidiary's inadequate capitalization; or
- a lack of adhering to corporate formalities.[151]

The different objectives of competition law and the demands of the principle of effectiveness may lead to the acceptance of other criteria of manifestation of control, presumably less demanding than those required by corporate law. This tendency, which is obvious in the case law and which we will examine in the following section, has been criticized by some authors for 'entirely' depriving the organizational form of a corporate group of its 'flexibility' and for 'attributing a higher legal standard to the objective of 'effective cartel enforcement' than the 'fundamental principle of a confinement of entrepreneurial risk'.[152] Yet, one may argue that as long as the principle of effective competition law enforcement does not directly run against the objective of corporate law to protect the interest of creditors, it would be preferable to pursue both objectives.[153]

In the following Section we will examine how the concept of the single economic entity was implemented in the context of complex corporate groups, in particular with regard to the relation between a parent company and its subsidiary.

4.3.2. THE SINGLE ENTITY DOCTRINE AND ITS APPLICATION IN COMPETITION LAW

A physical person, as well as an entity having a legal personality, such as a corporate group or a single subsidiary may be considered an undertaking for the purposes of competition law enforcement. The complexity of relationships within intra-corporate groups, with a number of activities often undertaken by a subsidiary, led the jurisprudence of the EU Courts, at least since the *Akzo Nobel v Commission* case,[154] to adopt the 'single economic unit doctrine', thus favouring the principle of enterprise liability as opposed to the liability of the subsidiary only. The doctrine plays both a 'defensive' and a 'prosecutorial' function: 'The single entity concept is inherently double-edged. On the one hand, single entity claims exonerate or shield market behaviour from competition law sanctions. On the other, they also potentially extend the reach of competition law fines to related legal entities.'[155]

The doctrine addresses the following distinct legal issues:

- Determining if the intra-group relation could fall within the scope of Article 101 TFEU in case this was conduct of two separate legal entities benefitting from organizational autonomy or if it was the conduct of a single economic entity, thus escaping the Article 101(1) TFEU prohibition, despite the existence of separate legal entities.

151 Ibid, 208. 152 Ibid, 209.

153 We will examine separately the issue of bankruptcy following the imposition of financial penalties as a result of a competition law infringement.

154 For an interesting discussion of the practice before *Akzo*, see A Kalintiri, 'Revisiting Parental Liability in EU Competition Law' (2018) 43(2) *European L Rev* 145 (noting that the case law focused on situations where subsidiaries were used as vehicles for implementing an anti-competitive plan of their parent companies, which masterminded the infringement of competition law, thus establishing 'a connection between the control exercised by the parent company over the subsidiary and the transgression in question before imputing the latter's act to the former').

155 P van Cleynenbreugel, 'Single Entity Tests in U.S. Antitrust and EU Competition Law' (21 June 2011), available at http://ssrn.com/abstract=1889232.

- Attributing liability for the illegal conduct to one or the other member of the corporate group.
- Assessing the market shares of the undertaking involved in the infringement of competition law, either this being in the context of merger control, or in the context of an abuse of a dominant position, or in order to determine the existence of a single undertaking for the application of a Block Exemption regulation.

This Section will focus on the first two issues.

4.3.2.1. The single economic entity doctrine and intra-corporate group relations

4.3.2.1.1. Group of companies, single-entity doctrine, and the application of Article 101(1) TFEU

In the *Centrafarm* cases,[156] the CJEU held that Article 101(1) TFEU 'does not apply to agreements or concerted practices between undertakings belonging to the same concern (group of companies) in the form of parent company and subsidiary, if the undertakings form an economic unit within which the subsidiary does not have real autonomy in determining its line of conduct on the market and if the agreements or practices have the aim of establishing an internal distribution of tasks between the undertakings'.[157]

In *Viho*, the CJEU seems to have put more emphasis on the first condition, omitting to mention that the agreement between affiliated undertakings served the internal assignment of tasks and responsibilities'. The Court held that a parent company detaining 100 per cent of the shares of its subsidiaries forms a single economic unit 'within which the subsidiaries do not enjoy real autonomy in determining their course of action in the market, but carry out the instructions issued to them by the parent company controlling them' and thus the two legal entities do not constitute two undertakings from the perspective of competition law.[158] The CJEU thus excluded such instructions from the scope of Article 101 TFEU, as a subsidiary must expect a direct instruction of its parent company, which sets the general strategy of the group of companies to which the subsidiary participates.

The CJEU explained the rationale of the single economic entity doctrine in *Hydrotherm*, where it held, with regard to undertakings having identical interests and controlled by the

[156] Case 15/74, *Centrafarm BV and Adriaan de Peijper v Sterling Drug Inc* [1974] ECR 1147 [hereinafter *Centrafarm I*]; Case 16/74, *Centrafarm BV and Adriaan De Peijper v. Winthrop BV* [1974] ECR 1183 [hereinafter *Centrafarm II*]. These cases built on some past decisional practice of the Commission and jurisprudence of the CJEU. See also *Christiani and Nielsen* (Case IV/22.548) Commission Decision [1969] OJ L 165/12 (applying for the first time the doctrine of the single economic entity to a market sharing arrangement that the parent had signed with its wholly owned subsidiary, because a wholly owned subsidiary is not an economic entity that can compete with its parent company in view of their economic interdependence, the doctrine being, however, constructed narrowly the anti-competitive effects in this case being internal to the corporate group, the Commission focusing on the condition of restriction of competition); *Kodak* (Case IV/24055) Commission Decision [1970] OJ L 147/24 (applying the doctrine to the parallel market conduct of several subsidiaries controlled by the same parent company, because the subsidiaries depended completely on the parent company which had issued detailed instructions to them and thus lacked any economic autonomy, the Commission focused this time on the absence of an agreement or concerted practice between non-economically autonomous entities that were commonly controlled by the same parent company); Case 22/71, *Béguelin Import Co v SAGL Import Export* [1971] ECR 949 (also insisting on the lack of economic independence of the subsidiary, one company being 'economically wholly dependent from the other' (para 4), hence negating the possibility of a distortion of competition).

[157] Case 15/74, *Centrafarm I* [1974] ECR 1147, para 41. See also C-30/87, *Corinne Bodson v SA Pompes funèbres des régions libérées* [1988] ECR 2479, para 19.

[158] Case C-73/95C, *Viho Europe v Commission* [1996] ECR I–5457, para 16.

same natural person which also participated in the collusive conduct, that 'in those circumstances competition between the persons participating together, as a single party, in the agreement in question is impossible'.[159] The underlying theory is that as the competitive order does not constitute the most appropriate organization form in this case, Article 101 TFEU should not intervene in order to regulate the specific conduct within the boundaries of an undertaking. As AG Lenz explained in his Opinion in *Viho*, 'there can be no competition between the parent company and its subsidiaries. Independent economic competitive measures by the subsidiaries are inconceivable where the parent company determines and controls their conduct completely [. . .]. Consequently, [Article 101 TFEU] is not applicable because there is no competition between the group companies which needs to be protected.'[160] However, applying the single entity doctrine does not provide complete immunity under competition law, as Article 102 TFEU may still apply to a unilateral conduct adopted by an 'undertaking'.

Intra-enterprise conspiracy in US antitrust law

A similar presumption that a parent corporation and its wholly owned subsidiary constitute a single economic entity has been explicitly recognized in US antitrust law in *Copperweld Corporation v Independence Tube Corporation* (1984).[161] The US Supreme Court explained this choice of antitrust immunity under Section 1 of the Sherman Act for the coordinated conduct between a parent company and a wholly owned subsidiary (as well as for coordinated conduct among officers or employees of the same company) by the fact that these do not constitute separate economic actors pursuing separate economic interests but have a 'complete unity of interest', their objectives being 'common, not disparate'; Their general corporate objectives are guided or determined 'not by two separate corporate consciousnesses, but one', the US Supreme court making an analogy with 'a multiple team of horses drawing a vehicle under the control of a single driver'.[162] The US Supreme Court linked this approach to the fact that the Sherman Act establishes a distinction between coordinated conduct subject to section 1 of the Sherman Act and unilateral conduct, which may fall under section 2 of the Sherman Act. Section 2 of the Sherman Act is the only one of these two provisions that could potentially apply to coordinated market behaviour between a parent company and a wholly owned subsidiary or between two entities controlled by the same person, the conduct being immune from the point of view of section 1 of the Sherman Act. According to the US Supreme Court, '[. . .] Congress made a purposeful choice to accord different treatment to unilateral and concerted conduct. Had Congress intended to outlaw unreasonable restraints as such, Section 1's requirement of a contract, combination or conspiracy would be superfluous, as would the entirety of Section 2'.[163] The 'identity of interests' between the two entities constitutes the main reason for recognizing

[159] Case 170/83, *Hydrotherm Gerätebau GmbH v Compact del Dott Ing Mario Andreoli & C Sas* [1984] ECR 2999, para 11.

[160] Opinion of AG Lenz in Case C-73/95 P, *Viho Europe v Commission* [1996] ECR I–5457, para 16.

[161] *Copperweld Corporation v Independence Tube Corporation*, 467 US 752 (1984). US antitrust law had initially applied the intra-enterprise conspiracy doctrine finding that a section 1 restraint may result 'as readily from a conspiracy among those who are affiliated or integrated under common ownership as from a conspiracy of those who are otherwise independent': *United States v Yellow Cab Co*, 67 S Ct 1565 (1947), intra-enterprise conspiracy claims being assessed under a rule of reason approach.

[162] *Copperweld Corporation v Independence Tube Corporation*, 467 US 752, 771 (1984).

[163] Ibid, 775.

this presumption of per se legality of coordinated action between a parent company and a wholly owned undertaking under Section 1 of the Sherman Act. The idea behind is that such coordination promotes competition with other entities with which there is no 'identity of interests'.[164] As was explained in the dissenting Opinion of Justice Stevens in *Copperweld* such coordinated action between a parent company and its wholly owned subsidiary '[does] not eliminate competition that would otherwise exist, but rather enhance the ability to compete'.[165]

Under the single entity doctrine, several legal persons may form an economic entity if a control relationship exists between them. Hence, the application of the doctrine presupposes the exercise of 'control' or 'decisive influence' by the parent company to the subsidiary.

Article 3(2) of EU Merger Regulation 139/2004 defines the acquisition of control as following:

> Control shall be constituted by rights, contracts or any other means which, either separately or in combination and having regard to the considerations of fact or law involved, confer the possibility of exercising decisive influence on an undertaking, in particular by
>
> (a) ownership or the right to use all or part of the assets of an undertaking
>
> (b) rights or contracts which confer decisive influence on the composition, voting or decisions of the organs of an undertaking.[166]

In the context of EU merger control, decisive influence does not necessarily entail absolute control over the totality of the capital of the other entity, the acquisition of a less than half the shares when the other shares are widely spread being sufficient for this purpose. This may also occur by holding rights providing direct operational control over the other entity (target undertaking of the merger), as control may also be exercised *de facto*, for instance on the basis of rights, contracts or equivalent direct influence on the composition, voting or decisions of the organs of an undertaking. The concepts of 'control' and 'decisive influence' have been interpreted broadly in order to expand the scope of the EU merger regulation and thus subject more merger operations to the assessment of the European Commission. Nevertheless, an acquisition of a shareholding in a competitor that does not procure decisive influence, is not subject to EU merger control, even if it allows the acquiring entity to influence the commercial activities of the acquired entity.

However, before the implementation of the EU Merger Control Regulation, the jurisprudence of the CJEU and the Commission adhered to a somewhat restrictive interpretation of the concept of 'control' and 'decisive influence'. This enabled the application of Articles 101 and 102 TFEU to acquisitions of a shareholding in a competitor, following the principles set by

164 See eg *Waste Conversion Sys, Inc v Greenstone Indus, Inc*, 33 SW3d 779, 781–2 (Tenn 2000).

165 Ibid, 778.

166 Council Regulation (EC) No 139/2004 on the control of concentrations between undertakings [2004] OJ L 24/1. See also EU Merger Regulation 139/2004, Article 3(3):

> Control is acquired by persons or undertakings which:
>
> (a) are holders of the rights or entitled to rights under the contracts concerned; or
>
> (b) while not being holders of such rights or entitled to rights under such contracts, have the power to exercise the rights deriving therefrom.

the CJEU's judgment in *Philip Morris*, where the CJEU held that Article 101(1) TFEU applied to an acquisition of a minority shareholding in a competitor if they may 'serve as an instrument for *influencing* the commercial conduct of the companies in question so as to restrict or distort competition'.[167]

In this case, Philip Morris directly controlled 24.9 per cent of the voting rights in Rothmans International including an important part of its capital (equity) and held 50 per cent of Rothman's International's convertible bonds (debt). Although the issue of the relation between the two entities was not examined as such, the Court considered that the two entities constituted in fact two separate undertakings, thus accepting the application of Article 101 TFEU in this context. The Court focused on the assessment of the condition of a restriction of competition, and the possibility of a minority shareholding leading to the acquisition of influence over another company to constitute a distortion of competition by object or effect. The CJEU found that Philip Morris could not influence the commercial activities of Rothmans, despite controlling 24.9 per cent voting interest and holding 50 per cent of Rothman's convertible bonds, because it did not have any board representation and because of the existence of various Chinese Walls insulating Rothmans from any influence.

It follows that holding a considerable part of a company's debt in conjunction with passive investments through some minority shareholding do not lead to 'influence', and presumably not to 'decisive influence'.[168]

Although we do not focus in this Chapter on the personal scope of the EU (or UK) merger control rules, but only on the EU (or UK) antitrust provisions, the concept of control, perceived as 'decisive influence', seems to indicate the contours of the single entity doctrine and thus the applicability of Articles 101 and 102 TFEU. Whatever happens within the sphere over which the 'single entity' exercises a decisive influence is outside the scope of Article 101 TFEU, which applies to collusive conduct involving more than one undertakings. Article 102 TFEU can, however, apply to unilateral conduct, but when the 'undertaking' or economic entity in question abuses a dominant position on a relevant market. Hence, it seems that when an entity does not exercise a 'decisive influence' but just 'some influence' or even 'influence' over another, the two entities do not constitute a single economic entity. Consequently, Article 101 TFEU may apply to a conduct jointly adopted by them, in view of the fact they are considered as two separate 'undertakings' for the purposes of Article 101 TFEU.

Setting the boundaries between 'significant influence' and 'influence' fulfils, however, an opposite aim in the context of Article 101 TFEU from that in EU merger control. Indeed, here the finding of 'significant influence' will exclude the specific conduct from the scrutiny of the competition authorities, rather than include it, as is case for EU merger control. One should also take into account that the 'control' thresholds have undoubtedly shifted, after the EU adopted a merger control regulation, in comparison to the period before the adoption of the first EC Merger Regulation 4064/89.[169] One may also question the need for a consistent

[167] Joined Cases 142 & 156/84, *British-American Tobacco Company Ltd and RJ Reynolds Industries Inc v Commission* [1987] ECR 4487.

[168] Although in *Gillette*, the Commission seems to have accepted that a company held a non-voting minority equity interest and a significant percentage of the total debt of another company (13.6 per cent) constituted evidence of 'some influence' over the second entity's commercial activities, for the purposes of the application of Article 102 TFEU, it did not conclude that this amounted to 'decisive influence': *Warner-Lambert/Gillette and Others* (Case IV/33.440) and *BIC/Gillette and Others* (Case IV/33.486), Commission Decisions [1993] OJ L 116/21.

[169] Making the point as to the situation of minority shareholdings, BE Hawk & HL Huser, 'Controlling the Shifting Sands: Minority Shareholdings under EEC Competition Law' (1993) 17(2) *Fordham Int'l LJ* 294.

interpretation of the concept of 'single economic entity' in the jurisprudence of the CJEU on antitrust and that of 'control' in the EU Merger Control.[170]

As explained earlier in this chapter, according to well-established jurisprudence of the EU Courts, 'the term "undertaking" must be understood as designating an economic unit even if in law that economic unit consists of several natural or legal persons, and that when such an economic entity infringes the competition rules, it is for that entity, according to the principle of personal responsibility, to answer for that infringement'.[171]

Although the principle of personal responsibility 'is of particular importance especially as regards liability in the sphere of civil law, it cannot be relevant for defining the perpetrator of an infringement of competition law, which is concerned with the actual conduct of undertakings', as '[t]he authors of the Treaties chose to use the concept of an undertaking to designate the perpetrator of an infringement of competition law, who is liable to be punished pursuant to [. . .] Articles 101 TFEU and 102 TFEU, and not the concept of a company or firm or of a legal person, used in Article 48 EC, currently Article 54 TFEU'; consequently, fines will be imposed to the legal entity/person found liable for the competition law infringement.[172]

The requirements of the principle of effectiveness of competition law are so strong that although a sanction may be imposed on an undertaking found liable following the unlawful action of a person who is generally authorized to act on behalf of the undertaking, the Court has accepted that the undertaking may be found liable even in the situation in which the authorized employee was also employed by another undertaking. Indeed, it would be too easy for an undertaking guilty of an infringement to avoid any penalty 'if it could validly raise against such a finding the fact that its employee was in reality acting at those meetings on behalf of another company', thus allowing 'the companies participating in cartels to avoid any liability by creating situations of dual employment with a company not involved in the cartel, by claiming that the joint employee acted solely on behalf of that other company'.[173]

4.3.2.1.2. Corporate groups and imputation of the anti-competitive conduct

Corporate groups raise questions also as to the imputation of the anti-competitive conduct and consequently the evaluation of the fine that may be imposed. Would anti-competitive conduct by a subsidiary be imputable to the parent company, in which case the fine will be evaluated as a proportion of the parent's turnover? In other words, does liability

[170] For such an argument see, WPJ Wils, 'The Undertaking as Subject of E.C. Competition Law and the Imputation of Infringements to Natural and Legal Persons', (2000) 25(2) *European L Rev* 99.

[171] Case C-90/09 P, *General Química and Others v Commission* [2011] ECR I–1, paras 34–5; Joined Cases C-201/09 & 216/09 P, *ArcelorMittal Luxembourg v Commission* and *Commission v ArcelorMittal Luxembourg and Others* [2011] ECR I–2239, para 95

[172] Case C-501/11 P, *Schindler Holding Ltd & Others v Commission*, ECLI:EU:C:2013:522, paras 101–2. See also Case C-231/11 P, *European Commission v Siemens AG Österreich and Others*, ECLI:EU:C:2014:256, para 42. For a criticism of this case law, see A Kalintiri, 'Revisiting Parental Liability in EU Competition Law' (2018) 43(2) *European L Rev* 145 (noting that it may deprive undertakings of the protection afforded to them by the Charter of Fundamental Rights [hereinafter Charter] and the general principles of EU law). However, in our view, this criticism related to the Charter is not appropriately substantiated. It does not also take into account the value of deterrence (which is related to economic efficiency) that may be promoted by a more extensive application of the single economic entity doctrine. See C Koenig, 'An Economic Analysis of the Single Economic Entity Doctrine in EU Competition Law' (2017) 13(2) *J Competition L & Economics* 281.

[173] Case T-551/08, *H&R ChemPharm v Commission*, ECLI:EU:T:2014:1081, para 131.

under EU competition law require that the legal entity in question has participated in the breach of competition law or is it sufficient that it has at least exercised some form of influence regarding the conduct in question, for instance by encouraging or passively tolerating the anti-competitive conduct of its subsidiary? The existence of a single economic entity in this context derives from the control exercised by the parent company to its subsidiaries.[174]

Parent company and wholly owned subsidiaries

In a series of cases concerning the question of the attribution of liability, the EU Courts held that there is a rebuttable legal presumption that the parent company actually exercises decisive influence over the subsidiary's commercial policy and market conduct if the parent company controls a 100 per cent shareholding of the subsidiary, thus presuming the actual exercise of the parent company's power of control from its ability to exert decisive influence on its subsidiary's distribution and pricing policies following the control of the totality or the quasi-totality of its shares.[175]

In *Bolloré*, the General Court deviated from the previous case law observing that a 100 per cent shareholding 'is not in itself sufficient to attribute liability to the parent for the conduct of its subsidiary [. . .] Something more than the extent of the shareholding must be shown, but this may be in the form of indicia',[176] thus adopting the so called '100 per cent + *X* rule' requiring some plus factors (*X*) in addition to the evidence of the complete ownership of the shares of the subsidiary by the parent company.[177]

However, the CJEU held in *Akzo Nobel* that, in the absence of evidence to the contrary, the legal presumption meant that the Commission or the claimant could rely on the control of 100 per cent shareholding of the subsidiary by its parent company, without the need to further substantiate its assumption that the parent company had actually exerted a decisive influence, thus rejecting the '100%+X rule'.[178]

[174] Starting with Case C-48/69, *Imperial Chemical Industries Ltd. v Commission of the European Community* [1972] ECR 619, paras 132, 133, and 135 (with regard to the application of Article 101 TFEU to a parent company for the activities of its subsidiary); Joined Cases 6 & 7/73, *Istituto Chemioterapico Italiana SpA and Commercial Solvents v Commission of the European Community* [1974] ECR 223 (with regard to the determination of the market shares in order to determine a corporate group's dominant position and attribute the market conduct of the subsidiary to its parent company, holding them jointly and severally liable for the anti-competitive conduct. In this case the parent company controlled the absolute majority (51 per cent) of the voting stock and had a 50 per cent representation on the affiliated company's executive committee. According to the CJEU, for a subsidiary to be treated as a single undertaking 'there must be (1) a power of direction of the parent company over the subsidiary and (2) also the actual exercise of the parent's control to such an extent that the subsidiary does not determine its behavior on the market in an autonomous manner, but essentially carries out the instructions given to it by the parent company' (Joined Cases 6 & 7/73, *Istituto Chemioterapico Italiana SpA and Commercial Solvents v Commission of the European Community* [1974] ECR 223, 323)).

[175] Starting with Case C-107/82, *AEG-Telefunken AG v Commission* [1983] ECR 3151, para 50. See also C-286/98 P, *Stora Kopparsberg Bergslag AB v Commission of the European Community* [2000] ECR I- 9925, paras 26–8.

[176] Joined Cases T-109, 118, 122, 125–6, 128–9, 132 & 136/02, *Bolloré v Commission* [2007] ECR II–947, para 132, partly set aside in Joined Cases C-322, 327 & 338/07 P, *Papierfabrik August Koehler and Others* v *Commission* [2009] ECR I–7191.

[177] According to the expression of AG Kokott in Case C-97/08 P, *Akzo Nobel and Others v Commission* [2009] ECR I–8237, para 68.

[178] See also Case C-90/09 P, *General Química and Others v Commission* [2011] ECR I–1, para 39; Joined Cases C-201 & 216/09 P, *ArcelorMittal Luxembourg v Commission* and *Commission v ArcelorMittal Luxembourg and Others* [2011] ECR I–2239, para 97.

Case C-97/08 P, *Akzo Nobel and Others v Commission*
[2009] ECR I–8237 (footnotes omitted)

Following a leniency application from an American producer, the Commission initiated an investigation into the global choline chloride industry, and found that a cartel was implemented at both the global and the European levels. The Commission adopted a decision finding a number of undertakings liable for an infringement of Article 101 TFEU in a series of agreements and concerted practices concerning price fixing, market sharing and concerted actions against competitors. The Commission decided to address the contested decision to AKZO Nobel, notwithstanding the fact that it had not itself participated in the cartel, because some of its subsidiaries were directly involved in the infringement. The Commission found that AKZO Nobel and its subsidiaries constituted a single economic unit with the other legal persons in the AKZO Nobel group and that it is that economic unit which participated in the cartel. The Commission concluded that that company was in a position to exert decisive influence over the commercial policy of its subsidiaries, in which it held, directly or indirectly, all of the shares, and that it could be assumed that it in fact did so. The Commission therefore concluded that AKZO Nobel's subsidiaries lacked commercial autonomy. AKZO Nobel and its subsidiaries appealed the Commission's decision before the General Court of the EU (then Court of First Instance), arguing that despite the presumption that a wholly owned subsidiary carries out the instructions of its parent company, in order to find the subsidiary liable, the claimant should bring evidence that the subsidiary determines its commercial policy largely on its own and that the parent company did in fact exercise a decisive influence in the specific case. The General Court rejected the appeal finding that '[i]n a specific case of a parent company holding 100% of the capital of a subsidiary which has committed an infringement, there is a simple presumption that the parent company exercises decisive influence over the conduct of its subsidiary [. . .], and that they therefore constitute a single undertaking within the meaning of Article [101 TFEU]'.[179] Hence, the decisive influence of the parent company over the subsidiary is presumed by the mere fact that the entire capital of a subsidiary is held by the parent company. The burden then shifts to the parent company which may rebut that presumption by adducing evidence to establish that its subsidiary was independent and that it did not, in essence, comply with the instructions issued by the parent company and, as a consequence, acted autonomously on the market. The General Court found that 'it is for the parent company to put before the Court any evidence relating to the economic and legal organizational links between its subsidiary and itself which in its view are apt to demonstrate that they do not constitute a single economic entity', the Court taking into account all the evidence adduced by the parties.[180] AKZO Nobel and its subsidiaries appealed the judgment of the General Court to the Court of Justice of the EU arguing, among others, that the Commission should have relied on more evidence than just the fact that the subsidiary's shares were whole owned by the parent company in order to infer the existence of a decisive influence of the latter to the former; that the rebuttal of that presumption was only permitted in narrow circumstances; and, finally, that extending the concept of commercial policy beyond the conduct of the subsidiary on the market would amount to introducing a strict liability regime, which would be contrary to the principle of personal responsibility under EU law.

57. The infringement of (EU) competition law must be imputed unequivocally to a legal person on whom fines may be imposed and the statement of objections must be

[179] Case T-112/05, *Akzo Nobel NV and Others v Commission* [2007] ECR II–5049, para 60.
[180] Ibid, para 65.

addressed to that person. It is also necessary that the statement of objections indicate in which capacity a legal person is called on to answer the allegations.

58. It is clear from settled case-law that the conduct of a subsidiary may be imputed to the parent company in particular where, although having a separate legal personality, that subsidiary does not decide independently upon its own conduct on the market, but carries out, in all material respects, the instructions given to it by the parent company, having regard in particular to the economic, organisational and legal links between those two legal entities.

59. [. . .] Thus, the fact that a parent company and its subsidiary constitute a single undertaking within the meaning of Article [101 TFEU] enables the Commission to address a decision imposing fines to the parent company, without having to establish the personal involvement of the latter in the infringement.

60. In the specific case where a parent company has a 100% shareholding in a subsidiary which has infringed the Community competition rules, first, the parent company can exercise a decisive influence over the conduct of the subsidiary and, second, there is a rebuttable presumption that the parent company does in fact exercise a decisive influence over the conduct of its subsidiary.

61. In those circumstances, it is sufficient for the Commission to prove that the subsidiary is wholly owned by the parent company in order to presume that the parent exercises a decisive influence over the commercial policy of the subsidiary. The Commission will be able to regard the parent company as jointly and severally liable for the payment of the fine imposed on its subsidiary, unless the parent company, which has the burden of rebutting that presumption, adduces sufficient evidence to show that its subsidiary acts independently on the market. [. . .]

63. It is clear from all those considerations that the Court of First Instance did not commit any error of law in holding that where a parent company has a 100% shareholding in its subsidiary there is a rebuttable presumption that that parent company exercises a decisive influence over the conduct of its subsidiary.

64. Accordingly, since the Commission is not required, as regards the imputation of the infringement, to submit, at the stage of the statement of objections, evidence other than proof relating to the shareholding of the parent company in its subsidiaries, the appellants' argument relating to the infringement of the rights of defence cannot be accepted. [. . .]

The CJEU notes that there is nothing which suggests that the possibility of rebutting the presumption is limited solely to cases where instructions have been issued by the parent company, the Court adopting the relatively open position of the General Court's judgment in that respect, holding, in particular, that it is for the parent company to put before the Court any evidence relating to the organizational, economic and legal links between its subsidiary and itself which are apt to demonstrate that they do not constitute a single economic entity.

72. [. . .] [T]he conduct of a subsidiary may be imputed to the parent company in particular where, although having a separate legal personality, that subsidiary does not decide independently upon its own conduct on the market, but carries out, in all material respects, the instructions given to it by the parent company.

73. It is clear [. . .] that the conduct of the subsidiary on the market cannot be the only factor which enables the liability of the parent company to be established, but is only one of the signs of the existence of an economic unit.

74. [. . .] [I]n order to ascertain whether a subsidiary determines its conduct on the market independently, account must be taken [. . .] of all the relevant factors relating

> to economic, organisational and legal links which tie the subsidiary to the parent company, which may vary from case to case and cannot therefore be set out in an exhaustive list. [. . .]

The CJEU dismissed the argument of the appellants that the General Court had committed an error of law as regards the sphere in which the parent company exercises influence over its subsidiary and concluded as following with regard to the argument of the appellants that the General Court had instituted a regime of strict liability in contravention of the principle of personal responsibility under EU law.

> 77. It must be observed in that connection that [. . .] (EU) competition law is based on the principle of the personal responsibility of the economic entity which has committed the infringement. If the parent company is part of that economic unit, which [. . .] may consist of several legal persons, the parent company is regarded as jointly and severally liable with the other legal persons making up that unit for infringements of competition law. Even if the parent company does not participate directly in the infringement, it exercises, in such a case, a decisive influence over the subsidiaries which have participated in it. It follows that, in that context, the liability of the parent company cannot be regarded as strict liability.

NOTES AND QUESTIONS ON AKZO NOBEL

1. *AKZO Nobel* is a case involving the issue of the attribution of liability between a parent company and its subsidiary for anti-competitive market behaviour. It expands the sphere of liability to the parent company exercising decisive influence on the commercial policy of its subsidiaries, even if it had not participated as such in the commission of the infringement (the prosecutorial function of the single entity doctrine). Because the parent company and its wholly owned subsidiary are presumed to have exercised a decisive influence over the commercial policy of the subsidiary and constitute a single economic entity for the purposes of Article 101 TFEU, unless the parent company, which has the burden of rebutting that presumption, adduces sufficient evidence to show that its subsidiary acts independently on the market. In case this presumption is not rebutted by the parent company, the Commission may address a decision imposing fines to the parent company, without having to establish the personal involvement of the latter in the infringement.[181] Should the claimant prove that the parent company has exercised decisive influence on its subsidiary in the particular case, or is it sufficient to raise the possibility that the parent company could exercise decisive influence over its wholly owned subsidiary? The evidential implications of the presumption resulting from the decisive influence that the parent company exercises towards its wholly owned subsidiary were explained by the CJEU in *AKZO Nobel*.[182]
2. This presumption was extended by the case law to situations 'where *almost all* the capital in the subsidiary is held by the parent company'.[183] Furthermore, 'in the specific case where a holding company holds 100% of the capital of an interposed company

[181] Ibid, para 59. [182] Ibid, para 61.

[183] Case C-508/11 P, *ENI SpA v Commission*, ECLI:EU:C:2013:289, para 47 (finding that Eni held, directly or indirectly, at least 99.97 per cent of the capital in the companies which were directly active within its group and therefore the *Akzo Nobel* presumption applied); Case C-289/11 P, *Legris Industries* v *Commission* [2012]

which, in turn, holds the entire capital of a subsidiary of its group which has committed an infringement of European Union competition law, there is also a rebuttable presumption that that holding company exercises a decisive influence over the conduct of the interposed company and also indirectly, via that company, over the conduct of that subsidiary'.[184]

3. If a subsidiary is not wholly owned in order to be able to impute the conduct of a subsidiary to the parent company, the Commission cannot merely find that the parent company is in a position to exercise decisive influence over the conduct of its subsidiary, but is also required to check whether the parent company actually exercised decisive influence over its subsidiary before imputing liability to the parent company.[185]

4. According to the jurisprudence of the CJEU, 'the presumption seeks precisely to find a balance between the importance, on the one hand, of the objective of penalising conduct contrary to the competition rules, in particular Article 101 TFEU, and to prevent its repetition and, on the other, the requirements of certain general principles of European Union law, such as, in particular, the principles of the presumption of innocence, that penalties should be applied only to the offender, legal certainty and the rights of the defence, including the principle of equality of arms. It is particularly for that reason that it is rebuttable'.[186] Hence, the fact that the presumption is rebuttable is a way to take into account the presumption of innocence, the personal nature of the liability, legal certainty, and rights of defence. Remark the relative importance awarded to the principle of effectiveness of competition law enforcement and to the objective of deterrence, as opposed to the principle of the presumption of innocence, in the way the balancing of these conflicting principles is configured, the presumption being that a parent company exercises decisive influence over its wholly owned subsidiary, absent proof to the contrary by the defendants.[187]

ECR, para 46; Case T-168/05, *Arkema SA v Commission* [2009] ECR II–180, para 70 (for parent companies that hold the totality or the quasi-totality of the capital of the subsidiary).

184 Case C-508/11 P, *ENI SpA v Commission*, ECLI:EU:C:2013:289, para 48.

185 See Case C-107/82, *AEG-Telefunken AG v Commission* [1983] ECR 3151, para 50. See also Joined Cases C-628 & 14/11 P, *Alliance One International and Standard Commercial Tobacco v Commission and Commission v Alliance One International and Others*, ECLI:EU:C:2012:479, paras 46–7.

186 Case C-508/11 P, *ENI SpA v Commission*, ECLI:EU:C:2013:289, para 50.

187 The balancing exercise between different principles was also noted by AG Kokott in her Opinion in Case C-97/08 P, *Akzo Nobel and Others v Commission* [2009] ECR I–8237:

> 39. The consequence of the *penal nature* of measures imposed by competition authorities for punishing cartel offences—in particular fines—is that the area is at least akin to criminal law. Therefore, what is decisive for the attribution of cartel offences is the *principle of personal responsibility*, which is founded in the rule of law and the principle of fault. Personal responsibility means that in principle a cartel offence is to be attributed to the natural or legal person who operates the undertaking which participates in the cartel; in other words, the principal of the undertaking is liable.
>
> 40. So far as the *purpose* of the measures imposed is concerned, it must be borne in mind that they serve the effective enforcement of competition rules in order to prevent distortions of competition (former Article 3(1)(g) EC Treaty); accordingly, they are intended to deter economic operators from committing cartel offences.
>
> 41. Taking personal responsibility as a reference point normally supports the effective enforcement of the competition provisions, given that the person conducting the undertaking also has decisive

5. The existence of property rights over assets and shares creates a presumption of decisive influence of the parent company over its subsidiary and provides therefore evidence of the existence of a single economic entity for the purposes of EU competition law. Although the concept of 'control' was not used by the CJEU in *AKZO Nobel*, one may argue that there is a presumption of decisive influence of the parent company on the subsidiary if the former exercises 'control' over the commercial policy of the latter. The 'decisive influence' follows from control.

   The concept of control is also used in merger control. The existence of property rights over assets and shares is not the only element to take into consideration when defining control and decisive influence, under Article 3(2)–(3) of the EU Merger Regulation. According to the Commission's Notice on the Concept of Concentration, 'purely economic relationships may also play a decisive role' in determining if there is control, observing that 'in exceptional circumstances, a situation of economic dependence may lead to control, on a *de facto* basis where, for example, very long-term supply agreements or credits provided by suppliers or customers, coupled with structural links, confer decisive influence.'[188]

   In the context of Article 101 TFEU, there is no equivalent presumption of control similar to that applying for a parent company holding 100 per cent shareholding of the subsidiary for entities that are not legally integrated through ownership rights but are solely economically integrated. In certain circumstances, however, it may be possible to take into account other factors than ownership of shares, but in this case there should be a case-by-case analysis in order to define if the two legal entities are in fact a single economic entity (see, for instance, for Commercial agency agreements, Chapter 10).
6. In your view, why did the CJEU decide not to expand the *AKZO Nobel* presumption to other instances of control outside the situation in which the parent company holds the totality or the quasi-totality of the capital of the subsidiary? Would this have led to expanding the prosecutorial function of the single entity doctrine too far, by extending the scope of the liability to other business participants than subsidiaries, when their contribution to the infringement may have been the product of economic coercion resulting from economic dependency? Why not, in this case, impose a higher fine to the controlling entity, by taking into account the turnover of the entities that were economically integrated with it? Should we take an equivalently narrow approach to the single entity doctrine when this is used in a defensive function? (See for instance, our discussion of commercial agency agreements in Chapter 10, an agreement between a principal and a genuine commercial agent escaping prohibition under Article 101(1) TFEU), because they form a single economic entity.)

influence over its market behaviour; the pressure of the penalties imposed should lead him to alter this conduct, such that in future the undertaking conducts itself in compliance with competition law. At the same time the penalty has general deterrent effect in that it also deters other economic participants from committing cartel offences.

188 Commission Notice on the Concept of Concentration [1998] OJ C 66/5, para 9.

Entities with a common owner (siblings or sister companies)

The *AKZO Nobel* presumption may also apply to entities with common owners (commonly referred to as 'siblings' or 'sister companies') with regard to their relation with their common owner.

In *Hydrotherm*, the Court examined the situation of two separate corporate legal entities with a common owner, a natural person, Mr Andreoli, who had complete control over the two corporate legal entities. The CJEU found that there was no possibility of competition between Mr Andreoli and the corporate legal persons he owned and thus it formed with each of them a single economic entity. Yet, the CJEU did not examine the question of the possibility of competition between the two corporate entities, but that between the owner and each of the corporate entities he owned.

But what about the relation between the two sister companies? Referring to some of the arguments presented by Viho at the CJEU in *Viho Europe v Commission*, Odudu and Bailey note that even corporate legal entities with a common owner may compete by charging different prices, applying different terms of warranty, undertaking different sales promotions at different times and in respect of different products, having different packaging, distribution methods and delivery criteria.[189] However, the authors note that the current position of the case law, although still ambivalent, is that separate legal entities with a common owner are presumed not to be capable of competing with each other and thus constitute a single economic entity. As is also explained by the Commission in its Guidelines on horizontal cooperation agreements,

> [w]hen a company exercises decisive influence over another company they form a single economic entity and, hence, are part of the same undertaking. The same is true for sister companies, that is to say, companies over which decisive influence is exercised by the same parent company. They are consequently not considered to be competitors even if they are both active on the same relevant product and geographic markets.[190]

Some recent case law explains that '[. . .] the mere fact that the share capital of two separate commercial companies is held by the same person or the same family is insufficient, in itself, to establish that those two companies form an economic unit'. The existence of an economic unit could, instead by proven by a 'set of circumstances', such as the fact that 'certain persons had assumed responsibilities simultaneously within (the two separate commercial companies)'.[191] Indeed, it is clear from the case law that the fact of occupying key positions on the management bodies of various companies is a factor that may be taken into account in order to establish that those companies form an economic unit (on the competition assessment of interlocking directorates, in particular in the context of merger control, see Chapter 12).

Non-wholly owned subsidiaries

The question arises as to what happens in cases in which the subsidiary is not wholly owned or almost wholly owned by its parent. This may, for instance, be the case of a parent company holding a majority shareholding (less than 100 per cent or a significant percentage) in

[189] O Odudu and D Bailey, 'The Single Economic Entity Doctrine in EU Competition Law' (2014) 51(1) *Common Market L Rev* 1, 12–3.

[190] European Commission, Guidelines on horizontal cooperation agreements [2011] OJ C 11/1, para 11.

[191] Case T-91/10, *Lucchini SpA v Commission*, ECLI:EU:T:2014:1033, paras 223–4.

a subsidiary when the market behaviour under competition law scrutiny results from a joint venture that is jointly controlled by two separate economic entities, or more broadly for entities with no controlling stakes in each other but which appear to be economically integrated. These situations require a case by case analysis exploring all the relevant factors relating to 'economic, organisational and legal links which tie the subsidiary to the parent company', which, according to the CJEU in *AKZO Nobel*, 'may vary from case to case and cannot therefore be set out in an exhaustive list'.[192] This case law is also applicable to the imputation of liability to one or more parent companies for an infringement committed by their joint venture.[193]

Joint ventures with no majority shareholding

What about joint ventures that are jointly governed by two or several parent companies, where no majority shareholding by one of the companies exists? Should these be considered as forming a single economic entity with their parent companies, in which case many agreements concluded between the parent companies and the joint venture, in this 'trilateral' relationship, may not fall under Article 101 TFEU or its national equivalent, the single economic entity operating as a shield (the defensive dimension of the single economic entity doctrine)? Should the parent companies and the joint venture be considered a single economic entity, and hence any joint action adopted by them excluded from the application of Article 101(1) TFEU, or should they be considered two separate undertakings that may infringe Article 101(1) if their joint action has as its object or effect to restrict competition?

In *Dow Chemical v Commission*, two parent companies each had a 50 per cent shareholding in a joint venture company which had committed an infringement.[194] The Commission, and the General Court on appeal, held both parent companies of the joint venture jointly and severally liable for the infringing behaviour of that joint venture in so far as both did in fact exercise decisive influence over the joint venture's conduct on the specific market, the three entities constituting, in view of all the economic, legal, and organizational links between them, a single economic unit and therefore a single undertaking for the purposes of Article 101 TFEU. Interestingly, the General Court held that since any gains resulting from illegal activities accrue to the shareholders exercising a decisive influence, it is only fair that that those who have the power of supervision should assume liability for the illegal business activities of their subsidiaries, thus adopting a business participant approach to liability.[195] Dow Chemicals argued on the contrary that any eventual gains generated by a joint venture involved in a cartel would benefit, not the shareholders, but the joint venture and that the parent companies could only exercise in this context a negative power to reject the decisions of the other shareholders of the joint venture, which could not amount to a decisive influence.

The CJEU dismissed the appeal, confirming the finding that the joint venture and its parent companies formed a single economic entity, although it also indirectly criticized the General Court for referring to the indirect benefit accruing to the parent companies in their shareholder capacity as a ground that was included in the judgment purely for the sake of completeness. The CJEU held that 'decisive influence of one or more parent companies is not necessarily tied in with the day-to-day running of a subsidiary' and that 'evidence of such influence must be assessed having regard to all the economic, organisational and legal links

192 Case T-112/05, *Akzo Nobel NV and Others v Commission* [2007] ECR II-5049, para 74.

193 Joined Cases T-141–2 &145–6/07, *General Technic-Otis and Others v Commission* [2011] ECR II-4977, paras 52–6.

194 Case C-179/12 P, *The Dow Chemical Company v European Commission*, ECLI:EU:C:2013:605.

195 Case T-77/08, *The Dow Chemical Company v European Commission*, ECLI:EU:T:2012:47.

between the subsidiary and the parent company'.[196] It also explained that the autonomy that a joint venture enjoys within the meaning of Article 3(4) of the EU Merger Regulation 'does not mean that that joint venture also enjoys autonomy in relation to adopting strategic decisions, and that it is therefore not under the decisive influence of its parent companies for the purposes of Article [101 TFEU]'.[197]

4.3.2.2. Attributing liability within the corporate group: is there a way out of the *AKZO Nobel* presumption?

The possibility of rebuttal of the *AKZO Nobel* presumption, as well as the case law on the non-wholly owned subsidiaries, provides important clues as to the instances in which the corporate veil will be pierced and a parent company will be found not liable for anti-competitive conduct initiated and executed by one of its subsidiaries. This will occur if it provides evidence of the independence of their subsidiary and the autonomy of its conduct on the market. In this case, liability should solely be attributed to the subsidiary that committed or participated in the commitment of the competition law infringement. In reality, however, there are very few instances in which the presumption was rebutted, some authors even qualifying this as a form of '*probatio diabolica*'.[198] As AG Kokott recognized in her Opinion in *Akzo Nobel*, the presumption may be rebutted only in very specific circumstances, such as (a) the parent company is an investment company and behaves like a pure financial investor, (b) the parent company holds 100% of the shares in the subsidiary only temporarily and for a short period, and (c) the parent company is prevented for legal reasons from fully exercising its 100 per cent control over the subsidiary.[199] It is nevertheless important here to focus on the meaning of 'decisive influence', the absence of which may rebut the *AKZO Nobel* presumption, and on the situation of corporate re-organizations which may also raise the issue of the rebuttal.

4.3.2.2.1. The meaning of 'decisive influence'

In *AKZO Nobel*, the CJEU held that the decisive influence of the parent company on the subsidiary, or the absence of it, may be inferred from a vague set of indirect, circumstantial evidence on the 'economic, organizational and legal links' tying the parent company and its subsidiary. For (parent) companies controlling the totality or the quasi-totality of the shareholding of a subsidiary, there is a presumption of decisive influence, which may be rebutted in theory by the parent company. However, the standard of proof required by the parent company is high, the presumption being considered by some as practically irrefutable.[200]

The EU Courts have held that '[t]he fact that it is difficult to adduce the evidence necessary to rebut the presumption does not in itself mean than that presumption is in fact irrebuttable, especially where the entities against which the presumption operates are those best placed to seek that evidence within their own sphere of activity'[201] and have rejected most of the efforts

196 Case C-179/12 P, *The Dow Chemical Company v European Commission*, ECLI:EU:C:2013:605, para 64.

197 Ibid, paras 64–5.

198 A Svetlicinii, 'Parental Liability for the Antitrust Infringements of Subsidiaries: A Rebuttable Presumption or Probatio Diabolica?' (2011) 10 *European L Reporter* 288. See also the criticisms of A Kalintiri, 'Revisiting Parental Liability in EU Competition Law' (2018) 43(2) *European L Rev* 145, and the references cited.

199 Opinion of AG Kokott in Case C-97/08, *Akzo Nobel NV and Others v Commission*, ECLI:EU:C:2009:262, para 67.

200 NI Pauer, *The Single Economic Entity Doctrine and Corporate Group Responsibility in European Antitrust Law* (Kluwer Law International, 2014), 116.

201 Joined Cases C-93 and 123/13 P, *European Commission v Versalis SpA & Eni SpA*, ECLI:EU:C:2015:150.

by parent companies to rebut the presumption and adduce evidence of the independence of the subsidiary:

- The fact that the subsidiary has never implemented a specific policy of reporting to the parent company or that there were no orders or instructions by the parent company to the subsidiary cannot rebut establish that the subsidiary is independent of its parent company.[202]
- The fact that the subsidiary operates on a different market from the parent company and has no links in terms of customer-supplier relationship was found to be a division of tasks that constitutes a 'normal phenomenon' within a corporate group, thus not sufficient to rebut the presumption.[203]
- The fact that the parent company has been involved in the adoption of high-level strategy decisions for the whole corporate group, without being involved in the process of implementing these decisions in the commercial policy of the subsidiary was also not found sufficient to rebut the presumption.[204] On the contrary, '[t]he subsidiary's conduct on the market is, in general, also under the decisive influence of the parent company where the latter retains only the power to define or approve certain strategic commercial decisions, where appropriate by its representatives in the bodies of the subsidiaries, while the power to define the commercial policy *stricto sensu* of the subsidiary is delegated to the managers responsible for its operational management, chosen by the parent company and representing and promoting the parent company's commercial interests.'[205]
- The absence of interlocking directorates (joint memberships of the boards of directors of the companies) and the existence of separate governing and managing organs was also found insufficient for adducing evidence of the independence of the subsidiaries vis-à-vis their parent companies.[206] According to the GC, '[. . .] in the case of a single shareholder, all decisions—including those relating to the operational management of the subsidiary—are taken by managers nominated and appointed either directly or indirectly (by the bodies whose members have been appointed by the parent company) by the parent company alone. Likewise, in the absence of another shareholder, the only commercial interests to be found within the subsidiary are in principle the commercial interests of the sole shareholder. Thus, the Commission may presume the effective exercise of decisive influence even where the operational management is carried out autonomously by the managers of the subsidiary'.[207]
- The situation is different for joint ventures, when 'there are several shareholders and the decisions of the joint venture's bodies are taken by members representing the commercial interests of the various parent companies, which may coincide, but which may also diverge. Consequently, the question whether a parent company has exercised actual

202 Case T-168/05, *Arkema SA v Commission* [2009] ECR II–180, para 79; Case T-41/05, *Alliance One International v Commission* [2011] ECR II–7101, para 160.

203 Case T-168/05, *Arkema SA v Commission* [2009] ECR II–180, para 80.

204 Case T-190/06, *Total and Elf Aquitaine v Commission* [2011] ECR II–5513, appeal dismissed by Order of the CJEU, Case C-495/11 P, ECLI:EU:C:2012:571.

205 Case T-25/06, *Alliance One International v Commission* [2011] ECR II–5741, paras 138–9; Case T-543/08, *RWE AG, RWE Dea AG*, ECLI:EU:T:2014:627, para 31.

206 Joined Cases T-141–2 & T-145–6/07, *General Technic-Otis and Others* v *Commission* [2011] ECR II–4977, para 83.

207 Case T-543/08, *RWE & RWE Dea v Commission*, ECLI:EU:T:2014:627, para 121.

influence over the operational management of the joint venture, in particular through the managers appointed by it or who at the same time occupy positions in the parent company's management, continues to be relevant'.[208]

- The fact that a subsidiary has its own local management and its own resources 'does not prove, in itself, that that company decides upon its conduct on the market independently of its parent company', the GC noting that '[t]he division of tasks between subsidiaries and their parent companies and, in particular, the fact that a wholly-owned subsidiary is entrusted with the management of day-to-day activities' being 'normal practice in large undertakings composed of a multitude of subsidiaries ultimately owned by the same holding company'.[209] Hence, in the case of a wholly owned or virtually wholly owned subsidiary directly involved in the infringement, the evidence adduced in that regard is not capable of rebutting the presumption that decisive influence over the subsidiary's conduct was effectively exercised by the parent company.[210]
- The existence of formal written policies for compliance with competition law does not also allow the rebuttal of the presumption that parent companies are liable for the conduct of their wholly owned subsidiaries.[211] Indeed, '[t]he fact that such policies are deployed does not establish that those subsidiaries determined their commercial policy on the market independently' and the fact that the parent companies 'ensure the implementation of such policies' tends instead to support the proposition that the subsidiaries are not managed independently.[212]
- The fact that the competition law infringement resulted from certain employees that disobeyed the parent company's instructions, in particular by concealing their behaviour from their superiors in the subsidiary and the parent company, does not reverse the presumption that the subsidiaries concerned were not autonomous, as '[t]hose employees are, in relation to the [. . .] subsidiaries which employ them, in a relationship characterised by the fact that they work for and under the management of each of them and are, throughout the term of that relationship, integrated into those undertakings, thereby forming with each of them an economic unit'.[213]

There is also case law about situations in which the parent company does not take the form of the classic parent company, but that of a non-operating holding or foundation.

In *Arkema*, the parent company in question, Elf Aquitaine, argued that it constituted merely a 'non-operational holding company' that rarely intervened in the management of its subsidiaries, in order to establish the independence of its subsidiary and rebut the *AKZO Nobel* presumption of decisive influence. The General Court, confirmed by the CJEU, held that the claim that the parent company was merely a non-operational holding

[208] Case T-541/08, *Sasol, Sasol Holding, Sasol Wax International, Sasol Wax GmbH v Commission*, ECLI:EU:T:2014:628, para 112; Case T-543/08, *RWE & RWE Dea v Commission*, ECLI:EU:T:2014:627, para 102 (noting that the Commission may demonstrate the decisive influence of the parent company on the basis of factual evidence, including the accumulation of posts by the same natural persons in the management of the parent company and that of its subsidiary or joint venture); Joined Cases C-189, 202, 205–8 & 213/02 P, *Dansk Rørindustri and Others v Commission* [2005] ECR I–5425, paras 119–20.

[209] Case T-566/08, *Total Raffinage Marketing v Commission* ECLI:EU:T:2013:423, para 518.

[210] Ibid.

[211] Case C-501/11 P, *Schindler Holding Ltd & Others v Commission* ECLI:EU:C:2013:522, para 113.

[212] Joined Cases T-141–2 & 145–6/07, *General Technic-Otis and Others v Commission* [2011] ECR II–4977, para 85.

[213] Ibid, para 87.

company was 'not sufficient to rule out the possibility that it exercises decisive influence over the applicant's conduct by coordinating, inter alia, financial investments' within the Elf Aquitaine corporate group, as 'in the context of a group of companies, a holding company that coordinates, inter alia, financial investments within the group is in a position to regroup shareholdings in various companies and has the function of ensuring that they are run as one, including by means of such budgetary control'.[214]

In *Alliance One International*, World Wide Tobacco España (WWTE) was found to have implemented a cartel entered into for processing Spanish raw tobacco, to which a number of other companies, whose shares were totally or significantly controlled by US multinational parent companies, participated. The Commission relied on the legal presumption that a parent company exercises decisive influence over its wholly-owned subsidiary, but also made use of the 'dual basis' method requiring in addition evidence of other factual elements confirming the presumption, in view of the uncertainties at the time over the evidential weight of the presumption following the *Bolloré* precedent of the General Court.

Applying the presumption and the dual basis method, the Commission found the grand parent company, Alliance One International (AOI), jointly liable for the competition law infringement of its ultimate subsidiary, WWTE, through the interposition of some intermediate subsidiaries which it controlled. Two thirds of the capital of WWTE was held by Trans-Continental Leaf Tobacco Corporation (TCLT), the interposed subsidiary, which was a holding company that did not carry out any commercial activity, which was also a wholly owned subsidiary of Standard Commercial Tobacco Company (SCTC), itself a wholly owned subsidiary of Standard Commercial Corporation (SCC) (now Alliance One International), which formed the ultimate parent company, or the grandparent company. AOI's share in WWTE, through its participation in TCLT, was later increased to 86.94 per cent. As a number of parent companies of other processors involved in the cartel were not found jointly and severally liable, WWTE's parent companies brought an action for annulment of the Commission's decision to the General Court. The General Court found that 'none of the materials relied on by the Commission in its decision supported the conclusion that TCLT had exercised decisive influence over the conduct of WWTE', noting that the interposed subsidiary was 'a company with no activity of its own and whose interest in WWTE (was) purely financial', the attribution of certain purchases of tobacco carried out by WWTE to TCLT resulting from 'accounting and fiscal reasons'.[215] Hence, the existence of an economic interest in a subsidiary was not found enough to infer decisive influence.

Other instances in which parent companies relied on the fact that they constituted a financial holding company have not proved successful. In *Legris*, the CJEU rejected the argument that because it was a financial holding company, the parent company in question could not have exercised decisive influence over its subsidiary.[216] In *1. garantovaná*, the General Court confirmed the Commission's finding that the Slovak Investment company was jointly liable for the anti-competitive conduct of one of its portfolio companies.[217]

[214] Case T-168/05, *Arkema SA v Commission* [2009] ECR II–180, para 76; Case C-520/09 P *Arkema SA v Commission* [2011] ECR I–8901, para 48. See also Case T-38/07, *Shell Petroleum v Commission* [2011] ECR II–4383, para 70.

[215] Case T-24/05, *Alliance One International Inc, Standard Commercial Tobacco Co, Inc, Trans-Continental Leaf Tobacco Corp Ltd v Commission* [2010] ECR II–5329, paras 195–6.

[216] Case C-289/11 P, *Legris Industries v Commission* ECLI:EU:C:2012:270, paras 45–55. See also Case C-90/09 P, *General Química SA and Others v Commission* [2011] ECR I–1.

[217] Case T-392/09, *1. garantovaná a.s. v Commission*, ECLI:EU:T:2012:674.

In *Portielje*, the CJEU confirmed the decision of the Commission to find liable a foundation pulling together family shareholders in order to ensure a unity of management of a subsidiary involved in a cartel in the international removal services sector in Belgium, the legal form of foundation rather than one of a company being irrelevant.[218] Indeed, according to the CJEU, 'it is also irrelevant whether each individual legal entity comprising the undertaking is itself economically active and therefore individually constitutes an undertaking'.[219] Making a distinction between holding companies and other parent companies would have been contrary to the principle of equal treatment.[220]

The CJEU did not agree with the General Court's view that the parental liability presumption was applicable only when the parent company engages in an economic activity or at least interferes with the economic activity of its subsidiary, thus being an undertaking itself. It also disagreed with the General Court's conclusion that in case the foundation was an undertaking, it had successfully rebutted the parental liability presumption because its first board of directors' meeting was held only after the infringement decision, the shareholders' general assembly was not held during the relevant period, and the subsidiary's board members were appointed before the foundation had acquired its shares.[221] The CJEU plainly disagreed with these findings, criticizing the General Court for concluding on the rebuttal of the presumption 'purely on the basis of an analysis conducted by reference to company law', thus signifying that any assessment should focus on all the relevant factors relating to the economic, organizational and legal links which tie the parent company and its subsidiary.[222] The CJEU found no infringement of Article 47 of the Charter of Fundamental Rights of the European Union or Article 6 of the European Convention on the Protection of Human Rights and Fundamental Freedoms, when the presumption remains within acceptable limits 'so long as it is proportionate to the legitimate aim pursued' and 'it is possible to adduce evidence to the contrary', even if it admitted that the latter is 'difficult'.[223]

The possibility of rebuttal for 'purely financial investors' is also slim, as the General Court gave a very narrow definition of this concept in *1. garantovaná a.s.* observing that it refers 'to the case of an investor who holds shares in a company in order to make a profit, but who refrains from any involvement in its management and in its control'.[224]

In *Edison*, the parent company succeeded in rebutting the parental liability presumption.[225] The case involved Ausimont, a company whose 100 per cent capital share was indirectly held

218 Case C-440/11 P, *Commission v Stichting Administratiekantoor Portielje and Gosselin Group NV*, ECLI:EU:C:2013:514, para 42.

219 Case C-440/11 P, *Commission v Stichting Administratiekantoor Portielje and Gosselin Group NV*, ECLI:EU:C:2013:514, para 43.

220 Opinion of AG Kokott in Case C-440/11 P, *Commission v Stichting Administratiekantoor Portielje and Gosselin Group NV*, ECLI:EU:C:2012:763, para 54.

221 Joined Cases T-208–9/08, *Gosselin Group NV and Stichting Administratiekantoor Portielje v Commission* [2011] ECR II-3639, paras 55–7.

222 Case C-440/11 P, *Commission v Stichting Administratiekantoor Portielje and Gosselin Group NV*, ECLI:EU:C:2013:514, para 67. The CJEU castigated, for instance, the General Court for having examined the personal links that existed between the foundation and its subsidiary simply from a company law perspective, as 'the fact that a finding that the author of the infringement and its holding entity form an economic unit does not necessarily presuppose the adoption of formal decisions by statutory organs and that, on the contrary, that unit may also have an informal basis, consisting inter alia in personal links between the legal entities comprising such an economic unit' (ibid, para 68).

223 Case C-440/11 P, *Commission v Stichting Administratiekantoor Portielje and Gosselin Group NV*, ECLI:EU:C:2013:514, paras 71–2.

224 Case T-392/09, *1. garantovaná a.s. v Commission* ECLI:EU:T:2012:674, para 52.

225 Case T-196/06, *Edison SpA v Commission* [2011] ECR II-3149; Case C-446/11 P, *Commission v Edison SpA*, ECLI:EU:C:2013:798.

by the Edison group, which had participated in a cartel on the markets for hydrogen peroxide and sodium perborate that was found to constitute a competition law infringement by the Commission, both Edison and Aussimont being found jointly and severally liable. Edison argued that it was purely a financial holding with no involvement whatsoever in the management of Aussimont, the management of which, following a severe financial difficulties in 1993, was entirely replaced by a new team appointed by the creditor banks, which had become its principal shareholders. Given the small management resources of Edison, the fact that its subsidiary operated in the chemical sector, which was no longer considered strategic by Edison and henceforth was progressively divested, and its incapacity to manage in an integrated manner an extremely diversified group, as each operating subsidiary was to be managed in complete independence by its own management team regarding both their market strategies and their commercial behaviours, Edison argued that it had rebutted the parent liability presumption. The General Court agreed with Edison and quashed the Commission's decision to hold it jointly and severally liable with its subsidiary. The company had indeed, not only relied on 'the fact that it was a holding company managing its subsidiary as a straightforward financial investment, through an interposed holding company, but also pleaded a body of special circumstances characterizing the links between the companies concerned at the time of the infringement at issue'.[226] The CJEU upheld the first instance judgment, insisting on the duty of the Commission to state reasons for rejecting the arguments of the parent company attempting to rebut the parent liability presumption, a constant emphasis in some of the most recent case law of the EU Courts.[227]

In *Commission v Versalis*, the CJEU held that 'in the specific case where a person holds all or almost all of the capital of an interposed company which, in turn, holds all or almost all of the capital of a subsidiary of its group which has committed an infringement of EU competition law, there is also a rebuttable presumption that that holding company exercises a decisive influence over the conduct of the interposed company and indirectly, via the company, also over the conduct of that subsidiary'.[228]

Even if the jurisprudence of the EU Courts seems to pierce the corporate veil and the enterprise liability doctrine by holding parent companies liable for infringements committed by subsidiaries over which they exercise a decisive influence, it clearly excludes from the scope of liability, other business participants, such as creditors (debt holders) and equity holders, who are not involved in the management of the company but simply hold shares 'in order to make a profit'.

A distinction is thus established between situations of 'managerial operational control', which give rise to the presumption, and 'financial structural control' by passive investors (debt or equity holders), which may act against the presumption and rebut it.[229]

The scope of this exception from the parent liability presumption has little practical significance, in view of the fact that it seems unlikely that a passive investor will acquire a majority

[226] Case T-196/06, *Edison SpA v Commission* [2011] ECR II–3149, para 173.

[227] See eg Case C-521/09, *Elf Aquitaine SA v Commission* [2011] ECR I–8947; Case T-185/06, *L'Air liquide, société anonyme pour l'étude et l'exploitation des procédés Georges Claude v Commission* [2011] ECR II–2809.

[228] Joined Cases C-93 & 123/13 P, *European Commission v Versalis SpA & Eni SpA*, ECLI:EU:C:2015:150, para 43. In this case Eni was found to hold part directly and part indirectly, 99.93 per cent to 100 per cent of the capital of the companies responsible within its group and consequently the parental liability presumption was found to apply.

[229] On this distinction, see Section 4.3.1, EW Orts, *Business Persons—A Legal Theory of the Firm* (OUP, 2013), 86 and 88.

shareholding in a company, to the extent usually relied upon for the parental liability presumption to operate.

Nevertheless, the exception may not catch private equity investors and hedge funds, which are usually involved in the supervision of the companies in their portfolio, at least from a corporate law perspective.

In *Gigaset v Commission*, the General Court confirmed a Commission decision holding Arques (now Gigaset), a German private equity fund specializing in the direct acquisition and restructuring of companies in distress, jointly liable for a fine imposed on a company (SKW Stahl-Metallurgie), which had participated in a cartel involving calcium carbide and magnesium based reagents for the steel and gas industries.[230] During the period of the infringement Arques held first the totality, then 57 per cent of the capital of SKW Holding, which controlled 100 per cent of the capital of SKW Stahl-Metallurgie. The Commission, confirmed by the General Court, applied the presumption of parent liability for the first period of the infringement and then relied on other factors for the second period of infringement during which Arques held indirectly a majority shareholding in the company engaged in the competition law infringement. The General Court dismissed Arques' arguments that it was involved only in strategic and restructuring decisions and did not engage in portfolio company business decision, by observing the need for Arques' approval for strategic decisions directly affecting the profitability and growth potential of SKW, the representation of Arques in the board of directors of SKW and the regular reporting of information on SKW's economic performance to Arques.[231]

Most recently, the Commission found the private equity arm of Goldman Sachs liable for the anti-competitive conduct of one of its former portfolio companies, Prysmian, which had participated in the power cables cartel.[232] In 2005, GS Capital Partners had acquired 100 per cent of Prysmian through one of its funds and following an IP in 2007 it retained 54 per cent of Prysmian before fully divesting in 2010 its remaining interest. The Commission found that GS Capital Partners and ultimately Goldman Sachs exercised 'decisive influence' over Prysmian between 2005 and 2009, the date the infringement stopped. Indeed, Goldman Sachs held 100 per cent of the voting rights, was represented on the board of directors of Prysmian and obtained monthly reports on Prysmian's business, which proved the finding of its 'decisive influence'. Goldman Sachs appealed the decision of the Commission to the General Court.

The GC upheld the Commission's decision noting that, although GS's ownership of Prysmian was through a fund vehicle, the Commission has not erred in finding that Goldman Sachs was not a pure financial investor.[233] Hence, the GC accepted that the *Akzo* presumption can apply in cases where the parent has less than 100 per cent shareholding, in case it is able to exercise all the voting rights and thus conduct company business independently of any other interests in the company. The GC noted, in particular, that a 'pure financial investor' does not constitute a legal criterion but is an example of a circumstance in which it is

230 Case T-395/09, *Gigaset AG v Commission*, ECLI:EU:T:2014:23. See also, for a similar fact pattern also involving a private equity controlling a majority stake in a company having participated in the calcium carbide cartel, Case T-392/09, *1. garantovaná a.s. v Commission*, ECLI:EU:T:2012:674.

231 Case T-395/09, *Gigaset AG v Commission*, ECLI:EU:T:2014:23.

232 *Power Cables* (Case COMP/ANT.39.610) Commission Decision [2014] OJ 319/10, summary version only available.

233 Case T-419/14, *The Goldman Sachs Group v Commission*, ECLI:EU:T:2018:445.

open to a parent company to rebut the presumption of actual exercise of decisive influence'.[234] The GC found that '[i]n accordance with settled case-law, it is unnecessary to restrict the assessment of the exercise of decisive influence to matters relating solely to the subsidiary's commercial policy on the market *stricto sensu*'.[235] It found also relevant the other factors the Commission had taken into account to demonstrate the decisive influence of Goldman Sachs in Prysmian, such as the fact that Goldman Sachs had appointed all the boards of directors of the company during the infringement period and that its appointees sat on the company's strategic committee.[236]

The financialization of the global economy has been described as a recurrent trend affecting a number of markets.[237] Following up the transformation of corporate control since the 1970s with the development of the multiproduct firm, in which managers sought to spread risks across various product lines in order to achieve greater profitability and to grow through mergers financed by leveraged buyouts, private equity investing financed by junk bonds and other innovative financial techniques, the level of corporate (but also household) debt has considerably increased. The financialization of the modern corporation has been a remarkable feature of this evolution, with the prevalence of the principle of shareholder value, the focus on short-term share price, leveraging through debt, hybrid financial instruments, and the important role of institutional investors, in particular financial institutions but also sovereign wealth funds. In view of the leveraging it enables, debt financing raises the rate of return on equity capital, at least in the short-term. But it can also facilitate equity buybacks, thus raising the stock prices and through that the revenue collected by the company's management via stock options pay. Hence, stock options pay affects the incentives of managers, aligning their interests with those of the financial markets, including the most important creditors of their company, who share with equity owners the financial structural control of the company. This is particularly the case in circumstances of financial failure or severe stress (eg economic crisis).[238] As it is well explained by Eric Orts, '[m]anagers in heavily leveraged firms are probably better described as focusing on 'creditor primacy', given their need to meet periodic debt payments with little managerial slack'.[239] However, EU and UK competition law focus on managerial operational control and seem to ignore financial structural control.

Do you consider that the current state of EU and UK competition law regarding the definition of the concept of undertaking and consequently the scope of the application of the EU and UK antitrust law provisions takes account of the increasing financialization of the economy? What would have been your suggestions in order to remedy this disconnection? Would you have taken into account financial structural control in the definition of the boundaries of the 'single economic entity'? Which criteria or factors would you have relied upon?

234 Ibid, para 151. 235 Ibid, para 152. 236 Ibid, paras 154 and 180.

237 More generally, see GA Epstein, *Financialization and the World Economy* (Edward Elgar, 2005); RJ Shiller, *The New Financial Order. Risk in the 21st Century* (Princeton University Press, 2003); J Montgomerie and K Williams, 'Financialised Capitalism: After the Crisis and beyond Neoliberalism' (2009) 13 *Competition & Change* 99; E Engelen, 'The Case for Financialization' (2008) 12 *Competition & Change* 111; N van der Zwan, 'Making Sense of Financialization' (2014) 12 (1) *Socio-economic Rev* 99; RM Solow, 'How to Save American Finance from Itself: Has Financialization Gone Too Far?', *New Republic* (8 April 2013), available at http://www.newrepublic.com/article/112679/how-save-american-finance-itself.

238 EW Orts, *Business Persons—A Legal Theory of the Firm* (OUP, 2013), 88. 239 Ibid.

4.3.2.2.2. Corporate reorganization, corporate shapeshifting, and succession (economic continuity) of an entity

As it was previously explained, the principle of personal responsibility requires that liability is to be attributed to the legal person operating the undertaking at the time it committed the infringement.[240] However, as AG J Kokott acknowledges,

> 68. The fundamental problem of attributing [. . .] (competition law) offences [is] the fact that the addresses of the competition rules and the addressees of decisions by the competition authorities are not necessarily the same.
>
> 69. Specifically, whereas the competition rules are directed to *undertakings* and apply to them directly regardless of how they are organised and their legal nature, decisions by competition authorities penalizing breaches of competition rules can be directed only to *persons*, not least because such decisions must be enforced. For that reason, in every case in which a competition authority penalises a cartel offence the question arises as to the attribution of that conduct to a specific person [. . .].
>
> 73. Admittedly, reorganisations, disposals of undertakings and other changes can lead to the situation in which, at the time a cartel offence is penalised, the person who conducts an undertaking which participated in the cartel is not the person who conducted the undertaking at the time of the infringement. In that scenario it follows from the principle of personal responsibility that in principle the cartel offence is to be attributed to the natural or legal person who conducted the undertaking at the time of the infringement (*original operator*), even if at the time of the decision by the competition authorities a different person is responsible for its operation (*new operator*); if the undertaking continued the infringement under the responsibility of the new operator, the cartel offence is to be attributed to the new operator only from the time at which he took over the undertaking.[241]

Indeed, corporate shapeshifting, that is instances of transformation of the corporate form such as changes in the capital structure and the allocation of control rights in a corporation, eventually with the creation of a new corporate entity succeeding the previous one, or more generally corporate restructuring and changes in the allocation of corporate assets are quite common in the modern economy. In case there is some re-organization, would the liability of the infringing undertaking be attributed to the former entity? Similarly, once an entity/undertaking was found liable for a competition law infringement, will that liability be passed on to subsequent acquirers of the entity, even if these did not control the entity at the time of the infringement?

In *PVC*, the Commission explained:

> It is thus irrelevant that an undertaking may have sold its [. . .] business to another: the purchaser does not thereby become liable for the participation of the seller in the cartel. If the undertaking which committed the infringement continues in existence it remains responsible in spite of the transfer.

240 Case C-49/92 P, *Commission v Anic Participazioni SpA* [1999] ECR I-4215, para 145; Case C-280/06, *Autorità Garante della Concorrenza e del Mercato v Ente tabacchi italiani—ETI SpA and Others* [2007] ECR I-10893, paras 39–40.

241 Opinion in Case C-280/06, *Autorità Garante della Concorrenza e del Mercato v Ente tabacchi italiani—ETI SpA and Others* [2007] ECR I-10893, paras 68–9 and 73.

On the other hand, where the infringing undertaking itself is absorbed by another producer, its responsibility may follow it and attach to the new or merged entity.

It is not necessary that the acquirer be shown to have carried on or adopted the unlawful conduct as its own. The determining factor is whether there is a functional and economic continuity between the original infringer and the undertaking into which it was merged.[242]

In the above excerpt, the Commission distinguished situations where the subsidiary or assets involved in the infringement are acquired by another undertaking (an asset sale) from those where are absorbed in the form of a merger (share sale).

The principle of personal responsibility would require that where assets are sold (the first scenario), the company previously responsible for those assets should be liable as long as it remains in existence. However, the case law opposes '[a]n excessively formalistic application of the principle of personal responsibility'.[243] Following the criterion of 'economic continuity' and as an exception to the principle of personal responsibility, if the original operator no longer exists or does not carry on any significant economic activity, the new entity (the one acquiring the assets responsible for the competition law infringement) may attract liability.

For the criterion of economic continuity to apply, 'it is necessary, first, to find the combination of physical and human elements which contributed to the commission of the infringement and then to identify the person who has become responsible for their operation, so as to avoid the result that because of the disappearance of the person responsible for its operation when the infringement was committed the undertaking may fail to answer for it'.[244] This seems to be more an issue relating to retributive justice than to specific or general deterrence.[245] Subsequent case law has nevertheless adopted considerations of specific and general deterrence as a foundation for the criterion of 'economic continuity' noting that:

As to the circumstances in which an entity that is not responsible for the infringement can nevertheless be penalised for that infringement, it must be held first that this situation arises if the entity that has committed the infringement has ceased to exist, either in law [. . .] or

242 *PVC* (Case COMP IV/31.865) Commission Decision [1994] L 239/14, para 41.

243 Opinion of AG J Kokott in Case C-280/06, *Autorità Garante della Concorrenza e del Mercato v Ente tabacchi italiani—ETI SpA and Others* [2007] ECR I-10893, para 74.

244 Case T-6/89, *Enichem v Commission* [1991] ECR II-1623, para 237.

245 Yet, in her Opinion in Case C-280/06 *Autorità Garante della Concorrenza e del Mercato v Ente tabacchi italiani—ETI SpA and Others* [2007] ECR I-10893, para 80, Advocate General J Kokott proposed an additional justification for the criterion of economic continuity, specific deterrence:

> [I]t is only by attributing the cartel offence to the new operator of the undertaking that one can ensure that on the one hand the person made responsible is the one who gains from any profits and increases in value of the undertaking in consequence of participation in the cartel [*referring to the principle of retributive justice*], and on the other that the penalty as such is not ineffective. This is because it is only the economically active new operator who can have the undertaking conduct itself in future in compliance with competition law. A penalty would not have a comparable effect if it were imposed on the original operator of the undertaking who was no longer economically active. The general deterrent effect on other economic participants too would be at least less [*referring to the principle of deterrence*].

See also her remarks on the purpose of attributing offences in EU competition law, which is that 'the measures serve the effective enforcement of competition rules in order to prevent distortions of competition' (para 70), and her reference to specific and general deterrence when she notes that

> Taking personal responsibility as a reference point normally supports the effective enforcement of the competition provisions, given that the person conducting the undertaking also has decisive influence over its market behaviour; the pressure of the penalties imposed of the penalties imposed should lead

> economically. With regard to the latter, it is worth noting that a penalty imposed on an undertaking that continues to exist in law, but has ceased economic activity, is likely to have no deterrent effect.[246]

The departure from the principle of personal responsibility and the application of the criterion of economic continuity occurs in the presence of 'particular circumstances':

> First, the criterion of economic continuity is applied where the changes affect only the operator of the undertaking which participated in the cartel and have the result that it no longer exists in law. Thus, having regard to economic continuity ensures that legal persons cannot escape their responsibility under antitrust law merely by changing their legal form or their name. [. . .].
>
> Second, the case-law also applies the criterion of economic continuity to reorganisations within a group of companies in which the original operator does not necessarily cease to exist in law but no longer carries on any significant economic activity, not even on a market other than that affected by the cartel. Specifically, the existence of a structural link between the original operator of the undertaking which participated in the cartel and the new one may allow the persons concerned to escape their responsibility under antitrust law, whether intentionally or unintentionally, by means of the structural possibilities available to them. Thus, for example, an internal group restructuring may have the effect that the original operator of the undertaking is changed into an 'empty shell'. A penalty imposed on it under antitrust law would be ineffective.[247]

The deterrence rationale may lead to broader exceptions to the principle of personal responsibility and to the liability of the new entity in corporate restructuring within a corporate group, following the criterion of economic continuity, even for situations where the original entity has remained in existence and is still an economically active entity. According to the Court, 'if no possibility of imposing a penalty on an entity other than the one which committed the infringement were foreseen, undertakings could escape penalties by simply changing their identity through restructurings, sales or other legal or organisational changes'; this 'would jeopardise the objective of suppressing conduct that infringes the competition rules and preventing its reoccurrence by means of deterrent penalties'.[248]

A similar approach applies to a change of the legal form of an undertaking, or its name, as the successor entity may be found liable for the anti-competitive conduct of its predecessor, 'when, from an economic point of view, the two are identical'.[249] Certainly, as AG J Kokott has observed in her Opinion in *ETI*, 'the criterion of economic continuity is intended not to be a substitute for the principle of personal responsibility, but merely to supplement', reliance on this criterion

him to alter this conduct, such that in future the undertaking conducts itself in compliance with competition law. At the same time the penalty has general deterrent effect in that it also deters other economic participants from committing cartel offences.

246 Case C-280/06, *Autorità Garante della Concorrenza e del Mercato v Ente tabacchi italiani—ETI SpA and Others* [2007] ECR I-10893, para 40.

247 Opinion of AG J Kokott in Case C-280/06, *Autorità Garante della Concorrenza e del Mercato v Ente tabacchi italiani—ETI SpA and Others* [2007] ECR I-10893, paras 78–9.

248 Case C-280/06 *Autorità Garante della Concorrenza e del Mercato v Ente tabacchi italiani—ETI SpA and Others* [2007] ECR I-10893, para 41 and the jurisprudence cited. See also Opinion of AG J Kokott in Case C-280/06 *Autorità Garante della Concorrenza e del Mercato v Ente tabacchi italiani—ETI SpA and Others* [2007] ECR I-10893, paras 81–4.

249 Joined Cases 29 and 30/83, *CRAM and Rheinzink v Commission* [1984] ECR 1679, para 9.

'remaining the exception'.[250] However, '[t]his does not prevent new categories of cases from being recognised in addition to the 'particular circumstances' she defined above. She gave, for instance, the example of a possible application of the criterion of economic continuity and the attribution of the infringement to the new operator, even if there is no structural link between the original operator and the new operator if the undertaking has been transferred to the new entity '*abusively*, that is with the intention of avoiding the antitrust law penalties'.[251]

The criterion of economic continuity does not, however, apply if the undertaking's assets were acquired by the third party at arm's length, the original operator being also held liable in this case.[252] In *NMH*, the General Court recognized that 'in certain circumstances an infringement of the rules on competition may be imputed to the economic successor of the legal person responsible, so that the effectiveness of those rules will not be compromised owing to the changes to, *inter alia*, the legal form of the undertakings concerned'.[253] Here, even though the successor undertaking did not take over all the assets and staff of the infringing undertaking, 'it none the less took over the main part of those physical and human elements that were employed in the manufacture of beams (which was the market where the competition infringement took place) and therefore contributed to the commission of the infringement in question'.[254] In reaching this decision the Court had regard in particular to the fact that the applicant was formed for the specific purpose of guaranteeing the continuation of the undertaking involved in the infringement, and was formed before the infringement commenced and therefore could be considered as this undertaking's successor (successor undertaking theory). In *HFB*, the General Court distinguished its judgment from that in *NMH*, refusing to pass on the liability to the economic successor in this case, as the new entity did not exist at the time of the infringement and there was no evidence that the re-organization formed part of an attempt to circumvent liability.[255]

The second scenario (share sale) refers to an undertaking involved in a competition law infringement through the conduct of one of its wholly owned subsidiaries or business unit, but then sells the unit or subsidiary that was responsible for the infringement to a third legal person by way of share sale. One may here distinguish two possibilities: first, the subsidiary remains in existence (as a legal person) and continues its activity as a subsidiary company of the acquiring undertaking; second, following the share sale, the legal person that committed the infringement (eg subsidiary) ceases to exist and is instead 'absorbed' into the acquiring entity.

With regard to the first possibility, if the infringer wholly owned subsidiary or business unit was sold to another company, the subsidiary retains its liability in accordance with the principle of personal responsibility and the original parent company will also be held jointly liable if it still exists.[256] The succeeding parent company will be held liable only if the subsidiary (or acquired business unit) has continued the infringement after the share sale and during the period of its ownership, in accordance with the rules governing parental liability.[257]

250 Opinion of AG J. Kokott in Case C-280/06, *Autorità Garante della Concorrenza e del Mercato v Ente tabacchi italiani—ETI SpA and Others* [2007] ECR I-10893, para 81.

251 Ibid, para 82.

252 Ibid, para 83.

253 Case T-134/94, *NMH Stahlwerke GmbH v Commission* [1999] ECR II-239, para 127.

254 Ibid, para 130.

255 Case T-9/99, *HFB & others v Commission* [2002] ECR II-1487, para 106.

256 Case C-279/98 P, *Cascades v Commission* [2000] ECR I-9693, para 78 ('[i]t falls, in principle, to the legal or natural person managing the undertaking in question when the infringement was committed to answer for that infringement, even if, when the Decision finding the infringement was adopted, another person had assumed responsibility for operating the undertaking').

257 See Joined Cases C-247 & 253/11 P, *Areva SA & Alstom SA v Commission*, ECLI:EU:C:2014:257, the Commission having found in this case jointly liable (i) the original parent company of the subsidiary directly involved in the infringement at the time of the infringement (Alstom), (ii) the subsidiary directly involved in

With regard to the second possibility, if, following the share sale, the infringing company ceases to exist and is absorbed into the acquiring entity, the liability passes to the acquiring entity.[258]

Joined Cases C-93 & 123/13 P, *European Commission v Versalis SpA & Eni SpA*, ECLI:EU:C:2015:150 (most notes and references omitted)

In its chloroprene rubber (CR) *decision the Commission found a number of undertakings had participated in a cartel between 1993 and 2002. Eni was found jointly and severally liable with its subsidiary Polimeri (renamed Versalis) for a fine of €132.16 million in view of the participation of its CR business in the cartel. Eni had re-organized its CR business various times. From 1993 to October 1997, the CR business was integrated in EniChem Elastomeri, which was controlled by Eni through its subsidiary EniChem. Following the merger of Enichem and EniChem Elastomeri in November 1997, the new entity, EniChem, was directly controlled by Eni. In January 2002 and until October 2002, the CR business was transferred to Polimeri Europa, the latter company having been wholly owned by EniChem, which was itself controlled by Eni. Polimeri changed its name to Versalis in Apri 2012 and EniChem changed its business name in April 2003, the new name not being revealed in the Court of Justice's judgment (confidential). Eni and Versalis challenged the Commission's decision before the General Court, which confirmed that both companies were jointly and severally liable but decreased their fine. Both the Commission and Versalis appealed the General Court's judgment to the CJEU. One of the grounds of Eni's and Versalis' appeal was that the General Court had violated the principle of personal liability as EniChem, and not Versalis, should have been found responsible for the infringing behaviour. Enichem still existed. The General Court had rejected this argument, finding that the Commission was right to find Versalis liable, since that at the time of the decision the CR business, in view of the 'close economic and organizational links' between the various companies, which were controlled by the same person, Eni, the parent company holding more than 99 per cent of the share capital of all companies. The economic continuity between the transferor company involved in the cartel (EniChem) and the transferee, Versalis, led the Commission to fine Versalis for the illegal conduct of its CR business.*

52. Versalis and Eni's second ground of appeal [. . .] concerns the question of the succession of undertakings. [. . .] [I]t is settled case-law that EU competition law refers to

the infringement (Areva T&D SA), and (iii) the parent companies of the subsidiary directly involved in the infringement at the time of the Commission's decision with which the subsidiary active on the relevant market was merged (Areva T&D Holdings SA and, as the ultimate parent company, Areva). On appeal to the judgment of the General Court that had upheld the decision of the Commission on the distribution of liability, the CJEU partly quashed the Commission's decision but held that:

> Where the Commission intends to make a subsidiary that has committed an infringement jointly and severally liable with each of the parent companies with which it has, in succession, formed a separate undertaking during the infringement period, that principle requires that institution to fix separately, for each of the undertakings involved, the amount of the fine for which the companies forming part of the undertaking are jointly and severally liable, according to the gravity of the infringement for which each of the undertakings concerned is individually responsible and the duration of that infringement.

Ibid, para 133.

258 Joined Cases T-259–264 & 271/02, *Raiffeisen Zentralbank Österreich AG and Others v Commission* [2006] ECR II-5169, para 326 ('[w]hen the undertaking in question ceases to exist, upon being merged with a purchaser, the latter takes on its assets and liabilities for infringements of [EU] law [. . .]. In such cases, the liability for the infringement committed by the undertaking taken over may be attributed to the purchaser.').

the activities of undertakings and that the concept of an undertaking covers any entity engaged in an economic activity, irrespective of its legal status and the way in which it is financed. When such an entity infringes competition rules, it falls, according to the principle of personal responsibility, to that entity to answer for that infringement.

53. The Court has already held that, where two entities constitute one economic entity, the fact that the entity that committed the infringement still exists does not as such preclude imposing a penalty on the entity to which its economic activities were transferred. In particular, applying penalties in this way is permissible where those entities have been subject to control by the same person and have therefore, given the close economic and organisational links between them, carried out, in all material respects, the same commercial instructions [. . .].

54. In [. . .] the judgment under appeal, the General Court noted the links between the companies successively responsible for the CR business within the group and the direct or indirect holding by Eni, as the parent company, of more than 99% of the share capital of all those companies. In the light of those factors, the General Court was right to conclude [. . .] that there was economic continuity between the transferor company involved in the cartel, namely EniChem [. . .], and the transferee company, namely Polimeri Europa (now Versalis).

55. The General Court also held [. . .] that there was a risk that the original operator of the CR business within the Eni group, namely EniChem [. . .] would become an 'empty shell' following the internal restructuring of that group and that the penalty imposed on it under antitrust law would be ineffective in that case. That is an assessment of fact which it is not for the Court of Justice to review in an appeal.

56. Having regard to those considerations, the General Court did not commit an error of law in finding [. . .] that the Commission was correct to attribute all the anticompetitive conduct by EniChem [. . .] to Polimeri (now Versalis), irrespective of the fact that [*the predecessor entity which controlled EniChem*] still existed.

57. That finding cannot be called into question by the fact that the Court of Justice, in paragraph 144 of the judgment in *ThyssenKrupp Nirosta* v *Commission* [ECLI:EU:C:2011:191], held that the possibility referred to in paragraph 53 of the present judgment also applies in a situation where the entity that has committed the infringement has ceased to exist, either in law or economically, since a penalty imposed on an undertaking which is no longer economically active is likely to have no deterrent effect; it does not follow from that judgment that an infringement may be imputed to an entity which did not commit the infringement only in cases where the application of a penalty to the company which did commit the infringement would not achieve its objective of deterrence [. . .].

58. In the judgment in *ETI and Others* [ECLI:EU:C:2007:775] to which the Court of Justice expressly referred in paragraph 144 of the judgment in *ThyssenKrupp Nirosta* v *Commission* [ECLI:EU:C:2011:191], the Court of Justice held that the Commission was entitled to impute the infringement to a company which had not committed the infringement where the entity which had done so continued to exist as an economic operator on other markets (see judgment in *ETI and Others*, ECLI:EU:C:2007:775, paragraph 45). The Court of Justice based that assessment on the fact that, at the time of the infringement, the companies concerned were held by the same public entity [. . .].

59. It must also be noted that the scope of the judgment in *ETI and Others* [ECLI:EU:C:2007:775] is not limited, contrary to the submissions of Versalis and Eni, to cases in which the entities concerned are controlled by a public authority. In paragraph 44 of that judgment, the Court of Justice stated that the fact that the decision

to transfer an activity is taken not by individuals, but by the legislature in view of a privatisation, is equally irrelevant. The Court therefore took the view that there could be doubts as to the imputability of an infringement to the successor entity, where, at the very most, both were controlled by a public authority, but those doubts were dispelled by the Court. However, there can be no doubt as regards that imputability where that control, as in the present case, is exercised by a company under private law (see judgment in *Versalis* v *Commission*, EU:C:2013:386, paragraph 57).

60. In the light of the foregoing, the General Court therefore did not err in law by holding that the Commission was entitled to impute all the infringements in question to Versalis.

NOTES AND QUESTIONS ON VERSALIS

1. (Paragraph 55) How would you assess the argument of the General Court that for deterrence reasons it might be necessary to hold the parent company jointly liable as there might be some incentive to re-organize the corporate group in a way that the entity's whose conduct was found anti-competitive is an 'empty shell', with the consequence that the fine imposed is not deterrent enough? Would these deterrence reasons be absent in all other circumstances in which the successor and its existing predecessor do not have any structural links? Is the argument about specific or general deterrence?

2. In paragraph 59, the Court distinguishes between cases in which the successor entity is controlled by a public authority and instances in which control is exercised by a company under private law. Although, according to the CJEU, there may be doubts with regard to the imputability of the infringement to the successor entity in case this is controlled by a public authority, there are no doubts when control is exercised by a company under private law. How do you understand this distinction introduced by the CJEU?

   In *ETI & Others*, to which the CJEU referred to with regard to control by public authorities, the Italian Ministry of Finance owned at the time of the competition law infringement both AAMS—an autonomous entity answering to the Ministry of the Economy and Finance, without legal personality, entrusted, until February 1999, with managing the tobacco monopoly, carrying out public functions in the tobacco sector but also pursuing a commercial activity in the gambling sector, in particular lotteries)—and ETI—a public limited company which received the assets and liabilities of AAMS and was later privatized. The Italian Competition Authority (ICA) had found that companies in the Philip Morris group had, first with AAMS, then with ETI (which was later acquired by the British American Tobacco group), formed and implemented a cartel, which had as its object and effect the distortion of competition as regards the sale price of cigarettes on the Italian market between 1993 and 2001. ICA had attributed the conduct adopted by AAMS prior to 1 March 1999 to ETI, on the ground that AAMS ceased its manufacturing and sales activities in the tobacco sector, once ETI became operational. In those circumstances, although AAMS did not cease to exist, ETI was AAMS' successor in accordance with the principle of economic continuity. The Regional Administrative Court of Lazio annulled the ICA's decision, on the basis of the criterion of personal responsibility, in so far as it attributed responsibility to ETI for acts committed by AAMS, which, following the organizational change constituted a new entity. On appeal the Italian Council of State sent a preliminary reference to the CJEU, questioning it on the possibility of attributing the infringement to the original undertaking (AAMS) when this no longer operated as a commercial undertaking, or at least not in the economic sector affected by the penalty.

The CJEU found irrelevant the legal and organizational changes, which, do not 'necessarily create a new undertaking free of liability for the conduct of its predecessor that infringed the competition rules, when, from an economic point of view, the two are identical'. The fact that the decision to transfer the activities of AAMS to ETI in view of the latter's privatization was adopted by the public authorities (legislator) of a Member State did not also impede the CJEU from applying the principle of economic continuity. The CJEU concluded that 'in the case of entities answering to the same public authority, where conduct amounting to one and the same infringement of the competition rules was adopted by one entity and subsequently continued until it ceased by another entity which succeeded the first, which has not ceased to exist, that second entity may be penalised for the infringement in its entirety if it is established that those two entities were subject to the control of the said authority'.[259]

SELECTIVE BIBLIOGRAPHY

Books

Pauer, NI, *The Single Economic Entity Doctrine and Corporate Group Responsibility in European Antitrust Law* (Kluwer Law International, 2014).

Thepot, F, *The Interaction Between Competition Law and Corporate Governance* (Cambridge University Press, 2019).

Chapters in books

Odudu, O, 'The Meaning of Undertaking within 81 EC' (2004–5) 7 *Cambridge Yearbook of European Legal Studies* 211.

Townley, C, 'The Concept of "Undertaking": The Boundaries of the Corporation—A Discussion of Agency, Employees and Subdidiaries' in Amato, G, and Ehlermann, C-D (eds) *EC Competition Law: A Critical Assessment* (Hart 2007), 3.

Journal articles

Cooter, RD, and Siegel, NS, 'Collective Action Federalism: A General Theory of Article I, Section 8' (2010) 63(1) *Stanford L Rev* 115.

Iacobucci, EM, and Triantis, GG, 'The Economic and Legal Boundaries of Firms' (2007) 93(3) *Virginia L Rev* 515.

259 Case C-280/06, *Autorità Garante della Concorrenza e del Mercato v Ente tabacchi italiani—ETI SpA and Others* [2007] ECR I-10893, para 55.

Jones, A, 'The Boundaries of an Undertaking in EU Competition Law' (2012) 8(2) *European Competition J* 301.

Kalintiri, A, 'Revisiting Parental Liability in EU Competition Law', (2018) 43(2) *European L Rev* 145.

Koenig, C, 'An Economic Analysis of the Single Economic Entity Doctrine in EU Competition Law' (2017) 13(2) *J Competition L & Economics* 281.

Odudu, O, and Bailey, D, 'The Single Economic Entity Doctrine in EU Competition Law' (2014) 51(1) *Common Market L Rev* 1.

Wils, W, 'The Undertaking as Subject of E.C. Competition Law and the Imputation of Infringements to Natural and Legal Persons' (2000) 25(2) *European L Rev* 99.

THE ELEMENTS OF ARTICLE 101 TFEU/CHAPTER I OF THE UK COMPETITION ACT 1998: COLLUSION

5.1. FOUNDATIONS

The finding of an infringement under Articles 101 TFEU and Chapter I CA98 thus requires evidence of the following elements:

An agreement, concerted practice or decisions of an association of undertakings (the collusion element)

- which have as their object or effect the prevention, restriction or distortion of competition within the internal market, without that being justified under the exception regime under Article 101(3) TFEU (the restriction of competition element)
- (and) which may affect trade between Member States in the EU or which is, or is intended to be, implemented in the United Kingdom (which we will call the geographic element).

We will examine the different elements of Article 101 of the Treaty on the Functioning of the European Union (TFEU) and of Chapter I of the Competition Act of 1998 (CA98).

5.2. THE FORMS OF COLLUSION: AGREEMENT, CONCERTED PRACTICE, OR DECISIONS BY ASSOCIATION OF UNDERTAKINGS

It is clear from their reference to the concepts of 'agreement', 'concerted practice' and 'decisions by association of undertakings' that both Article 101 TFEU and Chapter I CA98 apply to collusive practices between two or more undertakings (the requirement of collusive conduct). Unilateral conduct is excluded from the material scope of this provision.

Economists usually perceive collusion as

> a situation where firms' prices are higher than some competitive benchmark. A slightly different definition would label collusion as a situation where firms set prices which are close enough to monopoly prices. In any case, in economics collusion coincides with an outcome (high-enough price), and not with the specific form through which that outcome is attained [. . .] collusion can occur both when firms act through an organised cartel (explicit collusion), or when they act in a purely non-cooperative way (tacit collusion).[1]

For economists, collusion entails a suppression of inter-firm rivalry that would lead to an outcome/equilibrium (higher prices, lower output, lower innovation levels) that would be inferior to the outcome of 'some competitive benchmark'. The latter concept is broad enough to cover perfect competition, workable competition or the outcome that would have existed, had the examined conduct not taken place. Hence, one may notice that the definition of collusion as a non-competitive market outcome may easily overlap with the question of defining the existence, or not, of a restriction of competition. This does not mean that the two questions are merged into one: the existence, or not, of a non-competitive outcome. It matters, of course, if this outcome is produced by unilateral effects or by coordinated effects, as economic theory distinguishes between the two types of effects. Yet, the definition of what is unilateral or coordinated/collusive in economics and in law may not be the same, in view of the emphasis put by economics on *effects* or *outcomes* and the relatively cautious approach of the legal system with regard to the requirement of some *form* of conduct. It is submitted that this difference of approach may have to do with the concept of legal causation, which requires a causal link to be established between specific events so that responsibility may be attributed, while economics take a broader perspective on causation and rely either on regularities (the regularities account of causality) or on underlying mechanisms (the mechanistic account of causality), the main function being to *explain* the causal process rather than to *attribute* responsibility.

Consequently, it is remarkable that Article 101 TFEU does not refer to the concept of collusion as such, but to the concepts of 'agreement', 'concerted practice' and 'decisions by associations of undertakings', thus indicating that the use of the word collusion in economics cannot be transplanted as such in competition law, the meaning of these concepts being autonomously determined in competition law. An implication of this dissociation of the economic concept of collusion and the legal concepts of 'agreement', 'concerted practice', and 'decisions by associations of undertakings' is that competition law distinguishes the issue of the existence of an 'agreement', for instance, from that of a restriction to competition, whereas in economics, collusion and restriction of competition are, to a certain degree, conflated issues. The autonomy of the legal concepts of 'agreement', 'concerted practice', and 'decisions by associations of undertakings' should not, however, conceal the links between the various elements of Article 101 TFEU. These are all integrated in the first paragraph of Article 101 TFEU and their interpretation will have implications as to the economy of the

[1] M Motta, *Competition Policy—Theory and Practice* (CUP, 1st ed, 2004), 138. See also GJ Werden, 'Economic Evidence on the Existence of Collusion: Reconciling Antitrust Law with Oligopoly Theory' (2004) 71(3) *Antitrust LJ* 9.

whole provision. Hence, regard must be taken of the interaction between the requirement of collusive conduct and the concept of the restriction of competition. Some authors would consider that the two should be interpreted in isolation to each other, distinguishing between the 'jurisdictional' function of the concept of collusive conduct and the 'substantive' function of the concept of restriction of competition.[2] Others consider that, while being separate concepts, the two should be interpreted in congruence to each other taking into account of the objectives pursued by the provision into which they are both integrated, Article 101 TFEU.[3]

5.3. THE CONCEPT OF 'AGREEMENT'

5.3.1. AGREEMENT AS 'CONCURRENCE OF WILLS': BETWEEN LAW AND ECONOMICS

Whereas economists perceive collusion as being a non-competitive market outcome, lawyers distinguish the issue of the existence of an agreement from that of a restriction to competition. This has different implications for horizontal (arrangements between competitors) and vertical agreements (arrangements between firms present at different stages of the production and commercialization process).

5.3.1.1. The concept of antitrust agreement: The distinction between horizontal and vertical relationships

In the context of a horizontal relationship, cooperation between firms substitutes common action for competition and, in principle may increases market power. The assumption is that, according to the model of perfect competition, in competitive markets, 'each economic operator must determine independently the policy which he intends to adopt', which precludes 'any direct or indirect contact between such operators, the object or effect whereof is either to influence the conduct on the market of an actual or potential competitor or to disclose to such a competitor the course of conduct which they themselves have decided to adopt or contemplate adopting on the market'.[4]

The finding of a horizontal agreement is not without relevance to the existence of a collusive outcome, according to the meaning of this term in economics. Recognizing this fact, the Commission and the European Courts made efforts to stretch the concept of agreement and concerted practice in order to cover situations of collusion as considered by economics.[5] It is clear that an expansive definition for the concept of agreement aims to improve the effectiveness of Article 101 TFEU as an instrument of tackling collusion perceived as a non-competitive market outcome. The legal concept of collusion does not cover, however, entirely the economic one, as the concepts of agreement and concerted practice under Article 101

[2] O Odudu, *The Boundaries of EC Competition Law: The Scope of Article 81* (OUP, 1st ed, 2006), 96.

[3] I Lianos, Collusion in Vertical Relations under Article81 EC, (2008) 45 *Common Market Law Review* 1027.

[4] Joined Cases 40–8, 50, 54–6, 111, 113–14/73, *Cooperatieve Vereniging 'Suiker Unie' UA v Commission* [1975] ECR 1663, paras 173–4.

[5] See Case 48/69, *ICI v Commission* [1972] ECR 619. However, the Court took a more restrictive approach in Joined Cases C-89, 104, 114, 116–17 & 125–9/85, *Ahlström Osakeyhtiö and Others v Commission* [1993] ECR I-1307 [hereinafter *Woodpulp II*].

TFEU have not been extended to tacit collusion in situations of oligopolistic interdependence, we will explain below.

In the seminal case of *Consten & Grundig v Commission* regarding an exclusive distribution agreement concluded between the German company Grundig-Verkaufs-GmbH and the French company Établissements Consten for the distribution of Grundig products in France and the Saar region, the Court of Justice of the European Union (CJEU) rejected the exclusion of vertical relations between undertakings from the scope of article 101 TFEU, thus confirming the reasoning that the European Commission had followed in its decision prohibiting the agreement under Article 101(1) TFEU.[6] Indeed, Grundig and Consten argued that the prohibition in Article 101(1) TFEU did not apply to vertical agreements, but that it applied exclusively to horizontal agreements, noting that the person entitled to the exclusive rights is not on the same commercial plane as the wholesalers and in consequence has no need to enter into competition with them for it is this person who normally supplies the wholesale trade.[7] The Commission opposed the argument advancing two main arguments.[8] First, 'the field of application of Article [101] TFEU is determined by criteria other than the distinction between vertical and horizontal agreements, particularly by the distortion of competition and of trade between Member States', thus indicating that the different types of cartel enumerated by Article 101 TFEU were defined in accordance with their object or their economic effects, and not by the nature of the agreements on which they were based. The Commission has therefore to examine whether the agreement in question restricts competition and whether it may affect trade between the Member States. Second, the Commission noted that agreements, such as exclusive distribution, 'have as their object not only vertical restrictions but also horizontal restrictions on competition' as the agreement concerning an exclusive right of distribution, with absolute territorial protection, has as its object the protection of the person entitled to the exclusive distribution rights from competition on the wholesale level for the goods in respect of which such rights are given. In other words, even 'vertical' agreements may have horizontal anti-competitive effects. The CJEU ignored the characterization of the agreement as being vertical or horizontal, thus indicating that the nature of the agreement is not a relevant criterion for the scope of application of the prohibition principle of Article 101(1) TFEU and that the same concept of agreement applies to both horizontal and vertical relations. Had the CJEU accepted the arguments of Consten and Grundig, vertical agreements would have been subjected only to control of abuse by a dominant company by virtue of Article 102 TFEU.

Following the reform of the competition policy for vertical restraints in the late 1990s,[9] the Commission has recognized the 'self-policing' character of vertical restraints, thus distinguishing them from horizontal restrictions:

> It is [. . .] generally recognized that vertical restraints are on average less harmful than horizontal competition restraints. The main reason for treating a vertical restraint more leniently than a horizontal restraint lies in the fact that the latter may concern an agreement between competitors producing substitute goods/services while the former concerns an agreement between a supplier and a buyer of a particular product/service. In horizontal situations the exercise

[6] Joined Cases 56 & 58/64, *Établissements Consten SA & Grundig-Verkaufs-GmbH v EEC Commission* [1966] ECR 299. See further Chapter 2.

[7] Joined Cases 56 & 58/64, *Établissements Consten SA & Grundig-Verkaufs-GmbH v EEC Commission* [1966] ECR 299, 342.

[8] Ibid, 307–8. [9] See Chapter 10.

> of market power by one company (higher prices of its products) will benefit its competitors. This may provide an incentive to competitors to induce each other to behave anti-competitively. In vertical situations the product of the one is the input for the other. This means that the exercise of market power by either the upstream or downstream company would normally hurt the demand for the product of the other. The companies involved in the agreement may therefore have an incentive to prevent the exercise of market power by the other.[10]

Contrary to horizontal agreements where the interests of the parties converge, as both will profit from a price increase, the interests of the parties are, theoretically, divergent in vertical agreements. If both the upstream and the downstream markets are competitive, the gains of suppliers will be losses for the distributors and vice versa. Nonetheless, if there is substantial market power in the upstream or downstream market, the vertical restriction may have been imposed by one of the parties on the other.

These 'conceptual differences' notwithstanding, neither EU nor UK competition law draw any distinction between horizontal and vertical relations when it comes to the definition of the concept of agreement.

The CJEU has authoritatively defined the concept of agreement in *Bayer* (a vertical agreement case):

> the concept of an agreement within the meaning of Article [101 TFEU] centres on the existence of a concurrence of wills between at least two parties, the form in which it is manifested being unimportant so long as it constitutes the faithful expression of the parties' intention.[11]

5.3.1.2. A broad conception of 'agreement' in competition law

The emphasis on the 'concurrence of wills' between more than two entities indicates that each of the entities should be capable of having an independent intention, meaning that it should be able to act as an independent economic entity on the marketplace. This will should also represent a 'faithful expression of the parties' intention', which leaves open the possibility that a concurrence of wills resulting from coercion may not be considered as constituting a faithful expression of that intention and thus the specific conduct not qualified as an agreement. We will come back to this issue later in this Section.

This definition presents similarities to the usual understanding of this concept in other areas of law: ie, agreement implies the existence of a concurrence of wills between at least two parties, or in other words the existence of a common intention.[12] The exchange of consent (offer and acceptance) between the parties usually reveals the existence of an agreement. In contract law, the existence of a mutual consent is also required for the formation of a contract. The communication of assent between the parties to the agreement may take different forms,

10 Communication from the Commission on the application of the Community competition rules to vertical restraints: Follow-up to the Green Paper on vertical restraints, COM(98) 544 final [1998] OJ C 365/3

11 Joined Cases C-2 & 3/01 P, *Bundesverband der Arzneimittel-Importeure eV & Commission v Bayer* [2004] ECR I–23, para 69.

12 The 'will theory' of contracts provides the theoretical background of this principle. On the emergence of the consensus (will) theory of contract, see PA Hamburger, 'The Development of the Nineteenth-Century Consensus Theory of Contract' (1989) 7(2) *L & History Rev* 241.

which will often depend on the context of their relationship. For example, failing to reply to an offer may operate as a tacit acceptance where, because of previous dealings, it is reasonable to infer that the offer has been accepted, absent contrary notification by the offeree.[13] The retreat to formalism in these circumstances may be justified by the need to take into account the more efficient solution for the parties to the agreement and reduce their transactions costs, which is one of the principal aims of contract law. What this example illustrates is that, in contract law, the concept of agreement has been framed according to the policy objectives of this area of law and that the formal element of mutual consent has been interpreted in accordance to those objectives. Consequently, it would be erroneous to assess the definition of the concept of agreement in competition law in disconnection to the aims pursued by Article 101 TFEU which implies that because the aims of competition law are not similar to those of contract law, the requirement of concurrence of wills or mutual consent fulfils a different objective and should therefore be interpreted differently from contract law. The reduction of transaction costs to the mutual benefit of the parties (transactional efficiency) is not the primary objective of competition law. Its main focus is to enhance allocative efficiency to the benefit of the consumers. In other words, the concept of agreement under Article 101 TFEU is independent from that of contract law, or from national law concepts.

An implication of this broader perspective is that Article 101(1) TFEU may also apply to collusive conduct that does not form legally binding contracts under civil or commercial law principles. 'Gentleman's agreements',[14] non-binding simple understandings (memorandum of understanding),[15] protocols,[16] verbal agreements,[17] general guidelines to which other persons adhere to,[18] general terms and conditions of sale in a standard-form contracts,[19] the constitution of a trade association[20] or of a European Economic Interest Grouping,[21] have been qualified as 'agreements' under Article 101(1) TFEU in the same way as a legal contract (including a sub-section of it), even if it was never implemented.[22] This, even if the agreement's duration has expired, as long as its effects are still felt.[23] Indeed, according to the General Court,

> [. . .] according to settled case-law, Article [101 TFEU] also applies to agreements which continue to produce effects after the agreements have formally ceased.

[13] A Katz, 'The Strategic Structure of Offer and Acceptance: Game Theory and the Law of Contract Formation' (1990) 89(2) *Michigan L Rev* 215, 249–72.

[14] Case 41/69, *ACF Chemiefarma NV v Commission* [1970] ECR 661.

[15] *National Panasonic* (Case IV/30.070) Commission Decision [1982] OJ L 354/28.

[16] *HOV SVZ/MCN* (Case IV/33.941) Commission Decision [1994] OJ L 104/34.

[17] Case 28/77, *Tepea v Commission* [1978] ECR 1391.

[18] *Anheuser-Busch Incorporated/Scottish & Newcastle* (Case IV/34.237/F3) Commission Decision [2000] OJ L 49/37.

[19] Case 277/87, *Sandoz Prodotti Farmaceutici SpA v Commission* [1990] ECR I–45.

[20] Joined Cases 209–15 & 218/78, *Heintz van Landewyck SARL and others v Commission* [1980] ECR 3125.

[21] *Twinning programme Engineering Group*, Commission Decision [1992] OJ C 148/8.

[22] *Brasseries Kronenbourg, Brasseries Heineken* (Case COMP/C.37.750/B2) Commission Decision (29 September 2004), available at http://ec.europa.eu/competition/elojade/isef/case_details.cfm?proc_code=1_37750.

[23] Case 243/83, *Binon* [1985] ECR 2015, para 17; Case T-14/89 *Montedipe v Commission* [1992] ECR II–1155, para 231; Joined Cases T-109, 118, 122, 125–6, 128–9, 132 & 136/02, *Bolloré and Others v Commission* [2007] ECR II–947, para 186

In particular, the Commission may lawfully find that a cartel continues to produce its effects after collusive meetings have formally ceased in so far as the price increases planned during those meetings are to be applied at a later time.[24]

For an agreement to exist there should be concurrence of wills on the very principle of a restriction of competition. The following case provides an illustration of the evidence usually required so that collusive activity between competitors may be qualified to an agreement under Article 101 TFEU.

Case T-566/08, *Total Raffinage Marketing v Commission*, ECLI:EU:T:2013:423 (notes omitted)

In 2008, the Commission found liable and fined a number of undertakings (eg Shell, Sasol, and Repsol) for participating in a horizontal price fixing agreement (cartel) on the candle wax market in the European Economic Area (EEA) and on the German market for slack wax.[25] Slack wax is the raw material required for the manufacture of paraffin waxes. It is produced in refineries as a by-product in the manufacture of base oils from crude oil. It is also sold to end-customers, producers of particle boards: for instance, Paraffin waxes are used in the production of a variety of products such as candles, chemicals, tyres, and automotive products, as well as in the rubber, packaging, adhesive, and chewing-gum industries. The Commission had begun its investigation after Shell Deutschland Schmierstoff informed it in 2005 of the existence of a cartel and submitted a leniency application and proceeded to inspections collecting evidence on the existence of the cartel. In the light of the evidence available to it, the Commission considered that the majority of the producers of paraffin waxes and slack wax in the EEA, had participated in a single, complex, and continuous infringement of Article 101 TFEU, the infringement consisting of agreements or concerted practices relating to price-fixing and the disclosure of sensitive business information affecting paraffin waxes, as well as customer-sharing or market-sharing. The unlawful practices occurred at anti-competitive meetings called 'technical meetings', or sometimes 'Blauer Salon' meetings, by the participants and at 'slack wax meetings' devoted specifically to questions relating to slack wax. The companies found liable for infringement of competition law appealed the Commission's decision to the General Court alleging, among other arguments, that the agreements and concerted practices concerning the fixing of prices of paraffin waxes could not be validly found in respect of the applicant on the basis of the evidence in the file and that that the economic analysis of sales prices which it supplied contradicted its alleged adherence to a price-fixing agreement. The Court proceeded to the examination of these arguments, by explaining first the concepts of agreement and/or concerted practice. We will focus here on the parts of the judgment concerning one of the defendants, Total, discussing the concept of agreement and its relation to that of concurrence of wills.

30. According to Article [101(1) TFEU], all agreements between undertakings, decisions by associations of undertakings and concerted practices which may affect trade between Member States and which have as their object or effect the prevention,

[24] Case T-186/06, *Solvay SA v European Commission* [2011] ECR II–2839, paras 174–5. See also Case T-434/08, *Tono v Commission*, ECLI:EU:T:2013:187, para 100

[25] *Candle Waxes* (Case COMP/39.181) Commission Decision C(2008) 5476 final (1 October 2008), available at http://ec.europa.eu/competition/antitrust/cases/dec_docs/39181/39181_1908_8.pdf.

restriction or distortion of competition within the common market are incompatible with the common market and prohibited.

31. In order for there to be an agreement within the meaning of Article [101(1) TFEU] it is sufficient that the undertakings in question should have expressed their joint intention to conduct themselves on the market in a specific way.

32. An agreement within the meaning of Article [101(1) TFEU] can be regarded as having been concluded where there is a concurrence of wills on the very principle of a restriction of competition, even if the specific features of the restriction envisaged are still under negotiation.

The Commission had inferred the existence of the agreement by the existence of corporate statements and contemporaneous handwritten notes of the technical meetings between the competitors, made either at a particular technical meeting or shortly afterwards, and describing the content of the discussions at the meeting. The General Court rejected the arguments of Total that even if the Commission had found that information on prices had been exchanged at those meetings and that there was some agreement to maintain the level of prices, it had not found evidence of an agreement on an increase of prices. According to the General Court, '[a]n agreement to maintain prices is also an agreement to fix prices, since there is a concurrence of wills of the participants on the application of a price level which they have fixed together'.[26] It also rejected Total's argument with regard to the absence of documentary evidence on the existence of an agreement to fix prices and the fact that the level of the increase and that of the minimum prices varied from one undertaking to another. According to the General Court, this 'does not affect the characterisation of that meaning as having given rise to a "price fixing" agreement, as the expression "price fixing" does not imply the application of a single price for all participants'.[27] The General Court insisted on the 'overall assessment' that needs to be made in order to infer the existence of an agreement.

147. In the first place, it should be observed that Shell, Sasol and Repsol have admitted that the prices of paraffin waxes had been discussed at the technical meetings with the general objective of reaching agreement on their level. According to the case-law [. . .] the fact of having such a common objective already constitutes an agreement within the meaning of [Article 101(1) TFEU], since a concurrence of wills on the very principle of the restriction of competition existed. In addition, those undertakings also stated that at several technical meetings the participants had in fact agreed on minimum prices or on price increases and sometimes even on the means of increasing prices. It should be emphasised that, in their statements, the undertakings also referred to Total's participation in the technical meetings and stated the names of the applicant's employees who had represented it at the meetings.

148. In the second place, it must be emphasised that the statements in question are corroborated by numerous handwritten notes contemporaneous to the technical meetings that the Commission found during the inspections, to which the applicant had access during the administrative procedure [. . .].

149. In the third place, it should be borne in mind that the applicant was present at 39 anti-competitive meetings out of a total of 51 held during the period of its participation in the cartel [. . .].

26 Case T-566/08, *Total Raffinage Marketing v Commission*, ECLI:EU:T:2013:423, para 89.
27 Ibid, para 99.

152. The applicant puts forward no specific argument to counter the statements of Sasol, Repsol and Shell, according to which the aim of the technical meetings was price fixing.

153. Thus, at least so far as the technical meetings [. . .] are concerned, the Commission had in its possession a body of irrefutable evidence from which it emerged that the participants had regularly exchanged information on their prices and on planned increases at technical meetings for more than 12 years. The applicant has provided no coherent explanation in respect of those activities that might call into question the Commission's assertion that the object of those practices was, in particular, price fixing. On the contrary, the long period over which the meetings were systematically held constitutes in itself an indicium that the participants had as their objective to harmonise their pricing policies, knowingly substituting cooperation between them for the risks of the market, putting in place concerted practices relating to the price of paraffin waxes, indeed, at least so far as the technical meetings [. . .] are concerned, price-fixing agreements.

154. For the sake of completeness, it should be observed that, according to the case-law [. . .], Article [101(1) TFEU] precludes any direct or indirect contact between economic operators of such a kind as either to influence the conduct on the market of an actual or potential competitor or to reveal to such a competitor the conduct which the operator concerned has decided to follow itself or contemplates adopting on the market, where the object or effect of those contacts is to restrict competition. In the present case, the applicant does not deny either having had such contact or having exchanged sensitive information at the technical meetings. [. . .]

156. As regards agreements of an anti-competitive nature which, as in the present case, become evident at meetings of competing undertakings, the Court of Justice has already held that an infringement of Article [101 TFEU] was constituted when those meetings had the object of restricting, preventing or distorting competition and were thus aimed at artificially organising the functioning of the market. In such a case, it is sufficient for the Commission to establish that the undertaking concerned participated in meetings during which agreements of an anti-competitive nature were concluded in order to prove that the undertaking participated in the cartel. Where participation in such meetings has been established, it is for that undertaking to put forward indicia to establish that its participation in those meetings was without any anti-competitive intention by demonstrating that it had indicated to its competitors that it was participating in those meetings in a spirit that was different from theirs [. . .].

157. The reason underlying that principle of law is that, having participated in the meeting without publicly distancing itself from what was discussed, the undertaking gave the other participants to believe that it subscribed to what was decided there and would comply with it [. . .].

158. However, the applicant, having regularly participated in the technical meetings, does not claim to have publicly distanced itself from what was discussed at the anti-competitive meetings.

159. In the fifth place, it should be noted that the explanations put forward by the applicant relate each time to a particular technical meeting. Thus, they are not capable of constituting a plausible explanation in respect of the body of evidence gathered by the Commission, which enabled it to establish the existence of a complex, single and continuous infringement.

160. In the light of all of the foregoing considerations, it must be concluded that the Commission was correct to find, in the contested decision, that the participants in the cartel, including the applicant, had committed an infringement consisting, in particular,

in 'agreements and/or concerted practices aimed at price-fixing and exchanging and disclosing commercially sensitive information'. [. . .]

184. According to the case-law, the fact of not complying with a cartel does not alter the existence of the cartel [. . .]. Even on the assumption that it is proved that certain participants in the cartel succeeded in misleading other participants by sending incorrect information and in using the cartel to their advantage, by not complying with it, the infringement committed is not eliminated by that simple fact [. . .].

NOTES AND QUESTIONS ON TOTAL

1. With regard to evidence of the existence of an agreement, under Article 101 TFEU, the jurisprudence of the EU courts is quite sensitive to the difficulties in unveiling the existence of secret cartels. The difficulty of collecting evidence and more broadly concerns about administrability may influence the courts in setting their evidential requirements. The EU Courts have recognized the inherent difficulties of the task of proving a cartel infringement and apportioned accordingly the evidential requirements, by establishing adequate presumptions enabling the Commission to make inferences. As the CJEU has observed,

   [. . .] in practice, the Commission is often obliged to prove the existence of an infringement under conditions which are hardly conducive to that task, in that several years may have elapsed since the time of the events constituting the infringement and a number of the undertakings covered by the investigation have not actively co-operated therein. Whilst it is necessarily incumbent upon the Commission to establish that an illegal market-sharing agreement was concluded [. . .], it would be excessive also to require it to produce evidence of the specific mechanism by which that object was attained [. . .]. Indeed, it would be too easy for an undertaking guilty of an infringement to escape any penalty if it was entitled to base its argument on the vagueness of the information produced regarding the operation of an illegal agreement in circumstances in which the existence and anti-competitive purpose of the agreement had nevertheless been sufficiently established [. . .].[28]

2. (Paragraphs 156–7, 184) Note that the General Court states that documentary evidence of the participation of undertakings in a meeting to discuss future prices constitutes *prima facie* evidence of an agreement under Article 101 TFEU 'when those meetings had the object of restricting, preventing or distorting competition and were thus aimed at artificially organising the functioning of the market'. Indeed, the EU Courts have long established the presumption that if competitors participate in a meeting to discuss prices or output levels and remain active in the market after that meeting, they are presumed to have taken into account in their future action in the market the information exchanged with their competitors when determining their

[28] Joined Cases C-403/04 P & C-405/04, *Sumitomo Metal Industries Ltd and Others v Commission*, [2007] ECR I–729, para 203. See also Joined Cases T-44/02 and T-54, 56, 60 & 61/02 OP, *Dresdner Bank AG and Others v Commission* [2006] ECR II–3567, para 58, noting the existence of 'the practical effect principle' to which the Commission's finding of evidence are subject to, the Court not going so far as to require that the documentary evidence upheld in the contested decision constitutes 'irrefutable evidence' of an infringement. The case law requires only the submission of sufficient evidence.

conduct on that market and hence they are presumed to have participated in a concerted practice (the so-called *Anic* presumption).[29] Should this presumption apply to meetings held, not between competitors, but between suppliers and distributors, thus undertakings whose relation is vertical?

3. It is well accepted that the vertical or horizontal nature of the alleged agreement cannot influence the standard of proof applied (at most this might influence the cogency of evidence required). For example, the Court of Justice held that the standard of proof required for the purposes of establishing the existence of an anti-competitive agreement in the framework of a vertical relationship was not higher than that required in the framework of a horizontal relationship. All other relevant factors should be looked at, including the economic and legal context of the case. Whether it could be inferred that an antitrust agreement had been concluded could not be addressed in abstract terms, according to whether the relationship involved was vertical or horizontal.[30] However, should we take into account the vertical or horizontal relation between the parties when exploring the context of the emergence of the concurrence of wills?
4. The jurisprudence of the EU Courts is constrained by the presumption of innocence, or the principle *in dubio pro reo* (literally: '[when] in doubt, in favour of the accused'), enshrined in Article 6(2) of the European Convention of Human Rights and Article 48(1) of the Charter of Fundamental Rights of the European Union, which requires that 'any doubt in the mind of the Court must operate to the advantage of the undertaking to which the decision finding an infringement was addressed', in particular for decisions imposing fines or periodic penalty payments.[31] An example of the importance of evidence matters in qualifying an agreement under Article 101 TFEU is provided by the following case.

Case T-348/08, *Aragonesas Industrias y Energía v Commission* [2011] ECR II–7583 (notes omitted)

98. In so far as concerns the types of evidence which may be relied on to establish an infringement of Article [101 TFEU], the prevailing principle of European Union law is the unfettered evaluation of evidence.

99. Consequently, an absence of documentary evidence is relevant only in the overall assessment of the body of evidence relied on by the Commission. It does not, in itself, enable the undertaking concerned to call the Commission's claims into question by submitting a different version of the facts. The applicant may do so only where the evidence submitted by the Commission does not enable the existence of the infringement to be established unequivocally and without the need for interpretation [. . .].

29 Case C-49/92 P, *Commission v Anic Partecipazioni* [1999] ECR I–4125, para 121; Case C-199/ P, *Hüls v Commission* [1999] ECR I–4287, paras 162 and 167; Case C-8/08, *T-Mobile Netherlands BV and Others v Raad van bestuur van de Nederlandse* [2009] ECR I–4259, paras 51–2.

30 C-260/09, *Activision Blizzard Germany GmbH (formerly CD-Contact Data GmbH) v European Commission* [2011] ECR I–419, paras 71–2.

31 Case T-44/02, *Dresdner Bank AG and Others v Commission* [2006] II–3567, paras 60–1; Case T-36/05, *Coats Holdings Ltd v Commission*, [2007] ECR II–110, para 69.

100. In addition, no provision or general principle of European Union law prohibits the Commission from relying, as against an undertaking, on statements made by other incriminated undertakings. If that were not the case, the burden of proving conduct contrary to Article [101 TFEU], which is borne by the Commission, would be unsustainable and incompatible with its task of supervising the proper application of those provisions.

101. However, an admission by one undertaking accused of having participated in a cartel, the accuracy of which is contested by several other undertakings similarly accused, cannot be regarded as constituting adequate proof of an infringement committed by the latter undertakings unless it is supported by other evidence, given that the degree of corroboration required may be lesser in view of the reliability of the statements at issue.

102. As regards the probative value of the various items of evidence, the sole criterion relevant in that evaluation is the reliability of the evidence.

103. According to the general rules relating to evidence, the credibility and, thus, the probative value, of a document depends on the person from whom it originates, the circumstances in which it came into being, the person to whom it was addressed and whether it appears sound and reliable.

104. As regards statements, particularly great probative value may also be attached to those which, first, are reliable, second, are made on behalf of an undertaking, third, are made by a person under a professional obligation to act in the interests of that undertaking, fourth, go against the interests of the person making the statement, fifth, are made by a direct witness of the circumstances to which they relate and, sixth, were provided in writing deliberately and after mature reflection.

105. Moreover, even if some caution as to the evidence provided voluntarily by the main participants in an unlawful agreement is generally called for, considering the possibility, in this case, that they might tend to play down the importance of their contribution to the infringement and maximise that of others, the fact of seeking to benefit from the application of the Leniency Notice in order to obtain a reduction in the fine does not necessarily create an incentive for the other participants in the offending cartel to submit distorted evidence. Indeed, any attempt to mislead the Commission could call into question the sincerity and the completeness of cooperation of the person seeking to benefit, and thereby jeopardise his chances of benefiting fully under the Leniency Notice.

106. The Court also notes, in that regard, that the potential consequences of the submission of distorted evidence to the Commission are even more serious since [. . .] a statement of an undertaking that is disputed must be corroborated by other evidence. That being so, the likelihood of the Commission and the other undertakings accused of participating in the infringement of detecting the inaccurate nature of those statements is increased.

5.3.2. AGREEMENT AND COERCION (PRIVATE AND PUBLIC)

The way coercion in the formation of an antitrust agreement is assessed under Article 101 TFEU provides evidence that competition law does not adopt a contract-law based definition of agreement. One may distinguish between two forms of coercion: that coming from another undertaking party to the agreement (private coercion) and that resulting from the compulsion of the State (public coercion).[32]

[32] D Geradin, A Layne-Farrar, and N Petit, *EU Competition Law and Economics* (OUP, 2012), 112–13.

5.3.2.1. Private coercion

With regard to private coercion, the EU Courts have held that coercion exercised by another undertaking, even if that takes the extreme form of fraud or violence, does not rule out the existence of a concurrence of wills and thus the qualification of an agreement under Article 101 TFEU. Thus finding the existence of a concurrence of wills does not involve, as in contract law, the free consent of the parties to the competition law 'agreement'. In *Tréfileurope v Commission*, the General Court rejected the argument of the undertaking that there was no agreement as it had participated in the (anti-competitive) meetings against its will, as it 'could have complained to the competent authorities about the pressure brought to bear on it and lodged a complaint with the Commission [. . .] rather than participating in such meetings'.[33] In *Chalkor AE Epexergasias Metallon v Commission*, the General Court repeated that 'the case-law shows that pressure which is brought to bear by undertakings and which is intended to lead other undertakings to participate in an infringement of competition law does not, however great, absolve the undertaking concerned from its responsibility for the infringement committed or in any way alter the gravity of the infringement [. . .] since the undertaking concerned could have reported any pressure to the competent authorities and made a complaint to them'.[34] A similar conclusion was reached with regard to the exercise of economic coercion, for instance resulting from a situation of economic dependence. As the General Court noted in *Caffaro Srl v Commission*,

> [i]t must be observed that acting in a situation of economic dependence is not in itself a circumstance which may exclude the responsibility of a party to the cartel. Such a circumstance need not necessarily be taken into account when determining the amount of the fine.
>
> It is also settled case-law that an undertaking which participates in meetings with an anti-competitive object, even under constraint from other participants with greater economic power, can always report the anti-competitive activities in question to the Commission rather than continue to participate in the meetings. Even if an undertaking is pressured into joining a cartel, it could always have informed the competent authorities instead of supporting the cartel.[35]

The European Commission has also held in its Article 101(3) TFEU Guidelines that 'coordination can take the form of obligations that regulate the market conduct of at least one of the parties as well as of arrangements that influence the market conduct of at least one of the parties by causing a change in its incentives. *It is not required that coordination is in the interest of all the undertakings concerned*'.[36]

The existence of coercion may, however, be taken into account when devising the appropriate remedial response, for instance either in determining the amount of the fine or in assessing the possible damages that can be imposed.

Yet, although it is true that coercion is neither a necessary nor a sufficient condition for the finding of an agreement under Article 101 TFEU,[37] it may constitute an additional

[33] Case T-141/89, *Tréfileurope v Commission* [1995] ECR II–791, para 58.

[34] Case T-21/05, *Chalkor AE Epexergasias Metallon v European Commission* [2010] ECR II–1895, para 72.

[35] Case T-192/06, *Caffaro Srl v European Commission* [2011] ECR II–3063, paras 41–2.

[36] Communication from the Commission—Notice—Guidelines on the application of Article 81(3) of the Treaty [2004] OJ C 101/97, para 15 (emphasis added).

[37] Case T-368/00, *General Motors Nederland BV, Opel Nederland BV/ Commission* [2003] ECR II–4491, para 101.

indication substantiating such a claim, along with other factors. This is particularly clear if one looks to the application of Article 101 TFEU to conduct that may at first sight look as unilateral, in particular in vertical cases.

5.3.2.2. Public coercion or the doctrine of State compulsion

Regarding public coercion, EU competition law has developed a defence of for the finding of an agreement under Article 101(1) TFEU.[38] According to the CJEU,

> Articles [101] and [102] of the Treaty apply only to anti-competitive conduct engaged in by undertakings on their own initiative. If anti-competitive conduct is required of undertakings by national legislation or if the latter creates a legal framework which itself eliminates any possibility of competitive activity on their part, Articles [101] and [102] do not apply. In such a situation, the restriction of competition is not attributable, as those provisions implicitly require, to the autonomous conduct of the undertakings.
>
> Articles [101] and [102] may apply, however, if it is found that the national legislation does not preclude undertakings from engaging in autonomous conduct which prevents, restricts or distorts competition.[39]

Most recently, the CJEU held in *Deutsche Telekom AG v Commission* that

> [. . .] it is only if anti-competitive conduct is required of undertakings by national legislation, or if the latter creates a legal framework which itself eliminates any possibility of competitive activity on their part, that Articles [101 TFEU] and [102 TFEU] do not apply. [. . .]
>
> The possibility of excluding anti-competitive conduct from the scope of Articles [101 TFEU] and [102 TFEU] on the ground that it has been required of the undertakings in question by existing national legislation or that the legislation has precluded all scope for any competitive conduct on their part has thus been accepted only to a limited extent by the Court of Justice [. . .].
>
> Thus, the Court has held that if a national law merely encourages or makes it easier for undertakings to engage in autonomous anti-competitive conduct, those undertakings remain subject to Articles [101 TFEU] and [102 TFEU].[40]

The doctrine may have been inspired by US antitrust law, which recognizes a State compulsion defence when the consent of the undertakings is influenced by the intervention of a State authority (domestic or foreign).[41] The compulsion of a sovereign constitutes an antitrust defence, potentially fully removing the liability from the party invoking it. In the EU, the defence is very narrowly applied and essentially requires that the conduct is compulsory, really

[38] For analysis, see FC de la Torre, 'State Action Defence in EC Competition Law' (2005) 28(4) *World Competition* 407; M Martyniszyn, 'A Comparative Look at Foreign State Compulsion as a Defence in Antitrust Litigation' (2012) 8(2) *Competition L Rev* 143.

[39] Joined Cases C-359 and C-379/95 P, *Commission of the European Communities and French Republic v Ladbroke Racing Ltd* [1997] ECR I-6265, paras 33–4. See also Case T-513/93, *Consiglio Nazionale degli Spedizionieri Doganali v Commission* [2000] ECR II-1807, para 42.

[40] Case C-280/08 P, *Deutsche Telekom AG v European Commission* [2010] ECR I-9555, paras 80–2.

[41] For the domestic State action defence, see *Parker v Brown*, 317 US 341, 351 (1943). For the foreign State action defence, see *Hardford Fire Insurance Co v California*, 509 US 764, 798 (1993); *Interamerican Refining Corp v Texaco Maracaibo, Inc*, 307 F Supp 1291 (D Del 1970); The Department of Justice, Antitrust Enforcement Guidelines for International Operations (1988) 55 Antitrust & Trade Reg Rep (BNA) No 1391, § 6.

limiting the margin of the undertaking for autonomous action as an economic operator.[42] Mere persuasion or support by State authorities is not enough.[43] Yet, the jurisprudence of the CJEU does not go as far as requiring the presence at all times of a binding regulatory provision imposing the anti-competitive conduct in question. The State compulsion defence may also apply 'if it appears on the basis of objective, relevant and consistent evidence that that conduct was unilaterally imposed upon them by the national authorities through the exercise of irresistible pressures, such as, for example, the threat to adopt State measures likely to cause them to sustain substantial losses'.[44]

The possibility of excluding specific anti-competitive conduct from the scope of Article 101(1) TFEU, on the ground that it was required of the undertakings in question by existing national legislation or that any possibility of competitive activity on their part has been eliminated, has been applied restrictively by the Community judicature.[45] The undertakings should provide evidence of State coercion in order to escape liability under Article 101 TFEU. In *Stichting Sigarettenindustrie*, the Court confirmed the Commission's refusal to accept the application of the State compulsion doctrine to various anti-competitive agreements in the tobacco business in the Netherlands, the undertaking in question alleging that Dutch authorities had 'decisively influenced' its conduct by threatening it to take measures in case the undertakings in question did not adapt their conduct to the objectives set by the authorities.[46] The Court found that the Dutch authorities had discussions with the undertakings concerned in the course of which the authorities indicated certain objectives which they wished to see achieved. However, according to the CJEU, 'it has not been proved that the authorities indicated that those objectives should be achieved by the conclusion of the agreements restrictive of competition which have been held to be illegal by the contested decision'.[47] The doctrine applies restrictively and requires an assessment by the court of the residual autonomy which benefits the undertakings in question. In *Strintzis Lines*, the General Court rejected the application of the doctrine.[48] Greek shipping companies alleged that the policy pursued by the Greek Ministry of Merchant Shipping decisively restricted their autonomy with regard to the fixing of tariffs applicable both on the domestic routes and on the international segment of routes between Greece and Italy and thus they 'found themselves obliged to contact each other, to consult and to negotiate in relation to the fundamental parameters of their commercial policy, such as their prices'.[49] The Court proceeded to determine 'whether the legislative and regulatory framework and the policy of the Greek Ministry of Merchant Shipping had the cumulative effect of robbing the undertakings of their autonomy in adopting a tariff policy for the routes between Greece and Italy and thus of removing any possibility of competition between them'.[50] After examination of the relevant facts, the Court concluded that the

42 Joined Cases 89, 104, 114, 116, 117 & 125–9/85, *Woodpulp II* [1988] ECR 5193, para 20.

43 *Aluminium Imports from Eastern Europe*, (Case IV/26.870) Commission Decision 85/206/EEC [1985] OJ L 92/1, section 10.

44 Case T-387/94, *Asia Motor France SA and others* v *Commission of the European Communities* [1996] ECR II–961, para 65 [hereinafter *Asia Motor III*].

45 Joined Cases 209–15 & 218/78, *Heintz van Landewyck SARL and Others v Commission of the European Communities* [1980] ECR 3125, paras 130 and 133; Case T-513/93, *Consiglio Nazionale degli Spedizionieri Doganali v Commission* [2000] ECR II–1807, para 60.

46 Joined Cases 240–2, 261–2 & 268–9/82, *Stichting Sigarettenindustrie and Others v Commission of the European Communities* [1985] ECR 3831, para 38.

47 Ibid, para 40.

48 Case T-65/99, *Strintzis Lines Shipping SA* v *Commission of the European Communities* [2003] ECR II–5433, paras 119–41.

49 Ibid, para 123.

50 Ibid, para 124.

authorities 'neither adopted measures nor employed any practice that could be deemed 'irresistible pressure' on the shipping companies compelling them to conclude tariff agreements'.[51] An 'encouragement' to adopt the allegedly anti-competitive conduct did not amount to 'unilaterally imposing such action on the companies', as it was 'open to the companies to resist the informal encouragement without thereby exposing themselves to any threat that State measures might be adopted'.[52] The legislation in question also did not deprive the undertakings of 'all margin of autonomy' but still left them 'a certain liberty to determine their tariff policy', of course under certain conditions.[53]

Although the defence may not be applicable in order to provide immunity to the undertakings from the scope of Article 101 TFEU, it can still be a mitigating factor taken into account at the penalty setting stage.[54] An interesting question may also arise as to the legal implications of finding that the State compulsion doctrine applies in a specific case. According to the General Court in *CIF*, if a national law precludes undertakings from engaging in autonomous conduct which prevents, restricts or distorts competition, the undertakings concerned cannot be exposed 'to any penalties, either criminal or administrative', in respect of their past conduct 'where the conduct was required by the law concerned',[55] but also, more generally, 'shields the undertakings concerned from all the consequences of an infringement of Articles 101 and 102 TFEU and does so vis-à-vis both public authorities and other economic operators'.[56]

5.4. THE CONCEPT OF 'DECISIONS OF ASSOCIATIONS OF UNDERTAKINGS'

The concept of 'association of undertakings' is interpreted broadly.[57] The objective of extending the application of Article 101 TFEU/Chapter I to 'associations of undertakings' is linked to their important role in economic activity.

OECD, Trade Associations, DAF/COMP(2007)45, 16 (footnotes omitted)

Cooperatives and trade groups can be traced back to the merchant guilds of the middle age. Since then, trade and business associations have played a key role in the development of professions and trading activities around the world and have contributed to the wealth and success of many economies. It is particularly in the nineteenth century, however, that trade associations played a key role in shaping the industrialization process. In both liberal-oriented and in State-governed markets, many associations were created to react to the roughness of

[51] Ibid, para 138.

[52] Ibid, para 139. See also Case C-198/01, *Consorzio Industrie Fiammiferi (CIF) v Autorità Garante della Concorrenza e del Mercato* [2003] ECR I–8055, para 56.

[53] Case T-65/99, *Strintzis Lines Shipping SA v Commission of the European Communities* [2003] ECR II–5433, para 140.

[54] Case T-513/93, *Consiglio Nazionale degli Spedizionieri Doganali v Commission* [2000] ECR II–1807, para 57.

[55] Ibid, para 53. [56] Ibid, para 54.

[57] See Case 209/78, *Heintz van Landewyck* [1980] ECR 3125; Joined Cases 96/82 etc, *NAVEWA v Commission* [1983] ECR 3369; Case 123/83, *BNIC v Clair* [1985] ECR 391. See also OFT 408, Trade associations, professions and self-regulating bodies (2004).

free market capitalism or to the invading presence of the state in the economy. Businesses started organizing themselves to promote self-regulation and mutually agreed rules of conduct to compensate for shortcomings of the market or to pre-empt public intervention in the economy.

Over time, associations became real service providers to their industry. Such tight cooperation, however, often favoured explicitly cooperative agreements between competitors which limited the ability of individual market players to determine their business strategy autonomously. These restrictions, which were often established and enforced by trade associations, eliminated the normal risk associated with business activity as it concerned prices, quantities and other competitive factors and raised considerable concerns in governments as they were seen as an incentive to collusion to the ultimate detriment of consumer welfare.

Many of the first competition laws were enacted as a reaction to this trend towards industry wide cooperation, in an effort to control 'combinations' and 'trusts' of businesses (hence the word 'antitrust'), which pursued joint profit maximization through coordinated industry-wide conduct. The adoption in the United States of the Sherman Act in 1890, for instance, is a good example of a government reacting to this trend in order to preserve the competitive process and channel it along socially productive lines. The business combinations or trusts of the late 19th century were viewed by Congress as artificial devices to control markets, restrict competition and ultimately exploit consumers. Similarly, many years later, the drafters of the competition provisions in the Treaty of Rome were well aware of the possible risks for competition posed by trade associations' activities and have extended the scope of Article [101 TFEU] on anti-competitive agreements to include '[. . .] *all agreements between undertakings, decisions by associations of undertakings and concerted practices* [. . .]'.

The concept of 'association of undertakings' enables competition law to tackle the transformation of economic activity from the atomistic conception of competition among traders acting independently from each other, where competition on price constitutes an important dimension, to the emergence of networks of traders who while competing between them also cooperate so as to develop institutions ensuring the performativity of the market on which they are all active, in terms of other parameters of competition than price, such as quality. One may distinguish two parallel stories that explain the emergence of 'associations of undertakings' as a discrete form of collusion in EU and UK competition law.

First, modern trade associations, the successors of guilds in the Middle Ages, developed as a result of the professionalization movement in the latter half of the nineteenth century which aimed to regulate each profession/industry by imposing restrictions on trading practices to all their members. Some recent work on sociology of professions highlights how the constitution of professional markets, a process that began in the nineteenth century, was an attempt to translate special knowledge and skills to social and economic monopolistic rewards. The first phase of professionalization came through the constitution of professional associations and the subsequent closure of the domain through accreditation and professional examinations. This is certainly a strategy that characterizes the rise of the traditional professions in the nineteenth century (law, medicine) and explains the emergence of self-regulation of the professions.[58] The concept of association of undertakings has therefore the potential to bring within the scope of Article 101 TFEU's prohibition the activity of professional organizations. Recent work by the European Commission on the opening of the

[58] See eg MS Larson, *The Rise of Professionalism: A Sociological Analysis* (University of California Press, 1977).

market for liberal professions, in particular since the 1980s,[59] highlights the role the concept of 'association of undertakings' has to play in competition law enforcement.[60]

Second, the emergence of a centrally planned economy in order to organize the war effort, during the period preceding or immediately following the First World War, led to the development of corporatism and the establishment of various industrial or trade associations that took on them the organization of economic production, a process that was favoured or even initiated by governments. For instance, during the First World War, the US War Industries Board (WIB) played a central role in the regulation of economic activities and price fixing. Although the WIB was dissolved after the end of the First World War, industry/trade associations continued to push for self-regulation and cooperation among competitors.[61] The Great Depression led the Roosevelt administration to promote in the National Industrial Recovery Act of 1933 formal intra-industrial cartels managed by industry associations. Some of these cartels were organized openly, as explicit agreements between competing undertakings, until the US Supreme Court effectively outlawed them in 1940 by subjecting them to a *per se* standard of illegality.[62] Trade association managed cartels were particularly prominent in Germany from the second half of the nineteenth century to the end of the Second World War. The German Imperial State (1870–1918) had indeed contracted out public functions to trade associations through a system of export controls managed by compulsory syndicates to which the various companies participated in order to promote the German balance of payments. The war effort's need for central planning also reinforced the grip of trade associations on the German economy.

The development of competition law in Europe post-Second World War, led to a greater intrusion of competition authorities in the inner workings of trade associations, professional associations, and self-regulating bodies. Membership rules, recommendation as to prices and charges, including discounts and allowances, information exchange programs, standard-setting and certification programmes, including through the adoption of codes of conduct or standard terms and conditions to be applied by its members, restrictions on marketing and advertising, whether relating to the amount, nature, or form of advertising, were amongst the practices that were subject to closer scrutiny by competition agencies.[63] Yet, as it also remarked in a recent OECD report,

59 The CJEU supported this effort of liberalizing the professional services market with some significant judgments being issues in the 1980s: see eg Case 311/85, *ASBL Vereniging van Vlaamse Reisbureaus v ASBL Sociale Dienst van de Plaatselijke en Gewestelijke Overheidsdiensten* [1987] ECR 3801. The Commission adopted a report on Competition in Professional Services in 2004 (Commission Communication COM(2004) 83 final), setting out its position on the need to reform or modernize specific professional rules. A follow-up report 'Scope for more reform' was adopted in 2005 (Follow-up to the Report on Competition in Professional Services. Commission Communication COM(2005) 405 final). Member States were asked to review and eliminate restrictions to competition in the area of professional services: see Commission Staff Working Document SEC(2005) 1064.

60 For analysis, see IE Wendt, *EU Competition Law and Liberal Professions: An Uneasy Relationship?* (Martinus Nijhoff, 2013); CD Ehlermann and I Atanasiu (eds) *European Competition Law Annual 2004: The Relationship between Competition Law and the (Liberal) Professions* (Hart, 2006). On the economic impact of the self-regulation of liberal professions, see the European Commission commissioned study by I Paterson, M Fin, A Ogus et al, 'Economic Impact of Regulation in the Field of Liberal Professions in Different Member States', Research Report (January 2003), available at http://ec.europa.eu/competition/sectors/professional_services/studies/prof_services_ihs_part_1.pdf.

61 OECD, Trade Associations, DAF/COMP(2007)45, at 19.

62 *United States v Socony Vaccum Oil Co*, 310 US 150 (1940).

63 OECD, Trade Associations, DAF/COMP(2007)45, at 15; OFT 408, Trade associations, professions and self-regulating bodies (2004).

> [t]oday, the importance of trade and professional associations in performing a great number of functions, which are extremely valuable not just to the associations' members but to society in general, is widely acknowledged by the business community and government agencies alike. Trade associations and their activities are viewed as the expression of economic, social and political freedoms, which are often constitutionally protected. In many countries, the right of association is expressly protected as one of the fundamental rights of both individuals and corporations. Other constitutionally recognised freedoms and rights, such as the freedom of speech, the freedom of association and the right to petition the government, apply directly to a number of trade associations' activities and may represent a limit to the enforcement of antitrust rules.[64]

Such assessment of the pro- and anti-competitive dimension of trade associations is, however, conducted under the restriction of competition element of Article 101 TFEU/Chapter I CA98, as we will examine below in the *Wouters* judgment of the CJEU. What we focus on for the time being is the possibility for collusive activity taken place in the context of trade associations to fall under the scope of Article 101 TFEU.

As indicated above, both EU and UK competition law adopt a broad understanding of the concept of 'association of undertakings', yet this does not extend to all forms of 'association' used in common language: unions, alliances, societies, fraternities, and groups or other combinations of businesses (eg joint ventures, mergers). For competition law to apply to an 'association of undertakings' as a separate entity than its members, two elements must be present: (i) the organizational element as the association should have some 'lasting corporate structure', although it is irrelevant if the association has legal personality or it is a profit-making organization, and (ii) the functional element, which indicates that the association's activities either are of economic nature, or its members' activities are of economic nature, that it is indeed an association of 'undertakings'.[65] The second element relates to the concept of 'undertaking', which was examined in Chapter 4, and which explains that a decision by a trade union representing its members, employees, who are not themselves undertakings, will not be subject to Article 101(1) TFEU. However, when the trade union is not acting as a representative of its members, but on its own merit, and the activities in question have an economic nature, it may be subject to Article 101(1) TFEU as a decision of association of undertakings.

A distinction should also be made between the by-laws or act of incorporation of the association, which may be considered as an 'agreement' between undertakings, the founding members of the association, in particular if the objectives of the association, as agreed by the founding members are anti-competitive,[66] and any decision,[67] recommendation,[68] oral exhortation, or other activity of the association, which may be considered as a decision of an association of undertakings. According to an OFT (now replaced by CMA) Guidance,

64 OECD, Trade Associations, DAF/COMP(2007)45, at 19. 65 Ibid, 20–1.

66 See, for instance, the Dutch construction and building cartel case, Case C-137/95, *SPO v Commission* [1996] ECR I-1611.

67 Decisions may be informal and non-binding. According to OFT 408, Trade associations, professions and self-regulating bodies (2004), '[t]he key consideration is whether the effect of the decision, whatever form it takes, is to limit the freedom of action of the members in some commercial matter'.

68 It is not necessary for the undertakings members of the association to have fully complied with them: see Case C-96/82, *IAZ International Belgium NV v Commission* [1983] ECR 3369. It is presumed that members of the association have agreed to empower the association to undertake obligations on their behalf: see *Fedetab* (Cases IV/28.852 and IV/29.127) Commission Decision 78/670/EEC [1978] OJ L 224/29.

The relationship of an association of undertakings with third parties is likely to be considered an agreement between undertakings for the purposes of Article [101 TFEU] and the Chapter I prohibition. The internal relationship between the undertakings which form the association is likely to be considered as a decision of that association, although this will depend upon the facts of the case. Other activities of an association of undertakings may also fall within Article [101 TFEU] and the Chapter I prohibition, either as a decision or because they constitute agreements (or both), and this too will depend upon the circumstances of the case [. . .]'[69].

It is, nonetheless, possible for the association to be found liable, along its members, if it has a separate role in suggesting, orchestrating or implementing an illegal conduct. However, if the association is not aware of the illegal conduct of its members, it should not be held liable and the illegal activity in question does not form a decision of an association of undertakings.[70]

The concept of 'decisions of association of undertakings' has been recently re-visited by the jurisprudence of the EU courts. In its *Mastercard* decision the European Commission delved into the inner workings of the Mastercard card payment system. Interchange fees, which are fees paid between banks for the acceptance of card based transactions, had collectively been determined by the Mastercard payment organization. This was originally a cooperative association representing the issuing banks, and henceforth it formed an 'association of undertakings'. However, in 2006, following an Initial Public Offering (IPO), Mastercard was floated on the New York Stock Exchange and was transformed to a corporation, independent from the banks and answerable to its shareholders, not the banks. The Commission found that it continued to act as an association of undertakings and the multilateral interchange fees (MIF) resulted from a decision of an association of undertakings that falls under the scope of Article's 101 TFEU prohibition. MasterCard contested that point in front of the General Court, which nonetheless confirmed the Commission's decision on this issue, holding that "follows from the case law of the Court of Justice that the existence of a commonality of interests or a common interest is a relevant factor for the purposes of assessing whether there is a decision by an association of undertakings'.[71] The GC found that, the retention, after the IPO, of the banks' decision-making powers within the MasterCard payment organization and the existence of a commonality of interests between that organization and the banks on the issue of the MIF, as the banks had an interest in the MIF being set at a high level, the Commission was 'fully entitled to characterise as decisions by an association of undertakings the decisions taken by the bodies of the MasterCard payment organisation in determining the MIF', as, in essence, despite the changes brought about by MasterCard's IPO, the MasterCard payment organization had continued to be an institutionalized form of coordination of the conduct of the banks.[72] MasterCard appealed to the CJEU, arguing that to infer from a mere coincidence of interests between two or more economic operators the existence of an association of undertakings would extend the scope of Article 101 TFEU. On the contrary, Advocate General (AG) Mengozzi found evidence of acquiescence of the banks, and thus collusion, from the simple fact that they participated in an 'association of undertakings' which by decision had adopted

69 OFT 408, Trade associations, professions and self-regulating bodies (2004), para 1.5.

70 For instance, association meetings are often used by cartelist as a vehicle to meet separately and organize their anti-competitive activities. These illegal activities should be considered an agreement or a concerted practice, not a decision of association of undertakings.

71 Case T-111/08, *MasterCard and Others v Commission*, ECLI:EU:T:2012:260, para 251.

72 Ibid, para 259.

the MIF, noting that 'such a classification [association of undertakings] cannot be precluded outright in a context such as that of the present case, where the undertakings in question pursued, over several years, the same objective of joint regulation of the market within the framework of the same organisation, albeit under different forms'.[73] The CJEU confirmed the judgment of the General Court, although it also relativized the emphasis provided over the criterion of the 'commonality of interests' for the finding of the existence of an association of undertakings.

Case C-382/12 P, *MasterCard and Others v Commission*, ECLI:EU:C:2014:2201

64. In the present case [. . .] it is undisputed that, before the IPO, MasterCard could be considered to be an 'association of undertakings' within the meaning of Article [101 TFEU]. It is also apparent from that paragraph that, in the context of their third plea at first instance, the appellants complained that the Commission, in particular, had not taken into account the changes made by the IPO to MasterCard's structure and governance. In those circumstances [. . .] the third plea before the General Court concerned the issue whether MasterCard could still be considered to be 'an institutionalised form of coordination of the banks' conduct' after the changes made by the IPO. [. . .]

68. In that regard, [. . .] the General Court essentially found in its definitive assessment of the facts, first, that, at the time of the adoption of the decision at issue, even though the MasterCard member banks were no longer taking part in the decision-making process within the bodies of that organisation in relation to the MIF, 'MasterCard ... seemed instead to be continuing to operate in Europe as an association of undertakings, in which the banks were not merely customers for the services provided but participated collectively and in a decentralised manner in all essential elements of the decision-making power'. It should be emphasised in that regard that [. . .] the General Court did ascertain that, at the date of the decision at issue, the banks were continuing, collectively, to exercise decision-making powers in respect of the essential aspects of the operation of the MasterCard payment organisation after the IPO, which meant that the conclusions to be drawn from the IPO were very much to be set in perspective. Secondly, [. . .] the General Court also found, in essence, that the Commission had been able properly to conclude that the MIF reflected the banks' interests, because there was, on that point, a commonality of interests between MasterCard, its shareholders and the banks.

69. Taken together, those two factors, [. . .] effectively explain why, according to the General Court, the setting of the MIF by MasterCard continued to operate, notwithstanding the changes arising from the IPO, as 'an institutionalised form of coordination of the conduct of the banks'. According to the logic of the General Court in the judgment under appeal, given that MasterCard's interests and those of the shareholders

[73] Opinion of AG Mengozzi in Case C-382/12 P, *MasterCard and Others v Commission*, ECLI:EU:C:2014:42, para 45 also noting that

> [. . .] it cannot be precluded outright that a body may be classified as an association of undertakings even where, as in MasterCard's case, the decisions which it adopts are not taken by a majority of the representatives of the undertakings in question or in their exclusive interest, if it follows from a global assessment of the circumstances of the case that those undertakings intend or at least agree to coordinate their conduct on the market by means of those decisions and that their collective interests coincide with those taken into account when those decisions are adopted.

of MasterCard Inc. converged with regard to the setting of the MIF, the participating banks were in a position to delegate the setting of those fees, while retaining decision-making powers in many other respects.

71. [. . .] [T]he General Court considered the existence of a commonality of interests to be relevant in this instance not only on the basis of a theoretical concurrence of the banks' interests and those of MasterCard, but also having taken into account, in its definitive assessment of the facts, specific factual circumstances in respect of which no allegation of distortion was made, including, first, [. . .] the fact that it was undisputed that MasterCard was acting in the interests of the banks before the IPO; secondly, [. . .] the developments after the IPO which indicate that that organisation is, in reality, continuing to take into account concrete banks' interests in setting the level of the MIF; and, thirdly, [. . .] the fact that the interests of MasterCard's shareholders do not conflict with those of the banks.

72. In those circumstances, it was open to the General Court to find, in the particular circumstances of the case and taking into account the arguments expounded before it, that both the banks' residual decision-making powers after the IPO on matters other than the MIF, and the commonality of interests between MasterCard and the banks, were both relevant and sufficient for the purposes of assessing whether, after the IPO, MasterCard could still be considered to be an 'association of undertakings', within the meaning of Article [101 TFEU].

73. [. . .] Contrary to what is suggested by the appellants, in recalling in that context that 'it follows from the case-law of the Court of Justice that the existence of a commonality of interests or a common interest is a relevant factor for the purposes of assessing whether there is a decision by an association of undertakings within the meaning of Article [101(1) TFEU], the General Court did not seek to impose a general criterion, much less an exclusive criterion. [. . .]

76. In the light of all the foregoing considerations, it must be held that [. . .] the appellants cannot maintain that a body such as MasterCard cannot be classified as an association of undertakings when adopting decisions relating to the MIF, since it is apparent from the foregoing that the General Court correctly found that, when those decisions are taken, those undertakings intend or at least agree to coordinate their conduct by means of those decisions and that their collective interests coincide with those taken into account when those decisions are adopted, particularly in circumstances where the undertakings in question pursued, over several years, the same objective of joint regulation of the market within the framework of the same organisation, albeit under different forms.

NOTES AND QUESTIONS ON 'DECISIONS OF ASSOCIATIONS OF UNDERTAKINGS'

1. The involvement of an association of undertakings in an infringement of Article 101 TFEU and/or of the Chapter I CA98 prohibition may result in financial penalties being imposed on the association itself, its members or both. Finding an association liable for infringing competition law may raise interesting issues as to the legal consequences of the finding of the infringement. Evaluating the fine may raise problems of deterrence, as associations are not active on the market affected by the infringement and their turnover is often limited to the membership fees charged to its members, which is certainly not a sufficient basis to estimate the fine. Hence, with regard to fines, Article 23 of Regulation 1/2003 allows the European Commission to impose a fine of up to

10 per cent of the 'sum of the total turnover of each member active on the market affected by the infringement of the association' provided that the 'infringement of an association relates to the activities of its members'. If the association is not solvent to pay for the fine, in particular if this is estimated on the basis of the turnover of its members, then the association is obliged to call for contributions from its members so as to cover the amount of the fine and, in the absence of any action from the association, the Commission may demand the payment of the fine directly from any of the members of the decision-making bodies of the association and subsequently, where necessary, to request payment of the balance from any of the members of the association. It is, however, possible for one or more members of the association to refuse payment if they show that they have not implemented the decision/recommendation found to be an infringement of competition law, were not aware of its existence and have actively distanced themselves from it before the beginning of the Commission's investigation. It is also possible for third parties adversely affected by a decision of an association of undertakings to take action in the courts to stop the behaviour and/or to seek damages.

2. In *OTOC*, the CJEU examined the system of compulsory training for chartered accountants put in place by OTOC, a professional association of accountants and found that the decision to set up a compulsory training programme constituted a decision by an association of undertakings, notwithstanding the fact that OTOC was required by law to adopt binding rules of general application in order to put into place a system of compulsory training for its members and that those rules did not directly affect the economic activity of the members of the association in question[74] and, consequently, did not directly contribute to the collusive activity among the members of the association. According to the CJEU, a decision by an association of undertakings, '[. . .] can be such as to prevent, restrict or distort competition within the meaning of Article 101(1) TFEU, not only on the market on which the members of a professional association practice their profession, but also on another market on which that professional association itself has an economic activity'.[75]
3. The UK Competition and Markets Authority (CMA) has also recently addressed an infringement of competition law by a trade association in *Showmen's Guild*.[76] The CMA decided to accept binding commitments from the Showmen's Guild on the basis that, if the CMA were to accept them, then in accordance with the Guild's rules, the Guild's membership would implement them by a vote at the Guild's Central Council.

5.5. THE CONCEPT OF 'CONCERTED PRACTICE'

The interpretation of the nebulous concept of concerted practice has given rise to an important jurisprudence of the European Courts which struggled to find a compromise between, on one side, an effective competition law enforcement that takes into account the different forms that collusion may take and the available evidence and, on the other side, the need to ensure that the concept is not unduly extended so as to render the scope of Article 101 TFEU practically

[74] Case C-1/12, *Ordem dos Técnicos Oficiais de Contas v Autoridade da Concorrência*, ECLI:EU:C:2013:127.
[75] Ibid, para 45.
[76] CMA, Showmen's Guild: Suspected Anti-competitive Practices (15 December 2015), https://www.gov.uk/cma-cases/leisure-sector-anti-competitive-practices.

unlimited and the distinction between collusive and unilateral practices practically and theoretically irrelevant.

The concept of 'concerted practice' has enabled the Commission to bring within the scope of Article 101 TFEU cartel activity that would have remained uncovered if one was able to only employ the concept of 'agreement'. Although the concept of concerted practice has been merely used in the context of horizontal collusion (between competitors), there are three circumstances in which the concept was employed in a vertical context: (a) the concerted practice sanctions an apparently unilateral practice that implements a pre-existing vertical agreement, not necessarily anti-competitive;[77] (b) there is no clear evidence of the existence of an agreement between the supplier and the distributor but there is at least evidence of some degree of collusion between them;[78] and (c) the concerted practice brings within the scope of Article 101 TFEU a vertical/horizontal hybrid type of conspiracy between the supplier and members of its distribution network ('hub and spoke conspiracy').[79]

The CJEU first clarified the concept in its *Dyestuffs* ruling,[80] holding that:

> Article [101 TFEU] draws a distinction between the concept of 'concerted practices' and that of 'agreements between undertakings' or of 'decisions by associations of undertakings'; the object is to bring within the prohibition of that article a form of coordination between undertakings which, without having reached the stage where an agreement properly so-called has been concluded, knowingly substitutes practical cooperation between them for the risks of competition.
>
> By its very nature, then, a concerted practice does not have all the elements of a contract but may *inter alia* arise out of coordination which becomes apparent from the behaviour of the participants.[81]

A 'concerted' practice requires some form of 'coordination' between undertakings, which breaks with the requirement of 'independent' conduct. The latter concept constitutes the backbone of competition law, coordination being considered as an antithesis to the concept of 'independent' conduct. In the *Sugar* cartel case, the Court held that for a concerted practice to be constituted, it is not necessary for the plaintiff to prove that there is an 'actual plan'. As it was explained by the CJEU in *Sugar*,

> The criteria of coordination and cooperation laid down by the case-law of the Court, which in no way require the working out of an actual plan, must be understood in the light of the concept inherent in the provisions of the Treaty relating to competition that each economic operator must determine independently the policy which he intends to adopt on the common market including the choice of the persons and undertakings to which he makes offers or sells.
>
> Although it is correct to say that this requirement of independence does not deprive economic operators of the right to adapt themselves intelligently to the existing and anticipated conduct of their competitors, it does however strictly preclude any direct or indirect contact between such operators, the object or effect whereof is either to influence the conduct on the market of an actual or potential competitor or to disclose to such a competitor the course of conduct which they themselves have decided to adopt or contemplate adopting on the market.[82]

77 Case T-43/92, *Dunlop Slazenger International Ltd v Commission*, [1994] ECR II–441.

78 *Souris/TOPPS* (Case COMP/C-3/37.980) Commission Decision 2006/895/EC [2004] OJ L 353/5.

79 See our analysis in Section 3.2.6.2.

80 See the detailed discussion in Chapter 11.

81 Case 48/69, *Imperial Chemical Industries Ltd v Commission* [1972] ECR 619, paras 64–5.

82 Joined Cases 40–8, 50, 54–6, 111, 113 & 114/73, *Coöperatieve Vereniging 'Suiker Unie' UA and others v Commission* [1975] ECR 1663, paras 173–4.

By referring to various forms of the same thing, 'coordination and cooperation' between undertakings, the CJEU indicated that Article 101 TFEU is built on a foundational opposition between conduct that may be considered as purely independent, which escapes from the scope of this provision, and conduct that emanates from some form of 'coordination' and 'cooperation', which is viewed with suspicion, 'in the light of the concept inherent in the provisions of the Treaty relating to competition that each economic operator must determine independently the policy which he intends to adopt on the common market'.[83] The UK Competition Appeal Tribunal (CAT) has also noted in *Tesco* that:

> There is, therefore, a clear and important difference between undertakings intelligently adapting their behaviour in light of the existing and anticipated conduct of competitors, which is legitimate [and therefore does not constitute a concerted practice], and co-ordination that has as its object or effect the influencing of a competitor's conduct on the market or disclosing the course of conduct which a competitor has decided to adopt, or is contemplating adopting, on the market, which is not permissible [and therefore constitutes a concerted practice].[84]

Collusion constitutes the antithesis of purely independent behaviour. Its contours are nebulously defined, as the concept may refer to different degrees of coordination, from explicit coordination, for instance a written or verbal agreement, to more tacit forms. Indeed, as the EU Courts have repeated many times,

> [. . .] comparison between [. . .] agreement and [. . .] concerted practice [. . .] shows that, from the subjective point of view, they are intended to catch forms of collusion having the same nature and are only distinguishable from each other by their intensity and the forms in which they manifest themselves.[85]

What is clear is that a concerted practice is a less formalized form of cooperation/coordination than agreement, which is an issue that ultimately relates to the available evidence:

> [. . .] In order to prove that there has been a concerted practice, it is therefore not necessary to show that the competitor in question has formally undertaken, in respect of one or several other competitors, to adopt a particular course of conduct or that the competitors have colluded over their future conduct on the market. It is sufficient that, by its statement of intention, the competitor eliminated or, at the very least, substantially reduced uncertainty as to the conduct to expect from it on the market.[86]

83 Ibid, para. 173.

84 *Tesco Stores Limited et al* [2012] CAT 31, para 47.

85 Case C-49/92 P, *Commission v Anic Partecipazioni SpA* [1999] ECR I–4125, para 131. See also Case T-186/06, *Solvay v Commission* [2011] ECR II–2839, para 90; Case T-191/06, *FMC Foret v Commission*, [2011] ECR II–2959, para 102; Case T-655/11, *FSL Holdings, Firma Léon Van Parys and Pacific Fruit Company Italy SpA v Commission*, ECLI:EU:T:2015:383, para 418.

86 Case T-82/08, *Guardian Industries and Guardian Europe v Commission*, ECLI:EU:T:2012:494 (partly set aside by the CJEU in Case C-580/12 P, *Guardian Industries Corp and Guardian Europe Sàrl v European Commission*, ECLI:EU:C:2014:2363, but only with regard to the fine); Joined Cases T-25–6, 30–2, 34–9, 42–6, 48, 50–65, 68–71, 87–8 & 103–4/95, *Cimenteries CBR and Others v Commission* [2000] ECR II–491, para 1852; Case T-53/03, *BPB v Commission* [2008] ECR II–1333, para 182.

The concept of cooperation or coordination should not, however, only be conceived in terms of *active* participation in some form of coordination or contacts with other undertakings. *Passive* participation may also negate the characterization of the conduct as being 'independent', as long as this eliminates, 'or at the very least', substantially reduces, 'uncertainty as to the conduct to expect of the other on the market'.

In *Cimenteries*, the Court of First Instance (now the General Court) considered various alleged collusive contacts involving a large part of the European cement industry and stated the following:

> [T]he concept of concerted practice does in fact imply the existence of reciprocal contacts ... That condition is met where one competitor discloses its future intentions or conduct on the market to another when the latter requests it or, at the very least, accepts it [. . .].
>
> In order to prove that there has been a concerted practice, it is not therefore necessary to show that the competitor in question has formally undertaken, in respect of one or several others, to adopt a particular course of conduct or that the competitors have colluded over their future conduct on the market [. . .]. It is sufficient that, by its statement of intention, the competitor should have eliminated or, at the very least, substantially reduced uncertainty as to the conduct to expect of the other on the market.[87]

If one considers that a concerted practice may result from a substantial reduction of the uncertainty an undertaking has as to the conduct to expect—that is, future conduct—of another undertaking on the market, this offers quite broad scope for intervention to the concept of concerted practice, that may be more extensive than the sphere of intervention of the concept of agreement. This may raise questions as to the common 'nature' of both concepts.

This question notwithstanding, it is well accepted that the concepts of 'agreement' and 'concerted practice' 'have partially different elements'; yet, the EU courts have also made it clear that they are not 'mutually incompatible'.[88] What do these 'partially different elements' consist of? According to the EU case law,

> [. . .] as is clear from the very terms of Article [101(1) TFEU], a concerted practice implies, besides undertakings' concerting together, conduct on the market pursuant to those collusive practices, and a relationship of cause and effect between the two.[89]

It follows that a concerted practice involves some subjective element (some form of concertation or 'mental consensus whereby practical cooperation is knowingly substituted for competition'[90]), a material element (conduct on the market pursuant to collusion), and a causal relation between the subjective and the material elements. Difficulties in collecting evidence and concerns about administrability have nevertheless influenced the EU courts in setting their evidential requirements. The EU Courts have recognized the inherent difficulties of the task of proving a cartel infringement and apportioned accordingly the evidential

[87] Joined Cases T-25/95 etc, *Cimenteries CBR v Commission* [2000] ECR II-491, paras 1849 and 1852 (references omitted).

[88] Case C-49/92 P, *Commission v Anic Partecipazioni SpA* [1999] ECR I-4125, para 132.

[89] Case C-49/92 P, *Commission v Anic Partecipazioni SpA* [1999] ECR I-4125, para 118; Case C-286/13 P, *Dole Food Company, Inc, Dole Fresh Druit Europe v Commission*, ECLI:EU:C:2015:184, para 126.

[90] R Whish and D Bailey, *Competition Law* (OUP, 8th ed, 2015), 118.

requirements, by establishing adequate presumptions enabling the Commission to make inferences with regard to the different elements of a concerted practice.[91]

5.5.1. THE SUBJECTIVE/INTENTIONAL ELEMENT

With regard to the subjective/intentional element, evidence of a 'meeting of minds' is not necessary for finding the existence of a concerted practice.[92] The EU courts have even established presumptions facilitating the evidence of the subjective element, although these presumptions cannot suppress the need to provide the material evidence altogether.

5.5.1.1. Meetings as evidence of the subjective element

For instance, when competitors meet to discuss future prices this may constitute evidence of the subjective element to engage in a cartel.[93]

Joined Cases C-204, 205, 211, 213, 217 & 219/00 P, *Aalborg Portland A/S and Others v Commission*

[2004] ECR I–123 (references omitted)

After carrying out investigations into European cement producers and trade associations, the European Commission found that Aalborg Portland had infringed what is now Article 101(1) TFEU by its anti-competitive conduct in participating in agreements and/or concerted practices having the same aim. The concerted practices related to the exchange between competitors of information on the supply and demand situation, in particular prices, including information on rebates, the whole scheme being designed to prevent incursions by competitors on respective national markets in the EU.[94] *The General Court confirmed most of the infringements found in the Commission's decision. The undertakings appealed to the CJEU contesting their participation in the cartel.*

81. According to settled case-law, it is sufficient for the Commission to show that the undertaking concerned participated in meetings at which anti-competitive agreements were concluded, without manifestly opposing them, to prove to the requisite standard that the undertaking participated in the cartel. Where participation in such meetings has been established, it is for that undertaking to put forward evidence to establish that its participation in those meetings was without any anti-competitive intention by demonstrating that it had indicated to its competitors that it was participating in those meetings in a spirit that was different from theirs [. . .].

[91] See also Joined Cases T-44/02 OP, T-54/02 OP, T-56/02 OP, T-60/02 OP & T-61/02 OP, *Dresdner Bank AG and Others v Commission*, [2006] ECR II–3567, para 58, noting the existence of the practical effect principle to which the Commission's finding of evidence are subject to, the Court not going so far as to require that the documentary evidence upheld in the contested decision constitutes 'irrefutable evidence' of an infringement. The case law requires only the submission of sufficient evidence.

[92] Case T-587/08, *Fresh Del Monte Produce, Inc v Commission*, ECLI:EU:T:2013:129, para 300.

[93] Case C-199/92 P, *Hüls v Commission* [1999] ECR I–4287, para 155; Joined Cases C-204, 205, 211, 213, 217 & 219/00 P, *Aalborg Portland and Others v Commission* [2004] ECR I–123, para 81; Joined Cases C-403 & 405/04 P, *Sumitomo Metal Industries and Nippon Steel v Commission* [2007] ECR I–729, para 47.

[94] *Cement* (Cases IV/33.126 and 33.322) Commission Decision 94/815/EC [1994] OJ L 343/1.

82. The reason underlying that principle of law is that, having participated in the meeting without publicly distancing itself from what was discussed, the undertaking has given the other participants to believe that it subscribed to what was decided there and would comply with it.

83. The principles established in the case-law cited at paragraph 81 of this judgment also apply to participation in the implementation of a single agreement. In order to establish that an undertaking has participated in such an agreement, the Commission must show that the undertaking intended to contribute by its own conduct to the common objectives pursued by all the participants and that it was aware of the actual conduct planned or put into effect by other undertakings in pursuit of the same objectives or that it could reasonably have foreseen it and that it was prepared to take the risk.

84. In that regard, a party which tacitly approves of an unlawful initiative, without publicly distancing itself from its content or reporting it to the administrative authorities, effectively encourages the continuation of the infringement and compromises its discovery. That complicity constitutes a passive mode of participation in the infringement which is therefore capable of rendering the undertaking liable in the context of a single agreement.

85. Nor is the fact that an undertaking does not act on the outcome of a meeting having an anti-competitive purpose such as to relieve it of responsibility for the fact of its participation in a cartel, unless it has publicly distanced itself from what was agreed in the meeting [. . .]

86. Neither is the fact that an undertaking has not taken part in all aspects of an anti-competitive scheme or that it played only a minor role in the aspects in which it did participate material to the establishment of the existence of an infringement on its part. Those factors must be taken into consideration only when the gravity of the infringement is assessed and if and when it comes to determining the fine. [. . .]

87. Where the liability of undertakings for anti-competitive conduct results, according to the Commission, from their participation in meetings having such conduct as their purpose, it is for the Court of First Instance to ascertain whether those undertakings had the opportunity, both during the administrative procedure and before that Court, to rebut the findings thus made and, where appropriate, to prove circumstances which cast the facts established by the Commission in a different light and thus allow another explanation of the facts to be substituted for the one adopted by the Commission.

NOTES AND QUESTIONS ON AALBORG PORTLAND

1. It is of paramount importance to understand the emphasis put by the jurisprudence of the EU Courts on the subjective element for a concerted practice to be constituted. This is, for instance, clear in paragraph 83 of the above excerpt, where the Court requires the claimants to prove that the undertaking to be held liable for participating in a concerted practice '*intended* to contribute by its own conduct to the common objectives pursued by all the participants and that it was *aware* of the actual conduct planned or put into effect by other undertakings in pursuit of the same objectives or that *it could reasonably have foreseen* it and that it was prepared to take the risk'. This is a constant also in the most recent jurisprudence of the EU courts.[95] See for instance, the following excerpts from some other judgments of the EU courts:

95 See eg Case C-194/14 P, *AC-Treuhand AG v Commission*, ECLI:EU:C:2015:717, para 30.

[...] an undertaking may be held liable for an overall cartel even though it is shown to have participated directly only in one or some of its constituent elements, *if it knew, or must have known*, that the collusion in which it participated, especially by means of regular meetings organised over several years, was *part of an overall plan intended to distort competition* and if that *overall plan* included all the constituent elements of the cartel.[96]

In addition,

[...] the Court of Justice has already held that Article [101(1) TFEU] is infringed where those meetings have as their object the restriction, prevention or distortion of competition and are thus *intended* to organise artificially the operation of the market [...]. In such a case, it is sufficient for the Commission to establish that the undertaking concerned participated in meetings during which agreements [or concerted practices] of an anti-competitive nature were concluded in order to prove that the undertaking participated in the cartel. Where participation in such meetings has been established, it is for the undertaking concerned to put forward indicia to establish that its participation in those meetings was without any anti-competitive *intention* by demonstrating that it had indicated to its competitors that it was participating in those meetings in a *spirit* that was different from theirs.[97]

We highlighted in italics some terms (eg 'must have known', 'overall plan') showing that the subjective element, that of the anti-competitive intent, is always present in the characterization of a conduct as constituting a concerted practice, although the EU Courts accept that this may be presumed from the participation of the undertakings in meetings 'of anti-competitive nature' with their competitors. Note that the CJEU in *Suiker Unie* held that 'the criteria of coordination and cooperation laid down by the case-law of the Court [...] in no way require the working out of an actual plan'.[98] This may be now understood as not requiring the claimants to bring evidence of the 'actual plan' itself, as the existence of the latter may be inferred from the behaviour of the undertakings, for instance their participation in meetings of 'anti-competitive nature'. We will examine in detail the concept of 'anti-competitive nature' when exploring the concept of restrictions of competition by object, but it is sufficient to conclude, for the time being, that participation of undertakings in meetings in which restrictions by object are plotted may be qualified as a concerted practice, in view of the fact that undertakings 'must have known' that their participation in such meetings led to a practical cooperation that substituted for competition.

2. Participation in meetings of 'anti-competitive nature' establishes an evidential presumption that the undertaking participated in the concerted practice. Two questions may arise here as to the subjective element of concerted practice. First, in how many meetings should the undertaking participate for the presumption to operate? This issue was resolved by subsequent case law, which held that even one meeting of 'anti-competitive nature' may ignite the presumption.[99] Second, does this evidential

[96] Case T-452/05, *Belgian Sewing Thread (BST) NV v Commission* [2010] ECR II–1373, para 32.

[97] Case T-59/07, *Polimeri Europa v Commission* [2011] ECR II–4687,

[98] Joined Cases 40–8, 50, 54–6, 111, 113 & 114/73, *Coöperatieve Vereniging 'Suiker Unie' UA and others v Commission* [1975] ECR 1663, para 173

[99] Case C-8/08, *T-Mobile Netherlands and Others* [2009] ECR I–4529, para 60.

presumption operate also with regard to the subjective, as well as for the material element of a concerted practice? In the *Bananas* case,[100] Dole, which was found liable for a concerted practice infringing Article 101(1) TFEU, challenged the Commission's decision, in particular with regard to the counting of the exchanges and meetings it had with its competitors, submitting that it was unclear if Dole knew whether a single discussion of pre-pricing information (eg price setting factors and price trends) amounted to a restriction of competition by object under Article 101(1) TFEU. The General Court held the following:

368. It must be borne in mind that, with respect to the conditions in which unlawful concerted action can be established in the light of the question of the number and regularity of the contacts between competitors, it is apparent from the case-law that the number, frequency, and form of meetings between competitors needed to concert their market conduct depend on both the subject-matter of that concerted action and the particular market conditions. If the undertakings concerned establish a cartel with a complex system of concerted actions in relation to a multiplicity of aspects of their market conduct, regular meetings over a long period may be necessary. If, on the other hand, the objective of the exercise is only to concert action on a selective basis in relation to a one-off alteration in market conduct with reference simply to one parameter of competition, a single meeting between competitors may constitute a sufficient basis on which to implement the anti-competitive object which the participating undertakings aim to achieve [. . .].

369. The Court of Justice has specified that what matters is not so much the number of meetings held between the participating undertakings as whether the meeting or meetings which took place afforded them the opportunity to take account of the information exchanged with their competitors in order to determine their conduct on the market in question and knowingly substitute practical cooperation between them for the risks of competition. Where it can be established that such undertakings successfully concerted with one another and remained active on the market, they may justifiably be called upon to adduce evidence that that concerted action did not have any effect on their conduct on the market in question. [. . .]

373. In so far as the Commission might have meant thereby that, on the assumption that its findings relating to the frequency of the communications and its conclusion that there was a consistent 'pattern' of communications are not upheld, the existence of a single pre-pricing communication between Dole and its competitors for each year from 2000 to 2002 would be sufficient to establish collusive conduct, that claim would have to be rejected in the light of the specific object of the coordination complained of and of the nature of the market which was organised in weekly cycles. However, conversely, the Commission cannot be required to prove the existence of a weekly pre-pricing communication throughout the infringement period, since proof that a number of exchanges did take place, from which it is possible to establish that there was a system for disseminating information, is sufficient [. . .].

400. [. . .] Dole's purely arithmetical approach, which is based solely on drawing a link between the total number of weekly meetings relating to the setting of quotation

100 For more details on the case see Chapter 7.

prices and the total number of bilateral communications, is not such as to contradict the Commission's conclusion that the communications in question were sufficiently consistent to constitute an established mechanism for circulating information.[101]

3. According to the CJEU and some well-established case law the presumption of the subjective element following the participation of an undertaking in a meeting of anti-competitive nature may be rebutted, when the undertaking publicly distances itself from the content (of the alleged anti-competitive meeting) or reports it to the administrative authorities.[102] Furthermore, as the CJEU explained in *Hüls AG v Commission*, if the Commission is able to establish that an undertaking has participated in meetings between undertakings of a manifestly anti-competitive nature, it is for this undertaking 'to put forward evidence to establish that its participation in those meetings was without any anti-competitive intention by demonstrating that it had indicated to its competitors that it was participating in those meetings in a spirit that was different from theirs'.[103] Hence, public distancing should be perceived as such by the other members of the cartel.[104]

The CJEU has recently clarified the conditions under which use may be made of the criterion of public distancing by the defendant undertaking in order to rebut the presumption.

Case C-634/13 P, *Total Marketing Services SA v Commission*, ECLI:EU:C:2015:614 (references omitted)

The Commission found the majority of paraffin wax and slack wax producers in the EEA to had participated in an infringement consisting in agreements or concerted practices relating to price-fixing and the exchange and disclosure of sensitive business information affecting paraffin waxes, which took place during some 'technical meetings' between the participants to the cartel.[105] *One of the undertakings involved, Total Marketing Services SA appealed to the General Court, which, however, rejected all its pleas. Total brought the case to the CJEU alleging that it did not participate in the last three meetings of the cartel. Total challenged the General Court's reliance on the absence of positive evidence that Total has distanced itself from the cartel to infer its participation in the infringement even for the period covered by the last three meetings (12 May 2004 to 29 April 2005) at which Total was not present. Total argued that such finding was reversing the burden of proof from the authority to the defendant undertaking.*

In his Opinion, Advocate General Wahl attempted to put some limits on the operation of the presumption by emphasizing that the Court's reference to no public distancing 'should not make up for the lack of evidence of participation, albeit passive (of the undertaking in question),

[101] Case T-588/08, *Dole Food and Dole Germany v Commission* [2013] ECLI:EU:T:2013:130, paras 368–9, 373, 400, appeal dismissed by Case C-286/13 P, *Dole Food Company, Inc, Dole Fresh Fruit Europe v Commission*, ECLI:EU:C:2015:184.

[102] See also Joined Cases T-25/95 etc, *Cimenteries CBR and Others v Commission* [2000] ECR II–491.

[103] Case C-199/92 P, *Hüls AG v Commission* [1999] ECR I–4287, para 155.

[104] Case C-290/11 P, *Comap v Commission*, EU:C:2012:271, paras 74–6.

[105] Candle waxes (Case COMP/39.181) Commission Decision (1 October 2008), available at http://ec.europa.eu/competition/antitrust/cases/dec_docs/39181/39181_1908_8.pdf.

in an anti-competitive meeting'.[106] *Indeed, according to the AG, 'the public distancing requirement makes sense only if the undertaking has actually participated in collusive meetings or, at the very least, if there is evidence of concerted practices over a certain period' and '[i]t should thus come into play only in circumstances where it is reasonable to presume, in the light of the evidence specifically gathered during the investigation, that the defendant undertaking has continued to participate in a cartel'.*[107] *Hence, 'the fact that an undertaking does not publicly distance itself from a cartel is not in itself such as to constitute evidence of its participation in it'.*[108]

18. The General Court ruled that it could not be concluded that an undertaking had definitively ceased to belong to a cartel unless it had publicly distanced itself from the content of the cartel and it added that the decisive criterion in that regard was the understanding that the other parties participating in the cartel had of that undertaking's intention.

19. Thus, as the General Court ruled, even if it is undisputed that an undertaking is no longer participating in the collusive meetings of a cartel, it must distance itself publicly from that cartel if it is to be considered as having discontinued its participation in it, and the evidence of that distancing must be assessed according to the perception of the other participants in that cartel.

20. It must be noted that, in accordance with the case-law of the Court, a public distancing is necessary in order that an undertaking which participated in collusive meetings can prove that its participation was without any anti-competitive intention. For that purpose, the undertakings must demonstrate that it had indicated to its competitors that it was participating in those meetings in a spirit that was different from theirs [. . .].

21. The Court has also held that an undertaking's participation in an anti-competitive meeting creates a presumption of the illegality of its participation, which that undertaking must rebut through evidence of public distancing, which must be perceived as such by the other parties to the cartel [. . .].

22. Therefore, the case-law of the Court requires a public distancing as necessary proof in order to rebut the presumption recalled in the previous paragraph only in the case of an undertaking that participated in anti-competitive meetings; however, it does not require in all circumstances that there be such a distancing that puts an end to participation in the infringement.

23. With regard to participation in an infringement that took place over several years rather than in individual anti-competitive meetings, it can be concluded from the case-law of the Court that the absence of public distancing forms only one factor amongst others to take into consideration with a view to establishing whether an undertaking has actually continued to participate in an infringement or has, on the contrary, ceased to do so [. . .].

24. Consequently, the General Court erred in law in considering [. . .] that public distancing constitutes the only means available to an undertaking involved in a cartel of proving that it has ceased participating in that cartel, even in the case where that company has not participated in anti-competitive meetings.

25. Nevertheless, that error of law by the General Court cannot invalidate the findings in the judgment under appeal concerning the appellant's participation in the infringement between 12 May 2004 and 29 April 2005.

106 Opinion of AG Wahl in C-634/13 P, *Total Marketing Services v Commission*, ECLI:EU:C:2015:208, para 56.

107 Ibid, para 58.

108 Ibid.

26. It is settled case-law that in most cases the existence of an anti-competitive practice or agreement must be inferred from a number of coincidences and indicia which, taken together, may, in the absence of another plausible explanation, constitute evidence of an infringement of the competition rules [. . .].

27. As regards, in particular, an infringement extending over a number of years, the Court has held that the fact that direct evidence of an undertaking's participation in that infringement during a specified period has not been produced does not preclude that participation from being regarded as established also during that period, provided that that finding is based on objective and consistent indicia [. . .].

28. Even if a public distancing is not the only means available to an undertaking implicated in a cartel of proving that it has ceased participating in that cartel, such distancing none the less constitutes an important fact capable of establishing that anti-competitive conduct has come to an end. The absence of public distancing forms a factual situation on which the Commission can rely in order to prove that an undertaking's anti-competitive conduct has continued. However, in a case where, over the course of a significant period of time, several collusive meetings have taken place without the participation of the representatives of the undertaking at issue, the Commission must also base its findings on other evidence. [. . .]

30. However, it must be pointed out that the rejection of this plea at first instance is not based just on the absence of the appellant's having publicly distanced itself from the cartel. It is apparent from [. . .] the decision at issue, [. . .] that there was other factual evidence on which the Commission had relied and which was not disputed by the appellant, such as the initial confirmation of the participation of the appellant's representative in the meeting of 3 and 4 November 2004 and the initial reservation by the organiser of the collusive meetings of a hotel room for the representative for the meeting of 23 and 24 February 2005.

31. Therefore, that factual evidence, in conjunction with the absence of the appellant's publicly distancing itself from the cartel and the perception of the organiser of the collusive meetings constituted consistent indicia permitting finding that the appellant had continued to participate in the cartel.

5.5.2.2. Passive participation, facilitation of anti-competitive conduct, and the boundaries of the subjective element of the concerted practice

The CJEU has also addressed the participation of an undertaking in anti-competitive meetings for which it has a subsidiary, accessory, or passive role.

Case C-194/14 P, *AC-Treuhand AG v Commission*, ECLI:EU:C:2015:717

The Commission had found AC-Treuhand, a consultancy firm based in Switzerland and offering business management and administrations services, liable, under Article 101(1) TFEU, for a cartel consisting in fixing prices, allocation of markets and customers, and exchange of commercially sensitive information between undertakings active in the heat stabilizers sector. Although AC-Treuhand did not trade on the relevant markets or on related markets, the Commission found that it played an essential role in the infringement (the heat stabilizers cartel), by organizing meetings for the cartel participants which it attended and in which it actively participated, collecting and supplying to the participants data on sales on the relevant markets, offering to act as moderator in case of tensions between the cartel participants, and encouraging the parties to find compromises.[109] *This was not the first time AC-Treuhand had run into trouble with competition law. During its investigation in Organic Peroxides,*[110] *the Commission found that AC-Treuhand had played an essential role in the cartel by organizing the meetings and covering up evidence of the infringement. For those reasons, the Commission concluded that AC-Treuhand had also infringed the competition rules and imposed a fine of €1,000. The fine was rather modest due to the novelty of the policy followed in that area.*

Coming back to the heat stabilizers cartel, on appeal, the General Court held that the fact that the consultancy firm was not active on the market on which the restriction of competition occurred does not exclude liability for the infringement as a whole.[111] *Indeed, the Court found that the mere fact that an undertaking has participated in a cartel only in a subsidiary, accessory, or passive way is not sufficient for it to escape liability for the entire infringement.*[112] *Following the dismissal of AC-Treuhand's appeal, the case was brought to the CJEU. The CJEU had to assess whether AC-Treuhand could be considered as a perpetrator of the infringement, in view of the fact that it was not present on the affected markets and could not thus be considered as constituting a competitive constraint for the members of the cartel in the heat stabilizer sector.*

Advocate General Wahl took the view that the Commission was not entitled to hold AC-Treuhand directly liable for the competition law infringement, essentially requiring that '[i]n order to have the capacity to restrict competition, the person or entity proceeded against much be able, under normal circumstances, to constitute, for the operators present on the market, a competition constraint which can be eliminated or reduced through collusion'.[113] *This was not the case for AC-Treuhand as it was not active on the relevant market or the markets linked to the cartel. Drawing inspiration from criminal law, AG Wahl considered the possibility to hold AC-Treuhand liable as an 'accomplice' to the competition law infringement, because it had 'through positive' and 'intentional conduct, aided or facilitated the commission of that offense'.*[114] *He did not, however, follow this route because EU law 'as it stands' does not offer an adequate legal basis. According to this approach, legal certainty would thus take precedence over the desire to promote the effectiveness of EU competition law enforcement. The CJEU did not follow its Advocate General and found AC-Treuhand directly liable for the commission of the infringement, finding that the subjective element of the offence was satisfied in this case. Note the way the CJEU addressed the tensions between the principle of legal certainty for undertakings and the requirements of the principle of effectiveness.*

26. It is necessary to determine in the present case whether a consultancy firm may be held liable for infringement of Article [101(1) TFEU] where such a firm actively contributes, in full knowledge of the relevant facts, to the implementation and continuation of a cartel among producers active on a market that is separate from that on which the undertaking itself operates.

27. With regard, first, to Article [101(1) TFEU], which provides that agreements between undertakings, decisions by associations of undertakings and concerted practices which have particular characteristics are incompatible with the common market and prohibited, it should be noted that there is nothing in the wording of that provision

[109] *Heat stabilisers* (Case COMP/38589) Commission Decision (11 November 2009), available at http://ec.europa.eu/competition/antitrust/cases/dec_docs/38589/38589_4440_3.pdf.

[110] *Organic Peroxides* (Case COMP/E-2/37.857) Commission Decision [2003] OJ L 110 44.

[111] Case T-99/04, *AC Treuhand v Commission* [2008] ECR II-1501, para 127.

[112] Ibid, para 131.

[113] C-194/14 P, *AC-Treuhand v Commission*, ECLI:EU:C:2015:350, para 62.

[114] Ibid, para 79.

that indicates that the prohibition laid down therein is directed only at the parties to such agreements or concerted practices who are active on the markets affected by those agreements or practices.

28. It should also be noted that, according to the Court's case-law, in order for there to be an 'agreement', there must be the expression of the concurrence of wills of at least two parties, the form in which that concurrence is expressed not being by itself decisive [. . .].

29. As regards the term 'concerted practice', it is apparent from the Court's case-law that Article [101(1) TFEU] makes a distinction between that term and, in particular, the terms 'agreement' and 'decision by an association of undertakings', with the sole intention of catching various forms of collusion between undertakings which, from a subjective point of view, have the same nature and are distinguishable from each other only by their intensity and the forms in which they manifest themselves [. . .].

30. When, as in the present case, the infringement involves anti-competitive agreements and concerted practices, it is apparent from the Court's case-law that the Commission must demonstrate, in order to be able to find that an undertaking participated in an infringement and was liable for all the various elements comprising the infringement, that the undertaking concerned intended to contribute by its own conduct to the common objectives pursued by all the participants and that it was aware of the actual conduct planned or put into effect by other undertakings in pursuit of the same objectives or that it could reasonably have foreseen it and that it was prepared to take the risk [. . .].

31. In that connection, the Court has held in particular that passive modes of participation in the infringement, such as the presence of an undertaking in meetings at which anti-competitive agreements were concluded, without that undertaking clearly opposing them, are indicative of collusion capable of rendering the undertaking liable under Article [101(1) TFEU], since a party which tacitly approves of an unlawful initiative, without publicly distancing itself from its content or reporting it to the administrative authorities, encourages the continuation of the infringement and compromises its discovery [. . .].

32. It is true that the Court has stated, when called upon to determine whether there was an 'agreement' within the meaning of Article [101(1) TFEU], that the issue was whether the parties had expressed their concurrent intention to conduct themselves on the market in a particular manner [. . .]. The Court has also held that the criteria of coordination and cooperation which are constituent elements of a 'concerted practice' within the meaning of that provision must be understood in the light of the concept inherent in the provisions of the Treaty relating to competition, to the effect that each economic operator must determine independently the policy which he intends to adopt on the common market [. . .].

33. However, it cannot be inferred from those considerations that the terms 'agreement' and 'concerted practice' presuppose a mutual restriction of freedom of action on one and the same market on which all the parties are present.

34. Moreover, it cannot be inferred from the Court's case-law that Article [101(1) TFEU] concerns only either (i) the undertakings operating on the market affected by the restrictions of competition or indeed the markets upstream or downstream of that market or neighbouring markets or (ii) undertakings which restrict their freedom of action on a particular market under an agreement or as a result of a concerted practice.

35. Indeed, it is apparent from the Court's well established case-law that the text of Article [101(1) TFEU] refers generally to all agreements and concerted practices

which, in either horizontal or vertical relationships, distort competition on the common market, irrespective of the market on which the parties operate, and that only the commercial conduct of one of the parties need be affected by the terms of the arrangements in question [. . .].

36. It should also be noted that the main objective of Article [101(1) TFEU] is to ensure that competition remains undistorted within the common market. The interpretation of that provision advocated by AC-Treuhand would be liable to negate the full effectiveness of the prohibition laid down by that provision, in so far as such an interpretation would mean that it would not be possible to put a stop to the active contribution of an undertaking to a restriction of competition simply because that contribution does not relate to an economic activity forming part of the relevant market on which that restriction comes about or is intended to come about.

After reviewing AC-Treuhand's contribution to the cartel, the CJEU makes the following assessment:

38 [. . .] [T]he conduct adopted by AC-Treuhand is directly linked to the efforts made by the producers of heat stabilisers, as regards both the negotiation and monitoring of the implementation of the obligations entered into by those producers in connection with the cartels, the very purpose of the services provided by AC-Treuhand on the basis of service contracts concluded with those producers being the attainment, in full knowledge of the facts, of the anti-competitive objectives in question, namely—as is apparent from paragraph 4 of the judgment under appeal—price-fixing, market-sharing and customer-allocation and the exchange of commercially sensitive information.

39. In those circumstances, contrary to what is claimed by AC-Treuhand, even though those service contracts were formally concluded separately from the commitments entered into by the producers of heat stabilisers among themselves, and notwithstanding the fact that AC-Treuhand is a consultancy firm, it cannot be concluded that the action taken by AC-Treuhand in that capacity constituted mere peripheral services that were unconnected with the obligations assumed by the producers and the ensuring restrictions of competition.

40. With regard, in the second place, to General Court's alleged infringement of the principle that offences and penalties must be defined by law, it should be observed that, according to the Court's case-law, that principle requires the law to give a clear definition of offences and the penalties which they attract. That requirement is satisfied where the individual concerned is in a position to ascertain from the wording of the relevant provision and, if need be, with the assistance of the courts' interpretation of it, what acts and omissions will make him criminally liable [. . .].

41. The principle that offences and penalties must be defined by law cannot therefore be interpreted as precluding the gradual, case-by-case clarification of the rules on criminal liability by judicial interpretation, provided that the result was reasonably foreseeable at the time the offence was committed, especially in the light of the interpretation put on the provision in the case-law at the material time [. . .].

42. The scope of the notion of foreseeability depends to a considerable degree on the content of the text in issue, the field it covers and the number and status of those to whom it is addressed. A law may still satisfy the requirement of foreseeability even if the person concerned has to take appropriate legal advice to assess, to a degree that is reasonable in the circumstances, the consequences which a given action may entail. This is particularly true in relation to persons carrying on a professional activity, who are used to having to proceed with a high degree of caution when pursuing their

occupation. Such persons can therefore be expected to take special care in evaluating the risk that such an activity entails [. . .].

43. In that context, even though at the time of the infringements which gave rise to the contested decision, the courts of the European Union had not yet had the opportunity to rule specifically on the conduct of a consultancy firm such as the conduct characterising the action taken by AC-Treuhand, that firm should have expected, if necessary after taking appropriate legal advice, its conduct to be declared incompatible with the EU competition rules, especially in the light of the broad scope of the terms 'agreement' and 'concerted practice' established by the Court's case-law.

NOTES AND QUESTIONS ON AC-TREUHAND

1. The literature on cartels has noted the operation in some horizontal price fixing conspiracies of an undertaking/agent, situated at a different relevant market than the one covered by the cartel, whose function is to serve as 'an intermediary that speaks individually to each of the competitors and then relays each competitor's agreement [. . .] to the other competitors in a series of one-to-one conversations'.[115] The main concern of the participants to these conspiracies is to facilitate the implementation of the cartel even if they do not benefit from its effects directly (although they might receive some other form of compensation from the cartel members). The presence of these intermediaries on vertically related upstream or downstream markets or on markets that are simply not related to the one the cartel operates may introduce some non-horizontal/triangular element in the collusion, thus making its qualification more complex, the concerted practice being indirect rather than direct. A common characteristic of these situations of indirect concerted practice is that the undertakings in this triangular relation are all concerned with the implementation of the horizontal collusion scheme. According to well-established case law, this intermediary may be found to infringe Article 101 TFEU, which strictly precludes 'any direct *or indirect* contact' between competitors.[116] This is particularly the case if, for instance, information on future prices is exchanged between competitors through this intermediary. According to the European Commission, even when information is disclosed 'indirectly through a common agency (for example, a trade association) or a third party such as a market research organization or through the companies' suppliers or retailers such conduct may well infringe competition law'.[117]
2. There are various examples where a cartel was structured so as to rely on a third party in an upstream or downstream market, which has been outsourced some typical cartel function (ensuring the logistics of the meetings, monitoring the implementation of a cartel). In *Musique Diffusion Française* the Commission found that three exclusive distributors of Pioneer electronic equipment had participated in a concerted practice with Pioneer Electronic with the aim of preventing imports in France and therefore

115 G Hay, 'Horizontal Agreements: Concept and Proof' (2006) 51(4) *Antitrust Bulletin* 877, 882

116 Joined Cases 40–8, 50, 54–6, 111 & 113–14/73, *Cooperatieve Vereniging 'Suiker Unie' UA v Commission* [1975] ECR 1663, para 174 (emphasis added).

117 Communication—Guidelines on the applicability of Article 101 of the Treaty on the Functioning of the European Union to horizontal co-operation agreements [2011] OJ C11/1.

to maintain a higher level of prices.[118] The distributors participated in a meeting with Pioneer in which the French distributor complained of the existence of parallel imports in France. The Commission found that there was a concerted practice between Pioneer and each of its exclusive distributors, as Pioneer had informed them of the complaints of the French distributor. Pioneer contested this finding claiming that forwarding this type of information formed part of the 'normal exchange of information between supplier and distributor concerning the market situation'.[119] The Court, however, rejected this argument, considering the active role that Pioneer played in the concerted practice, as it did not only call and preside over meetings on parallel imports with the exclusive distributors but it also incited some of them to discover the source of parallel imports and to put a stop to them. In *Deltafina v Commission*,[120] the General Court upheld the decision of the Commission finding Deltafina, the main purchaser of Spanish raw tobacco, liable under Article 101(1) TFEU for having participated in a cartel between four Spanish processors of raw tobacco, even though Deltafina did not operate at the same production level as the four Spanish processors, in view of Deltafina's 'very significant economic interest in the Spanish tobacco market, albeit as a purchaser rather than a first processor, which allowed it to play a pivotal role [...] in the establishment and implementation of the processors cartel'.[121] The General Court noted that an undertaking may infringe Article 101(1) where the purpose of its conduct, as coordinated with that of other undertakings, is to restrict competition on a specific relevant market, regardless of whether the undertaking is active on that relevant market itself.[122] The GC added that 'where an undertaking tacitly approves an unlawful initiative, its behaviour encourages the continuation of the infringement and so compromises its discovery', this amounting 'to passive participation in the infringement which is capable of rendering the undertaking liable'.[123] In these circumstances, the 'subjective condition [of agreement/concerted practice] is inherent in the criteria relating to tacit approval of the cartel and to the undertaking's failure to distance itself from the cartel'. Indeed, according to the Court, the undertaking 'intended to contribute through its own conduct to the common objectives of the cartel and was aware of the anti-competitive conduct, or could reasonably have foreseen the conduct, and was ready to accept the attendant risk'.[124]

3. Does the fact that it is irrelevant whether the communication related to the conduct of only one or more of the parties[125] introduce the concept of an attempt to restrict competition?

The CJEU further examined the boundaries of the subjective element of concerted practice with regard to passive participation in the context of a case involving travel agents that had coordinated the discount rate applicable to their clients through the actions of a third party, the owner and administrator of the Internet booking system used by the travel agents.

118 Joined Cases 100–3/80, *SA Musique Diffusion Française v Commission* [1983] ECR 1825, paras 75–6, 79.

119 Ibid, para 73.

120 Case T-29/05, *Deltafina v Commission* [2010] ECR II–04077.

121 *Raw tobacco—Spain* (Case COMP/C.38.238/B.2) Commission Decision, 20 October 2004 [2004] OJ L 102/14, para 368.

122 Case T-29/05, *Deltafina v Commission* [2010] ECR II–04077, para 87.

123 Ibid, para 59.

124 Ibid, para 62.

125 Case C-194/14 P, *AC-Treuhand AG v Commission*, ECLI:EU:C:2015:717, para 35.

Case C-74/14, *Eturas UAB et al v Lietuvos Respublikos konkurencijos taryba*, ECLI:EU:C:2016:42

The case was launched when the Lithuanian Competition Council found evidence that the director of Eturas, a common online travel booking system (called e-Turas), which is used by most travel agents, had sent an email to the travel agencies having an electronic account in the e-Turas system asking them to 'vote' on the appropriateness of reducing the discounts offered on booking made through that system from 4 per cent to 1–3 per cent. A few days after sending this message, the administrator of Eturas sent through the internal messaging system of e-Turas an additional message indicating that 'following the appraisal of the statements, proposals and wishes expressed by the travel agencies concerning the application of a discount rate', a capping of the discount rate will be introduced in order to 'help to preserve the amount of the commission and to normalize the conditions of competition'. Travel agencies, will be able to offer online discounts in the range of 0 per cent to 3 per cent. For travel agents offering more than 3 per cent, according to this message transmitted through E-turas, these were automatically reduced to 3 per cent. However, travel agents were not prevented from granting their customers greater discounts than 3 per cent, but in order to do so they were required to take additional technical steps. The Lithuanian Competition Council considered that the travel agents using the e-Turas booking system during the period in question had participated, along with Eturas, in an anti-competitive concerted practice, the e-Turas system being used as a tool for coordinating the travel agents' actions and eliminating the need for meetings. The travel agencies challenged the decision of the Council in front of the Supreme Administrative Court, arguing that the capping was a unilateral action of Eturas, for which they could not be held liable, and that some of them were not able to receive or read the message at issue, nor did they pay any attention to the technical modifications made by e-Turas. The Lithuanian court referred the case to the CJEU, noting that the principal piece of evidence supporting the finding of infringement was a 'mere presumption that the travel agencies concerned read or should have read the message at issue' and 'should have understood all of the consequences arising from the decision concerning the restriction of the discount rates on bookings'.[126] The referring court expressed some uneasiness as to the compatibility of such presumption of the subjective element of concerted practice with the presumption of innocence, although it also accepted that the travel agencies using the e-Turas system knew or ought to have known that their competitors also used that system.

The CJEU framed the case as involving a passive mode of participation in collusive activity; however not in meetings at which anti-competitive agreements were concluded, but rather through participation in a common computerized information system. The case also raised important questions as to the law applicable to standard of proof and evidential presumptions with regard to whether the dispatch of a message by Eturas may constitute sufficient evidence to establish that the travel agents using the e-Turas system were aware, or ought to have been aware of the content of the message. On this issue, the CJEU noted:

> 34. [. . .] [T]he answer to the question whether the mere dispatch of a message, such as that at issue in the main proceedings, may, having regard to all of the circumstances before the referring court, constitute sufficient evidence to establish that its addressees were aware, or ought to have been aware, of its content, does not follow from the concept of a 'concerted practice' and is not intrinsically linked to that concept. That question must be regarded as relating to the assessment of evidence

126 Case C-74/14, *Eturas UAB et al v Lietuvos Respublikos konkurencijos taryba*, ECLI:EU:C:2016:42, para 22.

and to the standard of proof, with the result that it is governed—in accordance with the principle of procedural autonomy and subject to the principles of equivalence and effectiveness—by national law.

Although the CJEU noted that 'the principle of effectiveness requires that an infringement of EU competition law may be proven not only by direct evidence, but also through indicia, provided that they are objective and consistent',[127] *it also referred to the presumption of innocence as a general principle of EU law that needs to be equally taken into account.*

39. The presumption of innocence precludes the referring court from inferring from the mere dispatch of the message at issue in the main proceedings that the travel agencies concerned ought to have been aware of the content of that message.

40. However, the presumption of innocence does not preclude the referring court from considering that the dispatch of the message at issue in the main proceedings may, in the light of other objective and consistent indicia, justify the presumption that the travel agencies concerned were aware of the content of that message as from the date of its dispatch, provided that those agencies still have the opportunity to rebut it.

41. In that regard, the referring court cannot require that those agencies take excessive or unrealistic steps in order to rebut that presumption. The travel agencies concerned must have the opportunity to rebut the presumption that they were aware of the content of the message at issue in the main proceedings as from the date of that message's dispatch, for example by proving that they did not receive that message or that they did not look at the section in question or did not look at it until some time had passed since that dispatch.

42. [. . .] [A]s regards the participation of the travel agencies concerned in a concerted practice within the meaning of Article 101(1) TFEU, it must be recalled, first, that under that provision, the concept of a concerted practice implies, in addition to the participating undertakings concerting with each other, subsequent conduct on the market and a relationship of cause and effect between the two [. . .].

43. Secondly, it must be pointed out that the case at issue in the main proceedings, as presented by the referring court, is characterised by the fact that the administrator of the information system at issue sent a message concerning a common anticompetitive action to the travel agencies participating in that system, a message which could only be consulted in the 'Notices' section of the information system in question and to which those agencies did not expressly respond. Following the dispatch of that message, a technical restriction was implemented which limited the discounts that could be applied to bookings made via that system to 3%. Although that restriction did not prevent the travel agencies concerned from granting discounts greater than 3% to their customers, it nevertheless required them to take additional technical steps in order to do so.

44. Those circumstances are capable of justifying a finding of a concertation between the travel agencies which were aware of the content of the message at issue in the main proceedings, which could be regarded as having tacitly assented to a common anticompetitive practice, provided that the two other elements constituting a concerted practice, noted in paragraph 42 above, are also present. Depending on the referring court's assessment of the evidence, a travel agency may

127 Ibid, para 37.

be presumed to have participated in that concertation if it was aware of the content of that message.

45. However, if it cannot be established that a travel agency was aware of that message, its participation in a concertation cannot be inferred from the mere existence of a technical restriction implemented in the system at issue in the main proceedings, unless it is established on the basis of other objective and consistent indicia that it tacitly assented to an anticompetitive action.

The CJEU then explains how it is possible to distance oneself from the finding of concerted practice:

46. [. . .] [I]t must be pointed out that a travel agency may rebut the presumption that it participated in a concerted practice by proving that it publically distanced itself from that practice or reported it to the administrative authorities. In addition, according to the case-law of the Court, in a case such as that at issue in the main proceedings, which does not concern an anticompetitive meeting, public distancing or reporting to the administrative authorities are not the only means of rebutting the presumption that a company has participated in an infringement; other evidence may also be adduced with a view to rebutting that presumption [. . .].

47. As regards the examination of whether the travel agencies concerned publicly distanced themselves from the concertation at issue in the main proceedings, it must be noted that, in particular circumstances such as those at issue in the main proceedings, it cannot be required that the declaration by a travel agency of its intention to distance itself be made to all of the competitors which were the addressees of the message at issue in the main proceedings, since that agency is not in fact in a position to know who those addressees are.

48. In that situation, the referring court may accept that a clear and express objection sent to the administrator of the E-TURAS system is capable of rebutting that presumption.

49. As regards the possibility of rebutting the presumption of participation in a concerted practice by means other than public distancing or reporting it to the administrative authorities, it must be held that, in circumstances such as those at issue in the main proceedings, the presumption of a causal connection between the concertation and the market conduct of the undertakings participating in the practice, referred to in paragraph 33 of the present judgment, could be rebutted by evidence of a systematic application of a discount exceeding the cap in question.

NOTES AND QUESTIONS ON ETURAS

1. The CJEU distinguished between: (i) the evidential presumption of the present case with regard to the existence of the subjective/intentional element of the concerted practice from the simple dispatch of a message in a common computerized information system, which the CJEU analysed as an issue affecting the assessment of evidence and thus subject to national law, and (ii) the presumption of a causal connection between a concertation and the market conduct of the undertakings participating in the practice, according to which those undertakings, where they remain active on that market, take account of the information exchanged with their competitors in determining their conduct on that market (the so-called *Anic* presumption), which is a matter of substantive EU competition law on the concept

of 'concerted practice'.[128] Although the CJEU refers to the evidential presumption of the present case as a matter for national law, it provides some detailed instructions to national judges, on the basis of the principle of effectiveness. The distinction between the two forms of presumption remains also clear in the analysis of the possibilities of rebutting the presumption. Paragraph 49 refers to the *Anic* presumption, regarding the material element of a concerted practice, while paragraphs 46–8 mainly refer to the evidential presumption establishing the subjective element that the users of the e-Turas system were aware of the system notice.

2. Would the CJEU have applied a similar approach with regard to a situation in which an undertaking would have participated in a collusive meeting? In the latter context, the undertaking involved has, according to the case law, two possibilities to dissociate itself from the alleged concerted practice: it may publicly distance itself from the content of the illicit practice or, otherwise, report it to the administrative authorities.
3. When the CJEU mentions, in paragraph 49 of its judgment, that the presumption of a causal connection between the concertation and the market conduct of the undertakings participating in the practice may be rebutted by evidence of a systematic application of a discount exceeding the cap in question does this refer to the evidential presumption of the subjective/intentional element of the concerted practice? Would a non-systematic application of the discount suffice for rebutting the presumption, or would one also require some form of public distancing? In his opinion AG Szpunar considers it insufficient as a way of rebuttal to oppose the practice by mere conduct on the market, even if systematic, and emphasizes the need for the undertaking concerned to state, with sufficient clarity, its disagreement with the initiative and its intention not to follow the practice. Indeed, according to the AG, 'without public opposition, such conduct could not be easily distinguished from mere cheating on other cartel members'.[129] As we will examine in Chapter 7, it is important to subject to the scope of Article 101 TFEU undertakings that participated in cartel activity, even if these do not implement the common policy decided by the cartel, essentially for deterrence purposes. By accepting that evidence of systematic non-application is sufficient to rebut the presumption, is the CJEU opening to undertakings participating in cartels a way

[128] Ibid, paras 33 and 34:

The Court has indeed held that the presumption of a causal connection between a concertation and the market conduct of the undertakings participating in the practice, according to which those undertakings, where they remain active on that market, take account of the information exchanged with their competitors in determining their conduct on that market, follows from Article 101(1) TFEU and consequently forms an integral part of the EU law which the national court is required to apply.

However, in contrast to that presumption, the answer to the question whether the mere dispatch of a message, such as that at issue in the main proceedings, may, having regard to all of the circumstances before the referring court, constitute sufficient evidence to establish that its addressees were aware, or ought to have been aware, of its content, does not follow from the concept of a 'concerted practice' and is not intrinsically linked to that concept. That question must be regarded as relating to the assessment of evidence and to the standard of proof, with the result that it is governed—in accordance with the principle of procedural autonomy and subject to the principles of equivalence and effectiveness—by national law.

[129] Opinion of AG Szpunar in Case C-74/14, *Eturas UAB et al v Lietuvos Respublikos konkurencijos taryba*, ECLI:EU:C:2015:493, para 90.

to escape the prohibition of Article 101 TFEU, in case their participation was passive and there is no other evidence of acquiescence/tacit consensus?

4. AG Szpunar also noted in his Opinion that 'the concept of a concerted practice does imply reciprocity' and 'concerted action is necessarily the result of a consensus', which equally encompasses 'tacit approval'.[130] The possibility of inferring such tacit approval 'and therefore of establishing the existence of a consensus to cooperate rather than compete, depends on the context of the communication'.[131] According to the AG, the 'unusual nature of the method of communication' in this case (the common IT platform, rather than a meeting between competitors) was 'counterbalanced by other circumstances'.[132] Among these, AG Szpunar finds of interest that the 'restriction of competition in question is clearly of a horizontal nature' and that, consequently, '[t]he application of a uniform maximum discount rate by competitors requires their mutual reliance', as 'an undertaking would comply with such an initiative only on the condition that the same restriction applies horizontally to its competitors'.[133] AG Szpunar then clearly cautions against drawing 'a useful analogy' from the Court's case-law specific to vertical restrictions, in which cases, as he remarks, the mere continuation of commercial relations does not amount to tacit acquiescence.[134] If the finding of tacit acquiescence or approval depends on the nature of the restriction, among other considerations, would one be wrong to think that the AG adopts the substantive view of the concept of concerted practice/agreement?
5. Following the judgment of the CJEU, the Supreme Administrative Court of Lithuania has considered whether each travel agency involved had knowledge about the discount restriction imposed in the e-Turas system and whether it had objected to the restriction or not or withdrawn from the concerted action by systematically giving additional discounts. The Lithuanian court distinguished between various categories of travel agencies: (i) those that knew about the imposed restriction and did not oppose it; (ii) those that knew about it and opposed the imposed restriction; and (iii) those for which the Lithuanian Competition Council had failed to gather sufficient evidence for asserting that they knew about the restriction imposed in the Eturas system. The Court lifted the fines imposed on the travel agencies of the second and third group, while travel agencies that knew about the restriction and did not oppose it were found to have taken part in a restriction of competition.[135]
6. The *Eturas* case hints at the possibility that the subjective element of concerted practice may be satisfied with various, even less common, ways of reciprocal contact. This may be indirect, through a third party, or through even an IT platform and algorithmic pricing. A recent case of price-fixing brought by the US Department of Justice's San Francisco division against an e-commerce executive, Mr Topkins, alleged that the defendant and his co-conspirators adopted specific pricing algorithms for the sale of certain posters at the Amazon Marketplace with the goal of coordinating changes to their respective prices and wrote computer code that instructed algorithm-based software to set prices in conformity with this agreement.[136] Uber's surge pricing also constitutes

130 Ibid, paras 46–7. 131 Ibid, para 48. 132 Ibid, para 61. 133 Ibid, para 64.
134 Ibid.
135 *Eturas*, Case No A-97-858/2016. Supreme Administrative Court of Lithuania, Judgment of 2 May 2016.
136 See US Department of Justice, 'Former E-Commerce Executive Charged with Price Fixing in the Antitrust Division's First Online Marketplace Prosecution', Press Release (6 April 2015), available at https://www.justice.gov/opa/pr/former-e-commerce-executive-charged-price-fixing-antitrust-divisions-first-online-marketplace.

another example in which an algorithm pushes up prices or, as Uber would argue, balances supply and demand when many cars are needed simultaneously.[137]

7. Ezrachi and Stucke have recently observed with regard to the impact of artificial intelligence to collusion:

   Computers may limit competition not only through agreement or concerted practice, but also through more subtle means. For example, this may be the case when similar computer algorithms promote a stable market environment in which they predict each other's reaction and dominant strategy. Such a digitalized environment may be more predictable and controllable. Furthermore, it does not suffer from behavioral biases and is less susceptive to possible deterrent effects generated through antitrust enforcement.[138]

   The authors note 'four non-exclusive categories of collusion—the "Messenger", "Hub and Spoke", "Predictable Agent" and "Autonomous Machine" '. According to Ezrachi and Stucke, '*Messenger*—concerns the use of computers to execute the will of humans in their quest to collude and restrict competition'; '*Hub and Spoke*—concerns the use of a single algorithm to determine the market price charged by numerous users'; '*Predictable Agent*—presents a more complex scenario', in which 'humans unilaterally design the machine to deliver predictable outcomes and react in a given way to changing market conditions', however, 'with awareness of likely developments of other machines used by its competitors' and finally the '*Autonomous Machine*' where 'the competitors unilaterally create and use computer algorithms to achieve a given target, such as profit maximization', the machines, 'through self-learning and experiment', determining 'independently the means to optimize profit'.[139]

8. Reflect on the possible use of the concept of 'concerted practice' and the presence of the subjective element of collusion in order to bring this type of practice under the scope of Article 101 TFEU/Chapter I of the UK Competition Act. There have been some concerns raised with regard to digital assistants, such as Watson, Deepmind, Alexa, or

137 For a more detailed analysis and further examples, see OECD, *Algorithms and Collusion: Competition Policy in the Digital Age* (14 September 2017), available at www.oecd.org/competition/algorithms-collusion-competition-policy-in-the-digital-age.htm.

138 A Ezrachi and ME Stucke, 'Artificial Intelligence & Collusion: When Computers Inhibit Innovation' [2017] *University of Illinois L Rev* 1775, 1782. See also A Ezrachi and ME Stucke, *Virtual Competition* (Harvard University Press, 2016). See also SK Mehra, 'Antitrust and the Robo-Seller: Competition in the Time of Algorithms' (2016) 100 *Minnesota L Rev* 1323.

139 A Ezrachi and ME Stucke, 'Artificial Intelligence & Collusion: When Computers Inhibit Innovation' [2017] *University of Illinois L Rev* 1775, 1783. Various scenarios of algorithmic collusion have also been examined by competition authorities: see, CMA94, Pricing Algorithms (8 October 2018), available at https://assets.publishing.service.gov.uk/government/uploads/system/uploads/attachment_data/file/746353/Algorithms_econ_report.pdf; Algorithms and Collusion - Note by the European Commission, submitted for the OECD Competition Committee Hearings on 21-23 June 2017, DAF/COMP/WD(2017)12. Concerns over algorithmic collusion were also raised by the members of the CJEU: See, Opinion of Advocate General Szpunar in Case C 434/15, *Asociación Profesional Elite Taxi v Uber Systems Spain SL*, ECLI:EU:C:2017:981, fn. 23 (noting that "the use by competitors of the same algorithm to calculate the price is not in itself unlawful, but might give rise to hub and spoke conspiracy concerns when the power of the platform increases"). Some recent economic literature has nevertheless raised questions on the capabilities of algorithms to solve the coordination problem and sustain collusion without some form of communication: see, K-U Kühn and S Tadelis 'Algorithmic Collusion, available at http://www.cresse.info/uploadfiles/2017_sps5_pr2.pdf; U Schwalbe, Algorithms, Machine Learning, and Collusion (June 1, 2018), available at SSRN: https://ssrn.com/abstract=3232631.

robo-selling to increase the power of oligopolists to charge supra-competitive prices.[140] Artificial intelligence (AI) may facilitate coordination between a large number of sellers, providing them a long-term perspective on their profits, rather than a short-term one that would provide them incentives to cheat, and could also enable a more effective monitoring of the collusive outcome, as AI may be able to identify the real causes of price decreases. AI and Big Data may also augment the anti-competitive strategies by combining different sources of information (and not just price), predicting the rivals' cost curves and establishing with greater accuracy what would be the optimal strategy in the specific market circumstances. However, the ability of discriminating between different groups of consumers, or even offer personalized pricing, may lead to products that are less homogeneous, may increase product differentiation, and consequently reduce the risks of price transparency and collusion.[141]

9. In a recent decision regarding an anti-competitive arrangement between Trod and GBE concerning retail sales of licensed sport and entertainment posters and frames sold by both Parties on Amazon UK, the CMA found that the two companies had infringed competition law by agreeing that they would not, in certain specified circumstances, undercut each other's prices for posters and frames sold on Amazon's UK website, by adjusting prices through pricing algorithms.[142]

The facilitation of anti-competitive conduct was also examined by the General Court in *ICAP v Commission*.

Case T-180/15, *ICAP v European Commission*, ECLI:EU:T:2017:795

The case concerned the manipulation of benchmarks in relation to Yen interest rate derivatives. In a 2013 settlement decision, the Commission had declared and sanctioned six bilateral agreements between banks, stating in the decision that ICAP had acted as a facilitator for these bilateral agreements (but also underlying that the facts accepted by the settling parties could not establish separately liability for ICAP). In February 2015, the Commission issued a separate decision addressed to ICAP, which had refused to settle, holding that ICAP facilitated six separate bilateral infringements of Article 101(1) TFEU of differing durations, and fining ICAP with €14 million. The Commission found that ICAP had facilitated anti-competitive agreements related to the Japanese currency-based London and Tokyo inter-bank offered rates, LIBOR and TIBOR. ICAP and other banks had indeed discussed the level of upcoming Japanese Yen LIBOR submissions, revealing their preferences for future movements of rates. ICAP appealed to the GC challenging, among others, the application by the Commission of the concept of 'facilitation'. The General Court upheld the Commission's finding of an anti-competitive restriction by object, noting that such coordination with the intention to influence the extent of the payments due by, or due to, the banks participating in the scheme, had clearly an anti-competitive object, and therefore it was not necessary to examine whether the other

[140] S Mehra, 'Antitrust and the Robo-Seller: Competition in the Time of Algorithms' (2015) 100 *Minnesota L Rev* 1323; A Ezrachi and ME Stucke, 'Is Your Digital Assistant Devious?', *Competition Policy International* (September 2016), available at https://www.competitionpolicyinternational.com/is-your-digital-assistant-devious/.

[141] We analyse these aspects in more detail in Chapter 11.

[142] *Online sales of posters and frames* (Case 50223) CMA Decision (12 August 2016), paras 3.85–3.87, available at https://assets.publishing.service.gov.uk/media/57ee7c2740f0b606dc000018/case-50223-final-non-confidential-infringement-decision.pdf.

conduct common to those infringements, namely the exchange of confidential information, was also capable of justifying such classification as a restriction by object.[143] *With regard to the finding of facilitation of the illegal arrangements, ICAP claimed that (i) the 'facilitation' test applied to ICAP was too broad and a novelty and therefore breached the principle of legal certainty; (ii) that the role played by ICAP did not meet the 'facilitation' tests set out by case-law; and (iii) the use by ICAP of its contacts with certain banks to try to influence their Japanese Yen LIBOR panel submissions was not proven. The GC referred to the* AC-Treuhand *case law*[144] *as the appropriate legal precedent, and continued by holding the following:*

> 120. In that regard, although it is apparent from the case-law [. . .] that it was open to the Commission to prove either (i) that Icap was aware of the participation of the other bank concerned in each of the four infringements at issue or (ii) that Icap could reasonably have foreseen such participation, that second possibility must be considered taking into account the context in which the exchanges between UBS, and then Citi, and Icap took place.
>
> 121. As the applicants essentially submit, the requests addressed by UBS, and then Citi, to Icap with the aim of manipulating the JPY LIBOR rates did not imply, by their very nature, the existence of prior concerted action with another bank. Such requests could be legitimately interpreted by Icap as being made by UBS, and then by Citi, for the purposes of manipulating those rates in pursuit of their interests alone. It must be held that that circumstance makes it harder for the Commission to prove that Icap should reasonably have inferred from the requests of UBS, and then of Citi, that those requests formed part of collusion with another bank. [. . .]

The General Court then observed that, in the context of the bilateral cartel between UBS and RBS in 2008, the Commission did not succeed in proving that ICAP was aware of RBS's role in that cartel. In the light of the available evidence, which could not be classified as firm, precise, and consistent and contained ambiguous language, it was not also possible for the Commission to reasonably conclude that Icap should have suspected that UBS's requests in 2008 were part of the implementation of collusion with another bank (RBS). The GC then annulled the part of the Commission's decision alleging that Icap participated in the bilateral cartel between UBS and RBS in 2008.[145]

The appeal was, however, rejected with regard to the interaction between the conduct of ICAP and the other banks.

> 171. [. . .] it is clear that there is a complementary relationship between the conduct of which Icap is accused and that of which the banks concerned are accused, since the JPY LIBOR rates are calculated on the basis of the submissions of the banks which are members of the JPY LIBOR panel. The alteration of those rates would therefore have had a much lesser probability of success if the four infringements [. . .] had been based only on the alignment of the submissions of the two banks concerned by each infringement. It follows that Icap had a key role in the implementation of those infringements by influencing some of the JPY LIBOR panel submissions in the direction desired by the banks concerned.

The GC also noted that 'Icap should have expected, if necessary after taking appropriate legal advice, its conduct to be declared incompatible with the EU competition rules, especially in the light of the broad scope of the terms 'agreement' and 'concerted practice' established by the case-law of the Court of Justice'.[146] *The GC also highlighted the significance*

[143] Case T-180/15, *ICAP v European Commission*, ECLI:EU:T:2017:795, paras 72–3.
[144] Case T-180/15, *ICAP v European Commission*, ECLI:EU:T:2017:795, paras 98–104.
[145] Ibid, paras 139–45. [146] Ibid, para 197.

of the participation of ICAP in the infringements, and compared its conduct with that of AC-Treuhand in the AC-Treuhand case.

198. As regards the applicants' line of argument aimed at playing down Icap's role in the infringements at issue by comparing it with the role attributed to AC-Treuhand in the cartels which were the subject of the cases which gave rise to the judgment of 8 July 2008, *AC-Treuhand* v *Commission* [. . .] and to the judgment of 6 February 2014, *AC-Treuhand* v *Commission* [. . .], it is necessary, on the contrary, to point out the significance of that participation for some of those infringements. In so far as JPY LIBOR rates are calculated on the basis of the submissions of the panel members, the influence exerted by Icap over its customers which were members of that panel [. . .] made it possible to amplify the manipulations of those rates to a much greater extent than if those manipulations had remained confined only to the submissions of the two banks concerned by each of those infringements.

5.5.2. THE MATERIAL ELEMENT

The Court has interpreted broadly the material element of the concerted practice:

[. . .] [A] concerted practice [. . .] is caught by Article [101(1) TFEU], even in the absence of anti-competitive effects on the market.

First, it follows from the actual text of that provision that, as in the case of agreements between undertakings and decisions by associations of undertakings, concerted practices are prohibited, regardless of their effect, when they have an anti-competitive object.

Next, although the very concept of a concerted practice presupposes conduct by the participating undertakings on the market, it does not necessarily mean that that conduct should produce the specific effect of restricting, preventing or distorting competition.[147]

Although the case law requires a causal link between the concerted practice and some market conduct of the undertakings participating in the practice, this is broadly interpreted and is often presumed by the nature of the conduct.

For instance, EU Courts often presume that undertakings that have participated in meetings where sensitive information was exchanged between competitors, have taken into account the information exchanged in their future conduct in the market, and thus fulfil both the intentional and material elements of the concept of concerted practice in EU competition law. Indeed, in *Commission v Anic Partecipazioni*, the Court of Justice affirmed the validity of a Commission decision finding that Anic had participated in an EU-wide cartel operating in the polypropylene production sector from 1977 to 1983 stating as to the relationship of cause and effect between undertakings concerting together and their subsequent conduct on the market that '[. . .] subject to proof to the contrary, which it is for the economic operators concerned to adduce, there must be a presumption that the undertakings participating in concerting arrangements and remaining active on the market take account of the information exchanged with their competitors when determining their conduct on that market, particularly when they concert together on a regular basis over a long period [. . .]'[148]

[147] Case C-199/92 P, *Hüls AG v Commission*, [1999] ECR I-4287, paras 163–5.

[148] Case C-49/92 P, *Commission v Anic Partecipazioni* [1999] ECR I-4125, para 121.

(the *Anic* presumption).[149] According to the jurisprudence of the EU courts, the important thing is that the participating undertakings were afforded

> [. . .] the opportunity to take account of the information exchanged with their competitors in order to determine their conduct on the market in question and knowingly substitute practical cooperation between them for the risks of competition. Where it can be established that such undertakings successfully concerted with one another and remained active on the market, they may justifiably be called upon to adduce evidence that that concerted action did not have any effect on their conduct on the market in question.[150]

In analysing the EU case law, the UK CAT provided the following explanation for this presumption:

> '[. . .] This presumption is justified by the commercial and economic reality that competing undertakings are likely to take into account how their competitors are planning to behave on the market when determining their own strategy and conduct. The disclosure of future pricing intentions significantly reduces, and may indeed eliminate, uncertainty as to competitors' future conduct on the market allowing an undertaking to alter its behaviour accordingly. As a result of the disclosure or exchange of information, the participating undertakings are likely to behave differently on the market than if they were required to rely only on their own perceptions, predictions and experience of the market. Accordingly, the likely outcome of such an exchange is that the market will not be as competitive as it might otherwise have been.[151]

This presumption may, of course, be rebutted by the undertakings, which may, in principle, provide an alternative explanation of the parallel conduct than concertation, thus denying that the material element exists (the conduct on the market not being related to the alleged concerted practice). If concertation is not the *only* plausible explanation for the parallel conduct, then no causal link should be presumed to exist between the conduct on the market and the concerted practice. The presence of an alternative *plausible* explanation denies the existence of a causal link and thus the finding of a concerted practice. Yet, it is not clear what 'plausible' means in this context, the standard of proof being left undetermined.[152]

The competition authorities and courts may explore the relative strength of each explanation (hypothesis 1 being that the parallel conduct is predominantly explained by concerted practice; hypothesis 2 being that the parallel conduct is 'satisfactorily' explained by other circumstances, such as the 'oligopolistic tendencies of the market' and 'the specific circumstances

149 See ibid, paras 121 and 126; Case C-199/92, *Hüls v Commission* [1999] I–4287, paras 162 and 167; Case C-8/08, *T-Mobile Netherlands BV and Others v Raad van bestuur van de Nederlandse Mededingingautoriteir* [2009] ECR I–4259, paras 51–3; Joined Cases 89, 104, 114, 116, 117, 125 & 129/85, *Woodpulp II* [1993] ECR I–1307, para 71, with regard to the presumption of a causal connection between the concerted practice and the market conduct of the undertakings participating in the practice. The Court noted that the presumption is intrinsic to the concept of concerted practice in Article 101(1) TFEU, and consequently—forms an integral part of applicable—substantive EU law (*Woodpulp II*, para 52).

150 Case C-8/08, *T-Mobile Netherlands BV v Raad van Bestuur van de Nederlandse Mededingingsautoriteit* [2009] ECR I–4529, para 61.

151 *Tesco Stores Limited et al* [2012] CAT 31, para 51.

152 The standard of proof is an issue governed by national law, in accordance with the principle of procedural autonomy and subject to the principles of equivalence and effectiveness. Consequently, the standard of proof should be determined according to the law of the forum.

prevailing in certain periods').[153] One may take a different evidence law perspective than relative plausibility theory with regard to the operation of this evidential presumption and the discharge of the standard of proof and argue that 'plausible' means probable.[154]

One may, however, observe that, while theoretically possible, the rebuttal of the presumption of a causal link may be particularly difficult, if not impossible, in the context of the finding that competitors have exchanged information on future prices or quantities (evidence of a concerted practice). For instance, if it is presumed that they have taken that information into account in their future conduct on the market, this may render this presumption irrefutable in practice (at least for the material element of the concerted practice).[155] Indeed, it might be difficult, if not impossible, to discharge circumstantial evidence that concertation through forbidden price information exchange occurred, with economic evidence on the existence of other plausible explanations than collusion of that practice. Hence, one may argue that the rebuttal through the finding of an alternative plausible explanation is only possible where the Commission or NCAs findings rely solely on the undertakings' conduct on the market.[156] In *Woodpulp II*, the Court left open the possibility to find a concerted practice on the basis of parallel conduct on the market if there was no other alternative plausible explanation than concertation.[157] One may expect the discharge of the standard of proof of the rebuttal of this presumption to be at the centre of litigation, in particular in view of the important role of the presumption of innocence and more generally of the European Convention on Human Rights (ECHR) and fundamental rights jurisprudence in EU competition law enforcement.[158]

The following case provides a rare illustration of an instance in which the presumption of a causal link between concerted practice and conduct on the market was rebutted by the undertakings involved.

Case T-434/08, *Tono v Commission*, ECLI:EU:T:2013:187 (some case references omitted)

The case forms part of a case saga involving anti-competitive conduct by the International Confederation of Societies of Authors and Composers (CISAC), a non-profit non-governmental organization representing collecting societies managing copyright related to musical works in a number of countries. Collecting societies grant exploitation rights to commercial users, such as broadcasters or organizers of live shows, the price paid for these licences constituting the royalties the authors receive after the management expenses of collecting societies have been

153 Joined Cases 89, 104, 114, 116, 117, 125 & 129/85, *Woodpulp II* [1993] ECR I-1307, para 126. In favour of a relative plausibility theoretical framework in competition law, see I Lianos, 'Judging Economists: Economic Expertise in Competition Litigation: A European View' in I Lianos and I Kokkoris (eds) *The Reform of EC Competition Law* (Kluwer, 2010), 185.

154 In the probabilistic framework, the fact-finder considers the probability of the facts being 'true' on the basis of the available evidence. For a discussion and in defence of a probabilistic approach, see A Kalintiri, *A Critical Analysis of Evidence Standards in EU Competition Enforcement* (PhD thesis, Queen Mary University, 2015) (on file with the author).

155 It remains possible for the undertakings to distance themselves from the concertation, thus refuting the intentional element of the concerted practice.

156 For this argument, see A Kalintiri, *A Critical Analysis of Evidence Standards in EU Competition Enforcement* (PhD thesis, Queen Mary University, 2015), at 198 (on file with author).

157 Joined Cases C-89, 104, 114, 116–17 & 125–9/85, *Woodpulp II* [1993] ECR I-1307.

158 See, generally, A Scordamaglia, 'Cartel Proof, Imputation and Sanctioning in European Competition Law: Reconciling Effective Enforcement and Adequate Protection of Procedural Guarantees' (2010) 7(1) *Competition L Rev* 5, in particular 21–32.

subtracted. Since 1936, CISAC operated on a non-binding model for reciprocal representation agreements between its members collecting societies, according to which each collecting society agrees reciprocally to confer the rights over its repertoire to all the other collecting societies for the purposes of conferring licences covering public performance rights of musical works in the respective territories of each collecting society. Thus, collecting societies manage not only the rights that are directly transferred to them by the authors but also those transmitted from another collecting society managing similar categories of rights in another country. They are able to offer a worldwide portfolio of musical works to commercial users for use only in their respective territory.

RTL, a broadcaster based in Luxembourg and Music Choice Europe, an Internet broadcaster, lodged complaints to the European Commission in 2000 and 2003 respectively, against CISAC claiming that the model contract infringed EU competition law, as well as the refusal by a member of CISAC to grant RTL an EU-wide licence for its music broadcasting activities. The Commission adopted an infringement decision in 2008 prohibiting twenty-four European collecting societies from restricting competition by refusing to offer their services to authors and commercial users outside their domestic territory with regard to the exploitation of copyright via the Internet, satellite and cable retransmission.[159] *The Commission prohibited, in particular, membership clauses in the model contract which restrict author's ability to join freely the collecting society of their choice and exclusivity clauses which provide an absolute territorial protection to collecting societies in the territory in which they are established with regard to the grant of licences to commercial users. The Commission also found the existence of a concerted practice between collecting societies according to which each of them limited in its reciprocal representation agreements (RRAs) the right to grant licences relating to its repertoire in the territory of another collecting society party to the agreement. Although the Commission did not impose a fine and did not challenge the use of standard reciprocal representation agreements between collecting societies, it found that including clauses that limited each licensor collecting society's right to grant licences of its repertoire in the territory of other collecting societies in all reciprocal representation agreements between them was inevitably the result of concertation and thus constituted a concerted practice infringing Article 101 TFEU. Hence the theory of harm behind the Commission's infringement finding was the collusive network effect of all reciprocal representation agreements setting national territorial limitations concerning the mandate included in the reciprocal representation agreements, and did not relate to the individual agreements as such (with the exception of course of the membership and exclusivity clauses, as was previously indicated). The finding of a concerted practice between collecting societies was therefore crucial for the success of the case. The Commission's findings were duly challenged by the collecting societies before the General Court, the appellants arguing that the Commission did not satisfy the required burden of proof with regard to concerted practices.*

64. The applicant claims that, in order to prove the existence of a concerted practice relating to the national territorial limitations, the Commission, in the contested decision, relied exclusively on the parallel conduct of the collecting societies, and not also on the facts. Therefore, the Commission should have proved that the alleged concertation was the only plausible explanation for that parallel conduct, which it did not do.

65. The Commission contends that, in establishing the existence of the concerted practice at issue, it relied not only on the parallel conduct of the collecting societies, but also on other factors, namely:

- the discussions between the collecting societies, held in the context of the activities managed by CISAC, on the scope of the mandates contained in the RRAs;

[159] *CISAC* (Case COMP/C2/38.698) Commission Decision C(2008) 3435 final (16 July 2008).

- the Santiago Agreement;
- the Sydney Agreement;
- the historical link between the exclusivity clause and national territorial limitations.

66. The factors referred to in the first, second, and fourth indents of the previous paragraph are expressly mentioned in recital 158 to the contested decision as considerations supporting the finding of a concerted practice. Before the Court, the Commission also referred to the Sydney Agreement to show that there had been multilateral discussions between the collecting societies as regards the territorial scope of the mandates.

67. According to the Commission, the factors referred to in paragraph 65 above constitute 'documents' within the meaning of Joined Cases T-305/94 to T-307/94, T-313/94 to T-316/94, T-318/94, T-325/94, T-328/94, T-329/94 and T-335/94 *Limburgse Vinyl Maatschappij and Others* v *Commission* [1999] ECR II–931, paragraph 727 ('*PVC II*') and it did not therefore have to examine the question of whether the collecting societies' conduct can be explained by reasons other than the existence of concertation.

68. It follows from Article 2 of Regulation No 1/2003 and from settled case-law that, in the field of competition law, where there is a dispute as to the existence of an infringement, it is incumbent on the Commission to prove the infringement found by it and to adduce evidence capable of demonstrating to the requisite legal standard the existence of the circumstances constituting an infringement [. . .].

69. In that context, any doubt of the Court must benefit the undertaking to which the decision finding an infringement was addressed. The Court cannot therefore conclude that the Commission has established the infringement at issue to the requisite legal standard if it still entertains any doubts on that point, in particular in proceedings for annulment of a decision imposing a fine [. . .].

70. It is necessary to take into account the principle of the presumption of innocence resulting in particular from Article 6(2) of the European Convention for the Protection of Human Rights and Fundamental Freedoms, signed in Rome on 4 November 1950, which is one of the fundamental rights which, according to the case-law of the Court of Justice, constitute general principles of the Union's legal order. Given the nature of the infringements in question and the nature and degree of severity of the penalties which may ensue, the principle of the presumption of innocence applies, inter alia, to the procedures relating to infringements of the competition rules applicable to undertakings that may result in the imposition of fines or periodic penalty payments [. . .].

71. That case-law, developed in cases where the Commission had imposed a fine, is also applicable where, as in the present case, the decision finding an infringement is ultimately not accompanied by the imposition of a fine. Moreover, in the present case the statement of objections did in fact envisage accompanying the finding of an infringement with a fine.

72. In addition, account must be taken of the non-negligible stigma attached to a finding of involvement in an infringement of the competition rules for a natural or legal person (see, to that effect, judgment of the EFTA Court of 18 April 2012 in Case E-15/10 *Posten Norge* v *ESA*, not yet published in the EFTA Court Report, paragraph 90).

73. Furthermore, it must be recalled that, although the Commission did not impose a fine in the contested decision, the finding of a concerted practice and the order to bring an end to that infringement contained in the contested decision nevertheless expose the applicant to significant consequences, such as the possibility of being fined under Article 24(1)(a) of Regulation No 1/2003.

74. Thus, the Commission must show precise and consistent evidence in order to establish the existence of the infringement [. . .] and to support the firm conviction that

the alleged infringement constitutes a restriction of competition within the meaning of Article [101(1) TFEU] [. . .].

75. However, it is not necessary for every item of evidence produced by the Commission to satisfy those criteria in relation to every aspect of the infringement. It is sufficient if the set of indicia relied on by the Commission, viewed as a whole, meets that requirement [. . .].

76. Since the prohibition on participating in anti-competitive practices and agreements and the penalties which offenders may incur are well known, it is normal for the activities which those practices and those agreements entail to take place clandestinely, for meetings to be held in secret, and for the associated documentation to be reduced to a minimum. Even if the Commission discovers evidence explicitly showing unlawful contact between operators, such as the minutes of a meeting, it will normally be only fragmentary and sparse, so that it is often necessary to reconstitute certain details by deduction. In most cases, the existence of an anti-competitive practice or agreement must be inferred from a number of coincidences and indicia which, taken together, may, in the absence of another plausible explanation, constitute evidence of an infringement of the competition rules [. . .].

77. In *PVC II*,[160] on which the Commission relies, the Court arrived at a solution which balances those principles. In that case, the Court confirmed that, in accordance with the case-law, where the Commission's reasoning is based on the supposition that the facts established in its decision cannot be explained other than by concertation between the undertakings, it is sufficient for the applicants to prove circumstances which cast the facts established by the Commission in a different light and thus allow another explanation of the facts to be substituted for the one adopted by the Commission. However, the Court specified that that case-law was not applicable where the proof of concertation between the undertakings is based not on a mere finding of parallel market conduct but on documents which show that the practices were the result of concertation. In those circumstances, the burden is on the applicants not merely to submit another explanation for the facts found by the Commission but to challenge the existence of those facts established on the basis of the documents produced by the Commission [. . .].

78. Before considering the existence of explanations for the parallel conduct other than concertation, it is necessary to examine the question of whether the Commission, as it claims, established the existence of an infringement in relation to the national territorial limitations by evidence other than the mere finding of parallel conduct, a claim which the applicant contests. It is necessary to examine that issue before examining whether or not the explanations other than concertation are well-founded, since, if the Court concludes that such evidence was provided in the contested decision, those explanations, even if they were plausible, would not invalidate the finding of the infringement. Moreover, it must be pointed out that the contested decision does not have the same structure, in two stages, as that put forward by the Commission before the Court, namely that, first, the concerted practice had been proved by documents, within the meaning of *PVC II*, and, secondly, in the light of those documents and their supposed evidential value, the other explanations of the parallel conduct were not decisive for the purposes of proving that practice.

160 Joined Cases T-305–7, 313–16, 318, 325, 328–9 & 335/94, *Limburgse Vinyl Maatschappij and Others v Commission* [1999] ECR II–931 [hereinafter *PVC II*]. The Court also cited to the same effect, Joined Cases 29 & 30/83, *Compagnie royale asturienne des mines and Rheinzink v Commission* [1984] ECR 1679, para 16; Joined Cases C-89, 104, 114, 116–17 & 125–9/85, *Woodpulp II* [1993] ECR I–1307, paras 71 and 126 (footnote added).

79. It is therefore necessary, first of all, to establish whether the Commission has proven the existence of a concerted practice by factors other than the parallel conduct of the collecting societies that are comparable to 'documents', within the meaning of *PVC II*, on which the Commission relies. In that respect, it must be borne in mind that, in establishing the origin of the cartel at issue in that judgment, the Commission relied on the wording of planning documents, the information given by one of the applicants concerning those documents in response to a request for information, and the close correlation between the practices envisaged in those documents and the practices witnessed on the market [. . .].

80. In the present case, it must be recalled that the factors capable of proving concertation between the collecting societies are those referred to in paragraph 65 above, namely the discussions on the scope of the mandates contained in the RRAs held between the collecting societies in the context of the activities managed by CISAC, the Santiago Agreement, the Sydney Agreement, and the historical link between the exclusivity clause and the national territorial limitations.

81. In that respect, it must be observed that the absence of documentary evidence relating specifically to the national territorial limitations is all the more striking in the light of the fact that the Commission admits that some collecting societies wished to abandon the national territorial limitations. It would have been in the interest of those collecting societies to cooperate with the Commission, by providing it with documentary evidence of the existence of concertation. Given that the Commission, in the statement of objections, had demonstrated its intention to impose a fine on all the addressees, the collecting societies concerned could have cooperated with it in order to reduce the risk that they would be fined, or, at the very least, to limit the amount of that fine. Moreover, those collecting societies could have submitted evidence to the Commission establishing that the other collecting societies had put pressure on them to maintain the national territorial limitations decided in concert, but they did not do so.

The GC examined the evidential value of the five elements put forward by the Commission. It noted that the 'the mere fact that collecting societies met in the context of the activities managed by CISAC and that there is a certain amount of cooperation between them does not constitute, as such, evidence of prohibited concertation', the Commission not providing any evidence that the meetings organized by CISAC, in which the applicant participated, concerned the restriction of competition relating to the national territorial limitations.[161] *The return to national territorial limitations by all collecting societies after the expiration of the Santiago Agreement in which they had agreed to grant licences covering all the territories and for all the repertoires to users with their economic residence in an European Economic Area (EEA) country, did not also provide of concertation but a simple return to the* status quo ante. *Similarly, the existence of the Sydney Agreement was found ineffective to prove concertation, the agreement having ceased to be applicable at the time of the Commission's investigations. Having found no evidence of the existence of a concerted practice between the collecting societies with regard to national territorial limitations, the Court also assessed the existence of other plausible explanations than concertation advanced by the collecting societies.*

111. The applicant claims that the national territorial limitations are the result of individual rational decisions on a practical and economic level, given the specific conditions of the market, and not the result of a concerted practice.

[161] Case T-434/08, *Tono v Commission*, ECLI:EU:T:2013:187, para 84.

112. The applicant's arguments relating to the existence of explanations—other than the existence of concertation—for the parallel behaviour of collecting societies are centred on the need, first, for a local presence to monitor effectively the exploitations of copyright, secondly, to ensure that the amount of royalties received by the authors does not diminish, thirdly, to maintain the existence of national 'one-stop shops' from which users may obtain licences in respect of the worldwide repertoire and, fourthly, to take account of the existence, in the Norwegian legal system, of 'extended licences', namely licences which cover not only the works of right holders represented by the collecting society which grants the licence, but also the works of right holders which are not members of that collecting society. [. . .]

115. It is necessary, in the present case, to examine whether the Commission was right to find that the presence in all the RRAs of national territorial limitations did not correspond to the normal conditions of the market. In that respect, according to the case-law, it is for the party or the authority alleging an infringement of the competition rules to prove its existence and it is for the undertaking or association of undertakings invoking the benefit of a defence against a finding of an infringement to demonstrate that the conditions for applying such defence are satisfied, so that the authority will then have to resort to other evidence. Thus, although according to those principles the legal burden of proof is borne either by the Commission or by the undertaking or association concerned, the factual evidence on which a party relies may be of such a kind as to require the other party to provide an explanation or justification, failing which it is permissible to conclude that the burden of proof has been discharged [. . .].

The Court accepted the alternative explanation provided by Tono for national territorial limitations in that they are needed in order to monitor remotely the use of licences. It found that the Commission's objections to such explanation were not capable of 'undermining the credibility of the applicant's argument in that respect' and that the availability of other technological solutions allowing remote monitoring unconvincing.

158. On the basis of the foregoing, it must be found that the Commission has not proved to a sufficient legal standard the existence of a concerted practice relating to the national territorial limitations, since it has neither demonstrated that the applicant and the other collecting societies acted in concert in that respect, nor provided evidence rendering implausible one of the applicant's explanations for the collecting societies' parallel conduct.

5.5.3. UNILATERAL CONDUCT AND ARTICLE 101(1) TFEU: VERTICAL PRACTICES

Defining the contours of agreement when there is direct (written or oral) evidence of an exchange of consent between a supplier and a distributor has never been a matter of controversy. Much of the case law struggled with the issue of apparently unilateral practices that take place in the context of an existing distribution network. By conceptualizing distribution networks as institutions governed by specific norms, which are the product of an implicit agreement between the members of the distribution network, the European Commission and the courts managed to infer the existence of an agreement under Article 101 TFEU, simply by focusing on the economic and legal contexts of the specific vertical relationship. The formation of an institution, such as a network, presupposes the existence of 'a self-sustaining system of shared beliefs' about the rules of the game. The operation of the distribution network is therefore based on formal and informal 'game rules' that have been progressively shaped by its members.[162]

One could consider that the 'social norms' of the network govern the interaction between the parties of the network as much as the text of the bilateral distribution contract between the supplier and the dealer. The need to extend the scope of Article 101 TFEU to vertical practices that challenge the objective of the Internal Market provided the policy justification for this expansive definition. It follows that a comprehensive analysis of the 'social norms' that govern the network is essential in order to have a complete picture of the practice in question. An apparently unilateral practice may qualify as an agreement under Article 101 TFEU if the existence of informal rules or social norms within the network will make it plausible to conclude that the practice in question is the product of collusion. In other words, the abstraction of the distribution network will curtail the assumption of the divergence of interests between manufacturers and distributors that underpins the theory of the self-policing character of vertical restraints. Being parts of the same network, the supplier and the dealer will have convergent interests, which will facilitate the inference of a concurrence of wills and therefore of a vertical agreement.

The abstraction of the distribution network has important implications, not only for finding an agreement but also for the assessment of the anti-competitive effect of the relevant practice. Following well-established case law, the Commission and the courts assess the anti-competitive object or effect of the agreement within its economic and legal context.[163] The 'distribution system' forms part of this legal and economic context: even if the agreement in question does not itself restrict competition, the distribution network of which it is part may contribute to a cumulative foreclosure effect.[164] In both situations, the abstraction of the distribution network, conceived as a set (nexus) of relationships forming a separate but uniform system of formal and informal rules, from the point of view of outsiders, will make possible the expansion of the scope of Article 101 TFEU.

Some tension may, however, emerge between the need to incorporate this more holistic perspective that takes into account the existence of the distribution network, thus ensuring the effectiveness of competition law enforcement, with the legal requirement that responsibility for the commission of competition law infringements is personal.[165]

Motivated by the need to ensure the effectiveness of competition law enforcement and its ability to tackle business practices that affect market integration, the Commission has progressively embraced an expansive definition of the concept of agreement and included 'apparently unilateral conduct' adopted in the context of a distribution network within the scope of Article 101 TFEU. The CJEU initially supported this strategy, and although it affirmed that Article 101 TFEU does not cover unilateral conduct, it also held that conduct which appears unilateral may constitute an agreement for the purposes of Article 101 TFEU if it is integrated in the operation of a distribution network. The CJEU accepted that if the unilateral conduct was part of a continuous business relation, governed by a general agreement established in advance, the conduct will fall within the scope of Article 101 TFEU.

In *AEG-Telefunke v Commission*, the CJEU held that AEG's refusal to accept dealers that were complying with the qualitative requirements of its selective distribution network, because the latter were not willing to follow its pricing policy, constituted an agreement under Article

162 M Aoki, *Toward a Comparative Institutional Analysis* (MIT Press, 1st ed, 2001), 10.

163 See our analysis in Chapter 6.

164 See our analysis in Chapter 6.

165 'Personal' meaning attached to the undertaking found to be liable. See further Chapter 4.

101 TFEU. The Court was able to infer the existence of tacit acceptance of AEG's pricing policy by the retailers from the simple fact that continuing adherence to a distribution network implies the acceptance, tacit or express, of the supplier's policy on the basis of the pre-existing contractual relation.[166] According to the Court, refusals to approve distributors, even if they satisfy the qualitative criteria, may provide evidence of the supplier's anti-competitive policy, 'if their number is sufficient to preclude the possibility that they are isolated cases not forming part of systematic conduct'.[167] The Court adopted an expansive definition of the concept of agreement with the aim of preventing the suppliers from achieving their anti-competitive aims through a series of unilateral practices, for example by making the admission of dealers to their network conditional on meeting anti-competitive criteria. In subsequent case law, the CJEU held that the admission of a dealer to the supplier's distribution network implied acceptance by the dealer of the policy pursued by the manufacturer and that even in the absence of any link between the apparently unilateral conduct and the pre-existing agreement between the supplier and the dealer, the dealer's acceptance could be tacit and inferred from its compliance with the terms of the supplier's invitation to collude.[168]

The expansive interpretation of the 'agreement' concept in Article 101 TFEU by the Commission finally backfired and led the General Court and the CJEU to clarify the previous case law. In a series of landmark cases, starting with *Bayer*, the Courts emphasized the jurisdictional character of the concept of agreement and underscored its formal element, the existence of an offer and an acceptance. The position of the European courts has progressively moved from a relatively instrumental conception of antitrust agreement to a more formalistic approach. The *Bayer* case offered the opportunity to the General Court (then Court of First Instance) and the Court of Justice to reconsider their expansive jurisprudence on the concept of agreement under Article 101 TFEU as applied to apparently unilateral practices in a vertical context.

The *Bayer* case

Bayer had developed a policy in order to limit parallel imports of its best-selling range of medicines. Because of an important price differential between Spain, France, and the UK, resulting from differences in the price regulation of the pharmaceutical industry, French and Spanish wholesalers started to export to the UK. As a result, Bayer's sales to its UK subsidiary fell considerably. Bayer reduced its sales of Adalat, one of its best-selling ranges of medicines, to the Spanish and French dealers, to the amount it thought that dealers needed for domestic

166 Case 107/82, *AEG-Telefunken v Commission* [1983] ECR 3151, paras 38–9. The assumption is that admission and participation to the distribution network implies acceptance of its social norms by the dealers and in particular of the supplier's policy. See also Joined Cases 32 & 36–82/78, *BMW Belgium and Others v Commission* [1979] ECR 2435, paras 28–30.

167 Case 107/82, *AEG-Telefunken v Commission* [1983] ECR 3151, para 39. In this case, thirteen out of 260 were found to be sufficient for finding a 'systematic conduct'.

168 See Joined Cases 25 & 26/84, *Ford Werke & Ford of Europe Inc v Commission* [1985] ECR 2725, paras 20–1. (In this case, Ford was applying its initial agreement with the dealers, which granted to the supplier the right to decide which car models should be delivered.) In Case C-277/87, *Sandoz prodoti farmaceutici SpA v Commission* [1990] ECR I–45, the Court held that constantly and systematically sending invoices to customers with the inscription 'Export prohibited' could not be considered as unilateral conduct if it formed part of a continuous business relationship and customers continued to place orders without protest on the same conditions. The repeated use of general conditions of sale printed on the invoices and other order forms would thus lead to the conclusion that the resellers have accepted the offer of the supplier, which amounted to an agreement within the meaning of Article 101 TFEU.

sales and informed each dealer of its maximum amount. The dealers continued, however, to export to the UK and tried to find ways to circumvent Bayer's policy.

Following complaints by some of the dealers, the Commission found that Bayer had imposed an export ban in their commercial relations with its wholesalers in France and Spain, which formed an agreement under Article 101 TFEU. The Commission based this conclusion on the following two findings.[169] *First, Bayer developed a system for detecting exporting wholesalers and subjected them to a permanent threat to reduce the quantities supplied if they did not comply with the export ban. Second, the export ban was incorporated into the continuous relations between Bayer and its respective wholesalers. The wholesalers acquiesced to Bayer's policy, as they were aware of Bayer's real motives and they reduced the amounts they ordered from Bayer to align themselves with the figures that Bayer considered normal for supplying the national markets. Some wholesalers even attempted to obtain greater supplies by indirect means, precisely because of the export bans imposed by Bayer. In sum, the fact that Bayer coerced its wholesalers to adopt a policy which was not in their interest did not impede the Commission's finding the existence of an agreement between them and Bayer.*

Bayer appealed the decision to the Court of First Instance (now General Court) on the ground that its conduct was unilateral and involved no collusion with the dealers. Collusion within the Bayer group was irrelevant, as parent and dependent subsidiary are treated as a single undertaking.[170] *The question was whether collusion between Bayer and individual French and Spanish wholesalers had taken place. The General Court considered the earlier case law on the concept of 'agreement' and concluded as follows:*

Case T-41/96, *Bayer v Commission* (Judgment)
[2000] ECR II–3383

69. [. . .] The concept of agreement [. . .] centres around the existence of a concurrence of wills between at least two parties, the form in which it is manifested being unimportant so long as it constitutes the faithful expression of the parties' intention.

70. In certain circumstances, measures adopted or imposed in an apparently unilateral manner by a manufacturer in the context of his continuing relations with his distributors have been regarded as constituting an agreement within the meaning of Article [101(1) TFEU] [. . .].

71. That case law shows that a distinction should be drawn between cases in which an undertaking has adopted a genuinely unilateral measure and thus without the express of implied participation of another undertaking, and those in which the unilateral character of the measure is merely apparent. Whilst the former do not fall within Article [101(1) TFEU], the latter must be regarded as revealing an agreement between undertakings and may therefore fall within the scope of that article. That is the case, in particular, with practices and measures in restraint of competition which, though apparently adopted unilaterally by the manufacturer in the context of its contractual relations with its dealers, nevertheless receive at least the tacit acquiescence of those dealers.

72. It is also clear from that case law that the Commission cannot hold that apparently unilateral conduct on the part of a manufacturer adopted in the context of the contractual relation which he maintains with his dealers, in reality forms the basis of

169 *Adalat and Bayer*, Commission Decision 96/478/EEC [1996] OJ L 201/1.

170 See Case C-73/95 P, *Viho Europe BV v Commission* [1996] ECR I 5457. See further Section 4.3.2.1.1.

an agreement between undertakings within the meaning of Article [101(1) TFEU] if it does not establish the existence of an acquiescence by the other partners express or implied, in the attitude adopted by the manufacturer [. . .].

Bayer admitted that it had 'introduced a unilateral policy designed to reduce parallel imports',[171] *but denied having planned and imposed an export ban or having discussions with dealers about an export ban, let alone making an agreement with them. Moreover, the dealers did not adhere in any way to its unilateral policy and had no wish to do so. The General Court went very carefully through the evidence in relation to each of Bayer's dealers. It found that although Bayer intended to restrain parallel trade it did not intend to impose an export ban on the French or Spanish dealers. It tried to work out how much Adalat each dealer needed for its domestic customers, but did not check how much was actually exported by each to the UK.*[172] *The General Court also found that the dealers did not agree, even tacitly, not to export. They tried to obtain all the Adalat they could by putting in many small orders as well as the large ones they had been submitting centrally and provided all the Adalat not needed domestically for export. The Court also found that the wholesalers did not have an interest in complying with the export ban, as there was no evidence that Bayer made that request and that, in the absence of any monitoring of the final destination of the products, the possibility of sanctions was remote.*[173] *The Court stated that the wholesalers are required to ensure the distribution of products on the national market in an appropriate and stable manner.*[174] *The General Court did not, however, treat this as discouraging the dealers from exporting so much Adalat that insufficient would remain for local consumption.*[175] *Finally, the General Court distinguished the facts of the current case from the case-law cited by the Commission.*[176] *Unlike in* Sandoz,[177] *the invoices sent after each order accepted did not state 'export prohibited'. In* Tipp-Ex v Commission,[178] *the CJEU found that the dealer had co-operated with the supplier's request to raise the price of exports so as to remove any incentive for the purchaser to buy in another Member State. The General Court also distinguished BMW, AEG, and Ford on the ground that it is not enough to find a context of a contractual relationship—cooperation by the dealers must be established. Nor was it sufficient for the Commission to find that the dealers did not break off contractual relationships.*[179] *The Commission appealed to the CJEU, which confirmed the General Court's concept of agreement requiring a concurrence of wills.*

Joined Cases C-2 & 3/01 P, *Bundesverband der Arzneimittel-Importeure eV & Commission v Bayer*
[2004] ECR I–23

The Court examined the need for a system of monitoring and penalties as a precondition for finding an agreement concerning an export ban. The CJEU held that:

83. [. . .] [T]he [General Court] did not in any event consider that the absence of a system of subsequent monitoring and penalties in itself implied the absence of an

[171] Case T-41/96, *Bayer v Commission* [2000] ECR II–3383, para 76.
[172] Ibid, paras 81–9 and 100. [173] Ibid, para 109. [174] Ibid, para 136.
[175] Ibid, para 141. [176] Ibid, paras 158–71.
[177] Case C-277/87, *Sandoz prodoti farmaceutici SpA v Commission* [1990] ECR I–45.
[178] Case C-279/87, *Tipp-Ex GmbH & Co KG v Commission* [1990] ECR I–261.
[179] Case T-41/96, *Bayer v Commission* [2000] ECR II–3383, paras 172–3.

agreement prohibited by Article [101(1) TFEU]. On the other hand, such an absence was regarded as one of the relevant factors in the analysis concerning Bayer's alleged intention to impose an export ban and, therefore, the existence of an agreement in this case. In that regard, although the existence of an agreement does not necessarily follow from the fact that there is a system of subsequent monitoring and penalties, the establishment of such a system may nevertheless constitute an indicator of the existence of an agreement. [. . .]

The CJEU then examined the need for the manufacturer to require a particular line of conduct from the wholesalers or to seek to obtain their adherence to its policy and concluded as follows:

96. It does not appear from the judgment under appeal that the [General Court] took the view that an agreement within the meaning of Article [101(1) TFEU] could not exist unless one business partner demands a particular line of conduct from the other.

97. On the contrary, [. . .] the [General Court] set out from the principle that the concept of an agreement within the meaning of Article [101(1) TFEU] centres around the existence of a concurrence of wills between at least two parties, the form in which it is manifested being unimportant so long as it constitutes the faithful expression of the parties' intention. The Court further recalled [. . .] that for there to be an agreement within the meaning of Article [101(1) TFEU] it is sufficient that the undertakings in question should have expressed their common intention to conduct themselves on the market in a specific way.

98. Since, however, the question arising in this case is whether a measure adopted or imposed apparently unilaterally by a manufacturer in the context of the continuous relations which it maintains with its wholesalers constitutes an agreement within the meaning of Article [101(1) TFEU], the [General Court] examined the Commission's arguments [. . .] to the effect that Bayer infringed that article by imposing an export ban as part of the [. . .] continuous commercial relations [of Bayer France and Bayer Spain] with their customers, and that the wholesalers' subsequent conduct reflected an implicit acquiescence in that ban [. . .].

99. Concerning the argument that the [General Court] wrongly considered it necessary to prove an express export ban on the part of Bayer, it is clear from the Court's analysis concerning the system for monitoring the distribution of the consignments of Adalat delivered [. . .] that it did not in any way require proof of an express ban.

100. Concerning the appellants' arguments that the [General Court] should have acknowledged that the manifestation of Bayer's intention to restrict parallel imports could constitute the basis of an agreement prohibited by Article [101(1) TFEU], it is true that the existence of an agreement within the meaning of that provision can be deduced from the conduct of the parties concerned.

101. However, such an agreement cannot be based on what is only the expression of a unilateral policy of one of the contracting parties, which can be put into effect without the assistance of others. To hold that an agreement prohibited by Article [101(1) TFEU] may be established simply on the basis of the expression of a unilateral policy aimed at preventing parallel imports would have the effect of confusing the scope of that provision with that of Article [102 TFEU].

102. For an agreement within the meaning of Article [101(1) TFEU] to be capable of being regarded as having been concluded by tacit acceptance, it is necessary that the manifestation of the wish of one of the contracting parties to achieve an anti-competitive goal constitute an invitation to the other party, whether express or implied, to fulfil that goal jointly, and that applies all the more where, as in this case,

such an agreement is not at first sight in the interests of the other party, namely the wholesalers.

103. Therefore, the [General Court] was right to examine whether Bayer's conduct supported the conclusion that the latter had required of the wholesalers, as a condition of their future contractual relations, that they should comply with its new commercial policy. [. . .]

The CJEU went on to distinguish the earlier case law.

141. In that respect, it is important to note that this case raises the question of the existence of an agreement prohibited by Article [101(1) TFEU]. The mere concomitant existence of an agreement which is in itself neutral and a measure restricting competition that has been imposed unilaterally does not amount to an agreement prohibited by that provision. Thus, the mere fact that a measure adopted by a manufacturer, which has the object or effect of restricting competition, falls within the context of continuous business relations between the manufacturer and its wholesalers is not sufficient for a finding that such an agreement exists. [. . .]

NOTES AND QUESTIONS ON BAYER

1. Do the judgments of the General Court and the CJEU reverse any of the earlier law?
2. Would it be easy to set up such a non-collusive arrangement? What would a firm have to do to ensure there was no collusion? Examine the strategies followed by GSK in the *Sot Lélos kai Sia v GSK* case.[180] If you were advising a pharmaceutical company that wanted to take advantage of the precedent, what advice would you give it, practical as well as legal?
3. In *Bayer*, the Court focused on the subjective element of the concept of agreement: the existence of a concurrence of wills between at least two parties 'so long as it constitutes the *faithful* expression of the parties' (common) intention'.[181] The lack of an implicit or explicit invitation from the supplier to the retailers to achieve the reduction of exports defeated any finding of agreement. The continuation of business relations by the retailers was not deemed sufficient evidence of acquiescence.[182] As far as there was no declared intention on the part of the retailers to join efforts with Bayer to prevent parallel trade, the Court did not confirm the existence of a concurrence of wills. Indeed, the dealers had attempted to circumvent Bayer's policy by simulating increases in national demand, thus indicating that nominal compliance to Bayer's policy was not a 'faithful expression' of their intentions. This subjectivist perception of the concept of agreement by the Court explains the significant role played by the analysis of the 'faithful' (true) intention of the parties in order to find an agreement for the purposes of Article 101 TFEU. Following the suggestions of its Advocate General,[183]

180 See Case C-468–78/06, *Sot Lélos kai Sia EE and Others v GlaxoSmithKline AEVE* [2008] ECR I-07139 and analysis in Chapter 2.

181 Joined Cases C-2 & 3/01 P, *Bundesverband der Arzneimittel-Importeure eV (BAI) & Commission v Bayer* [2004] ECR I–23, para 97 (emphasis added).

182 Ibid, para 141.

183 Opinion of AG Tizzano in Joined Cases C-2 & 3/01 P, *Bundesverband der Arzneimittel-Importeure eV & Commission v Bayer* [2004] ECR I–23, para 110.

the Court concentrated its analysis on the existence of a 'stated intention' or on the actual conduct of the dealers on the market as an indication of intention. Do you agree with the position followed by the CJEU? Do you think that a discussion of the will or conduct of the parties should be separated from the analysis of their (economic) incentives? How would the later be considered in the assessment of the 'agreement' element of Article 101 TFEU? Should the concept of agreement be assessed according to the 'legal and economic context' of the specific conduct under examination? How does a test focusing on the intention of the parties, as defined by a declaration of will or a pattern of conduct, relate to the primary function of Article 101 TFEU: the prohibition of a restriction of competition that harms consumers? Does the approach followed by the Court in finding an agreement in *Bayer* seem to be inspired by the 'jurisdictional' or the 'substantive' view on the function of the concept of agreement/collusion in Article 101 TFEU?

4. Following *Bayer*, the jurisprudence of the EU courts adopted a more restrictive definition of the concept of agreement,[184] a trend that was followed by national courts.[185] This jurisprudence was criticized by some authors who suggested a different approach that would recognize the need for instrumentalism in interpreting the different elements of Article 101 TFEU (advancing the 'substantive' view on the concept of agreement), while avoiding, at the same time, an arbitrary and boundless enforcement of Article 101 to all types of business practices.[186]

[184] See Case T-368/00, *General Motors Nederland BV, Opel Nederland BV v Commission* [2003] ECR II–4491 (affirmed in Case C-551/03 P, *General Motors BV v Commission* [2006] ECR I–3173), where the General Court observed that evidence of coercion alone cannot be a sufficient factor to prove the existence of an agreement under Article 101 TFEU, the Court refusing to find an agreement between Opel and twenty of its dealers as there was no evidence of an 'express undertaking' of these dealers to comply with Opel's policy. The emphasis put on the direct evidence of acquiescence by the dealers to the supplier's policy underscores the formalism of the General Court's approach in this case. See also Case T-208/01, *Volkswagen AG v Commission* [2003] ECR II–5141, para 35, where the Court highlighted the need to establish the existence of an explicit or tacit acquiescence by the dealers of the supplier's policy, in order to prove an agreement under Article 101 TFEU. The General Court required evidence of the actual acquiescence by the dealers to the policy of the suppliers. According to the General Court (Case T-208/01, *Volkswagen* [2003] ECR II–5141, paras 63–6), if the contract is drafted in 'neutral terms', in the sense that it is clear 'from the very terms' of the contract that 'it does not envisage in any way an anti-competitive variation', the only way to prove an agreement for the purpose of Article 101 TFEU is to bring independent evidence of actual acquiescence by the retailers. It follows that an unlawful variation of an otherwise neutral agreement cannot establish the existence of a concurrence of wills between the supplier and the retailers under Article 101, unless the plaintiff brings evidence of tacit acquiescence by the dealer following the modification of the agreement. This formalistic approach may be contrasted to that followed in the pre-*Bayer* case law of the EU courts. For instance, in *Sandoz*, the fact that the dealership agreement was drafted in neutral terms did not impede the Court from concluding that the invoices sent by Sandoz were tacitly accepted by the dealers, as 'they formed part of the general framework of commercial relationships which (Sandoz) undertook with its customers' (Case C-277/8, *Sandoz*, [1990] ECR I–45, para 10) and that the distributors failed to object to these new conditions and continued to place more orders with Sandoz subject to the same conditions.

[185] In the UK, the Court of Appeal refused to adopt a 'purposive' definition of the concept of agreement in *Unipart Group Ltd & O2 (UK) Ltd (formerly BT Cellnet Ltd)* [2004] EWCA Civ 1034, paras 93 and 105 (finding that giving notice of termination under a contract constitutes unilateral conduct and not an agreement, as it was possible for the supplier to implement the anti-competitive policy without the assistance and cooperation of the dealers).

[186] See I Lianos, 'Collusion in Vertical Relations under Article 81 EC' (2008) 45 *Common Market L Rev* 1027.

5. The recent Commission's Guidelines on vertical restraints provide more guidance on the concept of agreement in a vertical context and how this may be distinguished from a purely unilateral action.

European Commission, Guidelines on Vertical Restraints [2010] OJ C 130/1

25. For there to be an agreement within the meaning of Article 101 it is sufficient that the parties have expressed their joint intention to conduct themselves on the market in a specific way. The form in which that intention is expressed is irrelevant as long as it constitutes a faithful expression of the parties' intention. In case there is no explicit agreement expressing the concurrence of wills, the Commission will have to prove that the unilateral policy of one party receives the acquiescence of the other party. For vertical agreements, there are two ways in which acquiescence with a particular unilateral policy can be established. First, the acquiescence can be deduced from the powers conferred upon the parties in a general agreement drawn up in advance. If the clauses of the agreement drawn up in advance provide for or authorise a party to adopt subsequently a specific unilateral policy which will be binding on the other party, the acquiescence of that policy by the other party can be established on the basis thereof. Secondly, in the absence of such an explicit acquiescence, the Commission can show the existence of tacit acquiescence. For that it is necessary to show first that one party requires explicitly or implicitly the cooperation of the other party for the implementation of its unilateral policy and second that the other party complied with that requirement by implementing that unilateral policy in practice. For instance, if after a supplier's announcement of a unilateral reduction of supplies in order to prevent parallel trade, distributors reduce immediately their orders and stop engaging in parallel trade, then those distributors tacitly acquiesce to the supplier's unilateral policy. This can however not be concluded if the distributors continue to engage in parallel trade or try to find new ways to engage in parallel trade. Similarly, for vertical agreements, tacit acquiescence may be deduced from the level of coercion exerted by a party to impose its unilateral policy on the other party or parties to the agreement in combination with the number of distributors that are actually implementing in practice the unilateral policy of the supplier. For instance, a system of monitoring and penalties, set up by a supplier to penalise those distributors that do not comply with its unilateral policy, points to tacit acquiescence with the supplier's unilateral policy if this system allows the supplier to implement in practice its policy. The two ways of establishing acquiescence described in this paragraph can be used jointly.

5.5.4. UNILATERAL CONDUCT AND ARTICLE 101(1) TFEU: HORIZONTAL PRACTICES

Apparently unilateral conduct in a horizontal context may also fall within the scope of Article 101 TFEU in certain circumstances. Information 'exchanges' between competitors raise interesting issues of qualification of the specific conduct as being collusive and thus subject to Article 101 TFEU (or Chapter I CA98) or purely unilateral and thus escaping competition law scrutiny under the abovementioned provisions.

There are circumstances in which the collusive element will be predominant, as there is a real 'exchange' of information between competitors. This is, for instance, the case where one competitor discloses its future intentions or conduct on the market to another when the latter requests it or, at the very least, accepts it.[187] Similarly, mere attendance at a meeting where a company discloses 'strategic data,'[188] or a meeting between competitors where they discuss commercially sensitive information may be qualified as a concerted practice, as it presumed that the competitors attending to this meeting have accepted the information and adapted their market conduct accordingly unless they respond with a clear statement that they do not wish to receive such data (the *Anic* presumption).[189] It is pretty clear that such conduct will easily fall under the scope of the collusion requirement of Article 101(1) TFEU or Chapter I CA98 and will be examined under the restriction of competition element.

A more difficult scenario relates to a unilateral or individual public announcement of future intentions, for instance a company makes a unilateral public announcement through a newspaper of its future pricing intentions. Being unilateral in essence such conduct will not be qualified as a concerted practice within the meaning of Article 101 TFEU, unless it falls under two possible exceptions: unilateral information disclosure and invitations to collude. Yet, contrary to the situation of apparently unilateral conduct in a vertical context, which we previously explored, there is no long-term contractual or other relation between the various undertakings to which this 'apparently' unilateral conduct may ultimately be attached to, the interaction between the competitors being purely situational: the undertakings are active on the same relevant market. At most, there is evidence of a one-way communication, the public announcement, without being clear if this communication targeted the undertaking's competitors, or the general public. Assessing individual public announcements under the 'concerted practice' conceptual box may nevertheless be justified by the risk of anti-competitive effects of such conduct. Indeed, in certain types of transparent oligopoly markets an undertaking disclosing information on sensitive parameters of competition (eg prices, output) or indicating, unilaterally, its willingness to enter into a collusive arrangement, may produce similar effects than a situation in which there was a collusive arrangement between the various competitors on this market. One may argue that if one has to take seriously the principle of effectiveness of competition law enforcement, these apparently unilateral practices should fall at least under the 'concerted practice' characterization.

There exist, however, various objections to this line of thought. First, this may conflict with the fundamental principle of personal responsibility and the fact that some fault or negligence is usually required for holding an undertaking liable for infringing competition law. Expanding the concept of 'concerted practice' to cover unilateral information disclosure, in the absence of any indication of reciprocity of information disclosure or acceptance of the invitation to collude, may amount to some form of strict-liability regime activated by the sole fact that one of the undertakings on the market has proceeded to such conduct, without any evidence that the other undertakings present on this market have actively *contributed* to such conduct. This may be perceived as unacceptable from a presumption of innocence and rule

[187] Joined Cases T-25–6, 30–2, 34–9, 42–6, 48, 50–65, 68–71, 87–8 & 103–4/95, *Cimenteries CBR and Others v Commission* [2000] ECR II–491, para 1849.

[188] According to Commission's Guidelines on the applicability of Article 101 of the Treaty on the Functioning of the European Union to horizontal co-operation agreements [2011] OJ C 11/1, para 86 [hereinafter Horizontal Guidelines], strategic data is 'data that reduces strategic uncertainty in the market' and 'can be related to prices (for example, actual prices, discounts, increases, reductions or rebates), customer lists, production costs, quantities, turnovers, sales, capacities, qualities, marketing plans, risks, investments, technologies and R&D programmes and their results [. . .]. The strategic usefulness of data also depends on its aggregation and age, as well as the market context and frequency of the exchange'.

[189] Case C-49/92 P, *Anic Partezipazioni* [1999] ECR I–4125, para 121.

of law perspective, in particular as Article 101 TFEU and Chapter I CA98 only apply to collusive conduct. Second, unilateral information disclosure may in some circumstances lead to pro-competitive effects. For instance, information disclosure is essential in order to provide shareholders or investors information on the situation and strategy of the undertaking and thus ensure the efficient operation of capital markets. Similarly, information disclosure may enable customers to make informed choices. Subjecting individual public announcements to the scrutiny of the existence of a restriction of competition under Article 101(1) TFEU may have chilling effects and could potentially lead to false positives (type I errors). Of course, such pro-competitive reasons are absent in the situation of invitations to collude and largely depend on the context in which they are made and the characteristics of the market.

Because of these concerns, competition authorities tend to be cautious in expanding the concept of collusion to such unilateral conduct in a horizontal context, although there are also examples in which some authorities have proceeded more actively, either on the basis of an expansive interpretation of the collusion element in their competition legislation, or on the basis of specific tools developed ad hoc.

There is some well-established case law on individual public announcements by one undertaking on its future market conduct, when these are followed by its competitors' public announcements.

In *Woodpulp*, the Commission charged forty producers of bleached sulfate wood pulp used in paper manufacturing and three of their trade associations with colluding on prices.[190] In particular, the Commission had found that a system of quarterly announcements of future prices to the trade press or sales agents 'constituted in itself, at the very least, an indirect exchange of information on future market conduct', in particular in view of the fact that 'prices were published well in advance of their entry into effect at the beginning of a new quarter', which 'guaranteed that other producers had sufficient time to announce their own-corresponding-new prices before that quarter and to apply them from the beginning of the quarter'.[191] Hence, the 'producer could expect that the prices he announced would immediately reach his competitors, just as he himself would expect to be given details in the way of his competitor's prices'.[192] Everyone's announced price was the same with only minor deviations. This was not the only collusive conduct involved though as the Commission also found evidence that prices were exchanged at face-to-face meetings and through fax messages between some of the producers and also between US producers, members of two trade associations.[193] Notwithstanding these different kinds of direct and indirect exchange of information, and even evidence of meetings between some of the cartelists, the Commission relied primarily on parallel pricing, noting that this universal adoption of relatively uniform price increases could not be explained, either by the market structure, which was not concentrated, or by price leadership.

The CJEU reversed the Commission's decision, holding that the price announcements by themselves could not constitute an infringement of Article 101(1) TFEU, neither did they constitute evidence of collusion. With regard to the first issue, the Court held that the communications on future prices 'arise from the price announcements made to users' (not competitors), and that '[t]hey constitute in themselves market behaviour which does not lessen each undertaking's uncertainty as to the future attitude of its competitors', as '[a]t the time when each undertaking engages in such behaviour, it cannot be sure of the future conduct of the others'.[194]

190 *Wood Pulp* (Case IV/29.275) Commission Decision [1985] OJ L 85/1. 191 Ibid.
192 Ibid, para 108. 193 Ibid, paras 109–10.
194 Joined Cases C-89/85 etc, *Woodpulp II* [1993] ECR I–1307, para 64.

Although the Court made the above comments in order to reject the Commission's assertion that advance price announcements were an infringement of Article 101(1) TFEU, that is, an issue relating to the existence of a restriction of competition, its reference to the fact that there was no reduction of uncertainty on the future conduct of one's competitor(s), may also be understood as referring to the absence of any evidence of collusion, as uncertainty over the anticipated conduct of competitors may leave as only option independent behaviour.

The Commission also rejected other hard evidence of meetings and contacts, thus essentially leaving little more than evidence of parallel pricing. It then proceeded to the examination of this evidence, in isolation to the rest of the evidence that was dismissed, finding that there were other plausible explanations for the parallel pricing observed in the wood pulp market and found irrelevant their parallel timing, as this could have easily resulted from market transparency and the oligopolistic nature of the market.

The reduction of uncertainty over the conduct of competitors may serve as a distinguishing element between collusion and independent behaviour, as it has also been accepted in subsequent cases.[195] It is noteworthy that the reduction of uncertainty is not of paramount importance in a vertical context for the finding of collusion (concerted practice or agreement). We have previously explained that the distinguishing element between collusion and independent conduct, in a vertical context is the existence of coercion. In both circumstances the necessary element for establishing the existence of collusion relates to the substance of Article 101 TFEU, in particular the alleged restriction of competition to be subject to competition law assessment, which is different for vertical and horizontal arrangements, as we have illustrated above.

In its 2011 Guidelines on Horizontal Co-operation Agreements, the Commission provided some practical guidance as to the characterization of unilateral announcements by undertakings to 'concerted practice', taking a more interventionist stance than the CJEU as to the scope of Article 101 TFEU.

Communication from the Commission—Guidelines on the applicability of Article 101 of the Treaty on the Functioning of the European Union to horizontal co-operation agreements [2011] OJ C 11/1 (some footnotes included)

61. [. . .] [I]nformation exchange can constitute a concerted practice if it reduces strategic uncertainty [footnote 4: Strategic uncertainty in the market arises as there is a variety of possible collusive outcomes available and because companies cannot perfectly observe past and current actions of their competitors and entrants.] in the market thereby facilitating collusion, that is to say, if the data exchanged is strategic. Consequently, sharing of strategic data between competitors amounts to concertation, because it reduces the independence of competitors' conduct on the market and diminishes their incentives to compete.

62. A situation where only one undertaking discloses strategic information to its competitor(s) who accept(s) it can also constitute a concerted practice. [footnote 5: See for example Joined Cases T-25/95 and others, *Cimenteries*, [2000] ECR II–491,

[195] Joined Cases T-25/95 etc, *Cimenteries CBR v Commission* [2000] ECR II–491, para 1852 (references omitted); Case T-82/08, *Guardian Industries and Guardian Europe v Commission*, ECLI:EU:T:2012:494 (partly set aside by the CJEU in Case 580/12 P, *Guardian Industries Corp and Guardian Europe Sàrl v European Commission*, ECLI:EU:C:2014:2363, but only with regard to the fine).

paragraph 1849: '[. . .] the concept of concerted practice does in fact imply the existence of reciprocal contacts [. . .]. That condition is met where one competitor discloses its future intentions or conduct on the market to another when the latter requests it or, at the very least, accepts it'.] Such disclosure could occur, for example, through contacts via mail, emails, phone calls, meetings etc. It is then irrelevant whether only one undertaking unilaterally informs its competitors of its intended market behaviour, or whether all participating undertakings inform each other of the respective deliberations and intentions. When one undertaking alone reveals to its competitors strategic information concerning its future commercial policy, that reduces strategic uncertainty as to the future operation of the market for all the competitors involved and increases the risk of limiting competition and of collusive behaviour [. . .]. For example, mere attendance at a meeting [. . .] where a company discloses its pricing plans to its competitors is likely to be caught by Article 101, even in the absence of an explicit agreement to raise prices [. . .]. When a company receives strategic data from a competitor (be it in a meeting, by mail or electronically), it will be presumed to have accepted the information and adapted its market conduct accordingly unless it responds with a clear statement that it does not wish to receive such data [. . .].

63. Where a company makes a unilateral announcement that is also genuinely public, for example through a newspaper, this generally does not constitute a concerted practice within the meaning of Article 101(1). [footnote 10: This would not cover situations where such announcements involve invitations to collude.] However, depending on the facts underlying the case at hand, the possibility of finding a concerted practice cannot be excluded, for example in a situation where such an announcement was followed by public announcements by other competitors, not least because strategic responses of competitors to each other's public announcements (which, to take one instance, might involve readjustments of their own earlier announcements to announcements made by competitors) could prove to be a strategy for reaching a common understanding about the terms of coordination.

NOTES AND QUESTIONS ON THE HORIZONTAL GUIDELINES

1. It is clear from the excerpts of the Horizontal Guidelines reproduced above that the concept of concerted practice applies where there is some direct or indirect communication between competitors with the potential to harm competition, as the doctrine 'preclude(s) any direct or indirect *contact* between competitors' leading to 'a *common understanding* on the terms of coordination', 'even without an explicit agreement on coordination'.[196] Would a public individual announcement that involves disclosure of strategic information, without this being followed by public announcements by competitors, amount to a concerted practice?
2. Should one distinguish the situation above from that of a one-way disclosure included in a private conversation between two competitors, without there being any evidence of reciprocity? In this scenario there is no ambiguity as to the intention of the undertaking communicating the strategic information to its competitor(s), in contrast to the situation of a one-way disclosure included in a public announcement, which may be explained by other reasons, for instance because of an obligation a publicly listed

[196] Horizontal Guidelines, paras 81, 83, and 86 (emphasis added).

company has to disclose a range of information to the investing public. It is clear from paragraph 62 of the Horizontal Guidelines that the Commission may condemn seemingly unilateral disclosure in a private conversation context, as 'mere attendance at a meeting [...] where a company discloses its pricing plans to its competitors is likely to be caught by Article 101 TFEU, even in the absence of an explicit agreement to raise prices' and that '[w]hen a company receives strategic data from a competitor (be it in a meeting, by mail or electronically), it will be presumed to have accepted the information and adapted its market conduct accordingly unless it responds with a clear statement that it does not wish to receive such data'. Because of this presumption, the silence of the recipient of information may be found to constitute a *prima facie* indication of consent,[197] thus shifting the burden of proof to the undertaking who must respond 'with a clear statement that it does not wish to receive such data'[198] when it comes to disclosure of strategic information if he is to avoid being caught by Article 101 TFEU (or Chapter I CA98).[199]

3. Reflect on the following fact pattern: 'Best flight' is one of the top five airlines (in terms of turnover), operating throughout Europe. 'Best flight' has a very efficient ticketing system allowing it to keep costs below those of many of its rivals. During a down raid to 'Best flight''s offices, the following piece of evidence has been collected. It is a transcript of a phone conversation held between Jordan B (J.B.), 'Best flight''s chairman and Michael D (M.D.), chairman of 'Fly high', 'Best flight''s main competitor.

J.B.: I think it's dumb to sit here and compete and neither of us making a dime...
M.D.: Well...
J.B.: I mean, you know what is the point of it?
M.D.: Nobody asked 'Best flight' to serve Amsterdam. Nobody asked 'Best Flight' to serve Munich, and there were low fares in there, you know, before. So...

[197] See Case C-199/92 P, *Hüls* [1999] ECR I–4287, para 162; Case C-49/92 P, *Anic Partezipazioni* [1999] ECR I–4125, para 121. See also, in UK competition law, OFT Case CE/8950/08, *Loan pricing* (20 January 2011). The OFT found evidence that between October 2007 and February or March 2008 individuals in Royal Bank of Scotland's Professional Practices Coverage Team disclosed generic as well as specific confidential and commercially sensitive future pricing information to their counterparts at Barclays. The disclosures by RBS took place through a number of contacts on the fringes of social, client or industry events or through telephone conversations. The OFT found evidence of a concerted practice between RBS and Barclays, even if Barclays did not reciprocate and even blew the whistle to the OFT. In its decision, the OFT noted that the 'information shared, although sometimes limited, was sufficient to highlight to Barclays that there was less downward pressure on its prices than Barclays might otherwise have expected' (*Loan Pricing*, para 293). Indeed, the OFT considered that it was entitled to presume that information received from RBS was taken into account by Barclays when pricing future deals, finding with the assistance of this presumption, that the information provided by RBS was taken into account generally by Barclays when formulating its subsequent pricing. The OFT imposed a fine of £28.59 million on RBS. Barclays brought the matter to the OFT's attention and, under the OFT's leniency policy, was not fined.

[198] Horizontal Guidelines, para 62.

[199] One should thus distinguish the procedural implication of the shifting of the burden of proof in the context of a private communication, which the CJEU's jurisprudence accepts as one of the broad consequences of the *Anic* presumption, from the evidential inference that the passive listener has consented to the invitation to collude, which for the time being has not been accepted by the EU Courts and does not necessarily follow from the *Anic* presumption. See Joined Cases T-25/95 etc, *Cimenteries CBR v Commission* [2000] ECR II–491, para 1849, distinguishing this presumption of the existence of reciprocal contacts, which is subject to Article 101 TFEU, from the 'purely passive role of a recipient of information', in which case it is less clear that Article 101 TFEU could apply.

J.B.: You better believe it, Michael. But you know, the problem is here. We are not going to change anything, right. We can both live here and there isn't enough room for Luftair (a third airline). But there is no reason that I can see to put both companies out of business.
M.D.: But if you are going to overlay every route that 'Best flight''s on top of every route that 'Fly high' has, I can't just sit here and allow you to bury us without giving our best effort. Do you have a suggestion for me?
J.B.: Yes, I have a suggestion for you. Raise your goddamn fares twenty percent. I will raise mine the next morning.
M.D.: Jordan, we...
J.B.: You will make money and I will do.
M.D.: We can't talk about pricing.
J.B.: Oh bull*** Michael. We can talk about any goddamn thing we want to talk about.

Would such unilateral disclosure of strategic information in a private conversation be considered as an invitation to collude and be qualified as a 'concerted practice' under Article 101 TFEU?

4. The exchange above is a slightly modified transcript from the *American Airlines* US antitrust law litigation, which marks the first instance in which the US Department of Justice showed interest in suspected invitations to collude, this one being challenged successfully and found unlawful under section 2 of the Sherman Act, that is a statute aiming at unilateral as well as collusive conduct, as an act of *attempted* monopolization.[200] In addition, the Federal Trade Commission (FTC) has entered into consent agreements in several cases alleging that an invitation to collude through a private or public announcement, although unaccepted by the competitor, violated section 5 of the FTC Act.[201] The FTC explained this case law by the fact that it may be difficult to determine whether a particular solicitation has or has not been accepted, that even an unaccepted solicitation may facilitate coordinated interaction by disclosing the solicitor's intentions or preferences, and finally the deterrence effect against conduct that is potentially harmful and that serves no legitimate business purpose.
5. Section 5 of the FTC Act prohibits 'unfair or deceptive acts or practices in or affecting commerce' and does not require prior to its application evidence of collusive conduct, as Article 101 TFEU or Chapter I CA98 do require. In the absence of specific legislation regarding 'attempts' to collude or unilateral information disclosure conduct that

200 *United States v American Airlines*, 743 F.2d 1114, 1116 (5th Cir 1984). Beginning in 1990, the DOJ also obtained a series of criminal convictions for wire fraud for alleged attempts to fix prices using the telephone: *United States v Ames Sintering Co*, 927 F.2d 1114 (5th Cir 1984), cert. dismissed, 474 US 1001 (1985).

201 See *Quality Trailer Products Corp*, 115 FTC 944 (1992); *AE Clevite, Inc*, 116 FTC 389 (1993); *YKK (USA) Inc*, 116 FTC 628 (1993); *Precision Moulding Co*, 122 FTC 104 (1996); *Stone Container Corp*, 125 FTC 853 (1998); *In re MacDermid*, 129 FTC (C-3911) (2000); *Valassis Communications, Inc, Analysis of Agreement Containing Consent Order to Aid Public Comment*, 71 Fed Reg 13976, 13978–9 (20 March 2006); *In re U-Haul Int'l, Inc*, 150 FTC 1, 53 (2010); *In re McWane, Inc*, Docket No 9351, Opinion of the Commission on Motions for Summary Decision, 20–1 (FTC 9 August 2012) ('an invitation to collude is "the quintessential example of the kind of conduct that should be [...] challenged as a violation of Section 5"'); *In the Matter of Mr Jacob J Alifraghis, Also Doing Business as InstantUPCCodes.com*, and *In the Matter of 680 Digital, Inc, Also Doing Business as Nationwide Barcode, and Philip B Peretz*, File No 141-0036 (August 2014), available at https://www.ftc.gov/enforcement/cases-proceedings/141-0036/instantupccodescom-matter. In a case brought under a state's version of section 5, the First Circuit expressed support for the Federal Trade Commission's application of section 5 to invitations to collude: see *Liu v Amerco*, 677 F.3d 489 (1st Cir 2012).

may produce anti-competitive effects, should EU competition law expand the concept of 'concerted practice' in order to cover invitations to collude included in unilateral public announcements? Interestingly, although the horizontal co-operation agreements guidelines note that '[w]here a company makes a unilateral announcement that is also genuinely public, for example through a newspaper, this generally does not constitute a concerted practice within the meaning of Article 101(1)',[202] it is explained in a footnote that '[t]his would not cover situations where such announcements involve invitations to collude', thereby opening the possibility for public announcements to fall within the scope of Article 101(1) TFEU.

6. As indicated above, invitations to collude have been targeted by the US antitrust authorities, under section 5 of the FTC Act. In a first series of cases, the FTC alleged that a solicitation to fix prices through private communications constitutes an infringement of section 5 FTC Act, even if it has not been accepted by the solicited party.[203] This created, according to some commentators, a 'per se prohibition against solicitations to fix prices', which was justified by the need to deter price fixing, in particular as this prohibition would not chill pro-competitive behaviour.[204] The same authors, however, noted that extending this approach to solicitations to enter into agreements that were not illegal *per se*, but constituted a legitimate joint venture, or to public announcements, could inhibit pro-competitive communications 'that only incidentally conveyed information to competitors'.[205] In addition, it was noted that public announcements can be more easily detected than private communications and thus less likely to result in secret cartels. Hence, for public announcements it was crucial to conduct a market structure analysis and assess possible legitimate efficiency justifications.[206] The FTC has extended the scope of the prohibition of section 5 of the FTC Act to some recent price signalling cases involving one-way public disclosures of information, without any evidence of reciprocity from the competitors, with the following explanation:

> The Commission has concluded that the fact of public communication should not, without more, constitute a defense to an invitation to collude, particularly where market conditions suggest that collusion, if attempted, likely would be successful (here, a durable duopoly). Private negotiation—in a proverbial smoke-filled room—may well be the most efficient route for would-be cartelists wishing to reach an accommodation. But it is clear that anticompetitive coordination also can be arranged through public signals and public communications, including speeches, press releases, trade association meetings and the like. Given the obligation under the securities laws not to make false and misleading statements with regard to material facts, Valassis' invitation to collude, made in the context of a conference call with analysts, may have been viewed by News America [its competitor] as even more credible than a private communication. If such public invitations to collude were per se lawful, then covert invitations to collude would be unnecessary.

202 Horizontal Guidelines, para 63.

203 *Starting with Quality Trailer Products Corp*, 115 FTC 944 (1992). In *Stone Container Corp*, 125 FTC 853 (1998), the invitation to collude consisted of both public and private communications.

204 KJ Arquit, 'The Boundaries of Horizontal Restraints: Facilitating Practices and Invitations to Collude' (1993) 61 *Antitrust LJ* 531.

205 Ibid, 548.

206 L Fullerton, 'FTC Challenges to "Invitations to Collude"' (2011) 25(2) *Antitrust LJ* 30–35, 31.

In evaluating cartels, antitrust law does not afford immunity to agreements that are brokered in public; courts recognize that a public venue does not necessarily mitigate the threat to competition. The same approach should govern invitations to collude. Liability should depend upon the substance and context of the communication, including issues of intent, likely effect, and business justification, and should not turn solely on the arena in which the communication occurs.[207]

Do you think that the same reasons will play out in EU competition law as well? Is it possible to extend the scope of the concept of 'concerted practice' to similar fact-patterns? What would be the implications of that for EU competition law?

7. As it is clear from the *Valassis* case above, the essence of the invitation to collude inquiry resorts in identifying circumstances in which such one-way solicitation may facilitate naked price fixing or other cartel-like behaviour.[208] In *U-Haul*, the FTC extended the scope of application of section 5 FTC to 'less egregious conduct', noting that 'it is not essential that the Commission find repeated misconduct attributable to senior executives, or define a market, or show market power, or establish substantial competitive harm, or even find that the terms of the desired agreement have been communicated with precision'.[209] There is no need also to prove harm to competition, as 'an unaccepted invitation to collude may facilitate coordinated interaction by disclosing the solicitor's intentions and preferences'.[210] In the case of private communications, such solicitation is presumed to have an anti-competitive intent and is thus prohibited *per se*. For public communications, the liability will depend upon 'upon the substance and context of the communication, including issues of intent, likely effect, and business justification'. If one were to transpose the section 5 FTC Act practice on unilateral invitations to collude in the context of Article 101 TFEU, one would run into problems with the 'jurisdictional function' view of collusion. Indeed, for public communications to be caught by the concept of 'concerted practice', it would have been important to analyse a number of factors that are usually taken into account when examining the condition of 'restriction of competition' (eg intent; likely effect; business justifications: is there a less restrictive alternative to achieve these business justifications?). Hence, supporters of the 'jurisdictional function' view of the concept of 'concerted practice' are left with limited options. According to some commentators, the current concept of 'concerted practice' cannot be extended to cover invitations to collude, in view of the requirement of collusive behavior and consequently of some form of reciprocal conduct.[211] They suggest, instead, the adoption of a separate prohibition of unilateral action that aims at facilitating tacit collusion without being the least restrictive mean to further a legitimate objective, either on the basis of Article 103 TFEU, or through its inclusion in national competition law statutes, Article 3(2)

207 *Valassis Communications, Inc, Analysis of Agreement Containing Consent Order to Aid Public Comment*, 71 Fed Reg 13976, 13978–9 (20 March 2006).

208 This may, for instance, take the form of a unilateral solicitation to boycott, a unilateral solicitation to reduce output etc. A solicitation may also take different forms and may involve promises of benefits or threats as inducement to enter into anti-competitive behaviour.

209 *In re U-Haul Int'l, Inc, Analysis of Agreement Containing Consent Order to Aid Public Comment*, 75 Fed Reg 35034, 35035 (21 June 2010).

210 Ibid, 35035.

211 FW von Papp, 'Information Exchange Agreements' in I Lianos and D Geradin (eds) *Handbook on European Competition Law: Substantive Aspects* (Edward Elgar, 2013), 130, 168.

of Regulation 1/2003 not closing such option (as it does not apply to purely unilateral practices).[212] Alternatively, one may argue, on the basis of the 'substantive function' view of the concept of collusion, that such unilateral invitations to collude may constitute a form of 'concerted practice', when a conjunction of criteria is met: a tight oligopoly, clear indications on the intent of the undertaking regarding the terms of the solicitation (the competitor solicited is clearly identified and is the closest competitor of the soliciting undertaking, the references to future price strategies is specific, the announced prices will enter in effect only after the solicited competitors responded by raising their prices or the solicited competitor is threatened with lower prices in the absence of response), absence of any redeeming justification, etc. These factors will constitute the subjective element of the concerted practice, their proof reversing the burden of proof to the soliciting undertaking, which will be offered the possibility to explain its conduct, for instance by arguing that this unilateral disclosure of information is required by legislation (eg securities laws) or that it may be explained by other circumstances (eg the ordinary course of business, such as proposal to enter a legitimate joint venture, disclosures in connection to the acquisition of shares or assets, disclosures involving supply contracts between the parties, etc).

8. Some national competition authorities have cracked down on price signalling using the remedial discretion that they enjoy when issuing a commitment decision. While not finding any evidence of price-fixing agreements among the investigated mobile operators, the Netherlands Authority for Consumers and Markets has concluded that public statements on future market behaviour (made at conferences or in interviews in specialized industry magazines) could lead to coordinated behaviour in the market and could limit 'strategic uncertainty'. The ACM accepted the mobile operators' commitments to avoid such verbal and written public statements, indicating that this type of unilateral disclosure could fall under the scope of the 'concerted practice' under Article 101 TFEU (and its national equivalent). Similarly, in its cement market investigation, the UK Competition Commission (CoCo) (which has now been replaced by the CMA)

212 Von Papp refers to the possibilities offered by German Competition Law (ibid). One may also note the example of Australia which introduced under the Australian Competition and Consumer Act 2010 a price signalling prohibition which applies only to the banking sector, thus complementing section 45 of the Australian Competition and Consumer Act governing contracts, arrangements and understandings that affect competition. According to this legislation which entered into force on 6 June 2012, illegal price signalling occurs where 'there is a private disclosure to competitors and the information relates to a price, discount, allowance, rebate or credit in relation to their deposit taking or advance activities (other than disclosures made in the ordinary course of business)'; or 'there is any disclosure (private or public) of information relating to price, discounts, allowances, rebates or credits in relation to deposit taking or advance activities, the capacity to supply or acquire, or commercial strategy in relation to those activities, where that disclosure has the purpose of substantially lessening competition'. Hence, for public disclosures to fall under the prohibition rule, there should be an assessment as to if they have the purpose to substantially lessening competition. Such assessment is not necessary for all types of private disclosure. A number of general exceptions to this prohibition are included, such as the disclosure was formally authorized or notified to the Australian Competition and Consumer Commission (ACCC). This reform has not led to any litigation and its sector-specific scope was considered as being problematic. The Harper Report, reviewing the Australian competition law system, suggested instead of adopting a specific legislation on unilateral information disclosure, the expansion of section 45 of the Australian Competition and Consumer Act to 'concerted practices' that have the purpose, effect, or likely effect of substantially lessening competition: I Harper et al, 'Competition Policy Review', Final Report (March 2015), para 3.6, Recommendation 29, available at http://competitionpolicyreview.gov.au/files/2015/03/Competition-policy-review-report_online.pdf.

assessed a number of letters by which cement suppliers informed their customers of future/'aspirational' price increases, which served as a starting point for negotiations with customers and did not reflect actual price increases agreed with customers. These letters were found to be a way to of signalling future price intentions to competitors resulting in alignment in changes in average prices of the UK cement producers over time. The CoCo ordered a remedy consisting in the prohibition of generic price announcement letters sent by all suppliers in Great Britain of cement materials to their customers.[213]

9. A further option in the UK to act against invitations to collude is offered by section 188 of the Enterprise Act on the Cartel Offence, which includes the inchoate offences of conspiracy and attempt.[214]
10. Of particular interest are the recent European Commission's proceedings against contained liner shipping companies for making regular public announcements of their (intended) future increases of prices through press releases on their websites and in the specialized trade press. These announcements were made several times a year and included detailed information on the amount of the price increase and the date of implementation, which was generally similar for all announcing companies. The announcements were typically made by the companies successively three to five weeks before the announced implementation date. Furthermore, announced general rate increases (GRIs) have sometimes been postponed or modified by some parties, as they aligned their own increases with those announced by other parties. The Commission expressed concerns over the compatibility of this practice with Article 101 TFEU, as such announcements were of little value for customers, because they were not informing them of the new full price they would be asked to pay in the future but only of the amount of the intended increase. They also had 'limited committal value', as they were not enabling customers to rely on them for their purchasing decisions. In view of the Commission's concerns that such practices may allow the parties to explore each other's pricing intentions and to coordinate their behaviour, the parties offered commitments to stop publishing and communicating GRIs. Should they publish or communicate their prices, including precise information that could be of value to the customers and bind the parties as maximum prices, although the parties may be free to offer lower prices.[215]

5.6. A FUNCTIONAL DEFINITION OF THE COLLUSION ELEMENT?

Recent case law has moved towards less formalism in determining the collusion element in the enforcement of Article 101 TFEU and Chapter I CA98. First, the concept of 'single and continuous infringement' developed by the jurisprudence of the CJEU has relativized the need to qualify, at least under certain circumstances, each fact pattern as an 'agreement', a

[213] Competition Commission, Market Investigation into the Supply or Acquisition of Aggregates, Cement and Ready-Mixed Concrete, The Price Announcement Order 2016, available at https://assets.digital.cabinet-office.gov.uk/media/56a206e0ed915d474700003d/Price_Announcement_Order_2016.pdf.

[214] Criminal Attempts Act 1981, section 1.

[215] Communication of the Commission published pursuant to Article 27(4) of Council Regulation (EC) No 1/2003 in Case AT.39850—Container Shipping [2016] OJ C 60/7.

'concerted practice', or a 'decision of association of undertakings', offering the possibility of a multiple qualification, ie, of agreement and/or concerted practice, thus taking a global, and less compartmentalized, view on the element of collusion. Second, the concept of hub and spoke conspiracy blurs the importance of the distinction between horizontal and vertical collusion, by enabling competition authorities to catch horizontal collusion via a vertical link. Despite these incursions to instrumentalism, the EU Courts have been careful not to expand the external boundaries of collusion under Article 101 TFEU and Chapter I CA98 in order to cover situations of uniform prices resulting from oligopolistic interdependence. By enshrining the communications-based view of collusion, EU and UK competition law enforcers have resisted the sirens of a more effects-based approach in defining collusion, thus adhering to some form of legal formalism.

5.6.1. THE CONCEPT OF 'SINGLE AND CONTINUOUS INFRINGEMENT': BREAKING THE INTERNAL BOUNDARIES OF ARTICLE 101 TFEU/CHAPTER I CA98?

Starting with the *Polypropylene* case in the 1980s, the Commission, followed by the EU Courts, employed the concept of 'single and continuous infringement', qualifying it overall as 'an agreement and/or a concerted practice', without any need to specify which of the elements of the 'single infringement' constitute an agreement, and which a concerted practice.[216] In *Commission v Anic*, the CJEU held that 'the agreements and concerted practices found to exist, formed part of systems of regular meetings, target-price fixing and quota-fixing, and that those schemes were part of a series of efforts made by the undertakings in question in pursuit of a single economic aim, namely to distort the normal movement of prices'; it continued by stating that 'it would be artificial to split up continuous conduct, characterised by a single purpose, by treating it as consisting of several separate infringements, when what was involved was a single infringement which progressively manifested itself in both agreements and concerted practices'.[217] The concept of 'single and continuous infringement frequently consists of a series of acts which follow each other in time and which, in themselves, at the time when they occur, can also constitute an infringement of the competition rules', the 'distinctive feature of those acts' lying 'in the fact that they form part of an overall strategy'.[218]

The lack of formalism in the qualification of the complex fact patterns that usually compose cartel behaviour was initially perceived as a necessary compromise in order to enhance the ability of the Commission to focus on the essential, evidence of collusion, without being

[216] *Polypropylene* Commission Decision 86/398/EEC [1986] OJ L 230/1, upheld on appeal by Case T-1/89, *Rhône-Poulenc v Commission* [1991] ECR II–867, para 126, upheld on appeal by Case C-49/92 P, *Commission v Anic* [1999] ECR I–4125. For a similar position in UK law, see *JJB Sports plc v OFT* [2004] CAT 17, para 644 ('It is trite law that it is not necessary for the OFT [now CMA] to characterise an infringement as either an agreement or a concerted practice: it is sufficient that the conduct in question amounts to one or the other.').

[217] Case C-49/92 P, *Commission v Anic* [1999] ECR I–4125, para 82.

[218] Joined Cases T-456 & 457/05, *Gütermann AG and Zwicky & Co AG v Commission* [2010] ECR II–1443, para 46. The concept has also been introduced in UK competition law. See *Airline passenger fuel surcharges for long-haul passenger flights* (Case CE/7691-06) OFT decision (19 April 2012), paras 382–8. The OFT has however declined to use the 'single and continuous infringement' concept in a series of bid-rigging cartels in the construction sector, each of them being analysed as discrete infringements: see *Bid rigging in the construction industry in England* (Case CE/4327-04) OFT decision (21 September 2009), 1631–2, the OFT noting, *inter alia*, that 'for many Parties, their Infringements involved different counterparties, making it wholly artificial to treat these as a single Infringement'.

excessively occupied with the legal qualification of each element of such collusive conduct as an 'agreement' or as a 'concerted practice'. As the General Court also noted in *Solvay SA v Commission*,

> [i]n the context of a complex infringement which involved many producers seeking over a number of years to regulate the market between them, the Commission cannot be expected to classify the infringement precisely, as an agreement or concerted practice, as in any event both those forms of infringement are covered by Article [101(1) TFEU] [. . .].
>
> The twofold characterisation of the infringement as an agreement 'and/or' concerted practice must be understood as referring to a complex whole comprising a number of factual elements some of which were characterised as agreements and others as concerted practices for the purposes of Article [101(1) TFEU], which lays down no specific category for a complex infringement of this type.[219]

This 'twofold characterisation' is particularly helpful for cartels of long duration, in which various firms have taken in turn active and then more passive roles through this 'single' cartel period.[220] For instance, once the Commission categorizes the cartel in question as a single infringement, it is not required to establish, as part of that categorization, the various durations of the acts which related to the cartelized market alone and is not required to take account of that difference of duration of these acts when determining the duration of the infringement as a whole. Indeed, 'it would be artificial to split up continuous conduct, characterised by a single purpose, into a number of separate infringements on the ground that the collusive practices varied in their intensity according to the market concerned'.[221] For some, this jurisprudence also indicated the turn towards a less legalistic approach that would facilitate the evidential burden of the Commission, as it would be possible for it to analyse a series of collusive practices from different undertakings as falling within the narrative of a single cartel, rather than consisting in several discrete cartels.[222] The concept has since been used for a variety of purposes that do not only relate to the problem of qualification of the various practices that are covered by the qualification of 'single and continuous infringement', such as a series of cartel practices over a broad geographical area, cartel practices over a range of different products and/or a series of distinct cartel practices, making some authors conclude that the concept of 'single overall agreement' is preferable.[223]

The discussion over semantics notwithstanding, this concept has been used instrumentally for furthering the ability of the Commission, and other enforcers, to more effectively analyse cartel activity, while deterring cartel conduct by opening the possibility that even

219 Case T-186/06, *Solvay SA v Commission* [2011] ECR II–2839, paras 91–2. See also Case T-235/07, *Bavaria v Commission* [2011] ECR II–3229, para 183.

220 Although the General Court refers to the 'twofold characterisation' of 'agreement and/or concerted practice', subsequent jurisprudence of the EU Courts has made it clear that decisions of association of undertakings may also be included in the characterization: see Case T-410/09, *Almanet v Commission*, ECLI:EU:T:2012:676, para 152, the court noting that 'according to settled case-law, the concept of a single infringement can be applied to the legal characterisation of anti-competitive conduct consisting in agreements, in concerted practices and in decisions of associations of undertakings'.

221 Case T-186/06, *Solvay SA v Commission* [2011] ECR II–2839, paras 165–6.

222 For the first analysis of this trend see I Lianos, 'La "confusion des infractions" de l'article 81§1: Quelques interrogations sur l'utilité de la notion d'infraction unique' (2000) 2 *Revue trimestrielle de droit européen* 239.

223 D Bailey, 'Single, Overall Agreement in EU Competition Law' (2010) 47 *Common Market L Rev* 473; R Whish and D Bailey, *Competition Law* (OUP, 8th ed, 2015), 107.

some loose causal connection of a collusive practice by an undertaking with a 'single and continuous infringement' may carry responsibility for the overall cartel, even if the undertaking in question was not involved in every aspect of the cartel activity, or attended every meeting of the cartel.[224]

In *Team Relocations v Commission* and *Putters International v Commission* the General Court limited the use of this concept only if three cumulative conditions are satisfied.

'[. . .] [A]n undertaking that has taken part in an infringement through conduct of its own which fell within the scope of an agreement or concerted practice having an anti-competitive object for the purposes of Article [101(1) TFEU] and which was intended to help bring about the infringement as a whole is also responsible, throughout the entire period of its participation in that infringement, for conduct of other undertakings in the context of the same infringement [. . .]

It follows [. . .] that in order to establish that there has been a single and continuous infringement, the Commission must show that the undertaking intended to contribute by its own conduct to the common objectives pursued by all the participants and that it was aware of the conduct planned or put into effect by other undertakings in pursuit of the same objectives or that it could reasonably have foreseen it and that it was prepared to take the risk [. . .].

Restrictive practices can be regarded as constituent elements of a single anti-competitive agreement only if it is established that they form part of an overall plan pursuing a common objective. In addition, only where the undertaking knew, or ought to have known, when it participated in those practices, that it was taking part in the single agreement, can its participation in them constitute the expression of its accession to that agreement [. . .].

Thus, it is apparent from that case-law that three conditions must be met in order to establish participation in a single and continuous infringement, namely the existence of an overall plan pursuing a common objective, the intentional contribution of the undertaking to that plan, and its awareness (proved or presumed) of the offending conduct of the other participants.[225]

Although competition law enforcers do not enjoy an unbounded discretion in using the qualification of 'single overall infringement', the concept certainly offers them an important tool in their battle against cartel activity.

Case T-452/05, *BST v Commission*

[2010] ECR II–1373 (references omitted)

A number of undertakings, including BST, had participated in a set of agreements and concerted practices on the market in thread for industrial customers other than automotive customers in Benelux, and in Denmark, Finland, Norway, and Sweden. The Commission qualified these as a single and continuous infringement. BST admitted to having committed the infringement but argued that it should be distinguished from the infringements committed by

[224] On the instrumental use of the concept, see K Seifert, 'The Single Complex and Continuous Infringement—"Effect Utilitarianism"?' (2008) 29 *European Competition L Rev* 546; A Riley, 'Revisiting the Single and continuous Infringement of Article 101: The Significance of ANIC in a New Era of Cartel Detection and Analysis' (2014) 37 *World Competition* 293. The concept has also been discussed, more recently, in Case T-691/14, *Servier SAS and Others v European Commission*, ECLI:EU:T:2018:922, paras 1264–1290.

[225] Joined Cases T-204 & 212/08, *Team Relocations NV and Others v Commission* [2011] ECR II–3569, paras 34–7; Case T-211/08, *Putters International v Commission* [2011] ECR II–3729, paras 31–5.

the other undertakings, as it formed no part of the single and continuous infringement on this market. It appealed the Commission's decision to the General Court.

31. It is apparent, first of all, from the case-law that, given the nature of the infringements of the competition rules and the nature and degree of severity of the ensuing penalties, liability for those infringements is personal in nature. The agreements and concerted practices referred to in Article [101(1) TFEU] are necessarily the result of collusion on the part of a number of undertakings, all of which are co-perpetrators of the infringement, but whose participation can take different forms, varying, in particular, according to the characteristics of the market concerned and the position of each undertaking on that market, the aims pursued and the means of implementation chosen or envisaged. However, the mere fact that each undertaking takes part in the infringement in ways particular to it does not suffice to exclude its liability for the entire infringement, including its liability for conduct which, in practical terms, is put into effect by other participating undertakings, but which has the same anti-competitive object or effect [. . .].

32. Thus, an undertaking may be held liable for an overall cartel even though it is shown to have participated directly only in one or some of its constituent elements, if it knew, or must have known, that the collusion in which it participated, especially by means of regular meetings organised over several years, was part of an overall plan intended to distort competition and if that overall plan included all the constituent elements of the cartel [. . .]. Similarly, the fact that the roles played by various undertakings in pursuit of a common objective were different does not cancel out the fact that the anti-competitive objective, hence the infringement, was the same, provided that each undertaking has contributed, at its own level, to the pursuit of the common objective [. . .].

33. Lastly, since, by virtue of the fact that they shared the same object, the agreements and concerted practices found to exist formed part of systems of regular meetings, target-price fixing and quota fixing, schemes which in turn formed part of a series of attempts made by the undertakings concerned in pursuit of a single economic aim, namely to distort the normal movement of prices, it would be artificial to split up such continuous conduct, characterised by a single purpose, by treating it as a number of separate infringements when, on the contrary, what was involved was a single infringement which progressively manifested itself both in the form of agreements and in the form of concerted practices. An undertaking which has taken part in such an infringement through conduct, particular to it, which was covered by the notion of an agreement or concerted practice having an anti-competitive object, for the purposes of Article [101(1) TFEU], and which was intended to help bring about the infringement as a whole, is also liable—throughout the entire period of its participation in that infringement—for conduct put into effect by other undertakings in the context of the same infringement. That is the case where it is established that the undertaking in question was aware of the offending conduct of the other participants, or could reasonably have foreseen it, and that it was prepared to take the risk. That conclusion is not inconsistent with the principle that liability for such infringements is personal in nature. It reflects a conceptual approach which is widely followed in the legal orders of the Member States concerning the attribution of liability for infringements committed by a number of perpetrators according to their participation in the infringement as a whole, which is not regarded in those legal systems as incompatible with the personal nature of liability [. . .].

34. It must therefore be determined whether the facts complained of with regard to BST form part of an overall plan intended to distort competition on the industrial thread market in Benelux and the Nordic countries and, accordingly, form part of the single and continuous infringement, as constituted by the cartel on that market.

35. In that regard, BST does not deny taking part in the meetings concerning the industrial thread market in Benelux and the Nordic countries. Nor does it dispute the fact that, during those meetings, the participants exchanged price lists and information on rebates, on the application of increases in list prices, on reductions in rebates and on increases in the special prices charged to certain customers; that they made agreements on future price lists, maximum rates of rebate, reductions in rebates and increases in the special prices charged to certain customers, with a view to avoiding undercutting, to the advantage of the incumbent supplier, and to the arrangement of customer allocation; or that they established contacts designed to encourage suppliers which had not taken part in the meetings to do so.

36. Moreover, BST admits that, when it took part in those meetings, it was aware that the intention of those who organised the meetings was to involve it in anti-competitive agreements. BST even stated that it expected the Commission to find that it had committed an infringement.

37. Furthermore, according to the case-law, it is sufficient for the Commission to show that the undertaking concerned participated in meetings at which anti-competitive agreements were concluded, without manifestly opposing them, to prove to the requisite standard that the undertaking participated in the cartel. Where participation in such meetings has been established, it is for that undertaking to put forward evidence to establish that its participation in those meetings was without any anti-competitive intention, by demonstrating that it had indicated to its competitors that it was participating in those meetings in a spirit that was different from theirs [. . .]. That is also true of the participation of an undertaking in the implementation of a single agreement. In order to establish that an undertaking participated in such an agreement, the Commission must show that the undertaking intended to contribute by its own conduct to the common objectives pursued by all the participants and that it was aware of the actual conduct planned or put into effect by other undertakings in pursuit of those same objectives, or that it could reasonably have foreseen it, and that it was prepared to take the risk [. . .].

38. However, BST has not shown that it indicated to its competitors that it was participating in those meetings in a spirit that was different from theirs.

39. It follows from the above considerations that the Commission was correct in considering that BST was liable for the single infringement committed on the industrial thread market in Benelux and the Nordic countries [. . .].

NOTES AND QUESTIONS ON THE CONCEPT OF 'SINGLE AND CONTINUOUS INFRINGEMENT'

1. The legal implications of the finding of a single overall agreement are quite important. Whish and Bailey note:

   It means, first, that each infringing undertaking is responsible for the overall cartel [. . .]. Secondly, [. . .] [the Commission] is entitled to impose only one fine on the members of the cartel (as opposed to separate fines for different infringements. [. . .] Thirdly, [. . .] [the Commission may impose] fines in respect of illegal practices that would otherwise be time-barred. Fourthly, a single overall agreement may increase the duration of infringement, and thus result in a larger fine than would otherwise be the case. Fifthly, the different anti-competitive activities of an overall agreement may lead to higher fines if the Commission considers the overall agreement to be more serious than the sum of its individual parts. Sixthly, [. . .] it may affect the application of the other requirements of Article 101 [for instance, increase the probability of finding an effect on trade] [. . .]. Lastly, undertakings may be jointly and severally liable in damages for the losses caused by the single overall agreement [. . .].[226]

2. With regard to the condition of the existence of an overall plan pursuing a common objective, the General Court held in *Almanet v Commission* that a single overall agreement may be found even if the cartel extends to various products belonging to separate markets as 'it cannot be inferred from [the] case-law that [. . .] every single infringement must necessarily relate to one product or to substitutable products' as 'the case-law contains examples of single infringements of the competition rules relating to several products which are not substitutable'.[227] The General Court further explained that the concept of 'single infringement' covers 'a situation in which several undertakings participated in an infringement in which continuous conduct in pursuit of a single economic aim was intended to distort competition, and also individual infringements linked to one another by the same object (all the elements sharing the same purpose) and the same subjects (the same undertakings, who are aware that they are participating in the common object)'.[228] According to the General Court, '[t]hat interpretation cannot be challenged on the ground that one or several elements of that series of acts or continuous conduct could also constitute, in themselves, an infringement of Article [101 TFEU]'.[229]

3. In *Almanet v Commission*, the General Court observed that 'the concept of a single objective cannot be determined by a general reference to the distortion of competition on the market concerned by the infringement, since an impact on competition, whether it is the object or the effect of the conduct in question, constitutes an element inherent

[226] R Whish and D Bailey, *Competition Law* (OUP, 8th ed, 2015), 110.

[227] Case T-410/09, *Almanet v Commission*, ECLI:EU:T:2012:676, paras 172–3. According to the General Court (ibid, para 173),

> [I]n Case C-113/04 P *Technische Unie* v *Commission* [2006] ECR I–8831, paragraphs 4, 170, 171, 173, 180 and 185, the Court upheld the finding that the acts at issue, relating to the wholesale electrotechnical fittings market, were part of a single infringement. It must be pointed out that the notion of 'electrotechnical fittings' encompasses a number of products which are clearly not all substitutable. Likewise, in its judgment in Case T-334/94 *Sarrió* v *Commission* [1998] ECR II–1439, paragraphs 2 to 5, 158 and 164 to 175—those aspects of which were not set aside in Case C-291/98 P *Sarrió* v *Commission* [2000] ECR I–9991—the General Court upheld the Commission's finding that the acts it had identified, relating to three distinct types of product which were not substitutable, formed part of a single and continuous infringement of the competition rules.

[228] Case T-410/09, *Almanet v Commission*, ECLI:EU:T:2012:676, para 152.

[229] Ibid.

in any conduct covered by Article [101(1) TFEU].'[230] According to the General Court, '[s]uch a definition of the concept of a single objective is likely to deprive the concept of a single and continuous infringement of part of its meaning, since it would have the consequence that different instances of conduct which relate to a particular economic sector and are prohibited under Article [101(1) TFEU] would have to be systematically characterised as constituent elements of a single infringement.'[231] The General Court deemed necessary, for the purposes of characterizing various instances of conduct as a single and continuous infringement, to establish whether these various instances of conduct 'display a link of complementarity in that each of them is intended to deal with one or more consequences of the "normal pattern" of competition and whether, through interaction, they contribute to the attainment of the set of anti-competitive effects desired by those responsible, within the framework of a global plan having a single objective.'[232] According to the General Court, '[i]n that regard, it will be necessary to take into account any circumstance capable of establishing or of casting doubt on that link, such as the period of implementation, the content—including the methods used—and, correlatively, the objective of the various agreements and concerted practices in question.'[233] The requirement of 'complementarity' was, however, later abandoned by the CJEU in *Siemens v Commission*, the CJEU noting that the 'General Court is not in fact required to examine such an additional condition of complementarity.'[234] This opens up the possibilities of expanding the use of the concept of 'single overall agreement' to conduct that is not necessarily judged 'complementary' to the operation of the cartel. Would just a contribution to the 'overall plan' be considered sufficient for engaging the liability of an undertaking for committing a single and continuous infringement?

4. In view of the legal implications of the finding of a single overall agreement for the undertakings in question, it is important to circumscribe the use of this concept to situations in which there has, demonstrably, been an '*intentional* contribution of the undertaking to that plan'. This condition, arguably overlaps with that requiring the 'awareness (proved or presumed) of the offending conduct of the other participants', in particular as the undertaking found to have taken part in (or contributed to) a single infringement through its own conduct, will be found liable 'throughout the entire period of its participation in that infringement', 'for conduct put into effect by other undertakings in the context of the same infringement.'[235] What counts is the intention of the undertaking to 'help bring about the infringement as a whole.'[236] According to the General Court, '[t]hat is the case where it is established that the undertaking in question was *aware* of the offending conduct of the other participants or that it could *reasonably have foreseen* it and that it was prepared to take the risk.'[237] Hence, 'neither the principle of personal responsibility for such infringements nor the principle of individual analysis of the evidence adduced is [. . .] called into question.'[238]
5. In *Bananas*, the Commission had found the existence of a single and continuous infringement between various undertakings active in the banana trade that were

230 Ibid, para 154. 231 Ibid. 232 Ibid. 233 Ibid.
234 Joined Cases C-239, 489 & 498/11 P, *Siemens AG and Others v Commission*, ECLI:EU:C:2013:866, para 248.
235 Case T-410/09, *Almanet v Commission*, ECLI:EU:T:2012:676, para 153.
236 Ibid. 237 Ibid (emphasis added). 238 Ibid.

involved in pre-pricing communications during which they discussed banana price-setting factors. Chiquita and Dole were held responsible for the entire single and continuous infringement, while Weichert (and consequently the undertaking comprising Weichert and Del Monte) was held responsible only for the part of the infringement relating to the collusive agreements with Dole.[239] The General Court upheld the Commission's decision, noting that

> [. . .] the fact that an undertaking has not taken part—like the undertaking comprising Weichert and Del Monte in the present case—in all aspects of an anti-competitive scheme or that it played only a minor role in the aspects in which it did participate is not material to the establishment of the existence of an infringement on its part. Such a factor must be taken into consideration only when the gravity of the infringement is assessed and if and when it comes to determining the fine.[240]

Del Monte challenged the General Court's judgment to the CJEU, arguing that the fact that Weichert was not aware of those exchanges is not only a mitigating factor for the determination of the fine but is also a key element for determining whether a single and continuous infringement has been established. The CJEU confirmed the judgment of the General Court on this point, stating that:

> [I]f an undertaking has directly taken part in one or more of the forms of anti-competitive conduct comprising a single and continuous infringement, but it has not been shown that that undertaking intended, through its own conduct, to contribute to all the common objectives pursued by the other participants in the cartel and that it was aware of all the other offending conduct planned or put into effect by those other participants in pursuit of the same objectives, or that it could reasonably have foreseen all that conduct and was prepared to take the risk, the Commission is entitled to attribute to that undertaking liability only for the conduct in which it had participated directly and for the conduct planned or put into effect by the other participants, in pursuit of the same objectives as those pursued by the undertaking itself, where it has been shown that the undertaking was aware of that conduct or was able reasonably to foresee it and prepared to take the risk.[241]

Hence, 'the fact that Weichert was unaware of the exchange of information between Dole and Chiquita and did not have to know about it was not such as to alter the finding of a single and continuous infringement, even though liability could not be attributed to that company in respect of all that infringement'.[242] The CJEU thus established a distinction between (i) the existence of the single and continuous infringement and (ii) the issue of the liability of the various undertakings that have contributed to it.

6. An undertaking will be found liable for the whole infringement, only if the restrictive practice
   (i) forms part of an overall plan pursuing a common objective and the undertaking in question,

239 *Bananas* (Case COMP/39.188) Commission Decision (15 October 2008), para 258.
240 Case T-587/08, *Fresh Del Monte v Commission*, ECLI:EU:T:2013:129, para 648.
241 Joined Cases C-293–4/13 P, *Fresh Del Monte Produce, Inc v European Commission*, ECLI:EU:T:2013:129, para 159.
242 Ibid, para 160.

(ii) has intended to contribute,
(iii) by its own conduct,
(iv) to the common objectives pursued by all the participants, and
(v) was aware or could reasonably have foreseen the conduct.

This, even if the undertaking has not participated directly in all the forms of anti-competitive conduct comprising the single and continuous infringement, but has simply been aware of all the other unlawful conduct planned or put into effect by the other participants in the cartel in pursuit of the same objectives, or could reasonably have foreseen that conduct.[243]

7. In *ICAP v Commission*,[244] ICAP challenged the Commission's decision to the GC, arguing that the Commission had not shown that ICAP's participation in those infringements was of equivalent duration to that of the banks concerned and that that participation continued unabated between the dates for which the Commission held evidence. ICAP also argued that the Commission was required to demonstrate continued knowledge by ICAP of the offending conduct of the banks concerned throughout the period in question in respect of each of those infringements. The Commission had taken the view that the evidence adduced demonstrated the existence of regular contacts that occurred at intermittent periods based on the needs of the individual participants and concluded from this that it would be artificial to split them up into individual instances of a few days' duration, on the ground that the JPY LIBOR rate-setting process occurred on a daily basis. For the Commission, the awareness of contacts between the various banks also implied that ICAP was in a position to assume that all of its routine actions for the benefit of the specific banks could be in support of a scheme between these banks and the other banks concerned by those infringements. The GC delved into the meaning of the concept of an 'overall plan' and how this could be interpreted in conformity with the principle of legal certainty.

218. With regard to a continuous infringement, the concept of an overall plan means that the Commission may assume that an infringement has not been interrupted even if, in relation to a specific period, it has no evidence of the participation of the undertaking concerned in that infringement, provided that that undertaking participated in the infringement prior to and after that period and provided that there is no proof or indication that the infringement was interrupted so far as concerns that undertaking. In that case, it will be able to impose a fine in respect of the whole of the period of infringement, including the period in respect of which it does not have evidence of the participation of the undertaking concerned [. . .].

219. However, the principle of legal certainty requires that, if there is no evidence directly establishing the duration of an infringement, the Commission should adduce at least evidence of facts sufficiently proximate in time for it to be reasonable to accept that that infringement continued uninterruptedly between two specific dates. [. . .]

220. Although the period separating two manifestations of infringing conduct is a relevant criterion in order to establish the continuous nature of an infringement, the fact remains that the question whether or not that period is long enough to

[243] Ibid, para 158.
[244] Case T-180/15, *ICAP v European Commission*, ECLI:EU:T:2017:795.

constitute an interruption of the infringement cannot be examined in the abstract. On the contrary, it needs to be assessed in the context of the functioning of the cartel in question. [...]

221. Lastly, if the participation of an undertaking in the infringement may be regarded as having been interrupted and the undertaking may be regarded as having participated in the infringement prior to and after that interruption, that infringement may be categorised as repeated if—as in the case of a continuing infringement—there is a single objective which it pursued both before and after the interruption, a circumstance which may be deduced from the identical nature of the objectives of the practices at issue, of the goods concerned, of the undertakings which participated in the collusion, of the main rules for its implementation, of the natural persons involved on behalf of the undertakings and, lastly, of the geographical scope of those practices. The infringement is then single and repeated and, although the Commission may impose a fine in respect of the whole of the period of the infringement, it may not do so for the period during which the infringement was interrupted. [...]

224. [...] [P]roof of Icap's participation in single and continuous infringements and, therefore, the incurring of its liability for the whole of the infringement periods required the Commission to produce evidence of positive measures adopted by Icap, if not on a daily basis, at least sufficiently limited in time. Otherwise, it was for the Commission to find the existence of single and repeated infringements and not to include in the infringement periods found against Icap the intervals in respect of which it does not possess evidence of its participation.

8. The CMA's recent decision in relation to *restrictive arrangements in the estate and letting agents sector* in 2015 provides an example of the use of the concept of a 'single and continuous infringement' in UK competition law.[245] The CMA found that an association of estate and lettings agents in Hampshire, Three Counties Estate Agents Limited (Three Counties), three of its members (Waterfords (Estate Agents) Limited, Castles Property Services Limited and Hamptons Estates Limited), and a local newspaper (Trinity Mirror Southern Limited (TMS)) had breached the Chapter I prohibition of the Competition Act 1998, having entered into one or more agreements or concerted practices that they would not advertise their fees in the Surrey & Hants *Star Courier* (published by TMS) and that they would deter or prevent members of TMS from advertising their fees in the *Star Courier*. In addition, TMS, as the publisher of the *Star Courier*, became a party to the agreement(s) or concerted practice(s) with certain of Three Counties' members, including Waterfords and Hamptons International, to prevent agents (whether members or non-members of Three Counties) from advertising their fees in the *Star Courier*.[246]

245 Decision of the CMA in Case CE/9832/13 *Restrictive arrangements preventing estate and letting agents from advertising their fees in a local newspaper* (8 May 2015).

246 In relation to the involvement of TMS in the infringement the CMA notes ibid, para 5.28:

An undertaking may be party to an anti-competitive agreement where the purpose of its conduct. . .is to restrict competition on a specific relevant market, even if that undertaking is not active on that relevant market itself. In addition, an undertaking may also be party to an anti-competitive agreement where it does not restrict its own freedom of action on the market on which it is primarily active. Although it is

The CMA concluded that in this case there was an arrangement consisting of one or more agreements adopted by various parties in pursuit of a common objective.[247] According to the CMA, 'an arrangement may properly be viewed as a single infringement for the time frame in which it existed, covering a range of practices (whether properly characterised as agreements, concerted practices or decisions by associations of undertakings).'[248] Moreover, the CMA added that 'an infringement of the Chapter I prohibition need not be based on a single, isolated act, but may operate through a pattern of conduct involving a series of agreements, concerted practices or decisions by associations of undertakings entered into over a period of time. Such an infringement may be viewed as a single and continuous infringement where the practices at issue are interlinked in terms of pursuing a common anti-competitive objective.'[249]

5.6.2. HUB AND SPOKE CONSPIRACIES

The concept of 'hub and spoke conspiracy' is a form of indirect concerted practice, in particular through information disclosure among competitors, which combines a covert horizontal element and a vertical element, involving communications between suppliers and each of their customers.[250] However, it presents some 'peculiarities' when compared to other forms of indirect concerted practice in that

> essential to show the existence of a joint intention to act on (or in relation to) the market in a specific way in accordance with the terms of the agreement, it is not necessary to establish a joint intention to pursue an anti-competitive aim.

See also C-194/14 P, *AC-Treuhand v Commission*, ECLI:EU:C:2015:350. According to the CMA (Case CE/9832/13, para 5.133) 'the infringement constituted, in essence, an horizontal arrangement between competitors, notwithstanding the involvement (at a later stage of the Infringement) of TMS in a supporting and more peripheral role'.

> The fact that a party may have played only a limited part in setting up an agreement, or may not be fully committed to its implementation, or may have participated only under pressure from other parties, does not mean that it is not party to the agreement. Parties may show varying degrees of commitment to the common plan: the fact that a party does not abide by the outcome of meetings or does not act on or subsequently implement the agreement does not preclude the finding of its liability or relieve that undertaking of responsibility for it. In addition, the fact that a party comes to recognize that it can 'cheat' on the agreement at certain times does not preclude the finding of an infringement.

Case CE/9832/13, Annex paras A.38–A.39.

247 Decision of the CMA in Case CE/9832/13 *Restrictive arrangements preventing estate and letting agents from advertising their fees in a local newspaper* (8 May 2015), para 5.17. Also see ibid, paras 5.71–5.72: In the alternative, the CMA has also found that 'the arrangements described above amounted to a series of individual agreements, concerted practices, and a decision by an association of undertakings, for the purposes of the Chapter I prohibition'.

248 Ibid, para 5.11.

249 Ibid, para 5.70. See also Case CE/7691/06 *Airline passenger fuel charges for long-haul flights*, OFT Decision CA98/01/12 (19 April 2012), paras 382–4.

250 On this concept, see O Odudu, 'Indirect Information Exchange: The Constituent Elements of Hub and Spoke Collusion' (2011) 7(2) *European Competition J* 205; PJG Cayseele, 'Hub-and-Spoke Collusion: Some Nagging Questions Raised by Economists' (2014) 5(3) *J European Competition L & Practice* 164; GL Zampa and P Buccirossi, 'Hub and Spoke Practices: Law and Economics of the New Antitrust Frontier?' (2013) 9(1) *Competition Policy Int'l* 91; N Sahuguet and A Walckiers, 'Hub-and-Spoke Conspiracies: the Vertical Expression of a Horizontal Desire?' (2014) 5(10) *J European Competition L & Practice* 711; N Sahuguet and A Walckiers, 'Selling to a Cartel of Retailers: A Model of Hub-and-Spoke Collusion', CEPR Discussion Paper, No 9385 (2013).

> [. . .] they sit at the crossroads of various theories of harm: they may in fact be seen as nothing more than a spillover of normal vertical conduct; or considered as a sophisticated way in which horizontal cooperation or, at least, an exchange of information may be structured. They may equally be viewed as a practice having the same detrimental effects on competition as a cartel but without the typical characteristics of a cartel. Further, to add to their peculiar nature, [hub and spoke conspiracies] may equally affect intrabrand and interbrand competition.[251]

This hybrid horizontal/vertical nature of 'hub and spoke' conspiracies raises interesting issues of characterization of the cooperation between the undertakings involved (the collusion element) as well as their qualification as a restriction of competition (the restriction of competition element). In this Section, we will focus on the first aspect. However, as previously noted, the collusion element does not exercise only a jurisdictional function, but its interpretation and scope is profoundly linked to the concept of restriction of competition adopted by the specific legal system. This indicates that its function may also be substantive.

There are different scenarios of hub and spoke practices (H&SPs).

GL Zampa and P Buccirossi, 'Hub and Spoke Practices: Law and Economics of the New Antitrust Frontier?' (2013) 9(1) *Competition Policy Int'l* 91, 93–6

> By their very nature, H&SPs may become relevant in settings where there is a legitimate repeated interaction between economic players, which, whilst typically operating at different levels of the supply chain—the triangle-shaped dynamic, end up having clearly convergent interests. This last element is a necessary pre-condition for understanding whether what is going on is a potentially illegal H&SP or a legitimate supplier-distributor interaction and we believe that the relevance of this aspect is often underestimated.
>
> Indeed, far from being sufficient in itself to evidence illegal practices, in all cases where a convincing case could be made that there are convergent interests between a supplier and its distributors (or between a distributor and its suppliers) on increasing the wholesale or, as the case may be, the retail price, the related interaction would seem to deserve further scrutiny. Thus, whether vertically convergent interests are present represents a very useful preliminary filtering screen.
>
> The two typical scenarios in which H&SPs may most naturally be found are the following. In a first setting (scenario A), the supplier may be considered as operating as a hub for indirect communications and/or interaction between distributors. This dynamic is represented in Figure 5.1 [. . .]. An example of this is the relationship between a supplier and its distributors, which is the most common situation for the majority of the cases that have some hub and spoke elements.
>
> Whilst the necessary relationship between a supplier and a distributor is of a vertical nature, this qualification does not exhaust all the relevant aspects of the relationship. It is simply a fact that, in a number of industries, suppliers and their distributors maintain an on-going contractual relationship which renders them more akin to commercial partners than to economic players in the typical and abstract seller/purchaser dynamic with contrasting/opposed interests.
>
> Over time, suppliers and distributors may consolidate their relationship, trying to refine it in light of their respective interests and market positions. It is in the context of these necessarily

[251] GL Zampa and P Buccirossi, 'Hub and Spoke Practices: Law and Economics of the New Antitrust Frontier?' (2013) 9(1) *Competition Policy Int'l* 91, 92.

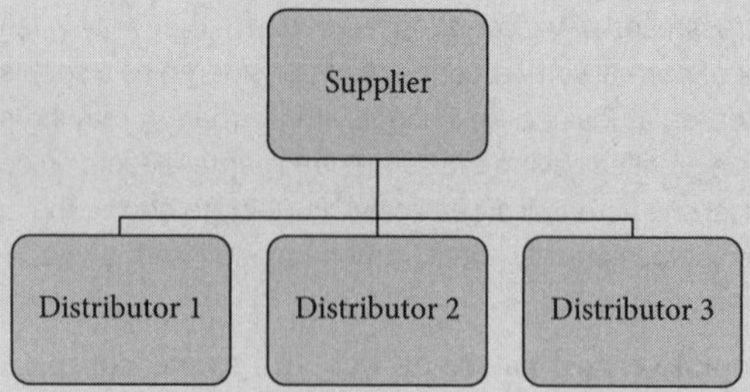

Figure 5.1

continuous contacts that H&SPs may find their origins: both the supplier and each of its distributors are inevitably aware that a similar interaction is at the same time occurring in parallel in relation to all other distributors. In other words, the distributor knows that the supplier is holding the same discussions, on the same commercial aspects, with its direct competitors (ie, the other distributors) and, symmetrically, the supplier is aware that the distributor knows it. This may or may not be exacerbated by what is typical in most industries, that is, the circulation of the employees of the parties between the various protagonists. Against this background, the question then becomes: what is made of this triangular situation? If and to the extent such a scenario evolves into an illegitimate H&SP essentially depends on what type of information is passed along this route.

A second typical situation (scenario B) is exactly the opposite; that is, when a distributor holds a number of parallel relationships with different suppliers. Here, somewhat symmetrically, each supplier knows that its competing suppliers have simultaneous analogous relationships with the distributor and the distributor is equally aware of it. Figure 5.2 [. . .] tries to visualize this second situation.

In both scenarios, a significant amount of information moves along the supplier-distributor axis, most of which is not only objectively necessary in the mechanics of the commercial relationship but also constitutes an integral part of the competitive process.

It is thus natural and, most importantly, fully legitimate, that a distributor and a supplier may exchange price information also in relation to other distributors and/or other suppliers. For example, in negotiating the wholesale price with the supplier, a distributor would naturally make reference to the retail price of its direct competitors (scenario A) and/or to the wholesale prices of other suppliers (scenario B). It would be rational for the distributor to benchmark the retail prices of the other distributors (ie, its direct competitors) with the wholesale price proposed

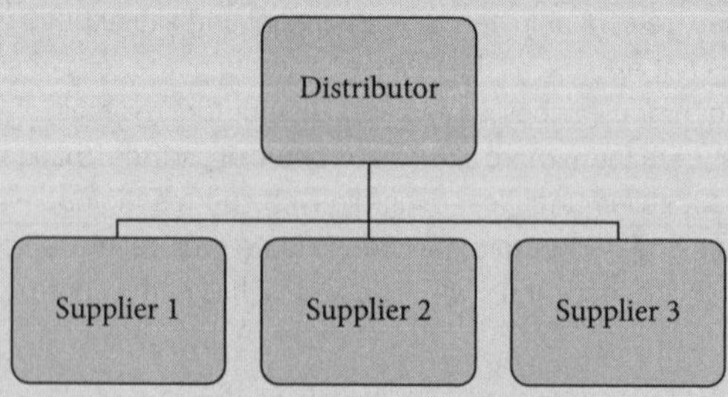

Figure 5.2

by the supplier in order to attempt to bid it down. The same would occur in scenario B, where the distributor has an incentive to show to each of its suppliers the wholesale price offered by other suppliers in order to play them off each other and as a result obtain better conditions and a lower procurement price. In scenario A, the distributor would thus put pressure on the supplier not to be offered worse terms and conditions than its competitors at the retail level. This could be the case in those markets where the retail prices typically provide some information on the level of the wholesale prices and this price data would typically be observed unilaterally through legitimate market intelligence. Equally rational would be the behaviour of a distributor in scenario B communicating to a supplier the wholesale prices of other suppliers, in order to play them off each other and obtain a better commercial deal.

Other types of perfectly normal and legitimate price information moving along the supplier-distributor route are, for example, the communication in advance by the supplier to the distributor of its intention to increase the wholesale price (ie, in order to test the waters and to give time to the distributor to budget for it) and the communication by the supplier to the distributor of the maximum or, more commonly, recommended retail prices. It is in fact a well-established principle on both sides of the Atlantic that suggested/recommended prices are compliant with antitrust laws. They are indeed a common feature of most of the industries producing goods for consumers. The supplier typically has more sophisticated marketing tools and is able to determine the profit-maximising price for both the retailers and the supplier, whilst allowing retailers full freedom to adhere or not to adhere to such recommended prices.

We have already noted above the self-policing character of the vertical relations between suppliers and retailers, as each aims to gain a higher share of the profits of the vertical chain, the product of one being the input of the other. This essentially preserves the best outcome for the final consumers, unless there is individual or collectively exercised market power at one or more levels of the vertical chain. The cooperation between producers and distributors and the exchange of information between them serves consumer sovereignty. Consumer preferences are not only about lower prices but also relate to the services that go along with the purchase and the consumption of the specific product. Dealers possess invaluable information on consumer preferences in different local markets, which explains why it is important for the manufacturers to reward the dealers' efforts and to provide the necessary incentives for them to accomplish their role. The self-policing character of vertical relationships will preserve the interests of the consumers, as each party will check that the other one is not remunerated more than the value (for the consumers) of their dispensed efforts.

However, H&SPs do not involve only bilateral cooperation between, for instance, a supplier and a retailer but also trilateral relations between two suppliers and a retailer or two retailers and a supplier. It is therefore difficult to systematically employ the self-policing character of the vertical dimension of the hub and spoke practice in this context. One may also note that the incentives of the parties to this triangular relation may differ from the textbook analysis of vertical relations.[252] In particular, in view of the repetitive and continuous nature of the relationship between suppliers and retailers in a specific supply chain, they may develop convergent interests and share any additional monopolistic profits they may extract from the final consumers, as this is explained in the excerpt below.

252 See Chapter 10.

GL Zampa and P Buccirossi, 'Hub and Spoke Practices: Law and Economics of the New Antitrust Frontier?' (2013) 9(1) *Competition Policy Int'l* 91, 97

For example, in scenario A considered above, where a distributor/retailer over time realises that the margins it obtains from the sale of the products of a supplier are modest or even absent, it would inevitably go back to the supplier to ask for a solution. It may request a reduction of the wholesale price or—and this is the same—demand other more favourable commercial terms or even threaten to de-list some of these low-margin items. If this low marginality is not imputable only to the retailers' strategies but can be attributed to the competitive dynamics at the retail level, the supplier would be faced with the alternative of having to reduce its own margins (by offering additional discounts/rebates, etc), being delisted or even losing an account or, possibly, trying to improve the complaining retailer's margins by making sure that other retailers understand that a retail price war is not in anyone's interest and that retail prices should be pushed up. Clearly, contributing to or facilitating the softening of retail competition would have a significant appeal to the supplier, as it would be (apparently) a zero cost proposition.

Correspondingly, in scenario B above, there may be a similar convergence between the supplier, which has a clear interest in increasing the wholesale price, and its distributors, which, under certain conditions, may view such an increase as an occasion for further (and more than proportionally) increasing their own prices downstream (ie, at the retail level). For example, in the relationships with its customers at the retail level, the distributor could 'put the blame' on the cost push derived from the suppliers' price increase, rationalising it as an objective fact outside of its control, and therefore having to pass on to them a new price increase. If all suppliers and, consequently, all distributors were to follow the same path, then a price increase would stand more chance to pass unchallenged by the ultimate end-user.

In both these scenarios, vertical relationships produced horizontal effects, upstream or downstream, which take either the form of horizontal collusive effects or the exercise of unilateral market power (by a powerful retailer or supplier). This horizontal effect has been noted as being equivalent to that often resulting from a minimum resale price maintenance agreement, which is addressed as a vertical collusive practice and treated quite harshly in EU competition law.[253] Other vertical practices that may also produce horizontal effects, include parity/MFN (most favoured nation or customer) clauses, single branding clauses etc.[254] These are often included in vertical agreements (ie between suppliers and retailers) and thus satisfying the collusion element of Article 101 TFEU. The horizontal effects of the practice are then examined under the restriction of competition element of Article 101(1) TFEU. For this reason, we do not examine these practices in this Section which focuses on the collusion element. Alternatively, in oligopolistic markets, these vertical arrangements having a horizontal effect may be considered as facilitating practice for the constitution or maintenance of a cartel. This relates to both the collusion and the restriction of competition elements and we examine this in Chapter 11.

Hub and Spoke conspiracies differ from these vertical practices producing horizontal effects in the fact that the hub (the supplier in scenario A) *voluntarily* participates in the conspiracy

253 N Sahuguet and A Walckiers, 'Hub-and-Spoke Conspiracies: the Vertical Expression of a Horizontal Desire?' (2014) 5(10) *J European Competition L & Practice* 711. See further Chapter 10.

254 See Chapter 10.

in order to improve the profits of the retailers downstream, by making their collusive scheme more stable and sharing with them any additional profits extracted from final consumers.[255] Remember that a vertical agreement may normally be inferred from the coercion of one party by the other one, and thus it is possible to find an agreement even if this is imposed by the stronger party in the relation (the dealer or retailer) and conflict with the interests of the other party. In case the supplier voluntarily participates in the conspiracy in order to share the additional profits made by the retailers downstream, this conduct will make sense if the market position of the retailers is stronger than that of the supplier, which indicates that the trilateral scheme was initiated by the dealers.[256] If the vertical restraint was adopted under dealer pressure, it will certainly reduce consumer welfare as it will increase the distribution mark up and will lead to higher prices for consumers, without this increase being justified by the provision of better distribution services. Hence, from a welfare perspective it may make sense to address this type of agreements as horizontal cartels and thus find the existence of a horizontal indirect collusion between the retailers.

However, one needs to be cautious about the alleged specificities of hub and spoke practices. First, under current law, there cannot be any prior analysis of the market position of the parties at the level of examining the existence of an agreement or concerted practice,[257] making it difficult to explore the bargaining position of the supplier vis-à-vis the retailers and determine the origin of the alleged restriction of competition. Second, one cannot presume the 'voluntary' participation of the supplier in the collusive scheme, just from the fact that it makes sense from an economics' perspective for the supplier to participate in such a scheme and share the additional profits brought by the dealer cartel which he helped making stable. The presumption of innocence and EU fundamental rights jurisprudence may raise obstacles to the development of inferences as to the participation of a supplier in a collusive scheme between retailers, simply because of some possible theorems developed by economic theory, without at least some evidence of intent to contribute to this collusive scheme. The case law on hub and spoke practices reflects this cautious approach that aims to balance the need for effectiveness in competition law enforcement against cartels and the requirements of the presumption of innocence.

The 'hub and spoke' concept is a US antitrust law import, although its use at the other side of the Atlantic has been relatively sparse.[258] The *E-Books* case provides some interesting insights on the distinction between the 'hub and spoke' qualification and a simple horizontal agreement to collude in US antitrust law and enables us to compare with the situation in Europe.

255 N Sahuguet and A Walckiers, 'Hub-and-Spoke Conspiracies: the Vertical Expression of a Horizontal Desire?' (2014) 5(10) *J European Competition L & Practice* 711, 715; N Sahuguet and A Walckiers, 'Selling to a Cartel of Retailers: A Model of Hub-and-Spoke Collusion', CEPR Discussion Paper No 9385(2013). For a criticism, see PJG Van Cayseele, 'Hub-and-Spoke Collusion: Some Nagging Questions Raised by Economists' (2014) 5(3) *J European Competition L & Practice* 164.

256 Market position is not similar to the concept of market power and may refer to a situation where the dealers dispose of a superior bargaining power, ie a situation where an important part of the supplier's turnover is realized with the particular dealer(s).

257 For a proposal in this sense, see I Lianos, 'Collusion in Vertical Relations under Article 81 EC' (2008) 45 Common Market L Rev 1027, 1071–5.

258 The first case considered as an example of hub and spoke conspiracy is *Intersate Circuit Inc v United States*, 306 US 208 (1939) concerning a collusive scheme between eight film distributors involving two movie theatre chains in order to control admission prices, where the Supreme Court held that even if there is no evidence of an agreement, an invitation to participate in a plan us sufficient to establish an unlawful conspiracy, if the parties knew about the plan, acted towards its commission and became aware that the others joined.

The e-books case in the US as an interesting case study distinguishing hub and spoke conspiracy and horizontal direct collusion

The case involved the implementation of a new business model regarding the distribution of e-books orchestrated, or at least facilitated by Apple that allegedly led to increased prices at retail level. Traditionally publishers sold books using a wholesale model. They would set a recommended retail price (RRP) and then sell those books to retailers at a wholesale price roughly half the price of that RRP. Retailers would then sell the books at whatever price they wanted, which would usually be around the RRP, but they could also sell below the RRP. When publishers started selling e-books they maintained the same wholesale model and established wholesale contracts with online distributors/malls, such as Amazon. Amazon detains a 90 per cent market share in e-books. It engaged in a loss-leading pricing, charging $9.99 for a best-seller in e-book format, several dollars below the wholesale price. Its strategy was through lower prices for books to promote its e-reader, the Kindle device, but also to attract demand for Amazon's vastly larger e-commerce business. Major publishing firms in the US found that such pricing strategy conflicted with their interests as it was 'cannibalizing new best-selling hardcovers' which were 'the mainstay of the publishing business'. Indeed, 'the bargain prices will lead consumers to conclude that books are worth only $10, or less, upsetting the pricing model that has survived for decades'.[259]

Some publishers reacted by delaying for several months the release of the electronic-book editions of their leading titles, taking a dramatic stand against the cut-rate by Amazon. The publishing industry was thus witnessing an important shift of power, as they were not able any more to create artificial scarcity by withholding content in one form and making it available later and lost control over pricing. Apple had developed a different distribution format (the agency model) with which it operated its iTunes and App Store which, contrary to Amazon's distribution model, put the content owner in control of pricing. When it launched the iBookstore and iPad in 2010, it signed contracts with the big publishers to use the agency model instead of the wholesale model. Under the agency model, the publishers set a retail price for e-books and Apple acts as an agent of these publishers and must sell at this retail price. However, it receives as a commission 30 per cent of the sale price. As a result of this model, customers pay the retail price set by the publishers, who keep control over the pricing of the books. As we

See also *Toys 'R' Us, Inc v FTC*, 221 F.3d 930 (7th Cir 2000); *Howard Hess Dental Labs Inc v Dentsply Int'l, Inc*, 602 F.3d 237, 255 (3d Cir 2010) (noting that a 'traditional hub-and-spoke conspiracy has three elements: (1) a hub, such as a dominant purchaser; (2) spokes, such as competing manufacturers or distributors that enter into vertical agreements with the hub; and (3) the rim of the wheel, which consists of horizontal agreements among spokes'); *United States v Apple, Inc*, 791 F.3d 290 (2nd Cir 2015) (finding a hub and spoke conspiracy between Apple Inc, which manufactures tablet computers and distributes electronic books (e-books), and several book publishers, alleging conspiracy to raise, fix, and stabilize retail prices for newly released and best-selling trade e-books in violation of the US Sherman Act and various state laws). For a more recent application of this concept, see *In Re: Musical Instruments and Equipment Antitrust Litigation*, 798 F.3d 1186 (9th Cir 2015) (where the Ninth Circuit analysed the hub-and-spoke conspiracy as 'simply a collection of vertical and horizontal agreements', making a 'key difference between a rimless hub-and spoke conspiracy (ie, a collection of purely vertical agreements) and a rimmed hub-and-spoke conspiracy (ie, a collection of vertical agreements joined by horizontal agreements)'. The Court also held that such a conspiracy should be 'broken into its constituent parts', which can each be analysed using the rule of reason (for vertical agreements) or under a *per se* analysis (for horizontal agreements). By distinguishing clearly between the two elements, the Court seems to acknowledge that allegations about vertical arrangements will not necessarily build up a story of horizontal collusion and could not substitute direct evidence of horizontal collusion).

[259] JA Trachtenberg, 'Two Major Publishers to Hold Back E-Books', *Wall Street J* (9 December 2009), available at http://www.wsj.com/articles/SB10001424052748704825504574584372263227740.

will examine in Chapter 10, vertical agency agreements of this sort may not be considered as agreements between two undertakings and thus not subject to Article 101 TFEU.

An additional but essential feature of these agency agreements was an MFN clause adopted by Apple *requiring* that the publishers adjust e-book prices in the iBookstore to match the lowest price offered by any other retailer—regardless of whether the publisher controlled the pricing in that retailer. Hence, Apple's iBookstore would always have the best wholesale price, and had the publishers decided to offer the e-book at a cheaper price, they should have lowered the price to Apple as well, the publishers (and not Apple) taking the whole loss of the reduction of the retail price. Under this model Apple was, however, maintaining its 30 per cent retail margin.

The US Department of Justice Antitrust Division argued that Apple and the publishers had colluded to raise the prices of e-books by switching to the agency model, finding evidence of meetings between publisher executives to discuss pricing issues and that Apple, which was vertically situated to the publishers, as it acted as distributor, had served as the intermediary and facilitator of the agreement between the publishers to switch to an agency distribution model. We will focus here on the second aspect, which is the way the US courts characterized Apple's assistance to the scheme (indirect horizontal concerted practice or agreement), absent evidence of the publishers' meetings (direct horizontal collusion). The district court judge found that '[. . .] [w]here a vertical actor is alleged to have participated in an unlawful horizontal agreement, plaintiffs must demonstrate both that a horizontal conspiracy existed, and that the vertical player was a *knowing* participant in that agreement and facilitated the scheme'.[260] The district court judge found 'overwhelming evidence' that 'Apple knew of the unlawful aims of the conspiracy and joined that conspiracy with the specific intent to help it succeed'.[261] The district court judge (at first instance) found that Apple was not only aware but had also facilitated the Publisher's collective action. Indeed, according to the district judge,

> [. . .] Apple's participation in the conspiracy proved essential. It assured each Publisher Defendant that it would move forward only if a critical mass of the major publishing houses agreed to its agency terms. It promised each Publisher Defendant that it was getting identical terms in its Agreement in every material way. It kept each Publisher Defendant apprised of how many others had agreed to execute Apple's Agreements. As [one of the witnesses] acknowledged at trial, 'I just wanted to assure them that they weren't going to be alone, so that I would take the fear awa[y] of the Amazon retribution that they were all afraid of.' As a result, the Publisher Defendants understood that each of them shared the same set of risks and rewards.[262]

Apple had thus reduced significantly uncertainty as to the conduct of the various Publishers, thus facilitating their horizontal collusion. The district court judge found irrelevant that Apple was not a dominant player in the relevant market as '[c]ourts have never found that the vertical actor must be a dominant purchaser or supplier in order to be considered a traditional "hub", only that this is generally the case'. Apple was indeed a new player in the e-books market, although it was expected that the launch of the iPad would have made Apple the dominant platform in e-readers.[263]

The Court of appeals for the second circuit confirmed the judgment of the district judge and rejected Apple's arguments that it was 'unwittingly facilitating' the Publisher's joint

260 *US v Apple Inc*, 952 F.Supp.2d 638, 690 (SDNY 2013) (emphasis added).
261 Ibid, 700.
262 Ibid, 693.
263 Ibid, 676, referring to some estimations by Apple's CEO at the time, Steve Jobs.

conduct, that is the shift to an agency model.[264] Apple was explaining that it had simply capitalized on the Publisher's 'preexisting incentives' and thus had not joined the alleged horizontal collusion between them. The Court disagreed, finding that Apple's contracts with the Publishers provided strong evidence that it had 'consciously orchestrated' a horizontal collusion between them, as the shifting to an agency model would not have been attractive individually for each Publisher, but *only* if they acted collectively. The Court of appeal indicated that as a 'sophisticated negotiator Apple was fully aware that its proposed Contracts would entice a critical mass of publishers only if these publishers perceived an opportunity collectively to shift' to an agency model.[265] This was, according to the Court, the purpose of the MFN clause. It was not also 'likely' that the 'near-simultaneous' signature of the agreements of the Publishers with Apple resulted from their independent decision and parallel decision-making.[266] The Court also relied on evidence that Apple had approached the publishers suggesting the agency model, had coordinated phone-calls between them and had kept them informed of the progress of negotiations, in particular updating them about how many of their peers had signed the contract with Apple, conduct which, as the Court noted, 'went well beyond legitimately exchanging information within the normal course of business'.[267] These facts indicated that Apple had played 'a key role in organizing their express collusion'.[268] The Court also indicated that vertical agreements, lawful in the abstract, can in context 'be useful evidence for a plaintiff attempting to prove the existence of a horizontal cartel [. . .] particularly, where multiple competitors sign vertical agreements that would be against their own interests were they acting independently'.[269] This was indeed the case here with the MFN clause which 'created a set of economic incentives pursuant to which the Contracts were only attractive to the Publishers [. . .] to the extent they acted collectively'.[270]

The European Commission opened competition law proceedings against Apple and five major publishers in 2011,[271] for the same practices and adopted a decision in 2013, accepting commitments by Apple and four major publishers, and reaching the preliminary assessment that each of the five publishers had engaged in direct and indirect (through Apple) contacts aimed at either raising the retail prices of e-books above those of Amazon (as was the case in the UK) or avoiding the arrival of such prices altogether (as was the case in France and Germany) in the EEA. According to the Commission, the joint switch for the sale of e-books from a wholesale model to an agency model with the same key pricing terms on a global basis amounted to a concerted practice with the object of either raising retail prices of e-books in the EEA or preventing the emergence of lower prices of e-books in the EEA.[272] The Commission noted that 'direct and indirect contacts had taken place between the Five Publishers and Apple'.[273] Furthermore, the joint conversion of the Publishers to the agency model was not possible unless each of the Five Publishers had disclosed to, and/or received information from the rest of the Five Publishers and/or Apple, regarding the future intentions of the Five Publishers with respect to entering into an agency agreement with Apple. Finally, both Apple and the Publishers shared the understanding that Apple's entry in the market for e-books on the agreed key agency model terms would have provided the global scale and framework

[264] *US v Apple Inc*, 791 F.3d 290 (2nd Cir 2015). [265] Ibid, 317. [266] Ibid, 318.
[267] Ibid, 319. [268] Ibid, 316. [269] Ibid, 340. [270] Ibid, 320.
[271] In the UK, the OFT had also opened investigations against Apple and the five publishers in January 2011, following a significant number of complaints, but the case was closed in December 2011 in view of the investigations initiated by the European Commission.
[272] *E-BOOKS* (Case AT.39847) Commission Decision C(2013) 4750 (25 July 2013).
[273] Ibid, para 76.

needed for the shift to this new model.[274] The Commission also took the view that 'the retail price MFN clause acted as a joint "commitment device" whereby each of the Five Publishers was in a position to force Amazon to accept changing to the agency model or otherwise face the risk of being denied access to the e-books of each of the Five Publishers, assuming that all Five Publishers had the same incentive during the same time period, and that Amazon could not have sustained simultaneously being denied access even to only a part of the e-books catalogue of each of the Five Publishers'.[275]

NOTES AND QUESTIONS ON E-BOOKS

1. Compare Apple's role in the e-books concerted practice with that of AC-Treuhand in the heat stabilizers cartel[276] and Pioneer in *Musique Diffusion Française*.[277] Was Apple present to a related market, downstream or upstream, of the market mainly affected by the horizontal collusion? Did the *AC-Treuhand* or *Musique Diffusion Française* cases involve any vertical practice, as the agency agreements and the MFN clause in e-books? What was the likelihood of type I and type II errors in each case?
2. In its decision in *E-Books* the Commission did not refer to the 'hub and spoke' concept but highlighted instead the 'direct and indirect (through Apple) contacts' between the five publishers. Do you think that by doing so the Commission ignored by design the complexity of the collusive scheme and its hybrid vertical-horizontal character, framing the issue as simply a form of direct (or indirect) horizontal concerted practice? How can one distinguish the *E-Books* case from the *Bananas* case[278] where it was found that an exchange of strategic information between competitors on price-setting factors or price trends constituted a concerted practice?
3. What would have made the e-books case a hybrid vertical-horizontal 'hub and spoke' case or a purely vertical case? Do you think that had the scheme not included a MFN clause, the Commission would have not qualified the conduct as a concerted practice between competitors? Is the nature of MFN, as a vertical practice producing horizontal effects, relevant for the qualification of the conduct as being a direct (or indirect) concerted practice between competitors?

Some National Competition Authorities have been at the frontline of the promotion of the concept of 'hub and spoke' conspiracy for hybrid, vertical and horizontal practices.[279] Of particular interest is the practice of *A-B-C* information exchanges, which arise when, for instance, a retailer *A* passes information to supplier *B*, in order for supplier *B* subsequently to pass this information on to retailer *C*.

274 Ibid, para 80. 275 Ibid, para 42.

276 Case C-194/14 P, *AC-Treuhand AG v Commission*, ECLI:EU:C:2015:717. See our analysis in Section 5.5.2.2.

277 Joined Cases 100–3/80, *SA Musique Diffusion Française v Commission* [1983] ECR 1825. See our analysis in Section 5.5.2.2.

278 *Bananas* (Case COMP/39.188) Commission Decision (15 October 2008), available at http://ec.europa.eu/competition/elojade/isef/case_details.cfm?proc_code=1_39188.

279 See, for instance, cases brought in Belgium, Italy, Bulgaria, Germany, Poland, Slovenia, Spain, among others.

In *Replica Football Kits*, the OFT (now replaced by the CMA) found that Umbro, a manufacturer of sport products, and a number of distributors were party to a series of agreements or concerted practices regarding the price fixing of replica football shirts of the England and other national league teams supplied by Umbro.[280] The objective of these agreements was to maintain the level of retail prices for some Umbro products and to avoid a price war between the different retailers. The resale price maintenance agreements involved not only the manufacturer and each of the distributors, but also had a horizontal component at the distribution level. Some agreements were indeed initiated by a distributor, JJB, which put pressure on Umbro to convince Sports Soccer, a retailer competitor, to raise its prices and to stop discounting. JJB had a considerable bargaining power in relation to Umbro which supplied JJB with much of its branded products. Following complaints from JJB and other retailers, Umbro requested that Sports Soccer stop discounting and gave Sports Soccer assurances as to the intentions of other retailers and in particular JJB on raising prices. The CAT confirmed the decision of the OFT as to the existence of a trilateral agreement or concerted practice between Umbro, Sport Soccer and the other major retailers, even if the reciprocal contact between one competitor and the other took place indirectly through Umbro, following JJB's complaints.[281]

The case was appealed, the Court of Appeal to determine whether the CAT 'failed to accord enough weight to the requirement of subjective consensus between all parties if an agreement or concerted practice between them is to be found'.[282] Because, in this case, the complaints were addressed indirectly by JJB to Umbro, the Court of Appeal found it necessary to examine 'JJB's state of mind in making the complaints',[283] thus implicitly requiring evidence of a subjective element of the parties adherence to an agreement or concerted practice. The conclusion of the Court of Appeal was that 'the level and the extent of the pressure' exercised on Umbro was such 'that JJB plainly did expect Umbro to do something in response, vis-à-vis Sports Soccer'.[284] Nevertheless, the Court considered that the CAT,

> may have gone too far [. . .] insofar as it suggests that if one retailer (A) privately discloses to a supplier (B) its future pricing intentions 'in circumstances where it is reasonably foreseeable that B might make use of that information to influence market conditions' and B then passes that pricing information on to a competing retailer (C) then A, B and C are all to be regarded as parties to a concerted practice having as its object or effect the prevention, restriction or distortion of competition. The Tribunal may have gone too far if it intended that suggestion to extend to cases in which A did not, in fact, foresee that B would make use of the pricing information to influence market conditions or in which C did not, in fact, appreciate that the information was being passed to him with A's concurrence.[285]

The Court's objective was to ensure that the scope of Article 101 TFEU would not be unduly extended so as to cast doubt on the freedom of discussion of actual or likely prices in a vertical context, between the manufacturers and their principal distributors, so long as they are conducted on a bilateral basis'.[286] The Court insisted, however, that its decision did not outlaw 'complaints by a wholesale customer to its supplier in general, especially if they are directed at getting better terms for the business between those two parties'.[287] The horizontal

280 CA 98/06/2003, *Price Fixing of Replica Football Kit* [2004] UKCLR 6.

281 *JJB Sports Plc* [2004] CAT 17, paras 657, 667.

282 *Argos Ltd, Littlewoods & OFT, JJB Sports & OFT* [2006] EWCA Civ 1318, para 32 (references omitted).

283 Ibid, para 82. 284 Ibid, para 89. 285 Ibid, para 91. 286 Ibid, para 106.

287 Ibid, para 106.

component of the discussions between Umbro and its retailers made this practice a 'far more serious' breach of the prohibition contained in Chapter I CA98 'than two unrelated vertical concerted practices, the customer party in each case being unaware of the fact or circumstances of the other'.[288]

Similarly, in *Toys*, the OFT found the existence of two bilateral vertical agreements or concerted practices between Hasbro, a toys manufacturer and two distributors, Argos and Littlewoods, and of a trilateral agreement 'with a horizontal component', between Hasbro, Argos, and Littlewoods with the aim to fix retail margins for certain Hasbro products.[289] Hasbro had published recommended retail prices and had also developed a 'pricing initiative' by inviting the distributors to maintain retail margins. None of the distributors would have committed to follow the pricing scheme without the assurance that its competitor would also adopt the same policy.[290] Finding that each of the companies 'was aware of the other's involvement and the nature of its intentions regarding its conduct in the relevant markets', the OFT concluded that 'this conduct constituted an overall agreement and/or concerted practice between these three undertakings'.[291]

The CAT confirmed the OFT's decision and found that there was an 'understanding' between Hasbro and the two distributors that prices would be at or near the RRP.[292] It also recognized that the agreement and/or concerted practice provided no guarantee that the distributors would follow the recommended prices. Referring to its case law in *Replica Football Kits*, the CAT assumed that by participating in discussions with Hasbro on their pricing intentions, each distributor 'must be taken to have known, or could at least have reasonably foreseen, that the information about pricing intentions which it was passing to Hasbro would be used by the latter in a way that would facilitate the maintenance of prices at RPRs in the market'.[293] This led the Court to conclude that the distributors had participated 'in indirect contacts with other economic operators the object or effect of which was to influence conduct in the market or to disclose future pricing intentions' and had thus infringed Chapter I CA98.[294]

Argos and Littlewoods challenged the CAT's conclusion by arguing that it did not adequately take into consideration the *Bayer* rule as there was no direct contact between the two distributors (the spokes in this case), or at least an invitation to collude. In the same judgment where it also examined the *Replica Football Kits* judgment of the CAT, the Court of Appeal dismissed the appeal but emphasized the need, following the *Bayer* rule, to prove that there was an invitation to collude, in other words, that the distributors (the spokes) *effectively knew* that the information they were giving to Hasbro (the hub) on their retail pricing strategy would be passed on to their competitor.[295] This seems to be a more restrictive approach than that of the CAT, which only required that it was 'reasonably foreseeable' that the competitor might make use of this information. Instead, the Court of appeal seems to require *actual knowledge* from A and C that the information has been used by B to

[288] Ibid, para 105.

[289] CA/98/8/2003 *Agreements between Hasbro UK Ltd, Argos Ltd & Littlewoods Ltd fixing the price of Hasbro toys and games* [2004] 4 UKCLR 717.

[290] Ibid, para 96. This was essential because of the retailing format of these two companies, as 'any "agreement" or "understanding" that the other catalogue retailer would price at an agreed price would not be seen to be implemented until much later when it would be too late to change one's own catalogue'.

[291] Ibid, para 108.

[292] *Argos Ltd, Littlewoods Ltd v OFT* [2004] CAT 24.

[293] Ibid, para 787.

[294] Ibid.

[295] *Argos Ltd, Littlewoods & OFT, JJB Sports & OFT* [2006] EWCA Civ 1318, para 140.

influence market conditions. The position of the Court of appeal was formulated by Lloyd LJ as follows:

> The proposition which, in our view, falls squarely within the *Bayer* judgment in the ECJ and which is sufficient to dispose of the point in the present appeal can be stated in more restricted terms: if (i) retailer A discloses to supplier B its future pricing intentions in circumstances where A may be taken to intend that B will make use of that information to influence market conditions by passing that information to other retailers (of whom C is or may be one), (ii) B does, in fact, pass that information to C in circumstances where C may be taken to know the circumstances in which the information was disclosed by A to B and (iii) C does, in fact, use the information in determining its own future pricing intentions, then A, B and C are all to be regarded as parties to a concerted practice having as its object the restriction or distortion of competition. The case is all the stronger where there is reciprocity: in the sense that C discloses to supplier B its future pricing intentions in circumstances where C may be taken to intend that B will make use of that information to influence market conditions by passing that information to (amongst others) A, and B does so.[296]

Evidence of the intent or the state of mind of the distributor (*B*) remained, however, largely speculative.[297]

The OFT (now CMA) also relied on the hub and spoke concept in its statement of objections in the *Tobacco* case in which it accused two tobacco manufacturers and ten retailers to have engaged in collusive practices with regard to retail prices for tobacco products in the UK, which involved the indirect exchange of information between competitors of future retail prices (hub and spoke), as well as arrangements between each manufacturer and each retailer that restricted the ability of each of these retailers to determine its selling prices independently, by linking the retail price of a manufacturer's brand to the retail price of a competing brand of another manufacture.[298] Although the OFT fined the manufacturers and the retailers for participation in an illegal cartel, it dropped the hub and spoke/indirect exchange of proposed future retail prices charges as it considered it had insufficient evidence to proceed to an infringement finding on this basis.[299] However, the CAT upheld appeals brought by six parties and quashed the OFT's Decision. The OFT decided not to appeal.[300]

The OFT (now CMA) also resorted to the hub and spoke concept in the *Dairy* case.

The *Dairy* case

By a decision adopted in 2011, also called 'Dairy retail price initiatives', the OFT had found that a number of retailers had in 2002 and 2003 indirectly exchanged their future retail pricing intentions in respect of certain dairy products, such as British-produced cheddar and territorial cheeses, as well as fresh liquid milk, via their common suppliers, and thus infringed the Chapter I prohibition of the Competition Act 1998.[301] *The OFT imposed fines*

296 Ibid, para 141.

297 The Court of appeal noting that 'it must have been apparent to Argos that, if Hasbro was feeding back to Argos Hasbro's views as to other retailers' pricing intentions, by the same token Hasbro would be feeding such views to other retailers, based on Hasbro's conversations with Argos': ibid, para 144.

298 OFT, Press Release 56/08, (25 April 2008), available at http://webarchive.nationalarchives.gov.uk/20140402142426/http://www.oft.gov.uk/news-and-updates/press/2008/56-08.

299 Case CE/2596-03 *Tobacco* OFT Decision CA98/01/2010 (15 April 2010).

300 *Imperial Tobacco Group Plc & Imperial Tobacco Limited v OFT* [2011] CAT 41.

301 Case CE/3094-03 *Dairy retail price initiatives* OFT Decision CA98/03/2011 (26 July 2011), para 7.44.

of almost £50 million on a number of supermarkets, including Tesco, which was the biggest purchaser, and retailer, of cheese in the UK at the time, and dairy processors finding a horizontal coordination between competitors which was achieved by supermarkets indirectly exchanging retail pricing intentions with each other via five dairy processors (Aria, Dairy Crest, McLelland, the Cheese Company, and Wiseman), the so-called A-B-C *information exchanges. Tesco appealed at the CAT. The CAT confirmed the OFT's decision, by finding that Tesco had been involved in three anti-competitive* A-B-C *information exchanges and had participated in a concerted practice, along other retailers and dairy suppliers* Tesco Stores and Others v OFT *[2012] CAT 31. The CAT spelled out the constitutive elements of a 'hub and spoke' collusion. Although the CAT noted that are no EU cases dealing specifically with the circumstances in which there can be a concerted practice by virtue of indirect contact between two or more undertakings via a common supplier, it examined the jurisprudence of the EU courts regarding the concept of concerted practice. It noted that '[a]lthough there is no EU authority on the point, it was common ground that the* Anic *presumption applied to the indirect exchange between competitors of confidential future pricing intentions'.*[302] *The CAT then went to examine the UK decisional practice and jurisprudence on 'hub and spoke' collusion, explaining the various limbs of the test and noting the 'the fact-specific nature of any assessment as to whether a concerted practice exists', as this is a 'versatile concept'.*[303]

Tesco Stores and others v OFT
[2012] CAT 31

57. [. . .] [A] retailer, supplier and another retailer may be properly regarded as parties to a concerted practice, having as its object the restriction of competition, in circumstances where:

(a) retailer A discloses to supplier B its future pricing intentions;

(b) A may be taken to intend that B will make use of that information to influence market conditions by passing that information to other retailers (of whom C is, or may be, one);

(c) B does, in fact, pass that information to C;

(d) C may be taken to know the circumstances in which the information was disclosed by A to B; and

(e) C does, in fact, use the information in determining its own future pricing intentions.

58. Thus, each of the 'A to B' and the 'B to C' communications comprises a conduct element and a mental element. There are, of course, two conduct elements necessary to establish an infringement: first, the transmission by one retailer of its future pricing intentions to a common supplier; and, secondly, the onward transmission by that supplier to, and receipt by, the competing retailer. Each conduct element must be accompanied by the requisite state of mind on the part of the relevant retailer.

[. . .]

302 *Tesco Stores and Others v OFT* [2012] CAT 31, para 53.

303 Ibid, para 56.

A to B: retailer A discloses its future pricing intentions to supplier B [Conduct element]

59. Disclosures of actual or likely retail prices by a customer to its supplier are often part of normal commercial dialogue. Suppliers may be better informed about the suitability of a particular retail price point, both in absolute terms and relative to the products of other suppliers, than a retailer. A supplier may be legitimately concerned that, without that information, the retailer will incorrectly position the supplier's goods in the market and that the supplier will be unable to negotiate appropriate cost prices. In *Toys and Kits*, the Court of Appeal was clearly of the view that bilateral, vertical discussions between a supplier and its customer in relation to matters such as '*actual or likely retail prices, profit margins and wholesale prices or terms of sale*' may be necessary and, therefore, permissible (see paragraph 106). The Court of Appeal was equally clear, however, that competition law concerns may arise where a retailer discloses such pricing information to its supplier, which uses it for anti-competitive purposes such as by disclosing it to other retailer-customers. This can amount to the knowing substitution of practical co-operation for the risks of competition by the retailers.

[. . .]

Retailer A's state of mind

Principles of attribution

60. Attribution of a mental state to a corporate entity depends on the interpretation of the legal rule that calls for the question of attribution to be decided [. . .]. The relevant legal rule in this case is the Chapter I prohibition. Hence, the state of mind to be attributed to an undertaking should be determined as a matter of UK and, by virtue of section 60(2) of the 1998 Act, EU competition law. Common law concepts of ostensible authority and/or vicarious liability are therefore not relevant [. . .]

The requisite state of mind

64. The state of mind that retailer A must have, at the time of disclosure, as to the use which supplier B makes of its future pricing intentions has been a central feature of this appeal. We have reached the following conclusions.

65. It is important to consider why the retailer's state of mind matters in a case of this kind. Where commercially sensitive information is disclosed directly by retailer A to retailer C, it is often unnecessary to go behind the fact of the disclosure in order to assess the parties' states of mind. The mere fact of a direct communication of future retail pricing intentions between horizontal competitors is almost invariably sufficient to demonstrate that each acted with the requisite state of mind (although it is conceivable that there may be rare situations where this is not the case). Where supplier B is interposed between A and C, however, there can be no presumption as to A's state of mind. The onward transmission of A's pricing intentions to one of A's competitors, C, is made by their common supplier, B. It is therefore incumbent on a competition authority to demonstrate that A acted with the relevant state of mind to avoid A being held strictly liable for the conduct of B, over whom it may have limited control.

66. [. . .] Establishing the requisite state of mind, namely that retailer A may be taken to have intended, or actually foresaw, that its future intentions would be conveyed to its competitor, retailer C, shows that dealings between a supplier and its customers

have gone beyond the legitimate framework of a vertical relationship and have given rise to an unlawful, albeit indirect, horizontal element. [. . .]

68. Establishing the state of mind of retailer A (and retailer C, of course) is a question of fact. A person's state of mind must be assessed by reference to all the circumstances. The subjective evidence of an individual witness, as to his or her own state of mind at the relevant time, perhaps given several years later, is undoubtedly relevant but is not necessarily conclusive. The Tribunal must consider all the relevant circumstances, of course including contemporaneous evidence, in order to determine whether retailer A may be taken to have intended that the information it was disclosing to its supplier would then be passed on by that supplier to other retailers.

The CAT found that 'the state of mind of retailer A may be inferred from the circumstances, taking into account all the available evidence on what must have been in A's mind at the relevant time'.[304] *According to the CAT, 'the court is entitled to draw inferences from what a person knew, said and did, both at the relevant time and later'.*[305] *The existence of reciprocity of information exchanges is not a necessary ingredient of an infringement but may nevertheless make the inference stronger.*[306] *The CAT also commented on the rejection of the reasonable foreseeability test with regard to the inference of the requisite state of mind of* A *with regard to its participation in the hub-and-spoke collusion.*

71. Furthermore, the OFT, in its written closing submissions, made much of the fact that in *Toys and Kits* the Court of Appeal sometimes referred to actual foresight that information '*would be passed on*' and sometimes to the prospect that it '*might be passed on*' (emphases added). The OFT argued that either would suffice for a finding that retailer A '*actually*' foresaw how its information would be treated by supplier B. The Tribunal does not consider that these differences in expression can bear the weight the OFT seeks to place on them. It is our view that the Court of Appeal's judgment must be read as a whole and in context, and applied with care. The proposition in paragraph 141 of the Court of Appeal's judgment is clear and we propose to apply it as we understand it. On that basis, we reject the submission that foresight that future retail pricing intentions '*might*' be passed on is sufficient to establish the requisite state of mind. For this reason we also reject the OFT's suggestion [. . .] that it is sufficient in law for retailer A '*to have a pretty good idea*' that supplier B would treat A's information in '*a cavalier fashion … which* might *include disclosure*' (emphasis in original) to one of A's competitors.

72. The absence of any legitimate commercial reason for a disclosure by retailer A of its future pricing intentions to supplier B may be indicative of the requisite state of mind, when viewed in light of all the circumstances known to the disclosing party at the time of the communication. In considering whether there is a legitimate reason in such circumstances, it is important to distinguish between communications to the effect that a retailer will reduce its prices, on the one hand, and that a retailer will maintain or increase its prices, on the other. In the case of a planned reduction in the retail price, the retailer might legitimately relay its intentions to the supplier, for example, in an attempt to secure a lower cost price to help fund the anticipated loss of margin. There may be fewer legitimate commercial reasons for the transmission of a retailer's intentions to maintain or increase its prices. [. . .]

304 Ibid, para 69. 305 Ibid. 306 Ibid, para 70.

73. Finally, there was considerable dispute as to whether a lesser state of mind than 'intend or may be taken to intend' can be sufficient for a finding of an unlawful concerted practice. [. . .]

This issue is addressed in more detail in paragraphs 350–4 of the judgment. In its submissions, the OFT was advancing the view that 'lesser states of mind' of A than outright evidence of actual knowledge or actual foresight (as in Toys *and* Replica Football Kits*) as to the transmission of the future retail pricing information by the common supplier* B *to* A*'s competitors was necessary. The OFT was open to accept the 'lesser' standard of 'foresight',*[307] *which encompasses 'a standard of 'recklessness' in the sense of actual awareness of risk'*[308] *and also ' 'suspicion' or 'foresight of the possibility'.*[309] *In its further submissions the OFT went even further to argue that it was 'entirely appropriate, and indeed logically necessary' to find an infringement of the Chapter I prohibition in 'any of the following circumstances: (i) where A did know or (ii) where A suspected or (iii) where A could have known or (iv) where A ought to have known' that supplier B 'would (or might)' pass its confidential future pricing intentions to another retailer, C'. Noting Loyd LJ's opinion in the Court of appeal judgment in Toys and Replica Football Kits that the CAT may have gone 'too far' in its previous case law on the inference of the intent of* A*, the CAT declined to determine the point directly although it indirectly accepted the possibility for the OFT (now CMA) to take a decision, 'primarily or in the alternative, on the basis that a lower standard of proof was sufficient to make out the infringements'.*[310]

74. In summary, we propose to adopt the following approach to the issue of state of mind of retailer A:

(a) acts of any employee may be attributed to his or her corporate employer, with whom they comprise the same undertaking;

(b) a retailer's state of mind is a subjective mental state but the law applies an objective standard as to whether that mental state existed or not;

(c) a retailer intends a particular result of its conduct if it actually foresees that result;

(d) a retailer may be taken to intend a particular result of its conduct, having regard to all the evidence placed before the Tribunal, including the evidence of the person alleged to have held the state of mind and the surrounding circumstances; and

(e) it is trite law that inadvertent or accidental disclosures are unlikely to constitute circumstances from which the requisite state of mind can be inferred.

[. . .]

B to C: Supplier B passes on retailer A's future pricing intentions to retailer C

75. The next limb of an infringement is that supplier B must be shown, as a matter of fact, to have transmitted retailer A's future pricing intentions to retailer C. This is a question, which will arise only if the conduct and mental elements of the A to B transmission have been established. [. . .]

79. In our judgement, the exchange of individualised data is more likely to facilitate co-ordination because it makes it easier for companies to reach a common understanding regarding future prices or sales. It also contributes to a more credible

[307] Ibid, para 352. [308] Ibid, para 351. [309] Ibid, para 352. [310] Ibid, para 354.

prospect of retaliation which disciplines the co-ordinating companies. Conversely, the exchange of aggregated data is less likely to lead to a collusive outcome since it is less likely to be indicative of specific competitors' future conduct or to lead to a common understanding of business behaviour. Even then, however, it cannot be excluded that the exchange of aggregated data may facilitate a collusive outcome, depending on the particular facts of the case. We take account of this distinction below, when considering whether the indirect exchanges of information found by the OFT eliminated, or substantially reduced, uncertainty on the market, with the result that competition was restricted.

[. . .]

Retailer C's state of mind

82. In our judgement, it is sufficient for the OFT to prove that retailer C may be taken to have known the circumstances in which A disclosed its future retail pricing intentions to B [. . .].

83. As we have said above, the relevant individual receiving the information at retailer C may state that he or she did not believe that the information communicated by supplier B was, in reality, confidential information belonging to retailer A, for example, because he thought B was simply engaging in market speculation. If that were true, then that would mean that retailer C could not be taken to have known the circumstances in which the information was disclosed by A to B. That, however, will be a matter of fact to be assessed by the Tribunal in light of the evidence. The circumstances known to the individual at retailer C will be a relevant consideration for that assessment. If, for example, that individual knows that his supplier, B, is in negotiations with retailer A about cost and retail price increases, and B subsequently tells him that A will be increasing its prices on a particular date, it will scarcely be credible for the individual at C to maintain that it never occurred to him that the information came from A.

The CAT then discusses the position of the Court of Appeal in Toys *and* Replica Football kits *that it is sufficient for the authority to prove that* C *may be taken to have known the circumstances in which the information was disclosed by* A *to* B.

85. [. . .] The key point is, in our view, that C must be shown to have appreciated the basis on which A provided the information to B, so that A, B and C can all be regarded as parties to a concerted practice.

[. . .]

Retailer C's use of Retailer A's future pricing intentions

86. The final element of the proposition formulated by Lloyd LJ in *Toys and Kits* is that retailer C does, in fact, use retailer A's future pricing intentions in determining its own future pricing intentions. In our view, the word '*use*' in this context is to be understood as referring to retailer C taking into account retailer A's future pricing intentions when making decisions as to its own future conduct on the market. There was no dispute that the *Anic* presumption [. . .] applies in these circumstances. Even where C's participation is limited to the mere receipt of information about the future conduct of a competitor, the law presumes that C cannot fail to take that information into account when determining its own future policy on the market. It is open, of course, for C to

seek to demonstrate that it determined independently the policies it pursued and did not act on the basis of A's future pricing intentions. [. . .]

NOTES AND QUESTIONS ON THE DAIRY *CASE AND 'HUB AND SPOKE' COLLUSION*

1. How does the CAT distinguish between a 'hub-and-spoke' collusion, which is addressed as a form of horizontal collusion, and situations in which there are independent bilateral vertical agreements? What is the nature of the interdependence between competitors in a hub and spoke context? Reflect with regard to the facts of the *Toys*, *Replica football kits*, and *Dairy* cases.
2. Remark how the CAT in *Dairy* distinguishes between the collusion element and the existence of a restriction of competition, when characterizing the facts of the case. For instance, once the indirect information exchange between *A* and *B* was found to be part of a hub and spoke collusion, then the courts need to explore whether it constitutes a restriction of competition, by either object or by effect.[311] As to the existence of a restriction of competition, the fact that a supplier (or retailer) *A* exchanges information (even on future prices) with retailer (or supplier) *B*, that is a simple bilateral vertical exchange of information, does not raise as such competition concerns and may be analysed as a simple vertical arrangement. Bilateral discussions between suppliers and retailers of wholesale prices are unlikely to be harmful and are often integral parts of the negotiation process. Retailers may even communicate a rival manufacturer's price to the manufacturer it is negotiating with in order to secure a better deal. A different situation, although still analysed as a vertical arrangement, may, however, arise from a bilateral discussion between a supplier and a retailer of retail prices, that is, the prices the retailers will sell the product to consumers. In contrast, the horizontal nature of a 'hub-and-spoke' collusion results from the finding that the information exchanged between *A* and *B* was or may be taken to be intended to be revealed to one or more of *A*'s competitors.[312] Hence, the intention of *A* transforms an apparently simple bilateral vertical exchange of information to a trilateral horizontal exchange of information. How is intention inferred? This intention may not be inferred from the fact that there is direct exchange of commercially sensitive information between competitors.[313] As the CAT notes, when supplier *B* is interposed between *A* and *C*, 'there can be no

[311] For an analysis of the distinction between object and effect to restrict competition, see Chapter 6.

[312] O Odudu, 'Hub and Spoke Collusion' in I Lianos and D Geradin (eds) *Handbook on European Competition Law* (Edward Elgar, 2013), 242, 247, noting that the case law requires that *A* has *knowledge* that its pricing intentions would be passed on by *B* to *C*.

[313] This may result from a reverse application of the *Anic* presumption, as one may consider that *A* is aware that *C* will take into account the commercially sensitive information to be communicated through *B*, in case of course this information is effectively communicated. One may also interpret the CJEU's judgment in Case C-557/12, *Kone AG and Others v ÖBB-Infrastruktur AG*, ECLI:EU:C:2014:1317, paras 29–30 that one (in this case undertakings profiting from an umbrella pricing effect) cannot 'disregard' the possibility that undertakings participating to a cartel, but also other competing undertakings 'set the price of its offer at an amount higher than it would have chosen under normal conditions of competition'. See also the Opinion of AG Kokott in the same case noting that 'any loss the incurrence of which the cartel members ought reasonably to take into consideration on the basis of practical experience is foreseeable (or ensues via an adequate causal link), unlike loss which results from an entirely extraordinary train of events and, therefore, ensues via an atypical causal chain'.

presumption as to *A*'s state of mind'.[314] The competition authority is thus required to bring evidence that *A* may be taken to have intended, or actually foresaw, that its future intentions would be conveyed to its competitor(s).[315] The existence of a 'bi-directional flow of information',[316] when there is a reciprocal exchange of information between *A* and *B*,[317] the fact that here is not any legitimate commercial reason for such disclosure[318] may indicate the requisite state of mind from the part of *A*.

3. How does the CAT interpret the evidential requirement for the anti-competitive intent?[319] Compare with the interpretation of these requirements by the Court of appeal in *Toys* and *Replica Football Kits*.[320] Does the CAT require 'actual knowledge' by A that the information will be passed on to its competitors or is it content with a 'reasonable foreseeability standard'? Which approach would be compatible with the approach followed by the EU courts in indirect concerted practice cases.[321]
4. The second limb in the 'hub and spoke' collusion assessment is that *B* passes *A*'s pricing intentions to *C*. This is a factual issue and 'will arise only if the conduct and mental elements of the *A* to *B* transmission have been established'.[322] The CAT refers to a traditional distinction in the law on information exchanges between competitors between the exchange of individualized, as opposed to aggregate data,[323] the former being considered as more risky, from a competition law perspective, than the latter.[324]
5. Although the CAT requires evidence of the state of mind of *A* and *C* (the spokes), there is no specific reference with regard to the state of mind of *B* (the hub), although the conduct element is part of the test (*B* should pass the strategic sensitive information from *A* to *C*). In some cases, it will be clear that *B* had an anti-competitive intent, in the sense of 'actual knowledge' of the indirect exchange of information between *A* and *C* (see eg the role of Apple in the *E-Books* case). But, what occurs if *B* has transmitted the strategic information on future prices by negligence? Or, in case *B* was reckless, in the sense that *B* was aware of the risks but still proceeded to sharing this information? Should one apply the same standard of intentionality as that required for *A* and *C*, or a higher standard as *B* (the hub) is not a competitor of *A* and *C*? It is reminded that responsibility for the commission of competition law infringements in personal.[325] The CJEU has also recently held in *AC-Treuhand v Commission* that 'in order to be able to find that an undertaking participated in an infringement and was liable for all the various elements comprising the infringement', one must prove that 'the undertaking concerned *intended* to contribute by its own conduct to the common objectives pursued by all the participants and that it was *aware of the actual conduct planned or put into effect* by other undertakings in pursuit of the same objectives or that it *could reasonably have foreseen it* and that it *was*

Indeed, 'the normal way of things' is that undertakings 'set their prices with an eye to the market behaviour of the undertakings belonging to the cartel' (ibid, paras 42, 46, and 47).

314 *Tesco Stores and Others v OFT* [2012] CAT 31, para 65. 315 Ibid, para 66.

316 O Odudu, 'Hub and Spoke Collusion' in I Lianos and D Geradin (eds) *Handbook on European Competition Law* (Edward Elgar, 2013), 242, 250.

317 *Tesco Stores and Others v OFT* [2012] CAT 31, para 70. 318 Ibid, para 72.

319 Ibid, paras 71, 73, 350–4.

320 CA 98/06/2003, *Price Fixing of Replica Football Kit* [2004] UKCLR 6, para 141 (Lloyd LJ).

321 See eg Case C-194/14 P, *AC-Treuhand AG v Commission*, ECLI:EU:C:2015:717.

322 *Tesco Stores and Others v OFT* [2012] CAT 31, para 75. 323 See Chapter 7.

324 *Tesco Stores and Others v OFT* [2012] CAT 31, para 79. 325 See Chapter 4.

prepared to take the risk.[326] The standard seems therefore to be satisfied with evidence of reckless behaviour (reasonable foreseeability). The CJEU also found in *AC Treuhand v Commission* that passive participation of an undertaking, through its presence in meetings between competitors at which anti-competitive agreements are concluded, without the undertaking distancing itself publicly from them reporting its content to administrative authorities, should be considered as evidence that the undertaking has contributed to the competition law infringement.[327] One may, however, question the application of this presumption concerning the participating in meetings between competitors to the 'hub and spoke' collusion context, as in this case it is normal for the hub (for instance supplier *B*) to enter into bilateral discussions on future retail prices (and eventually meet) with *A* and *C* (the distributors of its products), as this is essential for the coordination of the vertical value chain.[328] These cases may be distinguished from *AC-Treuhand v Commission* as in the latter case AC-Treuhand had no other reason to participate in meetings with the heat stabilizers cartel members than to organize their horizontal collusion. Indeed, according to the CJEU, AC-Treuhand's conduct was 'directly related to the efforts made by the producers of heat stabilisers, as regards both the negotiation and monitoring of the implementation of the obligations entered into by those producers in connection with the cartels, the very purpose of the services provided by AC-Treuhand on the basis of service contracts concluded with those producers being the attainment, *in full knowledge of the facts*, of the anti-competitive objectives in question'.[329]

6. The third limb in the 'hub-and-spoke' collusion test is that *C* uses the information on *A*'s future pricing intentions or at least that *C* took into account retailer *A*'s future pricing intentions when making decisions as to its own future conduct on the market. The CAT notes the application of the *Anic* presumption in this context. However, this presumption may be rebutted. Odudu distinguishes the situation in which disclosure of information was requested by *C*, in which case the rebuttal of the presumption seems unlikely and the presumption is conclusive, and that in which *C* did not request this information, in which cases *C* may rebut the presumption. This may, for instance, occur if *C* indicates that the information has not been requested at the first place, this reticence being recorded in internal document and the senior management of *B* being informed in writing, if *C* exits the market immediately after the exchange of that information, and any other evidence 'showing that an undertaking has repudiated the influence of the contact or communication in question and can show that it closed its mind to the knowledge otherwise gained', or for instance that the 'retail prices became publicly available before the knowledge and awareness obtained' by *C*, the information exchanged being 'verified by public sources more quickly than it could have been acted on' by *C* (in this case Tesco).[330] Odudu suggests the creation of 'an audit trail documenting how C's subsequent market conduct was determined and the source of information on which that market conduct was based', indicating that *C* acted independently of this information.[331]

326 Case C-194/14 P, *AC-Treuhand AG v Commission*, ECLI:EU:C:2015:717, para 30 (emphases added).
327 Ibid, para 31. 328 See Chapter 10.
329 Case C-194/14 P, *AC-Treuhand AG v Commission*, ECLI:EU:C:2015:717, para 38 (emphasis added).
330 *Tesco Stores and Others v OFT* [2012] CAT 31, para 277.
331 O Odudu, 'Hub and Spoke Collusion' in I Lianos and D Geradin (eds) *Handbook on European Competition Law* (Edward Elgar, 2013), 242, 257.

5.6.3. COMMUNICATIONS-BASED VERSUS EFFECTS-BASED APPROACHES IN DEFINING COLLUSION: BREAKING THE EXTERNAL BOUNDARIES OF ARTICLE 101 TFEU/CHAPTER I CA 98?

In some scholarly work dating from the 1960s, US judge and professor at the University of Chicago Law School Richard Posner famously argued that oligopolistic price coordination should be considered as an agreement and fall under the scope of section 1 of the Sherman Act.[332] Posner lamented 'the process by which the rule against price fixing was virtually emptied of any economic content, to become in effect a branch of the criminal law of conspiracies and attempts', as 'it rendered antitrust enforcers virtually helpless to deal with any case of collusive pricing in which the conspirators did not leave behind them a visible trail of communications or acts of concealment'.[333]

Posner criticized the position of economist Donald Turner, later an Assistant Attorney General in charge of the Antitrust Division of the US Department of Justice, who argued that oligopolistic pricing was inherent in the structure of highly concentrated markets and could not be prevented without changing market structure.[334] Turner was influenced by Edward Chamberlin's insights on the existence of oligopolistic interdependence,[335] who had put forward that conscious parallelism between competitors and identical prices were to be expected in an oligopoly situation, without 'overt communication or agreement, but solely through a rational calculation by each seller of what the consequences of his price decision would be, taking into account the probable or virtually certain reactions of his competitors'.[336] Turner explains that

> [i]n a significant sense, the behavior of the rational oligopolist in setting his price is precisely the same as that of the rational seller in an industry consisting of a very large number of competitors. Both are pricing their products and determining their output so as to make the highest profit, or suffer the least loss, that can be obtained in the market conditions facing them. The rational oligopolist simply takes one more factor into account- the reactions of his competitors to any price change that he makes. He must take them into account because his competitors will inevitably react [. . .] [I]t can fairly be said that the rational oligopolist is behaving in exactly

332 RA Posner, 'Oligopoly and the Antitrust Laws: A Suggested Approach' (1969) 21 *Stanford L Rev* 1562. It is reminded that section 1 of the Sherman Act forbids contracts, combinations, and conspiracies in restraint of trade.

333 RA Posner, 'Oligopolistic Pricing Suits, the Sherman Act, and Economic Welfare: A Reply to Professor Markovits' (1975) 28 *Stanford L Rev* 903, 904. According to Posner, 'whether a case involves oligopolistic pricing without explicit collusion, or overt conspiracy under such favorable conditions as to generate no evidence of conspiracy, is a distinction without a policy difference'.

334 DF Turner, 'The Definition of Agreement Under the Sherman Act: Conscious Parallelism and Refusals to Deal' (1962) 75(4) *Harvard L Rev* 655.

335 EH Chamberlin, *The Theory of Monopolistic Competition* (Harvard University Press, 1933, repr. 1948), 48, defined this situation as following: '[i]f each [seller] seeks his maximum profit rationally and intelligently, he will realize that when there are only two or a few sellers his own move has a considerable effect upon his competitors, and that this makes it idle to suppose that they will accept without retaliation the losses he forces upon them. Since the result of a cut by any one is inevitably to decrease his own profits, no one will cut, and although the sellers are entirely independent, the equilibrium result is the same as though there were a monopolistic agreement among them.'

336 DF Turner, 'The Definition of Agreement Under the Sherman Act: Conscious Parallelism and Refusals to Deal' (1962) 75(4) *Harvard L Rev* 655, 661.

> the same way as is the rational seller in a competitively structured industry; he is simply taking another factor into account, which he has to take into account because the situation in which he finds himself put in there.[337]

Similar reasons pushed Turner to agree with Carl Kaysen's view that there should not be agreement in the situation of price leadership, where each seller decides that it will be better for him to follow the single judgment of a price leader, or a succession of price leaders, which are usually the dominant and the low-cost firms, even if he disagrees with it.[338]

Turner considered that such behaviour may theoretically be qualified as either individual behaviour (although interdependent) or as an 'agreement'. Yet, he chose the first option, mainly for the following reasons. First, he thought it is 'questionable to call the behaviour of oligopolists in setting their prices unlawful when the behaviour in essence is identical to that of sellers in a competitive industry'.[339] Second, in view of the fact that monopoly and monopoly pricing are not unlawful *per se* under US antitrust law, 'neither should oligopoly and oligopoly pricing, absent agreement of the usual sort' as '[i]t would make no sense to deprive lawful oligopolists—those who have achieved their position by accidental events or estimable endeavor—of the natural consequence of their position if the lawful monopolist is left with his'.[340] Third, 'to hold unlawful the charging of a monopoly price by a monopolist, or the maintaining of noncompetitive prices by oligopolists, would be to invoke a purely public-utility interpretation of the Sherman Act', which Turner found objectionable, as it is implausible to conclude that Congress intended the courts, under the Sherman Act, to act as price regulators for all businesses possessing substantial monopoly power'.[341] Finally, for Turner, it was futile to expect an injunction against oligopolistic pricing to be effective, as such an injunction would command the oligopolists to behave irrationally by ignoring the effect of a price cut by one seller on the price and output of the others, would transform courts to public utility commissions and would impose 'immense' practical problems, as the courts would have to enjoin undertakings to produce at marginal costs, which are either 'theoretically indeterminate', in particular in cases of joint products,[342] or 'practically indeterminate'.[343]

One may also note the criticisms of Rahl who argued for a requirement of proving an actual agreement for section 1 to apply, in view of the fact that the Sherman Act is a penal statute.[344]

Turner was conscious of the fact that market power created by jointly acting oligopolists may escape the scope of section 1 of the Sherman Act.[345] However, he objected to the application of section 1 of the Sherman Act, in view of the difficulty to devise a limiting principle to the prohibition rule. According to Turner,

337 Ibid, 666. 338 Ibid, 664–5. 339 Ibid, 666. 340 Ibid, 668. 341 Ibid, 669.

342 These are products that are produced from the same process or operation (ie, beef meat and leather) and therefore share a common marginal cost curve.

343 DF Turner, 'The Definition of Agreement Under the Sherman Act: Conscious Parallelism and Refusals to Deal' (1962) 75(4) *Harvard L Rev* 655, 670.

344 J Rahl, 'Price Competition and the Price Fixing Rule-Preface and Perspective' (1962) 57 *Northwestern University L Rev* 137, 147.

345 In his seminal work with Carl Kaysen, in 1959, he concluded as following: '[t]he principal defect of present antitrust law is its inability to cope with market power created by jointly acting oligopolists [. . .]. [W]e believe it is safe to say that a considerable number of industrial markets exist in which oligopolists, acting jointly, possess substantial degrees of market power, which they exercise without engaging in conduct violating the Sherman Act': C Kaysen and DF Turner, *Antitrust Policy: An Economic and Legal Analysis* (Harvard University Press, 1959), 110.

> [c]hanging conditions and a growing economic sophistication have put heavy pressures on a statute drafted with different circumstances and simpler conceptions in mind; and there have been the usual counter-pressures to keep a statute, particularly a statute that is criminal as well as civil, within at least some traditional bounds. Inevitably the courts have had to struggle with the unhappy dilemma of either drawing lines between different forms of conduct having virtually identical results, or treating different forms of conduct as being the same despite the differences.[346]

He nevertheless considered that other institutional alternatives may offer a solution to this 'oligopoly problem', in particular by attacking such conduct with an unlawful 'attempt to monopolize' under section 2 of the Sherman Act, or with a violation of section 5 of the FTC Act, which proscribes unfair methods of competition.[347] An active merger policy could also provide some prophylactic remedies to the emergence of oligopolies and oligopolistic inter-dependence.[348] By rejecting inter-dependence as a criterion for the definition of the concept of 'agreement' (collusion) under Section 1 of the Sherman Act, Turner indirectly favoured the view that would find 'agreement' only if there has been some form of communication between the undertakings in question.[349]

Turner's view was compatible with the Structure-Conduct-Performance School dominant at the time in US antitrust. This favoured structural remedies, the break-up of monopolies, and a more expansive enforcement of section 5 of the FTC Act and section 2 of the Sherman Act, also to situations of 'shared monopoly'. On the basis of this declaration of the inability of section 1 of the Sherman Act to deal with the 'oligopoly problem' and the difficulties of expanding the scope of both section 5 of the FTC Act and section 2 of the Sherman Act, the White House Task Force on Antitrust Policy (The Neal report in 1968),[350] and Industrial Reorganization Act proposed by Senator Philip Hart in 1972[351] suggested the targeted breakup of tightly oligopolistic industries, a prospect that was heavily opposed by antitrust conservatives, influenced by the Chicago School of antitrust economics, whose intellectual influence began to rise in the 1970s.[352]

Richard Posner, as the rest of the Chicago School, were largely opposing the more regulatory approach of breaking up oligopolies followed by the Neal report and Senator Hart, and advanced the view that the oligopoly problem should be dealt under section 1 of the Sherman Act with behavioural remedies, which was thought of as a more acceptable, because more

346 DF Turner, 'The Definition of Agreement Under the Sherman Act: Conscious Parallelism and Refusals to Deal' (1962) 75(4) Harvard L Rev 655, 656.

347 Ibid, 682. Turner, however, accepts the application of section 1 of the Sherman Act to 'agreements or understandings designed to convert an imperfect oligopoly pricing pattern into a perfect one by eliminating uncertainties'. Ibid, 673.

348 C Kaysen and DF Turner, *Antitrust Policy: An Economic and Legal Analysis* (Harvard University Press, 1959), 132–3.

349 In his article, Turner distinguished the situation of horizontal and vertical agreements, his criticism over a theory based on inter-dependence only applying to horizontal collusion.

350 PC Neal, WF Baxter, RH Bork, and CH Fulda, 'Report of the White House Task Force on Antitrust Policy' (1968) 2 *Antitrust L and Economics Rev* 11.

351 S. 3832, 92nd Congress, 2nd Session (1972).

352 Turner was an antitrust moderate and did not necessarily adhere to the approach of the Neal Report and the proposed legislation by Senator Hart. Yet, because his article raised the issue of the 'gap' in the enforcement of section 1 of the Sherman Act that had initiated this process of reform of competition laws towards the sense of de-concentration through specific anti-oligopoly legislation, it was attacked by the antitrust conservatives of the Chicago School, such as Richard Posner.

limited, form of State intervention, in comparison to the structural break-up favoured by Turner and the antitrust hawks. Drawing on the work of Chicago economist George Stigler on oligopoly theory,[353] who showed that there are incentives to undercut any above-competitive price, as a rival may 'cheat' by lowering prices so as to 'steal' market share from its competitors before being detected, Posner argued that 'voluntary actions by the sellers are necessary to translate the bare condition of an oligopoly market into a situation of noncompetitive pricing.'[354] According to Posner, 'the attractiveness and feasibility of a price-fixing scheme to the sellers in a market are limited by the costs of bargaining to agreement and of enforcing the agreement to prevent cheating.'[355] Hence, contrary to what was thought by Turner, the oligopolist has a 'real choice' as it is not irrational for him to decide to set a price that approximates marginal cost, this not being unprofitable in view of the lag between 'cheating' (lowering the price to marginal costs) and detection by the other cartelists.[356]

Against the fatalism of the structuralist approach followed by Turner, as the action of the undertakings was pre-determined by the situation of the market, Posner espoused a behavioural approach that emphasized the role of individual agency, even in the context of oligopolistic markets.[357] Posner concluded that 'oligopolists cannot be presumed always or often to charge supracompetitive prices' but '[l]ike atomistic sellers they must [. . .] collude in one fashion or another' and that it seems 'improbable that prices could long be maintained above cost in a market, even a highly oligopolistic one, without *some* explicit acts of communication and implementation.'[358] Such acts do not only comprise explicit acts of collusion or enforcement, but also a tacit understanding or other forms of 'tacit collusion'. For Posner, as 'tacit collusion' is 'voluntary behaviour', it should be punished by 'appropriate punishment', like express collusion, as it is as a form of concerted rather than unilateral activity.[359] Yet, for both forms of collusion, section 1 of the Sherman Act emerges as *prima facie* the appropriate remedy.

The main difference between 'explicit cartels' and 'tacit collusion' is that the latter may be more easily concealed, that is a question of proof.[360] Although he concedes that proving tacit collusion will be difficult, he provides a laundry list of factors that, according to him, may provide evidence of tacit collusion and non-competitive pricing.[361] Posner nevertheless notes that courts will have to exercise extreme care in drawing inferences of tacit collusion from conduct and suggests to 'limit inquiry by and large to conduct-how the firms behave-and more narrowly still to conduct from which an absence of effective competition can be inferred: cartel-like conduct'. Turner's argument on the absence of an appropriate remedy under section 1 of the Sherman Act is also rejected as not being fatal to a rule forbidding tacit collusion under section 1 of the Sherman Act, in view of the deterrence provided by private treble-damage actions and other section 1 behavioural remedies. Posner criticized, however, structural remedies, such as the break-up of oligopolies, imposed either through specific legislation or through a more active merger policy against horizontal mergers.[362] In conclusion,

[353] GJ Stigler, 'A Theory of Oligopoly' (1964) 72(1) *J Political Economy* 44.

[354] RA Posner, 'Oligopoly and the Antitrust Laws: A Suggested Approach' (1969) 21 *Stanford L Rev* 1562, 1575.

[355] Ibid, 1571. [356] Ibid.

[357] Ibid, 1592, noting that '[t]acit collusion is not an unconscious state'. [358] Ibid, 1574.

[359] Posner was thus able to infer a 'meeting of the minds', referring to game theory. Through the element of conflict, mutual dependence, kind of collaboration and mutual accommodation the oligopoly 'game' leads undertakings to communicate by hint and by suggestive behaviour. RA Posner, 'Oligopoly and the Antitrust Laws: A Suggested Approach' (1968) 21 *Stanford L Rev* 1562, 1576 n 39.

[360] Ibid, 1575. [361] The different factors he takes into account are examined in Chapter 11.

[362] It is interesting to note Posner's assumptions justifying his preference for behavioural remedies: the fact that 'behavioral and prophylactic antitrust remedies such as penalties and injunction are swift and relatively

for Posner, 'if a firm raises price in the expectation that its competitors will do likewise, and they do, the firm's behavior can be conceptualized as the offer of a unilateral contract that the offerees accept by raising their prices.'[363]

The interpretation of section 1 of the Sherman Act by US courts has moved to a certain extent in the direction of Turner, although taking a more conservative approach as to the reach of US antitrust law in situations of 'tacit collusion'. Although in its seminal case *American Tobacco* in 1946 the US Supreme Court took a broad perspective on the concept of collusion, establishing the basis for an unlawful conspiracy to be inferred circumstantially from the conduct of the relevant oligopolists without direct evidence of formal agreements,[364] the Court refused so far to expand the scope of section 1 of the Sherman Act in order to cover 'mere interdependence' or 'tacit collusion'.[365] US antitrust law has not also taken the complementary steps suggested by Turner in order to fill this perceived 'gap', as some efforts to use section 5 of the FTC Act against 'shared monopoly' failed.[366] Yet, it is possible to bring in a Section 5 FTC case against 'facilitating practices' even in the absence of proof of conspiracy or, more generally communication, if conscious parallelism produces anti-competitive effects, under certain specific circumstances[367].

Why is this American debate over the scope of Section 1 of the Sherman Act relevant for EU competition law?

First, because the Turner–Posner discussion has exercised some influence on EU competition law. The discussion was ignited by an important judgment of the CJEU in the *ICI-Dyestuffs* case in which the CJEU explained that the prohibition of concerted practices under Article 101 TFEU has 'the object [. . .] to bring within the prohibition of that article a form of coordination between undertakings which, without having reached the stage where an agreement properly so-called has been concluded, knowingly substitutes practical cooperation between them for the risks of competition'.[368] As previously noted, the Court explained in this case that '[a]lthough parallel behavior may not itself be identified with a

costless compared to dissolution proceedings' and the idea that that market processes will usually eliminate an unmeritorious (single or joint) monopoly position: RA Posner, 'Oligopoly and the Antitrust Laws: A Suggested Approach' (1968) 21 *Stanford L Rev* 1562, 1597–8.

363 *In Re High Fructose Corn Syrup Antitrust Litigation Appeal of A & W Bottling Inc et al, US Court of Appeals*, 295 F.3d 652 (7th Cir 2002).

364 *American Tobacco Co v United States*, 328 US 781, 810 (1946), noting that conspiracy requires only 'a unity of purpose or a common design and understanding, or a meeting of minds in an unlawful arrangement'. See also *Interstate Circuit v United States*, 306 US 208, 226–7 (1939).

365 See eg *Theatre Enterprises v Paramount Film Distribution Corp*, 346 US 537 (1954); *Bell Atlantic Corp v Twombly*, 550 US 544, 554 (2007), the Supreme Court noting that 'the inadequacy of showing parallel conduct or interdependence, without more, mirrors the ambiguity of the behaviour, consistent with conspiracy, but just as much in line with a wide swath of rational and competitive business strategy unilaterally prompted by common perceptions of the market'. Furthermore, the Court has created a number of procedural hurdles to 'hedge against false inferences from identical behaviour at a number of points in the trial sequence'.

366 See, for instance, the Breakfast cereal case brought by the FTC in 1972 against the breakfast cereal oligopoly, alleging that the undertakings in question enjoyed a 'structural shared monopoly' position, maintained through the erection of barriers to entry by a number of marketing strategies employed by all the undertakings, such as the proliferation of brands or the promotion of trademarks through intensive advertising. The case was finally dismissed in 1981, following political opposition in Congress and by the Reagan administration.

367 See eg *EI Du Pont de Nemours & Co v FTC*, 729 F.2d 128 (2nd Cir 1984), where although the court of appeal dismissed the case, it acknowledged that section 5 of the FTC Act can be violated by 'non-collusive, non-predatory and independent conduct of a non-artificial nature, at least when it results in a substantial lessening of competition if "some indicial of oppressiveness" exist, such as evidence of anti-competitive intent, or the absence of an independent legitimate business reason for the conduct'.

368 Case 48/69, *Imperial Chemical Industries Ltd v Commission (Dyestuffs)* [1972] ECR 619, para 64.

concerted practice, it may however amount to strong evidence of such a practice if it leads to conditions of competition which do not respond to the normal conditions of the market [...]' and added that '[t]his is especially the case if the parallel conduct is such as to enable those concerned to stabilize prices at a level different from that to which competition would have led'.[369] Although the Court, and its Advocate General, did not refer to the Turner and Posner debate, and provided no detailed explanation for the rule, a number of commentators strongly criticised the Court's position, by proffering similar arguments than those used by Turner, on the grounds that CJEU's broad formulation opened the possibility that conscious parallelism may be qualified to concerted practice.[370]

A more frontal attack to this case law came from scholars insisting on the risks and perils of the more effects-based approach that presumably the CJEU adopted in *ICI-Dyestuffs* to the institutional structure of the EU system of protecting competition. According to them, this requires a 'rule-oriented approach' that would rely on evidence of the culpability of the competition law infringer (involving proof of an element of anti-competitive intent), rather than a 'result-oriented' approach, that would ignore the culpability of the parties involved and would focus merely on the effects of their behaviour.[371] It is reminded that at the time of the Court's judgment, there were no other institutional alternatives in EU competition law to deal with the issue of 'conscious' parallel pricing either in the context of Article 102 TFEU, the concept of collective dominant position making its appearance in EU competition law much later, and in the absence of a provision, such as section 5 of the FTC Act. The position of the CJEU may also be explained by the opposition of some national courts in interpreting their national competition law, to less formalism in the interpretation of the concept of collusion in competition law.[372]

369 Ibid, para 65–6.

370 See, for instance, the strong criticisms of R Joliet, 'Notion de pratique concertée et l'arrêt I.C.I dans une perspective comparative' (1974) 3(4) *Cahier de droit européen* 249; V Korah, 'Concerted Practices' (1973) 36 *Modern L Rev* 220. Both of these authors referred to the position of Turner, while ignoring that of Posner. These criticisms were somehow overstretched. As it is rightly noted by JM Joshua and S Jordan, 'Combinations, Concerted Practices and Cartels: Adopting the Concept of Conspiracy in European Community Competition Law Symposium on European Competition Law' (2004) 24(3) *Northwestern J Int'l L & Business* 647, 665, '[...] the Court's broad dictum has to be read in context: the judgment made it clear that standing on its own conscious parallelism could not be found unlawful'.

371 MR Pfeifer, 'Uniform Pricing in Concentrated Markets: Is Conscious Parallelism Prohibited by Article 85(1) of the Treaty of Rome' (1974) 7(2) *Cornell Int'l L J* 113, 120, '[t]here are two ways to regulate competition among enterprises. One may be termed a rule-oriented approach, the other a result-oriented approach. An interpretation of "concerted practice" requiring the Commission to prove that uniform pricing activities are the result of anticompetitive intent is most compatible with a rule-oriented approach. An interpretation which permits the Commission to impose a form of strict liability for uniform pricing practices best comports with a result-oriented approach.'

372 See, for instance, the position in Germany at the time, where the Federal Supreme Court held that an agreement within the meaning of section 1 of the German Act against restraints of competition (GWB) at the time could not be found to exist if the constituent elements of a private law contract were present. Initially, the 1973 Amendment of the GWB did not propose to prohibit concerted practices and suggested the use of section 22(2) of the Act on the abuse of a shared market dominating position to deal with this issue. This provision, or at least its interpretation at the time, provided only for a prohibition of abuses and does not touch on concerted action itself. However, 'at the last minute' the German Parliament enacted a prohibition of concerted action by adopting section 25(1) of the Act, according to which 'a concerted action of enterprises and association of enterprises which under this law may not be made the subject of a contractual restraint is prohibited'. For a discussion, see E-J Mestmäcker, 'Competition Policy and Antitrust: Some Comparative Observations' (1980) 136(3) *J Institutional and Theoretical Economics* 387, 395–6.

Subsequently, the CJEU moved to a position closer to that defended by Turner. In the *Sugar* case, although the CJEU rejected the idea that the concept of concerted practices presupposes 'a plan and the aim of removing in advance any doubt as to the future conduct of competitors' and found that collusion does not cover 'independent' behaviour, it also noted that 'this requirement of independence does not deprive economic operators of the right to adapt themselves intelligently to the existing and anticipated conduct of their competitors', thus raising some doubts as to the inclusion of conscious parallelism resulting from oligopolistic interdependence to the scope of the collusion element under Article 101(1) TFEU.[373] The Court drew the line between collusion and independent behaviour at 'direct or indirect contact [. . .] the object whereof is either to influence the conduct on the market of an actual or potential competitor or to disclose to such a competitor the course which they themselves have decided to adopt or contemplate adopting in the market'.[374] The Court seemed therefore open to attack oligopolistic interdependence, but only in the presence of some 'facilitating device', if we borrow from the US antitrust jargon, for instance the existence of direct or indirect contacts between competitors.[375]

In *Woodpulp II*, the CJEU moved even further towards the direction of Turner, by introducing a sort of oligopoly defence to the finding of collusion. Notwithstanding the presence of advance price announcements and the universal adoption of a basing point system, which could have facilitated the uniform price increases among the main producers supplying the Community pulp market, the CJEU annulled the Commission's findings, finding that concertation between competitors was not the only plausible explanation for the parallel conduct, which was explained by the high degree of market transparency and by the oligopolistic tendencies of the market as well as by the specific circumstances prevailing in certain periods.[376] 'Unnatural' parallel conduct therefore plays an evidential role as a 'form of economic evidence that substitutes for direct documentation of overt communication',[377] although it does not substitute for the requirement of conscious parallelism.

Since the *Woodpulp* case, it has become more difficult to attack tacit collusion with Article 101 TFEU, even indirectly through facilitating practices, although the Court's approach towards some type of facilitating practices of collusion, such as information exchange between competitors or Resale Price Maintenance clauses between suppliers and distributors, is rather strict, these practices being found anti-competitive by object. One should distinguish nevertheless between the cases where facilitating practices are assessed as a restriction of competition, and the cases where facilitating practices are considered as evidence of collusion. The point is clearly made by Kaplow:

> Facilitating practices may be relevant under competition law in two ways. First, their use provides a basis for inferring the existence of oligopolistic coordination. This inference is sensible when there exists no other plausible explanation for the practice. In contrast, practices

[373] Joined Cases 40–8, 50, 54–6, 111 & 113–14/73, *Re the European Sugar Cartel: Cooperatieve Vereniging 'Suiker Unie' UA v Commission* [1975] ECR 1663, paras 173–4.

[374] Ibid, para 174.

[375] JM Joshua and S Jordan, 'Combinations, Concerted Practices and Cartels: Adopting the Concept of Conspiracy in European Community Competition Law Symposium on European Competition Law' (2004) 24(3) *Northwestern J Int'l L & Business* 647, 658.

[376] Joined Cases C-89/85 etc, *Woodpulp II* [1993] ECR I–1307, para 126.

[377] JE Harrington, 'Developing Competition Law for Collusion by Autonomous Artificial Agents' (17 April 2018), 28 (on file with author).

that may facilitate oligopolistic interdependence but would likely be employed regardless are not directly probative. Second, facilitating practices may themselves be made a basis for liability.[378]

While EU competition law seems to have restricted, since the *Woodpulp* case, the first route, it seems more open to take the second route, at least with regard to some types of practices.

Second, it is clear that the issues raised by Turner and Posner with regard to the definition of collusion still haunt competition law scholarship and jurisprudence, at both sides of the Atlantic, but also beyond. The following excerpt describes what is at stake.

JE Harrington, Jr, 'Exploring the Boundaries of Unlawful Collusion: Price Coordination when Firms Lack Full Mutual Understanding', Working Paper (2012), 2

Given that mutual understanding is not something that is directly observed, the judicial approach is to focus on communications among firms and to infer a level of mutual understanding from those communications (while possibly supplementing it with market outcomes in drawing those inferences). From this assessment, the courts seek to determine whether the level of mutual understanding among firm is sufficient to produce (or have the capability to produce) coordinated behavior and thereby to be deemed an unlawful agreement. Express communication among firms involving an exchange of assurances (for example, one firm proposes to raise price and the other firm affirms) is clearly viewed as sufficient to conclude that firms have a 'meeting of minds' intended to produce a supracompetitive outcome. The real challenge is evaluating situations in which firms do not engage in such egregious and straightforward means for delivering the requisite mutual understanding.

Professor Louis Kaplow from Harvard University, criticized the 'communication-based' approach in defining collusion/agreement.[379] Kaplow advanced a different approach relying on game theory in order to infer a meeting of minds from oligopolistic interdependence, under certain circumstances.[380] He notes that in an infinitely repeated game, firms may develop strategic thinking allowing them to sustain a non-competitive price by predicting the equilibrium price, not by communicating with their competitors, but by simply relying on a general knowledge of the market and engaging in strategic estimation of their competitors' choice among a range of possible equilibria, their rivals' actions being also largely determined by their own strategic predictions as to the actions of their rivals, and so on. The selection of this non-competitive equilibrium is considered as an intersubjective process of mutual understanding among firms that price increases will be at least matched, which may give rise to a meeting of the minds and, consequently, collusion. Kaplow goes as far as denying that communication

378 L Kaplow, *Competition Policy and Price Fixing* (Harvard University Press, 2013), 276.

379 Ibid.

380 Ibid, 38–9, noting that 'interdependent behaviour [. . .] is taken to refer to behaviour that involves coordination with others [. . .] [T]he though process involved in such cases is iterative. One party is thinking about what the other is thinking: the second is thinking about what it is thinking, ad infinitum. This subjective state is commonly termed a meeting of the minds [. . .] In game-theoretic parlance, the situation constitutes an equilibrium.'

should be part of the definition of agreement or required for proof of collusion, focusing instead on the following question: are rivals behaving noncompetitively because they have achieved a meeting of minds about their course of action, or are they doing so because they are unilaterally pursuing the same profit-maximizing strategies?[381] Kaplow thus takes an effects-based approach in defining the scope of the collusion concept and links it to the issue of determining the pro or anti-competitive level of prices, which is an issue usually examined when determining the existence of a restriction of competition. By doing so, Kaplow emphasizes the need for a nexus between the requirement of collusion, which is a condition for the application of the prohibition rule, and the social harm that motivates the prohibition, for instance the social harm resulting from the elevation of prices as a result of the collusion. He questions the link between the communications-based approach and the social harm of collusion, by raising the 'paradox of proof'.

As we have briefly explained above, and will be exploring in more detail in Chapter 11, under the current communications-based approach adopted by both EU and US antitrust law, if the parallel behaviour of the undertakings in the market may be explained by the oligopolistic nature of the market, there is no collusion, as the behaviour of the undertakings is deemed a natural consequence of the competitive interplay in tight and transparent oligopoly markets. Kaplow finds that the communications-based prohibition is paradoxical, 'in the sense that it assigns liability to cases of moderate danger while exonerating defendants in cases posing the highest threat: where the expected likelihood, magnitude, and longevity of price elevation are the greatest'.[382] In contrast, an approach that will focus on the effects of the interaction between firms in an oligopolistic setting, when determining the existence of collusion, will escape the paradox as it will put the social objective motivating the legal prohibition at the centre of the analysis. Such an approach will certainly be incompatible with the 'jurisdictional' view of the concepts of agreement, concerted practice and decision of association of undertakings, as it will link the interpretation of the element of collusion to that of restriction of competition.

Notwithstanding the flexible interpretation of the collusion element of Article 101 TFEU and Chapter I CA98 by the EU and UK competition law enforcers, which challenged the view that it has a purely jurisdictional function, and the indirect influence of substantive legal policies in framing the concepts of 'agreement', 'concerted practice', and 'decision of association of undertakings', both EU and UK competition law have refused so far to consider, in a more direct way, the nexus between the concept of collusion and that of restriction of competition, for instance by developing a separate approach/definition for vertical collusion, as opposed to horizontal collusion, or offering a specific view of collusion in the context of oligopoly markets. The definition of the various forms of concertation under Article 101 TFEU and Chapter I CA98 applies horizontally, regardless of the type of commercial relation between the undertakings involved, the nature of the industry, or the prevailing market structure. One

381 Yet, Kaplow excludes mutual understanding over several equilibria from his suggested definition of collusion, even if there are achieved through a meeting of minds between oligopolists, in view of the possibility of errors. For instance, competitive equilibria should not be caught by section 1, even in the presence of a meeting of minds as enforcement should be limited to instances in which an undertaking has significantly elevated prices. This is also the case for certain non-competitive equilibria, such as monopoly pricing, which is tolerated in US antitrust law, Cournot oligopolies, which are one-shot games and thus cannot be classified as involving interdependent conduct, and Bertrand oligopolies, where firms sell differentiated products at prices above marginal cost, as this sort of pricing is independent, because each seller takes the actions of its rivals as given.

382 L Kaplow, *Competition Policy and Price Fixing* (Harvard University Press, 2013), 405.

may criticize this approach for ignoring the necessary nexus between the various elements of the prohibition rule in order to achieve more effectively the aims of Article 101 TFEU and/or Chapter I CA98.

Important developments in the global economy have shifted the structure of various industries towards rising levels of concentration: the large waves of mergers, acquisitions and take-overs, following the liberalisation of markets and the retreat of State monopolies in various economic sectors, the growing importance of financial capital with the recent 'rise of distorporation', major industrial empires being controlled by master limited partnerships (MLP) managed by a few global big-equity companies and institutional investors,[383] the global expansion of intellectual property rights and the need for extensive levels of cooperation between global competitors through cross-licensing arrangements or patent pools, the development of the Internet and consequently the importance of network effects and platform competition, have led to unprecedented levels of corporate consolidation at a global scale. Increasing levels of market concentration have become the rule, rather than the exception in various sectors of the American and European industry, in crucial, from a social welfare perspective, sectors such as agriculture, retailing, automobiles, banking and a number of manufacturing industries.[384] This is a very different environment than that at the time of the drafting of the EU Treaties, even more at the time of drafting of the US Sherman Act, when the levels of consolidation of various industries, in Europe, the US, and globally were not as important. This should not be considered as an argument for competition law intervention, but one may advance the view that oligopoly markets raise problems of their own. This is a topic we will explore in Chapter 11.

Advances in communication technologies may also change the dynamics of collusion. Information on prices, but also future pricing trends may be posted on web sites, making price signalling easier. Firm representatives may communicate through 'facially anonymous' blogs and chat-rooms or web-casts, enabling instant and less traceable communication, than 'old-fashioned' press conferences, conference meetings in 'smoke-filled rooms', etc.[385] Price fixing through algorithms may replace more classic forms of collusion. This may render detection more difficult for competition authorities which are, at the same time, subject to more extensive due process requirements, as a result of the extension of human/fundamental rights protection for corporate defendants. Other advances in communications, such as e-mails or digitilization, which facilitate record-keeping may assist competition authorities in the detection of collusive practices.

Firms' pricing decisions have also been increasingly delegated to software programs that incorporate the latest developments of artificial intelligence. But it is the most recent second

383 'Rise of the Distorporation', *The Economist* (26 October 2013). A recent study has also raised the related issue of horizontal shareholdings, a small group of institutions having acquired large shareholdings in horizontal competitors throughout various economic sectors, causing them to compete less vigorously with each other: E Elhauge, 'Horizontal Shareholding' (2016) 109 *Harvard L Rev* 1267. The author provides, among others, the example of the US airline industry, noting that 'from 2013-15, seven shareholders who controlled 60% of United Airlines also controlled big chunks of United's major rivals, including 27.5% of Delta Airlines, 22.3% of Southwest Airlines, and 20.7% of JetBlue Airlines. More generally, 77% of all airline stock is owned by institutional investors' and refers to an econometric study showing that 'this sort of horizontal shareholding has made average airline prices 3–10% higher than they otherwise would have been'.

384 For a number of examples drawing on the US markets, see B Linn, *Cornered: The New Monopoly Capitalism and the Economics of Destruction* (Wiley, 2010); White House Council of Economic Advisers Issue Brief, Benefits of Competition and Indicators of Market Power (April 2016).

385 L Kaplow, *Competition Policy and Price Fixing* (Harvard University Press, 2013), 437–8.

generation 'learning' pricing algorithms that pose concerns for the possible application of Article 101 TFEU. Calvano et al distinguish between two types of algorithms.[386] First-generation 'adaptive' pricing algorithms are those for which 'humans set rules that dictate optimal responses to specific contingencies', therefore leaving a detectable trace of human interaction and/or communication that could normally establish the existence of a meeting of minds and antitrust collusion in the traditional sense. Second-generation 'learning' pricing algorithms are largely based on neural networks, machine and deep learning, providing 'intelligent' algorithms the ability to learn that collusion is the most profitable strategy, even if they have not been specifically be designed to collude, and without any human intervention. These algorithms may also learn how to collude in the most effective (that is undetectable by competition authorities) way,[387] as they may learn to read the 'intentions' of the other 'intelligent' algorithms employed by competing undertakings.[388] For such algorithms, the traditional communications-based approach adopted in competition law may not work. Various regulatory options may be put forward: (i) take a wait and see approach collecting evidence about the real occurrence of algorithmic pricing and the risks for collusion; (ii) prohibit algorithmic pricing (a quite extreme option as pricing algorithms may also improve pricing decisions to the benefit of consumers); (iii) regulate price algorithms *ex ante* with some form of notification requirement and prior analysis by the Commission or national competition authorities, eventually using the procedure of regulatory sandbox;[389] and (iv) we may want to regulate them *ex post* through the application of competition law, although this time abandoning the classic communications-based approach to collusion for a different approach.[390] One may thus raise the question of the adequacy of the current legal framework in defining collusion under Article 101 TFEU and Chapter I CA98 with current market and technology realities.

SELECTIVE BIBLIOGRAPHY

Books

Ezrachi, A, and Stucke, M, *Virtual Competition* (Harvard University Press, 2016).

Filippelli, M, *Collective Dominance and Collusion: Parallelism in EU and US Competition Law* (Edward Elgar, 2013).

Harding, C, and Edwards, J, *Cartel Criminality: The Mythology and Pathology of Business Collusion* (Ashgate, 2015).

386 E Calvano, G Calzolari, V Denicolò, and S Pastorello, 'Algorithmic Pricing and Collusion: What Implications for Competition Policy?' (5 March 2018) (on file with author).

387 Competition authorities may also employ algorithms to unveil digital cartels, so it is difficult to predict who will be one step ahead from a technology perspective.

388 See B Salcedo, 'Pricing Algorithms and Tacit Collusion' (11 January 2015), available at http://brunosalcedo.com/docs/collusion.pdf

389 See A Ezrachi and ME Stucke, *Virtual Competition: The Promise and Perils of the Algorithm-Driven Economy* (Harvard University Press, 2016).

390 See JE Harrington, 'Developing Competition Law for Collusion by Autonomous Artificial Agents' (17 April 2018) (on file with author) (the author defines collusion as 'collusion is the situation when firms use strategies that embody a reward–punishment scheme which rewards a firm for abiding by the supracompetitive outcome and punishes it for departing from it'. The study defines liability and evidentiary standards for the application of competition law to collusion by autonomous agents).

Kaplow, L, *Competition Policy and Price Fixing* (Harvard University Press, 2013).

Marshall, RC, and Marx, LM, *The Economics of Collusion* (MIT Press, 2012).

Motta, M, *Competition Policy: Theory and Practice* (CUP, 1st ed, 2004).

Chapters in books

Odudu, O, 'Hub and Spoke Collusion' in Lianos, I and Geradin, D (eds) *Handbook on European Competition Law* (Edward Elgar, 2013).

Page, WH, 'Facilitating practices and concerted action under Section 1 of the Sherman Act' in Hylton, KN (ed) *Antitrust Law and Economics* (Edward Elgar, 2010).

Journal articles

Bailey, D, 'Single, Overall Agreement in EU Competition Law' (2010) 47 *Common Market L Rev* 473.

Elhauge, E, 'Horizontal Shareholding' (2016) 109 *Harvard L Rev* 1267.

Ghezzi, F, and, Maggiolino, M, 'Bridging EU Concerted Practices with U.S. Concerted Actions' (2014) 10 *J Competition L and Economics* 647.

Hay, G, 'Horizontal Agreements: Concept and Proof' (2006) 51(4) *Antitrust Bulletin* 877.

Hay, G, 'The Meaning of "Agreement" under the Sherman Act: Thoughts from the Facilitating Practices Experience' (2000) 16 *Rev Industrial Organization* 113.

Joliet, R, 'Notion de pratique concertée et l'arrêt I.C.I dans une perspective comparative' (1974) *Cahier de droit européen* 249.

Joshua, JM, and Jordan, S, 'Combinations, Concerted Practices and Cartels: Adopting the Concept of Conspiracy in European Community Competition Law Symposium on European Competition Law' (2004) 24 *Northwestern J Int'l L & Business* 647.

Lianos, I, 'Collusion in Vertical Relations under Article 81 EC' (2008) 45 *Common Market L Rev* 1027.

Martyniszyn, M, 'A Comparative Look at Foreign State Compulsion as a Defence in Antitrust Litigation' (2012) 8(2) *Competition L Rev* 143.

Odudu, O, 'Indirect Information Exchange: the Constituent Elements of Hub and Spoke Collusion' (2011) 7(2) *European Competition J* 205.

Riley, A, 'Revisiting the Single and continuous Infringement of Article 101: The Significance of ANIC in a New Era of Cartel Detection and Analysis' (2014) 37 *World Competition* 293.

Sahuguet, N, and Walckiers, A, 'Hub-and-Spoke Conspiracies: the Vertical Expression of a Horizontal Desire?' (2014) 5(10) *J European Competition L & Practice* 711.

Scordamaglia, A, 'Cartel Proof, Imputation and Sanctioning in European Competition Law: Reconciling Effective Enforcement and Adequate Protection of Procedural Guarantees' (2010) 7(1) *Competition L Rev* 5.

Siciliani, P, 'Should We Act *ex post* Against Tacit Collusion—and How?' (2014) 5 *J European Competition L & Practice* 26.

Stigler, GJ, 'A Theory of Oligopoly' (1964) 72(1) *J Political Economy* 44.

Turner, DF, 'The Definition of Agreement Under the Sherman Act: Conscious Parallelism and Refusals to Deal' (1962) 75 *Harvard L Rev* 655.

Werden, GJ, Economic Evidence on the Existence of Collusion: Reconciling Antitrust Law with Oligopoly Theory' (2004) 71(3) *Antitrust LJ* 719.

Whelan, P, '*CISAC*: How Difficult it is to Prove a Concerted Practice' (2013) 4 *J European Competition L & Practice* 486.

Zampa, GL, and Buccirossi, P, 'Hub and Spoke Practices: Law and Economics of the New Antitrust Frontier?' (2013) 9 *Competition Policy Int'l* 91.

6

THE ELEMENTS OF ARTICLE 101 TFEU/CHAPTER I OF THE UK COMPETITION ACT 1998: RESTRICTION OF COMPETITION

6.1. FOUNDATIONS

The finding of an infringement of Articles 101 of the Treaty on the Functioning of the European Union (TFEU) and Chapter I if the UK Competition Act 1998 (CA98) requires evidence that the agreement, concerted practice or decisions of association of undertakings (the *collusion* element), has as its *object* or *effect* the prevention, restriction or distortion of competition within the Internal Market, without that being justified by the exception regime, either under Article 101(3) TFEU, or sections 4, 9, and 10 of Chapter I CA98 (the *restriction of competition* element), and of course affects inter-State trade or is implemented in the UK (the *geographic* element). This Chapter focuses on the element of restriction of competition.

Article 101(1) TFEU stipulates that 'shall be prohibited as incompatible with the internal market: all agreements between undertakings, decisions by associations of undertakings and concerted practices which may affect trade between Member States and which have as their object or effect the prevention, restriction or distortion of competition within the internal market'. Article 101(3) TFEU establishes an exception to this prohibition by stipulating that the provisions of Article 101(1) TFEU, however, may be declared inapplicable if the collusive conduct in question contributes to (i) improving the production or distribution of goods or to promoting technical or economic progress, while (ii) allowing consumers a fair share of the resulting benefit, and which (iii) does not impose on the undertakings concerned restrictions which are not indispensable to the attainment of these objectives (iv) afford such undertakings the possibility of eliminating competition in respect of a substantial part of the products in question.

Chapter I CA98 has a similar structure and uses similar language. According to section 2(1) of the Act, 'agreements between undertakings, decisions by associations of undertakings or concerted practices which '(a) may affect trade within the United Kingdom, and (b) have as their object or effect the prevention, restriction or distortion of competition within the United Kingdom, are prohibited unless they are exempt in accordance with the provisions of this Part'. Section 3 of the Act provides for exclusions from the Chapter I prohibition,[1] while section 9 of the Act refers to the possibility of an individual exemption (also referred to in section 4) from the prohibition principle of any agreement which (a) contributes to

(i) improving production or distribution, or
(ii) promoting technical or economic progress, while allowing consumers a fair share of the resulting benefit;

but (b) does not

(i) impose on the undertakings concerned restrictions which are not indispensable to the attainment of those objectives; or
(ii) afford the undertakings concerned the possibility of eliminating competition in respect of a substantial part of the products in question.

Furthermore, section 6 CA98 provides the possibility for the Secretary of State to issue a 'block exemption order' following the recommendation by the CMA that the category of agreements included in the order satisfies the conditions of an exemption under section 9. Section 10 stipulates a system of 'parallel exemptions', according to which an agreement is exempt from the Chapter I prohibition if it is exempt from the prohibition of Article 101(1) TFEU, for instance, by virtue of a (block exemption) regulation, or because it has been given an individual exemption by the Commission.

The first implementing Regulation 17/1962[2] governed how the then Treaty establishing the European Community's (TEC) provisions on anti-competitive agreements and abuses of dominant position were enforced, until the 'modernization' of the EU competition policy,[3] with the implementation of Regulation 1/2003.[4] Regulation 1/2003 transformed the previous legal authorization system under Regulation 17/62 into a legal exception regime,

[1] See analysis in Section 4.2.5.

[2] Council Regulation No 17 (EEC): First Regulation implementing Articles 85 and 86 of the Treaty [1962] OJ 13/204.

[3] On the process of modernization, see White Paper on the Modernisation of the Rules implementing Articles 85 and 86 of the EC Treaty [1999] OJ C 132/1; For an analysis, see R Wesseling, *The Modernisation of EC Antitrust Law* (Hart, 2010).

[4] Council Regulation (EC) No 1/2003 of 16 December 2002 on the implementation of the rules on competition laid down in Articles 81 and 82 of the Treaty [2003] OJ L 1/1, as amended by Council Regulation (EC) No 411/2004 of 26 February 2004 repealing Regulation (EEC) No 3975/87 and amending Regulations (EEC) No 3976/87 and (EC) No 1/2003, in connection with air transport between the Community and third countries [2004] OJ L 68/1 and Council Regulation (EC) No 1419/2006 of 25 September 2006 repealing Regulation (EEC) No 4056/86 laying down detailed rules for the application of Articles 85 and 86 of the Treaty to maritime transport, and amending Regulation (EC) No 1/2003 as regards the extension of its scope to include cabotage and international tramp services [2006] OJ L 269/1.

where practices are found illegal only after a thorough analysis of their possible negative and positive effects to competition by the competition authorities and courts. The legal authorization regime relied on one integrated administrative authority, the European Commission, which alone had the possibility of implementing Article 101(3) TFEU, either by adopting individual exemptions, when the parties notified to it their agreement, or by issuing block exemption regulations. Parties to an agreement could also request negative clearance by the Commission certifying that their agreement did not infringe Article 101(1) TFEU. Although national courts could apply Article 101(1) TFEU, they did not have the power to implement Article 101(3) TFEU, as any exemption to the prohibition principle had to be authorized by the European Commission, this leading to a centralized enforcement system.

The legal exception regime, introduced by the implementing Regulation 1/2003, includes as full and equal actors in the enforcement process, national courts and national competition authorities, thus ending the legal monopoly of the European Commission in applying Article 101(3) TFEU. Although the reform of Regulation 1/2003 emphasized changes of procedural or, more broadly, institutional structure, its impact has been extremely important with regard to issues of evidence and proof of anti-competitive practices, as well as of substantive law.[5]

The Regulation abolished the system of prior authorization and centralized notification in favour of a directly applicable exception system with the stated objective of creating a more focused and efficient system of enforcement in which national competition authorities and courts would play a prominent role. The prior authorization and centralized notification system, which conferred on the Commission a monopoly in applying Article 101(3) TFEU, imposed excessive burdens on both companies and the Commission and had become unworkable in practice. Its abolition and replacement by a directly applicable exception system was therefore welcomed and has enabled the Commission to pursue a more proactive enforcement agenda. The system of notification of the agreements to the Commission was also gradually abandoned,[6] as it was no longer sustainable and prevented the Commission from engaging in investigations concerning 'serious' antitrust infringements.[7] Following the implementation of Regulation 1/2003 and the abolition of the notification system, the UK legislator also repealed sections 4, 5, and 12–16 of Chapter I CA98 which dealt with the notification of agreements under UK competition law.

[5] The distinction between an issue of evidence and one of substantive law issue may not be common in Continental civil law systems, but is well accepted in common law jurisdictions.

[6] The first step was Council Regulation (EC) No 1216/1999 of 10 June 1999 amending Regulation No 17: first Regulation implementing Articles 81 and 82 of the Treaty [1999] OJ L 148/5, which broadened the scope of the application of Article 4(2) of Regulation No 17/62, thus exempting all vertical agreements from the requirement that they be notified to the Commission prior to individual exemption. The notification system was finally set aside by the implementation of Regulation 1/2003.

[7] See White Paper on the Modernisation of the rules implementing Articles 85 and 85 of the EC Treaty [1999] OJ C132/1, paras 3–5. For commentary, see eg J Venit, 'Brave New World: The Modernisation and Decentralisation of Enforcement under Articles 81 and 82 EC Treaty' (2003) 40 *Common Market L Rev* 545, 55–6. See also C-D Ehlermann, 'The Modernisation of EC Antitrust Policy: A Legal and Cultural Revolution' (2000) 37 *Common Market L Rev* 537, 540, 544–5; R Wesseling, *The Modernisation of EC Antitrust Law* (Hart, 2001); A Riley, 'EC Antitrust Modernisation: The Commission Does Very Nicely, Thank You!—Part I' (2003) 24(11) *European Competition L Rev* 604; A Riley, 'EC Antitrust Modernisation: The Commission Does Very Nicely, Thank You!—Part II' (2003) 24(12) *European Competition L Rev* 657.

6.2. RULES, STANDARDS, AND THE CONCEPT OF RESTRICTION OF COMPETITION: A PERSPECTIVE OF DECISION THEORY

The respective role of paragraphs 1 and 3 of Article 101 TFEU in the assessment of agreements (refer to agreements, concerted practices, and decisions of associations of undertakings for reasons of brevity), has been at the centre of attention, at least until the implementation of Regulation 1/2003 in May 2004. One of the hot topics explored by competition law literature at the time was the introduction of a 'rule of reason', like the one followed in US antitrust law,[8] in the context of Article 101(1) TFEU that would qualify the *prima facie* finding of a restriction of competition and would enable the courts and competition authorities to take into account possible justifications for the restriction in question. Many authors criticized the 'formalistic' reasoning of the Commission, which had, according to them, adopted a very narrow approach in interpreting Article 101(1) TFEU, basically finding that any significant restriction of the freedom of the parties to an agreement would amount to a restriction of competition that fell within the scope of Article 101 TFEU's prohibition principle and could only be 'exempted' under Article 101(3) TFEU.[9] The institutional implication of such narrow view of the concept of restriction of competition is that the Commission, which had the monopoly of implementing Article 101(3) TFEU before Regulation 1/2003, would be the only institution able to determine and implement the policy analysis that is usually employed in the context of Article 101(3) TFEU.

In retrospect, one may advance two possible explanations for this approach: (i) the Commission was driven by the need to preserve the coherence and uniform application of EU competition law and policy, which could be jeopardized if national courts and/or authorities were able to justify a number of agreements under Article 101(1) TFEU, for which they shared the competence to implement with the European Commission; (ii) the Commission thought that a possible justification of *prima facie* restrictions of competition, for instance because it

[8] For a synopsis of a debate lasting more than a hundred years, see P Areeda, 'The "Rule of Reason" in Antitrust Analysis: General Issues', Federal Judicial Center (June 1981), available at https://www.fjc.gov/sites/default/files/2012/Antitrust.pdf; P Areeda, 'The Rule of Reason—A Catechism on Competition' (1986) 55 *Antitrust LJ* 193; ABA Section of Antitrust Law, *The Rule of Reason*, Monograph 23 (ABA, 1999); AI Gavil, 'Moving Beyond Caricature and Characterization: The Modern Rule of Reason in Practice' (2012) 85 *Southern California L Rev* 733.

[9] There are many contributions to this debate but, for some representative and influential views, see R Joliet, *The Rule of Reason in Antitrust Law. American, German and Common Market Laws in Comparative Perspective* (Nijhoff, 1967); V Korah, 'The Rise and Fall of Provisional Validity: The Need for a Rule of Reason in EEC Antitrust' (1981) 3 *Northwestern J Int'l L and Business* 320; E Steindorff, 'Article 85 and the Rule of Reason' (1984) 21(4) *Common Market L Rev* 639; I Forrester and C. Norall, 'The Laicization of Community Law: Self-help and the Rule of Reason. How Competition Law Is and Could Be Applied' (1984) 21(1) *Common Market L Rev* 11; V Korah, 'EEC Competition Policy—Legal Form or Economic Efficiency' (1986) 39 Current Legal Problems 85; R Whish and B Sufrin, 'Article 85 and the Rule of Reason' (1987) 7 *Yearbook of European L* 1; R Kovar, 'Le droit communautaire de la concurrence et la "règle de la raison"' (1987) 23(2) *Revue trimestrielle de droit européen* 237; J Peeters, 'The Rule of Reason Revisited: Prohibition on Restraints of Competition in the Sherman Act and the EEC Treaty' (1989) 37(3) *American J Comparative L* 521; P Manzini, 'La "rule of reason" nel diritto comunitario della concorrenza: Un'analisi giuridico-economica' (1991) 31(4) *Rivista di diritto europeo* 859; D Fasquelle, *Droit américain et droit communautaire des ententes: Étude de la règle de raison* (Joly éditions, 1993); T Ackermann, *85 Abs. 1 EGV und die rule of reason: Zur Konzeption der Verhinderung, Einschränkung oder Verfälschung des Wettbewerbs* (Heymanns, 1997); O Black, 'Per Se Rules and Rules of Reason: What are They?' (1997) 18(3) *European Competition L Rev* 145.

was a welfare-enhancing agreement, was an issue of policy, not law and, consequently, the Commission enjoyed some degree of discretion, in view of its role as a hybrid political/adjudicative body. If one wants to link this discussion on methods of assessment to that of the goals of competition law, the predominant goal of EU competition law at the time, economic freedom or freedom to compete of economic actors (suppliers, distributors), may be thought as more adjudication friendly, as it is the function of the courts to declare and adjudicate conflicting rights.

The competition law provisions with the strongest polycentric dimension, such as Article 101(3), were of the exclusive competence of the European Commission, as a result of the legal authorization system adopted by Regulation 17/62 and the obligation imposed to the parties to notify their agreements to the European Commission. Some have considered that the proponents of a 'rule of reason' approach in Article 101(1) TFEU were animated by the view that efficiency was the core value of EU competition law and were fervent supporters of the neoclassical paradigm, of competition law.[10] One of the arguments that was often opposed to the 'rule of reason' camp was that transposing the 'rule of reason' from US antitrust law is unnecessary in the EU as Article 101(3) provides the 'functional equivalent' of the 'rule of reason' and such a rule will blur the distinction between Articles 101(1), focusing on rivalry and freedom to compete, and 101(3), addressing efficiency as well as broader policy considerations.[11] Some authors have retorted to this argument that Article 101(1) and Article 101(3) may address different dimensions of efficiency, allocative efficiency for Article 101(1) TFEU and productive efficiency for Article 101(3).[12] A careful analysis of the case law of the EU courts shows nevertheless that the EU courts do not view the freedom of competition and efficiency narratives as mutually exclusive and that the specialization of paragraphs 1 and 3 of Article 101 TFEU in different dimensions of efficiency, not only misrepresents the case law of the EU Courts, but it would also be wrong from an economic theory perspective.[13]

Since May 2004, Article 101 TFEU is a provision that can be applied by all competition enforcement actors, including national courts. The principle of legal exception requires that Article 101 should be interpreted following a *global approach*,[14] which will take into account both anti-competitive and pro-competitive 'effects', before finding the existence of a competition law infringement and therefore adopting adequate remedies. By 'effects', we mean not only 'market effects' but effects to the decision criterion or criteria selected by the specific legal system, which may be many in the multi-goals approach followed in EU competition law or one in the mono-goal approach followed in UK competition law.

Following the adoption of a legal exception regime and of the global approach interpreting paragraphs 1 and 3 of Article 101 TFEU, the debate over the application of a rule of reason or balancing in the context of Article 101(1) TFEU and the interaction between paragraphs 1

[10] G Monti, *EC Competition Law* (CUP, 2007), 30, criticizing the proponents of the introduction of a rule of reason in Article 101(1) TFEU for advocating an exclusively economic analysis to competition policy and for being 'in favour of the neoclassical conception of competition'. We guess that being neoclassical at the level of Article 101(3) is perfectly all right, to the extent that as we will show below trade-off of benefits and harms under Article 101(3) TFEU is a rare bird.

[11] See eg R Whish and B Sufrin, 'Article 85 and the Rule of Reason' (1987) 7 *Yearbook of European L* 1; G Monti, *EC Competition Law* (CUP, 2007), 30.

[12] O Odudu, *The Boundaries of EC Competition Law: The Scope of Article 81 EC* (OUP, 2006).

[13] I Lianos, *La transformation du droit de la concurrence par le recours à l'analyse économique* (Bruylant, 2007), 707–8.

[14] Ibid, 806–8.

and 3 of Article 101 TFEU has lost some practical interest. It is now accepted that some form of balancing is taking place in the context of Article 101(1), although this does not amount to the US rule of reason type of balancing, and that although in principle balancing should take place in the context of Article 101(3), in practice little of that is happening, some authors referring to this disjunction between theory and practice, as the 'balancing myth'. It seems that similar concerns have been expressed about the enforcement of the US rule of reason in the context of section 1 of the Sherman Act, some authors advancing the view that balancing of costs and benefits of the specific practice to competition is performed in less than 4 per cent of all rule of reason cases.[15] Prominent academic commentators also argue that in rule of reason cases under the Sherman Act the courts do not balance costs and benefits, according to a uniform metric, and this is not what is usually done, as in particular the costs and benefits to trade-off may be different in kind, such as higher prices, from one side, and higher quality, from the other side.[16]

This global approach requires a unitary framework in the assessment of the *evidence* of an infringement. This unitary framework should promote the following objectives: (a) minimize the risk of error/thus enhancing the accuracy of the decision; (b) minimize the expenses that fact-finding and assessment procedures and decisions incur; and (c) apportion the risk of error and misdecision between parties to the litigation.[17] The bifurcation of Article 101 may therefore be considered as an issue of evidence, although it is clear that it will also have an impact on substantive law and the respective position of the defendant or plaintiff. The authors advocate a cost-effective way (in the sense of minimizing social costs) to address issues of evidence of consumer harm, under Article 101 TFEU.[18]

[15] See MA Carrier, 'The Real Rule of Reason: Bridging the Disconnect' [1999] 4 *Brigham Young U L Rev* 1266 (noting that 'courts rarely conduct the balancing for which the Rule (of Reason) is known' and that 'in 96% Rule of Reason cases, courts do not balance anything', reporting for the period 1977 to 1999); MA Carrier, 'The Rule of Reason: An Empirical Update for the 21st Century' (2009) 16(4) *George Mason L Rev* 827 (noting that balancing occurs 'in only 2% of cases', reporting for the period of 1999 to 2009). It is not, however, clear how many of these cases concerned 'mixed conduct': CS Hemphill, 'Less Restrictive Alternatives in Antitrust Law' (2016) 116(4) *Columbia L Rev* 927.

[16] According to H Hovenkamp, 'Antitrust Balancing' (2016) 12 *New York U J L & Business* 369,

> '[B]alancing' is a very poor label for what courts actually do. Balancing requires that two offsetting effects can each be measured by some common cardinal unit, such as dollars or tons or centimeters, and then weighed against each other. The factors that courts consider under the rule of reason rarely lend themselves to such treatment. For example, the decisions referenced above that discuss the need to balance 'patent rights' against the 'prohibitions of the Sherman Act' provide nothing in the way of a calculus for weighing either of these interests. At best, 'balancing' in such cases depends on a complex mixture of soft economic and even ideological judgments about the effectiveness and appropriate domain of the patent system against concerns about promoting competition.

This raises the issue of evaluation and commensuration, which is of particular interest for competition law regimes with multiple aims, such as EU competition law, and which we examine in depth at Chapter 2. See also R Haw Allensworth, 'The Commensurability Myth in Antitrust' (2016) 69(1) *Vanderbilt L Rev* 1 (arguing that costs and benefits to competition are usually incommensurate and balancing them under the Rule of Reason requires value judgments that often, economic science cannot supply). For a contrary position, among US scholars, see CS Hemphill, 'Less Restrictive Alternatives in Antitrust Law' (2016) 116(4) *Columbia L Rev* 927 (arguing that some form of balancing/trade-off between costs and benefits to competition occurs in the context of assessing the existence of a less restrictive to competition alternative).

[17] A Stein, *Foundations of Evidence Law* (OUP, 2005).

[18] This presentation draws on C Humpe, I Lianos, N Petit, and B Walle de Gelcke, 'The Effects Based Approach in Article 101 TFEU' in M Merola and D Waelbroeck (eds) *Towards an Optimal Enforcement of Competition Rules in Europe* (Bruylant 2010), 467 (first part written by I Lianos).

Social costs can be of two sorts: 'substantive costs' (error costs)[19] and 'procedural costs', also called costs of 'error-minimizing procedures' or decision costs).[20] There is a negative correlation between these two forms of costs, as in order to evaluate accurately the costs or benefits of specific conduct and thus minimize substantive errors (false positives or false negatives), which are costly, one would need to spend more time and resources gathering evidence and assessing it, thus increasing decision costs. False positives (or type I error) occur when the decision-maker finds violations although the conduct did not harm competition, while false negatives (or type II error) occur when the decision-maker does not find violations although the conduct harmed competition.

For instance, a full 'effects-based' approach that would have limited the likelihood of error costs increases the likelihood of decision costs (eg costs of information gathering and processing). Decision-makers employ a sequential information gathering process in order to reduce information and, more broadly, decision costs, while of course aiming to minimize the occurrence of substantive errors.[21] The decision to acquire more information is a trade-off between two types of costs: error costs, on the one hand, that is the decision-maker may mistakenly identify a pro-competitive practice as being anti-competitive or the opposite, and information or decision costs, on the other.[22] This trade-off is done incrementally, at each level of this sequential assessment.

However, this incremental trade-off/balancing of various forms of errors is not the only way forward. One may limit *ex ante* the instances this trade-off is performed incrementally by using an alternative legal technique to balancing, that of legal 'categorization'. 'Categorization' constitutes an alternative to balancing to the extent that the disputes focus on classification of facts within existing legal categories and the definition or redefinition of the boundaries of existing legal categories or the creation of new ones. Antitrust categories constitute the necessary analytical shortcuts that will ensure that the factual investigation and logical analysis performed are well focused. Categories will be based on experience, built over subsequent instances of balancing, over the social costs and likelihood of substantive and decision errors. This experience may instruct us that for certain categories of fact-patterns, one may assume that the balance between substantive costs and decision costs is optimal and that there is no need to continue performing incrementally the trade-off between substantive costs and decision costs.[23] Decision

[19] These are often the focus of competition law and economics commentators since the early 1970s and constitutes one of the principal contributions of the Chicago School of antitrust law and economics. As explained by J Baker, 'Taking the Error out of the "Error Cost" Analysis: What's Wrong with Antitrust Right?' (2015) 80(1) *Antitrust LJ* 1, 4, '[t]hat framework was first employed in the law and economics literature by Richard Posner during the 1970s and introduced into mainstream antitrust scholarship by Paul Joskow and Alvin Klevorick in 1979. Modern antitrust commentators often refer to Frank Easterbrook's adoption of the framework in a widely cited article published in 1984, but the idea is older': RA Posner, 'An Economic Approach to Legal Procedure and Judicial Administration' (1973) 2(2) *J Legal Studies* 399; PL Joskow and AK Klevorick, 'A Framework for Analyzing Predatory Pricing Policy' (1979) 89 *Yale LJ* 213; FH Easterbrook, 'The Limits of Antitrust' (1984) 63 *Texas L Rev* 1.

[20] A Stein, *Foundations of Evidence Law* (OUP, 2005), 1. One may also expand this category to 'transaction costs', which costs go beyond the costs of adjudication and information gathering but also include the costs of 'uncertainty about legal rules', which 'chills beneficial conduct or means that those rules fail to deter harmful conduct': J Baker, 'Taking the Error out of the "Error Cost" Analysis: What's Wrong with Antitrust Right' (2015) 80(1) *Antitrust LJ* 1, 5.

[21] CF Beckner III and SC Salop, 'Decision Theory and Antitrust Rules' (1999) 67(1) *Antitrust LJ* 41, 43.

[22] CF Beckner III and SC Salop, 'Decision Theory and Antitrust Rules' (1999) 67(1) *Antitrust LJ* 41, 46.

[23] The distinction between 'categorization' and 'balancing' is well known in constitutional law: A Barak, *Proportionality—Constitutional Rights and their Limitations* (CUP, 2012), 508–9:

> Methodologically speaking, thinking in legal categories stands in sharp contrast to legal thinking based upon specific, or ad hoc, balancing [. . .] The focus on categories was meant, among others, to prevent the

costs, therefore, set limits to the expansion of a full-effects based approach in Article 101 and call for some degree of categorical thinking. Categorical thinking may take the form of legal presumptions, that is rules that dispense any further factual investigation (relative presumptions) or, if these are absolute presumptions, any further logical analysis.

The allocation of the risk of error is 'always instrumental to the trade-off that reduces the aggregate sum of error costs and error-avoidance expenses' (decision costs).[24] The risk of error and of the corresponding decision cost must be allocated in a way that maximizes the number of correct decisions in the long run of cases. This criterion treats false positives and false negatives as equally harmful. However, there are instances where a particular type of error (eg false conviction) is considered to be more harmful than the opposite type of error.[25] This is decided according to the preferences expressed by the specific legal system.[26] Evidence suppressing rules will in this case skew the risk of error in the desired direction.

Decision-makers may be risk neutral or risk-averse. Risk neutral decision-makers weigh 'potential harms equally with potential benefits', while risk-averse decision-makers 'would even reject conduct with a higher expected value in light of the significant downside risk', in other words they will give additional weight to potential harms.[27] In this context, risk could be understood as uncertainty over the effects of the decision in the present case and in future cases.[28] For example, the fact that decision-makers give more weight to anti-competitive effects than to efficiency gains may indicate that they are risk-averse to possible errors of false negatives. A risk neutral decision-maker would have given the same weight to both effects. The asymmetry may also be closely related to the availability and the cost of evidence.[29] A lower standard of proof for anti-competitive effects than for efficiency gains may therefore seek to establish some degree of formal equality in the starting positions of the claimant and the defendant by compensating for the initial information disadvantage of the claimant. It remains, however, that this advantage, which may be real in the case of private enforcement, does not necessarily exist in the case of public enforcement of competition law.

After introducing the role of decision theory in framing competition law categories, we turn now to its implementation in the context of Article 101 TFEU. We argue that the objective of minimizing substantive error costs and decision costs constitutes the primary reason for

use of specific balancing in each case. The characterization of a set of facts as being attributed to a certain category led to a legal solution, without the need to conduct a specific balancing within that category [. . .] once the contours of the category [. . .] are determined, there is no room for additional balancing.

24 A Stein, *Foundations of Evidence Law* (OUP, 2005), 2. 25 Ibid, 16.

26 The respective social costs of type I and type II errors are something that depends on a choice made by the specific legal system and the prior beliefs or assumptions on which it is built on. For instance, one may consider that the costs of false positives may be higher than the costs of false negatives, if one holds the assumption that markets may self-correct, through entry of new competitors, that cartels are unstable and thus often break, that monopolists innovate or are constrained in their ability to exploit consumers, and that, in contrast, erroneous antitrust precedents are more durable than market power or that antitrust rules may be manipulated by competitors. However, all these assumptions may be subject to criticism: see J Baker, 'Taking the Error out of the 'Error Cost' Analysis: What's Wrong with Antitrust Right' (2015) 80(1) *Antitrust LJ* 1.

27 CF Beckner III and SC Salop, 'Decision Theory and Antitrust Rules' (1999) 67(1) *Antitrust LJ* 41.

28 Although the concepts of risk and that of uncertainty are not, in theory, similar, risk being considered as measurable uncertainty while uncertainty cannot be measured. See FH Knight, *Risk, Uncertainty and Profit* (Houghton Mifflin, 1921), 25, in this context the two terms will be used interchangeably.

29 See Commission Staff Working Paper on Damages Actions for Breach of the EC antitrust rules, SEC(2008) 404 (2 April 2008), available at http://ec.europa.eu/competition/antitrust/actionsdamages/files_white_paper/working_paper.pdf, remarking that competition cases are characterized by a very asymmetric distribution of the available information and the necessary evidence as it is often very difficult for claimants to produce the required evidence.

the bifurcation of Article 101 (in paragraphs 1 and 3). The bifurcation has therefore little to do with the fact that these provisions try to achieve different objectives or in other words that they refer to a different decision criterion, competitive rivalry or allocative efficiency for Article 101(1) TFEU and productive or dynamic efficiency for Article 101(3) TFEU, or transactional efficiency in Article 101(1) and other forms of efficiency in Article 101(3). We argue that the bifurcation of the competition law control is simply explained by the fact that Article 101 demands from competition law enforcers the application of two different 'decision procedures',[30] intuitive analysis for Article 101(1) TFEU and quantitative balancing of costs and benefits for Article 101(3) TFEU (cost–benefit analysis).[31] The objective of these procedures is to minimize the risk of both type of errors (substantive and procedural) and consequently total social costs.[32]

The competition assessment of a practice under Article 101(3) TFEU is particularly time- and resource-consuming, as the defendant will have to substantiate and quantify efficiency gains and the competition authority or the judicial decision-maker will have to balance these efficiency gains with anti-competitive effects (by performing a cost–benefit analysis), a particularly time and resources consuming assessment. Hence, in circumstances where there is no considerable uncertainty over the pro- or anti-competitive character of a practice, and the risk of error is not extremely high, the antitrust decision-maker will decide to adopt a lighter, in terms of decision costs, decision procedure (intuitive analysis instead of cost–benefit analysis). In all other circumstances, where there is considerable uncertainty over the impact of the practice on consumers or any other protected aim, cost–benefit analysis may become the most adequate procedure.

The principle of the presumption of innocence, under Article 6 of the European Convention on Human Rights (ECHR), signals the preference expressed in EU law that in most cases false positives will be considered more costly than false negatives. Allocating the burden of proof (burden of production of evidence) to the plaintiff is an attempt to mitigate that risk. In certain circumstances, however, the cost of false negatives will be considered as particularly prohibitive or the principle of the presumption of innocence will fade under clear indication of anti-competitive intent and purpose. In this case, it is possible to adopt evidence suppressing rules which will skew the risk of error towards the defendant. This situation explains essentially the development of presumptions, such as the concept of anti-competitive object. It should

30 MD Adler and EA Posner, *New Foundations of Cost-Benefit Analysis* (Harvard University Press, 1st ed, 2006), 64 ('a decision procedure is a technique for making choices').

31 This view was put forward for the first time by I Lianos, *La transformation du droit de la concurrence par le recours à l'analyse économique* (Bruylant, 2007); I Lianos, 'Commercial Agency Agreements, vertical restraint and the limits of Article 81(1) EC: Between Hierarchies and Networks' (2007) 3(4) *J Competition L* and Economics 625 (introducing, for the first time, the role of transactional efficiency in the context of Article 101 TFEU); C Humpe, I Lianos, N Petit, B Walle de Gelcke, 'The Effects Based Approach in Article 101 TFEU' in M Merola and D Waelbroeck (eds) *Towards an Optimal Enforcement of Competition Rules in Europe* (Bruylant, 2010), 467 (first part written by Ioannis Lianos). This view seems also supported by P Ibáñez Colomo, 'Market Failures, Transaction Costs and Article 101(1) TFEU Case Law' (2012) 37(5) *European L Rev* 541.

32 See also A Christiansen and W Kerber, 'Competition Policy with Optimally Differentiated Rules instead of 'Per se Rules versus Rule of Reason' (2006) 2(2) *J Competition L & Economics* 215, who also advance that an economic approach would aim to use economics for the formulation of appropriate competition rules. Showing that competition law rarely relies on case-by-case analysis of alleged anti-competitive practices, the authors advance an approach that would rely on an 'optimal differentiation of rules' through a deeper assessment of their advantages with regard to the reduction of decision errors of type I and II. They thus put forward a continuum of more or less differentiated rules that would largely depend on a marginalist-type analysis, comparing the marginal benefit of differentiation (the reduction of the sum of error costs), from one side, and the marginal costs of differentiation, from the other side.

remain theoretically possible for the defendant to argue efficiency gains in the context of the cost–benefit analysis under Article 101(3) TFEU,[33] but in this case, it is the defendant that will assume the risk of uncertainty (burden of proof) not the claimant or the plaintiff.

Employing monetized/quantitative cost–benefit analysis will also be dependent on the ability, or not, of that method to take into account a variety of public policy concerns. In areas such as environmental protection, the use of quantitative cost–benefit analysis has been generally accepted and collective environmental benefits have been quantified and compared to the costs following from environmental protection.[34] This evolution may explain the position adopted by the Commission in some recent cases to include collective environmental benefits in the assessment of a practice under Article 101(3) TFEU and to attempt to quantify them in order to compare them to other costs.[35] In other areas, such as social policy, however, this is not possible, as the monetized cost–benefit analysis has not yet been employed and quantification of benefits would be practically difficult and politically and/or morally reprehensible. This is the reason why these 'public interest' concerns are integrated in Article 101(1) TFEU and are examined according to the procedure of intuitive balancing[36] or simply excluded from the scope of Article 101(1) TFEU.[37] The allocation between intuitive assessment and cost–benefit analysis should therefore take into account this perspective.

One could refer as an example of the different methods of competition assessment the rules that apply to different types of distribution restraints. In applying Article 101(1) TFEU, the competition authorities and the courts should not focus only on the impact of the particular restriction to a single facet of efficiency (eg a price increase and consequently allocative efficiency). It is also important to take into account the organizational form of the particular transaction. It may appear that a market form of organization would present important deficiencies for the protection of the parties' investments from opportunistic behaviour or reputation externalities. This market organizational form's failure explains why it is necessary for the parties to incur additional administrative costs and establish a situation of hierarchy (vertical integration) or a network form of organization (franchise, selective distribution). This finding should have implications for the application of Article 101(1) TFEU. The latter should not apply in a situation of hierarchy.

A network form of organization will exclude from the scope of Article 101(1) TFEU the restrictions that are necessary for the implementation of the specific organizational form. It is important therefore that the competition authorities and the courts examine the characteristics of the specific transaction along with the consideration of its restrictive effects to allocative efficiency and exercise an intuitive analysis in order to decide if the restrictions are necessary for the operation of the organization form chosen by the parties. If this is the

33 Following the position in Case T-185/00, *Métropole television SA (M6) v Commission* [2002] ECR II–3805, para 86.

34 R Revesz and M Lievrmore, *Retaking Rationality* (OUP, 2008).

35 See *CECED* (Case IV.F.1/36.718) Commission Decision 2000/475/EEC [2000] OJ L 187/47.

36 See Case C-309/99, *Wouters and Others* [2002] ECR I–1577, and analysis in Section 6.3.4.2.1.

37 See eg Case C-67/96, *Albany International BV v Stichting Bedrijfspensioenfonds Textielindustrie* [1999] ECR I–5751, paras 54–64, where it was found that Article 101(1) does not apply to collective agreements between workers and employers in so far as those agreements related to the improvement of conditions of work and employment. The Court insisted on the fact that one of the Treaty's objectives was to achieve a high level of employment and social protection, which could be jeopardized if Article 101(1) applied to this type of agreements. This was not the case of the public interest objectives protected in Case C-309/99, *Wouters and Others* [2002] ECR I–1577 or Case C-519/04 P, *David Meca-Medina and Igor Majcen v Commission* [2006] ECR I–6991.

case, Article 101(1) TFEU should not apply.[38] Article 101(1) TFEU therefore takes indirectly into account the transactional efficiency gains resulting from this specific clause of the agreement, which implies the existence of an intuitive analysis of positive and negative effects on consumer harm, although this does not take the form of quantitative cost–benefit analysis of the effects of the specific clause under Article 101(3) TFEU.[39] If the characteristics of the transaction do not justify the particular clause, Article 101(1) TFEU will apply. However, it is possible for the parties to the agreement to advance cost or quality efficiency gains (productive or dynamic) that may outweigh its negative effects on competition and consumers. This will require a mostly quantitative cost–benefit analysis by the competition authorities and the courts under Article 101(3) TFEU. The burden of proof this time will be on the defendants who should identify and establish with cogent evidence the existence and the magnitude of productive efficiency gains that may within a reasonable period of time outweigh the negative effects of the agreement and thus benefit overall consumer welfare.[40]

This theory may provide a working explanation of the divide between the competition law assessment under paragraphs one and three of Article 101 and of the different regimes that may apply to vertical restraints integrated in different organizational forms, such as a parent firm–subsidiary relation, commercial agency agreements, franchise, or selective distribution.[41] The method of assessment of evidence of consumer harm is therefore what distinguishes the two paragraphs of Article 101 TFEU. Article 101(1) institutes a form of intuitive analysis approach that includes the effects of the practice on allocative efficiency, transactional efficiency gains, non-quantifiable dynamic efficiency gains, and other regulatory public interest objectives that correspond to the preferences of the specific consumers and that may justify restrictions to competition.

38 Although the plaintiff has the legal burden to prove that Article 101 is applicable, the defendants should have the evidential burden to find transactional efficiency gains in explaining their choice of the particular organization framework for their transaction. On the distinction between the legal and the evidential burden of proof, see *British Horseracing Board v Office of Fair Trading* [2005] CAT 29, para 132.

39 The evaluation in money terms of the cost efficiency gains is an important step of the cost–benefit analysis performed under Article 101(3) TFEU. See Communication from the Commission—Notice—Guidelines on the application of Article 101(3) (formerly Article 81(3)) of the Treaty [2004] OJ C 101/97, paras 55–6 [hereinafter Guidelines on Article 101(3) (formerly 81(3))].

40 Dynamic efficiency gains should not be excluded from the application of Article 81(1). In some cases, when a particular restriction is necessary for the penetration of an existing product to a new area (therefore the emergence of a new product for the consumers of the relevant geographic market), there is no restriction on Article 81(1): see Case 56/65, *Société Technique Minière v Maschinenbau Ulm* [1966] ECR 235, 249–50. In addition, dynamic efficiency gains may be taken into account in Article 81(3) when it is not possible to perform an intuitive (balancing) analysis of their effect. The performance of cost–benefit analysis for dynamic efficiencies is a thorny task because of the difficulty to evaluate in money terms 'qualitative' efficiency gains. However, nothing in theory excludes the possibility of measurement of these dynamic efficiencies and therefore the operation of a monetized cost–benefit analysis. See DG Enterprise and Industry, *Practical Methods to Assess Efficiency Gains in the Context of Article 81(3) of the EC Treaty (Final report)* (2006), 85–8, available at https://publications.europa.eu/en/publication-detail/-/publication/0cbd1037-04b5-41ee-a9e4-025bf02774f2. Nonetheless, the analysis of the second condition of Article 81(3), a fair share of the efficiency gains should pass on to consumers, is particularly complex for qualitative efficiencies or new products. In this case, the fourth condition of Article 81(3), the absence of a substantial elimination of competition, becomes an important criterion for the application of Article 101 and makes it possible to distinguish between the situation in which the qualitative efficiency gains will most likely be passed on to consumers and that in which the consumers will overall be worse off as a result of the vertical agreement. This re-introduces some qualitative analysis or value judgment. See P Nicolaides, 'The Balancing Myth: The Economics of Article 81(1) & 81(3)' (2005) 32 *Legal Issues of Economic Integration* 123, 136. See also Chapter IV of the Report on the concept of 'substantial elimination of competition'.

41 See I Lianos, 'Commercial Agency Agreements, Vertical Restraint and the Limits of Article 81(1) EC: Between Hierarchies and Networks' (2007) 3(4) *J Competition L and Economics* 625.

This analysis is performed only if there is no presumption of anti-competitive object: some types of commercial practices or facts may indeed be considered as being anti-competitive by their object. This presumption may be understood as having a dual purpose.

First, they may state a substantive rule, in the sense that a category of agreements, for example those establishing an absolute territorial protection or resale price maintenance, harm, by their nature, the interests protected by competition legislation (eg consumer interest, the public at large, the interest of the Union), or, as some authors have contended do not have 'any redeeming virtue' (we guess from the perspective of one or all the protected interests). This seems to be an irrebuttable presumption of anti-competitive object, dispensing of any further logical analysis under Article 101(1) TFEU (an *analytical* shortcut), as it is difficult to argue that an agreement, which constitutes a Resale Price Maintenance clause, is not a by object restriction. It is, however, possible for undertaking to argue justifications under Article 101(3) TFEU. It is also possible to argue that the specific agreement/conduct does not constitute a Resale Price Maintenance clause and thus characterize it differently, this time considered in the context of Article 101(1) TFEU, on the basis of the 'legal and economic context' of the agreement.

Second, one could infer from the content or the circumstances of a specific agreement (the basic fact or fact *A*) the proof of a fact *B* or presumed fact. Presumptions in this sense operate as a means of discharging evidential burdens of proof and the need for further evidence of the presumed fact (an *evidential* shortcut). For example, an interdiction of exports dispenses from the need to prove that parallel imports will be affected. From this perspective, one may consider that anti-competitive object may operate as a presumption of anti-competitive effects, of whatever nature these may be (effects on price, effects on parallel imports, effects on quality, effects on innovation, or even effects on competitors), the decision over the relevant effects to be considered as anti-competitive depending on the decision criterion or decision criteria adopted by the specific legislation. In this case, however, the presumption is not absolute or irrebuttable, as it should be possible for the other party to rebut this evidence by showing that it was in fact wrong to draw this particular inference from the proof of this fact. For example, one could argue that a reduction of parallel imports creates a presumption of consumer harm (if one focuses on consumer welfare), because less parallel imports may lead to a price increase, but that this presumption may be rebutted by the defendant, if the latter proves that the circumstances of the case or the conditions of the specific industry make that this normally drawn inference could not hold in reality, as only outcomes matter (a consequential rule). This presumption may, however, not be rebutted, if this type of conduct is deemed by object anti-competitive, because it harms the *process* of market integration and hence a reduction of the opportunity of parallel imports should be deemed unlawful (a deontological rule).

If the specific practice has no anti-competitive object and it is clear, after an abstract intuitive analysis, that it is likely to harm the interests protected by competition law, the expense of a more detailed inquiry under the cost–benefit analysis would be justified. The risk would in this case be on the defendant that argues this possibility of justification. The defendant should not only argue the defence but also substantiate it with quantitative and/or qualitative evidence proving that the consumers in the relevant market will not incur any harm. This is the essence of the second positive condition of Article 101(3) TFEU: that the situation of the specific consumer should not be worse off as a result of the specific agreement.[42]

This unitary framework for the assessment of evidence of consumer harm and the respective role of paragraphs 1 and 3 of Article 101 TFEU, may, however, be jeopardized by a

42 Guidelines on Article 101(3) (formerly 81(3)), para 85.

different form of institutional constraint. The OECD policy roundtable on *Presenting Complex Economic Theories to Judges*[43] noted that courts have generally experienced difficulties with basic economic assumptions and theories, and exposed a number of procedures that have been developed by some Member States to facilitate the assessment of economic evidence by courts. The relatively anaemic enforcement of Article 101(3) TFEU by national courts, in comparison to the enforcement of this provision by national competition authorities, brings forward the issue of the lack of economic expertise of judges as a central point in envisaging a more workable conceptualization of the bifurcation of Article 101 TFEU. The lack of experience in assessing economic evidence may explain the rare times Article 101(3) TFEU was enforced by national courts. The principle of procedural autonomy may constitute an obstacle to the development of a European framework for the assessment of evidence in competition cases. However, it is clear that, in some areas of competition law enforcement, procedural harmonization of national law has already started, following the need for greater effectiveness in the enforcement of Articles 101 and 102 TFEU.

6.3. OBJECT OR EFFECT TO RESTRICT COMPETITION UNDER ARTICLE 101(1) TFEU AND CHAPTER I CA98

6.3.1. OBJECT OR EFFECT: ALTERNATIVE REQUIREMENTS

6.3.1.1. Two views about by object restrictions to competition: The 'more analytical approach' versus the 'orthodox view'

According to a well-established case law of the EU courts, in order to be caught by the prohibition led down in Article 101(1) TFEU, an agreement, a decision by an association of undertakings or a concerted practice must have 'as [its] object or effect the prevention, restriction or distortion of competition within the internal market'.[44] Where the anti-competitive object of the agreement is established it is not necessary to examine its effects on competition. Where, however, an analysis of the content of the agreement does not reveal a sufficient degree of harm to competition, the effects of the agreement should then be considered and, for it to be caught by the prohibition, it is necessary to find that factors are present which show that competition has in fact been prevented, restricted or distorted to an appreciable extent.[45] The case law has long established that object and effect are alternative requirements for the application of Article 101(1) TFEU.[46]

Soon enough after the adoption of Regulation 17/62, the Court of Justice of the European Union (CJEU) indicated that the object and effect distinction meant that these were to be

[43] OECD, Presenting Complex Economic Theories to Judges (February 2008), 7–9, available at http://www.oecd.org/dataoecd/39/59/41776770.pdf.

[44] See, most recently, Case C-67/13 P, *CB v Commission*, ECLI:EU:C:2014:2204; Case C-345/14, *SIA Maxima Latvija v Konkurences padome*, ECLI:EU:C:2015:784.

[45] Case C-32/11, *Allianz Hungária Biztosító and Others*, ECLI:EU:C:2013:160, para 34; Case C-286/13 P, *Dole Food and Dole Fresh Fruit Europe v Commission*, ECLI:EU:C:2015:184, para 116.

[46] See Case-56/65, *Société Technique Minière (STM) v Maschinenbau Ulm (MBU)* [1966] ECR 235, 249; Joined Cases 56 & 58/64, *Consten and Grundig v Commission* [1966] ECR 299 (holding that once it has been shown that the object of an agreement is to restrict competition, 'there is no need to take account of the concrete effects of an agreement'); Case C-219/95 P, *Ferrière Nord v Commission* [1997] ECR I–4411 (confirming that the object or effect was disjunctive).

interpreted as alternative requirements and that therefore each of them requires separate consideration.

The seminal cases with regard to this issue are *Consten & Grundig*, where the CJEU (full court) held that absolute territorial protection has the object of restricting competition and, although it did consider the economic evidence for two whole pages, it concluded that there was no need to make a market analysis for restraints prohibiting active and passive parallel trade,[47] and *Société La Technique Minière v Maschinenbau Ulm*, parts of which are reproduced below.

6.3.1.1.1. Société La Technique Minière v. Maschinenbau Ulm GmbH: *The foundations of the 'more analytical approach'*

Case 56/65, *Société La Technique Minière v Maschinenbau Ulm GmbH*
[1966] ECR 235

The Court of Appeal for Paris asked for a preliminary ruling on an agreement similar to Consten*'s, save that there were no restrictions on export or any device based on a second trade mark. The agreement had not been notified so could not be exempted. The Court consisted of five of the same seven judges who sat in* Consten & Grundig. *After ruling that an agreement that had not been notified was not necessarily void and that to infringe Article [101(1) TFEU] there must be an agreement between undertakings that 'may affect trade between Member States', the Court continued:*

12. Finally, for the agreement at issue to be caught by the prohibition contained in Article [101(1) TFEU] it must have as its 'object or effect the prevention, restriction or distortion of competition within the Common Market'.

13. The fact that these are not cumulative but alternative requirements, indicated by the conjunction 'or', leads first to the need to consider the precise purpose of the agreement, in the economic context in which it is to be applied. This interference with competition referred to in Article [101(1) TFEU] must result from all or some of the clauses of the agreement itself. Where, however, an analysis of the said clauses does not reveal the effect on competition to be sufficiently deleterious, the consequences of the agreement should then be considered and for it to be caught by the prohibition it is then necessary to find that those factors are present which show that competition has in fact been prevented or restricted or distorted to an appreciable extent.

14. The competition in question must be understood within the actual context in which it would occur in the absence of the agreement in dispute. In particular it may be doubted whether there is an interference with competition if the said agreement seems really necessary for the penetration of a new area by an undertaking. Therefore, in order to decide whether an agreement containing a clause 'granting an exclusive right of sale' is to be considered as prohibited by reason of its object or of its effect, it is appropriate to take into account in particular the nature and quantity, limited or otherwise, of the products covered by the agreement,

[47] See our analysis in Chapter 2. Confirmed in Case 19/77, *Miller International Schallplatten GmbH v Commission* [1978] ECR 131 and followed in many Commission decisions.

the position and importance of the grantor and the concessionaire on the market for the products concerned, the isolated nature of the disputed agreement or, alternatively, its position in a series of agreements, the severity of the clauses intended to protect the exclusive dealership or, alternatively, the opportunities allowed for other commercial competitors in the same products by way of parallel re-exportation and importation.

NOTES AND QUESTIONS ON STM V MBU

1. The Italian text of Article 101 TFEU refers to 'object *and* effect', but in *Ferrière Nord v Commission*,[48] the CJEU in the light of the other language versions of the Treaty, construed this as 'object or effect.'
2. (Paragraphs 13 and 14). How was the Court in *Grundig* two weeks later able to avoid making the market analysis required? Was it due to the two additional judges altering the majority of the Court, to the attempts to prevent parallel trade or anything else? Note that the CJEU did devote two pages to the economic context of the agreement. Spell out the argument why an exclusive territory might be needed to penetrate another Member State.
3. (Paragraph 14). Note that the Court frequently refers in later cases to the *legal and economic context* of an agreement.
4. (Paragraphs 12 and 14). How did the CJEU construe the category of restrictions of competition by object? Does the Court exclude any economic analysis for restrictions of competition by object? Or is the CJEU also welcoming some form of economic analysis for both restrictions by object and restrictions by effect?
5. (Paragraph 14). The CJEU notes that '[t]he competition in question must be understood within the actual context in which it would occur *in the absence of the agreement in dispute*' (emphasis added). What type of analysis would such assessment require? Is this a form of counterfactual test,[49] or is the CJEU referring to the ancillary restraints doctrine?[50]
6. In your view, does the CJEU in *STM v MBU* consider that both 'object' and 'effect' seek to identify the same consequence of collusion: restriction of competition? Or, is the CJEU considering that each of these concepts should be considered as two separate categories, from an ontological perspective?

6.3.1.1.2. The 'orthodox' view of the Commission's Guidelines on Article 101(3) (formerly Article 81(3))

Following the judgment of the CJEU in *STM v MTB*, the decisional practice of the European Commission expanded the category of restrictions by object, occasionally omitting a thorough analysis of the legal and economic context of the agreement in question before concluding that it constituted a restriction of competition by object under Article 101(1) TFEU.

48 Case C-219/95 P, *Ferrière Nord v Commission* [1997] ECR I–4411, [1997] 5 CMLR 575, [1998] CEC 19.
49 See Section 6.3.3.1. 50 See Section 6.3.4.1.

The Commission addressed object restrictions as having 'by their very nature' at least the objective of restricting competition.[51]

The General Court (GC) moved to a similar direction in a number of cases, starting with *Montedipe SpA v Commission*, *Tréfilunion v Commission*, and *European Night Services v Commission*, where the GC held that the object-category consists of 'obvious restrictions of competition'.[52] The GC found that where an agreement contained these 'obvious' restrictions of competition, such as price-fixing, market-sharing or the control of outlets, there is no need to take into account 'of the actual conditions in which [the agreement] functions, in particular the economic context in which the undertakings operate, the products or services covered by the agreement and the actual structure of the market concerned',[53] although in in *European Night Services* it objected to the Commission for not taking into account the hypothetical. A possible interpretation of this case law is that all economic analysis is reserved for the consideration of the 'effects' of a practice, the category of 'object' restrictions, dispensing with the need to consider the economic impact of a practice. The aim of the 'object' restriction would in this case be to establish bright line rules for certain categories/types of 'obvious' restrictions to competition. Some authors have even gone as far as to claim that there is an 'object box', a list of practices that are considered as 'obvious' restrictions of competition.[54]

The Commission proceeded to an interpretation of the 'object' and 'effect' concepts and of their interaction in its Guidelines on the application of Article 101(3), adopted in 2004.[55] The Commission indicates that restrictions by object are those that 'by their nature have the potential to restrict competition' and for which it is not necessary to demonstrate any '*actual* effects' on the market (emphasis added). Why does the Commission refer only to 'actual' effects and not just to 'effects'? Does this mean that the Commission leaves open the possibility to consider potential effects when analysing restrictions of competition by object?

Some recent case law has examined in more detail the boundaries of the object and effect of restricting competition. The case law is characterized by some tension between cases which emphasize the need to consider the legal, but more crucially, also the economic context of the agreement, before concluding that this restricts competition by object, and cases which seem to consider that the existence of a restriction of competition results (or more accurately may

[51] See *Wm Teacher and Sons Ltd* (Case IV/28.859) Commission Decision 78/697/EEC [1978] OJ L 235/20 (finding that direct and indirect export prohibitions are likely by their nature to affect trade between Member States); *Flat glass* (Case IV/31. 906) Commission Decision 89/93/EEC [1989] OJ L 33/44, paras 65–6 (also referring to 'serious restrictions of competition' for price fixing among competitors); *Viho/Parker Pen* (Case IV/32.725) Commission Decision 92/426/EEC [1992] OJ L 233/27 (restriction of exports within the common market are by their nature a restriction of competition); *Pre-Insulated Pipe Cartel* (Case No IV/35.691/E-4) Commission Decision 1999/60/EC [1999] OJ L 24/1, para 165 ('[m]arket sharing and price fixing are by their nature a very serious violation of Article [101(1) TFEU'); *Graphite electrodes* (Case COMP/E-1/36.490) Commission Decision 2002/271/EC [2002] OJ L 100/1, para 131 (market-sharing and price-fixing practices are by their nature very serious violations of Article 101(1) TFEU); *Vitamins* (Case COMP/E-1/37.512) Commission Decision 2003/2/EC [2003] OJ L 6/1, para 663 (market sharing and price fixing practices are by their nature very serious violations of Article 101(1) TFEU).

[52] Case T-14/89, *Montedipe SpA v Commission* [1992] ECR II-1155; Case T-148/89, *Tréfilunion v Commission* [1995] ECR II-1063; Joined Cases T-374–5 & 384/94, *European Night Services v Commission* [1998] ECR II-3141. For a discussion, see S King, *Agreements that restrict competition by object under Article 101(1) TFEU: Past, Present and Future* (PhD thesis, London School of Economics, 2015), 32–4.

[53] Joined Cases T-374–5 & 384/94, *European Night Services v Commission* [1998] ECR II-3141, para 136. See also Case T-148/89 *Tréfilunion v Commission* [1995] ECR II-1063, para 109; Case T-14/89, *Montedipe SpA v Commission* [1992] ECR II-1155, para 265.

[54] R Whish and D Bailey, *Competition Law* (OUP, 8th ed, 2015), 123.

[55] Guidelines on Article 101(3) (formerly 81(3)), paras 19–21.

be presumed) when the agreement contains an 'obvious' restriction of competition, or a clause which seems 'by its very nature' to restrict competition.[56]

6.3.1.1.3. The Beef Industry Development Society rationalization agreement

Following the recommendations of the Beef Task Force, set up by the Irish Minister for Agriculture, concluded that there was an under-used slaughtering capacity in the beef industry in Ireland,[57] and that there were considerable benefits to be gained by a rationalization process leading to better matching of capacity with actual requirements. Consequently, the fifteen principal companies of the beef processing industry in Ireland, representing 93 per cent of the Irish market for the supply of beef, formed on 2 May 2002 the Beef Industry Development Society Limited (BIDS) with the purpose of implementing an arrangement on the rationalization of the production. BIDS prepared a draft rationalization plan which provided, *inter alia*, for a reduction in processing capacity of about 25 per cent, the equivalent of an annual volume of about 420 000 head of cattle. The BIDS suggested a decommissioning programme for some members of the BIDS (called the 'goers') who would voluntary agree to exit the beef market industry, by decommissioning their plants, and would sign a two year non-compete clause in relation to the processing of cattle in Ireland. In addition, land associated with the decommissioned plants of the goers would not be used for the purposes of beef processing for a period of five years. In exchange, the BIDS would set up a voluntary fund to compensate 'the goers' through loan agreements. The fund would receive payments from the 'stayers', the non-decommissioned plants, who would pay BIDS levies based upon an agreed formula in relation to stayers' existing traditional (percentage) cattle kill and cattle killed in excess of this traditional (percentage) kill. Furthermore, the equipment of goers for primary beef processing would be sold to stayers only for use as back-up equipment within three months. The parties notified the Irish Competition Authority of that agreement and the standard form of contract.

The Irish Competition Authority initiated an action against the BIDS agreement based on Article 4(1) of the 2002 Irish Competition Act and Article 101 TFEU, claiming that the object and/or effect of the BIDS agreement was to limit and control production and capacity on the market for the supply of beef, that it affected pricing and thus had the object or effect that the retail price to consumers was likely to rise. The parties to the agreement argued that the objective was to rationalize production, reduce overcapacity that was affecting the firms' profitability, their capacity to attain economies of scale and therefore their ability to stay on the market. They noted that the purpose of the arrangements was not adversely to affect competition or the welfare of consumers, but to rationalize the beef industry in order to make it more competitive by reducing, but not eliminating, production overcapacity.

The Irish High Court dismissed the claim of the Authority as it considered that no provision of the arrangements could be described as plainly or evidently limiting output, sharing

[56] For a discussion, see O Kolstad, *Object Contra Effect in Swedish and European Competition Law* (Konkurrensverket, 2009), 4 (noting that 'object' may be considered as a 'presumption-based rule', which means that '[f]or some agreements, the harmful effects are so clear that it should not be necessary for the competition authorities and the courts to expend resources on an exhaustive inquiry into the effects of the agreements. The finding of an anti-competitive object dispenses with costly proof requirements, such as proof of market power.'). For a similar view, see R Whish and D Bailey, *Competition Law* (OUP, 8th ed, 2015), 123–4.

[57] A consequence of the Common Agricultural Policy's interventions to guarantee farmers a floor or base price leading to 'a enormous increase in the number of factories being constructed and indeed also being upgraded' (*The Competition Authority v Beef Industry Development Society Limited and Barry Brothers (Carrigmore) Meats Limited* [2006] IEHC 294, para 9): That led to a 'widespread mismatch between output and capacity' (ibid, para 11).

markets or prohibiting investment and therefore there was no infringement of Article 101(1), thus not finding that such restriction was by object anti-competitive. The High Court examined in any case the application of Article 101(3) and found that the arrangements satisfied three of the conditions of Article 101(3), although BIDS have not managed to prove that they also allowed a fair share of the resulting benefits to consumers. The Authority appealed the decision of the High Court to the Supreme Court of Ireland,[58] which sent preliminary questions to the CJEU on the interpretation of Article 101(1) TFEU regarding restrictions of competition by object, in particular whether an agreement between undertakings representing 9 per cent of the producers to effect such a once-off reduction in capacity must be regarded as constituting a restriction by object of competition for the purpose of Article 101(1) TFEU and whether the ancillary restrictions on competition, and the use of land, the decommissioning and disposal of plant and/or the levy arrangements amounted, independently, to restrictions by object for the purposes of that provision.

Case C-209/07, *Competition Authority v Beef Industry Development Society Ltd and Barry Brothers (Carrigmore) Meats Ltd*
[2008] ECR I–8637

14. By its question, the national court asks, in essence, whether agreements with features such as those of the BIDS arrangements are to be regarded, by reason of their object alone, as being anticompetitive and prohibited by Article [101(1) TFEU] or whether, on the other hand, it is necessary, in order to reach such a conclusion, first to demonstrate that such agreements have had anti-competitive effects.

15. It must be recalled that, to come within the prohibition laid down in Article [101(1) TFEU], an agreement must have 'as [its] object or effect the prevention, restriction or distortion of competition within the common market'. It has, since the judgment in Case 56/65 LTM [1966] ECR 235, 249, been settled case-law that the alternative nature of that requirement, indicated by the conjunction 'or', leads, first, to the need to consider the precise purpose of the agreement, in the economic context in which it is to be applied. Where, however, an analysis of the clauses of that agreement does not reveal the effect on competition to be sufficiently deleterious, its consequences should then be considered and for it to be caught by the prohibition it is necessary to find that those factors are present which show that competition has in fact been prevented or restricted or distorted to an appreciable extent.

16. In deciding whether an agreement is prohibited by Article 101(1) TFEU, there is therefore no need to take account of its actual effects once it appears that its object is to prevent, restrict or distort competition within the common market [. . .]. That examination must be made in the light of the agreement's content and economic context [. . .].

17. The distinction between 'infringements by object' and 'infringements by effect' arises from the fact that certain forms of collusion between undertakings can be regarded, by their very nature, as being injurious to the proper functioning of normal competition.

The CJEU noted the conflicting positions of the interveners in this case: (i) those alleging that the object of the BIDS arrangements is obviously anti-competitive so that there is no need

[58] *The Competition Authority v The Beef Industry Development Society Limited and Another* [2008] ECC 6 (Supreme Court of Ireland).

to analyse their actual effects and that those arrangements were concluded in breach of the prohibition laid down in Article 101(1) TFEU, and (ii) those putting forward that the agreement should be analysed in the light of their actual effects on the market and arguing that the BIDS agreements were not anti-competitive in purpose and did not entail injurious consequences for consumers or, more generally, for competition, their purpose being 'to rationalise the beef industry in order to make it more competitive by reducing, but not eliminating, production overcapacity'. The Court clearly rejected the second position.[59]

21. In fact, to determine whether an agreement comes within the prohibition laid down in Article 101(1) TFEU, close regard must be paid to the wording of its provisions and to the objectives which it is intended to attain. In that regard, even supposing it to be established that the parties to an agreement acted without any subjective intention of restricting competition, but with the object of remedying the effects of a crisis in their sector, such considerations are irrelevant for the purposes of applying that provision. Indeed, an agreement may be regarded as having a restrictive object even if it does not have the restriction of competition as its sole aim but also pursues other legitimate objectives [. . .]. It is only in connection with Article 101(3) TFEU that matters such as those relied upon by BIDS may, if appropriate, be taken into consideration for the purposes of obtaining an exemption from the prohibition laid down in Article 101(1) TFEU.

22. BIDS argues, in addition, that the concept of infringement by object should be interpreted narrowly. Only agreements as to horizontal price fixing, or to limit output or share markets, agreements whose anti-competitive effects are so obvious as not to require an economic analysis come within that category. The BIDS arrangements cannot be assimilated to that type of agreement or to other forms of complex cartels. BIDS maintains that an agreement on the reduction of excess capacity in a sector cannot be assimilated to an agreement to 'limit production' within the meaning of Article 101(1)(b) EC. That concept must be understood as referring to a limitation of total market output rather than a limitation of the output of certain operators who voluntarily withdraw from the market, without causing a lowering of output.

23. However, as the Advocate General pointed out [. . .], the types of agreements covered by Article 101(1)(a) to (e) EC do not constitute an exhaustive list of prohibited collusion.

24. Therefore, it must be examined whether agreements with features such as those described by the national court have as their object the restriction of competition.

25. In BIDS' submission, if an agreement does not affect the total output on a market or obstruct operators' freedom to act independently, any anti-competitive effect can be excluded. In the main proceedings, the withdrawal of certain operators from the market is irrelevant, because the stayers are in a position to satisfy demand.

26. BIDS adds that the structure of the market does not allow the processors to influence it, since up to 90% of demand is from outside Ireland. On the Irish market, the power of the processors is largely counteracted by the purchasing power of the four major retailers. Account must also be taken of the competition which new operators entering the market concerned could bring about.

27. BIDS observes that the cases in which a limitation on output has been held to be infringement by object concerned agreements supplemental to horizontal

[59] Case C-209/07, *Competition Authority v Beef Industry Development Society Ltd (BIDS) and Barry Brothers (Carrigmore) Meats Ltd* [2008] ECR I–8637, para 20.

price or production fixing agreements [. . .] to which the BIDS arrangements are not comparable.

28. BIDS submits that the Commission's decision-making practice and the case-law do not permit the conclusion that there is a restriction by object [. . .].

29. The BIDS arrangements cannot be compared to the freezing of capacities proposed by the liner conferences [. . .], since the freezing was not sufficient to eliminate overcapacities in the sector.

30. Finally, the BIDS arrangements provide for neither the freezing nor the non-use of capacity, nor exchange of information, nor quotas or other measures intended to preserve the stayers' market shares.

31. In that regard, it is apparent from the documents before the Court and from the information provided by the national court that the object of the BIDS arrangements is to change, appreciably, the structure of the market through a mechanism intended to encourage the withdrawal of competitors.

32. The matters brought to the Court's attention show that the BIDS arrangements are intended to improve the overall profitability of undertakings supplying more than 90% of the beef and veal processing services on the Irish market by enabling them to approach, or even attain, their minimum efficient scale. In order to do so, those arrangements pursue two main objectives: first, to increase the degree of concentration in the sector concerned by reducing significantly the number of undertakings supplying processing services and, second, to eliminate almost 75% of excess production capacity.

33. The BIDS arrangements are intended therefore, essentially, to enable several undertakings to implement a common policy which has as its object the encouragement of some of them to withdraw from the market and the reduction, as a consequence, of the overcapacity which affects their profitability by preventing them from achieving economies of scale.

34. That type of arrangement conflicts patently with the concept inherent in the EC Treaty provisions relating to competition, according to which each economic operator must determine independently the policy which it intends to adopt on the common market. Article [101(1)TFEU] is intended to prohibit any form of coordination which deliberately substitutes practical cooperation between undertakings for the risks of competition.

35. In the context of competition, the undertakings which signed the BIDS arrangements would have, without such arrangements, no means of improving their profitability other than by intensifying their commercial rivalry or resorting to concentrations. With the BIDS arrangements it would be possible for them to avoid such a process and to share a large part of the costs involved in increasing the degree of market concentration as a result, in particular, of the levy [. . .] per head processed by each of the stayers.

36. In addition, the means put in place to attain the objective of the BIDS arrangements include restrictions whose object is anti-competitive.

37. As regards, in the first place, the levy [. . .] per head of cattle slaughtered beyond the usual volume of production of each of the stayers, it is, as BIDS submits, the price to be paid by the stayers to acquire the goers' clientele. However, it must be observed, [. . .] that such a measure also constitutes an obstacle to the natural development of market shares as regards some of the stayers who, because of the dissuasive nature of that levy, are deterred from exceeding their usual volume of production. That measure is likely therefore to lead to certain operators freezing their production.

38. As regards, secondly, restrictions imposed on the goers as regards the disposal and use of their processing plants, the BIDS arrangements also contain, by their very

object, restrictions on competition since they seek to avoid the possible use of those plants by new operators entering the market in order to compete with the stayers. As the Competition Authority pointed out in its written observations, since the investment necessary for the construction of a new processing plant is much greater than the costs of taking over an existing plant, those restrictions are obviously intended to dissuade any new entry of competitors throughout the island of Ireland.

39. Finally, the fact that those restrictions, as well as the non-competition clause imposed on the goers, are limited in time is not such as to put in doubt the finding as to the anti-competitive nature of the object of the BIDS arrangements. [. . .] [S]uch matters may, at the most, be relevant for the purposes of the examination of the four requirements which have to be met under Article [101(3) TFEU] in order to escape the prohibition laid down in Article [101(1) TFEU].

40. In the light of the foregoing considerations, the reply to the question referred must be that an agreement with features such as those of the standard form of contract concluded between the 10 principal beef and veal processors in Ireland, who are members of BIDS, and requiring, among other things, a reduction of the order of 25% in processing capacity, has as its object the prevention, restriction or distortion of competition within the meaning of Article [101(1) TFEU].

NOTES AND QUESTIONS ON BIDS

1. (Paragraph 17) The CJEU uses the expression 'as being injurious to the proper functioning of normal competition' to describe anti-competitive effects. This definition abstracts from the final outcome of the competitive process: that is, price, quantity and quality.
2. What do you think of the parties' arguments before the Irish Competition Authority[60] that the object of the agreement was not to restrict competition, but to increase competition by reducing costs? Do consumers ever benefit from agreements to reduce prices and costs by a mechanism agreed by market leaders that restricts production?
3. Is a national competition authority with regulatory powers able to impose a solution similar to BIDS to avoid a shortage of production in the long term? Should it be easily persuaded to do so?
4. (Paragraph 21) Whilst the CJEU describes this goal as a 'legitimate objective', it is maintained that such considerations are irrelevant for the purpose of applying the prohibition laid down in Article 101(1), whereas can be taken into consideration under Article 101(3).
5. (Paragraph 25) The defendant claims that the intended outcome of the agreement was not anti-competitive given that it was aimed at restricting total output. The aim was to coordinate an increase in concentration in order to achieve greater scale economies, and thus improve productive efficiency.
6. (Paragraph 25) Do consumers obtain a benefit if the demand is satisfied by members of a cartel at a higher level than if the agreement was condemned?
7. (Paragraph 26) Was BIDS' argument that demand from outside Ireland would have kept prices down to competitive levels cogent?

60 See ibid, para 19.

8. (Paragraph 35) The assessment of the anti-competitive nature of the agreement is based on a counterfactual analysis. The CJEU argues that absent the agreement the desired (and legitimate) increase in concentration could only have been reached through either exits or mergers. It must follow that these alternative means towards increased concentration are in line with the proper functioning of normal competition. Based on what explained above, could this type of assessment under Article 101(1) pre-empt the assessment under Article 101(3)? If so, under which one of the four cumulative criteria specifically?
9. (Paragraphs 36 and 37) What is the key difference between the rationalization element of the BIDS agreements discussed above and the two ancillary restrictions: a higher levy incurred to expand output, and a ban on disposal of existing facilities? Why is it more straightforward to conclude that the latter are anti-competitive 'by object'?

6.3.1.1.4. GlaxoSmithKline (dual pricing in Spain)

Case T-168/01, *GlaxoSmithKline Services Unlimited v Commission*
[2006] ECR II–2969

The facts of this case were examined in Chapter 2. GlaxoSmithKline (GSK), a producer of pharmaceutical products notified the Commission of a General Sales Conditions document sent to its Spanish wholesalers, which included in Clause 4 a 'dual pricing mechanism' distinguishing between prices charged from wholesalers for medicines sold domestically and higher prices charged in the case the drugs were exported to other Member States. The Commission found that Clause 4 had as its object and the effect the restriction of competition. The decision was appealed to the General Court, on a number of grounds, one of which concerned the interpretation of Article 101(1) TFEU and in particular the qualification of the clause restricting parallel trade as a restriction of competition by object. In GSK, the General Court highlighted that 'the objective assigned to Article 101(1), which constitutes a fundamental provision indispensable for the achievement of the missions entrusted to the Community, in particular for the functioning of the internal market [. . .], is to prevent undertakings, by restricting competition between themselves or with third parties, from reducing the welfare of the final consumer of the products in question'.[61] *The Court then concentrated its analysis on the nature of the presumption that the distinction between anti-competitive object and effect entails, before moving to consider the effects of the agreement in question. The General Court refused to accept that the mere existence of a clause (preventing parallel trade) which is in principle to be regarded as having as its object the restriction of competition allows the conclusion that such provision as such had indeed as its object the restriction of competition. The Court noted that:*

> 120. In *Consten and Grundig v Commission* [. . .] the Court of Justice, contrary to the Commission's contention in its written submissions, did not hold that an agreement intended to limit parallel trade must be considered by its nature, that is to say, independently of any competitive analysis, to have as its object the restriction of competition. On the contrary, the Court of Justice merely held, first, that an agreement between a producer and a distributor which might tend to restore the national divisions in trade

[61] Case T-168/01, *GlaxoSmithKline Services Unlimited v Commission* [2006] ECR II–2969, para 118.

between Member States might be of such a kind as to frustrate the most fundamental objectives of the Community [. . .], a consideration which led it to reject a plea alleging that Article 101(1) TFEU was not applicable to vertical agreements [. . .]. The Court of Justice then carried out a competitive analysis, abridged but real, during the course of which it held, in particular, that the agreement in question sought to eliminate any possibility of competition at the wholesale level in order to charge prices which were sheltered from all effective competition, considerations which led it to reject a plea alleging that there was no restriction of competition [. . .].

The analysis of the economic and legal context of the agreement may show that the agreement in question did not produce any harm to the final consumer. This is possible, precisely because the General Court conceived competition as essentially referring to an outcome defined by a set of parameters, such as price and quantity, which could affect the final consumers.[62] According to the General Court, 'the prices of the medicines concerned are to a large extent controlled by the public authorities, it cannot be taken for granted at the outset that parallel trade tends to reduce those prices and thus to increase the welfare of final consumers'; consequently, it cannot be presumed that limiting parallel trade, 'tends to diminish the welfare of final consumers'.[63] In the circumstances of this case, the GC therefore found that it could not be inferred from the presumed anti-competitive objective of the agreement that such agreement reveals by itself that it has as its object or effect to prevent, restrict or distort competition.

The Commission, GSK, and third interveners interjected appeals to the CJEU. Advocate General Trstenjak proceeded to the analysis of the concept of restriction of competition by object, arguing that some form of economic analysis is also necessary in this context and rejecting the linkage between the existence of a detriment to the final consumers and the finding a restriction of competition under Article 101(1) TFEU.[64]

Opinion of Advocate General Trstenjak in Joined Cases C-501, 513, 515 & 519/06 P, *GlaxoSmithKline Services Unlimited v Commission*, ECLI:EU:C:2009:409 (footnotes omitted)

90. A restrictive object must be considered to exist where agreements are by their very nature liable to restrict competition. That can be assumed to be the case where an agreement, having regard to its legal and economic context, has the specific capability and the tendency to have a negative impact on competition.

91. In this connection, regard must be had, in particular, to existing experience according to which, in all probability, certain types of agreement have a negative impact in the market and jeopardise the objectives pursued by the Community's competition legislation. Under this approach, the character of the restriction of competition by object as a form of inchoate offence becomes particularly clear, since certain types of agreement (such as price-fixing agreements, customer sharing or resale price maintenance) are classified, on the basis of existing experience, as restrictions of competition by

62 Ibid, para 167. 63 Ibid, para 147.

64 Opinion of Advocate General Trstenjak in Joined Cases C-501, 513, 515 & 519/06 P, *GlaxoSmithKline Services Unlimited v Commission*, ECLI:EU:C:2009:409.

object, without any specific analysis of their effects. This standardised approach certainly creates legal certainty. However, it is always subject to the proviso that the legal and economic context of the agreement to be examined does not preclude application of this standardised assessment.

92. The notion of restriction of competition by object is nevertheless not confined solely to certain types of agreement. It also covers agreements where a sufficiently deleterious effect on competition may be presumed on the basis of economic analysis. Such an assessment of an agreement presupposes that it is appraised in its legal and economic context. That situation therefore retains a certain closeness in content to the examination of the restrictive effects of the agreement. However, the difference compared with an examination of the restrictive effects of the agreement lies in the fact that, with a restriction of competition by object, the negative interference with market conditions is so clear that the agreement can be presumed, without any detailed market analysis, to have a restrictive effect.

93. In determining whether an agreement has a restrictive object, account must be taken, in particular, of the agreement's content, the objective aims pursued by the agreement, the agreement's legal and economic context and the conduct of the parties. The intention of the parties may also be taken into account as a circumstantial factor.

94. If the agreement does not have a restrictive object, it is then prohibited under Article [101(1) TFEU] only if it is argued and proved, on the basis of an analysis of the actual and/or potential effects of the agreement on the relevant market(s), that the agreement has the effect of restricting competition.

The CJEU adopted the following judgment:

Joined Cases C-501, 513, 515 & 519/06 P, *GlaxoSmithKline Services Unlimited v Commission*
[2009] ECR I–9291 (references omitted)

55. First of all, it must be borne in mind that the anti-competitive object and effect of an agreement are not cumulative but alternative conditions for assessing whether such an agreement comes within the scope of the prohibition laid down in Article 101(1) TFEU. According to settled case-law since the judgment in Case 56/65 *LTM* [1966] ECR 235, the alternative nature of that condition, indicated by the conjunction 'or', leads first to the need to consider the precise purpose of the agreement, in the economic context in which it is to be applied. Where, however, the analysis of the content of the agreement does not reveal a sufficient degree of harm to competition, the consequences of the agreement should then be considered and for it to be caught by the prohibition it is necessary to find that those factors are present which show that competition has in fact been prevented, restricted or distorted to an appreciable extent. It is also apparent from the case-law that it is not necessary to examine the effects of an agreement once its anti-competitive object has been established [. . .].

56. Secondly, to examine the anti-competitive object of the agreement before its anti-competitive effect is all the more justified because, if the error of law alleged by the Commission, Aseprofar and EAEPC turns out to be substantiated, GSK's appeal directed at the grounds of the judgment under appeal relating to the anti-competitive effect of the agreement will fall to be dismissed.

57. Consequently, it is appropriate to ascertain whether the General Court's assessment as to whether the agreement has an anti-competitive object [. . .] is in accordance with the principles extracted from the relevant case-law.

58. According to settled case-law, in order to assess the anti-competitive nature of an agreement, regard must be had inter alia to the content of its provisions, the objectives it seeks to attain and the economic and legal context of which it forms a part [. . .]. In addition, although the parties' intention is not a necessary factor in determining whether an agreement is restrictive, there is nothing prohibiting the Commission or the Community judicature from taking that aspect into account [. . .].

59. With respect to parallel trade, the Court has already held that, in principle, agreements aimed at prohibiting or limiting parallel trade have as their object the prevention of competition [. . .].

61. The Court has, moreover, held in that regard, in relation to the application of Article 101 TFEU and in a case involving the pharmaceuticals sector, that an agreement between producer and distributor which might tend to restore the national divisions in trade between Member States might be such as to frustrate the Treaty's objective of achieving the integration of national markets through the establishment of a single market. Thus on a number of occasions the Court has held agreements aimed at partitioning national markets according to national borders or making the interpenetration of national markets more difficult, in particular those aimed at preventing or restricting parallel exports, to be agreements whose object is to restrict competition within the meaning of that article of the Treaty [. . .].

The Court followed by rejecting the position of the General Court that, while it is accepted that an agreement intended to limit parallel trade must in principle be considered to have as its object the restriction of competition, that applies in so far as it may be presumed to deprive final consumers of the advantages of effective competition in terms of supply or price. According to the CJEU, 'by requiring proof that the agreement entails disadvantages for final consumers as a prerequisite for a finding of anti-competitive object and by not finding that that agreement had such an object, the General Court committed an error of law'[65] *as 'there is nothing in that provision to indicate that only those agreements which deprive consumers of certain advantages may have an anti-competitive object'.*[66] *Furthermore, 'Article 101 TFEU aims to protect not only the interests of competitors or of consumers, but also the structure of the market and, in so doing, competition as such' and 'consequently, for a finding that an agreement has an anti-competitive object, it is not necessary that final consumers be deprived of the advantages of effective competition in terms of supply or price'.*[67]

NOTES AND QUESTIONS ON GLAXOSMITHKLINE SERVICES UNLIMITED V COMMISSION

1. The CJEU agrees with Advocate General Trstenjak that the General Court erred in law by requirement that an 'object' infringement must be presumed to be harmful for final consumers. Advocate General Trstenjak further considered that such a requirement

[65] Joined Cases C-501, 513, 515 & 519/06 P, *GlaxoSmithKline Services Unlimited v Commission* [2009] ECR I-9291, para 64.

[66] Ibid, para 63. [67] Ibid.

would make it difficult to conclude that an agreement is anti-competitive 'by object' when it takes place at wholesale level, thus not directly affecting prices and supply to final consumers. Is this what the Commission and the General Court argued? Is there a difference between an argument that no anti-competitive effects could be established and an argument that no anti-competitive effects could be presumed?

2. Does the rejection of the defendant's claim that no anti-competitive effects, in terms of price and supply terms for final consumers, could be presumed suggest that an 'object' categorization is not rebuttable?

6.3.1.1.4. T-Mobile Netherlands

On 13 June 2001, representatives of mobile telecommunication operators offering mobile telecommunication services on the Netherlands market held a meeting. At that meeting they discussed, *inter alia*, the reduction of standard dealer remunerations for post-paid subscriptions on or about 1 September 2001. Five operators in the Netherlands had their own mobile telephone network, namely Ben Nederland ('Ben', now T-Mobile), KPN Dutchtone NV ('Dutchtone', now Orange), LibertelVodafone NV ('LibertelVodafone', now Vodafone), and Telfort Mobile BV (subsequently O2 (Netherlands) BV—'O2 (Netherlands)'—and now Telfort). In 2001, the market share held by the five operators amounted, respectively, to 10.6 per cent, 42.1 per cent, 9.7 per cent, 26.1 per cent, and 11.4 per cent. It was unforeseeable that a sixth mobile telephone network would be established because no further licences had been issued. Access to the market for mobile telecommunications services was therefore possible only through the conclusion of an agreement with one or more of those five operators.

By decision of 30 December 2002 ('the initial decision') the Dutch Competition Authority found that Ben, Dutchtone, KPN, O2 (Telfort), and Vodafone (formerly Libertel-Vodafone) had entered into a concerted practice relating to mobile telephone subscriptions, which restricted competition to an appreciable extent and was incompatible with both Article 101 TFEU and the equivalent Dutch competition law provision.

Following appeal actions by the undertakings concerned, the Administrative Court for Trade and Industry in the Netherlands referred a preliminary question to the CJEU stating that it was uncertain as to whether the object of the concerted practice of the operators in question, which relates to the remuneration paid to dealers for concluding subscription agreements, may be considered to be the prevention, restriction or distortion of competition within the meaning of Article 101(1) TFEU and that the competition case law of the Court may be interpreted as meaning that the object of an agreement or concerted practice is to restrict competition if experience shows that, by virtue of that agreement or that practice, irrespective of economic circumstances, competition is always, or almost always, prevented, restricted, or distorted. That was the case, according to the referring court, where the actual detrimental effects are unmistakable and will occur irrespective of the characteristic features of the relevant market. It would therefore be always necessary, according to the referring court, to examine the effects of a concerted practice in order to ensure that conduct is not regarded as pursuing the object of restricting competition when it is clear that it does not have any restrictive effects.

Advocate General Kokott's Opinion includes an interesting discussion of the distinction between restrictive object and effect under Article 101(1) TFEU.

Opinion of AG Kokott in Case C-8/08, *T-Mobile Netherlands BV, KPN Mobile NV, Orange Nederland NV and Vodafone Libertel NV v Raad van bestuur van de Nederlandse Mededingingsautoriteit*
[2009] ECR I–4529 (references omitted)

43. The prohibition of a practice simply by reason of its anti-competitive object is justified by the fact that certain forms of collusion between undertakings can be regarded, by their very nature, as being injurious to the proper functioning of normal competition. The per se prohibition of such practices recognised as having harmful consequences for society creates legal certainty and allows all market participants to adapt their conduct accordingly. Moreover, it sensibly conserves resources of competition authorities and the justice system.

44. Certainly, the concept of a restricted practice having an anti-competitive object may not be subject to unduly broad interpretation, given the serious consequences which may befall an undertaking in the case of an infringement of Article [101(1)TFEU]. However, nor may that concept be subject to unduly strict interpretation, if the primary law prohibition on 'infringement by object' is not to be erased through interpretation and, as a consequence, Article [101(1) TFEU] deprived of an element of its practical effectiveness. From the wording itself of Article [101(1) TFEU], it follows that both concerted practices having an anti-competitive object and those with anti-competitive effects are prohibited.

AG Kokott considered that anti-competitive object leads to an absolute presumption (not rebuttable) of incompatibility to Article 101(1);[68] *any other option, such as accepting that the presumption could be rebutted by proving in the specific case no negative impact for the operation on the market or the consumers would have mingled anti-competitive object and anti-competitive effect and therefore call into question the fact that a practice might be anti-competitive by object or by effect. There was thus no need to prove the existence of an anti-competitive effect. For AG Kokott, '[. . .] the prohibition on "infringements of competition by object" resulting from Article 101(1) TFEU is comparable to the risk offences (*Gefährdungsdelikte*) known in criminal law: in most legal systems, a person who drives a vehicle when significantly under the influence of alcohol or drugs is liable to a criminal or administrative penalty, wholly irrespective of whether, in fact, he endangered another road user or was even responsible for an accident. In the same vein, undertakings infringe European competition law and may be subject to a fine if they engage in concerted practices with an anti-competitive object; whether in an individual case, in fact, particular market participants or the general public suffer harm is irrelevant.'*[69]

56. [. . .] Even in the absence of a direct influence on consumers and the prices payable by them, a concerted practice may have an anti-competitive object.

57. From its wording alone, Article 101(1) TFEU is directed in general terms against the prevention, restriction or distortion of competition within the common market. Nor

68 Opinion of AG Kokott in Case C-8/08, *T-Mobile Netherlands BV, KPN Mobile NV, Orange Nederland NV and Vodafone Libertel NV v Raad van bestuur van de Nederlandse Mededingingsautoriteit* [2009] ECR I–4529, para 43 '. . . *per se* prohibition of such practices recognised as having harmful consequences for society creates legal certainty and allows all market participants to adapt their conduct accordingly'.

69 Ibid, para 47.

> do the various examples listed in subparagraphs (a) to (e) of Article 101(1) TFEU contain any restriction in terms such that only anti-competitive business practices having a direct impact on final consumers are prohibited.
>
> 58. Instead, Article 101 TFEU forms part of a system designed to protect competition within the internal market from distortions [Article 3(1)(g) EC, now repealed and replaced by Protocol No 27 and Article 3(3) TFEU]. Accordingly, Article 101 TFEU, like the other competition rules of the Treaty, is not designed only or primarily to protect the immediate interests of individual competitors or consumers, but to protect the structure of the market and thus competition as such (as an institution). In this way, consumers are also indirectly protected. Because where competition as such is damaged, disadvantages for consumers are also to be feared.
>
> 59. Thus, a concerted practice has an anti-competitive object not only where it is capable of having a direct impact on consumers and the prices payable by them, or—as T-Mobile puts it—on 'consumer welfare'. Instead, an anti-competitive object must already be assumed if the concerted practice is capable of preventing, restricting or distorting competition within the common market. That provides an indication that a concerted practice—indirectly, at least—may also have a negative impact on consumers.
>
> 60. To narrow the prohibition of Article [101(1) TFEU] simply to behaviour having a direct influence on consumer prices would deprive that provision, which is fundamental for the internal market, of much of its practical effect. [. . .]
>
> 72. A concerted practice pursues an anti-competitive object for the purposes of Article 101(1) TFEU where, according to its content and objectives and having regard to its legal and economic context, it is capable in an individual case of resulting in the prevention, restriction or distortion of competition within the common market. In that regard, neither the realisation of such prevention, restriction or distortion of competition nor a direct link between the concerted practice and retail prices is decisive. An exchange of confidential information between competitors is tainted with an anti-competitive object if the exchange is capable of removing existing uncertainties concerning the intended market conduct of the participating undertakings and thus undermining the rules of free competition.

Note that AG Kokott's Opinion also includes developments on the existence of a causal link between concerted practice and market conduct and on the presumption of a causal link should the concerted practice be an isolated event.

AG Kokott referred to the protection of competition as the main objective of Article 101.[70] She did not adopt, however, a deontological approach but suggested that competition is to the benefit of consumers and the 'public at large'. This seems to expanding the beneficiaries of the principle of competition enshrined in Article 101(1) beyond the category of final, or even intermediary, consumers. Nonetheless, it is not clear if this is a total welfare standard or something else. It seems a different position from that advanced by the European Commission in the Guidelines on Article 101(3), where the Commission had made an effort to link the recognition of restrictions which are anti-competitive by their object with the economic concept of 'consumer welfare'.[71] One could also consider that the outcome-based formulation of the principle of competition by the AG is a sham: the inclusion of consumers along with 'the

70 Ibid, para 71.

71 Guidelines on Article 101(3) (formerly 81(3)), para 21.

public at large', as beneficiaries of the principle of competition, aims in reality to legitimize a process-based view of competition.

It is not clear how this approach can accommodate the emphasis of the Commission on market power (and parameters of competition viewed from the point of the consumers) as a filter for the application of Article 101(1). In addition, it cannot offer any redemption under Article 101(1) to a restriction of competitive rivalry, even if it is absolutely clear that the final (or intermediary) consumers would benefit from it. It will still be presumed that the 'public at large' would suffer from the restriction of competitive rivalry. One may also, however, construct restrictively the position of AG as suggesting that the presumption applies only in case there is doubt over the effects of the practice on final (or intermediary) consumers.

Case C-8/08, *T-Mobile Netherlands BV, KPN Mobile NV, Orange Nederland NV and Vodafone Libertel NV v Raad van bestuur van de Nederlandse Mededingingsautoriteit*
[2009] ECR I–4529 (references omitted)

27. With regard to the assessment as to whether a concerted practice is anticompetitive, close regard must be paid in particular to the objectives which it is intended to attain and to its economic and legal context [. . .]. Moreover, while the intention of the parties is not an essential factor in determining whether a concerted practice is restrictive, there is nothing to prevent the Commission [. . .] or the competent [EU] judicature from taking it into account [. . .].

28. As regards the distinction to be drawn between concerted practices having an anti-competitive object and those with anti-competitive effects, it must be borne in mind that an anti-competitive object and anti-competitive effects constitute not cumulative but alternative conditions in determining whether a practice falls within the prohibition in Article [101(1) TFEU]. It has [. . .] been settled case-law that the alternative nature of that requirement, indicated by the conjunction 'or', means that it is necessary, first, to consider the precise purpose of the concerted practice, in the economic context in which it is to be pursued. Where, however, an analysis of the terms of the concerted practice does not reveal the effect on competition to be sufficiently deleterious, its consequences should then be considered and, for it to be caught by the prohibition, it is necessary to find that those factors are present which establish that competition has in fact been prevented or restricted or distorted to an appreciable extent [. . .].

29. Moreover, in deciding whether a concerted practice is prohibited by Article [101(1) TFEU], there is no need to take account of its actual effects once it is apparent that its object is to prevent, restrict or distort competition within the common market [. . .]. The distinction between 'infringements by object' and 'infringements by effect' arises from the fact that certain forms of collusion between undertakings can be regarded, by their very nature, as being injurious to the proper functioning of normal competition [. . .].

30. Accordingly, contrary to what the referring court claims, there is no need to consider the effects of a concerted practice where its anticompetitive object is established.

31. With regard to the assessment as to whether a concerted practice, such as that at issue in the main proceedings, pursues an anticompetitive object, it should be noted, first, as pointed out by the Advocate General [. . .] that in order for a concerted practice to be regarded as having an anticompetitive object, it is sufficient that it has the potential to have a negative impact on competition. In other words, the concerted practice must simply be capable in an individual case, having regard to the specific legal and economic context, of resulting in the prevention, restriction or distortion of competition within the common market. Whether and to what extent, in fact, such anti-competitive effects result can only be of relevance for determining the amount of any fine and assessing any claim for damages. [. . .]

36. [. . .] As to whether a concerted practice may be regarded as having an anticompetitive object even though there is no direct connection between that practice and consumer prices, it is not possible on the basis of the wording of Article [101(1) TFEU] to conclude that only concerted practices which have a direct effect on the prices paid by end users are prohibited.

37. On the contrary, it is apparent from Article [101(1)(a) TFEU] that concerted practices may have an anticompetitive object if they 'directly or indirectly fix purchase or selling prices or any other trading conditions'. In the present case, [. . .] the remuneration paid to dealers is evidently a decisive factor in fixing the price to be paid by the end user.

38. In any event, [. . .] Article [101 TFEU], like the other competition rules of the Treaty, is designed to protect not only the immediate interests of individual competitors or consumers but also to protect the structure of the market and thus competition as such.

39. Therefore, contrary to what the referring court would appear to believe, in order to find that a concerted practice has an anticompetitive object, there does not need to be a direct link between that practice and consumer prices. [. . .]

41. [. . .] [W]hile not all parallel conduct of competitors on the market can be traced to the fact that they have adopted a concerted action with an anti-competitive object, an exchange of information which is capable of removing uncertainties between participants as regards the timing, extent and details of the modifications to be adopted by the undertaking concerned must be regarded as pursuing an anti-competitive object, and that extends to situations, such as that in the present case, in which the modification relates to the reduction in the standard commission paid to dealers.

42. It is for the referring court to determine whether, in the dispute in the main proceedings, the information exchanged at the meeting [. . .] was capable of removing such uncertainties.

43. In the light of all the foregoing considerations, the answer to the first question must be that a concerted practice pursues an anti-competitive object for the purpose of Article [101(1) TFEU] where, according to its content and objectives and having regard to its legal and economic context, it is capable in an individual case of resulting in the prevention, restriction or distortion of competition within the common market. It is not necessary for there to be actual prevention, restriction or distortion of competition or a direct link between the concerted practice and consumer prices. An exchange of information between competitors is tainted with an anti-competitive object if the exchange is capable of removing uncertainties concerning the intended conduct of the participating undertakings.

NOTES AND QUESTIONS ON T-MOBILE

1. (CJEU judgment, paragraph 28). Note that the CJEU explains that the distinction between 'infringements by object' and 'infringements by effect' arises from the fact that certain 'forms of collusion between undertakings', that is kinds of arrangements, can be regarded, 'by their very nature, as being injurious to the proper functioning of normal competition', this assessment not necessarily being linked to the (actual) effects of the specific arrangement. The CJEU further notes in paragraph 31 that for a specific arrangement to be anti-competitive by object, it 'is sufficient that it has the *potential* to have a negative impact on competition' (emphasis added). Is the CJEU distinguishing between actual and potential effects? Are potential effects taken into account in identifying a restriction of competition by object?
2. (Opinion AG Kokott, paragraphs 56, 60, 62). Do you agree with the Advocate General that the presumption that restrictions by object infringe Article 101(1) TFEU should be absolute?
3. Contrary to Advocate General Kokott, the CJEU only refers to final consumer prices, but not to intermediate consumers. Does that leave open the possibility to rebut a presumption of anti-competitive effects by showing that the alleged 'object' infringement could not even result in anti-competitive effects in terms of prices and supply terms for intermediate consumers? Would the defendant have to argue that no anti-competitive effects could be established or that no anti-competitive effects could even be presumed?
4. How can an alleged object infringement harm consumers even indirectly where no anti-competitive effect could be presumed even at the level of intermediate consumers?

6.3.1.2. Legal and economic context: Blurring the distinction between object and effect?

The CJEU has longed recognized that each agreement should be examined in its 'economic and legal context' in order to infer an anti-competitive object or effect under Article 101(1) TFEU. This analysis was particularly important in *Consten and Grundig* where the Court inferred the existence of an anti-competitive object from the joint operation of the exclusive distribution agreement and the GINT trademark licence agreement.[72] The analysis of the legal and economic context does not always lead to an extension of the competition law liability for infringing Article 101 TFEU. It may operate also as a form of defence in certain circumstances.

Starting with *STM/MBU*, the EU Courts developed a more analytical approach in assessing restrictions of competition by object, putting emphasis on the legal and economic context of the agreement and introducing a multi-factor analysis that would look to the text of the agreement, the severity of the clauses included but also factors relating to the position of the parties, market structure, as well as the counterfactual test.

72 *Établissements Consten SA and Grundigverkaufs-GmbH v EEC Commission* [1966] CMLR 418, 474.

S King, *Agreements that Restrict Competition by Object under Article 101(1) TFEU: Past, Present and Future* (London School of Economics, PhD thesis, January 2015), 56–7 (references omitted)

The judgment in *STM* sets out a comprehensive test [. . .] in which to determine the object of an agreement and prescribes that:

(i) The 'precise purpose' of the agreement must be considered.

(ii) The consideration must be in the economic context in which the agreement is to be applied.

(iii) Such purpose (interference with competition) must result from some or all of the actual clauses of the agreement itself.

(iv) Should this analysis not 'reveal the *effect* on competition to be *sufficiently deleterious*, the consequences of the agreement should then be considered'.

(v) [When determining the purpose of the agreement] the competition must be understood within the actual context in which it would occur in the absence of the agreement in dispute [the counterfactual].

(vi) Whether a restriction is prohibited by reason of its object [or effect], it is appropriate to take account of:

a. the nature and quantity of the products covered by the agreement,

b. the position and importance of the supplier and distributor on the market for the products concerned,

c. the isolated nature of the disputed agreement or its position in a series of agreements, and

d. the severity of the clauses intended to protect the restriction or the opportunities allowed for other commercial competitors in the same products by way of parallel re-exportation and importation [. . .].

STM therefore lays the foundation for an analytical, economics-based approach towards determining whether the object of an agreement is to restrict competition. Under this methodology the standard of proof required to establish if an agreement is restrictive by object is considerably higher than that of the orthodox approach.

The most recent case law of the EU courts and the decisional practice of the Commission shows a tension between the 'orthodox' approach that establishes a clear distinction between restrictions by object and restrictions by effect, and seems to put forward the idea that a finding of anti-competitive object leads almost automatically to the prohibition of the agreement under Article 101(1) TFEU, and the more analytical approach that would emphasize more the analysis of the economic and legal context of the agreement, before concluding that it restricts competition, eventually also challenging the existence of a clear dichotomy between restrictions by object and restrictions by effect. We will explore the moving boundaries of the restrictions of competition by object and effect, before examining the most recent case law of the EU Courts, which seems to have reached some form of equilibrium on this issue.

6.3.1.2.1. Setting the moving boundaries of the object restriction: The battle between 'orthodoxy' and the 'more analytical approach'

The analysis of the decisional practice of the Commission and of the case law of the EU Courts on the distinction between restrictions by object and restrictions by effects illustrate the moving equilibrium between, on one side, the 'analytical' approach championed by the CJEU in *STM/MBU* and, on the other side, the 'orthodox' approach, that would reject any economic analysis in the context of the assessment of a restriction of competition by object.

It is not possible to identify clear historical patterns in the case law of the EU courts as to which approach was followed in various periods, as cases taking an 'orthodox' perspective co-existed with cases in which the EU Courts adopted the analytical approach. For instance, the EU Courts have accepted in *Coditel II, Erauw-Jacquery Sprl v La Hesbignonne Societé Coopérative*, and *Javico v Yves Saint Laurent* that absolute territorial protections and export bans, in the specific circumstances of these cases, did not constitute restrictions of competition by object.

Case 27/87, *Erauw-Jacquery Sprl v La Hesbignonne Société Coopérative*
[1988] ECR I–1983, [1988] CMLR 576

On a preliminary reference by the Tribunal de Commerce of Liège, the Court interpreted Article 101(1) TFEU in the context of an agreement granting a licence for the propagation and sale of certain varieties of cereal seeds protected by plant breeders' rights in Belgium. The agreement included a clause prohibiting the licensees from selling or exporting the basic seeds is compatible with Article 101(1) TFEU in so far as it is necessary to enable the breeder to select the licensed growers, as well as a clause requiring the licensee to respect minimum prices fixed by the breeder. It found that these clauses restrict competition within the Common Market and are covered by the prohibition in Article 101(1) TFEU if they have an appreciable effect on trade between Member States, which is a matter for the Belgian court to decide having regard to the legal and economic context of the agreement.

2. The question has arisen in the context of an action concerning certain clauses of an agreement whereby Société Louis Erauw-Jacquery, the owner of certain plant breeders' rights from their owner ('the breeder'), authorised the co-operative society La Hesbignonne ('the licensee') to propagate basic seeds and to sell the first or second generation seeds produced from these basic seeds and intended for the production of cereals ('reproductive seeds').

3. By this agreement, the licensee undertook (clause 2): (a) to propagate in Belgium the total quantity of E2 basic seeds or equivalent seeds supplied by the breeder [. . .] and not to sell or transfer E2 basic seeds or equivalent seeds of those varieties to propagating establishments, or to any other person except for the farmer propagating them, and not to export them to any country; [. . .] (f) not to export directly or indirectly, without prior written authorisation from the breeder, seeds of varieties for which the breeder is the owner or the agent of the owner of breeders' rights of any class whatever; [. . .]

5. According to the breeder, this sale compelled other propagating establishments to reduce their prices, thus incurring losses for which they sought compensation from the breeder. [. . .]

Compatibility with Article [101(1) TFEU] of the clause prohibiting the sale and export of E2 basic seeds

[. . .]

9. The Commission and the breeder contend that the clause prohibiting the sale and export of E2 basic seeds, which are supplied to propagating establishments only for the purpose of propagation, is not contrary to Article [101(1) TFEU]. Such a clause arises from the existence of plant breeders' rights.

10. On this point it should be emphasised that, as the Court found in Nungesser, [. . .] the development of basic lines may involve considerable financial sacrifices. Consequently, it should be accepted that anyone who makes considerable investments in developing basic seed varieties which may be the subject of plant breeders' rights must be able to obtain protection against improper handling of those seed varieties. For this purpose, the breeder must have the right to reserve propagation for the propagating establishments chosen by him as licensees. To that extent the clause prohibiting the licensee from selling and exporting basic seeds does not come within the prohibition laid down by Article [101(1) TFEU].

11. Therefore the answer to be given to the first part of the question submitted by the national court should be that a clause in an agreement concerning the propagation and sale of seeds, one of the parties to which is the owner or the agent of the owner of certain plant breeders' rights, and which prohibits the licensee from selling and exporting basic seeds, is compatible with Article [101(1) TFEU] if it is necessary to enable the breeder to select licensed propagating establishments. [. . .]

NOTES AND QUESTIONS ON ERAUW-JACQUERY

1. In his Opinion in *Louis Erauw-Jacquery*, Advocate General Mischo was concerned with export bans (and minimum resale price maintenance) of basic seed propagated by a licensed propagator. The AG noted with regard to the prohibition on selling and exporting basic seed:

   11. Basic seed is to a certain extent comparable to a manufacturing process protected by a patent, since certified seed of the first and second generation intended for sale to farmers for use in cereal production is produced from it. The breeder (or his agent) must therefore remain in a position to control the destination and the use of the basic seed; otherwise he would risk the *de facto* loss of the exclusive rights granted to him in respect of the new varieties which he has developed. The Commission is right to point out that the propagation agreement is an agreement where the identity of the other party is essential.

   12. The situation of a breeder or his agent therefore resembles in certain respects the situation of a franchisor, in respect of whom the Court has stated that he 'must be able to communicate his know-how to the franchisees and provide them with the necessary assistance in order to enable them to apply his methods, without running the risk that know-how and assistance might benefit competitors, even indirectly. It follows that provisions which are essential in order to avoid that risk do not constitute restrictions on competition for the purposes of Article [101(1) TFEU].

He concluded that 'Article [101(1) TFEU] does not preclude a provision prohibiting a grower from selling, assigning or exporting basic seed placed at his disposal by the breeder or his agent solely for the purpose of propagation'.[73] The Advocate General arrived at a different conclusion with regard to the provisions imposing minimum prices and prohibiting the exportation of other seed, qualifying them as restrictions of competition by object. He noted that:

> 24. [. . .] the prices imposed [in these cases] are applicable to certified seeds of all species, varieties and classes in respect of which Erauw-Jacquery is the breeder or agent. Consequently the provision covers even seed other than seed which La Hesbignonne propagates under its contract with Erauw-Jacquery.
>
> 25. It may therefore be concluded that the object of a minimum price provision in an agreement which is one of a cluster of identical agreements concluded by the same breeder or agent of foreign breeders and which is applicable even to seed not propagated under that agreement is to restrict competition.

2. The CJEU had come to a different conclusion with regard to absolute territorial protection clauses a few years earlier in *Nungesser*, where the CJEU distinguished between 'open' and 'closed' exclusive licences.[74] In contrast to the Commission's practice, the CJEU held that an 'open exclusive licence' is not in itself contrary to Article [101(1) TFEU]. French National Institute for Agricultural Research (INRA), financed by the French Minister of Agriculture, developed a commercially important F1 hybrid maize seed that could be grown in the colder climate of Northern Europe. For a few years, the variety was a great success, but was finally superseded by other varieties. INRA was not permitted by French law to exploit its discoveries commercially, so it licensed selected farmers in France to grow certified seed to be placed on the market. To exploit the German market, INRA made contracts in 1960 and 1965 with Eisele and later his firm, Nungesser (to be treated as a single undertaking), enabling Eisele to acquire the plant breeders' rights in the Federal Republic of Germany. INRA promised that it would try to prevent the seed grown in France from being exported to Germany save to Nungesser, and there were various other restrictions condemned by the Commission, such as minimum prices to be charged by Nungesser on the German market and an obligation to take two-thirds of its requirements of basic seed from the French growers. Nungesser arranged for the seeds to be grown and tested in Germany, and approved by a public authority for general sale. By 1972, the variety was already being superseded in France, and two dealers in Germany bought surplus quantities of certified seed from dealers in France. The Commission condemned the agreement without analysing the transaction to ascertain whether INRA could have arranged for the sale of its seed in Germany without granting what the Commission and Court treated as an exclusive licence. The CJEU, however, distinguished an open exclusive licence from one where absolute territorial protection is conferred. 'Open exclusive licence' is a novel term coined by the Court. It means an agreement:

> 53. [. . .] whereby the owner merely undertakes not to grant other licences in respect of the same territory and not to compete himself with the licensee in that territory.

[73] Opinion of AG Mischo in Case 27/87, *Erauw-Jacquery Sprl v La Hesbignonne Société Coopérative*, ECLI:EU:C:1987:538, para 13.

[74] Case 258/78, *LC Nungesser KG and Kurt Eisele v Commission*, [1982] ECR 2015.

According to the CJEU:

> 58. Having regard to the specific nature of the products in question, the Court concludes that, in a case such as the present, the grant of an open exclusive licence, that is to say, a licence which does not affect the position of third parties such as parallel importers and licensees for other territories, is not in itself incompatible with Article [101(1) TFEU].

3. The Court distinguished in the judgment the basic seed supplied to propagators from the certified seed sold to farmers. Even absolute territorial protection for the basic seed sent to propagating establishments for multiplication before sale to farmers was cleared, whereas in *Nungesser* such a clause in relation to certified seed was held to go too far even for an exemption. The Court's remarks in *Erauw-Jacquery* were confined to basic seed, but the reference to investment is of wide application, so the judgment might be extended to other protected products that need careful handling, such as software. One may construe the precedent more narrowly to relate only to basic and certified seed. Moreover, once a plant variety ceases to be distinct, uniform and stable, the intellectual property right is lost. This is not true of most other kind of intellectual property right.
4. The Court also accepted export restrictions in relation to a licence of performing rights in *Coditel II.*[75] It ruled that even absolute territorial protection may not infringe Article 101(1) TFEU in light of the commercial practice in the particular industry and the need for a film producer to obtain an adequate return. According to the CJEU, '[t]he characteristics of the cinematographic industry and of its markets in the Community, especially those relating to dubbing and subtitling for the benefit of different language groups, to the possibilities of television broadcasts, and to the system of financing cinematographic production in Europe serve to show that an exclusive exhibition licence is not, in itself, such as to prevent, restrict or distort competition.'[76]
5. In *Javico,*[77] before the accessions of Central and Eastern European countries to the EU in 2004, there were contractual restrictions forbidding a distributor in Eastern Europe from selling trademarked products in the EU. The CJEU held that such a ban did not necessarily have the object or effect of restricting competition within the EU. The legal and economic context was important. Such a restraint might have an effect in the Internal Market when the market was oligopolistic or where there was a significant difference in price between products inside and outside the Internal Market. It was for the national courts to decide the facts.

The jurisprudence of the CJEU also highlighted in a number of cases the need to take into account the economic context of an agreement when determining the existence of a restriction by object. In *CRAM and Rheinzink*, the CJEU observed:

> [. . .] [I]n order to determine whether an agreement has as its object the restriction of competition, it is not necessary to inquire which of the two contracting parties took the initiative

75 Case 262/81, *Coditel v Ciné Vog Films SA* [1982] ECR 3381 [hereinafter *Coditel II*].

76 Ibid, para 16.

77 Case C-306/96, *Javico International and Javico AG v Yves Saint Laurent Parfums SA (YSLP)* [1998] ECR I-1983.

in inserting any particular clause or to verify that the parties had a common intent at the time when the agreement was concluded. It is rather a question of examining the aims pursued by the agreement as such, in the light of the economic context in which the agreement is to be applied.[78]

In *ACF Chemiefarma v Commission*,[79] the Court dealt with a concerted practice involving price fixing and the allocation of markets. The case involved a contract fixing prices and quotas for supplying quinine to much of the world (the Quinine cartel), which expressly excluded the Common (Internal) Market, but the parties entered into a written 'gentlemen's agreement', enforceable by arbitration, to extend its application to the Common Market. This and the implementing oral and written arrangements were held to amount to 'agreements' within the meaning of Article [101(1) TFEU] even after they were put into mothballs by the parties, since they intended the prices fixed previously to continue in the Common Market. The CJEU noted that '[o]wing to the stringency of the restrictions imposed on undertakings from one Member State for the benefit of undertakings in other Member States and taking into account *the importance of such undertakings on the market in question*, these prohibitions clearly have as their object the restriction of competition within the Common Market and are capable of affecting trade between Member States.'[80]

The consideration of the economic and legal context may not operate only in order for a practice to escape the prohibition of Article 101(1) TFEU, as in *Louis Erauw-Jacquery*, but also to qualify some practices as a restriction of competition by object, as the following two examples illustrate. However, this expansion of the 'object' category led to a backlash, the Court signalling in *Groupement des cartes bancaires* the development of a more restrictive approach. The most recent judgments (in particular by the GC in *Lundbeck)* do not provide a clear picture as to the new equilibrium.

6.3.1.2.2. Pierre Fabre Dermo-Cosmetique

In *Pierre Fabre Dermo-Cosmetique (PFDC)*, the CJEU qualified as an object restriction of competition a ban on the sale of cosmetics and personal care products to end users via the Internet included in a selective distribution agreement.[81] Of particular interest is the Opinion of AG Mazák, who explored the distinction between restrictions of competition by object and hardcore restrictions.

Opinion of Advocate's General Mazák in Case C-439/09, *Pierre Fabre Dermo-Cosmetique SAS v Président de l'Authorité de la Concurrence, Ministre de l'Économie, de l'Industrie et de l'Emploi*, ECLI:EU:C:2011:113

23. According to the order for reference, the Decision found, inter alia, that the requirement in PFDC's distribution contracts that sales of the products in question be made in a physical space in the presence of a qualified pharmacist constituted a de facto ban on internet selling,

[78] Joined Cases C-29 & 30/83, *Compagnie Royal Asturienne des Mines and Rheinzink v Commission* [1984] ECR 1679, para 3 [hereinafter *CRAM and Rheinzink*].

[79] Case C-41/69, *ACF Chemiefarma v Commission* [1970] ECR 661.

[80] Ibid, para 155 (emphasis added).

[81] For a detailed analysis see Chapter 10.

is equivalent to a restriction of authorised distributors' active or passive sales and necessarily has the object of restricting competition. In addition, the ban was found to limit the commercial freedom of PFDC's distributors by excluding a means of marketing its products which also restricts the choice of consumers wishing to purchase online. [. . .]

24. I consider that a degree of confusion is apparent from the file before the Court with regard to the distinct concepts of a restriction of competition by object and a hard-core restriction. [. . .]

25. It is clear from the case law of the Court that vertical agreements may, in certain circumstances, have the object of restricting competition. The concept of a restriction by object flows, as indicated by PFDC, from the wording of art. [101(1) TFEU]. Where the anti-competitive object of the agreement is established it is not necessary to examine its effects on competition. However, while a finding of infringement by object with respect to an agreement will not require a demonstration of its anti-competitive effects in order to establish its anti-competitive nature, the Court has held that regard must be had, inter alia, to the content of the provisions of the agreement, the objectives it seeks to attain and the economic and legal context of which it forms a part.

26. The anti-competitive object of an agreement may not therefore be established solely using an abstract formula.

27. Thus while certain forms of agreement would appear from past experience to be prima facie infringements by object, this does not relieve the Commission or a national competition authority of the obligation of carrying out an individual assessment of an agreement. I consider that such an assessment may be quite truncated in certain cases, for example where there is clear evidence of a horizontal cartel seeking to control output in order to maintain prices, but it may not be entirely dispensed with.

28. The concept of a 'hard-core restriction' is not derived from the Treaty nor indeed Community legislation but is referred to in the Commission's Guidelines on Vertical Restraints ('Guidelines') which [include a list of 'hard-core restrictions which lead to the exclusion of the whole vertical agreement from the scope of application of (the vertical agreements block exemption regulation)]. Such hard-core restrictions thus include restrictions of the buyer's ability to determine its sale price, restrictions of the territory into which, or of the customers to whom, the buyer may sell the contract goods or services, the restriction of active or passive sales to end-users by members of a selective distribution system operating at the retail level of trade and the restriction of cross-supplies between distributors within a selective distribution system. In my view, while the inclusion of such restrictions in an agreement would give rise to concerns regarding the conformity of that agreement with art. [101(1) TFEU] and indeed, after examination of, inter alia, the particular agreement and the economic and legal context of which it forms a part, may in fact result in a finding of a restriction by object, there is no legal presumption that the agreement infringes Art. [101(1) TFEU].

29. In that regard, the Court has recently restated [. . .] the manner in which the distinct paragraphs of art. [101 TFEU] operate. Thus: 'where an agreement does not satisfy all the conditions provided for by an exempting regulation, it will be caught by the prohibition laid down in Article [101(1) TFEU] only if its object or effect is perceptibly to restrict competition within the common market and it is capable of affecting trade between Member States. In that latter case, and in the absence of individual exemption pursuant to Article [101(3)], that agreement would be automatically void under Article [101(2) TFEU].' In my view, the passage cited indicates that an agreement which does not satisfy all the conditions provided for by an exempting regulation does not necessarily have the object or effect of restricting competition pursuant to article [101 TFEU].

> 30. An individual examination is therefore required in order to assess whether an agreement has an anticompetitive object even where it contains a restriction which falls within the scope of [the Block Exemption Regulation on vertical agreements] thereby rendering the restrictive clause ineligible for exemption under that regulation.

The CJEU considered that in order to assess whether the contractual clause at issue involved a restriction of competition 'by object' within Article 101(1) TFEU, it was necessary to have regard to the content of the clause, the objectives it sought to attain and the economic and legal context of which it formed a part,[82] thus following the position of the CJEU in *GSK*.[83] It found that the contractual clause in the case considerably reduced the ability of an authorized distributor to sell the products to customers outside its contractual territory or area of activity, and was therefore liable to restrict competition. A contractual clause prohibiting *de facto* the Internet as a method of marketing, had, according to the CJEU, at the very least, the object of restricting such sales to end users who wished to purchase online and were located outside the physical trading area of the distributor. The Court even went as far as pronouncing that selective distribution agreements were 'restrictions by object' in the absence of 'objective justification'.[84] The approach of the CJEU is reminiscent of the 'orthodox' approach, as entire categories of collusive practices are declared presumptively restrictive of competition, without proceeding to an individual assessment as argued by the Advocate General who had noted that 'the mere fact that the selective distribution agreements in question [. . .] may restrict parallel trade may not in itself be sufficient to establish that the agreement has the object of restricting competition pursuant to Article 101(1)'.[85]

6.3.1.2.3. Allianz Hungária Biztosító Zrt.

In *Allianz Hungária*, the CJEU expanded the concept of anti-competitive object to include another series of vertical restrictions, on the basis of the more analytical approach and the specific economic context.

Case C-32/11, *Allianz Hungária Biztosító Zrt, Generali-Providencia Biztosító Zrt and Others v Gazdasági Versenyhivatal*, ECLI:EU:C:2013:160

> *The case arose out of a reference from the Hungarian Supreme Court under Article 267 TFEU and relates to a decision of the Hungarian Competition Authority finding that certain agreements in the Hungarian car insurance sector breached the Hungarian equivalent of Article 101 TFEU. Individual car dealers in Hungary had asked their trade association—GEMOSZ—to negotiate with car insurers annual framework agreements setting out the hourly labour charges*

[82] Case C-439/09, *Pierre Fabre Dermo-Cosmetique SAS v Président de l'Authorité de la Concurrence, Ministre de l'Économie, de l'Industrie et de l'Emploi* [2011] ECR I–9419.

[83] Joined Cases C-501, 513, 515 & 519/06 P, *GlaxoSmithKline Services Unlimited v Commission* [2009] ECR I-9291.

[84] Case C-439/09, *Pierre Fabre Dermo-Cosmetique* [2011] ECR I–9419, para 39.

[85] Opinion of AG Mazák in Case C-439/09, *Pierre Fabre Dermo-Cosmetique SAS v Président de l'Authorité de la Concurrence, Ministre de l'Économie, de l'Industrie et de l'Emploi*, ECLI:EU:C:2011:113, para 42.

that insurers would pay for repair work carried out by the car dealers. Insurers such as Allianz also had arrangements in place with the dealers pursuant to which the latter would act as intermediaries and offer Allianz car insurance to customers in exchange for a commission payment. Allianz entered into framework agreements with GEMOSZ, and related individual agreements with dealers, which provided that the hourly labour charges paid by Allianz would be increased where Allianz car insurance made up (more than) a certain percentage of the car insurance sold by the dealer. Allianz's fellow insurer, Generali, had agreements with GEMOSZ and individual car dealers that had a similar effect to Allianz's agreements (ie, they provided for increased hourly rates to be paid to dealers where Generali car insurance made up (more than) a certain percentage of the car insurance sold by the dealer). The Hungarian Supreme Court sent a preliminary question of the Court of Justice enquiring about the possibility for bilateral agreements between an insurance company and individual car repairers, or between an insurance company and a car repairers' association, under which the hourly repair charge paid by the insurance company to the repairer for the repair of vehicles insured by the insurance company depended, among other things, on the number and percentage of insurance policies taken out with the insurance company through the repairer, acting as the insurance broker for the insurance company in question, qualified as agreements which have as their object the prevention, restriction or distortion of competition, and thus contravene Article 101(1) TFEU. The parties to the agreement refuted this qualification as by object restrictions to competition.

Advocate General Cruz Villalón explored the distinction between restrictions by object and effect, noting the following:

> 64. The classification of an agreement or practice as restrictive of competition by object acts as a kind of 'presumption', since, if that agreement or practice is found to be restrictive, it will not be necessary to establish what effects it has on competition. Moreover, the prohibition may be adopted as a preventive measure without waiting until any effects which are detrimental to competition have actually occurred.

He referred to the approach followed by the Commission's Guidelines on the application of Article 101(3) TFEU (formerly Article 81(3)), and concluded that:

> 65. [. . .] To my mind, it follows from the foregoing that this category must be interpreted strictly and must be limited to cases in which a particularly serious inherent capacity for negative effects can be identified.

The AG first proceeded to the examination of the content of the agreement and its objectives, noting 'at the outset that these are vertical agreements, to which, as a general rule and subject to exceptions, Article 101(1) TFEU does not apply' and 'unlike horizontal agreements, where it is clearly easier to identify an object or effect restrictive of competition, vertical agreements are considerably more complex'.[86] *Finding that this was a series of vertical agreements, AG Cruz Villalón observed that '[a]s regards vertical agreements, the Court of Justice has hitherto classified only the following as restrictions of competition by object: the imposition of minimum resale prices, the prohibition of parallel trade between Member States through the establishment of absolute territorial protection, and, more recently, clauses prohibiting distributors from using the internet to sell certain products, unless that prohibition is*

[86] Opinion of AG Cruz Villalón in Case C-32/11, *Allianz Hungária Biztosító Zrt, Generali-Providencia Biztosító Zrt and Others v Gazdasági Versenyhivatal*, ECLI:EU:C:2012:663, para 69.

justified objectively as in the context of a selective distribution network'.[87] *He further noted that 'the agreements at issue in the present case do not in themselves have the capacity to restrict competition which those clauses had'.*[88] *The fact that the vertical block exemption provides that the exemption is not applicable to a particular kind of vertical agreement does not also mean, according to the AG, 'that such agreements should automatically be included in the category of restrictions by object', although he recognized that 'it is also true that the "black list" [in block exemption regulations] and the restrictions identified as "hardcore" by the Commission overlap to a large extent with the agreements and practices classified in the case-law as restrictions by object'.*[89] *Hence, 'although it is not a decisive criterion, it is clear that those lists can be used as an indication, in particular, of what is not a restriction by object'.*[90] *In addition, the AG noted that 'the case-law has analysed specific vertical agreements containing non-compete obligations of that kind, reaching the conclusion that they do not constitute restrictions of competition by object although it is necessary to analyse whether they have the effect of prohibiting, restricting or distorting competition'.*[91] *Consequently, the AG concluded that:*

> [I]n the light of their content and objectives, the capacity of the agreements at issue to restrict competition is not as high as that of the vertical agreements which the case-law has held in the past to be restrictions by object. Furthermore, their capacity to restrict competition also appears to be lower than that of vertical agreements which, in accordance with the case-law, do not constitute restrictions by object, although they might be capable of producing anti-competitive effects.[92]

In conclusion, the agreements did not constitute by object restrictions of competition, unless there was either collusion among the insurers or collusion among the car dealers.

Case C-32/11, *Allianz Hungária Biztosító Zrt, Generali-Providencia Biztosító Zrt and Others v Gazdasági Versenyhivatal*, ECLI:EU:C:2013:160

Interestingly, the CJEU did not follow the approach of its AG and adopted a more analytical approach focusing on the economic and legal context of the agreements and qualifying them as restrictions of competition by object. This case law highlights that the implementation of a more analytical approach does not necessarily lead the agreement in question to escape the qualification as a restriction by object, but has indeed the potential to expand the scope of the restrictions by object category.

> [. . .] 31. By its question, the referring court asks, in essence, whether Article 101(1) TFEU must be interpreted as meaning that agreements whereby car insurance companies come to bilateral arrangements, either with car dealers acting as car repair shops, or with an association representing the latter, concerning the hourly charge to be paid by the insurance company for repairs to vehicles insured by it, stipulating that that charge depends, inter alia, on the number and percentage of insurance contracts that the dealer has sold as intermediary for that company, can be considered a restriction of competition 'by object' within the meaning of that provision.

[87] Ibid, para 74. [88] Ibid, para 75. [89] Ibid, para 79. [90] Ibid. [91] Ibid, para 80.
[92] Ibid, para 81.

32. Allianz and Generali consider that such agreements do not constitute a restriction 'by object' and can therefore be treated as infringing Article 101(1) TFEU solely to the extent that it is shown that they are in fact likely to produce anti-competitive effects. By contrast, the Hungarian Government and the Commission suggest that the question submitted be answered in the affirmative. The EFTA Surveillance Authority considers that the answer to that question depends on the extent to which those agreements harm competition, which should be determined by the referring court.

33. It must first of all be recalled that, to be caught by the prohibition laid down in Article 101(1) TFEU, an agreement must have 'as [its] object or effect the prevention, restriction or distortion of competition within the internal market'. [. . .]

34. Accordingly, where the anti-competitive object of the agreement is established it is not necessary to examine its effects on competition. Where, however, the analysis of the content of the agreement does not reveal a sufficient degree of harm to competition, the effects of the agreement should then be considered and, for it to be caught by the prohibition, it is necessary to find that factors are present which show that competition has in fact been prevented, restricted or distorted to an appreciable extent [. . .].

35. The distinction between 'infringements by object' and 'infringements by effect' arises from the fact that certain forms of collusion between undertakings can be regarded, by their very nature, as being injurious to the proper functioning of normal competition [. . .].

36. In order to determine whether an agreement involves a restriction of competition 'by object', regard must be had to the content of its provisions, its objectives and the economic and legal context of which it forms a part [. . .]. When determining that context, it is also appropriate to take into consideration the nature of the goods or services affected, as well as the real conditions of the functioning and structure of the market or markets in question (see *Expedia*, Case C-226/11, *Expedia Inc v Autorité de la concurrence and Others*, ECLI:EU:C:2012:795, paragraph 21 and the case-law cited).

37. In addition, although the parties' intention is not a necessary factor in determining whether an agreement is restrictive, there is nothing prohibiting the competition authorities, the national courts or the Courts of the European Union from taking that factor into account [. . .].

38. The Court has, moreover, already held that, in order for the agreement to be regarded as having an anti-competitive object, it is sufficient that it has the potential to have a negative impact on competition, that is to say, that it be capable in an individual case of resulting in the prevention, restriction or distortion of competition within the internal market. Whether and to what extent, in fact, such an effect results can only be of relevance for determining the amount of any fine and assessing any claim for damages [. . .].

39. Concerning the agreements referred to in the question submitted, it should be noted that they relate to the hourly charge to be paid by the insurance company to car dealers, acting as repair shops, for the repair of cars in the event of accidents. They provide that that charge is increased in accordance with the number and percentage of insurance contracts that the dealer sells for that company.

40. Such agreements therefore link the remuneration for the car repair service to that for the car insurance brokerage. The linkage of those two different services is possible because of the fact that the dealers act in relation to the insurers in a dual capacity, namely as intermediaries or brokers, offering car insurance to their customers at the time of sale or repair of vehicles, and as repair shops, repairing vehicles after accidents on behalf of the insurers.

41. However, while the establishment of such a link between two activities which are in principle independent does not automatically mean that the agreement concerned has as its object the restriction of competition, it can nevertheless constitute an important factor in determining whether that agreement is by its nature injurious to the proper functioning of normal competition, which is the case, in particular, where the independence of those activities is necessary for that functioning.

42. Moreover, it is necessary to take account of the fact that such an agreement is likely to affect not only one, but two markets, in this case those of car insurance and car repair services, and that its object must be determined with respect to the two markets concerned.

43. In that regard, it must, first, be noted that, in contrast to the view apparently held by Allianz and Generali, the fact that both cases concern vertical relationships in no way excludes the possibility that the agreement at issue in the main proceedings constitutes a restriction of competition 'by object'. While vertical agreements are, by their nature, often less damaging to competition than horizontal agreements, they can, nevertheless, in some cases, also have a particularly significant restrictive potential. The Court has thus already held on several occasions that a vertical agreement had as its object the restriction of competition [. . .].

44. Next, with regard to determining the object of the agreements at issue in the main proceedings with respect to the car insurance market, it should be noted that, by such agreements, insurance companies such as Allianz and Generali aim to maintain or increase their market shares.

45. It is not disputed that, if there was a horizontal agreement or a concerted practice between those two companies designed to partition the market, such an agreement or practice would have to be treated as a restriction by object and would also result in the unlawfulness of the vertical agreements concluded in order to implement that agreement or practice. Allianz and Generali dispute however that they acted in agreement or concert and claim that the contested decision found that there was no such agreement or practice. It is for the referring court to check the accuracy of those claims and, to the extent that it is enabled under domestic law, to determine whether there is enough evidence to establish the existence of an agreement or concerted practice between Allianz and Generali.

46. Nevertheless, even if there is no agreement or concerted practice between those insurance companies, it will still be necessary to determine whether, taking account of the economic and legal context of which they form a part, the vertical agreements at issue in the main proceedings are sufficiently injurious to competition on the car insurance market as to amount to a restriction of competition by object.

47. That could in particular be the case where, as is claimed by the Hungarian Government, domestic law requires that dealers acting as intermediaries or insurance brokers must be independent from the insurance companies. That government claims, in that regard, that those dealers do not act on behalf of an insurer, but on behalf of the policyholder and it is their job to offer the policyholder the insurance which is the most suitable for him amongst the offers of various insurance companies. It is for the referring court to determine whether, in those circumstances and in light of the expectations of those policyholders, the proper functioning of the car insurance market is likely to be significantly disrupted by the agreements at issue in the main proceedings.

48. Furthermore, those agreements would also amount to a restriction of competition by object in the event that the referring court found that it is likely that, having regard to the economic context, competition on that market would be eliminated or

seriously weakened following the conclusion of those agreements. In order to determine the likelihood of such a result, that court should in particular take into consideration the structure of that market, the existence of alternative distribution channels and their respective importance and the market power of the companies concerned.

49. Finally, with regard to determining the object of the agreements at issue in the main proceedings with respect to the car repair service market, it is necessary to take account of the fact that those agreements appear to have been concluded on the basis of 'recommended prices' established in the three decisions taken by GÉMOSZ from 2003 to 2005. In that context, it is for the referring court to determine the exact nature and scope of those decisions [. . .].

51. In the light of all of the foregoing considerations, the answer to the question submitted is that Article 101(1) TFEU must be interpreted as meaning that agreements whereby car insurance companies come to bilateral arrangements, either with car dealers acting as car repair shops or with an association representing those dealers, concerning the hourly charge to be paid by the insurance company for repairs to vehicles insured by it, stipulating that that charge depends, inter alia, on the number and percentage of insurance contracts that the dealer has sold as intermediary for that company, can be considered a restriction of competition 'by object' within the meaning of that provision, where, following a concrete and individual examination of the wording and aim of those agreements and of the economic and legal context of which they form a part, it is apparent that they are, by their very nature, injurious to the proper functioning of normal competition on one of the two markets concerned.

NOTES AND QUESTIONS ON ALLIANZ HUNGÁRIA

1. (Paragraph 36) The CJEU held that in order to determine whether an agreement involves a restriction of competition 'by object', 'it is also appropriate to take into consideration the nature of the goods or services affected, as well as the real conditions of the functioning and structure of the market or markets in question'. Is this a departure from the previous case law on anti-competitive object? How would one now distinguish between anti-competitive object and effect, if it is also necessary to consider the '*real* conditions of the functioning and structure of the market or markets in question'?[93] Would this require a more *in concreto* analysis of the economic context of the specific agreement than the abstract analysis employed so far when examining the existence of a restriction of competition by object? According to paragraph 48 of the judgment, this analysis would also consider 'the existence of alternative distribution channels and [the] respective importance and the market power of the companies concerned'.
2. (Paragraph 36) The CJEU refers to paragraph 21 of the *Expedia* judgment,[94] which, however, does not deal specifically with by object restrictions of competition and concerns the question whether the agreement perceptibly restricts competition within the common market (effect on trade). This seems to relate more to the issue of the appreciability of the restriction of competition, than to its anti-competitive object, unless one considers object of restricting competition and appreciable restriction of competition as interrelated concepts. Indeed, the CJEU notes in paragraph

[93] Emphasis added. [94] See Section 6.3.3.2.1.

48 of the judgment that 'agreements would also amount to a restriction of competition by object in the event that the referring court found that it is likely that, having regard to the economic context, competition on that market would be *eliminated or seriously weakened* following the conclusion of those agreements' (emphasis added). According to the CJEU, '[i]n order to determine the likelihood of such a result, [national courts] should in particular take into consideration the structure of that market, the existence of alternative distribution channels and their respective importance and the market power of the companies concerned'.[95] Reflect on this issue by reading the judgment of the CJEU in *Groupement des cartes bancaires (CB) v Commission*.[96]

3. Do you think that the approach followed by the CJEU makes sense from the perspective of decision theory perspective? If information on the structure of the markets affected by the agreement is readily available (eg regulated industries for which this information is compiled by regulatory authorities) or quite easy to determine (eg a duopoly) would it not make sense to take this into account when considering the existence of a restriction of competition by object, before moving to the more elaborate analysis of anti-competitive effects, including the need to define a relevant market?
4. Does the CJEU perceive the concepts of anti-competitive object and effect as two distinct categories of restrictions or part of a continuum? If even non 'obvious' restrictions of competition, such as those in *Allianz Hungária* may be considered as restrictions of competition by object, when they lead to an appreciable restriction of competition, in view of the nature of the practice *and* the structure of the markets affected, would that not expand the use of the qualification of restrictions by object? What would be the incentive of competition authorities in this case to bring the more difficult and complex cases requiring evidence of anti-competitive effect?
5. If we accept that the CJEU relied in *Allianz Hungária* on the analysis of the structure of the markets affected, as part of its inquiry into the economic context of the agreement, to conclude that the specific practice constituted a restriction of competition by object, would not be possible for it to rely again on the economic context of the agreement in order to qualify an 'obvious' restriction of competition as not constituting a restriction of competition by object if, for instance, the structure of the markets affected was very competitive?
6. (Paragraphs 40–1) The CJEU views with suspicion the fact that the agreement in question establishes a link between two 'independent' activities. Although this fact alone does not lead the CJEU to qualify the practice as being by object anti-competitive, it is certainly an important factor when determining if it is by its nature injurious to the proper functioning of normal competition, in particular when the independence of these activities is necessary for the functioning of the market(s) in question. Does the CJEU refer to a form of bundling of car repair services to car insurance brokerage services? Note the reference in paragraph 47 of the CJEU's judgment to the *ratio legis* in the Hungarian domestic legislation, requiring that dealers acting as intermediaries or insurance brokers be independent from the insurance companies. Does the CJEU

[95] Case C-32/11, *Allianz Hungária Biztosító Zrt, Generali-Providencia Biztosító Zrt and Others v Gazdasági Versenyhivatal*, ECLI:EU:C:2013:160, para 48.

[96] Case C-67/13 P, *CB v Commission*, ECLI:EU:C:2014:2204. See further Section 6.3.1.2.4.

aim to ensure that the effectiveness of the Hungarian legislation is not jeopardized by the practices of the insurance companies and GÉMOSZ?

7. (Paragraph 42) How would you interpret the reference of the CJEU on the need to take into account the fact that the agreement in question is likely to affect two markets, and not just one, when considering the existence of an anti-competitive object? Does the CJEU link the analysis of anti-competitive object with the situation on the markets affected? Is this linkage helpful when considering the situation of multi-sided markets?[97]
8. The expansion of the qualification of restriction of competition by object also manifested itself in some other contemporary case law of the General Court, this time with regard to horizontal restrictions. In *Bananas*, the General Court held that 'pre-pricing' communications between competitors where they discussed price-setting factors relevant to the setting of future quotation prices consisted in an object restriction to competition, thus expanding the qualification of restrictions of competition by object to an information exchange between competitors.[98] In *Asnef-Equifax*, the CJEU had considered the nature and purpose of an exchange of information register between credit institutions in the context in which it was implemented and after noting that such register exists in numerous countries and brings positive effects to competition, it concluded that it did not constitute a restriction of competition by object and moved in assessing its effects.[99] In *Dole*, the CJEU confirmed the judgment of the General Court in *Bananas* noting that the exchange of information created abnormal conditions of competition, and that a practice may have an anti-competitive object even though there is no direct connection between that practice and consumer prices.[100]

6.3.1.2.4. *The swing of the pendulum?:* Groupement des cartes bancaires (CB)

In *CB*, the Commission took a more restrictive approach with regard to the pricing measures necessary for the operation of the system of payments by bank cards, finding that these constituted a restriction of competition by object,[101] a decision confirmed by the GC. However, the CJEU ultimately took a different approach, thus setting boundaries to an extension of the concept of restrictions of competition by object.

The *Cartes Bancaires* case

Groupement des Cartes Bancaires ('Groupement') manages the system of payments by 'CB' cards, which account for over 70 per cent of card payments in France. The system allows the use of bank cards issued by CB Group members ('issuing side') for payments to all affiliated merchants and for the withdrawal from ATMs controlled by any of the CB Group members

97 See the analysis of *CB* in Section 6.3.1.2.4.

98 Case T-588/08, *Dole Food Company, Inc and Dole Germany OHG v European Commission*, ECLI:EU:T:2013:130 [hereinafter *Bananas*].

99 Case C-238/05, *Asnef-Equifax, Servicios de Información sobre Solvencia y Crédito, SL v Asociación de Usuarios de Servicios Bancarios (Ausbanc)* [2006] ECR I–11125.

100 Case C-286/13 P, *Dole Food Company, Inc. and Dole Fresh Fruit Europe v European Commission*, ECLI:EU:C:2015:184 [hereinafter *Dole*]. For an analysis of these cases, see Chapters 7 & 11.

101 *Groupement des cartes bancaires 'CB'* (Case COMP/D1/38.606) Commission Decision C (2007) 5060 final (17 October 2007), available at http://ec.europa.eu/competition/antitrust/cases/dec_docs/38606/38606_611_1.pdf.

('acquiring side'). A CB card (Visa, MasterCard, etc) issued by a member can be used to make payments to all traders affiliated to the CB card system through any other member and/or can be used to make withdrawals from automatic teller machines (ATMs) operated by all other members. The Groupement, which had 148 members, was managed by the largest French banks. In 2002, the Groupement notified new regulations to the Commission for clearance or exemption under Regulation 17/1962, which was the preceding procedural regulation to Regulation 1/2003 and which permitted notifications to be made.

These rules concerned three pricing measures, involving certain fees to be paid by CB Groupement members depending on their card issuing/acquisition of merchants' ratio, with the aim to solve a free-riding problem on the issuing side. First, the MERFA (Mécanisme régulateur de la fonction acquéreur) which essentially aimed to encourage members that were issuers more than acquirers to expand their acquiring activities and to take financial account of the contributions of members whose acquiring activity was considerable in relation to their issuing activity (this involved a pricing formula that determined whether a fee of up to €11 on each card issued should be paid by member banks that were not sufficiently active in terms of the acquisition of merchants or the installation of ATMs). Second, new membership fees for the Groupement comprising, and in addition to a fixed sum of €50 000 levied on membership, a fee per active CB card issued in the three years following membership. Third, a mechanism known as a 'dormant member wake-up mechanism', which consisted in a fee per CB card issued, which was applicable to members that were inactive or not very active before the date of entry into force of the new pricing measures.

In October 2007, the Commission adopted a decision finding that the Groupement had infringed Article 101 TFEU. The Commission considered that the pricing measures introduced as part of the new regulations, had an anti-competitive object, in view of the actual formulas envisaged for those measures and the fact that they corresponded to the real objectives of those measures, namely the intention to impede competition for new entrants and to penalize them, the intention to safeguard the main members' revenue and the intention to limit the price reduction for CB cards. The measures had also the effect of restricting competition by increasing the cost of cards issued by new entrants, maintaining the price of cards in France above competitive levels and limiting the number of cards supplied at a competitive price. The Groupement argued that these measures were necessary in order to combat free-riding on the investments made by the main incumbent banks and to encourage new competitors of the major banks to acquire merchants and install ATMs, rather than simply engage in issuance. However, the Commission considered that the measures at issue could not be regarded as ancillary restraints, escaping the prohibition of Article 101(1) TFEU and could not be justified under Article 101(3) TFEU.

The Groupement appealed the Commission's decision to the General Court, which dismissed the Groupement's appeal in its entirety in a judgment issued in 2012. In relation to the Commission's consideration of the object and effect of the pricing measures, the Court concluded that the Commission was correct to consider that they limited the issue of cards by new entrants, on the basis that it was difficult for new entrants to develop sufficient acquiring activities to avoid the relevant fees. The Court considered that this was sufficient for the Commission to conclude that the measures had the object of restricting competition and so there was no need for the Court to consider the Groupement's arguments on the issue of the effect of the measures. The Groupement appealed to the CJEU.

Advocate General Wahl issued an Opinion, which is partly reproduced as it draws a useful summary of the discussion over the definition of anti-competitive object and its relation with anti-competitive effect and emphasizes the need to take into account the economic and legal context of the agreement, this concept enabling him to set boundaries to an extensive application of the restrictions by object category.

Opinion of Advocate General Wahl in Case C-67/13 P*, Groupement des cartes bancaires (CB) v Commission, *ECLI:EU:C:2014:1958

26. It is well established that any system to prohibit and penalise collusive practices covers conduct which has an effect that restricts competition.

27. In order to identify conduct which has an effect that restricts competition, two methodological approaches are generally conceivable.

28. The first is a casuistic approach involving a detailed and thorough examination of the actual and potential anticompetitive effects of the conduct of undertakings. Whilst such an approach has the considerable advantage of being directed precisely at practices which clearly have the effect of restricting competition, it involves the mobilisation of significant resources and is not a guarantee of procedural economy. It may thus ultimately represent an obstacle to detection of anticompetitive conduct.

29. These disadvantages have led to the adoption of a second approach, which is to some extent less tailored to individual cases, by reference also to conduct which is generally considered, on the basis of economic analysis, to have harmful effects on competition.

30. In such a system, there is no difference, from a substantive point of view, between the conduct of undertakings which is considered to restrict competition following an individual examination and conduct considered to be so on the basis of a standardised approach. Both are prohibited. The distinction which must be drawn is based, first and foremost, on procedural considerations relating to proof of the anticompetitive effects caused by the conduct in question.

31. By way of illustration, in US antitrust law, certain kinds of conduct are regarded as infringements per se. Undertakings that adopt such conduct are not able to challenge, either before the authority responsible for prosecuting competition infringements or before the courts, its classification as conduct restrictive of competition by proving that it has few harmful effects, and indeed some beneficial effects, on competition.

32. The reference in Article [101(1) TFEU] to agreements, decisions or concerted practices 'which have as their object or effect the prevention, restriction or distortion of competition within the common market' has comparable consequences, even though they are not identical.

33. First, where it is established that the conduct of undertakings has an anticompetitive 'object', that conduct is prohibited in principle, without any need to examine its effects.

34. Second, whilst it is conceivable to weigh pro- and anticompetitive effects in connection with the application of Article [101(3) TFEU], recourse to the concept of anticompetitive object nevertheless has a number of advantages in so far as it makes it easier to determine the restrictive impact of certain practices followed by the undertakings.

35. First of all, it undoubtedly provides predictability, and therefore legal certainty, for undertakings in that it enables them to know the legal consequences (including prohibitions and sanctions) of some of their actions, such as the conclusion of pricing agreements, and to modify their conduct accordingly. Second, identifying agreements, decisions and concerted practices which have the object of restricting competition also has a deterrent effect and helps to prevent anticompetitive conduct. Lastly, it furthers procedural economy in so far as it allows the competition authorities, when faced with certain forms of collusion, to establish their anticompetitive impact without any need for them to conduct the often complex and time-consuming examination of their potential or actual effects on the market concerned.

36. However, such advantages materialise only if recourse to the concept of restriction by object is clearly defined, failing which this could encompass conduct whose harmful effects on competition are not clearly established.

37. These considerations have a more solid foundation in the lessons which can be drawn from the Court's established case-law.

First, the AG cites the LTM v MBU *case law*[102] *on the alternative nature of the requirement relating to the existence of an agreement having 'as its object or effect' the restriction of competition. Second, the AG points out that the distinction between 'infringements by object' and 'infringements by effect' arises from the fact that 'certain forms of collusion between undertakings can be regarded, by their very nature, as being harmful to the proper functioning of normal competition', including a number of vertical agreements. The AG seems, however, to deny the existence of a clear dichotomy between object and effect, by insisting on the need to examine in all cases the legal and economic context of the agreement, an assessment that may involve some consideration of the economic impact of the specific type of arrangement.*

40. Third, the more standardised assessment resulting from recourse to the concept of restriction by object requires a detailed, individual examination of the agreement in question which must, however, be clearly distinguished from the examination of the actual or potential effects of the conduct of the undertakings concerned.

41. In this regard, the Court made clear, at a very early stage, that the examination of the question whether a contract had a restrictive object could not be divorced from the economic and legal context in the light of which it was concluded by the parties. It then held, and has ruled in settled case-law, that the clauses of the agreements in question had in fact to be examined in the light of their context, the underlying idea being that, in examining the compatibility of conduct with the provisions of the treaty with regard to agreements, decisions and concerted practices, purely theoretical and abstract considerations are difficult to defend.

42. To illustrate my remarks, I would refer to the example of an infringement which, in the light of experience, is presumed to cause one of the most serious restrictions of competition, namely a horizontal agreement concerning the price of certain goods. Whilst it is established that in general such a restrictive agreement is highly harmful for competition, that conclusion is not inevitable where, for example, the undertakings concerned hold only a tiny share of the market concerned. [. . .]

44. In my view, consideration of the economic and legal context in order to identify an anticompetitive object must, at the risk of introducing a shift that is detrimental to a proper reading of Article [101(1) TFEU] [. . .] be clearly distinguished from the demonstration of anticompetitive effects under that provision. Consideration of the context in identifying the anticompetitive object can only reinforce or neutralise the examination of the actual terms of a purported restrictive agreement. It certainly cannot remedy a failure actually to identify an anticompetitive object by demonstrating the potential effects of the measures in question.

45. In other words, and regardless of the conceptual similarities between the alternatives, recourse to the economic and legal context in identifying a restriction by object cannot lead to a classification to the detriment of the undertakings concerned in the case of an agreement whose terms do not appear to be harmful to competition.

[102] Case 56/65, *Société Technique Minière (LTM) v Maschinenbau Ulm GmbH (MBU)* [1966] ECR-337.

The AG recognizes that the case law to a certain extent, has been a source of differing interpretations and even of confusion. In particular, 'certain rulings seem to have made it difficult to draw the necessary distinction between the examination of the anti-competitive object and the analysis of the effects on competition of agreements between undertakings'[103] *and that 'in a number of cases, consideration of that context is similar to a genuine examination of the potential effects of the measures at issue'.*[104] *The AG gives as examples* GlaxoSmithKline v Commission *and* Allianz Hungária.[105] *With regard to* Allianz Hungária, *he continues as following:*

51. Here too, it is difficult to distinguish how the examination of the context advocated by the Court, which consists in evaluating the risk of competition on the market in question being eliminated or seriously weakened, having regard, in particular, to 'the structure of that market, the existence of alternative distribution channels and their respective importance and the market power of the companies concerned', differs from the examination of possible anticompetitive effects.

52. None the less, and despite the fact that, to some extent, case-law has contributed to blurring the boundary between the concepts of restriction by object or restriction by effect, I take the view that recourse to that concept must be more clearly defined.

53. Considering an agreement or a practice to restrict competition on account of its very object has significant consequences, at least two of which should be highlighted.

54. First of all, the method of identifying an 'anticompetitive object' is based on a formalist approach which is not without danger from the point of view of the protection of the general interests pursued by the rules on competition in the Treaty. Where it is established that an agreement has an object that is restrictive of competition, the ensuing prohibition has a very broad scope, that it is to say it can be imposed as a precautionary measure and thus jeopardise future contacts, irrespective of the evaluation of the effects actually produced.

55. This formalist approach is thus conceivable only in the case of (i) conduct entailing an inherent risk of a particularly serious harmful effect or (ii) conduct in respect of which it can be concluded that the unfavourable effects on competition outweigh the pro-competitive effects. To hold otherwise would effectively deny that some actions of economic operators may produce beneficial externalities from the point of view of competition. In my view, it is only when experience based on economic analysis shows that a restriction is constantly prohibited that it seems reasonable to penalise it directly for the sake of procedural economy

56. Only conduct whose harmful nature is proven and easily identifiable, in the light of experience and economics, should therefore be regarded as a restriction of competition by object, and not agreements which, having regard to their context, have ambivalent effects on the market or which produce ancillary restrictive effects necessary for the pursuit of a main objective which does not restrict competition.

57. Second, such classification relieves the enforcement authority of the responsibility for proving the anticompetitive effects of the agreement or the practice in question. An uncontrolled extension of conduct covered by restrictions by object is

[103] Opinion of Advocate General Wahl in Case C-67/13 P, *Groupement des cartes bancaires (CB) v Commission*, ECLI:EU:C:2014:1958, para 46.

[104] Ibid, para 47.

[105] Case T-168/01, *GlaxoSmithKline Services Unlimited v Commission* [2006] ECR II–2969; Case C-32/11, *Allianz Hungária Biztosító and Others*, ECLI:EU:C:2013:160.

dangerous having regard to the principles which must govern evidence and the burden of proof in relation to anticompetitive conduct.

58. Because of these consequences, classification as an agreement which is restrictive by object must necessarily be circumscribed and ultimately apply only to an agreement which inherently presents a degree of harm. This concept should relate only to agreements which inherently, that is to say without the need to evaluate their actual or potential effects, have a degree of seriousness or harm such that their negative impact on competition seems highly likely. Notwithstanding the open nature of the list of conduct which can be regarded as restrictive by virtue of its object, I propose that a relatively cautious attitude should be maintained in determining a restriction of competition by object.

59. Such caution is all the more necessary because the analytical framework that the Court is led to identify will be imposed both on the Commission and on the national competition authorities, whose awareness and level of expertise vary.

60. The advantage in terms of predictability and easing the burden of proof entailed by identifying agreements that are restrictive by object would appear to be undermined if that identification ultimately depends on a thorough examination of the consequences of that agreement for competition which goes well beyond a detailed examination of the agreement.

61. In any event, it should be noted that, despite the apparent extension of the conduct that is classified as restrictive by object, the Court has consistently held, from *LTM* to *Allianz Hungária Biztosító and Others*, that the analysis of the object must reveal 'a sufficient degree of harm'.

62. Lastly, I would observe that such an interpretation does not effectively 'immunise' certain conduct by exempting it from the prohibition under Article [101(1) TFEU]. Where it has not been established that a certain agreement is not specifically—that is to say in the light of its objectives and its legal and economic context—capable of preventing, restricting or distorting competition on the market, only recourse to the concept of restriction by object is ruled out. The competition authority will still be able to censure it after a more thorough examination of its actual and potential anticompetitive effects on the market.

Moving to the implementation of these principles in the specific case, the AG recognized that 'the case-law, which shows an ambivalence between the desire not to set out a closed list of restrictions by object and the need to respect the ratio legis *of Article [101(1) TFEU], which,* inter alia, *requires the conduct in question to present a certain degree of harm, does not always clearly answer the question whether or not the concept of restriction by object must be given a strict interpretation, even though certain Advocates General have supported one approach or the other'.*[106] *The AG criticized the judgment of the General Court for being 'wrong' in stating that the concept of object did not have to be given a strict interpretation.*[107] *The AG then explored the analytical framework used in the present case to establish the existence of a restriction by object:*

78. The Court must ascertain whether the General Court properly reviewed whether the Commission had sufficiently established, following a concrete and individual examination of the content, the aim and the economic and legal context of which they

[106] Opinion of Advocate General Wahl in Case C-67/13 P, *Groupement des cartes bancaires (CB) v Commission*, ECLI:EU:C:2014:1958, para 65.

[107] Ibid, paras 73–4.

formed a part, that the measures at issue achieved a degree of harm such that their negative effects on competition could be presumed.

79. To that end, experience is a perfectly relevant point of reference. 'Experience' must be understood to mean what can traditionally be seen to follow from economic analysis, as confirmed by the competition authorities and supported, if necessary, by case-law.

80. In the present context, it should be stated that the measures at issue are horizontal in nature and that, a priori, they could be considered to be quite capable of entailing an object that is restrictive of competition.

81. Whilst it is well established that certain horizontal agreements between undertakings include obvious restrictions of competition such as price fixing and market sharing and can therefore be regarded as entailing a restriction of competition by object, it is not apparent from the outset that the measures at issue are harmful to competition.

82. It should be examined, however, whether the General Court was justified in confirming the Commission's conclusion regarding the existence of a restriction by object, bearing in mind that that conclusion must be based on an overall assessment of the content of the measures, if necessary in the light of the aims objectively pursued and the economic and legal context.

The AG noted that the General Court failed to verify that the calculation formulas used in the measures at issue, included a mechanism that was anti-competitive by nature. He also held that it cannot be sufficient to show the existence of such an intention in order to conclude that the measures taken by them entail an anti-competitive object. Indeed, 'identification of an "anticompetitive object" requires a properly objective examination, irrespective of the will of the parties' and 'any intentions expressed by the participants in a supposed restrictive agreement, decision or concerted practice, like any legitimate objectives pursued by them, are not directly relevant in examining whether the agreement, decision or practice has an anticompetitive "object" '.[108] *Although the AG sided with the General Court that the justification proffered by the parties, the objective of fighting against free-riding 'did not, in general, have to be taken into account in the examination of the measures under Article [101(1) TFEU], but that it could be taken into consideration in the examination of the possibility of an exemption under Article [101(3) TFEU]', he explained that this conclusion 'appears to be meaningful only if it is clearly established, following a detailed examination, that the measures at issue have an anticompetitive object'.*[109]

125. Otherwise, that is to say in the case of a restriction by object which is not clearly established (as seems to be the case in this instance) it will be necessary to examine the anticompetitive effects and, in this framework, to assess the necessity and the proportionality of the measures in question having regard to the objective pursued.

He further added that it was difficult to see how the measures at issue present the degree of harm required by case-law.[110] *He moved then to the consideration of the legal and economic context of the agreement, reiterating the view that:*

139. [. . .] the elements relating to the economic and legal context surrounding the drafting of the measures at issue should not be capable in themselves of establishing the existence of an anticompetitive object. As I mentioned above, the examination of the context cannot remedy the failure actually to identify an anticompetitive object.

[108] Ibid, para 110. [109] Ibid, para 124. [110] Ibid, para 126.

Of particular interest was his assessment of the economic context of the agreement and, in particular, the argument of the appellant that the General Court ignored the characteristics of the CB card system and, in particular, the two-sided nature of the system.

147. In this respect, I take the view that, even assuming that it could be inferred from the terms and the objectives pursued by the measures at issue that they had an anticompetitive object, the context of the measures can weaken that conclusion.

148. In this connection, in order to establish the existence of a restriction by object, the Commission cannot simply conduct an abstract examination, in particular in the case of a restriction whose character is not evident.

149. In my view, consideration of the interactions between the 'issuing' aspect and the 'acquiring' aspect in the examination of the context of the measures with a view to identifying a restriction of competition by object seems quite distinct from the examination relating to the definition of the relevant market. It is not a question of challenging the assertion that the issuing and acquiring markets are distinct, but of examining whether sufficient account was taken of the economic context in which the measures were drafted.

150. In this case, and as the appellant mentioned before the General Court, the smooth operation of the CB card system requires issuing and acquiring activities to be performed in a balanced manner. With this in mind, it cannot be ruled out that the respective contributions of each member to the expansion of each of these functions can be taken into account. Whether it is already a member or a new entrant, a member of the Grouping that is active mainly or exclusively in issuing CB cards benefits from the investments made in order to expand the 'acquiring' aspect, which is a necessary pillar to the sustainability of the system.

The AG concluded by noting that the General Court erred in law, by reaching and adopting a non-restrictive interpretation of the concept of restriction by object and, by considering that the pricing measures presented a degree of harm such that their anti-competitive effects could be presumed. He then analysed the measures as restrictions of competition by effect, suggesting to the CJEU to set aside the judgment of the General Court that had confirmed the Commission's decision. The CJEU followed the suggestions of its AG.

CJEU Judgment in Case C-67/13 P, Groupement des cartes bancaires (CB) v Commission, *ECLI:EU:C:2014:2204*

49. [. . .] [I]t is apparent from the Court's case-law that certain types of coordination between undertakings reveal a sufficient degree of harm to competition that it may be found that there is no need to examine their effects.

50. That case-law arises from the fact that certain types of coordination between undertakings can be regarded, by their very nature, as being harmful to the proper functioning of normal competition.

51. Consequently, it is established that certain collusive behaviour, such as that leading to horizontal price-fixing by cartels, may be considered so likely to have negative effects, in particular on the price, quantity or quality of the goods and services, that it may be considered redundant, for the purposes of applying Article [101(1) TFEU], to prove that they have actual effects on the market. Experience shows that such behaviour leads to falls in production and price increases, resulting in poor allocation of resources to the detriment, in particular, of consumers.

52. Where the analysis of a type of coordination between undertakings does not reveal a sufficient degree of harm to competition, the effects of the coordination should, on the other hand, be considered and, for it to be caught by the prohibition, it is necessary to find that factors are present which show that competition has in fact been prevented, restricted or distorted to an appreciable extent

53. According to the case-law of the Court, in order to determine whether an agreement between undertakings or a decision by an association of undertakings reveals a sufficient degree of harm to competition that it may be considered a restriction of competition 'by object' within the meaning of Article [101(1)TFEU], regard must be had to the content of its provisions, its objectives and the economic and legal context of which it forms a part. When determining that context, it is also necessary to take into consideration the nature of the goods or services affected, as well as the real conditions of the functioning and structure of the market or markets in question.

54. In addition, although the parties' intention is not a necessary factor in determining whether an agreement between undertakings is restrictive, there is nothing prohibiting the competition authorities, the national courts or the Courts of the European Union from taking that factor into account.

The CJEU found that the General Court erred in law with regard to the definition of the relevant legal criteria in order to assess whether there was a restriction of competition by 'object' within the meaning of Article [101(1) TFEU]. The CJEU in particular lambasted the statement of the General Court that the concept of restriction of competition by 'object' must not be interpreted 'restrictively'. According to the CJEU:

58. [. . .] The concept of restriction of competition 'by object' can be applied only to certain types of coordination between undertakings which reveal a sufficient degree of harm to competition that it may be found that there is no need to examine their effects, otherwise the Commission would be exempted from the obligation to prove the actual effects on the market of agreements which are in no way established to be, by their very nature, harmful to the proper functioning of normal competition. The fact that the types of agreements covered by Article [101(1) TFEU] do not constitute an exhaustive list of prohibited collusion is, in that regard, irrelevant. [. . .]

Restrictions by object as restrictions with a sufficient degree of harm

69. However, although the General Court thereby set out the reasons why the measures at issue, in view of their formulas, are capable of restricting competition and, consequently, of falling within the scope of the prohibition laid down in Article [101(1) TFEU], it in no way explained [. . .] in what respect that restriction of competition reveals a sufficient degree of harm in order to be characterised as a restriction 'by object' within the meaning of that provision, there being no analysis of that point in the judgment under appeal

70. Although, as the General Court correctly found [. . .] the fact that the measures at issue pursue the legitimate objective of combatting free-riding does not preclude their being regarded as having an object restrictive of competition, the fact remains that that restrictive object must be established. [. . .]

75. Having acknowledged that the formulas for those measures sought to establish a certain ratio between the issuing and acquisition activities of the members of the Grouping, the General Court was entitled at the most to infer from this that those measures had as their object the imposition of a financial contribution on the members

of the Grouping which benefit from the efforts of other members for the purposes of developing the acquisition activities of the system. Such an object cannot be regarded as being, by its very nature, harmful to the proper functioning of normal competition, the General Court itself moreover having found [. . .] that combatting free-riding in the CB system was a legitimate objective.

Two-sided markets as an element to consider

76. In that regard, as the Advocate General observed at point 149 of his Opinion, the General Court wrongly held, [. . .] that the analysis of the requirements of balance between issuing and acquisition activities within the payment system could not be carried out in the context of Article [101(1) TFEU] on the ground that the relevant market was not that of payment systems in France but the market, situated downstream for the issue of payment cards in that Member State.

77. In so doing, the General Court confused the issue of the definition of the relevant market and that of the context which must be taken into account in order to ascertain whether the content of an agreement or a decision by an association of undertakings reveals the existence of a restriction of competition 'by object' within the meaning of Article [101(1) TFEU].

78. In order to assess whether coordination between undertakings is by nature harmful to the proper functioning of normal competition, it is necessary [. . .] to take into consideration all relevant aspects—having regard, in particular, to the nature of the services at issue, as well as the real conditions of the functioning and structure of the markets—of the economic or legal context in which that coordination takes place, it being immaterial whether or not such an aspect relates to the relevant market.

79. That must be the case, in particular, when that aspect is the taking into account of interactions between the relevant market and a different related market [. . .] and, all the more so, when, as in the present case, there are interactions between the two facets of a two-sided system.

80. Admittedly, it cannot be ruled out that the measures at issue [. . .] hinder competition from new entrants—in the light of the difficulty which those measures create for the expansion of their acquisition activity—and even lead to their exclusion from the system, on the basis, as BPCE argued at the hearing, of the level of fees charged pursuant to those measures.

81. However, [. . .] such a finding falls within the examination of the effects of those measures on competition and not of their object.

The CJEU observed that the General Court had in fact assessed the potential effects of the pricing measures, analysing the difficulties for the banks of developing acquisition activity on the basis of market data in order to consider that the measures at issue cannot be considered 'by their very nature' harmful to the proper functioning of normal competition and erred in finding that the measures at issue could be regarded as being analogous to those examined by the Court of Justice in BIDS, carefully distinguishing this jurisprudence from the present fact pattern.

84. By providing for a reduction of the order of 25% in processing capacity, the BIDS arrangements were intended, essentially, as their own wording makes clear, to enable several undertakings to implement a common policy which had as its object the encouragement of some of them to withdraw from the market and the reduction, as a consequence, of the overcapacity which affects their profitability by preventing

them from achieving economies of scale. The object of the BIDS arrangements was therefore to change, appreciably, the structure of the market through a mechanism intended to encourage the withdrawal of competitors in order, first, to increase the degree of concentration in the sector concerned by reducing significantly the number of undertakings supplying processing services and, secondly, to eliminate almost 75% of excess production capacity [. . .].

85. In the judgment under appeal, the General Court made no such finding, nor indeed was it argued before it that the measures at issue, like the BIDS arrangements, were intended to change appreciably the structure of the market concerned through a mechanism intended to encourage the withdrawal of competitors and, accordingly, that those measures revealed a degree of harm such as that of the BIDS arrangements.

86. Although the General Court found [. . .] that the measures at issue encouraged the members of the Grouping not to exceed a certain volume of CB card issuing, the objective of such encouragement was [. . .] not to reduce possible overcapacity on the market for the issue of payment cards in France, but to achieve a given ratio between the issuing and acquisition activities of the members of the Grouping in order to develop the CB system further.

87. It follows that the General Court could not, without erring in law, characterise the measures at issue as restrictions of competition 'by object' within the meaning of Article [101(1) TFEU].

The CJEU noted the general failure of analysis by the General Court, which erred by holding that the measures at issue had as their object a restriction of competition within the meaning of Article [101(1) TFEU], setting aside the judgment of the General Court.

97. [. . .] [I]t is therefore appropriate to ascertain whether, as the Commission found in the decision at issue, the agreements at issue have as their 'effect' the restriction of competition within the meaning of Article [101(1) TFEU].

98. However, that aspect of the case requires an examination of complex questions of fact based on elements which (i) were not assessed by the General Court in the judgment under appeal since it had found [. . .] that such an examination was superfluous [. . .] and (ii) were not discussed before the Court of Justice, with the result that the stage has not been reached where judgment can be given on that point.

99. Consequently, it is necessary to refer the case back to the General Court [. . .].

NOTES AND QUESTIONS ON CARTES BANCAIRES

1. (Paragraphs 28–9, AG Opinion) The AG establishes a distinction between two 'methodologies' in identifying 'conduct which has an effect that restricts competition', one being the individual analysis of the effects, which 'involves the mobilisation of significant resources and is not a guarantee of procedural economy', while the second one, a 'more standardized approach', is 'less tailored to individual cases', but still relying on some economic analysis, in this case at a more general level. Is this interpretation close to the decision-theory approach we highlighted above with regard to the distinction between restrictions 'by object' and restrictions 'by effect'?
2. (Paragraph 30, AG Opinion) Does the AG adopt a unified conception of restrictions 'by object' and 'by effect', both referring to the existence of some 'harm' to competition, the 'by object' restriction applying to 'certain *types* of coordination between

undertakings which reveal a *sufficient* degree of harm'? What is the nature of the distinction between 'by object' and 'by effect' restrictions of competition? Is this ontological, in the sense that each of these denotes a different kind/nature of harm? Is this cardinal, in the sense that the harm of a 'by object' restriction of competition is of a higher magnitude than that of a 'by effect' restriction of competition? Is this a difference relating to evidence matters, the restriction of competition 'by object' serving as a presumption of anti-competitive effects, the Commission being exempted from the obligation to prove the 'actual effects on the market of agreements' that are 'by their very nature' harmful? Would the last interpretation mean that restrictions of competition 'by effect' will require, from the plaintiff evidence of 'actual', and not just potential effects? How would the conception of the 'by object' and 'by effect' categories as referring to the same concept of restriction or harm to competition square with their consideration as alternative forms of qualification under Article 101(1) TFEU (anti-competitive by object *or* by effect)?

3. (Paragraphs 31–6, AG Opinion) The AG compares the 'by object' and 'by effect' distinction in EU Competition law with the 'per se prohibition' and 'rule of reason' distinction in US antitrust law. He notes, however, that there are some important differences between the two. Are you convinced by the analogy established by the AG? Can one consider 'by object' restrictions under Article 101(1) TFEU as equivalent to a 'prohibition *per se*'? Does this relate to the narrow interpretation and the relatively infrequent successful use of Article 101(3) TFEU in order to justify a restrictive to competition agreement?
4. (Paragraphs 36, 52–60, 79, AG Opinion). Note that according to the AG the concept of restriction by object should be clearly and narrowly defined, and encompass only conduct whose 'harmful effects on competition' are clearly established. Does the AG provide any indication as to how the 'harmful effects on competition' could be 'clearly' established? Would this be empirical evidence, economic theory, experience from past decisional practice of competition authorities? Is this compatible with the approach of the CJEU in *Allianz Hungária?* Are you convinced by the arguments of the AG in setting limits to the 'by object' category? Identify the winners and the losers of such an approach.
5. (Paragraphs 40–52, AG Opinion) Note that although the AG highlights the importance of economic analysis and the need to examine the legal and economic context of the agreement, he cautions against a confusion of genres between the analysis of the economic context, under a restriction 'by object' analysis, and that of effects in a restriction 'by effect' analysis. Can you identify and list the criteria distinguishing one from the other? Are you convinced by the arguments of the AG? How does he distinguish this case from *Allianz Hungária*? Is he suggesting to the CJEU to overrule *Allianz Hungária*?
6. (Paragraph 59, AG Opinion) National competition authorities (NCAs) have relied intensively on 'by object' restrictions of competition in their enforcement of Article 101 TFEU, bringing few restriction 'by effect' cases.[111] For AG Wahl, this is an argument to

[111] This impression results from reading the Commission's Staff Working Document, Ten Years of Antitrust Enforcement under Regulation 1/2003, SWD(2014) 230/2, which provides a statistical analysis of the enforcement of Article 101 TFEU by NCAs during the period May 2004–December 2013. A review of all the Commission's infringement decisions over this period also shows that almost all cases brought were framed in restriction 'by object' terms.

narrow down the 'by object' conceptual category and to be more 'cautious' in its use, even more so, as the NCAs' 'awareness and level of expertise' varies. Do you agree with the AG that the variable 'awareness and level of expertise' of NCAs in Europe should be an argument for limiting the use of 'by object' restrictions? Or, should it be considered as an argument in favour of a more expansive view of the 'by object' restriction category, in order to ensure a more uniform enforcement of competition law. How should one consider the variable resources of the different NCAs? Bringing an 'effects' case is expensive in terms of human and material resources and certainly not all NCAs have the capacity to bring an equivalent amount of such cases. Was this a factor taken into account by the AG? How would this influence the assessment of the need, or not, to limit an expansive use of the 'by object' category?

7. (Paragraph 139, AG Opinion) The AG seems to challenge the approach of the CJEU in *Allianz Hungária,* where the CJEU referred to the legal and economic context of the agreement to qualify it as a restriction of competition 'by object'? Do you think that the 'legal and economic context' should only be considered in order to exculpate an agreement from its characterization as a 'by object' restriction to competition? Or should it be also possible to rely on the economic and legal context in order to qualify an agreement as being restrictive 'by object'? How does the AG explain such asymmetry in the role of the 'legal and economic context'?
8. (Paragraphs 147–50, AG Opinion) The AG lambasted the General Court for not having considered the two-sided nature of CB's system, when considering the 'legal and economic context' of the agreement. Is this an element relating to the business model/practice followed by the undertaking(s) in question or a market characteristic? If it is the former, should it influence the assessment of a practice under Article 101(1) TFEU? If it is the latter, in what sense would this be different than taking account of the finding that the market structure is oligopolistic and/or that the undertaking in question disposes of market power? Does this relate to the availability of the information without a more detailed (and costly, from a procedural efficiency perspective) analysis? What if the information on the specific market structure or market power is easily available (eg in case the anti-competitive conduct takes place on a regulated market)?[112]
9. (Paragraphs 49–50, 69–70, CJEU Judgment) What does the CJEU mean by 'sufficient' degree of harm? Is this a quantitative or a qualitative test? Following the *Groupement des cartes bancaires* is the fact that an agreement simply has the potential to restrict competition sufficient to qualify it as a restriction of competition 'by object'? If not, what else is needed? Compare with the CJEU's ruling in *T-Mobile,*[113] where the CJEU accepted that for some conduct to be qualified as a 'by object' restriction of competition it 'must *simply be capable* in an individual case, having regard to the specific legal and economic context, of resulting in the prevention, restriction or distortion of competition'. According to the CJEU in *Groupement des cartes bancaires*, a finding that an agreement restricts competition 'by object' can be made where there is 'a sufficient degree of harm to competition' such that it can be regarded 'by [its] very nature as being harmful to the proper functioning of normal competition'.[114] This will be the

112 On two-sided markets, see Section 3.3.5.4.
113 Case C-8/08, *T-Mobile Netherlands and Others* [2009] ECR I-4529, paras 31–43.
114 Case C-67/13 P, *Groupement des cartes bancaires (CB) v Commission*, ECLI:EU:C:2014:2204, paras 49–50.

case where it has the object of 'changing appreciably the structure of the market', for example by causing competitors to leave the market and/or by reducing over-capacity.[115] This is certainly a narrower interpretation of restriction by object, particularly in comparison to the *T-Mobile* judgment where the anti-competitive object was sufficient to merely have 'the potential' or 'simply be capable' of having a negative impact on competition. *Cartes Bancaires* also held that 'where the analysis of a type of coordination between undertakings does not reveal a sufficient degree of harm to competition, the effects of the coordination should be considered, and for it to be caught, it is necessary to find that factors are present which show that competition has in fact been prevented, restricted, or distorted to an appreciable extent'.[116] One understanding of this is that where an agreement is not obviously restricted by object, then an effects-based assessment should take place because a categorization in the 'object box' would not be appropriate. Do you agree with this reading of the CJEU's judgment?

10. (Paragraphs 50–1, CJEU Judgment) Does the CJEU analyse anti-competitive object as a presumption of anti-competitive effects? Does the CJEU refer to the competitive process, or is it only addressing anti-competitive effects as only relating to the 'price, quantity or quality of the goods and services', thus focusing only on outcomes? Does the CJEU challenge the established view in the case law that restrictive object and effect are alternative forms of qualification of an infringement under Article 101(1) TFEU? In other words, if object is perceived as a presumption of effects, it is possible that there can be an object without effects? In other words, would it be now possible to argue that an object restriction to competition does not infringe Article 101(1) TFEU in case there is evidence that it does not produces any anti-competitive effects? Or, is the presumption of anti-competitive effects in this case irrefutable?
11. (Paragraph 53, CJEU Judgment) Note that the CJEU confirms that when exploring the economic and legal context, it is also necessary to take into consideration 'the nature of the goods or services affected, as well as the real conditions of the functioning and structure of the market or markets in question' citing to that effect its judgment in *Allianz Hungária*.[117]
12.. (Paragraphs 55–8, 61–77, CJEU Judgment) Identify the problems the CJEU had with the broad interpretation by the GC of the restriction of competition by object. Is this broad interpretation now over?
13. (Paragraph 75, CJEU Judgment). How do you understand the CJEU's reference to the fact that the agreement in question pursued a 'legitimate objective'? Does the CJEU mean that a mixed conduct could not be qualified as a restriction of competition 'by object'? Note that in *Pierre Fabre* the CJEU had found that 'in the absence of objective justification' an agreement constituting a selective distribution system may be a restriction of competition 'by object',[118] thus indicating that it is all-or-nothing: either the agreement has some legitimate objectives, in which case it is not characterized as a by object restriction of competition, or it does not have *any*, in which case it receives this qualification. In *Lundbeck* and *Servier*, however,

[115] Ibid, paras 84–5. [116] Ibid, para 52.
[117] Case C-32/11, *Allianz Hungária Biztosító and Others*, ECLI:EU:C:2013:160.
[118] Case C-439/09, *Pierre Fabre Dermo-Cosmetique* [2011] ECR I–9419, para 39.

the Commission classified under the 'by object' category an agreement having mixed effects.[119]

14. (Paragraphs 77–9, CJEU Judgment) Note the distinction made between the operation of examining the legal and economic context and that regarding market definition. Do you think that such distinction can be easily made in practice? What is the purpose of market definition? What is the purpose of examining the legal and economic context?

15. (Paragraphs 83–7, CJEU Judgment) How does the CJEU distinguish this situation from the *BIDS* case?[120] The CJEU explains that in *BIDS* the parties to the agreement 'intended to change appreciably the structure of the market concerned through a mechanism intended to encourage the withdrawal of competitors and, accordingly, that those measures revealed a degree of harm' that was not found with regard to the agreement in question in *Cartes Bancaires*. Indeed, the objective of the pricing measures was 'not to reduce possible overcapacity on the market for the issue of payment cards in France, but to achieve a given ratio between the issuing and acquisition activities of the members of the Grouping in order to develop the CB system further'. Does the reference to the 'degree of harm' indicate that for a *type* of agreement to be classified as a restriction 'by object', it should be capable of producing, or should be intended to produce, a *higher* degree of harm?

16. (Paragraphs 54, 64, 88, CJEU Judgment) What is the role of the intention of the parties to the anti-competitive agreement? Is this considered as a relevant element when defining anti-competitive object? Should it be?

17. The significance of *Cartes Bancaires* for the interpretation of the concept of restriction of competition by object cannot be overstated. The UK CAT has referred to the implications of this jurisprudence in *Sainsbury's v Mastercard*,

> 100. [. . .] For a period, it appeared that the legal threshold for an object restriction was becoming lower—in that it was becoming easier to establish restriction of competition by object. That trend appears to have been halted, and perhaps reversed, by the Court of Justice's decision in Cartes Bancaires.
>
> 101. It is clear that the essential criterion for discerning a restriction on competition 'by object' is that the agreement by its very nature reveals a sufficient degree of harm to competition, so as to obviate any need for an effects-based examination. Although the basic test—'a sufficient degree of harm to competition'—is not further defined, the following points can be made:
>
> [. . .] Given that a finding of object restriction obviates the need for a consideration of the anti-competitive effects of an agreement, *there is a symbiosis between restriction by object and restriction by effect. Restriction by object should not be used as a*

[119] *Lundbeck* (Case AT.39226) Commission Decision C(2013) 3803 final, available at http://ec.europa.eu/competition/antitrust/cases/dec_docs/39226/39226_8310_11.pdf; *Perindopril (Servier)* (Case AT.39612) Commission Decision C(2014) 4955 final, available at http://ec.europa.eu/competition/antitrust/cases/dec_docs/39612/39612_11972_5.pdf. Although the General Court partially annulled the Commission's decision in *Servier*, for having failed to prove an abuse of a dominant position, as the Commission made a series of errors in defining the relevant market and finding a dominant position, it confirmed the essence of the competition analysis under Article 101(1) TFEU and in particular the fact that the agreements entered into by Servier constituted restrictions of competition by object: see, Case T-691/14, *Servier SAS and Others v European Commission*, ECLI:EU:T:2018:922.

[120] Case C-209/07, *Beef Industry Development Society (BIDS)*, ECLI:EU:C:2008:643.

> *means of avoiding a difficult investigation of anti-competitive effects. In short, the harm to competition that might be expected in the case of an object restriction needs to be clear-cut and pronounced without an examination of the effects* [...].[121]

6.3.1.2.5. SIA Maxima Latvija

The *SIA Maxima Latvija* case provides an interesting example for the assessment of the anti-competitive object and effect.[122] The case concerned commercial lease agreements in shopping centres with a clause conferring on the tenant the right to approve the lease agreements that the property owner may conclude with third parties. Maxima Latvija is a major retailer in Latvia where it runs a chain of large shops and hypermarkets. It concluded a number of commercial lease agreements with owners of shopping centres to rent commercial spaces within such malls. Some of these agreements included a non-compete clause in favour of Maxima Latvija. As 'anchor tenant', Maxima Latvija was awarded the right to agree to the lessors letting third-parties other shops than those rented to Maxima Latvija in the same shopping centres where the tenant was already present. The CJEU was seized of a preliminary ruling question by the Latvian Supreme Court, which asked whether the commercial lease agreements including a non-compete clause in favour of the tenant amounted to a restriction of competition by object and in case it was not, if its effects restricted competition.

The Court noted that the contested agreement was a vertical agreement concluded by firms, a retailer and a property owner, that did not compete with each other, and although it found that this fact was not conclusive in itself, it nevertheless acknowledged that this *type* of agreement is not among those that may be considered, by their nature, as harmful to competition.[123] The CJEU's judgment indicates that Article 101 TFEU may apply to agreements involving the lease of land (land agreements). The CJEU cites both *CB* and *Allianz Hungária*, but distinguishes the specific vertical agreement from the latter case.

Case C-345/14, *SIA 'Maxima Latvija' v Konkurences padome*, ECLI:EU:C:2015:784

> 18. As regards the concept of restriction of competition 'by object', the Court has held that it must be interpreted restrictively and can be applied only to certain types of coordination between undertakings which reveal a sufficient degree of harm to competition that it may be found that there is no need to examine their effects (see, to that effect, judgment in *CB* v *Commission*, C-67/13 P, EU:C:2014:2204, paragraph 58). That case-law arises from the fact that certain types of coordination between undertakings can be regarded, by their very nature, as being harmful to the proper functioning of normal competition (judgment in *CB* v *Commission*, C-67/13 P, EU:C:2014:2204, paragraph 50 and the case-law cited).
>
> 19. It is established, in that regard, that certain collusive behaviour, such as that leading to horizontal price-fixing by cartels, may be considered by their nature as likely to have negative effects, in particular on the price, quantity or quality of the goods and services, so that it may be considered redundant, for the purposes of applying Article 101(1) TFEU, to prove that they have actual effects on the market (see, to that

121 *Sainsbury's Supermarkets Ltd v Mastercard* [2016] CAT 1, paras 100–1 (emphasis added).
122 Case C-345/14, *SIA Maxima Latvija v Konkurences padome*, ECLI:EU:C:2015:784.
123 Case C-345/14, *SIA Maxima Latvija v Konkurences padome*, ECLI:EU:C:2015:784, para 21.

> effect, in particular, judgment in *Clair*, 123/83, EU:C:1985:33, paragraph 22). Experience shows that such behaviour leads to falls in production and price increases, resulting in poor allocation of resources to the detriment, in particular, of consumers (judgment in *CB* v *Commission*, C-67/13 P, EU:C:2014:2204, paragraph 51).
>
> 20. In the light of the case-law which has just been cited, the essential legal criterion for ascertaining whether an agreement involves a restriction of competition 'by object' is therefore the finding that such an agreement reveals in itself a sufficient degree of harm to competition for it to be considered that it is not appropriate to assess its effects (see, to that effect, judgment in *CB* v *Commission*, C-67/13 P, EU:C:2014:2204, paragraph 57).
>
> 21. In the present case, it is apparent from the documents submitted to the Court that Maxima Latvija is not in a competitive situation with the shopping centres with which it has concluded the agreements at issue in the main proceedings. Although the Court has already held that a fact of that nature in no way precludes an agreement from containing a restriction of competition 'by object' (see, inter alia, judgment in *Allianz Hungária Biztosító and Others*, C-32/11, EU:C:2013:160, paragraph 43 and the case-law cited), it must, however, be stated that the agreements at issue in the main proceedings are not among the agreements which it is accepted may be considered, by their very nature, to be harmful to the proper functioning of competition.
>
> 22. Even if the clause at issue in the main proceedings could potentially have the effect of restricting the access of Maxima Latvija's competitors to some shopping centres in which that company operates a large shop or hypermarket, such a fact, if established, does not imply clearly that the agreements containing that clause prevent, restrict or distort, by the very nature of the latter, competition on the relevant market, namely the local market for the retail food trade.
>
> 23. Taking account of the economic context in which agreements, such as those at issue in the main proceedings are to be applied, the analysis of the content of those agreements would not, in the light of the information provided by the referring court, show, clearly, a degree of harm with regard to competition sufficient for those agreements to be considered to constitute a restriction of competition 'by object' within the meaning of Article 101(1) TFEU.
>
> 24. In the light of all the foregoing considerations, the answer to the first question is that Article 101(1) TFEU must be interpreted as meaning that the mere fact that a commercial lease agreement for the letting of a large shop or hypermarket located in a shopping centre contains a clause granting the lessee the right to oppose the letting by the lessor, in that centre, of commercial premises to other tenants, does not mean that the object of that agreement is to restrict competition within the meaning of that provision.

The Court then turned to the assessment of anti-competitive effects, applying the test it had employed in the *Delimitis* case, which requires a full analysis of the economic and legal context of the agreements and the competition conditions in the relevant market in order to establish whether the agreements have negative effects on competition.[124] The first part of the test consists 'in the examination of all the factors affecting the access to the relevant market for the purposes of assessing whether, in the catchment areas where the shopping centres which are covered by those agreements are located, there are real concrete possibilities for a new competitor to establish itself'.[125] According to the CJEU, 'it is appropriate in particular to take into

124 Case C-234/89, *Delimitis (Stergios) v Henninger Bräu* [1991] ECR I–935.

125 Case C-345/14, *SIA Maxima Latvija v Konkurences padome*, ECLI:EU:C:2015:784, para 27.

consideration the availability and accessibility of commercial land in the catchment areas concerned and the existence of economic, administrative or regulatory barriers to entry of new competitors in those areas'.[126] The second part of the test explores 'the conditions under which competitive forces operate on the relevant market', which includes 'not only the number and the size of operators present on the market, but also the degree of concentration of that market and customer fidelity to existing brands and consumer habits'.[127]

The analysis of the Court focuses on inter-brand competition, as the main point is to discover if access to that market is made difficult by all the similar agreements found on the market, and then to determine to what extent they contribute to any closing-off of that market, as only agreements which make an appreciable contribution to that closing-off are prohibited under Article 101 TFEU.[128]

NOTES AND QUESTIONS ON SIA MAXIMA LATVIJA V KONKURENCES PADOME

1. Note that the CJEU consistently cited *Cartes Bancaires* for almost all propositions with regard to the qualification of a practice as a 'by object' restriction to competition. *Allianz Hungária* is only cited once but its impact is immediately relativized in the specific context.
2. (Paragraphs 22–3) Note that the market foreclosure effect of the non-compete clause was not found of a 'sufficient' 'degree of harm' to constitute an object restriction. Is 'sufficient' and 'degree of harm' referring to a quantitative requirement? Or, is it a qualitative one? Note that the CJEU only refers to the 'content' of the agreement, and not its objectives and economic context, when assessing if there is a 'sufficient' 'degree of harm' to qualify the specific type of agreement as a restriction of competition 'by object'.
3. Should the distance from other clusters of retailers selling similar physical goods be relevant? If there are few shopping centres in remote areas nearby, such clauses may confer local monopolies on each retailer. Should this depend on whether one is considering object or effect?
4. If the distance of the shopping centre from others is relevant, would the validity of a clause not to let to competing retailers vary as populations move? Would such a clause be administrable?

6.3.1.2.6. Lundbeck v Commission and the Perindopril cases

The first was an action for annulment against the Commission's decision in *Lundbeck*.[129] Lundbeck had entered into six agreements with four undertakings active in the production and/or sale of generic medicinal products, competing with its blockbuster drug, citalopram, convening of payments of several millions of pounds (pay for delay settlements or reverse payment settlements[130]) as well as some additional conditions. The Commission imposed a

126 Ibid. 127 Ibid, para 28. 128 Ibid, para 29.

129 *Lundbeck* (Case AT.39226) Commission Decision C(2013) 3803 final, available at http://ec.europa.eu/competition/antitrust/cases/dec_docs/39226/39226_8310_11.pdf.

130 On the assessment of this practice in more detail see our analysis in I Lianos, *Competition Law and the Intangible Economy* (OUP, forthcoming 2019). This Section only focuses on the general part of the judgment relating to the interpretation of the main concepts of Article 101(1) TFEU.

total fine of €146 million on Lundbeck and four manufacturers of generic drugs. Lundbeck appealed to the General Court, which issued a judgment confirming the Commission's decision and rejecting the appeal entirely.

The GC's judgment contains several interesting paragraphs on the interpretation of the various concepts of Article 101(1) TFEU.

The applicants argued that the Commission's decision had misinterpreted the relevant case-law on establishing whether an agreement restricts potential competition, which according to them presupposes the existence of real concrete possibilities of entering the market in the absence of the agreement. The Commission had considered that challenging patents is an expression of potential competition in the pharmaceutical sector.

Case T-472/13, *H Lundbeck A/S and Lundbeck Ltd v Commission*, ECLI:EU:T:2016:449

The concept of potential competition

98. It must be noted, first of all, that, having regard to the requirements set out in Article 101(1) TFEU regarding effect on trade between Member States and repercussions on competition, that provision applies only to sectors open to competition (see judgment of 29 June 2012 in *E.ON Ruhrgas and E.ON* v *Commission*, T-360/09, ECR, EU:T:2012:332, paragraph 84 and the case-law cited). [. . .]

100. In order to determine whether an undertaking is a potential competitor in a market, the Commission is required to determine whether, if the agreement in question had not been concluded, there would have been real concrete possibilities for it to enter that market and to compete with established undertakings. Such a demonstration must not be based on a mere hypothesis, but must be supported by factual evidence or an analysis of the structures of the relevant market. Accordingly, an undertaking cannot be described as a potential competitor if its entry into a market is not an economically viable strategy (see judgment in *E.ON Ruhrgas and E.ON* v *Commission*, [. . .] [para] 86 and the case-law cited).

101. It necessarily follows that, while the intention of an undertaking to enter a market may be of relevance in order to determine whether it can be considered to be a potential competitor in that market, nonetheless the essential factor on which such a description must be based is whether it has the ability to enter that market (see judgment in *E.ON Ruhrgas and E.ON* v *Commission*, [. . .] [para] 87 and the case-law cited).

102. It should, in that regard, be recalled that whether potential competition—which may be no more than the existence of an undertaking outside that market—is restricted cannot depend on whether it can be demonstrated that that undertaking intends to enter that market in the near future. The mere fact of its existence may give rise to competitive pressure on the undertakings currently operating in that market, a pressure represented by the likelihood that a new competitor will enter the market if the market becomes more attractive (judgment in *Visa Europe and Visa International Service* v *Commission* [. . .] [para] 169).

103. Moreover, it also follows from the case-law that the very fact that an undertaking already present on the market seeks to conclude agreements or to establish information exchange mechanisms with other undertakings which are not present on the market provides a strong indication that the market in question is not impenetrable [. . .].

104. Although it follows from that case-law that the Commission may rely inter alia on the perception of the undertaking present on the market in order to assess whether other undertakings are potential competitors, nevertheless, the purely theoretical possibility of market entry is not sufficient to establish the existence of potential competition. The Commission must therefore demonstrate, by factual evidence or an analysis of the structures of the relevant market, that the market entry could have taken place sufficiently quickly for the threat of a potential entry to influence the conduct of the participants in the market, on the basis of costs which would have been economically viable (see, to that effect, judgment in *E.ON Ruhrgas and E.ON* v *Commission*, [. . .] [paras] 106 and 114).

The GC then moved to the discussion of the burden of proof and standard of proof/persuasion for a restriction on potential competition.

105. It follows from settled case-law, and from Article 2 of Regulation No 1/2003, that it is for the party or the authority alleging an infringement of the competition rules to prove its existence. Thus, where there is a dispute as to the existence of an infringement, it is incumbent on the Commission to prove the infringements which it has found and to adduce evidence capable of demonstrating to the requisite legal standard the existence of circumstances constituting an infringement (see judgment of 12 April 2013 in *CISAC* v *Commission*, T-442/08, ECR, EU:T:2013:188, paragraph 91 and the case-law cited).

106. In that context, any doubt on the part of the Court must operate to the advantage of the undertaking to which the decision finding an infringement was addressed. The Court cannot therefore conclude that the Commission has established the infringement in question to the requisite legal standard if it still entertains any doubts on that point, in particular in proceedings for annulment of a decision imposing a fine (see judgment in *CISAC* v *Commission*, [. . .] [para] 92 and the case-law cited).

107. It is necessary to take into account the principle of the presumption of innocence resulting in particular from Article 48 of the Charter of Fundamental Rights of the European Union. Given the nature of the infringements in question and the nature and degree of severity of the penalties which may ensue, the presumption of innocence applies, inter alia, to the procedures relating to infringements of the competition rules applicable to undertakings that may result in the imposition of fines or periodic penalty payments (see, to that effect, judgment in *CISAC* v *Commission*, [. . .] [para] 93 and the case-law cited).

108. In addition, account must be taken of the non-negligible stigma attached to a finding of involvement in an infringement of the competition rules for a natural or legal person (see judgment in *CISAC* v *Commission*, [. . .] [para] 95 and the case-law cited).

109. Thus, the Commission must show precise and consistent evidence in order to establish the existence of the infringement and to support the firm conviction that the alleged infringement constitutes a restriction of competition within the meaning of Article 101(1) TFEU (see judgment in *CISAC* v *Commission*, [. . .] [para] 96 and the case-law cited).

110. However, it is important to emphasise that it is not necessary for every item of evidence produced by the Commission to satisfy those criteria in relation to every aspect of the infringement. It is sufficient if the set of indicia relied on by the institution, viewed as a whole, meets that requirement (see judgment in *CISAC* v *Commission*, [. . .] [para] 97 and the case-law cited).

111. Lastly, it must be pointed out that, when the Commission establishes that the undertaking in question has participated in an anticompetitive measure, it is for that

undertaking to provide, using not only documents that were not disclosed but also all the means at its disposal, a different explanation for its conduct (see, to that effect, judgment of 7 January 2004 in *Aalborg Portland and Others* v *Commission*, C-204/00 P, C-205/00 P, C-211/00 P, C-213/00 P, C-217/00 P and C-219/00 P, ECR, EU:C:2004:6, paragraphs 79 and 132).

112. Nevertheless, where the Commission has documentary evidence of an anticompetitive practice, it is not sufficient for the undertakings concerned to prove circumstances which cast the facts established by the Commission in a different light and thus allow another explanation of the facts to be substituted for the one adopted by the Commission. In the presence of documentary evidence, the burden is on those undertakings not merely to submit another explanation for the facts found by the Commission but to challenge the existence of those facts established on the basis of the documents produced by the Commission (see, to that effect, judgment in *CISAC* v *Commission*, [. . .] [paras] 99 and 102 and the case-law cited). [. . .]

160. The case-law indeed indicates that the purely theoretical possibility of market entry is not sufficient to establish the existence of potential competition and that the Commission must demonstrate, by factual evidence or an analysis of the structures of the relevant market, that the market entry could have taken place sufficiently quickly for the threat of a potential entry to influence the conduct of the participants in the market, on the basis of costs which would have been economically viable (para. 104 above). [. . .]

163. [. . .] [I]t must be recalled that, in order to establish the existence of potential competition, the case-law requires only that the entry to the market take place within a reasonable period, without fixing a specific limit in that respect. The Commission therefore does not need to demonstrate with certainty that the entry of the generic undertakings to the market would have taken place before the expiry of the agreements at issue in order to be able to establish the existence of potential competition in the present case, particularly since, as the Court of Justice has already held, potential competition may be exerted long before the expiry of a patent [. . .].

The judgment also contains interesting analysis relating to the existence of a restriction of competition 'by object', the Commission having considered in its decision that the agreements at issue (a pay for delay agreements) constituted a restriction of competition 'by object'. The GC explained the general principles applying in this context for restrictions of competition by object.

339. In that regard, it is apparent from the case-law that certain types of coordination between undertakings reveal a sufficient degree of harm to competition for the examination of their effects to be considered unnecessary (judgment in *CB* v *Commission*, cited in paragraph 78 above, EU:C:2014:2204, paragraph 49; see also, to that effect, judgments of 30 June 1966 in *LTM*, 56/65, ECR, EU:C:1966:38, pp. 359 and 360, and 14 March 2013 in *Allianz Hungária Biztosító and Others*, C-32/11, ECR, EU:C:2013:160, paragraph 34).

340. That case-law arises from the fact that certain forms of coordination between undertakings can be regarded, by their very nature, as being injurious to the proper functioning of normal competition (judgment in *CB* v *Commission*, cited in paragraph 78 above, EU:C:2014:2204, paragraph 50; see also, to that effect, judgment in *Allianz Hungária Biztosító and Others*, [. . .] [para] 35 and the case-law cited).

341. Consequently, it is established that certain collusive behaviour, such as that leading to horizontal price-fixing by cartels or consisting in the exclusion of some

competitors from the market, may be considered so likely to have negative effects, in particular on the price, quantity or quality of the goods and services, that it may be considered redundant, for the purposes of applying Article 101(1) TFEU, to prove that they have actual effects on the market. Experience shows that such behaviour leads to falls in production and price increases, resulting in poor allocation of resources to the detriment, in particular, of consumers (see judgment in *CB* v *Commission*, [. . .] [para] 51 and the case-law cited; see also, to that effect, judgment of 20 November 2008 in *Beef Industry Development Society and Barry Brothers*, C-209/07, ECR, 'the *BIDS* judgment', EU:C:2008:643, paragraphs 33 and 34).

342. Where the analysis of a type of coordination between undertakings does not reveal a sufficient degree of harm to competition, the effects of the coordination should, on the other hand, be considered and, for it to be caught by the prohibition, it is necessary to find that factors are present which show that competition has in fact been prevented, restricted or distorted to an appreciable extent (judgments in *Allianz Hungária Biztosító and Others*, [. . .] [para] 34, and *CB* v *Commission*, [. . .] [para] 52).

343. In order to establish the anticompetitive nature of an agreement and assess whether it reveals a sufficient degree of harm to competition that it may be considered a restriction of competition by object for the purpose of Article 101(1) TFEU, regard must be had to the content of its provisions, its objectives and the economic and legal context of which it forms a part. When determining that context, it is also necessary to take into consideration the nature of the goods or services affected, as well as the real conditions of the functioning and structure of the market or markets in question (judgments in *Allianz Hungária Biztosító and Others*, [. . .] [paras] 36 and in *CB* v *Commission*, [. . .] [para] 53).

344. In addition, although the parties' intention is not a necessary factor in determining whether an agreement between undertakings is restrictive, there is nothing prohibiting the competition authorities, the national courts or the Courts of the European Union from taking that factor into account (judgments in *Allianz Hungária Biztosító and Others*, c[. . .] [paras] 37, and *CB* v *Commission*, [. . .] [para] 54 and the case-law cited) [. . .]

An interesting issue is the role of economics in the context of a restriction by 'object', the applicants claiming that an economic presumption, such as that put forward by the Commission with regard to this type of agreement, can be accepted only if it is based on robust empirical and theoretical foundations, and that the Commission can rely on an insufficiently clear presumption only if it has proved that that was the only plausible explanation. The GC rejected this argument.

386. [T]o accept the applicants' argument [. . .] would amount, ultimately, to considering that they could—by concluding agreements such as the agreements at issue with the generic undertakings—protect themselves against an irreversible price fall which, according to their own assertions, could not have been avoided even if they had been successful in infringement actions brought before the national courts. They could therefore, by concluding such agreements, maintain higher prices for their products, to the detriment of consumers and the healthcare budgets of States, even though such an outcome could not have been obtained if the national courts had confirmed the validity of their patents and the products of the generic undertakings had been held to be infringing. Such an outcome would be manifestly contrary to the objectives of the treaty provisions on competition, which are intended inter alia to protect consumers from unjustified price increases resulting from collusion between competitors

(see, to that effect, judgments of 19 March 2015 in *Dole Food and Dole Fresh Fruit Europe* v *Commission*, C-286/13 P, ECR, EU:C:2015:184, paragraph 115 and the case-law cited, and 9 July 2015 in *InnoLux* v *Commission*, C-231/14 P, ECR, EU:C:2015:451, paragraph 61). There is no reason to suppose that such collusion would be lawful in the present case, under the pretext that certain process patents were in dispute, when the defence of those patents before the national courts could not, even in the most favourable scenario for the applicants, have led to the same negative consequences for competition and, in particular, for consumers.

Comparison with *BIDS*

428 [. . .] [A]lthough it is true that, in the case that gave rise to the *BIDS* judgment, [. . .] the undertakings at issue were actual competitors, since the agreements in that case were intended to remove from the market undertakings which were already present on that market, whereas, in the present case, Lundbeck and the generic undertakings were merely potential competitors, it is nevertheless the case that, in the *BIDS* judgment, the Court of Justice did not require the Commission to demonstrate that, in the absence of those agreements, the undertakings would have stayed on the market. In the context of a restriction of competition by object, it is unnecessary to examine the effects of the agreements [. . .]. The Court merely found, in that case, that the agreements in question were intended to implement a common policy which had as its object the encouragement of some of them to withdraw from the market and the reduction, as a consequence, of the overcapacity which affected their profitability by preventing them from achieving economies of scale. It therefore held that that type of agreement conflicted patently with the concept inherent in the treaty provisions relating to competition, according to which each economic operator must determine independently the policy which it intends to adopt on the common market, noting that Article 101(1) TFEU is intended to prohibit any form of coordination which deliberately substitutes practical cooperation between undertakings for the risks of competition (see the *BIDS* judgment, [. . .] paras 33 and 34).

429. In the present case, the parties to the agreements at issue preferred to replace the risks inherent in the normal competitive process and the state of uncertainty surrounding the validity of Lundbeck's process patents and whether or not the products that the generic undertakings intended to market infringed those patents, with the certainty that those undertakings would not enter the market during the term of those agreements, in return for significant reverse payments which corresponded approximately to the profits that those undertakings would have made if they had entered the market. It is therefore irrelevant whether the undertakings would undoubtedly have entered the market during the term of the agreements at issue, since those agreements eliminated that very possibility, replacing it with the certainty that those undertakings would not enter the market with their products during that period. By doing so, the parties to the agreements at issue were able to share a part of the profits that Lundbeck continued to enjoy, to the detriment of consumers who continued to pay higher prices than those they would have paid if the generics had entered the market [. . .].

430 [. . .] As the Commission submitted, in both cases, the payments played a decisive role in that they induced the undertakings to withdraw from the market. Thus, in the case that gave rise to the *BIDS* judgment, [. . .] it is unlikely that the 'going' undertakings would have agreed to withdraw from the market in the absence of payments from the 'staying' undertakings. Likewise, in the present case, it can be seen from the

file that the generic undertakings would not have agreed to stay out of the market unilaterally, after having taken significant steps and having made significant investments, in the absence of reverse payments.

431. [. . .] In the present case, however, the Commission rightly considered that the reverse payments had played a decisive role, in that they had allowed Lundbeck to obtain commitments from the generic undertakings which they would not have been able to obtain in the absence of those payments, thereby delaying the market entry of those undertakings. [. . .]

The *Cartes bancaires* judgment narrowly interpreted

434. It must be observed that, by the judgment in *CB* v *Commission* [. . .] the Court of Justice did not call into question the basic principles concerning the concept of a restriction 'by object' set out in the previous case-law. It is true that, in its judgment, the Court of Justice rejected the General Court's analysis in the judgment of 29 November 2012 in *CB* v *Commission* (T-491/07, EU:T:2012:633), according to which the concept of restriction of competition 'by object' should not be interpreted in a restrictive manner. The Court of Justice noted that the concept of restriction of competition 'by object' could be applied only to certain types of coordination between undertakings which revealed a sufficient degree of harm to competition that it could be found that there was no need to examine their effects, otherwise the Commission would be exempted from the obligation to prove the actual effects on the market of agreements which were in no way established to be, by their very nature, harmful to the proper functioning of normal competition (judgment in *CB* v *Commission*, [. . .] [para] 58).

Analogy to market exclusion and restriction by object

435. It follows from the general scheme of the contested decision [. . .] that the agreements at issue were comparable to market exclusion agreements, which are among the most serious restrictions of competition. The exclusion of competitors from the market constitutes an extreme form of market sharing and of limitation of production. [. . .]

436. Accordingly, it must be held that the Commission correctly applied the case-law [. . .], which consists in determining whether an agreement may, by its very nature, be regarded as restricting competition in a sufficiently serious manner as to be classified as a restriction 'by object' in the case at hand [. . .].

437. Accordingly, the Commission was not required also to examine the specific effects of the agreements at issue on competition and, in particular, whether, in the absence of those agreements, the generic undertakings would have entered the market without infringing one of Lundbeck's patents, in order to be able to establish the existence of a restriction of competition by object, within the meaning of Article 101(1) TFEU, since those generic undertakings had real concrete possibilities in that respect and were potential competitors of Lundbeck at the time the agreements at issue were concluded (see the first plea in law above).

438. Moreover, contrary to what is claimed by the applicants, it is not necessary that the same type of agreement have already been censured by the Commission in order for them to constitute a restriction of competition by object. The role of experience, mentioned by the Court of Justice in paragraph 51 of the judgment in *CB* v *Commission*

[. . .] does not concern the specific category of an agreement in a particular sector, but rather refers to the fact that it is established that certain forms of collusion are, in general and in view of the experience gained, so likely to have negative effects on competition that it is not necessary to demonstrate that they had such effects in the particular case at hand. The fact that the Commission has not, in the past, considered that a certain type of agreement was, by its very object, restrictive of competition is therefore not, in itself, such as to prevent it from doing so in the future following an individual and detailed examination of the measures in question having regard to their content, purpose and context (see, to that effect, judgment in *CB* v *Commission*, [. . .] [para] 51; the Opinion of Advocate General Wahl in *CB* v *Commission*, C-67/13 P, ECR, EU:C:2014:1958, point 142, and the Opinion of Advocate General Wathelet in *Toshiba Corporation* v *Commission*, C-373/14 P, ECR, EU:C:2015:427, point 74).

NOTES AND QUESTIONS ON LUNDBECK

1. (Paragraphs 100–2) The GC indicates that an undertaking cannot be described as a potential competitor if its entry into a market is not an economically viable strategy and the undertaking does not have *the ability* to enter that market, but also explains that the 'mere fact 'of the existence of such an undertaking may give rise to competitive pressure on the undertakings currently operating in that market, and thus constitute potential competition and that there is no need to show that the undertaking has/had the intention to enter the market. Indeed, 'no more than the existence of an undertaking outside that market' is required. Note that the GC refers only to the *ability* of the undertaking outside the relevant market to enter, not to its *incentive*. Do you think that the GC's conception of 'potential competition' is broad, narrow or, just about right?
2. (Paragraphs 160, 163) Furthermore, the GC rejects the possibility that a 'purely theoretical possibility of market entry' would be sufficient to establish the existence of potential competition, and requires 'factual evidence or an analysis of the structures of the relevant market, that the market entry could have taken place sufficiently quickly for the threat of a potential entry to influence the conduct of the participants in the market, on the basis of costs which would have been economically viable'. However, as the case law does not fix a specific limit and 'requires only that the entry to the market take place within a reasonable period', Commission does not need to demonstrate 'with certainty' that the entry of the generic undertakings to the market would have taken place.
3. (Paragraphs 107–10) The CJEU mentions the principle of the presumption of innocence and the 'non-negligible stigma attached to a finding of involvement in an infringement of the competition rules for a natural or legal person', before noting, with regard to the standard of proof of a restriction to (actual or) potential competition, that the claimant 'must show precise and consistent evidence in order to establish the existence of the infringement and to support the firm conviction that the alleged infringement constitutes a restriction of competition within the meaning of Article 101(1) TFEU'. However, it also accepts that 'every item of evidence' produced by the Commission satisfies those criteria in relation 'to every aspect of the infringement', but that 'the set of indicia relied on' 'as a whole', meets this evidential requirement. Would that comply with a criminal standard of proof of beyond reasonable doubt? Would this indicate a lower standard of proof?

4. (Paragraph 112) Note, however, that documentary evidence of an anti-competitive practice cannot be countered by the defendant by simply proving circumstances which cast the facts established by the claimant/Commission in a different light and thus allow another explanation of the facts to be substituted for the one adopted by the claimant/Commission. In this case, undertakings must not merely submit another explanation for the facts found by the Commission but must challenge the existence of those facts.
5. (Paragraphs 339–44) In these paragraphs the GC explains the various steps needed for a *type* of coordination between undertakings to be considered as constituting a restriction of competition by object. First, these types of coordination should show a 'sufficient degree of harm' to competition for the examination of their effects to be considered unnecessary.[131] Second, there may be forms of coordination between undertakings, which can be regarded, by their very nature, as being injurious to the proper functioning of normal competition.[132] One may argue that anti-competitive object leads to a presumption of anti-competitive effects. On one hand, this may be based on 'experience' showing that 'such behaviour leads to falls in production and price increases, resulting in poor allocation of resources to the detriment, in particular, of consumers' (the GC referring here to horizontal price fixing), thus making "redundant" any analysis of actual effects.[133] On the other hand, this may (also) be based on some deontological principle that such *type* of coordination harms "by nature" the competitive process. For a restriction of competition by object, one needs to examine 'the content of its provisions, its objectives and the economic and legal context of which it forms a part'. With regard to the 'context' of the agreement, 'it is also necessary to take into consideration the nature of the goods or services affected, as well as the real conditions of the functioning and structure of the market or markets in question'.[134] The parties' intention is also an element eventually to consider but certainly not 'a necessary factor in determining whether an agreement between undertakings is restrictive'.[135] If the analysis of a *type* of coordination between undertakings does not reveal a sufficient degree of harm to competition, then 'the effects of the coordination should, on the other hand, be considered and, for it to be caught by the prohibition, it is necessary to find that factors are present which show that competition has in fact been prevented, restricted or distorted to an appreciable extent'.[136] Hence, the analysis of a restriction of competition by object, includes both an abstract assessment of the specific *type* of restrictive practice, with regard to past experience on the economic effects of the specific type of coordination, and a more concrete assessment of the context of the agreement in question, but only with regard to some limited factors: the content of its provisions, its objectives, the nature of the goods or services affected, as well as the real conditions of the functioning and structure of the market or markets in question. What is the difference between this analysis and that undertaken under the rubric of the restriction of competition by effect? Would that relate to the type of legal assessment, or more broadly to the choice of the specific decision procedure, rather than being related to the adoption of a decision criterion, such as economic efficiency?
6. (Paragraphs 386, 428) Is the assessment of a restriction of competition by object always related to past experience, from the point of view of welfare economics, that the

[131] Case T-472/13, *H Lundbeck A/S and Lundbeck Ltd v Commission*, ECLI:EU:T:2016:449, para 339.
[132] Ibid, para 340. [133] Ibid, paras 341–2. [134] Ibid, para 343. [135] Ibid, para 344.
[136] Ibid, para 342.

specific practice generates a sufficient degree of anti-competitive effects? Or, is it also possible to accommodate a deontological perspective that would find that a type of agreement is a restriction by object when it conflicts 'patently with the concept inherent in the treaty provisions relating to competition'?

7. (Paragraph 434) Do you consider that the GC's interpretation of a restriction of competition by object is compatible with the admonition of the CJEU following the GC's judgment in *CB v Commission* that the concept of restriction of competition 'by object' could be applied only to certain types of coordination between undertakings which '*revealed* [note the past tense] a sufficient degree of harm to competition'? How did the CJEU compare the specific fact pattern with the fact pattern in *BIDS*?[137] Do you find such comparison convincing?
8. (Paragraphs 435–6, 438) Did the GC perform an economic analysis of pay for delay settlements or reverse payment settlements before concluding that they could be characterized as a restriction of competition by object? Is the characterization of restriction of competition by object linked to some prior balancing of anti-competitive and pro-competitive effects of this type of coordination between undertakings? Does the GC adopt a categorization approach, reasoning by analogy to other similar types of restrictions of competition, that were previously found to constitute a restriction of competition by object? What if, there is no past experience with the specific *type* of coordination between undertakings? Examine the advantages and disadvantages of each option and critically assess the approach adopted by the GC.
9. An appeal is pending in front of the CJEU (Case C-591/16 P).

6.3.1.2.7. Summing up

The different categories of agreements which are deemed anti-competitive by their object are not immutable. They depend on the aims pursued by competition law. An abstract economic analysis of the effects of categories of agreements has been implicitly performed before their qualification as restrictions of competition by their object, at least at the level of the adoption of a block exemption regulation and the European Commission's Guidelines.

The characterization of an agreement as being restrictive of competition by object leads to a presumption of incompatibility to Article 101 TFEU. However, it is still possible for the parties to the agreement to justify it under Article 101(3) TFEU. Hence, anti-competitive object should not be confused with a per se prohibition rule.

When an agreement has an anti-competitive object, it is not necessary to examine its anti-competitive effect (actual or potential) before concluding on its incompatibility to Article 101(1) TFEU. However, the operation of assessing the anti-competitive object of an agreement is not automatic and involves the characterization or classification of the facts at issue as falling within one of the categories/*types* of coordination/collusion between undertakings having an anti-competitive object. This characterization step is always performed having regard to the past experience with regard to the *type* of the coordination but also with regard to the *economic and legal context* of the *specific* agreement. It is thus possible that an agreement that seems, at first sight, as being similar to a category of agreements that are

[137] See ibid, paras 428–31.

anti-competitive by object, is not qualified as a restriction of competition by object, because of the specific legal and economic context to which it forms part.

In order to assess whether specific conduct may be qualified as a by object restriction of competition, the analysis is performed at the level of the *type* of the agreement, taking consideration of the legal and economic context,[138] before looking to the nature of the *specific restriction* included in the agreement, also considered in its legal and economic context.[139] Indeed, in *CB*, the CJEU first explained that 'certain types of coordination between undertakings reveal a sufficient degree of harm to competition that it may be found that there is no need to examine their effects', and that these '*types* of coordination between undertakings can be regarded, by their very nature, as being harmful to the proper functioning of normal competition'.[140] The CJEU then described the factors that must be examined in order to determine whether an individual agreement may be considered a by object restriction: the content of its provisions, its objectives, the economic and legal context of which it forms part and the parties' intention. According to the CJEU, '[w]hen determining that context, it is also necessary to take into consideration the nature of the goods or services affected, as well as the real conditions of the functioning and structure of the market or markets in question'.[141] This does not, however, require the definition of a relevant market, but an overall abstract assessment of the general characteristics of the product and markets under consideration.[142] This assessment may also include the analysis of the ancillary nature of the *specific* alleged restriction to a generally positive to competition *type* of agreement.[143] The fact that a specific *type* of restriction may also have a legitimate aim will not, in some cases, be sufficient to escape a qualification as a restriction by object.[144] What counts for the characterization as a restriction of competition by object is the existence of a 'sufficient degree of harm to competition' of that type of conduct, 'irrespective of the actual, subjective aims of the parties involved, even if those aims are legitimate'.[145] Characterizing a type of conduct as a restriction of competition by object is only possible if the anti-competitive potential of this type of conduct outweighs any potential pro-competitive effects resulting from the economic and legal context of the agreement, as agreements which have ambivalent potential effects on the market cannot be qualified as restrictions of competition by object.[146]

138 In his Opinion in Case C-67/13 P, *CB v Commission*, ECLI:EU:C:2014:1958, paras 55–6, AG Wahl referred to a number of criteria forming this economic and legal context for the purposes of determining whether a specific type of agreement may fall be considered as by its object anti-competitive: sufficient experience (also from economic analysis) or other empirical evidence that the restriction in question will normally have an overall negative effect on competition and consumers.

139 L Peerperkorn, 'Defining by Object Restrictions' (2015) 3 *Concurrences* 40.

140 Case C-67/13 P, *CB v Commission*, ECLI:EU:C:2014:2204, paras 49–52 (emphasis added).

141 Ibid, paras 53–78.

142 Ibid, para 82. See also, T-691/14, *Servier SAS and Others v European Commission*, ECLI:EU:T:2018:922, para 221 (noting that the examination of the actual conditions and the structure of the market in question is not equivalent to assessing the effects of the conduct concerned, as otherwise the distinction between anti-competitive object and effect would be rendered ineffective).

143 See Section 6.3.2 on the ancillary restraints doctrine.

144 See, T-691/14, *Servier SAS and Others v European Commission*, ECLI:EU:T:2018:922, para 222; Case C-209/07, *Competition Authority v Beef Industry Development Society Ltd (BIDS)*, EU:C:2008:643, para 21. See also *PING Europe Limited v CMA* [2018] CAT 13, para 101, noting that 'even if the impugned measure had a pro-competitive purpose, this was "irrelevant" to an assessment of whether it constituted an object restriction for the purposes of Article 101(1)'.

145 Ibid, para 102. For a more detailed analysis of this case, see Section 10.4.4.3.1 and the discussion on online distribution bans in selective distribution systems.

146 See,T-691/14, *Servier SAS and Others v European Commission*, ECLI:EU:T:2018:922, paras 304, 306 & 996. Such analysis is not similar to the rule of reason under US antitrust law, as the consideration of potential effects is limited to what is necessary for establishing anti-competitive object (Ibid, paras 294 & 306).

If the *type* of the agreement and/or the *specific* clause are not anti-competitive by object, it is important to assess their effects, again in the economic and legal context the agreement occurs. This will require the analysis of the relevant market, any relevant counterfactuals, the appreciability of the restriction of competition, a possible combination with the effect of other similar restrictions to competition (cumulative effect).

6.3.2. RESTRICTIONS OF COMPETITION BY OBJECT

6.3.2.1. The definition of anti-competitive object by the Commission

The Commission's Guidelines on Article 101(3) explain in detail the operation of the 'by object' restriction of competition analysis.[147] In revising its *de minimis* Notice in 2014, following the *Expedia* judgment of the CJEU,[148] the European Commission published a *Guidance on restrictions of competition 'by object' for the purpose of defining which agreements may benefit from the De Minimis Notice*, which as a Commission Staff Working Document 'accompanies' the Commission's *de minimis* communication and as such does not have any binding effect and even less effect than the *de minimis* notice (which is published at the Official Journal of the EU and engages at least the Commission under the principle of legitimate expectations). However, the document provides some insights on the way the European Commission perceives the concept of anti-competitive object.

Commission Staff Working Document—Guidance on restrictions of competition 'by object' for the purpose of defining which agreements may benefit from the *De Minimis* Notice C(2014) 4136 final (some footnotes included)

[. . .] The distinction between 'restrictions by object' and 'restrictions by effect' arises from the fact that certain forms of collusion between undertakings can be regarded, by their very nature, as being injurious to the proper functioning of normal competition. Restrictions of competition 'by object' are those that by their very nature have the potential to restrict competition. These are restrictions which in the light of the objectives pursued by the Union competition rules have such a high potential for negative effects on competition that it is unnecessary for the purposes of applying Article 101(1) of the Treaty to demonstrate any actual or likely anti-competitive effects on the market. This is due to the serious nature of the restriction and experience showing that such restrictions are likely to produce negative effects on the market and to jeopardize the objectives pursued by the EU Union competition rules.

In order to determine with certainty whether an agreement involves a restriction of competition 'by object', regard must, according to the case law of the Court of Justice of the European Union, be had to a number of factors, such as the content of its provisions, its objectives and the economic and legal context of which it forms a part. In addition, although the parties' intention is not a necessary factor in determining whether an agreement restricts competition 'by object', the Commission may nevertheless take this aspect into account in its analysis.

The types of restrictions that are considered to constitute restrictions 'by object' differ depending on whether the agreements are entered into between actual or potential competitors or between non-competitors (for example between a supplier and a distributor). In the case of agreements between competitors (horizontal agreements), restrictions of competition by

147 Guidelines on Article 101(3) (formerly 81(3)), paras 22–3 (footnotes omitted).
148 Case C-226/11, *Expedia Inc v Autorité de la concurrence and Others*, ECLI:EU:C:2012:795.

object include, in particular, price fixing, output limitation and sharing of markets and customers. As regards agreements between non-competitors (vertical agreements), the category of restrictions by object includes, in particular, fixing (minimum) resale prices and restrictions which limit sales into particular territories or to particular customer groups.

The fact that an agreement contains a restriction 'by object', and thus falls under Article 101(1) of the Treaty, does not preclude the parties from demonstrating that the conditions set out in Article 101(3) of the Treaty are satisfied. However, practice shows that restrictions by object are unlikely to fulfil the four conditions set out in Article 101(3).

In exceptional cases, a restriction 'by object' may also be compatible with Article 101 of the Treaty not because it benefits from the exception provided for in Article 101(3) of the Treaty, but because it is objectively necessary for the existence of an agreement of a particular type or nature or for the protection of a legitimate goal, such as health and safety, and therefore falls outside the scope of Article 101(1) of the Treaty.

Types of practices that generally constitute restrictions of competition 'by object' can be found in the Commission's guidelines, notices and block exemption regulations. These refer to restrictions by object or contain lists of so-called 'hardcore' restrictions that describe certain types of restrictions which do not benefit from a block exemption on the basis of the nature of those restrictions and the fact that those restrictions are likely to produce negative effects on the market. Those so called 'hardcore' restrictions are generally restrictions 'by object' when assessed in an individual case. Agreements containing one or more 'by object' or hardcore restrictions cannot benefit from the safe harbour of the De Minimis Notice.

For the purpose of assisting undertakings in their assessment of whether agreements can benefit from the market share safe harbour of the De Minimis Notice, this document lists the restrictions of competition that are described as 'by object' or 'hardcore' in the various Commission regulations, guidelines and notices, supplemented with some particularly illustrative examples taken from the case law of the Court of Justice of the European Union and the Commission's decisional practice.

This document is without prejudice to any developments in the case law and in the Commission's decisional practice. It does not prevent the Commission from finding restrictions of competition by object that are not identified below. DG Competition intends to regularly update the examples listed below in the light of such further developments that may expand or limit the list of restrictions 'by object'. [. . .]

'By Object' Restrictions in Agreements between Competitors

The three classical 'by object' restrictions in agreements between competitors are price fixing, output limitation and market sharing (sharing of geographical or product markets or customers).

However, restrictions of that kind may not constitute restrictions 'by object' where they are part of a wider cooperation agreement between two competitors in the context of which the parties combine complementary skills or assets. For example, in the context of production agreements, it is not considered a 'by object' restriction where the parties agree on the output directly concerned by the production agreement (for example, the capacity and production volume of a joint venture or the agreed amount of outsourced products), provided that other parameters of competition are not eliminated. Another example is a production agreement that also provides for the joint distribution of the jointly manufactured products and envisages the joint setting of the sales prices for those products, and only those products, provided that the restriction is necessary for producing jointly, meaning that the parties would not otherwise have an incentive to enter into the production agreement in the first place. In those scenarios the agreement on output or prices will not be assessed separately, but will be assessed in the light of the overall effects of the entire production agreement on the market. [Footnote 12: For example, in the context of a joint-venture created by competitors, a non-compete clause with respect to the parties' activities after the expiry of the joint-venture agreement in markets where the joint-venture was not active has been considered a restriction 'by object' infringing Article 101 of the Treaty, whereas proportionate and objectively necessary non-compete clauses preventing the parties from competing on activities falling within the scope of joint-venture may be considered as not infringing Article 101 (See Case 39736 *Siemens/Areva*).]

[. . .]

'By Object' Restrictions in Agreements between non-competitors

Restrictions by object in agreements between non-competitors can be distinguished as to whether they relate to market partitioning by territory and/or customer group or to limitations on the buyer's ability to determine its resale price. The first category can be further divided into restrictions limiting the buyer's freedom to sell and restrictions limiting the supplier's freedom to sell. Moreover, the restrictions by object differ depending on whether they are agreed between a supplier and a buyer or between a licensor and a licensee.

6.3.2.2. The 'object box' and 'hardcore' restrictions

The Commission introduced the concept of 'hardcore restriction' in the Follow-up to the Green Paper on vertical restraints, published in 1998, where it was held that 'hardcore restraints are mainly related to resale price maintenance and to restrictions on resale which are deemed not to justify block-exemption in the light of the market integration objective'.[149] The term has been imported from the Organisation on Economic Co-operation and Development (OECD) Council Recommendation Concerning Effective Action Against Hard Core Cartels in 1998, which found 'hard core cartels' as 'the most egregious violations of competition law', 'that [. . .] injure consumers in many countries by raising prices and restricting supply, thus making goods and services completely unavailable to some purchasers and unnecessarily expensive for others'.[150] The terminology indicates that these practices will almost never be justified. The choice of the terminology of 'hardcore' restrictions in the Commission's Green paper in 1998 for vertical restraints may seem excessive, in particular in the context of Article 101 TFEU, as any type of agreement may theoretically be justified under Article 101(3). The terminology 'hardcore restriction' has also been employed in the context of the *de minimis* notice (in order to deny the *de minimis* immunity for this category of agreements), or in the horizontal cooperation agreements and the vertical agreements block exemption regulations

149 Communication from the Commission on the application of the Community competition rules to vertical restraints—Follow-up to the Green Paper on vertical restraints [1998] OJ C 365/3, esp 19.

150 OECD Council Recommendation Concerning Effective Action Against Hard Core Cartels (1998), 2. According to the recommendation (ibid, 3), 'a "hard core cartel" is an anticompetitive agreement, anticompetitive concerted practice, or anticompetitive arrangement by competitors to fix prices, make rigged bids (collusive tenders), establish output restrictions or quotas, or share or divide markets by allocating customers, suppliers, territories, or lines of commerce'. However,

> the hardcore cartel category does not include agreements, concerted practices, or arrangements that (i) are reasonably related to the lawful realisation of cost-reducing or output-enhancing efficiencies, (ii) are excluded directly or indirectly from the coverage of a Member country's own laws, or (iii) are authorised in accordance with those laws. However, all exclusions and authorisations of what would otherwise be hard core cartels should be transparent and should be reviewed periodically to assess whether they are both necessary and no broader than necessary to achieve their overriding policy objectives.

(in order to deny to this type of agreements the benefit of the block exemption regulation). However, as highlighted above, it remains theoretically possible to individually assess the possible application of Article 101(3), even for hardcore restrictions to competition.

Professor Richard Whish introduced the concept of the 'object' and 'effect boxes' to refer to the classification of agreements under Article 101 TFEU.[151] The 'object box' refers to practices for which there is a specific presumption that they infringe Article 101(1) TFEU. All other practices require a deeper assessment of qualitative evidence, as well as quantitative evidence before any conclusion is made as to their compatibility with Article 101(1) TFEU. This does not mean, however, that the contents of the 'box' will always stay as they are, the courts interpreting the provisions of Article 101 TFEU, eventually taking into account economic and empirical evidence of the economic impact of the types of arrangements, in particular when assessing various new commercial practices.

6.3.2.3. Examples of restrictions of competition by object

The Commission listed in a Staff Working Document the following restrictions by object, distinguishing between those included in agreements/concerted practices/decisions of associations of undertakings between competitors and non-competitors.[152]

6.3.2.3.1. Restrictions by object in agreements between competitors

Restrictions by object in agreements between competitors

Price fixing[153]

Restrictions whereby competitors agree to fix prices of products which they sell or buy are, as a matter of principle, restrictions by object. It is not necessary that the agreement expressly or directly fixes the selling or purchasing price: it is sufficient if the parties agree on certain parameters of the price composition, such as the amount of rebates given to customers.

151 R Whish, *Competition Law* (OUP, 6th ed, 2009), 118. See also R Wish and D Bailey, *Competition Law* (OUP, 2015).

152 Staff Working Document—Guidance on restrictions of competition 'by object' for the purpose of defining which agreements may benefit from the *De Minimis* Notice, SWD(2014) 198 final.

153 The Commission cited the following cases as relevant precedents for this type of practice: Joined Cases C-238, 244, 245, 247, 250–2 & 254/99 P, *ICI v Commission*, ECLI:EU:C:2002:582 (cartel in which target prices and target quotas were fixed, and there were concerted initiatives to raise price levels and monitor the operation of the collusive arrangements); Joined Cases C-125, 133, 135 & 137/07 P, *Österreichische Volksbanken v Commission*, ECLI:EU:C:2009:576 (a cartel in which banks fixed deposit and lending rates); Case T-208/08, *Gosselin Group v Commission*, ECLI:EU:T:2011:287 (a cartel on the international removal services market relating to the direct or indirect fixing of prices, market sharing and the manipulation of the procedure for the submission of tenders); Joined Cases T-217 & 245/03, *French Beef*, ECLI:EU:T:2006:391(agreement concluded by federations representing farmers and federations representing slaughterers aimed at fixing minimum prices for the purchase of cows by slaughterers and suspending beef imports); *Architectes Belges* (Case COMP/A.38549) Commission Decision 2005/8/EC [2005] OJ L 4/10 (recommended minimum fees of a national association of architects facilitating price coordination); *E-Books* (Case COMP/AT.39847) Commission Decision C(2012) 9288 (coordination between publishers and a distributor, to jointly switch from a wholesale model, in which retail prices were determined by retailers, to agency contracts, as part of a common strategy aimed at raising retail prices for e-books or preventing the introduction of lower retail prices on a global scale); *Visa Multilateral Interchange Fees* (Case COMP/39.398) Commission Decision C(2010) 8760 final (joint setting by banks of so-called Multilateral Interchange Fees (MIFs) in the payment card market was considered price fixing).

Market sharing[154]

Any arrangement by which competitors allocate markets (geographic markets or product markets) or customers is considered a restriction by object if it takes place in the context of a pure market sharing agreement between competitors (that is to say, a cartel not linked to any wider cooperation between the parties). If the conduct of the parties to an agreement (for example, a distribution agreement between actual or potential competitors) shows that their objective was to share the market, that objective may be taken into account in deciding whether the agreement is a restriction by object. Allocation of markets can also be achieved through restrictions on where the parties may sell (actively and/or passively) or through restrictions on production

Output restrictions[155]

Competitors agreeing to restrict the volume of their supply or production capacity (either for one or both of the parties) is seen as a restriction of output, which in turn is considered a restriction by object.

Bid rigging[156]

Bid-rigging occurs when two or more companies agree that, in response to a call for bids or tenders, one or more of them will not submit a bid, withdraw a bid or submit a bid at artificially high prices arrived at by agreement. This form of collusion is generally considered to restrict competition by object. It is a form of price fixing and market allocation which may, for example, take place in the case of public procurement contracts.

Collective boycott agreements[157]

A collective boycott occurs when a group of competitors agree to exclude an actual or potential competitor. This practice generally constitutes a restriction by object.

154 Case C-41/69, *ACF Chemie farma NV v Commission*, ECLI:EU:C:1970:71 (a cartel in which undertakings agreed to retain their respective domestic markets and fix prices and quotas for the export of quinine); Joined Cases 29 & 30/83, *CRAM v Commission*, ECLI:EU:C:1984:130 (market sharing cartel with a view to protect markets against parallel imports of certain products in the market for zinc); Cases T-370/09, *GDF Suez v Commission*, ECLI:EU:T:2012:333 and T-360/09, *E.ON Ruhrgas and E.ON v Commission*, ECLI:EU:T:2012:332 (agreement between competitors not to sell gas transported over a pipeline they co-constructed in each other's home markets and market sharing agreement after the liberalization of the gas market); *Lundbeck* (Case AT.39226) Commission Decision C(2013) 3803 final (a pay for delay agreement whereby a competitor pays a significant amount to an actual (or potential) competitor to stay out of a particular market); *Telefónica and Portugal Telecom* (Case AT.39839) Commission Decision C(2013) 306 final (a non-compete clause between competitors to stay out of each other's activities in a certain geographic area); *Fentanyl* (Case AT.39685) Commission Decision 8870 final (a 'co-promotion' agreement between potential competitors which provided for significant payments on a monthly basis for as long as the competitor stayed out of the market, a form of market exclusion)

155 Case C-209/07, *Beef Industry Development Society (BIDS)*, ECLI:EU:C:2008:643 (agreement to reduce production capacity within the context of a cartel on the market for beef and veal).

156 Case T-21/99, *Dansk Rorindustri v Commission*, ECLI:EU:T:2002:74 (a cartel agreement between producers of district heating pipes allocating individual projects to designated producers and manipulating the bidding procedure to ensure that the designated producer was awarded the assigned project).

157 Case C-68/12, *Protimonopolný úrad Slovenskej republiky v Slovenská sporiteľňa a.s.*, ECLI:EU:C:2013:71 (three banks monitored a competitor's activity, conferred with each other and decided, by common agreement, to terminate in a coordinated manner the contracts they had concluded with that competitor); *Pre-insulated pipes* (Case IV/35.691) Commission Decision [1999] OJ L 24/1 (competitors used norms and standards (agreed

Information sharing—future prices and quantities[158]

Information exchanges between competitors of individualized data regarding intended future prices or quantities are considered a restriction by object. Where information exchange is part of a monitoring or implementation mechanism for an existing cartel it will be assessed as part of that cartel (irrespective of whether it covers current/past or future prices or quantities).

Restrictions on carrying out R&D or using own technology

Restrictions in agreements between competitors which aim at restricting the parties' ability to carry out R&D or to continue to use their own technology for further R&D are also hardcore restrictions and generally considered a restriction by object.

Some recent case law seems also to include among the category of restrictions of competition by object the arrangements put in place by two competitors, which infringe EU rules giving rise to penalties, if this leads to the reduction of the competitive pressure on a relevant market. This case law seems to be conceptually close to some case law regarding the application of Articles 101 and 102 TFEU to conduct that restricts competition while also frustrating the objectives of other (regulatory) rules.[159]

Case C-179/16, *F Hoffmann-La Roche Ltd and Others v Autorità Garante della Concorrenza e del Mercato*, ECLI:EU:C:2018:25

The CJEU examined a preliminary reference by the Italian Consiglio di Stato (Council of State) concerning an arrangement put in place by pharmaceutical companies Roche and Novartis with which they designed to achieve an artificial differentiation between Avastin and Lucentis, two medicinal products developed by Genentech, a company which belongs to the Roche group, which had entrusted the commercial exploitation of Lucentis to the Novartis group by way of a licensing agreement, while it continued to market Avastin. Those medicinal products were authorized by the Commission and the European Medicines Agency (EMA). Lucentis was authorized for the treatment of eye diseases, while Avastin, was authorized only for

on by the industry) to prevent or delay the introduction of new technology which would result in price reductions); *Ordre national des pharmaciens en France* (Case 39510) Commission Decision C(2010) 8952 final (the association for pharmacists sanctioned groups of laboratories in the market for clinical laboratory testing with the aim of hindering the development of a new business format)

158 Joined Cases T-25–6, 30–2, 34–9, 42–6, 48, 50–65, 68–71, 87–8, 103 & 104/95, *Cimenteries CBR and Others*, ECLI:EU:T:2000:77 (Information exchange facilitating implementation of a cartel for cement); Case T-587/08, *Fresh Del Monte Produce v Commission*, ECLI:EU:T:2013:129 and Case T-588/08, *Dole Food and Dole Germany v Commission*, ECLI:EU:T:2013:130 (pre-pricing communications in which undertakings discussed price setting factors relevant to the setting of future quotation prices for bananas); Case T-380/10, *Wabco Europe and Others v Commission*, ECLI:EU:T:2013:449 (coordination of price increases and exchange of sensitive business information in a cartel—bathroom fixtures and fittings market); Case C-8/08, *T-Mobile Netherlands BV, KPN Mobile NV, Orange Nederland NV, Vodafone Libertel NV*, ECLI:EU:C:2009:343 (information exchange between competitors on future prices to be paid to sales representatives). See also Section 7.3.1.5.

159 Case C-32/11, *Allianz Hungária Biztosító Zrt and Others v Gazdasági Versenyhivatal*, ECLI:EU:C:2013:160, paras 46–7; Case C-457/10, *AstraZeneca v Commisson*, ECLI:EU:C:2012:770, paras 105–12.

the treatment of tumorous diseases, but was also frequently used 'off-label' to treat eye diseases because its price is lower than Lucentis. Avastin became the main competitor of Lucentis because of its widespread off-label use in Italy in the field of ophthalmology. The Autorità Garante della Concorrenza e del Mercato (AGCM, the Italian competition authority) found that the Roche group and the Novartis group entered into a market-sharing agreement, which constituted a restriction of competition by object. Although Avastin and Lucentis were equivalent in all respects for the treatment of eye diseases, Roche and Novartis produced and disseminated opinions which could give rise to public concern regarding the safety of Avastin when used in ophthalmology and to downplay the value of scientific opinions to the contrary, while Roche introduced amendment of the summary of Avastin's characteristics that were pending before the EMA and sent formal communication sent to healthcare professionals so as to limit the off-label use of Avastin. According to the AGCM, the arrangement had given rise to a drop in Avastin sales and had caused a shift in demand toward Lucentis, which resulted in a substantial cost increase for the national health service in Italy. In 2014, the AGCM imposed two fines, each amounting to over €90 million, on both Roche and Novartis. The actions brought by the parties were dismissed in first instance by the Regional Administrative Court, and following the parties' appeal, the Council of State referred the matter to the CJEU.

One of the issues raised was the definition of the arrangement put in place by the parties as a restriction of competition by object. The practice in question consisted in the dissemination of information relating to adverse reactions resulting from the off-label use of Avastin, which could not fit to the broader category of market sharing.

> 77. [. . .] [I]t must be considered that, by this question, the referring court is asking, in essence, whether Article 101(1) TFEU must be interpreted as meaning that an arrangement put in place between two undertakings marketing two competing products, which concerns the dissemination, in a context of scientific uncertainty on the matter, of information relating to adverse reactions resulting from the use of one of those medicinal products for indications not covered by its MA, with a view to reducing the competitive pressure resulting from that use on another medicinal product covered by an MA covering those indications, constitutes a restriction of competition 'by object' for the purposes of that provision.

The CJEU repeated its definition of a restriction of competition by object as applying 'only to certain types of coordination between undertakings which reveal a degree of harm to competition that is sufficient for it to be held that there is no need to examine their effects'[160] *and highlighted the elements that need to be taken into account for this analysis, such as the content of the arrangement's provisions, its objectives and the economic and legal context of which it forms a part, the latter including the nature of the goods or services affected, as well as the real conditions of the functioning and the structure of the market or markets in question.*[161] *In particular, the CJEU noted that '[w]here the question arises as to whether there is a cartel agreement in the pharmaceuticals sector, account must be taken of the impact of EU rules on pharmaceutical products'*[162] *citing by analogy, its judgment in* Lélos kai Sia and Others.[163] *The CJEU continued by observing that '[t]hose rules require that a medicinal product such as Avastin must be subject to a pharmacovigilance system under the control of the EMA in coordination with the competent national agencies for pharmaceutical*

[160] Case C-179/16, *F Hoffmann-La Roche Ltd and Others v Autorità Garante della Concorrenza e del Mercato*, ECLI:EU:C:2018:25, para 78.

[161] Ibid, paras 79–80.

[162] Ibid, para 80.

[163] Joined Cases C-468–78/06, *Lélos kai Sia and Others*, EU:C:2008:504, para 58.

matters' and obligations on the holder of the MA, first with regard to the collection of information on the risks of medicinal products as regards patients' or public health and, second the supply of accurate information and any new information to the EMA, to the Commission, and to the Member States, any violation of these rules carrying the risk of penalties by the Commission.[164]

89. With regard to the facts at issue in the main proceedings, which are a matter for the referring court alone, [. . .] the AGCM found that by adopting a common strategy to counteract the competitive pressure exerted on the sale of Lucentis by the use of Avastin for the treatment of eye diseases not covered by its MA, the undertakings concerned infringed Article 101 TFEU. According to that decision, the purpose of the arrangement put in place between Roche and Novartis was to create an artificial differentiation between those two medicinal products by manipulating the perception of the risks associated with the use of Avastin for the treatment of those diseases through the production and dissemination of opinions which, based on an 'alarmist' interpretation of available data, could give rise to public concern regarding the safety of certain uses of Avastin and influence the therapeutic choices of doctors, and by downplaying any scientific knowledge to the contrary.

90. [. . .] [T]his arrangement was also intended to disclose to the EMA information that could exaggerate the perception of the risks associated with that use in order to obtain the amendment of the summary of Avastin's characteristics and to be granted leave to send healthcare professionals a letter drawing their attention to such adverse reactions. [. . .]

91. In that regard, it should be noted, in the first place, before even examining the relevance for the purpose of establishing a restriction of competition by *object* under Article 101(1) TFEU of the misleading nature of the information supplied to the EMA and the general public, that the requirements for pharmacovigilance that might call for steps to be taken [. . .] rest [. . .] solely with the holder of the MA for that medicinal product and not with another undertaking marketing a competing medicinal product covered by a separate MA. Accordingly, the fact that two undertakings marketing competing pharmaceutical products collude with each other with a view to disseminating information specifically relating to the product marketed by only one of them might constitute evidence that the dissemination of information pursues objectives unrelated to pharmacovigilance.

92. In the second place, with regard to the misleading nature of the information at issue, it must be held that the information whose notification to the EMA and the general public, according to the AGCM's decision, was the subject of a cartel agreement between Roche and Novartis, are, failing compliance with the requirements of completeness and accuracy laid down in Article 1(1) of Regulation No 658/2007, to be regarded as misleading if the purpose of that information, which is a matter for the referring court to determine, was (i) to confuse the EMA and the Commission and have the adverse reactions mentioned in the summary of product characteristics so as to enable the MA holder to launch a communication campaign aimed at healthcare professionals, patients and other persons concerned with a view to exaggerating that perception artificially, and (ii) to emphasise, in a context of scientific uncertainty, the

[164] Case C-179/16, *F Hoffmann-La Roche Ltd and Others v Autorità Garante della Concorrenza e del Mercato*, ECLI:EU:C:2018:25, paras 81–8.

public perception of the risks associated with the off-label use of Avastin, given, inter alia, the fact that the EMA and the Commission did not amend the summary of characteristics of that product in respect of its 'adverse reactions' but merely issued 'Special warnings and precautions for use'.

93. However, in such a case, given the characteristics of the medicinal products market, it is likely that the dissemination of such information will encourage doctors to refrain from prescribing that product, thus resulting in the expected reduction in demand for that type of use. The provision of misleading information to the EMA, healthcare professionals and the general public [. . .] also constitutes an infringement of the EU rules governing pharmaceutical matters giving rise to penalties.

94. In those circumstances, an arrangement that pursues the objectives described in paragraph 92 above must be regarded as being sufficiently harmful to competition to render an examination of its effects superfluous.

6.3.2.3.2. Restrictions by object in agreements between non-competitors

Restrictions by object in agreements between non-competitors[165]

Sales restrictions on buyers[166]

A restriction on a buyer as to where (the territory) or to whom (the customers) the buyer can sell the contract products, actively and/or passively, is a hardcore restriction and generally considered a restriction by object. Such a restriction may result from direct obligations on the buyer but also from indirect measures aimed at inducing the buyer not to sell to particular customers or territories, such as refusal or reduction of bonuses or discounts, termination of supply, reduction of supplied volumes, requiring a higher price for products to be exported, limiting the proportion of sales that can be exported, etc. However restrictions which restrict the buyer's place of establishment are not hardcore restrictions.

165 The following section is a slightly modified version of the Staff Working Document—Guidance on restrictions of competition 'by object' for the purpose of defining which agreements may benefit from the *De Minimis* Notice.

166 Case C-70/93, *BMW v ALD Autoleasing* (a motor vehicle manufacturer with a selective distribution system was prohibiting its authorized dealers from delivering vehicles to independent leasing companies if those companies would make them available to lessees outside the contract territory of the dealer in question); Joined Cases 32, 36 & 82/78, *BMW Belgium v Commission* (a motor vehicle manufacturer issued circulars prohibiting its dealers from exporting vehicles to authorized dealers in other countries); Case C-439/09, *Pierre Fabre Dermo-Cosmetique* [2011] ECR I-9419 (a manufacturer of cosmetics and personal care products with a selective distribution system was prohibiting its authorised distributors from selling via the Internet; Case C-551/03 P, *General Motors BV v Commission* [2006] ECR I-3173 (a distribution agreement restricting or prohibiting dealers in one Member State from exporting to consumers in another Member State, not only through direct export prohibitions but also through indirect measures such as a restrictive supply or a bonuses policy which excludes exports to final consumers from retail bonus campaigns; *Yamaha* (Case COMP/37.975) Commission Decision (16 July 2003) (an obligation on authorised dealers operating in different Member States to sell exclusively to final consumers, with the object of preventing cross supplies within the network of dealers, thus restricting dealers from competing for sales to other dealers and impeding trade within the selective distribution network; Case C-501/06 P, *GlaxoSmithKline Services v Commission* [2009] ECR I-9291 (a pharmaceutical company's dual pricing policy according to which higher prices were charged to wholesalers for products to be exported to other Member States).

Sales restrictions on licensees[167]

In the case of technology transfer agreements, it is only restrictions of the licensee's passive sales (and not of its active sales) to a particular territory or customer group that are hardcore restrictions and which are generally considered restrictions by object. However, when the licensee is a member of a selective distribution system and operates at the retail level, restrictions of both the licensee's active and passive sales to end users are hardcore restrictions, without prejudice to the possibility of prohibiting a member of the system from operating out of an unauthorised place of establishment.

Sales restrictions on the supplier

Restrictions, agreed between a supplier of components and a buyer who incorporates those components, on the supplier's ability to sell the components as spare parts to end-users or to repairers or other service providers not entrusted by the buyer with the repair or servicing of its goods, are hardcore restrictions which are generally considered to be restrictions by object.

Certain hardcore restrictions are specific to the motor vehicle sector. A first type may arise in the context of an agreement between a manufacturer of motor vehicles which uses components for the initial assembly of motor vehicles, and a supplier of such components. In this context, restrictions on the supplier's ability to place its trade mark or logo effectively and in an easily visible manner on the components supplied or on spare parts are hardcore restrictions and generally considered restrictions by object. A second type of restrictions specific to the motor vehicle sector may arise in the context of an agreement between a supplier of spare parts, repair tools or diagnostic tools or other equipment and a manufacturer of motor vehicles. In this context, restrictions of the supplier's ability to sell those goods to authorised or independent distributors or to authorised or independent repairers or end users are considered hardcore restrictions.

Resale price maintenance[168]

Restrictions of a buyer's ability to determine its minimum sale price generally constitute restrictions by object.

Restrictions imposing maximum sale prices or recommending sale prices are not restrictions by object, provided that they do not amount to fixed or minimum sale prices as a result of pressure from, or incentives offered by, any of the parties.

As regards technology transfer agreements, any restrictions on the licensor's or the licensee's ability to determine their sale prices are hardcore restrictions which are generally

167 Joined Cases C-403 & 429/08, *Football Association Premier League and Others* [2011] ECR I–9083 (licence agreement prohibiting or limiting broadcasters from supplying decoder cards to television viewers seeking to watch the broadcasts outside the Member State for which the licence was granted, thus impeding broadcasters from effecting any cross-border provision of services and enabling each broadcaster to be granted absolute territorial exclusivity in the area covered by its licence).

168 Case 243/83, *SA Binon Cie v SA Agence et Messageries de la Presse* [1985] ECR 2015 (provisions which fix the prices to be observed in contracts with third parties); *Yamaha* (Case COMP/37.975) Commission Decision (16 July 2003) (imposition of minimum resale prices on distributors selling musical instruments either directly, by a prohibition on publishing, advertising or announcing prices different from the official price lists, or indirectly, by providing dealers with a formula for calculating their resale prices and with guidelines on recommended retail prices while making clear that advertising and promotion actions with more than 15 per cent rebates would not be considered normal, which *de facto* amounted to an obligation to respect minimum prices).

considered to be restrictions by object, without prejudice to the possibility of imposing a maximum sale price or recommending a sale price.

Fixing of prices or setting a minimum sale price may be directly imposed by means of a contractual provision but may also result from indirect measures. For example, an agreement may oblige the buyer to add a specific amount or percentage on top of its purchase price to establish its sale price. Similarly, an agreement may require that the buyer complies with maximum discount levels. Such indirect means of vertical price fixing also constitute restrictions by object.

6.3.3. RESTRICTIONS OF COMPETITION BY EFFECT

In examining the existence of an anti-competitive effect, courts and competition authorities have adopted a number of tests and filters in order to minimize the costs of a full-fledged competition assessment of a commercial practice. It is rare that all the anti-competitive and pro-competitive effects of an agreement are examined and this certainly does not take place in the context of an Article 101(1) TFEU assessment. We will examine successively the different tests and filters that have been developed in the case law of the EU Courts and the decisional practice of the European Commission.

When examining the possible existence of a restriction of competition by effect the CJEU has recognized that that existence of such a restriction must be assessed by reference to the 'actual circumstances' of the specific agreement.[169] These can be identified by examining the content of the provisions of the agreement, the objectives it seeks to attain and the economic and legal context of which it forms a part. With regard to the legal and economic, it is also appropriate to take into consideration the nature of the goods or services affected, as well as the real conditions of the functioning and the structure of the market or markets in question. Furthermore, the EU courts should not only consider how the specific agreement may affect actual competition, but also potential competition,[170] as long as this is based on the evidence at hand and 'represents a real, concrete possibility', rather than being purely speculative.[171] Effects may be demonstrated through a combination of empirical evidence and theories of harm based on economic models.

The relevance of the legal and economic context mentioned by the CJEU in *La Société Technique Minière (LTM)* for the assessment under Article 101(1) TFEU, applies also in the context of examining restrictions of competition by effect, and has enabled the CJEU to either clear a restriction on conduct as not infringing Article 101(1) TFEU, or to conclude that a particular agreement infringes Article 101(1) TFEU. Among the different methods used to assess the anti-competitive effect of conduct is the counterfactual test. Other methods include the *de minimis* test, the ancillary restraints doctrine, and different forms of intuitive balancing developed by the jurisprudence of the CJEU, as well as the cumulative effects doctrine, which, in contrasts to the previous doctrines, may lead to an expansion of the scope of restriction of competition under Article 101(1) TFEU.

169 Case 1/71, *Cadillon* [1971] ECR 351, para 8.

170 See eg Case T-504/93, *Tiercé-Ladbroke v Commission* [1997] ECR II–923; Case T-461/07, *Morgan Stanley v Visa International* [2011] ECR II–1279, paras 162–7.

171 Case T-374/94, *European Night Services v Commission* [1998] ECR II–3141, paras 139–47.

6.3.3.1. The counterfactual test: An issue relating to the causal link between conduct and effects?

Before concluding that an agreement is anti-competitive, the competition authorities and courts apply the counterfactual test. The counterfactual test compares the competitive situation resulting from the agreement and the situation that would have existed in its absence. In essence, the counterfactual test is a comparative analysis of two different outcomes with regard to the situation of consumers.

The counterfactual test forms part of the economic and legal context of the agreement. The Commission further explains the operation and the role of the counterfactual test in its Guidelines on the application of Article 101(3) TFEU.

Communication from the Commission—Notice—Guidelines on the application of Article 101(3) of the Treaty [2004] OJ C 101/97 (references omitted)

[. . .]

17. The assessment of whether an agreement is restrictive of competition must be made within the actual context in which competition would occur in the absence of the agreement with its alleged restrictions. In making this assessment it is necessary to take account of the likely impact of the agreement on inter-brand competition (i.e. competition between suppliers of competing brands) and on intra-brand competition (i.e. competition between distributors of the same brand). Article 101(1) prohibits restrictions of both inter-brand competition and intra-brand competition.

18. For the purpose of assessing whether an agreement or its individual parts may restrict inter-brand competition and/or intra-brand competition it needs to be considered how and to what extent the agreement affects or is likely to affect competition on the market. The following two questions provide a useful framework for making this assessment. The first question relates to the impact of the agreement on inter-brand competition while the second question relates to the impact of the agreement on intra-brand competition. As restraints may be capable of affecting both inter-brand competition and intra-brand competition at the same time, it may be necessary to analyse a restraint in light of both questions before it can be concluded whether or not competition is restricted within the meaning of Article 101(1):

(1) Does the agreement restrict actual or potential competition that would have existed without the agreement? If so, the agreement may be caught by Article 101(1). In making this assessment it is necessary to take into account competition between the parties and competition from third parties. For instance, where two undertakings established in different Member States undertake not to sell products in each other's home markets, (potential) competition that existed prior to the agreement is restricted. Similarly, where a supplier imposes obligations on his distributors not to sell competing products and these obligations foreclose third party access to the market, actual or potential competition that would have existed in the absence of the agreement is restricted. In assessing whether the parties to an agreement are actual or potential competitors the economic and legal context must be taken into account. For instance, if due to the financial risks involved and the technical capabilities of the parties it is unlikely on the basis of objective factors that each party would be able to carry out on its own the activities covered by the agreement

the parties are deemed to be non-competitors in respect of that activity. It is for the parties to bring forward evidence to that effect.

(2) Does the agreement restrict actual or potential competition that would have existed in the absence of the contractual restraint(s)? If so, the agreement may be caught by Article 101(1). For instance, where a supplier restricts its distributors from competing with each other, (potential) competition that could have existed between the distributors absent the restraints is restricted. Such restrictions include resale price maintenance and territorial or customer sales restrictions between distributors. However, certain restraints may in certain cases not be caught by Article 101(1) when the restraint is objectively necessary for the existence of an agreement of that type or that nature. Such exclusion of the application of Article 101(1) can only be made on the basis of objective factors external to the parties themselves and not the subjective views and characteristics of the parties. The question is not whether the parties in their particular situation would not have accepted to conclude a less restrictive agreement, but whether given the nature of the agreement and the characteristics of the market a less restrictive agreement would not have been concluded by undertakings in a similar setting. For instance, territorial restraints in an agreement between a supplier and a distributor may for a certain period of time fall outside Article 101(1), if the restraints are objectively necessary in order for the distributor to penetrate a new market. Similarly, a prohibition imposed on all distributors not to sell to certain categories of end users may not be restrictive of competition if such restraint is objectively necessary for reasons of safety or health related to the dangerous nature of the product in question. Claims that in the absence of a restraint the supplier would have resorted to vertical integration are not sufficient. Decisions on whether or not to vertically integrate depend on a broad range of complex economic factors, a number of which are internal to the undertaking concerned.

19. In the application of the analytical framework set out in the previous paragraph it must be taken into account that Article 101(1) distinguishes between those agreements that have a restriction of competition as their object and those agreements that have a restriction of competition as their effect. An agreement or contractual restraint is only prohibited by Article 101(1) if its object or effect is to restrict inter-brand competition and/or intra-brand competition.

The Commission's guidelines did not make it clear whether the counterfactual test applied to the assessment of both restrictions by object and effect.[172]

The EU courts have considered the application of the counterfactual test in examining the application of Article 101(1). In *GSK*,[173] the importance of the parameter of price in this market (the quality of the products imported by the parallel traders being by definition the same) led the General Court to emphasize the role of intra-brand competition on the markets of destination of the parallel trade,[174] and found that the Commission was right to infer that the specific agreement impeded that competition and blocked 'in substance the pressure which in its absence would have existed on the unit price of the medicines in question, to the

[172] Communication from the Commission—Notice—Guidelines on the application of Article 101(3) of the Treaty [2004] OJ C 101/97, para 19.

[173] Case T-168/01, *GlaxoSmithKline Services Unlimited v Commission* [2006] ECR II–2969.

[174] Ibid, para 182.

detriment of the final consumer'.[175] The Court did not proceed to a complex and sophisticated measurement and balancing of the advantages and disadvantages of the effects of this practice on final consumers, as it was clear enough that those of the country of destination of parallel imports would pay a higher price than what they would have paid in the absence of the agreement. On appeal, the CJEU did not examine this aspect of the judgment, probably because it rejected the analysis by the GC of the dual pricing arrangements as a restriction by effect, re-characterizing it as a restriction of competition by object.

The judgment of the General Court in *O2* provides a further illustration of the importance of the counterfactual test, again applied in the context of the assessment of a restriction by object.

Case T-328/03, *O2 (Germany) GmbH & Co OHG v Commission*
[2006] ECR-II 1231

T-Mobile, owned indirectly by Deutsche Telecom, the telecoms incumbent in Germany, provided digital mobile telecommunications network using GSM standards. T-Mobile and three others, including O2 had been had been awarded licences for network rollout of the next technical generation, G3. The regulatory framework for Germany and the licences required T-Mobile and O2 to cover half the population by the end of 2005. T-Mobile notified the Commission of a framework agreement for infrastructure sharing which would also permit each to roam on the other's network in Germany. The German regulator found that the agreement was in line with the national regulatory framework.

The Commission decided it had no grounds for action in relation to the site sharing and applied Article 101(3) TFEU to the provision for reciprocal roaming for specified periods. It took the view that T-Mobile had a 100 per cent share in the market for wholesale access to national roaming for the second generation of mobile telecommunications ('2G') in Germany and that, for 3G national roaming, the main actual or potential competitors in wholesale access and services markets were the two other licensees that planned to roll out 3G networks and services in Germany, namely D2 Vodafone and E-Plus. With regard to the markets for 3G retail services, the Commission found that the main competitors were D2 Vodafone and E-Plus and potential service providers such as Mobilcom and Debitel, on the basis of the available data relating to the situation for 2G retail services in respect of which the market shares were estimated in 2002 at 41.7 per cent for T-Mobile, 38.3 per cent for D2 Vodafone, 12.2 per cent for E-Plus, and 7.8 per cent for O2. Although the agreement was predominately a horizontal cooperation agreement between two competitors it also involved certain vertical aspects, the Commission finding that it did not have the object of restricting competition but it could have such an effect given that the parties to the agreement were competitors in the relevant markets. The Commission indeed noted that national roaming between network operators who are licensed to roll out and operate their own digital mobile networks by definition restricted competition between those operators on its key parameters.

O2 appealed against the decision in particular because the exemption provided by the Commission, under Article 101(3), was for limited periods. The main argument of O2 was that, while the agreement did not have as its object a restriction of competition, the Commission did not analyse the actual effects of the agreement on competition; in particular, it did not examine what the conditions of competition would have been in the absence of the agreement. Indeed,

175 Ibid, para 185.

for O2, the Commission's reasoning was based on an erroneous premise that national roaming was of itself restrictive of competition since the agreement enabled O2 to purchase wholesale services from T-Mobile, rather than providing those services itself and did not take into account the positive effects on competition of the agreement in question, in terms of population coverage, quality of services provided, transmission rates and prices. An important argument put forward was that, in the absence of the agreement, O2's competitive position would have been weakened and that it would probably have been unable to ensure, within the time frames provided for, the population coverage required for 3G services, something which the Commission seemed also to acknowledge in its decision. The agreement was also necessary and indispensable to enable O2 to be a competitive operator capable of offering coverage and quality services on the 3G mobile telecommunications market, to supplement its population coverage capacity, and therefore ultimately to benefit its market penetration rate and consequently competition.

The Commission opposed to this argument the fact that accepting O2's reasoning regarding the examination of the competition situation in the absence of the agreement would amount to applying a rule of reason to the provisions of Article 101(1) TFEU, in contradiction to the case-law, the agreement in question being concluded between two competitors, and therefore 'such as to influence their conduct with respect to key parameters of competition'.[176] *It also raised the issue of the dependence of O2's network on that of T-Mobile, which may 'completely undermines competition on national mobile communications markets'.*[177] *The GC did not accept the Commission's arguments.*

Findings of the Court

[. . .]

73. In order to take account of the two parts which this plea actually contains, it is therefore necessary to examine, first, whether the Commission did in fact consider what the competition situation would have been in the absence of the agreement and, second, whether the conclusions which it drew from its examination of the impact of the agreement on competition are sufficiently substantiated.

Concerning the examination of the competition situation in the absence of the agreement

74. The Decision cannot be criticised for not having carried out, in order to analyse the effects of the agreement, any comparison between the competitive structure introduced by the agreement and that which would prevail in the absence thereof. By contrast, as regards the terms of the comparison performed, it must be observed that the entire examination of the effects of the agreement is based on the idea that, whether there had or had not been an agreement, both the O2 and T-Mobile operators would have been present and competing on the relevant market. The hypothesis that, in the absence of the agreement, O2 might have been entirely or partially absent from the 3G mobile telephony market in Germany was at no time envisaged.

75. It follows implicitly but necessarily from the Decision that the Commission considered, first, that O2 would in any event be present on the market, which is apparent, for example, [. . .] from the projections concerning the 3G site infrastructure market

[176] Case T-328/03, *O2 (Germany) GmbH & Co OHG v Commission* [2006] ECR-II 1231, para 61.
[177] Ibid, para 62.

on the basis of the data relating to the 2G site infrastructure market and, second, that there would be no restriction of competition whereas the disputed agreement specifically brings about such restriction by reason of the national roaming for which it provides [. . .].

76. The Commission confirmed at the hearing that that was indeed its approach in the present case. [. . .]

77. Working on the assumption that O2 was present on the mobile communications market, the Commission did not therefore deem it necessary to consider in more detail whether, in the absence of the agreement, O2 would have been present on the 3G market. It must be held that that assumption is not supported in the Decision by any analysis or justification showing that it is correct, a finding that, moreover, the defendant could only confirm at the hearing. Given that there was no such objective examination of the competition situation in the absence of the agreement, the Commission could not have properly assessed the extent to which the agreement was necessary for O2 to penetrate the 3G mobile communications market. The Commission therefore failed to fulfil its obligation to carry out an objective analysis of the impact of the agreement on the competitive situation.

78. That lacuna cannot be deemed to be without consequences. It is apparent from the considerations set out in the Decision in the analysis of the agreement in the light of the conditions laid down in Article [101(3) TFEU] as regards whether it was possible to grant an exemption that, even in the Commission's view, it was unlikely that O2 would have been able, individually, without the agreement, to ensure from the outset better coverage, quality and transmission rates for 3G services, to roll out a network and launch 3G services rapidly, to penetrate the relevant wholesale and retail markets and therefore be an effective competitor [. . .]. It was because of those factors that the Commission considered that the agreement was eligible for exemption.

79. Such considerations, which imply some uncertainty concerning the competitive situation and, in particular, as regards O2's position in the absence of the agreement, show that the presence of O2 on the 3G communications market could not be taken for granted, as the Commission had assumed, and that an examination in this respect was necessary not only for the purposes of granting an exemption but, prior to that, for the purposes of the economic analysis of the effects of the agreement on the competitive situation determining the applicability of Article [101 TFEU]. [. . .]

Concerning the impact of the agreement on competition

[. . .]

85. It is apparent from those assessments that, for the Commission, the very nature of a roaming agreement, such as that concluded by the parties, brings about a restriction of competition by reason of the dependence on the visited operator which national roaming creates for the roaming operator. The restriction manifests itself in three ways: first, from the point of view of network coverage, because roaming constitutes an obstacle to the network roll-out of the operator which uses the network of its partner, second, as regards network and transmission quality, because the using operator depends on the technical and commercial choices of the visited operator and, third, as regards prices, because the wholesale rates of the roaming operator are a function of the wholesale price paid to the visited operator, which is the case in this instance.

86. Such general considerations, which could be formulated in respect of any national roaming agreement, are not based on any specific evidence showing that they are correct in the case of the agreement concluded between O2 and T-Mobile. [. . .]

The Court also objected to the lack of analysis of the effect of the agreement in other respects and concluded:

> 116. [. . .] that the Decision, in so far as it concerns the application of Article 101(1) TFEU [. . .], suffers from insufficient analysis, first, in that it contains no objective discussion of what the competition situation would have been in the absence of the agreement, which distorts the assessment of the actual and potential effects of the agreement on competition and, second, in that it does not demonstrate, in concrete terms, in the context of the relevant emerging market, that the provisions of the agreement on roaming have restrictive effects on competition, but is confined, in this respect, to a *petitio principii* and to broad and general statements.

NOTES AND QUESTIONS ON O2

1. This is one of only few judgments of the General Court on cooperative joint ventures.
2. Were the roaming provisions ancillary restraints reasonably necessary to enable O2 to enter the market? Consider *Métropole III*.[178] In what sense is the counterfactual test applied in this case different from the doctrine of ancillary restraints?[179] Is its purpose to explore the causal link between the specific conduct and the alleged anti-competitive effect?
3. Compare this judgment to the one in *BIDS*, which concerned a restriction of competition by object.[180] In *BIDS*, the CJEU concluded that the agreement to rationalize capacity was not in line with the proper function of normal competition. It did so by pointing out that in the absence of the agreement thereof, a reduction in capacity could only have come by as a result of exits or mergers. Did the CJEU apply something like a counterfactual test? Was this test exploring the existence of a causal link between the conduct and a restrictive effect on competition? Was there a need to do so, assuming that a restriction of competition by object has been considered as a presumption of anti-competitive effect? Should one arrive to a different conclusion, if the specific restriction by object did not result from an evidential shortcut (a presumption of anti-competitive effects) but from an analytical shortcut (that a type of restriction is by nature incompatible to Article 101(1) TFEU), such as a restriction on active and passive sales (absolute territorial protection). In the present case, the CJEU criticizes the Commission for failing to assess whether O2 would have been able to compete in the 3G market as effectively without national roaming. That is to say, the CJEU did not consider that the ability of O2 to roll out its own network in the absence of the agreement thereof could not be presumed. What do you think underpins this difference in how the CJEU assessed the application of the counterfactual test in the two cases?
4. What does this counterfactual analysis entail with respect to the assessment of Article 101(3) TFEU? Which of the four cumulative criteria is mainly affected? Is the fact that the same counterfactual analysis is of relevance to the assessment under both Articles 101(1) and 101(3) TFEU problematic, and why?

[178] Case T-112/99, *Métropole Télévision (M6) and Others v Commission* [2002] ECR II-2459 [hereinafter *Metropole III*]. See Section 6.3.4.1.2.

[179] See Section 6.3.4.1.

[180] Case C-209/07, *Beef Industry Development Society Ltd (BIDS)* [2008] ECR I-8637.

In *Lundbeck*,[181] the General Court confirmed (for some), or narrowed down (for others) the application of the counterfactual test to only restrictions of competition by effect.[182]

Case T-472/13, *H Lundbeck A/S and Lundbeck Ltd v Commission*, ECLI:EU:T:2016:449

472. [. . .] [I]nasmuch as the applicants submit that the Commission should have examined the counter factual scenario in the present case, it must be recalled that, as regards restrictions on competition by object, the Commission was only required to demonstrate that the agreements at issue revealed a sufficient degree of harm to competition, in view of the content of their provisions, the objectives that they are intended to achieve and the economic and legal context of which they formed part, without being required, however, to examine their effects [. . .].

473. The examination of a hypothetical counterfactual scenario—besides being impracticable since it requires the Commission to reconstruct the events that would have occurred in the absence of the agreements at issue, whereas the very purpose of those agreements was to delay the market entry of the generic undertakings [. . .]—is more an examination of the effects of agreements at issue on the market than an objective examination of whether they are sufficiently harmful to competition. Such an examination of effects is not required in the context of an analysis based on the existence of a restriction of competition by object [. . .].

474. Accordingly, even if some generic undertakings would not have entered the market during the term of the agreements at issue, as a result of infringement actions brought by Lundbeck, or because it was impossible to obtain an MA within a sufficiently short period, what matters is that those undertakings had real concrete possibilities of entering the market at the time the agreements at issue were concluded with Lundbeck, with the result that they exerted competitive pressure on the latter. That competitive pressure was eliminated for the term of the agreements at issue, which constitutes, by itself, a restriction of competition by object, for the purpose of Article 101(1) TFEU.

NOTES AND QUESTIONS ON LUNDBECK AND THE COUNTERFACTUAL TEST

1. Has the GC taken a different perspective on the counterfactual test in *Lundbeck* than in *O2*, or did it confirm that the counterfactual test applies only to restrictions of competition by effect?
2. Are you convinced by the Court's approach to apply the counterfactual test only for restrictions of competition by effect?
3. Note that in the previous paragraphs of its judgment (paragraphs 98–163) the GC examined if the generics could be considered as potential competitors, in particular assessing if their entry into a market was an economically viable strategy and if they

181 Cf Section 6.3.2.1.8.

182 The GC seems also to have adopted a similar position in Case T-691/14, *Servier SAS and Others v European Commission*, ECLI:EU:T:2018:922, paras 300, 1240-1247 (mentioning the position of the Commission without disapproving it and exploring the counterfactual test only in the context of the analysis of anti-competitive effects).

had *the ability* to enter that market. How would this analysis of the existence of a potential competition effect be different from the application of the counterfactual test in this case, had the GC not excluded the application of the counterfactual test because it qualified the conduct in question as a restriction of competition by object? Had the GC performed the counterfactual test when assessing the existence of a restriction of competition, it would have also analysed the *incentive* of the specific competitor to enter the market, in the absence of the agreement in question, and not just its *ability* to do so, as it does when assessing the existence of potential competition.[183] We make this hypothetical, in order to distinguish the type of assessment performed when assessing the existence of potential competition from the counterfactual test when assessing the existence of a restriction of competition (restriction counterfactual). These are two separate inquiries and should not be confused.

4. Is the GC's conception of the counterfactual test more claimant-friendly or more defendant-friendly?

6.3.3.2. Agreements of minor importance

6.3.3.2.1. The jurisprudence of the CJEU: Volk Vervaecke *and* Expedia Inc

The CJEU early confirmed an implied condition that to infringe Article 101 TFEU, the restriction of competition and the possible effect on trade between Member States should be appreciable. In *Völk v Vervaecke*, Völk made less than 1 per cent of the washing machines produced in Germany and the CJEU ruled that even absolute territorial protection granted to its exclusive distributor for Belgium and Luxembourg would not infringe Article 101(1) TFEU if it did not appreciably restrict competition and appreciably affect inter-State trade. The CJEU held that:

> An agreement falls outside the prohibition in Article [101] when it has only an insignificant effect on the markets, taking into account the weak position which the persons concerned have on the market of the product in question. Thus, an exclusive dealing agreement, even with absolute territorial protection, may, having regard to the weak position of the persons concerned on the market in the products in question in the area covered by the absolute protection, escape the prohibition laid down in Article 101(1).[184]

Taking into account the fact that the restriction in *Völk v Vervaecke* concerned an object restriction to competition (exclusive dealing with absolute territorial protection), one could have assumed that the requirement of 'appreciability' would apply to both object and effect restrictions. This was not, however, always clear, some NCAs and national courts examining the requirement of 'appreciability' in object cases, while others excluded such consideration in object cases.[185]

The Commission tried to reduce the uncertainty surrounding this *de minimis* rule by issuing a notice on Minor Agreements in 1970. The first *de minimis* Notices included a ceiling of turnover and applied to both the concepts of trade between Member States and of restriction of

183 See Section 6.3.1.2.6. 184 Case 5/69, *Völk v Vervaecke* [1969] ECR 295.

185 For a discussion, see FW von Papp, 'De Minimis: An Overview of EU and National Case Law', *Bulletin Concurrences* (Special Issue: De minimis) (6 May 2015).

competition. The most recent ones used a market share threshold, thus excluding the application of Article 101(1) TFEU to *de minimis* agreements concluded by large firms with small shares of particular markets, and focused only on the restriction of competition element, as the Commission adopted in 2004 a separate communication regarding the concept of the 'effect on trade'.[186] The notice has been reissued with alterations several times. Many NCAs adopted their own *de minimis* Notices.

A contentious issue has been the consideration of 'appreciability' when assessing restrictions of competition by object. The European Commission's previous 2001 Notice[187] excluded certain 'hardcore' restrictions, such as cartels (but not all restrictions by object), from the safe harbour of agreements of minor importance provided by the Notice (in case the market share of the undertakings concerned were below the thresholds denoting appreciability), but the *Völk v Vervaecke* precedent indicated that when the market share is quite low (less than 1 per cent), it would have been possible to conclude that a hardcore restriction would not be 'appreciable' and thus be subject to the prohibition principle of Article 101(1) TFEU. The 2001 De Minimis Notice was revised in 2014 in light of the CJEU *Expedia* case,[188] which altered the approach followed by the CJEU in *Völk v Vervaecke*.[189]

Case C-226/11, *Expedia Inc v Autorité de la concurrence and Others*, ECLI:EU:C:2012:795

The case was a preliminary reference from the French Cour de Cassation and arose out of a decision of the French Competition Authority's which imposed fines on Expedia and SNCF (France's State-owned railway company) for a partnership they had together created (a joint subsidiary called Agence VSC) in order to expand the sale of train tickets and travel over the Internet. In February 2009, the French Competition Authority found that the partnership constituted an agreement contrary to Article 101 TFEU and to Article L 420-1 of the French Commercial Code. The Competition Authority found that Expedia and SNCF were competitors in the market for on-line travel agency services, that their market shares were more than 10% and that, consequently, the de minimis *rule, as set out in paragraph 7 of the* de minimis *notice and Article L 464-2-1 of the Commercial Code, were not applicable. Consequently, the Authority imposed financial penalties on Expedia and SNCF. Expedia argued, on appeal before the Paris Cour d'Appel, that the Authority had overestimated the market share of Agence VSC. Without ruling on this point, the Cour d'Appel held that it was possible for the Competition Authority to bring proceedings against practices implemented by undertakings whose market share is below the thresholds specified by the relevant article in the French Commercial Code (setting a threshold equivalent to the Commission's* de minimis *notice) and by the Commission's* de minimis *notice. Subsequently, the Cour de Cassation made a preliminary ruling request to the Court of Justice and asked whether Article 101(1) TFEU and Article 3(2) of Regulation (EC) No 1/2003 must be interpreted as precluding the bringing of proceedings and the imposition of penalties by a national competition authority if the relevant*

[186] See Chapter 1.

[187] Commission Notice on agreements of minor importance which do not appreciably restrict competition under Article 81(1) of the Treaty establishing the European Community (de minimis) [2001] OJ C 368/13, which replaced the 1997 De Minimis Notice.

[188] Case C-226/11, *Expedia Inc v Autorité de la concurrence and Others*, ECLI:EU:C:2012:795.

[189] Case 5/69, *Völk v Vervaecke* [1969] ECR 295.

market share falls below the threshold. Essentially, the Court asked whether the thresholds specified by the Commission in the de minimis *notice were binding for the Member State authorities as well.*

14. By its question, the referring court seeks to know, essentially, whether Article 101(1) TFEU and Article 3(2) of Regulation No 1/2003 must be interpreted as precluding a national competition authority from applying Article 101(1) TFEU to an agreement between undertakings that may affect trade between Member States, but that does not reach the thresholds specified by the Commission in its *de minimis* notice.

15. It should be noted that Article 101(1) TFEU prohibits as incompatible with the internal market all agreements between undertakings, decisions by associations of undertakings and concerted practices which may affect trade between Member States and which have as their object or effect the prevention, restriction or distortion of competition within the internal market.

16. It is settled case-law that an agreement of undertakings falls outside the prohibition in that provision, however, if it has only an insignificant effect on the market (Case 5/69 *Völk* v *Vervaecke* [1969] ECR 295, paragraph 7 [. . .]).

17. Accordingly, if it is to fall within the scope of the prohibition under Article 101(1) TFEU, an agreement of undertakings must have the object or effect of perceptibly restricting competition within the common market and be capable of affecting trade between Member States [. . .].

The CJEU also notes that, in view of Article 3(2) of Regulation 1/2003, the NCAs can apply the provisions of national law prohibiting cartels to an agreement of undertakings which is capable of affecting trade between Member States within the meaning of Article 101 TFEU only where that agreement perceptibly restricts competition within the common market.

22. In its examination, the Court found, inter alia, that an exclusive dealing agreement, even with absolute territorial protection, has only an insignificant effect on the market in question, taking into account the weak position which the persons concerned have in that market [. . .]. In other cases, however, it did not base its decision on the position of the persons concerned in the market in question. [. . .]

23. It is apparent from paragraphs 1 and 2 of the *de minimis* notice that the Commission intends to quantify therein, with the help of market share thresholds, what is not an appreciable restriction of competition within the meaning of Article 101 TFEU and the case-law [. . .].

The CJEU notes that the 2004 de minimis *Notice indicates it has no binding nature, for both the competition authorities and the courts of the Member States and that it states that market share thresholds are used to quantify what is not an appreciable restriction of competition within the meaning of Article 101 TFEU, but that the negative definition of the appreciability of such restriction does not imply that agreements of undertakings which exceed those thresholds appreciably restrict competition.*

27. It also follows from the objectives pursued by the *de minimis* notice [. . .] that it is not intended to be binding on the competition authorities and the courts of the Member States.

28. It is apparent [. . .] first, that the purpose of that notice is to make transparent the manner in which the Commission, acting as the competition authority of the European Union, will itself apply Article 101 TFEU. Consequently, by the *de minimis* notice, the

Commission imposes a limit on the exercise of its discretion and must not depart from the content of that notice without being in breach of the general principles of law, in particular the principles of equal treatment and the protection of legitimate expectations [. . .]. Furthermore, it intends to give guidance to the courts and authorities of the Member States in their application of that article.

29. Consequently, and as the Court has already had occasion to point out, a Commission notice, such as the *de minimis* notice, is not binding in relation to the Member States [. . .].

30. Accordingly, that notice was published in 2001 in the 'C' series of the *Official Journal of the European Union*, which, by contrast with the 'L' series of the Official Journal, is not intended for the publication of legally binding measures, but only of information, recommendations and opinions concerning the European Union [. . .].

31. Consequently, in order to determine whether or not a restriction of competition is appreciable, the competition authority of a Member State may take into account the thresholds established in [. . .] the *de minimis* notice but is not required to do so. Such thresholds are no more than factors among others that may enable that authority to determine whether or not a restriction is appreciable by reference to the actual circumstances of the agreement.

32. Contrary to what Expedia argued during the hearing, the proceedings brought and penalties imposed by the competition authority of a Member State, on undertakings that enter into an agreement that has not reached the thresholds defined in the *de minimis* notice, cannot infringe, as such, the principles of legitimate expectations and legal certainty, having regard to the wording of paragraph 4 of that notice.

33. Furthermore, as the Advocate General [Kokott] pointed out in [. . .] her Opinion, the principle of the lawfulness of penalties does not require the *de minimis* notice to be regarded as a legal measure binding on the national authorities. Cartels are already prohibited by the primary law of the European Union, that is, by Article 101(1) TFEU.

34. In so far as Expedia, the French Government and the Commission have, in their written observations or during the hearing, questioned the finding made by the national court that it is not disputed that the agreement at issue in the main proceedings had an anti-competitive object, it should be remembered that, in proceedings under Article 267 TFEU, which is based on a clear separation of functions between the national courts and the Court of Justice, any assessment of the facts in the main proceedings is a matter for the national court [. . .].

35. Moreover, it should be noted that, according to settled case-law, for the purpose of applying Article 101(1) TFEU, there is no need to take account of the concrete effects of an agreement once it appears that it has as its object the prevention, restriction or distortion of competition [. . .].

36. In that regard, the Court has emphasised that the distinction between 'infringements by object' and 'infringements by effect' arises from the fact that certain forms of collusion between undertakings can be regarded, by their very nature, as being injurious to the proper functioning of normal competition [. . .].

37. It must therefore be held that an agreement that may affect trade between Member States and that has an anti-competitive object constitutes, by its nature and independently of any concrete effect that it may have, an appreciable restriction on competition.

38. In light of the above, the answer to the question referred is that Article 101(1) TFEU and Article 3(2) of Regulation No 1/2003 must be interpreted as not precluding a

national competition authority from applying Article 101(1) TFEU to an agreement between undertakings that may affect trade between Member States, but that does not reach the thresholds specified by the Commission in its *de minimis* notice, provided that that agreement constitutes an appreciable restriction of competition within the meaning of that provision.

NOTES AND QUESTIONS ON EXPEDIA

1. Do you agree with the Court in paragraph 37 that 'an agreement that may affect trade between Member States and that has an anti-competitive object constitutes, by its nature and independently of any concrete effect that it may have, an appreciable restriction on competition'? Should the Court have taken into account the economic context of the agreement? For example, would the effect of a cartel agreement between two undertakings holding together 1 per cent of the relevant market be substantial enough to justify the cost of competition law enforcement? What other considerations the Court might have taken into account to arrive to this result?
2. Note that the CJEU exempts from the consideration of the 'appreciable' nature of a restriction of competition all restrictions by object, and not just some hardcore restraints, as it was the case in the Commission's 2001 *de minimis* Notice.
3. Compare paragraph 37 of the CJEU with paragraphs 16 and 17, where the CJEU seems to acknowledge that *Völk v Vervaecke* is still a valid precedent and states that for a restriction of competition to fall within the prohibition of Article 101(1) TFEU it 'must have the *object* or effect of *perceptibly restricting competition*', thus indicating that the requirement of 'appreciability' still applies to object restrictions to competition. Note also that in *Pedro IV*, the CJEU noted that in order for a vertical price fixing scheme to be caught by Article 101(1) TFEU, *all* the conditions laid down in that provision must be met, including the requirement that 'the *object* or effect of the agreement is *perceptibly* to restrict competition within the common market'.[190] Is the CJEU in *Expedia* merely establishing a presumption of 'appreciability' for object restrictions of competition? Or, should the CJEU's judgment in *Expedia* be understood as mainly excluding object restrictions of competition from the benefit of the *de minimis* safe harbour, after some analysis of their economic and legal context, as it is also the case for restrictions of competition by object?
4. Does the CJEU establish a definitive distinction between the requirement that the restriction of competition is 'appreciable' and the requirement that that the restrictive agreement has to be capable of 'appreciably' affecting trade between Member States?
5. If you were the head of a competition authority, what would be the implications of this judgment for your enforcement strategy? Are you obliged to bring an action and prioritize restrictions of competition that are judged to be 'appreciable' in the sense of the Commission's *de minimis* Notice, following the interpretation of 'appreciability' provided by the CJEU in *Expedia*?

190 Case C-260/07, *Pedro IV Servicios SL v Total España SA* [2009] ECR I–2437, para 82 (emphases added).

6.3.3.2.2. The Commission's de minimis *Notice*

Communication from the Commission—Notice on agreements of minor importance which do not appreciably restrict competition under Article 101(1) of the Treaty on the Functioning of the European Union (De Minimis Notice) [2014] OJ C 291/01

1. Article 101(1) of the Treaty on the Functioning of the European Union prohibits agreements between undertakings which may affect trade between Member States and which have as their object or effect the prevention, restriction or distortion of competition within the internal market. The Court of Justice of the European Union has clarified that that provision is not applicable where the impact of the agreement on trade between Member States or on competition is not appreciable.

2. The Court of Justice has also clarified that an agreement which may affect trade between Member States and which has as its object the prevention, restriction or distortion of competition within the internal market constitutes, by its nature and independently of any concrete effects that it may have, an appreciable restriction of competition. This Notice therefore does not cover agreements which have as their object the prevention, restriction or distortion of competition within the internal market.

3. In this Notice the Commission indicates, with the help of market share thresholds, the circumstances in which it considers that agreements which may have as their effect the prevention, restriction or distortion of competition within the internal market do not constitute an appreciable restriction of competition under Article 101 of the Treaty. This negative definition of appreciability does not imply that agreements between undertakings which exceed the thresholds set out in this Notice constitute an appreciable restriction of competition. Such agreements may still have only a negligible effect on competition and may therefore not be prohibited by Article 101(1) of the Treaty.

4. Agreements may also fall outside Article 101(1) of the Treaty because they are not capable of appreciably affecting trade between Member States. This Notice does not indicate what constitutes an appreciable effect on trade between Member States. Guidance to that effect is to be found in the Commission's Notice on effect on trade, in which the Commission quantifies, with the help of the combination of a 5 % market share threshold and a EUR 40 million turnover threshold, which agreements are in principle not capable of appreciably affecting trade between Member States. Such agreements normally fall outside Article 101(1) of the Treaty even if they have as their object the prevention, restriction or distortion of competition.

[...]

8. The Commission holds the view that agreements between undertakings which may affect trade between Member States and which may have as their effect the prevention, restriction or distortion of competition within the internal market, do not appreciably restrict competition within the meaning of Article 101(1) of the Treaty:

(a) if the aggregate market share held by the parties to the agreement does not exceed 10 % on any of the relevant markets affected by the agreement, where the agreement is made between undertakings which are actual or potential competitors on any of those markets (agreements between competitors); or

(b) if the market share held by each of the parties to the agreement does not exceed 15 % on any of the relevant markets affected by the agreement, where the agreement is made between undertakings which are not actual or potential competitors on any of those markets (agreements between non-competitors).

9. In cases where it is difficult to classify the agreement as either an agreement between competitors or an agreement between non-competitors the 10 % threshold is applicable.

10. Where, in a relevant market, competition is restricted by the cumulative effect of agreements for the sale of goods or services entered into by different suppliers or distributors (cumulative foreclosure effect of parallel networks of agreements having similar effects on the market), the market share thresholds set out in point 8 and 9 are reduced to 5 %, both for agreements between competitors and for agreements between non-competitors. Individual suppliers or distributors with a market share not exceeding 5 %, are in general not considered to contribute significantly to a cumulative foreclosure effect. A cumulative foreclosure effect is unlikely to exist if less than 30 % of the relevant market is covered by parallel (networks of) agreements having similar effects.

11. The Commission also holds the view that agreements do not appreciably restrict competition if the market shares of the parties to the agreement do not exceed the thresholds of respectively 10 %, 15 % and 5 % set out in points 8, 9 and 10 during two successive calendar years by more than 2 percentage points 12. In order to calculate the market share, it is necessary to determine the relevant market. This consists of the relevant product market and the relevant geographic market. When defining the relevant market, reference should be had to the Notice on the definition of the relevant market. The market shares are to be calculated on the basis of sales value data or, where appropriate, purchase value data. If value data are not available, estimates based on other reliable market information, including volume data, may be used.

13. In view of the clarification of the Court of Justice referred to in point 2, this Notice does not cover agreements which have as their object the prevention, restriction or distortion of competition within the internal market. The Commission will thus not apply the safe harbour created by the market share thresholds set out in points 8, 9, 10 and 11 to such agreements. For instance, as regards agreements between competitors, the Commission will not apply the principles set out in this Notice to, in particular, agreements containing restrictions which, directly or indirectly, have as their object:

a) the fixing of prices when selling products to third parties;

b) the limitation of output or sales; or

c) the allocation of markets or customers.

Likewise, the Commission will not apply the safe harbour created by those market share thresholds to agreements containing any of the restrictions that are listed as hardcore restrictions in any current or future Commission block exemption regulation, which are considered by the Commission to generally constitute restrictions by object.

14. The safe harbour created by the market share thresholds set out in points 8, 9, 10 and 11 is particularly relevant for categories of agreements not covered by any Commission block exemption regulation. The safe harbour is also relevant for agreements covered by a Commission block exemption regulation to the extent that those

agreements contain a so-called excluded restriction, that is a restriction not listed as a hardcore restriction but nonetheless not covered by the Commission block exemption regulation.

NOTES AND QUESTIONS ON THE DE MINIMIS *NOTICE*

1. (Paras 1–4) Note that this notice does not deal extensively with the effect on trade between Member States. The Commission has issued separate guidelines on this concept: Guidelines on the effect of trade concept contained in Articles [101] and [102] of the Treaty [2004] OJ C 101/81.
2. (Paras 8–11) The ceilings have been raised from 5 per cent in the earlier notices. To decide whether the parties are actual or potential competitors, see Communication from the Commission, Guidelines on the Application of Article 101(3) of the Treaty [2004] OJ C 101/97, para 18.
3. (Para 10) See *Delimitis* examined below.
4. (Para 12) For the Notice on relevant market definition, see Chapter 3.
5. (Para 13) Note that this paragraph links object restrictions with the 'hardcore' restrictions listed in block exemption regulations.
6. (Paras 15–16). The Notice explains that for determining the applicability of the *de minimis* safe harbour one should also look to the market shares of the 'connected undertakings' to those that have concluded the agreement. For the purpose of the Notice 'connected undertakings' are:

   (a) undertakings in which a party to the agreement, directly or indirectly: (i) has the power to exercise more than half the voting rights, or (ii) has the power to appoint more than half the members of the supervisory board, board of management or bodies legally representing the undertaking, or (iii) has the right to manage the undertaking's affairs; (b) undertakings which directly or indirectly have, over a party to the agreement, the rights or powers listed in (a); (c) undertakings in which an undertaking referred to in (b) has, directly or indirectly, the rights or powers listed in (a); (d) undertakings in which a party to the agreement together with one or more of the undertakings referred to in (a), (b) or (c), or in which two or more of the latter undertakings, jointly have the rights or powers listed in (a); (e) undertakings in which the rights or the powers listed in (a) are jointly held by (i) parties to the agreement or their respective connected undertakings referred to in (a) to (d), or (ii) one or more of the parties to the agreement or one or more of their connected undertakings referred to in (a) to (d) and one or more third parties.
7. According to Whish and Bailey,[191] the *de minimis* doctrine does not exhaust all examples of non-appreciability of the restrictions of competition. They note a number of cases 'in which it was concluded that a restriction of competition was not appreciable, not because the parties to an agreement lacked market power (as indicated by the high market share), but because the restriction itself was insignificant in a qualitative sense'.[192] They cite, *inter alia, Pavel Pavlov v Stichting Pensioenfonds Medische*

[191] R Whish and D Bailey, *Competition Law* (OUP, 8th ed, 2015), 135–6. [192] Ibid.

Specialisten,[193] where the CJEU concluded that a decision by the members of a liberal profession to set up a pension fund responsible for the management of a supplementary pension scheme, did not restrict competition by object or by effect, even if it standardized in part the costs and supplementary pension benefits of medical specialists, and thus limited competition as far as concerns one cost factor of specialist medical services. The CJEU remarked that the restrictive effects of such a decision on the specialist medical services market were insignificant in comparison with other factors, such as medical fees or the cost of medical equipment, as the cost of the supplementary pension scheme had only a marginal and indirect influence on the final cost of the services offered by self-employed medical specialists.

6.3.3.3. Cumulative effect

In examining the economic and legal context of the agreement in order to assess its anticompetitive effect the European Court of Justice referred in its decision in *SA Brasserie de Haecht v Consorts Wilkin-Janssen* to the concept of cumulative effect on competition: this refers to the analysis of the combination of the effect of the examined agreement with the 'body of effects, whether convergent or not, surrounding their implementation' and the effect on competition of other similar agreements producing effects on the market they operate.[194] The concept of cumulative effect developed as a legal response to the important issue of vertical foreclosure, in most cases by an incumbent, of the market access of competitors, in particular those established in a different Member State when exercising their freedom of trade by distributing their product in the incumbent's territory. Its development thus serves a dual purpose: first, preserve the market access of foreign firms from private barriers to trade imposed by national incumbents (a market integration objective) and, second, avoid an anticompetitive vertical foreclosure that could harm consumers (the consumer interest objective). The *Delimitis* case provides an interesting illustration of both objectives.

6.3.3.3.1. *Exclusionary cumulative effect:* Stergios Delimitis v Henninger Bräu AG

Henninger Bräu let a beer house to Stergios Delimitis, subject to an obligation for Delimitis to buy all the beer sold there from Henninger Bräu and also to buy a fixed quantity of beer, but he was permitted to buy beer from anyone in other Member States. On the termination of the contract, a dispute arose concerning the amount of money Delimitis owed the brewery. The Community Court was asked to give a preliminary ruling in this test case on the application of Article 101(l) and the block exemption for exclusive purchasing, Regulation 1984/83 (now replaced).

The Court started by indicating the benefits of such an agreement for both parties. Delimitis obtained the premises, and in other cases a tied bar operator might obtain improvements to his premises or funding for them. Henninger Bräu in return obtained a regular outlet for its beer. The CJEU pointed to the benefits to both parties and concluded that the restriction did not have the 'object of restricting competition. It then required a national court to make a full

193 Joined Cases C-180–4/98, *Pavel Pavlov and Others v Stichting Pensioenfonds Medische Specialisten* [2000] ECR I-6451.

194 Case 23/67, *SA Brasserie de Haecht v Consorts Wilkin-Janssen* [1967] ECR (English special edition) 407, 415.

analysis of the market to appraise its effects: was it easy to enter at the retail level? If not, were so many outlets tied to one or other of the brewers for so long that insufficient free outlets remained or came on the market to take the supply of a new brewer of a viable size for distribution or for existing brewers to expand?

Case C-234/89, *Stergios Delimitis v Henninger Bräu AG*
[1991] ECR I–935, [1992] 5 CMLR 210, [1992] 2 CEC 530

13. If such agreements do not have the object of restricting competition within the meaning of Article 101(1), it is nevertheless necessary to ascertain whether they have the effect of preventing, restricting or distorting competition.

14. In its judgment in Case 23/67 *Brasserie De Haecht v Wilkin* [1967] ECR 407, the Court held that the effects of such an agreement had to be assessed in the context in which they occur and where they might combine with others to have a cumulative effect on competition. It also follows from that judgment that the cumulative effect of several similar agreements constitutes one factor amongst others in ascertaining whether, by way of a possible alteration of competition, trade between Member States is capable of being affected.

15. Consequently, in the present case it is necessary to analyse the effects of a beer supply agreement, taken together with other contracts of the same type, on the opportunities of national competitors or those from other Member States, to gain access to the market for beer consumption or to increase their market share and, accordingly, the effects on the range of products offered to consumers.

16. In making that analysis, the relevant market must first be determined. The relevant market is primarily defined on the basis of the nature of the economic activity in question, in this case the sale of beer. Beer is sold through both retail channels and premises for the sale and consumption of drinks. From the consumer's point of view, the latter sector, comprising in particular public houses and restaurants, may be distinguished from the retail sector on the grounds that the sale of beer in public houses does not solely consist of the purchase of a product but is also linked with the provision of services, and that beer consumption in public houses is not essentially dependent on economic considerations. The specific nature of the public house trade is borne out by the fact that the breweries organize specific distribution systems for this sector which require special installations, and that the prices charged in that sector are generally higher than retail prices.

17. It follows that in the present case the reference market is that for the distribution of beer in premises for the sale and consumption of drinks. That finding is not affected by the fact that there is a certain overlap between the two distribution networks, namely inasmuch as retail sales allow new competitors to make their brands known and to use their reputation in order to gain access to the market constituted by premises for the sale and consumption of drinks.

18. Secondly, the relevant market is delimited from a geographical point of view. It should be noted that most beer supply agreements are still entered into at a national level. It follows that, in applying the Community competition rules, account is to be taken of the national market for beer distribution in premises for the sale and consumption of drinks.

19. In order to assess whether the existence of several beer supply agreements impedes access to the market as so defined, it is further necessary to examine the nature

and extent of those agreements in their totality, comprising all similar contracts tying a large number of points of sale to several national producers (judgment in Case 43/69 *Bilger v Jehle* [1970] ECR 127). The effect of those networks of contracts on access to the market depends specifically on the number of outlets thus tied to national producers in relation to the number of public houses which are not so tied, the duration of the commitments entered into, the quantities of beer to which those commitments relate, and on the proportion between those quantities and the quantities sold by free distributors.

20. The existence of a bundle of similar contracts, even if it has a considerable effect on the opportunities for gaining access to the market, is not, however, sufficient in itself to support a finding that the relevant market is inaccessible, inasmuch as it is only one factor, amongst others, pertaining to the economic and legal context in which an agreement must be appraised (Case 23/67 *Brasserie De Haecht*, cited [in para 14] above). The other factors to be taken into account are, in the first instance, those also relating to opportunities for access.

21. In that connection it is necessary to examine whether there are real concrete possibilities for a new competitor to penetrate the bundle of contracts by acquiring a brewery already established on the market together with its network of sales outlets, or to circumvent the bundle of contracts by opening new public houses. For that purpose it is necessary to have regard to the legal rules and agreements on the acquisition of companies and the establishment of outlets, and to the minimum number of outlets necessary for the economic operation of a distribution system. The presence of beer wholesalers not tied to producers who are active on the market is also a factor capable of facilitating a new producer's access to that market since he can make use of those wholesaler's sales networks to distribute his own beer.

22. Secondly, account must be taken of the conditions under which competitive forces operate on the relevant market. In that connection it is necessary to know not only the number and the size of producers present on the market, but also the degree of saturation of that market and customer fidelity to existing brands, for it is generally more difficult to penetrate a saturated market in which customers are loyal to a small number of large producers than a market in full expansion in which a large number of small producers are operating without any strong brand names. The trend in beer sales in the retail trade provides useful information on the development of demand and thus an indication of the degree of saturation of the beer market as a whole. The analysis of that trend is, moreover, of interest in evaluating brand loyalty. A steady increase in sales of beer under new brand names may confer on the owners of those brand names a reputation which they may turn to account in gaining access to the public-house market.

23. If an examination of all similar contracts entered into on the relevant market and the other factors relevant to the economic and legal context in which the contract must be examined shows that those agreements do not have the cumulative effect of denying access to that market to new national and foreign competitors, the individual agreements comprising the bundle of agreements cannot be held to restrict competition within the meaning of Article 101(1) of the Treaty. They do not, therefore, fall under the prohibition laid down in that provision.

24. If, on the other hand, such examination reveals that it is difficult to gain access to the relevant market, it is necessary to assess the extent to which the agreements entered into by the brewery in question contribute to the cumulative effect produced

in that respect by the totality of the similar contracts found on that market. Under the Community rules on competition, responsibility for such an effect of closing off the market must be attributed to the breweries which make an appreciable contribution thereto. Beer supply agreements entered into by breweries whose contribution to the cumulative effect is insignificant do not therefore fall under the prohibition under Article 101(1).

25. In order to assess the extent of the contribution of the beer supply agreements entered into by a brewery to the cumulative sealing-off effect mentioned above, the market position of the contracting parties must be taken into consideration. That position is not determined solely by the market share held by the brewery and any group to which it may belong, but also by the number of outlets tied to it or to its group, in relation to the total number of premises for the sale and consumption of drinks found in the relevant market.

26. The contribution of the individual contracts entered into by a brewery to the sealing-off of that market also depends on their duration. If the duration is manifestly excessive in relation to the average duration of beer supply agreements generally entered into on the relevant market, the individual contract falls under the prohibition under Article 101(1). A brewery with a relatively small market share which ties its sales outlets for many years may make as significant a contribution to a sealing-off of the market as a brewery in a relatively strong market position which regularly releases sales outlets at shorter intervals.

27. The reply to be given to the first three questions is therefore that a beer supply agreement is prohibited by Article 101(1) of the EC Treaty, if two cumulative conditions are met. The first is that, having regard to the economic and legal context of the agreement at issue, it is difficult for competitors who could enter the market or increase their market share to gain access to the national market for the distribution of beer in premises for the sale and consumption of drinks. The fact that, in that market, the agreement in issue is one of a number of similar agreements having a cumulative effect on competition constitutes only one factor amongst others in assessing whether access to that market is indeed difficult. The second condition is that the agreement in question must make a significant contribution to the sealing-off effect brought about by the totality of those agreements in their economic and legal context. The extent of the contribution made by the individual agreement depends on the position of the contracting parties in the relevant market and on the duration of the agreement.

NOTES AND QUESTIONS ON THE JUDGMENT IN DELIMITIS

1. In paragraphs 10–12 (not reproduced here), the Court referred to the benefits to retailer and brewery of an exclusive purchasing obligation. Should the tie be limited to the period needed to make it worthwhile to build a brewery or distribution depot, or is this judgment not an example of the doctrine of ancillary restraints making viable a transaction not in itself anti-competitive?

2. (Paragraph 13) German was the authentic language of the case and the words 'even if' are a poor translation of '*wenngleich*', which means 'although'. The French translation, on which the deliberations of the judges would have taken place, is '*si*', which means either 'although' or 'if'. 'Although' is far stronger than 'if' in this context. In German, the Court was stating that because of the efficiencies it made possible, the exclusive

purchasing obligation did not have the object of restricting competition. This is the interpretation given by Fennelly AG in *DIP SpA*.[195]

4. (Paragraphs 16 and 17) Why does the Court confine the relevant market to beer sold in bars? Do you agree? If you were a foreign or new brewer and you wanted to enter the German market, how would you go about it? Would you enter into an agreement only with free houses, would you try to persuade tied houses to discontinue their ties with other brewers, and would you also sell your beer through retail, or all three? On the demand side, the two ways of marketing beer may not be substitutes, but on the supply side they are. The competitive danger of exclusive purchasing agreements is that they may keep out new entrants. So, all the ways of entering the market are important.
5. (Paragraph 18) The Court notes that most beer supply agreements are still entered into at a national level. Is it surprising that the Court does not seem concerned that beer supply agreements should be entered into at an EU level? In *Commission v Germany*,[196] the Court ruled that the German law defining the 'pure beer' which alone it was legal to sell in Germany infringed Articles [34 TFEU] and [36 TFEU], so it is now legal to import beer from Belgium or Luxembourg. Evidence was given in the *Delimitis* case that this rarely happens.
6. (Paragraph 21) Is the case concerned with inter- or intra-brand competition?
7. (Paragraphs 19–23) In what circumstances do exclusive purchasing obligations foreclose market entry?
8. If there was substantial foreclosure to which Henninger Bräu made a significant contribution, would it be able successfully to sue Delimitis (a) for failing to sell the minimum quantity of beer, or (b) for failure to pay for beer ordered for the bar? Where should such an action be brought?
9. Should the analysis be done under Article 101(1) or (3)? Why is the question important?[197]
10. Does the precedent apply only to an obligation to buy all the beer sold in a bar owned by the landlord; to buy any products from the same supplier; or to other exclusive agreements—exclusive distribution, exclusive franchising, exclusive licensing?
11. (Paragraphs 25–6) Was the Court right to say that the cumulative effect depended on the number of retailers tied or should it have looked at the cumulative market share of the retailers foreclosed?
12. The cumulative (foreclosure) effects approach was also used in *Neste Markkinointi Oy v Yötuuli*[198] and in *Van den Bergh Foods Ltd v Commission*.[199]

195 Joined Cases C-140–2/94, *DIP SpA and Others v Comune di Bassano del Grappa and Others* [1995] ECR I–3257, [1996] 4 CMLR 157, para 58.

196 Case 178/84, *Commission v Germany* [1987] ECR 1227.

197 Cf. Section 6.1.

198 Case C-214/99, *Neste Markkinointi Oy v. Yötuuli* [2000] ECR I–11121. On the importance of assessing the duration of the contracts in the context of the cumulative effect doctrine, see Order of the Court in Case C-506/07, *Lubricantes y Carburantes Galaicos SL v GALP Energía España SAU*, ECLI:EU:C:2009:504, para 32.

199 Case T-65/98, *Van den Bergh Foods Ltd v Commission* [2003] ECR II–4653, paras 75–119.

In *Neste Markkinointi Oy v Yötuuli*, the CJEU held that Article 101(1) TFEU does not apply to an exclusive purchasing agreement entered into by a motor-fuels supplier which the retailer may terminate upon one year's notice at any time where all that supplier's exclusive purchasing agreements, whether considered separately or as a whole, taken together with the network of similar agreements made by the totality of suppliers, have an appreciable effect on the closing-off of the market but where the agreements of the same kind as the agreement at issue in the main proceedings by reason of their duration represent only a very small part of the totality of one supplier's exclusive purchasing agreements, of which the majority are fixed term contracts entered into for more than one year. The short duration of the contracts and the possibility that they may be terminated upon one year's notice at any time should thus be considered and lead to the conclusion that these contracts do not make any significant contribution to the cumulative effect, for the purposes of the judgment in *Delimitis*.[200]

In *Van den Bergh Foods Ltd v Commission*, HB, a supplier dominant in the manufacture and supply of impulse ice creams—those that are individually packed for immediate consumption—supplied small retailers in Ireland with freezer cabinets free of charge and required them to be used only for its brands of individual ice creams. The Commission considered that this foreclosed other suppliers of impulse ice cream, such as Mars, from many retail outlets. Few shops in country areas would have the space or incentive to install a second freezer. *De facto* exclusivity creates concern as well as direct contractual provisions. Originally the Commission sent a comfort letter (a form of positive decision as to the compatibility of a practice to Article 101 TFEU) permitting the practice to continue, provided that the dominant firm allowed retailers to buy their cabinets on reasonable second-hand terms, including the possibility of hire purchase, and thereby become free of the tie. When Mars failed to make much headway in Ireland and complained again, the Commission changed its mind and prohibited freezer exclusivity by decision. On appeal, the CFI confirmed[201] that the Commission had carried out considerable market analysis in finding actual foreclosure when applying Article 101(1) TFEU. The General Court went on to consider the cumulative effect of other single branding agreements made with other manufacturers. The Commission had found that only 17 per cent of the small outlets were free of a tie. The General Court confirmed that the Commission's decision had adequately established the extent of foreclosure.[202] It referred to many of the points made by the Commission in its decision: the existence of other networks of single branding agreements, the large share HB enjoyed in the relevant market, the popularity of its brands, the inability of retailers with little space to use more than one cabinet. HB's conduct raised rivals' costs since they would also have to provide and service freezers without charge which would be proportionately more onerous since they had fewer brands and smaller shares of the market. The GC also found that HB enjoyed a dominant position. The CJEU upheld the GC's judgment.[203] As we will examine in Chapter 10, the parties to vertical agreements—those between suppliers at different levels of trade and industry that do not compete with each other, such as a supplier and its customer or a technology licensor and its licensee—contribute complementary products rather than substitutes. Each benefits from increased demand if the other lowers its

200 Case C-214/99, *Neste Markkinointi Oy v Yötuuli* [2000] ECR I–11121, paras 36 and 39.
201 Case T-65/98, *Van den Bergh Foods Ltd v Commission* [2003] ECR II–4653.
202 Ibid, paras 75–144.
203 Case C-552/03 P, *Unilever Bestfoods (Ireland) Ltd* [2006] 5 CMLR 27.

profit margin and increases its output. Collaboration between competitors should be judged more harshly, since each would benefit if the other produced less rather than more and at a higher price. This view was strongly endorsed by the Chicago School of economics. EU competition law treated, however, at the time vertical agreements quite harshly, because vertical agreements were perceived as having the aim to hamper market integration (dividing the EU Internal Market). Often an exclusive territory bounded by national frontiers was granted to the firm downstream. Moreover, agreements to handle the products only of a particular supplier or to buy exclusively or nearly exclusively from it may foreclose other suppliers. Views on vertical restraints started nevertheless changing in the late 1990s, vertical restraints being treated more leniently.

6.3.3.3.2. *Cumulative effect, facilitating practices, and collusion*

Most recently, the Commission has made reference to the concept of cumulative effect in order to bring within the scope of Article 101 TFEU, practices that facilitate collusion between undertakings (not just situations of foreclosure of competition).

Guidelines on vertical restraints [2010] OJ C 130/1 (emphases added)

> 20. An agency agreement may also fall within the scope of Article 101(1), even if the principal bears all the relevant financial and commercial risks, where it *facilitates collusion*. That could, for instance, be the case when *a number of principals use the same agents while collectively excluding others from using these agents*, or when they use the agents to collude on marketing strategy or to exchange sensitive market information between the principals. [. . .]
>
> 130. The possible competition risks of single branding are foreclosure of the market to competing suppliers and potential suppliers, softening of competition and *facilitation of collusion between suppliers in case of cumulative use* and, where the buyer is a retailer selling to final consumers, a loss of in-store inter-brand competition. Such restrictive effects have a direct impact on inter-brand competition. [. . .]

Although cumulative foreclosure effects are a well understood concept since *Delimitis* and widely used, the doctrine of cumulative collusive effects that underscores the above excerpts of the Commission's Vertical Restraints Guidelines seems quite tentative, not yet formalized as such, and not yet confirmed by the jurisprudence of the CJEU. It also relates to the interpretation of the element of the restriction of competition, once an agreement or a concerted practice is found to exist, and, in no way, enables the Commission to by-pass the need to establish collusion under Article 101(1) TFEU, as the concept kicks in once collusion under Article 101(1) TFEU has been found. However, it adds a possible theory of harm to the arsenal of the Commission or plaintiffs operating in markets where undertakings use similar types of vertical restraints leading to a likely restriction of competition through the development of collusive outcomes, either upstream or downstream.[204]

204 A similar approach focusing on 'parallel exclusion' has been put forward by some US-based authors with regard to US antitrust law: CS Hemphill and T Wu, 'Parallel Exclusion' (2013) 22 *Yale LJ* 1182.

Once an agreement or concerted practice is established between a supplier and a retailer (vertical agreement), it is possible to argue that the use by a significant number of suppliers or retailers of a 'similar' type of agreement may restrict competition, by facilitating collusion, either between suppliers or between retailers (horizontal dimension), or bring the agreement within the scope of the prohibition principle under Article 101(1) TFEU, the *de minimis* doctrine and other immunities from which may benefit the specific agreement (eg the commercial agency agreements immunity, see Chapter 10) not being able to clear the agreement in this case. This theory of harm may complement the finding that the specific vertical agreement restricts intra-brand competition or inter-brand competition (eg through foreclosure), by adding the possibility that it may also restrict competition by facilitating collusion.

6.3.4. INTUITIVE (ABSTRACT) BALANCING?

Although the assessment of the effects of an agreement focuses merely on evidence of negative effects to competition and consumer harm, often it includes some analysis of the positive effects of the agreement on competition, albeit at a very abstract and categorical level. The analysis of the legal and economic context of the agreement integrates the consideration of the positive effects the specific category of agreements to competition and consumers, as the following examples will illustrate. Of course, this does not amount to a deep or quantitative assessment of the positive effects of the commercial practice to competition, as this type of analysis is performed under Article 101(3) TFEU. We will employ the terminology of intuitive (abstract) balancing to distinguish this form of competition law assessment from that performed under Article 101(3).

The intuitive (abstract) balancing test has taken different forms. The ancillary restraints doctrine has been employed in order to consider business related justifications of restrictions of competition. Public policy considerations have also been taken into account in some cases, some authors referring to these cases as recognizing 'regulatory ancillarity'.[205]

6.3.4.1. Ancillary restraints doctrine (commercial ancillarity)

The dominant view at the Commission, prior to the adoption of the Green paper on vertical restraints, was that competition was essentially a process of rivalry, the Commission consequently adopting a restrictive approach to agreements between parties in a vertical relationship. Article 101(1) TFEU applied to any constraint or restriction imposed on the economic freedom of the distributor by its supplier which also affected inter-State trade. The agreement could be examined under Article 101(3) TFEU but the notification requirement dissuaded businesses to adopt contractual practices of vertical control. The broad interpretation of the scope of Article 101(1) did not only reflect the ideological underpinnings of competition policy in Europe but was also the result of the European Commission's exclusivity in the enforcement of Article 101(3). Bringing more agreements under the scope of Article 101(1) increased the role of the European Commission to the detriment of national courts and national competition authorities. The Commission frequently found that an exclusive agreement had at least the object or effect of restricting competition, even if it later exempted it under Article 101(3). Such an approach favoured vertical integration, which was either not

[205] R Whish and D Bailey, *Competition Law* (OUP, 8th ed, 2015), 138–42.

subject to competition law (integration by internal growth) or subject to a more lenient application of competition law (integration by external growth).

However, the CJEU and the General Court have often stated that an ancillary restriction, necessary to make a main transaction, such as franchising, viable, does not in itself restrict competition. Despite the formalistic approach followed then by the Commission, there were certain forms of restraints promoting welfare enhancing cooperation, either in the context of a vertical agreement or in that of a cooperative joint venture that could escape the prohibition principle of Article 101(1) TFEU, notwithstanding the fact that they restricted competitive rivalry. Initiated by the case law of the Court of Justice, subsequently followed by the Commission, these more lenient specific regimes for this welfare-enhancing cooperation may be explained as an attempt by the Court to loosen the straitjacket effect that a restrictive interpretation of Article 101(1) imposed on business as well as to curve the considerable administrative costs to the Commission, which had to deal with a great number of notifications, under the legal authorization regime of Regulation 17/62.

The ancillary restraints doctrine is expressed in more than one way. One is that the competition excluded was not possible without the restraint, for instance, that the firm could not have penetrated another Member State without cooperation from a local exclusive dealer who would not have invested in promotion without some protection from other dealers taking a free ride. Alternatively, an ancillary restraint may be one that is 'directly related and necessary to the implementation of the main operation'.

Non-competition clauses which are ancillary to the performance of a legitimate and welfare enhancing transaction, such as the transfer of business assets, have long being considered legal in the Common law of restraints of trade, under certain conditions. A similar rule applies in EU competition law. The doctrine of ancillary restraints was also developed from the judgment of the CJEU in *LTM v MBU*.[206] The CJEU ruled that if the dealer would not have made the investments necessary to organize distribution without being promised protection from free riders, then that protection would not infringe Article 101(1). A restriction of conduct that is necessary to make the main transaction viable and is not more extensive than necessary does not infringe Article 101(1) if the main transaction does not. The counterfactual is not the transaction without the restrictive provisions, but without the whole transaction including any restrictions.

The application of the ancillary restraints doctrine was extended to new forms of business practices that challenged the dominant neoclassical conception of the firm in series of cases in the late 1970s (on selective distribution) and 1980s (franchising), enabling the EU courts to take into consideration transactional efficiencies in the context of Article 101(1) TFEU.

There is more than one definition of ancillary restraints which do not infringe Article 101(1) provided that they are reasonable and no wider than necessary to support the basic transaction.

- The term may embrace provisions that make viable a transaction not in itself inherently anti-competitive, such as one leading to the penetration of a new market. This definition largely corresponds to comparing the present situation with the appropriate counterfactual.
- The Commission treats 'any restriction which is directly related and necessary to the implementation of a main operation' as an ancillary restraint. The General Court in *Métropole Télévision (M6) and Others v Commission*,[207] used the same definition, saying

[206] Case 56/65, *Société Technique Minière (LTM) v Maschinenbau Ulm GmbH (MBU)* [1966] ECR 337.
[207] Case T-112/99, *Métropole III* [2002] ECR II-2459.

that the analysis had to be somewhat abstract. This is not similar to the application of the counterfactual test.

- According to Enrique Gonzalez Diaz,[208], the ancillary restraints doctrine is 'used to justify restrictions that are necessary for the full preservation or full transfer of value in certain types of transaction'. This is narrower than the counterfactual test.

The judgments of the courts in Luxembourg have not always made it clear which definition is being applied, and they are not entirely consistent.

The origins of the ancillary restraints doctrine can be traced to the US case *Addyston Pipe*, where Judge Taft, on the basis of a meticulous review of English courts' decisions, held that restraints on trade are illegal, unless they are found to be merely ancillary to the main purpose of a lawful contract, as well as necessary for the protection of the parties' commercial interests.[209] The doctrine was endorsed by the CJEU.[210] Some of these cases relate to non-compete obligations imposed when it comes to agreements for the sale of business, which were found lawful as these aim to preserve the value of the assets transferred.[211] Others, as in the franchise context, immunize clauses that are 'objectively necessary' for making viable a transaction that is not in itself anti-competitive.[212]

The Commission deals with the issue of ancillary restraints in paragraphs 28–31 of its Guidelines on Article 101(3):

> In [EU] competition law the concept of ancillary restraints covers any alleged restriction of competition which is directly related and necessary to the implementation of a main non-restrictive transaction and proportionate to it. If an agreement in its main parts [. . .] does not have as its object or effect the restriction of competition, then restrictions, which are directly related to and necessary for the implementation of that transaction, also fall outside Article 101(1). These related restrictions are called ancillary restraints. A restriction is directly related to the main transaction if it is subordinate to the implementation of that transaction and is inseparably linked to it. The test of necessity implies that the restriction must be objectively necessary for the implementation of the main transaction and be proportionate to it.[213]

According to the Commission, in essence, the test of ancillary restraints is similar to the counterfactual test performed under Article 101(1) TFEU,[214] which asks if the agreement restrict(s) actual or potential competition that would have existed in the absence of the contractual restraint, this time, however, applying in all cases where the main transaction is not restrictive of competition, and not only its application being limited to determining the impact of the agreement on intra-brand competition. The General Court and, subsequently, the Commission have clarified that the requirement that an ancillary restraint be objectively necessary does not imply any balancing of pro- and anti-competitive effects, as the appraisal

[208] FE Gonzalez Díaz, 'The Notion of Ancillary Restraints Under EC Competition Law' (1995) 19(3) *Fordham Int'l LJ* 951.

[209] *United States v Addyston Pipe & Steel Co et al*, 85 Fed 271, 282 (6th Cir 1898).

[210] For examples, see FE Gonzalez Díaz, 'The Notion of Ancillary Restraints Under EC Competition Law' (1995) 19(3) *Fordham Int'l LJ* 951.

[211] Case 42/84, *Remia BV and Verenigde Bedrijven Nutricia NV v Commission* [1985] ECR 2545.

[212] Case 161/84, *Pronuptia de Paris GmbH v Pronuptia de Paris Irmgard Schillgallis* [1986] ECR 353.

[213] Guidelines on Article 101(3) (formerly 81(3)), para 29.

[214] Ibid, para 18(2). On the counterfactual test, see also Case T-328/03, *O2 (Germany) GmbH & Co OHG v Commission* [2006] ECR-II 1231.

of any alleged efficiency gains may be carried out only in the context of Article 101(3).[215] The assessment performed under the ancillary restraints doctrine is therefore narrower than the balancing of pro- and anti-competitive effects:

> The assessment of ancillary restraints is limited to determining whether, in the specific context of the main non-restrictive transaction or activity, a particular restriction is necessary for the implementation of that transaction or activity and proportionate to it. If on the basis of objective factors it can be concluded that without the restriction the main non-restrictive transaction would be difficult or impossible to implement, the restriction may be regarded as objectively necessary for its implementation and proportionate to it. If, for example, the main object of a franchise agreement does not restrict competition, then restrictions, which are necessary for the proper functioning of the agreement, such as obligations aimed at protecting the uniformity and reputation of the franchise system, also fall outside Article 101(1).[216]

The Commission's Notice on restrictions directly related and necessary to concentrations also provides some interesting insights on the ancillary restrictions test, in particular the requirements of 'direct relation' and 'necessity'. We replaced the term 'concentration' with that of 'main transaction', assuming that the meaning and assessment of the condition of ancillarity will not be different in the context of merger control than in the implementation of Article 101(1) TFEU:

> 11. The criteria of direct relation and necessity are objective in nature. Restrictions are not directly related and necessary to the implementation of a [main transaction] simply because the parties regard them as such.
>
> 12. For restrictions to be considered 'directly related to the implementation of the [main transaction]', they must be closely linked to the [main transaction] itself. It is not sufficient that an agreement has been entered into in the same context or at the same time as the [main transaction]. Restrictions which are directly related to the [main transaction] are economically related to the main transaction [. . .].
>
> 13. [The requirement of necessity] means that, in the absence of those agreements, the [main transaction] could not be implemented or could only be implemented under considerably more uncertain conditions, at substantially higher cost, over an appreciably longer period or with considerably greater difficulty. Agreements necessary to the implementation of [the main transaction] are typically aimed at protecting the value transferred, maintaining the continuity of supply after the break-up of a former economic entity, or enabling the start-up of a new entity. In determining whether a restriction is necessary, it is appropriate not only to take account of its nature, but also to ensure that its duration, subject matter and geographical field of application does not exceed what the implementation of the [main transaction] reasonably requires. If equally effective alternatives are available for attaining the legitimate aim pursued, the undertakings must choose the one which is objectively the least restrictive of competition.[217]

215 Case T-112/99, *Metropole III* [2001] ECR II–2459, para 107; Guidelines on Article 101(3) (formerly 81(3)), para 30.

216 Guidelines on Article 101(3) (formerly 81(3)), para 31.

217 Commission's Notice on restrictions directly related and necessary to concentrations [2005] OJ C 56/24.

This proportionality test does not require a full economic analysis of the market. Neither is it necessary to proceed to a quantitative and concrete analysis of the positive effect of the practice on consumers. The test only involves a qualitative and abstract analysis of its positive effects in the context of the relationship between the parties to the agreement. The legality of the ancillary restriction essentially depends on its connection with the main transaction and not on its independent impact on the market. However, as with the counterfactual test, to which the ancillary restraints test can be compared to, in order to make this determination, it is necessary to examine the competitive environment in the absence of these ancillary clauses,[218] without, nevertheless, this assessment going as far as proceeding to a detailed examination of the competitive situation in the relevant market before and after the transaction.

The analysis under the ancillary restraints doctrine also involves, according to the Commission, the assessment of the possibility of an alternative less restrictive of competition (which in any case forms part of the proportionality test in EU competition law[219]):

> Such exclusion of the application of Article [101(1) can only be made on the basis of objective factors external to the parties themselves and not the subjective views and characteristics of the parties. The question is not whether the parties in their particular situation would not have accepted to conclude a less restrictive agreement, but whether given the nature of the agreement and the characteristics of the market a less restrictive agreement would not have been concluded by undertakings in a similar setting.[220]

The alternative test of less restrictive to competition also constitutes an element for the application of Article 101(3) TFEU, in particular the third condition, that of the indispensability of the restrictions to achieve the improvement of the production or distribution of goods or the promotion of technical or economic progress (efficiency gains).[221] However, as explained below, the operation of the less restrictive to competition alternative test is different in the context of the ancillary restraints doctrine, under Article 101(1) TFEU, from in the context of the indispensability test, under Article 101(3) TFEU.

The ancillary restraints test does not proceed to a quantitative and concrete analysis of the positive effect of the practice on consumers but involves a qualitative and abstract analysis of its positive effects in the context of the relationship between the parties to the agreement.

There follow some examples where the ancillary restraints test was implemented by the Commission and the EU courts.

6.3.4.1.1. Remia

Nutricia sold its two subsidiaries: Remia, which produced sauces to Drs de Rooige and Luycks, which made pickles, to a subsidiary of Campbells. Nutricia required each purchaser not to compete in the products sold by the other business. In its decision, after examining the covenants not to compete, the Commission held that 'not every restriction of competition of this type which falls within Article [101(1) TFEU]' and that 'when the sale of a business

[218] Case 42/84, *Remia BV and Verenigde Bedrijven Nutricia NV v Commission* [1985] ECR 2545, para 18.

[219] Case C-331/88, *The Queen v Minister of Agriculture, Fisheries and Food and Secretary of State for Health, ex parte: Fedesa and others* [1990] ECR I–4023, para 13 (referring to the need to take into account the existence of a 'least onerous condition').

[220] Guidelines on Article 101(3) (formerly 81(3)), para 18(2).

[221] See Section 6.4.4.

involves the transfer not only of material assets but also of goodwill and clientele, it may be necessary to impose contractual restrictions of competition on the seller, these being considered 'a legitimate means of ensuring the performance of the seller's obligation to transfer the full commercial value of the business'.[222] The Commission, however, noted that 'the protection accorded to the purchaser cannot be unlimited' and 'must be kept to the minimum that is objectively necessary for the purchaser to assume, by active competitive behaviour, the place in the market previously occupied by the seller'.[223] The geographical scope of a non-competition clause also has to be limited to the extent which is objectively necessary to achieve the abovementioned goal. The Commission went on to find that a covenant not to compete with the businesses sold for ten years was excessive. Moreover, the covenant should have been limited to the countries where the businesses sold operated. The agreements were contrary to Article 101(l) only as to the excesses. It refused an exemption. The decision was appealed to the Court of Justice of the EU.

Case 42/84, *Remia BV and Verenigde Bedrijven Nutricia v Commission*
[1985] ECR 2545, [1987] 1 CMLR 1, CMR 14217

18. In order to determine whether or not [non-competition] clauses come within the prohibition in Article [101(1) TFEU], it is necessary to examine what would be the state of competition if those clauses did not exist.

19. If that were the case, and should the vendor and the purchaser remain competitors after the transfer, it is clear that the agreement for the transfer of the undertaking could not be given effect. The vendor, with his particularly detailed knowledge of the transferred undertaking, would still be in a position to win back his former customers immediately after the transfer and thereby drive the undertaking out of business. Against that background non-competition clauses incorporated in an agreement for the transfer of an undertaking in principle have the merit of ensuring that the transfer has the effect intended. By virtue of that very fact they contribute to the promotion of competition because they lead to an increase in the number of undertakings in the market in question.

20. Nevertheless, in order to have that beneficial effect on competition, such clauses must be necessary to the transfer of the undertaking concerned and their duration and scope must be strictly limited to that purpose. The Commission was therefore right in holding that where those conditions are satisfied such clauses are free of the prohibition laid down in Article [101(1)]. [. . .]

NOTES AND QUESTIONS ON REMIA

1. Note that in other contexts, neither Commission nor Court has applied the doctrine of ancillary restraints to export restraints. In *Miller*, the Commission, followed by the Court, treated export bans or deterrents as automatically infringing Article 101(1) TFEU.[224] The Court looked neither to whether restrictions on

222 *Nutricia* (Case IV/30.389) Commission Decision [1983] OJ L 376/22, paras 25–6.
223 Ibid, para 27.
224 Case 19/77, *Miller International Schallplatten GmbH v Commission,* [1978] ECR 131.

poaching were necessary to make viable a distribution system where retailers were required to provide facilities to browse, nor to whether there was strong inter-brand competition. In the extreme circumstances of *Distillers*,[225] the Advocate General would have reversed on substance the Commission's condemnation of the loss of a discount on exports, which was treated by the Commission as an export deterrent, had the agreement been notified, but the Court did not address the substantive issues.

2. Does the judgment correspond to the US doctrine of ancillary restraints necessary to make viable a transaction that is not in itself anti-competitive?
3. For other examples of early application of the ancillary restraint doctrine, see *Pronuptia*,[226] and the judgments of the EU Courts on intellectual property licensing in *Nungesser*,[227] *Coditel II*,[228] and *Louis Erauw Jacquery*,[229] or *Gøttrup-Klim*,[230] concerning cooperative purchasing associations in the agricultural sector. The question remains whether the doctrine of ancillary restraints is of general application or whether it applies only to the sale of a business as a going concern, franchising and intellectual property licensing. The Commission and General Court have also applied it to joint ventures, such as in *Métropole Télévision (M6)*.[231]
4. Reflecting again on the various definitions of the 'ancillary restraints' doctrine, highlighted above, the jurisprudence of the CJEU took various perspectives. In *Nungesser v Commission*, the CJEU held that an open exclusive licence of plant breeders' rights, one not granting absolute territorial protection, did not in itself infringe Article 101(1) TFEU because it was needed to induce the investment of both parties, and, in *Coditel II*, it held that in the light of the practice of the film industry, exclusive licences of performing rights did not do so, even though, in the circumstances, they conferred absolute territorial protection. These judgments seem to be based on the first definition of the ancillary restraints doctrine. In *Pronuptia*, the CJEU ruled that many restrictions on conduct do not infringe Article 101(1) TFEU where they are necessary to make a distribution franchising network viable, since franchising, in itself, does not restrict competition. In clearing clauses required to maintain a uniform image for the network as outside the prohibition of Article 101(1), the CJEU referred to the provisions being necessary to make distribution franchising work. This seems to be an application of the first definition of ancillary restraint; on the other hand, the analysis was abstract which corresponds more to the second definition. Certain provisions in the franchising contract are always valid, irrespective of market power, although few franchised networks, if any, have much market power.

225 Case 30/78, *Distillers Co Ltd v Commission* [1980] ECR 2229.

226 Case 161/84, *Pronuptia de Paris GmbH v Pronuptia de Paris Irmgard Schillgalis* [1986] ECR 353.

227 Case 258/78, *Nungesser (LG) KG and Kurt Eisele v Commission* [1982] ECR 2015.

228 Case 262/81, *Coditel II* [1982] ECR 3381.

229 Case 27/87, *Erauw-Jacquery (Louis) SPRL v La Hesbignonne SC* [1988] ECR 1919.

230 Case C-250/92, *Gøttrup-Klim ea Grovvareforeninger v Dansk Landbrugs Grovvareselskab AmbA* [1994] ECR I–5641.

231 Case T-206/99, *Métropole Télévision (M6) and Others v Commission* [2001] ECR II–1061 [hereinafter *Métropole I*].

6.3.4.1.2. Métropole Télévision (M6)

In *Métropole*, the General Court clearly adopted the second definition, which it took from the Commission's Guidelines. It stated that there should be no balancing between competitive benefits and detriments under Article 101(1) TFEU and any benefits should be considered under Article 101(3) TFEU. The GC construed the concept of ancillary restraints narrowly, to be applied in a relatively abstract manner.

Case T-112/99, *Métropole Télévision (M6) and Others v Commission* (*Métropole III*)
[2002] ECR II–2459

Six major TV companies in France entered into a partnership (TPS) for ten years. It was intended to break into the market for broadcasting satellite pay-TV programmes and services in digital mode. The Commission cleared a non-competition clause, for only three years and exempted for three years a clause giving TPS a right of priority and a right of first refusal for the production of special interest channels. The parties appealed on the ground that neither of these provisions infringed Article 101 or, alternatively, that they should have been exempted for ten years.

It is normal for the parties to a joint venture to agree not to compete with the joint venture as, otherwise, the other parties would not invest in the joint venture. The protection may well take the form of some limited exclusivity for the joint venture. TPS would have to compete with Canal+ which, with 70 per cent of the market by 1998, dominated it. So the investment must have been substantial and risky.

Were these provisions ancillary restrictions to be judged in the same way as the joint venture and cleared and, if not, should they be balanced against the pro-competitive aspects of an agreement to create a third supplier in the market? This was rejected by the General Court.

Findings of the Court

72. According to the applicants, as a consequence of the existence of a rule of reason in Community [EU] competition law, when Article [101(1) TFEU] is applied it is necessary to weigh the pro and anti-competitive effects of an agreement in order to determine whether it is caught by the prohibition laid down in that article. It should, however, be observed, first of all, that contrary to the applicants' assertions the existence of such a rule has not, as such, been confirmed by the Community courts. Quite to the contrary, in various judgments the Court of Justice and the General Court have been at pains to indicate that the existence of a rule of reason in Community competition law is doubtful [. . .].

73. Next, it must be observed that an interpretation of Article [101(1) TFEU], in the form suggested by the applicants, is difficult to reconcile with the rules prescribed by that provision.

74. Article [101 TFEU] expressly provides, in its third paragraph, for the possibility of exempting agreements that restrict competition where they satisfy a number of conditions, in particular where they are indispensable to the attainment of certain objectives and do not afford undertakings the possibility of eliminating competition in respect of a substantial part of the products in question. It is only in the precise framework of that provision that the pro and anti-competitive aspects of a restriction may be weighed [. . .] Article [101(3) TFEU] would lose much of its effectiveness if such an examination had to be carried out already under Article [101(1) TFEU].

75. It is true that in a number of judgments the Court of Justice and the General Court have favoured a more flexible interpretation of the prohibition laid down in Article [101(1) TFEU] [. . .].

76. Those judgments cannot, however, be interpreted as establishing the existence of a rule of reason in Community competition law. They are, rather, part of a broader trend in the case-law according to which it is not necessary to hold, wholly abstractly and without drawing any distinction, that any agreement restricting the freedom of action of one or more of the parties is necessarily caught by the prohibition laid down in Article [101(1) TFEU]. In assessing the applicability of Article [101(1)] to an agreement, account should be taken of the actual conditions in which it functions, in particular the economic context in which the undertakings operate, the products or services covered by the agreement and the actual structure of the market concerned [. . .].

77. That interpretation, while observing the substantive scheme of Article [101 TFEU] and, in particular, preserving the effectiveness of Article [101(3) TFEU], makes it possible to prevent the prohibition in Article [101(1)] from extending wholly abstractly and without distinction to all agreements whose effect is to restrict the freedom of action of one or more of the parties. It must, however, be emphasised that such an approach does not mean that it is necessary to weigh the pro- and anti-competitive effects of an agreement when determining whether the prohibition laid down in Article [101(1) TFEU].

78. In the light of the foregoing, it must be held that, contrary to the applicants' submission, in the contested decision the Commission correctly applied Article [101(1)] to the exclusivity clause and the clause relating to the special-interest channels inasmuch as it was not obliged to weigh the pro and anti-competitive aspects of those agreements outside the specific framework of Article [101(3) TFEU].

79. It did, however, assess the restrictive nature of those clauses in their economic and legal context in accordance with the case-law. Thus, it rightly found that the general-interest channels presented programmes that were attractive for subscribers to a pay-TV company and that the effect of the exclusivity clause was to deny TPS' competitors access to such programmes [. . .]. As regards the clause relating to the special-interest channels, the Commission found that it resulted in a limitation of the supply of such channels on that market for a period of 10 years [. . .].

80. This objection must therefore be rejected [. . .].

The alternative claim, alleging that the exclusivity clause and the clause relating to the special-interest channels are ancillary restrictions

[. . .]

103. It is necessary, first of all, to define what constitutes an ancillary restriction in Community competition law and point out the consequences which follow from classification of a restriction as ancillary. It is then necessary to apply the principles thereby established to the exclusivity clause and to the clause relating to the special-interest channels in order to determine whether, as the applicants' assert, the Commission committed an error of appraisal in not classifying those commitments as ancillary restrictions.

The concept of ancillary restriction

104. In Community competition law the concept of an ancillary restriction covers any restriction which is directly related and necessary to the implementation of a main operation [. . .]

105. In its notice on ancillary restrictions the Commission rightly stated that a restriction directly related to implementation of a main operation must be understood to be

any restriction which is subordinate to the implementation of that operation and which has an evident link with it [. . .]

106. The condition that a restriction be necessary implies a two-fold examination. It is necessary to establish, first, whether the restriction is objectively necessary for the implementation of the main operation and, second, whether it is proportionate to it [. . .]

107. As regards the objective necessity of a restriction, it must be observed that inasmuch as [. . .] the existence of a rule of reason in Community competition law cannot be upheld, it would be wrong, when classifying ancillary restrictions, to interpret the requirement for objective necessity as implying a need to weigh the pro and anti-competitive effects of an agreement. Such an analysis can take place only in the specific framework of Article [101(3) TFEU].

108. That approach is justified not merely so as to preserve the effectiveness of Article [101(3) TFEU], but also on grounds of consistency. As Article [101(1)] does not require an analysis of the positive and negative effects on competition of a principal restriction, the same finding is necessary with regard to the analysis of accompanying restrictions.

109. Consequently, as the Commission has correctly asserted, examination of the objective necessity of a restriction in relation to the main operation cannot but be relatively abstract. It is not a question of analysing whether, in the light of the competitive situation on the relevant market, the restriction is indispensable to the commercial success of the main operation but of determining whether, in the specific context of the main operation, the restriction is necessary to implement that operation. If, without the restriction, the main operation is difficult or even impossible to implement, the restriction may be regarded as objectively necessary for its implementation.

110. Thus, in the judgment in *Remia* v *Commission*, [. . .] the Court of Justice held that a non-competition clause was objectively necessary for a successful transfer of undertakings, inasmuch as, without such a clause, and should the vendor and the purchaser remain competitors after the transfer, it is clear that the agreement for the transfer of the undertaking could not be given effect. The vendor, with his particularly detailed knowledge of the transferred undertaking, would still be in a position to win back his former customers immediately after the transfer and thereby drive the undertaking out of business.

111. Similarly, in its decisions, the Commission has found that a number of restrictions were objectively necessary to implementing certain operations. Failing such restrictions, the operation in question could not be implemented or could only be implemented under more uncertain conditions, at substantially higher cost, over an appreciably longer period or with considerably less probability of success [. . .]

112. Contrary to the applicants' claim, none of the various decisions to which they refer show that the Commission carried out an analysis of competition in classifying the relevant clauses as ancillary restrictions. On the contrary, those decisions show that the Commission's analysis was relatively abstract. [. . .]

113. Where a restriction is objectively necessary to implement a main operation, it is still necessary to verify whether its duration and its material and geographic scope do not exceed what is necessary to implement that operation. If the duration or the scope of the restriction exceed what is necessary in order to implement the operation, it must be assessed separately under Article [101(3) TFEU] [. . .]

114. Lastly, it must be observed that, inasmuch as the assessment of the ancillary nature of a particular agreement in relation to a main operation entails complex

economic assessments by the Commission, judicial review of that assessment is limited to verifying whether the relevant procedural rules have been complied with, whether the statement of the reasons for the decision is adequate, whether the facts have been accurately stated and whether there has been a manifest error of appraisal or misuse of powers [. . .]

The consequences of classification as an ancillary restriction

115. If it is established that a restriction is directly related and necessary to achieving a main operation, the compatibility of that restriction with the competition rules must be examined with that of the main operation.

116. Thus, if the main operation does not fall within the scope of the prohibition laid down in Article [101(1) TFEU], the same holds for the restrictions directly related and necessary for that operation [. . .]. If, on the other hand, the main operation is a restriction within the meaning of Article [101(1)] but benefits from an exemption under Article [101(3) TFEU], that exemption also covers those ancillary restrictions.

117. Moreover, where the restrictions are directly related and necessary to a concentration [. . .] it follows [. . .] that those restrictions are covered by the Commission's decision declaring the operation compatible with the common market.

Classification of the exclusivity clause as an ancillary restriction

118. It is necessary to examine, in the light of the principles set out in paragraphs 103 to 114 above, whether in the present case the Commission committed a manifest error of assessment in not classifying the exclusivity clause as a restriction that was ancillary to the creation of TPS.

119. The applicants submit that the exclusivity clause is ancillary to the creation of TPS as the clause is indispensable to allow TPS to penetrate the pay-TV market in France because TPS does not enjoy any exclusive rights to films and sporting events of the first rank.

120. It must, however, be observed, first of all, that the fact that the exclusivity clause would be necessary to allow TPS to establish itself on a long-term basis on that market it is not relevant to the classification of that clause as an ancillary restriction.

121. As has been set out in paragraph 106 above, such considerations, relating to the indispensable nature of the restriction in the light of the competitive situation on the relevant market, are not part of an analysis of the ancillary nature of the restrictions. They can be taken into account only in the framework of Article [101(30 TFEU].

122. Next, it must be observed that although, in the present case, the applicants have been able to establish to the requisite legal standard that the exclusivity clause was directly related to the establishment of TPS, they have not, on the other hand, shown that the exclusive broadcasting of the general-interest channels was objectively necessary for that operation. As the Commission has rightly stated, a company in the pay-TV sector can be launched in France without having exclusive rights to the general-interest channels. That is the situation for CanalSatellite and AB-Sat, the two other operators on that market.

123. Even if the exclusivity clause was objectively necessary for the creation of TPS, the Commission did not commit a manifest error of assessment in taking the view that this restriction was not proportionate to that objective.

124. The exclusivity clause is for an initial period of 10 years. As the Commission [states] [. . .] such a period is deemed excessive as TPS [has] to establish itself on

the market before the end of that period. It is quite probable that the competitive disadvantage of TPS (principally with regard to access to exclusive rights to films and sporting events) will diminish over time [. . .]. It cannot, therefore, be ruled out that the exclusive broadcasting of the general-interest channels, although initially intended to strengthen the competitive position of TPS on the pay-TV market might ultimately allow it, after some years, to eliminate competition on that market.

125. Moreover, the exclusivity clause is also disproportionate in so far as its effect is to deprive TPS' actual and potential competitors of any access to the programmes that are considered attractive by a large number of French television viewers [. . .]. This excessiveness of the commitment is also reinforced by the existence of shadow zones. The television viewers living in those zones who wish to subscribe to a pay-TV company which also broadcasts the general-interest channels can turn only to TPS.

126. It must therefore be held that the Commission did not commit a manifest error of assessment in not classifying the exclusivity clause as a restriction that was ancillary to the creation of TPS.

127. That limb of the applicants' argument must, therefore, be rejected. [. . .]

130. It is clear from point 101 of the contested decision that the main reason why the Commission refused to classify the clause as an ancillary restriction was that it had a negative impact on the situation of third parties over quite a long period.

131. The applicants, despite having the burden of proof in that regard, have not adduced any evidence to invalidate that assessment.

132. They merely assert that on account of the exclusivity policy operated by CanalSatellite, the special-interest channels operated or created by them are the only channels to which TPS has access, so that the clause at issue is indispensable for its survival. Even accepting that such an assertion is correct, a consideration of that kind relating to the competitive situation of TPS cannot be taken into account for the purpose of classifying that clause as an ancillary restriction. As explained in paragraphs 107 to 112 above, the objectively necessary nature of the clause is established without reference to the competitive situation.

133. Furthermore, as the market for the operation of special-interest channels is enjoying rapid growth [. . .], the Commission did not commit a manifest error of assessment in taking the view that the obligation on the shareholders of TPS, for a period of 10 years, to offer their special-interest channels first to TPS exceeded what was necessary for the creation of TPS.

134. Finally, as the Commission has correctly submitted, the applicants are wrong in referring to the decisions in *Cégétel* and *Télécom développement* inasmuch as those decisions relate to different factual situations. Thus, the situation of TPS cannot be compared to that of a new entrant on a market dominated by a company with a long-standing monopoly and which requires access to essential infrastructure. Canal+ does not enjoy a long-standing monopoly on the market for the operation of the special-interest channels and entry onto that market does not require access to essential infrastructure. Furthermore, in the *Cégétel* and *Télécom développement* decisions, the effect of the clauses considered was not to deprive third-parties of any possibility of access to the services of the shareholders. It was merely a question of preferential treatment.

The CJEU continued by applying similar rules to the provisions about special interest channels.

NOTES AND QUESTIONS ON MÉTROPOLE III

1. What is the 'main operation' to which the restrictions of competition are 'ancillary'? Is this the establishment, that is the creation, of the joint venture TPS, or is it also its efficient (that is profitable) operation?
2. (Paragraphs 74–9) Did the CJEU balance the pro and anti-competitive effects in *Société Technique Minière* and *Remia*?
3. (Paragraph 105) How direct need the link be? Is the chain of causation broken by the protection of risky investment? The equivalent rule in the US refers to the ancillary restriction being 'reasonably necessary' for the joint venture to be viable.
4. (Paragraphs 107, 120) When is necessity not objective? Is there a distinction between provisions without which such classes of transactions would not be viable, and provisions that may be needed taking into account the size and risk of a particular transaction? Does Article 101 TFEU require firms to adopt the clauses usual in that class of transactions?
5. (Paragraph 131) Contrast with *European Night Services.*[232] Note that by virtue of Article 2 of Regulation 1/2003 the burden of proof under Article 101(3) is on the person claiming legality. On whom falls the burden in relation to ancillary restraints?

6.3.4.1.3. MasterCard v Commission

Case C-382/12P, *MasterCard Inc and Others v European Commission*, ECLI:EU:C:2014:2201

In a decision adopted in 2007, the Commission found that MasterCard's multilateral interchange fees (MIF) for cross-border payment card transactions within the European Economic Area (EEA) violated Article 101 TFEU,[233] the case being as old as 1992 when British retailers first complained about being overcharged for cross-border card transactions. MasterCard operates an 'open' (or 'four-part') payment card system, which unlike the 'closed' (or 'three-part') system owned by American Express (Amex) enables different financial institutions to participate in it under a common card trade-mark. Hence, this scheme is open for other members to join in the competition (creating competition within the brand, eg Visa, MasterCard). The system entails three levels of interaction: the first between the owner of the system and the affiliated banks; the second between the issuing banks (or issuers) and the acquiring banks (or acquirers); and the third between those banks and their respective customers, on one side of the market the cardholders and, on the other side, the merchants. The owner of the system has the function of coordinating the practices of the affiliated banks and may act as a network operator, providing an IT infrastructure for the transmission of the electronic messages that close the transaction, including invoicing fees and charges to banks for their participation in the system as well as fees for processing card payments. In the absence of

[232] Joined Cases T-374–5, 384 & 388/94 *European Night Services and Others v Commission* [1998] II–3141. See further Section 7.3.2.2.

[233] *MasterCard* (Case COMP/34.579), *EuroCommerce* (Case COMP/36.518), *Commercial Cards* (Case COMP/38.580) Commission Decision (2007), available at http://ec.europa.eu/competition/antitrust/cases/dec_docs/34579/34579_1889_2.pdf.

any bilateral agreement between the acquiring bank and the issuing bank, or of interchange fees set collectively at national level, MasterCard sets the MIFs which apply by default within the EEA or the euro area. The interchange fee is a charge levied on each payment at a retail outlet when the payment is processed. These fees are paid by the acquiring banks (merchants' banks) to the issuing banks (the cardholders' banks) for any transaction carried out by Master cards (under the MasterCard or Maestro brand) between Member States of the EEA or the euro area. Interchange fees for payments partly cover the costs of the issuing bank, in particular the expenses for infrastructure and operation (eg clearing, international network connections), investment in collective security measures, payment guarantee, and coverage of the risk of fraud). In principle, the interchange fees are included in full in the merchant service charges (MSC), which are the fees invoiced by the acquiring banks to merchants. The MSC may include all or part of the interchange fee and pay for remote collection, incoming payment, administration of accounts, etc. MSCs are freely negotiated between the merchant and its bank (acquiring bank) and may be adjusted according to the volume of activity, the risk, the extent of services provided, etc. The MIFs are a mechanism balancing cardholder and merchant demand in order to allocate the cost of delivering the service between the system's issuers and acquirer (see Figure 6.1).

The Commission considered that MasterCard's decision to set the MIFs was a decision of association of undertakings, which restricted price competition between banks and inflated the base on which acquiring banks set charges, thus establishing a price floor under the merchant fee. The Commission found that the absence of a MIF operating as a fall-back fee would not have made a card payment impossible, for instance if the cardholder made a purchase at

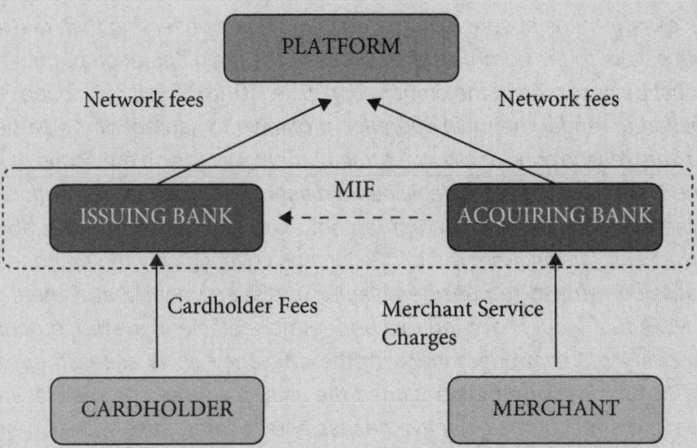

Figure 6.1. MIFs[a]

[a] The figure represents the classic four-party scheme, as this is operated by MasterCard and Visa. One should however note the existence of the 'closed' 'three-party' scheme, such as that operated by Amex or the Diners Club. In 'three-party' schemes the operator deals directly with cardholders and merchants. Hence, the issuer (having the relationship with the cardholder) and the acquirer (having the relationship with the merchant) is the same entity (operator). The operator issues the cards to cardholders, who pay the operator/issuer a fee and then also charges the merchant a fee. When the cardholder uses his card to buy goods or services from the merchant, the merchant is paid by the operator, the price less the merchant fee. The operator recovers the full price of the goods or services from the cardholder, thus clearing the transaction. In this context, there is no competition within the brand, but with other brands of payment system. For an analysis of the economics of the payment systems and their competition law implications, see J Tirole, 'Payment Card Regulation and the Use of Economic Analysis in Antitrust' (2011) 7(1) *Competition Policy Int'l* 137.

a merchant whose acquiring bank had no agreement with his issuing bank, as interchange fees were not necessary and the scheme could have functioned on the basis of the remuneration of the issuing bank by their cardholders and of the acquiring bank by the merchant. The Commission examined the competitive process that would have developed on the acquiring market in the absence of the MIF and concluded that, in the absence of the MIF and with a prohibition on ex post *pricing, the prices charged to merchants by acquirers 'would only be set taking into account the acquirer's individual marginal cost and his mark up', noting that '[t]he uncertainty of each individual acquirer about the level of interchange fees which competitors bilaterally agree to pay to issuers would exercise a constraint on acquirers', so that '[i]n the long run this process can be expected to lead to the establishment of inter-bank claims and debts at the face value of the payment, that is without deducting any interchange fees'.*[234] *According to the Commission, 'in the absence of a [MIF] the prices set by acquiring banks would be lower to the benefit of merchants and subsequent purchasers'.*[235] *Cash payers would not also have to share the cost of card transactions. The Commission did not find it important to qualify in a definitive way the practice as a restriction of competition by object or by effect, as it could clearly be established that it had anti-competitive effects.*

The Commission also took the view that the MIF could not qualify as legitimate ancillary restrictions, as they were not objectively necessary for the operation of an open payment card scheme. As previously mentioned, the scheme could function simply on the basis of the remuneration of issuing banks by cardholders, of acquiring banks by merchants, and of the owner of the scheme by the fees paid by the issuing and acquiring banks. Citing Métropole v Commission, Gottrup-Klim, *and* Wouters, *the Commission adopted a restrictive view of the objective necessity test of the ancillary restraints doctrine under Article 101(1) TFEU, noting that '[it] does not involve an assessment of whether the main operation would be commercially less successful in the absence of the restraint'*[236] *and observing that 'restrictive clauses desirable with a view to the commercial success of the main operation but not necessary for its viability must be assessed in the context of Article [101(3) TFEU]'.*[237] *Indeed, '[i]f a restraint is merely needed to render the main operation profitable for (some) of the parties involved, it is not for that very reason and "ancillary restraint" that falls outside the scope of Article [101(1) TFEU]'.*[238] *The Commission thus establishes a distinction between 'restrictions that are necessary for the implementation of an agreement and those which are desirable in terms of commercial success', the ancillary restraints doctrine covering only the first ones.*[239]

The Commission refused to consider MasterCard's argument that if there were default solutions to MIFs that would have led to a better (more efficient) system outcome than conflating the ancillary restraints doctrine with the efficiency gains assessment under Article 101(3) TFEU. The Commission thus excluded the analysis of the commercial success of the operation from the ambit of the objective necessity test. Interestingly, the Commission does not only cite Métropole v Commission *for this proposition, but also O2 (a counterfactual assessment case), observing that the consideration of whether the potentially restrictive agreement was 'indispensable/necessary' for O2 to enter the 3G market was 'another application of a pure objective necessity test, not a test of 'unchanged difficulty' or even of 'less efficiency'.*[240] *The Commission examined whether the restrictions were objectively necessary for the implementation of the main operation, which was the co-operation of banks in an open payment card scheme.*[241] *The Commission considered that MIFs were not objectively necessary for the establishment of an open payment system, as if there were no MIFs, the prices banks charge their customers will be established through competition rather than through*

[234] Ibid, paras 458–60. [235] Ibid, para 664. [236] Ibid, para 526. [237] Ibid, para 527.
[238] Ibid, para 525. [239] Ibid. [240] Ibid, para 546. [241] Ibid, para 547.

a multilateral agreement. The Commission noted the existence of a number of successful payment systems which are smaller than MasterCard and viable without MIF plan, which provided evidence that MIFs were not objectively necessary.[242] *The Commission also noted that in the absence of MIFs issuing banks will not raise cardholders' fees to the level that demand was insufficient for the viability of the scheme. The Commission did not find that there were any efficiency gains outweighing the anti-competitive effects in this case, under Article 101(3) TFEU. On appeal, the General Court upheld the Commission's decision, with regard to the objective necessity of the MIFs.*[243] *Mastercard appealed to the CJEU.*

89. It is apparent from the case-law of the Court of Justice that if a given operation or activity is not covered by the prohibition rule laid down in Article [101(1) TFEU], owing to its neutrality or positive effect in terms of competition, a restriction of the commercial autonomy of one or more of the participants in that operation or activity is not covered by that prohibition rule either if that restriction is objectively necessary to the implementation of that operation or that activity and proportionate to the objectives of one or the other [. . .]

90. Where it is not possible to dissociate such a restriction from the main operation or activity without jeopardising its existence and aims, it is necessary to examine the compatibility of that restriction with Article [101 TFEU] in conjunction with the compatibility of the main operation or activity to which it is ancillary, even though, taken in isolation, such a restriction may appear on the face of it to be covered by the prohibition rule in Article [101 TFEU].

91. Where it is a matter of determining whether an anti-competitive restriction can escape the prohibition laid down in Article [101 TFEU] because it is ancillary to a main operation that is not anti-competitive in nature, it is necessary to inquire whether that operation would be impossible to carry out in the absence of the restriction in question. Contrary to what the appellants claim, the fact that that operation is simply more difficult to implement or even less profitable without the restriction concerned cannot be deemed to give that restriction the 'objective necessity' required in order for it to be classified as ancillary. Such an interpretation would effectively extend that concept to restrictions which are not strictly indispensable to the implementation of the main operation. Such an outcome would undermine the effectiveness of the prohibition laid down in Article [101(1) TFEU].

92. However, that interpretation does not mean that there has been an amalgamation of, on the one hand, the conditions laid down by the case-law for the classification—for the purposes of the application of Article [101(1) TFEU]—of a restriction as ancillary, and, on the other hand, the criterion of the indispensability required under Article [101(3) TFEU] in order for a prohibited restriction to be exempted.

93. In that regard, suffice it to note that those two provisions have different objectives and that the latter criterion relates to the issue whether coordination between undertakings that is liable to have an appreciable adverse impact on the parameters of competition, such as the price, the quantity and quality of the goods or services, which is therefore covered by the prohibition rule laid down in Article [101(1) TFEU], can none the less, in the context of Article [101(3) TFEU], be considered indispensable to the improvement of production or distribution or to the promotion of technical or economic

242 Ibid, paras 555–647.

243 Case T-111/08, *MasterCard, Inc and Others v European Commission*, ECLI:EU:T:2012:260, paras 77–121 (objective necessity).

progress, while allowing consumers a fair share of the resulting benefits. By contrast, as is apparent from paragraphs 89 and 90 of the present judgment, the objective necessity test referred to in those paragraphs concerns the question whether, in the absence of a given restriction of commercial autonomy, a main operation or activity which is not caught by the prohibition laid down in Article [101(1) TFEU] and to which that restriction is secondary, is likely not to be implemented or not to proceed.

94. In ruling, in paragraph 89 of the judgment under appeal, that '[o]nly those restrictions which are necessary in order for the main operation to be able to function in any event may be regarded as falling within the scope of the theory of ancillary restrictions', and in concluding, in paragraph 90 of the judgment under appeal, that 'the fact that the absence of the MIF may have adverse consequences for the functioning of the MasterCard system does not, in itself, mean that the MIF must be regarded as being objectively necessary, if it is apparent from an examination of the MasterCard system in its economic and legal context that it is still capable of functioning without it', the General Court did not, therefore, err in law. [. . .]

The appellants also complained that the General Court had authorized the Commission to rely on a 'counterfactual hypothesis'—the prohibition of ex post *pricing—which would never in fact occur. They noted that the Commission's analysis was very different from an assessment of what would actually occur if the MIF were eliminated and amounted to the insertion of a fictional condition in the Commission's analysis, accepted by the GC—the prohibition of* ex post *pricing, which also assumed some degree of regulatory intervention. Hence, the appellants argued that the Commission did not assess the effects of the MIF on competition by comparison with what would actually occur in their absence. In essence, the argument was that the Commission had performed the wrong counterfactual test.*

107. It must be noted in that regard that, as is apparent from paragraphs 89 and 90 of the present judgment, in the context of the assessment, for the purposes of the application of Article [101(1) TFEU], of the ancillary nature of a given restriction of commercial autonomy in relation to a main operation or activity, it is necessary to consider not only whether that restriction is necessary for the implementation of the main operation or activity, but also whether that restriction is proportionate to the underlying objectives of that operation or activity.

108. It should be pointed out that, irrespective of the context or aim in relation to which a counterfactual hypothesis is used, it is important that that hypothesis is appropriate to the issue it is supposed to clarify and that the assumption on which it is based is not unrealistic.

109. Accordingly, in order to contest the ancillary nature of a restriction, as referred to in paragraphs 89 and 90 of the present judgment, the Commission may rely on the existence of realistic alternatives that are less restrictive of competition than the restriction at issue.

110. In that regard, as is apparent from paragraph 97 of the present judgment, the appellants also submit, in essence, that the General Court wrongly failed to penalise the Commission for not having tried, in the decision at issue, to understand how competition would function in the absence both of the MIF and of the prohibition of *ex post* pricing, a prohibition which the appellants would not have chosen to adopt without a regulatory intervention.

111. However, the alternatives on which the Commission may rely in the context of the assessment of the objective necessity of a restriction are not limited to the situation that would arise in the absence of the restriction in question but may also extend

to other counterfactual hypotheses based, inter alia, on realistic situations that might arise in the absence of that restriction. The General Court was therefore correct in concluding [. . .] that the counterfactual hypothesis put forward by the Commission could be taken into account in the examination of the objective necessity of the MIF in so far as it was realistic and enabled the MasterCard system to be economically viable. [. . .]

A further criticism of the GC's judgment and of the Commission's decision was that in assessing whether a decision has a restrictive effect on competition, the Commission relied on the premise of a MasterCard system operating without a MIF, on the basis of a rule prohibiting ex post *pricing, thus employing the same 'counterfactual hypothesis' it applied in order to examine whether the MIF could be regarded as an ancillary restriction. The CJEU disagreed with the GC on this point.*

163. [. . .] [T]he same 'counterfactual hypothesis' is not necessarily appropriate to conceptually distinct issues. Where it is a matter of establishing whether the MIF have restrictive effects on competition, the question whether, without those fees, but by the effect of prohibiting *ex post* pricing, an open payment system such as the MasterCard system could remain viable is not, in itself, decisive.

164. By contrast, the Court should, to that end, assess the impact of the setting of the MIF on the parameters of competition, such as the price, the quantity and quality of the goods or services. Accordingly, it is necessary, in accordance with the settled case-law [. . .] to assess the competition in question within the actual context in which it would occur in the absence of those fees. [. . .]

166. [. . .] [T]he scenario envisaged on the basis of the hypothesis that the coordination arrangements in question are absent must be realistic. From that perspective, it is permissible, where appropriate, to take account of the likely developments that would occur on the market in the absence of those arrangements.

167. In the present case, however, the General Court did not in any way address the likelihood, or even plausibility, of the prohibition of *ex post* pricing if there were no MIF, in the context of its analysis of the restrictive effects of those fees. In particular, it did not, as required by the case-law [. . .] address the issue as to how—taking into account in particular the obligations to which merchants and acquiring banks are subject under the Honour All Cards Rule, which is not the subject of the decision at issue—the issuing banks could be encouraged, in the absence of MIF, to refrain from demanding fees for the settlement of bank card transactions.

168. Admittedly, [. . .] the General Court was not obliged, in the context of the examination of the ancillary nature—as referred to in paragraphs 89 and 90 of the present judgment—of the MIF, to examine whether it was likely that the prohibition of *ex post* pricing would occur in the absence of such fees. Nevertheless, [. . .] the situation is different in the separate context of establishing whether the MIF have restrictive effects on competition.

169. In those circumstances, it is correctly submitted in the present case that, in relying on the single criterion of economic viability [. . .] to justify taking into consideration the prohibition of *ex post* pricing in the context of its analysis of the effects of the MIF on competition, and by failing therefore to explain in the context of that analysis whether it was likely that such a prohibition would occur in the absence of MIF otherwise than by means of a regulatory intervention, the General Court made an error of law.

170. It should be noted, however, that if the grounds of a decision of the General Court disclose an infringement of EU law but its operative part is shown to be well founded on

other legal grounds, such infringement is not one that should bring about the annulment of that decision and it is appropriate to carry out a substitution of grounds [. . .].

171. That is the case here. The appellants' arguments before the General Court in relation to the objective necessity of the MIF, as described in paragraph 94 of the judgment under appeal, which is not contested in the present appeal, were based in essence on the claim that, without MIF, acquirers would be put at the mercy of issuers, who would be able to determine the level of the interchange fee unilaterally, since merchants and acquirers would be bound to accept the transaction.

172. [. . .] [T]he General Court correctly considered [. . .] that the Commission was fully entitled to conclude that 'the possibility that some issuing banks might hold up acquirers who are bound by the [Honour All Cards Rule] could be solved by a network rule that is less restrictive of competition than MasterCard's current solution that, by default, a certain level of interchange fees applies. The alternative solution would be a rule that imposes a prohibition on *ex post* pricing on the banks in the absence of a bilateral agreement between them'.

173. It follows from this that [. . .] the only other option presenting itself at first instance as enabling the MasterCard system to operate without MIF was in fact the hypothesis of a system operating solely on the basis of a prohibition of *ex post* pricing. In those circumstances, that prohibition may be regarded as a 'counterfactual hypothesis' that is not only economically viable in the context of the MasterCard system but also plausible or indeed likely, given that there is nothing in the judgment under appeal to suggest, and it is common ground, that it was not in any way claimed before the General Court that MasterCard would have preferred to let its system collapse rather than adopt the other solution, that is to say, the prohibition of *ex post* pricing.

174. Consequently, even though the General Court wrongly considered that the economic viability of the prohibition of *ex post* pricing in the context of the MasterCard system was sufficient, by itself, to justify taking that prohibition into consideration in the analysis of the effects of the MIF on competition, in the circumstances of the present case, as described in the judgment under appeal, the General Court was entitled to rely in its analysis of the restrictive effects of the MIF on the same 'counterfactual hypothesis' it had used in the context of its analysis of the objective necessity of those fees, albeit for reasons other than those stated by the General Court [. . .]

The appellants also criticized the GC's assessment of anti-competitive effects, for having failed to consider the two-sided nature of the payment system.

177. As regards the argument [. . .] by which LBG accuses the General Court of having ruled the two-sided nature of the system to be relevant only in the context of Article [101(3)], it should be borne in mind that [. . .] the General Court was obliged to satisfy itself that the Commission had examined the alleged restriction of competition within its actual context. In order to determine whether coordination between undertakings must be considered to be prohibited by reason of the distortion of competition which it creates, it is necessary, according to the case-law [. . .] to take into account any factor that is relevant, having regard, in particular, to the nature of the services concerned, as well as the real conditions of the functioning and the structure of the markets, in relation to the economic or legal context in which that coordination occurs, regardless of whether or not such a factor concerns the relevant market. [. . .]

179. In those circumstances, the economic and legal context of the coordination concerned includes [. . .] the two-sided nature of MasterCard's open payment system, particularly since it is undisputed that there is interaction between the two sides of that system [. . .].

However, the CJEU noted that the criticism to the Commission's and the GC's failure to take the two-sided nature of the system into account framed in this case were merely highlighting the economic advantages that flow from the MIF and were not just arguing the need to consider the two-sided nature of the system. The CJEU rejected this criticism by observing that such advantages can be considered only in the context of Article 101(3) TFEU.

The CJEU also explored the distinction between the analysis of the restrictions of competition under Article 101(3) TFEU from the application of the ancillary restraints doctrine under Article 101(1) TFEU.

> 230. The Court must reject at the outset the argument that the General Court wrongly ignored the advantages to cardholders resulting from the MasterCard scheme. It will be recalled that any decision by an association of undertakings which proves to be contrary to the provisions of Article [101(1) TFEU] may be exempted under Article [101(3) TFEU] only if it satisfies the conditions in that provision, including the condition that it contribute to improving the production or distribution of goods or to promoting technical or economic progress [. . .]. Furthermore, as is apparent from paragraphs 89 and 90 of the present judgment, where it is not possible to dissociate a decision by an association of undertakings from the main operation or activity with which it is associated without jeopardising its existence and aims, it is appropriate to examine the compatibility of that decision with Article [101 TFEU] in conjunction with the compatibility of the main operation or activity to which it is ancillary.
>
> 231. By contrast, where it is established that such a decision is not objectively necessary to the implementation of a given operation or activity, only the objective advantages resulting specifically from that decision may be taken into account in the context of Article [101(3) TFEU].
>
> 232. In the present case, as is apparent from paragraphs 78 to 121 of the present judgment, it was open to the General Court to find in paragraph 120 of the judgment under appeal, without erring in law, that the MIF were not objectively necessary for the operation of the MasterCard system. In the light of that conclusion, the General Court also correctly concluded, in paragraph 207 of that judgment, that analysis of the first condition laid down in Article [101(3) TFEU] called for an examination of the appreciable objective advantages arising specifically from the MIF and not from the MasterCard system as a whole. It follows from this that the argument that the General Court wrongly ignored the advantages to cardholders resulting from the MasterCard scheme cannot be accepted. [. . .]

The CJEU's judgment concerned Mastercard's MIFs for cross-border transactions only and did not concern MIFs set at the national level. Note that the judgment provided momentum for the European Parliament and the European Council, following a proposal by the Commission in 2013, to adopt in 2015 a Regulation on interchange fees for card-based payment transactions, which introduces a cap on the level of interchange fees at 0.2 per cent for debit card payments and 0.3 per cent for credit card payments (cross-border or national).[244] As it is recognized at Recitals 10 and 14 of this Regulation, '[i]n addition to a consistent application of the competition rules to interchange fees, regulating such fees would improve the functioning of the internal market and contribute to reducing transaction costs for consumers', the Regulation being without prejudice to the application of Union and national competition rules.

244 Regulation (EU) 2015/751 of the European Parliament and of the Council of 29 April 2015 on interchange fees for card-based payment transactions [2015] OJ L 123/1, Articles 3–4.

6.3.4.1.4. Lundbeck v Commission

The concept of ancillary restraints was also examined by the GC in Lundbeck.

Case T-472/13, *H Lundbeck A/S and Lundbeck Ltd v Commission*, ECLI:EU:T:2016:449

The applicants had argued that the Commission's Lundbeck *decision had failed to recognize that the agreements at issue (including reverse payment settlements) were necessary in order to achieve a legitimate objective.*

451. [. . .] [A]ccording to the case-law, if a given operation or activity is not covered by the prohibition rule laid down in Article 101(1) TFEU, owing to its neutrality or positive effect in terms of competition, a restriction of the commercial autonomy of one or more of the participants in that operation or activity is not covered by that prohibition rule either if that restriction is objectively necessary to the implementation of that operation or that activity and proportionate to the objectives of one or the other (see judgment of 11 September 2014 in *MasterCard and Others* v *Commission*, C-382/12 P, ECR, EU:C:2014:2201, paragraph 89 and the case-law cited).

452. Where it is not possible to dissociate such a restriction from the main operation or activity without jeopardising its existence and aims, it is necessary to examine the compatibility of that restriction with Article 101 TFEU in conjunction with the compatibility of the main operation or activity to which it is ancillary, even though, taken in isolation, such a restriction may appear on the face of it to be covered by the prohibition rule in Article 101(1) TFEU (judgment in *MasterCard and Others* v *Commission*, [. . .] [para] 90).

453. Where it is a matter of determining whether an anticompetitive restriction can escape the prohibition laid down in Article 101(1) TFEU because it is ancillary to a main operation that is not anticompetitive in nature, it is necessary to inquire whether that operation would be impossible to carry out in the absence of the restriction in question. The fact that that operation is simply more difficult to implement or even less profitable without the restriction concerned cannot be deemed to give that restriction the 'objective necessity' required in order for it to be classified as ancillary. Such an interpretation would effectively extend that concept to restrictions which are not strictly indispensable to the implementation of the main operation. Such an outcome would undermine the effectiveness of the prohibition laid down in Article 101(1) TFEU (judgment in *MasterCard and Others* v *Commission*, [. . .] [para] 91).

454. The condition that a restriction be necessary therefore implies a two-fold examination. It is necessary to establish, first, whether the restriction is objectively necessary for the implementation of the main operation and, secondly, whether it is proportionate to it (see judgment in *E.ON Ruhrgas and E.ON* v *Commission*, [. . .] [para] 64 and the case-law cited).

455. Moreover, it must be emphasised that inasmuch as the existence of a rule of reason in EU competition law cannot be upheld, it would be wrong, when classifying ancillary restrictions, to interpret the requirement for objective necessity as implying a need to weigh the pro and anticompetitive effects of an agreement (see, to that effect, judgment in *E.ON Ruhrgas and E.ON* v *Commission*, [. . .] [para] 65 and the case-law cited). [. . .]

6.3.4.1.5. F Hoffmann-La Roche Ltd and Others v Autorità Garante della Concorrenza e del Mercato

Case C-179/16, *F Hoffmann-La Roche Ltd and Others v Autorità Garante della Concorrenza e del Mercato*, ECLI:EU:C:2018:25

We have summarized the facts of this case in Section 6.3.2.3.1. One of the other issues raised in the CJEU's judgment was the possible application of the ancillary restraints doctrine, the parties arguing that in the absence of the licensing agreement, it would not have been possible for Novartis to enter the relevant market within a short space of time and that although the licensing agreement did not include any restrictions, the parties could reasonably have provided in that agreement that Roche would not compete with Novartis, the licensee, on the relevant market. Such restriction, according to the parties, would not fall under the scope of Article 101(1) TFEU because Roche and Novartis could not be regarded as actual or potential competitors. Citing its judgment in MasterCard the CJEU rejected these arguments.

68. [. . .] [T]he referring court asks whether, in essence, Article 101(1) TFEU must be interpreted as meaning that any restrictions of competition agreed between the parties to a licensing agreement fall outside the scope of application of the first paragraph of that article even though the licensing agreement does not envisage any such restrictions on the ground that they are ancillary to that agreement.

69. In that regard, it is apparent from the case-law of the Court that if a given operation or activity is not covered by the prohibition laid down in Article 101(1) TFEU, owing to its neutrality or positive effects in terms of competition, a restriction of the commercial autonomy of one or more of the participants in that operation or activity is not covered by that prohibition either if that restriction is objectively necessary to the implementation of that operation or that activity and is proportionate to the objectives of one or the other [. . .].

70. Where it is not possible to dissociate such a restriction from the main operation or activity without jeopardising its existence and aims, it is necessary to examine the compatibility of that restriction with Article 101 TFEU in conjunction with the compatibility of the main operation or activity to which it is ancillary, even though, taken in isolation, such a restriction may appear on the face of it to be covered by the prohibition rule in Article 101(1) TFEU [. . .].

71. Where it is a matter of determining whether a restriction can escape the prohibition laid down in Article 101(1) TFEU because it is ancillary to a main operation that is not anticompetitive in nature, it is necessary to inquire whether that operation would be impossible to carry out in the absence of the restriction in question. The fact that that operation is simply more difficult to implement or even less profitable without the restriction concerned cannot be deemed to give that restriction the objective necessity required in order for it to be classified as ancillary. Such an interpretation would effectively extend that concept to restrictions which are not strictly indispensable to the implementation of the main operation. Such an outcome would undermine the effectiveness of the prohibition laid down in Article 101(1) TFEU [. . .].

72. In the present case, it should be noted that the conduct described in the AGCM's decision, which concerns the dissemination of allegedly misleading information relating to adverse reactions to Avastin where that product is administered for the treatment of eye diseases, was not designed to restrict the commercial autonomy of the parties to the licensing agreement regarding Lucentis but rather the conduct of third parties, in

particular healthcare professionals, with a view to preventing the use of Avastin for that type of treatment from interfering with the use of Lucentis for that same purpose.

73. Furthermore, while, admittedly, the file submitted to the Court contains no information that is capable of casting doubt on the favourable, or at least neutral, nature, in terms of competition, of the licence agreement concluded between Genentech and Novartis, it cannot be held that conduct such as that described in the preceding paragraph was objectively necessary for the implementation of the agreement. Indeed, that conduct was agreed upon several years after the agreement was concluded, and not in the agreement itself or upon its conclusion, with a view to eliminating the substitutability between the use of Avastin and that of Lucentis for the purpose of treating eye diseases, arising in particular from the prescribing practices of doctors.

74. The fact that the conduct penalised in the AGCM's decision was designed to reduce the use of Avastin and to increase the use of Lucentis so as to render more profitable the exploitation by Novartis of the technology rights over Lucentis granted to it by Genentech cannot mean, in the light of the case law [. . .] that that conduct is to be regarded as objectively necessary for the implementation of the licensing agreement at issue.

6.3.4.1.6. The UK MIFs cases: The various dimensions of the counterfactual in competition law assessment

Of particular interest for the application of the counterfactual test and the ancillary restraints doctrine are some recent judgments handed down by the CAT in *Sainsbury's v MasterCard.*[245] and the UK High Court in various actions brought by various large retailers (Asda, Arcadia, Next, B&Q, Comet, New Look, Iceland, Argos, WM Morrisons, and Debenhams) to claim damages from MasterCard[246] and Visa[247] for breach of EU and UK competition law.[248] The High Court in the *MasterCard* and *Visa* cases, and the CAT, adopted inconsistent approaches with regard to the lawfulness of MIF's under Article 101(1) TFEU, the interpretation of the counterfactual test and the ancillary restraints doctrine, and their application in these cases.[249] A recent judgment of the Court of Appeal, dealing with the three linked cases and involving supermarkets that brought claims against MasterCard and Visa held that in setting default multilateral interchange fees (MIFs) MasterCard and Visa have infringed Article 101(1) TFEU, thus allowing the merchants' appeals on this issue.[250] The Court of Appeal also remitted all three cases for reconsideration of the Article 101(3) TFEU exemption issue and for the evaluation of the quantum of damages.

Determining the proper counterfactual was an important issue in all cases.

In *Asda Stores Ltd & Others v MasterCard,*[251] the claimants alleged that MasterCard's EEA, UK, and Irish MIFs breached Article 101(1) TFEU and Chapter I CA98. The High Court

245 *Sainsbury's v MasterCard* [2016] CAT 11.

246 *Asda Stores Ltd & Others v Mastercard* [2017] EWHC 93 (Comm).

247 *Sainsbury's vs Visa* [2017] EWHC 3047 (Comm).

248 For a discussion, see C Veljanovski, 'Credit Cards, Counterfactuals and Antitrust Damages: The UK MasterCard Litigations' (2018) 9(3) *J European Competition L & Practice* 146.

249 They also took inconsistent approaches as to the implementation of Article 101(3) TFEU. See our analysis in Section 6.4.6.1.

250 *Sainsbury's v Mastercard / Arcadia v Mastercard / Sainsbury's v Visa* [2018] EWCA 1536 (Civ), para 74. The Court of Appeal heard together all three appeals relating to MIFs: one from the CAT which was decided in *Sainsbury's v MasterCard* [2016] CAT 1, the second was the High Court judgment in *Asda & Others v Mastercard* [2017] EWHC 93 (Comm) and the third one High Court judgment in *Sainsbury's v Visa* [2017] EWHC 3047 (Comm).

251 *Asda & Others v Mastercard* [2017] EWHC 93 (Comm).

focused on two uses of the counterfactual test with which it compared the specific restriction of competition under examination in order to assess if it fell under Article 101(1).

The first type is the 'restriction counterfactual', 'the appropriate counterfactual hypothesis against which to test whether the MIFs were a restriction on competition in the acquiring market compared with the position which would have obtained in such hypothetical counterfactual circumstances'.[252] According to the High Court, a 'restriction counterfactual must be such as *would be likely* to occur in the absence of the impugned agreement or practice and must be *realistic* [. . .]. In this respect, it is permissible, where appropriate, to take account of the likely developments that would occur on the market in the absence of the agreement in question.'[253]

The second type is the 'ancillary restraints counterfactual'. This is an essential step in the application of the ancillary restraints doctrine, requiring 'the court to consider counterfactual circumstances in which the ancillary restraint does not exist, in order to determine whether it is objectively necessary for the existence of the main operation compared with the potential existence of the main operation in the counterfactual circumstances'[254]. Referring to the CJEU's judgment in *MasterCard*, the High Court noted that:

> [T]he test for choosing the ancillary restraint counterfactual is slightly different from that which determines choice of the restriction counterfactual. The same counterfactual is not necessarily appropriate for conceptually distinct issues [. . .]. The ancillary restraint counterfactual can be one which *might* arise in the absence of the restraint, although it must be *realistic* [. . .].
>
> Thus, the test for choosing the counterfactual for the purposes of the ancillary restraint doctrine provides a lower threshold for the regulator or other person complaining of a restraint than the test for choosing the counterfactual for the purposes of establishing a restriction of competition within the prohibition of Article 101(1). For the ancillary restraint doctrine, it is enough for a person complaining of infringement to point to one or more counterfactuals which *might* arise, by comparison with which the ancillary restraint is not necessary for the survival of the main operation. By contrast, in order for the prohibition in Article 101(1) to bite on the restriction, it must be a restriction on competition by comparison with a restriction counterfactual which *likely would* arise. In both cases the counterfactual must also be realistic.[255]

The High Court analysed extensively the potentially realistic counterfactuals for consideration in the specific context without paying attention to the order to examination, restriction counterfactual first and ancillary restraints counterfactual next, or the inverse, finding that, in this case, this did not make any difference as to their final determination.[256]

In determining the restriction counterfactual, the courts (the CAT, the High Court, and the Court of Appeal) had to examine if 'the schemes' rules setting default MIFs restrict competition under Article 101(1) TFEU in the acquiring market, by comparison with a counterfactual without default MIFs, such as, for instance, where the schemes' rules provide for the issuer to settle the transaction at par [. . .] (i.e. to pay the acquirer 100% of the value of the transaction)'.[257] The 'realistic' counterfactual may depend on the way the competition law problem in this case is framed. If the essence of the alleged restriction of competition is that the MIFs are set collectively, the counterfactual would be pure bilateral agreements between acquiring and issuing banks or a decentralized system. If the essence of the competition law problem is that the MIFs have been set at too high levels, then the counterfactual would be settlement at par or a zero MIF.

252 *Asda Stores Ltd & Others v Mastercard* [2017] EWHC 93 (Comm), para 42.

253 Ibid, para 43. 254 Ibid, para 46 255 Ibid, paras 46–7. 256 Ibid, para 123.

257 *Sainsbury's v Mastercard / Arcadia v Mastercard / Sainsbury's v Visa* [2018] EWCA 1536 (Civ), para 7(i).

There were various potentially realistic counterfactuals, the CAT and the High Court disagreeing as to what would have actually happened in the counterfactual world: (i) a zero MIF (which is the same as no MIF); (ii) a positive MIF but lower than the maximum putatively lawful MIF;[258] (iii) a bilateral agreement on interchange fees between issuers and acquirers.[259] Interestingly, Popplewell J did not find that bilateral agreements was a realistic scenario, although the CAT had done so in *Sainsbury's v MasterCard*, showing that it is possible that courts may diverge in assessing 'realistic' counterfactual scenarios. The CAT had indeed found that if MasterCard transactions had been settled at par, which was equivalent to setting a default MIF of zero, its rival Visa would have maintained its MIFs as close to their then level. However, this would not have led banks to abandon the MasterCard scheme in order to benefit from the higher MIFs offered by Visa, but they would have sought bilaterally to agree interchange fees with the acquirers. These would have not rejected the offer as it was not in their common long-term interest for MasterCard scheme to collapse and for Visa to become a monopolist, or, for that matter, for some valuable features of the scheme to be withdrawn because of reduced MIFs. The bilateral agreements would have led some merchants to benefit from more favourable conditions than the traditional value per transaction basis.[260]

The High Court agreed with the CAT's starting point, that the proper counterfactual was that MasterCard transactions will be settled at par, but disagreed with the CAT's conclusion that bilateral agreements would have emerged in the counterfactual. According to the High Court, the merchants would not have thought about their common long-term interest to reject any offer that would have resulted in a zero MIF, basically for two reasons: they would have only considered their own interest, fearing that had they not done so their rivals would have acquired a competitive disadvantage (the free rider argument), and also because of the quite significant number of bilateral agreements among the various (non-overlapping) issuers and acquirers, which would have to be concluded, something that was thought to be practically unrealistic. Leaving aside for the moment the first issue, Popplewell J found the second argument irrelevant when determining the restriction counterfactual, concluding that the MasterCard MIFs did amount to a restriction of competition on the acquiring market by comparison with a counterfactual of no MIF or a lower putatively lawful MIF.[261] The MIFs imposed a floor below which the merchant service charge (MSC) could not fall, because acquirers had to pay at least that much to issuers and had to recoup it from the merchants, which in turn led to higher prices charged by acquirers to merchants through the MSC than if the MIF were lower or zero. The High Court found that such a floor restricted competition because it interfered with the ability of acquirers to compete for merchants' business by offering MSCs below such floor. According to the Court, it was no different in kind from a collective agreement by manufacturers to maintain inflated wholesale prices preventing wholesalers to compete on the retail market below those prices.[262]

However, Phillips J took a different perspective when assessing the compatibility of the Visa scheme with Article 101(1) TFEU, finding that Visa's UK MIFs did not restrict competition within the meaning of Article 101(1).[263] He did not follow the CAT's and Popplewell's approach in considering settlement at par as the proper restriction counterfactual, finding that a zero MIF or settlement at par counterfactual could also be considered as a 'floor', 'particularly in the context of a two-sided markets', as 'it prevents the possibility of market forces driving the MIF to a negative level (equivalent to a premium on settling the transaction

258 *Asda Stores Ltd & Others v Mastercard* [2017] EWHC 93 (Comm), para 155.
259 *Sainsbury's v MasterCard* [2016] CAT 1, paras 160–3. 260 Ibid, paras 267–9.
261 *Asda Stores Ltd & Others v Mastercard* [2017] EWHC 93 (Comm), para 156. 262 Ibid.
263 *Sainsbury's Supermarkets Ltd v Visa Europe Services LLC & Anor* [2017] EWHC 3047 (Comm), para 161.

price)'.[264] Consequently, Philips J found that there was no restriction of competition, as the counterfactual in question could have been considered as equally restrictive to competition, should the issue being the establishment of a 'floor' for MIFs.

Concerning the compatibility of the MasterCard scheme with Article 101(1) TFEU, MasterCard argued that the UK and Irish MIFs (but not the EEA MIFs) fell outside the scope of Article 101(1) under the ancillary restraint doctrine as they were objectively necessary to the main operation of the MasterCard scheme as a whole, which was neutral or positive in its competitive effect. It explained that if it had set its MIFs at zero, or even at a positive but significantly lower putatively lawful level, the MasterCard scheme would have collapsed. Indeed, assuming that Visa's MIF had been set at their actual levels and MasterCard had had a zero MIF, the issuing banks would have sought to maximise their revenues from the interchange and would have in a short period of time all switched to issuing Visa cards (the so called 'death spiral argument', which refers to the operation in reverse of the positive feedback loop of network effects, as a payment system that loses a critical mass of users eventually disappears).

Note that, as we have previously explained, MasterCard also claimed that the death spiral argument equally applied to the question of whether there was a restriction on competition falling within Article 101(1), because in operating the counterfactual test, one should take into account the fact that without the MIFs, Mastercard's scheme would not have had lower interchange fees (as it would have been driven from the market), and Visa's MIFs would also not have been lower, the potentially realistic counterfactuals in this case being the same for the restriction counterfactual as for the ancillary restraint counterfactual. With regard to the restriction counterfactual, the High Court rejected the submission that it should assume that, had MasterCard operated at a lower rate or at zero, Visa could have only lawfully operated at lower rates also, as it did not accept that the Visa and MasterCard schemes were materially identical. This was the same conclusion as that reached by the CAT on this issue, although the High Court applied different reasoning.

However, the High Court considered that the jurisprudence of the CJEU clearly established that the court can and must take account of competition facing the main operation when considering whether an ancillary restraint is objectively necessary to the main operation. Popplewell J held:

> In my judgment the CJEU jurisprudence clearly establishes that the court can and must take account of competition facing the main operation when considering whether the ancillary restraint is objectively necessary to the main operation [. . .]. In particular:
>
> (1) Paragraph 18 of *Remia* makes clear that competition is relevant. Indeed the essence of the whole passage from that decision which is quoted above is that it was the competition faced by the purchaser from the vendor which was capable of rendering a non-competition clause necessary as an ancillary restraint. [. . .] I can see no logical reason for confining the inquiry into the effect of competition to only one source of competition. If competition from the other party to the agreement is relevant in determining whether the ancillary restraint is necessary for the survival of the main operation, it is difficult to see why competition from third parties which makes it equally necessary should be irrelevant.
>
> (2) Similarly *Gottrup-Klim* makes clear at paragraph 31 that the inquiry must address 'the economic conditions prevailing on the markets concerned'. The prevailing economic conditions

264 Ibid, para 156.

will include those which are brought about by competitive activity. The whole passage quoted above illustrates that it was the competitive disadvantages which the cooperative might face if a rival cooperative were used which were capable of taking the restrictive provision outside the scope of Article 101(1).

(3) Equally the references in paragraph 111 of the CJEU *MasterCard* Judgment to 'economic viability' dictate that account is to be taken of the economic effect of competition.

(4) The General Court in *Métropole*:

(a) cited *Remia* but stated its reasoning and conclusion in terms which were simply inconsistent with that decision; and

(b) stated at paragraph 109 that the exercise is 'relatively abstract' without referring to Paragraph 31 of *Gottrup-Klim* which states in terms that the exercise is not an abstract one and makes clear that it requires examination of the actual economic circumstances.

(5) The CJEU in *MasterCard* reaffirmed that the principles were to be found in *Remia* and *Gottrup-Klim* and carefully did not approve the General Court's reliance on *Métropole* or its assertion that the competitive situation on the relevant market is not part of the analysis.

This conclusion seems to me to be consistent with the purpose of the ancillary restraint doctrine and its rationale within the framework of the control of anti-competitive activity laid down in Article 101. Where an operation has a neutral or positive competitive effect, it is not objectionable; therefore it ought not to be rendered unlawful by reason of some constituent element being a restriction if taken in isolation from the greater operation of which it forms a necessary part. If it is a necessary part of a desirable whole, the restraint 'escapes' the application of Article 101(1): it is simply outside the scope of the type of restraints which are offensive to EU competition law. The doctrine is aimed at permitting the main operation where it would be unable to function if the constituent part were removed. That involves choosing a counterfactual which is 'realistic'. If the main operation would be unable to survive in the realistic counterfactual world as a result of competition, the policy of the doctrine is engaged. There is no logic in drawing a distinction between non-survival which arises from something inherent in the structure of the main operation itself and non-survival arising from external pressures on the main operation in the realistic counterfactual world. It is clear from paragraph 111 of the *MasterCard* CJEU Judgment that the inquiry has to address whether the operation is 'economically viable'. To include economic consideration of all kinds other than competition is illogical, and moreover likely to be impractical in many cases. Further, such exclusion is inconsistent with the concept of the counterfactual being 'realistic'. An ancillary restraint counterfactual which ignores what would in fact happen when the counterfactual assumptions are made can hardly be regarded as realistic [. . .] [T]he approach dictated by *Remia* and *Gottrup-Klim* does not cut across the scheme of Articles 101(1) and 101(3) and does not require any weighing up of pro- and anti-competitive effects which is the function of Article 101(3). It requires an analysis of whether the main operation requires the ancillary restraint to be in place in order to be able to operate in the realistic counterfactual world. It starts from the premise that the main operation is desirable in competition terms because it has positive or neutral competitive effects. If that is so, the restrictive part falls outside the scope of Article 101 altogether if it is a necessary part of the desirable main operation. In deciding whether it is necessary, one examines what would happen realistically without it. If competition would kill off the main operation without the restriction being in place, the restriction is necessary for the main operation. That does not involve weighing pro and anti-competitive benefits, or making a value judgement in relation

> to such benefits; it is a binary question whether the main operation would survive at all in the realistic counterfactual world, taking account of such competitive pressures as would exist in that counterfactual world.[265]

The High Court noted that the question was not whether the scheme would have been commercially less successful, but whether it would have existed at all. The focus was upon survival of the MasterCard four party scheme in its existing form, adjusted only to change its MIF in the counterfactual world. Further, if the competitive pressures would have resulted in the extinction of the MasterCard scheme over the course of the claim period, then it was largely irrelevant how quickly that would have occurred. The High Court, therefore, concluded that in the zero MIF counterfactual world with Visa MIFs unconstrained, the MasterCard scheme would not have survived in the UK or Ireland in a materially and recognizably similar form.[266] The High Court then went on to examine the possibility for the MIF scheme outside Ireland and the UK to be exempted under Article 101(3) TFEU.[267]

As mentioned above, the CAT did not accept the 'death spiral argument' and in any case did not examine thoroughly the ancillary restraints counterfactual, simply noting that the MIFs were 'on no view inherently necessary to the MasterCard scheme which could operate better without MIFs'.[268] The 'death spiral' argument was also rejected by Phillips J finding, contrary to Popplewell J, that the CJEU case law did not require the courts to take into account competitors in both the restriction and the ancillary restraints counterfactuals.[269]

Following an appeal interjected against the High Court's judgment in *Asda Stores Ltd & Others v Mastercard*, the Court of Appeal found that the 'correct counterfactual' was a situation in which there were no MIFs and settlements between issuers and acquirers took place at par, with a prohibition on *ex post* pricing, this increasing competition between acquirers.[270] The Court of Appeal distinguished the issue of counterfactual with that of the application of the ancillary restraint doctrine, noting that the 'death spiral' argument was 'not relevant at this stage of the debate' (meaning when assessing the restriction counterfactual), and thus agreeing with Popplewell J that the rules of the MasterCard scheme providing for a default MIF in the absence of bilateral interchange fees infringed Article 101(1) TFEU.[271]

The Court of Appeal did not, however, accept Popplewell J's ancillary restraint 'death spiral' argument that led him to conclude that there was no restriction of competition for the MIF scheme in the UK and Ireland. It held, instead, that the High Court judge 'was wrong to conclude that the issue of whether, in the absence of the restriction in question, here the default MIF, the MasterCard scheme would survive in view of the competition from Visa, was one which could be considered under the ancillary restraint doctrine under article 101(1); and he was also wrong to hold that Métropole is contrary to other EU jurisprudence and had been implicitly disapproved by the CJEU's decision in MasterCard'.[272]

The Court of Appeal gave the following explanation for reaching this conclusion.

265 Ibid, paras 176–8. 266 Ibid, para 253. 267 See our analysis in Section 6.4.6.

268 *Sainsbury's v MasterCard* [2016] CAT 1, para 279.

269 *Sainsbury's Supermarkets Ltd v Visa Europe Services LLC & Anor* [2017] EWHC 3047 (Comm), paras 181–91.

270 *Sainsbury's v Mastercard / Arcadia v Mastercard / Sainsbury's v Visa* [2018] EWCA 1536 (Civ), para 185.

271 Ibid, paras 188 and 190. 272 Ibid, para 74.

Sainsbury's v Mastercard / Arcadia v Mastercard / Sainsbury's v Visa
[2018] EWCA 1536 (Civ)

67. We do not consider that there is anything in the judgment of the [General Court] in *Metropole* [Case T-112/99, *Métropole Télévision (M6) and Others v Commission* (*Metropole III*) [2002] ECR II–2459] that is inconsistent with the decisions of the CJEU in *Remia* [Case 42/84, *Remia BV and Verenigde Bedrijven Nutricia v Commission* [1985] ECR 2545] and *Gottrup-Klim*. So far as the decisions of the European Courts in *MasterCard* are concerned, we have already noted that the General Court approved the approach of the Court in *Métropole*. The only difference was that, whereas the Court in *Métropole* considered that it was sufficient for the main operation to be difficult to operate without the restriction, the General Court considered that, to be objectively necessary, the main operation had to be incapable of functioning without the restriction.

68. It was that narrow approach of the General Court to the objective necessity test which was the subject of one part of the appeal by MasterCard to the CJEU. As appears from [86] of the CJEU's decision, MasterCard relied upon [109] of *Métropole* as a correct statement of the law, contending that in limiting objective necessity to where it was impossible to operate the main operation, as opposed to where it was either difficult or impossible, the General Court had applied an incomplete test for objective necessity, which it had effectively amalgamated with the criterion of indispensability in the third condition of Article 101(3).

69. The CJEU said at [91] that the enquiry under the ancillary restraint doctrine is: 'whether that operation would be impossible to carry out in the absence of the restriction in question'. The CJEU then rejected at [92] the suggestion that there had been an amalgamation by the General Court of the ancillary restraint exception under article 101(1) with the criterion of indispensability under article 101(3).

Concerning the death spiral argument the Court of Appeal examined the implementation in this case of the legal principles of the ancillary restraint doctrine. It found that on that basis, Popplewell J was wrong to conclude that the issue of whether, in the absence of the default MIF, the MasterCard scheme would survive in view of the competition from Visa was one which could be considered under the ancillary restraint doctrine. According to the Court of Appeal, '[s]uch questions relating to the application of the so-called asymmetrical counterfactual are not for the ancillary restraint issue under article 101(1), but for the issue of exemption under article 101(3)'.[273] *This is of course an important issue, in view of the fact that the burden of proof for Article 101(1) TFEU rests on the plaintiff, while that for Article 101(3) TFEU on the defendant.*

Then the Court of Appeal continued:

199. We agree with the merchants that, if questions of the subjective necessity of a restriction for the survival of the particular main operation were relevant for the purposes of the ancillary restraint doctrine, it would enable failing or inefficient businesses that could not survive without a restrictive agreement or provision to avoid the effects of article [101(1) TFEU], which would undermine the effectiveness of that provision of EU law and the underlying competition policy.

[273] Ibid, para 198.

200. The only question in relation to the potential application of the ancillary restraint doctrine in the present context is whether, without the restriction of a default MIF (which is the relevant counterfactual), this type of main operation, namely a four-party card payment scheme, could survive. The short answer to that question is in the affirmative and the contrary was not suggested by MasterCard or Visa. There are a number of such schemes in other parts of the world which operate perfectly satisfactorily without any default MIF and only a settlement at par rule.

201. Even if Popplewell J had been correct in his conclusion that the decision of the Court of First Instance in *Métropole* was implicitly disapproved by the CJEU in *MasterCard*, so that it was appropriate to consider, in the context of the ancillary restraint doctrine the competitive effects of the removal of the restriction in question on the specific main operation, we consider that his adoption of the asymmetrical counterfactual was incorrect for two related reasons.

202. First, as the CJEU's decision makes clear at [108]–[109], the counterfactual must be a realistic one. The asymmetrical counterfactual which Popplewell J accepted assumes that MasterCard would be prevented from setting default MIFs but Visa would remain unconstrained. As Phillips J said at [168(ii)] of his first judgment, addressing the mirror argument made by Visa in that case, that situation is 'not merely unrealistic but seems highly improbable [. . .]'.

Then the Court of Appeal examined the findings made by the High Court judge in Sainsbury' v Visa[274] *and agreed with the conclusions made in this judgment that the two schemes are materially identical for the purposes of the Article 101(1) analysis and that:*

207. In those circumstances, even if Popplewell J had been correct that it was appropriate to consider, in the context of the ancillary restraint doctrine, the competitive effects of the removal of the restriction in question on the specific main operation, he should have gone on to conclude that the schemes were materially identical, so that in the counterfactual world Visa's MIFs would be constrained to the same extent as MasterCard's.[275]

As the ancillary 'death spiral' argument failed, the Court of Appeal examined the possible application of Article 101(3) TFEU to the restriction of competition.[276]

6.3.4.2. Intuitive balancing and public policy considerations

The GC's judgment in *Métropole III* may be difficult to reconcile with some later judgments, where the CJEU carefully analysed non-competitive justifications under Article 101(1) without referring to *Métropole III*, and performed some form of intuitive balancing analysis which may be explained as a separate flexible approach to Article 101(1) TFEU, based on national public interest.

274 *Sainsbury's v Visa* [2017] EWHC 3047 (Comm).

275 *Sainsbury's v Mastercard / Arcadia v Mastercard / Sainsbury's v Visa* [2018] EWCA 1536 (Civ), para 207.

276 See Section 6.4.6.

6.3.4.2.1. Wouters

Case C-309/99, *Wouters, Savelbergh and Price Waterhouse v Algemene Raad Van de Nederlandse Orde van Advocaten*
[2002] ECR I–1577

The CJEU held that a rule of the Dutch Bar Council forbidding lawyers to enter into multi-disciplinary partnership agreements with accountants restricted competition appreciably because some clients might want a single firm to advise them on the accounting as well as the legal aspects of a transaction. It might also affect trade between Member States.[277] *The rule amounted to a decision of an association of undertakings, because the lawyers were undertakings,*[278] *although the Bar Council was not.*[279] *The Court continued:*

> 97. However, not every agreement between undertakings or every decision of an association of undertakings which restricts the freedom of action of the parties or of one of them necessarily falls within the prohibition laid down in Article [101(1) TFEU]. For the purposes of application of that provision to a particular case, account must first of all be taken of the overall context in which the decision of the association of undertakings was taken or produces its effects. More particularly, account must be taken of its objectives, which are here connected with the need to make rules relating to organisation, qualifications, professional ethics, supervision and liability, in order to ensure that the ultimate consumers of legal services and the sound administration of justice are provided with the necessary guarantees in relation to integrity and experience [. . .]. It has then to be considered whether the consequential effects restrictive of competition are inherent in the pursuit of those objectives.
>
> 98. Account must be taken of the legal framework applicable in the Netherlands, on the one hand, to members of the Bar and to the Bar of the Netherlands, which comprises all the registered members of the Bar in that Member State, and on the other hand, to accountants.
>
> 99. As regards members of the Bar, it has consistently been held that, in the absence of specific Community rules in the field, each Member State is in principle free to regulate the exercise of the legal profession in its territory [. . .]. For that reason, the rules applicable to that profession may differ greatly from one Member State to another.

The CJEU notes that the Dutch legislation entrusts the Bar of the Netherlands with responsibility for adopting regulations designed to ensure the proper practice of the profession, is that the essential rules adopted for that purpose are, in particular, the duty to act for clients in complete independence and in their sole interest, the duty, mentioned above, to avoid all risk of conflict of interest and the duty to observe strict professional secrecy.

> 101. Those obligations of professional conduct have not inconsiderable implications for the structure of the market in legal services, and more particularly for the possibilities for the practice of law jointly with other liberal professions which are active on that market.

[277] Case C-309/99, *Wouters, Savelbergh and Price Waterhouse v Algemene Raad Van de Nederlandse Orde van Advocaten* [2002] ECR I-1577, paras 86–90.
[278] Ibid, paras 46–9. [279] Ibid, paras 112–15.

102. Thus, they require of members of the Bar that they should be in a situation of independence *vis-à-vis* the public authorities, other operators and third parties, by whom they must never be influenced. They must furnish, in that respect, guarantees that all steps taken in a case are taken in the sole interest of the client.

103. By contrast, the profession of accountant is not subject, in general, and more particularly, in the Netherlands, to comparable requirements of professional conduct.

104. As the Advocate General has rightly pointed out [. . .] there may be a degree of incompatibility between the advisory activities carried out by a member of the Bar and the supervisory activities carried out by an accountant. The written observations submitted by the respondent in the main proceedings show that accountants in the Netherlands perform a task of certification of accounts. They undertake an objective examination and audit of their clients' accounts, so as to be able to impart to interested third parties their personal opinion concerning the reliability of those accounts. It follows that in the Member State concerned accountants are not bound by a rule of professional secrecy comparable to that of members of the Bar, unlike the position under German law, for example.

105. The aim of the 1993 Regulation is therefore to ensure that, in the Member State concerned, the rules of professional conduct for members of the Bar are complied with, having regard to the prevailing perceptions of the profession in that State. The Bar of the Netherlands was entitled to consider that members of the Bar might no longer be in a position to advise and represent their clients independently and in the observance of strict professional secrecy if they belonged to an organisation which is also responsible for producing an account of the financial results of the transactions in respect of which their services were called upon and for certifying those accounts.

106. Moreover, the concurrent pursuit of the activities of statutory auditor and of adviser, in particular legal adviser, also raises questions within the accountancy profession itself [. . .]

107. A regulation such as the 1993 Regulation could therefore reasonably be considered to be necessary in order to ensure the proper practice of the legal profession, as it is organised in the Member State concerned.

108. Furthermore, the fact that different rules may be applicable in another Member State does not mean that the rules in force in the former State are incompatible with Community law [. . .] Even if multi-disciplinary partnerships of lawyers and accountants are allowed in some Member States, the Bar of the Netherlands is entitled to consider that the objectives pursued by the 1993 Regulation cannot, having regard in particular to the legal regimes by which members of the Bar and accountants are respectively governed in the Netherlands, be attained by less restrictive means [. . .]

109. In light of those considerations, it does not appear that the effects restrictive of competition such as those resulting for members of the Bar practising in the Netherlands from a regulation such as the 1993 Regulation go beyond what is necessary in order to ensure the proper practice of the legal profession [. . .]

110. Having regard to all the foregoing considerations, the answer to be given to the second question must be that a national regulation such as the 1993 Regulation adopted by a body such as the Bar of the Netherlands does not infringe Article [101(1) TFEU], since that body could reasonably have considered that that regulation, despite the effects restrictive of competition that are inherent in it, is necessary for the proper practice of the legal profession, as organised in the Member State concerned.

NOTES AND QUESTIONS ON WOUTERS

1. The CJEU considered that the rule did not infringe Article 101(1) TFEU: the Bar might reasonably have wanted to exclude the conflicts of interest that might arise from lawyers being in partnership with accountants and ensure the independence of the Bar.[280] The CJEU, therefore, cleared the rule as not infringing Article 101(1) TFEU.
2. (Paragraph 102) Did the CJEU consider that the Bar rules deserved an exemption because it was reasonable for the Bar Council to protect the independence of the Bar and its respect for the confidence of clients' information, or did it rule that the rule did not infringe Article 101(1)?
3. (Paragraphs 107 & 108) Was the rule objectively necessary if some Member States were entitled to allow such partnerships? The ethical rule in *Wouters* was clearly not an example of an ancillary restraint. It was not directly or reasonably necessary for the establishment of the Dutch Bar: as the CJEU stated, multidisciplinary partnerships might be permitted in other countries.[281]
4. The judgment enables national courts to balance non-competition objectives, national public interest, or otherwise, against a restriction of competition, and to conclude that the restriction does not fall under Article 101(1) TFEU if these restrictions are necessary for the accomplishment of these broader public interest regulatory objectives. Indeed, the Court found that broader public interest regulatory objectives may justify a restriction of competition (including a restriction of allocative efficiency: as the price of the good/service in question would have gone up because of the specific practice), if this is to the benefit of the ultimate consumer of these services and the sound administration of justice (which is also to the benefit of the ultimate consumer of judicial services).[282]
5. Does the CJEU second-guess the Dutch Council's assessment of the public interest in question and the possible regulatory aims pursued? Is this comparable with the assessment of efficiency gains undertaken under Article 101(3) TFEU? Does the CJEU proceed to a cost–benefit analysis, examining whether the regulatory benefits outweigh costs, or is the CJEU mainly conducting a means–end or a proportionality test? The means–end or proportionality tests do not involve any effort of quantifying the costs imposed by the restrictions to trade and comparing them to the benefits of the public interest objectives advanced by the Member State in question. Its objective cannot be to re-evaluate the need for State intervention, performing some form of cost–benefit analysis, that, besides technical difficulties, the courts do not have the information and legitimacy to conduct, but to unveil opportunistic and protectionist behaviour by States. The test might resort to intuitive analysis but it does not require the identification of a specific result of the trade-off, the net benefit in cost–benefit analysis jargon, as would a proper cost–benefit analysis test.[283]

280 Ibid, paras 97–110. 281 Ibid, para 108.

282 Ibid, para 97. For another example, see Joined Cases C-184–7, 194–5 & 208/13, *API v Ministero delle Infrastrutture e dei Transporti*, ECLI:EU:C:2014:2147, paras 47–57 (exploring if the restriction of competition in question could be justified by the 'legitimate objective' of the improvement of road safety).

283 For a different interpretation, see R Whish and D Bailey, *Competition Law* (OUP, 8th ed, 2015), 129.

6. It is not clear if the CJEU applies a means–end test or a proportionality test. A simple means–end rationality test, which will consider if the regulatory measures s chosen would indeed be a rational means to a purported end. This may amount to a simple suitability test, which would provide the decision-maker of a lot of discretion in adopting the specific regulatory measure, but with the limitation that the regulatory measure should be linked rationally with some limited ends. Hence, the test involves a list of limited ends, as it would make no sense to proceed to an analysis of means without having in mind the ends to which these means aim. Do you think that the CJEU limits somehow in the judgment the ends that the domestic regulatory measures may aim to achieve? Another possibility would be to assess the proportionality of the regulatory action. This intuitive trade-off device would inquire whether the means are proportionate to the ends. This exercise will involve in addition to considering if the means chosen are indeed a rational means to a purported end (step 1 of the test), some assessment of the possible excessive costs of the regulatory action in relation to its benefits (step 2) and whether the means chosen are the least restrictive to the affected interests' alternative (step 3). The last operation inquires whether there is a less restrictive (to the affected interests) reasonably available alternative to accomplish the same regulatory end. This test will not amount to a cost–benefit analysis, as it does not necessarily require that the benefits be more important than the costs: the costs may be more than the benefits but the decision-maker maintains some margin of appreciation to accept non-disproportional differences between costs and benefits in this case. A cost–benefit analysis test attempts to measure the costs and benefits of a remedial option or of alternative remedial options, before choosing the most appropriate one. This trade-off device requires of course a more intensive fact and evidence-gathering exercise by the decision-maker and the consideration of the values of the costs and benefits examined.

6.3.4.2.2. Meca-Medina

Case C-519/04 P, *David Meca-Medina and Igor Majcen v Commission*
[2006] ECR I–6991

As part of its policy of forbidding performance-enhancing drugs taken by athletes, the International Olympic Committee had ruled that the percentage of nandrolone (an anabolic substance) in an athlete's urine should not exceed a specified amount. Two swimmers tested negative after coming first and second in a race and were suspended for four years. The problem is that the human body produces nandrolone endogenously and the swimmers stated that the consumption of boar's meat in their home country increased that production. The International Swimming Federation (FINA) suspended them under the Olympic Movement's Anti-Doping Code for four years, a term subsequently reduced to two years by the Court of Arbitration for Sport. The two athletes filed a complaint with the European Commission, alleging that the International Olympic Committee's rules on doping control were not compatible with the EU rules on competition and freedom to provide services. The Commission rejected the complaint on the ground that the rule had the object not of restricting competition, but of controlling drug taking, and was justified, reasonable and balanced. The GC considered that all rules relating to sport were outside Article 101(1),[284] but the CJEU's judgment was less general.[285] It stated that the competition rules do apply in so far as rules or agreements relate to an economic activity, but not to rules of purely sporting interest provided that they remain limited to their proper objective.[286] The judgment uses several phrases from the judgment in Wouters *to which it referred.*

7. [. . .] [T]he [General Court] held, on the basis of case-law of the Court of Justice, that while the prohibitions laid down by Articles [45 TFEU] and [56 TFEU] apply to the rules adopted in the field of sport that concern the economic aspect which sporting activity can present, on the other hand those prohibitions do not affect purely sporting rules, that is to say rules relating to questions of purely sporting interest and, as such, having nothing to do with economic activity.

8. The [General Court] observed [. . .] that the fact that purely sporting rules may have nothing to do with economic activity, with the result that they do not fall within the scope of Articles [45] and [56 TFEU], means, also, that they have nothing to do with the economic relationships of competition, with the result that they also do not fall within the scope of Articles [101 TFEU] and [102 TFEU].

9. [. . .] [T]he [General Court] held that the prohibition of doping is based on purely sporting considerations and therefore has nothing to do with any economic consideration. It concluded that the rules to combat doping consequently cannot come within the scope of the Treaty provisions on the economic freedoms and, in particular, of Articles [56, 101, and 102 TFEU].

10. The [General Court] held [. . .] that the anti-doping rules at issue, which have no discriminatory aim, are intimately linked to sport as such. It found furthermore, in paragraph 57 of the contested judgment, that the fact that the IOC might possibly, when adopting the anti-doping rules at issue, have had in mind the concern, legitimate according to the present appellants themselves, of safeguarding the economic potential of the Olympic Games is not sufficient to alter the purely sporting nature of those rules.

11. The [General Court] further stated [. . .] that since the Commission concluded in the decision at issue that the anti-doping rules at issue fell outside the scope of Articles [101 TFEU] and [102 TFEU] because of their purely sporting nature, the reference in that decision to the method of analysis in *Wouters and Others* cannot, in any event, bring into question that conclusion. The Court held in addition, [. . .] that the challenging of those rules fell within the jurisdiction of the sporting dispute settlement bodies.

12. The [General Court] also dismissed the third plea put forward by the present appellants, holding, in paragraph 68 of the contested judgment, that since the anti-doping rules at issue were purely sporting, they did not fall within the scope of Article [56 TFEU]. [. . .]

18. In the appellants' submission, the [General Court] misinterpreted the case-law of the Court of Justice according to which sport is subject to Community law only in so far as it constitutes an economic activity. In particular, contrary to what was held by the [General Court], purely sporting rules have never been excluded generally by the Court of Justice from the scope of the provisions of the Treaty. While the Court of Justice has held the formation of national teams to be a question of purely sporting interest and, as such,

284 Case T-313/02, *Meca-Medina and Majcen v Commission* [2001] ECR II–3291.

285 Case C-519/04 P, *David Meca-Medina and Igor Majcen v Commission* [2006] ECR I–6991.

286 Ibid, paras 25 and 26.

having nothing to do with economic activity, the [General Court] could not infer therefrom that any rule relating to a question of purely sporting interest has, as such, nothing to do with economic activity and thus is not covered by the prohibitions laid down in Articles [45, 56, 101, 102 TFEU]. The concept of a purely sporting rule must therefore be confined solely to rules relating to the composition and formation of national teams.

19. The appellants further contend that the [General Court] was wrong in finding that rules of purely sporting interest are necessarily inherent in the organisation and proper conduct of competitive sport, when, according to the case-law of the Court of Justice, they must also relate to the particular nature and context of sporting events. The appellants also submit that, because professional sporting activity is, in practical terms, indivisible in nature, the distinction drawn by the [General Court] between the economic and the non-economic aspect of the same sporting activity is entirely artificial.

20. In the Commission's submission, the [General Court] applied correctly the case-law of the Court of Justice according to which purely sporting rules are, as such, not covered by the rules on freedom of movement. This does therefore involve an exception of general application for purely sporting rules, which is thus not limited to the composition and formation of national teams. Nor does the Commission see how a rule of purely sporting interest and relating to the specific nature of sporting events could fail to be inherent in the proper conduct of the events.

[. . .]

36. The appellants advanced three pleas in support of their action. They criticised the Commission for having found, first, that the IOC was not an undertaking within the meaning of the [EU] case-law, second, that the anti-doping rules at issue were not a restriction of competition within the meaning of Article [101 TFEU] and, finally, that their complaint did not contain facts capable of leading to the conclusion that there could have been an infringement of Article [56 TFEU]. [. . .]

40. The appellants contend that in rejecting their complaint the Commission wrongly decided that the anti-doping rules at issue were not a restriction of competition within the meaning of Article [101 TFEU]. They submit that the Commission misapplied the criteria established by the Court of Justice in *Wouters and Others* in justifying the restrictive effects of the anti-doping rules on their freedom of action. According to the appellants, first, those rules are, contrary to the Commission's findings, in no way solely inherent in the objectives of safeguarding the integrity of competitive sport and athletes' health, but seek to protect the IOC's own economic interests. Second, in laying down a maximum level of 2 ng/ml of urine which does not correspond to any scientifically safe criterion, those rules are excessive in nature and thus go beyond what is necessary in order to combat doping effectively.

41. It should be stated first of all that, while the appellants contend that the Commission made a manifest error of assessment in treating the overall context in which the IOC adopted the rules at issue like that in which the Netherlands Bar had adopted the regulation upon which the Court was called to rule in *Wouters and Others*, they do not provide any accompanying detail to enable the merits of this submission to be assessed.

42. Next, the compatibility of rules with the Community rules on competition cannot be assessed in the abstract [. . .]. Not every agreement between undertakings or every decision of an association of undertakings which restricts the freedom of action of the parties or of one of them necessarily falls within the prohibition laid down in Article [101(1) TFEU]. For the purposes of application of that provision to a particular case, account must first of all be taken of the overall context in which the decision of

the association of undertakings was taken or produces its effects and, more specifically, of its objectives. It has then to be considered whether the consequential effects restrictive of competition are inherent in the pursuit of those objectives (*Wouters and Others*, paragraph 97) and are proportionate to them.

43. As regards the overall context in which the rules at issue were adopted, the Commission could rightly take the view that the general objective of the rules was, as none of the parties disputes, to combat doping in order for competitive sport to be conducted fairly and that it included the need to safeguard equal chances for athletes, athletes' health, the integrity and objectivity of competitive sport and ethical values in sport.

44. In addition, given that penalties are necessary to ensure enforcement of the doping ban, their effect on athletes' freedom of action must be considered to be, in principle, inherent itself in the anti-doping rules.

45. Therefore, even if the anti-doping rules at issue are to be regarded as a decision of an association of undertakings limiting the appellants' freedom of action, they do not, for all that, necessarily constitute a restriction of competition incompatible with the common market, within the meaning of Article [101 TFEU], since they are justified by a legitimate objective. Such a limitation is inherent in the organisation and proper conduct of competitive sport and its very purpose is to ensure healthy rivalry between athletes.

46. While the appellants do not dispute the truth of this objective, they nevertheless contend that the anti-doping rules at issue are also intended to protect the IOC's own economic interests and that it is in order to safeguard this objective that excessive rules, such as those contested in the present case, are adopted. The latter cannot therefore, in their submission, be regarded as inherent in the proper conduct of competitive sport and fall outside the prohibitions in Article [101 TFEU].

47. It must be acknowledged that the penal nature of the anti-doping rules at issue and the magnitude of the penalties applicable if they are breached are capable of producing adverse effects on competition because they could, if penalties were ultimately to prove unjustified, result in an athlete's unwarranted exclusion from sporting events, and thus in impairment of the conditions under which the activity at issue is engaged in. It follows that, in order not to be covered by the prohibition laid down in Article [101(1) TFEU], the restrictions thus imposed by those rules must be limited to what is necessary to ensure the proper conduct of competitive sport [. . .].

48. Rules of that kind could indeed prove excessive by virtue of, first, the conditions laid down for establishing the dividing line between circumstances which amount to doping in respect of which penalties may be imposed and those which do not, and second, the severity of those penalties.

49. Here, that dividing line is determined in the anti-doping rules at issue by the threshold of 2 ng/ml of urine above which the presence of Nandrolone in an athlete's body constitutes doping. The appellants contest that rule, asserting that the threshold adopted is set at an excessively low level which is not founded on any scientifically safe criterion.

50. However, the appellants fail to establish that the Commission made a manifest error of assessment in finding that rule to be justified.

51. It is common ground that Nandrolone is an anabolic substance the presence of which in athletes' bodies is liable to improve their performance and compromise the fairness of the sporting events in which they participate. The ban on that substance is accordingly in principle justified in light of the objective of anti-doping rules.

52. It is also common ground that that substance may be produced endogenously and that, in order to take account of this phenomenon, sporting bodies, including the

IOC by means of the anti-doping rules at issue, have accepted that doping is considered to have occurred only where the substance is present in an amount exceeding a certain threshold. It is therefore only if, having regard to scientific knowledge as it stood when the anti-doping rules at issue were adopted or even when they were applied to punish the appellants, in 1999, the threshold is set at such a low level that it should be regarded as not taking sufficient account of this phenomenon that those rules should be regarded as not justified in light of the objective which they were intended to achieve.

53. It is apparent from the documents before the Court that at the material time the average endogenous production observed in all studies then published was 20 times lower than 2ng/ml of urine and that the maximum endogenous production value observed was nearly a third lower. While the appellants contend that, from 1993, the IOC could not have been unaware of the risk reported by an expert that merely consuming a limited quantity of boar meat could cause entirely innocent athletes to exceed the threshold in question, it is not in any event established that at the material time this risk had been confirmed by the majority of the scientific community. Moreover, the results of the studies and the experiments carried out on this point subsequent to the decision at issue have no bearing in any event on the legality of that decision.

54. In those circumstances, and as the appellants do not specify at what level the threshold in question should have been set at the material time, it does not appear that the restrictions which that threshold imposes on professional sportsmen go beyond what is necessary in order to ensure that sporting events take place and function properly.

55. Since the appellants have, moreover, not pleaded that the penalties which were applicable and were imposed in the present case are excessive, it has not been established that the anti-doping rules at issue are disproportionate.

The CJEU dismissed the plea.

NOTES AND QUESTIONS ON MECA-MEDINA

1. Compare the *Meca-Medina* jurisprudence with the approach of the CJEU in *Wouters*. Does the CJEU apply a means–end, a proportionality test, or something else when assessing the justification of the restriction?
2. Can it be argued that in *Meca-Medina* the Court had also in mind the ultimate consumer of sporting competition activities when it insisted on the need for 'competitive sport' to be conducted fairly, thus guaranteeing the 'quality' of the spectacle offered to the final consumer of sporting events? Viewed from this perspective, would that be considered as a non-competition related broader public interest consideration?
3. Following up the *Meca-Medina* precedent,[287] the European Commission found that the International Skating Union's (ISU) Eligibility rules constituted a decision of an

[287] Already in the Communication from the Commission to the European Parliament, the Council, the European Economic and Social Committee and the Committee of the Regions 'Developing the European Dimension in Sport', COM(2011) 12 final (18 January 2011), 11, the Commission made it clear that it will follow the *Meca-Medina* judgment of the CJEU in assessing the legitimacy of the objectives pursued by the sporting rules, whether any restrictive effects of those rules are inherent in the pursuit of the objectives and whether those rules are proportionate to such objectives.

association of undertakings restricting competition by object (also having an effect on (potential) competition), and infringed Article 101 TFEU.[288] The rules banned skaters from international speed skating events such as the Olympic Games or the World Championship, if they participate in international speed skating events that are not approved by the ISU. If skaters broke these rules, they could face up to a lifetime ban. The ISU could impose these penalties at its own discretion, even if the independent competitions posed no risk to legitimate sports objectives, such as the protection of the integrity and proper conduct of sport, or the health and safety of athletes. The Commission's view was that the rules restricted the athletes' commercial freedom unduly and resulted in a situation where they are not willing to participate in speed skating events other than those organized by the ISU or its members (national federations). This prevented new entrants from organizing alternative international speed-skating events because they were unable to attract top athletes, but it also deprived athletes of additional sources of income during their relatively short speed-skating careers. Despite some changes to the eligibility rules, introduced in June 2016, the Commission found that the system of penalties set out by the eligibility rules remained disproportionately punitive and prevented the emergence of independent international speed skating competitions. The Commission did not impose a fine but asked the ISU to change these rules.

4. Of particular interest is also the judgment of the CJEU in *Ordem dos Técnicos Oficiais de Contas*.[289] The proceedings arose out of a decision by the Portuguese competition authority that OTOC had put in place an anti-competitive system of compulsory training for chartered accountants. The authority said that OTOC had infringed Article 101, which prohibits not just anti-competitive agreements between undertakings but also anti-competitive decisions by an association of undertakings. In appeal proceedings against the authority's decision, the national courts referred a number of questions to the CJEU; it asked whether

   (1) OTOC was to be regarded as an association of undertakings and, if so, whether binding rules that such a body might lay down in relation to training were subject to Article 101 TFEU;

   (2) whether the fact that the laying down of the rules was required by legislation rendered Article 101 TFEU inapplicable (perhaps bringing the rules within the scope of Article 56 instead);

   (3) whether the rules could still be caught by Article 101 although they had no effect on the economic activity of OTOC's members; and

   (4) whether rules that reserved training to OTOC alone were permissible.

   The CJEU considered first that OTOC was an association of undertakings. Its members are undertakings (being engaged in economic activity). In respect of the decision in question, OTOC's rules did belong to the 'sphere of economic activity', even though they may not have affected the chartered accountants, as they had a direct impact on the market for compulsory training for chartered accountants (on which OTOC itself was active).

[288] *International Skating Union's Eligibility rules* (Case AT.40208) Commission Decision C(2017) 8240 final.

[289] Case C-1/12, *Ordem dos Técnicos Oficiais de Contas (OTOC)*, ECLI:EU:C:2013:127.

Second, it concluded that the Portuguese legislation requiring OTOC to lay down training rules did not permit OTOC to escape from the application of Article 101 TFEU. The legislation did not give OTOC the exclusive right to provide the shorter training sessions, nor did it set out what the rules must be. The rules were therefore adopted solely by OTOC, in its own discretion, without any input from the State.

Finally, the CJEU ruled that rules which reserved for OTOC a significant part of the market of compulsory training for chartered accountants (the rules required chartered accountants in Portugal to obtain all short training (of less than 16 hours) from OTOC itself) were likely to distort competition on the market of compulsory training for chartered accountants and were anti-competitive in breach of Article 101 TFEU. The rules did not ensure equality of opportunity between the various economic operators, eliminated competition for the shorter training sessions and were not necessary to guarantee the quality of the services offered.

5. Another interesting judgment is *Consiglio nazionale dei geologi v Autorità garante della concorrenza e del mercato*.[290] In Italy, geologists must be entered on a register administered by the National Association of Geologists. Geologists entered in that register constitute the Association and elect the National Council of Geologists (CNG). The CNG is responsible for ensuring compliance with professional regulations and qualifications. The CNG may also take disciplinary action against a registered person who fails to act in a manner consistent with the integrity or dignity of the profession. The CNG's Code of Conduct contains provisions relating to the criteria for determining fees. In particular, this provides that a geologist engaging in professional activity in whatever form (as an individual, as a member of a company or a partnership) must always ensure that the fee charged is commensurate with the scale and difficulty of the task to be performed, the dignity of the profession, technical knowledge and the commitment required.

In June 2010, the Italian Competition Authority found that the Association had breached Article 101 TFEU by encouraging its members to adopt a standard commercial approach by applying a scale of professional fees. It considered, in particular, that the requirements in the Code of Conduct to determine fees in accordance with general standards (such as the integrity and dignity of the profession), in the absence of criteria that characterize those standards by specific reference to the determination of fee scales for professional services might also lead to the assumption that the professional scale is to be regarded as compulsory, so preventing independent behaviour in the market. The CNG challenged the Authority's decision before the Italian courts. During the course of an appeal, the CNG asked the Italian court to refer to the CJEU several questions concerning the compliance of the provisions of Italian law and the Code of Conduct with EU competition law.

The Italian court asked whether Article 101 TFEU precludes a professional association, such as the National Association of Geologists in Italy, from adopting rules of professional conduct that lay down as criteria for determining remuneration, in addition to the quality and scale of the work to be performed, the dignity of the profession, with the result that, where fees are set below a certain level (a situation comparable to

290 Case C-136/12, *Consiglio nazionale dei geologi v Autorità garante della concorrenza e del mercato*, ECLI:EU:C:2013:489.

that in which minimum fees are fixed) that may be penalized on grounds of breach of those rules.

The CJEU held that rules (such as those in the Code of Conduct), which establish the dignity of the profession, in addition to the quality and scale of the work to be performed, as criteria for determining remuneration constitute a decision by an association of undertakings within the meaning of Article 101(1) TFEU, which may have the effect of restricting competition within the Internal Market. However, the CJEU held that it is for the referring court to assess whether this is in fact the effect of the rules, with regard to the overall context in which the Code of Conduct produces its effects, including the national legal framework in its entirety and the manner in which that Code is applied in practice by the National Association of Geologists. The national court must also verify whether the rules in the Code of Conduct (in particular in so far as they apply the criterion based on the dignity of the profession) may be regarded as necessary for the implementation of the legitimate objective of providing guarantees to consumers of geologists' services.

6. In *CHEZ Elektro Bulgaria AD*, the CJEU was referred preliminary questions from Bulgarian courts with regard to the application of competition law to the prerogative granted to the Bulgarian Supreme Council of the Legal Profession (SCLP) to set a minimum level of legal fees could infringe Article 101(1) TFEU, read in conjunction with Article 4(3) TEU.[291] The CJEU found that this could be the case here, as the SCLP was considered to be an association of undertakings within the meaning of Article 101 TFEU when adopting regulations determining the minimum amounts of lawyers' remuneration and that the fixing of minimum amounts for lawyers' remuneration, made mandatory by national legislation, was capable of restricting competition under Article 101(1) TFEU.[292] Citing *Wouters, Meca-Medina*, and *Consiglio Nazionale dei Geologi*, the Court, however, continued by considering if the regulation had legitimate objectives[293] noting that 'it is important to verify whether the restrictions thus imposed by the rules at issue in the main proceedings are limited to what is necessary to ensure the implementation of legitimate objectives.'[294] The CJEU instructed the referring court to assess, in the light of the overall context in which the regulation issued by the SCLP was taken or applies, if the restriction could be deemed necessary for the implementation of a legitimate objective.[295]

6.3.5. UK COMPETITION LAW AND THE ANTI-COMPETITIVE OBJECT/EFFECT DISTINCTION

Similar to Article 101(1) TFEU, Chapter I CA98 prohibits agreements, decisions of associations of undertakings and concerted practices that have 'the object or effect the prevention, restriction or distortion of competition' (the Chapter I prohibition).[296] As for Article 101(1)

[291] Joined Cases C-427 & 428/16, *CHEZ Elektro Bulgaria AD v Yordan Kotsev and FrontEx International EAD v Emil Yanakiev*, ECLI:EU:C:2017:890.

[292] See our analysis in Chapter 1.

[293] Joined Cases C-427 & 428/16, *CHEZ Elektro Bulgaria AD v Yordan Kotsev and FrontEx International EAD v Emil Yanakiev*, ECLI:EU:C:2017:890, paras 53–4.

[294] Ibid, para 55.

[295] Ibid, paras 56–7.

[296] Competition Act 1998 c 41, Chapter I, sections 2(1) and 2(8)

TFEU, section 2(2) provides an identical list of the sorts of agreements that would infringe Chapter I CA 98. The concepts are understood in a similar way as Article 101(1) TFEU, having regard to the Commission's Guidelines on the application of Article 101(3) TFEU.[297]

If an agreement has as its object the prevention, restriction or distortion of competition, it is not necessary to prove that the agreement has had, or would have, any anti-competitive effects in order to establish an infringement. Actual effects need not be considered where it is apparent that the object of the agreement is to prevent, restrict or distort competition.

A recent decision of the CMA on *Online resale price maintenance in the commercial refrigeration sector* provides a useful summary of the main principles:[298]

> A.33. The object of an agreement is to be identified primarily from an examination of objective factors, such as the content of its provisions, its objectives and the legal and economic context of the agreement. When determining that context, it is also necessary to take into consideration the nature of the goods or services affected, as well as the real conditions of the functioning and structure of the market or markets in question. Where appropriate, the way in which the coordination (or collusive behaviour) is implemented may be taken into account.
>
> A.34. Anti-competitive subjective intentions on the part of the parties can also be taken into account in the assessment, but they are not a necessary factor for a finding that there is an anti-competitive restrictive object.
>
> A.35. Furthermore, the fact that an agreement pursues other legitimate objectives does not preclude it being regarded as having a restrictive object. [. . .].[299]

The impact of the agreement and/or concerted practice on competition should be appreciable for it to be prohibited under Chapter I CA 98.[300] In its decision on *Online resale price maintenance in the commercial refrigeration sector*, the CMA held that the principle established in *Expedia* applies also to its analysis of appreciable effect under the prohibition of Chapter I.[301] However, unlike the position under Article 101(1) TFEU, there is no requirement that the effect on trade within the UK should be appreciable. This was clarified by the CAT in *Aberdeen Journals*.[302]

The category of restrictions by object in UK law is similar to that of Article 101(1) TFEU: price fixing, market sharing, collusive tendering, export bans. Although the UK NCA defines 'object infringements' as 'those forms of collusion between undertakings that are, by

297 *Cityhook Limited v Office of Fair Trading* [2007] CAT 18, para 269; *Bookmakers'Afternoon Greyhound Services v Amalgamated Racing*, [2008] EWHC 1978 (Ch).

298 See more on this case in Chapter 10.

299 Decision of the CMA, Case CE/9856/14, *Online resale price maintenance in the commercial refrigeration sector* (24 May 2016), (Annex) paras A.33–A.35; see also recent case on online RPM: Case CE/9857/14, *Online resale price maintenance in the bathroom fittings sector* (10 May 2016), paras 6.42.1–6.42.3 and Case CE/9827/2014, *Restrictive arrangements preventing estate and letting agents from advertising their fees in a local newspaper* (8 May 2015) para A.80.

300 *North Midland Construction plc v Office of Fair Trading* [2011] CAT 14, paras 45 and 52ff.

301 Decision of the CMA, Case CE/9856/14, *Online resale price maintenance in the commercial refrigeration sector* (24 May 2016), (Annex) para. A.63.

302 *Aberdeen Journals v Director General of Fair Trading* [2003] CAT 11, paras 459–60. See also *North Midland Construction plc v Office of Fair Trading* [2011] CAT 14, para 62: 'Effect on trade within the UK is a purely jurisdictional test to demarcate the boundary line between the application of EU competition law and national competition law. The CAT has clarified that given a close nexus between appreciable effect on competition and appreciable effect on trade within the United Kingdom, if one was satisfied, the other was likely to be so.'

their very nature, detrimental to competition',[303] the OFT and now CMA seem to take an open perspective on the category of by object restrictions of competition.

In *Roma-branded mobility scooters*, the OFT found that an agreement/concerted practice between the producer of mobility scooters and retailers, which prohibited retailers from the online advertising of below-recommended retail prices (RRPs) in respect of certain Pride mobility scooters set by Pride, had the object of preventing, restricting or distorting competition in the supply of mobility scooters in the UK or a part of the UK.[304] The OFT cited for this finding earlier case law of the European Commission that had found that an advertising prohibition issued by the Institute of Professional Representatives before the European Patent Office limited the commercial freedom of members and had implicitly the object of restricting competition between members of the profession, as the Commission did not require any effects analysis.[305] It also referred to other cases of the European Commission and the EU Courts that provided similar contractual rights to suppliers to prohibits retailers to advertise.[306] However, in addition to these references to past jurisprudence with relatively close fact-patterns, the OFT analysed the economic effects of Below-RRP Online Price Advertising Prohibitions, but also considered the following key factors 'which provide relevant context in which the agreements and/or concerted practices operated': the fact that intra-brand competition was already restricted as a result of quantitative selection criteria, the fact that intra-brand competition was already restricted as a result of qualitative selection criteria, the fact that consumers in this sector are often first-time buyers and that RRPs in the sector are somewhat arbitrary and/or are generally set at levels significantly higher than actual selling prices and finally that end-consumers' restricted mobility may make it more difficult for them physically to shop around.[307]

In *R (Cityhook Ltd) v OFT*, the High Court pronounced itself for the first time on the discretion of the OFT to close a case for lack of administrative priority.[308] The case involved a collective boycott of Cityhook's technology, the company exploiting a patented invention of a foreshore ducting system, by the members of United Kingdom Cable Protection Committee (UKCPC) which included British Telecommunications. Level 3 Communications and Global Crossing Ltd. After opening an investigation, the OFT closed the file in view of its administrative priorities. Cityhook appealed to the CAT, but as its appeal was found inadmissible, it made an application for judicial review at the High Court. The High Court Judge found that 'concerted collective boycott of a supplier who offers an innovative and cost-saving alternative approach to an established area of commercial activity would suggest a restriction of competition as its object', such an approach being 'the logical one to have taken in this case' as well as having 'the attraction of simplicity'. The High Court considered that 'it may take time for a particular form of apparently anti-competitive activity to emerge and be identified as a true

303 *Mobility scooters supplied by Pride Mobility Products Limited: prohibition on online advertising of prices below Pride's RRP* (Case CE/9578-12) OFT Decision (27 March 2014), Annex, para A.42.

304 Ibid, paras 3.194 ff.

305 *EPI code of conduct* (Case IV/36.147) Commission Decision [1999] OJ L 106/14, paras 39–41, confirmed by Case T-144/99, *Institute of Professional Representatives before the European Patent Office v Commission* [2001] ECR II–1090.

306 The OFT referred to, *Hasselblad*, Commission Decision [1982] OJ L 161/18, confirmed by Case 86/82, *Hasselblad v Commission* [1984] ECR 883; *Yamaha* (Case COMP/37.975) Commission Decision (16 July 2003) (unpublished but available at the DG Comp website).

307 *Mobility scooters supplied by Pride Mobility Products Limited: prohibition on online advertising of prices below Pride's RRP* (Case CE/9578-12) OFT Decision (27 March 2014), para 3.205.

308 *R (Cityhook Ltd) v OFT* [2009] EWHC 57 (Admin), paras 131–5.

object-based activity' and was reluctant to add a new restriction by object, finding 'tenable' that the OFT was reasonably entitled to hold the view that this was not a by object restriction of competition.[309]

The CMA's decision in relation to *Restrictive arrangements in the estate and letting agents sector* in 2015 described the authority's thinking and findings in relation to the concept of 'effect restrictions of competition'.[310] The CMA concluded that the objective of the arrangements (concerted practice) was to prevent Three Counties' members and, as subsequently extended, any agents, from advertising their fees in the Star Courier. The objective was to deny them the opportunity to use an important local media channel, in the process of competing with each other, to communicate their fees to potential vendors or lessors, and thus to reduce price competition between them and reduce downward pressure on the market price. In its assessment, the CMA took into account the fact that the market(s) for residential sales and lettings services are two sided markets with the estate agent acting as the intermediary between the vendors/lessors and the purchasers/tenants on each side of the market. An agent needs to attract a sufficient number of vendors' or lessors' instructions in order to be attractive to potential purchasers or tenants. Similarly, agents need to attract sufficient purchasers or tenants in order to be attractive to vendors or lessors. In this situation, marketing and advertising are important elements of competition, as establishing a brand and reputation is crucial for winning new instructions.[311]

Before reaching its conclusion the CMA also considered the parties' arguments that the true purpose of these arrangements was to raise the quality (whether relating to physical characteristics or its perceived 'image') of the newspaper, Star Courier.[312] The CMA found that each of the agreements, concerted practices and decision by an association of undertakings had the object or the potential effect of preventing, restricting or distorting competition in the market(s) for residential sales and lettings services in the UK or a part of the UK.[313]

According to the CMA, 'the assessment of the actual or potential effect of an agreement must be conducted by reference to the counterfactual; that is, the hypothetical position that would pertain in the absence of the agreement containing the restriction of competition'.[314] The focus on potential competition aims to ascertain 'whether, in the light of the structure of the market and the economic and legal context within which it functions, there are real concrete possibilities for the undertakings concerned to compete among themselves or for a new competitor to penetrate the relevant market and compete with the undertakings already established'.[315] Indeed, when compared to the counterfactual, the arrangements in place had the potential effect of preventing, restricting or distorting competition in the market(s) for residential sales and lettings services in the Three Counties Area by (a) reducing price competition between actual competitors, and (b) reducing price competition from potential competitors.[316]

Note that Schedule 3, paragraph 7, empowers the Secretary of State to make an order and exclude an agreement or a category of agreements from the application of Chapter I CA 98

[309] *Bookmakers' Afternoon Greyhound Services Limited v Amalgamated Racing Limited* [2008] EWHC 1978 (Ch) upheld on appeal [2009] EWCA Civ 750.

[310] Decision of the CMA in Case CE/9832/13, *Restrictive arrangements preventing estate and letting agents from advertising their fees in a local newspaper* (8 May 2015).

[311] Ibid, para 6.21. [312] Ibid, paras 5.106–5.111. [313] Ibid, para 5.74.

[314] Ibid, para 5.116. [315] Ibid.

[316] Decision of the CMA in Case CE/9832/13, *Restrictive arrangements preventing estate and letting agents from advertising their fees in a local newspaper* (8 May 2015), paras 5.116–5.130.

where there are 'exceptional and compelling reasons of public policy for doing so'. Such an order may be retrospective. This provides an additional possibility for UK competition authorities to introduce public policy concerns in the enforcement of Chapter I, in comparison to EU competition law, which can either qualify some activities as non-economic and therefore escaping Article 101 TFEU which may only apply to undertakings, or assess public policy concerns in the context of the regulatory ancillarity doctrine under Article 101(1) TFEU and, arguably, under the cost–benefit analysis test of Article 101(3) TFEU.[317] This possibility for exclusion from CA98 has nevertheless been sparingly used, essentially in relation to the defence industry[318] and the supply of fuel (oil and petroleum products) in the event of significant disruption or a threat of significant disruption to the normal supply of fuel.[319] Such orders do not serve to disapply EU competition law where the agreement also affects trade between EU Member States.[320]

Public policy concerns, such as those taken into account in *Wouters*, could also lead to an exclusion of the application of Chapter I prohibition, under Schedule 4, paragraph 1(1), which provided that the Chapter I prohibition did not apply to designated professional rules served to protect the public. However, the efforts of liberalizing the professions in the early 2000s led the OFT (now replaced by CMA) to recommend the repeal of the exclusion,[321] which finally occurred with section 207 of the Enterprise Act 2002. It is possible, however, to use the *Wouters* jurisprudence for taking into account this type of public policy concerns.[322]

A recent judgment by the CAT provides some interesting insights into the approach followed by the UK courts and competition authorities with regard to the object/effect distinction in Chapter I CA98. The case is particularly important as it may shed light on the approach followed by the UK courts in the aftermath of Brexit, assuming that they may be inclined to follow a different path from the approach of the EU Courts in interpreting Article 101 TFEU.

Agents' Mutual Limited v Gascoigne Halman Limited (T/A Gascoigne Halman)
[2017] CAT 15

Agents Mutual is a mutual association owned by its estate agent members. The case arose following a complaint by Gascoigne Halman claiming that Agents Mutual, a mutual association owned by its estate agent members, had breached the Chapter I prohibition by virtue of adopting (i) a rule by which an estate agent member may list its properties on no more than one other portal (the One Other Portal Rule); (ii) a rule restricting membership of Agents' Mutual to full-service office-based estate or letting agents, as opposed to agents operating only online (the Bricks and Mortar Rule); and (iii) a rule requiring members to promote only OnTheMarket and not any other property portal (the Exclusive Promotion Rule). Gascoigne Halman also argued that the One Other Portal Rule formed part of a wider arrangement

317 See our analysis in Sections 5.4.2. and 5.4.3.

318 Competition Act 1998 (Public Policy Exclusion) Order 2006, SI 2006/605 (maintenance and repair of worships); Competition Act 1998 (Public Policy Exclusion) Order 2008, SI 2008/1820 (nuclear submarines).

319 Competition Act 1998 (Public Policy Exclusion) Order 2012 (2012 No 710).

320 OFT 1389, Public Bodies and Competition Law (December 2011), para 3.5.

321 OFT 328, Competition in professions (March 2001), available at http://webarchive.nationalarchives.gov.uk/20140402172414/http://oft.gov.uk/shared_oft/reports/professional_bodies/oft328.pdf.

322 For general guidance, see OFT 408, Trade Associations, professions and self-regulating bodies (December 2004), available at https://www.gov.uk/government/uploads/system/uploads/attachment_data/file/284404/oft408.pdf.

between Agents' Mutual and others collectively to boycott the Zoopla and/or Rightmove website portals, contrary to the Chapter I prohibition.

The CAT found that the One Other Portal Rule did not infringe the Chapter I prohibition either by object or by effect. The rule was, in any event, objectively necessary to the various rules which bind members of Agents' Mutual (the listing agreement, articles of association and membership rules) as a whole, which were pro-competitive. Further, the rule did not form part of a wider concerted practice to 'boycott' Zoopla and was not invalid on that account. Further, the CAT found that neither the Bricks and Mortar Rule nor the Exclusive Promotion Rule infringed the Chapter I prohibition by object.

It is worth setting out the framework under which the CAT considered the alleged breach as a by object or a by effect restriction.

Restrictions of competition by object or by effect

The CAT stated that its approach would be to examine the agreement or provision in question to see whether by its very nature, having regard to the economic and legal context, it clearly and unambiguously reveals a sufficient degree of harm to competition to make any examination of its effects unnecessary. It then drew the following propositions from the statement of the case law with regard to restrictions by object:

149. [. . .]

(1) For an agreement to be held to restrict competition 'by object' it must by its very nature reveal a sufficient degree of harm to competition, having regard to its specific legal and economic context. It is not enough for it to be merely capable of resulting in the prevention, restriction or distortion of competition.

(2) In determining whether an agreement reveals a sufficient degree of harm, the CAT must look at the content of its provisions, its objectives and its economic and legal context. In determining that context, it must consider the nature of the services that are the subject of the agreement and the structure and functioning of the market or markets in question. The parties' intentions may be relevant, but the CAT is not obliged to take these as determinative.

(3) This evaluation of harm is not the same as considering the economic effects of the agreement, which is a quite distinct exercise, only necessary if restriction 'by object' is not established. Nevertheless the agreement must be capable of having some impact on the market or markets in question. Assessing this possible impact is a strictly limited exercise not involving a full examination of market effects, or any balancing of pro- or anti-competitive effects.

(4) The concept of restriction 'by object' should be interpreted restrictively in the sense that it should only be applied to those categories of agreement whose harmful nature is easily identifiable in the light of experience and well-established economic analysis.

150. Whether a given provision constitutes a restriction of competition 'by effect' requires extensive analysis of the agreement in its market context. This involves:

(1) Identifying the relevant agreement or provision said to constitute a restriction on competition. In this case, the only provision alleged by Gascoigne Halman to have an anti-competitive effect was the one other portal rule.

(2) Having identified the relevant provision, identifying the market or markets in which the effect of that provision is to be gauged. In this case, the relevant markets are linked.

The present case involves two or more relevant markets (property portals and estate agents), at least one of which (the property portals market) is 'two-sided'. The effects of the alleged anti-competitive practice may differ on the different sides of this market.

(3) To help the assessment, a theory of harm may be presented, and then tested against the evidence. In a public enforcement case, that is done by the competition authority; in a private action, it is the party alleging illegality which must make out its case and put forward the necessary evidence in support.

(4) The allegedly harmful effect must then be assessed and the effects that are alleged to occur tested against the evidence.

(5) In assessing the alleged restrictive effect of the various agreements and provisions, it is helpful to consider what the position would have been in their absence and then to compare the two situations.

Objective necessity

Where it is a matter of determining whether an anti-competitive restriction can escape the prohibition laid down in the Chapter I prohibition because it is ancillary to a main operation that is not anti-competitive in nature, it is necessary to inquire whether that operation would be impossible to carry out in the absence of the restriction in question. According to the CAT:

153. This exception to the Chapter I prohibition is best considered in stages:

(1) First, there must be a given 'operation' or 'activity' that is not caught by the prohibition because of its neutrality or positive effect in terms of competition. In this case, that 'operation' or 'activity' is the OnTheMarket portal.

(2) Second, there must be inherent to this operation or activity, but ancillary to it, a restriction of commercial activity that would, but for its relation to that operation or activity, be caught by the Chapter I prohibition. In this case, these comprise the various restrictions identified by Gascoigne Halman.

(3) Third, the relationship between the 'operation' or 'activity' not prohibited and the restriction that would otherwise be prohibited must be such that, without the restriction, the primary operation or activity could not be carried out. It is necessary to inquire whether that operation would be impossible to carry out in the absence of the restriction in question.

(4) Fourthly, the restriction must not only be necessary for the implementation of the main operation or activity: it must also be proportionate to the underlying objectives of that operation or activity.

The One Other Portal Rule

The CAT rejected the allegation that a rule by which an estate agent member may list its properties on no more than one other portal is a by object restriction of competition.

First, the CAT considered that the One Other Portal Rule was a restriction freely accepted by an estate agent as part of the price of accessing OnTheMarket.[323] *The nature of the restriction,*

[323] *Agents' Mutual Limited v Gascoigne Halman Limited (T/A Gascoigne Halman)* [2017] CAT 15, para 181.

which binds the moment the estate agent becomes a Member both in terms of its horizontal and vertical effects, is to impose on all participating estate agents a measure of exclusivity in relation to portals in general. The rule was not one of absolute exclusivity, as estate agents were not required to purchase their 'portal' advertising only from OnTheMarket. It was a variant on the exclusivity theme. Participating estate agents must advertise their properties through OnTheMarket and can choose to do so through one other (but only one other) portal. The CAT also found that the one other portal rule should be characterized, in terms of its nature, as 'a semi-exclusive purchasing obligation: that is an obligation to purchase advertising from a given portal, not to the exclusion of all other portals, but to the exclusion of all other portals but one', and that its economic and legal context strongly suggested that its nature and purpose were not to harm competition.[324]

Second, the CAT found that the One Other Portal Rule does not reveal a clear and obvious harm to competition to the extent that the limited exclusivity provided by the One Other Portal Rule did not clearly and unambiguously have the object of restricting competition.[325] *Having regard to the economic context in which the provision was intended to operate, that is, in a market with two-sided platforms, the CAT found that the nature of the provision suggested a pro-competitive object. The Tribunal added that the fact that the One Other Portal Rule was not exclusive but permitted Members (if they wished) to use or continue to use one other portal appeared to create competition between the two established portals. The evidence showed that the One Other Portal Rule was likely to increase competition between Rightmove and Zoopla in that both Rightmove and Zoopla would pay greater attention to the demands of estate agents subscribing or thinking of subscribing to Agents' Mutual because they appreciated that membership of Agents' Mutual entailed one or other of them being dropped. Moreover, the One Other Portal Rule was a provision whose object could be seen as pro-competitive, providing as it was a means of new market entry, and it did not obviously fit any previously established category of object restrictions. The CAT added that the overriding purpose of Agents' Mutual in launching its new Portal was to compete with the established property portals and provide cost reduction benefits to its Members, these aims not showing a clearly anti-competitive purpose.*

The One Other Portal Rule also imposed a vertical restraint on the ability of each Member to list its properties on more than one property portal.[326] *However, the CAT did not qualify this as a by object restriction. Indeed, the One Other Portal Rule formed part of a vertical agreement not concluded between direct competitors, but between undertakings at different levels of trade. Such agreements commonly contain restrictions on behaviour, but, according to the CAT, it cannot be presumed that such restrictions are anti-competitive, and vertical agreements are generally presumed to be pro-competitive. Furthermore, Agents' Mutual did not have market power either in the property portals market, where it was a new entrant, or in the estate agents market, where its Members, though significant in terms of numbers of estate agency branches, accounted for only a small share of relevant purchase revenues. The One Other Portal Rule, if seen as a semi-exclusive purchasing commitment not exceeding five years in duration, would not appear to fall within the categories of hardcore restriction excluded from the EU vertical agreements block exemption.*

With regard to these vertical arrangements producing a restriction of competition by effect, the CAT noted that Gascoigne Halman's theory of harm was that the entry onto the market of Agents' Mutual (with the One Other Portal Rule) caused a very material number of agents

[324] Ibid, para 182. [325] Ibid, para 184. [326] Ibid, paras 186ff.

to cease listing properties on Zoopla (with comparatively fewer leaving Rightmove). This, according to Gascoigne Halman, was because Rightmove was perceived as being the 'must have' portal, with Zoopla as the 'also-ran'. The consequence was that Rightmove's position in the market was strengthened, and Zoopla's ability to constrain Rightmove's apparent dominance was undermined. Gascoigne Halman did not base its theory of harm on the fact that Zoopla had been harmed (although that was a necessary part of its argument), but that this harm to Zoopla adversely affected consumers in the estate agents' market by adversely affecting Zoopla's ability to constrain Rightmove. However, the CAT found that George Halman provided insufficient data to make its analysis either robust or sound.[327] *In view of this finding, the CAT considered that it was not necessary to balance the pro- and anti-competitive effects of the One Other Portal Rule in the relevant markets, although it held that these pro-competitive effects existed.*[328] *Indeed, in this case there was no need to decide whether an outright exclusivity rule would have been objectively necessary, as Agents' Mutual One Other Portal Rule constituted a form of 'semi-exclusivity', and in light of 'the circumstances of this case, and the circumstances of the market [. . .] and given the beneficial central purpose of the new property portal, this apparently restrictive provision was objectively necessary to achieve the purpose of market entry'.*[329]

The Bricks and Mortar Rule

The question for the CAT was whether a rule restricting membership of Agents' Mutual to full-service office-based estate or letting agents, as opposed to agents operating only online is a 'by object' restriction.

Gascoigne Halman argued that the Bricks and Mortar Rule is an overtly protectionist provision seeking to deny non-bricks and mortar estate agents access to OnTheMarket. However, the CAT did not consider that Gascoigne Halman had demonstrated that the Bricks and Mortar Rule is, by its very nature, sufficiently harmful to competition as to remove any need for an effect-based examination of the provision.

The CAT found that the purpose of the Bricks and Mortar Rule was to enable like-minded undertakings to combine to provide a service ancillary to their business that they all need in order to do their business.[330] *The Bricks and Mortar Rule had the purpose of defining the nature and scope of the business created by Agents' Mutual, rather than clearly having the object of harming competition from or as between those undertakings not covered by its terms. It might possibly have such an effect, but this had not been alleged by Gascoigne Halman, which argued for this to be characterized as a restriction of competition by object. Remarkably, the CAT also noted the following:*

> 253. [. . .]
>
> (5) We decline to regard such a provision—particularly when contained in the rules of an undertaking that clearly has little or no market power—as anti-competitive 'by object'. Viewing the rule as a vertical restraint (ie, as between each Member and Agents' Mutual) leads to the same conclusion.

The fact that the CAT linked its refusal to characterize the restriction in question as a restriction of competition by object to the little or no market power of the undertaking in question, in both a horizontal and vertical relation context, is remarkable and may indicate a different approach than that followed by EU competition law under Article 101 TFEU.

327 Ibid, para 239. 328 Ibid, para 240. 329 Ibid, para 248. 330 Ibid, para 253.

The Exclusive Promotion Rule

The CAT then considered whether a rule requiring members to promote only OnTheMarket and not any other property portal constituted a 'by object' restriction to competition.[331] *Gascoigne Halman did not advance a 'by effect' case. Agents' Mutual contended that the provision was objectively necessary. The CAT did not consider that the Exclusive Promotion Rule is properly to be characterized as a 'by object' infringement, taking into account its duration. It commented that it failed to understand how a provision whereby a new entrant to a market is favoured in terms of advertising by its own members is anti-competitive by object, whether viewed as a horizontal or vertical restriction. However, it did not consider that the Exclusive Promotion Rule, if anti-competitive, could be justified as objectively necessary. There was no sufficient evidence to suggest that, if this rule had been abandoned from the Arrangements, Agents' Mutual would have been unable to launch or promote the Portal in the manner that it did.*

The Collective Boycott Allegation

Gascoigne Halman also alleged that estate agents and/or Members of Agents' Mutual and/or Agents' Mutual had substituted practical cooperation as to the portals they would use for the risks of competition. In these terms, this allegation appeared to amount to no more than an assertion that Agents' Mutual and/or its Members co-ordinated to establish in the market a new portal, OnTheMarket.

The CAT did not consider such a co-ordinated approach to be harmful, but probably more beneficial to competition. The CAT stated that:

> 260. In some circumstances horizontal co-operation even between competitors can be perfectly acceptable in competition terms; and the use of exclusivity requirements—like the One Other Portal Rule—can be similarly acceptable, either because competition law is not infringed at all (as here) or because an anti-competitive restriction is objectively necessary.

The CAT also commented that, during the course of the hearing, it became clear that Gascoigne Halman's Collective Boycott Allegation really amounted to a contention that there was a wider arrangement between estate agents and/or Members of Agents' Mutual and/or Agents' Mutual that Zoopla would be boycotted and Rightmove preferred when the time came for estate agents who were Members of Agents' Mutual to choose the 'one other portal' they would subscribe to in addition to OnTheMarket.[332] *The CAT did not consider that this contention was borne out by the facts.*

6.4. EXEMPTIONS AND EXCEPTIONS TO THE PROHIBITION PRINCIPLE

6.4.1. THE BASICS OF ARTICLE 101(3) TFEU

Not all agreements that perceptibly restrict competition and may affect inter-State trade are prohibited. Some forms of collaboration restrictive of competition may have

331 Ibid, paras 256–7. 332 Ibid, para 261.

beneficial effects and, by virtue of Article 101(3) TFEU the prohibition in Article 101(1) may be declared inapplicable to any agreements if they satisfy the following *cumulative*[333] conditions:

- The agreement contributes to improving the production or distribution of goods or to promoting technical or economic progress,
- while allowing consumers a fair share of the resulting benefit,

and which does not

- impose on the undertakings concerned restrictions which are not indispensable to the attainment of these objectives
- afford such undertakings the possibility of eliminating competition in respect of a substantial part of the products in question.

As a matter of principle, any agreement, having an anti-competitive object or effect, may be justified under Article 101(3) provided that all of those four conditions are met.[334]

In the enforcement system of Regulation 1/2003, Article 101(3) TFEU operates as a defence that undertakings may put forward with regard of agreements that are caught by Article 101(3) TFEU and are covered by a block exemption regulation. Note that prior to the implementation of the legal exception regime with Regulation 1/2003, the Commission used to adopt up to four individual exemptions a year. Only the Commission had power to grant individual exemptions under Regulation 17 (now repealed). Notification ended in May 2004 and the procedures have changed drastically, and Article 101(3) has direct effect in national courts and competition authorities.

Since Regulation 1/2003 came into effect, the notification system has come to an end and the Commission is unlikely often to apply Article 101(3) TFEU except when important new issues arise. Indeed, Regulation 1/2003 created a new type of decision in its Article 10 which empowers the Commission to adopt decisions finding that an agreement or practice does not infringe Article 101 (or 102) TFEU, where the Community public interest so requires. The Commission, acting on its own initiative, may by decision find that Article 101 TFEU is not applicable in a certain case, either because the conditions of Article 101(1) TFEU are not fulfilled or because the conditions of Article 101(3) TFEU are satisfied.[335] Such decisions have binding effect on national competition authorities and national courts. However, to the date of writing, the Commission has not adopted any decisions under Article 10. Some authors have suggested that the Commission should use the possibility to adopt positive decisions under Article 10 of Regulation 1/2003, as otherwise the application of Article 101(3) TFEU may become obsolete, in view of the

[333] See Case T-185/00 etc, *Métropole Télévision SA (M6)* [2002] ECR II–3805, para 86; Case T-17/93, Matra [1994] ECR II–595, para 85; and Joined Cases 43 & 63/82, *VBVB and VBBB* [1984] ECR 19, para 61.

[334] Satisfaction of which is 'both necessary and sufficient': Case 42/84 *Remia and Others v Commission* [1985] ECR 2545, para 38; Case T-17/93, *Matra Hachette SA v Commission* [1994] ECR II–595, para 104; Joined Cases C-501, 513, 515 & 519/06 P, *GlaxoSmithKline Services Unlimited v Commission* [2009] ECR I–9291.

[335] This is also illustrated in Recital 38 of Regulation 1/2003, which specifically contemplates the possibility that parties should be able to seek and obtain informal guidance from the Commission in cases giving rise to genuine uncertainty because they present novel or unresolved questions (see also the subsequent Notice on informal guidance in which the Commission outlined the policy it intended to adopt in granting such guidance). See Notice on informal guidance relating to novel questions concerning Articles 81 and 82 of the EC Treaty that arise in individual cases (guidance letters, [2004] OJ C 101/78.

reticence of national courts to enter into the complex economic assessments required by Article 101(3) TFEU.[336]

The Commission clearly opposed this view in its Report on the implementation of Regulation 1/2003[337] and the accompanying Staff Working Paper[338] regarding the (non)application of Article 10, taking the view that Article 10 was 'principally' created to ensure consistency, ie '(i) to "correct" the approach of a national competition authority; or (ii) to send a signal to the European Competition Network ("ECN") about how to approach a certain case'.[339] The Commission noted that 'the extensive efforts of the ECN in promoting the coherent application of the EC antitrust rules have made its use unnecessary to date', in view of '[t]he extent to which the ECN has proven to be a successful forum to discuss general policy issues was not anticipated at the time of the adoption of Regulation 1/2003'.[340] Certainly, achieving consistency within the ECN can be such a case of public interest, but this should not be the only hypothesis where Article 10 can be applied. All stakeholders, including undertakings and national courts, have an interest in the clarification of the law that may be brought by a positive decision, under Article 10 of Regulation 1/2003.

The Commission also noted the existence of a few prohibition decisions which also included some in-depth analysis of Article 101(3) TFEU.[341] The implementation of Article 101(3) TFEU by NCAs and national courts has been limited by various factors. Some studies regarding the enforcement of Article 101(3) by NCAs and National Courts indicate that few cases proceeded to an in-depth analysis of the conditions of Article 101(3) TFEU and even fewer, if any at all, have concluded that the Article 101(3) conditions were fully satisfied and that the restrictive agreement did not infringe Article 101 TFEU.

C Humpe, I Lianos, N Petit, and B Walle de Gelcke, 'The Effects-based Approach in Article 101 TFEU' in M Merola and D Waelbroeck (eds) *Towards an optimal Enforcement of Competition Rules in Europe* (Bruylant, 2010), 467, paras 41–2 (references omitted)

The development of case-law by national competition authorities [. . .] and courts applying Article [101(3) TFEU] is inherently limited by two main factors. First, as regards NCAs (and specialized courts entrusted with the review of NCA decisions), the legal exception regime and the competences set forth by Article 5 of the Regulation [1/2003] prevent the NCAs from adopting 'positive decisions' in the sense of clearance or exemption decisions.

336 C Humpe, I Lianos, N Petit, and B Walle de Gelcke, 'The Effects-based Approach in Article 101 TFEU' in M Merola and D Waelbroeck (eds) *Towards an Optimal Enforcement of Competition Rules in Europe* (Bruylant, 2010), 467.

337 Communication from the Commission to the European Parliament and the Council, Report on the functioning of Regulation 1/2003, COM(2009) 206 final [SEC(2009)574] (29 April 2009), para 15 [hereinafter Commission Report].

338 Commission Staff Working Paper accompanying the Communication from the Commission to the European Parliament and the Council, Report on the functioning of Regulation 1/2003, COM(2009) 206 final, (29 April 2009), para 113.

339 Ibid. 340 Ibid, para 116.

341 The Commission cited MasterCard (Case COMP/34.579) Commission Decision; *Morgan Stanley/Visa* (Case COMP/37.860) Commission Decision; *Groupement des Cartes Bancaires* (Case COMP/38.606) Commission Decision; *CISAC* (Case COMP/38.698) Commission Decision, which explored if the conditions of Article 101(3) TFEU were satisfied by the specific restrictions to competition.

Some NCAs take the view that therefore no decisions applying Article [101(3) TFEU] can be adopted. Such an interpretation of Article 5 would lead to a situation where, in cases where an investigated agreement or practice complies with the conditions of Article [101(3)], the case is terminated without decision. Such position seems to rest on too narrow an interpretation of Article 5. [. . .] Nevertheless, [. . .] the correct interpretation of Article 5 of the Regulation is indeed that NCAs, when deciding that there are no grounds for action on their part, can and should declare the reasons for such decision, which means that such decision should state the reasons—in the relevant cases—why the conditions of Article [101(3)] are met. Such decisions have in that respect only a declaratory and not a constitutive value, but will contribute to the positive enforcement of Article [101]. [. . .] [M]ost NCAs do state the reasons why Article [101(3)] applies or not. The most explicit decisions in that respect, are those where agreements or practices are, however, partly considered to be justified under Article [101(3)] not in respect of other provisions. [. . .] However, because NCAs apply Article [101(3)] only when it is invoked as a defence, the analysis is in most cases rather succinct (e.g. because it suffices that one condition is not complied with to deny the benefit of that provision).

The situation of national courts is not fundamentally different. Although the courts now have full jurisdiction to apply Article [101(3)], the judicial implementation of that provision remains poor. This is because, in the context of private litigation, the exemption provision is equally invoked as a defence against allegations of infringement of Article [101(1)] and of ensuring invalidity of agreements and/or damage claims. In such procedural situation, and bearing in mind that the burden of proof is entirely on the defendant, courts will only exceptionally proceed to a thorough assessment of the conditions of Article [101(3)]. Our overview of the case-law has not provided convincing examples of such assessments, and certainly not to the standards recommended by the Commission's Guidelines on Article [101(3)].

It does not seem that the situation has drastically changed since these lines were written.

In *Tele 2/Polska*, a case concerning the implementation of Article 102 TFEU by a NCA, the CJEU held that the NCAs authority is limited to the adoption of a decision stating that there are no grounds for action, and not that there has been no breach of a Treaty provisions (thus also including Article 101 TFEU). According to the CJEU, such negative decision on the merits would risk undermining the uniform application of the competition rules set up by the Treaty, which is one of the objectives of Regulation 1/2003, since such a decision might prevent the Commission from finding subsequently that the practice in question amounts to a breach of those rules.[342] One may venture that for the same reasons NCAS are prevented from adopting a decision clearing a restriction of competition because it satisfies the conditions of Article 101(3) TFEU (positive decision).

Although the Commission (and NCAs) do not provide detailed information on the way the various conditions of Article 101(3) TFEU will be implemented in practice, undertakings may rely on the various block exemption regulations, detailing how the various conditions of Article 101(3) are to be applied to categories of agreements, concerted practices and decisions of associations of undertakings, and/or the various soft law interpretative guidelines published by the European Commission, some accompanying the block exemption regulations,

342 Case C-375/09, *Prezes Urzędu Ochrony Konkurencji i Konsumentów v Tele2 Polska sp z o.o, devenue Netia SA* [2011] ECR I-3055, paras 28 and 30.

while others, such as the Commission's Guidelines on the application of Article 101(3) TFEU, are of general application.

The Commission (and the various NCAs and national courts) have an important discretion in implementing Article 101(3) TFEU, subject of course to the judicial review of the General Court and on points of law by the Court of Justice (for the Commission) and the general directions of the jurisprudence of the CJEU. By virtue of Article 1 of Regulation 1/2003, Article 101(3) will now have direct effect and can be applied by national courts and competition authorities. National courts and competition authorities will not be authorized to make decisions that conflict with those made by the Commission or envisaged in proceedings that it has already initiated (Article 16 of Regulation 1/2003 and *Masterfoods*).[343] As we have previously explained, the end of the notification system, the abandonment of the system of legal authorization and the adoption of a system of legal exception had profound implications on decision-making under Article 101(3) TFEU. Since May 2004, when Regulation 1/2003 entered into force, undertakings need to proceed to a self-assessment of their agreement, under both Articles 101(1) and 101(3) TFEU. This involves a more complex assessment of the economic and legal context than what was routinely undertaken under Article 101(1) TFEU, as the undertakings may need to be aware of their market position and of the possible efficiency gains of their agreement, as well as of their potential anti-competitive effects.

The move towards a more economic approach in implementing Article 101(3) TFEU means that undertakings may not escape an Article 101(1) prohibition, or their agreements being 'exempted' under Article 101(3), if they adopt the specific types of agreements that are explicitly exempted by the block exemption regulations, as it was the case in the past. A declaration by a court or competition authority under Article 101(3) differs from the old exemptions under Regulation 17/62. Exemptions used to be constitutive acts—for a specified period an agreement would not be subject to Article 101(1). The exemption might have to be renewed. Now the institution will declare that at the date in issue Article 101 does not apply to an agreement. Conditions may change, and the declaration may be of little use if they do. It is, therefore, probably wrong to refer to such clearances as exemptions: they are exceptions to the prohibition, or may be treated as limiting it.

The CJEU held in *Consten and Grundig* that the exercise of the Commission's powers under Article 101(3) necessarily involved complex evaluations of economic matters and judicial review was limited.[344] The judicial review performed on the Commission's decisions implementing Article 101(3) TFEU will be reviewed in the companion volume on enforcement. An additional reason for the margin of discretion allowed to the Commission is that it is the institution entrusted with the orientation of competition policy.[345] EU Courts can annul discretionary decisions when they do not conform with the legal framework, but cannot substitute their own discretion for that of the European Commission.[346] Until 1996,

343 Case C-344/98, *Masterfoods* [2000] ECR I–1136.

344 Case 56 & 58/64, *Établissements Consten SàRL and Grundig-Verkaufs-GmbH v Commission* [1966] ECR 299, 347.

345 As the Court held in Case C-344/98, *Masterfoods Ltd v HB Ice Cream Ltd* [2000] ECR I–11361, para 46, '[t]he Commission, entrusted by Article [105(1) TFEU] with the task of ensuring application of the principles laid down in Articles [101 and 102 TFEU], is responsible for defining and implementing the orientation of Community competition policy.'

346 On the limits of the judicial review in the context of Article 101(3) TFEU, or more broadly in EU competition law, see JC Laguna de Paz, 'Understanding the Limits of Judicial Review in European Competition Law' (2014) 2(1) *J Antitrust Enforcement* 203.

the EU Courts had never quashed an exemption granted by the Commission. Their jurisdiction under Article 263 TFEU to entertain an appeal over a decision addressed to someone else is limited. The appellant must establish that it is directly and individually concerned. This was narrowly construed by the CJEU in *Plaumann v Commission*,[347] but is being interpreted more widely in EU law and competition cases these days.[348]

In *Métropole I*,[349] the Commission had exempted a joint venture, the European Broadcasting Union, between most European state owned television companies whereby, through the Eurovision link, the members were entitled to transmit sports and other programmes made by the others. Several private television stations were excluded from the joint venture and appealed to the General Court against the decision of exemption. Some had taken part in the Commission's proceedings and others had not. The GC held that the appellants competed directly with the members of the EBU and were excluded from the benefits of the joint venture.[350] So, they were individually concerned by the decision, whether or not they had complained during the Commission's proceedings. They were also directly concerned by the exemption, since there was a direct causal link between it and their exclusion from the benefits. Consequently, the GC had jurisdiction to consider the appeal. For the first time, the GC annulled an exemption decision:

> 102. By failing to examine first whether the membership rules were objective and sufficiently determinate and capable of uniform, non-discriminatory application in order next to assess whether they were indispensable within the meaning of [Article101(3)], the Commission based its decisions on an erroneous interpretation of that provision.

Several exemptions granted to third parties have been considered by the GC since then. A third party damaged by an agreement that was cleared should be able to appeal to the GC when the clearance comes from the Commission. When it comes from a national court, a reference may be made to the CJEU under Article 267 TFEU, and when from a national competition authority, an appeal may be possible under national law; and when the case reaches a court, the court can make a reference to the CJEU under Article 267 TFEU. The remedy is less helpful if the clearance was granted by a national authority, as the CJEU is supposed to explain the law rather than apply it and most problems under the competition rules relate to the application of the law. The remedy is less helpful if the clearance was granted by a national authority, as the CJEU is supposed to explain the law rather than apply it and most problems under the competition rules relate to the application of the law.

Under Article 2 of Regulation 1/2003, the legal burden of proof for Article 101(3) is on the person alleging legality.[351] If, however, a good case is made, the Commission must examine the arguments and the evidence, and may have to provide an explanation if it dismisses them. Where an agreement is covered by an EU block exemption regulation the parties to the restrictive agreement are relieved of the burden of showing that their agreement satisfies the

[347] Case 25/62, *Plaumann & Co v Commission* [1963] ECR 95, 107.

[348] On judicial review, see H Schweitzer, 'Judicial Review in EU Competition Law' in I Lianos and D Geradin (eds) *Handbook on European Competition Law*, vol 2 (Edward Elgar, 2013), 491; and the companion volume, I Lianos, *Competition Law Enforcement and Procedure* (OUP, forthcoming 2019).

[349] Case T-206/99, *Métropole I* [2001] ECR II–1059. [350] Ibid, paras 59–64.

[351] See Joined Cases C-501, 513, 515 & 519/06 P, *GlaxoSmithKline Services and Others v Commission*, ECLI:EU:C:2009:610, para 82.

conditions in Article 101(3) TFEU. They only have to prove that the restrictive agreement is block exempted. Furthermore, the CJEU held in *Pedro IV* that:

> While it is indeed true that the block exemption regulations apply in so far as agreements contain restrictions on competition caught by Article [101(1) TFEU], it is nevertheless often more practical to ascertain first whether those regulations apply to a given agreement, in order to avoid—if those regulations do apply—a complex economic and legal assessment to determine whether the conditions for the application of Article [101(1) TFEU] are met.[352]

By virtue of Article 103(2)(b) TFEU, the Council may provide the authority to the Commission to issue block exemption regulations. Until 1965, the Commission probably had the power to grant exemption only to individual agreements. By Regulation 19/65, however, the Council empowered it to make regulations exempting from Article 101(1) classes of exclusive distribution and exclusive purchasing agreements and of agreements licensing intellectual property rights.[353] The following block exemption regulations were adopted on the basis of this authorization:

- Regulation 330/2010 on vertical agreements,[354] examined in Chapter 10;
- Regulation 461/2010 on vertical agreements relating to the motor vehicle aftermarket,[355] examined in Chapter 10;
- Regulation 316/2014 on technology transfer agreements,[356] examined in a companion volume *on Competition Law and the Intangible Economy*.

With Regulation 2821/71, the Council authorized the Commission to grant block exemptions to standardization agreements, research and development agreements and specialization agreements. On the basis of this authorization, the Commission adopted the following regulations, which are now in force:

- Regulation 1217/2010 on research and development agreements,[357] examined in Chapter 7;
- Regulation 1218/2010 on specialization agreements,[358] examined in Chapter 7.
- Council Regulation 1534/91 authorized the Commission to grant exemption in the insurance sector. This led to the following Commission Regulation currently in force:[359]
    - Regulation 267/2010.[360]

352 Case C-260/07, *Pedro IV Servicios SL v Total España SA* [2009] ECR I–2437, para 36.

353 Council Regulation 19/65 [1965] OJ 36/533, amended by Regulation 1215/99 [1999] OJ L 148/1.

354 Commission Regulation 330/2010 [2010] OJ L 102/1.

355 Commission Regulation No 461/2010 on the application of Article 101(3) TFEU to categories of vertical agreements and concerted practices in the motor vehicle sector [2010] OJ L129/52.

356 Commission Regulation No 316/2014 on the application of Article 101(3) TFEU to categories of technology transfer agreements [2014] OJ L 93/17 [hereinafter Regulation 316/2014].

357 Commission Regulation No 1217/2010 on the application of Article 101(3) TFEU to certain categories of research and development agreements [2010] OJ L 335/36.

358 Commission Regulation No 1218/2010 on the application of Article 101(3) TFEU to certain categories of specialisation agreements [2010] OJ L 335/43.

359 Council Regulation No 1534/91 on the application of Article 85(3) of the Treaty to certain categories of agreements, decisions and concerted practices in the insurance sector [1991] OJ L 143/1.

360 Commission Regulation No 267/2010 on the application of Article 101(3) TFEU to certain categories of agreements, decisions and concerted practices in the insurance sector [2010] OJ L 83/1. The Commission also issued an explanatory communication: Communication from the Commission on the application of

- Council Regulation 169/2009 provides for a block exemption to certain agreements from rules of competition to transport by rail, road and inland waterway.[361]
- Council Regulation 246/2009 authorizes the Commission to provide bloc exemption to consortia between liner shipping companies.[362] This led to the following Commission Regulation currently in force:
  - Regulation 906/2009.[363]
- Council Regulation 487/2009 authorizes the Commission to grant block exemptions for certain agreements in the air transport sector.[364]

Some of these Commission's regulations will be analysed in the following chapters. The old practice for group exemptions was to define the kinds of agreements that can come within them (distribution, technology licences, cooperation in R&D or whatever), then provide for permissible clauses in a 'white list' and in one or two 'black lists' to define the provisions that prevent the application of the exemption. The new generation of block exemption regulation, starting with Regulation 2790/99 adopted in 1999, and most recently replaced by Regulation 330/2010 relating to distribution agreements, include widely drafted exemptions, do not white-list categories of agreements, any provisions that are not black-listed being permissible, and apply a market share ceiling under which agreements that are not black-listed are permitted. Block exemption regulations explicitly exclude hardcore restrictions from the benefit of the block exemption. Although as a matter of principle all restrictive agreements that fulfil the four conditions of Article 101(3) are covered by the exception rule, hardcore restrictions that are usually black-listed in block exemption regulations or identified as hardcore restrictions in Commission guidelines and notices 'generally fail (at least) the two first conditions of Article 101(3)' as '(t)hey neither create objective economic benefits nor do they benefit consumers'.[365]

By virtue of Article 29 of Regulation 1/2003, the Commission may withdraw the benefit of a group exemption on its own initiative or on a complaint when it finds that in a particular case the agreement is not compatible with Article 101(3). When the collusion has effects in a Member State or part of it and that territory constitutes a distinct geographic market, the NCA of that State may also withdraw the benefit of the group exemption.

The Commission has exercised similar powers prior to Regulation 1/2003 under the group exemptions in *Langnese*.[366] The Commission is far more likely to threaten to withdraw an exemption, at which point the parties are under considerable pressure to modify their

Article 101(3) TFEU to certain categories of agreements, decisions and concerted practices in the insurance sector,[2010] OJ C 82/20.

361 Council Regulation No 169/2009 applying rules of competition to transport by rail, road and inland waterway [2009] OJ L 61/1.

362 Council Regulation No 246/2009 on the application of Article 81(3) of the Treaty to certain categories of agreements, decisions and concerted practices between liner shipping companies (consortia) [2009] OJ L 79/1.

363 Commission Regulation No 906/2009 on the application of Article 81(3) of the Treaty to certain categories of agreements, decisions and concerted practices between liner shipping companies (consortia) [2009] OJ L 256/31, as amended by Commission Regulation No 697/2014 [2014] OJ L 184/3.

364 Council Regulation No 487/2009 on the application of Article 81(3) of the Treaty to certain categories of agreements and concerted practices in the air transport sector [2009] OJ L 148/1. Previous Commission regulations specific to air transport have been gradually repealed and no such regulation is in force today.

365 Guidelines on Article 101(3) (formerly 81(3)), para 46.

366 *Langnese-Iglo GmbH & Co KG* (Case IV/34.072), Commission Decision 93/406/EEC [1993] OJ L 183/19. The final appeal did not consider much of the substance Case C-279/95 P, *Langnese-Iglo GmbH v Commission* [1998] ECR I–5609.

agreement so as to satisfy the Commission. In *Langnese*, the GC limited the withdrawal of the exemption to agreements already entered into, and held that Langnese was still entitled to benefit from the group exemption for subsequent agreements. Some regulations provide additional opportunities for flexibility, such as Article 6 of Regulation 330/2010 giving power to the Commission to withdraw by regulation the benefit of the bloc exemption from an entire sector, where parallel networks of similar vertical restraints cover more than 50 per cent of a relevant market.[367]

Block exemption regulations always contain an expiry date. Every time a new regulation is adopted it includes a transitional period.

The system of block exemptions remained in effect, even after the move to a legal exception regime. As the Commission explains in its Guidelines on Article 101(3) TFEU, Regulation 1/2003 does not affect the validity and legal nature of block exemption regulations, which have direct effect: 'agreements covered by block exemption regulations are legally valid and enforceable even if they are restrictive of competition within the meaning of Article [101(1) TFEU]'.[368] Indeed, 'such agreements can only be prohibited for the future and only upon formal withdrawal of the block exemption by the Commission or the appropriate national competition authority'.[369] National courts cannot hold that block exemption regulations are invalid; nor can NCAs. The Commission has published detailed guidelines in order to interpret the provisions of block exemption regulations and provide detailed information that could help undertakings to self-assess their agreements.

When an agreement can be framed to benefit from one of these group exemptions, the risk of illegality and nullity is avoided until the regulation expires or is not renewed and the task of the parties' advisers is far easier. There is no need to analyse the market or to consider whether ancillary restraints are wider than necessary to ascertain whether Article 101(1) is infringed, either when negotiating the agreement or when enforcing it. There are, however, disadvantages in having to bring a transaction within a block exemption. Certainly, more recent block exemptions have rather shorter black lists than the older ones and have replaced many formalistic provisions with a ceiling of market share, which is economically more sensible as, in the absence of an indication of market power, contractual restrictions are unlikely to affect competition. Nevertheless, at the time a commitment is made to invest, which market will be selected by a competition authority or court is not always predictable.

The following sections explore how these different conditions have been interpreted by the EU courts' case law, the Commission's guidance and decisional practice. The following chapters will engage with the application of Article 101(3) to various forms of collusive practices and will explore more in detail the implementation of the different block exemption regulations.

6.4.2. AN IMPROVEMENT IN THE PRODUCTION OR DISTRIBUTION OF GOODS OR IN TECHNICAL OR ECONOMIC PROGRESS

The interpretation of this condition has given rise to controversy between those that would favour a narrow definition of what may constitute an 'improvement in the production or

367 See also Regulation 316/2014, Article 7.

368 Guidelines on Article 101(3) (formerly 81(3)), para 2. 369 Ibid.

distribution of goods or in technical or economic progress', which would conceptualize these 'benefits' as merely gains in economic efficiency, while others favour a broader definition that would also include in this category broader public policy benefits, even if these are not conducive to just economic efficiency considerations. To be more precise, gains in economic efficiency are often conceptualized in terms of an increase of output, a reduction of prices or costs, but also in terms of an increase in quality and innovation. Broader public policy considerations may relate to the so called 'non-competition' concerns, such as industrial policy, the protection of the environment, the protection of employment, economic and social cohesion among regions, the promotion of cultural diversity, the protection of public health, to name a few.

The definition of eligible 'improvements' is of course of paramount importance, in particular as these have the potential to justify a restriction of competition so that the agreement (or other collusive practice) in question does not fall under the prohibition principle of Article 101 TFEU. Article 101(3) TFEU is quite clear that this condition forms part of a number of other *cumulative* conditions that the specific restrictive agreement should satisfy, if it is to be justified under Article 101(3). Hence, the interpretation of this condition should not be disconnected to the function it exercises in the context of Article 101 TFEU, that of justifying a restriction of competition under Article 101(1) TFEU, and to the way the other conditions of Article 101(3) are interpreted.

In a number of cases dating before the adoption of Regulation 1/2003, the EU Courts recognized the discretion of the Commission in taking into account public interest objectives when implementing Article 101(3).[370] On the basis of this case law, the Commission has taken into account public interest considerations, such as employment policy and the protection of workers,[371] cultural policy,[372] environmental policy,[373] the protection of public health,[374] among others, when implementing Article 101(3) TFEU. Since the adoption of Regulation

370 Case C-26/76, *Metro v Commission* [1977] ECR 1875, para 21 [hereinafter *Metro I*]:

> The powers conferred upon the Commission under [Article 101(3)] show that the requirements for the maintenance of workable competition may be reconciled with the safeguarding of *objectives of different nature* and to this end *certain restrictions of competition are permissible, provided they are essential to the attainment of those objectives* and they do not result in the elimination of competition for a substantial part of the common market. (emphasis added)

See also Joined Cases T-538, 542, 543 & 546/93, *Métropole Télévision v Commission* [1996] ECR II–649, para 118: 'in the context of an overall assessment, the Commission is entitled to base itself on considerations connected with the pursuit of the public interest in order to grant exemption under Article [101(3)]'.

371 *Ford/Volkswagen* (Case IV/33.814) Commission Decision 93/49/EEC [1992] OJ L 20/14, para 23 (considering the employment implications in the context of Article 101(3), although with additional efficiency gains); *Stichting Baksteen* (Case IV/34.456) Commission Decision 94/296/EC [1994] L 131/15, para 27; Case T-193/02, *Laurent Piau v Commission* [2005] ECR II–209, para 100, upheld by Case C-171/05 P, *Piau v Commission* [2006] ECR I–37 (protecting football players who have a short playing career from the risks incurred in the event of poorly negotiated transfers).

372 , *VBBB/VBVB* (Case IV/428) Commission Decision 82/123/EEC [1982] OJ L 54/36, paras 49–63 (the resale price maintenance agreement was not accepted).

373 *Philips/Osram* (Case IV/34.252) Commission Decision 94/986/EC [1994] OJ L 378/37, para 27: '[t]he use of cleaner facilities will result in less air pollution, and consequently in direct and indirect benefits for consumers from reduced negative externalities'; *CECED* (Case IV.F.1/36.718) Commission Decision 2000/475/EC [1999] OJ L 187/47, paras 55–7; *DSD* (Cases COMP/34493 etc) Commission Decision 2001/837/EC [2001] L 319/1, para 148: 'consumers will likewise benefit as a result of the improvement in environmental quality sought, essentially the reduction in the volume of packaging'.

374 *Pasteur-Mérieux/Merck* (Case IV/34.776) Commission Decision 94/770/EC [1994] OJ L 309/1, paras 89 and 108 (noting that the technical progress and improvements in distribution achieved by the anti-competitive agreement responded on top to 'a genuine public health concern').

1/2003, and the end of the Commission's monopoly in enforcing Article 101(3) TFEU, the Commission seems to have moved towards a more restrictive position, as to the eligible 'improvements' to take into account.

This approach also relates to the conceptualization of Article 101(3) by the Commission as encompassing a balancing decision procedure, involving the consideration of 'trade-offs' between various anti-competitive effects and pro-competitive benefits. The balancing or 'trade-off' metaphor used by the Commission seems to have been influenced by the turn towards a more economic approach, which took hold of US antitrust law in the 1970s, and which promoted a narrow view of the benefits to take into account when performing the trade-off.[375] The conceptualization of the decision-procedure of Article 101(3) as a trade-off between various 'effects' (pro-competitive and anti-competitive) indicates that Article 101(3) may only include commensurable values, that is values that can be compared, and in this case measured within a common metric, so as to conclude that there is a 'net' positive or negative effect. The Commission explained the operation of the 'trade-off' under Article 101(3) TFEU as follows.

[375] A classic article putting forward the narrow 'trade-off' approach was published by the Nobel laureate in economics Oliver Williamson completed when he was Special Economic Assistant to the Assistant Attorney General for Antitrust, US Department of Justice: O Williamson, 'Economics as an Anti-Trust Defense: The Welfare Trade-offs' (1968) 58(1) *American Economic Rev* 18. Although the article focused on horizontal mergers and argued that one should not prohibit them before taking into account the efficiencies that may result from the merger, the 'Williamsonian trade-off', as it was called, took hold of the imagination of competition law enforcers in the US and on this side of the Atlantic, and expanded into antitrust. In essence, assuming a merger or agreement between competitors enables them because of economies of scale or other synergies the trade-off, to reduce their production costs, and thus to increase their producer surplus, this benefit should be considered, along with the possible negative effects of the merger or the agreement, which by reducing competition may have led to an increase of the prices paid by consumers and thus to a fall of consumer surplus. The trade-off focuses on the 'social (total) surplus' generated by the merger or agreement on the specific market, which depends on whether the increase in producer surplus due to lower production costs is larger or smaller than the fall in consumer surplus due to higher prices. Williamson concluded that government regulators confronted to these mergers (or agreements) should examine their costs and benefits on a case-by-case basis. His model also put more weight on the gains of producer surplus than on the losses of consumer surplus, as he assumes that it does not take a large decrease in cost for producer surplus to exceed consumer surplus losses.

The 'Williamsonian trade-off' model has been criticized for relying on a number of improbable assumptions, for instance, that the pre-merger price is competitive, which if relaxed may change the conclusions of the model: for instance, if pre-merger one may observe a distorted supra-competitive price, then an even small increases in price can cause significant reductions in welfare: see the criticisms of MD Whinston, 'Antitrust Policy Toward Horizontal Mergers' in M Armstrong and RH Porter (eds) *Handbook of Industrial Organization*, vol 3 (North Holland, 2007), 2369, 2373–4.

This approach may also be criticized for not taking into account the distributional effects of the specific merger or agreement as changes in the producer and consumer surplus are treated symmetrically, and considers only the effect on prices, and not any other parameter of competition. It is also interesting to note that Williamson did not ignore that distributional effects may be considerable and should also be considered. He explained in this article that 'the income redistribution which occurs [as a result of a merger] is usually large relative to the size of the deadweight loss' and that 'attaching even a slight weight to income distribution effects can sometimes influence the overall valuation significantly' (Williamson, 'Economics as an Anti-Trust Defense', 28). He even puts forward an argument not to exclude such concerns from the analysis noting that

> the transfer involved [by a merger] could be regarded unfavorably not merely because it redistributes income in an undesirable way (increases the degree of inequality in the size distribution of income), but also because it produces social discontent. This latter has serious efficiency implications that the [traditional] analysis does not take explicitly into account (ibid).

Hence, for Williamson, 'distinguishing social from private costs in this respect may be the most fundamental reason for treating claims of private efficiency gains sceptically' (ibid). Yet, his final conclusion is in favour of a simple efficiency trade-off, as he claims that other policies, such as taxation, may take care of the distributive effects of mergers (or anti-competitive agreements). As we explained in Chapter 2, this assumption is also questionable.

European Commission, Guidelines on the application of Article 101(3) (references omitted)

32. The assessment of restrictions by object and effect under Article [101(1)] is only one side of the analysis. The other side, which is reflected in Article [101(3)], is the assessment of the positive economic effects of restrictive agreements.

33. The aim of the [EU] competition rules is to protect competition on the market as a means of enhancing consumer welfare and of ensuring an efficient allocation of resources. Agreements that restrict competition may at the same time have pro-competitive effects by way of efficiency gains Efficiencies may create additional value by lowering the cost of producing an output, improving the quality of the product or creating a new product. When the pro-competitive effects of an agreement outweigh its anti-competitive effects the agreement is on balance pro-competitive and compatible with the objectives of the Community competition rules. The net effect of such agreements is to promote the very essence of the competitive process, namely to win customers by offering better products or better prices than those offered by rivals. This analytical framework is reflected in Article [101(1)] and Article [101(3)]. The latter provision expressly acknowledges that restrictive agreements may generate objective economic benefits so as to outweigh the negative effects of the restriction of competition.

Indeed, the Commission conceptualizes the 'positive economic effects' of the agreement as 'efficiency gains', thus adopting a narrow perspective in the type of benefits included in the assessment. As the Commission explains in paragraphs 42 and 43 of the Guidelines on the application of Article 101(3) TFEU,

42. [. . .] The four conditions of Article [101(3)] are also exhaustive. When they are met the exception is applicable and may not be made dependant on any other condition. Goals pursued by other Treaty provisions can be taken into account to the extent that they can be subsumed under the four conditions of Article [101(3)].

43. [. . .] The assessment under Article [101(3)] of benefits flowing from restrictive agreements is in principle made within the confines of each relevant market to which the agreement relates. The Community competition rules have as their objective the protection of competition on the market and cannot be detached from this objective [. . .].

In addition to the CJEU's judgment in *Metro*,[376] the Commission cites the judgment of the General Court in *Matra Hachette* in order to support this proposition.[377]

According to a well-established principle in the jurisprudence of the CJEU,

[t]he question whether there is an improvement in the production of distribution of the goods in question, which is required for the grant of exemption, is to be answered in accordance with the spirit of Article [101 TFEU]. First, this improvement cannot be identified with all the advantages which the parties to the agreement obtain from it in their production or distribution activities. These advantages are generally indisputable and show the agreement as in all respects indispensable to an improvement as understood in this sense. This subjective method, which makes the content of the concept of 'improvement' depend upon the special features of the contractual

376 Case 26/76, *Metro I* [1977] ECR 1875, para 43.

377 Case T-17/93, *Matra Hachette* [1994] ECR II–595, para 139.

> relationships in question, is not consistent with the aims of Article [101]. Furthermore, the very fact that the Treaty provides that the restriction of competition must be 'indispensable' to the improvement in question clearly indicates the importance which the latter must have. This improvement must in particular show appreciable objective advantages of such a character as to compensate for the disadvantages which they cause in the field of competition'.[378]

Consequently, an increase in profitability because of cost savings arising out of the exercise of market power, for instance when companies agree to fix prices or share markets, cannot be taken into account; in other words, there 'efficiency gains' should result from the 'creation of value through an integration of assets and activities'.[379]

The balancing function of efficiency gains also makes the Commission conclude that 'it is necessary to verify what is the *link* between the agreement and the claimed efficiencies' (the requirement of a *causal link*, although the Commission will not exclude from consideration wider efficiency enhancing effects as long as these occur within the specific relevant market).[380] The causal link should be 'direct', as '[c]laims based on indirect effects are as a general rule too uncertain and too remote to be taken into account'.[381] This also involves the *evaluation* of efficiency gains (the Commission should explore 'what is the value of these efficiencies') and their *substantiation*, by the defendant, who bears the burden of proof under Article 101(3) TFEU. The Commission subjects undertakings to strict requirements for the *evaluation* and *substantiation* of efficiency gains:

> In the case of claimed *cost efficiencies* the undertakings invoking the benefit of Article [101(3)] must as accurately as reasonably possible calculate or estimate the value of the efficiencies and describe in detail how the amount has been computed. They must also describe the method(s) by which the efficiencies have been or will be achieved. The data submitted must be verifiable so that there can be a sufficient degree of certainty that the efficiencies have materialised or are likely to materialise.[382]

These requirements are less stringer for 'efficiencies in the form of new or improved products and other non-cost based efficiencies', for which the undertakings should just 'describe and explain in detail what is the nature of the efficiencies and how and why they constitute an objective economic benefit'.[383] The substantiation should lead to the *verification* of efficiency gains, and in particular:

> (a) The *nature* of the claimed efficiencies;
>
> (b) The *link* between the agreement and the efficiencies;

[378] Joined Cases 56 & 58/64, *Consten SaRL & Grundig Verkaufs-GmbH v Commission* [1966] ECR 299. The Commission's Guidelines are also clear that 'only objective benefits can be taken into account' and that 'efficiencies are not assessed from the subjective point of view of the parties': Guidelines on Article 101(3) (formerly 81(3)), para 49.

[379] Guidelines on Article 101(3) (formerly 81(3)), para 49.

[380] Ibid, para 50.

[381] Ibid, para 54. The Commission gives as an example of an indirect causal link a case where it is claimed that a restrictive agreement allows the undertakings concerned to increase their profits, enabling them to invest more in research and development to the ultimate benefit of consumers. According to the Commission, '[w]hile there may be a link between profitability and research and development, this link is generally not sufficiently direct to be taken into account in the context of Article [101(3)]'.

[382] Ibid, para 56 (emphasis added).

[383] Ibid, para 57.

(c) The *likelihood* and *magnitude* of each claimed efficiency; and

(d) *How* and *when* each claimed efficiency would be achieved.[384]

The Guidelines establish a distinction between different categories of efficiency gains: (i) cost efficiencies and efficiencies of a qualitative nature whereby value is created in the form of new or improved products, greater product variety, etc, although the Commission also adds that these categories are only examples and are not intended to be exhaustive.[385] As we have previously explained the latter are subject to a more lenient 'evidence' regime, with regard to the requirements of evaluation. The Guidelines on the application of Article 101(3) include a more detailed analysis of each of these categories of efficiency gains.[386]

The EU Courts and the Commission have generally applied strictly the evidential requirements for efficiency gains.[387] For instance, in *Lundbeck*, the parties claimed that the litigation settlements concluded between the generics and the brand drug manufacturers would have 'avoided costly, duplicative litigation in multiple jurisdictions' and thus reduce the litigation costs for the parties.[388] The Commission rejected this argument, noting, first, that there was no clear link between the agreements and the avoidance of any litigation costs, and, second, that mere cost savings for the parties concerned from avoided litigation did not constitute an efficiency gain within the meaning of Article 101(3), as benefits are not assessed from the subjective point of view of the parties and the parties should have substantiated how the agreement contributed to improving the production or distribution of goods or to promoting technical or economic progress. The GC upheld the Commission's decision.[389]

In *Fentanyl*, after some extensive analysis of the documentary and economic evidence at hand, the Commission found that the claimed benefits of approaching the pharmacists in order to indirectly influence what product was to be prescribed by the physicians was not substantiated by the way the co-promotion agreement was negotiated, implemented and evaluated and rejected the application of Article 101(3) TFEU.[390]

In *MasterCard*,[391] after the Commission found that an association of banks restricted competition under Article 101(1) TFEU by deciding on multilateral interchange fees, MasterCard invoked Article 101(3) claiming that a revenue transfer (such as the MIF) was needed from the acquiring side to the issuing side to correct an asymmetry of costs between them and

[384] Ibid, para 51. [385] Ibid, para 63.

[386] Ibid, paras 64–9 (cost efficiencies, eg the development new production technologies and methods which provide the potential for substantial cost savings, synergies resulting from an integration of existing assets, economies of scale, economies of scope, cost reductions from better planning of production) and ibid, paras 69–72 (quality efficiencies, eg quality improvements, new or improved goods and services, combinations of productive assets leading to better quality and novel products or the rapid dissemination of technology, better distribution services, etc).

[387] On the need for arguments and evidence to be 'convincing', see Joined Cases 43 & 63/82, *VBVB and VBBB v Commission* [1984] ECR 19, para 52; Joined Cases C-204, 205, 211, 213, 217 & 219/00 P, *Aalborg Portland and Others v Commission* [2004] ECR I–123, para 78.

[388] *Lundbeck* (Case AT.39226) Commission Decision C(2013) 3803 final, paras 1221–3.

[389] Case T-472/13, *H Lundbeck A/S and Lundbeck Ltd v Commission*, ECLI:EU:T:2016:449.

[390] *Fentanyl* (Case AT.39685) Commission Decision C(2013) 8870 final, para 414 (discussion in paras 406–39), available at http://ec.europa.eu/competition/antitrust/cases/dec_docs/39685/39685_1976_7.pdf.

[391] *MasterCard* (Case COMP/34.579) Commission Decision (2007), available at http://ec.europa.eu/competition/antitrust/cases/dec_docs/34579/34579_1889_2.pdf.

that it generated efficiencies in the form of increased output of the system. The Commission analysed the first condition of Article 101(3) TFEU by notably verifying whether the model underlying MasterCard's MIF was founded on realistic assumptions, whether the methodology used to implement that model could be considered objective and reasonable and whether the MIF had indeed led to the positive effects claimed. It found that MasterCard failed to submit empirical evidence to demonstrate the positive effects of its MIF on the merchants' market. Indeed, the Commission mentioned that the efficiency argument in this context should not be determined 'in a general manner by economic theory alone', but that it also depends 'on the concrete evidence brought forward by the parties',[392] as any claim that a MIF creates efficiencies should not rely on 'a general assertion that the balancing of the demand of cardholders and merchants through a MIF leads to a better performance of the MasterCard's system', but 'founded on a detailed, robust and compelling analysis that relies in its assumptions and deductions on empirical data and facts'.[393]

In contrast, in its *Visa* decision, also involving MIFs, which were found by the Commission to constitute a restriction of competition by effect under Article 101(1) TFEU, the Commission took the view that they qualified for an exemption under Article 101(3) TFEU as they satisfied all the conditions of Article 101(3) TFEU.[394] With regard to the first condition of Article 101(3) TFEU,[395] the Commission accepted that Visa's MIF scheme generated positive network effects, as it promoted a large scale international payment system with positive network externalities.[396] In the absence of the scheme, there would be fewer Visa cardholders and fewer merchants accepting Visa cards. On 31 December 2007, this Article 101(3) TFEU exemption expired, and in 2008, the Commission announced that it had initiated formal proceedings against Visa Europe Ltd in relation to its MIFs for cross-border point of sale transactions. Visa Europe offered commitments to cap its debit card MIFs at 0.20 per cent, which the Commission made binding in December 2010.[397] The proceedings regarding consumer credit MIFs continued, the Commission objecting to the interchange fees set by Visa for transactions with consumer credit cards in the EEA applying to international and cross-border transactions and rules on 'cross-border acquiring' in the Visa system that limited the possibility for a merchant to benefit from better conditions offered by banks established elsewhere in the Internal Market. Visa offered commitments, a final version of which was accepted and made binding by a Commission's Article 9 of Regulation 1/2003 decision in 2014.[398] These include a cap on the weighted average MIF for consumer credit card transactions at 0.30 per cent per transaction for all transactions where it sets the fee, as well as reform of its cross-border acquiring rules, so that banks will be able to apply either the domestic rate or a reduced cross-border interchange fee of 0.2 per cent and 0.3 per cent, respectively for both debit and credit transactions when they compete for clients cross-border.

The EU Courts nevertheless require from the Commission some serious analysis of the efficiency gains put forward by the parties, as the following cases illustrate.

392 Ibid, para 730. 393 Ibid, para 732.

394 *Visa International* (Case COMP/29.373) Commission Decision [2002] OJ L 318/17.

395 Ibid, paras 79–91. 396 Ibid, para 83.

397 *VISA EUROPE* (Case COMP/39.398) Commission Commitments Decision (2010), available at http://ec.europa.eu/competition/elojade/isef/case_details.cfm?proc_code=1_39398.

398 *VISA MIF* (Case AT.39398) Commission Decision C(2014) 1199 final.

Case T-168/01, *Glaxo-SmithKline Services Unlimited v Commission*
[2006] ECR II–2629

The facts of the case have been discussed in Section 2.3.3.1. Recall that the Commission found that Clause 4 of the General Sales Conditions issued by GlaxoSmithKline to its Spanish wholesalers had both the object and the effect of restricting competition by limiting parallel trade between Spain and other Member States. The Commission rejected Glaxo's request for an exemption under Article 101(3) TFEU. The decision of the Commission was appealed to the General Court on a number of grounds, including one relating to the interpretation and application of Article 101(3) TFEU by the Commission.

In its decision, the Commission had concentrated its examination on the first condition for the application of Article 101(3) TFEU and considered that the factual arguments and the evidence submitted by GSK did not demonstrate that that condition was satisfied. All other factual arguments and the evidence submitted by GSK on the second and other conditions of Article 101(3) TFEU were rejected by way of consequence. It was only subsequently, and solely in the interest of completeness, that the Commission responded to certain of the arguments put forward by GSK with regard to the second condition of Article 101(3) TFEU. The third and fourth conditions for the application of Article 81(3) EC were also examined summarily, and were also essentially rejected by way of consequence.

The General Court examined whether the General Sales Conditions satisfied the first condition of Article 101(3) TFEU, taking into account the fact that 'dealing with an application for annulment of a decision applying Article [101(3) TFEU] carries out, in so far as it is faced with complex economic assessments, a review confined, as regards the merits, to verifying whether the facts have been accurately stated, whether there has been any manifest error of appraisal and whether the legal consequences deduced from those facts were accurate'.[399]

Evidence of a gain in efficiency

247. In order to be capable of being exempted under Article [101(3) TFEU], an agreement must contribute to improving the production or distribution of goods or to promoting technical or economic progress. That contribution is not identified with all the advantages which the undertakings participating in the agreement derive from it as regards their activities, but with appreciable objective advantages, of such a kind as to offset the resulting disadvantages for competition [. . .].

248. It is therefore for the Commission, in the first place, to examine whether the factual arguments and the evidence submitted to it show, in a convincing manner, that the agreement in question must enable appreciable objective advantages to be obtained [. . .], it being understood that these advantages may arise not only on the relevant market but also on other markets [. . .].

249. That approach may entail a prospective analysis, in which case it is appropriate to ascertain whether, in the light of the factual arguments and the evidence provided, it seems more likely either that the agreement in question must make it possible to obtain appreciable advantages or that it will not [. . .].

250. In the affirmative, it is for the Commission, in the second place, to evaluate whether those appreciable objective advantages are of such a kind as to offset the disadvantages identified for competition in the context of the examination carried out under Article [101(1) TFEU] [. . .].

399 Case T-168/01, *Glaxo-SmithKline Services Unlimited v Commission* [2006] ECR II–2629.

251. In the present case, GSK claimed that Clause 4 of the General Sales Conditions would make it possible to secure advantages both upstream of the relevant market, by encouraging innovation, and on the market itself, by optimising the distribution of medicines. As those markets correspond to different stages of the value chain, the final consumer likely to benefit from those advantages is the same.

252. The Court must therefore determine, first of all, whether the Commission was entitled to conclude that GSK's factual arguments and evidence, examination of which entailed a prospective analysis, did not demonstrate, with a sufficient degree of probability, that Clause 4 of the General Sales Conditions would make it possible to obtain an appreciable advantage of such a kind as to offset the disadvantage which it entailed for competition, by encouraging innovation.

The GC first examined the existence of an appreciable objective advantage by the Commission. GSK put forward the view that the dual pricing mechanism would enable innovation to be encouraged by claiming that, first, parallel trade in medicines marketed in Spain leads to a loss in efficiency for inter-brand competition, in so far as it reduces GSK's capacity for innovation and, second, that such mechanism will lead to a gain in efficiency for inter-brand competition in so far as it will enable GSK's capacity for innovation to be increased. In order to support these arguments GSK put forward a number of items of economic or econometric evidence demonstrating, first, the loss in efficiency. For instance, innovation in this market is ensured by a level of R&D expenditure which is both substantial and higher than that which characterizes most other industries (around 14 per cent of the turnover of GSK, representing at the time £1.3 billion). As investment in R&D is costly, high-risk and long-term, it is mainly financed from the undertaking's own funds rather than by borrowing, the capacity for financing largely depending on some very successful medicines. R&D financing is thus dependent on current returns and also on anticipated returns and as parallel trade has the effect of reducing the returns of the pharma company concerned, it had the effect of reducing the capacities of GSK for financing R&D. GSK also claimed that the dual pricing mechanism will lead to a gain in efficiency, in particular in view of the fact that the differentiated pricing system provided for will make it possible to cover the cost of R&D by ensuring that the prices are set, on each national market, at the level corresponding to the preferences of the final consumer, that is to say, ultimately of the Member State concerned, while the strong competitive pressure by innovation which prevails in the sector would ensure that GSK will act as a rational economic operator by transforming, in so far as necessary, those additional profits into investment in R&D. In contrast, the Commission found that there was no proof that parallel trade had a negative impact on GSK's R&D activities and, in any event, that it was not proved that parallel trade had an appreciable negative effect on those activities. The Commission essentially examined if parallel trade gave rise to a loss of efficiency, and having not found any, it did not consider it necessary to examine in detail whether it was demonstrated that the dual pricing mechanism entailed a gain in efficiency. The GC criticized the Commission for not examining the gains in efficiency and for not also taking into account the possible losses in efficiency associated with parallel trade. The GC found that '[t]he factual arguments and the supporting evidence submitted by GSK appear to be relevant, reliable and credible, having regard to their content [. . .] which is itself corroborated on a number of significant aspects by documents originating with the Commission',[400] all of which emphasized the importance of R&D to innovation and the need to achieve a sufficient level of profitability to be able to devote the necessary resources to R&D to develop innovative products.[401]

400 Ibid, para 263. 401 Ibid, para 264.

The GC noted the following with regard to the loss of efficiency associated with parallel trade:

269. The Court notes that the conclusion that it has not been shown that parallel trade leads to a loss in efficiency by altering GSK's capacity for innovation is based on an examination [. . .] which does not take into consideration all the factual arguments and evidence pertinently submitted by GSK, contrary to what the Commission maintained in its written submissions, and is not supported by convincing evidence. While the Commission is clearly not required to examine all the arguments submitted to it, it must, on the other hand, in accordance with the case-law [. . .] adequately examine all the evidence which is relevant and, so far as necessary, refute it by means of evidence capable of substantiating its conclusion.

270. Taken as a whole, those arguments revealed that the competitive problem faced by GSK and the solution which it had sought to apply were, according to GSK, as follows.

271. First, the medicines sector is characterised by the importance of competition by innovation. R&D is costly and risky. Its cost is simultaneously a fixed cost (it is not connected with the number of medicines sold), a joint cost (it is incurred upstream from production and distribution and, in part, is not linked with a particular medicine) and a global cost (it is not connected with a particular country). It is most frequently financed from an undertaking's own funds rather than from borrowing. It therefore requires an optimum flow of income. The optimisation of income may be ensured by adapting the prices of medicines to the preferences of final consumers, where those preferences differ. Price differentiation thus allows the cost of R&D to be recovered from the final consumers who are prepared to pay for it. That practice of differentiated prices, which is presented here in a simplified form, is known to economists as 'Ramsey Pricing'.

272. Second, the implementation of that practice in the medicines sector is characterised by certain particular traits. When medicines are protected by patents, their price may be maintained, in the particular interest of the producer, at a higher level than the marginal cost throughout the life of the patent. However, when those medicines are reimbursed by the national sickness insurance schemes, their price must, in the general interest, be maintained directly (price control) or indirectly (control of benefits) at a level which is not excessively higher than the marginal cost. The extent of that excess reflects the preference of the final consumer, that is to say, essentially, the national sickness insurance scheme. If the latter is relatively sensitive to the price of the medicine, the excess will tend to be small; if it is relatively insensitive to that price, the excess will tend to be significant. In practice, that degree of sensitivity depends on various parameters, such as the standard of living or the state of public finances. The fraction of the cost of R&D recovered by producers of medicines therefore varies from one Member State to another, according to the income which the applicable price makes available. In the present case, it is in the United Kingdom that GSK could, owing to the regulations applicable, recuperate the global and joint part of its R&D costs.

273. Third, parallel trade has the effect of reducing that income, to an uncertain but real degree. That practice, which economists know as 'free riding', is characterised by the fact that the intermediary leaves the role which he traditionally plays in the value chain and becomes an arbitrageur and thus obtains a greater part of the profit. The legitimacy of that transfer of wealth from producer to intermediary is not in itself of interest to competition law, which is concerned only with its impact on the welfare of the final consumer. In so far as the intermediary participates in intrabrand competition, parallel trade may have a pro-competitive effect. In the medicines sector, however, that

activity is also seen in a special light, since it does not bring any significant added value for the final consumer.

274. Fourth, Clause 4 of the General Sales Conditions seeks to optimise income and to neutralise parallel trade. It limits the possibilities previously afforded to GW's wholesalers to sell, outside Spain, medicines bought at the price set with a view to reimbursement by the Spanish sickness insurance scheme. It therefore allows sales in other Member States to be made at the price determined with a view to reimbursement by their respective national sickness insurance schemes. The fact that the profit is retained by the producer will in all likelihood give rise to a gain in efficiency by comparison with the situation in which the profit is shared with the intermediary, because a rational producer which is able to ensure the profitability of its innovations and which operates in a sector characterised by healthy competition on innovation has every interest in reinvesting at least a part of its surplus profit in innovation.

275. However, [. . .] the Decision shows that the Commission, after acknowledging the importance of competition by innovation in the relevant sector, failed to undertake a rigorous examination of the factual arguments and the evidence submitted by GSK concerning the nature of the investments in R&D, the characteristics of the financing of R&D, the impact of parallel trade on R&D and the applicable regulations, but confined itself [. . .] to observations which, to say the least, are fragmentary and, as GSK rightly claims, of limited relevance or value.

276. Such an omission is particularly serious where the Commission is required to determine whether the conditions for the application of Article [101(3) TFEU] are satisfied in a legal and economic context, such as that characteristic of the pharmaceutical sector, where competition is distorted by the presence of national regulations. That circumstance obliges the Commission to examine with particular attention the arguments and evidence submitted to it by the person relying on Article [101(3) TFEU]. [. . .]

279. In those circumstances, the question of the degree of correlation between parallel trade and R&D could not be dealt with without a more thorough examination or be satisfied by the lapidary conclusion that it was not proved that there was a causal link between parallel trade (or its limitation) and R&D [. . .].

With regard to the gain in efficiency associated with Clause 4 of the General Sales Conditions the GC held:

294. It must be observed that, as GSK correctly maintains, the Commission carried out no serious examination of its factual arguments and its evidence relating, not to the disadvantages of parallel trade, but to the advantages of Clause 4 of the General Sales Conditions.

295. In the light of the structure of GSK's arguments and also of the discussion of that point during the administrative procedure, the Decision could not avoid examining, first of all, whether parallel trade led to a loss in efficiency for the pharmaceutical industry in general, and for GSK in particular. Only in the absence of any dispute in that regard could the Commission validly dispense with such an examination [. . .].

296. However, a comparison of the evidence provided by GSK with the other evidence invoked by the Commission in the Decision clearly reveals that in the medicines sector the effect of parallel trade on competition is ambiguous, since the gain in efficiency to which it is likely to give rise for intrabrand competition, the role of which is limited by the applicable regulatory framework, must be compared with the loss in efficiency to which it is likely to give rise for interbrand competition, the role of which is central.

297. In those circumstances, the Commission could not refrain from examining, second, whether Clause 4 of the General Sales Conditions could enable GSK's capacity for innovation to be reinstated and thus could give rise to a gain in efficiency for interbrand competition.

298. That, moreover, formed the very core of the prospective analysis which the Commission was under a duty to carry out in order to respond to GSK's request for an exemption. According to the consistent case-law [. . .] it is necessary to determine whether the agreement prohibited on account of the disadvantage which it represents for competition (Article [101(1) TFEU]) presents an advantage of such a kind as to offset that disadvantage (Article [101(3) TFEU]).

299. The Commission was therefore still required to examine GSK's arguments relating to the advantages expected of Clause 4 of the General Sales Conditions. [. . .]

301. The Commission could not merely reject those arguments outright on the ground that the advantage described by GSK would not necessarily be achieved [. . .] but was required, in accordance with the case-law, also to examine, as specifically as possible, in the context of a prospective analysis, whether, in the particular circumstances of the case and in the light of the evidence submitted to it, it seemed more likely that the advantages described by GSK would be achieved or, on the contrary, that they would not [. . .]. It was not entitled to consider, in a peremptory manner and without providing proper arguments, that the factual arguments and the evidence submitted by GSK must be regarded as hypothetical, as it maintained most recently at the hearing.

The GC concluded:

303. [. . .] [T]he Decision is vitiated by a failure to carry out a proper examination, as the Commission did not validly take into account all the factual arguments and the evidence pertinently submitted by GSK, did not refute certain of those arguments even though they were sufficiently relevant and substantiated to require a response, and did not substantiate to the requisite legal standard its conclusion that it was not proved, first, that parallel trade was apt to lead to a loss in efficiency by appreciably altering GSK's capacity for innovation and, second, that Clause 4 of the General Sales Conditions was apt to enable a gain in efficiency to be achieved by improving innovation.

The analysis by the GC of Article 101(3) TFEU in *GSK* was confirmed by the CJEU, after this part of the judgment was challenged, among others by the Commission, but also by GSK itself and number of other parties, such as the European Association of Euro Pharmaceutical Companies (EAEPC).

Case C-501/06 P, *GlaxoSmithKline Services Unlimited v Commission*
[2009] ECR I–9291

The Commission argued that the General Court misapplied the case-law relating to the allocation of the burden of proof and the standard of proof required in relation to Article [101(3) TFEU], criticizing the GC for having referred to the case law, criteria, and principles applicable to the review of concentrations, although, for the Commission, no such analogy should be drawn between the examination of the anti-competitive effects of a concentration and that of the application of Article 101(3) TFEU. The CJEU rejected this argument.

83. The burden of proof [. . .] falls on the undertaking requesting the exemption under Article [101(3) TFEU]. However, the facts relied on by that undertaking may be such as to oblige the other party to provide an explanation or justification, failing which it is permissible to conclude that the burden of proof has been discharged [. . .].

The Commission further claimed that the GC committed an error of law in finding that it is sufficient that an undertaking wishing to obtain an exemption under Article 101(3) TFEU show that it is probable that gains in efficiency may occur. This argument was also rejected by the CJEU.

93. [. . .] [A]n exemption granted for a specified period may require a prospective analysis regarding the occurrence of the advantages associated with the agreement, and it is therefore sufficient for the Commission, on the basis of the arguments and evidence in its possession, to arrive at the conviction that the occurrence of the appreciable objective advantage is sufficiently likely in order to presume that the agreement entails such an advantage.

94. The [General Court] therefore committed no error of law [. . .] in holding that the Commission's approach may entail ascertaining whether, in the light of the factual arguments and the evidence provided, it seems more likely either that the agreement in question must make it possible to obtain appreciable advantages or that it will not.

95. Moreover, the [General Court] made no error of law [. . .] in observing that it was necessary to determine whether the Commission was entitled to conclude that GSK's factual arguments and evidence, examination of which entailed a prospective analysis, did not demonstrate with a sufficient degree of probability that Clause 4 of the agreement would, by encouraging innovation, make it possible to obtain an appreciable objective advantage of such a kind as to offset the disadvantage which it entailed for competition.

The Commission also argued that the General Court had imposed a high standard on it for the analysis of GSK's arguments, on the ground that the situation faced by that company is structural. The CJEU also rejected this argument noting that the examination of the agreement under Article 101(3) 'must be undertaken in the light of the factual arguments and evidence provided in connection with the request for exemption':

103. Such an examination may require the nature and specific features of the sector concerned by the agreement to be taken into account if its nature and those specific features are decisive for the outcome of the analysis. Taking those matters into account, moreover, does not mean that the burden of proof is reversed, but merely ensures that the examination of the request for exemption is conducted in the light of the appropriate factual arguments and evidence provided by the party requesting the exemption.

The Commission further criticized the General Court for having misapplied the causal link necessary for the application of Article 101(3) TFEU in holding that the restriction of competition contributes to the promotion of technical progress because increased profits benefit the manufacturer and not the wholesaler. The Commission noted that it is necessary to determine whether the restriction actually does contribute to the promotion of technical progress and not whether it gives rise to increased profits which may, if the undertakings wish, be invested in R&D. Indeed, it is not sufficient that part of the increase in profits go to R&D expenditure and that it benefits manufacturers and not intermediaries. The Commission thus argued that the GC had committed an error of law in allowing the condition relating to the improvement in the distribution of goods or in the promotion of technical progress to be satisfied without there being any specific link between the restriction of competition and the advantage claimed. The CJEU also rejected this argument, noting that it does not result from the case law 'that the existence of an appreciable objective advantage necessarily supposes that all of the additional funds must be invested in R&D'.[402]

A further argument, this time by EAEPC, related to the lack of sufficient proof that the causal link between the reduction in parallel trade resulting from the insertion of Clause 4 of the agreement and the increase in innovation resulting from an increase in R&D expenditure. The CJEU dismissed the argument noting that it cannot be inferred from the judgment that the GC inferred a direct connection between parallel trade and expenditure on R&D.

The function of Article 101(3) being to justify a restriction of competition identified under Article 101(1) TFEU, the examination of efficiencies has to occur within the same analytical framework undertaken for the analysis of the anti-competitive effects of the agreement.[403] This has been interpreted by the Commission's Guidelines on Article 101(3) TFEU as requiring that the efficiency gains should be 'generated' within the context of the relevant market on which the anti-competitive effects were produced,[404] in view of the requirement of the second condition of Article 101(3) TFEU that the agreement should allow consumers 'a fair share of the resulting benefit'. We will examine more closely this condition in the subsequent section. One should, however, note that the Commission has exceptionally taken into account as efficiency gains benefits that were not generated on the specific relevant market, where the anti-competitive effects were felt, but also 'collective environmental benefits' that were not necessarily limited to the relevant market in question.[405] The EU Courts have also considered efficiency gains generated outside the specific confines of the relevant market identified under Article 101(1) TFEU. In *CGM v Commission*, with regard to some price fixing agreements that led to a price increase on the inland transport services market but brought benefits through intermodal transport of cargo in containers between Northern Europe and the Far East to the maritime transport services market, the General Court held that,

> [f]or the purposes of examining the merits of the Commission's findings as to the various requirements of Article [101(3) TFEU] [. . .], regard should naturally be had to the advantages arising from the agreement in question, not only for the relevant market, namely that for inland transport services provided as part of intermodal transport, but also, in appropriate cases, for every other market on which the agreement in question might have beneficial effects, and even, in a more general sense, for any service the quality or efficiency of

402 Case C-501/06 P, *GlaxoSmithKline Services Unlimited v Commission* [2009] ECR I–9291, para 120.

403 Case T-131/99, *Michael Hamilton Shaw and Others v Commission* [2002] ECR II–2023, para 163.

404 Guidelines on Article 101(3) (formerly 81(3)), para 43.

405 See *CECED* (Case IV.F.1/36.718) Commission Decision 2000/475/EC [1999] OJ L 187/47, paras 55–7. See also *P&I Clubs* (Cases IV/D-1/30.373 and IV/D-1/37.143) Commission Decision 1999/329/EC [1999] OJ L 125/12, noting that the agreements in question relating to the direct marine insurance market will not only benefit shipowners (the immediate customers of the protection and indemnity (P&I) clubs) and the final customers of shipowners, be they passengers or goods carriers, who also benefit from the provision of such a level of insurance, but also 'any other third person that could suffer from extra-contractual damages produced by a shipowner (such as marine pollution)'.

which might be improved by the existence of that agreement. [. . .] [Article 101(3) TFEU] envisage[s] exemption in favour of, amongst others, agreements which contribute to promoting technical or economic progress, without requiring a specific link with the relevant market.[406]

Although in most cases, the aggregation of efficiency gains across relevant markets was justified by the fact that, as the Commission notes in paragraph 43 of its Guidelines, 'the group of consumers affected by the restriction and benefiting from the efficiency gains [on a different market] are substantially the same', this has not always been the case, as some of the examples above illustrate. One may also argue that in the event of a restriction of competition by object, no relevant market is defined in the context of Article 101(1) TFEU.

6.4.3. ALLOWING CONSUMERS A FAIR SHARE OF THE RESULTING BENEFIT

This is arguably one of the most contentious conditions in Article 101(3) TFEU in the sense that its interpretation has given rise to controversy. A literal interpretation of this condition, in particular by reference to the French version of the Treaty, indicates that an equitable share of the profits generated by the efficiency gains should be passed on to users ('*tout en réservant aux utilisateurs une partie équitable du profit qui en résulte*'). As we have highlighted in Chapter 2, it is unclear if this condition would require an *actual* and *total* compensation for the consumers of the relevant market affected by the restriction of competition, or if an *hypothetical* compensation would be sufficient to the extent that it compensates at least *a part* of the loss to consumers resulting from the specific restriction of competition, and/or the specific anti-competitive conduct leads to higher output and lower prices in the long run than in comparison to a situation in which the specific restrictive conduct would not have taken place. As we have explained in Chapter 2, if one takes the first approach, Article 101 TFEU would be considered as a consumer interest provision, mandating that consumers should be better off following the restriction of competition (an objective of distributive justice). If one adopts the second approach, what would count is the increase in economic efficiency (wealth maximization), irrespective of the amount of that benefit that is effectively passed on to consumers. The Commission's Guidelines on Article 101(3) TFEU seem to adopt the first approach:

[406] Case T-86/95, *Compagnie Générale Maritime v Commission* [2002] ECR II-1011, para 343; Case T-213/00, *CMA CGM SA v Commission* [2003] ECR II-913, para 227. See also Case T-168/01, *GlaxoSmithKline Services Unlimited v Commission* [2006] ECR II-2629, paras 247–8 noting:

247. In order to be capable of being exempted under Article [101(3) TFEU], an agreement must contribute to improving the production or distribution of goods or to promoting technical or economic progress. That contribution is not identified with all the advantages which the undertakings participating in the agreement derive from it as regards their activities, but with appreciable objective advantages, of such a kind as to offset the resulting disadvantages for competition [. . .].

248. It is therefore for the Commission, in the first place, to examine whether the factual arguments and the evidence submitted to it show, in a convincing manner, that the agreement in question must enable appreciable objective advantages to be obtained [. . .] it being understood that these advantages may arise not only on the relevant market but also on other markets [. . .].

European Commission, Guidelines on the application of Article 101(3) (references omitted)

85. The concept of '*fair share*' implies that the pass-on of benefits must at least compensate consumers for any actual or likely negative impact caused to them by the restriction of competition found under Article [101(1) TFEU]. In line with the overall objective of Article [101] to prevent anti-competitive agreements, the net effect of the agreement must at least be neutral from the point of view of those consumers directly or likely affected by the agreement. If such consumers are worse off following the agreement, the second condition of Article [101(3)] is not fulfilled. The positive effects of an agreement must be balanced against and compensate for its negative effects on consumers. When that is the case consumers are not harmed by the agreement. Moreover, society as a whole benefits where the efficiencies lead either to fewer resources being used to produce the output consumed or to the production of more valuable products and thus to a more efficient allocation of resources.

86. It is not required that consumers receive a share of each and every efficiency gain identified under the first condition. It suffices that sufficient benefits are passed on to compensate for the negative effects of the restrictive agreement. In that case consumers obtain a fair share of the overall benefits ([para] 82). If a restrictive agreement is likely to lead to higher prices, consumers must be fully compensated through increased quality or other benefits. If not, the second condition of Article [101(3)] is not fulfilled.

The concept of 'consumer' is defined broadly by the Commission's Guidelines, as 'the customers of the parties to the agreement and subsequent purchasers', thus encompassing 'all direct or indirect users of the products covered by the agreement, including producers that use the products as an input, wholesalers, retailers, and final consumers, i.e. natural persons who are acting for purposes which can be regarded as outside their trade or profession.'[407] Indeed, EU competition law protects all consumers at each segment of the value chain, and not just final consumers.[408] For instance, in *GlaxoSmithKline v Commission*, the General Court and the CJEU treated as consumers both the final buyer of the medicines and the health funds who reimbursed or paid the cost.[409]

407 Guidelines on Article 101(3) (formerly 81(3)), para. 84.

408 The General Court adopted a different position in Case T-168/01, *GlaxoSmithKline Services Unlimited v Commission* [2006] ECR II–2969, the GC held that 'the objective assigned to Article [101(1) TFEU], which constitutes a fundamental provision indispensable for the achievement of the missions entrusted to the Community, in particular for the functioning of the internal market [. . .] is to prevent undertakings, by restricting competition between themselves or with third parties, from reducing the welfare of the final consumer of the products in question' (ibid, para 118), and concluded that Article 101(1) TFEU 'requires an analysis designed to determine whether it has as its object or effect the prevention, restriction or distortion of competition on the relevant market, to the detriment of the final consumer' (ibid, para 42). On appeal, the CJEU found that 'neither the wording of Article 101(1) TFEU nor the case-law lend support to such a position', the Court clearly announcing that 'Article [101 TFEU] aims to protect not only the interests of competitors or of consumers, but also the structure of the market and, in so doing, competition as such. Consequently, for a finding that an agreement has an anti-competitive object, it is not necessary that final consumers be deprived of the advantages of effective competition in terms of supply or price': Joined Cases C-501, 513, 515 & 519/06 P, *GlaxoSmithKline Services Unlimited v Commission* [2009] ECR I–9291, para 63.

409 T-168/01, *GlaxoSmithKline Services Unlimited v Commission* [2006] ECR II–2969; Joined Cases C-501, 513, 515 & 519/06 P, *GlaxoSmithKline Services Unlimited v Commission* [2009] ECR I–9291.

The concept of 'consumers' should be understood as a sociological category, rather than referring to the situation of individual consumers as such. The Commission explains in its Guidelines that '[t]he decisive factor is the overall impact on consumers of the products within the relevant market and not the impact on individual members of this group of consumers'.[410] The EU Courts fully acknowledge this:

> [I]t is the beneficial nature of the effect on *all* consumers in the relevant markets that must be taken into consideration, not the effect on each member of that category of consumers.[411]

Hence, it cannot be excluded that some individual consumers may be worse off as a result of an agreement justified by Article 101(3) TFEU.

Furthermore, the concept of consumers should not be understood as referring only to current customers of the undertakings in question in the relevant market, but also to 'subsequent purchasers'.[412] The Guidelines stipulate the method to be used for assessing these benefits for the future consumers in this relevant market:[413]

European Commission, Guidelines on the application of Article 101(3) (references omitted)

> 88. In making this assessment it must be taken into account that the value of a gain for consumers in the future is not the same as a present gain for consumers. The value of saving 100 euro today is greater than the value of saving the same amount a year later. A gain for consumers in the future therefore does not fully compensate for a present loss to consumers of equal nominal size. In order to allow for an appropriate comparison of a present loss to consumers with a future gain to consumers, the value of future gains must be discounted. The discount rate applied must reflect the rate of inflation, if any, and lost interest as an indication of the lower value of future gains.

The trade-off may also be presented as being between static versus dynamic efficiency, which is an issue we explore more in depth in Chapter 13.

The second condition of Article 101(3) thus seems to rely on the principle of compensation of consumers conceived as an abstract sociological category, rather than on the effective compensation of individual consumers that have been harmed by the restrictive practice. However, there are limits to how abstract the category of 'consumers' may be drawn. As we previously explained, paragraph 43 of the Commission's Guidelines on the application of Article 101(3) TFEU states that

> effects on consumers in one geographic market or product market cannot normally be balanced against and compensated by positive effects for consumers in another unrelated geographic market or product market. However, where two markets are related, efficiencies

410 Guidelines on Article 101(3) (formerly 81(3)), para 87.

411 Case C-238/05, *Asnef-Equifax, Servicios de Información sobre Solvencia y Crédito SL v Asociación de Usuarios de Servicios Bancarios (Ausbanc)* [2006] ECR I–11125, para 70.

412 Guidelines on Article 101(3) (formerly 81(3)), para 81.

413 On this issue, see also C Townley, 'Inter-generational Impacts in Competition Analysis: Remembering Those Not Yet Born' (2011) 11 *European Competition L Rev* 580.

> achieved on separate markets can be taken into account provided that the group of consumers affected by the restriction and benefiting from the efficiency gains are substantially the same.

One may claim that the assessment should not be limited to the benefit to actual (or future) consumers of the specific relevant market, but should extend overall in order to assess *all* the benefits of the conduct found restrictive of competition under Article 101(1) TFEU, without only limiting the assessment to those related to the specific relevant market. The General Court of the EU has made such a suggestion in *Compagnie Générale Maritime v Commission* where it held that:

> [R]egard should naturally be had to the advantages arising from the agreement in question, not only for the relevant market [. . .] but also, in appropriate cases, for every other market on which the agreement in question might have beneficial effects, and even, in a more general sense, for any service the quality or efficiency of which might be improved by the existence of that agreement [. . .] without requiring a specific link with the relevant market.[414]

Adopting a 'wide' definition of benefits accruing to the 'consumers', which expands the assessment of Article 101(3) TFEU to other markets than the relevant one, would nevertheless require some limiting principle, even if this assessment concerns only benefits to 'consumers' and not benefits to all other actors involved. Although the Commission has explicitly rejected any balancing of negative effects on consumers in one geographic or product market with positive effects for consumers in unrelated markets, in its *Star Alliance* decision, the Commission has taken into account 'out of market efficiencies' in view of 'objective factual elements specific to this case', such as 'a certain discrepancy between market definition on the demand-side and supply-side, two-way flow of efficiencies and considerable commonality between passenger groups travelling on the route of concern and related behind and beyond routes.'[415]

Some recent case law of the EU courts accepts the position of the Commission as reflected in paragraph 43 of its Guidelines on Article 101(3) TFEU. The Commission's

[414] Case T-86/95*Compagnie Générale Maritime v Commission of the European Communities* [2002] ECR II–1011; [2002] 4 CMLR 29, para 343. See also Case T-213/00*CMA CGM SA v Commission of the European Communities* [2003] ECR II–913; [2003] 5 CMLR 4, para 227.

[415] *Star Alliance* (Case COMP/AT.39595) Commission Decision, paras 57–8, available at http://ec.europa.eu/competition/antitrust/cases/dec_docs/39595/39595_3012_4.pdf. For an analysis, see A Italianer, 'Competitor Agreements under EU Competition Law', Speech (26 September 2013), available at http://ec.europa.eu/competition/speeches/text/sp2013_07_en.pdf, noting however that this happened 'in view of the specificity of the airline sector' and that this test does not substitute the standard test for consumer benefits but simply complements it. According to Italianer, 'the broadened test does not weigh the harm to one consumer group against the benefits to another, completely unrelated, consumer group' (ibid, 11–12). The degree of commonality expected for this trade-off to occur is high. For instance, the harm to actual consumers in a specific relevant market cannot be compensated by the benefits to future consumers in a related market. As the Commission explained in its *Star Alliance* decision, 'the assessment takes into account *only* those out-of-market efficiencies that are enjoyed by the passengers who travel *both* on the Frankfurt–New York route of concern and related behind and beyond routes—while the out-of-market efficiencies enjoyed by the passengers on related behind and beyond routes, who do not travel on the route of concern, are disregarded—this assessment does not balance competitive harm to one customer group against benefits to another customer group' (*Star Alliance* (Case COMP/AT.39595), para 61).

MasterCard decision was criticized by the appellants for not taking into account the benefits for cardholders resulting from the MIF, the Commission only focusing on the objective benefits that accrued to merchants, the other side of this multi-sided market. The General Court, citing the *Compagnie Générale Maritime v Commission* judgment, held that 'appreciable objective advantages to which the first condition of Article [101(3) TFEU] relates may arise not only for the relevant market but also for every other market on which the agreement in question might have beneficial effects, and even, in a more general sense, for any service the quality or efficiency of which might be improved by the existence of that agreement'.[416] However, the General Court also added (without citing any authority for this proposition) that '[...] as merchants constitute one of the two groups of users affected by payment cards, the very existence of the second condition of Article [101(3) TFEU] necessarily means that the existence of appreciable objective advantages attributable to the MIF must also be established in regard to them'.[417] The General Court also used language to indicate that the benefits compensating the restriction of competition should not be abstract and general, but that they should aim the category of consumers affected by the restrictive practice.

The General Court indeed distinguished the *MasterCard* case, where no exemption was granted under Article 101(3) TFEU, from the *Visa II* decision where exemption was granted, noting that the Commission admitted in this case that

> the utility of the Visa scheme for each category of user (merchants or cardholders) depended on the number of users belonging to the other category, (and that) [. . .] it was difficult to determine the average marginal utility of a Visa card payment to each category of user, (the Commission referring) to the need to find an acceptable proxy which met its concerns, including its concern that the MIF is set at a 'revenue-maximising' level [. . .]. Accordingly, while Visa's MIF was granted an exemption, this was not only on the basis of its contribution to the increase in system output but because it was determined by reference to three categories of costs corresponding to services that could be regarded as being provided, at least in part, for the benefit of merchants [. . .].[418]

In his Opinion, following the appeal of the General Court's judgment in *MasterCard* at the CJEU, AG Mengozzi held the following with regard to this issue:

> 153.[. . .] [The] appellants claim, in essence, that the General Court erred in ignoring the advantages which the MIF provide for cardholders, direct users of the services provided on the issuing market, whereas those advantages could potentially have compensated for the restrictive effects arising from the MIF for merchants, direct users of the services provided on the acquiring market.
>
> 154. The point of law underlying that complaint is therefore whether, in order for the exemption provided for in Article [101(3) TFEU] to be applicable in such a context, it is necessary that the fair share of the profit resulting from the advantages arising from the agreement, as provided for in Article [101(3) TFEU], be reserved for the direct consumers of the services provided on the market on which the restrictive effects for competition are produced—in this case, in particular, merchants—or whether it can be considered that the

416 Case T-111/08, *MasterCard, Inc and Others v European Commission*, ECLI:EU:T:2012:260, para 228.
417 Ibid. 418 Ibid, para 224.

restrictive effects harming those consumers may be compensated by the advantages produced for consumers of the services provided on a related market, namely, in this case, cardholders. [. . .]

156. In that regard, it should be observed, first, that the consumers referred to in that provision must be considered to be the direct or indirect consumers of the goods or services covered by the agreement. Second, it is apparent from consistent case-law that, in order for an agreement restrictive of competition to be capable of being exempted under Article [101(3) TFEU], the appreciable objective advantages created by that agreement must be of such a character as to compensate for the disadvantages which they cause for competition. It may be inferred from that case-law that, in order for a restrictive agreement to be able to benefit from the exemption, the advantages resulting from that agreement must ensure that consumers are compensated in full for the actual or probable adverse effects that they must bear owing to the restriction of competition resulting from the agreement. In other words, the benefits arising from the restrictive agreement must counterbalance its negative effects.

157. To my mind, however, that compensation must apply to consumers who are directly or indirectly affected by the agreement. It is the consumers that suffer the harm caused by the restrictive effects of the agreement at issue that must, in principle, be allowed, as compensation for that harm, the fair share of the benefit resulting from the agreement referred to in Article [101(3) TFEU].

158. In fact, if it were possible to take into consideration the advantages resulting from an agreement for *one* category of consumers of certain services in order to counterbalance the negative effects on *another* category of consumers of other services on a different market, that would amount to allowing the former category of consumers to be favoured to the detriment of the latter category. However, distributive logic of that type seem to me, in principle, to have no connection with the practical scope of competition law. Competition law is intended to protect the structure of the market, and thus competition, in the interest of competitors and, ultimately, consumers in general. Conversely, it is not intended to favour one category of consumers to the detriment of a different category.

159. In that regard, I must further observe that those considerations are not necessarily inconsistent with the settled case-law of the General Court, referred to (the *Compagnie Générale Maritime v Commission* judgment) according to which it is not excluded that it may be possible to take into consideration the advantages resulting from the agreement that occur on a different market from that on which the agreement produces the restrictive effects. Such advantages may be taken into consideration where, for example, the category of consumers affected by the agreement on the two separate markets is the same.

160. In the present case, the General Court considered that, in order for the exemption provided for in Article [101(3) TFEU] to be applicable, it is necessary that the existence of appreciable objective advantages arising from the MIF is, in any event, proved for merchants. In so far as merchants constitute the category of consumers that directly suffer the restrictive effects of the MIF on the market on which those effects are produced, I consider that the General Court did not err in law.

161. [. . .] Last, it also follows from the foregoing that, contrary to the contention of the main appellants, the General Court did not consider at paragraphs 228 and 229 of the judgment under appeal that where two or more categories of consumers are affected, *all* those categories must benefit from *the same share* of the profit resulting from a restriction of competition in order for the restriction to be considered to be compatible with Article [101 TFEU]. It considered only that objective advantages flowing from the MIF must be established in regard to merchants.

You will note the reference of the AG to the requirement that the same *category* of consumers is affected by the agreement, which is quite similar to the approach put forward by the Commission in its Article 101(3) TFEU Guidelines. The CJEU confirmed the General Court's judgment.

Case C-382/12 P, *MasterCard Inc and Others v Commission*, ECLI:EU:C:2014:2201

237. It follows from this that, in the case of a two-sided system such as the MasterCard scheme, in order to assess whether a measure which in principle infringes the prohibition laid down in Article [101(1) TFEU]—in so far as it creates restrictive effects in regard to one of the two groups of consumers associated with that system—can fulfil the first condition laid down in Article [101(3) TFEU], it is necessary to take into account the system of which that measure forms part, including, where appropriate, all the objective advantages flowing from that measure not only on the market in respect of which the restriction has been established, but also on the market which includes the other group of consumers associated with that system, in particular where, as in this instance, it is undisputed that there is interaction between the two sides of the system in question. To that end, it is necessary to assess, where appropriate, whether such advantages are of such a character as to compensate for the disadvantages which that measure entails for competition.

239. Likewise, the General Court also took into account the two-sided nature of the system when examining the advantages flowing from the MIF that are enjoyed by merchants, [. . .] in which it recognised that the increase in the number of cards in circulation may increase the utility of the MasterCard system as far as merchants are concerned, even though, in its definitive assessment of the facts, the General Court concluded that the risk of adverse effects for merchants is higher the greater the number of cards in circulation.

240. In particular, as regards the argument by which LBG complains that the General Court did not take into account the advantages flowing from the MIF for cardholders, it must be held that [. . .] the General Court was, in principle, required, when examining the first condition laid down in Article [101(3) TFEU], to take into account all the objective advantages flowing from the MIF, not only on the relevant market, namely the acquiring market, but also on the separate but connected issuing market.

241. It follows from this that, should the General Court have found that there were appreciable objective advantages flowing from the MIF for merchants, even if those advantages did not in themselves prove sufficient to compensate for the restrictive effects identified pursuant to Article [101(1) TFEU], all the advantages on both consumer markets in the MasterCard scheme, including therefore on the cardholders' market, could, if necessary, have justified the MIF if, taken together, those advantages were of such a character as to compensate for the restrictive effects of those fees.

242. [. . .] However [. . .] examination of the first condition laid down in Article [101(3) TFEU] raises the question whether the advantages derived from the measure at issue are of such a character as to compensate for the disadvantages resulting therefrom. Thus, where, as in the present case, restrictive effects have been found on only one market of a two-sided system, the advantages flowing from the restrictive measure on a separate but connected market also associated with that system cannot, in themselves, be of such a character as to compensate for the disadvantages resulting from that measure in the absence of any proof of the existence of appreciable objective advantages attributable to that measure in the relevant market, in particular [. . .] where the consumers on those markets are not substantially the same.

> 243. In the present case, and without any distortion having been claimed in that regard, the General Court concluded [. . .] that there was no proof of the existence of objective advantages flowing from the MIF and enjoyed by merchants. In those circumstances, it was not necessary to examine the advantages flowing from the MIF for cardholders, since they cannot, by themselves, be of such a character as to compensate for the disadvantages resulting from those fees. The General Court was therefore fully entitled to find [. . .] that 'the [appellants'] criticism that insufficient account was taken of the advantages of the MIF for cardholders is, in all events, ineffective'. [. . .]
>
> 248. Lastly, in so far as the appellants complain that the General Court did not explain why all the categories of consumers must benefit from the same share of the profit resulting from the MIF, suffice it to note that that complaint is based on a misreading of the judgment under appeal. The General Court did not in any way find that each group of consumers should benefit from the same share of that profit, but merely indicated that, as merchants constitute one of the two groups of users affected by payment cards, they should also enjoy appreciable objective advantages attributable to the MIF. Thus, by using the word 'also' in paragraph 228 of its judgment, the General Court correctly indicated that merchants had to enjoy the MIF 'as well as' cardholders, and not 'to the same extent' as them.

It is not clear if this signifies that the CJEU accepts the requirement that the category of consumers to which flow the benefits of the agreement must be substantially the same as those affected by its restrictive effects.[419]

As explained above, the Commission has occasionally considered *collective* benefits that accrue to other parties than the consumers of the specific relevant market even if these benefits cannot be subsumed to narrow efficiency gains and may consist in broader public interests. This broader balancing may transform Article 101(3) TFEU to some form of cost–benefit analysis, as long as the concept of 'consumer' may be expanded to include future consumers of the relevant market or consumers in related markets.

OFT, Article 101(3)—A Discussion of Narrow versus Broad Definitions of Benefits (12 May 2010) (text withdrawn from the OFT Archives/CMA website, on file with author) (excerpts)

> 1.4. Whilst there are many interesting questions that may be raised in the context of the exemption criteria, this paper restricts itself to three main questions.
>
> 1.5. First, what exactly are the benefits that contribute to improving the production or distribution of goods or contribute to promoting technical and economic progress? How broadly should benefits arising from improvements in production or distribution or from promotion of technical and economic progress be defined? For example, should environmental benefits be included within the definition?
>
> 1.6. Second, should one consider benefits and costs within each individual affected relevant market separately or should one aggregate across all affected markets? For example, if an agreement benefits consumers in two geographic markets but harms them in a third geographic market, should the agreement as a whole not be exempted?

[419] For an interesting discussion of 'out-of-market efficiencies' in a multi-sided markets setting see F Ducci, 'Out-of-Market Efficiencies, Two-Sided Platforms and Consumer Welfare: A Legal and Economic Analysis', (2016) 12(3) *Journal of Competition Law and Economics* 591.

1.7. Third, does 'consumers' in the second condition only refer to current consumers (that is, within the time dimension of the market definition) or should beneficiaries extend to future consumers? For example if an agreement will benefit tomorrow's consumers but harms today's consumers should it be possible to weigh these against each other and exempt the agreement if the future benefits outweigh today's harm?

1.8. Our main points for discussion regarding these three questions are as follows:

Broadening the definition of benefits to include indirect economic and non-economic benefits may have the following advantages:

- Where the benefits of an agreement overlap with wider government policy objectives, it ensures that competition policy is not regarded as a block on desirable social goals.
- Even where benefits of an agreement do not overlap with government objectives, broadening the definition of benefits ensures consumers are not denied real and significant benefits.
- It would bring the Article 101(3) assessment in line with standard cost–benefit analysis, in which all benefits are considered.
- It supports market integration and the harmonious development of the EU by allowing for greater alignment of competition and wider EU policy objectives.

However, broadening the definition of benefits to include indirect economic and non-economic benefits may also have the following disadvantages:

- Only measuring wider benefits and not wider costs would be inconsistent, and potentially allow agreements that are detrimental to society.
- Including wider benefits risks the distinction between competition and industrial policy becoming blurred.
- There are questions as to how one quantifies the benefits and whether difficulties in measuring them will increase the possibility of mistakes.

Aggregating both costs and benefits across different relevant affected markets may have the following advantages:

- It avoids erroneous conclusions in two-sided markets where consumers who benefit and those who are harmed are different but aggregate benefits across the entire market outweigh the harm.
- It is consistent with UK merger guidelines in allowing for the consideration of benefits in markets other than the relevant affected market.

However, aggregating both costs and benefits across different relevant affected markets may also have the following disadvantages:

- It raises issues of distributional equity.
- It may raise institutional issues and damage the support for competition regimes.

Widening direct economic benefits to include intergenerational benefits may have the following advantages:

[. . .]

- It recognises the generation of future efficiencies from dynamic competition (for example, through R&D innovation).

However, widening direct economic benefits to include intergenerational benefits may also have the following disadvantages:

- Determining the discount rate and time lag to be applied when including future benefits is not straightforward.
- In trading off benefits across different groups of consumers, competition authorities may not be best placed to make the subjective and inter-personal evaluations required.
- There is a danger that agreements permitted on the basis of expected future benefits may have an overall anti-competitive effect if these benefits are not realised.

One may raise concerns over the difficulties of measurement that such a broad consideration of benefits to actual and future consumers entails. With regard to the trade-off between various types of benefits to consumers and anti-competitive effects, the Commission notes in its Article 101(3) TFEU Guidelines that the second condition of Article 101(3) TFEU incorporates a 'sliding scale': '[t]he greater the restriction of competition found under Article [101(1)] the greater must be the efficiencies and the pass-on to consumers'.[420] According to the Commission, this sliding scale approach 'implies that if the restrictive effects of an agreement are relatively limited and the efficiencies are substantial it is likely that a fair share of the cost savings will be passed on to consumers', hence making it possible, in such cases, not to engage in a detailed analysis of the second condition of Article 101(3), provided that the three other conditions for the application of this provision are fulfilled.[421] However, if the restrictive effects of the agreement are substantial and the cost savings are relatively insignificant, 'it is very unlikely that the second condition of Article [101(3)] will be fulfilled', therefore indicating that 'the impact of the restriction of competition depends on the intensity of the restriction and the degree of competition that remains following the agreement'.[422]

The Commission's Guidelines also include detailed explanations as to the implementation of the trade-off and the necessary evaluation or measurement of the various efficiency gains that may be passed on to consumers by distinguishing between 'cost efficiencies' and 'qualitative efficiencies'.

Cost efficiencies may be passed on to consumers if the undertakings in question can increase profits by expanding output, and thus reaching out (for instance, by price discrimination) to consumers that would not have otherwise bought the product. The Commission will in this case consider 'two opposing forces resulting from the restriction of competition and the cost efficiencies': '[o]n the one hand, any increase in market power caused by the restrictive agreement gives the undertakings concerned the ability and incentive to raise price [. . .][;] [o]n the other hand, the types of cost efficiencies that are taken into account may give the undertakings concerned an incentive to reduce price'.[423] This does not seem to require in practice the quantification of costs and benefits, as the Commission indicates that it will be using a number of parameters, some of which have to do with the characteristics and the structure of the relevant market (the 'greater the degree of residual competition the more likely it is that individual undertakings will try to increase their sales by passing on cost efficiencies'), the nature and magnitude of the efficiency gains, the elasticity of demand (as the pass-on rate depends on the extent to which consumers respond to changes in price), the magnitude of the restriction of competition.[424]

Qualitative efficiencies may take the form of 'new and improved products, creating sufficient value for consumers to compensate for the anticompetitive effects of the agreement, including a price increase'.[425] For instance, it is possible that an agreement leading to higher

420 Guidelines on Article 101(3) (formerly 81(3)), para 90. 421 Ibid. 422 Ibid, para 91.
423 Ibid, para 101. 424 Ibid, para 96. 425 Ibid, para 102.

prices for consumers may be justified if consumers are compensated through other parameters of competition, such as increased quality or innovation.[426] The Commission recognizes that '[a]ny such assessment necessarily requires value judgment' as '[i]t is difficult to assign precise values to dynamic efficiencies of this nature'.[427] Indeed,

> [a]s long as the increase in value stemming from such improvements exceeds any harm from a maintenance or an increase in price caused by the restrictive agreement, consumers are better off than without the agreement and the consumer pass-on requirement of Article [101(3)] is normally fulfilled. In cases where the likely effect of the agreement is to increase prices for consumers within the relevant market it must be carefully assessed whether the claimed efficiencies create real value for consumers in that market so as to compensate for the adverse effects of the restriction of competition.[428]

This is particularly vague of course and indicates the Commission's discretion in assessing the trade-off.

The Guidelines do not include any guidance as to the evaluation of the trade-off between wider efficiency gains or the public interest and the restriction of competition. In *CECED*, the only case so far where such trade-off was performed, the Commission proceeded as follows.[429] The Commission considered that the restrictive agreement between the producers of washing machines led to a reduction of consumer choice, as all not energy efficient machines were removed from the market. This would have inevitably led to a price increase for washing machines overall. The consumer benefits took two different forms: first, individual consumers benefitted from the lower energy and water bills, which enabled the consumers to compensate for the price increase of the washing machines in less than a year;[430] second, there were collective benefits caused by the decrease of emissions of carbon dioxide and other environmentally damaging substances, as a result of the agreement, thus leading to social benefits that were evaluated in money terms to be seven times larger than the price increase of washing machines. As their name indicates, these benefits were not limited to the consumers of washing machines but accrued to all. Nonetheless, because of their importance and the fact that the price increase was largely compensated by the economies of energy supply it was clear that the restrictive agreement was a net benefit even for the consumers of the relevant market of washing machines. The consumers of energy, water and washing machines were largely overlapping categories and the collective benefits also accrued to the consumers of washing machines.

'Collective benefits' may be valued in various ways, either on the basis of revealed preferences, by using a market approach or through hedonic pricing and proxy goods if there is no market. Alternatively, a stated preferences approach may be used, in particular contingent valuation (CV). The approach followed may be similar to that adopted in the context of impact assessment/cost–benefit analysis.[431] With the exception of *CECED*, the European

426 Ibid, para 86; *MasterCard* (Case COMP/34.579) Commission Decision (2007), para 734, available at http://ec.europa.eu/competition/antitrust/cases/dec_docs/34579/34579_1889_2.pdf.

427 Guidelines on Article 101(3) (formerly 81(3)), para 103. 428 Ibid, para 104.

429 *CECED* (Case IV.F.1/36.718) Commission Decision 2000/475/EC [1999] OJ L 187/47.

430 Ibid, para 52.

431 For a description of these methodologies, see HM Treasury, The Magenta Book—Guidance for Evaluation (April 2011), available at https://www.gov.uk/government/uploads/system/uploads/attachment_data/file/220542/magenta_book_combined.pdf.

Commission has never proceeded to a cost–benefit analysis of anti-competitive effects and wider benefits.

Some national competition authorities put more emphasis on public policy concerns, such as sustainability. Netherlands is an excellent example of this wider approach to the justification of restrictive to competition agreements, by calling upon the Dutch Competition Authority to take into account sustainability benefits when assessing an otherwise anti-competitive agreement.[432] This may, for instance, include 'animal welfare', leading the competition authority to accept that an agreement that may raise consumer prices but at the same time enhance animal welfare may be justified if the gains in sustainability offset the price increase resulting from the agreement.[433] Of course, integrating sustainability in the trade-off raises interesting evaluation challenges, as it may be difficult to evaluate quantitatively the full array of benefits generated by sustainability.

Some may even claim that such trade-off is impossible in view of the incommensurability problem, the benefits and costs being of different kind, or in other words, qualitatively different. Commensuration is indeed 'the expression or measurement of characteristics normally represented by different units according to a common metric',[434] that being utility, price, efficiency, and competition. However, the trade-offs involved between static and dynamic efficiency (actual and future consumers), or those between price and quality, or even between the different individual consumers of the group of consumers affected by the specific restrictive conduct in the 'relevant market' may equally be described as conducive to the incommensurability problem.[435] Balancing various social values is also an exercise routinely undertaken by constitutional and administrative courts, sometimes involving issues of greater complexity than the more confined type of economic balancing needed in the context of a competition

432 On 23 December 2015, the Dutch Minister of Economic Affairs published a Draft Policy Rule on competition and sustainability for consultation. This Draft Policy Rule provides guidelines on the assessment of whether agreements relating to sustainability are exempted from the prohibition of cartels. The Rules replace the previous rules on competition and sustainability adopted in 2014. See Vision Document of the ACM on Competition and Sustainability (9 May 2014), available at https://www.acm.nl/en/publications/publication/13077/Vision-document-on-Competition-and-Sustainability/.

433 The Dutch NCA, the Authority on Competition and Markets (ACM) took into consideration sustainability concerns in agreements involving supermarkets, poultry farmers, and broiler meat processors concerning the selling of chicken meat produced under animal welfare friendly conditions in a decision adopted in 2015. In particular, the agreement looked to replace the regular chicken with the Chicken of Tomorrow, a chicken raised in a more animal-friendly manner. In examining the benefits of these agreements, the ACM explored if the measures concerned were valued by consumers and found that the improvements came at a cost higher than the consumers were willing to pay. The ACM concluded that the potential advantages did not outweigh the reduction in consumer choice and potential price increases. See ACM, ACM's analysis of the sustainability arrangements concerning the 'Chicken of Tomorrow' (26 January 2015), available at https://www.acm.nl/en/publications/publication/13789/ACMs-analysis-of-the-sustainability-arrangements-concerning-the-Chicken-of-Tomorrow/. Similar sustainability concerns were taken into account with regard to agreements between energy producers to close down coal-fired plants. See ACM, 'Private arrangement in Energy Agreement to withdraw production capacity from the market restricts competition' (26 October 2003), available at https://www.acm.nl/en/publications/publication/12194/Private-arrangement-in-Energy-Agreement-to-withdraw-production-capacity-from-the-market-restricts-competition/. One may make similar arguments with regard to an agreement between undertakings to limit the alcohol content of their drinks so as to reduce binge-drinking. For a discussion of the theoretical framework for such an approach, inspired by the capabilities approach of Amartya Sen and Martha Nussbaum, see R Claassen and A Gerbrandy, 'Rethinking European Competition Law: From a Consumer Welfare to a Capability Approach' (2016) 12(1) *Utrecht L Rev* 1.

434 W Nelson Espeland and ML Stevens, 'Commensuration as a Social Process' (1998) 24 *Annual Rev Sociology* 313, 315.

435 See the excellent analysis of R Haw Allensworth, 'The Commensurability Myth in Antitrust' (2016) 69(1) Vanderbilt L Rev 1.

law dispute.[436] The alleged incommensurability problem also ignores that commensuration is a social process, by essence deeply political.[437] Comparison is excluded between the values thought to be incommensurables. However, the choice of finding that values are incommensurable might also indicate that each of these values relies on justifications characterized by different logics, or different 'orders of worth'.[438] In this case, other decision procedures than balancing may be more appropriate, such as lexicographic (or lexical) ordering (so that certain values may take priority with respect to other values without this leading, however, to the suppression of the second ordered value), trumping (some values trumping others), combinations of trumping with balancing, etc.

6.4.4. INDISPENSABILITY OF THE RESTRICTIONS

Although this is listed as the third condition of Article 101(3) TFEU, it is usually examined before the assessment of the existence of a fair share for consumers. Indeed, such issue will not arise if the restrictions are not indispensable. The Commission explains in its Guidelines on Article 101(3) TFEU:

> 73. This condition implies a two-fold test. First, the restrictive agreement as such must be reasonably necessary in order to achieve the efficiencies. Secondly, the individual restrictions of competition that flow from the agreement must also be reasonably necessary for the attainment of the efficiencies.
>
> 74. [. . .] [T]he decisive factor is whether or not the restrictive agreement and individual restrictions make it possible to perform the activity in question more efficiently than would likely have been the case in the absence of the agreement or the restriction concerned. The question is not whether in the absence of the restriction the agreement would not have been concluded, but whether more efficiencies are produced with the agreement or restriction than in the absence of the agreement or restriction.

The Commission requires that 'the efficiencies be specific to the agreement in question in the sense that there are no other economically practicable and less restrictive means of achieving the efficiencies', taking into account the market conditions and business realities facing the parties to the agreement. This does not mean that the Commission will second-guess the

436 Ibid.

437 W Nelson Espeland and ML Stevens, 'Commensuration as a Social Process' (1998) 24 *Annual Rev Sociology* 313.

438 L Boltanski and L. Thévenot, *On Justification: Economies of Worth* (Princeton University Press, 2006), arguing that justifications fall into six main logics: civic (Rousseau), market (Adam Smith), industrial (Saint-Simon), domestic (Bossuet), inspiration (Augustine), and fame (Hobbes). Of particular interest for our purposes is the distinction made between the civic, market, and industrial logics. The Commission's interpretation of Article 101(3), a provision enabling the justification of restrictions of competition, focuses on the market logic and excludes the civic or the industrial logics from legitimate grounds of justification. Interpreting Article 101(3) TFEU more broadly would have widened the types of justification proffered against restrictive agreements. If Article 101(3) TFEU is to be interpreted broadly, then it is necessary to take into account these other forms of justification through different means. This is usually done in the context of Article 101(1) TFEU with the exclusion of some activities from the scope of competition law (see our analysis of the concept of 'undertaking'), or with intuitive balancing and the theory of regulatory ancillarity (see our analysis in Section 6.3.4). Some authors believe this is not enough and argue for the addition of an Article 101(4) TFEU that would enable public policy considerations to be balanced against the restriction of competition: G Monti, 'Article 81 EC and Public Policy' (2002) 39(5) *Common Market L Rev* 1057.

business judgment of parties' to the agreement, but that it would 'only intervene where it is reasonably clear that there are realistic and attainable alternatives'.[439] The onus is then on the parties to 'explain and demonstrate why such seemingly realistic and significantly less restrictive alternatives to the agreement would be significantly less efficient'.[440] The 'less restrictive to competition alternative test' does not only enable competition authorities to determine if the efficiencies are specific to the agreement in question but also to determine if the individual restrictions of competition resulting from the agreement are indispensable. The Commission explains in its Guidelines on Article 101(3) TFEU:

> 79. A restriction is indispensable if its absence would eliminate or significantly reduce the efficiencies that follow from the agreement or make it significantly less likely that they will materialise. The assessment of alternative solutions must take into account the actual and potential improvement in the field of competition by the elimination of a particular restriction or the application of a less restrictive alternative. The more restrictive the restraint the stricter the test under the third condition. Restrictions that are black listed in block exemption regulations or identified as hardcore restrictions in Commission guidelines and notices are unlikely to be considered indispensable
>
> 80. The assessment of indispensability is made within the actual context in which the agreement operates and must in particular take account of the structure of the market, the economic risks related to the agreement, and the incentives facing the parties. The more uncertain the success of the product covered by the agreement, the more a restriction may be required to ensure that the efficiencies will materialise. Restrictions may also be indispensable in order to align the incentives of the parties and ensure that they concentrate their efforts on the implementation of the agreement. A restriction may for instance be necessary in order to avoid hold-up problems once a substantial sunk investment has been made by one of the parties.

According to the Commission, if 'in some cases a restriction may be indispensable only for a certain period of time', the exception of Article 101(3) TFEU will only apply during this period. In any case, 'it is necessary to take due account of the period of time required for the parties to achieve the efficiencies justifying the application of the exception', which, in cases where the benefits cannot be achieved without considerable investment, should include the period of time required to ensure an adequate return on such investment.[441]

The indispensability requirement in Article 101(3) TFEU must be distinguished from the 'objective necessity test' employed in the context of ancillary restraints under Article 101(1) TFEU.[442] As the CJEU clearly explained in *MasterCard*:

> [. . .] [T]hose two provisions have different objectives and that the latter criterion relates to the issue whether coordination between undertakings that is liable to have an appreciable adverse impact on the parameters of competition, such as the price, the quantity and quality of the goods or services, which is therefore covered by the prohibition rule laid down in Article [101(1) TFEU], can none the less, in the context of Article [101(3) TFEU], be considered indispensable to the improvement of production or distribution or to the promotion of technical or economic progress, while allowing consumers a fair share of the resulting benefits. By contrast, [. . .] the objective necessity test [under Article 101(1) TFEU] concerns the question whether, in the

439 Guidelines on Article 101(3) (formerly 81(3)), para 75. 440 Ibid. 441 Ibid, para 81.

442 See our analysis in Section 6.3.4.1.

> absence of a given restriction of commercial autonomy, a main operation or activity which is not caught by the prohibition laid down in Article [101(1) TFEU] and to which that restriction is secondary, is likely not to be implemented or not to proceed.[443]

One may venture that the CJEU requires less restrictive factual conditions for finding that a restriction of competition is indispensable to the achievement of efficiency gains, under Article 101(3) TFEU, eventually accepting even restrictions of competition that would not eliminate, but also significantly reduce the efficiencies, than those required for the application of the 'objective necessity test' under the ancillary restraints doctrine in the context of Article 101(1) TFEU, where the CJEU seems to go as far as demand that in the absence of the restriction, the efficient main operation or activity 'is likely not to be implemented or not to proceed'.

6.4.5. NO ELIMINATION OF COMPETITION IN A SUBSTANTIAL PART OF THE MARKET

This condition ensures that some degree of residual competition will always exist on a specific market, regardless of the existence of efficiency gains. It shows that there are instances in which competitive rivalry is valued as such, even if efficiency gains may compensate the consumers affected by the conduct fund restrictive to competition. Indeed, as the Commission explains in its Guidelines on Article 101(3) TFEU:

> 105. [. . .] Ultimately the protection of rivalry and the competitive process is given priority over potentially pro-competitive efficiency gains which could result from restrictive agreements. The last condition of Article 81(3) recognises the fact that rivalry between undertakings is an essential driver of economic efficiency, including dynamic efficiencies in the shape of innovation. In other words, the ultimate aim of Article 81 is to protect the competitive process. When competition is eliminated the competitive process is brought to an end and short-term efficiency gains are outweighed by longer-term losses stemming *inter alia* from expenditures incurred by the incumbent to maintain its position (rent seeking), misallocation of resources, reduced innovation and higher prices.

The concept of elimination of competition in respect of a substantial part of the products concerned is an autonomous EU law concept specific to Article 101(3) TFEU.[444] Article 101(3) may thus be used by an undertaking in a dominant position to justify conduct falling under

443 Case C-382/12 P, *MasterCard Inc and Others v Commission*, ECLI:EU:C:2014:2201, para 93.

444 See Guidelines on Article 101(3) (formerly 81(3)), para 106; Joined Cases T-191, 212 & 214/98, *Atlantic Container Line (TACA)* [2003] ECR II-3275, para 939 (the General Court holding that '[a]lthough eliminating competition may preclude the application of the block exemption [provided in this case by the old Block Exemption for maritime conferences], the mere holding of a dominant position has no effect in that regard. As the concept of eliminating competition is narrower than that of the existence or acquisition of a dominant position, an undertaking holding such a position is capable of benefiting from an exemption [. . .]. Thus, [. . .] it is only where a liner conference abuses its dominant position that the Commission may withdraw the benefit of the block exemption provided for in [a block exemption] regulation. Furthermore, unlike the possibility of eliminating competition, the mere holding of a dominant position is not in itself prohibited by the competition rules laid down in the Treaty, since only the abuse of that position is prohibited'); Case T-395/94, *Atlantic Container Line* [2002] ECR II-875, para 330.

Article 101(1) to the extent that this does not amount to an abuse of a dominant position, that is, a competition law infringement under Article 102 TFEU.[445]

Indeed, 'since Articles [101] and [102] both pursue the aim of maintaining effective competition on the market, consistency requires that Article [101(3)] be interpreted as precluding any application of this provision to restrictive agreements that constitute an abuse of a dominant position.'[446] The group exemptions are made under Article 101(3) TFEU and do not exempt an agreement made by a firm that is later found to be dominant from infringing Article 102 TFEU.[447]

According to settled case law, the application of Article 101(3) cannot prevent the application of Article 102 TFEU.[448] An agreement exempted by Article 101(3) may still fall under the scope of Article 102 if the conditions of this provision are satisfied. The practical implication of this is that undertakings need to comply to both Articles 101 and 102 TFEU.[449] As the Commission notes, 'not all restrictive agreements concluded by a dominant undertaking constitute an abuse of a dominant position.'[450] The Commission provides the example of a case where a dominant undertaking is party to a non-full function joint venture, which is found to be restrictive of competition but at the same time involves a substantial integration of assets.

While it is clear that the concept should not be confused with dominance, its contours remain nebulous. The Commission's Guidelines on Article 101(3) TFEU, nevertheless provide some broader directions of the inquiry:

- Whether competition is being eliminated depends on the degree of competition existing prior to the agreement and on the impact of the restrictive agreement on both actual and potential competition.[451]
- Market shares are relevant, but as the Commission recognizes in its Guidelines on Article 101(3) TFEU 'the magnitude of remaining sources of actual competition cannot be assessed exclusively on the basis of market share.'[452] Indeed, a 'more extensive qualitative and quantitative analysis is normally called for'. This will include an assessment of the capacity of actual competitors to compete and their incentive to do so.[453]
- One should examine the influence of the restrictive agreement on the various parameters of competition, in particular 'the most important expressions of competition', that is, 'price competition' and 'or competition in respect of innovation and development of new products.'[454]

445 In that respect, the Guidelines on Article 101(3) (formerly 81(3)), para 106, re-interpreted some references in some older Guidelines regarding vertical restraints and horizontal cooperation agreements which stated that in principle restrictive agreements concluded by dominant undertakings cannot be exempted. It is only if the dominant undertaking abuses of its dominant position that for this conduct it may not use Article 101(3) TFEU.

446 Guidelines on Article 101(3) (formerly 81(3)), para 106.

447 T-51/89 *Tetra Pak* [1990] ECR II–309, at paras 21–5.

448 Joined Cases C-395 & 396/96 P, *Compagnie Maritime Belge* [2000] ECR I–1365, para 130.

449 As stated in the Guidelines on Article 101(3) (formerly 81(3)) n 90: '[s]imilarly, the application of Article [101(3)] does not prevent the application of the Treaty rules on the free movement of goods, services, persons and capital. These provisions are in certain circumstances applicable to agreements, decisions and concerted practices within the meaning of Article [101(1) TFEU] citing to that effect Case C-309/99, *Wouters* [2002] ECR I–1577, para 120.'

450 Guidelines on Article 101(3) (formerly 81(3)), para. 106.

451 Ibid, para. 108.

452 See also Case T-168/01, *GlaxoSmithKline Services Unlimited v Commission* [2006] ECR II–2969, para 313.

453 Guidelines on Article 101(3) (formerly 81(3)), para 109.

454 Ibid, para 110.

- Market conduct can be an important clue as to the existence of an elimination of competition. The Commission explains that if following the conclusion of the agreement the parties have implemented and maintained substantial price increases or engaged in other conduct indicative of the existence of a considerable degree of market power, this is an indication that the parties are not subject to any real competitive pressure and that competition has been eliminated with regard to a substantial part of the products concerned.[455]
- If the restrictive agreement removes the competitive constraint exercised by a maverick undertaking or changes its competitive incentives having thus an impact on future competitive interactions that may be a major source of concern.[456]
- The more the products of the parties to the agreement are close substitutes the greater the likely restrictive effect of the agreement.[457]
- The existence of barriers to entry eliminating potential competition, including any real possibility for new entry on a significant scale.[458]

6.4.6. EXEMPTIONS TO THE PROHIBITION PRINCIPLE: UK COMPETITION LAW

6.4.6.1. Individual assessment

As it is also the case for Article 101 TFEU, section 9 CA98 provides a 'legal exception' to the Chapter I prohibition. Section 9 CA98 mirrors the four conditions of Article 101(3) TFEU.[459] Note that the CMA has stated in its Guidance that it will have regard to the Commission's Guidelines on Article 101(3) TFEU in interpreting these conditions.[460] Accordingly, severe restrictions of competition are unlikely to benefit from individual exemption as such restrictions generally fail the first two conditions for exemption (objective economic benefits and benefits to consumers) and the third condition (indispensability). In the presence of hardcore restrictions, it is unlikely that the agreement can be exempted under Article 101(3) TFEU. The burden of proving that the conditions of Article 101(3) TFEU are met is on the party against which the allegations of infringement of the competition rules is made.[461]

In one of the older decisions,[462] the predecessor of the CMA, the OFT confirmed that payment card networks such as the MasterCard scheme provided benefits to customers by facilitating easy payment due to the fact that MasterCard was very widely accepted. In the absence of the MasterCard Members Forum (MMF) agreement, every issuing and every acquiring

455 Ibid, para 111. 456 Ibid, para 112. 457 Ibid, para 113. 458 Ibid, paras 114–15.

459 The wording of section 9(1) is similar to that of Article 101(3) TFEU except that in the first condition in section 9(1) the phrase 'of goods' is not included. The omission of these words is intended to make clear (and consistently with the practice of the European Commission in relation to Article 101(3)) that improvements in production or distribution in relation to services may also satisfy the first condition in section 9(1).

460 OFT 401, Agreements and concerted practices (December 2004), para 5.5. See also *Tobacco* (Case CE/2596-03) OFT Decision (15 April 2010), para 7.50. In this case, the parties did not demonstrate that the agreements contributed to improving production or distribution, or promoting technical or economic progress, or that the restrictions of competition were indispensable to the attainment of the efficiencies claimed (ibid, para 7.54).

461 *Online resale price maintenance in the bathroom fittings sector* (Case CE/9857/14) OFT Decision (10 May 2016), Annex, paras A.88–A.89.

462 *Investigation of the multi-lateral interchange fees provided for in the UK domestic rules of MasterCard UK members Forum Limited* (Case CA98/05/05) OFT Decision (6 September 2005).

bank would have had to enter into bilateral arrangements, relatively difficult and costly process. Therefore, the MMF multilateral interchange fee agreement reduced the costs of entry into the MasterCard scheme and the costs of operating the scheme and in principle could benefit consumers and meet the criteria for exemption under section 9 of the Competition Act or Article 101(3) TFEU. However, this would only be the case where the MIF was set at a level which was no greater than the costs of the payment transmission services and did not allow for the recovery of extraneous costs. The OFT therefore decided that as the MMF MIF allowed recovery of extraneous costs, it was set at a level which was higher than it would have been in the absence of the MMF MIF agreement. Accordingly, consumers did not receive a fair share of any benefits arising from the agreement (the extra costs were passed on to them) and the resultant distortion of competition was not necessary for the achievement of the beneficial objectives intended by the agreement.

More recently, in the *Mobility aids sector* decision the OFT (now CMA) recognized the importance, in the context of purchase of mobility scooters, of consumers having access to the right level of pre-sales and post-sales services and advice in order to ensure that end-consumers purchase products that are suitable to their needs. However, it did not consider that the Below-RRP Online Price Advertising Prohibition was indispensable to the achievement of these benefits. Even if it were established that the Below-RRP Online Price Advertising Prohibition was capable of ensuring that retailers provided pre-sales and post-sales services and advice, there were less restrictive means of achieving these benefits. Retailers who sell online (including by advertising their product and price information online) are capable of providing pre-sales and post-sales services and advice through their showrooms and/or are finding innovative, less restrictive, ways to provide pre-sales and post-sale services to their customers (including at the consumer's location).[463]

The CMA had also the opportunity to consider the section 9 exception in its recent decision in *Ophthalmology*.[464] The CMA issued a decision to Consultant Eye Surgeons Partnership Limited (CESP), confirming its breach of the Chapter I prohibition of the Competition Act 1998 and Article 101(1) TFEU (subsequently the case was settled). CESP, the membership organization of private consultant ophthalmologists, was found to infringe competition law, in particular, by:

(a) Recommending that its members refuse to accept lower fees offered by an insurer, and that they charge insured patients higher self-pay fees,

(b) Circulating amongst its members detailed price lists for ophthalmic procedures such as cataract surgery to be used with insurers. These collectively set prices did not pass on lower local costs (such as cheaper hospital fees) and made it harder for insurers and patients to obtain lower prices, and

(c) Facilitating the sharing of consultants' future pricing and business intentions such as whether to sign up to a private hospital group's package price, which enabled members to align their responses.

The CMA did not accept arguments that the joint setting of a price either fell outside the scope of the Chapter I prohibition or, alternatively, met the criteria for individual exemption. The CESP had argued to the CMA that the agreement in place was a commercialization

463 *Mobility aids sector: investigation into anti-competitive agreements* (Case CE/9587-12) OFT Decision (30 October 2014), paras 3.229–3.243.

464 *Conduct in the Ophthalmology sector* (Case CE/9784-13) OFT Decision (20 August 2015), paras 4.134–4.143.

agreement and that setting a collective price was objectively necessary to provide the private medical insurer (PMI) provider with national coverage.

A commercialization agreement is normally not likely to give rise to competition concerns if is objectively necessary to allow one party to enter a market it could not have entered individually or with a more limited number of parties than are effectively taking part in the co-operation, for example, because of the costs involved.

However, the CMA considered that this was not the case here. Consultants have a number of routes to the privately insured market which do not involve package prices set by a consultant group. The joint offering of ophthalmic services under this Inclusive Private Patient Package (IPPP) agreement, was therefore, not objectively necessary to enter this market. Further, most consultants offer their services to the privately insured market without using the IPPP agreement. In addition, the largest PMI provider has not found it necessary to enter to this agreement with CESP. There was also evidence that some CESP LLPs did not regularly use IPPP agreements.

The CMA also did not consider that it was necessary to achieve national coverage to be active on the market. Although PMI providers must be able to offer national coverage to their customers, they do so from a range of providers, and range of locations depending on the size and geographic coverage of the provider. It did not accept that there was a separate market for offering packaged ophthalmic services with national coverage. Even if there was, it would not be objectively necessary for there to be a single national price.

Therefore, the CMA concluded that the collective setting of IPPP prices is not objectively necessary to the extent that it would fall outside the scope of the Chapter I prohibition.

The CMA also analysed the IPPP infringement against the general efficiencies associated with joint selling agreements. It found that the reduction in administrative costs resulting from the PMI provider receiving only one invoice rather than separate invoices is not a direct benefit of the collectively set IPPP, but rather of the concept of a package price in general. Further, the creation of revenues for CESP LLPs that could be reinvested was a result of efficiencies at the CESP LLP level rather than of a collectively set IPPP price.

The CMA viewed the IPPP as a 'disguised cartel', which is unlikely to fulfil the conditions for exemption. In any event, it would have been difficult to prove that the direct benefits of the IPPP outweigh the significant level of the IPPPs agreed by CESP when compared to, for example, the lower package price offered by a certain LLP without coordination by CESP. There was no evidence that the efficiency savings for PMI providers were of significant size to outweigh the adverse effects on competition resulting from the IPPP.[465]

With regard to the application of Article 101(3) TFEU by UK courts, of particular interest is the different approaches followed by UK courts in analysing the implementation of Article 101(3) TFEU to MIFs.

MIFS and individual exemption under Article 101(3) TFEU

The UK MIFs cases (see Section 6.3.4.1.6) provide an illustration of the difficulty in implementing Article 101(3) TFEU in complex cases involving multi-sided markets and the different interpretative approaches that may be taken by various courts. The divergent approaches by the CAT and the High Court judges in these cases, led the intervention of the Court of Appeal.

465 Ibid, paras 4.149–4.163.

Sainsbury's v Mastercard
[2016] CAT 1 on exemption

Having concluded that on the counterfactual hypothesis, bilateral Interchange Fees would have been agreed between Issuing and Acquiring Banks the CAT considered that these bilateral Interchange Fees would have involved the development of novel charging structures between Issuing Banks and Acquiring Banks/Merchants and that one of the reasons why bilateral Interchange Fees were not agreed in the 'real' world was because of the existence of the UK MIF. For this reason, it was very difficult to see how the UK MIF as actually set could possibly be exempted under Article 101(3) TFEU.[466] *Indeed, the CAT considered that none of the four conditions of exemptability under Article 101(3) TFEU were met:*[467]

- *The UK MIF does not contribute to improving the production or distribution of goods, or to promoting technical or economic progress as it is not necessary to the operation of the MasterCard Scheme. It does not, in fact, make any contribution to the Scheme, beyond the saving of the transaction costs that would be incurred in negotiating bilateral agreements and the UK MIF as set in fact acts as an inhibitor to economic progress, frustrating bilateral negotiations between Issuing Banks and Acquiring Banks/Merchants, creating upward pressure on Merchant Service Charges, and preventing new charging structures from arising.*
- *There are no 'resulting benefits' to share with consumers.*
- *The UK MIF is not indispensable to the operation of the MasterCard Scheme, even though the MasterCard Scheme itself is highly beneficial.*
- *The UK MIF has the effect of precluding or inhibiting competition.*

Asda Stores Ltd & Others v Mastercard
[2017] EWHC 93 (Comm) on exemption

In contrast, in Asda Stores Ltd and Others v Mastercard, the High Court accepted the arguments advanced by MasterCard under Article 101(3) to justify the MIFs that were considered a restriction of competition (MIFs in the EEA with the exception of those in the UK and Ireland which were found not to constitute a violation of Article 101(1) TFEU).[468] *With regard to efficiency gains, the High Court noted that the relevant benefits should be causally linked to the MIF and that it was not sufficient to identify benefits which resulted from the use of cards generally or the MasterCard scheme generally. However, it also held that assessment should not be confined to benefits arising solely on the acquiring market but that, subject to the important proviso that the benefits must have a direct causal link with the MasterCard MIFs (not just the scheme), one could take into account benefits to all consumers on both sides of the market, merchants and cardholders as well as wider benefits by way of technical and economic progress. However, this assessment excludes benefits to the parties to the restrictive agreement (such as profits). The High Court found that there was no room for consideration in this case of some more general social benefits beyond those to the MasterCard merchants and cardholders, due to the causation requirement. For example, the wider social costs of*

466 *Sainsbury's v Mastercard* [2016] CAT 1, para 287. 467 Ibid, para 288.

468 *Asda Stores Ltd & Others v Mastercard* [2017] EWHC 93 (Comm), paras 262–92. The application of Article 101(3) TFEU was also explored by the High Court even if this was not necessary in view of Popplewell J's conclusion as to the compatibility of the MasterCard scheme with Article 101(1) TFEU.

cash, such as tax evasion or the cost of printing money, which are reduced by card use, are to a significant extent charged by banks to users through bank charges. There is no element which can be quantified as being a direct result of the MIF. Accordingly, the relevant benefits to be considered in this case were only those conferred on merchants and cardholders.

With regard to the fair share requirement of Article 101(3) TFEU, the High Court held that it is not material that the benefits produced by a restrictive agreement do not entirely compensate each particular consumer if the average consumer does enjoy that compensation and the agreement therefore produces a beneficial or neutral effect on the market generally. Two alternative methodologies were canvassed before the High Court as potential ways in which to quantify the exemptible level of the MIF:

- The merchant indifference test (MIT), also known as the tourist test, which takes its name from the premise that the only benefit to merchants of taking cards justifying an interchange fee is the amount that would make the merchant indifferent to whether the customer paid in cash or by card. To avoid taking account of the advantages of repeat trade, the customer is assumed to be a tourist. The premise is that the merchant's incremental cost of processing a cash payment is greater than that of processing a card payment, and it is the difference between the two which makes him indifferent to the method of payment if it has to be paid by way of a MIF.
- A benefit–cost balancing approach. This involves trying to identify the costs of producing the benefits to merchants which the MIF confers, based on the costs incurred by issuers in creating those benefits or at least some of them.

The High Court concluded that the best available approach to quantifying an exempt or exemptible level of MIF was to use the MIT methodology on the basis of the results of a 2015 European Commission Survey of merchants' costs of accepting cash and cards adequately adjusted to take account of other relevant benefits to merchants.

If a MIF at a particular level satisfied the fair share requirement, it would only be indispensable if the benefits could not be provided by a realistic alternative to a MIF. On the basis of these considerations, Popplewell J found that MIFs for all UK and Irish domestic transactions, as well as for cross-border EEA credit card transactions, could lawfully have been set higher than the average rates actually set by MasterCard, and that therefore the exemptible rate for cross-border EEA debit card transactions was below the level set by MasterCard during the contentious period, thus concluding that the MIFs were exempt under Article 101(3) TFEU.

Sainsbury's v Visa
[2018] EWHC 355 (Comm) on exemption

With regard to the Visa MIF scheme, Phillips J held in a High Court judgment in 2017 that Visa's UK MIFs did not restrict competition under Article 101(1) TFEU.[469] *In a subsequent judgment,*[470] *Phillips J held that if Visa's UK MIF did in fact infringe Article 101(1), Visa's UK MIF did not merit exemption under Article 101(3) TFEU.*[471]

469 *Sainsbury's Supermarkets Ltd v Visa Europe Services LLC & Anor* [2017] EWHC 3047 (Comm).

470 After having been asked by the parties to determine what levels of UK MIFs (if any) would or could have qualified for exemption under Article 101(3) on the basis that (contrary to his conclusion) the UK MIFs did restrict competition within the meaning of Article 101(1) and, contrary to his finding in *Sainsbury's v Visa* (ibid), were not objectively necessary.

471 *Sainsbury's Supermarkets Ltd v Visa Europe Services LLC* [2018] EWHC 355 (Comm).

7. [. . .] [E]xemption will only be granted to restrictive agreements which give rise to net economic benefits or increases in value: to the extent that a restriction simply benefits one group at the expense of the other (a 'zero sum game'), that restriction is not generating an efficiency, but merely transferring value which already exists in the economy. For example, the fact that accepting a payment card enables Merchants to win business from competitors who do not accept that card (referred to as 'Business Stealing') is a benefit for the accepting Merchants but not, in itself, for the economy as a whole: their competitors suffer an equal and opposite loss, achieving no more than transferring business from one to the other with no net gain [. . .].

8. It is not in dispute that the Scheme as a whole gives rise to several net economic benefits which would be capable of being 'efficiencies' for the purpose of Article 101(3), including some or all of the following aspects. The judge referred to the efficiency of payment card transactions, cost savings as a result of fewer payment transactions, facilitation of distance transactions, increase in aggregate sales by merchants.

However, all these efficiencies would arise even if the Scheme did not provide for MIFs (the no-MIF/default SAP counterfactual): they are inherent in any payment card scheme (for which, it must be assumed at this stage, a MIF is not objectively necessary).

9. [. . .] The questions which arise, therefore, are:

(a) whether the UK MIFs contribute to the achievement of cost or qualitative efficiencies beyond those which would be generated by the Scheme in any event, that is to say, whether the first condition of Article 101(3) is satisfied;

(b) whether, if and to the extent that UK MIFs do contribute to additional or greater efficiencies, 'consumers' receive a fair share of such benefits, that is to say, whether the second condition of Article 101(3) is satisfied; and

(c) whether the UK MIFs are indispensable to the achievement of any efficiencies to which they contribute, or whether they could reasonably be achieved by other less restrictive means, that is to say, whether the third condition of Article 101(3) is satisfied.

It is common ground that the fourth condition of Article 101(3) need not be considered: it is not suggested that the UK MIFs have the effect of eliminating competition.

On the first condition whether the UK MIFs contribute to benefits or efficiencies the High Court examined two issues:

(i) *MIFs as an incentive to Issuers to further stimulate card usage.*

The High Court found no evidence of a real, observable and measurable link between MIFs and actions taken by Issuers to stimulate card usage.

(ii) *Stimulation of more card usage.*

Philips J found it difficult to observe the alleged effect of MIFs on the steps taken by Issuers to stimulate card usage (including making cards more beneficial generally), as it was entirely impossible to discern and demonstrate, the alleged increase in card usage arising from such increased stimulation (as opposed to the pre-existing stimulation).[472]

Phillips J also commented on the conclusions made by the High Court judge in Asda v Mastercard *as 'the broadest of assumptions as to the level of MIFs passed through to*

472 Ibid, para 47.

Cardholders by Issuers, based on equally broad estimates of Issuers' overall profit margins' were made and noted:

51. I have no confidence that that type of exercise would produce anything approximating a true valuation of the allegedly pro-competitive effects of MIFs across the whole of the UK in the real economy. It would be a remarkably unsatisfactory and surprising way of assessing whether an agreement at a particular level is unlawful under a statute. In my judgment, neither EU nor UK competition law anticipates such open-textured assessment of whether an agreement is lawful: the strictures set out in the Article 101(3) Guidelines as to the approach to the proof of efficiencies speak to a far more rigorous approach.

The High Court judge then continued and assessed the other two conditions and concluded that (a) the fair share requirement was, in itself, a legal and logical barrier to Visa establishing an exempt level of MIF,[473] *(b) that none of those proposed alternatives of incentivizing cardholders or generating benefits under the Scheme seemed to be a remotely reasonable alternative but that if Visa's case was otherwise valid, UK MIFs at some level would, effectively by definition, be indispensable.*[474]

Sainsbury's v Mastercard / Arcadia v Mastercard / Sainsbury's v Visa
[2018] EWCA 1536 (Civ) on exemption (emphases added)

Fair share to the users and the existence of a causal link between efficiency gains passed on to consumers and the restriction of competition from which they suffer.

The parties alleged that the Guidelines on Article 101(3) TFEU[475] *did not require a direct causal link. The Court took a different perspective:*

87. [. . .] We do not read this part of the CJEU's judgment in that way. The Guidelines at [para 54] do not say that there must always be a direct causal link, but that it must normally be direct, because indirect effects are normally too remote and uncertain. The Guidelines then give a specific example of an indirect effect in the form of increased profits enabling more investment in research and development, in effect the *GlaxoSmithKline* case. Whilst it is true that the Guidelines say that such an indirect link is generally not sufficiently direct to be taken into account, they do not exclude that possibility if there is convincing evidence of the link. All the CJEU in that case was saying was that, in effect, an indirect causal link will be sufficient if it is established by convincing evidence. We see no inconsistency between the Guidelines and that decision.

88. [. . .] [I]n the context of these specific cases, establishing the requisite causal link involves two critical stages: (i) that the default MIFs in each case incentivise the issuers to take steps they would not otherwise have taken; and (ii) that the steps taken did indeed increase card usage or increase the efficiencies of transactions which would have been card transactions anyway. [. . .]

89. In order to satisfy the benefits requirement, a *balancing exercise* is required, namely that the restriction under consideration 'must in particular display appreciable objective advantages [for the relevant consumers] of such a character as to

[473] Ibid, para 64. [474] Ibid, para 66. [475] Guidelines on Article 101(3) (formerly 81(3)).

compensate for the disadvantages which [the restriction] entails for competition' (the CJEU's decision in *MasterCard* [Case C-382/12 P, *MasterCard Inc and Others v Commission*, ECLI:EU:C:2014:2201, para 234] citing its previous decision in *Consten and Grundig v Commission* [1966] ECR 299, para 348). The CJEU rejected an argument by MasterCard that the wider system output of the scheme, in the sense of benefits to society as a whole, should be considered under the first condition. The CJEU held [. . .] that in a two-sided system, such as the MasterCard scheme, regard must be had for the purposes of that first condition to the net advantages not only for the consumers on the acquiring market on which the restriction was established, but also for the consumers on the other side of the system, in the issuing market. In other words, for the purposes of the benefits requirement, the court is looking at *net advantages to both cardholders and merchants* [. . .].

90. It follows that, in order to establish the requisite causal link, the schemes have to satisfy the court that, when the balancing exercise is undertaken, the objective advantages of the default MIFs to both cardholders and merchants from increased card usage and efficiencies outweigh the disadvantages of the restriction. In the case of cardholders, the specific 'disadvantage' would be the fact that not all MIF income is passed through to them, but rather some is retained by the issuers as profit. In the case of merchants, a specific disadvantage would be the cost to them of default MIFs, which they always have to bear, even on transactions where the cardholder would have used a scheme card anyway, irrespective of the MIF.

91. [. . .] As [para 43] of the Guidelines [Guidelines on Article 101(3) (formerly 81(3))] makes clear, for the purposes of the first two conditions, where a restriction affects more than one market, its effect on all such markets must be considered. The effect of the default MIF must, therefore, be considered in both the issuing market (as regards cardholders) and the acquiring market (as regards merchants). It is also made clear in [para 43], however, that where overall there are negative effects on consumers in one market, those cannot be balanced against and compensated by positive effects on consumers in another market, unless the group of consumers in each market is substantially the same, which is not the case here. [. . .]

104. We consider [. . .] that nothing in the judgments of the European Courts in *MasterCard* alters the established position under the fair share requirement, that the consumers in the specific market, here the merchants in the acquiring market, will only receive a fair share of the benefits if the advantages to them caused by the restriction outweigh the disadvantages, so that, as Popplewell J said, they are no worse off. On this point we consider that his analysis was correct and that of Phillips J was wrong.

The indispensability requirement

105. [. . .] The party seeking exemption has to prove that the restriction in question, here the default MIF, was indispensable to the attainment of the relevant benefits or efficiencies. This condition only arises if the first two conditions are satisfied. Both the Commercial Court judges below proceeded on the basis that, if the first two conditions were satisfied in relation to the MIFs, then the MIFs were indispensable by definition. It seems to us that that approach ignores that a restriction will only be indispensable if there are no other less restrictive means of achieving the same benefits or efficiencies [see para 75 of the Guidelines on Article 101(3) (formerly 81(3))]. In the context of the MIFs it follows that the schemes have to prove that the particular level of MIF for which they contend was indispensable to achieving the relevant benefits or efficiencies.

The Court of Appeal then went on to examine each appeal. It concluded that regarding the Asda v Mastercard *High Court judgment,*[476] *'despite the obvious care and detail devoted by the judge to the article 101(3) issue, there were a number of flaws'.*[477] *First, in considering the first critical stage in the causation analysis, namely whether the issuers were incentivized to increase card usage to a greater extent than they would have been anyway. Second, the judge hardly addressed the second critical stage of the causation analysis, namely the extent to which card usage actually increased as a consequence of the steps taken by the issuers to incentivize it; and, third, the judge failed to carry out the balancing exercise to establish that overall the restriction, here the MIF, provided appreciable objective advantages for the relevant consumers of such a character as to compensate for the disadvantages which the restriction entailed for competition and, in this context, the burden it imposed on merchants.*

Regarding the Sainsbury's v Visa *High Court judgment,*[478] *the Court of Appeal found that the judge had overlooked evidence which went beyond economic theory and that he was wrong to say that Visa had produced no empirical evidence or data or factual evidence to support its case on the benefits requirement and the causal link between the MIF and increased card usage. It therefore set aside the judge's order and decided to remit the case for renewed consideration.*[479]

Regarding the Sainsbury's v Mastercard *CAT judgment,*[480] *the Court of Appeal noted that the CAT did not deal with the issue of exemption under Article 101(3) TFEU in any detail at all and that 'such limited analysis of whether the existing MasterCard MIFs were exempt by reference to the four conditions to be satisfied under article 101(3) was tied to its finding that there would have been bilateral agreements as to interchange fees in the article 101(1) counterfactual'.*[481] *Therefore the case was remitted to the CAT for reconsideration.*

In *Socrates Training Limited v The Law Society of England and Wales*,[482] the CAT assessed the conveyancing quality scheme (CQS), a scheme operated by the Law Society which provides a form of accreditation for firms of solicitors engaged in residential conveyancing. The CQS had incorporated for a number of years an element of mandatory training, including training in mortgage fraud and anti-money laundering. Socrates, provider of training courses, including training in anti-money laundering, contended that the requirement under the terms of the CQS that members of the scheme must obtain certain training courses exclusively from the Law Society was an anti-competitive agreement contrary to the Chapter I prohibition in the CA98 (as well as an abuse contrary to Chapter II CA98 and Article 102 TFEU). The CAT analysed if the restrictions could be justified under Article 9(1) CA98, noting that it would apply the same approach as that for assessing objective justifications under Chapter II CA98. The burden on establishing objective justification was on the defendant, the Law Society in this case, a position consistent for both Chapters I and II CA98.[483] The Law Society argued that the mandatory training was essential to ensure the quality of training which was essential in order to retain the confidence of mortgage lenders, and thus objectively justified.[484]

476 *Asda Stores Ltd & Others v Mastercard* [2017] EWHC 93 (Comm).
477 *Sainsbury's v Mastercard / Arcadia v Mastercard / Sainsbury's v Visa* [2018] EWCA 1536 (Civ), para 242.
478 *Sainsbury's v Visa* [2018] EWHC 355 (Comm).
479 *Sainsbury's v Mastercard / Arcadia v Mastercard / Sainsbury's v Visa* [2018] EWCA 1536 (Civ), para 291.
480 *Saisnbury's v Mastercard* [2016] CAT 1.
481 *Sainsbury's v Mastercard / Arcadia v Mastercard / Sainsbury's v Visa* [2018] EWCA 1536 (Civ), para 305.
482 *Socrates Training Limited v The Law Society of England and Wales* [2017] CAT 12.
483 Ibid, paras 88 and 166. 484 Ibid, paras 98 and 167.

Socrates identified three alternative approaches to achieve the same aim, of which Roth J dismissed two.[485] The third model was that the Law Society could set standards and authorise or accredit training providers. The Law Society submitted this would be extremely costly and would be administratively burdensome.[486] However, Roth found, 'as regards costs, the Law Society had not made any attempt to estimate what the costs might be'[487] and '[a]s regards auditing, we do not see that it would necessarily involve monitoring the content of every course [. . .] [t]hat is hardly a complex exercise'.[488] He concluded that 'the evidence on practical difficulties was scant and unpersuasive [. . .] it seems clear, on all the evidence we saw and heard, that it was simply never considered'.[489] Consequently, the CAT rejected 'the Law Society's case on objective justification, ie that there was no reasonable alternative to the mandatory training by the Law Society itself'.[490] As the conditions for exemption set out in section 9(1) CA98 are cumulative, Roth J found that the restriction of training provision to the Law Society was not 'indispensable' and accordingly, the restriction did not qualify for exemption.[491]

Undertakings should self-assess these conditions for the application of the exception. As for Article 101(3) TFEU, an undertaking claiming the benefit of section 9(1) bears the burden to prove that each of the conditions of this provision are satisfied. Any restrictive agreement or other collusive practice, even those by object, may be exempted under section 9(1) CA98.

Agreements and/or concerted practices, which have as their object the restriction of competition, are very unlikely to benefit from individual exemptions.[492]

The CMA has also adopted a 'short-form' opinion procedure on a trial basis in order to provide undertakings confidential and informal advice on how the law applies to prospective horizontal and vertical agreements. This procedure may be used in genuinely novel or unresolved questions the clarification of which would benefit a wider audience.[493] Opinions are not conclusive as to the application of competition law.

6.4.6.2. Block exemption regulations

As it was indicated in Chapter 1, section 6 CA98 allows the Secretary of State, acting upon a recommendation of the CMA, to adopt domestic block exemptions that specify particular categories of agreement which are likely to be exempt from the Chapter I prohibition as a result of section 9(1). The procedure for such block exemptions is set at section 8 CA98. An agreement which falls within a category specified in the block exemption will not be prohibited under the Chapter I prohibition. Only one block exemption regulation has been adopted so far.[494]

485 Ibid, para 170. 486 Ibid, para 171. 487 Ibid, para 172. 488 Ibid, para 173.
489 Ibid, para 174. 490 Ibid, para 176. 491 Ibid, paras 184–5.

492 CMA, Case CE/9856/14, *Online resale price maintenance in the commercial refrigeration sector* (24 May 2016), para 6.81.

493 CMA27, Guidance—CMA's approach to Short-form Opinions (April 2014), available at https://www.gov.uk/government/publications/guidance-on-the-cmas-approach-to-short-form-opinions.

494 Competition Act 1998 (Public Transport Ticketing Schemes Block Exemption) Order 2001, SI 2001/319, amended by the (Public Transport Ticketing Schemes Block Exemption) (Amendment) Order 2005, SI 2005/3347; CMA53con, CMA Draft Guidance, The public transport ticketing schemes block exemption (April 2016), available at https://www.gov.uk/government/uploads/system/uploads/attachment_data/file/516082/public-transport-ticketing-schemes-block-exemption-draft-guidance.pdf.

6.4.6.3. Parallel exemptions

Section 10 CA98 also provides for parallel exemptions for agreements that benefit from an EU Block Exemption, a finding of inapplicability of Article 101 TFEU by the Commission or to which was granted an individual exemption prior to 1 May 2004 under EU competition law, as well as for agreements that fall within the scope of a block exemption regulation but which do not affect inter-State trade and therefore are not subject to EU competition law. The practical implication is that for parties falling within the scope of an EU block exemption regulation, they do not need a domestic block exemption. The CMA may impose, or remove, conditions and obligations for providing the benefit of the parallel exemption, or may even cancel a parallel exemption, even retrospectively before the date of the CMA's decision. This discretion should, however, be exercised within the confined limits set by Article 3(2) of Regulation 1/2003, according to which, as a matter of EU law, the CMA cannot impose stricter standards than those envisaged by Article 101(3) TFEU. As we have previously explained, the CMA may, as any NCA, withdraw the benefit of an EU block exemption, under specific circumstances, under Article 29(2) of Regulation 1/2003.

SELECTIVE BIBLIOGRAPHY

Books

Gerard, D, Merola, M, Meyring, B, (eds), *The Notion of Restriction of Competition* (Bruylant, 2017).

Ibáñez Colomo, P, *The Shaping of EU Competition Law* (CUP, 2018).

Lianos, I, *La transformation du droit de la concurrence par le recours à l'analyse économique* (Bruylant, 2007).

Odudu, O, *The Boundaries of EC Competition Law: The Scope of Article 81 EC* (OUP, 2006).

Chapters in books

Humpe, C, Lianos, I, Petit, N, and Walle de Gelcke, B, 'The Effects Based Approach in Article 101 TFEU' in Merola, M, and Waelbroeck, D (eds) *Towards an Optimal Enforcement of Competition Rules in Europe* (Bruylant, 2010), 467.

Journal articles

Andreangeli, A, 'From Mobile Phones to Cattle: How the Court of Justice Is Reframing the Approach to Article 101 (Formerly 81 EC Treaty) of the EU Treaty' (2011) 34(2) *World Competition* 215.

Bailey, D, 'Restrictions of Competition by Object under Article 101 TFEU' (2012) 49(2) *Common Market L Rev* 559.

Christiansen, A, and Kerber, W, 'Competition Policy with Optimally Differentiated Rules instead of "Per se Rules versus Rule of Reason"' (2006) 2(2) *J Competition L & Economics* 215.

Ehlermann, CD, 'The Modernisation of EC Antitrust Policy: A Legal and Cultural Revolution' (2000) 37 *Common Market L Rev* 537.

Hemphill, CS, 'Less Restrictive Alternatives in Antitrust Law' (2016) 116(4) *Columbia L Rev* 927.

Hawk, B, 'The American (Anti-trust) Revolution: Lessons for the EEC?' (1988) 9(1) *European Competition L Rev* 53.

Haw Allensworth, R, 'The Commensurability Myth in Antitrust' (2016) 69(1) *Vanderbilt L Rev* 1.

King, S, 'How Appreciable Is Object? The *de minimis* doctrine and Case C-226/11 *Expedia Inc v Autorité de la concurrence*' (2015) 11(1) *European Competition L J* 1.

Kovar, J-P, Kovar, R, 'L'object anti-concurrentiel au sens de l'Article 101, paragraphe 1, du TFEU: Un Object Difficile á Identifier' (2016) *Revue Concurrences* N° 1-2016, Art. N° 77266, 48.

Monti, G, 'Article 81 EC and Public Policy' (2002) 39(5) *Common Market L Rev* 1057.

Nazzini, R, 'Article 81 EC Between Time Present and Time Past: A Normative Critique of "Restriction of Competition" in EU Law' (2006) 43(2) *Common Market L Rev* 497.

Nicolaides, P, 'The Balancing Myth: The Economics of Article 81(1) & 81(3)' (2005) 32 *Legal Issues of Economic Integration* 123.

Peerperkorn, L, 'Defining by Object Restrictions' (2015–13) *Concurrences* 40.

Townley, C, 'Inter-generational Impacts in Competition Analysis: Remembering Those Not Yet Born' (2011) 11 *European Competition L Rev* 580.

Whish, R, and Sufrin, B, 'Article 85 and the Rule of Reason' (1987) 7 *Yearbook of European L* 1.

7

HORIZONTAL RESTRICTIONS OF COMPETITION

7.1. COOPERATION BETWEEN COMPETITORS, COLLUSION, AND COMPETITION LAW

We have explained in Chapter 2 that both EU and UK competition law are built on a presumption in favour of competition as the default organization method for economic production. Competition law is generally hostile to collusion between competitors, as this is seen as a way for businessmen to increase prices, while competition encourages them to cut prices and costs or to improve the quality of their products. As Adam Smith's famous dictum goes:

> People of the same trade seldom meet together, even for merriment and diversion, but the conversation ends in a conspiracy against the public, or in some contrivance to raise prices. It is impossible indeed to prevent such meetings, by any law which either could be executed, or would be consistent with liberty and justice. But though the law cannot hinder people of the same trade from sometimes assembling together, it ought to do nothing to facilitate such assemblies; much less to render them necessary.[1]

Smith was not in favour of adopting competition law against these type of restraints, yet it is clear that the fact that collusion between competitors may raise prices was clearly understood by him as an implication of collusion between competitors (or horizontal collusion). To this 'economic' or utilitarian foundation of competition law's hostility to horizontal collusion, the US Sherman Act added a more political dimension: the opposition to concentration of economic power in few hands. It was felt that no person in democracy should have power

[1] A Smith, *An Inquiry into the Nature and Causes of the Wealth of Nations* (Methuen & Co Ltd, 5th ed, 1904), bk 1, ch 10, para 82.

over the things the people want to buy or over their opportunities to work unless he has been elected and is subject to constitutional checks.

The Sherman Act itself was seen as deriving from populist opposition to the industrial concentration occurring the late nineteenth century, with the development of various trusts controlling a sizable part of the booming US economy.[2] Antitrust was meant to put a rein on the growing power of 'robber barons', such John D Rockefeller, Cornelius Vanderbilt, Grenville Dodge, Leland Stanford, Henry Villard, James J Hill, who controlled the vitally important railroads, the network industry of the time, and the rapidly emerging oil sector, which using a *Dune* metaphor will become the 'spice' of modern economy during the twentieth century. Developing checks to political and economic power, freedom of access to job opportunities and commerce were also the stepping stones of economic and political liberalism, which was emerging as the dominant ideology in the United States and in Europe, following the American War of Independence and the French Revolution.

This systematic presumption against horizontal 'collusion' and in favour of competition, in the way industry was organized, following the adoption of the Sherman Act in 1890, was something relatively new, as much of the world, but also national, economy was regulated, quite openly until the mid-twentieth century, by a number of cartels, or more broadly structures implementing cooperation between competitors on several parameters of competition, including price, quantity, quality, etc.[3] Business history teaches us that cooperation between competitors was an important feature of various industries, some of them at the global level, and that, following up medieval guilds, associations of competitors, or various forms of inter-firm horizontal cooperation persisted for long periods of time, sometimes several decades, between the same firms.[4] Cartels, the practice targeted by the Sherman Act were but a 'subset of inter-firm cooperation, which ranges from highly, fluid spot markets with no individual market power to fully integrated enterprise hierarchies' (see Figure 7.1).[5]

The choice of the terms 'collusion' or 'conspiracy', which have a negative connotation, instead of 'collaboration', 'coordination', or 'cooperation', in order to refer to inter-firm relations between competitors, exemplifies the significant shift in ethics that occurred with the passage of the Sherman Act and the implementation of criminal sanctions against cartels, now perceived as a form of robbery of the general public and consumers.[6] The criminalization

[2] The 'agrarian movement' and other progressive/populist movements in the late nineteenth century are generally considered as having been instrumental in the emergence of modern antitrust law in the US. See H Thorelli, *The Federal Antitrust Policy: Origination of an American Tradition* (John Hopkins University Press, 1955); W Letwin, *Law and Economic Policy in America: The Evolution of the Sherman Antitrust Act* (Random House, 1965). But see G Stigler, 'The Origin of the Sherman Act' (1985) 14(1) *J Legal Studies* 1 (contesting the populist rationale and the influence of the agrarian movement).

[3] It has been reported that at the end of the Second World War, almost 40 per cent of world trade was governed by cartels: United Nations, Department of Economic Affairs, *International Cartels: A League of Nations Memorandum* (Lake Success, 1947).

[4] See G Symeonidis, *The Effects of Competition: Cartel Policy and the Evolution of Strategy and Structure in British Industry* (CUP, 2002), 69–71 finding that in the UK in the 1950s, 36 per cent of industries self-reported having collusive agreements and another 26 per cent reported some form of coordination.

[5] J Fear, 'Cartels and Competition: Neither Markets nor Hierarchies' (Harvard Business School, 2006, 07-011), 6–7.

[6] On a critical analysis of the impact of criminalization movement in the 'ethical' case against cartels, but also more broadly on their conceptualization as a distinctively nasty form of horizontal 'collusion' and the expansion of the legal rules leading to their prohibition, see C Harding and J Joshua, *Regulating Cartels in Europe* (OUP, 2nd ed, 2010), 11–6 (noting that the concept of 'cartel' is relatively modern); C Beaton-Wels and A Ezrachi (eds) *Criminalising Cartels: Critical Studies of an International Regulatory Movement* (Hart, 2011); B Wardaugh, *Cartels, Markets and Crime—A Normative Justification for the Criminalisation of Economic Collusion* (CUP, 2014); C Harding and J Edwards, *Cartel Criminality: The Mythology and Pathology of Business Collusion* (Ashgate, 2015).

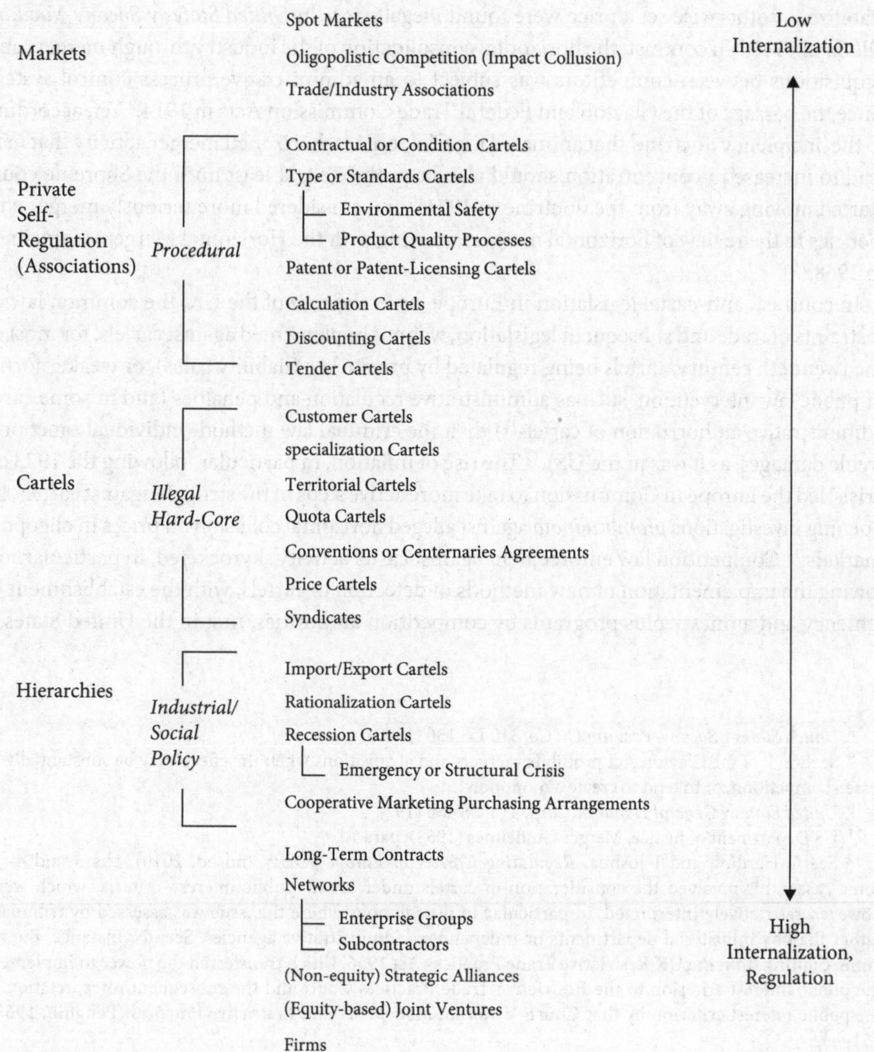

Figure 7.1. A spectrum of inter-firm cooperation.
Source: J Fear, 'Cartels and Competition: Neither Markets nor Hierarchies' (Harvard Business School, 2006, 07-011), 6–7.

of certain forms of cooperation between competitors was instrumental in establishing the moral opprobrium against cartel activity, which is prominent nowadays, at least in the United States.[7] This effort of criminalization was facilitated by the adoption of a clear prohibition rule against certain forms of agreements between competitors. Agreements to fix, raise, lower,

[7] The situation seems to be somewhat different in the UK and possibly the rest of Europe: see A Stephan, 'Survey of Public Attitudes to Price-Fixing and Cartel Enforcement in Britain' (2008) 5 *Competition L Rev* 123 (noting that although respondents demonstrated understanding that price-fixing is harmful and should be punished, less than 10 per cent were in favour of imprisonment for cartelists).

stabilize, or otherwise set a price were found illegal *per se* in *United States v Socony-Vacuum Oil Co* in 1940.[8] In contrast, the horizontal consolidation of the industry through mergers and acquisitions between competitors was subject to an administrative process control system since the passage of the Clayton and Federal Trade Commission Acts in 1914.[9] Yet, according to the 'incipiency doctrine' that animated the Clayton Act, horizontal merger activity that may lead to increase in concentration should also be prohibited, at least until the Supreme court started moving away from the doctrine in 1974[10] and considered more seriously merger efficiencies in the review of horizontal mergers, starting with the Horizontal Mergers Guidelines in 1968.[11]

In contrast, anti-cartel legislation in Europe, or in the case of the UK, the common law of restraints of trade and subsequent legislation, was not implemented against cartels, for most of the twentieth century, cartels being regulated by private law (liability rules), or weaker forms of public law intervention, such as administrative regulation and penalties (and in some cases administrative authorization of cartels[12]) than the criminal law method (individual sanctions, treble damages, as it was in the US).[13] The rise of inflation, in particular following the 1973 oil crisis, led the European Commission to take more active steps in the struggle against cartels, by opening investigations *promptu moto* against alleged horizontal collusion on prices in oligopoly markets.[14] Competition law enforcement against cartel activity skyrocketed, in particular following the implementation of new methods of detection of cartels, with the establishment of leniency and amnesty plus programs by competition authorities, first in the United States,[15]

8 *United States v Socony-Vacuum Oil Co*, 310 US 150 (1940).

9 Section 7 of the Clayton Act prohibits mergers and acquisitions when the effect 'may be substantially to lessen competition, or to tend to create a monopoly'.

10 *United States v General Dynamic Corp*, 415 US 486 (1974).

11 US Department of Justice, Merger Guidelines (1968), para 10.

12 See C Harding and J Joshua, *Regulating Cartels in Europe* (OUP, 2nd ed, 2010), chs 3 and 4. In some cases, this involved the consideration of cartels under broad 'public interest' criteria, which were, however, restrictively interpreted, in particular in jurisdictions where the issue was assessed by tribunals, rather than by ministerial departments or independent administrative agencies. See, for instance, the regime resulting from the UK Restrictive Trade Practices Act 1956, which transferred the power to implement the public interest criterion to the Restrictive Trade Practices Court and the subsequent interpretation of the public interest criterion by that Court: V Korah, *Monopolies and Restrictive Practices* (Penguin, 1968), 151–83.

13 C Harding and J Edwards, *Cartel Criminality: The Mythology and Pathology of Business Collusion* (Ashgate, 2015), 3.

14 The quinine and dyestuffs cases constitute the first example of European prosecutions of cartels, as the Commission mainly dealt with supplier cartels in the 1960s that were notified to it, as part of the legal authorization system of administrative enforcement under Regulation No 17: First Regulation implementing Articles 85 and 86 of the Treaty [1962] OJ 13/204. See *International Quinine Cartel* (Case IV/26.623) Commission Decision [1969] OJ L 192/5, on appeal Case C-41/69, *ACF Chemiefarma v Commission* [1970] ECR 661; Case C-44/69, *Buchler v Commission* [1970] ECR 733; Case C-45/69, *Boehringer Mannheim GmbH v Commission* [1970] ECR 769, and for the *Dyestuffs* case, *Matières colorants (dyestuffs)* (Case IV/26.267) Commission Decision [1969] JO L 195/11, on appeal Case C-48/69 *Imperial Chemical Industries v Commission* [1972] ECR 619. More on these cases in Chapter 11.

15 The original version of the US Corporate Leniency Program dates back to 1978, although it was rarely used. The Antitrust Division revised its Corporate Leniency Programme in 1993, the programme becoming an extremely successful US legal export. US Department of Justice, Antitrust Division, *Corporate Leniency Policy* (1993), available at http://www.justice.gov/atr/public/guidelines/0091.htm. On the evolution of the US leniency programme, which was an essential ingredient in the development of the US policy against cartels, see S Hammond, 'The Evolution of Criminal Antitrust Enforcement Over the Last Two Decades' (25 February 2010), available at https://www.justice.gov/atr/file/518241/download (noting that while in 1990,

then in Europe[16] leading to the uncovering of a number of cartels by whistle blowers, eager to benefit from immunity or a reduction of the sanctions imposed.[17] Penalties also considerably increased in both the US and Europe. As noted in Chapter 1, the cartel offence was adopted with a reform of UK competition law rules in 2002 and most recently reinforced with the 2013 reforms. It seems, therefore, that this criminalization movement of cartels has now expanded to Europe as well,[18] although, this mainly takes, at the EU level, the form of 'quasi-criminal' financial penalties against undertakings, rather than individual sanctions, such as imprisonment or other freedoms-preventing sanctions, or exemplary damages, as it is possible in UK competition law. The EU, however, lacked a proper system of EU merger control before 1989, thus leaving relatively undisturbed an important amount of merger activity between competitors, at least until the administrative system of EU Merger Regulation was adopted in 1989.[19]

This relatively strict approach in the US against certain forms of collusion between competitors, was essentially driven by the increasing recourse to economics in competition law enforcement. First, a restriction of rivalry between competitors, with the formal organization of sellers or buyers that agree to fix selling prices, purchase prices, or reduce production using a variety of tactics, is thought to provide them with the possibility of determining their output and price so that they jointly face a downward-sloping market demand curve, like that faced by a monopolist. As explained below, the cartel price will be determined by the market demand curve at the level of output chosen by the cartel. Cartelists become price-setters, thus challenging the principle of consumer sovereignty, which forms the essence of the principle of perfect competition, the economics backbone of competition law. Neoclassical price theory associated cartels to monopoly power, and derived from this negative association of cartels with monopoly, a policy of identification and elimination of cartels.[20] As with monopoly, cartels are perceived as an *abnormal* setting that breaks with the *normal* competitive process of the market order. This parallelism with monopoly, led, however, to some perceiving them, like monopoly, as a stable arrangement, which can only be defeated through the systematic de-concentration of the industry.

University of Chicago economist George Stigler challenged this conclusion, by showing in a seminal article published in 1964 that, contrary to monopoly, cartels are unstable.[21] Stigler's research question was how a cartel price, which is above the competitive level and even as high as the monopoly level, may be sustained? Accepting that members of a cartel collude to maximize profits, he examined the incentives each of them has to cheat on the agreement by undercutting any above-competition price, so as to steal customers from the other cartel members. He determined that an incentive to cheat will exist if the cheater may steal considerable sales

only one jurisdiction had a leniency programme, the US, by 2010 more than fifty jurisdictions had adopted such programme).

16 Europe adopted its own leniency programme in 1996. This was revised in 2002 and 2006, the last version being amended in 2015: European Commission Notice on Immunity from fines and reduction of fines in cartel cases [2006] OJ C 298/17, amended by [2015] OJ C 256/1.

17 Leniency programmes EU and the UK are examined in more detail in the companion volume, see I Lianos, *Competition Law Enforcement and Procedure* (OUP, forthcoming 2019).

18 P Whelan, *The Criminalization of European Cartel Enforcement: Theoretical, Legal and Practical Challenges* (OUP, 2014).

19 Council Regulation No 4064/89 on the control of concentrations between undertakings [1990] OJ L 257/13.

20 For a discussion, see JR Kinghorn and R Nielsen, 'A Practice Without Defenders: The Price Effects of Cartelization' in PZ Grossman (ed) *How Cartels Endure and How They Fail: Studies of Industrial Collusion* (Edward Elgar, 2004), 130.

21 GJ Stigler, 'A Theory of Oligopoly' (1964) 72 *J Political Economy* 44.

before being detected by the members of the cartel. These incentives, according to Stigler, and the resulting self-enforcing (because it is not possible to implement a cartel agreement as it is illegal) equilibrium of higher prices, depend on the circumstances under which cheating is possible, which in turn depends on the existence of a significant lag between cheating and detection. It is essentially an issue of information: if it easy for members of a cartel to identify the cheater to the (secret) agreement before the ink dries, then the 'dominant strategy' will be to sustain collusion. If, on the contrary, the quality of information available to the players is poor and cheating cannot be detected and eventually punished, the dominant strategy will be cheating, the cartel will be unstable and will eventually break. Stigler assumes that participation in a cartel involves a rational cost–benefit analysis of the various sellers and a comparison of the present value of cheating with the costs of adherence to the cartel price. By showing that cartels were unstable, Stigler questioned the reliance of neoclassical price theory until then on industry structure in order to assume the existence of deviations to competition. Relying on game theory, he emphasized instead behavioural, rather than structural elements, thus giving a new direction to competition law inquiry with regard to issues of horizontal collusion and sapping the case for regulatory, instead of the more light-touch antitrust intervention. By highlighting the implicit cost–benefit analysis undertaken by would-be cartelists, Stigler adhered to the neoclassical price theory on the assumption that undertakings behave as rational profit-maximizers when they reach a decision to enter a cartel, having weighed the expected gains from the cartel against the costs of participation. He derived from this principles of public action against cartels revolving around the need to enhance deterrence, according to the precepts of the optimal enforcement theory the Chicago School of law and economics was also developing at the time.[22] This assumption of rationality is crucial in order to understand the interplay between the criminalization of cartels, high financial penalties, and the emergence of new methods for detecting of cartels (eg leniency policy).[23]

Stigler's stimulating intellectual contribution notwithstanding, the reality of cartels is more complex than what is assumed in this rational choice theory intellectual framework. Behavioural economics may challenge the assumption of rationality of market players and lead to take into account other factors that may explain cartel stability, in particular dispositional and situational factors, including the corporate culture of the firm.[24] More importantly, business history studies and more empirical research show that cartels have been surprisingly and variably stable, independently from the factors explained in Stigler's theory. Despite the rise of anti-cartel policy in the US and Europe the last decades, cartels may still be pervasive and operate in sophisticated intermediary goods industries, including chemicals, coals, electrical equipment and other manufacturing machinery, textiles, paper, glass, to name a few sectors.[25] Research has shown that cartels break less easily than what was initially thought.[26] According to some empirical research, competition law enforcement and leniency

22 See our analysis in Section 7.2.

23 JM Connor and RH Lande, 'Cartels as Rational Business Strategy' (2012) 34(2) *Cardozo L Rev* 427.

24 See M Stucke, 'Am I a Price Fixer? A Behavioural Economics Analysis of Cartels' in C Beaton-Wels and A Ezrachi (eds) *Criminalising Cartels: Critical Studies of an International Regulatory Movement* (Hart, 2011), ch 12, 263.

25 See J Connor, *Global Price Fixing* (Springer, 2nd ed, 2008); MC Levestein and VY Suslow, 'Cartels and Collusion—Empirical Evidence' in RD Blair and DD Sokol (eds) *The Oxford Handbook of International Antitrust Economics*, vol 2 (OUP, 2015), ch 18, 442.

26 See MC Levenstein and VY Suslow, 'What Determines Cartel Success?' (2006) 44(1) *J Economic Literature* 43.

applications may explain a significant percentage of cartel breakup.[27] Yet, it was also reported that anti-cartel legislation led to the discovery and the dissolution of a large number of relatively weak cartels between smaller firms, but cartel-like behaviour was maintained in industries with a strong history of cooperation. The resulting increase in competition raised subsequently concentration levels through merger activity.[28] This indicates the complementary character of anti-cartel policy and merger control.

As explained above inter-firm cooperation between competitors may take various forms, some of which are considered benign in view of their positive effects to innovation, total or long-term consumer welfare. To cite a few, firms enter in arrangements to set quality standards, or codes of behaviour regarding environmental, labour, or safety regulations. Specialization agreements between competitors clarify the division of labour and the more efficient use of companies' capabilities, R&D agreements, and joint-ventures may enable companies to invest in innovative activities or technological diffusion. These agreements do not suppress all competition between the undertakings, which continue to compete on different parameters from the one they agree upon, but aim to regulate competition between them. Some business historians go even as far as seeing in horizontal agreements (including cartels) one of the first trans-national methods of economic governance, and consider them as a subset of horizontal networks assuring the performativity of the market by 'stabilizing' them.[29] Some have advanced that competition law may inhibit 'socially responsible collaboration' between competitors, in particular in order to tackle global environmental problems, such as, for instance environmental certification or ethical standards for production and agreements to preserve natural resources from overharvest and waste.[30]

These claims are of course as old as competition law or antitrust exists.[31] One may object that EU and UK competition law disposes of flexible tools in order to accommodate these concerns. Contrary to the US Sherman Act there is no *per se* prohibition of any specific category of agreement in theory, as it is always possible to use Article 101(3) of the Treaty on the Functioning of the European Union (TFEU) or the exclusion rules under UK competition law. Furthermore, there are a number of block exemption regulations (BERs) and guidelines providing a certain degree of flexibility in the implementation of competition law rules, allowing the consideration of efficiency gains of various categories of inter-firm cooperation and providing legal certainty to undertakings engaged in horizontal 'cooperation' agreements.

27 MC Levenstein and VY Suslow, 'Breaking up is Hard to Do: Determinants of Cartel Duration' (2011) 54 *J L and Economics* 455.

28 G Symeonidis, *The Effects of Competition: Cartel Policy and the Evolution of Strategy and Structure in British Industry* (CUP, 2002) (examining the effect of the Restrictive Trade Practice Act 1956, which, he found, led to a decline of explicit price-fixing cartels, which the Act outlawed).

29 J Fear, 'Cartels and Competition: neither Markets nor Hierarchies', Harvard Business School Working Paper 07-011 (2006), 25 (noting that cartels did not abolish competition but recast it in different parameters than price and finding in cartels a 'richer set of motivations' than just the desire to raise prices).

30 See, most recently, I Scott, 'Antitrust and Socially Responsible Collaboration: A Chilling Combination?' (2016) 53(1) *American Business LJ* 97. The private sector complies to various national and international regulations regarding consumer protection, food safety, and quality, imposing, for instance, the traceability of food, feed, at all stages of production, processing, and distribution by establishing standards (eg organic agriculture ISO-9000) and specific codes of conduct managed by industry associations formed by competing suppliers. For some examples, see ibid.

31 Similar arguments were made with regard to the net social benefits of an output-reducing monopoly in the presence of negative externalities, such as the extinction of animal species: see CW Park, 'Profit Maximization and the Extinction of Animal Species' (1973) 81(4) *J Political Economy* 950.

Hence, undertakings may achieve these objectives, while employing the least restrictive to competition alternative.

Drawing the line between categories of legitimate horizontal cooperation and illegal cartels, is not, however, an easy and straightforward task. The operation of presumptions of illegality, enabled by concept of by object restriction to competition under Article 101(1) TFEU, may provide competition authorities an appropriate tool for deterring *prima facie* anti-competitive conduct, while offering the possibility for a more careful consideration of possible efficiency gains under Article 101(3) TFEU. Block exemption regulations may also set safe harbours (presumptions of legality) for practices that appear *prima facie* pro-competitive, while the withdrawal of the benefit of the exemption may preserve from type II errors. Yet, this rigid architecture cannot conceal the important tensions between the competing narratives of 'collusion' and 'cooperation' in the step of the characterization of the alleged restriction, undertaken with the assistance of its legal and economic context. Such context, in our view, must take into account the emergence of new business models in a period of disruptive innovation, such as that we are living in. Collaborative innovation pushes firms to experiment new models of collaboration, while they position themselves as part of a 'fluid ecosystem of value creation.'[32] Companies are shifting from hierarchical structures to 'more networked and collaborative models', sharing assets and establishing platforms that partly operate as collaborative eco-systems to which also contribute some of their competitors.[33] Industry convergence through the digital transformation of the economy and the blurring of the digital, physical and biological dimensions, with digital companies expanding to the 'real' economy and 'real'-economy companies expanding to digital, will also inevitably transform the competitive positioning of companies, bringing them in close competition to former suppliers or customers.[34]

Professors Brandeburger's and Nalebuff's concept of 'co-opetition' may characterize the future of competitive interactions in the economy, where businesses become more competitive by cooperating with each other and developing unique capabilities that add value and complement those of their competitors.[35] Others have put forward the concept of 'semicollusion' to refer to situations where firms collude in one (or several) choice variable(s) and compete in others.[36] This is increasingly the case in highly R&D intensive industries. For instance, the Monsanto and Novozymes Bio-ag alliance was formed with the aim to discover, develop and sell microbial solutions that enable farmers worldwide to increase crop yields with less input by combining Novozymes' established product portfolio and strengths within microbial discovery, application development and fermentation with Monsanto's seeds and traits discovery, field-testing, and extensive commercial network. However, the companies maintained independent research contracts, competing on various dimensions of R&D, even if they cooperate on others. According to the literature, established models of semi-collusion refer to firms (i) colluding on prices while competing on capacities, (ii) colluding on some aspects of R&D while competing on others, but also

[32] K Schwab, *The Fourth Industrial Revolution* (World Economic Forum, 2016), 56. [33] Ibid, 58.

[34] See, for instance, the announced Google's and Apple's entry in the car market, for an example of the first, and the buy-out of Climate Corporation, a data analytics company by Monsanto, a global seed and chemicals company, for an example of the second.

[35] A Brandenburger and BJ Nalebuff, *Co-opetition* (Doubleday, 1997).

[36] A Brod and R Shivakumar, 'Advantageous Semicollusion' (1999) 47 *J Industrial Economics* 221; For a literature review, see F Steen and L Sørgard, 'Semicollusion' (2010) 5(3) *Foundations and Trends® in Microeconomics* 153 (citing the example of the liner shipping industry which forms cartels (conferences) for almost all major international route, where the companies collude on prices and compete along other dimensions of competition).

colluding on prices, or (iii) colluding on prices but competing on advertising, the objective of these practices being to deter entry.

We will first explore the boundaries of the cartel category and the underlying economic theory explaining their assessment in competition law. We will then delve into the assessment of horizontal anti-competitive cooperation by Article 101(1) TFEU, before moving to examining possible justifications for horizontal restrictions to competition.

7.2. CARTELS

7.2.1. WHAT IS A CARTEL?

Cartels constitute the archetypical restriction of competition. The term usually refers to 'a cooperative arrangement between hostile parties' and connotes the idea of a 'truce between rivals or disputants'.[37] Although cartels have been a topic thoroughly examined by economic literature, this literature does not provide a definition of what type of activity may constitute a cartel, other than the widely held view that cartels consist in competitors fixing prices together. The term 'cartel' is used neither in the EU Treaties, nor in the UK Competition Act 1998 (CA98). Nor is it referred to among the practices that are listed as examples of anti-competitive agreements, concerted practices, or decisions of association of undertakings in EU Article 101(1) or Chapter I CA98. These provisions refer instead to practices that '(a) directly or indirectly fix purchase or selling prices or any other trading conditions; (b) limit or control production, markets, technical development, or investment; (c) share markets or sources of supply', which are widely considered as practices constituting a cartel. The OECD Recommendation concerning Effective Action Against Hard Core Cartels provided[38] the first attempt to define the concept of 'cartel' with the aim to ensure convergence among various competition law regimes. The recommendation made use of the expression 'hardcore' cartel and confined it to certain categories of practices only.

OECD, Recommendation to the Council concerning Effective Action Against Hard Core Cartels, C(98)35/FINAL (25 March 1998)

For purposes of this Recommendation:

a) A 'hard core cartel' is an anticompetitive agreement, anticompetitive concerted practice, or anticompetitive arrangement by competitors to fix prices, make rigged bids (collusive tenders), establish output restrictions or quotas, or share or divide markets by allocating customers, suppliers, territories, or lines of commerce;

b) The hard core cartel category does not include agreements, concerted practices, or arrangements that (i) are reasonably related to the lawful realization of cost-reducing or output-enhancing efficiencies, (ii) are excluded directly or indirectly from the coverage of a Member country's own laws, or (iii) are authorised in accordance with those laws.

[37] C Harding and J Edwards, *Cartel Criminality: The Mythology and Pathology of Business Collusion* (Ashgate, 2015).

[38] OECD, Recommendation to the Council concerning Effective Action Against Hard Core Cartels, C(98)35/FINAL (25 March 2008), 3.

> However, all exclusions and authorizations of what would otherwise be hard core cartels should be transparent and should be reviewed periodically to assess whether they are both necessary and no broader than necessary to achieve their overriding policy objectives. After the issuance of this Recommendation, Members should provide the Organization annual notice of any new or extended exclusion or category of authorization.

It appears from this text that the definition of what constitutes a 'hardcore' cartel is not clearly delimited and that the category does not include collusive action, even between competitors, when this is 'reasonably related to the lawful realisation of cost-reducing or output-enhancing efficiencies' in particular. We will examine further below how this definitional problem regarding cartels has been resolved in EU, UK, and US competition law.

7.2.2. THE HARM CAUSED BY CARTELS

As explored in Chapter 3, cartels increase prices and reduce consumer surplus, in addition to possibly discouraging innovation. The following chart summarizes the standard treatment of cartels in economic literature.

The increase in prices above the competitive price *c*, induced by a cartel, leads to an increase in profits for the firm (π) above competitive level that is denoted by PS (*producer surplus*) in the Figure 7.2. However, at the same time there are social costs imposed by this change in prices. These social costs are represented by the area of the triangle marked as 'Net loss in SW' (*net loss in total social welfare*). There is obvious damage to the consumers, since they lose part of the consumer surplus as a consequence of the price-fixing activities of the firm. In addition, there is a clear reduction in total welfare, since due to the increase in price above competitive level the reduction of the consumer surplus exceeds the increase in producer surplus. Hence, the net effect is always negative, and it is necessary to block the cartel in order to reduce this damage.

In addition to this theoretical literature, there is a rich body of recent empirical literature on the subject of the aggregate harm caused by cartels to society. John Connor has constructed the most exhaustive data base on cartels throughout the world and in his joint work with

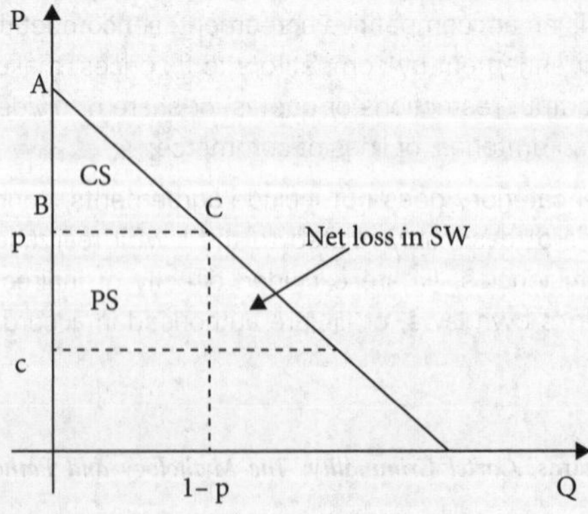

Figure 7.2. Harm caused by cartels (a static picture)

Lande has examined the design of optimal presumptions of harm for cartels.[39] In doing so, in conformity with the economic theory of deterrence, Connor has estimated both the average overcharge of cartels and the probability of such cartels being caught.

In their seminal paper on the size of cartel overcharge in the US and the EU, Connor and Lande argued that in the United States, cartels overcharged on an average of 18 per cent to 37 per cent of their total sales, depending upon the data set and methodology employed in the analysis and whether mean or median figures are used. With respect to European cartels, the overcharge was found to be in the 28 per cent to 54 per cent range. Finally, the authors looked at cartels that had effects solely within a single European country and found that overcharges averaged between 16 per cent and 48 per cent. The authors then compared these overcharges with the level of criminal or administrative fines imposed on those cartels and found that, on average, the cartel overcharges were significantly larger than the criminal fines in both the European Union and the United States. They concluded that since in those jurisdictions the cartel fines did not cover even the overcharge of the cartels, the United States and—especially—the European Union should increase their penalties for hard core collusion substantially.

Connor also assessed the antitrust fines and private penalties imposed on the participants of 260 international cartels discovered during 1990–2005, using four indicators of enforcement effectiveness.[40] Among other things, he found that median government antitrust fines average less than 10 per cent of affected commerce, but rises to about 35 per cent in the case of multi-continental conspiracies; that civil settlements in jurisdictions where they are permitted are typically 6 to 12 per cent of sales; and that global cartels prosecuted in Europe and North America typically paid less than single damages.

In a more recent paper, JM Connor surveys more than 700 published economic studies and judicial decisions that contain 2,041 quantitative estimates of overcharges of global hard-core cartels.[41] His primary findings are the following:

> (1) the median average long-run overcharge for all types of cartels over all time periods is 23.0%; (2) the mean average is at least 49%; (3) overcharges reached their zenith in 1891–1945 and have trended downward ever since; (4) 6% of the cartel episodes are zero; (5) median overcharges of international-membership cartels are 38% higher than those of domestic cartels; (6) convicted cartels have on average been 19% more effective at raising prices than unpunished cartels; (7) bid-rigging conduct displays 25% lower mark-ups than price-fixing cartels; (8) when cartels operate at peak effectiveness, price changes are 60% to 80% higher than the whole episode; and (9) laboratory and natural market data find that the Cartel Monopoly Index (CMI) varies from 11% to 95%.[42]

He finally concludes that 'historical penalty guidelines aimed at optimally deterring cartels are likely to be too low'.[43]

39 See eg JM Connor and RH Lande, 'How High Do Cartels Raise Prices—Implications for Optimal Cartel Fines' (2005) 80 *Tulane L Rev* 513; JM Connor and RH Lande, 'The Size of Cartel Overcharges: Implications for U.S. and E.U. Fining Policies' (2006) 51(4) *Antitrust Bulletin* 983, available at <http://ssrn.com/abstract=988722>; JM Connor and RH Lande, 'Cartel Overcharges and Optimal Cartel Fines' (2008) 3 *Issues in Competition L & Policy, ABA Section of Antitrust Law* 2203, available at http://ssrn.com/abstract=1285455.

40 JM Connor, 'Effectiveness of Antitrust Sanctions on Modern International Cartels' (2006) 6(3) *J Industry, Competition and Trade* 195.

41 JM Connor, 'Price-Fixing Overcharges', Working Paper (3rd revised ed, 2014). An earlier version of this paper was published as JM Connor, 'Price-fixing Overcharges: Legal and Economic Evidence' (2007) 22 *Research in L & Economics* 59..

42 JM Connor, 'Price-Fixing Overcharges', Working Paper (3rd revised ed, 2014), 1.

43 Ibid.

The work by Connor and Lande has inspired a number of authors to undertake studies refining their methodology in order to assess the level of overcharges from cartels. One such study was prepared for the European Commission by Oxera and a multi-jurisdictional team of lawyers and economists in December 2009.[44] Oxera removed from the Connor data set a large number of observations based on a number of criteria, in particular focusing only on estimates obtained from peer-reviewed academic articles and chapters in published books. It also refined the sample of cartels examined by Connor, by considering only cartels that started after 1960 (thus taking into account only more recent cartels), for which an estimate of the average overcharge was available (rather than only an estimate of the highest or lowest overcharge) and for which the relevant background study explicitly explained the method for calculating the average overcharge estimate.

In the distribution of cartel overcharges across this adjusted data set of 114 observations (out of more than 1000 initially), the overcharge range with the greatest number of observations is 10–20 per cent. Oxera found that in this data set the median overcharge was 18 per cent of the cartel price, which is not far from the 20 per cent found by Connor and Lande. Since the variation in observed overcharges is large, however, the authors considered the distribution of overcharges and not only the median or average. In 93 per cent of the past cartel cases in the sample, the overcharge as a percentage of the cartel price was above zero. This supports the theory that, in most cases, the cartel overcharge can be expected to be positive, although it also indicates that there is a small but significant proportion of cartels (7 per cent) where there is no overcharge.

In another study, Posner presents the overcharges for twelve cartel cases, with a median value of 28 per cent of the cartel price.[45] Elsewhere, Levenstein and Suslow, based on their review of sixteen cartel case studies, find that 'virtually every cartel case study surveyed reports that the cartel was able to raise prices immediately following cartel formation.'[46]

A 2002 OECD study based on a limited survey of fourteen cartel cases conducted by its members between 1996 and 2000 finds that the median overcharge was between 15 and 20 per cent.[47] The OECD report adds: 'At the very least it seems clear that the gain from cartel agreements can vary significantly from case to case, and sometimes it can be very high. Moreover, since the actual loss to consumers includes more than just the gain transferred to the cartel . . ., the total harm from cartels—is significant indeed.' Werden has reviewed thirteen other studies, and arrives at a median overcharge of 15 per cent of the cartel price.[48] Conducting a meta-analysis of cartel overcharge estimates, Boyer and Kotchoni found a mean and median overcharge estimate of 15.76 per cent and 16.43 per cent.[49]

44 OXERA, *Quantifying Antitrust Damages: Towards Non-Binding Guidance for Courts*, Study prepared for the European Commission, DG COMP (December 2009), available at http://ec.europa.eu/competition/antitrust/actionsdamages/quantification_study.pdf.

45 RA Posner, *Antitrust Law: An Economic Perspective* (2nd ed, University of Chicago Press, 2001), 303–4.

46 MC Levenstein and VY Suslow, 'What Determines Cartel Success?' (2006) 64 *J Economic Literature* 43, cited by Commission Staff Working Document, *Practical Guide Quantifying Harm in Actions for Damages Based on Breaches of Article 101 or 102 of the Treaty on the Functioning of the European Union*, C(2013) 3440, 89. .

47 OECD Competition Committee Report on the Nature and Impact of Hard Core Cartels and Sanctions against Cartels under National Competition Laws, DAFFE/COMP(2002)7 (9 April 2002), available at http://www.oecd.org/competition/cartels/2081831.pdf.

48 G Werden, 'The Effect of Antitrust Policy on Consumer Welfare: What Crandall and Winston Overlook', Economic Analysis Group Discussion Paper (January 2003), cited by Commission Staff Working Document, *Practical Guide Quantifying Harm in Actions for Damages Based on Breaches of Article 101 or 102 of the Treaty on the Functioning of the European Union*, C(2013) 3440, 90.

49 M Boyer and R Kotchoni, 'How Much Do Cartels Overcharge?, (2015) 47(2) *Rev Industrial Organization* 119.

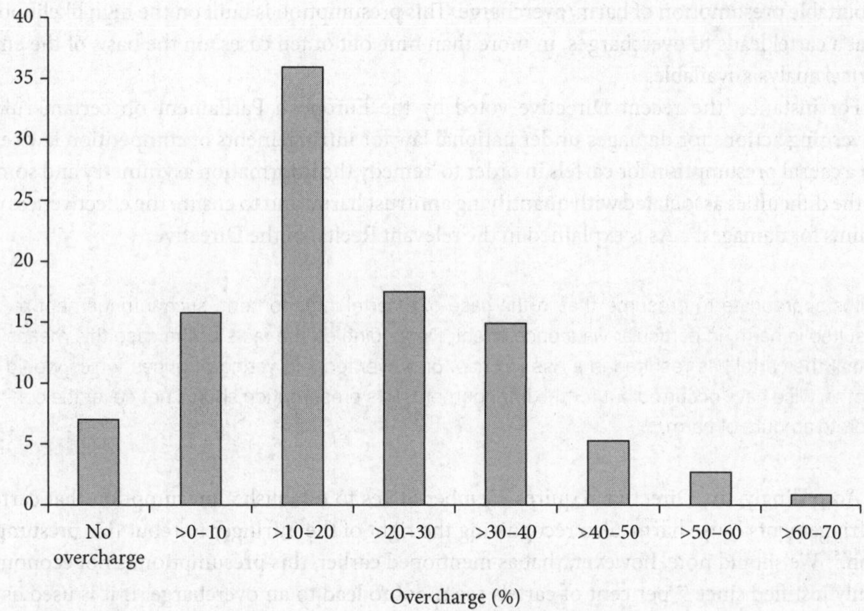

Figure 7.3. Distribution of cartel overcharges in empirical studies of past cartels
Indicative results from new sample selected by Oxera, based on Connor and Lande (2008). Imported from Commission Staff Working Document, *Practical Guide Quantifying Harm in Actions for Damages Based on Breaches of Article 101 or 102 of the Treaty on the Functioning of the European Union* C(2013) 3440.

Altogether these studies are highly consistent with one other on several points.[50] In only 7 per cent of the cases there is no overcharge. In more than 90 per cent of the cases cartels result in an overcharge. The median overcharge by cartels is between 10 and 20 per cent of the cartel price. However, there is a wide distribution of results across cartels and hence a case by case study is in order.

This literature has given rise to presumptions of cartel overcharge used in the context of either setting financial penalties in the context of public enforcement or in order to compute damages in the context of private enforcement.

In the context of private enforcement, the nature of the presumption is causal, as its aim is to facilitate the burden of proof of the claimants in damages cases against cartelists, in order to establish that claimants have been harmed as a result of a specific cartel (hence this relates to the individual harm of the specific cartel to the claimant). The claimant is not expected to bring forward concrete evidence of harm and overcharge, in order to establish the causal link between the cartel and the harm suffered, when a cartel has been found, but may rely on a

50 See also Y Bolotova, 'Cartel overcharges: An empirical analysis' (2009) 70(1–2) *J Economic Behavior & Organization* 321; G Symeonides, 'Collusion, profitability and welfare: Theory and evidence' (2018) 145 *J Economic Behavior & Organization* 530, 542 (exploring evidence from a natural experiment, the introduction of cartel law in the UK in the late 1950s, and finding that '[t]he econometric estimates suggest average decreases in price–cost margins following the breakdown of collusive pricing in 1960s Britain of at least 15% in low-capital and larger-sized relative to capital-intensive and smaller-sized industries, respectively'. He further notes that '[t]here is weak evidence of a price-cost margin fall in advertising-intensive and consumer good relative to low-advertising and producer good industries').

rebuttable presumption of harm/overcharge. This presumption is built on the high likelihood that a cartel leads to overcharges, in more than nine out of ten cases, on the basis of the empirical analysis available.

For instance, the recent Directive voted by the European Parliament on certain rules governing actions for damages under national law for infringements of competition law sets up a causal presumption for cartels in order to 'remedy the information asymmetry and some of the difficulties associated with quantifying antitrust harm, and to ensure the effectiveness of claims for damages'.[51] As is explained in the relevant Recital of the Directive,

> it is appropriate to presume that in the case of a cartel infringement, such infringement resulted in harm, in particular via a price effect. Depending on the facts of the case this means that the cartel has resulted in a rise in price, or prevented a lowering of prices which would otherwise have occurred but for the infringement. This presumption should not cover the concrete amount of harm.[52]

Accordingly, the Directive requires Member States to establish a presumption that cartel infringements cause harm, also recognizing the right of the infringer to rebut this presumption.[53] We should note, however, that as mentioned earlier, this presumption is not economically justified since 7 per cent of cartels seem not to lead to an overcharge. If it is used as a device to simplify the work of antitrust authorities or courts, it should remain a rebuttable presumption.

In the context of public enforcement, competition authorities most often make use of presumptions of harm, again on the basis of the empirical evidence on the average overcharge of cartels. For instance, the United States Sentencing Guidelines recommend a basic fine of 10 per cent of the affected volume of commerce to a firm convicted of cartel collusion, plus another 10 per cent for the harms 'inflicted upon consumers who are unable or for other reasons do not buy the product at the higher price'. This generates a fine of 20 per cent of the affected volume of commerce, subject to further adjustments for aggravating and mitigating circumstances. The Sentencing Commission, which adopted the Sentencing Guidelines in 1987 explained the choice of this 20 per cent by the fact that it doubled the figure representing the average overcharge of cartels (10 per cent) in order to account for losses, including customers who are priced out of the market (counterfactual customers). In the EU, the basic fine is set in a range up to 30 per cent of the relevant turnover over the duration of the infringement, presumably also taking into account empirical evidence that the median overcharge of cartels is between 15 and 20 per cent, in more than 40 per cent of the population of cartels in these studies having an overcharge of more than 30 per cent, as well as the need to factor in deterrence.

By being a step in the fine-setting process, such a presumption entails the risk that it will be used mechanically without taking into account the likely real harm that the specific cartel may have caused. As cartels are considered anti-competitive by their object in the EU and *per se* prohibited in the US, there is no effort made by the competition authorities to determine the harm caused by the cartel when establishing the existence of the competition law

[51] Council Directive 2014/104/EU of 26 November 2014 on certain rules governing actions for damages under national law for infringements of the competition law provisions of the Member States of the European Union [2014] OJ L 349/1, Article 17(2) [hereinafter Damages Directive].

[52] Ibid, Recital 47.

[53] Ibid, Article 17(2).

infringement, with the result that this information is unavailable at the stage of setting the fine. The use of presumptions facilitates the work of competition authorities at this stage, at the price, however, of accuracy and a better linkage between the harm caused (including the need for general and specific deterrence) and the sanction, as would have implied the reference to the principle of proportionality of sanctions. This preference for a formalistic approach explains also the institution of statutory maximum fines. The attraction of this form-based approach consists in saving the administrative costs and human resources that would have been required for the assessment of the harm of the cartel. As it is rightly explained by Harrington:

> [European Commission's] fines are tied to revenue in the affected markets and not to incremental profits or customer losses, so the penalty does not scale up with the overcharge. If we take these estimates on face value, the only cartels that will form are those with abnormally high overcharges which are the ones imposing the largest losses on consumers. The problem here resides in the formula for the penalty not being proportional to the additional profits from colluding. [. . .] That is the case in the U.S. as well. Though U.S. Sentencing Guidelines have a maximum of 'not more than the greater of twice the gross gain or twice the gross loss,' apparently that sort of calculation is not standard practice when the U.S. Department of Justice sets a fine. That cartel profits are not taken account of in setting or negotiating fines is a criticism of both the competition authority and the body that sets their budget.
>
> One defense of this practice is that it is too costly to calculate those profits. That does not seem credible. There are many plaintiffs who perform exactly that exercise for much smaller markets involving much smaller sums. If a plaintiff can engage in a cost-effective calculation of the impact of collusion on profits when hundreds of thousands of dollars of claims are at stake then a competition authority should be able to do so when millions of dollars of fines are at stake. A second defense is that a competition authority has limited resources and it is better for it to use those resources to develop additional cases. That is a valid point but then the argument should be made to increase the competition authority's budget so they can engage in the proper setting of fines. We must remember that the ultimate goal is not to convict and penalize cartels but rather to deter their formation, and that requires tying penalties to illicit profits. This point is worth emphasizing as competition authorities may attach too much weight to disabling cartels relative to deterring cartels.[54]

7.2.3. EFFECTS-BASED APPROACHES VERSUS FORMALISM IN ASSESSING THE COMPETITIVE IMPLICATIONS OF CARTELS

It is widely accepted that cartels almost always produce negative effects on welfare, if one takes a welfare perspective[55] and always produce negative effects if one focuses on the competitive

[54] J Harrington, 'Are Penalties for Cartels Excessive and, if They Are, Should We Be Concerned?' (13 February 2014) (on file with author).

[55] It was reported that in very rare circumstances cartels may be total welfare enhancing. I Bos and E Pot, 'On the Possibility of Welfare Enhancing Hard-core Cartels' (2012) 107(3) *J Economics* 199, 201–3 cite three strands in this literature (footnotes and references excluded):

> One strand of work argues that a cartel can have a welfare-enhancing effect when it is ancillary to cooperative productive activity engaged in by the cartel members (so-called 'non-naked' cartel agreements). This is essentially the view of the Chicago school of economics. The key argument is that when business practices such as price-fixing or market division form an essential part of a bigger arrangement

process. Hence, many competition law systems prohibit cartels, without the need to estimate their anti-competitive effects or to examine their effects on welfare. In other words, there is a presumption that cooperation between competitors amounting to a cartel is illegal, from the perspective of competition law. The rule against cartels may take different forms:

(i) It may constitute an irrebuttable presumption of illegality. Cooperation between competitors characterized as a cartel is to be prohibited as such, irrespective of any consideration of the concrete effects of the specific cartel on the market or consumers. This is the option chosen by US antitrust law, which applies a *per se* prohibition rule against activity characterized as a cartel. Cartels are illegal at any time and are subject to criminal prosecution, regardless of the economic effects of the specific cartels. This was not always the case in US antitrust law history. As it was explained by former Assistant Attorney General Christine Varney, cartels were accepted during the period of the Great Depression in the 1930s:

> [T]he onset of the Great Depression in the US did not cause the nation to reconsider the damaging effects of cartelization on economic performance. Instead of reinvigorating antitrust enforcement, the Government took the opposite tack. Legislation was passed in the 1930s that effectively foreclosed competition. The National Industrial Recovery Act ('NIRA'), which created the National Recovery Administration ('NRA'), allowed industries to create a set of industrial codes.
>
> These 'codes of fair competition' set industries' prices and wages, established production quotas, and imposed restrictions on entry. At the core of the NIRA was the idea that low profits in the industrial sectors contributed to the economic instability of those times. The purpose of the industrial codes was to create 'stability'—ie, higher profits—by fostering coordinated action in the markets. The codes developed following the passage of the NIRA governed many of America's major industrial sectors: lumber, steel, oil, mining, and automobiles. Under this legislation, the Government assisted in the enforcement of the codes if firms contributed to a coordinated effort by permitting unionization and engaging in collective bargaining.
>
> What was the result of these industrial codes? Competition was relegated to the sidelines, as the welfare of firms took priority over the welfare of consumers. It is not surprising that the

between firms, then a cartel could potentially increase productive efficiency more than it reduces allocative efficiency. For instance, a cartel between sellers may increase social welfare when participating firms advertise jointly using media that they cannot afford individually, even though this requires an agreement upon the prices that will be advertised. In fact, deterring or prosecuting efficient cartels could result in higher market prices as unit production costs will be higher in absence of the cartel.

A second strand of literature highlights the possibility that unrestricted competition may not necessarily lead to a competitive equilibrium. Most notably, a competitive equilibrium may be absent in industries with large fixed costs and decreasing long-run average costs. That is, with increasing returns markets may have an empty core. This basically means that, even when firms are willing to compete, competition is not viable in certain markets. As a result, some sort of strategic coordination between firms is required to maintain an industry, thereby contributing to social welfare. One particular solution for this type of market is to allow sellers to establish sales quotas. Such a hardcore cartel would be welfare-enhancing as it saves a surplus generating business that would not exist with unrestricted competition. It is noteworthy that the cost conditions under which the core may be empty sometimes seem to describe quite closely the cost structure in manufacturing industries such as cement and steel; industries that repeatedly have witnessed hard core cartel behaviour.

A third strand of work shows that naked cartels may result in higher welfare standards even in markets with constant or decreasing returns. Taking a dynamic approach, it can be argued that cartels may (temporarily) lead to an increase (or stabilization) instead of a decrease in industry output [. . .]. The reason is that the additional profits that result from the cartel either encourages entry or provides cartel members with the incentive to invest in production capacity.

industrial codes resulted in restricted output, higher prices, and reduced consumer purchasing power. It was not until 1937, during the second Roosevelt Administration, that the country saw a revival of antitrust enforcement.[56]

(i) The US antitrust law system does not include any crisis cartel exemption and cartels are found illegal and prohibited *per se*, irrespective of the economic circumstances of the economic sector or industry they concern. Although the US Sentencing Guidelines, which apply to criminal sanctions in federal cases, state that financial limitations on a defendant's ability to pay a fine may be taken into account, these provisions do not reflect a positive view on cartels in times of economic crisis but are based on the financial condition of the particular individual or firm. Yet, as we will examine below, US antitrust law has not characterized as cartels conduct that although it leads to the fixing of prices it is reasonably related to the lawful realization of cost-reducing or output-enhancing efficiencies.[57]

(ii) It might constitute a rebuttable presumption of illegality. For instance, activity characterized as a cartel will be considered illegal, although the defendant would be allowed a possibility to put forward pro-competitive justifications for the cartel or to explain the positive effects of the cartel on welfare. This is the case in Europe and the United Kingdom, where cartels are considered as anti-competitive and are prohibited by Article 101(1) TFEU or Chapter I CA98 as restrictions of competition by object. Yet, cartelists can put forward economic justifications for the constitution of the cartel and argue for the exception from the principle of prohibition that is provided by Article 101(3) TFEU or section 9 of Chapter I CA98. Note that according to Article 2 of Regulation 1/2003, the party claiming the benefit of Article 101(3) TFEU shall bear the burden of proving that the above four conditions are likely to be fulfilled. It is practically impossible for such justification to be forward successfully for cartels, as the Commission has nevertheless accepted in certain limited circumstances that '*crisis cartels*' which aim to reduce industry overcapacity may justified, in case of course they satisfy the four conditions of Article 101(3) TFEU.

(iii) It might consist of assessing the anti-competitive effects of the allegedly anti-competitive agreement and balancing these with alleged positive effects to welfare, before finding them illegal under the competition law provisions. This is not an option chosen by the major competition law systems in the world and most notably by the EU, UK, and US ones.

Neither EU nor UK competition law requires the assessment of the effects of the cartel before reaching the conclusion that it infringes competition law. Cartels constitute an archetypical example of restrictions of competition by object. There is no need to estimate the cartel overcharge, the profits gained by the cartel or the loss the cartel caused, except when calculating the damages in a private action. The characterization of a relation between undertakings as forming a cartel leads practically to the enforcement of the prohibition principle of Article 101 TFEU or Chapter I CA98.

56 C Varney, Assistant Attorney General, Antitrust Division, US Department of Justice, 'Vigorous Antitrust Enforcement in this Challenging Era', Remarks as Prepared for the Center for American Progress (12 May 2009), available at http://www.justice.gov/atr/speech/vigorous-antitrust-enforcement-challenging-era.

57 See below our discussion of *Broadcast Music v Columbia Broadcasting System*, 441 US 1 (1979).

The characterization of a fact pattern as a 'cartel' or any other restriction of competition by object, as in the EU and the UK, or a practice prohibited *per se*, as in the US, involves, however, some analysis of the economic and legal context of the agreement. As seen in Chapter 3, this leaves some discretion to the decision-makers in order to frame the category of practices that may fall under the prohibition principle. Even rules, such as *per se* prohibitions, are not self-defining, but require interpretation by the decision-maker based on background assumptions and purposes, a task which ultimately relies on interpretative rules.[58] The category of cartels may be extended or limited according to the background, prior beliefs and purposes of the decision-makers.

For instance, in the US, although cartels are prohibited *per se*, the Supreme Court has found that some practices involving price fixing may escape the characterization as cartel and the *per se* prohibition rule, if the conduct is related to efficiencies.

Characterization and the *BMI* precedent of the US Supreme Court

The TV network CBS brought an action against the American Society of Composers, Authors and Publishers (ASCAP) and Broadcast Music, Inc (BMI), and their members and affiliates, alleging, inter alia, *that the issuance by ASCAP and BMI to CBS of blanket licences to copyrighted musical compositions at fees negotiated by them is illegal price fixing under the antitrust laws. Blanket licences provide licensees the right to perform any and all of the compositions owned by the members or affiliates as often as the licensees dispose for a stated term. Fees for blanket licences are ordinarily a percentage of total revenues or a flat amount, and do not directly depend on the amount or type of music used. ASCAP was established by composers (the copyright holders) as those who performed copyrighted music for profit 'were so numerous and widespread, and most performances so fleeting, that as a practical matter it was impossible for the many individual copyright owners to negotiate with and license the users and to detect 'unauthorized uses', hence the need for a 'clearinghouse' for copyright owners and users to solve the transaction costs associated with the licensing of music. BMI was a non-profit corporation owned by members of the broadcasting industry with the same purpose as the ASCAP. While the majority of the Supreme Court found that these licensees amounted to fixing prices 'in a literal sense', as 'the composers and publishing houses have joined together into an organization that sets its price for the blanket license it sells',[59] it also noted that:*

> It is not a question simply of determining whether two or more potential competitors have literally 'fixed' a 'price'. As generally used in the antitrust field, 'price fixing' is a shorthand way of describing certain categories of business behavior to which the per se rule has been held applicable. The [. . .] literal approach does not alone establish that this particular practice is one of those types or that it is 'plainly anticompetitive' and very likely without 'redeeming virtue'. Literalness is overly simplistic and often overbroad. When two partners set the price of their goods or services they are literally 'price fixing', but they are not per se in violation of the Sherman Act. [. . .] Thus, it is necessary to characterize the challenged conduct as falling within or without that category of behaviour to which we apply the label 'per se price fixing'. That will often, but not always, be a simple matter.[60]

[58] D Crane, 'Rules versus Standards in Antitrust Adjudication' (2007) 64(1) *Washington & Lee L Rev* 49.
[59] Ibid, 8. [60] *Broadcast Music v Columbia Broadcasting System*, 441 US 1, 8–9 (1979).

The majority of the Court further noted the following:

> The blanket license, as we see it, is not a 'naked restrain[t] of trade with no purpose except stifling of competition', [. . .] but rather accompanies the integration of sales, monitoring, and enforcement against unauthorized copyright use. [. . .] As already indicated, ASCAP and the blanket license developed together out of the practical situation in the marketplace: thousands of users, thousands of copyright owners, and millions of compositions. Most users want unplanned, rapid, and indemnified access to any and all of the repertory of compositions, and the owners want a reliable method of collecting for the use of their copyrights. Individual sales transactions in this industry are quite expensive, as would be individual monitoring and enforcement, especially in light of the resources of single composers. Indeed, [. . .] the costs are prohibitive for licenses with individual radio stations, nightclubs, and restaurants [. . .] and it was in that milieu that the blanket license arose.
>
> A middleman with a blanket license was an obvious necessity if the thousands of individual negotiations, a virtual impossibility, were to be avoided. Also, individual fees for the use of individual compositions would presuppose an intricate schedule of fees and uses, as well as a difficult and expensive reporting problem for the user and policing task for the copyright owner. Historically, the market for public-performance rights organized itself largely around the single-fee blanket license, which gave unlimited access to the repertory and reliable protection against infringement. When ASCAP's major and user-created competitor, BMI, came on the scene, it also turned to the blanket license.
>
> With the advent of radio and television networks, market conditions changed, and the necessity for and advantages of a blanket license for those users may be far less obvious than is the case when the potential users are individual television or radio stations, or the thousands of other individuals and organizations performing copyrighted compositions in public. But even for television network licenses, ASCAP reduces costs absolutely by creating a blanket license that is sold only a few, instead of thousands of times, and that obviates the need for closely monitoring the networks to see that they do not use more than they pay for. ASCAP also provides the necessary resources for blanket sales and enforcement, resources unavailable to the vast majority of composers and publishing houses. Moreover, a bulk license of some type is a necessary consequence of the integration necessary to achieve these efficiencies, and a necessary consequence of an aggregate license is that its price must be established.[61]

After examining this economic context, the Supreme Court re-characterized the agreements in question as not involving price fixing prohibited *per se*, noting the following:

> Not all arrangements among actual or potential competitors that have an impact on price are per se violations of the Sherman Act or even unreasonable restraints. Mergers among competitors eliminate competition, including price competition, but they are not per se illegal, and many of them withstand attack under any existing antitrust standard. Joint ventures and other cooperative arrangements are also not usually unlawful, at least not as price-fixing schemes, where the agreement on price is necessary to market the product at all.
>
> Here, the blanket-license fee is not set by competition among individual copyright owners, and it is a fee for the use of any of the compositions covered by the license. But the blanket license cannot be wholly equated with a simple horizontal arrangement

[61] Ibid, 20–1.

among competitors. ASCAP does set the price for its blanket license, but that license is quite different from anything any individual owner could issue. [. . .]

With this background in mind, which plainly enough indicates that over the years, and in the face of available alternatives, the blanket license has provided an acceptable mechanism for at least a large part of the market for the performing rights to copyrighted musical compositions, we cannot agree that it should automatically be declared illegal in all of its many manifestations. Rather, when attacked, it should be subjected to a more discriminating examination under the rule of reason. It may not ultimately survive that attack, but that is not the issue before us today.[62]

On these considerations, the Court of appeal's judgment, applying the *per se* prohibition rule was set aside by the Supreme Court.

NOTES AND QUESTIONS ON BMI

1. The structure of the Sherman Act is such that once some conduct is found to fall under the *per se* rule, there is no possibility of escaping prohibition. Hence, the only means for conduct that presents redeeming efficiencies to avoid the prohibition rule is to be characterized as within a category that is subject to the rule of reason standard. This was what occurred in this case to a certain extent, as the Supreme Court adopted a flexible approach on the interpretation of section 1, by refusing to follow a literal interpretation of this provision and took pains to examine the economic context of the agreements, from which it inferred that the application of the *per se* prohibition rule was not desirable. It then proceeded in re-characterizing the fact pattern as not involving a cartel, conduct which is found by essence to infringe section 1 of the Sherman Act and prohibited *per se*, but a category of conduct that needs to be examined under the rule of reason. Would the same strategy be necessary in the context of the enforcement of Article 101 TFEU, which provides the possibility to benefit from an exception to the prohibition principle, provided, of course, that the conditions of Article 101(3) are satisfied?
2. What can be the limiting principle for such a flexible approach? Do you think that it may provide a way out for any type of conduct that amounts to price fixing to escape the prohibition principle, if it is reasonably related to some efficiency enhancing activity? Does the consideration of the economic context in which the restriction of competition is integrated and the possible efficiency gains achieved amounts to applying the rule of reason to price fixing activity? Is the analysis performed in the context of this characterization step of the *per se* prohibition principle similar to that undertaken under the rule of reason?
3. The choice for a rule of *per se* prohibition or for the categorization of cartels as among the types of competition law infringements that are anti-competitive by object is not due to the impossibility of estimating the effects of cartels. Various methods of estimating cartel overcharge have been advanced in the literature, and they are frequently used for the computation of the quantum of damages following a competition law infringement.[63] The European Commission Staff has also prepared a practical guide

[62] Ibid, 23–4.

[63] For an excellent summary, see J Baker and DL Rubinfeld, 'Empirical Methods in Antitrust Litigation: Review and Critique' (1999) 1(1) *American L and Economics Rev* 386; OXERA, *Quantifying Antitrust Damages Towards*

quantifying harm in actions for damages, which provides a detailed and non-technical analysis of the different methodologies employed in economic research to quantify harm.[64] There are various examples of an individual assessment of the amount of overcharge, in particular in the context of private enforcement for damages, as in both US and EU law, cartels are prohibited *per se* or by their object, hence there is no need to establish the existence and the likely amount of consumer harm in order to apply section 1 of the Sherman Act or Article 101 TFEU. Some analysis of the effects of the cartel is also performed in the context of determining fines.

4. However, both EU and UK competition law have opted for option (ii), that is a presumption that conduct characterized as a cartel should be considered illegal and infringes Article 101(1) TFEU and Chapter I CA98. The presumption is in theory rebuttable. In practice, however, it is excessively difficult, almost impossible to justify cartels under Article 101(3) TFEU or Section 8 of the UK Competition Act.[65]

In view of the negative effects of cartel activity, deterrence of cartels is considered as a more important objective than ensuring a more accurate analysis of their effects on competition, in view of the costs of substantive errors or procedural costs (see our analysis on decision theory and optimal rules in Chapter 6). This principle is also accepted by scholars arguing that in exceptional circumstances cartels may be welfare-enhancing, as discriminating between efficient and inefficient cartels is not 'an easy task' and '[i]t is, however, a priori unclear whether and in what way relaxing the per se rule would indeed lead to higher welfare standards'.[66] By providing the theoretical possibility that cartels may be justified under exceptional circumstances, both the EU and the UK competition law systems seem to make an optimal choice of rules.

7.3. THE APPLICATION OF ARTICLE 101(1) AND CHAPTER I CA98 TO HORIZONTAL RESTRICTIONS

7.3.1. COLLUSION BETWEEN COMPETITORS AND RESTRICTIONS OF COMPETITION BY OBJECT

As was noted in Chapter 6, in its recent *Guidance on restrictions of competition by object*, the Commission seems to equate restrictions of competition by object with hardcore restrictions, often excluded from the benefit of the block exemption regulations adopted for the implementation of Article 101(3) TFEU. An analysis of the jurisprudence of the European Courts and the decisional practice of the European Commission shows that the category of restrictions by object is evolving and it may include types of collusion between

Non-Binding Guidance for Courts, Study prepared for the European Commission, DG COMP (2009), v (comparative table).

64 European Commission Staff Working Document, Practical Guide, *Quantifying harm in actions for damages based on breaches of Articles 101 or 102 of the Treaty on the Functioning of the European Union*, SWD(2013) 205, available at http://ec.europa.eu/competition/antitrust/actionsdamages/quantification_guide_en.pdf.

65 See Communication from the Commission—Notice—Guidelines on the application of Article 101(3) (formerly Article 81(3)) of the Treaty [2004] OJ C 101/97, paras 46 & 79 [hereinafter Guidelines on Article 101(3) (formerly 81(3))].

66 I Bos and E Pot, 'On the Possibility of Welfare Enhancing Hard-core Cartels' (2012) 107(3) *J Economics* 199.

competitors that are not included in the category of 'hardcore cartels', as this was defined by the OECD Recommendation of 1998. Hence, in our view, the two concepts should be distinguished.[67]

7.3.1.1. Horizontal price fixing and output restrictions

Collusive conduct that expressly or directly fixes the selling or purchasing price or by which parties agree on certain parameters of the price composition, such as the amount of rebates given to customers, constitutes a restriction of competition by object under both Articles 101(1) TFEU and Chapter I of the UK Competition Act.

Joined Cases T-217 & 245/03, *French Beef* [2006] ECR II–04987

French federations representing cattle breeders and slaughterers had participated in an arrangement aiming at fixing minimum prices for the purchase of cows by slaughterers and suspending beef imports. The agreement was found by the Commission to infringe Article 101 TFEU. Note that in the Irish beef case the Court of Justice found that an output restriction also constituted an agreement to restrict competition by object.[68]

82. It must be observed, first, that the commitment in the disputed agreement to suspend imports had, in particular, the object of preventing the entry into France of beef at prices below those of the price scale decided upon by the applicants, in order to ensure the sale of the production of French farmers and the effectiveness of the price scale. It necessarily follows that the object of the disputed agreement was to partition off the French national market and in that way to restrict competition in the single market.

83. Second, with regard to the establishment of a price scale, it must be borne in mind that Article [101(1) TFEU] expressly provides that measures which directly or indirectly fix purchase or selling prices constitute restrictions of competition. It has consistently been held that price fixing is a patent restriction of competition [. . .].

84. In the present case, the applicants agreed on a slaughterhouse entry price scale for certain categories of cattle, which provided for a list of prices per kilogram of carcass for certain categories of cows and the method of calculating the price to be applied to other categories, by reference inter alia to the price fixed by the Community authorities in the framework of the special purchase scheme. Contrary to what the applicants claim, it is clear from the actual wording of the relevant stipulations of the disputed agreement that the prices were not recommended or target prices, but minimum prices to which the signatory federations undertook to secure adherence. The agreement provided that 'the contributions should at least be consistent with this scale.' [. . .]

85. By its very nature, an agreement such as that in the present case, concluded by federations representing farmers and federations representing slaughterers and fixing minimum prices for certain categories of cows, with the aim of making them binding on all traders in the markets in question, has the object of restricting competition in those markets (see, to that effect, Case 123/83 *BNIC* [1985] ECR 391,

[67] See Chapter 6. [68] See our comments in Section 6.3.1.1.3.

paragraph 22), inter alia by limiting artificially the commercial negotiating margin of farmers and slaughterers and distorting the formation of prices in the markets in question.

86. This conclusion cannot be undermined by the applicants' argument that the agricultural markets are regulated markets where the competition rules do not automatically apply and where the formation of prices quite often does not answer to the free operation of supply and demand. No doubt the agricultural sector has certain specific features and is the object of very detailed regulation which is frequently rather interventionist. However, it must be observed that the Community competition rules apply to the markets for agricultural products, even if certain exceptions are provided for to take account of the particular situation of those markets, and this will be examined in the context of the third plea.

87. Likewise, the applicants cannot use the argument that the prices of the disputed scale were not restrictive because they were fixed by reference to the prices of the special purchase scheme which were laid down by the Commission itself. The comparative tables produced by the parties at the request of the Court show that, although the prices laid down by the agreement for cows of average or inferior quality were fixed by reference to the prices given in the framework of the special purchase scheme, the prices fixed by the agreement for cows of superior quality (which accounted for 30% of the number slaughtered in 2001) were appreciably higher than the abovementioned intervention prices. In any case, the disputed agreement does not cease to be restrictive merely because the minimum prices are fixed by reference to the government intervention price. Reference to the latter price does not mean that the disputed scale loses its anti-competitive object consisting in fixing directly and artificially a predetermined market price or that it can be treated in the same way as the various government support and intervention schemes in the common organisation of the agricultural markets which have the object of stabilising markets characterised by excess supply by means of withdrawing a part of production. [. . .]

89. With regard to the applicants' allegation that they could not compel their members to adhere to the minimum prices decided upon, it must be said that, for an agreement between undertakings to fall within the ambit of Article [101(1) TFEU], it is not necessary for the associations in question to be able to compel their members to fulfil the obligations imposed on them by the agreement [. . .]. Furthermore, it must be noted that the reference to the judgment in *Wouters and Others*, is irrelevant here because the factual circumstances and the legal problems raised by that case, which concerned the regulation by a professional association of the practice of the profession of lawyer and its organisation, are not comparable with those of the present case.

90. Furthermore, the applicants cannot justify the disputed agreement by pleading the crisis in the beef sector at the material time, which particularly affected French farmers of adult cattle. This circumstance cannot, on its own, lead to the conclusion that the conditions for applying Article [101(1) TFEU were not fulfilled [. . .].

92. Likewise, with regard to the role of the French Minister for Agriculture in the conclusion of the agreement of 24 October 2001, suffice it to note that, according to settled case-law, the fact that conduct on the part of undertakings was known, authorised or even encouraged by national authorities has no bearing, in any event, on the applicability of Article [101 TFEU].

93. Lastly, the applicants' argument that the Commission failed to show that the disputed agreement had any effect on imports or on market prices must also be rejected. It has consistently been held that, for the purposes of application of Article [101(1) TFEU], there is no need to take account of the actual effects of an agreement when it has as its object the prevention, restriction or distortion of competition within the common market. Consequently, it is not necessary to show actual anti-competitive effects where the anti-competitive object of the conduct in question is proved [. . .]. As has just been found, the Commission proved that the disputed agreement had the object of restricting competition in the markets in question [. . .]. The Commission was therefore not required to examine the actual effects of those measures on competition within the common market, particularly in France.

7.3.1.2. Market sharing

Case C-41/69, *ACF Chemie farma NV v Commission*
[1970] ECR-661

A cartel in which undertakings agreed to retain their respective domestic markets and fix prices and quotas for the export of quinine.

This dispute involved the activity of certain undertakings related to the production and sale of quinine and quinidine and of their salts and compounds, products used in particular in the manufacture of medicines for the treatment of malaria and certain cardiac diseases. Nedchem (of which ACF Chemie farma NV is the successor) together with five other Dutch undertakings entered into an agreement in 1958 with Boehringer and Buchler & Co, whereby they retained their respective domestic markets and fixed prices and quotas for the export of quinine and quinidine. Following the intervention of the German Competition Authority (Bundeskartellamt), Boehringer and Nedchem amended the agreement excluding deliveries to EU Member States. In 1960 a new cartel was established by them and shortly was extended to French and British undertakings. This cartel was based on an export agreement and an agreement for fixing prices and rebates relating to quinine and quinidine exports and the allocation of export quotas supported by a system of compensation depending on whether the export quotas were exceeded or fulfilled. Moreover, a 'gentlemen's agreement' between them extended these provisions to all the sales within the Common Market, establishing the principle of the protection of domestic markets in favour of each other producer and bound the French members of the cartel to refrain from manufacturing synthetic quinidine.

The Commission condemned these agreements as restrictions by object and imposed a fine by decision in 1969. The applicant appealed the Commission's decision on the grounds, amongst others, that the 'gentlemen's agreement' did not constitute an agreement within the meaning of Article 101(1) TFEU. The Court of Justice considered that the 'gentlemen's agreement' had as its object the restriction of competition, since it amounted to the expression of the parties' joint intention with regard to their conduct in the Common Market and it guaranteed the protection of each producer's domestic market. According to the Court, the sharing out of domestic markets has as its object the restriction of competition and trade within the Common Market and the fact that there was a threatened shortage in raw materials could in no way alter this finding.

Joined Cases C-29 & 30/83, *CRAM v Commission*
[1984] ECR-1679

This case addressed concerted action on market allocation with a view to protect markets against parallel imports of certain products in the market for zinc (cartel). It involved certain major producers of rolled zinc products in France, Germany, and Belgium. The infringements which were the subject of this dispute concerned measures to protect markets taken by French producer CRAM and German producer RZ in 1976 on the one hand, and a reciprocal assistance contract concluded in 1974 between these two and a third Belgian producer (Vieille Montagne). More specifically, the Belgian producer Schiltz had concluded agreements with both the French producer CRAM and the German producer RZ, whereby Schiltz would resell rolled zinc products only to a specific non-member country so as to limit the risks of parallel imports into the EU, an agreement which the Commission found to be an infringement of competition by object. Moreover, concerted action in the form of parallel refusal to supply products to Schiltz was adopted in 1976 by CRAM and RZ with a view to protecting the German market against parallel imports effected by Schiltz.

The Court of Justice, in its judgment on the alleged concerted action, held that concertation should be seen against the background of measures taken to protect markets and those measures were prompted by the fact that at that time the prices charged by those producers of rolled zinc products were higher in Germany and in France than in other Member States and in particular Belgium. Those price differences favoured the activity of importers who bought rolled zinc in a country where prices were low in order to resell them in a country where prices were higher. The concerted action taken by CRAM and RZ was thus designed to prevent such parallel imports. However, the Court annulled the decision on the basis that the Commission has not managed to produce sufficiently precise and coherent evidence to justify that the parallel behaviour of these two producers was the result of concerted actions.

7.3.1.3. Bid rigging/collusive tendering

Collusion at auctions by bidding rings also constitutes a violation of Article 101 TFEU and Chapter I CA98. Bid rigging aims to suppress competition at the procurement/auction level. It involves deciding who should win a contract in a competitive tender process and at what price. Usually, the ring members will not bid against one another. The collusive gain is later allocated between the members of the bid rigging cartel through side payments or inter-company arrangements, like subcontracts or shared ownership. Side-payments may sometimes occur through post-auction litigation settlements for unrelated to the procurement (bogus) disputes between the members of the ring.[69] Bid rigging may be relevant to public sector purchases in view of their obligations to organize a procurement process.[70] Detecting bid ringing may be a difficult endeavour. Yet, competition authorities have identified some patterns followed by bid ringers that provide a sign of bid ringing: for instance, when there is an 'obvious pattern of rotation of successful bidders', or 'a unusually high margin between the winning and

69 For a description of a bidding ring narrative, see RC Marshall and LM Marx, *The Economics of Collusion* (MIT, 2012), 55–70.

70 European Directive 2014/24/EU of the European Parliament and of the Council of 26 February 2014 on public procurement [2014] OJ L 94/65; European Directive 2014/25/EU of the European Parliament and of the Council of 26 February 2014 on procurement by entities operating in the water, energy, transport and postal services sectors [2014] OJ L 94/243.

unsuccessful bids', 'when all bid prices drop when a potential new bidder who is not a member of the cartel comes on the scene' etc.[71]

In its *Bid-rigging in the construction industry in England* decision, the Office of Fair Trading (OFT, now Competition and Markets Authority, CMA) imposed fines totalling £129.2 million on 103 construction firms in England which it had found had colluded with competitors on building contracts.[72] The infringements affected building projects across England worth in excess of £200 million including schools, universities, hospitals, and numerous private projects from the construction of apartment blocks to housing refurbishments. The OFT found that the firms engaged in illegal anti-competitive bid-rigging activities on 199 tenders from 2000 to 2006, mostly in the form of 'cover pricing'. According to the OFT,

> [c]over pricing or cover bidding occurs when a supplier/bidder (Bidder A) submits a price for a contract that is not intended to win the contract; rather, it is a price that has been decided upon in conjunction with another supplier/bidder (Bidder B) that wishes to win the contract. It therefore only gives an impression of competitive bidding, as the token bid submitted by Bidder A is higher than the bid of Bidder B who seeks to win the contract. Whether or not the decision by Bidder A not to submit a genuine competitive bid was taken in conjunction with Bidder B, the level of the uncompetitive bid submitted by Bidder A was set using commercially sensitive price information obtained from Bidder B. Furthermore, a cover pricing arrangement may also include the payment by Bidder B to Bidder A of an agreed amount of money or other consideration to 'compensate' Bidder A for the fact that Bidder A has no prospect of winning the contract and/or to compensate for tendering costs already accrued by Bidder A (*the compensation payment*) [. . .].[73]

The OFT also noted the existence of compensation payment arrangements (without cover pricing) which occur 'where two suppliers/bidders each prepare and submit their own bids, but agree that the winning party will pay the losing party an agreed sum of money, again often expressed by the parties as a payment to compensate for lost tendering costs [. . .]; unlike cover bidding, both parties may still be hoping to win the tender, the level of bids is above the competitive level as a result of these arrangements.'[74]

The OFT found that some of the cover pricing infringements also constituted forms of price fixing (including the compensation arrangements), as price fixing may involve fixing either the price itself or the components of a price and it does not necessarily eliminate all competition. Interestingly, the OFT noted that price fixing and bid rigging are not mutually exclusive categories and that 'an agreement or concerted practice may, depending on the particular facts of the case in question, be categorised as one or more of price fixing, customer/market sharing, bid rigging, information exchange'.[75]

Following a well-established EU jurisprudence,[76] the OFT found that '[a]ny tenders submitted as the result of collusion between prospective suppliers, which reduce the uncertainty of the outcome of the tender process, are likely to have an appreciable effect on competition'

[71] OFT 435, Cartels and the Competition Act 1998 (2004) 7.

[72] *Bid rigging in the construction industry in England* (Case CE/4327-04) OFT Decision (21 September 2009).

[73] Ibid, para III.74. [74] Ibid. [75] Ibid, paras III.76–III.80.

[76] See eg *European Sugar Industry* (Case COMP IV/26.918) Commission Decision 73/109/EEC [1973] OJ L 140/17 upheld by Joined Cases C-40/73 etc, *Suiker Unie v Commission* [1975] ECR 1663 and *Pre-Insulated Pipe cartel* (Case COMP IV/35.691/E.4) Commission Decision [1999] OJ L 24/1, upheld by Case T-9/99, *HFB Holding and Others v Commission* [2002] ECR II-1487.

and concluded that 'bid rigging agreements and/or concerted practices, by their very nature, restrict competition to an appreciable extent', finding that they were restrictions by object.[77] Indeed, according to the OFT,

> [c]over bidding is at a minimum capable of leading to a reduction of consumer welfare as it suppresses the competitive process which would otherwise exist (either if the party taking a cover price submitted a properly estimated bid, or if it withdrew from the tender process and enabled the customer to seek a replacement bid). It also deceives the customer into believing that tender prices have been independently determined, when they have not, thereby giving him a distorted view of the market.[78]

On appeal, the companies argued for a reduction of the fines imposed to them noting that the OFT's analysis of cover pricing as equivalent in seriousness than bid rigging was erroneous. The CAT agreed that cover pricing did not produce similar effects to a 'hardcore cartel' and, consequently, considerably reduced the total fine imposed by the OFT. However, it did accept the analysis by the OFT of cover pricing as a by object restriction of competition, thus signifying that by object restrictions and hardcore restrictions may not be one and the same thing. The CAT also noted that while considering effects is not relevant for determining the existence of a by object restriction, it is necessary when assessing the level of the penalty.

Kier Group PLC and others v OFT
[2011] CAT 3

> 94. There is no doubt that 'simple' cover pricing constitutes an infringement of the Chapter I prohibition, but in our view the practice is materially distinct from 'bid rigging' as ordinarily understood. Bid rigging implies an agreement or arrangement which determines, or assists in the determination of, the price which will actually be charged to the purchaser. Cover pricing is less serious than conduct of that kind. [. . .]
>
> 99. [. . .] [C]over pricing is certainly not an innocuous activity [. . .]. It is an unlawful practice which at the very least may deceive the customer about the source and extent of the competition which exists for the work in question, and which is capable of having anti-competitive effects on the particular tendering exercise and on future exercises. [. . .]
>
> 100. All that being said, it also needs to be recognised that 'simple' cover pricing is a bilateral arrangement in the context of a multi-partite tendering exercise. Its purpose is not (as in a conventional price-fixing cartel) to prevent competition by agreeing the price which it is intended the client should pay. Indeed, its purpose is quite the reverse, namely to identify a price which the client will not be willing to pay. Nor is its purpose to reach an agreement that the recipient of the cover price will cease to be a contender—it is strongly argued by the Present Appellants, and not disputed by the OFT, that in a case of 'simple' cover pricing the recipient has already made its own unilateral decision not to compete for the work before the request for a cover price is made.

[77] OFT, Case CE/4327-04, *Bid rigging in the construction industry in England* (21 September 2009), para III.72. On collusive tendering, see also *Makers UK Ltd v OFT* [2007] CAT 11.

[78] *Bid rigging in the construction industry in England* (Case CE/4327-04) OFT Decision (21 September 2009), para III.110.

101. To the extent that cover pricing is capable of compromising the immediate tendering exercise, the most serious aspects are: the possible exclusion of a substitute tenderer in place of the one who has received a cover; and the risk that the whole tendering exercise may be subverted if a large number of covers are given. We consider it unlikely, although it is not inconceivable, that where some but not all competitors have been provided with covers, the cover provider may be encouraged to price his own tender a little higher on that account. The likelihood is that, even with the knowledge that only one genuine opponent remains, a tenderer who wishes to win will still put forward its keenest bid. It is therefore unsurprising that in none of the 'simple' cover pricing infringements in the Present Appeals, indeed in none of infringements of that kind in the Decision, is there a case where the price paid by the customer was found, or even alleged, to have been directly affected by the infringement. It is also perhaps worth noting that it would be the receipt of a request for a cover which might embolden a tenderer, for that is the source of his knowledge that the requester does not wish to win the work and is not a serious contender. He has this knowledge whether or not he agrees to supply a cover price.

102. Although the possibility cannot be excluded that the endemic nature of simple cover pricing in the construction industry may sometimes have raised prices and harmed clients, the harm is likely to be small by comparison with hard-core cartels. The typical profit margins in the construction industry, said to be about 2%, do not support the existence of substantial overcharges. Moreover, to the extent that the adverse effects of cover pricing on competition are indirect and prospective rather than direct and immediate, they are likely to be more evident to those trained in competition law or economics than to the operators of construction companies.

After noting the practice of the industry, the CAT concluded:

107. Whilst the industry's general perceptions and motivations as described above do not affect the unlawfulness of cover pricing, they do seem to us to have a bearing on the seriousness of the infringements in question, and to provide significantly more mitigation generally than has been recognised by the OFT in the Decision. [. . .]

7.3.1.4. Collective boycott agreements

In *Pre-insulated pipes*, the Commission found that competitors using norms and standards (agreed by the industry) to prevent or delay the introduction of new technology which would result in price reductions infringed Article 101(1) TFEU.[79] Producers of pre-insulated pipes for district heating had in concert divided national markets and eventually the whole European market amongst themselves on the basis of quotas, allocated national markets to particular producers and arranged the withdrawal of others, agreed prices for the product and for individual projects, allocated individual projects to designated producers and manipulated the bidding procedure for those projects in order to ensure that the assigned producer was awarded the contract in question and in order to protect the cartel from competition from the only substantial non-member, Powerpipe AB: they took concerted measures to hinder its

[79] *Pre-Insulated Pipe cartel* (Case COMP IV/35.691/E-4) Commission Decision 1999/60/EC [1999] OJ L 24/1.

commercial activity, damage its business or drive it out of the market altogether. They also used quality norms to keep up prices and delay the introduction of new cost-saving technology. The undertakings found to infringe Article 101 TFEU by the Commission appealed to the General Court, which approved the Commission's decision. They appealed the General Court's judgment at the Court of Justice.

Joined Cases C-189, 202 & 205–8/02, *Dansk Rorindustri A/S v Commission and Others*
[2005] ECR I–5425

After dismissing most of the procedural pleas some of them in the light of the judgments of the European Court of Human Rights, the CJEU came to consider whether conduct of some individuals could be attributed to one of the appellants.[80] *Then CJEU came to the substantive issues. It confirmed many of the findings of the Commission, approved by the General Court, about firms represented at meeting to discuss anti-competitive conduct.*

145. For the purposes of applying Article [101(1)] of the Treaty, it is sufficient that the object of an agreement should be to restrict, prevent or distort competition irrespective of the actual effects of that agreement. Consequently, in the case of agreements reached at meetings of competing undertakings, that provision is infringed where those meetings have such an object and are thus intended to organise artificially the operation of the market. In such a case, the liability of a particular undertaking in respect of the infringement is properly established where it participated in those meetings with knowledge of their object, even if it did not proceed to implement any of the measures agreed at those meetings. The greater or lesser degree of regular participation by the undertaking in the meetings and of completeness of its implementation of the measures agreed is relevant not to the establishment of its liability but rather to the extent of that liability and thus to the severity of the penalty (see Joined Cases C238/99 P, C-244/99 P, C-245/99 P, C-247/99 P, C250/99 P to C252/99 P and C-254/99 P *Limburgse Vinyl Maatschappij and Others* v *Commission* [2002] ECR I–8375, paragraphs 508 to 510).

146. It follows that the fact put forward by Brugg that it did not implement, and indeed was not capable of implementing, the boycott agreed at the meeting of 24 March 1995 cannot discharge its liability for having participated in that measure, unless it publicly distanced itself from what was agreed at the meeting, which Brugg does not claim to have done.

147. It is true, as Brugg maintains, and contrary to the finding made by the Court of First Instance at paragraph 62 of the judgment in *BruggRohrsysteme* v *Commission*, that it is irrelevant in that regard whether Brugg had an interest in any boycott of one of its direct competitors by other participants in the cartel (see, to that effect, *Aalborg Portland and Others* v *Commission*, paragraph 335).

148. However, that is a complaint directed against a ground included in the judgment purely for the sake of completeness which cannot lead to the judgment being set aside and is therefore nugatory (see, in particular, Case C-184/01 P *Hirschfeldt* v *EEA* [2002] ECR I–10173, paragraph 48 and the case-law cited).

80 Joined Cases C-189, 202 & 205–8/02, *Dansk Rorindustri A/S v Commission and Others* [2005] ECR I–5425, paras 103–52.

149. In Brugg's case, moreover, it is apparent from the contested decision that, contrary to Brugg's contention, the Commission did not regard its participation in the boycott of Powerpipe as an aggravating circumstance, since the only aggravating circumstance found in its case consisted in its having continued the infringement after the investigations.

150. Likewise, in the light of the case-law [. . .] the fact, put forward by the Henss/Isoplus group, that the participation in the cartel of dominant or particularly powerful undertakings in a position to take retaliatory measures against other, much less powerful, participants should the latter publicly distance themselves from what was decided at meetings having an anti-competitive object, has no effect on the liability of those undertakings for their participation in the anti-competitive measure, but may, where appropriate, have consequences for the determination of the level of the penalty.

151. As the Commission appositely observes, the opposite argument would be unacceptable, as the consequence would be that Article [101(1)] of the Treaty would be applied differently depending on the size of the undertakings, since the less powerful undertakings would be favoured.

NOTES AND QUESTIONS ON COLLECTIVE BOYCOTT AGREEMENTS

1. Sending a representative to a meeting known to be going to discuss anti-competitive conduct is risky. Even a small firm, which does not implement the anti-competitive decisions and which is frightened in the presence of an important competitor, known to act aggressively against price cutters, may be liable to fines, although these points could possibly mitigate the infringement.
2. (Paragraphs 145, 150) Whose objective is relevant: that of the conveners of the meeting or that of the small firm too frightened to object loudly? What should such a small firm do to avoid being fined?

7.3.1.5. Certain kinds of information exchange—on future prices and quantities

Information exchange may occur at the initial steps of forming a cartel, as the cartelists will need to identify the parameters of their cooperation and the selection of the cooperative equilibrium, for instance by determining the price or output level of the cartel or of its individual members, but may also facilitate the maintenance of the stability of a cartel by supporting the monitoring of any possible deviations from the cartel equilibrium reached by the parties.

7.3.1.5.1. Information exchange as an object restriction

For article 101 TFEU to apply, the *information exchange should result from some form of collusive action*, which can take the form of an agreement, concerted practice or a decision of an association of undertakings.

Communication from the Commission—Guidelines on the applicability of Article 101 TFEU to horizontal co-operation agreements [2011] OJ C 11/1 (footnotes omitted)

55. [. . .] Information exchange can take various forms. Firstly, data can be directly shared between competitors. Secondly, data can be shared indirectly through a common agency (for example, a trade association) or a third party such as a market research organisation or through the companies' suppliers or retailers.

56. Information exchange takes place in different contexts. There are agreements, decisions by associations of undertakings, or concerted practices under which information is exchanged, where the main economic function lies in the exchange of information itself. Moreover, information exchange can be part of another type of horizontal co-operation agreement (for example, the parties to a production agreement share certain information on costs). The assessment of the latter type of information exchanges should be carried out in the context of the assessment of the horizontal co-operation agreement itself.

59. Moreover, communication of information among competitors may constitute an agreement, a concerted practice, or a decision by an association of undertakings with the object of fixing, in particular, prices or quantities. Those types of information exchanges will normally be considered and fined as cartels. Information exchange may also facilitate the implementation of a cartel by enabling companies to monitor whether the participants comply with the agreed terms. Those types of exchanges of information will be assessed as part of the cartel.

Concerted practice

60. Information exchange can only be addressed under Article 101 if it establishes or is part of an agreement, a concerted practice or a decision by an association of undertakings. The existence of an agreement, a concerted practice or decision by an association of undertakings does not prejudge whether the agreement, concerted practice or decision by an association of undertakings gives rise to a restriction of competition within the meaning of Article 101(1). In line with the case-law of the Court of Justice of the European Union, the concept of a concerted practice refers to a form of coordination between undertakings by which, without it having reached the stage where an agreement properly so-called has been concluded, practical cooperation between them is knowingly substituted for the risks of competition. The criteria of coordination and cooperation necessary for determining the existence of a concerted practice, far from requiring an actual plan to have been worked out, are to be understood in the light of the concept inherent in the provisions of the Treaty on competition, according to which each company must determine independently the policy which it intends to adopt on the internal market and the conditions which it intends to offer to its customers.

61. This does not deprive companies of the right to adapt themselves intelligently to the existing or anticipated conduct of their competitors. It does, however, preclude any direct or indirect contact between competitors, the object or effect of which is to create conditions of competition which do not correspond to the normal competitive conditions of the market in question, regard being had to the nature of the products or services offered, the size and number of the undertakings, and the volume of the said

market. This precludes any direct or indirect contact between competitors, the object or effect of which is to influence conduct on the market of an actual or potential competitor, or to disclose to such competitor the course of conduct which they themselves have decided to adopt or contemplate adopting on the market, thereby facilitating a collusive outcome on the market. Hence, information exchange can constitute a concerted practice if it reduces strategic uncertainty in the market thereby facilitating collusion, that is to say, if the data exchanged is strategic. Consequently, sharing of strategic data between competitors amounts to concertation, because it reduces the independence of competitors' conduct on the market and diminishes their incentives to compete.

62. A situation where only one undertaking discloses strategic information to its competitor(s), who accept(s) it, can also constitute a concerted practice. Such disclosure could occur, for example, through contacts via mail, emails, phone calls, meetings etc. It is then irrelevant whether only one undertaking unilaterally informs its competitors of its intended market behaviour, or whether all participating undertakings inform each other of the respective deliberations and intentions. When one undertaking alone reveals to its competitors strategic information concerning its future commercial policy, that reduces strategic uncertainty as to the future operation of the market for all the competitors involved and increases the risk of limiting competition and of collusive behaviour. For example, mere attendance at a meeting where a company discloses its pricing plans to its competitors is likely to be caught by Article 101, even in the absence of an explicit agreement to raise prices. When a company receives strategic data from a competitor (be it in a meeting, by mail or electronically), it will be presumed to have accepted the information and adapted its market conduct accordingly unless it responds with a clear statement that it does not wish to receive such data.

63. Where a company makes a unilateral announcement that is also genuinely public, for example through a newspaper, this generally does not constitute a concerted practice within the meaning of Article 101(1). However, depending on the facts underlying the case at hand, the possibility of finding a concerted practice cannot be excluded, for example in a situation where such an announcement was followed by public announcements by other competitors, not least because strategic responses of competitors to each other's public announcements (which, to take one instance, might involve readjustments of their own earlier announcements to announcements made by competitors) could prove to be a strategy for reaching a common understanding about the terms of coordination.

7.3.1.5.2. Woodpulp II

The case involved a European Commission investigation into the European wood pulp industry in 1977 concerning the conduct of firms since 1973. This investigation led to a Commission decision finding the wood pulp producers had infringed Article 101(1) TFEU by colluding on price announcements and transaction prices, as well as an independent infringement of Article 101(1) TFEU for the exchange of price information between firms. The core argument examined by the Court related to the evidence of collusion, which was challenged in view of the expert reports commissioned by the CJEU which found that the parallel conduct by wood pulp producers was explained by the characteristics of the market and not by collusive conduct. This issue is discussed in Section 5.5.2. The Commission found that an information exchange agreement by itself constituted an infringement of Article 101(1) TFEU, even in the absence of evidence for collusion on prices. We will focus here on the different kinds of information exchanged in this case.

First, there were quarterly pre-sales price announcements made to buyers taking place simultaneously or almost simultaneously by the wood pulp producers. These were either direct private announcements to downstream customers or agents or public announcements through the trade press. These public price announcements generally conformed with the transactions prices, that is, there were no revisions of prices after public announcements in the trade press.

Second, there were instances in which wood pulp producers communicated among themselves, before making their price announcements. Kai-Uwe Kühn and Xavier Vives note for these practices the following:

> [T]he general mechanisms for information exchange may have been used to coordinate price announcements and monitor whether firms conformed with previous agreements. This evidence was sufficient for the Court of Justice to uphold the charge of collusion in some cases. However, there also seems to be some evidence that some coordination of price announcements went on through direct communications between firms. These information exchanges *prior* to price announcement should be considered as the central competition policy problem, not the price announcements in themselves. Information exchange should only be of interest when it helps to sustain tacit collusion among producers.[81]

Third, it results from the expert's report, that there was information exchange between the customers about the transaction prices they were obtaining from wood pulp producers. This had, according to Kai-Uwe Kühn and Xavier Vives, 'the explicit goal that paper producers could monitor each other's input costs and relax competition between them in the market for paper'.[82]

The CJEU examined whether the public exchange of information constituted an independent (from collusion on prices) infringement of Article 101(1) TFEU in the following paragraphs of the judgment.[83]

Joined Cases C-89, 104, 114, 116, 117 & 125–9/85, _A Ahlström Osakeyhtiö and Others v Commission_
[1993] ECR I–1307

> 57. In its first question, the Court asked whether the system of quarterly price announcements called in question by the Commission was to be regarded as constituting in itself an infringement of the Treaty or whether that system was merely evidence of concertation on announced prices which took place at an earlier stage. The

81 K-U Kühn and X Vives, 'Information Exchanges among Firms and their Impact on Competition' (December 1994), 89, available at https://blog.iese.edu/xvives/files/2011/09/Information-Exchanges-and-their-Impact-on-Competition.pdf.

82 Ibid, 91.

83 Professor Joliet, however, was concerned not to make it illegal without a clear evidence of concertation. See R Joliet, 'La notion de pratique concertée et l'arrêt I.C.I. dans une perspective comparative' (1974) *Cahier de droit européen* 249.

Commission's replies did not make it possible to choose between those two interpretations and so both must be considered. [. . .]

The system of quarterly price announcements constitutes in itself the infringement of Article [101] of the Treaty

59 According to the Commission's first hypothesis, it is the system of quarterly price announcements in itself which constitutes the infringement of Article [101 TFEU].

60. First, the Commission considers that that system was deliberately introduced by the pulp producers in order to enable them to ascertain the prices that would be charged by their competitors in the following quarters. The disclosure of prices to third parties, especially to the press and agents working for several producers, well before their application at the beginning of a new quarter gave the other producers sufficient time to announce their own, corresponding, new prices before that quarter and to apply them from the commencement of that quarter.

61. Secondly, the Commission considers that the implementation of that mechanism had the effect of making the market artificially transparent by enabling producers to obtain a rapid and accurate picture of the prices quoted by their competitors.

62. In deciding on that point, it must be borne in mind that Article [101(1) TFEU] prohibits all agreements between undertakings, decisions by associations of undertakings and concerted practices which may affect trade between Member States and which have as their object or effect the prevention, restriction or distortion of competition within the Common Market.

63. According to the Court's judgment in *Suiker Unie* [at paragraphs 26 and 173], a concerted practice refers to a form of coordination between undertakings which, without having been taken to the stage where an agreement properly so-called has been concluded, knowingly substitutes for the risks of competition practical cooperation between them. In the same judgment, the Court added that the criteria of coordination and cooperation must be understood in the light of the concept inherent in the provisions of the Treaty relating to competition that each economic operator must determine independently the policy which he intends to adopt on the Common Market.

64 In this case, the communications arise from the price announcements made to users. They constitute in themselves market behaviour which does not lessen each undertaking's uncertainty as to the future attitude of its competitors. At the time when each undertaking engages in such behaviour, it cannot be sure of the future conduct of the others.

65 Accordingly, the system of quarterly price announcements on the pulp market is not to be regarded as constituting in itself an infringement of Article [101(1) TFEU of the Treaty. [. . .]

The assessment by the CJEU of the second hypothesis explored by the Commission, the fact that the infringement arises from concertation on announced prices, is examined in Section 11.6.3. The CJEU did not discuss extensively, from a substantive competition law perspective, the other forms of information exchange. It noted, however, the following with regard to the information exchange of transaction prices taking place within the trade associations KEA and FIDES:

130. So far as concerns concertation on announced prices and the exchange of information on transaction prices, reference must be made first of all to Article IIa of the Policy Statement of the Pulp Group. According to that provision, the members of the group are to meet from time to time in order to fix unanimously prices for sales of pulp, known as 'KEA recommended prices', and they agree to announce those prices to

their customers. If, subsequently, the members of the association deviate from those prices-as they continue to be free to do—they are required to give advance notification to the manager of the group, who may decide, if necessary, to convene a further meeting of the group in order to discuss appropriate action.

131. Since the producers met from time to time in order to agree the 'KEA recommended price', it is clear that the producers belonging to KEA concerted within that association on announced prices for wood pulp. Similarly, it should be noted that, by undertaking to notify in advance any price deviating from that which they had fixed by common agreement, they established a system for the exchange of information on their future conduct that was such as to restrict competition.

132. That much is self-evident and the applicants' objection that in practice the 'KEA recommended price' fixed by the group was not always adhered to by its members is to no avail. That argument implicitly concedes that, at least some of the time, the applicants announced KEA recommended prices and therefore concerted on those prices. [. . .]

Note that the CJEU distinguished between the issues of market transparency for customers and market transparency for sellers. The issue of horizontal versus vertical transparency is examined further below. On this issue, Kai-Uwe Kühn and Xavier Vives remarked the following:

Market transparency for customers is essential for having competition in a market. If customers cannot make informed price comparison firms can essentially act as monopolists even in markets with many firms. The reason is that price cuts are simply never observed by customers so that they cannot react to them. As we have stated earlier, we know from the literature on informative advertising that the possibility of price announcements (through advertisements) will generally intensify competition. Market transparency on the producer side has several aspects. First, information about past prices will help in sustaining collusive outcomes. Secondly information about the costs or demands for the goods of competitors helps in allocating cartel quotas and detecting collusion via secret price cuts. Therefore, public announcements of prices increase both types of market transparency, while private exchange between producers of cost and quantity data only increases market transparency on the side of producers. This distinction is very important for policy conclusions. There is no sense in which one can come to policy conclusions about 'market transparency' without distinguishing between the two sides of the market.[84]

7.3.1.5.3. Cimenteries

Joined Cases T-25–6, 30–2, 34–9, 42–6, 48, 50–65, 68–71, 87–8, 103 & 104/95, *Cimenteries CBR and Others*
[2000] ECR II–491

By a decision adopted on 30 November 1994, the Commission held that the European Cement Association (Cembureau), eight national cement associations, and thirty-three European cement producers had infringed Article 101 TFEU by participating from 1983 in

84 K-U Kühn and X Vives, 'Information Exchanges Among Firms and their Impact on Competition' (December 1994), 93, available at https://blog.iese.edu/xvives/files/2011/09/Information-Exchanges-and-their-Impact-on-Competition.pdf.

a general market-sharing agreement, transnational restrictive practices, and restrictive practices relating to exports (market allocation and exchanges of information), in particular by agreements and concerted practices. The Commission had relied on documentary evidence in order to prove the existence of the Cembureau cartel agreement. The Cembureau agreement promoted the principle of not transhipping to internal European markets. The Commission found information on the premise of the cement producers that this principle was underpinned by concerted practices involving the exchange of information on prices. The aim of this exchange of information was to reduce price differences between the various countries so as to remove any temptation to export and so as to get those producers who did export to align their prices on those of local producers and thus avoid disrupting the market in the importing country.

In addition, the Commission found that at several meetings, the Portuguese and Spanish producers, represented by their associations, monitored cement exports between the two countries so as to ensure that markets were divided by exchanging information and refusing to sell to certain customers. A similar agreement existed between certain French and German firms. Some of these practices were aimed to curb the threat of low-price Greek cement exports to a number of Member States after the Greeks had lost important markets in the Middle East.

A number of meetings were organized between several producers where a common policy was devised in order to prevent Greek cement exports, in which meetings numerous items of information were exchanged. A number of large European manufacturers set up information and coordination bodies such as the European Cement Export Committee (ECEC) and the European Export Policy Committee (EPC), which had various aims and activities: including the monitoring of exports and export forecasts, the comparison of supply and demand on home and export markets, and the exchange of information on prices. White-cement producers also entered into restrictive practices involving non-trans-shipment to home markets and the channelling of production surpluses to third countries, exchanging information on their individual production capacities, sales and prices.

The Court noted that the Commission found that various measures governed and conditioned by the Cembureau agreement had been taken by various undertakings and associations of undertakings and it took the view that all the following were measures implementing the Cembureau agreement, in particular the specific and periodic exchanges of information on prices within the framework of Cembureau, which had an object similar to the agreement found to be a cartel, namely the common rule on non-transhipment to home markets, the exchange of information being merely considered as measures to implement or back up that rule. The Court also noted that the participants were also identical and accepted the view of the Commission that 'the whole of the arrangements adopted within the framework of Cembureau and the bilateral and/or multilateral meetings and contacts [. . . had] constituted a 'single and continuous agreement'.

Of particular interest are the following passages of the General Court's judgment with regard to the existence of concerted practices between cement producers in order to share markets:

> 1849. In that connection, the Court points out that the concept of concerted practice does in fact imply the existence of reciprocal contacts [. . .]. That condition is met where one competitor discloses its future intentions or conduct on the market to another when the latter requests it or, at the very least, accepts it. [. . .] [T]he meeting was held at the behest of Lafarge. Moreover, there is nothing in those minutes drawn up by Lafarge which shows that its representative expressed any reservations or

objections whatsoever [. . .]. In those circumstances, the applicants cannot seek to reduce Lafarge's attitude during the meeting in question to the purely passive role of a recipient of the information which Buzzi unilaterally decided to pass on to it, without any request by Lafarge.

1850. It may be inferred therefrom that the contacts between Lafarge and Buzzi were motivated by the element of reciprocity essential to a finding of concerted practice. Accordingly, the applicants' arguments must be rejected.

1851. , Buzzi denies the existence of an anti-competitive concerted practice claiming, first, that the views which it expressed to Lafarge during the meeting in question only concerned present and past circumstances, rather than anticipating future actions, and, secondly, that it had not given any undertaking to Lafarge as to its future conduct on the market in the Côte d'Azur.

1852. The Court points out in this regard that any direct or indirect contact between economic operators of such a nature as to disclose to a competitor the course of conduct which they themselves have decided to adopt or contemplate adopting on the market, where the object or effect of such contact is to create conditions of competition which do not correspond to the normal conditions of the market in question, constitutes a concerted practice prohibited by Article [101(1)] of the Treaty [. . .]. In order to prove that there has been a concerted practice, it is not therefore necessary to show that the competitor in question has formally undertaken, in respect of one or several others, to adopt a particular course of conduct or that the competitors have colluded over their future conduct on the market [. . .]. It is sufficient that, by its statement of intention, the competitor should have eliminated or, at the very least, substantially reduced uncertainty as to the conduct to expect of the other on the market [. . .].

1865. [. . .] [A]lthough, as is clear from the very terms of Article [101(1) TFEU], a concerted practice implies, besides undertakings' concerting together, conduct on the market pursuant to those collusive practices, and a relationship of cause and effect between the two, it must be held, subject to proof to the contrary, which the parties concerned must adduce, that the concerted action in question influenced the parties' conduct on the market [. . .].

While the passages of the judgment of the Court refer to the existence of a concerted practice between undertakings, they raise the question of the prohibition under Article 101(1) TFEU of the participation of undertakings in one meeting where they disclosed information on their future intentions or conduct on the market. This issue was examined in *T-Mobile*. Price signalling and other more indirect forms of communication were examined in *Bananas*.

7.3.1.5.4. T-Mobile

Case C-8/08, *T-Mobile Netherlands BV, KPN Mobile NV, Orange Nederland NV, Vodafone Libertel NV v Raad van bestuur van de Nederlandse Mededingingsautoriteit*
[2009] ECR I–4529

The facts of this case were examined in Section 6.3.1.1.4. In a nutshell, the case involved the organization of a meeting between the representatives of mobile telecommunications operators offering mobile telecommunications services in the Netherlands. At that meeting they discussed, inter alia, *the reduction of standard dealer remunerations for post-paid subscriptions and exchanged confidential information concerning their planned reductions in certain commissions payable to their respective dealers. That resulted in coordination of their market conduct in relation to reductions in certain commission payments to their respective dealers.*

Opinion of Advocate General Kokott (footnotes omitted)

51. Such exchange of confidential commercial information between competitors concerning their intended market behaviour is capable, in principle, of generating an anti-competitive impact because it reduces or removes the degree of uncertainty as to the operation of the market in question with the result that competition between undertakings is restricted. In that connection, it is irrelevant whether such an exchange of information constituted the main purpose of the contact or simply took place in the framework (or under the auspices) of a contact which in itself had no unlawful object. [. . .]

52. Regard must be had to the fact that independence of economic participants constitutes one of the basic requirements for competition to function. Accordingly, the provisions of the Treaty relating to competition are based on the concept that each economic operator must determine independently the policy which he intends to adopt on the common market. That requirement of independence precludes any direct or indirect contact between economic operators by which an undertaking influences the conduct on the market of its competitors or discloses to them its decisions or deliberations concerning its own conduct on the market, if as a result conditions of competition may apply which do not correspond to the normal conditions of the market in question.

53. That applies a fortiori when the exchange of information concerns a highly concentrated oligopolistic market. Precisely that structure appeared to characterise the Netherlands market for mobile telecommunication services in 2001: as is evident from the reference for a preliminary ruling, at that time only five undertakings in that country had their own mobile telephone networks, with one of them, KPN, even attaining a market share in excess of 40% whilst development of further independent networks was precluded in the absence of available licences.

54. It is irrelevant in that connection whether only one undertaking unilaterally informs its competitors of its intended market behaviour or whether all participating undertakings inform each other of their respective deliberations and intentions. Simply when one undertaking alone breaks cover and reveals to its competitors confidential information concerning its future commercial policy, that reduces for all participants uncertainty as to the future operation of the market and introduces the risk of a diminution in competition and of collusive behaviour between them.

Judgment of the CJEU

32. [. . .] [W]ith regard to the exchange of information between competitors, it should be recalled that the criteria of coordination and cooperation necessary for determining the existence of a concerted practice are to be understood in the light of the notion inherent in the Treaty provisions on competition, according to which each economic

operator must determine independently the policy which he intends to adopt on the common market (see *Suiker Unie and Others* v *Commission*, paragraph 173; Case 172/80 *Züchner* [1981] ECR 2021, paragraph 13; *Ahlström Osakeyhtiö and Others* v *Commission*, paragraph 63; and Case C7/95 P *Deere* v *Commission* [1998] ECR I3111, paragraph 86).

33. While it is correct to say that this requirement of independence does not deprive economic operators of the right to adapt themselves intelligently to the existing or anticipated conduct of their competitors, it does, none the less, strictly preclude any direct or indirect contact between such operators by which an undertaking may influence the conduct on the market of its actual or potential competitors or disclose to them its decisions or intentions concerning its own conduct on the market where the object or effect of such contact is to create conditions of competition which do not correspond to the normal conditions of the market in question, regard being had to the nature of the products or services offered, the size and number of the undertakings involved and the volume of that market (see, to that effect, *Suiker Unie and Others* v *Commission*, paragraph 174; *Züchner*, paragraph 14; and *Deere* v *Commission*, paragraph 87).

34. At paragraphs 88 et seq. of *Deere* v *Commission*, the Court therefore held that on a highly concentrated oligopolistic market, such as the market in the main proceedings, the exchange of information was such as to enable traders to know the market positions and strategies of their competitors and thus to impair appreciably the competition which exists between traders.

35. It follows that the exchange of information between competitors is liable to be incompatible with the competition rules if it reduces or removes the degree of uncertainty as to the operation of the market in question, with the result that competition between undertakings is restricted (see *Deere* v *Commission*, paragraph 90, and Case C-194/99 P *Thyssen Stahl* v *Commission* [2003] ECR I10821, paragraph 81). [. . .]

The CJEU further considers that there is a causal connection between the concerted practice and the market conduct of the undertakings participating in the practice and, subject to proof to the contrary, which it is for the undertakings concerned to adduce, national courts should apply a presumption that if the undertakings participating in the concerted practice remain active on that market, they are presumed to take account of the information exchanged with their competitors (presumption of a causal link). The applicants challenged the existence of a causal connection in case the concerted practice results from a single meeting between the undertakings in which they exchanged confidential information.

54. [. . .] [T]he referring court asks essentially whether, when applying the concept of concerted practices in Article [101(1) TFEU], there is in all cases a presumption of a causal connection between the concerted practice and the market conduct of the undertakings concerned, even if the concerted action is the result of a single meeting.

55. Vodafone, TMobile and KPN essentially take the view that it cannot be inferred from *Commission* v *Anic Partecipazioni* or *Hüls* that the presumption of a causal connection is applicable in all cases. In their view, that presumption should be applied only in cases in which the facts and circumstances are the same as those in those cases. In essence, they submit that it is only where the undertakings concerned meet on a

regular basis, in the knowledge that confidential information has been exchanged in the course of previous meetings, that those undertakings can be presumed to have been guided in their market conduct on the basis of the concerted action. Moreover, they consider that it is irrational to take the view that an undertaking should base its market conduct on information exchanged in the course of just one meeting, in particular where, as in the case in the main proceedings, the meeting has a legitimate purpose.

56. On the other hand, the Netherlands Government and the Commission submit that it is evident from the caselaw, in particular *Commission* v *Anic Partecipazioni* and *Hüls*, that the presumption of a causal connection is not dependent on the number of meetings which gave rise to the concerted action. They observe that such a presumption is justified if the contact which took place, regard being had to its context, content and the frequency with which it occurred, is sufficient to result in coordination of conduct on the market that is capable of preventing, restricting or distorting competition within the meaning of Article [101(1) TFEU] and if, moreover, the undertakings concerned remain active on the market.

57. According to the Netherlands Government, the action in the main proceedings is a perfect illustration of the fact that a single meeting is sufficient for concerted action to be established. [. . .]

58. It is evident from paragraph 162 of *Hüls* and paragraph 121 of *Commission* v *Anic Partecipazioni* that the Court found that that presumption applied only where there was concerted action and where the undertaking concerned remained active on the market. The addition of the words 'particularly when they concert together on a regular basis over a long period', far from supporting the argument that there is a presumption of a causal connection only if the undertakings meet regularly, must necessarily be interpreted as meaning that that presumption is more compelling where undertakings have concerted their actions on a regular basis over a long period.

59. Any other interpretation would be tantamount to a claim that an isolated exchange of information between competitors could not in any case lead to concerted action that is in breach of the competition rules laid down in the Treaty. Depending on the structure of the market, the possibility cannot be ruled out that a meeting on a single occasion between competitors, such as that in question in the main proceedings, may, in principle, constitute a sufficient basis for the participating undertakings to concert their market conduct and thus successfully substitute practical cooperation between them for competition and the risks that that entails.

60. As the Netherlands Government correctly pointed out, [. . .] the number, frequency, and form of meetings between competitors needed to concert their market conduct depend on both the subject-matter of that concerted action and the particular market conditions. If the undertakings concerned establish a cartel with a complex system of concerted actions in relation to a multiplicity of aspects of their market conduct, regular meetings over a long period may be necessary. If, on the other hand, as in the main proceedings, the objective of the exercise is only to concert action on a selective basis in relation to a one-off alteration in market conduct with reference simply to one parameter of competition, a single meeting between competitors may constitute a sufficient basis on which to implement the anti-competitive object which the participating undertakings aim to achieve.

61. In those circumstances, what matters is not so much the number of meetings held between the participating undertakings as whether the meeting or meetings which took place afforded them the opportunity to take account of the information exchanged with their competitors in order to determine their conduct on the market in question and knowingly substitute practical cooperation between them for the risks of competition. Where it can be established that such undertakings successfully concerted with one another and remained active on the market, they may justifiably be called upon to adduce evidence that that concerted action did not have any effect on their conduct on the market in question.

62. In the light of the foregoing, the answer to the third question must be that, in so far as the undertaking participating in the concerted action remains active on the market in question, there is a presumption of a causal connection between the concerted practice and the conduct of the undertaking on that market, even if the concerted action is the result of a meeting held by the participating undertakings on a single occasion.

The CJEU found that the exchange of information in this context constituted a restriction of competition by object.

7.3.1.5.5. Bananas

Case C-286/13 P, *Dole Food Company Inc and Dole Fresh Fruit Europe v European Commission*, ECLI:EU:C:2015:184 (*Dole*) (references omitted)

This case involved pre-pricing communications in which undertakings discussed price setting factors relevant to the setting of future quotation prices for bananas. In October 2008, the Commission found that two importers of bananas, Dole and Weichert, operated an illegal price cartel in breach of Article 101 TFEU and imposed to them a fine of €60.3 million. The cartel was discovered because a third importer, Chiquita blew the whistle. Chiquita escaped the fines as it benefitted from full immunity under the Commission's Leniency Notice. The banana importers were found by the Commission to have engaged in bilateral pre-pricing communications for a period of two years, engaging in pre-price (before setting their own quotation price) communications on 'price setting factors and price trends and or indications of quotation prices for the up-coming week'. Further, they exchanged information on quotation prices, once set, thus being able to monitor each other's pricing decisions in the light of the pre-pricing communications. According to the Commission, quotation prices served at least as market signals, trends, or indications as to the intended development of banana prices, and they were relevant for the banana trade and prices obtained, as in some transactions actual prices were directly linked to quotation prices. In its decision, the Commission found that the purpose of these pre-pricing communications was to reduce uncertainty as to the parties' conduct in respect of their weekly quotation prices and therefore gave rise to a concerted practice having an anti-competitive object. It also rejected the parties' defences based on the nature of the information exchanged, the regulatory framework of the banana sector and the lack of relevance of the quotation prices to the setting of actual sales prices for bananas. The parties interjected an appeal at the General Court. The same facts were at issue in Fresh Del Monte Produce, Inc v European Commission.[85]

[85] Case T-587/08, *Fresh Del Monte Produce, Inc v European Commission*, ECLI:EU:T:2013:129.

With regard to the content of the pre-pricing communications exchanged, the parties alleged that this was common knowledge in the market, both to ripeners and multiples, and that the Commission ignored in the contested decision the fact that this market intelligence was shared with the customers as well. According to the companies, the mere assertion that it was well known that the importers occasionally spoke amongst themselves about general market conditions, which is based on general statements by customers which in turn are not founded on any direct statement but on public rumour alone, does not permit the inference that all market participants were aware of the exact scope of the pre-pricing communications identified by the Commission, and that banana suppliers other than Chiquita, Dole, and Weichert were participating in those communications. The General Court did not accept this argument and noted that the Commission was right to rely 'on the necessary distinction between, on the one hand, competitors gleaning information independently or discussing future pricing with customers and third parties and, on the other hand, competitors discussing price-setting factors and the evolution of prices with other competitors before setting their quotation prices'.[86] *Indeed, '[t]he individual assessment by a banana importer of a climatic event affecting a region of production, information which is public and available, should not be confused with the joint evaluation by two competitors of that event, in combination, as the case may be, with other information on the state of the market, and of its impact on the development of the sector, very shortly before their quotation prices are set'.*[87]

With regard to the timing and frequency of the exchanges of information, which the applicants alleged were occasional and rare, the General Court noted that 'the number, frequency, and form of meetings between competitors needed to concert their market conduct depend on both the subject-matter of that concerted action and the particular market conditions' and that 'if the objective of the exercise is only to concert action on a selective basis in relation to a one-off alteration in market conduct with reference simply to one parameter of competition, a single meeting between competitors may constitute a sufficient basis on which to implement the anti-competitive object which the participating undertakings aim to achieve'.[88] *According to the General Court, 'Dole's explicit statements on the content and purpose of the pre-pricing communications also rule out the possibility of a bilateral discussion that might be limited to mere harmless gossip on the industry in general, even if the employees of the undertakings concerned might have raised, on certain occasions, in addition to factors relevant to the setting of quotation prices, price trends or price indications, an innocuous subject concerning the personnel of the undertakings which were active on the market'.*[89]

On this issue, the Court concluded that 'the significant number of communications recognized by Dole and Weichert, the similar content of those communications, the fact that they regularly involved the same persons with a virtually identical modus operandi in terms of timing and means of communication, the fact that they continued for at least three years and

[86] Case T-588/08, *Dole Food Company, Inc and Dole Germany OHG v Commission*, ECLI:EU:T:2013:130, para 291. See also Case T-587/08, *Fresh Del Monte Produce, Inc v European Commission*, ECLI:EU:T:2013:129, para 344.

[87] Case T-588/08, *Dole Food Company, Inc. and Dole Germany OHG v Commission*, ECLI:EU:T:2013:130, para 293. See also Case T-587/08, *Fresh Del Monte Produce, Inc v European Commission*, ECLI:EU:T:2013:129, para 346.

[88] Case T-588/08, *Dole Food Company, Inc and Dole Germany OHG v Commission*, ECLI:EU:T:2013:130, para 368. See also Case T-587/08, *Fresh Del Monte Produce, Inc v European Commission*, ECLI:EU:T:2013:129, para 351.

[89] Case T-588/08, *Dole Food Company, Inc and Dole Germany OHG v Commission*, ECLI:EU:T:2013:130, para 382. See also Case T-587/08, *Fresh Del Monte Produce, Inc v European Commission*, ECLI:EU:T:2013:129, para 363.

that none of the undertakings claims that there was any interruption in the exchanges, and Dole's statements on the relevance of the information exchanged for the setting of quotation prices are all evidence from which it may be concluded that the Commission was right to find that there had been a pattern or system of communications to which the undertakings concerned were able to resort according to their needs'.[90] *For the Court, '[t]hat mechanism made it possible to create a climate of mutual certainty as to their future pricing policies [. . .], a climate that was further reinforced by the subsequent exchanges of quotation prices'.*[91] *Furthermore, '[a]lthough certain information exchanged could be obtained from other sources, the exchange system established enabled the undertakings concerned to become aware of that information more simply, rapidly and directly [. . .] and to undertake an updated joint assessment of that information.'*[92]

The applicants also alleged that the object of the conduct in question had be assessed in the economic context in which it took place and noted that the banana market had specific characteristics, in particular, as it was highly transparent, in that all producers and customers had access to arrival volumes each week, and heavily regulated, with a licensing regime that predetermined the number of bananas imported into Europe each quarter.[93] *According to them, '[t]he importance of that legislation, which was applicable throughout the infringement period, with regard to the level of supply and the fact that it contributes to a certain degree of transparency on the market permits the conclusion that the formation of prices on the banana market did not answer completely to the free operation of supply and demand'.*[94] *The Court dismissed the argument mentioning that 'this finding is not [. . .] incompatible with the Commission's conclusion that the practice at issue had an anti-competitive object'.*[95] *The applicants also sought to establish that the communications between importers pursued, in the light of the specific nature of the relevant product, a legitimate purpose, namely enhanced market efficiency. They alleged that the product was highly perishable, thus leading importers to seek as much information as possible about conditions on the market from their own intelligence, from customers, and in some cases other suppliers, so that they could make sure their prices were set at the right level to achieve rapid market clearance. The Court again dismissed the argument, noting that 'according to the case-law, it is immaterial whether the undertakings acted in concert for reasons that were partially legitimate' and that 'the Court of Justice has held that an agreement may be regarded as having a restrictive object even if it does not have the restriction of competition as its sole aim but also pursues other legitimate objectives'.*[96]

[90] Case T-588/08, *Dole Food Company, Inc and Dole Germany OHG v Commission*, ECLI:EU:T:2013:130, para 401. See also Case T-587/08, *Fresh Del Monte Produce, Inc v European Commission*, ECLI:EU:T:2013:129, para 367.

[91] Case T-588/08, *Dole Food Company, Inc and Dole Germany OHG v Commission*, ECLI:EU:T:2013:130, para 402. See also Case T-587/08, *Fresh Del Monte Produce, Inc v European* Commission, ECLI:EU:T:2013:129, para 368.

[92] Case T-588/08, *Dole Food Company, Inc and Dole Germany OHG v Commission*, ECLI:EU:T:2013:130, para 403. See also Case T-587/08, *Fresh Del Monte Produce, Inc v European Commission*, ECLI:EU:T:2013:129, para 369.

[93] Case T-588/08, *Dole Food Company, Inc and Dole Germany OHG v Commission*, ECLI:EU:T:2013:130, para 301. See also Case T-587/08, *Fresh Del Monte Produce, Inc v European Commission*, ECLI:EU:T:2013:129, para 377.

[94] Case T-588/08, *Dole Food Company, Inc. and Dole Germany OHG v Commission*, ECLI:EU:T:2013:130, para 303. See also Case T-587/08, *Fresh Del Monte Produce, Inc v European Commission*, ECLI:EU:T:2013:129, para 382.

[95] Case T-588/08, *Dole Food Company, Inc and Dole Germany OHG v Commission*, ECLI:EU:T:2013:130, para 304. See also Case T-587/08, *Fresh Del Monte Produce, Inc v European* Commission, ECLI:EU:T:2013:129, para 383.

[96] Case T-588/08, *Dole Food Company, Inc and Dole Germany OHG v Commission*, ECLI:EU:T:2013:130, para 322. See also Case T-587/08, *Fresh Del Monte Produce, Inc v European Commission*, ECLI:EU:T:2013:129, para 425.

In addition, the applicants argued that the Commission failed to take account of the market structure and the market dynamics, and ignored the context in which the exchange of information had taken place and the fact that a large number of importers had not participated in the alleged pre-pricing communications. The General Court held in Case T-587/08, Fresh Del Monte Produce, Inc v European Commission, *as follows.*[97]

429. It must be noted that the Commission's view that the market structure is not relevant for the purposes of establishing an infringement in the present case is based on a misinterpretation of *Tate & Lyle and Others* v *Commission*[98] [. . .], inasmuch as the passages of that judgment [. . .] do not relate to the establishment of the infringement, but instead to the amount of the fine imposed.

430. It should be borne in mind that, according to the case-law, each economic operator must determine independently the policy which he intends to adopt on the common market and that, while it is correct to say that this requirement of independence does not deprive economic operators of the right to adapt themselves intelligently to the existing or anticipated conduct of their competitors, it does, none the less, strictly preclude any direct or indirect contact between such operators by which an undertaking may influence the conduct on the market of its actual or potential competitors or disclose to them its decisions or intentions concerning its own conduct on the market where the object or effect of such contact is to create conditions of competition which do not correspond to the normal conditions of the market in question, regard being had to the nature of the products or services offered, the size and number of the undertakings involved and the volume of that market [. . .].

431. If supply on a market is highly concentrated, the exchange of certain information may, according in particular to the type of information exchanged, be liable to enable undertakings to be aware of the market position and commercial strategy of their competitors, thus distorting rivalry on the market and increasing the probability of collusion, or even facilitating it. On the other hand, if supply is fragmented, the dissemination and exchange of information between competitors may be neutral, or even positive, for the competitive nature of the market [. . .].

432. The Court of Justice has also made clear that an information exchange system may constitute a breach of competition rules even where the relevant market is not a highly concentrated oligopolistic market [. . .].

433. In the present case, the intervener merely claims that the Commission ignored the fact that a large number of importers had not participated in pre-pricing communications, without providing further details or specific evidence to support its allegations.

434. It must be pointed out that, in the contested decision, the Commission states that, in addition to Chiquita, Weichert and Dole, Del Monte (in relation to its own activities as a supplier of bananas), Fyffes and Van Parys had significant banana sales in Northern Europe and that, in addition to those undertakings, a large number of other companies selling bananas were active in the Northern European region. Most of these were small companies that concentrated on a limited geographical area (particularly Germany) [. . .].

[97] Case T-587/08, *Fresh Del Monte Produce, Inc v European Commission*, ECLI:EU:T:2013:129, paras 429–35. We refer to this case here in view of the clarity of the drafting, the similar passages in Case T-588/08, *Dole Food Company, Inc and Dole Germany OHG v Commission*, ECLI:EU:T:2013:130 being less explicit.

[98] Joined Cases T-202, 204 & 207/98, *Tate & Lyle and Others v Commission* [2001] ECR II–2035, para 113.

> 435. The Commission states, however, that the parties had a substantial share of the market and were the suppliers of the three leading brands of bananas.

The General Court noted that the parties' combined share of banana sales by value accounted for approximately 45 to 50 per cent of banana sales in Northern Europe, the geographic relevant market, or 40 to 45 per cent of apparent consumption of fresh bananas in Northern Europe.

> 440. It follows from the foregoing considerations that the Commission did in fact take account of the structure of the market when assessing the impugned conduct, and that it was right to consider and take into account the fact that Dole, Chiquita and Weichert had a substantial—and not low, as Weichert merely claims—share of the relevant market, which, although it cannot be described as oligopolistic, cannot be characterised by supply of a fragmented nature.

Finally, the applicants questioned the alleged causal link between the quotation prices and final market prices, claiming that the quotation price was not the actual price and therefore that there was no collusion on actual prices. In contrast, for the Commission the quotation prices operated as market signals as to the intended development of the actual price. This raised the issue of the existence of a causal link between the collusion of the undertakings concerned and conduct on the market following that collusion. The General Court dismissed this argument as well. It found that the commission was right to find that quotation prices were relevant in the banana sector, by observing that they served at least as market signals, trends or indications as to the intended development of banana prices and that they were relevant for the banana trade and the prices obtained.[99] It also held that 'the Commission did not "mainly" rely on that presumption of a causal link between unlawful collusion and conduct on the market in order to establish, in the present case, the existence of a concerted practice having an anti-competitive object, since that conclusion was based on an assessment of the characteristics of the exchanges in question and of their legal and economic context, in accordance with the requirements of the caselaw'.[100]

Coming back to the Dole Food case, t he General Court concluded that by means of the pre-pricing communications, Dole and Weichert, who were among the main suppliers of bananas, 'coordinated the setting of their quotation prices instead of deciding on them independently'. During those bilateral discussions, Dole and Weichert 'disclosed the course of action which they contemplated adopting or at least enabled the participants to estimate competitors' future behaviour with regard to their quotation prices to be set and to anticipate their intended course of action'. These actions have 'decreased uncertainty concerning competitors' future decisions on quotation prices, with the result that competition between undertakings was restricted' and henceforth, that the Commission was right to conclude that the pre-pricing communications which took place between Dole and Weichert concerned the fixing of prices and that they gave rise to a concerted practice having as its object the restriction of competition within the meaning of Article 101 TFEU.[101]

The companies interjected an appeal at the CJEU. The issue of information exchanges as a by object restriction of competition was discussed mainly in the Dole appeal. The Dole

[99] Case T-587/08, *Fresh Del Monte Produce, Inc v European* Commission, ECLI:EU:T:2013:129, para 559.

[100] Case T-587/08, *Fresh Del Monte Produce, Inc v European* Commission, ECLI:EU:T:2013:129, para 582.

[101] Case T-588/08, *Dole Food Company, Inc and Dole Germany OHG v Commission*, ECLI:EU:T:2013:130, para 584. See also Case T-587/08, *Fresh Del Monte Produce, Inc v European Commission*, ECLI:EU:T:2013:129, para 585.

companies alleged, inter alia, *that by finding that the pre-pricing communications constitute a restriction of competition by object, the General Court erred in its legal characterization of the facts as the exchange of information which took place cannot be regarded as capable of removing uncertainty as to the intended conduct of the participating undertakings as regards the setting of actual prices. First, the pre-pricing communications were carried out by employees who were not responsible for setting quotation prices. Second, as those communications concerned quotation price trends, they were not capable of removing uncertainty as to actual prices. The applicants added that all the market participants involved in the Commission's investigation stated that quotation prices were far removed from actual prices. Dole also noted that it results from the case-law that the mere fact that an exchange of information might have a certain influence on prices is not sufficient to establish the existence of a restriction of competition by object. The Commission was unable to put forward such evidence, however, in view of the fact that there is no reliable connection between quotation price movements and those of actual prices. Dole argued that in the light of the relevant case-law, it was not possible to characterize the exchange of views on weather conditions as a restriction of competition by object, as such discussions are so far removed from the setting of actual price that they cannot reduce uncertainty and facilitate coordination of the prices of the products in question. The Court held as follows:*

117. According to the case-law of the Court, in order to determine whether a type of coordination between undertakings reveals a sufficient degree of harm to competition that it may be considered a restriction of competition 'by object' within the meaning of Article [101(1) TFEU], regard must be had, inter alia, to its objectives and the economic and legal context of which it forms a part. When determining that context, it is also necessary to take into consideration the nature of the goods or services affected, as well as the real conditions of the functioning and structure of the market or markets in question [. . .].

118. In addition, although the parties' intention is not a necessary factor in determining whether a type of coordination between undertakings is restrictive, there is nothing prohibiting the competition authorities, the national courts or the Courts of the European Union from taking that factor into account [. . .].

119. In so far as concerns, in particular, the exchange of information between competitors, it should be recalled that the criteria of coordination and cooperation necessary for determining the existence of a concerted practice are to be understood in the light of the notion inherent in the Treaty provisions on competition, according to which each economic operator must determine independently the policy which he intends to adopt on the common market [. . .].

120. While it is correct to say that this requirement of independence does not deprive economic operators of the right to adapt themselves intelligently to the existing or anticipated conduct of their competitors, it does, none the less, strictly preclude any direct or indirect contact between such operators by which an undertaking may influence the conduct on the market of its actual or potential competitors or disclose to them its decisions or intentions concerning its own conduct on the market where the object or effect of such contact is to create conditions of competition which do not correspond to the normal conditions of the market in question, regard being had to the nature of the products or services offered, the size and number of the undertakings involved and the volume of that market [. . .].

121. The Court has therefore held that the exchange of information between competitors is liable to be incompatible with the competition rules if it reduces or removes

the degree of uncertainty as to the operation of the market in question, with the result that competition between undertakings is restricted [. . .].

122. In particular, an exchange of information which is capable of removing uncertainty between participants as regards the timing, extent and details of the modifications to be adopted by the undertakings concerned in their conduct on the market must be regarded as pursuing an anticompetitive object [. . .].

123. Moreover, a concerted practice may have an anticompetitive object even though there is no direct connection between that practice and consumer prices. Indeed, it is not possible on the basis of the wording of Article [101(1) TFEU] to conclude that only concerted practices which have a direct effect on the prices paid by end users are prohibited [. . .].

124. On the contrary, it is apparent from Article [101(1) TFEU] that concerted practices may have an anticompetitive object if they 'directly or indirectly fix purchase or selling prices or any other trading conditions' [. . .].

125. In any event, Article [101 TFEU], like the other competition rules of the Treaty, is designed to protect not only the immediate interests of individual competitors or consumers but also to protect the structure of the market and thus competition as such. Therefore, in order to find that a concerted practice has an anticompetitive object, there does not need to be a direct link between that practice and consumer prices [. . .].

126. Lastly, it should be pointed out that the concept of a concerted practice, as it derives from the actual terms of Article [101(1) TFEU], implies, in addition to the participating undertakings concerting with each other, subsequent conduct on the market and a relationship of cause and effect between the two [. . .].

127. In that regard, the Court has held that, subject to proof to the contrary, which the economic operators concerned must adduce, it must be presumed that the undertakings taking part in the concerted action and remaining active on the market take account of the information exchanged with their competitors in determining their conduct on that market. In particular, the Court has concluded that such a concerted practice is caught by Article [101(1) TFEU], even in the absence of anticompetitive effects on the market [. . .].

129. As observed by the Advocate General [. . .], it is apparent from the extremely detailed findings of the General Court, first, that bilateral pre-pricing communications were exchanged between the Dole companies and other undertakings in the banana sector and, as part of those communications, the undertakings discussed their own quotation prices and certain price trends. Moreover, the Dole companies do not contest that finding.

130. Second, the General Court found [. . .] that quotation prices were relevant to the market concerned, since, on the one hand, market signals, market trends or indications as to the intended development of banana prices could be inferred from those quotation prices, which were important for the banana trade and the prices obtained and, on the other, in some transactions the actual prices were directly linked to the quotation prices.

131. Third, [. . .] the General Court found that the Dole employees involved in the pre-pricing communications participated in the internal pricing meetings.

132. Furthermore, those findings of the General Court are to a large extent based on statements made by Dole Food and the Dole companies have not alleged any form of distortion in that regard.

133. Accordingly, the General Court was entitled to take the view, without erring in law, that the conditions for the application of the presumption referred to at paragraph 127 above were fulfilled in the present case, with the result that the Dole companies' claims that that court infringed the principle governing the burden of proof and the presumption of innocence are unfounded.

134. It also follows that the General Court was entitled to take the view [. . .] that it was permissible for the Commission to conclude that, as they made it possible to reduce uncertainty for each of the participants as to the foreseeable conduct of competitors, the pre-pricing communications had the object of creating conditions of competition that do not correspond to the normal conditions on the market and therefore gave rise to a concerted practice having as its object the restriction of competition within the meaning of Article [101 TFEU].

7.3.1.5.6. Guidelines on horizontal cooperation agreements

In its 2011 Guidelines on horizontal cooperation agreements ('Horizontal Guidelines'), the Commission provided some guidance on information exchange that may have an anticompetitive object.

Communication from the Commission—Guidelines on the applicability of Article 101 TFEU to horizontal co-operation agreements [2011] OJ C 11/1 (footnotes omitted)

Restriction of competition by object

72. Any information exchange with the objective of restricting competition on the market will be considered as a restriction of competition by object. In assessing whether an information exchange constitutes a restriction of competition by object, the Commission will pay particular attention to the legal and economic context in which the information exchange takes place. To this end, the Commission will take into account whether the information exchange, by its very nature, may possibly lead to a restriction of competition.

73. Exchanging information on companies' individualised intentions concerning future conduct regarding prices or quantities is particularly likely to lead to a collusive outcome. Informing each other about such intentions may allow competitors to arrive at a common higher price level without incurring the risk of losing market share or triggering a price war during the period of adjustment to new prices [. . .]. Moreover, it is less likely that information exchanges concerning future intentions are made for pro-competitive reasons than exchanges of actual data.

74. Information exchanges between competitors of individualised data regarding intended future prices or quantities should therefore be considered a restriction of competition by object. In addition, private exchanges between competitors of their individualised intentions regarding future prices or quantities would normally be considered and fined as cartels because they generally have the object of fixing prices or quantities. Information exchanges that constitute cartels not only infringe Article 101(1), but, in addition, are very unlikely to fulfil the conditions of Article 101(3).

NOTES AND QUESTIONS ON INFORMATION EXCHANGE AGREEMENTS IN EU COMPETITION LAW

1. Consider *Woodpulp II*. Does paragraph 63 lead to the parallel announcement in the trade press of future prices being illegal? Would economists consider this to be collusion in the absence of evidence of an intent to influence competitors? Should they? If it is so considered, is there any way an important firm in a concentrated industry can raise its prices when costs increase or otherwise? In a concentrated market, when faxes could not be sent to multiple customers all at once, as when *Woodpulp II* was decided, individual price lists could not be sent out *en masse*. Please answer, after reading the excerpt by Kai-Uwe Kühn and Xavier Vives in Section 7.3.1.5.2.
2. Once the information exchange results from collusive action, the next step is to examine if it leads to a restriction of competition, by object or effect. The case law has generally found that information exchange restricts competition by object, when this is closely associated to a cartel, for instance an exchange of information in order to proceed to fixing prices. A similar conclusion has been reached with regard to an exchange of information that is ancillary to a market-sharing concerted practice.[102] The following case illustrates the distinction between information exchange associated to a cartel arrangement and a practice of 'pure' information exchange.
3. Do you consider that the Commission's Guidance provides a narrower interpretation of the concept of object restriction than the jurisprudence of the EU Courts in *Bananas*?
4. In particular, would the Commission accept that where it is not possible technologically to inform multiple customers simultaneously of price changes, no intention to collude should be inferred?
5. Note that, in *Bananas*, the General Court found that the quotation prices were relevant to the market concerned because it was possible to infer market signals, trends, or indications as to the intended development of banana prices from them. The fact that the link to consumer prices was indirect did not impede the General Court, confirmed by the CJEU, to conclude that the practice had an anti-competitive object. The CJEU referred to its case law on anti-competitive object, according to which 'certain types of coordination between undertakings can be regarded, by their very nature, as being harmful to the proper functioning of normal competition', in view of the fact that 'they reveal a sufficient degree of harm to competition that it may be found that there is no need to examine their effects'.[103] Hence, the Court concluded that price signals removing the degree of uncertainty as to the behaviour of competitors on the market in question may be seen as of having a sufficient degree of harm to competition to be considered as by object restrictions. As examined in Chapter 5, price signalling may fall under the scope of Article 101 TFEU/Chapter I CA98 in case there is evidence of collusion. In *Bananas*, this was not an issue, as there was ample evidence of bilateral and private pre-pricing communication between Dole and Weichert, even if these

[102] Joined Cases C-40–8, 50, 54–6, 111, 113 & 114/73, *Coöperatieve Vereniging 'Suiker Unie' UA and Others v Commission* [1975] ECR I–1663.

[103] Case C-286/13 P, *Dole Food Company Inc and Dole Fresh Fruit Europe v European Commission*, ECLI:EU:C:2015:184, paras 113–14.

conversations were of more generic nature and touched on market trends, weather conditions in Europe and in the countries where bananas were produced, and other factors influencing supply and demand. Yet, the Commission, in a decision upheld by both the General Court and the CJEU, found that there was a sufficient causal link between these practices and a possible effect, not only on prices for consumers, but more generally on the integrity of the competitive process, since 'the pre-pricing communications had the object of creating conditions of competition that do not correspond to the normal conditions on the market'. It is interesting to note that in its guidelines the Commission arrived at a similar conclusion as to the anti-competitive object of such prices, but the reasons for reaching this conclusion were related to the fact that the communication allowed the competitors to set a common higher price level and there were no pro-competitive reasons explaining these information exchanges.[104]

6. The Commission has initiated proceedings against fifteen container shipping companies, which have regularly announced their intended (future) increases of prices for containerized shipping services by sea, at least on routes from Far East Asia to Northern Europe and the Mediterranean, on their websites, via the press, or in other ways (also called General Rate Increase Announcements). These announcements did not indicate the fixed final price for the service concerned, but only the amount of the increase in US dollars per transported container unit, the affected trade route, and the planned date of implementation. The Commission expressed concerns that these announcements may be of very little value for customers, as stating only the amount of an intended increase may not inform customers of the new full price they will be asked to pay in the future. Furthermore, it noted that these announcements may have only limited committal value and thus, customers may not be able to rely on them for their purchasing decisions. According to the Commission, this practice may allow the parties to explore each other's pricing intentions and to coordinate their behaviour, thus constituting a concerted practice in violation of Article 101 TFEU. Indeed, the practice may enable the parties to 'test', without incurring the risk of losing customers, whether they can reasonably implement a price increase and thereby may reduce strategic uncertainty for container shipping companies involved and diminish the incentives to compete. The liner shipping companies offered commitments, which were accepted by the Commission.[105]

7. The dividing line between information that is confidential and that which was not was considered by the General Court in *Koninklijke Philips NV v Commission*.[106] The appellant had argued in this case that the information the parties had exchanged was inaccurate and misleading and that it was not, overall, competitively sensitive. Consequently, it did not remove strategic uncertainty to a sufficient extent to constitute a restriction of competition by object. The General Court referred to *Dole*[107]

[104] Communication from the Commission—Guidelines on the applicability of Article 101 of the Treaty on the Functioning of the European Union (TFEU) to horizontal co-operation agreements [2011] OJ C 11/1, para 73 [hereinafter Horizontal Guidelines].

[105] Communication of the Commission published pursuant to Article 27(4) of Council Regulation EC No 1/2013 in Case AT.39850 [2016] C 60/7.

[106] Case T-762/14, *Koninklijke Philips NV v Commission* ECLI:EU:T:2016:738 [hereinafter *Smart Chips*].

[107] Case C-286/13 P, *Dole Food Company Inc and Dole Fresh Fruit Europe v European Commission*, ECLI:EU:C:2015:184.

as authority for the proposition that an exchange of information which is capable of removing uncertainty between participants as regards the timing, extent and details of the modifications to be adopted by the undertakings in their conduct on the market must be regarded as pursuing an anti-competitive object.[108] In analysing the nature of the price information exchange in that case, the Commission had found that the parties had discussed, at the very least, the price that a named customer had requested from them for 2004, the intention of Samsung and of the applicants not to offer the price requested by that customer (that is $.80 per chip) and of their intention not to offer the product for a price less than $1.0. The General Court held that such an exchange of information relating to the future pricing strategy of the undertaking in general and of a customer in particular was capable of affecting normal competition.

7.3.1.5.7. Information exchange as an object restriction: The UK perspective

Decision of the Office of Fair Trading No CA98/05/2006, *Exchange of information on future fees by certain independent fee-paying schools,* Case CE/2890-03 (20 November 2006) (footnotes omitted)

The Office of Fair Trading, the CMA's predecessor, found that during the period from 1 March 2001 to June 2003, fifty fee-charging independent schools infringed Chapter I CA98 by participating in an agreement and/or concerted practice having as its object the prevention, restriction, or distortion of competition in the relevant markets for the provision of educational services. The Participant schools engaged in the exchange of specific information regarding future pricing intentions on a regular and systematic basis. The information exchanged concerned the Participant schools' intended fees and fee increases for both boarding and day pupils, which were set annually with effect from the beginning of each academic year in September. The information exchange was organized by the bursar of one of the participant schools to whom the other schools submitted details of their current fee levels, proposed fee increases (expressed as a percentage) and the resulting intended fee levels, the bursar subsequently circulated this information amongst the schools participating in the information exchange in tabular form as a survey. This took place between January and June each year, and was timed to provide the participant schools with information on competitor fee increases early in their budgetary cycles. Indeed, schools decided their fee increases for September in May or June of the same calendar year; the earliest date by which any of the Participant schools decided their fees for September was March of the same calendar year. As a result, each of the Participant schools received at least one version of the survey before it finalized its own fee increase(s) for the new academic year starting in September. Equally, each school participating in the agreement/concerted practice submitted information regarding its own intended fee increase(s) for inclusion in the survey before the other Participant schools had finalized their fee increase(s) for the new academic year. The OFT found that through their participation in the survey, the Participant schools exchanged on a regular and systematic basis highly confidential information regarding each other's pricing intentions for the coming academic year that was not made available to parents of pupils at the Participant schools or published more generally. The OFT decided the following:

108 Case T-762/14, *Smart Chips*, ECLI:EU:T:2016:738, para 62.

1354. [. . .] The exchange of pricing information is particularly sensitive from a competition law perspective. Indeed, the mere disclosure of such information to competitors will almost certainly be anti–competitive where it is capable of influencing their future conduct on the market, as will its receipt [. . .].

1356. The threat to effective competition is especially obvious where an arrangement involves the regular and systematic exchange of specific information as to future pricing intentions between competitors. The exchange of such information reduces uncertainties inherent in the competitive process and facilitates the coordination of the parties' conduct on the market

1357. The OFT therefore considers that the unilateral disclosure or exchange of future pricing information between competitors (in particular the private exchange, or unilateral disclosure, amongst competitors of specific future pricing intentions, especially where this is on a regular and systematic basis) has as its obvious object the prevention, restriction or distortion of competition. Accordingly, in order to establish an infringement of the Chapter I prohibition in such circumstances it is not necessary for the OFT to demonstrate that it also had this effect.

1358. Such exchange of information risks facilitating parallel price increases whilst at the same time reducing, or even eliminating, the risk of losing customers to more efficient competitors that might not otherwise have increased their prices. Indeed, it is hard to envisage what legitimate purpose could be served by the exchange of such information, in particular in circumstances where the information remains otherwise confidential and is not shared with customers.

1371. [. . .] [T]he OFT considers that, the exchange of specific information regarding future pricing intentions between competitors, particularly where it is done on a regular and systematic basis, constitutes an obvious restriction of competition and, as such, has as its 'object' the prevention, restriction or distortion of competition. In these circumstances, it is not necessary to examine the specific economic context of the information exchange or the structure of the relevant market.

1372. By participating in the Sevenoaks Survey, the Participant schools took part in the exchange of specific information regarding future pricing intentions. This was done on a regular and systematic basis.

1373. In light of the above, the OFT considers that the Participant schools were party to an agreement and/or concerted practice having as its object the prevention, restriction or distortion of competition. The OFT considers that this amounts to a serious infringement of the Chapter I prohibition.

1374. [It] follows that, for the purposes of establishing an infringement of the Chapter I prohibition, there is no need for the OFT also to show that the arrangement had an anti-competitive effect. The OFT, therefore, makes no finding as to whether the arrangement, as well as having as its object the prevention, restriction or distortion of competition, also had an effect on the fee levels of the Participant schools

1376. The OFT considers that, as in the case of price fixing or market sharing agreements, an agreement or concerted practice amongst competitors which has as its object the co-ordination of prices in breach of the Chapter I prohibition, by its very nature, restricts competition to an appreciable extent.

1377. The overall agreement and/or concerted practice between the Participant schools had as its object the prevention, restriction or distortion of competition and concerned the exchange of sensitive information relating to future pricing intentions. The OFT therefore considers that the agreement and/or concerted practice has an appreciable effect on competition irrespective of whether or not the Parties' combined market share in the relevant market falls below 10 per cent. The OFT therefore takes the view that the agreement and/or concerted practice in this case prevents, restricts or distorts competition to an appreciable extent.

1378. The OFT notes that, in any event, the Parties' combined market shares, at least in the market for boarding services, are well above the level at which their conduct, even had it not consisted in the exchange of information on future fees, could be expected to have an appreciable effect on the market.

The OFT decided, however, to limit the penalties imposed to each participant school to a fixed amount of £10 000, in view of the following 'exceptional features of the case', which led it to depart from its penalty guidance:[109] *the voluntary admission on behalf of the participant schools, the fact that the schools participating in the information exchange had agreed to make an* ex gratia *payment to fund a £3 million educational trust fund for the benefit of pupils who attended the specific schools during the academic years in respect of which fee information was exchanged, thus indirectly benefiting those whose interests the Act is designed to protect and, third, that the Participant schools were all non-profit making charitable bodies.*

Motor insurers' data exchange **(commitment decision)**

In January 2010, the OFT launched a formal investigation against a large number of insurance companies operating in the broker insurance market, suspecting that they were indirectly exchanging commercially sensitive price information through certain third party providers of IT software, facilitated by third party service providers, and that such arrangements might have the object or effect of preventing, restricting or distorting competition. The information exchange occurred indirectly between a large number of insurers operating in the broker insurance market through the use of several products used for data analysis. The OFT identified an increased risk of price coordination in view of the use by the insurers of a specialist market analysis tool called 'Whatif? Private Motor', which enabled the insurers to access not only the pricing information they themselves provided to brokers but also pricing information supplied by other competing insurers. The OFT accepted the commitments of the insurers to no longer being able to access each other's individual pricing information through 'Whatif? Private Motor'. The insurers committed to exchange pricing information through the analysis tool only if that information met certain principles, such as that the pricing information is anonymized, aggregated across at least five insurers.[110]

Conduct in the modelling sector

In December 2016, the CMA found that five model agencies and their trading association (the Association of Model Agents, AMA) that had put in place an exchange of information scheme in the UK modelling sector had infringed Article 101 TFEU and Chapter I CA98 (restriction of competition by object), the CMA imposing fines totalling £1 533 500.[111] *The CMA found that*

109 *Exchange of information on future fees by certain independent fee-paying schools* (Case CE/2890-03) OFT Decision CA98/05/2006 (20 November 2006), para 1425.

110 OFT 1395, Decision to accept binding commitments to modify a data exchange tool used by Motor Insurers (December 2011).

111 *Conduct in the modelling sector* (Case CE/9859-14) CMA Decision (16 December 2016).

the parties had regularly and systematically exchanged confidential, competitively sensitive information, including future pricing information, in the context of negotiations with particular customers, those including well-known high-street chains, online fashion retailers and consumer goods brands, and in some instances agreed a common approach to pricing. The AMA also played an important role in the coordination of prices by seeking to influence other AMA members, by regularly issuing email circulars, known as 'AMA Alerts', to resist downward pressure on prices for the supply of modelling services. The CMA therefore found that the information was shared indirectly through the AMA Alerts circulated by the AMA, and directly through discussions and/or email correspondence prior to and after the release of one or more AMA Alerts, and through other instances of more protracted and detailed contact between the parties in relation to particular customers or usage types. According to the CMA, the agreement and/or concerted practice in question had 'an appreciable potential impact on competition for the supply of modelling services in particular in view of the market position and importance of the parties', as the AMA had seventeen members, 'including most of the larger and most prestigious UK model agencies, and the market share of the Parties is materially above 10%'.[112] *The CMA's investigation did not concern the services of 'top models' but extended to a wide range of modelling assignments—from fashion magazine shoots offering model fees of a few hundred pounds to advertising campaigns offering over £10 000.*

Galvanized steel water tanks—information exchange

In December 2016, the CMA found that Balmoral, a supplier of galvanized steel water tanks, along with three other businesses, had breached competition law by taking part in an exchange of competitively sensitive information on prices and pricing intentions, which constituted a concerted practice contrary to Article 101(1) TFEU and to the Chapter 1 CA98, and fined Balmoral £130,000.[113] *The other parties to the exchange were fined as a result of another infringement decision the same day concerning a cartel involving bid rigging, price-fixing and market sharing in relation to the supply of galvanized steel water tanks in the UK. The information exchange took place at a single meeting in July 2012 at which Balmoral was invited to join a long-running price-fixing cartel. Balmoral refused to take part in the price-fixing cartel, but exchanged competitively-sensitive information with its competitors. This meeting was secretly recorded by the CMA. Citing the EU precedents in T-Mobile and Dole, the CAT confirmed the CMA's decision on appeal.*[114]

7.3.2. COLLUSION BETWEEN COMPETITORS AND RESTRICTIONS OF COMPETITION BY EFFECT

The general principles and methodology are explained in the Commission's general Guidelines on the application of Article 101(3) and its Horizontal Guidelines.

[112] Ibid, para 4.122.

[113] *Galvanised steel tanks for water storage information exchange infringement* (Case CE/9691/12) CMA Decision (19 December 2016).

[114] *Balmoral Tanks Limited & Balmoral Group Holdings Limited* [2017] CAT 23.

We will focus here on information exchange agreements that are not found to be anti-competitive by object.

7.3.2.1. Information exchange agreements

An information exchange is assessed under Article 101 TFEU as a restriction of competition by effect, if it has passed the dual filter of resulting from some form of collusive action (an agreement, a concerted practice, a decision of association of undertakings) and it does not constitute a restriction of competition by object.

The CJEU has dealt with information exchanges as a restriction of competition by effect in a number of judgments. The main difficulty with information exchanges between competitors that are not attached to a cartel is the fact that their effect is ambivalent. They may produce anti-competitive effects, as well as achieve considerable efficiencies. Hence, competition authorities and the Courts should proceed to a case-by-case analysis of these agreements and of their economic and legal context in order to distinguish the agreements producing overall anti-competitive effects from those that have pro-competitive effects.

Nevertheless, while more accurate in principle, a case-by-case approach may run into the following problems:

M Bennett and P Collins, 'The Law and Economics of Information Sharing: The Good, the Bad and the Ugly' (2010) 6(2) *European Competition J* 311, 313

[A] case-by-case analysis implies that every situation would require a full investigation of all the economic facts and circumstances to determine whether the conduct in question is providing a net benefit or net harm to consumers. Such investigations take substantial time and resources. In a world in which there are no budget constraints, either for firms or the competition authorities, such an analysis would clearly be optimal. However, since investigations involve commitment of time and money for both firms and competition authorities, looking at every situation on a case-by-case analysis has two negative impacts.

First, a case-by-case analysis places a high cost and burden on firms, which may not be in a position, let alone wish, to carry out complex economic analysis for every individual situation. A requirement to undertake such an analysis for every situation may mean that firms simply do not engage in certain activities, even though some may provide benefits (Type I errors). So, quite apart from cost and practicalities, a case-by-case approach runs the risk of chilling beneficial firm activity, and thus being detrimental to a competitive economy.

Secondly, a case-by-case approach places a high burden on competition authorities and private claimants in bringing cases, which could result in under-enforcement and therefore insufficient deterrence of anti-competitive behaviour (Type II errors). Such concerns are likely to be more significant for less mature competition regimes or authorities with tight resource constraints, but nevertheless of concern to all regimes as they run the risk of detriment to a competitive economy.

With regard to anti-competitive effects, it is recognized that information exchange may (i) facilitate coordinated effects (tacit collusion) and/or (ii) may also lead to non-coordinated effects, such as the foreclosure of competitors. These two types of anti-competitive effects are examined below.

Communication from the Commission—Guidelines on the applicability of Article 101 TFEU to horizontal co-operation agreements [2011] OJ C 11/1

64. Once it has been established that there is an agreement, concerted practice or decision by an association of undertakings, it is necessary to consider the main competition concerns pertaining to information exchanges.

Collusive outcome

65. By artificially increasing transparency in the market, the exchange of strategic information can facilitate coordination (that is to say, alignment) of companies' competitive behaviour and result in restrictive effects on competition. This can occur through different channels.

66. One way is that through information exchange companies may reach a common understanding on the terms of coordination, which can lead to a collusive outcome on the market. Information exchange can create mutually consistent expectations regarding the uncertainties present in the market. On that basis companies can then reach a common understanding on the terms of coordination of their competitive behaviour, even without an explicit agreement on coordination. Exchange of information about intentions concerning future conduct is the most likely means to enable companies to reach such a common understanding.

67. Another channel through which information exchange can lead to restrictive effects on competition is by increasing the internal stability of a collusive outcome on the market. In particular, it can do so by enabling the companies involved to monitor deviations. Namely, information exchange can make the market sufficiently transparent to allow the colluding companies to monitor to a sufficient degree whether other companies are deviating from the collusive outcome, and thus to know when to retaliate. Both exchanges of present and past data can constitute such a monitoring mechanism. This can either enable companies to achieve a collusive outcome on markets where they would otherwise not have been able to do so, or it can increase the stability of a collusive outcome already present on the market [. . .].

68. A third channel through which information exchange can lead to restrictive effects on competition is by increasing the external stability of a collusive outcome on the market. Information exchanges that make the market sufficiently transparent can allow colluding companies to monitor where and when other companies are attempting to enter the market, thus allowing the colluding companies to target the new entrant. This may also tie into the anti-competitive foreclosure concerns discussed in paragraphs 69 to 71. Both exchanges of present and past data can constitute such a monitoring mechanism.

Anti-competitive foreclosure

69. Apart from facilitating collusion, an exchange of information can also lead to anti-competitive foreclosure.

70. An exclusive exchange of information can lead to anti-competitive foreclosure on the same market where the exchange takes place. This can occur when the exchange of commercially sensitive information places unaffiliated competitors at a significant competitive disadvantage as compared to the companies affiliated within the exchange system. This type of foreclosure is only possible if the information

concerned is very strategic for competition and covers a significant part of the relevant market.

71. It cannot be excluded that information exchange may also lead to anti-competitive foreclosure of third parties in a related market. For instance, by gaining enough market power through an information exchange, parties exchanging information in an upstream market, for instance vertically integrated companies, may be able to raise the price of a key component for a market downstream. Thereby, they could raise the costs of their rivals downstream, which could result in anti-competitive foreclosure in the downstream market.

The fact that information exchange may promote the external stability of collusion[115] between competitors has been criticized.

M Bennett and P Collins, 'The Law and Economics of Information Sharing: The Good, the Bad and the Ugly' (2010) 6(2) *European Competition J* 311, 324 (footnotes omitted)

The Cheap Talk Critique

The above theory regarding information sharing to support coordination has been criticized as being vulnerable to the 'cheap talk' critique: in particular, with regard to the ability of private sharing of information to facilitate coordination via the provision of a focal point and monitoring. For example when considering whether to share information to allow monitoring, a firm has no incentive to cheat on a tacit agreement and then disclose this fact through the shared information. The firm always has an incentive to disclose information to its rivals which says it is not cheating, regardless of whether it is cheating or not. Knowing this, its rivals who receive the information will discount it as worthless and it becomes simply 'cheap talk'. The same applies to information sharing in the context of finding focal prices.

As discussed previously, differences in firms' underlying costs result in differences in the optimal price or quantity on which to coordinate. For example, all else being equal, a low-cost firm will prefer a lower price than a high-cost firm. If a firm can influence the focal point by sharing information, the firm will have an incentive to provide whatever information moves the equilibrium closest to its own optimum. Knowing this, a rational firm will ignore any information that is not strictly compatible with the disclosing firm's incentives.

The literature suggests that communications between firms may have little value in facilitating coordination unless the information is verifiable. However, there is also evidence that personal friendship and trust play important roles in sustaining collusion. Economists have postulated that communication between firms can play an important role in creating and sustaining these relationships, thus overcoming the problems of trust. For this reason, even 'cheap talk' may pose a danger to reaching and sustaining coordination.

With regard to the benefits of information exchange between competitors, one should be careful to distinguish between the benefits of vertical transparency from those of horizontal transparency. While the former may improve the position of consumers by providing them information facilitating their consumption choice according to their preferences, this

115 Horizontal Guidelines, para 68.

consideration does not apply to exchange of information leading to horizontal transparency. On this distinction, read the following:

FW von Papp, 'Information Exchange Agreements' in I Lianos and D Geradin (eds) *Handbook on European Competition Law: Substantive Aspects* (Edward Elgar, 2013), 130, 147–9

Crucial to this categorization is the differentiation between the flow of information on the horizontal level—i.e., between competitors—('horizontal transparency'), and the vertical flow of information along the distribution chain ('vertical transparency'). While the significance of this distinction should be obvious to every competition lawyer, vertical transparency is not always sufficiently distinguished from horizontal transparency.

On the most fundamental level, this omission to distinguish between horizontal and vertical transparency may result in a category mistake (or the attempt to induce such a category mistake in others). In enumerating the pre-conditions for perfect competition, 'market transparency' or 'perfect information' are usually high on the list. This has been employed as an argument that information exchanges are necessarily benign, because they increase market transparency and make information more perfect. This deduction is logically fallacious for two separate reasons.

First, [. . .] in real-life markets the other conditions for perfect competition (such as zero transaction costs, an infinite number of buyers and sellers, instantaneous adaptation and a perfectly horizontal demand curve) are not present; and where not *all* of the pre-conditions are present, it is unclear whether it is desirable to improve an imperfection affecting just *one* of the pre-conditions in isolation. The second imperfection could even be beneficial—it could be the 'remedial imperfection' to counterbalance the first imperfection.

Secondly, and more pertinently to the present context, for the model of perfect competition to work, it is not necessary that firms have *horizontally* perfect information about the terms their competitors demand. It is sufficient that customers have perfect information about the terms offered by the suppliers (and vice versa) in the *vertical* relationship, so that search costs are zero. The fact that we need perfect vertical transparency in the model of perfect competition tells us nothing about the desirability of horizontal transparency. The distinction between vertical and horizontal transparency becomes especially clear in the context of auctions. While it is important that the bidders have sufficient information about outside options and their resulting willingness to pay for the auction prize (vertical transparency), auctioneers take great care that horizontal transparency is kept to a minimum where tacit collusion could otherwise result, while bidders try their best to circumvent the precautions taken by the auctioneer.

There are several benefits from increasing vertical transparency through the exchange of information. In some circumstances the disclosure of information among competitors has been mandated by competition authorities as a way to promote the interests of consumers. For instance, in its investigation on *Payment Protection Insurance* (*PPI*) in the UK, the Competition Commission required that all PPI providers should be required to provide information on pricing of PPI policies to the Financial Services Authority (now FCA) and third parties for comparison tables. Yet, promoting horizontal transparency may also provide some benefits.

M Bennett and P Collins, 'The Law and Economics of Information Sharing: The Good, the Bad and the Ugly' (2010) 6(2) *European Competition J* 311, 318–20

[. . .] [I]nformation sharing can also be beneficial in situations where it is not directly targeted at customers.

First, information dissemination and sharing can allow firms to benchmark themselves in critical areas against other firms, including actual or potential competitors. This can promote innovation and best practice and enhance efficiency, which can drive competition in sectors. For example, comparing business processes and performance against best practices within a sector or across sectors may allow firms to develop plans on how to make improvements in quality or to adapt specific practices with the aim of doing things better, faster and cheaper.

Second, information sharing can help improve allocative efficiency— ensuring that scarce resources are allocated to those who want or need them most. [. . .]

Third, information sharing can allow companies to understand market trends and experience and hence better plan to match supply with demand. This is particularly the case in markets where demand fluctuates significantly, where a market is undergoing significant technological change or where consumer tastes and preferences are rapidly changing. Having information about other firms' experiences and performance on the market may be better than just having your own. The more you can verify your experience and performance, the more likely it is that your plans will be well founded. This is particularly the case if each firm has access to only a portion of the entire information. By pooling their information together, firms may individually be able to make better business and investment plans.

Fourth, information sharing on individual consumers' risks can also be important in reducing the problems of adverse selection (where firms cannot tell good consumers from bad consumers) and moral hazard (where a consumer who is protected from risk may behave differently than if fully exposed to the risk).

For example, in the insurance industry, it is important to have a large database of past claimants in order to be able to predict claim rates on a particular insurance product. The larger the database, the more accurate the prediction is. [*This justification is particularly prevalent in the insurance sector*].

Fifth, in certain sectors, in recognition of the difficulties of sustaining services, transparency and communication amongst suppliers, including information sharing, may be sanctioned. For example, the EU has granted block exemptions for information exchanges that facilitate the coordination of activities for liner shipping consortia. The exemptions were aimed at allowing firms to capture the benefits from synchronization, rationalization and achieving economies of scale.

Sixth, it is worth noting that information sharing may also be necessary in the context of other types of beneficial horizontal agreements, eg pro-innovation/pro-competitive cooperation agreements on R&D to share technical information on the 'next generation' of products (say mobile phones) in order to enable suppliers to design standard components and enable finished products to interconnect. Another example is information shared for the purpose of standardization, eg sharing information on the patents necessary to achieve a standardization objective.

The assessment under Article 101(1) TFEU takes into account a number of factors. We will first explore the case law of the EU courts before examining the Commission's guidelines.

7.3.2.1.1. UK Agricultural Tractor Registration Exchange

The tractor makers in the UK entered into an agreement to exchange information, but not about price. From at least 1975, the exchange had identified the volume of retail sales and market shares of eight manufacturers and importers of agricultural tractors on the UK market. There were no other regular suppliers and the market was oligopolistic. The exchange was managed by AEA (the Agricultural Engineers Association), a trade association open to all manufacturers and importers of agricultural tractors in the United Kingdom, which at the material time had about 200 members. Processing of the data was entrusted to the data-processing company Systematics International Group of Companies Limited (SIL), to which the United Kingdom Ministry of Transport passed the information obtained when agricultural tractors were registered as fit to be driven on UK roads. SIL invoiced the cost of its services to each of the members of the agreement, under individual contracts concluded between SIL and those members. The Commission did not consider it necessary to include SIL in the proceedings. The Commission analysed both the structure of the market and the detailed terms of the scheme, indicating what information the parties were able to obtain. V55/5 forms provided to AEA by the Ministry of Transport enabled the members to discover exactly which models were sold in each small area of the UK and to discover parallel imports. After receiving the Commission's statement of objections, the parties suspended the operation of the exchange, but four, later three, of the parties notified a modified information scheme which they did not implement while the Commission's proceedings were continuing.

By a decision[116] upheld by the General Court (then Court of First Instance) and the CJEU, the Commission found that the part of the information exchange identifying the sales of the individual members, led to restrictions of competition.

First because it created a degree of market transparency between the suppliers in a highly concentrated market which is likely to destroy what hidden competition there remains between the suppliers in that market on account of the risk and ease of exposure of independent competitive action. The Commission noted that where there is a low degree of concentration, market transparency can increase competition in so far as consumers benefit from choices made in full knowledge of what is on offer but the United Kingdom tractor market was neither a low concentration market nor is the transparency in question in any way directed towards, or of benefit to, consumers. Indeed, four firms dominated the UK market with a combined market share of approximately 80 per cent, and these four firms had created an information exchange with other well-known suppliers capable of challenging their market position, with the effect that the conditions of a narrow oligopoly have been artificially created between the best-established competitors on this market by giving them information of any change in volumes and market shares at manufacturer and dealer level. The market was also protected from competition from outside the United Kingdom through high barriers to entry. Demand was very dispersed, with numerous buyers, the majority of whom did not have the possibility of purchasing tractors in other Member States. The Commission noted that in the absence of the exchange, firms would have to compete in a market with some measure of uncertainty as to the exact place, degree and means of attack by rivals. Uncertainty would lead the firms to compete more strongly than if they knew exactly how much of a response was necessary to meet competition. The information exchange reduced uncertainty by revealing the actions and reactions of all participating competitors.

116 *UK Agricultural Tractor Registration Exchange* (Cases COMP IV/31.370 and 31.446) Commission Decision [1992] OJ L 68/19.

Second, the Commission found that the information exchange did not only lessen competition between members of the Exchange and between their dealers, but also restricted competition between members and non-members of the information exchange scheme, even if in principle any manufacturer or importer could be admitted to the information exchange. Detailed knowledge of the sales pattern for tractors on the United Kingdom market improved the members' ability to defend their positions vis-à-vis non-members. According to the Commission, the Exchange favoured the big suppliers who already belonged to it, by enabling them to become aware of the existence of new entry and instantly to detect the market penetration by any such new member and thus containing the expansion of other suppliers on the United Kingdom market who were not members of the Exchange. The Commission also found that AEA provided its members with a forum for contacts facilitating a high price policy.

Among other arguments the parties submitted that the information related only to past transactions as opposed to future planned actions and therefore had no impact on competition in the market concerned. The Commission did not accept this argument finding that in a market where demand is stable or declining as is the case for the agricultural tractor market in the United Kingdom, forecasts of competitors' future actions can largely be determined on the basis of past transactions. However, it also accepted that the more accurate and the more recent the information on quantities sold and on market shares, the more impact this information has on future behaviour of the firms in the market and that from a certain point in time, market information relating to past transactions may become truly historic and no longer have any real impact on future behaviour. A safe harbour was recognized for an annual exchange of one-year-old sales figures of individual competitors in the United Kingdom, as commercial data with no appreciable distorting effect on competition between the manufacturers or between the dealers operating on the UK market. Yet, the Commission went on to reject the argument that no restriction of competition resulted from the scheme. Potential effects were relevant. Moreover, the parties' market shares had remained relatively stable during the existence of the exchange. The Commission prohibited the continuation of the exchange, but did not impose fines, probably because this was the first decision where the information exchange did not relate to prices.

Case T-35/92, *John Deere Ltd v Commission of the European Communities*
[1994] ECR II–957

In its judgments on two unsuccessful appeals from this decision, the General Court confirmed the approach of the Commission to agreements to exchange information in concentrated markets. The judgment of the CJEU was largely concerned with admissibility and jurisdiction. It did not add greatly to the theory about information exchange agreements, other than to approve the reasoning of the General Court.

[. . .]

51. The Court observes that, as the applicant points out, the Decision is the first in which the Commission has prohibited an information exchange system concerning sufficiently homogeneous products which does not directly concern the prices of those products, but which does not underpin any other anti-competitive arrangement either. As the applicants correctly argues, on a truly competitive market transparency between traders is in principle likely to lead to the intensification of competition between

suppliers, since in such a situation, the fact that a trader takes into account information made available to him in order to adjust his conduct on the market is not likely, having regard to the atomized nature of the supply, to reduce or remove for the other traders any uncertainty about the foreseeable nature of its competitors' conduct. On the other hand, the Court considers that, as the Commission argues this time, general use, as between main suppliers and, contrary to the applicant's contention, to their sole benefit and consequently to the exclusion of the other suppliers and of consumers, of exchanges of precise information at short intervals, identifying registered vehicles and the place of their registration is, on a highly concentrated oligopolistic market such as the market in question and on which competition is as a result already greatly reduced and exchange of information facilitated, likely to impair substantially the competition which exists between traders [. . .]. In such circumstances, the sharing, on a regular and frequent basis, of information concerning the operation of the market has the effect of periodically revealing to all the competitors the market positions and strategies of the various individual competitors.

52. Furthermore, provision of the information in question to all suppliers presupposes an agreement, or at any rate a tacit agreement, between the traders to define the boundaries of dealer sales territories by reference to the United Kingdom postcode system, as well as an institutional framework enabling information to be exchanged between the traders through the trade association to which they belong and, secondly, having regard to the frequency of such information and its systematic nature, it also enables a given trader to forecast more precisely the conduct of its competitors, so reducing or removing the degree of uncertainty about the operation of the market which would have existed in the absence of such an exchange of information. Furthermore, the Commission correctly contends [. . .] that whatever decision is adopted by a trader wishing to penetrate the United Kingdom agricultural tractor market, and whether or not it becomes a member of the agreement, that agreement is necessarily disadvantageous for it. Either the trader concerned does not become a member of the information exchange agreement and, unlike its competitors, then forgoes the information exchanged and the market knowledge which it provides; or it becomes a member of the agreement and its business strategy is then immediately revealed to all its competitors by means of the information which they receive.

53. It follows that the plea that the information exchange agreement at issue is not of such a nature as to infringe the Community competition rules must be dismissed.

The applicants alleged that the Commission had failed to fulfil its obligation to adduce proof of the alleged anti-competitive effects and that assessment of it under Article 101(1) TFEU ought to be based solely on the assessment of its actual effects and not simply its potential effects. They were also arguing that in the absence of actual anti-competitive effects, any doubt ought to benefit the parties making the notification. The General Court noted the following:

61. The Court finds that, contrary to the applicant' s submission, the fact that the Commission is unable to establish that the practice at issue produces an actual anti-competitive effect on the market in question, which could be accounted for by the fact inter alia that the agreement in its general form has been in force since 1975, has no bearing on the outcome of the case since Article [101(1) TFEU] prohibits both actual anti-competitive effects and purely potential effects, provided that they are sufficiently appreciable [. . .] which they are in the present case, having regard to the characteristics of the market).

On the existence of an agreement under Article 101 TFEU, the Court noted the following:

66. As has already been stated previously [. . .] the Court considers that the provision of information collected upon registration of every vehicle presupposes an agreement, or at any rate a tacit agreement, between the traders concerned to define the boundaries of dealer sales territories by reference to the United Kingdom postcode system, as well as an institutional framework enabling information to be exchanged between traders through the trade association to which they belong. If such an agreement did not exist, the information disseminated could not be exploited in the same way by its addressees. By acting in concert in that way, the traders participating in the information exchange system on the United Kingdom agricultural tractor market have necessarily restricted their ability to make independent decisions in ways which may have consequently affected competition between those traders. That being so, the applicant cannot argue that the members of the information exchange agreement did not infringe Article [101(1) TFEU] when by common accord they agreed to such methods of organizing the respective sales territories of their dealers. [. . .]

With regard to the restriction of competition as a result of the dissemination of data on the sales of each competitor.

68. This plea has three parts. The applicant submits, first, that there is no restriction of competition resulting from the alleged 'prevention of hidden competition'; secondly, that there is no restriction of competition resulting from the alleged reinforcement of barriers to entry into the market for competitors who are not members of the agreement; and, thirdly, that there is no effect on competition resulting from the meetings of the AEA committee.

With regard to the first issue, the Court noted that there was no manifest error in the Commission's assessment, which, having regard to the extent to which the products were sufficiently homogenous, rightly defined the relevant market as the agricultural tractor market in the United Kingdom, displaying the characteristics of a closed oligopoly, the aggregate market share of the four main suppliers representing between 75 and 80 per cent of the market, the market being also characterized by relative stability of the competitors' positions and by high barriers to entry. The General Court also noted the following:

81. [. . .] with regard to the type of information exchanged, the Court considers that, contrary to the applicant's contention, the information concerned, which relates in particular to sales made in the territory of each of the dealerships in the distribution network, is in the nature of business secrets. Indeed, this is admitted by the members of the agreement themselves, who strictly defined the conditions under which the information received could be disseminated to third parties, especially to members of their distribution network. The Court also observes that, as stated above [. . .] having regard to its frequency and systematic nature the exchange of information in question makes the conduct of a given trader's competitors all the more foreseeable for it in view of the characteristics of the relevant market as analyzed above, since it reduces, or even removes, the degree of uncertainty regarding the operation of the market, which would have existed in the absence of such an exchange of information, and in this regard the applicant cannot profitably rely on the fact that the information exchanged does not concern prices or relate to past sales. Accordingly, the first part of the plea, to the effect that there is no restriction of competition as a result of alleged 'prevention of hidden competition', must be dismissed.

The General Court then explored if there was any restriction of competition through alleged increased barriers to market entry for manufacturers who are not members of the agreement and noted the following:

84. The Court considers that, contrary to the applicant's assessment, the Commission correctly contends [. . .] that whatever decision is adopted by a trader wishing to penetrate the United Kingdom agricultural tractor market and whether or not it becomes a member of the agreement, the agreement is necessarily disadvantageous for it, regardless of whether, having regard to its modest cost and its membership rules, the information exchange system is in principle open to all. Either the trader concerned does not become a member of the information exchange agreement and, unlike its competitors, it then forgoes the information exchanged and a particularly reliable source of market knowledge; or it becomes a member of the agreement and its business strategy is then immediately revealed to all its competitors by means of the information which they receive [. . .]. In that regard, it is not significant that the number of traders entering the relevant market is in fact high. Accordingly, the second part of the plea, to the effect that the information exchange system at issue does not discriminate against new competitors wishing to penetrate the United Kingdom agriculture tractor market, must be dismissed.

Finally, the General Court examined if there restrictions of competition resulted from the AEA meetings, observing the following:

87. [. . .] the Court considers that the provision to suppliers of information collected upon the registration of every vehicle presupposes the existence of an institutional framework enabling information to be exchanged between traders through the trade association to which they belong. By acting in concert in that way, the traders participating in the information exchange system on the United Kingdom agricultural tractor market have necessarily restricted their ability to make independent decisions in ways which are likely to have influenced competition between them. That being so, the applicant cannot argue that the members of the information exchange agreement did not agree, within the trade association to which they belong, on certain organizational rules for the information exchange at issue [. . .]. It should, however, be pointed out that every contact made within the AEA is not necessarily to be considered as contrary to Article [101(1) TFEU] and that the Commission has never argued the contrary.

The applicants also relied on a counterfactual in order to prove that no restriction of competition resulted from dissemination of data concerning the sales of each member's dealers, disputing that it was possible, by means of the information exchange system at issue, to identify the sales of a competitor. The General Court noted the following:

92. Article [101 TFEU] prohibits agreements, decisions and concerted practices which have an anti-competitive object or effect. In the present case it is not contended that the information exchange system in question has an anti-competitive object. Accordingly, any objection to it can be based only on its effects on the market (see, a contrario, the judgment of the Court of Justice in Joined Cases 56 and 58/64 Consten and Grundig v Commission [1966] ECR 299). According to settled case-law, in such a case any anti-competitive effects of the agreement should be assessed by reference to the competition which would in fact occur 'in the absence of the agreement in dispute' (judgment in Société Technique Minière v Machinenbau Ulm [Case 56/65, *STM v MBU* [1966] ECR 337]). In that regard, the fact that the Commission is not able to demonstrate that the information exchange system at issue produces an actual anti-competitive effect on the United Kingdom agricultural tractor market does not affect the outcome

of the case since Article [101(1) TFEU] prohibits both actual anti-competitive effects and purely potential effects, provided that they are sufficiently appreciable. That is the case here, having regard to the characteristics of the market as previously analysed [. . .] and the fact that, in certain cases, the information disseminated is not sufficiently aggregated, so that it enables sales to be identified. The applicant is therefore not justified in claiming that the Commission, which, without committing any manifest error of assessment, was entitled to set at ten units the number of vehicles sold in a given dealer territory as the figure below which it is possible to identify sales made by each of the competitors, has not sufficiently demonstrated that to that extent the information exchange system at issue falls foul of Article [101(1) TFEU].

The General Court finally examined the application by the Commission of Article 101(3) TFEU. The applicant alleged that the Commission's decision wrongly refused to apply Article 101(3) TFEU since the information exchange system at issue provided considerable pro-competitive benefits.

105. The Court observes, first, that it has been consistently held that the four conditions laid down in Article [101(3) TFEU] for an individual exemption to be granted in respect of an agreement properly notified to the Commission are cumulative, so that if one of them is not satisfied the Commission may lawfully reject the application made to it. Furthermore, it is primarily for the undertakings notifying an agreement for an exemption to present to the Commission the evidence to show that the conditions laid down in Article [101(3) TFEU] are fulfilled [. . .]. In the present case, the Decision finds that the restrictions of competition resulting from the exchange of information are not indispensable, since 'own company data and aggregate industry data are sufficient to operate in the agricultural tractor market' in the United Kingdom. [. . .] The applicant does not show that the restrictions of competition resulting from the information exchange system, as previously analysed [. . .] are indispensable, particularly with regard to the objectives of contributing to economic progress and equitable distribution of benefits. Furthermore, the applicant cannot profitably argue that, in the absence of the system at issue, information equivalent to that provided by the system at issue could be obtained by traders active on the agricultural tractor market in the United Kingdom from market research producing information which would be in particular out of date, isolated and not as frequent as the information provided by the system at issue, it not even being necessary in this regard to take into consideration the costs of gaining access to such information. Consequently, the information exchange system, which does not, in particular, fulfil the third of the four conditions laid down in Article [101(3) TFEU], does not satisfy that article.

NOTES AND QUESTIONS ON JOHN DEERE

1. Did the Commission allege a secret cartel to stabilize market shares or a facilitating device making it easier for each firm to protect its own market share? If the latter, did the Commission have to find any collusion other than the agreement to exchange information to establish an infringement of Article 101(1) TFEU?
2. Note that some facilitating devices may not be collusive. Is there any way that the Commission can attack non-collusive facilitating devices? Does the concept of joint/collective dominance help?[117] Should an offense of attempt to restrict competition be introduced into the law?

[117] Cf Chapter 8.

3. The information was not made available to buyers. Why should this be relevant?
4. Why is aggregate information permitted but not more detailed information?
5. How can an agreement to exchange information about market conduct avoid intense price competition? Commodity and stock exchanges release detailed information. Perfect competition assumes complete transparency. Why should the rule be different for concentrated markets?
6. Did the information exchanged include prices?
7. Could the Commission have brought action against the UK authorities for making available to the industry registration data identifying the sales of individual competitors in a given market as opposed to aggregate data not identifying individual companies? The CJEU noted with regard to this question the following:

   58. [T]he Court finds that it is clear from [the decision of the Commission] that in certain circumstances the practices in question could at the same time amount to an infringement by the undertakings concerned of Article [101 TFEU] and an infringement of Articles [3(f) then, modified by the Treaty of Lisbon], [Article 4(3) TEU, then Article 5 TEC] and [101 TFEU] of the Treaty by the Member State on whose territory such practices occur, without the conduct of the national authorities being in any event capable of exonerating the traders from the consequences of their infringement of Article [101(1) TFEU]. Furthermore, it is apparent from point 49 of its grounds that the Decision expressly refrains from ruling on the question whether the practice in question is capable of constituting an infringement of the obligations which Article 5 of the Treaty places on the United Kingdom authorities. Consequently, the submission that the practice in question does not constitute an infringement of [Article 4(3) TEU] must be dismissed in any event.

9. Did the information disseminated relate to future or past transactions?
10. Do you think that the court mostly relied on the reduction of uncertainty regarding the operation of the market to infer anti-competitive effects? Would you agree with such an approach? Compare with the Commission's Horizontal Guidelines.
11. Subsequent case law held that some form of information may escape from liability under Article 101(1) TFEU. See, for instance, *BPB de Eendracht NV v Commission*, where the General Court noted that 'the exchange of purely statistical information [. . .] is not in, or capable of being put into, the form of individual information on the ground that the information exchanged might be used for anti-competitive purposes' and that 'the mere fact that a system for the exchange of statistical information might be used for anti-competitive purposes does not make it contrary to Article [101(1) TFEU], since in such circumstances it is necessary to establish its actual anti-competitive effect'.[118] In other cases, however, the EU Courts have taken a stricter approach as to the existence of a safe harbour for information exchange, by noting, for instance, that '[. . .] an information exchange may constitute a breach of competition rules even where the relevant

[118] Case T-311/94, *BPB de Eendracht NV v Commission* [1998] ECR II–1129, para 286.

market is not a highly concentrated oligopolistic market [. . .] the only general principle applied in relation to the market structure being that supply must not be atomized'.[119]

7.3.2.1.2. Asnef-Equifax

Case C-238/05, *Asnef-Equifax, Servicios de Información sobre Solvencia y Crédito, SL v Asociación de Usuarios de Servicios Bancarios* (*Ausbanc*)
[2006] ECR I–11125

A preliminary ruling reference by the Spanish Supreme Court to the CJEU. The case involved a register run by Asnef-Equifax—a group of financial organizations which exchanged solvency and credit information about their customers in order to evaluate the risks undertaken when engaging in credit or lending activities. The CJEU was asked to rule on whether such an agreement infringed Article 101(1) TFEU, in particular if its effect was to restrict competition in the financial and credit institutions sector, and whether such an agreement could be authorized by a national competition authority under Article 101(3) TFEU if implementation of the agreement could benefit consumers. An issue relating to Article 101 TFEU discussed by the CJEU but omitted in this chapter concerned the existence of an effect on intra-EU trade.

The existence of a restriction of competition

46. It is common ground that the essential object of credit information exchange systems, such as the register, is to make available to credit providers relevant information about existing or potential borrowers, in particular concerning the way in which they have previously honoured their debts. The nature of the information available may vary according to the type of system in use. In the main proceedings, the register contains [. . .] negative information, such as non-payment, as well as positive information, such as outstanding credit balances, collateral, guarantees and security, leasing transactions or temporary disposal of assets.

47. Such registers, which, as the Polish Government observes, exist in numerous countries, increase the amount of information available to credit institutions on potential borrowers, reducing the disparity between creditor and debtor as regards the holding of information, thus making it easier for the lender to foresee the likelihood of repayment. In doing so, such registers are in principle capable of reducing the rate of borrower default and thus of improving the functioning of the supply of credit.

48. As registers such as that in issue in the main proceedings do not thus have, by their very nature, the object of restricting or distorting competition within the common market within the meaning of Article [101(1) TFEU], it is for the national court to determine whether they have the effect of doing so.

49. In that regard, it should be emphasised that the appraisal of the effects of agreements or practices in the light of Article [101 TFEU] entails the need to take into consideration the actual context to which they belong, in particular the economic and legal context in which the undertakings concerned operate, the nature of the goods or services affected, as well as the real conditions of the functioning and the structure

[119] Case C-194/99 P, *Thyssen Stahl v Commission* [2003] ECR I–10821, para 86 (steal beams).

of the market or markets in question (see, to that effect, Case C250/92 *DLG* [1994] ECR I5641, paragraph 31; Case C399/93 *Oude Luttikhuis and Others* [1995] ECR I4515, paragraph 10; and *Javico*, paragraph 22).

50. However, while Article [101(1) TFEU] does not restrict such an assessment to actual effects alone, as that assessment must also take account of the potential effects of the agreement or practice in question on competition within the common market, an agreement will, however, fall outside the prohibition in Article [101 TFEU] if it has only an insignificant effect on the market (Case 5/69 *Völk* v *Vervaecke* [1969] ECR 295, paragraph 7; *John Deere* v *Commission*, paragraph 77; and *Bagnasco and Others*, paragraph 34).

51. According to the case-law on agreements on the exchange of information, such agreements are incompatible with the rules on competition if they reduce or remove the degree of uncertainty as to the operation of the market in question with the result that competition between undertakings is restricted (*John Deere* v *Commission*, paragraph 90, and Case C194/99 P *Thyssen Stahl* v *Commission* [2003] ECR I–10821, paragraph 81).

52. In effect, it is inherent in the Treaty provisions on competition that every economic operator must determine autonomously the policy which it intends to pursue on the common market. Thus, according to that case-law, such a requirement of autonomy precludes any direct or indirect contact between economic operators of such a kind as either to influence the conduct on the market of an actual or potential competitor or to reveal to such a competitor the conduct which an operator has decided to follow itself or contemplates adopting on the market, where the object or effect of those contacts is to give rise to conditions of competition which do not correspond to the normal conditions of the market in question, taking into account the nature of the products or the services provided, the size and number of the undertakings and also the volume of the market (see *Commission* v *Anic Partecipazioni*, paragraphs 116 and 117, as well as the case-law cited).

53. However, that requirement of independence does not deprive economic operators of the right to adapt themselves intelligently to the existing or anticipated conduct of their competitors (*John Deere* v *Commission*, paragraph 87; *Commission* v *Anic Partecipazioni*, paragraph 117; and *Thyssen Stahl* v *Commission*, paragraph 83).

54. Accordingly, as follows from paragraph 49 of this judgment, the compatibility of an information exchange system, such as the register, with the Community competition rules cannot be assessed in the abstract. It depends on the economic conditions on the relevant markets and on the specific characteristics of the system concerned, such as, in particular, its purpose and the conditions of access to it and participation in it, as well as the type of information exchanged—be that, for example, public or confidential, aggregated or detailed, historical or current—the periodicity of such information and its importance for the fixing of prices, volumes or conditions of service.

55. As indicated at paragraph 47 of this judgment, registers such as the one at issue in the main proceedings, by reducing the rate of borrower default, are in principle capable of improving the functioning of the supply of credit. As the Advocate General observed, in substance [. . .] if, owing to a lack of information on the risk of borrower default, financial institutions are unable to distinguish those borrowers who are more likely to default, the risk thereby borne by such institutions will necessarily be increased and they will tend to factor it in when calculating the cost of credit for all borrowers, including those less likely to default, who will then have to bear a higher cost than they would if the institutions were in a position to evaluate the probability of repayment more precisely. In principle, registers such as that mentioned above are capable of reducing such a tendency.

56. Furthermore, by reducing the significance of the information held by financial institutions regarding their own customers, such registers appear, in principle, to be capable of increasing the mobility of consumers of credit. In addition, those registers are apt to make it easier for new competitors to enter the market.

57. None the less, whether or not there is in the main proceedings a restriction of competition within the meaning of Article [101(1) TFEU] depends on the economic and legal context in which the register exists, and in particular on the economic conditions of the market as well as the particular characteristics of the register.

58. In that regard, first of all, if supply on a market is highly concentrated, the exchange of certain information may, according in particular to the type of information exchanged, be liable to enable undertakings to be aware of the market position and commercial strategy of their competitors, thus distorting rivalry on the market and increasing the probability of collusion, or even facilitating it. On the other hand, if supply is fragmented, the dissemination and exchange of information between competitors may be neutral, or even positive, for the competitive nature of the market (see, to that effect, *Thyssen Stahl* v *Commission*, paragraphs 84 and 86). In the present case, it is common ground, as may be seen from paragraph 10 of this judgment, that the referring court premissed its reference for a preliminary ruling on the existence of 'a fragmented market', which it is for that court to verify.

59. Secondly, in order that registers such as that at issue in the main proceedings are not capable of revealing the market position or the commercial strategy of competitors, it is important that the identity of lenders is not revealed, directly or indirectly. In the present case, it is apparent from the decision for referral that the Tribunal de Defensa de la Competencia imposed on Asnef-Equifax, which accepted it, a condition that the information relating to lenders contained in the register not be disclosed.

60. , it is also important that such registers be accessible in a non-discriminatory manner, in law and in fact, to all operators active in the relevant sphere. If such accessibility were not guaranteed, some of those operators would be placed at a disadvantage, since they would have less information for the purpose of risk assessment, which would also not facilitate the entry of new operators on to the market.

61. It follows that, provided that the relevant market or markets are not highly concentrated, that the system does not permit lenders to be identified and that the conditions of access and use by financial institutions are not discriminatory, an information exchange system such as the register is not, in principle, liable to have the effect of restricting competition within the meaning of Article [101(1) TFEU].

62. While in those conditions such systems are capable of reducing uncertainty as to the risk that applicants for credit will default, they are not, however, liable to reduce uncertainty as to the risks of competition. Thus, each operator could be expected to act independently and autonomously when adopting a given course of conduct, regard being had to the risks presented by applicants. Contrary to Ausbanc's contention, it cannot be inferred solely from the existence of such a credit information exchange that it might lead to collective anti-competitive conduct, such as a boycott of certain potential borrowers.

63. Furthermore, since, as the Advocate General observed, in substance, at point 56 of his Opinion, any possible issues relating to the sensitivity of personal data are not, as such, a matter for competition law, they may be resolved on the basis of the relevant provisions governing data protection. In the main proceedings, it is apparent from the documents before the Court that, under the rules applicable to the register, affected consumers may, in accordance with the Spanish legislation, check the information concerning them and, where necessary, have it corrected, or indeed deleted.

The applicability of Article [101(3) TFEU]

64. Only if the referring court finds, in the light of the considerations set out at paragraphs 58 to 62 of this judgment, that there is indeed in the dispute before it a restriction of competition within the meaning of Article [101(1) TFEU] will it be necessary for that court to carry out an analysis by reference to Article [101(3) TFEU] in order to resolve that dispute.

65. The applicability of the exemption provided for in Article [101(3) TFEU] is subject to the four cumulative conditions laid down in that provision. First, the arrangement concerned must contribute to improving the production or distribution of the goods or services in question, or to promoting technical or economic progress; secondly, consumers must be allowed a fair share of the resulting benefit; thirdly, it must not impose any non-essential restrictions on the participating undertakings; and, fourthly, it must not afford them the possibility of eliminating competition in respect of a substantial part of the products or services in question (see, to that effect, Joined Cases 43/82 and 63/82 *VBVB and VBBB* v *Commission* [1984] ECR 19, paragraph 61, as well as *Remia and Others* v *Commission*, paragraph 38).

66. It is clear from the documents before the Court, and in particular from the second question referred by the national court, that that court seeks an answer from the Court in respect of, in particular, the second of those conditions, which provides that consumers are to be allowed a fair share of the profit resulting from the agreement, decision or practice in question. The national court asks, in essence, whether, where all consumers do not derive a benefit from the register, the register might none the less benefit from the exemption provided for in Article [101(1) TFEU].

67. Apart from the potential effects described at paragraphs 55 and 56 of this judgment, registers such as the one at issue in the main proceedings are capable of helping to prevent situations of over indebtedness for consumers of credit as well as, in principle, of leading to a greater overall availability of credit. In the event that the register restricted competition within the meaning of Article [101(1) TFEU], those objective economic advantages might be such as to offset the disadvantages of such a possible restriction. It would be for the national court, if necessary, to verify that.

68. Admittedly, in principle it is not inconceivable that, as Ausbanc suggests, certain applicants for credit will, owing to the existence of such registers, be faced with increased interest rates, or even be refused credit.

69. However, without its being necessary to decide whether such applicants would none the less benefit from a possible credit discipline effect or from protection against over indebtedness, that circumstance cannot in itself prevent the condition that consumers be allowed a fair share of the benefit from being satisfied.

70. Under Article [101(3) TFEU], it is the beneficial nature of the effect on all consumers in the relevant markets that must be taken into consideration, not the effect on each member of that category of consumers.

71. Moreover, as follows from paragraphs 55 and 67 of this judgment, registers such as the one at issue in the main proceedings are, under favourable conditions, capable of leading to a greater overall availability of credit, including for applicants for whom interest rates might be excessive if lenders did not have appropriate knowledge of their personal situation.

72. In the light of all of the foregoing, the questions referred to the Court should be answered as follows:

Article [101(1) TFEU] must be interpreted as meaning that a system for the exchange of information on credit between financial institutions, such as the register, does not, in principle, have as its effect the restriction of competition within the meaning of that provision, provided that the relevant market or markets are not highly concentrated, that that system does not permit lenders to be identified and that the conditions of access and use by financial institutions are not discriminatory, in law or in fact.

In the event that a system for the exchange of information on credit, such as that register, restricts competition within the meaning of Article [101(1) TFEU], the applicability of the exemption provided for in Article [101(3) TFEU] is subject to the four cumulative conditions laid down in that provision. It is for the national court to determine whether those conditions are satisfied. In order for the condition that consumers be allowed a fair share of the benefit to be satisfied, it is not necessary, in principle, for each consumer individually to derive a benefit from an agreement, a decision or a concerted practice. However, the overall effect on consumers in the relevant markets must be favourable.

NOTES AND QUESTIONS ON ASNEF-EQUIFAX

1. (Paragraphs 46–8) What reasons led the Court not to find the existence of an anti-competitive object? Does this reason relate to the economic effects of the agreement?
2. (Paragraphs 51–2) Does the Court consider that reducing uncertainty in the market constitutes in itself an anti-competitive effect? Does the Court identify any other anti-competitive effects?
3. (Paragraphs 49, 50, 54, 57–61) Which factors does the Court include in the 'economic and legal context of the agreement', in order to assess the existence of an anti-competitive effect?
4. (Paragraphs 55–6) Consider the pro-competitive effects of the information exchange identified by the Court. How these relate to the considerations taken into account in paragraph 47 to reject the allegation that the exchange of information in this case had an anti-competitive object?
5. (Paragraph 56) In this respect, it is worth noticing that the Small Business, Enterprise and Employment Act 2015 has mandated greater sharing among small- and medium-sized enterprise (SME) lenders of information about the creditworthiness of UK SMEs based on performance indicators summarising SME's usage of business current accounts. Specifically, Credit Reference Agencies are now required to provide access to these indicators of creditworthiness of potential SME borrowers also to non-bank lenders who do not provide business current accounts (ie, and thus are not able to reciprocate the same access to data).
6. (Paragraphs 64–71) Provide a similar assessment (as in question 4 above) with regard to the benefits allegedly brought by that agreement in the context of Article 101(3) TFEU.

7.3.2.1.3. The European Commission's Guidelines on Information Exchange Agreements

The European Commission included a section on 'Information Exchange Agreements' in its revised Guidelines on the applicability of Article 101 TFEU to horizontal co-operation agreements. The Guidelines take an economic approach and attempt to reconcile this approach with the existing case law of the European Courts, eventually pushing the law further. On the relation between the case law and the Guidelines, read the following:

VHSE Robertson, 'A Counterfactual on Information Sharing: The Commission's Horizontal Guidelines 2011 Applied to the Leading Cases' (2013) 36(4) *World Competition*, 459, 484–5 and 487–8 (footnotes omitted)

[. . .] Generally, one could say that the case law of the Court of Justice with regard to information exchanges contains two major weaknesses that make its application to newly arising facts somewhat difficult: The ambiguous distinction between pure and merely ancillary information exchanges, and the special market characteristics present in many of the leading cases.

First, the Commission and the Court did not always clearly differentiate between a pure information exchange and information that is exchanged within the realm of other anti-competitive conduct. This makes it difficult to deduce under which circumstances a pure information exchange would be contrary to Article 101 TFEU. For instance, in the late 1990s the Commission pointed out that what had been at issue in *John Deere* was not simply the information exchange, but equally the use made of that information for collusive purposes. However, what one could and perhaps should gather from this statement is not that *John Deere* was not a case of pure information sharing—which indeed it was! Instead, what the Commission presumably meant was that the harm in *John Deere* did not lie in the simple fact that the undertakings concerned had exchanged information, but that this information was liable to lead to a collusive outcome (in the economic sense). Nevertheless, such statements can be misleading.

In *Thyssen Stahl*, the Commission held that the information exchange in question was not a separate infringement but had to be seen as part of wider infringements, notably price-fixing and market-sharing agreements. The Court, however, rejected this argument and stated that, based on the Commission's own decision, the information exchange of itself was a separate competition law infringement. This shows that it is not always clear to what extent an information exchange can be a stand-alone infringement of Article 101(1) TFEU, and at which point it becomes part of another anti-competitive conduct. After all, a cartel agreement will also require the exchange of business secrets. [. . .]

The Guidelines, though aware of this important issue, cannot give any clear answers. As this aspect of the case law on information sharing is particularly controversial, the Guidelines do not undertake to restate or summarize it, nor do they provide actual guidance—presumably for the simple reason that a theoretical approach to this issue is doomed to fail. Instead, it will be those analysing a given set of facts that need to draw the appropriate line anew in every single case. Perhaps the lessons learned in recent years can be of guidance in this respect.

Turning to the second weakness of the Court's case law on information sharing, one can notice that the cases that came before the Court often occurred under market circumstances that easily led to the conclusion that the information exchange was anti-competitive. Without such 'extreme' market characteristics present, it is difficult to anticipate whether or not an information exchange would be held to be anti-competitive. It can therefore easily be seen that some guidance on pure information sharing was urgently needed for day-to-day business.

It has been argued that in the area of pure information exchange agreements, the Horizontal Guidelines draw heavily on the Court's case law as it was established in *John Deere*, Asnef-Equifax, *T-Mobile Netherlands*, and other cases. However, [. . .] one must conclude that the Guidelines also introduce several novelties for analysing information sharing agreements. In particular, the question of when an anti-competitive object will be found can now be answered with much more precision, as this category has been substantially narrowed. In most cases, the analysis by the Commission will now concentrate on the effects of an information exchange and take real efficiencies into account, as is strongly suggested by economists. In this sense, it goes beyond the established case law. [. . .]

Following *T-Mobile Netherlands*, companies and their competition lawyers were apprehensive about the prospect of many information agreements being too quickly seen as a restriction of competition by object, making individual exemption under Article 101(3) TFEU very unlikely. Based on this assumption, companies would then no longer engage in information exchanges even if the latter yielded substantial efficiencies and benefits for consumers—the exact opposite of what competition law wants to achieve! The Guidelines, it would seem, have managed to counter these fears. While the distinction between pure and ancillary information sharing remains blurry, the Guidelines now draw a clear line between restrictions by object and restrictions by effect, thereby settling an issue that has long been debated by economists and lawyers. In addition, by limiting their 'object' approach to a very narrow and precise set of cases, the Commission's Guidelines signal that information sharing will now rarely be caught as having an anti-competitive object, meaning that the analysis will focus more on the efficiencies that can be generated through exchanges of information. While the Guidelines do not answer all questions, one can hope that they will provide companies in the internal market with incentives to share those kinds of information that will indeed enhance efficiencies and ultimately benefit consumers.

Communication from the Commission—Guidelines on the applicability of Article 101 TFEU to horizontal co-operation agreements [2011] OJ C 11/1

Restrictive effects on competition

75. The likely effects of an information exchange on competition must be analysed on a case-by-case basis as the results of the assessment depend on a combination of various case specific factors. The assessment of restrictive effects on competition compares the likely effects of the information exchange with the competitive situation that would prevail in the absence of that specific information exchange. For an information exchange to have restrictive effects on competition within the meaning of Article 101(1), it must be likely to have an appreciable adverse impact on one (or several) of the parameters of competition such as price, output, product quality, product variety or innovation. Whether or not an exchange of information will have restrictive effects on competition depends on both the economic conditions on the relevant markets and the characteristics of information exchanged.

76. Certain market conditions may make coordination easier to achieve, sustain internally, or sustain externally. Exchanges of information in such markets may have more restrictive effects compared to markets with different conditions. However, even where market conditions are such that coordination may be difficult to sustain before

> the exchange, the exchange of information may change the market conditions in such a way that coordination becomes possible after the exchange—for example by increasing transparency in the market, reducing market complexity, buffering instability or compensating for asymmetry. For this reason it is important to assess the restrictive effects of the information exchange in the context of both the initial market conditions, and how the information exchange changes those conditions. This will include an assessment of the specific characteristics of the system concerned, including its purpose, conditions of access to the system and conditions of participation in the system. It will also be necessary to examine the frequency of the information exchanges, the type of information exchanged (for example, whether it is public or confidential, aggregated or detailed, and historical or current), and the importance of the information for the fixing of prices, volumes or conditions of service. The following factors are relevant for this assessment.

Read paragraphs 77–104 of the Guidelines on the 'multi-factor'[120] analysis that will be performed by the Commission. We reproduce some key paragraphs from the Guidelines.

Market characteristics

Communication from the Commission—Guidelines on the applicability of Article 101 TFEU to horizontal co-operation agreements [2011] OJ C 11/1

> 77. Companies are more likely to achieve a collusive outcome in markets which are sufficiently transparent, concentrated, non-complex, stable and symmetric. In those types of markets companies can reach a common understanding on the terms of coordination and successfully monitor and punish deviations. However, information exchange can also enable companies to achieve a collusive outcome in other market situations where they would not be able to do so in the absence of the information exchange. Information exchange can thereby facilitate a collusive outcome by increasing transparency in the market, reducing market complexity, buffering instability or compensating for asymmetry. In this context, the competitive outcome of an information exchange depends not only on the initial characteristics of the market in which it takes place (such as concentration, transparency, stability, complexity etc.), but also on how the type of the information exchanged may change those characteristics).
>
> 78. [. . .] The lower the pre-existing level of transparency in the market, the more value an information exchange may have in achieving a collusive outcome. An information exchange that contributes little to the transparency in a market is less likely to have restrictive effects on competition than an information exchange that significantly increases transparency. Therefore it is the combination of both the pre-existing level of transparency and how the information exchange changes that level that will determine how likely it is that the information exchange will have restrictive effects on competition. The pre-existing degree of transparency, inter alia, depends on the number of market participants and the nature of transactions, which can

120 FW von Papp, 'Information Exchange Agreements' in I Lianos and D Geradin (eds) *Handbook on European Competition Law: Substantive Aspects* (Edward Elgar, 2013), 130–73.

range from public transactions to confidential bilateral negotiations between buyers and sellers. [. . .]

79. Tight oligopolies can facilitate a collusive outcome on the market as it is easier for fewer companies to reach a common understanding on the terms of coordination and to monitor deviations. [. . .]

82. A collusive outcome is more likely in symmetric market structures. When companies are homogenous in terms of their costs, demand, market shares, product range, capacities etc., they are more likely to reach a common understanding on the terms of coordination because their incentives are more aligned. [. . .]

85. Overall, for a collusive outcome to be sustainable, the threat of a sufficiently credible and prompt retaliation must be likely. Collusive outcomes are not sustainable in markets in which the consequences of deviation are not sufficiently severe to convince coordinating companies that it is in their best interest to adhere to the terms of the collusive outcome. [. . .]

Characteristics of the information exchange

The Guidelines distinguish between different types of information: strategic, market coverage, aggregated/individualized data, age of data, frequency of the information exchange, public/non-public information, public/non-public exchange of information.

Type of information	Implications
Strategic information (Horizontal Guidelines, para 86) Strategic information can be related to prices (for example, actual prices, discounts, increases, reductions or rebates), customer lists, production costs, quantities, turnovers, sales, capacities, qualities, marketing plans, risks, investments, technologies and R&D programmes and their results. Generally, information related to prices and quantities is the most strategic, followed by information about costs and demand. The strategic usefulness of data also depends on its aggregation and age, as well as the market context and frequency of the exchange.	More likely to produce restrictive effects to competition and be caught by Article 101 than exchanges of other types of information.
Market coverage (Horizontal Guidelines, para 87) The companies involved in the exchange have to cover a sufficiently large part of the relevant market.	Market coverage below the market share threshold of 20 per cent of the relevant market set by the Guidelines and the relevant block exemption regulation or 10 per cent of the *De Minimis* Notice pertaining to the type of agreement in question will usually not be large enough for the information exchange to give rise to restrictive effects on competition.

Type of information	Implications
Aggregated data (Horizontal Guidelines, para 89) Data for which the recognition of individualized company level information is sufficiently difficult eg sales data, data on capacities or data on costs of inputs and components	Unless it takes place in a tight oligopoly, the exchange of aggregated data is unlikely to give rise to restrictive effects on competition. Nevertheless, the possibility cannot be excluded that even the exchange of aggregated data may facilitate a collusive outcome in markets with specific characteristics. Namely, members of a very tight and stable oligopoly exchanging aggregated data who detect a market price below a certain level could automatically assume that someone has deviated from the collusive outcome and take market-wide retaliatory steps. In other words, in order to keep collusion stable, companies may not always need to know who deviated, it may be enough to learn that 'someone' deviated.
Individualized data (Horizontal Guidelines, para 89) eg Company-level data	The exchange of individualized data facilitates a common understanding on the market and punishment strategies by allowing the coordinating companies to single out a deviator or entrant.
Historic data (Horizontal Guidelines, para 90) There is no predetermined threshold when data becomes historic, that is to say, old enough not to pose risks to competition. Whether data is genuinely historic depends on the specific characteristics of the relevant market and in particular the frequency of price re-negotiations in the industry. For example, data can be considered as historic if it is several times older than the average length of contracts in the industry if the latter are indicative of price re- negotiations. Moreover, the threshold when data becomes historic also depends on the data's nature, aggregation, frequency of the exchange, and the characteristics of the relevant market.	Historic data is unlikely to lead to a collusive outcome as it is unlikely to be indicative of the competitors' future conduct or to provide a common understanding on the market. It is also unlikely to facilitate monitoring of deviations.
Frequent information exchange (Horizontal Guidelines, para 91)	Frequent exchanges of information that facilitate both a better common understanding of the market and monitoring of deviations increase the risks of a collusive outcome.

Type of information	Implications
Infrequent information exchange (Horizontal Guidelines, para 91)	Infrequent exchanges would not tend to be sufficient to achieve a collusive outcome in markets with short-term contracts indicative of frequent price re-negotiations. However, the frequency at which data needs to be exchanged to facilitate a collusive outcome also depends on the nature, age and aggregation of data. Furthermore, in markets with long-term contracts (which are indicative of infrequent price re-negotiations) a less frequent exchange of information would normally be sufficient to achieve a collusive outcome.
Genuine public information (Horizontal Guidelines, para 92) Genuinely public information is information that is generally equally accessible (in terms of costs of access) to all competitors and customers. This should include situations where information is available to the public at little cost. Even if the data exchanged between competitors is what is often referred to as being 'in the public domain', it is not genuinely public if the costs involved in collecting the data deter other companies and customers from doing so. A possibility to gather the information in the market, for example to collect it from customers, does not necessarily mean that such information constitutes market data readily accessible to competitors.[121]	Exchanges of genuinely public information are unlikely to constitute an infringement of Article 101 TFEU. Even if there is public availability of data (for example, information published by regulators), the existence of an additional information exchange by competitors may give rise to restrictive effects on competition if it further reduces strategic uncertainty in the market. In that case, it is the incremental information that could be critical to tip the market balance towards a collusive outcome.

121 Note the Italian competition authority's decision in Case *Ras-Generali-IAMA Consulting* (30 September 2004), where the Italian Competition Authority (Autorità Garante della Concorrenza e del Mercato, AGCM) objected to a database set up by an independent consultant, *IAMA*, which collated and disseminated detailed information on life assurance and pension insurance products. This information was public in that it was disclosed to customers (as required by Italian regulation) and often available on the web. The AGCM, did not find that the fact that the information was public brought the practice outside the scope of the competition law provisions on collusion, noting that it was not public domain information. Indeed, the information was provided directly by the participants to *IAMA*, making it more trustworthy than information collected on the web. The AGCM also considered that each insurance company did not have the resources to implement a similar database without collaboration from its competitors. The AGCM found that the information exchange amounted to a concerted practice which, even though it recognized that the market was not concentrated, restricted competition by object. Therefore, it was not necessary to analyse the effects. The *Tribunale Amministrativo Regionale de Lazio* (TAR) annulled the AGCM's decision, stating that the exchange of information available on the market cannot restrict competition *per se* and that the AGCM's distinction between public information and public domain information is unsatisfactory given that information that is '*immediately accessible by anyone without incurring significant costs*' does not exist in practice. The TAR did not exclude that the exchange of non-sensitive information could restrict competition, but in such a case it requires the AGCM to provide evidence of

Type of information	Implications
Public exchange of information (Horizontal Guidelines, para 94) An information exchange is genuinely public if it makes the exchanged data equally accessible (in terms of costs of access) to all competitors and customers.	The fact that information is exchanged in public may decrease the likelihood of a collusive outcome on the market to the extent that non- coordinating companies, potential competitors, as well as costumers may be able to constrain potential restrictive effect on competition. However, the possibility cannot be entirely excluded that even genuinely public exchanges of information may facilitate a collusive outcome in the market.

Assessment under Article 101(3) TFEU

Communication from the Commission—Guidelines on the applicability of Article 101 TFEU to horizontal co-operation agreements [2011] OJ C 11/1

Efficiency gains

95. Information exchange may lead to efficiency gains. Information about competitors' costs can enable companies to become more efficient if they benchmark their performance against the best practices in the industry and design internal incentive schemes accordingly. [. . .]

99. Information exchange that is genuinely public can also benefit consumers by helping them to make a more informed choice (and reducing their search costs). Consumers are most likely to benefit in this way from public exchanges of current data, which are the most relevant for their purchasing decisions. Similarly, public information exchange about current input prices can lower search costs for companies, which would normally benefit consumers through lower final prices. [. . .]

100. Exchanging present and past data is more likely to generate efficiency gains than exchanging information about future intentions. [. . .]

Indispensability

101. Restrictions that go beyond what is necessary to achieve the efficiency gains generated by an information exchange do not fulfil the conditions of Article 101(3). For fulfilling the condition of indispensability, the parties will need to prove that the data's subject matter, aggregation, age, confidentiality and frequency, as well as coverage, of the exchange are of the kind that carries the lowest risks indispensable for creating the claimed efficiency gains. [. . .] Finally, it is generally unlikely that the sharing of individualised data on future intentions is indispensable, especially if it is related to prices and quantities.

tangible effects on competition. The TAR's ruling was reversed by the *Consiglio di Stato*, which considered that the exchange of information which is publicly available but not '*genuinely public*' must be presumed to facilitate collusion and to amount to a restriction of competition by object.

102. Similarly, information exchanges that form part of horizontal co-operation agreements are also more likely to fulfil the conditions of Article 101(3) if they do not go beyond what is indispensable for the implementation of the economic purpose of the agreement (for example, sharing technology necessary for an R&D agreement or cost data in the context of a production agreement).

Pass-on to consumers

103. Efficiency gains attained by indispensable restrictions must be passed on to consumers to an extent that outweighs the restrictive effects on competition caused by an information exchange. The lower is the market power of the parties involved in the information exchange, the more likely it is that the efficiency gains would be passed on to consumers to an extent that outweighs the restrictive effects on competition.

No elimination of competition

104. The criteria of Article 101(3) cannot be met if the companies involved in the information exchange are afforded the possibility of eliminating competition in respect of a substantial part of the products concerned.

7.3.2.2. Cooperative joint ventures

Communication from the Commission—Guidelines on the applicability of Article 101 TFEU to horizontal co-operation agreements [2011] OJ C 11/1

21. The analysis of horizontal co-operation agreements has certain common elements with the analysis of horizontal mergers pertaining to the potential restrictive effects, in particular as regards joint ventures. There is often only a fine line between full-function joint ventures that fall under the Merger Regulation and non-full-function joint ventures that are assessed under Article 101. Hence, their effects can be quite similar.

Until 1986 the Commission had never cleared a joint venture as not infringing Article 101(1) TFEU on the ground that neither parent could have undertaken its tasks on its own, but had always exempted them or terminated proceedings with a comfort letter, thereby creating a risk for the parties to joint ventures that did not receive a formal decision that they might not be able to enforce important contractual provisions allocating the benefits of the joint venture and enabling each party to reap the benefit of its investment.[122]

Three important judgments of the General Court and the Court of Justice in the late 1990s and early 2000s paved the way for a more flexible competition assessment of joint ventures under Article 101(1) TFEU and the consideration of their positive effects, under the ancillary restraints doctrine.[123] We have already examined *Metropole* III and *O2 v Commission*. We focus here on *European Night Services*.

122 *BP/Kellog* 85/561/EEC Commission Decision [1985] OJ L 369/6.

123 See Chapter 6.

Joined Cases T-374, 375, 384 & 388/94, *European Night Services Ltd (ENS) et al v Commission*

[1998] ECR II–3141 (some references to case law are omitted)

European Night Services (ENS) is a company formed by four railway undertakings, British Rail (BR), Deutsche Bundesbahn (DB), Nederlandse Spoorwegen (NS), and Société Nationale des Chemins de Fer Français (SNCF), to provide overnight passenger services between the UK and Continental Europe through the Channel Tunnel. The parent companies agreed to provide services to their joint venture, including traction over their individual networks, locomotives and train crews and notified their agreement to the Commission, as was required by the rules applicable at the time (before the implementation of Regulation 1/2003 disposing of notification requirements and the monopoly of the Commission in enforcing Article 101(3) TFEU). The Commission found that the agreement infringed Article 101(1) TFEU and granted an exemption for a period of eight years under Regulation 1017/68[124] *subject to conditions that the parents grant to any other international grouping of railway operators paths under the English Channel, special locomotives for very fast trains capable of running over the tracks of different parents and the channel tunnel as well as the crew to drive them. The General Court treated the decision like a boxer's punch ball. It quashed it for failure to make a proper analysis on many grounds, although any one of them would have sufficed. On some points, it went further and found the Commission's findings to be manifest error. The case marked a turning point for the competition assessment of joint ventures under Article 101(1) TFEU.*[125]

9. The first agreement notified concerned the formation, by the four railway undertakings mentioned above—BR, SNCF, DB and NS—either directly or through subsidiaries owned by them, of ENS, a company established in the United Kingdom whose business was to consist of providing and operating overnight passenger rail services between points in the United Kingdom and the Continent through the Channel Tunnel, on the following four routes: London–Amsterdam, London–Frankfurt/Dortmund, Glasgow/Swansea–Paris and Glasgow/Plymouth–Brussels. [. . .]

12. The second group of agreements notified comprised the operating agreements concluded by ENS with the railway undertakings concerned and with SNCF under which each of them agreed to provide ENS with certain services, including traction over its network (locomotive, train crew and path), cleaning services on board, servicing of equipment and passenger-handling services. EPS and SNCF further agreed to provide traction through the Channel Tunnel. [. . .]

14. In the notification, ENS and the railway undertakings concerned stated that, on the market for the service in question, in competition with air, coach, ferry and car transport, ENS could achieve an overall market share of some 2.4% of the business segment and 5% of the leisure segment. Even if that market were defined more narrowly, taking account only of the routes concerned, ENS's overall market shares would remain insignificant. None of the railway undertakings concerned could operate alone a comparable service on the routes served by ENS, nor was there any indication that any other group had expressed an interest in, or could derive any profit from, the same activity. The notifying parties further gave the assurance that the ENS agreements did

124 Regulation (EEC) No 1017/68 of the Council of 19 July 1968 applying rules of competition to transport by rail, road and inland waterway [1968] OJ L 175/1.

125 V Korah, '*European Night Services*, the First Judgment of a Joint Venture Adopted a Realistic Approach to Effects on Competition' (2002) 6 *Competition LJ* 331

not create any barriers to entry additional to those already in place for any other undertakings wishing to provide similar services, which could constitute international groupings' within the meaning of Article 3 of Directive 91/440; such groupings would thus gain access to railway infrastructures—train-paths on the relevant lines—and would have no difficulty in finding qualified staff and suitable rolling stock. [. . .]

The Commission distinguished two relevant service markets: the market for the transport of business travellers, for whom scheduled air travel, high-speed rail travel, and the rail services to be operated by ENS are interchangeable modes of transport, and the market for the transport of leisure travellers, for whom substitute services may include economy-class air travel, train, coach, and possibly private motor car, the geographic market been confined to the four routes actually to be served by ENS, namely London–Amsterdam, London–Frankfurt/Dortmund, Paris–Glasgow/Swansea, and Brussels–Glasgow/Plymouth. The Commission further noted that ENS's parent undertakings were not withdrawing permanently from the relevant market, since their technical and financial resources could easily enable them to set up an international grouping and to provide overnight passenger transport services. Indeed, they continued to operate primarily on a market upstream from ENS's market, namely the market in necessary rail services which the railway undertakings sell to transport operators such as ENS. The Commission found that the ENS joint venture constituted an agreement caught by Article 101 TFEU, as do the operating agreements between it and each of its parent undertakings and SNCF.

The agreement gave rise to the following restrictions of competition.

First, those agreements had eliminated or appreciably restricted, as between ENS's parent undertakings, the scope for competition. For instance, any of ENS's parent undertakings could itself take on the role of transport operator, or set up a subsidiary specialising as a transport operator, and provide international transport services by buying the necessary rail services from the railway undertakings concerned.

Second, given the commercial strength of the parent undertakings, the formation of ENS might impede access to the market by transport operators in a position to compete with it. Indeed, as was noted by the Commission, ENS's parent undertakings continue to hold a dominant position in the supply of rail services in their Member States of origin, especially as regards special locomotives for the Channel Tunnel and in view of ENS's direct access to those services and of its special relationship with its parent undertakings, other operators could be placed at a disadvantage in competition for necessary rail services. In addition, BR and SNCF control a significant proportion of available paths for international trains through the Channel Tunnel, by virtue of the usage contract concluded with Eurotunnel.

Third, those restrictions of competition were enhanced by the fact that ENS forms part of a network of joint ventures between the parent undertakings. BR/EPS, SNCF, DB, and NS take part to varying degrees in a network of joint ventures for the operation of goods and passenger transport services, in particular through the Channel Tunnel. Nevertheless, the Commission exempted the agreement from prohibition under Article 101(3) TFEU, as the formation of ENS is likely to favour economic progress by, inter alia, *providing competition between modes of transport, and users will benefit directly from the new services offered. The restrictions were, moreover, found indispensable in view of the fact that the services involved are completely new, entailing substantial financial risks which could be borne by a single undertaking only with great difficulty. The Commission concluded that subject to the imposition of a condition to ensure the presence on the market of rail transport operators competing with ENS, the formation of ENS did not eliminate all competition on the relevant market and Article 101(1) TFEU was declared inapplicable for a period of eight years to the agreement subject to the condition that the railway undertakings party to the ENS agreements should supply to any international grouping of railway undertakings or any transport operator wishing to operate night passenger trains through the Channel Tunnel the same necessary rail services they had agreed to supply to ENS. These services consisted of the provision of the locomotive, train crew and path on each national network and in the Channel Tunnel. The railway undertakings had to supply these services on their networks on the same technical and financial terms as they allow to ENS.*

The General Court went on to decide various procedural questions before delving into the substance, examining the pleas of the applicants who submitted that the contested decision should be annulled for, among other reasons, not establishing the constituent elements of the conduct prohibited by Article [101(1) TFEU], since the ENS agreements did not restrict competition, and the decision was therefore vitiated by inaccurate and incomplete assessment of the facts, manifest error in law, and a failure to state reasons. This plea was divided in two parts: first, that the relevant market was wrongly defined and that the ENS agreements had no appreciable effect on trade between Member States and, second, that those agreements had no restrictive effect on competition.

Relevant market and market shares

93. It is to be noted here that the contested decision makes no reference to the market shares of ENS or of any other operators competing with ENS and also present on the various intermodal markets taken by the Commission as the relevant markets for the purposes of applying Article [101(1) TFEU]. Consequently, even if—contrary to the applicants' submission—the ENS agreements were to restrict competition, the Court is not in a position, in the absence of any such data concerning the analysis of the relevant market in the contested decision, to make any finding as to whether the supposed restrictions on competition had an appreciable effect on trade between Member States and were thus caught by Article [101(1) TFEU], having regard, in particular, to the intermodal competition which is, according to the decision itself, a feature of the two service markets in question. [. . .]

95. It is settled law that whilst, in stating the reasons for the decisions which it takes to enforce the rules on competition, the Commission is not required to discuss all the issues of fact and law and the considerations which have led it to adopt its decision, it is none the less required [. . .] to set out at least the facts and considerations having decisive importance in the context of the decision in order to make clear to the Court and the persons concerned the circumstances in which it has applied the Treaty [. . .]. It is also clear from the case-law that, other than in exceptional circumstances, the statement of reasons must be contained in the decision itself, and it is not sufficient for it to be explained subsequently for the first time before the Court [. . .].

96. It follows from the abovementioned case-law that when a Commission decision applying Article [101(1) TFEU] suffers from serious omissions, such as the absence of any reference to the market shares of the undertakings concerned, the Commission may not remedy that defect by adducing for the first time before the Court figures and other analytical data from which it may be concluded that the essential elements of a situation in which Article [101(1) TFEU] applies are in fact present unless none of the parties had challenged the analytical data in question during the prior administrative procedure.

97. Here, according to the estimates put forward by the applicants in the notification, ENS's market shares were not expected to exceed 4%, and it was only on the basis of a narrower market definition that they might reach 7% for the business travel market

and 8% for the leisure travel market [. . .], without even then having an appreciable effect on competition. [. . .]

102. In any event, even if, as noted above, ENS's share of the tourist travel market was in fact likely to exceed 5% on certain routes, attaining 7% on the London–Amsterdam route and 6% on the London–Frankfurt/Dortmund route [. . .], it must be borne in mind that, according to the case-law, an agreement may fall outside the prohibition in Article [101(1)] of the Treaty if it has only an insignificant effect on the market, taking into account the weak position which the parties concerned have on the product or service market in question (Case 5/69 *Volk v Vervaecke* [1969] ECR 295, paragraph 7). [. . .].

103. That being so, where, as in the present case, horizontal agreements between undertakings reach or only very slightly exceed the 5% threshold regarded by the Commission itself as critical and such as to justify application of Article [101(1) TFEU], the Commission must provide an adequate statement of its reasons for considering such agreements to be caught by the prohibition in Article [101(1) TFEU]. Its obligation to do so is all the more imperative here, where, as the applicants stated in their notification, ENS has to operate on markets largely dominated by other modes of transport, such as air transport, and where, on the assumption of an increase in demand on the relevant markets and having regard to the limited possibilities for ENS to increase its capacity, its market shares will either fall or remain stable. [. . .].

105. It must be concluded from the foregoing that the contested decision does not contain a sufficient statement of reasons to enable the Court to make a ruling on the shares held by ENS on the various relevant markets and, consequently, on whether the ENS agreements have an appreciable effect on trade between Member States, and the decision must therefore be annulled on that ground.

[. . .]

Concerning the assessment of the restrictive effects of the ENS agreements on competition, the General Court noted the following:

135. According to the contested decision, the ENS agreements have effects restricting existing and potential competition (a) among the parent undertakings, (b) between the parent undertakings and ENS and (c) *vis-à-vis* third parties; furthermore (d), those restrictions are aggravated by the presence of a network of joint ventures set up by the parent undertakings.

136. Before any examination of the parties' arguments as to whether the Commission's analysis as regards restrictions of competition was correct, it must be borne in mind that in assessing an agreement under Article [101(1) TFEU], account should be taken of the actual conditions in which it functions, in particular the economic context in which the undertakings operate, the products or services covered by the agreement and the actual structure of the market concerned (judgments in *Delimitis* [Case C-234/89, Stergios Delimitis v Henninger Bräu AG, [1991] ECR I–935], *Gottrup-Klim*, [Case C-250/92, *Gøttrup-Klim e.a. Grovvareforeninger v Dansk Landbrugs Grovvareselskab AmbA* [1994] ECR I–5641], paragraph 31, Case C-399/93 *Oude Luttikhuis and Others v Verenigde Cooperatieve Melkindustrie* [1995] ECR I–4515, paragraph 10, and Case T-77/94 *VGB and Others v Commission* [1997] ECR II–759, paragraph 140), unless it is an agreement containing obvious restrictions of competition such as price-fixing, market-sharing or the control of outlets (Case T-148/89 *Trefilunion v Commission* [1995] ECR II–1063, paragraph 109). In the latter case, such restrictions may be weighed against their claimed pro-competitive effects only in the context of Article [101(3) TFEU], with a view to granting an exemption from the prohibition in Article [101(1)].

137. It must also be stressed that the examination of conditions of competition is based not only on existing competition between undertakings already present on the relevant market but also on potential competition, in order to ascertain whether, in the light of the structure of the market and the economic and legal context within which it functions, there are real concrete possibilities for the undertakings concerned to compete among themselves or for a new competitor to penetrate the relevant market and compete with the undertakings already established (*Delimitis*, cited above, paragraph 21). [. . .] The assumption of potential competitive circumstances presupposes that each parent alone is in a position to fulfil the tasks assigned to the joint venture and that it does not forfeit its capabilities to do so by the creation of the joint venture. An economically realistic approach is necessary in the assessment of any particular case [. . .].

138. It is in the light of those considerations, therefore, that it is necessary to examine whether the Commission's assessment of the restrictive effects of the ENS agreements was correct.

The General Court examined the restrictions on competition, focusing first on those among the parent undertakings and exploring if there were possibilities of competition between the parent undertakings in the absence of the agreement, thus conducting some form of counterfactual analysis. For instance, the Court noted that:

[. . .] it would be unrealistic, given the novelty and the specific features of the night rail services in question, for the parent undertakings to set up other subsidiaries in other Member States having the status of railway undertakings for the sole purpose of forming a new joint venture to compete with ENS. The prohibitive cost of the investment required for such services through the Channel Tunnel and the fact that there are no economies of scale in the operation of a single route, as opposed to the four routes to be operated together by ENS, show how unrealistic potential competition is among the parent undertakings and between them and ENS.[126]

The Court then examined the existence of restrictions on competition vis-à-vis third parties, in particular the finding in the Commission's decision that 'third-party access to the relevant markets was likely to be impeded by the existence of a special relationship between ENS and its parent undertakings, placing other operators at a disadvantage in competition for the necessary rail services provided by the parent undertakings, and by the Channel Tunnel usage agreement entered into by BR, SNCF and Eurotunnel, which allows BR and SNCF to retain a significant proportion—75 per cent—of the path capacity reserved for international train services'.[127] *The Court made the following observations.*

150. With regard, first, to the special relationship between ENS and the railway undertakings concerned, it must be noted that the Commission's analysis is based on the premiss that the market for rail passenger transport is split into two parts: an upstream market in the provision of necessary rail services' (train paths, special locomotives and train crews) and a downstream market in passenger transport, on which transport operators such as ENS operate alongside railway undertakings. According to the decision, the parent undertakings could abuse their dominant position on the upstream market by refusing to provide necessary rail services to third parties competing with ENS on the downstream market.

[126] Joined Cases T-374, 375, 384 & 388/94, *European Night Services Ltd (ENS) et al v Commission* [1998] ECR II-3141, para 145.

[127] Ibid, para 149.

This raised the question whether the services provided to ENS by the parent undertakings may be categorized as 'necessary or essential facilities'.

One of the pleas of the applicants against the Commission's decision referred to Article 2 of the decision which required the notifying parties to supply to other international groupings or transport operators the same necessary rail services as they supply to ENS. The applicants argued that the Commission had misapplied the essential facilities doctrine. It was alleged that such an obligation had the effect not merely of undermining the railway undertakings' efforts in setting up international groupings but also of obliging them to share the benefits of their cooperation with third parties without those third parties having to bear any of the commercial risks involved. It was also submitted that the economic effect of obliging the railway undertakings to make necessary services available to transport operators on terms which they cannot freely decide amounted, moreover, to an expropriation. The General Court noted:

205. [. . .] the aim of the condition imposed in Article 2 of that decision is that of preventing the restrictions of competition from going beyond what is 'indispensable'.

206. However, as the Court has concluded [. . .], the Commission must be regarded as not having made a correct and adequate assessment in the contested decision of the economic and legal context in which the ENS agreements were concluded. It has thus not been demonstrated that those agreements restrict competition within the meaning of Article [101(1) TFEU] and that they therefore need to be exempted under Article [101(3)]. Consequently, since the contested decision did not contain the relevant analytical data concerning the structure and operation of the market on which ENS operates, the degree of competition prevailing on that market or, therefore, the nature and extent of the alleged restrictions on competition, the Commission was not in a position to assess whether the condition imposed by Article 2 of the contested decision was or was not indispensable for the purpose of granting a possible exemption under Article [101(3) TFEU].

207. However, even if the Commission had made an adequate and correct assessment of the restrictions of competition in question, it would be necessary to consider whether it was a proper application of Article [101(3)] to impose on the notifying parties the condition that train paths, locomotives and crews must be supplied to third parties on the same terms as to ENS, on the ground that they are necessary or that they constitute essential facilities, as discussed by the parties in their pleadings and at the hearing.

208. In that regard, it follows from the case-law on the application of Article [102 TFEU] that a product or service cannot be considered necessary or essential unless there is no real or potential substitute (Joined Cases C-241/91P and C-242/91 P *RTE and ITP v Commission* (*Magill*) [1995] ECR I–743, paragraphs 53 and 54, and Case T-504/93 *Tiércé Ladbroke v Commission* [1997] ECR II–923, paragraph 131).

209. Consequently, with regard to an agreement such as that in the present case, setting up a joint venture, which falls within Article [101(1)] of the Treaty, the Court considers that neither the parent undertakings nor the joint venture thus set up may be regarded as being in possession of infrastructure, products or services which are necessary or essential for entry to the relevant market unless such infrastructure, products or services are not interchangeable and unless, by reason of their special characteristics—in particular the prohibitive cost of and/or time reasonably required for reproducing them—there are no viable alternatives available to potential competitors of the joint venture, which are thereby excluded from the market.

210. The question whether the Commission could validly regard the supply of (a) train paths, (b) locomotives and (c) crews to ENS by its parent undertakings as necessary or

essential services which had to be made available to third parties on the same terms as to ENS and whether, in so doing, it provided a valid statement of reasons for its decision must be examined in the light of the above considerations and by analogy with the case-law [. . .].

The GC found that the Commission's assessment of the necessary or essential nature of the special locomotives, thus, the obligation imposed on the parent undertakings to supply such locomotives to third parties was insufficiently reasoned. It also accepted the arguments of the applicants against the limitation of the duration of the exemption provided under Article 101(3) TFEU and annulled the Commission's decision.

NOTES AND QUESTIONS ON EUROPEAN NIGHT SERVICES

1. (Paragraph 137) Is a joint venture with a large initial market share inevitably contrary to Article 101(1)? Should potential competition be considered when defining the market, or when appraising the market power of a firm within the market as defined.
2. (Paragraphs 137, 146) If you were arguing that none of the parents was in a position to operate the night services individually, what facts would you stress (a) prior to directive and (b) after it was in force?
3. (From paragraph 205) If the Commission had not given adequate reasons for deciding that Article 101(1) was infringed, was it necessary to consider the exemption? Why do you think the court did so?
4. (From paragraph 205) In what other contexts have the Courts considered the essential facilities doctrine (see Chapter 9). Does the General Court apply the concept widely or narrowly here? Why?
5. Compare with *Métropole III* and *O2 v Commission*, the other General Court judgments on JVs.
6. Everyone is talking of *ENS* as a break through. Does it amount to a rule of reason? Do you think the General Court was divided about the application of a rule of reason (see our discussion of *Métropole III* in Chapter 6).

7.4. POSSIBLE JUSTIFICATIONS AND EXCEPTION FROM THE PRINCIPLE OF PROHIBITION

In view of the delicate balance between cooperation and competition that, in some circumstances, needs to be achieved in order to promote total and consumer welfare, which may not be adequately reflected in the analysis performed under Article 101(1) or its national equivalent, both EU and UK competition law have developed flexible mechanisms for the implementation of competition law provisions against horizontal cooperation agreements, either for situations of economic 'crisis', or, more broadly, for certain categories of agreements, which while restrictive of competition, that may produce overall positive effects to competition, or more generally collective benefits. The situation of State-imposed horizontal restrictions to competition should also be examined. The final sections of this Chapter and its Supplement explore case studies in various economic sectors.

7.4.1. CRISIS CARTEL

EU competition law confronted situations of economic crisis and structural overcapacity after the first and, more intensively, after the second oil shock in the mid to late 1970s. This led to some calls to suspend the application of Article 101 TFEU under certain circumstances, or to apply generously Article 101(3) TFEU to 'crisis cartels'.[128] The Commission resisted such calls, but gave consideration in a number of its decisions applying Article 101(3) to situations of structural overcapacity. The current economic downturn, following the global financial crisis of 2007–8, indicates that the topic of crisis cartels is still a hot one. The Commission has explained its position in the following report submitted to one of the roundtables on Best Practices organized by the OECD Competition Committee.

European Commission Comments, OECD, *Crisis Cartels* DAF/COMP/GF(2011)11 (18 October 2011), 109–11 (footnotes omitted)

In the context of the current economic downturn, a number of undertakings in various industries across Europe are seeking to justify agreements restricting competition by invoking overcapacity problems or economic crises in their respective sectors. The schemes falling under the notion of 'industrial restructuring agreements' (sometimes referred to as 'crisis cartels') usually involve scenarios where a significant number of industry players get together to find a joint solution to their common difficulties in times of crisis. This may be achieved by, for example, reducing overcapacity and/or by agreeing on a 'fair' price level to avoid that some companies would go bankrupt and leave the market. [. . .]

The term 'crisis cartels' is misleading as it may create expectations that competition authorities might envisage to allow cartels in order to protect industry from an economic crisis in general. However, the discussion of industrial restructuring agreements should not be related to the current, or any other, cyclical economic crisis and the recession induced fall in demand. In a properly functioning market economy it should normally be price that influences the changing relationship between supply and demand, and when demand falls it is likely that price would follow as well. If the consequence of a recession is that some undertakings go bankrupt, it would normally be those least adapted to the crisis for a number of reasons. Hence, it can generally be assumed that competition would correct the problem of overcapacity available and, over time, it would bring the market back to equilibrium. Therefore, until this adjustment takes place prices must not be artificially maintained at a high level by means of a cartel. In line with this fundamental economic law of supply and demand, the case law of the Court of Justice of the European Union [. . .] generally concludes that a cyclical overcapacity in principle cannot justify the formation of cartels.

Irrespective of the existence of a general crisis, however, more long lasting overcapacity problems could exist in industries in decline due, for example, to technological changes in the market, or in industries where firms have been substantially overinvesting for a prolonged period of time. For instance, such difficulties could arise in industries that have been granted state aids for a long time, or where state control prevented the closure of plants because of overriding social or other political factors, such as unemployment. The relevant question to ask in such situations is whether market forces alone would be able to solve the problem or

[128] For a critical discussion of these proposals, see T Sharpe, 'The Commission's Proposals on Crisis Cartels' (1980) 17(1) *Common Market L Rev* 75; R Joliet, 'Cartelisation, Dirigism and Crisis in the European Community' (1981) 3(4) *World Economy* 403.

whether some kind of intervention by the affected undertakings in the market concerned is necessary.

There may indeed be market situations where the problem of overcapacity may not be remedied by market forces alone, which would imply that overcapacity is of a structural nature.

There are economic reasons explaining why in situations of overcapacity the problems cannot always be remedied by the free interplay of market forces and the mechanisms of competition alone. This can be best explained by the notion of '*war of attrition*'. This refers to a situation where the object of firms is to induce the rivals to give up and, consequently, they would wait and suffer economic losses for a while until their rivals would effectively exit the market. In such a context, firms try to avoid closing plants and giving up market shares as thereby they would increase their costs. This situation is especially likely to occur in industries characterised by increasing returns to scale and/or high fixed or sunk costs (and thereby high costs of exit and entry).

The undertakings involved in a 'war of attrition' expect that sooner or later some firms will leave the market and, therefore, they may not want to close their unused capacity as they would hope to be able to utilize it for production in the future. The persistence of such a situation can be illustrated with the *theory of a public good*, where more production and corresponding investment in capacity than would be socially optimal takes place because of a '*free riding*' problem. In such situations, even though unilateral or coordinated reduction of overcapacity would be beneficial for everyone in the industry, firms would prefer not to make the first move of reducing their own capacity. Instead, it is possible that they would prefer to wait for other competitors to reduce capacity in order to benefit from the overall fall in capacity in the sector concerned, without incurring the costs of reducing it themselves.

However, this situation, which in game theory is referred to as a '*prisoner's dilemma*',[129] is generally considered to be sustained in very specific circumstances, such as stable, transparent and symmetric market structures. This is because if it is expected that one firm will suffer more than its competitors from the persistence of overcapacity problems, its incentives to reduce capacity would be higher and it would be more likely to reduce capacity first. Moreover, where there is no symmetry in size and competitiveness, the weaker firms could foresee that they will have to exit first (as soon as they empty their pockets) and therefore it is unlikely that they remain in the wasteful 'war'. Thereby, in heterogeneous market structures with firms of different sizes and cost structures the problem of overcapacity would normally not persist. The waste of economic resources caused by the '*war of attrition*' may significantly impair the industry's competitiveness which could ultimately result in consumer harm. In this very rare type of situation, and assuming all conditions of Article 101(3) are met [. . .] such industrial restructuring agreement could possibly be exempted.

These principles describe the practice of the European Commission in a number of decisions applying Article 101(3) TFEU and the approach followed by the European Courts when applying the conditions of Article 101(3) TFEU. It is clear that most restructuring agreements involve some restructuring, which constitutes a restriction of competition by object under Article 101(1) TFEU.[130] The agreement should thus be assessed under Article 101(3) TFEU.

(i) The restructuring should first contribute to improving the production or distribution of goods or contribute to promoting technical or economic progress. The Commission

129 See the analysis in Section 11.2.

130 See Case C-209/07, *Competition Authority v Beef Industry Development Society Ltd and Barry Brothers (Carrimore) Meats Ltd (BIDS)* [2008] ECR I-8637.

has already considered that restructuring agreements may bring efficiency gains, if they remove inefficient capacity from the market.[131] This requires that the 'restructuring agreement should provide sufficient indication of what capacity will be removed', for instance by specifying which firms should reduce capacity or leave the market, or at least the criteria under which the parties will assess the capacity to exit the market, but also that the undertakings remaining in the market are able to increase capacity utilization and subsequently output. Hence, agreements that lead efficient plants to exit the market, cannot be justified. Nor can agreements that contain limitations on increases of output increases, for similar reasons. The efficiency gains need to be substantiated and examined on a case-by-case basis, in order to distinguish exit by efficient or inefficient plants.

(ii) The restrictions should be indispensable to the attainment of these objectives. This requires a finding of structural over-capacity that market forces alone could not have solved within a reasonable time period. The assessment of this condition is further explained by the Commission.[132]

(iii) Finally, the consumers should receive a fair share of any pro-competitive benefits and a residual degree of competitive constraint should be also be maintained in the market. This may come out of the remaining undertakings and/or the existence of buying power.

An important part of the analysis of the impact on competition relates to the existence of alternative solutions less restrictive of competition, such as state subsidies, mergers and acquisitions, specialization agreements, among others. In comparison with crisis cartels, such practices are not secret and are usually notified to competition or other public authorities, which may assess them.

Merger control explicitly provides for the possibility of restructuring through consolidation of undertakings and industries facing structural problems due to over-capacity, through the 'failing firm defence'. The conditions for such defence may apply where 'the competitive structure of the market would deteriorate to a lesser extent if the concentration did not proceed'.[133] In order to prove that the undertakings in question should provide evidence that '[f]irst, the allegedly failing firm would in the near future be forced out of the market because of financial difficulties if not taken over by another undertaking; second, there is no less anti-competitive alternative purchase than the notified merger; third, in the absence of a merger, the assets of the failing firm would inevitably exit the market.'[134]

[131] See eg *Synthetic Fibres* (Case IV/30.810) Commission Decision [1984] OJ L 207/17, para 39 ('The Agreement also ensures that the shake-out of capacity will eliminate the non-viable and obsolete plant that could only have survived at the expense of the profitable plant through external subsidies or loss financing within a group, and will leave the competitive plants and businesses in operation.'); *Stichting Baksteen (Dutch Bricks)* (Case IV/34.456) Commission Decision [1994] OJ L 131/15, para 26 ('As the capacity closures concern production units that are the least suitable and least efficient because of obsolescence, limited size or outdated technology, production will in future be concentrated in more modern plants which will then be able to operate at higher capacity and productivity levels.') and para 29.

[132] European Commission Comments, OECD, *Crisis Cartels* DAF/COMP/GF(2011)11 (18 October 2011), 109–11.

[133] Joined Cases C-68/94 & C-30/95, *French Republic and Société commerciale des potasses et de l'azote (SCPA) and Entreprise minière et chimique (EMC) v Commission of the European Communities* [1998] ECR I-1375, para 114 [hereinafter *Kali and Salz*].

[134] European Commission, Guidelines on the assessment of horizontal mergers under the Council Regulation on the control of concentrations between undertakings [2004] OJ C 31/5, para 90, applying the criteria devised by the CJEU in Joined Cases C-68/94 & C-30/95, *Kali and Salz* [1998] ECR I-1375.

The notifying parties should provide 'in due time all the relevant information necessary to demonstrate that the deterioration of the competitive structure that follows the merger is not caused by the merger'.[135]

Block Exemption Regulation No 1218/2010 for specialization agreements also enables competing undertakings to enter into agreements by virtue of which one or more parties agree to cease production of certain products while the other party agrees to produce these products. This possibility is confined to the specific conditions set by that Regulation: (i) the parties should not have a combined market share in excess of 20 per cent; (ii) that the party continuing the manufacturing of the product in question agrees to supply the other parties which remain active in the downstream selling market; (iii) that the agreement is not widespread to all competitors in the market but consists in an agreement between industry players resolving the structural over-capacity through specialization.[136] Such approaches may less restrict competition less than a crisis cartel. The latter leads more to the closure of plants, which reduces fixed costs, while specialization agreements may focus on variable costs. However, it could be also argued that both solutions may lead to the closure/mothballing of the less efficient plants, thus typically entailing both a reduction in fixed costs (ie, avoiding duplication) and variable ones (ie, production is concentrated in the more efficient plants). Consumers are more likely to receive a fair share of the resulting cost pro-competitive benefits in the case of reductions of variable costs than in the case of reductions of fixed costs, because pricing decisions are often based on marginal cost.

In conclusion, EU competition law seems to take an inhospitable approach towards crisis cartels. The restrictive interpretation of the conditions of Article 101(3) TFEU, in particular that of indispensability, renders the success of such defence unlikely. The EU Courts have also rejected such defences in a number of cases. In *Raiffeisen Zentralbank Österreich v Commission*, the General Court rejected the argument that the crisis in the banking sector justified widespread meetings between Austrian banks and a regular system of information exchange between them ('the Lombard network') with respect to the essential factors of competition in the Austrian market in banking products and services, noting that 'the Commission is not required to treat the poor financial health of the sector in question as a mitigating circumstance' and that 'the fact that in previous cases the Commission took account of the economic situation in the sector as a mitigating circumstance does not mean that it must necessarily continue to follow that practice'.[137]

135 European Commission, Guidelines on the assessment of horizontal mergers under the Council Regulation on the control of concentrations between undertakings [2004] OJ C 31/5, para 91.

136 European Commission Comments, OECD, *Crisis Cartels* DAF/COMP/GF(2011)11 (18 October 2011), 118.

137 Joined Cases T-259–64 & 271/02, *Raiffeisen Zentralbank Österreich AG and Others v Commission* [2006] ECR II–5169, para 510. See also the restrictive interpretation by the General Court of the decisions of the Commission in *Synthetic Fibres* and *Dutch Bricks* in Case T-148/89 *Tréfilunion SA v Commission of the European Communities* [1995] ECR II–1063, para 117, the Court noting that '[. . .] the applicant' s alleged restructuring plan cannot be regarded as an agreement for the coordinated reduction of overcapacity and that, in any event, it was open to the producers to notify their agreements to the Commission under Article [101(3) TFEU], which would have enabled the Commission, if appropriate, to rule as to whether they met the criteria laid down by that provision. Since the applicant did not avail itself of that opportunity, it cannot rely on the crisis to justify setting up secret agreements contrary to Article [101(1) TFEU]'. This argument may be understood under the previous legal authorization regime, which required the notification of all agreements conducive to violating what is now Article 101(1) TFEU for Article 101(3) TFEU to enter into play. It is doubtful if such a restrictive interpretation of Article 101(3) TFEU in the circumstances of a crisis cartel will be maintained in a legal exception regime, such as in force since the implementation of Regulation 1/2003.

7.4.2. ARTICLE 101(3)

Communication from the Commission—Guidelines on the applicability of Article 101 TFEU to horizontal co-operation agreements [2011] OJ C 11/1 (footnotes omitted)

Article 101(3)

[. . .]

50. In the area of horizontal co-operation agreements there are block exemption regulations based on Article 101(3) for research and development and specialisation (including joint production) agreements. Those Block Exemption Regulations are based on the premise that the combination of complementary skills or assets can be the source of substantial efficiencies in research and development and specialisation agreements. This may also be the case for other types of horizontal co-operation agreements. The analysis of the efficiencies of an individual agreement under Article 101(3) is therefore to a large extent a question of identifying the complementary skills and assets that each of the parties brings to the agreement and evaluating whether the resulting efficiencies are such that the conditions of Article 101(3) are fulfilled.

51. Complementarities may arise from horizontal co-operation agreements in various ways. A research and development agreement may bring together different research capabilities that allow the parties to produce better products more cheaply and shorten the time for those products to reach the market. A production agreement may allow the parties to achieve economies of scale or scope that they could not achieve individually.

52. Horizontal co-operation agreements that do not involve the combination of complementary skills or assets are less likely to lead to efficiency gains that benefit consumers. Such agreements may reduce duplication of certain costs, for instance because certain fixed costs can be eliminated. However, fixed cost savings are, in general, less likely to result in benefits to consumers than savings in, for instance, variable or marginal costs.

Recognizing the positive effect of certain horizontal cooperation agreements to competition, the Commission adopted two block exemption regulations for the application of Article 101(3) TFEU: Regulation No 1217/2010 of 14 December 2010 on categories of research and development agreements,[138] *Regulation No 1218/2010 on categories of specialization agreements,*[139] *and Guidelines on horizontal cooperation agreements, which in addition to a part presenting the general framework for the application of Article 101 to horizontal agreements include chapters on specific types of agreements: information exchange; research and development agreements; production agreements; purchasing agreements; agreements on commercialization; and standardization agreements. We will briefly summarize the main principles applying to these different types of agreements, with the exception of information exchange examined in Section 7.3.1.5.*

138 Commission Regulation No 1217/2010 of 14 December 2010 on the application of Article 101(3) TFEU to categories of research and development agreements [2010] OJ L 335/36.

139 Commission Regulation No 1218/2010 of 14 December 2010 on the application of Article 101(3) TFEU to categories of specialization agreements [2010] OJ L 335/43 [hereinafter Block Exemption Regulation 1218/2010].

Although the Guidelines are structured according to the different categories of horizontal cooperation agreements, specific provisions are included on mixed horizontal cooperation arrangements, combining different stages of cooperation.

Communication from the Commission—Guidelines on the applicability of Article 101 TFEU to horizontal co-operation agreements [2011] OJ C 11/1 (footnotes omitted)

13. Horizontal co-operation agreements may combine different stages of co-operation, for example research and development ('R&D') and the production and/or commercialisation of its results. Such agreements are generally also covered by these guidelines. When using these guidelines for the analysis of such integrated co-operation, as a general rule, all the chapters pertaining to the different parts of the co-operation will be relevant. However, where the relevant chapters of these guidelines contain graduated messages, for example with regard to safe harbours or whether certain conduct will normally be considered a restriction of competition by object or by effect, what is set out in the chapter pertaining to that part of an integrated co-operation which can be considered its 'centre of gravity' prevails for the entire co-operation.

14. Two factors are in particular relevant for the determination of the centre of gravity of integrated co-operation: firstly, the starting point of the co-operation, and, secondly, the degree of integration of the different functions which are combined. For example, the centre of gravity of a horizontal co-operation agreement involving both joint R&D and joint production of the results would thus normally be the joint R&D, as the joint production will only take place if the joint R&D is successful. This implies that the results of the joint R&D are decisive for the subsequent joint production. The assessment of the centre of gravity would change if the parties would have engaged in the joint production in any event, that is to say, irrespective of the joint R&D, or if the agreement provided for a full integration in the area of production and only a partial integration of some R&D activities. In this case, the centre of gravity of the co-operation would be the joint production.

We will examine in the following sections the regime of specific categories of horizontal cooperation arrangements.

7.4.2.1. Research and development (R&D) agreements

Communication from the Commission—Guidelines on the applicability of Article 101 TFEU to horizontal co-operation agreements [2011] OJ C 11/1 (footnotes omitted)

111. R&D agreements vary in form and scope. They range from outsourcing certain R&D activities to the joint improvement of existing technologies and co-operation concerning the research, development and marketing of completely new products. They may take the form of a co-operation agreement, of a jointly controlled company

> or an arrangement with a research institute or university. This chapter applies to all forms of R&D agreements, including related agreements concerning the production or commercialisation of the R&D results.

R&D agreements may infringe Article 101(1) TFEU, either by object, if they disguise a cartel,[140] or by their effect,[141] by reducing competition on product and technology markets or competition in innovation and new product markets.[142]

The assessment of the effects of the agreement requires the definition of the relevant markets in order to 'identify those products, technologies or R&D efforts that will act as the main competitive constraints on the parties'.[143] At one end of the spectrum of possible situations, the decision maker should assess the effects of the agreement on innovation that may result in a product (or technology) which competes in an existing product (or technology) market. At the other end, the focus may be on the effects of the agreement on innovation that may result in an entirely new product which creates its own new product market.[144] The calculation of market shares in each of these cases will be different. For product markets, market shares are calculated on the basis of the sales value of the existing products. For technology markets, one should calculate market shares 'on the basis of each technology's share of total licensing income from royalties, representing a technology's share of the market where competing technologies are licensed'.[145] Because of the absence of clear information on royalties or the use of royalty free cross-licensing, this method may not always work and hence the Commission adopts an alternative approach relying on the sales of products or services incorporating the licensed technology on downstream product markets.[146] As it explained in the Guidelines, '[u]nder that approach all sales on the relevant product markets are taken into account, irrespective of whether the product incorporates technology that is being licensed'.[147] The nature of the cooperation also plays a significant role.[148]

If the agreement is found to infringe Article 101(1) TFEU, it may be exempt if it falls within the scope of Regulation 1217/2010. The Regulation defines R&D agreements (Article 1) and grants them exemption from the application of Article 101(1) TFEU provided they meet certain conditions (Articles 2–4). The benefit of the exemption is excluded for the whole agreement if it includes a 'hardcore restriction' (Article 5). Some 'excluded restrictions' in an agreement may not benefit from the exemption, although the Regulation may continue to apply to the rest of the agreement (Article 6).

Regulation 1217/2010 covers only 'research and development' agreements. These are defined in Article 1(1)(a) and include

> an agreement entered into between two or more parties which relates to the conditions under which those parties pursue:
>
> (i) joint research and development of contract products or contract technologies and joint exploitation of the results of that research and development;

140 Horizontal Guidelines, para 128. 141 Ibid, paras 129–40. 142 Ibid, para 127.
143 Ibid, para 112. 144 Ibid. 145 Ibid, paras 123–4. 146 Ibid, para 125.
147 Ibid, para 125. 148 Ibid, paras 129–39.

(ii) joint exploitation of the results of research and development of contract products or contract technologies jointly carried out pursuant to a prior agreement between the same parties;

(iii) joint research and development of contract products or contract technologies excluding joint exploitation of the results;

(iv) paid-for research and development of contract products or contract technologies and joint exploitation of the results of that research and development;

(v) joint exploitation of the results of paid-for research and development of contract products or contract technologies pursuant to a prior agreement between the same parties; or

(vi) paid-for research and development of contract products or contract technologies excluding joint exploitation of the results.[149]

These agreements benefit from an exemption whose contours are described in Articles 2–4 of Regulation 1217/2010 and which applies to 'research and development agreements containing provisions which relate to the assignment or licensing of intellectual property rights to one or more of the parties or to an entity the parties establish to carry out the joint research and development, paid-for research and development or joint exploitation, provided that those provisions do not constitute the primary object of such agreements, but are directly related to and necessary for their implementation'.[150] Article 2(2) sets the boundaries between the scope of Regulation 1217/2010 and Regulation 316/2014 on the Transfer of Technology.[151] Licensing agreements are covered by Regulation 1217/2010 only to the extent that they are ancillary to a specialization agreement, which involves as was indicated in Article 1(1)(a) Regulation 1217/2010 obligations (unilateral or reciprocal) to purchase the products resulting from the specialization agreement. According to Article 3 of Regulation 1217/2010, the exemption applies subject to a number of conditions, including that 'the research and development agreement must stipulate that all the parties have full access to the final results of the joint research and development or paid-for research and development, including any resulting intellectual property rights and know-how, for the purposes of further research and development and exploitation, as soon as they become available' and that 'research and development agreement may foresee that the parties compensate each other for giving access to the results for the purposes of further research or exploitation, but the compensation must not be so high as to effectively impede such access'. The R&D Block Exemption Regulation also provides for a specific exception to the rule that all the parties should have full access to the final results of the joint R&D development or paid for R&D in the case of academic bodies, research institutes or specialized companies which provide R&D as a service and which are not active in the industrial exploitation of the results of R&D.

Different conditions apply to agreements between competitors or agreements between non-competitors. Article 4(1) applies to agreements between non-competitors, while Article 4(2) applies to agreements between competitors.

149 Commission Regulation No 1217/2010 of 14 December 2010 on the application of Article 101(3) TFEU to categories of research and development agreements [2010] OJ L 335/36.

150 Ibid, Article 2(2).

151 See further Chapter 13.

Commission Regulation No 1217/2010 of 14 December 2010 on the application of Article 101(3) TFEU to categories of research and development agreements [2010] OJ L 335/36

Article 4

Market share threshold and duration of exemption

1. Where the parties are not competing undertakings, the exemption provided for in Article 2 shall apply for the duration of the research and development. Where the results are jointly exploited, the exemption shall continue to apply for 7 years from the time the contract products or contract technologies are first put on the market within the internal market.

2. Where two or more of the parties are competing undertakings, the exemption provided for in Article 2 shall apply for the period referred to in paragraph 1 of this Article only if, at the time the research and development agreement is entered into:

(a) in the case of research and development agreements referred to in point (a)(i), (ii) or (iii) of Article 1(1), the combined market share of the parties to a research and development agreement does not exceed 25 % on the relevant product and technology markets; or

(b) in the case of research and agreements referred to in point (a)(iv), (v) or (vi) of Article 1(1), the combined market share of the financing party and all the parties with which the financing party has entered into research and development agreements with regard to the same contract products or contract technologies, does not exceed 25 % on the relevant product and technology markets.

3. After the end of the period referred to in paragraph 1, the exemption shall continue to apply as long as the combined market share of the parties does not exceed 25 % on the relevant product and technology markets.

Agreements that contain hardcore restrictions are nevertheless excluded from the benefit of the exemption.

Commission Regulation No 1217/2010 of 14 December 2010 on the application of Article 101(3) TFEU to categories of research and development agreements [2010] OJ L 335/36

Article 5

Hardcore restrictions

The exemption provided for in Article 2 shall not apply to research and development agreements which, directly or indirectly, in isolation or in combination with other factors under the control of the parties, have as their object any of the following:

(a) the restriction of the freedom of the parties to carry out research and development independently or in cooperation with third parties in a field unconnected with that to which the research and development agreement relates or, after the completion of the joint research and development or the paid-for research and development, in the field to which it relates or in a connected field;

(b) the limitation of output or sales, with the exception of: (i) the setting of production targets where the joint exploitation of the results includes the joint production of the contract products; (ii) the setting of sales targets where the joint exploitation of the results includes the joint distribution of the contract products or the joint licensing of the contract technologies within the meaning of point (m)(i) or (ii) of Article 1(1); (iii) practices constituting specialisation in the context of exploitation; and (iv) the restriction of the freedom of the parties to manufacture, sell, assign, or license products, technologies, or processes which compete with the contract products or contract technologies during the period for which the parties have agreed to jointly exploit the results;

(c) the fixing of prices when selling the contract product or licensing the contract technologies to third parties, with the exception of the fixing of prices charged to immediate customers or the fixing of licence fees charged to immediate licensees where the joint exploitation of the results includes the joint distribution of the contract products or the joint licensing of the contract technologies within the meaning of point (m)(i) or (ii) of Article 1(1);

(d) the restriction of the territory in which, or of the customers to whom, the parties may passively sell the contract products or license the contract technologies, with the exception of the requirement to exclusively license the results to another party;

(e) the requirement not to make any, or to limit, active sales of the contract products or contract technologies in territories or to customers which have not been exclusively allocated to one of the parties by way of specialisation in the context of exploitation;

(f) the requirement to refuse to meet demand from customers in the parties' respective territories, or from customers otherwise allocated between the parties by way of specialisation in the context of exploitation, who would market the contract products in other territories within the internal market;

(g) the requirement to make it difficult for users or resellers to obtain the contract products from other resellers within the internal market.

Furthermore, although the inclusion of 'excluded restrictions' in a R&D agreement will not lead to the exclusion of the benefit of the exemption for the whole agreement, according to Article 6 of Regulation 1217/2010, specific clauses will not benefit from the exemption (excluded restrictions). Issues may arise as to whether what is left in the agreement suffices to found a defence of force majeure or similar doctrine under the relevant national law.

Commission Regulation No 1217/2010 of 14 December 2010 on the application of Article 101(3) TFEU to categories of research and development agreements [2010] OJ L 335/36

Article 6

Excluded restrictions

The exemption provided for in Article 2 shall not apply to the following obligations contained in research and development agreements:

(a) the obligation not to challenge after completion of the research and development the validity of intellectual property rights which the parties hold in the internal market and which are relevant to the research and development or, after the expiry of the research and development agreement, the validity of intellectual property rights which the parties hold in the internal market and which protect the results of the research and development, without prejudice to the possibility to provide for termination of the research and development agreement in the event of one of the parties challenging the validity of such intellectual property rights;

(b) the obligation not to grant licences to third parties to manufacture the contract products or to apply the contract technologies unless the agreement provides for the exploitation of the results of the joint research and development or paid-for research and development by at least one of the parties and such exploitation takes place in the internal market vis-à-vis third parties.

If the R&D agreement does not benefit from the block exemption regulation, it is assessed under the four conditions of Article 101(3) TFEU. The Commission's horizontal cooperation guidelines discuss the application of each of these conditions in detail.[152] According to the Commission's Guidelines it is unlikely that agreements including the hardcore restrictions enumerated in Article 5 of Regulation 1217/2010 may satisfy the indispensability condition of Article 101(3) TFEU.[153] The Guidance takes an economic perspective advocating an *ex ante* approach that would consider the incentives of the parties to invest.

Communication from the Commission—Guidelines on the applicability of Article 101 TFEU to horizontal co-operation agreements [2011] OJ C 11/1 (footnotes omitted)

145. [. . .] When applying Article 101(3) in accordance with those principles it is necessary to take into account the initial sunk investments made by any of the parties and the time needed and the restraints required for making and recouping an efficiency enhancing investment. Article 101 cannot be applied without taking due account of such *ex ante* investment. The risk facing the parties and the sunk investment that must be made to implement the agreement can thus lead to the agreement falling outside Article 101(1) or fulfilling the conditions of Article 101(3), as the case may be, for the period of time needed to recoup the investment. Should the invention resulting from the investment benefit from any form of exclusivity granted to the parties under rules specific to the protection of intellectual property rights, the recoupment period for such an investment will generally be unlikely to exceed the exclusivity period established under those rules.

Note that the Commission takes into account only the period of time needed to recoup the investment, which may appear narrow, as one may argue that we should also take into account

152 Horizontal Guidelines, paras 141–9.

153 Ibid, para 142.

the period which, after allowing for the recoupment for the risk of investment, was necessary in order to induce the investment.[154]

7.4.2.2. Production agreements

The Commission adopted specific rules for 'production agreements' too. This category includes a large array of agreements.

Communication from the Commission—Guidelines on the applicability of Article 101 TFEU to horizontal co-operation agreements [2011] OJ C 11/1 (footnotes omitted)

150. Production agreements vary in form and scope. They can provide that production is carried out by only one party or by two or more parties. Companies can produce jointly by way of a joint venture, that is to say, a jointly controlled company operating one or several production facilities or by looser forms of co-operation in production such as subcontracting agreements where one party (the 'contractor') entrusts to another party (the 'subcontractor') the production of a good.

151. There are different types of subcontracting agreements. Horizontal subcontracting agreements are concluded between companies operating in the same product market irrespective of whether they are actual or potential competitors. Vertical subcontracting agreements are concluded between companies operating at different levels of the market.

152. Horizontal subcontracting agreements comprise unilateral and reciprocal specialisation agreements as well as subcontracting agreements with a view to expanding production. Unilateral specialisation agreements are agreements between two parties which are active on the same product market or markets, by virtue of which one party agrees to fully or partly cease production of certain products or to refrain from producing those products and to purchase them from the other party, which agrees to produce and supply the products. Reciprocal specialisation agreements are agreements between two or more parties which are active on the same products market or markets, by virtue of which two or more parties agree, on a reciprocal basis, to fully or partly cease or refrain from producing certain but different products and to purchase those products from the other parties, which agree to produce and supply them. In the case of subcontracting agreements with a view to expanding production the contractor entrusts the subcontractor with the production of a good, while the contractor does not at the same time cease or limit its own production of the good.

With regard to the application of Article 101(3) TFEU some of these agreements enter into the scope of the Block Exemption Regulation 1218/2010 of 14 December 2010 on the application of Article 101(3) TFEU to certain categories of specialization

154 On the importance of reward and incentives in promoting innovation, see Chapter 13.

agreements,[155] while some vertical sub-contracting agreements at different stages of the market may fall under the vertical Guidelines or the Notice on sub-contracting agreements.[156]

The main competitive concerns raised by these agreements consist in:

- restricting competition between the parties, as parties directly align output levels and quality, the price at which the joint venture sells on its products, or other competitively important parameters;[157]
- Coordinating parties' behaviour to the extent parties dispose of market power and the market characteristics are conducive to such coordination. For instance, production agreement may increase the parties' commonality of costs (that is to say, the proportion of variable costs which the parties have in common) to a degree which enables them to achieve a collusive outcome.[158] Yet, as the Commission notes in its Guidelines, '[c]ommonality of costs increases the risk of a collusive outcome only if only if production costs constitute a large proportion of the variable costs concerned'.[159]
- It is also possible that a production agreement can give rise to restrictive effects on competition if it involves an exchange of commercially strategic information which can lead to a collusive outcome or anti-competitive foreclosure. Yet, the Guidelines observe that '[w]hether the exchange of information in the context of a production agreement is likely to lead to restrictive effects on competition should be assessed according to the guidance given in Chapter 2 [of the Horizontal Guidelines]'.[160]
- Anti-competitive foreclosure of third parties in a related market. For instance, by engaging in joint production in an upstream market the parties may gain enough market power to be able to raise the price of a key component for a market downstream, thus using the joint production to follow a raising rival's cost strategy against their rivals downstream and, ultimately, force them off the market, thus increasing their market power downstream and enabling them to sustain prices above the competitive level or otherwise harm consumers. However, the Guidelines note that 'for this kind of foreclosure to have anti-competitive effects, at least one of the parties must have a strong market position in the market where the risks of foreclosure are assessed'.[161]

These agreements may restrict competition by their object or effect, and consequently be prohibited by Article 101(1) TFEU, unless exempted individually or by group exemption. However, it is noted that although agreements which involve price-fixing, limiting output, or sharing markets or customers restrict competition by object, in the context of production agreements this does not apply where 'the parties agree on the output directly concerned by the production agreement' (for instance, the capacity and production volume of a joint venture or the agreed amount of outsourced products), as long as the other parameters of competition are not eliminated; or where 'a production agreement that also

155 Block Exemption Regulation 1218/2010.

156 See Horizontal Guidelines, para 153. See further Chapter 10.

157 Horizontal Guidelines, para 157. 158 Ibid, para 158. 159 Ibid, para 178.

160 Ibid, para 181. 161 Ibid, para 159.

provides for the joint distribution of the jointly manufactured products envisages the joint setting of the sales prices for those products, and only those products, provided that that restriction is necessary for producing jointly, meaning that the parties would not otherwise have an incentive to enter into the production agreement in the first place'.[162]

The first step in the assessment of anti-competitive effects consists in defining the relevant market.[163] Then, the decision-maker should assess the likely anti-competitive effects, including a number of parameters.[164] The approach followed involves the performance of a counter-factual test and the consideration of the nature of the agreement, as well as its likely effects.[165]

Concerning the application of Article 101(3) TFEU, the Block Exemption Regulation 1218/2010 applies to three types of specialization agreements, unilateral specialization agreements, reciprocal specialization agreements, and joint production agreements.[166] The scope of BER 1218/2010 is defined in Articles 1 and 2. Article 3 includes the market share threshold (cap), the exemption applying on condition that the combined market share of the parties does not exceed 20 per cent on any relevant market, Article 4 lists the hardcore restrictions (the fixing of prices when selling the products to third parties, the limitation of output or sales with some exceptions and the allocation of markets or customers). Article 5 explains the calculation of the market share threshold. Note that according to Article 2(2) of Regulation 1218/2010, the assignment or licensing of IP rights is covered by the exemption only to the extent that it is ancillary to a specialization agreement. If it is the primary object of the agreement, it would need to fall under the scope of Regulation 316/2014 on the Transfer of Technology[167] in order to be exempt.

If the agreement is not covered by the Block Exemption Regulation, there is still the possibility for an individual application of Article 101(3) TFEU. The Commission's Horizontal Guidelines describe the individual assessment. Production agreements enabling undertakings to put together their technologies may provide efficiency gains in the form of cost savings or better production technologies, reducing their marginal costs, bringing economies of scale, increasing product variety, and improving product quality.[168] However, the restrictions of competition included in the agreement should be indispensable: for instance, if the restrictions imposed relate to output outside the co-operation, these will

162 Ibid, paras 160–1 (the Commission noting that in these two cases the agreement on output or prices 'will not be assessed separately, but in the light of the overall effects of the entire production agreement on the market').

163 Ibid, paras 155–6. 164 Ibid, paras 162–82. 165 Ibid, paras 163 and 167.

166 According to Article 1(1) of Regulation 1218/2010 on the application of Article 101(3) of the Treaty on the Functioning of the European Union to certain categories of specialisation agreements [2010] OJ L 335/43, 'unilateral specialisation agreement' is 'an agreement between two parties which are active on the same product market by virtue of which one party agrees to fully or partly cease production of certain products or to refrain from producing those products and to purchase them from the other party, who agrees to produce and supply those products', a 'reciprocal specialisation agreement' constitutes 'an agreement between two or more parties which are active on the same product market, by virtue of which two or more parties on a reciprocal basis agree to fully or partly cease or refrain from producing certain but different products and to purchase these products from the other parties, who agree to produce and supply them', and a 'joint production agreement' means 'an agreement by virtue of which two or more parties agree to produce certain products jointly'.

167 Commission Regulation No 316/2014 of 21 March 2014 on the application of Article 101(3) TFEU to categories of technology transfer agreements [2014] OJ L 93/17. See further Chapter 13.

168 Horizontal Guidelines, para 183.

normally not be considered to be indispensable; likewise for setting prices jointly when the production agreement does not involve joint commercialization.[169] The efficiency gains must be passed on to consumers in the form of lower prices or better product quality or variety to an extent outweighing the restriction of competition[170] and without eliminating competition in respect of a substantial part of the products in question.[171]

7.4.2.3. Purchasing agreements

Competing undertakings may also conclude agreements for the joint purchase of products. These can take different forms: they 'can be carried out by a jointly controlled company, by a company in which many other companies hold non-controlling stakes, by a contractual arrangement or by even looser forms of co-operation (collectively referred to as "joint purchasing arrangements")', the later agreements usually aiming 'at the creation of buying power which can lead to lower prices or better quality products or services for consumers'.[172] One form of joint purchasing agreement is an 'alliance', which is an association of undertakings formed by a group of retailers for the joint purchasing of products.[173]

Joint purchasing arrangements were assessed under Article 101(1) TFEU by the CJEU in *Gøttrup-Klim* regarding an agricultural cooperative purchasing association that forbade its members to participate in other forms of organized cooperation which were in direct competition with it.

Case C-250/92, *Gøttrup-Klim ea Grovvareforeninger v Dansk Landbrugs Grovvareselskab AmbA*
[1994] ECR I–5641

The case involved a preliminary reference from a Danish court for questions of EU law arising out of proceedings between, as plaintiffs, a number of local cooperative associations specializing in the distribution of farm supplies and, as a defendant, DLG, a Danish cooperative association distributing farm supplies. The main proceedings concerned the compatibility with Article 101 TFEU of an amendment made by DLG to its statutes, which allegedly led to the exclusion of the plaintiffs. The claimants were members of DLG, before being excluded from it. Indeed, dissatisfied with the prices charged by DLG on the sale of fertilizers and plant protection products, the claimants took the initiative and began themselves to cooperate in order to import those products, forming another cooperative association, named LAG. By amending its statutes, DLG sought to prohibit any of its members to participate in, associations, societies or other forms of cooperative organization in competition with it on the wholesale market, with regard to the purchase and sale of fertilizers and plant protection products, practically expelling the local cooperatives participating in LAG. The expelled local cooperatives brought an action before a Danish court against DLG, arguing that by closing the Danish market to a wide variety of foreign suppliers, the amendment to DLG's statutes is contrary to Articles 101 and 102 TFEU.

169 Ibid, para 184. 170 Ibid, para 185. 171 Ibid, para 186. 172 Ibid, para 194.
173 Ibid, para 196.

28. In the second set of questions, the national court seeks to ascertain whether a provision in the statutes of a cooperative purchasing association, the effect of which is to forbid its members to participate in other forms of organized cooperation which are in direct competition with it, is caught by the prohibition in Article [101(1) TFEU].

29. The plaintiffs in the main proceedings claim that the object or effect of such an amendment to the statutes is to restrict competition, inasmuch as the objective pursued was to put an end to 'B' members purchasing through LAG in competition with DLG, and thus to acquire a dominant position on the markets concerned.

30. A cooperative purchasing association is a voluntary association of persons established in order to pursue common commercial objectives.

31. The compatibility of the statutes of such an association with the Community rules on competition cannot be assessed in the abstract. It will depend on the particular clauses in the statutes and the economic conditions prevailing on the markets concerned.

32. In a market where product prices vary according to the volume of orders, the activities of cooperative purchasing associations may, depending on the size of their membership, constitute a significant counterweight to the contractual power of large producers and make way for more effective competition.

33. Where some members of two competing cooperative purchasing associations belong to both at the same time, the result is to make each association less capable of pursuing its objectives for the benefit of the rest of its members, especially where the members concerned, as in the case in point, are themselves cooperative associations with a large number of individual members.

34. It follows that such dual membership would jeopardize both the proper functioning of the cooperative and its contractual power in relation to producers. Prohibition of dual membership does not, therefore, necessarily constitute a restriction of competition within the meaning of Article [101(1) TFEU] and may even have beneficial effects on competition.

35. Nevertheless, a provision in the statutes of a cooperative purchasing association, restricting the opportunity for members to join other types of competing cooperatives and thus discouraging them from obtaining supplies elsewhere, may have adverse effects on competition. So, in order to escape the prohibition laid down in Article [101(1) TFEU], the restrictions imposed on members by the statutes of cooperative purchasing associations must be limited to what is necessary to ensure that the cooperative functions properly and maintains its contractual power in relation to producers.

36. The particular features of the case at issue in the main proceedings, which are referred to in the questions submitted by the national court, must be assessed in the light of the foregoing considerations. In addition, it is necessary to establish whether the penalties for non-compliance with the statutes are disproportionate to the objective they pursue and whether the minimum period of membership is unreasonable.

37. First of all, the amendment of DLG's statutes is restricted so as to cover only fertilizers and plant protection products, the only farm supplies in respect of which a direct relationship exists between sales volume and price.

38. Furthermore, even after DLG has amended its statutes and excluded the plaintiffs, it is open to 'non-members' of the association, including the plaintiffs, to buy from it the whole range of products which it sells, including fertilizers and plant protection products, on the same commercial terms and at the same prices as members, except that 'non-members' are obviously not entitled to receive a yearly discount on the amount of the transactions carried out.

39. Finally, DLG's statutes authorize its members to buy fertilizers and plant protection products without using DLG as an intermediary, provided that such transactions are carried out otherwise than through an organized consortium. In that context, each member acts individually or in association with others but, in the latter case, only in making a one-off common purchase of a particular consignment or shipload.

40. Taking all those factors into account, it would not seem that restrictions laid down in the statutes, of the kind imposed on DLG members, go beyond what is necessary to ensure that the cooperative functions properly and maintains its contractual power in relation to producers.

41. As regards the penalties imposed on the plaintiffs as a result of their exclusion for infringing DLG's rules, these would not appear to be disproportionate, since DLG has treated the plaintiffs as if they were members exercising their right to withdraw.

42. So far as concerns the membership period, this has been reduced from ten to five years, which does not seem unreasonable.

43. It is significant, in the last analysis, that after their exclusion, the plaintiffs succeeded, through LAG, in competing vigorously with DLG, with the result that in 1990 their market share was similar to DLG's.

44. The other matters mentioned in the second set of questions referred by the national court are not such as to affect the analysis of the problem.

45. The answer to the second set of questions referred by the national court must therefore be that a provision in the statutes of a cooperative purchasing association, forbidding its members to participate in other forms of organized cooperation which are in direct competition with it, is not caught by the prohibition in Article [101(1) TFEU], so long as the abovementioned provision is restricted to what is necessary to ensure that the cooperative functions properly and maintains its contractual power in relation to producers.

NOTES AND QUESTIONS ON GØTTRUP-KLIM

1. The CJEU also found that even if the cooperative purchasing association holds a dominant position on a given market, an amendment of its statutes prohibiting its members from participating in other forms of organized cooperation which are in direct competition with it does not constitute an abuse of a dominant position contrary to Article 102 TFEU, so long as the abovementioned provision is limited to what is necessary to ensure that the cooperative functions properly and maintains its contractual power in relation to producers.[174] Indeed, the CJEU recognized that cooperative purchasing associations may encourage more effective competition on some markets.
2. In *Coberco*, the CJEU also considered a combination of clauses in the statutes of cooperative associations in the agricultural sector requiring exclusive supply and payment of excessive fees on withdrawal, thus tying the members to the association for long periods and thereby depriving them of the possibility of approaching competitors.[175] The CJEU referred to *Gøttrup-Klim,* noting that 'the restrictions imposed on members by the statutes of cooperative associations intended to secure their loyalty

[174] Case C-250/92, *Gøttrup-Klim ea Grovvareforeninger v Dansk Landbrugs Grovvareselskab AmbA* [1994] ECR I-5641, para 52.

[175] Case C-399/93, *HG Oude Luttikhuis and Others & Verenigde Coöperatieve Melkindustrie Coberco BA (Coberco)* [1995] ECR I-4520.

must be limited to what is necessary to ensure that the cooperative functions properly and in particular to ensure that it has *a sufficiently wide commercial base and a certain stability in its membership*'.[176] The CJEU considered that national courts must take into account, before reaching a decision as to the compatibility of such practices to Article 101(1) TFEU, 'the object of the agreement providing for such fees, the effects of that agreement and whether it affects intra-Community trade, taking into account the economic context in which the undertakings operate, the products or services covered by the agreement, the structure of the market concerned and the actual conditions in which it functions'.[177] Valentine Korah notes that the rumour around the Court at the time was that *Coberco* was a good chance to undermine *Gøttrup-Klim*. Note also the *Dutch cheese* purchasing agreement, where a cooperative of producers in the diary sector which required all its members to buy exclusively cheese from each other. The Commission with its decision[178] condemned this agreement on the basis that the members of the cooperative accounted for over 90 per cent of the Dutch market, this provision having the object and the effect of helping to preserve a non-competitive structure in this market. The decision was also upheld by the Court of Justice.[179]

3. The General Court also examined a joint purchasing arrangement in *Métropole v Commission*, regarding Métropole's complaint about the European Broadcasting Union's (EBU) practices concerning the acquisition of TV rights to sporting events.[180] Following the development of pay-TV in the 1980s and its reliance on premium content, such as sports, public broadcasters reacted and formed the EBU in order to join forces for the acquisition of sports broadcasting rights.[181] The EBU rejected Métropole's membership request several times.

While its rules on the acquisition of TV rights to sporting events were notified to the Commission and exempted, the Commission's decision was annulled by the General Court on appeal by Métropole.[182] The Commission's revised *Eurovision* decision[183] was again challenged by Métropole in the GC.[184] The controversy concerned the importance granted by the Commission in assessing the EBU's rules under Article 101(3) TFEU to the sub-licensing scheme included in the EBU's rules, which granted access to Eurovision rights to major sporting events to third parties, competitors of EBU members. Because of this sub-licensing scheme, the Commission found that there was not a substantial restriction of competition and thus the EBU rules satisfied the fourth condition of Article 101(3) TFEU. Métropole disagreed.

While the GC acknowledged that purchase of televised rights for an event is not in itself a restriction of competition and may be justified by particular characteristics of the product or the market, the acquisition of exclusive TV rights to certain major

176 Ibid, para 14 (emphasis added). 177 Ibid, para 20.

178 *Rennet* (Case COMP IV/29.011) Commission Decision 80/234/EEC [1980] OJ L 51/19.

179 Case C-61/80, *Coöperatieve Stremsel- en Kleurselfabriek v Commission* [1981] ECR 851.

180 Joined Cases T-185, 216, 299 & 300/00, *Métropole Télévision SA (M6) and Others v Commission* [2002] ECR II-3805.

181 B Van Rompuy and K Donders, 'The EBU's Eurovision System Governing the Joint Buying of Sports Broadcasting Rights: Unfinished Competition Business' (2013) 9(1) *Competition Law Rev* 7.

182 Cases T-528, 542, 543 & 546/93 *Métropole Télévision SA (M6) & others v Commission* [1996] ECR II–649.

183 *Eurovision* (Case IV/32.150) Commission Decision 2000/400/EC [2000] OJ L 151/18.

184 Joined Cases T-185, 216, 299 & 300/00, *Métropole Télévision SA (M6) and Others v Commission* [2002] ECR II-3805.

sporting events may have a strong impact on the downstream television markets on which the sporting events are broadcast, as well as the market in sponsorship and advertising, which is the main source of revenue for TV channels which broadcast free-to-air.[185] These effects were 'accentuated' in this case by the level of vertical integration of the EBU and its members (as these were buyers of TV rights but also TV operators broadcasting the rights purchased) and the geographic extent of the EBU, whose members broadcast in all the countries of the EU.[186] Hence, 'when the EBU acquired transmission rights for an international sporting event, the access to that event is in principle automatically precluded for all non-member operators'.[187] In view, however, of the sub-licensing scheme committing the EBU and its members to grant non-member broadcasters access to Eurovision sports programmes for which the rights had been acquired through collective negotiations the GC examined whether third-party access to the Eurovision system counterbalanced the restrictions on competition and avoided their exclusion from competition.[188]

Exploring the sub-licensing scheme, the GC found, however, that, in practice, an EBU member need only reserve the live transmission of the majority of the competitions of an event for non-members competing for the same market to be refused sub-licences for live transmission of the entire event, including competitions in that event which no EBU member will transmit live.[189] Nothing in the rules and modes of implementation of the scheme enabled competitors of EBU members to obtain sub-licences for the live broadcast of unused Eurovision rights. The GC concluded even if the exclusivity from which benefit the members of the EBU in transmitting live the programmes purchased by it was necessary in order to guarantee the economic value of a given sports programme in terms of viewing figures and advertising revenues, none of these reasons justified the extension of that right to all the competitions which are part of the same event.[190] Although the Commission's decision was again annulled, a third decision was never issued and the European Commission closed the case observing that the EBU had lost significant buying power as it was no longer the sole buyer of premium international sports rights, as rights owners tend to diversify the sale pattern of their media rights.[191]

4. The issue of collective buying of premium international sports rights attracted attention aagain following the judgment of the CJEU in *Football Association Premier League*.[192] The CJEU found that the contractual provision with which Premier League prevented broadcasters, which acquired the rights, from offering services to subscribers outside the Member State for which they held the licence prohibited the broadcasters from effecting any cross-border provision of services that related to those matches and thus enabled all competition between broadcasters in the field of those services to be eliminated.[193] The CJEU, however, did not call into question the actual grant of exclusive licences for the broadcasting of Premier League matches.[194]

185 Ibid, paras 64–5. 186 Ibid, para 67. 187 Ibid. 188 Ibid, para 68.
189 Ibid, para 71. 190 Ibid, para 73.
191 Commission, *Report on Competition Policy 2007* (2008), 114.
192 Joined Cases C-403 & 429/08, *Football Association Premier League Ltd and Karen Murphy* [2011] ECR I-9083. The case is also examined in Chapter 10.
193 Joined Cases C-403 & 429/08, *Football Association Premier League Ltd and Karen Murphy* [2011] ECR I-9083, para 142.
194 Ibid, para 141.

Importantly, the judgment addressed only the anti-competitive object of the contractual territorial protection clauses. The CJEU did not call into question the principle of granting exclusive licences.

This case law may lead to some rethinking of the implementation of competition law to joint purchasing arrangements involving the broadcasting of sports. As B van Rompuy and K Donders note '[. . .] the appraisal of the joint acquisition of sports rights by the EBU will always be tied to deliberations about broad and free access to the broadcasting of major international sports events. This necessarily involves a balancing exercise between economic considerations and broader public interest considerations.'[195] The same authors observe that '[t]he acquisition of exclusive broadcasting rights to a certain major sporting event (such as the Olympic Games or the FIFA World Cup) strongly impacts the downstream markets in sponsorship and advertising, which is the main source of income for free-to-air TV. Because of the widespread appeal and the economic importance of the international sporting events addressed by the Eurovision system, the Commission made clear that any restriction on the acquisition, sharing or exchange of the Eurovision rights among the European broadcasters will *de facto* be appreciable under the purposes of Article 101(1) TFEU'.[196] Although, the authors note that 'the EBU sublicensing rules in their current format no longer provide that an event is considered to be transmitted live when the majority of the principal competitions constituting it are transmitted live', risks of foreclosure of third-parties still exist, as all depends on the implementation of sublicensing systems in a way that grants access to third-parties.[197]

There is no block exemption regulation for joint purchasing arrangements. The Commission's Horizontal Guidelines explain their assessment under Articles 101(1) and 101(3) TFEU.

If joint purchasing arrangements involve both horizontal and vertical agreements, a two-step analysis will be necessary. First, the competition authorities should assess the horizontal agreements between the companies engaging in joint purchasing according to the principles of the Commission's Horizontal Guidelines and only if that assessment leads to the conclusion that the joint purchasing arrangement does not give rise to competition concerns, a further assessment will be necessary to examine the relevant vertical agreements, according to the rules of the Block Exemption Regulation on Vertical Restraints and the Guidelines on Vertical Restraints (Chapter 10).[198]

Joint purchasing arrangements may restrict competition by object if they do not truly concern joint purchasing, but serve as a tool to engage in a disguised cartel.[199] This may, for instance, be the case for arrangements involving the fixing of selling prices. However, with regard to the fixing of purchase prices, the Commission notes in its Guidelines that the principle that agreements which involve the fixing of purchase prices can have the object of restricting competition

> [. . .] does not apply where the parties to a joint purchasing arrangement agree on the purchasing prices the joint purchasing arrangement may pay to its suppliers for the products subject to the supply contract. In that case an assessment is required as to whether the

[195] B Van Rompuy and K Donders, 'The EBU's Eurovision System Governing the Joint Buying of Sports Broadcasting Rights: Unfinished Competition Business' (2013) 9(1) *Competition L Rev* 7, 23.

[196] Ibid, 26. [197] Ibid, 27. [198] Horizontal Guidelines, para 195. [199] Ibid, para 205.

agreement is likely to give rise to restrictive effects on competition within the meaning of Article 101(1). In both scenarios the agreement on purchase prices will not be assessed separately, but in the light of the overall effects of the purchasing agreement on the market.

With regard to anti-competitive effects, joint purchasing arrangements may affect two markets: (i) the market or markets with which the joint purchasing arrangement is directly concerned (the relevant purchasing market or markets); (ii) the market or markets downstream where the parties to the joint purchasing arrangement are active as sellers (the selling market or markets).[200] For purchasing markets, substitutability has to be defined from the viewpoint of supply and not from the viewpoint of demand. The decision-maker should thus analyse the suppliers' alternatives in order to identify the competitive constraints on purchasers, for instance, by examining the suppliers' reaction to a small but non-transitory price decrease.[201] Selling markets should be defined following the approach in the Market Definition Notice of the European Commission.[202] If the parties to the joint purchasing agreement are competitors on one or more selling markets, those markets are also relevant for the assessment.[203]

Joint purchasing arrangements may produce restrictive effects on competition on the purchasing and/or downstream selling market or markets, such as increased prices, reduced output, product quality or variety, or innovation, market allocation, or anti-competitive foreclosure of other possible purchasers.[204] This depends on the existence of significant selling or buying power. First, if the parties have a significant degree of market power (even below dominance) on the selling market or markets, the lower purchase prices achieved by the joint purchasing arrangement are likely not to be passed on to consumers.[205] Second, if the parties have a significant degree of market power on the purchasing market (buying power) there is a risk that they may force suppliers to reduce the range or quality of products they produce, which may bring about restrictive effects on competition such as quality reductions, lessening of innovation efforts, or ultimately sub-optimal supply.[206] Third, buying power of the parties to the joint purchasing arrangement may also be used to foreclose competing purchasers by limiting their access to efficient suppliers, in particular, if there are a limited number of suppliers and there are barriers to entry on the supply side of the upstream market.[207] Yet, buying power is not enough, as in any case the likelihood of anti-competitive effects depends on the market power of the parties to the agreement on the selling market or markets.[208] Fourth, joint purchasing agreements may facilitate the coordination of the parties' behaviour on the selling market(s) and thus lead to collusive outcomes.[209] This can be the case if the parties achieve a high degree of commonality of costs through joint purchasing, provided the parties have market power and the market characteristics are conducive to coordination.[210]

This may also be achieved through an exchange of commercially sensitive information, such as purchase prices and volumes, unless spill-over effects from the exchange of commercially sensitive information, for example, can be minimized through Chinese walls, for instance where data is collated by a joint purchasing arrangement which does not pass on the information to the parties.[211] The Guidelines note, however that any negative effects arising from the exchange of information will not be assessed separately but in the light of the overall effects of the agreement, according to the guidance provided in the section of the Guidelines

200 Ibid, para 197. 201 Ibid, para 198. 202 See Section 3.3.3.
203 Horizontal Guidelines, para 199. 204 Ibid, para 200. 205 Ibid, para 201.
206 Ibid, para 202. 207 Ibid, para 203. 208 Ibid, para 204. 209 Ibid, para 213.
210 Ibid, para 214. 211 Ibid, para 215.

on information exchange agreements. It is, however, indicated that '[i]f the information exchange does not exceed the sharing of data necessary for the joint purchasing of the products by the parties to the joint purchasing arrangement, then even if the information exchange has restrictive effects on competition within the meaning of Article 101(1), the agreement is more likely to meet the criteria of Article 101(3) than if the exchange goes beyond what was necessary for the joint purchasing.'[212]

Note also that joint sales agreements between small competitors, even if outside the group exemption, are unlikely to restrict competition—our comments above on *Coberco* and *Gottrieb Klim*.

The Guidelines also provide a safe harbour for joint purchasing arrangements.

Communication from the Commission—Guidelines on the applicability of Article 101 TFEU to horizontal co-operation agreements [2011] OJ C 11/1

208. There is no absolute threshold above which it can be presumed that the parties to a joint purchasing arrangement have market power so that the joint purchasing arrangement is likely to give rise to restrictive effects on competition within the meaning of Article 101(1). However, in most cases it is unlikely that market power exists if the parties to the joint purchasing arrangement have a combined market share not exceeding 15 % on the purchasing market or markets as well as a combined market share not exceeding 15 % on the selling market or markets. In any event, if the parties' combined market shares do not exceed 15 % on both the purchasing and the selling market or markets, it is likely that the conditions of Article 101(3) are fulfilled.

A joint purchasing arrangement which does not fall within that safe harbour requires a detailed assessment of its effects on the market(s) involving, but not limited to, factors such as market concentration and possible countervailing power of strong suppliers.[213] Anti-competitive buying power is also likely to arise if a joint purchasing arrangement accounts for a sufficiently large proportion of the total volume of a purchasing market so that access to the market may be foreclosed to competing purchasers.[214] Assessing buying power does not only involve the analysis of the parties' market shares in the purchasing side of the market. The Guidelines also note that in the analysis of whether the parties to a joint purchasing arrangement have buying power, account should be taken of the number and intensity of links (for example, other purchasing agreements) between the competitors in the market.[215]

If the joint purchasing arrangement involves the cooperation of competing purchasers who are not active on the same relevant selling market (for example, retailers which are active in different geographic markets aiming with that agreement to gain a better bargaining position vis-à-vis their suppliers and thus cannot be regarded as potential competitors between each other), the joint purchasing arrangement is unlikely to have restrictive effects on competition unless the parties have a position in the purchasing markets that is likely to be used to harm the competitive position of other players in their respective selling markets.[216]

The Horizontal Guidelines also examine the application of the four conditions of Article 101(3). They recognize the efficiency gains that may be brought by joint purchasing

[212] Ibid, para 216. [213] Ibid, para 209. [214] Ibid, para 210. [215] Ibid, para 211.
[216] Ibid, para 212.

arrangements: cost savings such as lower purchase prices or reduced transaction, transportation, and storage costs, qualitative efficiency gains.[217] They accept that an obligation to purchase exclusively through the cooperation may, in certain cases, be indispensable to achieve the necessary volume for the realization of economies of scale.[218] It is also observed, with regard to the requirement that efficiency gains should be passed on to consumers (the parties' customers), that lower purchasing prices resulting from the mere exercise of buying power are not likely to be passed on to consumers if the purchasers together have market power on the selling markets, and thus do not meet the criteria of Article 101(3) TFEU.[219] Finally, the parties should not be afforded the possibility of eliminating competition in respect of a substantial part of the products in question, in both the purchasing and selling markets.

7.4.2.4. Agreements on commercialization

Commercialization agreements, also covered by the Commission's Horizontal Guidelines, involve cooperation between competitors in the selling, distribution, or promotion of their substitute products. This may go from a joint determination of all commercial aspects related to the sale of the product, including price, to more limited agreements that address only one specific commercialization function, such as distribution, after-sales service, or advertising.[220]

The Guidelines also clarify the rules applying to distribution agreements, in this context, as these may also fall within the scope of the Vertical Block Exemption Regulation and Guidelines (Chapter 10).

Communication from the Commission—Guidelines on the applicability of Article 101 TFEU to horizontal co-operation agreements [2011] OJ C 11/1

226. An important category of those more limited agreements is distribution agreements. The Block Exemption Regulation on Vertical Restraints and Guidelines on Vertical Restraints generally covers distribution agreements unless the parties to the agreement are actual or potential competitors. If the parties are competitors, the Block Exemption Regulation on Vertical Restraints covers only non-reciprocal vertical agreements between competitors, if (a) the supplier is a manufacturer and a distributor of goods, while the buyer is a distributor and not a competing undertaking at the manufacturing level or, (b) the supplier is a provider of services at several levels of trade, while the buyer provides its goods or services at the retail level and does not provide competing services at the level of trade where it purchases the contract services.

227. If competitors agree to distribute their substitute products on a reciprocal basis (in particular if they do so on different geographic markets) there is a possibility that the agreements have as their object or effect the partitioning of markets between the parties or that they lead to a collusive outcome. The same can be true for non-reciprocal agreements between competitors. Reciprocal agreements and non-reciprocal agreements between competitors thus have first to be assessed according to the principles set out in this Chapter. If that assessment leads to the conclusion that co-operation between competitors in the area of distribution would in principle be acceptable, a further assessment will be necessary to examine the vertical restraints included in such

217 Ibid, para 217. 218 Ibid, para 218. 219 Ibid, para 219. 220 Ibid, para 225.

> agreements. That second step of the assessment should be based on the principles set out in the Guidelines on Vertical Restraints in chapter 10.
>
> 228. A further distinction should be drawn between agreements where the parties agree only on joint commercialisation and agreements where the commercialisation is related to another type of co-operation upstream, such as joint production or joint purchasing. When analysing commercialisation agreements combining different stages of co-operation it is necessary to determine the centre of gravity of the co-operation [. . .].

This is done according to the principles set in paragraphs 13 and 14 of the Horizontal Guidelines.

Commercialization agreements may give rise to the following theories of harm:

- Price-fixing.[221]
- Commercialization agreements may facilitate output limitation, because the parties may decide on the volume of products to be put on the market, thereby restricting supply.[222]
- They may become a means to divide the markets or allocate orders or customers.[223]
- They may lead to an exchange of strategic information relating to aspects within or outside the scope of the co-operation or to commonality of costs which may result in a collusive outcome.[224]
- A joint commercialization agreement that does not involve price fixing may also give rise to restrictive effects on competition if it increases the parties' commonality of variable costs to a level which is likely to lead to a collusive outcome.[225] Hence, if prior to the agreement the parties already have a high proportion of their variable costs in common, the additional increment emanating from the commercialization costs of the product subject to the agreement can tip the balance towards a collusive outcome. As the Horizontal Guidelines note, the likelihood of a collusive outcome depends on the parties' market power and the characteristics of the relevant market, and increases if the commercialization costs constitute a large proportion of the variable costs related to the products concerned, for instance products which entail costly commercialization, for example, high costs of distribution or marketing.[226]
- Similar concerns about a likely collusive outcome may also result from information exchange among the parties to the agreement. As some degree of information exchange is required in order to implement a commercialization agreement, it is necessary to verify whether the information exchange can give rise to a collusive outcome with regard to the parties' activities within and outside the cooperation, the likely restrictive effects on competition of information exchange depending on the characteristics of the market and the data shared.[227] The assessment should follow the principles applicable to information exchange agreements, examined above.

Agreements limited to joint selling generally have the object of coordinating the pricing policy of competing manufacturers or service providers and are therefore likely to restrict competition by object, irrespective of the fact that the agreement is non-exclusive and the parties are free to sell individually outside the agreement, as

221 Ibid, para 230. 222 Ibid, para 231. 223 Ibid, para 232. 224 Ibid, para 233.
225 Ibid, para 242. 226 Ibid, para 233. 227 Ibid, paras 244–5.

long as it can be concluded that the agreement will lead to overall coordination of the prices charged by the parties.[228] Likewise, distribution arrangements between parties which are active in different geographic markets may become an instrument of market division and thus restrict competition by object.[229] For instance, a reciprocal distribution agreement to distribute each other's products, thus eliminating actual or potential competition between them by deliberately allocating markets or customers, is likely to have as its object a restriction of competition unless the market is very competitive. According to the Horizontal Guidelines, if the agreement is not reciprocal, the risk of market partitioning is less pronounced. However, one should also examine whether the agreement constitutes the basis for a mutual understanding to avoid entering each other's markets.[230]

With regard to the assessment of anti-competitive effects, the Horizontal Guidelines note that this should not only be conducted for the relevant product market(s) directly concerned by the cooperation, but also neighbouring markets, as a commercialization agreement in one market may also affect the competitive behaviour of the parties in a market which is closely related to the market directly concerned by the cooperation, which should also be defined. The neighbouring market may be horizontally or vertically related to the market where the cooperation takes place.[231]

Although they produce restrictive effects in some circumstances commercialization agreements may escape the prohibition of Article 101(1) TFEU.

Communication from the Commission—Guidelines on the applicability of Article 101 TFEU to horizontal co-operation agreements [2011] OJ C 11/1

237. A commercialisation agreement is normally unlikely to give rise to competition concerns if it is objectively necessary to allow one party to enter a market it could not have entered individually or with a more limited number of parties than are effectively taking part in the co-operation, for example, because of the costs involved. A specific application of this principle would be consortia arrangements that allow the companies involved to participate in projects that they would not be able to undertake individually. As the parties to the consortia arrangement are therefore not potential competitors for implementing the project, there is no restriction of competition within the meaning of Article 101(1).

238. Similarly, not all reciprocal distribution agreements have as their object a restriction of competition. Depending on the facts of the case at hand, some reciprocal distribution agreements may, nevertheless, have restrictive effects on competition. The key issue in assessing an agreement of this type is whether the agreement in question is objectively necessary for the parties to enter each other's markets. If it is, the agreement does not create competition problems of a horizontal nature. However, if the agreement reduces the decision-making independence of one of the parties with regard to entering the other parties' market or markets by limiting its incentives to do so, it is likely to give rise to restrictive effects on competition. The same reasoning applies to non-reciprocal agreements, where the risk of restrictive effects on competition is, however, less pronounced.

228 Ibid, paras 234–5. 229 Ibid, para 236. 230 Ibid. 231 Ibid, para 229.

There is no specific Block Exemption Regulation for commercialization agreements. The Commission's Horizontal Guidelines, however, provide for a safe harbour.

Communication from the Commission—Guidelines on the applicability of Article 101 TFEU to horizontal co-operation agreements [2011] OJ C 11/1

> 240. Commercialisation agreements between competitors can only have restrictive effects on competition if the parties have some degree of market power. In most cases, it is unlikely that market power exists if the parties to the agreement have a combined market share not exceeding 15 %. In any event, if the parties' combined market share does not exceed 15 % it is also likely that the conditions of Article 101(3) are fulfilled.

If the commercialization agreement is found to infringe Article 101(1) TFEU and the parties' market share exceeds 15 per cent, it may still be possible to justify the agreement, if it satisfies the four conditions of Article 101(3) TFEU. The Commission notes that commercialization agreements can give rise to significant efficiency gains.[232]

The agreements should of course be indispensable (a condition which can only be satisfied under exceptional circumstances by agreements involving price fixing or market allocation).[233] Efficiency gains should also be passed on to consumers, something that is presumed for agreements between parties disposing of a combined market share of below 15 per cent.[234] Finally, the parties should not be afforded the possibility of eliminating competition either in the relevant market to which the products subject to the cooperation belong or to possible spill-over markets.[235]

7.2.4. STANDARDIZATION AGREEMENTS

This category includes agreements relating to the standardization of technical or quality requirements and agreements relating to standard terms and conditions of sale or purchase.

Communication from the Commission—Guidelines on the applicability of Article 101 TFEU to horizontal co-operation agreements [2011] OJ C 11/1 (footnotes omitted)

> 257. Standardisation agreements have as their primary objective the definition of technical or quality requirements with which current or future products, production processes, services or methods may comply. Standardisation agreements can cover various issues, such as standardisation of different grades or sizes of a particular product or technical specifications in product or services markets where compatibility and interoperability with other products or systems is essential. The terms of access to a particular quality mark or for approval by a regulatory body can also be regarded as a standard. Agreements setting out standards on the environmental performance of products or production processes are also covered by this chapter [. . .].

232 Ibid, paras 246–8. 233 Ibid, para 249. 234 Ibid, para 250. 235 Ibid, para 251.

259. In certain industries companies use standard terms and conditions of sale or purchase elaborated by a trade association or directly by the competing companies ('standard terms'). Such standard terms are covered by these guidelines to the extent that they establish standard conditions of sale or purchase of goods or services between competitors and consumers (and not the conditions of sale or purchase between competitors) for substitute products. When such standard terms are widely used within an industry, the conditions of purchase or sale used in the industry may become *de facto* aligned. Examples of industries in which standard terms play an important role are the banking (for example, bank account terms) and insurance sectors.

260. Standard terms elaborated individually by a company solely for its own use when contracting with its suppliers or customers are not horizontal agreements and are therefore not covered by these guidelines.

The Commission's Horizontal Guidelines note that from an economic perspective 'standardisation agreements usually produce significant positive economic effects', for instance the promotion of economic interpenetration on the EU Internal Market and the development of new and improved products or markets and improved supply conditions.[236] The effects may not be only for the specific parties to the agreement but to 'economies as a whole', in view of the lower output and sales' costs, as well as the maintenance and the enhancement of quality, the provision of information and inter-operability or compatibility, which provide value to the consumers. Yet, they may also produce anti-competitive effects, in particular by potentially restricting price competition and limiting or controlling production, markets, innovation or technical development.[237] The Horizontal Guidelines identify the following theories of harm/anti-competitive scenarios:

- If companies were to engage in anti-competitive discussions in the context of standard-setting, this could reduce or eliminate price competition in the markets concerned, thereby facilitating a collusive outcome on the market.[238]
- Standards that set detailed technical specifications for a product or service may limit technical development and innovation, as once one technology has been chosen and the standard has been set, competing technologies and companies may face a barrier to entry and may potentially be excluded from the market. This is particularly the case for standards requiring that a particular technology is used exclusively or which prevent the development of other technologies by obliging the members of the standard-setting organization to exclusively use a particular standard.[239] This may occur in the context of standardization agreements involving intellectual property (IP) rights.[240]
- Standardization may lead to anti-competitive results by preventing certain companies from obtaining effective access to the results of the standard-setting process, either by being completely prevented from obtaining access to the result of the standard, or by being granted access on prohibitive or discriminatory terms.[241] This is also something occurring in the context of standardization agreements involving IP rights.

236 Ibid, para 263. 237 Ibid, para 264. 238 Ibid, para 265. 239 Ibid, para 266.
240 See our analysis in I Lianos, *Competition Law and the Intangible Economy* (OUP, forthcoming 2019).
241 Horizontal Guidelines, para 268.

- Similarly, standard terms can give rise to restrictive effects on competition by limiting product choice and innovation, in particular if a large part of an industry adopts the standard terms and chooses not to deviate from them in individual cases (or deviates from them only in exceptional cases of strong buyer-power), thus obliging customers to accept the conditions in the standard terms, as they would not dispose of any other option. This is only likely in cases where the standard terms define the scope of the end-product and do not concern classical consumer goods, as standard terms of sale generally do not limit innovation of the actual product or product quality and variety.[242]
- Standard terms relating to price may also restrict price competition and risk affecting the commercial conditions of the final product.[243]
- Anti-competitive effects may also arise when the standard terms become industry practice and thus access to them may be vital for entry into the market. Refusing access to the standard terms could risk causing anti-competitive foreclosure, hence the need for standard terms to remain effectively open for use by anyone which wishes to have access to them.

The Commission notes that in certain circumstances standardization agreements may restrict competition by object, in particular if the standard is used as part of a broader restrictive agreement aimed at excluding actual or potential competitors, as a support to an object restriction of competition (eg cartel). The Guidelines cite the example of the *Pre-insulated pipes* decision of the Commission, which involved a Europe-wide secret market-sharing, price-fixing, and bid-rigging cartel in district heating pipes, which involved a highly formalized structure of collaboration beginning in late 1990 among Danish producers and to which producers in other Member States, in particular Germany, Switzerland, Finland, Italy, and Austria, covering the whole of the EU, as well as the non-EU Baltic States and several Eastern European markets. The Managing Directors of the cartelists met regularly in secret meetings, often held just after legitimate trade association meetings. The Commission found that part of the infringement of Article 101 TFEU consisted in using norms and standards in order to prevent or delay the introduction of new technology which would result in price reductions.[244] Another example consists in a national association of manufacturers which sets a standard and puts pressure on third parties not to market products that do not comply with the standard.[245]

Standard terms may also form part of a broader restrictive agreement aiming to exclude actual or potential competitors and support a restriction of competition by object (eg a cartel), the Horizontal Guidelines citing the example of a trade association which does not allow a new entrant access to its standards terms, the use of which is vital to ensure entry to the market.[246] Furthermore, any standard terms containing provisions which directly influence the prices charged to customers (that is to say, recommended prices, rebates, etc) constitute restrictions of competition by object.

The assessment of the restrictive effects of standard-setting should take into account their legal and economic context with regard to their actual and likely effect

[242] Ibid, para 270. [243] Ibid, para 271.

[244] *Pre-insulated pipes* (Case COMP IV/35.691) Commission Decision 1999/60/EC [1999] OJ L 24/1, para 147.

[245] Horizontal Guidelines, para 273. [246] Ibid, para 275.

on competition and should, in particular, focus on the following relevant markets: (i) the product or service market or markets to which the standard or standards relates; (ii) the technology market, where the standard-setting involves the selection of technology, and where the rights to intellectual property are marketed separately from the products to which they relate; (iii) the market for standard-setting if different standard-setting bodies or agreements exist; or (iv) a distinct market for testing and certification.[247]

As regards standard terms, the effects are, in general, felt on the downstream market where the companies using the standard terms compete by selling their product to their customers.[248]

According to the Commission's Horizontal Guidelines, in the absence of market power, a standardization agreement is not capable of producing restrictive effects on competition and restrictive effects are most unlikely in a situation where there is effective competition between a number of voluntary standards.[249] For those standard-setting agreements which risk creating market power, the Guidelines set out a safe harbour, enumerating a series of conditions under which such agreements would normally fall outside the scope of Article 101(1) TFEU.[250] It is, however, noted that the non-fulfilment of any or all of these conditions will not lead to any presumption of a restriction of competition within Article 101(1), but it will require self-assessment to establish whether the agreement falls under Article 101(1) and, if so, whether the conditions of Article 101(3) are fulfilled.[251] The Horizontal Guidelines are open to the existence of different models for standard-setting, recognizing that competition within and between those models is a positive aspect of a market economy and leave the standard-setting organizations entirely free to put in place rules and procedures that do not violate competition rules although different from these conditions. These are described in detail in paragraphs 280–6 of the Horizontal Guidelines and summarized in paragraph 280 reproduced below.

Communication from the Commission—Guidelines on the applicability of Article 101 TFEU to horizontal co-operation agreements [2011] OJ C 11/1 (footnotes omitted, emphases added)

280. Where participation in standard-setting is *unrestricted* and the procedure for adopting the standard in question is *transparent*, standardisation agreements which contain *no obligation to comply* with the standard and provide *access to the standard on fair, reasonable and non-discriminatory terms* will normally not restrict competition within the meaning of Article 101(1).

The conditions are examined in detail in the companion volume on the application of competition law to IP rights.[252]

For standardization agreements that depart from the principles set out in paragraphs 280 to 286, and so do not benefit from the safe harbour provided by the Guidelines, the assessment

[247] Ibid, para 261. [248] Ibid, para 262. [249] Ibid, para 277. [250] Ibid, para 278.
[251] Ibid, para 279.
[252] I Lianos, *Competition Law and the Intangible Economy* (OUP, forthcoming 2019).

of each standardization agreement must take into account the likely effects of the standard on the markets concerned and in particular the following considerations (again, we exclude from the following excerpt the parts dedicated to standardization in the context of licensing of IP rights).

Communication from the Commission—Guidelines on the applicability of Article 101 TFEU to horizontal co-operation agreements [2011] OJ C 11/1 (footnotes omitted)

293. Whether standardisation agreements may give rise to restrictive effects on competition may depend on whether the members of a standard-setting organisation remain free to develop alternative standards or products that do not comply with the agreed standard. For example, if the standard-setting agreement binds the members to only [*sic*] produce products in compliance with the standard, the risk of a likely negative effect on competition is significantly increased and could in certain circumstances give rise to a restriction of competition by object. In the same vein, standards only covering minor aspects or parts of the end-product are less likely to lead to competition concerns than more comprehensive standards.

294. The assessment whether the agreement restricts competition will also focus on access to the standard. Where the result of a standard (that is to say, the specification of how to comply with the standard [. . .]) is not at all accessible, or only accessible on discriminatory terms, for members or third parties (that is to say, non-members of the relevant standard-setting organisation) this may discriminate or foreclose or segment markets according to their geographic scope of application and thereby is likely to restrict competition. However, in the case of several competing standards or in the case of effective competition between the standardised solution and non-standardised solution, a limitation of access may not produce restrictive effects on competition.

295. If participation in the standard-setting process is open in the sense that it allows all competitors (and/or stakeholders) in the market affected by the standard to take part in choosing and elaborating the standard, this will lower the risks of a likely restrictive effect on competition by not excluding certain companies from the ability to influence the choice and elaboration of the standard. The greater the likely market impact of the standard and the wider its potential fields of application, the more important it is to allow equal access to the standard-setting process. However, if the facts at hand show that there is competition between several such standards and standard-setting organisations (and it is not necessary that the whole industry applies the same standards) there may be no restrictive effects on competition. Also, if in the absence of a limitation on the number of participants it would not have been possible to adopt the standard, the agreement would not be likely to lead to any restrictive effect on competition under Article 101(1). In certain situations the potential negative effects of restricted participation may be removed or at least lessened by ensuring that stakeholders are kept informed and consulted on the work in progress. The more transparent the procedure for adopting the standard, the more likely it is that the adopted standard will take into account the interests of all stakeholders.

296. To assess the effects of a standard-setting agreement, the market shares of the goods or services based on the standard should be taken into account. It might not always be possible to assess with any certainty at an early stage whether the standard will in practice be adopted by a large part of the industry or whether it will only be a

standard used by a marginal part of the relevant industry. In many cases the relevant market shares of the companies having participated in developing the standard could be used as a proxy for estimating the likely market share of the standard (since the companies participating in setting the standard would in most cases have an interest in implementing the standard). However, as the effectiveness of standardisation agreements is often proportional to the share of the industry involved in setting and/or applying the standard, high market shares held by the parties in the market or markets affected by the standard will not necessarily lead to the conclusion that the standard is likely to give rise to restrictive effects on competition.

297. Any standard-setting agreement which clearly discriminates against any of the participating or potential members could lead to a restriction of competition. For example, if a standard-setting organisation explicitly excludes upstream only companies (that is to say, companies not active on the downstream production market), this could lead to an exclusion of potentially better technologies.

The Horizontal Guidelines also include information on the competitive assessment of standard terms.

Communication from the Commission—Guidelines on the applicability of Article 101 TFEU to horizontal co-operation agreements [2011] OJ C 11/1 (footnotes omitted, emphases added)

301. As long as participation in the actual establishment of standard terms is *unrestricted* for the competitors in the relevant market (either by participation in the trade association or directly), and the established standard terms are *non-binding* and *effectively accessible* for anyone, such agreements are not likely to give rise to restrictive effects on competition (subject to the caveats set out in paragraphs 303, 304, 305 and 307).

302. Effectively accessible and non-binding standard terms for the sale of consumer goods or services (on the presumption that they have no effect on price) thus generally do not have any restrictive effect on competition since they are unlikely to lead to any negative effect on product quality, product variety or innovation. There are, however, two general exceptions where a more in-depth assessment would be required.

303. Firstly, standard terms for the sale of consumer goods or services where the standard terms define the scope of the product sold to the customer, and where therefore the risk of limiting product choice is more significant, could give rise to restrictive effects on competition within the meaning of Article 101(1) where their common application is likely to result in a *de facto* alignment. This could be the case when the widespread use of the standard terms *de facto* leads to a limitation of innovation and product variety. For instance, this may arise where standard terms in insurance contracts limit the customer's practical choice of key elements of the contract, such as the standard risks covered. Even if the use of the standard terms is not compulsory, they might undermine the incentives of the competitors to compete on product diversification.

304. When assessing whether there is a risk that the standard terms are likely to have restrictive effects by way of a limitation of product choice, factors such as existing competition on the market should be taken into account. For example if there is a large

number of smaller competitors, the risk of a limitation of product choice would seem to be less than if there are only a few bigger competitors. The market shares of the companies participating in the establishment of the standard terms might also give a certain indication of the likelihood of uptake of the standard terms or of the likelihood that the standard terms will be used by a large part of the market. However, in this respect, it is not only relevant to analyse whether the standard terms elaborated are likely to be used by a large part of the market, but also whether the standard terms only cover part of the product or the whole product (the less extensive the standard terms, the less likely that they will lead, overall, to a limitation of product choice). Moreover, in cases where in the absence of the establishment of the standard terms it would not have been possible to offer a certain product, there would not be likely to be any restrictive effect on competition within the meaning of Article 101(1). In that scenario, product choice is increased rather than decreased by the establishment of the standard terms.

305. Secondly, even if the standard terms do not define the actual scope of the end-product they might be a decisive part of the transaction with the customer for other reasons. An example would be online shopping where customer confidence is essential (for example, in the use of safe payment systems, a proper description of the products, clear and transparent pricing rules, flexibility of the return policy, etc). As it is difficult for customers to make a clear assessment of all those elements, they tend to favour widespread practices and standard terms regarding those elements could therefore become a *de facto* standard with which companies would need to comply to sell in the market. Even though non- binding, those standard terms would become a *de facto* standard, the effects of which are very close to a binding standard and need to be analysed accordingly.

306. If the use of standard terms is binding, there is a need to assess their impact on product quality, product variety and innovation (in particular if the standard terms are binding on the entire market).

307. Moreover, should the standard terms (binding or non-binding) contain any terms which are likely to have a negative effect on competition relating to prices (for example terms defining the type of rebates to be given), they would be likely to give rise to restrictive effects on competition within the meaning of Article 101(1).

There is no specific block exemption regulation for standardization agreements. The Commission's Horizontal Guidelines nevertheless provide some guidance on the assessment of the four conditions of Article 101(3) for standardization agreements and agreements on standard terms.

With regard to the condition relating to the presence of efficiency gains the Commission notes that the development of European Union wide standards may facilitate market integration and allow companies to market their goods and services in all Member States, leading to increased consumer choice and decreasing prices. Additional efficiency gains relate to standardization enhancing technical inter-operability and compatibility which often encourages competition on the merits between technologies from different companies and helps prevent lock-in to one particular supplier. The fact that standards may reduce transaction costs for sellers and buyers is also put forward. The Commission also highlights the positive effects of the development of standards on quality, safety and environmental aspects of a product to consumer choice and product quality, as well as their role for innovation, in particular by reducing the time it takes to bring a new technology to the market and by allowing companies to build on top of agreed solutions.[253] Yet, the Horizontal Guidelines note that to achieve those efficiency gains the information necessary to apply the standard must be effectively available to those wishing to enter the market.[254] Dissemination of a standard can also be enhanced by marks or logos certifying compliance which provide certainty to customers.[255] Yet, the Horizontal Guidelines consider that agreements for testing and certification go beyond the primary objective of defining the standard and would normally constitute a distinct agreement and market.[256] Compatibility on a horizontal level between different technology platforms may promote innovation and give rise to efficiency gains.[257]

Standard terms can bring efficiency gains also by making it easier for customers to compare the conditions offered and thus facilitate switching between companies, as well as efficiency gains in the form of savings in transaction costs or as facilitators of entry in certain sectors where the contracts are of a complex legal structure. Standard terms may also increase legal certainty for the contract parties.[258] The higher the number of competitors on the market, the greater the efficiency gain of facilitating the comparison of conditions offered.[259]

The restrictions of competition included in the agreement should be indispensable for the achievement of these efficiency gains, standardization agreements covering no more than what is necessary to ensure their aims, whether this is technical inter-operability and compatibility or a certain level of quality[260] and standard-setting being normally open to all competitors in the market or markets affected by the standard unless the parties demonstrate significant inefficiencies of such participation or recognized procedures are foreseen for the collective representation of interests.[261] Restrictions in a standardization agreement making a standard binding and obligatory for the industry are in principle not indispensable.[262] This also applies to agreements on standard terms.[263] Similarly, for standardization agreements that entrust certain bodies with the exclusive right to test compliance with the standard, which go beyond the primary objective of defining the standard and may also restrict competition. In these cases, the standardization agreement should include adequate safeguards to mitigate possible risks to competition resulting from exclusivity (eg a certification fee which needs to be reasonable and proportionate to the cost of the compliance testing).[264]

The assessment of the condition of the likely passing on of the efficiency gains to the consumers involves, in this context, examining whether the procedures are used to guarantee that the interests of the users of standards and end consumers are protected.[265] The passing on is presumed for standards facilitating technical interoperability and compatibility or competition between new and already existing products, services and processes.[266] A similar presumption applies in the context of agreements on standard terms for certain efficiency gains, such as increased comparability of the offers on the market, facilitated switching between providers, and legal certainty of the clauses set out in the standard terms, while for others, such as lower transaction costs, it is necessary to make an assessment on a case-by-case basis and in the relevant economic context whether these are likely to be passed on to consumers.[267]

The assessment of the fourth condition of Article 101(3) TFEU, that there is no substantial elimination of competition, also involves some careful analysis of the sources of competition in the relevant markets and the level and impact of the competitive constraint they impose on the parties to the agreement. The Commission notes that while market shares are relevant for

253 Horizontal Guidelines, para 308.
254 Ibid, para 309.
255 Ibid, para 310.
256 Ibid.
257 Ibid, para 311.
258 Ibid, para 312.
259 Ibid, para 313.
260 Ibid, para 317.
261 Ibid, para 316.
262 Ibid, para 318.
263 Ibid, para 320.
264 Ibid, para 319.
265 Ibid, para 321.
266 Ibid, para 321.
267 Ibid, para 323.

that analysis, the magnitude of remaining sources of actual competition cannot be assessed exclusively on the basis of market share except in cases where a standard becomes a *de facto* industry standard.[268]

Intercompany agreements: Companies may decide to organize standards among themselves in order to achieve environmental objectives set by law. These agreements will provide assurance that all of them are going to behave the same way, thus avoiding a prisoners' dilemma. There are, however, obvious risks for competition (collusion).

The Commission has examined environmental agreements in the context of Article 101(1) and 101(3) TFEU.

7.4.3. PUBLIC POLICY CONCERNS AND COLLECTIVE BENEFITS

In some circumstances, horizontal cooperation agreements between undertakings restricting competition may provide benefits, not only directly to the category of consumers affected by the anti-competitive practice, as this results from the relevant market definition, but also to the economy and the 'public at large'. These benefits relate to broader public interests, linked either to existing regulations, or more broadly to values and principles animating public policy at a more general level. For instance, policies in favour of the protection of the environment may conflict with the emphasis placed by competition law on price competition. The application of competition law, in particular Articles 101 and 102 TFEU, to business practices relating to the protection of the environment raises interesting questions as to the interaction between competition law and the public policy to protect the environment, in view of the principle of integration of Article 11 TFEU, calling for environmental concerns to be taken into account in all EU policies.[269] The EU and its Member States actively promote the protection of the environment through different means: (i) direct (command and control) regulation based on coercive measures such as permits, zoning, regulatory standards; (ii) incentive regulation with the use of taxes and/or charges to induce environmental friendly behaviour from the firms, such as the organization of a market for tradable permits; (iii) the promotion of self-regulation by undertakings; (iv) mixed intervention, such as voluntary agreements, that is, formal, bilateral commitments between the authorities and industry which set forth environmental objectives and the means to achieve them; and (v) inter-company agreements concluded by undertakings without being coerced or induced by the State. Article 101 TFEU, on its own, may catch anti-competitive practices resulting from categories (v), (iii), and (iv), as the undertakings involved in voluntary agreements are not coerced by the State to restrict competition, but act as autonomous entities on the market.[270] One should of course keep in mind the possibility that dominant firms may impose their technical standards and environmental management systems on their competitors, in which case the practice may fall under Article 102 TFEU. Both competition law and environmental protection are policies of the Union.

268 Ibid, para 324.

269 For a thorough analysis of the interaction between competition law and environmental regulation, see S Kingston, *Greening EU Competition Law and Policy* (Cambridge University Press, 2011).

270 The list is taken from OECD, *Competition Policy and Environment*, OCDE/GD(96)22 (13 February 1996), 6–9.

With regard to Article 101 TFEU, the Commission's 2011 horizontal cooperation guidelines do not include a separate section on 'environmental agreements', as did their 2000 version,[271] which was, however, careful not to refer to the existence of 'collective benefits' arising out of these agreements and was referring instead to 'economic benefits', 'either at individual or aggregate *consumer* level'.[272]

At the level of individual decisions enforcing Article 101 TFEU, the Commission has dealt with practices involved in the waste management systems sector. In *Duales System Deutschland (DSD)*, the Commission examined not only from the perspective of Article 102 TFEU, but also under Article 101 TFEU, of the practices of DSD the only undertaking that operated a comprehensive packaging collection and recycling system in Germany (thus holding a dominant position on this market).[273] DSD's system aimed at enabling manufacturers and retailers to meet the requirements of the EU and national regulation on packaging and packaging wastes, which required manufacturers and retailers to take back sales packaging. DSD's system relied on 'trademark agreements' concluded with the manufacturers/retailers, under which DSD provided them with a collection and recycling service which satisfied their legal obligations. The agreement also supported the method of collecting refuse by use of the Green Dot trademark on the packaging and the fee to be paid to DSD for the service, which exempted manufacturers and retailers from their legal obligations under the packaging and packaging wastes regulation. It might have been simpler to object to the tie, that customers could not use other services for collecting their waste packaging without double payment. That might have been justified by economies of scale, but that would have had to be established by strong evidence.

With regard to payment, the 'trademark agreements' included a provision obliging DSD's clients to pay for all the sales packaging brought on the German market bearing the Green Dot trademark, even if DSD did not actually provide that service, thus leading to a situation of double payment for clients wishing to use the services of competitors for parts of their packaging. DSD also sub-contracted the packaging waste service to local collecting companies, with which it concluded 'services agreements'. In 1992, DSD (thus before the implementation of Regulation 1/2003 and the establishment of a legal exception regime) notified its system to the European Commission as involving potentially anti-competitive agreements seeking confirmation that this did not infringe Article 101(1) TFEU and, in case it did, was exempted under Article 101(3) TFEU. Following the complaints of a competing waste disposal firm and certain hair-care product manufacturers, the Commission objected to the payment provision in the 'trademark agreements' as an abuse of a dominant position, infringing Article 102 TFEU. The Commission requested DSD not to charge a fee for the part of packaging bearing the Green Dot which was performed by a competing service provider.[274] The Commission

[271] Commission Notice—Guidelines on the applicability of Article 101 of the EC Treaty to horizontal cooperation agreements [2001] OJ C 3/2, paras 179–98, defining environmental agreements as 'those by which the parties undertake to achieve pollution abatement, as defined in environmental law, or environmental objectives, in particular, those set out in [. . .] the Treaty. Therefore, the target or the measures agreed need to be directly linked to the reduction of a pollutant or a type of waste identified as such in relevant regulations. [. . .] Environmental agreements may set out standards on the environmental performance of products (inputs or outputs) or production processes.'

[272] Commission Notice—Guidelines on the applicability of Article 81 of the EC Treaty to horizontal cooperation agreements [2001] OJ C 3/2, para 193 (emphasis added). The Commission also noted that '[w]here consumers individually have a positive rate of return from the agreement under reasonable payback periods, there is no need for the aggregate environmental benefits to be objectively established' (ibid, para 194).

[273] *DSD* (Case COMP D3/34493) Commission Decision 2001/463/EC [2001] OJ L 166/1.

[274] *DSD* (Case COMP D3/34493) Commission Decision 2001/463/EC [2001] OJ L 166/1.

also adopted a second decision, this time on the application of Article 101 TFEU finding no restriction of competition for the remaining parts of the system, with the exception of the 'services agreements'.[275] These were declared incompatible to Article 101 (1) TFEU, because of the exclusivity they provided in favour of one collector per collection area in view of the long duration of the agreement. Yet, the restriction of competition was exempted under Article 101(3) TFEU for a limited period of time under the obligation for DSD not to prevent its collectors from contracting with competitors and to provide them unrestricted access to the collection infrastructure of the collectors it collaborated with. The Commission noted that the agreement 'seeks to give effect to national and Community environmental policy with regard to the prevention, recycling and recovery of waste packaging'[276] and that 'consumers [affected] will likewise benefit as a result of the improvement in environmental quality sought, essentially the reduction in the volume of packaging',[277] the benefits thus being assessed at the individual consumer level. DSD appealed against both Articles 101 and 102 TFEU decisions.

The General Court dismissed both appeals, first recognizing that that DSD restricted competition by imposing a licence fee provision which ignored the principle of 'no service, no fee'[278] and, second, accepting the exemption conditions set by the Commission.[279] The Commission has published guidance on the application of competition law to waste management systems.[280]

Of particular interest for the individual assessment of environmental agreements under Article 101(3) TFEU is the Commission's decision in *CECED*, concerning an agreement between washing machine manufacturers to cease production and importation of less energy efficient machines.[281] The Commission found that the restrictions of production and imports of less efficient washing machines included in the agreement prevented manufacturers and importers from competing throughout the full range of energy categories, as they did before the agreement, reducing diversity and consumer choice and distorting price competition, as well as reducing electricity demand (restriction of output). Notwithstanding the fact, however, that the agreement was found restrictive by object falling under the prohibition of Article 101(1) TFEU, the Commission exempted it under Article 101(3) TFEU. The Commission considered among the positive effects of the agreement on economic or technical progress and benefits to the consumer, 'collective environmental benefits' which appeared to be more than seven times greater than the increased purchase costs to consumers of more energy-efficient washing machines. According to the Commission, '[s]uch environmental results for society would adequately allow consumers a fair share of the benefits even if no benefits accrued to individual purchasers of the machine'.[282]

275 *DSD et al*, Commission Decision 2001/837/EC [2001] OJ L 319/1.

276 Ibid, para 143.

277 Ibid, para 148.

278 Case T-151/01, *Der Grüne Punkt—Duales System Deutschland GmbH v Commission* [2007] ECR II-1607, confirmed by C-385/07 P, *Der Grüne Punkt—Duales System Deutschland GmbH v Commission* [2009] ECR I-6155.

279 Case T-289/01 *Der Grüne Punkt—Duales System Deutschland GmbH v Commission* [2007] ECR II-1691.

280 See DG Competition Paper Concerning Issues of Competition in Waste Management Systems (2005), available at http://ec.europa.eu/competition/sectors/energy/waste_management.pdf. See also *Eco-Emballages* (Case COMP/39.450) Commission Decision 2001/663/EC [2001] OJ L 233/37, approving the contracts concluded by the company Eco-Emballages SA concerning its system of selective collection and recovery of household packaging waste and defining for the first time the principles of competition with which such collective systems must comply.

281 *CECED* (Case IV.F.1/36.718) Commission Decision 2000/475/EC [2000] OJ L 187/47.

282 Ibid, para 56.

SELECTIVE BIBLIOGRAPHY

Books

Beaton-Wels, C, and Ezrachi, A (eds) *Criminalising Cartels: Critical Studies of an International Regulatory Movement* (Hart, 2011).

Brandenburger, A, and Nalebuff, BJ, *Co-opetition* (Doubleday, 1997).

Connor, J, *Global Price Fixing* (Springer, 2nd ed, 2008).

Harding, C, and Joshua, J, *Regulating Cartels in Europe* (OUP, 2nd ed, 2010).

Harding, C, and Edwards, J, *Cartel Criminality: The Mythology and Pathology of Business Collusion* (Ashgate, 2015).

Kingston, S, *Greening EU Competition Law and Policy* (CUP, 2011).

Marshall, RC and Marx, LM, *The Economics of Collusion* (MIT Press, 2012).

Morais, L, *Joint Ventures and EU Competition Law* (Hart, 2013).

Nowag, J, *Environmental Integration in Competition and Free-Movement Laws* (OUP, 2016).

Wardaugh, B, *Cartels, Markets and Crime: A Normative Justification for the Criminalisation of Economic Collusion* (CUP, 2014).

Whelan, P, *The Criminalization of European Cartel Enforcement: Theoretical, Legal and Practical Challenges* (OUP, 2014).

Chapters in books

Kühn, K-U, and Vives, X, 'Information Exchanges Among Firms and their Impact on Competition' (December 1994), available at http://blog.iese.edu/xvives/files/2011/09/Information-Exchanges-and-their-Impact-on-Competition.pdf.

Levestein, MC, and Suslow, VY, 'Cartels and Collusion—Empirical Evidence' in Blair, RD, and Sokol, DD (eds) *The Oxford Handbook of International Antitrust Economics*, vol 2 (OUP, 2015), ch 18.

Wagner von Papp, F, 'Information Exchange Agreements' in Lianos, I, and Geradin, D (eds) *Handbook on European Competition Law: Substantive Aspects* (Edward Elgar, 2013), 130–73.

Journal articles

Bennett, M, and Collins, P, 'The Law and Economics of Information Sharing: The Good, the Bad and the Ugly' (2010) 6(2) *European Competition J* 311.

Bos, I, and Pot, E, 'On the Possibility of Welfare Enhancing Hard-core Cartels' (2012) 107(3) *J Economics* 199.

Connor, JM, and Lande, RH, 'Cartels as Rational Business Strategy' (2012) 34(2) *Cardozo L Rev* 427.

Connor JM, 'Effectiveness of Antitrust Sanctions on Modern International Cartels' (2006) 6 *J Industry, Competition and Trade* 195.

Connor, JM and Lande, RH, 'How High Do Cartels Raise Prices—Implications for Optimal Cartel Fines' (2005) 80 *Tulane Law Review* 513.

Joliet, R, 'Cartelisation, Dirigism and Crisis in the European Community' (1981) 3(4) *The World Economy* 403.

Korah, V, '*European Night Services*, the First Judgment of a Joint Venture Adopted a Realistic Approach to Effects on Competition' (2002) 6 *Competition LJ* 331.

Levenstein, MC, and Suslow, VY, 'What Determines Cartel Success?' (2006) 44 *J Economic Literature* 43.

Scott, I, 'Antitrust and Socially Responsible Collaboration: A Chilling Combination?' (2016) 53 *American Business LJ* 97.

Sharpe, T, 'The Commission's Proposals on Crisis Cartels' (1980) 17 *Common Market L Rev* 75.

Stephan, A, 'Price Fixing in Crisis: Implications of an Economic Downturn for Cartels and Enforcement' (2012) 35(3) *World Competition* 511.

Stephan, A, 'An Empirical Evaluation of the Normative Justifications for Cartel Criminalisation', (2017) 37(4) *Legal Studies* 621.

Wardhaugh, B, 'Crisis Cartels: Non-Economic Values, the Public Interest and Institutional Considerations' (2014) 10(1) *European Competition J* 311.

ABUSE OF DOMINANT POSITION: MAIN ELEMENTS

8.1. RELEVANT LAWS

Competition law not only punishes collusive practices and provides remedies, like those examined in the previous chapters of this book, but also prohibits unilateral conduct. In EU competition law, unilateral conduct may infringe Article 102 of the Treaty on the Functioning of the European Union (TFEU). Under UK competition law, unilateral conduct of undertakings may infringe Chapter II CA98.

These provisions apply only if a dominant undertaking has abused its dominant position. They prohibit the *abuse* of a dominant position, but not the dominant position itself. An undertaking that does not have a dominant position can therefore adopt unilateral conduct without incurring the risk of the prohibition of Article 102 TFEU and/or Chapter II CA98. The situation is different in US law.

US law

The scope of US antitrust law is theoretically wider as it does not establish control over the abuse of a dominant position. Section 2 of the Sherman Act was interpreted by the courts to cover three types of violations:

(a) The *monopolization offence* has two elements: (1) the possession of monopoly power in the relevant market and (2) the wilful acquisition or maintenance of that power as distinguished from growth or development as a consequence of a superior product, business acumen, or historic accident.[1]

[1] *United States v Grinnell Corp*, 384 US 563, 570–1 (1966).

(b) The *attempted monopolization offence* requires proof of three elements: (1) that the defendant has engaged in predatory or anti-competitive conduct with (2) a specific intent to monopolize and (3) a dangerous probability of achieving monopoly power.[2]

(c) The offence of *conspiracy to monopolize*: requires evidence of (1) conspiracy, (2) a specific intent to monopolize, and (3) an overt act in furtherance of the conspiracy.[3] It is not necessary to bring evidence of actual market power or of the existence of anti-competitive effects. In addition, conduct might be found to violate Sherman Act section 2 even though it does not violate Sherman Act section 1.

US antitrust law includes also a prohibition of unilateral conduct when this is an unfair method of competition under section 5 of the Federal Trade Commission (FTC) Act.

The discrepancy between the EU and the US is obvious with regard to the absence in the EU of an attempted monopolization (or abuse of dominance) offence.

Herbert Hovenkamp, 'The Legal Periphery of Dominant Firm Conduct', University of Iowa Legal Studies Research Paper No 07-21 (1 September 2007) (footnotes omitted)

One possible rationale for the presence of an attempt offense under U.S. law but not the law of the European Union lies in the differing standards of conduct that the two bodies of law impose on dominant firms. In general, the rules for pricing (high, predatory, discounting practices) in the EU are more aggressive than in the U.S., as are the rules for unilateral refusals to deal or abuses of IP rights. One could justifiably say that the U.S. has a more 'structural' approach that attempts to pre-empt the conditions that give rise to the abuses, rather than remedying the abuses themselves.

That explanation does find support in the fact that much of EU law respecting unilateral dominant firm conduct does seem to be more aggressive than United States law. Perhaps more significantly in considering the wisdom of a separate offence of attempt to monopolize, EU law has also expressed a willingness to condemn high prices, which are defined as prices that are excessive in relation to the firm's costs. By contrast, the United States position is unambiguously that once the monopolist has attained its position it may charge any price that the market will bear.

8.2. THE ROLE OF THE PROHIBITION OF THE ABUSE OF A DOMINANT POSITION

8.2.1. SPECIFIC AIMS OF THE PROHIBITION OF THE ABUSE OF A DOMINANT POSITION

As was indicated in Chapter 2, EU and UK competition law follow a variety of aims. As one of the two main provisions of EU and UK competition law, the prohibition of the abuse of a dominant position contributes to the achievement of these aims. Nevertheless, more than for any

2 *Spectrum Sports v McQuillan*, 506 US 445, 456 (1993).
3 *NYNEX Corp v Discon, Inc*, 525 US 128 (1998).

other provision of competition law, the prohibition of abusive conduct has been a subject of intense controversy among jurisdictions.[4] A recent survey by the Unilateral Conduct Working Group of the International Competition Network (ICN) among thirty-three competition authorities on the objectives of provisions prohibiting the abuse of a dominant position noted the plurality of aims followed by unilateral conduct competition law provisions, such as ensuring an effective competitive process, promoting consumer welfare, maximizing efficiency, ensuring economic freedom, ensuring a level playing field for small and medium size enterprises, promoting fairness and equality, promoting consumer choice, achieving market integration, facilitating privatization and market liberalization, and promoting competitiveness in international markets.[5] According to the results of this survey, the objectives of EU competition law are ensuring an effective competitive process as a goal and/or a means, of promoting consumer welfare, maximizing efficiency, and achieving market integration. On the contrary, the following objectives were not mentioned as important in EU competition law: ensuring economic freedom, ensuring a level playing field for small- and medium-sized enterprises (SMEs), promoting fairness and equality, promoting consumer choice, achieving market integration, facilitating privatization and market liberalization, and promoting competitiveness in international markets. For the UK, the main objectives cited were ensuring an effective competitive process as a goal and/or a means, promoting consumer welfare, and maximizing efficiency. Of course, such survey gives only some form of vague impression about the belief of authorities on the aims they are attempting to achieve in enforcing provisions on abusive conduct, but it illustrates the variety of approaches that competition authorities and courts adopt in this area of competition law.

In the EU, the debate has been between those arguing that the aim of this provision is the protection of the competitive process, the institution of competition, and those advocating a 'more economic approach' that would interpret Article 102 TFEU in conformity with neo-classical price theory and the overall objective of consumer welfare. Both groups, however, recognize the importance of the objective of market integration in the interpretation and application of Article 102 TFEU.[6] The first view was advanced by the 'ordoliberal' group, essentially German academics linked with the University of Fribourg.[7] For ordoliberal writers, the objective of competition law, as well as of all State regulation, is to promote the competitive process, perceived as an institution (*Institutionsschutztheorie*), and not to protect individuals

[4] See the documents published by the International Competition Network (ICN) Unilateral Conduct Working Group, available at www.internationalcompetitionnetwork.org/working-groups/current/unilateral.aspx. The OECD has also published various documents comparing national practices with regard to the interpretation and application of the prohibition of an abuse of a dominant position. See OECD Policy Roundtable *Abuse of Dominance and Monopolisation* (1996), www.oecd.org/competition/abuse/2379408.pdf.

[5] ICN, *Report on the Objectives of Unilateral Conduct Laws, Assessment of Dominance/Substantial Market Power, and State-Created Monopolies*, Unilateral Conduct Working Group, Doc No 353, available at www.internationalcompetitionnetwork.org/uploads/library/doc353.pdf.

[6] For a discussion, see H Schweitzer, 'The History, Interpretation and Underlying Principles of Section 2 Sherman Act and Article 82 EC' in CD Ehlermann and M Marquis (eds) *European Competition Annual 2007: A Reformed Approach to Article 82 EC* (Hart, 2008), 128–38.

[7] For a discussion, see DJ Gerber, 'Constitutionalizing the Economy: German Neo-liberalism, Competition Law and the "New" Europe' (1994) 42 *American J Comparative L* 25; H Rieter and M Schmolz, 'The ideas of German Ordoliberalism 1938–45: Pointing the Way to a New Economic Order' (1993) 1 *European J History of Economic Thought* 87; W Möschel, 'Competition Policy from an Ordo Point of View' in A Peacock and H Willgerodt (eds) *German Neo-Liberals and the Social Market Economy*, (London: Macmillan, 1989). For an English translation of the views of one of the principal authors of the ordoliberal group, see W Eucken, *The Foundations of Economics: History and Theory in the Analysis of Economic Reality* (Springer, 1992 [1939]).

or specific groups (*Individualschutztheorie*), such as consumers or the competitors of the dominant firm. In her Opinion in *British Airways*, Advocate General Kokott has made forcefully this point:

> [Article 102] forms part of a system designed to protect competition within the internal market from distortions (Article 3(1)(g) EC). Accordingly, Article [102 TFEU], like the other competition rules of the Treaty, is not designed only or primarily to protect the immediate interests of individual competitors or consumers, but to protect the *structure of the market* and thus *competition as such (as an institution)*, which has already been weakened by the presence of the dominant undertaking on the market. In this way, consumers are also indirectly protected. Because where competition as such is damaged, disadvantages for consumers are also to be feared.[8]

The focus of the ordoliberal authors is not so much on specific outcomes but on the protection of the competitive process from the abuse of power.[9] The concept of 'complete competition' (*vollständige Konkurrenz)* that is advanced by the ordoliberals, aims to characterize a market situation where no market participant (firms, consumers) has the power to coerce others. Nevertheless, this concept creates an anomaly in the ordoliberal setting, as it may give the impression that the ordoliberals were taking an outcomes-driven perspective and were thus requiring the intervention of competition law every time the market situation was not compatible with the ideal of 'complete competition', a position more or less similar to some neoclassical price theory that perceives the ideal of 'perfect competition' and equates it to economic efficiency. The use of the concept of 'performance competition' (*Leistungswettbewerb*), by some of these authors, is a source of additional ambivalence, as it seems to refer to outcomes, rather than the competitive process as such. This is, however, meant in a process-oriented way, as requiring the preservation of *competition on the merits*, although it seems that the benefit to consumers is the ultimate justification for the policy.[10]

One should nevertheless be careful to consider that the views often expressed over the 'ordoliberal approach' to competition law are vitiated by errors and misrepresentations. For this reason, we will use the expression 'received ordoliberal approach' when we refer to the dominant perception of 'ordoliberal' competition law, as represented in the Anglo-American competition law literature,[11] for the reason that opposition to that approach has been an important rallying argument of the proponents of the 'more economic approach' in EU competition law, which we will expose in the next paragraphs. However, as is explained by the following article, the 'received ordoliberal approach' is far away from the research programme and the intellectual positions ordoliberal authors were really putting forward.

8 Opinion of AG J Kokott in Case C-95/04, *British Airways v Commission* [2006] ECR I-2336, para 68.

9 See also the discussion in D Zimmer, 'On Fairness and Welfare: The Objectives of Competition Policy', in CD Ehlermann and M Marquis, *European Competition Annual 2007: A Reformed Approach to Article 82 EC* (Hart, 2008), 103–7.

10 See the lucid analysis of VJ Vanberg, *The Freiburg School: Walter Eucken and Ordoliberalism*, Freiburg Discussion Papers on Constitutional Economics 04/11 (2011), 13–14.

11 See eg DJ Gerber, *Law and Competition in Twentieth Century Europe: Protecting Prometheus* (Clarendon Press, 1998); P Akman, *The Concept of Abuse in EU Competition Law: Law and Economic Approaches* (Hart, 2012), 49–105.

P Behrens, 'The Ordoliberal Concept of "Abuse" of a Dominant Position and its Impact on Article 102 TFEU' (9 September 2015), in P Nihoul and I Takahashi (eds) *Abuse Regulation in Competition Law: 10th ASCOLA Conference* (forthcoming), 2, 12, available at https://ssrn.com/abstract=2658045 (footnotes omitted)

[T]he ordoliberal school was far from monolithic and it was not at all static. After World War II, especially in the 1950ies, its adherents represented already a much larger group of intellectuals some of whom introduced neoliberal ideas (such as Friedrich von Hayek) whereas others (such as Alfred Müller-Armack) developed the famous concept of a 'social market economy' which then became the general model for Germany. Consequently, there were differences among ordoliberals on crucial issues; and, even more importantly, over time ordoliberal thinking underwent considerable adjustments and refinements which must be taken into account when it comes to an assessment of its impact on the drafting of Article 86 of the Rome Treaty [now Article 102 TFEU] in the 1950ies. [. . .]

The constituent elements of ordoliberalism may [. . .] be summarized as follows:

- Competition results from individual freedom of producers to choose what they want to offer and of consumers to choose what they want to buy.
- Competition is understood as a dynamic system (process) of interaction between choice-making individuals who by making their choices reveal their preferences and produce the kind of information that other individuals need to make their choices.
- It is the fundamental role of the system of private law to provide individuals with legal rights the unrestricted use of which forms the basis of competitive rivalry among producers and of consumers' freedom of choice among alternative sources of supply.
- It is the task of the state to provide laws against restraints of such competitive rivalry and to enforce them as rules of the game with which market participants have to comply. These basic elements are generally shared by ordoliberals of all generations even though many of them have added, one way or another, further refinements. [. . .]

The opponents of the 'received ordoliberal view' often argue that focusing on 'fairness' instead of 'welfare' does not provide helpful operational criteria for the enforcement of Article 102 TFEU. They note the possible shift to active enforcement of competition law protecting essentially the interest of competitors from more efficient dominant firms, which do not take into account the possible efficiency gains of conduct that might compensate for its anti-competitive effects. They often rely on false positive errors, as explained in Chapter 6 and hint about their concern that there may be false positives (type I errors) that an active and unfocused enforcement of Article 102 TFEU might lead to. For the proponents of a 'more economics approach', neoclassical price theory may provide a necessary limiting principle to the intervention of competition law in these circumstances.[12]

The textual support in the Treaty for either approach is ambivalent. For example, Article 102(b) advances 'limiting production, markets or technical development to the prejudice

[12] See C Ahlborn and J Padilla, 'From Fairness to Welfare: Implications for the Assessment of Unilateral Conduct under EC Competition Law' in C Ehlermann and M Marquis (eds) *European Competition Law Annual 2007: A Reformed Approach to Article 82* EC (Hart, 2008), 97–8, (noting the existence of what they call 'Brussels consensus', which relies on 'two key propositions'. 'First, the goal of Article [102] [. . .] should be aggregate consumer welfare, second, the existing form-based or economics-based approach to Article [102] needs to be replaced by an effects-based or economics-based approach to the assessment of unilateral conduct.'

of consumers', as the primary concern, while Article 102(c) aims to apply to business-to-business relations and protects undertakings, not consumers, against competitive disadvantages). Article 102(a) refers to unfairness of prices and trading conditions, while Article 102(d) seems to focus on preserving contracting parties from coercion resulting from 'making the conclusion of contracts subject to acceptance by the other parties of supplementary obligations which, by their nature or according to commercial usage, have no connection with the subject of such contracts'. The original absence of a proper merger control system seeking to preserve *ex ante* the competitive process and to ensure benefits for consumers, until 1990, also indicates the interpretation of Article 102 TFEU would evolve over time.

The proponents of these two approaches have opposed each other since the early 1970s (see our developments below on the distinction between exploitative and exclusionary conduct). However, the tide began to turn in the mid-2000s, at least at the level of the European Commission. Following up the process of reform already engaged for Article 101 TFEU and merger control, the Commission attempted to introduce more economic analysis in the interpretation and application of Article 102 TFEU. It organized a group of economic experts who adopted a Report advocating the need for a 'more economic approach' in Article 102 TFEU.[13]

Economic Advisory Group for Competition Policy (EAGCP), *An Economic Approach to Article 82 EC*, Report (July 2005) (excerpts)

An economic approach to Article [102] focuses on improved consumer welfare. In so doing, it avoids confusing the protection of competition with the protection of competitors and it stresses that the ultimate yardstick of competition policy is in the satisfaction of consumer needs. Competition is a process that forces firms to be responsive to consumers needs with respect to price, quality, variety, etc.; over time it also acts as a selection mechanism, with more efficient firms replacing less efficient ones. Competition is therefore a key element in the promotion of a faster growing, consumer-oriented and more competitive European economy.

An economics-based approach requires a careful examination of how competition works in each particular market in order to evaluate how specific company strategies affect consumer welfare [. . .].

An economics-based approach to the application of article [102] implies that the assessment of each specific case will not be undertaken on the basis of the form that a particular business practice takes (for example, exclusive dealing, tying, etc.) but rather will be based on the assessment of the anti-competitive effects generated by business behaviour. This implies that competition authorities will need to identify a competitive harm, and assess the extent to which such a negative effect on consumers is potentially outweighed by efficiency gains. The identification of competitive harm requires spelling out a consistent business behaviour based on sound economics and supported by facts and empirical evidence. Similarly, efficiencies and how they are passed on to consumers should be properly justified on the basis of economic analysis and grounded on the facts of each case.

The Commission advanced this 'more economics approach' in a DG Competition Staff's *Discussion Paper on the Application of Article 82 of the Treaty to Exclusionary Abuses*[14] and its Guidance on the Commission's enforcement priorities in Applying Article 82 EC

[13] Economic Advisory Group for Competition Policy (EAGCP), *An Economic Approach to Article 82 EC*, Report (July 2005), available at http://ec.europa.eu/dgs/competition/economist/eagcp_july_21_05.pdf.

[14] DG Competition, 'Discussion Paper on the Application of Article 82 of the Treaty to Exclusionary Abuses' (December 2005), available at http://ec.europa.eu/competition/antitrust/art82/discpaper2005.pdf.

Treaty [now Article 102 TFEU] to abusive exclusionary conduct by dominant undertakings.[15] As it will become apparent from the following developments, this position is not entirely shared by the case law of the Court of Justice of the EU (CJEU) and the General Court (GC) on Article 102, its recent case law putting some limits to the Commission's initiative towards a more economic approach and raising some doubts as to the continuation of this process of 'reform' although this trend may have been reversed by the recent judgment of the CJEU in *Intel v Commission.*[16] It is also clear that the Commission's Guidance on its enforcement priorities in applying Article 102 TFEU does not produce any binding effect vis-à-vis the EU and national courts or NCAs, something that is already acknowledged in Recitals 2 and 3 of the Guidance, and it is highly unlikely that it could bind the European Commission, for instance through the operation of the principle of legitimate expectations, as this is not a formal Guidance about the interpretation of the law, but Guidance on the Commission's enforcement priorities, that is, a matter of policy.[17]

The starting point has been different in the UK. The history of the UK competition law in modern times with regard to monopolies' conduct starts with the Monopolies and Restrictive Practices (Inquiry and Control) Act 1948, which put in place an investigative system relying heavily on administrative authorities, following the 'Labour Government's' impetus in the aftermath of the Second World War 'to orient corporate power towards serving general social interests and ensure full employment by discouraging anticompetitive practices by monopolies'.[18] The Restrictive Trade Practices Act 1956 established a distinction between restrictive practices that were subject to strict scrutiny and a registration requirement and monopolies, which were

[15] Communication—Guidance on the Commission's enforcement priorities in applying [Article 102 TFEU] to abusive exclusionary conduct by dominant undertakings [2009] OJ C 45/7 [hereinafter Commission Guidance on Article 102].

[16] Such (initial) reaction was anticipated by some authors: see eg I Lianos, *La Transformation du droit de la Concurrence par le recours à l'analyse économique* (Bruylant, 2007); G Monti, 'Article 82 EC: What Future for the Effects-Based Approach?' (2010) 1 *J European Competition L & Practice* 1.

For some authors, the *Intel* judgment of the General Court (Case T-286/09, *Intel Corp v Commission*, ECLI:EU:T:2014:547), constituted the swan song of the 'more economic approach': P Nihoul, 'The Ruling of the General Court in Intel: Towards the End of an Effectbased Approach in European Competition Law?' (2014) 5 *J European Competition L & Practice* 521; JS Venit, 'Case T-286/09 *Intel v Commission*—The Judgment of the General Court: All Steps Backward and No Steps Forward' (2014) 10 *European Competition J* 203; W Wils, 'The Judgment of the EU General Court in *Intel* and the so-called "More Economic Approach" to Abuse of Dominance' (2014) 37 *World Competition* 405.

Others have called for a more cautious perspective on this case law, see R Whish, '*Intel v Commission*: Keep Calm and Carry on!' (2015) 6 *J European Competition L & Practice* 1; P Ibáñez Colomo, 'Intel and Article 102 TFEU Case Law: Making Sense of a Perpetual Controversy', LSE Law, Society and Economy Working Paper No 29/2014. Some relied on the *Post Danmark I* case law of the CJEU (Case C-209/10, *Post Danmark A/S v Konkurrencerådet*, ECLI:EU:C:2012:172) and to a certain extent *Post Danmark II* (Case C-23/14, *Post Danmark A/S v Konkurrencerådet*, ECLI:EU:C:2015:651, where the CJEU requires some evidence of anti-competitive impact, although it accepted that this may be just 'probable', there being 'no need to show that it is of a serious or appreciable nature') to put forward the view that the 'more economic approach' in Article 102 TFEU is alive and kicking: see eg E Rousseva & M Marquis, 'Hell Freezes Over: A Climate Change for Assessing Exclusionary Conduct under Article 102 TFEU' (2012) 4 *J European Competition L & Practice* 32; OXERA, 'The Post *Danmark II* Judgment: Effects Analysis in Abuse of Dominance Cases' (October 2015).

Finally, some have taken the view that the General Court's judgment in the *Intel* case 'retracts from, but does not nullify', the more economic approach. Yet, they criticize the 'non-welfarist' perspective that the General Court seems to have adopted in this case: N Petit, 'Intel, Leveraging Rebates and the Goals of Article 102 TFEU' (2015) 11(1) *European Competition J* 26.

However, the fact that the judgment of the GC has been set aside by the CJEU in Case C-413/14 P, *Intel Corp v European Commission*, ECLI:EU:C:2017:632, may indicate that the 'more economic approach' may be still alive and kicking. For a detailed analysis of this case, see Section 8.4.5.3.3.

[17] See, Case T-827/14, *Deutsche Telekom AG v European Commission*, ECLI:EU:T:2018:930, para 114.

[18] A Scott, 'The Evolution of Competition Law and Policy in the United Kingdom', LSE Law, Society and Economy Working Paper No 9/2009, 6–7 available at www.lse.ac.uk/collections/law/wps/WPS2009-09_Scott.pdf.

left to the regime of the 1948 Act. The Competition Act 1980 attempted to put in place a more active control of monopolistic practices, but with little success. Following a Green Paper in 1992, examining various options, including the suggestion to implement in the UK a provision prohibiting the abuse of a dominant position, following the EU model, in 1995, a House of Commons Select Committee inquiry into monopoly controls identified the pitfalls of the monopoly investigation system. The change of government from conservatives to Labour in 1997 led to the adoption of the Competition Act 1998, which, in its Chapter II, prohibited the abuse of a dominant position. The main aim of the Competition Act 1998 (CA98) was to align the UK regime to EU competition law, as is also illustrated by section 60 of the Act, so Chapter II CA98 follows the structure and wording of Article 102 TFEU. Yet, because of its short history, the fact that economists have been quite influential in the authorities put in place to implement Chapter II, and the lack of objectives such as market integration, the UK has been at the forefront of adopting an economic approach in the interpretation and application of the concept of abuse of a dominant position, less rule-based and focusing more on the economic analysis of single cases, thus adopting a more effects-based approach in Chapter II cases.[19] Moreover, the UK has been vocal in the EU for the adoption of a more economics approach focusing on consumer welfare.[20] Brexit may thus influence the direction of EU competition law and policy away from the 'more economic approach' in the context of Article 102 TFEU, if the jurisdiction that most actively championed this approach in Article 102 TFEU exits the EU.

The evolution towards a more economic approach raises the question of the role of Article 102 TFEU in the competition law system of the Treaty and in particular its interaction with Article 101 TFEU.

8.2.2. THE DICHOTOMY BETWEEN UNILATERAL AND COLLUSIVE CONDUCT

The competition provisions of the TFEU, the UK Competition Act, as well as those of the Sherman Act in the United States, are all based on the dichotomy between collusive and unilateral conduct. The classification is not, however, always clear-cut. One can easily distinguish an agreement between competitors from a refusal by an undertaking to deal with its competitors. There are, however, more difficult cases. Although a distribution practice or agreement may involve more than one undertaking, the combination might be based on the unilateral exercise of the economic or bargaining power by one of the parties. Should the specific practice be classified in this case as unilateral? What is the degree of constraint (and exercise of power) that is needed in order to qualify a practice as unilateral? More importantly, what is the purpose of distinguishing unilateral from collusive practices, if the competition authority follows an effects-based approach?

The classification between unilateral and collusive behaviour may nevertheless serve the purpose of providing a safe harbour for those activities that would otherwise be costly, in terms of risks of enforcement error. The *Colgate* exception in US antitrust law, or the *Bayer* rule in EU competition law satisfy this objective.[21] Unilateral behaviour by non-dominant firms benefits from forbearance, in other words *per se* legality, regardless of the effects of

[19] See S Pilsbury and H Jenkins, 'The Evolution of Effects-based analysis under the Competition Act 1998' (2010) 9 *Competition L Rev* 216.

[20] See eg OFT 414a, Assessment of Conduct (April 2004), available at http://webarchive.nationalarchives.gov.uk/20140402142426/http://www.oft.gov.uk/shared_oft/business_leaflets/competition_law/oft414a.pdf.

[21] See the analysis in Section 5.5.3.

the commercial practice on consumers. This 'gap' in Article 102 essentially constitutes a form-based approach. Unilateral conduct by non-dominant firms is exempt from antitrust scrutiny, even if it may harm consumers by leading to the acquisition or exercise of market power.

Merger control in the EU has recently integrated the analysis of unilateral effects, in the absence of dominance by a single undertaking. This has not yet been the case under Article 102 TFEU, although it is easier to identify consumer harm with greater precision *ex post* rather than *ex ante*. The cost of error is more likely in the context of an *ex ante* control, which relies on prospective analysis, in comparison to an *ex post* control, which would focus on a finding of anti-competitive effects. This paradox highlights that the main justification for the 'gap' in Article 102 is essentially a value judgment: expansion of market power by merger is perceived as less meritorious than expansion by unilateral commercial practices. John Vickers has critically observed with regard to the idea that there should not be a 'gap' in Article 102, that:

> Competition policy would then fail to discriminate between the accumulation of market power by successful product market competition and, on the other hand, the acquisition of market power by merger. It is one thing to win customers over time by serving them well in the product market, quite another to acquire them at a stroke in the stock market [. . .]. From the point of view of the economic incentives of firms, and on general grounds, that would seem rather odd. The threshold of market power that triggers intervention to maintain competitive incentives by preventing anti-competitive structural changes in markets ought to be lower than that which triggers liability for the breach of competition law prohibitions on firms that have become dominant [. . .]. Put differently, merger regulation would seem logically to be a closer relative of Article 101 than Article 102. A merger is the ultimate agreement between firms.[22]

Another reason why there is a lower bar under merger control on an *ex-ante* basis may be because the concern is mainly about exploitative anti-competitive effects, whereby the risk of costly false convictions is very high even on an *ex-post* basis.

Article 102 TFEU can apply to either collusive or unilateral conduct.[23] It is possible to use both provisions, if the firm has a dominant position, in order to sanction different components of a single antitrust offence.[24] For example, in *Van den Bergh Foods*, Unilever's distribution practices were found to infringe both Articles 101 and 102 TFEU. Article 101 applied to the exclusivity clause that was included in the distribution agreements concerning the use of the freezer cabinets provided by Unilever (then HB Ice Cream) to members of its distribution network. Article 102 applied to the practice of *inducing* the retailers who did not have a freezer cabinet to enter into freezer-cabinet agreements with HB, subject to a condition of exclusivity.[25] The later practice could not fall within the scope of Article 101 as it was a purely

[22] J Vickers, 'How to Reform the EC Merger Test?', OFT (8 November 2002), available at http://webarchive.nationalarchives.gov.uk/20140402142426/http://www.oft.gov.uk/shared_oft/speeches/spe0802.pdf.

[23] For conduct in oligopoly markets, see our analysis Chapter 9 (tacit collusion and collective dominance).

[24] See Case C-85/76, *Hoffmann-La Roche*, ECLI:EU:C:1979:36, para 116 ('[. . .] the fact that exclusive agreements may fall within the scope of Article 101 does not preclude the application of Article 102 since this latter Article is expressly aimed in fact at situations which clearly originate in contractual relations [. . .]').

[25] Case T-65/98, *Van den Bergh Foods Ltd v Commission* [2003] ECR II-4653, para 118 (Article 101), paras 159–60 (Article 102).

unilateral conduct: an invitation to participate in an agreement, which naturally pre-dates the conclusion of the agreement itself. This interpretation is supported by the explicit reference of the Court to the retailers that did *not* have their own freezer cabinets or cabinets available by other suppliers, that is, retailers that had *not yet* concluded a distribution agreement with HB.[26] Both the General Court and the CJEU rejected Unilever's argument that the Commission and the General Court had recycled the same arguments for the purposes of applying Articles 101 and 102 TFEU and affirmed that these claims involved a 'separate analysis'.[27]

The distinction between unilateral and collusive conduct was not an important issue in this case, as the Court had to examine thoroughly, in both situations, the effect of HB's conduct on consumer welfare. It made no difference, from the point of view of the judicial test applied, if this was an Article 101 or an Article 102 case. In both situations, the plaintiff had first the burden to prove the existence of an anti-competitive effect. The alleged anti-competitive conduct could then be justified by objective justifications and/or efficiency gains. It follows that it is highly unlikely that the litigants will concentrate the most important part of their efforts in contesting the qualification of the practice as an agreement or concerted practice, when they can either prove that it does not produce any anti-competitive effect or that it generates efficiency gains.

The finding of collusion has nevertheless important practical implications when the specific practice is by its nature anti-competitive and prohibited by its object under Article 101(1) TFEU. The characterization of the practice as unilateral or collusive will in this case be decisive as, if there is collusion, the conduct will automatically be found to infringe Article 101 TFEU, without the need to further examine its actual or potential effect on consumer welfare. The definition of what constitutes collusion (agreement or concerted practice) will therefore have important implications on the analysis of the restriction of competition. If the courts adopt a broad interpretation of the concept of agreement, a greater number of practices will be found to infringe Article 101 TFEU. A narrower interpretation of this concept will have the opposite effect.

8.3. THE CONCEPT OF DOMINANT POSITION

The concept of dominance has been one of the first few concepts in EU competition law to be interpreted by reference to economic analysis, in particular industrial economics (the economics of monopoly or market power). However, this does not mean that it is a concept that has the same meaning across legal systems, just because it is defined with reference to the same economic input.[28]

[26] According to the General Court (para 159), the infringement of Article 102 'takes the form, in this case, of an *offer* to supply freezer cabinets to the retailers and to maintain the cabinets free of any direct charge to the retailers'. This important element is not taken into account by E Rousseva, *Rethinking Exclusionary Abuses in EU Competition Law* (Hart, 2010), 636, who concludes that inducement was not a 'meaningful point of distinction' between Article 101 and Article 102 and that the reasoning of the Court 'was a mere recycling of the arguments made under Article 101'.

[27] Order of 28 September 2006 in Case C-552/03, *Unilever Bestfoods (formerly Van den Bergh Foods) v Commission* [2006] ECR I–909, para 136.

[28] ICN Unilateral Conduct Group, Doc. No. 752, Chapter 3: Assessment of dominance (May 2011), 4–6, available at www.internationalcompetitionnetwork.org/uploads/library/doc752.pdf.

8.3.1. THE RELATION OF DOMINANT POSITION AND MARKET POWER

There are different conceptions of market power in competition law and in economics. The neoclassical definition of market power has always focused on the ability of a firm to raise prices profitably and reduce output for a significant period of time, which essentially fits with the competition as an efficient outcome approach.[29] The legal definition of market or monopoly power has, on the contrary, insisted on the ability of the firm to exclude competitors and to affect the competitive process, a definition that fits well with the conception of competition as a process of rivalry.

The right to exclude is the cornerstone of the legal conception of 'monopoly', before the more economic concept of market power was finally accepted. Indeed, during the most active period of antitrust enforcement that started in United States in the 1930s, the legal definition of what constituted 'monopoly' was still predominant and diverged from the definition of this term by economists.[30]

In a seminal study, in 1937, Edward Mason explained the dissimilarities between the legal and the economic concepts of monopoly power.[31] According to Mason, lawyers and economists use the term of monopoly power with different meanings. For lawyers, monopoly power means restriction of the freedom to compete. For economists, it illustrates the control of the market. According to Mason,

> [t]he antithesis of the legal conception of monopoly is *free* competition, understood to be a situation in which the freedom of any individual or firm to engage in legitimate economic activity is not restrained by the state, by agreements between competitors or by the predatory practices of a rival. But free competition thus understood is quite compatible with the presence of monopoly elements in the *economic* sense of the word monopoly. For the antithesis of the economic conception of monopoly is not *free* but *pure* competition, understood to be a situation in which no seller or buyer has any control over the price of his product. Restriction of competition is the legal content of monopoly; control of the market is its economic substance. And these realities are by no means equivalent.[32]

The legal definition of market power emphasizes, on the contrary, restriction of trade and exclusion.

> It was not incumbent upon the courts to show that prices had actually been raised or quality of the product deteriorated in order to be able to hold that a monopoly existed contrary to the common law. Monopoly meant exclusion from a certain trade by legal dispensation and no examination of control of the market was necessary to establish this fact.[33]

The result of this definition of monopoly power was that the courts were finding illegal 'every contract limiting competition among the contracting competitors regardless of the effect or

29 See Chapters 2 and 3.

30 *Continental paper Bag Co v Eastern Paper Bag Co*, 210 US 405 (1908).

31 ES Mason, 'Monopoly in Law and Economics' (1937) 47 *Yale LJ* 34.

32 Ibid, 36.

33 Ibid, 37.

probable effect of such a contract on control of the market [. . .] (and) without examination of the extent of its (firm's) control of the market'.[34]

The concept of dominant position in EU competition law has been predominately inspired by the second approach, as it insists on the ability of the firm to maintain independent behaviour from the other actors of the market system rather than focusing on market outcomes.

Dominance for the purposes of EU competition law has been defined by the CJEU in the *United Brands* and *Hoffman-La Roche* and many other cases as:

> [A] position of economic strength enjoyed by an undertaking which enables it to prevent effective competition being maintained on the relevant market by affording it the power to behave to an appreciable extent independently of its competitors, customers and ultimately of its consumers.[35]
>
> [S]uch a position does not preclude some competition [. . .] but enables the undertaking [. . .] if not to determine, at least to have an appreciable influence on the conditions under which that competition will develop, and in any case to act largely in disregard of it so long as such conduct does not operate to its detriment.[36]

The definition of dominance appears thus to contain two conditions rather than one:

- The ability to prevent effective competition being maintained on the relevant market; and
- The power to behave to an appreciable extent independently of competitors, customers, and consumers. This differs from the economists' idea of a firm whose conduct is not closely constrained by competing products.

It is not entirely clear how these two conditions relate to one another, if at all.

D Geradin, P Hofer, F Louis, N Petit, and M Walker, 'The Concept of Dominance in EU Competition Law', Global Competition Law Centre, College of Europe, Research Paper on the Modernization of Article 82 EC (2005), 3 (footnotes omitted)

> Certain authors have seen two elements in this definition, namely (i) the power to behave independently of competitors, customers and consumers; and (ii) the ability to prevent effective competition being maintained on the relevant market. However, [. . .] it seems that on the legal ground, these elements are simply one and the same thing. This is confirmed by the rulings of the Community Courts which have never drawn any distinction between these elements.
>
> Nonetheless, the formulation used by the CJEU is not entirely satisfactory. The concept of 'acting independently' does not provide an adequate basis for discriminating between dominant firms and non-dominant firms. No firm can act to an appreciable extent independently, since every firm will be constrained by its respective demand curve. First, every firm is limited in its commercial behaviour to some extent by competitors since the presence of these competitors affects the firm's demand curve. Although this is by definition true for firms operating

[34] Ibid, 46.

[35] Case C-27/76, *United Brands company and United Brands Continental v Commission* [1978] ECR 207, para 65; and Case C-85/76, *Hoffman-La Roche & Co v Commission* [1979] ECR 461, para 38.

[36] Case C-27/76, *United Brands* [1978] ECR 207, para 113; Case C-85/76, *Hoffman-La Roche* [1979] ECR 461, para 39.

in a competitive market, it is also true for a dominant firm. All firms, including those that are held to be dominant, will increase prices to the point at which further price increases would be unprofitable. In this sense, competitors do constrain the behaviour of firms so that even a dominant firm does not act independently of its competitors. Second, an individual firm's demand curve is equally affected by the behaviour and preferences of its customers. Firms typically face downward sloping demand curves, indicating that a higher price comes at the expense of fewer sales: it is not generally open to a firm to raise prices and sell the same quantity as before. Again, this is true of a dominant firm just as much as it is true of a non-dominant firm.

There is, of course, one important sense in which a dominant firm can act to an appreciable extent independently of its competitors. A dominant firm can increase its price above the competitive level and so can to some extent act independently at the *competitive price*. As Professor Whish notes, 'the ability to restrict output and increase price derives from independence or, to put the matter another way, freedom from competitive constraint.' However, there is a measurement problem here: how can one measure whether a firm has the ability to price above the competitive price level? The competitive price level is virtually always impossible to calculate (on both conceptual and data grounds). More fundamentally, if it could be routinely calculated then the identification of a dominant position would become redundant, since one could simply adopt the rule that all market participants are required to price at the competitive level. [. . .]

For these reasons, a better economic test for identifying a dominant position lies in the other part of the definition of dominance, i.e. a firm's ability to engage in business activities that 'prevent effective competition from being maintained'.

From an economic perspective, competition can be said to be effective when no firm, either acting individually or in concert, is able to exercise substantial *market power*. The standard definition of market power is the ability to profitably raise price (through the restriction of output) above the level that would prevail under competitive conditions. This definition is already used by a number of competition authorities. For instance, the European Commission considers that 'market power is essentially measured by reference to the power of the undertaking concerned to raise prices by restricting output without incurring a significant loss of sales or revenues'. The UK Office of Fair Trading (hereafter, the 'OFT') has also adopted a close definition. It refers to market power as 'the ability to raise prices consistently and profitably above competitive levels'.

However, the existence of market power is not a zero-one matter. Market power is a continuum and a very large number of firms possess *some* degree of market power.

Dominance should therefore apply only to those firms that possess substantial market power or a very high degree of market power. It is worth noting that the equating of dominance with *substantial* (or significant) market power is already made in the definition of dominance formulated by the CJEU. The reference to the ability for a firm to behave independently to an 'appreciable extent' indicates that Article [102 TFEU] is not concerned with the minimal amount of market power that most firms enjoy. A similar principle has been recognized in sector specific legislation where the Council and the Parliament explicitly use 'significant market power' and dominance as synonyms. Furthermore, in the UK the OFT has indicated that 'an undertaking is unlikely to be dominant if it does not have substantial market power'.

The Commission and the courts have relied largely on *market share* when deciding whether a firm is dominant. We will consider the CJEU's appraisal of dominant positions case by case as we deal with the concept of abuse.

The broad definition of dominant position as essentially an ability to behave independently because of a variety of sources of economic power, including the power to exclude competitors (exclusionary economic power) or purely relational economic power because of the existence of a situation of obligatory partner and economic dependence may constitute an alternative option in defining a dominant position, enabling competition authorities to diversify their sources of wisdom beyond neoclassical price theory (NPT) and economics. This may be particularly appealing as the static analysis of the effects of a specific conduct on the consumers of a relevant market has been criticized as being inadequate to understand the broader sources of *economic power* (not necessarily *market power*) in the modern economy.

The position of EU competition law has evolved. Article 2 of the former EC Merger Regulation 4064/89 employed the concept of dominant position but linked it more directly than the previous case law on Article 102 TFEU to the concept of effective competition. In order to define the existence of effective competition, one should look to indications of performance as well as of market structure. In other words, effects on the market count. The Commission has attempted to extend considerably the definition of the concept of dominant position in the application of Article 102 TFEU and in EU merger control by creating the concept of collective dominant position, which aims to include in the scope of the EU competition law oligopolistic situations which may produce anti-competitive effects (because of tacit collusion).[37] The implementation of a new substantive test in EU merger control—the significant impediment of effective competition test—led to a reduction of the importance of the criterion of dominant position in EU merger control. According to Regulation 139/2004 on the control of concentrations between undertakings, the criterion of dominant position serves now as a simple indication of a significant impediment of effective competition and therefore of the existence of a potential harm to consumers.[38]

In its most recent documents, the Commission embraced this more economics-oriented definition of the concept of dominant position in other areas than EU merger control, by equating dominant position to substantial market power.[39]

Communication from the Commission—Guidance on the Commission's enforcement priorities in applying Article [102 TFEU] to abusive exclusionary conduct by dominant undertakings [2009] OJ C 45/7 (excerpts)

10. Dominance has been defined under Community law as a position of economic strength enjoyed by an undertaking, which enables it to prevent effective competition being maintained on a relevant market, by affording it the power to behave to an appreciable extent independently of its competitors, its customers and ultimately of consumers. This notion of independence is related to the degree of competitive constraint exerted on the undertaking in question. Dominance entails that these competitive constraints are not sufficiently effective and hence that the undertaking in question enjoys substantial market power over a period of time. This means that the undertaking's decisions are largely insensitive to the actions and reactions of competitors, customers

[37] See Chapter 11.

[38] Council Regulation (EC) No 139/2004 on the control of concentrations between undertakings [2004] OJ L 24/1, Article 2(2) [hereinafter EU Merger Regulation].

[39] See also Communication from the Commission—Notice—Guidelines on the application of Article 101(3) (formerly Article 81(3)) of the Treaty [2004] OJ C 101/97, para 26 [hereinafter Guidelines on Article 101(3)]; DG Competition, *Discussion Paper on the Application of Article 82 of the Treaty to Exclusionary Abuses* (December 2005), para 23.

> and, ultimately, consumers. The Commission may consider that effective competitive constraints are absent even if some actual or potential competition remains. In general, a dominant position derives from a combination of several factors which, taken separately, are not necessarily determinative.
>
> 11. The Commission considers that an undertaking which is capable of profitably increasing prices above the competitive level for a significant period of time does not face sufficiently effective competitive constraints and can thus generally be regarded as dominant. In this Communication, the expression 'increase prices' includes the power to maintain prices above the competitive level and is used as shorthand for the various ways in which the parameters of competition—such as prices, output, innovation, the variety or quality of goods or services—can be influenced to the advantage of the dominant undertaking and to the detriment of consumers.
>
> 12. The assessment of dominance will take into account the competitive structure of the market, and in particular the following factors:
>
> - constraints imposed by the existing supplies from, and the position on the market of, actual competitors (the market position of the dominant undertaking and its competitors),
> - constraints imposed by the credible threat of future expansion by actual competitors or entry by potential competitors (expansion and entry),
> - constraints imposed by the bargaining strength of the undertaking's customers (countervailing buyer power).

Market power, in particular *substantial market power*, operates as the unifying concept for the application of Articles 101 and 102 TFEU and the introduction of a more economics-oriented approach in justifying antitrust intervention on the marketplace. A capacity of independent behaviour with regard to competitors and consumers is not a sufficient criterion for a finding of a dominant position.[40]

The convergence of the economic and the legal definition of monopoly power or dominant position is not, however, complete. While the definition of the concept of market power adopted by the Commission's Guidance on Article 102 as well as the non-horizontal merger guidelines presents similarities to the economic concept of market power, its scope is broader. In a similar formulation for Articles 101 and 102 TFEU and EU merger control purposes, the Commission defines market power as 'the ability of one or more firms to profitably increase prices, reduce output, choice or quality of goods and services, diminish innovation, or otherwise negatively influence parameters of competition'.[41]

This broad definition accommodates the emphasis of EU competition law on the protection of the competitive process and consumer sovereignty. Although the ability to increase price remains the primary concern of competition law, in conformity with the NPT approach, the emphasis on parameters of competition other than price, in particular consumer choice, epitomizes the broad definition of what constitutes a restriction of competition under EU competition law and the recognition of the importance of quality and variety investment

[40] Commission Guidance on Article 102.

[41] Guidelines on the assessment of non-horizontal mergers under the Council Regulation on the control of concentrations between undertakings [2008] OJ C 265/6, para 10; Guidelines on Article 101(3), para 25; DG Competition, 'Discussion Paper on the Application of Article 82 of the Treaty to Exclusionary Abuses' (December 2005), para 24, available at http://ec.europa.eu/competition/antitrust/art82/discpaper2005.pdf; Commission Guidance on Article 102, para 11.

competition instead of just price competition.[42] For this reason, it is important to examine the different dimensions of a dominant position.

8.3.2. THE VARIOUS DIMENSIONS OF THE DOMINANT POSITION

One can distinguish four dimensions of the concept of market power and dominant position, should this concept be equated to 'substantial market power'. Their relative influence has depended on the evolution of EU competition law towards a more economic approach.

8.3.2.1. Neoclassical market power: Power over price

The first dimension is closely linked to the neo-classical price paradigm, which we have exposed in Chapter 3. Based on A Marshall's partial equilibrium theory,[43] this approach conceives the ability of a firm to increase prices with regard to those that would apply in a situation of perfect competition in the context of a specific market, in abstraction of all other markets. If one defines dominant position as 'substantial market power' in the neo-classical theory way, then one should necessarily focus on the undertaking's 'power over price'.[44] This concept is formalized in the so-called 'Lerner index', which measures the proportional deviation of price at the firm's profit-maximizing output from the firm's marginal cost at that output, without measuring the firm elasticity of demand.[45] However, this index is quite difficult to establish as, even assuming price is observable, marginal costs (the effect on total costs of a small change in output) are quite difficult to determine in practice, especially by the methods of litigation.[46] Hence, if the firm's elasticity of demand is unknown, one may rely on market shares to compute market power, the firm's elasticity of demand, and hence its market power, being derived by combining the firm's market share with other factors such as the market elasticity of demand.[47] However, one should exercise some caution in inferring market power from high market shares. As Landes and Posner explain:

[42] Competition based on quality (*Q*) or variety (*V*) increasing investment is equally important than price competition. Richard Markovits defines *QV* investment competition as 'the process through which rival sellers compete away their potential supernormal profits by introducing additional QV investments until even the most profitable project in the relevant area of product space generates just a normal rate of return': R Markovits, *Truth or Economics. Is economic efficiency a sound basis upon which to make public policy or legal decisions?* (Yale University Press, 2008), 90. The importance of this type of competition has been recognized by the European Court of Justice in Case C-26/76, *Metro SB-Großmärkte GmbH & Co KG v Commission* [1977] ECR 1875, para 21. See Chapter 10.

[43] See Section 3.2.

[44] WM Landes and RA Posner, 'Market Power in Antitrust Cases' (1981) 94 *Harvard L Rev* 937.

[45] A Lerner, 'The Concept of Monopoly and the Measurement of Monopoly Power' (1934) 1 *Rev Economic Studies* 157. The equation is the following: $L = \frac{P - MC}{P}$ where *P* is the market price set by the firm and *MC* is the firm's marginal costs. The index ranges from a high of 1 to a low of 0, with higher numbers implying greater market power. In a perfectly competitive firm (where $P = MC$), the Lerner index will equal 0, thus showing that the firm has no market power.

[46] WM Landes and RA Posner, 'Market Power in Antitrust Cases' (1981) 94 *Harvard L Rev* 937.

[47] Ibid.

> [. . .] Although the formulation of the Lerner index [. . .] provides an economic rationale for inferring market power from market share, it also suggests pitfalls in mechanically using market share data to measure market power. Since market share is only one of three factors [. . .] that determine market power, inferences of power from share alone can be misleading. In fact, if market share alone is used to infer power, the market share measure [. . .], which is determined without regard to market demand or supply elasticity (separate factors in the equation), will be the wrong measure. The proper measure will attempt to capture the influence of market demand and supply elasticity on market power. [. . .].[48]

Furthermore, market share may not be a good indicator of market power, in particular because it does not take into account the possible entry of new competitors.

The operation of defining the market is a crucial step in the definition of market power. Landes and Posner also note another possible approach to determining market power when elasticities are unknown, the use of 'guesstimates' of elasticities in defining the market in the first place, the adjustment for elasticities coming not after a market share is calculated but when the market is defined. They note that this is the dominant judicial method of taking account of elasticities of demand and supply. Crucially, however, evidence of market power from the economic perspective does not indicate the existence of a dominant position or monopoly power from a legal perspective.

Adopting the 'power over price' neoclassical theory conception of market power may present several shortcomings in the European context as Landes & Posner note:

> The concept of 'power over price' is [. . .] not entirely satisfactory. First, it underplays the fact that substantial market power can be exercised on many other factors such as, for instance, quality, service and innovation. Thus, a definition of substantial market power should also encompass the ability to lower quality or reduce the pace of innovation. Second, the suggested definition of this concept requires the identification of the competitive price level which is a notoriously daunting task. It is indeed virtually impossible to determine the competitive price level, and if that was possible, there would be no need to be concerned with the concept of dominance. Hence, a test articulated on the 'ability of a firm to restrict output substantially in the market place, below its current level' would probably be better suited for the purpose of identifying a substantial market power. If a firm is able to restrict significantly total output in the market by restricting its own output, this indicates that other firms are unable to replace the supply taken away by the allegedly dominant firm. This implies that there are both barriers to entry and barriers to expansion, which suggests that a firm with a large market share may well have substantial market power.[49]

Remarkably, EU competition law perceives the definition of a dominant position as a two-step process, which includes: (i) market definition and (ii) estimating the dominant position of the undertaking based on a number of criteria, such as market shares, entry barriers, etc. How close is this methodology to the neo-classical conception of market power of 'power over price'?

48 Ibid.

49 D Geradin, P Hofer, F Louis, N Petit, and M Walker, 'The Concept of Dominance in EU Competition Law', Global Competition Law Centre, College of Europe, Research Paper on the Modernization of Article 82 EC (2005), 3.

8.3.2.2. Exclusionary market power and dominant position

The second dimension is linked to the traditional legal conception of monopoly power as conferring a power of exclusion and has exercised considerable influence on the enforcement of Article 102 TFEU. Preserving the market access of EU based firms from private barriers to entry imposed by national incumbents and monopolies was one of the main objectives of the enforcement of EU competition law during the first decades of European integration. Competition law operated during these years, and for some still operates, as a complement to the Internal Market rules in achieving a greater economic integration of the European economies. The evolution towards an economic approach has not weakened the appeal of the exclusionary conception of monopoly power. New industrial economics have focused on the possibility of incumbents to employ strategic barriers to entry in order to exclude or marginalize rivals and thus be able to raise prices and harm consumers.[50] Professors Krattenmaker, Lande, and Salop have argued that there are two methods of exercising market power corresponding, respectively, to the 'power to control price' and 'power to exclude competitors' distinction:[51]

> First, the firm or group of firms may raise or maintain price above the competitive level directly by restraining its own output ('control price'). The power to control price by restraining one's own output is the usual focus of Chicago School antitrust analysts. For this reason, we denote the power to control price profitably, directly by restraining one's own output, as classical [. . .] market power.
>
> Second, the firm or group of firms may raise price above the competitive level or prevent it from falling to a lower competitive level by raising its rivals' costs and thereby causing them to restrain their output ('exclude competition'). Such allegations are at the bottom of most antitrust cases in which one firm or group of firms is claimed to have harmed competition by foreclosing or excluding its competitors. We denote this power as exclusionary [. . .] market power. Consumer welfare is reduced by the exercise of either [classical] or [exclusionary] market power. [. . .]
>
> Exercising either type of power reduces allocative efficiency and transfers wealth from consumers to the owners of the firms exercising monopoly power. In addition, for [exclusionary] market power, production efficiency also is reduced.[52]

The distinction is important as 'anticompetitive, exclusionary, market power occurs when an excluding firm successfully achieves two related goals': first 'by denying inputs to its rivals, the excluding firm materially raises its rivals' costs'; second, 'by thus precluding the competitive check on its price and output decisions that those rivals provide, the excluding firm thereby gains the power to price in its output market above the competitive level. [. . .]'.[53] Proof of either power should, according to the same authors, lead to the finding of market power or a dominant position.

An important implication of exclusionary market power concept is that it leads to a different approach from neo-classical market power or 'power over price' in order to estimate the existence of a dominant position, the competition authority first identifying the allegedly

[50] See A Jacquemin, *Sélection et pouvoir dans la nouvelle économie industrielle* (Economica, 1985), 118.

[51] TG Krattenmaker, RH Lande, and SC Salop, 'Monopoly Power and Market Power in Antitrust Law' (1987) 76 *Georgetown LJ* 241, 248.

[52] Ibid, 248–53. [53] Ibid.

exclusionary conduct, and then analysing market power. Krattenmaker, Lande, and Salop note: '[exclusionary] power cannot be evaluated in a vacuum, independent of and prior to analysis of the allegedly exclusionary conduct. It is the exclusionary conduct that creates the market power being evaluated, not the other way around'.[54] According to these authors, 'the use of a threshold market power test in exclusion cases is unwarranted'.[55]

Do you agree with the authors that market power (or the analysis of structural conditions) should come after the identification of the conduct? Should that imply that the analysis under Article 102 TFEU should start by examining the conduct, then the existence of dominant position and, finally, the interplay of the dominant position and the conduct, that could lead to an abuse? Would this interpretation be compatible with the text of Article 102 TFEU? Shouldn't such an approach also apply to exclusionary collusive practices that can fall under Article 101 TFEU? How would the two provisions be reconciled in this case? Compare this approach with that advocated by Judge Easterbrook on the need to adopt filters in the competition law assessment, such as market power, before examining in detail the anti-competitive effects of the conduct. In the words of Judge Easterbrook, 'no power, no problem'.[56]

8.3.2.3. Relational market power and dominant position

The third dimension of market power is linked to the idea that firms may be able to harm consumers because they have acquired a position of strength towards other economic actors (suppliers, retailers, consumers) that provides them the power to behave independently and to harm consumers.

In some cases, the existence of this power is linked to the difficulty undertakings would have in extracting themselves from an investment, because of sunk costs, leading to their partner's power to impose costs or confer benefits in day-to-day transactions. Look, for instance, to the relation between a franchisor and a franchisee: the franchisee has sunk costs (that he may not recover if terminates the relation with the franchisor), for instance 'a non refundable franchise fee paid to the franchisor or to unrecoverable costs of designer decorating, or equipping the franchise outlet',[57] or power emanating from the various non-compete obligations that a franchisor may impose on the franchisee joined with the fact that the franchisor rents the premises to the franchisee, the latter having concluded a long-term lease agreement with the result that he would need to vacate the commercial premises, should the relationship with the franchisor break up.

One could also distinguish between the power over price which may result from a high degree of market concentration, as in the economic model of monopoly, from the power over price sometimes available to sellers from market imperfections that exist in all markets, regardless of the degree of concentration at the seller's or buyer's side. Only structural market power affects overall industry price and output levels. 'Nonstructural' market power is limited to a particular firm. This type of market power might be present in aftermarkets, as consumers might be locked in, because of sunk costs and information asymmetry between them and the seller, with regard to a certain primary product, as they often do not consider, when purchasing the primary product, the possibility that they might be exploited by the undertaking in question in the provision of after-sale services or replacement parts.

54 Ibid, 255 55 Ibid.

56 F Easterbrook, 'The Limits of Antitrust' (1984) 63 *Texas L Rev* 1, 21.

57 LA Sullivan and WS Grimes, *The Law of Antitrust: An Integrated Handbook* (West, 2000), 460.

8.3.2.3.1. The theory of non-structural market power

The theory of non-structural market power has been criticized by some authors as not being sufficiently substantial to constitute market power under competition law, and that it should therefore be excluded from competition law assessment.[58] Two reasons are advanced for this criticism: (i) enforcement agency budgets and judicial resources are scarce and thus, it does not make sense to squander them in attacks on market power over low sales volumes, as it is the case for relational market power and (ii) there are no procedures or specific methodology for measuring the extent of market imperfections, thus permitting the intervention of the competition authority in situations of significant relational market power.

Despite these criticisms, the concept of relational market power is integrated in modern competition law assessment in two ways. First, the competition law of some Member States takes directly into account the existence of a situation of 'economic dependency' in the enforcement of competition law, even in the absence of neoclassical market power.[59] Second, non-structural factors might be taken into account indirectly, in assessing the existence of a dominant position, either by narrowing down the relevant market definition (excluding the price constraints imposed on the specific after-sales services by competing manufacturers under the assumption that consumers take into account the cost of after-sales services when they purchase a product) or by considering it as an additional factor reinforcing the finding of a dominant position, even if the firm does not have high market shares (theory of obligatory partner in EU competition law).

Non-structural market power in EU competition law: Virgin/British Airways

In Virgin/British Airways, *the Commission found that British Airways (BA) had a dominant position in the market for air transport, based on BA's market shares, that were not conclusive, and the fact that it was an obligatory business partner for travel agents.*

***Virgin/British Airways* (Case IV/D-2/34.780) Commission Decision [2000] OJ L 30/1**

92. BA's position on the markets for air transport makes it an obligatory business partner for travel agents. As BA has pointed out, the IATA passenger agency programme may oblige it to deal with all travel agents who meet certain objective criteria. However what makes BA dominant is the fact that travel agents are in a situation where an extremely large proportion of the air tickets they sell will be BA tickets, and hence a similar proportion of their sales of air travel agency services will be to BA. This allows BA, in its purchases of air travel agency services, to act independently of the other airlines who purchase air travel agency services. Regardless of the conditions on which BA buys these services from travel agents, agents have to deal with BA and accept that a large portion of their income from these services will be that generated by the sale of BA tickets.

58 B Klein, 'Market Power in Antitrust: Economic Analysis After Kodak (1994) 3 *Supreme Court Economic Rev* 43.

59 See German Act against Restraints of Competition, section 20(2); French Commercial Code, Article L 420-2.

The Commission examined this element of the dominant position of BA, when discussing BA's relative dominant position with regard to its immediate competitors, the 'top 10 airlines'.

93. This overall statistic including all travel agencies and all airlines may conceal the extent of BA's influence in key areas. In 1998 BA accounted for 39.7% of all air ticket sales through travel agents, but 57% of sales by top 10 airlines. In 1998 BA accounted for 43.7% of the sales of air tickets through the 10 largest travel agents in the United Kingdom. In other words, BA enjoys a particularly powerful position relative to its leading rival airlines, and with respect to the most important travel agencies.

The importance of the BA brand for travel agents might be considered as an element reinforcing the market share criterion and thus leading to the finding of a dominant position.

The General Court (then Court of First Instance) confirmed the position of the Commission on this point.

Case T-219/99, *British Airways v Commission*
[2003] ECR II–5925[60]

BA argued that:

184. Contrary to what the Commission maintains in recital 92 of the contested decision, the fact that a single airline accounts for a large proportion of the tickets sold by a travel agency does not mean that that airline is 'an obligatory business partner' for that agency. In practice, BA argues, every agency needs to offer the tickets of a broad range of airlines. In fact, agencies have substantial bargaining power and the final choice of agent is a matter for the customer.

185. Unlike distributors [. . .], travel agents do not normally hold stocks of tickets or need actually to sell BA's tickets. Since the routes served by BA are also served by other airlines, agents are able to offer the choice that passengers demand as long as they are in a position to sell BA tickets.

The Court concluded:

215. As a whole, the services operated by BA on routes to and from United Kingdom airports have the cumulative effect of generating the purchase by travellers of a preponderant number of BA air tickets through travel agents established in the United Kingdom, and, correspondingly, at least as many transactions between BA and those agents for the purposes of supplying air travel agency services, particularly in the distribution of BA air tickets.

216. It necessarily follows that those agents substantially depend on the income they receive from BA in consideration for their air travel agency services.

217. BA is therefore wrong to deny that it is an obligatory business partner of travel agents established in the United Kingdom and to maintain that those agents have no actual need to sell BA tickets. BA's arguments are not capable of calling into question

[60] See also Case T-229/94, *Deutsche Bahn v Commission* [1997] ECR II–1689, para 57, finding the dominant position of the German railway operator, because of its statutory monopoly, which placed 'those seeking the services in a position of economic dependence on the supplier'.

the finding, in recital 93 of the contested decision, that BA enjoys a particularly powerful position in relation to its nearest rivals and the largest travel agents.

On appeal, the Court of Justice did not discuss this issue.[61]

8.3.2.3.2. Non-structural market power in national competition law: Economic dependency

Starting with Germany in 1973,[62] several EU Member States have adopted provisions in their competition laws prohibiting the abuse of economic dependency or of a superior bargaining power position.[63] Recital 8 of Regulation 1/2003 explicitly mentions provisions regulating the abuse of economic dependency and superior bargaining power in order to explain the possibility opened by Article 3(2) of Regulation 1/2003 to Member States to enact competition law provisions that are stricter than Article 102 TFEU for unilateral conduct.[64] The inclusion of the abuse of economic dependency or abuse of superior bargaining power in competition law raises important concerns discussed by the following article by Judge Frederic Jenny.

F Jenny, 'The "Coming Out" of Abuse of Superior Bargaining Power in the Antitrust World' (15 July 2008), 3–5, available at http://unctad.org/sections/ditc_ccpb/docs/ditc_ccpb0008_en.pdf (excerpts)

In the neoclassical price-theory paradigm consumers and suppliers enter transactions only to the extent that their satisfaction is enhanced by the transaction, thus the assumption is that, absent market power or other market failures/imperfections, transactions are mutually beneficial.

61 Case C-95/04 P, *British Airways v Virgin* [2007] ECR I-2331.

62 Gesetz gegen Wettbewerbsbeschränkungen [German Act Against Restraints of Competition], section 20(2), available at http://www.gesetze-im-internet.de/englisch_gwb/ [hereinafter GWB]. An important case implementing the abuse of economic dependency in Germany is *Rossignol*, where the German Federal Court found that Rossignol had the duty to supply its distributors, although its market share was 8 per cent, partly because of the importance of the Rossignol brand: KZR 1/75 (Rossignol, 20 November 1975) WuW/E BGH 1391. The German case law distinguishes between two broad situations of abuse of economic dependence: (i) *Sortimentsbedingte Abhänginkeit*, referring to the existence of a situation of economic dependency because of the importance of the brand and the impossibility of the distributor in question to have access to other important brands, and (ii) *Unternehmensbedingte Abhänginkeit* for cases where the undertakings have been in a continuous long term commercial relationship with important sunk costs incurred by one of them, thus making the termination of the commercial relationship particularly harmful for the undertaking found economically dependent. France has also a distinctive tradition in the application of the theory of the abuse of economic dependency. For an analysis, see I Lianos, *La Transformation du droit de la concurrence par le recours à l'analyse économique* (Bruylant, 2007), 370–80.

63 For an overview, see Commission Staff Working Paper accompanying the Report on the Functioning of Regulation 1/2003 SEC(2009) 574 final, paras 162–9, available at http://eur-lex.europa.eu/LexUriServ/LexUriServ.do?uri=SEC:2009:0574:FIN:EN:PDF, noting that '[b]esides rules concerning specifically the abuse of economic dependence, some national provisions regulate behaviour labelled as "abuse of superior bargaining power" or "abuse of significant influence". The aim of these kinds of rules is essentially to regulate disparities of bargaining power in distribution relationships, including where neither the supplier nor the distributor holds a dominant position on a specific market' (ibid, para 162).

64 At the international level, see ICN Special Program for Kyoto Annual Conference, Report on Abuse of Superior Bargaining Position, prepared by Task Force for Abuse of Superior Bargaining Position, ICN 7th Annual Conference, Kyoto, Japan, 14–16 April, 2008, available at http://www.internationalcompetitionnetwork.org/uploads/library/doc386.pdf, reporting a number of jurisdictions worldwide having equivalent provisions to the abuse of economic dependence or superior bargaining power and discussing different national approaches.

[. . .] What is more rarely discussed in economic literature is what happens when some operators are coerced into entering a transaction (or a type of transaction). This problem is not completely ignored by competition enforcers who recognize that there are circumstances (for example when an operator owns an essential facility) when the result of a transaction (for example the price charged for the use of the essential facility) or the refusal to enter a transaction (for example a refusal to interconnect) must be monitored to ensure that they do not distort market competition.

But a more general question is rarely addressed in the literature on competition. What happens when transactions (or a subset of transactions) on a competitive market are not mutually beneficial for the parties but one party is coerced into entering the transaction?

This general question can be subdivided into several sub-questions:

- Can coercion be defined in an economically meaningful way?
- Can we relate superior bargaining power to coercion?
- Is coercion possible in structurally competitive markets?
- If coercion occurs in individual transactions or in a subset of transaction on an otherwise competitive market, will the market adjustment process send signals consistent with welfare maximisation?

[Countries with provisions on the abuse of economic dependency or superior bargaining position] generally define the situation of the dependent firm as characterized by a lack of economic alternative and they describe the prohibited abuses of dependency or of superior bargaining power as practices which are closely related to the concept of coercion as we have defined it previously. [. . .]

The condition for successful coercion is also familiar to countries where competition law enforcers deal with competition problems related to essential facilities.

In the case of 'essential facilities' the rationale for antitrust enforcers or regulators' intervention is precisely that the potential entrants are powerless vis-à-vis the owner of the essential facility since they do not have any other choice besides access to the essential facility in order to enter the market. This complete lack of alternative exposes them to the risk of either being excluded from the market altogether, if the owner of the essential facility refuses to give them access, or of being the victims of extortionist demands.

But, in the case of an essential facility, the lack of alternative for the potential entrants is established by reference to the fact that there is and can be only one facility to which they need to be connected. Thus, lack of access and/or the lack of access on 'fair terms' for the entrants will mean that the owner of the essential facility will have (or rather keep) a monopoly on the market on which the entrants are trying to enter.

The question arises of whether it is only when they are faced with a problem of access to a (unique) essential facility that operators lack reasonable choice or alternative and therefore can be subject to coercion.

If there are other situations where coercion is possible, as is suggested by countries which have a specific provision against abuse of dependency or abuse of superior bargaining power, the question is then to define what standard should be applied to establish that the coercee has no reasonable choice but to bow to the pressure of the coercer. Is it sufficient that the coercee believed that it did not have any alternative? Is the lack of alternative defined by an objective fact such as that the coercee would be worse off if it did not accept the least preferred alternative offered by the threat maker or does one have to establish that irreparable harm would have come to him?

An answer suggested by the case law of countries which have provisions prohibiting abuse of superior bargaining power or abuse of dependency is that it is not sufficient to entering into a contract with the coercor that the latter was likely to exercise threats in the course of their contractual relationship. Such a case could happen if, for example, the coercor had a well-documented history of threatening firms with which it had entered into contractual agreements. In such an instance, one could argue that by choosing to ignore the reputation of the coercor the coercee deliberately exposed himself to the possibility of being faced with a threat or, at the very least, did not exercise sufficient caution to avoid the threat.

Whatever the standard used to define a coercive threat, one must ask what are the possible consequences of the exercise of coercion in order to establish whether coercion should be an antitrust concern. [. . .]

In addition to their distributional impact, the author notes that coercive threats may also produce negative effects on efficiency.

First, as mentioned earlier, through coercion retailers can shift over to suppliers the burden of some functions that would otherwise be theirs as retailers. They have an interest in doing so, irrespective of whether or not the suppliers are more or less efficient at providing those functions than they are. Thus burden shifting may take place, even if it means a loss of productive efficiency.

Second, and more importantly, when faced with the prospect that retailers will capture their efficiency gains through additional coercive threats and demands, upstream firms will be discouraged from seeking productivity gains, from investing or even from staying in the industry. The only firms that will consider staying in the industry at the upstream level are firms which for some reason (the strength of their brand, for example) have a countervailing bargaining power. New entrants or small firms will usually not have such a countervailing bargaining power in the initial stages of their entry on a market and will therefore be at a disadvantage. As a result, bargaining power on the retailer side is likely to create or increase barriers to entry in the upstream industry, and to lead to an increase in concentration and a decrease in consumer choice and competition. There are allegations in Europe that the increase in concentration in the European food industry is partly a response to concentration (and buyer power) at the retail level.

It has been argued that powerful retailers are unlikely to engage in coercion since by doing so they would promote concentration among their suppliers and thereby undermine their own interests. But they will do so because of the externality involved. In an oligopolistic situation in the retail sector; a large scale retail chain cannot be sure that its competitors will not engage in coercive practices which might ultimately lead to more concentration of suppliers, irrespective of whether or not it engages in such practices itself. Yet if the others do not engage in such practices, each oligopolist retailer has an incentive to engage in such practices since it will gain competitive advantage by shifting some costs to suppliers).

In this scenario, even if we assume that consumers may benefit in the short run (if, for example, the additional advantages secured through coercion are passed on to them), they will ultimately bear the cost of the increase in concentration (and therefore the decrease in the intensity of competition) between the suppliers in the medium to long run.

Overall, coercive practices, which may be defined relatively easily, which always have a distributional impact and may or may not have an effect on competition, make entry on the market where the coerced firm operates more costly. If coercive practices have a negative effect on competition and efficiency, it is likely to be a long-term effect rather than a short term effect. It is possible that even if they have a negative effect on competition and efficiency in the long run, coercive practices may have a positive effect on consumer surplus in the short run (if the benefits obtained through coercion are passed on to consumers by the coercers). It is likely that the occurrence of coercive threats will be greater when the coercers are in an oligopolistic market. [. . .]

The author then critically examines the arguments against the inclusion of the superior bargaining position theory in competition law analysis

Three arguments are often invoked against the introduction of specific provisions against abuse of superior bargaining power in antitrust laws. The concept of superior bargaining power is vague; the alleged 'abuses' of superior bargaining power in most cases do not raise competition issues; civil courts are better equipped to deal with contractual disputes than competition authorities.

The first argument seems to be the weakest. Indeed, as we saw earlier the ability to coerce can be defined fairly precisely. There is room for some discussion as to what standard should be applied to assess the existence of coercion (should it be whether the least preferred alternative is worse than what would have been the situation of the alleged victim in 'normal' circumstances or 'if the proposal had not been made' or 'if competition' had prevailed? Should one consider only '*ex ante*' dependency? What to do when the coercee should have expected to be confronted with a coercive threat?).

However, as the recent discussion at the EU level on abuse of dominance has clearly shown, even when rigorous analysis is applied, economists can differ on the appropriate standard to assess a particular behaviour. The assessment of economic coercion does not seem to present insuperable problems.

The second argument (alleged abuses of superior bargaining power do not raise competition issues in many cases) requires closer scrutiny. First, the fact that a practice does not always restrict competition does not mean that it should not be part of competition law. It is well known that vertical restrictive agreements may in certain circumstances be pro-competitive rather than anti-competitive and the same applies to low prices by dominant firms. Yet, they typically fall within the purview of antitrust or competition laws. However, the ambiguous effect of such practices on market competition means that these practices should be examined under a rule of reason approach rather than being prohibited per se.

However, there are some differences worth noting between vertical restraints and low prices by a firm having a dominant position on the one hand and coercive practices on the other hand.

Vertical restrictive agreements typically link an upstream firm with a set of downstream firms (or vice versa) and low prices by dominant firms is a practice undertaken by firms having market power. In both cases the presumption that such practices may have an effect on the market is reasonable, even if the precise nature of this effect is subject to close scrutiny in each case.

Coercion, or abuse of superior bargaining position, because it is defined purely in terms of the ability of a firm to inflict harm on another firm seems to potentially cover a very large number of practices, each of which is unlikely to affect market competition or efficiency, even if one recognizes that the cumulative effect of abuses of superior bargaining power may be to significantly lower efficiency.

Thus, the argument against the inclusion of provisions against abuse of superior bargaining power in competition laws does not rest on the fact that such abuses have no effect on competition and efficiency but on the fact that they do not reach the threshold which would warrant intervention by competition authorities in each case of abuse. [. . .]

Another argument often invoked against the inclusion of provisions against abuses of superior bargaining position in competition laws states that even if it is true that such abuses may undermine the foundations of a competitive market system, civil courts are better equipped to deal with contractual disputes than competition authorities.

The relevance of this argument must be assessed with consideration for local conditions and the nature of coercion.

It may well be that in some countries, for example in developed countries, where the civil court system is reasonably efficient, firms that are victims of coercive practices can successfully argue that they were coerced into accepting contractual obligations that they would not have accepted had they been in a position to exercise their free will and that they should either be released from their commitments or fairly compensated for the injury they have suffered.

Yet in other countries, particularly in some developing countries, the judicial system may not be in a position to handle such claims effectively for a variety of reasons, such as the fact that it is underfunded, overworked, corrupt, lacks the necessary expertise, etc. Thus, one cannot presume that in all cases the judicial system will be more effective than competition authorities in discouraging the abuse of superior bargaining power.

Even in countries where civil courts are well-equipped to deal with contractual disputes, it is not obvious that abuse of superior bargaining power will be discouraged. Victims may be reluctant to bring cases to courts precisely because they are in an inferior bargaining position and may fear retaliation if they lodge a claim against the firm on which they are dependent.

Thus, relying entirely on private right of actions in countries with well-developed civil law systems may not be sufficient to deter abuses of superior bargaining power to protect the market mechanism against the externality generated by such practices. There may be a need for a public enforcement as well and the competition authority may be the appropriate institution for undertaking this task.

NOTES AND QUESTIONS

1. The UK does not have equivalent provisions prohibiting the abuse of economic dependency or superior bargaining position.[65] Chapter II of the UK Competition Act 1998 can only be enforced in the presence of a dominant position. According to the UK competition authorities, '[a]n undertaking will not be dominant unless it has substantial market power'. The later concept is defined as 'the ability profitably to sustain prices above competitive levels or to restrict output or quality below competitive levels'.[66] The UK authorities thus adopt the neoclassical definition of market power as power over price. The assessment of dominance focuses on the price constraints imposed by existing and potential competitors in a defined relevant market and strong buying power from the undertaking's customers. The latter does not rely on relational sources of market power.[67] Thus, relational or non-structural sources of market power are not taken into account.[68]
2. Would you be in favour for the UK to adopt provisions prohibiting the abuse of economic dependency or superior bargaining power? Consider the position of the UK competition authorities with regard to some alleged anti-competitive practices in the groceries sector. Would these practices have been dealt more efficiently if the UK had a provision prohibiting the abuse of economic dependency or superior

[65] See, however the proposals of Lord Tyrie, the CMA chairman, who in a recent letter to the Secretary of State (BEIS) indicated that in the process of the review of substantive provisions of UK competition law in the context of the digital economy (as part of the Furman review), the CMA is examining 'whether explicit prohibitions on unilateral conduct that exploits economic dependence or inequality of bargaining power, even in the absence of an established dominant market position', may be needed in the UK competition law regime. Letter to the Secretary of State for Business, Energy and Industrial Strategy from Lord Tyrie (February 21, 2019), available at https://assets.publishing.service.gov.uk/government/uploads/system/uploads/attachment_data/file/781151/Letter_from_Andrew_Tyrie_to_the_Secretary_of_State_BEIS.pdf, fn 23 p 14.

[66] OFT 402, Abuse of a dominant position (2004), para 4.14, available at https://assets.publishing.service.gov.uk/government/uploads/system/uploads/attachment_data/file/284422/oft402.pdf (Guidance adopted by the CMA).

[67] See our discussion in Section 8.3.4.3. on buyer power.

[68] See OFT 402, Abuse of Dominant Position (2004), 13–16.

bargaining position being adopted? Examine the pros and cons of establishing such a prohibition in the UK.

3. Should competition law be interested in the effects of superior bargaining power on small and medium enterprises? Would this be compatible with economic efficiency?

8.3.2.3.3. Superior bargaining power and the limits of competition law

Concerns over the rising power of retailers in the food sector have led many competition authorities to use existing rules or adopt new rules on superior bargaining power, these rules either forming part of competition law statutes or of other functional equivalents.[69], [70] These different rules stay relatively opaque as to the definition of the concept of superior bargaining power, the common characteristic (and presumably) advantage of these provisions being that they may potentially impose competition law related duties to undertakings not disposing of a dominant position or a significant market power, for unilateral conduct, which would have otherwise not been subject to competition law related duties under the traditional rules of abuse of a dominant position. The concept of superior (or unequal) bargaining power is also well-known in the fields of contract law and unfair competition law,[71] where it has given rise to a considerable literature attempting to unveil its theoretical underpinnings.[72] Authors usually contrast the use of this concept in these areas of law, where the focus is on the unfairness of the process of exchange, with the efforts to integrate this rule in the field of competition law, where

69 This Section partly draws in part on I Lianos and C Lombardi, 'Superior Bargaining Power and the Global Food Value Chain: The Wuthering Heights of Holistic Competition Law?' (2016-I) *Concurrences* 22.

70 For a comparative analysis of rules on superior bargaining power, see ICN, Report on Abuse of Superior Bargaining Position (2008), available at http://www.internationalcompetitionnetwork.org/uploads/library/doc386.pdf.

71 See, for instance, for contract law, at the EU level, the Principles of European Contract Law 2002, Article 4:109 (ex-Article 6.109) on excessive benefit or unfair advantage, because at the time of the conclusion of the contract 'was dependent on or had a relationship of trust with the other party, was in economic distress or had urgent needs, was improvident, ignorant, inexperienced or lacking in bargaining skill'; the Draft Common Frame of Reference (DCFR), Principle 10, concerning restrictions to the principle of the freedom of contract because of inequality of bargaining power (even in the context of business-to-business (B2B) relations); and the contract law sub-doctrines that explicitly or implicitly incorporate bargaining power, such as unconscionability, duress, undue influence, the parole evidence rule, and public policy. On unfair competition, again at the EU level, see Green Paper on unfair trading practices in the business-to-business food and non-food supply chain in Europe COM(2013) 37; Communication of the Commission—Tackling unfair trading practices in the business-to-business food supply chain, COM(2014) 472 final. See also the doctrines of 'unconscionable conduct', economic duress, and undue influence in contract law in England & Wales, in particular the concept of economic duress, as vitiating elements for a contract. This type of duress 'arises where one party uses his superior economic power in an "illegitimate" way so as to coerce the other contracting party to agree to a particular set of terms': E McKendrick, *Contract Law* (Palgrave Macmillan, 2005), 358.

72 See in particular the seminal cases *Lloyds Bank Ltd v Bundy* [1974] EWCA Civ 8 (EWCA (Civ)); *Macaulay v Schroeder Publishing Co Ltd* [1974] 1 WLR; and the following critical and explanatory appraisal by SN Thal, 'Inequality of Bargaining Power Doctrine: The Problem of Defining Contractual Unfairness' (1988) 8 *Oxford J Legal Studies* 17; MJ Trebilcock, 'The Doctrine of Inequality of Bargaining Power: Post-Benthamite Economics in the House of Lords' (1976) 26(4) *U Toronto LJ* 359; LA DiMatteo, Equity's Modification of Contract: An Analysis of the Twentieth Century's Equitable Reformation of Contract Law (1998) 33 *New England L Rev* 265; and, more recently, A Choi and G Triantis, 'The Effect of Bargaining Power on Contract Design' (2012) 98 *Virginia L Rev* 1665.

the emphasis is usually put on outcomes, such as efficiency or consumer welfare.[73] The underlying objective of contract law or unfair competition statutes consists in regulating the contest between contracting parties and ensuring a relatively equalized landscape of bargaining capacity, bargaining power being interpreted as the interplay of the parties' actual power relationship in an exchange transaction.[74] On the contrary, competition law defines bargaining power more generally, in terms of the ability of an undertaking to introduce a deviation from the price or quantity obtained from the competitive situation in the market in which the transaction takes place. In this context, buying power denotes the ability of a buyer to achieve more favourable terms than those available to other buyers or what would otherwise be expected under normal competitive conditions. This approach emphasizes the gain resulting from the presence of bargaining power relative to a situation in which it is absent (not necessarily that of perfect competition),[75] focusing on market structure and concentration.[76]

European competition authorities are careful to distinguish between the respective fields of contract law, when issues of unconscionability, economic duress, and undue influence are examined, and that of competition law, noting that 'most of certain practices linked to imbalances of bargaining power between market players that are deemed unfair [. . .] do not fall within the scope of competition rules at EU level or in most Member States, as they did not affect consumer welfare'.[77] The debate usually takes a more philosophical dimension, the main argument put forward by the opponents to the integration of the concept of 'superior bargaining power' in competition law assessment, being that competition law aims exclusively at the maximization of welfare effects, and should not include considerations of fairness, allegedly served by the doctrines of economic duress, unconscionability and undue influence in English contract law.

The opposition to this conceptual contagion of competition law from fairness considerations prominent in the elaboration of these doctrines in contract law may take several forms. It may consist in the effort to clearly distinguish the dimension of economic power that should be the focus of competition law ('market power') from its dimension that may be of concern for contract law ('superior bargaining power'), by narrowing the definition of the concept of 'dominant position' in EU competition law so as to exclude the latter from its scope. It may also take the form of framing the relevant tests for determining the existence of an 'abuse' in such as way as to exclude any risk of expanding the scope of the prohibition principle of Article 102 TFEU to 'unfair' commercial practices that do not reduce consumer welfare or efficiency.

With regard to the definition of the relevant concept of economic power, some scholars have tried to draw a clear boundary between bargaining power, which is considered a contract law issue, and monopoly power, which is viewed as a competition law issue, what we will call the separability thesis. In particular, Trebilcock believes that it is fundamental to differentiate

73 See P Akman, *The Concept of Abuse in EU Competition Law: Law and Economic Approaches* (Hart, 2012), 170–84.

74 Yet, it is important to note that regulatory interventions in order to rebalance contractual inequality are still designed as exceptions to the principle of the freedom of contract and the certainty of the contract, especially in B2B contracts, where a very limited power to rebalance the contractual arrangement is generally left to the discretion of the judge.

75 See R Clarke, S Davies, PW Dobson, and M Waterson, *Buyer Power and Competition in European Food Retailing* (Edward Elgar, 2002).

76 JT Dunlop and B Higgins, 'Bargaining Power and Market Structures' (1942) 50(1) *J Political Economy* 1, 4–5; RG Noll, '"Buyer Power" and Economic Policy' (2005) 72 *Antitrust Law J* 589.

77 European Competition Network (ECN) Activities in the Food Sector (May 2012), para 26.

'situational monopolies' from 'structural monopolies'.[78] Situational monopolies are transitory states of imbalance in the bargaining position of the parties to an agreement, which can be subject to exploitation. The 'situational monopolist' (in Trebilcock's terms) may take advantage of the business partner by charging prices that are higher than its 'reference price'. For instance, Trebilcock imagines a situation where 'A has violated his own reference price in opportunistically taking advantage of B's temporary dependency'.[79] For Trebilcock, these monopolies should be regulated by contract law. On the other hand, structural monopolies are those that antitrust law should target, as the dominance of the monopolist is market-wide and non-transitory. Here, the dominant firm enjoys market power that precedes the negotiation of a specific bargain and which impacts on all the market actors.[80] However, it has already been noted that when the relevant market is narrowly defined, as it may happen in EU competition law, the two situations are indistinguishable and therefore the distinction may lose significance.[81] Trebilcock maintains that while the problem of competition law is to determine and remedy to market failures, contract deals with contracting failures, which in the particular case of duress, relates to the coercion of voluntariness that may happen in 'situational monopolies'. This is particularly the case for long-term contracts where exploitation of a 'bilateral monopoly' is likely to occur.[82]

With regard to the second issue, the text of Article 102 TFEU may be source of confusion, as in its second paragraph identifies four exemplary cases of abuse and relentlessly refers to unfair conducts or conditions and the imposition of conditions, the focus on exploitative abuses being similar to the type of conduct targeted by these doctrines in contract law.[83] Furthermore, Article 102 'is expressly aimed [. . .] at situations which clearly originate in contractual relations'.[84] In the Courage case, the UK Court of Appeal went even further by saying that the prohibition of abuse of dominant position 'expressly protects against the consequences of unequal bargaining power and, in terms, prohibits 'unfair trading terms'.[85] Inequality of bargaining power has also been used by the European Commission in several cases, especially to deal with situations of economic dependence.[86] Here the point made by the Commission,

78 MJ Trebilcock, *The Limits of Freedom of Contract* (Harvard University Press, 1997); MJ Trebilcock, 'The Doctrine of Inequality of Bargaining Power: Post-Benthamite Economics in the House of Lords' (1976) 26(4) *University of Toronto LJ* 359.

79 MJ Trebilcock, *The Limits of Freedom of Contract* (Harvard University Press, 1997), 94.

80 Ibid, 96.

81 P Akman, 'The Relationship between Economic Duress and Abuse of a Dominant Position' [2014] *Lloyd's Maritime and Commercial L Q* 99, 113.

82 Ibid, 111. In this connection, Akman recalls Hovenkamp arguing that '[s]imple bilateral monopoly is not an antitrust problem because bilateral monopoly has no consequences for market prices and output' in Herbert Hovenkamp, 'Harvard, Chicago, and Transaction Cost Economics in Antitrust Analysis' (2010) 57 *Antitrust Bulletin* 613, 614.

83 These abuses indeed consist in:

(a) directly or indirectly imposing unfair purchase or selling prices or other unfair trading conditions;
(b) limiting production, markets or technical development to the prejudice of consumers;
(c) applying dissimilar conditions to equivalent transactions with other trading parties, thereby placing them at a competitive disadvantage;
(d) making the conclusion of contracts subject to acceptance by the other parties of supplementary obligations which, by their nature or according to commercial usage, have no connection with the subject of such contracts.

84 Case 85/76, *Hoffmann-La Roche & Co AG v EC Commission* [1979] ECR 461, para 116.

85 *Courage Ltd v Crehan* [1999] ECC 455, para 19.

86 See *General Motors* (Case IV/28.851) Commission Decision [1974] OJ L 29/14; *ABG/Oil companies operating in the Netherlands* (Case IV/28.841) Commission Decision [1977] OJ L 117/1; *Hugin/Liptons*

was that the situation of relative dominance enjoyed by one of the parties, made possible the exploitation of the economic dependence of the other. According to Akman, '[t]he lack of freedom to choose between different suppliers as a result of the dominant undertaking's conduct is indeed a concern in many Article 102 cases'.[87] Akman identifies two main problems that may arise of the interplay between competition law and the contract law doctrine of economic duress:

> First, there is a danger that pure contract cases are litigated as competition cases, even where there is no harm to competition. This has already happened in some cases before the English courts and has led to an increase (often wastefully) in the money and time invested in resolving the case due to proceedings being protracted to examine the competition issues and subsequent appeals. Such use of competition law is particularly a possibility where contract (re) negotiations fail and one of the parties claims that this involves a breach of competition law, for example by a refusal to contract or by charging an excessive price. Such litigation could be avoided if one explicitly required harm to competition in Article 102 cases, but this has not always been the case in the jurisprudence. This concern has been aggravated by the fact that markets have historically been defined narrowly, leading to findings of dominance rather easily in the context of Article 102. Secondly, competition cases can be litigated as contract cases. [. . .] In fact, some economic duress cases that were decided by the English courts could also have been pursued as cases of abuse of dominance [. . .].[88]

Adopting a separability thesis, which aims to establish clear boundaries for the application of competition law and contract law, Akman argues that 'pure exploitative practices where there are no issues of exclusion are more appropriately dealt with by contract law rather than by competition law'.[89]

In conclusion, two views are usually advanced with regard to the interaction of provisions focusing on superior bargaining power and competition law. First, considerable effort has been spent in order to mould the concept of superior bargaining power into the competition law and economics traditional framework by bringing adjustments to traditional competition law concepts such as relevant market and market power[90] or focusing competition

(Case IV/29132) Commission Decision [1978] OJ L 22/23; *Magill TV Guide* (Case IV/31851) Commission Decision [1989] OJ L 78/43.

87 The author cites the following cases: Case 322/81, *Michelin v EC Commission* [1983] ECR 3461, para 73 [hereinafter *Michelin I*]; Case T-228/97, *Irish Sugar Plc v EC Commission* [1999] ECR II–2696, para 214; Case T-203/01, *Manufacture française des pneumatiques Michelin v EC Commission* [2003] ECR II–4071, paras 62 and 240 [hereinafter *Michelin II*]; Case C-95/04, *British Airways Plc v EC Commission* [2007] ECR I–2331, para 67; Case C-280/08 P, *Deutsche Telekom AG v European Commission* [2010] ECR I–9555, paras 175, 181–3; Case T-155/06, *Tomra Systems ASA and Others v European Commission* [2010] ECR I–4361, para 209. See also P Akman, 'The Relationship between Economic Duress and Abuse of a Dominant Position' [2014] *Lloyd's Maritime and Commercial L Q* 99, 102, who also noted that 'the level of competition on a market and the objectionability of the contracts entered into on that market may be related' (ibid, 101–2).

88 P Akman, 'The Relationship between Economic Duress and Abuse of a Dominant Position' [2014] *Lloyd's Maritime and Commercial L Q* 99, 102–3, who also notes that because of the richer array of remedies in the context of competition law (damages, behavioural remedies including the possibility to *make* the other party enter into a contract), it may make sense for claimants to also try the competition law route under Article 102 TFEU.

89 P Akman, 'The Relationship between Economic Duress and Abuse of a Dominant Position' [2014] *Lloyd's Maritime and Commercial L Q* 99, 108–9.

90 See eg the German Act against Restraints of Competition, section 20 on 'relative and superior market power' (*relative und absolute Marktmach*).

law enforcement on 'buying power'. Second, new provisions on superior bargaining power or economic dependence, introduced in the competition law statutes by some jurisdictions, are typically examined from the perspective of efficiency and consumer welfare and usually relegated to the outer boundaries of competition law provisions on abuse of a dominant position, for instance on the basis of an error cost analysis,[91] or the perception that fairness concerns have little role to play in modern competition law.[92] Provisions on superior bargaining power are examined from a public choice perspective as a by-product of the political pressure of organized interests of small and medium undertakings or farmers, leading to the adoption of mainly redistributive statutes that restrict competition and presumably economic efficiency.

We consider that the 'superior bargaining power' concept is too easily dismissed by competition law scholarship. First, from a normative perspective, the role this concept may play in competition law enforcement becomes particularly significant, should one abandon a narrow neoclassical price theory efficiency or consumer welfare driven perspective for an approach that would seek to preserve the competitive process or even one that will be inspired by broader political economy considerations. Second, from a descriptive perspective, we note that legislators and competition authorities do not share the antitrust law pessimism usually displayed by authors inspired by the NPT paradigm towards the concept of superior bargaining power, and have increasingly engaged with it, in the context of traditional competition law enforcement with regard to retail consolidation through buying alliances or mergers, in particular in the context of vertical restraints. That said, we do not consider that the concept should dispense from an analysis, probably at a latter stage in the competition law assessment, of the existence of harm to competition as a result from the specific conduct, the simple exploitation of a situation of superior bargaining power not being equated to harm to competition.[93] The main added value of our approach is that it will not exclude outright from consideration exclusionary or exploitative conduct resulting from a situation of superior bargaining power, because of the simple fact that the undertaking in question does not dispose of substantial market power, defined as power over price (neoclassical market power), the latter concept functioning as a filter dispensing any further analysis under Article 102 TFEU. Such an approach will also break the artificial dichotomy between the step of determining

[91] See eg FW von Papp, 'Unilateral Conduct by Non-dominant Firms: A Comparative Reappraisal', Paper presented at the 10th ASCOLA Conference, Tokyo, 21–3 May 2015, available at http://ascola-tokyo-conference-2015.meiji.jp/conference_working_papers.html, conducting an 'error cost analysis' and advancing the view that dominance, and consequently the definition of a relevant market, is a necessary condition for a superior bargaining power to be considered as a competition law problem and recognizing the countervailing impact that subsidiary contract law enforcement would have on error costs. An error cost analysis conducted *in abstracto* may underestimate the transaction costs associated with the use of the specific legal process, which may vary from jurisdiction to jurisdiction and in some cases may be less important in the context of competition law enforcement than other alternatives. Error cost analysis may also lead to the 'sin of single institutional analysis', see KN Komesar, *Law's Limits* (CUP, 2001), as it will emphasize the defects of one institutional alternative (eg competition law) on some aspects to argue for an expansive role of another, probably equally defective in some other aspects, institutional choice: contract law or unfair competition law statutes.

[92] See eg P Akman, *The Concept of Abuse in EU Competition Law* (Hart, 2012), ch 4.

[93] With regard to this issue we agree with P Akman, 'The Relationship between Economic Duress and Abuse of a Dominant Position' [2014] *Lloyd's Maritime and Commercial LQ* 99, 130, who argues that 'demonstration of 'harm to competition' over and above harm to trading partners or competitors in all abuse cases may go some way in bringing clarity to the distinction between these two doctrines [economic duress and abuse of a dominant position]'.

the existence of a dominant position and that of identifying the abuse, thus enabling a more purposive definition of each element, enabling the claimant to put forward an overall theory of harm to competition resulting from the alleged abuse of a dominant position, which may eventually be rebutted by the defendant.

Recourse to the concept of 'superior bargaining power' may also expand the sources of market power taken into account in competition law. The attention of the competition law enforcers usually lingers on size and market share or concentration of the negotiating parties in order to define their power relations.[94] However, scholarly studies on contracts and negotiations take a game/bargaining theory approach arguing that, for the outcome of negotiation, even more important than market shares or the size of negotiating parties is the existence of 'threat points' enabling one of the parties to seek a 'best alternative to a negotiated agreement' (BATNA).[95] Indeed, the negotiating party holding a BATNA has the possibility to resort to a valid alternative to the negotiation in progress or to the contract concluded, preventing hold-up and threats to cease negotiation. In conceiving the bargaining model, one may take a Nash cooperative bargaining solution as the axiomatic starting point,[96] or resort to a non-cooperative or sequential bargaining model which will attempt to factor in the costs of the delay to agreement, and extend this analysis from bilateral bargaining to n-person bargaining.[97] Although it is not clear if the results will be the same under each of these models, their common feature, in contrast to industrial organization theory, is that bargaining power is perceived as a concept that can be measured with reference to a specific bargaining relation in a specific context and it is not dependent on structural analysis (for instance the existence of monopsony or oligopsony). Bargaining power may also impact on price as well as on non-price terms.[98] Measuring bargaining power may be considered as a difficult exercise, although not necessarily more complex than that of measuring market power. It is encouraging that some competition law enforcers have tried to engage with the measurement task, adopting diverse approaches.[99]

The issue may take more centre-stage as in the modern digital and algorithmic economy, we observe very different processing and evaluation capabilities among firms, as a number

[94] This is for instance the approach by the Commission in, European Commission, DG Comp, The Economic Impact of Modern Retail on Choice and Innovation in the EU Food Sector: Final Report, available at http://ec.europa.eu/competition/publications/KD0214955ENN.pdf.

[95] A Renda et al, Study on the Legal Framework Covering Business-to-Business Unfair Trading Practices in the Retail Supply Chain, Final Report, DG MARKT/2012/049/E 25 (26 February 2014), available at http://ec.europa.eu/internal_market/retail/docs/140711-study-utp-legal-framework_en.pdf; I Ayres and BJ Nalebuff, 'Common Knowledge as a Barrier to Negotiation' (1996) 44 *U California Los Angeles L Rev* 1631.

[96] Most of these studies have relied on this type of model so far.

[97] See eg J Sutton, 'Non-Cooperative Bargaining Theory: An Introduction' (1986) 53 *Rev Economic Studies* 709–24; K Binmore, MJ Osborne, and A Rubinstein, 'Non-Cooperative Models of Bargaining' in R Aumann and S Hart (eds) *Handbook of Game Theory with Economic Applications*, vol 1 (Elsevier, 1992), 179.

[98] A Choi and G Triantis, 'The Effect of Bargaining Power on Contract Design' (2012) 98 *Virginia L Rev* 1665.

[99] See Bundeskartellamt, Sektoruntersuchung Nachfragemacht Im Lebensmitteleinzelhandel (2014) B2-15/11 BKartA, available at http://www.bundeskartellamt.de/Sektoruntersuchung_LEH.pdf?__blob=publicationFile&v=7 [hereinafter Bundeskartellamt Food Retail Report]. The conditions adopted for this analysis were not only price terms but also non-price terms, such as deadline for payment and agreements on delivery. A fundamental stage of the Bundeskartellamt's assessment was the reckoning of the importance of a retailer for its suppliers and the evaluation of the 'outside options' of both parties. For a discussion, see I Lianos and C Lombardi, 'Superior Bargaining Power and the Global Food Value Chain: The Wuthering Heights of Holistic Competition Law?' (2016-I) *Concurrences* 22.

of economic actors may be considered as holding 'asymmetrical bargaining power' vis-à-vis their suppliers or buyers, through the collection of Big Data and the use of algorithms.[100] Some authors have even coined the term of 'algorithmic power'[101] in order to convey an additional, quite important, source of market power, in the sense that this is based on the 'technological dependence'[102] of economic actors that work and consume in an increasingly complex computational environment. It is also based on the capability of some actors to control the 'agenda' of decision-making,[103] for instance through the gate-keeping role of their digital platforms as the most important gateway of businesses to consumers,[104] or for the storage and processing of data,[105] the 'oil' of the new economy,[106] or for the provision of artificial intelligence services. This is exemplified by, for instance, control over the choice architecture which frames individual choice in the context of an economic transaction.[107] These economic actors will therefore be in a position to exploit their superior 'algorithmic power' and/or 'manipulate' the choice and eventually the preferences of their suppliers and buyers,[108] thus enabling then to restrict vertical competition with negative effects for productivity, the overall economy and consumer welfare.

100 See F Pasquale, *The Black Box Society: The Secret Algorithms that Control Money and Information* (Havard University Press, 2015), ch 2; A Ezrachi and M Stucke, *Virtual Competition* (Harvard University Press, 2016), 125, 225 (discussing 'asymmetric bargaining power').

101 See T Bucher, 'Want To Be On the Top? Algorithmic Power and the Threat of Invisibility on Facebook' (2012) 14(7) *New Media and Society* 1164.

102 See the Opinion of AG Whatelet in Case C-170/13, *Huawei Technologies Co Ltd v ZTE Corp and ZTE Deutschland GmbH* [2015] ECLI:EU:C:2014:2391, paras 71 and 74, who coined the term. The AG found in this case that the incorporation of a patent-protected element into the industry standard and the fact that a licence to use that patent was therefore indispensable had created a relationship of dependence between the Standards Essential Patents-holder and the undertakings which produce products and services in accordance with that standard. According to the AG, '[t]hat technological dependence leads to economic dependence'.

103 On the various definitions of 'power' in economics and sociology, see M Granovetter, *Society and Economy* (Harvard University Press, 2017), ch 4.

104 One may, for instance, refer to the Amazon Marketplace.

105 This could, for instance, be access to the cloud that is highly important for the Internet of Things. See B Lundqvist, 'Standardization for the Digital Economy: The Issue of Interoperability and Access Under Competition Law' 62(4) *Antitrust Bulletin* 710.

106 'The World's Most Valuable Resource is no Longer Oil, but Data', *The Economist* (6 May 2017).

107 See, for instance, a recent report.

108 See the literature on market manipulation, providing evidence that firms take advantage of the specific characteristics of consumers and manipulate their cognitive biases, which ma be extended to platform to business transactions, when digital platforms dispose of superior bargaining power: JD Hanson and DA Kysar, 'Taking Behavioralism Seriously: Some Evidence of Market Manipulation' (1999) 112 *Harvard L Rev* 1420; R Calo, 'Digital Market Manipulation' (2014) 82 *George Washington L Rev* 995; E Kamenica, S Mullainathan, and R Thaler, 'Helping Consumers Know Themselves' (2011) 101(3) *American Economic Rev: Papers & Proceedings* 417, 418 (noting that 'when the seller has more information about expected usage than the customer, they may try to exploit this information by targeting specific offers to specific consumers' and raising the problem of 'adverse targeting', that is the ability of sellers 'to use this informational advantage to construct special offers that the consumers will overvalue'; Ph Hacker and B Petkova, 'Reining in the Big Promise of Big Data: Transparency, Inequality, and New Regulatory Frontiers' (2017) 15(1) *Northwestern J Technology and Intellectual Property*, available at https://scholarlycommons.law.northwestern.edu/njtip/vol15/iss1/1/. See the recent ideas to regulate from a fairness perspective platform to business relations: Inception Impact Assessment, Fairness in Platform to Business Relation, Ares(2017)5222469, available at https://ec.europa.eu/info/law/better-regulation/initiatives/ares-2017-5222469_en (raising interesting questions as to the interaction of competition law and other forms of economic regulation in order to tame the superior bargaining power of digital platforms).

8.3.3. MARKET DEFINITION AND DOMINANT POSITION

In determining the existence of a dominant position, it is first necessary to identify the relevant product and geographic markets.[109]

8.3.4. STRUCTURAL FACTORS AND DOMINANT POSITION

The most usual indicators of a dominant position are structural factors, such as market shares and barriers to entry or expansion. One may, ore broadly distinguish, between three broad categories of assessments used in order to determine the existence of a dominant position:[110]

- Quantitative assessments of market structure (this comes essentially to market definition and evaluating the undertaking's market shares);
- Qualitative assessments of market characteristics (which includes barriers to entry, other characteristics of markets affecting the intensity of competition, and countervailing buyer power); and
- Direct assessment of prices or profits.

Competition authorities make an often use of the first two approaches, although they have also recently proceeded to a direct assessment of prices and profits when sufficient data is available (this is mainly in consumer markets where scanner data have been collected).

8.3.4.1. Market shares

The primary indicator of dominance is usually the market share of the undertaking on the relevant market (ie the percentage that the sales of the undertaking represent in relation to the whole market turnover). The Court of Justice held in *Hoffmann-La Roche* that

> the existence of a dominant position may derive from several factors which taken separately are not necessarily determinative but among these factors a highly important one is the existence of very large market shares.[111]

Market shares provide a starting point for the assessment of the existence of a dominant position. Very high market shares provide in themselves virtually conclusive evidence that a firm is dominant.

The CJEU stated in *Hoffmann-La Roche* that:

> although the importance of the market shares may vary from one market to another the view may legitimately be taken that very large market shares are in themselves, and save in exceptional circumstances, evidence of the existence of a dominant position.[112]

109 See Chapter 3 on market definition and the Commission's Notice on market definition.

110 A Coscelli and G Edwards, 'Dominance and Market Power in EU Competition Law Enforcement' in I Lianos and D Geradin, *Research Handbook in EU Competition Law* (Edward Elgar, 2012), ch 8.

111 Case C-85/76, *Hoffmann-La Roche v Commission* [1979] ECR 461, para 39

112 Ibid, para 41.

The following case may also provide an illustration of the role of market share in inferring the existence of a dominant position.

Case C-62/86, *AKZO Chemie BV v Commission*
[1991] ECR I–3359

55. The Commission considers that AKZO has a dominant position within the organic peroxides market. It bases its view on AKZO' s market share and on the existence of a number of factors which, combined with that market share, is said to give it a marked predominance.

[. . .]

57. AKZO disputes the assessment of its market share and also the existence or relevance of the other factors mentioned in the decision. In particular, it claims that its market share was evaluated wrongly because the Commission should not have regarded the organic peroxides market as a single market. It maintains, moreover, that the fact that it offers a wider range of products than its competitors cannot constitute evidence of a dominant position.

58. Those arguments cannot be accepted. Since the organic peroxides market was rightly regarded as the relevant market, it follows that AKZO's market share had to be calculated by taking organic peroxides as a whole. In that light, it is obvious that the fact that AKZO offered a range of products wider than that of its main rivals was one of the factors that assured for AKZO a dominant position in that market.

59. It should be further observed that according to its own internal documents AKZO had a stable market share of about 50% from 1979 to 1982 [. . .]. Furthermore, AKZO has not adduced any evidence to show that its share decreased during subsequent years.

60. With regard to market shares the Court has held that very large shares are in themselves, and save in exceptional circumstances, evidence of the existence of a dominant position (judgment in Case 85/76 *Hoffman-La Roche v Commission* [1979] ECR 461, paragraph 41). That is the situation where there is a market share of 50% such as that found to exist in this case.

61. Moreover, the Commission rightly pointed out that other factors confirmed AKZOs predominance in the market. In addition to the fact that AKZO regards itself as the world leader in the peroxides market, it should be observed that, as AKZO itself admits, it has the most highly developed marketing organization, both commercially and technically, and wider knowledge than that of their competitors with regard to safety and toxicology [. . .].

NOTES AND QUESTIONS ON AKZO CHEMIE BV

1. In paragraph 60 of its judgment, the CJEU established a presumption of dominant position if the undertaking in question disposes of a market share of more than 50 per cent of the relevant market. Do you agree with such a presumption? Is a market share of 50 per cent high or not high enough in order to find the existence of a dominant position? Does this depend on the specific economic sector? For example, in some high technology sectors competition takes place for the market, not in the market and dominant undertakings usually have a very high market share.

2. In comparison, in US antitrust law, there is no finding of monopoly power for undertakings having a market share below 65–70 per cent of the relevant market. Why is EU competition law adopting a more interventionist approach in the enforcement of Article 102 TFEU with regard to the definition of a dominant position?

In other cases, the Court has inferred from the very high market shares of the undertaking in question a super-dominant position.[113] This introduces a sliding scale approach to the determination of dominance. It might also indicate that certain categories of conduct would be found abusive when engaged in by undertakings occupying a position of particular strength on a market but not when engaged in by other undertakings.[114] In *Compagnie Maritime Belge Transports SA v Commission* the Court suggested that the same conduct, price discrimination might not be abusive if it was engaged in by a firm or group of firms that did not hold a position comparable to the 90 per cent market share held by the shipping conference in this case.

In his opinion, AG Fennelly endorsed a sliding scale approach to the assessment of dominance and its relation with the concept of abuse.

Opinion of AG Fennelly in Joined Cases C-395/96 P and C-396/96 P, *Compagnie Maritime Belge Transports SA v Commission*
[2000] ECR I–1365

137. [. . .] To my mind, Article 102 cannot be interpreted as permitting monopolists or quasi-monopolists to exploit the very significant market power which their superdominance confers so as to preclude the emergence either of a new or additional competitor. Where an undertaking, or group of undertakings whose conduct must be assessed collectively, enjoys a position of such overwhelming dominance verging on monopoly, comparable to that which existed in the present case at the moment when G & C entered the relevant market, it would not be consonant with the particularly onerous special obligation affecting such a dominant undertaking not to impair further the structure of the feeble existing competition for them to react, even to aggressive price competition from a new entrant, with a policy of targeted, selective price cuts designed to eliminate that competitor. Contrary to the assertion of the appellants, the mere fact that such prices are not pitched at a level that is actually (or can be shown to be) below total average (or long-run marginal) costs does not, to my mind, render legitimate the application of such a pricing policy.

The Commission has also taken a similar position.[115] According to paragraph 14 of the Commision's Guidance on Article 102, the Commission suggests that a market share of less

113 The expression refers to a situation of a firm benefiting from an overwhelming dominant position in the market. See Joined Cases, C-395/96 and 396/96 P, *Compagnie Maritime Belge Transports SA v Commission* [2000] ECR I–1365, paras 114–20.

114 See also Case C-333/94, *Tetra-Pak v Commission* [1996] ECR I–5951, para 24, where the CJEU indicated that the extent of the special responsibility imposed on a firm under Article 102 TFEU must be considered in the light of the particular circumstances of each case.

115 Commission Guidance on Article 102, paras 13–15.

than 40 per cent is not a proxy for the finding of dominance. However, this should not be perceived as a safe harbour, as there have been cases where the Commission, approved by the Court, found that there was a dominant position with less than 40 per cent market shares.[116] In other documents, the Commission seems to suggest a safe harbour for the finding of dominance.

Commission Guidelines on market analysis and the assessment of significant market power under the Community regulatory framework for electronic communications networks and services [2002] OJ C 165/6 (excerpts)

75. [. . .] a dominant position is found by reference to a number of criteria and its assessment is based, as stated above, on a forward-looking market analysis based on existing market conditions. Market shares are often used as a proxy for market power. Although a high market share alone is not sufficient to establish the possession of significant market power (dominance), it is unlikely that a firm without a significant share of the relevant market would be in a dominant position. Thus, undertakings with market shares of no more than 25 % are not likely to enjoy a (single) dominant position on the market concerned. In the Commission's decision-making practice, single dominance concerns normally arise in the case of undertakings with market shares of over 40 %, although the Commission may in some cases have concerns about dominance even with lower market shares, as dominance may occur without the existence of a large market share. According to established case-law, very large market shares—in excess of 50 %—are in themselves, save in exceptional circumstances, evidence of the existence of a dominant position. An undertaking with a large market share may be presumed to have [substantial market power] SMP, that is, to be in a dominant position, if its market share has remained stable over time. The fact that an undertaking with a significant position on the market is gradually losing market share may well indicate that the market is becoming more competitive, but it does not preclude a finding of significant market power. On the other hand, fluctuating market shares over time may be indicative of a lack of market power in the relevant market.

The UK Competition authorities also rely on market shares for the finding of a dominant position for the purposes of applying Chapter II of the 1998 Competition Act.[117] Despite the role of market shares in inferring the existence of substantial market power, the OFT also noted circumstances in which market shares might not be reliable indicators of market power.

116 *Virgin/British Airways* (Case IV/D-2/34.780) Commission Decision [2000] OJ L30/1; Case T-219/99, *British Airways plc v Commission* [2003] ECR II-5917, paras 189–225; Case C-95/04 P *British Airways plc v Commission* [2007] ECR I-2331. BA was held to be dominant in the UK market for procurement of air travel agency services with a market share of 39.7 per cent. The General Court agreed with the Commission's qualification and considered that BA was an 'obligatory business partner for travel agents'.

117 OFT 402, Abuse of Dominant Position (2004), 14–15, available at www.gov.uk/government/uploads/system/uploads/attachment_data/file/284422/oft402.pdf.

OFT 415, Assessment of Market Power (2004), 11–13, available at www.gov.uk/government/uploads/system/uploads/attachment_data/file/284400/oft415.pdf (footnotes excluded)

4.4. Nevertheless, market shares alone might not be a reliable guide to market power, both as a result of potential shortcomings with the data (discussed in the next section) and for the following reasons:

- *Low entry barriers*—An undertaking with a persistently high market share may not necessarily have market power where there is a strong threat of potential competition. If entry into the market is easy, the incumbent undertaking might be constrained to act competitively so as to avoid attracting entry over time by potential competitors [. . .].
- *Bidding markets*—Sometimes buyers choose their suppliers through procurement auctions or tenders. In these circumstances, even if there are only a few suppliers, competition might be intense. This is more likely to be the case where tenders are large and infrequent (so that suppliers are more likely to bid), where suppliers are not subject to capacity constraints (so that all suppliers are likely to place competitive bids), and where suppliers are not differentiated (so that for any particular bid, all suppliers are equally placed to win the contract). In these types of markets, an undertaking might have a high market share at a single point in time. However, if competition at the bidding stage is effective, this currently high market share would not necessarily reflect market power.
- *Successful innovation*—In a market where undertakings compete to improve the quality of their products, a persistently high market share might indicate persistently successful innovation and so would not necessarily mean that competition is not effective.
- *Product differentiation*—Sometimes the relevant market will contain products that are differentiated. In this case undertakings with relatively low market shares might have a degree of market power because other products in the market are not very close substitutes.
- *Responsiveness of customers*—Where undertakings have similar market shares, this does not necessarily mean that they have similar degrees of market power. This may be because their customers differ in their ability or willingness to switch to alternative suppliers (see also the discussion of buyer power).
- *Price responsiveness of competitors*—Sometimes an undertaking's competitors will not be in a position to increase output in response to higher prices in the market. For example, suppose an undertaking operates in a market where all undertakings have limited capacity (e.g. are at, or close to, full capacity and so are unable to increase output substantially). In this case, the undertaking would be in a stronger position to increase prices above competitive levels than an otherwise identical undertaking with a similar market share operating in a market where its competitors were not close to full capacity.

4.5. Therefore, while consideration of market shares over time is important when assessing market power, an analysis of entry conditions and other factors is equally important. [. . .]

The existence of high market shares does not establish as such the existence of a dominant position. In *National Grid*, the CAT 'treated market shares as high as 90 per cent as one indicator of market power but not raising a presumption of dominance'.[118] In *NCNN 500*, the OFCOM has also found the existence of a dominant position with a market share of 31 per cent, in the presence of additional factors of dominance.[119]

Recent case law has also raised questions about the use of market shares as a proxy for assessing market power in dynamic markets. Although these are merger cases, they provide insights that could also be relevant in the context of abuse of dominance cases. Market shares have been used as a proxy for the assessment of market power in dynamic markets in *Microsoft/Yahoo! Search Business*[120] and *Google/DoubleClick*.[121] However, in *Microsoft/Skype*, the Commission paid less attention to market shares as the market was expected to grow immensely with the number of users.[122] In *Cisco*, it was established that market shares may not necessarily be good indicators of dominance in markets of fast-growing nature and with short innovation cycles.[123] The fact that a company has high market shares and there is a high degree of concentration on the 'narrow market' identified by the Commission 'is not indicative of a degree of market power which would enable the new entity to significantly impede effective competition'.[124] The General Court found relevant the fact that the existing value chain of PCs was the 'most used platform for consumer video communication', but that 'a substantial and growing share of new demand for those services originates from users of tablets and smartphones, sales of those appliances having overtaken those of PCs in Western Europe', that is other value chains, on the basis of smartphone technology, and that 'any attempt by the new entity to exert any market power on the narrow market would risk reinforcing that trend to the detriment of the new entity', the new entity being 'less present on those other platforms and faces strong competition from other operators'.[125] The 'weak presence' of the new entity in the growing market for tablets and smartphones, would not allow it 'to respond to that new demand and therefore reduces its commercial attractiveness'.[126] One may consider that the GC was referring here to disruptive innovation by a new value chain (smart phones), with few possibilities for a company dominant in the disrupted value chain, that of PCs, to react.

8.3.4.2. Barriers to entry and expansion

The second most important structural factor examined by the EU competition law jurisprudence in the definition of a dominant position is the existence of barriers to entry. We have already examined the economic definition of barriers to entry in Chapter 2. With regard to the role of barriers to entry in the definition of a dominant position, the Commission's Guidance on Article 102 provides the following:

118 Case 1099/1/2/08, *National Grid plc v the Gas and Electricity Markets Authority* [2009] CAT 14, CompAR 282, para 51, cited by R Whish and D Bailey, *Competition Law* (OUP, 7th ed, 2011), 365.

119 OFCOM decision *NCNN 500* [2008] UKCLR 501, paras 5.1–5.166.

120 *Microsoft/Yahoo!* (Case COMP/M. 5727) Commission Decision [2010] OJ C 20/32, paras 112–30.

121 *Google/DoubleClick* (Case COMP/M.4731) Commission Decision [2008] OJ C 184/10, paras 96–118.

122 *Microsoft/Skype* (Case COMP/M.6281) Commission Decision [2011] OJ C 341/2, paras 70–2.

123 Case T-79/12, *Cisco Systems, Inc and Messagenet SpA v Commission*, ECLI:EU:T:2013:635, para 69, the Commission noting that 'the consumer communications sector is a recent and fast-growing sector which is characterised by short innovation cycles in which large market shares may turn out to be ephemeral'.

124 Ibid, para 74. 125 Ibid, para 70. 126 Ibid, para 71.

Communication from the Commission—Guidance on the Commission's enforcement priorities in applying Article [102 TFEU] to abusive exclusionary conduct by dominant undertakings [2009] OJ C 45/7 (footnotes omitted)

(b) Expansion or entry

16. Competition is a dynamic process and an assessment of the competitive constraints on an undertaking cannot be based solely on the existing market situation. The potential impact of expansion by actual competitors or entry by potential competitors, including the threat of such expansion or entry, is also relevant. An undertaking can be deterred from increasing prices if expansion or entry is likely, timely and sufficient. For the Commission to consider expansion or entry likely it must be sufficiently profitable for the competitor or entrant, taking into account factors such as the barriers to expansion or entry, the likely reactions of the allegedly dominant undertaking and other competitors, and the risks and costs of failure. For expansion or entry to be considered timely, it must be sufficiently swift to deter or defeat the exercise of substantial market power. For expansion or entry to be considered sufficient, it cannot be simply small-scale entry, for example into some market niche, but must be of such a magnitude as to be able to deter any attempt to increase prices by the putatively dominant undertaking in the relevant market.

17. Barriers to expansion or entry can take various forms. They may be legal barriers, such as tariffs or quotas, or they may take the form of advantages specifically enjoyed by the dominant undertaking, such as economies of scale and scope, privileged access to essential inputs or natural resources, important technologies or an established distribution and sales network. They may also include costs and other impediments, for instance resulting from network effects, faced by customers in switching to a new supplier. The dominant undertaking's own conduct may also create barriers to entry, for example where it has made significant investments which entrants or competitors would have to match, or where it has concluded long-term contracts with its customers that have appreciable foreclosing effects. Persistently high market shares may be indicative of the existence of barriers to entry and expansion.

The Commission's expansive definition of barriers to entry and expansion joins the expansive definition of barriers to entry by the courts in the enforcement of Article 102 TFEU.

A Coscelli and G Edwards, 'Dominance and Market Power in EU Competition Law Enforcement' in I Lianos and D Geradin, *Research Handbook in EU Competition Law* (Edward Elgar, 2012), ch 8, 366–70 (excerpt, most footnotes omitted, emphasis original)

Access to key inputs or distribution networks. Entry can be more difficult when it requires access to scarce inputs or distribution networks. Established firms that already have agreements for the supply of key upstream inputs or downstream distribution, or that are vertically integrated upstream or downstream, may have advantages over entrants that must either enter themselves at all functional levels or develop relationships with input suppliers or a network of distributors. In *United Brands* the CJEU pointed to United Brands' integration at all stages in the banana supply chain, from planting to sea transport to packaging and presentation in support of its finding of dominance.[127] In *Hilti*, the [European Commission (EC)] pointed to Hilti's 'strong and well-organized distribution system' as a factor strengthening Hilti's dominant position.[128] The EC also emphasized superior sales and distribution networks in *Michelin II*.[129]

Entry is particularly difficult when established firms control access to key inputs or infrastructure that cannot easily be duplicated. For example, in *Commercial Solvents* the dominant firm's control over European production of two chemicals that were essential for the production of ethambutol represented a barrier to firms wishing to enter and supply ethambutol.[130] Intellectual property rights (IPRs) can be a form of key input for entry to or effective competition in a market. However, the fact that one firm on a market has IPRs does not necessarily preclude entry into and competition in the market from firms with differentiated products that do not rely on those IPRs. Moreover, IPRs may be seen as pro-competitive, providing appropriate rewards to innovation. Care should therefore be taken before finding that an IPR represents a barrier to entry. [. . .]

Technological superiority of established firms. A number of cases have suggested that an established firm's superior technology or knowhow represents a barrier to entry when looking at competition in the market at a particular point in time. In *United Brands* the CJEU found that United Brands' superior R&D could not be matched by potential competitors and that this represented a barrier to entry (among many others in that case).[131] Similarly, superior R&D and technological advantages were referenced as factors pointing to dominance by the EC in *Hilti* and *Michelin II*.[132] On the other hand, in many industries (such as pharmaceuticals) competition takes place over time through innovation and R&D capability can be a critical factor for competition rather than a barrier to entry per se.

Network effects. Some products and services have the characteristic that the more they are used, the more valuable they are to any individual user. Such products and services are said to benefit from network effects. A classic example of network effects is telecommunications; the value of a telephone depends on how many other people have telephones that you can then speak to. If only a handful of people had telephones, the value to any one of them would be limited compared to when telephones are ubiquitous. A more complex example is where markets are two-sided, such as in advertising. A newspaper will not convince many advertisers to place advertisements in it unless it can establish a substantial base of readers. Network effects may represent entry barriers since established firms that already benefit from them will have a clear advantage over entrants that have smaller customer bases (at least if there are product compatibility issues). The EC [European Commission] relied heavily upon network effects as a barrier to entry in finding Microsoft to be dominant in personal computer operating systems, noting that the more widespread an operating system is among users, the more applications that developers will write for it and, in turn, the more popular it will become.[133]

[127] See Case C-27/76, *United Brands Company and United Brands Continental BV v Commission* [1978] ECR 207, paras 70–84 and 122.

[128] *Eurofix-Bauco v Hilti* (Case IV/30.787) Commission Decision [1988] OJ L 65/19, para 69.

[129] *Michelin* (Case COMP/E-2/36.041/PO) Commission Decision [2002] OJ L 143/1, paras 191–5.

[130] See Joined Cases C-6 & 7/73, *Istituto Chemioterapico Italiano SpA and Commercial Solvents Corporation v Commission* [1974] ECR 223.

[131] Case C-27/76, *United Brands Company and United Brands Continentaal BV v Commission* [1978] ECR 207, paras 84 and 122.

[132] *Eurofix-Bauco v Hilti* (Cases IV/30.787 and 31.488) Commission Decision 88/138/EEC [1988] OJ L 65/19 para 69 and *Michelin* (Case COMP/E-2/36.041/PO) Commission Decision [2002] OJ L 143/1, paras 182–4.

[133] *Microsoft/W2000* (Case COMP/C-3/37.792) Commission Decision C(2004)900 final (24 March 2004), paras 448–59, available at ec.europa.eu/competition/antitrust/cases/dec_docs/37792/37792_4177_1.pdf. See also ibid, paras 515–22 in relation to work group server operating systems.

Switching costs. Costs faced by customers when switching suppliers can also act as a barrier to entry or expansion. Switching costs can be exogenous—that is, inherent in the nature of the product being supplied and/or in the existing switching process. Switching costs can also be influenced by the choices of firms in the market, sometimes as a strategic effort to restrict competition. Switching costs as barriers to entry were mentioned in the findings of dominance in the *IMS* and *Microsoft* cases.[134] To the extent that entrants may need to compensate customers in order to encourage them to switch, these compensation efforts may also be seen as a barrier to entry in the form of sunk costs. Switching costs can be particularly problematic for entry and expansion when the incumbent firm can price discriminate between 'inactive' and 'active' customers by offering lower prices to 'active' customers who are more likely to switch. [. . .]

Financial and economic strength. Economic and financial strength can be a barrier to entry, in so far as it can provide an established firm with an advantage over potential competitors with respect to easier access to finance. This would not be the case if capital markets were perfect. However, in reality capital markets are often imperfect, for example due to information asymmetries between lenders and borrowers. This means that an established firm may well have lower costs of raising finance for risky projects, whether internally or externally.

Easier access to finance, or 'deep pockets', can also assist an established firm to maintain a credible threat that any entry will be met by a predatory price war.

Strategic barriers to entry. Some of the barriers to entry and expansion [. . .] are not always exogenous and are susceptible to manipulation by established firms. A clear example is switching costs. An established firm's choice of technology or a strategy to make its product incompatible with others is capable of raising artificial barriers to entry and expansion. More generally, there is a myriad of ways in which established firms can raise barriers to entry and expansion through strategic behaviour. For example, investment in significant spare capacity can act as a credible threat to expand output and reduce prices if entry is attempted. Indeed, an incumbent firm's excess capacity was accepted by the CJEU in *Hoffman-La Roche* as a factor relevant to a finding of dominance.[135] Established firms in markets characterised by economies of scale may also find ways to credibly commit to maintain their pre-entry output levels, ensuring that entry would be unprofitable. Established firms with advantages in access to finance may develop a reputation for predation, which may act as a barrier to entry. And in the *Microsoft* case, the European Commission regarded Microsoft's behaviour in withholding interoperability information as an (artificial) barrier to entry.[136] Other examples include long-term contracts, fidelity discounts and selective price discounting (eg the use of MFN [most favoured nation] clauses).

Legal or administrative barriers to entry. The barriers to entry discussed above are all in the nature of economic reasons why entry might be difficult. Quite apart from the economic characteristics of a market or established firms within it, there may be legal or administrative barriers to entry. Legislation or regulation can limit the number of players on a market, either explicitly (eg the granting of exclusive rights to statutory monopolies) or implicitly (eg through onerous licensing requirements or standard-setting processes). Intellectual property laws can also be seen as legal barriers to entry, since they prevent other firms from replicating an innovative product or technology for a period of time. Intellectual property rights as barriers to entry are discussed above.

[134] Case C-418/01 *IMS Health GmbH & Co v NDC Health GmbH & Co*, [2004] ECR I-5039 [hereinafter *IMS v NDC*]; *Microsoft/W2000* (Case COMP C-3/37.792) Commission Decision C(2004)900 final (24 March 2004), para 900.

[135] See Case C-85/76, *Hoffman-La Roche & Co AG v Commission* [1979] ECR 461, para 48.

[136] *Microsoft/W2000* (Case COMP/C-3/37.792) Commission Decision C(2004)900 final (24 March 2004), para 524.

Barriers to entry featured heavily in *Google Search (Shopping)* as part of the Commission assessment of Google dominance in the general search market (see our analysis in Section 8.4.5.3.2). Specifically, the Commission took into consideration the positive feedback loops between the two sides of the general search platform: the advertisers' and the users' sides.

Case AT.39740, *Google Search (Shopping)* (2017) not yet published

Barriers to entry and expansion

285. The Commission concludes that the national markets for general search services are characterised by the existence of a number of barriers to entry and expansion.

286. First, the establishment of a fully-fledged general search engine requires significant investments in terms of time and resources. For example, each year since at least 2009, Microsoft has invested [a significant amount] in R&D and capital expenditure in the development and maintenance of the latest version of its general search engine launched in June 2009 under the brand name 'Bing'. Other companies indicate that the costs associated with the establishment of a fully-fledged general search engine constitute a barrier to entry. For example, [. . .] argues that it only operates its own general search technology for [. . .] language websites because 'investments are too large to develop such technology for [. . .] language websites'. [. . .] says that 'the incremental costs of converting [. . .] into a viable, competitive broad search service would [. . .] require years of development'. As for [. . .], a company that already has substantial server capacities in place [. . .], it says: 'Investment in equipment and personnel would likely be the primary costs, and they would be very high. In addition, obtaining the large quantity of data necessary to develop an effective [general] search engine (e.g., the information upon which relevancy algorithms can be built and improved) would be a significant barrier to entry'.

287. Second, because a general search service uses search data to refine the relevance of its general search results pages, it needs to receive a certain volume of queries in order to compete viably. The greater the number of queries a general search service receives, the quicker it is able to detect a change in user behaviour patterns and update and improve its relevance. This is supported by internal Google documents and by evidence from a number of other general search services.

288. A general search service also needs to receive a certain volume of queries in order to improve the relevance of its results for uncommon ('tail') queries. Tail queries are important because users evaluate the relevance of a general search service on a holistic basis and expect to obtain relevant results for both common ('head') and uncommon tail queries. The greater the volume of data a general search service relevant results for all types of queries.

289. In that regard, there may be diminishing returns to scale in terms of improvements in relevance once the volume of queries a general search service receives exceeds a certain volume. It may also be that the lower success and relevance of a general search service can be explained by other reasons, such as the fact that it does not localise its search results in different countries, that its web index is more limited in depth, or that it is slower in updating its index in order to deliver fresh content to users. Regardless of the veracity of such arguments, however, they remain of limited relevance for the assessment of barriers to entry and expansion on the national markets

for general search services because of the underlying fact that a general search service has to receive at least a certain minimum volume of queries in order to compete viably.

290. The relevance of scale is also not called into question by the fact that in the late 1990s, Google was able to overtake the former market leaders, AltaVista and Lycos. At that time, scale was less of a critical factor because the indexing technology of general search engines was not yet able to assess user behaviour.

291. Third, general search services constantly invest to improve their product and a new entrant would have no choice but to attempt to match these investments. [. . .]

292. Fourth, the existence of positive feedback effects on both sides of the two-sided platform formed by general search services and online search advertising creates an additional barrier to entry.

293. The positive feedback effects on the online search advertising side are due to the link between the number of users of a general search service and the value of the online search advertisement shown by that general search engine. The higher the number of users of a general search service, the greater the likelihood that a given search advertisement is matched to a user and converted into a sale. This in turn increases the price that a general search engine can charge advertisers if their search advertisements are clicked on. The general search engine can then reinvest that revenue in seeking to attract new users of its general search service.

294. As regards the positive feedback effects on the general search side of the general search engine platform, they derive from both direct and indirect network effects.

295. the direct network effects stem from the fact that a substantial minority of users of a general search service derive a benefit from search advertisements. The fact that advertisers are willing to bid for AdWords results on Google's general search results pages is evidence that at least some users value these advertisements. [. . .]

296. The indirect network effects stem from the link between the attractiveness of the online search advertising side of a general search engine platform and the revenue of that platform. The higher the number of advertisers using an online search advertising service, the higher the revenue of the general search engine platform; revenue which can be reinvested in the maintenance and improvement of the general search service so as to attract more users (see also recital 293). [. . .]

The Commission summarily dismissed Google's argument about the fact that users do not pay for the general search service.

319. The Commission concludes that a finding of dominance is not precluded by Google's claim that it offers its general search services free of charge.

320. First, that claim is misleading. While users do not pay a monetary consideration for the use of general search services, they contribute to the monetisation of the service by providing data with each query.

321. Second, and in any event, the free nature of a service is only one '*relevant factor in assessing [. . .] market power*'. Other equally, if not more, relevant factors in this case include the following.

322. In the first place, Google has enjoyed strong and stable market shares by volume across the EEA since 2008, and there has been no effective entry in any EEA country during that period.

323. In the second place, the national markets for general search services are characterised by the existence of a number of barriers to entry and expansion.

324. In the third place, because of the infrequency of user multi-homing and the existence of brand effects, Google could alter the quality of its general search service to

> a certain degree without running the risk that a substantial fraction of its users would switch to alternative general search engines.
>
> *By the same token, the Commission rejected the criticism that a SSNIP test hadn't been carried out.*
>
> 242. [. . .] [T]he Commission was not required to carry out a SSNIP test.
>
> 243. In the first place, the SSNIP test is not the only method available to the Commission when defining the relevant market.
>
> 244. In the second place, the Commission is required to make an overall assessment of all the evidence and there is no hierarchy between the types of evidence that the Commission can rely upon.
>
> 245. In the third place, the SSNIP test would not have been appropriate in the present case because Google provides its search services for free to users.
>
> 246. The Commission thus concludes that comparison shopping services constitute a distinct relevant product market, which does not include merchant platforms. Google claims that the relevant product market comprises both comparison shopping services and merchant platforms. [. . .]

Barriers to entry are also considered in the UK for the finding of a dominant position.[137]

8.3.4.3. Buyer power

Both the EU Commission Guidance on Article 102 and the UK Competition Authorities take into consideration buyer power. A typical definition of buyer power is the following one provided by Roger Noll:

> '[B]uyer power' refers to the circumstances in which the demand side of a market is sufficiently concentrated that buyers can exercise market power over sellers. A buyer has market power if the buyer can force sellers to reduce price below the level that would emerge in a competitive market. Thus buyer power arises from monopsony (one buyer) or oligopsony (a few buyers), and is the mirror image of monopoly or oligopoly[138].

In the standard model of monopsony, the supply side of a market is perfectly competitive and is represented by an upward-sloping supply curve. As a mirror image of a monopolist's behaviour, a monopsonist can take advantage of his market power by reducing his demand. The lower price obtained by the buyer reflects the lower marginal cost of supply.

What are the competitive effects of buyer power and monopsony power?[139] With regard to the upstream side, as the monopsonist restricts its input purchases to reduce prices below competitive levels, there might be allocative inefficiency and the buyer may extract supplier surplus. With regard to the downstream side, there is no allocative inefficiency if the monopsonist discriminates perfectly. Consumers do not benefit though from reduced input prices as these do not lead to reduced output prices that are passed to output buyers, to the

137 OFT 415, Assessment of Market Power (2004), 15–16.

138 RG Noll, '"Buyer Power" and Economic Policy' (2005) 72 *Antitrust LJ* 589.

139 For a detailed analysis, see RD Blair and JL Harrison, *Monopsony in Law and Economics* (CUP, 2010).

extent that 'the monopsonist may control the *price* it pays for an input but cannot control the *quantity* of the input offered for sale at that price'.[140] Buyer power may also result in 'waterbed effects' or 'spiralling effects'. The '*waterbed effects*' may result, for instance, from the fact that buyer power could lead to a reduction of marginal costs and lower input prices for the entity with buyer power, which sees its output rising, while at the same time buyer power raises the input prices of the competitors of the entity which do not dispose of buyer power, as the reduction of prices has to be passed on to someone else, which may lead them to increase their prices, thus affecting the final consumers.[141]

Although monopsony is considered as the mirror image of monopoly, buyer-side conduct is regularly treated more leniently than equivalent conduct on the selling side. This relies on the idea that serving large buyers may involve lower distribution costs and lower production costs, leading to important discounts, as the larger the buyer the more credible would be its threat to integrate backwards and produce the good itself.[142]

One may also distinguish between buyer power, which denotes the ability of buyers to obtain advantageous terms of trade from their suppliers and countervailing power, which characterizes the presence of strong buyers mitigating or even fully averting adverse consequences for consumer surplus or total welfare that would otherwise arise from the exercise of market power at the supply side. Countervailing power on the buyer side may be an important force offsetting suppliers' increased market power.[143] The economic analysis of bilateral monopoly or oligopoly, the situation where a lawful monopolist confronts a lawful monopsony, does not offer clear directions. While some authors argue that bilateral monopoly produces welfare effects that are superior to those of monopoly or monopsony and that it does not raise any competition concerns,[144] others doubt on the possibility of bilateral bargaining to reliably reach an efficient outcome, because of the pervasive presence of private information and incomplete contracts.[145]

The concept of 'buyer power' and that of 'countervailing buyer power' have been discussed in competition authorities' soft law, either focusing on the role of buyer power in the assessment of market power (or dominant position) or on 'countervailing buyer power'.

140 JL Harrison, 'Complications in the Antitrust Reponse to Monopoly' in I Lianos and D Sokol (eds) *The Global Limits of Competition Law* (Stanford University Press, 2012), 54, 58.

141 On the '*waterbed effects*', see R Inderst and T Valletti, 'Buyer Power and the "Waterbed Effect"' (2011) 59(1) *J Industrial Economics* 1; P Dobson and R Inderst, 'Differential Buyer Power and the Waterbed Effect: Do Strong Buyers Benefit or Harm Consumers?' (2007) 28(7) *European Competition L Rev* 393; A Majumdar, 'Waterbed Effects and Buying Mergers', CCP Working Paper 05-7 (2007), available at https://ssrn.com/abstract=911574.

142 D Sheffman and P Spiller, 'Buyers' Strategies, Entry Barriers, and Competition' (1992) 30 *Economic Inquiry* 418.

143 The term was first coined by John Kenneth Galbraith to describe the power developed on one side of the market as a way to counter the market power on the other side of the market. John Kenneth Galbraith, *American Capitalism: The Concept of Countervailing Power* (1952). See also T von Ungern-Sternberg, 'Countervailing Power Revisited' (1996)14 *Int'l J Industrial Organization* 507; PW Dobson and M Waterson, 'Countervailing Power and Consumer Prices' (1997) 107 *Economic J* 418; Z Chen, 'Dominant Retailers and Countervailing Power Hypothesis' (2003) 34 *Rand J Economics* 612.

144 T Campbell, 'Bilateral Monopoly in Mergers' (2007) 74 *Antitrust LJ* 521; RD Blair and C Depasquale, 'Bilateral Monopoly and Antitrust Policy' in RD Blair and D Sokol (eds) *Oxford Handbook of International Antitrust Economics*, vol 1 (Oxford University Press, 2015), 364, 377.

145 JB Baker, J Farrell, and C Shapiro, 'Merger to Monopoly to Serve a Single Buyer', (2008) 75(2) *Antitrust LJ* 637.

OFT 415, Assessment of Market Power (2004), 24–5

Buyer power

6.1. The strength of buyers and the structure of the buyers' side of the market may constrain the market power of a seller. Size is not sufficient for buyer power. Buyer power requires the buyer to have choice.

6.2. The analysis of buyer power requires an understanding of the way that buyers interact with suppliers. Buyer power is most commonly found in industries where buyers and suppliers negotiate, in which case buyer power can be thought of as the degree of bargaining strength in negotiations. A buyer's bargaining strength might be enhanced if the following conditions hold:

- the buyer is well informed about alternative sources of supply and could readily, and at little cost to itself, switch substantial purchases from one supplier to another while continuing to meet its needs.
- the buyer could commence production of the item itself or 'sponsor' new entry by another supplier (e.g. through a long-term contract) relatively quickly and without incurring substantial sunk costs
- the buyer is an important outlet for the seller (i.e. the seller would be willing to cede better terms to the buyer in order to retain the opportunity to sell to that buyer)
- the buyer can intensify competition among suppliers through establishing a procurement auction or purchasing through a competitive tender.

6.3. In general, buyer power is beneficial in two circumstances:

(i) when there are large efficiency gains that result from the factors (e.g. size) that give the buyer its power and these are passed on to the final consumer (e.g. through downstream competition), and (ii) when it exerts downward pressure on a supplier's prices and the lower prices are passed on to the final consumer.

6.4. However, buyer power does not always benefit the final consumer. First, where only some buyers are powerful, for example, a supplier with market power might harm downstream competition through actions which lead to weaker buyers facing higher input prices. Second, buyer power might be weakened as a result of the agreement or behaviour under investigation. Third, where the buyer also has market power as a seller in the downstream market, it may not pass on lower prices to the final consumer. Fourth, conduct by a dominant buyer may harm competition. A careful analysis of vertical relationships in the market, on a case-by-case basis, is therefore often required to assess buyer power.

Communication from the Commission—Guidance on the Commission's enforcement priorities in applying Article [102 TFEU] to abusive exclusionary conduct by dominant undertakings [2009] OJ C 45/7 (footnotes omitted)

(c) Countervailing buyer power

18. Competitive constraints may be exerted not only by actual or potential competitors but also by customers. Even an undertaking with a high market share may not be able

to act to an appreciable extent independently of customers with sufficient bargaining strength. Such countervailing buying power may result from the customers' size or their commercial significance for the dominant undertaking, and their ability to switch quickly to competing suppliers, to promote new entry or to vertically integrate, and to credibly threaten to do so. If countervailing power is of a sufficient magnitude, it may deter or defeat an attempt by the undertaking to profitably increase prices. Buyer power may not, however, be considered a sufficiently effective constraint if it only ensures that a particular or limited segment of customers is shielded from the market power of the dominant undertaking.

NOTES AND QUESTIONS

1. What is the function of (countervailing) buying power in the finding of a dominant position? Is it considered as a constraint to the capacity of the 'dominant' undertaking to act independently from its customers, if we adopt the standard definition of the dominant position by EU courts?
2. The OFT (now CMA) has noted that 'buyer power does not always benefit the final consumer'.[146] Why? Does the OFT take a different perspective on buyer power from the EU Commission on the role of buyer power in finding the existence of a dominant position?

8.3.4.4. Other criteria

Both the EU and the UK competition authorities and courts take into account several other indicia of dominant position or substantial market power (SMP), such as:

- the nature of competition;
- evidence of behaviour and performance; or
- regulation by government.

A Coscelli and G Edwards, 'Dominance and Market Power in EU Competition Law Enforcement' in I Lianos and D Geradin (eds) *Research Handbook in EU Competition Law* (Edward Elgar, 2012), ch 8, 371–2 (excerpt, some footnotes omitted)

Nature of competition

[E]ven if there are barriers to entry and the firm under investigation has a very high market share, in some instances the nature of competition with other firms in the market may be such as to deny any power over price. A well-established instance of this is where competition takes the form of periodical bidding in auctions or tenders for large contracts. In bidding markets, even a firm that has close to 100% of a market characterised by high barriers to

146 OFT 415, Assessment of Market Power (2004), para 6.4.

entry may not have SMP if there are a number of other firms in the market that are capable of competing on an equal footing for the next set of contracts. [. . .].

High barriers to entry may also be less important in markets that are characterised by what is called 'innovation competition'. Innovation competition may be seen as a form of competition 'for' the market, rather than competition 'in' the market. Markets characterised by innovation competition may experience a series of firms with very high market shares, but any market power that any of those firms has will be transitory, since the markets can swing quickly to an entrant with a superior technology or idea. Many new media markets are said to exhibit these characteristics. As the EC has observed in its SMP Guidelines: 'high barriers to entry may become less relevant with regard to markets characterised by on-going technological progress. In electronic communications markets, competitive constraints may come from innovative threats from potential competitors that are not currently in the market. In such markets, the competitive assessment should be based on a prospective, forward-looking approach'.[147] [. . .]

Other market features may point against any finding of dominance despite some forms of barriers to entry. For example, where demand is expected to grow significantly (taking the size of the barriers to entry as given), entry should be more feasible.[148]

OFT 415, Assessment of Market Power (2004), 25–26

Evidence on behaviour and performance

6.5. An undertaking's conduct in a market or its financial performance may provide evidence that it possesses market power. Depending on other available evidence, it might, for example, be reasonable to infer that an undertaking possesses market power from evidence that it has:

- set prices consistently above an appropriate measure of costs, or
- persistently earned an excessive rate of profit.

6.6. High prices or profits alone are not sufficient proof that an undertaking has market power: high profits may represent a return on previous innovation, or result from changing demand conditions. As such, they may be consistent with a competitive market, where undertakings are able to take advantage of profitable opportunities when they exist. However, persistent significantly high returns, relative to those which would prevail in a competitive market of similar risk and rate of innovation, may suggest that market power does exist. This would be especially so if those high returns did not stimulate new entry or innovation.

Economic regulation

6.7. In some sectors the economic behaviour of undertakings (such as the prices they set or the level of services they provide) is regulated by the government or an industry sector regulator, and an assessment of market power may need to take that into account. Although an undertaking might not face effective constraints from existing competitors, potential competitors

[147] Commission Guidelines on market analysis and the assessment of significant market power under the Community regulatory framework for electronic communications networks and services [2002] OJ C 165/6, para 78.

[148] The EC has pointed to mature markets as a factor reinforcing a firm's dominance: see eg *Eurofix-Bauco v Hilti* (Cases IV/30.787 and 31.488) Commission Decision 88/138/EEC [1988] OJ L 65/19, para 69.

or the nature of buyers in the market, it may still be constrained from profitably sustaining prices above competitive levels by an industry sector regulator. However, that is not to say that market power cannot exist when there is economic regulation. It is feasible, for example, that regulation of the average price or profit level across several markets supplied by an undertaking may still allow for the undertaking profitably to sustain prices above competitive levels in one (or more) of these markets and/or to engage in exclusionary behaviour of various kinds.

8.3.5. DIRECT EVIDENCE OF MARKET POWER AND DOMINANT POSITION

As we have already seen in Chapter 3, direct evidence of market power and anti-competitive effect, without the need to define a relevant market, is generally acceptable in the application of Article 101 TFEU and Chapter I CA98. Whether the conduct has increased (in a retrospective case) or is likely to increase (in a prospective case) market power, it is possible that economic methods may be used to assess changes in market power, examining a historical counterfactual without the challenged practices in order to decide if a conduct has increased market power (a retrospective analysis in the situation of an agreement or abusive conduct), or providing an analysis of the change in incentives (a prospective analysis for instance regarding mergers) in order to examine of the conduct is likely to increase market power.[149] Profitability level assessment, however, presents serious challenges for decision-makers.

A Coscelli and G Edwards, 'Dominance and Market Power in EU Competition Law Enforcement' in I Lianos and D Geradin (eds) *Research Handbook in EU Competition Law* (Edward Elgar, 2012), ch 8, 375 (excerpt)

[. . .] [A] difficulty with profitability assessments is the necessity in most cases to work with accounting data and the lack of a close correspondence between accounting measures of costs and profitability and economic concepts relevant to competition law.[150]

In the *Microsoft* case the EC concluded its discussion of barriers to entry by pointing to Microsoft's high profits as 'consistent with its near-monopoly position in the client PC operating system market'.[151] [. . .] We believe that evidence of significant profits by market leaders in dynamic industries can be regarded as supportive of a dominance finding even if the nature of competition in the industry will be a relevant factor in assessing whether any alleged abuse of dominance by the firm in question has actually occurred.[152] On the other

149 JB Baker and T Bresnahan, 'Economic Evidence in Antitrust: Defining Markets and Measuring Market Power' in Paolo Buccirossi (ed) *Handbook of Antitrust Economics* (MIT Press, 2008), 1, 15

150 For a discussion of the use of profitability analysis in market power assessments, see OXERA, 'Assessing Profitability in Competition Policy Analysis', OFT Economic Discussion Paper 6 (July 2003).

151 *Microsoft/W2000* (Case COMP/C-3/37.792) Commission Decision C(2004)900 final (24 March 2004), para 464.

152 Different price-cost margin metrics may be used. A prominent one is the Lerner index. The Lerner index describes a firm's market power. It is defined by $L = (P - MC)/P$ where P is the market price set by the firm and MC is the firm's marginal cost. The index ranges from a high of 1 to a low of 0, with higher numbers implying greater market power. See also Section 3.2 of this volume.

hand, while evidence of low profits tends to suggest that there is no market power, in some cases low profits can co-exist with SMP, and one should therefore not be too hasty to rule out dominance in such cases. First, it is possible that the reason for low profits is that high potential profitability has been eroded by *x*-inefficiency that is sometimes a characteristic of dominant firms (that is, the very lack of competitive pressure may sometimes lead to managerial slack and wasted opportunities to realize high profits). This might be more likely when the firm is State-owned, rather than privately held. Second, where the abusive conduct is predatory pricing, the abuse itself necessitates low profits, at least for a temporary period. For this reason the CJEU in *Michelin I* rejected an argument that because Michelin was making losses it was not dominant.[153] The CJEU considered that the losses were a temporary state of affairs and did not contradict a finding, based on a range of other factors, that Michelin was dominant. Finally, a dominant firm might also engage in rent seeking behaviour that dissipates profits.

It is not, however, clear that it is possible to pass the definition of a relevant market in order to find the existence of a dominant position, even if UK competition authorities do not exclude the measurement of profitability as an alternative means of inferring the existence of a dominant position.

For the reasons explained below, the definition of a relevant market is an important filter in order to test the coherence of the consumer harm story advanced by the plaintiff and to provide the first analytical step in the definition of a dominant position. It is also important to distinguish between cases where the conduct examined is the result of the collusion between firms or their merger (which constitutes the absolute agreement) and cases involving unilateral conduct. The risks of type I errors might be more important in unilateral conduct cases, as an intrusive application of competition law might affect the incentives of the firms to compete vigorously on the marketplace. It follows that market definition should be an indispensable analytical step in assessing the existence of a dominant position.

NOTES AND QUESTIONS

1. 'Many businesses operate in complex ecosystems. Their success depends on providers of complementary products as well as providers of substitutes and on a variety of vertical relationships. Reducing competitive constraints these businesses face to a list of demand- and supply-side substitutes can eliminate many important nuances about the environment in which these businesses operate. A number of industries, including many businesses that involve software or the Web, are centered on multisided platforms (also known as two sided markets) that serve as intermediaries between several groups of customers and providers of complementary products.'[154] Taking into account the complexity of the task and the various elements to take into account, should competition authorities attempt to define the existence of dominant position directly, or should judges and competition authorities adopt a narrative approach, in

[153] Case C-322/81, *NV Nederlandsche Baden-Industrie Michelin v Commission* [1983] ECR 3461, paras 54–5.

[154] D Evans, 'Lightening up on Market Definition', in E Elhauge (ed) *Research Handbook on the Economics of Antitrust Law* (Edward Elgar, 2012), ch 3, 84.

which the step of the definition of a relevant market constitutes a pre-requisite of the finding of a dominant position?

2. Compare the possibilities opened for the direct estimation of anti-competitive effects and thus the exercise of substantial market power in the context of the abuse of a dominant position with the development of the unilateral effects doctrine in merger control.[155] Do you think that the type of analysis performed is similar? Should it be?
3. Discussing a positive aspect of profitability as an indicator of market power, Niels, Jenkins, and Kavanagh note that '[. . .] the difficulties of profitability analysis are overstated. The theoretical framework for such an analysis has been developed [. . .] and, perhaps, exceptionally in economics, a whole lot of good financial data is out there, in published company accounts, management accounts, and financial markets.'[156] Thousands of business and investment decisions are made every day based on this data by the very companies that we scrutinize under competition law. It would be a waste if this data were completely ignored in the competition analysis. Measurement and interpretation problems are also prevalent in other economic techniques, such as the estimation of demand elasticities for market definition or the use of game theory to assess market conduct. Do you agree with the conclusions reached by the authors? Is data often available for the whole European Union, or only for some mature national markets in larger Member States? Would the absence of data challenge the use of profitability analysis in the assessment of dominant position?

8.3.6. DOMINANT POSITION IN AFTERMARKETS

The economic analysis of market definition in aftermarkets is provided in Chapter 3.[157] The issue has been raised in cases where the producer of the original equipment has prevented independent third parties from servicing the equipment or from selling replacement parts.[158] The classic example is a printer manufacturer selling printers at (or below) cost and charging high mark-ups over cost on proprietary printer ink cartridges. It has been argued that, in these circumstances,

> concerns about market power arise because, once a consumer buys a copier or a complicated computer system, the consumer may to some extent be locked in, because the 'switching costs' involved in selling the computer and buying a new one from another manufacturer can be significant. Therefore, it is possible for the seller of the original equipment to charge prices above costs for all future services to the good. In simple economic models, prices above costs generate a reduction in social welfare because of the deadweight loss associated with market power. Concerns would not arise if it were possible to write detailed enforceable contracts that specify the conditions and costs of every possible future action of the seller and the buyer.

155 See Section 12.3.5.

156 See G Niels, H Jenkins, and J Kavanagh, *Economics for Competition Lawyers* (OUP, 2011), 150–3 and 165.

157 See Section 3.3.5.1.

158 A Coscelli and G Edwards, 'Dominance and Market Power in EU Competition Law Enforcement' in I Lianos and D Geradin (eds) *Research Handbook in EU Competition Law* (Edward Elgar, 2012), ch 8.

However, in practice such contracts are usually too costly or otherwise not feasible (and even if they were, it is questionable that they would resolve concerns in practice, for example because of behavioural economics considerations.[159]

Everything will depend in this case on the market structure of the original equipment market. If it is competitive, the demand for the product by future customers will be negatively affected by the prices charged for aftermarket services; hence there will be little incentive for the producer of the original equipment to charge prices above competitive levels. However, manufacturers face two sorts of customers: those that have already bought the product and are thus 'locked-in', for which producers may charge high prices in the aftermarkets, and future customers that may take this strategy into account when making their purchase, thus inflicting the producer a reputational cost. Before adopting a strategy concerning aftermarkets, the producer will thus explore the trade-off between the reputation costs and the benefits arising out of the exploitation of 'locked-in' customers.

The trade-off will be affected by possible imperfections relating to the flow of information from the primary to secondary markets (or aftermarkets), 'an inherently empirical question',[160] the main question being whether 'customers purchasing a system (for example, accounting software and support services) can directly protect themselves when they purchase the product in the main market'.[161] Shapiro and Teece argue that the markets more 'conducive to *ex post* exploitation by a firm of its customer base' in the following situations: (a) in a declining market, so future sales are less important relative to the size of the installed base; (b) for a firm that is having trouble competing in the market, so it discounts the importance of future sales; (c) for products that are marginally profitable or unprofitable on a life-cycle basis, so that future sales are not likely to generate significant profits, even when viewed on a life-cycle basis; (d) for a firm with few other products whose goodwill will be hurt; or (e) for a firm in financial distress, or one with a very high cost of capital, which places unusual weight on current profits relative to future profits.[162]

In the EU, the Commission and the Courts have been rather open in finding the existence of a dominant position in aftermarkets. Consider the analysis in *Hugin*.

8.3.6.1. *Hugin*

Case C-22/78, *Hugin Kassaregister AB and Hugin Cash Registers Ltd v Commission* [1979] ECR 1869

The case was an action for annulment of a decision adopted by the Commission in application of Article 102 TFEU against Hugin Kassaregister and its British subsidiary company Hugin Cash Registers Ltd. Hugin manufactured cash registers and similar equipment detaining a market share of 12–14 per cent in the UK as well as in the EU Internal Market at

159 Ibid. 160 Ibid.

161 C Shapiro and DJ Teece, 'Systems Competition and Aftermarkets: An Economic Analysis of Kodak' (1994) 39(1) *Antitrust Bulletin* 135.

162 Ibid, 153.

the time, the market shares of other manufacturers being 34–36 per cent, 15–18 per cent, and 13–16 per cent. Hugin was thus not the market leader. The maintenance and repair of Hugin cash registers was exclusively carried out by technicians in the service of Hugin or its subsidiaries and main distributors and thus independent maintenance and repair undertakings were excluded from this field of activity. Liptons, a UK independent repairer of cash registers of most makes, entered an agreement with Hugin retaining responsibility for after sales service for Hugin cash registers, while continuing to provide after-sales service in the context of its own business. After Liptons rejected the contract offered by Hugin for insufficient commercial margins, the latter refused to supply spare parts for Hugin cash registers. Following a complaint from Liptons, the Commission declared that Hugin AB and Hugin UK had infringed Article 102 TFEU by refusing to supply spare parts for Hugin cash registers to Liptons and imposed a fine on the two undertakings. The Court of Justice reviewed the decision of the Commission

Opinion of AG Gerhard Reischl

The applicants [. . .] take the view primarily that the Commission relied on too narrow a definition of the relevant market—the supply of Hugin spare parts and the servicing of Hugin machines. In reality those services should be viewed in conjunction with the market for cash registers. In that market they are but *one* element of competition which, as is shown by Hugin's share of the market and the growing success of Japanese producers in the Common Market, is extremely fierce. Accordingly it is not possible to assume that the Hugin group holds a dominant position as regards purchasers of Hugin cash registers even with regard to spare parts and after-sales service. This is also confirmed by Hugin's conduct on the market which has not led to detrimental effects for customers because after-sales service and supplies of spare parts are provided at very low prices and even at a loss for Hugin. It is said to be quite wrong to restrict the examination to the question whether a dominant position as against undertakings such as Liptons can be taken to exist. [. . .] In this dispute it can hardly be denied that the supply of spare parts and the servicing of cash registers are elements of competition on the market in cash registers which naturally are of importance for customers when they acquire cash registers. [. . .] It is therefore certainly possible to describe after-sales service in a certain sense as an activity which is *accessory* to the sale of cash registers. On the other hand, in my view this does not necessarily lead to the conclusion that such services are *only* to be viewed in conjunction with the market for cash registers and that they do not have *any* independent significance, thus denying the existence of a particular market for spare parts and servicing. If a customer has acquired a cash register which is said to have an average life of eight years, there is then for a considerable period demand only for spare parts and servicing from the purchaser. A considerable proportion of customers (according to the applicants, more than one third) do not make use of the possibility of concluding maintenance contracts with Hugin but ask for servicing and the supply of spare parts as they need them. Similarly, the fact should not be over-looked that there exist independent workshops engaged in such activities—in the United Kingdom there are apparently some 40 other undertakings apart from Liptons—and that, because other manufacturers of cash registers do not have the same after-sales policy as Hugin, spare parts are supplied by them to independent repair undertakings. [. . .] I am therefore of the opinion that the Commission was right to assume that there is a particular market for spare parts and after-sales service for cash registers and to raise the question whether Hugin occupies a dominant position on a market defined in that way. [. . .] It can therefore in fact be said that Hugin has a monopoly for the supply of Hugin spare parts and therefore holds a dominant position [. . .] One important factor is the value of spare parts in relation to the value of cash registers and the value of maintenance service. According to the applicant's turnover figures, as the Commission has shown, spare parts cost on average 3 per cent. of the price of the cash register; their value is also relatively small in comparison with the cost of the annual servicing for which the applicants charge £25, that is to say roughly one eighteenth of the price of the cash register. In view of that situation it can certainly be assumed that even relatively substantial increases in the price of spare parts are possible without affecting the customers' choice of a make of cash register. [. . .] [A]s the Commission correctly assumes, there exists a separate category of customers for spare parts, that of the independent servicing undertakings, which may be taken to be even more genuinely dependent on Hugin, which in turn leaves considerable scope for the independent fixing of prices. [. . .]

Judgment of the Court of Justice

Hugin's position on the market

3. As regards the question whether Hugin occupies a dominant position on the market the Commission takes the view that the facts of the case have shown that while Hugin has only a relatively small share of the cash register market—which is very competitive—it has a monopoly in spare parts for machines made by it and that consequently it occupies a dominant position for the maintenance and repair of Hugin cash registers in relation to independent companies which need a supply of Hugin spare parts. As regards the reconditioning of used machines and the renting out of such machines the Commission also takes the view that Hugin occupies a dominant position as regards cash registers of its own manufacture, since undertakings engaged in such activities depend on supplies of Hugin spare parts.

4. Hugin contests the validity of the Commission's findings on these various points. In its principal argument it states that the supply of spare parts and of maintenance services is certainly not a separate market but is an essential parameter of competition in the market for cash registers as a whole. It states that on that market after-sales service and the quality of repair and maintenance services, including the supply of spare parts, constitute such a significant competitive factor that Hugin runs those services at a loss.

5. To resolve the dispute it is necessary, first, to determine the relevant market. In this respect account must be taken of the fact that the conduct alleged against Hugin consists in the refusal to supply spare parts to Liptons and, generally, to any independent undertaking outside its distribution network. The question is, therefore, whether the supply of spare parts constitutes a specific market or whether it forms part of a wider market. To answer that question it is necessary to determine the category of clients who require such parts.

6. In this respect it is established, on the one hand, that cash registers are of such a technical nature that the user cannot fit the spare parts into the machine but requires the services of a specialised technician and, on the other, that the value of the spare parts is of little significance in relation to the cost of maintenance and repairs. That being the case, users of cash registers do not operate on the market as purchasers of spare parts, however they have their machines maintained and repaired. Whether they

avail themselves of Hugin's after-sales service or whether they rely on independent undertakings engaged in maintenance and repair work, their spare part requirements are not manifested directly and independently on the market. While there certainly exists amongst users a market for maintenance and repairs which is distinct from the market in new cash registers, it is essentially a market for the provision of services and not for the sale of a product such as spare parts, the refusal to supply which forms the subject-matter of the Commission's decision.

7. On the other hand, there exists a separate market for Hugin spare parts at another level, namely that of independent undertakings which specialise in the maintenance and repair of cash registers, in the reconditioning of used machines and in the sale of used machines and the renting out of machines. The role of those undertakings on the market is that of businesses which require spare parts for their various activities. They need such parts in order to provide services for cash register users in the form of maintenance and repairs and for the reconditioning of used machines intended for re-sale or renting out. Finally, they require spare parts for the maintenance and repair of new or used machines belonging to them which are rented out to their clients. It is, moreover, established that there is a specific demand for Hugin spare parts, since those parts are not interchangeable with spare parts for cash registers of other makes.

8. Consequently the market thus constituted by Hugin spare parts required by independent undertakings must be regarded as the relevant market for the purposes of the application of Article [102 TFEU] to the facts of the case. It is in fact the market on which the alleged abuse was committed.

9. It is necessary to examine next whether Hugin occupies a dominant position on that market. In this respect Hugin admits that it has a monopoly in new spare parts. For commercial reasons any competing production of spare parts which could be used in Hugin cash registers is not conceivable in practice. Hugin argues nevertheless that another source of supply does exist, namely the purchase and dismantling of used machines. The value of that source of supply is disputed by the parties. Although the file appears to show that the practice of dismantling used machines is current in the cash register sector it cannot be regarded as constituting a sufficient alternative source of supply. Indeed the figures relating to Liptons' turnover during the years when Hugin refused to sell spare parts to it show that Liptons' business in the selling, renting out and repairing of Hugin machines diminished considerably, not only when expressed in absolute terms but even more so in real terms, taking inflation into account.

10. On the market for its own spare parts, therefore, Hugin is in a position which enables it to determine its conduct without taking account of competing sources of supply. There is therefore nothing to invalidate the conclusion that it occupies, on that market, a dominant position within the meaning of Article [102 TFEU].

The Court found that Hugin was abusing its dominant position but did not apply Article 102 TFEU as the trade between Member States was not affected and thus annulled the decision of the Commission.

NOTES AND QUESTIONS

1. Did the Court's definition of a relevant market and finding of a dominant position focus on the exploitation of final consumers and if this was the case, which were the consumers protected? Further, did the Court emphasize instead the access of

independent repairers (intermediary consumers) to Hugin's spare parts? What was the objective of the Court in defining such a narrow relevant market?

2. In its most recent *Guidelines on Vertical Restraints*, the European Commission notes the following:

   Where a supplier produces both original equipment and the repair or replacement parts for that equipment, the supplier will often be the only or the major supplier on the after-market for the repair and replacement parts. This may also arise where the supplier (original equipment manufacturer, OEM) subcontracts the manufacturing of the repair or replacement parts. The relevant market for application of the Block Exemption Regulation may be the original equipment market including the spare parts or a separate original equipment market and after-market depending on the circumstances of the case, such as the effects of the restrictions involved, the lifetime of the equipment and importance of the repair or replacement cost. In practice, the issue is whether a significant proportion of buyers make their choice taking into account the lifetime costs of the product. If so, it indicates there is one market for the original equipment and spare parts combined.[163]

   How does this position compare with the one the CJEU adopted in *Hugin*? Is the Commission's position closer to the analysis of aftermarket power in economics?

3. The OFT explicitly discussed aftermarkets in its Market Definition Guidelines (now adopted by the CMA).[164] The discussion closely mirrors the European Commission's approach and the relevant economic literature. The OFT recognized that the main issue in cases involving secondary products would be to assess whether the customer takes account of the whole-life cost of the product before purchasing. Nonetheless, the OFT accepted that it will not be necessary that all customers take into account the whole-life cost of the product. So long as the manufacturer cannot discriminate between those customers that do and those that do not, the manufacturer would be prevented from exploiting any monopoly position in the secondary market.

8.3.6.2. Follow-ups: *Pelikan/Kyoecera*, *Info-Lab/Ricoh*, and *EFIM*

The Commission set the principles of its aftermarkets analysis in its *Pelikan/Kyoecera*, *Info-Lab/Ricoh*, and *EFIM* decisions, relating to complaints regarding the market for toners for

[163] See also Commission Notice on the definition of relevant market for the purposes of Community competition law [2007] OJ C 372/5, para 56 on the method of defining primary and secondary markets:

> The method of defining markets in these cases is the same, i.e. assessing the responses of customers based on their purchasing decisions to relative price changes, but taking into account as well, constraints on substitution imposed by conditions in the connected markets. A narrow definition of market for secondary products, for instance, spare parts, may result when compatibility with the primary product is important. Problems of finding compatible secondary products together with the existence of high prices and a long lifetime of the primary products may render relative price increases of secondary products profitable. A different market definition may result if significant substitution between secondary products is possible or if the characteristics of the primary products make quick and direct consumer responses to relative price increases of the secondary products feasible.

[164] OFT 403, Market Definition (December 2004), available at www.gov.uk/government/uploads/system/uploads/attachment_data/file/284423/oft403.pdf.

printers and toners for photocopiers.[165] In its Notice on market definition, the Commission explained this approach by noting the need when defining a market not only to assess the responses of customers based on their purchasing decisions when relative prices change, but also constraints on substitution imposed by conditions in the connected markets.[166] If the issue of compatibility between the spare parts and the primary product is important for consumers and the primary product has a long lifespan, there might be the risk that charging higher prices to the 'locked in' the brand customers may be a profitable strategy, hence leading to the definition of a narrow secondary product market (eg spare parts, after-sales services). However, according to the Commission's Notice, 'a different market definition may result if significant substitution between secondary products is possible or if the characteristics of the primary products make quick and direct consumer responses to relative price increases of the secondary products feasible'. As it is further explained in the Commission's vertical restraints guidelines, '[i]n practice, the issue to decide is whether a significant proportion of buyers make their choice taking into account the lifetime costs of the product. If so, this indicates there is one market for the original equipment and spare parts combined'.[167]

Traditionally economic analysis on aftermarkets has emphasized whether consumers 'full cost' at the outset in order to distinguish between the different cases.[168] A similar approach was adopted by the US Supreme Court in *Eastman Kodak*, which has been perceived as animated by post-Chicago principles that market imperfections (eg information imperfections) may lead 'unsophisticated' market participants to be exploited in aftermarkets for products they are locked in, even if the primary market is competitive.[169,170]

165 *Pelican/Kyocera* (Case COMP IV/34.330) Commission Decision (22 September 1995), para 6 (noting that the Commission will consider the following four elements: 'the extent that a customer (i) can make an informed choice including lifecycle-pricing, knowing of the warranty restrictions of the various manufacturers, that he (ii) is likely to make such choice accordingly, and that, in case of an apparent policy of exploitation being pursued in one specific aftermarket, a (iii) sufficient number of customers would adapt their purchasing behavior at the level of the primary market (iv) within a reasonable time'); *Info-Lab/Ricoh* (Case IV/E 2/36.431) Commission Decision (1999), paras 37ff; *EFIM* (Case COMP/C-3/39.391) Commission Decision, Doc C(2009)4125, para 16. For cases where similar issues were raised, see *Varta/Bosch* (Case COMP IV/M.12) Commission Decision 91/595/EEC [1991] OJ L 320, para 26; *Caterpillar/Perkins Engines* (Case COMP IV/M.1094) Commission Decision [1998] OJ C 94/28, para 23; and *Lucas/Varity* (Case COMP IV/M.768) Commission Decision [1996] OJ C 266/6, para 6.

166 Commission Notice on the definition of the relevant market for the purposes of Community competition law [1997] OJ C 37/5, para 56.

167 Commission Guidelines on Vertical Restraints [2010] C 130/1, para 91. See also DG Competition, 'Discussion Paper on the Application of Article 82 of the Treaty to Exclusionary Abuses' (December 2005), paras 257–8, available at http://ec.europa.eu/competition/antitrust/art82/discpaper2005.pdf (focusing on switching costs for customers to shift their demand to another primary product).

168 See P Davis, L Coppi, and P Kalmus, 'The Economics of Secondary Product Markets', OFT Discussion Paper (2012).

169 *Eastman Kodak Co v Image Technical Services, Inc*, 504 US 451 (1992). The judgment of the Supreme Court was criticized by some scholars, eg H Hovenkamp, *The Antitrust Enterprise Principle and Execution* (Harvard University Press, 2005), 310 (calling for the overruling of the Kodak precedent), and lauded by others, eg WS Grimes, 'Antitrust Tie-in Analysis After Kodak: Understanding the Role of Market Imperfections' (1994) 62 *Antitrust LJ* 263. Controversy notwithstanding, the *Eastman Kodak* precedent seems still to be good law, at least for some district courts: see, most recently, *Avaya, Inc v Telecom Labs, Inc*, 1:06-cv-2490(JEI) (DNJ, 2006) (27 March 2014).

170 On aftermarkets see also the judgment of the CJEU in Case C-56/12 P, *European Federation of Ink and Ink Cartridge Manufacturers (EFIM) v Commission*, ECLI:EU:C:2013:575, para 37, which confirmed the approach followed so far by the Commission.

8.3.7. COLLECTIVE (JOINT) DOMINANT POSITION

Article 102 TFEU prohibits the abuse 'by one or more undertakings' of a dominant position. Based on this textual reference, the Commission, supported by the Courts, developed the concept of 'collective dominance' or 'joint dominant position'. The aim followed by the Commission was to extend the scope of applicability of Article 102 TFEU to oligopolistic market settings, where some anti-competitive effects may occur.[171] In 1965, a group of academics were appointed by the European Commission to reflect on 'the Concentration of Enterprises in the Common Market': they adopted a report advocating the possibility to apply the concept of abuse of dominance to oligopolistic price leadership.[172] Influential figures, such as judge (then professor) R Joliet have been arguing since the early 1970s that Article 102 should apply to joint dominance in order to cover situations of oligopolistic interdependence.[173] Nevertheless, in *Hoffman-La Roche*, the Court distinguished the concept of dominant position from that of oligopolistic interdependence: 'a dominant position must also be distinguished from parallel courses of conduct which are peculiar to oligopolies in that in an oligopoly the courses of conduct interact, while in the case of an undertaking occupying a dominant position the conduct of the undertaking which derives profits from that position is to a great extent determined unilaterally'.[174] Despite the negative predisposition of the CJEU towards the concept of collective dominance in a number of cases,[175] the European Courts reconsidered their position in subsequent cases.

8.3.7.1. *Società Italiana Vetro SpA v Commission* (*Italian Flat Glass*)

In its decision in *Flat Glas*, the Commission found a horizontal cartel between three makers of flat glass in Italy contrary to Article 101, but added a further count that the three had presented a common face to the outside world, so together enjoyed a dominant position within the common market and abused it through their cartel.[176]

The newly established General Court (then Court of First Instance) quashed parts of the decision relating to Article 102 and denied that the Commission had adequately established that Italy was the appropriate geographic market. The case is included here only on the question whether Article 102 applies to several firms who abuse a collective dominant position by parallel conduct.

171 See Chapter 11.

172 For a summary, see 'Concentration of Enterprises in the Common Market' (January 1966), 3, available at http://aei.pitt.edu/15718/1/P_1_66.pdf.

173 R Joliet, *Monopolization and Abuse of a Dominant Position: A Comparative Study of the American and European Approaches to the Control of Economic Power* (Martinus Nijhoff, 1970), 239.

174 Case C-85/76, *Hoffmann-La Roche & Co v Commission* [1979] ECR 461, para 39.

175 Case C-243/83, *SA Binon et Cie v SA Agences et messageries de la presse* [1985] ECR 2015; Case C-66/86, *Ahmed Saeed Flugreisen et Silver Line Reisebüro GmbH v Zentrale zur Bekämpfung unlauteren Wettbewerbs eV* [1989] ECR 803; Case C-247/86 *Société alsacienne et lorraine de télécommunications et d'électronique (Alsatel) v SA Novasam* [1988] ECR 5987.

176 *Flat Glass (Italy)* (Case COMP IV/31.906) Commission Decision [1989] OJ L 33, para 44.

Joined Cases T-68, 77 & 78/89, *Società Italiana Vetro SpA v Commission (Italian Flat Glass)*

[1992] ECR II–1403, [1992] 5 CMLR 302, [1992] 2 CEC 33 (full references omitted)

357. The Court notes that the very words of the first paragraph of Article 102 provide that 'one or more undertakings' may abuse a dominant position. It has consistently been held, as indeed all the parties acknowledge, that the concept of agreement or concerted practice between undertakings does not cover agreements or concerted practices among undertakings belonging to the same group if the undertakings form an economic unit. It follows that when Article 101 refers to agreements or concerted practices between 'undertakings', it is referring to relations between two or more economic entities which are capable of competing with one another.

358. The Court considers that there is no legal or economic reason to suppose that the term 'undertaking' in Article 102 has a different meaning from the one given to it in the context of Article 101. There is nothing, in principle, to prevent two or more independent economic entities from being, on a specific market, united by such economic links that, by virtue of that fact, together they hold a dominant position vis-à-vis the other operators on the same market. This could be the case, for example, where two or more independent undertakings jointly have, through agreements or licences, a technological lead affording them the power to behave to an appreciable extent independently of their competitors, their customers and ultimately of their consumers judgment (judgment of the Court in *Hoffmann-la Roche* cited above, paragraphs 38 and 48).

359. The Court finds support for that interpretation in the wording of Article 8 of Council Regulation (EEC) No 4056/86 of 22 December 1986 laying down detailed rules for the application of Articles 81 and 82 of the Treaty to maritime transport (Official Journal L 378, p.4). Article 8(2) provides that the conduct, of a liner conference benefiting from an exemption from a prohibition laid down by Article 101(1) of the Treaty may have effects which are incompatible with Article 102 of the Treaty. A request by a conference to be exempted from the prohibition laid down by Article 101(1) necessarily presupposes an agreement between two or more independent economic undertakings.

360. However, it should be pointed out that for the purposes of establishing an infringement of Article 102 of the Treaty, it is not sufficient, as the Commission's agent claimed at the hearing, to 'recycle' the facts constituting an infringement of Article 101, deducing from them the finding that the parties to an agreement or to an unlawful practice jointly hold a substantial share of the market, that by virtue of that fact alone they hold a collective dominant position, and that their unlawful behaviour constitutes an abuse of that collective dominant position. Amongst other considerations, a finding of a dominant position, which is in any case not in itself a matter of reproach, presupposes that the market in question has been defined. The Court must therefore examine, firstly, the analysis of the market made in the decision and, secondly, the circumstances relied on in support of the finding of a collective dominant position.

361. With regard to the definition of the market, the Court recalls that the section of the factual part of the decision entitled 'The market' (points 2 to 17) is almost entirely

descriptive and that, moreover, it contains a number of errors, omissions and uncertainties which have already been examined by the Court. [. . .]

366. It follows that, even supposing that the circumstances of the present case lend themselves to application of the concept of 'collective dominant position' (in the sense of a position of dominance held by a number of independent undertakings), the Commission has not adduced the necessary proof. The Commission has not even attempted to gather the information necessary to weigh up the economic power of the three producers against that of Fiat, which could cancel each other out.

NOTES AND QUESTIONS ON ITALIAN FLAT GLASS

1. (Paragraphs 357–9) Does the General Court deny the possibility of collective dominance? Is it hostile to the idea?
2. In the Court's ruling the finding of a collective dominance position is conditional on the fact that the undertakings found collectively dominant are united 'by such economic links that, by virtue of that fact, together they hold a dominant position vis-à-vis the other operators on the same market'. What did the Court have exactly in mind? Are the 'economic links' the Court refers to constitutive of a situation of oligopolistic interdependence? How can we reconcile this position with that taken by the Court in *Hoffmann-La Roche*?
3. Should a competition authority be more concerned about a market protected by entry barriers where (1) one firm supplies 80 per cent of a product and the other firms are fragmented, or (2) where two firms supply 40 per cent each, or (3) three firms each supply over 25 per cent? Why? Should non-collusive conduct to exclude others be subject to Article 102 in all three cases? For an analysis of the conditions in which non-collusive action might be anti-competitive when a merger led to concentrated supply, see Chapter 11.
4. If the Commission wanted to establish power to control exclusionary conduct by more than one dominant firm, do you think it was sensible of it to argue for a concept of collective dominance in a case where a charge under Article 102 added nothing to one under Article 101 TFEU?
5. See *Gencor*,[177] where the General Court accepted the concept of joint dominance in relation to mergers. See especially paragraphs 199–238 where it considered the factors likely to lead to collective dominance.
6. The decisional practice of the Commission in applying the concept of joint or collective dominance closely follows the paradigm it set in the application of this concept in merger control. For more details, see Chapter 12. The link between the case law on collective dominance in the context of Article 102 TFEU and that in the context of merger control has been made more clearly in *Compagnie Maritime Belge*.

[177] Case T-102/96, *Gencor v Commission* [1999] ECR II-753. For an analysis of the case, see Chapter 12.

8.3.7.2. *Compagnie Maritime Belge*

Case C-395/96 P, *Compagnie Maritime Belge* [2000] ECR I–1365, [2000] 4 CMLR 1076

The members of a shipping conference took steps through conference committees to exclude their only competitor on the conference routes, G & C. Since there was a Council regulation granting a block exemption to liner shipping conferences, most of these collective activities did not infringe Article 101 TFEU. The Commission took a decision imposing fines on the members of the conference for an infringement of Article 102 TFEU. It determined that the firms enjoyed a collective dominant position and abused it by taking the various steps taken to exclude G & C. The decision of the Commission was appealed to the General Court (then Court of First Instance), which upheld the decision on this point.[178]

32. The second and third grounds of appeal, which should be examined together, relate essentially to the issue whether the Commission is entitled to base a finding that there is abuse of a dominant position solely on circumstances or facts which would constitute an agreement, decision or concerted practice under Article [101(1)] TFEU, and therefore be automatically void unless exempted under Article [101(3) TFEU].

33. It is clear from the very wording of Articles [101(1)(a), (b), (d), and (e)] and [102(a) to (d) TFEU] that the same practice may give rise to an infringement of both provisions. Simultaneous application of Articles [101] and [102] [TFEU] cannot therefore be ruled out *a priori*. However, the objectives pursued by each of those two provisions must be distinguished.

34. Article [101 TFEU] applies to agreements, decisions and concerted practices which may appreciably affect trade between Member States, regardless of the position on the market of the undertakings concerned. Article [102 TFEU], on the other hand, deals with the conduct of one or more economic operators consisting in the abuse of a position of economic strength which enables the operator concerned to hinder the maintenance of effective competition on the relevant market by allowing it to behave to an appreciable extent independently of its competitors, its customers and, ultimately, consumers.

35. In terms of Article [102 TFEU], a dominant position may be held by several 'undertakings'. The Court of Justice has held, on many occasions that the concept of 'undertaking' in the chapter of the Treaty devoted to the rules on competition presupposes the economic independence of the entity concerned.

36. It follows that the expression 'one or more undertakings' in Article [102 TFEU] implies that a dominant position may be held by two or more economic entities legally independent of each other, provided that from an economic point of view they present themselves or act together on a particular market as a collective entity. That is how the expression 'collective dominant position', as used in the remainder of this judgment, should be understood.

37. However, a finding that an undertaking has a dominant position is not in itself a ground of criticism but simply means that, irrespective of the reasons for which it has such a dominant position, the undertaking concerned has a special responsibility not to allow its conduct to impair genuine undistorted competition on the common market [. . .].

[178] Joined Cases T-24-6 & 28/93, *Compagnie maritime belge transports SA and Compagnie maritime belge SA, Dafra-Lines A/S, Deutsche Afrika-Linien GmbH & Co and Nedlloyd Lijnen BV v Commission* [1996] ECR II–1201.

38. The same applies as regards undertakings which hold a collective dominant position. A finding that two or more undertakings hold a collective dominant position must, in principle, proceed upon an economic assessment of the position on the relevant market of the undertakings concerned, prior to any examination of the question whether those undertakings have abused their position on the market.

39. So, for the purposes of analysis under Article [102 TFEU], it is necessary to consider whether the undertakings concerned together constitute a collective entity vis-à-vis their competitors, their trading partners and consumers on a particular market. It is only where that question is answered in the affirmative that it is appropriate to consider whether that collective entity actually holds a dominant position and whether its conduct constitutes abuse. [. . .]

41. In order to establish the existence of a collective entity as defined above, it is necessary to examine the economic links or factors which give rise to a connection between the undertakings concerned.

42. In particular, it must be ascertained whether economic links exist between the undertakings concerned which enable them to act together independently of their competitors, their customers and consumers [. . .].

43. The mere fact that two or more undertakings are linked by an agreement, a decision of associations of undertakings or a concerted practice within the meaning of Article [101(1) TFEU] does not, of itself, constitute a sufficient basis for such a finding.

44. On the other hand, an agreement, decision or concerted practice (whether or not covered by an exemption under Article [101(3) TFEU]) may undoubtedly, where it is implemented, result in the undertakings concerned being so linked as to their conduct on a particular market that they present themselves on that market as a collective entity vis-à-vis their competitors, their trading partners and consumers.

45. The existence of a collective dominant position may therefore flow from the nature and terms of an agreement, from the way in which it is implemented and, consequently, from the links or factors which give rise to a connection between undertakings which result from it. Nevertheless, the existence of an agreement or of other links in law is not indispensable to a finding of a collective dominant position; such a finding may be based on other connecting factors and would depend on an economic assessment and, in particular, on an assessment of the structure of the market in question.

46. Under Article 1(3)(b) of Council Regulation (EEC) No 4056/86 of 22 December 1986 laying down detailed rules for the application of Articles 81 and 82 of the Treaty to maritime transport (OJ 1986 L 378, p. 4), a liner conference is 'a group of two or more vessel-operating carriers which provides international liner services for the carriage of cargo on a particular route or routes within specified geographical limits and which has an agreement or arrangement, whatever its nature, within the framework of which they operate under uniform or common freight rates and any other agreed conditions with respect to the provision of liner services.'

47. The eighth recital in the preamble to that regulation states that such conferences 'have a stabilising effect, assuring shippers of reliable services; [. . .] they contribute generally to providing adequate efficient scheduled maritime transport services and give fair consideration to the interests of users; [. . .] such results cannot be obtained without the cooperation that shipping companies promote within conferences in relation to rates and, where appropriate, availability of capacity or allocation of cargo for shipment, and income; [. . .] in most cases conferences continue to be subject to effective competition from both non-conference scheduled services and, in certain circumstances, from tramp services and from other modes of transport; [. . .] the mobility of fleets, which is

a characteristic feature of the structure of availability in the shipping field, subjects conferences to constant competition which they are unable as a rule to eliminate as far as a substantial proportion of the shipping services in question is concerned.'

48. It emerges from those provisions that, by its very nature and in the light of its objectives, a liner conference, as defined by the Council for the purposes of qualification for block exemption under Regulation No 4056/86, can be characterised as a collective entity which presents itself as such on the market vis-à-vis both users and competitors. So seen, it was logical for the Council to lay down in Regulation No 4056/86 the provisions necessary to avoid a liner conference having effects incompatible with Article [102 TFEU] (see, in particular, Article 8 of that regulation).

49. That in no way prejudges the question whether, in a given situation, a liner conference holds a dominant position on a particular market or, *a fortiori*, has abused that position. As is clear from Article 8(2) of Regulation No 4056/86, it is by its conduct that a conference holding a dominant position may have effects which are incompatible with Article [102 TFEU].

50. It is in the light of those considerations that the merits of the second and third grounds of appeal must be examined. [. . .]

52. Admittedly, in Section II(A) of the preamble to the contested decision, entitled 'Applicability of Article [102] to shipping conferences,' the Commission merely stated, in point 49, that Article 8 of Regulation No 4056/86 deals with the possibility of an abuse of a dominant position by shipping conferences, that the General Court had cited shipping conferences as an example of agreements between economically independent entities enabling economic links to be formed which could give those entities jointly a dominant position in relation to other operators on the same market, and that the agreement between the members of Cewal constituted such an agreement. According to point 50, the fact that some of Cewal's activities were covered by a block exemption did not prevent [Article 102 TFEU] from being applied to the activities of the conference. [. . .]

54. However, it does not follow that the General Court must be deemed to have considered that [. . .] the Commission would not have been entitled to find that the Cewal conference constituted a collective entity capable of holding a dominant position on the relevant market. On the contrary, the reasoning [. . .] is intended to show, in response to the appellants' arguments, that implementation of the Cewal agreement resulted in the conference members presenting themselves on the market as a collective entity. [. . .]

58. In those circumstances, it is not necessary to rule on the question whether the conduct of the members of a shipping conference must always be assessed collectively for the purpose of applying Article [102] of the Treaty [. . .]

NOTES AND QUESTIONS ON THE JUDGMENT IN COMPAGNIE MARITIME BELGE

1. (Paragraph 33) Can Article 102 TFEU apply to agreements that are subject to Article 101 TFEU?
2. (Paragraph 36) The Court defines the concept of collective dominant position. This definition has been repeated by the General Court in *Atlantic Container Line*.[179]

[179] Joined Cases T-191 & 212–14/98, *Atlantic Container Line AB and Others v Commission* [2003] ECR II–3275, para 595.

Two steps are required for the finding of a dominant position: (i) the existence of a collective entity and (ii) the existence of a dominant position.

a. With regard to the first issue, in *Laurent Piau v Commission*, the General Court held that:

Three cumulative conditions must be met for a finding of collective dominance: first, each member of the dominant oligopoly must have the ability to know how the other members are behaving in order to monitor whether or not they are adopting the common policy; second, the situation of tacit coordination must be sustainable over time, that is to say, there must be an incentive not to depart from the common policy on the market; thirdly, the foreseeable reaction of current and future competitors, as well as of consumers, must not jeopardise the results expected from the common policy.[180]

The Court cited its *Airtours v Commission*[181] judgment, where the General Court defined the conditions for finding a collective dominant position in the context of merger control.[182] The Court established thus a direct link between the interpretation of the concept of collective dominance in the context of Article 102 TFEU and that in merger control. However, the scope of collective dominance in Article 102 is larger than in merger control, as it may not only cover situations of oligopolistic tacit collusion. In *Laurent Piau*, the Court found that football clubs held a collective dominant position by virtue of their membership of FIFA. The reference of the Court to 'tacit coordination' (that is a situation of tacit collusion) could therefore be understood as making the point that the concept of collective dominance in Article 102 TFEU covers *also* situations of tacit collusion. However, there has been no case so far, where the Courts found the existence of a collective dominant position under Article 102 TFEU by relying only on tacit collusion. One could also ask if the *Airtours* criteria, which apply to merger control, are relevant in the context of the *ex post* competition law enforcement of Article 102 TFEU, where the competition analysis relies merely on past events. Should the standard of proof be similar to the one applied for the largely prospective analysis of merger control? Should the Commission benefit from the same margin of discretion?

b. With regard to the second issue, it has been noted that reliance on market shares may not be appropriate in the context of collective dominant position. Even if the undertakings detain jointly high market shares, they might not be able to exercise collectively market power by adopting common strategies on the market: G Monti noted that 'while a single dominant firm can be presumed to have market power if it has a very large market share, the same presumption cannot be made with respect to oligopolists because other factors are relevant to determine whether the oligopolists can act as a group independently of other competitors, customers and consumers. For example, if two firms producing differentiated products in a market where there is no price transparency jointly have 60% of the market, then the market is one where tacit coordination is more difficult and the ability to exercise market power is diminished.'[183] Do you agree with this statement?

180 Case T-193/02, *Laurent Piau v Commission* [2005] ECR II–209, para 111.

181 Case T-342/99 *Airtours v Commission* [2002] ECR II–2585, para 62.

182 See Chapter 9.

183 G Monti, 'The Scope of Collective Dominance under Articles 82 EC' (2001) 38(1) *Common Market L Rev* 131, 137.

Weren't these factors taken already into account in assessing the first element of the offense, the existence of a collective entity? In its decision in *Irish Sugar*,[184] the Commission found that a supplier and a distributor collectively held a dominant position, although this, by definition, was on different markets: the supplier was present in the production market for industrial granulated sugar in Ireland, while the distributor in the retail market. The Commission found that in view of Irish Sugar's equity holding in its retailer, its representation on the retailer's boards, the structure of policy-making of the companies and the communication process established to facilitate it, 'there were direct economic ties between the companies', which 'created a clear parallelism of interest of the two companies vis-à-vis third parties', thus permitting the finding of a joint dominant position. The Commission's finding was upheld by the General Court in *Irish Sugar v Commission*.[185] Do you agree with the Commission's extension of the use of collective dominant position in a vertical (supplier-retailer) setting? Should it be possible to find a collective dominant position on different markets? Should it be possible to aggregate the dominant position undertakings hold in distinct but related markets in order to find a collective dominant position? What other types of related market can you think of? Would the related markets be not only referring to product markets, but also geographical markets?[186]

3. (Paragraphs 41–5) How far are economic links (a) relevant and (b) decisive to a finding of joint dominance?
4. Should the finding of collective dominance require the elimination of *all* effective competition between the undertakings held to be jointly dominant? Is it also possible to find the existence of a collective dominant position, when the undertakings still compete on some parameters of competition? In *Atlantic Container Line v Commission*, the General Court noted that 'there can be no requirement, for the purpose of establishing the existence of such a dominant position, that the elimination of effective competition must result in the elimination of all competition between the undertakings concerned'.[187] Hence, it is possible that the undertakings might be competing on parameters other than price? For example, should their common position on the market relate to the price they charge consumers? How different is this than the degree of competition between undertakings forming a cartel?
5. (Paragraphs 47) In what ways are shipping conferences different from cartels? In what ways do they resemble them?
6. (Paragraph 51) Should the market be defined in terms of particular routes when a ship can be brought from one route to another? Was this relevant to the Court?

[184] *Irish Sugar* (Cases IV/34.621, 35.059/F-3) Commission Decision 97/624/EC [1997] OJ L 258/1.

[185] Case T-228/97, *Irish Sugar plc v Commission* [1999] ECR II–2969, [1999] 5 CMLR 1300.

[186] See eg Case C-393/92, *Gemeente Almelo and others v Energiebedrijf Ilsselmij* [1994] ECR I–1477.

[187] Joined Cases T-191 & 212–14/98, *Atlantic Container Line AB and Others v Commission* [2003] ECR II–3275, para 654

8.3.7.3. Collective dominant position in Article 102 TFEU and merger control

Since the expansion of the concept of collective dominant position in merger control and the development of the decisional practice of the Commission and the case law of the Courts on tacit collusion in the merger regulation context,[188] the concept of collective dominant position has faded in the context of Article 102 TFEU. In the *Discussion paper on the application of Article 82 EC of the Treaty to exclusionary abuses*, published by the staff of the DG Comp in 2005, the concept of collective dominant position was examined in a number of paragraphs (see excerpt below). However, in the final version of the Commission Guidance on Article 102, the concept was just referred once, the Commission focusing entirely on single dominant positions.

Communication from the Commission—Guidance on the Commission's enforcement priorities in applying Article [102 TFEU] to abusive exclusionary conduct by dominant undertakings [2009] OJ C 45/7 (footnotes omitted)

4. Article [102 TFEU] applies to undertakings which hold a dominant position on one or more relevant markets. Such a position may be held by one undertaking (single dominance) or by two or more undertakings (collective dominance). This document only relates to abuses committed by an undertaking holding a single dominant position.

NOTES AND QUESTIONS

1. Do you think the above excerpt indicates that the Commission will not be using the concept of collective joint dominance in exclusionary cases (on the distinction see Section 8.4.1)? Would the concept be used only for exploitative practices?
2. In any case, the DG Discussion Paper of 2005 includes some interesting analysis of collective dominance, which it will be useful to reproduce as a summary of the latest thinking at the Commission on applying this concept in Article 102 TFEU cases. It is clear that the Commission was inspired by the same tacit collusion doctrine that applies in the context of merger control (see Chapter 12).[189]

8.4. THE CONCEPT OF ABUSE

8.4.1. INTRODUCTORY NOTE: THE CONCEPT OF ABUSE AND EXPLOITATION OF CONSUMERS

When the first cases on Article 102 TFEU arrived at the Court of Justice in the early 1970s, there was a sharp divide in the literature on the scope of Article 102 TFEU and the different

188 On coordinated effects, see Chapter 12.

189 DG Competition, 'Discussion paper on the application of Article 82 of the Treaty to exclusionary abuses' (December 2005), paras 45–50, available at http://ec.europa.eu/competition/antitrust/art82/discpaper2005.pdf.

forms abuse of dominant position could take. René Joliet, who was later appointed a judge at the CJEU, argued that the abuse of dominant position should not cover exclusion of competitors that did not lead to the exploitation of consumers.[190] At the opposite side of the spectrum, some German scholars, such as Arved Derringer and Ernst-Joachim Mestmäcker, defended the view that Articles 102 TFEU could also apply to conduct excluding competitors without that leading necessarily to exploitative consumer effects.[191] On the opposition of these two views, see the enlightening comments of Heike Schweitzer.

H Schweitzer, 'The History, Interpretation and Underlying Principles of Section 2 Sherman Act and Articles 82 EC' in CD Ehlermann and M Marquis (eds) *European Competition Law Annual 2007: A Reform Approach to Article 82 EC* (Hart, 2008), 138–9 (footnotes omitted)

Before *Continental Can*, commentators' ideas about the meaning and relevance of Article [102] sharply diverged. Representative of the uncertainties surrounding Article [102] is the monograph by René Joliet on monopolization and abuse of dominance, published in 1970. Contrasting Article [102] with the (at that time) strongly structural approach towards monopoly power under Section 2 Sherman Act, Joliet hypothesized that Article [102] lacked any structural component and took a purely behavioural stance. According to Joliet, the application of Article [102] was limited to controlling exploitative abuses, and would not extent to exclusionary abuses. In concentrating on exploitation, the Treaty of Rome exhibited a purely regulatory character:

> The EEC Treaty [. . .] tends to curb only the abuses of power and thus to regulate the market behavior of dominant firms. The approach taken by Article [102] is based upon an attitude of neutrality toward the existence of market dominant positions. It does not try to break up monopolistic positions, but instead, is confined to supervising the conduct and performance of dominant firms. Remedies are thus behavioral rather than structural. In cases of abuses, the enforcement agency could go as far as to set prices at which dominant firms can sell or to fix the quantities which they must produce. The EEC approach amounts to a kind of public utility regulation.

Joliet concluded that the main preoccupation of the Treaty of Rome was not the maintenance of a competitive system. Rather, 'the major objective of Article [102] is to ensure that dominant firms do not use their power to the detriment of utilizers and consumers'.

Mestmäcker—at that time special advisor to DG IV (now DG Competition) and an influential voice in the development of EC competition law—took a radically different view. In preparing the Commission's position in the *Continental Can* case, he started with the assertion that Article [102] had to be interpreted with a view to the overriding purpose of the competition rules, i.e., the aim of protecting a system of undistorted competition in the common market against distortions. Actions of dominant firms that are objectively incompatible with a system of undistorted competition must therefore be prohibited by Article [102]. However, abuses of dominance cannot be defined based on the effects of a dominant firm's actions on third parties alone. Article [102] prohibits a certain type of market *conduct*, not a certain type of market

190 R Joliet, *Monopolization and Abuse of Dominant Position* (Martinus Nijhoff, 1970), 250–1.

191 A Deringer, *The Competition Law of the European Economic Community: A Commentary on the EEC Rules of Competition (Articles 85 to 90) Including the Implementing Regulations and Directives* (Commerce Clearing House, 1968), 1.

structure as such. Yet an abuse of a dominant position can lie in the restriction of (residual) competition, in defending a dominant position against current or potential competition, especially by hampering market entry, or in expanding a dominant position into adjacent markets. The fact that Article [102] does not oppose the formation of dominant firms does not preclude a finding of abuse in the case of a further strengthening of market dominance. Rather, by covering the maintenance and strengthening of dominance (other than by means of performance), Article [102] covers the most widespread, typical and dangerous exclusionary acts. Mestmäcker went on to establish certain guiding principles for the interpretation of Article [102]. First of all, he stressed the close links between competition policy and the protection of open markets within the Community. The competition which the competition rules protect results from the opening up of the markets of the Member States.

In *Continental Can*, the Court of Justice examined the scope of Article 102 TFEU.

8.4.1.1. *Continental Can Europemballage Corporation and Continental Can Company Inc v Commission*

Case C-6/72, *Continental Can Europemballage Corporation and Continental Can Company Inc v Commission*
[1973] ECR 215

Continental Can Co (CCC) was an American company with considerable technology relating to the making of metal cans and the machines with which canners could close the cans after filling them. CCC granted technology licences to most of the European manufacturers of cans who did not have a licence from its competitor, American Can. Licensees included Metal Box, the leading can maker in the UK, Carnaud, the leading maker in France, and Thomassen, the leading producer in the Netherlands. In 1969, Continental Can acquired 85.8 per cent of the shares in Schmalbach, a maker of cans and closing machines in West Germany. Continental Can planned through Europemballage, a wholly owned subsidiary still in the process of being formed under Belgian law, to acquire several other major can makers in Europe: Thomassen, Carnaud, and Metal Box. Carnaud refused for commercial reasons and the Commission sent letters stating that it would challenge the remaining mergers under Article 102 if they were consummated. The acquisition of only Thomassen proceeded. Having failed to persuade the parties to desist voluntarily, the Commission adopted a decision, finding that through its shareholding in Schmalbach Continental Can held a dominant position in North West Germany in respect of light packaging for meat and fish and of metal caps for glass jars. By acquiring a majority shareholding in its potential competitor, Thomassen, in the Netherlands, Continental Can's dominant position had been reinforced to such an extent that competition had 'practically' ceased. This, the Commission concluded, amounted to the abuse of its dominant position.

On appeal, Advocate General Roemer stated the generally accepted view that mergers were rarely contrary to what is now Article 102 TFEU. The Court decided to the contrary.

On the competence of the Commission

14. The applicants argue that according to the general principles of international law, Continental, as an enterprise with its registered office outside the Common Market, is

neither within the administrative competence of the Commission nor under the jurisdiction of the Court of Justice. The Commission, it is argued, therefore has no competence to promulgate the contested decision with regard to Continental and to direct to it the instruction contained in Article 2 of that decision. Moreover, the illegal behaviour against which the Commission was proceeding should not be directly attributed to Continental, but to Europemballage.

15. The applicants cannot dispute that Europemballage, founded on 20 February 1970, is a subsidiary of Continental. The circumstance that this subsidiary company has its own legal personality does not suffice to exclude the possibility that its conduct might be attributed to the parent company. This is true in those cases particularly where the subsidiary company does not determine its market behaviour autonomously, but in essentials follows directives of the parent company.

16. It is certain that Continental caused Europemballage to make a take-over bid to the shareholders of TDV in the Netherlands and made the necessary means available for this. On 8 April 1970 Europemballage took up the shares and debentures in TDV offered up to that point. Thus this transaction, on the basis of which the Commission made the contested decision, is to be attributed not only to Europemballage, but also and first and foremost to Continental. Community law is applicable to such an acquisition, which influences market conditions within the Community. The circumstance that Continental does not have its registered office within the territory of one of the Member States is not sufficient to exclude it from the application of Community law. [. . .]

On Article [102] of the Treaty and abuse of a dominant position

18. In Articles 1 and 2 of the Commission's decision of 9 December 1971 Continental Can is blamed for having infringed Article 102 of the EC Treaty by abusing the dominant position which it allegedly held through Schmalbach Lubeca Werke AG of Brunswick (hereinafter called SLW) in a substantial part of the Common Market in the market for light metal containers for meat, meat products, fish and crustacea as well as in the market for metal closures for glass jars. According to Article 1 the abuse consists in Continental having acquired in April 1970, through its subsidiary Europemballage, about 80% of the shares and debentures of TDV. By this acquisition competition in the containers mentioned was practically eliminated in a substantial part of the Common Market.

19. The applicants maintain that the Commission by its decision, based on an erroneous interpretation of Article [102] of the [TFEU] Treaty, is trying to introduce a control of mergers of undertakings, thus exceeding its powers. Such an attempt runs contrary to the intention of the authors of the Treaty, which is clearly seen not only from a literal interpretation of Article [102] of the [TFEU] Treaty, but also from a comparison of the [. . .] Treaty and the national legal provisions of the Member States. The examples given in Article [102] of abuse of a dominant position confirm this conclusion, for they show that the Treaty refers only to practices which have effects on the market and are to the detriment of consumers or trade partners. Further, Article [102] reveals that the use of economic power linked with a dominant position can be regarded as an abuse of this position only if it constitutes the means through which the abuse is effected. But structural measures of undertakings—such as strengthening a dominant position by way of merger—do not amount to abuse of this position within the meaning of Article [102] of the Treaty. The decision contested is, therefore, said to be void as lacking the required legal basis.

20. [. . .] The question is whether the word 'abuse' in Article 102 refers only to practices of undertakings which may directly affect the market and are detrimental to production or sales, to purchasers or consumers, or whether this word refers also to changes in the structure of an undertaking, which lead to competition being seriously disturbed in a substantial part of the Common Market.

21. The distinction between measures which concern the structure of the undertaking and practices which affect the market cannot be decisive, for any structural measure may influence market conditions, if it increases the size and the economic power of the undertaking.

22. In order to answer this question, one has to go back to the spirit, general scheme and wording of Article [102], as well as to the system and objectives of the Treaty. These problems thus cannot be solved by comparing this Article with certain provisions of the ECSC Treaty [*now suppressed*].

23. Article [102] is part of the chapter devoted to the common rules on the Community's policy in the field of competition. This policy is based on Article 3(g) of the Treaty [*now replaced by Protocol no 27*] according to which the Community's activity shall include the institution of a system ensuring that competition in the Common Market is not distorted. The applicants' argument that this provision merely contains a general programme devoid of legal effect, ignores the fact that Article 3 considers the pursuit of the objectives which it lays down to be indispensable for the achievement of the Community's tasks. As regards in particular the aim mentioned in (f), the Treaty in several provisions contains more detailed regulations for the interpretation of which this aim is decisive.

24. But if Article 3(g) [*now replaced by Protocol no 27*] provides for the institution of a system ensuring that competition in the Common Market is not distorted, then it requires *a fortiori* that competition must not be eliminated. This requirement is so essential that without it numerous provisions of the Treaty would be pointless. Moreover, it corresponds to the precept of Article 2 of the Treaty according to which one of the tasks of the Community is 'to promote throughout the Community a harmonious development of economic activities'. Thus the restraints on competition which the Treaty allows under certain conditions because of the need to harmonize the various objectives of the Treaty, are limited by the requirements of Articles 2 and 3. Going beyond this limit involves the risk that the weakening of competition would conflict with the aims of the Common Market.

25. With a view to safeguarding the principles and attaining the objectives set out in Articles 2 and 3 of the Treaty, Articles [101] to [102] have laid down general rules applicable to undertakings. Article [101] concerns agreements between undertakings, decisions of associations of undertakings and concerted practices, while Article [102] concerns unilateral activity of one or more undertakings. Articles [101] and [102] seek to achieve the same aim on different levels, *viz.* the maintenance of effective competition within the Common Market. The restraint of competition which is prohibited if it is the result of behaviour falling under Article [101], cannot become permissible by the fact that such behaviour succeeds under the influence of a dominant undertaking and results in the merger of the undertakings concerned. In the absence of explicit provisions one cannot assume that the Treaty, which prohibits in Article [101] certain decisions of ordinary associations of undertakings restricting competition without eliminating it, permits in Article [102] that undertakings, after merging into an organic unity, should reach such a dominant position that any serious chance of competition is practically rendered impossible. Such a diverse legal treatment

would make a breach in the entire competition law which could jeopardize the proper functioning of the Common Market. If, in order to avoid the prohibitions in Article [101], it sufficed to establish such close connections between the undertakings that they escaped the prohibition of Article [101] without coming within the scope of that of Article [102], then, in contradiction to the basic principles of the Common Market, the partitioning of a substantial part of this market would be allowed. The endeavour of the authors of the Treaty to maintain in the market real or potential competition even in cases in which restraints on competition are permitted, was explicitly laid down in Article [101(3)(b)] of the Treaty. Article [102] does not contain the same explicit provisions, but this can be explained by the fact that the system fixed there for dominant positions, unlike Article [101(3)], does not recognize any exemption from the prohibition. With such a system the obligation to observe the basic objectives of the Treaty, in particular that of Article 3(g) [now replaced by Protocol no 27], results from the obligatory force of these objectives. In any case Articles [101] and [102] cannot be interpreted in such a way that they contradict each other, because they serve to achieve the same aim.

26. It is in the light of these considerations that the condition imposed by Article [102] is to be interpreted whereby in order to come within the prohibition a dominant position must have been abused. The provision states a certain number of abusive practices which it prohibits. The list merely gives examples, not an exhaustive enumeration of the sort of abuses of a dominant position prohibited by the Treaty. As may further be seen from letters (c) and (d) of Article [102(2)], the provision is not only aimed at practices which may cause damage to consumers directly, but also at those which are detrimental to them through their impact on an effective competition structure, such as is mentioned in Article 3(g) [now replaced by Protocol no 27] of the Treaty. Abuse may therefore occur if an undertaking in a dominant position strengthens such position in such a way that the degree of dominance reached substantially fetters competition, i.e. that only undertakings remain in the market whose behaviour depends on the dominant one.

27. Such being the meaning and the scope of Article [102] of the [TFEU] Treaty, the question of the link of causality raised by the applicants which in their opinion has to question exist between the dominant position and its abuse, is of no consequence, for the strengthening of the position of an undertaking may be an abuse and prohibited under Article [102] of the Treaty, regardless of the means and procedure by which it is achieved, if it has the effects mentioned above.

On the facts set forth in the statement of reasons in the decision

28. The Commission based its decision, *inter alia*, on the thesis that the acquisition of the majority holding in a competing company by an undertaking or a group of undertakings holding a dominant position may, in certain circumstances, amount to an abuse of this position. This is the case, according to the Commission, if an undertaking in a dominant position strengthens such position through a merger in such a way that real or potential competition in the goods concerned is in practice eliminated in a substantial part of the Common Market.

29. If it can, irrespective of any fault, be regarded as an abuse if an undertaking holds a position so dominant that the objectives of the Treaty are circumvented by an alteration to the supply structure which seriously endangers the consumer's freedom of action in the market, such a case necessarily exists, if practically all competition is

eliminated. Such a narrow precondition as the elimination of all competition need not exist in all cases. But the Commission, basing its decision on such elimination of competition, had to state legally sufficient reasons or, at least, had to prove that competition was so essentially affected that the remaining competitors could no longer provide a sufficient counterweight.

30. In order to justify its thesis the Commission viewed the consequences of the disputed merger from various angles. In this respect a distinction has to be made in the statement of reasons for its decision between four essential elements:

(a) the present market share of the combined undertakings in the products concerned,

(b) the relative proportions of the new unit created by the merger compared to the size of potential competitors in this market,

(c) the economic power of the purchasers vis-à-vis that of the new unit, and

(d) the potential competition of either the manufacturers of the same products, who are situated in geographically distant markets, or of other products made by manufacturers situated in the Common Market.

In examining these various factors the decision on the one hand is based on the very high market share already held by SLW in metal containers, on the weak competitive position of the competitors remaining in the market, on the economic weakness of most of the consumers in relation to that of the new unit and on the numerous legal and factual links between Continental and potential competitors; and, on the other hand, on the financial and technical difficulties involved in entering a market characterized by a strong concentration.

31. The applicant contests the exactitude of the data on which the Commission basis its decision. It cannot be concluded from SLW's market share, amounting to 70 to 80% in meat cans, 80 to 90% in cans for fish and crustacea and 50 to 55% in metal closures with the exception of crown corks percentages which moreover are too high and could not be proved by the defendant, that this undertaking dominates the market for light metal containers. The decision, moreover, excluded the possibility of competition arising from substitute products (glass and plastic containers) relying on reasons which do not stand up to examination. The statements about possibilities of real and potential competition as well as about the allegedly weak position of the consumers are therefore, in the applicants' view, irrelevant.

32. For the appraisal of SLW's dominant position and the consequences of the disputed merger, the definition of the relevant market is of essential significance, for the possibilities of competition can only be judged in relation to those characteristics of the products in question by virtue of which those products are particularly apt to satisfy an inelastic need and are only to a limited extent interchangeable with other products.

The Court also noted that in its decision the Commission had defined three markets: a 'market for light containers for canned meat products', a 'market for light containers for canned seafood', and a 'market for metal closures for the food packing industry, other than crown corks', all allegedly dominated by SLW and in which the disputed merger threatened to eliminate competition. However, according to the CJEU, the Commission's decision had not provided any details of how these three markets differed from the general market for light metal containers. It was also held by the CJEU that a dominant position on the market for light metal containers for meat and fish cannot be decisive, as long as it has not been proved that competitors from other sectors of the market for light metal containers are not in a position to enter this market, by a simple adaptation, with sufficient strength to create a serious counterweight (potential competition). The Court found contradictions in the Commission's reasoning, thus annulling the decision.

NOTES AND QUESTIONS ON CONTINENTAL CAN

1. Did the Court adopt the position of Joliet or that of Deringer and Mestmäcker? Did the Court extend the scope of Article 102 TFEU to exclusionary abuses (those that affect the competitive structure of the market and thus harm consumers) or limited only its application to exploitative abuses (those that harm directly the consumers). Explain your conclusions.
2. Do you think that the diplomats negotiating the EC Treaty intended Article 86 at the time (now Article 102 TFEU) to cover mergers?[192] Do you think the Community Court should construe the EU Treaties in accordance with the probable intentions of the negotiators or in accordance with the needs, as it perceives them, of the common market?[193]
3. Article 102 TFEU includes no provision for exemption like Article 101(3). On the other hand, it is only an 'abusive exploitation' that is forbidden. A national court, and not only the Commission, can apply this criterion. Is it desirable for prohibitions to be drawn broadly and to provide for administrative exemptions? If Article 102 were to be interpreted to control mergers, would it be only those that led to substantial market power that would be forbidden? Should efficiencies be a defence?
4. The Commission was in a dilemma. Continental Can's licensees were exchanging market information with each other. In subsequent cases, such systems have been held to be anti-competitive in concentrated markets but, at that time, the Commission had had no experience with them. This made it difficult for the Commission to establish that Schmalbach and Thomassen were potential competitors. Had it dealt with the exchange of information under Article 101 TFEU before attacking the merger, it might have been difficult to unscramble the companies, as Continental Can's personnel would have discovered Thomassen's business secrets. The Court refers at paragraph 35 to the lack of competition between the firms and the Advocate General at paragraphs 40–1. For agreements between competitors to exchange detailed marketing information see Chapter 7.
5. Would it be more difficult for a new entrant to develop the technology and find the capital than it was for Continental Can? Is the Court concerned with power over price or something else and, if so, what? Why did the Court not raise the possibility of a new entrant using American Can's technology?
6. (Judgment, paragraphs 22–4) Is the Court taking power to legislate under the more general provisions of the preliminary articles, which constrain it less than the articles that crystallize the general principles?

[192] On this issue see Chapter 12.

[193] For an interesting analysis of the drafting history of Article 102 on this point, see P Akman, 'Searching for the Long-Lost Soul of Article 82EC' (2009) 29 *Oxford J Legal Studies* 267; H Schweitzer, 'The History, Interpretation and Underlying Principles of Section 2 Sherman Act and Articles 82 EC' in CD Ehlermann and M Marquis (eds) *European Competition Law Annual 2007: A Reformed Approach to Article 82 EC* (Hart, 2008), 128.

8.4.1.2. The distinction between exploitative and exclusionary abuses

In general, exploitation abuses refer to practices by a 'dominant undertaking taking advantage of its market power to extract rents from consumers that would not have been possible for a non-dominant undertaking or to take advantage of consumers in some other way'.[194] This can either manifest itself either through pricing behaviour (eg excessive prices, price discrimination) or through some form of non-pricing behaviour (eg the exploitation of a strong dominant position to enjoy a quiet life and act inefficiently).[195] They are distinguished from exclusionary abuses, which relate to practices by a dominant undertaking taking advantage of its market power to exclude other competitors and thus harm *indirectly* consumers. The CJEU defined the concept of exclusionary abuse in *Hoffmann-La Roche*, as 'a behaviour which, through recourse to methods different from those which condition normal competition in products or services on the basis of transactions of commercial operators, has the effect of hindering the maintenance of the degree of competition still existing in the market or the growth of that competition'.[196] The concept of 'normal competition' has been defined as referring to 'competition on the merits'.[197]

The concept of 'normal competition' is also employed in UK competition law, along with that of 'competition on the merits' for exclusionary abuses.

National Grid Plc v Gas and Electricity Markets Authority
[2009] CAT 14

> 90. 'Normal competition' [. . .] means the parameters which affect a customer's choice in a situation where the customer is free to choose from amongst the products which make up the relevant market. In conditions of normal competition, a buyer will base his purchasing decisions on his assessment of who offers the best price and the best quality product or service. He might, on the basis of these criteria, choose the dominant firm's product and thereby maintain or increase the dominant firm's market share. That does not involve an abuse because the dominant firm has won that business because its product is the better overall offer from the customer's point of view. If the customer subsequently discovers that another company offers a better, cheaper product he will switch his custom to the new supplier—he may switch back again if the dominant undertaking then improves its offer.

[194] R O'Donoghue and AJ Padilla, *The Law and Economics of Article 82 EC* (Hart, 1st ed, 2006), 174.

[195] See P Akman, 'The Role of Exploitation under Article 82 EC' (2009) 11 *Cambridge Yearbook of European Legal Studies* 165.

[196] Case C-85/76, *Hoffman-La Roche v Commission* [1979] ECR 461, para 91.

[197] Case T-65/98, *Van den Bergh Foods Ltd v Commission* [2003] ECR II–4653, para 157:

> It is settled case-law that the concept of abuse is an objective concept relating to the behaviour of an undertaking in a dominant position which is such as to influence the structure of the market where, as result of the very presence of the undertaking in question, the degree of competition is weakened and which, through recourse to methods different from those which condition *normal competition* in products or services on the basis of the transactions of commercial operators, has the effect of hindering the maintenance of the degree of competition still existing in the market or the growth of that competition. It follows that Article [102 TFEU] prohibits a dominant undertaking from eliminating a competitor and from strengthening its position by recourse to means other than those based on *competition on the merits*. The prohibition laid down in that provision is also justified by the concern not to cause harm to consumers. (Emphasis added.)

Exploitative abuses are assessed according to different criteria (see Chapter 9). For a recent reminder of the importance of the distinction between exclusionary and exploitative abuses:

Case C-52/09, *Konkurrensverket v TeliaSonera Sverige AB*
[2011] ECR I–527 (footnotes excluded)

20. Article 3(3) TEU states that the European Union is to establish an internal market, which, in accordance with Protocol No 27 on the internal market and competition, annexed to the Treaty of Lisbon (OJ 2010 C 83, p. 309), is to include a system ensuring that competition is not distorted.

21. Article 102 TFEU is one of the competition rules referred to in Article 3(1)(b) TFEU which are necessary for the functioning of that internal market.

22. The function of those rules is precisely to prevent competition from being distorted to the detriment of the public interest, individual undertakings and consumers, thereby ensuring the well-being of the European Union. [. . .]

23. Accordingly, Article 102 TFEU must be interpreted as referring not only to practices which may cause damage to consumers directly, but also to those which are detrimental to them through their impact on competition. Whilst Article 102 TFEU does not prohibit an undertaking from acquiring, on its own merits, the dominant position in a market, and while, a fortiori, a finding that an undertaking has a dominant position is not in itself a ground of criticism of the undertaking concerned, it remains the case that, in accordance with settled case-law, an undertaking which holds a dominant position has a special responsibility not to allow its conduct to impair genuine undistorted competition in the internal market.

There are two different interpretations of the relationship between these two forms of abuse. On one side, that each abuse forms an autonomous concept. If competitors are excluded by the dominant firm, this is enough to infer, in specific circumstances, consumer harm. It is not necessary to prove that exclusionary abuses will lead to exploitative effects. On the other side, modern claims of anti-competitive effect are, however, always supplemented with an 'explanatory link' between an exclusionary and an exploitative element: the assumption is that the exclusionary abuse will most likely lead to exploitative effects, that is some form of consumer harm. This does not, however, go as far as requiring empirical evidence of anti-competitive effects or consumer harm. It may instead take the form of a *theory* of consumer harm, which aims to establish a relationship of causality between the specific practice and potential consumer detriment. The explicit introduction of a consumer harm element in exclusionary abuses further weakens the importance of the distinction between exclusionary and exploitative abuses, one of the main differences being that in exploitative abuses there is already evidence of an actual consumer detriment, which could, for example, be 'excessive' pricing (as compared to a competitive level pricing).

Nevertheless, most of the cases brought under Article 102 TFEU and Chapter II of the Competition Act 1998 are exclusionary abuse cases.[198] Courts have applied Articles 102(a),

[198] See E Paulis, 'Article 82 and Exploitative Conduct' in CD Ehlermann and M Marquis (eds) *European Competition Law Annual 2007: A Reformed Approach to Article 82 EC* (Hart, 2008), 515. See, however, the recent resurgence of exploitative abuse cases in certain NCAs, in particular in the pharma sector in the UK, eg CMA, 'Liothyronine Tablets: Suspected Excessive and Unfair Pricing' (25 October 2016), available at

102(b), and 102(c) to prohibit unfair prices, unfair trading conditions, the limitation of production, markets or technical development to the detriment of consumers and exploitative discriminatory prices.[199] It is also observed in the Commission's Enforcement Priorities Guidance on exclusionary abuses that the Commission will focus on those 'types of conduct that are most harmful to consumers' excluding 'conduct which is directly exploitative of consumers'.[200] This lack of interest on exploitative abuses and emphasis on exclusionary abuses has been criticized by some authors as being paradoxical.

B Lyons, 'The Paradox of the Exclusion of Exploitative Abuse', CCP Working Paper No 08-1 (December 2007), available at http://ssrn.com/abstract=1082723 (footnotes omitted)

Despite the textbook monopoly abuse being high prices, most competition economists (and probably also most competition lawyers) have a profound distaste for the direct control of exploitative abuse under Article [102]. It conjures images of detailed interventions throughout the economy, when most would argue that regulation should be reserved for cases of genuine natural monopoly (eg those parts of privatised utilities which cannot be structured competitively due to network economies). The latter require specific, well informed regulators, and these cannot be put in place for all corners of the economy in which a firm may be dominant. Far better, the argument goes, to concentrate on maximising the chances for the competitive process to throw up a new competitor; hence, the focus on exclusionary abuse.

So, we have a strong consensus that an exclusionary practice, whereby a dominant firm hurts rivals, is only an abuse when the consequence is that consumers are expected to be harmed So, we can summarise on exclusionary abuse: while hurting one or more rivals is necessary for an exclusionary abuse, it is not sufficient: to be an abuse, exclusion also requires an expectation of eventual consumer harm (i.e. exploitation). And on exploitative abuse: many eminent economists and lawyers say that Article [102] should not deal with such abuses. This results in our paradox: it is good to prohibit only those exclusionary practices which can be expected to result (indirectly) in an exploitative abuse [. . .] but at the same time it is bad to prohibit directly exploitative practices!

Usually, this caution to prosecute exploitative abuses is explained by the following difficulties.[201] First, a 'measurement issue', as it is difficult to identify all the costs of the undertakings and to measure how high a particular price is in relation to the cost, while establishing that these high profits are not the result of competition on the merit. Hence, there is a high risk of false positives. Second, competition authorities are not always the best equipped to understand broader market dynamics and the role of high prices as an incentive to investment and innovation. Third, focusing the analysis on the exploitation

https://www.gov.uk/cma-cases/pharmaceutical-sector-anti-competitive-conduct or some related to big data in Germany: Bundeskartellamt, 'Bundeskartellamt Initiates Proceeding against Facebook on Suspicion of Having Abused its Market Power by Infringing Data Protection Rules' (2 March 2016), available at https://www.bundeskartellamt.de/SharedDocs/Meldung/EN/Pressemitteilungen/2016/02_03_2016_Facebook.html.

199 See our analysis in Chapter 9.

200 Commission Guidance on Article 102, para 7.

201 See B Lyons, 'The Paradox of the Exclusion of Exploitative Abuse', CCP Working Paper No 08-1 (December 2007), available at http://ssrn.com/abstract=1082723; R O'Donoghue and AJ Padilla, *The Law and Economics of Article 82 EC* (Hart, 2006), 621; DS Evans and AJ Padilla, 'Excessive Prices: Using Economics to Define Administrative Legal Rules' (2005) 1 *J Competition L & Economics* 97.

occurring in one relevant market might not take into account the complexity of multi-sided platforms that operate across various relevant markets, with the result that any competition assessment looking to one relevant market only or one set of 'exploited' consumers is partial.[202] Fourth, the difficulty of devising effective remedies for exploitative practices and the difficulty of administering such remedies in a court setting, price regulation being more under the remit of regulatory agencies. However, although exclusionary abuses have at their core an exploitative abuse element, for the aforementioned reasons, competition authorities are less inclined to bring exploitative abuse cases.

8.4.2. THE DISTINCTION PRICE/NON-PRICE BASED EXCLUSIONARY ABUSES

The most important new classification introduced by the Commission's Guidance on Article 102, is the distinction between price and non-price related exclusionary abuses.

Communication from the Commission—Guidance on the Commission's enforcement priorities in applying Article [102 TFEU] to abusive exclusionary conduct by dominant undertakings [2009] OJ C 45/7 (footnotes omitted)

C. Price-based exclusionary conduct

23. The considerations in paragraphs 23 to 27 apply to price-based exclusionary conduct. Vigorous price competition is generally beneficial to consumers. With a view to preventing anti-competitive foreclosure, the Commission will normally only intervene where the conduct concerned has already been or is capable of hampering competition from competitors which are considered to be as efficient as the dominant undertaking [para 17].

24. However, the Commission recognises that in certain circumstances a less efficient competitor may also exert a constraint which should be taken into account when considering whether particular price-based conduct leads to anti-competitive foreclosure. The Commission will take a dynamic view of that constraint, given that in the absence of an abusive practice such a competitor may benefit from demand-related advantages, such as network and learning effects, which will tend to enhance its efficiency.

25. In order to determine whether even a hypothetical competitor as efficient as the dominant undertaking would be likely to be foreclosed by the conduct in question, the Commission will examine economic data relating to cost and sales prices, and in particular whether the dominant undertaking is engaging in below-cost pricing. This will require that sufficiently reliable data be available. Where available, the Commission will use information on the costs of the dominant undertaking itself. If reliable information on those costs is not available, the Commission may decide to use the cost data of competitors or other comparable reliable data.

26. The cost benchmarks that the Commission is likely to use are average avoidable cost (AAC) and long-run average incremental cost (LRAIC) [18]. Failure to cover AAC

202 On the problems raised by 'one sided logic' in a two sided markets framework, see J Wright, 'One-sided Logic in Two-sided Markets' (2004) 3(1) *Rev Network Economics* 44.

> indicates that the dominant undertaking is sacrificing profits in the short term and that an equally efficient competitor cannot serve the targeted customers without incurring a loss. LRAIC is usually above AAC because, in contrast to AAC (which only includes fixed costs if incurred during the period under examination), LRAIC includes product specific fixed costs made before the period in which allegedly abusive conduct took place. Failure to cover LRAIC indicates that the dominant undertaking is not recovering all the (attributable) fixed costs of producing the good or service in question and that an equally efficient competitor could be foreclosed from the market [para 19].
>
> 27. If the data clearly suggest that an equally efficient competitor can compete effectively with the pricing conduct of the dominant undertaking, the Commission will, in principle, infer that the dominant undertaking's pricing conduct is not likely to have an adverse impact on effective competition, and thus on consumers, and will therefore be unlikely to intervene. If, on the contrary, the data suggest that the price charged by the dominant undertaking has the potential to foreclose equally efficient competitors, then the Commission will integrate this in the general assessment of anti-competitive foreclosure (see Section B [. . .]), taking into account other relevant quantitative and/or qualitative evidence.

The distinction between price and non-price exclusionary conduct permeates all other distinctions between various forms of abuse, in the sense that the legal standards are profoundly different depending on the characterization of a restriction as being related to price or non price exclusionary conduct. If the efficiency of the undertaking is a major concern for price restraints, it remains a secondary one for non-price restraints, for which even the exclusion of a less efficient competitor could be a matter of concern.[203] The adoption of cost-based tests as filters for antitrust enforcement in the area of price-based exclusionary conduct is a direct consequence of this classification.[204] The price-cost test excludes from the scope of Article 102 TFEU conduct that is exclusionary, may harm consumers (by raising prices or affecting quality and more broadly consumer choice) for the simple reason that the excluded company is a less efficient firm.

We think that the distinction between price and non-price abuses introduces a conceptual anomaly in the framework of Article 102. Back in 2005, the DG Competition staff Discussion Paper recognized that price and non-price abuses may lead to 'similar foreclosure effects' and that they are substitutable, from the point of view of dominant firms, although it also advanced a different theoretical framework for assessing pricing behaviour from non-price based exclusionary conduct.[205] The Commission Guidance on Article 102 provides a rather short explanation of this fundamental dichotomy: 'vigorous price competition is generally beneficial to consumers', thus implying that if a cost-based filter did not apply, the costs of false positives could be prohibitive.[206] The Commission does not adopt a cautious approach for non-price-related exclusionary conduct, which either indicates that there is a higher probability of false positives for price-based conduct than for non-price-based conduct, or that the cost of false positives in the context of price-related conduct is higher than the cost of false positives in the context of non-price-based conduct. No empirical evidence is, however, advanced to support either of these two claims. The use of cost benchmarks basically subsumes identification of practice and anti-competitive effects

[203] Commission Guidance on Article 102, para 22 (interpreted *a contrario*). [204] Ibid, para 24.
[205] Ibid, para 63. [206] Ibid, para 22.

thanks to the as-efficient competitor test. This combined standard is not available for non-price abuses.

Nevertheless, the Commission's Guidance on Article 102 makes clear that the cost-benchmark is necessary but not sufficient, in that it is still necessary to meet the foreclosure standard, ie, similarly to non-price abuses. One may argue that this price/cost test is not needed for non-price abuses where the identification of the conduct (ie, exclusivity) is uncontroversial (ie, once the facts are established), so the investigation will focus on anti-competitive effects. In addition, the Court of Justice states quite clearly that the only reasonable as efficient competitor test is the one based on the defendant downstream costs,[207] and this is because this is the only formulation that makes sure there is certainty as to what constitute compliance of a pricing practice (ie, since the dominant firm doesn't know the level of rivals' costs, or those of a reasonably efficient competitor). This level of certainty is not available with non-price alleged abuses, alas, and therefore self-assessment is solely based on risk of foreclosure. From a practitioner point of view the need to do a price-cost test increases the probatory hurdle for the plaintiff, just think on how tricky is to identify the 'contestable share of demand' in order to calculate the effective price in a loyalty rebate scheme [. . .] or to deal with the tricky issue of how to treat scale/scope economies in a price–cost test.[208]

The General Court echoed the dichotomy between price and non-price exclusionary conduct in *Deutsche Telekom*: following the Commission's position, it chose to emphasize the likelihood that the pricing practices of the dominant undertaking would have the effect of removing from the market an economic operator that was just as efficient as the dominant firm, in order to determine whether the pricing practices were abusive.[209] The General Court cited, *inter alia*, the case law of the CJEU in *AKZO*[210] as an authority for the proposition that 'the abusive nature of a dominant undertaking's pricing practices is determined in principle on the basis of its own charge and costs, rather than on the basis of the situation of actual or potential competitors'.[211] As it is well explained in the judgment:

> [A]ny other approach could be contrary to the general principle of legal certainty. If the lawfulness of the pricing practices of a dominant undertaking depended on the particular situation of competing undertakings, particularly their cost structure—information which is generally not known to the dominant undertaking—the latter would not be in a position to assess the lawfulness of its own activities.[212]

However, in other parts of the judgment the General Court was less clear on the choice of the benchmark for assessing the efficiency of the competing undertakings. It simply indicated

207 Case C-280/08 P, *Deutsche Telekom v Commission* [2010] ECR I–9555, para 202.

208 On the other hand, in the *Cardiff Bus* (Case CE/5281/04) OFT Decision CA98/01/2008 (18 November 2008) the easiest thing was to meet the price-cost test, since bus patronage fell a lot short of expectations (so revenue was lower than bus costs). However, the defendant argued that lower revenue were unexpected given demand uncertainty, so the failure of the price cost test was meaningless. This actually forced the OFT to prove foreclosure effects by looking at all the evidence 'in the round', which was far more challenging than simply relying on the *AKZO* price–cost test.

209 Case C-280/08 P, *Deutsche Telekom AG v European Commission* [2010] ECR I–9555, paras 187 and 199. See also Case T-5/97, *Industrie des poudres sphériques SA v Commission* [2000] ECR II–3755, para 180.

210 Case C-62/86, *AKZO Chemie BV* v *Commission* [1991] ECR I–3359.

211 Case C-280/08 P, *Deutsche Telekom AG v European Commission* [2010] ECR I–9555, para 188.

212 Ibid, para 192.

that the legality of the dominant firm's practice is determined not only on the basis of its own costs but that the situation of the rival companies could also serve as a relevant benchmark.[213] The Commission's Guidance on Article 102 is more explicit as to the benchmark: this is the long-run average incremental cost (LRAIC) of the downstream division of the integrated dominant firm. Only when it is not possible clearly to allocate the dominant firm's costs to downstream and upstream operations will the LRAIC of a non-integrated competitor downstream be used.[214]

The underlying principle of this case law is that price-related abuses should be dealt with more leniently than non-price-related abuses. However, neither the Commission, nor the Court provides any explanation for such a distinction. Some authors have advanced the view that enforcing Article 102 to price-related behaviour leads to a high risk of false positives, while prohibiting exclusionary contracts does not have the same effect: 'unlike low prices, exclusionary contracts do not always benefit consumers in the short term, regardless of their long-term effect on competition.'[215]

This assumption may be questioned. Competition based on quality (*Q*), variety (*V*), or increasing investment is equally important. This may be defined as 'the process through which rival sellers compete away their potential supernormal profits by introducing additional QV investments until even the most profitable project in the relevant area of product space generates just a normal rate of return.'[216] The importance of this type of competition has been recognized by the CJEU in *Metro*.[217] It may have also justified the more lenient antitrust regime for vertical restraints, as these could be conceived as contract enforcement mechanisms that ensure the quality of distribution services provided to consumers, even if this has also the effect to reduce intra-brand price competition.[218] There is no specific reason advanced to explain why price competition is more important as an antitrust concern than *QV* investment competition. It has been argued by some economists that a cost-based standard should also apply to technological and contractual tying.[219] There is a risk (which for some could represent a desirable objective) that the efficiency-based standard for price exclusionary practices will expand to non-price exclusionary practices, thus replacing the consumer interest oriented anti-competitive foreclosure standard. This appears incompatible with a real effects-based approach. There are instances where a bundled discount may produce the same degree of exclusivity as contractual tying.[220] A rule that would adopt a more lenient standard for price-related

213 Ibid, para 198, where the General Court emphasizes the need to provide equal opportunities to the various economic operators, in particular if the later have different costs and revenue structures. See S Gevenaz, 'Margin Squeeze after *Deutsche Telekom*', *Global Competition Policy Magazine* (May 2008), 21–3, available at https://www.competitionpolicyinternational.com/file/view/5320. The General Court seems to employ a not (yet) as efficient as test.

214 Commission Guidance on Article 102, para 79.

215 ML Popofsky and H Ehrman, 'Drawing a Line Between Bundling and Contractual Exclusion under the Sherman Act', *Global Competition Policy Magazine* (June 2008), 5–6, available at https://www.competitionpolicyinternational.com/file/view/5386.

216 R Markovits, *Truth or Economics: On the Definition, Prediction, and Relevance of Economic Efficiency* (Yale University Press, 2008), 90.

217 Case C-26/76, *Metro SB-Großmärkte GmbH & Co KG v Commission* [1977] ECR 1875, para 21.

218 B Klein and K Murphy, 'Vertical Restraints as Contract Enforcement Mechanisms' (1988) 31(2) *J L & Economics* 265.

219 J Tirole, 'The Analysis of Tying Cases: A Primer' (2005) 1 *Competition Policy Int'l* 1.

220 See N Economides and I Lianos, 'The Elusive Antitrust Standard on Bundling in Europe and in the United States at the Aftermath of the Microsoft Cases' (2009) 76 *Antitrust LJ* 483, section 2.3.2.2. It is well accepted in EC competition law that *de facto* exclusivity (which could take the form of financial inducement through rebates) is considered as harmful as *de jure* exclusivity: Case T-65/98, *Van den Bergh Foods Ltd v*

bundling practices as opposed to non-price related ones might therefore produce false negatives. What is clear, is that the distinction between price and non-price exclusionary practices has been introduced in order to create a safe harbour for dominant undertakings.

However, the link between the classification of price and non-price related conduct and the interpretation of the concept of consumer harm (which is the reference point to measure effects) is missing. The Commission defines the concept of consumer harm broadly as covering, not only restraints that affect competition through lower prices, but also those affecting the possibility for consumers to benefit from better quality products and wider choice of new or improved goods and services.[221] The underlying objectives of Article 102, in particular its emphasis on preserving consumer choice, may explain the relatively strict antitrust standards that apply to technical tying, in comparison with contractual tying.[222] It is clear that the Commission does not establish a hierarchy between these different aspects of consumer harm. The distinction between price and non-price based exclusionary conduct seems incompatible with the objectives of EC competition law and should be re-examined. The introduction of the price/non-price abuses dichotomy in EC competition law is also at odds with recent developments in US antitrust law. In *Pacific Bell v Linkline*, the US Supreme Court made clear that 'there is no reason to distinguish between price and non-price components of a transaction' and consequently found that its reasoning in *Trinko* (involving an insufficient assistance claim by a competitor) applied 'with equal force to price squeezing claims'.[223] What counts is the effect of the specific conduct on consumers, not the price or non-price label attached to it by the plaintiff/claimant or the defendant.

The Court of Justice of the EU has recently confirmed the validity of the distinction between non-price and some price related exclusionary abuses, the latter being subject to the prohibition of Article 102 TFEU only if they lead to the exclusion of at least as efficient as competitors.

Case C-209/10, *Post Danmark A/S v Konkurrencerådet*, ECLI:EU:C:2012:172

20. It is apparent from case-law that Article [102 TFEU] covers not only those practices that directly cause harm to consumers but also practices that cause consumers harm through their impact on competition. It is in the latter sense that the expression 'exclusionary abuse' appearing in the questions referred is to be understood.

21. It is settled case-law that a finding that an undertaking has such a dominant position is not in itself a ground of criticism of the undertaking concerned. It is in no way the purpose of Article [102 TFEU] to prevent an undertaking from acquiring, on its own merits, the dominant position on a market. Nor does that provision seek to ensure that competitors less efficient than the undertaking with the dominant position should remain on the market.

22. Thus, not every exclusionary effect is necessarily detrimental to competition. Competition on the merits may, by definition, lead to the departure from the market or the marginalisation of competitors that are less efficient and so less attractive to consumers from the point of view of, among other things, price, choice, quality or innovation.

Commission [2003] ECR II-4653, para 118 (Article 101), paras 159–60 (Article 102); confirmed by Case C-552/03, *Unilever Bestfoods (formerly Van den Bergh Foods) v Commission* [2006] ECR I-909.

221 Commission Guidance on Article 102, para 5.

222 Ibid, para 52. The main justifications provided for this classification is that technical tying is costly to reverse and that it also reduces the opportunities for resale of individual components.

223 *Pacific Bell Telephone Company v Linkline Communications Inc*, 555 US 438, 129 S Ct 1109 (2009), para 10.

> [. . .]
>
> 25. Thus, Article [102 TFEU] prohibits a dominant undertaking from, among other things, adopting pricing practices that have an exclusionary effect on competitors considered to be as efficient as it is itself and strengthening its dominant position by using methods other than those that are part of competition on the merits. Accordingly, in that light, not all competition by means of price may be regarded as legitimate.

A number of other recent cases on price-related exclusionary abuses also arrived at the same conclusion.[224]

However, in a remarkable judgment in the *Intel* case, the General Court revisited the distinction between price and non-price abuses and, surprisingly, qualified a rebate as a non-price restriction, because of the fact that the specific rebate was a conditional rebate on the condition of exclusive or quasi-exclusive supply from the undertaking in a dominant position. According to the General Court, 'such rebates are designed, through the grant of a financial advantage, to prevent customers from obtaining their supplies from competing producers'.[225]

The General Court examined the argument of the applicants against the Commission's decision of the need in the case of exclusionary rebates to carry out an analysis of the circumstances of the case in order to establish at least a potential foreclosing effect, before concluding in the existence of an abuse of a dominant position.

Case T-286/09, *Intel Corp v European Commission*, ECLI:EU:T:2014:547

> 98. Second, the applicant relies on Case C-280/08 P *Deutsche Telekom* v *Commission* [2010] ECR I–9555 ('Case C-280/08 P *Deutsche Telekom*'), paragraph 175, *TeliaSonera* [Case C-52/09 *TeliaSonera Sverige* [2011] ECR I-527], paragraph 28, and [C-209/10] *Post Danmark* [ECLI:EU:C:2012:172], paragraph 26. In those judgments, the Court of Justice held that, 'in order to determine whether the undertaking in a dominant position has abused such a position by its pricing practices, it is necessary to consider all the circumstances [. . .]'.
>
> 99. However, the scope of that case-law is limited to pricing practices and does not affect the legal characterisation of exclusivity rebates. Case C-280/08 P *Deutsche Telekom*, paragraph 98 above, and *TeliaSonera* [. . .] concerned margin squeeze practices and *Post Danmark* [. . .] concerned low price practices, so that those three cases

224 Case C-280/08, *Deutsche Telekom AG v European Commission* [2010] ECR I–9555, paras 198–9, 'in order to assess whether the pricing practices of a dominant undertaking are likely to eliminate a competitor contrary to Article [102 TFEU], it is necessary to adopt a test based on the costs and the strategy of the dominant undertaking itself [. . .] a dominant undertaking cannot drive from the market undertakings which are perhaps as efficient as the dominant undertaking but which, because of their smaller financial resources, are incapable of withstanding the competition waged against them'; Case C-52/09, *Konkurrensverket v TeliaSonera Sverige AB* [2011] ECR I–527, para 31: 'A margin squeeze [a price related exclusionary abuse, see Section 9.4], in view of the exclusionary effect which it may create for competitors who are at least as efficient as the dominant undertaking, in the absence of any objective justification, is in itself capable of constituting an abuse within the meaning of Article 102 TFEU.' See also, Case T-827/14, *Deutsche Telekom AG v European Commission*, ECLI:EU:T:2018:930, paras 163–5 and 206–8.

225 Case T-286/09, *Intel Corp v European Commission*, ECLI:EU:T:2014:547, para 77, citing Case C-85/76, *Hoffman-La Roche & Co v Commission* [1979] ECR 461, para 90, and Case T-155/06, *Tomra Systems ASA and Others v European Commission* [2010] ECR I–4361, para 210.

> concerned pricing practices. However, the present case does not relate to a pricing practice. As regards the rebates granted to the various OEMs, the complaint made against the applicant in the contested decision is not based on the exact amount of the rebates and thus on the prices charged by the applicant, but on the fact that the grant of those rebates was conditional on exclusive or quasi-exclusive supply. Different treatment of exclusivity rebates and pricing practices is justified by the fact that, unlike an exclusive supply incentive, the level of a price cannot be regarded as unlawful in itself.
>
> 100. In that regard, it is also necessary to reject the applicant's argument, put forward at the hearing, that *Post Danmark* [. . .] deals with loyalty rebates comparable to those of the case in point. In that case, the proceedings before the Court of Justice concerned the practice of Post Danmark of charging its main competitor's former customers rates different from those that it charged its own pre-existing customers without being able to justify those significant differences in its rate and rebate conditions by considerations relating to its costs, a practice described by the Danish Competition Authority as 'primary-line price discrimination' (*Post Danmark* [. . .], paragraph 8). That presentation of the anti-competitive practices contains no reference to an exclusivity rebate system. On the contrary, the proceedings which gave rise to the reference for a preliminary ruling concerned solely whether there was an abuse by means of selectively low prices (*Post Danmark* [. . .], paragraphs 15 to 17). Thus, in reply to the question referred to it for a preliminary ruling, the Court only replied to the question in which circumstances a policy of charging low prices had to be considered to amount to an exclusionary abuse, contrary to Article 82 EC (*Post Danmark* [. . .], paragraph 19).

The characterization of an allegedly abusive conduct as being price or non-price related does not depend on the fact that it concerns a commercial pricing strategy on prices or commercial practice that does not involve prices, as the Commission envisaged the distinction in its Guidance on Article 102 with regard to exclusionary abusive conduct. The important criterion is whether the claim concerns the exact amount of the rebate and thus the level of the prices charged, in which case it will be considered as a price-related conduct, or the fact that the grant of those rebates was conditional on exclusive or quasi-exclusive supply, in which case it will be considered as a non-price related conduct. According to the General Court, this '[d]ifferent treatment of exclusivity rebates and pricing practices is justified by the fact that, unlike an exclusive supply incentive, the level of a price cannot be regarded as unlawful in itself'.[226] Are you convinced by the Court's effort to categorize rebates as non-price restraints? Would that take outside the scope of the price-related category all loyalty rebates, as by definition they are aimed to promote exclusivity? Pronouncing itself on appeal in the *Intel* case, the CJEU did not seem to agree with the qualification of loyalty rebates as non-price practices, although the language employed is muddled.[227]

The distinction between price and non-price related exclusionary abuses holds also in UK competition law, following section 60 CA98 with regard to 'questions arising in relation to competition', which imports to UK competition law the principles set for the interpretation of Article 102 TFEU by the jurisprudence of the Court of Justice, and the recent case law of the CJEU adopting this distinction. Nevertheless, this distinction might have less impact in UK competition law, following the relatively more flexible approach in UK courts on formal distinctions between different types of abuse.[228]

226 Case T-286/09, *Intel Corp v European Commission*, ECLI:EU:T:2014:547, para 99.

227 Case C-413/14 P, *Intel Corp. v European Commission*, ECLI:EU:C:2017:632.

228 *National Grid plc v Gas and Electricity Markets Authority* [2010] EWCA Civ 114, [2010] UKCLR 386, para 54, challenging 'the need for any finding of abuse to be based on a benchmark'. According to the Court:

8.4.3. THE 'SPECIAL RESPONSIBILITY' OF THE DOMINANT FIRM

EU competition law recognizes the existence of a 'special responsibility' of the dominant firm not to harm the competitive process. Based on this 'special responsibility' the case law has frequently found (i) an inference of consumer harm from the fact that the structure of the market has been affected or from the fact that competitors have been excluded and (ii) has developed a rather strict burden of proof rule for dominant undertakings, shifting the burden of production of exculpatory evidence of an abuse to the dominant undertaking once some inference of likely anti-competitive effect is made.

The CJEU first employed this concept in *Michelin I* at the part of the judgment dealing with the existence of a dominant position.

Case C-322/81, *Nederlandsche Banden-Industrie Michelin NV v Commission*
[1983] ECR 3461 (*Michelin I*)

The Dutch subsidiary of Michelin granted annual rebates to those dealers who sold sufficient tyres. Dealers' annual targets were fixed individually in advance and operated on total purchases, not just on the incremental ones above the target. Dealers were informed orally. Targets were usually set a little higher than the individual dealer's sales the year before but, in some years, account was taken of the proportion of Michelin tyres in the turnover of each. Nearly all dealers selling 3 000 tyres a year obtained the maximum rebate. Sometimes there were disputes at the end of the year about what the target was. The Commission adopted a decision that Michelin was dominant over the supply of tyres for heavy vehicles in the Netherlands to retailers for the replacement market, to the exclusion of retreads. The incentive rebates were found to constitute an abuse of that position. On appeal, the Court of Justice of the EU confirmed the Commission's decision.

> 55. [. . .] in order to assess the relative economic strength of Michelin NV and its competitors on the Netherlands market the advantages which those undertakings may derive from belonging to groups of undertakings operating throughout Europe or even the world must be taken into consideration. Amongst those advantages, the lead which the Michelin group has over its competitors in the matters of investment and research and the special extent of its range of products, to which the Commission referred in its decision, have not been denied. In fact in the case of certain types of tyre the Michelin group is the only supplier on the market to offer them in its range.
>
> 56. That situation ensures that on the Netherlands market a large number of users of heavy-vehicle tyres have a strong preference for Michelin tyres. As the purchase of tyres represents a considerable investment for a transport undertaking and since much time is required in order to ascertain in practice the cost-effectiveness of a type

It is true that benchmarks of a kind have been applied in certain pricing contexts, such as in drawing a dividing line between competitive low pricing and abusive predatory pricing, and that according to para 21 of its guidance document the Commission's own approach to assessing anti-competitive foreclosure is *usually* to make a comparison with an appropriate counterfactual. There is, however, no rule requiring the use of a benchmark in every case, let alone a benchmark that will tell one precisely where the line between lawful and unlawful conduct is to be drawn. The question whether an abuse exists is highly fact-sensitive and dependent upon an evaluation of a wide range of factors, in the light of the general principles expressed in *Hoffmann-La Roche* and other cases. (Ibid.)

> or brand of tyre, Michelin NV therefore enjoys a position which renders it largely immune to competition. As a result, a dealer established in the Netherlands normally cannot afford not to sell Michelin tyres.
>
> 57. [. . .] A finding that an undertaking has a dominant position is not in itself a recrimination but simply means that, irrespective of the reasons for which it has such a dominant position, the undertaking concerned has a special responsibility not to allow its conduct to impair genuine undistorted competition on the common market.

Since then, the term has been repeated a number of times by the CJEU,[229] including in the Guidance on Article 102.

Communication from the Commission—Guidance on the Commission's enforcement priorities in applying Article [102 TFEU] to abusive exclusionary conduct by dominant undertakings [2009] OJ C 45/7 (footnotes omitted, emphasis added)

> 1. Article [102 TFEU] prohibits abuses of a dominant position. In accordance with the case-law, it is not in itself illegal for an undertaking to be in a dominant position and such a dominant undertaking is entitled to compete on the merits. However, the undertaking concerned has a *special responsibility* not to allow its conduct to impair genuine undistorted competition on the common market. Article [102 TFEU] is the legal basis for a crucial component of competition policy and its effective enforcement helps markets to work better for the benefit of businesses and consumers. This is particularly important in the context of the wider objective of achieving an integrated internal market.
>
> [. . .]
>
> 9. The assessment of whether an undertaking is in a dominant position and of the degree of market power it holds is a first step in the application of Article [102 TFEU]. According to the case-law, holding a dominant position confers a *special responsibility* on the undertaking concerned, the scope of which must be considered in the light of the specific circumstances of each case.

The function of this concept is unclear. According to Advocate General Kokott in *British Airways v Commission*:

> Within the scope of the application of Article [102 TFEU], a dominant undertaking is subject to certain limitations that do not apply to other undertakings in the same form. Because of the presence of the dominant undertaking, competition on the market in question is weakened. Therefore, whatever the causes of its dominant position—that undertaking has a particular responsibility to ensure that its conduct does not undermine effective and undistorted competition in the common market. A practice which would be unobjectionable under normal circumstances can be an abuse if applied by an undertaking in a dominant position.[230]

[229] See eg Case T-201/04, *Microsoft Corp v Commission* [2007] ECR II–3601, para 775; Case T-203/01, *Michelin II* [2003] ECR II–4071, para 97; Case C-280/08, *Deutsche Telekom AG v European Commission* [2010] ECR I–9555, para 176; Case C-52/09, *Konkurrensverket v TeliaSonera Sverige AB* [2011] ECR I–527, para 24.

[230] Opinion of AG Kokott in Case C-95/04P *British Airways v Commission* [2007] ECR I–2331, para 23.

For example, the GC found in *Michelin II* that 'discounts granted by an undertaking in a dominant position *must* be based on a countervailing advantage which may be economically justified'.[231] In comparison, non-dominant undertakings are able to grant discounts even if these are not based on the economic justifications envisioned by the court, such as economies of scale, and even if the result of these discounts will be the acquisition of a dominant position. Nevertheless, once the threshold of dominance has been reached, the undertaking will not be able to maintain these rebates, unless they provide an economic justification for 'the discount rates chosen for the various steps in the rebate system in question' (quantity discounts).

The case law does not, however, make explicit the theoretical and practical reasons that impose this special responsibility on dominant firms. The likelihood of anti-competitive effects does not seem to be the main reason for this special responsibility. If this were the case, all firms holding market power, not just dominant firms, would bear a special responsibility to preserve the competitive process.

The concept of special responsibility means that dominant firms' commercial freedom is restricted in comparison to non-dominant undertakings.[232] The latter remain free to use commercial practices that are different from those governing normal competition.[233] The focus of the test seems to be the protection of 'free competition' or 'complete competition' and 'open markets'.[234] The underlying theoretical assumption is that rivalry brings variety in the marketplace, in the sense that entrepreneurs test a certain number of hypotheses on the parameters of the 'product' (price, quality, service, and so on) that they think will satisfy consumers' demands; variety ultimately preserves the choice of the consumers and their ability to test the solutions adopted by the entrepreneurs.[235] The variety of 'products' (or solutions suggested by the entrepreneurs) therefore are not the outcome of the 'natural' selection process of the marketplace but result from a process of 'artificial selection' by formal and informal institutions that 'channel the competitive process and give it a certain direction' and select 'at the same time, artificially, which entrepreneurial hypotheses will survive'.[236] Dominant firms are in a position to influence directly the market activities of other economic agents and therefore may constitute an informal institution that can indirectly affect the ultimate choice of the consumers.

Their freedom of action is restricted to 'performance competition', offering better terms to consumers, and does not extend to 'impediment competition', where commercial practices such as loyalty rebates or predatory pricing hinder the ability of rivals to compete, in other words, to offer their own set of solutions to the essential problem of productive activity: what 'products' do the consumers prefer?[237]

231 Case T-203/01 *Manufacture française des pneumatiques Michelin v Commission (Michelin II)* [2003] ECR II–4071, para 100.

232 Case T-201/04, *Microsoft Corp v Commission* [2007] ECR II–3601, para 1096. See also *Streetmap Limited v Google Inc* [2016] EWHC 253 (Ch), para 83.

233 This may be seen as the 'system of variable thresholds' ('*System beweglicher Schranken*', ie, the concept that behaviour which may be unproblematic for competition law purposes in the hands of a firm in a competitive market need not be harmless in the hands of a dominant firm).

234 W Eucken, 'Die Wettbewerbsordnung und ihre Verwirklichung' (1949) 2 *Ordo: Jahrbuch für die Ordnung von Wirtschaft und Gesellschaft* 1, translated in W Eucken, 'The Competitive Order and Its Implementation' (2006) 2(2) *Competition Policy Int'l* 219.

235 C Matzavinos, *Individuals, Institutions and Markets* (CUP, 2004), 193–203.

236 Ibid, 174.

237 The distinction between 'performance competition' and 'impediment competition' was suggested as an element distinguishing abusive from non-abusive practices by professor Peter Ulmer of the University of Heidelberg and was influential in the enforcement of the GWB. DJ Gerber, *Law and Competition in Twentieth Century Europe: Protecting Prometheus* (Clarendon Press, 1998) 313. For a criticism from other

The concept of special responsibility of dominant firms may be explained by the emphasis of EU competition law on consumer sovereignty. Consumer sovereignty can be preserved by the ability of consumers to influence price, quality, variety, and subsequently the competitive (or innovation) process according to their own preferences. The emphasis on the special responsibility of dominant firms to protect the competitive process should therefore be understood as a proxy for consumer sovereignty: open and contestable markets are a prerequisite for the empowerment of consumers.

The special responsibility of the dominant undertakings was also an important factor taken into account in the recent *Intel* case of the General Court, where the GC noted that '[a]lthough exclusivity conditions may, in principle, have beneficial effects for competition, so that in a normal situation on a competitive market, it is necessary to assess their effects on the market in their specific context, those considerations cannot be accepted in the case of a market where, precisely because of the dominant position of one of the economic operators, competition is already restricted', that approach being justified 'by the special responsibility that an undertaking in a dominant position has not to allow its conduct to impair genuine undistorted competition in the common market and by the fact that, where an economic operator holds a strong position in the market, exclusive supply conditions in respect of a substantial proportion of purchases by a customer constitute an unacceptable obstacle to access to the market'.[238] Although it set aside the judgment of the GC, the CJEU re-affirmed the 'special responsibility' of dominant undertakings.[239]

8.4.4. ABUSE IN A LINKED MARKET, THE (CAUSAL) LINK BETWEEN THE ABUSE AND THE DOMINANT POSITION, AND COUNTERFACTUALS

Article 102 TFEU does not address the issue of the existence of a causal link between the dominant position and the abuse. It is, however, expected that there should be some causal link between the dominant position and the abuse, as otherwise the scope of the prohibition rule would have been extremely wide. This reading of Article 102 TFEU may also fit well the tort-like structure (and effects) of the prohibition. There are two broad concepts in analysing causation: in a nutshell, causation in law is attributive and establishes the responsibility of agents for the outcomes that follow their actions, while causation in fact is merely used for explanatory purposes instantiating in the concrete circumstances if event *X* is a factual cause of event *Y*, by exploring for instance if event *Y* actually occurred, and if event *X* is a necessary condition for event *Y* to occur, the point of the inquiry being to separate 'causes' from 'mere circumstances or conditions'.[240] One may thus distinguish between causation in law, which in this case concerns the (causal) relation between the concept of dominant position and that of abuse, and causation in fact that would attempt to establish a causal link between the dominant position, the undertaking's conduct and the effects of the conduct found abusive in the concrete case. As we will explore below, the EU Courts have taken a very liberal approach as

ordoliberals of the 'impediment competition' concept, see E Hoppmann, 'Behinderungsmißbrauch und Nichtleistungswettbewerb' [1980] 30 *Wirtschaft und Wettbewerb* 811.

[238] Case T-286/09, *Intel Corp v European Commission*, ECLI:EU:T:2014:547, paras 89–90.

[239] Case C-413/14 P, *Intel Corp v European Commission*, ECLI:EU:C:2017:632, para 135. See also, Case T-827/14, *Deutsche Telekom AG v European Commission*, ECLI:EU:T:2018:930, para 86.

[240] The utility of the distinction has been criticised by tort scholars but it is still widely employed by courts and the literature.

to the interpretation of causation in law, and may not even always require evidence of causation in fact.

Starting with the need to establish a causal link between the dominant position and the abuse, the issue was flagged up by AG Roemer in his Opinion in *Continental Can*, who noted:

> [. . .] The wording of Article [102 TFEU], first paragraph, with its expression 'abuse [. . .] of a dominant position within the Common Market', appears to hint that its application can be considered only if the position on the market is used as an *instrument* and is used in an objectionable manner; these criteria are therefore essential prerequisites of application of the law. If this is indeed so, then the application of Article [102 TFEU] to the present case must certainly be excluded since, as has already been stated, even the Commission takes the view that the applicant Continental did not in connection with the acquisition of the Thomassen shares use their market strength acquired through Schmalbach, as an instrument.[241]

The applicants were arguing that the Commission's decision in this case, which expanded the scope of Article 102 TFEU to also cover the strengthening of a dominant position through merger activity, lacked the required legal basis because 'the use of economic power linked with a dominant position can be regarded as an abuse of this position only if it constitutes the mean through which the abuse is effected'.[242] Hence, they argued that it was indispensable to provide evidence of a causal link between the dominant position, the conduct, and its effects. Their interpretation of the causal link was narrow, as they referred to a means-end test in order to include under the scope of Article 102 TFEU only conduct that could have produced the anti-competitive effects because of the existence of a dominant position, in other words a 'but-for' causality test. The CJEU did not pronounce itself directly on this issue. Holding that Article 102 TFEU 'is not only aimed at practices which may cause damage to consumers directly, but also at those which are detrimental to them through their impact on an effective competition structure', the CJEU continued stating that '[s]uch being the meaning and the scope of Article [102 TFEU], the question of the causal link raised by the applicants which in their opinion has to question exist between the dominant position and its abuse, is of no consequence, for the strengthening of the position of an undertaking may be an abuse and prohibited under Article [102 TFEU], regardless of the means and procedure by which it is achieved, if it has the effects mentioned above'.[243] It seems therefore that for the CJEU a dominant firm could be found responsible for an infringement of Article 102 when the specific conduct had our could strengthened its dominant position even if using its dominant position to achieve this result was not necessary. This substantially widens the scope of the prohibition under Article 102 TFEU. Similarly, in *Hoffman-La Roche*, the CJEU stated that 'the interpretation suggested by the applicant that an abuse implies that the use of the economic power bestowed by a dominant position is the means whereby the abuse has been brought about cannot be accepted'.[244]

The question of the requirement of a link between the dominant position and the abuse was also raised in *Télémarketing*.[245] The case concerned a subsidiary of Radio and Television

241 Opinion of AG Roemer in Case 6/72, *Europemballage Corporation and Continental Can Company Inc v Commission*, ECLI:EU:C:1972:101, para 20.

242 Case 6/72, *Europemballage Corporation and Continental Can Company Inc v Commission*, ECLI:EU:C:1973:22, para 19.

243 Ibid, para 27.

244 Case C-85/76, *Hoffmann-La Roche* [1979] ECR 461, para 91.

245 Case 311/84, *Centre belge d'études de marché—Télémarketing (CBEM) v SA Compagnie luxembourgeoise de télédiffusion (CLT) and Information publicité Benelux (IPB)*, ECLI:EU:C:1985:394.

Luxembourg, which had ceased to accept spot advertisements involving an invitation to make a telephone call for further information unless its telephone number was used. The national court before which this practice was challenged stated that Radio and Television Luxembourg and its subsidiary were dominant over television advertising in the French-speaking parts of Belgium and that telemarketing was a separate market from general TV advertising. The second question of the referring national court concerned whether an undertaking holding a dominant position in a particular market, by reserving to itself or to an undertaking belonging to the same group, to the exclusion of any other undertaking, an ancillary activity which could be carried out by another undertaking as part of its activities on a neighbouring but separate market, abuses its dominant position within the meaning of Article 102. Here the abuse and the conduct were in separate markets. The Court considered that Article 102 TFEU could apply '[i]f [. . .] telemarketing activities constitute a separate market from that of the chosen advertising medium, *although closely associated with it*',[246] thus indicating some requirement of a link between the relevant market on which the dominant position lies and that where the abuse takes place, the CJEU accepting by the same that the dominant position does not have to be over the same market as the abuse. The terminology chosen indicates that the CJEU required a causal link that would be sufficiently strong between the dominant position and the abuse, the case concerning conduct that would have enabled the leveraging of a dominant position in one market in order to gain a dominant position in another 'closely associated' relevant market. However, it did not explain how one may prove the existence of such causal link.

In *Tetra Pak II*, the Commission condemned an abuse in a market over which Tetra Pak was not found to be dominant when the market was linked to one over which it was found to be dominant.[247] Tetra Pak was found to be dominant over the supply of cartons for keeping milk and fruit juice fresh for 6 months and over the machinery for filling them—the aseptic sector. It also supplied some 55 per cent of the cartons for pasteurised milk and fruit juice and machinery for filling them—the non-aseptic sector—but was not found to be dominant over it, although in *AKZO* the CJEU held that there is a rebuttable presumption of dominance at 50 per cent. The General Court had confirmed that Tetra Pak was dominant over the aseptic sector and had a very strong position in the non-aseptic sector, strengthened by links between the two.

However, the Commission's decision condemned not only conduct in the aseptic markets, where Tetra Pak had been held to be dominant, but also conduct in the linked non-aseptic market, where it had not been held to be dominant. This was a considerable extension of the existing case law. In *Commercial Solvents*,[248] the Court upheld a decision condemning the use of a dominant position in an upstream market to monopolize one downstream and, as we highlighted above, in *Télémarketing*, it condemned the use of a dominant position to monopolize an ancillary activity. In *Tetra Pak*, however, the Commission alleged only that the profits made in the aseptic market enabled Tetra Pak to practise predatory or discriminatory pricing for non-aseptic machines and cartons in the view of links which it found between the two sectors. In the earlier cases, the dominant position in a market had been used to monopolize the other. Tetra Pak argued:

246 Ibid, para 26 (emphasis added).
247 *Tetra Pak II* (Case IV/31043) Commission Decision [1992] OJ L 72/1.
248 Joined Cases 6 & 7/73, *Commercial Solvents* [1974] ECR 223.

104. [. . .] that in this case the Commission has not demonstrated that there is a causal link between the abuses allegedly committed in the non-aseptic sector and Tetra Pak's dominant position in the aseptic sector. The applicant rejects in particular the Commission's allegation that profits made in the aseptic sector enabled it to practice [*sic*] predatory or discriminatory pricing for non-aseptic machines and cartons. It also disputes the existence of any link between its dominant position in the aseptic sector and the allegedly unfair contractual terms which it is said to have imposed in the non-septic sector. In its view, those terms are justified by the need to ensure the proper functioning of the packaging systems and were incorporated in contracts for the supply of non-aseptic machines well before the aseptic equipment was perfected. . . .

After reciting Article 102 TFEU,[249] *Michelin*, *Hoffman-La Roche*, and *Vitamins*, the GC held that Article 102 'imposed on an undertaking in a dominant position, irrespective of the reasons for which it had such a dominant position, a special responsibility not to allow its conduct to impair genuine undistorted competition on the common market'.[250] The GC went on to consider other cases in which either the abuse had been in the monopolized market, or where a refusal to supply the monopolized product without the secondary product led to monopolizing the latter. It went on to consider the 'associative links' alleged by the Commission:

Case T-83/91, *Tetra Pak International SA v Commission*, ECLI:EU:T:1994:246

121. It follows that the Commission was entitled to find that the above-mentioned links between the two aseptic markets and the two non-aseptic markets reinforced Tetra Pak's economic power over the latter markets. The fact that Tetra Pak held nearly 90% of the markets in the aseptic sector meant that, for undertakings producing both fresh and long-life liquid food products, it was not only an inevitable supplier of aseptic systems but also a favoured supplier of non-aseptic systems. Moreover, by virtue of its technological lead and its quasi-monopoly in the aseptic sector, Tetra Pak was able to focus its competitive efforts on the neighbouring non-aseptic markets, where it was already well established, without fear of retaliation in the aseptic sector, which meant that it also enjoyed freedom of conduct compared with the other economic operators on the non-aseptic markets as well.

120. In relation, next, to the alleged associative links between the relevant markets, it is common ground that they are due to the fact that the key products packaged in aseptic and non-aseptic cartons are the same and to the conduct of manufacturers and users. Both the aseptic and the non-aseptic machines and cartons at issue in this case are used for packaging the same liquid products intended for human consumption, principally dairy products and fruit juice. Moreover, a substantial proportion of Tetra Pak's customers operate both in the aseptic and the non-aseptic sectors. In its written observations submitted in reply to the statement of objections, confirmed in its written observations before the Court, the applicant thus stated that in 1987 approximately 35% of its customers had purchased both aseptic and non-aseptic systems. Furthermore, the Commission correctly noted that the conduct of the principal manufacturers of carton-packaging systems confirmed the link between the aseptic and the non-aseptic markets, since two of them, Tetra Pak and PKL, already operate on all four

249 Case T-83/91, *Tetra Pak International SA v Commission*, ECLI:EU:T:1994:246, para 112.
250 Ibid, para 114.

> markets and the third, Elopak, which is well-established in the non-aseptic sector, has for some considerable time been trying to gain access to the aseptic markets.
>
> 122. It follows from all the above considerations that, in the circumstances of this case, Tetra Pak's practices on the non-aseptic market are liable to be caught by Article [102TFEU], without its being necessary to establish the existence of a dominant position on those markets taken in isolation, since the undertaking's leading position on the non-aseptic markets, combined with the close associative links between those markets and the aseptic markets, gave Tetra Pak freedom of conduct compared with the other economic operators on the non-aseptic markets, such as to impose on it a special responsibility under Article [102TFEU] to maintain genuine undistorted competition on those markets.
>
> 123. It follows from all the above that the first limb of the third plea relied on by the applicant must be rejected. [. . .]

The CJEU at paragraphs 21–33 confirmed the GC's judgment that conduct in the linked market might be condemned without finding a dominant position over the non-aseptic sector.[251] The CJEU stated:

> 27. It is true that application of Article [102 TFEU] presupposes a link between the dominant position and the alleged abusive conduct, which is normally not present where conduct on a market distinct from the dominated market produces effects on that distinct market. In the case of distinct, but associated, markets, as in the present case, application of Article [102 TFEU] to conduct found on the associated, non-dominated market and having effects on that associated market can only be justified by special circumstances.

The CJEU went on to indicate that Tetra Pak was the leading firm in the non-aseptic markets and concluded that 'the relevance of the associative links which the GC thus took into account cannot be denied'. The alleged links were that dairies needed equipment and cartons for both markets and 35 per cent of Tetra Pak's customers bought both systems. It is important to note, however, that the CJEU confirmed the judgment of the GC only on the basis of cumulative factors. Where there is less market power in the linked market, the result may be different.

It is difficult to see how the alleged link increased the market power of Tetra Pak in either market. The Commission found abuses in both the aseptic and the non-aseptic market. Was it right to do this, when the dominant position had been established only on the aseptic market? Should the associative links[252] have led to a finding that Tetra Pak was dominant in both markets rather than to extending the law under Article 102 TFEU to markets where the firm has not used its dominance to extend its market power in that or another market? Note that, in *Hilti*, each pair of products was complementary, but the Court treated the nail-gun as in a separate market from the cartridges used with it. Is the notion of 'associative links' consistent with the treatment of complementary products as being in separate markets? Did the complementarity of the aseptic and non-aseptic markets increase Tetra Pak's power in the non-aseptic? Should the Commission have established dominance over the latter, rather than that action in the latter abused a dominant position in the aseptic markets?

[251] Case C-333/94 P, *Tetra Pak International SA v Commission*, ECLI:EU:C:1996:436, paras 21–3.

[252] See *Tetra Pak II* (Case IV/31043) Commission Decision [1992] OJ L 72/1, para 121.

In conclusion, in *Tetra Pak II* the CJEU extended the earlier case law. There was no earlier judgment condemning the abuse in a linked market not vertically related to that dominated, although a refusal to supply a raw material or component may affect competition downstream. In that event, a firm supplying raw materials may be dominant also over the final product, if there are no substitutes for making the input.[253] Similarly, in *Microsoft*, the General Court held that the abuse may involve the use of the undertaking's power on the dominated market to leverage its position in an adjacent market, the specific theory of harm, leveraging, implying the existence of a causal link between the relevant market where the dominance was held, and that on which the abuse produced its effects.[254]

Some authors referred to the *AstraZeneca*[255] and *Rambus*[256] cases as casting 'further doubts on whether some plausible connection between the position of dominance and the act(s) of abuse is necessary under Article 102 TFEU'.[257] They note, for instance, that in *AstraZeneca* the abuse in question, the obtention of the patent by misrepresentation to the patent office was not 'facilitated or enables by the dominance itself: any form can misstate the position, if it so chooses'.[258] The Commission also considered that Rambus 'may have engaged in intentional deceptive conduct in the context of the standard-setting process by not disclosing the existence of the patents and patent applications which it later claimed were relevant to the adopted standard', falling under Article 102 TFEU, even if at the time of the alleged conduct Rambus was not dominant. This cannot, however, be considered as negating the existence of a causal link, as the Commission may have considered that Rambus conduct and its dominant position were somehow interlinked, when it asserted that 'Rambus held a dominant position on the market at the point when it started asserting its patents and has continued to hold that dominant position since'.[259]

Assuming that EU Courts require the existence of some causal link between dominant position and the abusive conduct, it remains important to explore if the claimant should prove the existence of a causal link between the conduct of the undertaking in a dominant position and the effects of the concrete abusive conduct (causation in fact). In *Intel*, the appellants argued that the Commission was wrong not to take into account the absence of actual anti-competitive effects of the applicant's practices and that the Commission had to establish 'a causal link between the practices complained of and effects on the market'. Again, in this case, as in *Hofmann-La Roche*, the potential anti-competitive effect of the rebate scheme operated by the dominant undertaking was on the market where the undertaking was dominant. The GC rejected the appellants' interpretation of Article 102 TFEU, holding that 'given that it is not necessary to prove actual effects of the rebates, it follows necessarily from this that the Commission is also not required to prove a causal link between

253 Joined Cases 6 & 7/73, *Commercial Solvents* [1974] ECR 223.

254 Case T-201/04, *Microsoft Corp v Commission* [2007] ECR II–3601, para 1344, noting that the Commission took issue with Microsoft for having used, by leveraging, its quasi-monopoly on the client PC operating systems market to influence the work group server operating systems market for the abusive refusal to supply, and similarly for the market for streaming media players.

255 *AstraZeneca* (Case COMP/A.37.507/F3) Commission Decision [2006] OJ L 332/24; on appeal case T-321/05, *AstraZeneca v Commission*, ECLI:EU:T:2010:266; Case C-457/10P, *AstraZeneca v Commission*, ECLI:EU:C:2012:770.

256 *RAMBUS* (Case COMP/38.636) Commission Decision [2010] OJ C 30/17.

257 R O'Donoghue and J Padilla, *The Law and Economics of Article 102 TFEU* (Hart, 2013), 264.

258 Ibid.

259 *RAMBUS* (Case COMP/38.636) Commission Decision [2010] OJ C 30/17, para 26. One may indeed argue that the misrepresentation was a step towards the ultimate aim of acquiring or reinforcing Rambus' dominant position/market power.

the practices complained of and actual effects on the market'.[260] It further noted that 'a fortiori, the Commission is not required to prove either direct damage to consumers or a causal link between such damage and the practices at issue in the contested decision [as it] is apparent from the case-law that Article [102 TFEU] is aimed not only at practices which may cause damage to consumers directly, but also at those which are detrimental to them through their impact on an effective competition structure'.[261] Of course, what the GC rejected in this case was the requirement of evidence of a causal link between the dominant position, the conduct and its anti-competitive effects, these anti-competitive effects being presumed as a result of the abusive conduct. Hence, a causal presumption replaces the concrete analysis of the link between the dominant position, the conduct in question and the negative effects of such an abuse on the specific relevant market, for instance by employing a counterfactual test. Such an interpretation is compatible with the fact that the use of the counterfactual test was rejected in the context of restrictions of competition by object under Article 101(1) TFEU.[262]

Where does this leave us as to the need for a causal link between dominance and the abuse? In our view, although this link is not explicitly required, one may consider that it is assumed, where dominance and the abuse are situated in the same relevant market, as well as also in situations where dominance and abuse are situated in vertically related markets. In all other situations, there must be some 'associative links' between the two relevant markets, that of the dominance and that where the abusive conduct occurred or where the effects of the abuse were felt. What constitutes an 'associative link' does not, however, seem to depend on the theory of harm, or more generally some economic justification. It certainly does not seem to require proof that the dominant position was one of the necessary conditions for the occurrence of the abusive conduct, what could have been tested using the notorious 'but-for test'. If a causal link is inherent in Article 102 TFEU and explains the interaction of dominance and abuse in these cases, this seems to be a quite broadly defined one, a simple contribution of the dominant position to the abuse being considered as sufficient. This is also how one may understand the statement of Roth J in *Streetmap v Google*, writing that '[i]t is clear as a matter of principle that conduct which might infringe Article 102 when started might no longer constitute an infringement several years later: e.g. if the undertaking involved no longer held a dominant position', which seems to attach a great importance to the concomitant temporal existence of both dominance and abuse as a an element to take into account in determining if an undertaking is responsible for the infringement of Article 102 TFEU.[263]

With regard to causation in fact when anti-competitive effects are not presumed, as this seems to be the case for certain categories/types of abuse,[264] and there is need to assess the anti-competitive effects of the specific conduct, there must be some evidence of a causal link between the alleged abuse and the anti-competitive effects observed or theorised (likely effects). This relates to the implementation of the causation in fact test to the specific conduct alleged to be an abuse, the law considering that in these situations dominant undertakings are liable under Article 102 TFEU/or Chapter II CA98, only if their conduct produces

260 Case T-286/ 09, *Intel Corp v European Commission*, ECLI:EU:T:2014:547, para 104.

261 Ibid, paras 104–6.

262 See Chapter 6.

263 *Streetmap Limited v Google Inc* [2016] EWHC 253 (Ch), para 91.

264 Our discussion of the distinction between anti-competitive object and effect in the context of Article 102 TFEU in Section 7.4.5.1.

anti-competitive effects. In order to establish this causal link, the Commission's priorities guidance makes use of the counterfactual test. It states that in these cases '[t]his assessment will usually be made by comparing the actual or likely future situation in the relevant market (with the dominant undertaking's conduct in place) with an appropriate counterfactual, such as the simple absence of the conduct in question or with another realistic alternative scenario, having regard to established business practices' (the so-called counterfactual test).[265] This calls for a comparison with a benchmark situation (the counterfactual), with the purpose of testing whether the specific conduct has the actual or likely effect of hindering competition.[266] What should be the benchmark situation is, however, not explained, other than the Commission requiring that regard should be paid 'to established business practices'.

In *Post Danmark II*, the CJEU mentioned that if 'there are anti-competitive effects *attributable* to [the dominant undertaking], [. . .] it is nevertheless open to a dominant undertaking to provide justification for behaviour liable to be caught by the prohibition set out in Article 102 TFEU]'.[267] Determining if the effects of the conduct are 'attributable' to the dominant undertaking may call for an application of the counterfactual test, but this is not the only alternative on offer, the jurisprudence of the CJEU staying relatively silent on the adequate causation in fact test. Even assuming that the counterfactual is the appropriate causation in fact test may not necessarily lead to a uniform interpretation by the courts and/or competition authorities, in particular as the benchmark scenario cannot be determined in advance. Indeed, as Richards LJ explained in *National Grid*:

> There is, however, no rule requiring the use of a benchmark in every case, let alone a benchmark that will tell one precisely where the line between lawful and unlawful conduct is to be drawn. The question whether an abuse exists is highly fact-sensitive and dependent upon an evaluation of a wide range of factors, in the light of the general principles expressed in *Hoffmann-La Roche* and other cases [. . .].
>
> The use of counterfactuals as a tool of appraisal is plainly permissible and of potential value. What is appropriate by way of counterfactual, however, is a matter of judgment for the decision-maker. There is no rule of law that the counterfactual has to take a particular form. The Commission's guidance document refers to a range from 'the simple absence of the conduct in question' to 'another realistic alternative scenario, having regard to established business practices'. It does not say that the alternative scenario must be based on alternative arrangements that the parties to the contracts in issue would or might realistically have made instead, and there is no principle requiring the adoption of such a restrictive approach. The purpose of the counterfactual is simply to cast light on the effect of the conduct in issue. It is for the decision-maker to determine whether a counterfactual is sufficiently realistic to be useful, and to decide how much weight to place on it. This is an area of appreciation, not of legal rules.[268]

265 Commission Guidance on Article 102, para 21.

266 See also Roth J in *Streetmap Limited v Google Inc* [2016] EWHC 253 (Ch), para 100, noting that '[i]n addressing the effect of particular conduct, it is necessary to have in mind the alternative position against which that effect falls to be assessed: i.e. what is usually referred to as the counterfactual', the latter concept being described as 'the only practical way to proceed' (ibid, para 101).

267 Case C-23/14, *Post Danmark II*, ECLI:EU:C:2015:651, para 47 (emphasis added).

268 *National Grid plc v Gas and Electricity Markets Authority* [2010] EWCA Civ 114, paras 54 and 57.

8.4.5. RESTRICTION OF COMPETITION AND ABUSE OF A DOMINANT POSITION

8.4.5.1. Is there a distinction between anti-competitive object and anti-competitive effect in the context of the abuse of a dominant position?

Certain forms of practices, such as loyalty rebates, predatory prices and exclusive dealing obligations imposed by dominant firms were often analysed as being anti-competitive and therefore infringing Article 102 TFEU by their 'nature' and 'effect'.[269] It is true that the case law does not always require the examination of the existence of actual anti-competitive effects, as these follow from the qualification of the conduct as being a loyalty rebate or a predatory pricing, for example.[270] This classification or characterization process that precedes the assessment of the anti-competitive effects of the conduct plays an important role and raises the issue of the existence of the distinction between an anti-competitive object and anti-competitive effect, also for the purposes of Article 102 TFEU, although the text of this provision does not refer to such a distinction, as is the case for Article 101(1) TFEU. It is also difficult in practice to advance objective justifications or efficiency gains for certain types of conduct. The question thus arises whether there are hardcore restrictions, prohibited *per se*, in the context of Article 102 TFEU.

In *Sot Lélos Kai Sia v GlaxoSmithKline*, Advocate General Colomer referred to two reasons explaining why there should not be a *per se* prohibition in Article 102 TFEU. First, Article 102 TFEU does not have an equivalent provision to Article 101(3) TFEU. The absence of an exception provision indicates that the analysis of abusive behaviour always requires a 'dialectical debate' between the dominant undertaking and the competent authorities, whether national or EU, as well as interested parties.[271] According to AG Colomer, if certain types of practice were to give rise to an irrebuttable presumption of abuse, dominant firms would be denied the right of defence. Article 102(a)–(d) do not contain examples of *per se* abuses. The examples of abuses that are cited constitute presumptions *iuris tantum* in order to shift the burden of proof from the claimant to the defendant.[272] Further, the institution of *per se* abuses would be contrary to the need to decide each case on the basis of its economic and legal context. A *per se* approach would amount to excessive formalism.[273]

AG Colomer also noted that, although there are two different types of abuses: those that affect consumers (exploitative abuses) and those that affect actual or potential competitors (exclusionary abuses), there is no hierarchy between these two categories. Dominant firms should be able to defend themselves on the basis of economic results obtained.[274] According to the AG, a balancing test will determine the existence of positive and negative effects to

[269] Opinion of AG Colomer in Joined Cases C-468–78/06, *Sot Lelos kai Sia v GlaxoSmithKline* [2008] ECR I–7139, para 50 [hereinafter *GSK*]; Case T-203/01, *Michelin II* [2003] ECR II–4071, para 241: '[f]or the purposes of applying Article [102 TFEU], establishing the anti-competitive object and the anti-competitive effect are one and the same thing [. . .]. If it is shown that the object pursued by the conduct of an undertaking in a dominant position is to limit competition, that conduct will also be liable to have such an effect.'

[270] Case T-203/01, *Michelin II* [2003] ECR II–4071, para 239 (loyalty rebates); Case T-340/03, *France Télécom SA v Commission* [2007] ECR II–107, [2007] 4 CMLR 21, paras 195 and 197 (predatory pricing). See also Case T-66/01, *Imperial Chemical Industries Ltd v Commission* [2010] ECR II–2631, paras 297–9; Case T-155/06, *Tomra v Commission* [2010] ECR II–4361, para 289 (loyalty rebates and exclusive agreements).

[271] Opinion of AG Colomer in Joined Cases C-468–78/06, *GSK* [2008] ECR I–7139, para 69.

[272] Ibid, para 70. [273] Ibid, para 72. [274] Ibid, para 74.

competition for the consumers and other economic operators that exploit 'the same relevant market'. Consequently, AG Colomer suggested that the Court should declare without ambiguity that Article 102 TFEU does not apply before examining the existence of positive effects/defences, even if it is clear that the facts of the case do not leave any doubt as to the anti-competitive intent of the parties.[275] This denies the existence of a *per se* prohibition rule in Article 102 TFEU.

Of particular interest is the discussion of the role of the analysis of the anti-competitive intent of the dominant firm, which according to the AG, is an aggravating circumstance for the finding of an abuse.[276] In particular, he advanced the view that there are two possible aspects of intent: first, subjective intent which may in certain circumstances indicate the existence of an abuse; second, objective intent when a dominant firm adopts conduct that tends to restrict competition. In the latter situation, the qualification of intent does not depend on subjective elements but on the nature of the conduct of the dominant firm: there is a strong presumption that categories of conduct that grossly ignore the objectives of the Treaty constitute a serious infringement of Article 102 TFEU and could be presumed abusive.[277]

The finding of anti-competitive intent should not, however, lead to a *per se* prohibition under Article 102 TFEU.[278] Courts and competition authorities should systematically examine the positive and negative effects of the practice, even if there is a clear intent to restrict competition. AG Colomer distinguishes between different categories of conduct, some of them being so grossly anti-competitive that they may justify a different allocation of the burden of proof (eg if there is a restriction of parallel trade, the burden of proof may shift to the defendant). Other practices will require from the claimant a more complete substantiation of anti-competitive effects before moving to the next step of the analysis, the examination of possible defences.[279] Categorical thinking seems therefore, compatible with an effects-based approach as it may introduce a different allocation of the burden of proof for certain categories of practice.

The position of AG Colomer, with regard to the non-existence of *per se* prohibitions under Article 102 TFEU, leaves place to the introduction of a distinction between object and effect in the context of Article 102, with anti-competitive object being a concept different from a *per se* prohibition, as it would be possible to justify a conduct having an anti-competitive object with efficiency gains.[280] One could therefore interpret the reference by the European Commission in its Guidance on Article 102 to circumstances where it would not be necessary to carry out a detailed assessment before concluding that the conduct in question is likely to result in consumer harm as not excluding the theoretical possibility of an efficiency defence.[281] It is true that the Commission considers that in this case the anti-competitive effect will be inferred, as it appears that the conduct can only raise obstacles to competition and creates no efficiencies. One could argue, however, that this paragraph does not affect the theoretical possibility for

275 Ibid, para 76. 276 Joined Cases C-468–78/06, *GSK* [2008] ECR I–7139, paras 47–54.
277 Ibid, para 54. 278 Ibid, para 61. 279 Ibid, para 70.

280 This seems to be contrary to the interpretation of the anti-competitive object concept (in the context of Article 101(1) TFEU) by AG Kokkott in Case C-8/08, *T-Mobile Netherlands BV, KPN Mobile NV, Orange Nederland NV and Vodafone Libertel NV v Raad van bestuur van de Nederlandse Mededingingsautoriteit* [2009] ECR I–4529, para 43 [hereinafter *T-Mobile and Others*], who seems to consider that anti-competitive object and *per se* prohibition refer to the same concept. This is plainly wrong as a matter of law, as, in a legal exception regime, conduct which is anti-competitive by object may still be justified under Article 101(3) TFEU and therefore not prohibited *per se*. In other words, there could be no prohibition under Article 101 TFEU before the antitrust decision-maker has examined the possible application of Article 101(3) TFEU.

281 Commission Guidance on Article 102, para 22. The Commission provides some non-exhaustive examples, such as conduct through which the dominant undertaking prevents its customers from testing the conduct of competitors or pays a distributor or a customer to delay the introduction of a competitor's product.

dominant undertakings to invoke efficiencies, in particular as it remains possible for conduct leading to anti-competitive foreclosure to be justified by the defences of objective necessity and efficiencies, before finding the existence of an abuse of a dominant position. The Commission does not explicitly exclude these practices from section D of the report on objective necessity and efficiencies that follows, although, in practice, it seems unlikely that the alleged efficiencies will be accepted, for failure to comply at least with the first two cumulative conditions of the efficiency defence.

The judgment of the CJEU in *GSK* did not discuss the general framework of Article 102 TFEU. The Court preferred to start its analysis by referring to the familiar case law on refusals to deal, which opens the door for the defendants to argue objective justifications and escape the finding of an abuse of a dominant position.[282] The Court's decision seems nevertheless implicitly to recognize that certain types of conduct, such as a restriction of parallel trade may create a presumption of negative effects on consumers, and therefore may shift the burden of proof to the defendant, without it being necessary for the claimant to bring additional evidence as to the causal link between the specific conduct and consumer harm.[283] According to the Court,

> In the light of the abovementioned Treaty objective (avoid national divisions in the Internal Market trade) as well as that of ensuring that competition in the internal market is not distorted, *there can be no escape* from the prohibition laid down in Article [102 TFEU] for the practices of an undertaking in a dominant position which are aimed at avoiding *all* parallel exports from a Member State to other members States, practices which, by partitioning the national markets, neutralise the benefits of effective competition in terms of the supply and the prices that those exports would obtain for final consumers in the other Member States.[284]

Despite the language employed, however, the Court immediately qualified this statement by accepting that this does not amount to an absolute presumption of consumer harm or a *per se* prohibition rule. The presumption of anti-competitive effects may still be rebutted by the defendant in limited circumstances: a company must be 'in a position to take steps that are reasonable and in proportion to the need to protect its own commercial interests'.[285] This is a more limited array of objective justifications than those contemplated by AG Colomer in his opinion. The full array of objective justifications may not apply in this case (only reasonable and proportionate protection of commercial interests).[286] The Court thus introduces a degree of categorical analysis in Article 102, as it implies that some restrictions of competition are so severe that only a limited range of objective justifications may enter into consideration. Furthermore, the Court immediately qualified the possibility of dominant firms justifying restrictions on parallel trade by indicating that it is limited to circumstances where (a) State intervention is one of the factors liable to create the opportunities for parallel trade in the first place[287] and (b) where a

[282] Joined Cases C-468–78/06, *GSK* [2008] ECR I–7139, paras 34, 69, and 76.
[283] Ibid, paras 56–7. [284] Ibid, para 66 (emphases added). [285] Ibid, para 69.
[286] The content of this concept is unclear. A restrictive definition of the concept will cover only a meeting competition defence, thus excluding the consideration of efficiency gains. The interpretation of this expression is not clear. See E Rousseva, 'The Concept of "Objective Justification" of an Abuse of a Dominant Position: Can it Help to Modernise the Analysis under Article 82?' (2006) 2 *Competition L Rev* 27, 33–4, who observes the following: '[. . .] the question is what a legitimate commercial interest of a dominant undertaking is: does this interest mean only a right of a dominant undertaking to survive on the market, i.e., to prevent its inefficient operation, or does it also mean a right to carry out a profit oriented policy? How does the prerogative of a dominant firm to protect its interest fit with the essential goal of competition to serve consumers' interests? These are questions on which views diverge.'
[287] Joined Cases C-468–78/06, *GSK* [2008] ECR I–7139, para 67.

different interpretation of Article 102, rejecting any possibility of justification, would have left dominant firms only the choice 'not to place its medicines on the market at all in a Member State where the prices of those products are set at a relatively low level'.[288]

The EU Commission's Guidance on Article 102 adopts an effects-based approach and does not employ language that suggests the existence of an object restriction of competition under Article 102 TFEU. More importantly, the Commission does not establish any distinction with regard to the type of abusive conduct as to the possible efficiency gains/objective justifications that dominant undertakings may argue against the finding of an abuse of dominant position. Furthermore, some recent case law of the CJEU includes analysis of the anti-competitive effects of the conduct.[289] Yet, one may advance that these cases related to types of abuses (margin squeeze) that were not generally found as creating a presumption of anti-competitive effect. The *Intel* case also provides some useful insights with regard to the possibility of the so called 'naked restraints' adopted by Intel to be considered anti-competitive 'by object' (in this case Intel had granted payments to the Original Equipment Manufacturers (OEMs) in order that the OEMs delay, cancel or in some other way restrict the marketing of the products of its competitor AMD).[290]

8.4.5.2. Freedom of competition, competitive structure, and 'consumer welfare': Three roads for interpreting the concept of abuse of a dominant position

Commentators analysing the case law on Article 102 TFEU often have recourse to different overall narratives, in their attempt to synthesize the concept of abuse and explain the past case law in this area. Some oppose the old case law of the European Courts focusing on the principle of the 'freedom to compete' and the need to preserve a competitive market structure with the more economics and welfare oriented approach chosen by the European Commission. The idea is that the turn towards a 'more economics approach' is antithetical to the case law and thus not legitimate.[291] The underlying assumption is that the principle of freedom of competition does not accommodate the 'economic', 'effects-based' approach, of the Commission's Guidance on Article 102, as (i) it is more 'forms-based', (ii) it does not look to economic efficiency and the possible efficiency gains resulting from the dominant undertaking's conduct, (iii) it perceives the objective of the law as the protection of the interests of the competitors of the dominant undertaking, rather than the interests of the consumers, (iv) it does not require evidence of 'consumer harm' for the application of Article 102 TFEU, but rather relies on the likely exclusion of competitors for the finding of an abuse. In contrast, the 'economics' 'effects-based' approach (i) requires evidence of consumer harm (directly or indirectly) for the application of Article 102 TFEU, (ii) focuses on the likely anti-competitive effects of the

288 Ibid, para 68.

289 Case C-280/08 P, *Deutsche Telekom AG v European Commission* [2010] ECR I–9555; Case C-52/09, *Konkurrensverket v TeliaSonera Sverige AB* [2011] ECR I–527; Case T-398/07, *Spain v Commission*, ECLI:EU:T:2012:173.

290 Case T-286/09, *Intel Corp v European Commission*, ECLI:EU:T:2014:547, para 204 (noting that '(t)he only interest that an undertaking in a dominant position may have in preventing in a targeted manner the marketing of products equipped with a product of a specific competitor is to harm that competitor. Consequently, by applying naked restrictions vis-à-vis HP, Lenovo and Acer, the applicant pursued an anti-competitive object'. The fact that the CJEU quashed the judgment of the GC (with regard to the characterization of loyalty rebates) [Case C-413/14 P, *Intel Corp. v European Commission*, ECLI:EU:C:2017:632] does not challenge the analysis of 'naked restraints' as by restrictions of competition 'by object' in the context of Article 102 TFEU.

291 L Lovdahl-Gormsen, 'Why the European Commission's Enforcement Priorities on Article 82 EC should be Withdrawn' (2010) 31 *European Competition L Rev* 45; P Akman, 'The European Commission's Guidance on Article 102 TFEU: From *Inferno* to *Paradiso*?' (2010) 73 *Modern L Rev* 605.

conduct, rather than on its form, (iii) integrates efficiency considerations as a possible justification of the anti-competitive effects of consumers, and (iv) perceives the objective of the law as the promotion of 'consumer welfare'.

8.4.5.3. The different approaches followed in practice

The case law of the Courts and the decisional practice of the European Commission have never followed a unique perspective but, combined to different degrees, elements from various theoretical approaches: the 'freedom to compete'/ordoliberal approach, the structuralist approach and the consumer welfare approach.[292] One could distinguish between different phases. From the early 1970s to mid-2000s, the European Commission and the European Courts followed an approach combining elements of the 'freedom to compete' approach with a structuralist approach. However there have also been cases where the Courts signalled the development of a new approach that would seem closer to the positions of the effects-based 'consumer welfare' perspective. Since the Commission's turn towards a more 'effects-based' approach, starting with the publication of a DG Competition Staff Discussion paper in 2006, the tide has turned and the effects-based 'consumer welfare' approach became if not dominant, at least prevalent.

8.4.5.3.1. *The early case law and the development of two doctrines for Article 102 TFEU*

In *Continental Can*, the Court held that an infringement to Article 102 TFEU is committed if an undertaking in a dominant position strengthens such position in such way that the degree of dominance substantially fetters competition, ie that only undertakings remain in the market whose behaviour depends on the dominant one; in this case, 'the objectives of the Treaty are circumvented by an alteration of the supply structure which seriously endangers the *consumers*' freedom of action in the market'.[293] In this case, the Court might have referred to the principle of consumer sovereignty, mentioned above, interpreting it to mean that consumers' freedom of action should always be preserved in the marketplace. This is not seen from the demand side (ensuring consumers an adequate revenue to enable them to consume), but simply from the supply side (ensuring that the supply structure provides consumers enough alternatives to exercise their freedom to act in the market—by preserving undertakings whose action, and thus the products and services they offer, including the price they offer them, is independent from the decision of the dominant undertaking).

In *United Brands v Commission*,[294] The CJEU confirmed a Commission's decision finding that United Brands, a multi-national controlling the Chiquita bananas brand, had abused its dominant position by having recourse to a number of commercial practices, including a prohibition to its distributors/ripeners to resell bananas that were still green to other retailers, the related discontinuation of supplies of green bananas to a retailer/ripener for having distributed and invested effort in the promotion of a competitor's branded bananas, price discrimination practices and alleged excessive prices. The Court applied for the first two exclusionary practices a proportionality standard. It held that it is possible for an undertaking to select retailers according to objective criteria, as long as the effect of such policy does not go beyond the objective pursued.[295] A dominant undertaking is also free to counterattack its competitors

[292] See Section S.8.4.5.2.

[293] Case C-6/72, *Continental Can v Commission* [1973] ECR 223, paras 26 and 29.

[294] Case C-27/76, *United Brands v Commission* [1978] ECR 207.

[295] Ibid, para 158.

and protect its 'own commercial interests', yet the Court noted that the attack must 'still be proportionate to the threat taking into account the economic strengths of the undertakings confronting each other'.[296] The Court referred for all these exclusionary practices to the existence of a 'prejudice to consumers', but seemed to presume this from the nature of the abuse, should the proportionality test not be able to justify the competition distortion. The Court also found that discontinuing the supplies to a retailer for the simple reason that the latter prefers to promote more the products of a competitor amounts 'to a serious interference with the independence of small and medium sized firms in their commercial relations with the undertaking in a dominant position and this independence implies the right to give preference to competitors' goods'.[297] Unlike in *Continental Can*, the fact that this discontinuation would have allowed only firms 'dependent upon the dominant undertaking to stay in business' was deemed by the Court as an important element to conclude in the existence of an abuse.[298]

In *Hoffmann-La Roche*,[299] the CJEU reviewed a Commission's decision imposing fines under Article 102 TFEU on Hoffmann-La Roche for excluding its competitors by entering into supply contracts with its largest customers providing for exclusivity or by giving fidelity rebates. After examining the extent and the duration of the exclusivity arrangements of Hofmann La Roche, the Court concluded that 'an undertaking which is in a dominant position on a market and ties purchasers—even if it does so at their request—by an obligation or promise on their part to obtain all or most of their requirements exclusively from the said undertaking' or by fidelity rebates, 'that is to say discounts conditional on the consumer's obtaining all or most of its requirements—whether the quantity of its purchases be large or small—from the undertaking in a dominant position', abuses its dominant position.[300] According to the CJEU:

> Obligations of this kind to obtain supplies exclusively from a particular undertaking, whether or not they are in consideration of rebates or of the granting of fidelity rebates intended to give the purchaser an incentive to obtain his supplies exclusively from the undertaking in a dominant position, are incompatible with the objective of undistorted competition within the Common Market, because—unless there are exceptional circumstances which may make an agreement between undertakings in the context of Article [101 TFEU] and in particular of paragraph (3) of that article, permissible—they are not based on an economic transaction which justifies this burden or benefit but are *designed to deprive the purchaser of or restrict his possible choices of sources of supply and* to *deny other producers access to the market*.[301]

For the Court, 'these practices by an undertaking in a dominant position and especially on an expanding market tend to consolidate this position by means of a form of competition which is not based on the transactions effected and is therefore distorted'.[302] Thus, the Court based the finding of abuse not on any demonstration of consumer prejudice, but presumed

296 Ibid, paras 189 and 190. 297 Ibid, para 193.

298 Ibid, para 194. See also Joined Cases 6 & 7/73, *Istituto Chemioterapico Italiano SpA and Commercial Solvents Corporation v Commission* [1974] ECR 223 (where the Court found that the discontinuation by a dominant undertaking of supply to an existing customer amounted to an abuse of a dominant position. In this case the dominant undertaking was the supplier of raw material and made the decision to vertically integrate in the downstream market. At the same time it refused to supply this raw material to its competitor downstream, thus leading to its exclusion from the downstream market).

299 Case C-85/76, *Hoffmann-La Roche* [1979] ECR 461. 300 Ibid, para 89.

301 Ibid, para 90 (emphasis added). 302 Ibid.

the existence of abuse from the simple fact that the practice deprived or restricted intermediary consumers (the retailers) from possible choices of sources of supply *and* by the fact that through these practices Hofmann La Roche denied its competitors access to the market, by foreclosing with requirement contracts and loyalty rebates a substantial part of it (more than 90 per cent of their needs). What is more interesting is that for the Court, 'any further weakening of the structure of competition may constitute an abuse of a dominant position'.[303]

This evolution towards more restrictive standards for dominant firms and emphasis on their duty to preserve competition found its apogee in *Michelin I*.[304] The Dutch subsidiary of Michelin granted annual rebates to those dealers who sold sufficient tyres. Dealers' annual targets were fixed individually in advance and operated on total purchases, not just on the incremental ones above the target. Dealers were informed orally. Targets were usually set a little higher than the individual dealer's sales the year before but, in some years, account was taken of the proportion of Michelin tyres in the turnover of each. Nearly all dealers selling 3 000 tyres a year obtained the maximum rebate. Sometimes there were disputes at the end of the year about what the target was. The Commission adopted a decision that Michelin was dominant over the supply of tyres for heavy vehicles in the Netherlands to retailers for the replacement market, to the exclusion of retreads. The incentive rebates constituted an abuse of that position. The Court confirmed the decision of the Commission, finding that the discount system applied by Michelin NV constituted an abuse because it was based on the fixing of individual and selective sales targets not clearly defined in writing, thus tying tyre dealers to Michelin NV, and thus depriving the customers of any choice as regards their sources of supply. Michelin contested this finding arguing that a rebate system based on sales targets should not be prohibited *per se*. The Court noted that Article 102 TFEU applies to practices which are likely to affect the structure of a market where, as a direct result of the presence of the dominant undertaking in question, competition has already been weakened and which, through recourse to methods different from those governing normal competition in products or services based on traders' performance, have the effect of hindering the maintenance or development of the level of competition still existing on the market.[305] According to the Court, this does not mean that holding a dominant position is in itself a recrimination but simply means that, 'irrespective of the reasons for which it has such a dominant position, the undertaking concerned has a special responsibility not to allow its conduct to impair genuine undistorted competition on the common market'.[306] The Court found important to examine if the loyalty rebate tended to 'remove or restrict the buyer's freedom to choose his sources of supply, to bar competitors from access to the market, to apply dissimilar conditions to equivalent transactions with other trading parties or to strengthen the dominant position by distorting competition'.[307] No independent assessment of consumer harm was made. On the contrary, the Court focused on the limitation of the dealers' choice of supplier, thus making access to the market more difficult for competitors: '[n]either the wish to sell more nor the wish to spread production more evenly can justify such a restriction of the customer's freedom or choice and independence'.[308]

This case law seems to have relied on a two-step process in defining the existence of an abuse:

> Article [102] covers practices which are *likely* to affect the structure of a market where, as a direct result of the presence of the undertaking in question, competition has already been

[303] Ibid, para 123. [304] Case C-322/81, *Michelin I* [1983] ECR 3461. [305] Ibid, para 70.
[306] Ibid, para 57. [307] Ibid, para 73. [308] Ibid, para 85.

> weakened and which, through recourse to methods different from those governing normal competition in products or services based on traders' performance, have the effect of hindering the maintenance or development of the level of competition still existing on the market.[309]

As a first step, the abuse test involves assessing whether the conduct was of a type 'likely' or 'such as' to affect the structure of an otherwise concentrated market and which constitutes a (business) method 'different from those governing normal competition in products or services based on traders' performance' (abstract/categorical analysis) that would initially require the classification of the practice into a specific antitrust category. In the second step, the competition authority or judge will examine the anti-competitive effects of the specific practice (fact-based analysis). The first prong of this abuse test, abstract/categorical analysis, implies that, for certain practices, there is a presumption of anti-competitive or pro-competitive effect when the firm has a dominant position (see our remarks earlier for the possible existence of *per se* restrictions of competition in Article 102 TFEU). Yet also, the second step might not mean much, should the existence of anti-competitive effects be presumed from the simple exclusion of a competitor from the market.

In theory, many commercial practices may have the effect of excluding rivals from the market or substantially of hindering their ability to compete. The test is unworkable without a limiting principle that could provide dominant undertakings the ability to identify, *ex ante*, if their commercial practices would be considered illegal. The comparative analysis of the *Michelin II*[310] and the *British Airways*[311] rebates cases may provide an example of how a form-based approach could be different from a more effects-based test. In *Michelin II*, the General Court spent a number of paragraphs examining whether the specific target rebate scheme could be characterized as loyalty inducing, which did not require the court to analyse the concrete effects of the specific scheme on consumers. The General Court conducted instead an abstract/categorical analysis of the facts of the case to find out if the quantity rebate system, put in place by Michelin, fit the characterization of 'loyalty inducing' rebates.[312] The General Court considered that quantity rebates that are justified by a 'countervailing advantage' that is 'economically justified' do not constitute in general loyalty-inducing rebates and therefore would escape the prohibition of Article 102.[313] The Court subjected this economic justification of the rebate to a high standard of proof,[314] and, in the absence of an objective justification, the General Court concluded that the rebate system was loyalty inducing.[315] As a result of its loyalty-inducing character, the quantity rebate scheme 'limited the dealers' choice of supplier and made access to the market more difficult for competitors'.[316] The anti-competitive effect of this practice was thus presumed from the simple characterization of the rebate scheme as

309 Case C-322/81, *Michelin I* [1983] ECR 3461, para 70. Compare with the terminology used by the CJEU in Case C-85/76, *Hoffman-La Roche & Co v Commission* [1979] ECR 461, para 91; Case C-95/04, *British Airways plc v Commission* [2007] ECR I-2331, para 66: Article 102 'refers to conduct *which is such as to influence the structure of a market* where, as a result of the very presence of the undertaking in question, the degree of competition is already weakened.' (emphasis added). The difference between 'likely to affect' and 'conduct which is such as to influence' may indicate a difference in the degree of probability of the occurrence of the outcome ('affect' or 'influence' the structure of the market) as a result of the specific conduct.

310 Case T-203/01, *Michelin II* [2003] ECR II-4071.

311 Case C-95/04, *British Airways plc v Commission* [2007] ECR I-2331

312 Case T-203/01, *Michelin II* [2003] ECR II-4071, para 95. The Court concluded that the rebate scheme offered by Michelin 'has the characteristics of a loyalty-inducing discount system'.

313 Ibid, para 100. 314 Ibid, para 108–9. 315 Ibid, para 113.

316 Ibid, paras 110, 240.

loyalty inducing without any analysis of anti-competitive effects and possible consumer detriment. One could compare this approach to a quasi-*per se* illegality test for loyalty-inducing rebates.

The position of the General Court, confirmed by the CJEU, seems to have slightly evolved in *British Airways* towards a more flexible approach in the form-based/effects-based continuum. First, the Court found that even if the specific schemes had a 'fidelity building' effect, they could escape the application of Article 102 if they were based on an 'economically justified consideration'.[317] It would be possible for the dominant undertaking to justify these fidelity-inducing rebates by referring to efficiency justifications.[318] The consideration by the General Court of the existence of objective economic justifications did not aim to determine whether the rebate scheme has a loyalty inducing effect, as it was the case in *Michelin II*, but followed the characterization step of the rebate scheme as having a fidelity-building character. Thus, it formed part of the second prong of the abuse test, after the identification of the practice as being the assessment of anti-competitive foreclosure under a cost benefit analysis test.[319] Moreover, the second prong of the abuse test may include countervailing efficiency gains that benefit consumers.[320] In *British Airways*, General Court concluded that the loyalty rebates schemes should not only be examined under the first prong of the abuse test, but instead that the competition assessment should include an analysis of their anti-competitive effects under the second part of the test. This is closer to a structured rule of reason approach than to a quasi-*per se* illegality rule. The CJEU confirmed the approach of the General Court in *British Airways* and adopted a standard resembling to a structured rule of reason approach: It has to be determined whether the exclusionary effect arising from such a system, which is disadvantageous for competition, may be counterbalanced, or outweighed, by advantages in terms of efficiency which also benefit the consumer. If the exclusionary effect of that system bears no relation to advantages for the market and consumers, or if it goes beyond what is necessary in order to attain those advantages, that system must be regarded as an abuse.[321] Second, in contrast to *Michelin II*, the Court emphasized the existence of a consumer prejudice, an indication that it placed its analysis under the second prong of the abuse test under Article 102 TFEU.[322]

The consideration of anti-competitive effects and consumer harm constitutes the main difference between the decision of the GC in *Michelin II* and that of the CJEU in *British Airways*. Nonetheless, examining the existence of exclusionary effects does not necessarily mean that evidence of anti-competitive effects and consumer detriment is required. In other words, the analysis of possible economic justifications of a discount with a fidelity-building effect does not necessarily amount to the adoption of a full effects-based approach that would require empirical evidence of actual consumer prejudice. As the Court noted in *British Airways v Commission*:

[317] Case T-219/99, *British Airways plc v Commission* [2003] ECR II–5917, para 271.

[318] Ibid, para 280. This included efficiency gains.

[319] One could refer to this step as an equivalent to an Article 101(3) defence. Article 101 identifies two analytical steps: the prohibition principle of Article 101(1), which is a quick look establishing the existence of anti-competitive effects, and the exception principle of Article 101(3), which integrates a more detailed assessment of the practice under a cost benefit to consumers test. No such distinction is however mentioned in the context of Article 102 TFEU.

[320] Case T-219/99, *British Airways plc v Commission* [2003] ECR II–5917, paras 279–80 (not just public policy type of justifications).

[321] Case C-95/04, *British Airways plc v Commission* [2007] ECR I–2331, para 86

[322] Ibid, para 106.

> Article [102 TFEU] is aimed not only at practices which may cause prejudice to consumers directly, but also at those which are detrimental to them through their impact on an effective competition structure [. . .].[323]

The preservation of the competitive process constitutes thus an important objective of EU competition law. Advocate General Kokott has explained this position in *British Airways*:

> The starting-point here must be the protective purpose of Article [102 TFEU]. The provision forms part of a system designed to protect competition within the internal market from distortions [then Article 3(1)(g) of the EC Treaty, now Protocol no 27]. Accordingly, Article [102 TFEU], like the other competition rules of the Treaty, is not designed only or primarily to protect the immediate interests of individual competitors or consumers, but to protect the *structure of the market* and thus *competition as such (as an institution)*, which has already been weakened by the presence of the dominant undertaking on the market. In this way, consumers are also indirectly protected. Because where competition as such is damaged, disadvantages for consumers are also to be feared.[324]

At the same time, the Court was taking a different perspective in some refusal to supply or licence cases, where it was subjecting the finding of an abuse to some stricter standards. This may be due, in this area of competition law, to the direct collision with property rights, either on tangibles or intangibles (intellectual property rights). As R Nazzini rightly notes,

> the limitation of freedom of contract and proprietary rights inherent in the prohibition of abusive refusal to supply poses an acute enforcement problem because it may discourage investments both by the dominant undertaking and by other market participants. Therefore, EU law requires a higher intervention threshold for refusal to supply.[325]

The same author observes that 'an element in common to all types of refusals to supply is that the input must be 'indispensable for the customer', the case law also requiring 'a particularly severe exclusionary effect, with formulations ranging from the elimination of the competitor requesting access to the elimination of all competition on the downstream market'.[326] The Court held that a refusal to supply an IP rights is abusive only in 'exceptional circumstances'.[327] Exceptional circumstances consist of the following: (i) access is indispensable, (ii) the refusal to license prevented the appearance of a new product for which there was potential consumer demand, (iii) there was no justification for such refusal, and (iv) the

323 Case C-95/04, *British Airways plc v Commission* [2007] ECR I–2331, para 106.

324 Opinion of AG Kokott in Case C-95/04, *British Airways plc v Commission* [2007] ECR I–2331, para 68.

325 R Nazzini, 'Abuse of Dominance: Exclusionary Non-Pricing Abuses' in I Lianos and D Geradin (eds) *Handbook on EU Antitrust Law* (Edward Elgar Publishing, 2013), 473, 489, referring to the Opinion of AG Jacobs in Case C-7/97, *Oscar Bronner GmbH & Co KG v Mediaprint Zeitungs- und Zeitschriftenverlag GmbH & Co KG* [1998] ECR I–7791, para 57 [hereinafter *Oscar Bronner*]; Case C-418/01, *IMS v NDC* [2004] ECR I–5039, para 48.

326 R Nazzini, 'Abuse of Dominance: Exclusionary Non-Pricing Abuses' in I Lianos and D Geradin (eds) *Handbook on EU Antitrust Law* (Edward Elgar Publishing, 2013), 473, 489.

327 Joined Cases C-241 and 242/91 P, *RTE & ITP v Commission* [1995] ECR I–743, para 50; Case C-418/01, *IMS v NDC* [2004] ECR I–5039, paras 34–5; Case T-201/04 *Microsoft v Commission* [2007] ECR II–3601, para 331.

refusal to license excluded all competition on the secondary market. The requirement that the refusal to license prevented the sale of a new kind of product for which there was unsatisfied demand indicates that the Court aimed to protect innovation on the market. In comparison to general refusal to supply cases, the test applied for refusals to licence seems to require that all *effective* competition on the market be eliminated as a result of the refusal to licence. It adds also the condition that the refusal to supply must cause consumer harm in the form of the prevention of the emergence of a new product for which there is consumer demand or deterrence of innovation.[328]

In *Oscar Bronner*, a case on refusals to supply, the Court took a restrictive view of the obligation of a dominant undertaking to grant access to its facilities by imposing a number of conditions.[329] The refusal 'must be likely to eliminate all competition' on the part of the competitor requesting access; the access should be indispensable, not merely make it harder for the requesting undertaking to compete, and; the refusal should not be capable of objective justification. The case is well known for Advocate General Jacob's opinion. He emphasized with force, for the first time so explicitly, that 'the primary purpose of Article [102 TFEU] is to prevent distortion of competition—and in particular to safeguard the interests of consumers—rather than to protect the position of particular competitors'.[330] The importance of the incentives of dominant firms to innovate and the need to balance 'the interest in free competition with that of providing an incentive for research and development and for creativity' was another theme explored in the highly influential Opinions of Advocate General Jacobs, which signalled a different, more effects-based approach oriented, point of reference for the case law of the Court.[331] The Opinions of Advocate General Jacobs and the case law of the Court in the area of refusals to licence or refusals to deal marked a new point in the evolution towards a more 'effects-based' consumer welfare oriented approach in the application of Article 102 TFEU. With respect to the indispensability condition,[332] the Court held that access would have been indispensable only if it was not economically viable to create a home-delivery system for a newspaper with a comparable circulation to that of the dominant firm.[333]

One could argue that the conditions in *Bronner* set the outer boundaries of the special responsibility of a dominant firm and consequently the corresponding duty, under Article 102 TFEU, to abstain from any action that would be likely to exclude rivals from the market. The excluded rival would be granted access only if it is impossible for an undertaking with a comparable output to the dominant firm to develop such facility, which indicates that the Court applies a not yet as efficient as test, similar in essence to that applied for predatory pricing cases, since its *AKZO* case in 1991.[334] In this case, the Court held that there is no abuse if the

[328] Case T-201/04, *Microsoft Corp v Commission* [2007] ECR II–3601, para 647.

[329] Case C-7/97, *Oscar Bronner GmbH & Co KG v Mediaprint* [1998] ECR I–7791, para 41.

[330] Opinion of AG Jacobs in Case C-7/97, *Oscar Bronner GmbH & Co KG v Mediaprint* [1998] ECR I–7791, para 58.

[331] See also his highly influential Opinion in Case C-53/03, *Synetairismos Farmakopoion Aitolias & Akarnanias (Syfait) and Others v GlaxoSmithKline plc and GlaxoSmithKline AEVE* [2005] ECR I–4609 (noting the importance of investment and R&D).

[332] According to R Nazzini, 'Abuse of Dominance: Exclusionary Non-Pricing Abuses' in I Lianos and D Geradin (eds) *Handbook on EU Antitrust Law* (Edward Elgar Publishing, 2013), 473, 490, 'the term "indispensable" was first used by the Court of Justice in the *Télémarketing* case'.

[333] Case C-7/97, *Oscar Bronner GmbH & Co KG v Mediaprint* [1998] ECR I–7791, paras 45–6.

[334] Case C-62/86, *AKZO Chemie BV v Commission* [1991] ECR I–3359.

dominant firm is pricing above its average total costs and under certain conditions its average variable costs. The Court thus established a price cost screen for predatory pricing claims, with the aim to filter claims of exclusion by non-efficient competitors and thus to ensure that only claims leading to the exclusion of less efficient competitors will be considered.[335] In *Magill* and in *IMS*, the Court confirmed that indispensability was not limited to the legal or technical impossibility to replicate the input but included cases in which to replicate the input is 'not economically viable for production on a scale comparable to that of the undertaking which controls the existing product or service'.[336]

8.4.5.3.2. The turn towards an 'effects-based' approach?

The Commission's Guidance on Article 102

The European Commission began in 2005 a reflection on the policy underlying Article 102 TFEU and the way in which it should enforce that policy. The broad lines of that reform were spelled out by Commissioner Neelie Kroes in a speech delivered at the Fordham Corporate Law Institute in September 2005, in which she highlighted that 'the objective of Article [102 TFEU] is the protection of competition on the market as a means of enhancing consumer welfare and ensuring an efficient allocation of resources' and that the Commission's enforcement policy was 'to give priority to so-called exclusionary abuses, since exclusion is often at the basis of later exploitation of customers', leaving exploitative abuses for a second round of policy review.[337] Some months earlier, the Economic Advisory Group on Competition Policy had delivered a report, suggesting 'an economic approach' to Article 102 TFEU.[338] The Staff of the DG Competition followed with a Discussion Paper, published in December 2005, adopting a new analytical approach for the application of Article 102 TFEU to exclusionary abuses that relied on 'consumer welfare' rhetoric.[339]

During the same period, there was some reflection in the US on the modernization of US antitrust enforcement, in particular with regard to the application of section 2 of the Sherman Act. An Antitrust Modernization Commission (AMC) was created in 2002: the Commission was active from 2004 to 2007 and a Report was adopted in 2007 and communicated to Congress and the President.[340] The AMC Report examined whether it was necessary to adopt different tests for particular types of conduct or if a single test could apply to all types of exclusionary conduct of a dominant firm (US antitrust law does not cover exploitative conduct by dominant firms).[341] Some US authors have consistently argued for a general standard that would apply to all types of conduct, although there was no agreement over the

335 Ibid, para 72 (the Court noting that 'such prices can drive from the market undertakings which are perhaps as efficient as the dominant undertaking').

336 Case C-418/01 *IMS v NDC* [2004] ECR I-5039, para 28. See also *Magill*; Joined Cases C-241 & 242/91 P, *Radio Telefis Eireann (RTE) and Independent Television Publications Ltd (ITP) v Commission* [1995] ECR I-743.

337 N Kroes, 'Preliminary Thoughts on Policy Review of Article 82' (23 September 2009), available at http://europa.eu/rapid/pressReleasesAction.do?reference=SPEECH/05/537&format=HTML&aged=0&language=EN&guiLanguage=en.

338 EAGCP, *An Economic Approach to Article 82*, Report (July 2005), available at http://ec.europa.eu/dgs/competition/economist/eagcp_july_21_05.pdf.

339 DG Competition, 'Discussion Paper on the Application of Article 82 of the Treaty to Exclusionary Abuses' (December 2005), available at http://ec.europa.eu/competition/antitrust/art82/discpaper2005.pdf.

340 Antitrust Modernization Commission, *Report and Recommendations* (April 2007), available at http://govinfo.library.unt.edu/amc/report_recommendation/amc_final_report.pdf.

341 Ibid, 91–4.

test to apply.[342] However, it is not clear whether a unique standard will take into account all the complexities of the competition law assessment of unilateral practices. The Antitrust division of the US Department of Justice (DOJ) published a Single Firm Conduct Report in 2008, withdrawn in 2009,[343] where it recommended the development of different tests for different types of conduct, 'depending, among other things, on the scope of harm likely to result from the practice; the relative costs of false positives, false negatives, and enforcement; the ease of application; and other concerns about administrability'.[344] It also recommended, however, the application of a disproportionality test as the default test for types of conduct for which there is no specific standard. This test is essentially a cost benefit analysis test which gives considerably more weight to pro-competitive effects than to anti-competitive effects: 'conduct that potentially has both procompetitive and anticompetitive effects is anticompetitive under section 2 if its likely anticompetitive harms substantially outweigh its likely precompetitive benefits'.[345] This bias in favour of defendants may be explained by the perceived higher risk of private antitrust litigation and the procedural specificities of the US enforcement system. Such a test may not correspond to the institutional and procedural context of EU competition law.

The discussion generated by the AMC's work in the US and the European Commission's review process for Article 102 TFEU continued at the OECD level, which debated the concept of 'competition on the merits' in 2005.[346] The report identified a number of liability standards or tests, proposed by US academics or judges, in order to assist the decision-makers in distinguishing good conduct ('competition on the merits') from exclusionary conduct, thus showing that an effects-based approach is not one-dimensional, but might take very different perspectives.

342 E Elhauge, 'Defining Better Monopolization Standards' (2003) 56 *Stanford L Rev* 253, 330; AD Melamed, 'Exclusive Dealing Agreements and Other Exclusionary Conduct: Are There Unifying Principles?' (2006) 73 *Antitrust LJ* 375, 389; SC Salop, 'Exclusionary Conduct, Effect on Consumers, and the Flawed Profit-Sacrifice Standard' (2006) 73 *Antitrust LJ* 311, 341.

343 US DOJ, *Competition and Monopoly: Single-Firm Conduct under Section 2 of the Sherman Act* (2008), available at www.justice.gov/atr/public/reports/236681.htm. The other US federal antitrust enforcer, the Federal Trade Commission (FTC) also released a statement, which was critical of some of the views expressed by the US DOJ: 'Statement of Commissioners Harbour, Leibowitz and Rosch on the Issuance of the Section 2 Report by the Department of Justice' (8 September 2008), available at www.ftc.gov/sites/default/files/attachments/press-releases/ftc-commissioners-react-department-justice-report-competition-monopoly-single-firm-conduct-under/080908section2stmt.pdf [hereinafter FTC Statement]. FTC Chairman William E Kovacic did not join in the FTC Statement and wrote separately. See WE Kovacic, 'Modern U.S. Competition Law and the Treatment of Dominant Firms: Comments on the Department of Justice and Federal Trade Commission Proceedings Relating to Section 2 of the Sherman Act', Statement of FTC Chairman (8 September 2008), available at www.ftc.gov/sites/default/files/attachments/press-releases/ftc-commissioners-react-department-justice-report-competition-monopoly-single-firm-conduct-under/080908section2stmtkovacic.pdf. The US DOJ *Single-Firm Conduct Report* was withdrawn by the new US DOJ leadership, following the election of President Obama, in May 2009: see DOJ, 'Justice Department Withdraws Report on Antitrust Monopoly Law' (11 May 2009), available at www.justice.gov/opa/pr/2009/May/09-at-459.html.

344 US DOJ, *Competition and Monopoly: Single-Firm Conduct under Section 2 of the Sherman Act* (2008), 46, available at www.justice.gov/atr/public/reports/236681.htm.

345 Ibid, 45.

346 OECD, *Competition on the Merits*, Policy Roundtable, DAF(COMP)2005 (30 March 2006), 27, available at www.oecd.org/competition/abuse/35911017.pdf

OECD, *Competition on the Merits*, Policy Roundtable, DAF(COMP)2005 (30 March 2006), 27

(3) ***Dissatisfaction with both the ambiguity of some jurisdictions' competition statutes and the lack of clear definitions for terms like competition on the merits has prompted a number of specific tests that aim to detect abusive conduct.***

Over the years, scholars searching for more principled ways to sort out pro-competitive conduct from anti-competitive conduct have proposed a number of tests that agencies and courts can apply in abuse of dominance and monopolisation cases. These include the profit sacrifice test [no predation test], the no economic sense test, the equally efficient firm test, and various consumer welfare balancing tests. There is general agreement that no single test is suitable for every type of case, but there is also some variation with respect to the test that different delegates tend to favour.

Each of the four major types of tests has been used by courts and agencies. Other tests [. . .] have been proposed from time to time as scholars continue trying to pinpoint what competition on the merits is. Each of the tests has certain strengths and weaknesses.

(2) ***The profit sacrifice test states that conduct should be considered unlawful when it involves a profit sacrifice that would be irrational if the conduct did not have a tendency to eliminate or reduce competition.***

One form of this test is useful for capturing predatory pricing conduct, but it does not appear to be a good test in other types of cases because it is both over-inclusive and under-inclusive. It is over-inclusive because it can capture certain types of behaviour that increase consumer welfare even though they also exclude competitors. For example, research and development costs for a new drug may be so high that an investment in developing the drug can be profitable only if the drug is so effective that it excludes competitors and gives the innovating firm market power. But is it sound policy to discourage such investments? On the other hand, some conduct may entail no short run profit sacrifice at all yet still be harmful to competition. In addition, the profit sacrifice test is not well-suited to difficult cases in which the conduct at issue can be both beneficial and harmful.

(5) ***The no economic sense test states that conduct should be unlawful if it would make no economic sense without a tendency to eliminate or lessen competition.***

This test avoids under-inclusiveness because it does not require profit sacrifice. The test can be used offensively, *i.e.*, to argue that conduct was exclusionary because it made no economic sense, and defensively, *i.e.*, to demonstrate that conduct should not be condemned because it did make economic sense. It seems, however, that over-inclusiveness and an inability to deal well with conduct that has mixed effects are characteristic of this test, too.

(6) ***The equally efficient firm test states that conduct should be unlawful if it would be likely to exclude a rival that is at least as efficient as the dominant firm is.***

The equally efficient firm test (which is also known as the as efficient competitor test) is geared toward distinguishing harm to competition from harm to competitors, and it relies on the fact that without bad conduct by a dominant firm, equally efficient rivals cannot be eliminated. The test may be too lenient, though, if it is interpreted as allowing the elimination of new firms that are currently less efficient but that would eventually become equally or more efficient than the incumbent if they are able to survive long enough. Furthermore, an equally efficient firm might be able to enter a market and survive, but that does not always mean it would be able to exert competitive pressure. The mere fact that it could survive, therefore, is not necessarily enough to preserve competition.

(7) ***Consumer welfare balancing tests determine whether conduct should be unlawful by requiring decision-makers to weigh the positive and negative effects that the conduct has on consumer welfare.***

There are several varieties of consumer welfare tests. They all have a certain amount of appeal because they attempt to use consumer welfare effects themselves, rather than indirect factors such as profit sacrifice, as the gauge of dominant firm conduct. Unfortunately, although it may be possible to determine whether conduct enhances or reduces consumer welfare in some cases, it can be quite challenging, if not impossible, to measure the magnitude of those changes. Yet when conduct has both positive and negative effects on consumer welfare, a balancing step is necessary to determine which effect is stronger. It is therefore difficult to have confidence that balancing tests can be applied accurately, objectively, and consistently. Furthermore, it is not clear what the appropriate time horizon should be when applying this test, but that choice has very important implications for dynamic strategies such as predatory pricing.

These tests generated an extensive academic debate, in both the US and Europe, for different types of practices and focalized the attention of economic and legal commentators. The debate obviously influenced DG Comp at the European Commission, which also used the terminology of 'tests' in its Discussion Paper[347] and suggested the use of the 'hypothetical as efficient competitor test' for price-based exclusionary practices.[348]

The publication of the Discussion Paper by the DG Comp staff was followed by a period of uncertainty, as the Commission did not follow up this text with Guidelines, probably in view of the rather critical views of the Court of Justice and the General Court at the time on a 'consumer welfare' approach.[349] In a number of Opinions for both Articles 102 TFEU and 101 TFEU cases, Advocate General Kokott, emphasized the importance of preserving a competitive market structure, the protection of consumers being a side-effect of a competitive market structure, and thus not the principal aim of EU competition law:[350]

347 DG Competition, 'Discussion Paper on the Application of Article 82 of the Treaty to Exclusionary Abuses' (December 2005), para 56, available at http://ec.europa.eu/competition/antitrust/art82/discpaper2005.pdf.

348 Ibid, para 63.

349 See eg Case C-95/04, *British Airways plc v Commission* [2007] ECR I–2331; Case T-271/03, *Deutsche Telekom AG v Commission* [2008] ECR II–477.

350 Opinion AG Kokott J in Case C-95/04, *British Airways plc v Commission* [2007] ECR I–2331, paras 68, 86, and 125 [Article 102 TFEU]; Opinion AG Kokott J in Case C-8/08, *T-Mobile and Others* [2009] ECR I–4529, para 58:

> Article [101 TFEU], *like the other competition rules of the Treaty*, is not designed only or primarily to protect the immediate interests of individual competitors or consumers, but to protect the structure of the market and thus competition as such (as an institution). In this way, consumers are also indirectly protected. Because where competition as such is damaged, disadvantages for consumers are also to be feared. (Emphasis added.)

Opinion of AG Kokott J in Case C-95/04 *British Airways plc v. Commission*
[2007] ECR I–2331

> 68. [Article 102 TFEU] forms part of a system designed to protect competition within the internal market from distortions [formerly Article 3(1)(g) EC, now Protocol no 27]. Accordingly, Article [102 TFEU], like the other competition rules of the Treaty, is not designed only or primarily to protect the immediate interests of individual competitors or consumers, but to protect the *structure of the market* and thus *competition as such (as an institution)*, which has already been weakened by the presence of the dominant undertaking on the market. In this way, consumers are also indirectly protected. Because where competition as such is damaged, disadvantages for consumers are also to be feared. [. . .]
>
> 86. Article [102 TFEU] is not designed only or primarily to protect the immediate interests of individual competitors or consumers, but to protect the structure of the market and thus competition as such (as an institution) [. . .]

The Commission may have also been waiting the outcome of the General Court's judgment in the *Microsoft* case.[351]

The Commission finally published a Communication—Guidance on Article 102 in December 2008.[352] The Guidance on Article 102 is a softer law instrument than guidelines: it is complementary to the Commission's specific enforcement decisions. The choice of the instrument of guidance on enforcement priorities offers to the Commission more leeway in presenting its approach for Article 102 TFEU. The Commission could not have adopted guidelines contrary to the rulings of the European Courts.[353] The Commission Guidance on Article 102 takes resolutely a more consumer welfare oriented approach than the previous case law, although some commentators noted that it did not go as far as to adopt the resolutely effects-based approach advocated by the EAGCP report.[354] The Commission Guidance on Article 102 focuses only on exclusionary abuses. It employs in some parts of the text a 'consumer welfare' rhetoric, but still maintains language that would be reminiscent of the other two approaches for the interpretation of Article 102 TFEU: for example, it observes the

351 Case T-201/04, *Microsoft Corp v Commission of the European Communities* [2007] ECR II–3601.

352 Commission Guidance on Article 102.

353 For a recent reminder, see Opinion of AG Kokott J in Case C-8/08, *T-Mobile and Others* [2009] ECR I–4529, para 29, 'communications from the Commission are not legally binding and, therefore, are incapable of anticipating interpretation by the Court [. . .]'. See also *Intel* (Case COMP/C-3/37.990) Commission Decision [2009] OJ C 227/13, para 916:

> The guidance paper [ie, Guidance on Article 102] is not intended to constitute a statement of the law and is without prejudice to the interpretation of Article 82 by the Court of Justice or the Court of First Instance. As a document intended to set priorities for the cases that the Commission will focus upon in the future, it does not apply to proceedings that had already been initiated before it was published, such as this case.

354 See, for some critical discussion, P Akman, 'The European Commission's Guidance on Article 102 TFEU: From *Inferno* to *Paradiso?*' [2010] 73 *Modern L Rev* 605; V Korah, 'Radical Reforms of the Commission's Approach to EU Competition Law . . . From Protecting Freedom to Enter a market to an Efficient Allocation of Resources to Increase Consumer Welfare?' in G Ajani, A Gambaro, M Graziadei, R Sacco, V Vigoriti, and M Waelbroeck (eds) *Studi in Onore di Aldo Frignani: Nuovi Orizzonti del Diritto Comparato Europeo e Transnazionale* (Jovene Editore, 2011), 620; N Petit, 'From Formalism to Effects? The Commission's Communication on Enforcement Priorities in Applying Article 82 EC' (2009) 4 *World Competition* 485.

special responsibility of a dominant firm to preserve competition,[355] it maintains the focus on the 'competitive structure', at least at the level of the appreciation of dominance,[356] it values the protection of rivalry and the competitive process.[357] The focus of Article 102 TFEU is on 'consumer harm', defined broadly as covering all practices restricting competition in the form of higher prices, lower innovation, and/or narrower consumer choice.[358] Consumer harm seems to be a different concept than consumer welfare, as this concept is traditionally understood in economics. The Commission's approach is impressionistic: sometimes the guidance refers to consumer harm, other times to consumer welfare: no definition is provided.[359]

The Commission's Guidance advances a new analytical framework for the identification of an abuse under Article 102 TFEU, based on the concept of 'anti-competitive foreclosure'. This concept appeared in the jargon of the Commission in its Guidelines on non-horizontal mergers in 2004, where the Commission distinguished the concept of 'foreclosure', which is used to describe the restriction of the rivals' access to the market from the concept of 'anti-competitive foreclosure', which denotes exclusion or marginalization of competitors that leads to 'consumer harm' or to some form of 'consumer detriment'.[360] The analytical framework of the Commission is reproduced below:

Communication—Guidance on the Commission's enforcement priorities in applying [Article 102 TFEU] to abusive exclusionary conduct by dominant undertakings [2009] OJ C 45/7

B. Foreclosure leading to consumer harm ('anti-competitive foreclosure')

19. The aim of the Commission's enforcement activity in relation to exclusionary conduct is to ensure that dominant undertakings do not impair effective competition by foreclosing their competitors in an anti-competitive way, thus having an adverse impact on consumer welfare, whether in the form of higher price levels than would have otherwise prevailed or in some other form such as limiting quality or reducing consumer choice. In this document the term "anti-competitive foreclosure" is used to describe a situation where effective access of actual or potential competitors to supplies or markets is hampered or eliminated as a result of the conduct of the dominant undertaking whereby the dominant undertaking is likely to be in a position to profitably increase prices to the detriment of consumers. The identification of likely consumer harm can rely on qualitative and, where possible and appropriate, quantitative evidence. The Commission will address such anti-competitive foreclosure either at the intermediate level or at the level of final consumers, or at both levels.

355 Commission Guidance on Article 102, paras 1 and 9. 356 Ibid, para 12.

357 Ibid, para 30. 358 Ibid, para 5.

359 Y Katsoulacos, 'Some Critical Comments on the Commission's Guidance Paper on Art. 82 EC', *Competition Policy Int'l* (February 2009), section I, available at https://www.competitionpolicyinternational.com/file/view/5806.

360 Guidelines on the assessment of non-horizontal mergers under the Council Regulation on the control of concentrations between undertakings [2008] OJ C 256/6, para 18:

> The term 'foreclosure' will be used to describe any instance where actual or potential rivals' access to supplies or markets is hampered or eliminated as a result of the merger, thereby reducing these companies' ability and/or incentive to compete. As a result of such foreclosure, the merging companies—and, possibly, some of its competitors as well—may be able to profitably increase the price charged to consumers. These instances give rise to a significant impediment to effective competition and are therefore referred to hereafter as 'anticompetitive foreclosure.

20. The Commission will normally intervene under Article [102 TFEU] where, on the basis of cogent and convincing evidence, the allegedly abusive conduct is likely to lead to anti-competitive foreclosure. The Commission considers the following factors to be generally relevant to such an assessment:

- the position of the dominant undertaking: in general, the stronger the dominant position, the higher the likelihood that conduct protecting that position leads to anti-competitive foreclosure,
- the conditions on the relevant market: this includes the conditions of entry and expansion, such as the existence of economies of scale and/or scope and network effects. Economies of scale mean that competitors are less likely to enter or stay in the market if the dominant undertaking forecloses a significant part of the relevant market. Similarly, the conduct may allow the dominant undertaking to 'tip' a market characterised by network effects in its favour or to further entrench its position on such a market. Likewise, if entry barriers in the upstream and/or downstream market are significant, this means that it may be costly for competitors to overcome possible foreclosure through vertical integration,
- the position of the dominant undertaking's competitors: this includes the importance of competitors for the maintenance of effective competition. A specific competitor may play a significant competitive role even if it only holds a small market share compared to other competitors. It may, for example, be the closest competitor to the dominant undertaking, be a particularly innovative competitor, or have the reputation of systematically cutting prices. In its assessment, the Commission may also consider in appropriate cases, on the basis of information available, whether there are realistic, effective and timely counterstrategies that competitors would be likely to deploy,
- the position of the customers or input suppliers: this may include consideration of the possible selectivity of the conduct in question. The dominant undertaking may apply the practice only to selected customers or input suppliers who may be of particular importance for the entry or expansion of competitors, thereby enhancing the likelihood of anti-competitive foreclosure. In the case of customers, they may, for example, be the ones most likely to respond to offers from alternative suppliers, they may represent a particular means of distributing the product that would be suitable for a new entrant, they may be situated in a geographic area well suited to new entry or they may be likely to influence the behaviour of other customers. In the case of input suppliers, those with whom the dominant undertaking has concluded exclusive supply arrangements may be the ones most likely to respond to requests by customers who are competitors of the dominant undertaking in a downstream market, or may produce a grade of the product—or produce at a location—particularly suitable for a new entrant. Any strategies at the disposal of the customers or input suppliers which could help to counter the conduct of the dominant undertaking will also be considered,
- the extent of the allegedly abusive conduct: in general, the higher the percentage of total sales in the relevant market affected by the conduct, the longer its duration, and the more regularly it has been applied, the greater is the likely foreclosure effect,
- possible evidence of actual foreclosure: if the conduct has been in place for a sufficient period of time, the market performance of the dominant undertaking and its competitors may provide direct evidence of anti-competitive foreclosure. For reasons attributable to the allegedly abusive conduct, the market share of the dominant undertaking may have risen or a decline in market share may have been slowed. For similar reasons, actual competitors may have been marginalised or may have exited, or potential competitors may have tried to enter and failed,

> – direct evidence of any exclusionary strategy: this includes internal documents which contain direct evidence of a strategy to exclude competitors, such as a detailed plan to engage in certain conduct in order to exclude a competitor, to prevent entry or to pre-empt the emergence of a market, or evidence of concrete threats of exclusionary action. Such direct evidence may be helpful in interpreting the dominant undertaking's conduct.
>
> 21. When pursuing a case the Commission will develop the analysis of the general factors mentioned in paragraph 20, together with the more specific factors described in the sections dealing with certain types of exclusionary conduct, and any other factors which it may consider to be appropriate. This assessment will usually be made by comparing the actual or likely future situation in the relevant market (with the dominant undertaking's conduct in place) with an appropriate counterfactual, such as the simple absence of the conduct in question or with another realistic alternative scenario, having regard to established business practices.
>
> 22. There may be circumstances where it is not necessary for the Commission to carry out a detailed assessment before concluding that the conduct in question is likely to result in consumer harm. If it appears that the conduct can only raise obstacles to competition and that it creates no efficiencies, its anti-competitive effect may be inferred. This could be the case, for instance, if the dominant undertaking prevents its customers from testing the products of competitors or provides financial incentives to its customers on condition that they do not test such products, or pays a distributor or a customer to delay the introduction of a competitor's product.

To this analytical framework, the Commission added a complementary one for 'price-based exclusionary conduct'. According to the Commission's Guidance on Article 102:

> 23. Vigorous price competition is generally beneficial to consumers. With a view to preventing anti-competitive foreclosure [for price-based exclusionary conduct], the Commission will normally *only* intervene where the conduct concerned has already been or is capable of hampering competition from competitors which are considered to be as efficient as the dominant undertaking.

We have commented previously on the distinction between price and non-price based exclusionary conduct.[361] The Commission introduces a dichotomy in its analytical framework for exclusionary abuses. For non-price exclusionary conduct, the test is that of 'anti-competitive foreclosure'. The Commission looks to the possible effects of the conduct on consumers, by examining a number of variables. From this perspective, even if the conduct can exclude or marginalize a less efficient competitor than the dominant firm, it might be prohibited by Article 102 TFEU in case it worsens the situation of consumers (intermediary or final). Excluding less efficient rivals may produce a negative consumer welfare effect if that removes a competitive constraint on the market power of the defendant and thus allows the defendant to raise prices and reduce consumer surplus while the effects on total surplus are ambiguous.[362]

361 See Section 8.4.2.

362 M de la Mano and B Durand, 'A Three-Step Structured Rule of Reason to Assess Predation under Article 82', Office of the Chief Economist, Discussion Paper (12 December 2005), available at http://ec.europa.eu/dgs/competition/economist/pred_art82.pdf; SC Salop, 'Exclusionary Conduct, Effect on Consumers, and the Flawed Profit-Sacrifice Standard' (2006) 73 *Antitrust LJ* 311, 328.

In contrast, for price-based exclusionary conduct, the Commission introduces an efficiency filter, based on a price–cost test. According to the Commission's Guidance on Article 102:

> 27. If the data clearly suggest that an equally efficient competitor can compete effectively with the pricing conduct of the dominant undertaking, the Commission will, in principle, infer that the dominant undertaking's pricing conduct is not likely to have an adverse impact on effective competition, and thus on consumers, and will therefore be unlikely to intervene. If, on the contrary, the data suggest that the price charged by the dominant undertaking has the potential to foreclose equally efficient competitors, then the Commission will integrate this in the general assessment of anti-competitive foreclosure, taking into account other relevant quantitative and/or qualitative evidence.

However, the 'as efficient competitor' test introduced by the Commission in this paragraph does not establish a safe harbour for dominant firms. The Guidance also notes the following:

> 24. [. . .] the Commission recognises that in certain circumstances a less efficient competitor may also exert a constraint which should be taken into account when considering whether particular price-based conduct leads to anti-competitive foreclosure. The Commission will take a dynamic view of that constraint, given that in the absence of an abusive practice such a competitor may benefit from demand-related advantages, such as network and learning effects, which will tend to enhance its efficiency.

This is compatible with some case law of the Court of Justice of the EU that found that even prices above costs might lead to anti-competitive foreclosure in specific circumstances.[363]

The Google Search *case of the Commission in 2017*

The recent *Google Search* case of the Commission is remarkable in the sense that although it may be considered as focusing on the effects of the specific conduct in question, it does not seem to be inspired by the principle of economic efficiency, as the Commission's Guidance on Article 102, but by that of equality of opportunity.[364]

The European Commission initiated in November 2010 an investigation against Google's parent company, Alphabet, with regard to its general search results on its search engine Google. Relying on a large body of evidence, the Commission issued a decision in June 2017 finding that Google has abused its market dominance as a search engine by giving an illegal advantage to another Google product, its comparison shopping service and fining Alphabet €2.42 billion, the largest fine in EU competition law history.[365]

This case is the most significant episode so far in the Google Search investigation saga, following the initiation of the investigation in November 2010, the first statement of objections sent to Alphabet in April 2015,[366] the commitments offered by Google apparently not fully

363 Joined Cases C-395–6/96 P, *Compagnie Maritime Belge Transports SA v Commission* [2000] ECR I–1365. For an analysis of above-cost predation, see Chapter 9.

364 See our analysis of this principle in Chapter 2.

365 *Google Search (Shopping)* (Case AT.39740) Commission Decision (26 June 2017), available at http://ec.europa.eu/competition/elojade/isef/case_details.cfm?proc_code=1_39740.

366 Ibid.

addressing the Commission's concerns.[367] The Commission sent a supplementary Statement of Objections in July 2016. During these different steps of the procedure Google opposed these allegations by putting forward the argument that it is not in its interests to bias the presentation of search results, as end users may detect this reduction of the quality of the search engine (in terms of relevance) and then turn to competing search engines, a claim that has been questioned by some authors as the reduction of the quality of search may not be detectable to consumers and the two-sided nature of the market may reinforce these quality effects.[368]

Relying on Google's high market shares which exceeded 90 per cent in most countries, the Commission found that Google was dominant in general Internet search markets in all thirty-one countries of the European Economic Area (EEA), since 2008, with the exception of the Czech Republic where it has been dominant since 2011.[369] It was also noted that almost 90 per cent of Google's revenues stem from adverts, such as those it shows consumers in response to a search query, which indicates that the Commission took into account the paying side of the platform, thus connecting market share on the search side with revenues on the advertising side.[370] The Commission also found that there are also high barriers to entry in these markets, in part because of network effects, as the more consumers use a search engine, the more attractive it becomes to advertisers, the profits generated being used to attract even more consumers. The Commission also noted the importance of the data a search engine gathers about consumers, which can in turn be used to improve results and thus make the search engine more attractive to them.

Google's abusive conduct concerned the 'separate market of comparison shopping in Europe', to which it first entered in 2004. Its 'Google Shopping' website offered consumers the opportunity to compare products and prices online and find deals from online retailers of all types, including online shops of manufacturers, platforms (such as Amazon and eBay), and other re-sellers. Despite the fact that Google's comparison shopping business' performance was relatively poor, according to the Commission, Google was able to reverse that trend and attract considerable traffic as it began in 2008 to implement in European markets a fundamental change in strategy to push its comparison shopping service. Attracting traffic is, of course, very important, since it brings bigger advertising revenue. The Commission found that this strategy relied on Google's dominance in general Internet search, instead of competition on the merits in comparison shopping markets and apparently involved the following conduct:

- Google has, according to the Commission, systematically given prominent placement to its own comparison-shopping service, its results being displayed at or near the top of the search results.
- Google has allegedly included a number of criteria in its generic search algorithms, as a result of which rival comparison shopping services were demoted in its search results. In contrast, Google's own comparison-shopping service were not subject to Google's generic search algorithms, and thus were not subject to such demotions.[371]

367 See European Commission (EC), Commitments in Case COMP/C-3/39740 (3 April 2013); EC, 'Antitrust: Commission Obtains from Google Comparable Display of Specialised Search Rivals', MEMO/14/87 (5 February 2014).

368 I Lianos and E Motchenkova, 'Market Dominance and Search Quality in the Search Engine Market' (2013) 9(2) *J Competition L & Economics* 419.

369 On dominance and market shares, see *Google Search (Shopping)* (Case AT.39740) Commission Decision (26 June 2017), paras 271–84.

370 Ibid, paras 7.2 and 344.

371 Ibid, paras 344 and 512.

As a result of these practices, Google's comparison shopping service became much more visible to consumers in Google's search results, whilst rival comparison shopping services were much less visible. As the Commission found evidence showing that consumers click far more often on results that are more visible, that is the results appearing higher up in Google's search results, this being particularly the case on mobile devices given the much smaller screen size, Google's alleged conduct conferred to its own comparison shopping service a significant competitive advantage compared to rivals.

Noting the special responsibility of dominant undertakings not to abuse their powerful market position by restricting competition, either in the market where they are dominant or in separate markets, the Commission found that Google's conduct amounted to an abuse of Google's dominant position in general Internet search.[372] According to the Commission:

> The Conduct is abusive because it constitutes a practice falling outside the scope of competition on the merits as it: (i) diverts traffic in the sense that it decreases traffic from Google's general search results pages to competing comparison shopping services and increases traffic from Google's general search results pages to Google's own comparison shopping service; and (ii) is capable of having, or likely to have, anti-competitive effects in the national markets for comparison shopping services and general search services.[373]

In its decision the Commission seems to focus on both the form of the conduct in question, which consisted in leveraging and discrimination, and on its effects on the Google's rivals.

According to the Commission, '(a) system of undistorted competition can be guaranteed only if equality of opportunity is secured as between the various economic operators'.[374] The Commission focused on market structure holding that Article 102 not only prohibits abusive practices 'which may cause damage to consumers directly, but also those which harm them indirectly through their impact on an effective competition structure'.[375] It then emphasized the form of the conduct, noting hat Article 102 TFEU 'not only' prohibits practices by an undertaking in a dominant position which tend to strengthen that position, but also the conduct of an undertaking with a dominant position in a given market that tends to extend that position to a neighbouring but separate market by distorting competition',[376] noting that it is not necessary that the dominance, the abuse and the effects of the abuse are all in the same market'.[377]

With regard to effects, the Commission first noted that Article 102 TFEU prohibits 'behaviour that tends to restrict competition or is capable of having that effect, regardless of its success' and that occurs 'not only where access to the market is made impossible for competitors, but also where the conduct of the dominant undertaking is capable of making that access more difficult, thus causing interference with the structure of competition on the market'. Although this seems at first sight as aiming to protect competitors, the Commission noting that 'competitors should be able to compete on the merits for the entire market and not just for a part of it', it could also benefit consumers, the Commission also observing that '[c]ustomers and users should have the opportunity to benefit from whatever degree of competition is possible on the market'.[378] The Commission found that Google's conduct had stifled competition on the merits in comparison shopping markets, by decreasing in

372 Ibid, para 331. 373 Ibid, para 341. 374 Ibid, para 331. 375 Ibid, para 332.
376 Ibid, para 334. 377 Ibid. 378 Ibid, para 339.

generic search traffic from Google's general search results pages to almost all competing comparison shopping services,[379] which accounted for a large proportion of traffic to competing comparison shopping services, and had allowed Google's comparison shopping service to make significant gains in traffic at the expense of its rivals, which have suffered very substantial losses of traffic on a lasting basis,[380] as they were not able to find viable alternatives to replace generic search traffic from Google's general search result pages. The conduct was also to the detriment of European consumers as it deprived them, according to the Commission, of 'genuine choice and innovation'.[381] We explore in more detail the Commission's approach in Chapter 9.

In addition to the €2.42 billion fine, calculated on the basis of the value of Google's revenue from its comparison shopping service in the countries affected, the Commission also required Google to stop its illegal conduct within 90 days of the decision and refrain from any measure that has the same or an equivalent object or effect. What is particularly significant is that the decision orders Google to comply with the simple principle of giving equal treatment to rival comparison shopping services and its own service, meaning that 'Google has to apply the same processes and methods to position and display rival comparison shopping services in Google's search results pages as it gives to its own comparison shopping service.'[382]

8.4.5.3.3. The case law of the European Courts post-Guidance on Article 102

In a number of subsequent recent judgments, most of them relating to decisions of the Commission adopted before the publication of the Commission's Guidance on Article 102, the CJEU and the General Court confirmed that a shift towards a 'consumer welfare' approach is not to be expected any time soon. The Courts took care not to employ the term of 'consumer welfare', preferring that of detriment to consumers, and used language that would indicate an effort of synthesis between the three different approaches previously mentioned.

Konkurrensverket v TeliaSonera

In *Konkurrensverket v TeliaSonera*, the CJEU was seized by a preliminary ruling on the interpretation of Article 102 TFEU with regard to a pricing practice imposed by TeliaSonera, a vertically integrated Swedish fixed telephony network operator. The practice consisted in applying a spread between the sale price of ADSL input services intended for wholesale users and the sale prices of broadband connection services offered by TeliaSonera to end users, with the result that the retail price was not sufficient to cover the costs TeliaSonera itself had to incur in order to distribute those broadband connection services to the end users.[383]

379 Ibid, para 462. 380 Ibid, paras 342 and 462.

381 This is mentioned in the press release published by the Commission: European Commission, 'Antitrust: Commission fines Google €2.42 Billion for Abusing Dominance as Search Engine by Giving Illegal Advantage to own Comparison Shopping Service', Press Release (27 June 2017), available at http://europa.eu/rapid/press-release_IP-17-1784_en.htm. In the text of the decision, the only clear reference to consumer harm is included in *Google Search (Shopping)* (Case AT.39740) Commission Decision (26 June 2017), para 593, where it is noted that the conduct 'has the potential to foreclose competing comparison shopping services, which may lead to higher fees for merchants, higher prices for consumers, and less innovation'.

382 Ibid, paras 699 and 700.

383 Case C-52/09, *Konkurrenverket v TeliaSonera Sverige AB* [2011] ECR I–527.

Case C-52/09, *Konkurrenverket v TeliaSonera Sverige AB*
[2011] ECR I–527 (some references omitted)

The objectives of Article 102 TFEU

21. Article 102 TFEU is one of the competition rules referred to in Article 3(1)(b) TFEU which are necessary for the functioning of that internal market.

22. The function of those rules is precisely to prevent competition from being distorted to the detriment of the public interest, individual undertakings and consumers, thereby ensuring the well-being of the European Union. [. . .]

24. Accordingly, Article 102 TFEU must be interpreted as referring not only to practices which may cause damage to consumers directly, but also to those which are detrimental to them through their impact on competition. Whilst Article 102 TFEU does not prohibit an undertaking from acquiring, on its own merits, the dominant position in a market, and while, a fortiori, a finding that an undertaking has a dominant position is not in itself a ground of criticism of the undertaking concerned, it remains the case that, in accordance with settled case-law, an undertaking which holds a dominant position has a special responsibility not to allow its conduct to impair genuine undistorted competition in the internal market. [. . .]

27. The concept of abuse of a dominant position prohibited by that provision is an objective concept relating to the conduct of a dominant undertaking which, on a market where the degree of competition is already weakened precisely because of the presence of the undertaking concerned, through recourse to methods different from those governing normal competition in products or services on the basis of the transactions of commercial operators, has the effect of hindering the maintenance of the degree of competition still existing in the market or the growth of that competition.

28. In order to determine whether the dominant undertaking has abused its position by the pricing practices it applies, it is necessary to consider all the circumstances and to investigate whether the practice tends to remove or restrict the buyer's freedom to choose his sources of supply, to bar competitors from access to the market, to apply dissimilar conditions to equivalent transactions with other trading parties, or to strengthen the dominant position by distorting competition. [. . .]

The CJEU adopted the as efficient competitor test focusing its attention on the exclusionary effect which a practice may create for competitors who are at least as efficient as the dominant company.

40. Where an undertaking introduces a pricing policy intended to drive from the market competitors who are perhaps as efficient as that dominant undertaking but who, because of their smaller financial resources, are incapable of withstanding the competition waged against them that undertaking is, accordingly, abusing its dominant position.

The price cost test

41. In order to assess the lawfulness of the pricing policy applied by a dominant undertaking, reference should be made, as a general rule, to pricing criteria based on the costs incurred by the dominant undertaking itself and on its strategy (see, to that effect, Case C-62/86 *AKZO* v *Commission* [1991] ECR I–3359, paragraph 74, and *France Télécom* v *Commission*, paragraph 108).

This test relates to the emphasis put on the actual or potential exclusion of as efficient as competitors. (This test is examined further in Section 8.4.5.3.2.)

Special responsibility

53. The special responsibility which a dominant undertaking has not to allow its conduct to impair genuine undistorted competition in the internal market concerns specifically the conduct, by commission or omission, which that undertaking decides on its own initiative to adopt.

Classification of abuses

54. TeliaSonera maintains, in that regard, that, in order specifically to protect the economic initiative of dominant undertakings, they should remain free to fix their terms of trade, unless those terms are so disadvantageous for those entering into contracts with them that those terms may be regarded, in the light of the relevant criteria set out in Case C-7/97 *Bronner* [1998] ECR I–7791, as entailing a refusal to supply.

55. Such an interpretation is based on a misunderstanding of that judgment. In particular, it cannot be inferred from paragraphs 48 and 49 of that judgment that the conditions to be met in order to establish that a refusal to supply is abusive must necessarily also apply when assessing the abusive nature of conduct which consists in supplying services or selling goods on conditions which are disadvantageous or on which there might be no purchaser.

Actual or potential effects?

This aspect is examined in Section 9.4.3.2.

The importance of market strength

78. The referring court seeks to ascertain, fourthly, whether the degree of market dominance held by the undertaking concerned is relevant to establishing whether the pricing practice in question constitutes an abuse.

79. As stated in paragraph 23 of this judgment, the dominant position referred to in Article 102 TFEU relates to a position of economic strength enjoyed by an undertaking which enables it to prevent effective competition being maintained on the relevant market by affording it the power to behave to an appreciable extent independently of its competitors, its customers and ultimately of consumers.

80. Accordingly, that provision, as stated by the Advocate General in point 41 of his Opinion, does not envisage any variation in form or degree in the concept of a dominant position. Where an undertaking has an economic strength such as that required by Article 102 TFEU to establish that it holds a dominant position in a particular market, its conduct must be assessed in the light of that provision.

81. Of course, that does not mean that an undertaking's strength is not relevant to the assessment of the lawfulness of the conduct in the market of such an undertaking in the light of Article 102 TFEU. The Court itself has based its analyses on the fact that an undertaking enjoyed a position of super-dominance or a quasi-monopoly. Nonetheless the degree of market strength is, as a general rule, significant in relation

to the extent of the effects of the conduct of the undertaking concerned rather than in relation to the question of whether the abuse as such exists.

82. It follows that the application of a pricing practice resulting in margin squeeze by an undertaking may constitute an abuse of a dominant position where that undertaking has such a position, and, as a general rule, the degree of dominance in the market concerned is not relevant in that regard.

Causality between dominance and abuse

This aspect is examined in Section 8.4.4.

No predation test

This aspect is examined in Section 8.4.5.3.2.

New technologies and the enforcement of Article 102 TFEU

104. The eighth and last issue raised by the Stockholms tingsrätt concerns the relevance, for that same purpose, of the fact that the markets concerned are growing rapidly and involve new technology which requires high levels of investment.

105. In that regard, it must first be observed that the degree to which the markets affected by the exploitation of an undertaking's dominant position are mature is not a point on which Article 102 TFEU makes any distinction.

106. Next, in a rapidly growing market, the competitive advantage flowing from the possession of a dominant position in a second neighbouring market may distort the course of competition in the first market, taking into consideration the fact that in that first market, as stated by TeliaSonera itself, the operators may be inclined to operate for some time at a loss or while accepting lower levels of profitability.

107. It is in precisely such circumstances that the further reduction in the ability of an operator to trade profitably which results from the squeeze of his margins imposed by the pricing practice at issue may prevent the establishment or development on the market concerned of normal conditions of competition.

108. Moreover, taking into account the objective of the competition rules, as stated in paragraph 22 of this judgment, their application cannot depend on whether the market concerned has already reached a certain level of maturity. Particularly in a rapidly growing market, Article 102 TFEU requires action as quickly as possible, to prevent the formation and consolidation in that market of a competitive structure distorted by the abusive strategy of an undertaking which has a dominant position on that market or on a closely linked neighbouring market, in other words it requires action before the anti-competitive effects of that strategy are realised.

109. That is therefore all the more true of a market, such as that of supplying high speed internet access services, which is closely linked to another market, such as the local loop access market in the telecommunications sector. Not only is that market in no way new or emerging, but its competitive structure is also still highly influenced by the former monopolistic structure. The possibility that undertakings may exploit their dominant position in that market in such a way as to impair the development of competition in a rapidly growing neighbouring market means that no derogation from the application of Article 102 TFEU can be tolerated. [. . .]

NOTES AND QUESTIONS ON TELIA SONERA

1. The General Court also applied the 'as efficient competitor' test to a margin squeeze case in *Kingdom of Spain v Commission.*[384] This case followed up an appeal by Spain against a decision of the Commission finding Telefonica to have abused its dominant position by applying tariffs to the supply of wholesale broadband access that squeezed its competitors out of the retail broadband access services market. The Court also considered the argument that the Commission should have applied the *Oscar Bronner* criteria for refusals to supply, such as the indispensability of access test:

   73. [. . .] [W]hile the Kingdom of Spain claims that, if the margin between the national and regional wholesale products, on the one hand, and the retail product, on the other, was so close that it amounted to being negative, with the result that no other operator could use those wholesale products, the conduct under examination ought then to be analysed as a refusal of access which should then be regarded as abusive only by reference to the criteria stated in Case C-7/97 *Bronner* [1998] ECR I–7791, such an argument must also fail.

   74. The Court of Justice has made it clear that it cannot be inferred from *Bronner* that the conditions to be met in order to establish that a refusal to supply is abusive must necessarily also apply when assessing the abusive nature of conduct which consists in supplying services or selling goods on conditions which are disadvantageous or on which there might be no purchaser. Such conduct may, in itself, constitute an independent form of abuse distinct from that of refusal to supply.

   75. If *Bronner* were to be interpreted otherwise, that would amount to a requirement that before any conduct of a dominant undertaking in relation to its terms of trade could be regarded as abusive the conditions to be met to establish that there was a refusal to supply would in every case have to be satisfied, and that would unduly reduce the effectiveness of Article [102 TFEU].

2. The case also contains some interesting developments on the requirement to prove actual anti-competitive effects:

   90. The effect referred to in the case-law cited in the preceding paragraph does not necessarily relate to the actual effect of the abusive conduct complained of. For the purposes of establishing an infringement of Article [102 TFEU], it is sufficient to show that the abusive conduct of the undertaking in a dominant position tends to restrict competition or, in other words, that the conduct is capable of having, or likely to have, that effect. The pricing practice concerned must have an anti-competitive effect on the market, but the effect does not necessarily have to be concrete, and it is sufficient to demonstrate that there is an anti-competitive effect which may potentially exclude competitors who are at least as efficient as the dominant undertaking.

   91. It is apparent from the case-law of the Court of Justice, cited in paragraph 51 above that, in order to determine whether the undertaking in a dominant position has abused such a position by its pricing practices, it is necessary to consider all the circumstances and to investigate whether the practice tends to remove or restrict the buyer's freedom to choose his sources of supply, to bar competitors from

[384] Case T-398/07, *Kingdom of Spain v European Commission*, ECLI:EU:T:2012:173, para 68.

access to the market, to apply dissimilar conditions to equivalent transactions with other trading parties, thereby placing them at a competitive disadvantage, or to strengthen the dominant position by distorting competition.

92. Since Article [102 TFEU] thus refers not only to practices which may cause damage to consumers directly, but also to those which are detrimental to them through their impact on competition, a dominant undertaking has a special responsibility not to allow its conduct to impair genuine undistorted competition on the common market.

93. It follows from this that Article [102 TFEU] prohibits a dominant undertaking from, inter alia, adopting pricing practices which have an exclusionary effect on its equally efficient actual or potential competitors, that is to say practices which are capable of making market entry very difficult or impossible for such competitors, and of making it more difficult or impossible for its co-contractors to choose between various sources of supply or commercial partners, thereby strengthening its dominant position by using methods other than those which come within the scope of competition on the merits. From that point of view, therefore, not all competition by means of price can be regarded as legitimate.

It is noteworthy that the Court rejects any requirement of evidence of actual or concrete anti-competitive effects, but also insists on the need for the plaintiff to prove that the practice of the dominant firm would potentially exclude competitors who are at least as efficient as the dominant undertaking.

Post Danmark v Konkurrecerädet (Post Danmark I)

In a preliminary ruling case in *Post Danmark v Konkurrecerädet*, the CJEU had to examine a targeted policy of price reductions, practised by Post Danmark, a dominant firm on the Danish market for the distribution of unaddressed mail, with the aim to ensure the loyalty of its customers.[385] These prices did not allow Post Danmark to cover its average total costs, although it allowed it to cover its average incremental costs. Post Danmark brought an against the decision of the national court claiming that the practice could be considered an abuse only if the plaintiff proved that the dominant firm had the intention to drive a competitor from the market, relying on the authority of the *AKZO* case of the Court on predatory pricing. In essence, Post Danmark was requiring the application of the predatory standard based on *AKZO*, which, according to its interpretation, required evidence of anti-competitive intent for Article 102 TFEU to apply. The Court relied on the language of the *TeliaSonera* case and the as efficient competitor test:

21. [i]t is in no way the purpose of Article [102 TFEU] to prevent an undertaking from acquiring, on its own merits, the dominant position on a market. Nor does that provision seek to ensure that competitors less efficient than the undertaking with the dominant position should remain on the market.

22. Thus, not every exclusionary effect is necessarily detrimental to competition. Competition on the merits may, by definition, lead to the departure from the market or the marginalisation of competitors that are less efficient and so less attractive to consumers from the point of view of, among other things, price, choice, quality or innovation.

385 Case C-209/10, *Post Danmark I*, ECLI:EU:C:2012:172.

Although the Court also repeated that 'a dominant undertaking has a special responsibility not to allow its behaviour to impair genuine undistorted competition on the internal market',[386] it also held that

> 25. Article [102 TFEU] prohibits a dominant undertaking from, among other things, adopting pricing practices that have an exclusionary effect on competitors considered to be as efficient as it is itself and strengthening its dominant position by using methods other than those that are part of competition on the merits. Accordingly, in that light, not all competition by means of price may be regarded as legitimate.

The protection of the 'buyer's freedom as regards choice of sources of supply' or the protection of competitors' access to the market, were among the elements examined by the Court.[387] The Court gave a particular emphasis on the possibility for a competitor as efficient as the dominant undertaking 'to compete with those prices without suffering losses that are unsustainable in the long run'.[388]

Tomra v Commission

In *Tomra* the CJEU reviewed a decision of the Commission finding Tomra had abused its dominant position by implementing an exclusionary strategy involving exclusivity agreements, individualized quantity commitments and individualized retroactive rebates.[389] The Commission found that the rebates were granted for individualized quantities corresponding to the entire or almost entire demand, that they were established on the basis of the customer's estimated requirements and/or purchasing volumes achieved in the past and that they induced the customer to purchase all or virtually all its requirements from Tomra. The judgment of the Court includes some useful information on the role of intent in defining the existence of an abuse:

> 19. It must be observed in that regard that where the Commission undertakes an assessment of the conduct of an undertaking in a dominant position, that assessment being an essential prerequisite of a finding that there is an abuse of such a position, the Commission is necessarily required to assess the business strategy pursued by that undertaking. For that purpose, it is clearly legitimate for the Commission to refer to subjective factors, namely the motives underlying the business strategy in question.
>
> 20. Accordingly, the existence of any anti-competitive intent constitutes only one of a number of facts which may be taken into account in order to determine that a dominant position has been abused.
>
> 21. However, the Commission is under no obligation to establish the existence of such intent on the part of the dominant undertaking in order to render Article [102 TFEU] applicable.
>
> 22. In that regard, the General Court correctly stated, in paragraph 36 of the judgment under appeal, that it was perfectly legitimate for the contested decision to concentrate primarily on Tomra's anti-competitive conduct, since it was precisely that conduct which it was the Commission's task to establish. The existence of an intention to compete on the merits, even if it were established, could not prove the absence of abuse.

[386] Ibid, para 23. [387] Ibid, para 26. [388] Ibid, para 38.

[389] Case C-549/10, *Tomra Systems ASA v Commission*, ECLI:EU:C:2012:221.

Post Danmark A/S v Konkurrencerådet (Post Danmark II)

The case involved conditional, standardized (as they were based on the volume supplied, all customers being entitled to receive the same rebate on the basis of their aggregate purchases over an annual reference period) and retroactive volume rebates offered in 2007 and 2008 by Post Danmark, the Danish postal incumbent, which was responsible for the one-day delivery universal postal service, throughout Danish territory, for letters and parcels, including bulk mail, to its direct-mail customers.[390] Allegedly, this had contributed to the exit of Bring Citymail, which was its only serious competitor on the bulk mail market.

The CJEU started with a categorical approach, noting that the rebate scheme at issue was not a simple quantity rebate, which linked solely to the volume of purchases, since the rebates at issue were not granted in respect of each individual order, thus corresponding to the cost savings made by the supplier, but on the basis of the aggregate orders placed over a given period.[391] It then noted that '[h]aving regard to the particularities of the present case, it is also necessary to take into account, in examining *all the relevant circumstances*, the extent of Post Danmark's dominant position and the particular conditions of competition prevailing on the relevant market'.[392] The Court then proceeded in specifying the relevant test holding that

> it first has to be determined whether those rebates can produce an exclusionary effect, that is to say whether they are capable, first, of making market entry very difficult or impossible for competitors of the undertaking in a dominant position and, secondly, of making it more difficult or impossible for the co-contractors of that undertaking to choose between various sources of supply or commercial partners' and it 'then has to be examined whether there is an objective economic justification for the discounts granted.[393]

This may look like accepting to analyse the effects of the conduct, however the CJEU's 'exclusionary effect' analysis relies on categorical thinking, the Court making inferences as to the existence of an exclusionary effect from the characteristics of the rebates (the fact that they are retroactive, that they do not relate solely to the growth in purchases of products of that undertaking made by those co-contractors during the period under consideration, but extend also to those purchases in aggregate, or the fact that they are standardized).

The analysis then turns structural, the Court noting that Post Danmark held 95 per cent of that market, a very high share protected by high barriers and which was characterised by the existence of significant economies of scale, also finding that Post Danmark enjoyed structural advantages because of its statutory monopoly, concluding that competition on that market was already very limited.[394] The 'impact on the market' of the scheme is also assumed from the fact that it covers the majority of customers on the market, this bearing out bear out the likelihood of an anti-competitive exclusionary effect, although the CJEU is also careful to note that this does not in itself constitute evidence of abusive conduct by that undertaking.[395] The Court also accepts that the dominant undertaking may put forward objective justifications, counterbalancing, or outweighing the exclusionary effects.[396] Yet, the CJEU refuses to consider as necessary to perform a price-cost test in order to determine if the excluded competitors were as efficient as the dominant undertaking, holding that 'prices below cost prices,

390 Case C-23/14 P, *Post Danmark II*, ECLI:EU:C:2015:651. 391 Ibid, para 28.
392 Ibid, para 30. See also ibid, para 29 (emphasis added). 393 Ibid, para 31.
394 Ibid, paras 39–41. 395 Ibid, paras 44–6. 396 Ibid, para 48.

to customers is not a prerequisite of a finding that a retroactive rebate scheme operated by a dominant undertaking is abusive.'[397]

However, this does not mean that the as efficient as competitor test is outright rejected by the CJEU, as it takes care to note that its conclusion with regard to the relevance of the test in this case 'ought not to have the effect of excluding, on principle, recourse to the as-efficient-competitor test in cases involving a rebate scheme for the purposes of examining its compatibility with Article [102 TFEU].'[398] It is therefore the facts of the specific case, in which the dominant undertaking held a very large market share and benefitted from structural advantages, and the scope of the rebate which applied to 70 per cent of mail on the relevant market, that made the CJEU conclude that 'the as-efficient-competitor test is of no relevance inasmuch as the structure of the market makes the emergence of an as-efficient competitor practically impossible.'[399] After all, '[t]he as-efficient-competitor test [AEC test] must thus be regarded as one tool amongst others for the purposes of assessing whether there is an abuse of a dominant position in the context of a rebate scheme.'[400]

The language of the CJEU may sound like music to the ears of the proponents of the 'effects-based' approach. In the final part of the judgment, the CJEU notes with regard to the evidence of the exclusionary effect and ultimately of the abuse that 'in order to establish whether such a practice is abusive, that practice must have an anti-competitive effect on the market, but the effect does not necessarily have to be concrete, and it is sufficient to demonstrate that there is an anti-competitive effect which may potentially exclude competitors who are at least as efficient as the dominant undertaking', the Court further explaining that '[s]uch an assessment seeks to determine whether the conduct of the dominant undertaking produces an actual or likely exclusionary effect, to the detriment of competition and, thereby, of consumers' interests.'[401] However, this part also includes some language that indicates that the Court may maintain its loyalties to the more 'formalistic' approach, or at least rejects the option of a purely quantitative 'effects-based' approach. For instance, the scope seems to take a broad view of what may constitute an exclusionary effect, as it simply rejects 'purely hypothetical'[402] anti-competitive effects, but seems to be open to anything more than that, the Court indicating that it is important to examine 'whether that rebate tends to remove or restrict the buyer's freedom to choose his sources of supply, to bar competitors from access to the market, to apply dissimilar conditions to equivalent transactions with other trading parties or to strengthen the dominant position by distorting competition.'[403] This tendency is confirmed in the last part of the judgment that deals with the existence of a 'serious or appreciable nature of the anticompetitive effect'. The CJEU is clear in rejecting such an additional evidential requirement, which could be interpreted as a *de minimis* threshold in the context of Article 102 TFEU. First, such a requirement may create tensions with the fact that 'a dominant undertaking has a special responsibility not to allow its behaviour to impair genuine, undistorted competition on the internal market.'[404] Second, 'since the structure of competition on the market has already been weakened by the presence of the dominant undertaking, *any* further weakening of the structure of competition may constitute an abuse of a dominant position.'[405] Consequently, 'fixing an appreciability (*de minimis*) threshold for the purposes of determining whether there is an abuse of a dominant position is not justified' as '[t]hat anticompetitive practice is, by its very nature, liable to give rise to not insignificant restrictions

[397] Ibid, para 56. [398] Ibid, para 58. [399] Ibid, paras 59–60. [400] Ibid, para 61.
[401] Ibid, paras 66 and 69. [402] Ibid, para 65. [403] Ibid, para 64. [404] Ibid, para 71.
[405] Ibid, para 72 (emphasis added).

of competition, or even of eliminating competition on the market on which the undertaking concerned operates'.[406] The last paragraph of the judgment adds the final nail in the coffin of a purely quantitative 'effects-based approach, noting that 'the anticompetitive effect of a rebate scheme operated by a dominant undertaking must be probable, there being no need to show that it is of a serious or appreciable nature'.[407] However, the judgment of the CJEU in *Post Danmark* does not seem to reject a qualitative 'effects-based' approach, which would not necessarily require a quantitative assessment of the welfare effects of the conduct to consumers' interests, or more broadly to the competitive process.

Intel v Commission

The General Court's judgment

In its judgment on the *Intel* case, the General Court seems to have backtracked from the trend inaugurated in the most recent case law of the Court of Justice to inject some form of economic reasoning inspired by the neoclassical price theory paradigm in the assessment of abusive conduct.[408] The case involved an action for annulment by Intel of the decision of the European Commission declaring its rebate system and payments made to original equipment manufacturers (OEMs) as constituting conditional rebates and 'naked restrictions' infringing Article 1022 TFEU and imposing fines. The case will be considered in more detail in the next Chapter.

The General Court characterized the rebates as being 'de facto conditional' upon the OEMs purchasing all or almost all of their requirements in central processing units (CPUs) of the x86 architecture, the relevant product market at least in a certain segment, from Intel. Drawing on the previous case law of the CJEU in *Michelin I* and *British Airways*,[409] the General Court held that '[a]s regards in particular whether the grant of a rebate by an undertaking in a dominant position can be characterised as abusive, a distinction should be drawn between three categories of rebates', thus adopting an approach based on categorical thinking.[410]

In particular, the Court distinguished between (i) quantity rebate systems ('quantity rebates'), which are linked solely to the volume of purchases made from an undertaking occupying a dominant position and which are generally considered not to have the foreclosure effect prohibited by Article 102 TFEU, as they are deemed to reflect gains in efficiency and economies of scale made by the undertaking in a dominant position; (ii) exclusivity or 'fidelity' rebates, that is rebates the grant of which is conditional on the customer's obtaining all or most of its requirements from the undertaking in a dominant position; (iii) other rebate systems where the grant of a financial incentive is not directly linked to a condition of exclusive or quasi-exclusive supply from the undertaking in a dominant position, but where the mechanism for granting the rebate may also have a fidelity-building effect ('rebates falling within the third category').[411] That category of rebates includes *inter alia* rebate systems depending on the attainment of individual sales objectives which do not constitute exclusivity rebates, since those systems do not contain any obligation to obtain all or a given proportion of supplies from the dominant undertaking. According to the GC, in examining whether the application of such a rebate constitutes an abuse of dominant position, it is necessary to

406 Ibid, para 73. 407 Ibid, para 74.

408 Case T-286/09, *Intel Corp v European Commission*, ECLI:EU:T:2014:547.

409 Case 322/81, *Michelin I* [1983] ECR 3461, paras 71–3; Case C-95/04 P, *British Airways v Commission* [2007] ECR I-2331, paras 62–3, 65, 67–8.

410 Case T-286/09, *Intel Corp v European Commission*, ECLI:EU:T:2014:547, para 74.

411 Ibid, paras 75–9.

consider *all* the circumstances, particularly the criteria and rules governing the grant of the rebate, and to investigate whether, in providing an advantage not based on any economic service justifying it, that rebate tends to remove or restrict the buyer's freedom to choose his sources of supply, to bar competitors from access to the market, or to strengthen the dominant position by distorting competition. According to the Court, 'the question whether an exclusivity rebate can be categorised as abusive does not depend on an analysis of the circumstances of the case aimed at establishing a potential foreclosure effect'.[412]

The Court characterized the rebates offered by Intel to the OEMs as rebates falling within the second category, namely exclusivity rebates, as those rebates were conditional upon customers' purchasing from Intel, at least in a certain segment, either all their x86 CPU requirements, or most of their requirements, in this case between 95 per cent and 80 per cent. It concluded that that type of rebate constituted an abuse of a dominant position if there was no objective justification for granting it. The GC refused to assess *all* the circumstances of the case, noting that this is necessary only in the case of rebates falling within the third category,[413] but not in the case of exclusivity rebates falling within the second category.[414] The explanation provided by the GC exemplifies the categorical approach inspiring the judgment, the GC noting that 'exclusivity rebates granted by an undertaking in a dominant position are by their very nature capable of restricting competition,'[415] as 'the capability of tying customers to the undertaking in a dominant position is inherent in exclusivity rebates',[416] and moreover 'exclusivity rebates granted by an undertaking in a dominant position are by their very nature capable of foreclosing competitors', as the 'financial advantage granted for the purpose of inducing a customer to obtain all or most of its requirements from the undertaking in a dominant position means that that customer has an incentive not to obtain, in respect of the part of its requirements concerned by the exclusivity condition, supplies from competitors of the undertaking in a dominant position'.[417] The Court then examined the positive effects of exclusivity conditions but dismissed them altogether from the analysis. Note that the GC compared this approach with the more 'effects-based' approach it follows in exclusive dealing cases in the context of Article 101 TFEU, such as *Delimitis*, the Court noting that this more favourable approach to exclusivity cannot be transposed in the context of Article 102 TFEU.[418] Again, the special responsibility of dominant undertakings was put forward as a justification for this more aggressive approach in order to protect the 'structure of competition on the market' from further interference. The GC very clearly rejected the need to prove actual anti-competitive effects, the GC making it clear that the 'Commission must only show that a practice is capable of restricting competition,'[419] and is not required to prove direct damage to consumers or a causal link between such damage and the practices at issue.[420] According to the GC, the Commission is not required to demonstrate the foreclosure capability of exclusivity rebates on a case-by-case basis for exclusivity rebates,[421] and for this reason recourse to the as efficient competitor test is not necessary. But the GC goes even further and challenges the essentiality of performing the AEC test, even in the case of rebates falling within the third category, for which an examination of the circumstances of the case is necessary, noting that the case law of the CJEU (referring to *Michelin I*) accepts the characterization of a rebate as being a 'loyalty' rebate 'without requiring proof, by means of a quantitative test, that competitors had been forced to sell at a loss in order to be able to compensate the rebates falling

[412] Ibid, para 80. [413] Ibid, para 82. [414] Ibid, para 84. [415] Ibid, para 85.
[416] Ibid, para 86. [417] Ibid, para 87. [418] Ibid, para 89. [419] Ibid, para 103.
[420] Ibid, paras 104–5. [421] Ibid, para 143.

within the third category granted by the undertaking in a dominant position', or more generally charge 'negative prices', that is 'prices lower than the cost price'.[422]

Indeed, the GC gives a broad meaning to the concept of 'foreclosure effect', noting that this does not only occur 'where access to the market is made impossible for competitors', but 'it is sufficient that that access be made more difficult', something that the AEC is unable to verify, as even 'a positive AEC test result would not be capable of ruling out the potential foreclosure effect'.[423]

Furthermore, the GC seems profoundly attached to categorical thinking. Eager to ensure consistency between its own position and that of the CJEU in *TeliaSonera* and *Post Danmark I*, it distinguishes the more 'effects-based' approach followed in these cases from the more formalistic it adopted in *Intel* by explaining that the obligation to carry out price and cost analyses in these cases was attributable to the fact that 'it is impossible to assess whether a price is abusive without comparing it with other prices and costs', as '(a) price cannot be unlawful in itself'. However, the GC notes 'in the case of an exclusivity rebate, it is the condition of exclusive or quasi-exclusive supply to which its grant is subject rather than the amount of the rebate which makes it abusive'.[424] In holding so, the GC went counter the position adopted by the Commission's Guidance on its enforcement priorities in applying Article [102] to abusive exclusionary conduct by dominant undertakings, but found unnecessary to consider whether the contested decision is in line with the Guidance. The Commission had performed an AEC test in this case, 'for the sake of completeness', but according to the GC this 'did not constitute a necessary element to show that the practices at issue were illegal'.[425]

Finally, the GC accepted the Commission's characterization of 'naked restrictions' as an infringement of Article 102 TFEU. Intel contested this characterization noting that before reaching this conclusion, the Commission was 'required to demonstrate that the practices are capable of restricting competition "in economic terms"'.[426] Intel argued that this was even more so the case, as the practices characterized by the Commission as 'naked restrictions' were markedly different from those adopted in the GC's precedent in *Irish Sugar v Commission*, with the result that the Commission had 'wrongly created a new type of abuse falling within Article [102 TFEU]'.[427] The GC rejected these arguments, referring to the broad definition it previously gave to the concept of 'foreclosure effect', which includes situations where competitor's access is made more difficult, and holding that 'for the purposes of applying Article [102 TFEU], showing an anti-competitive object and an anti-competitive effect may, in some cases, be one and the same thing', merely indicating the existence of a presumption of 'foreclosure effect', for certain types of conduct, such as the grant of payments to customers in consideration of restrictions on the marketing of products equipped with a product of a specific competitor, which is conduct falling 'outside the scope of competition on the merits'.[428] Similarly, '(a) marketing restriction which targets a competitor's products undermines the competition structure, since it impedes in a targeted manner the placing on the market of that competitor's products'.[429] The GC seems to reason in terms of object/effect distinction, this time transposed to Article 102 TFEU.[430] Again, reference was made to the 'special responsibility of the dominant undertaking'.[431] However, the GC also refused that it relied exclusively on the anti-competitive object of the three naked restrictions in reaching

422 Ibid, paras 144–5. 423 Ibid, paras 149 and 151. 424 Ibid, para 152.
425 Ibid, para 159. 426 Ibid, para 200.
427 Ibid. See Case T-228/97, *Irish Sugar v Commission* [1999] ECR II-2969.
428 Case T-286/09, *Intel Corp v European Commission*, ECLI:EU:T:2014:547, para 205.
429 Ibid, para 207. 430 Ibid, para 203. 431 Ibid, para 205.

its conclusion that the practices were illegal under Article 102 TFEU. In a cryptic paragraph, it noted that 'it relied on additional circumstances confirming the capability of the naked restrictions to restrict competition, even though reference to such circumstances is not essential in order to characterise them as abusive under Article [102 TFEU]': 'characterisation of a naked restriction as abusive depends solely on the capability to restrict competition, and that characterisation does not therefore require proof of an actual effect on the market or of a causal link'.[432] This does not provide much information on how to determine 'the capability to restrict competition', other than that evidence of actual effects is not necessary. The discussion by the GC of the possibility for the Commission to establish 'new' types/categories of abuses further demonstrates the categorical approach followed by the GC in this judgment.[433]

Intel interjected an appeal to the CJEU, which set aside the judgment of the GC, referring back the case to the GC in order for it to examine the arguments put forward by Intel concerning the capacity of the rebates at issue to restrict competition.[434] The case is of great importance, in view of the Opinion of AG Wahl who attacked the theoretical tenets of the judgment of the GC and put forward a different vision of Article 102 TFEU.

The Opinion of Advocate General N Wahl

In an Opinion issued in October 2016, Advocate General N. Wahl explicitly embraced the theoretical tenets of the 'more economic' approach in the context of Article 102, opting for its most extreme version, that of economic efficiency, although the formulation he employed remains ambiguous as he focuses on the detriment to consumers, without explaining if this relates to the loss of consumer surplus (dead-weight loss), or also covers wealth transfers from consumers to the dominant undertaking. According to the AG:

> From the outset, EU competition rules have aimed to put in place a system of undistorted competition, as part of the internal market established by the EU. In that regard, it cannot be over-emphasised that protection under EU competition rules is afforded to the competitive process as such, and not, for example, to competitors. In the same vein, competitors that are forced to exit the market due to fierce competition, rather than anti-competitive behaviour, are not protected. Therefore, not every exit from the market is necessarily a sign of abusive conduct, but rather a sign of aggressive, yet healthy and permissible, competition. *This is because, given its economic character, competition law aims, in the final analysis, to enhance efficiency.* The importance placed on efficiency is also in my view clearly reflected in the case-law of the EU Courts.
>
> From that emphasis it naturally follows that dominance as such is not considered to be at variance with Article 102 TFEU. Rather, only behaviour which constitutes an expression of market power to the detriment of competition and, thus, to consumers is prohibited and accordingly sanctioned as an *abuse* of dominance.[435]

On the basis of these foundations for Article 102 TFEU, AG Wahl took a diametrically different approach than that of the GC and recommended to the CJEU to set aside the judgment of the GC, castigating the type of categorical thinking adopted by the GC in this judgment. In a

[432] Ibid, para 212. [433] Ibid, paras 219–20.
[434] Case C-413/14 P, *Intel Corp v European Commission*, ECLI:EU:C:2017:632.
[435] Opinion of AG N Wahl in Case C-413/14 P, *Intel Corp v European Commission*, ECLI:EU:C:2016:788, paras 41–2. The first emphasis is added.

nutshell, the Advocate General criticized the GC for proceeding to the tripartite classification of the rebates in question, criticizing the 'assumption' of the GC that the so-called 'exclusivity rebates' 'result always, and without exception, in anticompetitive foreclosure', thus making it unnecessary to explore 'the capability of the conduct to have anticompetitive effects'.[436] The AG noted that the previous case law of the CJEU had consistently taken into account 'all the circumstances' when determining whether the impugned conduct amounted to an abuse of a dominant position. According to the AG, even in the seminal *Hoffmann-La Roche* case, the CJEU had examined the economic context before proceeding to tis characterization of the dominant undertaking's conduct. Hence, the GC should not have concluded that 'not even context can save 'exclusivity rebates' from condemnation'.[437] The AG noted that the CJEU's reasoning in *Hofmann-La Roche* did not exclude any consideration of context in its analysis, although, on what may seem as *prima facie* contradictory, he criticized the GC for applying '*verbatim*' the *Hoffman-La Roche* precedent.[438] Nonetheless, the AG noted that '[r]eiterating a statement of principle concerning a presumptive abusiveness is, as shown in the Court's case-law, however, not the same thing as failing to consider the circumstances in a *concrete case*'.[439]

Hence, economic analysis may potentially form part of the competition assessment of rebates at least at two levels. First, at the level of designing relevant antitrust categories to which specific analytical presumptions may be attached (such as loyalty rebates are presumptively abusive, a reasoning focusing at the level of a specific *type* of anti-competitive conduct); second, at the level of the concrete assessment of the specific conduct and its probable anti-competitive effects (that is, the specific anti-competitive effects of the rebate granted by Intel).

The AG gave four reasons why the design of the 'exclusionary rebates' category by the GC as being presumptively unlawful should not be accepted. The first problem is that '[a]n assumption of unlawfulness by virtue of form cannot be rebutted', in particular as, according to the AG, this makes it problematic to invoke efficiency gains or objective justifications as 'irrespective of the effects, the form remains the same'.[440] Second, '[e]xperience and economic analysis do not unequivocally suggest that loyalty rebates are, as a rule, harmful or anticompetitive, even when offered by dominant undertakings', 'because rebates enhance rivalry, the very essence of competition'.[441] Third, 'contemporary economic literature commonly emphasises that the effects of exclusivity are context-dependent'.[442] Fourth, 'the case-law relating to pricing and margin squeeze practices requires, as the appellant rightly points out, consideration of all the circumstances in order to determine whether the undertaking in question has abused its dominant position', '[s]ound and coherent legal categorization' requiring that a similar approach is taken for loyalty rebates.[443]

The AG makes it clear in his Opinion that loyalty rebates, margin squeeze and predatory pricing are different forms of 'price-based exclusion', dismissing the distinction effectuated by the GC which considered, because of the exclusivity condition, that the 'exclusionary rebates' sub-category was closer to the exclusive dealing category than to 'price-related' abuses.[444] According to the AG, 'such a distinction is a distinction without a difference (given that the

436 Ibid, para 47. 437 See, in particular, ibid, paras 52, 54, 66–8, 70.

438 Compare, for instance, ibid, paras 66 and 75 with para 70. 439 Ibid, para 70.

440 Ibid, paras 86–8.

441 Ibid, paras 89–93. The AG challenges the conclusion of the GC that rebates 'conditional on the customer purchasing all (or a substantial part) of its requirements from it' produce specific restrictive effects that require a stricter approach than other sub-types of loyalty rebates, providing 'no objective reason why category 2 rebates should receive a stricter treatment than those falling under category 3'.

442 Ibid, paras 94–100. 443 Ibid, para 103. 444 Ibid, para 102.

difference lies in form rather than effects)' and, assuming these rebates are considered as 'price-based exclusion, 'such a reading of that judgment would stand in contrast to the approach of the Court—sitting in Grand Chamber—in *Post Danmark I*, where it held that in so far as pricing practices are concerned, all the circumstances must be considered'.[445]

It is our understanding that the AG's criticism of the approach of the GC may relate to two issues: first, the GC is criticized for having dispensed any analysis of the economic considerations when it established its tripartite categorization of rebates, and in particular when it created the category of 'exclusionary rebates'. Second, it is our understanding from the AG's Opinion, that the AG would have criticized as well the GC's judgment, even if the latter had designed the category of 'exclusionary rebates' after analysis of the economic effects of this specific type of conduct (at the abstract level), when this effort of categorical thinking has the effect of dispensing any concrete analysis of 'all the circumstances' of the specific/concrete conduct. Hence, the AG would have opposed any rule of *per se* illegality (we borrow this term from US antitrust law) or 'blanket prohibition' (we borrow this term from the AG's Opinion) in the context of Article 102 TFEU. Indeed, according to the AG, such 'blanket prohibition would risk catching and penalising pro-competitive conduct', and something he is not ready to accept for Article 102 TFEU.[446] The AG therefore expresses a clear concern for false positives.[447]

The AG did not, however, oppose categorical thinking. His main opposition to the approach followed by the GC is that it established a tripartite categorization, rather than a bipartite one, that he would have favoured, and which represents, in his view, the approach followed by the CJEU. Such bipartite categorization distinguishes between volume-based rebates that are 'presumptively lawful' and loyalty rebates for which would apply a 'presumption of unlawfulness'. Crucially, however, there should be a possibility for this presumption of illegality to be rebutted after analysis of 'all the circumstances' of the specific rebate (in the concrete case).[448]

The interpretation by the AG of the previous case law and his proposal for a bipartite categorization for rebates may be plausible. However, we do not consider that the AG has provided anywhere in his Opinion an explanation for his outright rejection of the third 'subcategory' of loyalty rebates established by the GC, that of 'exclusionary rebates', even if the GC would have arrived at such a categorization after performing some economic analysis, at the level of the design of the antitrust category. There are various reasons that would have explained a non-rebuttable presumption for 'exclusionary rebates': the fact that there are no redeeming efficiencies for this *type* of conduct and therefore it does not make sense to perform an *in concreto* analysis as this will increase enforcement costs.[449] Indeed, it seems rather odd that the AG does not express any concern about false negatives resulting from the presumption of legality for volume-based rebates, or indicates that this presumption should be a rebuttable one. Does this mean that he considers the weight of a type I error (false positive) to be more important than the weight of a type II error (false negative)? This is a classic characteristic of the Chicago School of antitrust, but seems, somehow odd in the context of

[445] Ibid, para 105. [446] Ibid, para 78. [447] See also ibid, para 119.

[448] Ibid, paras 81, 82, 84, and 198.

[449] One may indeed imagine, if someone takes an economic efficiency approach, as it seems AG Wahl does, a situation in which the increase in enforcement costs of implementing the *in concreto* analysis of the context of each 'exclusionary rebate' will be more important than the decrease of the substantive error costs resulting from a false positive, therefore indicating that the most optimal decision rule in this case may be an irrebuttable presumption of illegality.

Article 102 TFEU, in view of the emphasis put by the jurisprudence of the CJEU on the 'special responsibility' of dominant undertakings.[450]

One may also object that economic considerations should not be the only ones, and are not the only ones, inspiring the classification of abuses under Article 102 TFEU, the EU Courts occasionally integrating other values and broader concerns, eventually also being able to adopt a more deontological perspective in designing appropriate antitrust categories, in view, for instance, of the principle of 'equality of opportunity'.[451]

Concluding this first part of his Opinion, the AG stated that the General Court erred in finding that 'exclusivity rebates' constituted a separate and unique category of rebates that require no consideration of all the circumstances in order to establish an abuse of dominant position.

In the second part of his Opinion, AG Wahl explained why the General Court has also erred in law in its alternative assessment of capability of restricting competition by failing to establish, on the basis of 'all the circumstances', that the rebates and payments offered by the appellant had, in all likelihood, an anti-competitive foreclosure effect. Although the AG accepts that 'evidence of actual effects does not need to be presented', because 'it is sufficient, in relation to conduct that is presumptively unlawful, that the impugned conduct be capable of restricting competition', he also explains that 'capability cannot merely be hypothetical or theoretically possible',[452] something more is required. This analysis focuses on 'the *use* of loyalty rebates'[453] in the specific case and tries to determine if they have an anti-competitive foreclosure effect. Indeed, '[t]he aim of the assessment of capability is to ascertain whether, in all likelihood, the impugned conduct has an anticompetitive foreclosure effect'.[454]

For the AG, what is required is a 'likelihood' and 'likelihood must be considerably more than a mere possibility that certain behaviour may restrict competition', even 'more likely than not is simply not enough'.[455] In order to avoid the risk of over-inclusion resulting from categorical thinking, the assessment of capability concerning presumptively unlawful behaviour must be understood, according to the AG, 'as seeking to ascertain that, having regard

450 Interestingly, AG Wahl mentions the special responsibility of dominant undertakings (Opinion of AG N Wahl in Case C-413/14 P, *Intel Corp v European Commission*, ECLI:EU:C:2016:788, paras 60 & 118), but he does not seem to derive any conclusions with regard to the step of the design of antitrust categories for rebates, or that of the characterization of the specific abuse as falling within a specific antitrust category, but only mentions it when examining the separate step of assessing the anti-competitive effects of the specific practice. He then simply argues that 'that responsibility cannot be taken to mean that the threshold for the application of the prohibition of abuse laid down in Article 102 TFEU can be lowered to such an extent as to become virtually non-existent'. On the Chicago School of antitrust and the considerable weight given to false positives, the excellent analysis of J Baker, 'Taking the Error out of "Error Cost" Analysis: What's Wrong with Antitrust Right?' (2005) 80 *Antitrust LJ* 1.

451 See I Lianos, 'Categorical Thinking in Competition Law and the "Effects-based" Approach in Article 82 EC' in A Ezrachi (ed) *Article 82 EC: Reflections on its Recent Evolution* (Hart, 2009), 19.

452 Opinion of AG N Wahl in Case C-413/14 P, *Intel Corp v European Commission*, ECLI:EU:C:2016:788,, para 114.

453 Ibid, para 115.

454 Ibid, para 117.

455 Ibid. It is unclear if the AG refers here to the standard of proof, requiring a higher standard than that of the balance of probabilities. One may criticize his narrow conception of the standard of proof as essentially a probability enquiry, as one may put forward a relative plausibility approach, something that the jurisprudence of the CJEU is compatible with: see I Lianos, '"Judging Economists": Economic Expertise in Competition Litigation: A European View' in I Lianos and I Kokkoris (eds) *Towards an Optimal Competition Law System* (Kluwer International, 2009), 185; I Lianos and C Genakos, 'Econometric Evidence in EU Competition Law: An Empirical and Theoretical Analysis' in I Lianos and D Geradin (eds) *Handbook on European Competition Law* (Edward Elgar, 2013), 1, esp 94–5.

to all circumstances, the behaviour in question does not just have ambivalent effects on the market or only produce ancillary restrictive effects necessary for the performance of something which is pro-competitive, but that its presumed restrictive effects are in fact confirmed', and in the absence of 'such a confirmation, a fully-fledged analysis has to be performed'.[456] The AG explains that he draws inspiration by the framework offered by Article 101 TFEU regarding restrictions of competition by object. He notes:

> [I]n a somewhat similar fashion to the enforcement shortcut concerning restrictions by object under Article 101 TFEU, the assessment of all the circumstances under Article 102 TFEU involves examining the context of the impugned conduct to ascertain whether it can be confirmed to have an anticompetitive effect. If any of the circumstances thus examined casts doubt on the anticompetitive nature of the behaviour, a more thorough effects analysis becomes necessary.[457]

This will necessarily involve an analysis of the actual or potential effects of that conduct.[458] In performing this assessment the AG finds relevant to examine, 'at the very least' (i) the market coverage of the rebates, (ii) their duration, and (iii) '[i]n addition, it may be necessary to consider other circumstances that may differ from case to case', such as, in this case, the as efficient competitor test.[459] Interestingly, he notes that a 14% market coverage is 'inconclusive', explicitly rejecting any quantitative threshold or presumption for determining the existence of an anti-competitive foreclosure,[460] without, however, saying much as to the contribution of this factor in the finding of anti-competitive effects. Similarly, the assessment of duration is also deemed inconclusive, the AG expressing his reticence to adopt clear thresholds for the duration of the rebate that would structure the analysis of anti-competitive effects by generating rebuttable presumptions of legality or illegality.[461]

However, the AG finds that the AEC test may be a relevant factor in assessing the existence of an exclusionary effect. Indeed, 'given that an exclusionary effect is required, the AEC test cannot be ignored'.[462] For the AG, the test may operate a useful dual function: (i) first, it 'serves to identify conduct which makes it economically impossible for an as-efficient competitor to secure the contestable share of a customer's demand', thus helping to 'identify conduct that has, in all likelihood, an anticompetitive effect'; (ii) second, it may disculpate conduct from being considered as abusive, as 'where the test shows that an as-efficient competitor is able to

[456] Opinion of AG N Wahl in Case C-413/14 P, *Intel Corp v European Commission*, ECLI:EU:C:2016:788, para 120.

[457] Ibid, para 135. [458] Ibid, para 136. [459] Ibid, para 172.

[460] Ibid, paras 142–3. He also considered irrelevant the fact that according to the GC, Intel was 'an unavoidable trading partner on the CPU market', dismissing this as an element proving that 'the impugned conduct has, in all likelihood, an anticompetitive effect'. The opposition of the AG to the relevance of the finding that the dominant undertakings is an 'unavoidable trading partner' may be explained by the fact that this is a categorical concept, either one is an unavoidable trading partner or not, and not a scalar concept, that can potentially be measured, such as anti-competitive effects in terms of price, quality, or output, for instance. Although the AG notes that 'defining the level of market coverage that may cause anticompetitive effects is by no means an arithmetic exercise', rejecting a simple quantitative threshold for anti-competitive foreclosure, such as the one used in the context of Article 101 TFEU for certain vertical restraints (eg tying), he seems to embrace an 'arithmetic approach' or, more accurately, a 'measurement' approach, when he indicates that a higher probability of anti-competitive effects is required than the balance of probabilities approach.

[461] Opinion of AG N Wahl in Case C-413/14 P, *Intel Corp v European Commission*, ECLI:EU:C:2016:788, paras 147–57.

[462] Ibid, para 165.

cover its costs, the likelihood of an anticompetitive effect significantly decreases', and '[t]hat is why, from the perspective of capturing conduct that has an anticompetitive foreclosure effect, the AEC test is particularly useful',[463] although he is careful to also stress that 'there is no legal obligation to make use of that test'.[464] The AG refers to the *Post Danmark II* case law of the CJEU considering that this 'case demonstrates that the case-law pertaining to *other types* of price-based exclusion cannot simply be disregarded in the context of rebate cases'.[465] Although the AEC test is not obligatory, 'precisely because that test was carried out by the Commission in the decision at issue, cannot be ignored in ascertaining whether the impugned conduct is capable of having an anticompetitive foreclosure effect'.[466]

In the third part of his Opinion, AG Wahl reiterates his view that no separate category of 'exclusivity rebates' exists and alternatively he opines that, should the CJEU disagree with this interpretation of the case law, the GC's judgment should still be set aside on the basis that 'only rebates which are conditional upon the customer purchasing 'all or most' of the customer's requirements from the dominant undertaking would fall under the umbrella of "exclusivity rebates" ', which is not satisfied in the circumstances of this case.[467] Indeed, he notes that OEMs could still purchase 'significant quantities' of 86 CPUs from Intel's competitor, AMD.

The judgment of the Court of Justice in Intel v Commission

The judgment of the CJEU is a monument of ambiguity.[468] First, although not explicitly embracing the economic efficiency perspective of its AG, the CJEU seems to have been inspired by the principle of economic efficiency, when noting that 'it is in no way the purpose of Article 102 TFEU to [. . .] ensure that competitors less efficient than the undertaking with the dominant position should remain on the market' and that '[c]ompetition on the merits may, by definition, lead to the departure from the market or the marginalisation of competitors that are less efficient and so less attractive to consumers from the point of view of, among other things, price, choice, quality or innovation'.[469] The CJEU, however, also referred to the special responsibility of dominant undertakings 'not to allow its behaviour to impair genuine, undistorted competition on the internal market'.[470]

Second, the CJEU seems to have limited the scope of prohibition Article 102 TFEU for pricing practices to those 'that have an exclusionary effect on competitors considered to be *as efficient as* it is itself' but also added pricing practices 'strengthening' the dominant company's (Domco) 'dominant position by using methods other than those that are part of competition on the merits', noting that 'not all competition by means of price may be regarded as legitimate'.[471] A possible interpretation of this paragraph is that the exclusion of less efficient rivals through pricing practices will not fall under the prohibition of Article 102 TFEU unless it is the result of a method of competition that is not judged to be 'competition on the merits'. The CJEU provides such examples of competition not being 'on the merits' in the following paragraph referring (i) to the situation of 'an undertaking which is in a dominant position on a market and ties purchasers—even if it does so at their request—by an obligation or promise on their part to obtain all or most of their requirements exclusively from that undertaking' 'whether the obligation is stipulated without further qualification

463 Ibid, para 165. 464 Ibid, para 167.

465 Ibid, para 166. Note that the AG challenges the GC's conclusion that loyalty rebates are not 'price-related' restraints.

466 Ibid, para 172. 467 Ibid, para 200.

468 Case C-413/14 P, *Intel Corp v European Commission*, ECLI:EU:C:2017:632.

469 Ibid, paras 133–4. 470 Ibid, para 135. 471 Ibid, para 136 (emphasis added).

or whether it is undertaken in consideration of the grant of a rebate', and (ii) if the Domco in question, 'without tying the purchasers by a formal obligation, applies, either under the terms of agreements concluded with these purchasers or unilaterally, a system of loyalty rebates, that is to say, discounts conditional on the customer's obtaining all or most of its requirements—whether the quantity of its purchases be large or small—from the undertaking in a dominant position'.[472] It is unclear if the examples of rebates conducive to imposing exclusivity conditions that lead to a significant foreclosure effect constitute according to the CJEU practices that do not constitute 'competition on the merits' and therefore could be of concern for competition law even if they exclude less efficient rivals, but such an interpretation is possible. If this is true, the CJEU juxtaposes to the principle of economic efficiency another unnamed principle/value that seems to expand the scope of Article 102 TFEU. Would that be the principle of 'equality of opportunity'.

Third, the CJEU feels important to qualify the previous statement by further clarifying that 'where the undertaking concerned submits, during the administrative procedure, on the basis of supporting evidence, that its conduct was not capable of restricting competition and, in particular, of producing the alleged foreclosure effects', '[i]n that case, the Commission is not only required to analyse, first, the extent of the undertaking's dominant position on the relevant market and, secondly, the share of the market covered by the challenged practice, as well as the conditions and arrangements for granting the rebates in question, their duration and their amount' but 'is also required to assess the possible existence of a strategy aiming to exclude competitors that are at least as efficient as the dominant undertaking from the market'.[473] The CJEU seems therefore to narrow again the scope of Article 102 TFEU, this time when evaluating foreclosure effects to the exclusion of undertakings 'at least as efficient as the dominant undertaking', although it seems that it envisions before this evaluative step, some *prima facie* evidence, brought by the dominant undertaking that its conduct was not capable of producing the alleged foreclosure effects.

This initiates a form of four steps approach, which seems arguably to apply to all forms of exclusionary pricing practices, such as rebates. The Commission has first to show that either the practice excludes an as efficient competitor *or* that it constitutes a practice that is not judged to be 'competition on the merits', namely conditional rebates on the requirement that the customer obtains 'all or most of its requirements' by the dominant undertaking. Second, if the Commission chooses the second option, the undertaking may put forward evidence denying the capability of its conduct to restrict competition and produce the alleged foreclosure effects. Third, in this case, the Commission needs to proceed to a more detailed analysis of the rebates scheme, including 'the possible existence of a strategy aiming to exclude competitors that are at least as efficient as the dominant undertaking from the market', the CJEU referring here to the as efficient competitor (AEC) test. Fourth, the undertaking may put forward objective justifications in order to escape from Article 102 TFEU prohibition for a rebate scheme

472 Ibid, para 137.

473 Ibid, paras 138–9. To support this proposition the CJEU cites 'by analogy', C-209/10, *Post Danmark I*, ECLI:EU:C:2012:172, para 29. This paragraph examined the anti-competitive strategy of Post-Danmark noting that in this case it could not be established if Post-Danmark had deliberately sought to drive out their competitor. It seems unclear to us how this paragraph which refers broadly to the anti-competitive intent of the dominant undertaking could be relevant for the AEC test, but a possible interpretation is that for the CJEU the AEC test may operate as a way to determine the anti-competitive intent of the undertaking, to the extent that evidence that a AEC could be excluded by the rebate scheme could indicate the existence of a anti-competitive strategy to 'deliberately drive out' that efficient competitor.

that is disadvantageous for competition and produces exclusionary effects, if these effects are 'counterbalanced, or outweighed, by advantages in terms of efficiency which also benefit the consumer'.[474] In order to show that this is a separate step than that of assessing in detail the capability of the conduct to foreclose an as efficient competitor, the CJEU notes that the 'balancing of the favourable and unfavourable effects of the practice in question on competition can be carried out in the Commission's decision *only after* an analysis of the intrinsic capacity of that practice to foreclose competitors which are at least as efficient as the dominant undertaking'.[475]

This may seem to be clear, but the CJEU indicates in the following paragraph that '[i]f, in a decision finding a rebate scheme abusive, the Commission carries out such an analysis, the General Court must examine all of the applicant's arguments seeking to call into question the validity of the Commission's findings concerning the foreclosure capability of the rebate concerned',[476] the important thing here being the conditional 'if'. Could that be understood as opening the possibility for the Commission not to follow the four steps approach? This seems a plausible interpretation, as the CJEU notes in the following paragraph that:

> In this case, while the Commission emphasised, in the decision at issue, that the rebates at issue were by their very nature capable of restricting competition such that an analysis of all the circumstances of the case and, in particular, an AEC test were not necessary in order to find an abuse of a dominant position [. . .] it nevertheless carried out an in-depth examination of those circumstances, setting out [. . .] a very detailed analysis of the AEC test, which led it to conclude [. . .] that an as efficient competitor would have had to offer prices which would not have been viable and that, accordingly, the rebate scheme at issue was capable of having foreclosure effects on such a competitor.[477]

The CJEU castigates the GC for not attaching any importance to the AEC test carried out by the Commission and, accordingly, not addressing Intel's criticisms of that test, '[i]n its examination of the circumstances of the case, carried out for the sake of completeness'.[478] Interestingly, the CJEU does not take issue with the fact that the GC thought that it was not necessary for the Commission to apply in this case the AEC test, but with the fact that the GC did not address Intel's arguments on the absence of foreclosure, even if the Commission applied an in-depth examination of the rebates and proceeded to a detailed analysis of the AEC, which 'played an important role in the Commission's assessment of whether the rebate scheme at issue was capable of having foreclosure effects on as efficient competitors'.[479] The important element in the judgment of the CJEU that explains why it set aside the judgment of the GC seems therefore to be that the latter 'wrongly failed to take into consideration Intel's line of argument seeking to expose alleged errors committed by the Commission in the AEC test'.[480]

The judgment may thus give rise to two possible interpretations: either it is a judgment of principle emphasizing the need for the Commission to apply an AEC test before finding that a rebate scheme is capable to foreclose competition and to produce foreclosure effects, stepping in this respect the approach followed by the CJEU in *Post Danmark I* that the marginalization and/or exclusion of less efficient rivals following competition on the merits should not be of concern for Article 102 TFEU, a case which is cited approvingly by the CJEU in *Intel*,[481]

474 Case C-413/14 P, *Intel Corp v European Commission*, ECLI:EU:C:2017:632, para 140.

475 Ibid, para 140 (emphasis added).

476 Ibid, para 141.

477 Ibid, para 142.

478 Ibid, para 146.

479 Ibid, para 143.

480 Ibid, para 147.

481 It is remarkable that the CJEU did not cite *PostDanmark II* in the part of the judgment containing its analysis of the case. The case had relativized the use of the AEC test, which was not found to be a 'necessary

or it is a judgment that does not aim to bring into the complex equation of assessing loyalty rebates the AEC test, but simply indicates that in case the Commission relies in its decision on an AEC test, the GC needs to examine the arguments of the dominant undertaking to deny that the rebate scheme could exclude an as efficient competitor.

Some thoughts about the concepts/slogans of 'more economic approach' and 'effects-based' approach

The quest for an optimal test or tests that would identify with more precision the anti-competitive nature of a single firm conduct should not conceal the fact that the choice to be made depends on the underlying objective(s) of the specific competition law system. It is also the outcome of a difficult balance between the need for sophistication in view of the complexity of the real economy and the need for predictability of the rules/standards that are essential for legal certainty. The aim of this quest for the optimal test is to find the optimal rule or standard producing, comparatively, the less possible substantive error costs and enforcement costs, including compliance costs from undertakings.[482]

With regard to the underlying objective(s) of competition law, choosing an 'as efficient competitor' test for all types of unilateral conduct may indicate that the primary aim of the competition law system is to preserve economic efficiency. A 'consumer welfare' or 'consumer choice' standard may signal that the law integrates some distributive justice concerns, although that depends on the interpretation (including long-term or short-term time frame) one gives to the concept of 'consumer welfare'.[483]

Focusing on the objective(s) pursued by the legal system assumes that any discussion of the principles that apply at the doctrinal stage, that of designing appropriate categories/tests, or at the adjudicative stage, that of implementing these tests in concrete cases, should include a discussion of the meta-principles applying at the jurisprudential stage, where the values *justifying* a specific legal practice or 'order of worth' are posited. These values are made explicit by the interpretative work of the courts and that of competition authorities. On the basis of this work, a *decision criterion* will emerge and will guide the decision-making process at the doctrinal stage, that is, at the level of designing appropriate antitrust categories, as well as at the adjudicative stage, the implementation of this decision criterion in specific cases.

The 'more economic approach' seems to be animated by a decision criterion that emphasizes the role of economic efficiency in determining which conduct is 'worthy' from an economic efficiency perspective, or lawful (if one considers that economic efficiency and lawfulness are one and the same thing), and which is not. This may refer to the output produced or the price level, resulting from the specific practice, but this needs not be always the case. The 'more economic approach' may not be, exclusively or even partially, inspired by neoclassical price theory (NPT), but may also be influenced by other approaches in economics: classical school approaches, behavioural economics, neo-Keynesianism, etc. It is a testimony of the dominance of NPT in modern competition law that the 'more economic approach' is usually perceived as uniquely referring to a more NPT-consistent approach.

condition for a finding to the effect that a rebate scheme is abusive' and its application was considered 'of no relevance', the test constituting 'one tool amongst others for the purposes of assessing whether there is an abuse of a dominant position in the context of a rebate scheme': Case C-23/14, *Post Danmark A/S v Konkurrencerådet*, ECLI:EU:C:2015:651, paras 61–2.

482 See our analysis of the decision theoretic approach in designing competition law rules and categories in Chapter 6.

483 See Chapter 2.

The jurisprudential and the doctrinal stages should not however be conflated: one may indeed imagine a situation where economic efficiency does not constitute the only value adopted at the jurisprudential stage, fairness in distribution being an additional value, but economic efficiency, narrowly defined as in NPT, may remain the main source of inspiration for the decision criterion at the doctrinal stage, due to various practical considerations, for instance the greater ability of economics (and economic efficiency) to integrate other values and achieve a better balance between sophistication and predictability, in view of the superiority of the evaluative technology of modern economics.

To this more 'economic approach', one may oppose various other approaches, that may adopt different decision criteria than economic efficiency. These may in turn lead to different sources of wisdom than economics in determining the decision criteria at the doctrinal stage. For instance, one may be inspired by analytical philosophy (the 'more philosophical approach'), sociology ('the more sociological approach'), democratic theory emphasizing the values of liberty, equality, and justice ('the more democratic approach'), and so forth, and develop decision criteria that correspond to these different 'orders of worth'.[484] Again, the choice made will depend on the comparative ability of these other approaches to offer a better balance, than NPT, between sophistication and predictability. Multiple orders of worth may also co-exist in a society/legal system, though they may not enjoy equal persuasive power, again because of a compromise between the opposite dynamics of sophistication and predictability.

The issue of determining the decision criterion should be distinguished from that of choosing *decision procedures*, by that we mean a technique for making choices. One may opt, for instance, for an approach focusing on the 'effects' of the specific conduct, proceeding to its assessment on a case-by-case basis (a 'full-blown rule of reason approach' if we employ the US antitrust terminology). Alternatively, it is possible to opt for an approach that would focus on categorical thinking, proceeding to categorize different types of business practices. These different categories may be determined according to the 'effects' of these practices, conduct producing similar 'effects' being grouped under the same category (thus they will be 'effects-based'), or according to some formal criterion, on the basis of an ontological principle (eg the protection of the freedom of undertakings to compete). Various other approaches and combinations are also possible. The terminology 'effects-based' approach may thus cover both decision procedures that rely on categorical thinking that is strictly based on the effects of the practices included in the same category, and approaches that only focus on the effects of each specific practice, eventually performing a balancing of pro- and anti-competitive effects, before concluding on the lawfulness, or not, of the specific conduct. The concept of 'effects' may also take various meanings, depending on the decision criterion adopted at the first place. One may expect a different definition of 'effect' if one takes a narrow economic efficiency NPT perspective than if one takes a distributive justice approach or an approach emphasizing innovation. All this seems of course quite complex and may be criticized as allowing for vagueness, but at the same time it provides the necessary 'breathing space' for the discipline of competition law to integrate new values and concerns when these come to the fore because of political circumstances and broader intellectual trends linked to technological transformations in economic production.

484 On 'orders of worth', see L Boltanski and L Thévenot, 'On Justification: Economies of Worth' (Princeton University Press, 2006), who explain that these constitute legitimate/universal evaluative standards used to adjudicate competing claims to resources, legitimacy, and other goods that characterize social life.

8.4.6. OBJECTIVE ECONOMIC JUSTIFICATIONS

8.4.6.1. The concept of 'objective economic justification'

Article 102 TFEU has long been interpreted as including the possibility for the dominant undertaking to justify its conduct and thus avoid the finding of an abuse.[485] The concept of 'objective economic justification' has been used by the Court in the past to indicate the existence of specific defences that can be argued by a dominant undertaking.[486] These have taken different forms in the jurisprudence of the CJEU and the General Court.

- In *United Brands*, but also in subsequent cases, the CJEU found that an undertaking in a dominant position cannot be deprived of its entitlement to protect its own commercial interests when these are attacked.[487] According to the Court, 'such an undertaking must be conceded the right to take such reasonable steps as it deems appropriate to protect its said interests'.[488] The Court also added that '[e]ven if the possibility of a counterattack is acceptable that attack must still be proportionate to the threat taking into account the economic strength of the undertakings confronting each other.'[489]
- In *AKZO*,[490] the CJEU found that meeting competition could be considered a defence for predatory pricing, but only when the alignment of the price with the prices offered by the competitor was a defensive measure. Yet, the meeting competition defence is available only where the undertaking in question is not super-dominant.[491]
- In *Hilti*[492] and *Tetra Pak II*,[493] the CJEU found that consumer safety and health can be legitimate interests that can operate as an objective justification for the finding of an abuse.
- In *Microsoft*,[494] the analysis of objective (or efficiency) justifications constituted a necessary complement to the analysis of the existence of an anti-competitive foreclosure. The concept of 'efficiency' indicates some form of trade of between the anti-competitive effects and the efficiency gains (objective justification). The consideration of 'efficiency

485 For a discussion, see A Albors-Llorens, 'The Role of Objective Justifications and Efficiencies in the Application of Article 82 EC' (2007) 44 *Common Market L Rev* 1727; E Rousseva, 'Abuse of Dominant Position Defences—Objective Justification and Article 82 EC in the Era of Modernization' in G Amato and CD Ehlermann (eds) *EC Competition Law: A Critical Assessment* (Hart, 2007) 377.

486 Case C-95/04 P, *British Airways plc v Commission* [2007] ECR I–2331, para 69.

487 The content of this concept is unclear. A restrictive definition of the concept will not cover efficiency gains. The interpretation of this expression is not yet clear. See E Rousseva, 'The Concept of "Objective Justification" of an Abuse of a Dominant Position: Can it Help to Modernise the Analysis under Article 82?' (2006) 2 *Competition L Rev* 27, 33–4, who observes that:

> [. . .] the question is what a legitimate commercial interest of a dominant undertaking is: does this interest mean only a right of a dominant undertaking to survive on the market, i.e., to prevent its inefficient operation, or does it also mean a right to carry out a profit oriented policy? How does the prerogative of a dominant firm to protect its interest fit with the essential goal of competition to serve consumers' interests? These are questions on which views diverge.

488 Case C-27/76, *United Brands* [1978] ECR 207, para 189. See also Joined Cases C-468–78/06, *GSK* [2008] ECR I–7139, para 50.

489 Case C-27/76, *United Brands* [1978] ECR 207, para 190.

490 Case C-62/86, *AKZO Commission* [1991] ECR 3359, para 156.

491 Joined Cases C-395 & 396/96 P, *Compagnie Maritime Belge* [2000] ECR I–1365, para 119.

492 Case T-30/89, *Hilti AG v Commission* [1990] ECR II–163; Case C-53/92 P, *Hilti AG v Commission* [1994] ECR I–667.

493 Case T-83/91, *Tetra Pak International SA v Commission* [1994] ECR II–755; Case C-333/94 P, *Tetra Pak International SA v Commission* [1996] ECR I–5951.

494 Case T-201/04, *Microsoft v Commission* [2007] ECR II–3601.

gains' was one of the core suggestions of the EAGCP Group's report on the 'economic approach' to Article 102 TFEU.[495] In *British Airways v. Commission*, the CJEU also employed the term of 'efficiency gains':

> Assessment of the economic justification for a system of discounts or bonuses established by an undertaking in a dominant position is to be made on the basis of the whole of the circumstances of the case. It has to be determined whether the exclusionary effect arising from such a system, which is disadvantageous for competition, may be counterbalanced, or outweighed, by advantages in terms of efficiency which also benefit the consumer. If the exclusionary effect of that system bears no relation to advantages for the market and consumers, or if it goes beyond what is necessary in order to attain those advantages, that system must be regarded as an abuse.[496]

It has been contended that objective justifications should not be considered as a 'defence', as what they simply do is to prevent the finding of an infringement under Article 102 TFEU. These authors criticize the 'two-stage' model of Article 102 TFEU, first identifying the anticompetitive conduct, and then exploring the defence of 'objective justification', noting that efficiency gains and justifications should be take into account *before* a finding of abuse is made.[497]

Despite the theoretical possibility to argue different forms of objective justifications, the European Courts have practically never accepted such a defence. Several reasons have been advanced for this:

JF Bellis and T Kasten, 'Will Efficiencies Play an Increasingly Important Role in the Assessment of Conduct under Article 102 TFEU?' in F Etro and I Kokkoris (eds) *Competition Law and the Enforcement of Article 102* (OUP, 2010), 130–1.

> Why has it been so difficult to justify conduct under Article 102 TFEU? Perhaps one reason is that arguments based on efficiencies and other objective justifications are generally presented as a defence against an existing claim of anticompetitive conduct [. . .]. However, when such an allegation is made, it can be just as difficult for a dominant undertaking to justify conduct that is already seen as foreclosing competition as it would be to justify a hard-core cartel. In effect, efficiency-based arguments are treated as a request for an exemption, an almost impossible burden to meet. [. . .] This approach of considering efficiencies only after establishing that conduct is liable to foreclose competition has become firmly established in the case law. [. . .]
>
> Another reason why dominant undertakings have found it historically difficult to justify conduct on the grounds of efficiencies, particularly cost-based efficiencies, may be that the traditional

495 EAGCP, *An Economic Approach to Article 82*, Report (July 2005), 3, available at http://ec.europa.eu/dgs/competition/economist/eagcp_july_21_05.pdf.

496 Case C-95/04 P, *British Airways plc v Commission* [2007] ECR I–2331, para 86.

497 See R O'Donoghue and J Padilla, *The Law and Economics of Article 102 TFEU* (Hart, 2nd ed, 2013), 283, noting that '[t]he defence of objective justification is in some ways a tautology' and citing as supporting this view the position of AG Jacobs in Case C-53/03, *Synetairismos Farmakopoion Aitolias & Akarnanias and Others v GlaxoSmithKline plc*, ECLI:EU:C:2004:673, para 72 [hereinafter *Syfait*], noting that '[. . .] it is therefore more accurate to say that certain types of conduct on the part of a dominant undertaking do not fall within the category of abuse at all'. See also P Akman, 'Searching for the Long-Lost Soul of Article 82 EC' (2009) 29 *Oxford J Legal Studies* 267, 288–9.

definition of a 'dominant position'; can only generate scepticism over whether any efficiencies will be passed onto customers. By definition, a dominant undertaking is able 'to behave to an appreciable extent independently of its competitors, its customers and ultimately of consumers'. Under that view, it is not clear that a dominant undertaking would necessarily pass on efficiencies to customers. This reasoning may explain, at least in part, the historically very sceptical view taken by the Commission and European Courts in response to efficiency arguments.

It is also possible to argue that may be the Commission is already performing an analysis of potential objective justifications prior to opening an investigation under Article 102 TFEU, with the result that the picture provided by the Commission's decisions implementing Article 102 TFEU, and their judicial review by the EU Courts, may be distorted and fail to represent the real weight given to objective justifications in guiding the enforcement action of the Commission regarding Article 102 TFEU. This claim should of course be verified empirically.

The Commission included a substantial part of its Guidance on Article 102 on the concept of objective justifications.

Communication—Guidance on the Commission's enforcement priorities in applying [Article 102 TFEU] to abusive exclusionary conduct by dominant undertakings [2009] OJ C 45/7 (footnotes omitted)

D. Objective necessity and efficiencies

28. In the enforcement of Article 82, the Commission will also examine claims put forward by a dominant undertaking that its conduct is justified. A dominant undertaking may do so either by demonstrating that its conduct is objectively necessary or by demonstrating that its conduct produces substantial efficiencies which outweigh any anti-competitive effects on consumers. In this context, the Commission will assess whether the conduct in question is indispensable and proportionate to the goal allegedly pursued by the dominant undertaking.

29. The question of whether conduct is objectively necessary and proportionate must be determined on the basis of factors external to the dominant undertaking. Exclusionary conduct may, for example, be considered objectively necessary for health or safety reasons related to the nature of the product in question. However, proof of whether conduct of this kind is objectively necessary must take into account that it is normally the task of public authorities to set and enforce public health and safety standards. It is not the task of a dominant undertaking to take steps on its own initiative to exclude products which it regards, rightly or wrongly, as dangerous or inferior to its own product.

30. The Commission considers that a dominant undertaking may also justify conduct leading to foreclosure of competitors on the ground of efficiencies that are sufficient to guarantee that no net harm to consumers is likely to arise. In this context, the dominant undertaking will generally be expected to demonstrate, with a sufficient degree of probability, and on the basis of verifiable evidence, that the following cumulative conditions are fulfilled:

- the efficiencies have been, or are likely to be, realised as a result of the conduct. They may, for example, include technical improvements in the quality of goods, or a reduction in the cost of production or distribution,

- the conduct is indispensable to the realisation of those efficiencies: there must be no less anti-competitive alternatives to the conduct that are capable of producing the same efficiencies,
- the likely efficiencies brought about by the conduct outweigh any likely negative effects on competition and consumer welfare in the affected markets,
- the conduct does not eliminate effective competition, by removing all or most existing sources of actual or potential competition. Rivalry between undertakings is an essential driver of economic efficiency, including dynamic efficiencies in the form of innovation. In its absence the dominant undertaking will lack adequate incentives to continue to create and pass on efficiency gains. Where there is no residual competition and no foreseeable threat of entry, the protection of rivalry and the competitive process outweighs possible efficiency gains. In the Commission's view, exclusionary conduct which maintains, creates or strengthens a market position approaching that of a monopoly can normally not be justified on the grounds that it also creates efficiency gains.

31. It is incumbent upon the dominant undertaking to provide all the evidence necessary to demonstrate that the conduct concerned is objectively justified. It then falls to the Commission to make the ultimate assessment of whether the conduct concerned is not objectively necessary and, based on a weighing-up of any apparent anti-competitive effects against any advanced and substantiated efficiencies, is likely to result in consumer harm.

NOTES AND QUESTIONS

1. Note that the Commission does not mention the concept of 'meeting competition', nor that of 'protecting its own commercial interests', but only those of 'objective necessity' and 'efficiencies' or 'efficiency gains'. The DG Comp Staff Discussion Paper included the 'meeting competition' defence as a variance of possible defences-objective justifications (in addition to objective necessity, efficiency gains, for dominant undertakings to avoid the qualification of their conduct as an abuse).[498]
2. The Commission Guidance on Article 102, section on objective necessity and efficiencies, illustrates the similarities with the 'efficiency defence' under Article 101(3) by applying similar cumulative requirements for the acceptance of the alleged efficiency gains in Article 102 with the conditions the Treaty requires in the context of Article 101(3). The Commission Guidance employs a slightly different formulation of the third requirement by not explicitly requiring that 'a fair share of the resulting benefit' be passed on to consumers. However, this requirement was interpreted restrictively by the Guidelines on Article 101(3) (the net effect of the

[498] DG Competition, 'Discussion Paper on the Application of Article 82 of the Treaty to Exclusionary Abuses' (December 2005), paras 81–3, noting that:

> [T]he meeting competition defence is only applicable in relation to behaviour which otherwise would constitute a pricing abuse. It can in addition only apply to individual and not to collective behaviour to meet competition. For this second type of objective justification it is necessary to apply a proportionality test. The Community Courts have considered that defending its own commercial and economic interests in the face of action taken by certain competitors may be a legitimate aim. (Ibid, para 81).

According to the DG Discussion paper, 'meeting competition' and the protection of 'legitimate interests' should thus be conflated to the same concept.

agreement must at least be neutral from the point of view of those consumers directly or likely affected by the agreement).[499] The requirement in the Commission's Guidance on Article 102 that 'the likely efficiencies brought about by the conduct outweigh any likely negative effects on competition and *consumer welfare* in the affected markets'[500] may have a similar meaning. Furthermore, according to the Guidelines on Article 101(3):

> Rivalry between undertakings is an essential driver of economic efficiency, including dynamic efficiencies in the form of innovation. In its absence the dominant undertaking will lack adequate incentives to continue to create and *pass on* efficiency gains.[501]

3. According to the Commission Guidance on Article 102, 'the conduct is indispensable to the realisation of those efficiencies: there must be no less anti-competitive alternatives to the conduct that are capable of producing the *same efficiencies*'.[502] How would a dominant undertaking bring evidence of such a condition? D Waelbroeck has criticized this condition for the purpose of assessing efficiencies under Article 102 TFEU:

> [I]n the context of Article 101, agreements are reached between the parties in full transparency and with full information as to what restrictions are indeed needed to achieve the efficiencies in question (for instance the question of whether territorial protection is indeed the only way to encourage investment by the distributors in a distribution system, or whether a non-compete clause is necessary etc). This is, however, not the case for dominant companies assessing the impact of their conduct on competition in the market: they do not have detailed knowledge about the prices, costs, or general strategy of their competitors. And indeed, they are not even supposed to have this information, as having it generally would result from an infringement of Article 101.[503]

Discuss.

4. In his Opinion in *Syfait*, Advocate General Jacobs observed:

> [I]t is clear that the Community case-law provides dominant undertakings with the possibility of demonstrating an objective justification for their conduct, even if it is *prima facie* an abuse, and I now turn to the issue of objective justification. I would add that the two-stage analysis suggested by the distinction between an abuse and its objective justification is to my mind somewhat artificial. Article [102 TFEU], by contrast with Article [101 TFEU], does not contain any explicit provision for the exemption of conduct otherwise falling within it. Indeed, the very fact that conduct is characterised as an 'abuse' suggests that a negative conclusion has already been reached, by contrast with the more neutral terminology of 'prevention, restriction, or distortion of competition' under Article [101 TFEU]. In my view, it is therefore more accurate to say that certain types of conduct on the part

[499] Guidelines on Article 101(3), para 85. [500] Ibid, para 30 (emphasis added).
[501] Ibid (emphasis added). [502] Commission Guidance on Article 102, para 30.
[503] D Waelbroeck, 'The Assessment of Efficiencies under Article 102 and the Commission's Guidance Paper' in F Etro and I Kokkoris (eds) *Competition Law and the Enforcement of Article 102* (OUP, 2010), 115.

of a dominant undertaking do not fall within the category of abuse at all. However, given that the Commission has, in the light of some previous Community case-law, developed its submissions in terms of objective justification, it may be convenient for present purposes to assume that structure.[504]

Do you think that in its Guidance on Article 102, the Commission takes into account the concerns of AG Jacobs? The structure of the defence under the Commission's Guidance on Article 102 is not 'to deny a claim of anticompetitive foreclosure but rather to exonerate the conduct in question despite its established negative effects on the market'.[505] Does the methodology and the structure of the defence fit the text and purpose of Article 102 TFEU? Does the Commission's Guidance on Article 102 go as far as creating an Article 102(3), thus contravening the letter of the Treaty?

5. How would efficiencies argued in the context of Article 102 TFEU pass the condition that the conduct should not 'eliminate effective competition', 'by removing all or most existing sources of actual or potential competition'. By definition, as objective justifications are argued after the plaintiff has brought evidence of actual or likely anti-competitive effect, 'effective competition' might have already been eliminated.
6. An important difference with the efficiency defence under Article 101(3) could be the allocation of the burden of proof between claimants and defendants. Article 2 of Regulation 1/2003 provides that:

   In any national or Community proceedings for the application of Articles [101] and [102] of the Treaty, the burden of proving an infringement of Article [101(1)] or of Article [102] of the Treaty shall rest on the party or the authority alleging the infringement. The undertaking or association of undertakings claiming the benefit of Article 101(3) of the Treaty shall bear the burden of proving that the conditions of that paragraph are fulfilled.

   This provision refers only to Article 101(3), when it mentions the exception to the rule that it is on the claimant to prove the existence of a competition law infringement. The absence of an equivalent provision to Article 101(3) in the context of Article 102 could be interpreted as indicating that it is on the claimant to prove that the conduct produces anti-competitive effects and that it cannot be justified by efficiency gains. This does not, however, take into account Recital 5 of Regulation 1/2003, which shifts the burden of proof to the defendant not only in the context of Article 101(3) but, more generally, for all circumstances where justifications are advanced. It does not also take into account decision theoretic concerns, such as the fact that it is most cost effective, in terms of enforcement, to ask the dominant undertakings to substantiate possible efficiency gains/objective justifications, as they (a) possess this information already, (b) have the incentive to provide it in order to escape liability, and (c) it is less costly for them to produce (in terms of search costs and economies of scale if there are multiple claimants and a number of alleged infringements). Some national courts distinguish between the legal burden of proof and the evidentiary burden of proof to make the point that, although there is no equivalent to Article 101(3) in the context of the prohibition of an abuse of dominant position, it is still for the defendant to advance

504 Opinion AG Jacobs in Case C-53/03, *Syfait* [2005] ECR I–4609, para 72.

505 E Rousseva, *Rethinking Exclusionary Abuses in EU Competition Law* (Hart, 2010), 37.

justifications of conduct producing anti-competitive effects.[506] The General Court has also recognized in *Microsoft* that

> although the burden of proof of the existence of the circumstances that constitute an infringement of Article [102] is borne by the Commission, it is for the dominant undertaking concerned, and not for the Commission, before the end of the administrative procedure, to raise any plea of objective justification and to support it with arguments and evidence. It then falls to the Commission, where it proposes to make a finding of an abuse of a dominant position, to show that the arguments and evidence relied on by the undertaking cannot prevail and, accordingly, that the justification put forward cannot be accepted.[507]

The dominant undertaking bears the evidentiary burden of proof with regard to the existence of objective justifications, while the legal burden of proof of the existence of an abuse falls on the Commission or the claimant. That is, the claimant or the Commission bears the risks of the doubt in finding the existence of an abuse although it is on the defendant to produce evidence of efficiencies and objective justifications. It follows that, if the defendant produces 'with a sufficient degree of probability', 'verifiable' evidence of efficiencies which conforms with the cumulative requirements set in the Guidance,[508] if there is still a doubt following a balance of probabilities test (therefore a 50–50 per cent situation), this doubt should benefit to the dominant undertaking. That could establish a slight difference between Articles 101 and 102, as the legal burden of proof for an Article 101(3) defence, that is the risks of a doubt on the existence of efficiency gains, are bore by the defendant.

7. Is there a difference with regard to the standard of proof for possible objective justifications/efficiency gains between Articles 101 and 102 TFEU? The first step of the competition assessment under Article 101 establishes the existence of an anti-competitive object or effect. The competition authority or the claimant bears the legal burden of proof. The standard of proof required in the first step of the analysis is relatively low. First, it is possible to prove the existence of an anti-competitive object by referring to the nature of the conduct and by characterizing it as falling within the 'object box'.[509] Second, the existence of potential negative effects on consumers, in the form of higher prices, reduced innovation and variety and lower output, may also be sufficient to identify a practice as being restrictive of competition.[510] However, even in this case, the competition assessment is not a fully effects-based. The enforcement of Article 101(1) largely emphasizes structural elements, such as high market shares or barriers to entry.[511] The burden then shifts to the defendant, except in circumstances where

[506] On the distinction between the legal and the evidential burden of proof, see *British Horseracing Board v Office of Fair Trading* [2005] CAT 29, para 132. In the context of Article 82, see R Nazzini, 'The Wood Began to Move: An Essay on Consumer Welfare, Evidence and Burden of Proof in Article 82 EC Cases' (2006) 31 *European L Rev* 518.

[507] Case T-201/04, *Microsoft v Commission* [2007] ECR II–3601, para 1144.

[508] Commission Guidance on Article 102, para 30.

[509] This highly evocative (in terms of categorical thinking) term has been introduced by R Whish, *Competition Law* (OUP, 6th ed, 2009) 118.

[510] Guidelines on Article 101(3), para 24.

[511] For an interesting analysis, see M Lankhorst, 'Improving Accuracy in Effects-based analysis: An Incentive-oriented approach', Amsterdam Centre for Law and Economics Working Paper No 2007-1 (12 January 2007), available at https://ssrn.com/abstract=956330.

the specific commercial practice is covered by a block exemption regulation. The defendant may claim efficiency gains that would outweigh the anti-competitive effects under Article 101(3). However, there are strict requirements for substantiating efficiency gains.[512] In conclusion, an essential characteristic of the framework of Article 101 is the marked asymmetry between the standard of proof that is required from the claimant and the standard of proof required by the defendant, to the benefit of the former. The situation is not very different when it comes to the application of Article 102. In practice, it would be very difficult for a dominant undertaking to prove the existence of objective justifications, the control and the conditions for such a defence being at least as restrictive as the conditions of Article 101(3) TFEU[513] In contrast, the standard of proof for consumer harm is particularly low, as there is no need to prove the existence of an actual or direct consumer detriment.[514] The Court noted in *Microsoft* that consumer choice would be affected if rival products of equal or better quality cannot compete on equal terms.[515] Nevertheless, in other parts of the decision, the Court interprets this condition as requiring only the preservation of the market access of competitors without requiring that the claimant produce evidence that competitors that are excluded from the market are, or would likely to, produce better quality products than those of the dominant firm. Consumer choice seems to have been equated in this case to the preservation of competitive rivalry on the marketplace.[516] The standard of proof for harm to competition and possible defences in Article 102 is therefore also asymmetrical, although there might be some difference of degree in the asymmetry: it is generally more difficult for efficiency gains and other objective justifications to outweigh the anti-competitive effects in the context of Article 102 than in Article 101(3).[517]

8. There are different reasons that may explain this asymmetry. Beckner and Salop note, in a different context, that decision makers may be risk neutral or risk averse. Risk neutral decision makers weigh 'potential harms equally with potential benefits', while risk-averse decision makers 'would even reject conduct with a higher expected value in light of the significant downside risk', in other words they will give additional weight to potential harms.[518] In this context, risk could be understood as uncertainty over the effects of the decision in the present case and in future cases.[519] The fact that decision makers give more weight to anti-competitive effects than to efficiency gains may indicate that they are risk averse to possible errors of false negatives. As a matter of comparison, the recent report of the US Department of Justice on Single-Firm Conduct adopts the exact opposite standard: 'conduct should be unlawful under section 2 if its anticompetitive effects are shown to be substantially disproportionate to any associated precompetitive effects'.[520] The asymmetry between the weight attached to

512 Guidelines on Article 101(3), para 51.

513 See eg Case C-95/04 P, *British Airways plc v Commission* [2007] ECR I–2331, para 86.

514 Ibid, para 106. 515 Ibid, para 652. 516 Ibid, para 664.

517 See G Monti, *EC Competition Law* (CUP, 1st ed, 2007), 203, observing that 'no firm has yet managed to defend itself successfully under Article 82 EC'.

518 CF Beckner III and SC Salop, 'Decision Theory and Antitrust Rules' (1999) 67(1) *Antitrust LJ* 41.

519 Although the concepts of risk and that of uncertainty are not, in theory, similar, risk being considered as measurable uncertainty while uncertainty cannot be measured. See FH Knight, *Risk, Uncertainty and Profit* (Houghton Mifflin Company, 1921), 25. In this context, the two terms will be used interchangeably.

520 US DOJ, *Competition and Monopoly: Single-Firm Conduct under Section 2 of the Sherman Act* (2008), ix and 45–6, available at www.usdoj.gov/atr/public/reports/236681.pdf

anti-competitive effects and that to pro-competitive effects indicates that the US DOJ is risk-averse to false positives following the enforcement of section 2 Sherman Act. A risk neutral decision maker would have given the same weight to both effects. The asymmetry is also closely related to the availability and the cost of evidence. According to the Commission's staff working paper on damages competition cases are characterized by a very asymmetric distribution of the available information and the necessary evidence: it is often very difficult for claimants to produce the required evidence, since many of the relevant facts are in the possession of the defendant or of third persons and are often not known to claimants in sufficient detail.[521] A lower standard of proof for anti-competitive effects than for efficiency gains may therefore seek to establish some degree of formal equality in the starting positions of the claimant and the defendant by compensating for the initial information disadvantage of the claimant.

9. Can objective justifications (efficiencies) be argued for any type of abuse? In his Opinion in *Sot Lélos Kai Sia*, AG Colomer observed that, although there are two different types of abuses: those that affect consumers (exploitative abuses) and those that affect actual or potential competitors (exclusionary abuses), dominant undertakings should be able to defend themselves on the basis of economic results obtained for both types of abuses.[522] A balancing test will determine the existence of positive and negative effects to competition for the consumers and other economic operators that are situated 'in the same relevant market'. Consequently, AG Colomer suggested that the Court declares without ambiguity that Article 102 TFEU does not apply before examining the existence of positive effects/defences, even if it is clear that the facts of the case do not leave any doubt as to the anti-competitive intent of the parties.[523] One could interpret the reference by the European Commission in its Guidance on Article 102 to circumstances where it would not be necessary to carry out a detailed assessment before concluding that the conduct in question is likely to result in consumer harm as not necessarily excluding the theoretical possibility of an efficiency defence.[524] It is true that the Commission considers that the anti-competitive effect will be inferred in this case, as that type of conduct can only raise obstacles to competition without adding any efficiency gain. One could argue, however, that this paragraph does not affect the theoretical possibility for dominant undertakings to invoke efficiencies, in particular as it remains possible for conduct leading to anti-competitive foreclosure to be justified by the objective necessity defence and efficiencies, before finding the existence of an abuse of a dominant position. The Commission does not explicitly exclude these practices from Section D of the report on objective necessity and efficiencies that follows, although, in practice, it seems unlikely that the alleged efficiencies will be accepted, for failure to comply at least with the first two cumulative conditions of the efficiency defence. In *GSK*, the CJEU seems to have implicitly recognized that certain types of conduct, such as a restriction of parallel trade, 'there

[521] Commission Staff Working Paper on Damages Actions for Breach of the EC antitrust rules, SEC (2008) 404 (2 April 2008), available at http://ec.europa.eu/comm/competition/antitrust/actionsdamages/documents.html.

[522] Ibid, para 74.

[523] Opinion of AG Colomer in Joined Cases C-468–78/06, *GSK* [2008] ECR I-7139, para 76.

[524] Commission Guidance on Article 102, para 22. The Commission provides some non-exhaustive examples, such as conduct through which the dominant undertaking prevents its customers from testing the conduct of competitors or pays a distributor or a customer to delay the introduction of a competitor's product.

can be *no escape* from the prohibition laid down in Article [102 TFEU]'.[525] Despite, however, the language employed, the Court immediately qualified this statement by accepting that this does not amount to an absolute presumption of consumer harm or a *per se* prohibition rule. The presumption of anti-competitive effects may still be rebutted by the defendant in limited circumstances: a company must be 'in a position to take steps that are reasonable and in proportion to the need to protect its own commercial interests'.[526] The full array of objective justifications may not apply in this case (only reasonable and proportionate protection of commercial interests).[527] The Court introduces a degree of categorical analysis in Article 102 TFEU, as it implies that some restrictions of competition are so severe that only a limited range of objective justifications may enter into consideration. Furthermore, the Court immediately qualifies the possibility of dominant firms justifying restrictions on parallel trade by indicating that it is limited to circumstances where (a) State intervention is one of the factors liable to create the opportunities for parallel trade in the first place[528] and (b) where a different interpretation of Article 102 TFEU, rejecting any possibility of justification, would have left dominant firms only the choice 'not to place its medicines on the market at all in a Member State where the prices of those products are set at a relatively low level'.[529] This passage indicates that a possible interpretation of the Court's position would be that dominant firms may justify restrictions on parallel trade falling under Article 102 only in a *Distillers* type situation:[530] following the prohibition of the differential pricing system by the Commission, Distillers withdrew Johnnie Walker Red label from the UK market.[531] This implies that some restrictions of competition are so severe that only a limited range of objective justifications may enter into consideration and only under specific circumstances.

8.4.6.2. Some recent case law in the EU

Some recent cases of the European Courts provide some guidance as to the scope and modalities of the efficiency defence in the context of Article 102 TFEU. The Court seems to

525 Opinion of AG Colomer in Joined Cases C-468–78/06, *GSK* [2008] ECR I–7139, para 66 (emphasis added).

526 Ibid, para 69.

527 The content of this concept is unclear. A restrictive definition of the concept will cover only a meeting competition defence, thus excluding the consideration of efficiency gains. The interpretation of this expression is not yet clear. See E Rousseva, 'The Concept of "Objective Justification" of an Abuse of a Dominant Position: Can it Help to Modernise the Analysis under Article 82?' (2006) 2 *Competition L Rev* 27, 33–4, who observes the following:

> [. . .] the question is what a legitimate commercial interest of a dominant undertaking is: does this interest mean only a right of a dominant undertaking to survive on the market, i.e., to prevent its inefficient operation, or does it also mean a right to carry out a profit oriented policy? How does the prerogative of a dominant firm to protect its interest fit with the essential goal of competition to serve consumers' interests? These are questions on which views diverge.

528 Joined Cases C-468–78/06, *GSK* [2008] ECR I–7139, para 67. 529 Ibid, para 68.

530 *The Distillers Co Ltd (Conditions of Sales and Price Terms)* (Case IV/26.528) Commission Decision [1978] OJ L 50/16. See the criticisms of AG Warner in Case C-30/78 *Distillers Co v Commission* [1980] ECR 2229; V Korah, 'Goodbye Red Label: Condemnation of dual pricing by Distillers' (1979) *European L Rev* 1.

531 Similar issues of differential pricing under Article 101 have been dealt by the CJEU: Joined Cases C-501, 513, 515 & 519/06 P, *GlaxoSmithKline Services Unlimited v Commission*, ECLI:EU:C:2009:610, appeal of Case T-168/01, *GlaxoSmithKline Services v Commission* [2006] ECR II–2969.

apply a proportionality test instead of a trade-of between the efficiency gains and the anti-competitive effects.

Case C-52/09, *Konkurrenverket v TeliaSonera Sverige AB*
[2009] ECR I–527 (references omitted)

75. [. . .] It must be borne in mind that an undertaking remains at liberty to demonstrate that its pricing practice, albeit producing an exclusionary effect, is economically justified.

76. The assessment of the economic justification for a pricing practice established by an undertaking in a dominant position which is capable of producing an exclusionary effect is to be made on the basis of all the circumstances of the case. In that regard, it has to be determined whether the exclusionary effect arising from such a practice, which is disadvantageous for competition, may be counterbalanced, or outweighed, by advantages in terms of efficiency which also benefit the consumer. If the exclusionary effect of that practice bears no relation to advantages for the market and consumers, or if it goes beyond what is necessary in order to attain those advantages, that practice must be regarded as an abuse.

Case C-209/10, *Post Danmark A/S v Konkurrencerådet (Post Danmark I)*, ECLI:EU:C:2012:172 (references omitted)

40. If the court making the reference, after carrying out that assessment, should nevertheless make a finding of anti-competitive effects due to Post Danmark's actions, it should be recalled that it is open to a dominant undertaking to provide justification for behaviour that is liable to be caught by the prohibition under Article [102 TFEU].

41. In particular, such an undertaking may demonstrate, for that purpose, either that its conduct is objectively necessary, or that the exclusionary effect produced may be counterbalanced, outweighed even, by advantages in terms of efficiency that also benefit consumers.

42. In that last regard, it is for the dominant undertaking to show that the efficiency gains likely to result from the conduct under consideration counteract any likely negative effects on competition and consumer welfare in the affected markets, that those gains have been, or are likely to be, brought about as a result of that conduct, that such conduct is necessary for the achievement of those gains in efficiency and that it does not eliminate effective competition, by removing all or most existing sources of actual or potential competition.

8.4.6.3. *Streetmap Limited v Google (UK) and Google Search (EU)*

Of particular interest is the application of the objective justification defence by the English High Court (Roth J) in *Streetmap v Google*, which constitutes an example of a careful assessment of the objective justifications put forward by the defendant and of the operation of the proportionality test in the context of Article 102 TFEU. The case also involved some interesting parts on the concept of anti-competitive foreclosure. The case attracted a lot of interest Europe-wide in view of the pending investigations of the Commission against Google, one of which is on a similar type of abuse as the one alleged in the *Streetmap* case.[532] Roth J distinguished the facts of the case from the CJEU's judgments in *Hoffmann-La Roche* and *Post Danmark II*, which involved conduct by the dominant undertaking on the market where it was dominant and where no appreciable effect had to be shown because the relevant market was already weakened by the presence of the dominant undertaking, with the case in hand, where the effect of the allegedly anti-competitive conduct was on a separate market where the undertaking was not dominant, and for which it was necessary (for the claimant) to bring evidence that there was an appreciable effect. Roth J made a thorough analysis of the effects of the specific conduct on competition in the market for online mapping services and proceeded to a unique in depth analysis of the objective justifications put forward by the parties. An important part of the assessment of the objective justifications by the High Court was the proportionality question: was there a less distortive alternative available that could provide the same benefits without imposing a disproportional/unreasonable burden on Google?

In contrast, in *Google Search* the European Commission rejected the objective justifications put forward by Google.[533] The Commission noted that the exclusionary effect produced 'may be counterbalanced, outweighed even, by advantages in terms of efficiency gains that also benefit consumers'[534] but considered that the arguments put forward by Google, either did not understand the theory of harm employed by the Commission in this case, which was the discriminatory application of mechanisms, and the discriminatory displays of results by Google, or *inter alia* did not take into account the 'freedom of competing comparison shopping services and other economic operators to conduct a business', and 'the right of users to receive information from competing comparison shopping services.'[535]

SELECTIVE BIBLIOGRAPHY

Books

Akman, P, *The Concept of Abuse in EU Competition Law: Law and Economic Approaches* (Hart, 2012).

Etro, F, and Kokkoris, I (eds) *Competition Law and the Enforcement of Article 102* (OUP, 2010).

Filippelli, M, *Collective Dominance and Collusion: Parallelism in EU and US Competition Law* (Edward Elgar, 2013).

Fumagalli, C, Motta, M, and Calcagno, C, *Exclusionary Practices: The Economics of Monopolisation and Abuse of Dominance* (CUP, 2018).

Joliet, R, *Monopolization and Abuse of a Dominant Position: A Comparative Study of the American and European Approaches to the Control of Economic Power* (Martinus Nijhoff, 1970).

532 See European Commission, 'Antitrust: Commission sends Statement of Objections to Google on comparison shopping service; opens separate formal investigation on Android', Press Release IP/15/4780 (15 April 2015), available at http://europa.eu/rapid/press-release_IP-15-4780_en.htm.

533 *Google Search (Shopping)* (Case AT.39740) Commission Decision (26 June 2017), paras 653–71.

534 Ibid, para 653.

535 Ibid, paras 669 and 670.

Nazzini, R, *The Foundations of European Union Competition Law: The Objective and Principles of Article 102* (OUP, 2011).

O'Donoghue, R, and Padilla, J, *The Law and Economics of Article 102 TFEU* (Hart, 2nd ed, 2013).

Pace, LF (ed) *European Competition Law: The Impact of the Commission's Guidance on Article 102* (Edward Elgar, 2011).

Rousseva, E, *Rethinking Exclusionary Abuses in EU Competition Law* (Hart, 2010).

Chapters in books

Coscelli, A, and Edwards, G, 'Dominance and Market Power in EU Competition Law Enforcement' in Lianos, I, and Geradin, D (eds) *Handbook on European Competition Law* (Edward Elgar, 2013), 350.

Gal, M, 'Abuse of Dominance – Exploitative Abuses' in Lianos, I and Geradin, D (eds) *Handbook on European Competition Law* (Edward Elgar, 2013), 385.

Jones, A, and Gormsen, LL, 'Abuse of Dominance–Exclusionary Pricing Abuses' in Lianos, I, and Geradin, D, *Handbook on EU Competition Law: Substantive Aspects* (Edward Elgar, 2013), 423.

Lianos, I, 'Categorical Thinking in Competition Law and the "Effects-based" Approach in Article 82 EC' in Ezrachi, A (ed) *Article 82 EC: Reflections on its recent Evolution* (Hart, 2009), 19.

Mestmäcker, EJ, 'The Development of German and European Competition Law with Special Reference to the EU Commission's Article 82 Guidance of 2008' in Pace, LF (ed) *European Competition Law: The Impact of the Commission's Guidance on Article 102* (Edward Elgar, 2011), 25.

Journal articles

Akman, P, 'The European Commission's Guidance on Article 102 TFEU: From *Inferno* to *Paradiso*?' (2010) 73 *Modern L Rev* 605.

Akman, P, 'The Relationship between Economic Duress and Abuse of a Dominant Position' [2014] *Lloyd's Maritime and Commercial L Q* 99.

Geradin, D, 'Limiting the Scope of Article 82 EC: What Can the EU Learn from the US Supreme Court's Judgment in "Trinko" in the Wake of "Microsoft", "IMS" and "Deutsche Telekom"?' (2004) 41(6) *Common Market L Rev* 1519.

Ibáñez Colomo, P, 'Beyond the "More Economics-Based. Approach": A Legal Perspective on Article 102 TFEU Case Law' (2016) 53(3) *Common Market L Rev* 709.

Lianos, I, and Lombardi, C, 'Superior Bargaining Power and the Global Food Value Chain: The Wuthering Heights of Holistic Competition Law?' (2016-I) *Concurrences* 22.

Lovdhal-Gormsen, L, 'Why the European Commission's Enforcement Priorities on Article 82 EC should be Withdrawn' (2010) 31 *European Competition L Rev* 45.

Monti, G, 'Article 82 EC: What Future for the Effects-Based Approach?' (2010) 1 *J European Competition L & Practice* 1.

Nazzini, R, 'The Wood Began to Move: An Essay on Consumer Welfare, Evidence and Burden of Proof in Article 82 EC Cases' (2006) 31 *European L Rev* 518.

Petit, N, 'Intel, Leveraging Rebates and the Goals of Article 102 TFEU' (2015) 11(1) *European Competition J* 26.

Rey, P and Venit J, 'An Effects-Based Approach to Article 102: A Response to Wouter Wils', (2015) 38 *World Competition* 1.

Rousseva, E, and Marquis, M, 'Hell Freezes Over: A Climate Change for Assessing Exclusionary Conduct under Article 102 TFEU' (2012) 4 *J European Competition L & Practice* 32.

Temple Lang J, 'How Can this Problem of Exclusionary Abuses under Article 102 TFEU Be Resolved?, (2012) 37 European L Rev 136

Wils, W, 'The Judgment of the EU General Court in *Intel* and the so-called "More Economic Approach" to Abuse of Dominance' (2014) 37 *World Competition* 405.

ABUSE OF A DOMINANT POSITION (SPECIFIC ABUSES)

9.1. ACQUISITION OF COMPETITORS AND EXCLUSIVE RIGHTS

In *Continental Can v Commission*, the Court of Justice of the European Union (CJEU) found that the acquisition of a competitor might be abusive if it strengthens a dominant position.[1] The Court also held that the list of abuses included in Article 102 of the Treaty on the Functioning of the European Union (TFEU) is not exhaustive.

In *Tetra Pak Rausing v Commission*,[2] Tetra Pak Rausing, a group specializing mainly in equipment for packaging fresh or UHT treated milk in cartons, had acquired through its acquisition of a group of companies (Liquipak), an exclusive patent licence relating to a new process for packaging UHT milk in cartons. The aseptic packaging machines on the market were adapted for either 'brick' or 'gable-top' cartons. Elopak, a competitor of Tetra Pak in the supply of 'gable-top' cartons, was also the exclusive distributor for Liquipak's machines for pasteurized milk and for any machine Liquipak might develop or acquire for UHT-treated milk. It had assisted Liquipak in its efforts to develop a new packaging machine incorporating the process protected by the exclusive patent licence at issue in this case.

[1] Case C-6/72, *Europemballage Corporation and Continental Can Co Inc v Commission* [1973] ECR 215. See Section 7.4.1.1.

[2] Case T-51/89, *Tetra Pak Rausing SA v Commission* [1990] ECR II–309.

Following a complaint by Elopak, the Commission found that the acquisition by Tetra Pak Rausing of the exclusive licence from Liquipak infringed Article 102 TFEU. Its acquisition by Tetra Pak had the effects of strengthening Tetra Pak's dominant position in the market for aseptic milk-packaging machines, further weakening existing competition and making the entry of any new competition even more difficult. Tetra Pak commenced an action for annulment of the Commission's decision before the Court of First Instance (now General Court, GC) on the ground that the Commission's decision was contrary to Articles 101(3) and 102 TFEU, as the Commission cannot treat an agreement enjoying a block exemption under Article 101(3) as prohibited by Article 102 TFEU because Articles 101 and 102 TFEU both pursue the same objective. The argument was that as the exclusive licensee would have enjoyed the benefit of the current block exemption regulation on patent licensing agreements, under Article 101(3) TFEU, it did not make sense to find that the acquisition of exclusivity afforded by the licence through takeover of a competing company should be treated differently, as both practices have the same restrictive effects on competition.

The CJEU rejected this argument. First, it explained that the applicability to an agreement of Article 101 does not preclude application of Article 102, as both provisions may apply to the same conduct. Second, the CJEU tried to reconcile the application of Article 102 with an exemption under Article 101(3). The CJEU noted:

> Articles [101] and [102] are complementary inasmuch as they pursue a common general objective [. . .] which provides that the activities of the Community are to include 'the institution of a system ensuring that competition in the common market is not distorted'. But they none the less constitute, in the scheme of the Treaty, two independent legal instruments addressing different situations. [. . .][3]

Hence, 'in principle, the grant of exemption cannot preclude application of Article [102 TFEU]'.[4] The Court further made a distinction between individual and block exemptions.

> [. . .] The grant of individual exemption presupposes that the Commission has found that the agreement in question complies with the conditions set out in Article [101(3)]. So, where an individual exemption decision has been taken, characteristics of the agreement which would also be relevant in applying Article [102] may be taken to have been established. Consequently, in applying Article [102], the Commission must take account, unless the factual and legal circumstances have altered, of the earlier findings made when exemption was granted under Article [101(3)].
>
> Now it is true that regulations granting block exemption, like individual exemption decisions, apply only to agreements which, in principle, satisfy the conditions set out in Article [101(3)]. But unlike individual exemptions, block exemptions are, by definition, not dependent on a case-by-case examination to establish that the conditions for exemption laid down in the Treaty are in fact satisfied. In order to qualify for a block exemption, an agreement has only to satisfy the criteria laid down in the relevant block-exemption regulation. The agreement itself is not subject to any positive assessment with regard to the conditions set out in Article [101(3)]. So a block exemption cannot, generally speaking, be construed as having effects similar to negative clearance in relation to Article [102]. The result is that, where agreements to which

[3] Ibid, para 22. [4] Ibid, para 26.

> undertakings in a dominant position are parties fall within the scope of a block-exemption regulation (that is, where the regulation is unlimited in scope), the effects of block exemption on the applicability of Article [102] must be assessed solely in the context of the scheme of Article [102].[5]

The Court also examined the standard applying to the conduct in question, holding that the mere fact that an undertaking in a dominant position acquires an exclusive patent licence does not as such constitute an abuse within the meaning of Article 102 TFEU and that for the purpose of applying Article 102 TFEU, the circumstances surrounding the acquisition, and in particular its effects on the structure of competition in the relevant market, must be taken into account. In particular, the Court noted that 'licence was alone capable of giving an undertaking the means of competing effectively with the applicant in the field of the aseptic packaging of milk' and that '[t]he takeover [. . .] was no more than the means—to which the Commission has attached no particular significance in applying Article [102]—by which the applicant acquired the exclusivity of the [. . .] licence, the effect of which was to deprive other undertakings of the means of competing with the applicant. [. . .]'[6]

9.2. UNILATERAL REFUSALS TO SUPPLY/GRANT ACCESS TO ASSETS

According to Article 17(1) of the Charter of Fundamental Rights (legally binding since the Treaty of Lisbon):

> Everyone has the right to own, use, dispose of and bequeath his or her lawfully acquired possessions. No one may be deprived of his or her possessions, except in the public interest and in the cases and under the conditions provided for by law, subject to fair compensation being paid in good time for their loss. The use of property may be regulated by law insofar as is necessary for the general interest.

However, in some circumstances, a unilateral refusal to supply may restrict competition. We will briefly examine some economic theories which may suggest that unilateral refusals to supply could, in specific circumstances, produce anti-competitive effects and harm consumers.

9.2.1. THE ECONOMICS OF UNILATERAL REFUSALS TO SUPPLY (FORECLOSURE)

Economists have advanced a number of theories of anti-competitive effects explaining why even a unilateral practice (including a refusal to supply) may raise competition law concerns, in particular vertical foreclosure. Even if these theories apply to different settings, we will examine here the main economic principles that emerge from these different theories.[7]

[5] Ibid, paras 28–9. [6] Ibid, para 23. [7] On vertical foreclosure see also Section 9.4.2.

We focus here on practices that produce anti-competitive effects and consumer harm by excluding competitors (exclusionary practices). This Section does not concern practices that produce directly consumer harm, without the exclusion of a competitor (eg excessive prices, price discrimination), the so-called exploitative abuses.[8]

9.2.1.1. The leverage theory

A controversial doctrine of anti-competitive effects is the leverage theory, which explains that, by refusing to supply/deal the monopolists seek to extend their monopoly power to a related market, upstream or downstream.[9] This theory was criticized by authors of the Chicago School of antitrust economics, who argued that an upstream monopolist has no interest in leveraging its monopoly power to a related market because it is possible to gain only one monopoly profit overall (the single monopoly profit theorem).[10] As a result, the leverage theory has lost its appeal as an autonomous basis for action in the United States,[11] although it still retains some significance in Europe. The economic grounding of the single monopoly profit theorem has nevertheless been revisited lately.[12] Other authors have criticized the narrow assumptions of the single monopoly profit theorem, noting that in reality it almost never holds.[13] The leverage theory has also inspired the recent *Google Search* (Shopping) case of the Commission regarding practices of self-referencing. See our analysis in Section 9.8.6.2.

9.2.1.2. Raising rivals' costs

A distinct theory of anti-competitive effects is that dominant firms may refuse to deal in order to create barriers to entry and raise the costs of their rivals.[14] As a result, they will be able to increase profitably their prices, up to the level of their rivals and exercise market power, or they would be able to profitably undercut rivals' prices and drive them out of the market.

In certain circumstances, these strategies will have the advantage of requiring little or no short-run sacrifice of profit to achieve the desired long-term goal of lessening competition in the market. They may nonetheless achieve anticompetitive foreclosure. This will have the effect of limiting their rivals' choice and reducing their incentives to innovate, thus restraining competition in the final product market.

9.2.1.3. Maintenance of monopoly

The theories of anti-competitive effects set out in this Section do not only relate to strategies that erode the competitive advantage of the dominant firm's rivals in a related market with the aim of expanding the dominant firm's market power in that related secondary market. An

8 See Section 7.4.1.2.

9 L Kaplow, 'Extension of Monopoly Power Through Leverage' (1985) 85 *Columbia L Rev* 515.

10 W Bowman, 'Tying Arrangements and the Leverage Problem' (1957) 67 *Yale LJ* 19; R Posner, *Antitrust Law* (University of Chicago Press, 2001), 198–200. See our detailed analysis in Section 8.8.1.

11 *Verizon Communications, Inc v Law Offices of Curtis V Trinko, LLP*, 540 US 398 (2004) [hereinafter *Trinko*].

12 See our analysis in Section 9.8.1.

13 See E Elhauge, 'Tying, Bundled Discounts, and the Death of the Single Monopoly Profit Theory' (2009) 123 *Harvard Law Review* 397 (criticizing the single monopoly profit theorem from a welfare perspective); H. First, 'No Single Monopoly Profit, No Single Policy Prescription?' (2009) 5(2) *Competition Policy Int'l* 199 (criticizing the theory from a non-economic perspective).

14 TG Krattenmaker and SC Salop, 'Anticompetitive Exclusion: Raising Rivals' Costs to Achieve Power Over Price' (1986) 96 *Yale LJ* 209.

alternative claim of anti-competitive effect is that the dominant firm will seek to *maintain* its monopoly power on the primary market.[15]

Having introduced some of the economic theories inspiring competition law enforcement against refusals to supply/grant access to assets by a dominant undertaking, we will develop the various sub-legal categories of such type of abuse, established by the jurisprudence of the CJEU.

9.2.2. REFUSAL TO SUPPLY AN EXISTING CUSTOMER

9.2.2.1. *Commercial Solvents*

Case C-6/73, *Istituto Chemioterapico Italiano SpA and Commercial Solvents Corp v Commission*

[1974] ECR 223 (*Commercial Solvents*)

Commercial Solvents Corporation (CSC) was the only undertaking in the world producing nitropropane and aminobutanol on a commercial scale. There were barriers to entry consisting of the knowhow needed to make nitropropane. From nitropropane it was comparatively easy to produce aminobutanol. Aminobutanol was an intermediate product used to emulsify paint, as well as to make ethambutol, a drug used for the cure from tuberculosis. Zoja had been buying aminobutanol to make ethambutol specialities from Istituto, CSC's 51 per cent joint venture. It discovered that it could obtain aminobutanol more cheaply from distributors to paint emulsifiers and, in 1970, Zoja asked Istituto to cancel its order. This was agreed but CSC arranged for the supply of the intermediate products to dry up. When Zoja asked for supplies to be resumed, CSC refused. CSC was already supplying aminobutanol to Istituto, and to American Cyanamid who were producing ethambutol.

After further fruitless attempts to obtain supplies, Zoja complained to the Commission that the refusal to resume supply infringed Article [102 TFEU]. The Commission adopted an interim decision Zoja v Commercial Solvents Corp *[1973] CMLR D50, [1973] OJ L 299/51 at the end of that year, jointly and severally requiring CSC and Istituto to supply 30.00 kg of aminobutanol to Zoja to meet its most urgent needs at a price not exceeding the maximum price previously charged for those two products and imposed a fine. CSC and Istituto appealed to the CJEU for annulment of the decision and its suspension meanwhile.*

22. Contrary to the arguments of the applicants it is in fact possible to distinguish the market in raw material necessary for the manufacture of a product from the market on which the product is sold. An abuse of a dominant position on the market in raw materials may thus have effects restricting competition in the market on which the derivatives of the raw material are sold and these effects must be taken into account in considering the effects of an infringement, even if the market for the derivative does not constitute a self-contained market. [. . .]

25. However, an undertaking being in a dominant position as regards the production of raw material and therefore able to control the supply to manufacturers of derivatives cannot, just because it decides to start manufacturing these derivatives (in

[15] See DW Carlton and M Waldman, 'The Strategic Use of Tying to Preserve and Create Market Power in Evolving Industries' (2002) 33 *Rand J Economics* 194, building on the work of MD Whinston, 'Tying, Foreclosure, and Exclusion' (1990) 80 *American Economic Rev* 837, analysed in Section 8.1.

competition with its former customers), act in such a way as to eliminate their competition which, in the case in question, would have amounted to eliminating one of the principal manufacturers of ethambutol in the Common Market. Since such conduct is contrary to the objectives expressed in [Article 3(1)(g) of the Treaty, now moved to Protocol no 27] and set out in greater detail in Articles [101] and [102], it follows that an undertaking which has a dominant position in the market in raw materials and which, with the object of reserving such raw material for manufacturing its own derivatives, refuses to supply a customer, which is itself a manufacturer of these derivatives, and therefore risks eliminating all competition on the part of this customer, is abusing its dominant position within the meaning of Article [102]. In this context it does not matter that the undertaking ceased to supply in the spring of 1970 because of the cancellation of the purchases by Zoja, because it appears from the applicants' own statement that, when the supplies provided for in the contract had been completed, the sale of aminobutanol would have stopped in any case.

26. It is also unnecessary to examine, as the applicants have asked, whether Zoja had an urgent need for aminobutanol in 1970 and 1971 or whether this company still had large quantities of this product which would enable it to reorganise its production in good time, since that question is not relevant to the consideration of the conduct of the applicants.

27. Finally Commercial Solvents Corp. states that its production of nitropropane and aminobutanol ought to be considered in the context of nitration of paraffin, of which nitropropane is only one of the derivatives and that, similarly, aminobutanol is only one of the derivatives of nitropropane. Therefore, the possibilities of producing the two products in question are not unlimited but depend in part on the possible sales outlets of the other derivatives.

28. However, the applicants do not seriously dispute the statement in the decision in question to the effect that 'in view of the production capacity of the Commercial Solvents Corp. plant it can be confirmed that Commercial Solvents Corp. can satisfy Zoja's needs, since Zoja represents a very small percentage (approximately 5–6 per cent) of Commercial Solvents Corp.'s global production of nitropropane'. It must be concluded that the Commission was justified in considering that such statements could not be taken into account.

29. These submissions must therefore be rejected.

NOTES AND QUESTIONS ON COMMERCIAL SOLVENTS

1. This is the first case where the Commission, confirmed by the Court of Justice, held that a refusal to supply a former customer amounted to the abuse of a dominant position. In later cases, the CJEU has referred to the doctrine of essential facilities. The owner of an essential facility may be required to grant access to its customers, but only in certain circumstances. Note the strength of CSC's dominant position and that Zoja had previously been a customer downstream.
2. Why should the previous contractual arrangement be relevant?
3. Perceived *ex post*, after CSC has developed the technology, the market would be more competitive if its competitors had access to the essential facility. Perceived *ex ante*, before CSC developed the technology, would one arrive to the same conclusion? The issue may not have arisen in this case. It seems that a new use was found for the raw materials which had previously been used for less lucrative purposes.

4. (Paragraph 25) This is the most quoted paragraph in the judgment. Note that this judgment was delivered shortly after *Continental Can* and before *United Brands*.[16] At that time, undertakings were not lightly considered to enjoy a dominant position. In his Opinion, AG Warner noted that '[a] crucial finding in the decision of the Commission was that ethambutol could not be manufactured competitively on an industrial scale from any raw materials other than nitropropane and aminobutanol'.[17]
5. (Paragraph 25) Can you distinguish between competition on the merits and eliminating competitors? Does the CJEU draw such a distinction?
6. (Paragraph 25) Was the CJEU protecting the competitors of CSC or those paying for the treatment of tubercular patients? Which should it protect?
7. (Paragraph 28) Does the fact that Zoja currently requires only 5–6 per cent of CSC's global production demonstrate that it has sufficient capacity to supply Zoja? To what should the Commission have looked? When by products are involved it may be very expensive to increase the supply of one unless outlets can be found for the others.
8. (Paragraphs 42–50) If CSC does not want to supply the raw materials, how should the price be set? Here the order was interim and the raw materials had recently been sold voluntarily, so the old price could be taken. If there were no previous sales, how should the price be set: at the monopoly level, or the cost of supply? Should the cost or value of the original technology be considered? Consider your answer to Question 3. Note that this is one of the main reasons for limiting any duty to supply.

9.2.2.2. *United Brands*

Case C-27/76, *United Brands Co and United Brands Continentaal BV v Commission*
[1978] ECR 207

In United Brands v Commission, *a company (UBC) with a dominant position in the production of bananas, which it marketed under the brand name 'Chiquita', among other anti-competitive practices cut off supplies to a Danish ripener-distributor when the latter, following a disagreement with UBC, began promoting a competitor's bananas and allegedly taking less care in the ripening of UBC's bananas. UBC was not present in the distribution market (which distinguishes this case from Commercial Solvents).*[18] *UBC claimed that they were defending themselves against the commercial attack of the Dole brand, which aimed to oust them from the Danish market.*

182. In view of these conflicting arguments it is advisable to assert positively from the outset that an undertaking in a dominant position for the purpose of marketing a product—which cashes in on the reputation of a brand name known and valued by the consumers—cannot stop supplying a long standing customer who abides by regular commercial practice, if the orders placed by this customer are in no way out of the ordinary.

[16] Cf Case C-6/72, *Europemballage Corporation and Continental Can Co Inc v Commission* [1973] ECR 215; Case 27/76, *United Brands Co v Commission* [1978] ECR 207.

[17] Opinion of AG Warner in Joined Cases 6 & 7/73, *Istituto Chemioterapico Italiano SpA and Commercial Solvents Corporation v Commission* [1974] ECR 259, 268.

[18] UBC took care of distribution and risk of fluctuating prices up to the point when the boat was four days from the port of arrival. The ripeners took the risk from the time they told UBC how many bananas it they wanted from each ship load. The ripener whose supplies were reduced was the exclusive distributor in Denmark for the rival Dole bananas.

183. Such conduct is inconsistent with the objectives laid down in [Article 3(f) of the Treaty, now replaced by Protocol No 27], which are set out in detail in Article [102], especially in paragraphs (b) and (c), since the refusal to sell would limit markets to the prejudice of consumers and would amount to discrimination which might in the end eliminate a trading party from the relevant market.

184. It is therefore necessary to ascertain whether the discontinuance of supplies by UBC in October 1973 was justified. [. . .]

189. Although it is true, as the applicant points out, that the fact that an undertaking is in a dominant position cannot disentitle it from protecting its own commercial interests if they are attacked, and that such an undertaking must be conceded the right to take such reasonable steps as it deems appropriate to protect its said interests, such behaviour cannot be countenanced if its actual purpose is to strengthen this dominant position and abuse it.

190. Even if the possibility of a counterattack is acceptable that attack must still be proportionate to the threat taking into account the economic strength of the undertakings confronting each other.

191. The sanction consisting of a refusal to supply by an undertaking in a dominant position was in excess of what might, if such a situation were to arise, reasonably be contemplated as a sanction for conduct similar to that for which UBC blamed Olesen.

192. [. . .] by acting in this way it would discourage its other ripener/distributors from supporting the advertising of other brand names and that the deterrent effect of the sanction imposed on one of them would make its position of strength on the relevant market that much more effective.

193. Such a course of conduct amounts therefore to a serious interference with the independence of small and medium sized firms in their commercial relations with the undertaking in a dominant position and this independence implies the right to give preference to competitors' goods.

194. In this case the adoption of such a course of conduct is designed to have a serious adverse effect on competition on the relevant banana market by only allowing firms dependent upon the dominant undertaking to stay in business.

NOTES AND QUESTIONS ON UNITED BRANDS

1. How far may a dominant firm decide (a) with whom it may deal initially; (b) to cut off an existing customer-what should a dominant firm do before terminating an unsatisfactory dealer?
2. Would this judgment affect the willingness of a firm entering Europe to appoint an exclusive dealer?

9.2.3. REFUSAL TO SUPPLY A NEW CUSTOMER AND THE ESSENTIAL FACILITIES DOCTRINE

9.2.3.1. The essential facilities doctrine

The essential facilities doctrine emerged in US antitrust law.[19] Although never explicitly accepted by the US Supreme Court, the lower courts have set the conditions for the application of

[19] Although the Supreme Court did not refer to it, some commentators perceive *United States v Terminal Railroad Association*, 24 US 383 (1912) as being the first illustration of the essential facilities doctrine. The case involved a group boycott case by the Terminal Railroad Association, established by fourteen railroad

the doctrine as requiring from the plaintiff proof of the following four elements: (1) control of the essential facility by a firm with market power; (2) a competitor's inability practically or reasonably to duplicate the essential facility; (3) the denial of the use of the facility by a competitor; (4) the feasibility of the dominant undertaking duplicating the facility.[20] The Supreme Court has recently marginalized the doctrine of essential facilities and it seems that the use of the doctrine in US law has fallen in desuetude.[21] In any case there is room for interpretation with regard to the second element of the doctrine, starting from the view that duplication of the facility should be physically impossible, and ending to the one that access to the essential facility need not be indispensable and 'it is sufficient if duplication of the facility would be economically infeasible and if denial of its use inflicts a severe handicap on potential market entrants'.[22] This would be, for example the case, only if the facility is a natural monopoly, in which event duplication would be wasteful from a social welfare perspective. There is also disagreement as to need for the plaintiff to prove that the monopolist uses the facility to control a vertically related distinct market and that the plaintiff is at least a potential competitor in either the upstream or the downstream market, some authors arguing that it should be possible to apply the doctrine even in situations involving one market and monopolist attempts to protect its position in that market.[23]

In EU competition law, the Commission first used the concept of 'essential facilities' in some decisions on interim measures involving the opening of port facilities to competition. In *Sea Containers v Stena Sealink*,[24] Sealink managed Holyhead Harbour, a focal point for ferry services between the central part of the UK and Dublin, There were other routes further North or South. Sealink also operated ferries from the harbour. A rival ferry company which also operated at Holyhead, B&I, complained that Sealink, as manager of the harbour, modified the sailing schedule of its own ferry operator in such a way that it interfered with B&I's loading and unloading of ferries. Sealink alleged that the facility was not indispensable because there was a technical solution available to B&I. Moreover, the bow wave that would be created would require Sealink to suspend its service for 20 minutes whenever the sailings were close to each other in time. It is doubtful whether Sealink retains a dominant position over the central corridor, as the ferryboats are now fast catamarans, for which the UK terminal at Liverpool is

companies, which controlled terminal facilities essential for the transportation of freight in the area of St Louis. The case was not a unilateral conduct case, it involved the application of section 1 of the Sherman Act, but it lent support to the idea that an entity controlling an essential facility has a duty to deal with firms needing access to it on reasonable and non-discriminatory terms. Since the parties had voluntarily agreed to build the bridge across the Mississippi, settling the price for an involuntary sale was less difficult than in a case where the refusal is unilateral. The mandated sale could be for the price charged initially for voluntary access. One could not predict the price precisely, but would not be left with no criterion to apply. See also *Associated Press v United States*, 326 US 1 (1945) (also a group boycott case involving the application of section 1 of the Sherman Act).

20 *MCI Communications Corp v AT&T*, 708 F 2d 1081, 1132–3 (7th Cir 1983).

21 See, for instance, the position of the Supreme Court in *Trinko*, 540 US 398 (2004). The Court noted that there are several problems with imposing a duty to deal and with regard to the essential facilities doctrine, it found 'no need either to recognize it here or to repudiate it here' (ibid, 411) noting that the doctrine applies if access is unavailable. That was not the case as the 1996 Telecommunications Act already mandated access. Some lower courts have nevertheless continued to apply the essential facilities doctrine after the *Trinko* decision. For a critical perspective on the Supreme Court's Opinion in *Trinko*, see N Economides, 'Vertical Leverage and the Sacrifice Principle: Why the Supreme Court Got *Trinko* Wrong' (2005) 61(3) *New York University Annual Survey of American Law* 379.

22 *Hecht v Pro-Football, Inc*, 570 F 2d 982, 992 (DC Cir 1977).

23 R Pitofsky, D Patterson, and J Hooks, 'The Essential Facilities Doctrine under US Law' (2002) 70 *Antitrust LJ* 443.

24 *Sea Containers v Stena Sealink* (Case COMP IV/34.689) Commission Decision [1994] OJ L 15/8. See also *B&I Line plc v Sealink Harbours Ltd and Sealink Stena Ltd* (Case COMP IV/34.174) Commission Decision [1992] CMLR 255.

available. The Commission found that an undertaking which occupies a dominant position in the provision of an essential facility and itself uses that facility (ie, a facility or infrastructure, without access to which competitors cannot provide services to their customers), and which refuses other companies access to that facility without objective justification or grants access to competitors only on terms less favourable than those which it gives to its own services, infringes Article 102 if the other conditions of that article are met.

Some commentators have noted that the Commission defined the relevant market very narrowly as referring to the 'central corridor' of ferry journeys between Great Britain and Ireland, within which Holyhead was the only available British port, hinting that the possibility that Sea Containers might have found an alternative port to operate in the central corridor and raising the question of the existence of sufficient differences between the central, northern and southern corridors to justify the definition of separate markets for each.[25] This brings to the fore the importance of the operation of defining relevant markets, as a narrowly defined market might inevitably lead to the finding that the dominant undertaking controls an essential facility and should thus be subject to a duty to deal.

The 'essential facilities doctrine' has assumed some importance in a number of decisions reached by competition authorities throughout the world because of the liberalization of utilities, which feature a number of possible essential facilities and the desire of governments to contain the power of those controlling these facilities from extending it in the related services markets linked to the use of these 'facilities'. Modern and efficient essential facilities are a key infrastructure feature fundamental to economic growth in both developed and developing economies. An essential facility may be defined as a facility to which access is essential for the provision of goods or services in a related market and where it is not economically efficient or feasible for a new entrant to replicate the facility. The concept has extended beyond infrastructure (railways, including track and stations, airports, including slot allocation, ground handling services; utility distribution networks, eg, electricity wires and gas pipelines, bus stations, ports) to airline computer reservations systems and in some cases intellectual property (IP) rights.

There is some debate over the practical use of this doctrine and its added value in view of the interventionist approach of competition authorities and courts in Europe in imposing a duty to deal, in comparison to the United States. Some authors have gone as far as analysing all the case law of the European Courts on unilateral refusals to deal from the prism of the essential facilities doctrine.[26]

On one side, an expansive view of the doctrine is a matter for concern: forcing a monopolist to share the essential facilities will reduce the incentives of the dominant undertaking and of the undertaking demanding access to invest on the facility. First, decreasing the monopolist's profit *ex post* by applying Article 102 TFEU will affect the incentives to invest in creating the facility at the first place. Second, it will reduce the incentives of the undertaking seeking access to invest and create its own facility. Applying Article 102 TFEU and imposing a duty to deal will thus increase allocative efficiency but risks reducing dynamic efficiency.[27]

Imposing a duty to deal under Article 102 TFEU will not also necessarily improve the situation of consumers in the absence of an obligation to provide access at a competitive price.

25 D Ridyard, 'Essential Facilities and the Obligation to Supply Competitors under UK and EC Competition Law' (1996) 8 *European Competition L Rev* 438.

26 See J Temple Lang, 'Defining Legitimate Competition: Companies' Duties to Supply Competitors, and Access to Essential Facilities' (1994) 18(2) *Fordham Int'l LJ* 437.

27 For a similar argument, see Opinion AG Jacobs in Case C-7/97, *Oscar Bronner GmbH & Co KG v Mediaprint Zeitungs- und Zeitschriftenverlag GmbH & Co KG* [1998] ECR I–7791 [hereinafter *Oscar Bronner*].

Indeed, assuming that a monopolist controls a pipeline that delivers gas to customers and that the competitive price and output will be £1 per unit and 100 units, and that whereas the monopolist's price and output is £1.5 and 80 units, requiring the monopolist to sell 20 units to the plaintiff and 60 to its other customers, will not make a difference if the monopolist still sells each unit at £1.5.[28] As it has been noted by some commentators, '[r]equiring the firm to share access to the facility with a competitor creates an incentive for the two to set output levels no higher than before'. Hence, '[t]he result may simply be a redistribution of monopoly profits or rents between the owner of the facility and the plaintiff'.[29] There is thus need for courts or competition authorities to determine the competitive price and retain some on-going supervision over the remedy of compulsory access at the competitive price. Mandating access might be more effective and will not require supervision by competition authorities or courts in the presence of a sector-specific regulator. However, in this context, it might make sense to delegate the task to the sector-specific regulator at the first place and the matter to be dealt under regulatory law.

On the other side, in some circumstances, applying the essential facilities doctrine might be a 'second best solution'. Cotter notes:

> [. . .] if the government grants to a firm a monopoly over some asset for which there are no good substitutes, and the prospect of new entry is bleak, applying the essential facilities doctrine may increase social welfare by reducing the short-term costs of the monopoly (though, again, only if the price is thereafter regulated). Given the government's initial assistance, the risk of discouraging ex ante investment may be relatively small in such a case. Of course, a first-best solution might be to avoid granting the monopoly in the first place.[30]

It has also been observed, that 'in some cases, forced access may enable competitors to survive and prosper long enough to develop their own, competing facilities in the longer term'; indeed, some degree of forced sharing may actually increase competition 'by enabling new entrants to gain the foothold necessary to develop their own facilities over time'.[31]

QUESTIONS ON THE ESSENTIAL FACILITIES DOCTRINE

1. Are you concerned that the duration of dominant company's (Domco) market power may be short lived in view of further technical developments? Is there any machinery for Sealink to be free to refuse a sailing slot now that voyages to Liverpool are feasible. Sealink is probably no longer dominant over the central corridor, and the facility at Holyhead no longer indispensable. Moreover, permitting entry by B&I forced Sealink to cancel the fourth trip per day that it had already announced.
2. Was B&I's complaint an example of raising rivals' costs? Should the Commission speculate whether the service by Sealink or by B&I was preferable to passengers?

[28] TF Cotter, 'The Essential Facilities Doctrine' in KN Hylton (ed) *Antitrust Law and Economics* (Edward Elgar, 2010), 157, 169, quoting an example from P Areeda and H Hovenkamp, *Antitrust Law* (Aspen, 2nd ed, 2002), 172, para 771b.

[29] TF Cotter, 'The Essential Facilities Doctrine' in KN Hylton (ed) *Antitrust Law and Economics* (Edward Elgar, 2010), 157, 169.

[30] Ibid.

[31] TF Cotter, 'The Essential Facilities Doctrine' in KN Hylton (ed) *Antitrust Law and Economics* (Edward Elgar, 2010), 157, 171.

3. The modern data-driven economy may give rise to some demand over the use of the essential facilities doctrine.[32] Indeed, competitors of a dominant undertaking may face important barriers to access to personal or non-personal data, when these are an important input in the production process (of a good or a service).[33] The importance of access to data and the need for open access has been recognized by the European Commission in multiple occasions.[34] Should these data be covered by some form of intellectual property protection, on the basis of the database directive,[35] or protected as a trade secret,[36] the relevant standard for the application of Article 102 TFEU has been set by a well-established jurisprudence of the EU Courts regarding IP rights, granting access only under 'exceptional circumstances' (this case law is examined in detail in the companion volume).[37] One may also cite the restrictive interpretation of the duty to deal (also for access to non-IP protected inputs) in *Oscar Bronner*.[38] Some national competition authorities (NCAs) have concluded that the requirements of this case law 'would only be met, if it is demonstrated that the data owned by the incumbent is truly unique and that there is no possibility for the competitor to obtain the data that it needs to perform its services'.[39] Discriminatory access to data may also constitute a competition law problem dealt under the refusal to supply category, if there is a refusal to provide access to the input, although access is provided to other undertakings,[40] but could also be addressed under a different category of abuse, such as exclusionary (price or non-price) discrimination (see Section 9.7).

32 Autorité de la Concurrence and Bundeskartellamt, 'Competition Law and Data' (10 May 2016), 17–18, available at http://www.autoritedelaconcurrence.fr/doc/reportcompetitionlawanddatafinal.pdf.

33 DL Rubinfeld and M Gal, 'Access Barriers to Big Data' (2017) 59 *Arizona L Rev* 339.

34 See eg Commission Staff Working Document on the free flow of data and emerging issues of the European data economy, SWD(2017) 2 final (10 January 2017), 21, available at https://ec.europa.eu/digital-single-market/en/news/staff-working-document-free-flow-data-and-emerging-issues-european-data-economy. Specific rules mandating access to data have been inserted for in-vehicle data in after-sale services markets (see the recent proposed Draft Regulation amending Regulation (EC) No 715/2007 of the European Parliament and of the Council of 20 June 2007 on type-approval of motor vehicles with respect to emissions from light passenger and commercial vehicles (Euro 5 and Euro 6) and on access to vehicle repair and maintenance information [2007] OJ L 171/1) or for access to payment information (Directive 2015/2366 of the European Parliament and of the Council of 25 November 2015 on payment services in the internal market, amending Directives 2002/65/EC, 2009/110/EC and 2013/36/EU and Regulation (EU) No 1093/2010, and repealing Directive 2007/64/EC, [2015] OJ L337/35). See https://ec.europa.eu/info/law/better-regulation/initiatives/ares-2018-1297632_en.

35 Directive 96/9 of the European Parliament and of the Council of 11 March 1996 on the legal protection of databases [1996] OJ L 177/20.

36 Directive 2016/943 on the protection of undisclosed know-how and business information (trade secrets) against their unlawful acquisition, use and disclosure [2016] OJ L 157/1.

37 I Lianos, *Competition Law and the Intangible Economy* (OUP, forthcoming 2019). The most significant cases are: Case C-418/01, *IMS Health GmbH & Co OHG v NDC Health GmbH & Co KG*, ECLI:EU:C:2004:257, paras 34–52 and Case T-201/04, *Microsoft Corp v Commission*, ECLI:EU:T:2007:289, paras 320–36, according to which an undertaking may request access to a facility if the dominant undertaking's refusal to grant access concerns an input which is indispensable for carrying on the business in question, if the refusal prevents the emergence of a new product for which there is a potential consumer demand (this condition being only applicable in the context of the exercise of an intellectual property right), if it is not justified by objective considerations and if it is likely to exclude all competition in the secondary market.

38 Case C-7/97, *Oscar Bronner* [1998] ECR I-7791. See Section 9.2.3.2.

39 Autorité de la Concurrence & Bundeskartellamt, 'Competition Law and Data' (10 May 2016), 18.

40 Ibid, 18–19 (citing the example of the *Cegedim* case of the French Competition Authority, Decision no 14-D-06 (8 July 2014), where Cegedim, which controlled the leading medical information database in France, refused to sell its main database to customers using the software of one of its competitors on the adjacent market for customer relationship management (CRM) software in the health sector, but would sell it to other customers).

9.2.3.2. *Oscar Bronner*

The Court of Justice set the boundaries of the extension of Article 102 TFEU by imposing liability for unilateral refusals to supply in *Oscar Bronner*.[41] The case provides important insights on the tensions that occasionally exist between the protection of the principle of competition and consumers, from one side, and that of the freedom of contract/economic freedom or the needs to maintain the dominant undertaking's incentives to invest, from the other side. Any solution reached should also not result in implementing administrable rules that would compromise the adjudicative function of courts.

Oscar Bronner GmbH & Co KG ('Oscar Bronner') was the publisher of the daily newspaper *Der Standard*. In 1994, *Der Standard*'s share of the Austrian daily newspaper market was 3.6 per cent of circulation and around 6 per cent of advertising revenues. Oscar Bronner wanted to use the nationwide home-delivery service for daily newspapers owned by the Mediaprint group for the distribution of its newspaper (the only nationwide network offering delivery to every address in Austria) against payment of reasonable remuneration but Mediaprint refused to provide Oscar Bronner any access. Mediaprint was the publisher of two newspapers, which in 1994 disposed of a combined market share of 46.8 per cent of total circulation and 42 per cent of total advertising revenues. In addition, they reached 53.3 per cent of the population from the age of fourteen in private households and 71 per cent of all newspaper readers.

The Advocate General's Opinion and the Court's judgments in *Oscar Bronner* should be seen in the context of the position adopted by the CJEU in the *Magill* judgment, regarding a refusal to license an IP right, IP referring to a property right on an intangible.[42]

The CJEU held that the exercise of an exclusive right by the intellectual property owner might, in 'exceptional circumstances', involve abusive conduct. Exceptional circumstances consist of the following: (i) access is indispensable; (ii) the refusal to license prevented the appearance of a new product for which there was potential consumer demand; (iii) there was no justification for such refusal; (iv) the refusal to license excluded all competition on the secondary market. By insisting on the requirement that the refusal to license prevented the sale of a new kind of product for which there was unsatisfied demand, the CJEU appeared to consider the necessity to protect innovation in the market. In *Magill*, the refusal to license had impeded the emergence of a new product, a composite TV guide, which the holders of the intellectual property right did not offer and for which there was a potential demand. The weak and questionable nature of the IP right that was involved in this case, a copyright protection granted on simple TV listings under a 'sweet of the brow' standard, may explain the position of the Court, in particular as access to these data was indispensable for the emergence of the new product. The judgment was also unclear as to the cumulative or alternative character of these exceptional circumstances and some confusion resulted from a subsequent case of the General Court, which treated conditions (i) and (ii) of *Magill* as alternative rather than cumulative.[43]

41 Case C-7/97, *Oscar Bronner* [1998] ECR I–7791.

42 Joined Cases C-241 & 242/91, *Radio Telefis Eireann v Commission* ECR [1995] I–743 [hereinafter *Magill*]. On this judgment and the case law on refusals to license, see the companion volume I Lianos, *Competition Law and the Intangible Economy* (OUP, forthcoming 2019).

43 Case T-504/93, *Tiercé Ladbroke SA v Commission* [1995] ECR II–923.

9.2.3.2.1. *The Opinion of Advocate General Jacobs*

Opinion of Advocate General Jacobs in Case C-7/97, *Oscar Bronner GmbH & Co KG v Mediaprint Zeitungs- und Zeitschriftenverlag GmbH & Co KG*, ECLI:EU:C:1998:264

33. The key issue raised by the referring court's first question is whether refusal by an undertaking in Mediaprint's position to allow a competitor access to its nation-wide home-delivery system constitutes an abuse. Bronner, referring to what is known as the 'essential facilities' doctrine, considers that Mediaprint is obliged to grant such access since it is a prerequisite for effective competition on the market in daily newspapers. [. . .]

The AG first examines the possible application of the essential facilities doctrine in EU competition law.

50. It is [. . .] clear that the Commission considers that refusal of access to an essential facility to a competitor can of itself be an abuse even in the absence of other factors, such as tying of sales, discrimination *vis-à-vis* another independent competitor, discontinuation of supplies to existing customers or deliberate action to damage a competitor (although it may be noted that in many of the cases with which it has dealt such additional factors are to a greater or lesser extent present). An essential facility can be a product such as a raw material or a service, including provision of access to a place such as a harbour or airport or to a distribution system such as a telecommunications network. In many cases the relationship is vertical in the sense that the dominant undertaking reserves the product or service to, or discriminates in favour of, its own downstream operation at the expense of competitors on the downstream market. It may however also be horizontal in the sense of tying sales of related but distinct products or services.

51. In deciding whether a facility is essential the Commission seeks to estimate the extent of the handicap and whether it is permanent or merely temporary. The test to be applied has been described by one commentator as 'whether the handicap resulting from the denial of access is one that can reasonably be expected to make competitors' activities in the market in question either impossible or permanently, seriously and unavoidably uneconomic'[. . .]. The test applied is an objective one, concerning competitors in general. Thus a particular competitor cannot plead that it is particularly vulnerable. [. . .]

53. The laws of the Member States generally regard freedom of contract as an essential element of free trade. Nevertheless, the competition rules of some Member States explicitly provide that an unjustified refusal to enter a binding contract may constitute an abuse of a dominant position. [. . .] As regards essential facilities in particular, in some Member States specific legislative provisions prohibit enterprises which control them from unjustifiably refusing to enter contracts to supply those facilities. [. . .] In other Member States the notion of essential facilities has begun to develop from more general principles to require enterprises controlling such facilities not to refuse access to them without justification [. . .].

55. It is clear from the above discussion that that question raises a general issue which can arise in a variety of different contexts. While it would not be appropriate, on the facts of the present case, to attempt to provide comprehensive guidance on that issue, a number of general points should be made before I turn more specifically to the present case.

56. First, it is apparent that the right to choose one's trading partners and freely to dispose of one's property are generally recognised principles in the laws of the Member States, in some cases with constitutional status. Incursions on those rights require careful justification.

57. Secondly, the justification in terms of competition policy for interfering with a dominant undertaking's freedom to contract often requires a careful balancing of conflicting considerations. In the long term it is generally pro-competitive and in the interest of consumers to allow a company to retain for its own use facilities which it has developed for the purpose of its business. For example, if access to a production, purchasing or distribution facility were allowed too easily there would be no incentive for a competitor to develop competing facilities. Thus while competition was increased in the short term it would be reduced in the long term. Moreover, the incentive for a dominant undertaking to invest in efficient facilities would be reduced if its competitors were, upon request, able to share the benefits. Thus the mere fact that by retaining a facility for its own use a dominant undertaking retains an advantage over a competitor cannot justify requiring access to it.

58. Thirdly, in assessing this issue it is important not to lose sight of the fact that the primary purpose of Article [102 TFEU] is to prevent distortion of competition—and in particular to safeguard the interests of consumers—rather than to protect the position of particular competitors. It may therefore, for example, be unsatisfactory, in a case in which a competitor demands access to a raw material in order to be able to compete with the dominant undertaking on a downstream market in a final product, to focus solely on the latter's market power on the upstream market and conclude that its conduct in reserving to itself the downstream market is automatically an abuse. Such conduct will not have an adverse impact on consumers unless the dominant undertaking's final product is sufficiently insulated from competition to give it market power. [. . .]

61. It is on the other hand clear that refusal of access may in some cases entail elimination or substantial reduction of competition to the detriment of consumers in both the short and the long term. That will be so where access to a facility is a precondition for competition on a related market for goods or services for which there is a limited degree of interchangeability.

62. In assessing such conflicting interests particular care is required where the goods or services or facilities to which access is demanded represent the fruit of substantial investment. That may be true in particular in relation to refusal to license intellectual property rights. Where such exclusive rights are granted for a limited period that in itself involves a balancing of the interest in free competition with that of providing an incentive for research and development and for creativity. It is therefore with good reason that the Court has held that the refusal to license does not of itself, in the absence of other factors, constitute an abuse [Case 238/87, *Volvo v Veng* [1988] ECR 6211].

63. The ruling in *Magill* can in my view be explained by the special circumstances of that case which swung the balance in favour of an obligation to license [. . .].

64. While generally the exercise of intellectual property rights will restrict competition for a limited period only, a dominant undertaking's monopoly over a product, service or facility may in certain cases lead to permanent exclusion of competition on a related market. In such cases competition can be achieved only by requiring a dominant undertaking to supply the product or service or allow access to the facility. If it is so required the undertaking must however in my view be fully compensated by

allowing it to allocate an appropriate proportion of its investment costs to the supply and to make an appropriate return on its investment having regard to the level of risk involved. I leave open the question whether it might in some cases be appropriate to allow the undertaking to retain its monopoly for a limited period.

65. It seems to me that intervention of that kind, whether understood as an application of the essential facilities doctrine or, more traditionally, as a response to a refusal to supply goods or services, can be justified in terms of competition policy only in cases in which the dominant undertaking has a genuine stranglehold on the related market. That might be the case for example where duplication of the facility is impossible or extremely difficult owing to physical, geographical or legal constraints or is highly undesirable for reasons of public policy. It is not sufficient that the undertaking's control over a facility should give it a competitive advantage.

66. I do not rule out the possibility that the cost of duplicating a facility might alone constitute an insuperable barrier to entry. That might be so particularly in cases in which the creation of the facility took place under non-competitive conditions, for example, partly through public funding. However, the test in my view must be an objective one: in other words, in order for refusal of access to amount to an abuse, it must be extremely difficult not merely for the undertaking demanding access but for any other undertaking to compete. Thus, if the cost of duplicating the facility alone is the barrier to entry, it must be such as to deter any prudent undertaking from entering the market. In that regard it seems to me that it will be necessary to consider all the circumstances, including the extent to which the dominant undertaking, having regard to the degree of amortisation of its investment and the cost of upkeep, must pass on investment or maintenance costs in the prices charged on the related market (bearing in mind that the competitor, who having duplicated the facility must compete on the related market, will have high initial amortisation costs but possibly low maintenance costs).

67. It is in my view clear that in the present case there can be no obligation on Mediaprint to allow Bronner access to its nation-wide home-delivery network. Although Bronner itself may be unable to duplicate Mediaprint's network, it has numerous alternative—albeit less convenient—means of distribution open to it. That conclusion is borne out by the claims made in *Der Standard* itself that the 'Standard' is enjoying spectacular growth in terms of both new subscriptions [. . .] and placement of advertisements [. . .]. Such a claim hardly seems consistent with the view that Mediaprint's home-delivery system is essential for it to compete on the newspaper market.

68. Moreover, it would be necessary to establish that the level of investment required to set up a nation-wide home distribution system would be such as to deter an enterprising publisher who was convinced that there was a market for another large daily newspaper from entering the market. It may well be uneconomic, as Bronner suggests, to establish a nation-wide system for a newspaper with a low circulation. In the short term, therefore, losses might be anticipated, requiring a certain level of investment. But the purpose of establishing a competing nation-wide network would be to allow it to compete on equal terms with Mediaprint's newspapers and substantially to increase geographical coverage and circulation.

69. To accept Bronner's contention would be to lead the Community and national authorities and courts into detailed regulation of the Community markets, entailing the fixing of prices and conditions for supply in large sectors of the economy. Intervention on that scale would not only be unworkable but would also be

anti-competitive in the longer term and indeed would scarcely be compatible with a free market economy.

70. It seems to me therefore that the present case falls well short of the type of situation in which it might be appropriate to impose an obligation on a dominant undertaking to allow access to a facility which it has developed for its own use. [. . .]

NOTES AND QUESTIONS ON THE OPINION OF AG JACOBS IN BRONNER

1. (Paragraph 58) This is one of the clearest statements by the CJEU that competition is for the benefit of customers or users rather than competitors.
2. (Paragraphs 56–8) Note the reasons for limiting the doctrine of essential facilities to extreme cases. Was this also the view of the Commission?
3. (Paragraph 66) Should the authorities be more willing to require access when the original investment was made at public expense and the industry is regulated?
4. (Paragraphs 59, 65) Does AG Jacobs limit the remedy of a duty to deal to cases where there was market power downstream?
5. (Paragraphs 58, 61–5) Why is competition downstream important?
6. (Paragraphs 57, 62) Why does it become important to assess whether there has been substantial investment by the owner of the facility? Investment in the past is water under the bridge, but undertakings contemplating substantial investment in some other market, might be deterred. If an undertaking had a very bright idea that enabled it to acquire or build the facility cheaply and that could not be duplicated, should it be required to grant access? Should the Court of Justice distinguish between the monopolist who first uses the only path through the mountains and the first to build a tunnel through them? Why?
7. (Paragraph 63) Would Advocate General Jacobs have decided *Magill*[44] in the same way as the CJEU for the same reasons? Note that television broadcasting is regulated, so one might expect a duty to supply. Did the CJEU make the point in *Magill?* Should a regulatory practice be passed on to competition cases?
8. (Paragraph 66) Why is public funding relevant?
9. (Paragraphs 67–8) Advocate General Jacobs advances an objective test for determining if the facility can be duplicated by examining if, without that facility, 'it is extremely difficult not merely for the undertaking demanding access but for *any* other undertaking to compete'.[45] Hence, if the cost of duplicating the facility alone is the barrier to entry, 'it must be such as to deter any prudent undertaking from entering the market'. How will it be possible to determine if a prudent undertaking would be deterred from entering the market? The AG suggests that the CJEU should consider all the circumstances: (i) the extent to which the dominant undertaking, having regard to the degree of amortization of its investment and the cost of upkeep, must pass on investment or maintenance costs in the prices charged on the related market, bearing in mind that the competitor, who having duplicated the facility must compete on the related market and will have high initial amortization costs but possibly low

[44] See Section 9.2.4.

[45] Emphasis added.

maintenance costs; (ii) the level of investment required to set up a nationwide home distribution system would be such as to deter an enterprising publisher who was convinced that there was a market for another large daily newspaper from entering the market. How would it be possible for the plaintiff to carry his burden of proof? What type of evidence should be brought? Compare the evidence required by the plaintiff in this context with that required in a margin squeeze case.

10. Does the AG suggest transforming the requirement of indispensability to an 'as-efficient-competitor test'?[46] Examine the interpretation given by the Court to paragraph 68 of the Advocate's General Opinion at paragraph 46 of the Judgment: 'it is not economically viable to create a second home-delivery scheme for the distribution of daily newspapers with a circulation comparable to that of the daily newspapers distributed by the existing scheme'.
11. (Paragraph 69) What is the third economic reason given by the Advocate General for narrowing the doctrine of essential facilities? Do you agree with his concern about administrability?

9.2.3.2.2. *CJEU Judgment in* Oscar Bronner

Case C-7/97, *Oscar Bronner GmbH & Co KG v Mediaprint Zeitungs- und Zeitschriftenverlag GmbH & Co KG*
[1998] ECR I–7791

37. [. . .] [I]t would need to be determined whether the refusal by the owner of the only nationwide home-delivery scheme in the territory of a Member State, which uses that scheme to distribute its own daily newspapers, to allow the publisher of a rival daily newspaper access to it constitutes an abuse of a dominant position within the meaning of Article [102 TFEU], on the ground that such refusal deprives that competitor of a means of distribution judged essential for the sale of its newspaper.

38. Although in *Commercial Solvents v EC Commission* and *CBEM*, the Court of Justice held the refusal by an undertaking holding a dominant position in a given market to supply an undertaking with which it was in competition in a neighbouring market with raw materials [. . .] and services [. . .] respectively, which were indispensable to carrying on the rival's business, to constitute an abuse, it should be noted, first, that the Court did so to the extent that the conduct in question was likely to eliminate all competition on the part of that undertaking.

39. Secondly, in *Magill* [. . .] the Court held that refusal by the owner of an intellectual property right to grant a licence, even if it is the act of an undertaking holding a dominant position, cannot in itself constitute abuse of a dominant position, but that the exercise of an exclusive right by the proprietor may, in exceptional circumstances, involve an abuse. [. . .]

41. Therefore, even if that case-law on the exercise of an intellectual property right were applicable to the exercise of any property right whatever, it would still be necessary, for the *Magill* judgment to be effectively relied upon in order to plead the

46 Cf Chapter 8.

existence of an abuse within the meaning of Article [102 TFEU] in a situation such as that which forms the subject-matter of the first question, not only that the refusal of the service comprised in home delivery be likely to eliminate all competition in the daily newspaper market on the part of the person requesting the service and that such refusal be incapable of being objectively justified, but also that the service in itself be indispensable to carrying on that person's business, inasmuch as there is no actual or potential substitute in existence for that home-delivery scheme.

42. That is certainly not the case even if, as in the case which is the subject of the main proceedings, there is only one nationwide home-delivery scheme in the territory of a member state and, moreover, the owner of that scheme holds a dominant position in the market for services constituted by that scheme or of which it forms part.

43. In the first place, it is undisputed that other methods of distributing daily newspapers, such as by post and through sale in shops and at kiosks, even though they may be less advantageous for the distribution of certain newspapers, exist and are used by the publishers of those daily newspapers.

44. Moreover, it does not appear that there are any technical, legal or even economic obstacles capable of making it impossible, or even unreasonably difficult, for any other publishers of daily newspapers to establish, alone or in co-operation with other publishers, its own nationwide home-delivery scheme and use it to distribute its own daily newspapers.

45. It should be emphasised in that respect that, in order to demonstrate that the creation of such a system is not a realistic potential alternative and that access to the existing system is therefore indispensable, it is not enough to argue that it is not economically viable by reason of the small circulation of the daily newspaper or newspapers to be distributed.

46. For such access to be capable of being regarded as indispensable, it would be necessary at the very least to establish, as the Advocate General has pointed out at paragraph 68 of his Opinion, that it is not economically viable to create a second home-delivery scheme for the distribution of daily newspapers with a circulation comparable to that of the daily newspapers distributed by the existing scheme.

47. In the light of the foregoing considerations, the answer to the first question must be that the refusal by a press undertaking which holds a very large share of the daily newspaper market in a member state and operates the only nationwide newspaper home-delivery scheme in that member state to allow the publisher of a rival newspaper, which by reason of its small circulation is unable either alone or in co-operation with other publishers to set up and operate its own home-delivery scheme in economically reasonable conditions, to have access to that scheme for appropriate remuneration does not constitute abuse of a dominant position within the meaning of Article [102 TFEU] of the Treaty.

NOTES AND QUESTIONS ON THE JUDGMENT IN OSCAR BRONNER

1. (Paragraph 41) Does *Magill* apply to other intellectual property rights such as patents? Does it apply to the ownership of property in physical things like the raw materials in *Commercial Solvents*?
2. (Paragraph 43) Should substitutes be considered when defining the relevant market or when considering abuse?

3. Has the CJEU followed the Advocate General? Has it helped to define the meaning of an essential facility? Has it limited the concept as used by the Commission?
4. (Paragraphs 43 and 44) Is the CJEU refusing to adopt a narrow market definition in order to find that a facility is essential?
5. If the dominant firm grants access to one undertaking independent of it, is it required to grant access to other undertakings? Should the dominant firm discriminate in favour of a single firm?
6. Once one firm has access, is all competition downstream eliminated? Is the relevant criterion all competition on the part of the person seeking access? Which should it be?

9.2.3.3. Refusal to supply in aftermarkets

We have previously examined the possibility that a dominant position may be found in an aftermarket (or secondary market).[47] In these cases, the refusal to supply may be found abusive. The DG Competition staff had examined this question in more detail in their discussion paper on the application of Article 102 TFEU to exclusionary abuses. The Commission's priority guidance does not, however, focus on this topic, although the DG Staff Discussion paper touched upon this topic, noting that excluding competitors from a dominant undertaking's aftermarket may be done through either tying or a refusal to deal.[48]

9.2.4. REFUSAL TO LICENSE

Both EU and UK competition law start from the general rule that a duty to deal with a competitor should be rarely imposed to dominant undertakings.[49] Consequently, there is no obligation for the IP holder to license the use of their IP rights to others. This rule may be explained for four main reasons, all accepted as significant in both EU and UK competition law, the first three relating to any type of refusal to deal, the fourth one being specific for a refusal to deal/license an IP right. First, undertakings should have the right to choose their trading partners and to dispose freely of their property.[50] Second, existence of an obligation to license, even for a fair remuneration, 'may undermine undertakings' incentives to invest and innovate and, thereby, possibly harm consumers'.[51] Third, this cautious approach may

47 See Section 8.3.5. and our *Notes and questions* on the *Hugin* case.

48 DG Competition, 'Discussion Paper on the Application of Article 82 of the Treaty to Exclusionary Abuses' (December 2005), paras 264–5, available at http://ec.europa.eu/competition/antitrust/art82/discpaper2005.pdf [hereinafter DG Comp Discussion Paper].

49 See Chapter 8.

50 Communication from the Commission—Guidance on the Commission's enforcement priorities in applying [Article 102 TFEU] to abusive exclusionary conduct by dominant undertakings [2009] OJ C 45/7, para 75 [hereinafter Commission Guidance on Article 102]. See also, in US antitrust law, *United States v Colgate & Co*, 250 US 300, 307 (1919): '[i]n the absence of any purpose to create or maintain a monopoly, the [Sherman Act] does not restrict the long recognized right of [a] trader or manufacturer engaged in an entirely private business, freely to exercise his own independent discretion as to parties with whom he will deal.'

51 Commission Guidance on Article 102, para 75. See also, in US antitrust law, *Trinko*, 540 US 398, 407 (2004):

Firms may acquire monopoly power by establishing an infrastructure that renders them uniquely suited to serve their customers. Compelling such firms to share the source of their advantage is in some tension

also be explained by a concern over the administrability of competition law. As AG Jacobs put it in *Oscar Bronner*, a duty to deal will lead Community and national authorities and courts into 'detailed regulation of the Community markets, entailing the fixing of prices and conditions for supply in large sectors of the economy', the AG noting that 'such intervention on that scale would not only be unworkable but would also be anti-competitive in the longer term and indeed would scarcely be compatible with a free market economy'.[52] The same concern animates US antitrust law regarding refusals to deal, the Supreme Court noting in *Trinko* that 'an antitrust court is unlikely to be an effective day-to-day enforcer of these detailed sharing obligations', should a duty to license be imposed more frequently.[53] Fourth, economists generally believe that Coasesian bargaining over licensing produces efficiency by creating a market to transfer IP rights to the actor who values them most, as determined by a party's ability to use the right productively. Forced licensing has the potential to reduce efficiency by altering the incentives of IP owners: Compulsion to license on equal or fair terms reduces the incentive to license at all.

9.2.4.1. *Volvo v Veng* and *CICRA v Renault*

In the context of EU competition law, the application of Article 102 TFEU, prohibiting the abuses by an undertaking of its dominant position, to unilateral refusals to license IP rights has been an important issue since the judgments of the CJEU in *Volvo v Veng* and *CICRA v Renault*, both cases presenting a similar pattern of facts.[54] In *CICCRA/Renault* and *Volvo/Veng*, concerning the refusal by the automobile manufacturers to deliver to independent repairers the spare parts they were producing, the Court emphasized that 'the right of the proprietor of a protected design to prevent third parties from manufacturing and selling or importing, without its consent, products incorporating the design constitutes the very subject-matter of his exclusive right', finding that 'an obligation imposed upon the proprietor of a protected design to grant to third parties in return for a reasonable royalty, a licence for the supply of products incorporating the design would lead to the proprietor thereof being deprived of the substance of his exclusive right, and that a refusal to grant such a licence cannot in itself constitute an abuse of a dominant position'.[55] The Court noted, however, that the 'exercise' of an exclusive right could be subject to Article 102 TFEU in 'exceptional circumstances' if there was 'certain abusive conduct' and provided three examples of situations where Article 102 TFEU could be applicable: in this case (i) the excessive pricing of the patented products, (ii) the refusal to supply independent repair shops and (iii) failure to continue production of parts for car models still in circulation.[56] The concepts of 'subject matter' and 'essential function' of IP rights have been used in these cases as a shield to competition law enforcement. However, by opening the door for 'certain abusive conduct' to fall under Article 102 TFEU the Court sapped the practical relevance of the 'existence'/'exercise' distinction.

with the underlying purpose of antitrust law, since it may lessen the incentive for the monopolist, the rival, or both to invest in those economically beneficial facilities.

52 Opinion of AG Jacobs in Case C-7/97, *Oscar Bronner* [1998] ECR I–7791, para 69.

53 In *Trinko*, 540 US 398, 415 (2004), the Court was cautious in finding exceptions to the general rule of no duty to aid a rival, precisely 'because of the uncertain virtue of forced sharing and the difficulty of identifying and remedying anticompetitive conduct by a single firm' (ibid, 408).

54 Case C-53/87, *CICCRA v Renault* [1988] ECR 6039; Case C-238/87, *Volvo v Veng* [1988] ECR 6211.

55 Case 238/87, *Volvo v Veng* [1988] ECR 6211, para 8; Case 53/87, *CICCRA v Renault* [1988] ECR 6039.

56 Case 238/87, *Volvo v Veng* [1988] ECR 6211, para 9.

9.2.4.2. *Magill*

In *Magill*, the CJEU held that the exercise of an exclusive right by the intellectual property owner might, in 'exceptional circumstances', involve abusive conduct.[57]

Joined Cases C-241 & 242/91 P, *Radio Telefis Eireann v Commission*
[1995] ECR I–743 (*Magill*)

The three television stations that could be heard in Ireland and Northern Ireland each published its own weekly guide of programmes in advance. Each also permitted newspapers to publish weekly highlights of the programmes and daily lists. When Magill started to publish a comprehensive guide to the three stations, however, each sued it successfully for copyright infringement. The Commission adopted a decision stating that this amounted to an abuse of a dominant position and required each to provide Magill with the information and to permit it to publish. This decision was affirmed by the General Court.

The CJEU confirmed that mere ownership of an intellectual property right does not confer a dominant position,[58] but that, since the stations were the only source of programme information to a company publishing a comprehensive guide to television programmes, they each enjoyed a dominant position over that information. The CJEU also confirmed that, in the absence of standardization or harmonization, the scope of intellectual property rights was a matter for national law, but added that 'the exercise of an exclusive right by the proprietor may, in exceptional circumstances, involve abusive conduct'.[59] It then went through the various criteria mentioned by the GC and found that the exercise of copyright against Magill was abusive. There were no substitutes for the information; the GC had found that the weekly highlights and daily programmes or the individual guides published by the stations were not sufficient substitutes. The CJEU has no jurisdiction on questions of fact. The producer of a comprehensive weekly guide was dependent on the stations.

50. [. . .] it is [. . .] clear from [Case 238/87, *Volvo*, para 9] that the exercise of an exclusive right by the proprietor may, in exceptional circumstances, involve abusive conduct.

51. In the present case, the conduct objected to is the appellants' reliance on copyright conferred by national legislation so as to prevent Magill—or any other undertaking having the same intention—from publishing on a weekly basis information (channel, day, time and title of programmes) together with commentaries and pictures obtained independently of the appellants.

52. Among the circumstances taken into account by the General Court in concluding that such conduct was abusive was, first, the fact that there was, according to the findings of the General Court, no actual or potential substitute for a weekly television guide offering information on the programmes for the week ahead. On this point, the Court of First Instance confirmed the Commission's finding that the complete lists of programmes for a 24-hour period—and for a 48-hour period at weekends and before public holidays—published in certain daily and Sunday newspapers, and the television sections of certain magazines covering, in addition, 'highlights' of the week's programmes, were only to a limited extent substitutable for advance information to viewers on all the week's programmes. Only weekly television guides containing comprehensive listings for the week ahead would enable users to decide in advance which

[57] Joined Cases C-241 & 242/91 P, *Magill* [1995] ECR I–743. [58] Ibid, para 46.
[59] Ibid, para 49.

programmes they wished to follow and arrange their leisure activities for the week accordingly. The [General Court] also established that there was a specific constant and regular potential demand on the part of consumers

53. Thus the appellants—who were, by force of circumstance, the only sources of the basic information on programme scheduling which is the indispensable raw material for compiling a weekly television guide—gave viewers wishing to obtain information on the choice of programmes for the week ahead no choice but to buy the weekly guides for each station and draw from each of them the information they need to make comparisons.

54. The appellants' refusal to provide basic information by relying on national copyright provisions thus prevented the appearance of a new product, a comprehensive weekly guide to television programmes, which the appellants did not offer and for which there was a potential consumer demand. Such refusal constitutes an abuse under heading (b) of the second paragraph of Article [102 TFEU].

55. Second, there was no justification for such refusal either in the activity of television broadcasting, or in that of publishing television magazines [. . .]

56. Third, and finally, as the Court of First Instance also held, the appellants, by their conduct, reserved to themselves the secondary market of weekly television guides by excluding all competition on that market [. . .] since they denied access to the basic information which is the raw material indispensable for the compilation of such a guide.

57. In the light of all those circumstances, the Court of First Instance did not err in law in holding that the appellants' conduct was an abuse of a dominant position within the meaning of Article 82 of the Treaty.

58. It follows that the plea in law alleging misapplication by the [General Court] of the concept of abuse of a dominant position must be dismissed as unfounded [. . .].

The CJEU adopted the 'new product' rule where it held that the exercise of an exclusive right by the intellectual property owner might, in 'exceptional circumstances', involve abusive conduct.[60] Exceptional circumstances consist of the following: (i) access is indispensable; (ii) the refusal to license prevented the appearance of a new product for which there was potential consumer demand; (iii) there was no justification for such refusal; and (iv) the refusal to license excluded all competition on the secondary market. By insisting on the requirement that the refusal to license prevented the sale of a new kind of product for which there was unsatisfied demand, the CJEU appeared to consider the necessity to protect innovation in the market. In *Magill*, the refusal to license had impeded the emergence of a new product, a composite TV guide, which the holders of the intellectual property right did not offer and for which there was a potential demand. The weak and questionable nature of the IP right that was involved in this case, a copyright protection granted on simple TV listings under a 'sweet of the brow' standard, may explain the position of the Court, in particular as access to these data was indispensable for the emergence of the new product. The judgment was not also clear as to the cumulative or alternative character of these exceptional circumstances and some confusion resulted from a subsequent case of the General Court, which treated conditions (i) and (ii) of Magill as alternative rather than cumulative.[61]

In *Tiércé Ladbroke*,[62] the *Magill* judgment was construed narrowly by both the GC and the CJEU. The GC held that the judgment did not apply to the refusal by the copyright

60 Ibid, para 10.

61 Case T-504/93, *Tiércé Ladbroke SA v Commission* [1995] ECR II-923.

62 Ibid.

holders in horse races to enable Ladbroke to screen the films in its Belgian betting shops. Ladbroke was not endeavouring to enter a market: it was the largest operator of betting shops in Belgium.[63] A licence was not essential, nor were betting shops a new product.[64] Nevertheless, the GC construed paragraph 54 of *Magill* to contain alternative rather than cumulative conditions. This was not necessary to its judgment, nor argued, so is but a weak precedent as the GC has no jurisdiction to go beyond the pleadings. Moreover, the GC observed that the copyright holders were not protecting their own activities in Belgium by not exploiting their copyright. This hostility to discrimination downstream seems to amount to the protection of competitors. Consumers, those betting on the horse races, would be better off with one firm providing the excitement of live films than with no one.

In the meantime, the CJEU in *Oscar Bronner*, a case which did not involve a refusal to license but the refusal by a dominant firm to share its distribution network with a competitor, interpreted the four conditions of *Magill* as being cumulative and narrowed down the duty to deal doctrine in EU competition law, by interpreting the indispensability condition as requiring evidence from the undertaking requesting access that it should not be economically viable for an undertaking with a comparable size with the dominant firm to develop its own facility or input.[65] A plaintiff likely will satisfy the indispensability prong if the State originally invested in the essential facility.[66] High switching costs also suggest indispensability.[67]

The CJEU had to opportunity to revisit the application of the *Magill* doctrine in its *IMS/NDC Health* judgment.

9.2.4.3. *IMS Health v NDC Health*

Case C-418/01, *IMS Health GmbH & Co OHG v NDC Health GmbH & Co KG*
[2004] ECR I–5039

IMS and NDC engaged in tracking sales of pharmaceutical and healthcare products. IMS provides data on regional sales of pharmaceutical products in Germany to pharmaceutical laboratories formatted according to the brick structure. Since January 2000, it has provided studies based on a brick structure consisting of 1860 bricks, or a derived structure consisting of 2847 bricks, each corresponding to a designated geographic area. Those bricks were created by taking account of various criteria, such as the boundaries of municipalities, postcodes, population density, transport connections and the geographical distribution of pharmacies and doctors' surgeries. NDC tried to enter the market in competition with IMS but its customers were unwilling to have NDC's data based on different geographic areas. So it used the zones worked out by IMS Health and its customers. IMS had set up a working group in which participated undertakings in the pharmaceutical industry that are clients of IMS. That working group made suggestions for improving and optimising market segmentation. The extent of the working group's contribution to the determination of market segmentation was a subject of dispute between IMS and NDC. IMS did not only market its brick structures, but also

63 Ibid, para 130. 64 Ibid, para 131. 65 Case C-7/97, *Oscar Bronner* [1998] ECR I–7791.

66 See V Korah, *Intellectual Property Rights & the EC Competition Rules* (Hart, 2006), 143 (citing Opinion of AG Jacobs in Case C-7/97, *Oscar Bronner* [1998] ECR I–7791, para 66).

67 See V Korah, *Intellectual Property Rights & the EC Competition Rules* (Hart, 2006), 144.

distributed them free of charge to pharmacies and doctors' surgeries. Arguably, that practice had helped those structures to become the normal industry standard to which its clients adapted their information and distribution systems

IMS obtained an interim injunction against copyright infringement from a German trial court, which also sent a number of preliminary questions to the CJEU. Meanwhile, NDC complained to the Commission. An interim decision of the Commission required IMS to license its copyright in what was claimed to be a de facto *industry standard, a set of maps on the basis of which IMS provided localized data to its clients, the pharmaceutical laboratories. IMS had obtained an interim injunction from a German court to restrain NDC and another firm from infringing its copyright in the maps. The decision suggested that where a* de facto *industry standard is protected by an IP right and prevents all competition in a neighbouring market, the holder is required to grant a licence. Where an industry standard necessary for a newcomer to enter a market is protected by an IP right it may be sensible to require a licence. Often there is no way around an industry standard.*

The appeal of the Commission's decision to the General Court was suspended and later set aside when the injunction from the German Court was quashed on appeal on the grounds that IMS was not the sole holder of the copyright, but entitled only to restrain slavish imitation. The Commission withdrew its decision and the General Court abandoned the case.

The German trial court that had granted the injunction has sought guidance from the CJEU on various preliminary questions relating to the application of Article 102 TFEU.

28. It is clear from paragraphs 43 and 44 of *Bronner* that, in order to determine whether a product or service is indispensable for enabling an undertaking to carry on business in a particular market, it must be determined whether there are products or services which constitute alternative solutions, even if they are less advantageous, and whether there are technical, legal or economic obstacles capable of making it impossible or at least unreasonably difficult for any undertaking seeking to operate in the market to create, possibly in cooperation with other operators, the alternative products or services. According to paragraph 46 of *Bronner*, in order to accept the existence of economic obstacles, it must be established, at the very least, that the creation of those products or services is not economically viable for production on a scale comparable to that of the undertaking which controls the existing product or service.

29. It is for the national court to determine, in the light of the evidence submitted to it, whether such is the case in the dispute in the main proceedings. In that regard [. . .] account must be taken of the fact that a high level of participation by the pharmaceutical laboratories in the improvement of the 1860 brick structure protected by copyright, on the supposition that it is proven, has created a dependency by users in regard to that structure, particularly at a technical level. In such circumstances, it is likely that those laboratories would have to make exceptional organisational and financial efforts in order to acquire the studies on regional sales of pharmaceutical products presented on the basis of a structure other than that protected by the intellectual property right. The supplier of that alternative structure might therefore be obliged to offer terms which are such as to rule out any economic viability of business on a scale comparable to that of the undertaking which controls the protected structure.

30. [. . .] [F]or the purposes of examining whether the refusal by an undertaking in a dominant position to grant a licence for a brick structure protected by an intellectual property right which it owns is abusive, the degree of participation by users in the development of that structure and the outlay, particularly in terms of cost, on the part of potential users in order to purchase studies on regional sales of pharmaceutical

products presented on the basis of an alternative structure are factors which must be taken into consideration in order to determine whether the protected structure is indispensable to the marketing of studies of that kind.

The CJEU then proceeded in answering the first question of the referring court relating to the refusal to grant a licence.

34. According to settled case-law, the exclusive right of reproduction forms part of the rights of the owner of an intellectual property right, so that refusal to grant a licence, even if it is the act of an undertaking holding a dominant position, cannot in itself constitute abuse of a dominant position. [. . .]

35. Nevertheless, as is clear from that case-law, exercise of an exclusive right by the owner may, in exceptional circumstances, involve abusive conduct [. . .].

36. The Court held that such exceptional circumstances were present in the case giving rise to the judgment in *Magill*, in which the conduct of the television channels in a dominant position which gave rise to the complaint consisted in their relying on the copyright conferred by national legislation on the weekly listings of their programmes in order to prevent another undertaking from publishing information on those programmes together with commentaries, on a weekly basis.

37. According to the summary of the *Magill* judgment made by the Court at paragraph 40 of the judgment in *Bronner*, the exceptional circumstances were constituted by the fact that the refusal in question concerned a product (information on the weekly schedules of certain television channels), the supply of which was indispensable for carrying on the business in question (the publishing of a general television guide), in that, without that information, the person wishing to produce such a guide would find it impossible to publish it and offer it for sale [. . .] the fact that such refusal prevented the emergence of a new product for which there was a potential consumer demand [. . .], the fact that it was not justified by objective considerations [. . .], and was likely to exclude all competition in the secondary market. [. . .]

38. It is clear from that case-law that, in order for the refusal by an undertaking which owns a copyright to give access to a product or service indispensable for carrying on a particular business to be treated as abusive, it is sufficient that three cumulative conditions be satisfied, namely, that that refusal is preventing the emergence of a new product for which there is a potential consumer demand, that it is unjustified and such as to exclude any competition on a secondary market. [. . .]

40. In that regard, it is appropriate to recall the approach followed by the Court in the *Bronner* judgment, in which it was asked whether the fact that a press undertaking with a very large share of the daily newspaper market in a Member State which operates the only nationwide newspaper home-delivery scheme in that Member State refuses paid access to that scheme by the publisher of a rival newspaper, which by reason of its small circulation is unable either alone or in cooperation with other publishers to set up and operate its own home-delivery scheme under economically reasonable conditions, constitutes abuse of a dominant position. [. . .]

42. [. . .] [T]he Court held [*in Oscar Bronner*] that it was relevant, in order to assess whether the refusal to grant access to a product or a service indispensable for carrying on a particular business activity was an abuse, to distinguish an upstream market, constituted by the product or service, in that case the market for home delivery of daily newspapers, and a (secondary) downstream market, on which the product or service in question is used for the production of another product or the supply of another service, in that case the market for daily newspapers themselves.

43. The fact that the home-delivery service was not marketed separately was not regarded as precluding, from the outset, the possibility of identifying a separate market.

44. It appears, therefore [. . .] that, for the purposes of the application of the earlier case-law, it is sufficient that a potential market or even hypothetical market can be identified. Such is the case where the products or services are indispensable in order to carry on a particular business and where there is an actual demand for them on the part of undertakings which seek to carry on the business for which they are indispensable.

45. Accordingly, it is determinative that two different stages of production may be identified and that they are interconnected, inasmuch as the upstream product is indispensable for the supply of the downstream product.

46. Transposed to the facts of the case in the main proceedings, that approach prompts consideration as to whether the 1860 brick structure constitutes, upstream, an indispensable factor in the downstream supply of German regional sales data for pharmaceutical products.

47. It is for the national court to establish whether that is in fact the position, and, if so be the case, to examine whether the refusal by IMS to grant a licence to use the structure at issue is capable of excluding all competition on the market for the supply of German regional sales data on pharmaceutical products.

The CJEU then examined the first condition, relating to the emergence of a new product.

48. [. . .] [T]hat condition relates to the consideration that, in the balancing of the interest in protection of the intellectual property right and the economic freedom of its owner against the interest in protection of free competition, the latter can prevail only where refusal to grant a licence prevents the development of the secondary market to the detriment of consumers.

49. Therefore, the refusal by an undertaking in a dominant position to allow access to a product protected by an intellectual property right, where that product is indispensable for operating on a secondary market, may be regarded as abusive only where the undertaking which requested the licence does not intend to limit itself essentially to duplicating the goods or services already offered on the secondary market by the owner of the intellectual property right, but intends to produce new goods or services not offered by the owner of the right and for which there is a potential consumer demand

50. It is for the national court to determine whether such is the case in the dispute in the main proceedings.

As to the second condition, relating to whether the refusal was unjustified, the CJEU held:

51. As to that condition, on whose interpretation no specific observations have been made, it is for the national court to examine, if appropriate, in light of the facts before it, whether the refusal of the request for a licence is justified by objective considerations.

The CJEU concluded:

52. [. . .] [T]he refusal by an undertaking which holds a dominant position and owns an intellectual property right in a brick structure indispensable to the presentation of regional sales data on pharmaceutical products in a Member State to grant a licence to use that structure to another undertaking which also wishes to provide such data in the same Member State, constitutes an abuse of a dominant position within the meaning of Article [102 TFEU] where the following conditions are fulfilled:

- the undertaking which requested the licence intends to offer, on the market for the supply of the data in question, new products or services not offered by the owner of the intellectual property right and for which there is a potential consumer demand;
- the refusal is not justified by objective considerations;
- the refusal is such as to reserve to the owner of the intellectual property right the market for the supply of data on sales of pharmaceutical products in the Member State concerned by eliminating all competition on that market.

The CJEU followed *Magill*, reaffirming the cumulative character of these conditions and explained that the 'new product or service' rule limits the finding of abuse for a refusal to licence '*only* where the undertaking which requested the licence does not intend to limit itself essentially to duplicating the goods or services already offered on the secondary market by the owner of the copyright, but intends to produce new goods or services not offered by the owner of the right and for which there is a potential consumer demand'.[68] Note that in *Renault* and *Volvo*, both of which involved rights of design on spare parts, the exceptional circumstances were held to exist even if the refusal to license did not impede the emergence of a new product. The CJEU noted in that the duty to supply arises only if there are separate markets, one upstream and the other downstream, but it followed AG Tizzano,[69] adding that 'it is sufficient that a potential market or even hypothetical market can be identified':[70] a question for the national court to answer. The identification of two different but interconnected stages of production is also important, as it is only if the upstream products or services are an indispensable input for the supply of the downstream product that a refusal to licence may fall within the scope of Article 102 TFEU. Yet, as the Court noted, it is sufficient to identify a captive, potential or hypothetical input market, for example by distinguishing between the different stages of the innovation process, the intellectual property right being one of them.[71] The CJEU stated that it was also for the national court to decide whether access to the brick structure was essential.

9.2.5. REFUSAL TO PROVIDE INTEROPERABILITY

Refusals to provide interoperability are assessed in the EU competition law under the broader category of refusals to supply.[72] The Commission applied Article 102 TFEU to the refusal by Microsoft to supply Sun Microsystems the necessary information to establish interoperability between their work group server operating systems and Microsoft's PC operating system Windows.[73] Microsoft was ordered to disclose interoperability information in a reasonable, non-discriminatory, and timely way. While the Commission did not contemplate compulsory disclosure of the source code of Windows and the disclosure measure only covered interface specifications, it acknowledged that 'it cannot be excluded that ordering Microsoft to disclose such specifications and allow such use of them by third parties restricts the exercise of

[68] Case C-418/01, *IMS Health GmbH & Co OHG v NDC Health GmbH & Co KG* [2004] ECR I-5039, para 49 (emphasis added).

[69] Ibid, para 42 (citing Opinion of AG Tizzano in Case C-418/01, *IMS Health GmbH & Co OHG v NDC Health GmbH & Co KG*, ECLI:EU:C:2003:537, paras 56–9).

[70] Case C-418/01, *IMS Health GmbH & Co OHG v NDC Health GmbH & Co KG* [2004] ECR I-5039, para 44.

[71] Ibid, paras 44–5. [72] Ibid, para 78.

[73] *Microsoft/W2000* (Case COMP/C-3/37.792) Commission Decision C(2004)900 final (24 March 2004), available at ec.europa.eu/competition/antitrust/cases/dec_docs/37792/37792_4177_1.pdf. See further Chapter S.4.

Microsoft's intellectual property rights'.[74] Microsoft's conduct was not necessarily impeding the emergence of an identifiable new product. Microsoft's conduct had nevertheless, according to the Commission, the effect of reducing the incentives of its competitors to innovate (and produce new products in the future) and therefore to limit consumer choice.

The Commission affirmed that intellectual property rights cannot as such constitute a 'self-evident objective justification' for Microsoft's refusal to supply and employed a balancing test examining if the possible negative impact of an order to supply on Microsoft's incentives to innovate could be outweighed by its positive impact on the level of innovation of the whole industry (including Microsoft). Taking the view that 'Microsoft's research and development efforts are [. . .] spurred by the innovative steps its competitors take in the work group server operating' system market that 'were such competitors to disappear, this would diminish Microsoft's incentives to innovate', the Commission concluded that the costs outweighed the benefits in this case.

The GC (at the time the Court of First Instance) confirmed the Commission's Microsoft decision in 2007.[75] While it reaffirmed the four criteria of the CJEU in *Magill* and *IMS/NDC Health* it also adopted a more open-ended interpretation for some of these conditions. First, the Court used language that implied that these conditions were not the only exceptional circumstances in which the exercise of the exclusive right by the owner of the intellectual property rights may give rise to such an abuse, although it noted that the requirement 'that the refusal prevents the appearance of a new product for which there is consumer demand is found only in the case-law on the exercise of an intellectual property right'.[76] Second, the Court gave also a broad interpretation to the 'new product rule' of *IMS/NDC Health*, finding that consumer injury may arise where there is a limitation not only of production or markets, but also of technical development.[77] The expansion of the 'new product' prong to incorporate technological efficiency perhaps has collapsed this element into indispensability.[78] A new product finding generally might follow a determination of indispensability and the fact that the plaintiff requests a licence.[79]

Contrary to *Magill* and *IMS/NDC Health*, Microsoft's conduct did not impede the emergence of identifiable new products but affected the competitive process that would have brought about these new products in the future. Third, the Court interpreted 'consumer harm' broadly noting that consumer choice would be affected if rival products of equal or better quality would not be able to compete on equal terms at the market.[80]

The General Court would not sanction the approach of balancing the incentives of various market participants to innovate, but it nevertheless considered the following factors relevant to the objective justification inquiry: 'the value of the underlying investment, the value of the information concerned for the organization of the dominant undertaking and the value transferred to competitors in the event of disclosure'.[81]

74 *Microsoft/W2000* (Case COMP/C-3/37.792) Commission Decision C(2004)900 final (24 March 2004), paras 546 and 1004.

75 Case T-201/04, *Microsoft v Commission* [2007] ECR II-3601.

76 Ibid, paras 332–4.

77 Ibid, para 647.

78 See V Korah, *Intellectual Property Rights & the EC Competition Rules* (Hart, 2006), 147.

79 See BC Gallego, 'Unilateral Refusal to License Indispensable Intellectual Property Rights—U.S. & EU Approaches' in J Drexl (ed) *Research Handbook on Intellectual Property & Competition Law* (Edward Elgar 2008), 226.

80 Case T-201/04, *Microsoft v Commission* (2007) ECR II-3601, para 652.

81 Ibid, para 207.

A licensee still must pay consideration for the right to use the IP right. The level of this royalty theoretically could encourage or discourage innovation. The result further may depend on the productive capability of the licensor and who else licenses the technology.[82] By contrast, when a court finds patent misuse, it issues a compulsory licence 'freely available to everyone'.[83] The patentee loses the right to continue to enforce the patent. This result clearly represents a more severe and costly penalty than ordering 'a paid compulsory license to only one party'.[84]

9.2.5.1. The Commission's Guidance on Article 102 on refusal to supply

The Commission takes a wide perspective on the 'concept of refusal to supply', noting that it may cover a broad range of practices, such as a refusal to supply products to existing or new customers, refusal to license intellectual property rights, including when the licence is necessary to provide interface information, or refusal to grant access to an essential facility or a network.[85] This broad perspective also explains why the Commission 'does not regard it as necessary for the refused product to have been already traded', as it is sufficient 'that there is demand from potential purchasers and that a potential market for the input at stake can be identified'.[86] These practices will constitute priorities of the Commission's enforcement policy if all the following circumstances are satisfied, the aim being to limit the likelihood that type I errors (over-enforcement) may occur:

- 'the refusal relates to a product or service that is objectively necessary to be able to compete effectively on a downstream market';
- 'the refusal is likely to lead to the elimination of effective competition on the downstream market';
- 'the refusal is likely to lead to consumer harm'; and
- the conduct cannot be justified on efficiency grounds.[87]

Of particular interest is the category of 'naked exclusion', for which the abovementioned conditions are not considered, the risk of type I error being quite limited in these circumstances and other types of costs (administrative costs) being more manageable, thus shifting the balance towards enforcement of Article 102 TFEU.

Communication from the Commission—Guidance on the Commission's enforcement priorities in applying Article [102 TFEU] to abusive exclusionary conduct by dominant undertakings [2009] OJ C 45/7 (footnotes omitted)

Naked exclusion

82. In certain specific cases, it may be clear that imposing an obligation to supply is manifestly not capable of having negative effects on the input owner's and/or other operators'

82 See D Kallay, *The Law & Economics of Antitrust & Intellectual Property: An Australian Approach* (Edward Elgar, 2004), 125.

83 Ibid.

84 Ibid.

85 Commission Guidance on Article 102, para 78.

86 Ibid, para 79.

87 Ibid, paras 81, 83–9.

incentives to invest and innovate upstream, whether ex ante or ex post. The Commission considers that this is particularly likely to be the case where regulation compatible with Community law already imposes an obligation to supply on the dominant undertaking and it is clear, from the considerations underlying such regulation, that the necessary balancing of incentives has already been made by the public authority when imposing such an obligation to supply. This could also be the case where the upstream market position of the dominant undertaking has been developed under the protection of special or exclusive rights or has been financed by state resources. In such specific cases there is no reason for the Commission to deviate from its general enforcement standard of showing likely anti-competitive foreclosure, without considering whether the three circumstances referred to in paragraph 81 are present.

NOTES AND QUESTIONS ON THE COMMISSION'S GUIDANCE ON ARTICLE 102

1. (Paragraphs 81, 83) What is meant by 'objectively necessary to be able to compete effectively downstream'?
2. (Paragraphs 81, 83) Does the second condition mean that the complainant eliminates all competition in the downstream market or only effective competition? The case law is not consistent.
3. Should regulation and competition be kept separate? Why? If the regulator has imposed a duty to supply, should there be any need to turn to competition law to provide supply. Are the criteria and their objectives usually applied by regulators the same as those for competition law?
4. (Paragraph 84) If the dominant company had previously supplied the firm wanting supply, it will be harder to argue that it is not a fit and proper person to handle the supply. It may also be harder for the Domco to show that it is unable to supply effectively.
5. (Paragraph 89) Should the question be whether the incumbent is making sufficient profit on its investment or whether at the time the investment was made it looked likely that the incumbent would profit in the future? Give reasons.

9.2.5.2. UK case law

Atheraces Ltd v British Horseracing Board
[2005] EWHC 3015 (Ch)

The case concerned a dispute between the British Horseracing Board Ltd (the BHB) (the administrator and governing body of British horseracing) and Attheraces Ltd (ATR) (a broadcaster whose output largely consisted of information concerning British races). Pursuant to the Orders and Rules of Racing issued by the BHB and the Jockey Club, race organisers and others involved in British racing were required to submit, in advance of any race, certain pre-race information to 'Weatherbys', a company engaged by the BHB to collate that information and to distribute it to persons authorized by the BHB to receive it. This 'pre-race data' included the details of each race, the names of the horses entered and each declared runner together with its saddlecloth and stall number, age, weight, official rating, jockey, owner, and trainer.

The pre-race data supplied by Weatherbys was the authoritative source of such information, which it was essential for bookmakers to provide in betting shops to punters. In view of the abolition of the horserace-betting levy from which BHB benefitted, BHB sought to exploit commercially the right to receive the pre-race data. This was denied by the CJEU, ruling on a separate case, which found that the sort of pre-race data at issue did not qualify for protection under the European Database Directive. ATR sought to negotiate with the BHB to be supplied with that data for the purposes of two relatively new broadcasted services which ATR was supplying to bookmakers outside of the UK and Republic of Ireland. BHB refused to supply the data except in return for a 50 per cent share of ATR's profits from the two services. BHB had nevertheless agreed to provide pre-race data to another broadcaster to overseas bookmakers ('Phumelela') in return for a profit share of only 30 per cent (which was still viewed by ATR as excessive). ATR then commenced proceedings in the Chancery Division, alleging that the BHB had abused its dominant position in the market for supply of pre-race data in respect of British races in violation of Article 102 and Chapter II of the Competition Act 1998 (CA98), alleging an unreasonable refusal to supply the data to ATR, the excessive and unfair pricing of that data, and discriminatory pricing of that data.

The trial court accepted the allegations of ATR,[88] *but the decision was reversed by the Court of appeal (however, only on the ground relating to lack of evidence of the excessive character of the rates asked).*[89] *The trial court's judgment contains some interesting analysis of the 'essential facilities doctrine' and refusals to supply, which have not been reversed in the Court of Appeal's judgment.*

Opinion of Mr Justice Etherton in *Attheraces Ltd v British Horseracing Board* [2005] EWHC 3015 (Ch)

Unreasonable refusal to supply data

[. . .]

244. The parties are not agreed on the relevant legal principles applicable to that claim.

245. BHB contends that, in order to succeed on this head of claim, ATR must show that it is an existing customer of BHB or alternatively that pre-race data is an essential facility controlled by BHB, and that BHB has refused to supply or has constructively refused to supply the data, and that has resulted in a total elimination of competition, and such conduct of BHB has no objective justification. BHB submits that, in addition to a total elimination of competition, ATR must show that it is in competition, or potential competition, with BHB in the downstream market.

246. BHB contends that ATR is not an existing customer of BHB; BHB's data is not an essential facility; BHB has not refused to supply anything; there is no evidence of total elimination of competition, or even a partial elimination of competition, arising from BHB's actions; BHB is not in competition, or potential competition, with ATR;

88 *Attheraces Ltd v British Horseracing Board* [2005] EWHC 3015 (Ch).

89 *Attheraces Ltd & Attheraces Ltd UK v British Horseracing Board & British Horseracing Board UK* [2007] EWCA Civ 38.

and, even if BHB had refused to supply with ATR, it would have been objectively justified in doing so by ATR's refusal to agree reasonable terms.

247. I accept ATR's submission that refusing to supply an existing customer will amount to an abuse of a dominant position, even if the dominant undertaking is contractually entitled to do so, unless the act is 'objectively justified' [. . .].

248. Furthermore, I accept the submission of ATR that where a person who is dominant in the market is the owner or controller of a facility, which is an essential facility, it will be an abuse within Article [102TFEU] and s.18 of the 1998 Act if he refuses access to it and the refusal has no objective justification, whether or not the party seeking access is an existing or a new customer: *Oscar Bronner* at paras 42–43.

249. In my judgment, unreasonable refusal, including constructive refusal, to supply may amount to an abuse of a dominant position within Article [102 TFEU] and s.18 of the 1998 Act whether or not the supplier is in competition, or potential competition, with the purchaser.

250. Standing back from any detailed legal analysis, there is no reason why the absence of such direct competition should preclude unreasonable refusal to supply falling within the mischief of Article [102TFEU] and s.18 of the 1998 Act. Irrespective of such competition, the effect may be, for example, to deter others from entering into the market, or to encourage the purchaser to leave the market, or to curtail the purchaser's activities within the market, in each case whether in the upstream market or the downstream market.

251. There is no authority which has been cited to me which authoritatively determines that either in the case of the refusal to supply an existing customer or of the refusal to grant access to an essential facility to an existing or new customer, there is an additional requirement that the supplier is refusing to supply a competitor or potential competitor: cf para 47 of the Opinion of AG Jacobs in *Oscar Bronner* summarising the US essential facilities doctrine.

252. BHB relies on the decision of the ECJ in *Oscar Bronner*, especially at paras 38–42; but in those passages, as on the actual facts of *Oscar Bronner*, the court was considering a case in which the parties were in fact competitors. No authoritative general statement was made by the court which would preclude the doctrine applying on the facts of the present case. I agree with ATR that *Irish Continental Group v CCI Morlaix* Case IV/35.388 [1995] 5 CMLR 177 (port authority refusing a ferry operator access to the port facilities) indicates the contrary.

253. I do not accept BHB's submission that, for present purposes, ATR is not an existing customer of BHB. BHB's case is that ATR has refused to negotiate an agreement with BHB as to the terms on which ATR can receive BHB's pre-race data, and so ATR is at most a former customer (under ATR).

254. I consider that, for present purposes, whether ATR is to be regarded as an existing customer or as a former customer is to be resolved as a matter of substance, rather than form, and having regard to the mischief at which Article [102TFEU] and s.18 of the 1998 Act are aimed. [. . .] The substance and commercial reality is that ATR has continued to be BHB's customer, both indirectly and directly, since 29 March 2004, but has been unable to agree what amount, if any, it should pay to BHB in respect of BHB's pre-race data in addition to the amounts paid by ATR to PA.

255. Even if that analysis of the relationship between BHB and ATR is incorrect, it is clear, in my judgment, that BHB's pre-race data is an essential facility for present purposes. BHB claims that the data is not an essential facility since ATR could obtain the data from public sources albeit not as conveniently as, and possibly of a lower quality than, the supply from BHB, through PA.

256. At para 47 of *Oscar Bronner* AG Jacobs summarised the US case law requirements for an essential facility (from which the concept of essential facility originates) as follows: 'a competitor is unable practically or reasonably to duplicate the essential facility. It is not sufficient that duplication would be difficult or expensive, but absolute impossibility is not required'.

257. At para 65 of that case he said: '. . .intervention of that kind, whether understood as an application of the essential facilities doctrine or, more traditionally, as a response to a refusal to supply goods or services, can be justified in terms of competition policy only in cases in which the dominant undertaking has a genuine stranglehold on the related market. That might be the case for example where duplication of the facility is impossible *or extremely difficult* owing to physical, geographic or legal constraints or is highly undesirable for reasons of public policy' (my emphasis). See also para 41 of the ECJ's judgment ('. . .no actual or potential substitute in existence. . .').

258. It is clear that BHB's pre-race data satisfies that test. The data is essential to ATR's business. There is no substitute for it. No one, other than BHB, is currently a supplier of that data in the market. It would be prohibitively expensive and difficult, and quite impractical, for any other person to collate and supply the same data. [*Further evidence is provided for this allegation.*] [. . .] ATR would be eliminated from the market if it could not obtain access to the data. There would be no competition in the overseas countries in which ATR's services are provided. [. . .]

279. As the Commission has said, the concept of refusal to supply covers not only outright refusal but also situations, which it calls constructive refusal, where the dominant firm makes supply subject to objectively unreasonable conditions: *Deutsche Post AG and British Post Office* Comp/C-1/36.915 25 July 2001.

Justice Etherton rejected the objective justifications alleged by BHP and found that its conduct constituted an unreasonable refusal to supply, infringing Article 102 TFEU and Chapter II of the Competition Act 1998.

NOTES AND QUESTIONS ON ATTHERACES

1. Do you agree with Mr Justice Etherton (paragraph 249) that a refusal to deal/supply amounts to an abuse of a dominant position even if the supplier is not an actual or potential competitor with the purchaser? What would be the harm to competition protected by competition law in these circumstances?
2. According to Mr Justice Etherton, would the theory of essential facilities step in if the purchaser was not an actual or potential competitor to the supplier? What are the shortcomings of such an expansive view of the doctrine? What are the benefits that such an expansive view will enable competition authorities to achieve?

ME Burgess, JJ Burgess and SJ Burgess (trading as JJ Burgess & Sons) v Office of Fair Trading

[2005] CAT 25

The case involved an appeal from the OFT's refusal to find an abuse by W Austin and Sons Limited ('Austin') of its dominant position. JJ Burges and Austin were both funeral directors; Austin also owned and controlled a crematorium regularly used by the applicant. The alleged abuse derived from a refusal by Austin to give the applicant direct and indirect (ie through other funeral firms) access to the crematorium. The CAT first began by analysing the relevant geographical market for funeral directing services and crematorium services respectively. After defining the relevant geographical area as that of Stevenage/Knebworth, the CAT held that Austin was dominant because of its high market share (over 75 per cent) and the barriers to entry in the market.

With regards to the crematorium services' geographical market, the CAT found that Austin crematorium had practically virtual exclusivity in relation to cremations within its catchment area. The high share for cremations in this market (90 per cent), the high barriers of entry caused by the difficulty of opening another crematorium, the ability of Austin to act independently of the reactions of its competitors and customers, all showed a dominant position in the relevant geographical market.

The CAT proceeded to discuss the issue of abuse of a dominant position. Relying on *United Brands* and *Oscar Bronner*, it was held to be an abuse to refuse to supply a long standing customer who abided by normal commercial practice, at least where the refusal to sell would limit markets to the prejudice of consumers and eliminate a trading party from the relevant market. Moreover, Austin could be held to abuse its dominance in crematoria services by refusing to supply those services to J Burges where this would result in eliminating the competition from J Burges in the closely associated market of funeral directing services where Austin also competed and was dominant, per *Commercial Solvents* and *Télémarketing*. Austin had abused its dominant position in crematoria services, funeral directing, or both, and there was no objective justification for such conduct.

Chemistree Homecare Limited v Abbvie Ltd
[2013] EWHC 264 (Ch)

The case dealt with the distribution of a patented drug, Kaletra. The claimant provided homecare services for hospitals and was also a licensed drugs wholesaler. During the contractual relationship the claimant requested increased quantities of the drug, failing to disclose the wholesale side of sales. When the defendant learnt about the wholesale side of sales it decided to limit the quantities of drug supplied, leading to an action by the claimant for abuse of dominant position.

In analysing the issue of dominance, the High Court found it possible for a single patented drug to be dominant in a market and for such a drug to constitute a distinct market of its own. However, the instances where this occurred would be rare, per Genzyme Ltd.[90]

In the present situation, the defendant showed the possibility for patients to switch to other drugs within the same category. No evidence was provided by the claimant showing the share of the market for which Kaletra was a 'must have' drug. Thus no real prospect for dominance could be argued.

Despite the claimant's failure in proving the issue of dominance, the High Court proceeded to discuss whether there could be an abuse. A dominant undertaking's refusal to supply could be abusive, even where the refusal was not absolute but qualified to wholesale for example, per Sot Lelos v GlaxoSmithKline. *In the present case, however, the High Court declined to find an abuse in relation to the defendant's refusal, in view of the disproportionate quantities requested by the claimant compared to previous supplies. This finding was strengthened by the fact that the defendant did not entertain an outright complete refusal and the claimant's behaviour throughout the commercial relation was found to be disingenuous.*

90 *Genzyme Limited and the Office of Fair Trading* [2004] CAT 4.

9.3. PREDATION: PREDATORY PRICING AND SELECTIVE LOW PRICING

9.3.1. THE ECONOMICS OF PREDATION

The concept of predation is not clearly defined and could refer to any practice by a dominant undertaking to exclude a rival from the market and reduce social welfare.[91] A predatory practice may involve a sacrifice of profits, the dominant firm reducing, during a period of time (*T*), its prices below a certain measure of its costs, with the expectation that its rivals will be excluded from the market, thus enabling it to increase its prices, at period $T + 1$ when it is not facing any effective competition from the defendant or from anyone. A predatory practice may also consist of conduct that excludes an equally efficient competitor, again with the expectation of increasing the prices to consumers. Predation often takes the form of lower prices to all customers (predatory pricing) or to some of the customers of the dominant undertaking (selective low pricing). The predatory firm first lowers its price until it is below the average cost of its competitors. The competitors must then lower their prices below average cost, thereby losing money on each unit sold. If they fail to cut their prices, they will lose virtually all their customers; if they do cut their prices, they will eventually go bankrupt. After the competitor has been forced out of the market, the predatory firm raises its price, compensating itself for the money it lost while it was engaged in predatory pricing, and earns monopoly profits for ever after.

As cutting prices constitutes at first sight good news for consumers, one might wonder why such a practice may fall under the scope of Article 102 TFEU, if the objective of the latter provision is to protect consumers. However, the claim of predatory pricing is not lower prices as such but the potential increase of the price level, post-exclusion, to a higher level than if competitors hadn't been excluded. From this perspective, predatory pricing and selective price-cutting may harm consumers.

There are divergent views in economic literature over the occurrence of predatory pricing in real markets. At one side of the spectrum, there are economists advancing that predatory pricing is rare, as there is a low likelihood of success of these practices and the exclusion of competitors from the market. First, even if a dominant undertaking can use its 'deep pockets' to price below costs and outlast its less powerful rivals, a rival firm may be able to survive if it receives outside capital enabling it to stay in the market up to the moment when prices will have to rise back above predatory levels.[92] Second, re-entry may be facilitated from the fact that the prey's production facilities will still be available and can be bought by a new entrant at liquidation prices, thus being able to enter with a lower cost base. Any gains from induced exclusion may be therefore short-lived. This may be particularly the case given that predator's losses during the predatory pricing period will be typically larger than those of its prey. Indeed, if the firms have symmetric costs, if price is set below average cost, the dominant

[91] This Section draws upon the excellent overviews of the economics of predatory pricing by B Kobayashi, 'The Law and Economics of Predatory Pricing' in KN Hylton (ed) *Antitrust Law and Economics* (Edward Elgar, 2010), 116; A Edlin, 'Predatory Pricing' in E Elhauge (ed) *Research Handbook on the Economics of Antitrust Law* (Edward Elgar, 2012), 144. See also C Fumagalli, M Motta, and C Calcagno, *Exclusionary Practices—The Economics of Monopolisation and Abuse of Dominance* (Cambridge University Press, 2018), 14–125; M Funk and C Jaag, 'The More Economic Approach to Predatory Pricing' (2018) 14(2) *J Competition L & Economics* 292.

[92] J McGee, 'Predatory Price Cutting: The *Standard Oil* (N.J.) Case' [1958] 1(1) *J L & Economics* 137.

firm will incur the largest losses by virtue of having the largest volume of sales (any reduction on prices would apply to a higher volume of sales compared to the prey). Consequently, it is implausible that the predator will pursue this practice. The prospect of incurring losses indefinitely in the hope of being able at some point to charge monopolistic prices is thus extremely risky, as the prey knows that the practice is more costly to the predator and thus has incentives to persist.[93] Predation may succeed only under specific conditions: the price is sufficiently low to induce rivals to exit, the strategy of the predator of keeping prices low as long as it takes must be credible enough, and there must be no possibility of re-entry, once the predator tries to recoup its losses from predation by increasing the price. A price war may also expand in neighbouring markets, thus complicating the strategy of the predator. Third, there was some empirical literature in the 1970s suggesting that there have been few successful cases of predation.[94]

At the other side of the spectrum, there are economists arguing that predatory pricing is a plausible strategy and might be used strategically to exclude rivals from the market and reduce consumer welfare. First, they note that predation might succeed if the firms have asymmetric financial resources. A predator with a long purse may outlast the prey and deter its entry to the market.[95] Moreover, where the prey relies on external finance, investors may withdraw their financial support due to the uncertainty as to whether the prey's losses are a result of predation or merely inferior product offering. Second, the predator may develop a reputation of aggressive predatory strategies, by systematically preferring to predate rather than accommodate new entrants, thus deterring entry.[96] Third, low prices may signal to new entrants that the incumbent's costs are lower than theirs. Assuming that each firm knows its own costs but not those of its rivals, that strategy might lead the predator's rivals to reconsider their entry in the market.[97] Similarly, the predator's low prices might be taken as a signal of insufficient demand. Fourth, recent empirical studies have found evidence of successful predatory pricing, challenging the findings of earlier literature.[98]

The identification of predatory pricing that may harm competition and consumers also requires the development of a methodology that would enable the authority's decision to minimize the sum of enforcement costs (which includes the cost of administering the rule and those emanating from litigation) and error costs. Error costs include the costs of false positives (type I errors, wrongfully condemning pro-competitive practices) and false negatives (type II errors, wrongfully allowing anti-competitive predatory pricing). In view of the lower prices from which consumers benefit, extra care should be taken before qualifying price-cutting as predatory pricing, with the risk of chilling pro-competitive behaviour that greatly benefits

93 R Bork, *The Antitrust Paradox: A Policy at War with Itself* (Basic Books, 1978), 154; F Easterbrook, 'Predatory Strategies and Counterstrategies' (1981) 48 *U Chicago L Rev* 263.

94 R Koller II, 'The Myth of Predatory Pricing: An Empirical Study' (1971) 4 *Antitrust L & Economics Rev* 105.

95 L Telser, 'Cutthroat Competition and the Long Purse' (1966) 9 *J L & Economics* 259.

96 P Milgrom and J Roberts, 'Predation, Reputation and Entry Deterrence' (1982) 27 *J Economic Theory* 280; J Ordover and G Saloner, 'Predation, Moopolization and Antitrust' in R Schmalensee and RD Willig (eds) *Handbook of Industrial Organization*, vol 1 (North-Holland, 1989), 538.

97 G Saloner, 'Predation, Mergers and Incomplete Information' (1987) 18 *Rand J Economics* 165.

98 B Yamey, 'Predatory Price Cutting: Notes and Comments' (1972) 15 *J L & Economics* 129; R Zerbe and D Cooper, 'An Empirical and Theoretical Comparison of Alternative Predation Rules' (1982) 61 *Texas L Rev* 655; R Zerbe and M Mumford, 'Does Predatory Pricing Exist? Economic Theory and the Courts after Brooke Group' (1996) 41 *Antitrust Bulletin* 949. See the extensive discussion of the empirical literature in B Kobayashi, 'The Law and Economics of Predatory Pricing' in KN Hylton (ed) *Antitrust Law & Economics* (Edward Elgar, 2010), 124.

consumers. For this reason, applying a welfare test that would have examined the effects of a predatory strategy on consumers would have led to type I errors. Hence, decision-makers rely on alternative tests for predatory pricing, in particular cost-price tests enabling the filtering of predatory pricing claims.

The best-known test is that suggested by professors Areeda and Turner in a seminal article in 1975.[99] Areeda and Turner defined predation as selling below costs, in particular short run marginal costs.[100] Their assumption is that in a situation of competitive equilibrium, prices will be driven down to marginal costs (MC) and that any price below MC indicates that the predatory firm sacrifices profits. As it is difficult to observe and measure marginal costs, Areeda and Turner suggested using the proxy of average variable costs (AVC), which are more easily observable. According to their theory, prices below AVC should be presumptively unlawful.

Other authors have suggested the use of average avoidable costs (AAC) as the price threshold. AAC includes marginal costs but also fixed costs that are not sunk (see Table 9.1).[101] Firms are expected to be able to leave the market once their costs are below AAC, so prices below AAC involve a profit sacrifice but also indicate the point an equally efficient rival (with no exclusionary intentions) would have left the market.

Table 9.1. Costs

Total Cost	Total cost of production—fixed costs (that do not vary or change with output) and variable costs (that vary with output, such as fuel and labour). In the long run, most fixed costs become variable.
Average Total Cost (ATC)	Total cost involved in production of one unit (total cost, divided by the number of units produced).
Long-Run Average Incremental Costs (LRAIC)	The total long-run average cost of supplying an extra unit (the average cost of producing the predatory increment), whenever such costs are incurred. It includes product specific fixed costs, even if they have been sunk before the period of predatory pricing.
Avoidable Cost	The costs that would be avoided if the firm ceases a particular operation.
Average Avoidable Cost (AAC)	Avoidable cost involved in the production of one unit. It includes variable costs and product-specific fixed costs that could have been avoided by not producing the predatory unit. It omits costs that were sunk before the time of predation and so are generally lower than LRAIC.
Average Variable Cost (AVC)	Variable cost involved in production of one unit (excludes all fixed costs). This constitutes the AVC of the entire output, not just the incremental output involved in the predatory strategy.
Marginal Cost	The increase in total cost of increasing output by one unit. Short-run marginal cost is the marginal costs based on the firm's existing plant and equipment (and does not include fixed costs). Although Areeda and Truner preferred a test-based on marginal cost, they accepted that marginal costs are very hard to determine in practice. Conventional accounting methods do not provide the information necessary to calculate marginal costs.

99 P Areeda and D Turner, 'Predatory Pricing and Related Practices under Section 2 of the Sherman Act' (1975) 88 *Harvard L Rev* 697.

100 For an explanation of the different costs see Table 9.1.

101 W Baumol, 'Predation and the Logic of the Average Variable Cost Test' (1996) 39(1) *J L & Economics* 49.

Some authors are in favour of a more structural test (instead of a price–cost test) that would include as the first step of the inquiry proxies for market power, such as the predator's market shares and their stability, the size of other firms, the predator's profit history, the residual elasticity of demand. The second step will include the analysis of factors relating to the conditions of entry into the market. The third step would be to examine the dynamic effects of entrants on the market conditions. Those advocating these tests question the administrability of a price–cost test, put in place a structural filter instead and remain open to the possibility that prices below average total costs (ATC) are predatory, thus establishing a presumption of illegality for prices below ATC, prices above ATC being presumed legal unless the price cut was reversed within a reasonable period of time (eg two years).[102]

This discussion of predation assumes one-sided traditional markets, with one set of sellers supplying one set of buyers. The two-sided markets context may, however, complicate the identification of predation, as it is well known that in this context the two-sided platform may often choose to charge only one side of the platform, providing services for free to the other side or even subsidizing the consumers of the other side (negative prices). In multi-sided platforms, products or services are interconnected and complementary, thus leading to strategies for multi-sided markets to increase revenue. For example, a company managing a search engine may decide to offer services to consumers for free (eg providing free mapping services through the search engine) while benefiting from the increase of traffic on its website to gain additional advertising revenues at the other side of the market. Hence, it is frequent that in the framework of a two-sided market, firms can rationally choose to price one side below marginal cost. A proper assessment of predatory pricing claims in this context requires the decision-maker to take into account the prices charged at both sides of the market to ensure that undertakings are not falsely accused of predatory pricing when they are simply charging only one side of the market, offering the service for free or subsidizing the other side of the market.

Temporary below-cost prices may be justified for promotional purposes. This can be particularly the case where there are network effects, so that the utility/desirability of a product depends on how many customers have already adopted the new product. Under these circumstances, there is a strong case for subsidising early adopters with below-cost prices, in order to quickly reach a 'critical mass', which would signal confidence to late adopters that the product will be commercially successful.

Another issue raised by some authors is the possibility of above-cost pricing to be anti-competitive. Dynamic predation theories advance that incumbents may behave strategically and price aggressively in response to entry in the market in order to induce exit of their rivals and then quickly reverse the price cut by increasing prices.[103] Some authors have even suggested a price freeze that would make any price cuts quasi-permanent, thus punishing the predator by impeding any recoupment of the lost profits.[104] In subsequent cases involving hub and spoke airlines, the US Department of Justice alleged that some airlines behaved unlawfully by expanding capacity and thus selectively cutting price in response to a rival's entry,

[102] P Joskow and A Klevorick, 'A Framework for Analyzing Predatory Pricing Policy' (1979) 89 *Yale LJ* 213. For other proposals focusing on market structure, see P Bolton, J Brodley, and M Riordan, 'Predatory Pricing: Strategic Theory and Legal Policy' (2000) 88 *Georgetown LJ* 2239.

[103] O Williamson, 'Predatory Pricing: A Strategic and Welfare Analysis' (1977) 87 *Yale LJ* 284.

[104] W Baumol, 'Quasi-Permanence of Price Reductions: A Policy for Prevention of Predatory Pricing' (1979) 89 *Yale LJ* 1.

even if the price charged by the airlines exceeded all relevant measures of cost. Following the rapid exit of the entrant, incumbents increased their prices to their higher pre-entry level. The case led to a debate between those favouring the application of competition law to selective price-cutting by dominant firms, even if this is done above ATC, and those opposing such an expansive application of competition law. The first group criticizes the price–cost test for being under-inclusive for anti-competitive markets where entrants may not be for the time being as efficient as the incumbent but may reduce their costs in the long run with economies of scale or learning by doing. In addition, as a result of the application of competition law to above-cost selective price cuts, the dominant firms may decide to adopt a policy of limit pricing *ex ante*, thus deterring any new entrant, without at the same time incurring any risk of being found to infringe competition law. Hence, consumers will benefit from lower prices in both short and long term. Some authors have advanced a 'consumer betterment standard', which would challenge a practice if 'it is likely in the circumstances to exclude from the defendant's market a competitor who would provide consumers a better deal than they get from the monopoly'.[105] Aaron Edlin, the main proponent of this standard explains:

> The consumer betterment standard focuses on increases in consumer surplus, asking: is a better deal for consumers excluded from the market? The better deal might be a lower price or higher quality. This approach flows fairly directly from the view [. . .] that [competition law] is intended to protect consumer welfare. [. . .] In fact, it seems odd that the main stream of monopolization thinking interprets competition on the merits as equivalent to the triumph of the firm with the greater productive merits, regardless of whether those merits will be passed on to consumers.[106]

This approach reflects the value of the competitive process and of maintaining in the market even inefficient rivals, as these may constrain the pricing of the dominant firm to levels that are lower than those in their absence. Edlin explains the differences between the consumer betterment standard and the as-efficient-competitor standard:

A Edlin, 'Predatory Pricing' in E Elhauge (ed) *Research Handbook on the Economics of Antitrust Law* (Edward Elgar, 2012), 162, 164

> [C]onsider an efficient incumbent that sells at high prices but forestalls entry (from less efficient firms) because it 'advertises' a credible threat (or makes a contractual promise) to cut prices post-entry to levels below average costs of entrants but above its own avoidable costs. If entrants would otherwise provide consumers with better deals, then this incumbent monopolizes according to the consumer betterment standard. The incumbent does not monopolize according to the equally efficient competitor standard because the excluded entrants are inefficient.
>
> Entrants in this example stand willing to provide consumers with a better deal than the incumbent actually gives consumers, but entrants don't do so because the efficient incumbent would drive them from the market. Those worried solely about productive efficiency

105 A Edlin, 'Predatory Pricing' in E Elhauge (ed) *Research Handbook on the Economics of Antitrust Law* (Edward Elgar, 2012), 162.

106 Ibid, 163.

are not concerned about productively inefficient firms, of course, but why should antitrust focus on the exclusion of productively efficient firms if consumer welfare is its ultimate consequentialist goal? [. . .] The consumer betterment standard is largely a process-based rule, protecting the competitive process, rather than a standard demanding an ultimate consumer welfare calculus.

Other authors have opposed the application of competition law to above-cost pricing.[107] First, they argue that restricting efficient pricing behaviour may create disincentives and affect firms' investment decisions: that is, not only by the defendant, but also by potential competitors whose incentives to invest in state-of-the-art production facilities would be blunted under a protection standard that is more generous than the as-efficient-competitor test. Second, in view of the common costs incurred, as firms produce several products and may have fixed or variable costs that are common to several of its products, undertakings may 'charge high demand buyers higher prices to get them to cover a disproportionate share of recurring common costs', while 'charging low-demand customers lower prices that are closer to firm's marginal costs once these common costs are incurred'.[108] Third, entrants that are not yet as efficient as the incumbent because of economies of scale may obtain the necessary funding from capital markets to withstand any above-cost price-cutting campaign led by the dominant undertaking, if their cost curve is the same or better than that of the incumbent/dominant firm. However, this assumes that the entrants can easily attract capital from the markets. Fourth, some argue that competition authorities should be particularly careful to prohibit above-cost price cuts, as the gains from the application of competition law are in the future (hence discounted) and highly uncertain, while the benefits of price cuts are present and observable.

Having in mind these economic principles, we will now focus on the case law of the European Courts and the decisional practice of the European Commission with regard to predatory pricing and above-cost price-cutting.

9.3.2. PRICING BELOW COSTS (PREDATORY PRICING)

The European Courts have established the standards for predatory pricing claims to succeed in three subsequent cases: *AKZO*, *France Telecom*, and *Post Danmark*. We will examine the three cases before analysing the position of the European Commission in its Guidance on Article 102.

9.3.2.1. *AKZO*

Case C-62/86, *AKZO v Commission*
[1991] ECR I–03359

AKZO produces organic peroxides for use in making plastics. ECS is a small English firm that makes the same chemicals for use in the English flour industry. When ECS started to sell also

[107] See, notably, E Elhauge, 'Why Above-Cost Price Cuts to Drive Out Entrants are not Predatory—And the Implications for Defining Costs and Market Power' (2003) 112 *Yale LJ* 681.
[108] Ibid, 686–7.

to plastics producers, AKZO threatened to drive ECS out of the market for flour additives, and began to offer deep discounts to ECS' major customers. The Commission found that AKZO was dominant in the supply of organic peroxides generally, and not only for plastic production, and that it had abused its position by predatory pricing. On appeal, the Court of Justice of the EU held:

The dominant position

59. It should be further observed that according to its own internal documents AKZO had a stable market share of about 50% from 1979 to 1982 [. . .]. Furthermore, AKZO has not adduced any evidence to show that its share decreased during subsequent years.

60. With regard to market shares the Court has held that very large shares are in themselves, and save in exceptional circumstances, evidence of the existence of a dominant position Judgment in Case 85/76 *Hoffman-La Roche v Commission* [1979] ECR 461, paragraph 41. That is the situation where there is a market share of 50% such as that found to exist in this case.

61. Moreover, the Commission rightly pointed out that other factors confirmed AKZO's predominance in the market. In addition to the fact that AKZO regards itself as the world leader in the peroxides market, it should be observed that, as AKZO itself admits, it has the most highly developed marketing organization, both commercially and technically, and wider knowledge than that of their competitors with regard to safety and toxicology [. . .]

The existence of an abuse of a dominant position

63. According to the contested decision (point 75) AKZO had abusively exploited its dominant position by endeavouring to eliminate ECS from the organic peroxides market mainly by massive and prolonged price-cutting in the flour additives sector.

64. According to the Commission, Article 82 does not make costs the decisive criterion for determining whether price reductions by a dominant undertaking are abusive (point 77). Such a criterion does not take any account of the general objectives of the EC competition rules as defined in [Article 3(1)(g) of the Treaty, now replaced by Protocol No 27] and in particular the need to prevent the impairment of an effective structure of competition in the common market. A mechanical criterion would not give adequate weight to the strategic aspect of price-cutting behaviour. There can be an anti-competitive object in price-cutting whether or not the aggressor sets its prices above or below its own costs, whatever the manner in which those costs are understood (point 79).

65. A detailed analysis of the costs of the dominant undertaking might, however, according to the Commission, be of considerable importance in establishing the reasonableness or otherwise of its pricing conduct. The exclusionary consequences of a price-cutting campaign by a dominant producer might be so self-evident that no evidence of intention to eliminate a competitor is necessary. On the other hand, where the low pricing could be susceptible of several explanations, evidence of an intention to eliminate a competitor or restrict competition might also be required to prove an infringement (point 80).

66. AKZO disputes the relevance of the criterion of lawfulness adopted by the Commission, which it regards as nebulous or at least inapplicable. It maintains that the Commission should have adopted an objective criterion based on its costs.

67. In that respect, it states that the question of the lawfulness of a particular level of prices cannot be separated from the specific market situation in which the prices were fixed. There is no abuse if the dominant undertaking endeavours to obtain an optimum selling-price and a positive coverage margin. A price is optimum if the undertaking may reasonably expect that

the offer of another price or the absence of a price would produce a less favourable operating profit in the short term. Furthermore, a coverage margin is positive if the value of the order exceeds the sum of the variable costs.

68. According to AKZO, a criterion based on an endeavour to obtain an optimal price in the short term cannot be rejected on the grounds that it would jeopardize the viability of the undertaking in the long term. It is only after a certain time that the undertaking in question could take measures to eliminate the losses or withdraw from a loss-making branch of business. In the meantime the undertaking would have to accept 'optimum orders' in order to reduce its deficit and to ensure continuity of operation.

69. It should be observed that, as the Court held in its judgment in Case 85/76 *Hoffmann-La Roche v Commission* [1979] ECR 461, paragraph 91, the concept of abuse is an objective concept relating to the behaviour of an undertaking in a dominant position which is such as to influence the structure of a market where, as a result of the very presence of the undertaking in question, the degree of competition is weakened and through recourse to methods which, different from those which condition normal competition in products or services on the basis of the transactions of commercial operators, has the effect of hindering the maintenance of the degree of competition still existing in the market or the growth of that competition.

70. It follows that Article [102] prohibits a dominant undertaking from eliminating a competitor and thereby strengthening its position by using methods other than those which come within the scope of competition on the basis of quality. From that point of view, however, not all competition by means of price can be regarded as legitimate.

71. Prices below average variable costs (that is to say, those which vary depending on the quantities produced) by means of which a dominant undertaking seeks to eliminate a competitor must be regarded as abusive. A dominant undertaking has no interest in applying such prices except that of eliminating competitors so as to enable it subsequently to raise its prices by taking advantage of its monopolistic position, since each sale generates a loss, namely the total amount of the fixed costs (that is to say, those which remain constant regardless of the quantities produced) and, at least, part of the variable costs relating to the unit produced.

72. Moreover, prices below average total costs, that is to say, fixed costs plus variable costs, but above average variable costs, must be regarded as abusive if they are determined as part of a plan for eliminating a competitor. Such prices can drive from the market undertakings which are perhaps as efficient as the dominant undertaking but which, because of their smaller financial resources, are incapable of withstanding the competition waged against them. [. . .]

NOTES AND QUESTIONS ON AKZO

1. (Paragraphs 59–61) Does a market share of 50 per cent establish dominance, is it a rebuttable presumption or merely one factor to be taken into account?
2. Had AKZO been found dominant over organic peroxides for use only in the plastics industry, would an abuse in the flour additives market have infringed Article 102?[109]
3. (Paragraph 65) Note the reference of the CJEU to intent.
4. (Paragraph 69) Note how the CJEU frequently quotes from its earlier judgments almost as if they were statutes. 'Normal competition in products or services on the basis

[109] Cf Case C-311/84, *Centre belge d'études de marché—Télémarketing (CBEM) v Compagnie luxembourgeoise de télédiffusion SA (CLT) & Information publicité Benelux SA* [1985] ECR 3261, paras 25–7 [hereinafter *Télémarketing*].

of the transactions of commercial operators' is the same poor translation of the concept of 'competition on the merits'. Is the definition of abuse the same as in any of the earlier cases?

5. (Paragraph 71) What are marginal costs? How do they differ from variable or avoidable costs? Variable over what time period? Note that marginal cost may vary immensely. For instance they are large when an extra passenger turns up to take a plane and the existing one is full. Which passenger is marginal, the last to book, or the last to turn up, or the first to turn up after the plane is full? Average variable costs are less volatile. Average avoidable costs are those that could be saved by supplying less.
6. (Paragraph 71) Can you think of any other reasons for predation? Might it be to obtain a reputation for predating, which might discourage competitors in other markets, or even in the same market, competing aggressively with the dominant company?
7. (Paragraph 72) Is having a strategic plan the same as intention?
8. Would it be better to consider long-term incremental costs? These are the cost of creating new capacity and using it: the cost, in the long term, of increasing production. It may include some sunk costs. Where technology is improving, long-run average incremental cost (LRAIC) does not permit the full recovery of historical costs of the investment made in older technology.
9. Note that in some industries average variable costs are virtually zero—telecoms once the wires have been installed, freight once a ship has been designated for sailing from a specific place, at a specified time and has space in its hold.
10. Does the use of any of these cost concepts enable a dominant firm to exclude a firm that will have significant overheads if it enters?
11. (Paragraph 71) Are prices below average variable costs illegal *per se*? Think of situations and arguments both ways. Are these arguments inconsistent with the Judgment, or does it leave scope for them?
12. List the conditions in which predatory pricing might be commercially sensible if it were legal. Note that charging lower prices than a monopolist might charge in the short term will increase demand and the total demand must be met if a competitor is to be driven from the market. Then the competitor's plant must be acquired from its liquidator or it may be bought up cheaply by someone else. New competitors must be excluded if the predator is to recoup the foregone profits.
13. Average variable costs may be a better test than marginal costs, as the marginal cost may be immense when it is necessary to install more capacity. It is often arbitrary to decide which item is the marginal one. See Question 7.
14. (Paragraph 71, second sentence) What concept of cost should be used: historic or opportunity cost? The historic cost is the money that was spent on something in the past. The opportunity cost is what it costs to take advantage of the opportunity. If land has become more valuable since it was acquired, the opportunity cost of using it, is what could otherwise be got for its use. If a product is no longer worth what it cost, the opportunity cost of using it, is what it would fetch minus the costs of selling it. Often stocks are not worth as much as they cost. The purchase may have been mistaken, the stock may have become obsolescent or unfashionable.

Would it be predatory to sell it at less than its original cost if that is as much as can be obtained? The Court looked to historic costs later in its judgment, but the products were being replaced, so the historic and opportunity costs may well have been the same in the case.

15. (Paragraph 72) There are more occasions when prices below average total costs are commercially sensible without hoping to recoup. In a cyclical industry, is the dominant company over-pricing during the upturn and predating in the downturn contrary to Article 102? It is possible to ascertain average total costs or is there a range of possibilities?
16. Where there are common costs for several operations, how should a dominant firm be required to apportion them? These questions did not arise in *AKZO*. Does the language of the Judgment help you to answer?
17. (Paragraph 72) If 'abuse' is an objective concept, why should a plan to eliminate a competitor be relevant? Is a plan different from intention to exclude?
18. Is a test based on intention sensible? Do not normal competitors each plan and hope to excel over the others? What is normal competition on the basis of performance? Does it include selling on a low margin?
19. (Paragraphs 71, 72) Can you read into the words a condition that the dominant undertaking has hopes of recoupment? Is such a condition desirable?[110]

9.3.2.2. *France Télécom* (the *Wanadoo* case)

In 2003, the European Commission found that Wanadoo Interactive SA (Wanadoo) had pursued a predatory pricing policy in relation to its Pack eXtense and Wanadoo ADSL services, as part of a plan to exclude competitors in the high-speed Internet access market, and had thereby infringed Article 102 TFEU. At the time, Wanadoo was part of the France Télécom group. The French State owned 56 per cent of the shares in France Telecom, which indirectly held over 70 per cent of the shares in Wanadoo. Wanadoo and France Télécom merged in 2004. France Telecom supplied high-speed Internet access through ADSL modems by wholesale and sold these to Wanadoo on more favourable terms than to other retailers. Wanadoo's customers paid fees to both Wanadoo and France Telecom. The Commission defined the market as high-speed Internet access for residential customers and found that, from 1999 to 2002, Wanadoo's services were marketed at prices below its average costs (until August 2001, prices were considerably below average variable costs and from August 2001 until October 2002, prices were approximately equal to variable costs, but below total costs) and imposed fines on Wanadoo. When balancing Wanadoo's costs and revenues, the Commission ignored the profit made by France Telecom from providing the ADSL service and other streams of revenue such as advertising opportunities. The Commission also sought to bring evidence that the conduct of Wanadoo was part of a plan to exclude competition, by relying on direct documentary evidence of the exclusionary intent (internal documents to the company). Wanadoo appealed to the General Court,[111] which dismissed the appeal in its entirety. France Télécom then appealed to the CJEU.

110 See Opinion of AG Fennelly in Case C-395/96 P, *Compagnie Maritime Belge Transports SA v Commission* [2000] ECR I–1365, para 136, discussed in Section 9.3.3.1 below.

111 Case T-340/03, *France Télécom v Commission* [2007] ECR II–107.

Case C-202/07 P, *France Télécom v Commission*
[2009] ECR I–2369

Price alignment (Meeting competition defence)

42. It must be stated, as the Commission contends, that the [General Court] in the present case responded amply to the arguments put forward by WIN at first instance seeking, essentially, to justify the pricing practice concerned on the basis of the right of every economic operator, irrespective of its position on the market, to align its prices on those of its competitors. [. . .]

46. To that end, the Court refers in paragraphs 185 and 186 of the judgment under appeal to the Community caselaw according to which Article [102 TFEU] imposes specific obligations on undertakings in a dominant position. In particular, the Court recalled that, although the fact that an undertaking is in a dominant position cannot deprive it of the right to protect its own commercial interests if they are attacked and such an undertaking must be allowed the right to take such reasonable steps as it deems appropriate to protect those interests, it is not possible, however, to countenance such behaviour if its actual purpose is to strengthen that dominant position and abuse it.

47. [. . .] WIN cannot rely on any absolute right to align its prices on those of its competitors in order to justify its conduct where that conduct constitutes an abuse of its dominant position. [. . .]

Recoupment

103. In considering the merits of the first part of this ground of appeal, it is necessary to note at the outset that, according to settled caselaw, Article [102 TFEU] is an application of the general objective of European Community action laid down by Article 3(1)(g) EC [now Protocol No 27], namely, the institution of a system ensuring that competition in the common market is not distorted. Thus, the dominant position referred to in Article [102 TFEU] relates to a position of economic strength enjoyed by an undertaking which enables it to prevent effective competition being maintained on the relevant market by affording it the power to behave to an appreciable extent independently of its competitors, its customers and ultimately of the consumers (Case 85/76 *Hoffmann-La Roche* v *Commission* [1979] ECR 461, paragraph 38). [. . .]

104. In that context, in prohibiting the abuse of a dominant market position in so far as trade between Member States is capable of being affected, Article [102 TFEU] refers to conduct which is such as to influence the structure of a market where the degree of competition is already weakened and which, through recourse to methods different from those governing normal competition in products or services on the basis of the transactions of commercial operators, has the effect of hindering the maintenance of the degree of competition still existing in the market or the growth of that competition [. . .].

105. Therefore, since Article [102 TFEU] refers not only to practices which may cause damage to consumers directly, but also to those which are detrimental to them through their impact on an effective competition structure (Case 6/72 *Europemballage and Continental Can* v *Commission* [1973] ECR 215, paragraph 26), an undertaking which holds a dominant position has a special responsibility not to allow its behaviour to impair genuine undistorted competition on the common market (*Nederlandsche Banden-Industrie-Michelin* v *Commission*, paragraph 57).

106. As the Court has already stated, it follows that Article [102 TFEU] prohibits a dominant undertaking from eliminating a competitor and thereby strengthening its position by using methods other than those which come within the scope of competition on the basis of quality.

From that point of view, not all competition by means of price can be regarded as legitimate (*AKZO* v *Commission*, paragraph 70).

107. In particular, it must be found that an undertaking abuses its dominant position where, in a market the competition structure of which is already weakened by reason precisely of the presence of that undertaking, it operates a pricing policy the sole economic objective of which is to eliminate its competitors with a view, subsequently, to profiting from the reduction of the degree of competition still existing in the market.

108. In order to assess the lawfulness of the pricing policy applied by a dominant undertaking, the Court, in paragraph 74 of *AKZO* v *Commission*, relied on pricing criteria based on the costs incurred by the dominant undertaking and on its strategy.

109. Thus, the Court of Justice has held, first, that prices below average variable costs must be considered prima facie abusive inasmuch as, in applying such prices, an undertaking in a dominant position is presumed to pursue no other economic objective save that of eliminating its competitors. Secondly, prices below average total costs but above average variable costs are to be considered abusive only where they are fixed in the context of a plan having the purpose of eliminating a competitor (see *AKZO* v *Commission*, paragraphs 70 and 71, and *Tetra Pak* v *Commission*, paragraph 41).

110. Accordingly, contrary to what the appellant claims, it does not follow from the caselaw of the Court that proof of the possibility of recoupment of losses suffered by the application, by an undertaking in a dominant position, of prices lower than a certain level of costs constitutes a necessary precondition to establishing that such a pricing policy is abusive. In particular, the Court has taken the opportunity to dispense with such proof in circumstances where the eliminatory intent of the undertaking at issue could be presumed in view of that undertaking's application of prices lower than average variable costs (see, to that effect, *Tetra Pak* v *Commission*, paragraph 44).

111. That interpretation does not, of course, preclude the Commission from finding such a possibility of recoupment of losses to be a relevant factor in assessing whether or not the practice concerned is abusive, in that it may, for example where prices lower than average variable costs are applied, assist in excluding economic justifications other than the elimination of a competitor, or, where prices below average total costs but above average variable costs are applied, assist in establishing that a plan to eliminate a competitor exists.

112. Moreover, the lack of any possibility of recoupment of losses is not sufficient to prevent the undertaking concerned reinforcing its dominant position, in particular, following the withdrawal from the market of one or a number of its competitors, so that the degree of competition existing on the market, already weakened precisely because of the presence of the undertaking concerned, is further reduced and customers suffer loss as a result of the limitation of the choices available to them.

113. The Court of First Instance was right therefore to hold, in paragraph 228 of the judgment under appeal, that demonstrating that it is possible to recoup losses is not a necessary precondition for a finding of predatory pricing.

NOTES AND QUESTIONS ON CJEU'S JUDGMENT IN FRANCE TÉLÉCOM V COMMISSION

1. (Paragraphs 42–66) The Court of Justice confirmed the position of the General Court on the defence of meeting competition and price alignment.
2. According to paragraph 66 of the judgment of the CJEU, the decisional practice of the Commission and the General Court's judgments take 'the costs simply as they appear

in the undertaking's accounts'. Do you agree with such an approach? Should opportunity costs also be considered? In the airline predatory pricing cases in the United States, the courts considered measures of opportunity cost instead of accounting based measures of costs.[112] In this case, the airlines have expanded capacity as a response to a rival's entry, the later claiming that this additional capacity and lowering of the price should be qualified as predatory pricing. As it is noted by B Kobayashi, '[o]ne of the proposed cost measures used the forgone profits that resulted from the diversion of capacity (an aircraft) from another, more profitable, route as the appropriate measure of the opportunity costs of the aircraft rather than using leasing costs or other accounting measures of cost.'[113]

3. Recoupment is not an essential element of predation but the Court recognizes that it may play some role in finding an abuse.[114] Compare the position of the Court with the Opinion of Advocate General Fennelly in the *Compagnie Maritime Belge* case of the CJEU.[115] The Opinion of AG Fennelly has not carried the Court, which rejected the recoupment requirement first in *Tetra Pak II* and then in *France Télécom*.
4. Do you think the Commission should be concerned about the recoupment of sunk costs?

9.3.2.3 *Post Danmark A/S v Konkurrencerådet (Post Danmark I)*: Implications for predatory pricing

As the case[116] raises issues with regard to above-cost selective price-cutting and the interaction of the predatory price–cost standard of *AKZO* and a standard more focused on exclusion, it will be examined in Section 9.3.3.2. Yet, we include some information on this case and its follow up, which might be relevant to cases on predatory pricing.

A Jones and L Lovdahl Gormsen, 'Abuse of Dominance- Exclusionary Pricing Abuses' in I Lianos and D Geradin (eds) *Handbook in EU Competition Law: Substantive Issues* (Edward Elgar, 2013), ch 10, 434 (footnotes omitted)

This case indicates that the Court will be flexible about the costs standards adopted by the Commission and appears to accept that in specified cases there might be better ways of estimating marginal cost than using AVC. It also reiterates that although pricing between AVC (or AAC/AIC) and ATC can be abusive, it cannot be presumed to be so. Rather it will only be abusive where it can be demonstrated to form part of a deliberate strategy to exclude a competitor *or* where anti-competitive effects can be demonstrated.

112 See *Spirit Airlines v Northwest Airlines, Inc*, 431 F 3d 917 (6th Cir 2005).

113 B Kobayashi, 'The Law and Economics of Predatory Pricing' in KN Hylton (ed) *Antitrust Law & Economics* (Edward Elgar, 2010), 116, 146. In *US v AMR Corp*, 355 F 3d 1109 (10th Cir 2003), the Court of Appeal rejected this approach because of the difficulty of courts to search for hypothetical, more profitable investments a firm could have made in order to identify 'opportunity costs'.

114 Case C-202/07 P, *France Télécom v Commission* [2009] ECR I–2369, para 111.

115 See Opinion of AG Fennelly in Case C-395/96 P, *Compagnie Maritime Belge Transports SA v Commission* [2000] ECR I–1365, para 136.

116 Case C-209/10, *Post Danmark A/S v Konkurrencerådet*, ECLI:EU:C:2012:172 [hereinafter *Post Danmark I*].

Hence, while the *AKZO* presumption for prices below AVC, AAC, or AIC (average incremental costs) is still valid, the *Post Danmark* case law raises the possibility for prices between AIC or AAC and ATC to be found abusive, either because there is, as in *AKZO*, evidence of a plan for eliminating a competitor (anti-competitive intent established by documentary evidence) or in case there is a potential exclusionary effect.[117]

9.3.2.4. The Commission's Guidance on Article 102

Read paragraphs 63–74 and answer the following questions.

> ***NOTES AND QUESTIONS ON THE COMMISSION'S GUIDANCE ON ARTICLE 102***
>
> 1. (Paragraph 63) The Commission also noted in a footnote to this paragraph that
>
>   [it] may also pursue predatory practices by dominant undertakings on secondary markets on which they are not yet dominant. In particular, the Commission will be more likely to find such an abuse in sectors where activities are protected by a legal monopoly such as an IPR or a franchise from the government or a regulator. While the dominant undertaking does not need to engage in predatory conduct to protect its dominant position in the market protected by legal monopoly, it may use the profits gained in the monopoly market to cross-subsidize its activities in another market and thereby threaten to eliminate effective competition in that other market.
>
> 2. (Paragraph 62) Should the Commission rely on documentary evidence provided by the Domco?

9.3.2.5. UK competition law

There have been few cases of predatory pricing under Chapter II CA98.

In *Napp Pharmaceuticals*,[118] the OFT imposed a penalty of £3.2 million on Napp Pharmaceuticals ('Napp'), a Cambridge-based pharmaceutical company, for abusing its dominant position in the market for the supply of sustained release morphine tablets and capsules in the United Kingdom. Sustained release morphine is commonly used in the treatment of cancer-related pain. Napp was found to have supplied its sustained release morphine product, MST, to patients in the community at excessively high prices while supplying hospitals at less than direct cost (a proxy for AVC) with the effect of eliminating competition in the relevant market The OFT found that Napp had offered important discounts when tendering for hospital contracts. In addition, Napp had targeted these discounts at other sustained release morphine products produced by its competitors with the result that, in at least one instance, a competitor was forced to leave the market. Napp argued that below-cost sales to hospitals were justified, as Napp would be able to recover the full price from follow-on sales to patients in the community, because the prescribing practices of GPs were found to be strongly

[117] See Section 9.3.3.2 for our analysis of *Post Danmark I*, esp paras 37–9 and 41 of the Judgment, and Question No 11 on the Judgment in *Post Danmark I*.

[118] *Napp Pharmaceutical Holidings Ltd* [2001] UKCLR 597.

influenced by the brands used in hospitals. The OFT rejected that argument noting that Napp's justification for pricing below AVC was 'circular' and that 'Napp can earn high compensating margins in the community segment' precisely 'because its discount policy in the hospital segment has hindered competition in the community segment'.

On appeal, the CAT confirmed the decision of the OFT on this point.[119] Napp objected arguing that its hospital sales have in fact always been profitable when one takes account of the 'net revenue' resulting from both the sale in the hospital and the 'follow-on' sales in the community to which the hospital sales give rise. This argument was rejected by the CAT for providing no yardstick for distinguishing between what is legitimate, and what is abusive, behaviour on the part of a dominant undertaking, as in most cases of predatory pricing, the predator is willing to forego short-term profits, in the hope of recouping its losses on subsequent, more profitable, sales. According to the CAT, 'arguments based on a "net revenue test" *may* be relevant to show that the dominant undertaking had "no plan to eliminate competition" so as to fall within the exception to the *AKZO* test but not otherwise'.[120] It also rejected the argument of Napp claiming that hospital and community prices were 'system prices, as an essential aspect of the legitimate use of system pricing is that the buyer is in a position to evaluate the life-time, or system-wide costs, and so make a rational choice between competing possibilities. However, that was not the case here as during the period of infringement in this case, there were two separate groups of buyers, the hospital authorities, and the GPs respectively, rather than a single buyer.

In *Aberdeen Journals*, the CAT set aside the first decision of the OFT for problems in market definition.[121] The OFT adopted a second decision concluding that Aberdeen Journals had sold advertising in one of its newspapers at less than AVC and hence was guilty of predatory pricing.[122] On appeal against the second decision the CAT made some interesting comments on predatory pricing, in particular on the concept of variable and fixes costs:

Aberdeen Journals Ltd v OFT
[2003] CAT 11

353. One particular aspect of the distinction between average variable costs and average total costs, not yet explored in the case law, but relevant in the present case, is the period of time over which costs are to be assessed as 'fixed' rather than 'variable'. The longer the period that is taken, the more likely it is that cost will be classified as variable since, for example, over a longer timescale, employees can be dismissed or plant closed in response to changes in output. Indeed, in the long run, almost all costs are 'variable'.

354. The Director suggests, at paragraph 4.6 of OFT 414, referred to in paragraph 175 of the decision, that the period to be used for determining which costs are to be treated as 'variable' and which 'fixed', is 'the time period over which the alleged predatory price or set of prices prevailed or could reasonably be expected to prevail'. Despite some possible circularity in this approach, paragraph 4.6 of OFT 414 seems to us to be a useful starting point. What the Director should do, in the first instance, is to

119 *Napp Pharmaceutical Holdings Limited and Subsidiaries v Director General of Fair Trading* [2002] CAT 1.
120 Ibid, para 262.
121 *Aberdeen Journals Ltd v Director general of Fair Trading* [2002] CAT 4, setting aside OFT decision of 16 July 2001 in *Aberdeen Journals Ltd* CA98/5/2001 [2001] UKCLR 856.
122 *Aberdeen Journals Ltd—remitted case* [2002] UKCLR 740.

identify provisionally the period over which pricing below cost is suspected. He should then take that period and examine whether costs are variable over that period. We do not exclude the possibility of the Director taking other periods, for example a year or a period of months, or even less, as a cross check, if to do so would be reasonable from a business perspective. Whether the period taken is a reasonable period will be a matter of fact and degree, to be judged in the circumstances of each particular case.

355. The consequence is that the longer a dominant undertaking prices at some level below total costs, the more likely it is that costs which might be treated as 'fixed' in the short run should be treated as 'variable' for the purpose of applying the *AKZO* test. In applying the Chapter II prohibition that would not seem to us an unreasonable approach. In order to survive in the market a competitor needs to cover total costs, including overheads. The longer a dominant undertaking prices below total costs, the more likely it is that an equally efficient competitor will be forced to exit the market. That risk is not averted simply because the dominant firm may be covering its average variable costs as measured on a short-run basis.

356. Similarly, it seems to us, the longer the prices of a dominant undertaking remain below total costs the easier it is likely to be to infer an intent to eliminate competition, in accordance with the *AKZO* test, absent special circumstances such as recessionary conditions. Such an intention may be inferred, of course, from other circumstances, such as selective price cutting.

In *Cardiff Bus*, the OFT found that Cardiff Bus had engaged in predatory pricing intended to eliminate its rival bus company 2 Travel from the market.[123] Cardiff Bus operated bus services on a number of routes in and around Cardiff City Centre. These services were branded with the Cardiff Bus livery ('liveried service'). 2 Travel had a number of contracts with Cardiff schools to provide before and after school bus services for pupils. The buses and drivers used to provide these school bus services were largely unutilized during school hours. 2 Travel operated a no frills bus service on certain routes within Cardiff; the service was operated on an 'in-fill' basis, that is to say it was operated during school hours and using the same buses that 2 Travel used to provide school bus services ('the in-fill service'). The in-fill service routes overlapped with some of the routes used by Cardiff Bus' liveried service, but offered lower fares on those routes than the liveried service. Cardiff Bus reacted by operating an unbranded bus along the same routes as the in-fill service—this was known as the 'White Service' as the buses used were white and otherwise unmarked. The White Service operated in addition to Cardiff Bus' existing liveried services on those routes; it charged fares that were the same as or slightly lower than those charged by the 2 Travel in-fill service and it timed its buses to depart just before the scheduled departure time of corresponding in-fill service buses. The Cardiff Bus White Service ceased to operate shortly after the 2 Travel in-fill service had ceased to operate and 2 Travel went into liquidation. The defendant claimed that the price–cost test was misleading, given that there was (*ex ante*) uncertainty as to the potential level of demand for 'no-frills' services, whereas the costs incurred were mainly fixed once the new scheduled services had been committed to. The defendant also claimed that the decision to withdraw its White Service was motivated by the realization (*ex post*) that the level of demand for 'no-frills' services was lower than initially expected. The OFT found that Cardiff Bus' sole purpose in running the White Service was not to market test the demand for and profitability of a 'no-frills' service, as Cardiff Bus had earlier claimed, but to exclude 2 Travel from

123 *Cardiff Bus* [2009] UKCLR 332.

the relevant market by depriving its in-fill service of passengers and, therefore, of revenues. Accordingly, the OFT decided that running the White Service at all—as opposed to running it in a particular way—amounted to abuse of a dominant position and infringed the Chapter II CA98 prohibition.

Cardiff Bus [2009] UKCLR 332

7.22. For a company to choose to launch new services that are likely to result in its generating losses (i.e. making lower profits overall than it would have done had it not launched those services) would not normally be commercially rational conduct on its part. Cardiff Bus submitted in its representations, however, that: '. . .the OFT's retrospective actual revenue based approach is not appropriate because the financial test applied cannot serve as an obvious indicator of the intention of Cardiff Bus when setting its prices. It was by no means obvious to Cardiff Bus when it started operating its white services that these would not be profitable'. In summary, therefore, Cardiff Bus has submitted that its white services were launched as a trial and, accordingly, it did not know whether these services would be commercially successful.

7.23. The OFT has given careful consideration to Cardiff Bus' explanation for its launch and operation of the white services. In that regard, the OFT accepts that, in principle, for the purposes of assessing whether a dominant undertaking's conduct was predatory, the rationality of the decision to engage in, or continue, that conduct should be judged on the basis of the facts as they would have appeared to the dominant company at that time. Depending on the circumstances of the case, therefore, it may not be appropriate to infer that conduct was predatory if there was a genuine attempt to market test new services which were considered to have a realistic prospect of success, but which ultimately proved not to be commercially successful.

7.24. On the other hand, the OFT also considers that claims by a dominant undertaking that conduct on its part at around the time of new entry into the market by a competitor was unintentionally loss-making cannot be taken at face value, and should be considered in the light of all the available evidence with a view to determining whether those claims are credible.

7.25. The OFT has therefore considered it appropriate to evaluate the explanation offered by Cardiff Bus [. . .] that its white services were launched as part of a genuine attempt to test the market. In doing so, as noted above, the OFT has considered the overall conduct of Cardiff Bus in introducing and operating the white services in the light of all the available evidence, including Cardiff Bus' pricing and contemporaneous internal and public documents.

7.26. The OFT would have considered it reasonable to give appropriate weight to any internal documents, produced by Cardiff Bus in the lead-up to its decision to launch the white services, credibly evidencing the 'market testing' motive and/or demonstrating an internal view that the launch of those services could be profitable for Cardiff Bus.

7.27. [. . .] [H]owever, Cardiff Bus has been able to provide little in the way of contemporaneous documents to support its explanation that the white services were introduced to test market demand for no-frills services rather than merely to divert passengers from 2 Travel. It has produced only very limited evidence to the contrary, and in particular could provide no contemporaneous internal documentary evidence that it planned a genuine market test, nor that it had any expectation that the test might prove that white services would lead to its making more, or at least no less, profit overall, nor that it subsequently assessed the outcomes of such a test. In the OFT's view, it would be very unlikely for a company like Cardiff Bus to launch and to continue a market test of this kind without generating any internal documents making the business case for carrying out that test, or seeking to evaluate its results. In particular, there is no evidence that Cardiff Bus conducted any predictive assessment of whether the introduction of its no-frills services would have been profitable.

7.28. Section E also identifies evidence that contradicts Cardiff Bus' explanation that it was conducting a market test. This includes evidence that Cardiff Bus planned to launch no-frills white services in order to divert potential customers away from 2 Travel. There is also evidence that Cardiff Bus publicly disparaged the concept of no-frills services and avoided promoting them. In the OFT's view, the evidence considered as a whole does not support Cardiff Bus' explanation for its launch of the white services.

7.29. Further to this, the OFT has identified evidence that gives rise to a strong inference that Cardiff Bus launched its white service with exclusionary intent—in other words, with the intention of diverting prospective customers away from 2 Travel and thereby forcing 2 Travel out of the market, thus protecting Cardiff Bus' dominant position, and not with the intention of competing on the merits or carrying out a genuine market test. Section E assesses the coincidence in the timing and routes of the white services with those offered by 2 Travel. In particular, the Section presents evidence of the substantial preparations made by Cardiff Bus to respond aggressively to 2 Travel's entry, as well as ongoing assessment by Cardiff Bus of the threat posed by 2 Travel. The Section demonstrates that Cardiff Bus' white services were planned as a retaliatory reaction to new entry by a competitor, with the intention of forcing that new entrant out of the market and thereby restoring the market to its previous state.

7.30. [The evidence submitted], in the OFT's view, is sufficient to demonstrate that the launch and continued operation of the white services was loss-making for Cardiff Bus. In other words, that by launching and continuing the white services, Cardiff Bus was making less money than it would have done had it not launched or continued those services.

7.31. There is little evidence that Cardiff Bus ever considered the likely impact on its profits of launching the white services. Rather, the contemporaneous evidence suggests that Cardiff Bus simply wanted to divert passengers away from 2 Travel and did not consider whether or not the white services would be profitable in their period of operation. In the OFT's view, this failure to consider whether the white services would be profitable does not undermine, but rather supports, a conclusion that the launch of those services was motivated by predatory intent. Once the white services were running, it would have quickly become evident to any objective observer in the position of Cardiff Bus that the services as run were loss-making and a commercial failure.

7.32. In all the circumstances, the OFT concludes that the evidence is sufficient to demonstrate that the white services were not launched as a market test, but were launched and operated simply for the purpose of driving out 2 Travel, rather than making profits for Cardiff Bus or fulfilling any other legitimate commercial strategy.

7.33. In the OFT's view, Cardiff Bus' conduct did not constitute 'normal competition on the merits', but instead was predatory and an abuse of Cardiff Bus' dominant position.

9.3.3. ABOVE-COST SELECTIVE PRICE-CUTTING

Are there any instances in which prices above-cost may be held to infringe Article 102 TFEU? Imagine a fact pattern in which an incumbent hub airline carrier, a dominant undertaking, supplies a new customer on a particular route at lower prices when a new airline carrier decides to compete with it on this route. Should this selective price cut offered by the incumbent dominant undertaking to consumers be considered anti-competitive, because it may exclude from the market a new entrant and lead eventually to the return of the prices to their higher pre-entry level, even if the price set is above the dominant firm's ATC?

This question may depend on one's view about the benefits of assisting the Domco's rival to enter and maintain its position on the market thus providing consumers further choice and also increased competition in the long term as opposed to the costs consumers incur immediately or short-term by foregoing the lower prices offered by the Domco. The topic is hotly debated also in the United States, following a price war between major airlines and claims that incumbents have attempted to drive new entrants out of the market exploiting the advantages offered by operating a hub.[124] For a discussion of the economic arguments with regard to the competitive effects of selective price-cutting see the following OFT report:

OFT 804, Selective price cuts and fidelity rebates, Economic Discussion Paper (July 2005)

1.6. When distinguishing an exclusionary abuse from normal price competition, the following high level principles are important.

1.7. First, low prices and pricing freedom should generally be encouraged. The pervasive use of price cuts and non-cost-related discounts by firms without market power demonstrates that there are many non-exclusionary motives for using discount schemes. The same motives apply for dominant firms as well. Economic theory does not suggest that dominant firms usually use selective price cuts and discounts that give rise to anti-competitive outcomes.

1.8. Second, the competition concern raised by selective price cuts and fidelity rebates is usually foreclosure. The analysis of foreclosure is the main competition issue and is, therefore, the principal focus of our report. The appropriate definition of foreclosure must distinguish between behaviour that leads to a rival's lower market share (or exit) without harming competition versus harmful exclusionary outcomes that are ultimately bad for consumers. We define foreclosure as a practice by a firm with market power that harms consumers in the long run (a) by marginalising and weakening existing competition in markets where entry barriers exist; and/or (b) by raising entry barriers to markets where existing competition is not effective. [. . .]

1.23. Selective price cuts occur where a supplier selects a group of customers and charges different prices to that group compared to another group, even though both groups purchase the same product. Usually the concern is that lower prices have

124 For opposing views in the US, see A Edlin, 'Stopping Above-Cost Predatory Pricing' (2002) 111 *Yale LJ* 941, 952 (advancing the view that when the new entrants have higher costs than the incumbent and expect to be competed out upon entry, then, consumers would be worse off than if the monopoly firm did not exist, because they must pay higher prices than entrants would charge if they entered. Hence, cutting dramatically prices in response to new entry, even if they are still above costs, might discourage entry and should fall within the scope of section 2 of the Sherman Act) and E Elhauge, 'Why Above-Cost price Cuts to Drive Out Entrants Are Not Predatory—And the Implications for Defining Costs and Market Power' (2003) 112 *Yale LJ* 681 (arguing that restricting above-cost pricing will often penalize efficient pricing behaviour by limiting undertakings to maximize their ability to incur common costs—and thus create output—by differentiating between high-demand buyers who will be charged higher prices and low-demand customers who are charged lower prices that are close to the firm's marginal costs once these common costs are incurred).

been targeted at a group of customers to induce them not to switch to a potential new entrant, whilst other customers who are less likely to switch continue to pay the undiscounted prices. [. . .]

1.25. There is no support in economic theory for a presumption that when an incumbent responds to the threat of new entry by selectively lowering prices that this will necessarily harm competition and consumers. Further, models that show how exit might occur rarely offer practical guidance on when intervention to protect rivals is appropriate or on what the remedies should be. [. . .]

1.40. A contentious issue with the application of the equally efficient competitor test to selective price cuts is that a potential entrant has not yet incurred any sunk costs that are required to enter the market. Thus, even if the entrant would be as efficient as the rival if it enters, the incumbent might be able profitably to exclude the entrant by pricing above its own avoidable cost but below that of its rival.

1.41. This has been dubbed 'above cost predation'. It begs the questions of whether the incumbent's advantage should be treated as a legitimate cost advantage (and thus the entrant is simply not equally efficient) and whether competition can be improved through seeking to 'manage' the entry of less efficient rivals.

1.42. In theory, we can devise models which show how intervening to protect a less efficient entrant can be either good or bad for consumers. While intervention may be good for consumers if the counterfactual is no entry at all, consumers may suffer if a rule against above cost exclusion means that the entrant finds it more profitable to enter at a 'high' cost rather than invest further and enter with a lower cost (or better) product. This highlights the problem: intervening against 'above cost predation' could discourage innovation and protect inefficient production.

1.43. There are also practical problems. How do we measure the incumbent's cost advantage and thereby 'handicap' the incumbent appropriately? If the incumbent had to price at the entrant's cost level, it would probably not know these costs and hence what was a lawful price and what was not. It would be inappropriate to punish the dominant firm for pricing below a level that it could not observe. Further, a rival could 'game' the system by inflating its own costs, making it more likely that the dominant firm is punished and regulated (eg: by the imposition of a price floor). Complaining could become more profitable than competing.

1.44. Further, finding and monitoring the appropriate remedy is also difficult. For example, if the dominant firm is not permitted to lower price for a certain amount of time, can it increase quality instead? If the authorities prevent firms from making quality improvements, would this harm innovation?

1.45. In short, intervention against above cost predation would generate the real risk that a precedent is established which creates an unintended chilling effect on price competition in other markets. Even where there is a good case for intervention in a specific case, there is still the possibility that this creates precedent that affects other markets, although this could be dampened where the intervention is widely understood to be case specific (eg: where the authorities make statements to 'ring-fence' precedent or, in some regulated industries, where interventions are understood to be at most sector specific).

QUESTIONS ON THE OFT DISCUSSION PAPER (JULY 2005)

1. (Point 1.7) Consider some commercial reasons other than excluding a new competitor, why a non-dominant firm might want to make selective price cuts.

2. (Point 1.23) Should this apply when the costs of supplying the new entrant are lower than those of supplying other customers?
3. (Point 1.44) Would it have been simpler if the OFT had defined a lower price to include lower quality or any of the other parameters of competition?

The Commission and the European Courts have examined the issue of selective price-cutting in *Irish Sugar*[125] and the *Compagnie Maritime Belge* cases.

9.3.3.1. *Compagnie Maritime Belge v Commission* and the development of the EU approach against above-cost selective price-cutting

Case C-395/96 P, *Compagnie Maritime Belge Transports SA v Commission*
[2000] ECR I–1365

The members of a shipping conference took steps through conference committees to exclude their only competitor on the conference routes, which G&C had recently entered. Since there was a Council regulation granting a block exemption for liner shipping conferences, most of these collective activities did not infringe Article 101 TFEU. The Commission took a decision imposing fines on the members of the conference for an infringement of Article 102 TFEU. It determined that the firms enjoyed a collective dominant position and abused it by taking the various steps to exclude G&C, by cutting the conference freight rates either to match or to be lower than those charged by G&C for ships sailing at the same or similar dates, a practice known as 'fighting ships'. The Commission found that although this practice was not predatory pricing, as the prices charged by the liner shipping companies, members of the maritime conference, were still above their costs, it was nonetheless abusive. The case came to the Court of Justice on appeal from the judgment of the General Court, then known as the Court of First Instance, which had dismissed the action for annulment of the Commission's decision.

Opinion of Advocate General Fennelly on 'fighting ships'

The abusive nature of the 'fighting ships' conduct

131. It is clear that the abuse of which the appellants have been found guilty does not figure on the non-exhaustive list contained in Article [102](a) to (d). In *Continental Can* the Court confirmed (in the context of the acquisition of a competitor) that the practices prohibited by Article [102] were not only 'those which are detrimental to [consumers directly] through their impact on an effective competition structure' but also those which cause the dominant position of the undertaking to be strengthened 'in such a way that the degree of dominance reached substantially fetters competition, i.e. that only undertakings remain in the market whose behaviour depends on the dominant one'. In *AKZO* the Court observed (paragraph 70) that 'not all competition by means of price [could] be regarded as legitimate', having regard to the special obligations of dominant

125 Case T-228/97, *Irish Sugar Plc v Commission of the European Communities* [1999] ECR II–2969.

undertakings. However, it would, in my opinion, potentially significantly impair the pursuit of the objective of Article 3(g) [TEU] [now replaced by the Protocol on Internal Market and Competition] of ensuring the establishment of an internal market in which competition is not distorted, if the Court were to regard a threshold such as total average (or long-run marginal) costs as an absolute yardstick against which all possible abusive or exclusionary pricing practices had to be assessed. The Court in *Tetra Pak II* approved the view taken by the Court of First Instance in that case '. . . that the actual scope of the special responsibility imposed on a dominant undertaking must be considered in the light of the specific circumstances of each case which show a weakened competitive situation.'

132. I would, on the other hand, accept that, normally, non-discriminatory price cuts by a dominant undertaking which do not entail below-cost sales should not be regarded as being anti-competitive. In the first place, even if they are only shortlived, they benefit consumers and, secondly, if the dominant undertaking's competitors are equally or more efficient, they should be able to compete on the same terms. Community competition law should thus not offer less efficient undertakings a safe haven against vigorous competition even from dominant undertakings. Different considerations may, however, apply where an undertaking which enjoys a position of dominance approaching a monopoly, particularly on a market where price cuts can be implemented with relative autonomy from costs, implements a policy of selective price cutting with the demonstrable aim of eliminating all competition. In those circumstances, to accept that all selling above cost was automatically acceptable could enable the undertaking in question to eliminate all competition by pursuing a selective pricing policy which in the long run would permit it to increase prices and deter potential future entrants for fear of receiving the same targeted treatment.

133. There are peculiar features of certain markets such as maritime transport where costs may be an unreliable guide to the reasonableness of competitive strategies adopted by dominant firms. In the first place, once a ship has been designated to sail on a particular day, then, provided capacity is available, the cost of transporting an additional container shipped as a result of a reduced-rate offer may be close to zero. More generally, freight rates will largely be determined not by the marginal cost for the shipping line of providing the service but by the price elasticity of demand for the product shipped.

134. The fundamental question posed in the present case is whether, at the material time, the adverse potential effects of the conduct undertaken by CEWAL members, in reaction to the competitive threat posed by the entrance of G & C, on the structure of competition on the market at issue were such as, having regard to the extent of the market power collectively enjoyed by them, to be sufficient to constitute an abuse.

135. Certain specific features of the 'fighting ships' practice and its setting in the current case can be recalled. CEWAL enjoyed not merely a dominant position but, as it says, a *de facto* monopoly. The practice flowed from CEWAL's unjustified claim to maintain a monopoly on the relevant market which it had sought to enforce via the Ogefrem Agreement and was incontestably designed not merely to beat competition but to eliminate the competitor. At the same time, CEWAL was in a position to devise a scheme of selective designation of sailings for the rate reductions. The resulting loss of revenue was shared between conference members. Both because of the selectivity of the reductions and their very large market share, the members could spread and absorb the loss of revenue. Furthermore, as the Commission suggests (point 82 of the Decision), the very fact that CEWAL was able to set the fighting rates at or above cost may suggest in itself that the normal rates were substantially above cost, or, I would observe, that marginal cost was, in any event, very low.

136. The sharing of loss of revenues prompts me to revert briefly to the possible need to establish an intention or a possibility of recoupment. The process of sharing revenue losses is in essence a form of recoupment. The strategic purpose of the fighting rates carries with it the unspoken implication that rates will not be reduced for any sailings, current or future, where that is not necessary to meet competition. Furthermore, once the competitor was eliminated, they would clearly no longer be justified. Thus, to the extent that it is necessary, I believe that the present case passes the test of recoupment. At the same time, I would say that some such requirement should be part of the test for abusively low pricing by dominant undertakings. It is implied in the first paragraph of the quotation from *AKZO* (see paragraph 126). It is inherent in the *Hoffmann-La Roche* test (see paragraph 124). The reason for restraining dominant undertakings from seeking to hinder the maintenance of competition by, in particular, eliminating a competitor is that they would thus be enabled to charge abusively *high* prices. Thus, an inefficient monopoly would be reinstated and consumers would benefit only in the short run. If that result is not part of the dominant undertaking's strategy it is probably engaged in normal competition.

137. In all these circumstances, the Court of First Instance committed no error of law in finding that the response of CEWAL members to the entrance of G & C was not 'reasonable and proportionate' [paragraph 148]. To my mind, Article [102] cannot be interpreted as permitting monopolists or quasi-monopolists to exploit the very significant market power which their superdominance confers so as to preclude the emergence either of a new or additional competitor. Where an undertaking, or group of undertakings whose conduct must be assessed collectively, enjoys a position of such overwhelming dominance verging on monopoly, comparable to that which existed in the present case at the moment when G & C entered the relevant market, it would not be consonant with the particularly onerous special obligation affecting such a dominant undertaking not to impair further the structure of the feeble existing competition for them to react, even to aggressive price competition from a new entrant, with a policy of targeted, selective price cuts designed to eliminate that competitor. Contrary to the assertion of the appellants, the mere fact that such prices are not pitched at a level that is actually (or can be shown to be) below total average (or long-run marginal) costs does not, to my mind, render legitimate the application of such a pricing policy.

138. In this case the Court of First Instance has, rightly in my view, upheld the Commission's finding that CEWAL members devised a strategy, for the sole and exclusive aim of eliminating G & C, their only competitor. The Commission has demonstrated that the appellants sought, by targeting G & C sailings with fighting rates equal to or lower than those offered by G & C in respect of its sailings, to inflict the maximum damage to G & C while minimising the losses of revenue thereby incurred through the operation of their revenue pool system. To my mind, the Commission was manifestly correct to take the view that, even if G & C were as efficient a shipping line as the members of CEWAL, it could not be expected to 'resist' such 'competition practised in a concerted and abusive manner by a powerful group of shipowners operating together in a shipping conference' (point 82). In other words, the 'fighting ships' practice was designed to drive G & C out of the market with the minimum of cost for CEWAL members, so as to restore them to their previous position of virtual monopoly and accordingly permit them to return their rates to the level of the published conference tariff.

139. Consequently, I recommend that the appeal against the decision of the Court of First Instance to uphold the Commission's characterisation as abusive of the 'fighting ships' conduct undertaken by CEWAL members be dismissed in its entirety.

NOTES AND QUESTIONS ON THE OPINION OF AG FENNELLY IN COMPAGNIE MARITIME BELGE

1. (Paragraphs 132, 135, 137) Is there a heavier responsibility on super-dominant firms? Compare with the position of the CJEU in its judgment.[126]
2. (Paragraph 132) Was Mr Fennelly concerned with protecting consumers or G & C? Compare with Jacobs AG in paragraph 58 of *Oscar Bronner*. Is this a change from the case law of the 1970s?
3. (Paragraph 133) Can you think of other products for which average variable cost is likely to be close to zero? If a dominant firm is permitted to price down to the average variable cost of such a product, would it be likely to enjoy a monopoly in the long term? Spell out your reasons.
4. Under the Ogefram Agreement, the African government was required to reserve half the trade on the conference routes to members of CEWAL. Can governments be expected not to restrict competition to their nationals through regulation? There were also other exclusionary practices such as exclusive dealing agreements with shippers and loyalty discounts.
5. (Paragraph 136) The relevance and importance of recoupment are controversial. The only thing about predatory pricing on which economists are agreed is that it does no harm unless recoupment is expected to be possible after driving out the competitor. Consumers benefit from the lower prices as long as they last, and if the predator has no power to raise prices later over the level they would have reached without the price war, there is no countervailing detriment.
6. (Paragraph 136) Does the concept of recoupment from other members of the cartel support the same view, or is it different?
7. (Paragraph 136) Should the Advocate General be interested in intention? Was the GC (formerly Court of First Instance) picking up the view of the Court's in *AKZO* about a plan to exclude?
8. (Paragraphs 137) Are the restraints the Domco is allowed to impose stricter than those permitted to a non-dominant company?

Case C-395/96 P, Compagnie Maritime Belge Transports SA v Commission
[2000] ECR I–1365

114. Furthermore, the actual scope of the special responsibility imposed on a dominant undertaking must be considered in the light of the specific circumstances of each case which show that competition has been weakened (Case C-333/94 P, *Tetra Pak v Commission* [1996] ECR I–5951, paragraph 24).

115. The maritime transport market is a very specialised sector. It is because of the specificity of that market that the Council established, in Regulation No 4056/86, a

[126] Case C-395/96 P, *Compagnie Maritime Belge Transports SA v Commission* [2000] ECR I–1365, paras 114 and 119.

set of competition rules different from that which applies to other economic sectors. The authorisation granted for an unlimited period to liner conferences to cooperate in fixing rates for maritime transport is exceptional in light of the relevant regulations and competition policy.

116. It is clear from the eighth recital in the preamble to Regulation No 4056/86 that the authorisation to fix rates was granted to liner conferences because of their stabilising effect and their contribution to providing adequate efficient scheduled maritime transport services. The result may be that, where a single liner conference has a dominant position on a particular market, the user of those services would have little interest in resorting to an independent competitor, unless the competitor were able to offer prices lower than those of the liner conference.

117. It follows that, where a liner conference in a dominant position selectively cuts its prices in order deliberately to match those of a competitor, it derives a dual benefit. First, it eliminates the principal, and possibly the only, means of competition open to the competing undertaking. Second, it can continue to require its users to pay higher prices for the services which are not threatened by that competition.

118. It is not necessary, in the present case, to rule generally on the circumstances in which a liner conference may legitimately, on a case by case basis, adopt lower prices than those of its advertised tariff in order to compete with a competitor who quotes lower prices, or to decide on the exact scope of the expression 'uniform or common freight rates' in Article 1(3)(b) of Regulation No 4056/86.

119. It is sufficient to recall that the conduct at issue here is that of a conference having a share of over 90% of the market in question and only one competitor. The appellants have, moreover, never seriously disputed, and indeed admitted at the hearing, that the purpose of the conduct complained of was to eliminate G & C from the market.

120. The Court of First Instance did not, therefore, err in law, in holding that the Commission's objections to the effect that the practice known as 'fighting ships,' as applied against G & C, constituted an abuse of a dominant position were justified. It should also be noted that there is no question at all in this case of there having been a new definition of an abusive practice.

121. The grounds of appeal concerning fighting ships must therefore be rejected as inadmissible or unfounded.

NOTES AND QUESTIONS ON THE JUDGMENT IN COMPAGNIE MARITIME BELGE

1. (Paragraph 114–21) The concept of the 'special responsibility' of the Domco comes from *Michelin I.*[127] It is habitually relied upon by the Commission and Court of Justice in cases on exclusionary abuse.
2. (Paragraph 115) Why do you think the Council grated a group exemption for agreements about liner shipping?
3. (Paragraph 119) This is one of the few indications by the CJEU that the special responsibility of the Domco may be larger when the dominance is extreme.

[127] Case 322/81, *Michelin v EC Commission* [1983] ECR 3461 [hereinafter *Michelin I*].

4. Do you think that the CJEU is applying the predation theory of harm, which involves evidence of a profit sacrifice and then recoupment, or that of anti-competitive foreclosure, which focuses on the exclusion of competitors and the likely consumer harm that may follow?

The issue of selective price-cutting was also examined in the context of the *Post Danmark* case (examined in the following section).

9.3.3.2. *Post Danmark A/S v Konkurrencerådet* (*Post Danmark I*)

Post Danmark was a monopolist by law in the market for the delivery of addressed letters and parcels not exceeding a certain weight. The company was subject to a universal service obligation across Denmark and had established for this purpose a nationwide distribution network, which simultaneously enabled the company to operate on the liberalized market for unaddressed mail on which Post Danmark enjoyed a dominant position because of its market share of around 50 per cent and its special position due to its nation-wide distribution network which can be maintained, because of the universal service obligation in respect of the distribution of mail, without the distribution of unaddressed mail. Forbruger-Kontakt (FK) was the main competitor of Post Danmark in the unaddressed mail sector (folders, brochures, telephone directories, local newspapers, etc). In 2004, Post Danmark poached three major customers (the supermarkets SuperBest, Spar, and Coop) from its main competitor in the distribution of unaddressed mail by offering them rates lower than those it charged to its traditional customers. The offer made by Post Danmark to Coop allowed Post Danmark to cover its average incremental costs of delivery but not its total costs. Post-Danmark's offers to SuperBest and Spar were above its ATC. FK accused Post Danmark of having abused its dominant position on the Danish market for the distribution of unaddressed mail by having resorted to targeted price reductions and engaged in price discrimination practices, ie, by having charged new customers 'rates different from those it charged its own pre-existing customers without being able to justify those significant differences in its rate and rebate conditions by considerations relating to its costs'.[128] *The complainant prevailed before the Danish Competition Council on the count of second line price discrimination, which was found an abuse under Article 102(c) TFEU, but not on that of selective low pricing. The Competition Council could not establish that Post Danmark had intentionally sought to eliminate competition, the second step of the AKZO test in situations of predatory pricing between AVC and ATC.*[129] *The Danish Competition Complaints Board upheld the infringement decision. Only the part of the judgment on selective low pricing was appealed to the Danish High Court and the case ended up before the Danish Supreme Court, which sought guidance from the CJEU on the following question: 'Is Article [102 TFEU] to be interpreted as meaning that selective price reductions on the part of a dominant postal undertaking that has a universal service obligation to a level lower than the postal undertaking's average total costs, but higher than the provider's average incremental costs, constitutes an exclusionary abuse, if it is established that the price was not set at that level for the purpose of driving out a competitor?'*[130]

[128] Case C-209/10, *Post Danmark A/S v Konkurrencerådet* (*Post Danmark I*), ECLI:EU:C:2012:172, para 8.

[129] On these concepts see Section 9.3.1 and Table 9.1.

[130] Case C-209/10, *Post Danmark A/S v Konkurrencerådet* (*Post Danmark I*), ECLI:EU:C:2012:172, para 18.

The preliminary question sent to the CJEU thus focused only on selective low pricing (or primary line price discrimination), but not on secondary line price discrimination, the decision of the Danish Competition Authority being final with regard to this practice.

Advocate General Mengozzi's Opinion provides an insightful analysis of the challenges raised by above-cost pricing.

Opinion of Advocate General Mengozzi in Case C-209/10, *Post Danmark AS v Konkurrencerådet*, ECLI:EU:C:2011:342 (*Post Danmark I*) (excerpt)

53. Much of the dispute between the interested parties turns on the interpreting of the implications of a series of judgments of the Court of Justice and the General Court in which selective pricing on the part of dominant undertakings has been examined. On both sides the judgments support the views expressed in the observations submitted to the Court. [. . .]

56. [. . .] [W]hile the prohibition of the abuse of a dominant position may, quite naturally, be intended to ensure the direct welfare of consumers, it is also justified by the need to protect and maintain competition, the pursuit of that objective being presumed in some way to benefit consumers.

57. So far as pricing is concerned, while the special responsibility of the dominant undertaking has led the Court to state that not all competition by means of price may be regarded as legitimate, that statement means that such competition is generally authorised, or even recommended, subject to exceptions. Competition by price being generally beneficial, it is not, as a matter of principle, to be prohibited for undertakings with a dominant position on a given market.

58. Nevertheless, the question whether the pricing practices of an undertaking with a dominant position in a given market lead to abuse of that position within the meaning of Article [102 TFEU] must be determined by considering all the circumstances and calls for examining whether those practices tend to bar competitors from access to the market or to strengthen the dominant position by distorting competition.

59. As some of the interested parties have pointed out, the case-law refers to several cases in which the Union judicature has found that a selective reduction in prices by one or more undertakings with a dominant position conflicted with the prohibition laid down by Article [102 TFEU]. [. . .]

The AG explored the approach followed by the CJEU in AKZO, *where AKZO's selective price offers were associated with predatory pricing conduct, and the Court inferred from AKZO's selective pricing that it did not have the effect of driving out the competitor, but merely an intention to do so, and in particular Compagnie Maritime Belge and Irish Sugar, which directly concerned selective price-cutting conduct. He then explored the implications of these cases.*

86. First, as I have already mentioned, they are instances of a judicial approach according to which a selective reduction in prices by a dominant undertaking is held to be contrary to Article [102 TFEU], without the prices having been considered in relation to the costs of the undertaking and when it is apparent that the prices had not been fixed below the average total costs.

87. Second, whereas in *Akzo* v *Commission* the Court deduced, from the selective discounts offered to customers of Akzo's main competitor, that Akzo intended to drive out competitors, in the abovementioned cases of *Compagnie maritime belge*

transports and Others v *Commission* and *Irish Sugar* v *Commission* the Union judicature adopted a different approach. The Court took the view that the pricing practices in question gave effect to the intention of driving out the competitor, that intention being evidenced, not by the selective pricing, but by internal documents of the dominant undertakings concerned or other documents in the case file.

88. In that connection, it must be observed that, in the two latter cases, the fact that the practices in question did not have the desired effect, that is to say, that they did not lead to the withdrawal of the competitor, was not considered decisive with regard to the finding that there was no abuse of a dominant position. [. . .].

89. That conclusion appears to mean that the pricing practices in question are anti-competitive in object but not in effect. However, when read outside its context, it could also come up against the consideration that dominant undertakings are not, in principle, deprived of the right to compete by price.

90. The explanation for the Union judicature's approach in *Compagnie maritime belge transports and Others* and *Irish Sugar* could, in my opinion, be due to three aspects, of a rather factual nature, common to the situations giving rise to the judgments of the Court of Justice and the General Court.

91. First, as I have already observed, in both cases the dominant undertaking's intention to drive out a competitor was inferred, not from selective pricing, but from other circumstances. Therefore, selective pricing was not considered to be the concrete form of that intention.

92. Second, it must be observed that the economic strength of the dominant undertakings concerned was close to that of a monopoly because their respective market shares were almost 90%. Consequently there were barriers to entering the market because of a 'super-dominance', of which Advocate General Fennelly was aware in his Opinion in *Compagnie maritime belge transports and Others*.

93. Finally, the selective pricing practices formed part of a series of other practices which constituted abuses, whether in relation to prices or not, all of which had a cumulative effect which may have been significant.

94. These considerations lead me to think that *Compagnie maritime belge transports* and *Irish Sugar* are only marginally relevant with regard to the reply to be given to the referring court, even if only because, in the case in the main proceedings, it is established that no intention to drive out a competitor was proved by either the Danish competition authorities or the Danish courts, and because there is no indication at all in the documents in the file that Post Danmark was in a position of 'super-dominance'. Furthermore, with regard to *Irish Sugar* in particular, on which the Commission based some of its observations at the hearing, it must be observed that, first, in that case the dominant undertaking was trying to keep its customers by offering selective discounts to its distributors who were exposed to competition from other sugar producers and not, as in the main proceedings here, trying to attract customers from its main or only competitor. Secondly, the discounts in question were aimed at limiting the influence of the pricing policy of operators active principally on an adjacent national market on that of operators active on another national market, a practice which has in fact been held to constitute an obstacle to the achievement of the common market.

95. It seems to me that the Court's case-law must be interpreted as meaning that, where the (relatively exceptional) conditions of the *Compagnie maritime belge transports* and *Irish Sugar* cases are not fulfilled, and in particular where no intention on the part of the dominant undertaking to drive out a competitor or competitors can be inferred from the circumstances other than offers of selective prices, a selective price reduction must be examined by reference to the costs of the dominant undertaking,

following the example of the criterion used in paragraphs 114 and 115 of *Akzo* v *Commission*.

96. That interpretation allows a consistent reading of the case-law. It may also provide greater legal certainty for undertakings with a dominant position when they offer selective price reductions. Moreover, in so far as a dominant undertaking knows its own costs and prices, and not those of its competitors, for the competition authorities and the courts to take into account the structure of the competitor's costs may run counter to the principle of legal certainty, for it would not allow the dominant undertaking to assess the legality of its own conduct, save for special circumstances.

97. In that respect, regardless of the sector in which it operates, I think that a dominant undertaking which offers different prices, but all, nevertheless, higher than its average total costs, depending on whether they are offered to its regular customers or to its competitor's customers, cannot, in principle, even if its pricing is selective and discriminatory, cause the removal of the equally efficient competitor.

98. That competitor will, in principle, always be able to respond to such competition by prices because selling at such prices covers the average variable costs and fixed costs. Those sales will therefore be profitable and it would, in theory, be inconceivable for the competitor to be driven from the market. The result could be different if, in spite of everything, the competitor's prices were higher than the average total costs of the dominant undertaking. However, in that situation, the competitor will probably be less efficient than the dominant undertaking. The competitor's removal will therefore be only the normal result of competition on merits, in which dominant undertakings must also be able to participate in spite of their special responsibility.

99. It is true that the behaviour of the dominant undertaking may still be found contrary to Article [102](c) TFEU in so far as it may entail a competitive disadvantage for certain customers of the dominant undertaking ('secondary-line discrimination'). However, its behaviour must not, in principle, cause its competitor to be driven out.

100. When applied to the facts of the main proceedings, the assessment in paragraphs 96 to 98 above should, in my opinion, lead the referring court to find that the prices offered by Post Danmark to Spar and Superbest, two of FK's three customers whose situations were mentioned in the order for reference and in the observations of the interested parties, could not in principle result in FK's being driven from the market because it is established, as I have already said, that those prices were higher than Post Danmark's average total costs. In addition, the referring court has not informed the Court of FK's cost structure.

101. It remains to be considered whether a dominant undertaking such as Post Danmark may wrongfully drive out its competitor if it, Post Danmark, offers a selective reduction in prices to a large customer of its competitor when those prices are higher than the average incremental costs of the dominant undertaking, but less than its average total costs.

102. First of all, I do not think that the mere fact that the price offers in question were made to a single customer of the main or only competitor can lead to rejecting a finding of abuse of a dominant position. Such a customer may indeed account for a significant volume of purchases and a significant market share, as appears to have been the case of Coop in the main proceedings.

103. Secondly, it would be tempting to extend by analogy the Court's reasoning at paragraphs 113 to 115 of *Akzo* v *Commission*, as the Commission suggested at the hearing.

104. Taking that approach, it would follow that the fact that the dominant undertaking offered its competitor's customer prices lower than its average total costs, while charging its regular customers prices higher than that average, would enable it, at least partly, to offset 'the losses' arising on sales to the competitor's customer with the

profits on sales to its regular customers. If there were no economic justification, such a practice would amount to driving the competitor from the market.

105. In the main proceedings, that approach would in all likelihood lead the referring court to find that Post Danmark had abused its dominant position in the national market for the distribution of unaddressed mail, in so far as the Danish competition authorities found that Post Danmark had not shown that the selective offer to Coop, one of FK's main customers, was justified by economies of scale, and that finding was not overruled by the Danish court in its order for reference.

106. While that does not necessarily affect the finding of abuse of a dominant position by Post Danmark, I nevertheless hesitate to suggest a line of reasoning strictly based on that in paragraphs 113 to 115 of *Akzo* v *Commission*, as the Commission proposed at the hearing.

107. That line of reasoning seems to me to over-simplify, at the very least, the problem of selective price offers by a dominant undertaking operating at one and the same time on a partly reserved market, where it has a universal service obligation, and on a market totally open to competition, where no operator is burdened by universal service constraints.

108. First, the fact that the prices offered to the competitor's main customer are higher than the average incremental costs of the dominant undertaking must not, in my view, be regarded as a situation in which sales give rise to 'losses', but rather as characterised by sales which do not maximise the earnings of that undertaking. In principle, such sales remain profitable because the earnings from them cover the costs engendered in carrying on the specific business on the competitive market, namely, in the present case, the distribution of unaddressed mail.

109. Therefore, whether the dominant undertaking can charge prices at that level does not depend, in my opinion, on a set-off of the price of sales to regular customers on the market open to competition, with regard to which it maximises its earnings, against the price of sales to the competitor's main customer on the same market, with regard to which the dominant undertaking does not maximise earnings. In order to maintain the price level offered to the competitor's customer, the dominant undertaking does not, in principle, need to set off in that way.

110. However, in a market where there is no other constraint on the regular customers of the dominant undertaking who are victims of the difference in pricing, the latter are perfectly able in principle to find a competitor capable of offering them equivalent services at a price less than that charged by the dominant undertaking.

111. Secondly, on the other hand, in so far as incremental costs take little or no account of the fixed costs common to business carried out on both markets on which the dominant undertaking is present, in particular, the fixed costs of maintaining the capacity of its distribution network used, as in the main proceedings, both for its (partly reserved) operations in fulfilling universal service obligations, and also for its unaddressed mail business, the dominant undertaking could, even while charging a price higher than its average incremental cost, in the final analysis, cause the customers of the partly reserved operations in the market in which it has a universal service obligation to bear the cost of the distribution network capacity mobilised by the dominant undertaking for its unaddressed mail business.

112. In other words, it is perfectly possible, taking the average incremental cost as the yardstick, for the dominant undertaking to be able to charge a price slightly higher than that average (thus preventing the price from being automatically regarded as predatory) by causing all or part of the common fixed costs to be borne by the partly reserved operations in the market in which it has a universal service obligation, and those operations therefore subsidise the price offered on the market which is open to

competition. Whether selective or not, such a practice could eventually lead to driving competitors from the liberalised market, that is to say, in the main proceedings here, those operating in the Danish market for the distribution of unaddressed mail which, of course, do not benefit from the same cross-subsidy arrangement.

113. I consider, therefore, that the fact that a dominant undertaking, such as Post Danmark, charges a selective price higher than the average incremental cost does not make it impossible, contrary to what was in essence suggested by Post Danmark and the Czech Government in their observations before the Court, that such a price level may entail a risk of driving out that undertaking's competitor, since the price is likely to be subsidised by the earnings from the partly reserved business of the dominant undertaking on the market on which it operates while carrying out universal service obligations.

114. In order to ascertain whether that is so, I think it would be necessary to establish the 'stand-alone' cost of the services provided by the dominant undertaking in the market in which it carries out universal service obligations and to determine whether the earnings generated by those services exceed such cost. If so, it would probably have to be found that there was a cross-subsidy of sales on the market open to competition, for which the price charged is less than the average total cost. In view of the particular responsibility of an undertaking in a dominant position for maintaining the competition structure of the market, the use of such cross-subsidies would eventually involve a real risk of driving out the competitor and would, in my view, justify preventive action by the competition authorities.

115. Depending on how long that practice was employed, such a risk may be inferred from the competitor's loss of market share.

116. In the main proceedings it seems, however, [. . .] that the Danish competition authorities were unable to find that there were unlawful cross-subsidies in favour of Post Danmark's distribution business for unaddressed mail. However, the referring court will have to satisfy itself on that point.

117. At this stage, it is still uncertain whether the price offer made by Post Danmark to one of the main customers of its only or main competitor in the unaddressed mail market is proportionate. The question can be considered from two angles.

118. First, it may be asked whether, in view of the particular responsibility of the dominant undertaking in the market, it did not fall to the latter to refrain from offering, in a selective manner, a price higher than its incremental costs, so as to pursue a non-discriminatory pricing policy in relation to its regular customers. Secondly, there is a question as to the reasons why a dominant undertaking such as Post Danmark should make different price offers to its competitor's customers.

119. On the first point, I think that to compel a dominant undertaking to offer the same prices to its regular customers and to those of its competitor, that is to say, in the main proceedings, to offer a uniform price higher than average incremental costs, could no doubt prevent 'secondary-line discrimination' between the trading partners of that undertaking, but would not have a positive influence on the potential effect of driving out the competitor. While it is possible that uniform pricing cannot be maintained for as long as in the context of selective pricing, on the other hand the level of the prices offered by the dominant undertaking to its competitor's customer remains unchanged, irrespective of whether the price is offered selectively or in the context of a uniform rate.

120. With regard to the second point, in so far as the competitor's customers to whom different prices were offered are considered to be in a comparable situation, I find it difficult to understand the reasons why a dominant undertaking such as Post Danmark should vary its offers in such a way that two of them (those to Spar and SuperBest) cover Post Danmark's total average costs, while the other (Coop) does not, although in

the first case the offers, which, as I have said, entail no risk of removal of the competitor, are always below the competitor's prices. Consequently even a price offer at the level of that made to Spar and SuperBest could have been sufficiently attractive for a customer like Coop because, it seems, it was less than the prices offered by FK without, however, having the possible effect of driving out the competitor. Nevertheless, whether that effect actually materialises will depend above all on whether the dominant undertaking can subsidise the prices offered to Coop from its own (partly reserved) business operations in the sector in which it has a universal service obligation.

121. To conclude, the approach which I have just proposed, which is to give priority to considering an at least potential effect of driving out a competitor, rather than an intention to do so, as in *Akzo* v *Commission*, also seems to me more appropriate in view of the circumstances of the main proceedings. Unlike the situation in *Akzo* v *Commission*, the referring court is not confronted by a number of unlawful practices on the part of one and the same undertaking, some of which clearly have the object of removing its competitor, which in my eyes may explain why the Court, when considering Akzo's selective pricing, merely inferred that undertaking's intention to damage its competitor.

122. The result of adopting an approach based on the intention of excluding a competitor rather than on the effects of so doing would be to regard any selective pricing as an abuse intended to drive out competitors, because the prices of the dominant undertaking are less than its average total costs, unless that is justified economically. However, as I have explained in the foregoing arguments, that presumption seems to me neither well founded from the economic and legal aspects, nor appropriate. It cannot be automatically inferred from a difference in the price treatment of regular customers of the dominant undertaking and the customer or customers of its competitor.

123. For all those reasons, I consider that Article [102 TFEU] is to be interpreted as meaning that the conduct of a dominant undertaking constitutes abuse of a dominant position when that undertaking thereby offers a selective reduction in prices, at a level higher than the average incremental costs but lower than the average total costs of that undertaking, to the main customer of its main or only competitor on the national market for the distribution of unaddressed mail, which is fully open to competition, if the selective price offer is likely to be subsidised by the earnings from the dominant undertaking's operations, which are partly reserved, on the market for postal services on which it operates by carrying out universal service obligations, so having the effect of driving that competitor from the market. In that connection, in order to establish the existence of unlawful cross-subsidisation of the dominant undertaking's unaddressed mail business, it is necessary to determine whether the earnings generated by its services in the postal services market on which it carries out universal service obligations exceed the 'stand-alone' cost of those services. It is for the national court to determine whether such is the case in the dispute in the main proceedings.

NOTES AND QUESTIONS ON THE OPINION OF AG MENGOZZI IN POST DANMARK I

1. (Paragraph 57) Note that despite mentioning the Domco's special responsibility the Advocate General establishes a presumption that competition by price is generally beneficial and that 'as a matter of principle' does not fall under Article 102 TFEU.

2. (Paragraph 65) Note the generally positive view by the Advocate General of secondary-line discrimination, finding that such a practice may create some competitive disadvantage for some customers but that 'it is less certain that such a practice, considered in isolation, may lead to the elimination of an equally efficient competitor' and hence should fall under Article 102 TFEU.
3. (Paragraphs 66–7) The Advocate General attempts to explain the 'harshness' of the *AKZO* case law for dominant undertakings by observing that AKZO's selective price offers were associated with a number of other unlawful practices, such as predatory pricing, and that there is no economic justification for adopting selective price-cutting practices, as uniform low prices, even if predatory, benefit consumers in the short run. Indeed, selective price-cutting is detrimental to the dominant undertaking's own customers. Do these paragraphs refer to the existence of a presumption of an anti-competitive intent for selective price-cutting, if prices are below the ATC of the dominant undertaking? Why should we adopt the threshold of ATC rather than that of AVC? The Advocate General notes: 'By taking as its point of reference the undertaking's average total costs, that is to say, including fixed costs and variable costs, the Court condemns selectiveness even though the sale of an additional unit to the dominant undertaking's own customers covers the variable costs of the unit produced and at least part of the fixed costs attributable to that unit.'[131]
4. (Paragraph 66) Should intent be considered in assessing the anti-competitive effects of a conduct? What is the function exercise by the concept of intent in AG's Opinion? Is it functionally equivalent to the concept of 'plan or strategy of eliminating competition'?
5. (Paragraphs 69–89) The Advocate General contrasts the position of the Court in *AKZO* with that followed in *Irish Sugar* and *Compagnie Maritime Belge*, noting that in the later cases the Court did not employ a price-cost test, as in *AKZO*. He derives from this the conclusion that according to these cases, selective price-cutting at a level above ATC was anti-competitive by object, and not by effect. Do you agree with this statement?
6. (Paragraph 87) Should the authorities be concerned about 'smoking guns' or does this lead to a useless search through the documents without much economic analysis?
7. (Paragraphs 87–9) Is the Advocate General concerned about the effects of selective price differences or their objective?
8. (Paragraphs 66, 90–4) In *Post Danmark I* the Advocate General also limited the scope of the *Irish Sugar* and the *Compagnie Maritime Belge* case law by linking the approach followed by the Court with the specific factual background of these cases. He identifies three 'exceptional circumstances' in these cases: (i) the dominant undertaking's intention to drive out a competitor was not inferred only from selective pricing but also from other circumstances. Is this different from the position of the Court in *AKZO*? (ii) Where the undertakings concerned enjoyed a super-dominant position—more than 90 per cent of the market. In AKZO? (iii) The 'selective pricing practices formed part of a series of other practices which constituted abuses, whether in relation to

[131] Opinion of Advocate General Mengozzi in Case C-209/10, *Post Danmark A/S v Konkurrencerådet*, ECLI:EU:C:2011:342, para 65.

prices or not, all of which had a cumulative effect which may have been significant'.[132] None of these exceptional circumstances was present in the *Post Danmark I* case,[133] hence these precedents are 'marginally pertinent' in this case. The Advocate General observes that if the exceptional circumstances of *Irish Sugar* and the *Compagnie Maritime Belge* are not present then the Court should apply the *AKZO* test.[134] Selective price-cutting can thus only be assessed by reference to the relevant costs of the dominant firm. Would that create a safe harbour for certain dominant undertakings adopting selective price-cutting?[135] Note the possibility of applying Article 102(c) to price discrimination.[136]

9. (Paragraphs 104–105). What are the advantages and disadvantages of applying the *AKZO* price–cost test to selective price-cutting? What would have been the outcome in this case if the price–cost test of *AKZO* were applied?
10. (Paragraphs 108–12) Note that the Commission had suggested in this case to follow the *AKZO* test holding that prices below average incremental costs can be deemed abusive when the 'losses' incurred as a result thereof are offset by the above average cost prices charged to traditional clients and there is no apparent economic justification. At paragraph 111 of his Opinion, the Advocate General rejected this position for essentially two reasons: (i) as long as prices are above average incremental costs, they are not 'loss-making' but rather 'non-profit maximizing' and hence profitable, because the earnings from the sales cover the costs engendered in carrying on the specific business on the competitive market; (ii) in so far as incremental costs do not sufficiently account for the fixed costs common to business carried out on both markets on which the dominant undertaking is present, a price higher than the dominant undertaking's average incremental cost could be charging part of the common fixed costs on the reserved market. Such prices may have an exclusionary effect, because they would be subsidized by the revenue earned in the reserved market. In these cases it would be necessary to identify the stand-alone cost of providing the universal service and to examine whether those costs were exceeded by the earnings generated by these services in order to prove the existence of 'unlawful cross-subsidization'.
11. Note that the Advocate General refers to long run average incremental costs in order to refine the *AKZO* predatory pricing test (based on AVC and ATC) when an undertaking operates simultaneously in a liberalized market and fulfils universal service obligations in another market closed to competition.
12. (Paragraph 121) The Advocate General gives priority to the 'potential effect of driving out a competitor, rather than an intention to do so, as in *AKZO* v *Commission*'. Is this approach more favourable to dominant undertakings than the AKZO approach? Note that according to AKZO, any selective price cuts below ATC would have been considered abusive, unless objectively justified.
13. Remember that the Commission believes that the burden of proof under Article 102(c) is on the Domco, and that this has been interpreted widely, which makes it almost impossible to establish efficiencies that might outweigh detriments to consumers.

[132] Opinion of AG Mengozzi in Case C-209/10, *Post Danmark I*, ECLI:EU:C:2011:342, para 93.
[133] Ibid, para 94.
[134] Ibid, para 95. [135] Ibid, para 97. [136] Ibid, para 99.

Case C-209/10, Post Danmark A/S v Konkurrencerådet ECLI:EU:C:2012:172 (*Post Danmark I*)

19. By its questions, which may appropriately be examined together, the court making the reference asks, in essence, what the circumstances are in which a policy, pursued by a dominant undertaking, of charging low prices to certain former customers of a competitor must be considered to amount to an exclusionary abuse, contrary to Article [102 TFEU], and, in particular, whether the finding of such an abuse may be based on the mere fact that the price charged to a single customer by the dominant undertaking is lower than the average total costs attributed to the business activity concerned, but higher than the total incremental costs pertaining to the latter.

20. It is apparent from case-law that Article [102 TFEU] covers not only those practices that directly cause harm to consumers but also practices that cause consumers harm through their impact on competition (see Case C52/09 *TeliaSonera Sverige* [2011] ECR I–527, paragraph 24 and case-law cited). It is in the latter sense that the expression 'exclusionary abuse' appearing in the questions referred is to be understood.

21. It is settled case-law that a finding that an undertaking has such a dominant position is not in itself a ground of criticism of the undertaking concerned (Case 322/81 *Nederlandsche Banden-Industrie-Michelin* v *Commission* [1983] ECR 3461, paragraph 57, and Joined Cases C395/96 P and C396/96 P *Compagnie maritime belge transports and Others* v *Commission* [2000] ECR I1365, paragraph 37). It is in no way the purpose of Article [102 TFEU] to prevent an undertaking from acquiring, on its own merits, the dominant position on a market (see, inter alia, *TeliaSonera Sverige*, paragraph 24). Nor does that provision seek to ensure that competitors less efficient than the undertaking with the dominant position should remain on the market.

22. Thus, not every exclusionary effect is necessarily detrimental to competition (see, by analogy, *TeliaSonera Sverige*, paragraph 43). Competition on the merits may, by definition, lead to the departure from the market or the marginalisation of competitors that are less efficient and so less attractive to consumers from the point of view of, among other things, price, choice, quality or innovation.

23. According to equally settled case-law, a dominant undertaking has a special responsibility not to allow its behaviour to impair genuine, undistorted competition on the internal market (Case C202/07 P *France Telecom* v *Commission* [2009] ECR I2369, paragraph 105 and case-law cited). When the existence of a dominant position has its origins in a former legal monopoly, that fact has to be taken into account.

24. In that regard, it is also to be borne in mind that Article [102 TFEU] applies, in particular, to the conduct of a dominant undertaking that, through recourse to methods different from those governing normal competition on the basis of the performance of commercial operators, has the effect, to the detriment of consumers, of hindering the maintenance of the degree of competition existing in the market or the growth of that competition (see, to that effect, *AKZO* v *Commission*, paragraph 69; *France Télécom* v *Commission*, paragraphs 104 and 105; and Case C280/08 P *Deutsche Telekom* v *Commission* [2010] ECR I0000, paragraphs 174, 176 and 180 and case-law cited).

25. Thus, Article [102 TFEU] prohibits a dominant undertaking from, among other things, adopting pricing practices that have an exclusionary effect on competitors considered to be as efficient as it is itself and strengthening its dominant position by using methods other than those that are part of competition on the merits. Accordingly, in that light, not all competition by means of price may be regarded as legitimate (see, to that effect, *AKZO* v *Commission*, paragraphs 70 and 72; *France Télécom* v *Commission*, paragraph 106; and *Deutsche Telekom* v *Commission*, paragraph 177).

26. In order to determine whether a dominant undertaking has abused its dominant position by its pricing practices, it is necessary to consider all the circumstances and to examine whether those practices tend to remove or restrict the buyer's freedom as regards choice of sources of supply, to bar competitors from access to the market, to apply dissimilar conditions to equivalent transactions with other trading parties, thereby placing them at a competitive disadvantage, or to strengthen the dominant position by distorting competition (see, to that effect, *Deutsche Telekom* v *Commission*, paragraph 175 and case-law cited).

27. In *AKZO* v *Commission*, in which the issue was to determine whether an undertaking had practised predatory pricing, the Court held, in the first place, at paragraph 71, that prices below the average of 'variable' costs (those that vary depending on the quantities produced) must, in principle, be regarded as abusive, inasmuch as, in charging those prices, a dominant undertaking is deemed to pursue no economic purpose other than that of driving out its competitors. In the second place, it held, at paragraph 72, that prices below average total costs, but above average variable costs, must be regarded as abusive if they are part of a plan for eliminating a competitor.

28. Thus, in order to assess the lawfulness of a low-price policy practised by a dominant undertaking, the Court has made use of criteria based on comparisons of the prices concerned and certain costs incurred by the dominant undertaking, as well as on the latter's strategy (*AKZO* v *Commission*, paragraph 74, and *France Télécom* v *Commission*, paragraph 108).

29. As to whether Post Danmark pursued an anti-competitive strategy, it can be seen from the documents before the Court that the complaint at the source of the main proceedings was based on the suggestion that Post Danmark, by a policy of low prices directed at certain of its competitor's major customers, might drive that competitor from the market in question. However, as is apparent from the order for reference, it could not be established that Post Danmark had deliberately sought to drive out that competitor.

30. Moreover, contrary to the line of argument put forward by the Danish Government, which has submitted observations in these proceedings in support of the Konkurrencerådet's position in the main proceedings, the fact that the practice of a dominant undertaking may, like the pricing policy in issue in the main proceedings, be described as 'price discrimination', that is to say, charging different customers or different classes of customers different prices for goods or services whose costs are the same or, conversely, charging a single price to customers for whom supply costs differ, cannot of itself suggest that there exists an exclusionary abuse.

31. In the present case, it emerges from the case-file that, for the purpose of carrying out a price-cost comparison, the Danish competition authorities had recourse, not to the concept of 'variable costs' mentioned in the case-law stemming from *AKZO* v *Commission*, but to another concept, which those authorities termed 'incremental costs'. In this respect, it can be seen from, in particular, the written observations of the Danish Government and its written replies to the questions asked by the Court, that those authorities defined 'incremental costs' as being 'those costs destined to disappear in the short

or medium term (three to five years), if Post Danmark were to give up its business activity of distributing unaddressed mail'. In addition, that government stated that 'average total costs' were defined as being 'average incremental costs to which were added a portion, determined by estimation, of Post Danmark's common costs connected to activities other than those covered by the universal service obligation'.

32. However, as the Danish Government stated in its written replies to those questions, a notable feature of the case in the main proceedings is that there are considerable costs related both to the activities within the ambit of Post Danmark's universal service obligation and to its activity of distributing unaddressed mail. These 'common' costs are due, in particular, to the fact that, at the material time, Post Danmark was using the same infrastructure and the same staff for both the activity of distributing unaddressed mail and the activity reserved to it in connection with its universal obligation for certain addressed items of mail. That government states that, according to the Konkurrencerådet, because Post Danmark's unaddressed mail activity used the undertaking's 'common distribution network resources', the costs of its universal service obligation activities could be reduced over a period of three to five years if Post Danmark were to give up distributing unaddressed mail.

33. In those circumstances, it emerges from the case-file, and in particular from paragraphs 148 to 151 and 200 of the Konkurrencerådet's decision of 24 November 2004, mentioned in paragraph 13 above, that for the purpose of estimating what it described as 'average incremental costs', the Konkurrencerådet included, among other things, not only those fixed and variable costs attributable solely to the activity of distributing unaddressed mail, but also elements described as 'common variable costs', '75% of the attributable common costs of logistical capacity' and '25% of non-attributable common costs'.

34. In the specific circumstances of the case in the main proceedings, it must be considered that such a method of attribution would seem to seek to identify the great bulk of the costs attributable to the activity of distributing unaddressed mail.

35. When that estimation was completed, it was found, among other things, that the price offered to the Coop group did not enable Post Danmark to cover the average total costs attributed to the activity of unaddressed mail distribution taken as a whole, but did enable it to cover the average incremental costs pertaining to that activity, as estimated by the Danish competition authorities.

36. Moreover, it is common ground that, in the present case, the prices offered to the Spar and SuperBest groups were assessed as being at a higher level than those average total costs, as estimated by those authorities. In those circumstances, it cannot be considered that such prices have anti-competitive effects.

37. As regards the prices charged the Coop group, a pricing policy such as that in issue in the main proceedings cannot be considered to amount to an exclusionary abuse simply because the price charged to a single customer by a dominant undertaking is lower than the average total costs attributed to the activity concerned, but higher than the average incremental costs pertaining to the latter, as respectively estimated in the case in the main proceedings.

38. Indeed, to the extent that a dominant undertaking sets its prices at a level covering the great bulk of the costs attributable to the supply of the goods or services in question, it will, as a general rule, be possible for a competitor as efficient as that undertaking to compete with those prices without suffering losses that are unsustainable in the long term.

39. It is for the court making the reference to assess the relevant circumstances of the case in the main proceedings in the light of the finding made in the previous

paragraph. In any event, it is worth noting that it appears from the documents before the Court that Forbruger-Kontakt managed to maintain its distribution network despite losing the volume of mail related to the three customers involved and managed, in 2007, to win back the Coop group's custom and, since then, that of the Spar group.

40. If the court making the reference, after carrying out that assessment, should nevertheless make a finding of anti-competitive effects due to Post Danmark's actions, it should be recalled that it is open to a dominant undertaking to provide justification for behaviour that is liable to be caught by the prohibition under Article [102 TFEU] (see, to this effect, Case 27/76 *United Brands and United Brands Continentaal* v *Commission* [1978] ECR 207, paragraph 184; Joined Cases C241/91 P and C242/91 P *RTE and ITP* v *Commission* [1995] ECR I743, paragraphs 54 and 55; and *TeliaSonera Sverige*, paragraphs 31 and 75).

41. In particular, such an undertaking may demonstrate, for that purpose, either that its conduct is objectively necessary (see, to that effect, Case 311/84 *CBEM* [1985] ECR 3261, paragraph 27), or that the exclusionary effect produced may be counterbalanced, outweighed even, by advantages in terms of efficiency that also benefit consumers (Case C95/04 P *British Airways* v *Commission* [2007] ECR I2331, paragraph 86, and *TeliaSonera Sverige*, paragraph 76).

42. In that last regard, it is for the dominant undertaking to show that the efficiency gains likely to result from the conduct under consideration counteract any likely negative effects on competition and consumer welfare in the affected markets, that those gains have been, or are likely to be, brought about as a result of that conduct, that such conduct is necessary for the achievement of those gains in efficiency and that it does not eliminate effective competition, by removing all or most existing sources of actual or potential competition.

43. In the present case, it is enough to state, with regard to the considerations set out at paragraph 11 above, that the mere fact that a criterion explicitly based on gains in efficiency was not one of the factors appearing in the schedules of prices charged by Post Danmark cannot justify a refusal to take into account, where necessary, such gains in efficiency, provided that that their actual existence and their extent have been established in accordance with the requirements set out in paragraph 42 above.

44. Having regard to all the foregoing considerations, the answer to be given to the questions referred is that Article [102 TFEU] must be interpreted as meaning that a policy by which a dominant undertaking charges low prices to certain major customers of a competitor may not be considered to amount to an exclusionary abuse merely because the price that undertaking charges one of those customers is lower than the average total costs attributed to the activity concerned, but higher than the average incremental costs pertaining to that activity, as estimated in the procedure giving rise to the case in the main proceedings. In order to assess the existence of anti-competitive effects in circumstances such as those of that case, it is necessary to consider whether that pricing policy, without objective justification, produces an actual or likely exclusionary effect, to the detriment of competition and, thereby, of consumers' interests.

NOTES AND QUESTIONS ON THE JUDGMENT OF THE COURT OF JUSTICE IN POST DANMARK I

1. Do you think that the judgment of the Court in *Post Danmark* has replaced or completed the framework for predatory pricing established in the *AKZO* case? Does the Court's judgment touch upon the presumption of anti-competitive effect for prices

below average avoidable costs? In this case, it was explained by the reference of the national court which stated that Post Danmark's costs were above its average incremental costs which, according to paragraph 31 of the Court's judgment, included the costs 'destined to disappear in the short or medium term (three to five years), if Post Danmark were to give up its business activity of distributing unaddressed mail'. These costs included not only the variable cost for the service in question but also (part of) the necessary fixed costs for this to operate and hence were higher than the average avoidable costs. Following the predatory test of *AKZO*, the plaintiff in Post Danmark should have established the existence of an exclusionary intent.

2. The Court used Average Incremental Costs instead of Average Variable Costs. In his Opinion AG Mengozzi explained the reason for this:

> 33. The fact that the order for reference mentions Post Danmark's incremental costs as constituting the relevant costs to be taken into account in the main proceedings, and not the variable costs, as in *Akzo* v *Commission*, appears to be explained, according to the documents in the file, by the coexistence, within one undertaking, of, on the one hand, reserved and non-reserved operations the carrying on of which, in either case, is subject to universal service obligations and, on the other hand, purely commercial operations which take place on the liberalized market for unaddressed mail.
>
> 34. A comparison of prices with the variable costs of a dominant undertaking entrusted with a task of general economic interest (public service or universal service) proves to be inappropriate. On the one hand, it could entail an overestimate of losses because the undertaking's task of general economic interest entails higher costs than those of its competitors for the part of its business operations accounted for in the market open to competition. Conversely, to take the variable costs of the dominant undertaking as the only criterion could also lead to an overestimate of its costs if it operates with high fixed costs (for example, the costs of utilisation of its network) and small variable costs.
>
> 35. In those circumstances, it appears appropriate to take into account a different cost criterion, namely incremental costs, which take account of the fixed costs and variable costs of the specific operations in the market which is open to competition.'

3. In *Deutsche Post*,[137] the Commission had also relied on the LRAIC incurred by Deutsche Post to provide its parcel service activity to determine if it had engaged in predatory pricing for the provision of such service. In that case, the German postal incumbent had abused its dominant position by using revenues from its profitable letter-post monopoly to finance a strategy of below-cost selling in the liberalized commercial parcel market. Deutsche Post had to incur costs in order to maintain a capacity reserve large enough to respond to its universal service obligations under German Law, which required Deutsche Post to provide each potential postal user over the counter parcel services at a prescribed quality and uniform prices. However, the Commission took into account the average incremental costs. These comprise only the average fixed and variable costs of providing the service exposed to competition. It thus excluded the common fixed costs, those which do not depend on the provision of a single service.

137 *Deutsche Post AG* (Case COMP/35.141) Commission Decision [2001] OJ L 125/27.

According to the Commission, the costs attributable to a specific service must not be burdened with the common fixed cost of providing network capacity, incurred as a result of the universal service obligation finding that Deutsche Post could not cross-subsidize from the regulated markets to the liberalized ones and that it should cover the costs attributable to or incremental to producing the liberalized service.

The referring court concentrated only on Post Danmark's selective reduction of prices ('primary-line discrimination'). Hence the question was not the discrimination between the terms of business with the three supermarkets (secondary-line discrimination) but the exclusion of Post Danmark competitor (FK). In his Opinion, Advocate General Mengozzi endorsed the distinction between primary-line and secondary-line discrimination:

> The distinction made by the Danish authorities and courts between 'primary-line' and 'secondary-line' discrimination seems to me expedient and it is, furthermore, strongly supported by certain commentators. Although the list of abusive practices in Article [102 TFEU] is not an exhaustive enumeration of the kinds of abuses of a dominant position prohibited by that Article, the distinction makes it possible, in my opinion, to clarify the relationship between discriminatory pricing practices under Article [102(c)], that is to say, those whose anticompetitive effects are produced in the market or markets of 'trading parties', thereby 'placing them at a competitive disadvantage', which corresponds to what is known as secondary discrimination because, by definition, those parties cannot be the competitors of the undertaking which is abusing its dominant position, and the effects that are produced on the market on which the dominant undertaking and its competitors operate and which fall within other situations, including that of limiting production, markets or technical development to the prejudice of consumers, referred to by Article [102(b)], and which have the effect of driving out or excluding those competitors.[138]

4. Commenting on the *Post Danmark* case, Ekaterina Rousseva and Mel Marquis observed that with the preliminary reference in *Post Danmark*,

> a window of opportunity opened up for the European Court of Justice [CJEU], and the Court—sitting in its Grand Chamber formation—could have clung to the hallowed paragraphs of the past but it chose instead to experiment with newer lines of thinking. This choice potentially marks a critical juncture in abuse of dominance law, and it might signal a new partnership between the [CJEU] and the European Commission whereby these two institutions bring about, in their interpretations of the Treaty and in the Commission's policy initiatives, a bolder, more enlightened analysis of unilateral pricing practices by dominant firms, an analysis guided ultimately by consumer's interest (ie, their interests in terms of price, choice, quality, or innovation). A fundamental jurisprudential shift is by no means a foregone conclusion, and we would not be surprised to see judgments occasionally expressing more traditional habits of mind. Nevertheless, we expect that pockets of resistance in abuse of dominance law are destined ultimately to erode and give way to a more transversal and coherent set of analytical rules to govern unilateral conduct

[138] Opinion of Advocate General Mengozzi in Case C-209/10, *Post Danmark I*, ECLI:EU:C:2011:342, para 46. The text of the Opinion refers to Article 102(c) instead of Article 102(c), but the former seems the correct formulation as this article refers to 'limiting production, markets or technical development to the prejudice of consumers'.

in the European Union, with cascading consequences for the application of abuse of dominance law in the EU Member States.[139]

Do you agree with the assessment by these authors of the 'jurisprudential shift' of the Court? Give reasons.

5. The Court refers to the exclusion of an as efficient competitor as a relevant factor in the analysis. Is this a requirement for Article 102 TFEU to apply? Does this substitute or complement the price–cost test? What is the role of other factors mentioned in paragraph 26 of the judgment?
6. In this case, there was no documentary evidence that Post Danmark had the intention to drive its competitors from the market. Hence, the facts of the case did not fit the second criterion of the *AKZO* jurisprudence (a plan to eliminate competition). How would the case have been decided, if there was evidence of anti-competitive intent?
7. The Court in paragraph 30 notes that price discrimination does not automatically lead to the finding of an abuse. Compare with the older case law of the Court on price discrimination.[140]
8. In paragraph 33 of the judgment, the Court noted that the Danish competition authority included in the definition of 'average incremental costs', among other things, 'not only those fixed and variable costs attributable solely to the activity of distributing unaddressed mail, but also elements described as "common variable costs", "75% of the attributable common costs of logistical capacity" and "25% of non-attributable common costs"'. Common costs are those that are common to the production of several products or services and it is a common feature in markets with multi-product or multi-services providers. For example, a postal operator may provide regular mail service, parcels delivery, express mail, banking services. These services will all rely on the same personnel and offices, hence personnel and offices will constitute common costs in this example. According to the Opinion of Advocate General Mengozzi in *Post Danmark I*, in *Deutsche Post*,

> the Commission found that Deutsche Post had abused its dominant position by offering the services in question at prices below its incremental costs, so that it had offered predatory prices. The Commission defined those costs as the costs arising solely from the provision of a specific service, which depend on the quantity supplied and which would disappear if the service were discontinued, which implies that the common fixed costs, which do not depend on the provision of a single service, are not included in the incremental costs. It also appears from that decision, which on that point clearly guided the Danish competition authorities in the main proceedings, that the costs attributable to a specific service must not be burdened with the common fixed cost of providing network capacity, incurred as a result of the universal service obligation. Therefore the average incremental costs
>
> comprise only the average fixed and variable costs of providing the service exposed to competition.[141]

[139] E Rousseva and M Marquis, 'Hell Freezes Over: A Climate Change for Assessing Exclusionary Conduct under Article 102 TFEU' (2012) 4(1) *J European Competition L & Practice* 32, 32–3.

[140] See Section 9.7.

[141] Opinion of AG Mengozzi in Case C-209/10, *Post Danmark I*, ECLI:EU:C:2011:342, para 37.

9. The Advocate General excludes from consideration any common costs, focusing only on the costs that are truly incremental to the product or service the dominant firm is accused of selling at predatory prices ('the incremental cost approach'). The problem with this approach is, as Geradin, Layne-Farrar, and Petit explain, 'that it penalizes competitors that only sell one product and which therefore have to cover all the stand-alone costs of producing that product'.[142] An alternative approach would 'require the dominant firm to allocate its common costs on an acceptable basis between the several products it produces' (the 'fully allocated costs' approach), which is, however, difficult as there are no generally acceptable methodologies to allocate common costs.[143] In *Post Danmark II*, the Danish Competition Authority adopted a 'fully allocated costs' approach by determining the percentage of common versus non-common costs to attribute. Who is favoured by this approach? The dominant firm? The competitors of the dominant firm? Bear in mind that an incremental cost approach enables the dominant firm to allocate all their common costs to the service on which they enjoy substantial market power and hence escape liability under predatory pricing. The issue is of importance, as if one includes common costs and adopts a 'fully allocated costs approach', this might favour dominant undertakings and incentivize them to adopt exclusionary strategies marginalizing their competitors. Could they escape liability with regard to above-cost selective price-cutting?[144]
10. (Paragraph 36) What is the test for selective low pricing above ATC? Can this conduct be found to constitute an abuse, and in which circumstances? The CJEU notes that selective price-cutting above ATC cannot have anti-competitive effects and hence Post Danmark's prices to its customers SuperBest and Spar could not be considered an abuse of a dominant position.
11. (Paragraphs 37–9, 41) The CJEU examined the selective law pricing below ATC/AIC in relation to Post Danmark pricing policy to its customer Coop, and held that if a dominant undertaking prices below ATC but above AVC (or AAC or AIC), then selective price-cutting may be found an abuse if it 'produces an actual or likely exclusionary effect, to the detriment of competition and, thereby, of consumers' interests' and there is no objective justification by the Domco, without that requiring the claimant to show the Domco's exclusionary intent. In any case, in *Post Danmark I*, there was no exclusionary intent. The CJEU examined the existence of an 'actual or likely' anti-competitive effect by referring to the as 'efficient competitor test'.[145] This limits the scope of the previous test applying to above-cost selective price cuts in *Compagnie Maritime Belge* and *Irish Sugar*, which led to the possible finding of an abuse under Article 102 TFEU, even if the excluded competitor was not as efficient as the Domco. The Domco may also defend its selective price-cutting conduct and refute the allegation of abuse

[142] D Geradin, A Layne-Farrar, and N Petit, *EU Competition Law and Economics* (OUP, 2012), 242.
[143] Ibid.
[144] See Opinion of AG Mengozzi in Case C-209/10, *Post Danmark I*, ECLI:EU:C:2011:342, paras 111–16, suggesting to the court to examine if there are any unlawful cross-subsidies between the reserved business (eg the market on which the dominant undertaking carries out universal service obligations) and that open to competition, in which case even an above-cost selective price-cutting could lead to anti-competitive exclusion.
[145] Case C-209/10, *Post Danmark I*, ECLI:EU:C:2012:172, para 38.

by showing that its prices on average cover a 'great bulk of the costs attributable to the supply of the goods or services in question'.[146] In any case, in the absence of evidence of exclusionary intent, the evidential presumption of *AKZO* for the finding of abuse does not apply and the claimant and the defendant are both in equality of arms to argue for the existence (or not) of anti-competitive effects. In the presence of evidence of exclusionary intent, the *AKZO* presumption still holds and it would not be possible, in principle, to the Domco to rebut it by employing a cost-based argumentation with the aim to prove that the excluded competitor is not as efficient as the Domco or arguing the absence of actual or likely anti-competitive effects.

12. At no part of the judgment does the CJEU indicate that it reverses its previous holdings in *Irish Sugar* and *Compagnie Maritime Belge*? If these cases are still good law, how can they be reconciled with *Post Danmark*? Lundqvist and G Skovgaard Ølykke note the specific characteristics of *Compagnie Maritime Belge* and *Irish Sugar*, the fact that both cases dealt with super-dominant firms that engage in pricing practices with the aim to 'fend off specific competitors', adopting elaborate practices aimed at specific competitors, such as fighting ships in *Compagnie Maritime Belge (CMB)* and 'a rather sophisticated pricing scheme, where the prices decreased the closer geographically the customers where to Northern Ireland and, thus, to the access to English sugar'.[147] According to the authors, '*CMB* and *Irish Sugar* concern specific and rather unique circumstances and should, thus, be considered to be overruled only with regard to the finding of anti-competitive effect when selective low pricing above ATC is employed. Still, for example, the strategy of "fighting ships" may in itself be conduct which is to be considered an abuse, because it is not competition on the merits', noting the 'dichotomy between competition on the merits and anticompetitive effect proven under the "as efficient" competitor test'.[148] Discuss.

13. Following up the preliminary ruling of the CJEU in *Post Danmark*, the Danish NCA dropped its claims concerning the customers of Post Danmark who were charged a price above Post Danmark's ATC and focused on the claims involving pricing below ATC: Post-Danmark's conduct relating to Coop.[149] The following box provides a summary of the findings of the Danish Supreme Court. Note that the CJEU has also been seized by the Danish courts for a preliminary ruling in *Post Danmark II*[150] regarding rebate schemes with a standardized volume threshold imposed by Post Danmark to several of its customers, which is analysed in Section 9.6.4.2.

146 Ibid.

147 See B Lundqvist and G Skovgaard Ølykke, '*Post Danmark*, now concluded by the Danish Supreme Court: Clarification of the Selective Low Pricing Abuse and Perhaps the Embryo of a New Test under Article 102 TFEU?' (2013) 34(9) *European Competition L Rev* 484, 486.

148 Ibid.

149 Danish Competition and Consumer Authority, Sag 2/2008 *Højesterets dom Post Danmark A/S mod Konkurrencerådet afsagt* (15 February 2013), 43.

150 Case C-23/14, *Post Danmark A/S v Konkurrencerådet*, ECLI:EU:C:2015:651 [hereinafter *Post Denmark II*].

B Lundqvist and G Skovgaard Ølykke, '*Post Danmark*, now concluded by the Danish Supreme Court: Clarification of the Selective Low Pricing Abuse and Perhaps the Embryo of a New Test under Article 102 TFEU?' (2013) 34(9) *European Competition L Rev* 484, 485 (footnotes omitted)

The Danish Supreme Court followed the CJEU, and stated that price discrimination in itself cannot constitute an exclusionary abuse. Then, it stated that exclusionary abuse cannot exist where the price is above ATC. Moreover, the dominant undertaking is not necessarily committing an exclusionary abuse when it uses a price which is between ATC and AIC (or AVC) to conquer a competitor's customers. The Danish Supreme Court continued to state that, in the absence of an objective justification, such pricing behaviour constitutes abuse, if an as efficient competitor actually or likely will be eliminated by the conduct to the detriment of competition and consumers. Thus, the Danish Supreme Court recited the 'as efficient' competitor test, analysed average prices and costs of Post Danmark, stating that if the dominant undertaking covers its costs, an as efficient competitor would be able to compete. The Danish Supreme Court considered whether exclusionary effects of Post Danmark's pricing behaviour would be likely, and found that this was not the case. It emphasized that, on average, Post Danmark's prices to all customers were above ATC, and that an 'as efficient' competitor would be able to compete on those terms; it also noted that Forbruger-Kontakt had been able to uphold its distribution network in spite of the loss of customers. Hence, the Danish Supreme Court set aside the decision on exclusionary selective low pricing.

9.3.4. UK CASE LAW

Claymore Dairies Limited and Arla Foods UK PLC v Office of Fair Trading
[2005] CAT 30

Claymore brought an appeal in the CAT against the OFT's finding that Wiseman had not abused its dominant position.

Wiseman had been found to be dominant in the supply of fresh processed milk to middle-ground retailers in Scotland.

The CAT dealt with predatory pricing issues. In particular, it found errors in the OFT's original figure for ATC in addition to discrepancies between the figures and Wiseman's management or statutory accounts, and inconsistencies with the fact that Wiseman had been found selling to two large customers at a price below total cost by the Competition Commission. These elements and further omissions and errors, regarding timeframe for the calculations for example, rendered the OFT figures for total costs unreliable. This, in turn, undermined the OFT's conclusion that Wiseman's prices were above total costs.

The CAT also had some criticism regarding the approach by the OFT in calculating AVC; however, it was not provided with evidence to conclude that Wiseman's prices were below AVC.

The CAT also assessed, in line with AKZO, *whether there was 'an intention to eliminate a competitor', necessary to prove predation where prices were between AVC and ATC. The CAT referred to drawing such intention where a dominant firm had prices below ATC for a significant amount time without offering any explanation, per* Aberdeen Journals. *In the present situation, however, the CAT could not make a useful finding regarding intent in the absence of useful evidence by the OFT.*

9.4. MARGIN SQUEEZE

9.4.1. DEFINITION

Margin squeeze is a vertical leveraging practice by which a dominant firm exploits its dominant position in an input market with the aim of restricting competition in a competitive downstream market. The practice should now be distinguished from price discrimination and refusal to deal.

Imagine a market over which firm *A* is dominant in an input market *X*, which is essential for the production of an output *Y*. Firm *A* delivers units of this input *X* to its own vertically integrated subsidiary *B* as well as to a rival competitor *C*. *B* and *C* are both present in the downstream market *Y*. In this configuration, the dominant firm may decide to discriminate in favour of its own downstream business by charging its own subsidiary *B* a wholesale price lower than it charges a rival competitor *C*—thus causing a secondary line injury.[151] It may also decide to refuse to supply downstream rival *C* with any unit of the input. A refusal to supply refers to a situation where a vertically integrated firm that is dominant in an upstream input market denies access to that input (unilateral refusal to deal) or proceeds to a constructive refusal to deal by imposing terms that that it is impossible for the other party to accept (provide low quality inputs).

A margin squeeze relates to the situation where a dominant undertaking in an upstream input market raises the price of the input compared to the price it charges on the downstream market to a level that (i) its downstream competitors (which are not active in the upstream market) are unable to cover their costs (they are operating at loss) or, more broadly, (ii) their margin is squeezed to a level that an equally efficient competitor would not be able to trade profitably in the downstream market on a lasting basis. By 'margin' we refer to the difference between retail price and wholesale price. Situation (i) indicates a negative margin, in which the downstream costs exceed the difference between upstream and downstream prices, while situation (ii) also covers a positive margin, that is, the downstream costs do not exceed the difference between upstream and downstream prices.

9.4.2. THE ECONOMICS OF MARGIN SQUEEZE

From an economic perspective, margin squeeze supposes the existence of a vertically integrated firm with a dominant position in an upstream market and which prevents its (non-vertically integrated) rival in a downstream market from achieving 'an economically viable price-cost margin'[152] (see Figure 9.1).

A predation theory of harm would involve a profit sacrifice in the first phase and recoupment in the second phase. This is the only available theory of harm in case the wholesale price is set by regulators on a strictly cost-basis. Application of a predatory pricing theory of harm would involve that the competition authority or court examine 'whether the dominant firm's own downstream business would be profitable if it had to pay the same actual input prices as third parties', that is, 'a test of downstream predatory pricing in the context of vertical integration'.[153] The focus here would be on the analysis of downstream competition between the dominant undertaking and its competitor(s).

151 See Section 9.7.

152 R O'Donoghue and J Padilla, *The Law and Economics of Article 102 TFEU* (Hart, 2nd ed, 2013), 366.

153 R O'Donoghue and J Padilla, *The Law and Economics of Article 102 TFEU* (Hart, 2nd ed, 2013), 397.

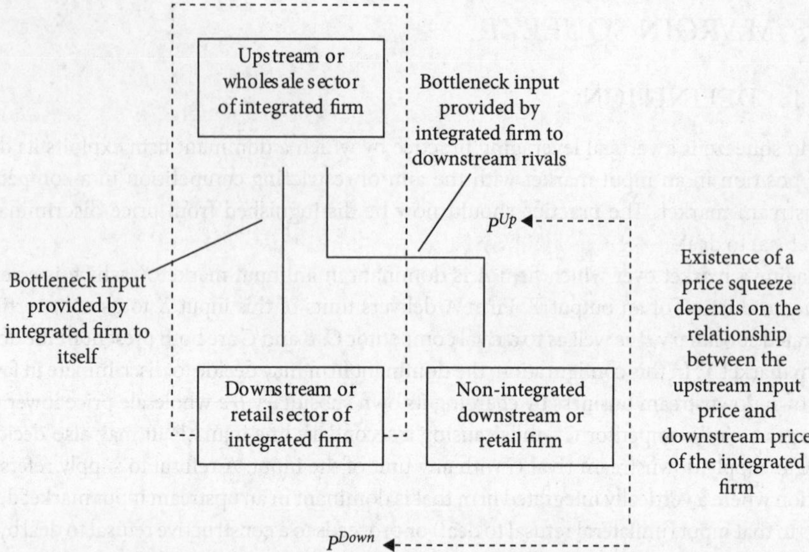

Figure 9.1. Classic market structure in which a margin squeeze might arise Economists identify different rationales/theories of harm for (anti-competitive) margin squeeze. First, the behaviour may be the result of an exclusionary practice, which may either be based on predation, or on anti-competitive foreclosure.
OECD, Margin Squeeze, DAF/COMP(2009)36, 25.

There are, however, also notable differences between margin squeeze and predatory pricing: first, although in predation cases competition authorities look to all costs of the dominant undertaking, they only look at the costs in the downstream market and the upstream price for margin squeeze; second, margin squeeze does not involve that the dominant undertaking is losing money overall, as it might be able to gain profits upstream rather than downstream and the margin squeeze may be overall profitable for the vertically integrated undertaking. Hence, it is not necessary to examine the recoupment of this 'sacrifice' by the dominant undertaking, as it may well be that the undertaking recoups its losses more or less simultaneously throughout the period of the abuse of margin squeeze.[154] The existence of a 'sacrifice' in margin squeeze cases may, however, take different forms, such as the opportunity cost for each unit not sold to downstream competitors, because of the high price of the bottleneck input, this opportunity cost being sometimes quite large if the wholesale price is above the upstream marginal cost (eg in presence of large economies of scale).

An anti-competitive foreclosure theory of harm may involve a vertical foreclosure, which would arise when 'the bottleneck good is either used as an input (eg an infrastructure) by a potentially competitive downstream industry (input foreclosure) [. . .], or when the bottleneck is needed to access final consumers (customer foreclosure)'.[155] A distinct possibility is horizontal foreclosure, which 'arises when the monopolized good is sold directly to customers, who use it in conjunction with complementary goods (eg system goods or after-sale services)',

[154] Ibid, 398.

[155] B Jullien, P Rey, and C Saavedra, 'The Economics of Margin Squeeze', Institut d'économie industrielle Report (March 2014), 11, available at http://idei.fr/sites/default/files/medias/doc/by/jullien/Margin_Squeeze_Policy_Paper_revised_March_2014.pdf.

involving scenarios in which the integrated undertaking attempts to protect its upstream monopoly or core market from potential competition by downstream customers or its market position in an adjacent market.[156]

Although most of the scenarios involving margin squeeze examined by EU and national competition authorities and courts involved vertical foreclosure, as 'margin squeeze allegations are typically made in network industries where a vertically integrated operator supplies access to its network to downstream competitors', one cannot exclude the horizontal foreclosure scenario as well. Vertical foreclosure may involve the leverage theory of harm, the margin squeeze being explained by the anti-competitive motive to monopolize the downstream market, or to dampen competition in the downstream market.

The vertical foreclosure theory was subject to criticism by the Chicago School of antitrust economics, arguing that there is a single monopoly profit to be made overall from end to end in the vertically integrated structure, and that the bottleneck monopolist may earn the entire monopoly profit simply by charging the monopoly margin at the upstream (bottleneck input) level and, consequently, leveraging market power from the bottleneck input market to the downstream market is not the main rationale for adopting such practices, and that these may be explained by efficiency reasons.[157]

The single monopoly profit theorem was criticized by post-Chicago School antitrust economists, observing the very strict assumptions under which it may apply and the fact that in the absence of exclusionary practices the upstream monopolist cannot fully exert its monopoly power.[158] The horizontal foreclosure argument will often take the form of maintenance of monopoly theory of harm or defensive leveraging.

Second, margin squeeze may arise as 'a by-product of pure exploitation of upstream market power by a vertically integrated firm', the upstream monopolist raising prices above the competitive level in order to 'appropriate some of the value created by downstream firms'.[159] By raising its price upstream, the bottleneck monopolist will reduce the profits of downstream competitors which will be captured by the monopolist upstream (excessive pricing theory of harm). Of course, the monopolist should never charge prices that are so high as to eliminate its downstream rivals, because this will eliminate the wholesale profits made by selling the bottleneck input to them, the vertically integrated undertaking deriving revenue from two sources: the wholesale level and the retail level. This exploitative strategy makes sense in particular when the downstream rivals are differentiated from the vertically integrated firm's downstream unit. For example, downstream rivals may preside a niche market segment, or may offer better customer service, thus being able to sell at a premium compared to the vertically integrated firm's downstream price. Yet, exploitative wholesale pricing may reduce the competitiveness of downstream competitors, thus providing the monopolist a 'price umbrella', enabling him to raise prices at the downstream level, or increase the profits of its downstream unit (raising rivals costs theory).

In addition to these anti-competitive harm narratives, economists also acknowledge that a margin squeeze conduct may also generate plausible efficiency gains, such as dynamic pricing in markets with network effects and switching costs, promotional efforts for experience or

[156] Ibid, 11–12. [157] More on the 'single monopoly profit' argument, see Section 9.2.1.2.

[158] See our analysis in Section 9.8.1.

[159] B Jullien, P Rey, and C Saavedra, 'The Economics of Margin Squeeze', Institut d'économie industrielle Report (March 2014), 19, available at http://idei.fr/sites/default/files/medias/doc/by/jullien/Margin_Squeeze_Policy_Paper_revised_March_2014.pdf. In contrast, Chicago School of economics would disagree with the characterization of such conduct as abusive behaviour. The single-monopoly profit theorem posits that the upstream monopolist can extract its rent by charging downstream rivals. So it is hard to claim this is about abuse of dominance to the extent that that is what they would expect a dominant operator to do.

credence goods, emergent markets, or even the motivation to use margin squeeze in order to meet competition. It is also often argued that the likelihood of error in identifying a margin squeeze is high as competition authorities and courts may not take into account other possible justification for the finding that downstream costs exceed the difference between upstream and downstream prices, such as industry shakeouts or temporary responses to bad market conditions, or the fact that the company may be undertaking legitimate investments in order to enhance its future profitability.

As it is not possible to always observe the price at which the firm sells its bottleneck input to its downstream sector, or because of the possibility of a fully integrated firm to shift apparent profits around within the upstream and downstream components of the same firm (through transactions or transfer pricing), the price at which the integrated firm sells its bottleneck input are inferred or imputed. The process is explained in the following excerpt:

R O'Donoghue and J Padilla, *The Law and Economics of Article 102 TFEU* (Hart, 2nd ed, 2013), 376

The most important element of a margin squeeze concerns the methodology to be applied to identify (or impute) an abuse. This raises several issues. First, what legal test should be applied to determine whether the dominant firm's upstream and downstream prices cause the activities of a downstream rival to be uneconomic, i.e. either loss-making or insufficient to provide a 'reasonable profit'. The most commonly applied test is whether the dominant firm's own downstream operations would make a profit if they had to pay the same input price as rivals. A second, related issue is whether a different test based on the costs of a 'reasonably efficient entrant' can also be applied. Third, the relevant cost standard to be applied to the dominant firm's downstream operations needs to be identified. Fourth, because margin squeeze concerns the price spread, or margin, one must look not only at costs but also at profitability, and it is necessary to apply a specific methodology in this regard. Finally, it needs to be ensured that the compared inputs, costs, and downstream revenues are truly comparable. [. . .]

A number of alternative tests could be envisaged in order to ascertain whether the dominant firm's prices would unlawfully exclude downstream rivals: (1) whether the dominant firm's own downstream operations could trade profitably on the basis of the wholesale price charged to third parties for the relevant input; (2) whether the dominant firm's downstream rivals could trade profitably on the basis of the wholesale price charged by the dominant firm; (3) whether some notional or hypothetical 'reasonably efficient operator' could trade profitably on the basis of the dominant firm's input prices; or (4) a combination of some or all of the preceding tests.

With regard to the above imputation tests, the one focusing on the dominant firm's own costs is only concerned with margin squeeze conduct that may exclude firms that are as efficient as the dominant undertaking, that it the excluded rivals have costs than the dominant firm (the Domco's own costs test). The test is practical as the dominant firm cannot know its rivals' costs but only its own costs.[160] Another imputation test would focus on the costs of a reasonably efficient competitor, which will find abusive a margin that is insufficient to allow a reasonably

[160] However, it could be argued that the Domco can observe downstream rivals' prices. This may be relevant where the downstream rival is differentiated and able to sell at a premium compared to the downstream price charged by the Domco. Under these circumstances, failure to pass the AEC test might not necessarily establish

efficient competitor to obtain a normal profit, for instance the downstream rival's costs (the reasonable efficient competitor test). The second test may lead to the application of Article 102 TFEU if the margin squeeze excludes a less efficient rival than the dominant firm, as long as this is a 'reasonably efficient' competitor.[161] Hence, the test involves a crucial choice as to the degree of efficiency it is reasonable to expect from rivals and emphasizes the competitive process, rather than efficiency as such, as the test facilitates the maintenance of competitors even less efficient than the dominant undertaking in the market.

The application of the equally efficient competitor test involves the consideration of all product-specific costs that the dominant firm incurs at the downstream market, exploring whether given these cost the dominant undertaking would remain profitable on the basis of the bottleneck input price it charges its competitors. Long-run average incremental costs constitute the most commonly applied cost benchmark in margin squeeze cases and refer to the product-specific costs linked with the total volume of output of the relevant product. As it is explained by the Commission, the choice of this cost benchmark

> [. . .] is in accordance with economic theory and the Commission's decisional practice where the ability of competitors to operate profitably in the long term was assessed. In order to assess whether the prices that the dominant firm applies over time are such that they can foreclose equally efficient competitors the costs considered must include the total costs which are incremental to the provision of the product/service. These are also the prices which form the basis of the firm's decision to invest.[162]

Finally, margin squeeze claims involve some profitability analysis, which 'entails assessing whether the vertically integrated dominant firm's own downstream operations could operate profitably on the basis of the upstream price charged to its competitors by its upstream operating arm'.[163] This is performed either by employing a 'period by period' approach, which 'compares for every year (or for shorter periods) the observed revenues and costs extracted from the dominant firm's accounts in which investment expenditure have been amortised over appropriate periods', or by using a discounted cash flow (DCF) approach, which 'consists in assessing the overall profitability over an adequate period (in general several years) in order to take account not only of current revenues but also of future revenues flowing from current investments'.[164]

9.4.3. MARGIN SQUEEZE AS A STAND-ALONE/SEPARATE CATEGORY OF ABUSE

The European Commission spelled out the criteria for a margin squeeze abuse in the *Nappier Brown/British Sugar* case.[165] The Commission found in this case that British Sugar was dominant

exclusionary intent, as the higher wholesale price charged to the downstream rival might be aimed at extracting the premium thereof, thus being exploitative in nature.

161 Where there are downstream economies of scale (ie, due to large fixed advertising costs), for example, the domco's downstream costs might be adjusted upward to reflect the fact that the rival is operating at a lower scale. However, this treatment of downstream scale economies may amount to consider them as an anticompetitive entry barrier, which may be contentious.

162 European Commission, Contribution to the OECD, *Margin Squeeze*, DAF/COMP/WP2/WD(2009)32, 6.

163 Ibid. 164 Ibid, 7.

165 The concept of margin squeeze was also mentioned in the *National Carbonising* interim measures decision of the Commission: *National Carbonising*, Commission Decision 76/185/ECSC [1976] OJ L 35/6.

in both the market for raw material (bulk/industrial sugar) and the derived product downstream (retail sugar) and that it had engaged to a strategy of maintaining a margin between the price it charged for the raw material (bulk sugar), its competitors in the derived product market and the price which it charged for retail sugar to a level that did not reflect its own costs of transformation (eg repackaging). According to the Commission, this conduct restricted competition in the downstream market for retail sugar and constituted an abuse of a dominant position.

The Commission shed some light on the different forms of margin squeeze ('price squeeze') in its Notice on the application of the competition rules to access agreements in the telecommunications sector:

Commission—Notice on the application of the competition rules to access agreements in the telecommunications sector—framework, relevant markets and principles [1998] OJ C 265/2

117. Where the operator is dominant in the product or services market, a price squeeze could constitute an abuse. A price squeeze could be demonstrated by showing that the dominant company's own downstream operations could not trade profitably on the basis of the upstream price charged to its competitors by the upstream operating arm of the dominant company. A loss-making downstream arm could be hidden if the dominant operator has allocated costs to its access operations which should properly be allocated to the downstream operations, or has otherwise improperly determined the transfer prices within the organisation. The Commission Recommendation on Accounting Separation in the context of Interconnection addresses this issue by recommending separate accounting for different business areas within a vertically integrated dominant operator. The Commission may, in an appropriate case, require the dominant company to produce audited separated accounts dealing with all necessary aspects of the dominant company's business. However, the existence of separated accounts does not guarantee that no abuse exists: the Commission will, where appropriate, examine the facts on a case-by-case basis.

118. In appropriate circumstances, a price squeeze could also be demonstrated by showing that the margin between the price charged to competitors on the downstream market (including the dominant company's own downstream operations, if any) for access and the price which the network operator charges in the downstream market is insufficient to allow a reasonably efficient service provider in the downstream market to obtain a normal profit (unless the dominant company can show that its downstream operation is exceptionally efficient).

In *Industrie des poudres sphériques* (*IPS*), the General Court recognized that an abuse by margin squeeze could take place if there was an imbalance between an upstream and a downstream price, without any need to demonstrate either that the wholesale price was excessive in itself or that the retail price was predatory in itself.[166] Pechiney Electrometallurgie (PEM) was the sole EU producer of low oxygen calcium metal, which was transformed and marketed as broken calcium metal. Industrie des Poudres Sphériques (IPS), PEM's competitor in the derivative market for broken calcium metal, complained

166 Case T-5/97, *Industrie des poudres sphériques SA v Commission*, [2000] ECR II–3755, para 179.

that the price for the low oxygen calcium metal was abnormally high and that combined with a very low price for the derivative broken calcium metal, PEM's competitors in the derivative market were driven to sell at a loss. The Court examined the existence of a margin squeeze claim:

Case T-5/97, *Industrie des poudres sphériques v Commission*
[2000] ECR II–3755

178. The applicant [. . .] contends that PEM proceeded to apply what is known as 'price squeezing'. Price squeezing may be said to take place when an undertaking which is in a dominant position on the market for an unprocessed product and itself uses part of its production for the manufacture of a more processed product, while at the same time selling off surplus unprocessed product on the market, sets the price at which it sells the unprocessed product at such a level that those who purchase it do not have a sufficient profit margin on the processing to remain competitive on the market for the processed product.

179. None the less, it must be held that, in view of the arguments put forward above to the effect that the additional costs included in the price proposed by PEM in its offer of 21 June 1995 are justified, the applicant's complaints concerning the alleged exclusion effect of the price proposed by PEM must be rejected in view of the fact that the applicant has failed to prove even the very premiss on which its argument is predicated, namely, the existence of abusive pricing of the raw material. In the absence of abusive prices being charged by PEM for the raw material, namely low-oxygen primary calcium metal, or of predatory pricing for the derived product, namely broken calcium metal, the fact that the applicant cannot, seemingly because of its higher processing costs, remain competitive in the sale of the derived product cannot justify characterising PEM's pricing policy as abusive. In that regard, it must be pointed out that a producer, even in a dominant position, is not obliged to sell its products below its manufacturing costs.

180. Moreover, the applicant has not shown that the price of low-oxygen calcium metal is such as to eliminate an efficient competitor from the broken calcium metal market.

Although the Court refers to the composite character of the margin squeeze claim (a claim of abusive excessive prices and that of predatory prices), it applied a single test, since it asks the plaintiff to prove that the price of the primary market product is such as to eliminate an efficient competitor from the secondary product market.[167] Hence, margin squeeze constitutes a different type of abuse than excessive pricing and predatory pricing. The approach followed in EU competition law may be contrasted to the position of some US courts and commentators that margin squeeze should not constitute an independent doctrine of antitrust liability.[168]

The more recent case law has delved into the relationship between the doctrine of margin squeeze and that of refusal to deal. This question may not arise in situations where the

[167] Ibid, para 180.

[168] See G Sidak, 'Abolishing the Price Squeeze as a Theory of Antitrust Liability' (2008) 4 *J Competition L & Economics* 279; DW Carlton, 'Should "Price Squeeze" be a Recognized Form of Anticompetitive Conduct?' (2008) 4 *J Competition L & Economics* 271; *Covad Communications Company v Bell Atlantic Corp*, 398 F 3d 666 (DC Cir 2005) (US). See, however, *Linkline Communications, Inc v SBC California, Inc*, 503 F 3d 876 (9th Cir 2007) (US), accepting antitrust liability for margin squeeze.

dominant undertaking has a regulatory duty to deal, but may be an important issue in other cases. It is possible to argue that the claimant in a margin squeeze case should provide evidence that access to the upstream input was indispensable for rivals and, more generally, for effective competition in the downstream level.[169] After all, a firm that has the ability to refuse to deal should also be able to decide to deal on unattractive terms. Other authors advance, nevertheless, the view that 'margin squeeze case law is less concerned with the 'indispensable' nature of the relevant upstream input than with the existence of alternative upstream supplies at competitors' disposal that could allow them to compete'.[170]

The question is of particular interest in view of the restrictive conditions of the *Oscar Bronner* case law of the EU Court, in particular the requirement that access is indispensable or 'objectively necessary' for the abuse of refusal to supply to be constituted.

The Commission Guidance on Article 102 establishes a parallel between the margin squeeze doctrine and that of refusals to deal: both are treated under the same chapter and as essentially practices that are substitutable for dominant firms.[171]

The Commission Guidance on Article 102 does not provide a detailed explanation as to the application of the *Oscar Bronner* conditions also to margin squeeze cases. One view might be that the *Oscar Bronner* conditions, in particular the fact that the claimant should prove that the refusal to deal or margin squeeze relates to a product or service that is 'objectively necessary' for the non-dominant firm to be able to compete effectively on a downstream market, also apply to margin squeeze cases.[172] Another view would take a broader perspective and will try to integrate the indispensability test of *Oscar Bronner* in the operation of the as-efficient-competitor (AEC) test. With regard to unilateral refusals to deal, the indispensability test led down by the European Court of Justice and Advocate General Jacobs in *Oscar Bronner* requires from the plaintiff to prove that it would not be economically viable for a competitor with a comparable turnover to create the facilities/input his rivals are requesting access to. The test integrates a (not-yet) AEC test, as it is only if the input or facility would not be economically viable,[173] 'in the sense that it would not generate enough revenue to cover its costs',[174] that a duty to deal may be imposed under Article 102. The test involves comparing relevant costs and revenues. The dominant firm's costs in running the upstream facility are employed as the comparator for the evaluation of the costs, hence the implicit introduction of an AEC test. This illustrates

[169] See R O'Donoghue, 'Regulating the Regulated: *Deutsche Telekom v European Commission*', *Global Competition Policy Magazine* (May 2008), 19, referring to Case T-271/03, *Deutsche Telecom*, para 237, where the GC observes that '[h]aving regard to the fact that the applicant's wholesale services are thus *indispensable* to enabling a competitor to enter into competition with the applicant on the downstream market in retail access services, a margin squeeze between the applicant's wholesale and retail charges will in principle hinder the growth of competition in the downstream markets' (emphasis added).

[170] S Genevaz, 'Margin Squeeze after Deutsche Telekom', *Global Competition Policy Magazine* (May 2008), 1, 26.

[171] Commission Guidance on Article 102, part D. See also ibid, para 80.

[172] The decision of the majority of the US Supreme Court in *Pacific Bell Telephone Company v Linkline Communications, Inc*, 555 US 438 (2009), is of particular interest here as the Supreme Court held that no price-squeeze claim could be brought under section 2 of the Sherman Act in the absence of an antitrust duty to deal. The Supreme Court considered that a margin squeeze claim is essentially a composite antitrust liability claim, comprising a refusal to deal claim and a predatory pricing claim. It follows that it is only if the conditions of a refusal to deal claim are present that a plaintiff could bring a margin squeeze case in the US, a notoriously difficult claim to bring in the US.

[173] *Pacific Bell Telephone Company v Linkline Communications, Inc*, 555 US 438 (2009), paras 43–6. AG Jacobs Opinion in Case C-7/97, *Oscar Bronner* [1998] ECR I–7791, para 68.

[174] DG Comp Discussion Paper, para 229.

how the debate over the application (or not) of the *Oscar Bronner* indispensability condition in margin squeeze cases is misconceived. The Court is already applying an AEC test, which constitutes the first step of the margin squeeze analysis.[175] There is no need therefore to introduce on the top of it an indispensability condition. The question if margin squeeze is a separate type of abuse than pricing abuses or refusal to supply has been examined by the case law.

9.4.3.1. *Deutsche Telekom*

Case T-271/03, *Deutsche Telekom AG v Commission*
[2008] ECR II–477

Since 1998, Deutsche Telekom (DT) was obliged to provide competitors with local access to its network. The retail and wholesale prices DT was entitled to charge for such access were subject to a strict regulatory scheme. Wholesale prices were fixed by the-then German telecoms regulator, RegTP, and retail prices were subject to a price cap. By a decision adopted on 21 May 2003, the Commission found that DT had abused a dominant position because, from 2002, there was an insufficient margin between the prices which it charged its competitors for unbundled broadband access at the wholesale level and those it charged its subscribers for access. The difference between retail and wholesale prices was insufficient to cover the product-specific costs to DT of providing its own retail services on the downstream market. Consequently, even an equally efficient competitor to DT would have had its profit margins squeezed. The Commission did not allege that the wholesale prices were excessive, but that DT's retail prices were too low, hence DT could have reduced the margin squeeze by increasing its charges to end-customers.

An interesting issue raised in this decision is the interaction between competition law and sector-specific regulation, as the rates proposed by DT were approved by the German telecommunications regulator. DT's argument was that the Commission should have acted against Germany under Article 258 TFEU. The Commission rejected this argument and confirmed that 'competition rules may apply where the sector-specific legislation does not preclude the undertakings it governs from engaging in autonomous conduct that prevents, restricts or distorts competition'.[176]

DT appealed the decision of the Commission to the General Court, which confirmed the approach followed by the Commission with regard to the methodology for margin squeeze and the position of the Commission with regard to the interaction between competition and sector-specific regulation.

Read in particular paragraphs 166–8, 186–94 of the Judgment.

On appeal, the CJEU confirmed the judgment of the GC.

Case C-280/08 P, *Deutsche Telekom AG v Commission*
[2010] ECR I–9555

Concerning the relevance of the margin squeeze test for the purpose of establishing an abuse within the meaning of Article 102 TFEU.

175 Case T-271/03, *Deutsche Telekom AG v Commission*, paras 194, 199, and 237. See also *Nappier Brown/British Sugar* (Case COMP IV/30.178) Commission Decision [1988] OJ L 284/41, para 65.

176 *Deutsche Telekom AG* (Cases COMP/C-1/37.451, 37.578, 37.579) Commission Decision [2003] OJ L 263/9, para 54.

169. [. . .] [I]n order to consider whether the present complaint is well founded, the Court must consider whether the General Court was right [. . .] to find that, even if the appellant does not have scope to adjust its wholesale prices for local loop access services, its pricing practices can nevertheless be categorised as an abuse within the meaning of Article [102 TFEU] where, irrespective of whether those wholesale prices and the retail prices for end-user access services are, in themselves, abusive, the spread between them is unfair, namely, according to that judgment, where that spread is either negative or insufficient to cover the appellant's product-specific costs of providing its own services, so that a competitor who is as efficient as the appellant is prevented from entering into competition with the appellant for the provision of end-user access services. [. . .]

177. [. . .] Article [102 TFEU] prohibits a dominant undertaking from, inter alia, adopting pricing practices which have an exclusionary effect on its equally efficient actual or potential competitors, that is to say practices which are capable of making market entry very difficult or impossible for such competitors, and of making it more difficult or impossible for its co-contractors to choose between various sources of supply or commercial partners, thereby strengthening its dominant position by using methods other than those which come within the scope of competition on the merits. From that point of view, therefore, not all competition by means of price can be regarded as legitimate (see, to that effect, *Nederlandsche Banden-Industrie-Michelin* v *Commission*, paragraph 73; *AKZO* v *Commission*, paragraph 70; and *British Airways* v *Commission*, paragraph 68).

178. In the present case, it must be noted that the appellant does not deny that, even on the assumption that it does not have the scope to adjust its wholesale prices for local loop access services, the spread between those prices and its retail prices for end-user access services is capable of having an exclusionary effect on its equally efficient actual or potential competitors, since their access to the relevant service markets is, at the very least, made more difficult as a result of the margin squeeze which such a spread can entail for them.

179. At the hearing the appellant submitted, however, that the test applied in the judgment under appeal for the purpose of establishing an abuse within the meaning of Article [102 TFEU] required it, in the circumstances of the case, to increase its retail prices for end-user access services to the detriment of its own end-users, given the national regulatory authorities' regulation of its wholesale prices for local loop access services.

180. It is true, [. . .] that Article [102 TFEU] aims, in particular, to protect consumers by means of undistorted competition (see Joined Cases C-468/06 to C-478/06 *Sot. Lélos kai Siaand and Others* [2008] ECR I7139, paragraph 68).

181. However, the mere fact that the appellant would have to increase its retail prices for end-user access services in order to avoid the margin squeeze of its competitors who are as efficient as the appellant cannot in any way, in itself, render irrelevant the test which the General Court applied in the present case for the purpose of establishing an abuse under Article [102 TFEU].

182. By further reducing the degree of competition existing on a market—the end-user access services market—already weakened precisely because of the presence of the appellant, thereby strengthening its dominant position on that market, the margin squeeze also has the effect that consumers suffer detriment as a result of the limitation of the choices available to them and, therefore, of the prospect of a longer-term reduction of retail prices as a result of competition exerted by competitors who are at least as efficient in that market [. . .].

183. In those circumstances, in so far as the appellant has scope to reduce or end such a margin squeeze [. . .] by increasing its retail prices for end-user access services, the General Court correctly held in paragraphs 166 to 168 of the judgment under appeal that that margin squeeze is capable, in itself, of constituting an abuse within the meaning of Article [102 TFEU] in view of the exclusionary effect that it can create for competitors who are at least as efficient as the appellant. The General Court was not, therefore, obliged to establish, additionally, that the wholesale prices for local loop access services or retail prices for end-user access services were in themselves abusive on account of their excessive or predatory nature, as the case may be.

184 It follows from this that the appellant's complaint that the test applied by the General Court in order to establish an abuse within the meaning of Article [102 TFEU] was erroneous must be rejected as, in part, inadmissible and, in part, unfounded. [. . .]

The adequacy of the method of calculating the margin squeeze

186. The appellant submits that, in its analysis of the method used by the Commission to calculate the margin squeeze, the judgment under appeal is vitiated by several errors of law, in so far as the General Court relies, in respect of several key aspects of the issue, on criteria which are not compatible with Article [102 TFEU]. The appellant puts forward two complaints concerning, first, the misapplication of the as-efficient-competitor test and, second, an error of law in that call services and other telecommunications services were not taken into account in calculating the margin squeeze. [. . .]

198. In that regard, it must be borne in mind that the Court has already held that, in order to assess whether the pricing practices of a dominant undertaking are likely to eliminate a competitor contrary to Article [102 TFEU], it is necessary to adopt a test based on the costs and the strategy of the dominant undertaking itself (see *AKZO* v *Commission*, paragraph 74, and *France Télécom* v *Commission*, paragraph 108).

199. The Court pointed out, inter alia, in that regard that a dominant undertaking cannot drive from the market undertakings which are perhaps as efficient as the dominant undertaking but which, because of their smaller financial resources, are incapable of withstanding the competition waged against them (see *AKZO* v *Commission*, paragraph 72).

200. In the present case, since [. . .] the abusive nature of the pricing practices at issue in the judgment under appeal stems in the same way from their exclusionary effect on the appellant's competitors, the General Court did not err in law when it held [. . .] that the Commission had been correct to analyse the abusive nature of the appellant's pricing practices solely on the basis of the appellant's charges and costs.

201. As the General Court found, [. . .] since such a test can establish whether the appellant would itself have been able to offer its retail services to end-users otherwise than at a loss if it had first been obliged to pay its own wholesale prices for local loop access services, it was suitable for determining whether the appellant's pricing practices had an exclusionary effect on competitors by squeezing their margins.

202. Such an approach is particularly justified because, as the General Court indicated, in essence [. . .] it is also consistent with the general principle of legal certainty in so far as the account taken of the costs of the dominant undertaking allows that undertaking, in the light of its special responsibility under Article [102 TFEU], to assess the lawfulness of its own conduct. While a dominant undertaking knows what its own costs and charges are, it does not, as a general rule, know what its competitors' costs and charges are.

203. Those findings are not affected by what the appellant claims are the less onerous legal and material conditions to which its competitors are subject in the provision of their telecommunications services to end-users. Even if that assertion were

proved, it would not alter either the fact that a dominant undertaking, such as the appellant, cannot adopt pricing practices which are capable of driving equally efficient competitors from the relevant market, or the fact that such an undertaking must, in view of its special responsibility under Article [102 TFEU], be in a position itself to determine whether its pricing practices are compatible with that provision.

204. The appellant's complaint concerning the misapplication of the as-efficient-competitor test must, therefore, be rejected. [. . .]

With regard to the effects of the margin squeeze

250. With regard to the third part of the second ground of appeal, it must be held at the outset that [. . .] the General Court correctly rejected the Commission's arguments to the effect that the very existence of a pricing practice of a dominant undertaking which leads to the margin squeeze of its equally efficient competitors constitutes an abuse within the meaning of Article [102 TFEU], and that it is not necessary for an anti-competitive effect to be demonstrated.

251. It should be borne in mind that, in accordance with the case-law [. . .], by prohibiting the abuse of a dominant position in so far as trade between Member States is capable of being affected, Article [102 TFEU] refers to the conduct of a dominant undertaking which, through recourse to methods different from those governing normal competition in products or services on the basis of the transactions of commercial operators, has the effect of hindering the maintenance of the degree of competition still existing in the market or the growth of that competition.

252. The General Court therefore held [. . .], without any error of law, that the anti-competitive effect which the Commission is required to demonstrate, as regards pricing practices of a dominant undertaking resulting in a margin squeeze of its equally efficient competitors, relates to the possible barriers which the appellant's pricing practices could have created for the growth of products on the retail market in end-user access services and, therefore, on the degree of competition in that market.

253. [. . .] [A] pricing practice such as that at issue in the judgment under appeal that is adopted by a dominant undertaking such as the appellant constitutes an abuse within the meaning of Article [102 TFEU] if it has an exclusionary effect on competitors who are at least as efficient as the dominant undertaking itself by squeezing their margins and is capable of making market entry more difficult or impossible for those competitors, and thus of strengthening its dominant position on that market to the detriment of consumers' interests.

254. Admittedly, where a dominant undertaking actually implements a pricing practice resulting in a margin squeeze of its equally efficient competitors, with the purpose of driving them from the relevant market, the fact that the desired result is not ultimately achieved does not alter its categorisation as abuse within the meaning of Article [102 TFEU]. However, in the absence of any effect on the competitive situation of competitors, a pricing practice such as that at issue cannot be classified as exclusionary if it does not make their market penetration any more difficult.

NOTES AND QUESTIONS ON DEUTSCHE TELEKOM V COMMISSION

1. (GC, paragraph 166) Note that the case concerned a margin squeeze practice leading to negative margins.

2. (GC, paragraphs 167–8; CJEU, paragraph 169) Note that the abusive conduct is confined to the unfairness of the spread between wholesale prices and the retail prices, 'unfair' in the sense that 'a competitor who is as efficient as the appellant is prevented from entering into competition with the appellant for the provision of end-user access services', and not from the 'the abusive nature of its retail prices'. Note the difference and compare with the distinction made by the General Court in *Intel*[177] between price and non-related abuses, classifying loyalty rebates to the latter and margin squeeze to the former: According to the distinction established by the General Court in *Intel*, if the issue relates to the level of price, then it is a price restraint. If it is not linked to the level of price, then it is a non-price restraint. Assess the criteria of this distinction and the way the General Court and the CJEU defined the abusive nature of margin squeeze. Do they seem compatible to you?
3. (GC, paragraphs 186–7; CJEU, paragraphs 177–8) Note that both the GC and the CJEU refer to the 'as efficient as actual or potential competitor' test when examining the possible anti-competitive effects of the margin squeeze conduct. It is only if the margin squeeze conduct is 'capable of making market entry very difficult or impossible for such competitors, and of making it more difficult or impossible for [the Domco's] co-contractors to choose between various sources of supply or commercial partners, thereby strengthening its dominant position by using methods other than those which come within the scope of competition on the merits',[178] that Article 102 TFEU may apply. Does this heighten the burden of the claimant in margin squeeze cases? Discuss.
4. (GC, paragraphs 188–93; CJEU, paragraphs 198–200) Both the GC and the CJEU adopt the Domco's own costs test when identifying the abuse. They seem to reject the other imputation test relying on a reasonably efficient competitor, which was put forward in the Commission's Notice on the application of the competition rules to access agreements in the telecommunications sector—framework, relevant markets and principles [1998] OJ C 265/2. Would the objectives of general competition law be different from those pursued by the regulatory framework on the telecom sector? Note that telecom regulation aims to incentivize new entry in order to curb the power of the incumbent. Would arguments of legal certainty be more prevalent in the context of the general enforcement of Article 102 TFEU than with regard to the implementation of the telecom regulatory framework?
5. (CJEU, paragraphs 183, 250) Note that the CJEU does not require from the claimants evidence of anti-competitive effects (actual or likely, including a consumer harm story), but that the margin squeeze leads to the exclusion of an equally efficient competitor.
6. (CJEU, paragraphs 253–4) The CJEU further indicates that the test it applies for margin squeeze does not require the demonstration of any actual or likely anti-competitive effects, but that it suffices to prove that the practice of margin squeeze makes the market penetration of as efficient as actual or likely competitors 'any more difficult' or 'impossible'.

177 Case T-286/09, *Intel Corp v European Commission*, ECLI:EU:T:2014:547, paras 98–9.
178 Case C-280/08, *Deutsche Telekom AG v Commission* [2010] ECR I-9555, para 177.

9.4.3.2. *TeliaSonera*

Case C-52/09, *Konkurrensverket v TeliaSonera Sverige AB*
[2011] ECR I–527

TeliaSonera Sverige AB ('TeliaSonera') is the historical operator of the fixed telephone network in Sweden. TeliaSonera has long been the owner of a local metallic access network to which almost all Swedish households are connected. In addition to offering retail broadband services, TeliaSonera also offers wholesale access to its network to other operators who are also active in the retail market, either through local loop unbundling in compliance with EU regulations, or voluntarily, and under no regulatory obligations, through a particular input for ADSL connections. The Swedish Competition Authority brought proceedings before the Stockholm District Court against TeliaSonera alleging that it had abused its dominant position on the wholesale market by applying a margin between the wholesale price for input ADSL products and the retail price for ADSL services it offers to consumers, which would not have been sufficient to cover TeliaSonera's incremental costs on the retail market. The Stockholm District Court referred ten preliminary questions to the CJEU as to the preconditions under which the pricing policy of a vertically integrated dominant undertaking qualifies as a margin abuse under Article 102 TFEU. After repeating its well established case law that 'Article 102 TFEU must be interpreted as referring not only to practices which may cause damage to consumers directly but also to those which are detrimental to them through their impact on competition', the Court examined the abusive nature of the conduct.

25. As regards the abusive nature of pricing practices such as those in the main proceedings, it must be noted that subparagraph (a) of the second paragraph of Article 102 TFEU expressly prohibits a dominant undertaking from directly or indirectly imposing unfair prices.

26. Furthermore, the list of abusive practices contained in Article 102 TFEU is not exhaustive, so that the list of abusive practices contained in that provision does not exhaust the methods of abusing a dominant position prohibited by EU law [. . .].

31. A margin squeeze, in view of the exclusionary effect which it may create for competitors who are at least as efficient as the dominant undertaking, in the absence of any objective justification, is in itself capable of constituting an abuse within the meaning of Article 102 TFEU [. . .].

32. In the present case, there would be such a margin squeeze if, inter alia, the spread between the wholesale prices for ADSL input services and the retail prices for broadband connection services to end users were either negative or insufficient to cover the specific costs of the ADSL input services which TeliaSonera has to incur in order to supply its own retail services to end users, so that that spread does not allow a competitor which is as efficient as that undertaking to compete for the supply of those services to end users.

33. In such circumstances, although the competitors may be as efficient as the dominant undertaking, they may be able to operate on the retail market only at a loss or at artificially reduced levels of profitability.

34. It must moreover be made clear that since the unfairness, within the meaning of Article 102 TFEU, of such a pricing practice is linked to the very existence of the margin squeeze and not to its precise spread, it is in no way necessary to establish that the wholesale prices for ADSL input services to operators or the retail prices for broadband connection services to end users are in themselves abusive on account of their excessive or predatory nature, as the case may be [. . .].

35. In addition, as maintained by TeliaSonera, before the spread between the prices of those services can be regarded as squeezing the margins of competitors of the dominant undertaking, account must be taken not only of the prices of services supplied to competitors which are comparable to the services which TeliaSonera itself must obtain to have entry to the retail market, but also of the prices of comparable services supplied to end users on the retail market by TeliaSonera and its competitors. Similarly, a comparison must be made between the prices actually applied by TeliaSonera and its competitors over the same period of time. [. . .]

37. However, as regards the criteria an interpretation of which is requested by that court to enable it correctly to assess whether TeliaSonera did infringe Article 102 TFEU by committing an abuse of a dominant position in the form of a margin squeeze, the following points can be made.

The prices to be taken into account

38. The Stockholms tingsrätt seeks to ascertain, first, whether, for that purpose, account should be taken not only of the retail prices applied by the dominant undertaking for services to end users, but also those applied by competitors for those services.

39. It must be recalled, in that regard, that the Court has already made clear that Article 102 TFEU prohibits a dominant undertaking from, inter alia, adopting pricing practices which have an exclusionary effect on its equally efficient actual or potential competitors [. . .]

40. Where an undertaking introduces a pricing policy intended to drive from the market competitors who are perhaps as efficient as that dominant undertaking but who, because of their smaller financial resources, are incapable of withstanding the competition waged against them, that undertaking is, accordingly, abusing its dominant position [. . .].

41. In order to assess the lawfulness of the pricing policy applied by a dominant undertaking, reference should be made, as a general rule, to pricing criteria based on the costs incurred by the dominant undertaking itself and on its strategy [. . .].

42. In particular, as regards a pricing practice which causes margin squeeze, the use of such analytical criteria can establish whether that undertaking would have been sufficiently efficient to offer its retail services to end users otherwise than at a loss if it had first been obliged to pay its own wholesale prices for the intermediary services [. . .].

43. If that undertaking would have been unable to offer its retail services otherwise than at a loss, that would mean that competitors who might be excluded by the application of the pricing practice in question could not be considered to be less efficient than the dominant undertaking and, consequently, that the risk of their exclusion was due to distorted competition. Such competition would not be based solely on the respective merits of the undertakings concerned.

44. Furthermore, the validity of such an approach is reinforced by the fact that it conforms to the general principle of legal certainty, since taking into account the costs and prices of the dominant undertaking enables that undertaking to assess the lawfulness of its own conduct, which is consistent with its special responsibility under Article 102 TFEU [. . .]. While a dominant undertaking knows its own costs and prices, it does not as a general rule know those of its competitors [. . .].

45. That said, it cannot be ruled out that the costs and prices of competitors may be relevant to the examination of the pricing practice at issue in the main proceedings. That might in particular be the case where the cost structure of the dominant undertaking is not precisely identifiable for objective reasons, or where the service supplied to competitors consists in the mere use of an infrastructure the production cost of which has already been written off, so that access to such an infrastructure

no longer represents a cost for the dominant undertaking which is economically comparable to the cost which its competitors have to incur to have access to it, or again where the particular market conditions of competition dictate it, by reason, for example, of the fact that the level of the dominant undertaking's costs is specifically attributable to the competitively advantageous situation in which its dominant position places it.

46. It must therefore be concluded that, when assessing whether a pricing practice which causes a margin squeeze is abusive, account should as a general rule be taken primarily of the prices and costs of the undertaking concerned on the retail services market. Only where it is not possible, in particular circumstances, to refer to those prices and costs should those of its competitors on the same market be examined. [. . .]

[The *Oscar Bronner* conditions]

53. The special responsibility which a dominant undertaking has not to allow its conduct to impair genuine undistorted competition in the internal market concerns specifically the conduct, by commission or omission, which that undertaking decides on its own initiative to adopt [. . .].

54. TeliaSonera maintains, in that regard, that, in order specifically to protect the economic initiative of dominant undertakings, they should remain free to fix their terms of trade, unless those terms are so disadvantageous for those entering into contracts with them that those terms may be regarded, in the light of the relevant criteria set out in Case C7/97 *Bronner* [1998] ECR I–7791, as entailing a refusal to supply.

55. Such an interpretation is based on a misunderstanding of that judgment. In particular, it cannot be inferred from paragraphs 48 and 49 of that judgment that the conditions to be met in order to establish that a refusal to supply is abusive must necessarily also apply when assessing the abusive nature of conduct which consists in supplying services or selling goods on conditions which are disadvantageous or on which there might be no purchaser.

56. Such conduct may, in itself, constitute an independent form of abuse distinct from that of refusal to supply.

57. Moreover, it must be observed that since the Court was, in the said paragraphs of *Bronner*, called upon, in essence, only to interpret Article [Article 102 TFEU] with regard to the conditions under which a refusal to supply may be abusive, the Court did not make any ruling on whether the fact that an undertaking refuses access to its home-delivery scheme to the publisher of a rival newspaper where the latter does not at the same time entrust to it the carrying out of other services, such as sales in kiosks or printing, constitutes some other form of abuse of a dominant position, such as tied sales.

58. Moreover, if *Bronner* were to be interpreted otherwise, in the way advocated by TeliaSonera, that would, as submitted by the European Commission, amount to a requirement that before any conduct of a dominant undertaking in relation to its terms of trade could be regarded as abusive the conditions to be met to establish that there was a refusal to supply would in every case have to be satisfied, and that would unduly reduce the effectiveness of Article 102 TFEU.

59. It follows that the absence of any regulatory obligation to supply the ADSL input services on the wholesale market has no effect on the question of whether the pricing practice at issue in the main proceedings is abusive. [. . .]

Whether an anti-competitive effect is required and whether the product offered by the undertaking must be indispensable

60. The referring court seeks to ascertain, thirdly, whether the abusive nature of the pricing practice in question depends on whether there actually is an anti-competitive effect and, if so, how that effect can be determined. Moreover, it seeks to ascertain whether the product offered by TeliaSonera on the wholesale market must be indispensable for entry onto the retail market.

61. It must be observed in that regard that, bearing in mind the concept of abuse of a dominant position, the Court has ruled out the possibility that the very existence of a pricing practice of a dominant undertaking which leads to the margin squeeze of its equally efficient competitors can constitute an abuse within the meaning of Article 102 TFEU without it being necessary to demonstrate an anti-competitive effect [. . .].

62. The case-law has furthermore made clear that the anti-competitive effect must relate to the possible barriers which such a pricing practice may create to the growth on the retail market of the services offered to end users and, therefore, on the degree of competition in that market [. . .].

63. Accordingly, the practice in question, adopted by a dominant undertaking, constitutes an abuse within the meaning of Article 102 TFEU, where, given its effect of excluding competitors who are at least as efficient as itself by squeezing their margins, it is capable of making more difficult, or impossible, the entry of those competitors onto the market concerned [. . .].

64. It follows that, in order to establish whether such a practice is abusive, that practice must have an anti-competitive effect on the market, but the effect does not necessarily have to be concrete, and it is sufficient to demonstrate that there is an anti-competitive effect which may potentially exclude competitors who are at least as efficient as the dominant undertaking.

65. Where a dominant undertaking actually implements a pricing practice resulting in a margin squeeze on its equally efficient competitors, with the purpose of driving them from the relevant market, the fact that the desired result, namely the exclusion of those competitors, is not ultimately achieved does not alter its categorisation as abuse within the meaning of Article 102 TFEU.

66. However, in the absence of any effect on the competitive situation of competitors, a pricing practice such as that at issue in the main proceedings cannot be classified as an exclusionary practice where the penetration of those competitors in the market concerned is not made any more difficult by that practice [. . .].

67. In the present case, it is for the referring court to examine whether the effect of TeliaSonera's pricing practice was likely to hinder the ability of competitors at least as efficient as itself to trade on the retail market for broadband connection services to end users.

68. In that examination that court must take into consideration all the specific circumstances of the case.

69. In particular, the first matter to be analysed must be the functional relationship of the wholesale products to the retail products. Accordingly, when assessing the effects of the margin squeeze, the question whether the wholesale product is indispensable may be relevant.

70. Where access to the supply of the wholesale product is indispensable for the sale of the retail product, competitors who are at least as efficient as the undertaking which dominates the wholesale market and who are unable to operate on the retail market other than at a loss or, in any event, with reduced profitability suffer a

competitive disadvantage on that market which is such as to prevent or restrict their access to it or the growth of their activities on it [. . .].

71. In such circumstances, the at least potentially anti-competitive effect of a margin squeeze is probable.

72. However, taking into account the dominant position of the undertaking concerned in the wholesale market, the possibility cannot be ruled out that, by reason simply of the fact that the wholesale product is not indispensable for the supply of the retail product, a pricing practice which causes margin squeeze may not be able to produce any anti-competitive effect, even potentially. Accordingly, it is again for the referring court to satisfy itself that, even where the wholesale product is not indispensable, the practice may be capable of having anti-competitive effects on the markets concerned.

73. Secondly, it is necessary to determine the level of margin squeeze of competitors at least as efficient as the dominant undertaking. If the margin is negative, in other words if, in the present case, the wholesale price for the ADSL input services is higher than the retail price for services to end users, an effect which is at least potentially exclusionary is probable, taking into account the fact that, in such a situation, the competitors of the dominant undertaking, even if they are as efficient, or even more efficient, compared with it, would be compelled to sell at a loss.

74. If, on the other hand, such a margin remains positive, it must then be demonstrated that the application of that pricing practice was, by reason, for example, of reduced profitability, likely to have the consequence that it would be at least more difficult for the operators concerned to trade on the market concerned.

75. That said, it must be borne in mind that an undertaking remains at liberty to demonstrate that its pricing practice, albeit producing an exclusionary effect, is economically justified [. . .].

76. The assessment of the economic justification for a pricing practice established by an undertaking in a dominant position which is capable of producing an exclusionary effect is to be made on the basis of all the circumstances of the case [. . .]. In that regard, it has to be determined whether the exclusionary effect arising from such a practice, which is disadvantageous for competition, may be counterbalanced, or outweighed, by advantages in terms of efficiency which also benefit the consumer. If the exclusionary effect of that practice bears no relation to advantages for the market and consumers, or if it goes beyond what is necessary in order to attain those advantages, that practice must be regarded as an abuse [. . .].

77. It must then be concluded that, in order to establish that a pricing practice resulting in margin squeeze is abusive, it is necessary to demonstrate that, taking into account, in particular, the fact that the wholesale product is indispensable, that practice produces, at least potentially, an anti-competitive effect on the retail market which is not in any way economically justified [. . .].

The extent of the dominant position

83. The referring court seeks to ascertain, fifthly, whether the fact that the undertaking concerned has a dominant position solely in the wholesale market for ADSL input services is sufficient for the practice in question to be considered abusive, or whether, rather, it is necessary, for that purpose, that that undertaking also has such a position in the retail market for broadband connection services to end users.

84. It must be stressed, in that regard, that Article 102 TFEU gives no explicit guidance as to what is required in relation to where on the product markets the abuse took place. Accordingly, the actual scope of the special responsibility imposed on a

dominant undertaking must be considered in the light of the specific circumstances of each case which show that competition has been weakened [. . .].

85. It follows that certain conduct on markets other than the dominated markets and having effects either on the dominated markets or on the non-dominated markets themselves can be categorised as abusive [. . .].

86. While the application of Article 102 TFEU presupposes a link between the dominant position and the alleged abusive conduct, which is normally not present where conduct on a market distinct from the dominated market produces effects on that distinct market, the fact remains that in the case of distinct, but associated, markets, the application of Article 102 TFEU to conduct found on the associated, non-dominated, market and having effects on that associated market can be justified by special circumstances [. . .].

87. Such circumstances can arise where the conduct of a vertically integrated dominant undertaking on an upstream market consists in attempting to drive out at least equally efficient competitors in the downstream market, in particular by applying margin squeeze to them. Such conduct is likely, not least because of the close links between the markets concerned, to have the effect of weakening competition in the downstream market.

88. Further, in such a situation, in the absence of any other economic and objective justification, such conduct can be explained only by the dominant undertaking's intention to prevent the development of competition in the downstream market and to strengthen its position, or even to acquire a dominant position, in that market by using means other than reliance on its own merits.

89. Consequently, the question whether a pricing practice introduced by a vertically integrated dominant undertaking in the wholesale market for ADSL input services and resulting in the margin squeeze of competitors of that undertaking in the retail market for broadband connection services to end users is abusive does not depend on whether that undertaking is dominant in that retail market.

The relevance of the fact that the supply concerned is to a new customer

[. . .]

91. [. . .] the abusiveness of a pricing practice resulting in a margin squeeze on competitors who are at least as efficient as the dominant undertaking resides, in essence, in the fact that [. . .] such a practice may prevent normal competition in a market neighbouring the dominated market in so far as it may have the effect of driving out that undertaking's competitors from that market.

92. In that regard, as correctly maintained by the Commission, whether the operators concerned are existing or new customers of the dominant undertaking can be of no relevance.

93. Moreover, the fact that the new clients concerned are not yet active on the market concerned can also be of no relevance.

94. The point must be made that the abusiveness of a pricing practice such as that at issue in the main proceedings must be assessed not only with regard to the possibility that the effect of that practice may be that equally efficient operators who are already active in the relevant market may be driven from it, but also by taking into account any barriers which the practice is capable of creating in the way of operators who are potentially equally efficient and who are not yet present on the market [. . .].

95. Consequently, whether the pricing practice at issue is liable to drive out from the market concerned existing clients of the dominant undertaking or rather new clients of that undertaking is not, as a general rule, relevant to the assessment of whether the practice is abusive.

The opportunity to recoup losses

96. The seventh issue raised by the referring court is whether, in order for the pricing practice in question to be considered abusive, it is necessary that the dominant undertaking be able to recoup the losses caused by that practice.

97. It must be borne in mind in that regard that [. . .] a margin squeeze is in itself capable, in the absence of any objective justification, of constituting an abuse within the meaning of Article 102 TFEU.

98. However, a margin squeeze is the result of the spread between the prices for wholesale services and those for retail services and not of the level of those prices as such. In particular, that squeeze may be the result not only of an abnormally low price in the retail market, but also of an abnormally high price in the wholesale market.

99. Consequently, an undertaking which engages in a pricing practice which results in a margin squeeze on its competitors does not necessarily suffer losses.

100. In any event, even if the dominant undertaking suffers losses in order to squeeze the margins of its competitors, there can be no requirement that, in order to establish the existence of an abuse, evidence must be produced of the capacity to recoup any such losses.

101. The possibility that competitors may be driven from the market does not depend on either the fact that the dominant undertaking suffers losses or the fact that that undertaking may be capable of recouping its losses, but depends solely on the spread between the prices applied by the dominant undertaking on the markets concerned, the result of which may be that it is not the dominant undertaking itself which suffer losses but its competitors.

102. Lastly, in the event that the dominant undertaking were nonetheless to apply a price on the retail market which was so low that sales would engender losses, beyond the fact that such conduct is likely to constitute an autonomous form of abuse, namely the application of predatory prices, the Court has in any event already rejected the argument that, even in such a case, proof of the possibility of recoupment of losses suffered by the application, by an undertaking in a dominant position, of prices lower than a certain level of costs constitutes a necessary precondition to establishing that such a pricing policy is abusive [. . .].

103. It follows that whether the dominant undertaking is able to recoup any losses suffered as a result of applying the pricing practice at issue has no relevance to the matter of establishing whether that pricing practice is abusive. [. . .]

112. Having regard to all of the foregoing, the answer to the questions referred is that, in the absence of any objective justification, the fact that a vertically integrated undertaking, enjoying a dominant position on the wholesale market for ADSL input services, applies a pricing practice of such a kind that the spread between the prices applied on that market and those applied in the retail market for broadband connection services to end users is not sufficient to cover the specific costs which that undertaking must incur in order to gain access to that retail market may constitute an abuse within the meaning of Article 102 TFEU.

113. When assessing whether such a practice is abusive, all of the circumstances of each individual case should be taken into consideration. In particular:

- as a general rule, primarily the prices and costs of the undertaking concerned on the retail services market should be taken into consideration. Only where it is not possible, in particular circumstances, to refer to those prices and costs should those of competitors on the same market be examined, and
- it is necessary to demonstrate that, taking particular account of whether the wholesale product is indispensable, that practice produces an anti-competitive effect, at least potentially, on the retail market, and that the practice is not in any way economically justified.

114. The following factors are, as a general rule, not relevant to such an assessment:
- the absence of any regulatory obligation on the undertaking concerned to supply ADSL input services on the wholesale market in which it holds a dominant position;
- the degree of dominance held by that undertaking in that market;
- the fact that that undertaking does not also hold a dominant position in the retail market for broadband connection services to end users;
- whether the customers to whom such a pricing practice is applied are new or existing customers of the undertaking concerned;
- the fact that the dominant undertaking is unable to recoup any losses which the establishment of such a pricing practice might cause, or
- the extent to which the markets concerned are mature markets and whether they involve new technology, requiring high levels of investment.

NOTES AND QUESTIONS ON TELIASONERA

1. (Paragraphs 25–6, 34) The Court notes that the unfairness of the practices that may fall under Article 102(a) is linked to the 'very existence' of margin squeeze.
2. (Paragraphs 32–3) There is margin squeeze if the spread between the wholesale prices upstream and the retail prices to end users downstream practices by the Domco were either negative or insufficient to cover the specific costs at the upstream level which the Domco has to incur in order to supply its own retail services to end users, so that that spread does not allow a competitor which is as efficient as that undertaking to compete for the supply of those services to end users, leading the Domco's actual or potential equally efficient rivals to operate on the retail market only at a loss or at artificially reduced levels of profitability. Hence margin squeeze covers both situations of negative and positive margins.
3. The Court clearly distinguishes the margin squeeze abuse from those of predatory pricing and excessive pricing. First, the margin squeeze relates to the spread between the wholesale and the retail prices rather than to the price level, as is the case for predatory and excessive pricing.[179] Second, margin squeeze entails some comparison between the prices the dominant undertaking charges at the wholesale level to its own subsidiary in the retail market with the prices of services supplied to competitors, but also between the prices TeliaSonera and its competitors charge for comparable services supplied to end users on the retail market.[180]
4. Note that Article 102 TFEU applies only if the margin squeeze may exclude an equally efficient competitor. The Court refers to pricing criteria based on the costs incurred by the dominant undertaking itself and on its strategy rather than to the undertaking's rivals requesting access to the input at the upstream market. What is the main reason explaining the Court's choice?
5. (Paragraph 45) Although the CJEU opts for the Domco's own costs rule, it also opens the possibility for the application of a different imputation test, that of the reasonably efficient competitor. This is the case (i) 'where the cost structure of the dominant undertaking is not precisely identifiable for objective reasons', or (ii) 'where the service supplied to competitors consists in the mere use of an infrastructure the

179 Case C-52/09, *Konkurrensverket v TeliaSonera Sverige AB* [2011] ECR I–527, para 34.
180 Ibid, para 35.

production cost of which has already been written off, so that access to such an infrastructure no longer represents a cost for the dominant undertaking which is economically comparable to the cost which its competitors have to incur to have access to it', or (iii) 'where the particular market conditions of competition dictate it', for instance, 'the level of the dominant undertaking's costs is specifically attributable to the competitively advantageous situation in which its dominant position places it'.

6. (Paragraphs 53–9) The CJEU maintains that margin squeeze is a stand-alone and separate category of abuse, as applying the *Oscar Bronner* criteria would have led to requiring claimants to establish the conditions for a refusal to supply abuse for any alleged abuse of margin squeeze.
7. The Court requires evidence of anti-competitive effect, ruling out the possibility that the simple existence of a margin squeeze of a Domco excluding its equally efficient competitors can constitute an abuse without prior demonstration of anti-competitive effects.[181] These anti-competitive effects need not be concrete and in any case, there is no need to show that the exclusion of the as efficient competitors finally materialized. In the examination of the anti-competitive effects, the court must take into account 'all the specific circumstances of the case',[182] a point that applies to other types of abuses as well. First, the functional relationship (indispensability) of the wholesale product to the retail product constitutes a factor that, if present, may lead to some evidential presumption.[183] If access to the bottleneck input is indispensable for the sale of the retail product, leading to the exclusion of an equally efficient competitor, the anti-competitive effects of margin squeeze are 'probable'.[184] If the wholesale product is not indispensable to the supply of the retail product, the presumption is that margin squeeze may not be able to produce any anti-competitive effects, even potentially.[185] Second, the degree of margin squeeze of competitors at least as efficient as the Domco matters. If the practice of margin squeeze leads to a negative margin, that is, the wholesale price is higher than the retail price to end users, 'an effect which is at least potentially exclusionary is probable'.[186] However, if such margin remains positive, it is on the plaintiff to demonstrate that the application of the margin squeeze pricing practice was by reason of 'reduced profitability "likely" to have the consequence that it would be at least more difficult for the operators concerned to trade on the market concerned'.[187] It is unclear from the CJEU's judgment how this higher degree of difficulty for competitors to trade will be assessed, and what would be the precise counterfactual.
8. (Paragraphs 75–77) Note that the CJEU stipulates the possibility for a Domco to claim some economic justification for using the specific pricing practice. In paragraph 77, the CJEU envisages the absence of economic justification as part of the margin squeeze test.
9. (Paragraphs 83–9) Note that the Court does not require a dominant position on both the wholesale (upstream) and the retail (downstream) markets if the two markets are 'associated'. This association is presumed to exist between vertically related markets, in particular where the conduct of a vertically integrated dominant undertaking on an upstream market consists in attempting to drive out at least equally efficient competitors in the downstream with a margin squeeze practice. What happens in cases where the party controlling the bottleneck input is not vertically integrated?

181 Ibid, para 61.
182 Ibid, para 68.
183 Ibid, para 69.
184 Ibid, paras 70–1.
185 Ibid, para 72.
186 Ibid, para 73.
187 Ibid, para 74.

10. (Paragraphs 91–5) The CJEU dismisses the importance for finding a margin squeeze abusive of the distinction between an exclusionary practice aimed at an existing customer or a new customer. It is reminded that this distinction is employed in order to assess the refusal to supply category of abusive conduct, the CJEU having established in *Commercial Solvents*[188] a presumption that a refusal to supply existing customers by a Domco constitutes an abuse. This distinction is not adopted here, the CJEU noting the importance of existing as well as potential efficient competitors that may enter the market on which the Domco's abusive conduct effects are felt.
11. (Paragraph 96–103) The CJEU confirms that in order for a margin squeeze practice to be abusive, it is not necessary that the dominant undertaking be able to recoup the losses caused by this practice.

9.4.3.3. *Telefónica*

Case T-398/07, *Kingdom of Spain v Commission* ECLI:EU:T:2012:173

The case arose out of a complaint to the Commission from France Télécom against Telefónica for margin squeeze practices. Telefónica, a legal monopoly before the liberalization of the Spanish telecommunications sector in 1998, controlled the only fixed-line telecommunication network in the country. The Commission investigated Telefónica's conduct during the period 2001–6. Telefónica constituted a 'vertically integrated operator', as it was active at both the wholesale (upstream) and the retail (downstream) level. The Commission found that the margin between the wholesale prices Telefónica's subsidiaries charged their competitors downstream for wholesale broadband access in Spain and the retail prices they charged end users was not sufficient to enable Telefónica's competitors to compete effectively at the retail level. Telefónica refuted these allegations, arguing that it has never charged abusively high (monopoly) prices to competing entities for wholesale broadband access, nor priced their products predatorily at the retail level, hence its conduct did not constitute an abuse under Article 102 TFEU. An important aspect of the case was if in order for Article 102 TFEU to apply the Commission had to demonstrate that access to Telefónica's network was essential to its competitors to provide retail broadband services. Telefónica argued that the Oscar Bronner *conditions should apply in this case, interpreting the allegation of margin squeeze as a form of constructive refusal to deal: (i) there were real and/or potential alternatives to the regional and national wholesale access services of Telefónica (eg wholesale access to cable networks), (ii) the regional and national wholesale access services of Telefónica can be replicated, and (iii) the alleged conduct was not likely to eliminate all competition on the downstream market.*

The Commission held in its decision that 'in the light of the specific factual, economic and legal context of the case, in particular the fact that wholesale access at regional level is mandated since March 1999 and wholesale access at national level is mandated since April 2002 and the fact that the former monopoly's ex ante *incentives to invest in its infrastructure are not at stake in the present case, the legal test applied by the European Court of Justice in Oscar Bronner is not applicable'.*[189] *What would have been the case, however, if access was not mandated or if the dominant firm did not benefit from the investments of a former legal monopoly*

188 Case C-6/73, *Istituto Chemioterapico Italiano SpA and Commercial Solvents Corp v Commission* [1974] ECR 223
189 *Wanadoo España v Telefónica* (Case COMP/38.784) Commission Decision [2007] OJ C 3196, para 309.

and therefore its incentives to invest would have been jeopardized by antitrust liability? Would the Oscar Bronner *conditions have applied in this case? This issue was examined by the General Court, in light of the CJEU's judgment in* TeliaSonera, *in a judgment confirming the European Commission's decision but providing more information on this issue.*

63. In the light of the principles stated above, the Court must examine whether the Commission has committed the manifest errors of assessment claimed by the Kingdom of Spain.

64. First, the Kingdom of Spain claims that it is a requirement of the caselaw that, before there can be a margin squeeze between a wholesale product and a retail product contrary to Article [102 TFEU], as found by the contested decision, that the wholesale product should be indispensable for the provision of the retail service, which is not true in the present case.

65. In response to questions at the hearing on the meaning and scope of its argument, particularly in the light of the judgment in *TeliaSonera*, the Kingdom of Spain reiterated that its position was that where, as in the present case, there existed a regulatory obligation to supply a wholesale product, it was the duty of the Commission, in order to establish the existence of a margin squeeze contrary to Article [102 TFEU], to demonstrate that that product was indispensable to the provision of the retail product. The Kingdom of Spain also stated that the reasoning of *TeliaSonera* applied only where the wholesale products at issue had been voluntarily placed on the market, in the absence of any regulatory obligation.

66. [. . .] [I]n order to determine whether the dominant undertaking has abused its position by the pricing practices it applies, it is necessary to consider all the circumstances and to investigate whether the practice tends to remove or restrict the buyer's freedom to choose his sources of supply, to bar competitors from access to the market, to apply dissimilar conditions to equivalent transactions with other trading parties, or to strengthen the dominant position by distorting competition.

67. In particular, a pricing practice adopted by a vertically integrated dominant undertaking which is unfair because it effectively squeezes the margins of its competitors on the retail market, because of the spread between the prices of its wholesale products and the prices of its retail products, may constitute an abuse of a dominant position contrary to Article [102 TFEU] [. . .].

68. A margin squeeze, in view of the exclusionary effect which it may create for competitors who are at least as efficient as the dominant undertaking, in the absence of any objective justification, is in itself capable of constituting an abuse within the meaning of Article [102 TFEU] [. . .].

69. In that regard, the Kingdom of Spain's argument, presented at the hearing, that the reasoning of *TeliaSonera* applies only where the wholesale products at issue have been voluntarily placed on the market, in the absence of any regulatory obligation, must also be rejected.

70. In *TeliaSonera* the Court of Justice held in effect that Article [102 TFEU] applies only to anti-competitive conduct engaged in by undertakings on their own initiative. If anti-competitive conduct is required of undertakings by national legislation or if the latter creates a legal framework which itself eliminates any possibility of competitive activity on their part, Article [102 TFEU] does not apply. In such a situation, the restriction of competition is not attributable, as that provision implicitly requires, to the autonomous conduct of the undertakings (see *TeliaSonera*, paragraph 49 and case-law cited).

71. On the other hand, Article [102 TFEU] may apply if it is found, as in the present case [. . .] that the national legislation preserves the possibility that undertakings may

engage in autonomous conduct which prevents, restricts or distorts competition (see, to that effect, *TeliaSonera*, paragraph 50 and case-law cited).

72. The Court has stated that, notwithstanding such legislation, if a dominant vertically integrated undertaking has scope to adjust even its retail prices alone, the margin squeeze may on that ground alone be attributable to it [. . .]

73. Moreover, while the Kingdom of Spain claims that, if the margin between the national and regional wholesale products, on the one hand, and the retail product, on the other, was so close that it amounted to being negative, with the result that no other operator could use those wholesale products, the conduct under examination ought then to be analysed as a refusal of access which should then be regarded as abusive only by reference to the criteria stated in Case C7/97 *Bronner* [1998] ECR I–7791, such an argument must also fail.

74. The Court of Justice has made it clear that it cannot be inferred from *Bronner* that the conditions to be met in order to establish that a refusal to supply is abusive must necessarily also apply when assessing the abusive nature of conduct which consists in supplying services or selling goods on conditions which are disadvantageous or on which there might be no purchaser. Such conduct may, in itself, constitute an independent form of abuse distinct from that of refusal to supply [. . .].

75. If *Bronner* were to be interpreted otherwise, that would amount to a requirement that before any conduct of a dominant undertaking in relation to its terms of trade could be regarded as abusive the conditions to be met to establish that there was a refusal to supply would in every case have to be satisfied, and that would unduly reduce the effectiveness of Article [102 TFEU] (see, to that effect, *TeliaSonera*, paragraph 58).

76. It follows that the Kingdom of Spain cannot claim that the Commission was obliged, in the contested decision, in order to establish the very existence of a margin squeeze, to demonstrate that the wholesale products concerned were indispensable for the operators who had concluded contracts for them. The Kingdom of Spain's arguments designed to demonstrate that, in the contested decision, the Commission considered that the regional and national wholesale products were necessary on the basis of a misconceived interpretation of the theory of scale of investments, must therefore also fail. [. . .]

The analysis of the effect of the anticompetitive conduct

89. In that regard, it must be borne in mind that, in accordance with the caselaw, in prohibiting the abuse of a dominant position, in so far as trade between Member States is capable of being affected, Article [102 TFEU] refers to the conduct of a dominant undertaking which, on a market where the degree of competition is already weakened precisely because of the presence of the undertaking concerned, through recourse to methods different from those governing normal competition in products or services on the basis of the transactions of commercial operators, has the effect of hindering the maintenance of the degree of competition still existing in the market or the growth of that competition [. . .].

90. The effect referred to in the case-law cited in the preceding paragraph does not necessarily relate to the actual effect of the abusive conduct complained of. For the purposes of establishing an infringement of Article [102 TFEU], it is sufficient to show that the abusive conduct of the undertaking in a dominant position tends to restrict competition or, in other words, that the conduct is capable of having, or likely to have, that effect [. . .]. The pricing practice concerned must have an anti-competitive effect on the market, but the effect does not necessarily have to be concrete, and it is sufficient

to demonstrate that there is an anti-competitive effect which may potentially exclude competitors who are at least as efficient as the dominant undertaking [. . .].

91. It is apparent from the case-law of the Court of Justice [. . .] that, in order to determine whether the undertaking in a dominant position has abused such a position by its pricing practices, it is necessary to consider all the circumstances and to investigate whether the practice tends to remove or restrict the buyer's freedom to choose his sources of supply, to bar competitors from access to the market, to apply dissimilar conditions to equivalent transactions with other trading parties, thereby placing them at a competitive disadvantage, or to strengthen the dominant position by distorting competition.

92. Since Article [102 TFEU] thus refers not only to practices which may cause damage to consumers directly, but also to those which are detrimental to them through their impact on competition, a dominant undertaking has a special responsibility not to allow its conduct to impair genuine undistorted competition on the common market [. . .].

93. It follows from this that Article [102 TFEU] prohibits a dominant undertaking from, inter alia, adopting pricing practices which have an exclusionary effect on its equally efficient actual or potential competitors, that is to say practices which are capable of making market entry very difficult or impossible for such competitors, and of making it more difficult or impossible for its co-contractors to choose between various sources of supply or commercial partners, thereby strengthening its dominant position by using methods other than those which come within the scope of competition on the merits. From that point of view, therefore, not all competition by means of price can be regarded as legitimate [. . .].

NOTES AND QUESTIONS ON TELEFÓNICA

1. (Paragraphs 69–71) In comparison to the fact pattern in *TeliaSonera*, where the dominant undertaking had provided voluntarily access to its network at wholesale, Telefónica was under a regulatory obligation to supply a wholesale product, although it engaged in the margin squeeze on its own initiative. Does it make any difference for the application of Article 102 TFEU?
2. (Paragraphs 73–5) The General Court re-affirmed the independence of the margin squeeze by rejecting the application of the *Oscar Bronner* conditions. Indeed, in its decision, the Commission took the view that in the circumstances of that case it did not have to prove that these conditions were satisfied, arguing, first, that Spanish and EU telecommunications law already imposed on Telefónica an obligation to supply and it was clear, from the considerations underlying such regulation, that the necessary balancing of incentives had already been made by the public authority when imposing such an obligation to supply and, second, that Telefónica's infrastructure was to a large extent the fruit of investments that were undertaken well before the advent of broadband in Spain and were undertaken in a context where Telefónica was benefiting from special or exclusive rights that shielded it from competition. Do you agree with the approach followed by the Commission and confirmed by the General Court?[190]

[190] For a critical perspective on this judgment, see D Geradin, 'Refusal to Supply and Margin Squeeze: A Discussion of Why the "*Telefonica* Exceptions" are Wrong', TILEC Discussion Paper No 2011-009 (16 February 2011), 8–12, available at https://ssrn.com/abstract=1762687.

3. In its decision in *Telefónica*, the Commission considered that profitability should be assessed on the basis of the dominant company's downstream costs (the 'equally efficient competitor test'). There are two options to assess the margin squeeze. The first is to look to the costs of the dominant firm's downstream business, in line with the equally efficient competitor test. This test is also known as the 'imputation test' because the costs of the as efficient competitor are imputed from those of the dominant undertaking. The second is to use the costs of a hypothetical reasonably efficient competitor in order to take into account the fact that a dominant company may have a lower downstream unit cost because of economies of scale or an installed customer base that smaller 'not yet efficient' rivals may not benefit from. The Commission adopted the imputation or 'equally efficient competitor' test. That is, the detrimental effect of a margin squeeze can be described in terms of the foreclosure of competitors that are able to provide downstream services as efficiently as the dominant firm. Thus the relevant test is whether Telefónica would have been able to offer downstream services without incurring a loss if, during the period under investigation, it had had to pay the upstream access price charged to competitors as an internal transfer price for its own retail operations. The essence of the test is whether a competitor having the same cost function as the downstream arm of the vertically integrated company is able to be profitable in the downstream market given the wholesale and retail prices levied by the vertically integrated company.
4. What are the pros and cons of the 'equally efficient competitor test'? Which test is more favourable to Telefónica? As it is explained in the Commission's Decision,

   > Given the economies of scale and scope of Telefónica, its unit costs can be expected to be lower than those of its reasonably efficient competitors. A reasonably efficient competitor sharing the same cost structure as Telefónica's own downstream businesses but not enjoying the same economies of scale as those enjoyed by Telefónica during the period under investigation inevitably has higher unit network costs. At the same time, through its presence and leadership position in all the telecommunications markets [. . .] Telefónica has economies of scope enabling it to spread some costs (administration, advertising, commercial network) over a much broader set of operations than a reasonably efficient operator with a narrower range of activities. The importance of economies of scale and scope in this industry entails that Telefónica can price above cost in the downstream market and still foreclose entry and growth in this market.[191]

   Which of the two tests enables dominant undertakings to comply more easily with EU competition law?
5. Does the General Court require evidence by the plaintiff of the anti-competitive effect of the margin squeeze, or the abuse of dominance can be found solely from the finding of a margin squeeze of an equally efficient competitor?[192] Does it make sense to require additional evidence of anti-competitive effects in case it has been already established that the margin between the wholesale and the retail price would have excluded an equally efficient competitor? Would the consideration of the actual and potential

191 *Wanadoo España v Telefónica* (Case COMP/38.784) Commission Decision [2007] OJ C 31/96, para 314, available at http://ec.europa.eu/competition/antitrust/cases/dec_docs/38784/38784_311_10.pdf.

192 Case T-398/07, *Kingdom of Spain v Commission* ECLI:EU:T:2012:173, paras 89–93.

anti-competitive effects of the margin squeeze have reduced the risk of false positives in view of the practical problems with the imputation of the costs to the specific activity from which the rivals have been excluded?

6. The appropriate cost standard used for assessing margin squeeze is the LRAIC. In order to assess the profitability of prices which are to be applied over time by an operator, and which will form the basis of that operator's decisions to invest, the costs considered must include the total costs which are incremental to the provision of the service. As it is explained by the Commission, '[t]he long run incremental cost of an individual product refers to the product-specific costs associated with the total volume of output of the relevant product. It is the difference between the total costs incurred by the firm when producing all products, including the individual product under analysis, and the total costs of the firm when the output of the individual product is set equal to zero, holding the output of all other products fixed. Such costs include not only all volume sensitive and fixed costs directly attributable to the production of the total volume of output of the product in question but also the increase in the common costs that is attributable to this activity.'[193] The use of a long-run cost measure implies that any cost that is incremental in the long run due to the activity should be included in the margin squeeze test. The idea is that, if the revenues associated with the downstream activity fall below LRAIC, a rational and profit-maximizing firm, enjoying the same economies of scale and scope would have no economic interest in offering downstream services in the medium term. The Commission has analysed profitability on the basis of two methods: namely, the period-by-period method and the discounted cash flow method. The period-by-period approach measures profitability in each year, while the DCF model measures profitability over an adequate period (in general several years), across the lifetime of an investment, and is better suited to dynamic markets. In *Telefónica*, the Commission applied both tests and obtained the same results.
7. For dominant undertakings offering a wide range of retail broadband products with a correspondingly wide range of prices, a possible question is the aggregation level at which the margin squeeze test should be applied either at the highest level of detail (ie, at the level of each individual offer) or at the aggregate portfolio level (ie, at the level of the mix of services marketed on the retail market). In *Telefónica*, the margin squeeze price was calculated across the full range of products offered by the dominant undertaking in the relevant retail market. According to the Commission, this 'is based on the principle that competitors must at least be able to profitably replicate Telefónica's product pattern. This is the approach most favourable to Telefónica, since it gives it maximal flexibility to spread the costs that are common to its retail products (provided that the margin squeeze test yields a positive result with the aggregated approach). The aggregated approach is consistent with a new entrant's internal decision-making process in that it assesses the profitability of its investment in a network by considering the complete range of products that it is able to offer in the relevant downstream market.'[194]

[193] *Wanadoo España v Telefónica* (Case COMP/38.784) Commission Decision [2007] OJ C 31/96, para 319.
[194] Ibid, para 388.

Most recently, the Commission imposed fines on *Slovak Telekom* and its parent *Deutsche Telekom* for an abusive strategy to shut out competitors from the Slovak market for broadband services, in breach of Article 102 TFEU. In particular, the Commission concluded that Slovak Telekom refused to supply unbundled access to its local loops to competitors, and imposed a margin squeeze on alternative operators, the Commission making use of the equally efficient competitor test for the assessment of margin squeeze.[195] By two recent judgments, the GC partially annulled the Commission's decision reducing the amount of the fines imposed.[196] The GC did not disagree with the broader framework used by the Commission in this case to find an infringement. First, the GC held that the Commission was not required to demonstrate that access to Slovak Telekom's local loop was indispensable for potential competitors of that company, noting that given that the relevant regulatory framework for telecommunications clearly acknowledged the need for access to the domco's local loop, in order to allow the emergence and development of effective competition in the Slovak market for high-speed internet services, 'the demonstration, by the Commission, that such access was indeed indispensable [...] [as it was required for refusals to deal in Oscar Bronner] was not required'.[197] According to the GC, 'the existence of such a regulatory obligation is a relevant aspect of the economic and legal context' in which it is necessary to assess whether the conduct could be classified as abusive for the purposes of Article 102 TFEU.[198] Second, the GC referred to Telia Sonera for the proposition that the conditions to be met in order to establish that a refusal to supply is abusive according to Oscar Bronner must not necessarily also apply for independent forms of abuse distinct from that of refusal to supply, as otherwise that 'would unduly reduce the effectiveness of Article 102 TFEU'.[199] According to the GC, the approach followed by the CJEU in Telia Sonera not to require evidence that access is indispensable for the exercise of the activity of competitor operators, before finding an infringement under Article 102 TFEU, did not only concern the practice of margin squeeze, but more generally 'other business practices capable of producing unlawful exclusionary effects for current or potential competitors', such as, for instance, 'an implicit refusal to supply access' to Slovak Telekom's local loop.[200] However, the GC accepted Slovak Telekom's criticism of the application by the Commission of the case law on margin squeeze to the facts of the case. The Commission had indeed mostly relied on a multi-period approach in order to assess if an equally efficient competitor using wholesale access to Slovak Telekom's local loop was faced with negative margins and could not

195 *Slovak Telekom* (Case AT.39523) Commission Decision (15 October 15), paras 828–30. The Commission used the LRAIC as the relevant cost measure for the assessment of a margin squeeze in the telecommunications sector. The calculations in the Decision took account of the data of Slovak Telekom (ST) and showed that an equally efficient competitor using ST's unbundled local loops (ULL) wholesale access was facing significant negative margins and could not replicate profitably the retail broadband portfolio of ST on a lasting basis. The Commission found that ST's margin squeeze and overall exclusionary behaviour artificially raised barriers to entry on the retail market, deprived alternative operators of the possibility to compete effectively with ST and other players by relying on ULL access and engaging in the competition on the retail mass market for fixed broadband services thus making it more difficult for alternative operators to compete effectively with ST on the retail market, including competition based on alternative operators ' own networks (infrastructure-based competition).

196 See, Case T-827/14, *Deutsche Telekom AG v European Commission*, ECLI:EU:T:2018:930; Case T-851/14, *Slovak Telekom, a.s. v European Commission*, ECLI:EU:T:2018:929.

197 Case T-851/14, *Slovak Telekom, a.s. v European Commission*, ECLI:EU:T:2018:929, para 121.

198 Ibid, paras 151–3.

199 Ibid, paras 123–4.

200 Ibid, paras 126–8.

replicate profitably its retail broadband portfolio, finding that overall the margins have been negative, while had it relied on a 'period-by-period' (year-by-year) approach, it would have found that margins were positive during four months in 2005.[201] The Commission did not find that this fact questioned its conclusions, as 'an entry over four months could not be considered as entry on a lasting basis'.[202] While the GC agreed with the overall approach of the Commission to use a multi-period approach, it nevertheless held that the Commission had not demonstrated the existence of a practice resulting in a margin squeeze for the period of time in which there was a positive margin, as in this case the Commission was subject to a specific obligation with regard to the proof of exclusionary effects of the practice of a margin squeeze. Indeed, according to the GC, while 'if a margin is positive, it is not ruled out that the Commission can, in the context of the examination of the exclusionary effect of a pricing practice, demonstrate that the application of that practice was, by reason, for example, of reduced profitability, likely to have the consequence that it would be at least more difficult for the operators concerned to trade on the market concerned', the Commission had not shown exclusionary effects for the four months positive margins period, 'such a demonstration [being] required particularly' in the presence of positive margins.[203] Consequently, the GC found that the Commission had failed to demonstrate that Slovak Telekom's pricing practice had led to those exclusionary effects before 1 January 2006, partially annulling the Commission's decision and reducing the fine.

9.4.4. UK CASE LAW

Genzyme Limited v Office of Fair Trading
[2004] CAT 4

Genzyme was the manufacturer of a drug called Cerezyme and the only United Kingdom supplier. Genzyme entered into a distribution agreement with Healthcare at Home, the sole distributor of Cerezyme in the UK. After terminating the agreement, Genzyme launched its own delivery and home care services operation for the drug while Healthcare at Home continued to provide the same service. Healthcare at Home complained to the OFT that the pricing policy by Genzyme was abusive, because it bundled the price of the drug with that of home care services, and because it supplied the drug only at the full list price, affecting the margins of any third party supplier of home care services.

The OFT found Genzyme to have abused its dominant position, and Genzyme appealed to the CAT against this decision. In terms of the relevant upstream market, this was held to be the supply of drugs for the treatment of Gaucher disease in the United Kingdom in light of demand-side substitutability. Any treatment that did not treat Gaucher disease would be of no use to a patient or consumer in connection to that disease.

The CAT found Genzyme to be dominant in upstream based on a high market share (90–100 per cent), significant barriers of entry related to the creation of a new drug, and the lack of statutory (or other) mechanisms strengthening the countervailing buyer power of the National Health Service (NHS).

201 Ibid, paras 240–51.
202 Ibid, para 251.
203 Ibid, para 260.

The CAT also identified the relevant downstream market as the supply of home care services to Gaucher patients, due to the lack of any demand-side substitution and the constraints of supply-side substitution deriving from Genzyme's patent rights.

The CAT then discussed the abuse of dominant position; on the bundling issues, Genzyme's practice of including the price of Homecare Services in the NHS list price for Cerezyme could be theoretically defined as bundling; however the effects could not be described as having a significant adverse effect on competition.

With regards to the margin squeeze, it was found that Genzyme's price policy for Cerezyme offered no effective margin to providers of home care services to Gaucher patients, regardless of the efficiency of any undertaking in the downstream market. Following Commercial Solvents, Napier Brown/British Sugar, *and* Télémarketing, *the CAT agreed that the margin squeeze was meant to monopolize the downstream market in favour of Genzyme, and thus eliminate any competition.*

Lastly, the CAT held that potential objective justifications were not meant to benefit a dominant undertaking but would have to be aimed at the general interest, with particular reference to customers and consumers. In Genzyme's case there was no objective justification for the margin squeeze abuse.

Albion Water Limited & Albion Water Group Limited v Water Services Regulation Authority (Dwr Cymru/Shotton Paper)

[2006] CAT 23; [2006] CAT 36; [2008] EWCA Civ 536

Albion was appointed to supply non-potable water to Shotton Paper, a paper-making plant previously supplied by Dwr Cymru Welsh Water (DCWW). Albion planned to purchase water from a supplier and use the piping network of DCWW to transport it to Shotton Paper. DCWW's pricing policy only maintained a small difference between the price of carriage of water and the price of purchasing the water.

Albion brought a case against DCWW claiming that the latter had abused its dominant position by imposing a margin squeeze and by charging an excessive price. The claim was rejected by the Director General of Water Services, and therefore Albion brought an appeal at the CAT against the decision of the regulator.

In addition to the finding of excessive prices, the CAT also found DCWW to have adopted a margin squeeze. The efficient component pricing rule (ECPR) methodology and the approach used by the Director General of Water Services had not followed the OFT and European Commission. In particular, it was held that the margin between DCWW's retail price and the price it had imposed on Albion would not have permitted the latter, any other efficient competitor or a notional retail arm of DCWW to make any form of profit. This would have allowed DCWW to block any competition and preserve its dominance, prejudicing ultimately the end consumer. The CAT's approach to margin squeeze was also subsequently confirmed by the Court of Appeal, where emphasis was placed on the 'as-efficient-competitor' test. The key question was whether the dominant undertaking would be able to trade profitably if it had to pay the upstream price as an internal transfer price for its own downstream operation. If there was no profit then there was a potentially anti-competitive price policy requiring justification. The use of the costs by the dominant undertaking downstream activities, however, did not mean that actual displacement of the dominant undertaking's activities in the downstream market or the saving of costs associated with those activities were necessary features of the margin squeeze test per Deutsche Telekom *and* Wanadoo España.

9.5. EXCLUSIVE PURCHASING/DEALING

The category of exclusive purchasing/dealing as an abuse of a dominant position covers an array of commercial practices.

International Competition Network, *Unilateral Conduct Workbook*, Chapter 5: 'Exclusive Dealing', paras 1–4

The term 'exclusive dealing' is generally used to describe an arrangement through which an upstream seller's goods are sold to a distributor or retailer under the condition that the distributor or retailer does not sell similar competing products. The term exclusive dealing may also describe an arrangement by which a downstream purchaser requires an upstream seller not to sell its product to any competing downstream purchasers. This Chapter focuses on the first type of exclusive dealing arrangement [*the second is related to non-compete clauses*].

Exclusive dealing arrangements can take a number of forms. One possibility is a contract between the seller and buyer that requires the buyer to purchase all units of a particular product from the seller (sometimes called a 'requirements contract'). More typically, however, a reseller agrees to sell only the product sold by the seller or a downstream manufacturer agrees to use only the seller's input in goods sold downstream. The exclusivity need not be expressly stated in a formal agreement but may rather be the *de facto* result of agreements or a seller's policy not to deal with a purchaser that purchases its rivals' products.

Among the practices [. . .] under the rubric of 'exclusive dealing arrangements' are those that do not contractually require total exclusivity but have many of the same characteristics. Such arrangements include provisions that require a distributor or retailer to purchase a high percentage (rather than all) of its needs for a particular good and/or provide for limited exceptions to selling only the product of the upstream seller. For example, this may be the case with a stocking requirement or a minimum purchase requirement.

In addition, exclusive dealing may be enforced through creating direct or indirect disincentives to turn to alternative sources of supply or distribution channels, for example if discounts are made conditional on exclusivity, either explicitly or in effect.

It follows that exclusive dealing arrangements may cover situations in which the exclusivity results from a contractual clause or commitment (*de jure* exclusivity) and also situations in which buyers have strong inducements, for instance through the provision of financial or other incentives, not to purchase from alternative sources of supply even where no specific obligation not to do so exists.[204] An arrangement may also be considered as exclusive dealing

[204] As the Commission explains in its Guidance on Article 102, para 32 n 4:

> The notion of exclusive dealing also includes exclusive supply obligations or incentives with the same effect, whereby the dominant undertaking tries to foreclose its competitors by hindering them from purchasing from suppliers. The Commission considers that such input foreclosure is in principle liable to result in anti-competitive foreclosure if the exclusive supply obligation or incentive ties most of the efficient input suppliers and customers competing with the dominant undertaking are unable to find alternative efficient sources of input supply.

According to the Commission, '[c]ertain other obligations, such as stocking requirements, which appear to fall short of requiring exclusive purchasing, may in practice lead to the same effect' (ibid, para 33).

even if it does not cover the entirety of the purchases or sales of the dominant firm's business partner. The important element is the anti-competitive foreclosure that even a partial exclusivity (not covering the entirety of the purchases or sales of the dominant firm's business partner) may produce.

9.5.1. THE ECONOMICS OF EXCLUSIVE DEALING

Exclusive dealing may raise competitive concerns if its effect is to prevent a sufficient number of supplier's competitors from distributing their products to a sufficient number of customers in a cost-effective way, this resulting to a restriction of competition. This may raise rivals' costs by forcing them to utilize significantly more costly or less efficient avenues of distribution or manufacturing, it may also facilitate anti-competitive coordination among the remaining distributors, it may limit the potential market shares of new firms entering the market or deter a new entry altogether, it may constrain the output of existing rivals and limit their ability to gain market share by denying them access to critical inputs or outlets. The rivals may not be forced out of the market but through exclusive dealing a dominant undertaking may affect their ability to compete, because of the costs increases resulting from their reduced output and thus their reduced ability to benefit from economies of scale. Consumers are likely to be harmed from exclusive dealing if this enables a dominant undertaking to gain the power to raise or maintain supra-competitive prices or to face less competitive pressure to reduce its prices, in the absence of sufficient competition from other non-excluded competitors. Consequently, overall output may be reduced.

Exclusive dealing constitutes an example of horizontal foreclosure, the dominant undertaking attempting to exclude discipline or marginalize a rival at its own level in the supply chain (upstream rival) by foreclosing its access to customers (customers foreclosure).[205]

Figure 9.2 provides an example, where *A* is dominant in the upstream market and tries to foreclose access of an actual or potential upstream rival *B* to customers such as *X* and *Z* in the downstream market.[206]

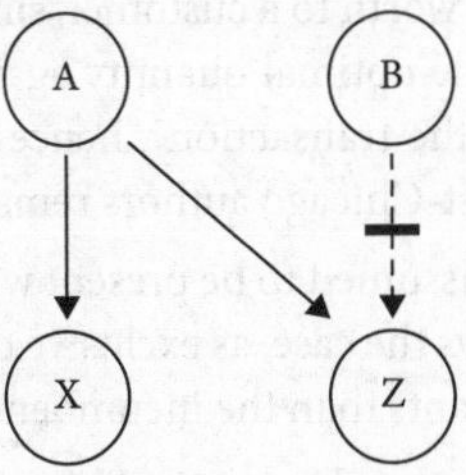

Figure 9.2. Anti-competitive foreclosure

205 Tying/bundling, predatory pricing and rebates also constitute examples of horizontal foreclosure. Refusal to deal or margin squeeze in which the dominant undertaking is attempting to exclude a downstream competitor, for instance by refusing to grant access to a bottleneck good which is either used as an input by a potentially competitive downstream industry or when access to the bottleneck is needed in order to reach final consumers (customer foreclosure) give rise to vertical foreclosure. Refusal to deal may, however, be used also as a horizontal foreclosure strategy if the bottleneck is integrated.

206 DG Comp Discussion Paper, para 70.

The Chicago School of antitrust economics has put forward some justifications for exclusive dealing. The starting point is that there is a single source of monopoly profit to be made, that is the demand from downstream customers, which correlates to their willingness to pay for the product. Hence, if the supplier wants to impose exclusivity to a retailer who does not want it, it will have to bribe the retailer by charging less than it would otherwise have been able to thus 'purchasing' the retailer's acquiescence. In view of this fact, the supplier has no incentive to offer an exclusive contract unless exclusivity is efficient. As it is explained by O'Donoghue and Padilla, 'unless properly compensated, a customer would never agree to sign a contract which stifles competition and gives the exclusive supplier the power to raise future prices at its detriment', hence, the exclusive dealing is unprofitable for the supplier unless it also has efficiency justifications.[207] What are these possible pro-competitive/efficiency justifications for exclusive dealing? First, exclusive dealing may secure retailer investment and effort, by avoiding the risk of free riding by other suppliers on the promotional assistance, machinery, training, quality control, or other complementary services provided by the supplier to the retailer. A lot of these investments are relation-specific, that is, if the business relation between the specific retailer and the supplier is terminated, the supplier will not be able to use this in order to supply other customers. Hence, by exclusive dealing the supplier ensures he has a return on his investment. Otherwise, he would have never made this investment in the first place. A long term exclusive dealing also increases the supplier's incentives to invest in order to achieve economies of scale or it may also be necessary in order to protect the value of the supplier's brand, by avoiding that retailers may free ride on the supplier's superior brand reputation in order to pass off an inferior product as the supplier's own.[208] In essence, the argument goes that exclusive dealing aligns the distributor's and manufacturer's interests, increases the distributor's investments, and hence increases their total surplus.[209]

This positive narrative on exclusive dealing was challenged by post-Chicago School theories of exclusive dealing. These theories criticized the number of (unrealistic) assumptions made by the Chicago School to arrive at the conclusion that exclusive dealing is for the most part efficient. The criticized assumptions include:[210]

(i) firms are assumed to be able to use nonlinear pricing (that is a price structure with a fixed fee upfront plus a unit price per quantity purchased), in which case 'they may extract what the product is worth to a customer, simply by offering each customer the possibility of purchasing the optimal quantity against a fixed fee, equal to the entire surplus brought about by the transaction', hence if they use exclusive dealing only when this is efficient.[211] Post-Chicago authors remark that this is not always possible.

(ii) that all affected agents are assumed to be present when the exclusive contracts are negotiated, which is not always the case, as exclusive dealing may aim to deter the future entry of more efficient entrants than the incumbent.

(iii) that a dominant firm entering such a contract has to compensate all its retailers, which is rebutted by the possible use of exclusive dealing with some retailers only in order to impede a potential entrant from achieving a minimum viable scale.

207 R O'Donoghue and J Padilla, *The Law and Economics of Article 102 TFEU* (Hart, 2013), 424–5.

208 R O'Donoghue and J Padilla, *The Law and Economics of Article 102 TFEU* (Hart, 2013), 426.

209 The seminal argument was made by H Marvel, *Exclusive Dealing* (1982) 25(1) *J L & Economics* 1.

210 The discussion draws on R O'Donoghue and J Padilla, *The Law and Economics of Article 102 TFEU* (Hart, 2013), 426–8.

211 Ibid, 426.

Post-Chicago theories have raised possibility theorems, advancing hypothesis under which exclusive dealing may be anti-competitive. Some post-Chicago economists argued that if a firm entering a market has to trade with a sufficient number of buyers in order to achieve economies of scale and be competitive, the incumbent dominant undertaking may opt to use exclusive contracts to deter efficient entry, as the 'purchase' or 'bribing' by the new entrant of the remaining buyers may not be sufficient to cover the minimum efficient scale of the entrant, thus deterring entry.[212]

Even those retailers who have not entered into exclusive dealing contracts with the incumbent supplier may refuse to distribute the excluded product in any case. This may be the case if they are concerned that rival suppliers might turn out to be commercially unsuccessful unless they reach a sufficient scale, which is essential because of either supply-side scale economies, or demand-side network effects. Under these circumstances, exclusive dealing is instrumental to generate the coordination failure among retailers, who might be better off collectively if they sponsor the entry of a rival supplier, potentially even more efficient than the incumbent one.[213]

9.5.2. THE POSITION OF THE EU COURTS

In *Hoffmann-La Roche*, the CJEU found that a dominant undertaking that had offered customers financial incentives for purchasing all or most of their annual requirements from it had abused its dominant position.[214] These exclusivity contracts were found illegal although they were concluded upon the request of the purchasers. The CJEU held that in a situation of dominance, competition is already weakened and thus any further interference to the structure of the market is likely to eliminate all competition. According to the Court, '[a]n undertaking which is in a dominant position on a market and ties purchasers—even if it does so at their request—by an obligation or promise on their part to obtain all or most of their requirements exclusively from the said undertaking abuses its dominant position within the meaning of Article [102 TFEU], whether the obligation in question is stipulated without further qualification or whether it is undertaken in consideration of the grant of a rebate'.[215] Indeed, 'the concept of an abuse [. . .] in principle includes any obligation to obtain supplies exclusively from an undertaking in a dominant position which benefits that undertaking'.[216] Subsequent case law of the General Court and the CJEU in *British Plasterboard* confirmed this restrictive approach.[217]

The *Van den Bergh Foods* case was the first one in which the General Court and the CJEU looked carefully at the individual circumstances of the exclusive dealing obligation and its potential market effects, instead of inferring directly these by the fact that a dominant undertaking entered into exclusive dealing arrangements. What is particularly interesting in this case is that the exclusive dealing arrangements in this context did not only take the form of a formal *de jure* exclusivity, as did the requirement contracts offered by Hoffmann-La Roche to

212 EB Rasmusen, JM Ramseyer, and JS Wiley, 'Naked Exclusion' (1991) 81 *American Economic Rev* 1137.

213 C Fumagalli and M Motta, 'Exclusive Dealing and Entry, when Buyers Compete' [2006] 96 *American Economic Rev* 785.

214 Case C-85/76, *Hoffmann-La Roche and Co AG v Commission* [1979] ECR 461.

215 Ibid, para 89. 216 Ibid, para 121.

217 Case T-65/89, *BPB Industries and British Gypsum Ltd v Commission* [1993] ECR II–389; Case C-310/93 P, *BPB Industries plc and British Gypsum Ltd v Commission* [1995] ECR 865.

its customers (although some of them also included some form of financial inducement via rebates), but also consisted in a *de facto* exclusivity.

Case T-65/98, *Van den Bergh Foods Ltd v Commission*
[2003] ECR II–4653

Van Den Bergh Foods, formerly HB Ice Cream Ltd ('HB') was a wholly owned subsidiary of Unilever plc and the main manufacturer of impulse ice-cream products (single-wrapped ice-creams for immediate consumption) in Ireland holding a dominant position in this market its market share exceeding 75 per cent. Van den Bergh Foods supplied retailers with freezer cabinets, in which it retained ownership, for no direct charge on the condition that the cabinets were used exclusively for the sale of HB products. Masterfoods (a subsidiary of Mars, Inc) decided to enter the Irish market and attempted to persuade some retailers to include its products in the freezers provided by HB, as a result of which HB decided to include exclusivity contracts in its distribution agreements.

This greatly affected Masterfoods whose share dropped from 42 to 20 per cent. Masterfoods decided to bring an action in the Irish High Court claiming that HB's exclusivity clause infringed Articles 101 and 102 TFEU as well as the Irish equivalents. It also complained to the European Commission, which adopted a decision in 1998 finding that the exclusivity arrangements in HB's distribution agreements infringed both Articles 101 and 102 TFEU and refused to provide an exemption under Article 101(3) TFEU.[218] *The Irish High Court nevertheless rejected Masterfoods' action and the case was appealed to the Irish Supreme Court, which sent a preliminary reference to the CJEU. The CJEU found that when considering issues already subject to a Commission's decision, national courts should not reach a judgment which conflicts with that decision.*[219] *In the meantime, HB seized the General Court with an action for annulment of the Commission's decision, the GC upholding the decision.*

According to the General Court, Article 101 applied to the exclusivity clause that was included in the distribution agreements concerning the use of the freezer cabinets provided by Unilever (then HB Ice Cream) to members of its distribution network.[220] *Article 102 TFEU applied to the practice of inducing the retailers who did not have a freezer cabinet to enter into freezer-cabinet agreements with HB, subject to a condition of exclusivity.*[221] *The latter practice could not fall within the scope of Article 101 TFEU as it was purely unilateral conduct—an invitation to participate in an agreement, which naturally pre-dates the conclusion of the agreement itself. This interpretation is supported by the explicit reference of the Court to the retailers that did not have their own freezer cabinets or cabinets from other suppliers, ie retailers that had not yet concluded a distribution agreement with HB. Both the GC and the CJEU rejected Unilever's argument that the Commission and the GC had recycled the same arguments for the purposes of applying Articles 101 and 102, the CJEU confirming that these claims involved a 'separate analysis'.*[222]

The GC examined the foreclosure effects of the de facto *exclusive dealing in the same way it did in* Delimitis *for exclusive dealing contractual clauses when applying Article 101 TFEU, thus*

[218] *Van den Bergh Foods Ltd* (Cases COMP IV/34.073, IV/34.395, and IV/35.436) Commission Decision [1998] OJ L 246/1.

[219] Case C-344/98, *Masterfoods Ltd v HB Ice Cream Ltd* [2000] ECR I–11369.

[220] Case T-65/98, *Van den Bergh Foods Ltd v Commission* [2003] ECR II–4653, para 118.

[221] Ibid, paras 159–60.

[222] Order of the Court in Case C-552/03, *Unilever Bestfoods (Ireland) Ltd v Commission* [2006] ECR I–9091, para 136.

accepting that de facto *exclusivity (which could take the form of financial inducement through rebates) is considered as harmful as de jure exclusivity.*[223]

154. It is settled case-law that very large market shares are in themselves, and save in exceptional circumstances, evidence of the existence of a dominant position. An undertaking which has a very large market share and holds it for some time, by means of the volume of production and the scale of the supply which it stands for—without holders of much smaller market shares being able to meet rapidly the demand from those who would like to break away from the undertaking which has the largest market share—is by virtue of that share in a position of strength which makes it an unavoidable trading partner and which, because of this alone, secures for it, at the very least during relatively long periods, that freedom of action which is the special feature of a dominant position [. . .]. Moreover, a dominant position is a position of economic strength enjoyed by an undertaking which enables it to prevent effective competition being maintained on the relevant market by giving it the power to behave to an appreciable extent independently of its competitors, customers and ultimately of its consumers [. . .].

155. The Court notes, first, that the contested decision defines the relevant market as the market for single wrapped items of impulse ice-cream in Ireland [. . .] and that HB does not dispute that definition. HB, whilst not challenging the Commission's assertion [. . .] that its share, in volume and in value, of the relevant market exceeds 75% and that it has retained that share over several years, submits that it does not hold a dominant position on that market. When the contested decision was adopted, HB's share of the relevant market was 89% [. . .]. It must also be pointed out that the other suppliers of impulse ice-cream present on that market, such as Mars and Nestlé, have very small market shares [. . .], despite the fact that they are major players on the neighbouring markets for confectionery and chocolate and sell those products in the same outlets as those in question in the present case. Furthermore, Mars and Nestlé have well-known brands for their products and the experience and financial capacity to enter new markets. HB therefore not only has an extremely large share of the relevant market but there is a considerable gap between its market share and those of its immediate competitors.

156. Moreover, it is clear from the documents before the Court that HB has the most extensive and most popular range of products on the relevant market, that it is the sole supplier of impulse ice-creams in approximately 40% of outlets in the relevant market, that it is part of the multinational Unilever group which has been producing and marketing ice creams for many years in all the Member States and many other countries, in which undertakings in the group are very often the major supplier in their respective market, and that the HB brand is very well-known. The Court therefore finds that the Commission correctly held that HB is an unavoidable partner for many retailers on the relevant market and that it has a dominant position on that market.

157. It is necessary, next, to ascertain whether the Commission was correct to conclude in the contested decision that HB had abused its dominant position on the relevant market. It is settled case-law that the concept of abuse is an objective concept relating to the behaviour of an undertaking in a dominant position which is such as to influence the structure of the market where, as result of the very presence of the undertaking in question, the degree of competition is weakened and which,

223 Case C-234/89, *Stergios Delimitis v Henniger Bräu* [1991] ECR I–935. See Section 10.4.4.4.1..

through recourse to methods different from those which condition normal competition in products or services on the basis of the transactions of commercial operators, has the effect of hindering the maintenance of the degree of competition still existing in the market or the growth of that competition [. . .]. It follows that Article [102 TFEU] prohibits a dominant undertaking from eliminating a competitor and from strengthening its position by recourse to means other than those based on competition on the merits. The prohibition laid down in that provision is also justified by the concern not to cause harm to consumers [. . .].

158. Consequently, although a finding that an undertaking has a dominant position is not in itself a recrimination, it means that, irrespective of the reasons for which it has such a dominant position, the undertaking concerned has a special responsibility not to allow its conduct to impair genuine undistorted competition on the common market [. . .].

159. The Court finds, as a preliminary point, that HB rightly submits that the provision of freezer cabinets on a condition of exclusivity constitutes a standard practice on the relevant market [. . .]. In the normal situation of a competitive market, those agreements are concluded in the interests of the two parties and cannot be prohibited as a matter of principle. However, those considerations, which are applicable in the normal situation of a competitive market, cannot be accepted without reservation in the case of a market on which, precisely because of the dominant position held by one of the traders, competition is already restricted. Business conduct which contributes to an improvement in production or distribution of goods and which has a beneficial effect on competition in a balanced market may restrict such competition where it is engaged in by an undertaking which has a dominant position on the relevant market. With regard to the nature of the exclusivity clause, the Court finds that the Commission rightly held in the contested decision that HB was abusing its dominant position on the relevant market by inducing retailers who, for the purpose of stocking impulse ice-cream, did not have their own freezer cabinet, or a cabinet made available by an ice-cream supplier other than HB, to accept agreements for the provision of cabinets subject to a condition of exclusivity. That infringement of Article [102 TFEU] takes the form, in this case, of an offer to supply freezer cabinets to the retailers and to maintain the cabinets free of any direct charge to the retailers.

160. The fact that an undertaking in a dominant position on a market ties de facto—even at their own request—40% of outlets in the relevant market by an exclusivity clause which in reality creates outlet exclusivity constitutes an abuse of a dominant position within the meaning of Article [102 TFEU]. The exclusivity clause has the effect of preventing the retailers concerned from selling other brands of ice cream (or of reducing the opportunity for them to do so), even though there is a demand for such brands, and of preventing competing manufacturers from gaining access to the relevant market. It follows that HB's contention [. . .] that the percentage of outlets potentially likely to be inaccessible owing to the provision of freezer cabinets does not exceed 6%, is incorrect and must be rejected.

161. Furthermore, HB's reference to the Opinion of Advocate General Jacobs in the judgment in *Bronner*, is irrelevant in the present case because, as the Commission correctly submits in its pleadings, it did not claim in the contested decision that HB's freezer cabinets were an essential facility, which is the issue examined in his Opinion, and it is not necessary for HB to transfer an asset or to conclude contracts with persons which it has not selected in complying with the contested decision.

NOTES AND QUESTIONS ON VAN DEN BERGH FOODS

1. Note that the GC did not find the freezer exclusivity as being abuse *per se* but further examined if it led to anti-competitive foreclosure, considering the effects on the market quite carefully. Compare the analysis of the GC with the analysis of the CJEU in *Delimitis*.[224]
2. (Paragraphs 155–6, 160) The GC examines both the market share of HB on the relevant market for single wrapped items of impulse ice-cream in Ireland (where HB's share exceeds 75 per cent) and the share of outlets in the relevant market for which HB is the sole supplier (40 per cent of the outlets). The GC also noted that HB was an unavoidable partner for many retailers on the relevant market and that it had a dominant position. Which of these factors was considered more significant by the GC in order to reach its decision?
3. (Paragraph 160) HB was challenging the Commission's position on market foreclosure as unsustainable, claiming that the percentage of outlets with the potential for foreclosure by reason of HB cabinet provision was no more than 6 per cent. For HB only the percentage of outlets in which the retailer wishes to change brand but is unable to do so should have been taken into account. According to HB, in all the cases in which vertical exclusivity has been held to be an abuse the Court of Justice or the General Court had expressly or implicitly applied a threshold or a *de minimis* test of market foreclosure.[225] Should the foreclosure effect be 6 per cent, the materiality threshold for an abuse alleged to consist of market foreclosure through the use of an exclusivity clause was not achieved in this case. The GC refuted these factual allegations of HB. It noted that the provision of a freezer 'without charge', the evident popularity of HB's ice cream, the breadth of its range of products and the benefits associated with the sale of them are very important considerations in the eyes of retailers when they consider whether to install an additional freezer cabinet in order to sell a second, possibly reduced, range of ice cream or, *a fortiori*, to terminate their distribution agreement with HB in order to replace HB's freezer cabinet either by their own cabinet or by one belonging to another supplier, which would, in all probability, be subject to a condition of exclusivity. In determining the percentage of outlets foreclosed by HB GC relied on the 'commercial dependence of retailers on HB' in view of the abovementioned factors.[226]
4. (Paragraph 161) Note that the GC excludes the application of the *Oscar Bronner* criteria (in particular the one on indispensability) in this case, with the explanation that the freezer cabinets were not essential facilities and that it was not necessary for HB to transfer an asset or to conclude contracts with persons which it has not selected in complying with the contested decision. Do you agree with the GC's approach? Is the *Oscar Bronner* precedent confined to the above-mentioned circumstances?
5. Note that the European Commission has adopted a series of Article 9 commitment decisions in view of the anti-competitive effects of the exclusive dealing

224 Case C-234/89, *Stergios Delimitis v Henninger Bräu AG* [1991] ECR I–935.

225 Case 85/76, *Hoffmann-La Roche v Commission* [1979] ECR 461; Case C-62/86, *AKZO v Commission* [1991] ECR I–3359; Case 322/81, *Michelin I* [1983] ECR 3461; Case T-65/89, *BPB Industries and British Gypsum v Commission* [1993] ECR II–389.

226 Case T-65/98, *Van den Bergh Foods Ltd v Commission* [2003] ECR II–4653, para 104.

arrangements. In *DeBeers/Alrosa*, the Commission objected to a five year trade agreement between De Beers, the world's biggest diamond miner controlling over 80 per cent of the world production of rough diamonds in all ranges either from its mines in southern Africa or through contracts to sell diamonds for Russia and Canada, and Alrosa, a Russian State-owned miner and the second largest at the time diamond producer in the world, providing that De Beers would buy the vast majority of Alrosa's rough diamonds destined for export from Russia and thereby continue its *de facto* exclusive distribution of Alrosa rough diamonds sold on the world market.[227] The Commission took the view in its statement of objections that this long-term relation between De Beers and Alrosa and De Beers' purchases hindered Alrosa from competing fully with De Beers and from acting as an alternative and independent supplier on the rough diamond market. De Beers gave commitments to gradually reducing its purchases and to stop purchasing Alrosa diamonds altogether. Although the commitments were found disproportional and infringing the freedom of contract by the GC, seized by Alrosa with an action for annulment, the CJEU set aside the GC judgment.[228]

6. Other important decisions involving exclusive dealing arrangements concern the energy sector and in particular long term exclusive supply commitments by vertically integrated energy suppliers.[229]

9.5.3. THE COMMISSION'S GUIDANCE ON ARTICLE 102

Communication from the Commission—Guidance on the Commission's enforcement priorities in applying Article [102 TFEU] to abusive exclusionary conduct by dominant undertakings [2009] OJ C 45/7 (footnotes omitted)

34. In order to convince customers to accept exclusive purchasing, the dominant undertaking may have to compensate them, in whole or in part, for the loss in competition resulting from the exclusivity. Where such compensation is given, it may be in the individual interest of a customer to enter into an exclusive purchasing obligation with the dominant undertaking. But it would be wrong to conclude automatically from this that all exclusive purchasing obligations, taken together, are beneficial for customers overall, including those currently not purchasing from the dominant undertaking, and the final consumers. The Commission will focus its attention on those cases where it is likely that consumers as a whole will not benefit. This will, in particular, be the case if there are many customers and the exclusive purchasing obligations of the dominant undertaking, taken together, have the effect of preventing the entry or expansion of competing undertakings.

227 *De Beers* (Case COMP/B-2/38.381) Commission Decision [2006] OJ L 205/24, available at http://ec.europa.eu/competition/antitrust/cases/dec_docs/38381/38381_1065_1.pdf.

228 Case T-170/06, *Alrosa v Commission* [2007] ECR II-2601; Case C-441/07 P, *Commission v Alrosa* [2010] ECR I-5949.

229 See eg *Distrigaz* (Case COMP/37.966) Commission Decision [2007] OJ C9/5; *RWE Gas Closure* (Case COMP/39.402) Commission Decision [2009] OJ C 133/8. For an extensive commentary, see K Talus, 'Long-term Natural Gas Contracts and Antitrust Law in the European Union and the United State' (2011) 4(3) *J World Energy L & Business* 260.

The Commission noted that in addition to the usual factors for assessing anti-competitive foreclosure (paragraph 20 of the Commission's Guidance on Article 102), that is factors for non-price-related abuses, the following factors will generally be of particular relevance in determining whether the Commission will intervene in respect of exclusive purchasing arrangements:

> 36. The capacity for exclusive purchasing obligations to result in anti-competitive foreclosure arises in particular where, without the obligations, an important competitive constraint is exercised by competitors who either are not yet present in the market at the time the obligations are concluded, or who are not in a position to compete for the full supply of the customers. Competitors may not be able to compete for an individual customer's entire demand because the dominant undertaking is an unavoidable trading partner at least for part of the demand on the market, for instance because its brand is a 'must stock item' preferred by many final consumers or because the capacity constraints on the other suppliers are such that a part of demand can only be provided for by the dominant supplier. If competitors can compete on equal terms for each individual customer's entire demand, exclusive purchasing obligations are generally unlikely to hamper effective competition unless the switching of supplier by customers is rendered difficult due to the duration of the exclusive purchasing obligation. In general, the longer the duration of the obligation, the greater the likely foreclosure effect. However, if the dominant undertaking is an unavoidable trading partner for all or most customers, even an exclusive purchasing obligation of short duration can lead to anti-competitive foreclosure. [. . .]
>
> 46. Provided that the conditions set out in Section III D [objective justifications] are fulfilled, [. . .] the Commission will consider evidence demonstrating that exclusive dealing arrangements result in advantages to particular customers if those arrangements are necessary for the dominant undertaking to make certain relationship-specific investments in order to be able to supply those customers.

9.5.4. EXCLUSIVITY PAYMENTS

In its recent *Qualcomm* decision, the Commission fined €997 million the US producer of baseband chipsets enabling smartphones and tablets to connect to cellular networks, which are used both for voice and data transmission.[230] According to the Commission, Qualcomm has paid billions of US dollars to Apple, a key customer on the condition that Apple would exclusively use Qualcomm's baseband chipsets in all its iPhones and iPads. Qualcomm is the world's largest supplier of baseband chipsets that comply with the 4G Long-Term Evolution (LTE) standard. It held a dominant position in this market in the EU, in view of its high market shares, amounting to more than 90 per cent, and the important barriers to entry, in particular R&D expenditure. Intel (the largest supplier for chipsets used in computers) is also present in this market and has tried to challenge and compete with Qualcomm for customers. Qualcomm concluded an exclusivity agreement with Apple, which was a key customer for LTE baseband chipsets, and renewed it in 2016. According to the terms of the agreement, in case Apple commercially launched a device with a chipset supplied by a rival, it should have

230 European Commission, 'Antitrust: Commission Fines Qualcomm €997 Million for Abuse of Dominant Market Position', Press Release (24 January 2018), see http://europa.eu/rapid/press-release_IP-18-421_en.htm.

had to return to Qualcomm a large part of the payments it had received in the past, thus creating a disincentive to switch suppliers and denying Qualcomm's rivals the possibility to compete effectively for Apple's significant business. At the time of writing, the text of the decision has not been made public. The Commission's press release mentions that the Commission rejected Qualcomm's price-cost test, although there is no information if this type of test is required for exclusionary payments but was wrongly performed by Qualcomm, or was not necessary to prove anti-competitive foreclosure. The issue is further examined in the subsequent section on the *Intel* case regarding loyalty rebates.

9.5.5. UK CASE LAW

National Grid PLC v The Gas and Electricity Markets Authority
[2009] CAT 14; [2010] EWCA Civ 114

National Grid held a monopoly over gas transportation and the supply of gas meters and ancillary services in the United Kingdom. It installed, and retained ownership of, gas meters in domestic properties and provided a gas metering service to the gas suppliers. The contractual relationship between the National Grid and gas suppliers established no up-front fees for the installation of meters which were to be covered instead by monthly payments. The liberalization of the market and a decline in rental payments for meters led National Grid to negotiate new contracts whereby there would be additional payments to National Grid by gas suppliers if the number of meters rented fell below a prescribed minimum. Separate contracts covered any new and replacement meters installed after the date of the legacy agreement.

The CAT and the Court of Appeal did not find any issues with OFGEM's treatment of relevant market and dominance. They also confirmed that the contractual provisions constituted an abuse—the provisions had a clear foreclosing effect in discouraging gas suppliers from moving more of their business to competing gas meter operators, slowing the liberalisation and market-share reduction of National Grid. While it was acknowledged that National Grid had incurred sunk costs for the installation of meters to gas suppliers without requiring up-front fees in exchange, this did not justify the additional charges which had been prescribed in the new contractual arrangements. In normal competition conditions, National Grid could have protected itself against the sunk costs issues through other methods. Contracts that tied a buyer to continuing to trade with a particular undertaking, even if a competitor offered a better, cheaper product affected the competitive process per Hoffman-La Roche *and* Michelin.

Arriva the Shires Ltd v London Luton Airport Operations Ltd
[2014] EWHC 64 (Ch)

Arriva had an agreement to operate a coach service between Luton Airport and London; this lasted until Luton Airport decided to award the provision of the service under an auction-style process. A different coach company was awarded the agreement and the new contract granted a seven-year exclusivity period that precluded the grant of another concession for the operation of the same service, with a small exception for another bus company (Easybus).

Arriva brought a claim in the High Court against Luton Airport on the basis that the selection procedure was unfair, and the grant of exclusivity, including the exception to Easybus, amounted to an abuse.

The trial proceeded with the assumption that Luton Airport held a dominant position, due to the 100 per cent share in the relevant market for the supply of facilities at the airport bus station. The High Court did not find an abuse in the selection process adopted by Luton Airport in choosing a new coach service provider.

With regards to the grant of exclusivity, the High Court found the case to be unusual from others like Hoffman-La Roche *and* Tomra*: normally it was the customer that was foreclosed to competitors of the supplying dominant undertaking. In the present situation, however, the dominant undertaking was limiting its own ability to supply the competitors of its downstream customer. The High Court found no requirement for a dominant undertaking to gain some commercial benefit from its conduct before that conduct could be condemned as abusive,* Aeroports de Paris v Commission*. The judge also rejected a requirement that the economic or commercial interest of the dominant undertaking had to derive from it being active itself on the downstream market; Luton Airport was gaining a significant economic benefit from the terms of the new agreement despite not being active in the operation of the coaches. The new agreement therefore gave Luton Airport a stake in the downstream market, sufficient to favour one downstream coach company over another in order to maximize its returns under the new agreement.*

The High Court found that a lengthy grant of exclusivity to a downstream provider had a distortive effect on competition where other downstream competitors could not enter the market, per Joint Selling of Media Rights to the FAPL*. In the present case, the distortive effect was compounded by three elements in the new agreement: its duration, which would cover a period of expansion of the airport's bus station, a right of first refusal to the new coach company, and the discrimination in favour of Easybus.*

On the potential of objective justifications, the judge rejected the arguments in relation to the congestion of the airport's bus stations and it was held that a coach service could be accommodated without disruption to other coach services or other risks.

9.6. CONDITIONAL/LOYALTY REBATES OR DISCOUNTS

9.6.1. THE ECONOMICS OF LOYALTY REBATES

The abuse category of 'loyalty' rebates covers practices involving 'pricing structures offering lower prices, in return for a buyer's agreed or *de facto* commitment to source a large and/or increasing share of his requirements with the discounter'.[231] One should thus distinguish loyalty rebates, which involve some degree of conditionality based on a reference to rivals,[232] the discount being conditional upon the customer receiving a certain share of sales from the Domco, and unconditional price cuts, which may be assessed under the predatory pricing abuse category or the discrimination one, should the criteria for these categories of abuse being satisfied.[233] The anti-competitive effects of loyalty rebates hinge on the existence of a non-contestable portion of the overall demand faced by rivals, in the sense that they anticipate

231 OECD, *Loyalty and Fidelity Discounts and Rebates*, DAFFE/COMP(2002)21 (4 February 2003), 19, available at http://www.oecd.org/competition/abuse/2493106.pdf.

232 FM Scott Morton, 'Contracts that Reference Rivals' (2013) *Antitrust Magazine* 27, 72.

233 R O'Donoghue and J Padilla, *The Law and Economics of Article 102 TFEU* (Hart, 2nd ed, 2013), 461.

that it would not be possible for them to entice buyers to switch more than the complementary contestable portion of demand away from the Domco, that is, even if they offered a substantially lower price.[234]

DG Comp 'Discussion Paper on the application of Article 82 of the Treaty to exclusionary abuses' (December 2005), available at http://ec.europa.eu/competition/antitrust/art82/discpaper2005.pdf

[On the distinction between conditional and unconditional rebates]

137. A basic distinction for rebates is between unconditional rebates and conditional rebates. Unconditional rebates, while granted to certain customers and not to others, are granted for every purchase of these particular customers, independently of their purchasing behaviour. For instance, a rebate that is offered only to customers that might more easily switch to foreign suppliers because they are located in the border region. Unconditional rebates differentiate the purchase price between customer groups. Conditional rebates are granted to customers to reward a certain (purchasing) behaviour of these customers. The latter type of rebates may depend on a number of aspects of the customer's behaviour, such as the amount purchased in a preceding period from the same supplier or the percentage of total requirements purchased in a preceding period from the same supplier or the supply of a certain service by the customer. These conditional rebates differentiate the purchase price for each customer depending on its behaviour. Although not necessarily so, this may also lead to a differentiation in purchase price between buyers.

The case law has also distinguished loyalty or 'loyalty-inducing' rebates, which fall under the prohibition of abuse of dominance, and quantitative rebates, which are compatible with competition law.

The fact that the rebate is conditional on the satisfaction of a specific commitment/target to purchase a certain share or a quantity of sales from the Domco, pose similar concerns than those encountered when we examined the category of exclusive dealing. Indeed, 'the ultimate objection to problematic rebate practices is that they create conditional pricing structures that may lead to *de facto* exclusive dealing. In other words, the conditions attached to the rebate may lead to the rebate operating in a manner that is equivalent to where a non-compete clause is expressly specified.'[235] Hence, the 'objectionable feature' of loyalty rebates is not the level of price as such but the condition to purchase a share of its sales or a quantity from the supplier.[236]

An alternative interpretation is that loyalty rebates can be exploitative in nature, to the extent that they induce rivals to renounce to expand their volumes of sales by pricing aggressively, given that the price that would need to be set to compensate buyers from the loss of the loyalty discount is unsustainably too low. Therefore, rivals prefer to sell only to the residual portion of demand that is left to them by setting higher prices. This in turn allows

[234] FM Scott Morton and Z Abrahamson, 'A Unifying Analytical Framework for Loyalty Rebates' (2016), available at https://ssrn.com/abstract=2833563.

[235] R O'Donoghue and J Padilla, *The Law and Economics of Article 102 TFEU* (Hart, 2nd ed, 2013), 461.

[236] Ibid, 461–2.

the Domco to set the discounted price at a high level, so that prices across the board can be higher compared to the 'but for' counterfactual without the loyalty rebates.[237]

Economists advance various pro-competitive or efficiency enhancing reasons for using loyalty rebates.[238]

Discounts may bring prices more in line with marginal costs leading to greater allocative efficiency (ie reduced 'dead-weight losses') and enhanced resource savings in, either production, or distribution, as well as dynamic efficiency since discounts may be used in order to convince buyers to try new products.[239] The claimed allocative efficiencies, however, require that the wholesale discounted price be lower than the wholesale price that would have been set in the counterfactual without the alleged practice. The claimed dynamic efficiencies require that the wholesale discount granted by the supplier to the retailer is then passed on to consumers by the latter. Neither of these two conditions is to be taken for granted. Rebates may be justified when the production involves significant fixed costs, as they may assist the undertaking in recovering more easily its fixed costs by charging a high price to consumers whose demand is inelastic (the assured base of sales), while charging a lower price (by offering a discount) to the part of the demand whose elasticity is high, thus expanding the output sold overall. This is equivalent to some form of price discrimination, leading to an increase of the Domco's profits. However, this argument rests on the assumption that retailers pass on the wholesale discount only to the elastic part of their demand, rather than charging a uniform price. As was highlighted above, economists have a positive view on price discrimination, when this leads to increase output. Lawyers may object to discrimination on ethical or other grounds.

Rebates may also provide a further mechanism to incentivize retailers and to align the suppliers' and retailers' interests, as regards the effort that needs to be made for an efficient distribution of the supplier's product. By increasing the retailers' distribution margin and reducing its share (wholesale price) in the overall profit of the vertical chain, the supplier aims to provide retailers good incentives to promote the product and expand sales. Retailers usually provide pre-sale advice, such as (local) advertising, showroom facilities, and after-sale services, such as cashiers, parking facilities, etc. From that perspective, the supplier has the choice between various incentives schemes, some involving vertical contractual restraints, others direct payments to the retailers (eg slotting allowances). Yet, these schemes require an efficient contract between the supplier and the retailer, specifying the required effort from the retailer and, eventually, enforcement costs, should the contract not be implemented. Loyalty rebate schemes constitute a much simpler and effective option to align the interests of suppliers and retailers.

As is also the case for other practices dealing with the supplier/retailer relations, loyalty rebates may reduce the adverse effects of double marginalization, a situation occurring when because of the externalities from the decentralization of the decision variables to the supplier and retailer, in the sense that each firm, when setting its mark-up, does not take into account the impact of this decision on the other firm's profit. For instance, when setting the final price, the retailer trade-offs an increase in its distribution margin against a decrease in the quantity

237 E Elhauge and AL Wickelgren, 'Robust Exclusion Through Loyalty Discounts' (2015) 43 *Int'l J Industrial Organization* 111. See also N Economides, 'Tying, Bundling, and Loyalty/Requirement Rebates' in E Elhauge (ed) *Research Handbook of the Economics of Antitrust Law* (Edward Elgar, 2012), 136.

238 The following paragraphs summarize the discussion in R O'Donoghue and J Padilla, *The Law and Economics of Article 102 TFEU* (Hart, 2nd ed, 2013), 465–8.

239 OECD, *Loyalty and Fidelity Discounts and Rebates*, DAFFE/COMP(2002)21 (4 February 2003), 26.

sold but does not take into account the reduction in the producer's profits, which decrease as the quantity sold decreases. This problem may be resolved through vertical integration of the upstream and downstream level or contractual vertical restraints (eg a fixed resale price ceiling downstream) that lead to an optimal sharing of the joint profits of suppliers and retailers. It may also be solved through non-linear pricing (eg rebates or two-part tariffs). Note that the double marginalization justification for vertical restraints works only in case there is market power at both levels of the vertical chain.

As any other conduct of single-branding (eg exclusive dealing, non-compete clauses), royalty rebates may also resolve the 'hold up' problem, which arises because of client-specific investments made by either the supplier or the buyer in order to satisfy a particular requirement of one of his customers. For instance, the supplier may not wish to invest in training the sales force of its retailers, if part of the knowledge transferred to them may be used by the retailer to promote the sales of competing products rather than its own. The investor, here the supplier, may not commit the necessary investments before being assured that the retailer will concentrate all efforts in the promotion of his own products. This may be achieved by providing retailers the right incentives for making these complementary investments.

Finally, loyalty rebates may be preferred to quantity based discounts when the supplier intends to stimulate competition among asymmetric competing buyers by allowing smaller ones to benefit from the same discount as the larger ones; whereas with a quantity based discount, subject to a common volume threshold, the smaller buyer would be disadvantaged because of the lower procurement volumes.[240]

Loyalty rebates may also produce anti-competitive effects. By anti-competitive effects we mean (i) negative effects to any of the parameters of consumer welfare, including higher prices; lower quantity, quality and innovation; where quality encompasses both vertical quality differentiation (ie, basic as well as upmarket versions) and horizontal one (ie, more variety); or (ii) negative effects to consumer choice, should a legal system elevate this decision criterion as a stand-alone driver for the kind of harm competition law focuses on.

OECD, *Loyalty and Fidelity Discounts and Rebates,* DAFFE/COMP(2002)21 (4 February 2003), 25–6

The probability that a fidelity discount will have anticompetitive tendencies essentially depends on whether, and to what degree, the discounts:

1. reduce price transparency; and/or
2. exclude actual or potential competitors, thereby facilitating anticompetitive co-ordination or creating/strengthening a dominant position.

These factors cannot be assessed without considering the exact details of the discount and the characteristics of markets they arise in.

In terms of the discounts themselves, special attention should be paid to: the degree of nonlinearity (i.e. how rapidly and smoothly do the discounts increase as a buyer sources more of his requirements with the discounter); the fixed price versus fixed percentage nature of the

240 A Heimler, 'Below-Cost Pricing and Loyalty-Inducing Discounts: Are They Restrictive and, If So, When?' (2005) 1 *Competition Policy Int'l* 149.

discount; the length of reference period; and the degree to which reference periods are synchronised or staggered across buyers.

A buyer receiving fidelity discounts is less likely to switch to a competitor the further along in a reference period he happens to be. Longer reference periods could therefore aggravate any anticompetitive effects associated with a fidelity discount. A related effect is the degree to which reference periods are non-synchronised across buyers.

In the presence of significant economies of scale in an industry, non-synchronised reference periods would augment any anticompetitive effects associated with a fidelity discount.

Achieving minimum efficient scale could be considerably delayed if new entrants, to take an extreme example, could only compete for one out of every 365 buyers on any given day of the year. They would tend to be in a better position if all reference periods began and ended on the same day for all buyers in the market.

Turning to market characteristics, the most important thing to determine is whether there is a significant asymmetry differentiating the fidelity discounter(s) from actual or potential competitors. The kind of asymmetry we have in mind is any advantage enjoyed by the fidelity discounter(s) which will grow considerably more important if competition switches from rivalry conducted continually at the margin, towards buyer by buyer contests to supply something approaching the buyer's total requirements. Where there is such an asymmetry, fidelity discounts are likely to restrict actual or potential competitors beyond what they are already because of the advantage possessed by fidelity discounter. Whether such harm will translate into harm to competition depends on things like: the initial market power of the firm or firms introducing fidelity discounts; the degree to which fidelity discounts are widespread in the market; and the existence and importance of economies of scale, network effects, and buyer switching costs. It also requires considering any procompetitive effects of fidelity discounts.

Although economists accept that different forms of conditional rebates may produce different effects, they emphasize that relying only on the form of rebates may produce misleading results.

G Federico, 'The Antitrust Treatment of Loyalty Discounts in Europe: Towards a More Economic Approach' (2011) 2 *J European Competition L & Practice* 277, 278.

The insight that a given conduct can have a significant impact on its effects in the market place is correct. Economic [. . .] theory suggests that discounts that are both individualized and retrospective can give rise to strong incentives for buyers to procure from a dominant seller. They can also make it cheaper for the dominant firm to obtain loyalty from buyers, by targeting the marginal purchasing decisions of each customer.

However, the form of a given [. . .] structure [form of rebate] is typically not sufficient to conclude that it is likely to lead to anticompetitive effects. A coherent economic evaluation of the likely effects of a loyalty discount scheme should contain two additional elements: (i) economic evidence that efficient rivals to the dominant firm are not able to match the discounts offered to buyers, and (ii) a coherent theory of how the exclusion of rivals can result in consumer harm (even if actual adverse effects on consumers might be difficult to identify or have not materialized yet.

Conditional rebates may take various forms, different types of rebates having different effects and requiring a different type of analysis.

As we explained above, the core of the economic story on the anti-competitive effects of loyalty rebates relies on the existence of actual or likely welfare effects, in the form of reduced efficiency (as efficient rivals being excluded or marginalized from the market) or some form of consumer harm (eg higher prices, lower quantity and quality and less innovation). For instance, the exclusion of actual or potential competitors should not be sufficient as such, to lead to the finding of an abuse, but it needs to be connected to an economic narrative, for example, facilitating anti-competitive coordination (coordinated effect) or creating/strengthening a dominant position (unilateral effect).

However, requiring that loyalty rebates produce actual or likely anti-competitive effects may also take different forms, according to the emphasis put on efficiency or the interests of final consumers and the theory of harm that is selected. Economists diverge as to which theory of harm, predation, or anti-competitive foreclosure through leveraging, should guide the competition law assessment of loyalty rebates.

Giulio Federico, 'The Antitrust Treatment of Loyalty Discounts in Europe: Towards a More Economic Approach' (2011) 2 *J European Competition L & Practice* 277, 281.

Predation is in many ways a natural candidate theory of harm for loyalty discounts. A predatory theory of harm posits that a dominant firm prices below cost in the short-run in order to induce the exit or marginalization of a rival competitor. According to this theory the resulting harm to competitors allows the dominant firm to raise prices in the future, thus also injuring consumers (assuming the presence of barriers to reentry or to expansion by rival firms once prices go up). This theory of harm is dynamic, in the sense that in the short-run consumers are better off and the dominant firm is worse off (ie it incurs a profit sacrifice), but in the medium-run the converse is the case. The conditions identified in the economic literature for a predatory theory [. . .] include the presence of uncertainty on the costs of the dominant firm (which can induce a firm to signal the existence of low costs through low prices); the possibility for the predator to establish a reputation for aggressive behaviour (which may benefit a dominant operator across multiple markets); and financing constraints on the prey.

A retroactive rebate can be interpreted as the application of predatory pricing 'in disguise'. That is, the retroactive structure hides the existence of very low prices on contestable volumes by the application of the discount on all of the volumes sold by the dominant firm (including non-contestable or infra-marginal volumes). In reality, however, if the dominant firm truly has some non-contestable sales, it faces no incentives to discount these volumes below the monopoly price. The loyalty rebate can therefore be correctly reinterpreted as a two-part pricing structure: a monopoly price on non-contestable sales; and a potentially much lower effective price on the contestable sales. The latter is computed by applying the entire retroactive discount only on the contestable units. [. . .] If this effective price is below cost, then it can be seen as predatory and it may result in consumer harm in the future.

The predation theory of harm supposes some form of price–cost test that would identify if the 'effective price' is below cost, in which case it might be considered as entailing a sacrifice, the first step in a predatory strategy claim, and, according to the specific circumstances of the case, amount to an abuse of a dominant position. A further characteristic of the predation theory of harm is that consumer detriment occurs in the long term and derives from the exclusion of equally efficient actual or potential competitors and a less intensive level of competition in this market. In the short term predation may lead to lower prices for consumers, which is a positive thing, of course if the predatory strategy ultimately fails! By insisting, however, on the long term nature of the anti-competitive effects, predation theory undermines to a certain degree the strength of the anti-competitive story advanced by the claimant, as long term effects are usually discounted and are subject to considerable uncertainty. The application of the predation theory of harm to loyalty rebates may lead to a risk of false negatives.

The leveraging theory of anti-competitive foreclosure suggests that anti-competitive effects may arise even without a profit sacrifice, the loyalty rebate being leveraged by the dominant company from its non-contestable portion or 'assured base' (monopoly) into the contestable portion (competition) allowing it to exclude rivals from the market, even if its overall average price is higher than that of its rivals. This can be especially the case where the rival supplier is forced to set high prices because foreclosure prevents it from lowering its costs by expanding output. That is, the exclusionary aim of loyalty rebates leads to exploitative effects, whereby the foreclosed rival is not utterly excluded, but merely marginalized and forced to set high prices that facilitate the Domco to impose high prices in turn.[241]

The crucial characteristic of the anti-competitive foreclosure through leveraging theory of harm is that it acknowledges the *short* and *long* term effects of loyalty rebates. By foreclosing the contestable share of the market, the Domco reduces the opportunity of its customers to benefit from whatever degree of competition is possible on the contestable part of the market and limits consumer choice. There are different variants of the leveraging theory of harm:[242] (i) rebates may be considered as a form of obtaining *de facto* exclusive purchasing from a final buyer (see our comments above); (ii) rebates may be used in order to 'bribe' intermediaries, such as wholesalers, with the aim to provide them incentives to influence the choice of their customers to the benefit of the Domco's products; (iii) rebates may be perceived as bundled discounts between a monopoly product (non-contestable share of the market) and a competitive product (contestable share of the market), which may lead to the exclusion of a rival from the competitive product without a loss of profit for the dominant firm. According to G Federico, '[c]onsumer harm only follows if the dominant firm can threaten to increase the standalone price of the non-contestable good above the monopoly level', which 'requires the dominant firm to be able to credibly commit to a high standalone price' and 'assumes that this commitment mechanism cannot be implemented independently of the bundled offer'.[243] This last theory may be relevant for multiproduct rebates (or bundled rebates), yet it may also apply in the context of single-product rebates. Leverage can be defensive in nature, whereby the Domco pre-empts the rival supplier from gradually establishing its brand as a credible alternative, thus ultimately growing the contestable share of demand.

In none of these theories of consumer harm it is required to show a 'sacrifice', or even to use a price–cost test. Contrary to predation theory, the leveraging theory may also catch practices that lead to the exclusion of less efficient competitors than the Domco, if this has the effect to reduce the competitive constraints on the Domco.

One may of course attempt to find a compromise between the two theories: for instance, focus on both short-term and long-term effects by applying the theory of anti-competitive foreclosure through leveraging, but also apply a price–cost test with the aim to identify if

241 E Elhauge, 'How Loyalty Discounts Can Perversely Discourage Discounting' (2009) 5 *J Competition L & Economics* 189.

242 G Federico, 'The Antitrust Treatment of Loyalty Discounts in Europe: Towards a More Economic Approach' (2011) 2 *J European Competition L & Practice* 277, 282–3.

243 Ibid, 283.

the excluded rivals are less efficient than the Domco, limiting the scope of competition law intervention to foreclosure practices against equally efficient competitors. The long-term effects can also result from the fact that the marginalized rival has weaker incentives to keep on investing in future product improvements unless there is a reasonable expectation regarding the ability to expand beyond the residual share of demand beyond the loyalty threshold. Therefore, over time the level of quality of the rival firm might worsen, thus entrenching the Domco's position. Arguably, for this long-term effect to arise there is no need for the Domco to incur a profit sacrifice.

In any case, those in favour of a more economic approach stress the importance of a separate analysis of the economic (welfare) effects of the practice prior to its qualification to an abuse of a dominant position.

Economic evidence may, nevertheless, also be relevant when examining the effect of the condition of purchasing a certain share or a quantity of sales from the Domco, inherent in loyalty rebates, on the incentives of customers to switch to competing suppliers, the so-called 'suction effect'. This suction effect should be distinguished from the welfare effects discussed above, as it constitutes a metric of the strength of the conditionality or exclusivity engendered by the loyalty rebate. Hence, it can be relevant, even if one does not focus on the economic/welfare effects of loyalty rebates and the existence or likelihood of consumer harm, but focuses instead on the loyalty-inducing nature of the rebate, as is currently the case in the case law of EU Courts (see our analysis to follow). Loyalty being something that cannot be observed or measured, except after the fact, and in view of the prospective nature of the assessment, as competition authorities do not only focus on past effects but also on likely effects in the future, the suction test aims to provide some proxy and seemingly objective measure of the loyalty-inducing effect of rebates. It is rational choice-based as it assumes that undertakings will only aim to maximize their short and long term profits, which as regards customers is to stick, when passing orders, with the cheapest option they dispose, and consequently any behaviour deviating from this rational choice model would be ignored. The suction test involves four stages:

(i) Determining the size of the contestable market and of the relevant range

That would first involve assessing on what proportion the sales or products of the Domco are necessary, that is, the minimum proportion of its products that retailers must have, the dominant undertaking being an 'unavoidable partner'. This will also require some analysis, on the supply side, of the ability of rivals to respond to consumer demand and the consideration of the eventual capacity constraints they may face. From the demand side, one might want to examine the existence of high switching costs with regard to some proportion of the demand.

The consideration of the relevant time period on which customers base their decision to switch may also be a key factor in the analysis and may make a difference. If the time frame is long, then a larger proportion of the demand is considered contestable than if a short time frame is selected.

Determining the contestable portion of the demand constitutes a difficult exercise that is highly dependent on the theory of harm, case-specific information and the availability of data. As is noted in the Commission Guidance Article 102, the relevant range depends on the specific facts of each case and the form of the specific rebate practices:

> For incremental rebates, the relevant range is normally the incremental purchases that are being considered. For retroactive rebates, it will generally be relevant to assess in the specific market context how much of a customer's purchase requirements can realistically be switched

> to a competitor (the 'contestable share' or 'contestable portion'). If it is likely that customers would be willing and able to switch large amounts of demand to a (potential) competitor relatively quickly, the relevant range is likely to be relatively large. If, on the other hand, it is likely that customers would only be willing or able to switch small amounts incrementally, then the relevant range will be relatively small. For existing competitors their capacity to expand sales to customers and the fluctuations in those sales over time may also provide an indication of the relevant range. For potential competitors, an assessment of the scale at which a new entrant would realistically be able to enter may be undertaken, where possible. It may be possible to take the historical growth pattern of new entrants in the same or in similar markets as an indication of a realistic market share of a new entrant.[244]

The *Intel* case offers some interesting insights on the complexity of the analysis required.[245]

(ii) Calculating the effective price over the contestable proportion of the market.

This step examines what would be the average price per unit that the buyer pays over the contestable range of the market, also called effective price. This is determined by the following formula:

Effective price = (Payment of incremental sales in the contestable market minus
Rebate the customer received on its assured base) divided
by quantity provided over the contestable market.

According to the Commission's Enforcement Priorities Guidance on Article 102,

> [t]he Commission will estimate what price a competitor would have to offer in order to compensate the customer for the loss of the conditional rebate if the latter would switch part of its demand ('the relevant range') away from the dominant undertaking. The effective price that the competitor will have to match is not the average price of the dominant undertaking, but the normal (list) price less the rebate the customer loses by switching, calculated over the relevant range of sales and in the relevant period of time. The Commission will take into account the margin of error that may be caused by the uncertainties inherent in this kind of analysis.[246]

The effective price may indicate the level of compensation the competitor will need to provide to customers to convince them to switch, and thence the cost of loyalty to the competitor.

(iii) Calculating the effective cost of sales over the contestable proportion of the market.

This involves the choice of cost that enables (as efficient as) rivals to stay in the market. The Commission's Guidance on Article 102 advocates calculating both the AAC and LRAIC.[247] This step does not concern the suction effect as such, but the possible effects of the condition on the exclusion of equally efficient competitors, and thus on efficiency (welfare effects). It is

244 Commission Guidance on Article 102, para 42. 245 See Section 9.6.4.

246 Commission Guidance on Article 102, para 41.

247 The LRAIC benchmark is to be preferred when competition is dynamic in nature, in the sense that rivals must continuously invest to improve their product offerings (as in R&D intensive industries). Under these circumstances, even if the effective price is above the AAC related to the current generation of products, unless the rival has a reasonable expectation to be able to recover the fixed costs needed to develop the next generation of products. See FM Scott Morton and Z Abrahamson, 'A Unifying Analytical Framework for Loyalty Rebates' (2016), available at https://ssrn.com/abstract=2833563.

based on the assumption that avoiding the exclusion of less efficient rivals than the Domco from the market should not be a concern under EU competition law.

(iv) Comparing the effective price with the effective cost of sales

This step examines the competitive disadvantage the competitors suffer in the contestable portion of the market, as measured by the effective price they would need to compete with in the contestable portion of the market, and of their 'worthiness', in being protected from exclusion, through enforcement of competition law. This step (as well as the previous one) does not concern the suction effect as such, but the possible effects of the condition on the exclusion of equally efficient competitors, and thus on efficiency (welfare effects). It is based on the assumption that avoiding the exclusion of less efficient rivals than the Domco from the market should not be a concern under EU competition law.

For this reason, the suction-effect test may be criticized for not taking into account the emphasis put by EU competition law on the competitive process, rather than on outcomes or the attainment of an equilibrium that is better than the one achieved prior to the rebate. The suction effect is also vulnerable to consumer preferences: the more heterogeneous consumer preferences are, the less likely suction effect would lead to an effective foreclosure.

If one takes a different approach and values the competitive constraint that even less efficient rivals may impose to Domcos, then the focus should be on foreclosure and the relevant question should be how much customer foreclosure is necessary to achieve entrant foreclosure. This may be set in the form of a presumption that a certain threshold of customer foreclosure (eg 40 per cent of customers) constitutes anti-competitive foreclosure, or would require a more elaborate analysis *in concreto*. Another possibility would be to focus on the capacity of competitors to impose a competitive constraint to the Domco medium to long term, even if they are less efficient now, in view of technological or other capabilities they dispose. The role of the suction effect if such an approach is chosen will be limited.

Fiona Scott Morton and Zachary Abrahamson propose an amended version of the test that does not take into consideration the cost structure of an as-efficient competitor, but merely measure the discount that a rival would have to offer over its current volume of sales in order to compensate buyers for the discount that would be lost if they no longer qualified for the Domco's loyalty rebate because they bought a larger quantity from the rival. The label this yardstick the 'effective entrant burden'.[248]

Measuring the suction-effect test is not the only tool available for determining the loyalty-inducing character of rebates. An alternative option would be to rely on the form/nature of the rebates, some of which present characteristics which, theoretically (at a level of abstraction), may more easily induce loyalty from the customers. The literature distinguishes four different types of rebates.

R O'Donoghue and J Padilla, *The Law and Economics of Article 102 TFEU*
(Hart, 2nd ed, 2013), 472

The first is rebates linked to an express or *de facto* exclusive dealing requirement, i.e. where the rebate is conditional upon the customer sourcing all or most of its requirements from the dominant firm. Such rebates have obviously strong parallels with outright non-compete

[248] FM Scott Morton and Z Abrahamson, 'A Unifying Analytical Framework for Loyalty Rebates' (2016), available at https://ssrn.com/abstract=2833563.

or single-branding obligations [. . .]. Indeed, non-compete, clauses and rebates conditioned upon exclusivity will often be applied in parallel [. . .].

The second category is where the rebate is linked to an individualised volume target usually expressed to cover a period of time representing multiple different purchases, whether monthly, quarterly, or annually. Under such schemes, a dominant firm offers customers meeting a quantity or other threshold (e.g. percentage growth in the dominant firm's sales relative to a past period) a rebate that applies not only on the additional units above the particular threshold, but also to all past sales below the threshold. Usually, there will be a series of thresholds, with each threshold containing an all-unit discount. And typically the period in which the all-unit discount applies is longer than normal purchase frequencies in the market concerned.

A third category is 'incremental rebates'. This is similar to the second category except that the rebate applies only to the additional units purchased above a given threshold (expenditure or quantity). In contrast to an all-unit, or retroactive, discount, the rebate is applied 'per tranche' e.g. a 1% rebate for units 1–10; 1.1% for units 11–20; 1.2% for units 21–30 and so on.

The final category is standardised all-unit discounts. These are the same as the second scheme, but, crucially, are not tailored to individual customer's needs or growth, but apply generally to all customers. [. . .] Again, it bears emphasis that the above categories are not necessarily hard and fast, and that their effects can obviously vary depending on the circumstances.

The above typology of rebates classifies rebates according to the degree of their resemblance to *de facto* exclusive dealing producing a single branding effect. The first category of rebates represents one pole of the *continuum*, where the resemblance to *de facto* exclusivity is the most striking, standardized discounts representing the opposite pole, where the exclusivity resemblance seems the weakest. Although the idea of building a typology around the criterion of the resemblance to *de facto* exclusivity seems, at first sight arbitrary, it may be justified by the various degrees of suction each of these forms of rebate generates, as it is demonstrated below.

Alternatively, one may distinguish two families of discounts, individualized and standardized, each of them including two sub-categories of all-unit (retroactive) discounts or incremental discounts,[249] the distinguishing criterion this time being the influence exercised by the Domco on the choice architecture of its customers. The effects of each may be different, as is described below.

N Economides, 'Tying, Bundling, and Loyalty/Requirement Rebates' in E Elhauge (ed) *Research Handbook on the Economics of Antitrust Law* (Edward Elgar, 2012), 121, 132–3.

We should be much more concerned about individualized loyalty/requirement discounts than about standardized discounts. Individualized discounts can be tailored to exclude rivals. If the same discount is available to all buyers who buy the same quantity (or combinations of quantities of A and B), a quantity-based price discount will leave some consumer surplus with buyers when buyers vary in their demand for the product(s). But an individualized loyalty requirement pricing scheme with a condition based on the percentage sales by the monopolist of the needs of a buyer can be tailored to extract more surplus for the monopolist. A loyalty/requirement program can be written so that the discount will apply to different buyers according to the percentage of their purchases from the dominant firm, and therefore it can

[249] N Economides, 'Tying, Bundling, and Loyalty/Requirement Rebates' in E Elhauge (ed) *Research Handbook on the Economics of Antitrust Law* (Edward Elgar, 2012), 121.

affect different units for each buyer. For example, a discount based on a 90% requirement/loyalty program affects different units when applied to a buyer of 100 units than when applied to a buyer of 1000 units. Of course, pricing that depends on an individual buyer's demand and gives the same discount to one buyer for say unit number 100 while to another buyer for unit 1000 is very hard to justify on efficiency considerations. Finally, a volume discount will tend to be less restrictive since it will not require that fewer purchases be made from the rival(s) and leaves open the possibility for the buyer to buy from the rival(s) at competitive prices. [. . .]

One needs also to be more concerned with retroactive (all-unit) discounts, rather than with incremental discounts, as the following example shows. Retroactive rebates can lead to effective prices below the rebated price level, thus generating a suction effect.

Numerical example: Incremental versus retroactive rebates

Under retroactive rebate schemes customers obtain a discount on all the quantities purchased if a certain level of purchases is met (ie, a volume threshold). Consider a retroactive rebate scheme under which a seller offers a 5 per cent rebate on a unit price of €1 if quantity purchased is 1000 units or greater. Under this scheme, expenditure falls from €999 to €950 as demand increases from 999 to 1000 units (ie, average unit price of €0.95). Therefore, the retroactive nature of the rebate means that the incremental price is negative when the quantity purchased moves above the threshold at which the rebate kicks in.

Now let's assume that the non-contestable share of demand is 750 units. If the customer had sourced only this share from the Domco, the corresponding revenue would have been 750. This entails that the effective unit price for the contestable share (ie, up to 1000 units) under the retroactive rebate scheme is 0.8 = (950–750) ÷ 250. That is, the difference between the average unit price paid under the Domco's scheme and the effective price represent the compensation for the lost discount over the non-contestable share of demand: (0.95–0.8) × = (1–0.95) × 750.

This is equivalent to an incremental rebate scheme with a unit price of 1 up to 750 units and a discounted unit price of 0.8 for volumes above 750 units. If the unit cost of production is 0.85 per unit, the discounted price under the incremental rebate scheme would fail a predatory price-cost test, even though the average unit price under retroactive rebate scheme is 0.95, that is, well above unit costs with a profit mark-up of around 10 per cent.

The Domco will set the thresholds differently if the discount is incremental or retroactive (all-unit). For incremental rebates the threshold is set at the point at which the demand for the Domco's product becomes more elastic (for the part of the volume that is more contestable), while for retroactive rebates the threshold is set at the volume the firm actually wants to sell.

The typology of rebates in Table 9.2 may also indicate the different degrees of intrusion that each 'category' or rebate involved in the choice architecture on which customers/consumers ground their decisions. Its underlying idea is that consumers should be left free to exercise their preferences and make choices without any interference from the Domcos, whatever form this might take: contractual obligation, incentive etc. Domcos may seek to influence consumer choice by establishing a specific choice architecture favouring their products. Hence, the customers' choice to continue purchasing the Domco's products, will not represent their real preferences as to the correspondence of the characteristics of the specific product (and its price) and their wants but will be the by-product of an elaborate choice architecture imposing a penalty to those customers that are not staying 'loyal' to the Domco (or an incentive to purchase the Domco's product if one views the other side of the coin).

Table 9.2. Type of loyalty/requirement discounts.

Qualifier/Requirement	To Which Units the Discount Applies	
	Discount on Incremental Units	**Discount on All Units**
Standardized Quantity Discounts	Not a concern if after-discount price is above unit cost. Concern on the effects on rivals if after-discount price is below unit cost.	Concern if after-discount prices are below unit cost for some users.
Individualized Buyer-Specific Share or Buyer-Specific Quantity Discounts	May be a concern if tailored to exclude rivals.	Major concern since this type of discount is typically aimed at excluding rivals.

Source: N Economides, 'Tying, Bundling, and Loyalty/Requirement Rebates' in E Elhauge (ed) *Research Handbook on the Economics of Antitrust Law* (Edward Elgar, 2012), 121–43.

This can be especially the case if the Domco's customers were competing with each other and where the discounted product is considered 'must have' by final consumers; that is, the price on offer for the Domco's product is taken into consideration by final consumers as a reference price in order to infer the overall level of convenience of the Domco's customers. Under these circumstances, peer pressure among Domco's customers means that unilaterally breaking away from the common course of conduct—where everyone stays loyal to the Domco—is risky.

Hence, another possibility is to establish different presumptions and decision procedures for the various categories of rebate. For instance, the characterization of a discount as a quantity rebate may give rise to a negative presumption that this is not an abuse of a dominant position. In contrast, a rebate of the first category (conditional rebate linked to exclusive or near-exclusive dealing) will give rise to a positive, although rebuttable, presumption of an abuse. Intermediary forms of rebates may be subject to some form of structured balancing analysis, building on rebuttable presumptions or, at least, inferences that certain 'categories' of rebates lead to specific anti-competitive effects.

In the following sections, we will examine the case law of the EU Courts and the decisional practice of the European Commission.

9.6.2. THE EMERGENCE OF THE EU RULE AGAINST LOYALTY REBATES

In *Suiker Unie*, the CJEU distinguished between true quantity rebates and loyalty rebates, only the latter being a concern for Article 102 TFEU purposes:

> [. . .] the rebate at issue is not to be treated as a quantity rebate exclusively linked with the volume of purchases from the producer concerned but has rightly been classified by the Commission as a 'loyalty' rebate designed, through the grant of a financial advantage, to prevent customers obtaining their supplies from competing producers.[250]

250 Cases C-40/73, *Coöperatieve Vereniging 'Suiker Unie' UA and Others v Commission* [1975] ECR 1663, para 518.

9.6.2.1. Rebates linked to an express or *de facto* exclusive dealing requirement: *Hoffmann-La Roche v Commission*

A similar approach was followed in *Hoffmann-La Roche v Commission*.[251]

Case C-85/76, *Hoffmann-La Roche v Commission*
[1979] ECR 461

Roche, the leading global producer of multiple vitamins, was found to have a dominant position in each of several vitamins (eg going from 47 per cent in vitamin A to 95 per cent of the market, for vitamin B6). Roche also had a technological lead over its competitors because of its pioneering of the synthesis of various vitamins and the existence of a very extensive and highly specialized sales network. Roche had contracted with twenty-two large purchasers, including Merck and Unilever, for the sale of vitamins to them, these purchasers undertaking to obtain all or most of their requirements of vitamins or certain vitamins exclusively from Roche (exclusive purchase contracts) or Roche giving them a strong incentive to do so by including a promise of a discount (conditional rebates). These rebates became effective to all past purchases when the buyer passed certain thresholds representing portions of the requirements of the buyer. The rebates varied in general between 1 per cent and 5 per cent. However, Roche had also entered into several contracts with large purchasers tailored to the parties' needs. Merck agreed to absorb Roche's additional capacity of vitamin B6 and Roche agreed to give Merck a 20 per cent discount. Merck agreed not to resell the vitamins purchased at this discount. This fidelity rebate, unlike quantity rebates exclusively linked with the volume of purchases from the producer concerned, was designed through the grant of a financial advantage to prevent customers from obtaining their supplies from competing producers. The rebates applied cumulatively to the purchase of more than one kind of vitamin (bundled rebates). Roche also offered its customers the so-called English clauses: if a customer received a better offer from a competitor and Roche refused to lower its price to meet the better offer, the customer was free to obtain supplies from the competitor without losing the benefit of the rebate. The better terms had to be offered by another competitor operating in Europe and on the same scale as Roche, and the offer had to be comparable. A number of internal documents confirmed the main features of the 'fidelity system' implemented by Roche and the benefits which it derived therefrom.

The Commission found that these practices constituted an abuse of a dominant position because they limited markets distorting competition between producers by depriving customers of the undertaking in a dominant position of the opportunity to choose their sources of supply (infringing Article 102(d) and (b)) and, on the other hand, because their effect was to apply dissimilar conditions to equivalent transactions with other trading partners, thereby placing them at a competitive disadvantage, in that Roche offered two purchasers two different prices for an identical quantity of the same product depending on whether these two buyers agree or not to forego obtaining their supplies from Roche's competitors (infringing Article 102(c)). The Commission's decision was confirmed by the CJEU.

Exclusive purchase contracts and conditional rebates

89. An undertaking which is in a dominant position on a market and ties purchasers—even if it does so at their request—by an obligation or promise on their part to obtain all or most of their requirements exclusively from the said undertaking abuses its

[251] Case C-85/76, *Hoffmann-La Roche v Commission* [1979] ECR 461.

dominant position within the meaning of Article [102 TFEU], whether the obligation in question is stipulated without further qualification or whether it is undertaken in consideration of the grant of a rebate.

The same applies if the said undertaking, without tying the purchasers by a formal obligation, applies, either under the terms of agreements concluded with these purchasers or unilaterally, a system of fidelity rebates, that is to say discounts conditional on the customer's obtaining all or most of its requirements—whether the quantity of its purchases be large or small—from the undertaking in a dominant position.

90. Obligations of this kind to obtain supplies exclusively from a particular undertaking, whether or not they are in consideration of rebates or of the granting of fidelity rebates intended to give the purchaser an incentive to obtain his supplies exclusively from the undertaking in a dominant position, are incompatible with the objective of undistorted competition within the Common Market, because—unless there are exceptional circumstances which may make an agreement between undertakings in the context of [Article 101(3)] of that article, permissible—they are not based on an economic transaction which justifies this burden or benefit but are designed to deprive the purchaser of or restrict his possible choices of sources of supply and to deny other producers access to the market.

The fidelity rebate, unlike quantity rebates exclusively linked with the volume of purchases from the producer concerned, is designed through the grant of a financial advantage to prevent customers from obtaining their supplies from competing producers.

Furthermore the effect of fidelity rebates is to apply dissimilar conditions to equivalent transactions with other trading parties in that two purchasers pay a different price for the same quantity of the same product depending on whether they obtain their supplies exclusively from the undertaking in a dominant position or have several sources of supply.

Finally these practices by an undertaking in a dominant position and especially on an expanding market tend to consolidate this position by means of a form of competition which is not based on the transactions effected and is therefore distorted. [. . .]

The English clause

102. All the contracts in question except five (the Animedica International, Guyomarc'h, Merck B6, Protector and Upjohn contracts) contain a clause, called the English clause, under which the customer, if he obtains from competitors offers at prices which are more favourable than those under the contracts at issue may ask Roche to adjust its prices to the said offers; if Roche does not comply with this request, the customer, in derogation from his undertaking to obtain his requirements exclusively from Roche, is entitled to get his supplies from the said competitor without for that reason losing the benefit of the fidelity rebates provided for in the contracts in respect of the other purchases already effected or still to be effected by him from Roche.

103. In the applicant's view this clause destroys the restrictive effect on competition both of the exclusivity agreements and of the fidelity rebates. In particular in the case of those contracts which do not contain an express undertaking by the purchaser to obtain his requirements exclusively from Roche the English clause eliminates 'the attractive effect' of the rebates at issue since the customer does not have to choose between acceptance of Roche's less attractive offers or losing the benefit of the fidelity rebates on all purchases which he has already effected from Roche.

104. There is no doubt whatever that this clause makes it possible to remedy some of the unfair consequences which undertakings by purchasers to obtain their requirements exclusively

from Roche or the provision for fidelity rebates on all purchases accepted for relatively long periods, might have in so far as those purchasers are concerned. Nevertheless it is necessary to point out that the purchaser's opportunities for exploiting competition for his own benefit are more restricted than appears at first sight. [. . .]

106. Furthermore the English clause does not remove the discrimination resulting from the fidelity rebates between purchasers in similar circumstances depending on whether or not they reserve their freedom to choose their suppliers.

107. It is particularly necessary to stress that, even in the most favourable circumstances, the English clause does not in fact remedy to a great extent the distortion of competition caused by the clauses obliging purchasers to obtain their requirements exclusively from Roche and by the fidelity rebates on a market where an undertaking in a dominant position is operating and where for this reason the structure of competition has already been weakened.

In fact the English clause under which Roche's customers are obliged to inform it of more favourable offers made by competitors together with the particulars above mentioned—so that it will be easy for Roche to identify the competitor—owing to its very nature, places at the disposal of the applicant information about market conditions and also about the alternatives open to, and the actions of, its competitors which is of great value for the carrying out of its market strategy.

The fact that an undertaking in a dominant position requires its customers or obtains their agreement under contract to notify it of its competitor's offers, whilst the said customers may have an obvious commercial interest in not disclosing them, is of such a kind as to aggravate the exploitation of the dominant position in an abusive way. Finally by virtue of the machinery of the English clause it is for Roche itself to decide whether, by adjusting its prices or not, it will permit competition.

108. It is able in this way, owing to the information which its own customers supply, to vary its market strategy in so far as it affects them and its competitors.

It follows from all these factors that the Commission's view that the English clauses incorporated in the contracts at issue were not of such a kind as to take them out of the category of abuse of a dominant position has been arrived at by means of a proper construction and application of Article [102 TFEU].

NOTES AND QUESTIONS ON HOFFMAN-LA ROCHE

1. (Paragraphs 89–90) How do exclusive purchasing obligations restrict or distort competition? How do fidelity rebates do so? How do progressive discounts? In what circumstances?
2. Could competitors operate similar rebate schemes? Would that make a difference? Could those supplying a smaller range of vitamins buy in others to be in a position to supply the full range?
3. Are quantity discounts necessarily cost justified? Do they foreclose as much as a fidelity-rebate system?
4. Is the discrimination mentioned in paragraph 90, third sentence, the kind of discrimination exemplified in Article 102? Is it discriminatory to charge lower prices to those who take a large part of their requirements from Roche even if their orders are no larger in absolute terms? Are the transactions equivalent, and do they harm competition downstream?
5. (Paragraph 90) Should the Court distinguish sharply between loyalty and quantity discounts? Should progressive quantity discounts be found abusive unless roughly justified by cost savings?

6. (Paragraph 91) 'Competition in products or services on the basis of the transactions of commercial operators' is a poor translation from the Judgment, which was originally written in German, meaning 'competition on the merits' or 'on the basis of performance'.
7. (Paragraphs 102–8) What is an English clause? In what way is it competitive? In what way is it anti-competitive? Consider agreements between competitors to exchange information.[252]
8. Note that the CJEU made no distinction between the exclusive dealing obligation and the conditional rebates system included in the contracts between Roche and its customers, noting the following: 'it must be borne in mind that, even if, as Roche submits, the purchaser's non-compliance with his undertaking to obtain his requirements exclusively from Roche did not make him liable to be sued for breach of contract but only caused him to lose the benefit of the promised rebates, such contracts nevertheless contain a sufficient incentive to reserve to Roche the sole right to supply the purchaser for them to be, for this reason alone, an abuse of a dominant position'.[253]
9. Subsequent case law of the CJEU applied and extended the *Hoffman-La Roche* rule against conditional rebates,[254] in particular in presence of internal documents demonstrating that the exclusion of competitors from the contestable share of the market constituted the strategic objective of the rebates put in place.[255] In contrast, quantity discounts were found compatible with Article 102 if they were not discriminatory (therefore not infringing Article 102(c)) and were justified on objective grounds.[256]

9.6.2.2. Other types of rebates

In *Michelin I*, the CJEU applies Article 102 TFEU to individualized volume all-unit target rebates[257]. In *Michelin II*, the scope of the prohibition of Article 102 TFEU expanded to also cover individualized and standardized all-unit rebates,[258] the EU Courts taking a formalistic approach, focusing on the form of rebates rather than on their economic effects.[259] The *British Airways v Commission* case provides an illustration of the paucity of economic effects-based analysis in the EU case law concerning the application of Article 102 TFEU on rebates.

252 See Section 7.3.2.1.

253 Case C-85/76, *Hoffmann-La Roche v Commission* [1979] ECR 461, para 111.

254 See eg Case T-228/97, *Irish Sugar plc v Commission* [1999] ECR II–2969, confirmed on appeal by Case C-497/99 P, *Irish Sugar plc v Commission* [2001] ECR I–5333, regarding rebates conditional on the customer buying more quantity than in a previous period, the rebates being calculated in such a way so as to be only available to customers who purchased the totality or the near-totality of their requirements with Irish Sugar.

255 *Soda-Ash/ICI* (Case IV/33.133d) Commission Decision [1991] OJ L 152/40, overturned on procedural grounds and re-adopted in *Soda-Ash/ICI* (Case IV/33.133) Commission Decision [2003] OJ L 10/33, on appeal Case T-66/01, *Imperial Chemical Industries Ltd v Commission* [2010] ECR II–2631; *Soda-Ash/Solvay* (Case IV/33.133d) Commission Decision [1991] OJ L 152/21, overturned on procedural grounds and re-adopted *Soda Ash/Solvay* (Case IV/33.133c) Commission Decision [2003] OJ L 10/10.

256 Case C-163/99, *Portugal v Commission* (Landing Fees at Portuguese Airports) [2001] ECR I–2613.

257 Case C-322/81, *Michelin I* [1983] ECR 3461.

258 Case T-203/01, *Michelin v Commission* [2003] ECR II–4071 [hereinafter *Michelin II*]. See the discussion in J Kallaugher and B Sher, 'Rebates Revisited: Anti-Competitive Effects and Exclusionary Abuse Under Article 82' (2004) *European Competition L Rev* 263.

259 This case law is discussed in Section S.9.6.2.2.

Case C-95/04, *British Airways plc v Commission of the European Communities*
[2007] ECR I–2331

In its Virgin/British Airways *decision of July 1999, the European Commission condemned a rebate scheme granted by British Airways (BA) to travel agents as a 'loyalty discount' contrary to Article 102 TFEU.*[260] *BA was found to be in a dominant position in the UK as a buyer in the market for air travel agency services, although it had a market share of 39.7 per cent, which was in decline (as it fell from 47.7 per cent at the beginning of the 1990s to 39.7 per cent), the shares of other carriers, notably Virgin and British Midland, having grown rapidly.*

The Commission objected to three schemes to encourage travel agents to sell BA tickets:

- *'The marketing agreements', which provided for payment to agents selling at least £500,000 of an addition to their basic commission calculated on a sliding scale for selling tickets to a greater value than in a previous period.*
- *'The global agreements', entitled three agents to additional commission calculated by reference to the growth of BA's share in their world-wide sales, and 'the new performance reward scheme', which reduced the basic commission but provided additional commission depending on whether the total revenue from the sales of BA tickets issued by an agent in a particular calendar month was greater than that achieved during the corresponding month in the previous year.*

The rebates scheme offered by BA therefore included financial compensation to travel agents in return for meeting or for exceeding their previous year's sales of BA tickets. Once the targets were met, the travel agents received an increase in commission not just on the tickets sold thereafter but also on all the tickets sold in the reference period. So effectively the scheme amounted to a retroactive (all-units) rebates system as it 'rolled back' in the reference period. The Commission noted the following:

> This means that when a travel agent is close to one of the thresholds for an increase in commission rate[,] selling relatively few extra BA tickets can have a large effect on his commission income. Conversely a competitor of BA who wishes to give a travel agent an incentive to divert some sales from BA to the competing airline will have to pay a much higher rate of commission than BA on all of the tickets sold by it to overcome this effect.[261]

In other words, the Commission identified a 'disloyalty penalty' for travel agents that refused to buy a BA flight once they were close to the retroactive rebate target. BA's competitor needed therefore to overcome this 'disloyalty penalty' if they were to convince the travel agents to purchase air travel from them instead. The Commission found that, given BA's dominant position, these commission schemes represented loyalty discounts (condemned in the Michelin I *and* Hoffmann-La Roche *cases) and abusive discrimination between travel agents (condemned under Article 102(c)), even if the market share of BA's competitors increased during this period. According to the Commission, 'it can only be assumed that competitors would have had more success in the absence of these abusive commission schemes'.*[262]

The General Court upheld the Commission's decision, noting the following:

> 263. (a) rebate granted by an undertaking in a dominant position by reference to an increase in purchases made over a certain period, without that rebate being capable of

[260] *Virgin/British Airways* (Case COMP IV/D-2/34.780) Commission Decision [2000] OJ L 30/1.
[261] *Virgin/BA* (Case COMP IV/D-2/34.780) Commission Decision [2000] OJ L30/1, para 29.
[262] *Virgin/BA* (Case COMP IV/D-2/34.780) Commission Decision [2000] OJ L 30/1, para 107.

being regarded as a normal quantity discount, constitutes an abuse of that dominant position, since such a practice can only be intended to tie the customers to which it is granted and place competitors in an unfavourable competitive position.

264. Article [102 TFEU] does not require it to be demonstrated that the conduct in question had any actual or direct effect on consumers. Competition law concentrates upon protecting the market structure from artificial distortions because by doing so the interests of the consumer in the medium to long term are best protected [. . .].

272. Concerning, first, the fidelity-building character of the schemes in question, the Court finds that, by reason of their progressive nature with a very noticeable effect at the margin, the increased commission rates were capable of rising exponentially from one reference period to another, as the number of BA tickets sold by agents during successive reference periods progressed [. . .].

293. Finally, BA cannot accuse the Commission of failing to demonstrate that its practices produced an exclusionary effect. In the first place, for the purposes of establishing an infringement of Article [102 TFEU], it is not necessary to demonstrate that the abuse in question had a concrete effect on the markets concerned. It is sufficient in that respect to demonstrate that the abusive conduct of the undertaking in a dominant position tends to restrict competition, or, in other words, that the conduct is capable of having, or likely to have, such an effect.[263]

BA appealed the judgment of the General Court (then Court of First Instance) to the Court of Justice, which issued a judgment confirming that of the General Court four years later. In the meantime, the European Commission was considering a move towards a more 'effects-based' analysis of rebates and more generally exclusionary abuses and two reports by a group of economic advisors (the EAGCP Report)[264] and DG Comp staff[265] were published advocating the move towards a more economic approach in assessing the exclusionary effects of rebates.

The first plea, alleging error of law in the Court's assessment of the exclusionary effect of the bonus schemes at issue. The first part of the first plea, concerning the criterion for assessing the possible exclusionary effect of the bonus schemes at issue. The CJEU repeated its previous case law.

67. In order to determine whether the undertaking in a dominant position has abused such a position by applying a system of discounts [. . .] the Court has held that it is necessary to consider all the circumstances, particularly the criteria and rules governing the grant of the discount, and to investigate whether, in providing an advantage not based on any economic service justifying it, the discount tends to remove or restrict the buyer's freedom to choose his sources of supply, to bar competitors from access to the market, to apply dissimilar conditions to equivalent transactions with other trading parties or to strengthen the dominant position by distorting competition [. . .].

68. It follows that in determining whether, on the part of an undertaking in a dominant position, a system of discounts or bonuses which constitute neither quantity discounts or bonuses nor fidelity discounts or bonuses within the meaning of the judgment in *Hoffmann-La Roche* constitutes an abuse, it first has to be determined whether those discounts or bonuses can produce an exclusionary effect, that is to say whether they are capable, first, of making market entry very difficult or impossible for competitors of the undertaking

[263] Case T-219/99, *British Airways v Commission* [2003] ECR II-5925.

[264] Economic Advisory Group for Competition Policy (EAGCP), An Economic Approach to Article 82, Report (July 2005), 34–8, available at http://ec.europa.eu/dgs/competition/economist/eagcp_july_21_05.pdf.

[265] DG Comp Discussion Paper, paras 134–76.

in a dominant position and, secondly, of making it more difficult or impossible for its co-contractors to choose between various sources of supply or commercial partners.

69. It then needs to be examined whether there is an objective economic justification for the discounts and bonuses granted. [. . .] [A]n undertaking is at liberty to demonstrate that its bonus system producing an exclusionary effect is economically justified.

70. With regard to the first aspect, the case-law gives indications as to the cases in which discount or bonus schemes of an undertaking in a dominant position are not merely the expression of a particularly favourable offer on the market, but give rise to an exclusionary effect.

71. First, an exclusionary effect may arise from goal-related discounts or bonuses, that is to say those the granting of which is linked to the attainment of sales objectives defined individually [. . .]

72. It is clear from the findings of the [. . .] judgment under appeal that the bonus schemes at issue were drawn up by reference to individual sales objectives, since the rate of the bonuses depended on the evolution of the turnover arising from BA ticket sales by each travel agent during a given period.

73. It is also apparent from the case-law that the commitment of co-contractors towards the undertaking in a dominant position and the pressure exerted upon them may be particularly strong where a discount or bonus does not relate solely to the growth in turnover in relation to purchases or sales of products of that undertaking made by those co-contractors during the period under consideration, but extends also to the whole of the turnover relating to those purchases or sales. In that way, relatively modest variations—whether upwards or downwards—in the turnover figures relating to the products of the dominant undertaking have disproportionate effects on co-contractors [. . .].

The CJEU confirmed the findings of the GC that the bonus schemes at issue had a fidelity-building effect capable of producing an exclusionary effect.

The second part of the first plea concerned the assessment by the General Court of the relevance of the objective economic justification for the bonus schemes at issue.

84. Discounts or bonuses granted to its co-contractors by an undertaking in a dominant position are not necessarily an abuse and therefore prohibited by Article [102 TFEU]. According to consistent case-law, only discounts or bonuses which are not based on any economic counterpart to justify them must be regarded as an abuse [. . .].

86. Assessment of the economic justification for a system of discounts or bonuses established by an undertaking in a dominant position is to be made on the basis of the whole of the circumstances of the case [. . .]. It has to be determined whether the exclusionary effect arising from such a system, which is disadvantageous for competition, may be counterbalanced, or outweighed, by advantages in terms of efficiency which also benefit the consumer. If the exclusionary effect of that system bears no relation to advantages for the market and consumers, or if it goes beyond what is necessary in order to attain those advantages, that system must be regarded as an abuse.

The CJEU rejected the second plea, alleging an error of law in that the General Court did not examine the probable effects of the commissions granted by BA and did not take into account the evidence that the commissions had no material effect on competing airlines.

The third plea, claiming that the General Court had not examined whether BA's conduct involved a 'prejudice [to] consumers' within the meaning of sub-paragraph (b) of the second paragraph of Article 102 TFEU, was also dismissed as 'unfounded'.

105. It should be noted first that [. . .] discounts or bonuses granted by an undertaking in a dominant position may be contrary to Article [102 TFEU] even where

they do not correspond to any of the examples mentioned in the second paragraph of that article.

106. Moreover, as the Court has already held in paragraph 26 of its judgment in *Europemballage and Continental Can*, CB Article [102 TFEU] is aimed not only at practices which may cause prejudice to consumers directly, but also at those which are detrimental to them through their impact on an effective competition structure, such as is mentioned in [Article 3(1)(g) EC, now Protocol No 27].

107. The [General Court] was therefore entitled, without committing any error of law, not to examine whether BA's conduct had caused prejudice to consumers within the meaning of subparagraph (b) of the second paragraph of Article [102 TFEU], but to examine [. . .] whether the bonus schemes at issue had a restrictive effect on competition and to conclude that the existence of such an effect had been demonstrated by the Commission in the contested decision.

NOTES AND QUESTIONS ON LOYALTY REBATES AND BRITISH AIRWAYS

1. Retrospective rebates are frequently given by firms with virtually no market power. Do you think that they always foreclose, or are there some circumstances that make foreclosure more or less likely?
   - The retrospective nature of the discount reduces the income to be made for the goods actually sold while, on the other hand, more produce may be shifted. The likelihood of foreclosure may depend on a trade-off between the extents of these influences.
   - Unless the target is set close to the likely purchases of the customer it is unlikely to foreclose.
   - Are there other routes to the final buyer, such as wholesalers? Is the market contestable?
   - How many customers are substantially locked into the Domco? Should a captive base be presumed?
2. (Paragraphs 67–8) Should it suffice to establish an abuse that the conduct can be or is capable of foreclosing? Should it also have to be established that it is likely to do so? Compare with paragraph 20 of the Commission Guidance on Article 102.
3. (Paragraph 67) According to the CJEU, for conditional rebates of the type of *Michelin I*[266] it is necessary to consider 'all the circumstances'. Does the CJEU require something equivalent for conditional rebates of the type of *Hoffmann-La Roche*?[267] Does the Court imply that conditional rebates of the type of *Hoffmann-La Roche* are abusive by their nature, irrespective of the 'circumstances'? Compare with the classification of rebates by the General Court in *Intel*.[268]
4. (Paragraphs 68 and 69) According to the CJEU rebates of both types (*Hoffmann-La Roche, Michelin I*) should be assessed in the light of two criteria: (i) 'whether those discounts or bonuses can produce an exclusionary effect, that is to say whether they are

266 Case 322/81, *Michelin I* [1983] ECR 3461 para 65, not reproduced.
267 Case C-85/76, *Hoffmann-La Roche v Commission* [1979] ECR 461, para 62, not reproduced.
268 See Section 9.6.4.3.

capable, first, of making market entry very difficult or impossible for competitors of the undertaking in a dominant position and, secondly, of making it more difficult or impossible for its co-contractors to choose between various sources of supply or commercial partners';[269] (ii) 'whether there is an objective economic justification for the discounts and bonuses granted'.[270] Does the reference in (i) on 'exclusionary effects' require the analysis of the welfare effects of the practice, or is it just a legal discrimination test establishing the existence of a differential burden between the dominant incumbent and its competitors? Does the CJEU say anything about 'as efficient as competitors' or is it simply referring to *any* competitor, even less efficient than the dominant undertaking? How would (ii) operate in this assessment? Is this an exception to the rule that rebates producing an 'exclusionary effect' fall under Article 102 TFEU? Does it operate instead as a trade-off device (either balancing or a proportionality test)?

5. (Paragraph 86) Is it possible reliably to balance the disadvantage of foreclosing competition against the benefit derived from greater efficiency? Can either be quantified?
6. (Paragraphs 105–7) Does the CJEU consider that evidence of significant consumer harm is necessary when establishing an abuse of a dominant position?
7. The position of the CJEU in *British Airways* is remarkable not only because the court applied an anti-competitive foreclosure test, but also because in a quite similar case involving the same parties the US Second Circuit rejected Virgin's attempted monopolization claim based on British Airways' bundling of its ticket sales for corporate customers on routes between the United Kingdom and the United States.[271] The plaintiff's expert had advanced a 'predatory foreclosure' theory, according to which British Airways had priced below its *own* costs in certain routes by adding additional flights to deter or delay its rival Virgin's expansion and the costs incurred by British Airways were immediately recouped by setting prices substantially above cost on other routes.[272] The Second Circuit found that Virgin failed to bring evidence of below cost pricing because, *inter alia*, the correct measure of costs was average avoidable costs calculated on all of the British Airways routes in the geographical market (and not only an incremental sales test as was argued by Virgin's expert).[273] The Second Circuit also refused to find that there was recoupment, as Virgin did not indicate how much above its costs British Airways priced the non-competitive routes. Thus, the court adopted a predatory standard test, noting that 'low prices are a positive aspect of a competitive marketplace and are encouraged by antitrust laws', and it considered that, '[a]s long as low prices remain above predatory levels, they neither threaten competition nor give rise to an antitrust injury'.[274] Although the test of 'predatory foreclosure' applied by the Second circuit imposes an even higher standard of proof on the plaintiff than some other case law of the US courts,[275] the case indicates that had the EU court followed a price cost test, it is probable that British Airways target rebates would have been found compatible to Article 102 TFEU.

[269] Case C-85/76, *Hoffmann-La Roche v Commission* [1979] ECR 461, para 68.

[270] Ibid, para 69.

[271] *Virgin Atl Airways Ltd v British Airways plc*, 257 F 3d 256 (2d Cir 2001).

[272] Ibid, 266.

[273] Ibid, 271–2.

[274] Ibid, 269.

[275] N Economides and I Lianos, 'The Elusive Antitrust Standard on Bundling in Europe and in the United States in the Aftermath of the *Microsoft* Cases' (2009) 76 *Antitrust LJ* 483.

9.6.3. THE COMMISSION'S GUIDANCE ON ARTICLE 102

The European Commission followed up the DG Comp Staff Discussion Paper's new methodology for assessing rebates with the publication of a Guidance on the enforcement priorities applying Article 102 TFEU to abusive exclusionary conduct by dominant undertakings, operationalizing the emphasis put on (i) the exclusion of as efficient as competitors, (ii) the actual or potential welfare effects of the rebates scheme, and (iii) the application of a price-cost test in order to assess the suction effect.

According to this document, conditional rebates constitute an example of price-based exclusionary conduct, hence the focus on the possible anti-competitive foreclosure of only as-efficient competitors.[276] Hence, in addition to the factors usually examined in order to establish anti-competitive foreclosure (the position of the dominant undertaking, the conditions on the relevant market, the position of the dominant undertaking's competitors, the position of the customers or input suppliers, the extent of the allegedly abusive conduct, possible evidence of actual foreclosure, direct evidence of any exclusionary strategy),[277] if a hypothetical competitor as efficient as the dominant undertaking would be likely to be foreclosed by the conduct in question, by examining economic data relating to cost and sales prices, and in particular whether the dominant undertaking is engaging in some form of below-cost pricing.[278]

Communication from the Commission—Guidance on the Commission's enforcement priorities in applying Article [102 TFEU] to abusive exclusionary conduct by dominant undertakings [2009] OJ C 45/7

41. When applying the methodology explained in paragraphs 23 to 27 [the price–cost test], the Commission intends to investigate, to the extent that the data are available and reliable, whether the rebate system is capable of hindering expansion or entry even by competitors that are equally efficient by making it more difficult for them to supply part of the requirements of individual customers. In this context the Commission will estimate what price a competitor would have to offer in order to compensate the customer for the loss of the conditional rebate if the latter would switch part of its demand ('the relevant range') away from the dominant undertaking. The effective price that the competitor will have to match is not the average price of the dominant undertaking, but the normal (list) price less the rebate the customer loses by switching, calculated over the relevant range of sales and in the relevant period of time. [. . .]

As explained above, the Commission will examine the 'contestable' and 'non-contestable' portion of a customer's demand and a 'relevant range', the main concern being the possible leverage through the use of the non-contestable portion of the demand to decrease the price of the contestable portion. The Commission will apply a price–cost test in order

276 Commission Guidance on Article 102, para 23. However, the Commission recognized (ibid, para 24) that 'in certain circumstances a less efficient competitor may also exert a constraint which should be taken into account when considering whether particular price-based conduct leads to anti-competitive foreclosure', giving as example a competitor that may benefit from demand-related advantages, such as network and learning effects, which will tend to enhance its efficiency in a dynamic perspective.

277 Ibid, para 20. 278 Ibid, para 25.

to calculate the effective price the competitor has to match in order to compensate the customer for the loss of the rebate and assess if an as efficient competitor may compete profitably notwithstanding the rebate. According to the Commission, if the effective price remains above the dominant undertaking's LRAIC, 'the rebate is normally not capable of foreclosing in an anti-competitive way'.[279] *If the effective price is below the AAC of the dominant undertaking, 'as a general rule the rebate scheme is capable of foreclosing even equally efficient competitors'.*[280] *If the effective price is between AAC and LRAIC, 'the Commission will investigate whether other factors point to the conclusion that entry or expansion even by equally efficient competitors is likely to be affected', for instance whether and to what extent competitors have realistic and effective counterstrategies at their disposal, such as a capacity to also use a 'non contestable' portion of their buyers' demand as leverage to decrease the price for the relevant range.*[281] *If such counterstrategies are not available, the Commission will consider that the rebate scheme is capable of foreclosing equally efficient competitors.*[282]

> 45. [. . .] [T]his analysis will be integrated in the general assessment, taking into account other relevant quantitative or qualitative evidence. It is normally important to consider whether the rebate system is applied with an individualised or a standardised threshold. An individualized threshold—one based on a percentage of the total requirements of the customer or an individualized volume target—allows the dominant supplier to set the threshold at such a level as to make it difficult for customers to switch suppliers, thereby creating a maximum loyalty enhancing effect. By contrast, a standardized volume threshold—where the threshold is the same for all or a group of customers—may be too high for some smaller customers and/or too low for larger customers to have a loyalty enhancing effect. If, however, it can be established that a standardised volume threshold approximates the requirements of an appreciable proportion of customers, the Commission is likely to consider that such a standardized system of rebates may produce anti-competitive foreclosure effects.

The Commission will also consider cost or other advantages that are passed on to customers.

NOTES AND QUESTIONS ON THE COMMISSION'S GUIDANCE ON ARTICLE 102 REGARDING REBATES

1. Are the Commission's Guidance on Article 102 emphasis on as-efficient competitors and reliance on the price–cost test compatible with the position of the CJEU in *British Airways/Commission*?
2. How easy or complex is the Commission's Guidance on Article 102 test in comparison to the CJEU's approach? Are the benefits in terms of accuracy of the test and consideration of economic effects outweighing the costs?
3. Some authors have criticized the test for being quite difficult to apply, in particular calculating in an accurate way the contestable share of the demand, or collecting information and analysing the possible counter-strategies available to rivals.[283]

[279] Ibid, para 43. [280] Ibid, para 44. [281] Ibid. [282] Ibid.

[283] See eg L Kjølbe, 'Rebates Under Article 82 EC: Navigating Uncertain Waters' (2010) *European Competition L Rev* 66, 73.

4. In paragraph 37 of the Commission Guidance on Article 102, not reproduced here, the Commission notes that conditional rebates have actual or potential foreclosure effects similar to exclusive purchasing obligations, without necessarily entailing a sacrifice for the dominant undertaking. Hence, one may distinguish conditional rebates from predatory pricing, which involves a sacrifice of profits. Should this have implications as to the classification of rebates as price-related abuses? Should they be instead classified as non-price abuses, as any other exclusive purchasing obligation?

9.6.4. THE CASE LAW OF THE EU COURTS AND DECISIONAL PRACTICE OF THE COMMISSION POST-GUIDANCE ON ARTICLE 102

In its most recent decisions on rebates after the publication of the Guidance on Article 102, the Commission applied the principles of the enforcement priorities guidance in the following two cases: *Tomra* and *Intel*. Both decisions have been appealed to the General Court and the CJEU issued a judgment in the *Tomra* case, a more recent one in *Post Danmark II* on a preliminary reference by a Danish court as well as a judgment in *Intel*. The judgments of the General Court and the CJEU illustrate the distance that still exists between the Commission's economic approach regarding rebates in its Guidance on Article 102 and the more values-driven approach followed by the European judiciary.

9.6.4.1. *Tomra*

In March 2006, the Commission found that Tomra, an undertaking whose market shares in various national markets in Europe in the supply of reverse vending machines (RVM) used by supermarkets to collect empty drink containers had continuously exceeded 70 per cent in the years before 1997 and even 95 per cent the period thereafter and which were many times larger than those of their competitors, had abused its dominant position. The Commission had received a complaint from Prokent AG a competitor active in the empty beverage-container collection sector and the supply of related products and services, which alleged that Tomra prevented it from entering the market. After investigating the Commission concluded that Tomra had been implementing an exclusionary strategy in the national RVM markets in Germany, the Netherlands, Austria, Sweden, and Norway, involving exclusivity and preferred supplier agreements and a system of individualized quantity commitments and individualized retroactive rebate schemes, applying the rebate to every product bought by the customer during a particular reference period (also called 'high-volume block orders') and rebates that conditional on customers purchasing all or most of their requirements from the dominant supplier, thus foreclosing competition on these markets. Indeed, the agreements foreclosed on average, about 39 per cent of total demand in the market.

According to the Commission's decision, 'Tomra resorted to such practices, in particular, in anticipation of expected market entry, whether due to the planned introduction of new legislation introducing a deposit system or otherwise, or as a reaction to the implementation of such legislation, being aware that competitors needed to achieve certain sales volumes in order to become profitable'.[284] The Commission also found documentary evidence that the

284 *Prokent/Tomra* (Case COMP/E-1/38.113) Commission Decision [2008] OJ C 219/11, para 13.

exclusionary conduct was discussed extensively within the group on various occasions, be it at meetings and conferences or in correspondence, for instance, e-mail. The Commission found that the retroactive rebates granted by Tomra, the so-called high-volume block orders, was 'not a strategy confined to the normal competitive process and the selection resulting from it', but it was designed 'to interfere with this process and prevent it from eroding the dominant position of the undertaking'.[285] The Commission noted that following *Michelin II* and *British Airways*, it could have been sufficient to 'show that the abusive conduct of the undertaking in a dominant position tends to restrict competition or, in other words, that the conduct is capable of having that effect', yet it also completed an analysis of the likely suction effects of Tomra's practices on the RVMs market by applying the principles of the Guidance on Article 102. It also found that such practices produced negative welfare effects, noting the link between the size of the tied market and the high market share of Tomra as well as the link between the tied market demand and the changes in position of the market players, with Tomra maintaining the leading position and a situation in which the situation where 'the prices of the products did not go down and the choice of the products did not change significantly'.[286] It arrived at the conclusion that such practices constituted an abuse of a dominant position and fined Tomra €24 million.

Tomra appealed to the General Court arguing, among other things, that the Commission had wrongfully applied the test for rebates and that it was ambiguous if certain type of abuse practices were *per se* illegal or not, the Commission having failed to explain the test or criteria used when assessing whether the agreements were capable of restricting or foreclosing competition. It was also alleged that the total demand covered by the rebates in the national RVM markets was insufficient to foreclose Tomra's competitors, as these would have none the less remained free to seek the customers of other undertakings than Tomra, this point raising the issue of the portion of the demand that was incontestable. Furthermore, the applicants argued that the assumptions used as the basis for the assessment of the capability of the retroactive rebates to foreclose competition were wrong. They argued in particular that where retroactive rebates lead to positive prices, it cannot be presumed that they will necessarily be capable of producing exclusionary effects and criticized the Commission's decision for not evaluating the prices resulting from their rebates against any benchmark or workable objective criterion.

The General Court did not accept these allegations and confirmed the Commission's decision.[287] The judgment of the General Court was nevertheless quite ambiguous as to the first point made by the applicants regarding the *per se* prohibition of loyalty rebates.[288] Tomra appealed to the CJEU, which confirmed the General Court's judgment and provided some clarification.

Case C-549/10 P, *Tomra Systems ASA v European Commission*, ECLI:EU:C:2012:221

With regard to the argument of the applicant for an alleged error of law and failure to provide adequate reasoning concerning the portion of total demand which the agreements had to cover in order to constitute abuse.

37. The second ground of appeal concerns, in essence, the question whether the General Court was well founded in its assessment of the relevant part of the market

[285] Ibid, para 14. [286] Ibid, para 344.

[287] Case T-155/06, *Tomra Systems ASA, Tomra Europe AS, Tomra Systems GmbH v Commission* [2010] ECR II-4361.

[288] Ibid, paras 211–15, 238–42.

at issue which had to be covered by the agreements at issue before it could be established that those agreements were capable of foreclosing competition on the market.

38. As regards the level of domination of a specific market by the undertaking concerned necessary to establish the existence of abuse by that undertaking, it is clear from paragraph 79 of *TeliaSonera* that the dominant position referred to in Article 102 TFEU relates to a position of economic strength enjoyed by an undertaking which enables it to prevent effective competition being maintained on the relevant market by affording it the power to behave to an appreciable extent independently of its competitors and its customers.

39. Moreover, it is clear from paragraphs 80 and 81 of *TeliaSonera* that Article 102 TFEU does not envisage any variation in form or degree in the concept of a dominant position. Where an undertaking has an economic strength such as that required by Article 102 TFEU to establish that it holds a dominant position in a particular market, its conduct must be assessed in the light of that provision. None the less, the degree of market strength is, as a general rule, significant in relation to the extent of the effects of the conduct of the undertaking concerned rather than in relation to the question of whether the abuse as such exists.

40. It is true that, as is stated in [. . .] the judgment under appeal, the Commission did not establish a precise threshold beyond which the practices of the Tomra group would be capable of excluding its competitors from the market in question.

41. However, [. . .] the General Court properly approved the Commission's reasoning that, by foreclosing a significant part of the market, the Tomra group had restricted entry to one or a few competitors and thus limited the intensity of competition on the market as a whole.

42. In fact, and as stated by the General Court [. . .] the foreclosure by a dominant undertaking of a substantial part of the market cannot be justified by showing that the contestable part of the market is still sufficient to accommodate a limited number of competitors. First, the customers on the foreclosed part of the market should have the opportunity to benefit from whatever degree of competition is possible on the market and competitors should be able to compete on the merits for the entire market and not just for a part of it. Second, it is not the role of the dominant undertaking to dictate how many viable competitors will be allowed to compete for the remaining contestable portion of demand.

43. Further, the General Court stated [. . .] that only an analysis of the circumstances of the case, such as the analysis carried out by the Commission in the contested decision, may make it possible to establish whether the practices of an undertaking in a dominant position are capable of excluding competition. It would, however, be artificial to establish without prior analysis the portion of the tied market beyond which the practices of a dominant undertaking may have an exclusionary effect on competitors.

44. The General Court accordingly determined, following that analysis of the circumstances of this case [. . .] that a considerable proportion (two fifths) of total demand during the period and in the countries under consideration was foreclosed to competition.

45. That conclusion of the General Court cannot be regarded as containing any error of law.

46. As regards the appellants' argument that the Commission should have applied the 'minimum viable scale' test, suffice it to observe that, first, the General Court was correct to hold that the determination of a precise threshold of foreclosure of the market beyond which the practices at issue had to be regarded as abusive was not required for the purposes of applying Article 102 TFEU and, secondly, in the light of the findings

made [. . .], it was, in any event, in the present case, proved to the requisite legal standard that the market had been closed to competition by the practices at issue. [. . .]

The CJEU also examined the findings of the General Court with regard to the retroactive rebates awarded by Tomra.

67. As regards the substance, it must be observed that, according to the Commission, the failure in the judgment under appeal to examine the arguments on whether the prices charged by the Tomra group were lower than their long-run average incremental costs had no effect on the conclusion reached by the General Court that the Commission's analysis of the abusive nature of the rebates applied by Tomra was well founded.

68. The General Court was correct to observe [. . .] that, for the purposes of proving an abuse of a dominant position within the meaning of Article 102 TFEU, it is sufficient to show that the abusive conduct of the undertaking in a dominant position tends to restrict competition or that the conduct is capable of having that effect.

69. As regards rebates granted by a dominant undertaking to its customers, the Court has stated that those may infringe Article 102 TFEU, even where they do not correspond to any of the examples mentioned in the second paragraph of that Article 102 [. . .].

70. In the event that an undertaking in a dominant position makes use of a system of rebates, the Court has ruled that that undertaking abuses that position where, without tying the purchasers by a formal obligation, it applies, either under the terms of agreements concluded with these purchasers or unilaterally, a system of loyalty rebates, that is to say, discounts conditional on the customer's obtaining—whether the quantity of its purchases is large or small—all or most of its requirements from the undertaking in a dominant position [. . .].

71. In that regard, it is necessary to consider all the circumstances, particularly the criteria and rules governing the grant of the rebate, and to investigate whether, in providing an advantage not based on any economic service justifying it, the rebates tend to remove or restrict the buyer's freedom to choose his sources of supply, to bar competitors from access to the market, or to strengthen the dominant position by distorting competition [. . .].

72. As regards the present case, it is clear [. . .] that a rebate system must be regarded as infringing Article 102 TFEU if it tends to prevent customers of the dominant undertaking from obtaining their supplies from competing producers.

73. Contrary to what is claimed by the appellants, the invoicing of 'negative prices', in other words prices below cost prices, to customers is not a prerequisite of a finding that a retroactive rebates scheme operated by a dominant undertaking is abusive.

74. As the General Court was fully entitled to observe, [. . .] the third part of the second and fourth pleas in law submitted at first instance was based on an incorrect premiss. The fact that the retroactive rebate schemes oblige competitors to ask negative prices from Tomra's customers benefiting from rebates cannot be regarded as one of the fundamental bases of the contested decision in showing that the retroactive rebate schemes are capable of having anticompetitive effects. Further, the General Court correctly stated [. . .] that a whole series of other considerations relating to the retroactive rebates operated by Tomra underpinned the contested decision as regards its conclusion that those types of practices were capable of excluding competitors in breach of Article 102 TFEU.

75. In that regard, the General Court observed, more particularly, that, according to the contested decision, in the first place, the incentive to obtain supplies exclusively or almost exclusively from Tomra was particularly strong when thresholds, such as those applied by Tomra, were combined with a system whereby the achievement of the bonus threshold or, as the case may be, a more advantageous threshold benefited all the purchases made by the customer during the reference period and not exclusively the purchasing volume exceeding the threshold concerned [. . .]. Secondly, the rebate schemes were individual to each customer and the thresholds were established on the basis of the customer's estimated requirements and/or past purchasing volumes and represented a strong incentive for buying all or almost all the equipment needed from Tomra and artificially raised the costs of switching to a different supplier, even for a small number of units [. . .]. Third, the retroactive rebates often applied to some of the largest customers of the Tomra group with the aim of ensuring their loyalty [. . .]. Lastly, Tomra failed to show that their conduct was objectively justified or that it generated significant efficiency gains which outweighed the anti-competitive effects on consumers [. . .].

76. Accordingly, it is apparent from all the reasoning [. . .] of the judgment under appeal, referred to above, that the General Court came to the conclusion that the third part of the second and fourth pleas in law submitted at first instance was based on an incorrect premiss as regards the evidential value, in respect of whether the rebates scheme at issue was anti-competitive, of the specific characteristics of that scheme, irrespective of the precise level of prices charged.

77. The General Court took its reasoning further by stating [. . .] that the Commission, in the contested decision, first, did not state that the rebate schemes automatically resulted in negative prices and, second, did not maintain that showing that is a prerequisite to finding those rebate schemes to be abusive.

78. The General Court added, in that regard [. . .] that the exclusionary mechanism represented by retroactive rebates does not require the dominant undertaking to sacrifice profits, since the cost of the rebate is spread across a large number of units. If retroactive rebates are given, the average price obtained by the dominant undertaking may well be far above costs and ensure a high average profit margin. However, retroactive rebate schemes ensure that, from the point of view of the customer, the effective price for the last units is very low because of the 'suction effect'. The General Court therefore rejected as ineffective the claims made by Tomra that there were errors of fact in the analysis within the contested decision of the level of prices charged by them.

79. The General Court was therefore justified in ruling, in essence [. . .] that the loyalty mechanism was inherent in the supplier's ability to drive out its competitors by means of the suction to itself of the contestable part of demand. When such a trading instrument exists, it is therefore unnecessary to undertake an analyse of the actual effects of the rebates on competition given that, for the purposes of establishing an infringement of Article 102 TFEU, it is sufficient to demonstrate that the conduct at issue is capable of having an effect on competition [. . .].

80. That being the case, the alleged absence, in the judgment under appeal, of an examination of the arguments raised by the applicants at first instance, on the need to compare the prices charged by them with their costs, which underlies both the complaint of a procedural irregularity and that of an error of law, cannot mean that the judgment under appeal is vitiated by an error of law. The Commission established the existence of an abuse of a dominant position by relying on the other considerations [. . .] and the General Court correctly found that that analysis was adequate and sufficient to establish the existence of that abuse. Accordingly, neither the Commission nor the

General Court was obliged to examine the question of whether the prices charged by the Tomra group were or were not lower than their long-run average incremental costs, and accordingly this ground of appeal must fail in the context of the present appeal.

81. The appellants' arguments that the Commission's Guidance [. . .] provides for a comparative analysis of prices and costs cannot invalidate that conclusion. As the Advocate General observes in point 37 of his Opinion, the Guidance, published in 2009, has no relevance to the legal assessment of a decision, such as the contested decision, which was adopted in 2006.

NOTES AND QUESTIONS ON TOMRA

1. (GC, paragraphs 238–42; CJEU, paragraphs 30–46) How do the EU Courts examine Tomra's argument with regard to the contestable portion of the demand? Do the Courts conflate market foreclosure and customer foreclosure? How significant should customer foreclosure be in order to be considered anti-competitive? Do the EU Courts provide an answer to this question?
2. (GC, paragraph 242; CJEU, paragraph 42) How would you understand both courts' dictum that 'the customers on the foreclosed part of the market should have the opportunity to benefit from whatever degree of competition is possible on the market and competitors should be able to compete on the merits for the entire market and not just for a part of it'? Does this mean that, as a matter of principle, markets should always be fully contestable at all times? How can one achieve such an objective in practice?
3. (GC, paragraphs 213–14; CJEU, paragraphs 68, 70, 71) Do both EU Courts accept the *per-se* illegality of certain forms of rebates? Or do they require that for each type of rebate, even those of Hofmann-La Roche, there should be an assessment of 'all the circumstances'? What do these 'circumstances' refer to? The term has been used in various non-rebates cases, such as *Oscar Bronner, TeliaSonera*, and *Post Danmark I*; however, in using the same expression in rebates-related cases, the EU Courts add the following sentence: 'particularly the criteria and rules governing the grant of the discount'. Is this addition significant? Does this refer to the economic and legal context of the practice—which the Courts also examine, as we described in Chapter 6—relating to object restrictions of competition under Article 101 TFEU? Would this refer to the 'nature' of the restriction?
4. (CJEU, paragraphs 73–4) The CJEU rejects the argument of the parties that negative prices is a prerequisite for the practice to be considered as foreclosing a competitor. The CJEU took a similar approach in margin-squeeze cases (see *TeliaSonera*, which finds '*exclusionary*' margin-squeeze abuses when the rivals' margins are 'positive', for instance because of '*reduced profitability*'[289]). The CJEU subjected, however, positive margin squeezes to higher evidential standards in comparison to margin squeezes with negative margins in which cases the exclusionary effect is presumed to exist and does not have to be separately established. Does the CJEU seem to take a similar approach here, or is the CJEU rejecting a distinction between positive and negative prices with regard to rebates?

289 Case C-52/09, *Konkurrensverket v TeliaSonera Sverige AB* [2011] ECR I-527, paras 73–4.

5. (CJEU, paragraphs 75–6) Does the CJEU imply that the practice was found illegal because of some concrete analysis of its likely potential or actual welfare effects? What are the elements the Court relies upon to arrive to the finding that the rebates in question constituted an abuse of a dominant position?
6. (CJEU, paragraph 78) Does the CJEU reject the profit sacrifice test as an appropriate test for the assessment of rebates under Article 102 TFEU? What are the implications of rejecting the requirement of a sacrifice and focusing instead on 'suction effects'? Does this also have implications on the way the CJEU will assess the suction effects?
7. (CJEU, paragraphs 79–80) How does the CJEU assess the existence of 'suction effects'? Compare with the approach followed by the Commission's Guidance on Article 102 (Section 9.6.3).
8. Do the GC and the CJEU discuss at any point the theory of harm with respect to consumers in this case? Is there a direct link between the fact that specific rebates are 'capable' of excluding competition and consumer harm?

9.6.4.2. *Post Danmark II*

The case follows up the litigation between Post Danmark, the former Danish State monopoly that controls the market for bulk mail in Denmark, and the Danish competition authority, which had brought a case against Post Danmark alleging, among others, that it had excluded from the bulk mail market in Denmark its competitor Bring Citymail, which was a subsidiary of the Norwegian State undertaking Posten Norge AS, and which after a short foray into the market between 2007 and 2010, it withdrew suffering heavy losses. Post Danmark held a share of the bulk mail market in Denmark that was approximately 95 per cent. Some 70 per cent of the bulk mail market was covered by the exclusive right exercised by Post Danmark as a regulated undertaking for the purposes of providing universal service. Of the bulk mail market, direct advertising mail, that is, addressed advertising mail sent simultaneously to a large number of recipients, formed a segment representing 12 per cent of the overall market in 2007 and 7 per cent in 2008, a proportion of this direct advertising mail not been covered by Post Danmark's statutory monopoly (that was 15 per cent in 2007 and 9 per cent in 2008). Post Danmark granted rebates of up to 16 per cent on the distribution of direct advertising mail provided that its customers reached certain standardized volume or turnover thresholds over a reference period of one year. The rebate was retroactive, thus applying to all direct advertising mail distributed for the customers concerned throughout the reference period. The rebate did not make a distinction as to whether the mailings were covered by Post Danmark's monopoly or whether there was a competitor present in the area in question.

In particular, the rebate scheme included eight levels, the first rebate threshold attracting a 6 per cent rebate, on the condition that the customer had commissioned a minimum number of letters, as well as reached a specific gross postage value of its mailings, during the reference year. According to the Opinion of AG Kokott, 'the variation in the rebates granted was most pronounced among medium-sized customers, whereas large customers usually qualified for the highest level of rebate anyway on account of the volume of orders placed by them'.[290]

290 Opinion of AG Kokott, in Case C-23/14, *Post Danmark A/S v Konkurrencerådet*, ECLI:EU:C:2015:343, para 11.

The rebate scheme operated as following: at the beginning of each reference year, the price payable by a given customer was determined on a provisional basis by reference to the volume which that customer was expected to order during that year. However, at the end of the reference period, the prices were retroactively adjusted according to the volume of mail actually sent for that customer during the year. It was thus possible that the customer could be required to reimburse Post Danmark if the actual volume ordered fell short of the volume forecast and the rebate estimated and granted at the beginning of the year had therefore been too high. The rebates could therefore be characterized as both conditional on a standardized volume threshold and retroactive.

The Danish competition authority found that the rebate scheme had tied customers to Post Danmark, thus foreclosing the bulk mail market. In reaching this conclusion the Danish NCA did not carry out a price–cost analysis in the form of an AEC test, but relied on the position of Post Danmark, finding that it was an unavoidable trading partner and that the market was characterized by high barriers to entry. The Danish Competition Appeal Tribunal confirmed the decision of the NCA. Pronouncing itself on appeal, the Danish Maritime and Commercial Court sent a preliminary ruling reference to the CJEU asking in particular the criteria to be applied in the assessment of the rebates, the relevance of the AEC test, and whether a rebate scheme must generate probable and/or appreciable exclusionary effects to fall under Article 102 TFEU.

Opinion of AG Kokott in Case C-23/14, *Post Danmark A/S v Konkurrencerådet*, ECLI:EU:C:2015:343

AG Kokott agreed with the Commission that 'rebates granted by dominant undertakings sometimes conceal anti-competitive practices which are only superficially the expression of a favourable offer, closer inspection showing them to have little to do with genuinely low prices, and can be very damaging to competition',[291] although she also mentioned that the category of rebates 'do[es] not attract a general assumption of abuse which those undertakings must disprove'.[292] According to the AG, 'what matters is whether the dominant undertaking grants rebates which are capable of producing on the relevant market an exclusionary effect *which is not economically justified', this 'effect' being explained as a distortion of competition resulting from the fact that the 'rebates seek to remove or restrict the buyer's freedom to choose his sources of supply, to bar competitors from access to the market, or to strengthen the dominant position'.[293] It is interesting that 'effects' is not meant in the way economists usually refer to this term, as market/welfare effect. The AG also noted an additional theory of harm for rebates resulting from Article 102(c) which prohibits dominant undertakings from granting discriminatory rebates applying dissimilar conditions to equivalent transactions with other trading parties, although she notes that this was not the case here, thus focusing the assessment on the existence, or not, of an exclusionary effect.*

The AG highlights the need to take into account all the circumstances of the specific rebate, each market and each rebate scheme having features which are peculiar to it.[294] Among the criteria and rules governing the grant of the rebate, the AG finds relevant the fact that retroactive rebates produce a higher suction effect. The existence of anti-competitive intent is also a

291 Opinion of AG Kokott in Case C-23/14, *Post Danmark A/S v Konkurrencerådet*, ECLI:EU:C:2015:343, para 26.

292 Ibid, para 27.

293 Ibid, para 29.

294 Ibid, para 34.

factor to take into account, without, however, that being a mandatory precondition for a finding of infringement of Article 102 TFEU. Furthermore, according to the AG, 'invoicing of 'negative prices', in other words prices below cost prices, to customers is not *a prerequisite of a finding that a retroactive rebates scheme operated by a dominant undertaking is abusive', explaining that '[b]ecause of its appreciably higher turnover, the dominant undertaking can usually continue to cover its costs even though it is offering substantial rebates. It can therefore, through its rebates, trigger an exclusionary effect without necessarily having to go into the red itself'.*[295]

With regard to conditions of competition prevailing on the relevant market and the position of the dominant undertaking on that market, AG Kokott, 'account must be taken not only of the market shares held by the dominant undertaking and its competitors, but also the origin of the dominant undertaking's position and any existing statutory monopoly which it has over all or some of the market'.[296] *This is particularly damning for the rebate in this case, in view of the fact that Post Danmark controlled 95 per cent of the market and that 70 per cent of the market was closed to competition from the outset, because of Post Danmark's statutory monopoly, thus making Post Danmark an 'unavoidable trading partner'.*[297] *These findings make the AG conclude that the rebate scheme is capable of producing considerable exclusionary effects.*

With regard to AEC test, the AG states that Article 102 TFEU 'does not *support the inference of any legal obligation requiring that a finding to the effect that a rebate scheme operated by a dominant undertaking constitutes abuse must always be based on a price–cost analysis such as the AEC test'.*[298] *It dismisses the approach followed in the Enforcement Priorities Communication of the Commission noting that '[s]uch an administrative practice by the Commission is not, of course, binding on the national competition authorities and courts'.*[299] *Although the AG notes that it is not 'inconceivable, in theory, to make a finding of price-based exclusionary conduct routinely conditional on the carrying out of an AEC test',*[300] *she opposes such a 'reorientation' of the case law. She notes the following:*

> 66. On the one hand, the added value of expensive economic analyses is not always apparent and can lead to the disproportionate use of the resources of the competition authorities and the courts, which are then unavailable for the purposes of effectively enforcing the competition rules in other areas. The methodology applied can [. . .] prompt considerable differences of opinion. What is more, the data available for use as a basis for such analyses are not always reliable and presuppose that the dominant undertaking is genuinely ready to cooperate with the competition authorities and the courts, which, as the German Government has pointed out, is not always necessarily the case.
>
> 67. On the other hand, it is wrong to suppose that the issue of price-based exclusionary conduct can be managed simply and in such a way as to ensure legal certainty by applying some form of mathematical formula based on nothing more than the price and cost components of the businesses of the undertakings concerned. As I have already said, corporate data is not uncommonly open to different interpretations.
>
> 68. In particular, however, a finding of abuse in the context of Article [102 TFEU], as in other contexts, always requires an evaluation which takes into account all the relevant circumstances of the individual case in question and must not be confined to an examination of price and cost components alone. On the contrary, there are many other factors, such as the specific *modus operandi* of a rebate scheme and certain characteristics of the market on which the dominant undertaking operates, that may

[295] Ibid, para 41. [296] Ibid, para 42. [297] Ibid, paras 45–6.
[298] Ibid, para 61 (original emphasis). [299] Ibid, para 60. [300] Ibid, para 65.

also be relevant to a finding of abuse. In fact, they may be much more informative than a price/cost analysis. [. . .]

72. [. . .] [I]t would from the outset make no sense to carry out some form of price/cost analysis in order to examine whether the rebate scheme operated by the dominant undertaking has an exclusionary effect on a purely hypothetical as-efficient competitor. If no competitor can be as efficient as the dominant undertaking, then, by extension, an AEC test will not provide any reliable conclusions as to whether or not there are likely to be any exclusionary effects on the market.

73. On the contrary, on a market in which competition is so weakened by the presence of a dominant undertaking that as-efficient competitors cannot even establish themselves there, the competitive pressure exerted even by less efficient undertakings must not be underestimated. Maintaining that pressure is one of the fundamental objectives pursued by Article [102 TFEU]. It is after all essential to ensure that the market structure and the choices available to customers do not deteriorate further because of the commercial conduct of the dominant undertaking.

With regard to the need to prove 'appreciable anti-competitive effects', the AG raised the importance of a uniform application of EU competition law throughout the Union, noting that this is a matter of substantive law and thus should not be appropriately dealt with the principle of procedural autonomy with regard to issues of evidence law.[301] *She distinguishes the issue of the likelihood of the presence of the anti-competitive effect from that of the 'seriousness' or 'appreciability' of the likely anti-competitive effect.*

With regard to the first issue, she noted that the rebates 'schemes in question must be capable not only in the abstract *but also* in practice *of making it difficult or impossible for the dominant undertaking's competitors to gain access to the market and for its co-contractors to choose between various sources of supply or trading partners', without, however, going as far as requiring evidence of 'actual effects', potential effects being also sufficient. Indeed, she finds 'inappropriate to set a higher bar for assuming the existence of an abuse that is incompatible with Article [102 TFEU] and, for example, to require that the presence of an exclusionary effect must be "very likely" or "particularly likely" or must be assumed to be "beyond reasonable doubt" '.*[302] *Dominant undertakings have a 'special responsibility to ensure that their conduct does not undermine effective and undistorted competition' and thus 'must [. . .] refrain from all commercial practices which are likely to produce an exclusionary effect, not just those in the case of which such an effect seems "very likely" or "particularly likely" or must be assumed to be "beyond reasonable doubt" '.*[303]

With regard to the second issue, the AG notes some translation error of the judgment of the General Court in Post Danmark I, *which led some to consider that the CJEU called for an appreciability criterion or* de minimis *threshold to apply to rebate schemes operated by dominant undertakings. Indeed, in AG Kokott's view, 'abuse within the meaning of Article [102 TFEU] is to be regarded as being constituted by all rebate schemes operated by dominant undertakings which are capable of producing an exclusionary effect, not just those whose effects on competition are or may be "serious" or "appreciable" '.*[304] *Among the reasons put forward for the rejection of a* de minimis *test is that 'it is not the role of the dominant undertaking to dictate how many viable competitors will be allowed to compete for the remaining contestable portion of demand',*[305] *a statement that shows the structuralist overtone of AG Kokott's Opinion. The CJEU followed some of the suggestions included in the AG's Opinion.*

[301] Ibid, para 77. [302] Ibid, para 83. [303] Ibid, para 84. [304] Ibid, para 90.
[305] Ibid, para 92.

Case C-23/14, *Post Danmark A/S v Konkurrencerådet*, ECLI:EU:C:2015:651

26. As regards the application of Article [102 TFEU] to a rebate scheme, it should be recalled that, in prohibiting the abuse of a dominant market position in so far as trade between Member States could be affected, that article refers to conduct which is such as to influence the structure of a market where, as a result of the very presence of the undertaking in question, the degree of competition is already weakened and which has the effect of hindering the maintenance of the degree of competition still existing in the market or the growth of that competition (see, to that effect, judgments in *Nederlandsche Banden-Industrie-Michelin* v *Commission*, 322/81, EU:C:1983:313, paragraph 70, and *British Airways* v *Commission*, C95/04 P, EU:C:2007:166, paragraph 66).

27. It is also settled case-law that, in contrast to a quantity discount linked solely to the volume of purchases from the manufacturer concerned, which is not, in principle, liable to infringe Article [102TFEU], a loyalty rebate, which by offering customers financial advantages tends to prevent them from obtaining all or most of their requirements from competing manufacturers, amounts to an abuse within the meaning of that provision (see judgments in *Nederlandsche Banden-Industrie-Michelin* v *Commission*, 322/81, EU:C:1983:313, paragraph 71, and *Tomra Systems and Others* v *Commission*, C549/10 P, EU:C:2012:221, paragraph 70).

28. So far as the rebate scheme at issue in the main proceedings is concerned, it must be observed that that scheme cannot be regarded as a simple quantity rebate linked solely to the volume of purchases, since the rebates at issue are not granted in respect of each individual order, thus corresponding to the cost savings made by the supplier, but on the basis of the aggregate orders placed over a given period. Moreover, it was not coupled with an obligation for, or promise by, purchasers to obtain all or a given proportion of their supplies from Post Danmark, a point which served to distinguish it from loyalty rebates within the meaning of the case-law referred to in paragraph 27 above.

29. In those circumstances, in order to determine whether the undertaking in a dominant position has abused that position by applying a rebate scheme such as that at issue in the main proceedings, the Court has repeatedly held that it is necessary to consider all the circumstances, particularly the criteria and rules governing the grant of the rebate, and to investigate whether, in providing an advantage not based on any economic service justifying it, the rebate tends to remove or restrict the buyer's freedom to choose his sources of supply, to bar competitors from access to the market, to apply dissimilar conditions to equivalent transactions with other trading parties or to strengthen the dominant position by distorting competition (judgments in *British Airways* v *Commission*, C95/04 P, EU:C:2007:166, paragraph 67, and *Tomra Systems and Others* v *Commission*, C549/10 P, EU:C:2012:221, paragraph 71). [. . .]

31. In that regard, it first has to be determined whether those rebates can produce an exclusionary effect, that is to say whether they are capable, first, of making market entry very difficult or impossible for competitors of the undertaking in a dominant position and, secondly, of making it more difficult or impossible for the co-contractors of that undertaking to choose between various sources of supply or commercial partners. It then has to be examined whether there is an objective economic justification for the discounts granted (judgment in *British Airways* v *Commission*, C95/04 P, EU:C:2007:166, paragraphs 68 and 69).

32. As regards, in the first place, the criteria and rules governing the grant of the rebates, it must be recalled that the rebates at issue in the main proceedings were 'retroactive', in

the sense that, if the threshold initially set at the beginning of the year in respect of the quantities of mail was exceeded, the rebate rate applied at the end of the year applied to all mailings presented over the reference period and not only to mailings exceeding the threshold initially estimated. On the other hand, a customer whose volume of mailings proved to be lower than the quantity estimated had to reimburse Post Danmark.

33. It is apparent from the case-law that the contractual obligations of co-contractors of the undertaking in a dominant position and the pressure exerted upon them may be particularly strong where a discount does not relate solely to the growth in purchases of products of that undertaking made by those co-contractors during the period under consideration, but extends also to those purchases in aggregate. In that way, relatively modest variations in sales of the products of the dominant undertaking have disproportionate effects on co-contractors (see, to that effect, judgment in *British Airways* v *Commission*, C95/04 P, EU:C:2007:166, paragraph 73).

34. In addition, it must be pointed out that the rebate scheme at issue in the main proceedings was based on a reference period of one year. However, any system under which discounts are granted according to the quantities sold during a relatively long reference period has the inherent effect, at the end of that period, of increasing the pressure on the buyer to reach the purchase figure needed to obtain the discount or to avoid suffering the expected loss for the entire period (judgment in *Nederlandsche Banden-Industrie-Michelin* v *Commission*, 322/81, EU:C:1983:313, paragraph 81).

35. Consequently, [. . .] such a rebate scheme is capable of making it easier for the dominant undertaking to tie its own customers to itself and attract the customers of its competitors, and thus to secure the suction to itself of the part of demand subject to competition on the relevant market. That suction effect is further enhanced by the fact that, in the case in the main proceedings, the rebates applied without distinction both to the contestable part of demand and to the non-contestable part of demand, that is to say, in the latter case, to addressed advertising mail weighing less than 50 grams covered by Post Danmark's statutory monopoly. [. . .]

36. In the case in the main proceedings, according to the file placed before the Court, for 25 of Post Danmark's largest customers, representing approximately one-half of the volume of transactions on the relevant market during the period at issue, approximately two-thirds of mail sent in the form of direct advertising mail not covered by the monopoly could not be transferred from Post Danmark to Bring Citymail without an adverse impact on the scale of the rebates. If that were established, a matter which it is for the referring court to ascertain, the incentive to obtain all or a substantial proportion of their supplies from Post Danmark would be particularly strong, reducing significantly customers' freedom of choice as to their sources of supply.

37. Moreover, as regards the standardisation of the rebate scale, whereby all customers were entitled to receive the same rebate on the basis of their aggregate purchases over the reference period, such a characteristic admittedly supports the conclusion that, in principle, the rebate scheme implemented by Post Danmark did not result in the application of dissimilar conditions to equivalent transactions with other trading parties, within the meaning of Article [102(c) TFEU].

38. However, the mere fact that a rebate scheme is not discriminatory does not preclude its being regarded as capable of producing an exclusionary effect on the market, contrary to Article [102 TFEU]. [. . .]

The CJEU finds that the large market share of Post Danmark makes it an unavoidable trading partner, this fact supporting the conclusion that 'competition on that market was already very limited'. However, the Court also noted:

44. The fact that the rebates applied by Post Danmark concern a large proportion of customers on the market does not, in itself, constitute evidence of abusive conduct by that undertaking. [. . .]

46. However, the fact that a rebate scheme, such as that at issue in the main proceedings, covers the majority of customers on the market may constitute a useful indication as to the extent of that practice and its impact on the market, which may bear out the likelihood of an anticompetitive exclusionary effect.

47. Lastly, should the referring court find that there are anticompetitive effects attributable to Post Danmark, it should be recalled that it is nevertheless open to a dominant undertaking to provide justification for behaviour liable to be caught by the prohibition set out in Article [102 TFEU].

The Court repeated the principles of its jurisprudence on assessing objective justifications referring to British Airways *and* TeliaSonera *and concluded that:*

50. [. . .] in order to determine whether a rebate scheme, such as that at issue in the main proceedings, implemented by a dominant undertaking is capable of having an exclusionary effect on the market contrary to Article [102 TFEU], it is necessary to examine all the circumstances of the case, in particular, the criteria and rules governing the grant of the rebates, the extent of the dominant position of the undertaking concerned and the particular conditions of competition prevailing on the relevant market. The fact that the rebate scheme covers the majority of customers on the market may constitute a useful indication as to the extent of that practice and its impact on the market, which may bear out the likelihood of an anticompetitive exclusionary effect.

It then explored the application of the AEC test and its relevance in the competition assessment under Article 102 TFEU.

53. The application of the as-efficient-competitor test consists in examining whether the pricing practices of a dominant undertaking could drive an equally efficient competitor from the market.

54. That test is based on a comparison of the prices charged by a dominant undertaking and certain costs incurred by that undertakings as well as its strategy (see judgment in *Post Danmark*, C209/10, EU:C:2012:172, paragraph 28). [. . .]

56. As regards the comparison of prices and costs in the context of applying Article 82 EC to a rebate scheme, the Court has held that the invoicing of 'negative prices', that is to say, prices below cost prices, to customers is not a prerequisite of a finding that a retroactive rebate scheme operated by a dominant undertaking is abusive (judgment in *Tomra Systems and Others* v *Commission*, C549/10 P, EU:C:2012:221, paragraph 73). In that same case, the Court specified that the absence of a comparison of prices charged with costs did not constitute an error of law (judgment in *Tomra Systems and Others* v *Commission*, C-549/10 P, EU:C:2012:221, paragraph 80). [. . .]

58. Nevertheless, that conclusion ought not to have the effect of excluding, on principle, recourse to the as-efficient-competitor test in cases involving a rebate scheme for the purposes of examining its compatibility with Article [102 TFEU].

The AG noted that in a market where competition is already limited, as in the situation of Post Danmark, applying the AEC test may be of no relevance to the extent that the structure of the market makes the emergence of an as-efficient competitor practically impossible. The CJEU agreed with the AG that preserving less efficient competitors may be an aim to pursue in such circumstances.

60. [. . .] [I]n a market such as that at issue in the main proceedings, access to which is protected by high barriers, the presence of a less efficient competitor might contribute to intensifying the competitive pressure on that market and, therefore, to exerting a constraint on the conduct of the dominant undertaking.

The Court notes that the AEC is just a tool amongst others for the purposes of assessing whether there is an abuse of a dominant position in the context of a rebate scheme.

The likelihood of anticompetitive effects

66. The Court has [. . .] held that, in order to establish whether such a practice is abusive, that practice must have an anticompetitive effect on the market, but the effect does not necessarily have to be concrete, and it is sufficient to demonstrate that there is an anticompetitive effect which may potentially exclude competitors who are at least as efficient as the dominant undertaking (judgment in *TeliaSonera Sverige*, C52/09, EU:C:2011:83, paragraph 64). [. . .]

68. In that regard, the assessment of whether a rebate scheme is capable of restricting competition must be carried out in the light of all relevant circumstances, including the rules and criteria governing the grant of the rebates, the number of customers concerned and the characteristics of the market on which the dominant undertaking operates.

69. Such an assessment seeks to determine whether the conduct of the dominant undertaking produces an actual or likely exclusionary effect, to the detriment of competition and, thereby, of consumers' interests (judgment in *Post Danmark*, C209/10, EU:C:2012:172, paragraph 44).

The appreciability of anticompetitive effects—*de minimis* rejected

70. As regards, in the second place, the serious or appreciable nature of an anticompetitive effect, although it is true that a finding that an undertaking has a dominant position is not in itself a ground of criticism of the undertaking concerned (judgment in *Post Danmark*, C-209/10, EU:C:2012:172, paragraph 21), the conduct of such an undertaking may give rise to an abuse of its dominant position because the structure of competition on the market has already been weakened (see, to that effect, judgments in *Hoffmann-La Roche v Commission*, 85/76, EU:C:1979:36, paragraph 123, and *France Télécom* v *Commission*, C-202/07 P, EU:C:2009:214, paragraph 107).

The CJEU notes the special responsibility of the dominant undertaking and the fact that as the 'structure of competition on the market' is already weakened because of the dominant undertaking, 'any further weakening of the structure of competition may constitute an abuse of a dominant position'.[306]

73. It follows that fixing an appreciability (*de minimis*) threshold for the purposes of determining whether there is an abuse of a dominant position is not justified. That anticompetitive practice is, by its very nature, liable to give rise to not insignificant restrictions of competition, or even of eliminating competition on the market on which the undertaking concerned operates.

74. It follows from the foregoing considerations that Article [102 TFEU] must be interpreted as meaning that, in order to fall within the scope of that article, the anticompetitive effect of a rebate scheme operated by a dominant undertaking must be probable, there being no need to show that it is of a serious or appreciable nature.

306 Case C-23/14, *Post Danmark II*, ECLI:EU:C:2015:651, para 72.

NOTES AND QUESTIONS ON POST DANMARK II

1. Do you think that the judgment of the CJEU adheres to the more formalistic perspective in the implementation of Article 102 TFEU, or that it also contains elements of an 'effects-based' approach? Is this 'effects-based' approach looking similar to a market/welfare effects-based approach?
2. (Paragraph 27) Does the CJEU conclude that loyalty rebates are abusive by object?
3. (Paragraph 28) Can retroactive rebates be part of the 'quantity rebates' category, thus being presumptively lawful and escaping liability under Article 102 TFEU? Are retroactive rebates on aggregate orders placed over a given period, as in this case those adopted by Post Danmark categorized as quantity rebates? Are they categorized as loyalty rebates?
4. (Paragraphs 29, 50, 68). How should retroactive rebates on aggregate orders be assessed? Note that the CJEU requires the consideration of 'all the circumstances' of the specific rebate. Does the Court adopt the suggestions of its Advocate General concerning this issue, who also highlighted the need to take into account all the circumstances of the specific rebate, each market and each rebate scheme having features which are peculiar to it?[307] Is this compatible with a restriction of competition by object or a restriction of competition by effect assessment?
5. These factors include the criteria and rules governing the grant of the rebate,[308] but also the extent of the dominant position and the particular conditions of competition on the market.[309] Are these factors similar to those taken into account by the previous case law of the CJEU?
6. (Paragraphs 69, 74) Does the Court distinguish between the concepts of 'actual or likely exclusionary effect, to the detriment of competition and, *thereby*, of consumers' interests' and that of 'probable' anti-competitive effect?[310] Are the two concepts one and the same thing? If this is the case, would you consider that evidence of likely exclusionary effect, resulting out of the suction effect produced by a rebate would be sufficient to be considered as 'probable', without the need to prove that this leads to consumer harm? Note that the Court mentions harm to consumers' interest as following up from the existence of a detriment of competition (thereby), but does not seem to require independent evidence of consumer harm, this being merely assumed by the existence of a detriment to competition. Is this compatible with a market/welfare effects-based approach?
7. (Paragraphs 70 and 73) Would the rejection of the *de minimis* test make sense if the CJEU was adopting a market/welfare effects-based approach? Does the CJEU adopt the conclusions of the Opinion of its Advocate General on this issue as well?

9.6.4.3. *Intel*

In May 2009, the European Commission adopted a decision finding that Intel had infringed Article 102 TFEU and fining the undertaking €1.06 billion for conduct vis-à-vis five major

307 See Opinion of AG Kokott, in Case C-23/14, *Post Danmark A/S v Konkurrencerådet*, ECLI:EU:C:2015:343, para 34.

308 Case C-23/14, *Post Danmark II*, ECLI:EU:C:2015:651, paras 32–6.

309 Ibid, paras 40–6.

310 Ibid, para 69 (emphasis added).

original equipment manufacturers (OEMs)—namely: Dell, Hewlett-Packard (HP), Acer, NEC, and IBM—with the aim to foreclose its competitor Advanced Micro Devices (AMD).[311] This decision was first appealed by Intel to the General Court, which issued its judgment in June 2014, and then to the CJEU, whose judgment was adopted in September 2017. The products concerned by the Decision are central processing units (CPUs) of the x86 architecture. The CPU is a key component of any computer, both in terms of overall performance and in terms of cost. It is often referred to as a computer's 'brain'. The x86 architecture is a standard designed by Intel for its CPUs. It can run both the Windows and Linux operating systems. The decision of the Commission noted that since 2000, Intel and AMD are essentially the only two companies still manufacturing x86 CPUs. The Commission's enquiry led to the conclusion that the relevant product market was not wider than the worldwide market of x86 CPUs, leaving open the question whether the relevant product market definition could be subdivided between x86 CPUs for desktop computers, notebook computers and servers since, as the Commission remarked, given Intel's market shares under either definition, there is no difference to the conclusion on dominance. On the basis of Intel's market shares and the barriers to entry and expansion, the Commission concluded that Intel held a dominant position in the market during the period of the infringement. Intel had adopted two types of conduct: vis-à-vis its trading partners: conditional rebates and so-called naked restrictions. The description of the practices follows in the following excerpt of the General Court's judgment, which confirmed the approach followed by the Commission.[312]

Case T-286/09 *Intel Corp v European Commission*, ECLI:EU:T:2014:547

Facts

27. The contested decision describes two types of Intel conduct vis-à-vis its trading partners, namely conditional rebates and 'naked restrictions'.

28. First, according to the contested decision, Intel awarded four OEMs, namely Dell, Lenovo, HP and NEC, rebates which were conditioned on these OEMs purchasing all or almost all of their x86 CPUs from Intel. Similarly, Intel awarded payments to MSH, which were conditioned on MSH selling exclusively computers containing Intel's x86 CPUs.

29. The contested decision concludes that the conditional rebates granted by Intel constitute fidelity rebates. With regard to Intel's conditional payments to MSH, the contested decision establishes that the economic mechanism of these payments is equivalent to that of the conditional rebates to OEMs.

30. The contested decision also conducts an economic analysis of the capability of the rebates to foreclose a hypothetical competitor as efficient as Intel (as-efficient-competitor test; 'the AEC test'), albeit not dominant. More precisely, the test establishes at what price a competitor as efficient as Intel would have had to offer CPUs in order to compensate an OEM for the loss of an Intel rebate. The same kind of analysis was conducted for the Intel payments to MSH.

31. The evidence gathered by the Commission led it to the conclusion that Intel's conditional rebates and payments induced the loyalty of the key OEMs and of MSH.

311 *Intel* (Case COMP/C-3/37.990) Commission Decision (summary) [2009] OJ C 227/13. On this case, see also our analysis in Section 8.4.5.3.3.

312 See Section S.9.6.4.3.

> The effects of these practices were complementary, in that they significantly diminished competitors' ability to compete on the merits of their x86 CPUs. Intel's anti-competitive conduct thereby resulted in a reduction of consumer choice and in lower incentives to innovate.
>
> 32. Second, with regard to naked restrictions, the Commission states that Intel awarded three OEMs, namely HP, Acer and Lenovo, payments which were conditioned on these OEMs postponing or cancelling the launch of AMD CPU-based products and/or putting restrictions on the distribution of those products. The contested decision concludes that Intel's conduct also directly harmed competition, and did not constitute normal competition on the merits.
>
> 33. The Commission concludes in the contested decision that, in each instance, Intel's conduct vis-à-vis the OEMs mentioned above and MSH constitutes an abuse under Article [102 TFEU], but that each of those individual abuses are also part of a single strategy aimed at foreclosing AMD, Intel's only significant competitor, from the market for x86 CPUs. Those individual abuses are therefore part of a single infringement of Article [102 TFEU].

On appeal, the CJEU set aside the GC's judgment with regard to the assessment of the rebate scheme.[313]

We have already commented on the appeal to the CJEU by Intel and the Opinion of Advocate General N Wahl.[314] We include here some excerpts from the Opinion of AG Wahl before exploring the CJEU's judgment. Parts of the Opinion relating to the general philosophy of Article 102 TFEU, are not produced here as they are commented on in Section 8.4.5.3.3. We only include the parts relating to the characterization of the rebates and the test employed for their assessment. Note that AG Wahl adopts an economic efficiency perspective for competition law and that for him 'effects' means welfare effects, not just exclusionary effects or 'fidelity-inducing effects'.[315] The Advocate general also uses the term 'exclusionary effect', but this seems not to be considered as a synonym to 'anti-competitive effect', as it indicates the exclusionary potential of a rebate, because of its 'fidelity-inducing effect', but this, in his opinion, is not sufficient to prove the existence of anti-competitive effects bringing the rebate under the scope of a prohibition under Article 102 TFEU.[316] The AG seems also inspired by the distinction introduced at the European Commission's Non-Horizontal Merger Guidelines between 'foreclosure effect' (which could be considered as a synonym to 'exclusionary effect') and 'anti-competitive foreclosure effect' (which refers to welfare effects, not just exclusionary effects), only the latter counting for him as evidence of an infringement of Article 102 TFEU. This different conception of 'effects' makes AG Wahl disagree with AG Kokott, and in our view also with the jurisprudence of the CJEU in *Post Danmark II*, on the rejection of a *de minimis* test in Article 102 TFEU.

Reinforcing the impression of a trend towards a unified conceptual structure of Articles 101 and 102 TFEU, the Opinion of AG Wahl embraces the distinction between object and effect in the context of Article 102 TFEU, while emphasizing the need to take into account the 'legal and economic context' in all cases, as it is also happening within the context of Article 101 TFEU.

313 Case C-413/14 P, *Intel Corp v European Commission*, ECLI:EU:C:2017:632.

314 See Section 4.5.3.3.5.

315 See Opinion of AG N Wahl in Case C-413/14 P, *Intel Corp v European Commission*, ECLI:EU:C:2016:788, paras 40–3.

316 See the way this term is used ibid, paras 117–18.

This leads him to conclude that there cannot be a presumption of anti-competitive effect and illegality for any *type* of rebate (even loyalty rebates), as the economic and legal context (or 'all the circumstances' of the specific rebate, which is the expression mostly used in the context of Article 102 TFEU, for saying the same thing than the 'economic and legal context' for Article 101 TFEU purposes always plays a role in the assessment).

The Opinion of AG Wahl manifests a different conception than that of AG Kokott on the interpretation and enforcement of Article 102 TFEU to rebate schemes. Identify the main differences and reflect on the deeper disagreements they reflect on the intellectual foundations of Article 102 TFEU and, more generally, competition law (welfare versus competitive process; economic efficiency versus multi-values/goals approach; rules versus standards).

Opinion of Advocate General N Wahl in Case C-413/14 P, *Intel Corp v European Commission*, ECLI:EU:C:2016:788

[The importance of taking into account 'all the circumstances' of the rebate, in particular its 'legal and economic context']

54. [. . .] [T]he basic tenets of the relevant case-law will be set out to illustrate that the case-law requires an assessment of all the circumstances. [. . .]

60. On a general note, the case-law of the Court displays a mistrust of a variety of different rebate mechanisms offered by dominant undertakings. This may be explained by the fact that it is generally considered that dominant undertakings have a special responsibility not to allow their conduct to impair competition on the internal market. From this special responsibility it follows that mechanisms which in one way or another tie customers to source supplies from the dominant undertaking are regarded as loyalty-inducing and, thus, presumptively abusive.

61. It follows from the line of authority devolving from the seminal *Hoffmann-La Roche* judgment that rebates that are conditional on the customer purchasing all or most of its requirements from the dominant undertaking are presumptively unlawful. The same presumption of unlawfulness applies to other rebates which also induce loyalty, even though they are not formally based on exclusivity. Rebates, be they retroactive and individualised, as in the cases of *Michelin I, British Airways* and *Tomra* or market-share based and individualised as in *Hoffmann-La Roche*, have been regarded as anticompetitive by the Court. So far, the only type of rebate that has escaped the presumption of unlawfulness is one which is volume-based. Those rebates are linked solely to the volume of purchases made from an undertaking in a dominant position.

62. The rebates and payments offered by Intel can be described as market-share-based loyalty rebates. To be eligible for a discount, the customer must source a certain percentage of its requirements from the dominant undertaking. As explained, relying on the statement of the Court in *Hoffmann-La Roche*, the General Court considered that, where a rebate is an exclusivity rebate falling under category 2, there is no need to consider the capability of such a rebate to restrict competition on the basis of the circumstances of the case.

63. *Hoffmann-La Roche* dealt with a market-share-based rebate scheme which was conditional on the customer purchasing a certain percentage of its requirements from the dominant undertaking. More specifically, the rebates were incremental depending on the percentage of the turnover reached by the purchases. In that case, the Court held that, save in exceptional circumstances, loyalty rebates are not based on an economic

transaction which justifies this burden or benefit. Instead, they are, in the Court's view, designed to remove or restrict the purchaser's freedom to choose its sources of supply and to deny other producers access to the market. According to the Court, therefore, 'an undertaking which is in a dominant position on a market and ties purchasers ... by an obligation or promise on their part to obtain all or most of their requirements exclusively from that undertaking abuses its dominant position within the meaning of Article [102 TFEU], whether the obligation in question is stipulated without further qualification or whether it is undertaken in consideration of the grant of a rebate'. The Court went on to hold that the 'same applies if the said undertaking, without tying the purchasers by a formal obligation, applies, either under the terms of agreements concluded with these purchasers or unilaterally, a system of loyalty rebates, that is to say, discounts conditional on the customer's obtaining—whether the quantity of its purchases is large or small—all or most of its requirements from the undertaking in a dominant position'.

64. In making that seminal statement, the Court made no mention of the need to consider all the circumstances when determining whether an abuse of a dominant position had been established to the requisite legal standard.

65. Seen in that light, it is perhaps not surprising that the General Court concluded as it did.

66. However, it should be pointed out already here that in *Hoffmann-La Roche* the conclusion concerning the unlawfulness of the rebates in question was, nevertheless, based on a thorough analysis of, inter alia, the conditions surrounding the grant of the rebates and the market coverage thereof. It was on the basis of that assessment that the Court held that the loyalty rebates in question were, in that case, intended, by granting a financial advantage, to prevent customers from obtaining their supplies from competing producers.

67. Since *Hoffmann-La Roche*, as the General Court rightly pointed out, the case-law has mainly centred on devising the appropriate criteria for determining whether an undertaking has abused its dominant position by making use of rebate schemes that are not directly linked to exclusive or quasi-exclusive supply. These are the rebates that, in the taxonomy employed in the judgment under appeal, fall within category 3.

68. In that subsequent case-law, the Court has constantly reiterated the statement of principle stemming from *Hoffmann-La Roche* concerning the presumptive abusiveness of loyalty rebates. Yet, as ACT correctly pointed out at the hearing, in practice it has consistently taken into account 'all the circumstances' in ascertaining whether the impugned conduct amounts to an abuse of a dominant position contrary to Article 102 TFEU. [. . .]

70. Reiterating a statement of principle concerning a presumptive abusiveness is, as shown in the Court's case-law, however, not the same thing as failing to consider the circumstances in a concrete case. In fact, the judgment under appeal constitutes one of the very few cases where the Court's statement in *Hoffmann-La Roche* has been applied *verbatim*, without examining the circumstances of the case, before concluding that an undertaking has abused its dominant position. To justify that strict approach to 'exclusivity rebates', the General Court considered in the judgment under appeal that the rebates and payments made by Intel were conditional on exclusivity (in a similar, yet not identical manner as in *Hoffmann-La Roche*, given the lack of a formal exclusivity obligation). That circumstance served to distinguish the present case from those mentioned in the previous point.

71. It could, therefore, easily be concluded that, on its face, the judgment under appeal simply reaffirms the existing case-law and applies it to Intel's conduct.

72. However, such a conclusion would overlook the importance of the legal and economic context in accordance with that same case-law. [. . .]

The circumstances of the case as a means to determine whether the impugned conduct has a likely effect on competition

74. Even a brief perusal of the cases discussed above (points 66 to 69), shows that the case-law does not omit to look at the legal and economic context of the conduct—or, to employ the standard formula in Article 102 TFEU cases, 'all the circumstances'—in order to determine whether an undertaking has abused its dominant position. That is the case for both rebates conditioned on exclusivity and other types of loyalty inducing arrangements.

75. Accordingly, in my view, the General Court's interpretation of *Hoffmann-La Roche* misses an important point. Contrary to what was held in the judgment under appeal, in *Hoffmann-La Roche* the Court considered several circumstances relating to the legal and economic context of the rebates in finding that the undertaking in question had abused its dominant position. True, that judgment does not explicitly state that an analysis of all the circumstances is crucial for determining whether the impugned conduct amounts to an abuse of a dominant position. Nevertheless, as noted above (point 66), a closer look at the judgment shows that the Court examined in commendable detail the particularities of the pharmaceutical market in question, the market coverage of the rebates, as well as the terms and conditions of the contracts between the dominant undertaking and its customers. On the basis of that detailed analysis of the legal and economic context of the rebates, namely the conditions for the grant of the rebates, the market coverage thereof, as well as the duration of the rebate arrangements, the Court reached the conclusion that loyalty rebates are unlawful, save in exceptional circumstances.

76. [. . .] [A]part from *Hoffmann-La Roche*, I am not aware that the Court has dealt with other cases pertaining to exclusive supply obligations similar to those at issue there. Unsurprisingly, therefore, the need to consider all the circumstances was yet again reiterated in *Post Danmark II*, a preliminary ruling handed down after the judgment under appeal was delivered, in relation to retroactive rebates that are not tied to an exclusivity obligation.

77. But what does an assessment of 'all the circumstances' *entail*?

78. As I see it, the analysis of 'context'—or 'all the circumstances', as it is termed in the Court's case-law—aims simply but crucially to ascertain that it has been established, to the requisite legal standard, that an undertaking has abused its dominant position. Even in the case of seemingly evident exclusionary behaviour, such as pricing below cost, context cannot be overlooked. Otherwise, conduct which, on occasion, is simply not capable of restricting competition would be caught by a blanket prohibition. Such a blanket prohibition would also risk catching and penalising pro-competitive conduct.

79. That is why context is essential.

There are only two categories of rebates according to the case-law

80. For the purposes of Article 102 TFEU, loyalty rebates constitute—as I see it—a near-equivalent to a restriction by object under Article 101 TFEU. This is because loyalty rebates, like restrictions by object, are presumptively unlawful. However, as already noted above (point 61), loyalty rebates must be understood as encompassing not only those conditional on the customer sourcing all or most of its requirements with the dominant undertaking, but also other pricing structures conditional upon the customer reaching a particular target.

81. Contrary to what the General Court held in the judgment under appeal, the case-law distinguishes between *two, not three*, categories of rebates. On the one hand, some rebates are presumptively lawful, such as volume-based rebates. Any

investigation into the (un)lawfulness of such rebates necessarily requires a full examination of their actual or potential effects. Those rebates are not at issue here.

82. On the other hand, for loyalty rebates (which are presumptively unlawful), whether those rebates are directly conditional upon exclusivity or not, the Court employs an approach that displays certain similarities with the approach to restrictions by object under Article 101 TFEU. That is because, under that provision too, in order to ascertain whether certain conduct constitutes a restriction by object, the legal and economic context of the impugned conduct must first be examined so as to exclude any other plausible explanation for that conduct. In other words, the particular context of the impugned conduct is never ignored.

83. As already mentioned above, in *Hoffmann-La Roche* the Court did consider all the circumstances. [. . .] The purpose of an analysis of all the circumstances is to ascertain whether an abuse of dominance has been established to the requisite legal standard and whether, as a consequence, the rebates are capable of anticompetitive foreclosure.

84. In the judgment under appeal, however, the General Court went one step further. By applying the statement of the Court in *Hoffmann-La Roche* to the letter, without placing that statement in its proper context, it distinguished one sub-type of loyalty rebate, which it termed 'exclusivity rebates', from other types of rebates that induce loyalty. In doing so, it created a 'super category' of rebates for which consideration of all the circumstances is not required in order to conclude that the impugned conduct amounts to an abuse of dominance contrary to Article 102 TFEU. More importantly, the abusiveness of such rebates is assumed in the abstract, based purely on their form.

85. That is by no means a methodologically self-evident step to take. The following four reasons explain why.

An assumption of unlawfulness by virtue of form cannot be rebutted

[. . .]

88. [Firstly] [. . .] [T]here is no efficiency or other consideration that can assist an undertaking in justifying the use of 'exclusivity rebates' where the prohibition is concerned with form, rather than effects. Indeed, irrespective of the effects, the form remains the same. That is problematic. The dominant undertaking should be able, as the General Court rightly pointed out in the judgment under appeal, (and as the Commission itself accepted in its written pleadings, to justify the use of a rebate scheme by providing evidence that the exclusionary effect produced may be counterbalanced or even outweighed by advantages in terms of efficiency.

Loyalty rebates are not always harmful

89. Secondly, creating a 'super-category' of rebates is warranted only if it is considered that there can be no redeeming features relating to arrangements that are conditioned on exclusivity, irrespective of the individual circumstances of the particular case. Paradoxically, however, the General Court itself admitted that exclusivity conditions can also have beneficial effects. Yet, it rejected any need to look into those effects on the ground that, owing to the dominant position of the undertaking on the market, competition is already and irrefutably restricted.

90. Experience and economic analysis do not unequivocally suggest that loyalty rebates are, as a rule, harmful or anticompetitive, even when offered by dominant undertakings. That is because rebates enhance rivalry, the very essence of competition.

91. It is true, however, that the greatest competitive concern in relation to rebates is said to arise where the customers of a dominant undertaking must carry a percentage of its products and/or where the discount is conditional on the customer purchasing all (or a substantial part) of its requirements from it. That could be seen as an argument in favour of treating 'exclusivity rebates' more strictly. Yet, other types of rebates can have a similar distorting effect. This is so even where the scheme is not explicitly linked to exclusivity.

92. Indeed, as the case-law clearly illustrates, a mechanism that induces loyalty may take different forms. As was the case in *Hoffmann-La Roche* and *Tomra*, the loyalty mechanism can be inherent in the requirement that the customer purchase all or most of its material requirements from the dominant undertaking. It can also take the form of individualised sales targets or bonuses, which are not necessarily tied to a particular proportion of requirements or sales.

93. Seen in that light, there is no objective reason why category 2 rebates should receive a stricter treatment than those falling under category 3.

The effects of loyalty rebates are context-dependent

94. Thirdly, contemporary economic literature commonly emphasises that the effects of exclusivity are context-dependent. Conversely, few commentators would deny that loyalty rebates in particular can—depending on the circumstances—have an anticompetitive foreclosure effect. [. . .]

100. If anything, the difference between the rebates at issue in *Tomra* and *Hoffmann-La Roche* is one of degree rather than kind. The same can be said about *Post Danmark II*, a case in which the relevance of context and all the circumstances in determining whether the impugned conduct amounts to an abuse of a dominant position was recently confirmed.

Related practices require consideration of 'all the circumstances'

101. Fourthly, and lastly, the case-law relating to pricing and margin squeeze practices requires, as the appellant rightly points out, consideration of all the circumstances in order to determine whether the undertaking in question has abused its dominant position.

102. The General Court dismissed the relevance of that case-law on the ground that, unlike an incentive to exclusive supply, a particular price cannot be abusive in and of itself. Yet, the judgment under appeal considers Intel's rebates to be anticompetitive on account of price. To my mind, dismissing the relevance of that case-law is problematic: it results in an unwarranted distinction between different types of pricing practices. Indeed, loyalty rebates, margin squeeze practices as well as predatory pricing possess the common feature of constituting 'price based exclusion'.

103. It goes without saying that it is of the utmost importance that legal tests applied to one category of conduct are coherent with those applied to comparable practices. Sound and coherent legal categorisation benefits not only undertakings in terms of increased legal certainty, but also assists competition authorities in the enforcement of competition law. Arbitrary categorisation does not.

104. The Court seems to agree. Most recently in *Post Danmark II*, the Court applied the case-law relating to pricing and margin squeeze practices to support its findings in relation to a rebate scheme offered by a dominant undertaking. It is true, however, that *Post Danmark II* could also be read as supporting the view that, in so far as 'exclusivity rebates' are concerned, there might be no need to consider all the circumstances. The reason for this is that, in that case, the Court distinguished the rebates in question

from those based on an exclusivity obligation before holding that all the circumstances must be considered to determine whether the dominant undertaking has abused its dominant position. Indeed, if anything, the retroactive rebates considered by the Court in that case resembled those that were considered, in the judgment under appeal, to be fidelity-inducing rebates belonging to category 3.

105. As explained above, such a distinction is a distinction without a difference (given that the difference lies in form rather than effects). More fundamentally, however, such a reading of that judgment would stand in contrast to the approach of the Court—sitting in Grand Chamber—in *Post Danmark I*, where it held that in so far as pricing practices are concerned, all the circumstances must be considered. Tellingly in fact, the Court reiterated, at a different point in its judgment in *Post Danmark II*—and there without distinguishing between different types of rebates schemes—that 'the assessment of whether a rebate scheme is capable of restricting competition must be carried out in the light of all relevant circumstances'. Assuredly it did so in order to ensure a coherent jurisprudential approach to the assessment of conduct falling under the purview of Article 102 TFEU.

The AG then reached the following conclusion.

106. Having regard to the above, 'exclusivity rebates' should not be regarded as a separate and unique category of rebates that requires no consideration of all the circumstances in order to determine whether the impugned conduct amounts to an abuse of a dominant position. Accordingly, in my opinion, the General Court erred in law in considering that 'exclusivity rebates' can be categorised as abusive without an analysis of the capacity of the rebates to restrict competition depending on the circumstances of the case.

107. That said, the General Court proceeded, in the alternative, to assess in detail whether the rebates and payments offered by the appellant were capable of restricting competition. That is to say, it investigated 'all the circumstances'. That is why the finding regarding an error in law made in the previous point does not necessarily entail the setting aside of the judgment under appeal. [. . .]

The AG continues assessing the way the GC considered 'all the circumstances' of the rebate.

Capability and/or likelihood [of anti-competitive foreclosure]

114. Certainly, evidence of actual effects does not need to be presented. This is because it is sufficient, in relation to conduct that is presumptively unlawful, that the impugned conduct be capable of restricting competition. Importantly, however, that capability cannot merely be hypothetical or theoretically possible. Otherwise, there would be no need to consider all the circumstances in the first place.

115. True, there is some discrepancy in the case-law regarding the terminology employed. The case-law refers to capability and likelihood, sometimes even interchangeably. It is my understanding that those terms designate one and the same compulsory step in an analysis seeking to determine whether the use of loyalty rebates amounts to an abuse of a dominant position.

116. But what degree of probability of anticompetitive foreclosure is required? That question is at the core of the disagreement between the appellant and the Commission regarding the adequacy of the General Court's assessment of capability: whereas the Commission believes that the assessment was adequate, Intel claims that the General Court failed to verify that the appellant's conduct could, in the circumstances of the case, restrict competition.

117. The aim of the assessment of capability is to ascertain whether, in all likelihood, the impugned conduct has an anticompetitive foreclosure effect. For that reason, likelihood must be considerably more than a mere possibility that certain behaviour may restrict competition. Contrariwise, the fact that an exclusionary effect appears more likely than not is simply not enough.

118. Although it is certainly true that in its case-law the Court has consistently emphasised the special responsibility of dominant undertakings, that responsibility cannot be taken to mean that the threshold for the application of the prohibition of abuse laid down in Article 102 TFEU can be lowered to such an extent as to become virtually non-existent. That would be the case if the degree of likelihood required for ascertaining that the impugned conduct amounts to an abuse of a dominant position was nothing more than the mere theoretical possibility of an exclusionary effect, as seems to be suggested by the Commission. If such a low level of likelihood were accepted, one would have to accept that EU competition law sanctions form, not anticompetitive effects.

119. Clearly, that would considerably hamper the attainment of the objectives of EU competition law. To assume the existence of an abuse on the basis that, on balance, anticompetitive foreclosure seems more likely than not risks capturing not only isolated instances of practices, but a non-negligible number of practices that may, in reality, be pro-competitive. The cost of error of such an approach would be unacceptably high due to over-inclusion.

120. To avoid over-inclusion, the assessment of capability as concerns presumptively unlawful behaviour must be understood as seeking to ascertain that, having regard to all circumstances, the behaviour in question does not just have ambivalent effects on the market or only produce ancillary restrictive effects necessary for the performance of something which is pro-competitive, but that its presumed restrictive effects are in fact confirmed. Absent such a confirmation, a fully-fledged analysis has to be performed. [. . .]

[Intent and capability to restrict competition]

128. While a strategy of foreclosure may certainly provide an indication of a subjective intent to foreclose competitors, the mere will to do so does not translate into capability to restrict competition. [. . .]

Other circumstances [context]

135. As already explained, in a somewhat similar fashion to the enforcement shortcut concerning restrictions by object under Article 101 TFEU, the assessment of all the circumstances under Article 102 TFEU involves examining the context of the impugned conduct to ascertain whether it can be confirmed to have an anticompetitive effect. If any of the circumstances thus examined casts doubt on the anticompetitive nature of the behaviour, a more thorough effects analysis becomes necessary.

Market coverage

140. As explained, the focus of EU competition rules has consistently been on effects, not form. Viewed in that light, the size of the tied part of the market is equally relevant, irrespective of the form of the scheme. That is why it is generally accepted that the likelihood of negative effects on competition increases in line with the size of the tied market share.

141. That said, defining the level of market coverage that may cause anticompetitive effects is by no means an arithmetic exercise. Unsurprisingly, therefore, the Court has rejected the idea that a precise threshold of foreclosure of the market must be determined, beyond which the practices at issue can be regarded as abusive for the purposes of applying Article 102 TFEU. This was confirmed by the Court in *Tomra*.

142. It is certainly true that thresholds may prove problematic due to the specificities of different markets and the circumstances of each individual case. For example, where loyalty rebates target customers that are of particular importance for competitors to enter or expand their share of the market, even modest market coverage *can* certainly result in anticompetitive foreclosure. Whether that is the case will depend on a number of factors specific thereto.

143. Seen in that light, a market coverage of 14% may or may not have an anticompetitive foreclosure effect. What is certain, however, is that such market coverage cannot rule out that the rebates in question *do not* have an anticompetitive foreclosure effect. This is so even assuming that the rebates and payments in question target key customers. Quite simply, 14% is inconclusive.

144. [. . .] [A]ccording to the General Court, the fact that an undertaking constitutes an unavoidable trading partner indicates, at the very least, that an 'exclusivity rebate' or payment offered by such an undertaking is capable of restricting competition.

145. That conclusion is only correct if it is accepted that the degree of likelihood required does not amount to anything more than the mere possibility that certain behaviour has anticompetitive effects. As previously explained, however, the assessment of all the circumstances seeks to ascertain that the impugned conduct has, in all likelihood, an anticompetitive effect.

Duration

[. . .]

151. Where, as here, exclusivity hinges, in the final analysis, on the *choice* of the customer to source the majority of supplies from the dominant undertaking, it cannot simply be assumed—*ex post facto*—that the cumulation of short-term agreements shows that those rebates are capable of restricting competition. [. . .]

153. First, unlike in a situation of exclusive dealing, there is no penalty involved in switching suppliers. [. . .]

154. More specifically, in an *ex post* analysis of duration, as here, it is necessary to determine whether another supplier could have compensated for the loss of the rebates. [. . .]

155. Plainly, it cannot simply be assumed, on the basis of a customer's choice to stay with the dominant undertaking, that that choice constitutes an expression of abusive behaviour. That is because there may be other plausible explanations for that choice. Those include, but are not limited to, quality concerns, the security of supply, and the preference of end-users.

156. Second, a long overall duration of the arrangement can certainly point to a loyalty-inducing effect of the rebate mechanism at the level of the individual customer. However, unless further compelling evidence to that effect has been presented, the fact that a customer has decided to stay with the dominant undertaking cannot suffice to establish that the rebates offered are capable of restricting competition to the requisite standard. [. . .]

157. Therefore, I consider that the assessment of duration undertaken in the judgment under appeal—which was limited to considering the overall duration of the arrangements scrutinised—is inconclusive. Quite simply, that assessment does not assist in ascertaining that that conduct has, in all likelihood, an anticompetitive effect.

The AEC test

164. [. . .] The foreclosure capability must be demonstrated in each individual case. Certainly, the AEC test can be dismissed as irrelevant if one accepts that a mere hypothetical or theoretical possibility that the impugned conduct has an anticompetitive foreclosure effect suffices to establish an abuse. Indeed, in theory, any rebate offered by a dominant undertaking can, in some circumstances, have an anticompetitive effect.

165. However, given that an exclusionary effect is required, the AEC test cannot be ignored. As the General Court noted, the test serves to identify conduct which makes it economically impossible for an as-efficient competitor to secure the contestable share of a customer's demand. In other words, it can help identify conduct that has, in all likelihood, an anticompetitive effect. By contrast, where the test shows that an as-efficient competitor is able to cover its costs, the likelihood of an anticompetitive effect significantly decreases. That is why, from the perspective of capturing conduct that has an anticompetitive foreclosure effect, the AEC test is particularly useful.

166. As regards the second and the third considerations, I have explained above (points 101 to 105) why the case-law relating to pricing practices and margin squeeze practices should not be disregarded. In any event, any remaining uncertainty in that regard has disappeared with *Post Danmark II*. That case demonstrates that the case-law pertaining to other types of price-based exclusion cannot simply be disregarded in the context of rebate cases. As the Court confirmed, by reference inter alia to that case-law, the AEC test may prove useful in the context of assessing a rebate scheme too. [. . .]

168. In that sense, it would certainly seem tempting to conclude that, in the present case, there is no need to have recourse to an AEC test. Following that logic, as argued by the Commission, the assessment of capability carried out by the General Court would not contain an error in law in having disregarded the AEC test as irrelevant.

169. However, that standpoint overlooks two issues. Unlike in *Tomra*, the Commission did in fact carry out an extensive AEC analysis in the decision at issue. More fundamentally still, the other circumstances assessed by the General Court do not unequivocally support a finding of an effect on competition. In those circumstances, it is clear to me that the AEC test cannot simply be ignored as an irrelevant circumstance. [. . .]

172. The circumstances considered in that assessment cannot confirm an effect on competition. At most, that assessment shows that an anticompetitive foreclosure effect of the impugned conduct is theoretically possible, but the effect as such has not been confirmed. As a matter of principle, an assessment of all the circumstances must, at the very least, take into account the market coverage and duration of the impugned conduct. In addition, it may be necessary to consider other circumstances that may differ from case to case. In the present case, the AEC test, precisely because that test was carried out by the Commission in the decision at issue, cannot be ignored in ascertaining whether the impugned conduct is capable of having an anticompetitive foreclosure effect. The assessment of the relevant circumstances should, taken as a whole, allow us to ascertain, to the requisite degree of likelihood, that the undertaking in question has abused its dominant position contrary to Article 102 TFEU. Absent such a confirmation due to, for example, low market coverage, short duration of the impugned arrangements or a positive result of an AEC test, a more thorough economic assessment of the actual or potential effects on competition is necessary for the purposes of establishing an abuse. [. . .]

Classification of certain rebates as 'exclusivity rebates'

The appellant argued that the General Court should not have classified the rebate arrangements with HP and Lenovo as 'exclusivity rebates'. Indeed, '[a]lthough those rebates covered 95% of HP's corporate desktops and 80% of Lenovo's notebooks, they constitute a minority of the CPU purchases of those two undertakings taken as a whole' and hence, 'the General Court erred in considering that that has the same effect as the supply of "all or most" of the customer's total requirements.'[317]

> 198. I have explained above why there is no separate category of 'exclusivity rebates'. A presumption of unlawfulness applies to loyalty rebates, including (but not limited to) those termed by the General Court as 'exclusivity rebates'. One of the possible reasons why a rebate is considered a loyalty rebate is that it is based on the requirement that the customer purchases 'all or most' of its requirements from the dominant undertaking. However, form alone does not determine the fate of such rebates. That is because all the circumstances must be considered before it can be concluded that the impugned conduct amounts to an abuse of a dominant position. Therefore, if the Court allows the appellant's appeal on the first ground as I suggest, it is not necessary to consider the third.
>
> 199. However, the third ground remains significant if the Court were to dismiss the first ground and consider that 'exclusivity rebates' must be distinguished from other types of loyalty rebates.
>
> 200. If the Court were to reach that conclusion, the 'all or most' requirement assumes a crucial role in the assessment of those rebates. That is because only rebates which are conditional upon the customer purchasing 'all or most' of the customer's requirements from the dominant undertaking would fall under the umbrella of 'exclusivity rebates'.

The AG noted that although this condition seemed at first to refer to all or most of the customer's total requirements, the 95 per cent appear to correspond to approximately 28 per cent of HP's total CPU requirements. The AG notes that the Commission's decision established no distinction between CPUs used in corporate computers and those used in consumer computers. The General Court had found that such condition would have restricted considerable the 'purchasing choice of the OEMs in question' 'in the segment concerned' of the relevant market, the CPUs being interchangeable for either corporate computers or computers used by non-corporate consumers.[318] *The GC thus seemed to aim to protect the freedom of choice of the OEMs.*[319] *However, the AG noted the following:*

> 209. Indeed, a point that must be emphasised is that we are dealing with exclusionary conduct vis-à-vis the appellant's competitor AMD, not exploitation of the appellant's customers. What counts, from the perspective of AMD (and hence, for the purposes of determining whether the impugned conduct constitutes an exclusionary abuse of a dominant position contrary to Article 102 TFEU), is the overall percentage of requirements that are tied as a result of Intel's rebates and payments.
>
> 210. [. . .] [I]t does not matter whether some requirements are purchased for one particular segment. What matters is whether the OEMs in question can still purchase significant quantities from Intel's competitors. Here, that appears to be the case: HP and Lenovo could still purchase significant quantities of x86 CPUs from AMD. The question of whether an undertaking has abused its dominant position by excluding a competitor cannot depend on a seemingly arbitrary segmentation of the market.
>
> 211. Seen in that light, it seems difficult to argue that, as regards HP, the requirement pertaining to exclusivity on 95% of corporate desktops would amount to anything

[317] Ibid, para 195. [318] Ibid, para 206. [319] Ibid, para 208.

more than 28% of HP's overall requirements. By the same logic, exclusivity in Lenovo's notebooks does not equal exclusivity *overall*. Quite simply, the 'all or most' requirement cannot be satisfied in such circumstances.

212. At the risk of stating the obvious, the approach adopted in the judgment under appeal leads to a result which is hardly warranted: even an 'exclusivity rebate' concerning a segment of the relevant market that covers an insignificant part of the customer's overall requirements (let us say, for the sake of argument, 3%) could be condemned automatically.

213. Therefore, I conclude that the General Court erred in law regarding its classification of the rebates offered by the appellant to HP and Lenovo.

NOTES AND QUESTIONS ON AG WAHL'S INTEL *OPINION*

1. Note that, contrary to what was suggested by some commentators criticizing the 'formalistic' approach of the General Court in *Intel*,[320] the AG is careful not to seem to suggest an overruling of the now almost sacrosanct *Hoffman-La Roche* jurisprudence of the CJEU. In fact, he is suggesting to ignore the letter of this case law, and to re-interpret it a way as to integrate some analysis of the economic and legal context of the rebate scheme. Would such reading of the *Hofmann-La Roche* case be compatible with the 'spirit' of this case law?
2. The AG does not abandon the effort of classification of the various abuses. He even argues that the GC got this classification wrong by distinguishing between three categories, while there are only two: quantity rebates which are *per se* legal and loyalty rebates which may be found anti-competitive after an analysis of 'all of the circumstances' of the specific rebate scheme. One of the arguments put forward by the AG is that related types of practices require consideration of 'all the circumstances', referring to pricing and margin squeeze practices, criticizing the approach of the GC, which distinguished exclusionary rebates from these pricing practices. AG embraced categorical thinking in Article 102 TFEU, however, he highlighted the risks of 'arbitrary categorization',[321] loyalty rebates presenting the common feature to margin squeeze practices as well as predatory pricing of constituting 'price based exclusion'.[322]
3. One may, however, criticize the AG's categorization as also being arbitrary. If one looks to the United States' case law, US courts have employed various analogies comparing rebate schemes with other restrictive practices, when assessing the theoretical framework to apply to rebates (reasoning by analogy to related categories), considering as 'related practices' predatory pricing, tying, and exclusive dealing.[323] Each of these specific analogies makes perfect sense, from a specific perspective.[324] Some economists

320 D Geradin, 'Loyalty Rebates after *Intel*: Time for the European Court of Justice to Overrule *Hoffman-La Roche*' (2015) 11(3) *J Competition L & Economics* 579.

321 Opinion of AG N Wahl in Case C-413/14 P, *Intel Corp v European Commission*, ECLI:EU:C:2016:788, para 102.

322 Ibid.

323 FM Scott Morton and ZG Abrahamson, 'A Unifying Analytical Framework for Loyalty Rebates' (2016), esp 34–7, available at https://ssrn.com/abstract=2833563.

324 Reasoning by analogy in both EU and US antitrust jurisprudence and the 'battle of standards' in Article 102 TFEU was already analysed as the most promising theoretical framework in understanding the case law on unilateral practices at both sides of the Atlantic by I Lianos, 'Categorical Thinking in Competition Law and the "Effects-based" Approach in Article 82 EC' in A Ezrachi (ed) *Article 82 EC: Reflections on its Recent Evolution*

even consider that the best analogy for rebates is that of tying, as [a]nticompetitive loyalty schemes function by binding a product for which no substitutes exist—non-contestable demand—to a product on which competition occurs—contestable demand [. . .] [a]nd like ties, loyalty schemes exclude only when a "substantial volume of commerce is foreclosed": that is, when loyalty thresholds exceed levels of non-contestable share.'[325] As we will explain in Section 9.8, the standards for contractual tying employed by dominant undertakings are particularly harsh in EU competition law, and essentially come close to some form of quasi-*per se* illegality test, or at the best-case scenario to a rebuttable presumption of anti-competitive effects.

4. Although the corporate segment accounted for only around 30 per cent of HP (Hewlett Packard) overall procurement needs, this was the upmarket segment, in the sense that corporate customers had on average a stronger preference for quality in terms of CPU performance and were therefore less price-sensitive than individual consumers. What does this entail with respect to relative importance attributed to the short-term and long-term foreclosure effects and, accordingly, with respect to the choice of the proper cost benchmark to be used in the AEC test?

Case C-413/14 P, *Intel v Commission*, ECLI:EU:C:2017:632

It is important to point out that this judgment was adopted by the Grand Chamber. After rejecting the fourth and fifth grounds of appeal regarding, respectively, Intel's right of defence and an issue on the extra-territorial application of EU competition law, the CJEU proceeded with the main substantive issue under the first ground of appeal where Intel submitted that the General Court erred in law by failing to examine the rebates at issue in the light of all the relevant circumstances.

129. In the first place, [. . .], Intel [. . .] argues, in essence, that the General Court accepted that the practices at issue could be considered an abuse of a dominant position within the meaning of Article 102 TFEU without first examining all of the circumstances of the present case and without assessing the likelihood of that conduct restricting competition.

130. In the second place [. . .], Intel criticises the General Court's analysis, carried out for the sake of completeness [. . .] concerning the capacity of the rebates and payments granted to Dell, HP, NEC, Lenovo and MSH to restrict competition in the circumstances of the case.

131. In that context, Intel challenges, inter alia, the General Court's assessment of the relevance of the AEC test applied by the Commission in the present case.

132. It submits, in particular, that, since the Commission applied that test, the General Court should have examined Intel's line of argument alleging that the application of that test was badly flawed and that, had it been correctly applied, it would have led to the conclusion contrary to that which the Commission reached, namely that the rebates at issue were not capable of restricting competition.

(Hart, 2009), 19; N Economides and I Lianos, 'The Elusive Standard on Bundling in Europe and in the United States in the Aftermath of the Microsoft Cases' (2009) 76(2) *Antitrust LJ* 483.

325 FM Scott Morton and ZG Abrahamson, 'A Unifying Analytical Framework for Loyalty Rebates' (2016), esp 39, available at https://ssrn.com/abstract=2833563.

133. In that respect, it must be borne in mind that it is in no way the purpose of Article 102 TFEU to prevent an undertaking from acquiring, on its own merits, the dominant position on a market. Nor does that provision seek to ensure that competitors less efficient than the undertaking with the dominant position should remain on the market (see, inter alia, judgment of 27 March 2012, *Post Danmark*, C-209/10, EU:C:2012:172, paragraph 21 and the case-law cited).

134. Thus, not every exclusionary effect is necessarily detrimental to competition. Competition on the merits may, by definition, lead to the departure from the market or the marginalisation of competitors that are less efficient and so less attractive to consumers from the point of view of, among other things, price, choice, quality or innovation (see, inter alia, judgment of 27 March 2012, *Post Danmark*, C-209/10, EU:C:2012:172, paragraph 22 and the case-law cited).

135. However, a dominant undertaking has a special responsibility not to allow its behaviour to impair genuine, undistorted competition on the internal market (see, inter alia, judgments of 9 November 1983, *Nederlandsche Banden-Industrie-Michelin* v *Commission*, 322/81, EU:C:1983:313, paragraph 57, and of 27 March 2012, *Post Danmark*, C-209/10, EU:C:2012:172, paragraph 23 and the case-law cited).

136. That is why Article 102 TFEU prohibits a dominant undertaking from, among other things, adopting pricing practices that have an exclusionary effect on competitors considered to be as efficient as it is itself and strengthening its dominant position by using methods other than those that are part of competition on the merits. Accordingly, in that light, not all competition by means of price may be regarded as legitimate (see, to that effect, judgment of 27 March 2012, *Post Danmark*, C-209/10, EU:C:2012:172, paragraph 25).

137 In that regard, the Court has already held that an undertaking which is in a dominant position on a market and ties purchasers—even if it does so at their request—by an obligation or promise on their part to obtain all or most of their requirements exclusively from that undertaking abuses its dominant position within the meaning of Article 102 TFEU, whether the obligation is stipulated without further qualification or whether it is undertaken in consideration of the grant of a rebate. The same applies if the undertaking in question, without tying the purchasers by a formal obligation, applies, either under the terms of agreements concluded with these purchasers or unilaterally, a system of loyalty rebates, that is to say, discounts conditional on the customer's obtaining all or most of its requirements—whether the quantity of its purchases be large or small—from the undertaking in a dominant position (see judgment of 13 February 1979, *Hoffmann-La Roche* v *Commission*, 85/76, EU:C:1979:36, paragraph 89).

138. However, that case-law must be further clarified in the case where the undertaking concerned submits, during the administrative procedure, on the basis of supporting evidence, that its conduct was not capable of restricting competition and, in particular, of producing the alleged foreclosure.

139. In that case, the Commission is not only required to analyse, first, the extent of the undertaking's dominant position on the relevant market and, secondly, the share of the market covered by the challenged practice, as well as the conditions and arrangements for granting the rebates in question, their duration and their amount; it is also required to assess the possible existence of a strategy aiming to exclude competitors that are at least as efficient as the dominant undertaking from the market (see, by analogy, judgment of 27 March 2012, *Post Danmark*, C-209/10, EU:C:2012:172, paragraph 29).

140. The analysis of the capacity to foreclose is also relevant in assessing whether a system of rebates which, in principle, falls within the scope of the prohibition laid down

in Article 102 TFEU, may be objectively justified. In addition, the exclusionary effect arising from such a system, which is disadvantageous for competition, may be counterbalanced, or outweighed, by advantages in terms of efficiency which also benefit the consumer (judgment of 15 March 2007, *British Airways* v *Commission*, C-95/04 P, EU:C:2007:166, paragraph 86). That balancing of the favourable and unfavourable effects of the practice in question on competition can be carried out in the Commission's decision only after an analysis of the intrinsic capacity of that practice to foreclose competitors which are at least as efficient as the dominant undertaking.

141. If, in a decision finding a rebate scheme abusive, the Commission carries out such an analysis, the General Court must examine all of the applicant's arguments seeking to call into question the validity of the Commission's findings concerning the foreclosure capability of the rebate concerned.

142. In this case, while the Commission emphasised, in the decision at issue, that the rebates at issue were by their very nature capable of restricting competition such that an analysis of all the circumstances of the case and, in particular, an AEC test were not necessary in order to find an abuse of a dominant position [. . .] it nevertheless carried out an in-depth examination of those circumstances, setting out [. . .] a very detailed analysis of the AEC test, which led it to conclude [. . .] that an as efficient competitor would have had to offer prices which would not have been viable and that, accordingly, the rebate scheme at issue was capable of having foreclosure effects on such a competitor.

143. It follows that, in the decision at issue, the AEC test played an important role in the Commission's assessment of whether the rebate scheme at issue was capable of having foreclosure effects on as efficient competitors.

144. In those circumstances, the General Court was required to examine all of Intel's arguments concerning that test.

145. It held, however [. . .] that it was not necessary to consider whether the Commission had carried out the AEC test in accordance with the applicable rules and without making any errors, and that it was also not necessary to examine the question whether the alternative calculations proposed by Intel had been carried out correctly.

146. In its examination of the circumstances of the case, carried out for the sake of completeness, the General Court therefore attached no importance [. . .] to the AEC test carried out by the Commission and, accordingly, did not address Intel's criticisms of that test.

147. Consequently, without it being necessary to rule on the second, third and sixth ground of appeal, the judgment of the General Court must be set aside, since, in its analysis of whether the rebates at issue were capable of restricting competition, the General Court wrongly failed to take into consideration Intel's line of argument seeking to expose alleged errors committed by the Commission in the AEC test.

NOTES AND QUESTIONS ON THE CJEU'S INTEL *JUDGMENT*

1. Note that, in contrast to the General Court and the AG, the CJEU did not engage in the effort of classification of the various forms of rebates, but merely restated the *Hoffmann-La Roche* case law (paragraph 137) that a rebate that ties purchasers to obtain all or most of their requirements exclusively from the dominant undertaking is presumptively abusive.

2. In addition, the Court rejected (at paragraph 136) the General Court's characterization of exclusivity rebates as a non-pricing practice. In doing so, the Court relied on *Post Danmark II* to elevate the AEC test as the common standard to be applied to prove that the pricing practice is capable of restricting competition.
3. However, the Court merely stated that (paragraphs 138–9) the Commission must apply the AEC test (in addition to taking into consideration all the relevant circumstances such as the extent of market coverage and duration of the contested practice) in response to the defendant's argument that its conduct was not capable of producing the alleged foreclosure. Is this a mute point, or a genuine reversal of the burden of proof? Will the Commission wait for the defendant's counterargument before applying the AEC test, or shall it apply it straight away? See our analysis of the case in 8.4.5.3.3.
4. To note that the Court did not opine on the argument advanced by the General Court that a negative outcome of the AEC test (ie, indicating that an as efficient competitor would have to set 'negative' prices to compensate customers for the loss of the rebate received by the dominant undertaking) is a sufficient but not necessary condition for a finding that the rebate is capable of anti-competitive foreclosure, in that it is sufficient to establish that the grant of exclusivity rebates by an undertaking in a dominant position makes it *more difficult* (albeit not *impossible*) for a competitor to supply its own goods to customers of that dominant undertaking. Does that mean that a positive outcome of the AEC test is a necessary, but not sufficient condition for the defendant's rebuttal of the presumption that an exclusivity rebate is capable of producing the alleged foreclosure?
5. (Paragraphs 137, 139) The Court seems to indicate that although rebates conducive to imposing exclusivity conditions that lead to a significant foreclosure effect may not constitute 'competition on the merits', the Commission may be required 'to assess the possible existence of a strategy aiming to exclude competitors that are at least as efficient as the dominant undertaking from the market'. Note that the CJEU excludes from the scope of the rule rebates that tie the purchasers by a formal obligation, as presumably these will be considered as tying/bundling and the AEC test is not explicitly required for tying.[326]

9.6.5. UK CASE LAW

In the UK case law there are a few decisions dealing with fidelity rebates. One of them is a decision of the Office or Rail and Road (formerly Office of Rail Regulation) (ORR), *English Welsh & Scottish Railway Ltd.*[327] English Welsh & Scottish Railway (EWS), the dominant supplier of rail freight services in England, Wales and Scotland, was alleged to have foreclosed access by competitors to the market for the supply of coal to UK industrial users, particularly the power sector. The ORR found that EWS abused its dominant position by entering into agreements with industrial users of coal for the haulage of coal by rail. The ORR's assessment

326 See Section 9.8.

327 *English Welsh & Scottish Railway Ltd*, ORR Decision of 17 November 2006 [2007] UKCLR 937.

of these agreements was supported by contemporaneous documentary evidence of EWS's exclusionary intent. Some of the agreements were found to be restrictive due to the type and level of discounts. The ORR found that 'EWS's discounting structure is designed and operates so as to induce loyalty from [EWS's customers] to concentrate [their] marginal tonnage requirements for coal haulage with EWS to the exclusion of potential competitors and new entrants'.[328]

In assessing the discount arrangements in EWS's contracts, the ORR applied the following legal definition of loyalty rebates as those which: 'by offering customers financial advantages, tend to prevent them from obtaining their supplies from competing suppliers. Accordingly, rebates, which depend on a purchasing target being achieved by the customer, will normally be contrary to Article [102 TFEU]'.[329] According to the decision, quantity rebates are:

> [. . .] linked solely to the volume of purchases from a dominant undertakings are, in themselves, generally considered not to have the foreclosure effect prohibited by Article [102TFEU]. If increasing the quantity supplied results in lower costs for the supplier, the latter is entitled to pass on that reduction to the customer in the form of a more favourable tariff. Quantity rebates are therefore deemed to reflect gains in efficiency and economies of scale made by the undertaking in a dominant position. Quantity rebates will not infringe Article [102TFEU] unless the criteria and rules for granting the rebate reveal that the system is not based on an economically justified countervailing advantage but tends to prevent customers from obtaining their supplies from competitors.[330]

The Decision sets out to the test for exclusionary effect:

> A100. The potential for foreclosure effects with uniform discounts is most acute when marginal prices are below cost, or in the extreme, negative. ORR uses the concept of marginal price to denote the additional expenditure (per tonne) that the customer would incur, under the discount scheme, if it were to purchase additional volume. This marginal price depends on both the volume that the customer has already taken (or expects to take) from EWS and the additional volume that the customer would be purchasing.
>
> A101. Marginal prices are relevant to the analysis of foreclosure since it is marginal prices against which alternative suppliers compete. For example, in the case of new business, if the increase in volumes purchased takes the customer to a new discounted price, then the marginal price is calculated as the increase in expenditure from new purchases (i.e. new discounted price multiplied by the increase in quantity) minus the reduction in expenditure on existing sales (i.e. price reduction multiplied by existing sales), all divided by the increase in quantity purchased.
>
> A102. If the marginal price is less than average variable costs, then an equally efficient competitor will be unable to compete effectively for that specific volume of new business. However, because competitors will need to recover fixed costs in order to justify continuing in the market, such exclusion can take place even when the marginal price is above the level of variable costs.

The ORR also assessed and rejected the argument from EWS that its conduct was justified by a legitimate commercial rationale, in that the discounts were stipulated by the customer to

[328] Ibid, para A87. [329] Ibid, para A88(a). [330] Ibid, para A88(b).

protect it from being stranded with high, non-volume related rates, doe to a lack of contemporaneous evidence of its actual motivation.[331]

In *Claymore v OFT*,[332] Claymore appealed the OFT's decision to close its investigation into Wiseman diaries on the basis that, whilst it is likely that Wiseman has a dominant position in relation to the supply of milk to middle ground retailers in Scotland, the OFT did not believe that further investigation would produce evidence of any abuse of that position. The applicants were producers and suppliers of milk and had complained to the OFT about Wiseman. Claymore argued that it was abusive for Wiseman to offer customers such as CWS and Aberness contracts covering the whole of Scotland as this had the effect of excluding it from supplying the Highlands outlets of these customers, despite the fact that Claymore's prices were competitive with those of Wiseman. The OFT, however, had concluded that Wiseman had not acted abusively in offering a single price for supplying milk to all the outlets of a particular retailer. It considered that it had not found clear or compelling evidence that Wiseman had ever made supply in any area or to any outlet conditional on supply on an all Scotland basis or that Claymore had been excluded from competing.

The CAT noted in that respect that on the basis of established case law, there is an abuse by a dominant undertaking where it ties purchasers (even at the customer's request) by an obligation or promise on the part of the customer to obtain all or most of their requirements exclusively from the dominant supplier, whether or not the obligation is conditional on the grant of a rebate. Due to the asymmetries in the size of Claymore and Wiseman, Claymore was not able to offer comparable deals covering the whole of Scotland, though it was able to compete effectively in the Highlands. Therefore, Wiseman's offer of 'All Scotland' deals could threaten Claymore's viability and lead to its elimination. The CAT considered that it is arguable that Wiseman's deal with CWS could, therefore, be seen to be *de facto* exclusionary and could have had the effect of driving out Wiseman's local competition so giving it a *de facto* monopoly. The CAT therefore considered that there was, at least, a serious case for investigation under the Chapter II prohibition in relation to the CWS contract and that the OFT failed to conduct a proper investigation into these issues.

The CAT also noted that 'a "gentleman's agreement" whereby a dominant firm offers, and the customer accepts, an inducement to be "loyal" to the dominant firm, is likely in principle to be abusive for the purposes of the Chapter II prohibition, even if the arrangement concerns a major part, but not the whole, of the customer's requirements'.[333]

The OFT (the CMA's predecessor) has also emphasized the need of evidence of foreclosure from case-closure decisions:

(a) In *British Airways*,[334] the OFT closed its investigation into whether British Airways (BA) was abusing its dominant position through offering non-linear discounts in its corporate deals contrary to the Chapter II CA98 prohibition and Article 102 TFEU. The deals typically included a combination of upfront route-specific discounts (URDs) and backend aggregate rebates (BARs). The OFT was concerned that the deals had a foreclosure effect, *inter alia*, because the provisions in some contracts allowed BA to 'claw back' URDs and/or reduce or withdraw URDs if targets were not met. However,

331 Ibid, para A174. 332 *Claymore v OFT* [2005] CAT 30

333 *Claymore v OFT* [2005] CAT 30, paras 305–7.

334 OFT, *British Airways: alleged abuse of a dominant position in corporate deals* (Case CE/4875/04), Case closure decision (30 April 2007), available at www.gov.uk/cma-cases/british-airways-alleged-abuse-of-a-dominant-position-in-corporate-deals.

without reaching a conclusion on this and other issues, the OFT decided to close the file, primarily because of 'a lack of evidence indicating that BA's corporate deals were likely to have a substantial foreclosure effect'.[335]

(b) In *Walkers Snacks Limited*,[336] the OFT closed its investigation into whether Walkers Snacks Limited (WSL) was abusing a dominant position in the relevant market in the UK through a range of practices including growth rebates, financial inducements, and *solus* agreements. In particular, it was alleged that 'WSL's growth rebates foreclosed the market by linking the discount customers received on WSL products to the percentage increase in the annual volumes they purchased from WSL.'[337] Again, however, the OFT decided not to continue with the investigation, after obtaining extensive evidence, on the basis that 'the investigation uncovered no evidence that the WSL rebates had a material impact on customer decision making or on the process of competition generally.'

More recently, in 2014, the CMA opened an investigation into a suspected loyalty-inducing discount scheme in the pharmaceutical sector for a potential breach of Chapter II CA98 and Article 102 TFEU.

After several months of information gathering, the CMA concluded that further investigation of the conduct would have limited benefit to consumer welfare. In accordance with its own prioritization principles, the CMA issued a statement announcing the closure of its investigation without any substantive finding as to whether the conduct at issue was lawful or unlawful.[338] However, the CMA emphasized that this did not mean that it would not look into 'suspected loyalty-inducing discount schemes in the future'.

The CMA sent a warning letter to the company concerned and issued further guidance for pharmaceutical businesses in relation to the use of discounts and rebates.

According to the CMA guidance, this type of scheme may be capable of inducing customer loyalty (and thus being unlawful) where the following three conditions are met:

(i) There are units that a customer has no choice but to buy from the dominant company (so-called 'non-contestable sales');

(ii) There are also units which the customer needs and which the customer may be willing and able to purchase either from the dominant company or from a competitor of the dominant company (so-called 'contestable sales'); and

(iii) The discount or rebate scheme targets the contestable sales—the customer will be entitled to a discount or rebate if it purchases units from the dominant company that it might otherwise have chosen to buy from a competitor. The economic theory is that dominant firms are unavoidable trading partners such that their customers will always need to purchase a certain (high) percentage of their purchasing requirements for the

335 See *British Airways*, CMA Closure Decision (30 April 2007), available at https://www.gov.uk/cma-cases/british-airways-alleged-abuse-of-a-dominant-position-in-corporate-deals.

336 *Walkers Snacks Ltd: Alleged Abuse of a Dominant Position* (Case CE/1604-02), OFT Case closure decision (3 May 2007), available at www.gov.uk/cma-cases/walkers-snacks-ltd-alleged-abuse-of-a-dominant-position.

337 https://www.gov.uk/cma-cases/walkers-snacks-ltd-alleged-abuse-of-a-dominant-position

338 See the summary closure decision in the CMA case, *Conduct in the pharmaceutical sector investigation* (Case CE/9855-14): CMA, 'Statement regarding the CMA's decision to close an investigation into a suspected breach of competition law in the pharmaceutical sector on the grounds of administrative priority' (June 2015), available at assets.publishing.service.gov.uk/media/558c2743e5274a1559000004/Pharmaceutical_sector_investigation_closure_statement.pdf.

relevant products or services from that firm. With respect to pharmaceuticals, this scenario is more likely to surface in connection with patented drugs or drugs coming off patent, that is, when a rapid erosion of sales is anticipated due to generic entry or the entry of drugs for which customers or doctors have a therapeutic preference.

The CMA has indicated that the three conditions set out in its guidance are not exhaustive and that it is also likely to intervene where the prices (after the discount or rebate) for contestable sales are below average variable cost of production and the customer would be able to reduce its overall spending on the dominant company's products by increasing the volume of contestable sales.

9.7. (EXCLUSIONARY) PRICE AND NON-PRICE DISCRIMINATION

Although discrimination may take different forms and may affect different parameters of competition, price discrimination has attracted the attention of economists and competition authorities.

9.7.1. THE ECONOMICS OF PRICE DISCRIMINATION

Economists consider that a firm price discriminates when two 'similar' products are sold at prices that are different ratios to their respective marginal costs.[339] For economists, a simple difference in price of the same product to various customers does not constitute price discrimination if the difference of price reflects a difference in costs—for example, different distribution costs. Price discrimination may be a competition law concern in various circumstances.

P Papandropoulos, 'How Should Price Discrimination Be Dealt With by Competition Authorities?' (2007) 3 *Concurrences* 34, 34 para 3

Under European competition policy, price discrimination constitutes a worry for three different reasons. First, price discrimination by dominant firms may reduce consumer welfare by extracting consumer surplus (without any exclusionary impact on competitors).[340] This is generally referred to as 'exploitative' price discrimination. Second, the pursuit of the Internal Market objective has given mandate to DG Competition to defeat attempts by private firms to erect barriers to trade between Member States which allows them to price discriminate across countries (the issue of geographic price discrimination is particularly prominent in the area of car sales and pharmaceuticals). Finally, price discrimination can lead to exclusionary

[339] GJ Stigler, *The Theory of Price* (Macmillan, 1987). Different marginal costs for 'similar' products may be the result of 'versioning'—for example, a watched offered with strap of different material, more and less prestigious. A narrower definition is that price discrimination occurs where two similar products with the same marginal costs are sold by the same firm at two different prices: see CM Armstrong, 'Recent Developments in the Economics of Price Discrimination' in R Blundell, WK Newey, and T Persson (eds) *Advances in Economics and Econometrics: Theory and Applications, Ninth World Congress of the Econometric Society*, vol 2 (CUP, 2006), ch 4.

[340] See our analysis of the effects of market power in Chapter 3.

effects. Such exclusionary effects can either affect the dominant firm's rivals (primary line discrimination) [or first-degree discrimination] or the dominant firm's downstream customers (secondary line discrimination) [or second-degree discrimination].

Economists agree that price discrimination may have ambiguous effects—it may increase or reduce welfare—depending on the way it is implemented.[341] In this part of the book we only focus on price discrimination that leads to exclusionary effects and market distortions. We will examine exploitative price discrimination and geographic price discrimination in Sections 9.10.2 and 9.11.2.

With regard to market-distorting exclusionary price discrimination, it is important to distinguish between primary line (or first-degree) discrimination and secondary line (or second-degree) discrimination.

Primary line (or first-degree) price discrimination may involve for instance the implementation of 'targeted' predatory pricing (the dominant undertaking implementing selective and predatory price cuts in the customer segment where if faces entry) and mixed bundling or tying strategies in order to exclude the products of its competitors. The foreclosure effects that may arise in these cases relate to the specific conduct giving rise to price discrimination, for instance the predatory pricing, the selective price-cutting or mixed bundling, without the need to consider price discrimination as a separate type of abuse.

Secondary line (or second-degree) price discrimination raise less competition law concerns, as the discrimination only concerns a downstream market in which the dominant undertaking allegedly committing the abuse is not active. The concern here is that the dominant undertaking should not distort competition on an upstream or a downstream market, as 'co-contractors of such undertakings must not be favoured or disfavoured in the area of the competition which they practise amongst themselves'.[342] The duties such provision imposes to dominant undertakings is particularly interesting if one thinks of the role some undertakings have in controlling or influencing 'ecosystems' composed by a number of business partners, and would be competitors, should one also take into account 'vertical competition', in particular vertical innovation competition, seriously.[343]

An important element to consider in applying Article 102(c) is if the dominant undertaking is vertically integrated.

P Papandropoulos, 'How Should Price Discrimination Be Dealt With by Competition Authorities?' (2007) 3 *Concurrences* 34, 37 paras 17–18

[A] crucial distinction arises whether the dominant firm is vertically integrated or not. In fact, whereas price discrimination may constitute a device to exclude downstream rivals by an integrated supplier, the opposite situation arises when the supplier is not vertically integrated. Indeed, a non-integrated supplier would in fact benefit from a ban in price discrimination as pricing to intermediaries is often the result of bilateral negotiations (rather than posted

341 D Bergeman, B Brooks, and S Morris, 'The Limits of Price Discrimination' (2015) 105(3) *American Economic Rev* 921.

342 Opinion AG N Wahl in Case C-525/16, *Meo—Serviços de Comunicações e Multimédia v Autoridade da Concorrência*, ECLI:EU:C:2017:1020, para 74.

343 See our analysis in Section 3.1.1.

prices). Indeed, if price discrimination is possible in the context of secret negotiations, each downstream firm will ask for secret price cuts. Taking the other contracts as given, the supplier and each downstream firm will maximize their joint profit and this will lead to efficient pricing (as in the case of vertical integration). With a competitive downstream market, prices to consumers will end up being lower. In this context, price discrimination has the effect of eroding the upstream supplier's market power as it cannot commit not to offer secret price cuts in bilateral negotiations. [. . .]

When the upstream supplier is vertically integrated, things are very different. Indeed, while vertical integration may lead to efficient pricing (i.e. elimination of double marginalization), a vertically integrated dominant supplier may have incentives to exclude downstream rivals by raising their costs or engaging in margin squeeze. These insights are particularly relevant for the application of Article [102](c). They suggest that price discrimination should primarily be of concern in cases where the dominant firm is vertically integrated whereas price discrimination is considerably less likely to negatively affect competition when the upstream supplier faces a competitive downstream market and is not vertically integrated. A cautious approach is therefore advocated in the latter case.

9.7.2. EU COMPETITION LAW

Under Article 102(c) TFEU, dominant undertakings are prohibited from 'applying dissimilar conditions to equivalent transactions with other trading parties, thereby placing them at a competitive disadvantage'. This provision prohibits price discrimination by a supplier between two competing purchasers, as a higher price to one customer might well be deemed to competitively disadvantage it vis-à-vis the other. This requires three conditions to be established: (i) that there are equivalent transactions; (ii) that the dominant undertaking applies to these transactions dissimilar conditions; and (iii) that the dominant undertaking by this conduct places downstream undertakings at a competitive disadvantage. All three of Article 102(c)'s conditions must be satisfied.

Article 102(c) can thus include secondary line (or second-degree) price discrimination, in the separate category of price discrimination abuse in EU competition law, Article 102(c) not requiring the dominant undertaking and the undertaking in the downstream market to be direct competitors for Article 102 TFEU to apply. The Commission, confirmed by the EU Courts, has also applied Article 102(c) in cases of exclusionary abuses involving primary line (or first-degree) discrimination, such as rebates and selective price-cutting (*Hoffmann-La Roche*,[344] *Michelin I*,[345] *Irish Sugar*,[346] *BPB Industries*,[347] *British Airways*,[348] and *Clearstream*[349]), or other forms of price discrimination, sometimes combining first degree and second degree

344 Case C-85/76, *Hoffmann-La Roche/ Commission* [1979] ECR 461.

345 Case C-322/81, *Michelin I* [1983] ECR 3461, paras 90–1, where the CJEU annulled the Commission's finding of price discrimination contrary to Article 102(c).

346 Case T-228/97, *Irish Sugar plc v Commission* [1999] ECR II–2969; Case C-497/99 P, *Irish Sugar plc v Commission* [2001] ECR I–5333.

347 Case T-65/89, *BPB Industries and British Gypsum Ltd v Commission* [1993] ECR II–389; Case C-310/93 P, *BPB Industries plc and British Gypsum Ltd v Commission* [1995] ECR I–865.

348 Case C-95/04, *British Airways v Commission* [2007] ECR I–2331.

349 Case T-301/04, *Clearstream Banking AG and Clearstream International SA v Commission* [2009] ECR II–3155.

price discrimination.[350] However, there is no consensus in the literature with regard to the application of Article 102(c) to primary line (or first-degree) discrimination, in particular if this produces foreclosure effects, as the specific conduct may satisfy the criteria of other categories of abuses, some authors considering the category of abusive price discrimination redundant.[351]

The Commission's Guidance on Article 102 does not mention discriminatory exclusionary practices although the topic was discussed in the DG Competition Staff Discussion Paper.[352]

However, Article 102(c) has been applied to both vertically integrated and non-vertically integrated undertakings. The CJEU found that *United Brands* failed to comply with Article 102(c) by selling bananas to national distributors at non-uniform prices. The Court did not require direct competition between distributors, since each resold the product in separate local markets.[353]

In *Hoffman-La Roche*, the Court struck down under Article 102(c) varying fidelity rebates offered to customers that bought all or a pre-determined percentage of their requirements from the dominant seller, Hoffman-La Roche. Preventing inter-brand harm to competition, or primary-line effects, motivated the Court's decision, since price discrimination inhibited rivals from selling to Hoffman's customers.[354]

In *British Airways*, the General Court focused on whether a dominant undertaking could offer a cost justification for a given rebate. Absent a link to costs, the Court held competition authorities reasonably might view the discount as a fidelity rebate aimed at preventing rivals from competing on the merits for the business of a dominant undertaking's customers.[355]

In its recent *Meo—Serviços de Comunicações e Multimédia SA*, the CJEU applied Article 102(c) in the context of a case where there was no first-degree price discrimination, the allegedly dominant company (GDA) discriminating between customers active in a market (Meo and NOS) in which it was not itself active.[356]

Beyond Article 102(c), courts have held selective price-cuts as a more general abuse of dominance when used to deter entry or exclude rivals. As we have examined in Section 9.3.3, *Post Danmark I* has limited the extension of price discrimination law, at least in primary-line cases, to price-cuts below average total cost.[357] Some authors have discussed the existence of a more general theory of exclusionary discrimination and in particular of a 'general duty not to discriminate against rivals', but they suggested that there is no such general duty and put forward instead a case-by-case effects-based approach.[358]

350 See eg Case T-229/94, *Deutsche Bahn v Commission*, EU:T:1997:155, confirmed by the order of the Court in Case C-436/97 P, *Deutsche Bahn AG v Commission*, ECLI:EU:C:1999:205.

351 D Geradin and N Petit, 'Price Discrimination under EC Competition Law: Another Antitrust Doctrine in Search of Limiting Principles?' (2006) 2 *J Competition L & Economics* 479 (advancing the view that Article 102(c) should only apply to the limited circumstances where a non-vertically integrated dominant firm price discriminates between customers with the effect of placing one or several of them at a competitive disadvantage vis-à-vis other customers, or in situations of geographic price discrimination).

352 DG Comp Discussion Paper, paras 140–1.

353 Case 27/76, *United Brands Co v Commission of the European Communities* [1978] ECR 207.

354 Case 85/76, *Hoffman-La Roche & Co v Commission* [1979] ECR 461, para 90.

355 Case T-219/99, *British Airways plc v Commission* [2003] ERC II–5917, paras 46–7.

356 Case C-525/16, *Meo—Serviços de Comunicações e Multimédia v Autoridade da Concorrência*, ECLI:EU:C:2018:270.

357 Case C-209/10, *Post Danemark I*, ECLI:EU:C:2012:172, para 25. On this case, see JM Strader, '*Post Danmark*'s Recoupment Element' (2014) 10(2) *Competition L Rev* 205, 211.

358 See P Ibáñez Colomo, 'Exclusionary Discrimination under Article 102 TFEU' (2014) 51 *Common Market L Rev* 141, 151–61.

We examine some examples of cases involving the application of Article 102(c) to price discrimination.

9.7.2.1. *Clearstream*

Case T-301/04, *Clearstream Banking AG and Clearstream International SA v Commission*
[2009] ECR II–3155

By a 2004 decision, the Commission found that Clearstream Banking AG (also known as Clearstream Banking Frankfurt or CBF), an undertaking enjoying a dominant position in the market for the provision of 'primary' clearing and settlement services for securities issued under German law to central securities depositories in other Member States and to international central securities depositories.[359] Central securities depositories are entities holding and administering securities and enabling securities transactions to be processed ('primary clearing' and settlement services). The Commission had found that Clearstream (CBF) had discriminated against Euroclear Bank by charging a higher per transaction price to Euroclear Bank, one of its customers, than to national central securities depositories outside Germany for a period of two years. The Commission had also found that Clearstream had also infringed Article 102 by denying Euroclear Bank (EB) clearing and settlement services again for a period of two years. EB was a direct competitor to CBL, a sister company of CBF and the only other international central securities depositories in the European Union, on the downstream market for clearing and settlement of cross-border securities transactions. The Commission examined in detail the content of the services and the costs of providing them and concluded that the price differences were not justified by the costs. It also found that the alleged price discrimination raised EB's costs and ultimately the prices paid by its customers. CBF and CBL argued that there was no abusive discrimination in the setting of prices for EB, as the combinations of requested services and the costs attributable to them differed, as well as the volume of transactions and the Commission had not examined whether the setting of the prices charged to EB by the applicants led to a competitive disadvantage for EB. The General Court rejected the applicants' argument that the content of primary clearing and settlement services for cross-border transactions provided by CBF to the CSDs and the ICSDs was not equivalent or not justified. It then examined the applicant's argument that the Commission had not examined the existence of a competitive disadvantage between CBF's customers.

192. As pointed out by the Court of Justice, the specific prohibition of discrimination in subparagraph (c) of the second paragraph of Article [102 TFEU] forms part of the system for ensuring, in accordance with Article [3(1)(g) EC now Protocol No 27], that competition is not distorted in the internal market. The commercial behaviour of the undertaking in a dominant position may not distort competition on an upstream or a downstream market, in other words, between suppliers or customers of that undertaking. Co-contractors of that undertaking must not be favoured or disfavoured in the area of the competition which they practise amongst themselves. Therefore, in order for the conditions for applying subparagraph (c) of the second paragraph of Article [102 TFEU] to be met, there must be a finding not only that the behaviour of an undertaking

[359] *Clearstream Banking AG and Clearstream International SA* (Case COMP/38.096) Commission Decision C(2004)1958 final (2 June 2004).

in a dominant market position is discriminatory, but also that it tends to distort that competitive relationship, in other words, to hinder the competitive position of some of the business partners of that undertaking in relation to the others (Case C-95/04 P *British Airways* v *Commission* [2007] ECR I-2331, paragraphs 143 and 144).

193. In that regard, there is nothing to prevent discrimination between business partners who are in a relationship of competition from being regarded as abusive as soon as the behaviour of the undertaking in a dominant position tends, having regard to the whole of the circumstances of the case, to lead to a distortion of competition between those business partners. In such a situation, it cannot be required in addition that proof be adduced of an actual quantifiable deterioration in the competitive position of the business partners taken individually (*British Airways* v *Commission*, paragraph 192 above, paragraph 145).

194. In the present case, the application to a trading partner of different prices for equivalent services continuously over a period of five years and by an undertaking having a de facto monopoly on the upstream market could not fail to cause that partner a competitive disadvantage.

NOTES AND QUESTIONS ON CLEARSTREAM

1. (Paragraphs 192–3) Note that the General Court only requires evidence of the tendency of the specific price discrimination to distort the competitive relationship between the various business partners of the dominant undertaking (including its downstream unit) and not 'any proof of an actual quantifiable deterioration in the competitive position of the business partners taken individually'. Does this deny (on) the condition of the 'competitive disadvantage' any limiting principle?
2. (Paragraph 194) May this precedent be explained by the specific circumstances of the case? EFB enjoyed a *de facto* monopoly position in the relevant market and the Commission aimed to actively promote a pan-European settlement and clearing market, considered regulatory action and had adopted in 2006 a Code of Conduct on clearing and settlement.

9.7.2.2. *Soda-Ash/Solvay*

In *Soda Ash*,[360] the European Commission condemned Solvay's pricing structure which consisted of offering rebates where the basic tonnage in soda ash was sold at the normal price, but the additional quantities that the customer might otherwise have bought from another supplier—the 'top slice'—were offered at a substantial discount. The Commission found that the rebates were exclusionary but also applied Article 102(c), finding that the rebates were discriminatory. Solvay appealed to the General Court arguing that there was no factual basis for the finding that its practices were discriminatory (in addition to being found exclusionary) and that while soda ash is the most important raw material used in the manufacture of glass, it represents only 2 to 6 per cent of the average selling price

360 *Soda Ash/Solvay* (Case COMP/33.133-c) Commission Decision [2003] OJ L 10/10.

of the glass and a difference in the amount of a rebate on the price of soda ash cannot therefore have a significant impact on the competitive position of the glass manufacturers concerned.

Case T-57/01, *Solvay SA v Commission*
[2009] ECR II–4261

Relating to the discriminatory nature of the impugned practices

396. According to the case-law of the Court of Justice, an undertaking occupying a dominant position is entitled to offer its customers quantity discounts linked solely to the volume of purchases made from it. However, the rules for calculating such discounts must not result in dissimilar conditions being applied to equivalent transactions with other trading parties within the meaning of subparagraph (c) of the second paragraph of Article [102 TFEU]. In that connection, it should be noted that it is of the very essence of a system of quantity discounts that larger purchasers of a product or users of a service enjoy lower average unit prices or—which amounts to the same—higher average reductions than those offered to smaller purchasers of that product or users of that service. It should also be noted that even where there is a linear progression in quantity discounts up to a maximum discount, initially the average discount rises (or the average price falls) mathematically in a proportion greater than the increase in purchases and subsequently in a proportion smaller than the increase in purchases, before tending to stabilise at or near the maximum discount rate. The mere fact that the result of quantity discounts is that some customers enjoy in respect of specific quantities a proportionally higher average reduction than others in relation to the difference in their respective volumes of purchase is inherent in this type of system, but it cannot be inferred from that alone that the system is discriminatory. None the less, where as a result of the thresholds of the various discount bands, and the levels of discount offered, discounts (or additional discounts) are enjoyed by only some trading parties, giving them an economic advantage which is not justified by the volume of business they bring or by any economies of scale they allow the supplier to make compared with their competitors, a system of quantity discounts leads to the application of dissimilar conditions to equivalent transactions. In the absence of any objective justification, having a high threshold in the system which can only be met by a few particularly large partners of the undertaking occupying a dominant position, or the absence of linear progression in the increase of the quantity discounts, may constitute evidence of such discriminatory treatment (Case C163/99 *Portugal* v *Commission* [2001] ECR I–2613, paragraphs 50 to 53).

397. In the present case, as already indicated in the context of the examination of the first part of the fifth pea, the applicant does not dispute the findings relating to the system of rebates set up in France.

398. The rebate system set up by the applicant did not follow a linear progression by reference to quantities, even among undertakings benefiting from such rebates. It follows from the contested decision that the rebates granted to Durant and Perrier were of different amounts (recitals 75 and 76).

399. Accordingly, for that reason alone, contrary to the applicant's assertion, the objection relating to the existence of discriminatory practices was based on elements of fact set out in the contested decision. [. . .]

401. The applicant also refers to the low costs of soda ash. However, that assertion is unsubstantiated and is not of such a kind as to call in question the discriminatory nature of the applicant's practices.

NOTES AND QUESTIONS ON SODA-ASH/SOLVAY

1. (Paragraphs 396, 298) The case concerned a primary-line (or first-degree) discrimination against Solvay's competitors in the supply of soda ash. Yet, the Commission, confirmed by the General Court, found that, in addition, these financial inducements provided to Solvay's customers (glass manufacturers) gave rise to pure secondary-line discrimination and thus was contrary to Article 102(c). What is the constitutive element of this abuse?
2. In its decision, the Commission had found that the discrimination had a considerable effect on the cost of the affected undertakings. In the glass sector (which accounts for the majority of soda ash consumption) soda ash was, after fuel costs, the most expensive single item in the manufacturing process and accounted for up to 70 per cent of the raw material batch cost, thus affecting the profitability and competitive position of glass manufacturers.[361] The Commission concluded from this finding that the discriminatory practices were not only placing at a competitive disadvantage glass manufacturers who might not take their full or the major part of their requirement from Solvay (only a few did not do so) but also to discriminate as between customers who did. Indeed, the Commission noted that a large customer could pay substantially more per tonne than a smaller producer, even though both were buying their total requirement from Solvay. This finding led the Commission that the condition of the existence of a competitive disadvantage was satisfied. Padilla and O'Donoghue note that a distinction should be established between a disadvantage and a competitive disadvantage:

   Article 102(c) does not state that there is discrimination when one party pays more, or received better terms, than another trading party. They key phrase is a 'competitive' disadvantage. This raises an important issue, not yet addressed in the decisional practice or case law: the need to differentiate between an impact on profitability and an impact on competitiveness, i.e. whether there is a need to also show a *distortion of competition*. All else equal, a trading party paying more for a purchased good or service will have higher costs than a trading party paying less. But it does not follow that even if the difference in treatment is significant there is a material impact on overall profits, still less that an impact on profits would affect the competitiveness of the disfavoured party (and still less again an impact on competition in the relevant market). Profitability and competitiveness are two different things and an impact on a single firm may or may not have an impact on competition. It would all depend on the state of inter- and intra-brand competition that remained.[362]

361 Ibid, para 185.

362 R O'Donoghue and J Padilla, *The Law and Economics of Article 102 TFEU* (Hart, 2013), 801–2 (original emphasis).

3. Did the Commission and the General Court examine in this case intra-brand and inter-brand competition? Should they have done so and what role, if any, plays the fact that the practice in question is adopted by a dominant undertaking?

9.7.2.3. *Aéroports de Paris*

Case T-128/98, *Aéroports de Paris v Commission*
[2000] ECR II–3929

Aéroports de Paris (ADP) was dominant on the market for the provision of airport management services at the Paris airports (legal monopoly) and licensed undertakings to carry out ground-handling services. ADP charged different levels of commercial fees in the Paris airports of Orly and Roissy–Charles de Gaulle on suppliers or users engaged in ground-handling or self-handling activities relating to catering (including the loading and unloading of food and beverages on aircraft), to the cleaning of aircraft and to the handling of cargo, depending on whether the services were provided by an undertaking to another undertaking member of the same group (self-handling) or by an undertaking to third parties (third party ground-handling), self-handling being charged a lower fee. The fees also varied from undertaking to undertaking. These transactions were found by the Commission to be equivalent as when an airline or one of its specialized subsidiaries is authorized by ADP to self-handle a specific category of services and is also authorized to supply the same services to third parties, ADP provides it with exactly the same airport management services as it provides for all its handling activities.[363] On this basis, the Commission concluded that the different levels of commercial fees on users licensed only to self-handle gives them a discriminatory advantage in terms of costs with regard to their self-handling activities and, therefore, with regard to air transport self-handle, with the result that the cost of ADP's management services supplied to all ground-handlers, including self-handlers, are passed on to suppliers of services for third parties, thus making ground-handling services for third parties more expensive than self-handling services. The market-distorting effect took place on a downstream market on which the dominant undertaking was not present. Hence, there was no leveraging strategy put in place, nor had the undertaking any incentive to harm undertakings downstream. The practice was discriminatory without a clear exclusionary purpose. In order to find that the practice infringed Article 102(c), the Commission relied on the following: (i) the commercial fee was an important part of a suppliers' cost structure, adding to the unit cost of the services in question; (ii) it had a significant effect on competition between suppliers to third parties, the Commission finding that a supplier paying the highest rate could not offer competitive prices whilst maintaining the same profit margin, with the result that either he would lose customers or reduce its profit margin in order to quote a competitive price which would compensate for the difference in the commercial fee.[364] ADP appealed to the General Court.

ADP argued at the General Court that Article 102 TFEU could not apply as ASP was not present on the markets in respect of which the Commission found that competition was affected. The General Court noted:

[363] *Alpha Flight Services/Aéroports de Paris* (Case COMP IV/35.613) Commission Decision [1998] OJ L 230/10, para 117.

[364] *Alpha Flight Services/Aéroports de Paris* (Case COMP IV/35.613) Commission Decision [1998] OJ L 230/10, paras 109–10.

164. [. . .] The Court of Justice quite clearly stated in Case C-333/94 P *Tetra Pak* v *Commission* [. . .] that *Commercial Solvents* v *Commission* [. . .] and *CBEM* v *CLT and IPB* [. . .] provide examples of abuses having effects on markets other than the dominated markets. There is no doubt, therefore, that an abuse of a dominant position on one market may be censured because of effects which it produces on another market. It is only in the different situation where the abuse is found on a market other than the dominated market that Article [102] of the Treaty is inapplicable except in special circumstances [. . .]

165. In the present case, although the conduct of ADP to which the contested decision objects, namely the application of discriminatory fees, has effects on the market in groundhandling services and, indirectly, on the market in air transport, the fact remains that it takes place on the market in the management of airports, where ADP occupies a dominant position. Furthermore, where the undertaking in receipt of the service is on a separate market from that on which the person supplying the service is present, the conditions for the applicability of Article [102 TFEU] are satisfied provided that, owing to the dominant position occupied by the supplier, the recipient is in a situation of economic dependence *vis-à-vis* the supplier, without their necessarily having to be present on the same market. It is sufficient if the service offered by the supplier is necessary to the exercise by the recipient of its own activity. [. . .]

173. In that regard, it should be recalled that the concept of abuse is an objective concept and implies no intention to cause harm. Accordingly, the fact that ADP has no interest in distorting competition on a market on which it is not present, and indeed that it endeavoured to maintain competition, even if proved, is in any event irrelevant. It is not the arrival on the market in groundhandling services of another supplier that is in issue, but the fact that at the time of the adoption of the contested decision, the conditions applicable to the various suppliers of those services were considered by the Commission to be objectively discriminatory.

The judgment of the General Court was confirmed by the CJEU.[365]

NOTES AND QUESTIONS ON ADP

1. The General Court found that ADP had abused its dominant position even if it was not vertically integrated in the downstream markets of ground-handling services or air transport that were directly or indirectly affected by the abuse. The aim of the practice was not therefore to provide a competitive advantage to ADP at the downstream markets, as ADP was not present in any of those. Nor was there any indication that the abuse would assist ADP in maintaining its dominant position in the upstream market. The GC noted that there can be an abuse of a dominant position if 'the recipient is in a situation of economic dependence *vis-à-vis* the supplier, without their necessarily having to be present on the same market. It is sufficient if the service offered by the supplier is necessary to the exercise by the recipient of its own activity'.[366] Is there any limiting principle in the application of Article 102 TFEU to such a configuration of a

365 Case C-82/01 P, *Aéroports de Paris v Commission* [2002] ECR I-9297.
366 Case T-128/98, *Aéroports de Paris v Commission* [2000] ECR II-3929, para 165.

non-vertically integrated undertaking? Note that the GC used the term 'necessary' and not 'indispensable' (as in *Oscar Bronner* for refusals to deal), thus indicating that it is sufficient for the claimant to prove that he needs to use the service offered by the supplier at the upstream market. Can the GC's judgment be understood as being limited to circumstances in which there is an economic dependence between the supplier at the upstream market and the undertaking at the downstream market, because the former benefits from an exclusive right? Would that correspond to the situation described in the Commission's Guidance on its enforcement priorities in applying Article 102 TFEU to abusive exclusionary conduct by dominant undertakings where the Commission notes concerning refusals to deal that it would not consider imposing an obligation to supply as being capable of having negative effects on the input owner's and/or other operators' incentives to invest and innovate upstream 'if the market position of the dominant undertaking has been developed under the protection of special or exclusive rights or has been financed by state resources'?[367]

2. It is clear that the existence of a discriminatory effect may be an indication for an abuse but absence of such an effect does not place a rebates system out of the reach of Article 102 TFEU. See, for instance, *Michelin I*, where the CJEU found a breach of Article 102 TFEU although it did not uphold the Commission's complaint that the rebates were discriminatory.[368]

9.7.2.4. *British Airways v Commission*

In addition to the finding that the rebates practised were exclusionary, in *British Airways/Virgin* there was also discrimination by a dominant undertaking between intermediaries (pure secondary line discrimination).[369] British Airways, which had a dominant position in the UK as a buyer in the market for air travel agency services, paid a bonus commission to travel agents who had increased their sales and achieved their targets relative to sales in a past reference period. The Commission found that the bonus scheme was discriminatory since two travel agents selling the same amount of tickets would receive different commissions if one of the travel agents had achieved the targets set with regard to the increase of sales by a greater proportion that his past sales relative to the other agent. The General Court confirmed the decision of the Commission.[370] The CJEU addressed, among other things, the requirement relating to the finding of a competitive disadvantage under Article 102(c) TFEU and suggested that it might not be necessary to show that there has been 'an actual quantifiable deterioration in the competitive position of the business partners taken individually'.[371]

367 Commission Guidance on Article 102, para 82.
368 Case C-322/81, *Michelin I* [1983] ECR 3461.
369 *Virgin/BA* (Case COMP IV/D-2/34.780) Commission Decision [2000] OJ L 30/1.
370 Case T-219/99 *British Airways v Commission* [2003] ECR II–5917, para 217.
371 Case C-95/04 P, *British Airways plc v. Commission* [2007] ECR I–2331, para 145. On 'competitive disadvantage', see also Case C-52/07, *Kanal 5 Ltd v Föreningen Svenska Tonsättares Internationella Musikbyrå (STIM) upa*, ECLI:EU:C:2008:703, para 46, which interprets the requirement of 'competitive disadvantage' as requiring that the trading partners subject to discrimination form part of the 'same market'.

Case C-95/04 P, *British Airways plc v. Commission*
[2007] ECR I–2331

142. In the second part of its fifth plea, BA argues that, for the purposes of correctly applying subparagraph (c) of the second paragraph of Article [102 TFEU] the mere finding of the [General Court] [. . .] that travel agents, in their capacity to compete with each other, are 'naturally affected by the discriminatory conditions of remuneration inherent in BA's performance reward schemes' is not sufficient, since concrete evidence of a competitive disadvantage was required.

143. The specific prohibition of discrimination in subparagraph (c) of the second paragraph of Article [102 TFEU] forms part of the system for ensuring, in accordance with [Article 3(1)(g) EC, now Protocol No 27], that competition is not distorted in the internal market. The commercial behaviour of the undertaking in a dominant position may not distort competition on an upstream or a downstream market, in other words between suppliers or customers of that undertaking. Co-contractors of that undertaking must not be favoured or disfavoured in the area of the competition which they practise amongst themselves.

144. Therefore, in order for the conditions for applying subparagraph (c) of the second paragraph of Article [102 TFEU] to be met, there must be a finding not only that the behaviour of an undertaking in a dominant market position is discriminatory, but also that it tends to distort that competitive relationship, in other words to hinder the competitive position of some of the business partners of that undertaking in relation to the others [. . .].

145. In that respect, there is nothing to prevent discrimination between business partners who are in a relationship of competition from being regarded as being abusive as soon as the behaviour of the undertaking in a dominant position tends, having regard to the whole of the circumstances of the case, to lead to a distortion of competition between those business partners. In such a situation, it cannot be required in addition that proof be adduced of an actual quantifiable deterioration in the competitive position of the business partners taken individually.

146. [. . .] [The General Court] found that travel agents in the United Kingdom compete intensely with each other, and that that ability to compete depended on two factors, namely 'their ability to provide seats on flights suited to travellers' wishes, at a reasonable cost' and, secondly, their individual financial resources.

147. Moreover, in the part of the judgment under appeal relating to the examination of the fidelity-building effect of the bonus schemes at issue, the [General Court] found that the latter could lead to exponential changes in the revenue of travel agents.

148. Given that factual situation, the [General Court] could, in the context of its examination of the bonus schemes at issue having regard to subparagraph (c) of the second paragraph of Article [102 TFEU], move directly, without any detailed intermediate stage, to the conclusion that the possibilities for those agents to compete with each other had been affected by the discriminatory conditions for remuneration implemented by BA.

9.7.2.5. *Meo v Autoridade da Concorrência*

The case involved the main TV broadcasters in Portugal (Meo and NOS) and GDA, a collecting society in Portugal. In 2014, Meo complained to the Portuguese competition authority that GDA had abused of its dominant position by charging Meo a higher royalty rate for audio-visual content than its competitor NOS. The royalty rate for licensing resulted from an arbitration decision, GDA and NOS having resorted to arbitration when their bilateral negotiations proved unsuccessful. As previously mentioned, the case involved a second-degree price discrimination, the dominant undertaking in question, GDA, not being present in the downstream market (TV broadcasting). After examining Meo's average costs and profitability, the Portuguese competition authority dismissed the complaint on the grounds that the rate difference was not sufficient to compromise Meo's competitive position vis-à-vis NOS. On appeal, the Portuguese Competition, Regulation and Supervision Court referred a preliminary question to the CJEU, providing it with the opportunity to clarify its position with regard to the application of the third element of the abusive price discrimination test, the concept of 'competitive disadvantage'. The CJEU emphasized the importance of examining thoroughly the third element of the test, which was somehow interpreted loosely by some older case law of the CJEU. For instance, in the *British Airways* case, the CJEU had accepted that the third prong of the test is satisfied if the price discrimination 'tends to distort [the] competitive relationship, in other words, to hinder the competitive position of some of the business partners of [the allegedly dominant] undertaking in relation to the others'.[372]

The case was also of particular interest as it could indicate that the trend started by *Intel* to examine all relevant circumstances, including the possible exclusion of as efficient competitors, before concluding that the conduct constitutes an abuse, may continue and expand in other types of abuse. However, the case can also be considered as a much-needed correction to the quite broad interpretation the CJEU has given in the past to the concept of 'competitive disadvantage', in particular in second-degree price discrimination cases. The approach followed in this case may not apply in other, less controversial—from the perspective of the economics of competition law—types of abuses.

Indeed, in his Opinion in this case Advocate General Niels Wahl, emphasized the need to clarify the case law of the CJEU on the practice of price differentiation, noting that '[. . .] it cannot be assumed that price differentiation practices create a "competitive disadvantage" without examining all of the circumstances of the case at hand, especially when what is at issue is so-called "second degree" discrimination'.[373] The AG noted that 'the disadvantage which Meo allegedly suffered in terms of the sums it paid in order to make use of works protected by copyright and related rights did not result in any decrease in its market share', Meo's market share increasing from 25 to 40 per cent during the period of the infringement.[374] Drawing on his general view of competition law as merely a legal tool aiming to promote economic efficiency, a personal opinion he also defended in *Intel*,[375] AG Wahl also made some general remarks on the category of price discrimination as a type of abuse under Article 102 TFEU:

> 61. [. . .] It is important to bear in mind that discrimination, including discrimination in the charging of prices, is not in itself problematic from the point of view of competition law. The reason for that is that price discrimination is not always harmful to competition. On the contrary, as is evidenced in particular by the (vain) official attempts made in the United States to repeal the

372 Case C-95/04 P *British Airways* v *Commission* [2007] ECR I–2331, para 144.

373 Opinion AG N Wahl in Case C-525/16, *Meo—Serviços de Comunicações e Multimédia v Autoridade da Concorrência*, ECLI:EU:C:2017:1020, paras 4 and 59.

374 Ibid, para 39.

375 Opinion of AG N Wahl in Case C-413/14 P, *Intel Corp v European Commission*, ECLI:EU:C:2016:788, paras 40–3

provision in the Robinson-Patman Act of 1936[376] which prohibits such discrimination, purely and simply prohibiting price discrimination may prove injurious to economic efficiency and the well-being of consumers.

62. Indeed, it is well established that a practice of discrimination, and a differential pricing practice in particular, is ambivalent in terms of its effects on competition. Such a practice may have the consequence of increasing economic efficiency and thus the well-being of consumers. These are goals which, to my mind, should not be overlooked in the application of the rules of competition law, and they are, in any event, quite distinct from considerations of fairness. As the Court has repeatedly held, the rules of competition law are designed to safeguard competition, not to protect competitors.

63. It should only be possible to penalise price discrimination, either under the law applicable to cartels or under the law applicable to abuses of a dominant position, if it creates an actual or potential anticompetitive effect. The identification of such an effect must not be confused with the disadvantage that may immediately be experienced, or suffered, by operators that have been charged the highest prices for goods or services. Accordingly, the fact that an undertaking has been charged a higher price when purchasing goods or services than that applied to one or more of its competitor undertakings may be characterised as a disadvantage, but it does not necessarily result in a 'competitive disadvantage'.

64. Therefore, even where an undertaking is charged higher prices than those applied to other undertakings and, as a result, suffers (or considers that it suffers) discrimination, the conduct in question will be caught by Article 102 TFEU only if it is established that it is likely to restrict competition and diminish the well-being of consumers'.[377]

Note the ambivalent language of the AG with regard to the 'well-being of consumers'. Are these 'consumers' the customers of the dominant undertaking who are charged higher prices compared to their rivals in the downstream market, or the final consumers of the downstream market, here the customers of Meo and NOS, that may be affected by the 'competitive disadvantage' from which suffers Meo because of the discriminatory practice of GDA and, in particular from the impact this practice may have on the intensity of competition between Meo and NOS in the downstream market? An interesting point is also that, by embracing the efficiency approach and dismissing fairness considerations, the AG seems to adopt a narrow perception of 'consumer well-being', what economists would qualify as 'consumer surplus',[378] rather than a broader view of 'consumer well-being' that would also take into account wealth transfers from producers to consumers, or broader distributional effects. Regardless of the need for the case law on Article 102(c) to be streamlined, in particular for second-degree price discrimination, do you think that this narrow view on 'consumer well-being' is normatively justified and fits the facts of the case?

The AG also argued that the legal test for price discrimination under Article 102(c) TFEU should also reflect the distinction 'between undertakings that are vertically integrated and

376 Robinson–Patman Act of 1936 (or Anti-Price Discrimination Act) Pub L No 74-692, 49 Stat 1526, 15 USC § 13. The Act prohibits, under certain conditions, a seller from charging competing buyers different prices for the same 'commodity' or discriminating in the provision of 'allowances'. On a discussion about the recent efforts to reform or repeal the Act, see JB Kirkwood, 'Reforming the Robinson–Patman Act to Serve Consumers and Control Powerful Buyers' (2015) 60(4) *Antitrust Bulletin* 358.

377 Opinion AG N Wahl in Case C-525/16, *Meo—Serviços de Comunicações e Multimédia v Autoridade da Concorrência*, ECLI:EU:C:2017:1020, paras 61–4.

378 See our discussion in Section 3.2.3.

will therefore have an interest in displacing competitors on the downstream market and those that have no such interest'.[379] If, for the first, the situation is very similar to first-degree price discrimination and indirectly affects the rivals of the dominant undertaking, for the second-degree price discrimination, when the undertaking in a dominant position is not in competition with its customers on the downstream market, according to the AG, 'it is not easy to determine the reasons which might lead that undertaking to apply discriminatory prices, other than the direct exploitation of its customers' as it might be 'somewhat irrational for it to reduce the competitive pressure which exists among its trading partners on the downstream market'.[380] According to the AG, Article 102(c) TFEU 'cannot be interpreted as requiring an undertaking in a dominant position on a given market to apply, in all circumstances and independently of any analysis of the effects on competition of the conduct complained of, uniform prices to all its trading partners'.[381] This brought him to emphasize the importance of proving the existence of a 'competitive disadvantage', which he was careful to distinguish from the 'existence of "disadvantages between competitors", or even of a disadvantage pure and simple'.[382] This requires evidence that the disadvantage suffered is 'sufficiently significant as to have consequences for the competitive position of the undertaking discriminated against' and that 'the discriminatory prices have a tendency to distort the competitive relationship between the trading partners on the downstream market'.[383] This analysis requires to take into account 'all of the circumstances of the case' rather than 'evaluate the impact of the discriminatory practice on a specific trading partner'.[384] Hence, 'possible differences in treatment which have no impact, or only a very minor impact on competition cannot constitute an abuse',[385] in particular for practices, such as second degree price discrimination, which are not 'intrinsically harmful'.[386] The AG suggested a number of factors competition authorities and courts may take into account in performing analysis of 'all of the circumstances' of the case,[387] these also been retained by the CJEU, and listed in the excerpt of the judgment.

Case C-525/16, *Meo—Serviços de Comunicações e Multimédia v Commission*, ECLI:EU:C:2018:270

24. In accordance with the case-law of the Court, the specific prohibition of discrimination under subparagraph (c) of the second paragraph of Article 102 TFEU is intended to ensure that competition is not distorted in the internal market. The commercial behaviour of the undertaking in a dominant position may not distort competition on an upstream or a downstream market, in other words, between suppliers or customers of that undertaking. Co-contractors of such undertakings must not be favoured or disfavoured in the area of the competition which they practise amongst themselves (judgment of 15 March 2007, *British Airways* v *Commission*, C-95/04 P, EU:C:2007:166, paragraph 143). Thus, it is not necessary that the abusive conduct

[379] Opinion AG N Wahl in Case C-525/16, *Meo—Serviços de Comunicações e Multimédia v Autoridade da Concorrência*, ECLI:EU:C:2017:1020, para 76.

[380] Ibid, para 79. The AG noted in particular that cases of 'pure' second degree discrimination', are 'extremely rare'. Ibid, para 80.

[381] Ibid, para 87. [382] Ibid, para 95. [383] Ibid, para 97. [384] Ibid, para 98.

[385] Ibid, para 105. [386] Ibid, para 102. [387] Ibid, paras 106–10.

affects the competitive position of the dominant undertaking itself on the same market in which it operates, compared with its own potential competitors.

25. In order for the conditions for applying subparagraph (c) of the second paragraph of Article 102 TFEU to be met, there must be a finding, not only that the behaviour of an undertaking in a dominant market position is discriminatory, but also that it tends to distort that competitive relationship, in other words, to hinder the competitive position of some of the business partners of that undertaking in relation to the others (judgment of 15 March 2007, *British Airways* v *Commission*, C-95/04 P, EU:C:2007:166, paragraph 144 and the case-law cited).

26. In order to establish whether the price discrimination on the part of an undertaking in a dominant position vis-à-vis its trade partners tends to distort competition on the downstream market, as the Advocate General submitted, in essence, in paragraph 63 of his Opinion, the mere presence of an immediate disadvantage affecting operators who were charged more, compared with the tariffs applied to their competitors for an equivalent service, does not, however, mean that competition is distorted or is capable of being distorted.

27. It is only if the behaviour of the undertaking in a dominant position tends, having regard to the whole of the circumstances of the case, to lead to a distortion of competition between those business partners that the discrimination between trade partners which are in a competitive relationship may be regarded as abusive. In such a situation, it cannot, however, be required in addition that proof be adduced of an actual, quantifiable deterioration in the competitive position of the business partners taken individually (judgment of 15 March 2007, *British Airways* v *Commission*, C-95/04 P, EU:C:2007:166, paragraph 145).

28. Therefore, as the Advocate General submitted in paragraph 86 of his Opinion, it is necessary to examine all the relevant circumstances in order to determine whether price discrimination produces or is capable of producing a competitive disadvantage, for the purposes of subparagraph (c) of the second paragraph of Article 102 TFEU.

29. With regard to the issue whether, for the application of subparagraph (c) of the second paragraph of Article 102 TFEU, it is necessary to take into account the seriousness of a possible competitive disadvantage, it must be pointed out that fixing an appreciability (*de minimis*) threshold for the purposes of determining whether there is an abuse of a dominant position is not justified (see, to that effect, judgment of 6 October 2015, *Post Danmark*, C-23/14, EU:C:2015:651, paragraph 73).

30. However, in order for it to be capable of creating a competitive disadvantage, the price discrimination referred to in subparagraph (c) of the second paragraph of Article 102 TFEU must affect the interests of the operator which was charged higher tariffs compared with its competitors.

31. When it carries out the specific examination referred to in paragraph 28 above, the competition authority or the competent national court is required to take into account all the circumstances of the case submitted to it. It is open to such an authority or court to assess, in that context, the undertaking's dominant position, the negotiating power as regards the tariffs, the conditions and arrangements for charging those tariffs, their duration and their amount, and the possible existence of a strategy aiming to exclude from the downstream market one of its trade partners which is at least as efficient as its competitors (see, by analogy, judgment of 6 September 2017, *Intel* v *Commission*, C-413/14 P, EU:C:2017:632, paragraph 139 and the case-law cited).

The CJEU referred the analysis of facts to the national court. It noted, however, that MEO and NOS had certain negotiating power vis-à-vis GDA, that the difference in tariffs between MEO and NOS represented an amount that was a relatively low percentage of the total costs borne by MEO and thus had a limited effect on MEO's profits, the impact of the practice thus being not significant and not capable of having any effect on the competitive position of the discriminated undertaking in the downstream market. Finally, the Court noted that the dominant undertaking had no interest in excluding one of its trade partners from the downstream market, thus raising the bar for bringing a second degree price discrimination case.

NOTES AND QUESTIONS ON MEO

1. How does the CJEU analyse 'competitive disadvantage'? Is an individual prejudice suffered by an undertaking downstream enough for Article 102(c) TFEU to apply?[388]
2. In his Opinion, AG Wahl made a distinction between situations of first degree discrimination and pure second degree price discrimination, 'followed by a non-vertically integrated dominant undertaking', which is not a conduct that may be considered as 'intrinsically harmful', thus implying a restriction of competition, but a conduct 'the actual repercussions of which must be examined more thoroughly if a finding is to be made that there is a restriction of competition'.[389] The distinction between practices that are 'inherently harmful', which do not require an analysis of the effects and all the relevant circumstances in relation to the transactions at issue and the characteristics of the market on which the trading partners of the dominant undertaking operate, and practices for which a more thorough analysis of effects is required, is reminiscent to the distinction between restrictions of competition by object and effect in Article 101 TFEU. Although the CJEU does not explicitly adopt the categorization suggested by the AG, in its discussion of the legal principles applying to price discrimination, it refers in paragraph 35 to the fact that in the situation in question (the second degree price discrimination), the dominant undertaking had no interest in excluding one of its trading partners from the downstream market.
3. Note that the CJEU held that there is no need to adduce evidence that the price discrimination has led to an 'actual, quantifiable deterioration in the competitive position of the business partners taken individually'.[390] The CJEU also rejected the adoption of a requirement of appreciability of the effects (*de minimis*) for a conduct to be characterized as an abuse of a dominant position. Once it is established that there a competitive disadvantage is likely, then even conduct producing non-appreciable effects may fall under Article 102 TFEU.
4. However, this does not mean that a small price differential will not be considered as one of the factors taken into account for the analysis of the existence of a competitive disadvantage, the conditions and arrangements of the tariffs, as well as their duration and amount, are among the factors the CJEU requires national courts to take into account.[391] Other factors include the undertaking's dominant position, the negotiating power with regard to tariffs, and 'the possible existence of a strategy aiming to exclude from the downstream market one of its trade partners which is at least as efficient as its competitors'.[392]

[388] See C-525/16, *Meo—Serviços de Comunicações e Multimédia v Commission*, ECLI:EU:C:2018:270, paras 26–7.

[389] Opinion AG N Wahl in Case C-525/16, *Meo—Serviços de Comunicações e Multimédia v Autoridade da Concorrência*, ECLI:EU:C:2017:1020, para 102.

[390] Case C-525/16, *Meo—Serviços de Comunicações e Multimédia v Commission*, ECLI:EU:C:2018:270, para 27.

[391] Ibid, para 31.

[392] Ibid.

5. When using the as efficient as competitor concept in paragraph 31, the CJEU referred 'by analogy' to its judgment in *Intel*.[393] This seems to imply that the as-efficient-as-competitor test could set the outer boundaries of Article 102 TFEU, with competition authorities taking action only if the exclusionary conduct has the potential to exclude as efficient competitors. This may provide hints as to the possible interpretation of the CJEU's *Intel* judgment by the General Court, as the CJEU employed in this judgment quite ambivalent language as to the need for the Commission to rely on the AEC test for proving that a loyalty rebate infringed Article 102 TFEU.[394]

9.7.3. UK CASE LAW

One example of price discrimination can be found in *Napp*.[395] The OFT (now replaced by the CMA) decided that Napp had abused a dominant position in breach of the Chapter II CA98 prohibition by supplying sustained release morphine tablets and capsules to patients in the community at excessively high prices while supplying hospitals at discount levels that foreclose competition and imposed a fine of £3.21 million. However, the OFT assessed these practices under the predatory and excessive pricing forms of abusive conduct.

Another example of a case in which price discrimination was considered is *Attheraces v BHB*.[396] The dispute arose between Attheraces Ltd. ('ATR'), a group of companies supplying websites, television channels and other audio-visual media relating to British racing to bookmakers and punters, against British Horseracing Board, the administrator and governing body of British horseracing, and its commercial arm, BHB Enterprises PLC ('BHB') concerning ATR's access to pre-race data about British horse races, compiled and controlled by BHB.

ATR accused BHB of refusing to supply pre-race data to ATR, an existing customer, without objective justification. ATR also alleged that BHB was demanding an excessive and discriminatory price, by seeking to obtain from ATR a higher price than that paid by other broadcasters. The Court held that BHB had abused a dominant position in the market for supply of the pre-race data by unreasonably refusing to supply the data to an existing customer, ATR, charging excessive, unfair, and discriminatory prices to ATR.

On appeal, the Court of Appeal overturned all the abuse findings. With regards to discriminatory pricing, the Court of Appeal stated:

> There is plenty of evidence, if evidence were needed, that differential pricing is not necessarily abusive and may be benign. It becomes abusive where, for example, a dominant supplier refuses arbitrarily to supply an established customer, or for no acceptable reason charges different prices in different member states for the same product, distorting competition by—for example—obstructing the free movement of goods, oppressing the less powerful of their customers within the EU or partitioning national markets.[397]

393 Ibid. See Case C-413/14 P, *Intel v Commission*, ECLI:EU:C:2017:632, para 139.

394 See our analysis in Section 9.6.4.3.

395 *Napp Pharmaceutical Holdings Limited and subsidiaries*, OFT Decision CA/2/2001 (March 2011), available at www.gov.uk/cma-cases/napp-pharmaceutical-holdings-ltd-alleged-abuse-of-a-dominant-position.

396 *Attheraces v BHB* [2007] EWCA Civ 38.

397 Ibid, para 267.

The Court of Appeal also noted:

> [. . .] It is correct that both Article [102(c) TFEU] and s. 18(2)(c) of the [1998 Act] give as an example of abuse 'applying dissimilar conditions to equivalent transactions with other trading parties, thereby placing them at a competitive disadvantage'. The formulation requires the court to decide which transactions are in this sense 'equivalent' and what amounts to a competitive disadvantage.
>
> We are prepared to accept, as the judge did, that the transactions by which ATR found itself paying considerably more per race meeting than [a broadcaster operating in another jurisdiction] did were equivalent transactions. But how did this place ATR at a competitive disadvantage? Certainly it made ATR's operation less profitable than it would otherwise have been, but ATR's ability to compete with [the other broadcaster] (or, so far as material, with others) remained intact. Although they impact on each other, profitability and competitiveness are two different things, and the latter, which is critical to the case, was not addressed in terms by the Judge.[398]

More recently, OFCOM found Royal Mail in breach of Section 18 (Chapter II) CA98 and Article 102 TFEU, for issuing contractual notices to change its wholesale prices for other postal operators to access its delivery network, by charging a higher price per letter to competitors, such as Whistl, that wished to start delivering 'bulk mail' (business letters) in some parts of the UK, in comparison to the rate charged per letter to companies that used Royal Mail to deliver across the whole UK. In view of Royal Mail's near-monopoly in delivery services, OFCOM found that Royal Mail's conduct was reasonably likely to put other companies at a competitive disadvantage and to have a material impact on their profits, making it significantly harder for new companies to enter the 'bulk mail' delivery market.[399]

9.8. BUNDLING/TYING

Article 102(d) provides tying/bundling as an example of an abuse when it subjects to Article 102 TFEU a dominant undertaking when 'making the conclusion of contracts subject to acceptance by the other parties of supplementary obligations which, by their nature or according to commercial usage, have no connection with the subject of such contracts'. We will first briefly explore the economics of tying/bundling before focusing on the case law and the decisional practice of the Commission.

9.8.1. THE ECONOMICS OF BUNDLING/TYING

Tying and bundling are pervasive business practices:[400] for example, hotels offer breakfast, fast food diners offer 'happy meals', football teams sell season tickets. Bundling/tying can take many different forms (eg contractual or technical tying; financial or mixed bundling through rebates), which in turn has led competition authorities and courts to develop specific competition law

[398] Ibid, paras 269–70.

[399] Royal Mail fined £50m for breaking competition law (14 August 2018), available at https://www.ofcom.org.uk/about-ofcom/latest/features-and-news/royal-mail-whistl-competition-law.

[400] This Section draws substantially on N Economides and I Lianos, 'Google Dominance and Tying for Android', CLES Research Paper No 9/2018, forthcoming. On the economics of tying/bundling, see also C Fumagalli, M Motta, and C Calcagno, *Exclusionary Practices—The Economics of Monopolisation and Abuse of Dominance* (Cambridge University Press, 2018), 350–464.

standards for each category. These different standards may be explained by the need to take into account the risk of enforcement errors and the likelihood of exclusionary effects, which may be different for each form of bundling/tying. It is important, therefore, to develop coherent competition law standards so that any similarity or difference in the treatment of these practices is adequately explained. It is also important to acknowledge that competition law is concerned with a forced or heavily incentivized combination or package sale, but non-forced or incentivized combinations are not illegal. For instance, sellers may refuse to sell shoes unless the customer agrees to purchase a pair of them or to sell automobiles without their tires. The various categories of abusive conduct are not clear cut: it is possible to present the facts of a case as fitting within more than one specific category/type of abuse. The Commission's Guidance on Article 102 explains that '[t]ying usually refers to situations where customers that purchase one product (the tying product) are required also to purchase another product from the dominant undertaking (the tied product)', while 'bundling usually refers to the way products are offered and priced by the dominant undertaking'.[401] The difference between tying and bundling is the fact that in the former customers are 'required' to purchase the two products together, while in bundling such requirement may not exist. According to this understanding, a simple incentive to buy products together would not amount to a 'requirement' and thus not to tying.[402] Legal economists also distinguish between three types of bundling/tying practices:[403]

- *Pure bundling*: in this case, none of the package components is offered individually, and each of them can only be acquired as part of the bundle. Often, the products are offered in fixed proportions.
- *Tying*: some of the goods contained in the package are offered on their own (tied product) whereas others are not available individually (tying products). Consumers of the latter are forced (coerced) to acquire the former (tied products). The requirement to buy the two products together may result from *contractual tying* or *technical tying*. According to the Commission's Guidance on Article 102, '[t]echnical tying occurs when the tying product is designed in such a way that it only works properly with the tied product (and not with the alternatives offered by competitors). Contractual tying occurs when the customer who purchases the tying product undertakes also to purchase the tied product (and not the alternatives offered by competitors).'[404]
- *Mixed bundling (or financial tying)*: a practice of selling each product as part of a package, as well as individually (à-la-carte). Yet, consumers are incentivized to purchase the different products as a package, as the bundle price is lower than the sum of individual prices (eg round-trip airline tickets is cheaper than buying separately the outward and the inward flight). This, for instance, may take the form of a bundled rebate: the customer benefits from a discount if he buys two products from the same seller, compared to the situation he buys only one of them.

401 Commission Guidance on Article 102, para 48.

402 This establishes a distinction between coercion and incentive, the latter being thought to be less intrusive to individual autonomy of consumers than the former. According to this conception, the competitive order is thought as preserving individual autonomy in the sense that the price system relies on the expression of each person's preferences on the market when making purchasing decisions (revealed preferences). Yet, individual autonomy should also be recognized to sellers, when making decisions over the characteristics of the products (the product bundles) they offer on the marketplace, as long as the market is a competitive one and consumers have the possibility to choose different product bundles.

403 R O'Donoghue and J Padilla, *The Law and Economics of Article 102 TFEU* (Hart, 2nd ed, 2013), 596–7.

404 Commission Guidance on Article 102, para 48 n 2.

Distinguishing tying from other categories of abuse is not always easy. For instance, one may conceive tying as a form of conditional refusal to sell one product unless the buyer also purchases from the seller another product. Additionally, it is not always easy to distinguish between tying/bundling and perfectly legal business decisions over the characteristics of the product an undertaking offers to consumers. Competition law only addresses a combination or package sale that is forced or incentivized through illegal means, but certainly does not engage with every decision of an undertaking to combine two allegedly separate products into one. For instance, automobiles are sold with tires, even if one may buy tires separately. This example shows that competition law should not engage with combinations, packaged sales, or the imposition of supplementary obligations that may be explained, in the terms of Article 102(d), by their 'nature' or 'according to commercial usage'. For instance, it is not in the commercial usage to sell cars without tires. One could also advance that nowadays it is not in the commercial usage to sell cars without car-audio equipment or a GPS navigation device. This was certainly not in the commercial usage a few years ago. Reliance on 'commercial usage' or the 'nature' of the transactions seems therefore a fairly fuzzy concept, to the extent that perceptions of the nature of the transaction and what constitutes, or not, a 'supplementary obligation' and 'commercial usage' may change.

A closely related issue is on the evidence one may rely upon in order to uncover 'commercial usage' or how 'natural' the link is between the 'supplementary obligations' and the 'subject' of the contractual transaction. Should one rely on information on historic (or actual) patterns in the demand and the supply side? Should one instead develop a forward-looking approach that would engage with information on the possible development of 'new' products and packages sales, as this transpires from the business strategy of the various firms competing for consumers of a relevant market? Should one rely on the views/strategies of the dominant undertaking, or primarily take into account the views of its competitors? How does the step of market definition relate to that of deciding over the normality of the link between the allegedly 'distinct' products and 'commercial usage?' These are some critical questions to have in mind before exploring the economic assessment of tying/bundling practices and the legal approach.

To a certain extent, competition economists do not engage with these semantic questions as their principal focus is to assess the welfare consequences of tying or bundling practices. For economists, the distinction between tying and bundling carries no normative effect on its own but is used as a description of the various forms a tying or bundling practice might take. The crucial issue examined by economists is to identify the possible anti-competitive (welfare-reducing) effects of tying/bundling practices and their possible pro-competitive (welfare-increasing) effects they may have. Economists have indeed presented various theories of harm that tying/bundling practices may bring, as well as theories relying on efficiency justifications for the same practices.

Without entering into a detailed analysis of the history of the evolution of economic thought in this area, suffice is to say that for a long time competition law perceived tying/bundling practices with suspicion as it was thought as a practice dominant undertakings could use in order to leverage their market power from the tying product market to the tied product market by also imposing to consumers a bundle of products that did not correspond to the consumers' preferences.[405] The theory denotes the possibility that tying could be used

[405] On the leverage theory and tying, see L Kaplow, 'Extension of Monopoly Power Through Leverage' (1985) 85 *Columbia L Rev* 515. On the ordoliberal perspective on tying, see C Ahlborn and C Grave, 'Walter Eucken and Ordoliberalism: An Introduction from a Consumer Welfare Perspective' (2006) 2 *Competition Policy Int'l* 197, which explain that ordoliberal theory inspired authors would have classified tying as a form of 'impediment competition' and thus presumptively an anticompetitive practice.

in order to maintain or extend monopoly power in the tied product market, as well as, if one takes a broader perspective, to achieve a competitive advantage in the tied product market. In any case, tying leads to a possible increase of prices or a reduction of output in the tied product market and thus to deadweight loss.

In the late 1970s prominent scholars of the Chicago school (Richard Posner, Frank Easterbrook, Robert Bork) proposed that tying should be *per se* legal, and only in exceptional circumstances can there be antitrust liability.[406] Their reasoning was based on early work by Director and Levy which has become known as the Chicago School 'one surplus theory'.[407] Indeed, the Chicago School of economics criticized the leveraging theory by arguing that there is only one monopoly profit to be made, which cannot be increased by tying. This theory essentially stated that a monopolist in good *A* has no reason to tie product *B* except when there are cost savings or other efficiencies in the joint production or distribution of *A* and *B*. In the Chicago School line of reasoning, tying only occurs when it is efficient (because of cost savings), and therefore tying should be allowed in principle, and only occasionally and in special circumstances might be found illegal. At the heart of the Chicago School analysis, the first question is 'why does the monopolist want a second monopoly?'[408] The seller cannot earn a double monopoly profit and force consumers to pay even more that what they would pay but for tying, as monopoly prices are determined at the final output level of each product and there is a single profit-maximizing price for each final product. Hence, the total amount of restriction that the monopolist may profitably be able to impose is fixed: the monopolist cannot increase prices in a secondary market without losing profits in its primary market and therefore has no incentive to use tying for anti-competitive purposes.

Clearly, the Chicago School is correct to state that cost savings in production and distribution are a possible reason for any firm, even a monopolist, to want a second monopoly, not for the second monopoly's revenue and profits, but for the cost savings created in selling the combination of the two goods. However, the Chicago School's proposition that cost savings in joint production and distribution are the *only* reason for tying and bundling is incorrect.

The question 'why does a monopolist want a second monopoly' is insufficient to describe the incentives of a monopolist to impose tying and bundling. The key to understanding the motives behind the decision to tie or bundle is that a monopolist can extract surplus in varying degrees from buyers. Thus, the word 'monopoly' does not describe sufficiently the extent of extraction of consumer surplus by the seller.[409] In some markets, monopolists are able to extract all consumer surplus by selling each unit to every buyer at his/her willingness to pay, a practice called perfect price discrimination. In most markets, this very complex pricing is unfeasible. Perfect price discrimination may be unfeasible for at least three reasons: (i) the seller does not know the willingness to pay for each unit that every buyer may be willing to buy; (ii) the pricing schedule to be implemented is very complex; and (iii) resale among the users (arbitrage) makes price discrimination unfeasible.

406 See R Bork, *The Antitrist Paradox* (Basic Books, 1978), 375; RA Posner and F Easterbrook, *Antitrust Cases, Economic Notes and Other Materials* (West Publishing, 2d ed, 1981), 802–10.

407 See A Director and EH Levi, 'Law and the Future: Trade Regulation' (1956) 51 *Northwestern U L Rev* 281, 290.

408 See RA Posner and F Easterbrook, *Antitrust Cases, Economic Notes and Other Materials* (West Publishing, 2d ed, 1981), 802..

409 Consumer surplus is the difference between what consumers are cumulatively willing to pay and what they cumulatively actually pay in a market. It represents the net benefit to consumers from the existence of the market. As long as a consumer or different consumers have varying valuations for different units of a good, and the good is sold at a single price, consumer surplus is positive.

The incentive of a monopolist to impose tying or bundling practices depends on the extent to which he is able to extract surplus from each buyer and on the extent to which each buyer is left with some consumer surplus before tying or bundling is imposed. In particular, if a monopolist is able to extract *all* consumer surplus from every buyer without imposing tying or bundling, there is no incentive for tying or bundling that does not create a substantial foreclosure share in the tied product except in the presence of cost savings from joint production and distribution.[410] Therefore, in this very special setting where the monopolist is able to extract *all* consumer surplus from every buyer and the tie does not foreclose a substantial share of the tied product market, the Chicago School theory is correct.[411]

However, extracting *all* consumer surplus from every buyer is very unlikely to occur in practice, and thus, the Chicago School's theory fails most of time. The Chicago School theory is developed under the assumption of a homogeneous monopolized good and a homogeneous tied good. If there is consumer demand for variety or quality product differentiation, the Chicago School theory can easily fail because entry of even an inefficient rival in new variety or quality can add to consumer surplus. Besides extracting additional consumer surplus from its current degree of tying market power, a monopolist might be able to gain if it forecloses a substantial share of the tied product and that (1) gives the firm tied market power it can use against tied product buyers who were not subject to the tie, or (2) increases the degree of tying market power.

The specific inabilities of a monopolist to extract the full consumer surplus from all buyers define a roadmap of how tying and/or bundling without a substantial foreclosure share can profitably be used by a monopolist to extract additional surplus in the absence of joint production and distribution cost savings. If buyers buy one unit each but vary in willingness to pay, a single-price monopolist will fail to extract all consumer surplus. The monopolist can then use tying and/or bundling mechanisms to extract more surplus from buyers. If a buyer buys more than one unit and values each unit differently, again a single-price monopolist will fail to extract all consumer surplus, and can use tying and bundling practices to extract more surplus from buyers. Typically, each buyer buys more than one unit of varying valuations *and* buyers differ in their valuations, so even sophisticated nonlinear pricing by the monopolist will have a very hard time extracting *all* surplus from *all* buyers. Then the availability of tying and bundling strategies increase the ability of a monopolist to extract consumer surplus.

Note that the Chicago School accepted that tying might be used to price discriminate, although this should not raise competition concerns, in particular because of the view that price discrimination may not be anti-competitive as it can increase total welfare. However, it is rather indisputable that price discrimination may decrease the welfare of final consumers although this was not a concern for the Chicago School of antitrust, which focused on efficiency and total welfare, rather than the welfare of the final consumers, and thus included the

410 Full consumer surplus can be extracted when each buyer buys only one unit and the seller is able to sell to each buyer at the price that buyer is willing to pay, thereby leaving no consumer surplus for any buyer. Or, more generally, a seller sells many units to each buyer, but is able to offer very sophisticated, individually tailored pricing, that extracts all consumer surplus from all units bought by each buyer.

411 Even with full consumer surplus extraction by the seller and tying not creating substantial foreclosure in the tied product, the Chicago School theory can fail if a buyer has made complementary investments that require the use of a certain amount of the relevant goods. By manipulating the prices and ratios of tied goods in the tying contract, the monopolist can effectively threaten not to sell the amounts that the buyer counted on buying when making the complementary investments, and thereby the buyer can extract even more surplus. In this case, the buyer would be willing to give up more surplus so as not to lose the value of the complementary investments.

additional benefits appropriated by the monopolist through the wealth transfer from the final consumers in their welfare analysis. In addition to increasing tied power, as tying can impair the competitiveness of rivals in the tied market in ways that increase tied product prices and profits, and 'increasing tying power' if the tying market is not competitive, tying may lead to 'intra-product price discrimination', in case the buyers use varying amounts of the tied product.[412]

Post-Chicago economists did not only criticize the validity of the single monopoly profit theorem. They also offered a number of possibility theorems according to which tying may be used in an anti-competitive way. They argued a number of reasons/settings that provide an incentive to a monopolist to impose tying restrictions that go beyond cost savings, as described above. I assume no cost savings from joint distribution and production and no substantial foreclosure share and look for other reasons that may drive a monopolist in good *A* to tie product *B* or to create a bundling contract that involves *A* and *B*. If cost savings from joint distribution and production exist, they can be taken into consideration as efficiencies to counterbalance consumer losses, but cost savings are not a necessary cause for a dominant firm to profitably introduce tying and/or bundling.

Post-Chicago economists developed a number of stylized models in order to prove that if the tied product market is oligopolistic, and not perfectly competitive, undertakings might have an incentive to tie for anti-competitive reasons. For instance, some authors argued that it might be profitable for an undertaking with a monopoly in the tying product market to tie a distinct product when the tied product market is subject to economies of scale, the leveraging successfully inducing the exit or deterring the entry of competitors in the tied market. Whinston criticized the assumptions of the Chicago School and argued that, in certain circumstances, a monopolist in a market *A* may follow a leveraging strategy by using tying practices as a commitment device in order to signal to its actual or potential competitors in the downstream market *B* that they will face aggressive competitive behaviour, which will eventually decrease their profits.[413] The potential rivals will thus be less inclined to enter the market or be excluded from it, if they were present. This strategy is profitable if the tied goods are complements in fixed proportions to the goods in market *A*.[414] In some scenarios tying will make it necessary for a prospective competitor in one of the products to enter the market for both products at the same time. Choi and Stefanadis developed a model in which the incumbent firm may have the interest to extend its monopoly from one market to another if the two products are complements and the new entrant can effectively enter the market for one of the two product only if it has successfully innovated in both markets.[415] The cumulative innovators would therefore be prevented from capturing the social value of their innovation in one market before they also innovate in the second market. This will decrease their incentives to

412 E Elhauge, 'Tying, Bundled Discounts, and the Death of the Single Monopoly Profit Theory' (2009) 123 *Harvard L Rev* 397.

413 MD Whinston 'Tying, Foreclosure and Exclusion' (1990) 80 *American Economic Rev* 837.

414 Ibid (noting that a monopolist committed to a price war at the tied product market and thus charging low prices would be able to recoup some of his profitability losses because of the drop in the prices of the tied product by the effect of an increased output in the tying product market, while his competitors at the tied product market would not, the impact of a price drop in the tied product market being far greater for his competitors); B Nalebuff, 'Bundling', Yale ICF Working Paper No 99-14 (22 November 1999), available at https://ssrn.com/abstract=185193 (noting that tying may deny competitors in the tied product market of an adequate scale to develop).

415 JP Choi, 'Preemptive R&D, Rent Dissipation and the 'Leverage Theory' (1996) 110 *Q J Economics* 1153; JP Choi and C Stefanadis, 'Tying, Investment, and the Dynamic Leverage Theory' (2001) 32 *Rand J Economics* 52.

engage in innovation at the first place with the result that the dominant firm's strategy will pre-empt the emergence of cumulative innovation.

It is also possible that tying is not a strategy aiming that erode the competitive advantage of the dominant firm's rivals in a related market with the aim of extending the dominant firm's market power in that related secondary market, but is strategically used by a dominant firm seeking to maintain its monopoly power on the primary market.

Carlton and Waldman give the example of a two-period setting with a firm that operates in a primary market and a market for a complementary product good.[416] Under this example, owing to an exclusive right, for example a patent, the firm has, in a first period, a dominant position in the primary market. However, in a second period, the incumbent monopolist faces the risk of entry by an alternative producer into the primary market. According to their model, although the alternative producer has a superior complementary product in both periods, its primary product is of equivalent quality only in the second period.

The strategy of the alternative producer will be to use the profits earned by selling units in the complementary market to cover its fixed costs of entering the primary market. The incumbent monopolist can react by increasing the costs of entry of his rivals in the complementary market. It will achieve this goal by tying the primary product to the complementary product. As a result, the entry of the alternative producer in the primary market at the second period will be deterred. It is not the objective of the strategy to extend monopoly power in the market of the complementary product but simply to preserve market power in the primary product. Consequently, less innovation will take place in either the primary or complementary products markets.

These different models suggest that, in certain circumstances, dominant firms may have the interest to deter dynamic innovation that could render obsolete their technological standard.[417] This situation is exacerbated in a network setting, as the dominant form will have more incentives to engage in exclusionary practices in order to control the standard of the network.[418]

Both Chicago School and post-Chicago economists would agree that tying permits price discrimination when the buyers do not always use the tied product in fixed proportions to the tying product (think for instance of printers and ink cartridges). Consumers using more cartridges derive greater value from their printer than consumers that print less and thus use fewer cartridges. Tying would serve in this case as a metering device to charge more users that derive greater value from the printers. Of course, undertakings may opt for a direct discrimination between categories of consumers, according to their use, yet this is in most cases not practical, as undertakings cannot devise before a printer is sold of the value the customer would derive from its use.[419] Furthermore, the pricing schedule to be implemented may be very complex and resale among the users (arbitrage) make defeat price discrimination.[420] Such price discrimination will reduce consumer welfare

416 DW Carlton and M Waldman, 'The Strategic Use of Tying to Preserve and Create Market Power in Evolving Industries' (2002) 33 *Rand J Economics* 194, building on the work of MD Whinston, 'Tying, Foreclosure, and Exclusion' (1990) 80 *American Economic Rev* 837.

417 DW Carlton and RH Gertner, 'Intellectual Property, Antitrust and Strategic Behavior', NBER Working Paper No 8976 (June 2002), available at www.nber.org/papers/w8976.

418 H Hovenkamp, *The Antitrust Enterprise: Principle and Execution* (Harvard University Press, 2005), 277–304.

419 For a Chicago perspective, see WS Bowman, Jr, 'Tying Arrangements and the Leverage Problem' (1957) 67 *Yale LJ* 19, 33.

420 N Economides, 'Tying, Bundling, and Loyalty/Requirement Rebates' in E Elhauge (ed) *Research Handbook on the Economics of Antitrust Law* (Edward Elgar, 2012), 121.

and, in most cases, also total welfare, as tying only offers an imperfect mechanism to price discriminate.[421]

Post-Chicago economists also emphasize the possibility that tying be used to maintain monopoly power at the tying product market (defensive leveraging).[422] In this context, the undertaking's dominant position in the tying product market may be vulnerable to future entry or expansion by a competitor in the tying or the tied product market. The tied product may be a partial substitute to the tying product (not necessarily in the same product market) and tying may enhance the dominant undertaking's dominant position in the tying product market by, for instance, erecting barriers to entry to actual or potential competitors.

Tying may finally be used in order to extend monopoly to an unregulated activity and thus escape the consequences of regulation.

In most of the scenarios above, tying will lead to anti-competitive effects, essentially because of price discrimination or because of the substantial foreclosure effects it will have on the tied or tying markets.

(i) One scenario is that tying would help the dominant undertaking to extract more consumer surplus of product *A* than what it would have been able to extract through single-price monopoly of good product *A*, as absent tying the monopolist in product *A* would have been unable to implement perfect price discrimination and extract all the consumer surplus of product *A* as its profits.[423] In this context tying 'implicitly reveals the willingness to pay of a buyer of A if the willingness to pay for A is highly positively correlated with use of (tied product) B'.[424]

(ii) (The dominant undertaking may also use tying in order to induce buyers that purchase multiple units of the tying product and value units differently to purchase from him the tied product.[425] In the first two scenarios, tying is used to extract more consumer surplus from a single monopolized market.

(iii) However, it is also possible that tying is used in order to extract consumer surplus in the second (tied product) market, in particular, but not exclusively, 'in the presence of substantial market power in the tying market, when consumers buy two goods and their demands do not have very strong positive correlation'.[426]

(iv) Tying may also be used to substantially foreclose rivals, reduce their scale of operations, and thereby increase their unit costs.[427]

With the exception of (iv), where a substantial share of the tied product market should be foreclosed for the conduct to achieve its anti-competitive aims, tying may produce anti-competitive effects even in the absence of substantial foreclosure of the tied product market.[428]

Of course, the likelihood of leveraging (offensive or defensive) should not automatically lead to a finding of an abuse of a dominant position. Tying may also have positive consequences. It may lower costs and increase economies of scale and scope in production and

421 ER Elhauge, 'Tying, Bundled Discounts, and the Death of the Single Monopoly Profit Theory' (2009) 123 *Harvard L Rev* 397.

422 R Cooper Feldman, 'Defensive Leveraging in Antitrust' (1999) 87 *Georgetown LJ* 2079.

423 N Economides, 'Tying, Bundling, and Loyalty/Requirement Rebates' in E Elhauge (ed) *Research Handbook on the Economics of Antitrust Law* (Edward Elgar, 2012), 121, 125–6.

424 Ibid, 126. 425 Ibid. 426 Ibid, 129. 427 Ibid.

428 ER Elhauge, 'Rehabilitating Jefferson Parish: Why Ties Without a Substantial Foreclosure Share Should Not Be Per Se Legal' (2016) 80 *Antitrust LJ* 463.

distribution. Indeed, two products may be cheaper to make or distribute together, or they may be more valuable to the buyer if the seller bundles them than if the buyer does not. Making separate offers may not also be justified in view of commercial usage: although some consumers would prefer buying separately their car and the tires it is delivered with, most prefer that such choice be made by the manufacturer. Tying may also ensure that consumers use compatible consumables for the primary product they purchased, thus ensuring the reputation of the manufacturer of the tying product, in particular if this is a technically complex product for which it is possible that the consumer will make a poor choice of complements, unless the choice is made upfront by the manufacturer. Although informing the buyer might be a less restrictive to competition option, this may not always be available and equally effective in guaranteeing quality. Tying reduces also search costs for the most appropriate combinations of the tying and tied products. It is also possible that the metering function of tying could be consumer welfare-enhancing if for instance a machine has maintenance or user costs which may vary with the intensity of its use, tying offering the opportunity to meter the machine's use so that each of the lessees pays the maintenance costs that result from his use.[429] Finally, it is possible that a firm monopolizing the markets for two complementary products may charge lower prices than would two separate monopolists in each market (double marginalization), a monopoly provider of two goods at different levels of supply maximizing its profits across the two goods, 'while separate providers will price each good at the individual profit-maximizing price.'[430]

9.8.2. CONTRACTUAL TYING

The CJEU dealt with contractual tying in two leading cases, *Hilti* and *Tetra Pak II*, which found tying when used by a dominant undertaking an abuse of a dominant position unless objectively justified. Both cases concerned tying of consumables tied to a primary product. Contractual tying may also be subject to Article 101 TFEU. According to Article 2(1), read in conjunction with Article 3, of Regulation 330/2010 on vertical agreements when the market share of the supplier on both the market of the tied product and the market of the tying product does not exceed 30 per cent. Above these market shares, an individual assessment should occur under Article 101(3) TFEU.[431]

9.8.2.1. *Hilti*

Hilti was the largest European producer of nail guns, nails, and cartridge strips. Eurofix and Bauco complained that Hilti was excluding them from the market in nails compatible with Hilti's products by refusing to sell Hilti-cartridges without Hilti-nails to distributors and by cutting off the supply of Hilti-cartridges to rival nail makers. The Commission found that nail-guns, cartridges, and nails each constituted a separate relevant product market and Hilti had power on the markets for Hilti-compatible cartridge strips and nail guns. The Commission found evidence that Hilti had tied cartridge strips and nails by carrying out a policy of

429 See N Economides, 'Tying, Bundling, and Loyalty/Requirement Rebates' in E Elhauge (ed), *Research Handbook on the Economics of Antitrust Law* (Edward Elgar, 2012), 121.

430 C Ahlborn, DS Evans, and AJ Padilla, 'The Antitrust Economics of Tying: A Farewell to Per Se Illegality' (2004) 49 *Antitrust Bulletin* 287.

431 See Chapter 10.

supplying cartridge strips to certain end users or distributors only when such cartridge strips were purchased with the necessary complement of nails. Hilti had also attempted to block the sale of competitors' nails by a policy of reducing discounts for orders of cartridges without nails, thus imposing a penalty when the customer was purchasing competitors' nails or more broadly by imposing discriminatory discounts. Hilti had also given instructions to its independent distributors not to fulfil certain export orders that would have enabled its competitors to obtain supplies of Hilti cartridges. Hilti had a policy of not supplying cartridges to independent producers of nails and was unwilling to provide any licence to any cartridge strip technology that would have enabled its competitors to arrange for their own independent supply of cartridges strips. It had also adopted a policy of refusing to honour the guarantees on its tools when non-Hilti nails were used. The Commission found that Hilti had abused of its dominant position through its attempts to prevent or limit the entry of independent producers of Hilti-compatible consumables into these markets, which 'went beyond the means legitimately available to a dominant company'.[432] The decision was upheld by the General Court[433] and the CJEU.[434]

9.8.2.2. *Tetra Pak II*

Before the accession of Sweden, the Commission fined Tetra Pak, a multinational firm, originally Swedish but with its head office in Switzerland, for abusing a dominant position in two product markets. It found that Tetra Pak had been charging very different prices in different Member States, discriminating ad hoc, tying the sale of cartons to the equipment for filling them, setting predatory prices and imposing on its customer contractual restrictions that the Commission said had no connection with the contract in those and linked product markets.

In the 1950s and 1960s, Tetra Pak developed a process and the machinery required for packaging milk, fruit juice, and other liquid or semi-liquid foodstuffs. The Commission accepted that this invention 'proved to be particularly well suited for aseptic packaging techniques'.[435] Originally, it was used only for pasteurized milk but, later, it was used more for aseptic packaging techniques for liquid foods expected to last for six months without refrigeration. The basic patents expired long ago, but Tetra Pak continued to develop improvements and habitually obtained patent protection for these.

There were substitutes in the non-aseptic markets that would enable pasteurized milk to be kept for a few days. That market was oligopolistic. Tetra Pak supplied about 50–55 per cent, Elopak 27 per cent, and PKL 11 per cent. The other suppliers were small.

Substitutes had not been fully developed in the aseptic market for packaging long-life milk and Tetra Pak supplied 90–95 per cent of this market. The rest was supplied by PKL.

The Commission decided that Tetra Pak was dominant over the markets for cartons and the equipment for filling them aseptically.[436] Although, in *AKZO*, the Court of Justice noted that a dominant position might be presumed with a market share of 50 per cent but that other factors were relevant, the Commission did not find that Tetra Pak was dominant over the oligopolistic non-aseptic market for cartons and equipment used for pasteurized liquids. Nevertheless,

432 *Eurofix-Bauco/Hilti* (Case COMP IV/30.787) Commission Decision [1988] OJ L 65/19.
433 Case T-30/89, *Hilti v Commission* [1991] ECR II–1439.
434 Case C-53/92 P, *Hilti AG v EC Commission* [1994] ECR I–667, para 74.
435 *Elopak Italia/Tetra Pak* (Case COMP IV-31.043) Commission Decision [1991] OJ L 72/1, para 14.
436 Ibid.

owing to the links between the aseptic and non-aseptic markets—dairies and fruit juice producers needed both—the Commission condemned conduct which it considered abusive not only on the aseptic, but also on the non-aseptic markets.

The General Court confirmed the decision as a whole,[437] and, on appeal, the CJEU confirmed the GC's judgment.[438]

The GC confirmed the separation of the aseptic market both from the non-aseptic and from other kinds of packaging. It observed that it would be difficult for the producers of non-aseptic cartons and machinery to switch to making aseptic cartons and equipment and that the aseptic sector was more attractive on the demand side. It was easier to distribute the liquids, since they lasted and did not have to be kept refrigerated.[439] Finally, until the end of the relevant period, aseptic packaging into plastic was not possible[440] and in the non-aseptic markets, consumers were used to cartons.[441] The Court added that cartons were separate from the machines for filling them.[442] Elopak had started to make cartons only for non-aseptic packaging. Although Tetra Pak had required some of its customers for machines to take only Tetra Pak cartons, the GC considered that commercial usage does not support the conclusion that the machinery for packaging a product is indivisible from the cartons. For a considerable period of time there have been independent manufacturers who specialize in the manufacture of non-aseptic cartons designed for use in machines manufactured by other concerns and who do not manufacture machinery themselves.[443] The GC also found that considerations of public health cannot be used to infer the existence of an integrated packaging systems market.[444] These findings were confirmed by the CJEU.[445]

With regard to the existence of an abuse of a dominant position, the Commission's decision condemned not only conduct in the aseptic markets, where Tetra Pak had been held to be dominant, but also conduct in the linked non-aseptic market, where it had not been held to be dominant. This was a considerable extension of the existing case law. In *Commercial Solvents*,[446] the Court upheld a decision condemning the use of a dominant position in an upstream market to monopolize one downstream and, in *Télémarketing*,[447] it condemned the use of a dominant position to monopolize an ancillary activity. In *Tetra Pak*, however, the Commission alleged only that the profits made in the aseptic market enabled Tetra Pak to practise predatory or discriminatory pricing for non-aseptic machines and cartons in the view of links which it found between the two sectors (cross-subsidizing between the different markets). In the earlier cases, the dominant position in a market had been used to monopolize the other. Tetra Pak argued that 'the Commission has not demonstrated that there is a causal link between the abuses allegedly committed in the non-aseptic sector and Tetra Pak's dominant position in the aseptic sector' and rejected the Commission's allegation that profits made in the aseptic sector enabled it to practice predatory or discriminatory pricing for non-aseptic machines and cartons. It also disputed the existence of any link between its dominant position in the aseptic sector and the allegedly unfair

437 Case T-83/91, *Tetra Pak International SA v Commission* [1994] ECR II–755 [hereinafter *Tetra Pak II*].
438 Case C-333/94 P, *Tetra Pak International SA v Commission* [1996] ECR I–5951.
439 Case T-83/91, *Tetra Pak II* [1994] ECR II–755, para 69.
440 Ibid, para 71
441 Ibid, para 72.
442 Ibid, para 82.
443 Ibid.
444 Ibid, paras 83–4.
445 Case C-333/94 P, *Tetra Pak International SA v Commission* [1996] ECR I–5951, para 19.
446 Joined Cases 6 & 7/73, *Istituto Chemioterapico Italiano SpA and Commercial Solvents Corporation v Commission* [1974] ECR 223.
447 Case 311/84, *Telemarketing* [1985] ECR 3261.

contractual terms which it is said to have imposed in the non-septic sector, alleging that these terms were justified by the need to ensure the proper functioning of the packaging systems and were incorporated in contracts for the supply of non-aseptic machines well before the aseptic equipment was perfected.[448]

After reciting Article 102, *Michelin I*, and *Hoffman-La Roche*, the General Court mentioned the special responsibility of the dominant undertakings and went on to consider other cases in which either the abuse had been in the monopolized market, or where a refusal to supply the monopolized product without the secondary product led to monopolizing the latter, in particular the 'associative links' alleged by the Commission.

Case T-83/91, *Tetra Pak II*
[1994] ECR II–755

> 120. In relation, next, to the alleged associative links between the relevant markets, it is common ground that they are due to the fact that the key products packaged in aseptic and non-aseptic cartons are the same and to the conduct of manufacturers and users. Both the aseptic and the non-aseptic machines and cartons at issue in this case are used for packaging the same liquid products intended for human consumption, principally dairy products and fruit juice. Moreover, a substantial proportion of Tetra Pak's customers operate both in the aseptic and the non-aseptic sectors. In its written observations submitted in reply to the statement of objections, confirmed in its written observations before the Court, the applicant thus stated that in 1987 approximately 35% of its customers had purchased both aseptic and non-aseptic systems. Furthermore, the Commission correctly noted that the conduct of the principal manufacturers of carton-packaging systems confirmed the link between the aseptic and the non-aseptic markets, since two of them, Tetra Pak and PKL, already operate on all four markets and the third, Elopak, which is well-established in the non-aseptic sector, has for some considerable time been trying to gain access to the aseptic markets. [. . .]
>
> 122. It follows from all the above considerations that, in the circumstances of this case, Tetra Pak's practices on the non-aseptic market are liable to be caught by Article 82 of the Treaty, without its being necessary to establish the existence of a dominant position on those markets taken in isolation, since the undertaking's leading position on the non-aseptic markets, combined with the close associative links between those markets and the aseptic markets, gave Tetra Pak freedom of conduct compared with the other economic operators on the non-aseptic markets, such as to impose on it a special responsibility under Article 82 to maintain genuine undistorted competition on those markets.

The CJEU confirmed the judgment of the General Court that conduct in the linked market might be condemned without finding a dominant position over the non-aseptic sector.[449] The CJEU noted that 'it is true that application of Article [102 TFEU] presupposes a link between the dominant position and the alleged abusive conduct, which is normally not present where conduct on a market distinct from the dominated market produces effects on that distinct market. In the case of distinct, but associated, markets, as in the present case, application of

448 Case T-83/91, *Tetra Pak II* [1994] ECR II–755, para 104.
449 Case C-333/94 P, *Tetra Pak International SA v Commission* [1996] ECR I–5951, paras 22–33.

Article [102 TFEU] to conduct found on the associated, non-dominated, market and having effects on that associated market can only be justified by special circumstances'.[450] Indeed, Tetra had 78 per cent of the overall market in packaging in both aseptic and non-aseptic cartons (leading position in the non-aseptic market) and a quasi-monopolistic position in the dominant aseptic cartons market. Tetra's customers in one sector are also potential customers in the other. Finally, Tetra and its most important competitor, PKL, were present on all four markets.

Tetra Pak argued that its practice of requiring buyers to use on its machines only Tetra Pak cartons bought from Tetra Pak should not be regarded as the tie of the cartons to the machines as 'packaging systems are complete and indivisible systems, comprising the machine, the packaging material, training and after-sale service'.[451] Elopak, the complainant, supplied complete packaging systems in the non-aseptic sector. In the US, where Tetra Pak did not impose a tie, all the buyers of its machines also bought their cartons from it. Tetra Pak also required dairies acquiring machines to accept certain maintenance services. These enabled Tetra Pak to enter the premises of the dairies and check that the contract was being performed. The General Court found that tying constituted an overall strategy aiming to make the customer totally dependent on Tetra Pak for the entire life of the machine once purchased or leased, thereby excluding in particular any possibility of competition at the level both of cartons and of associated products.[452] The General Court examined if the resulting system of tied sales was objectively justified in the light of commercial usage and the very 'nature' of the products in question within the meaning of Article 102(d) TFEU holding that

> [. . .] the tied sale of filling machines and cartons cannot be considered to be in accordance with commercial usage. Moreover, [. . .] [e]ven a usage which is acceptable in a normal situation, on a competitive market, cannot be accepted in the case of a market where competition is already restricted.[453]

The General Court also rejected the argument based on public health by referring to its judgment in *Hilti*, in which it held that it was 'clearly not the task of an undertaking in a dominant position to take steps on its own initiative to eliminate products which, rightly or wrongly, it regards as dangerous or at least as inferior in quality to its own products'.[454] The General Court also alleged that hygienic standards could be assured by disclosing the specifications for compatible products to those using Tetra Pak's machines and that 'even if using another brand of cartons on Tetra Pak machines involved a risk it was for the applicant to use the possibility afforded it by the relevant national legislation in the various Member States'.[455] It concluded that

> [i]n those circumstances, it is clear that the tied-sale clauses and the other clauses referred to in the Decision went beyond their ostensible purpose and were intended to strengthen Tetra Pak's dominant position by reinforcing its customers' economic dependence on it. Those clauses were therefore wholly unreasonable in the context of protecting public health, and also went beyond the recognized right of an undertaking in a dominant position to protect its commercial interests. [. . .] Whether considered in isolation or together they were unfair.[456]

450 Ibid, para 27.
451 Case T-83/91 *Tetra Pak II* [1994] ECR II–755, para 122.
452 Ibid, para 135.
453 Ibid, para 137.
454 Case T-30/89 *Hilti v Commission* [1991] ECR II–1439, para 118.
455 Case T-83/91 *Tetra Pak II* [1994] ECR II–755, para 139.
456 Ibid, para 140.

The findings were confirmed by the CJEU, which noted in particular that

> [f]or a considerable time there have been independent manufacturers who specialize in the manufacture of non-aseptic cartons designed for use in machines manufactured by other concerns and who do not manufacture machinery themselves. That assessment, itself based on commercial usage, rules out the existence of the natural link claimed by Tetra Pak stating that other manufacturers can produce cartons for use in Tetra Pak's machines [. . .] [a]ny independent producer is quite free, as far as Community competition law is concerned, to manufacture consumables intended for use in equipment manufactured by others, unless in doing so infringes a competitor's intellectual property right.
>
> [. . .] [E]ven where tied sales of two products are in accordance with commercial usage or there is a natural link between the two products in question, such sales may still constitute abuse within the meaning of Article [102] unless they are objectively justified.[457]

NOTES AND QUESTIONS ON TETRA PAK II

1. Tetra Pak had used a complex series of practices. This involved predatory pricing as the Commission had condemned Tetra Pak for selling Tetra Rex cartons in Italy for non-aseptic milk below cost, although the Commission had not alleged that Tetra Pak was dominant over these. Tetra Pak argued that the Commission had not established any exclusionary intent. At the hearing, Tetra Pak cited a recent judgment of the United States Supreme Court,[458] which held that sales at a loss are exclusionary only when the undertaking in question has a reasonable prospect of recouping its losses: the market in non-aseptic cartons was competitive. Moreover, the low prices for the cartons had not eliminated Elopak—it had doubled its market share during the period. The General Court referred to the Judgment in *AKZO*[459] and observed that sales from 1976–82 constantly at prices below variable direct cost sufficed to establish predatory intent.[460] Moreover, the prices were 20–50 per cent below the prices charged in other Member States. It referred to statements by the board of Tetra Pak's Italian subsidiary about the need to make financial sacrifices, but did not state with what the profits were being compared. The CJEU confirmed that the Commission was not required to establish that the dominant firm would be able to recoup the loss of profits made in Italy. Tetra Pak had also imposed predatory machine prices in the UK. Tetra Pak alleged that in the UK it could not cross-subsidize its sales of non-aseptic equipment from the profits on aseptic equipment, as only 10 per cent of the milk sold in the UK was UHT. In any case, cross-subsidization would not of itself have contravened Article 102 TFEU. The General Court rejected the argument and noted Tetra Pak's leading position in the non-aseptic sector in conjunction with the link between that sector and the aseptic sector, finding that sufficient for Article 102 TFEU to apply, without being necessary to prove that there was cross-financing between the two sectors.
2. The Commission had also found that Tetra Pak had charged discriminatory machine and carton prices in different Member States. Tetra Pak admitted that its prices for

457 Case C-333/94 P, *Tetra Pak International SA v Commission* [1996] ECR I-5951, paras 36–7.
458 *Brooke Group v Brown & Wilkinson Tobacco*, 409 US 209, 125 L Ed 2d 168, 113 S Ct 2578 (1993).
459 Case C-62/86, *AKZO Chemie BV v Commission* [1991] ECR I-3359.
460 Case T-83/91, *Tetra Pak II* [1994] ECR II-755, para 150.

cartons between 1981 and 1984 were low in Italy, but said that otherwise, taking the carton prices with those for equipment, there was no discernible pattern. The General Court examined the possible application of Article 102(c) on price discrimination.[461]

3. The Commission found abuses in both the aseptic and the non-aseptic market. Was it right to do this, when the dominant position had been established only on the aseptic market? Should the associative links have led to a finding that Tetra Pak was dominant in both markets rather than to extending the law under Article 102 TFEU to markets where the firm has not used its dominance to extend its market power in that or another market?
4. Each pair of products was complementary, but in *Hilti* the Court treated the nail gun as in a separate market from the cartridges used with it. Is the notion of 'associative links' consistent with the treatment of complementary products as being in separate market?
5. What is a tie? Would you say that the requirement to use only Tetra Pak cartons and other services with the machines amounted to a tie? What may be anti-competitive about a tie? Why might Tetra Pak have tied the sale of the cartons to its machines?
6. The Commission, the General Court, and the CJEU found that the safety argument raised by Tetra Pak was not justified. Must a firm not dominant over the non-aseptic market take the risk to its reputation and possibly incur liability for defective products? What measures could it have taken to reduce the risk?
7. Tetra Pak's machines were to some extent protected by improvement patents. Would it have been anti-competitive for Tetra Pak to have charged not only for the purchase or hire of the machines, but also a royalty for their use so as to charge more to those who used the machines intensively and were likely to have valued them more? Might Tetra Pak have had difficulty in monitoring the use to ensure that royalties were correctly paid? How would such a system of charging have differed from a tie?
8. Of particular interest is the comparison of the EU rule on contractual tying with US antitrust law. Although judicial decisions were often developed without much concern for analysing anti-competitive effects, the more recent case law in the United States requires the examination of the anti-competitive effects of the practice before concluding whether there is illegal tying. In *Jefferson Parish*, the Supreme Court adopted a modified *per se* test for contractual tying.[462] There was a presumption of anti-competitive effects whenever a firm with market power employed bundling practices that had the effect of foreclosing rivals from significant market shares in the tied product market,[463] of extracting consumer surplus,[464] or of raising barriers to entry in both the tying and the tied markets.[465] However, in *United States v Microsoft*, the DC Circuit moved to a rule of reason test for software bundles (technological tying) that require plaintiffs to demonstrate that the benefits of the tying practice are outweighed by the harms in the tied product market.[466] In comparison to this case law, the CJEU

461 See Section 9.7.

462 *Jefferson Parish Hosp Dist No 2 v Hyde*, 466 US 2, 12–18 (1984) [hereinafter *Jefferson Parish*].

463 *Fortner Enters v US Steel Corp*, 394 US 495 (1969).

464 *Jefferson Parish*, 466 US 2, 14–15 (1984) (market power in the tying market is employed to 'impair competition on the merits in another market', thus 'increasing monopoly profits over what they would be absent the tie').

465 *Eastman Kodak Co v Image Technical Servs, Inc*, 504 US 451 (1992).

466 *United States v Microsoft Corp*, 253 F 3d 34, 95–7 (DC Cir 2001). Pro-competitive justifications for tying were also considered in *Illinois Tool Works*, 547 US 28, 36 (2006).

position in *Hilti* and *Tetra Pak II* seems to adopt a quasi-*per se* illegality approach for contractual tying employed by dominant undertakings. According to this case law, if the two products are found to be distinct, that is, in most cases, if there are independent producers in the tied product market, it is required that dominant undertakings abstain from any conduct, such as contractual tying, that would have the effect of restricting the freedom of these independent producers to compete in the tied market. The EU court has not examined the actual or likely anti-competitive effects of tying but simply presumed the abuse from dominance, tying, and the absence of any objective justifications. Dominant undertakings may argue the existence of an objective justification for their conduct. Early case law has, however, restrictively interpreted this concept as not including any efficiency defence, but only broad non-economic public policy concerns, such as safety or health factors related to the dangerous nature of the product in question. However, the EU *Microsoft I* case offered the opportunity to the Commission and the General Court to clarify the role of objective justifications in the tying test. We examine this case law briefly in Section 9.8.3.

9.8.3. TECHNICAL TYING: *MICROSOFT I* AND *MICROSOFT II*

In 2004, the European Commission adopted a decision declaring that Microsoft had violated Article 102 TFEU by committing two abuses of its dominant position on the market for PC operating systems (EU *Microsoft I*).[467] Microsoft was held to have abused its dominant position by refusing to supply competitors with certain interoperability information and to allow them to use it for the purpose of developing and distributing competing products on the market for work group server operating systems. It also found that Microsoft had infringed Article 102 TFEU by making supply of its client PC operating system Windows conditional on the simultaneous acquisition of its Windows Media Player (WMP). The European Court of First Instance (GC), now the general Court of the EU, affirmed the decision of the Commission in 2007.[468]

When examining the tying of the operating system Windows with WMP by Microsoft, the European Commission opted for a different approach than the quasi-*per se* illegality rule of the 'classical' contractual tying case law noting that:

> There are indeed circumstances relating to the tying of WMP which warrant closer examination of the effects that tying has on competition in this case. While in classical tying cases, the Commission and the Courts considered the foreclosure effect for competing vendors to be demonstrated by the bundling of a separate product with the dominant product, in the case at issue, users can and do to a certain extent obtain third party media players through the internet, sometimes for free. There are therefore indeed good reasons not to assume without further analysis that tying WMP constitutes conduct which by its very nature is liable to foreclose competition.[469]

467 *Microsoft/W2000* (Case COMP/C-3/37.792) Commission Decision C(2004)900 final (24 March 2004).
468 Case T-201/04, *Microsoft Corp v Commission* [2007] ECR II-3601. The EU *Microsoft I* case will be further examined in the companion volume I Lianos, *Competition Law and the Intangible Economy* (OUP, forthcoming 2019).
469 *Microsoft/W2000* (Case COMP/C-3/37.792) C(2004)900 final (24 March 2004), para 841.

The tying part of the investigation was largely driven by RealNetworks, another US company and the instigator of a similar investigation in Korea, which criticized the integration of Windows and WMP. The Commission found that Microsoft had made the availability of Windows client PC operating systems conditional on the simultaneous acquisition of WMP and that, therefore, since 1999 Microsoft had tied the Windows streaming Media Player to Windows contrary to Article 102(d) TFEU.

First, Microsoft had a dominant position on the client PC operating systems market. Second, streaming media players and client PC operating systems constituted separate products. The Commission defined the relevant market to include only streaming (downloads content as it plays it) MPs, to the exclusion of software for downloading music as well as classical playback devices such as CDs and DVDs.[470] Third, Microsoft did not give consumers the opportunity to buy Windows without WMP. Finally, the tie restricted competition on the media players market. The Commission found four elements to a tying claim: (i) the tying and the tied products are two separate products; (ii) the undertaking concerned is dominant in the market for the tying product; (iii) the undertaking concerned does not give customers a choice to obtain the tying product without the tied product; and (iv) the practice in question forecloses competition.[471] The Commission also examined the objective justifications of the conduct that were advanced by Microsoft and referred to this condition as the fifth step of the analysis.[472] The Commission thus applied a structured rule of reason approach by examining the anti-competitive effects of the practice, including the efficiency justifications argued by Microsoft and Microsoft's incentives to foreclose, before concluding that Microsoft's conduct infringed Article 102 TFEU.

With reference to the first element, the Commission found that the WMP and operating systems were separate products, although the WMP was integrated into the software for PCs.[473] The test adopted by the CJEU in *Hilti*[474] and *Tetra Pak II*[475] was not technical integration but a contractual restraint. It sufficed that independent companies provided the tied product separately from the tying product, which indicated separate demand. The second element of tying is that the undertaking concerned is dominant in the tying product market. Microsoft no longer denied that it was dominant over the tying product. Regarding the third element, Microsoft gave customers no choice to obtain Windows without the WMP,[476] although no charge was made for it. Under Microsoft's standard licence to manufacturers of computers, they were required to pre-install the WMP when licensing Windows for PCs. They were free to install other media players only in addition. Their customers were in turn unable to decide whether to have the WMP. The fourth element of tying is foreclosure.[477] The Commission considered the judgments on loyalty-inducing rebates (which we examined in Section 9.6) and, while noting that the GC in *BA* and *Michelin II* had stated that conduct that tends to foreclose is abusive whether or not it has such an effect,[478] went on, in some detail, to analyse the foreclosure in this case. With a 93.8 per cent share of the operating system market for PCs, the WMP was ubiquitous. In 2002, 121 million client PC operating systems were shipped and the player came pre-installed on 114 million.[479] The Commission analysed the possibility of selling media players through the Internet and other channels, and found that they were far less satisfactory than pre-installation. Just as most software applications

470 Ibid, paras 407–25. 471 Ibid, para 794. 472 Ibid, para 794

473 Ibid, paras 800–25. 474 Case C-53/92 P, *Hilti AG v Commission* [1994] ECR I–667.

475 Case C-333/94 P, *Tetra Pak International SA v Commission* [1996] ECR I–5951.

476 *Microsoft/W2000* (Case COMP/C-3/37.792) C(2004)900 final (24 March 2004), paras 826–34.

477 Ibid, paras 835–954. 478 Ibid, para 838. 479 Ibid, paras 843–8.

are designed by third parties to work on the most popular operating system, the content providers tend to target the most popular media player as their platform.[480] Microsoft's share of the player market increased hugely after it started to tie its player to its operating system. The Commission did not accept that this was the result of competition on the merits. It compared various commercial reviews, which often concluded that other media players were better. The Commission concluded[481] that Microsoft had used the Windows operating system for PCs to distribute the MWP leaving its competitors at a disadvantage. Tying raises the content and applications barriers to entry that protect Windows and will facilitate the erection of such a barrier for WMP. A position of strength in a market with network effects is sustainable. This shields Microsoft from effective competition from potentially more efficient vendors of media players. It reduces the talent and capital invested in media players, including its own. Moreover, tying enables Microsoft anti-competitively to expand its position in adjacent media-related software markets. It sends messages that deter innovation in any technologies in which Microsoft could conceivably take an interest and tie with Windows PCs in the future.

The Commission found that through tying WMP with Windows, Windows was used by Microsoft as 'a distribution channel to anti-competitively ensure for itself a significant competition advantage in the media player market', putting Microsoft's competitors *a priori* at a disadvantage irrespective of whether their competing products to WMP 'were potentially more attractive on the merits'.[482] In particular, Microsoft interfered with the 'normal competitive process', 'which would benefit users in terms of quicker cycles of innovation due to unfettered competition on the merits' by raising, through the tying, content and applications barrier to entry which protects Windows, or facilitating the erection of such a barrier for WMP, in a market with important network effects, which generally work in favour of a company which has gained a decisive momentum and amount to entry barriers for potential competitors.[483] According to the Commission, tying WMP with Windows would bring the following effects:

> This shields Microsoft from effective competition from potentially more efficient media player vendors which could challenge its position. Microsoft thus reduces the talent and capital invested in innovation of media players, not least its own and anti-competitively raises barriers to market entry. Microsoft's conduct affects a market which could be a hotbed for new and exciting products springing forth in a climate of undistorted competition.
>
> Moreover, tying of WMP allows Microsoft to anti-competitively expand its position in adjacent media-related software markets and weaken effective competition to the eventual detriment of consumers
>
> Microsoft's tying of WMP also sends signals which deter innovation in any technologies which Microsoft could conceivably take interest in and tie with Windows in the future [. . .]
>
> There is therefore a reasonable likelihood that tying WMP with Windows will lead to a lessening of competition so that the maintenance of an effective competition structure will not be ensured in the foreseeable future [. . .].[484]

Microsoft was not allowed to offer any technological, commercial, or contractual term or inducement to make the bundled version the more attractive, and a monitoring trustee

480 Ibid, paras 879–96. 481 Ibid, para 978. 482 Ibid, para 979.
483 Ibid, para 980. 484 Ibid, paras 981–4.

was required to ensure that the unbundled version of Windows works as well as the bundled version.[485]

In essence, the Commission Decision took the view that Microsoft had violated Article 102 TFEU, in particular because of the possible leveraging of its quasi-monopolistic position in the PC operating systems market to the media player market.

The Commission's Decision imposed one of the largest at the time fine for a single undertaking in EU competition law history, €497 million, as well as a series of behavioural remedies, including the distribution of an unbundled version of Windows, without WMP.[486]

The General Court confirmed the legality of the substantive parts of the Commission's decision in *Microsoft*, accepting the approach followed by the Commission. However, it used language that limits the scope of the structured rule of reason approach in situations of technological tying. The GC mentioned that

> while it is true that neither [the] provision nor, more generally, Article [102 TFEU] as a whole contains any reference to the anti-competitive effect of bundling, the fact remains that, in principle, conduct will be regarded as abusive only if it is capable of restricting competition.[487]

The GC referred to *Michelin II* to substantiate this point, a case standing for the proposition that 'establishing the anticompetitive object and the anti-competitive effect are one and the same thing'.[488] The GC also noted the following:

> [T]he applicant cannot claim that the Commission relied on a new and highly speculative theory to reach the conclusion that a foreclosure effect exists in the present case. As indicated at [. . .] the contested decision, the Commission considered that, in light of the specific circumstances of the present case, it could not merely assume, *as it normally does in cases of abusive tying*, that the tying of a specific product and a dominant product has by its nature a foreclosure effect. The Commission therefore examined more closely the actual effects which the bundling had already had on the streaming media player market and also the way in which that market was likely to evolve.[489]

It follows that although the GC did not reject the structured rule of reason approach of the Commission with regard to technical tying, it maintained its previous quasi *per se* illegality approach for all other forms of bundling (essentially contractual tying). In the French version of the same paragraph, the GC even uses the expression '*effet d'exclusion sur le marché per se*' (bundling of two products by a dominant undertaking leads to an exclusionary effect *per se*) when it refers to the 'normal' approach for abusive tying cases. In sum, in examining the existence of the fourth step of a tying claim, the GC did not presume that there was foreclosure of competition from the simple fact that a dominant undertaking tied two distinct products in the absence of objective justifications, as in the contractual tying cases. Instead, it found that one had to determine if the foreclosure of competitors led to anti-competitive effects and if

485 Ibid, paras 1011–12.

486 On the remedies, see N Economides and I Lianos, 'A Critical Appraisal of Remedies in the E.U. Microsoft Cases' (2010) 2 *Columbia Business L Rev* 346.

487 Case T-201/04, *Microsoft Corp v Commission* [2007] ECR II–3601, para 867.

488 Case T-203/01, *Michelin II* [2003] ECR II–4071, paras 239 and 241.

489 Case T-201/04, *Microsoft Corp v Commission* [2007] ECR II–3601, para 868 (emphasis added).

there were objective justifications (efficiencies). This in turn implicitly injects a structured rule of reason approach into the analysis of technological tying.[490]

The Commission's Guidance on Article 102 seems nevertheless to consider that technical tying should be subject to a stricter competition law regime than contractual tying, by providing the following explanation:

> The risk of anti-competitive foreclosure is expected to be greater where the dominant undertaking makes its tying or bundling strategy a lasting one, for example through technical tying which is costly to reverse. Technical tying also reduces the opportunities for resale of individual components.[491]

A few years later, the Commission also opened investigations, following complaints in December 2007 by Opera, the Norwegian Internet browser maker, against Microsoft, sending a Statement of Objection in January 2009, alleging a violation by Microsoft of Article 102 TFEU for tying its web browser, 'Internet Explorer' (IE), to its dominant client PC operating system, 'Windows' (*Microsoft II*). To terminate the Commission's investigation in the Internet Explorer case, Microsoft initially announced that it would not distribute the standard Windows 7 in Europe. Instead, it intended to produce and distribute in Europe a special edition of Windows 7 called Windows 7-E which would not have Internet Explorer or any other browser pre-installed. Microsoft thus adopted the removal approach of the Windows-N remedy imposed by the Commission in the WMP case as the sole version of Windows in Europe. Computer manufacturers (OEMs) would have the option to install an Internet browser of their choice as the default as well as include other browsers before the PC reaches the final consumers. As part of the initial proposal of Microsoft, European consumers who would buy an upgrade to Windows 7 for Windows Vista or XP, as well as those consumers who would buy Windows 7 and install it themselves from scratch on a 'naked' computer (that comes from the manufacturer without an operating system) would be given a version of Windows 7-E that would include a file transfer protocol (FTP) link to a web site from which they could download and install IE.

Despite the similarities with the unbundling remedy adopted in *Microsoft I*, the Commission was nevertheless not convinced. Based on the Commission's public feedback as well as on private discussions, Microsoft withdrew its unilateral plan of distributing Windows 7-E and proposed a final resolution that would commit it to (i) distribute a 'ballot screen' or 'choice screen' through software update to EEA users of Windows XP, Windows Vista, Windows 7, and Windows Client PC Operating Systems, by means of Windows Update; and (ii) allow both computer manufacturers and users to turn on or off IE.193 Thus, the remedy does not only concern Windows 7. This remedy (the ballot or choice screen) aimed to give those users who have set Internet Explorer as their default web browser an opportunity to choose whether and which competing web browser(s) to install in addition to the one(s) they already have. The design of the choice screen attempted to represent as best as possible actual consumer preferences. At the same time, it did not provide an excessively large choice that would have occupied a lot of disk space. The Commission accepted Microsoft's commitments to make available the choice screen for five years (until 2014) with an Article 9 of Regulation 1/2003 decision in 2009.[492]

490 N Economides and I Lianos, 'The Elusive Antitrust Standard on Bundling in Europe and in the United States in the Aftermath of the Microsoft Cases' (2009) 76 *Antitrust LJ* 483.

491 Commission Guidance on Article 102, para 53.

492 *Microsoft (tying)* (Case COMP/C-3/39.530) Commission Decision (16 December 2009), para 60, available at http://ec.europa.eu/competition/antitrust/cases/dec_docs/39530/39530_2671_3.pdf.

In contrast, 'technological' tying is subject to the rule of reason in US law, whereas contractual tying falls under the quasi-*per se* rule of *Jefferson Parish*. The position of the European Commission cannot be explained by the case law of the GC, which does not establish such a distinction between contractual and technical tying. It is not also compatible with consumer welfare, as in most cases technical tying bundles products in fixed proportions and is thus more likely to be motivated by efficiency gains rather than by an anti-competitive aim.

The *Microsoft* cases put network economics to prominence in competition law, with an important part of the debate in this case revolving around network effects. A market exhibiting network externalities is one where the value of being in the network is increased as others join it. Microsoft licenses more than 90 per cent of the operating systems for personal computers (PCs). Consequently, there is a big incentive for consumers to use the Microsoft operating system, so that they can benefit from complementary activities of other users of the OS. Moreover, firms writing application programs, such as media players, to be used with an operating system will target the most popular system so as to increase their potential client base. It is costly in time and money to design an application to be compatible with additional operating systems. Consequently, more applications are written to be compatible with Microsoft Windows and, in turn, this increases the inducement for consumers to use Windows.

Once an undertaking has achieved a very large share of a 'network market,' it becomes very difficult for competitors to challenge it, even if their technology is superior, as fewer applications are designed to be used with the new operating system and there are fewer users to benefit from. The market 'tips' in favour of the incumbent. If only part of an industry is a natural monopoly, it may be possible to keep the rest of the market competitive. A competition authority has a strong incentive to act to prevent the monopolist of one part of the system extending its market power to other parts before those markets tip, too. If all the adjacent markets are supplied mainly by the same firm, it will be very difficult for a newcomer to challenge the original monopoly.

A possible way out of the dilemma is the creation of middleware: a platform or software interface designed to be compatible with several operating systems, which can support many applications software. In that way, the applications compatible with the middleware can be 'ported' or used with any operating system. Besides being an operating system, Windows was a middleware platform; but there were also other platforms that relied on different operating systems, such as Linux, Mac OS, and web servers/browsers which could be used to write software applications while bypassing Windows. The core of the allegations against Microsoft was that the Redmond-based company sought through exclusionary practices and predatory pricing to create a high barrier to entry in the platform market as it perceived a threat to its Windows monopoly from other middleware/platforms, in particular web server/web browser platforms. In the US *Microsoft* case, US Department of Justice alleged that Microsoft had made it difficult for Netscape and Java, which might have become middleware and challenge Windows, to expand sufficiently. Different views were expressed by economic experts on the possible effects of these practices on consumers and innovation.[493]

493 For an interesting early analysis of the different economic views put forward by the experts hired by the parties in the US litigation, see D Evans, FM Fisher, DL Rubinfeld, and RL Schmalensee, *Did Microsoft Harm Consumers? Two Opposing Views* (AEI-Brookings Joint Center for Regulatory Studies, 2000). See also R Gilbert and M Katz, 'An Economist's Guide to U.S. v. Microsoft' (2001) 15(2) *J Economic Perspectives* 25.

An important dimension of competition in these cases was to preserve the interoperability between the various applications/middleware running on various platforms. This was not an issue at the early 1980s in view of the fact that the computer industry was vertical integrated and there was competition between various vertically integrated platforms (eg IBM, Digital, Unisys, ICL). Things, however, changed with the emergence of the personal computer (PC), the rising importance of the operating system and software vis-à-vis hardware, as the main source of value added and revenues in this sector, vertical disintegration and the emergence of a more heterogeneous environment for the computer industry in early to mid-2000s, with different companies being present in various segments of the computer industry value chain.[494] Microsoft was prominent in the application system's segment, while also expanding its presence in applications, tools and networking, and became the lead firm of the personal computer industry value chain, replacing IBM, the former vertically integrated hardware manufacturer, which dominated the computer industry value chain in the 1970s and early 1980s, but which had, quite unexpectedly, decided in early 1980s to buy out the microprocessor and the operating system software from outside vendors, thus leading to vertical disintegration and the emergence of competition in the software and, to a lesser extent, the microprocessors' markets, to the exception of the operating system segment, which was controlled by Microsoft. Original Equipment Manufacturers, such as Apple, Hewlett-Packard (HP), Dell, and Compaq competed in the PC markets, part of which was controlled by no-name brands produced by firms ranging from very small local shops to the large distributors. Microprocessor firms, such as Intel, AMD, Sun, and Texas Instruments were competing in the processors' segment of the value chain.

The important commercial success of Microsoft spearheaded by the development of the Windows operating system gave the company a gatekeeping role in the software market and transformed it to the personal computer industry uncontested leader, being the only firm with the capacity to integrate or control the entire value chain. Microsoft encouraged competition at the other segments of the value chain, ensuring that no other rival lead firm could develop with the capacity to control the PC value chain, thus indicating the 'vertical competition' for rents that exists between firms present at different parts of the value chain to increase their share of the total surplus value of the chain.[495] We believe that this value chain approach may provide a better understanding of the exclusionary practices adopted by Microsoft, which were ultimately punished by the European Commission.

9.8.4. *GOOGLE (ANDROID)*

The Commission also opened a separate antitrust investigation into Google's conduct as regards the mobile operating system Android exploring whether Google has entered into anti-competitive agreements or abused a possible dominant position in the field of operating

[494] M Kenney and J Curry, 'The Internet and the Personal Computer Value Chain' in BRIE-IGCC E-conomy Project (ed) *Tracking a Transformation* (Brookings Institution Press, 2001), 151.

[495] Ibid, 153. See also TF Bresnahan, 'New Modes of Competition: Implications for the Future Structure of the Computer Industry' in JA Eisenach and TM Lenard (eds) *Competition, Innovation and the Microsoft Monopoly: Antitrust in the Digital marketplace* (Springer, 1999), 155; T Bresnahan and S Greenstein, 'Technological Competition and the Structure of the Computer Industry' (27 May 1997), 22, available at www-siepr.stanford.edu/workp/swp97028.pdf, explaining that there is vertical competition at every link of the chain for control of a platform 'among the sellers of its various components', which arises 'only in situations of divided technical leadership'.

systems, applications and services for smart mobile devices.[496,497] These restrictions are included in the Google Mobile Services (GMS) agreements between Google and OEMs (smartphone manufacturers). GMS is a bundle of applications, including the Google Play store, a digital distribution platform operated by Google (originally called the Android Market), which allows users to browse and download applications developed with the Android Software development kit, Google Search (the search engine of Google) and Google Chrome (the browser developed by Google), among other software. Each service in GMS is complementary to the Android Operating System, which is the dominant operating system in Europe for mobiles and tablets. Note that there are a number of competing third party apps for each app in GMS. The alleged abuse relates to the conditions in the GMS agreements. Indeed, if an OEM installs GMS, Google's contract obliges the OEM to pre-install all the apps in the GMS bundle, which includes Google Play (the tying product on which Google has a dominant position), tied to other apps in GMS including Google Search, and Chrome, to pre-install Google Search as the default for Internet search, pre-install Google's browser Chrome and the obligation to not pre-install apps that compete with GMS apps (such as third-party 'store' and third party 'search') on any other of the specific OEM's devices running other versions of Android (Android forks) (the so-called anti-fragmentation clause). The result of these contractual conditions is that an OEM cannot produce some devices with GMS on the 'standardized Google version of Android' and some without it on another version of Android (Android fork).

The Commission opened proceedings concerning Google's conduct as regards the Android operating system and applications in 2015 alleging that Google has imposed conditions on those manufacturers and mobile network operators accepting its GMS Agreements, that is the non-open source part its' Android Platform.

Although there are a number of competing third party apps for each app in GMS, which the OEMs (and ultimate consumers) may install in the devices, there is no other digital distribution platform than the Google Play store that may be installed in Android GMS devices.

The Commission found dominance in three markets: (i) national markets for general search services (not just mobile)—just as in the *Google Shopping* case; (ii) the worldwide market (excluding China) for the licensing of smart mobile Operating Systems (OS); (iii) the worldwide market (excluding China) for Android app stores. The Commission found that Google was dominant in all these three markets.

The Commission took issue with three types of conduct by Google. First, Google's mobile application distribution agreements (MADA), Google's licensing contract, raised competition concerns in view of the fact that it oblige the OEM deciding to install GMS to pre-install all the apps in the GMS bundle. Therefore, Google Play (the tying product) is contractually tied to other apps in GMS, such as Google Search and Chrome (tied products), which are pre-installed as defaults. Note that MADA requires non-exclusive pre-installation, meaning that OEMs may also install rival apps, although it is not clear if they can install them as a default. Users can also disable Google apps.

However, the foreclosure effects are reinforced by the second conduct found to constitute an abuse, Google's anti-fragmentation agreements (AFA) which prohibit manufacturers from selling smart mobile devices with non-compatible Android forks. Google licensed Play Store

[496] This Section draws substantially on N Economides and I Lianos, 'Google Dominance and Tying for Android', CLES Research Paper No 9/2018 forthcoming.

[497] Commission, 'Antitrust: Commission Sends Statement of Objections to Google on Android Operating System and Applications', Press Release No IP/16/1492 (20 April 2016), available at http://europa.eu/rapid/press-release_IP-16-1492_en.htm.

and other apps only if OEMs entered into an AFA, which prevented OEM distributing devices based on an incompatible Android fork, a form of tying. OEMs were obliged not to 'fork' Android and thus not to distribute even one device based on a 'fork' to the extent that the AFAs applied to the entire portfolio of an OEM, ie not only to devices which pre-install Google proprietary apps.

The third conduct relates to the revenue share agreements (RSAs). The Commission alleged that Google has provided for the period 2011–14 significant financial incentives to some of the largest smartphone and tablet manufacturers as well as mobile network operators on condition that they exclusively pre-install Google Search on their devices. These conditional payments constituted according to the Commission an infringement of competition.

By a decision adopted on 18 July 2018, the Commission found that Google infringed Article 102 TFEU by imposing 'illegal restrictions on Android device manufacturers and mobile network operators to cement its dominant position in general internet search', fining Google €4.34 billion and requiring Google to bring the illegal conduct to an end and to refrain from any measure that has the same or an equivalent object or effect.[498] Although, at the time of writing, the text of the decision has not yet been published, the Commission's press release provides a good summary of the main issues. The Commission found anticompetitive conduct the fact that:

- Google has required manufacturers to pre-install the Google Search app and browser app (Chrome), as a condition for licensing Google's app store (the Play Store).

According to the Commission's press release, 'the Play Store is a "must-have" app, as users expect to find it pre-installed on their devices', in particular 'because they cannot lawfully download it themselves'.[499] By tying the Play Store with the Google Search app, Google is able to establish a bottleneck as Google Search is an important entry point for search queries on mobile devices. The Commission has found this practice illegal since 2011, which is the date Google became dominant in the market for app stores for the Android mobile operating system. By tying the Google Chrome browser with the Play Store, Google's strategy was to ensure that the mobile browser is pre-installed on practically all Android devices sold in the EEA. This also adds another bottleneck, as browsers represent an important entry point for search queries on mobile devices and Google Search is the default search engine on Google Chrome. According to the Commission, this pre-installation of these two apps may create a '*status quo* bias',[500] first of OEMs, which have limited interest in duplicating apps, because of transaction costs, the need to preserve user experience, and that it might be difficult for Google's competitors to arrange for a similar pre-installation, and second of the users, as users are likely to stick to these apps. There was also evidence that users do not download competing apps in order to offset the competitive advantage, in terms of distribution, from which benefits Google. There is indeed evidence that users of Android devices make most of their search queries through Google search, while most users of Windows mobile devices prefer Microsoft's Bing search engine, which is also pre-installed to their device. According to the Commission, this pre-installation reduced the ability of rivals to compete effectively with Google. Indeed, pre-installation provides a considerable competitive advantage as this is demonstrated by Google's Search high market share when there is pre-installation (95 per

498 European Commission, 'Antitrust: Commission fines Google €4.34 billion for illegal practices regarding Android mobile devices to strengthen dominance of Google's search engine', Press Release No IP/18/4851 (18 July 2018), available at http://europa.eu/rapid/press-release_IP-18-4581_en.htm.

499 Ibid. 500 Ibid.

cent) and the relatively lower market share when there is no pre-installation (25 per cent in Microsoft devices). The Commission also found that tying was not necessary for the survival of the business model of Google, as the Google Play Store earns Google billions of dollars in annual revenues, and thanks to the app, Google harvests a lot of data that is valuable to Google's search and advertising business from Android devices, and may boost its revenue from search advertising. Google's Search market share is also higher on mobile than desktop, where no such tying and pre-installation arrangements are imposed.

- Google made payments to certain large manufacturers and mobile network operators on condition that they exclusively pre-installed the Google Search app on their devices.

These payments were made on condition of exclusivity of pre-installation of Google Search across their entire portfolio of Android devices. Indeed, OEMs and mobile network operators (MNOs) were offered portfolio-based revenue shares on condition that they do not pre-install competing search services on Android devices. The portfolio effect also led to the possibility that, if a customer wanted to launch just one device with a rival pre-installed, Google Search would lose the revenue share across all devices. The Commission based its analysis of the potential harm to competition on a quantitative analysis, finding that in view of the market share of Google devices, an equally efficient rival search engine would have been unable to compensate a device manufacturer or mobile network operator for the loss of the revenue share payments from Google across all of its devices and still make profits. The Commission analysed these payments drawing on the principles of the *Intel* judgment of the CJEU on loyalty rebates.[501] The Commission relied on the as-efficient competitor test as well as contemporaneous evidence that the OEMs/MNOs would have wished to pre-install competing search services, but were deterred by the RSAs (in combination with MADA). The Commission rejected Google's argument that such incentives were necessary to convince device manufacturers and mobile network operators to produce devices for the Android ecosystem.

- Finally, Google has prevented manufacturers wishing to pre-install Google apps from selling even a single smart mobile device running on alternative versions of Android that were not approved by Google (the so-called 'Android forks').

This conduct exercised impact on the competitive opportunities for devices running on Android forks to be developed and sold, in particular the devices based on Amazon's Android fork called 'Fire OS'. This tying directly foreclosed rival open source operating systems, in particular as Google is dominant in the market for Android app stores and in the markets for general search services and both Play Store and the Google Search app cannot be obtained without entering into AFAs. This also impeded competitors from benefiting from an important channel to introduce apps and services, in particular general search services, which could be pre-installed on Android fork, thus reducing innovation and consumer choice. The Commission also rejected Google's justifications that these restrictions were necessary for preventing a fragmentation of the Android ecosystem, to the extent that no technical incompatibilities between Android forks and Google apps. The Commission found that these three practices formed 'part of an overall strategy by Google to cement its dominance in general internet search, at a time when the importance of mobile internet was growing

[501] Case C-413/14 P, *Intel Corp v European Commission*, ECLI:EU:C:2017:632. See our analysis in Section 9.6.4.3.

significantly', denying rival search engines the possibility to compete on the merits and restricting the development of Android forks as competing platforms for rival search engines and other apps. For the Commission, 'Google's practices also harmed competition and further innovation in the wider mobile space, beyond just internet search' by preventing other mobile browsers to compete with Google Chrome and the development of Android forks.[502]

The case may be compared, to a certain extent, to *Microsoft*. Here, the dominant company (Google) imposes acceptance of Google Search and making it a default by tying it with Google Play. This is very similar to Microsoft tying Windows Media Player with Windows and making WMP the default. In an alternative theory of harm, here the dominant company (Google) enhances and preserves its monopoly in search through tying search with the very desirable Google Play. Google is more forceful in the way it imposes the unlawful tying compared to Microsoft tying Internet Explorer with the Windows OS. Google gives OEMs an 'all or nothing' choice, knowing full well that 'nothing' is not a commercially viable option given the dominant position of Google's apps and related online services in certain markets (eg Google Search, Google Play, or YouTube). Thus, if an OEM wishes to pre-install even a single Google app which users consider 'must-have', it must pre-install the entire suite of Google apps including those for which there are potentially better alternatives from rival providers. For example, for the user to receive updates to the operating system on his device, the device should be equipped with Google Play, which therefore would mean that the entire suite of Google apps should be pre-installed. Even if OEMs had the chance to preload additional apps of their choice, Google imposes placement requirements on them, which place Google's apps in prominent positions on the devices making other apps less discoverable by the user.

Users may download and install apps of their choice on their Android phones, but limited memory space makes it harder for them to download multiple applications. Therefore, even if OEMs have the right to pre-install additional apps, they are less likely to do so, especially because it's much harder to erase Google's pre-installed apps and change the default settings. Moreover, in view of Google's placement requirements imposed on OEMs in relation to its own apps, which are placed prominently on the phone's home screen or one screen away, it becomes more difficult for users to access the apps of their choice, which when downloaded are only accessible by scrolling multiple screens.

9.8.5. MIXED BUNDLING, FINANCIAL TYING, AND BUNDLED REBATES

The first issue, with regard to bundled rebates or mixed bundling, is to classify them as a form of either rebate or tying, in view of applying the different criteria to each category of abuse. The case law of the EU Courts is not clear as to the proper characterization of bundled rebates. In *Hilti*, the Commission considered that reducing discounts for orders of cartridges without nails, thus imposing a penalty when the customer was purchasing competitors' nails, amounted to illegal tying, a decision upheld on appeal.[503] The CJEU examined Hoffman-La Roche's rebates offered to customers which acquired the whole range of its vitamins or groups

502 European Commission, 'Antitrust: Commission fines Google €4.34 billion for illegal practices regarding Android mobile devices to strengthen dominance of Google's search engine', Press Release No IP/18/4851 (18 July 2018), available at http://europa.eu/rapid/press-release_IP-18-4581_en.htm.

503 *Eurofix-Bauco/Hilti* (Case COMP IV/30.787) Commission Decision [1988] OJ L 65/19, para 75.

of vitamins, finding that 'having regard to the fact [. . .] that the various groups of vitamins are products which are not interchangeable and represent separate markets, this system of rebates on overall purchases is furthermore an abuse within the meaning of subparagraph (d) of the second paragraph of Article [102 TFEU] in that it aims at making the conclusion of contracts subject to acceptance by the other parties of supplementary obligations which, by their nature or according to commercial usage, have no connexion with the subject of such contracts'.[504] In *Coca-Cola*, the Commission accepted commitments from Coca Cola not to offer anymore rebate to its customers who committed to buy less popular products together with its more best-selling brands, thus indicating that the practice of multi-product rebates in order to leverage market power is incompatible with Article 102 TFEU.[505]

The DG Competition's Staff Discussion Paper on the application of Article [102] to Exclusionary Abuses examined together mixed bundling and tying practices and considered mixed bundling as a form of 'commercial' tying.[506] The main difference between tying and mixed bundling was therefore the form of restricting the choice for consumers to obtain the tying product without the tied product. In contractual and technical tying, the DG Competition Staff considered that coercion generally takes a direct form, while for mixed bundling, coercion is indirect and often takes the form of an inducement of the customers to purchase the tied product through granting bonuses, rebates, discounts or any other commercial advantage. Yet, the DG Competition Staff paper distinguished the two forms of bundling (tying and mixed bundling) when it examined the foreclosure effect of these practices, by advocating a cost–price measure for mixed bundling practices, while adopting an anti-competitive foreclosure standard for tying cases. The DG Comp Discussion Paper separately categorized mixed bundling practices or bundled discounts that produce effects on *other* markets or on different products of the same market than single product rebates, analysing the former in the section of the Discussion Paper devoted to tying practices, although there were also classified in the Discussion Paper as a pricing abuse.[507] The Discussion Paper acknowledges that these may have effects on competition similar to tying and that the distinction between mixed bundling and pure bundling is not 'necessarily clear-cut' as mixed bundling may come close to pure bundling when the prices charged for the individual offerings are high.[508] Nonetheless, the Discussion Paper recognized that both practices have similar foreclosure effects: mixed bundling constitutes an indirect measure to achieve the same result as contractual tying 'by *inducing* customers to purchase the tied product through granting bonuses, rebates, discounts or any other commercial advantage'.[509] In this sense, the Discussion Paper seemed to recognize that coercion and inducement may produce the same effects on customer choice. However, the Discussion Paper differentiated between commercial tying and contractual tying when it examined the existence of a market-distorting foreclosure effect. It is only if the discount was so large that 'efficient competitors offering only some but not all of the components, cannot compete against the discounted bundle' that a bundled discount was found to infringe Article 8102 TFEU.

The Commission's Enforcement Priorities Guidance on Article 102 follows a similar approach by including 'multiproduct rebates' within the tying/bundling category.[510] This does

504 Case C-85/76, *Hoffman-La Roche & Co v Commission* [1979] ECR 461, para 111.

505 *Coca Cola* (Case COMP/A.39.116/B2) Commission Decision [2005] OJ C 253/21, para 33, available at http://ec.europa.eu/competition/antitrust/cases/dec_docs/39116/39116_258_4.pdf.

506 DG Comp Discussion Paper, para 182. 507 Ibid, para 142. 508 Ibid, para 177 n 112.

509 Ibid, para 182. 510 Commission Guidance on Article 102, paras 59–61.

not imply, however, that both practices are subject to a similar competition law regime. In this case, the distinction is not between commercial and contractual tying but between price-based and non-price-based exclusionary conduct. For price-related conduct, only the exclusion of competitors at least equally as efficient as the dominant firm triggers antitrust intervention. Hence, according to the Commission's Guidance on Article 102, multi-product rebates are anti-competitive (on the tying or the tied market) if they are so large 'that equally efficient competitors offering only some of the components cannot compete against the discounted bundle'.[511] The Commission takes into account the incremental price that customers pay for each of the dominant undertaking's products in the bundle and assesses whether this price remains above the LRAIC of the dominant undertaking when this product is included in the bundle.[512] If this is the case, the Commission will not intervene 'since an equally efficient competitor with only one product should in principle be able to compete profitably against the bundle'.[513] Where both the dominant undertaking and its competitor offer identical bundles, 'the Commission will generally regard this as a bundle competing against a bundle, in which case the relevant question is not whether the incremental revenue covers the incremental costs for each product in the bundle, but rather whether the price of the bundle as a whole is predatory'.[514] The exclusion of less-efficient competitors remains nevertheless an important concern for non-price based exclusionary conduct, such as tying. Indeed, the Commission Guidance on Article 102 does not exclude further analysis of the practice to detect anti-competitive foreclosure once the other two conditions for the application of Article 102 TFEU are fulfilled, which are (i) the undertaking is dominant in the tying market, and (ii) the tying and the tied product are distinct products.

Overall, the Commission's approach for bundling/tying seems inconsistent. The Commission adopts different standards for the various forms of bundling (contractual, technological, and commercial/bundled rebates), strict standards for contractual tying, stricter standards for technological tying, and lenient standards for bundled rebates, all without clearly explaining how these fit with the overall objectives and aims of Article 102 TFEU. It is important to acknowledge that, in an effects-based approach, the antitrust standards applied should be coherent, meaning that any similarity or difference in the treatment of these practices should be adequately explained. For example, there is a fine line between characterizing the Windows Media Player in the *Microsoft* case as a bundled discount and considering it as a case of tying. The WMP was offered for free, which may formally correspond to a bundled discount, a practice that entails the offering by the supplier to the distributor of a discount (zero price in this case) for accepting a bundle of different products or services. The fact that the Courts analysed the facts of the case as tying should not conceal the importance of developing a coherent conceptual framework for all types of bundling.

It seems also that the re-qualification by the General Court in *Intel* of loyalty rebates as non-price related conduct will have implications for the characterization of mixed bundling/bundled discounts practices, which allegedly cannot be classified any more as price related conduct, if even single-product unconditional rebates are thought of constituting a non-price related conduct, 'as the level of price cannot be unlawful in itself'.[515] The essential element of a tying/bundling abuse is the leveraging of the power of the dominant

511 Ibid, para 59.
512 Ibid, para 60.
513 Ibid, para 60.
514 Ibid, para 61.
515 Case T-286/09, *Intel Corp v European Commission*, ECLI:EU:T:2014:547, para 99.

undertaking from an uncontested part of the market (or an uncontested market) on which the undertaking holds a dominant position to a contested one, the same way one can analyse loyalty rebates. Hence, it is likely that the AEC test advanced by the Commission in its Guidance on Article 102 for mixed bundling will not apply for the assessment of bundled rebates, as a result of the *Intel* case law of the General Court.

9.8.6. LEVERAGING AS A STAND-ALONE COMPETITION LAW CONCERN? *TÉLÉMARKETING* AND *GOOGLE SEARCH*

Although the economic theory of leveraging provides the theoretical foundation for the hostility of competition law to tying practices, as well as some other types of abusive conduct, it remains an open question if it constitutes a stand-alone type of abusive practice, from a legal perspective. This issue is less of a concern for US antitrust law, where there are no clear boundaries between the various types of conduct that may fall under the monopolization offence,[516] the attempted monopolization offence,[517] or the conspiracy to monopolize offence,[518] which constitute the various forms that may take an infringement of section 2 of the Sherman Act. Although US courts usually rely on specific tests framed by legal precedents, they also tend to analyse the facts of the case through the perspective of possible theories of harm. The situation is different in the EU, where the classification of the fact pattern in a specific category of abuse forms a distinct and quite important step in the assessment of the allegedly illegal conduct, before the likely effects of that conduct are analysed. In Europe, the CJEU found that a leveraging practice may constitute a stand-alone competition law concern that could fall under Article 102 TFEU in *Télémarketing*. The Commission seems to have followed a similar approach in is recent decision on *Google Search (Shopping)*.

9.8.6.1. *Télémarketing*

The CJEU found also that a leveraging practice may constitute a stand-alone competition law concern that could fall under Article 102 TFEU in *Télémarketing*.[519] A subsidiary of Radio and Television Luxembourg (RTL) ceased to accept spot advertisements involving an invitation to make a telephone call for further information unless its telephone number was used. A national court before which this practice was challenged stated that RTL and its subsidiary were dominant over television advertising in the French-speaking parts of Belgium. At that time, it was illegal for Belgian television to carry advertisements. The national judge had found that telemarketing was a separate market from general TV advertising. The referent national court asked, among other questions, whether an undertaking holding a dominant position on a particular market could abuse of its dominant position by reserving to itself or to an undertaking belonging to the same group an ancillary activity which could be carried out by another undertaking as part of its activities on a neighbouring but separate market. The CJEU referred to the *Commercial Solvents* jurisprudence and observed that '[e]ven if the conduct in issue in the main proceedings were to be regarded not as a refusal to supply but as the imposition of a contractual condition, it would, in the Commission's view, be contrary' to Article 102 TFEU', further noting that the dominant undertaking in question imposed on all other undertakings

516 *United States v Grinnell Corp*, 384 US 563, 570–71 (1966).
517 *Spectrum Sports v McQuillan*, 506 US 445, 456 (1993).
518 *NYNEX Corp v Discon, Inc*, 525 US 128 (1998).
519 Case C-311/84, *Télémarketing* [1985] ECR 3261.

for telemarketing operations 'a condition which it does not impose on itself for the same operations, namely the condition that it must not use its own telephone number; that is an unfair trading condition within the meaning of Article [102(a) TFEU]' and subjected 'the conclusion of contracts to the acceptance of supplementary obligations which have no connection with the subject of the contracts', and that is contrary to Article [102(d) TFEU].[520] The CJEU concluded that notwithstanding the presence of a refusal to deal, an abuse of a dominant position is committed where, 'without any objective necessity an undertaking holding a dominant position on a particular market reserves to itself or to an undertaking belonging to the same group an ancillary activity which might be carried out by another undertaking as part of its activities on a neighbouring but separate market, with the possibility of eliminating all competition from such undertaking'.[521] The broad approach followed by the CJEU may be explained by the specificities of the case, the dominant position of the undertaking in question, RTL, being due not to the activities of the undertaking itself but to the fact that by reason of provisions laid down by law there can be no competition or only very limited competition on the market.

9.8.6.2. *Google Search*: A 'leveraging' abuse?[522]

As indicated in Section 8.4.5.3.2, the European Commission initiated in November 2010 an investigation against Google's parent company, Alphabet, with regard to its general search results on its search engine Google. Relying on a large body of evidence, the Commission issued a 215-page decision in June 2017 (published in December 2017),[523] finding that Google has abused its market dominance as a search engine by giving an illegal advantage to another Google product, its comparison shopping service. We include here some excerpts of the Commission's decision on market definition/dominant position and abuse.

Google Search (Shopping) (Case AT.39740) Commission Decision—Summary
[2018] C 9/11

Market definition and dominance

3. The Decision concludes that the relevant product markets for the purpose of this case are the market for general search services and the market for comparison shopping services.

---

520 Ibid, para 24. 521 Case C-311/84, *Télémarketing* [1985] ECR 3261, para 27.

522 This investigation of the European Commission has led to a number of publications on this issue (many of which have been sponsored or supported in kind by Google or its competitors so some caution should be exercised when reviewing their arguments). See B Vesterdorf, 'Theories of Self-Preferencing and Duty to Deal—Two Sides of the Same Coin' (2015) 1(1) *Competition L & Policy Debate* 4; AD Chirita, 'Google's Anti-Competitive and Unfair Practices in Digital Leisure Markets' (2015) 11(1) *Competition L Rev* 109; A Renda, 'Searching for Harm or Harming Search? A Look at the European Commission's Antitrust Investigation Against Google', CEPS Special Report No 118 (September 2015), available at https://www.ceps.eu/system/files/AR Antitrust Investigation Google.pdf; FW von Papp, 'Should Google's Secret Source Be Organic?' (2015) 16(2) *Melbourne J Int'l L* 609; R Nazzini, 'Google and the (Ever-stretching) Boundaries of Article 102 TFEU' (2015) 6(5) *J European Competition L & Practice* 301; JT Lang, 'Comparing Microsoft and Google: The Concept of Exclusionary Abuse' (2016) 39(1) *World Competition* 5; P Akman, 'The Theory of Abuse in *Google Search*: A Positive and Normative Assessment under EU Competition Law' [2017] *U Illinois J L, Technology and Policy* 301, available at http://illinoisjltp.com/journal/wp-content/uploads/2017/12/Akman.pdf.

523 *Google Search (Shopping)* (Case AT.39740) Commission Decision, C(2017) 4444 final (27 June 2017), available at http://ec.europa.eu/competition/antitrust/cases/dec_docs/39740/39740_14996_3.pdf.

4. The provision of general search services constitutes a distinct product market, because (i) it constitutes an economic activity; (ii) there is limited demand-side substitutability and limited supply-side substitutability between general search services and other online services; and (iii) this conclusion does not change if general search services on static devices versus mobile devices are considered.

5. The provision of comparison shopping services constitutes a distinct relevant product market. This is because comparison shopping services are not interchangeable with the services offered by: (i) search services specialised in different subject matters (such as, for example, flights, hotels, restaurants, or news); (ii) online search advertising platforms; (iii) online retailers; (iv) merchant platforms; and (v) offline comparison shopping tools.

6. The Decision concludes that the relevant geographic markets for general search services and comparison shopping services are all national in scope.

Google's dominant position in general search

7. The Decision concludes that since 2007, Google has held a dominant position in each national market for general search in the EEA, apart from in the Czech Republic, where Google has held a dominant position since 2011.

8. This conclusion is based on Google's market shares, the existence of barriers to expansion and entry, the infrequency of user multi-homing and the existence of brand effects and the lack of countervailing buyer power. The conclusion holds notwithstanding the fact that general search services are offered free of charge and regardless of whether general search on static devices constitutes a distinct market from general search on mobile devices.

Abuse of a dominant position

9. The Decision concludes that Google commits an abuse in the relevant markets for general search services in the EEA by positioning and displaying more favourably, in its general search results pages, its own comparison shopping service compared to competing comparison shopping services.

10. Google's conduct is abusive because it: (i) diverts traffic away from competing comparison shopping services to Google's own comparison shopping service, in the sense that it decreases traffic from Google's general results pages to competing comparison shopping services and increases traffic from Google's general search results pages to Google's own comparison shopping service; and (ii) is capable of having, or likely to have, anti-competitive effects in the national markets for comparison shopping services and general search services.

Google's conduct: more favourable positioning and display in its general search result pages of its own comparison shopping service

11. The Decision explains the way in which Google positions and displays more favourably, in its general search results pages, its own comparison shopping service compared to competing comparison shopping services.

12. First, it is explained how competing comparison shopping services are positioned and displayed in Google's general search results pages. In relation to their positioning, the Decision explains how certain dedicated algorithms make competing comparison shopping services prone to having their ranking reduced in Google's

general search results pages and how this has affected their visibility in Google's general search results pages. In relation to their display, the Decision explains the format in which competing comparison shopping services can be displayed in Google's general search results.

13. Second, it is explained how Google's own comparison shopping service is positioned and displayed in Google's general search results pages. In relation to its positioning, the Decision explains that Google's service is positioned prominently and not subject to the dedicated algorithms that make competing comparison shopping services prone to having their ranking reduced in Google's general search pages. In relation to its display, the Decision explains that Google's own comparison shopping service is displayed with enhanced features at or near the top of the first general search page, while such features are inaccessible to its rivals.

Google's more favourable positioning and display of its own comparison shopping service diverts traffic from competing comparison shopping services

14. The Decision first analyses the influence of the positioning and display of generic search results on user behaviour. It shows that users tend to click more on links which are more visible on the general search results page.

15. The Decision then analyses the actual evolution of traffic to competing comparison shopping services, which confirms its findings on user behaviour.

16. First, there is evidence that shows the immediate influence of the ranking of generic search results in Google Search on the click-through rates on these search results.

17. Second, the Commission compared the evolution of the visibility of important competing comparison shopping services as calculated by the independent company Sistrix and the evolution of generic search traffic from Google to these services.

18. Third, evidence in the Commission's file indicates that the more favourable positioning and display of Google's comparison shopping service in its general search results pages has led to an increase in traffic to that service.

19. Fourth, evidence in the file on the actual evolution of traffic to Google's comparison shopping service confirms that the more prominently positioned and displayed it is within Google' general search results pages, the more it gains traffic.

Generic search traffic from Google's general search results pages represents a large proportion of competing comparison shopping services' traffic and cannot easily be replaced

20. The Decision concludes that generic search traffic from Google's general search results pages, i.e. the source of traffic diverted from competing comparison shopping services, accounts for a large proportion of traffic to those services.

21. It also concludes that none of the existing alternative sources of traffic currently available to competing comparison shopping services, including traffic from AdWords, mobile applications and direct traffic, can effectively replace the generic search traffic from Google's general search results pages.

Google's conduct has potential anti-competitive effects

22. The decision concludes that Google's conduct has a number of potential anti-competitive effects.

23. First, Google's conduct has the potential to foreclose competing comparison shopping services, which may lead to higher fees for merchants, higher prices for consumers, and less innovation.

24. Second, Google's conduct is likely to reduce the ability of consumers to access the most relevant comparison shopping services.

25. Third, Google's conduct would also have potential anti-competitive effects even if comparison shopping services did not constitute a distinct relevant product market, but rather a segment of a possible broader relevant product market comprising both comparison shopping services and merchant platforms.

It is worth noting that, notwithstanding the fact that the Commission relied on the argument that the loss of traffic from Google's general search results pages represents a large proportion of competing comparison shopping services' traffic which could not effectively be replaced, the Commission framed this case under a standard leverage theory of harm, rather than the more challenging refusal to supply access to an essential facility, or even under a broader theory of exclusionary discrimination under Article 102(c) TFEU. Indeed, the Commission relied on *TeliaSonera* and *Intel* to argue that it is sufficient to establish that Google's conduct was capable of making it more difficult (ie, short of impossible) for competing comparison shopping services to access their separate but adjacent markets.[524] This hurdle is clearly lower than a requirement to prove that access to Google's general search pages is indispensable that would have been required had Google's conduct be qualified as a vertical foreclosure case akin to a refusal to supply (the *Oscar Bronner* conditions).

Follow some excerpts from the text of the Decision.

Google Search (Shopping) **(Case AT.39740) Commission Decision,** C(2017) 4444 final (27 June 2017)

Abuse of a dominant position—Principles

331. Dominant undertakings have a special responsibility not to impair, by conduct falling outside the scope of competition on the merits, genuine undistorted competition in the internal market. A system of undistorted competition can be guaranteed only if equality of opportunity is secured as between the various economic operators. The scope of the special responsibility of the dominant undertaking has to be considered in light of the specific circumstances of the case. [. . .]

334. Article 102 of the Treaty and Article 54 of the EEA Agreement prohibit not only practices by an undertaking in a dominant position which tend to strengthen that position, but also the conduct of an undertaking with a dominant position in a given market that tends to extend that position to a neighbouring but separate market by distorting competition. Therefore, the fact that a dominant undertaking's abusive conduct has its adverse effects on a market distinct from the dominated one does not preclude the application of Article 102 of the Treaty or Article 54 of the EEA Agreement. It is not necessary that the dominance, the abuse and the effects of the abuse are all in the same market.

[524] *Google Search (Shopping)* (Case AT.39740) Commission Decision, C(2017) 4444 final (27 June 2017), para 339.

335. Article 102 of the Treaty and Article 54 of the EEA Agreement list a number of abusive practices. [. . .] The legal characterisation of an abusive practice does not depend on the name given to it, but on the substantive criteria used in that regard. The specific conditions to be met in order to establish the abusive nature of one form of conduct covered by Article 102 of the Treaty and Article 54 of the EEA Agreement must not necessarily also apply when assessing the abusive nature of another form of conduct covered by those articles.

336. In order to determine whether the undertaking in a dominant position has abused such a position, it is necessary to consider all the circumstances and to investigate whether the practice tends, for example, to bar competitors from access to the market, to apply dissimilar conditions to equivalent transactions with other trading parties, thereby placing them at a competitive disadvantage, or to strengthen the dominant position by distorting competition. [. . .]

Abusive conduct

341. The Commission concludes that the Conduct constitutes an abuse of Google's dominant position in each of the thirteen national markets for general search services where Google either launched the Product Universal or, if the Product Universal was never launched in that market, the Shopping Unit. The Conduct is abusive because it constitutes a practice falling outside the scope of competition on the merits as it: (i) diverts traffic in the sense that it decreases traffic from Google's general search results pages to competing comparison shopping services and increases traffic from Google's general search results pages to Google's own comparison shopping service; and (ii) is capable of having, or likely to have, anti-competitive effects in the national markets for comparison shopping services and general search services.

Potential anticompetitive effects on several markets

The Commission had found that the conduct decreased traffic from Google's general results pages to competing comparison shopping services and increased traffic from Google's general search results pages to Google's own comparison shopping service. The Commission concluded that generic search traffic from Google's general search results pages accounts for a large proportion of traffic to competing comparison shopping services and cannot be effectively replaced by other sources currently available to comparison shopping services. Consequently, the conduct was capable of having, or likely to have, anti-competitive effects, in the national markets for comparison shopping services.

[. . .]

593. First, the Conduct has the potential to foreclose competing comparison shopping services, which may lead to higher fees for merchants, higher prices for consumers, and less innovation for the reasons explained below.

594. In the first place, the Conduct is capable of leading competing comparison shopping services to cease providing their services. This would allow Google to impose and maintain higher fees on merchants for participation in its own comparison shopping service. These higher costs for merchants are capable of leading to higher product prices for consumers.

595. In the second place, the Conduct is likely to reduce the incentives of competing comparison shopping services to innovate. Competing comparison shopping services will have an incentive to invest in developing innovative services, improving the relevance of their existing services and creating new types of services, only if they can reasonably expect that their services will be able to attract a sufficient volume of user traffic to compete with Google's comparison shopping service. Moreover, even if

competing comparison shopping services may try to compensate to some extent the decrease in traffic by relying more on paid sources of traffic, this will also reduce the revenue available to invest in developing innovative services, improving the relevance of their existing services and creating new types of services.

596. In the third place, the Conduct is likely to reduce the incentives of Google to improve the quality of its comparison shopping service as it does not currently need to compete on the merits with competing comparison shopping services.

597. Second, the Conduct is likely to reduce the ability of consumers to access the most relevant comparison shopping services. This is for two reasons.

598. In the first place [. . .] users tend to consider that search results that are ranked highly in generic search results on Google's general search results pages are the most relevant for their queries and click on them irrespective of whether other results would be more relevant for their queries. [. . .] Google started the Conduct even though as a result, it did not always show to users the most relevant results (as ranked by its generic search algorithms) at least for certain queries.

599. In the second place, Google did not inform users that the Product Universal was positioned and displayed in its general search results pages using different underlying mechanisms than those used to rank generic search results. As for the Shopping Unit, while the 'Sponsored' label may suggest that different positioning and display mechanisms are used, that information is likely to be understandable only by the most knowledgeable users [. . .].

600. The Conduct therefore risks undermining the competitive structure of the national markets for comparison shopping services. The prospects of commercial success of Google's comparison shopping service are enhanced not because of the merits of that service, but because Google applies different underlying mechanisms on the basis of the advantages provided to it by its dominant position in the national markets for general search services. [. . .]

602. [. . .] [T]he Commission is not required to prove that the Conduct has the actual effect of leading certain competing comparison shopping services to cease offering their services. Rather, it is sufficient for the Commission to demonstrate that the Conduct is capable of having, or likely to have, such an effect.

605. [. . .] [T]he Commission's conclusion is not called into question by Google's claim that the Commission has failed to demonstrate, as part of its analysis of anticompetitive effects, a causal link between, on the one hand, the Conduct and the decrease in traffic to competing comparison shopping services and, on the other hand, the Conduct and the increase in traffic to Google's comparison shopping service.

606. [. . .] [T]he Commission is not required to prove that the Conduct has the actual effect of decreasing traffic to competing comparison shopping services and increasing traffic to Google's comparison shopping service. Rather, it is sufficient for the Commission to demonstrate that the Conduct is capable of having, or likely to have, such effects.

607. In the second place, and in any event, the Commission has demonstrated by 'tangible evidence' that the Conduct decreases traffic to competing comparison shopping services and increases traffic to Google's own comparison shopping service.

Google's arguments with regard to the applicable legal test

644. Google claims that the Conduct cannot amount to an abuse of a dominant position on the facts of the case.

645. First, Google claims that the Conduct could be considered abusive only if the criteria established in the *Bronner* case are fulfilled. By failing to apply those criteria,

the Commission is imposing on Google a duty to promote competition by allowing competing comparison shopping services to have access to a significant proportion of its general search results pages, despite access to those pages not being indispensable in order to compete.

646. Second, Google claims that there is no precedent for characterising the Conduct as an abuse: even if 'Article 102 TFEU does not establish a closed list of abusive conducts, new abuse categories must be consistent with the legal framework of Article 102 TFEU', and the 'rules must be knowable in advance'.

647. Third, Google claims that the Product Universal and the Shopping Unit constitute product design improvements, which are a form of competition on the merits and 'therefore, can be found abusive only in exceptional circumstances'.

648. Google's arguments are unfounded.

649. First, it is not novel to find that conduct consisting in the use of a dominant position on one market to extend that dominant position to one or more adjacent markets can constitute an abuse. [. . .] Such a form of conduct constitutes a well-established, independent, form of abuse falling outside the scope of competition on the merits.

650. Second, the Conduct does not concern a passive refusal by Google to give competing comparison shopping services access to a proportion of its general search results pages, but active behaviour relating to the more favourable positioning and display by Google, in its general search results pages, of its own comparison shopping service compared to comparison shopping services. [. . .] (i) Google's own comparison shopping service is not subject to the same ranking mechanisms as its competitors, including adjustment algorithms such as [. . .] and Panda; and (ii) when triggered, Google positions results from its own comparison shopping service on its first general results page in a highly visible place (i.e. either above all generic search results or, in the majority of cases, within or at the level of the first generic search results).

651. Third, the *Bronner* criteria are irrelevant in a situation, such as that of the present case, where bringing to an end the infringement does not involve imposing a duty on the dominant undertaking to 'transfer an asset or enter into agreements with persons with whom it has not chosen to contract'. While the Decision requires Google to cease the Conduct, it does not require it either to transfer any asset or to enter into agreements with one or more competing comparison shopping services.

652. Fourth, there is no indication in the case law that alleged improvements in product designs should be assessed under a different legal standard to that developed to assess the use of a dominant position on one market to extend that dominant position to one or more adjacent markets. [. . .]

NOTES AND QUESTIONS ON GOOGLE SEARCH (SHOPPING)

1. In addition to the €2.42 billion fine, Google is required to stop its illegal conduct within 90 days of the decision and refrain from any measure that has the same or an equivalent object or effect. What is particularly significant is that the decision orders Google to comply with the simple principle of giving *equal treatment* to rival comparison shopping services and its own service, meaning that Google has to apply the same processes and methods to position and display rival comparison shopping services in Google's search results pages as it gives to its own comparison shopping service. The simplest way for Google to comply would be to subject its own product to the same treatment under its general search, as implied by the Commission's argument that, in

contrast to the *Bronner* case law, Google is not required to enter into agreements with one or more competing comparison shopping services.

2. Nevertheless, in case Google decided to retain prominence for its own comparison shopping service, it would be required to provide similar treatment to rivals. In particular, this would presumably entail the imposition of margin-squeeze requirements on the fees rivals would be charged for sharing the prominent spot on Google's general search page. Therefore, it could be argued that, ultimately, this decision decisively blurs the distinction between the leverage and the margin-squeeze theories of harm.
3. The Commission argued that although Google adopted a 'Sponsored' label which may suggest that different positioning mechanisms (from those applicable to competing comparison shopping services) are used, that information is likely to be understandable only by the most knowledgeable users.[525] Could Google have escaped liability by proactively seeking user consent to give preferential treatment to its own comparison shopping service?
4. The Commission argued that Google's conduct constitute an abuse of a position of dominance regardless of the fact that its intention was to improve its services. Does that mean that the principle of special responsibility for an integrated dominant undertaking extends to a requirement not to pursue an improvement of the products or services offered if the improvement thereof is capable of making it more difficult for a competitor to access the market? Did the changes made to Google's search algorithms in 2011 bring innovation to the market benefiting consumers, or was their main effect to steer traffic away from competitors and in favour of Google, thus limiting consumer choice?
5. The Commission considers that Google's conduct raises a vertical foreclosure concern in the downstream market of comparison shopping services, or of shopping services and merchant platforms, should these be considered a separate market.[526] Could the Chicago one-monopoly-profit theorem apply in this case and deny any possible anti-competitive rationale behind Google's strategy? Note the importance here of the role of Google's general search engine platform that connects two distinct user groups which interact together through this platform. In other words, it constitutes a two-sided platform. The two-sidedness of the platform has impact on the analysis of vertical foreclosure as a plausible anti-competitive strategy in this case. As the Commission explains:

   At least for one of these users groups, the value obtained from the platform depends on the number of users of the other class. General search services and online search advertising constitute the two sides of a general search engine platform. The level of advertising revenue that a general search engine can obtain is related to the number of users of its general search service: the higher the number of users of a general search service, the more the online search advertising side of the platform will appeal to advertisers.[527]

   This means that 'the typical Chicago school critique would not be profitable because a dominant firm would make more money by appropriately pricing its products or services does not apply here: given its business model, Google does not charge consumers, nor comparison services for inclusion in its search pages the monetisation of

[525] *Google Search (Shopping)* (Case AT.39740) Commission Decision, C(2017) 4444 final (27 June 2017), para 536.

[526] Ibid, paras 608–13. [527] Ibid, para 159.

its search services would come only when consumers go to its [. . .] "Google Product Search" webpage and click on a merchant post; or when they click on the image of a merchant in its "Google shopping" service'.[528]

6. Assess if the Commission has sufficiently proven consumer harm, or if the finding of consumer harm is mainly assumed from the marginalization and exclusion of rival websites downstream. The Commission finds that consumers may suffer from a reduction of their choice of comparison websites and/or less innovation. Its findings rely on the idea that 'generic search results generate significant traffic to a website when they are ranked within the first three to five generic search results on the first general search results page'[529] and that consumers typically look to the generic search results on the first general search results page before clicking to shopping comparison websites and then merchant websites. Is this a plausible assumption about users' behaviour? Or is the Commission aiming to protect non-knowledgeable users of the Internet who would not have developed a brand loyalty to a merchant website or a price comparison website so as to type its web address directly on the white address bar at the top of the page, but prefer instead to search for these on the Google search bar?
7. Google has appealed to the GC against the Commission's decision. Note that the Google decision of the Commission was adopted a few months before the CJEU rendered its judgment in *Intel v Commission.*[530] How would this judgment impact, if at all, on the categorization of Google's conduct and the competition assessment completed? Do you think it plausible that the GC may require, in view of the CJEU's judgment in *Intel* that the Commission applies in Google the AEC test, when assessing foreclosure effects, by exploring if the comparison websites marginalized by Google's conduct were equally efficient? How could this test apply in the context of a market where consumers pay a zero monetary price? Is it relevant that the CJEU in *Intel* seems to have excluded tying practices through the imposition of a formal condition from the application of the AEC test? Could the leveraging conduct in *Google* qualify as equivalent to the imposition of a 'formal obligation'?
8. In addition to leveraging, which is the category of abuse put forward by the Commission, and vertical foreclosure through conduct conducive to a refusal to supply (which was not put forward), the Commission could have conceptualized this conduct under a broader theory of exclusionary discrimination under Article 102(c) TFEU, to the extent that it imposes a 'general duty not to discriminate against rivals'.[531] The case law on exclusionary discrimination does not require the Commission to adduce evidence of an actual quantifiable deterioration in the competitive position of the business partners taken individually. Note that similar concerns with regard to Google's conduct in taking advantage of the gatekeeping role of its search engine were identified by the French Competition Authority which, in its Navx decision, and relying on Article 102(c)

[528] C Fumagali, M Motta, and C Calcagno, *Exclusionary Practices: The Economics of Monopolisation and Abuse of Dominance* (CUP, 2018), 5.

[529] *Google Search (Shopping)* (Case AT.39740) Commission Decision, C(2017) 4444 final (27 June 2017), para 159

[530] See Section 9.6.4.3.

[531] On a discussion of a more general theory of exclusionary discrimination see, P Ibáñez Colomo, 'Exclusionary Discrimination under Article 102 TFEU' (2014) 51 *Common Market L Rev* 141, 151–61.

TFEU, found that the sudden closure of Navx's AdWords account by Google for violation of its content policy without warning was discriminatory and non-transparent and asked Google to re-establish Navx's account and to ensure the transparency of its content policy with specific commitments by Google as to the transparency of the content policy of its advertising platform AdWords.[532] Explain the advantages and disadvantages for the Commission for choosing one or the other category of abuse in this case.

9.8.7. UK CASE LAW

Streetmap.Eu Limited v Google Inc, Google Ireland Limited, Google UK Limited
[2016] EWHC 253 (Ch)

Streetmap claimed that the combination of Google's prominent display of its map in its search engine results page (SERP) in response to certain geographic queries, with the relegation of other maps to a secondary position represented an abuse of Google's dominant position in the market for online search.

The High Court deemed that the analysis of abuse should be conducted on the basis that Google was dominant in the market for general online search.

Streetmap put forward two heads in relation to the abuse: the first concerned the bundling of Google Search and Google Maps, the second a preferential display of Google Maps, through a thumbnail map, compared to other map providers. The first argument was said to be an atypical allegation of bundling, since there was no payment for either the search engine or the maps, nor was there an obligation to use Google Maps. In respect of the second argument, the issue was not the display of a thumbnail map per se*: the complete lack of such functionality, as a matter of fact, would have affected negatively the interests of consumers.*

The High Court emphasized how the categories of abuse were not restricted within those enumerated in Article 102 TFEU, and how abuse could have anti-competitive effects on associated or related markets to those where the undertaking was dominant.

In deciding whether Google's conduct had the potential or actual effect of foreclosing competitors in the online maps, the High Court held that where, such as in the present circumstances, the conduct was pro-competitive on the dominant market but potentially anti-competitive on a non-dominated market then a de minimis *threshold would apply. Thus, Google's disputed conduct would be abusive if it were reasonably likely to have a serious or appreciable effect in the market for on-line maps. This, however, was not held to be the case; the introduction of the new Google Maps functionality did not in itself have an appreciable effect in taking custom away from Streetmap, which was more likely due to the changes in technical advancements and cost-savings to customers. Google's conduct therefore was not found to give rise to anti-competitive foreclosure.*

The High Court also assessed the potential for objective justification under the hypothesis that Google's conduct was an abuse of its dominant position. Per Post Danmark*, the dominant undertaking would have to show outweighing positive effects, proportional to the conduct in question. Technical efficiencies, such as the provision of a thumbnail map, were considered capable of falling within the test for objective justification. None of the alternative options to Google's approach were capable of rendering Google's conduct disproportional.*

[532] Autorité de la concurrence, Decision 10-D-30 of 28 October 2010 on Internet advertising, available at http://www.autoritedelaconcurrence.fr/pdf/avis/10d30.pdf.

Socrates Training Limited v The Law Society of England and Wales
[2017] CAT 10

The facts of this case have been summarized in Section 6.4.6.1. Although it was argued in the alternative that the scheme infringed Chapter I CA 98, Socrates mainly argued that the requirement under the terms of the CQS that members of the scheme must obtain these training courses exclusively from the Law Society constituted an abuse of a dominant position ('tying') contrary to Chapter II CA 98. The CAT found that the Law Society abused its dominant position by tying its anti-money laundering (AML) training to its accreditation scheme for conveyancing lawyers (the Conveyancing Quality Scheme (CQS)).

The Tribunal defined two separate product markets: (a) an upstream market, in which the Law Society supplies the CQS (the supply of accreditation to law firms providing residential conveyancing in England and Wales); and (b) a downstream market, in which Socrates and others supply training courses in AML, mortgage fraud and financial crime to firms that require AML training under the ML Regulations.[533] *The Tribunal defined the relevant market as the upstream market of the supply of accreditation to solicitors. The economic expert of the defendant put forward the idea that the relevant upstream market was a two-sided platform serving two distinct customer groups: on the one side, the provision of quality assurance to mortgage lenders with regard to solicitors that offered residential conveyancing services, on the other side, access to the panels of mortgage lenders for solicitors offering such services.*[534] *The Tribunal noted that even if that were the correct analysis, it is only the market power and anti-competitive effect as regards solicitors which is at issue. In addressing those questions, the focus is therefore on that side of a putative two-sided market, and the fact that there may be another side serving a distinct group of customers is relevant only if that provides a competitive constraint.*[535] *The CAT then found that the Law Society's ability to set its charges under the CQS to an appreciable extent independently of the solicitor customers indicated that it was dominant.*[536]

With regard to the analysis of the abuse, the CAT found two distinct products, as the supply of the training course itself was thought to be clearly different from the supply of accreditation and the two were functionally distinct. With regard to the assessment of anti-competitive effects, the CAT referred to the Streetmap *judgment and the High Court's finding that 'the impugned conduct must be reasonably likely to harm the competitive structure of the market' and that '[i]n determining that question, the court will take into account, as a very relevant consideration, evidence as to what the actual effect of the conduct has been'. However, the CAT noted that the latter observation must be seen in the context of the factual situation in that case.*[537] *The CAT found inappropriate to consider the actual effect on any independent provider like Socrates, holding the degree to which conduct has* actually *had (or not had) an anti-competitive effect as only evidential. Hence,* demonstration of a potential effect *was thought to be sufficient, provided that the conduct was* reasonably likely *to have an effect, and even if the effect had not yet been realized.*[538] *The CAT also referred to the requirement of an appreciable effects resulting from* Streetmap. *The CAT concluded that the meaning of an 'appreciable' effect should be the same in the context of the Chapter II CA98 prohibition (or Article 102 TFEU) as it has for the Chapter I CA98 prohibition (or Article 101 TFEU), where the*

533 *Socrates Training Limited v The Law Society of England and Wales* [2017] CAT 10, paras 112 and 118.

534 Mortgage lenders play a critical role in the legal conveyancing market—it is important for a conveyancing solicitor to be on the panels of as many mortgage lenders as possible since if a firm is not on the panel it cannot act for that lender in a conveyancing transaction.

535 *Socrates Training Limited v The Law Society of England and Wales* [2017] CAT 10, para 111.

536 Ibid, para 134. 537 Ibid, para 149. 538 Ibid, para 150.

requirement to show an appreciable effect (actual or potential) is well-established. Accordingly, appreciable does not mean substantial: it means more than de minimis *or insignificant.*[539]

The Tribunal concluded that once the CQS became a must-have product to which close to 60 per cent of firms active in residential conveyancing subscribed, it was satisfied that by reserving at least a significant part of the demand from such firms for AML/mortgage fraud training from at least a significant number of those firms at any one time, potential competition from other suppliers of such training was actually or potentially impaired, and that this could discourage entry by other suppliers into this segment of the market.[540] *Hence, the anti-competitive effect was appreciable, ie more than* de minimis. *The CAT found no objective justifications for the conduct (the analysis was the same as for section 9(2) CA98 examined in Section 6.4.6.1).*

9.9. ABUSIVE (VEXATIOUS) LITIGATION AND ABUSE OF THE REGULATORY PROCESS

9.9.1. GENERAL PRINCIPLES

Dominant firms have been found to abuse the regulatory and litigation system with the aim to raise the costs of their rivals, exclude competition, and ultimately harm consumers.[541]

9.9.2. VEXATIOUS LITIGATION

This type of practices is particular salient in the context of IP rights litigation.[542] The abuse may consist in instigating litigation with the collateral purpose of inflicting an anti-competitive injury. In the context of patent litigation, this conduct may take the form of competition law (antitrust) counterclaims to patent infringement claims, what is generally referred to as 'sham litigation' in the US or 'vexatious litigation' in Europe. These practices are analysed in detail in the companion volume relating to the interaction between competition law and IP rights.[543] In its seminal *ITT Promedia v Commission* judgment, the GC accepted that vexatious litigation may 'in wholly exceptional circumstances' constitute an abuse of a dominant position, contrary to article 102 TFEU,[544] a principle that was most recently confirmed in *Protégé International Ltd v Commission.*[545] The key piece of evidence in identifying sham litigation is the absence of genuine interest in receiving judicial relief. Establishing the genuine motive of the plaintiff, therefore, has been the central issue to much of the case law on sham litigation.

539 Ibid, para 154. 540 Ibid, para 164.

541 For a general discussion, see D Bailey, 'The New Frontiers of Article 102 TFEU: Antitrust Imperialism or Judicious Intervention?' (2018) 6(1) *J Antitrust Enforcement* 25. See also, I Lianos, *Competition Law and the Intangible Economy* (OUP, forthcoming 2019) (examining in detail practices such as unilateral and collusive conduct involving patent litigation, pay for delay and early entry practices, evergreening, misrepresentation in the context of the patent process).

542 For a detailed discussion, see I Lianos and P Regibeau, 'Sham Litigation—When Can It Arise and How Can It Be Reduced?' (2017) 62(4) *Antitrust Bulletin* 643.

543 I Lianos, *Competition Law and the Intangible Economy* (OUP, forthcoming 2019).

544 Case T-111/96, *ITT Promedia NV v Commission* (1998) ECR II–2937.

545 Case T-119/09, *Protégé International Ltd v European Commission*, ECLI:EU:T:2012:421 (available only in French).

According to *ITT Promedia v Commission*, bringing legal proceedings may constitute an abuse only in 'exceptional circumstances', namely (i) where the action cannot reasonably be considered as an attempt to establish the rights of the undertaking concerned and would therefore serve only to 'harass' the opposite party and (ii) the action is part of a plan whose aim is to eliminate competition.[546] According to the Court, when applying the first criterion, 'it is the situation existing when the action in question is brought which must be taken into account in order to determine whether that criterion is satisfied'.[547] Furthermore, 'when applying that criterion, it is not a question of determining whether the rights which the undertaking concerned was asserting when it brought its action actually existed or whether that action was well founded, but rather of determining whether such an action was intended to assert what that undertaking could, at that moment, reasonably consider to be its rights'.[548] This is 'satisfied solely when the action did not have that aim, that being the sole case in which it may be assumed that such action could only serve to harass the opposing party'.[549] Once the first part of the test is satisfied, it becomes important to consider whether the action was conceived in the framework of a plan whose goal was to eliminate competition. In *Protégé International Ltd v Commission*, the GC noted that the two conditions of the *ITT Promedia* case law should be interpreted restrictively in order not to jeopardize the application of the general principle of EU law on access to justice and that the conditions are cumulative.[550]

9.9.3. ABUSE OF THE REGULATORY PROCESS

A Commission's decision in 2005 found that Astra Zeneca had infringed Article 102 TFEU by (i) submitting misleading information to national patent offices in order to acquire supplementary protection certificates (SPCs) which would extent the patent protection for Losec and then defending those in court and (ii) for misusing national rules by launching a tablet form of the drug and withdrawing authorizations for the original version of its drug Losec in certain national markets where patents or SPCs were due to expire.[551] The General Court and the CJEU confirmed the Commission's decision on appeal.[552] According

546 Case T-111/96, *ITT Promedia NV v Commission* [1998] ECR II-293, paras 55 and 57.

547 Ibid, para 72.

548 Ibid, para. 73 549 Ibid.

550 Case T-119/09, *Protégé International Ltd v European Commission*, ECLI:EU:T:2012:421, paras 49 and 63 (available only in French). The case law on 'vexatious litigation' was singled out in Case T-480/15, *Agria Polska sp z oo and Others v European Commission*, ECLI:EU:T:2017:339, as being of 'exceptional nature' (ibid, para 71). The GC noted that, in the case of vexatious litigation, as well as that involving the abuse of regulatory procedures (see Section 9.9.3),

> the administrative and judicial authorities seized by the undertakings in a dominant position concerned *had no discretion* as to whether it was appropriate to follow up or otherwise the applications made by those undertakings, whether that was a counterclaim brought before a national court or the decision of an undertaking to withdraw its application for authorisation to place a medicinal product on the market. (Case T-480/15, *Agria Polska sp z oo and Others v European Commission*, ECLI:EU:T:2017:339, para 70, emphasis added.)

Indeed, 'the court to which that counterclaim was made was required to rule on it' (ibid). Hence, the case law of the EU courts does not seem to qualify as vexatious litigation situations in which the public authorities whose process may serve as the means of the abuse can adopt their decision independently of the information supplied by the defendants (ibid, para 71) and/or exercise some discretion.

551 *AstraZeneca* (Case COMP/A.37.507/F3) Commission Decision 2006/857/EC [2006] OJ L 332/24.

552 Case T-321/05, *Astra Zeneca v Commission* [2010] ECR II-2805; Case C-457/10 P, *Astra Zeneca v Commission* [2012] ECLI:EU:C:2012:770.

to this case law, an undertaking which holds a dominant position cannot use 'regulatory procedures' in such a way as to prevent or make more difficult the entry of competitors on the market, in the absence of grounds relating to the defence of the legitimate interests of an undertaking engaged in competition on the merits or in the absence of objective justification.[553] This case law is analysed in detail in the companion volume relating to the interaction between competition law and IP rights.

9.9.4. ANTI-COMPETITIVE USE OF INJUNCTIONS

Some recent decisions of the European Commission[554] and some case law of the CJEU[555] envision the possibility that the threat, or seeking, of injunctions in circumstances where a dominant undertaking, which is holding standard essential patents (SEPs), has given a fair, reasonable, and non-discriminatory (FRAND) commitment, could be found to be an abuse. This case law is discussed in detail in the companion volume.[556] Suffice to note that in *Huawei v ZTE*, the CJEU, examined the relevant issue, not only from the perspective of competition law, but also of IP law.[557] In contrast to the previous case law of the CJEU regarding refusals to license, where an abuse may only be found in exceptional circumstances, the CJEU distinguished this case, noting (i) that the essential nature of the SEP makes it indispensable to all manufacturers of standard-compliant products and (ii) that the SEP-holder took a commitment to the SSO, in this case ETSI, to grant licences on FRAND terms, thus creating legitimate expectations for implementers. These very broad conditions have been and will be interpreted by the jurisprudence of the national courts.[558]

9.10. ABUSES AFFECTING THE INTERNAL MARKET

9.10.1. PRACTICES LIMITING PARALLEL TRADE

As explained in Chapter 2, the objective of market integration may explain why EU competition law has consistently found all practices limiting the opportunities of parallel trade as infringing either Article 101(1) TFEU or Article 102 TFEU. The practices may take

553 Case T-321/05, *Astra Zeneca v Commission* [2010] ECR II–2805, paras 672 & 817; Case C-457/10P *Astra Zeneca v Commission* [2012] ECLI:EU:C:2012:770, para. 134.

554 *Motorola—Enforcement of GPRS standard essential patents* (Case AT.39985) Commission Decision (29 April 2014); *Samsung—Enforcement of UMTS standard essential patents* (Case COMP/C-39939) Commission Decision (29 April 2014).

555 Case C-170/13, *Huawei Technologies Co Ltd v ZTE Corp., ZTE Deutschland GmbH*, ECLI:EU:C:2015:477.

556 I Lianos, *Competition Law and the Intangible Economy* (OUP, forthcoming 2019).

557 Case C-170/13, *Huawei Technologies Co Ltd v ZTE Corp and ZTE Deutschland GmbH*, ECLI:EU:C:2015:477.

558 See, for instance, the recent case of the UK Patent Court in *Unwired Planet International Ltd v Huawei Technologies Co Ltd* [2017] EWHC 711 (Pat), para 744, where Briss J interpreted the CJEU's judgment in *Huawei v ZTE* as follows:

> (i) In the judgment the CJEU has set out a scheme which both the patentee and implementer can be expected to follow in the context of a dispute about a patent declared essential to a standard and subject to a FRAND undertaking.
>
> (ii) In stating that the implementer and patentee must express a willingness to conclude a licence on FRAND terms, the CJEU is referring to a willingness in general terms. The fact that concrete proposals are also required does not mean it is relevant to ask if those proposals are actually FRAND or not.

different forms. In *British Leyland*, the CJEU confirmed the Commission's decision finding that British Leyland had abused its dominant position by adopting a strategy aimed at discouraging parallel imports of left-hand drive cars in the UK.[559] The dispute arose as to the requirement of UK law that a person who wishes to register a vehicle for use on the UK roads, must present a certificate of conformity, unless he is importing the vehicle for personal use. That certificate of approval was awarded by the manufacturer of the vehicle or the holder of a primary minister's approval certificate. According to the CJEU, as a manufacturer, British Leyland benefitted from an 'administrative monopoly' in the ancillary to the sale of vehicles relevant market of services indispensable for dealers to be able to sell British Leyland's vehicles. The CJEU further found that British Leyland had abused this dominant position by refusing to issue certificates of conformity in order to impede re-importations to the UK from other Member States and thus protect its selective distribution network in the UK. The CJEU also found that the fees charged by British Leyland for the award of the certificates was 'excessive' as it was disproportionate to the economic value of the service.[560]

Similarly in *AAMS v Commission*, the General Court confirmed the Commission's decision finding that AAMS, an undertaking with a dominant position on the Italian market for the wholesale distribution of cigarettes, had abused its dominant position by imposing standard distribution agreements to certain cigarette manufacturers, under which the latter made AAMS responsible for the introduction and wholesale distribution on Italian territory of cigarettes which they manufactured in another Member State.[561] AAMS had also adopted unilateral actions limiting parallel trade in cigarettes.

Of particular interest for this line of cases on parallel trade is the judgment of the CJEU on a preliminary question from the Athens Appeal Court in *Sot. Lélos kai Sia EE and others v GlaxoSmithKline AEVE*.[562] GlaxoSmithKline Plc, a pharmaceutical research and

(iii) If the patentee complies with the scheme prior to starting a claim for infringement of that patent which includes a claim for an injunction, then bringing such a claim will not be abusive under Art 102. That is the *ratio* of the CJEU's decision.

(iv) In the circumstances contemplated by the CJEU, bringing a claim for infringement of a SEP which includes a claim for an injunction without prior notice of any kind will necessarily be an abuse of dominant position. Insofar as the decision identifies what is abusive rather than what is not, the decision does not go further than that.

(v) Bringing a claim for infringement which includes a claim for an injunction even with sufficient notice is capable of being an abuse of dominant position. However the judgment does not hold that if the circumstances diverge from the scheme set out in any way then a patentee will necessarily abuse their dominant position by starting such a claim. In those circumstances the patentee's conduct may or may not be abusive. The scheme sets out standard of behaviour against which both parties behaviour can be measured to decide in all the circumstances if an abuse has taken place.

(vi) Nor does it follow that if the patentee complies with the scheme such that bringing the action is not *per se* abusive, the patentee can behave with impunity after issue. Again, the scheme sets out standards of behaviour against which both parties' behaviour can be measured to decide if an abuse has taken place.

(vii) If the patentee does abuse its dominant position in bringing the claim or in its conduct after issue, that affords a defence to the claim for an injunction. In other words the proper remedy is likely to be refusal of an injunction even though a patent has been found to be valid and infringed and the implementer has no licence.

559 Case C-226/84, *British Leyland Public Limited Company v Commission* [1986] ECR 3263.

560 See Section 9.11.1 on excessive pricing.

561 Case T-139/98, *Amministrazione Autonoma dei Monopoli di Stato (AAMS) v Commission* [2001] ECR II-3413.

562 Joined Cases C-468–78/06, *Sot Lelos kai Sia EE and Others v GlaxoSmithKline AEVE Farmakeutikon Proionton* [2008] ECR I-7139.

manufacturing company established in the UK, distributed and warehoused its products in Greece through its subsidiary GSK AEVE (collectively referred to as GSK), which holds the parent company's marketing authorization for the products in Greece. The appellants in the main proceedings had for a number of years acquired these medicines in various forms as intermediary wholesalers in order to supply them both to the Greek and to other markets, particularly Germany and the United Kingdom (parallel exporters). Citing a shortage of the three medicinal products referred to above, for which it declined to take any responsibility, GSK changed its system of distribution in Greece at the end of October 2000. It stopped meeting the appellants' orders and supplied the products to hospitals and pharmacies through the company Farmacenter AE. Then in 2001, GSK reinstated normal supplies and resumed supplying the drugs to the wholesalers, albeit to a limited extent. The wholesalers attacked at the Greek competition authority arguing an infringement of Article 102 TFEU, which referred certain questions relating to the interpretation of Article 102 TFEU to the CJEU for a preliminary ruling. The Court's judgment did not address the substance of the dispute because it found that it had no jurisdiction to answer questions referred by a body which is not a court or tribunal.[563] Parallel proceedings involving the same parties were launched in front of Greek courts, the Athens Appeal Court deciding to ask the CJEU for a preliminary ruling on the issues raised by the case.

Joined Cases C-468–78/06, *Sot Lelos kai Sia EE and Others v GlaxoSmithKline AEVE Farmakeutikon Proionton*
[2008] ECR I–7139

33. Article [102 TFEU] prohibits any abuse by one or more undertakings of a dominant position within the common market or in a substantial part of it as incompatible with the common market in so far as it may affect trade between Member States. According to point (b) of the second paragraph of that article, such abuse may, in particular, consist in limiting production, markets or technical development to the prejudice of consumers.

34. The established case-law of the Court shows that the refusal by an undertaking occupying a dominant position on the market of a given product to meet the orders of an existing customer constitutes abuse of that dominant position under Article 82 EC where, without any objective justification, that conduct is liable to eliminate a trading party as a competitor (see, to that effect, Joined Cases 6/73 and 7/73 *Istituto Chemioterapico Italiano and Commercial Solvents* v *Commission* [1974] ECR 223, paragraph 25, and Case 27/76 *United Brands and United Brands Continentaal* v *Commission* [1978] ECR 207, paragraph 183).

35. With regard to a refusal by an undertaking to deliver its products in one Member State to wholesalers which export those products to other Member States, such an effect on competition may exist not only if the refusal impedes the activities of those wholesalers in that first Member State, but equally if it leads to the elimination of effective competition from them in the distribution of the products on the markets of the other Member States.

563 Case C-53/03, *Synetairismos Farmakopoion Aitolias & Akarnanias (Syfait) and Others v GlaxoSmithKline plc and GlaxoSmithKline AEVE* [2005] ECR I–4609.

36. [. . .] [I]t is common ground between the parties in the main proceedings that, by refusing to meet the Greek wholesalers' orders, GSK AEVE aims to limit parallel exports by those wholesalers to the markets of other Member States in which the selling prices of the medicinal products in dispute are higher.

37. In respect of sectors other than that of pharmaceutical products, the Court has held that a practice by which an undertaking in a dominant position aims to restrict parallel trade in the products that it puts on the market constitutes abuse of that dominant position. [. . .] Indeed, parallel imports enjoy a certain amount of protection in Community law because they encourage trade and help reinforce competition. [. . .]

39. In order to determine whether the refusal by a pharmaceuticals company to supply medicinal products to such wholesalers indeed falls within the prohibition laid down in Article 82 EC, in particular at point (b) of the second paragraph of that article, it must be examined whether, as GSK AEVE maintains, there are objective considerations based on which such a practice cannot be regarded as an abuse of the dominant position occupied by that undertaking (see, to that effect, *United Brands and United Brands Continentaal* v *Commission*, paragraph 184, and Case C95/04 P *British Airways* v *Commission* [2007] ECR I2331, paragraph 69).

GSK argued that a dominant undertaking is not under an obligation to honour orders that are out of the ordinary, citing United Brands and the possibility recognized to a dominant undertaking to take reasonable steps in order to protect its legitimate commercial interests. It also noted that pharmaceutical companies do not control the prices of their products, those prices being fixed at various levels by the public authorities, which 'prevents the manufacturers of medicines from developing their activities in normal competitive conditions'. In addition, the public authorities which fix the prices are at the same time buyers of the medicines wherever there are national health systems. Producers are also subject to precise obligations with regard to distribution as they are required by law to deliver their products in all Member States where they are authorized to do so. According to GSK, parallel trade has negative consequences for the planning of production and distribution of medicines, it reduces the profits that pharmaceutical companies can invest in research and development activities and finally does not provide any genuine benefit to the ultimate consumers since 'the greater part of the price difference which makes the business profitable is taken up by intermediaries'.[564] *Hence, parallel trade does not result in genuine pressure on the prices of medicines in the Member States where those prices are higher.*

49. It should be recalled that in paragraph 182 of its judgment in *United Brands and United Brands Continentaal* v *Commission* the Court held that an undertaking in a dominant position for the purpose of marketing a product—which cashes in on the reputation of a brand name known to and valued by consumers—cannot stop supplying a longstanding customer who abides by regular commercial practice, if the orders placed by that customer are in no way out of the ordinary. In paragraph 183 of the same judgment, the Court held that such conduct is inconsistent with the objectives laid down in [former Article 3(1)(g) EC, now Protocol no 27], which are set out in detail in Article [102 TFEU], particularly in points (b) and (c) of the second paragraph of that article, since the refusal to sell would limit the markets to the prejudice of consumers and would amount to discrimination which might in the end eliminate a trading party from the relevant market.

564 Joined Cases C-468–78/06, *Sot. Lélos kai Sia EE and Others v GlaxoSmithKline AEVE Farmakeftikon Proïonto* [2008] ECR I–7139, para 45.

50. In paragraph 189 of the judgment in *United Brands and United Brands Continentaal v Commission*, the Court stated that, although the fact that an undertaking is in a dominant position cannot deprive it of its right to protect its own commercial interests if they are attacked, and that such an undertaking must be conceded the right to take such reasonable steps as it deems appropriate to protect those interests, such behaviour cannot be accepted if its purpose is specifically to strengthen that dominant position and abuse it. [. . .]

The Court moved then to the analysis of the consequences of parallel trade for ultimate consumers.

[. . .]

53. In that connection, it should be noted that parallel exports of medicinal products from a Member State where the prices are low to other Member States in which the prices are higher open up in principle an alternative source of supply to buyers of the medicinal products in those latter States, which necessarily brings some benefits to the final consumer of those products. [. . .]

55. [. . .] [T]he attraction of the other source of supply which arises from parallel trade in the importing Member State lies precisely in the fact that that trade is capable of offering the same products on the market of that Member State at lower prices than those applied on the same market by the pharmaceuticals companies.

56. As a result, even in the Member States where the prices of medicines are subject to State regulation, parallel trade is liable to exert pressure on prices and, consequently, to create financial benefits not only for the social health insurance funds, but equally for the patients concerned, for whom the proportion of the price of medicines for which they are responsible will be lower. At the same time, as the Commission notes, parallel trade in medicines from one Member State to another is likely to increase the choice available to entities in the latter Member State which obtain supplies of medicines by means of a public procurement procedure, in which the parallel importers can offer medicines at lower prices. [. . .]

The CJEU then analysed the impact of State price and supply regulation in the pharmaceuticals sector.

61. [T]he control exercised by Member States over the selling prices or the reimbursement of medicinal products does not entirely remove the prices of those products from the law of supply and demand.

64 [. . .] [W]here a medicine is protected by a patent which confers a temporary monopoly on its holder, the price competition which may exist between a producer and its distributors, or between parallel traders and national distributors, is, until the expiry of that patent, the only form of competition which can be envisaged

65 In relation to the application of Article [101 TFEU], the Court has held that an agreement between producer and distributor which might tend to restore the national divisions in trade between Member States might be such as to frustrate the objective of the Treaty to achieve the integration of national markets through the establishment of a single market. Thus on a number of occasions the Court has held agreements aimed at partitioning national markets according to national borders or making the interpenetration of national markets more difficult, in particular those aimed at preventing or restricting parallel exports, to be agreements whose object is to restrict competition within the meaning of that Treaty article (see, for example, Joined Cases 96/82 to 102/82, 104/82, 105/82, 108/82 and 110/82 *IAZ International Belgium and Others v Commission* [1983] ECR 3369, paragraphs 23 to 27; Case C306/96 *Javico* [1998]

ECR I1983, paragraphs 13 and 14; and Case C551/03 P *General Motors* v *Commission* [2006] ECR I3173, paragraphs 67 to 69).

66. In the light of the abovementioned Treaty objective as well as that of ensuring that competition in the internal market is not distorted, there can be no escape from the prohibition laid down in Art. [102TFEU] for the practices of an undertaking in a dominant position which are aimed at avoiding all parallel exports from a Member State to other Member States, practices which, by partitioning the national markets, neutralise the benefits of effective competition in terms of the supply and the prices that those exports would obtain for final consumers in the other Member States.

67. Although the degree of price regulation in the pharmaceuticals sector cannot therefore preclude the Community rules on competition from applying, the fact none the less remains that, when assessing, in the case of Member States with a system of price regulation, whether the refusal of a pharmaceuticals company to supply medicines to wholesalers involved in parallel exports constitutes abuse, it cannot be ignored that such State intervention is one of the factors liable to create opportunities for parallel trade.

68. Furthermore, in the light of the Treaty objectives to protect consumers by means of undistorted competition and the integration of national markets, the Community rules on competition are also incapable of being interpreted in such a way that, in order to defend its own commercial interests, the only choice left for a pharmaceuticals company in a dominant position is not to place its medicines on the market at all in a Member State where the prices of those products are set at a relatively low level.

Is this a per se *prohibition rule? Not really . . .*

69. It follows that, even if the degree of regulation regarding the price of medicines cannot prevent any refusal by a pharmaceuticals company in a dominant position to meet orders sent to it by wholesalers involved in parallel exports from constituting an abuse, such a company must nevertheless be in a position to take steps that are reasonable and in proportion to the need to protect its own commercial interests.

70. [. . .] [I]t is necessary for pharmaceuticals companies to limit parallel exports in order to avoid the risk of a reduction in their investments in the research and development of medicines, it is sufficient to state that, in order to appraise whether the refusal by a pharmaceuticals company to supply wholesalers involved in parallel exports constitutes a reasonable and proportionate measure in relation to the threat that those exports represent to its legitimate commercial interests, it must be ascertained whether the orders of the wholesalers are out of the ordinary.

71. Thus, although a pharmaceuticals company in a dominant position, in a Member State where prices are relatively low, cannot be allowed to cease to honour the ordinary orders of an existing customer for the sole reason that that customer, in addition to supplying the market in that Member State, exports part of the quantities ordered to other Member States with higher prices, it is none the less permissible for that company to counter in a reasonable and proportionate way the threat to its own commercial interests potentially posed by the activities of an undertaking which wishes to be supplied in the first Member State with significant quantities of products that are essentially destined for parallel export.

72. In the present cases, the orders for reference show that, in the disputes which gave rise to those orders, the appellants in the main proceedings have demanded not that GSK AEVE should fulfil the orders sent to it in their entirety, but that it should deliver them quantities of medicines corresponding to the monthly average sold during the first 10 months of 2000. In 6 of the 11 actions in the main proceedings, the

appellants asked for those quantities to be increased by a certain percentage, which was fixed by some of them at 20%.

73. In those circumstances, it is for the referring court to ascertain whether the abovementioned orders are ordinary in the light of both the previous business relations between the pharmaceuticals company holding a dominant position and the wholesalers concerned and the size of the orders in relation to the requirements of the market in the Member State concerned.

74. Those considerations equally deal with the argument raised by GSK AEVE, namely the impact of State regulation on the supply of medicinal products, and more particularly the argument that undertakings that engage in parallel exports are not subject to the same obligations regarding distribution and warehousing as the pharmaceuticals companies and are therefore liable to disrupt the planning of production and distribution of medicines.

75. It is true that in Greece, as is apparent from paragraph 8 of this judgment, national legislation places pharmaceuticals wholesalers under an obligation to supply the needs of a defined geographical area with a range of pharmaceutical products. It is equally true that, in cases where parallel trade would effectively lead to a shortage of medicines on a given national market, it would not be for the undertakings holding a dominant position but for the national authorities to resolve the situation, by taking appropriate and proportionate steps [. . .].

76. However, a producer of pharmaceutical products must be in a position to protect its own commercial interests if it is confronted with orders that are out of the ordinary in terms of quantity. Such could be the case, in a given Member State, if certain wholesalers order from that producer medicines in quantities which are out of all proportion to those previously sold by the same wholesalers to meet the needs of the market in that Member State.

77. In view of the foregoing, the answer to the questions referred should be that Article [102 TFEU] must be interpreted as meaning that an undertaking occupying a dominant position on the relevant market for medicinal products which, in order to put a stop to parallel exports carried out by certain wholesalers from one Member State to other Member States, refuses to meet ordinary orders from those wholesalers is abusing its dominant position. It is for the national court to ascertain whether the orders are ordinary in the light of both the size of those orders in relation to the requirements of the market in the first Member State and the previous business relations between that undertaking and the wholesalers concerned.

NOTES AND QUESTIONS ON SOT LÉLOS

1. In his Opinion in the *Syfait* case, the preliminary reference from the Hellenic Competition Commission, on the same facts and parties, Advocate General Jacobs noted the following:[565]

89. [. . .] [I]t is also relevant to consider some of the economic factors affecting the commercial policy of pharmaceutical undertakings. Innovation is an important parameter of competition in the pharmaceuticals sector. Substantial investment is typically required in the research and development of a new pharmaceutical

[565] Opinion of AG Jacobs in Case C-53/03, *Synetairismos Farmakopoion Aitolias & Akarnanias (Syfait) and Others v GlaxoSmithKline plc and GlaxoSmithKline AEVE* [2005] ECR I-4609.

product. The production of a pharmaceutical product is usually characterised by high fixed costs (to research and develop the product) and comparatively low variable costs (to manufacture the product once developed). The decision whether to invest in developing a new pharmaceutical product will obviously depend in part upon whether the producer expects to be able to make sufficient profits to recoup the cost of investment. Once the investment is made, however, that cost is sunk. It is therefore rational for an undertaking to supply its products on any market where the price is fixed above variable cost. The mere fact that a product is marketed on a given market at a given price does not mean that a pharmaceuticals undertaking could recoup its total costs if that price were generalised across the whole of the Community. The issue could be tested if the national court were able to establish whether the price obtained by the dominant undertaking in a particular Member State did allow it to cover its fixed and variable costs and make a reasonable profit.

90. Those factors provide some insight into the possible consequences of prohibiting any restriction of supply by dominant pharmaceutical undertakings intended to limit parallel trade.

91. There would clearly be an incentive for such undertakings not to market products which might win for them a dominant position in Member States in which prices are fixed at a low level. As discussed above, the legal and moral obligations upon undertakings might render it difficult for them to withdraw products already marketed in those States. More credibly, they might delay the launch of new products in those States. The levels of output and consumer welfare generated by some pharmaceutical products would therefore fall within the Community.

92. Similarly, the regulatory negotiation of prices in low-price Member States would almost certainly become more difficult. There would be considerable pressure for prices to rise in those States if they were to be generalised, by process of parallel trade, across the Community. Such price rises as were agreed would again reduce output and consumer welfare in the States where they occurred. Moreover, they would effectively result in a redistribution of resources from consumers in the low-price Member States to those in the high-price Member States.

93. If low-price Member States were able to resist the pressure for price rises, and pharmaceuticals undertakings did not withdraw or delay products, the revenue generated by products in respect of which dominance was found would be cut. The incentive for a pharmaceutical undertaking to invest in research and development would to that extent be reduced, given the lower returns which such an undertaking could expect to enjoy during the period of its patent protection.

94. The Commission suggests that pharmaceutical undertakings have a choice as to whether to market a product at a given price, and if they choose to do so, it must be assumed that the price in question is commercially viable. As explained above, that conclusion in my view goes too far. An undertaking may agree to a price in one Member State, despite the limited opportunity which that price offers for the recoupment of the fixed costs associated with the development of a given pharmaceutical product, provided that variable production costs are met and that the price will not be generalised across the Community, eliminating the revenues generated in other Member States.

95. As a consequence, it is entirely conceivable that, if they cannot negotiate a price increase in low-price Member States, dominant pharmaceutical undertakings

would respond to an obligation to supply parallel traders within a given Member State by removing existing products from the market in that State, if they were able to do so, and by delaying the launch of new products there. Price differentials would be replaced by a greater fragmentation of the market, with a differing range of products available from State to State.

The Advocate General suggested to answer the question of the referring Greek competition authority as following: (i) '[a] pharmaceutical undertaking holding a dominant position does not necessarily abuse that position by refusing to meet in full the orders sent to it by pharmaceutical wholesalers only by reason of the fact that it aims thereby to limit parallel trade' and (ii) '[s]uch a refusal is capable of objective justification, and thus of not constituting an abuse, where the price differential giving rise to the parallel trade is the result of State intervention in the Member State of export to fix the price there at a level lower than that which prevails elsewhere in the Community, given the combined circumstances of the European pharmaceutical sector at the current stage of its development, and in particular

- the pervasive and diverse State intervention in the pricing of pharmaceutical products, which is responsible for price differentials between the Member States,
- the regulation by the Community and the Member States of the distribution of pharmaceutical products, which establishes nationally demarcated obligations upon pharmaceutical undertakings and wholesalers to ensure the availability of adequate stocks of those products,
- the potentially negative consequences of parallel trade for competition, the common market, and incentives to innovate, given the economic characteristics of the pharmaceutical industry,
- the fact that end consumers of pharmaceutical products may not in all cases benefit from parallel trade and that public authorities in the Member States, as the main purchasers of such products, cannot be assumed to benefit from lower prices, given that they are themselves responsible for fixing prices within their territories'.

Hence, the approach of AG Jacobs was favourable to pharmaceutical companies which, were not found to have abused their dominant position, even if there was evidence that they aimed to limit parallel trade (thus requiring from the plaintiff evidence of anti-competitive effects and consumer harm) and had this evidence being brought forward, pharmaceutical companies were still able to argue objective justifications, in particular the fact that the price differential was the result of State intervention in the pricing of pharmaceutical products. AG Jacob's Opinion was followed by the Hellenic Competition Commission in its decision on the merits of the case, finding that Article 102 TFEU was inapplicable due to State interventionism in the price-fixing of pharmaceuticals, the percentage by which the quantities supplied by the dominant undertaking exceeded national consumption, the effect of parallel trade on the profit of the dominant undertaking, the lack of any benefit for the end consumer entailed by parallel trade and the overall economic and regulatory context of the decision.[566]

566 Hellenic Competition Authority, *Synetairismoi Farmakopoion kai Farmakapothikes v Glaxo*, Decision 318/V/2006 (1 September 2006).

Compare the approach suggested by AG Jacobs in *Syfait* with that followed by the CJEU in *Sot Lélos*. Do you think that the CJEU has taken a more restrictive approach to dominant pharmaceutical companies than that promoted by AG Jacobs? Which of the two approaches seems more sensible to you?

2. The judgment is of particular interest for the question of the existence of an object/effect restriction of competition in the context of Article 102 TFEU and more generally the existence of *per se* prohibitions in the context of Article 102, in the absence of an equivalent to Article 101(3) TFEU. Advocate General Colomer cited, in his Opinion two reasons that explain why there should not be a *per se* prohibition in Article 102 TFEU. First, the absence of an exception provision, such as Article 101(3) TFEU, indicates that the analysis of abusive behaviour always requires a 'dialectical debate' between the dominant undertaking and the competent authorities, whether national or EU, as well as interested parties. According to AG Colomer, if certain types of practice were to give rise to an irrebuttable presumption of abuse, dominant firms would be denied the right of defence. Article 102(a)–(d) does not contain examples of *per se* abuses. The examples of abuses that are cited constitute presumptions *iuris tantum* in order to shift the burden of proof from the claimant to the defendant. Further, the institution of *per se* abuses would be contrary to the need to decide each case on the basis of its economic and legal context. A *per se* approach would commit the sin of excessive formalism. AG Colomer also noted that although there are two different types of abuses—those that affect consumers (exploitative abuses) and those that affect actual or potential competitors (exclusionary abuses)—there is no hierarchy between these two categories. Dominant firms should be able to defend themselves on the basis of economic results obtained. According to the AG, a balancing test will determine the existence of positive and negative effects to competition for the consumers and other economic operators that are situated 'in the same relevant market'. Consequently, AG Colomer suggested that the Court declare without ambiguity that Article 102 TFEU does not apply before examining the existence of positive effects/defences, even if it is clear that the facts of the case do not leave any doubt as to the anti-competitive intent of the parties. This is a particularly strong statement, which denies the existence of a *per se* prohibition rule in Article 102 TFEU. AG Colomer nevertheless distinguished between different categories of conduct, some of them being so grossly anti-competitive that they may justify a different allocation of the burden of proof (for example, if there is a restriction of parallel imports, the burden of proof may shift to the defendant). Other practices will require from the claimant a more complete substantiation of anti-competitive effects before moving to the next step of the analysis, the examination of possible defences. Has the CJEU followed AG Colomer in any of his suggestions?

3. (Paragraph 49) Why does the CJEU cite the *United Brands* case law? Is it a refusal to deliver to an existing or a new customer?

4. Could one consider in this case that there was intention to limit parallel trade? Was partitioning the market the primary objective of the patent holder, or the consequence of Member States' pricing rules? Should the existence of intent be relevant?

5. (Paragraphs 53, 55–6) How did the CJEU link the benefit of the ultimate (final) consumers with the protection of the Internal Market objective and market integration?

The Court noted that parallel exports of medicinal products from a Member State where the prices are low to other Member States in which the prices are higher 'open up in principle an alternative source of supply to buyers of the medicinal products in those latter States, which *necessarily* brings some benefits to the final consumer of those products'.[567] It further specified the nature of that consumer benefit by observing that 'the attraction of the other source of supply which arises from parallel trade in the importing Member State lies precisely in the fact that that trade is capable of offering the same products on the market of that Member State at *lower prices* than those applied on the same market by the pharmaceuticals companies' and '[a]t the same time [. . .] parallel trade in medicines from one Member State to another is likely to *increase the choice* available to entities in the latter Member State'.[568]

6. (Paragraphs 61, 64–8) Had the CJEU adequately considered State intervention in fixing the price of pharmaceuticals in the design of the appropriate legal standard in this case? Is parallel trade is the only way the governments of the Member States with high prices to reduce the price of prescription medicines? Ian Forrester and Anthony Dawes note that States may impose unilateral profit reductions on all prescription medicines delivered by pharmaceutical, or may adopt 'claw back' regulations in order to recover part of the windfall profits earned by pharmacies and wholesalers via parallel trade.[569] Is this an adequate solution to the problem, or will this increase regulatory divergence among Member States? How relevant should it be that Greece had set the prices at the lowest level in the EU? How is it possible to determine a 'reasonable' level of profit of pharmaceutical companies so that future consumers are not harmed by the lack of Research and Development and innovation, due to the lack of investment?
7. Are we certain that the additional profits earned by the pharmaceutical companies will be used for Research and Development? Marianna Mazzucato notes that a significant part of the profits of the pharmaceutical companies are not invested in R&D but in stock repurchase programmes which increase ownership and earnings per share, and thus boost the CEO's and other company executives' pay and cash to shareholders.[570] Who should have the burden to prove that lower profits might affect R&D? The competition authority/plaintiff or the dominant undertaking? How did the CJEU deal with this issue in the context of Article 102 TFEU?
8. (Paragraphs 70–7) How is it possible to ascertain that the orders of the wholesalers are 'out of the ordinary'? Should one rely on information on past consumer demand in the specific relevant market? What if this is a new pharmaceutical product? Would that require determining the past demand from the specific wholesaler to whom the pharmaceutical company refuses to deliver or imposes a quota? What if this is a refusal to deliver or a quota to a new customer?

567 Joined Cases C-468–78/06, *Sot Lélos kai Sia EE and Others v GlaxoSmithKline AEVE Farmakeftikon Proïonto* [2008] ECR I-7139, para 53 (emphasis added).

568 Ibid, para 56.

569 I Forrester and A Dawes, 'Parallel Trade in Prescription Medicines in the European Union: The Age of Reason?' (2008) 1 *Yearbook of Antitrust and Regulatory Studies* 9, 11–12.

570 M Mazzucato, *The Entrepreneurial State* (Anthem Press, 2013), ch 3.

9.10.2. NATIONALITY-BASED OR GEOGRAPHIC PRICE DISCRIMINATION

The objective of market integration also leads EU competition law to find nationality-based price discrimination or certain forms of geographical price discrimination to be incompatible with Article 102(c) TFEU, prohibiting a dominant undertaking from 'applying dissimilar conditions to equivalent transactions with other trading parties, thereby placing them at a competitive disadvantage'.

Discriminations based on nationality are a no-brainer for EU law and explicitly prohibited by Article 18 TFEU. The prohibition covers both direct discrimination on nationality or indirect discrimination, on the basis of suspicious criteria, such as domicile or the place of establishment. For instance, in *GVL*, the CJEU found that a refusal by a dominant undertaking, in this case a collecting society having a *de facto* monopoly in Germany, to provide services based on the nationality or the residence of the client constituted an abuse of a dominant position.[571] Indeed, according to the CJEU, the collecting society in question conducted its activities in such a way that any foreign artist who was not resident in Germany was not in a position to benefit from rights of secondary exploitation, even if he could show that he held such rights either because German law was applicable or because the law of some other State recognized the same rights.

Geographic price discrimination may result from the situation of a dominant undertaking charging different prices in different Member States. This case law is nevertheless less clear than nationality-based direct or indirect discrimination, as in all cases involving geographic price discrimination in the context of Article 102 TFEU, there was conduct that supported the market-partitioning effect of price discrimination. Hence, it was not price discrimination *per se* that was found anti-competitive.

Case C-27/76, *United Brands v Commission*
[1978] ECR 207

In addition to restricting its distributors from reselling its bananas while still green, thus limiting the opportunities of trade between Member States (as the opportunities of reselling ripe bananas are limited to a specific period of time) and to refusing to supply Danish distributor Olesen as a sanction to its participation in a Dole (a rival brand) advertising campaign, United Brands had also charged differential prices to distributors in different Member States. UBC generally delivered the bananas to distributors in Rotterdam and Bremerhaven, where unloading costs only differ by a few cents and were resold, with some exceptions, subject to the same conditions of sale and terms of payment after they have been loaded on the buyers' wagons or lorries in these ports. Hence, the CJEU found that there were equivalent transactions and explored whether the policy of charging differing prices according to the Member States for which the bananas were intended was prohibited by Article 102(c). According to the CJEU, the greatest difference in price was 138 per cent between the delivered Rotterdam price charged by UBC to its customers in Ireland and the freight on road (f.o.r.) Bremerhaven price charged by UBC to its customers in Denmark, that is to say the price paid by Danish customers was 2.38 times the price paid by Irish customers. UBC argued that its prices were determined by market forces and thus could not therefore be discriminatory, the prices being calculated so as to reflect as much

[571] Case C-7/82, *Gesellschaft zur Verwertung von Leistungsschutzrechten mbH (GVL) v Commission* [1983] ECR 483.

as possible the anticipated yellow market price (the average anticipated final market price) in the following week for each national market, and after discussions with the ripeners/distributors, taking into account the different competitive context in which they were operating in each country. Price differences were also due to fluctuating market factors such as the weather, different availability of seasonal competing fruit, holidays, strikes, Government measures, and currency denominations. Indeed, UBC argued that as long as the EU institutions have not set up the machinery for a single banana market and the various markets remain national and respond to their individual supply/demand situations differences in prices between them cannot be prevented. The CJEU addressed UBC's arguments as following:

225. [. . .] [T]he bananas sold by UBC are all freighted in the same ships, are unloaded at the same cost in Rotterdam or Bremerhaven and the price differences relate to substantially similar quantities of bananas of the same variety, which have been brought to the same degree of ripening, are of similar quality and sold under the same 'Chiquita' brand name under the same conditions of sale and payment for loading on to the purchaser's own means of transport and the latter have to pay customs duties, taxes and transport costs from these ports. [. . .]

227. Although the responsibility for establishing the single banana market does not lie with the applicant, it can only endeavour to take 'what the market can bear' provided that it complies with the rules for the regulation and coordination of the market laid down by the Treaty.

228. Once it can be grasped that differences in transport costs, taxation, customs duties, the wages of the labour force, the conditions of marketing, the differences in the parity of currencies, the density of competition may eventually culminate in different retail selling price levels according to the Member States, then it follows those differences are factors which UBC only has to take into account to a limited extent since it sells a product which is always the same and at the same place to ripener/distributors who—alone—bear the risks of the consumers' market.

229. The interplay of supply and demand should, owing to its nature, only be applied to each stage where it is really manifest.

230. The mechanisms of the market are adversely affected if the price is calculated by leaving out one stage of the market and taking into account the law of supply and demand as between the vendor and the ultimate consumer and not as between the vendor (UBC) and the purchaser (the ripener/distributors).

231. Thus, by reason of its dominant position UBC, fed with information by its local representatives, was in fact able to impose its selling price on the intermediate purchaser. This price and also the 'weekly quota allocated' is only fixed and notified to the customer four days before the vessel carrying the bananas berths.

232. These discriminatory prices, which varied according to the circumstances of the Member States, were just so many obstacles to the free movement of goods and their effect was intensified by the clause forbidding the resale of bananas while still green and by reducing the deliveries of the quantities ordered.

233. A rigid partitioning of national markets was thus created at price levels, which were artificially different, placing certain distributor/ripeners at a competitive disadvantage, since compared with what it should have been competition had thereby been distorted.

234. Consequently the policy of differing prices enabling UBC to apply dissimilar conditions to equivalent transactions with other trading parties, thereby placing them at a competitive disadvantage, was an abuse of a dominant position.

NOTES AND QUESTIONS ON UNITED BRANDS

1. (Paragraphs 229–31) The CJEU emphasizes the importance of competition for each stage between the vendor and the ultimate consumer. Hence, it is not possible to 'leave out one stage of the market', here the retail level. Hence, discrimination was at a level of trade before the final customer, but based on what final customers would pay. What is the benefit of competition at the retail level if the dominant supplier takes into account the 'law of supply and demand' between him and the final consumer? Is it that we do not trust a dominant supplier to take into account the interplay of supply and demand directly? What if this dominant supplier decided to vertically integrate at the retail level? Should discrimination at the retail level be treated differently? (See Question 3 below on *Tetra Pak II.*)
2. (Paragraphs 232–3) The CJEU notes that the effect of the price discrimination was to establish obstacles to the free movement of goods. Yet, it also observes that their effect was 'intensified' by the other two clauses: the prohibition of resale of green bananas and the reduction of the deliveries of the quantities ordered. The result of the combination of these clauses was a 'rigid partitioning of national markets'. Do you think the CJEU should have reached the same conclusion, if charging different prices was not supported by other clauses, with the result that that its effect on market integration might have been less pronounced? Actually, simple price discrimination, without further clauses partitioning markets, would have led to an increase of trade in goods, as arbitrageurs often take advantage of price differences among Member States.
3. Of particular interest is also the judgment of the General Court in *Tetra Pak II.*[572] Among the different practices examined in this case, it was found by the Commission that Tetra Pak's prices for cartons and machines displayed a 'wide disparity' among Member States. Tetra Pak argued that the wide differences were not discriminatory as there is some correlation between machine and carton prices, linked to competition on the local market, so that the decisive factor is the cost of the system as a whole, this equilibrium between carton and machine prices varying from one Member State to another. The price divergences were, according to Tetra Pak, due to a complex interaction of historical factors, local market conditions which varied considerably from one State to the other, dairy industry structures, local cost considerations and Tetra Pak's policy of allowing maximum autonomy to its local subsidiaries. In contrast, he Commission argued that the differences observed were too great to be explained by the objective material differences between the products. The GC rejected the Tetra's argument that each product should have been examined separately, and remarked that, in any case, the price differences would have still been significant if the whole system of machine and cartons were considered, instead. The average price differences were found to be substantial, from 20 to as much 70 per cent. The GC proceeded to examine if the price differences found could not be justified by objective economic factors. The GC concluded the following: 'the appreciable differences found in the prices of machines and cartons occurred in the context of a partitioning of national markets by the tied-sale clauses in the contracts, reinforced by Tetra Pak's autonomous production and distribution system and by the group's quasi-monopoly on the aseptic markets in

572 Case T-83/91, *Tetra Pak II* [1994] ECR II-755, paras 153–73.

the Community. In those circumstances, it is clear that those price differences could not be due to normal competitive forces [. . .].' The GC also refuted the specificity of the conditions on local markets, in view of the definition of a single geographical market encompassing the entire EU, by virtue in particular of the marginal nature of transport costs. The conclusion of the GC was reinforced by the finding that Tetra Pak had an overall strategy of partitioning markets. Such a strategy was inferred from the policies implemented by Tetra Pak, in particular as to the contracts, throughout the EU and shown by direct documentary evidence produced by the Commission with regard to the communication between the Tetra Pak group and its subsidiary, Tetra Pak Italiana. The General Court confirmed the finding of the Commission as to the existence of discriminatory pricing contrary to Article 102(c). The CJEU judgment on appeal did not discuss discriminatory pricing. It is noteworthy that price discrimination was not considered on its own as constituting an abuse but in conjunction with a number of other practices adopted by Tetra Pak.

9.11. EXPLOITATIVE PRICES

9.11.1. EXCESSIVE PRICES OR UNFAIRLY LOW PRICES

Excessive prices (royalties) may be found to infringe Article 102(a) TFEU which may apply to purely exploitative conduct (exploiting consumers directly without any requirement to prove any exclusionary conduct), in particular conduct that is 'directly or indirectly imposing unfair purchase or selling prices or other unfair trading conditions'. This provision has been considered as one of the most intriguing features of EU competition law. The economic rationales for the excessive pricing abuse follow from the finding that monopoly engenders social costs, of which higher prices and the reduction of allocative that follows is a noticeable example.[573] However, some authors have also emphasized the historical underpinnings of this prohibition.

M Gal, 'Abuse of Dominance: Exploitative Abuses' in I Lianos and D Geradin (eds) *Handbook on European Competition Law: Substantive Aspects* (Edward Elgar, 2013) 385, 422–4 (footnotes omitted)

The EU rule against excessive pricing is based on fairness, as indicated in the language of the law. The question to be asked is unfair in what sense and to whom. To answer this question one must focus on conceptions of fairness and how they apply to monopoly pricing. Fairness is not a single-valued concept. Rather, it is a flexible one that can incorporate different meanings, depending on the ideology and the goals that are sought to be achieved. Fairness ties into deep notions of morality and justice, often stemming from different religious, sociological and political concepts of how societal interactions should be conducted. For example, fairness can relate to distributive justice. Alternatively, it might ensure a level playing field. Fairness is thus derived from the perceived rules of the market game and may vary among

[573] See Chapter 3. For an excellent law and economics analysis of excessive and unfair pricing see, P Davis and V Mani, 'The Law and Economics of Excessive and Unfair Pricing: A Review and a Proposal', 2018 63(4) *The Antitrust Bulletin* 399.

cultures and time periods. It is part of one's jurisculture. The question is on what grounds excessive pricing breaches notions of fairness. [. . .]

An important source of influence is the German Ordoliberal concept of economic constitution. [. . .]

Yet the notion that a high price might be unfair is not a 20th century invention. Rather, it has long historical and ideological roots. Aristotle's theory of justice in exchange established that to maintain stability and avoid uncontrolled re-distribution of wealth in society, the transacting parties are to exchange goods of equal value. A relation between price and value also appears in the Roman Digest. An edict of Emperor Diocletian establishes the principle known as *laesio enormis*, according to which if land is 'sold for less than its value', the purchaser 'should pay you what is lacking of the just price [. . .]. A price is considered too little if one half of the true value is not paid.' The rule's importance stems from assuming that there is an objective just price, which is not necessarily equal to the price agreed upon by the parties, which is based on the market price of the land. The principle of *laesio* remained in force as a legal norm throughout the middle ages, and was extended to include additional goods and services.

During medieval times the concepts of 'usury' and 'just price' emerged. The prohibition against usury was based on the biblical prohibition not to take biting interest from the defenseless poor. It applied to situations in which the parties did not have equal bargaining power and one side exploited the need, carelessness or inexperience of another, in order to gain a pecuniary advantage which disproportionately exceeded the value of the performance granted in return. Usury was perceived as dishonest conduct, and therefore intrinsically unlawful. It limited the ability to achieve private gain based on exploiting the economic weaknesses of others.

The doctrine of just price was based on exploitation of market conditions, which was labeled morally wrong and abhorrent to the religious tenets of society. The concept of just price was developed into a comprehensive theory in the middle ages, mainly through the works of the scholastics. The scholastics' idea of a just price was not of a fixed benchmark. Rather, they identified it with the ongoing market price, set by the free interplay of supply and demand. Having the just price determined by the common market price meant that a seller was not allowed to take advantage of an individual buyer's dire need, carelessness or inexperience. In the absence of a system of supply and demand curves, the market price was the result of a common estimation, taking into account factors such as need, scarcity and costs of production. These concepts were partly incorporated into the Corpus Juris Civilis which served as a basis for law and legal education throughout much of Europe from the 11th century until well into the 19th century. They helped set the stage for the modern prohibition of unfair monopoly prices. It is noteworthy, however, that past prohibitions did not apply specifically to monopolists. [. . .]

Several additional motivations for prohibiting excessive pricing may be relevant. The signatories of the Treaty recognized that the emerging common market needed companies of bigger size than those prevailing, to achieve optimal scales once barriers to trade between Member States were reduced. Yet they were less confident than their U.S. counterparts that high prices will attract sufficient entrants to lead to lower prices. Accordingly, price regulation was seen as necessary to protect customers until competition develops more fully. This need was strengthened by the fact that the Treaty did not directly apply to the acquisition of a dominant position by way of internal expansion, thereby justifying a stricter policy towards the consequences of market power, once achieved. In addition, the rampant inflation after World War II experienced by many European countries naturally led to a strong interest in an economic policy that ensured lower prices. The fact that many dominant firms were created, controlled or protected by national governments might also have played a role, as such monopolies were not likely to be eliminated by market forces.

But more fundamentally, we should attempt to understand the prohibition in light of the basic aim of the EU, to open markets all across the Community and create a common market. The driving paradigm behind the Treaty was the substitution of age-old rivalries with the merging of essential interests, to create a basis for a broader and deeper understanding among Members. Accordingly, the Treaty sought to achieve not only economic efficiency and a free market economy, but also broader social and political goals, most notably the creation of a single, integrated European market. The prohibition should thus be explored in light of these goals.

In *United Brands*, the Court of Justice held that a price may be found excessive if it has no reasonable relation to the economic value of the product supplied.[574] According to the Court, this excess could, *inter alia*, be determined objectively if it were possible for it to be calculated by making a comparison between the selling price of the product in question and its cost of production, which would disclose the amount of the profit margin.[575] A two-step analysis is carried out: it has to be determined 'whether the difference between the costs actually incurred and the price actually charged is excessive, and, if the answer to this question is in the affirmative, whether a price has been imposed which is either unfair in itself or when compared to competing products'.[576] These two conditions (steps) are cumulative. Evidence of an excessive profit margin is not sufficient in itself to prove an abuse. The EU competition authorities employ a cost–price approach in order to determine the excessive character of a profit margin.

Case C-27/76, *United Brands v Commission*
[1978] ECR 207

UBC was the largest seller of bananas in the world through its well known Chiquita brands. According to the Commission, UBC had abused its dominant position by charging its customers in various Member States of the EU unfair prices, which in the circumstances it considered are excessive in relation to the economic value of the product supplied. For instance, the prices in Germany were sometimes 100 per cent higher than the prices charged to customers in Ireland and produced for UCB a substantial and excessive profit in relation to the economic value of the product supplied. There was also a 20–40 per cent difference between the price of Chiquita and unbranded bananas, although the Commission also recognized that the quality of unbranded was lower than that of labelled bananas. The Commission advanced that UBC should proceed to a reduction of its price levels to prices at least 15 per cent below the prices it charged its customers in the relevant market, except in Ireland. UBC argued that the difference in the price of branded and unlabelled bananas was justified, because the precautions taken between cutting and sale to the consumer fully explained the price differential, there were genuine differences between UBC bananas and other branded bananas which explained the price difference of 7.4 per cent and prices also changed every week so the 15 per cent reduction would have been quite difficult to achieve.

248. The imposition by an undertaking in a dominant position directly or indirectly of unfair purchase or selling prices is an abuse to which exception can be taken under Article [102 TFEU].

574 Case C-27/76, *United Brands v Commission* [1978] ECR 207.
575 Ibid, para 251.
576 Ibid, para 252.

249. It is advisable therefore to ascertain whether the dominant undertaking has made use of the opportunities arising out of its dominant position in such a way as to reap trading benefits which it would not have reaped if there had been normal and sufficiently effective competition.

250. In this case charging a price which is excessive because it has no reasonable relation to the economic value of the product supplied would be such an abuse.

251. This excess could, *inter alia*, be determined objectively if it were possible for it to be calculated by making a comparison between the selling price of the product in question and its cost of production, which would disclose the amount of the profit margin; however the Commission has not done this since it has not analysed UBC's costs structure.

252. The questions therefore to be determined are whether the difference between the costs actually incurred and the price actually charged is excessive, and, it the answer to this question is in the affirmative, whether a price has been imposed which is either unfair in itself or when compared to competing products.

253. Other ways may be devised—and economic theorists have not failed to think up several—of selecting the rules for determining whether the price of a product is unfair.

254. While appreciating the considerable and at times very great difficulties in working out production costs which may sometimes include a discretionary apportionment of indirect costs and general expenditure and which may vary significantly according to the size of the undertaking, its object, the complex nature of its set up, its territorial area of operations, whether it manufactures one or several products, the number of its subsidiaries and their relationship with each other, the production costs of the banana do not seem to present any insuperable problems.

256. The Commission was at least under a duty to require UBC to produce particulars of all the constituent elements of its production costs.

257. The accuracy of the contents of the documents produced by UBC could have been challenged but that would have been a question of proof.

258. The Commission bases its view that prices are excessive on an analysis of the differences—in its view excessive—between the prices charged in the different Member States and on the policy of discriminatory prices which has been considered above. [. . .]

UBC counter-argued that the prices were such that it had not made a profit for the past five years, although the CJEU also noted that no specific accounting documents provided evidence to support this allegation.

264. However unreliable the particulars supplied by UBC may be [. . .], the fact remains that it is for the Commission to prove that the applicant charged unfair prices.

265. UBC's retractation, which the Commission has not effectively refuted, establishes beyond doubt that the basis for the calculation adopted by the latter to prove that UBC's prices are excessive is open to criticism and on this particular point there is doubt which must benefit the applicant, especially as for nearly 20 years banana prices, in real terms, have not risen on the relevant market.

266. Although it is also true that the price of Chiquita bananas and those of its principal competitors is different, that difference is about 7%, a percentage which has not been challenged and which cannot automatically be regarded as excessive and consequently unfair.

267. In these circumstances it appears that the Commission has not adduced adequate legal proof of the facts and evaluations which formed the foundation of its finding that UBC had infringed Article [102 TFEU] by directly and indirectly imposing unfair selling prices for bananas.

With regard to the measurement of the 'excessive' nature of the prices, a possible option is to determine an adequate cost measure to measure profit (adopt a cost-plus approach), compare that to the price and then to assess the excessiveness of the profit margin, the last operation involving the definition of some benchmarks. However, the definition of the relevant costs becomes a daunting task in the context of IP rights related conduct, as developing new technology involves R&D expenses, thus high fixed costs, which it would be difficult to assess, as firms engage in multiple projects and intense cross-subsidization between successful and unsuccessful projects. Common costs used for the development and production of different technologies (particularly in situations of cumulative innovation), makes the operation even harder.[577]

In *Scandlines*, the Commission rejected a cost-plus approach (add to marginal cost a reasonable profit calculated as a percentage of a production cost) for an approach that would look to whether the price had a reasonable relation to the economic value of the service supplied and would integrate additional costs (eg sunk costs, opportunity costs) and factors not reflected in the audited profits and costs (eg intangible value of the assets).[578] How much profit margin will be deemed excessive is another important issue. In *United Brands*, the Court held that a profit margin of 7 per cent is not sufficient.[579] Some profit margin would also be entirely justified in dynamic industries or industries with network effects.

As to the adequate benchmark prices that would define the 'unfair' character of the prices charged, a comparison with the prices charged by competitors might be a possible option (although one should be cautious, as price differences may indicate quality differences). In *United Brands* the Court noted that 'other ways may be devised—and economic theorists have not failed to think up several—of selecting the rules for determining whether the price of a product is unfair'.[580] Other options include the comparison with the price of the product over different geographic markets.[581]

Joined Cases C-395/87 & 110, 241–2/88, *Ministère Public v Jean Louis Tournier, François Lucazeau and Others v Société des Auteurs, Compositeurs et Editeurs de Musique Jean Verney (SACEM)*
[1989] ECR 2565

SACEM is a French copyright-collecting society to which most French copyright holders have assigned their right to exploit their performing rights. Discotheques complained that SACEM was charging too much for licences.

577 See the analysis in the companion volume, I Lianos, *Competition Law and the Intangible Economy* (OUP, forthcoming 2019).

578 *Scandlines Sverige AB v Port of Helsingborg* (Case COMP/A-36.568/D3) Commission Decision (23 July 2004), paras 209, 224, 226–7, 234–5, available at http://ec.europa.eu/competition/antitrust/cases/dec_docs/36568/36568_44_4.pdf. See also, in an IP context, *Attheraces Limited v The British Horseracing Board Limited* [2007] EWCA Civ 38, where the Court of Appeal held that the High Court had been wrong to regard the 'economic value' of the pre-race data as limited to the product of the cost and formula.

579 Case C-27/76, *United Brands v Commission* [1978] ECR 207, para 266.

580 Ibid, para 253.

581 Ibid, para 239; Case C-395/87, *Ministère Public v Tournier* [1989] ECR 2521; Case C-110/88, *Lucazeau v SACEM* [1989] ECR 2811, the last two cases concerning the level of royalties charged by the French collecting society SACEM for playing recorded music in discotheques (acknowledging that important price differentials between Member States could indicate an abuse, unless the undertaking justifies the difference by reference to objective dissimilarities between the situation in the Member State concerned and the situation prevailing in all the other Member States).

34. It must be observed at the outset that by virtue of the very terms of Article [102 TFEU], the imposition of any unfair trading conditions by an undertaking holding a dominant position constitutes an abuse of that position. [. . .]

38. When an undertaking holding a dominant position imposes scales of fees for its services which are appreciably higher than those charged in other Member States and where a comparison of the fee levels has been made on a consistent basis, that difference must be regarded as indicative of an abuse of a dominant position. In such a case it is for the undertaking in question to justify the difference by reference to objective dissimilarities between the situation in the Member State concerned and the situation prevailing in all the other Member States.

39. SACEM has claimed that certain circumstances justify that difference. It referred to the high prices charged by discotheques in France, the traditionally high level of protection provided by copyright in France, and the peculiar features of French legislation whereby the playing of recorded musical works is subject not only to a performing right but also to a supplementary mechanical reproduction fee.

40. Circumstances of that kind cannot account for a very appreciable difference between the rates of royalty charged in the various Member States. The high level of prices charged by discotheques in a particular Member State, even if substantiated, may be the result of several factors, one of which might, in turn, be the high level of royalties payable for the use of recorded music. As regards the level of protection provided by national legislation, it must be noted that copyright in musical works includes in general a performing right and a reproduction right, and the fact that a 'supplementary reproduction fee' is payable in some Member States including France, in the event of public dissemination does not imply that the level of protection is different. As the Court held in its judgment in Case 402/85 *Basset v Sacem* [1987] ECR 1747, the supplementary reproduction fee may be seen, disregarding the concepts used by French legislation and practice, as constituting part of the payment for an author's rights over the public performance of a recorded musical work and therefore fulfills a function equivalent to that of the performing right charged on the same occasion in another Member State.

41. SACEM also contends that the customary methods of collection are different, in that certain copyright-management societies in the Member States tend not to insist on collecting royalties of small amounts for small users spread over the country, such as discotheque operators, dance organisers and cafe proprietors. The opposite tradition has developed in France, in view of the wish of authors to have their rights fully observed.

42. That argument cannot be accepted. It is apparent from the documents before the Court that one of the most marked differences between the copyright-management societies in the various Member States lies in the level of operating expenses. Where—as appears to be the case here, according to the record of the proceedings before the national court—the staff of a management society is much larger than that of its counterparts in other Member States and, moreover, the proportion of receipts taken up by collection, administration and distribution expenses rather than by payments to copyright holders is considerably higher, the possibility cannot be ruled out that it is precisely the lack of competition on the market in question that accounts for the heavy burden of administration and hence the high level of royalties.

43. It must therefore be concluded that a comparison with the situation in other Member States may provide useful indications regarding the possible abuse of a dominant position by a national copyright-management society. Accordingly, the answer to the third question must be in the affirmative.

NOTES AND QUESTIONS ON THE JUDGMENT IN SACEM

1. In *United Brands*, the Court referred to the test of cost-plus. Why is this unsatisfactory in this case?
2. In *BEMIM v Commission*,[582] the General Court accepted the Commission's decision not to pursue SACEM's unfair pricing policy further than to require a report making international comparisons between the charges of the different copyright collecting societies on the ground of lack of Community interest in a problem that was centred in France. The French Conseil de la Concurrence then condemned the charges as excessive.[583]
3. (Paragraphs 38–43) What are the different tests of unfair prices that may apply? Were any of these applicable in the SACEM litigation?
4. In *Kanal 5*, the remuneration model applied by the Swedish Copyright Management Organization (STIM), relating to the broadcast of musical works protected by copyright, which calculated the amount of royalties on the basis of the revenue of companies broadcasting those works and the amount of music broadcast, was found to be an abuse for the simple reason that another method would have enabled the use of those musical works and the audience to be identified and quantified more precisely.[584]

Case C-177/16, *AKKA/LAA v Konkurences padome (Latvian copyright)*, ECLI:EU:C:2017:689 (some references omitted)

This case resulted from a series of appeals relating to a decision that the Latvian Competition Council (LCC) took over conduct of the Consulting Agency on Copyright and Communications (AKKA)/Latvian Authors' Association (LAA), the Latvian collective management organization handling copyright licences for (Latvian and foreign) musical works in Latvia. The 2013 infringement decision found that the AKKA/LAA had abused its dominant position by imposing excessive music licence fees for music played in Latvian retailers and service providers. The Latvian Supreme Court referred a number of questions to the CJEU regarding the concept of excessive pricing, the CJEU giving useful guidance on the concept of what is an appropriate and sufficient comparator, the threshold of an excessive price ('appreciability') and how excessive prices can be still justified.

Question relating to the comparison between the prices (rates) in the market in question and the prices (rates) in neighbouring markets and the methodologies used.

In his Opinion, AG Wahl highlighted the variety of different methods that could be used in order to determine whether a price is excessive, concluding that that the proper approach is to 'combine

582 Case T-114/92, *Bureau Européen des Médias de l' Industrie Musicale (BEMIM) v Commission* [1995] ECR II-188.

583 Conseil de la concurrence, Avis 93-A-05 (20 April 1993).

584 Case C-52/07, *Kanal 5 Ltd and TV 4 AB v Föreningen Svedska Tonsättares Internationella Musikbyrå (STIM) UPA* [2009] ECR I-9275.

several methods' where possible, so as to avoid errors.[585] *Should only one of these methods of determining the benchmark price be available or suitable, AG Wahl suggested 'consider[ing] other indicators which may corroborate or, conversely, cast doubt on the result of that method',*[586] *such as the presence of high barriers to entry or expansion (the AG being 'convinced that unfair prices under Article 102 TFEU can only exist in regulated markets, where the public authorities exert some form of control over the forces of supply and, consequently, the scope for free and open competition is reduced'),*[587] *the presence of a sectoral regulation (antitrust intervention being 'mainly confined to cases of error or, more generally, to regulatory failures'),*[588] *or the presence of powerful buyers. Referring to the presumption of innocence,*[589] *AG Wahl considered that an abuse can be established where there is a 'sufficiently complete and reliable set of elements which point in one and the same direction',*[590] *such that 'almost no doubt remains' as to the abusive nature of the conduct.*[591] *This is a very high standard of proof. It is not clear if this is based on a serious economic analysis of the effects of this type of abuse, or mainly ideology.*

The CJEU did not follow the AG's recommendations and re-affirmed the validity of the United Brands *approach, without requiring that any other methods be combined to alleviate any doubt.*[592] *Note also that the CJEU found that there was no minimum threshold above which a rate must be regarded as 'appreciably higher' for the cross-market price comparison for Article 102 TFEU to apply, thus relaxing the standards for the finding of abusive pricing.*[593]

> 38. [. . .] [A]ccording to the case-law of the Court, a method based on a comparison of prices applied in the Member State concerned with those applied in other Member States must be considered valid. It is apparent from that case-law that, when an undertaking holding a dominant position imposes scales of fees for its services which are appreciably higher than those charged in other Member States, and where a comparison of the fee levels has been made on a consistent basis, that difference must be regarded as indicative of an abuse of a dominant position (judgments of 13 July 1989, *Tournier*, 395/87, EU:C:1989:319, paragraph 38, and of 13 July 1989, *Lucazeau and Others*, 110/88, 241/88 and 242/88, EU:C:1989:326, paragraph 25).
>
> 39. However, having regard to the fact that, in the cases that led to the judgments referred to in the previous paragraph, the rates charged by a copyright management organisation of a Member State had been compared with those in force in all other Member States at that time, the referring court is unsure whether a comparison, such as that made by the Competition Council in the main proceedings between the rates applied by the AKKA/LAA in Latvia and those charged in Lithuania and Estonia, supported by a comparison with the rates charged in other Member States adjusted in accordance with the PPP index [*Purchase Price Parity index based on gross domestic product*], is sufficiently representative.
>
> 40. In that regard, it should first be noted that a comparison cannot be considered to be insufficiently representative merely because it takes a limited number of Member States into account.
>
> 41. On the contrary, such a comparison may prove relevant, on condition [. . .] that the reference Member States are selected in accordance with objective, appropriate

585 Opinion of AG Wahl in Case C-177/16, *Biedrība 'Autortiesību un komunicēšanās konsultāciju aģentūra—Latvijas Autoru apvienība' v Konkurences padome*, ECLI:EU:C:2017:286, para 45 [hereinafter *AKKA/LAA v Konkurences padome (Latvian copyright)*].

586 Ibid, para 46. 587 Ibid, para 48. 588 Ibid, para 49.

589 Ibid, para 52. 590 Ibid, para 54. 591 Ibid, para 112.

592 Case C-177/16, *AKKA/LAA v Konkurences padome (Latvian Copyright)*, ECLI:EU:C:2017:689.

593 Ibid, para 55.

and verifiable criteria. Therefore, there can be no minimum number of markets to compare and the choice of appropriate analogue markets depends on the circumstances specific to each case.

42. Those criteria may include, inter alia, consumption habits and other economic and sociocultural factors, such as gross domestic product per capita and cultural and historical heritage. It will be for the referring court to assess the relevance of the criteria applied in the case in the main proceedings, while taking into account all the circumstances of the case. [. . .]

44. Next, it should be borne in mind that a comparison between the prices applied in the Member State concerned and those applied in other Member States must be made on a consistent basis [. . .]

46. In that last regard, it should be noted [. . .] that there are, as a general rule, significant differences in price levels between Member States for identical services, those differences being closely linked with the differences in citizens' purchasing power, as expressed by the PPP index. The ability of shop or service centre operators to pay for the services of the copyright management organisation is influenced by living standards and purchasing power. Thus the comparison, for an identical service, of the rates in force in several Member States in which living standards differ necessarily implies that the PPP index must be taken into account. [. . .]

49. It falls to the competition authority concerned to make the comparison and to define its framework, although it should be borne in mind that that authority has a certain margin of manoeuvre and that there is no single adequate method. For example, it should be noted that, in the cases which led to the judgments of [*Tournier* & *Lucazeau and Others*] [. . .] the comparison related to fees collected in several Member States from discothèques with certain specific features, one of which was the surface area.

50. Thus, it is permissible to make a comparison within one or several specific segments if there are indications that the possibly excessive nature of the fees affects those segments, this being a matter for the referring court to verify.

Question regarding the threshold of appreciability for the difference between the rates compared to be considered excessive and possibilities to demonstrate that those rates are not excessive.

53. It should first be recalled that, when an undertaking holding a dominant position imposes scales of fees for its services which are appreciably higher than those charged in the other Member States, that difference must be regarded as indicative of an abuse of a dominant position [. . .].

54. However, in the present case, as indicated by the referring court, the difference between the rates charged in Latvia and those charged in the other reference Member States is not as large as the differences observed between the fees in certain Member States in the cases that led to the judgments of [*Tournier* & *Lucazeau and Others*] [. . .]. In that regard, the referring court notes that, according to the findings of the Competition Council, for surface areas of between 81 m^2 and 201-300 m^2, rates in Latvia were at least twice as high as those applied in Estonia and in Lithuania. As for the comparison made with the rates applied in the other Member States [. . .] that court found that the rates applicable in Latvia were between 50% and 100% higher than the average level of EU rates [. . .].

55. Nonetheless, it cannot follow from the judgments of [*Tournier* & *Lucazeau and Others*] [. . .] that differences such as those observed in the case in the main proceedings can never be qualified as 'appreciable'. There is in fact no minimum threshold

above which a rate must be regarded as 'appreciably higher', given that the circumstances specific to each case are decisive in that regard. Thus, a difference between rates may be qualified as 'appreciable' if it is both significant and persistent on the facts, with respect, in particular, to the market in question, this being a matter for the referring court to verify.

56. It should be emphasised in this regard that [. . .] the difference must be significant for the rates concerned to be regarded as 'abusive'. Furthermore, that difference must persist for a certain length of time and must not be temporary or episodic.

57. Next, it should be noted that these factors are merely indicative of abuse of a dominant position. It may be possible for the copyright management organisation to justify the difference by relying on objective dissimilarities between the situation of the Member State concerned and that of the other Member States included in the comparison [. . .].

58. In order to justify such a difference, certain factors can be taken into consideration, such as the relationship between the level of the fee and the amount actually paid to the rightholders. When the proportion of fees taken up by collection, administration and distribution expenses rather than by payments to copyright holders is considerably higher, the possibility cannot be ruled out that it is precisely the lack of competition on the market in question that accounts for the heavy burden of administration and hence for the high level of fees [. . .].

61. It follows [. . .] that the difference between the rates compared must be regarded as appreciable if that difference is significant and persistent. Such a difference is indicative of abuse of a dominant position and it is for the copyright management organisation holding a dominant position to show that its prices are fair by reference to objective factors that have an impact on management expenses or the remuneration of rightholders.

Unfairly low prices may also be a concern for the application of Article 102(a). This does not concern predatory prices, but situations in which a dominant buyer purchases inputs at unfairly low prices. These are determined according to a comparison between the price paid and the economic value of the service provided. In *CICCE*, the Court examined an action for annulment against a decision of the Commission relating to conduct by some French television stations holding exclusive broadcasting rights to pay low licence fees for the rights of films and accepted that Article 102(a) could apply in these circumstances, although in this case the Commission had not found an abuse, as it was impossible, in view of the variety of the films and the different criteria for assessing their value, to determine an administrable yardstick valid for all firms, since each film is different.[594]

There has been a lot of discussion recently on targeting purely exploitative behaviour, such as excessive royalties, through the means of Article 102(a) and the issue of royalty stacking occurring in the context of standard-setting and eventual hold up situations.[595]

594 Case C-298/83, *Comité des industries cinématographiques des Communautés européennes v Commission* [1985] ECR 1105.

595 See M Motta and A de Streel, 'Exploitative and Exclusionary Excessive Prices in EU Law' in CD Ehlermann and I Atanasiu (eds) *What is an Abuse of a Dominant Position?* (Hart, 2006), 91; E Paulis, 'Article 82 EC and Exploitative Conduct' in CD Ehlermann and M Marquis (eds) *European Competition Law Annual 2007: A Reformed Approach to Article 82 EC* (Hart, 2008), 515; LH Röller, 'Exploitative Abuses' in CD Ehlermann and

One should bear in mind that the Commission Guidance on Article 102 does not cover exploitative abuses. Commentators have expressed a number of reservations on this issue:

(i) Assessing excessive pricing may be hard. What should be the right benchmark: a competitive price? But what does this mean? Duopoly? Perfect or imperfect competition? How can it be calculated? If one allows some margin above competitive price, what is the magnitude of this margin? How to establish reasonable return on investment?

(ii) Setting clear rules for compliance in dynamic markets is even harder. How should these rules apply in dynamic markets, where there is upfront investment for the future? Should one require high *ex post* margins to incentivise *ex ante* risky investments (eg in R&D)? It is important to acknowledge that high margins on some activities may be required to cover fixed costs that are common across activities;

(iii) Remedies for excessive pricing can equate to price regulation (either implicitly or explicitly);

(iv) Price regulation can be distortive to competition, investment and R&D; Price regulation can inhibit entry/expansion by competitors, can distort investment incentives, can distort incentives for marketing and R&D—ie 'portfolio pricing' approach (in view of the fact that the majority of R&D projects fail), may distort pricing incentives; Proponents of this view suggest that there may need to be explicit regulation for certain areas of natural monopoly—such as utilities—but this should be done carefully by sector-specific regulators. The rest of the economy should be left alone—since the risks of careless and ill-informed intervention outweigh any potential benefits;

(v) The problem will typically solve itself, since high profits encourage entry;

(vi) Defining what constitutes an excessive price is too complicated for competition authorities or the courts, which are not the adequate institutions for this task.

Commentators have also suggested a number of limiting principles to the application of Article 102(a) to purely exploitative practices. This should apply only in narrow circumstances. There is wide agreement as to possibility to apply Article 102(a) when: (i) there are very high and long lasting barriers to entry (and expansion); and (ii) the firms (near) monopoly position has not been the result of past innovation or investment. Yet, some authors propose additional conditions. For example, Evans and Padilla suggest that as well as meeting the first two conditions it is necessary that (iii) the prices charged by the firm widely exceed its average total costs; and (iv) there is a risk that those prices may prevent the emergence of new goods and services in adjacent markets.[596] Geradin, Layne-Farrar, and Petit add that there needs to be some form of an exclusionary element or deceptive practice.[597] Röller would have applied it only to situations of 'enforcement gap'.[598] Motta and De Streel argue that 'there should be no sector-specific regulator'.[599] Paulis disagrees with the sector

M Marquis (eds) *European Competition Law Annual 2007: A Reformed Approach to Article 82 EC* (Hart, 2008), 525; DS Evans and JA Padilla, 'Excessive Prices: Using Economics to Define Administrable Legal Rules' (2005) 1 *J Competition L & Economics* 97; M Furse, 'Excessive Prices, Unfair Prices and Economic Value: The Law of Excessive Pricing under Article 82 and the Chapter II Prohibition' (2008) *European Competition J* 59; A Ezrachi and D Gilo, 'Are Excessive Prices Really Self-Correcting?' (2009) 5 *J Competition L & Economics* 249.

596 DS Evans and JA Padilla, 'Excessive Prices: Using Economics to Define Administrable Legal Rules' (2005) 1 *J Competition L & Economics* 97.

597 D Geradin, A Layne-Farrar, and N Petit, *EU Competition Law and Economics* (OUP, 2012), 289.

598 LH Röller, 'Exploitative Abuses' in CD Ehlermann and M Marquis (eds) *European Competition Law Annual 2007: A Reformed Approach to Article 82 EC* (Hart, 2008), 525.

599 M Motta and A de Streel, 'Exploitative and Exclusionary Excessive Prices in EU Law' in CD Ehlermann and I Atanasiu (eds) *What is an Abuse of a Dominant Position?* (Hart, 2006), 91.

regulator point, noting that the Commission should maintain the option to intervene when a national regulator is not acting or is taking decisions that are not in conformity with Community law.[600] One could, however, challenge the requirement that the exploitative practice results from some form of deceptive practice or exclusionary conduct to be *contra legem*, as the text of Article 102(a) envisages unfair prices as a separate violation than the abuse of 'other unfair trading conditions'. We could apply Article 102(a) only to practices that involve an element of exclusionary or deceptive conduct that would jeopardize the full effect of Article 102(a) and the type of practices the article is aimed at. The strength of the case for intervention will of course vary and will be stronger if all these conditions are present. Others have criticized the assumption often made that markets are self-correcting and that high prices encourage entry.[601]

One could also oppose the argument over the incapacity of courts and competition authorities to define what constitutes an excessive price by referring to the role of the courts in evaluating damages in the context of competition disputes or IP infringement cases. The Commission has published detailed non-binding guidance on the different methodologies available for evaluating competition law damages.[602] Similar guidance may be published for exploitative practices. US courts proceed quite often to the examination of complex econometric evidence in antitrust disputes.

Competition authorities and courts are also involved in the policing of compulsory licensing remedies and assess the reasonableness of royalties required. Following the decision of the European Commission finding that Microsoft's refusal to provide interoperability infringed Article 102 TFEU, Microsoft was required to grant access to and authorize the use of the interoperability information on reasonable and non-discriminatory terms. The European Commission suggested that the assessment of the reasonableness of Microsoft's prices depended on 'whether there is innovation in the protocols, and if there is, what is charged for comparable technologies in the market'.[603] According to the Commission, 'such a remuneration should not reflect the strategic value, stemming from Microsoft's market power'. In this case, the benchmark for the calculation of royalties was the incremental value of Microsoft's protocols over the prior art and the royalties agreed among third parties for comparable technologies. Following the remedy imposed by the Commission, Microsoft submitted its remuneration schemes, containing principles for pricing the interoperability information, as these were negotiated by the parties. The Commission found that some of the remunerations charged by Microsoft for non-patented information were unreasonable and imposed periodic penalties.[604] The General Court confirmed the control effectuated by the Commission of the reasonableness of the royalties' rate charged.[605]

600 E Paulis, 'Article 82 EC and Exploitative Conduct' in CD Ehlermann and M Marquis (eds) *European Competition Law Annual 2007: A Reformed Approach to Article 82 EC* (Hart, 2008), 515.

601 A Ezrachi and D Gilo, 'Are Excessive Prices Really Self-Correcting?' (2009) 5 *J Competition L & Economics* 249.

602 Commission Staff Working Document, Practical Guidance, *Quantifying harm in actions for damages based on breaches of Article 101 or 102 of the TFEU*, SWD(2013) 205, available at http://ec.europa.eu/competition/antitrust/actionsdamages/quantification_guide_en.pdf.

603 *Microsoft/W2000* (Case COMP/C-3/37.792) C(2004)900 final (24 March 2004), paras 1005–9.

604 *Microsoft* (Case COMP/C-3/37.792) Commission Decision [2009] OJ C 166/20.

605 Case T-167/08, *Microsoft Corp v European Commission*, ECLI:EU:T:2012:323 (noting that the distinction between the strategic value and the intrinsic value of the technologies covered is a basic premise of the assessment of the reasonableness of any remuneration charged).

Following a period with relatively little enforcement activity against excessive and unfair pricing, in particular in the pharmaceutical sector, the Commission has opened in May 2017 an investigation in relation to Aspen Pharma's pricing practices for cancer medicines.[606]

9.11.2. ALGORITHMIC DISCRIMINATION AND PERSONALIZED PRICING

The practice of *behavioural pricing* or *personalized price discrimination*, which comes tantamount to first degree price discrimination (or person-specific pricing), is now possible in view of Big Data and algorithmic pricing as practiced in online commerce, as sellers charge different prices depending upon a buyers' search history, or 'digital shadow'.[607] Firms may actively manipulate the choice of consumers.[608] Recent calls for intervention against 'behavioural pricing' (or personalized price discrimination),[609] which may be considered as a form of algorithmic discrimination, illustrate the broader societal concerns (if not only economic) that are raised with regard to the perceived manipulation of consumers by companies, something as old as

606 European Commission, 'Antitrust: Commission opens formal investigation into Aspen Pharma's pricing practices for cancer medicines', Press Release No IP/17/1323 (15 May 2017).

607 M Gal, 'Algorithmic-facilitated Coordination: Market and Legal Solutions', *Competition Policy International* (15 May 2017), available at https://www.competitionpolicyinternational.com/algorithmic-facilitated-coordination-market-and-legal-solutions/ (noting that '[a]s more data is gathered about each consumer's preferences, a personalized "digital profile" can be created by algorithms, which calculates and updates each consumer's elasticity of demand in real-time. This digital shadow can then be used by suppliers to increase their profits even further, if they can price-differentiate between the offers they make to different consumers.').

608 See JD Hanson and DA Kysar, 'Taking Behavioralism Seriously: The Problem of Market Manipulation' (1999) 74 *New York U L Rev* 630. For the first study in EU competition law raising this problem, see N Economides and I Lianos, 'The Elusive Antitrust Standard on Bundling in Europe and in the United States in the Aftermath of the Microsoft Cases' (2009) 76 *Antitrust LJ* 483, 542.

609 See Autorité de la Concurrence & Bundeskartellamt, 'Competition Law and Big Data' (10 May 2016), 21–22, noting that although the application of EU competition law to these practices may be debated, in Germany, the Federal Supreme Court found that the national provision against the abuse of a dominant position can include a consumer protection dimension as regards price discrimination, see German Federal Supreme Court (BGH), 'Entega II', KZR 5/10, judgment of 07.12.2010. For a discussion of 'personalized pricing', see P Coen and N Timan, 'The Economics of Online Personalised Pricing', OFT (2013), available at http://webarchive.nationalarchives.gov.uk/20140402154756/http://oft.gov.uk/shared_oft/research/oft1488.pdf; Oxera, 'Behavioural Economics and Its Impact on Competition Policy' (June, 2013), available at https://www.oxera.com/publications/behavioural-economics-and-its-impact-on-competition-policy/; TJ Richards, J Liaukonyte, and NA Streletskaya, 'Personalized Pricing and Price Fairness' (15 September 2015), available at https://courses.cit.cornell.edu/jl2545/papers/personalized_Pricing_IJIO.pdf; A Ezrachi and M Stucke, 'The Rise of Behavioural Discrimination' (2016) 37 *European Competition L Rev* 484; A Ezrachi and M Stucke, *Virtual Competition* (Harvard University Press, 2016), ch 11 (distinguishing 'near perfect' discrimination, involving the categorization of consumers through the harvesting of personal information collected with the help of Big Data and self-learning algorithms, from 'behavioural' discrimination, which is led with the aim to trigger consumer biases and increase consumption); M Bourreau, A De Streel, and I Graaf, 'Big Data and Competition Policy: Market Power, Personalised Pricing and Advertising', CERRE Project Report (February 2017), available at https://researchportal.unamur.be/en/publications/big-data-and-competition-policy-market-power-personalised-pricing; CMA 94 Pricing Algorithms (8 October 2018), available at https://assets.publishing.service.gov.uk/government/uploads/system/uploads/attachment_data/file/746353/Algorithms_econ_report.pdf (defining personalized pricing, at section 7.3, as 'the practice where businesses may use information that is observed, volunteered, inferred, or collected about individuals' conduct or characteristics, to set different prices to different consumers—whether individuals or groups—based on what the business thinks they are willing to pay').

advertising exists.[610] In the era of 'machine learning' and artificial intelligence (AI) assisted pricing, the risks of 'digital' consumer manipulation may admittedly increase at an industrial scale.[611] Digital markets exacerbate the above risks, in view of the possibilities they offer of 'a vast psychological audit, discovering and representing the desires of society'[612] and of each individual separately, offering sophisticated evaluation methods that are closely linked to the direct observation of consumer preferences, but also more broadly of a whole range of preferences expressed in social, and private life, through the means of sociometric analysis.[613] Big data enable us to observe, allegedly more accurately, the inner mental states of people and potentially influence the way these form their core preferences. Such manipulative potential, and of course the possibility that this may occur at a larger scale, in view of the possibilities offered by algorithms, data analysis, and artificial intelligence, is clearly motivating public authorities to action.

This can later feed in the companies' commercial strategies that may, for instance, develop personalized pricing strategies, which may be considered a form of price discrimination. Price discrimination may be of different types:

- *First-degree price discrimination*: it enables the producer to set individualized prices for each customer, relying on its knowledge of *individual* preferences
- *Second-degree price discrimination*: The producer doesn't know the individual preferences and proposes a menu of options to consumers, letting the consumers choose their preferred one.
- *Third-degree price discrimination*: The producer doesn't know the individual preferences, but charges different prices to groups of consumers with different observable characteristics.

There is price discrimination when two transactions of the same good occur at different prices despite having the same cost. Successful, from the company's perspective price discrimination (that is one that cannot be defeated by consumers switching to other producers) requires some conditions, including (i) market power, (ii) the ability to distinguish customers, and (iii) the ability to prevent resale. Personalized pricing improves the ability to distinguish customers and may lead to first degree price discrimination, as well as third degree price discrimination, when it is possible for the firms to apply group pricing, discriminating between groups of consumers. Subjecting to price discrimination final users may enable the producer to capture the entire consumer surplus, generate unequal treatment of various individual consumers or groups of consumers, and affect competition with other producers (not necessarily of the same relevant market), in the sense that by enabling the producer to charge a specific consumer as high as his willingness to pay, reduces the available income of the consumer to make other purchases. Different producers compete for the limited resources/budget of a consumer or a group of consumers.

610 See I Lianos, 'Brands, Product Differentiation and EU Competition Law' in D Desai, I Lianos, and S Weber Waller (eds) *Brands, Competition Law and IP* (CUP, 2015), 146 (discussing the 'persuasive view' of advertising in economic literature).

611 R Calo, 'Digital Market Manipulation' (2014) 82 *George Washington L Rev* 995.

612 W Davies, *The Happiness Industry: How the Government & Big Business Sold Us Wellbeing* (Verso, 2015), 15.

613 Ibid.

Personalized pricing or 'price targeting' has been observed in various markets.[614] To the extent that this manipulation may result in welfare losses for individuals, or group of consumers, in the sense that the specific individual, or the specific group of consumers, could find its/their situation worse off, in comparison to a counterfactual where no such digital manipulation would have taken place, it can be argued that these deviations from the counterfactual situation need to be corrected through State intervention, eventually by competition law enforcement. But this is a matter for debate. One may argue that personalized pricing should not be considered as a form of 'manipulation', but as a technological opportunity to charge each consumer as much as her/his willingness to pay is. This may, for instance, enable some consumers that would not have been able to purchase the specific product, if a uniform price would have been implemented and would have been higher than their willingness, to pay for the product. 'Personalized pricing' may have ambiguous welfare effects, depending on market structure and the trade-off between the market 'appropriation' effect on consumer with high willingness to pay and the 'market expansion' effect on consumers with low willingness to pay the targeted pricing.[615]

Nevertheless, economic theory suggests that the use of price discrimination under competition may squeeze profits to the benefit of consumers.[616] For example, if with the use of data analytics firms are able to identify consumers who are loyal to a rival brand, the use of price discrimination among rival firms based on heterogeneous brand preferences among consumers will tend to reduce prices. Under this circumstances competitors face a prisoner's dilemma, in that they would be collectively better off without the use of price discrimination, but each one of them has a unilateral incentive to adopt it. There are other circumstances where the use of price discrimination under competition can be inconsequential. For example, if two firms have the same information regarding a consumer's high willingness to pay, none of them might be able to charge a higher price because of the threat of being undercut by the rival. However, firms would be able to exploit information about consumer search costs. That is to say, the use of price discrimination augmented by superior data analytics may be particularly detrimental towards vulnerable consumers who, for whatever reason, face high search costs. Finally, it is

614 See the analysis and examples provided in M Bourreau, A De Streel, and I Graaf, 'Big Data and Competition Policy: Market Power, Personalised Pricing and Advertising', CERRE Project Report (February 2017), 40–1, available at https://researchportal.unamur.be/en/publications/big-data-and-competition-policy-market-power-personalised-pricing, and the empirical studies they refer to. See also European Commission, 'Consumer market study on online market segmentation through personalised pricing/offers in the European Union', Final Report (June 2018), available at https://ec.europa.eu/info/sites/info/files/aid_development_cooperation_fundamental_rights/aid_and_development_by_topic/documents/synthesis_report_online_personalisation_study_final_0.pdf; CMA 94, Pricing Algorithms (October 2018), available at https://assets.publishing.service.gov.uk/government/uploads/system/uploads/attachment_data/file/746353/Algorithms_econ_report.pdf with references (also noting, ibid, para 7.27, that 'algorithms could make personalised pricing less resource intensive and more accurate'. For personalized pricing to occur it is important that firms should be able to 'observe or possess information about each customer's willingness to pay; and [. . .] prevent resale between customers or customer segments'): ibid, para 7.30.

615 For a discussion, see OFT 1488, 'The Economics of Online Personalised Pricing' (May 2013), available at http://webarchive.nationalarchives.gov.uk/20140402142426/http:/www.oft.gov.uk/shared_oft/research/oft1488.pdf; M Bourreau, A De Streel, and I Graaf, 'Big Data and Competition Policy: Market Power, Personalised Pricing and Advertising', CERRE Project Report (February 2017), 43–5, available at https://researchportal.unamur.be/en/publications/big-data-and-competition-policy-market-power-personalised-pricing; CMA 94, Pricing Algorithms (October 2018), available at https://assets.publishing.service.gov.uk/government/uploads/system/uploads/attachment_data/file/746353/Algorithms_econ_report.pdf.

616 M. Armstrong, 'Recent Developments in the Economics of Price Discrimination' in R Blundell, WK Newey, and T Persson (eds) Advances in Economics and Econometrics: Theory and Applications: Ninth World Congress, vol 2 (CUP, 2003), 97.

intriguing to consider how personalized pricing would rule out the use of price-parity clauses such as MFN, RPM, and price-matching guarantees. As the use of price-parity restraints is often alleged to be aimed at softening pricing rivalry, both inter and intra-brand, the inability to adopt these practices due to the use of personalised pricing may end up being a welcome development from a consumer perspective. This is particularly so if one considers that consumers will also be able to take advantage of digital shopping assistants capable of searching and comparing prices and other quality attributes more comprehensively on behalf of consumers.

In *Asnef-Equifax*, when examining the possible efficiency gains brought by a restrictive to competition information exchange, the CJEU held that when performing the trade-off under Article 101(3) TFEU '[. . .] it is the beneficial nature of the effect on *all* consumers in the relevant markets that must be taken into consideration, not the effect on *each member* of that category of consumers.'[617]

One may also argue that EU competition law's focus on distributive justice, in particular its emphasis on the position of 'consumers', who should not be worse of following the specific conduct,[618] may justify competition law intervention if the additional benefits from personalized pricing are not passed on to consumers, either in the form of lower prices, or in the form of better quality and/or innovative products. Competition law intervention may also be motivated by fairness considerations (value ethics), in particular if personalized pricing is not transparent and thus consumers are not informed, or the need to limit an extensive use by the firms practising algorithmic discrimination of consumers' sensitive personal data, in view of the purpose limitation and data minimization requirements in the Data Protection regulation.[619] These practices may also raise more conventional competition law concerns, as they discourage consumer search by making it harder or more expensive to return to buy after a search for alternatives, with the effect that the matching of products to consumers is sub-optimal and that consumers, on aggregate, may finish paying higher prices.[620]

In a recent report, the CMA has flagged up the risks factors for personalised pricing to become a competition law issue.

CMA 94, Pricing Algorithms (October 2018), para 8.8, available at https://assets.publishing.service.gov.uk/government/uploads/system/uploads/attachment_data/file/746353/Algorithms_econ_report.pdf

[. . .] [P]ersonalised pricing was more likely to be harmful to consumer welfare when:

(a) There is a lack of competition in the market (i.e. a monopolist). [. . .]

(b) Discrimination is particularly complex (several different consumer groups) or opaque to consumers [. . .].

617 Case C-238/05, *Asnef-Equifax, Servicios de Información sobre Solvencia y Crédito, SL v Asociación de Usuarios de Servicios Bancarios (Ausbanc)*, ECLI:EU:C:2006:734, para 70 (emphasis added).

618 See Chapter 6 for our analysis of the way the Commission interprets the third condition of Article 101(3) TFEU.

619 Regulation (EU) 2016/679 of the European Parliament and of the Council of 27 April 2016 on the protection of natural persons with regard to the processing of personal data and on the free movement of such data, and repealing Directive 95/46/EC [2016] L 119/1, Article 5(1) [hereinafter GDPR]. See also Article 9(1) GDPR and section 2 of the Data Protection Act 1998 which require the data controller when processing personal data to obtain a specific and explicit consent to process these categories of data.

620 M Armstrong and J Zhou, 'Search Deterrence' (2016) 83 *Rev Economic Studies* 26.

(c) It is very costly to firms, because if firms incur significant costs to price discriminate, then they will need to recover these costs through higher prices [. . .].

(d) Consumers lose trust in the market and, as a result of their lack of confidence that they are receiving a good or fair price, they may withdraw their demand or decline to participate in the market (and potentially, in other similar online markets) [. . .].

There are different ways to deal with personalized pricing, from a competition law perspective.[621] It is possible that such practices will be qualified as a form of price discrimination under Article 102(c).[622] Article 101(1)(d) TFEU also prohibits agreements that 'apply dissimilar conditions to equivalent transactions with other trading parties, thereby placing them at a competitive disadvantage'. Article 102(c) utilizes almost identical language to inhibit dominant undertakings from engaging in price discrimination. EU competition authorities have focused price discrimination enforcement on dominant undertakings. Among the conditions for the application of this provision, there is the requirement that the 'other trading partners' are placed at a 'competitive disadvantage', which may suggest that this provision may not apply to discrimination on price or other parameters of competition against final consumers. However, this language has not impeded the Commission to apply Article 102(c) to final consumers in *Deutsche Post*, in particular consumers of postal services, which due to the behaviour of Deutsche Post were affected negatively by having to pay prices for these services which were 'higher than those charged to other senders and by having their mailings delayed significantly' The Commission noted that

> Article [102 TFEU] may be applied even in the absence of a direct effect on competition between undertakings on any given market. This provision may be also be applied in situations where a dominant undertakings behaviour causes damage directly to consumers.[623]

Also note that the case law does not require evidence of a competitive disadvantage, which in some cases has been presumed.[624]

Would you be in favour of extending Article 102(c) to personalized pricing or to situations of algorithmic discrimination?

Alternatively, personalized pricing may be attacked through Article 102(a) if it can be qualified as 'directly or indirectly imposing unfair purchase or selling prices or other unfair

[621] For a discussion, see C Townley, E Morrison, and K Yeung, 'Big Data and Personalised Price Discrimination in EU Competition Law' (2017) 36(1) *Yearbook of European L* 683; M Maggiolino, 'Personalized Prices in European Competition Law', Bocconi Legal Studies Research Paper No 2984840 (12 June 2017), available at https://ssrn.com/abstract=2984840. On the UK approach, see OFT 1489, Personalised Pricing (May 2013), available at http://webarchive.nationalarchives.gov.uk/20140402165101/http:/oft.gov.uk/shared_oft/markets-work/personalised-pricing/oft1489.pdf; CMA94, Pricing Algorithms (October 2018), available at https://assets.publishing.service.gov.uk/government/uploads/system/uploads/attachment_data/file/746353/Algorithms_econ_report.pdf.

[622] See Autorité de la Concurrence & Bundeskartellamt, Competition Law and Big Data (10 May 2016), 21–2, noting that although the application of EU competition law to these practices may be debated, in Germany, the Federal Supreme Court found that the national provision against the abuse of a dominant position can include a consumer protection dimension as regards price discrimination, see German Federal Supreme Court (BGH), 'Entega II', KZR 5/10, judgment of 7 December 2010.

[623] *Deutsche Post AG* (COMP/C.1/36.915) Commission Decision [2001] OJ L 331/40 (not appealed), para 133.

[624] See Section 9.7.2.

trading conditions', for instance because it has led to the imposition of a higher price (or lower quality) than what would have been the case but for the specific digital manipulation and enables the producer to capture the entire consumer surplus. Of course, should this route be followed, it would be important to design a test with more specific conditions than just the fact that there is no reasonable relation between the price charged to the consumer and the 'economic value' of the product supplied, as personalized pricing aims precisely to set the price at the exact level the specific consumer thinks is the 'economic value' of the product (subjective perception of value that corresponds to the subjective willingness to pay of this specific consumer), which from an economic efficiency perspective should not be problematic. However, one may argue that the principle of 'open market economy' would require that economic value should be set in the context of a competitive process taking place on a market, where various actors, consumers and suppliers interact, in view of the fact that 'competition is, by its very essence, determined by price.'[625] Hence, charging a consumer a personalized price that would correspond to her/his willingness to pay, without him being aware of this and without enabling the specific consumer to benefit from the competitive process taking place at the 'open market' and the source of information this may provide so as to enable informed comparison with regard to the situation of other consumers may contravene to 'the principle of an open market economy with free competition.'[626] This is particularly important as one may argue that consumers value the competitive process as such, and not just the fact that the price of a product is within the range of their willingness to pay, which is also something that cannot be set in advance, but essentially cultivated in the context of a market involving continuous interactions between buyers and sellers. That said, it is important to explore if competition law is the best legal instrument to deal with welfare-reducing targeted pricing, or if other alternatives, such as consumer protection law, data protection and privacy rules, anti-discrimination law, unfair commercial practices law, free movement law, regulation, may prove to be more appropriate, following a detailed comparative institutional analysis.[627]

9.11.3. NON-PRICE EXPLOITATION

The exploitation of consumers may not only take the form of higher prices, but may also include a reduction of the quality of the services provided and other exploitative effects, such as the extraction of personal data without the user's consent.

A recent case brought by the German competition authority (*Bundeskartellamt*) against Facebook raises interesting issues as to the possible extension of Article 102 to cover abuses

625 Opinion of AG Szpunar in Case C-148/15, *Deutsche Parkinson Vereinigung eV v Zentrale zur Bekämpfung unlauteren Wettbewerbs eV*, ECLI:EU:C:2016:394, para 18.

626 This principle is mentioned in Articles 119, 120, and 127 TFEU.

627 See M Bourreau, A De Streel, and I Graaf, 'Big Data and Competition Policy: Market Power, Personalised Pricing and Advertising', CERRE Project Report (February 2017), 45–7, available at https://researchportal.unamur.be/en/publications/big-data-and-competition-policy-market-power-personalised-pricing, noting restrictions on personalized pricing from data protection rules (the need to have the explicit consent of the data subject involved), consumer protection rules (disclosure to consumers about the prices and how they are calculated), unfair commercial practices (prohibiting in certain circumstances consumer profiling and considering this as a misleading commercial practice), free movement law (the Services' directive prohibitions to discrimination based on the service recipient's nationality or residence), as well as specific regulations on geo-blocking (see Proposal for a Regulation of the European Parliament and of the Council on addressing geo-blocking and other forms of discrimination based on customers' nationality, place of residence or place of establishment within the internal market and amending Regulation (EC) No 2006/2004 and Directive 2009/22/EC, COM(2016) 289 final), or the application of competition law provisions against geo-blocking (see Section 2.3.3.3).

resulting from the exploitation of consumers by digital platforms when harvesting consumer (personal) data.[628] The Bundeskartellamt differentiated between user data that are generated through the use of Facebook and user data obtained from third party sources and not generated by the use of Facebook's social network itself. According to the Bundeskartellamt, 'on principle, competition concerns do not arise where, as part of a business model which is based on a company offering a product or service for free and monetising this through targeted advertising, data that are generated through the use of the product or service are used for advertising activities', as 'users have to expect a certain processing of their data if they use such a free service' and within the network 'they may considerably influence the extent to which their data are being collected by paying attention to the way they use the network and the content they post'.[629] This is not, however, the case with data harvested off-Facebook network use. Facebook held a dominant position in the German market for social networks, in view of its high market shares, direct and indirect network effects, and because of the absence of multi-homing, other Professional networks such as LinkedIn and Xing, as well as messaging services such as WhatsApp and Snapchat or other social media such as YouTube or Twitter not being part of the relevant product market.[630] The Bundeskartellamt raised concerns with regard to the possible existence of an abuse of a dominant position as Facebook made the use of its service conditional upon the user granting the company extensive permission to use his or her personal data, even those generated off-Facebook, leading the users to lose control as they were no longer able to control how their personal data was used. The Bundeskartellamt noted that Facebook's users were oblivious as to which data from which sources were merged to develop a detailed profile of them and their online activities. Considering that Facebook's merging of the data constituted a violation of the users' constitutionally protected right to informational self-determination, the Court decided that section 19 of the Gesetz gegen Wettbewerbsbeschränkungen (GWB) [German Act Against Restraints of Competition] could apply noting that this provision applies in cases where one contractual party is so powerful that it is practically able to dictate the terms of the contract and the contractual autonomy of the other party is abolished. The Bundeskartellamt also examined whether Facebook's data processing terms were admissible including in the assessment the principles of the harmonised European data protection rules (EU General Data Protection Regulation), thus indicating that a violation of EU data protection law could give rise to an abuse of a dominant position. The Bundeskartellamt was careful to envisage in this case only the application of national (German) competition law, leaving Article 102 TFEU aside, but the case raises interesting questions as to the possibility to expand Article 102 to cover these practices to the extent that final consumers may be affected. The Bundeskartellamt confirmed this approach in its final decision in February 2019 and imposed on Facebook far-reaching restrictions in the processing of user data, the German competition authority finding that to the extent to which Facebook collects, merges and uses data in user accounts from third party sources, including Facebook-owned services such as Instagram or WhatsApp, but also third party websites which include interfaces such as the "Like" or "Share" buttons, without users giving their voluntary consent, Facebook has abused its dominant position on the market for social networks in Germany.[631]

628 Bundeskartellamt, Preliminary assessment in Facebook proceeding: Facebook's collection and use of data from third-party sources is abusive (19 December 2017), available at http://www.bundeskartellamt.de/SharedDocs/Meldung/EN/Pressemitteilungen/2017/19_12_2017_Facebook.html.

629 Ibid. 630 Ibid.

631 Bundeskartellamt, Bundeskartellamt prohibits Facebook from combining user data from different sources, available at https://www.bundeskartellamt.de/SharedDocs/Meldung/EN/Pressemitteilungen/2019/07_02_2019_Facebook.html..

9.11.4. UK CASE LAW—EXCESSIVE AND UNFAIR PRICES

Albion Water Limited & Albion Water Group Limited v Water Services Regulation Authority (Dwr Cymru/Shotton Paper) [2008] CAT 31

One of the arguments brought forward by Albion against DCWW in the CAT concerned the latter's excessive pricing.

On the issue of excessive price, the CAT held that the price charged by DCWW was excessive: the distribution cost of the water on an average accounting basis had not been investigated nor evidenced properly. Further, the ECPR methodology adopted in the case should not have been used as the retail price used was not cost related, the evidence pointed to an excessive retail price, and the use of this methodology would have effectively precluded any competition.

The CAT followed the United Brands' test to prove an abuse of unfair pricing; this required proof that the price was not only excessive but also unfair. A revised accounting methodology (AAC+) showed that the price charged by DCWW was excessive as it was approximately 46.8 per cent above the costs reasonably attributable to the supply of water. The price charged was also unfair because it had, irrespective of comparable indicators, no reasonable relation to the economic value of the services to be supplied. This insulated DCWW from the competitive process and allowed it to exploit end consumers.

CMA, Case CE/9742-13, Unfair pricing in respect of the supply of phenytoin sodium capsules in the UK

The CMA issued a decision against Pfizer and Flynn finding that they each abused their dominant position by charging excessive and unfair prices in the UK for phenytoin sodium capsules, an anti-epilepsy drug, violating Chapter II CA98 and Article 102 TFEU and fining them nearly £90 million. The CMA has also ordered the companies to reduce their prices. Pfizer manufactures the capsules and then supplies them to Flynn Pharma, which then distributes them to UK wholesalers and pharmacies. Patent protection for this drug had expired and the drug was superseded by newer drugs, very few newly diagnosed epilepsy patients being prescribed the specific drug. Although the sales of the drug were declining, they still represented at the time of the decision approximately 10 per cent of epilepsy patients in the UK. There were only two companies manufacturing and supplying phenytoin sodium capsules to the UK: Pfizer, which branded the drug as Epanutin, and NRIM Limited. The prices of Epanutin were regulated as part of Pfizer's portfolio of branded drugs under the National Health Service's (NHS) Pharmaceutical Price Regulation Scheme (PPRS).

In 2012, Pfizer and Flynn entered into agreements under which Pfizer transferred its marketing authorizations (MAs) for Epanutin to Flynn for £1. Pfizer continued to manufacture its phenytoin sodium capsules which it exclusively supplied to Flynn for distribution in the UK. Following this transfer, Flynn de-branded ('genericized') Epanutin and began distributing the product under a different name (Phenytoin), without any discernible change to the supply chain. As the product was de-branded, the product was also withdrawn from the PPRS, such that it was no longer subject to price regulation and both Pfizer's average selling price to Flynn and Flynn's prices were increased substantially.

The CMA concluded that Pfizer and Flynn have each abused their respective dominant positions by charging unfair prices for each capsule strength of phenytoin sodium capsules. This qualification concerned both the prices Pfizer charges to Flynn and those charged by Flynn to its customers, after Pfizer sold the UK distribution rights for this drug to Flynn Pharma, which de-branded it and started selling it on to customers at prices which were between 25 and 27 times higher than those historically charged by Pfizer. Pfizer also continued to manufacture the drug selling it to Flynn at prices that were eight to seventeen times higher than its historic prices. The prices were considered by the CMA as 'excessive', and 'unfair', the prices increasing by up to 2 600 per cent overnight after the drug was deliberately de-branded in September 2012.

Pharmacies' adherence to the principle of Continuity of Supply has resulted in Pfizer and Flynn effectively having a captive customer base. Flynn (directly) and Pfizer (indirectly) were, according to the CMA unavoidable trading partners for the NHS. The CMA found that the average selling price for each of the four capsule were excessive for both Pfizer and Flynn as they materially exceed their costs plus a reasonable rate of return (the theoretical benchmark of cost plus 6 per cent). The CMA concluded that the new price was first excessive and then unfair 'in itself' because it exceeded the cost-plus benchmark. In the absence of any non-cost related factors that should increase the economic value of the products, the very excessiveness of a price can, according to the CMA, be sufficient to establish that the price bears no reasonable relation to the economic value of the product being supplied. The prices were also considered unfair in themselves in view of a range of factors, including the fact that there was a substantial disparity between the economic value of each party's products the prices they charge, that both parties had each been able to sustain excessive prices because they were shielded from effective competition and had a captive market of patients, the fact that their respective excessive prices have been sustained for over four years and was unlikely to be reduced through market forces in the near future, the fact that costs had increased dramatically and resources had to be diverted from other services and treatments to meet those increased costs. In reaching this conclusion, the CMA also took into account he characteristics of phenytoin sodium capsules—in particular, the age of the product, the fact it has long been off-patent and has been genericized, the fact it has not been subject to any recent innovation, and the fact that the arrangement between Pfizer and Flynn had not produced any benefits for patients. The CMA also noted that the drug was cheaper in other EU Member States than in the UK.

The decision was appealed by both parties, which challenged, among others, the CMA's conclusion on dominance and market definition, the application of the cost plus benchmark of a return on sales (ROS) of 6 per cent test for excessive pricing, as well as CMA's methodology for allocating common costs on the basis of sales volumes.

In view of the fact that Flynn (and Pfizer) were directed to reduce their prices, Flynn applied for interim relief to the CAT arguing that there was significant and irreparable harm in the form of financial loss and major business upheaval (as it would be required to change its business model) and there was great uncertainty as to what a reasonable price would be. The CAT rejected the application finding that Flynn would not suffer irreparable harm if forced to comply with the directions, as 'there must be something more such as a demonstrable threat to the applicant's continuation in business', and financial loss alone was not enough.[632] *According to the CAT, public harm from allowing Flynn to continue charging higher prices for the drug outweighed the harm Flynn may suffer as a result of the CMA's order, in particular taking into account, not just the financial loss to the NHS but also the 'consequent effect on the health and well-being of affected patients and hence to public health overall and the public interest'.*[633]

[632] *Flynn Pharma Ltd v CMA* [2017] CAT 1, para 78.

[633] Ibid, para 105.

Flynn Pharma Limited, Flynn Pharma Holdings Limited v CMA
[2018] CAT 11

On appeal,[634] *the CAT accepted the CMA's narrow definition of the market and that Pfizer and Flynn each held dominant positions. It disagreed, however, with the CMA's approach with regard to the finding of abuse and the application of the* United Brands *test for excessive pricing. The judgment also includes some broader reflections of the CAT on excessive pricing, the CAT interpreting quite narrowly the case law of the CJEU both in* United Brands *and, more recently, in* AKKA/LAA (Latvian Copyright). *Interestingly, the CAT referred approvingly to the Opinion of AG Wahl, as being 'eminently sensible', although this was not followed by the CJEU.*[635] *The CAT held that*

> [the] CMA's conclusions on abuse of dominance were in error. The CMA did not correctly apply the legal test for finding that prices were unfair; it did not appropriately consider what was the right economic value for the product at issue; and it did not take sufficient account of the situation of other, comparable, products, in particular of the phenytoin sodium tablet. This means that the CMA's findings on abuse of dominance in this case cannot be upheld.[636]

In the absence of a factual analysis by the CMA that would have enabled the CAT to substitute the CMA's conclusion with its own, the CAT provisionally decided to send the case back to the CMA for further consideration in line with its judgment.

The CAT expressed concerns as to the methodology followed by the CMA, for both the excessiveness and the unfairness prongs of the United Brands *test.*

On excessiveness the CAT noted that the CMA's comparison analysis was wrong in law, as it has not established 'a benchmark price (or range) that would have pertained in circumstances of normal and sufficiently effective competition ["real competition"] using the evidence more widely available'.[637] *For the CAT, the CMA could have further explored alternative methodologies.*

> 318. In this case, the CMA's almost total reliance on a reasonable rate of return approach is unconvincing. Quite apart from the criticism that may be made of how it arrived at a 6% ROS as a reasonable rate, which we discuss below, it is clear that the CMA's approach owes more to a theoretical concept of idealised or near perfect competition, than to the real world (where normal, effective competition is the most that should be expected). It has on the whole avoided making comparisons with other products or companies and made little significant attempt, other than by invoking the Price Comparison over Time, to place Pfizer's and Flynn's prices in their commercial context during the Relevant Period. [. . .]
>
> 323. [. . .] Finding a minimum return on capital for investors was merely another manifestation of using a Cost Plus approach to calculate the excess, and was subject to the same basic error as with finding a reasonable return on sales (of not focussing, as a start point, on the prices that would have pertained in circumstances of normal and sufficiently effective competition). [. . .]
>
> 360. [. . .] [T]he CMA's approach to aspects of its Cost Plus analysis for Flynn is affected by its failure to set a benchmark price or range in circumstances of normal and sufficiently effective competition. If it had approached the analysis in this way, it would

634 *Flynn Pharma Limited, Flynn Pharma Holdings Limited v CMA* [2018] CAT 11.
635 Ibid, para 307. 636 Ibid, para 464. 637 Ibid, para 310.

have examined the conditions of a competitive market more closely. That may in turn have affected the way it examined possible comparator products and companies and its view of the PPRS, and to have taken a less rigid view of what was an appropriate rate of return.

With regard to unfairness, the CAT examined the two alternatives of the unfair limb of the United Brands *test, that is, first, that the price is 'unfair in itself', and second, unfairness compared to competing products, providing guidance as to the relation between the two alternatives. Referring to the principle of presumption of innocence, the CAT noted:*

367. In our view, it cannot be right that an authority can simply ignore a *prima facie* valid argument that a price is fair under one Alternative and proceed to find an infringement of Article 102 solely on the basis of the other Alternative establishing that prices are unfair. That is not to say that the authority cannot find that there is an infringement where one Alternative demonstrates unfairness and the other does not since it does not need to succeed on both heads. However, the authority must consider whether a *prima facie* case of fairness under one Alternative undermines the basis for the finding of unfairness under the other Alternative and produce a reasoned basis for determining that the Unfair Limb is satisfied.

In this case, the CMA had exercised its discretion and, although it did consider 'for completeness' if a comparison with other products could be established, having considered parallel imports and the production of phenytoin sodium tablets (Pfizer and Flynn selling capsules), it concluded that there were no products that would provide a meaningful comparison for the purpose of the second alternative of the unfair limb test of United Brands.[638] *This conclusion was not accepted by the CAT, which interpreted the words 'competing products' in the second limb of the* United Brands *test as not meaning 'products in the same relevant market for the purpose of competition law'.*[639] *The CAT found that phenytoin sodium tablets were competing products and were sold to the NHS at considerably higher prices than the price of the capsules, thus questioning the conclusion reached by the CMA with regard to the unfairness of the scheme. The CAT also criticized the CMA for not sufficiently considering economic value. This term was defined as being 'a legal rather than an economic concept' and including cost of production, but also non-cost considerations, such as elements of value to the purchaser, in this case patient benefits.*[640] *In making an overall assessment of unfairness, competition authorities should take into account that 'simple percentages expressed as absolute mark-ups are not sufficient'.*[641] *The CAT concluded by putting forward a number of principles to be considered by competition authorities (and claimants) bringing an excessive pricing case.*

442. We recognise the difficulties inherent in seeking to formulate a generally applicable framework or test for abuse by unfair pricing, and we are conscious that, as *United Brands* itself states, there may be other ways than the two-limb test set out in that case for establishing an abuse. Nonetheless, if an authority chooses to proceed to apply the two-limb test in a structured way, as the CMA has purported to do in this case, a sensible framework would, in our view, and in light of the requirements and factors we have already set out above, be as follows.

443. In our assessment, to apply Article 102 through the two-limb test of United Brands, in circumstances where the only alleged infringement is one of excessive

[638] Ibid, para 371. [639] Ibid, para 373. [640] Ibid, para 407. [641] Ibid, para 425.

pricing and the dominance of an undertaking in a given market has been established, a competition authority should:

(1) consider a range of possible analyses, reflecting market conditions and the extent and quality of the data that can be obtained, to establish a benchmark price, or range, that reflects the price that would pertain under conditions of normal and sufficiently effective competition. On the facts of a particular situation, there might be only one basis of analysis that was credible, but the authority is not entitled to select one basis of analysis and ignore others that are also credible. The criteria for selection and application must be objective, appropriate and verifiable. The analysis must also be done on a consistent basis;

(2) compare that price (or range) with the price that has been charged in practice and determine whether that is excessive;

(3) for that purpose, form an assessment, for the purpose of the Excessive Limb, of whether that differential is sufficiently significant and persistent to be excessive, as a matter of its own discretion, exercised fairly and reasonably, in the light of such factors as:

(i) the absolute size and stability of that differential

(ii) the reasons for it, taking account of the fact that the conditions for excessive pricing will only usually occur where the market is one where regulation, or some similar feature, or other barriers to entry, protect it from competition, or where there is regulatory failure and the relevant regulator has not intervened;

(iii) previous decisions finding other differentials excessive, weighted for the markets applicable in those cases;

(iv) the wider market conditions, including the evolution of pricing over time.

(4) where there is a conclusion that the differential is excessive, then proceed to consider whether it is unfair under the Unfair Limb;

(5) be free to use either Alternative 1 (unfair in itself) or Alternative 2 (unfair compared to competing products) to determine unfairness but give due consideration to any *prima facie* convincing argument that the pricing is actually fair under either Alternative and take that into account in reaching a decision under either Alternative 1 or 2;

(6) if there is a finding of unfairness under the Unfair Limb, assess what is the economic value of the product, and whether the price charged in practice bears no reasonable relation to it;

(7) give appropriate consideration to any objective justification advanced by the dominant undertaking;

(8) make a finding of an infringement of Article 102 if all the conditions above are fulfilled; and: (i) the price bears no reasonable relation to the economic value; (ii) the dominant undertaking is reaping trading benefits that it would not reap under conditions of normal and sufficiently effective competition.

444. It is for the competition authority to determine, when considering comparators, either for the application of Alternative 2 or for considering whether there are *prima facie* issues raised under Alternative 2 that need to be considered before proceeding under Alternative 1, or indeed if they are relevant to the Excessive Limb, what weight to be applied to them in the light of market conditions and their suitability, as comparators, for the product concerned. In making that determination, it must, but need only, act in a manner which is objective, appropriate and verifiable. It has a substantial margin of appreciation, but must recognise the presumption of innocence in favour of the undertaking under investigation.

In 2016, the CMA also opened a new investigation, this time for excessive and unfair pricing of Hydrocortisone tablets, in particular for substantial hikes in the price of 20 mg hydrocortisone tablets (by nearly 9 500 per cent compared to the previous branded price), once the drug was de-generecized and thus not subject any more to price regulation.[642] The recent judgment of the CAT in *Pfizer v Flynn* may have an impact on the CMA's investigations on excessive pricing and indicate some difference of approach between the UK and the EU on this type of abuse, which may be accentuated post-Brexit. It is quite significant that the CAT does not seem to limit its analysis of the unfair nature of the price of the second limb of the *United Brands* test to 'competing products' which are in the same relevant market. Does this sufficiently protect the consumers of the 'competing products' in the same relevant market? Does it make sense to have a broader view of 'competing products' beyond the relevant market for the purposes of applying Article 102 TFEU, if the purpose of the analysis of the relevant market is precisely to determine the users/consumers that may suffer from the anti-competitive conduct? Wouldn't this broad construction of the concept of 'competing product' deny these consumers protection from exploitation?

9.12. UNFAIR COMMERCIAL TERMS AND CONDITIONS

Exceptionally, the Commission and the European Courts have found that the imposition of unfair trading conditions may constitute an abuse of a dominant position.

In *BRT v SABAM*, the CJEU examined if a collecting society had imposed through its statutes or contracts concluded with its members, directly or indirectly, unfair conditions on members or third parties in the exploitation of works, the protection of which has been entrusted to it.[643] The CJEU examined if the collecting society in question adopted conduct which exceeded the limit absolutely necessary for the attainment of its object, the protection of the rights and interests of its individual members against, in particular, major exploiters and distributers of musical material, such as radio broadcasting bodies and record manufacturers, 'with due regard also to the interest which the individual author may have that his freedom to dispose of his work is not limited more than need be'.[644] The CJEU found that 'a compulsory assignment of all copyrights, both present and future, no distinction being drawn between the different generally accepted types of exploitation, may appear an unfair condition, especially if such assignment is required for an extended period after the member's withdrawal', noting that, in any case, 'the inequitable nature of such provisions must be determined by the relevant court, bearing in mind both the intrinsic individual effect of those clauses and their effect when combined'.[645]

Similarly in *AAMS v Commission*, the General Court confirmed the Commission's decision finding that AAMS, an undertaking with a dominant position on the Italian market for the wholesale distribution of cigarettes, had abused its dominant position by imposing standard distribution agreements to certain cigarette manufacturers, some of which were found to constitute unfair trading conditions.[646] The contracts included clauses relating to time limits for the

642 See CMA, Hydrocortisone tablets: suspected excessive and unfair pricing: Case timetable, available at https://www.gov.uk/cma-cases/pharmaceutical-sector-anti-competitive-practices#case-timetable.

643 Case C-127/73, *Belgische Radio en Televisie v SN SABAM and NV Fonior* [1974] ECR 313.

644 Case C-127/73, *Belgische Radio en Televisie v SN SABAM and NV Fonior* [1974] ECR 313, para 11.

645 Ibid, paras 12–13.

646 Case T-139/98, *Amministrazione Autonoma dei Monopoli di Stato (AAMS) v Commission* [2001] ECR II–3413.

introduction of new cigarette brands and imposing maximum quantities of new cigarette brands and cigarettes allowed into the market. It is noteworthy that the GC rejected AAMS reliance on the reasoning of the CJEU in *Oscar Bronner*, pointing out that that judgment was not relevant as 'the Commission does not accuse AAMS of refusing to grant certain foreign firms access to its distribution network but of making access to the network conditional upon the firms accepting unfair terms in the distribution agreement', thus narrowing down the scope of the *Oscar Bronner* defence in refusal to supply cases only.[647] While the GC accepted that an undertaking having a dominant position on a market should not be deprived of its entitlement to protect its own commercial interests when they are attacked may take such reasonable steps as it deems appropriate to protect its interests, it noted that AAMS had not proved to the requisite legal standard that the abovementioned clauses were necessary to protect its commercial interests.[648] Such types of abuse may become more popular in the context of 'unfair' commercial practices adopted by dominant digital platforms and affecting other businesses, in addition to the regulatory remedies envisaged in the recent draft regulation on the fairness of platform-to-business (P2B) trading practices in the online platform economy.[649] One may analyze the Bundeskartellamt's Facebook case (see 9.11.3.) as also fitting this category of abuse, to the extent that Facebook's users were confronted to a take-it-or-leave-it exchange, where they had little choice, in view of the dominant position of Facebook, than to consent to the use of their data by Facebook and third-parties with which Facebook shared their data. This 'consent' cannot be considered as voluntary, therefore Facebook's conduct may be found to constitute an 'unfair' commercial practice.

SELECTIVE BIBLIOGRAPHY

Books

Akman, P, *The Concept of Abuse in EU Competition Law: Law and Economic Approaches* (Hart, 2012).

Joliet, R, *Monopolization and Abuse of a Dominant Position: A Comparative Study of the American and European Approaches to the Control of Economic Power* (Martinus Nijhoff, 1970).

Nazzini, R, *The Foundations of European Union Competition Law: The Objective and Principles of Article 102* (OUP, 2011).

O'Donoghue, R, and Padilla, J, *The Law and Economics of Article 102 TFEU* (Hart, 2nd ed, 2013).

Rousseva, E, *Rethinking Exclusionary Abuses in EU Competition Law* (Hart, 2010).

Chapters in books

Gal, M, 'Abuse of Dominance—Exploitative Abuses' in Lianos, I, and Geradin, D (eds) *Handbook in EU Competition Law: Substantive Aspects* (Edward Elgar, 2013), ch 9.

Jones, A, and Gormsen, LL, 'Abuse of Dominance-Exclusionary Pricing Abuses' in Lianos, I, and Geradin, D, *Handbook in EU Competition Law: Substantive Aspects* (Edward Elgar, 2013), ch 10.

647 Ibid, para 76.
648 Ibid, para 79.
649 Proposal for a Regulation on promoting fairness and transparency for business users of online intermediation services, COM(2018) 238 final.

Motta, M, '*Michelin II*: The Treatment of Rebate' in Lyons, B (ed) *Cases in European Competition Policy: The Economic Analysis* (CUP, 2009) 29–49.

Motta, M, and De Streel, A, 'Exploitative and Exclusionary Excessive Prices in EU Law' in Ehlermann, CD, and Atanasiu, I (eds) *What is an Abuse of a Dominant Position?* (Hart, 2006) 91–126.

Journal articles

Areeda, P, and Turner, D, 'Predatory Pricing and Related Practices under Section 2 of the Sherman Act' (1975) 88 *Harvard L Rev* 697.

Bowman Jr, WS, 'Tying Arrangements and the Leverage Problem (1957) 67 *Yale LJ* 19.

Carlton, DW, and Waldman, M, 'The Strategic Use of Tying to Preserve and Create Market Power in Evolving Industries' (2002) 33 *Rand J Economics* 194.

Choi, JP, and Stefanadis, C, 'Tying, Investment, and the Dynamic Leverage Theory' (2001) 32 *Rand J Economics* 52.

Cooper Feldman, R, 'Defensive Leveraging in Antitrust' (1999) 87 *Georgetown LJ* 2079.

Economides, N, and Lianos, I, 'The Elusive Antitrust Standard on Bundling in Europe and in the United States in the Aftermath of the Microsoft Cases' (2009) 76 *Antitrust LJ* 483

Edlin, A,' Stopping Above-Cost Predatory Pricing' (2002) 111 *Yale LJ* 941, 952

Elhauge, E, and Einer, R, 'Tying, Bundled Discounts, and the Death of the Single Monopoly Profit Theory' (2009) 123 *Harvard L Rev* 397.

Elhauge, E, 'Why Above-Cost price Cuts to Drive Out Entrants Are Not Predatory—And the Implications for Defining Costs and Market Power' [2003] 112 *Yale LJ* 681.

Evans, DS, and Padilla, JA, 'Excessive Prices: Using Economics to Define Administrable Legal Rules' (2005) 1 *J Competition L & Economics* 97.

Ezrachi, A, and Gilo, D, 'Are Excessive Prices Really Self-Correcting?' (2009) 5 *J Competition L & Economics* 249.

Ezrachi, A and Stucke, M, 'The Rise of Behavioural Discrimination' (2016) 37 *European Competition L Rev* 484.

Federico, G, 'The Antitrust Treatment of Loyalty Discounts in Europe: Towards a more Economic Approach' (2011) 2 *J European Competition L & Practice* 277.

Geradin, D, 'Loyalty Rebates after *Intel*: Time for the European Court of Justice to Overrule *Hoffman-La Roche*' [2015] 11 *J Competition L & Economics* 579.

Geradin, D, and Petit, N, 'Price Discrimination under EC Competition Law: Another Antitrust Doctrine in Search of Limiting Principles?' (2006) 2 *J Competition L & Economics* 479.

Ibáñez Colomo, P, 'Exclusionary Discrimination under Article 102 TFEU' (2014) 51 *Common Market L Rev* 141.

Kaplow, L, 'Extension of Monopoly Power Through Leverage' (1985) 85 *Columbia L Rev* 515.

Krattenmaker, TG, and Salop, SC, 'Anticompetitive Exclusion: Raising Rivals' Costs to Achieve Power Over Price' (1986) 96 *Yale LJ* 209.

Marvel, H, 'Exclusive Dealing' (1982) 25(1) *J L & Economics* 1.

Pitofsky, R, Patterson, D, and Hooks, J, 'The Essential Facilities Doctrine Under US Law' (2002) 70 *Antitrust LJ* 443.

Rasmusen, EB, Ramseyer, JM, and Wiley, JS, 'Naked Exclusion' (1991) 81 *American Economic Rev* 1137.

Rousseva, E, and Marquis, M, 'Hell Freezes Over: A Climate Change for Assessing Exclusionary Conduct under Article 102 TFEU' (2012) 4(1) *J European Competition L & Practice* 32.

Temple Lang, J, 'Defining Legitimate Competition: Companies' Duties to Supply Competitors, and Access to Essential Facilities' (1994) 18 *Fordham Int'l LJ* 437.

Whinston, MD, 'Tying, Foreclosure and Exclusion' (1990) 80 *American Economic Review* 837.

Zenger, H, 'Loyalty Rebates and the Competitive Process' (2012) 8 *J Competition L & Economics* 717.

DISTRIBUTION AGREEMENTS

10.0. FOUNDATIONS

Firms exercise choices about how to get their products or services to the final consumers.

A supplier of products is confronted to six problems:

1. how to find customers,
2. how to obtain the materials or components it needs to make its products,
3. how to make the product,
4. how to get the finished product to its customers,
5. how to finance its operations and
6. how to provide against the unknown.[1]

A firm may perform all six functions itself, this amounting to a situation of 'vertical integration'. Direct sales to end users could be made through an Internet website, catalogues, and through employed salespersons. In this case, there will be no intermediaries between the firms and the end users. The firm's own employees will provide point-of-sale or after-sale service to consumers. Instead, or in addition, to selling directly to

[1] V Korah and D O'Sullivan, *Distribution Agreements under the EC Competition Rules* (Hart, 2002), 1.

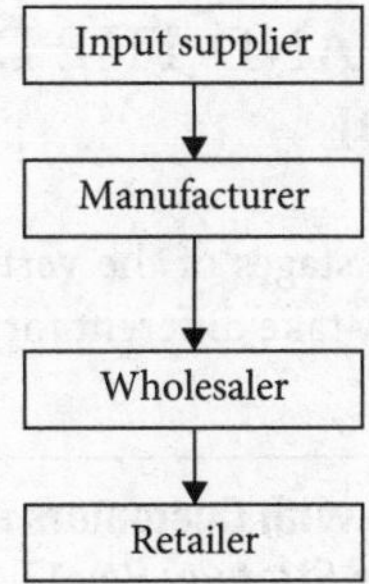

Figure 10.1. The vertical supply chain.

final consumers, the firm may choose to sell through intermediaries (distributors). These can be either wholesalers or retailers. The firm's relationship with its distributors will be governed by a contract, which may be written, oral, and occasionally subject to statutory provisions for the protection of distributors. Firms may therefore agree with other independent firms that they should carry out some, or all, of these tasks (vertical distribution by independent retailers). They may also entrust an agent who will be vested with the power to negotiate and/or conclude on behalf of the supplier (the principal), either in the agent's name or in the principal's name for the purchase of goods and services by the principal or the sale of goods and services supplied by the principal (commercial agency).

Perceived in this way, distribution is a service that may be bought by the supplier, the cost of which must be included in the final price to consumers. In some situations, it is more efficient to perform the functions within the firm, in others to buy in the distribution services market. The mainstream view, since the introduction of economic analysis in EU competition law enforcement, is that unless there is good reason, businessmen should be left to select the most cost-effective method with as little distortion as possible induced by the competition rules and other kinds of legal measure.

In this Chapter we will examine the application of Article 101 of the Treaty on the Functioning of the European Union (TFEU) to restraints included in the distribution of products,[2] including the specific block exemption regulation (BER) on vertical restraints,[3] and the vertical restraints guidelines,[4] which set the principles applying in this context.

[2] Restrictions included in agreements concerning the distribution of digital content over the Internet and included in licensing agreements involving intellectual property (IP) rights are examined in detail in the companion volume I Lianos, *Competition Law and the Intangible Economy* (OUP, forthcoming 2019).

[3] Commission Regulation (EU) No 330/2010 on the application of Article 101(3) of the Treaty on the Functioning of the European Union to categories of vertical agreements and concerted practices [2010] OJ L 102/1 [hereinafter Regulation 330/2010]. Guidelines on Vertical Restraints [2010] OJ C 130/1 [hereinafter Vertical Restraints Guidelines 2010].

[4] Ibid, para 19.

10.1. SUPPLY CHAINS AND THE DIFFERENT FORMS OF VERTICAL CONTROL

Coordination between the different stages of the vertical chain requires some degree of vertical control. Vertical control may take different forms.

JA Kay, 'Managing Relationships with Customers and Suppliers: Law, Economics And Strategy' (1991) 2(1) *Business Strategy Rev* 17, 17–18

> Vertical relationships describe the contracts between firms and their customers or suppliers. Traditionally, the supply chain was divided clearly into *two* or three stages—corresponding, for example, to manufacture, wholesale, and retail. Indeed, it is still common to talk about primary, secondary and tertiary stages of production. [. . .] Each firm undertakes a discrete series of activities and then sells its output on for further processing. But supply chains within industries look like that less and less frequently. Firms at each stage of production are involved in the value systems of their customers and their suppliers. Sometimes, and most familiarly, this is achieved through ownership and control. The outcome is then complete vertical integration. Another development has been the growth of intermediate forms of relationship. A firm may exercise extensive control and influence over a supplier, or a retailer, which falls short of outright ownership and management.
>
> Private label retailing, where a manufacturer produces goods to a specification laid down by a retailer who himself brands the product, is one example. The converse is franchising, where an independent retailer owns and operates his shop to a specification and format dictated by his supplier. Another common form of interrelationship is one in which wholesalers own retail premises which they rent to independent agents; petrol and beer are generally sold in this way in many countries. Firms attempt to determine the conditions under which their product is sold. They impose exclusive dealing requirements, or impose territorial exclusivity; they effect resale price maintenance, or sell only through a network of authorized distributors; they offer incentives to distributors to promote their products through aggregated rebates, full-line forcing, or override commissions. In entering such arrangements, firms have two principal groups of motive. They may believe they are selling composite products, where the purchaser is buying both the commodity itself and the conditions under which it is sold. This is very obvious for, as example, a pint of beer purchased in a bar; the customer obtains a package which includes both the beer itself and the environment of the bar. The same is true of the Macdonald's product, or the St Michael brand. But firms are also concerned with effects on the structure of the industry, and by controlling channels of supply and distribution they can expect to gain advantages relative to their competitors and over potential entrants to their industry.

10.1.1. FROM VERTICAL INTEGRATION TO VERTICAL COOPERATION: THE TRANSACTION COSTS ECONOMICS FOUNDATIONS OF MODERN COMPETITION LAW TOWARDS VERTICAL RESTRAINTS

Vertical control may take different forms, going from a rigid mechanism of control within a hierarchy (vertical integration), which is based on control through the exercise of *power*, to more loose forms of coordination of economic activity (vertical control through contractual arrangements)[5] and 'take-it-or-leave-it exchange', that are only based on *trust* (or coercion), rather than a legally binding commitment.[6] This Chapter's focus is on 'vertical restraints' arising in the context of distribution arrangements. These should be distinguished from the standard sale contract in the context of 'take it or leave-it exchange'.

J Church and R Ware, *Industrial Organization: A Strategic Approach* (McCraw-Hill, 2000), 688

Vertical restraints can be defined as any economic exchange that differs from the standard sale contract observed in perfect competition. In that contract, when a buyer purchases a good or service, complete legal control transfers to the buyer. The buyer may resell the good at any price, to any purchaser of its choice, in any location. The most commonly observed vertical restraints are restrictions on the flexibility of the buyer, where the buyer is usually a distributor or retailer, and the restriction is imposed by the manufacturer.

Hierarchy			Market
Vertical integration	Quasi-integration	Vertical contractual arrangements (vertical cooperation)	Take-it-or-leave-it exchange

There might be different reasons explaining the choice between vertical integration and vertical contractual arrangements. The starting point is transaction costs economics (TCE) and more broadly contractual theories of vertical integration is the work of Ronald Coase, Oliver Williamson and Paul Joskow.[7] According to TCE, the coordination of economic activities may take place either through the market or through some form of hierarchical control imposed by the entrepreneur within the boundaries of a hierarchy. One of the main reasons for incurring the costs of organization within a hierarchy are the costs that are imposed by employing the market mechanism, due to a number of market imperfections, such as the absence of perfect information that would enable the economic operator to select the best available partner (as an example of transaction costs).[8] As we have explored in Chapter 3, the governance of these costly (if one uses the market mechanism) transactions would require either the constitution of a hierarchical organization under the control of the entrepreneur,

[5] MK Perry, 'Vertical Integration: Determinants and Effects' in R Schmalensee and RD Willig (eds) *Handbook of Industrial Organization*, vol 1 (North Holland, 1989), 183, 186. A vertical control 'arises from a contract between two firms at different stages which transfers control of some, but not all, aspects of production or distribution'.

[6] Ibid, 188. The distinction between power and trust as the defining characteristic of the opposition between hierarchy and market is inspired by N Luhmann, *Trust and Power* (Wiley, 1979).

[7] RH Coase, 'The Nature of the Firm' (1937) 16(4) *Economica* 386; O Williamson, *The Economic Institutions of Capitalism* (Free Press, 1985); P Joskow, 'The New Institutional Economics: Alternative Approaches' (1995) 151(1) *J Institutional and Theoretical Economics* 248; P Joskow, 'Transaction Cost Economics, Antitrust Rules and Remedies' (2002) 18(1) *J L Economics and Organization* 95. For a brief discussion, see Chapter 2.

[8] EG Furubont and R Richter, *Institutions and Economic Theory: The Contribution of the New Institutional Economics* (University of Michigan Press, 1999).

who will integrate these activities in its existing hierarchy, or the selection of (independent) partners, their relation being managed by (long-term) contractual arrangements. Relying on vertical control, instead of the pure market exchange mechanism, may also be explained by the bounded rationality of economic agents. US economist Herbert Simon once explained that 'it is only because individual human beings are limited in knowledge, foresight, skill, and time that organizations are useful investments for the achievement of human purpose'.[9]

Transaction costs economics and the bounded rationality of economic agents explain the constitution of different forms of organization of economic activity promoting efficiency-enhancing collaboration. One option is to vertically integrate, in order to achieve a durable integration of the assets of different economic agents. Another option would be to put in place a flexible form of coordination that avoids any risk of opportunistic behaviour by the agents.

In some cases, the realization of the objectives of the economic agents will require the elaboration of a long-term agreement. A long-term agreement may create a risk of opportunism as each party will commit some specific assets necessary for the completion of the common objective ('asset specificity') and will thus incur a sunk cost, that is, a cost that could not be recovered if the company exited the market. Whenever a firm has to make an investment in something that has no other equally valuable use, it needs contractual protection from opportunistic behaviour by its suppliers. The costs sunk in the investment create an inequality in bargaining power and hence allow unilateral appropriation of the benefit of that investment ('hold up') unless the investor protects himself by means of an enforceable contract. This is a major justification for imposing contractual vertical control. There are different tools ensuring vertical control in relations of vertical cooperation. These arrangements may impose 'vertical restraints', that is, 'agreements and contractual provisions between vertically related firms'.[10]

10.1.2. MARKETS, HIERARCHIES AND NETWORKS: THE ROLE OF TRANSACTIONAL EFFICIENCY

Markets and Hierarchies are not distinct concepts but different poles of a *continuum*.[11] This led Oliver Williamson to introduce a third category in his taxonomy, falling between Markets and Hierarchies, for organizational forms that do not correspond to the characteristics of those two forms. He called this category 'Hybrids'.[12] This term, still highly imprecise, covers a variety of organizational forms, such as alliances, collective trademarks, networks, partnerships, and relational contracts,[13] which do not institute hierarchies, as each of the participants retains its autonomy, and do not institute markets, as there are formal or informal mechanisms that are set in order to facilitate a long-term coordination and cooperation between the different entities forming the hybrid.[14]

[9] HA Simon, *Models of Man* (Wiley, 1957), 199.

[10] M Motta, *Competition Policy: Theory and Practice* (CUP, 2004), 302.

[11] Part of this Section draws on I Lianos, 'Commercial Agency Agreements, Vertical Restraints, and the Limits of Article 81(1) EC: Between Hierarchies and Networks' (2007) 3 *J Competition L & Economics* 625.

[12] O Williamson, 'Comparative Economic Organization: The Analysis of Discrete Structural Alternatives' (1991) 36 *Administrative Science Q* 269.

[13] S Deakin et al, '"Trust" or Law? Towards an Integrated Theory of Contractual Relations Between Firms' (1994) 21 *J L & Society* 329, 334–5; IR MacNeil, 'Contracts: Adjustment of Long-Term Economic Relations Under Classical, Neoclassical, and Relational Contract Law' (1978) 72 *Northwestern U L Rev* 854, 857.

[14] C Ménard, 'The Economics of Hybrid Organizations' (2004) 160 *J Institutional and Theoretical Economics* 345, 347–50.

According to Williamson, each of these organizational forms presents different characteristics and is supported by different forms of contract law.[15] The identity of the parties is irrelevant in transactions in spot markets and the price mechanism is the only way to allocate tasks and rights of control. However, it becomes an important element if the transaction involves specific investments, since its long duration creates uncertainty regarding the *ex post* sharing of joint profits, which induces the risk of opportunistic behaviour from the parties. Because of the difficulty of considering *ex ante* all the possible 'consequential disturbances' that may happen in the future, the contract will inevitably be incomplete.[16] 'Long-term incomplete contracts require special adaptive mechanisms to effect realignment and restore efficiency when beset by unanticipated disturbances'.[17] Although these adaptive mechanisms perfect the contract between the parties, at the same time, they impose important restrictions on their autonomy in the market. If the specific investments are important and there is an important risk of opportunism, the transaction costs will be important and a hierarchy will emerge.

Property rights theories of the firm acknowledge the importance of vertical restraints as control mechanisms for complementary assets,[18] even in the absence of asset specificity. As Hart pointed out, 'in a world of transaction costs and incomplete contracts, *ex post* residual rights of control will be important because through their influence in asset usage, they will affect *ex post* bargaining power and the division of *ex post* surplus in a relationship', division which will, in turn, 'affect the incentives of actors to invest in that relationship'.[19]

The degree of control (ownership versus contractual commitment) will of course depend on a number of variables.

JA Kay, 'Managing Relationships With Customers and Suppliers: Law, Economics And Strategy' (1991) 2 *Business Strategy Rev* 17, 22

Many forms of relationship between supplier and customer exist which lie between the extremes of complete independence and outright ownership. Petrol wholesaling and retailing provides a clear instance. Many wholesalers have company-managed sites, on which the staff are simply employees of an oil major. That company determines prices, hours of opening, layout of store in much the same way as any other multiple retailer. At the opposite end of the spectrum, leading supermarket chains put out tenders to supply petrol on their sites to several leading oil companies. Intermediate relationships include commission agency—the company owns the site and the stock and pays the station operator a royalty on product sold. There are tenants of company-owned sites who fix their own selling prices and negotiate buying prices or price support with the owner of the service station. And there are independent retailers who obtain favourable terms in return for a long-term exclusive supply relationship. There is a complete spectrum of relationship, and almost every feasible relationship is to be found.

15 O Williamson, *The Economic Institutions of Capitalism: Firms, Markets, Relational Contracting* (Free Press, 1985), 68–72; O Williamson, *The Mechanisms of Governance* (OUP, 1996), 93.

16 O Williamson, 'Comparative Economic Organization: The Analysis of Discrete Structural Alternatives' (1991) 36 *Administrative Science Q* 269, 271.

17 O Williamson, *The Mechanisms of Governance* (OUP, 1996), 96.

18 O Hart and J Moore, 'Property Rights and the Nature of the Firm' (1990) 98 *J Political Economy* 1119.

19 O Hart, 'An Economist's Perspective on the Theory of the Firm' (1989) 89 *Columbia L Rev* 1757, 1766.

For the proponents of TCE, the legal regime should take account of the specificities of each of these forms of organization and the existence of transaction costs that would justify, from an economic efficiency perspective, a more integrated form of control and coordination between the parties to the transaction. Accordingly, the law applicable to the internal organization of the firm or hierarchy should be forbearance. Williamson explains: 'whereas courts routinely grant standing to contracts between firms should there be disputes over prices, the damages to be ascribed to delays, failures of quality, and the like, the courts have the good sense to refuse to hear disputes between one internal division and another over identical technical issues. Access to the courts being denied, the parties must resolve their differences internally, which is to say that the firm becomes its own court of ultimate appeal.'[20]

There are two reasons that mainly justify the law of forbearance:

> (1) parties to an internal dispute have deep knowledge—both about the circumstances surrounding a dispute as well as the efficiency properties of alternative solutions—that can be communicated to the court at great cost, and (2) permitting the internal disputes to be appealed to the court would undermine the efficacy an integrity of hierarchy.[21]

The identification of these different forms of organization and of their corresponding regimes of contract law has important implications for competition law analysis. Vertical restraints may be considered as governance tools that are used in order to avoid organizational failures that arise in situations of hierarchy or hybrid (networks): they thus bring transactional efficiencies. In the absence of significant market power, competition law should not intervene in a situation of hierarchy, as this will compromise the internal organization of this form of governance and the transactional efficiencies this may bring. The scope of competition law intervention may be more important in the situation of a network.

The distinction between network and hierarchies should not, however, be overstated. Networks may evolve towards a loose form of hierarchy as they are subject to cyclical developments following which the most powerful participants may bring the network itself under control and create a situation of hierarchy.[22] Consequently, it is important for competition law to recognize the specificities of these different organizational forms and adopt a flexible approach, which will not affect the choice of the most efficient organizational structure by the parties to the transaction, in the absence of significant market power.[23]

10.1.3. VERTICAL RESTRAINTS BEYOND TRANSACTIONAL EFFICIENCY

Both TCE and property rights theories of the firm view vertical restraints as an efficient response to contracting frictions.[24] The first one treats each transaction in isolation, focusing

[20] O Williamson, 'The Economics of Governance' (2005) 95 *American Economic Rev* 1, 10.

[21] O Williamson, *The Mechanisms of Governance* 100.

[22] HB Thorelli, 'Networks: Between Markets and Hierarchies' (1986) 7 *Strategic Management J* 37.

[23] C Ménard, 'Maladaptation of Regulation to Hybrid Organizational Forms' (1999) 18 *Int'l Rev L and Economics* 403, 414–16.

[24] T Bresnahan and J Levin, 'Vertical Integration and Market Structure', NBER Working Paper No 17889 (March 2012).

on the transaction's characteristics and the market structure of the markets affected by the vertical restraint (in terms of horizontal competition), while recognizing that vertical integration allows the firm to protect specific investments and avoid potential hold-ups. The second one views firms as a collection of physical assets, associating vertical integration with shifts in asset ownership that strengthen the bargaining position of the parties in the event of a breakdown, and therefore ensuring the stability of the relationship over time. These are not the only theories that put forward a positive perception of vertical integration: one may also cite the decision rights approach, which focuses on vertical integration as a way to avoid the double marginalization problem (see Section 10.5.1.1), or the principal–agent model that aims to ensure a better coordination and alignment of incentives (including financial incentives) between the various segments of a vertical value chain (see Section 10.5.1.3). A more dynamic perspective will also view vertical integration and vertical restraints as a way for firms to leverage their internal capabilities in related markets or to exploit their superior management capabilities.[25]

However, under certain circumstances, vertical integration and vertical restraints may also form part of a strategic effort to limit competition by raising barriers and marginalising competitors through strategic foreclosure, thus limiting horizontal competition and leading to an exercise of market power. Empirical evidence for each of these theories is relatively ambiguous and quantifying the effects of integration decisions remains challenging.[26] These approaches emphasize horizontal competition as the main source of competitive constraint that merits to be preserved by competition law, to the extent that in case there is intense horizontal competition exists, vertical integration, and vertical restraints are more likely to serve benign rather than malign objectives. Certainly, vertical integration or vertical restraints may limit vertical competition (on this concept, see Section 3.1.1) but it is thought that vertical competition relates more to distributional effects (relating to the allocation of the surplus value) or 'pecuniary externalities' that, according to neoclassical price theory (NPT), should be ignored if one focuses on economic efficiency.[27] However, one may take a non-economic efficiency-based perspective for competition law, promoting other values such as fairness, in which case the distribution of the total surplus value between the different segments of the value chain may become an important concern for competition law, either because of considerations relating to equality of opportunity concerns, or because substantial restrictions to vertical competition may impact on productivity, as an overwhelming percentage of the total surplus value is captured by 'superstar' large firms that enjoy tremendous levels of profitability, without however these accumulated profits being used for productive investments, that could ultimately generate value for consumers.

Taking a resource-based view of the firm the Global Value Chain (GVC) approach focuses on different key determinants of governance patterns than TCE to explain the prevalence of certain forms of organization, in particular the complexity of transactions, the codifiability of information, and the capability of suppliers, while TCE only focuses on the determinants of asset specificity and the frequency of the transactions as the driving forces for organizational choice.[28] Adopting the GVC approach may therefore change our current understanding of vertical tools of control and coordination.

25 Ibid. citing literature in business strategy, taking the perspective of the resource-based view of the firm: see, in particular, B Wernerfelt, 'A Resource-Based View of the Firm' (1984) 5(2) *Strategic Management* 171.

26 T Bresnahan & J Levin, Vertical Integration and Market Structure, NBER Working Paper No 17889 (2012).

27 This is the main lesson of the so-called Coase theorem, which assumes a world of zero transaction costs and individuals that are able to bargain and internalize technological externalities, leaving aside pecuniary externalities: RG Holcombe and RS Sobel, 'Public Policy Toward Pecuniary Externalities' (2001) 29(4) *Public Finance Rev* 304.

28 Gary Gereffi, John Humphrey and Timothy Sturgeon, 'The governance of global value chains', (2005) 12(1) *Review of International Political Economy* 78–104.

EU competition law is quintessentially following the NPT rulebook by focusing on horizontal competition, but one may also observe tensions, in particular in specific economic sectors between the economic efficiency and the fairness perspectives (see Section S.10.8.2.1 on competition law enforcement in the food sector).

10.2. A TYPOLOGY OF VERTICAL RESTRAINTS

Massimo Motta, *Competition Policy—Theory and Practice* (CUP, 2004), 302–4 (footnotes omitted)

[. . .] [C]onsider the classical example of the vertical relationship between a manufacturer and a retailer which distributes its products. In general, both the manufacturer and a retailer decide on different actions and what is an optimal action for one is not necessarily optimal for the other. As a result, a party can try to use contracts and clauses so as to restrain the choice of the other and induce an outcome which is more favourable to itself. (To put it another way, each party's actions create an externality on the other. Vertical contracts might be used to try to control for these externalities.)

For instance, the manufacturer would like the retailer to make a lot of effort in marketing its products (such as advertise its products, put them in evidence on shelves, employ specialized personnel who assist potential customers, offer post-sale assistance and so on), but the latter might have a lower incentive to do so, as effort and services are costly to provide. The manufacturer might then decide to use contractual provisions (that is, vertical restraints) in order to induce higher marketing effort from its retailer. To continue the example, it might assign an exclusive area of competence to the retailer so that it would fully appropriate the benefits of the services provided (if other retailers carry the same brand within the same region there is a free-riding problem that further reduces the incentive to provide those services); or it might use a non-linear contract such that the retailer would have a discount if it buys a large number of units, in order to encourage its sales effort; or it might simply oblige the retailer to sell a minimum number of units of the good, which again would increase its effort; or it might convince the retailer not to carry competing brands, to stimulate its sales efforts; or it might simply take over the retailer so as to make coordination of actions easier.

The garden variety vertical restraints include both price restraints, which impose conditions on the price that the downstream firm can charge for the good that is purchased from the upstream firm, and non-price restraints.

Massimo Motta, *Competition Policy—Theory and Practice* (CUP, 2004), 302–4 (footnotes omitted)

- *Non-linear pricing.* (Also called franchise fee or two-part tariff contracts). In the simplest possible relationship between two agents, one buys from the other on the basis of a 'linear pricing' rule, that is, the total payment is proportional to the number of units involved in the transaction. Whether one buys one unit or one hundred units, the unit price would be the same. A simple vertical restraint is then 'non-linear pricing', a contract which specifies a fixed amount independent of the number of units bought (the 'franchise fee') plus a variable component. For instance, to sell a given clothes producer's brand, a shop might have to pay 1,000 euro per year plus 10 euro for each T-shirt it buys. The effect of such a contract is that the unit cost effectively paid by the shop decreases with the number of units bought from the same producer. The effect is to encourage the retailer to buy more units.

- *Quantity discounts.* Quantity discounts or progressive rebates have the same effect as non-linear pricing contracts, as the larger the quantity bought the cheaper the transaction on average.
- *Resale price maintenance* (RPM). The manufacturer might have different perceptions from the retailer as to which price final customers should be charged for the product. As a consequence, the former might want to affect the price decisions of the latter. In its most extreme form, RPM simply consists of the price at which the retailer should sell the product. But it might also be a recommended price, or it might establish either a minimum resale price (price floor) or a maximum resale price (price ceiling).
- *Quantity fixing.* The manufacturer might want to specify the number of units that the retailer should buy. Again, this might also take different forms, such as *quantity forcing* [or requirement contracts] (the retailer cannot buy less than a certain amount) or *quantity rationing* (it cannot buy more than a certain amount).
- *Exclusivity clauses.* Manufacturer and retailer might also sign exclusivity agreements. For instance, an *exclusive territory* clause would imply that there is only one retailer who can sell a certain brand within a certain geographical area (or to a certain type of customers). Under *exclusive dealing* a retailer agrees to carry only the brand of a certain manufacturer. *Selective distribution* clauses allow only a certain type of retailers—usually specified in objective terms—to carry a manufacturer's brand. For instance, a luxury good producer might want to provide its product only to high-street retailers and not to supermarkets or discount stores, fearing that the latter might undermine the quality or luxury image associated with its product.

It is important to notice that in any given market—due to the nature of the transactions, or due to institutional constraints—some of these vertical restraints might be effective whereas others might not be. For instance, RPM makes sense only insofar as the effective price paid by final customers can be observed by the manufacturer. For mass products this might be the case; but in other circumstances there might be a bargaining process between the retailer and the final buyer whose outcome might be difficult to observe. If discounts on prices cannot be observed by the manufacturer, RPM loses its restraining power, and a manufacturer might want to rely on other restraints to achieve a certain objective. For instance, quantity fixing might be a substitute for RPM.

Other common vertical restraints comprise the following:

- *Bundling or tying.* The supplier requires from or offers incentives to the distributor to purchase a second distinct tied product (or service) as a condition for purchasing the first (tying) product. Bundling or tying may take different forms: it might be contractual (if it is imposed by a contract), technological (when this results from the integration of the second distinct product to the tying product, the two products not being available separately), or commercial/financial (called also mixed bundling when the where products or services are offered undiscounted a la carte as well as at a discounted price only to a retailer committing to buy at least *x* percent of his needs in all the bundled products from the same supplier).

- *Non-compete obligations*. According to the European Commission, 'a non-compete obligation means any direct or indirect obligation causing the buyer not to manufacture, purchase, sell or resell goods or services which compete with the contract goods or services, or any direct or indirect obligation on the buyer to purchase from the supplier or from another undertaking designated by the supplier more than 80 % of the buyer's total purchases of the contract goods or services and their substitutes on the relevant market, calculated on the basis of the value or, where such is standard industry practice, the volume of its purchases in the preceding calendar year'.[29]
- *Price protection clauses*. Price protection clauses aim to ensure that the margins at a certain level of the vertical chain (usually the retail level) will be protected from competition and that retailers will be able to maintain the pricing level that corresponds to their agreed level of compensation by the supplier for the provision of retail services. It may take different forms.
- *Most-favoured-nation (MFN)* clauses, also called most-favoured-customer (MFC) or anti-discrimination clauses, is a promise by one party to the vertical relationship, a supplier, to treat a buyer as well as the supplier treats its best, most-favoured customer. The supplier commits to a specific retailer to lower the price in order to match any reduction of the price to another retailer. The clauses protect the retailers from subsequent price reductions that might be given to other firms.
- *Minimum advertised pricing* (*MAP*) clauses restrict the dealer from advertising below some minimum price determined by its supplier.
- *Discount pass-through* or *promotional pass-through* arrangements condition any discounts granted to a certain level of the commercialization chain (eg wholesaler) to passing through the lower price to the next level of the commercialization chain (dealer or end-consumer).
- *Restrictions on advertising*. These include *MAP* clauses as well as *cooperative advertising programs*. Sponsored by the suppliers (through an allowance or other mechanism of sharing the costs), these programs restrict the freedom of retailers, for example by precluding them from including any information on pricing in the advertisement.
- *Upfront access payments*. According to the Vertical Restraints Guidelines, '[u]pfront access payments are fixed fees that suppliers pay to distributors in the framework of a vertical relationship at the beginning of a relevant period, in order to get access to their distribution network and remunerate services provided to the suppliers by the retailers. This category includes various practices such as *slotting allowances* (fixed fees that manufacturers pay to retailers in order to get access to their shelf space), the so-called *pay-to-stay fees* (lump sum payments made to ensure the continued presence of an existing product on the shelf for some further period), *payments to have access to a distributor's promotion campaigns*, etc.'[30] Upfront access payments put in place a three-part tariff, combining a negative upfront payments made by the manufacturer even if the retailer does not buy anything afterwards with a two part-tariff scheme (the supplier charging wholesale prices and the retailers paying conditional fixed fees on the products they actually purchased).

29 Regulation 330/2010, Article 1(1)(d).

30 Vertical Restraints Guidelines 2010, para 203 (emphasis added).

10.3. VERTICAL CONTROL BY OWNERSHIP, VERTICAL CONTROL BY CONTRACT, AND COMPETITION LAW

Competition law has traditionally distinguished restrictions of competition that find their source in vertical control by ownership (vertical integration) and in vertical control by contract ('vertical restraints').

Vertical integration by new entry and vertical integration by merger occur when the owner of one level of the production and commercialization process takes ownership of a second level as well.

Vertical control by contract occurs when firms owned and controlled separately enter into long-term commitments on their freedom of economic action or their resources to a specific, vertically related partner.

10.3.1. THE ORIGINS OF A DIFFERENTIATED APPLICATION OF COMPETITION LAW TO VERTICAL INTEGRATION AND VERTICAL CONTRACTUAL RESTRAINTS

Because of the relatively narrow conception of the firm as having essentially a productive function in economic literature until the late 1960s, vertical integration and vertical contractual arrangements were subject to a relatively tight competition law regime. However, vertical control by ownership has been generally treated more leniently than vertical control by contract.[31]

10.3.2. A DIFFERENTIATED REGIME FOR VERTICAL INTEGRATION AND VERTICAL RESTRAINTS IN EUROPE

In Europe, vertical integration through internal growth is not subject to competition law, unless the firm is found to abuse its dominant position. Vertical integration through external growth was also viewed more positively than vertical control by contract, as the EU did not dispose of a proper system of merger control until 1990 (see Chapter 12). This was due to the view that firms should take advantage of the considerable economies of scale that flowed from the EU Internal Market integration.

National merger control was of course enforced against mergers between competitors (horizontal mergers). In the UK, there was no provision for the control of mergers until the Monopolies and Mergers Act 1965.[32] The first proposal for the adoption of merger control in the UK concerned only horizontal mergers,[33] although vertical mergers were later added to the final version of the Act. The Fair-Trading Act 1973 also included vertical mergers, but very few mergers were referred to the Monopolies and Mergers Commission (MMC), the

[31] H Hovenkamp, 'The Law of Vertical Integration and the Business Firm: 1880–1960' [2010] 95 *Iowa L Rev* 863.

[32] See V Korah, 'Legal Regulation of Corporate Mergers in the United Kingdom' (1969) 5 *Texas Int'l L Forum* 71.

[33] White Paper, 'Monopolies, Mergers and Restrictive Practices', Cmnd 2299 (1963).

decision-making body at the time, for further investigation. Although the MMC expressed concern about the effects upon competition of some vertical mergers, it took a relatively positive stance and considered that the possible harm to competition could be offset by other benefits.[34]

Vertical contractual restraints in distribution have been, however, almost immediately subject to the strict scrutiny of EU competition law. In *Consten & Grundig*,[35] *LTM v MBU*,[36] and *Italian Republic v Council and Commission*[37] the CJEU confirmed the application of Article 101 TFEU to agreements between suppliers and retailers.[38] The Commission, followed occasionally by the Court, adopted aggressive competition law enforcement against vertical control by contract by considering that any restriction on the economic freedom of the parties to the agreement could be a restriction of competition, notwithstanding the absence of any actual or potential effect on consumers.

UK competition law's starting point was diametrically different, as it had initially considered that distribution agreements were benign from a competition law perspective.[39] Other vertical agreements were largely ignored by the Resale Prices Act 1976 and the Restrictive Trade Practices Act 1976, although the enactment of the 1980 Competition Act marked an evolution towards a more restrictive approach against vertical restraints in distribution agreements.[40] Distribution agreements, in particular exclusive purchasing, were also subject to the restraints of trade doctrine of the common law, although courts consistently saved them from

34 R Whish, *Competition Law* (Butterworths, 1985), 522–3.

35 Joined Cases C-56 & 58/64, *Établissements Consten et Grundig Verkaufs GmbH* [1966] ECR 430.

36 Case C-56/65, *Société Technique minière (LTM) v Maschinenbau ULM GmbH (MBU)* [1966] ECR 235.

37 Case C-32/65, *République italienne v Council of the EEC and Commission of the EEC* [1966] ECR 389.

38 This followed a number of decisions of the Commission, see *Grossfilex/Fillistord* (Case IV/61) Commission Decision 64/233/EEC [1964] OJ L 64/915; *Bendix/Mertens et Straet* (Case IV/12868) Commission Decision 64/344/EEC [1964] OJ L 64/1426; *Nicholas Frères/Vitapro* (Case IV/95) Commission Decision 64/502/EEC [1964] OJ L 64/2287; *Consten/Grundig* (Case IV/3344) Commission Decision 64/566/EEC [1964] OJ L 64/2545; *DECA* (Case IV/71) Commission Decision 64/599/EEC [1964] OJ L 64/2761; *DRU/Blondel* (Case IV/3036) Commission Decision 65/366/EEC [1965] OJ L 65/2581; *Hummel/Isbecque* (Case IV/2702) Commission Decision 65/426/EEC [1965] OJ L 65/2581.

39 With the exception, however, of resale price maintenance clauses, which were found to be illegal *per se* since 1956 for 'collective' RPM and 1964 for 'individual' RPM clauses. A clause is considered as an 'individual' RPM when a single manufacturer stipulates the resale price for its own products. In 'collective' RPM agreements RPM schemes are widely used by various competing manufacturers, commonly within the framework of an association of undertakings. Part II of the Restrictive Trade Practice Act 1956 prohibited only the collective enforcement of Resale Price Maintenance clauses. In return, suppliers were given a new statutory right to enforce their Resale Price Maintenance conditions against price-cutters irrespective of whether the price-cutters were in direct contractual relations with the Supplier; Jeremy Lever, 'The Development of British Competition Law: A Complete Overhaul and Harmonization', Discussion Paper FS IV 99 (4 March 1999), 23–4, available at https://bibliothek.wzb.eu/pdf/1999/iv99-4.pdf. However, the industry devised methods of circumventing the prohibition of the Act, by adopting individual RPM clauses, which were not prohibited by the legislation (*White Paper on Monopolies, Mergers and Restrictive Practices*, 1964, Cmnd. 2299). See V Korah, 'Resale Price Maintenance and the Restrictive Trade Practices Act 1956 S. 25' (1961) 24(2) *Modern L Rev* 219. The government did not manage to impose a absolute ban on individual RPM but subjected them to the jurisdiction of the Registrar and the Restrictive Practices Court, providing that the later could exempt certain classes of goods if it appeared that enforcement of these clauses could result in certain specific injuries to consumers, including reduced product quality, product unavailability, prices increases, lessened product safety, and reduced service in connection with the product. RPM was not made a criminal offence but enforcement was simply guaranteed through civil proceedings by an injured trader or the Crown. See V Korah, 'Statutes: Resale Prices Act 1964' (1965) 28(2) *Modern L Rev* 193. Only the areas of drugs and books was exempted from the application of RPM clauses.

40 R Whish, *Competition Law* (Butterworths, 1985), 429–33.

a finding of unreasonableness.[41] The 1998 Competition Act (CA98) repealed the Restrictive Trade Practice Act as well as specific legislation relating to resale price maintenance. Vertical agreements were nevertheless excluded from the scope of the prohibition of Chapter I CA98 until 30 April 2005 (Land and Vertical Agreements Exclusion Order).[42] Article 4 of the Order provided that the exclusion from the prohibition

> [could] not apply where the vertical agreement, directly or indirectly, in isolation or in combination with other factors under the control of the parties has the object or effect of restricting the buyer's ability to determine its sale price, without prejudice to the possibility of the supplier imposing a maximum sale price or recommending a sale price, provided that these do not amount to a fixed or minimum sale price as a result of pressure from, or incentives offered by, any of the parties.

The Vertical Agreements Exclusion Order was repealed in 2004, following the enactment of EU Regulation 1/2003. Following this date, vertical restraints in distribution agreements are caught by the prohibition of Chapter I CA98. The prohibition should be interpreted consistently with EU law, according to section 60 CA98 and in accordance with the Vertical Block Exemption Regulation by virtue of section 10 CA98, providing a system of parallel exemptions (an agreement exempted under EU Competition Law should also be exempted under UK Competition Law). Because of the important similarities between the EU and the UK competition law regime for vertical restraints, these will not be examined separately, but included in our analysis of the application of Article 101 to vertical restraints. That said, it is quite likely that the area of vertical restraints will lead to some divergence between UK and EU competition law following Brexit.

The distinction between the legal regimes of vertical control by ownership and vertical control by contract has been attenuated after the adoption of Regulation 139/2004 on merger control, which established the significant impediment of effective competition test that is broader than the previous dominant test. Furthermore, the non-horizontal merger guidelines follow an analytical approach more similar to vertical mergers than to the Block Exemption Regulation on vertical agreements or the vertical restraints guidelines.[43]

10.4. THE APPLICATION OF ARTICLE 101(1) TFEU TO VERTICAL RESTRAINTS

Article 101(1) TFEU applied to vertical restraints that emanate from

- an agreement, a concerted practice, or a decision of association of undertakings (Section 10.4.2)

[41] *Esso Petroleum Co Ltd v Harper's Garage (Stourport) Ltd* [1968] AC 269, [1967] 1 All ER 699; *Texaco Ltd v Mulberry Filling Station Ltd* [1972] 1 All ER 513, [1972] 1 WLR 814.

[42] Competition Act 1998 (Land and Vertical Agreements Exclusion) Order 2000, SI 2000/310. The purpose of the land and vertical agreements exclusion order was to remove any need to notify such agreements to the OFT or regulators on a precautionary basis, while putting in place mechanisms to deal with any agreements within the categories that raised competition concerns. In addition, the UK legislator did not share the Commission's concern that vertical agreements could divide the single market on national grounds, which was not relevant to the chapter I prohibition. In almost every case in which the Commission has acted against vertical agreements, single market considerations have been the predominant, or the only, concerns.

[43] See Chapter 12.

- or between two undertakings (Section 10.4.1),
- the object *or* effect of which is to restrict competition (Section 10.4.4),
- and which affect trade between Member States (Section 10.4.3).

10.4.1. SINGLE ENTITY DOCTRINE AND THE APPLICATION OF ARTICLE 101(1) TFEU

Article 101 applies only to collusive practices between undertakings. The concept of undertaking was defined in Chapter 4 as 'every entity engaged in an economic activity, regardless of the legal status of the entity and the way in which it is financed'.[44] The concept of 'economic entity' has been defined broadly to include both natural and legal persons. Article 101 TFEU could thus potentially apply to all transactions between the different parts of the distribution chain.

Adopting such an approach may nevertheless have considerable shortcomings. First, it will subject to Article 101 TFEU all forms of vertical control (including vertical integration that occurred by internal growth in the absence of a dominant position). Second, it may burden considerably the inner workings of the vertical chain, as because of the broad approach that was followed by the Commission in the interpretation of Article 101(1), any restriction of the economic freedom of the parties would have been subject to Article 101(1) and thus in need for exemption under Article 101(3) (and notification under the legal authorization regime before the adoption of Regulation 1/2003). EU competition law has thus developed the single entity doctrine, according to which Article 101 TFEU does not apply to agreements or concerted practices between firms that constitute a single economic entity.

10.4.1.1. Vertical control within the boundaries of the firm (parent companies and subsidiaries)

10.4.1.1.1. The single entity doctrine in a vertical context: Viho

As seen in Chapter 4, an agreement between a parent company and a subsidiary, or between two companies which are under the common control of a third, does not fall within Article 101(1) TFEU if the companies form an economic unit, within which the subsidiary cannot independently determine its course of action on the market. Since entities which form part of the same economic unit cannot be expected to compete with one another, relations between such entities, although these entities have separate legal personalities, cannot give rise to an agreement or concerted practice that restricts competition.

The doctrine first materialized in *Consten & Grundig* when the European Court of Justice held that the wording of Article 101 TFEU causes the prohibition to apply, provided that the other conditions are met, to an agreement between several undertakings. It does not apply where a sole undertaking integrates its own distribution network into its business organization.[45] According to the Court:

[44] Case C-41/90, *Klaus Höfner and Fritz Elser v Macrotron GmbH* [1991] ECR I–1979, para 21.

[45] Joined Cases C-56 & 58/64, *Établissements Consten SA and Grundigverkaufs-GmbH v EEC Commission* [1966] ECR 299.

> The wording of Article [101 TFEU] causes the prohibition to apply, provided that the other conditions are met, to an agreement between several undertakings. Thus it does not apply where a sole undertaking integrates its own distribution network into its business organization. It does not thereby follow, however, that the contractual situation based on an agreement between a manufacturing and a distributing undertaking is rendered legally acceptable by a simple process of economic analogy—which is in any case incomplete and in contradiction with the said article. Furthermore, although in the first case the Treaty intended in Article [101 TFEU] to leave untouched the internal organization of an undertaking and to render it liable to be called in question, by means of Article [102 TFEU], only in cases where it reaches such a degree of seriousness as to amount to an abuse of a dominant position, the same reservation could not apply when the impediments to competition result from agreement between two different undertakings which then as a general rule simply require to be prohibited.[46]

This approach was consistent with the fact that there was no EU merger control for vertical integration by ownership, at least until 1990, and with the adoption of a substantive criterion linked to the creation or strengthening of a dominant position until the enactment of the new Merger Regulation 139/2004. The Court seemed to accept that undertakings could have been able to adopt through vertical integration practices that would have a similar effect as territorial restrictions imposed by a supplier to retailers, the latter being prohibited under Article 101(1). The constitution of vertically integrated, Europe-wide firms was not considered as being equally harmful to the Internal Market objective than vertical contractual restraints imposing barriers to trade.

The Court later extended this exception to the application of Article 101 TFEU to intra-group agreements between a parent company and its subsidiaries. It held in *Centrafarm BV v Sterling Drug* that Article 101 does not apply to agreements or concerted practices between undertakings belonging to the same group ('concern') and having the status of parent company and subsidiary, 'if the undertakings form an economic unit within which the subsidiary has no real freedom to determine its course of action on the market, and if the agreements or practices are concerned merely with the internal allocation of tasks as between the undertakings'.[47] While the two companies in question may constitute separate legal entities, in reality they constitute a single entity, since the parent company controls the subsidiary.

Although the regime of immunity to Article 101 TFEU covered at the beginning only those practices that related to the internal allocation of tasks between the parent company and its subsidiaries, the Court finally abandoned this condition in *Viho*.[48]

Case C-73/95 P, *Viho Europe BV v Commission*
[1996] ECR I–5457

> *Parker Pen imposed on its subsidiaries a certain number of practices, which aimed to maintain and partition national markets by means of absolute territorial protection. The Court had condemned practices of this kind before as violating by their nature the objectives of EU*

46 Ibid, 340.

47 Case C-15/74, *Centrafarm BV v Sterling Drug Inc* [1974] ECR 1147. See also C-75/84, *Metro-SB-Grossmärkte GmbH & Co KG v Commission (No 2)* [1986] ECR 3021, para 84 [hereinafter *Metro II*], where the Court ignored the market share of a parent company that did not exert close control over its subsidiary.

48 Case C-73/95 P, *Viho Europe BV v Commission* [1996] ECR I–5457 [hereinafter *Viho*].

competition law. Viho complained to the Commission that the subsidiaries and independent distributors of Parker Pen were restrained by Parker from selling outside their respective territories. The Commission started to investigate and found that Viho was able to obtain Parker products from any of the independent distributors. It rejected the complaint in part on the ground that Article 101 does not apply to relations within a corporate group. The General Court confirmed this[49] and the CJEU was concerned with the appeal therefrom.

15. It should be noted, first of all, that it is established that Parker holds 100 per cent of the shares of its subsidiaries in Germany, Belgium, Spain, France and the Netherlands and that the sales and marketing activities of its subsidiaries are directed by an area team appointed by the parent company and which controls, in particular, sales targets, gross margins, sales costs, cash flow and stocks. The area team also lays down the range of products to be sold, monitors advertising and issues directives concerning prices and discounts.

16. Parker and its subsidiaries thus form a single economic unit within which the subsidiaries do not enjoy real autonomy in determining their course of action in the market, but carry out the instructions issued to them by the parent company controlling them [. . .].

17. In those circumstances, the fact that Parker's policy of referral, which consists essentially in dividing various national markets between its subsidiaries, might produce effects outside the ambit of the Parker group which are capable of affecting the competitive position of third parties cannot make Article [101](1) applicable [. . .]. On the other hand, such unilateral conduct could fall under Article [102 TFEU] of the Treaty if the conditions for its application, as laid down in that Article, were fulfilled.

18. The Court of First Instance was therefore fully entitled to base its decision solely on the existence of a single economic unit in order to rule out the application of Article [101](1) to the Parker group.

NOTES AND QUESTIONS ON THE JUDGMENT IN VIHO

1. Is it only instructions from the parent allocating tasks to each subsidiary that escape the prohibition of Article 101(1) TFEU, as stated in *Centrafarm v Sterling*, or also other instructions from the parent and agreements between the subsidiaries?
2. How much control must be exercised by the parent? Does this depend on shareholdings, on the practices of management generally or in relation to the particular course of conduct? Should the Court's case law on imputing the behaviour of the subsidiary to its foreign parent for the purpose of establishing liability be relevant? (See Chapter 4).
3. Note that Article 101 TFEU did not apply to these practices because Parker Pen held 100 per cent of the shares of its subsidiaries and controlled their marketing activities.[50] However, the Court did not exclude the application of article 102 TFEU.[51]
4. Although the ownership of the shares of the subsidiary were considered important, the Court also insisted on the more general concepts of independence of decision-making and real autonomy or absence of control in delineating the scope of the concept of single economic entity. It was therefore able to extend the application of the single economic unit doctrine to a combination of employees or departments of the

[49] Case T-102/92, *Viho v Commission* [1995] ECR II-17.
[50] Case C-73/95 P, *Viho* [1996] ECR I-5457, para 15.
[51] Ibid, para 17.

same firm.[52] Both of these situations refer to the existence of a right of control and therefore establish a situation of hierarchy. We refer to our discussion of the concept of undertaking in Chapter 4 for further details on the application of these criteria and the imputation of anti-competitive conduct to subsidiaries.

UK competition law follows a similar approach with regard to the application of Chapter I CA98.[53]

10.4.1.1.2. Searching for the economic foundations of the single entity doctrine: Transaction cost economics and property rights theories of vertical integration

As explained in Chapter 3, since the seminal contribution of Ronald Coase, contractual theories of vertical integration aim to understand why and how economic activity divides between firms and markets. To the extent that these theories have influenced the approach of competition law (in the US and in Europe) with regard to vertical restraints, TCE, and property tights theories of vertical integration may provide useful insights in order to understand the nature of the immunity for the application of Article 101 TFEU, from which benefit certain vertical restraints, such as those included between parent companies and their subsidiaries. Situations of 'hierarchy' in the nomenclature of transaction costs economics correlate with the finding of a single economic entity in competition law.

One may explain this correlation referring to the property rights model of vertical integration. The existence of property rights over assets creates a presumption that the owner has residual rights of control over these assets and can therefore determine their use. The emphasis is put on incentives to invest. Property rights over assets exist because of the large relation-specific investments incurred by the parties to the transaction and because of the fact that, due to the long duration of the relationship, contracts will necessarily be incomplete. It is therefore important to establish the existence of property rights over assets in order to avoid situations of opportunism *ex post* that may arise because of hold up situations but also in order to give parties incentives to invest. As Oliver Hart explains, '[i]n a world of transaction costs and incomplete contracts, ex post residual rights of control will be important because, through their influence on asset usage, they will affect ex post bargaining power and the division of ex post surplus in a relationship. This division in turn will affect the incentives of actors to invest in that relationship.'[54]

One may argue that hierarchy emerges because its efficiency with respect to these particular transactions is superior to that of a market form of organization concerning these particular transactions. A mechanism of central coordination may achieve faster results than the decentralized method of the market in adapting the relationship to new contingencies. It may also constrain opportunism, as property rights confer residual rights of control over assets that the other party to the relationship cannot use without prior authorization. It would also be possible to avoid the litigation costs of settling disputes between the different parties to the relationship, as hierarchy will be the final arbiter of any dispute. It follows that a parent company should be able to freely exercise its control over the assets used by its subsidiary.

A situation of hierarchy may certainly produce negative effects on third parties, by excluding non-owners from the use of these assets. However, these negative effects are not

52 Case C-22/98, *Jean Claude Becu* [1999] ECR I-5665.

53 See *Sepia Logistics Ltd (formerly Double Quick Supplyline Ltd) v Office of Fair Trading* [2007] CAT 13, [2007] Comp AR 747.

54 O Hart, 'An Economist's Perspective on the Theory of the Firm' (1989) 89 *Columbia L Rev* 1757, 1766.

enough to justify public intervention and the application of Article 101 TFEU. First, the cost of the intervention will be prohibitive, as it will have the effect of undermining hierarchy leading to a comparatively less efficient mode of organizing the particular transaction, which will now take place in the context of a market. However, the decision to organize the transaction through a hierarchy instead of a market is already the outcome of a comparative institutional analysis undertaken by the parties to the transaction. Presumably, the parties have more information than the public authorities on the benefits and costs of each mode of organization. Second, it will involve a re-allocation of the rights of control over the assets, which is a process that could entail significant costs. Indeed, if hierarchy is the most efficient mode of organization for the transaction, sooner or later it will re-emerge. Thus, public intervention would simply have the effect of replacing a situation of one hierarchy with another. The costs of enforcing competition law will not be the only deadweight loss. More significant will be the costs ensuing from the disincentive of the owners of the assets to invest. The more the holder of residual control rights faces an expropriation risk, the more the cost of investment in these assets will increase, as the existence of a risk involves additional costs. The concept of hierarchy may therefore mark the boundaries of Article 101 TFEU.

The same method could also apply to Article 102 TFEU. However, the Court preferred a different approach. One possible explanation is the fact that Article 102 focuses on the unilateral practices of a single economic unit. Article 102 imposes a burden on dominant firms to take into consideration the effects of their business practices on consumer welfare. Hierarchy does not exempt any more from the application of competition law, which explains the absence of a regime exempting these practices from the application of Article 102.[55]

A similar trade-off between transactional efficiency and allocative efficiency operates with regard to commercial agency agreements, which also benefit from a specific regime in EU competition law.

10.4.1.2. Commercial agency agreements

Commercial agency agreements 'cover the situation in which a legal or physical person (the agent) is vested with the power to negotiate and/or conclude contracts on behalf of another person (the principal), either in the agent's own name, or in the name of the principal for the purchase of goods or services by the principal or the sale of goods or services supplied by the principal.'[56] Those agreements benefit from a limited exception from the application of Article 101(1). We will briefly examine the origins of such a specific regime, its current application, and its economic rationale.[57]

[55] Case C-66/86, *Ahmed Saeed Flugreisen et Silver Line Reisebüro GmbH/ Zentrale zur Bekämpfung unlauteren Wettbewerbs* [1989] ECR 803, para 35:

> [. . .] according to the case-law of the Court Article 85 (now art 81) does not apply where the concerted practice in question is between undertakings belonging to a single group as parent company and subsidiary if those undertakings form an economic unit within which the subsidiary has no real freedom to determine its course of action on the market [. . .]. However, the conduct of such a unit on the market is liable to come within the ambit of Article [102].

See also Case C-73/95 P, *Viho* [1996] ECR I-5457, para 17.

[56] European Commission—Notice on Guidelines on Vertical Restraints [2000] OJ C 291/1, para 12 [hereinafter Vertical Restraints Guidelines 2000].

[57] For a more extensive analysis, see I Lianos, 'Commercial Agency Agreements, Vertical Restraints, and the Limits of Article 81(1) EC: Between Hierarchies and Networks' [2007] 3 *J Competition L & Economics* 625.

10.4.1.2.1. The origins of the specific regime for commercial agency agreements

It has been a consistent trend in EU competition law that certain restrictive clauses of commercial agency agreements fall outside the scope of Article 101 TFEU. This specific immunity regime for commercial agency agreements was laid down for the first time in a 1962 Commission Notice,[58] well before the European Court of Justice affirmed the applicability of Article 101(1) TFEU to vertical agreements in *Consten & Grundig*.

The Notice did not cover all the different types of agency agreements.[59] It provided, however, that the characterization of an agreement as a commercial agency was not enough in order to confer immunity. The Commission made a distinction between the effect of the agency agreement on the market for agency services and the effect of the agreement on the market for the products of the principal and it gave two different theoretical foundations for the competition law regime that it applied to them. The Notice further established a distinction between agency agreements, which benefit from an immunity regime, and those concluded by independent traders, which are subject to the prohibition of Article 101(1).[60] What distinguishes an agent from an independent trader is that the latter incurs a number of financial risks bound up with the sale or Notice on Exclusive Dealing with the performance of the contract. By contrast, a commercial agent should not normally assume any financial risk of the transaction, for then his function would become 'economically akin to that of an independent trader' and the agreement would fall within the scope of Article 101(1) TFEU.[61] The fact that the agent bears risks proves his economic autonomy vis-à-vis the principal and identifies him as an independent market participant.[62] The Commission did not advance a specific theoretical justification for the immunity regime but simply affirmed that these contracts have 'neither the object nor the effect of preventing, restricting or distorting competition'.[63] The allocation of the risks between the parties became an important criterion.

The Commission's policy on commercial agency agreements received implicit support from the Court of justice in *Consten/Grundig*. In this case, the Court established explicitly a distinction between the competition law regime for vertical integration and unilateral conduct and that for vertical agreements between independent traders. Only the latter may fall within the scope of Article 101 TFEU.

> It is pointless to compare on the one hand the situation, to which Article [101] applies, of a producer bound by a sole distributorship agreement to the distributor of his products with on the other hand that of a producer who includes within his undertaking the distribution of his own products by some means, for example, by commercial representatives, to which Article [101] does not apply. These situations are distinct in law and, moreover, need to be

[58] European Commission—Notice on Exclusive Dealing Contracts with Commercial Agents [1962] OJ 139/2921. In this Notice, the Commission explained that 'contracts made with commercial agents in which those agents undertake, for a specified part of the territory of the common market, to negotiate transactions on behalf of an enterprise, do not fall under the prohibition in Article [101(1) TFEU]'.

[59] For instance, it did not include agents that acted in their own name, but on behalf of the principal. See F Wijckmans, F Tuytschaever, and A Vanderelst, *Vertical Agreements in EC Competition Law* (OUP, 2011), 225.

[60] Notice on Exclusive Dealing Contracts with Commercial Agents, [1962] OJ 139/2921, para II.

[61] Ibid, para I.

[62] The Notice excluded the *del credere* clauses for the consideration of the allocation of financial risks between the agent and the principal, even though this has the effect to shift some financial risks to the agent.

[63] European Commission—Notice on Exclusive Dealing Contracts with Commercial Agents [1962] OJ 139/2921, para II.

assessed differently, since two marketing organizations, one of which is unintegrated into the manufacturer's undertaking whilst the other is not, may not necessarily have the same efficiency.[64]

The Court advanced the concept of the single economic unit doctrine in order to justify the existence of the two distinct regimes. Article 101 TFEU should not touch the internal organization of an 'undertaking', this concept being synonymous to that of a single economic entity. The Court did not adopt a formalist approach concerning the concept of single economic entity and was indifferent to the fact that the entities have separate legal forms. Consequently, the focus of the Court moved from the allocation of risks to the integration of the agent with the principal's business. This offered a convenient and plausible theoretical justification for the specific regime for commercial agencies, but it also led to the adoption of a different criterion than the allocation of risks between the parties.

In *Sugar*,[65] the CJEU focused its analysis on the 'real economic function' of the agent. The Court reaffirmed the importance of the criterion of the allocation of risks as an element distinguishing the situation of a commercial agent from that of an independent trader, but avoided examining the allocation of risks between the parties. It focused instead on the economic function of the representatives and concluded that the agreements were not genuine commercial agencies and could infringe Article 101(1). The Court stressed two elements, in particular. First, the agents were large business houses and were undertaking 'a very considerable amount of business for their own account' by exporting sugar to third countries.[66] It could be inferred from this that the agents acted as independent dealers.[67] Second, the fact that the agents were integrated into the sale organization of the principals did not rule out the possibility of their competing with independent traders when their principal permitted to do so.[68] These elements created, according to the Court, 'an ambivalent relationship', that could not be considered a genuine commercial agency agreement.[69]

The Court used two criteria to define the scope of the agency agreement regime. First, the agent should not bear any financial risk of the transaction. Second, the agent should not engage in the activities of both agent and one of independent trader in respect of the same market. The aim of the test is to verify the degree of autonomy of the agent with respect to the principal, which is determined according to the criterion of economic dependency. Being economically dependent or independent does not only result from the economic size of the agent or the fact that he also acts as an independent trader in respect of the same product market. It may also be implied by other circumstances, such as the fact that the agent works for other principals.[70]

The CJEU expressed doubts on the criterion of economic dependence in *Volkswagen*,[71] by emphasizing the allocation of risks between the principal and the agent, although the Court

[64] Joined Cases C-56 & 58/64, *Établissements Consten SA and Grundigverkaufs-GmbH v EEC Commission* [1966] ECR 299, 340.

[65] Joined Cases C-40–8, 50, 54–6, 111, 113 & 114/73, *Coöperatieve Vereniging 'Suiker Unie' UA and Others v Commission* [1975] ECR-1663 [hereinafter *Suiker Unie*].

[66] Ibid, para 544. [67] Ibid, para 545. [68] Ibid, para 546. [69] Ibid, para 547.

[70] See Case C-311/85, *ASBL Vereniging van Vlaamse Reisbureaus v ASBL Sociale Dienst van de Plaatselijke en Gewestelijke Overheidsdiensten* [1987] ECR 3801, para 20.

[71] See Case C-266/93, *Bundeskartellamt v Volkswagen AG and VAG Leasing GmBH* [1995] ECR I–3477. The first step of the analysis would be to determine if the agreement could be characterized as a 'typical' commercial agency, by looking to the criterion of financial risks. If this was the case, then the second step would be to ascertain if the particular clause of the contract is necessary on account of its legal/economic nature.

did not question the theoretical foundation of the immunity, the single economic entity doctrine. The Commission followed by definitively abandoning the economic dependence criterion in the 2000 Vertical Restraints Guidelines for that of the allocation of risks.[72] The 2010 Vertical Restraints Guidelines adopted a similar approach.

10.4.1.2.2. The application of Article 101(1) TFEU to commercial agency agreements

The Vertical Restraints Guidelines

The 2010 Vertical Restraints Guidelines include a number of paragraphs on the application of Article 101(1) TFEU to commercial agency agreements. According to the Commission,

> The determining factor in defining an agency agreement for the application of Article 101(1) is the financial or commercial risk borne by the agent in relation to the activities for which he has been appointed as an agent by the principal. In this respect it is not material for the assessment whether the agent acts for one or several principals. Neither is material for this assessment the qualification given to their agreement by the parties or national legislation.[73]

The Commission identifies three types of financial or commercial risk that are material to the definition of an agency agreement for the application of Article 101(1):

- *contract-specific risks*, which are 'directly related to the contracts concluded and/or negotiated by the agent on behalf of the principal, such as financing of stocks';
- *risks related to market-specific investments*, which are 'investments specifically required for the type of activity for which the agent has been appointed by the principal, i.e. which are required to enable the agent to conclude and/or negotiate this type of contract'. According to the Commission, such investments are usually 'sunk', that is, 'upon leaving that particular field of activity the investment cannot be used for other activities or sold other than at a significant loss';
- *risks related to other activities undertaken in the same product market*, 'to the extent that the principal requires the agent to undertake such activities, but not as an agent on behalf of the principal but for its own risk'.[74]

The Commission then acknowledges that

> For the purposes of applying Article 101(1) the agreement will be qualified as an agency agreement if the agent *does not bear any, or bears only insignificant, risks* in relation to the contracts concluded and/or negotiated on behalf of the principal, in relation to market-specific investments for that field of activity, and in relation to other activities required by the principal to be undertaken in the same product market.[75]

However, it is further noted that 'risks that are related to the activity of providing agency services in general, such as the risk of the agent's income being dependent upon his success as an agent or general investments in for instance premises or personnel, are not material to this assessment'.[76]

72 Vertical Restraints Guidelines 2000, paras 12–20. 73 Ibid, para 13. 74 Ibid, para 14.
75 Ibid, para 15 (emphasis added). 76 Ibid.

An important element to take into account in determining the commercial agency immunity is also where property in the contract goods bought or sold are not vested in the agent, or the agent does not himself supply the contract services, which along with a number of other risks, when these are not undertaken by the agent, indicate the existence of a 'genuine' commercial agency relationship.[77] However, even if the agent incurs one or more of the risks or costs listed in the Guidelines, the agreement between agent and principal will not necessarily be qualified as an agency agreement, as, for the Commission, the question of risk must be assessed on a case-by-case basis, and with regard to the economic reality of the situation rather than the legal form.[78] This risk analysis starts with the assessment of the contract-specific risks an in the event that contract-specific risks are incurred by the agent, this may be found sufficient to conclude that the agent is an independent distributor.[79] However, 'if the agent does not incur contract-specific risks, then it will be necessary to continue further the analysis by assessing the risks related to market-specific investments'.[80] The analysis includes not just contract-specific risks, but also risks related to market-specific investments, and finally, risks related to other required activities within the same product market, all of which need to be considered.[81]

In applying Article 101(1) TFEU to agency agreements, the Commission notes that if the principal bears the commercial and financial risks related to the selling and purchasing of the contract goods and services 'all obligations imposed on the agent in relation to the contracts concluded and/or negotiated on behalf of the principal fall outside Article 101(1)'.[82] In contrast, where the agent bears 'one or more of the relevant risks', 'the agreement between agent and principal does not constitute an agency agreement for the purpose of applying Article 101(1)' and in 'that situation the agent will be treated as an independent undertaking and the agreement between agent and principal will be subject to Article 101(1) as any other vertical agreement'.[83]

The Guidelines provide a list of obligations on the agent's part are considered to form an 'inherent part of an agency agreement, and therefore are covered by the commercial agency immunity, as each of them relates to the ability of the principal to fix the scope of activity of the agent in relation to the contract goods or services, which is essential if the principal is to take the risks and therefore to be in a position to determine the commercial strategy', such as 'limitations on the territory in which the agent may sell these goods or services', 'limitations on the customers to whom the agent may sell these goods or services', 'the prices and conditions at which the agent must sell or purchase these goods or services'.[84]

However, the Guidelines distinguish the above-mentioned clauses from clauses, also often included in commercial agency agreements, concerning the relationship between the agent and the principal, such as a provision preventing the principal from appointing other agents in respect of a given type of transaction, customer or territory (exclusive agency provisions) and/or a provision preventing the agent from acting as an agent or distributor of undertakings which compete with the principal (single branding provisions). With regard to these clauses, the agent is considered as a separate undertaking from the principal, that is the commercial agency immunity does not apply, and they may therefore be found to infringe Article 101(1) TFEU.[85] Although it is noted in the Guidelines that exclusive agency provisions 'will in general not lead to anti-competitive effects', 'single branding provisions and post-term non-compete provisions, which concern inter-brand competition, may infringe Article 101(1) if they lead

[77] Ibid, para 16. [78] Ibid, para 17. [79] Ibid, para 17. [80] Ibid. [81] Ibid.
[82] Ibid. [83] Ibid, para 21. [84] Ibid, para 18. [85] Ibid, para 19.

to or contribute to a (cumulative) foreclosure effect on the relevant market where the contract goods or services are sold or purchased'.[86] These provisions may nevertheless benefit from the Block Exemption Regulation, or be individually justified by efficiencies under Article 101(3) TFEU, as per other vertical restraints. Another limitation to the commercial agency immunity, leading to the possible application of Article 101(1), even in situations where the principal bears all the relevant financial and commercial risks, is when the commercial agency agreement facilitates collusion, for instance 'when a number of principals use the same agents while collectively excluding others from using these agents, or when they use the agents to collude on marketing strategy or to exchange sensitive market information between the principals'.[87]

The DaimlerChrysler *case: Single economic entity and the criterion of the allocation of risks*

The Commission issued a decision in 2001 against DaimlerChrysler finding that by adopting measures preventing the members of its distribution network from selling to consumers outside their contractual territory, and by contributing to a resale price maintenance scheme, its brand, Mercedes-Benz, had infringed Article 101(1).[88] Although Mercedes-Benz' dealers were commercial agents according to the provisions of the German Commercial Code, the Commission applied Article 101(1) because it considered that they exercised an independent commercial or economic activity and bore the financial risks of the transactions.[89] The agents bore a considerable share of the price risk associated with the sale of vehicles as any price concession or discount granted to a customer was deducted from the agent's commission.[90] They also bore the transport costs risks, as they had to deliver the new vehicles to their customers if the latter did not wish to collect them at the factory.[91] They dedicated their resources to sales promotion 'to a very considerable extent' and assumed part of the cost for setting an after-sales service.[92] They were finally required to maintain a workshop for carrying out works on vehicles and to acquire replacement parts on their own cost.[93] DaimlerChrysler objected that the agents were selling exclusively Mercedes-Benz vehicles and that they formed an integral part of its business. The Commission rejected this argument and affirmed that 'the criterion of integration is, unlike risk allocation, not a separate criterion for distinguishing a commercial agent from a dealer'.[94]

DaimlerChrysler brought an action for annulment against the Commission's decision before the Court of First Instance.[95] Its main arguments were that the agents bore only those risks relevant to their activities as intermediaries, which in any case were negligible, and that they were an integral part of the Mercedes-Benz business. Although the Commission did not deny that the allocation of risks and the integration of the agent to the principal's business were cumulative conditions for triggering the application of the commercial agency agreements' immunity regime, it insisted that the criterion of integration should not be examined independently from that of the allocation of risks. According to the Commission, if the agent bears risks, he should be able to keep his freedom of action in order to deal with those risks, without being restricted by obligations that would exceed what is necessary for the defence of his mutual interest with the principal.[96]

None of the parties questioned the fact that the condition of the integration of the agent to his principal's business was an important element in determining the existence of a genuine

86 Ibid. 87 Ibid, para 20.
88 *Mercedes-Benz* (Case COMP/36.264) Commission Decision 2002/758/EEC [2001] OJ L 257/1.
89 Ibid, para 123. 90 Ibid, paras 155–6. 91 Ibid, para 157. 92 Ibid, para 158.
93 Ibid, para 159. 94 Ibid, para 163.
95 Case T-325/01, *DaimlerChrysler AG v Commission* [2005] ECR II-3319. 96 Ibid, paras 70–1.

agency agreement. They both disagreed, however, on the idea that an independent evidential value should be given to the criterion of integration. The Commission advocated a more restrictive approach limiting the scope of the immunity, whereas DaimlerChrysler's approach would have extended the scope of the immunity, as the simple fact that the agent bore some risks would not be enough to denying to the agreement the benefit of the immunity regime, if he was integrated with his principal's business.

Although the Court did not arrive at the same conclusion as the Commission, with respect to the allocation of risks between the parties, and although it ultimately annulled the decision, its approach is not different from that advocated by the Commission. The Court's ruling underlines the importance of the concept of undertaking and economic unit theory as the foundation of the specific regime for commercial agency agreements.

Case T-325/01, *DaimlerChrysler AG v Commission*
[2005] ECR II–3319 (references omitted)

83. It is clear from the wording of [. . .] article [101 TFEU] that the prohibition thus laid down concerns exclusively conduct that is coordinated bilaterally or multilaterally, in the form of agreements between undertakings, decisions by associations of undertakings and concerted practices. It follows that the concept of an agreement within the meaning of Article [101(1) TFEU], as interpreted in case-law, centres around the existence of a joint intention between at least two parties.

84. It follows that, where a decision by a manufacturer constitutes unilateral conduct of the undertaking, that decision escapes the prohibition laid down in Article [101(1) TFEU].

85. It is also settled case-law that in competition law the term 'undertaking' must be understood as designating an economic unit for the purpose of the subject-matter of the agreement in question, even if in law that unit consists of several persons, natural or legal. The Court of Justice has emphasised that, for the purposes of applying the competition rules, formal separation of two companies resulting from their having distinct legal identity, is not decisive. The test is whether or not there is unity in their conduct on the market. Thus, it may be necessary to establish whether two companies that have distinct legal identities form, or fall within, one and the same undertaking or economic entity adopting the same course of conduct on the market.

86. The case-law shows that this sort of situation arises not only in cases where the relationship between the companies in question is that of parent and subsidiary. It may also occur, in certain circumstances, in relationships between a company and its commercial representative or between a principal and its agent. In so far as application of Article [101 TFEU] is concerned, the question whether a principal and its agent or 'commercial representative' form a single economic unit, the agent being an auxiliary body forming part of the principal's undertaking, is an important one for the purposes of establishing whether given conduct falls within the scope of that article. Thus, it has been held that 'if . . . an agent works for the benefit of his principal he may in principle be treated as an auxiliary organ forming an integral part of the latter's undertaking, who must carry out his principal's instructions and thus, like a commercial employee, forms an economic unit with this undertaking'.

87. The position is otherwise if the agreements entered into between the principal and its agents confer upon the agent or allow him to perform duties which from an economic point of view are approximately the same as those carried out by an independent dealer, because they provide for the agent accepting the financial risks of selling or of the performance of the contracts entered into with third parties. It has

therefore been held that an agent can lose his character as independent economic operator only if he does not bear any of the risks resulting from the contracts negotiated on behalf of the principal and he operates as an auxiliary organ forming an integral part of the principal's undertaking.

88. Accordingly, where an agent, although having separate legal personality, does not independently determine his own conduct on the market, but carries out the instructions given to him by his principal, the prohibitions laid down under Article 101(1) TFEU do not apply to the relationship between the agent and the principal with which he forms an economic unit.

The existence of a separate legal personality should not be an obstacle in recognizing that the principal and the agent form a single economic unit. The Court gives the example of the case law on the relations between parent companies and their subsidiaries and establishes a parallelism between this situation and that of commercial agents and principals.[97] The agent is an auxiliary organ integrated into the firm of the principal and follows his instructions, just as employees follow the instructions of their employer.[98] Even if the agent and the principal each have distinct legal personalities, Article 101(1) does not apply to the relations between them when the agent does not act autonomously on the market but just applies the instructions of the principal.[99] The agent loses his economic independence and autonomy only if the principal bears all of the risks associated with the contract negotiated on his behalf and the agent acts as an auxiliary integrated into the principal's business.[100]

The Court's decision shifts the focus of the analysis from the concept of integration to that of control or authority. Both of the concepts are linked. An agent that is integrated into his principal's business loses the control of the contractual assets, which are then under the control of the principal who should therefore be the only one with authority to make decisions as to their use. The criterion of integration is therefore more circumscribed than before. It is only if the principal retains residual rights of control that the agreement is considered a commercial agency. Situations of economic dependency are therefore implicitly excluded from the analysis of the auxiliary nature of the 'agent'.

This explains why the Court focuses its analysis on two issues: first, external manifestations of authority, like the absence of authority for the agent to pass orders, to conclude the final terms of the transactions or to set the sale price and grant discounts;[101] second, the allocation of risks between the agent and principal that will determine which party should have the right of residual control on the assets. The Court's conclusion was that although the agents incurred a certain degree of costs and bore risks,[102] these were not significant enough, and that in any case the risks concerned activities related to separate markets. Consequently, for a vertical agreement to be considered as a genuine commercial agency, it is not necessary that the principal bears all the risks of the transaction. In addition, the Court drew a distinction between the concept of risk and the obligations that are often imposed on distributors by their suppliers, mainly in order to protect goodwill or assets whose use has been temporary transferred to the distributor, such as trademarks,[103] thus making more explicit the distinction between commercial agency and other types of vertical agreements between independent traders.

97 Ibid, para 86. 98 Ibid. 99 Ibid, para 88. 100 Ibid, para 87.

101 Ibid, paras 93–4.

102 In particular, because they participated in transport costs, they were obliged to maintain a stock of vehicles, ensure the after-sales service, and establish a workshop for carrying out works.

103 Case T-325/01, *DaimlerChrysler AG v Commission* [2005] ECR II–3319, para 115.

Although the Court's decision in *DaimlerChrysler* makes clear that the single economic unit doctrine constitutes the theoretical basis of the specific regime for commercial agency agreements, the case did not examine the regime that applies to non-compete clauses. The Guidelines on Vertical Restraints exclude non-compete provisions from the scope of the immunity to Article 101(1) TFEU whenever there is a foreclosure effect.[104]

The Repsol *and CESPA cases: Non-compete clauses included in commercial agency agreements*

In *Repsol*, the European Commission examined a series of agreements for the exclusive purchase of fuel between Repsol, one of the most important distributors of fuel for motor vehicles in Spain, and some operators of petrol stations.[105] The agreements contained non-compete clauses for fuel and clauses relating to the setting of a maximum fuel retail price. There were eight different categories of distribution agreement, depending on the type of the tenure of the service stations and the nature of the commercial relationship between Repsol and the distributors, the latter having the status either of agent or of an independent retailer.[106] The Commission followed the same approach as that in the 2000 Vertical Restraints Guidelines and affirmed the importance of the criterion of the allocation of financial risks in determining the existence of a genuine agency agreement.[107] However, it also affirmed that the question of the status of the operators of Repsol's service stations had no bearing on the application of Article 101(1) to non-compete clauses. According to the Commission, '[. . .] whatever the agent's situation in the light of these criteria, the non-compete clauses agreed with him may be problematic owing to their effects on inter-brand competition. This is the case if such clauses lead to foreclosure on the relevant market where the contract goods or services are sold or purchased.'[108]

Indeed, some of Repsol's distribution agreements could contribute to a significant foreclosure effect in the market, in particular because of the significant vertical integration of operators, the cumulative effect of the parallel networks of vertical restraints and other barriers. It follows that the characterization of the agreement as a genuine commercial agency should not make any difference with respect to the application of Article 101(1) in case of a significant foreclosure of the market. However, while applying Article 101(1), the Commission considered that the non-compete clauses integrated in distribution agreements in which Repsol owned the service stations did not contribute to the foreclosure effect because, 'at the end of the contractual relationship, it is invariably the supplier in his capacity as owner of the service station, and not the tenant-operator, who decides what products will be sold through the sales outlet concerned'.[109] Non-compete clauses that are integrated in agreements in which the petrol station operators (either independent retailers or agents) retain the property of the service station (land and buildings) were on the contrary found to infringe Article 101(1) if they significantly foreclose competition on the market. The commitments offered by Repsol were nevertheless sufficient to address the competition concerns raised by these agreements.[110]

[104] Vertical Restraints Guidelines 2010, para 19.

[105] European Commission—Notice Pursuant to Article 27(4) of Council Regulation 1/2003 concerning Case COMP/B-1/38348—*Repsol CPP SA* [2004] OJ C 258/7.

[106] Ibid, para 13. [107] Ibid, para 16.

[108] Ibid, para 17. See also ibid, para 22 (non-compete clauses may foreclose the market by excluding others suppliers or raising barriers to entry and therefore weaken inter-brand competition but 'whether service station operators are described in the agreement as agents or retailers is immaterial in this respect').

[109] Ibid, para 25.

[110] *Repsol CPP* (Case COMP/B-1/38.348) Commission Decision 2006/446/EEC [2006] OJ L 176/104.

The regime of commercial agency agreements has been recently re-examined in *CESPA*,[111] a preliminary ruling request from the Supreme Court of Spain to the Court of Justice of the European Union (CJEU). CESPA, a Spanish oil company, had imposed on the service stations which it supplied fixed prices for the sale of its fuel to consumers as well as other conditions restrictive to competition (such as exclusive distribution and non-competition clauses). The service station operators had the status of commercial agent and the Spanish Supreme Court therefore raised a question as to the applicability of Article 101(1) to commercial agency agreements. The fact that the agent constitutes a separate undertaking from his principle is an important element in finding the existence of an agreement.

Advocate General Kokott made a considerable effort to rationalize the previous case law and practice, but her opinion constituted in some respects a departure from the Commission's approach in the 2000 Vertical Restraints Guidelines. The Advocate General reintroduced the distinction made by the 1962 Notice between the situation of the agent in the market for agency services and that of the agent in the market for his principal's products, which was not mentioned in the 2000 Vertical Restraints Guidelines. In the first situation, the agent is considered 'normally' to be an independent trader and therefore constitutes an undertaking for Article 101 purposes.[112] Exclusive agency provisions or non-compete provisions that are eventually included in these agreements are restrictions of competition that may only be justified under Article 101(3). This is contrary to the position adopted by the Commission in its 1962 Notice,[113] which applied the ancillary restraints doctrine in order to exclude these clauses from the application of Article 101(1). In the second situation, the agent is not considered a separate entity from his principle but this presumption can be rebutted if the agent assumes 'some' of the financial risks of the transaction.[114] The criterion of the allocation of risks between the agent and the principal is therefore a decisive element in deciding if the agreement constitutes a genuine or a non-genuine agency.

In addition, the Advocate General considered that the criterion of the assimilation (integration) of the agent to the business of the principal is not a different, independent criterion than that of the allocation of risks but that they both constitute 'two sides of the same coin'.[115] As explained previously, this conclusion is compatible with the previous case law and with the position adopted by the Commission. However, the Advocate General relied also on the distinction between product market and market for agency services in affirming that the assimilation of the agent to the principal's business may be a criterion to determining the existence of a commercial agency when it comes to the market for the agent's service.[116] Although, according to the Advocate General, there is a presumption that an agent is 'normally' regarded as an independent operator in the market for agency services, this presumption may be overcome if the agent is assimilated into the principal's business. Both of the criteria (allocation of risks and integration) serve the same objective: to define the scope of the immunity for agency agreements, even if it is important in all circumstances to verify that the agent does not bear

[111] Case C-217/05, *Confederación Española de Empresarios de Estaciones de Servicio v Compañia Española de Petróleos, SA* [2006] ECR I–11987.

[112] Opinion of AG Kokott in Case C-217/05 *Confederación Española de Empresarios de Estaciones de Servicio v Compañia Española de Petróleos, SA* [2006] ECR I–11987, para 44.

[113] European Commission—Notice on Exclusive Dealing Contracts with Commercial Agents [1962] OJ 139/2921.

[114] Opinion of AG Kokott in Case C-217/05 *Confederación Española de Empresarios de Estaciones de Servicio v Compañia Española de Petróleos, SA* [2006] ECR I–11987, para 49.

[115] Ibid, para 48 n 52. [116] Ibid.

significant risks.[117] Nonetheless, the Advocate General does not explain whether it is the concept of economic unit or the concept of ancillary restraints that justifies this specific regime. She avoids addressing the issue as this is 'a purely theoretical problem and on the ground that in practice it makes no difference if the exclusion of the application of Article 101 is based on the concept of 'undertaking' or that of 'restriction of competition'.[118]

As for determining the actual allocation of risks between agents and their principals, the Advocate General rejects the proposition that the designation of the intermediary in the contract is a relevant factor and instead proposes an economic approach, which focuses on the analysis of the allocation of risks. The consideration of the allocation of risks takes the form of a *continuum*. If the agent bears part of the risks arising out of the transactions he negotiates, his position becomes closer to that of an independent trader. If he bears no risks or only risks that are insignificant, he is regarded as a proper agent and an auxiliary to the principal. According to the Advocate General, if the analysis of the risk allocation leads to the conclusion that the service-station proprietors form an economic unit with the principal, then 'there is no agreement between independent undertakings and the disputed provisions in the service-station contracts are accordingly not within the scope of Article [101 TFEU] at all'.[119] Although this paragraph of the Opinion refers to the price-fixing provisions of the agreement, it implies that any restrictive position may benefit from the same immunity regime.

As indicated above, in its Guidelines on Vertical Restraints, the Commission explicitly excluded non-competition clauses of genuine commercial agency agreements from the scope of the immunity if these had the effect of significantly foreclosing the market. The Advocate General discussed the possibility of foreclosure only with respect to the situation of non-genuine commercial agreements. The position of the Advocate General is compatible with a strict interpretation of the implications of finding that the agent is auxiliary to his principal. Indeed, if there is a genuine agency, there is no agreement between undertakings and therefore Article 101 should not apply. It follows that the immunity regime should not only cover resale price maintenance clauses but all different types of obligations, including non-compete clauses, imposed by the principals on their agents. However, the CJEU did not accept this position,[120] although its references to the concept of undertaking seem to explain that the theoretical foundations of the commercial agency immunity are similar than those of the single economic entity doctrine for the parent–subsidiary relationship.

Case C-217/05, *Confederación Española de Empresarios de Estaciones de Servicio v Compañia Española de Petróleos, SA*
[2006] ECR I–11987 (references omitted)

38. [. . .] [V]ertical agreements such as the agreements between CEPSA and service-station operators are covered by Article [101 TFEU] only where the operator is regarded as an independent economic operator and there is, consequently, an agreement between two undertakings.

39. It is settled case-law that, in Community competition law, the definition of an 'undertaking' covers any entity engaged in an economic activity, regardless of the legal status of that entity and the way in which it is financed.

40. The Court has also stated that, in the same context, the term 'undertaking' must be understood as designating an economic unit for the purpose of the subject-matter

[117] Ibid, para 51 *in fine*. [118] Ibid. [119] Ibid, para 66. [120] See ibid, para 62.

of the agreement in question even if in law that economic unit consists of several persons, natural or legal.

41. The Court has furthermore made clear that for the purposes of applying the rules on competition the formal separation between two parties resulting from their separate legal personality is not conclusive, the decisive test being the unity of their conduct on the market.

42. In certain circumstances, the relationship between a principal and his agent may be characterised by such economic unity.

43. In that connection, it is clear, however, from the case-law that agents can lose their character as independent traders only if they do not bear any of the risks resulting from the contracts negotiated on behalf of the principal and they operate as auxiliary organs forming an integral part of the principal's undertaking.

44. Therefore where an intermediary, such as a service-station operator, while having separate legal personality, does not independently determine his conduct on the market since he depends entirely on his principal, such as a supplier of fuel, because the latter assumes the financial and commercial risks as regards the economic activity concerned, the prohibition laid down in Article [101(1) TFEU] is not applicable to the relationship between that intermediary and the principal.

45. Conversely, where the agreements concluded between a principal and its intermediaries confer on or allow them functions which, from an economic point of view, are approximately the same as those carried out by an independent economic operator, because they make provision for those intermediaries to assume the financial and commercial risks linked to sales or the performance of contracts entered into with third parties, such intermediaries cannot be regarded as auxiliary organs forming an integral part of the principal's undertaking, so that a clause restricting competition which they have entered into may be an agreement between undertakings for the purposes of Article [101] of the Treaty.

46. It follows that the decisive factor for the purposes of determining whether a service-station operator is an independent economic operator is to be found in the agreement concluded with the principal and, in particular, in the clauses of that agreement, implied or express, relating to the assumption of the financial and commercial risks linked to sales of goods to third parties. As the Commission rightly submitted in its observations, the question of risk must be analysed on a case-by-case basis, taking account of the real economic situation rather than the legal classification of the contractual relationship in national law.

47. In those circumstances, an assessment must be made as to whether or not, in the context of agreements having the characteristics described by the national court, the service-station operators assume certain financial and commercial risks linked to the sale of fuel to third parties.

48. An analysis of how those risks are allocated must be made in the light of the factual circumstances of the case in the main proceedings. [. . .] [T]he file submitted to the Court does not provide full information as to the way in which that allocation operates under the agreements concluded between CEPSA and the service-station operators.

49. In that context, it must be recalled that the Court has no jurisdiction to give a ruling on the facts in an individual case or to apply the rules of Community law which it has interpreted to national measures or situations, since those questions are matters within the jurisdiction of the national court.

50. Nevertheless, in order to give a useful answer to the national court, it is appropriate to set out the criteria enabling an assessment to be made as to the actual allocation of the financial and commercial risks between service-station operators and the

fuel supplier under the agreements at issue in the main proceedings, for the purposes of determining whether Article [101 TFEU] is applicable to them.

51. In that connection, the national court should take account, first, of the risks linked to the sale of the goods, such as the financing of fuel stocks and, second, of the risks linked to investments specific to the market, namely those required to enable the service-station operator to negotiate or conclude contracts with third parties.

52. First, as regards the risks linked to the sale of the goods, it is likely that the service-station operator assumes those risks when he takes possession of the goods at the time he receives them from the supplier, that is to say, prior to selling them on to a third party.

53. Likewise, the service-station operator who assumes, directly or indirectly, the costs linked to the distribution of those goods, particularly the transport costs, should be regarded as thereby assuming part of the risk linked to the sale of the goods.

54. The fact that the service-station operator maintains stocks at his own expense could also be an indication that the risks linked to the sale of the goods are transferred to him.

55. Furthermore, the national court should determine who assumes responsibility for any damage caused to the goods, such as loss or deterioration, and for damage caused by the goods sold to third parties. If the service-station operator were responsible for such damage, irrespective of whether or not he had complied with the obligation to keep the goods in the conditions necessary to ensure that they undergo no loss or deterioration, the risk would have to be regarded as having been transferred to him.

56. It is also necessary to assess the allocation of the financial risk linked to the goods, in particular as regards payment for the fuel should the service-station operator not find a purchaser, or where payment is deferred as a result of payment by credit card, on the basis of the rules or practices relating to the payment system for fuel.

57. In that connection, it is apparent from the order for reference that the service-station operator is required to pay CEPSA the amount corresponding to the sale price of the fuel nine days after the date of delivery and that, by the same date, the service-station operator receives commission from CEPSA, in an amount corresponding to the quantity of fuel delivered.

58. In those circumstances, it is for the national court to ascertain whether the payment to the supplier of the amount corresponding to the sale price of the fuel depends on the quantity actually sold by that date and, as regards the turnover period for the goods in the service-station, whether the fuel delivered by the supplier is always sold within a period of nine days. If the answer is in the affirmative it would have to be concluded that the commercial risk is born by the supplier.

59. As regards the risks linked to investments specific to the market, if the service-station operator makes investments specifically linked to the sale of the goods, such as premises or equipment such as a fuel tank, or commits himself to investing in advertising campaigns, such risks are transferred to the operator.

60. It follows from the foregoing that, in order to determine whether Article [101] of the Treaty is applicable, the allocation of the financial and commercial risks between the service-station operator and the supplier of fuel must be analysed on the basis of criteria such as ownership of the goods, the contribution to the costs linked to their distribution, their safe-keeping, liability for any damage caused to the goods or by the goods to third parties, and the making of investments specific to the sale of those goods.

61. However, as the Commission rightly submits, the fact that the intermediary bears only a negligible share of the risks does not render Article [101] of the Treaty applicable.

62. Nevertheless, it must be pointed out that, in such a case, only the obligations imposed on the intermediary in the context of the sale of the goods to third parties on

behalf of the principal fall outside the scope of that article. As the Commission submitted, an agency contract may contain clauses concerning the relationship between the agent and the principal to which that article applies, such as exclusivity and non-competition clauses. In that connection it must be considered that, in the context of such relationships, agents are, in principle, independent economic operators and such clauses are capable of infringing the competition rules in so far as they entail locking up the market concerned.

63. If, following examination of the risks assumed by the service-station operators involved in the case in the main proceedings, the obligations imposed on them in the context of the sale of goods to third parties were not to be regarded as agreements between undertakings within the meaning of Article [101] of the Treaty, the obligation imposed on those service-station operators to sell fuel at a specific price would fall outside that provision and would thus be inherent in CEPSA's ability to delimit the scope of the activities of its agents. [. . .]

The Court's position may be explained if one focuses on the necessary trade-off between transactional efficiency and the allocative inefficiencies resulting from the restrictive clauses included in commercial agency agreements.[121] In some circumstances, for instance cumulative foreclosure effect or a high collusion risk, in particular affecting inter-brand competition, the right decision procedure cannot be the exclusion of all restrictions from the scope of the prohibition of Article 101(1) TFEU (the immunity approach), which would have put more emphasis on transactional efficiency, even to the price of some allocative inefficiency, but a case-by-case analysis of the specific clauses, as for all other forms of vertical arrangements.

Commercial agency agreements and the e-Books case

The Commission also examined commercial agency agreements in the *e-Books* case (see Chapter 5) concerning the switch of five major publishers of e-books to a commercial agency distribution model after each of them signed a contract with Apple, whereby the latter would distribute the e-books as an agent of each publisher, in conjunction with a most-favoured-nation (MFN)/most-favoured-customer (MFC) clause.[122] Under an MFN (or MFC) clause, a seller agrees that a buyer will benefit from terms (eg prices) that are at least as favourable as those offered by the seller to any other buyer.

Each of the five publishers was, in principle, free to set the retail price for its e-books titles, but each agency agreement contained a clause setting the maximum retail price points either for all titles or for newly released e-books. The Commission focused on the horizontal element of the collective switch to an agency model, finding that there was parallel behaviour between the Five Publishers and Apple, including, *inter alia*, in relation to the process of negotiation and the content of the agency agreements which fell under the scope of Article 101(1) TFEU and thus not focusing on the 'genuine' (or not) character of the commercial agency agreements concluded between each of the Publishers and Apple. One of the commitments accepted by the Commission concerned the termination of the commercial agency agreements for any such agreement that restricts, limits, or impedes an e-book retailer's/agent's ability to set, alter,

121 For a more expansive development of the argument, see I Lianos, 'Commercial Agency Agreements, Vertical Restraints, and the Limits of Article 81(1) EC: Between Hierarchies and Networks' [2007] 3 *J Competition L & Economics* 625.

122 *E-BOOKS* (Case AT.39.847) C(2013) 4750 (25 July 2013), available at ec.europa.eu/competition/antitrust/cases/dec_docs/39847/39847_27536_4.pdf.

or reduce the retail price or to offer any other form of promotions, or contains an MFN clause regarding price. The problem highlighted by these conditions is of course the horizontal collusion, which as we know would have anyway led to the application of Article 101(1) TFEU, even in the presence of a 'genuine' commercial agency agreement, as the situation seems close to what the Commission envisages in paragraph 20 of the Guidelines on Vertical Restraints (when 'genuine' commercial agency agreements facilitate collusion).

In conclusion, it appears that the scope of the immunity under Article 101(1) TFEU for commercial agency agreements is narrower than that for agreements between parent companies and subsidiaries. The legal regime of non-compete obligations in commercial agency agreements can be contrasted with the approach adopted by the Court and the Commission with respect to combinations between parent companies and their subsidiaries. These are considered to be outside the scope of Article 101(1), even if they produce a significant foreclosure effect.

10.4.1.3. The application of Article 101(1) TFEU to sub-contracting agreements

Sub-contracting agreements are one form of production agreement, where one party (the contractor) entrusts the production of a good to another party (subcontractor) putting at its disposal productive assets, such as intellectual property rights, know-how, and equipment, while obtaining from its subcontractor a commitment that the transferred assets will not be used for any other purpose than for the supply of the products under contract.[123] The other two are joint production agreements and specialization agreements, which have been examined in Chapter 7, when these are concluded between companies operating in the same product market irrespective of whether they are actual or potential competitors (horizontal cooperation agreements).[124] However, vertical subcontracting agreements are not covered by the Horizontal Guidelines, but may fall within the scope of the Guidelines on Vertical Restraints and, subject to certain conditions, and eventually benefit from the Block Exemption Regulation on Vertical Restraints, as well as the Notice on sub-contracting agreements.[125]

The legal regime of sub-contracting agreements is therefore complex: no less than four legal frameworks might be applicable: (i) Regulation 330/2010 and the guidelines on vertical restraints (on vertical sub-contracting agreements); (ii) Regulation 1218/2010 (on horizontal specialization agreements[126]) and the Horizontal Guidelines; (iii) Regulation 316/2014 on Technology Transfer Agreements and the technology transfer agreements guidelines for horizontal or vertical sub-contracting agreements involving the licensing of a technology in as much as the licensing constitutes the primary object of the agreement;[127] and (iv) the Notice on sub-contracting agreements, adopted in 1978 and which continues to apply to the present

[123] F Wijckmans, F Tuytschaever, and A Vanderelst, *Vertical Agreements in EC Competition Law* (OUP, 2011), 246.

[124] Communication from the Commission—Guidelines on the applicability of Article 101 TFEU to horizontal co-operation agreements [2011] OJ C 11/1, para 151 [hereinafter Horizontal Guidelines].

[125] Ibid, para 154.

[126] Commission Regulation (EU) No 1218/2010 of 14 December 2010 on the application of Article 101(3) of the Treaty on the Functioning of the European Union to certain categories of specialisation agreements [2010] OJ L 335/43. On this BER, see Chapter 6.

[127] Commission Regulation (EU) No 316/2014 of 21 March 2014 on the application of Article 101(3) of the Treaty on the Functioning of the European Union to categories of technology transfer agreements [2014] OJ L 93/17. On this BER, see Chapter 13.

day.[128] This Notice provides a limited immunity for the application of Article 101(1) to certain clauses included in sub-contracting agreements, which resembles to that for commercial agency agreements. The immunity to Article 101(1) can thus be justified for the same reasons as for commercial agency agreements: these restrictions do not fall within the scope of Article 101(1) TFEU on condition that the contractor provides the subcontractor with technology or equipment that, without access to them, the sub-contractor would not have been capable of being an independent supplier in the market for the contract products. The nature of the immunity is thus related to the single economic entity doctrine, at least for this type of restriction.

The most recent guidelines on vertical restraints reiterate the nature and scope of this limited immunity for vertical sub-contracting agreements, noting that 'subcontracting agreements whereby the subcontractor undertakes to produce certain products exclusively for the contractor generally fall outside the scope of Article 101(1) provided that the technology or equipment is necessary to enable the subcontractor to produce the products', while also accepting that 'other restrictions imposed on the subcontractor such as the obligation not to conduct or exploit its own research and development or not to produce for third parties in general may fall within the scope of Article 101'.[129] These restrictions may benefit from the vertical BER in case the conditions for its applicability are satisfied, in particular if this is not an agreement between competitors, and the subject matter of the agreement falls within the scope of the exemption.

10.4.2. VERTICAL RESTRAINTS AND THE UNILATERAL/ COLLUSIVE PRACTICES DICHOTOMY IN COMPETITION LAW

Vertical restraints are not only included in specific distribution agreements but may also be unilaterally imposed by the supplier or the retailer. Article 101 (or Chapter I CA98) applied only when there is a vertical agreement or a vertical concerted practice.[130] The UK competition authorities also employed the concept of hub and spoke conspiracy for the application of UK competition law to vertical restraints.[131]

As explained in Chapter 5, the legal regime for vertical collusion differs from that on vertical unilateral practices. For example, a unilateral minimum resale-price policy can escape the prohibition of Article 101(1), in the absence of any evidence of collusion, and thus be found compatible with competition law. In contrast, an RPM clause in a collusive context is a hardcore restriction under Article 101(1) TFEU. Nonetheless, there is a fine line in distinguishing between the two forms of conduct. Judge Richard Posner highlighted the irrelevance of the distinction between unilateral conduct and collusion in a vertical context with regards to the concept of the restriction of competition when he remarked that vertical restraints are 'unilateral abuses of market power'.[132]

While it is not possible to apply Article 101 TFEU to unilateral vertical practices, both unilateral and vertical practices may fall under Article 102 TFEU. This is particularly the case for certain vertical restraints that restrict inter-brand competition (eg exclusive dealing, rebate

128 Commission—Notice concerning the assessment of certain subcontracting agreements in relation to Article 85(1) of the EEC Treaty [now Article 101(1) TFEU] [1979] OJ C 1/2.

129 Vertical Restraints Guidelines 2010, para 22.

130 On the difficulties of defining the collusive or unilateral character of vertical restraints and the concept of agreement and concerted practice, see Chapter 5.

131 See our analysis of the hub-and-spoke conspiracy in Chapter 5.

132 RA Posner, 'Vertical Restraints and Antitrust Policy' (2005) 72 *U Chicago L Rev* 229.

systems and contractual tying). Intra-brand competition restraints are usually examined under Article 101 TFEU only.

The joint-applicability of Articles 101 and 102 to vertical restraints is a matter of controversy. Some authors advance the view that vertical restraints should be assessed only under Article 101 TFEU.[133] Different arguments are advanced in support of this view, such as that (i) the methodology of assessing the competitive impact of vertical restraints does not differ substantially in Article 101, in comparison to Article 102, treating all vertical restraints under Article 101 will increase the consistency of the enforcement of competition law to vertical restraints, (ii) there is an argument to be made in favour of transposing the as efficient as competitor test the Commission adopted in the context of Article 102 for price restrictions to all types of vertical restraints (unilateral and collusive), (iii) treating all vertical restraints under Article 101 will increase legal certainty and is likely to reduce the administrative costs of the litigation process.

A similar view could be advanced with regard to the application of only Article 102 (or Chapter II CA98) to vertical restraints. This follows Judge Posner's intuition that all vertical restraints constitute a unilateral abuse of market power, as they are often imposed either by a supplier or by a distributor with bargaining power. In arguing for the necessary simplification of US antitrust law, Judge Posner suggested the repeal of either section 1 of the Sherman Act or section 2 of the Sherman Act. In the former scenario, US antitrust law would only prohibit monopolization, without regard to the form that this might take (unilateral practice or collusion). The prohibition will thus bring within the scope of US antitrust law 'acontractual exclusionary practices, although these also 'invariably violate other laws with heavy penalties'.[134] In the European context, enforcing only Article 102 TFEU to vertical practices will exclude from the scope of EU competition law vertical restraints from non-dominant firms, notwithstanding their anti-competitive effects.

There are a number of criticisms that can be addressed to the thesis of the unique applicability of Articles 101 or 102 TFEU (or equivalent national competition law provisions) to vertical restraints: (i) this integrates in the analysis a formalistic criterion, for example concerning the application of only Article 101 TFEU that of the existence of an agreement or a concerted practice; (ii) it will lead to under-enforcement: if only Article 101 TFEU applies, non-collusive vertical restraints will be excluded from the scope of the prohibition; if only Article 102 applies, then only dominant firms will be precluded from employing vertical restraints; (iii) the establishment of a coherent regime for vertical restraints under both Articles 101 and 102, by developing a categorization of abuses more compatible with an effects-based approach,[135] constitutes a superior alternative than reducing the arsenal of competition authorities to combat vertical restrictive practices and adopting formalistic distinctions. Competition authorities have, on the contrary, employed an array of competition law tools to regulate anti-competitive vertical restraints, in complement to Articles 101 and 102 TFEU (or their equivalent national provision).

10.4.3. EFFECT ON TRADE BETWEEN MEMBER STATES AND VERTICALS

The effect on trade is central to the application of Article 101 TFEU and more generally the application of EU competition law. In case there is no effect on trade, the restraints of

133 E Rousseva, *Rethinking Exclusionary Abuses in EU Competition Law* (Hart, 2010), 472–3.

134 RA Posner, *Antitrust Law* (University of Chicago Press, 2001), 260.

135 See our analysis in Chapter 8.

competition that were included in the distribution agreement will be assessed exclusively under the national competition law. Following section 60 CA98, national competition law should apply to the clauses of the distribution agreement in a manner that is consistent with the treatment of corresponding questions arising in EU competition law. Furthermore, national courts must have regard to relevant decisions and statements by the European Commission, including the Commission's guidelines. Should the agreement be found to have an appreciable effect on trade, it will fall within the scope of Article 101(1). National competition law may also apply. In the UK, Chapter I CA98 will apply if the 'relevant arrangement is or is intended to be implemented in the UK'. Following Article 3(2) of Regulation 1/2003, the application of national competition law may not lead to the prohibition of collusive practices which may affect trade between Member States but which do not restrict competition within the meaning of Article 101(1) of the Treaty or which fulfil the conditions of Article 101(3) or which are covered by a regulation for the application of Article 101(3). Inversely, if the agreement is incompatible with Article 101(1), then it would not be possible to rely on national competition law in order to save the specific restriction or agreement. This was of particular interest in UK competition law, because of the exclusion of vertical agreements from the application of Chapter I CA98 until May 2004.[136] Vertical agreements are further dealt under the Guidelines on the effect on trade concept.[137]

10.4.4. VERTICAL RESTRAINTS AND ARTICLE 101(1) TFEU: TOWARDS AN ECONOMIC APPROACH

Vertical restraints have been the principal terrain of the application of the economic approach to the interpretation of Article 101 TFEU.

As noted in Chapter 1, having obtained control over decisions on competition in Regulation 17 of 1962 (since revoked) by taking exclusive power to grant exemptions, the Commission continued, with few exceptions, to decide that any exclusive agreement that is important on the market has the object or effect of restricting competition. Since it lacked the manpower to grant more than a very few exemptions each year, it resorted to group exemptions so as to dispose of many cases opened by notification.

V Korah and D O'Sullivan, *Distribution Agreements under the EC Competition Rules* (Hart, 2002), 114 (footnotes omitted)

Some 30,000 exclusive dealing agreements were notified to the Commission under Regulation 17 (the regulation in force prior to Regulation 1/2003) and 27/62[138] with requests for clearance or exemption in the 1960s, shortly after the Regulations introduced a system of notification for agreements which citizens wanted exempted.

The Commission might have dealt with the problem by deciding that agreements involving parties which did not have significant market power did not infringe Article [101(1)] and needed

136 For an analysis of the condition of the effect on trade in general and the concept of appreciability, see Chapter 1.

137 Guidelines on the effect on trade concept contained in Articles 81 [now 101 TFEU] and 82 [now 102 TFEU] of the Treaty [2004] OJ C 101/7, paras 61–3, 70–2, 77, 86–92.

138 Since replaced by Commission Regulation 3385/94 [1994] OJ L 377/28.

no exemption, or that ancillary restrictions necessary to enable a firm to penetrate the market in another member state did not infringe the prohibition. Instead, it decided to reduce the number of pending files by granting group exemptions. [. . .]

Already, by 1965 [. . .] the Commission had decided not to operate through broad economic principles and to control only those agreements that might give cause for concern, but to treat all significant exclusive contracts as contrary to Article [101(1)] and provide group exemptions for specified kinds of agreement into which Community businessmen are expected to distort their agreements.

The Commission adopted successive block exemption regulations exempting distribution agreements: there have been regulations for exclusive dealing agreements, exclusive purchasing agreements, franchising outlets, specific regulations for exclusive distribution agreements for vehicles, beer, and petrol distribution.[139]

V Korah and Denis O'Sullivan, *Distribution Agreements under the EC Competition Rules* (Hart, 2002), 116 (footnotes omitted)

In 1994, the Commission set in train a long internal and external consulting process including economic studies which led to the Green paper with radical ideas differing from its earlier view. The Commission was concerned that monitoring notifications was a waste of resources both its own and those of business. Moreover, thinking has been transformed by the experience of the merger task force. This included officials, many seconded from member states and other departments of the Commission, who were educated in economics or had worked closely with economists. An economist, David Deacon, was appointed to head the policy directorate of the competition department and he was in charge of the team producing the Green paper.

In the Green paper, the Commission analyzed the drawbacks of the current system: made it clear that vertical restraints were less harmful than horizontal ones, that vertical restraints had anti-competitive effects, but also solved some possible causes of market failure. [. . .]

Starting with the Green Paper on Vertical Restraints in 1997,[140] the Commission attempted to respond to the criticisms addressed to its 'legalistic' and 'formalistic' approach that considered that every restriction on the commercial freedom of distributors could fall within the scope of Article 101(1) by adopting a more 'economic approach'.[141] The shift towards an economic analysis of vertical restrictions was completed with the publication of a Follow-up Report to the Green Paper[142] and the adoption of the Vertical Block Exemption Regulation 2790/99[143]

[139] See V Korah and W Rothnie, *Exclusive Distribution and the EEC Competition Rules: Regulations 1983/83 and 1984/83* (Sweet & Maxwell, 2nd ed, 1992); V Korah, *Franchising and the EEC Competition Rules—Regulation 4078/88* (Sweet & Maxwell, 1989).

[140] Commission of the European Communities, Green Paper on Vertical Restraints in EC Competition Policy COM (96) 721 final (22 January 1997).

[141] For a strong and influential criticism of the Commission's vertical restraints policy, see BE Hawk, 'System Failure: Vertical Restraints and EC Competition Law' [1995] 32 *Common Market L Rev* 973. See also D Deacon, 'Vertical Restraints under EU Competition Law: New Directions' [1995] *Fordham Corporate L Institute* 307.

[142] Communication from the Commission on the application of the Community competition rules to vertical restraints—Follow-up to the Green Paper on vertical restraints, COM/98/0544 final [1998] OJ C 365/3.

[143] Commission Regulation (EC) No 2790/1999 of 22 December 1999 on the application of Article 81(3) of the Treaty to categories of vertical agreements and concerted practices [1999] OJ L336/21.

and of detailed vertical restraints guidelines[144] in 1999 that examine not only the application of Article 101(3) but also that of Article 101(1) to 'vertical restraints'. The regulatory framework was revised in 2010 with the adoption of a new Block Exemption Regulation 330/2010 on the application of Article 101(3) of the Treaty to categories of vertical agreements and concerted practices[145] and of the new Guidelines on Vertical Restraints, which replaced respectively Regulation 2790/99 and the vertical restraints guidelines of 1999. These texts are also relevant for the application of Article 101(1) to vertical restraints. The Commission has recently launched the review process of the Vertical Block Exemption Regulation 330/2010 as this expires on 31 May 2022.[146]

Guidelines on Vertical Restraints [2010] OJ C 130/1

5. Article 101 applies to vertical agreements that may affect trade between Member States and that prevent, restrict or distort competition ('vertical restraints').[147] Article 101 provides a legal framework for the assessment of vertical restraints, which takes into consideration the distinction between anti-competitive and pro-competitive effects. Article 101(1) prohibits those agreements which appreciably restrict or distort competition, while Article 101(3) exempts those agreements which confer sufficient benefits to outweigh the anti-competitive effects.[148]

The Commission no longer has power to grant individual exemptions since Regulation 1/2003 has entered into force. As it was explained in Chapters 1 and 6, EU competition law has moved from a legal authorization regime to a legal exception regime with the adoption of Regulation 1/2003. Distribution agreements should no longer be notified to the European Commission in order to benefit from Article 101(3) TFEU.[149] The assessment under Article 101 TFEU follows a global approach that combines the analysis of the existence of a restriction of competition under Article 101(1), before a more thorough analysis is performed under Article 101(3). The legal burden of proof under Article 101(1) falls on the plaintiff or the competition authority. The legal burden of proof under Article 101(3) falls on the defendant.

Although this Section will focus on the application of Article 101(1) to vertical restraints, one should not forget that a restriction of competition under Article 101(1) (practice having as its object or effect the restriction of competition) might be found legal if the defendant successfully carries her burden of proof by providing evidence that the specific agreement fulfils the four cumulative conditions of Article 101(3). Both Articles 101(1) and 101(3) are thus relevant for vertical restraints.

144 Vertical Restraints Guidelines 2000.

145 Regulation 330/2010.

146 See, https://ec.europa.eu/info/law/better-regulation/initiatives/ares-2018-5068981_en.

147 See eg judgments of the Court of Justice in Joined Cases C-56 & 58/64, *Grundig-Consten v Commission* [1966] ECR 299; Case C-56/65, *Technique Minière v Maschinenbau Ulm* [1966] ECR 235; and the judgment of the GC in Case T-77/92, *Parker Pen v Commission* [1994] ECR II–549.

148 See Communication from the Commission—Notice—Guidelines on the application of Article 101(3) (formerly Article 81(3)) of the Treaty [2004] OJ C 101/97, para 26 [hereinafter Guidelines on Article 101(3)] for the Commission's general methodology and interpretation of the conditions for applying Article 101(1) and in particular Article 101(3).

149 Vertical restraints were liberated from the requirement of notification earlier than the enactment of Regulation 1/2003, with the adoption of Regulation 1215/99 [1999] OJ L 148/1.

The reform of EU competition law on vertical restraints de-regulated a significant part of vertical restraints that were previously subject to strict notification requirements and to the assessment of the Commission and the Courts. The aim of the reform was to liberate resources at the European Commission level for the enforcement of competition law to cartels that were considered the most dangerous forms of commercial practices from the consumer's perspective. Enforcing competition law to vertical restraints required considerable resources with a high risk of over-enforcement of competition law and the chilling competition effects that this might have. The Commission believed that vertical restraints should be dealt by private litigation or by public competition law enforcement at the national level. The reform thus shifted the financial burden of applying competition law to vertical restraints to private litigants and national competition authorities. The economic approach adopted by the Commission was not thus only related to the substance of EU competition law (the way vertical restraints were assessed) but also to the structure of competition law enforcement to vertical restraints (and more specifically to the question of who should incur the costs of competition law enforcement).

The main contributions of the economic approach towards the assessment of vertical restraints under Article 101(1) are the following (i) the introduction of distinction between vertical and horizontal restrictions (Section 10.4.3.1), (ii) the focus on inter-brand competition (Section 10.4.3.2), and the (iii) consideration of the effects of vertical practices on competition before resuming to the application of Article 101(1) TFEU (Section 10.4.3.3).

10.4.4.1. The vertical/horizontal restraints dichotomy

The turn towards a more economic approach manifests itself first with the official adoption of the vertical/horizontal restraints dichotomy as an important conceptual category in EU competition law. Undertakings are found to be in a vertical relation when they are present in different levels of the commercialization process, ie supply and distribution. They are found to be in a horizontal relation in situations where they are actual or potential competitors and produce substitutable products or services.

The emergence of the vertical/horizontal dichotomy is fairly recent in competition law. US antitrust law was particularly influential from this perspective. The US Supreme Court employed for the first time the expression 'vertical agreement' in *White Motors Co v US*, which involved territorial restrictions imposed contractually by a manufacturer on retailers.[150] The Court found the concept broad enough to cover forms of cooperation raising issues different from horizontal cooperation arrangements (or cooperation between competitors) as well as from resale price maintenance schemes (that is, vertical price restraints considered equivalent to a horizontal collusion between retailers), both of which were then prohibited per se at the time under section 1 of the *Sherman Act*.[151] The Court rejected any extension of the per se illegality rule to non-price vertical agreements, noting that 'we need to know more than we do about the actual impact of these arrangements on competition to decide whether they have such a pernicious effect on competition and lack of redeeming virtue'.[152] Subsequent

150 *White Motors Co v US*, 372 US 253 (1963).

151 The latter since the seminal decision in *Dr Miles Medical Co v John D. Park & Sons*, 220 US 373 (1911). The Court has recently reversed this decision in *Leegin Creative Leathers Products, Inc v PSKS, Inc*, 551 US 877 (2007), 127 S Ct 2705 (2007).

152 *White Motors Co v US*, 372 US 253, 263 (1963).

antitrust cases adopted a more hostile approach towards vertical contractual integration. The expression 'vertical restraints', that is vertical agreements found to be infringing competition law, was employed for the first time in *Motor Co v Webster Auto Sales* for both non-price and price-related practices in a vertical relation.[153] The scope of the per se rule was extended to cover customer and territorial restrictions by the US Supreme Court a year later in *Schwinn*.[154] The Court's aim was to prohibit restrictions on the freedom of retailers to compete against each other (intra-brand competition), even if the effect of those restrictions was to enhance competition between different suppliers (inter-brand competition), the Court applying the same analysis to vertical and horizontal restrictions.

However, under the joint influence of the Chicago School of antitrust economics, which insists on the role of inter-brand competition and market power as filters to antitrust enforcement,[155] and new institutional economics, which drew attention to the economic motives of vertical contractual integration,[156] the US Supreme Court overruled *Schwinn* in *Continental TV, Inc v GTE Sylvania*.[157] The Court held that vertical customer and territorial restrictions should be assessed according to a cost benefit analysis under the rule of reason.[158] Horizontal territorial restrictions should on the contrary be subject to a per se prohibition approach.[159] The characterization of a restriction or agreement as being horizontal or vertical has therefore important implications on the outcome of a competition law case.

A number of competition authorities have followed US antitrust law in adopting the vertical/horizontal classification as a shortcut to the antitrust assessment of anti-competitive effects. Different presumptions seem to apply, depending on the characterization of a restriction as being vertical or horizontal.

The issue of the applicability of the provision on collusive practices of the Treaty of Rome to distribution restraints in EU competition law was raised for the first time in *Bosch*, where the CJEU had to examine if a contractual restriction on exports integrated in a distribution agreement infringed Article 101 TFEU.[160] The Court followed the Opinion of its Advocate General Lagrange and considered that interdictions on exports fall within the scope of Article 101(1), without distinguishing between vertical or horizontal agreements.

The European Commission first referred to the vertical/horizontal agreements dichotomy in the Green Paper on Vertical Restraints.[161] The Commission stressed the need to take into account the economic effects of vertical agreements before the finding of an infringement of Article 101. Although the economic approach has been also extended to horizontal

153 *Motor Co. v Webster Auto Sales* 361 F 2d 874 (1st Cir 1966).

154 *United States v Arnold, Schwinn & Co*, 388 US 365 (1967).

155 See F Easterbrook, 'The Limits of Antitrust' (1984) 63(1) *Tex L Rev* 1.

156 See O Williamson, 'Assessing Vertical Market Restrictions: Antitrust Ramifications of the Transaction Cost Approach' [1979] 127 *U Pennsylvania L Rev* 953.

157 *Continental TV Inc v GTE Sylvania Incorporated*, 433 US 36 (1977) [hereinafter *Sylvania*].

158 Ibid, 49: '[. . .] the true test of legality is whether the restraint imposed is such as merely regulates and perhaps thereby promotes competition or whether it is such as may suppress or even destroy competition.'

159 *United States v Sealy Corp*, 388 US 350, 352 (1967).

160 Case C-13/61, *Geus en Uitdenbogerd v Bosch and Others* [1962] ECR 45.

161 Commission of the European Communities, Green Paper on Vertical restraints in EC Competition Policy COM (96) 721 final (22 January 1997), para 2. See also Vertical Restraints Guidelines 2000, para 6 ('[f]or most vertical restraints, competition concerns can only arise if there is insufficient inter-brand competition, ie if there is some degree of market power at the level of the supplier or the buyer or at both levels. If there is insufficient inter-brand competition, the protection of inter- and intra-brand competition becomes important').

agreements,[162] the distinction between horizontal and vertical restraints still plays an important role when it comes to the drafting of block exemption regulations. There are now specific rules applying to vertical agreements and the characterization of an agreement as being vertical usually triggers the use of a higher market share threshold for benefitting of the exception under Article 101(3) than for horizontal restrictions.[163]

The effect of vertical restraints on consumers is ambiguous and largely depends on the economic context and the specific circumstances of each case. Contrary to horizontal restraints, which are considered with suspicion, vertical restraints came to be seen more favourably in competition law. The classification of a restraint as being horizontal or vertical has therefore important implications on competition law enforcement. The Guidelines on Vertical Restraints recognize that vertical restraints are less harmful to competition than horizontal restraints and may provide 'substantial scope for efficiencies'.[164]

10.4.4.2. Vertical 'restraints' and intra-brand versus inter-brand restrictions of competition

Different forms of vertical restraints affect intra-brand and inter-brand competition. Vertical restraints affect intra-brand competition when they affect competition between sellers of the same brand. Typically, this takes the form of authorizing the distributors to sell only from specific locations, within a specific geographic area, or by imposing to all distributors to resell at the same price, thus diminishing competition between them. By granting an exclusive distribution territory to Consten, Grundig was restricting intra-brand competition between Consten and other distributors that could also theoretically resell from the same geographic area. Inter-brand vertical restraints limit competition between different brands (eg between Grundig and another TV manufacturer). Typically, the distributors will be prohibited by their suppliers from carrying competing brands (eg exclusive dealing) with the result that a competing manufacturer cannot have access to the single-brand retailer.

The distinction between intra-brand and inter-brand restrictions of competition has been an important categorical distinction in US antitrust law, following the Chicago School antitrust 'revolution' that valued only the protection of inter-brand competition.[165] It also gained some prominence in EU competition law as an analytical tool of the effect of vertical restrictions on competition, perceived as competitive rivalry. In *Consten & Grundig*, Advocate General Roemer referred to the distinction in order to refute the thesis that EU competition law emphasized only inter-brand competition:

[162] See Commission Notice—Guidelines on the applicability of Article 81 of the EC Treaty [now 101 TFEU] to horizontal cooperation agreements [2001] OJ C 3/2, para 7; Guidelines on Article 101(3), para 25.

[163] See the analysis in Section 10.6.2.1.

[164] Vertical Restraints Guidelines 2010, paras 6–7.

[165] While both intra-brand and inter-brand competition were equally valued in *United States v Topco Associates, Inc*, 405 US 596, 612 (1972), the Supreme Court recognized in *Sylvania*, 433 US 36 (1977) noting the redeeming virtues of vertical restrictions on inter-brand competition and advancing a more lenient application of competition law despite their effects on intra-brand competition. For a similar evolution with regard to vertical restrictions on resale price, see *State Oil Co v Khan*, 522 US 3, 15 ('the antitrust laws' primary purpose . . . is to protect interbrand competition'); *Leegin Creative Leather Products, Inc v PSKS, Inc*, 551 US 877, 896 (2007) ('[t]he antitrust laws primarily are designed to protect interbrand competition from which lower prices can later result').

> The principle of freedom of competition concerns the latter's different stages and aspects. Although competition between producers is generally more visible than that between distributors of the same brand, it does not thereby follow that an agreement which tends to restrict the latter should escape the prohibition of Article [101](1) merely because it might increase the former.[166]

The importance that the Commission attached to intra-brand competition largely explains the quite broad application of Article 101(1) TFEU to vertical restraints included in distribution agreements the first forty years of EU competition law.

The reform of EU competition policy on vertical restraints in 1997, in particular the Green Paper on Vertical Restraints made a number of suggestions for a more economics-oriented approach, including a prioritization of the protection of inter-brand competition.

Green Paper on Vertical Restraints in EC Competition Policy, COM(96)721 final (22 January 1997)

> 54. Current economic thinking stresses the importance of market structure in determining the impact of vertical restraints on competition. The fiercer is interbrand competition the more likely are the pro-competitive and efficiency effects to outweigh any anti-competitive effects of vertical restraints. The inverse is true when interbrand competition is weak and there are significant barriers to entry. [. . .]
>
> 65. For policy purposes, it is necessary to translate the conclusions from economic analysis into workable tools that are both consistent with EC competition rules and relatively easy to implement with the necessary legal certainty for undertakings. One element has emerged as crucial in analysing the impact of vertical restraints: the degree of interbrand competition. [. . .]
>
> 85. This chapter presented a sketch of the findings of the recent economic analysis about vertical restraints. There are a number of conclusions that may be made: i. Anti-competitive effects of vertical restraints are likely to be insignificant in competitive markets. Rather their efficiency enhancing effect and benefit to consumers is likely to dominate. Anti-competitive effects are only likely where interbrand competition is weak and there are barriers to entry.

The importance of inter-brand competition was also recognized by the Commission in the 2000 Vertical Restraints Guidelines.[167]

The most recent Vertical Restraints Guidelines, adopted in 2010,[168] employ sparingly the conceptual categories of inter-brand and intra-brand competition. The categorical thinking across the lines of inter-brand versus intra-brand competition has lost its prominent role in favour of a more realistic economic approach that takes into account the effect of vertical restraints on the competition at both levels of the vertical chain (eg supply and retail level).

166 Opinion of AG Roemer in Joined Cases C-56 & 58/64, *Établissements Consten SA and Grundigverkaufs-GmbH v EEC Commission* [1966] CMLR 418, 473.

167 Vertical Restraints Guidelines 2000, para 6.

168 Vertical Restraints Guidelines 2010.

10.4.4.3. The scope of the prohibition of a restriction of competition under Article 101(1)

Article 101(1) TFEU prohibits collusive practices that have as their object or effect to restrict competition.

The first step in finding the existence of a restriction of competition under Article 101(1) is to find out if the specific vertical restraint has as its object the restriction of competition (Section 10.4.3.3.1).

In the absence of an anti-competitive object, it is important to analyse the anti-competitive effect of the vertical agreement (Section 10.4.3.3.2).

10.4.4.3.1. Vertical restrictions having as their object the restriction of competition

We will not repeat here our remarks on the concept of anti-competitive object in Chapter 6, but will simply remind the relevant guidelines of the Commission.

Communication from the Commission—Notice—Guidelines on the application of [Article 101 TFEU] [2004] OJ C 101/97 (footnotes omitted)

> 23. Non-exhaustive guidance on what constitutes restrictions by object can be found in Commission block exemption regulations, guidelines and notices. Restrictions that are black-listed in block exemptions or identified as hardcore restrictions in guidelines and notices are generally considered by the Commission to constitute restrictions by object. [. . .] As regards vertical agreements the category of restrictions by object includes, in particular, fixed and minimum resale price maintenance and restrictions providing absolute territorial protection, including restrictions on passive sales.

Resale price maintenance

RPM practices requiring buyers to observe fixed or minimum resale prices are found to be restrictive by object of competition. This covers both collective and individual RPMs.[169] The Commission was initially concerned about market integration. It found that in many trades RPM was national and protected by export bans. RPM may take different forms. Sometimes an individual manufacturer imposes minimum prices on its dealers and enforces them by contract (vertical, individual RPM). Frequently, a trade association requires its members to impose individual resale prices but enforces the agreements for its members (collective enforcement of individual RPM). Such a system is less likely to be justified by free rider arguments. Some trade associations whose members sold homogenous products went further and themselves imposed resale prices (collective RPM). Collective RPM denotes the situation where several sellers or their trade association agree to impose the same resale prices on their dealers, the effect being close to that of a cartel.

Article 101(1)(a) TFEU provides for a non-exhaustive list of the kinds of agreement that are likely to have the object or effect of restricting competition, and include those that directly

169 The following paragraphs draw on V Korah and D O'Sullivan, *Distribution Agreements under the EC Competition Rules* (Hart, 2002), 104–10.

or indirectly fix purchase or selling prices or any other trading conditions. This is not expressly limited to horizontal agreements—those made between competitors or imposed by trade associations—and applies equally to vertical agreements. Contrary to the position of various national competition laws,[170] the Commission did not make a distinction between individual and collective RPM.[171] The practice was often confined to a single Member State and the Commission saw it as reinforcing the isolation of national markets. The Commission nevertheless took the view that the practice usually escaped the prohibition of Article 101(1), yet it attacked individual RPM indirectly, for instance when it was associated with exclusive distribution. The Commission also objected to individual RPM in its decisions on selective distribution. For instance, it did not object to SABA being able to find out its dealers' gross income provided it did not enforce resale prices or offer incentives to dealers to sell only at recommended prices.[172] The CJEU also has objected to measures taken by suppliers to maintain prices in judgments such as *Metro v Commission*[173] and *Allgemeine Elektricitäts-Gesellschaft AEG-Telefunken AG v Commission.*[174] In *Pronuptia*,[175] the CJEU treated as contrary to Article 101(1) not only individual RPM, but also any control over the prices at which franchisees might advertise, but it treated recommended prices as outside the prohibition of Article 101(1). In *Louis Erauw-Jacquery v La Hesbignonne*,[176] the parties argued only that the maintenance of prices at which propagators might sell did not affect trade between Member States, not that it did not have the object or effect of restricting competition. The need to protect licensees of plant breeders' rights in basic seed against free riders was not raised and, on the basis of the first example given in Article 101(1), the CJEU assumed that the practice has the object of restricting competition without considering the possibility of free riders. The Court ruled that the maintenance of minimum resale prices would be unlawful if, in the context of other agreements concluded between the breeder and other licensees, the agreements might have an appreciable effect on trade between Member States.

Collective RPMs were condemned in *FEDETAB*.[177] The collective enforcement of RPM was found anti-competitive by object in *VBVB and CBBB*.[178] An agreement between two trade associations of publishers, one in Belgium and the other in the Netherlands, and others was binding on the members of each. Members were forbidden to give discounts on retail prices except to recognized parties and required to abide by the retail prices. The Commission decided that the object and effect of the agreement was to restrict competition and the CJEU confirmed that various defences raised by the parties were not effective, such as the cultural interest accepted by governments in keeping specialized bookshops in business.

170 For analysis, see I Apostolakis, *Resale Price Maintenance and the Limits of Article 101 TFEU: Reconsidering the Application of EU Competition Law to Vertical Price Restraints* (PhD thesis, University of Glasgow, 2015), Appendix.

171 R Joliet, 'Resale Price Maintenance under EEC Antitrust Law' (1971) 16 *Antitrust Bulletin* 589.

172 *SABA (I)* (Case IV/847) Commission Decision 76/159/EEC [1976] OJ L 28/19, [1976] 1 CMLR D61; *SABA (II)* (Case IV/29.598) Commission Decision 83/672/EEC [1983] OJ L376/41, [1983] 1 CMLR 676.

173 Case C-26/76, *Metro SB-Großmärkte GmbH & Co KG v Commission* (No 1) [1977] ECR 1875 [hereinafter *Metro I*].

174 Case C-107/82, *Allgemeine Elektrizitäts-Gesellschaft AEG-Telefunken AG v Commission* [1983] ECR 3151.

175 Case C-161/84, *Pronuptia de Paris GmbH v Pronuptia de Paris Irmgard Schillgallis* [1986] ECR 353 [hereinafter *Pronuptia*].

176 Case C-27/87, *Louis Erauw-Jacquery v La Hesbignonne* [1988] ECR 1919, para 20.

177 Joined Cases C-209–15 & 218/78, *Heintz van Landewyck Sàrl, Fédération Belgo-Luxembourgeoise des Industries du Tabac Asbl v Commission* [1980] ECR 3125.

178 Joined Cases C-43 & 63/82, *Vereniging ter Bevordering van het Vlaamse Boekwezen (VBVB) and Vereniging ter Bevordering van de Belangen des Boekhandels (VBBB) v Commission* [1984] ECR 19.

In the UK, two types of products were exempted from the RPM ban in 1997: books and branded, over-the-counter medicaments. Under the Net Book Agreement (NBA), a collective RPM scheme, publishers were allowed to set the retail prices of books, any retailer refusing to abide by the price risking to be refused supply of future books by all publishers. The NBA came into effect on 1 January 1900 and was operational until it was declared against the public interest and therefore illegal by the Restrictive Practices Court in March 1997.[179] Following the end of RPM in the book sector, UK book retailers became free to set retail prices, yet the publishers continue to set recommended retail prices (RRPs) the retailers then bargaining with publishers over wholesale price discounts on the RRP. A report commissioned by the OFT examined the effects of the breakdown of the NBA, finding that the total sales of books increased, there has been a significant increase in retail diversity with the entry of supermarkets and Internet sellers (in the retail sector making a positive contribution to industry productivity, the situation being overall better that the situation in other jurisdictions where the RPM was authorized for books (such as Germany).[180]

In *Replica Football Kits* and *Toys*, the OFT, the CAT, and subsequently the Court of Appeal were confronted to a hybrid horizontal/vertical restraints as the cases involved bilateral vertical agreements or concerted practices between the supplier(s) and the retailer(s), including RPM clauses, with 'a horizontal component', in view of the finding that each of the competitors 'was aware of the other's involvement and the nature of its intentions regarding its conduct in the relevant markets'.[181] The horizontal collusion dimension of the arrangement was therefore found predominant, RPM being found to have facilitated collusion downstream.

The OFT also found that two tobacco manufacturers (Imperial Tobacco and Gallaher) and ten retailers (Asda, The Co-operative Group, First Quench, Morrisons, One Stop Stores (formerly T&S Stores), Safeway, Sainsbury's, Shell, Somerfield, and TM Retail) engaged in unlawful practices in relation to retail prices for tobacco products in the UK.[182] The OFT concluded that each manufacturer had a series of individual arrangements with each retailer whereby the retail price of a tobacco brand was linked to that of a competing manufacturer's brand. Indeed, the retailer was to price particular brands of the manufacturer's tobacco products at retail prices which implemented that manufacturer's desired pricing relativities between its brands and the brands of a competing manufacturer (these requirements being commonly referred to as manufacturer's parity and differential requirements). The agreements also involved a combination of various elements: the manufacturer's strategy in relation to the retailer's retail prices (namely to achieve the parity and differential requirements between competing tobacco brands that were set by the manufacturer); written trading agreements between the supplier and the retailer under which the retailer agreed that it would price a number of the manufacturer's brands according to the parity and differential requirements stipulated by the manufacturer; contacts between the manufacturer and the retailer regarding the retail prices

[179] The Restrictive Trade Practices Court had approved the RPM scheme in 1962, putting forward the specific characteristics of books and broader social and cultural aspects. On the history of the NBA, see BS Yamey, 'The Net Book Agreement' (1963) 26 *Modern L Rev* 691.

[180] OFT 981, An evaluation of the impact upon productivity of ending resale price maintenance on books—Report prepared for the OFT by S Davies and M Olczak of the Centre for Competition Policy, University of East Anglia (2008).

[181] For a discussion of these cases, see Section 5.6.2.

[182] *Tobacco* (Case CE/2596-03) OFT Decision (15 April 15), available at webarchive.nationalarchives.gov.uk/20140402142426/http://www.oft.gov.uk/shared_oft/ca98_public_register/decisions/tobacco.pdf. For a commentary, see A Jones and A Turati, 'The UK *Tobacco* Case: Identifying Restrictions by Object in Vertical Agreements' (2012) *J European Competition L & Practice* 287.

for manufacturer's brands; the retail prices for the manufacturer's competitor's brands and the retail prices charged by the retailer's competitors; the payment or withdrawal of bonuses and other incentives (whether financial or other) by the manufacturer to incentivize the retailer to set its retail prices in accordance with the abovementioned retail pricing strategy and frequent and detailed monitoring; as well as evidence of complaints by the manufacturer and subsequent alignment of the retailer's retail prices to ensure compliance with the retail pricing strategy. According to the OFT,

> [. . .] a maximum differential requirement restricts the ability of a retailer to determine its resale prices. Specifically, the retailer is obliged to ensure that the difference in the retail price of two competing brands does not exceed a certain level (such that the retail price of brand X is not at a level which exceeds the relative price ceiling determined by the relevant differential requirement). Thus, in the example where the retail price of brand X must be no higher than that of brand Y, once the retailer has determined the price of brand X, it could in principle still choose to set the price of the competing brand Y at a higher level, but it is restricted in its freedom to set it at a lower level relative to brand X. If a retailer wants to increase the price of brand X and that brand's retail price is at the relative price ceiling, it could only do so if it increased the price of brand Y at the same time. Conversely, if the retailer wanted to reduce the retail price of the competing manufacturer's brand Y, and brand X was already at its price ceiling relative to brand Y, the retailer could only do so if it reduced the price of brand X at the same time. Therefore, a maximum differential requirement imposes as a corollary a minimum retail price on brand Y, relative to the retail price of brand X.[183]

The OFT considered that each of the infringing agreements was, by its very nature, capable of restricting competition, as it restricted the retailer's ability to determine its retail prices for competing linked brands, finding the existence of a restriction of competition by object and imposed fines totalling £225m. The CAT annulled the decision of the OFT on different grounds without pronouncing itself on the categorization of the practice as an object restriction.[184]

The views of economists diverge as to the characterization of RPM as by object restrictions to competition. Some authors argue that 'there is not yet sufficient evidence to justify moving RPM out of the EU's "presumed illegality" or "object" box and into a case-by-case assessment of "effect" box', but also recognize the possibility of such standard to produce false positives.[185] The framework they put forward does not, however, go as far as establishing a sort of per se prohibition for RPM, as in any case it is possible to justify them under Article 101(3) TFEU, the presumption of illegality being 'truly rebuttable', including the requirement that the authority should set out at least one plausible 'theory of harm' consistent with the specific fact-pattern. A prioritization of enforcement against RPM based on screens, such as unilateral market power or concentration upstream, the existence of significant downstream buyer power or concentration, and of other networks of RPM agreements involving a number of upstream suppliers who account for a significant share of the upstream market, complete the suggested framework.

183 *Tobacco* (Case CE/2596-03) OFT Decision (15 April 2010), para 6.232.
184 *Imperial Tobacco Group plc and Others* [2011] CAT 41.
185 M Bennett, A Fletcher, E Giovannetti, and D Stallibrass, 'Resale Price Maintenance: Explaining the Controversy, and Small Steps Towards a More Nuanced Policy' [2010] 33 *Fordham Int'l LJ* 1278.

Others put forward a more lenient approach to RPM, advancing the view that the theoretical or empirical literature is ambiguous whether the anti-competitive or the pro-competitive effects of RPM are more important, that, in any case, firms with little market share are unlikely to give rise to significant anti-competitive effects and that the smaller the market power possessed by a firm the smaller the efficiency gain required for RPM to have a positive effect, and that finally RPM is less likely to harm if it is an isolated practice. They conclude:

> The presumption that RPM is welfare detrimental and that it is unlikely that an exemption would be granted even to firms enjoying less than 30% market share should be replaced by a statement that 'the larger market power the stronger should be the demonstrated efficiency gains' with a concrete rule that states: (1) the de minimis rule applies also for RPM (i.e., a firm with less than 15% market share can engage in RPM); (2) for a firm with a share above 15%, the burden of proving that RPM will have beneficial effects on competition is resting upon it; (3) it is unlikely that a firm with a share in excess of 30% will be able to show that RPM will have a net beneficial effect.[186]

Absolute territorial protection and restrictions on parallel imports

Vertical territorial practices may be qualified as object restrictions to competition when they lead to a situation of absolute territorial protection, that is suppress both opportunities of active and passive sales.[187] Furthermore, according to the CJEU's case law 'by its very nature, a clause prohibiting exports constitutes a restriction on competition, whether it is adopted at the instigation of the supplier or of the customer since the agreed purpose of the contracting parties is the endeavour to isolate a part of the market'.[188]

In *Erauw-Jacquery (Louis) SPRL v La Hesbignonne SC*,[189] however, in view of the substantial sunk costs incurred by the holder of plant breeders' rights in developing a plant variety and the need for careful handling of basic seed, the CJEU cleared a restraint on the licensee selling and exporting basic seed although it conferred absolute territorial protection. The Commission applies the judgment only in relation to basic seed. It is generally agreed that the judgment creates a very narrow exception and may be due to the fragility of plant breeders' rights which expire once the variety ceases to be distinct, uniform, stable, and useful.

The CJEU has accepted limited restrictions on cross border trade as not infringing Article 101(1) in view of the investments made by both parties in *Nungesser (LG) KG and Kurt Eisele v Commission*.[190] The CJEU has also accepted in relation to Article 101(1) that even absolute territorial protection was necessary to support investment by permitting absolute territorial protection in relation to copyright in performing rights in *Coditel v Ciné Vog Films (No 2)*.[191]

As we have examined in Chapter 2, in the Spanish *GlaxoSmithKline* (*GSK*) case, the EU Courts dealt with the GSK's general sales conditions for its wholesalers in Spain, which in their Article 4 provided that GSK could charge different prices for the pharmaceutical products to

[186] M Motta, P Rey, F Verboven, and N Vettas, 'Hardcore Restrictions under the Block Exemption Regulation on Vertical Agreements: An Economic View', available at ec.europa.eu/dgs/competition/economist/hardcore_restrictions_under_BER.pdf.

[187] See Chapter 6.

[188] Case C-19/77, *Miller International Schallplatten GmbH v Commission* [1978] ECR 131.

[189] Case C-27/87, *Erauw-Jacquery (Louis) SPRL v La Hesbignonne SC* [1988] ECR 1919, paras 10–11.

[190] Case C-258/78, *Nungesser (LG) KG and Kurt Eisele v Commission* [1982] ECR 2015.

[191] Case C-262/81, *Coditel v Ciné Vog Films (No 2)* [1982] ECR 3381, para 20.

be sold on the domestic market and those for exports (practice of 'dual pricing').[192] According to the Commission, '[i]n so doing, GSK aimed to restrict parallel trade in its medicines in which Spanish intermediaries were engaging on account of the price differentials between Spain and other Member States.'[193] The General Court overturned the Commission's decision finding that, in view of the legal and economic context in which GSK's General Sales Conditions were applied, and in particular the intervention of State regulation into the prices of reimbursable medicines in Spain, which, 'to a large extent', shielded them from 'the free play of supply and demand', it was necessary for the Commission to undertake an effects-based analysis of these clauses, thus rejecting the usual qualification of restrictions of parallel trade to restrictions of competition by object.[194] The CJEU reversed the judgment of the General Court on this issue and maintained the traditional position of EU competition law that restrictions to parallel imports should be characterized as restrictions of competition by object.[195] The CJEU acknowledged that even restrictions to parallel trade may be justified by Article 101(3) TFEU.

Other forms of territorial restrictions were also found to constitute restrictions of competition by object, as the following case illustrates.

Joined Cases C-403 & 429/08, *Football Association Premier League Ltd and Others v QC Leisure and Others and Karen Murphy v Media Protection Services Ltd*
[2011] ECR I–9083

The recent judgments of the CJEU with regard to territorial restrictions in media rights licensing and imported satellite decoder cards illustrate the strict stand of EU competition law to territorial restrictions. In order to protect such territorial exclusivity and to prevent the public from receiving broadcasts outside the relevant Member State, each broadcaster undertakes, in the licence agreement concluded with the Football Association Premier League (FAPL), to encrypt its satellite signal and to transmit the signal, so encrypted, by satellite solely to subscribers in the territory which it has been awarded. Consequently, the licence agreement prohibits the broadcasters from supplying decoder cards to persons who wish to watch their broadcasts outside the Member State for which the licence is granted.

In this case, certain pubs in the United Kingdom have begun to use foreign decoder cards, issued by a Greek broadcaster to subscribers residing in Greece, to access Premier League matches. The pubs buy a card and a decoder box from a dealer at prices lower than those of Sky, the holder of the broadcasting rights in the United Kingdom. The FAPL took the view that such activities undermine the exclusivity of the television broadcasting rights and the value of those rights; it is seeking to bring them to an end by means of legal proceedings. The first

192 For a more detailed analysis, see A Komninos and A Dawes, 'EC Competition Law and Parallel Trade in Pharmaceutical Products' in I Lianos and I Kokkoris (eds) *The Reform of EC Competition Law, New Challenges, The Reform of EC Competition Law: New Challenges* (Kluwer Law International, 2010), 377, 389ff, noting that the qualification of 'dual pricing' in this case is a 'misnomer' as GSK had agreed with its wholesalers only on the higher prices for the medicines that were not reimbursable under Spanish legislation, as for those that were reimbursable by the Spanish healthcare system, the price was set by the Spanish State, not GSK.

193 *GSK Spain* (Case IV/36.957/F3) Commission Decision 2001/791/EC [2001] OJ L 302/1, para 189.

194 Case T-168/01, *GlaxoSmithKline Services Unlimited v Commission* [2006] ECR II–2969, paras 122 and 147.

195 Joined Cases C-501, 513, 515 & 519/06 P, *GlaxoSmithKline Services v Commission* [2009] ECR I–9291, paras 59, 62–4.

case (C-403/08) concerns a civil action brought by the FAPL against pubs that have screened Premier League matches by using Greek decoder cards and against the suppliers of such decoder cards to those pubs. The second case (C-429/08) has arisen from criminal proceedings against Karen Murphy, the landlady of a pub that screened Premier League matches using a Greek decoder card. In those two cases, the High Court of Justice of England and Wales has referred a number of questions concerning the interpretation of European Union law to the Court of Justice. The Court's judgment applied the free movement provisions of the Treaty (free provision of services) and competition law. With regard to the first set of EU law rules, it held that national legislation which prohibits the import, sale, or use of foreign decoder cards is contrary to the freedom to provide services and cannot be justified either in light of the objective of protecting intellectual property rights or by the objective of encouraging the public to attend football stadiums. The Court found that payment by the television stations of a premium in order to ensure themselves absolute territorial exclusivity goes beyond what is necessary to ensure the right holders appropriate remuneration, because such a practice may result in artificial price differences between the partitioned national markets. Such partitioning and such an artificial price difference are irreconcilable with the fundamental aim of the Treaty, which is completion of the Internal Market. The Court also applied the competition law provisions of the Treaty. Here are the relevant paragraphs of the case:

243. [. . .] With regard to the application of the prohibition of anti-competitive practices under Article 101(1) TFEU, the referring courts are seeking to ascertain whether it is sufficient that a licence agreement concerning the territorially limited transmission of a broadcast has the object of preventing, restricting or distorting competition or whether an actual impairment of competition must be shown.

244. A concerted practice pursues an anti-competitive object for the purpose of Article 101(1) TFEU where, according to its content and objectives and having regard to its legal and economic context, it is liable in an individual case to result in the prevention, restriction or distortion of competition within the common market. It is not necessary for there to be actual prevention, restriction or distortion of competition or a direct link between the concerted practice and consumer prices. It is thus not necessary to examine the effects of an agreement in order to establish its anti-competitive object.

245. It must therefore be examined in the present cases whether licence agreements pursue an anti-competitive object where a programme content provider enters into a series of exclusive licences, each for the territory of one or more Member States, under which the broadcaster is licensed to broadcast the programme content only within that territory (including by satellite) and a contractual obligation is included in each licence requiring the broadcaster to prevent its satellite decoder cards which enable reception of the licensed programme content from being used outside the licensed territory.

246. In order to assess the anti-competitive object of an agreement, regard must be had, in particular, to the content of its provisions, the objectives which it seeks to attain and the legal and economic context of which it forms a part.

247. An agreement between a producer and a distributor which might tend to restore the national divisions in trade between Member States might be such as to frustrate the Treaty's objective of achieving the integration of national markets through the establishment of a single market. Thus, on a number of occasions, the Court has held agreements aimed at partitioning national markets according to national borders or making the interpenetration of national markets more difficult, in particular those aimed at preventing or restricting parallel exports, to be agreements the object of which is to restrict competition within the meaning of Article 101(1) TFEU.

248. A contractual obligation linked to a broadcasting licence requiring the broadcaster to prevent its satellite decoder cards which enable reception of the licensed programme content from being used outside the licensed territory has the same effect as agreements to prevent or restrict parallel exports. Such an obligation is intended to prevent any competition between broadcasters through a reciprocal compartmentalisation of licensed territories. Such licences with absolute territorial protection are incompatible with the internal market. There is therefore no reason to treat such agreements any differently from agreements intended to prevent parallel trade.

249. The examination of freedom to provide services confirms this conclusion since conflicting assessments of the fundamental freedoms and competition law are to be avoided in principle.

250. It must also be pointed out that an anti-competitive agreement within the meaning of Article 101(1) TFEU can be justified pursuant to Article 101(3) TFEU. However, a person who relies on that provision must demonstrate, by means of convincing arguments and evidence, that the conditions for obtaining an exemption are satisfied. In this connection, it would appear that similar considerations should apply as in the examination of whether a restriction of freedom to provide services is justified.

251. [. . .] [W]here a programme content provider enters into a series of exclusive licences each for the territory of one or more Member States under which the broadcaster is licensed to broadcast the programme content only within that territory (including by satellite) and a contractual obligation is included in each licence requiring the broadcaster to prevent its satellite decoder cards which enable reception of the licensed programme content from being used outside the licensed territory, such licence agreements are liable to prevent, restrict or distort competition. They are therefore incompatible with Article 101(1) TFEU; it is not necessary to show that such effects have actually occurred.

NOTES AND QUESTIONS ON FOOTBALL ASSOCIATION PREMIER LEAGUE

1. According to this judgment, is exclusive territorial licensing problematic as such with regard to Article 101(1) TFEU? On the other hand, did the Court accepted it in principle, but subjected it to some conditions?
2. In this case, the CJEU did not condemn the exclusive licences granted by the FAPL, but only what it regarded as the additional obligations on broadcasters not to supply decoding devices with a view to their use outside the territory covered by the licence agreement. This was on the basis that these provisions 'prohibit broadcasters from effecting any cross-border provision of services', 'granted absolute territorial exclusivity', and eliminated 'all competition between broadcasters'.
3. With regard to the application of Article 101(3) TFEU, the CJEU referred to the proportionality which it applied for the free movement provisions part of the judgment. The Court did not accept the objective justifications put forward, in particular that the restrictions had the objective of encouraging the public to attend football stadiums (in connection with the prohibition on broadcasting football matches in the UK during the Saturday afternoon 'close period'); and the objective of protecting intellectual property (or similar) rights, by ensuring that rights-holders are appropriately remunerated, remarking that the restrictions were not necessary in order to ensure

appropriate remuneration for the rights-holders, as the rights-holder in this case was remunerated for the broadcasting of the protected subject-matter (in the country of origin). The 'premium' paid by rights-holders for absolute territorial protection was thus not necessary to ensure appropriate remuneration for exploitation of the rights, in particular as such absolute territorial exclusivity results in the partitioning of national markets and artificial price differences between markets, which is irreconcilable with the fundamental aims of the TFEU and the remuneration agreed between a rights-holder and broadcaster could be set so as take account of the potential audience in other Member States.

4. It remains an open question as to how the CJEU's reasoning in respect of the broadcasting of football matches will be applied to other markets where digital rights are often licensed on a territorial basis (for example computer software, music, e-books, or films made available via the Internet, as envisaged by Advocate General Kokott in her opinion). No guidance was given by the Court in this regard. Do you think that the same principles should apply? See our analysis about geo-blocking in Section 2.3.3.3.

It is noteworthy that in its 2010 Vertical Restraints Guidelines, the Commission acknowledges that in exceptional circumstances hardcore restrictions may be objectively necessary for an agreement of a particular type or nature and therefore fall outside Article 101(1) TFEU.[196]

Guidelines on Vertical Restraints [2010] OJ C 130/1

61. A distributor which will be the first to sell a new brand or the first to sell an existing brand on a new market, thereby ensuring a genuine entry on the relevant market, may have to commit substantial investments where there was previously no demand for that type of product in general or for that type of product from that producer. Such expenses may often be sunk and in such circumstances the distributor may not enter into the distribution agreement without protection for a certain period of time against (active and) passive sales into its territory or to its customer group by other distributors. [. . .] Where substantial investments by the distributor to start up and/or develop the new market are necessary, restrictions of passive sales by other distributors into such a territory or to such a customer group which are necessary for the distributor to recoup those investments generally fall outside the scope of Article 101(1) during the first two years that the distributor is selling the contract goods or services in that territory or to that customer group, even though such hardcore restrictions are in general presumed to fall within the scope of Article 101(1).

62. In the case of genuine testing of a new product in a limited territory or with a limited customer group and in the case of a staggered introduction of a new product, the distributors appointed to sell the new product on the test market or to participate in the first round(s) of the staggered introduction may be restricted in their active selling outside the test market or the market(s) where the product is first introduced without falling within the scope of Article 101(1) for the period necessary for the testing or introduction of the product.

196 2010 Vertical Restraints Guidelines, para 60.

This flexibility under Article 101(1) TFEU for what would have otherwise be considered as a restriction of active and passive sales and therefore a restriction of competition by object may be understood as related to a possible application of the ancillary restraints doctrine and therefore should be interpreted restrictively.[197] Note that there is no such flexibility for the application of Article 101(1) TFEU in the context of RPM clauses. Do you find this sensible? Do RPM clauses produce more anti-competitive effects?[198]

M Motta, P Rey, F Verboven, and N Vettas, *Hardcore Restrictions under the Block Exemption Regulation on Vertical Agreements: An Economic View,* available at ec.europa.eu/dgs/competition/economist/hardcore_restrictions_under_BER.pdf (references omitted)

There are at least two questions that the current treatment of territorial restrictions raises: (i) Is it reasonable to prevent firms with little market power from using territorial restrictions clauses? (ii) Is it reasonable to treat in such a different way active and passive sales?

(i) It is well established that even firms with little market power will have an incentive to try and discriminate prices across consumer groups (or countries), for the very principle indicated above. However, it is clear that the lower their market power the smaller the effect their price discrimination will have on the market. Since it is also unclear whether this effect is positive or negative, it would be hard to justify on economic grounds a prohibition of territorial restrictions for such firms.

(ii) From an economic perspective, it is not clear to us why active and passive sales should be treated in different ways, as both have the same effect, which is to lead to price uniformity. The distinction between active and passive sales is also increasingly fuzzier given that online sales become more important, and given the Guidelines' interpretation that general advertising and promotion on the Internet amount to passive sales. Furthermore, it is not clear why the parallel trade activities of large wholesalers should be treated as if they were purchases of individual consumers. It is questionable, therefore, whether such a distinction should be given such an important role in competition policy. Rather than resorting to a formal and to a large extent arbitrary approach aiming to classify active v. passive sales, it may be worth using a more "effect-based" approach according to which the treatment of firms which use territorial restrictions would depend of the market share they hold and the possible efficiency justifications associated with such restrictions.

Given these considerations, we would advocate for territorial clauses a similar approach as for RPM. (1) A de minimis rule should apply for territorial restrictions of the parallel trade

197 I Apostolakis, 'Resale Price Maintenance and Absolute Territorial Protection: Single Market Integration, the Ancillary Restraints Doctrine and the Application of Article 101 TFEU to Vertical Agreements' (2015) 38 *World Competition L & Economics Rev* 215.

198 Ibid, 231 (noting that in reality the opposite occurs, as '[. . .] the allocation of exclusive territories eliminates all types of competition between dealers, while RPM leave non-price competition unaffected'). See, however, P Rey and T Vergé, 'Resale Price Maintenance and Interlocking' (2010) 58 *J Industrial Economics* 928, 930–1 (noting that RPM allows manufacturers to avoid inter-brand competition (dampen competition) 'even when, due to retailers' differentiation strategies meeting consumer demand makes it undesirable to grant exclusive territories and exclude some of the established retailers', thus hinting to the possibility that RPM may be used in order to achieve a broader array of anti-competitive strategies than exclusive territories). See also J Asker and B-I Heski, 'Raising Retailers' Profits: On Vertical Practices and the Exclusion of Rivals' (2014) 104(2) *American Economic Rev* 672 (highlighting the exclusionary and foreclosure potential of RPM).

activities of firms (be they wholesalers or retailers active in other territories); (2) firms holding a market share between 15% and 30% will have the burden of proving the efficiency gains associated with territorial restriction clauses; (3) it is unlikely that firms which hold a market share in excess of 30% will be able to show that clauses limiting parallel trade have a net beneficial impact on competition.

This policy—which uses market share criteria to interpret the effects of territorial restrictions—would be in line with economic efficiency objectives. To guarantee the rights of citizens not to be discriminated against on the basis of their location or nationality, it may be established that individual purchases could never be restricted. This would amount to redefine the prohibition of restricting passive sales as the prohibition to restrict sales to individual consumers only.

Pierre Fabre: *Absolute online distribution bans*

In *Pierre Fabre*, the CJEU included among the restrictions that are considered by object anti-competitive under Article 101(1) TFEU and also hardcore restrictions under Article 101(3) TFEU, the absolute prohibition of Internet sales by retailers members of a selective distribution system.

C-439/09, *Pierre Fabre Dermo-Cosmétique SAS v Président de l'Autorité de la concurrence and Ministre de l'Économie, de l'Industrie et de l'Emploi*

[2011] ECR I–9419

Pierre Fabré Dermo-Cosmétique (PFDC) manufactures and markets cosmetics and personal care products and has several subsidiaries, including the Klorane, Ducray, Galenic, and Avene laboratories, whose cosmetic and personal care products are sold under those brands. In 2007, the Pierre Fabre group had 20 per cent of the French market for those products. For the sale of their products on both the French and European market, PFDC has created a selective distribution system. Even though these products are not classified as medicines, the distribution contracts for these products only allow sales in a physical space and in the presence of a qualified pharmacist, and therefore de facto *bans all Internet sales. Distribution contracts for those products in respect of the Klorane, Ducray, Galénic, and Avène brands stipulate that such sales must be made exclusively in a physical space, in which a qualified pharmacist must be present. Hence, those requirements exclude* de facto *all forms of selling by Internet. PFDC explained that the products at issue, by their nature, require the physical presence of a qualified pharmacist at the point of sale during all opening hours, in order that the customer may, in all circumstances, request and obtain the personalized advice of a specialist, based on the direct observation of the customer's skin, hair and scalp. On 29 October 2008, the French Competition Authority (l'Autorité de la concurrence, hereinafter 'Authority') decided that PFDC's ban on all Internet sales was contrary to competition law and thus prohibited. PFDC was ordered to remove the restrictive clauses from their distribution contracts. In the contested decision, the Authority noted first of all that the ban on Internet sales amounted to a limitation on the commercial freedom of PFDC's distributors by excluding a means of marketing its products. Moreover, that prohibition restricted the choice of consumers wishing to purchase online and ultimately prevented sales to final purchasers who are not located in the 'physical' trading area of the authorized distributor. According to the Authority, that limitation necessarily had the object of restricting competition, in addition to the limitation inherent in the manufacturer's very choice of a selective distribution system, which limits the number of distributors authorized to distribute the product and prevents distributors from selling the goods to non-authorized distributors. The Authority rejected PFDC's argument that the ban on Internet sales at issue contributes to improving the distribution of dermo-cosmetic products whilst avoiding the risks of counterfeiting and of free-riding between authorized pharmacies. PFDC's choice of a selective distribution system, with the presence of a pharmacist at the place of sale, guaranteed that an advisory service is provided at all authorized pharmacies and that each of them bears the cost. In response to PFDC's argument on the need for a pharmacist to be physically present when the products at issue are purchased, in order to ensure the consumer's well-being, the Competition Authority noted that the products concerned were not medicines. In this respect, the specific legislation by which they are governed concerns rules which apply to their manufacture and not to their distribution which is free, and, moreover, a pharmacist does not have the power to make a diagnosis, only a doctor being authorized to do so. According to the decision of the Authority, PFDC also failed to demonstrate in what way visual contact between the pharmacist and the users of the product ensures 'cosmeto-vigilance', which requires health-care professionals to record and communicate any adverse reactions to cosmetic products. Indeed, any negative effects of the products at issue will become apparent only after the product has been used and not when it is purchased. In the event of problems linked to its use, the patient will tend to consult a doctor. The Competition Authority did not find the fact that Internet distribution does not lead to a reduction in prices to be relevant. The benefit for the consumer lies not only in the reduction of prices, but also in the improvement of the service offered by the distributors including,* inter alia, *the possibility of ordering the products at a distance, without time restrictions, with easy access to information about the products and allowing prices to be compared. PFDC challenged the decision before the Paris Court of Appeals and claimed that the presence of a pharmacist is necessary to guarantee that the customer can at all times request and obtain advice from a specialist. It also argued that the Competition Authority wrongly denied PFDC the benefit of the block exemption or an individual exemption. In 2009, the Paris Court of Appeals asked the CJEU for a preliminary ruling on the arguments put forward by PFDC. The case was brought under the regime of former Regulation 2790/99. The CJEU's judgment follows.*

32. It is to be observed at the outset that neither Article 101 TFEU nor Regulation No 2790/1999 refer to the concept of 'hardcore' restriction of competition.

33. In those circumstances, the question referred for a preliminary ruling must be understood as seeking to ascertain, firstly, whether the contractual clause at issue in the main proceedings amounts to a restriction of competition 'by object' within the meaning of Article 101(1) TFEU, secondly, whether a selective distribution contract containing such a clause—where it falls within the scope of Article 101(1) TFEU—may benefit from the block exemption established by Regulation No 2790/1999 and, thirdly, whether, where the block exemption is inapplicable, the contract could nevertheless benefit from the exception provided for in Article 101(3) TFEU. [. . .]

The classification of the restriction in the contested contractual clause as a restriction of competition by object

36. The selective distribution contracts at issue stipulate that sales of cosmetics and personal care products by the Avène, Klorane, Galénic and Ducray brands must be made in a physical space, the requirements for which are set out in detail, and that a qualified pharmacist must be present.

37. According to the referring court, the requirement that a qualified pharmacist must be present at a physical sales point *de facto* prohibits the authorised distributors from any form of internet selling.

38. As the Commission points out, by excluding *de facto* a method of marketing products that does not require the physical movement of the customer, the contractual clause considerably reduces the ability of an authorised distributor to sell the contractual products to customers outside its contractual territory or area of activity. It is therefore liable to restrict competition in that sector.

39. As regards agreements constituting a selective distribution system, the Court has already stated that such agreements necessarily affect competition in the common market (Case 107/82 *AEG-Telefunken* v *Commission* [1983] ECR 3151, paragraph 33). Such agreements are to be considered, in the absence of objective justification, as 'restrictions by object'.

40. However, it has always been recognised in the case-law of the Court that there are legitimate requirements, such as the maintenance of a specialist trade capable of providing specific services as regards high-quality and high-technology products, which may justify a reduction of price competition in favour of competition relating to factors other than price. Systems of selective distribution, in so far as they aim at the attainment of a legitimate goal capable of improving competition in relation to factors other than price, therefore constitute an element of competition which is in conformity with Article 101(1) TFEU (*AEG-Telefunken* v *Commission*, paragraph 33).

41. In that regard, the Court has already pointed out that the organisation of such a network is not prohibited by Article 101(1) TFEU, to the extent that resellers are chosen on the basis of objective criteria of a qualitative nature, laid down uniformly for all potential resellers and not applied in a discriminatory fashion, that the characteristics of the product in question necessitate such a network in order to preserve its quality and ensure its proper use and, finally, that the criteria laid down do not go beyond what is necessary (Case 26/76 *Metro SB-Großmärkte* v *Commission* [1977] ECR 1875, paragraph 20, and Case 31/80 *L'Oréal* [1980] ECR 3775, paragraphs 15 and 16).

42. Although it is for the referring court to examine whether the contractual clause at issue prohibiting *de facto* all forms of internet selling can be justified by a legitimate aim, it is for the Court of Justice to provide it for this purpose with the points of interpretation of European Union law which enable it to reach a decision (see *L'Oréal*, paragraph 14).

43. It is undisputed that, under Pierre Fabre Dermo-Cosmétique's selective distribution system, resellers are chosen on the basis of objective criteria of a qualitative nature, which are laid down uniformly for all potential resellers. However, it must still be determined whether the restrictions of competition pursue legitimate aims in a proportionate manner in accordance with the considerations set out at paragraph 41 of the present judgment.

44. In that regard, it should be noted that the Court, in the light of the freedoms of movement, has not accepted arguments relating to the need to provide individual advice to the customer and to ensure his protection against the incorrect use of products, in the context of non-prescription medicines and contact lenses, to justify a ban on internet sales [. . .].

45. Pierre Fabre Dermo-Cosmétique also refers to the need to maintain the prestigious image of the products at issue.

46. The aim of maintaining a prestigious image is not a legitimate aim for restricting competition and cannot therefore justify a finding that a contractual clause pursuing such an aim does not fall within Article 101(1) TFEU.

47. In the light of the foregoing considerations, the answer to the first part of the question referred for a preliminary ruling is that Article 101(1) TFEU must be interpreted as meaning that, in the context of a selective distribution system, a contractual clause requiring sales of cosmetics and personal care products to be made in a physical space where a qualified pharmacist must be present, resulting in a ban on the use

of the internet for those sales, amounts to a restriction by object within the meaning of that provision where, following an individual and specific examination of the content and objective of that contractual clause and the legal and economic context of which it forms a part, it is apparent that, having regard to the properties of the products at issue, that clause is not objectively justified.

The possibility of a block exemption or an individual exemption

48. If it is established that an agreement or contractual clause restricts competition within the meaning of Article 101(1) TFEU, it will be for the referring court to examine whether the conditions in paragraph 3 of that article are met.

49. The possibility for an undertaking to benefit, on an individual basis, from the exception provided for in Article 101(3) TFEU derives directly from the Treaty. It is not contested in any of the observations submitted to the Court. That possibility is also open to the applicant in the main proceedings.

50. However, in that regard, given that the Court does not have sufficient information before it to assess whether the selective distribution contract satisfies the conditions in Article 101(3) TFEU, it is unable to provide further guidance to the referring court.

51. As regards the possibility that the selective distribution contract may benefit from the block exemption of Regulation No 2790/1999, it should be noted that the categories of vertical agreements that are eligible have been defined by the Commission in that regulation, on the basis of the Council's authorisation contained in Council Regulation No 19/65/EEC [. . .].

52. Under Articles 2 and 3 of Regulation No 2790/1999, a supplier, in the context of a selective distribution system, may, in principle, benefit from an exemption, where its market share does not exceed 30%. It is apparent from the documents before the Court that Pierre Fabre Dermo-Cosmétique's market share does not exceed that threshold. However, that regulation, pursuant to Article 2 of Regulation No 19/65, has excluded certain types of restrictions that have severely anticompetitive effects, irrespective of the market share of the undertakings concerned.

53. Hence, it follows from Article 4(c) of Regulation No 2790/1999 that the exemption is not to apply to vertical agreements which directly or indirectly, in isolation or in combination with other factors under the control of the parties, have as their object the restriction of active or passive sales to end users by members of a selective distribution system operating at the retail level of trade, without prejudice to the possibility of prohibiting a member of the system from operating out of an unauthorised place of establishment.

54. A contractual clause such as the one at issue in the main proceedings, prohibiting *de facto* the internet as a method of marketing, at the very least has as its object the restriction of passive sales to end users wishing to purchase online and located outside the physical trading area of the relevant member of the selective distribution system.

55. According to Pierre Fabre Dermo-Cosmétique, the ban on selling the contractual products via the internet is equivalent however to a prohibition on operating out of an unauthorised establishment. It submits that, since the conditions for exemption laid down at the end of the provision, cited in paragraph 53, are thus met, Article 4 does not apply to it.

56. It should be pointed out that, by referring to 'a place of establishment', Article 4(c) of Regulation No 2790/1999 concerns only outlets where direct sales take place. The question that arises is whether that term can be taken, through a broad interpretation, to encompass the place from which internet sales services are provided.

57. As regards that question, it should be noted that, as an undertaking has the option, in all circumstances, to assert, on an individual basis, the applicability of the

exception provided for in Article 101(3) TFEU, thus enabling its rights to be protected, it is not necessary to give a broad interpretation to the provisions which bring agreements or practices within the block exemption.

58. Accordingly, a contractual clause, such as the one at issue in the main proceedings, prohibiting *de facto* the internet as a method of marketing cannot be regarded as a clause prohibiting members of the selective distribution system concerned from operating out of an unauthorised place of establishment within the meaning of Article 4(c) of Regulation No 2790/1999.

59. In the light of the foregoing considerations, the answer to the second and third parts of the question referred for a preliminary ruling is that Article 4(c) of Regulation No 2790/1999 must be interpreted as meaning that the block exemption provided for in Article 2 of that regulation does not apply to a selective distribution contract which contains a clause prohibiting *de facto* the internet as a method of marketing the contractual products. However, such a contract may benefit, on an individual basis, from the exception provided for in Article 101(3) TFEU where the conditions of that provision are met.

NOTES AND QUESTIONS ON PIERRE FABRE

1. Are restrictions on Internet sales considered as restrictions on active or on passive sales?
2. Are restrictions on Internet sales anti-competitive by object? Why is that?
3. Are restrictions on Internet sales hardcore restraints? What are the implications for the application of Article 101(3)?
4. According to the CJEU, '[t]he aim of maintaining a prestigious image is not a legitimate aim for restricting competition and cannot therefore justify a finding that a contractual clause pursuing such an aim does not fall within Article 101(1) TFEU.'[199] Do you agree or disagree with this statement? Explain your conclusions.
5. Was PFDC's selective distribution system a quantitative one or a qualitative one? Would it make any difference here?
6. The UK competition adjudicators have also recently examined the compatibility of online sales bans with Art. 101 TFEU and Chapter I CA98, when these are included in a selective distribution agreement.[200] In *Online sales ban in the golf equipment sector*,[201] the CMA considered whether the clauses imposing an online sales ban that were included in the distribution agreements concluded between Ping, a manufacturer of golf clubs, golf accessories and clothing, and two UK retailers, constituted a restriction of competition, or whether such clauses were objectively justified or could be exempted under Article 101(3) TFEU. The parties argued that the ban was justified and/or beneficial as its aim was to enable face-to-face custom fitting, which cannot take place online. They also claimed that the ban promoted intra-brand competition by increasing the overall quality and choice in golf club hardware and fitting and protected Ping's brand image. Crucially, they also claimed that it dealt with a free rider problem as in order to perform

[199] C-439/09, *Pierre Fabre Dermo-Cosmétique SAS v Président de l'Autorité de la concurrence and Ministre de l'Économie, de l'Industrie et de l'Emploi* [2011] ECR I–9419, para 46 [hereinafter *PFDC*].

[200] *PING Europe Limited v CMA* [2018] CAT 13.

[201] *Online Sales ban in the golf equipment sector* (Case 50230) CMA Decision (24 August 2017), available at https://www.gov.uk/cma-cases/sports-equipment-sector-anti-competitive-practices.

face-to-face custom fitting, the retailers had to invest in expensive equipment, make face-to-face investments and take careful measurements of the customers, as well as to perform a number of tests (eg swing, ball flight analysis), only for the consumer to leave and complete the purchase online because they never intended to make a purchase at the brick and mortar store in the first place. This would have, according to the parties to the agreement, caused retailers to either stop custom fitting or to go out of business.

After finding that the online sales ban constituted a restriction of competition, following *Pierre Fabre Dermo-Cosmétique*, the CMA went on to consider if the restrictive measure was objectively justified. The CMA decided to perform a full proportionality assessment relying on paragraph 43 of the CJEU judgment in *Pierre Fabre*, which states that the test is if the measure 'pursues legitimate aim in a proportionate manner'.[202] Although it found that the promotion of custom fitting constituted, in principle, a legitimate aim, and that the Internet policy was a suitable means to promote custom fitting, it held that the online sales ban policy was not necessary to pursue the promotion of custom fitting, that it was disproportionate to the promotion of custom fitting and thus not objectively justified. Ping appealed against the CMA's decision to the CAT.[203] The CAT rejected the CMA's approach with regard to the proportionality assessment before concluding that the absolute online ban in this case constituted a restriction of competition by object.

PING Europe Limited v CMA
[2018] CAT 13

Article 101(1) TFEU

95. The assessment of whether the ban satisfies the criteria in the *Metro* case (i.e. the first question) is a binary assessment: either the restriction is necessary for non-price competition to exist or it is not. It is not a balancing exercise. The Tribunal is not weighing up the likely pro- and anti- competitive effects of the restriction. Where a restriction is not strictly 'necessary' for non-price competition to exist, but it does promote non-price competition, then it is clear that such a clause may benefit from an individual exemption under Article 101(3).

96. It follows that the assessment of whether a restriction satisfies the *Metro* criteria, is conceptually distinct from that of whether the restriction is capable of being redeemed under Article 101(3). The Court of First Instance in *Métropole*, in the context of assessing an ancillary restraint argument, noted that the '*examination of the objective necessity of a restriction in relation to the main operation cannot but be relatively abstract*' (para 109, our emphasis). We consider that this applies equally in the context of the application of the *Metro* criteria. Moreover, the proper place to weigh up the pros and cons of a measure is in the framework of Article 101(3).

97. Under the CMA's approach the question of objective justification was bound up with the question of whether the policy constituted a 'by object' restriction. This assessment entails a detailed enquiry into the proportionality and effectiveness of the policy. The CMA contended that Ping's internet ban was not objectively justified

202 Case C-439/09, *PFDC* [2011] ECR I-9419.

203 *PING Europe Limited v CMA* [2018] CAT 13.

because it was not proportionate to the objective pursued and—on the facts of this case—such a finding meant that the policy would also be incapable of justification under Article 101(3). If correct, the CMA's approach to the law might risk the assessment under Article 101(3) being emptied of any real substance.

98. We accept Ping's submission that objective justification and proportionality are not in themselves relevant to an assessment of whether an agreement is an infringement by object. The law on 'object' is set out authoritatively by the Court of Justice in *Cartes Bancaires* which makes no reference to proportionality. We should emphasise that we do not see any contradiction between *Pierre Fabre* and *Cartes Bancaires.* In particular, we do not consider that it was the intention of the Court of Justice in *Pierre Fabre* to devise a special form of 'by object' assessment which incorporates proportionality considerations specifically for internet sales bans. On the contrary, it can be seen that the Court of Justice conducted a standard (albeit brief) assessment of the nature of the restriction in its relevant context at paras 35–38 of the judgment. The Court of Justice then went on to consider the separate question of 'objective justification' in paras 39–44 and concluded that the internet sales ban was unlikely to be proportionate. The reference to 'objective justification' at para 47 of the *Pierre Fabre* decision is, in our view, best understood as a reference back to the *Metro* criteria, compliance with which would take the internet sales ban outside the prohibition in Article 101(1).

99. We therefore consider that the CMA erred in law by conducting a full proportionality analysis as part of its assessment under Article 101(1) of whether Ping's internet policy was 'objectively justified'. An assessment of this type properly forms a part of the assessment under Article 101(3) and is necessary if—and only if—it has first been established that the impugned provision constitutes a restriction of competition 'by object' or 'by effect'.

100. Whilst the CMA has erred in law, this error would only be a material error requiring the Decision to be quashed if the Decision cannot stand in the light of that error and it cannot be supported on some other basis. In later parts of this judgment we conclude that the CMA's error made no difference to the overall conclusions reached by the CMA and is not a ground for quashing the Decision.

The CAT also rejected Ping's submission that the presence or absence of a 'plausibly pro-competitive rationale' is the key to identifying an infringement by object.[204] *Ping claimed that this reflected the law as stated by the Court of Justice in* Cartes Bancaires.[205] *The CAT disagreed noting that '[h]ad the Court of Justice considered it appropriate for national courts to limit their consideration as to the plausibility of the rationale underlying the relevant restrictions, it would have said so explicitly'.*[206] *The CAT relied on the CJEU's in* BIDS[207] *and* General Motors[208] *for the proposition that 'even if the impugned measure had a pro-competitive purpose, this was "irrelevant" to an assessment of whether it constituted an object restriction for the purposes of Article 101(1)'.*[209] *Indeed, 'the Tribunal approaches the issue of object infringement on the basis that an agreement revealing a sufficient degree of harm to competition may be deemed to be a restriction of competition "by object" irrespective of the actual, subjective aims of the parties involved, even if those aims are legitimate'.*[210]

[204] *PING Europe Limited v CMA* [2018] CAT 13, paras 103–4.

[205] Case C-67/13 P, *CB v Commission*, ECLI:EU:C:2014:2204. See further Section 6.3.1.2.4.

[206] *PING Europe Limited v CMA* [2018] CAT 13, para 101.

[207] Case C-209/07, *Competition Authority v Beef Industry Development Society Ltd*, ECLI:EU:C:2008:643, para 20

[208] Case C-551/03 P, *General Motors v Commission*, ECLI:EU:C:2005:639, para 64

[209] *PING Europe Limited v CMA* [2018] CAT 13, para 101.

[210] Ibid, para 102.

Limiting the scope of the Pierre Fabre case law in an online selective distribution system (partial online sales restrictions and restrictions on the use of marketplaces): Coty Germany GmbH v Parfümerie Akzente GmbH

This is a preliminary reference submitted in the context of a dispute between Coty Germany GmbH ('Coty Germany'), a leading supplier of luxury cosmetics in Germany, and Parfümerie Akzente GmbH ('Parfümerie Akzente'), an authorized distributor of those products (member of Coty's selective distribution system), concerning the prohibition on the use by the latter undertaking in a discernible way of non-authorized third undertakings for Internet sales of the contract goods.[211] Coty's new selective distribution system authorised online sales through an electronic shop window of the distributor and prohibited the use of different business names and involvement of third parties. Parfümerie Akzente refused to sign in this new system and started selling on Amazon.de. Coty sued and the case was sent to the CJEU by the national court. More specifically, the CJEU was asked whether and to what extent selective distribution systems relating to luxury and prestige products and designed mainly to preserve the 'luxury image' of those products, are aspects of competition that are compatible with Article 101(1) TFEU. In that connection, the Court was called upon to determine whether an absolute ban on members of a selective distribution system, who operate as retailers on the market, making use in a discernible way of third undertakings for Internet sales, is compatible with Article 101(1) TFEU, without consideration of whether there is any actual breach of the legitimate requirements of the manufacturer in terms of quality. In addition, the Court was requested to determine the application of Article 4(b) and (c) of Regulation No 330/2010, an issue that we will examine in Section 10.6.2.2.2. The judgment concerns restrictions in a selective distribution network, and takes the view that selective distribution has neutral or positive effects on competition. We explore in more detail restrictions included in selective distribution systems in Section 10.4.4.3.2.

We include a summary of the Opinion of AG Wahl and some excerpts from the CJEU's judgment.

Case C-230/16, *Coty Germany GmbH v Parfümerie Akzente GmbH*, ECLI:EU:C:2017:941

Coty Germany is one of Germany's leading suppliers of luxury cosmetics. It sells certain luxury cosmetic brands via a selective distribution network, on the basis of a distribution contract employed uniformly throughout Europe and supplemented by various special contracts designed to organize that network. Parfümerie Akzente had for many years distributed Coty Germany's products as an authorized retailer, both at brick-and-mortar locations and over the Internet, partly through its own online store and partly via the platform 'amazon.de'. In March 2012, Coty Germany revised the selective distribution network contracts and the supplemental agreement, stipulating that 'the authorised retailer is entitled to offer and sell the products on the Internet, provided, however, that that Internet sales activity is conducted through an 'electronic shop window' of the authorized store and the luxury character of the products is preserved'. The supplemental agreement also expressly prohibited the use of a different business name and the recognizable engagement of a third-party undertaking that is not an authorized retailer of Coty Prestige. A footnote to that clause stated that 'accordingly, the authorized retailer is prohibited from collaborating with third parties if such collaboration

[211] See Case C-230/16, *Coty Germany GmbH v Parfümerie Akzente GmbH*, ECLI:EU:C:2017:941.

is directed at the operation of the website and is effected in a manner that is discernible to the public'. Parfümerie Akzente refused to approve those amendments to the distribution contract and Coty Germany brought an action before a national court of first instance, seeking an order prohibiting Parfümerie Akzente from distributing products bearing the brand via the platform 'amazon.de'.

At first instance, the national court dismissed that action on the ground that the contractual clause infringed Article 101(1) TFEU and its equivalent in German competition law, finding that the objective of maintaining a prestigious image of the mark was not compatible with the Pierre Fabre case law of the CJEU, the clause also constituting a hardcore restriction under Article 4(c) of Regulation No 330/2010, and could not also benefit from an individual exemption, since the general prohibition on Internet sales via third-party platforms which it imposed did not result in efficiency gains of such a kind as to offset the disadvantages for competition that resulted from the restriction of the means of marketing, and was unnecessary, since there were other means which were also appropriate but less restrictive of competition, such as the application of specific quality criteria for the third-party platforms. Coty Germany brought an appeal against the judgment and the appeal court (Higher Regional Court, Frankfurt am Main) decided to stay the proceedings and to refer matter to the CJEU for a preliminary ruling, asking a number of questions relating to (i) the compatibility with Article 101(1) TFEU of a selective distribution system for luxury goods designed, primarily, to preserve the luxury image of those goods, (ii) the lawfulness under Article 101(1) TFEU of a general prohibition on Internet sales via third-parties, and (iii) its compatibility with Articles 4(b) and 4(c) of Regulation 330/2010.[212]

We include first some excerpts of the AG's N Wahl opinion before looking to the judgment of the CJEU.

Opinion of AG Wahl in Case C-230/16, *Coty Germany GmbH v Parfümerie Akzente GmbH*, ECLI:EU:C:2017:603

32. Generally, the competition rules—and Article 101 TFEU in particular—are designed to prevent distortions of 'competition', it being understood that competition, which is intended to promote economic efficiency and ultimately the welfare of consumers, must not only permit the introduction of the lowest possible prices but also be a vector for diversity in the choice of goods, the optimisation of the quality of goods and the services provided and also the stimulation of innovation. European competition law does not see price competition as the only possible model.

33. In that regard, the Court held at a very early stage that although price competition is important, it does not constitute the only effective form of competition or that to which absolute priority must in all circumstances be accorded. There are thus legitimate requirements, such as the maintenance of a specialist trade capable of providing specific services as regards high-quality and high-technology products, which may justify a reduction of price competition in favour of competition relating to factors other than price.

34. It is on the basis of that premiss that selective distribution systems should be seen.

[. . .]

212 The issue is discussed in Section 10.6.2.2.2.

45. Consequently, selective distribution systems may be considered, generally, to have neutral, or indeed beneficial, effects from the aspect of competition.

[. . .]

48. In that context, it must be emphasised that Article 101 TFEU is not intended to regulate or to proscribe certain freely consented contractual obligations, such as those arising from the contract between a distributor and its supplier, but relates essentially to the economic impacts of conduct viewed from the aspect of competition. Also, the fact that a selective distribution system may lead to contractual imbalance between the parties, in particular to the disadvantage of an authorised distributor, is not a relevant factor in the context of the examination of the restrictive effects that that agreement may have on competition.

[. . .]

The AG took care to distinguish this case from Pierre Fabre:

78. As regards, in the first place, the factual context of the judgment [. . .] Pierre Fabre Dermo-Cosmétique [. . .] I recall that the point at issue in that case was the obligation imposed by a manufacturer of cosmetics and personal care products on its selected distributors to supply evidence that there would be physically present at their respective outlets at all times at least one qualified pharmacist. According to the Court, which approved the assessment that had been made by the French competition authority, that requirement excluded de facto and absolutely any possibility that the products in question might be sold by authorised distributors via the internet.

79. As is clear from the question referred to the Court for a preliminary ruling in that case, the only point at issue was a contractual clause containing a general and absolute ban on internet sales of the contract goods to end users, imposed on authorised distributors within the framework of a selective distribution system. Conversely, the selective distribution system in its entirety was not at issue.

80. In the second place, as regards the reasoning expressly applied by the Court in the judgment in *Pierre Fabre Dermo-Cosmétique*, it relates only to the contractual clause containing, in particular, the ban on internet sales imposed by Pierre Fabre. The mere fact that the inclusion of that clause was based on the need to preserve the prestige image of the products in question was not regarded by the Court as constituting a legitimate objective for restricting competition. However, that does not mean that it was the Court's intention that distribution systems specifically designed to preserve the brand image of the products concerned must necessarily be caught by the prohibition of agreements and concerted practices referred to in Article 101(1) TFEU.

The AG also noted that Coty Germany only required its authorized distributors not to sell the contract products via third-party platforms, and such restriction was 'far from imposing an absolute prohibition on online sales' as in Pierre Fabre.[213] *Hence, in the present case, authorized distributors were still allowed to distribute the contract products via their own Internet sites and were not prohibited from making use of third-party platforms in a non-discernible manner in order to distribute those products.*[214]

We will not comment further on the Opinion of the AG as this was followed by the CJEU.

213 Opinion of AG Wahl in Case C-230/16, *Coty Germany GmbH v Parfümerie Akzente GmbH*, ECLI:EU:C:2017:603, para 109.

214 Ibid, para 110.

Case C-230/16, *Coty Germany GmbH v Parfümerie Akzente GmbH*, ECLI:EU:C:2017:941 (some references omitted)

The compatibility with Article 101(1) TFEU of a selective distribution system for luxury goods designed, primarily, to preserve the luxury image of those goods.

24. [T]he Court has ruled that the organisation of a selective distribution network is not prohibited by Article 101(1) TFEU, to the extent that resellers are chosen on the basis of objective criteria of a qualitative nature, laid down uniformly for all potential resellers and not applied in a discriminatory fashion, that the characteristics of the product in question necessitate such a network in order to preserve its quality and ensure its proper use and, finally, that the criteria laid down do not go beyond what is necessary [. . .]

25. With particular regard to the question whether selective distribution may be considered necessary in respect of luxury goods, it must be recalled that the Court has already held that the quality of such goods is not just the result of their material characteristics, but also of the allure and prestigious image which bestow on them an aura of luxury, that that aura is essential in that it enables consumers to distinguish them from similar goods and, therefore, that an impairment to that aura of luxury is likely to affect the actual quality of those goods [. . .].

27. In that context, the Court has in particular taken the view that the establishment of a selective distribution system which seeks to ensure that the goods are displayed in sales outlets in a manner that enhances their value contributes to the reputation of the goods at issue and therefore contributes to sustaining the aura of luxury surrounding them [. . .].

28. It thus follows from that case-law that, having regard to their characteristics and their nature, luxury goods may require the implementation of a selective distribution system in order to preserve the quality of those goods and to ensure that they are used properly.

29. A selective distribution system designed, primarily, to preserve the luxury image of those goods is therefore compatible with Article 101(1) TFEU on condition that the criteria mentioned in paragraph 24 of the present judgment are met.

30. Contrary to the claims of Parfümerie Akzente and the German and Luxembourg Governments, that conclusion is not invalidated by the assertion contained in paragraph 46 of the judgment of 13 October 2011, *Pierre Fabre Dermo-Cosmétique* (C-439/09, EU:C:2011:649).

31. That assertion must be read and interpreted in the light of the context of that judgment.

32. In that regard, it must be recalled that, in the case which gave rise to that judgment, the referring court was unsure as to whether a specific contractual clause imposing on authorised distributors, in the context of a selective distribution system, a comprehensive prohibition on the online sale of the contract goods complied with Article 101(1) TFEU, rather than whether such a system in its entirety was compliant. It must also be stated that the goods covered by the selective distribution system at issue in that case were not luxury goods, but cosmetic and body hygiene goods.

The national court had referred to paragraph 46 of the judgment in Pierre Fabre for the proposition that the need to preserve the prestigious image of cosmetic and body hygiene goods was not a legitimate requirement for the purpose of a selective distribution network. The CJEU proceeded to a different interpretation of this paragraph.

34. [. . .] The assertion in paragraph 46 of that judgment related [. . .] solely to the goods at issue in the case that gave rise to that judgment and to the contractual clause in question in that case.

35. By contrast, it cannot be inferred from the judgment of 13 October 2011, *Pierre Fabre Dermo-Cosmétique* (C-439/09, EU:C:2011:649) that paragraph 46 thereof sought to establish a statement of principle according to which the preservation of a luxury image can no longer be such as to justify a restriction of competition, such as that which stems from the existence of a selective distribution network, in regard to all goods, including in particular luxury goods, and consequently alter the settled case-law of the Court [. . .].

36. In view of the foregoing considerations, the answer to the first question is that Article 101(1) TFEU must be interpreted as meaning that a selective distribution system for luxury goods designed, primarily, to preserve the luxury image of those goods complies with that provision to the extent that resellers are chosen on the basis of objective criteria of a qualitative nature that are laid down uniformly for all potential resellers and applied in a non-discriminatory fashion and that the criteria laid down do not go beyond what is necessary. [. . .]

The lawfulness under Article 101(1) TFEU of a general prohibition on Internet sales via third-parties in a selective distribution system for luxury goods designed, primarily, to preserve the luxury image of those goods.

40. In the context of such a system, a specific contractual clause designed to preserve the luxury image of the goods at issue is lawful under Article 101(1) TFEU provided that the criteria mentioned in paragraph 36 of the present judgment are met.

41. While it is for the referring court to determine whether a contractual clause, such as that at issue in the main proceedings, which prohibits the use of third-party platforms for the online sale of the contract goods, meets those criteria, it is nevertheless for the Court of Justice to provide the referring court for this purpose with all the points of interpretation of EU law which will enable it to reach a decision [. . .].

The CJEU noted that the contractual clause at issue had the objective of preserving the image of luxury and prestige of the goods at issue, and looked objective and uniform, applying without discrimination to all authorized distributors.

43. It is therefore necessary to ascertain whether, in circumstances such as those at issue in the main proceedings, the prohibition imposed by a supplier on its authorised distributors of the use, in a discernible manner, of third-party platforms for the internet sale of the luxury goods at issue is proportionate in the light of the objective pursued, that is to say, whether such a prohibition is appropriate for preserving the luxury image of those goods and whether or not it goes beyond what is necessary to achieve that objective.

44. With regard, in the first place, to the appropriateness of the prohibition at issue in the main proceedings in the light of the objective pursued, it must be observed, first, that the obligation imposed on authorised distributors to sell the contract goods online solely through their own online shops and the prohibition on those distributors of using a different business name, as well as the use of third-party platforms in a discernible manner, provide the supplier with a guarantee, from the outset, in the context of electronic commerce, that those goods will be exclusively associated with the authorised distributors.

45. Since such an association is precisely one of the objectives sought when recourse is had to such a system, it appears that the prohibition at issue in the main

proceedings includes a limitation which is coherent in the light of the specific characteristics of the selective distribution system.

46. Consequently, if, as is apparent from the case-law of the Court, those characteristics make the selective distribution system an appropriate means by which to preserve the luxury image of luxury goods and therefore contribute to sustaining the quality of those goods [. . .] a limitation such as that stemming from the prohibition at issue in the main proceedings, the effect of which is inherent in those characteristics, must also be regarded as being such as to preserve the quality and luxury image of those goods.

47. Second, the prohibition at issue in the main proceedings enables the supplier of luxury goods to check that the goods will be sold online in an environment that corresponds to the qualitative conditions that it has agreed with its authorised distributors.

48. Non-compliance by a distributor with the quality conditions set by the supplier allows that supplier to take action against that distributor, on the basis of the contractual link existing between those two parties. The absence of a contractual relationship between the supplier and third-party platforms is, however, an obstacle which prevents that supplier from being able to require, from those third-party platforms, compliance with the quality conditions that it has imposed on its authorised distributors.

49. The internet sale of luxury goods via platforms which do not belong to the selective distribution system for those goods, in the context of which the supplier is unable to check the conditions in which those goods are sold, involves a risk of deterioration of the online presentation of those goods which is liable to harm their luxury image and thus their very character.

50. Third, given that those platforms constitute a sales channel for goods of all kinds, the fact that luxury goods are not sold via such platforms and that their sale online is carried out solely in the online shops of authorised distributors contributes to that luxury image among consumers and thus to the preservation of one of the main characteristics of the goods sought by consumers.

51. Consequently, the prohibition imposed by a supplier of luxury goods on its authorised distributors to use, in a discernible manner, third-party platforms for the internet sale of those goods is appropriate to preserve the luxury image of those goods.

52. With regard, in the second place, to the question of whether the prohibition at issue in the main proceedings goes beyond what is necessary for the attainment of the objective pursued, it must be noted, first, that, in contrast to the clause referred to in the case which gave rise to the judgment of 13 October 2011, *Pierre Fabre Dermo-Cosmétique* (C-439/09, EU:C:2011:649), the clause here at issue in the main proceedings does not contain an absolute prohibition imposed on authorised distributors to sell the contract goods online. Indeed, under that clause, the prohibition applies solely to the internet sale of the contract goods via third-party platforms which operate in a discernible manner towards consumers.

53. Consequently, authorised distributors are permitted to sell the contract goods online both via their own websites, as long as they have an electronic shop window for the authorised store and the luxury character of the goods is preserved, and via unauthorised third-party platforms when the use of such platforms is not discernible to the consumer.

54. Second, it must be noted that, as is apparent from the provisional results of the Preliminary Report on the E-commerce Sector Inquiry carried out by the Commission pursuant to Article 17 of Council Regulation (EC) No 1/2003 of 16 December 2002 on the implementation of the rules on competition laid down in Articles [101 and 102 TFEU] (OJ 2003 L 1, p. 1), adopted on 15 September 2016, despite the increasing importance

of third-party platforms in the marketing of distributors' goods, the main distribution channel, in the context of online distribution, is nevertheless constituted by distributors' own online shops, which are operated by over 90% of the distributors surveyed. That fact was confirmed in the final report relating to that inquiry, dated 10 May 2017.

55. Those factors support the view that it may be inferred that a prohibition, such as the prohibition which the applicant in the main proceedings imposed on its authorised distributors, on using, in a discernible manner, third-party platforms for the internet sale of luxury goods does not go beyond what is necessary in order to preserve the luxury image of those goods.

56. In particular, given the absence of any contractual relationship between the supplier and the third-party platforms enabling that supplier to require those platforms to comply with the quality criteria which it has imposed on its authorised distributors, the authorisation given to those distributors to use such platforms subject to their compliance with pre-defined quality conditions cannot be regarded as being as effective as the prohibition at issue in the main proceedings.

57. It follows that, subject to inquiries which it is for the referring court to make, such a prohibition appears to be lawful in relation to Article 101(1) TFEU.

58. Having regard to the foregoing considerations, the answer to the second question is that Article 101(1) TFEU must be interpreted as not precluding a contractual clause, such as that at issue in the main proceedings, which prohibits authorised distributors in a selective distribution system for luxury goods designed, primarily, to preserve the luxury image of those goods from using, in a discernible manner, third-party platforms for the internet sale of the contract goods, on condition that that clause has the objective of preserving the luxury image of those goods, that it is laid down uniformly and not applied in a discriminatory fashion, and that it is proportionate in the light of the objective pursued, these being matters to be determined by the referring court.

The Court seems to have set the record straight with regard to the interpretation of paragraph 46 of *Pierre Fabre*.[215] Without reversing *Pierre Fabre*, the CJEU interpreted *Pierre Fabre* in light of the context, the fact that the restriction in *Pierre Fabre* was about a total ban on online sales and that the products were not luxury goods, finding that paragraph 46 of *Pierre Fabre* provided 'interpretative elements' to the CJEU 'necessary to enable it to rule on the issue' but was not a 'statement of principle'.[216] Note that in his Opinion in *Coty*, AG Wahl referred to high-quality and high-technology products, which may raise questions as to the scope of *Coty* beyond genuine luxury products, although both the national court and the CJEU referred to luxury goods. In any case, it seems that specific restraints are to be evaluated in light of the same objective justification theory for selective distribution (the *Metro* criteria)[217] as the system as a whole. In conclusion, the Court held that a contractual clause in a selective distribution system that prohibiting authorized distributors from using, in a discernible manner, third-party platforms for the Internet sale of the goods is in line with Article 101 (1) if it has the objective of preserving the luxury image, it is laid down uniformly and applied non-discriminatory, and it is proportionate in the light of the objective pursued. These are, of course, matters that were left to be determined by the referring court, which will not, in case all these conditions are satisfied, find that the clauses restrict Article 101(1) TFEU when these do not lead to an outright online

215 Case C-439/09, *PFDC* [2011] ECR I–9419.

216 Case C-230/16, *Coty Germany GmbH v Parfümerie Akzente GmbH*, ECLI:EU:C:2017:941, para 33 and 35.

217 Case 26/76, *Metro I* [1977] ECR 1875.

ban, as was the case in *Pierre Fabre*. In the event these clauses are not proportional or any of the other conditions are not fulfilled (eg the product is not a luxury product for which such restrictions may be justified), Article 101(1) TFEU will apply, but the clause may be saved in case it is exempted by Regulation 330/2010 (if the conditions of the Reg. are satisfied) or through an individual exemption under Article 101(3) TFEU. We examine in detail the implications of the *Coty* judgment regarding partial online bans, such as restrictions on the use of marketplaces and/or price comparison websites in Section S.10.8.1.2.2.

Expanding and retracting the object category in verticals: Allianz Hungária *and* SIA Maxima Latvija

In *Allianz Hungária Biztosító and Others*,[218] the CJEU examined a series of bilateral vertical agreements concluded annually between a number of Hungarian insurance companies and car dealers which also operated as repair shops. The Hungarian competition authority brought proceedings against the insurer Allianz for having concluded a number of individual agreements with various dealers (which were also selling products from different insurers), pursuant to which their repair shops' hourly charge would increase if the motor insurance policies taken out with Allianz came to a specified percentage of the total number of insurance policies sold by the dealer concerned. The individual hourly repair rates charged by the repairers were based on prices agreed between Allianz and GÉMOSZ, the trade association for car repairers, in the context of a framework agreement, GÉMOSZ having anyway taken decisions recommending prices. A similar case was brought against another insurer, Generali-Providencia Biztosító Zrt, but this time there was no framework agreement with GÉMOSZ on the level of hourly repair rates. The Hungarian competition authority found that taken as a whole and individually, that bundle of agreements had as its object the restriction of competition in the insurance contracts market and the car repair services market. The decision was upheld on appeal and ended at the Hungarian Supreme Court which sent a preliminary reference to the CJEU, which found that such vertical agreements constituted a restriction of competition by object. According to the CJEU,

> 43. [. . .] [I]t must, first, be noted that, in contrast to the view apparently held by Allianz and Generali, the fact that both cases concern vertical relationships in no way excludes the possibility that the agreement at issue in the main proceedings constitutes a restriction of competition 'by object'. While vertical agreements are, by their nature, often less damaging to competition than horizontal agreements, they can, nevertheless, in some cases, also have a particularly significant restrictive potential. The Court has thus already held on several occasions that a vertical agreement had as its object the restriction of competition [. . .].

According to the CJEU, had this been an horizontal agreement or concerted practice between Allianz and Generali to adopt similar practices, there could be no dispute that it would have been treated as a restriction by object, this by the same effect resulting in the unlawfulness of the vertical agreements concluded in order to implement that agreement or practice.'[219]

[218] Case C-32/11, *Allianz Hungária Biztosító and Others*, ECLI:EU:C:2013:160. See our analysis in Chapter 6.

[219] Case C-32/11, *Allianz Hungária Biztosító and Others*, ECLI:EU:C:2013:160, para 45. This seems equivalent to the situation in the Commission's e-books investigation where the commercial agency (vertical) agreements had to be dropped as there was evidence of a parallel (horizontal) conduct between the five publishers (see Section 10.4.1.2.2).

The CJEU nevertheless noted that 'even if there is no agreement or concerted practice between those insurance companies, it will still be necessary to determine whether, taking account of the economic and legal context of which they form a part, the vertical agreements at issue in the main proceedings are sufficiently injurious to competition on the car insurance market as to amount to a restriction of competition by object',[220] finding that this was the case here in view of a number of factors, including the likelihood that competition would be eliminated or seriously weakened following the conclusion of such agreements, such likelihood being determined taking into account 'the structure of the market, the existence of alternative distribution channels and their respective importance and the market power of the companies concerned'.[221]

In its most recent judgment in *SIA Maxima Latvija*, the CJEU took a more favourable stance to vertical agreements.[222] The case concerned commercial lease agreements in shopping centres with a clause conferring on the tenant the right to approve the lease agreements that the property owner may conclude with third parties. Maxima Latvija is a major retailer in Latvia where it runs a chain of large shops and hypermarkets. It concluded a number of commercial lease agreements with owners of shopping centres to rent commercial spaces within such malls. Some of these agreements included a non-compete clause in favour of Maxima Latvija. As 'anchor tenant', Maxima Latvija was awarded the right to agree to the lessors letting third parties other shops than those rented to Maxima Latvija in the same shopping centres where the tenant was already present. The CJEU was seized of a preliminary ruling question by the Latvian Supreme Court, which asked whether the commercial lease agreements including a non-compete clause in favour of the tenant amounted to a restriction of competition by object and in the case it was not, if its effects restricted competition. The Court noted that the contested agreement was a vertical agreement concluded by firms, a retailer and a property owner, that did not compete with each other, and although it found that this fact is not conclusive in itself, it nevertheless acknowledged that this type of agreement is not among those which it is accepted may be considered, by their nature, to be harmful to competition.[223] The market foreclosure effect of the non-compete clause was not found sufficient to constitute an object restriction. The CJEU examined, instead, the agreement for the existence of an anticompetitive effect, following the *Delimitis* precedent.[224]

10.4.4.3.2. Vertical restrictions having as their effect the restriction of competition

The concept of restriction of competition under Article 101(1) seems to refer indirectly to the necessity of ensuring, at least, a residual level of competitive rivalry, which should not be jeopardized by practices of vertical control. However, as it has been explained in Chapter 6, any reduction of competitive rivalry should not fall automatically under the scope of the prohibition principle of Article 101(1) TFEU, at least in the absence of specific circumstances. This is the core of the economic approach in the application of Article 101(1) TFEU.

The objective of market integration largely inspired the Commission's approach to vertical restraints, its aim being to preserve market access of foreign producers from the possible

220 Case C-32/11, *Allianz Hungária Biztosító and Others*, ECLI:EU:C:2013:160, para 46.

221 Ibid, para 48.

222 Case C-345/14, *SIA Maxima Latvija v Konkurences padome*, ECLI:EU:C:2015:784.

223 Ibid, para 21.

224 Case C-234/89, *Delimitis (Stergios) v Henninger Bräu* [1991] ECR I-935. See also our analysis on *SIA Maxima Latvija* in Chapter 6.

foreclosing effect of vertical restraints and export bans. The dominant view, prior to the adoption of the Green Paper, was that competition was essentially a process of rivalry, the Commission consequently adopting a restrictive approach to agreements between parties in a vertical relationship. Article 101(1) TFEU applied to any constraint or restriction imposed on the economic freedom of the distributor by its supplier which also affected inter-State trade. The agreement could be examined under Article 101(3) TFEU. The notification requirement however dissuaded businesses to adopt contractual practices of vertical control. The broad interpretation of the scope of Article 101(1) did not only reflect the ideological underpinnings of competition policy in Europe but was also the result of the European Commission's exclusivity in the enforcement of Article 101(3). Bringing more agreements under the scope of Article 101(1) increased the role of the European Commission to the detriment of national courts and national competition authorities. In Chapter 6, we saw that the Commission frequently found that an exclusive agreement had at least the object or effect of restricting competition, even if it later exempted it from the prohibition of Article 101(1). Such an approach favoured vertical integration, which was either not subject to competition law (integration by internal growth) or subject to a more lenient application of competition law (integration by external growth).

However, the CJEU and the General Court have often stated that an ancillary restriction, necessary to make a transaction such as franchising viable, does not in itself restrict competition[225] and that, before finding that exclusive purchasing obligations foreclose, one must analyse the market.[226] Some of the cases concerned distribution and have been included in this Chapter, but they are important also for defining the scope of Article 101(1). Despite the formalistic approach followed by the Commission, there were certain forms of vertical agreements that escaped the prohibition principle of Article 101(1), even if they restricted the economic freedom of the distributors. These more lenient specific regimes for vertical restraints can be explained as an attempt by the Court to loosen the straitjacket effect that a restrictive interpretation of Article 101(1) imposed on business as well as to curve the considerable administrative costs to the Commission of the compulsory notification system.

However, one could also argue that business cooperation networks was a new economic phenomenon, after the era of vertical integration the first two post-war decades, and this new economic reality may have triggered the change of the approach towards a less formalistic interpretation of Article 101(1) TFEU with regard to vertical contractual arrangements. In its survey of the American business history in 1977, Chandler noted that vertical integration was the result of the nineteenth-century technical change in transportation and communication that made possible the collapse of geographical barriers and the emergence of larger markets.[227] This, in turn, increased economies of scale that led to mass distribution with the emergence of department stores, mail-order houses, and chain stores.[228] The position of the distributors in the value chain changed: independent wholesalers were increasingly replaced by in-house purchasing and marketing units. First, producers demanded increasingly higher volumes, thus eliminating 'one of the primary *raisons d'être*

[225] See eg Case 42/84, *Remia BV and Others v Commission* [1985] ECR 2545; Case 161/84, *Pronuptia* [1986] ECR 414.

[226] See eg Case 55/65, *LTM v MBU* [1966] ECR 337.

[227] AD Chandler, *The Visible Hand: The Managerial Revolution in American Business* (Harvard University Press, 1977), 79.

[228] Ibid, ch 7.

of wholesalers, the ability to work at higher volumes than one's customers.'[229] Second, the standardization of inputs and outputs required a relative specialization, rather than a more general ability to deal with a diverse set or products. Further, 'standardization of inputs and outputs militated against another of the merchant's comparative advantages, the ability to deal with a diverse set of products.'[230]

This period of vertical integration has been followed by a period of vertical disintegration. Large, vertically integrated firms were becoming less significant and were joining a richer mix of new organizational forms (eg franchise agreements, alliances, sub-contracting).[231] This followed the need for further specialization of functions coupled with the generalization of the capabilities of managers, which became detached from the specific product as their main function became to manage risks. This evolution is also linked to the emergence of a modular system of production, which relied on a vertically disintegrated production system and thus required looser forms of vertical control than ownership. The concept of network perfectly captures these intermediate forms of vertical control. The case law on franchise and selective distribution illustrates that EU competition law has recognized the importance of this form of organization of the transactions, alongside the specific competition law regime for hierarchies, and the neutrality of competition law towards the choice of different forms of organization of the transactions (Section 10.4.3.3.2). Similar considerations apply to network forms of organization in the horizontal cooperation context.

In addition to this case law on network forms of organization, EU competition law also took into account other considerations in framing the scope of Article 101(1)'s prohibition: (i) administrative costs in employing scarce resources (regulatory authorities and courts) to examine commercial practices that are not very harmful to the consumer, and (ii) the protection of small and medium enterprises. The limitations on the application of Article 101(1) to vertical restraints in this context will be examined separately further below.

Network forms of organization and Article 101(1): Franchise and selective distribution agreements

Contrary to the restrictive position of the Commission towards vertical restraints in distribution agreements and the application of Article 101(1) TFEU whenever an agreement restricted the economic freedom of one of the parties to compete, franchise and selective distribution agreements were treated more leniently. This Section explains the reason for this specific treatment under Article 101(1) TFEU.

What's different with franchise and selective distribution agreements?

The competition law regime applying to franchising and selective distribution systems has different characteristics from those applying to intra-group agreements or other vertical restraints.[232] Restrictions included in exclusive distribution agreements can only be justified under the cost-benefit analysis test of Article 101(3) TFEU, whereas restrictive clauses in franchising and selective distribution agreements often escape the Article 101(1) prohibition, thanks to the ancillary restraints doctrine.[233]

229 RN Langlois, 'The Vanishing Hand: The Changing Dynamics of Industrial Capitalism' (2003) 12 *Industrial and Corporate Change* 351, 369.

230 Ibid. 231 Ibid.

232 This sub-section partly draws on I Lianos, 'Commercial Agency Agreements, Vertical Restraints, and the Limits of Article 81(1) EC: Between Hierarchies and Networks' (2007) 3 *J Competition L & Economics* 625.

233 See Chapter 6.

It is easy to understand why non-compete obligations are compatible with Article 101(1) when it comes to agreements for the sale of business. The objective of these agreements is to transfer the right of control over specific assets, the most important of these assets being the clients of the business. If the vendor was able to compete with the purchaser after selling his business to him and could therefore attract his clients, this would affect the value of the assets transferred and would definitively undermine the property rights of the purchaser. However, the transfer of the rights of control over the assets shows that these are valued more by the purchaser than by the vendor. Indeed, if this were not the case, the purchaser would never have sought to acquire the property rights for the assets in the first place. It follows that it would counteract efficiency to undermine the property rights of the purchaser. Imposing non-compete obligations preserves the value of the assets and therefore their efficient allocation, which explains why these clauses escape the application of Article 101 TFEU.

There is a different explanation for the regime applying to restrictive clauses in franchising and selective distribution agreements. This does not relate to the protection of property rights *stricto sensu* but to the specific characteristics of these forms of distribution systems, which constitute a hybrid form of organization, falling between a hierarchy and the market.

Indeed, integration is not the only alternative to markets but hybrid forms of organization may constitute a distinct possibility in organizing transactions. Ménard provides the following definition of hybrids—networks being a particular form of a hybrid.

> A very preliminary notion of hybrids [. . .] includes all forms of inter-firm collaboration in which property rights remain distinct while joint decisions are made, requiring specific modes of co-ordination. The emphasis is on the commitment of distinct property rights holders, operating distinct legal entities, but organizing some transactions through governance forms mutually agreed upon.[234]

Three main characteristics distinguish hybrids from hierarchies and markets. First, the transaction involves important relation-specific investments and asset specificity, which raises the issue of *ex post* opportunistic behaviour and the emergence of a hold up situation. The transaction may also entail the bundling of resources and dynamic capabilities that one firm would be unable to provide or to get from the market.[235] However, integration under a hierarchy would also reduce flexibility and would have the effect of weakening incentives. The parties in this context therefore prefer to establish an intermediate governance structure. They will preserve their autonomy and will maintain residual control over their assets and resources, but they will also accept that the situation of mutual dependence that will arise will lead to the emergence of a coordination mechanism and will impose limits on their autonomy for their mutual advantage.

Second, hybrids involve 'relational contracting'.[236] As Ménard has explained, in this context 'the identity of the partners matters'.[237] Hybrid forms of organization are 'selective, not

[234] C Ménard, 'A New Institutional Approach to Organization' in C Ménard and M Shirley (eds) *Handbook of New Institutional Economics* (Springer, 2005), 281, 294.

[235] D Teece, G Pisano, and A Shuen, 'Dynamic Capabilities and Strategic Management' (1997) 18 *Strategic Management J* 509; S Winter, 'Understanding Dynamic Capabilities' (2003) 24 *Strategic Management J* 991.

[236] See, on relational contracts and vertical integration, G Baker, R Gibbons, and KJ Murphy, 'Contracts and the Theory of the Firm' (2002) 117 *Q J Economics* 39.

[237] C Ménard, 'A New Institutional Approach to Organization' in C Ménard and M Shirley (eds) *Handbook of New Institutional Economics* (Springer, 2005), 281, 296.

open systems'.[238] Participation in the network involves the acceptance of the norms that have emerged to ensure its identity. Accordingly, it should be possible to exclude participants that do not fulfil the conditions imposed by the network authorities.

Finally, contrary to the situation of hierarchy, hybrid forms are characterized by a certain degree of competition. There may be instances of competition between the different nodes of the network, as they may compete for activities not covered by the cooperation agreement. One distinct possibility would be the existence of competition with respect to sharing the profits between the different entities of the network (intra-network competition). Networks may also compete with other networks and hybrid forms or hierarchies (inter-network competition).

The existence of a governance mechanism distinguishes networks from markets. The governance of hybrids or networks may take different forms, from contract-based arrangements to more integrated modes of governance, depending on the degree of the risk of *ex post* opportunism and/or the mis-coordination of tasks.[239] The risk of opportunism depends on the specific investments made by the parties to the transaction. 'The more specific mutual investments are, the higher are the risks of opportunistic behaviour, and the tighter are the forms of control implemented.'[240] It may therefore be necessary to include in the agreement between the parties adaptation clauses, clauses determining quality standards, or safeguard clauses that will preserve the parties from the risk of opportunism and situations of hold up.[241] These clauses may restrict not only the autonomy of the parties to the transaction but also intra-network competition; but they are necessary in order to facilitate coordination between the different nodes of the network to their mutual benefit.[242] Competition law should take into account the specific characteristics of the network or hybrid forms of organization and avoid intervening any time these restrictions would have the effect of limiting the autonomy of the parties to the transaction. The existence of a network or hybrid form of organization may explain the specific competition law regime that applies to franchising and selective distribution agreements, with respect to the enforcement of article 101(1) TFEU.

Franchising: Pronuptia

Franchising constitutes an archetype of a hybrid form of organization.[243], [244] A common feature of franchise contract is the transfer of intellectual property rights (trademark) and know-how from the franchisor to the franchisee. This may create a risk of *ex post* opportunism.[245] Indeed, 'if one franchisee allows the quality of his establishment to deteriorate, he benefits by the full amount of the savings from reduced quality maintenance' but 'he loses only part of the costs, for part is borne by other franchisees'.[246] It follows that the franchisor will have to select his franchisees carefully, institute a quality control mechanism, and introduce early termination clauses in the franchising agreement. The franchisee may also decide to join a different

238 C Ménard, 'The Economics of Hybrid Organizations' (2004) 160 *J Institutional and Theoretical Economics* 345, 351.

239 C Ménard, 'A New Institutional Approach to Organization' in C Ménard and M Shirley (eds) *Handbook of New Institutional Economics* (Springer, 2005), 281, 299.

240 C Ménard, 'The Economics of Hybrid Organizations' (2004) 160 *J Institutional and Theoretical Economics* 345, 354–5.

241 Ibid, 362–3.

242 Ibid, 365.

243 This sub-section partly draws on I Lianos, 'Commercial Agency Agreements, Vertical Restraints, and the Limits of Article 81(1) EC: Between Hierarchies and Networks' (2007) 3 *J Competition L & Economics* 625

244 PH Rubin, 'The Theory of the Firm and the Structure of the Franchise Contract' (1978) 21 *J L & Economics* 223, 231.

245 Ibid, 228.

246 Ibid, 227.

network or use this valuable information and training himself. It is therefore important for the franchisor to limit this risk by imposing a non-compete obligation to the franchisee. The existence of externalities, such as the fact that 'some franchisees may attempt to free-ride off of the promotional efforts of others' explains why franchisors would have 'the incentive to extend their reach beyond the initial franchise awards to include constraints on the condition of supply'.[247] As Rubin explains, 'the franchisor would perform functions with costs which fall for a substantial level of output, while the franchisee will perform function whose average cost curve turns up relatively sooner'.[248]

The CJEU recognized the specific characteristics of franchise agreements in *Pronuptia*.[249] This was the first time that the issue of the compatibility of a franchise agreement with EU competition law, in particular Article 101 TFEU, was brought before the Court. Advocate General Van Themaat distinguished franchise agreements from commercial agency agreements and other distribution agreements that the Court had examined in the past. The franchisee is an independent undertaking that deals in its own name and at its own risk. By contrast, agents in commercial agency agreements do not normally acquire the property of the goods they sell and do not bear significant risks of the transaction. The risk of opportunistic behaviour is accordingly less important in a franchise agreement than in a commercial agency agreement. The franchisee has far more to lose than the commercial agent if the product sold is not successful with the consumers and there is a reduction in sales of the franchised good. Furthermore, the franchisees incur relation-specific investments to become part of the franchise network, which will be sunk if their relationship with the franchisor is to be terminated.

However, franchise agreements institute more a relationship of mutual dependence between the franchisor and the franchisee than other distribution agreements. In comparison with other members of the franchise network, there are very few factors allowing the individualization of a franchisee. Moreover, if a franchisee performs poorly, the effects will extend to the whole franchise network, thus producing important externalities. These are not fully internalized by the fact that the franchisee retains the property rights to the goods sold, as there are instances in which a situation of opportunistic behaviour will be profitable. This explains why it is important for the franchisor to intervene and 'regulate' the activity of the franchisee. The franchisee does not lose the property rights to the goods, for which he continues to retain the residual rights of control. However, his freedom of action is restricted by the need to protect the identity and reputation of the network and the value of the assets, such as the trademark, that are also used by the other members of the franchise network.

Case 161/84, *Pronuptia de Paris GmbH v Pronuptia de Paris Irmgard Schillgallis*
[1986] ECR 414

Pronuptia had developed in the Paris region a formula for selling wedding gowns and other clothing worn at weddings. Its German subsidiary granted Frau Schillgalis exclusive franchises under three standard contracts for Hamburg, Oldenburg, and Hanover. The franchisee was entitled to use the mark 'Pronuptia de Paris' for a shop at a designated address in each of the cities, and was subject to various restrictions on her conduct. The franchisee had paid

[247] O Williamson, *The Economic Institutions of Capitalism* (Free Press, 1985), 39.

[248] PH Rubin, 'The Theory of the Firm and the Structure of the Franchise Contract' (1978) 21 *J L & Economics* 223, 231.

[249] Case 161/84, *Pronuptia* [1986] ECR 414.

lump sums for each franchise, and was required to pay 5 per cent of her turnover for national advertising and a further 5 per cent for the marketing assistance Pronuptia promised to provide. She fell three years behind with the royalties and, when sued, alleged that the contract was void under Article 101(2) TFEU. This was accepted by the Court of Appeal in Germany. On appeal, the German Supreme Court asked the CJEU for a preliminary ruling on various questions and, in particular, whether franchising agreements infringed Article 101(1) TFEU and whether they could come within the group exemption granted at the time by Regulation 67/67, the original group exemption for agreements relating to the supply of good for resale. Many lawyers were concerned that the Court might not be familiar with franchising, and counsel advised the Court to confine its judgment to the kind of distribution franchising involved in the case. Both the Advocate General and the Court did so.

The Advocate General observed that franchising had developed rapidly in Europe since the 1970s as a way of bringing products to the market. There was no precise definition of such a contractual relationship, but its main features were the grant by the brand owner to an independent firm of the exclusive right to use a name, mark, or symbol to distribute contract products according to a formula and marketing assistance in return, usually, for a royalty. Since the franchisees were independent firms, he said that they could not be treated as exclusive agents to whom Article 101(1) TFEU might not apply, as distribution franchises were more similar to exclusive distribution contracts. He quoted Italy v Commission,[250] *to show that such agreements may restrict competition between the dealer and third parties. The Court in that case refused to equate exclusive distribution with agency. The Advocate General considered that the EU case law 'like the American case law, it appears to treat possible restrictions on horizontal competition as decisive for the application of Article [101(1) TFEU], rather than the mutual restrictions on their commercial freedom agreed to by the parties to a vertical relationship'.*[251] *He found that that conclusion was not affected by the CJEU's emphasis on intra-brand competition in* Consten & Grundig, *because a closer examination of this precedent showed that 'there too the Court was particularly concerned with restrictions of competition between the exclusive distributor and third parties (in that case, parallel importers of products of the same brand), that is, intentional restrictions on horizontal competition'.*[252]

He noted, however, that the EU case law ascribed 'greater importance to horizontal "intrabrand competition," especially where national markets are protected against parallel imports, than is the case in recent American judgments'.[253] *He found that franchises resemble more to beer contracts made by a large number of retailers with one of many brewers, than exclusive distribution agreements with a single distributor for a large area-the kind of agreement with which the Commission had been dealing. After noting the advantages of franchising agreements for franchisor, franchisee, and consumers, he set out the criteria for the application of Article 101(1). According to the AG, since it is the horizontal effects of vertical agreements that give rise to concern, 'the question whether or not a franchise agreement results in a fair division of costs and benefits as between franchisor and franchisee is not in itself relevant to the question whether Article [101(1) TFEU] is applicable'.*[254]

The AG observed that '[w]ith regard to such vertical obligations [. . .] Article [101(1) TFEU] can only apply when it can be shown in a particular case that they cause injury to third parties (competitors, suppliers or purchasers), which will seldom be the case where there are adequate alternative chains of distribution for similar products'.[255] *He concluded that '[i]f the main issue is thus the "horizontal" effects, or more correctly the results of the agreement for*

250 C-32/65, *Italy v Commission* [1966] ECR 389.
251 Opinion of AG Verloren van Themaat in Case 161/84, *Pronuptia* [1986] ECR 355, 363.
252 Ibid, 364. 253 Ibid. 254 Ibid, 369. 255 Ibid.

third parties, then, according to the judgments of the Court, particular attention must be paid to the questions whether (i) parallel imports remain possible [. . .] (ii) whether, having regard to the market position of the suppliers concerned, access to the market for other suppliers or dealers is restricted [. . .] and (iii) whether the agreement results in price increases [. . .] or involves price-fixing by means of contractual obligations or concerted practices on the part of the franchisor, its subsidiaries and its various franchisees'.[256]

With regard to resale price maintenance clauses and other forms of price agreement, the AG argued that an RPM is suspect only if the parties enjoy market power in local markets or where it is also applied by competitors, thus essentially limiting the application of Article 101(1) TFEU to collective RPM. The raising of prices due to the royalty payments should also be considered only when the franchisor, 'from one member-State, plays a role of price leader or otherwise occupies a position of economic strength in a significant number of local markets in a second member-State'.[257] *In conclusion, in the view of the Advocate General, Article 101(1) TFEU would apply only in very narrowly defined circumstances: there must be subsidiaries or franchisees in more than one Member State, the franchised network must have a significant market share and the agreements must either have the object or effect of restricting parallel trade or result in the establishment of local or regional monopolies.*

Judgment of the CJEU

13. It should be pointed out first of all that franchise agreements, the legality of which has not previously been put in issue before the Court, are very diverse in nature. It appears from what was said in argument before the Court that a distinction must be drawn between different varieties of franchise agreements. In particular, it is necessary to distinguish between (i) service franchises, under which the franchisee offers a service under the business name or symbol and sometimes the trade mark of the franchisor, in accordance with the franchisor's instructions, (ii) production franchises, under which the franchisee manufactures products according to the instructions of the franchisor and sells them under the franchisor's trade-mark, and (iii) distribution franchises, under which the franchisee simply sells certain products in a shop which bears the franchisor's business name or symbol. In this judgment the Court is concerned only with this third type of contract, to which the questions asked by the national court expressly refer.

14. The compatibility of franchise agreements for the distribution of goods with Article [101(1)] cannot be assessed *in abstracto* but depends on the provisions contained in such agreements. In order to make its reply as useful as possible to the Bundesgerichtshof the Court will concern itself with contracts such as that described above.

15. In a system of distribution franchises of that kind an undertaking which has established itself as a distributor on a given market and thus developed certain business methods grants independent traders, for a fee, the right to establish themselves in other markets using its business name and the business methods which have made it successful. Rather than a method of distribution, it is a way for an undertaking to derive financial benefit from its expertise without investing its own capital. Moreover, the system gives traders who do not have the necessary experience access to methods which they could not have learned without considerable effort and allows them to

256 Ibid. 257 Ibid, 370.

benefit from the reputation of the franchisor's business name. Franchise agreements for the distribution of goods differ in that regard from dealerships or contracts with incorporate approved retailers into a selective distribution system, which do not involve the use of a single business name, the application of uniform business methods or the payment of royalties in return for the benefits granted. Such a system, which allows the franchisor to profit from his success, does not in itself interfere with competition. In order for the system to work two conditions must be met.

16. First, the franchisor must be able to communicate his know-how to the franchisees and provide them with the necessary assistance in order to enable them to apply his methods, without running the risk that that know-how and assistance might benefit competitors, even indirectly. It follows that provisions which are essential in order to avoid that risk do not constitute restrictions on competition for the purposes of Article [101(1)]. That is also true of a clause prohibiting the franchisee, during the period of validity of the contract and for a reasonable period after its expiry, from opening a shop of the same or a similar nature in an area where he may compete with a member of the network. The same may be said of the franchisee's obligation not to transfer his shop to another party without the prior approval of the franchisor; that provision is intended to prevent competitors from indirectly benefiting from the know-how and assistance provided.

17. Secondly, the franchisor must be able to take the measures necessary for maintaining the identity and reputation of the network bearing his business name or symbol. It follows that provisions which establish the means of control necessary for that purpose do not constitute restrictions on competition for the purposes of Article [101(1)].

18. The same is true of the franchisee's obligation to apply the business methods developed by the franchisor and to use the know-how provided.

19. That is also the case with regard to the franchisee's obligation to sell the goods covered by the contract only in premises laid out and decorated according to the franchisor's instructions, which is intended to ensure uniform presentation in conformity with certain requirements. The same requirements apply to the location of the shop, the choice of which is also likely to affect the network's reputation. It is thus understandable that the franchisee cannot transfer his shop to another location without the franchisor's approval.

20. The prohibition of the assignment by the franchisee of his rights and obligations under the contract without the franchisor's approval protects the latter's right freely to choose the franchisees, on whose business qualifications the establishment and maintenance of the network's reputation depend.

21. By means of the control exerted by the franchisor on the selection of goods offered by the franchisee, the public is able to obtain goods of the same quality from each franchisee. It may in certain cases—for instance, the distribution of fashion articles—be impractical to lay down objective quality specifications. Because of the large number of franchisees it may also be too expensive to ensure that such specifications are observed. In such circumstances a provision requiring the franchisee to sell only products supplied by the franchisor or by suppliers selected. by him may be considered necessary for the protection of the network's reputation. Such a provision may not however have the effect of preventing the franchisee from obtaining those products from other franchisees;

22. Finally, since advertising helps to define the image of the network's name or symbol in the eyes of the public, a provision requiring the franchisee to obtain the

franchisor's approval for all advertising is also essential for the maintenance of the network's identity, so long as that provision concerns only the nature of the advertising.

23. It must be emphasized on the other hand that, far from being necessary for the protection of the know-how provided or the maintenance of the network's identity and reputation, certain provisions restrict competition between the members of the network. That is true of provisions which share markets between the franchisor and franchisees or between franchisees or prevent franchisees from engaging in price competition with each other.

24. In that regard, the attention of the national court should be drawn to the provision which obliges the franchisee to sell goods covered by the contract only in the premises specified therein. That provision prohibits the franchisee from opening a second shop. Its real effect becomes clear if it is examined in conjunction with the franchisor's undertaking to ensure that the franchisee has the exclusive use of his business name or symbol in a given territory. In order to comply with that undertaking the franchisor must not only refrain from establishing himself within that territory but also require other franchisees to give an undertaking not to open a second shop outside their own territory. A combination of provisions of that kind results in a sharing of markets between the franchisor and the franchisees or between franchisees and thus restricts competition within the network. As is clear from the judgment of 13 July 1966 (Joined Cases 56 and 58/64 *Consten and Grundig* v. *Commission* [1966] ECR 299), a restriction of that kind constitutes a limitation of competition for the purposes of Article [101(1)] if it concerns a business name or symbol which is already well-known. It is of course possible that a prospective franchisee would not take the risk of becoming part of the chain, investing his own money, paying a relatively high entry fee and undertaking to pay a substantial annual royalty, unless he could hope, thanks to a degree of protection against competition on the part of the franchisor and other franchisees, that his business would be profitable. That consideration, however, is relevant only to an examination of the agreement in the light of the conditions laid down in Article [101(3)].

25. Although provisions which impair the franchisee's freedom to determine his own prices are restrictive of competition, that is not the case where the franchisor simply provides franchisees which price guidelines, so long as there is no concerted practice between the franchisor and the franchisees or between the franchisees themselves for the actual application of such prices. It is for the national court to determine whether that is indeed the case.

26. Finally, it must be added that franchise agreements for the distribution of goods which contain provisions sharing markets between the franchisor and the franchisees or between the franchisees themselves are in any event liable to affect trade between Member States, even if they are entered into by undertakings established in the same Member State, in so far as they prevent franchisees from establishing themselves in another Member State.

27. In view of the foregoing, the answer to the first question must be that:

(1) The compatibility of franchise agreements for the distribution of goods with Article [101(1)] depends on the provisions contained therein and on their economic context.

(2) Provisions which are strictly necessary in order to ensure that the know-how and assistance provided by the franchisor do not benefit competitors do not constitute restrictions of competition for the purposes of Article Article [101(1)].

(3) Provisions which establish the control strictly necessary for maintaining the identity and reputation of the network identified by the common name or symbol do not constitute restrictions of competition for the purposes of Article [101(1)].

(4) Provisions which share markets between the franchisor and the franchisees or between franchisees constitute restrictions of competition for the purpose of Article [101(1)].

(5) The fact that the franchisor makes price recommendations to the franchisee does not constitute a restriction of competition, so long as there is no concerted practice between the franchisor and the franchisees or between the franchisees themselves for the actual application of such prices.

(6) Franchise agreements for the distribution of goods which contain provisions sharing markets between the franchisor and the franchisees or between franchisees are capable of affecting trade between Member States. [. . .]

NOTES AND QUESTIONS ON PRONUPTIA

1. Are restrictions on dealers imposed by their supplier as anti-competitive as restrictions relating to the same matters agreed in a horizontal agreement between the dealers? Why are the horizontal effects of vertical agreements less likely to restrict competition than horizontal agreements?
2. Was the Advocate General right to ignore considerations of fairness between the parties? If such a concept reduces the incentive to deal with those in a weaker bargaining position, does it make the position of the latter worse?
3. Is 'McDonald's' a distribution, service, or production franchise? Does the reasoning in *Pronuptia* apply to service or production franchises? The Court noted that *Pronuptia* was a distribution franchise. It seems likely that McDonald's may involve a service franchise, or business format franchise, if one considers that what McDonald's franchisees do is to provide a fast food service. The franchisor's involvement and the restrictions imposed on the franchisees are different in services franchises.
4. In the case of the *Computerland* franchise (distribution of microcomputer products), the Commission noted that the franchisor provided the franchisee with 'continuing support services including training, information, advice, guidance and know-how regarding the Computerland methods in store management, operation, financing, advertising, sales and inventory, based on Computerland's empirical experience in the area of retail sales of microcomputer products throughout the world [. . .] The franchisee received advance information on numerous brands of new products and how they could be used together [. . .] as well as advice as to which among the many new products were likely to succeed on the market.'[258]

   In *ServiceMaster*, the Commission granted exemption for a standard form service franchise agreement concerning the supply of housekeeping, cleaning and maintenance services to both commercial and domestic customers submitted to it by an English company. The following excerpt of the Commission's decision is particularly important for our purposes:

   The Commission considers that, despite the existence of specific matters, service franchises show strong similarities to distribution franchises and can therefore basically be treated in the same way as the distribution agreements already exempted by the Commission. This basic premise relies on the fact that the EEC competition

[258] *Computerland* (Case IV/32.034) Commission Decision 87/407/EEC [1987] OJ L 222/12.

rules apply without distinction to both products and services. This does not prevent the Commission from taking into account in individual cases certain specific characteristics relating to the provision of services.

In particular, know-how is often more important in the [*supply of services*] than in the supply of goods because each service requires the execution of particular work and creates a close personal relationship between the provider of the service and the receiver of the service. Therefore, the protection of the franchisor's know-how and reputation can be even more essential for service franchises than for distribution franchises where mainly the goods advertise the business by carrying the trademark of the producer or distributor. Also certain services, as for instance the ServiceMaster services, are executed at the customer's premises, while goods are usually sold at the premises of the retailer. Services of this type further reinforce the link between the provider of the services and the customer.[259]

More recently, some UK case law also confirmed that '[t]he principles which the Court went on to state [in *Pronuptia*] have, however, been applied more widely to other types of franchise, including service franchises'.[260]

5. One may also note that restrictions imposed in the context of services franchises, in particular the broader non-compete obligations and the restrictions to the franchisees' entrepreneurship, constitute particularly harmful restrictions, as they deprive the franchisee 'effectively of earning a livelihood in a field where he has acquired an expertise'.[261] This may serve as an argument to narrow down the application of the ancillary restraints doctrine in services franchises, in comparison to distribution franchises.
6. If you were drafting paragraph 14 would you add another criterion? Contrast with paragraph 27(1), which mentions also the legal and economic context of the agreement. Judge Joliet was the *juge rapporteur* and was a very careful draftsman. Conjecture why these points may differ.
7. (Paragraph 15) Should the view that franchising is generally desirable eliminate all concern under Article 101(1), even if the franchised network enjoys market power? Do you believe that many franchisors enjoy much market power?
8. (Paragraph 16) What clauses may be justified by the need for the franchisor to communicate marketing know-how without its becoming available to its competitors?
9. In an exclusive distribution transaction, can the supplier limit the retailers to whom the distributor may sell to those providing services at the point of retail sale?

259 *ServiceMaster* (Case IV/32.358) Commission Decision 88/604/EEC [1988] OJ L 332/38.

260 *Carewatch Care Services Limited & Focus Caring Services Limited* [2014] EWHC 2313 (Ch), para 153.

261 *Vendo plc v Adams* (2002) NICh 3. In this case, the High Court of Northern Ireland applying the restraints of trade doctrine under English and Welsh law (which sits alongside competition law and needs to be considered separately), distinguished between franchises for services and franchises for goods. C Lucey, *The Interface Between Competition Law and the Restraint of Trade Doctrine for Professionals: Understanding the evolution of problems and proposing solutions for courts in England and Wales* (Thesis, London School of Economics, 2012), 223, observes that: '[t]his distinction implicitly recognises that the franchisee's personal expertise plays a role in a service franchise (unlike a franchise for goods which sell themselves) and this personal dimension merits protection from undue restriction. Paying attention to the inherent skills of the individual (and accepting it needs protection) indicates the distinctively personal aspect of the [Restraints of Trade Doctrine's] objective and, for this reason, should be emphasized.'

10. Judge Joliet was the first and most cogent critic of *Consten & Grundig v Commission*. Did he manage to reduce its impact in any way in paragraph 24 of *Pronuptia*?
11. Is the early part of the judgment an example of the 'rule of reason' under US law or of an independent ancillary restraint doctrine? Is there any difference? See also our analysis in Section 6.3.4.1. Note that some of the clauses present in the agreement may likely not benefit from the ancillary restraints doctrine if there are less restrictive alternatives that could achieve the purposes of the agreement and the restrictive clauses appear disproportional with regard to the objectives sought.
12. Compare the Judgment with the cases on selective distribution (Section 9.4.4.3.2). The franchisor is permitted to choose his own franchisees (paragraph 20), so does not have to set up a system for approving those who want indirect supplies.
13. What is the best way of ensuring that only qualified retailers handle the goods of a prestigious brand owner? Can this judgment be reconciled with the position of the CJEU in *Pierre*, that 'the aim of maintaining a prestigious image is not a legitimate aim for restricting competition and cannot therefore justify a finding that a contractual clause pursuing such an aim does not fall within Article 101(1) TFEU'?[262]

The 2010 Guidelines on Vertical Restraints follow a similar approach for the application of Article 101(1) to franchise agreements, finding that a 'non-compete obligation on the goods or services purchased by the franchisee falls outside the scope of Article 101(1) where the obligation is necessary to maintain the common identity and reputation of the franchised network' and that '[i]n such cases, the duration of the non-compete obligation is also irrelevant under Article 101(1), as long as it does not exceed the duration of the franchise agreement itself'.[263]

Selective distribution

V Korah and D O'Sullivan, *Distribution Agreements under the EC Competition Rules* (Hart, 2002), 85

Brand owners may want to control their retail outlets in order to compete on presales service, location or ambience, for which it may be difficult to charge consumers, rather than on price. If so, they may well wish to limit the kinds of outlet selling their goods and to protect such expensive outlets from acute price competition. They may require the dealers to whom they sell their products to supply only the general public or authorised dealers. [. . .]

In *Metro I*,[264] the CJEU ruled that a restriction as to the dealers to whom an exclusive distributor may sell did not infringe Article 101(1) TFEU provided that the supplier specified objective, qualitative criteria for approval as to the premises and staff required and applied the criteria objectively without discrimination. The CJEU stressed that there might be competition not only over price, but also over service—Article 101 being concerned not only with perfect but also workable competition. Nevertheless, where there were limitations on

262 C-439/09, *PFDC* [2011] ECR I–9419, para 46.
263 Vertical Restraints Guidelines 2010, para 190.
264 Case 26/76, *Metro I* [1977] ECR 1875.

the number of dealers to be approved—quantitative criteria- the restraint on dealers selling to non-approved dealers would infringe Article 101(1).

In *AEG Telefunken v Commission*, the CJEU stated that 'it has always been recognized in the case law of the Court that there are legitimate requirements, such as the maintenance of a specialist trade capable of providing specific services as regards high-quality, high-technology products, which may justify a reduction of price competition in favour of competition relating to factors other than price' and provided that '[s]ystems of selective distribution, in so far as they aim at the attainment of a legitimate goal capable of improving competition in relation to factors other than price, therefore constitute an element of competition which is in conformity with Article [101](1).'[265] These limitations 'inherent in a selective distribution system are however acceptable only on condition that their aim is in fact an improvement in competition', the Court setting a certain number of conditions for such systems to be permissible:

> [F]irst, that the characteristics of the product in question necessitate a selective distribution system, in the sense that such a system constitutes a legitimate requirement having regard to the nature of the product concerned, in particular its high quality or technical sophistication, in order to preserve its quality and ensure its proper use; secondly, that resellers are chosen on the basis of objective criteria of a qualitative nature which are laid down uniformly for all potential resellers and are not applied in a discriminatory fashion; thirdly, that the system in question seeks to achieve a result which enhances competition and thus counterbalances the restriction of competition inherent in selective distribution systems, in particular as regards price; and, fourthly, that the criteria laid down do not go beyond what is necessary.[266]

According to the CJEU's case law, these four factors have been identified as the key elements of a qualitative (simple) selective distribution system and the question whether those conditions are fulfilled 'must be assessed objectively, taking account of the interests of consumers'.

Case T-19/92, *Leclerc v Commission* [1996] II–1851 (footnotes omitted)

> 112. According to the case-law of the Court of Justice, selective distribution systems constitute an element of competition which is in conformity with Article [101(1)] of the Treaty if four conditions are satisfied: first, that the characteristics of the product in question necessitate a selective distribution system, in the sense that such a system constitutes a legitimate requirement having regard to the nature of the product concerned, in particular its high quality or technical sophistication, in order to preserve its quality and ensure its proper use; secondly, that resellers are chosen on the basis of objective criteria of a qualitative nature which are laid down uniformly for all potential resellers and are not applied in a discriminatory fashion; thirdly, that the system in question seeks to achieve a result which enhances competition and thus counterbalances the restriction of competition inherent in selective distribution systems, in particular as regards price; and, fourthly, that the criteria laid down do not go beyond what is necessary. The question whether those conditions are fulfilled must be assessed objectively, taking account of the interests of consumers.

[265] Case 107/82, *Allgemeine Elektricitäts-Gesellschaft AEG-Telefunken AG v EC Commission* [1983] ECR 3151, para 33.

[266] Case T-19/92, *Leclerc v Commission* [1996] ECR II–1851, para 112. See also Case C-107/82, *Allgemeine Elektrizitäts-Gesellschaft AEG-Telefunken AG v Commission* [1983] ECR 3151, paras 34–5.

If these cumulative conditions are satisfied, the selective distribution system will be qualitative and the system as a whole, including the restriction on sales to unauthorized retailers, will generally fall outside the scope of Article 101(1), unless there is not sufficient inter-brand competition (circumstances related to the structure of the market).[267]

In the Final Report of the e-commerce Sector Inquiry the Commission found that the development of e-commerce has led to an 'increased recourse to selective distribution systems', the manufacturers acknowledging that this allows them a better control of their distribution networks, in terms of quality or price, this being a reaction to the growth of e-commerce.[268] The Commission noted that this did not call for a change in its general approach to qualitative and quantitative distribution as reflected in the Vertical Block Exemption Regulation (VBER) but it nonetheless recognized that '[s]elective distribution may [. . .] facilitate the implementation and monitoring of certain vertical restraints that may raise competition concerns and require scrutiny'.[269]

The nature of the product

Selective distribution must be justified by the requirements of the product concerned. The justification of this condition is to preserve the quality and ensure the proper use of the selective distribution system.[270] In *AE G v Telefunken v Commission*, the CJEU mentioned the high quality or technical complexity of the products as justifying the need for specialist services, which in turn justified the reduction of intra-brand price competition.[271] The use of selective distribution has been found to be justified in respect of the following technically complex products: consumer electronics,[272] photographic products,[273] automobiles,[274] personal computers,[275] ceramic tableware;[276] plumbing fixtures[277] and Swatch watches,[278] however, were denied the possibility of selective distribution. The General Court and the Commission have also extended the justification to luxury products, such as jewellery and fine flagrances for the sale of which ambience is important.[279]

The jurisprudence of the EU courts slightly moved from a product characteristic justification to an emphasis given on consumers' perception of the nature of the product.[280]

267 Vertical Restraints Guidelines 2010, paras 174–5.

268 European Commission, Final Report on the E-commerce Sector Inquiry, COM (2017) 229 final, para 15(ii).

269 Ibid, para 25.

270 Case C-31/80, *L'Oreal NV and l'Oreal SA v De Nieuwe AMCK PVBA* [1980] ECR 3775.

271 Case C-107/82, *Allgemeine Elektricitäts-Gesellschaft AEG-Telefunken AG v Commission* [1983] ECR 3151.

272 See eg *Grundig* (Case IV/3344) Commission Decision 85/404/EEC [1985] OJ L 233/1.

273 See eg *Kodak* (Case IV/24.055) Commission Decision 70/332/EEC [1970] OJ L 147/24.

274 See eg *BMW AG* (Case IV/14.650) Commission Decision 75/73/EEC [1975] OJ L 29/1.

275 See eg *IBM Personal Computer* (Case IV/30.849) Commission Decision 84/233/EEC [1984] OJ L 118/24.

276 See eg *Villeroy and Boch* (Case IV/30.665) Commission Decision 85/616/EEC [1985] OJ L 376 /15.

277 See eg *Ideal Standard's Distribution System* (Case IV/30.261) Commission Decision 85/45/EEC [1985] L 20/38.

278 Case C-31/85, *SA ETA Fabriques d'Ebauches v SA DK Investment and others* [1985] ECR 3933, para 16 (noting that 'the battery is expressly excluded from the guarantee' and 'its replacement does not pose any particular technical difficulties').

279 Case 99/79, *SA Lancôme and Cosparfrance Nederland BV v Etos BV and Albert Heyn Supermat BV* [1980] ECR 2511 (perfumes); Case T-19/92, *Leclerc v Commission* [1996] ECR II–1851 (perfumes); *Murat* (Case IV/ 32.736) Commission Decision 83/610/EEC [1983] OJ L 348/20 (jewellery); *Omega* (Cases IV/3213, 10.498, 11.546, 12.992, 17.394, 17.395, 17.971, 18.772, 18.888) Commission Decision 70/488/EEC [1970] OJ L 242/22 (luxury watches).

280 See also Case T-88/92 *Groupement d'achat Édouard Leclerc v Commission* [1996] ECR II–1961, para 11.

Case T-19/92, *Leclerc v Commission*
[1996] ECR II–1851 (references omitted)

113. While the Court of Justice has held in particular that such selective distribution systems based on qualitative criteria may be accepted in the sector covering production of high-quality and technically advanced consumer durables without infringing Article [101(1) TFEU], in particular in order to maintain a specialist trade capable of providing specific services for such products, it is also apparent from its case-law that selective distribution systems which are justified by the specific nature of the products or the requirements for their distribution may be established in other economic sectors without infringing Article [101(1) TFEU]. Likewise, the Court of Justice held in *Metro I* (paragraph 20) that the nature and intensiveness of the 'workable competition' necessary to attain the objectives of the Treaty could vary to an extent dictated by the products or services in question and the economic structure of the relevant market sectors, without offending against the principle in Articles 3 and 101 of the Treaty that competition is not to be distorted.

114. It is common ground, first, that luxury cosmetics, and in particular the luxury perfumes which constitute the bulk of the products at issue, are sophisticated and high-quality products which are the result of meticulous research, and which use materials of high quality, in particular in their presentation and packaging secondly, that those products enjoy a 'luxury image' which distinguishes them from other similar products lacking such an image and, thirdly, that that luxury image is important in the eyes of consumers, who appreciate the opportunity of purchasing luxury cosmetics, and luxury perfumes in particular. There is, in consumers' minds, only a low degree of substitutability between luxury cosmetic products and similar products falling within other segments of the sector.

115. Accordingly, the Court considers that the concept of the 'characteristics' of luxury cosmetics, within the meaning of the judgment in *L'Oréal*, cannot be limited to their material characteristics but also encompasses the specific perception that consumers have of them, in particular their 'aura of luxury'. This case is therefore concerned with products which, on the one hand, are of a high intrinsic quality and, on the other, have a luxury character arising from their very nature.

116. As to whether selective distribution constitutes a legitimate requirement in the case of products possessing such characteristics, the Court notes that the reasoning in the Decision on that point [. . .] is not based on the concept of a specialist trade capable of providing specific services for technically advanced products, as referred to in the judgments in *Metro I*, *Metro II* and *AEG*, but rather on two other principal considerations, namely (a) Yves Saint Laurent's interest as a producer of luxury cosmetic products in preserving its prestige brand image and safeguarding the fruits of its promotion activities and (b) the need to safeguard, in the consumer's mind, the 'aura of exclusivity and prestige' of the products at issue, in particular by ensuring 'appropriate marketing that brings out the specific aesthetic or function quality' of the products and 'a setting that is in line with the luxurious and exclusive nature of the products and a presentation which reflects the [. . .] brand image'.

117. Although a producer is free to choose his own marketing policy, Article [101(1) TFEU] of the Treaty must be taken into account where implementation of that policy results in agreements which impose on other independent economic operators obligations capable of restricting their freedom to compete to an extent that appreciably affects intra-Community trade. Accordingly, the mere fact that a producer has made significant efforts to promote his products does not in itself constitute an objective justification capable of rendering Article 101(1) inapplicable to a distribution network which limits the freedom to compete of participating undertakings and third parties. Were it otherwise, any manufacturer could justify the adoption of a selective

distribution system simply on the basis of his promotion efforts, and any restrictive selection criterion at all could be justified on the ground that it was necessary in order to protect the marketing policy desired by the manufacturer.

118. A selective distribution system thus falls outside the scope of Article [101(1) TFEU] only if it is objectively justified, account being also taken of the interests of consumers.

119. It is in the interests of consumers seeking to purchase luxury cosmetics that such products are appropriately presented in retail outlets. Since they are high- quality products whose luxury image is appreciated by consumers, criteria which seek only to ensure that they are presented in an enhancing manner pursue an objective which improves competition by preserving that luxury image and thus counterbalances the restriction of competition inherent in selective distribution systems. Such criteria thus constitute a legitimate requirement for the purposes of the case-law cited above.

120. In that regard, the Court considers that it is in the interests of consumers seeking to purchase luxury cosmetics that the luxury image of such products is not tarnished, as they would otherwise no longer be regarded as luxury products. The current segmentation of the cosmetics sector between luxury and non-luxury cosmetics reflects the varying needs of consumers and thus is not improper in economic terms. Although the 'luxury' nature of luxury cosmetics also derives, inter alia, from their high intrinsic quality, their higher price and manufacturers' advertising campaigns, the fact that they are sold through selective distribution systems which seek to ensure that they are presented in retail outlets in an enhancing manner also contributes to that luxury image and thus to the preservation of one of the main characteristics of the products which consumers seek to purchase. Generalized distribution of the products at issue, as a result of which Yves Saint Laurent would have no opportunity of ensuring that its products were sold in appropriate conditions, would entail the risk of deterioration in product presentation in retail outlets which could harm the 'luxury image' and thus the very character of the products. Consequently, criteria aimed at ensuring that the products are presented in retail outlets in a manner which is in keeping with their luxury nature constitute a legitimate requirement of such a kind as to enhance competition in the interests of consumers within the meaning of the case-law cited above.

121. That conclusion is not invalidated by the fact, established in the course of these proceedings, that in certain Member States, in particular the Netherlands but also the United Kingdom and France, a greater or lesser proportion of sales is by unauthorized distributors who obtain their supplies on the parallel market. It cannot be ruled out that consumers' interest in such sales has resulted in part from the luxury image whose preservation is due at least partly to selective distribution. It therefore does not follow that that luxury image would remain intact if there were no selective distribution.

122. However, while it is in the interests of consumers to be able to obtain luxury cosmetics which are suitably presented for sale and to ensure that their luxury image is preserved in that way, it is also in their interests that distribution systems founded on that consideration are not applied too restrictively and, in particular, that access to the products is not limited inordinately, as contended during the administrative procedure by the four consumer associations. Also, it is clear from the case-law of the Court of Justice that Yves Saint Laurent's system cannot be regarded as pursuing a legitimate objective counterbalancing the restriction of competition inherent in that system unless it is open to all potential retailers who are capable of ensuring that the products will be well presented to consumers in an appropriate setting and of preserving the luxury image of the products concerned. A selective distribution system which resulted in the exclusion of certain forms of marketing capable of being used to sell products in enhancing conditions, for example in a space or area adapted for that

purpose, would simply protect existing forms of trading from competition from new operators and would therefore be inconsistent with Article [101(1) TFEU].

123. It follows that, in the luxury cosmetics sector, qualitative criteria for the selection of retailers which do not go beyond what is necessary to ensure that those products are suitably presented for sale are in principle not covered by Article [101(1) TFEU], in so far as they are objective, laid down uniformly for all potential retailers and not applied in a discriminatory fashion.

Note the interesting link the CJEU establishes between the interests of the supplier and the consumers in this context. The choice of selective distribution was also extended to newspapers.[281]

It is clear that by restricting the choice of a selective distribution system to certain categories of products, EU competition law allocates the burden of proof to the supplier who has to provide justifications as to the use of selective distribution, in particular for products for which there is no established case law accepting this form of distribution. First, this assumes that the regulator or judge is more knowledgeable than the entrepreneur on the need to develop a selective distribution network for a specific product. The main justification for such a system is the perceived preference of the consumers to receive additional distribution services, such as information provided at the point of sale, a comfortable shopping environment that corresponds to the prestige of the brand, retail services post sale of the product than a lower price, in the absence of selective distribution. Consumers have heterogeneous preferences. Some value lower prices more than higher distribution services (consumers with low search costs—less wealthy consumers with a lower cost of time and better informed about the product). Others (impulse buyers), having higher search costs, would value distribution services and would more likely to be attracted by the image, shopping environment and distribution services. The retailers that want to attract customers away from other retailers are focused excessively on low-search-cost consumers and are therefore biased towards price competition. They do not have thus the incentive to provide valuable distribution services, unless they are pushed to do so by the supplier. Selective distribution is a supplier control mechanism with the aim to change the mix of price and services and thus to satisfy more adequately consumer preferences.

T Buettner, A Coscelli, T Vergé, and RA Winter, 'An Economic Analysis of the Use of Selective Distribution by Luxury Goods Suppliers' (2009) 5 *European Competition J* 201, 209

Selective distribution changes the mix towards higher prices and higher service through three mechanisms. First, by protecting the retail price margin from erosion through greater competition at the retail level, the distribution system increases the marginal benefit that each retailer obtains from attracting customers through service. If the retail margin is €10 per unit instead of €5, then the retailer has twice the incentive to attract more customers at the margin, and service in all of its dimensions will increase. Secondly, in cases where there is free-riding on services—by which we mean that a customer obtains pre-sales service (such as expert information, consultation or, say, sampling perfumes) at a high-priced outlet and then purchases the product at a low-priced outlet that provides no service—prohibiting low-priced, no-service outlets increases the incentive for other stores to provide the informational service since they retain all of the customers that they

281 Case 243/83, *SA Binon & Cie v SA Agence et messageries de la presse* [1983] ECR 2015.

inform. Thirdly, restraining intra-brand competition enhances the profits that outlets earn. If an upstream supplier contracts with outlets for high service and must monitor (at some cost) the provision of this service with the strategy of terminating dealers who under-provide the service, the additional profits represent a 'carrot' for the retailer that is lost with termination by the upstream supplier and therefore enhance the retailer's incentive to provide the service.

In addition, selective distribution is less likely to have anti-competitive effects, which justifies a generally lenient approach under Article 101(1) TFEU.

T Buettner, A Coscelli, T Vergé, and RA Winter, 'An Economic Analysis of the Use of Selective Distribution by Luxury Goods Suppliers'
(2009) 5 *European Competition J* 201, 201

[. . .] Selective distribution can play the role of enhancing retailer incentives to invest in promoting a product or in investing in enhancements to the product image. Moreover, within the context of a rule of reason, we suggest, the only potential concerns about restricted distribution relate to: (i) instances where the vertical restraints imposed by the suppliers are found to facilitate collusion (among suppliers or among retailers, including the situation where the vertical restraint is imposed as a result of pressure from a group of retailers); or (ii) instances where vertical restraints play a strategic, competition-dampening effect [. . .]. We find that selective distribution is unlikely to facilitate supplier collusion, leaving the competition-dampening effect or retailer-pressure/retailer-cartel as the main anti-competitive theories of selective distribution. In a case in which the incentive for selective distribution must be identified, the burden of proof, as in any vertical restraints case, should rest on the side of the regulator. That is, the appropriate burden rests not on the respondent to justify the use of selective distribution, but rather on the side of government intervention to demonstrate that the use of selective distribution is damaging to consumers or total welfare.

But why should selective distribution be only justified for certain categories of products? The following excerpt analyses the economic arguments in favour of selective distribution for luxury products.

T Buettner, A Coscelli, T Vergé, and RA Winter, 'An Economic Analysis of the Use of Selective Distribution by Luxury Goods Suppliers'
(2009) 5 *European Competition J* 201, 220

1. Image as a Component of the Products

The image of a luxury product is an essential component of the product. Expensive perfumes provide a perfect example. A perfume with a strong (and expensive) image that is purchased by a consumer is enjoyed by her—and perceived by her friends as an input into her own image—more than if it were sold as a chemical compound without any image whatsoever. The product is defined not simply by its chemical composition but by its image.

Suppliers choose to invest in image because this is what consumers demand. Chanel and Dior, for instance, have the option not to invest in image; but without investments in image, the demand for their products at any price would be much lower.

2. Retail Distribution Channels as Investment in Product Image

Luxury goods in general tend to be distributed by their suppliers through upmarket retailers. Whether the distribution systems are vertically integrated or not, greater expenditure is undertaken at the retail level on aspects such as sales assistance, an exclusive showroom, comfort for the shopper and a strong retail brand name. Some of this expenditure is designed to make the shopping experience more pleasant for the consumer. However, the main effect is to enhance the image of the product: if Chanel No 5 were sold in bulk over the Internet, without any image investment, it would be an entirely different product than the one sold in small bottles at upmarket perfumeries, advertised in expensive magazines, and so on.

The use of an upscale distribution channel is expensive for suppliers, in that the supplier needs to tolerate a retailer margin that allows the retailer to recover its investment cost. The benefit for the supplier is that the retailers' contribution to product image adds a component to the final product, as perceived by both the purchaser and those who interact with the purchaser. The choice of upmarket retailers as distribution channels is hence a costly investment in product image by the supplier.

3. The Need for Vertical Restraints on Distribution

Accepting that image is a valuable and expensive component of a product, and that one important investment into the overall product image takes place at the retail point-of-sale, the question is, why will the retail market not provide the supplier's desired investment in image? Why might an unfettered market, simply purchasing the supplier's product at a wholesale price and reselling to consumers, fail to provide the mix of low price and strong image? In the case of luxury goods, the two prominent reasons for the failure of the unrestrained market—for the price system itself—to provide the right incentives are free-riding among retailers and consumer heterogeneity [. . .]. For luxury products, restricting distribution is a means of enhancing investments in product image at the retail level that is a response to incentive incompatibilities in the retail distribution sector. Without such restraints, the investment in image by retailers will be fundamentally undersupplied from the supplier's point of view.

4. Normative Analysis

From an economist's perspective, the axiom of 'consumer sovereignty' takes consumer welfare as the values that are revealed by their choices. Consumers are evidently willing to pay high prices for goods with a strong luxury image. To the extent that a supplier uses a selective distribution restraint to enhance the retail sector's input into the image of a product, the supplier is adding to a valuable dimension. [. . .] [N]othing in the development of this perspective relies on competition among suppliers. Even in the case of a pure monopolist of luxury goods, a restriction on downstream competition or distribution channels is a means of investing in product image. If image were not important to consumers, the monopolist would be the first to enlist low-cost Internet retailers. The optimal competition policy towards distribution strategies of luxury good suppliers then follows directly from the normative analysis in the first section of this article: there is no basis for the position that manufacturers' choices of the mix of price and non-price dimensions, such as image at the retail level (whether implemented via restrictive distribution or not), systematically reduce consumers' welfare. Economic theory therefore suggests that legal prohibitions against selective distribution are no more justified than attempts by a regulator to micro-manage suppliers' advertising expenditures. Indeed, where potential retailer free-riding distortions explain the design of restrictive distribution systems, these distribution systems are welfare enhancing so legal constraints on the choice of such systems will reduce welfare. Because the burden of proof must lie on the regulator, and there is no basis for assuming that intervention will improve welfare, a laissez-faire policy towards the design of distribution systems is called for. [. . .]

These considerations may apply to a series of products, for which brands carry a specific value to consumers to the point of constituting a component of the product. The limitation as to the nature of the products in the EU competition law case law may also be explained by non-economic rationales. As the General Court noted in *Perfumes*, selective distribution agreements 'impose on other independent economic operators obligations capable of restricting their freedom to compete to an extent that appreciably affects intra-Community trade'.[282] This anti-competitive presumption explains why the burden of proof for justifying the use of selective distribution for only specific categories of products falls on the supplier. However, one could question the validity of such a presumption, following the move towards a more economic approach in the interpretation of Article 101(1) TFEU. Consequently, we suggest to abandon the condition of the nature of the product for selective distribution agreements.

Qualitative, objective, and non-discriminatory criteria of selection

In *Metro I*, the CJEU distinguished 'qualitative' from what it called 'quantitative' criteria. 'Qualitative' criteria relate to an aspect of quality in the reseller network (suitability of selling premises, training and qualification of staff, presentation of products, level of service in general provided to the customer) and they should not directly limit the number of resellers within the system.[283] For the restriction to escape the prohibition of Article 101(1), the criteria must be objective in two senses: first, the supplier must specify the qualitative criteria that are sensible in the particular trade and, second, it must apply them without discrimination, permitting any dealer who qualifies to be approved. A 'qualitative' criterion is open, in the sense that any retailer can form part of the distribution network, as soon as he fulfils the criterion. A 'quantitative' criterion restricts access to the distribution network for retailers that objectively fulfil the qualitative criteria.

In practice, it is difficult to distinguish between qualitative and quantitative criteria, as the case law has been inconsistent, finding certain criteria to be qualitative in one case and quantitative in another. The manufacturer or trademark owner may also have to provide protection to induce investment from the part of the retailers by adopting quantitative criteria, such as promising not to select any other retailers within a given distance, place a numerical cap on the number of resellers by reference to population density or purchasing power, or a requirement to effect minimum purchases or sales. These criteria will usually be found to be quantitative.[284] However, requirements concerning the holding of stock or the

282 Case T-19/9, *Leclerc v Commission* [1996] II–1851.

283 Case T-88/92, *Groupement d'achat Édouard Leclerc v Commission of the European Communities* [1996] ECR II–1961.

284 See the broad interpretation by the Court of a quantitative criterion in Case T-19/91, *Société d'Hygiène Dermatologique de Vichy v Commission of the European Communities* [1992] ECR II–415:

> [T]he criterion for admission to an exclusive or selective distribution system must be regarded as being quantitative in character [. . .] where its object or effect is, beyond the sphere of normal supply and demand, to impose a quantitative limitation on the number of sales outlets. If the limitation on the number of sales outlets is not a result of the normal functioning of the market, the criterion for admission to the distribution network adopted by the producer must be regarded as being quantitative in nature. It

advertising and promotion of products were found in some cases to be qualitative[285] and in others, quantitative.[286] Selective distribution systems should not also exclude a priori any category of retailers, such as hypermarkets[287] and self-service or cash-and-carry wholesalers at the wholesale level.[288] Selected distributors must be allowed to sell via the Internet, provided they also sell through fixed retail premises.[289] The requirement to have one or more brick and mortar shops or to provide specific services constitutes a qualitative selective distribution criterion.[290]

Resellers must be chosen on the basis of objective criteria of a qualitative nature which are laid down uniformly for all and made available to all potential resellers and are not applied in a discriminatory manner. Acceptance to the network should respect transparent procedures and within fixed limits.[291] Once accepted, the reseller can only be excluded from the network for breach of contract or closure of the distribution network, although the supplier may adopt new selection criteria compatible and require selected resellers to comply with these new criteria.

The criteria must be proportionate

The criteria must be appropriate to the distribution of the particular kind of product.[292] In *Vichy*, the Commission found that 'the status of dispensing chemist, which is a precondition for admission to the distribution network for Vichy products' was not necessary. Indeed, even if the criteria were found objective, the agreement would have infringed Article 101(1) TFEU because the qualitative criteria were not necessary to maintain quality and ensure a proper use of the prestige brands of cosmetics involved. There were national and Community rules governing cosmetic products for the protection of consumers' health, and the requirement that the prestige brands be sold through pharmacies was more stringent than necessary.

Market factors: *Metro II*

The earlier cases were largely concerned with the nature of the products for which selective distribution may not infringe Article 101(1). From *Metro II*, the CJEU has increasingly stressed the relevance of inter-brand competition and required a more elaborate analysis.

is therefore of little importance, in that regard, whether the limitation of the number of distribution outlets derives from a pre-existing situation created by legislation or solely from the intention of the producer, provided that the latter is, at least, in some way associated with that limitation.

285 See eg *Villeroy and Boch* (Case IV/30.665) Commission Decision 85/616/EEC [1985] OJ L 376/15, where the Commission found that the requirement to display and stock a sufficiently wide and varied range of products did not infringe Article 101(1).

286 See eg *Grundig* (Case IV/3344) Commission Decision 85/404/EEC [1985] OJ L 233/1 (where the Court found that the obligation to carry and stock a whole range of products went beyond what was necessary for the distribution of the products).

287 Case T-88/92, *Groupement d'achat Édouard Leclerc v Commission of the European Communities* [1996] ECR II-1961, paras 164–71.

288 Case 26/76, *Metro I* [1977] ECR 1875, para 50.

289 European Commission, 'Commission Approves Selective Distribution System for Yves Saint Laurent Perfume', Press Release IP/01/713 (17 May 2001).

290 Vertical Restraints Guidelines 2010, para 179.

291 *Parfums Givenchy* (Case IV/33.542) Commission Decision 92/428/EEC [1992] OJ L 236/11.

292 Case C-26/76, *Metro I* [1977] ECR 1875, paras 20–1; Case C-31/80 *L'Oréal v PVBA* [1980] ECR 3775, paras 15–16; Case C-107/82, *AE G* [1983] ECR 3151, para 35; Case T-19/91, *Vichy v Commission* [1992] ECR II-415, para 65.

Case C-75/84, *Metro-SB-Grossmärkte GmbH & Co. KG v Commission (No 2)*
[1986] ECR 3021 (*Metro II*)

In 1983, the Commission renewed the exemption it had granted in SABA.[293] *On appeal,* in Metro II, *the CJEU considered that the technology for colour television was sufficiently complex to justify specialized wholesalers and retailers and ruled that simple selective distribution systems based on objective criteria as to premises and staff are not necessarily incompatible with Article 101(1). The Court went on, however, to examine the possible effect on competition of networks of similar agreements tying up the market and leaving no room for other methods of distribution.*

40. It must be borne in mind that, although the court has held in previous Decisions that 'simple' selective distribution systems are capable of constituting an aspect of competition compatible with Article [101(1) TFEU], there may nevertheless be a restriction or elimination of competition where the existence of a certain number of such systems does not leave any room for other forms of distribution based on a different type of competition policy or results in a rigidity in price structure which is not counterbalanced by other aspects of competition between products of the same brand and by the existence of effective competition between different brands.

41. Consequently, the existence of a large number of selective distribution systems for a particular product does not in itself permit the conclusion that competition is restricted or distorted. Nor is the existence of such systems decisive as regards the granting or refusal of an exemption under Article [101(3)], since the only factor to be taken into consideration in that regard is the effect which such systems actually have on the competitive situation. Therefore the coverage ratio of selective distribution systems for colour television sets, to which Metro refers, cannot in itself be regarded as a factor preventing an exemption from being granted.

42. It follows that an increase in the number of 'simple' selective distribution systems after an exemption has been granted must be taken into consideration, when an application for renewal of that exemption is being considered, only in the special situation in which the relevant market was already so rigid and structured that the element of competition inherent in ' simple ' systems is not sufficient to maintain workable competition. Metro has not been able to show that a special situation of that kind exists in the present case. [. . .]

46. Therefore Metro's submission based on the growth of selective distribution systems in the consumer electronics sector must be rejected.

In *Lancôme v Etos*, the Court stressed the importance of market analysis under Article 101(1) TFEU.[294] However, in *Leclerc*,[295] the General Court noted that even if most manufacturers employ qualitative selective distribution systems, that does not lead automatically to the application of Article 101(1).[296]

Conclusions on selective distribution and Article 101(1) TFEU

The relatively lenient regime to selective distribution agreements under Article 101(1) TFEU pre-existed the publication of the Green Paper on Vertical Restraints and the subsequent

293 *SABA's EEC distribution system* (Case COMP IV/29.598) Commission Decision [1983] OJ L 376/41.

294 Case C-99/79, *SA Lancôme and Cosparfrance Nederland BV v Etos BV and Albert Heyn Supermart BV* [1980] ECR 2511, para 24.

295 Case T-19/92, *Leclerc v Commission* [1996] II–1851; Case T-88/92, *Groupement d'achat Édouard Leclerc v Commission of the European Communities* [1996] ECR II–1961.

296 Case T-19/92, *Leclerc v Commission* [1996] II–1851, paras 182–4.

reform process of the Block exemption regulation. It is still maintained in the most recent Guidelines on vertical restraints with the exception of some hardcore restrictions included in selective distribution agreements.[297] However, the nature of this specific regime for selective distribution is different from that for franchise agreements. In contrast to franchise, the establishment of a selective distribution system does not involve the transfer of any property rights or the protection of a common identity for the network. Selective distributors remain free to sell competing brands, which is never the case for franchise agreements. Distributors have a distinct identity from their supplier and the other members of the selective distribution network because, unlike with franchise networks, they do not have 'the use of a single mark' nor is there a uniform commercial method that applies to the whole network.[298] Selective distribution agreements are based on the idea of a process of selecting the distributors that form part of the network, which may show the existence of a relational contract. However, this is insufficient to create the degree of mutual interdependence, which characterizes a dense network form of organization. Consequently, the regime of selective distribution agreements differs from that of franchising when it comes to the application of Article 101(1).

The Court' approach is more restrictive when it comes to the application of Article 101(1) to selective distribution agreements. Here, only those clauses that relate to the process for selecting members of the network fall outside the scope of Article 101(1) (simple selective distribution). In addition, the selection criteria should be of a 'qualitative nature' and applied without discrimination.[299] The requirements should not go beyond what is necessary in order to protect the quality of the products. The possibility of suppliers imposing selection requirements for the members of their network is also limited to certain types of products of high quality or technical complexity. Subsequent case law extended the possibility of imposing qualitative requirements to other types of products and took into account the need to induce dealers to invest by giving them the possibility to appropriate their sunk costs. However, it should be for the supplier or the distributor to explain why the characteristics or the nature of the product render a selective distribution system necessary, in case this product or economic sector has not been previously considered.[300] Requirements concerning the premises and the staff of the distributors are almost always considered qualitative. Requirements as to the promotion of the goods or the fact that the distributors should maintain a stock are within the scope of Article 101(1) but they may benefit from an exemption under Article 101(3). However, even qualitative requirements in simple selective distribution systems may fall within the scope of Article 101(1) where there is significant foreclosure because of the existence of a cumulative effect of networks of similar agreements.[301] This is an important difference from the regime applying to franchise agreements.[302]

Other limitations for the application of Article 101(1) to vertical restraints:
De minimis *doctrine and small and medium undertakings*

The *de minimis* doctrine[303] applies also to vertical restraints, with the exception of hardcore restrictions. Small and medium undertakings are also excluded from the application of Article 101(1) TFEU. These exclusions are justified for administrative efficiency reasons.

297 See Sections 10.6.2.2.3 and 10.6.2.2.4.
298 Case T-19/92, *Leclerc v Commission* [1996] II–1851, para 15.
299 Case C-26/76, *Metro I* [1977] ECR 1875.
300 Case T-19/92, *Groupement d'Achat Edouard Leclerc v Commission* [1994] ECR II–441, para 113.
301 Case C-75/84, *Metro II* [1986] ECR 3021.
302 See Vertical Restraints Guidelines 2010, para 190(b).
303 See Chapter 6.

Guidelines on Vertical Restraints **[2010] OJ C 130/1 (references omitted)**

8. Agreements that are not capable of appreciably affecting trade between Member States or of appreciably restricting competition by object or effect do not fall within the scope of Article 101(1). The Block Exemption Regulation applies only to agreements falling within the scope of application of Article 101(1). These Guidelines are without prejudice to the application of Commission Notice on agreements of minor importance which do not appreciably restrict competition under Article 81(1) of the Treaty establishing the European Community *(de minimis)* or any future *de minimis* notice.

9. Subject to the conditions set out in the *de minimis* notice concerning hardcore restrictions and cumulative effect issues, vertical agreements entered into by non-competing undertakings whose individual market share on the relevant market does not exceed 15 % are generally considered to fall outside the scope of Article 101(1). There is no presumption that vertical agreements concluded by undertakings having more than 15 % market share automatically infringe Article 101(1). Agreements between undertakings whose market share exceeds the 15 % threshold may still not have an appreciable effect on trade between Member States or may not constitute an appreciable restriction of competition. Such agreements need to be assessed in their legal and economic context. [. . .]

Since the judgment of the CJEU in Expedia,[304] *the* de minimis *rule does not immunize hardcore restrictions, even for agreements between parties that hold less than the* de minimis *market share thresholds.*

11. In addition, the Commission considers that, subject to cumulative effect and hardcore restrictions, vertical agreements between small and medium-sized undertakings [. . .] are rarely capable of appreciably affecting trade between Member States or of appreciably restricting competition within the meaning of Article 101(1), and therefore generally fall outside the scope of Article 101(1). In cases where such agreements nonetheless meet the conditions for the application of Article 101(1), the Commission will normally refrain from opening proceedings for lack of sufficient interest for the European Union unless those undertakings collectively or individually hold a dominant position in a substantial part of the internal market.

For the application in the UK of the *de minimis* doctrine, the UK competition authorities 'will have regard' to the approach of the EU *de minimis* Notice.[305]

For the application of the *de minimis* doctrine, one needs to define first a relevant market in order to compute the market share of the parties to the agreement.[306]

A recent order of the CJEU in *Estación de Servicio Pozuelo 4, SL v GALP Energía España SAU*, concerning a long-term exclusive purchasing obligations gave the opportunity to explore again the application of the *de minimis* criterion in EU Competition law.[307] The case involved a forty-five-year-long term purchasing obligation committing Pozuelo, the operator of a gas station, to procure all its needs in petroleum products from Galp, an upstream supplier, which was granted a right known as a 'surface right' for the purpose of building a service station and

304 Case C-226/11, *Expedia Inc v Autorité de la concurrence and Others*, ECLI:EU:C:2012:79..

305 OFT 419, Vertical Agreements (December 2004), paras 2.2 and 2.3.

306 See the Commission's Notice on Market Definition [1997] OJ C 372/5, and our discussion in Section 3.3.2.

307 Order of the Court in Case C-384/13, *Estación de Servicio Pozuelo 4, SL v GALP Energía España SAU*, ECLI:EU:C:2014:2425.

letting it to the owner of the land for a period equivalent to the duration of the right. The case was referred to the CJEU by the Spanish Supreme Court, which enquired as to whether, despite its long duration that exceeded the average duration of contracts generally concluded on the relevant market, such exclusivity clause could not be caught under Article 101(1) TFEU because of the supplier's modest market share of less than 3 per cent, compared to the cumulative market share of about 70 per cent held by three other suppliers. The CJEU acknowledged that the *de minimis* notice of the Commission is not binding on national competition authorities (NCAs) and national courts which remain, however, free to take into account the thresholds put in place.[308] The Court also held that the fact that the duration of the clause in question exceeded the threshold set with regard to the duration of non-compete and exclusive dealing clauses to benefit from the VBER, which is five years, is not relevant in order to determine of the agreement constitutes an appreciable restriction of competition under Article 101(1) TFEU, the important element being the average duration of the contracts generally concluded on the relevant market.[309] The CJEU remarked that the clause in question was not forty-five years but thirty years and that the average duration of such clauses in this market was between twenty and 31.6 years. It nevertheless asked the referring court to verify if the duration of the contract was not manifestly excessive compared to the average duration of the contracts generally concluded on the relevant market. Further, in view of the supplier's modest market share the CJEU found that such clause did not have the effect of restricting competition appreciably and therefore escaped the prohibition set out in Article 101(1) TFEU.[310]

10.4.4.4. Towards a more economic approach in the application of Article 101(1) to vertical restraints

The case law of the Court moved gradually to the consideration of market factors in the application of Article 101(1), for restrictions that are not anti-competitive by their object. This new approach first manifested itself with the emergence of the doctrine of cumulative effect.[311]

Following the Green Paper on Vertical Restraints adopted by the Commission in 1997 and the reform process that followed, the Commission has also moved towards a consideration of market factors before finding that a vertical restraint constitutes an infringement of Article 101(1) TFEU.

10.4.4.4.1. The consideration of market factors under Article 101(1): The case law on cumulative effect

Delimitis

In *Delimitis*,[312] the CJEU used the concept of cumulative effect to rule that a single branding agreement did not have the object of restricting competition and would not have that effect unless all the agreements tying dealers to one or other of the suppliers kept other suppliers out of the market. This would be the case only if there where entry barriers at the level downstream and so many outlets were tied for so long to one or other of the suppliers that a new one would not be able to enter the market on an efficient scale for advertising. Even then the effect on competition would be appreciable only if the particular brewer made a significant contribution to the foreclosure. The Court required the national court to consider the agreement in its legal and economic context. Subsequent cases refined the concept of cumulative effect.

308 Ibid, paras 34–5. 309 Ibid, para 37. 310 Ibid, para 42. 311 See Chapter 6.

312 Case C-234/89, *Delimitis (Stergios) v Henninger Bräu* [1991] ECR I–935. See further Section 6.3.3.3.1.

The ice cream cases: Single branding agreements under Article 101(1) TFEU
Several cases concerned major manufacturers of ice cream, most of them subsidiaries of Unilever that supplied freezers free of charge to small retail outlets in return for an obligation to place in them only the supplier's brand of single unit ice cream, 'freezer exclusivity'. Sometimes retailers agreed to sell only the manufacturer's ice cream in the outlet, 'outlet exclusivity'. The narrow product definition by the Commission—single unit ice cream—excluded the supermarket trade in blocks of ice cream to be divided by consumers and resulted in high market shares.

Mars, which was trying to introduce its brand of single unit ice cream in various countries made several complaints to the Commission that as the result of these agreements it could not expand sales rapidly.

In *Schöller Lebensmittel GmbH (SLG) & Co KG, Schöller*,[313] SLG supplied freezers to many small retailers and petrol stations in Germany and required that all 'single item ice cream' sold in those outlets be acquired only from it. The Commission found that the agreements restrained each retailer from stocking the single item ice creams and thus precluded competition for the retailer between SLG and other suppliers of contract goods (restriction of inter-brand competition). These exclusive purchasing obligations 'make it more difficult or impossible to set up independent distribution structures such as are necessary if new entrants are to gain access to the relevant market or if an existing market is to be consolidated'.[314] The Commission found that SLG supplied over 20 per cent of the market of single item ice creams in Germany, although not all of it through outlets subject to a single branding restraint and concluded that it had appreciable effects. The Commission refused the exemption under Article 101(3). In an almost identical case involving *Langnese*, which had a slightly larger share of the German market, the Commission adopted a virtually identical decision.[315] In *Langnese v Commission*, the General Court confirmed the decision of the Commission but proceeded to a more extensive analysis of market factors under Article 101(1), and not Article 101(3) as did the Commission,[316] thus confirming the importance of market analysis under Article 101(1).

In *Mars*, the Commission had issued a statement of objections to HB Ice Cream, the largest producer of ice cream in Ireland. HB provided freezers to small retailers responsible for about 40 per cent of the sales of single unit ice cream in that country in return for an obligation that the retailer would stock only HB ice cream therein—'freezer exclusivity'. The Commission objected under Articles 101 and 102 to excluding competing suppliers from retailers that had room for only one freezer. HB then changed its policy and permitted retailers to whom it had lent a freezer to buy the cabinets outright or on hire purchase terms and thereby terminate the tie. After investigating further complaints, the Commission published a notice in the Official Journal (OJ) stating that it intended to take a favourable view of this compromise. HB obtained an injunction from the Irish High Court restraining Mars from persuading retailers to stock its ice cream in HB cabinets. Mars, which wished to enter the market by having its ices stocked in HB's cabinets, complained again to the Commission that few retailers were prepared to take advantage of the possibility of terminating the tie. So, the Commission reopened proceedings and condemned freezer exclusivity.[317]

313 *Schöller Lebensmittel GmbH & Co KG, Schöller* (Case IV/31.400) Commission Decision 93/405/EEC [1993] OJ L 183/1.

314 Ibid, paras 68–9.

315 *Langnese-Iglo GmbH* (Case IV/34.072) Commission Decision 93/406/EEC [1993] OJ L 183/19.

316 Case T-7/93, *Langnese Iglo GmbH v Commission of the European Communities* [1995] ECR II–1533, paras 99–113.

317 *Masterfoods Ltd and Valley Ice Cream (Ireland) Ltd v Van Den Bergh Foods Ltd (formerly HB Ice Cream Ltd)* (COMP Cases IV/34.073, IV/34.395, and IV/35.436) Commission Decision [1998] OJ L 246/1.

Meanwhile, the Irish judgment granting an injunction against Mars came before the Irish Supreme Court, which requested a preliminary ruling from the CJEU. Consequently, the General Court suspended its proceedings on the appeal from the Commission's decision.[318] The CJEU did not deal with the points of substance, but only with the procedural issues. It ruled that a national court may not give a judgment contrary to a Commission decision, although the original injunction Van den Bergh was attempting to enforce had been granted before the Commission's decision.[319]

The Commission accepted in its original statement of objections that supplying the freezers had contributed to an improvement of distribution by overcoming the lack of capital of many small retailers. Nevertheless, the first mover advantage was considerable. Many small retailers lacked the space for a second freezer, and if they entered into an alternative exclusive arrangement with Mars, they would have to give up the sale of their existing supplier's product. It would be harder for Mars to persuade small retailers to carry its brands than it had been for the first: Mars made only one kind of impulse ice cream, so the proportional cost of a freezer cabinet would have been greater for it than for the suppliers of a larger range of ice cream. The General Court eventually upheld the Commission's decision. It carefully considered the Commission's analysis for single wrapped items of impulse ice cream in Ireland under Article 101 TFEU.

Case T-65/98, *Van den Bergh Foods Ltd v Commission*
[2003] ECR II–4653 (references omitted)

83. In order to determine whether HB's exclusive distribution agreements fall within the prohibition contained in Article [101(1) TFEU], it is appropriate, in accordance with the case-law, to consider whether all the similar agreements entered into in the relevant market and the other features of the economic and legal context of the agreements at issue, show that those agreements cumulatively have the effect of denying access to that market to new competitors. If, on examination, that is found not to be the case, the individual agreements making up the bundle of agreements cannot impair competition within the meaning of Article [101(1) TFEU]. If, on the other hand, such examination reveals that it is difficult to gain access to the market, it is then necessary to assess the extent to which the agreements at issue contribute to the cumulative effect produced, on the basis that only those agreements which make a significant contribution to any partitioning of the market are prohibited [. . .].

84. It follows that, contrary to HB's submission, the contractual restrictions on retailers must be examined not just in a purely formal manner from the legal point of view, but also by taking into account the specific economic context in which the agreements in question operate, including the particular features of the relevant market, which may, in practice, reinforce those restrictions and thus distort competition on that market contrary to Article [101(1) TFEU].

85. In that regard, it must be remembered that the exclusivity clause in HB's distribution agreements was part of a set of similar agreements concluded by manufacturers on the relevant market and was an established practice not only in Ireland but also in other countries [. . .]

87. It is apparent from the file that the outlets which are the most important for the sale of impulse ice cream are generally small in area and have limited space. [. . .]

[318] Case T-65/98R, *Van den Bergh Foods Ltd v Commission* [2003] ECR II–4653.
[319] Case C-344/98, *Masterfoods v HB Ice Cream* [2000] ECR I–11369.

88, Furthermore it cannot be denied that the relevant product market is characterised by the need for each retailer to have at least one freezer—either owned by him or supplied by an ice creams manufacturer—in order to stock and display ice creams. Consequently, the decision that a retailer who sells products for immediate consumption, such as confectionary, crisps and carbonated drinks, has to take is different where, on the one hand, an ice creams manufacturer offers to sell him its products, as a replacement or supplement to an existing range, and, on the other hand, where a similar offer is made by a manufacturer of other products such as cigarettes or chocolate, which do not require a freezer cabinet but normal shelf space. A retailer cannot simply stock a new range of ice creams alongside other existing products for a trial period in order to establish whether there is sufficient demand for that range. He must first of all take a business decision as to whether the investment, risks and other disadvantages associated with the installation of a freezer or an additional freezer, including the displacement and decrease in the sales of other brands of ice creams and other products, will be outweighed by additional profit. It follows that a rational retailer will allocate space to a freezer in order to stock ice cream of a particular brand only if the sale of that brand is more profitable than the sale of impulse ice creams of other brands and of product for immediate consumption.

89. The Court finds that, in the circumstances set out [. . .], the provision of a freezer without charge, the evident popularity of HB's ice cream, the breadth of its range of products and the benefits associated with the sale of them are very important considerations in the eyes of retailers when they consider whether to install an additional freezer cabinet in order to sell a second, possibly reduced, range of ice cream or, *a fortiori*, to terminate their distribution agreement with HB in order to replace HB's freezer cabinet either by their own cabinet or by one belonging to another supplier, which would, in all probability be subject to a condition of exclusivity.

90. Moreover, HB has held a dominant position on the relevant market for several years. When the contested decision was adopted it had an 89 % share of the relevant market, both in volume and in value, the remainder being shared between several small suppliers.

97. In the light of the foregoing, the Court finds that the Commission has proved to the required legal standard that, notwithstanding the high degree of recognition of HB's products on the relevant market and the fact that it offers a complete range of ice creams, many of which are highly popular with consumers, there is objective and specific evidence demonstrating the existence of demand in Ireland for the ice creams of other manufacturers where they are available, even though those manufacturers have a smaller range of ice creams, namely the ice creams of manufacturers who, like Mars, occupy quite specific niches. The Commission has shown in that regard that a considerable number of retailers are prepared to stock impulse ice-creams from various manufacturers, provided that they may stock them in one and the same freezer and that they are not inclined to do so when they have to install an additional freezer of their own or one belonging to another manufacturer. Consequently, the Court cannot accept HB's argument that the reluctance of retailers to sell products of other ice-cream manufacturers must be attributed not to the exclusivity clause but rather to the fact that there is no demand for those products on the relevant market.

98. The Court also finds that the Commission rightly held, having regard to the specific features of the product in question and the economic context of this case, that the network of HB's distribution agreements together with the supply of freezer cabinets without charge subject to the condition of exclusivity, have a considerable dissuasive effect on retailers with regard to the installation of their own cabinet or that of another

manufacturer and operate de facto as a tie on sales outlets that have only HB freezer cabinets, that is to say 40% of sales outlets in the relevant market. Despite the fact that it is theoretically possible for retailers who have only an HB freezer cabinet to sell the ice creams of other manufacturers, the effect of the exclusivity clause in practice is to restrict the commercial freedom of retailers to choose the products they wish to sell in their sales outlets. [. . .]

The GC exercised the same care in confirming that in the light of all the circumstances the Commission had not made a manifest error in refusing to apply Article 101(1).

106. As regards HB's argument relating to application of the rule of reason in the present case, the Court would point out that the existence of such a rule in Community competition law is not accepted. An interpretation of Article [101(1) TFEU], such as suggested by HB, is moreover difficult to reconcile with the structure of the rules prescribed by Article [101 TFEU].

107. Article [101 TFEU] expressly provides, in its third paragraph, for the exemption of agreements that restrict competition where they satisfy a number of conditions, in particular where they are indispensable to the attainment of certain objectives and do not afford undertakings the possibility of eliminating competition in respect of a substantial part of the products in question. It is only within the specific framework of that provision that the pro and anti-competitive aspects of a restriction may be weighed [. . .]. Article [101(3) TFEU] would lose much of its effectiveness if such an examination had already to be carried out under Article [101(1) TFEU] [. . .].

108. Furthermore, it cannot be inferred with certainty from the sole fact that the identified part of the HB network of agreements involved around 40% of all sales outlets in the market, that that part is automatically capable of preventing, restricting or distorting competition appreciably. That implies, as HB contended at the hearing, that 60%, therefore a majority, of sales outlets in the relevant market are not foreclosed as result of the exclusivity clause.

109. When assessing the effects of such a network of distribution agreements, it is necessary to have regard to the economic and legal context in which it operates and in which it might combine with others so as to have a cumulative effect on competition [. . .].

Paragraphs 87–90 demonstrate the care taken by the General Court to examine the legal and economic context of the agreement. It was in the light of all these factors that it confirmed that the supply of freezers in return for exclusive dealing was abusive. Merely finding 40 per cent foreclosure was not sufficient.

The CJEU dismissed the appeal to the General Court's judgment by HB, considering that the assessment by the GC of the economic and legal context of the agreement constituted a question of fact and thus subject to a limited judicial control (only in case of clear distortion of facts and evidence). It held that the effects of an agreement on competition have to be assessed in the legal and economic context in which it occurs and where it might combine with others to have a cumulative effect on competition. Consequently, 'the contractual restrictions on retailers must be examined not just in a purely formal manner from the legal point of view'.[320]

320 Case C-552/03, *Unilever Bestfoods (Ireland) Ltd, formerly Van den Bergh Foods Ltd v Commission* [2006] ECR I-9091.

10.4.4.4.2. The consideration of market factors in the assessment of Article 101(1) TFEU: The Commission's approach

The Commission has moved towards the consideration of a number of market factors before applying the prohibition of Article 101(1). The Commission justified the existence of a more lenient regime for vertical agreements in the Follow-up to the Green Paper on Vertical Restraints that followed the publication of the Green Paper and a consultation process, in which the Commission also spelled out the reasons that led it to suggest a reform of the EU competition regime on vertical restraints. The reform is remarkable for introducing the concept of market power as an important factor in the application of Article 101(1) to vertical restraints.

Commission—Communication on the application of the Community competition rules to vertical restraints—Follow-up to the Green Paper on vertical restraints COM/98/0544 final [1998] OJ C 365/3

Community competition policy concerning vertical restraints has a history of nearly forty years. Although this policy has been successful a review is necessary. The reasons for this review were amply described in the Green Paper on Vertical Restraints. The Green Paper has identified a number of shortcomings in current policy, which can be summarised as follows.

First, the current Block-Exemption Regulations (BERs) comprise rather strict form-based requirements and as a result are considered too legalistic and work as a strait-jacket. This is especially awkward in the light of the major changes in methods of distribution that have taken place and still are taking place. For the vertical agreements that, sometimes with difficulty, do fall within the current BERs a compliance burden is created through unnecessary legal uncertainty. Companies without significant market power suffer unnecessary regulation and may even be prevented from using vertical restraints to improve their competitive position in the market.

Secondly, for those agreements that fall within the BERs there is the real risk that the Commission is exempting agreements that distort competition. As the BERs are form-based instead of effect-based and do not contain any market share limit, companies with significant market power can benefit from them. The sanction of withdrawal is in this respect not seen as a real deterrent because it works only with effect for the future. Thus, the present BERs exempt for instance, non-compete obligations up to 100% market share although these may cause serious foreclosure effects and allow the charging of exorbitant prices on the market to the detriment of consumers.

Thirdly, as the BERs only cover vertical agreements concerning the resale of final goods and not intermediate goods or services a significant part of all vertical agreements are not covered by the current BEs, even when the parties involved have no market power. This means that an unnecessarily large number of vertical restraints could in principle be scrutinised, resulting in legal uncertainty and unnecessary enforcement costs.

Need for a more economics-based approach

To remedy these three shortcomings and better protect competition, the primary objective of Community competition policy, a more economics based approach is required. Such an approach should be based on the effects on the market; vertical agreements should be analysed in their market context. It is only when inter-brand competition is weak and market power exists that it becomes important to control vertical agreements. This should facilitate a relaxation of the form-based requirements, ensure that fewer agreements are covered by Article [101](1) and afford a better scrutiny of agreements of companies having substantial market power. [. . .]

Most markets are fairly competitive, the companies not having market power. Therefore, the number of cases that may need scrutiny, as depicted below, will be relatively low. This is confirmed by an analysis of recent merger cases [. . .]

Economics of Verticals

Vertical restraints and market power

As indicated in the introduction, economics tells us that in the field of vertical restraints competition concerns can only arise if there is insufficient inter-brand competition, i.e. if there exists a certain degree of market power. On the one hand, the fiercer the inter-brand competition is, the more likely it is that vertical restraints have no negative effect or at least a net positive effect. On the other hand, the weaker the inter-brand competition, the more likely it is that vertical restraints have a net negative effect. This means that the same vertical restraint can have different effects depending on the market structure and on the market power of the company applying the vertical restraint.

In economics, market power is usually defined as the power to raise price above the competitive level (in the short run marginal cost, in the long run average total cost). In other words, a company has market power if it has a perceptible influence on the price against which it can sell and if by charging a price above the competitive level it is able, at least in the short term, to obtain supra-normal profits. Most economists would agree that there exists market power below the level of dominance as defined by the Court of Justice. This view was also expressed in the Green Paper, to indicate that vertical restraints can harm competition below the level of dominance and therefore that Article [102] and merger control will not suffice. Article [101] needs to be applied to vertical restraints, in particular in oligopolistic markets where none of the individual companies hold a dominant position.

It is also generally recognised that vertical restraints are on average less harmful than horizontal competition restraints. The main reason for treating a vertical restraint more leniently than a horizontal restraint lies in the fact that the latter may concern an agreement between competitors producing substitute goods/services while the former concerns an agreement between a supplier and a buyer of a particular product/service. In horizontal situations the exercise of market power by one company (higher price of its product) will benefit its competitors. This may provide an incentive to competitors to induce each other to behave anti-competitively. In vertical situations the product of the one is the input for the other. This means that the exercise of market power by either the upstream or downstream company would normally hurt the demand for the product of the other. The companies involved in the agreement may therefore have an incentive to prevent the exercise of market power by the other (so-called self-policing character of vertical restraints).

However, this self-restraining character should not be over-estimated. When a company has no market power it can only try to increase its profits by optimising its manufacturing and distribution processes, with or without the help of vertical restraints. However, when it does have market power it can also try to increase its profits at the expense of its direct competitors by raising their costs and at the expense of its buyers/consumers by trying to appropriate some of their surplus. This can happen when the upstream and downstream company share the extra profits or when one of the two imposes the vertical restraint and thereby appropriates all the extra profits.

The emphasis on market power for the application of Article 101(1) transcends the area of vertical restraints.

Communication from the Commission—Notice—Guidelines on the application of Article [101(3) TFEU] [2004] OJ C 101/97 (analysing the basic principles for assessing agreements under Article 101(1))

> 25. Negative effects on competition within the relevant market are likely to occur when the parties individually or jointly have or obtain some degree of market power and the agreement contributes to the creation, maintenance or strengthening of that market power or allows the parties to exploit such market power. Market power is the ability to maintain prices above competitive levels for a significant period of time or to maintain output in terms of product quantities, product quality and variety or innovation below competitive levels for a significant period of time. In markets with high fixed costs undertakings must price significantly above their marginal costs of production in order to ensure a competitive return on their investment. The fact that undertakings price above their marginal costs is therefore not in itself a sign that competition in the market is not functioning well and that undertakings have market power that allows them to price above the competitive level. It is when competitive constraints are insufficient to maintain prices and output at competitive levels that undertakings have market power within the meaning of Article [101(1)].
>
> 26. The creation, maintenance or strengthening of market power can result from a restriction of competition between the parties to the agreement. It can also result from a restriction of competition between any one of the parties and third parties, e.g. because the agreement leads to foreclosure of competitors or because it raises competitors' costs, limiting their capacity to compete effectively with the contracting parties. Market power is a question of degree. The degree of market power normally required for the finding of an infringement under Article [101(1)] in the case of agreements that are restrictive of competition by effect is less than the degree of market power required for a finding of dominance under Article [102 TFEU].

In addition to the market share thresholds (a proxy of market power) that define the boundaries of the block exemption, market power is also taken into account in the individual assessment of vertical restraints under Article 101(1) TFEU, along with a number of other market factors. The Guidelines make it clear that:

> In assessing cases above the market share threshold of 30 %, the Commission will undertake a full competition analysis. The following factors are particularly relevant to establish whether a vertical agreement brings about an appreciable restriction of competition under Article 101(1):
>
> (a) nature of the agreement;
>
> (b) market position of the parties;
>
> (c) market position of competitors;
>
> (d) market position of buyers of the contract products;
>
> (e) entry barriers;
>
> (f) maturity of the market;
>
> (g) level of trade;
>
> (h) nature of the product;
>
> (i) other factors.[321]

321 Vertical Restraints Guidelines 2010, para 111.

10.5. ECONOMIC ANALYSIS OF VERTICAL RESTRAINTS

The introduction of the vertical/horizontal dichotomy is consistent with economic learning. The currently dominant neoclassical economic paradigm recognizes that dealers have significant influence on consumer demand and that distribution services constitute an important input in the commercialization process of a product. It follows that the manufacturer has an interest to coordinate the distribution of its products, in particular as the dealers may have incentives that differ from those of the manufacturer. In this case, a principal–agent (coordination) problem may ensue.[322] Coordination problems may relate to the definition of an optimal level of services to be provided by the dealers, the price of the product and finally the allocation of risks between the upstream and the downstream level of the vertical relation. Vertical integration constitutes a possible solution to this problem.

Monitoring and coordination costs in a vertically integrated entity may, however, be significant.[323] Manufacturers could make instead the choice of independent dealers to distribute their products and may conclude with them contracts that will specify the required services. Writing contracts may nevertheless be insufficient to overcome the coordination problems in a vertical relationship, because of the different incentives of the parties and the difficulty of monitoring the performance of these contractual provisions.[324] This could be analysed as a classic principal–agent problem.

ACM Chen and KN Hylton, 'Procompetitive Theories of Vertical Control' (1999) 50(3) *Hastings LJ* 573, 580

[. . .] One of the features of a perfectly competitive market is that firms will compete based on perfect information. Under this assumption, a manufacturer effortlessly acquires knowledge regarding customer preferences, and uses that information to adjust its competitive strategies in order to offer more attractive terms or to provide better services than its rivals do. Moreover, perfect information enables the manufacturer to respond to any increase or decrease in market demand by entering or exiting the market without delay.

To be sure, this assumption may not always hold. In fact, most of the information necessary for decision making takes time to collect. When the resources required for information collection are significant, selling through an independent dealer who is already operating in the market and is familiar with regional demand conditions is frequently the less costly way of doing business for the manufacturer.

However, sale by independent dealers has its shortcomings too. For example, finding a qualified dealer and negotiating a contract acceptable to both parties is a time-consuming process. And due to the problem of imperfect information, the manufacturer may not be able to find

322 ACM Chen and KN Hylton, 'Procompetitive Theories of Vertical Control' (1999) 50(3) *Hastings LJ* 573, 581.

323 AA Alchian 'Production, Information Costs, and Economic Organization' (1972) 62(5) *American Economic Rev* 777; SJ Grossman and OD Hart 'The Cost and Benefits of Ownership: A Theory of Vertical Integration' (1986) 94(4) *J Political Economy* 691.

324 B Klein 'Transaction Cost Determinants of Unfair Contractual Arrangements' (1980) 70(2) *American Economic Rev* 356.

> out beforehand the dealer's hidden flaws, such as a tendency to renege on contractual obligations. Consequently, the manufacturer will need to constantly monitor the performance of the distribution agreement after sale responsibilities are assigned to the downstream firms. This problem complicates Coase's theory, in the sense that the tradeoff between the costs of direct sale and sale by a dealer becomes harder to assess. In cases where the required information for evaluating the tradeoff is unavailable, the outcome of agent sales could be sub-optimal for the manufacturer. The conflict between the need to use a distribution system and the uncertainty arising from informational asymmetry can be described as a principal–agent dilemma.

According to this view, vertical restraints constitute a mechanism to deal with externalities.

P Rey and T Vergé, 'Economics of Vertical Restraints' in P Buccirossi (ed) *Handbook of Antitrust Economics* (MIT Press, 2008), 360

> The vertical structure considered as a whole faces a number of decision variables: some affect the joint profit (retail prices, quantity sold to consumers, selling efforts, [. . .]) while others affect the way this joint profit is shared between the different parties (wholesale price, franchise fee, [. . .]). The decentralization of the decision variables that affect the joint profit (the 'targets') to the retailers can cause inefficiencies since they create externalities that have to be correctly accounted for. Vertical restraints can then be used as means to coordinate and restore the efficiency of the vertical structure. As we will now show, this does not necessarily mean that it is in the consumers' (or society as a whole) best interest to eliminate or correct these externalities.

There are conflicting stories on the motivation of the parties to impose vertical restraints. The parties will often employ vertical contracts in order to align their incentives, for example by making it possible for dealers to earn additional profits, which helps to encourage joint-maximizing behaviour.[325] Vertical contractual control may also bring a number of efficiencies, for example the mitigation of the effects of a successive monopoly, if monopoly power is present at both the upstream and the downstream level of the market (the double marginalization problem),[326] the protection of retailers' promotional and commercialization efforts from free riding or the appropriation of these investments from other dealers,[327] the integration by manufacturers of efficient dealers with a reputation in providing quality services in their distribution network,[328] or the protection of their suppliers' investments from appropriability.[329]

Vertical restrictions may also be adopted for anti-competitive purposes and may thus produce anti-competitive effects. They may raise rivals' costs,[330] eventually excluding rivals,[331] enabling

325 B Klein and KM Murphy, 'Vertical Restraints as Contract Enforcement Mechanisms' (1988) 31(2) *J L & Economics* 265.

326 JJ Spengler, 'Vertical Integration and Antitrust Policy' (1950) 58(4) *J Political Economy* 347.

327 LG Telser, 'Why Should Manufacturers Want Free Trade' (1960) 3 *J L & Economics* 86.

328 HP Marvel and S McCafferty, 'Resale Price Maintenance and Quality Certification' (1984) 15(3) *Rand J Economics* 346.

329 HP Marvel, 'Exclusive Dealing' (1982) 25(12) *J L & Economy* 1.

330 T Krattenmaker and SC Salop, 'Anticompetitive Exclusion: Raising Rivals' Costs to Achieve Power over Price' (1986) 96 *Yale LJ* 209; DT Scheffman and RS Higgins, '20 years of Raising Rivals' Costs: History, Assessment, and Future' (2003) 12(4) *George Mason L Rev* 371.

331 P Aghion and P Bolton, 'Contracts as a Barrier to Entry' (1987) 77(3) *American Economic Rev* 388.

the firm to exercise market power, or more generally reduce inter-brand competition.[332] It is widely accepted, however, that in the absence of market power (individual or collective) at the upstream or downstream market, vertical restraints will not produce consumer harm that will be enough to justify antitrust intervention, even if competition between retailers (intra-brand competition) will effectively be reduced.[333] The assumption is that horizontal competition between actual or potential rival suppliers (inter-brand competition) will make unprofitable any increase of the price of the good, or reduction of output, quality, and innovation.[334] Resale price maintenance clauses may also facilitate collusion and suppress competition among manufacturers[335] or among dealers (dampening competition effect).[336]

We will analyse first the pro-competitive theories of vertical control (Section 10.5.1) and their reception in EU competition law, before looking to anti-competitive theories of vertical control and their reception in EU competition law (Section 10.5.2). Each theory advances different motivations for the adoption of vertical restraints. Selecting which of the theories could explain the selection of the specific vertical restraint depends on the interpretation of the facts of the case. This raises the issue of the right legal policy towards vertical restraints: should we develop presumptions? Should we adopt a cost benefit analysis approach for every restraint (rule of reason test in the US)? What are the right inferences and the optimal allocation of the burden of proof between the opposing parties to a vertical restraints case? (Section 10.5.3)

10.5.1. PRO-COMPETITIVE THEORIES OF VERTICAL CONTROL

We have already examined the organizational efficiencies brought by vertical restraints in terms of transaction costs economics theory in Section 10.4.1.1.2. We have seen that these are taken into account in the interpretation of Article 101(1), as they do not require quantification and can be intuitively assessed by the competition authorities or the judiciary. This part will focus on the other aspects of efficiency that can also be affected by the adoption of vertical restraints (productive, allocative, and dynamic efficiency). The consideration of such efficiencies may be either intuitive and take place in the context of Article 101(1) or be more resource-intensive and take place in the context of Article 101(3) TFEU.

10.5.1.1. Double marginalization

This is also referred to as the 'successive monopoly problem'. The intuition is simple: one monopoly is better than two for consumer welfare. This justification assumes a non-competitive downstream (distribution) market and a non-competitive upstream (supply level). Each firm would the profit maximising price, thus at a mark-up over marginal costs. Price above marginal costs yields deadweight losses, which in this case are being incurred twice. The aggregate profits of the upstream and downstream level are also reduced in comparison to the monopoly

[332] P Rey and J Stiglitz 'The Role of Exclusive Territories in Producer's Competition' (1995) 26(3) *Rand J Economics* 431.

[333] M Motta, *Competition Policy: Theory and Practice* (CUP, 2004), 343.

[334] Ibid, 305–6.

[335] Ibid, 158.

[336] G Shaffer, 'Slotting Allowances and Resale Price Maintenance: A Comparison of Facilitating Practices' (1991) 22(1) *Rand J Economics* 120.

profit. The double marginalization problem is thus caused by externalities from the decentralization of the decision variables to the supplier and retailer:

> The externality arises from the fact that each firm, when setting its mark-up does not take into account the impact of this decision on the other firm's profit. For instance, when setting the final price, the retailer trades off an increase in its margin against a decrease in the quantity sold, but does not take into account the reduction in the producer's profit due to the increase in the quantity.[337]

A vertical integration of the upstream and downstream level may resolve the problem of double marginalization as it will lead to a centralization of the decision variables that affect the joint profit. Alternative solutions consist in controlling the retail price by imposing to the downstream level a fixed resale price (resale price maintenance) and then setting the wholesale price to the most optimal level for the sharing of the joint profits. A nonlinear tariff, such as two-part tariffs, could also yield a similar result. As it explained by JA Kay:

> Insurance agents are frequently offered override commissions—remuneration which increases more than proportionately with the total amount of business done with a particular company. Travel agents receive similar incentives, which may also be related to the increase in business over a base period. Aggregated rebates relate to the totality of business done with a supplier—thus Hoffman la Roche offered discounts based on the customer's purchases of all vitamins from the company. This strengthens the position of a supplier with a portfolio of products by making selective entry by competitors more difficult.[338]

The supplier may set the wholesale price at marginal costs, thus providing the incentive to the retailer to set the resale price at the monopoly level (but this time there is a single monopoly mark-up!), the supplier receiving a fixed fee (eg franchise fee) that will be used to share the joint profits as desired. Notice that the double marginalization justification for vertical restraints works only in case there is market power at both levels of the vertical chain. In addition, a fixed fee (franchise fee) may not solve the problem as the manufacturer and the dealer should have a high level of information to write or enforce a contract that specifies an optimal fee. Suppliers may also employ alternative restraints, such as quantity forcing, requiring the dealers to sell minimum numbers of units, providing the incentive to dealers to reduce their mark-up in order to achieve the required minimum number of units.[339]

P Rey and T Vergé, 'Economics of Vertical Restraints' in P Buccirossi (ed) *Handbook of Antitrust Economics* (MIT Press, 2008), 353, 361

> [. . .] [V]ertical restraints are not necessarily needed to solve the double-marginalisation problem. Introducing strong intra-brand competition (using several perfectly substitutable retailers) would remove the retail markup. [. . .] Different types of restraints (RPM, quotas,

337 P Rey and T Vergé, 'Economics of Vertical Restraints' in P Buccirossi (ed) *Handbook of Antitrust Economics* (MIT Press, 2008), 360.

338 JA Kay, 'Managing Relationships with Customers and Suppliers: Law, Economics And Strategy' (1991) 2(1) *Business Strategy Review* 17, 23.

339 ABA Section of Antitrust Law, *Antitrust Law and Economics of Product Distribution* (2006), 118.

nonlinear tariffs) appear as substitutes for a better efficiency. However, this equivalence vanishes when market conditions such as demand or distribution costs are uncertain and the retailer is risk-averse. A two-part tariff ensures that the distributor selects always the retail price that maximizes the aggregate profit of the vertical structure, but the distributor bears all the risk. RPM, on the other hand, does not allow the distributor to adjust the retail price after a demand or (retail) cost shock. This means that the vertical restraints do not perfectly solve the double-marginalization problem if there is uncertainty and are no longer equivalent. For instance, RPM is preferred to two-part tariffs when demand is uncertain, whereas two-part tariffs yield a higher joint profit than RPM under cost uncertainty.

10.5.1.2. The free rider rationale and retail services

The brand owner may wish to provide its dealers with incentives to invest in providing a range of pre-sale services that affect the demand for the product such as free delivery, investments in skilled personnel, demonstration models, pre-sale advice to potential buyers, showrooms, they may be required to sell fashion and glamorous articles in a luxurious ambience.[340] These efforts will not only produce 'vertical externalities' between the supplier and the retailers (as the supplier will benefit from an increased volume of sales of the product) but also 'horizontal externalities', as the benefits from these additional services will extend to other retailers distributing the same brand. It would be stupid for a dealer to agree to make such investments if it could not charge separately for the services and another dealer nearby does not supply the service and so can sell at lower prices. Many customers would make their selection at the expensive shop that provides the service, but order the main product from the cheaper shop that does not. The 'cheap' shop would be able to take a 'free ride' on the services provided at the 'expensive shop'. There may be no way that two kinds of retailer of high priced products for which pre-sales services are important can co-exist selling the same brands, one providing expensive services and the other not if their shops are nearby or if the brand is sold by mail order or the Internet. When consumers need, but are resistant to paying independently for, pre-sales services, the shop providing the services would have to cease doing so.

In case these dealer services are important for the demand of the product, the supplier has the incentive to reduce the risk of horizontal externality by imposing a vertical restriction: most often by granting exclusive territories to their dealers, which internalizes the horizontal externality by creating a property right for the retailer who invests on services that increase the demand for the supplier's product. Exclusive territories suppress all intra-brand competition within the allocated territory. An alternative is to impose a minimum resale price (resale price maintenance clause), which will restrict price competition but will maintain the possibility for non-price competition. The supplier could also buy these services directly by making a fixed-fee payment, in the form of an upfront fee or slotting allowances. For these vertical restraints to be effective, the supplier should be able to monitor the resale efforts of the dealers, in order to ensure compliance, as the latter may have the incentive to provide services that enhance their own profits, instead of those of the supplier. Monitoring costs are more important in the case of an upfront payment fee than for RPM, which enhance non-price competition among dealers, thus the service agreement becomes self-enforcing.

340 LG Telser, 'Why should Manufacturers want Free Trade' (1960) 3 *J Law & Economics* 86. The text in this sub-section is a modified version of V Korah and D O'Sullivan, *Distribution Agreements Under the EC Competition Rules* (Hart, 2002), 28, 29.

If the market is competitive, the brand owner has no interest in granting dealers more protection from other dealers than it thinks is necessary to induce the investment in services which it thinks is optimal. Indeed, its business may fail if it grants too much protection. The brand owner is more likely to get this assessment right that an official or court looking at the matter years later. It is risking its profits and livelihood when it makes decisions, so has an incentive to make them carefully. It probably understands the product and market conditions better than an official or a court.

10.5.1.3. Vertical restraints and principal–agent theory

Managing the vertical relation between a supplier and distributors is costly, in particular because of the barrier of imperfect information. For example, finding a qualified and trustworthy dealer and negotiating a contract acceptable to both parties are both time-consuming process.[341] One could explain these problems by employing the principal–agent terminology of adverse selection and moral hazard.

Adverse selection occurs when the supplier's product is not well known in the market and thus the distribution chain is composed by both high and low quality distributors. The distributors are generally better informed than the supplier on the value of the product, as they know the needs of the local consumers. This information asymmetry makes it difficult for the supplier to determine the distribution margin that will attract the best distributors in each market. They will set an average wholesale price, on the assumption that demand at each market will be medium, with the result that good distributors will be driven out of the market (the adverse selection problem). An exclusive distribution agreement will ensure that good quality distributors accept to carry the supplier's product. The product can be set differently, with distributors having to make a choice between the products of different suppliers. In this case, an exclusive dealing clause will ensure that the best suppliers will be chosen.

The issue can also be presented as a commitment problem when a monopolist manufacturer supplies several competing retailers. For example, the supplier may decide to provide exclusivity for a geographical region to one of the retailers and competitive bidding by the retailers would lead to set the price (reduced distribution margin or a franchise fee). If, however, offers are unobservable, the supplier can renege on its offer and secretly renegotiate with one of the retailers. This is particularly the case if the manufacturer contracts sequentially with competing retailers and thus has an incentive to cheat on early signing retailers when negotiating later deals. The other retailers would anticipate this move and if the manufacturer were unable to commit to this exclusivity, they would not accept the initial offer. The manufacturer thus needs to commit itself in a credible way to provide the territorial exclusivity only to one retailer for this region. The supplier can reduce retail competition and commit by granting an exclusive right or a RPM that will impose a price-floor. Because of this commitment problem, the supplier will not be able to appropriate all the monopoly profit and appropriate the monopoly power it potentially has.

Moral hazard refers to a situation of post-contractual opportunism that arises from the disparity between the manufacturer's and distributors' objectives. In the presence of incomplete information, each party may exploit the other party. This is particularly the case if there is a hold up problem because one of the parties made specific investments that have little residual

[341] On principal agency theory, see MC Jensen and WH Meckling, 'Theory of the Firm: Managerial Behavior, Agency Costs, and Capital Structure' (1976) 3 *J Financial Economics* 305.

value if the relationship is terminated (eg sunk costs). In this case, various vertical restraints may protect the parties' investments, such as an exclusive territory in order to protect the distributors' investments, or a non-compete or exclusive dealing provision, in case the aim is to protect the supplier.

10.5.1.4. Vertical restraints and quality certification

An additional justification for certain vertical restraints, in particular RPM, is that they are employed with the aim to attract high-end retailers to the vertical chain.

ABA Section of Antitrust Law, *Antitrust Law and Economics of Product Distribution* (2006), 69–70

It is apparent that distributors differ in their attractiveness both to customers and to suppliers. By visiting a distributor with a good reputation for discernment and selection, a consumer can gain information about the products the distributor stocks. But that information need not be accompanied by any special promotional efforts directed towards the product in question. The mere choice of the product may be all the promotion that is necessary, and all that is provided. Indeed, it may be more costly for a discerning retailer to evaluate products than for a less skilled counterpart to choose a retail assortment. However, the talented retailer will typically have a high-opportunity cost of shelf-space—consumers will visit it first and, without a good reason to go elsewhere, will purchase at that retailer rather than searching at a competitive outlet with less-valued selection ability.

Here, however, the high-end retailer is providing a service-information to guide choices—that is difficult to protect. The consumer can observe the stock of the prestige retailer, but if that stock consists of branded products, a purchase at a lower price elsewhere will be attractive. Consumers in such cases care where the product is sold but not where their particular units of the product are purchased. The result is a form of free-riding that is more akin to an adverse selection problem than one of moral hazard. A producer of a superior product whose quality is consonant with the image of a prestige retailer will fund its product deleted from that retailer's inventory if it is widely available elsewhere at lower prices. This quality certification argument differs from the presale services explanation for RPM in that there need be no tangible service associated with the sale of the product. It is merely the choice of the prestige retailer that matters to consumer and supplier, and it is nothing more than this choice that the supplier wants to protect with RPM.

Suppliers have thus an interest to impose a vertical restraint (such as RPM) that will protect dealers from free-riding and will provide them a sufficient margin for the certification services they provide.[342]

10.5.1.5. Vertical restraints ensuring retailers for demand uncertainty

According to this theory the suppliers would not prefer to have their products sold by discounters and would prefer to impose a uniform price to all retailers, which could take the

342 HP Marvel and S McCafferty, 'Resale Price Maintenance and Quality Certification' (1984) 15(3) *Rand J Economics* 346.

form of RPM, in order to preserve retailers from demand uncertainty.[343] This is particularly problematic in case the dealers set retail prices before observing demand, as retailers must order inventories prior to the resolution of demand uncertainty. In the absence of a uniform pricing, the retailers will be divided in two separate niches: discount retailers who will offer low prices but could not guarantee availability and high-end retailers who will set high prices and thus be able to sell profitably after the discounter's inventories run out and they risk to be stuck with unsold inventories. The efficient solution from the point of view of the vertical chain is for the supplier to place all retailers at the same level and by imposing a uniform price avoid discounting at a lower retail price and selling at an excessively high price.

10.5.1.6. Vertical restraints as contract-enforcement mechanisms and the 'promotional services theory' of vertical restraints

The standard free-rider rationale on pre-sale services for vertical restraints (in particular RPM) has been criticized for the reason that higher resale prices do not guarantee that retailers will compete on the non-price aspects of competition that are considered valuable from the point of view of the supplier. They may invest in promotional services that will attract additional customers from other dealers carrying the supplier's brand, not customers of other brands, by offering bundled discounts on other products or on future purchases. The standard theory on vertical restraints assumes that manufacturers will induce the supply of desired services by increasing the margin the retailers are able to charge consumers through RPM clauses or an exclusive contract. However, vertical restraints do not create an incentive to retailers to supply the desired services. As it was noted by Klein and Murphy, '[e]ven if the manufacturer fixes the retail price and does not permit price competition, retailers still have an incentive to free ride by supplying nonprice services that are not desired by the manufacturer but are of value to consumers.'[344] It is possible also that retailers take the additional margin from the vertical restraint and continue to free ride on other retailers, where desired dealer services are unobserved by consumers.

Klein and Murphy suggested an alternative theory that emphasizes the role of vertical restraints in inducing desired dealer services through a private enforcement mechanism. Drafting enforceable contracts that specify the desired dealer services to be provided is impractical because the dealer performance may be prohibitively costly to measure. Rather than relying on a third-party enforcer (courts), which is going to be highly impractical, an alternative will be to privately enforce some elements of dealer performance solely by the threat of termination of the transactional relationship and thus prevent the non-conforming retailer from the additional revenue stream (quasi-rent) provided by the vertical restraint. An RPM clause could thus reinforce a threat of termination. A retailer, which finds that carrying the product of the supplier imposing the vertical restraint is more valuable than its next best opportunity, is likely to provide the services desired by the supplier, in order to avoid termination. Thus, vertical restraints may be conceived as payments for additional services and effort from the retailers.

343 R Deneckere, HP Marvel, and J Peck, 'Demand Uncertainty, Inventories, and Resale Price Maintenance' (1996) 111 *Q J Economics* 885.

344 B Klein and KM Murphy, 'Vertical Restraints as Contract Enforcement Mechanisms' (1988) 31 *J Law & Economics* 265, 266.

This approach was further developed by Klein in subsequent articles on the 'promotional services theory' of vertical restraints.[345] According to this theory, the free riding rationale does not explain the adoption of vertical restraints, in particular RPM, by the suppliers to protect retailer services in products, such as vitamins, hair shampoo, jeans, pet foods, athletic shoes, underwear etc, in which there is no significant danger of free riding of the retailer's promotional efforts. Klein argues, on the contrary, that vertical restraints are tools for the supplier to encourage dedicated retailer promotion to his products. He questions the assumption of the standard free-riding theory, that consumer demand for some products is related to the pre-sale promotional services supplied by the retailers: additional pre-sale retailer services might not necessarily lead to an increase in the consumer demand for the supplier's products for the reason that retailers have no incentive to promote the additional pre-sale services favoured by the supplier: those that are targeted to marginal consumers who, absent the promotion, would have not purchased the supplier's product (this includes in most cases 'impulse' purchases, consumers who have no prior intent to purchase a product but do so if they see it on display, as opposed to infra-marginal consumers who are attached to a specific brand or make their decisions based on the size of the markdowns). For example, by offering brand (supplier)-specific retail services, such as displaying the products of a specific brand or a particular presentation by sales staff, the retailers will increase the supplier's incremental sales to the detriment of other competing brand products available for sale in their shop. The result is that manufacturers will in this case earn a significantly greater incremental profit margin than retailers and that 'a retailer's independent profit incentive to promote a particular manufacturer's products will be significantly less than the profit incentive of the manufacturer'.[346] Retailers have the incentive to provide non-brand specific resale services, such as free parking or fast check-out that would have inter-retailer demand effects and will attract consumers from other retailers. These are not, however, pre-sale services that the suppliers would like to promote, as they might benefit to other brands that are also sold by the retailer. The supplier puts in place self-enforcing vertical arrangements, such as RPM or exclusive territories, in order to compensate retailers for providing increased supplier-specific promotional efforts. The implications of such a theory are that vertical restraints, and free riding, are part of the normal competitive process. Suppliers will employ RPM in order to increase the number of retail outlets that will sell the supplier's products and will thus provide brand-specific pre-sale promotional services.

Note that the promotional services theory of vertical restraints assumed that the product has a low marginal cost and offers a high incremental profit margin, which makes the additional promotional services very valuable to the supplier. In addition, it assumes that it is more efficient to compensate the distributors' on a per unit sold basis than on a per service supplied basis, as in the former case there is an incentive for the retailer to invest in supplier-specific pre-sale promotional services.

[345] Ibid, 282ff; B Klein, 'Competitive Resale Price Maintenance in the Absence of Free Riding' (2009) 6 *Antitrust LJ* 431. See also B Klein and J D Wright, 'The Economics of Slotting Contracts' (2007) 50(3) *J L & Economics* 421.

[346] B Klein, 'Competitive Resale Price Maintenance in the Absence of Free Riding' (2009) 6 *Antitrust LJ* 431, 448.

10.5.1.7. The substitutability of vertical restraints

Guidelines on vertical restraints [2010] OJ C 130/1

106. It is important to recognise that vertical restraints may have positive effects by, in particular, promoting non-price competition and improved quality of services. When a company has no market power, it can only try to increase its profits by optimising its manufacturing or distribution processes. In a number of situations vertical restraints may be helpful in this respect since the usual arm's length dealings between supplier and buyer, determining only price and quantity of a certain transaction, can lead to a sub-optimal level of investments and sales. [. . .]

109. A large measure of substitutability exists between the different vertical restraints. As a result, the same inefficiency problem can be solved by different vertical restraints. For instance, economies of scale in distribution may possibly be achieved by using exclusive distribution, selective distribution, quantity forcing or exclusive sourcing. However, the negative effects on competition may differ between the various vertical restraints, which plays a role when indispensability is discussed under Article 101 (3).

The existence of less restrictive to competition vertical restraints that may provide a satisfactory solution to a vertical coordination problem should therefore be considered in the context of enforcing paragraphs one and three of Article 101 TFEU.

10.5.2. ANTI-COMPETITIVE THEORIES OF VERTICAL CONTROL

Vertical restraints can also produce consumer harm by reducing intra-brand or inter-brand competition. Both are important and their interrelation is highlighted in the excerpt below.

P Rey and T Vergé, 'Vertical restraints in European Competition Policy', (2014) 4 *Concurrences* 44, 47

Economic analysis does support the proposition that inter-brand competition is socially desirable, not only to ensure that products and services are provided at affordable prices, but also to foster product variety, encourage innovation, and so forth. There is less convergence, however, on the role and social desirability of intra-brand competition. [. . .]

[S]trong intra-brand competition ensures that the retail price for one product is mainly driven by the manufacturer's wholesale price (together with retail costs) rather than by a rival's prices. This results in head to-head competition between the rival manufacturers. By contrast, in case of weak intra-brand competition within a manufacturer's distribution network, the retail price for the manufacturer's product will respond only partially to the manufacturer's wholesale price, and is likely to respond as well to changes in the prices of the rival products. This, in turn, encourages a rival manufacturer to raise its own wholesale price, knowing that, although this will lead to an increase in the retail price and thus a reduced demand for its product, the rival manufacturers' retailers will now partially match this price increase, thereby attenuating the demand reduction.

In other words, limiting intra-brand competition within a manufacturer's distribution network reduces the sensitivity of the demand perceived by rival manufacturers, thus dampening inter-brand competition. As intra-brand competition becomes weaker, the initially direct, head-to-head competition among rival manufacturers becomes more indirect and, as a result, softer.

The important thing is to focus on the competitive harm story that a reduction of inter-brand or intra-brand competition may entail. These can be of various sorts.

P Rey, Vertical Restraints—An Economic Perspective (13 October 2012), 19 and 30, available at www.fne.gob.cl/wp-content/uploads/2013/11/Patrick-Rey.-Vertical-Restraints.pdf

In the short-term, that is, keeping the market structure constant, vertical restraints can impede competition in various ways: they can be used to maintain collusion either upstream (*facilitating practices*) or downstream (*sham cartels*), weaken interbrand competition when it is already imperfect (*competition dampening*), and allow firms with significant market power to exploit it more fully (by solving *commitment problems*); vertical restraints can also be used to foster the role of downstream firms in coordinating upstream rivals (*common agency*) and to avoid competition among these common agents when competing upstream firms rely on the same competing downstream firms to distribute their products (*interlocking relationships*). [. . .]

From a longer term perspective, and thus accounting for investment and entry/exit decisions, vertical restraints can foster potential competitors' incentives to enter a market (pro-competitive effects), and can also be used by incumbent to raise entry barriers (market foreclosure).

10.5.2.1. Vertical restraints as collusive devices

Vertical restraints, such as RPM and exclusive territories may be used by downstream firms (retailers) in order to circumvent the law prohibiting horizontal cartels and thus maintain a cartel agreement. The retailers will use such 'sham vertical agreements' with a 'pseudo upstream partner' in order to sustain a dealer cartel and extract profits at the expense of consumers and social welfare.[347] This may also occur when rivals adopt cross-licensing agreements to facilitate price-competition, or when they use their relationship with a common supplier to exchange information and facilitate collusion.[348] The suppliers do not have an *a-priori* interest to cooperate, as their aim is to increase the sales of their product and therefore to limit the distribution margin, unless the dealers are able, through their collective market power or because of a situation of economic dependence, to coerce them to cooperate. However, there can be no coercion if the supplier(s) has market power or if it is possible to use alternative distribution channels. A distinct possibility would be for the dealers to induce the suppliers to enforce the dealer cartel by agreeing to share the expected monopolistic return with them. It is difficult, however, to imagine circumstances in which the dealers will act in concert, if there

[347] P Rey, 'Vertical Restraints—An Economic Perspective' (13 October 2012), 19–20, available at www.fne.gob.cl/wp-content/uploads/2013/11/Patrick-Rey.-Vertical-Restraints.pdf.

[348] Ibid, 20.

are a fairly large number of them on the market, as this will increase the difficulty to police the eventual dealer cartel arrangement.

Vertical restraints may also facilitate collusion among suppliers, either by 'fostering coordination', for instance by identifying a desirable price or market share targets and more generally by simplifying the price structure, or by helping firms to 'sustain collusion' by making the market more transparent and therefore easing the detection of price deviations.[349] For instance, a RPM clause may enhance the stability of a cartel by eliminating retail price variation.[350] In the absence of RPM, retail prices would have been driven by wholesale prices, but also by local shocks on retailing costs or demand conditions, thus making it difficult for suppliers to perfectly infer the underlying wholesale prices and thus detect cheating from another supplier. Consequently, RPM may contribute to sustain the stability of the suppliers' cartel.

In any case, vertical restraints, such as RPM may be observed more easily than a secret cartel, hence limiting the incentives of dealers to enter this type of vertical/horizontal arrangement. Empirical studies on vertical restraints suggest that that the use of RPM as a collusive device is fairly uncommon as only 13.1 per cent of all cases involved a horizontal price fixing allegation.[351]

10.5.2.2. Vertical restraints as exclusionary devices

Vertical restraints may also be used as exclusionary mechanism to foreclose market access and prevent the entry of more efficient competitors, or more generally of competitors that would have exercised some downward pressure on pricing. For instance, locking up/tying the best distributors or locations into long-term exclusive contracts, or non-compete obligations may force competing suppliers to set up their own distribution systems, which may be costly and thus raise their costs, whenever there are significant economies of scope or scale in distribution.[352]

Raising rivals' costs may occur through certain types of vertical restraints (most usually of the single branding sort) aimed at forcing upon rivals higher costs than those borne by the firm employing the vertical practice, by increasing their distribution costs.[353] As a result of this practice, the profit-maximizing output of the rivals is decreased, and its prices eventually rise, thus enabling the firm to put in place the scheme to enjoy higher profits during the period the vertical restraints is implemented, but also to impose higher prices on consumers, as the effect of such a scheme is to create a price umbrella under which the firm employing the practice is

349 P Rey and F Caballero-Sanz, 'The Policy Implications of the Economic Analysis of Vertical Restraints', European Commission Economic Paper No 119 (1996), 17; F Mathewson and R Winter, 'The Law and Economics of Resale Price Maintenance' [1998] 13 *Rev Industrial Organization* 57; B Jullien and P Rey, 'Resale Price Maintenance and Collusion' [2007] 38 *Rand J Economics* 983; P Rey, 'Vertical Restraints—An Economic Perspective' (13 October 2012), 20, available at www.fne.gob.cl/wp-content/uploads/2013/11/Patrick-Rey.-Vertical-Restraints.pdf.

350 F Mathewson and R Winter, 'The Law and Economics of Resale Price Maintenance' (1998) 13 *Rev Industrial Organization* 57.

351 PM Ippolito, 'Resale Price Maintenance: Empirical Evidence from Litigation' (1991) 34(2) *J L & Economics* 263, 281.

352 P Rey, 'Vertical Restraints—An Economic Perspective' (13 October 2012), 30, available at www.fne.gob.cl/wp-content/uploads/2013/11/Patrick-Rey.-Vertical-Restraints.pdf.

353 For a discussion of this theory in the context of vertical contractual restraints, see T Krattenmaker and SC Salop, 'Anticompetitive Exclusion: Raising Rivals' Costs to Achieve Power over Price' (1986) 96 *Yale LJ* 209; SC Salop and DT Schefman, 'Raising Rivals' Costs' [1983] 73 *American Economic Rev* 267.

able to increase its returns. Such a strategy is not costly to the undertaking employing it, as is for instance predatory pricing, and hence the likelihood that this occurs in real life is higher. These practices may be used against actual competitors, reducing their market shares, marginalizing their competitive constraint, and eventually leading to their exclusion from the market. They may also be used to raise artificial entry barriers against potential competitors, preventing them from entering the market or delaying their entry, thus affecting the competitive conditions of the specific market long-term. Chicago School scholars have questioned the likelihood of these practices, by noting that distributors will also be hurt by such strategies (eg an exclusive dealing arrangement) and thus will not have incentives to agree to join them unless they receive compensation for their support, which will affect the profitability of the supplier employing such strategies in order to deter entry.

However, a number of studies have noted that incumbents may still have the incentives to employ vertical restraints as exclusionary strategies in order to deter the entry of a more efficient competitor.[354] For instance, the incumbent-supplier may be able to 'bribe' a number of customers-retailers into exclusive arrangements by sharing the rents it gets from exploiting monopoly power vis-à-vis the remaining customers, this strategy being successful when the monopoly rents exceed the benefits the targeted customers can hope to derive from entry of the competitor. Indeed, 'the service that (these) retailers provide is the exclusion of a potential entrant'.[355] Hence, the incumbent is playing customers against each other, by discriminating between various customers as exclusivity is only offered to some of them, relying on the poor coordination among its customers who would have been better off, had they been collectively able to reject the exclusivity contracts (or the rebates conditional on exclusivity). The supplier may also share its monopolistic rents with the retailers that assisted him in excluding rival brands by denying them shelf-space through periodic lump-sum payments to retailers (through slotting fees or loyalty rebates).[356] As a result, both suppliers and retailers gain from this practice. This compensation does not necessarily result out of an explicit exclusivity clause in an enforceable contract, but may also emerge out of an equilibrium understanding between an incumbent manufacturer and retailers.[357]

The compensation of the downstream firm (ie, retailer) entering into such exclusionary arrangements may also take the form of a commitment of the upstream incumbent to protect the downstream customer from downstream intra-brand competition (eg through an exclusive territory or RPM).[358] A vertically integrated incumbent may also want to protect its market power when the entry of a new competitor at one stage (upstream or downstream) triggers competition not only at that stage but also at the other stage, hence limiting the joint profit of the incumbent at both stages. By foreclosing entry at one stage, through exclusive

354 P Aghion and P Bolton, 'Contracts as a Barrier to Entry' (1987) 77(3) *American Economic Rev* 388; EB Rasmusen, MJ Ramseyer, and JS Wiley Jr, 'Naked Exclusion' (1991) 81 *American Economic Rev* 1137; IR Segal and MD Whinston, 'Naked Exclusion: A Comment' (2000) 90 *American Economic Rev* 296.

355 J Asker and B-I Heski, 'Raising Retailers' Profits: On Vertical Practices and the Exclusion of Rivals' (2014) 104(2) *American Economic Rev* 672.

356 G Shaffer, 'Slotting Allowances and Optimal Product Variety' (2005) 5 *Advances in Economic Analysis & Policy*, art 3; J Asker and B-I Heski, 'Raising Retailers' Profits: On Vertical Practices and the Exclusion of Rivals' (2014) 104(2) *American Economic Rev* 672

357 J Asker and B-I Heski, 'Raising Retailers' Profits: On Vertical Practices and the Exclusion of Rivals' (2014) 104(2) *American Economic Rev* 672.

358 P Rey, 'Vertical Restraints—An Economic Perspective' (13 October 2012), available at www.fne.gob.cl/wp-content/uploads/2013/11/Patrick-Rey.-Vertical-Restraints.pdf, 35; D O'Brien and G Shaffer, 'Vertical Control with Bilateral Contracts' (1992) 23 *Rand J Economics* 299.

dealing arrangements, the incumbent protects his monopolistic rents and their market power at both stages.[359]

The incumbent supplier may also employ vertical restraints in order to commit its retail customers to an aggressive attitude in the event of entry of a competitor. For instance, long-term exclusive dealing provisions, tying distributors to a specific brand, or exclusive territories for distributors enabling them to cut prices locally without taking into account the effect of the price cut in neighbouring areas, 'induce' distributors 'to engage in fiercer (interbrand) competition if competing products appear'.[360]

10.5.2.3. Vertical restraints as dampening competition devices

There is economic literature arguing that vertical restraints may damper/soften competition by enabling incumbent suppliers to credibly commit not to behave aggressively vis-à-vis their rivals, with the result that these may raise their prices and reduce their output.[361] This occurs in particular if the incumbent supplier uses independent distributors in downstream markets for the distribution of his products, delegating the pricing decisions to them, or reducing the intra-brand competition they are facing (for instance through exclusive territories) with the result that the retail price of the product will not reflect its wholesale price, as it would have been the case if these retailers were subject to intensive intra-brand competition. This 'strategic delegation' may have the effect of transforming 'direct, head-to-head interbrand competition into an indirect and less intense form of competition'.[362] Strong intra-brand competition may contribute to intensifying inter-brand competition between rival manufacturers.[363] However, an important factor is that the decision over prices is delegated to the downstream retailer, which indicates that the theory may not work for vertical restraints limiting the pricing discretion of the retailer, such as RPM. It is not also necessary for suppliers to hold bargaining power, as retailers may also use similar strategies (this time retailer-induced RPM and/or slotting fees) in order to soften competition on the retail market.[364]

Assuming that these independent retailers also distribute competing products, which is usually the case for most consumer goods, the suppliers may use the distributors as 'common agents' to eliminate inter-brand competition.[365] In case there is competition at the downstream level and 'common agents' distributors compete with each other, vertical restraints may still lead to a reduction of inter-brand competition. Hence, in markets characterized by interlocking relationships—that is, when the same rival suppliers use the same rival retailers

359 W Comanor and P Rey, 'Vertical Restraints and the Market Power of Large Distributors' (2000) 17 *Rev Industrial Organization* 135.

360 P Rey, 'Vertical Restraints—An Economic Perspective' (13 October 2012), 38, available at www.fne.gob.cl/wp-content/uploads/2013/11/Patrick-Rey.-Vertical-Restraints.pdf.

361 J Vickers, 'Delegation and the Theory of the Firm' (1985) 95 *Economic J* (Economic International Conference Supplement) 138; G Bonanno and J Vickers, 'Vertical Separation' (1988) 36 *J Industrial Economics* 257.

362 P Rey, 'Vertical Restraints—An Economic Perspective' (13 October 2012), 22, available at www.fne.gob.cl/wp-content/uploads/2013/11/Patrick-Rey.-Vertical-Restraints.pdf.

363 P Rey and JE Stiglitz, 'Vertical Restraints and Producers Competition' (1988) 32 *European Economic Rev* 561; P Rey and JE Stiglitz, 'The Role of Exclusive Territories in Producer's Competition' (1995) 26(3) *Rand J Economics* 431.

364 G Shaffer, 'Slotting Allowances and Resale Price Maintenance: A Comparison of Facilitating Practices' (1991) 22 *Rand J Economics* 120.

365 BD Bernheim and MD Whinston, 'Common Agency' (1986) 54 *Econometrica* 923.

for the distribution of their products—vertical restraints such as RPM may eliminate competition both upstream and downstream. The reduction of intra-brand competition among 'common agents' retailers enables suppliers to soften inter-brand competition. Hence, downstream competition between retailers has an important role to play in fostering upstream competition between suppliers.[366]

10.5.2.4. Vertical restraints affecting market integration

As we have previously examined in Section 2.1.6.2, one of the principal goals followed by EU competition law is to promote market integration and the completion of a single market for the EU. Vertical restraints, such as, for instance, territorial restrictions arising out of absolute territorial protection, dual pricing practices, or other practices interfering with parallel trade, in particular passive sales, are viewed with suspicion and most often are found to be anti-competitive. The 'political' objective of market integration exercises a considerable weight in EU competition policy with regard to vertical restraints. Economists take nevertheless a different perspective, as they focus exclusively on the welfare effects of vertical restraints and consumer surplus. They note that if a supplier is able to limit through vertical restraints the possibility of arbitrage by parallel importers between rich consumers, to whom the supplier charges high prices, and poor consumers, who pay low prices, the supplier may be pushed to increase the price for the poorer consumers.[367] For this reason, economists view geographic price discrimination positively and generally criticize, from a welfare perspective, the propensity of EU competition law to prohibit vertical practices limiting the possibilities of arbitrage, for instance by challenging an outright ban on absolute territorial restrictions. For EU lawyers inspired by the principle of market integration, this is a welfare cost they are ready to pay.

105.2.5. Vertical restraints are not always efficient and necessary

An important criticism to the use of vertical restraints by suppliers relates to their presumed efficiency and necessity. Proponents of the positive effects of vertical restraints, such as RPM to competition, often argue that higher margins to the retailers will incentivize them to increase their pre-sales services and will therefore lead output to expand and consumer welfare to increase.[368] Other authors have criticized this argument by showing that consumer welfare may decline even if output is increased, the net welfare consequence depending on the nature of the demand shift induced by the provision of pre-sale services and the magnitude of that shift.[369]

One may advance the familiar distinction between marginal and infra-marginal consumers. Marginal consumers value the additional pre-sale services provided by the retailers, hence they may switch to the specific product/service from other products/services with which the specific supplier competes in the market. The additional costs to the supplier generated by the

366 P Rey and T Vergé, 'Resale Price Maintenance and Interlocking Relationships' (2010) 58 *J Industrial Economics* 928.

367 M Armstrong 'Price Discrimination' in P Buccirossi (ed) *Handbook of Antitrust Economics* (MIT Press, 2008); P Rey and T Vergé, 'Vertical Restraints in European Competition Policy' (2014) 4 *Concurrences* 44, 50.

368 See RH Bork, 'Resale Price Maintenance and Consumer Welfare' (1968) 77 *Yale LJ* 950.

369 FM Scherer, 'The Economics of Vertical Restraints' (1983) 52 *Antitrust LJ* 687; WS Comanor, 'Vertical Price Fixing and Market Restrictions and the New Antitrust Policy' (1995) 98 *Harvard L Rev* 990.

higher retail margins will enhance consumer welfare. Infra-marginal consumers do not value these additional expenses generated by the additional pre-sale services, as they would have bought the product even in the absence of pre-sale services. They end up, however, paying a higher price for the product as a result of the RPM scheme. The additional investment on pre-sales services will not correspond to the infra-marginal consumers' preferences. The consumers mostly interested in pre-sale services are indeed those being indifferent whether they purchase or not.[370]

Manufacturers may, however, consider only marginal consumers and ignore infra-marginal consumers, depending on whether the demand curve shifts with this additional investment on pre-sales services and whether the consumer surplus generated is mainly captured by the consumers that value pre-sale services. It has also been noted that the reasons suppliers use some forms of vertical restraints, such as RPM may not be linked to their efficiency, but may simply be explained by the fact that suppliers are boundedly rational and follow what other suppliers or market leaders do, even in the absence of any credible pro-competitive justification for these practices.[371] They are thus prone to overuse RPM, at times harming consumers. This excessive reliance on RPM may slowly diminish over time, as biased manufacturers are taught or disciplined by the market. The slow demise of this practice, however, may entail significant efficiency losses over many years.

10.5.3. VERTICAL RESTRAINTS AND THE PROBLEM OF INFERENCE

JC Cooper, LM Froeb, D O'Brien, and MG Vita, 'Vertical Antitrust Policy as a Problem of Inference', Federal Trade Commission (18 February 2005)

The legality of non-price vertical practices in the U.S. is determined by their likely competitive effects. An optimal enforcement rule combines evidence with theory to update prior beliefs, and specifies a decision that minimizes the expected loss. Because the welfare effects of vertical practices are theoretically ambiguous, optimal decisions depend heavily on prior beliefs, which should be guided by empirical evidence. Empirically, vertical restraints appear to reduce price and/or increase output. Thus, absent a good natural experiment to evaluate a particular restraint's effect, an optimal policy places a heavy burden on plaintiffs to show that a restraint is anticompetitive. [. . .]

To assess the competitive effects of a vertical restraint, one must compare the world with the restraint—which is observed—to the world without the restraint, which typically is not. In general, it is possible to draw inferences about the unobserved state of the world in either of two ways. If a 'natural experiment' mimics the effect of the restraint, one can compare a 'control group' (without the restraint) to an 'experimental group' (with the restraint) to gauge the effect of the practice. Provided one can hold constant other factors that might affect price, output, or other relevant variables, one can estimate the competitive effects of the restraint.

370 J Cooper, L Froeb, D O' Brien, and M Vita, 'Vertical Restrictions and Antitrust Policy: What about the Evidence?' (2005) 1 *Competition Policy Int'l* 45, 49.

371 A Tor and WJ Rinner, 'Behavioral Antitrust: A New Approach to the Rule of Reason after Leegin' (2011) *U Illinois L Rev* 805

Absent a good natural experiment, one must instead use an economic model of the restraint to help assess its competitive impact; i.e., the analyst must posit a theory under which the restraint can harm competition, against alternatives where the restraint is benign or procompetitive, and then determine which theory best explains the evidence. [. . .]

The outcome-based approach to antitrust ushered in by *Sylvania* in the United States (and gaining momentum in the EU) requires enforcement officials to demonstrate likely adverse effects on welfare. We view this primarily as a problem of inference: given the evidence, what is the probability that a given practice is anticompetitive? One approach to the inference problem is to set up 'screens' based on structural conditions like market share, where harm is presumed if the conditions are met. Unfortunately, the search for a screen that works well in all but a few well specified instances has proved elusive.

A second approach is one based on an economic model of the restraint; i.e., posit a theory under which the restraint in question can harm competition, against alternatives in which the restraint is benign or procompetitive, and then determine which theory best explains the available evidence. In this paper, we have argued that it is difficult to distinguish welfare enhancing from welfare-reducing vertical practices based on evidence because the theory of vertical control tells us only that anticompetitive effects are possible. Until theory can be used to determine how likely it is that a restraint will lead to an anticompetitive outcome, it does not give us a way to interpret evidence in most cases. In this world, enforcement decisions should be guided by prior beliefs and loss functions. Our review of the empirical evidenc—which informs our priors—suggests that vertical restraints are likely to be benign or welfare enhancing.

An aggressive enforcement policy, therefore, would have to be justified by relatively large type II error costs.

Given the current state of knowledge, we suggest that enforcement policy should be guided by a third approach: draw inferences about the competitive effects of the restraint from a natural experiment. The quality of the experiment and how closely it mimics the effect of the restraint would be issues for the court or decision maker to resolve.

10.6. THE APPLICATION OF ARTICLE 101(3) TFEU TO VERTICAL RESTRAINTS

M Brenning-Louko, A Gurin, L Peeperkorn, and K Viertiö, 'Vertical Agreements: New Competition Rules for the Next Decade'
(June 2010) 1 *CPI Antitrust J*

[Background to Regulation 330/2010]

On 20 April 2010 the Commission adopted a new Block Exemption Regulation applicable to vertical agreements[372] (hereinafter 'the Regulation'). At the same time it adopted the contents of accompanying Guidelines on vertical restraints,[373] which were subsequently formally adopted in all official languages of the Union by Vice-President Almunia on behalf of

372 Regulation 330/2010. 373 Guidelines on vertical restraints [2010] OJ C 130/1.

the Commission on 10 May 2010. Both of these instruments [have been] applicable from 1 June 2010 [. . .].

The new rules were adopted following a review process that was launched in the spring of 2008 because of the expiry of the Block Exemption Regulation of 1999 ('the 1999 Regulation') on 31 May 2010. The Commission services took stock of enforcement with the national competition authorities and a consensus was quickly reached confirming that the architecture put in place in 1999 had worked well and only needed some up-dating and clarification. This was subsequently confirmed by a public consultation which elicited a very high response rate.

The 1999 Regulation and Guidelines on vertical restraints formed the very first package of a new generation of block exemption regulations and guidelines inspired by a more economic and effects-based approach, which was subsequently implemented in other antitrust areas. Under this approach, in order to conduct a proper assessment of a vertical agreement, it is necessary to analyse its likely effects on the market. For companies lacking significant market power (i.e. whose market share is below 30 percent), the 1999 Regulation provided for a block exemption, because it is presumed that vertical agreements concluded between such companies will either have no anticompetitive effects or, if they do, that the positive effects will outweigh any negative ones. In contrast, for vertical agreements concluded by companies whose market share exceeds 30 percent, there is no such safe harbour, but there is no presumption that the agreement is illegal either: it is necessary to assess the agreement's negative effects and positive effects on the market (under Article 101(1) and Article 101(3), respectively). The 1999 Regulation was accompanied by Guidelines which assist companies in making this assessment, and which have proved particularly important since the discontinuation, in 2004, of the former notification system whereby companies had to notify their agreements to the Commission in order to obtain an exemption.

It was decided to maintain this architecture, but to adapt and update it in the light of two major developments since 1999, namely a considerable increase in online sales, and enforcers' increased attention to and experience with the possible anticompetitive effects of a buyer's market power.

10.6.1. THE SCOPE OF APPLICATION OF REGULATION 330/2010—ARTICLE 2

The block exemption regulation applies to vertical agreements regarding (i) the purchase/sale/resale of goods/services and (ii) concluded by undertakings at different levels of the market. It follows that the block exemption regulation does not apply to vertical agreements between competitors, nor for agreements on intellectual property (IP) rights. In addition, Article 2(5) of Regulation 330/2010 states that the Block Exemption Regulation does 'not apply to vertical agreements the subject matter of which falls within the scope of any other block exemption regulation, unless otherwise provided for in such a regulation'.

Guidelines on Vertical Restraints [2010] OJ C 130/1 (references omitted)

24. Article 1(1)(a) of the Block Exemption Regulation defines a 'vertical agreement' as 'an agreement or concerted practice entered into between two or more undertakings each of which operates, for the purposes of the agreement or the concerted

practice, at a different level of the production or distribution chain, and relating to the conditions under which the parties may purchase, sell or resell certain goods or services'.

25. The definition of 'vertical agreement' referred to in paragraph (24) has four main elements:

(a) *The Block Exemption Regulation applies to agreements and concerted practices.* The Block Exemption Regulation does not apply to unilateral conduct of the undertakings concerned. Such unilateral conduct can fall within the scope of Article 102 which prohibits abuses of a dominant position. [. . .] [*On the concept of agreement and concerted practice, see Chapter 5.*] The agreement or concerted practice is between two or more undertakings.

(b) *Vertical agreements with final consumers not operating as an undertaking are not covered by the Block Exemption Regulation.* More generally, agreements with final consumers do not fall under Article 101(1), as that article applies only to agreements between undertakings, decisions by associations of undertakings and concerted practices of undertakings. This is without prejudice to the possible application of Article 102.

(c) *The agreement or concerted practice is between undertakings each operating, for the purposes of the agreement, at a different level of the production or distribution chain.* This means for instance that one undertaking produces a raw material which the other undertaking uses as an input, or that the first is a manufacturer, the second a wholesaler and the third a retailer. This does not preclude an undertaking from being active at more than one level of the production or distribution chain.

(d) *The agreements or concerted practices relate to the conditions under which the parties to the agreement, the supplier and the buyer, 'may purchase, sell or resell certain goods or services'. This reflects the purpose of the Block Exemption Regulation to cover purchase and distribution agreements.* These are agreements which concern the conditions for the purchase, sale or resale of the goods or services supplied by the supplier and/or which concern the conditions for the sale by the buyer of the goods or services which incorporate these goods or services. Both the goods or services supplied by the supplier and the resulting goods or services are considered to be contract goods or services under the Block Exemption Regulation. Vertical agreements relating to all final and intermediate goods and services are covered. The only exception is the automobile sector, as long as this sector remains covered by a specific block exemption [. . .]. The goods or services provided by the supplier may be resold by the buyer or may be used as an input by the buyer to produce its own goods or services.

26. *The Block Exemption Regulation also applies to goods sold and purchased for renting to third parties.* However, rent and lease agreements as such are not covered, as no good or service is sold by the supplier to the buyer. More generally, the Block Exemption Regulation does not cover restrictions or obligations that do not relate to the conditions of purchase, sale and resale, such as an obligation preventing parties from carrying out independent research and development which the parties may have included in an otherwise vertical agreement. In addition, Article 2(2) to (5) of the Block Exemption Regulation directly or indirectly excludes certain vertical agreements from the application of that Regulation.

NOTES AND QUESTIONS[374]

1. To come within the group exemption and, indeed, to infringe Article 101(1), there must be collusion between 'undertakings'. Vertical agreements with final purchasers are subject to the competition rules only when the purchaser constitutes an undertaking (2010 Vertical Restraints Guidelines, para 2). A vertical agreement to buy a television set for the home is unlikely to be an agreement between undertakings, but an agreement whereby a hotel buys identical television sets for guests' bedrooms would amount to an agreement between undertakings within the meaning of Article 101, although it would be unlikely to have appreciable effects on competition or trade between Member States. Unlike the position under the earlier group exemptions, an agreement to which more than two undertakings are party may be exempt. For instance, a single contract may be made between the holder of a trademark, the supplier of the product and the customer, or between a supplier, a distributor for a single Member State and a wholesaler for a smaller region.
2. A vertical agreement supposes that each of the parties is 'operating for the purpose of the agreement, at a different level of the production or distribution chain'.[375] Even if a supermarket chain manufactures its own brand of chocolate biscuits and arranges to buy a brand of plain biscuits to sell in its stores, the agreement on plain biscuits qualifies as vertical: 'for the purpose of the agreement, the parties operate at different level of trade'. Whether the supermarket's own brand of chocolate biscuits competes with the plain biscuits would be relevant under Article 2(4) of Regulation 330/2010.
3. The exemption is not expressly limited to distribution: it applies to agreements and concerted practices relating to the conditions under which the parties may purchase, sell or resell certain goods or services ('vertical agreements').[376] According to the Vertical Guidelines,

   > this reflects the purpose of the Block Exemption Regulation to cover purchase and distribution agreements. These are agreements which concern the conditions for the purchase, sale or resale of the goods or services supplied by the supplier and/or which concern the conditions for the sale by the buyer of the goods or services which incorporate these goods or services. Both the goods or services supplied by the supplier and the resulting goods or services are considered to be contract goods or services under the Block Exemption Regulation. Vertical agreements relating to all final and intermediate goods and services are covered. The only exception is the automobile sector, as long as this sector remains covered by a specific block exemption.[377]

   The exemption seems to relate to terms under which the parties are restrained from further purchases and sales, arguably a wider category than distribution agreements. There is no reason expressed why this should be done only in a contract of sale made between one party, *A* to the other party, *B*. B may agree in a contract not of sale but a

[374] The following notes and questions draw partly on V Korah and D O'Sullivan, *Distribution Agreements under the EC Competition Rules* (Hart, 2002), 130–53.

[375] Regulation 330/2010, Article 1(a).

[376] Ibid, Article 1(a).

[377] Vertical Restraints Guidelines 2010, para 26(d).

copyright or trade-mark licence under which *B* agrees to duplicate disks and sell them under *A*'s mark, not to sell brands other than *A*'s, or *A* may promise not to make any direct sales within a territory in which *B* is interested. If the phrase were intended to relate only to the transaction of sale, there would be no need to refer to 'the conditions under which the parties may [. . .]'. It is however clear that the conditions must relate to purchase or sale. If *B*, an Internet service provider, were to need inter-connection not to the local loop of a telecoms operator whose share of the wires market would probably exceed 30 per cent, but to the wires of a cable company with a share of wires in the locality of less than 30 per cent, would the agreement relate to the conditions on which *B* might buy interconnection services or sell Internet services? The agreement would have to specify the terms on which *B* could inter-connect and whether he might take unbundled services. Those conditions would relate to the purchase or sale of services.

4. Article 2(4) excludes from the benefit of the exemption a number of distribution agreements entered into between 'competing undertakings' as defined in Article 1(a) of Regulation 330/2010, which includes potential competitors (Article 1(c)). However, if the agreement is non-reciprocal, if the buyer's turnover is below €100 million, or if the agreement concerns so-called 'dual distribution' of goods or services[378] then the block exemption will still apply.[379] These conditions exclude most distribution agreements between telecoms and other utilities (operators), for example, since even where the agreement for the supply of services is non-reciprocal, the buyer is usually also a provider of services at the same level as the supplier.
5. Article 1(a) includes in the scope of the exemption vertical agreements that give rise to restraints also relating to the conditions under which the parties may buy, sell or resell *goods or services*. Hence, it may apply to the supply of goods, such as components or raw materials, for incorporation in other products as well as to the supply of services. Neither rental and leasing agreements nor bartering agreements are covered by the Regulation. According to the Guidelines:

   The Block Exemption Regulation also applies to goods sold and purchased for renting to third parties. However, rent and lease agreements as such are not covered, as no good or service is sold by the supplier to the buyer. More generally, the Block Exemption Regulation does not cover restrictions or obligations that do not relate to the conditions of purchase, sale and resale, such as an obligation preventing parties from carrying out independent research and development which the parties may have included in an otherwise vertical agreement. In addition, Article 2(2) to (5) of the Block Exemption Regulation directly or indirectly excludes certain vertical agreements from the application of that Regulation.[380]

   Article 101 TFEU (and Chapter I CA98) may nevertheless apply to vertical agreements which do not themselves relate to purchase, sale or resale, although these may not be covered by the VBER. The recent *SIA Maxima Latvija* case provides an interesting example indicating that Article 101 TFEU may apply to agreements involving the lease of land (land agreements).[381] Land agreements also fall within the

378 Vertical Restraints Guidelines 2010, para 27.
379 See Section 9.6.1.1.
380 Vertical Restraints Guidelines 2010, para 26.
381 Case C-345/14, *SIA Maxima Latvija v Konkurences padome* [2015] ECLI:EU:C:2015:784.

scope of Chapter I UK CA98, their exclusion from the scope of Chapter I (although not from that of Chapter II CA98) between May 2000 and April 2011 being revoked by the Competition Act 1998 (Land Agreements Exclusion Revocation) Order 2011 with effect from 6 April 2011.[382] The OFT (the predecessor of CMA) has published guidance on the application of competition law following the revocation of the exclusion of land agreements from Chapter I CA98.[383] Although the OFT recognized that 'a minority of restrictions' in land agreements may infringe competition law it also held that two main categories of restrictions in land agreements are more likely to restrict competition:

First, if the parties to a land agreement are competitors in a relevant market and a restriction regarding the use of land is aimed at sharing or carving-up markets between those parties, the agreement is very likely to constitute a serious infringement of the Chapter I prohibition.

Second, other types of restriction may fall within the Chapter I prohibition if they have the effect of restricting competition by raising barriers to entry (or expansion) in a particular market where a party to the agreement is carrying out an economic activity and a restriction makes access to that market by other competitors more difficult. These types of restriction are unlikely to appreciably restrict competition unless one or more of the parties to the agreement possess 'market power' in a related market. Market power is the ability to maintain prices above competitive levels or to maintain output in terms of product quantities, product quality, and variety or innovation below competitive levels for a not insignificant period of time.[384]

Usually, competition authorities are ready to take action in cases involving land agreements, such as the lease of the outlet from which the commercial activity is exercised, if any of the parties dispose of a market share exceeding 30 per cent on one of the relevant markets, either the upstream market for land, downstream, or related market involving the economic activity where the land affected by the agreement is used.[385]

6. Article 2(2) of Regulation 330/2010 exempts certain distribution agreements entered into between an association of retailers and its members or suppliers. This exemption is provided for without prejudice to the question of whether the association's horizontal activities are compatible with Article 101(1) or Article 101(3) TFEU.[386] Article 2(2) provides that *vertical* agreements entered into between such an association of retailers and its suppliers or its members may benefit from the block exemption under certain conditions.[387] The concept of retailers is defined by the 2010 Vertical Guidelines as 'distributors reselling goods to final consumers';[388] hence, any undertaking purchasing goods for its own use will not qualify as a retailer.

382 By virtue of the Competition Act 1998 (Land Agreements Exclusion Revocation) Order 2010 (SI 2010/1709). Planning obligations continue to benefit from exclusion from the Chapter I prohibition. One may find useful information for the definition of the relevant market when land agreements are involved in the OFT's (now CMA) Guidance on Land Agreements by virtue of CA98, Schedule 3, para 1.

383 See OFT 1280a, Land Agreements (March 2011), available at www.gov.uk/government/uploads/system/uploads/attachment_data/file/284406/land-agreements-guideline.pdf (also adopted by the UK CMA).

384 See ibid, paras 1.8 and 1.9.

385 See ibid, para 1.22 (also adopted by the UK CMA).

386 See Section 7.3.

387 See Section 9.6.1.1.

388 Vertical Restraints Guidelines 2010, para 29.

7. Unlike the block exemption regulations preceding Regulation 2790/99, the Regulation 330/2010 applies whether or not there are more than two undertakings, provided that none of them competes with any of the others. It is often sensible to have tripartite registered user agreements between a brand owner, a manufacturer, and a distributor. Additional parties no longer prevent the application of the exemption. As long as none of the parties is an actual or potential competitor at any level of trade, there is no reason of policy to exclude multipartite agreements. For the supplier to make a single agreement with two distributors, who each agree not to make active sales into the other's territory, however, would be excluded by Article 2(4) (agreements between competing undertakings). Two contracts independent of each other, one with each dealer, would not be excluded.
8. Paragraph 27 of the vertical restraints guidelines stipulates that the horizontal aspects of agreements between competitors fall to be considered under the Horizontal Guidelines, while the vertical aspects are dealt with in the Guidelines on Vertical Restraints. Paragraph 30 of the vertical restraints guidelines indicates the order in which the respective horizontal and vertical elements of agreements concerning a retailers' association should be assessed. In the Commission's opinion, one should first consider any horizontal elements, under the Horizontal Guidelines. If this assessment indicates that the cooperation as such is permissible, then the association's vertical agreements must be considered in the light of Regulation 330/2010 and of the Guidelines on Vertical Restraints. The Commission notes that '[o]nce that assessment leads to the conclusion that the horizontal agreement is not anticompetitive, an assessment of the vertical agreements between the association and individual members or between the association and suppliers is necessary.'

10.6.1.1. Vertical agreements between competitors

Guidelines on Vertical Restraints [2010] OJ C 130/1 (references omitted)

Read paragraphs 27–30 (association of retailers).

M Brenning-Louko, A Gurin, L Peeperkorn, and K Viertiö, 'Vertical Agreements: New Competition Rules for the Next Decade' (June 2010) (1) CPI Antitrust J

[. . .]

Vertical Agreements between Competitors

As a general rule, neither Regulation 2790/99, nor Regulation 330/2010 cover vertical agreements entered into between competitors. Agreements between competitors, also for the distribution of each others' products, are first and foremost assessed as horizontal agreements. However, the 1999 Regulation did cover a limited number of situations of non-reciprocal vertical agreements between competitors. There are two changes in the Regulation with regard to the coverage of vertical agreements between competitors, both of which set further limits on the scope of the Regulation. First, the 1999 Regulation covered situations in which a producer sold its products to a competing producer that distributed them, as long as the turnover of the latter did not exceed EUR 100 million. This exception has now been removed, because experience shows that, in certain markets, a EUR 100 million company may be the main local or national producer and thus a major competitor. As a result of this change, such agreements fall outside the scope of the Regulation and will have to be assessed as horizontal agreements. Secondly, not just for goods but also for services, the Regulation's coverage of vertical agreements between competitors is now limited to situations of dual distribution, i.e. where the buyer is active at the distribution level only.[389] For instance, if a brewer operates its own pubs and thus is active at the retail level, its agreements to supply its beer to independent pubs fall within the scope of the Regulation. The same applies to a franchisor's agreements providing services to its franchisees while also operating its own shops.

10.6.1.2. IP Rights involved in vertical agreements

Article 2 of Regulation 330/2010 sets out the various agreements which can benefit from the block exemption. By definition, other distribution arrangements fall outside the 'safe harbour' of this Regulation. Of these distribution arrangements which do not involve 'vertical agreements' as defined in the BER, two types in particular give cause for concern: (i) agreements in which intellectual property rights are an important element and (ii) (industrial) franchising of well-known brands.

Article 2(3) of Regulation 330/2010 exempts certain vertical agreements containing provisions as to IP rights assigned to or used by the buyer. This applies where those provisions are not the 'primary object' of the agreement, and where they relate to the use, sale, or resale of goods or services by the buyer or its customers. The provisions are exempted only in so far as they do not have the same object or effect as other vertical restraints not exempted by the BER. There are thus five grounds why an agreement with provisions concerning IP rights may fall outside the 'safe harbour'.

Guidelines on Vertical Restraints [2010] OJ C 130/1 (references omitted)

Vertical agreements containing provisions on intellectual property rights (IPRs)

31. Article 2(3) of the Block Exemption Regulation includes vertical agreements containing certain provisions relating to the assignment of IPRs to or use of IPRs by the buyer in its application and thereby excludes all other vertical agreements containing IPR provisions from the Block Exemption Regulation. The Block Exemption Regulation applies to vertical agreements containing IPR provisions where five conditions are fulfilled:

(a) The IPR provisions must be part of a vertical agreement, that is, an agreement with conditions under which the parties may purchase, sell or resell certain goods or services;

389 Previously, the requirement that the buyer is only active at the distribution level did not apply to services.

(b) The IPRs must be assigned to, or licensed for use by, the buyer;

(c) The IPR provisions must not constitute the primary object of the agreement;

(d) The IPR provisions must be directly related to the use, sale or resale of goods or services by the buyer or its customers. In the case of franchising where marketing forms the object of the exploitation of the IPRs, the goods or services are distributed by the master franchisee or the franchisees;

(e) The IPR provisions, in relation to the contract goods or services, must not contain restrictions of competition having the same object as vertical restraints which are not exempted under the Block Exemption Regulation.

32. Such conditions ensure that the Block Exemption Regulation applies to vertical agreements where the use, sale or resale of goods or services can be performed more effectively because IPRs are assigned to or licensed for use by the buyer. In other words, restrictions concerning the assignment or use of IPRs can be covered when the main object of the agreement is the purchase or distribution of goods or services.

33. The first condition makes clear that the context in which the IPRs are provided is an agreement to purchase or distribute goods or an agreement to purchase or provide services and not an agreement concerning the assignment or licensing of IPRs for the manufacture of goods, nor a pure licensing agreement. The Block Exemption Regulation does not cover for instance:

(a) agreements where a party provides another party with a recipe and licenses the other party to produce a drink with this recipe;

(b) agreements under which one party provides another party with a mould or master copy and licenses the other party to produce and distribute copies;

(c) the pure licence of a trade mark or sign for the purposes of merchandising;

(d) sponsorship contracts concerning the right to advertise oneself as being an official sponsor of an event;

(e) copyright licensing such as broadcasting contracts concerning the right to record and/or broadcast an event.

34. The second condition makes clear that the Block Exemption Regulation does not apply when the IPRs are provided by the buyer to the supplier, no matter whether the IPRs concern the manner of manufacture or of distribution. An agreement relating to the transfer of IPRs to the supplier and containing possible restrictions on the sales made by the supplier is not covered by the Block Exemption Regulation. That means, in particular, that subcontracting involving the transfer of know-how to a subcontractor does not fall within the scope of application of the Block Exemption Regulation. [. . .]. However, vertical agreements under which the buyer provides only specifications to the supplier which describe the goods or services to be supplied fall within the scope of application of the Block Exemption Regulation.

35. The third condition makes clear that in order to be covered by the Block Exemption Regulation, the primary object of the agreement must not be the assignment or licensing of IPRs. The primary object must be the purchase, sale or resale of goods or services and the IPR provisions must serve the implementation of the vertical agreement.

36. The fourth condition requires that the IPR provisions facilitate the use, sale or resale of goods or services by the buyer or its customers. The goods or services for use or resale are usually supplied by the licensor but may also be purchased by the licensee from a third supplier. The IPR provisions will normally concern the marketing of goods or services. An example would be a franchise agreement where the franchisor sells

goods for resale to the franchisee and licenses the franchisee to use its trade mark and know-how to market the goods or where the supplier of a concentrated extract licenses the buyer to dilute and bottle the extract before selling it as a drink.

37. The fifth condition highlights the fact that the IPR provisions should not have the same object as any of the hardcore restrictions listed in Article 4 of the Block Exemption Regulation or any of the restrictions excluded from the coverage of the Block Exemption Regulation by Article 5 of that Regulation [. . .].

38. Intellectual property rights relevant to the implementation of vertical agreements within the meaning of Article 2(3) of the Block Exemption Regulation generally concern three main areas: trade marks, copyright and know-how.

Trade mark

39. A trade mark licence to a distributor may be related to the distribution of the licensor's products in a particular territory. If it is an exclusive licence, the agreement amounts to exclusive distribution.

Copyright

40. Resellers of goods covered by copyright (books, software, etc.) may be obliged by the copyright holder only to resell under the condition that the buyer, whether another reseller or the end user, shall not infringe the copyright. Such obligations on the reseller, to the extent that they fall under Article 101(1) at all, are covered by the Block Exemption Regulation.

41. Agreements, under which hard copies of software are supplied for resale and where the reseller does not acquire a licence to any rights over the software but only has the right to resell the hard copies, are to be regarded as agreements for the supply of goods for resale for the purpose of the Block Exemption Regulation. Under that form of distribution, licensing the software only occurs between the copyright owner and the user of the software. It may take the form of a 'shrink wrap' licence, that is, a set of conditions included in the package of the hard copy which the end user is deemed to accept by opening the package.

42. Buyers of hardware incorporating software protected by copyright may be obliged by the copyright holder not to infringe the copyright, and must therefore not make copies and resell the software or make copies and use the software in combination with other hardware. Such use-restrictions, to the extent that they fall within Article 101(1) at all, are covered by the Block Exemption Regulation.

Know-how

43. Franchise agreements, with the exception of industrial franchise agreements, are the most obvious example of where know-how for marketing purposes is communicated to the buyer.[390] Franchise agreements contain licences of intellectual property rights relating to trade marks or signs and know-how for the use and distribution of goods or the provision of services. In addition to the licence of IPR, the franchisor usually provides the franchisee during the life of the agreement with commercial or

390 Paragraphs 43–5 apply by analogy to other types of distribution agreements which involve the transfer of substantial know-how from supplier to buyer.

technical assistance, such as procurement services, training, advice on real estate, financial planning etc. The licence and the assistance are integral components of the business method being franchised.

44. Licensing contained in franchise agreements is covered by the Block Exemption Regulation where all five conditions listed in paragraph (31) are fulfilled. Those conditions are usually fulfilled as under most franchise agreements, including master franchise agreements, the franchisor provides goods and/or services, in particular commercial or technical assistance services, to the franchisee. The IPRs help the franchisee to resell the products supplied by the franchisor or by a supplier designated by the franchisor or to use those products and sell the resulting goods or services. Where the franchise agreement only or primarily concerns licensing of IPRs, it is not covered by the Block Exemption Regulation, but the Commission will, as a general rule, apply the principles set out in the Block Exemption Regulation and these Guidelines to such an agreement.

45. The following IPR-related obligations are generally considered necessary to protect the franchisor's intellectual property rights and are, where these obligations fall under Article 101(1), also covered by the Block Exemption Regulation:

(a) an obligation on the franchisee not to engage, directly or indirectly, in any similar business;

(b) an obligation on the franchisee not to acquire financial interests in the capital of a competing undertaking such as would give the franchisee the power to influence the economic conduct of such undertaking;

(c) an obligation on the franchisee not to disclose to third parties the know-how provided by the franchisor as long as this know-how is not in the public domain;

(d) an obligation on the franchisee to communicate to the franchisor any experience gained in exploiting the franchise and to grant the franchisor, and other franchisees, a non-exclusive licence for the know-how resulting from that experience;

(e) an obligation on the franchisee to inform the franchisor of infringements of licensed intellectual property rights, to take legal action against infringers or to assist the franchisor in any legal actions against infringers;

(f) an obligation on the franchisee not to use know-how licensed by the franchisor for purposes other than the exploitation of the franchise;

(g) an obligation on the franchisee not to assign the rights and obligations under the franchise agreement without the franchisor's consent.

NOTES AND QUESTIONS

1. According to the first condition, in order to benefit from the block exemption, there must be a vertical agreement, which relates to the conditions under which the parties may purchase, sell, or resell goods or services. Pure licences of a trademark or know-how are not covered, as these do not relate to the conditions under which the parties purchase, sell, or resell goods or services, but just to the authorization of the use of the trademark or know-how. Such agreements will also be outside of the scope of the block exemption in view of Article 2(5) of the VBER, which prevents the application of Regulation 330/2010 where another block exemption is applicable and pure know how agreements are now covered by Block Exemption Regulation 316/2014 on transfer of technology agreements, in case these provisions are directly related to the

production of the contract products (also called ancillary provisions).[391] Paragraph 33 of the VBER gives five examples of agreements that would not benefit from the exemption under Regulation 330/2010.

2. According to the second condition, Article 2(3) VBER applies only where the supplier transfers IP rights to the buyer and not when the buyer transfers IP rights to the supplier. Sub-contracting agreements, where the buyer transfers IP rights to the supplier are not covered by the block exemption. However, if the buyer provides specifications to the supplier (not IP rights), the VBER is applicable.
3. The IP rights must be directly related to the use, sale, or resale of goods or services by the buyer or its customers. According to paragraphs 43–5 of the Guidelines on Vertical Restraints, Regulation 330/2010 may apply to franchise agreements, since the IP rights provisions are directly related to the use, sale or resale of goods and services by the franchisee. If a franchise agreement 'only or primarily' concerns licensing of IP rights, it would not be covered by the block exemption. Furthermore, according to the Commission's guidelines, industrial franchise agreements are not covered by the VBER. Industrial franchise agreements probably refer to trade-mark licence combined with a recipe or other secret, substantial, and recorded technical know-how, according to which the licensee produces something, as in *Moosehead/Whitbread.*[392] Since the franchisee will have to market that product, it could be argued that the trade-mark is related to the sale of goods by the buyer. It is not clear, however, that the trade-mark does 'not constitute the primary object of such agreements and are directly related to the [. . .] sale [. . .] of goods or services by the buyer or its customers' within the meaning of Article 2(3). They may, however, enter into the scope of the 316/2014 Block exemption regulation on transfer of technology agreements, in which case they will be excluded from the scope of Regulation 330/2010 by virtue of Article 2(5). The Guidelines provide in Paragraph 45 more information on a series of typical IP rights-related obligations found in franchise agreements that would benefit from the block exemption.

10.6.2. THE SCOPE OF THE EXEMPTION

In addition to these conditions, *three conditions* must be met for the Block Exemption to apply:

- absence of market power, that is, both parties to the agreement should have a market share below *30 per cent* (market share cap)—Article 3 of Regulation 330/2010;
- the agreement does not contain any '*hardcore*' restrictions (eg RPM)—Article 4 of Regulation 330/2010;
- any '*impermissible*' restrictions must be severable from the rest of the agreement (eg non-compete obligations)—Article 5 of Regulation 330/2010.

391 This is examined in the companion volume, I Lianos, *Competition Law and the Intangible Economy* (OUP, forthcoming 2019).

392 *Moosehead/Whitbread* (Case IV/32.736) Commission Decision 90/186/EEC [1991] OJ L 100/32, [1991] 4 CMLR 391.

10.6.2.1. The market share cap: Article 3 of Regulation 330/2010

The previous vertical restraints guidelines, adopted by the Commission in 2000, recognized that 'for most vertical restraints, competition concerns can only arise if [. . .] there is some degree of market power at the level of the supplier or the buyer or at both levels'.[393] The market position of the buyer was also one of the parameters considered in the analysis of vertical restraints under Article 101(1), the Commission noting that 'the effect of buying power on the likelihood of anti-competitive effects is not the same for the different vertical restraints' and it has particularly negative effects in case of restraints from the limited distribution and market partitioning groups such as exclusive supply, exclusive distribution, and quantitative selective distribution.[394] However, retailer power was not the focus of the analysis under the block exemption regulation: a vertical agreement between a powerful retailer and a weaker supplier could pass through the 30 per cent market share threshold that conditioned the application of the block exemption regulation, in the absence of hardcore restraints on competition.

One should make a distinction between the two dimensions of retailer market power, that is, their ability to affect one of the parameters of competition (price, quality, innovation, consumer choice) profitably. Retailers may dispose of buying power but also of selling power. Buying power is exercised upstream to suppliers. It is characterized as 'countervailing buying power' in case the supplier disposes of market power. If there is only one buyer, it takes the form of a monopsony.[395] Selling power is exercised downstream to the retailers' customers, for example final consumers. In most cases, buying and selling power are interlinked: a supermarket chain with selling power has also an important buying power, as it becomes the principal gateway for the suppliers' products. This is not always the case of course, as some retailers may have a local selling power, because they are the only retail outlet within a specific geographical community, but do not dispose buying power, because the supplier operates at the national level.

Regulation 330/2010 takes into account retailer market power. It adds in its Article 3 a second market share threshold for falling within the scope of the block exemption regulation, based not only on the market share held by the supplier, but also on that held by the buyer. In its first draft of the block exemption regulation, the Commission chose a general formulation of this rule and provided the exemption from the application of Article 101(1), 'on condition that the market share held by each of the undertakings party to the agreement does not exceed 30% *on any* of the relevant markets affected by the agreement'.[396] The block exemption regulation provides a safe harbour for agreements only if neither party (supplier, retailer) has a market share above 30 per cent. However, as some of the contributions to the consultation process noted, such a broad definition could encompass both dimensions of retailer market power and could indeed cover also circumstances of retailer selling power, adding the 'practical difficulty for a supplier to estimate the market share of each and every buyer forming part of its distribution system across the EU', as 'it is not unusual [. . .] for a supplier to appoint hundreds, if not thousands, of distributors in the E.U.' and 'it may often not be possible for the supplier just to assume, as a methodological short-cut, that the buyer operates on a relevant market with the same product and geographic scope as the supplier, given that downstream

393 Vertical Restraints Guidelines 2000, para 6.

394 Ibid, para 125.

395 See RD Blair and JL Harrison, *Monopoly in Law and Economics* (CUP, 2010).

396 Regulation 330/2010, Article 3.

distribution markets may frequently be broader in product terms but much narrower in geographic terms'.[397]

The final text of the block exemption regulation and the guidelines take into account some of these concerns. According to Article 3 of Regulation 330/2010, the exemption applies on condition that the market share held by the buyer does not exceed 30 per cent 'of the relevant market on which he *purchases* the contract goods or services'. The regulation thus emphasizes the buying dimension of retailer power, not its selling side, which would have led to practical difficulties for business in terms of compliance to the regulation. Block Exemption will only apply for as long as the market share threshold continues to be met. It becomes thus important to ensure on-going careful monitoring of relevant market shares. Regulation 330/2010 includes, however, some exceptions which cover temporary increases above 30 per cent threshold—see Article 7(d) and (e)—but these are only available in limited circumstances.

10.6.2.2. Hardcore restrictions: Article 4 of Regulation 330/2010

Article 4 of Regulation 330/2010 contains a list of hardcore restrictions, in particular restraints on the buyer's ability to determine its sale price and certain types of (re)sale restrictions. These are considered serious restrictions of competition that should in most cases be prohibited because of the harm they cause to consumers. The consequence of including such a hardcore restriction in an agreement is that the whole vertical agreement is excluded from the scope of application of the Regulation.[398] In addition, in these cases there is a double presumption, namely that the agreement will have actual or likely negative effects and therefore fall within Article 101(1), and it will not have positive effects that fulfil Article 101(3).

This is, however, rebuttable: in individual cases, the parties can bring forward evidence under Article 101(3) that their agreement leads, or is likely to lead to efficiencies that outweigh the negative effects.[399] Where this is the case, the Commission is required to effectively assess (rather than just presume) the likely negative impact on competition before making a final assessment of whether the conditions of Article 101(3) are fulfilled.

According to paragraph 47 of the Guidelines on Vertical Restraints,

> Article 4 of the Block Exemption Regulation contains a list of hardcore restrictions which lead to the exclusion of the whole vertical agreement from the scope of application of the Block Exemption Regulation.[400] Where such a hardcore restriction is included in an agreement, that agreement is presumed to fall within Article 101(1). It is also presumed that the agreement is unlikely to fulfil the conditions of Article 101(3), for which reason the block exemption does not apply. However, undertakings may demonstrate pro-competitive effects under Article 101(3) in an individual case.[401] Where the undertakings substantiate that likely efficiencies result from

397 I Van Bael and F Bellis, 'Comments on the Draft Vertical Agreements Block Exemption and Guidelines on Vertical Restraints', 1–2, available at ec.europa.eu/competition/consultations/2009_vertical_agreements/vanbaelbellis_en.pdf.

398 Vertical Restraints Guidelines 2010, para 47.

399 See, in particular, ibid, paras 63–4 that provide some examples of a possible efficiency defence for hardcore (re)sales restrictions; ibid, paras 106–9 that describe in general possible efficiencies related to vertical restraints; and ibid, section VI.2.10 on resale price restrictions. For general guidance on this, see Guidelines on Article 101(3).

400 This list of hardcore restrictions applies to vertical agreements concerning trade within the Union.

401 See Vertical Restraints Guidelines 2010, esp paras 106–9, describing in general possible efficiencies related to vertical restraints and section VI.2.10 on resale price restrictions. See for general guidance on this Guidelines on Article 101(3).

> including the hardcore restriction in the agreement and demonstrate that in general all the conditions of Article 101(3) are fulfilled, the Commission will be required to effectively assess the likely negative impact on competition before making an ultimate assessment of whether the conditions of Article 101(3) are fulfilled.[402]

This means that the usual order of bringing forward evidence is reversed in the case of a hardcore restriction.

Furthermore, according to the Guidelines on Vertical Restraints, '[t]his list of hardcore restrictions applies to vertical agreements concerning trade within the Union. In so far as vertical agreements concern exports outside the Union or imports/re-imports from outside the Union see judgment of the Court of Justice in *Javico v Yves Saint Laurent*.'[403] In that judgment the CJEU held in paragraph 20 that 'an agreement in which the reseller gives to the producer an undertaking that it will sell the contractual products on a market outside the Community cannot be regarded as having the object of appreciably restricting competition within the common market or as being capable of affecting, as such, trade between Member States.'[404] There are five types of hardcore restrictions:

- resale price maintenance;
- absolute territorial restraints or restraints on resale to customers;
- restraints on resale in a selective distribution system;
- restraints on cross supplies in a selective distribution system; and
- restraints on supply of spare parts.

If you include any hardcore restraint in a vertical agreement, then the whole agreement will be excluded from the Block Exemption.

10.6.2.2.1. Resale price maintenance: Article 4(a) of Regulation 330/2010

Guidelines on Vertical Restraints [2010] OJ C-130/1 (references omitted)

> 48. The hardcore restriction set out in Article 4(a) of the Block Exemption Regulation concerns resale price maintenance (RPM), that is, agreements or concerted practices having as their direct or indirect object the establishment of a fixed or minimum resale price or a fixed or minimum price level to be observed by the buyer. In the case of contractual provisions or concerted practices that directly establish the resale price, the restriction is clear cut. However, RPM can also be achieved through indirect means. Examples of the latter are an agreement fixing the distribution margin, fixing the maximum level of discount the distributor can grant from a prescribed price level, making the grant of rebates or reimbursement of promotional costs by the supplier subject to the observance of a given price level, linking the prescribed resale price to the resale prices of competitors, threats, intimidation, warnings, penalties, delay or suspension of deliveries or contract terminations in relation to observance of a given price level.

402 Although, in legal terms, these are two distinct steps, they may in practice be an iterative process where the parties and Commission in several steps enhance and improve their respective arguments.
403 Case C-306/96, *Javico v Yves Saint Laurent* [1998] ECR I–1983.
404 Vertical Restraints Guidelines 2010, para 47 n 5.

> Direct or indirect means of achieving price fixing can be made more effective when combined with measures to identify price-cutting distributors, such as the implementation of a price monitoring system, or the obligation on retailers to report other members of the distribution network that deviate from the standard price level. Similarly, direct or indirect price fixing can be made more effective when combined with measures which may reduce the buyer's incentive to lower the resale price, such as the supplier printing a recommended resale price on the product or the supplier obliging the buyer to apply a most-favoured-customer clause. The same indirect means and the same 'supportive' measures can be used to make maximum or recommended prices work as RPM. However, the use of a particular supportive measure or the provision of a list of recommended prices or maximum prices by the supplier to the buyer is not considered in itself as leading to RPM.
>
> 49. In the case of agency agreements, the principal normally establishes the sales price, as the agent does not become the owner of the goods. However, where such an agreement cannot be qualified as an agency agreement for the purposes of applying Article 101(1) (see paragraphs (12) to (21)) an obligation preventing or restricting the agent from sharing its commission, fixed or variable, with the customer would be a hardcore restriction under Article 4(a) of the Block Exemption Regulation. In order to avoid including such a hardcore restriction in the agreement, the agent should thus be left free to lower the effective price paid by the customer without reducing the income for the principal.[405]

Outside the safe harbour of the Block Exemption, the parties have to carry out a detailed assessment under Article 101(3). Indeed, the 2010 Guidelines recognize that in some circumstances RPM restrictions in a vertical agreement may lead to 'efficiencies' which outweigh any anti-competitive effects. Note, nonetheless, how difficult would the standard of proof be for the defendants, should they wish to benefit from an individual exemption under Article 101(3) TFEU.

Guidelines on Vertical Restraints [2010] OJ C 130/1 (references omitted)

> 223. As [previously] explained resale price maintenance (RPM), that is, agreements or concerted practices having as their direct or indirect object the establishment of a fixed or minimum resale price or a fixed or minimum price level to be observed by the buyer, are treated as a hardcore restriction. Where an agreement includes RPM, that agreement is presumed to restrict competition and thus to fall within Article 101(1). It also gives rise to the presumption that the agreement is unlikely to fulfil the conditions of Article 101(3), for which reason the block exemption does not apply. However, undertakings have the possibility to plead an efficiency defence under Article 101(3) in an individual case. It is incumbent on the parties to substantiate that likely efficiencies result from including RPM in their agreement and demonstrate that all the conditions of Article 101(3) are fulfilled. It then falls to the Commission to effectively assess the likely negative effects on competition and consumers before deciding whether the conditions of Article 101(3) are fulfilled.

405 See eg *Eirpage* (Case IV/32.737) Commission Decision 91/562/EEC [1991] OJ L 306/22, in particular Recital 6.

The Commission notes that RPM may restrict competition in a number of ways: (i) it may facilitate collusion between suppliers; (ii) it may eliminate intra-brand price competition, also facilitating collusion between the buyers, that is, at the distribution level; (iii) it may more generally soften competition between manufacturers and/or between retailers, in particular when manufacturers use the same distributors to distribute their products and RPM is applied by all or many of them; (iv) it may prevent some or all distributors from lowering their sales price for that particular brand, thus increasing the price; (v) it may 'lower the pressure on the margin of the manufacturer, in particular where the manufacturer has a commitment problem, that is, where it has an interest in lowering the price charged to subsequent distributors';[406] (vi) it may be implemented by a manufacturer with market power to foreclose smaller rivals; and, finally, (vii) it may reduce dynamism and innovation at the distribution level, by preventing more efficient retailers and new distribution formats, such as price discounters, from entering the market or acquiring sufficient scale with low prices.[407]

Although the communication of lists of recommended or maximum prices by the supplier to the retailers is not included in the black-listed hardcore restrictions, and therefore is exempted by the VBER, provided that the market share thresholds are not exceeded and this does not amount to a minimum or fixed retail price, resulting from pressure, threats and coercion, they may raise, in certain circumstances, some concerns with regard to Article 101 TFEU.[408] The development of e-commerce and the increased price transparency offered by price comparison websites may also allow companies to more easily monitor their prices at retail, most retailers also tracking the online prices of competitors through the use of automatic software programmes that help them adjust their own prices based on their competitors' observed prices. The recent Commission's Final Report on the e-Commerce Sector Inquiry recognizes that '[w]ith pricing software, detecting deviations from recommended retail prices takes a matter of seconds and manufacturers are increasingly able to monitor and influence retailers' price setting', the availability of 'real-time pricing information' being able to 'trigger automatized price coordination' that could raise competition concerns.[409] This increased online price transparency could also 'facilitate or strengthen collusion between retailers by making it easier to detect deviations from the collusive agreement' and 'reduce the incentives fro retailers to deviate from the collusive price.'[410]

The Commission also notes that minimum RPM may also bring efficiency gains, which need to be taken into account in the context of Article 101(3) TFEU (where a manufacturer introduces a new product or in the context of a coordinated short term low price campaign—two to six weeks in most cases—so as to allow retailers to provide (additional) pre-sales services, in particular in case of experience or complex products.[411]

In conclusion, as minimum RPM is a hardcore restriction, it does not benefit from the block exemption, there is a presumption of negative effects under Article 101(1) (as it is a restriction anti-competitive by object) and there is a presumption that it is unlikely that the conditions of Article 101(3) are fulfilled.[412]

406 Vertical Restraints Guidelines 2010, para 224. 407 Ibid.

408 Ibid, paras 226–9. The main concerns is that if a supplier has a strong market position, maximum or recommended resale prices may work as a focal point for the resellers and might be followed by most or all of them and/or that they may soften competition or facilitate collusion between suppliers. However, it is also recognized that they may be used to avoid double marginalization or to ensure that the brand in question competes more forcefully with other brands, including own label products, distributed by the same distributor.

409 European Commission, Final Report on the E-commerce Sector Inquiry, COM(2017) 229 final, para 13.

410 Ibid, para 33. 411 Vertical Restraints Guidelines 2010, para 225. 412 Ibid, para 47.

Nevertheless, paragraph 47 of the Guidelines on vertical restraints leaves open the possibility for undertakings to plead and substantiate an efficiency defence.[413] The order of bringing forward evidence and showing effects is reversed:

(i) likely efficiencies need to be shown by the firm

(ii) before the likely negative effects are shown by the authority.

The justification for such a rigorous competition law regime is that RPM produces some negative effects to competition (facilitation of collusion, elimination of intra-brand competition, loss of dynamism, and innovation from discounters).[414] There is also some empirical evidence that RPM lead to a sharp increase in retail prices, although it remains unclear if this by nature harms consumers, as this may be compensated by higher quality in distribution services.[415] By considering minimum RPM as a hardcore restriction, EU (and to a certain extent UK) competition law seems to acknowledge that the trade-off between higher prices, on one side, and higher quality, on the other side, is negative, in view of the existence of less restrictive alternatives to achieve higher distribution services. Hence, the choice of a

413 See eg ibid, para 225.

414 For a more detailed analysis of the economics of RPM, see OECD, *Resale Price Maintenance*, DAF/COMP(2008)37, available at www.oecd.org/daf/competition/43835526.pdf.

415 BS Yamey, *The Economics of Resale Price Maintenance* (Pitman, 1954) (finding that RPM has been associated primarily with dealer cartelization efforts); JF Pickering, *Resale Price Maintenance in Practice* (George Allen, 1966) (finding that following the passage the Restrictive Trade Practices Act, which led to a more prohibitive regime for RPM, in a sample of twenty-six food and non-food products, resale prices fell by 8 per cent for food products, the retail margins taken on certain branded groceries falling from about 20 to 14 or 15 per cent and that the resale prices on various non-food items fell by about 7 per cent); OFT 981, S Davies and M Olczak, An Evaluation of the Impact upon Productivity of Ending Resale Price Maintenance on Books, Report prepared for the OFT by the Centre for Competition Policy, University of East Anglia (February 2008) (finding that an industry wide agreement allowing publishers to set the retail prices of books caused harm by preventing the entry of innovative retail formats and protecting traditional retailers); P Biscourp, X Boutin, and T Vergé, 'The Effects of Retail Regulation on Prices: Evidence from the loi Galland' [2013] 123 *Economic J* 1279 (noting that a government regulation—the *loi Galland* in France—making it illegal for retailers to sell below cost and thus leading to an elimination of intra-brand competition, as do RPM clauses, led to an increase of prices); A MacKay and DA Smith, 'The Empirical Effects of Minimum Resale Price Maintenance on Prices and Output', Kilts Booth Marketing Series, Paper No 1-009 (16 June 2014), available at https://ssrn.com/abstract=2513533 (exploring the welfare effects of the rule of reason for RPM in some US states and finding that in states where RPM contracts were treated under the more relaxed rule-of-reason standard, prices increased and that, in aggregate, consumers were worse off in the rule-of-reason states); NJ Harris, 'Leegin's Effect on Price: An Empirical Analysis' [2013] 9 *J L Economic & Policy* 251 (finding evidence that the Leegin jurisprudence of the US Supreme Court increased prices for consumers although it also noted that increased prices did not harm consumers); T Overstreet, Bureau of Economics Staff Report to the FTC, 'Resale Price Maintenance: Economic Theories and Empirical Evidence' (November 1983), available at www.ftc.gov/sites/default/files/documents/reports/resale-price-maintenance-economic-theories-and-empirical-evidence/233105.pdf (finding that RPM in most cases increased the prices of products sold with RPM, although this was not always the case, but holding this evidence non conclusive as higher prices may not harm consumers and that concluding that RPM has been used in both socially desirable and undesirable ways.); PM Ippolito, 'Resale Price Maintenance: Empirical Evidence from Litigation' (1991) 34 *J L & Economics* 263 (finding that all of the cases reviewed appear to be consistent with at least one of the service-enhancing theories of minimum RPM); F Lafontaine and M Slade, 'Exclusive Contracts and Vertical Restraints: Empirical Evidence and Public Policy' (September 2005), available at https://warwick.ac.uk/fac/soc/economics/staff/academic/slade/wp/ecsept2005.pdf (finding that RPM lead to higher prices but also holding that when manufacturers choose to impose vertical restraints, they make themselves better off, but they also typically allow consumers to benefit from higher quality products and better service provision. In conclusion, 'the empirical evidence suggests that in fact a fairly relaxed antitrust attitude towards restraints may well be warranted').

presumptive illegality standard, that may nevertheless be rebutted under Article 101(3) TFEU if the defendant brings evidence that the conditions for individual exemption are satisfied.

10.6.2.2.2. Absolute territorial protection: Article 4(b) of Regulation 330/2010

The scope of the prohibited category

The condemnation of territorial restrictions under Article 101(1) TFEU was essentially motivated by the objective of achieving market integration[416] and the protection of intra-brand competition. Any form of territorial restriction could fall under the scope of EU competition law to the extent that all the constitutive elements of an infringement under Article 101 were established (in particular the existence of an agreement or a concerted practice).

Direct restrictions on exports, that is, provisions that oblige a reseller to sell only to customers in its contractual territory or prohibit them from selling to customers in other Member States outside its territory are considered, are by their nature, anti-competitive and an infringement of Article 101(1).[417] This is also the case for provisions preventing the reseller from advertising or offering the contractual good for sale, or establishing distribution outlets, in other Member States outside its territory. Territorial restrictions may also take the form of differential pricing (including by bonus schemes and discounts schemes) or 'dual pricing' clauses, with which the supplier charges its distributors different prices for the same or equivalent products dependent on their destination or place of sale within the EU,[418] product differentiation undertaken as part of an agreement[419] and restrictions as to the applicability of the manufacturer's warranty and after-sale services provision, if these are imposed by an

416 See our analysis in Chapter 2.

417 Case C-551/03 P, *General Motors BV v Commission* [2006] ECR I–3173; *PO/Yamaha* (Case IV/37.935) Commission Decision (16 July 2003), available at http://ec.europa.eu/competition/antitrust/cases/dec_docs/37975/37975_91_3.pdf.

418 Although the Commission prohibited 'dual pricing' practices in *Glaxo Wellcome and Others* (Cases COMP IV/36.957/F3, IV/36.997/F3, IV/37.121/F3, IV/37.138/F3, IV/37.380/F3) Commission Decision [2001] OJ L 302/1, qualifying the practice as a restriction of competition by object (although the Commission also examined the effects on the market of the dual pricing clauses). The qualification of such practice as a restriction of competition by object led to the annulment of the Commission's decision by the General Court in Case T-168/01, *GlaxoSmithKline Services* v *Commission* [2006] ECR II–2969. The GC focused instead on the possible anti-competitive effects of such a practice, finding that the Commission was right to find an anti-competitive effect, but that it had failed to carry out an adequate examination as to whether the conditions under Article 101(3)TFEU were met. On appeal, the CJEU, however, decided that the GC had made on this point an error of law, upholding the Commission's conclusion that the agreement was a restriction by object. However, the CJEU confirmed the GC's finding that the Commission had failed to conduct a full examination of the arguments put forward by GSK in relation to the exemption under Article 101(3) TFEU, and dismissed the appeal brought by the Commission. As a result of the judgment of the CJEU, the Commission Decision was rendered null and void, and the situation was to be regarded as if the Commission had never adopted it. The complainants, the European Association of Euro-Pharmaceutical Companies (EAEPC) and other stakeholders, formally requested that the Commission, on the basis of Article 265 TFEU, adopt a new decision in relation to the complaint in light of the CJEU judgment. The Commission assessed the complaint and, in view of its discretion to reject complaints that do not fall within its priorities, it reached the conclusion that the complaint lacked EU interest and thus had to be rejected (see *Glaxo Welcome* (Case COMP/AT.36957) Commission Decision C(2014) 3654 final, rejecting the complaint, available at http://ec.europa.eu/competition/antitrust/cases/dec_docs/36957/36957_612_6.pdf). Among the reasons that led it to take this decision, the Commission noted that the 'conduct at issue is not producing persisting effects' (ibid, 8). In a recent judgment, the General Court upheld the Commission's refusal to reinvestigate and its deprioritization of the complaint (Case T-574/14, *European Association of Euro-Pharmaceutical Companies (EAEPC) v Commission*, ECLI:EU:T:2018:605). National competition authorities have also stayed away from aggressive enforcement action against such dual pricing clauses in recent years.

419 Case T-43/92, *Dunlop Slazenger v Commission* [1994] ECR II–441.

agreement,[420] although restrictions on warranty may be valid within the context of a selective distribution system.[421]

Only contractual clauses imposing an 'absolute territorial protection' are considered as restrictive of competition by their nature and anti-competitive by their object. The distinction between absolute and relative territorial protection constitutes a rule of thumb in order to distinguish between those agreements that are most harmful to consumers. Absolute territorial protection leads to a complete elimination of intra-brand competition. It is impossible for any retailer established in another territory to resell the contractual goods to consumers established in the exclusive territory, either actively or passively (responding to orders by consumers). Relative territorial protection preserves some residual level of intra-brand competition on the market, as passive sales are still possible.

As a general rule, the Block Exemption will not apply where the agreement includes direct or indirect:

- restraints on the territory into which a buyer or distributor may sell the contract goods or services; or
- restraints on the customers to whom a buyer or distributor may sell the contract goods or services.

This is without prejudice to a restriction on the buyer's place of establishment (eg warehouses).

Guidelines on Vertical Restraints [2010] OJ C 130/1 (references omitted)

50. The hardcore restriction set out in Article 4(b) of the Block Exemption Regulation concerns agreements or concerted practices that have as their direct or indirect object the restriction of sales by a buyer party to the agreement or its customers, in as far as those restrictions relate to the territory into which or the customers to whom the buyer or its customers may sell the contract goods or services. This hardcore restriction relates to market partitioning by territory or by customer group. That may be the result of direct obligations, such as the obligation not to sell to certain customers or to customers in certain territories or the obligation to refer orders from these customers to other distributors. It may also result from indirect measures aimed at inducing the distributor not to sell to such customers, such as refusal or reduction of bonuses or discounts, termination of supply, reduction of supplied volumes or limitation of supplied volumes to the demand within the allocated territory or customer group, threat of contract termination, requiring a higher price for products to be exported, limiting the proportion of sales that can be exported or profit pass-over obligations. It may further result from the supplier not providing a Union-wide guarantee service under which normally all distributors are obliged to provide the guarantee service and are reimbursed for this service by the supplier, even in relation to products sold by other distributors into their territory.[422] Such practices are even more likely to be viewed as a restriction of the buyer's sales when used in conjunction with the implementation by the supplier of a monitoring system aimed

420 Case C-86/82, *Hasselblad (GB) Limited v Commission of the European Communities* [1984] ECR 883.

421 Case C-376/92, *Metro SB Grossmärkte GmbH & Co KG v Cartier SA* [1994] ECR I-15.

422 If the supplier decides not to reimburse its distributors for services rendered under the EU-wide guarantee, it may be agreed with these distributors that a distributor which makes a sale outside its allocated territory, will have to pay the distributor appointed in the territory of destination a fee based on the cost of the services (to be) carried out including a reasonable profit margin. This type of scheme may not be seen as a

> at verifying the effective destination of the supplied goods, such as the use of differentiated labels or serial numbers. However, obligations on the reseller relating to the display of the supplier's brand name are not classified as hardcore. As Article 4(b) only concerns restrictions of sales by the buyer or its customers, this implies that restrictions of the supplier's sales are also not a hardcore restriction [. . .]. Article 4(b) applies without prejudice to a restriction on the buyer's place of establishment. Thus, the benefit of the Block Exemption Regulation is not lost if it is agreed that the buyer will restrict its distribution outlet(s) and warehouse(s) to a particular address, place or territory.

There are, however, four exceptions to the general rule, depending on whether they authorize the supplier to restrict active and passive sales.

- '*Active*' sales involve directly approaching or specifically targeting particular customers.
- '*Passive*' sales involve responding to unsolicited requests from individual customers.[423]

The first exception in Article 4(b)(i) allows a supplier to restrict active sales by a buyer party to the agreement to a territory or a customer group which has been allocated exclusively to another buyer or which the supplier has reserved to itself. The supplier is allowed to combine the allocation of an exclusive territory and an exclusive customer group by for instance appointing an exclusive distributor for a particular customer group in a certain territory. Such protection of exclusively allocated territories or customer groups must, however, permit passive sales to such territories or customer groups. Hence, under this exception passive sales cannot be restricted

The other three exceptions allow for the restriction of *both* active and passive sales.

- It is permissible to restrict a wholesaler from selling to end users, which allows a supplier to keep the wholesale and retail level of trade separate. That exception does not exclude the possibility that the wholesaler can sell to certain end users, such as bigger end users, while not allowing sales to (all) other end users.
- It is permissible for a supplier to restrict an appointed distributor in a selective distribution system from selling, at any level of trade, to unauthorized distributors located in any territory where the system is currently operated or where the supplier does not yet sell the contract products (referred to as 'the territory reserved by the supplier to operate that system').
- The supplier is free to restrict a buyer of components, to whom the components are supplied for incorporation, from reselling them to competitors of the supplier. The term 'component' includes any intermediate goods and the term 'incorporation' refers to the use of any input to produce goods.

Restrictions on online sales

When Regulation 2790/1999 was adopted, Internet was still in its infancy, and is therefore mentioned nowhere in the Regulation and only mentioned in passing in the current Vertical Guidelines. At the moment of the adoption of Regulation 330/2010, it was ubiquitous, and has undoubtedly changed the distribution landscape as well as brought many advantages for

restriction of the distributors' sales outside their territory (see judgment of the Court of First Instance in Case T-67/01, *JCB Service v Commission* [2004] ECR II–49, paras 136–45).

423 See Vertical Restraints Guidelines 2010, para 51 on for a more extensive analysis of what constitutes an 'active' and a 'passive' sale.

the consumer and for competition. In the context of the review of the vertical rules, the treatment of Internet became a central topic. The starting point of the new Guidelines is that *every* distributor must be allowed to use the Internet to sell products. But there are a number of important exceptions: a supplier can, for example, restrict online sales in limited circumstances where an outright ban on online sales may be objectively necessary and fall outside the scope of Article 101 TFEU:

- The supplier can require 'quality standards' for the use of a website to resell his goods:

  This is relevant in particular for selective distribution although it is not entirely clear what will constitute acceptable 'quality standards'. What also about the use of third party platforms?
- The supplier can require distributors to have one or more brick and mortar shops as a condition for becoming a member of the distribution system, where the nature of the product requires it
- The supplier is allowed to impose restrictions on active sales by a distributor into an exclusive territory or to an exclusive customer group reserved to the supplier, or allocated to another distributor.

Guidelines on Vertical Restraints [2010] OJ C 130/1 (references omitted)

52. The internet is a powerful tool to reach a greater number and variety of customers than by more traditional sales methods, which explains why certain restrictions on the use of the internet are dealt with as (re)sales restrictions. In principle, every distributor must be allowed to use the internet to sell products. In general, where a distributor uses a website to sell products that is considered a form of passive selling, since it is a reasonable way to allow customers to reach the distributor. The use of a website may have effects that extend beyond the distributor's own territory and customer group; however, such effects result from the technology allowing easy access from everywhere. If a customer visits the web site of a distributor and contacts the distributor and if such contact leads to a sale, including delivery, then that is considered passive selling. The same is true if a customer opts to be kept (automatically) informed by the distributor and it leads to a sale. Offering different language options on the website does not, of itself, change the passive character of such selling. The Commission thus regards the following as examples of hardcore restrictions of passive selling given the capability of these restrictions to limit the distributor's access to a greater number and variety of customers:

(a) an agreement that the (exclusive) distributor shall prevent customers located in another (exclusive) territory from viewing its website or shall automatically re-rout its customers to the manufacturer's or other (exclusive) distributors' websites. This does not exclude an agreement that the distributor's website shall also offer a number of links to websites of other distributors and/or the supplier;

(b) an agreement that the (exclusive) distributor shall terminate consumers' transactions over the Internet once their credit card data reveal an address that is not within the distributor's (exclusive) territory;

(c) an agreement that the distributor shall limit its proportion of overall sales made over the Internet. This does not exclude the supplier requiring, without limiting the online sales of the distributor, that the buyer sells at least a certain absolute amount (in value or volume) of the products offline to ensure an efficient operation of its brick and mortar shop (physical point of sales), nor does it preclude the supplier from making sure that the online activity of the distributor remains consistent with the supplier's distribution model.[424] This absolute amount of required offline sales can be the same for all buyers, or determined individually for each buyer on the basis of objective criteria, such as the buyer's size in the network or its geographic location;

(d) an agreement that the distributor shall pay a higher price for products intended to be resold by the distributor online than for products intended to be resold offline. This does not exclude the supplier agreeing with the buyer a fixed fee (that is, not a variable fee where the sum increases with the realized offline turnover as this would amount indirectly to dual pricing) to support the latter's offline or online sales efforts.

53. A restriction on the use of the internet by distributors that are party to the agreement is compatible with the Block Exemption Regulation to the extent that promotion on the internet or use of the internet would lead to active selling into, for instance, other distributors' exclusive territories or customer groups. The Commission considers online advertisement specifically addressed to certain customers as a form of active selling to those customers. For instance, territory-based banners on third party websites are a form of active sales into the territory where these banners are shown. In general, efforts to be found specifically in a certain territory or by a certain customer group is active selling into that territory or to that customer group. For instance, paying a search engine or online advertisement provider to have advertisements displayed specifically to users in a particular territory is active selling into that territory.

54. However, under the Block Exemption the supplier may require quality standards for the use of the internet site to resell its goods, just as the supplier may require quality standards for a shop or for selling by catalogue or for advertising and promotion in general. This may be relevant in particular for selective distribution. Under the Block Exemption, the supplier may, for example, require that its distributors have one or more brick and mortar shops or showrooms as a condition for becoming a member of its distribution system. Subsequent changes to such a condition are also possible under the Block Exemption, except where those changes have as their object to directly or indirectly limit the online sales by the distributors. Similarly, a supplier may require that its distributors use third party platforms to distribute the contract products only in accordance with the standards and conditions agreed between the supplier and its distributors for the distributors' use of the internet. For instance, where the distributor's website is hosted by a third party platform, the supplier may require that customers do not visit the distributor's website through a site carrying the name or logo of the third party platform. [. . .]

56. [*Referring to Article 4(c) of Regulation 330/2010, but included here as it deals with restrictions on Internet sales*] [. . .] Within a selective distribution system the dealers should be free to sell, both actively and passively, to all end users, also with the help of the internet. Therefore, the Commission considers any obligations which dissuade appointed dealers from using the internet to reach a greater number and variety of customers by imposing criteria for online sales which are not overall equivalent to the criteria imposed for the sales from the brick and mortar shop as a hardcore restriction. This does not mean that the criteria imposed for online sales must be identical to those imposed for offline

424 See Vertical Restraints Guidelines 2010, paras 54 and 56.

> sales, but rather that they should pursue the same objectives and achieve comparable results and that the difference between the criteria must be justified by the different nature of these two distribution modes. For example, in order to prevent sales to unauthorised dealers, a supplier can restrict its selected dealers from selling more than a given quantity of contract products to an individual end user. Such a requirement may have to be stricter for online sales if it is easier for an unauthorised dealer to obtain those products by using the internet. Similarly, it may have to be stricter for offline sales if it is easier to obtain them from a brick and mortar shop. In order to ensure timely delivery of contract products, a supplier may impose that the products be delivered instantly in the case of offline sales. Whereas an identical requirement cannot be imposed for online sales, the supplier may specify certain practicable delivery times for such sales. Specific requirements may have to be formulated for an online after-sales help desk, so as to cover the costs of customers returning the product and for applying secure payment systems.

We have analysed in Section 10.4.4.3.1 how the scope of the expansive definition of the category of restrictions of competition by object that would include bans on Internet sales by retailers in a selective distribution system was narrowed down by the CJEU in *Coty*, where the Court held that suppliers of luxury goods can prohibit the members of their selective distribution system from making online sales through discernible third-party platforms, to the extent this is appropriate to preserve the luxury image of those goods, this prohibition being compatible with Article 101(1) TFEU and not a restriction of competition by object.[425] The CJEU distinguished between a platform ban which is permissible, as it only restricts a specific kind of online sale,[426] and an absolute ban on Internet sales, which is not permitted under Article 101(1) TFEU and which forms a restriction of competition by object following *Pierre Fabre*.[427] Part of the judgment of the CJEU (and of the Opinion of AG Wahl) concerned the interpretation of Article 4(b) and (c) of Regulation 330/2010, and how this could interact with the fact that a general clause prohibiting authorized distributors in a selective distribution system for luxury goods designed, primarily, to preserve the luxury image of those goods from using, in a discernible manner, third-party platforms for the online sale of the contract goods, was excluded by the CJEU from the scope of Article 101(1) TFEU.

Opinion of AG Wahl in Case C-230/16, *Coty Germany GmbH v Parfümerie Akzente GmbH*, ECLI:EU:C:2017:603

> 131. In effect, it must not be overlooked that the objective pursued by the exemption regulations adopted on the basis of Regulation No 19/65/EEC lies, in particular, in the need to allow the undertakings concerned to assess for themselves the compatibility of their conduct with the competition rules.

425 Ibid, para 51.

426 Ibid, para 52. See also the Opinion of AG Wahl in Case C-230/16, *Coty Germany GmbH v Parfümerie Akzente GmbH*, ECLI:EU:C:2017:603 (arguing that a supplier's restriction imposed on its authorized distributors in a selective distribution system to sell the contract products via third-party platforms, cannot, in the present state of development of e-commerce, be assimilated to an outright ban on or a substantial restriction of internet sales, in particular if authorized distributors are allowed to distribute the contract products via their own internet sites).

427 C-439/09, *PFDC* [2011] ECR I-9419.

132. The pursuit of that objective would be undermined if, for the purposes of classifying the measures adopted by undertakings as vertical agreements having as their 'object' the restriction of certain types of sales within the meaning of Article 4(b) and (c) of Regulation No 330/2010, those undertakings were required to conduct a sophisticated and thorough examination of the restrictive effects of those measures on competition in the light of the market situation and the position of those undertakings.

133. As I have already said, it is necessary to distinguish the exercise consisting in identifying a 'restriction of competition by object' within the meaning of Article 101(1) TFEU and the characterization, for the purposes of the application of a block exemption regulation, of certain types of conduct as hardcore restrictions—in this instance those referred to in Article 4(b) and (c) of Regulation No 330/2010.

134. The fact nonetheless remains that, in both cases, it is a matter of identifying the conduct that is presumed to be particularly harmful for competition by reference to the assessment of the immediate economic and legal context of the measures adopted by the undertakings.

135. In that regard, it should be borne in mind that the distinction between 'infringements by object' and 'infringements by effect' arises from the fact that certain forms of collusion between undertakings can be regarded, by their very nature, and taking the experience gained into account, as being harmful to the proper functioning of normal competition. As for the rationale of Article 4 of Regulation No 330/2010, which identifies a number of hardcore restrictions, it is based on the idea, set out in recital 10 of that regulation, that 'vertical agreements containing certain types of severe restrictions of competition such as minimum and fixed resale-prices, as well as certain types of territorial protection, should be excluded from the benefit of the block exemption established by this Regulation irrespective of the market share of the undertakings concerned'.

136. Thus, along the lines of the approach taken in the identification of a restriction by object within the meaning of Article 101(1) TFEU, it is necessary, in order to determine whether a contractual clause has as its 'object the restriction' of the territory into which, or of the customers to whom, the distributor may sell (Article 4(b) of Regulation No 330/2010), or of active or passive sales by the distributor to end users (Article 4(c) of that regulation), to refer to the terms of the contractual provisions concerned and to their objectives, examined in their immediate economic and legal context. I would point out, indeed, that the objective of facilitating the self-assessment exercise required of the undertakings concerned would be undermined if, in order to identify the hardcore restrictions within the meaning of Article 4 of Regulation No 330/2010, the undertakings had to carry out a thorough examination, employing, in particular, a counterfactual analysis, of the effects of the proposed measures on the structure and operational conditions of the market or markets concerned. [. . .]

138. [Article 4(b) of Regulation No 330/2010 and Article 4(c) of that regulation] must thus be seen as being intended to exclude from the benefit of the block exemption certain contractual clauses designed to restrict the territory into which, or the customers to whom, the distributor may sell. On the other hand, it seems to me that those provisions cannot be interpreted as excluding from the benefit of the block exemption restrictions that determine the methods whereby the products can be sold.

Having regard to the content, the objective, and the economic and legal context of the clause (paragraphs 145–9), the AG suggested that the prohibition imposed on the members of a selective distribution system who operate as retailers on the market from making use in a discernible manner of third undertakings for Internet sales does not constitute a restriction of the retailer's customers within the meaning of Article 4(b) of Regulation 330/2010.

Case C-230/16, *Coty Germany GmbH v Parfümerie Akzente GmbH*, ECLI:EU:C:2017:941

59. It is only if the referring court should find that a clause, such as that at issue in the main proceedings, restricts competition within the meaning of Article 101(1) TFEU that the question as to whether that clause can benefit from an exemption under Regulation No 330/2010 by reason of Article 101(3) TFEU may arise. It follows from the order for reference that the market share thresholds laid down in Article 3 of that regulation have not been exceeded. Therefore, that clause may benefit from the exemption provided for in Article 2 of that regulation.

60. However, Regulation No 330/2010 excludes from the benefit of the block exemption certain types of restrictions that are liable to have severely anticompetitive effects, irrespective of the market share of the undertakings concerned. Those restrictions are the hardcore restrictions set out in Article 4 of that regulation.

61. The block exemption provided for in Article 2 of Regulation No 330/2010 cannot, therefore, be applied to a prohibition such as that at issue in the main proceedings if it is one of those hardcore restrictions.

62. [. . .] [T]he referring court asks, in essence, whether Article 4 of Regulation No 330/2010 must be interpreted as meaning that, in circumstances such as those in the main proceedings, the prohibition imposed on the members of a selective distribution system for luxury goods, which operate as distributors at the retail level of trade, of making use, in a discernible manner, of third-party undertakings for internet sales constitutes a restriction of their customers, within the meaning of Article 4(b) of that regulation, or a restriction of passive sales to end users, within the meaning of Article 4(c) of that regulation.

63. In accordance with Article 4(b) and (c) of Regulation No 330/2010, the exemption laid down in Article 2 thereof does not apply to vertical agreements which have the object of restricting the territory into which, or the customers to which, a buyer party to the agreement can sell the contract goods or services, or restrict active or passive sales to end users by members of a selective distribution system operating at the retail level of trade.

64. It is therefore necessary to ascertain whether a contractual clause such as that at issue in the main proceedings restricts the customers to whom authorised distributors can sell the luxury goods at issue or whether it restricts authorised distributors' passive sales to end users.

65. In that respect, first of all, it must be recalled that, in contrast to the clause referred to in the case that gave rise to the judgment of 13 October 2011, *Pierre Fabre Dermo-Cosmétique* (C-439/09, EU:C:2011:649), the clause at issue in the present case does not prohibit the use of the internet as a means of marketing the contract goods [. . .]

66. Next, it is apparent from the documents before the Court that it does not appear possible to circumscribe, within the group of online purchasers, third-party platform customers.

67. Finally, it is also apparent from the documents before the Court that the selective distribution contract at issue in the main proceedings allows, under certain conditions, authorised distributors to advertise via the internet on third-party platforms and to use online search engines, with the result that [. . .] customers are usually able to find the online offer of authorised distributors by using such engines.

68. In those circumstances, even if it restricts a specific kind of internet sale, a prohibition such as that at issue in the main proceedings does not amount to a restriction of the customers of distributors, within the meaning of Article 4(b) of Regulation No 330/2010, or a restriction of authorised distributors' passive sales to end users, within the meaning of Article 4(c) of that regulation.

NOTES AND QUESTIONS ON ONLINE VERTICAL RESTRAINTS

1. The debate has focused very much on the requirements which suppliers can impose through selective distribution as regards Internet sales.[428] Currently, selective distribution authorizes suppliers to control both '*who is authorized*' as a reseller, and '*at what conditions*' he may sell. (This is so both for off-line and on-line sales.) Opponents of the current regime such as Internet platforms are reluctant to incur the costs implicit in a selective distribution system. They argue that the rules need to change. In their view, suppliers may otherwise deprive consumers of the benefits of the Internet, and the costs of the requirements of selective distribution will keep consumer prices high. They argue that
   - online restrictions of any kind should therefore be considered as hardcore restraints, and that
   - the 'consumer should have the choice', ie those who prefer buying products in a shop should go there, but there should equally be unrestricted possibilities to buy the product online without having to pay the costs inherent in the requirements of selective distribution. These arguments are largely reminiscent of those made years ago by cash-and carry shops, etc, against selective distribution.
2. Do you think there are any reasons (eg market integration) that a specific retail distribution channel—the Internet—were treated differently than the others (supermarkets, department stores, specialist traders, mail order, etc)? Former EU competition commissionaire Neelie Kroes, explained the essence of her approach at the time of the renewal of the Guidelines on Vertical Restraints as follows: 'The internet gives more power to the individual than any technological change in history. We cannot let that power be taken away.'[429]
3. In the context of the Digital Single Market strategy, the Commission launched a sector inquiry into e-commerce in the EU, on the basis of Article 17 of Regulation 1/2013.[430] This provision enables the Commission to open investigations into sectors of the economy and into types of agreements, if there are some indications that competition may be restricted. Although the Commission cannot adopt remedies, it publishes a report, which informs its subsequent enforcement action under Article 101 and/or 102 TFEU. The aim of the e-sector inquiry was to allow the Commission to gather data on the functioning of e-commerce markets so as to identify possible restrictions of competition, in particular with regard to cross-border online trade, the Commission's

428 See our further analysis in Section 10.8.1.

429 N Kroes, 'Making Online Commerce a Reality' (17 September 2008), available at http://europa.eu/rapid/press-release_SPEECH-08-437_en.htm.

430 See European Commission, Sector inquiry into e-commerce, available at ec.europa.eu/competition/antitrust/sector_inquiries_e_commerce.html.

findings being merely based on surveys of companies present in the sector. A Final report on the E-commerce Sector Inquiry was published in May 2017,[431] complemented by a lengthy Commission Staff Working Document analysing the findings of the Commission.[432] The Commission has also published in March 2016 a separate issues paper relating to geo-blocking,[433] a practice which has been examined in more detail in Chapter 2.

4. The Final Report and the Commission Staff Working Paper examine, among other things, whether restrictions on the use of marketplaces or price comparison tools can amount to a restriction of competition by object. The Report was published before the CJEU's judgment in *Coty* but the findings of the sector inquiry did not show that absolute marketplace bans generally amounted to a *de facto* prohibition to sell online and it was held that '[m]arketplace bans should not therefore be equated to a *de facto* prohibition to sell via the internet similar to the restriction at stake in the *Pierre Fabre* judgment, a position that is similar to that taken by the CJEU in *Coty*. The Staff Working Paper also took the view that restrictions on the use of marketplaces 'do not have as their object a restriction of the territory or the customers to whom the retailer in question may sell or the restriction of active or passive sales to end users', they are 'not aimed at segmenting markets in the internal market based on territory or customers',[434] and consequently an absolute ban on the use of marketplaces should not constitute a hardcore restriction under Article 4(b) or 4(c) of Regulation 330/2010.[435] However, the Staff Working Document also envisages the possibility that bans on the use of marketplaces may be found incompatible with EU competition law depending on the circumstances and notes that '[t]he Commission or a national competition authority may decide to withdraw the protection of the VBER in particular cases when justified by the market situation'.[436] The Commission cites as relevant circumstances the 'importance of marketplaces as an online sales channel in relation to the product and geographic market in question, the type of restrictions applied (absolute ban or qualitative criteria) as well as the credibility of brand protection considerations and the need for pre- and post-sale advice will be important elements in the analysis' or the fact that 'the manufacturer has accepted the marketplace operator as an authorised seller within its selective distribution agreement', the latter making brand protection considerations 'less convincing'.[437]

5. The e-commerce Sector Inquiry Report also considers the compatibility with Article 101 TFEU of bans to use price comparison tools, for which the Commission has not

431 European Commission, Final report on the E-commerce Sector Inquiry, COM(2017) 229 final (10 May 2017), available at http://ec.europa.eu/competition/antitrust/sector_inquiry_final_report_en.pdf.

432 European Commission, Commission Staff Working Document Accompanying the Report on the E-commerce Sector Inquiry, SWD(2017) 154 final [hereinafter Commission Staff Working Document E-commerce].

433 Commission Staff Working Document—Geo-blocking practices in e-commerce—Issues paper presenting initial findings of the e-commerce sector inquiry conducted by the Directorate-General for Competition, SWD(2016) 70 final (18 March 2016), available at http://ec.europa.eu/competition/antitrust/ecommerce_swd_en.pdf.

434 Commission Staff Working Document E-commerce, para 508. 435 Ibid, section 4.4.8.

436 European Commission, Final Report on the E-commerce Sector Inquiry, COM(2017) 229 final (10 May 2017), para 43.

437 Commission Staff Working Document E-commerce, paras 513–14.

taken a position in the Guidelines on Vertical Restraints.[438] Price comparison tools compare prices of different retailers and establish extensive price transparency in retail markets with standardized products. The actual sale takes place on the website of the (authorized) retailer. Their use can be prevented by absolute bans, or the prohibition of the use of brand names as search terms, among other practices. As it is noted in the Staff Working paper,

> [m]arketplaces and price comparison tools [. . .] differ in a number of respects, including the fact that no transaction takes place on the price comparison tool's website/app. Instead interested customers are being directed to the website of the (authorised) distributor from which the product can be purchased and which generally fulfils all the quality criteria requested by the manufacturer of the product (within its selective distribution system).
>
> Absolute price comparison tool bans may make it more difficult for (potential) customers to find the retailers' website and may thereby limit the (authorised) distributor's ability to effectively promote its online offer and generate traffic to its website. Such bans may also make it more difficult to attract (potential) customers outside the physical trading area of the retailer via online promotion. Absolute price comparison tool bans which are not linked to quality criteria therefore potentially restrict the effective use of the internet as a sales channel and may amount to a hardcore restriction of passive sales under Article 4 b) and 4 c) of the VBER. Restrictions on the usage of price comparison tools based on objective qualitative criteria are generally covered by the VBER.[439]

6. For a more extensive analysis of other forms of online vertical restraints, see Section S.10.8.1.

10.6.2.2.3. Restrictions on resale in a selective distribution system: Article 4(c) of Regulation 330/2010

The supplier cannot impose restraints in a selective distribution system, which prevents distributors from making active or passive sales to end users. However, he can prohibit a member of the system from operating out of an 'unauthorised place of establishment'. Remark that, following the case law of the CJEU in *Pierre Fabre Dermo-Cosmétique*, and the 2010 Guidelines on Vertical Restraints (paragraph 56), a website/the Internet will not be considered to be a 'place of establishment'.[440]

10.6.2.2.4. Restraints on cross-suppliers in a selective distribution system: Article 4(d) of Regulation 330/2010

According to the 2010 Vertical Restraints Guidelines, 'an agreement or concerted practice may not have as its direct or indirect object to prevent or restrict the active or passive selling of the contract products between the selected distributors'. This means that once distributors

438 Ibid, section 4.5.4. 439 Ibid, para 553.

440 On restrictions to the use of marketplaces in selective distribution systems, see subsection above on Article 4(b). See also the CJEU judgment in Case C-230/16, *Coty Germany GmbH v Parfümerie Akzente GmbH*, ECLI:EU:C:2017:941.

form part of a selective distribution network, they 'must remain free to purchase the contract products from other appointed distributors within the network, operating either at the same or at a different level of trade'. In practice, selective distribution cannot therefore be combined with 'vertical restraints aimed at forcing distributors to purchase the contract products exclusively from a given source'.[441]

10.6.2.2.5. Restraints that prevent or restrict end users, independent repairers, and service providers from obtaining spare parts directly from the manufacturer: Article 4(e) of Regulation 330/2010

This condition ensures that an agreement between a manufacturer of spare parts and a buyer that incorporates those parts into its own products (original equipment manufacturer (OEM)), may not, 'either directly or indirectly, prevent or restrict sales by the manufacturer of those spare parts to end users, independent repairers or service providers'.[442] An example of indirect restriction is when the supplier of the spare parts is restricted in supplying technical information and special equipment which are necessary for the use of spare parts by users, independent repairers or service providers. However, the OEM may require its own repair and service network to buy spare parts from it.

In these cases, the principle of severability will kick in: the Block Exemption can apply to the remaining part of the vertical agreement if it is severable from 'impermissible' restraints. Compare this outcome with the position with regard to hardcore restraints, where the whole agreement is excluded from the benefit of the Block Exemption regulation.

10.6.2.3. Severable, non-exempted obligations—Article 5 of Regulation 330/2010

Impermissible (but non-hardcore) restraints are listed in Article 5 of Regulation 330/2010. These include:

- any direct or indirect non-compete obligation, the duration of which is indefinite or exceeds five years (including tacit renewal). According to the Guidelines, '[n]on-compete obligations are arrangements that result in the buyer purchasing from the supplier or from another undertaking designated by the supplier more than 80 % of the buyer's total purchases of the contract goods and services and their substitutes during the preceding calendar year (as defined by Article 1(1)(d) of the Block Exemption Regulation), thereby preventing the buyer from purchasing competing goods or services or limiting such purchases to less than 20 % of total purchases'.[443]
- post-term non-compete obligations preventing the buyer from dealing in competing goods or services after the termination of the agreement, subject to certain exceptions.[444]
- restrictions concerning the sale of competing goods in a selective distribution system, in particular 'if the supplier prevents its appointed dealers, either directly or indirectly, from buying products for resale from specific competing suppliers, such an obligation cannot enjoy the benefit of the Block Exemption Regulation'. The aim pursued is to avoid a situation 'whereby a number of suppliers using the same selective distribution outlets

441 Vertical Restraints Guidelines 2010, para 58. 442 Ibid, para 59. 443 Ibid, para 66.
444 Ibid, para 68.

prevent one specific competitor or certain specific competitors from using these outlets to distribute their products (foreclosure of a competing supplier which would be a form of collective boycott).'[445]

The principle of severability will kick in: the Block Exemption can apply to the remaining part of the vertical agreement if it is severable from 'impermissible' restraints.[446] Compare this outcome with the position with regard to hardcore restraints, where the whole agreement is excluded from the benefit of the Block Exemption Regulation.

10.6.2.4. Flexibility tools: Withdrawal of the Block Exemption and disapplication regulations to deal with network agreements

In view of the changing circumstances of markets and their diversity, Regulation 3330/2010 includes some flexibility tools in order to enable the Commission and the NCAs to take into account the specific conditions of a relevant market. These tools are (i) the possibility to withdraw the benefit of the block exemption regulation and (ii) disapplication regulations to deal with network agreements.

Guidelines on Vertical Restraints [2010] OJ C 130/1 (references omitted)

Withdrawal procedure

74. The presumption of legality conferred by the Block Exemption Regulation may be withdrawn where a vertical agreement, considered either in isolation or in conjunction with similar agreements enforced by competing suppliers or buyers, comes within the scope of Article 101(1) and does not fulfil all the conditions of Article 101(3).

75. The conditions of Article 101(3) may in particular not be fulfilled when access to the relevant market or competition therein is significantly restricted by the cumulative effect of parallel networks of similar vertical agreements practised by competing suppliers or buyers. Parallel networks of vertical agreements are to be regarded as similar if they contain restraints producing similar effects on the market. Such a situation may arise for example when, on a given market, certain suppliers practise purely qualitative selective distribution while other suppliers practise quantitative selective distribution. Such a situation may also arise when, on a given market, the cumulative use of qualitative criteria forecloses more efficient distributors. In such circumstances, the assessment must take account of the anti-competitive effects attributable to each individual network of agreements. Where appropriate, withdrawal may concern only a particular qualitative criterion or only the quantitative limitations imposed on the number of authorised distributors.

76. Responsibility for an anti-competitive cumulative effect can only be attributed to those undertakings which make an appreciable contribution to it. Agreements entered into by undertakings whose contribution to the cumulative effect is insignificant do not fall under the prohibition provided for in Article 101(1) [The Guidelines refer to Judgment of the Court of Justice of 28 February 1991 in Case C-234/89, *Stergios*

445 Ibid, para 69. 446 Ibid, paras 70–1.

Delimitis v *Henninger Bräu AG* [1991] ECR I–935] and are therefore not subject to the withdrawal mechanism. [. . .]

77. Where the withdrawal procedure is applied, the Commission bears the burden of proof that the agreement falls within the scope of Article 101(1) and that the agreement does not fulfil one or several of the conditions of Article 101(3). A withdrawal decision can only have ex nunc effect, which means that the exempted status of the agreements concerned will not be affected until the date at which the withdrawal becomes effective.

78. [. . .] [T]he competition authority of a Member State may withdraw the benefit of the Block Exemption Regulation [see Recital 14 of VBER] in respect of vertical agreements whose anti-competitive effects are felt in the territory of the Member State concerned or a part thereof, which has all the characteristics of a distinct geographic market. The Commission has the exclusive power to withdraw the benefit of the Block Exemption Regulation in respect of vertical agreements restricting competition on a relevant geographic market which is wider than the territory of a single Member State. When the territory of a single Member State, or a part thereof, constitutes the relevant geographic market, the Commission and the Member State concerned have concurrent competence for withdrawal.

Disapplication of the Block Exemption Regulation

79. Article 6 of the Block Exemption Regulation enables the Commission to exclude from the scope of the Block Exemption Regulation, by means of regulation, parallel networks of similar vertical restraints where these cover more than 50 % of a relevant market. Such a measure is not addressed to individual undertakings but concerns all undertakings whose agreements are defined in the regulation disapplying the Block Exemption Regulation.

80. Whereas the withdrawal of the benefit of the Block Exemption Regulation implies the adoption of a decision establishing an infringement of Article 101 by an individual company, the effect of a regulation under Article 6 is merely to remove, in respect of the restraints and the markets concerned, the benefit of the application of the Block Exemption Regulation and to restore the full application of Article 101(1) and (3). Following the adoption of a regulation declaring the Block Exemption Regulation inapplicable in respect of certain vertical restraints on a particular market, the criteria developed by the relevant case-law of the Court of Justice and the General Court and by notices and previous decisions adopted by the Commission will guide the application of Article 101 to individual agreements. Where appropriate, the Commission will take a decision in an individual case, which can provide guidance to all the undertakings operating on the market concerned.

81. For the purpose of calculating the 50 % market coverage ratio, account must be taken of each individual network of vertical agreements containing restraints, or combinations of restraints, producing similar effects on the market. Article 6 of the Block Exemption Regulation does not entail an obligation on the part of the Commission to act where the 50 % market-coverage ratio is exceeded. In general, disapplication is appropriate when it is likely that access to the relevant market or competition therein is appreciably restricted. This may occur in particular when parallel networks of selective distribution covering more than 50 % of a market are liable to foreclose the market by using selection criteria which are not required by the nature of the relevant

goods or which discriminate against certain forms of distribution capable of selling such goods.

82. In assessing the need to apply Article 6 of the Block Exemption Regulation, the Commission will consider whether individual withdrawal would be a more appropriate remedy. This may depend, in particular, on the number of competing undertakings contributing to a cumulative effect on a market or the number of affected geographic markets within the Union.

83. Any regulation referred to in Article 6 of the Block Exemption Regulation must clearly set out its scope. Therefore, the Commission must first define the relevant product and geographic market(s) and, secondly, must identify the type of vertical restraint in respect of which the Block Exemption Regulation will no longer apply. As regards the latter aspect, the Commission may modulate the scope of its regulation according to the competition concern which it intends to address. For instance, while all parallel networks of single-branding type arrangements shall be taken into account in view of establishing the 50 % market coverage ratio, the Commission may nevertheless restrict the scope of the disapplication regulation only to non-compete obligations exceeding a certain duration. Thus, agreements of a shorter duration or of a less restrictive nature might be left unaffected, in consideration of the lesser degree of foreclosure attributable to such restraints. Similarly, when on a particular market selective distribution is practised in combination with additional restraints such as non-compete or quantity-forcing on the buyer, the disapplication regulation may concern only such additional restraints. Where appropriate, the Commission may also provide guidance by specifying the market share level which, in the specific market context, may be regarded as insufficient to bring about a significant contribution by an individual undertaking to the cumulative effect.

84. [. . .] [T]he Commission will have to set a transitional period of not less than six months before a regulation disapplying the Block Exemption Regulation becomes applicable. This should allow the undertakings concerned to adapt their agreements to take account of the regulation disapplying the Block Exemption Regulation.

85. A regulation disapplying the Block Exemption Regulation will not affect the exempted status of the agreements concerned for the period preceding its date of application.

According to paragraph 72 of the Guidelines on Vertical Restraints, where a supplier uses the same distribution agreement to distribute several goods/services some of these may, in view of the market share threshold, be covered by the Block Exemption Regulation while others may not. In that case, the Block Exemption Regulation applies to those goods and services for which the conditions of application are fulfilled. Furthermore, according to paragraph 73, in respect of the goods or services which are not covered by the Block Exemption Regulation, the ordinary rules of competition apply, which means:

- there is no block exemption but also no presumption of illegality;
- if there is an infringement of Article 101(1) which is not exemptible, consideration may be given to whether there are appropriate remedies to solve the competition problem within the existing distribution system;
- if there are no such appropriate remedies, the supplier concerned will have to make other distribution arrangements.

Such a situation can also arise where Article 102 applies in respect of some products but not in respect of others.

10.6.2.5. What happens if the Block Exemption Regulation does not apply?—Individual assessment of vertical restraints under Article 101(3)

Guidelines on Vertical Restraints [2010] OJ C 130/1 (references omitted)

Individual cases of hardcore sales restrictions that may fall outside the scope of Article 101(1) or may fulfil the conditions of Article 101(3)

60. Hardcore restrictions may be objectively necessary in exceptional cases for an agreement of a particular type or nature[447] and therefore fall outside Article 101(1). For example, a hardcore restriction may be objectively necessary to ensure that a public ban on selling dangerous substances to certain customers for reasons of safety or health is respected. In addition, undertakings may plead an efficiency defence under Article 101(3) in an individual case. [. . .]

61. A distributor which will be the first to sell a new brand or the first to sell an existing brand on a new market, thereby ensuring a genuine entry on the relevant market, may have to commit substantial investments where there was previously no demand for that type of product in general or for that type of product from that producer. Such expenses may often be sunk and in such circumstances the distributor may not enter into the distribution agreement without protection for a certain period of time against (active and) passive sales into its territory or to its customer group by other distributors. For example such a situation may occur where a manufacturer established in a particular national market enters another national market and introduces its products with the help of an exclusive distributor and where this distributor needs to invest in launching and establishing the brand on this new market. Where substantial investments by the distributor to start up and/or develop the new market are necessary, restrictions of passive sales by other distributors into such a territory or to such a customer group which are necessary for the distributor to recoup those investments generally fall outside the scope of Article 101(1) during the first two years that the distributor is selling the contract goods or services in that territory or to that customer group, even though such hardcore restrictions are in general presumed to fall within the scope of Article 101(1).

62. In the case of genuine testing of a new product in a limited territory or with a limited customer group and in the case of a staggered introduction of a new product, the distributors appointed to sell the new product on the test market or to participate in the first round(s) of the staggered introduction may be restricted in their active selling outside the test market or the market(s) where the product is first introduced without falling within the scope of Article 101(1) for the period necessary for the testing or introduction of the product.

63. In the case of a selective distribution system, cross supplies between appointed distributors must normally remain free (see paragraph (58)). However, if appointed wholesalers located in different territories are obliged to invest in promotional activities in 'their' territories to support the sales by appointed retailers and it is not practical to specify in a contract the required promotional activities, restrictions on active sales by the wholesalers to appointed retailers in other wholesalers' territories to overcome possible free riding may, in an individual case, fulfil the conditions of Article 101(3).

64. In general, an agreement that a distributor shall pay a higher price for products intended to be resold by the distributor online than for products intended to be resold

447 See Guidelines on Article 101(3), para 18.

> offline ("dual pricing") is a hardcore restriction (see paragraph (52)). However, in some specific circumstances, such an agreement may fulfil the conditions of Article 101(3). Such circumstances may be present where a manufacturer agrees such dual pricing with its distributors, because selling online leads to substantially higher costs for the manufacturer than offline sales. For example, where offline sales include home installation by the distributor but online sales do not, the latter may lead to more customer complaints and warranty claims for the manufacturer. In that context, the Commission will also consider to what extent the restriction is likely to limit internet sales and hinder the distributor to reach more and different customers.

The Commission and national competition authorities should in this case proceed to a cost-benefit analysis of the vertical restraint in question, by looking to its positive and negative effects, with the aim to apply the four conditions of Article 101(3) TFEU.

For the various positive and negative effects of vertical restraints that might be considered in the application of Article 101(3) read the Commission's vertical restraints guidelines[448] and our analysis in Section 10.5.

Of particular importance for the framework of analysis of vertical restraints is the acceptance of their self-policing character, which distinguishes them from horizontal restraints, although this characteristic should not be overestimated.

Guidelines on Vertical Restraints [2010] OJ C 130/1 (references omitted)

> 98. Vertical restraints are generally less harmful than horizontal restraints. The main reason for the greater focus on horizontal restraints is that such restraints may concern an agreement between competitors producing identical or substitutable goods or services. In such horizontal relationships, the exercise of market power by one company (higher price of its product) may benefit its competitors. This may provide an incentive to competitors to induce each other to behave anti-competitively. In vertical relationships, the product of the one is the input for the other; in other words, the activities of the parties to the agreement are complementary to each other. The exercise of market power by either the upstream or downstream company would therefore normally hurt the demand for the product of the other. The companies involved in the agreement therefore usually have an incentive to prevent the exercise of market power by the other.
>
> 99. Such self-restraining character should not, however, be over-estimated. When a company has no market power, it can only try to increase its profits by optimising its manufacturing and distribution processes, with or without the help of vertical restraints. More generally, because of the complementary role of the parties to a vertical agreement in getting a product on the market, vertical restraints may provide substantial scope for efficiencies. However, when an undertaking does have market power it can also try to increase its profits at the expense of its direct competitors by raising their costs and at the expense of its buyers and ultimately consumers by trying to appropriate some of their surplus. This can happen when the upstream and downstream company share the extra profits or when one of the two uses vertical restraints to appropriate all the extra profits. [. . .]

448 Ibid, paras 100–9.

The Guidelines provide further information on the relevant factors for the assessment of the trade-of between anti- and pro-competitive effects of vertical agreements under Article 101(3) TFEU.[449]

The judgment of the CJEU in *GlaxoSmithKline v Commission*[450] provides an excellent illustration of the real possibilities offered to the parties to the vertical agreement not benefiting from the Block Exemption Regulation to argue that the four conditions of Article 101(3) are fulfilled. It is reminded that in this judgment the Court annulled the Commission's decision to refuse to grant the benefit of the exception of Article 101(3) to a dual pricing scheme, contained in GSK's sales conditions providing for dual pricing for supplies in Spain, with a higher price being charged for sales for exports, so as to avoid the low prices imposed by Spanish regulation for the domestic market. The General Court, that first pronounced judgment on an action for annulment against the Commission's decision, found that the agreement infringed Article 101(1) (albeit by means of its restrictive *effect*), and on the basis that the anti-competitive object and effect of an agreement are not cumulative but alternative conditions for assessing whether an agreement is within the scope of Article 101, the Court concluded that GSK's claim that the agreement did not have an anti-competitive effect was unfounded. The General Court also annulled the Commission's decision as to the refusal to grant the benefit of the exception of Article 101(3) TFEU. The Commission asked the CJEU to review the General Court's judgment as to both the application of Articles 101(1) and 101(3). The CJEU found that the GC had committed an error of law in failing to conclude that GSK's agreements had an anti-competitive object and thus Article 101(1) applied, but also held that it had correctly interpreted Article 101(3) TFEU. The Commission alleged that the General Court had misapplied the case law relating to the allocation of the burden of proof and the standard of proof and the causal link necessary for the application of Article 101(3), as between the restrictive features of the agreement and the claimed advantages or efficiencies in terms of research and development or innovation. The Court disagreed with the Commission that the existence of an objective advantage for Article 101(3) purposes requires that all of the funding resulting from the operation of the GSK sales conditions must be invested in R&D and confirmed the GC's judgment on this point, which had considered sufficient that *part* of the increase in profits resulting from the restriction of parallel exports would go to R&D expenditure. Hence, the CJEU lowered the standard of proof for the condition of objective advantage to be fulfilled.

The UK CAT also examined the possibility that the restriction of competition resulting from the online sales ban in agreements between Ping, a manufacturer of golf clubs, golf accessories, and clothing and two UK retailers could be justified under Article 101(3) TFEU by performing an individual assessment of the agreement.[451] In *Online sales ban in the golf equipment sector*,[452] the CMA had found that the restrictive measure did not meet the exemption criteria as Ping had not established a sufficient causal link between the ban and the benefits associated with custom-fitting, the protection of its brand image, or the fact that the online sales ban was justified as a anti-free-riding measure. The measure was not also judged indispensable to achieving efficiency, as some customers can and do choose without custom-fitting.[453] Moreover, there were less restrictive alternatives than an absolute online

449 Vertical Restraints Guidelines 2010, paras 96–9, 122–7.

450 Joined Cases C-501, 513, 515 & 519/06 P, *GlaxoSmithKline Services Unlimited v Commission of the European Communities* [2009] ECR I–9291.

451 On the application of Article 101(1) TFEU in this case, see our analysis in Section 10.4.4.3.1.

452 *Online Sales ban in the golf equipment sector* (Case 50230) CMA Decision (24 August 2017), available at https://www.gov.uk/cma-cases/sports-equipment-sector-anti-competitive-practices.

453 Ibid, para 4.223.

sales ban (for instance, the main alternative would have been to permit retailers to sell online if they demonstrated their ability to promote custom-fitting in the online sales channel and to examine any additional conditions that Ping would have included in its selective distribution agreements). The CAT upheld the CMA's findings that Ping's Internet policy could not benefit from an individual exemption under Article 101(3).[454]

10.6.3. MOTOR-VEHICLE DISTRIBUTION

The distribution of motor vehicles has been the subject of frequent attention from the European Commission, in particular with regard to restrictions on selling cars cross-border, in view of the strong price differentials within the EU.[455] The distribution of motor vehicles has been covered, since 1985, by a separate block exemption regulation than that for vertical agreements generally, which was highly protective for dealers.[456] This specific regime was maintained even after the reform of the EU competition policy towards vertical restraints in the late 1990s.[457] One of the main concerns justifying the maintenance of this specific regime was the need to ensure multi-branding, as in order to benefit from the block exemption, a manufacturer's contracts had to allow its dealers to sell at least three different brands in the same showroom. The aim pursued was to avoid foreclosure of networks to new entrants by manufacturers. This concern seem nevertheless overstretched as new entrants have chosen to position their brands primarily through single-brand outlets, rather than placing them in existing show rooms of other brands. Regulation (EU) No 461/2010 extended the life of Regulation 1400/2002, which was due to expire on 31 May 2010, until 13 May 2013 with regards to vertical agreements relating to the conditions under which the parties may purchase, sell or resell new motor vehicles (primary market). The Commission has published *Supplementary Guidelines*, which complete the general vertical restraints guidelines.[458]

However, since 1 June 2013, these vertical agreements fall within the general vertical agreements block exemption regime set out in Regulation 330/2010, which allows single branding for a period of five years, the manufacturer being also able to oblige the downstream dealers to purchase up to 80 per cent of their requirements from the manufacturer. Manufacturers can also prohibit dealers to open additional sales outlets, by putting in place a quantitative selective distribution system, which are exempted if the selection criteria are 'specified', all parties' market shares are below 30 per cent and cross-supplies between approved dealers are

454 *PING Europe Ltd v CMA* [2018] CAT 13, para 211.

455 See the car prices reports periodically published by the European Commission, ec.europa.eu/competition/sectors/motor_vehicles/prices/archive.html.

456 Commission Regulation (EC) No 123/85 [1985] OJ L 15/1, which was replaced by Commission Regulation (EC) No 1475/95 [1995] OJ L 145/25. For an insightful analysis of the respective influence of dealer and consumer interests in this legislation, see C Joerges, 'Selective Distribution Schemes in the Motor-Car Sector: European Competition Policy, Consumer Interests and the Draft Regulation on the Application of Article 85(3) of the Treaty to certain Categories of Motor-Vehicle Distribution and Servicing Agreements' in M Goyens (ed) *EC Competition Policy and the Consumer Interest* (Cabay, 1985), 187.

457 Commission Regulation (EC) No 1400/2002 [2002] L203/30, which was replaced by Commission Regulation (EU) No 461/2010 [2010] OJ L 129/52. For a critical analysis, see D Gerard, '"Regulated Competition" in the Automobile Distribution Sector: A Comparative Analysis of the Car Distribution System in the US and the EU' (2003) 10 *European Competition L Rev* 518.

458 Commission Notice—Supplementary Guidelines on vertical restraints in agreements for the sale and repair of motor vehicles and for the distribution of spare parts for motor vehicles [2010] OJ C 138/16.

permitted. In interpreting the condition of 'specified' criteria, the CJEU held that suppliers operating selective distribution systems are under no obligation to publish the criteria used to appoint distributors, and that a car manufacturer using a selective distribution system based on quantitative criteria is under no obligation to apply these criteria in a uniform manner, or to ensure that these criteria are objectively justified, as such requirement would conflate the requirements of quantitative selective distribution (covered by the block exemption) with those of a qualitative selective distribution (which escapes the prohibition under Article 101(1) TFEU).[459] The *Supplementary Guidelines* continue to be in effect and contain a section dealing with single branding clauses and selective distribution.[460]

The new regime does not include conditions, such as a minimum two-year regular termination notice period and the requirement for detailed, objective, and transparent grounds for termination, which aimed to increase dealer independence from manufacturers, introducing more flexibility in the contractual regime of motor vehicle distribution agreements. Codes of conduct adopted by the motor vehicle manufacturers may nevertheless provide for such rules, the reform essentially aiming not to deregulate the relation between suppliers and retailers but to regulate it in a different way (self-regulation by codes of conduct, instead of command and control or incentives regulation).[461] This is a trend we have also observed in other distribution markets (see for instance our discussion of the Groceries Supply Code of Practice—GSCOP below).

Additionally, Article 3 of Regulation 461/2010 exempts from the application of Article 101(1) TFEU vertical agreements relating to the conditions under which parties may purchase, sell, or resell spare parts for motor vehicles or provide repair and maintenance services for motor vehicles (the aftermarket), which fulfil the requirements for an exemption under Regulation 330/2010 (the main BER for verticals), including the 30 per cent market share thresholds, and also do not contain any of the hardcore clauses listed in Article 5 of Regulation 461/2010. These agreements are subject to Regulation 461/2010 until 31 May 2023, the specific exemption aiming to ensure effective competition on the repair and maintenance markets.[462] As in most cases, the relevant market will be a brand-specific aftermarket, manufacturer-authorized repairers competing with independent repairers specializing in the specific brand, the Commission is particularly vigilant. The Supplementary Guidelines indicate that competition issues are likely to emerge, when, for instance, manufacturers prevent the access of independent repairers to technical information, when they misuse their legal and/or extended warranties to exclude independent repairers, and when they make access to authorized repairer networks conditional upon non-qualitative criteria (eg restrictions on the number of

459 Case C-158/11, *Auto 24 SARL v Jaguar Land Rover France SAS*, ECLI:EU:C:2012:351. The case concerned an authorized dealer of Land Rover in France, Auto 24's, which later became an authorized repairer, and whose application to be re-admitted as authorized dealer was rejected by land Rover on the basis of a '*numerus clausus*' which Land Rover had established and which foresaw the admittance of a limited number of dealers (quantitative selective distribution system). Auto 24 argued that these criteria were restrictive and could not be objectively justified as they did not apply in a uniform and non-discriminatory manner in all areas and to all participants. The French Court de Cassation sent a preliminary question to the CJEU, which inter alia found that a supplier is under no obligation to publish these criteria, as this may jeopardize business secrets, and even risk facilitating possible collusive behaviour.

460 Commission Notice—Supplementary Guidelines on vertical restraints in agreements for the sale and repair of motor vehicles and for the distribution of spare parts for motor vehicles [2010] OJ C 138/16, section IV.

461 Ibid, para 7.

462 See S Colino, 'Recent Changes in the Regulation of Motor Vehicle Distribution in Europe—Questioning the Logic of Sector-Specific Rules for the Car Industry' [2010] 10 *Competition L Rev* 203; GM Pelecanos, 'Europe's Reform of the Regulatory Framework of Motor Vehicle Distribution' (June 2010) 1 *CPI Antitrust J* 1.

authorized repairers or minimum sales requirements).[463] The importance of protecting independent repairers is still recognized as an important objective by the Commission:

> Independent repairers in particular provide vital competitive pressure, as their business models and their related operating costs are different from those in the authorised networks. Moreover, unlike authorised repairers, which to a large extent use car manufacturer- branded parts, independent garages generally have greater recourse to other brands, thereby allowing a motor vehicle owner to choose between competing parts. In addition, given that a large majority of repairs for newer motor vehicles are currently carried out in authorised repair shops, it is important that competition between authorised repairers remains effective, which may only be the case if access to the networks remains open for new entrants.[464]

One may expect that technological evolution, in particular the integration of big data technology in cars, driverless cars, personalized production, with limited needs to hold a large inventory of cars under stock, may push suppliers towards a more integrated distribution model, combining online distribution and manufacturer-owned brick and mortar stores in order to maintain ownership of distribution and repair, thus consequently raising questions as to a possible legal change in this sector.[465]

10.7. RETAILER POWER AND VERTICAL RESTRAINTS

10.7.1. VERTICAL RESTRAINTS—INTEGRATING THE RETAILER POWER STORY IN COMPETITION LAW

The antagonistic nature of the relationship between suppliers and retailers constitutes the main justification for adopting vertical restraints. It has been a constant feature of the dominant story on the competitive effects of vertical restraints that competition between vertical structures (inter-brand competition) will mitigate any anti-competitive exercise of market power by the manufacture imposing vertical restraints on her distributors and that it will eventually preserve consumers' interest.[466] This conclusion is based on the assumption that the interest of the manufacturer is to reduce the distribution margin of the retailer at the level which will be optimal for the consumer and which will guarantee the reward of the promotional efforts of retailers up to what is necessary to ensure quality distribution services.[467] This also constituted the conceptual foundation of the shift towards a more lenient antitrust

463 Commission Notice—Supplementary Guidelines on vertical restraints in agreements for the sale and repair of motor vehicles and for the distribution of spare parts for motor vehicles [2010] OJ C 138/16, paras 60–71.

464 Ibid, para 58.

465 For instance, US car manufacturer Tesla employs an online sales model coupled with company-owned stores to sell its cars.

466 The primacy of inter-brand competition is an important feature of the approach followed by US antitrust law on vertical restraints, the US Supreme Court recognizing in *Leegin Creative Leathers Products, Inc v PSKS, Inc*, 551 US 877, 890 (2007), that the promotion of inter-brand competition is important because 'the primary purpose of the antitrust laws is to protect [this type of] competition' (citing *State Oil Co v Khan*, 522 US 3, 15 (1997)).

467 R Posner, 'The Rule of Reason and the Economic Approach: Reflections on the *Sylvania* Decision' [1977] 45 *University of Chicago L Rev* 1; F Easterbrook, 'Vertical Arrangements and the Rule of Reason' (1984) 53 *Antitrust LJ* 135, 156–7.

regime for vertical restraints in Europe. The underlying assumption of the dominant story was that vertical restraints are generally imposed by the suppliers/producers to the dealers and that the downstream retail market is close to perfectly competitive.[468]

The reality of the marketplace is nevertheless different, as large multi-brand retailers may also take the initiative of suggesting or imposing vertical restraints to their suppliers, in particular as the balance of power between the different segments of the vertical chain has in recent years evolved in their favour.[469] The Commission noted in its Green Paper on vertical restraints,

> manufacturers are more and more dependent on distributors and grocery retail for getting their products to the consumers. Since the shelf space for new products is limited, conflicts arise between the increasing number of new product launches and the retailers' objective of profit optimization. The conflict has resulted in retailers asking for listing fees (key money) or for discount schemes which sometimes go beyond possible cost savings of the manufacturers.[470]

Furthermore, it is not always true that the interests of consumers and producers correspond, as it is likely that vertical restraints may lead to non-optimal distribution services for certain classes of consumers (in particular infra-marginal consumers), who will pay higher prices for services they feel they do not need.[471] In the absence of sufficient inter-brand competition, vertical restraints will therefore harm infra-marginal consumers. The need to ensure coordination between the different levels of the vertical chain will not always justify the adoption of vertical restraints.[472]

Individual or collective retailer power has been at the centre of the attention of public authorities in Europe,[473] with certain investigations being recently carried out at the national

468 For a criticism of this view, see W Comanor and P Rey, 'Vertical Restraints and the Market Power of Large Distributors' [2000] 17 *Rev Industrial Organization* 135; PW Dobson and M Waterson, 'Vertical Restraints and Competition Policy', OFT 177, Research Paper No 12 (December 1996), 23–5, available at http://webarchive.nationalarchives.gov.uk/20140402181333/http://www.oft.gov.uk/shared_oft/reports/comp_policy/oft177.pdf.

469 See OFT, 'Competition in Retailing', Research Paper 13 (September 1997), 46–7, available at http://webarchive.nationalarchives.gov.uk/20140402182835/http://www.oft.gov.uk/shared_oft/reports/comp_policy/oft195.pdf: 'over the last decade or so, retailers have tended to become a more important element in the overall value chain, partly at the expense of manufacturers. This change has occurred for various reasons, including: increased retailer size and retail concentration; increased importance of retailer image, which means that own-brand products have become more competitive with branded products; increased retailer information on consumers' preferences (partly as a result of scanner technology); and increased retailer command of technology.'

470 Commission Green Paper, COM(96) 721 final (January 1997), 66.

471 See WS Comanor, 'Vertical Price Fixing, Vertical Market Restrictions and the New Antitrust Policy' (1985) 98 *Harvard L Rev* 983; WS Comanor, 'The Two Economics of Vertical Restraints' (1992) 21 *Southwestern U L Rev* 1265.

472 FM Scherer, *Industrial Market Structure and Economic Performance* (Houghton Mifflin, 3rd ed, 1989), 554 criticized the quality certification argument for resale price maintenance:

> . . . what is the wider economic significance of a high-status image that comes from the high prices at which the product is sold, and not from the product intrinsic superiority? If an individual consumer derives utility from exclusiveness, and if the utility declines when a product enters mass distribution, there must be external diseconomies in consumption, violating one of the fundamental assumptions on the basis of which the efficiency of market processes is judged. The argument that product quality certification through resale price maintenance is efficiency-enhancing becomes even more dubious.

473 See the study commissioned by the OFT: P Dobson, M Waterson, and A Chu, 'The Welfare Consequences of the Exercise of Buyer Power', OFT 239, Research Paper 16 (September 1998), available at http://webarchive.nationalarchives.gov.uk/20140402181432/http://www.oft.gov.uk/shared_oft/reports/comp_policy/oft239.pdf; OECD, *Buying Power of Multiproduct Retailers*, Policy Roundtable, DAFFE/CLP(99)21 (1999), available at http://www.oecd.org/competition/abuse/2379299.pdf; European Commission, *Buyer Power and its Impact in*

level.[474] As a recent study commissioned by the European Commission shows, the top 10 European retailers have seen their market share grow from 26 per cent of total EU grocery market in 2000 to almost 31 per cent in 2011, the overall concentration of retailers increasing in virtually all Member States.[475] The international expansion of some retail brands across Europe, but also in non-European markets, has led to a general decrease in the importance of home markets for top European retailers in terms of the domestic share of European grocery banner sales.[476] Retailer power also manifests itself increasingly with the use of private labels, which compete directly with leading manufacturers' brands and other national brands and illustrate this shift in the balance of power between retailers and suppliers.[477]

However, empirical evidence of the negative welfare effects of private labels is lacking and is, at best, ambiguous, thus not giving clear directions to competition authorities for action. The emergence of commercial practices, such as slotting allowances and category management agreements are also illustrations of this increasing importance of retailer bargaining power that started to characterize the evolution of the distribution sector in the 1980s. Block Exemption Regulation 330/2010 and, in particular, the 2010 guidelines have taken on board this new reality and provide guidance for this type of retailer-induced vertical arrangements. We examine here three types of vertical restraints that may be considered as indicating the shift of the power balance from the suppliers to the distributors.[478]

10.7.2. PRIVATE LABELS

The development of private labels illustrates the emergence of a new equilibrium in the relations between suppliers and retailers that may question the validity of the assumptions of the Chicago School of antitrust economics on distribution restraints. Private label is a term referring to all products sold under a retailer's brand, which could be the retailer's own name (store brands) or a brand created by a manufacturer exclusively for the retailer, who defines the characteristics of the product (generic brands). Private label products are generally exclusively

the Food Retail Distribution Sector of the European Union, Final Report (1999); UK Competition Commission, *Supermarkets: A Report on the Supply of Groceries from Multiple Stores in the United Kingdom*, Cm 4842 (2000).

474 UK Competition Commission, *The Supply of Groceries in the UK: Market Investigation* (30 April 2008); OFT, *Grocery Market—Proposed Decision to Make a Market Investigation Reference* (March 2006), 42–9; A Svetlicinii, 'The Croatian Competition Authority Issues a Report on Competition on the Food Retail Market in 2008' *e-Competitions Bulletin* (16 July 2009) Article No 28749, available at https://www.concurrences.com/en/bulletin/news-issues/july-2009/The-Croatian-Competition-Authority-28749; HP Nehl, 'The Austrian Competition Authority Concludes General Inquiry in the Highly Concentrated Food Distribution Sector while Highlighting Indications of Strong Buyer Power (*Branchenuntersuchung Lebensmittelhandel*)', *e-Competitions Bulletin* (18 June 2007), Article No 13981, available at http://www.concurrences.com/en/bulletin/news-issues/june-2007/The-Austrian-competition-authority-13981.

475 European Commission, DG Comp, *The Economic Impact of Modern Retail on Choice and Innovation in the EU Food Sector*, Case Studies Report (September 2014), 50–2, available at ec.europa.eu/competition/publications/KD0214955ENN.pdf. This is driven by higher concentration of modern retail.

476 Ibid, 55.

477 DR Desai, I Lianos, and S Weber Waller, *Brands, Competition Law and IP* (CUP, 2015); A Ezrachi and U Bernitz, *Private Labels, Branded Goods and Competition Policy: The Changing Landscape of Retail Competition* (OUP 2009); A Ezrachi, 'Unchallenged Market Power? The Tale of Supermarkets, Private Labels, and Competition Law' (2010) 33(2) *World Competition* 257; A Foer, 'Introduction to Symposium on Buyer Power and Antitrust' (2005) 72 *Antitrust LJ* 505; L Vogel, 'Competition Law and Buying Power' (1998) 19 *European Competition L Rev* 4.

478 For a more extensive analysis of other implications in the rise of supermarket power see Section S.10.8.2. on the food retail case study.

distributed by the retailer along with national brand products, which are marketed by manufacturers throughout the national market, not only in the specific retailers' outlets. This brings a horizontal dimension in the relationship between suppliers and retailers, as private labels may compete for market share with national brands.[479] Private label brands' market share has been constantly growing, in particular in the food sector'[480] and represents a significant volume of retail sales in Europe. According to an economic report, recently commissioned by the European Commission, '[g]lobally, penetration of private labels is high in Europe, where they can exceed 40% market share in countries such as Switzerland and the UK, compared with an average in the US of 18% market share in 2011.'[481] Private labels are generally perceived by consumers as being lower in price and of inferior quality than national brands. In addition, national labels benefit from a 'reputation premium', as a result of more extensive advertising than private labels and brand-loyalty building. This leads to lower prices of private labels than equivalent, in terms of quality, national brand products. Despite this retail price differential, retailer's gross margins for private labels are more important in comparison to national brand products. It follows that the commercialization of this is more profitable for the retailers compared to that of national brands. This constitutes the main reason for the introduction of private labels by retailers and leads often to the exclusion of second-tier national brands from the market.[482]

Two reasons explain the higher retail gross margins for retailers. Steiner notes that retailers with strong private labels have more leverage with manufacturers and this helps them to increase their gross margins.[483] Private labels may also enhance consumer loyalty to retail brands and therefore reinforce the horizontal market power of the retailers. This will in turn

479 Although the issue of private labels being in the same market than national brands depends on a number of circumstances, recent case law has not excluded that private labels may be in the same relevant market than national brands at the retail level but not at the wholesale level because of differences in the functioning of the markets for national and private labels: *Kimberly/Clark-Scott* (Case IV/M.623) Commission Decision (16 January 1996); *SCA/Metsä Tissue* (Case COMP/M.2097) Competition Decision (31 January 2001), paras 20–8, available at ec.europa.eu/comm/competition/mergers/cases/decisions/m2097_en.pd.

480 MB Ward and others, 'Effects of the Private-Label Invasion in Foods Industries' [2002] 844 *American J Agricultural Economics* 961. This is also highlighted in the UK Competition Commission report into the grocery sector: UK Competition Commission, *Grocery's Market Investigation*, Final Report (30 April 2008), available at http://webarchive.nationalarchives.gov.uk/20140402194746/http://www.competition-commission.org.uk/our-work/directory-of-all-inquiries/groceries-market-investigation-and-remittal/final-report-and-appendices-glossary-inquiry [hereinafter Grocery's Market Report]. Some retailers have also developed a strong private-label identity as they sell only own-label goods (eg Aldi, Marks & Spencer) and the development of private labels constitutes an important aspect of their commercial strategy against other retailers. It seems that the development of private labels is an important aspect of horizontal competition between retailers: ibid, 71 n 2. See also ibid, Appendix 9.10 ('consumer research indicates that around 20 per cent of shoppers choose their grocery retailer on the basis of own-label ranges'). According to a recent economic report prepared for the European Commission, '[p]rivate labels are increasingly being seen by retailers as important tools for building client loyalty and strengthening banner image': European Commission, DG Comp, *The Economic Impact of Modern Retail on Choice and Innovation in the EU Food Sector*, Case Studies Report (September 2014), 54, available at ec.europa.eu/competition/publications/KD0214955ENN.pdf.

481 European Commission, DG Comp, *The Economic Impact of Modern Retail on Choice and Innovation in the EU Food Sector*, Case Studies Report (September 2014), 54, available at ec.europa.eu/competition/publications/KD0214955ENN.pdf. The Report notes (ibid, 25) that '[k]ey reasons for this likely include a perception among consumers that these products offer good value for money, the opportunity of higher margins for retailers, and a profitable way for manufacturers to make use of spare capacity.'

482 MB Ward and others, 'Effects of the Private-Label Invasion in Foods Industries' (2002) 84 *American J Agricultural Economics* 961, 963.

483 RL Steiner, 'The Nature and Benefits of National Brand/Private Label Competition' (2004) 24 *Rev Industrial Organization* 105, 113–14.

strengthen the retailers' vertical bargaining power against national brand manufacturers and will enable them to obtain better deals that will increase their profits.[484] These distributional outcomes are ambiguous from the point of view of the consumers. Steiner observes the generally positive effect of competition between private labels and national brands, what he calls the 'mixed regime':

> In this structure a group of (national brands) receive vigorous competition from the (private labels) of the major chain retailers—contest that tends to maximize social welfare in consumer goods industries. That is, it brings about a high level of total surplus while also stimulating innovation by manufacturers. It produces these benefits because of a combination of horizontal and vertical relationships that are unique to this structure.[485]

The commercialization of private labels obviously increases consumer choice by offering a lower price substitute to the consumers. The system may also introduce an effective countervailing power for retailers against the market power of national brand owners. Nevertheless, private labels may also produce important anti-competitive effects, in particular if they finish by dominating the market. Consumer choice and product variety may be affected if private labels exclude all but the leading national brand. This may also increase retail prices for consumers. Private labels will increase search costs for consumers and will therefore offer the opportunity for a higher mark-up at the supply or retail level.

Empirical studies have also shown that competition from private labels might not lead to lower prices for national brand products.[486] Consumers with a high degree of loyalty to the manufacturer's brand will not benefit from the introduction of private label products:

> The trade-off for the national brand producer facing a private label is between exploiting the loyal consumers with a high price and competing for the switching consumers with a lower price. When the fraction of loyals is high, the national brand will concentrate on the loyal segment and a private label will be introduced at a lower price. On the other hand, when the fraction of loyals is relatively low, the national brand finds it optimal to offer an exclusivity contract to the retailer at a low price and no private label is introduced [. . .]. If the national brand producer serves both loyal and switching consumers initially, the price of the national brand will be relatively low. In such a situation private label competition would lead to an increase in the price of the national brand. The reason is that the national brand producer decides not to serve the switching consumers to which the private label is offered and instead sets a high price to serve only loyal consumers [. . .]. Loyal consumers are worse off due to a higher price on the national brand, while switching consumers are better off when offered a low-price private label. It turns out that in some cases consumers on aggregate benefit from private label introduction, in other cases they are worse off.[487]

It follows that the effect of private labels on consumers is ambiguous and largely depends on the characteristics of consumer demand for the specific product. Restricting the commercial

[484] Ibid, 112–13. [485] Ibid.

[486] T Staahl Gabrielsen and L Sørgard, 'Private Labels, Price Rivalry, and Public Policy' (2007) 51 *European Economic Rev* 403, 404.

[487] Ibid, 406.

freedom of retailers may have, depending on the circumstances, a positive or a negative welfare effect for consumers.[488]

Private labels are not mentioned in Regulation 330/2010. According to the 2010 Vertical Restraints Guidelines, the existence of own brands including private labels and the brand image of the undertaking concerned amongst final consumers are elements to be considered in assessing if one of the undertaking's customers possesses buyer power.[489] Buyer power is viewed positively, as it 'may prevent the parties from exercising market power and thereby solve a competition problem that would otherwise have existed', which 'is particularly so when strong customers have the capacity and incentive to bring new sources of supply on to the market in the case of a small but permanent increase in relative prices'.[490] Private labels are also mentioned in the part on category management agreements, where the Commission stresses that they may lead to distortions of competition. According to the Guidelines on Vertical Restraints, 'in most cases the distributor may not have an interest in limiting its choice of products, when the distributor also sells competing products under its own brand (private labels), the distributor may also have incentives to exclude certain suppliers, in particular intermediate range products'.[491]

10.7.3. UPFRONT ACCESS PAYMENTS

According to the vertical restraints guidelines, upfront access payments are 'fixed fees that suppliers pay to distributors in the framework of a vertical relationship at the beginning of a relevant period, in order to get access to their distribution network and remunerate services provided to the suppliers by the retailers'.[492] The category includes practices, such as slotting allowances, pay-to-stay fees, and payments to have access to a distributor's campaigns.

There are conflicting stories on the rationale of upfront access payments. Some authors have advanced anti-competitive theories. Slotting fees might be a mechanism for manufacturers to raise rivals' costs: dominant suppliers aim to secure a sufficient amount of shelf space in order to increase the costs and impose barriers to entry to potential upstream competitors.[493] Upfront payments provide dominant manufacturers an instrument to leverage their power against potential competitors by raising their cost of entry. Economies of scale or scope must of course be present at the supplier level and the shelf space should be foreclosed for a significant amount of time for the raising rivals' costs strategy to succeed.[494] Small manufacturers are

488 For a more detailed analysis of the literature on the welfare effects of private labels and their assessment in competition law, see I Lianos, 'Some Reflections on the Vertical Restraints Antitrust Category' (2008) 4 *Concurrences* 17, available at www.concurrences.com/IMG/pdf/Colloque_UCL-IDC_Paris_230508_EN-2.pdf; A Ezrachi, 'Unchallenged Market Power? The Tale of Supermarkets, Private Labels, and Competition Law' (2010) 33(2) *World Competition* 257; C Doyle and R Murgatroyd, 'The Role of Private Labels in Antitrust' (2011) 7(3) *J Competition L & Economics* 631; A Ezrachi and K Ahuia, 'Private Labels, Brands and Competition Law Enforcement' in D Desai, I Lianos, and S Weber Waller (eds) *Brands, Competition Law and IP* (CUP, 2015), 179.

489 Vertical Restraints Guidelines 2010, para 116. 490 Ibid.. 491 Ibid, para 210.

492 Ibid, para 203.

493 For an overview, see PN Bloom, GT Gundlach, and JP Cannon, 'Slotting Allowances and Fees: Schools of Thought and the Views of Practising Managers' (2000) 64 *J Marketing* 92, 96–7.

494 B Klein and JD Wright, 'The Economics of Slotting Contracts' (2007) 50(3) *J L & Economics* 421, note however, that 'most slotting arrangements involve relatively short-term retailer shelf space commitments', usually a period of six months to a year. They also note that some large retailers, such as Wal-Mart prefer receiving the single best wholesale price that suppliers can offer instead of slotting fees.

also disadvantaged in comparison to large manufacturers because they lack adequate access to capital markets and thus may not be able to pay the large upfront fees that are demanded by the retailers. It has been argued that 'the dominant firm prefers to pay for scarce shelf space with slotting allowances rather than with wholesale price concessions because the former go directly to the retailers' bottom line, whereas the latter are mitigated by retail price competition'; 'by paying retailers with lump-sum money, the dominant firm can compensate retailers for their scarce shelf space without having to lower its wholesale price, which would reduce the overall available profit to be split'.[495] Slotting allowances make exclusion by dominant firms of their competitive fringe profitable: 'if the dominant firm had to pay for exclusion by offering retailers lower wholesale prices, exclusion would not be profitable'.[496] These theories of harm focus on the abuse of retailers' buying power by dominant manufacturers that aim to exclude their smaller rivals in the upstream market. A possible generalization would be that upfront payments are welfare reducing if they are initiated by dominant manufacturers and unlikely to lead to exclusion, when they are initiated by powerful buyers.

However, other theories emphasize the role of downstream market power in excluding competitors and limiting the distribution of small manufacturers' products. Marx and Shaffer have argued that upfront payments may allow a retailer with bargaining power to earn positive profits while it prevents small manufacturers from obtaining distribution from another retailer: 'the manufacturer will not want to trade with the rival retailer because of fears that if it did, the dominant retailer would cut back on some or all of its planned purchases'.[497] The welfare implications are that retail prices will be higher, because there is less competition at the retail level, and with fewer retailers buying from the small manufacturer, the choice in the marketplace will be reduced. Policy makers should thus be concerned when slotting allowances are initiated by powerful retailers and, in this case, should not only prohibit slotting allowances, but also other means to achieve exclusion, such as an explicit exclusive dealing provision.

Other authors advance the view that retailers employ three-part tariffs that combine slotting allowances (negative upfront payments made by the manufacturer even if the retailer does not buy anything afterwards) with two part-tariffs (the supplier charges wholesale prices and the retailers pay conditional fixed fees on actual trade) in order to achieve a monopolistic outcome and reduce retail competition.[498] This is not possible with a two-part tariff structure if the retailer has bargaining power, as in this case each retailer has an incentive to free-ride on its rival's revenue by reducing its own prices. The story goes as follows:

> Wholesale prices above costs maintain retail prices at the monopoly level, while large conditional payments (corresponding to the retailers' anticipated variable profits) protect retailers against opportunistic moves by their rivals: any price-cutting by one retailer would lead the others to 'opt out'; upfront payments by the manufacturer (slotting allowances) can then be used to give ex ante each retailer its full contribution to the industry profits.[499]

[495] G Shaffer, 'Slotting Allowances and Optimal Product Variety' (2005) 5(1) *Advances in Economic Analysis & Policy* 3.

[496] Ibid, 23.

[497] LM Marx and G Shaffer, 'Upfront Payments and Exclusion in Downstream Markets' (2007) 38 *Rand J Economics* 823, 838.

[498] P Rey, J Thal, and T Vergé, 'Slotting Allowances and Conditional Payments', Institut d'Économie Industrielle (IDEI) Working Paper (4 July 2006), available at http://idei.fr/sites/default/files/medias/doc/conf/fpi/papers_2006/verge.pdf.

[499] Ibid, 4–5.

Slotting allowances do not lead to the exclusion of efficient retailers but they allow firms to maintain monopoly prices in a situation in which competing manufacturers offer contracts to a common retailer.

Other authors have argued that slotting fees constitute a facilitating practice to increase profit levels at the expense of suppliers and final consumers.[500] As Shaffer explains,

> [i]n providing a means for retailers to commit contractually to high prices, a manufacturer indirectly raises retailer profits by eliminating their incentive for aggressive downstream pricing. Although manufacturers would prefer lower retail prices and hence greater sales, the competition among themselves for the scarce shelf space provides the incentive for such contracts.[501]

Some authors noted, however, that empirical evidence does not support this theory as retailer profits and prices did not increase, following the introduction of slotting allowances, and manufacturer profits did not fall, as they would have if retailers have been using slotting allowances to price discriminate.[502]

To these anti-competitive stories for slotting allowances one could oppose an efficiency rationale. Slotting allowances enable retailers to manage efficiently a scarce resource, shelf space, and allocate it to its best possible use. They might serve as a signalling device for new products and 'a basis for achieving efficient cost sharing and risk shifting among manufacturers and retailers'.[503] Slotting allowances moderate the risks of new product introductions and compensate retailers for the increasing costs of introducing and managing new products: they help equate an oversupply of new products with a less-than commensurate consumer demand for them.[504] Finally, some authors have advanced 'the promotional services theory of slotting contracts'.[505] Retail shelf space is thought as a means to create incremental or promotional sales that would not occur otherwise and for which infra-marginal consumers would not be willing to pay, as they will purchase the product without promotional shelf space. The manufacturers want greater retailer promotional shelf space supplied for their products but retailers have sub-optimal incentives to provide it, as they would not take into account of the manufacturer's profit margin on the incremental sales produced by the promotional shelf space, which is particularly problematic if the manufacturer is supplying a differentiated product. Upfront fees can thus be thought as a way to incentivize retailers to supply the optimal promotional shelf space and also as targeted discounts to marginal consumers, thereby increasing the marginal elasticity of demand. Manufacturers with the greatest profitability from incremental sales will be able to pay the most for shelf space and thus win the competition between suppliers for obtaining superior promotional shelf space.

But why choose upfront payments, instead of a wholesale price reduction, that could arguably achieve a similar result and provide more information on the value of the shelf space

[500] G Shaffer, 'Slotting Allowances and Resale Price Maintenance: A Comparison of Facilitating Practices' (1991) 22 *Rand J Economics* 120.

[501] Ibid, 121.

[502] MW Sullivan, 'Slotting Allowances and the Market for New Products' (1997) 40(2) *J L & Economics* 461, 490.

[503] LM Marx and G Shaffer, 'Upfront Payments and Exclusion in Downstream Markets' (2007) 38(3) *Rand J Economics* 93.

[504] MW Sullivan, 'Slotting Allowances and the Market for New Products' (1997) 40(2) *J L & Economics* 461.

[505] B Klein and JD Wright, 'The Economics of Slotting Contracts' (2007) 50(3) *J L & Economics* 421; JD Wright, 'Slotting Contracts and Consumer Welfare' (2007) 74 *Antitrust LJ* 439.

provided by the retailer? Klein and Wright explain that in the presence of inter-retailer price competition, retailers will be obliged to decrease their price more than they will increase incremental sales for the manufacturer, as they are selling to both marginal and infra-marginal consumers, the latter being ready to switch retailers if they find the product cheaper elsewhere, and thus any shelf payment through a lower wholesale price will be eroded.[506] The manufacturer will thus have to reduce even more considerably its wholesale price in order to create the equilibrium shelf space rental return. However, if the retailer competition is intense, Klein and Wright argue that there will be a point where a lower wholesale price will be an inappropriate way for a manufacturer to compensate retailers for the supply of promotional shelf space and the manufacturers will thus employ upfront payments.

The new guidelines on vertical restraints take into account these different anti-competitive and pro-competitive stories for slotting allowances. The guidelines indicate the anti-competitive effects that upfront access payments may have for other distributors, when such payments induce the supplier to channel its products through only one distributor. In this case upfront access payments may have the same downstream foreclosure effect as an exclusive supply obligation and, according to the Guidelines, should be assessed by analogy to the assessment of exclusive supply obligations.[507] The Guidelines add that 'exceptionally' upfront payments may also foreclose other suppliers, because of the increased barrier to entry. In this case, the assessment of that possible negative effect will be made in analogy to the assessment of single branding obligations.[508] It seems thus that the Commission considers that upfront access payments are more problematic, from the point of view of competition, if they are initiated by powerful retailers with the aim to dampen competition at the distribution market.

Upfront access payments may also soften competition and facilitate collusion between retailers. The Commission follows Shaffer's 1991 study, by indicating that slotting allowances are likely to increase the price charged by the supplier for the contract products and higher supply prices may reduce the incentive of the retailers to compete on price on the downstream market and increase the profits of the distributors. However, the final version of the guidelines added some limitations to this scenario by explicitly indicating that there should be a cumulative use of upfront access payments and that the distribution market should be highly concentrated.[509]

The Guidelines list also possible positive effects of slotting allowances. They note their contribution to the efficient allocation of shelf space for new products and as a means to prevent free riding by suppliers on distributors' promotional efforts, by shifting the risk of product failure back to the suppliers. However, no mention is made of the 'promotional services theory of slotting contracts'. Maybe a reason for this is that such theory would also lead to view more positively other mechanisms of shelf space compensation to prevent inter-retailer price competition, such as resale price maintenance clauses or rebates on a well-known product as a way to gain shelf space for another less well-known product, which was a 'no go' for the Commission.[510]

506 B Klein and JD Wright, 'The Economics of Slotting Contracts' (2007) 50(3) *J L & Economics* 421.

507 Vertical Restraints Guidelines 2010, para 204. 508 Ibid, para 205. 509 Ibid, para 206.

510 Resale price maintenance is considered a hardcore restraint in EU competition law and excluded from the benefit of the block exemption regulation under Commission Regulation (EU) 330/2010 [2010] OJ L 102/1, Article 4(a). The ability to provide rebates on sales of a well-known product as a way to gain shelf space for a less well-known product was limited in the Coca-Cola undertaking, *Coca-Cola* (Case COMP 39.116/B-2) Commission Decision (22 June 2005), 6, available at http://ec.europa.eu/competition/antitrust/cases/dec_docs/39116/39116_258_4.pdf.

The introduction of a section on upfront access payments in the text of the vertical restraints regulation constitutes an important novelty, but should be understood as responding to an increasing concern, justified or not, over retailer power in the different Member States. Some Member States have instituted prohibitions on slotting allowances in their unfair competition statutes. Other Member States, such as the UK and Ireland have recently adopted soft law instrument that also banned this practice.[511]

There is a considerable benefit in adopting provisions that integrate a competition test and that take into account both the benefits and the costs of slotting allowances for consumers. Bringing these issues within the realm of competition law and the scope of action of competition agencies accomplishes this objective and potentially reduces the pressure to institute per se prohibitions or formalistic bans on such practices at the Member States' level. The inclusion of this new section in the new vertical guidelines is a step towards that direction.

10.7.4. CATEGORY MANAGEMENT

Category management is a vertical partnership in which previously confidential information is shared between manufacturers and retailers in order to cut costs in distribution and increase the margin of both parties. The major impetus for this type of arrangement came from the supermarket industry as a response to the intense competition of warehouses and discounts stores. The category captain presents a plan-o-gram to the retailer suggesting a layout and a promotional plan for the entire category.

There are different forms of category management arrangements, going from strong ones, when the category captain has joint responsibility with the retailer for category development and is entrusted all category decisions, to loose forms of category management, where the retailer also received second opinions and recommendations from other category captains or the role of the category captain is an advisory one.[512]

Category management is efficiency-enhancing: it reduces the risk of retailers' out of stock and inventories, speeds up delivery times, enables the retailers to plan their production schedules. Suppliers and retailers have complementary information on consumers' needs and category management is a way to pool this information together for the benefit of consumers.[513] Alongside these various justifications, Klein and Wright have also advanced that category management is a way to ensure that the distributor provides a sufficient level of promotion desired by the supplier.[514] The story is similar than the promotional services theory advanced for slotting contracts. The distributors do not supply the sufficient level of promotion

511 See Section 10.8.2.

512 DM Desrochers, GT Gundlach, and AA Foer, 'Analysis of Antitrust Challenges to Category Captain Arrangements' (2003) 22 *J Public Policy & Marketing* 201, 204.

513 See *Workshop on Slotting Allowances and Other marketing Practices in the Grocery Industry*, FTC Report (2001), 46–55, 'the manufacturers may know things like the times of year when a product will best sell, the kind of promotion that are most effective in moving the product or the kinds of complementary goods that might be advantageously displayed in adjacent markets'. Retailers have point of sale data and knowledge of their promotional efforts. However, because retail outlets carry thousands of categories of products, the retailer cannot be expected to understand detailed aspects pertinent to the marketing of each category.

514 B Klein and JD Wright, 'Antitrust Analysis of Category Management: *Conwood v. United States Tobacco*' (Preliminary Draft 10 November 2006), available at www.justice.gov/atr/public/hearings/single_firm/docs/219951.htm. See also JD Wright, 'An Antitrust Analysis of Category Management: *Conwood Co. v. United States Tobacco Co.*' (2009) 17 *Supreme Court Economic Rev* 311.

desired by the supplier because they do not take into account of the supplier's marginal profit when deciding what level of promotion to supply. Shelf space is a particular type of promotional service. Klein and Wright argue that category management is a substitute contractual device to a limited exclusivity provision in the distribution contract. The fundamental limitation on the degree of exclusivity is that the category captain is obliged to place rival brands on its plan-o-grams and that the final decision regarding listing and the allocation of shelf space belongs to the retailer and not the category captain. The retailer has the incentive to hold up the manufacturer by providing insufficient shelf space and promotional effort. The suppliers provide payment to ensure sufficient shelf space, either by reducing their wholesale prices, or by paying upfront access fees (slotting allowances) or through the premium earned by the retailers because of an RPM clause. Category management allows the supplier to prevent retailer hold up, for example by selling the same shelf space twice, and ensures some return to the supplier in the form of a limited exclusive distribution for their products. There is, indeed, an implicit understanding that category captaincy is intended to privilege the brands of the category captain.

The 2010 Guidelines on Vertical Restraints do not embrace this conceptualization when they examine the possible positive effects of category management. It is certainly noted in the guidelines that category management is generally positive and can produce anti-competitive effects only in specific circumstances.[515] A similar positive assessment of the effects of such agreements on consumers was made by the Commission in its *Procter & Gamble* case in the context of EU merger control.[516] The Commission also notes in the vertical restraints guidelines that category management arrangements might also bring a number of efficiency gains: they may allow distributors to achieve economies of scale as they ensure that the optimal quantity of products is presented timely and directly on the shelves.[517] They may also enable suppliers to achieve economies of scale by allowing them to better anticipate demand and to tailor their promotions accordingly.[518] However, no effort is made to develop a more holistic view of this practice, such as the 'the promotional services theory' advanced by Klein and Wright. The reason might be that accepting this theory could provide room for a more lenient approach towards RPM, another mechanism of retailer promotional services' compensation,[519] which is something the Commission did not want to pursue in this revision of the Block Exemption Regulation on Vertical Agreements.

Category management may 'sometimes distort competition between suppliers, and finally result in anti-competitive foreclosure of other suppliers, where the category captain is able, due to its influence over the marketing decisions of the distributor, to limit or disadvantage the distribution of products of competing suppliers'.[520] This comes essentially from the conflict of

515 Vertical Restraints Guidelines 2010, para 210 ('in most cases category management agreements will not be problematic').

516 *Procter & Gamble/Gillette* (Case No COMP/M.3732) Commission Decision (15 July 2005), para 151, available at ec.europa.eu/competition/mergers/cases/decisions/m3732_20050715_20212_en.pdf, 'category management policy appears to provide an advantage to leading brands in general, and not only to the parties. This may be seen as largely pro-competitive, as it makes it easier for retailers to stock the most-demanded brands and easier for consumers to find them in sufficient quantities on the shelves. Hence, there is no elimination of competition.'

517 Vertical Restraints Guidelines 2010, para 209.

518 See also *Procter & Gamble/Gillette* (Case No COMP/M.3732) Commission Decision (15 July 2005), para 150, available at ec.europa.eu/competition/mergers/cases/decisions/m3732_20050715_20212_en.pdf.

519 See, most recently, B Klein, 'Competitive Resale Price Maintenance in the Absence of Free Riding' (2009) 76 *Antitrust LJ* 431.

520 Vertical Restraints Guidelines 2010, para 210.

interest between the supplier and the retailers, although the Commission notes that 'in most cases the distributor may not have an interest in limiting its choice of products'.[521] Category management might, however, produce exclusionary effects to other suppliers, in particular when the category captain is able, due to its influence over the marketing decisions of the distributor, to limit or disadvantage the distribution of products of competing suppliers. The US litigation in *Conwood v US Tobacco Co* provides an illustration of this risk for anti-competitive effects, although one should note that the factual circumstances of this case are exceptional.[522] This conflict of interest is particularly acute when the distributor also sells private labels, in which case he has incentives to exclude certain suppliers, in particular intermediate national brands, as this is also noted in the Commission's Vertical Restraints Guidelines.[523] The Commission will assess this upstream foreclosure effect by analogy to the assessment of single branding obligations, and will integrate factors such as the market coverage of these agreements, the market position of competing suppliers and the possible cumulative use of such agreements.[524]

The Commission also examines the possible collusive effects of category management agreements at the upstream and downstream level. This was an important concern in the UK Competition Commission (CoCo) supply of groceries in the UK market investigation.[525] The CoCo acknowledged that category management may provide increased opportunities to exchange information between suppliers, whether directly or indirectly via retailers. The report reviewed category management in two product categories—fresh fruit and yogurt—and found varying degrees of supplier interaction as a result of category management relationships.[526] The Commission concluded that 'the degree of interaction among suppliers arising from category management is a cause for concern'.[527]

The European Commission also recognizes in the vertical restraints guidelines that 'category management may also facilitate collusion between suppliers through increased opportunities to exchange, via retailers, sensitive market information, such as for instance information related to future pricing, promotional plans or advertising campaigns'.[528] The risk might be more significant if the retailers sell private labels and are thus competitors to the supplier/category captain. Direct information exchange between competitors is not

521 Ibid.

522 *Conwood Company, LP v United States Tobacco Co*, 290 F.3d 768 (6th Cir 2002) (finding maintenance of monopoly power through exclusionary conduct, including the destruction of competitors' promotional stands, payments for exclusive product display space).

523 Vertical Restraints Guidelines 2010, para 210. See, however, the more positive for category management analysis of the Commission in *Procter & Gamble/Gillette* (Case No COMP/M.3732) Commission Decision (15 July 2005), paras 143–5, available at ec.europa.eu/competition/mergers/cases/decisions/m3732_20050715_20212_en.pdf, where the Commission notes that there is little likelihood that category managers would provide biased recommendations to retailers, as 'the market investigation has shown that there is no significant information asymmetry between retailers and suppliers which could be abused' and that 'most of the parties' competitors and some of the retailers, through their private labels, provide a full range of oral care products, sometimes similar or even broader than the parties' range, which prevents the parties from forcing retailers to buy a full line of their own branded products'.

524 Vertical Restraints Guidelines 2010, referring to paras 132–41 (single-branding obligations).

525 UK Competition Commission, *The Supply of Groceries in the UK: Market Investigation* (30 April 2008).

526 Ibid, Appendix 8.1.

527 Grocery's Market Report, 151, para 8.19, noting that 'there were also some examples where suppliers offered information to grocery retailers regarding the future plans of competitors' and (ibid, 155, para 8.33), observing that '[o]ur review of the conditions necessary for tacit coordination to arise and be sustainable suggested that these conditions may be present in UK grocery retailing.'

528 Vertical Restraints Guidelines 2010, para 212.

covered by the Block Exemption Regulation on vertical agreements, as these constitute horizontal agreements that fall outside the scope of Regulation 330/2010, according to Article 2(4) of Reg. 330/2010.[529] The new information exchange agreements between competitors' section of the guidelines on horizontal cooperation agreements[530] provides more detailed information on the Commission's assessment of information exchange in a horizontal context. Any information exchange between the supplier/category captain and the retailer that carries its own private label should be carefully monitored, for example by the constitution of Chinese walls or firewalls and the separation of the category management and product sales functions.[531] It is also possible that trading negotiations between retailers and suppliers (vertical relations) might be qualified to horizontal collusion with anti-competitive information exchange.[532] Competition authorities in various Member States of the EU have increasingly employed the hub and spoke theory to bring indirect information exchanges between retailers via their suppliers in the context of vertical relations but facilitating collusion at the supply level within the realm of competition law.[533]

Furthermore, the Commission acknowledges in the Vertical Restraints Guidelines that category management agreements may facilitate collusion between distributors when the same supplier serves as a category captain for all or most of the competing distributors on a market and provides these distributors with a common point of reference for their marketing decisions.[534] One could question the possibility of this anti-competitive effect happening, unless there is a widespread adoption of the same category captain by all retailers. The category captain may also only provide advice about stocking and presentation of the category and is not involved in setting the retail selling price. As the UK Competition Commission noted in its report in the groceries market investigation, this concern might

529 Regulation 330/2010, Article 2(4): 'The exemption provided for in paragraph 1 shall not apply to vertical agreements entered into between competing undertakings.' See also Vertical Restraints Guidelines 2010, paras 27–8.

530 Horizontal Guidelines, paras 55–110.

531 See the recommendations in FTC, *Report on the Federal Trade Commission Workshop on Slotting Allowances and Other Marketing Practices in the Grocery Industry* (February 2001), available at www.ftc.gov/bc/slotting/index.shtm.

532 On the horizontal/vertical characterization for category management agreements, see K Glazer, BR Henry, and J Jacobson, 'Antitrust Implications for Category Management: Resolving the Horizontal/Vertical Characterization Debate', The Antitrust Source (July 2004), available at www.abanet.org/antitrust/at-source/04/07/Jul04-CatMgmt7=23.pdf. See also I Lianos, 'Collusion in Vertical Relations under Article 81 EC' (2008) 45 *Common Market L Rev* 1027; P Whelan, 'Trading Negotiations Between Retailers and Suppliers: A Fertile Ground for Anti-competitive Horizontal Information Exchange?' (2009) 5 *European Competition J* 823.

533 See the replica football kits and the toys sagas in the UK: CA/98/06/2003, *Price Fixing of Replica Football Kit* [2004] UKCLR 6; CA/98/8/2003 *Agreements between Hasbro UK Ltd, Argos Ltd & Littlewoods Ltd fixing the price of Hasbro toys and games* [2004] 4 UKCLR 717; *JJB Sports Plc* [2004] CAT 17; *Argos Ltd, Littlewoods Ltd v OFT* [2004] CAT 24; *Argos Ltd, Littlewoods & OFT, JJB Sports & OFT* [2006] EWCA Civ 1318; the recent *Dairy* investigation: 'OFT Update on Dairy Investigation', Press Release 45/10 (30 April 2010), available at http://webarchive.nationalarchives.gov.uk/20140403003905tf_/http://www.oft.gov.uk/news-and-updates/press/2010/45-10; and *Tobacco* (Case CE/2596-03) OFT Decision (15 April 2010), available at webarchive.nationalarchives.gov.uk/20140402142426/http://www.oft.gov.uk/shared_oft/ca98_public_register/decisions/tobacco.pdf (although the hub-and-spoke elements of the claim were dropped); D Desrochers, GT Grundlach, and AA Foer, 'Analysis of Antitrust Challenges to Category Captain Arrangements' (2003) 22 *J Public Policy & Marketing* 201, 206 note that '[a]s a result of the hub and spoke nature of Category Captain arrangements, rivals may learn about one another's pricing, merchandising, and promotion plans.' The same authors, however, acknowledge that 'no evidence of category captain facilitated collusion has been made public'. On hub and spoke, see Section 5.6.2.

534 Vertical Restraints Guidelines 2010, para 211.

be overstated as there was no evidence, from the case studies that category management activities were being used to facilitate, or had the effect of facilitating, collusion between grocery retailers.[535]

SELECTIVE BIBLIOGRAPHY

Books

Desai, DR, Lianos, I, and Weber Waller, S, *Brands, Competition Law and IP* (CUP, 2015).

Ezrachi, A, and Bernitz, U, *Private Labels, Branded Goods and Competition Policy: The Changing Landscape of Retail Competition* (OUP, 2009).

Korah, V, and O'Sullivan, D, *Distribution Agreements under the EC Competition Rules* (Hart, 2002).

Lianos, I, *La transformation du droit de la concurrence par le recours à l'analyse économique* (Bruylant, 2007).

Williamson, O, *The Mechanisms of Governance* (OUP, 1996).

Wijckmans, W, Tuytschaever, F, and Vanderelst, A, *Vertical Agreements in EC Competition Law* (OUP, 2011).

Chapters in books

M, De la Mano, and A, Jones, 'Vertical Agreements Under EU Competition Law: Proposals for Pushing Article 101 Analysis, and the Modernization Process, to a Logical Conclusion' in Healey, D and Jacobs, M (eds) *Research Methods in Competition Law* (Edward Elgar, forthcoming 2018), available at https://ssrn.com/abstract=2930943.

Rey, P, and Vergé, T, 'Economics of Vertical Restraints' in Buccirossi, P (ed) *Handbook of Antitrust Economics* (MIT Press, 2008), 360.

Journal articles

Apostolakis, I, 'Resale Price Maintenance and Absolute Territorial Protection: Single Market Integration, the Ancillary Restraints Doctrine and the Application of Article 101 TFEU to Vertical Agreements' (2015) 38(2) *World Competition* 215.

Baker, JB, 'Vertical Restraints with Horizontal Consequences: Competitive Effects of "Most-Favored-Customer" Clauses' (1996) 64(3) *Antitrust LJ* 517.

Bennett, M, Fletcher, A, Giovannetti, E, and Stallibrass, D, 'Resale Price Maintenance: Explaining the Controversy, and Small Steps Towards a More Nuanced Policy' (2010) 33(4) *Fordham Int'l L J* 1278.

Buccirossi, P, 'Vertical Restraints on e-Commerce and Selective Distribution' (2015) 11(3) *J Competition L and Economics* 747.

Buettner, T, Coscelli, A, Vergé T, and Winter, RA, 'An Economic Analysis of the Use of Selective Distribution by Luxury Goods Suppliers' (2009) 5(1) *European Competition J* 201.

535 Grocery's Market Report, Findings, Appendix 8.1, para 25. See also ibid, 151, para 8.18.

Evans, D, 'Economics of Vertical Restraints for Multi-sided Platforms' (2013) 9(1) *Competition Policy Int'l*, available at https://www.competitionpolicyinternational.com/assets/Uploads/CPI-Spring-2013-Evans.pdf.

González-Díaz, FE, and Bennett, M, 'The Law and Economics of Most-Favoured Nation Clauses' (2015) 1 *Competition L & Policy Int'l*, available at https://www.competitionpolicyinternational.com/wp-content/uploads/2016/03/Most-Favored-Nation-Clauses.pdf.

Hawk, BE, 'System Failure: Vertical Restraints and EC Competition Law' (1995) 32(4) *Common Market L Rev* 973.

Hederström, J, and Peeperkorn, L, 'Vertical Restraints in On-line Sales: Comments on Some Recent Developments' (2016) 7(1) *J European Competition L & Practice* 10.

Jones, A, Resale Price Maintenance: A Debate About Competition Policy in Europe? (2009) 5(2) *European Competition J* 479.

Lianos, I, 'Collusion in Vertical Relations under Article 81 EC' (2008) 45 *Common Market L Rev* 1027.

Lianos, I, 'Commercial Agency Agreements, Vertical Restraints, and the Limits of Article 81(1) EC: Between Hierarchies and Networks' (2007) 3(4) *J Competition L & Economics* 625.

Lianos, I, 'Some Reflections on the Vertical Restraints Antitrust Category' (2008-I) 4 *Concurrences* 17.

Lianos, I, and Lombardi, C, 'Superior Bargaining Power and the Global Food Value Chain: The Wuthering Heights of Holistic Competition Law?' (2016) 1 *Concurrences* 22

Monti, G, 'Restraints on Selective Distribution Agreements' (2013) 36(4) *World Competition* 489.

Rey, P, and Vergé, T, 'Vertical Restraints in European Competition Policy' (2014) 4 *Concurrences* 44.

Sahuguet, N, Steenbergen, J, Vergé, T, and Walckiers, A, 'Vertical Restraints: Towards Guidance to Iron Out Perceived Enforcement Discrepancies Across Europe?' (2016) 7(4) *J European Competition L & Practice* 274.

Van den Bergh, R, 'Vertical Restraints' (2016) 61(1) *Antitrust Bulletin* 167.

Vogel, L, 'The Recent Application of European Competition Law to Distribution Agreements: A Return to Formalism?' (2015) 6(6) *J European Competition L & Practice* 454.

Waelbroeck, D, and Davies, Z, 'Coty, Clarifying Competition Law in the Wake of Pierre Fabre' (2018) 9(7) *J European Competition L & Practice* 431.

Wright, JD, 'Slotting Contracts and Consumer Welfare' (2007) 74(4) *Antitrust LJ* 439.

THE OLIGOPOLY PROBLEM IN COMPETITION LAW

11.1. INTRODUCTION TO MAIN OLIGOPOLISTIC MODELS USED IN COMPETITION LAW AND GAME THEORY

Competition law enforcement is there to prevent the exploitation of market power by either preventing its creation through external growth *ex ante* or restoring competitive conditions *ex post*, whilst allowing the pursuit and maintenance of a position of substantial market power due to superior efficiency and/or quality. That is 'competition on the merits'.

Under EU competition law, a position of substantial market power is equated to dominance within the meaning of Article 102 of the Treaty on the Functioning of the European Union (TFEU). Dominance and, to a larger extent, the augmented version of 'super dominance' is based on the notion of independence, whereby the conduct of the dominant firm is 'largely insensitive to the actions and reactions of competitors, customers and, ultimately, consumers'.[1] This definition is clearly based on the monopoly model of static competition, where the dominant firm would at most face competition from a 'competitive fringe' made up of smaller firms who merely react to the former's decision. The smaller firms are

[1] European Commission, Guidance on the Commission's enforcement priorities in applying Article [102 TFEU, ex-Article 82 EC Treaty] to abusive exclusionary conduct by dominant undertakings [2009] OJ C 45/02, para 10 [hereinafter Commission Guidance on Article 102].

referred to as 'price takers'. They have no choice as to what price to charge or what quantity to produce. That is to say, the dominant firm acts as a monopolist over the 'residual demand' obtained after discounting the passive reactions of the price takers.[2]

Market failures due to market power are, however, not limited to the existence of an individual position of substantial market power. Indeed, the only other setting where firms are independent, in that their actions are insensitive to what rivals do, is the opposite of monopoly, *perfect competition*. This is the situation where no firm has any competitive advantage over rivals, neither in terms of productive efficiency, nor of quality differentiation. This indistinctiveness in terms of both production process and output, combined with the lack of entry barriers, leads to a fragmentation of the supply structure whereby firms are too small to be able to set their own price: in economic jargon, they are 'price takers'. That is to say, firms must align to prevailing market prices which are strictly based on costs. Therefore, under perfect competition, consumer surplus and allocative efficiency are maximized.

Nevertheless, there is a range of market outcomes between the two extremes of perfect competition and monopoly where firms are not independent, in that they are sensitive to the actions and reactions of rivals. Typically, there is a small number of firms each of which is large enough to affect the market outcome, but they also need to take into consideration rivals' actions. In economic jargon, there is strategic interaction amongst oligopolistic firms.

Strategic interaction among oligopolists can take two forms, depending on whether firms make decisions that are conditional on rivals not taking advantage of the 'soft' strategic stance adopted by the firm in question. As explained in Chapter 3 a 'soft' strategic stance increases rivals' profitability, for instance by reducing the quantity sold, thus making it easier for rivals to sell theirs, or increasing the price, thus making substitute products more convenient.

Normally, it would not make sense to adopt a 'soft' strategic stance unless there is an expectation that rivals would reciprocate, thus renouncing an aggressive reaction such as by increasing output to fill the gap left and keeping prices constant in order to steal business. Hence, there must be a reciprocal understanding among rivals that they can be collectively better off if each of them renounces conduct in its own best (self-)interest. Economists describe this state of mutual dependency as a *non-cooperative*,[3] *collusive/coordinated* outcome, whilst among legal practitioners the terms *cartel, collective dominance*, and *conspiracy* are prevalent. Collusion is considered to be a departure from the norm where firms' decisions are not conditional on rivals deviating from their best *unilateral* course of conduct. These two opposite competitive modes are discussed in some detail in the next two sections.

[2] For a technical discussion, see P Davis and E Garcés, *Quantitative Techniques for Competition and Antitrust Analysis* (Princeton University Press, 2010), 220–3.

[3] It is important not to confuse *cooperation* with *coordination*. In game theory, cooperative games are those where binding commitments are enforceable: in other words, if one party refused to discharge its obligations. Whereas, in non-cooperative games binding commitments are not possible since they are not enforceable for instance because they are illegal. Therefore, whilst the term cooperative refers to the rules of the game, the term coordination refers to the outcome of the game. Accordingly, there can be non-cooperative coordination, where firms manage to coordinate their conducts regardless of the impossibility of relying on binding commitment to secure compliance to the agreed common course of conduct.

11.2. THE ECONOMICS OF COLLUSION

The conditions underpinning collusion can be conveniently illustrated with a stylized two-dimensional pay-off matrix where two symmetric firms consider whether or not to raise prices, as shown in Table 11.1.[4]

In game theory, the configuration depicted above is known as 'prisoner's dilemma'. Under a 'prisoner's dilemma', the dominant course of conduct for players is not to coordinate their moves, even if by doing so they fail to maximize their pay-off collectively.

Accordingly, the two key conditions that need to hold are: (i) the unilateral decision to increase prices—whilst the other firm does not—yields worst possible pay-off (ie, 1 > 0); (ii) the unilateral decision not to increase prices—whilst the other firm does—yields the highest pay-off (ie, 5 > 3). The decision to trust the other player in selecting the mutually beneficial, common course of conduct (ie, increase prices) is risky. If the depicted game was played only once, the only sustainable outcome would be the one where none of the players raise their prices. In economics parlance, this is the only Nash equilibrium[5] of the 'prisoner's dilemma' game.[6]

Therefore, collusion is a game of trust which relies on a shared expectation that mutual benevolence among rivals can last over time. To this end, patience is the key virtue: firms must have a shared understanding that everyone is better-off sharing collusive profits potentially up to the monopoly profit over the long-term, rather than cheating unilaterally in order to earn a higher share of overall profits in the short-term, but then facing retaliation triggered by the breach of trust, typically, in the form of a prolonged period of intensive competitive rivalry.

Table 11.1. The 'prisoner's dilemma'.

	Don't raise	**Raise**
Don't raise	(1; 1)	(5; 0)
Raise	(0; 5)	(3; 3)

4 The first letter identifies the pay-off corresponding to the course of action in the corresponding row, conditional on the other agent opting for the course of action in the column—and vice versa.

5 In a two-person strategic interaction, a Nash equilibrium combination of strategies is such that each agent's strategy is that agent's best reply to the other agent's best reply to it. That is, no agent could do better by deviating from the equilibrium course of conduct assuming that the others will not change theirs. See M Motta, *Competition Policy: Theory and Practice* (CUP, 2004), 549. The fundamental assumptions of this model is (i) rationality, as players are assumed to be interested in maximizing their payoffs, that is their utility function. Firms, for the most part, are interested in maximizing profits, and (ii) common knowledge, as all players know the structure of the game and that their opponents are rational, that all players know that all players know the structure of the game and that their opponents are rational, and so on. One may distinguish between *cooperative games*, where the players may be able to make binding commitments to each other, and hence the players will honour agreements that are not incentive compatible- not in their self-interest, and *non-cooperative games*, where agreements are not binding, so a player cannot use them as mechanism to commit to ignore his self-interest. Therefore, the agreement will not change her incentives and behaviour.

6 Indeed, it can be shown that the non-coordinated outcome prevails as long as the game is played for a finite number of times.

This inter-temporal incentive constraint is enshrined in the 'folk theorem', called this way because its origin remains uncertain.[7]

That collusion is desirable to each of the few firms and sustainable, however, is not enough. Firms must first be able to reach a common understanding as to the terms of the collusive agreement, the coordination problem. Moreover, firms must be able to monitor rivals' compliance. In other words, they must be able to detect unilateral deviation in order to punish it.

Regarding the feasibility of collusion, the role of communication among colluding firms is ambivalent. Collusion is treated differently under competition law depending on whether there is evidence of past communication among alleged firms. If there is, collusion is treated as a cartel infringement under Article 101 TFEU and a criminal offence in many jurisdictions, such as in the UK. Otherwise, collusion amounts to a position of *collective dominance* within the meaning of Article 102 TFEU, which, under the mainstream approach, is not considered an abuse on its own.[8] Accordingly, economists have drawn a corresponding distinction between *explicit* and *tacit collusion*. In contrast, in the ex-ante assessment as to whether a merger increases the likelihood of collusion, called *coordinated effects*, there is normally no distinction between the two types, albeit both overt and tacit collusion can be contemplated.[9]

Nevertheless, given the non-cooperative nature of both explicit and tacit collusion owing to the collusive agreement not being legally binding and enforceable, any kind of communication among alleged firms should have no influence in the assessment of the feasibility and sustainability of collusion, since any statement would lack credibility due to its non-committal nature. In this sense, economists have coined the expression 'cheap talk'.[10]

Perhaps, a more nuanced view is that coordination cannot be simply spontaneous and 'it follows that the needed efforts at concurrence, coordination and compliance should yield sufficient smoking-gun-type evidence for conviction.'[11] That is to say, some sort of communication, even if 'cheap talk', is ultimately necessary to be able to reach a collusive agreement by signalling the intention to collude in the first place, and how collusion would work in practice, for instance how to allocate production quotas.[12] By the same token, cartel prosecution might, paradoxically, add credibility to 'cheap talk' given the implicit risk of being caught.[13]

Nevertheless, when assessing the feasibility and sustainability of collusion *ex ante*, or *ex post* with respect to tacit collusion: that is in the absence of communication among the alleged

[7] For less formal explanation, see F Jenny, 'Economic Analysis, Anti-trust Law and the Oligopoly Problem' (2000) 1(1) *European Business Organization L Rev* 41, 42–3.

[8] See eg R Whish, *Competition Law* (OUP, 6th ed, 2009), 565.

[9] See eg Competition Commission (CoCo) and Office of Fair Trading (OFT), Merger Assessment Guidelines, CC2 (revised)/OFT1254 (September 2010), para 5.5.4, available at https://www.gov.uk/government/publications/merger-assessment-guidelines:

> Coordination can be explicit or tacit. Explicit coordination is achieved through communication and agreement between the parties involved. Tacit coordination is achieved through implicit understanding between the parties, but without any formal arrangement. Both can be germane to an assessment of the effects of a merger.

[10] See J Farrell and M Rabin, 'Cheap Talk' (1996) *J Economic Perspective* 10, 103.

[11] GJ Werden, 'Economic Evidence on the Existence of Collusion: Reconciling Antitrust Law With Oligopoly Theory' (2004) 71 *Antitrust LJ* 719, 763.

[12] See, in this respect, WH Page, 'Neo-Chicago Approach to Concerted Action' (2011) 78 *Antitrust LJ* 173, 192 ('But the fact that cartelists choose to communicate and thus increase their risks of prosecution suggests that communication is necessary or at least worth the risk in most instances.')

[13] See, in this respect, M Armstrong and S Huck 'Behavioural Economics as Applied to Firms: A Primer' (2010) 6(1) *Competition Policy Int'l* 1, 11–12, available at http://else.econ.ucl.ac.uk/papers/uploaded/359.pdf ('Firms feel more committed to a collusive agreement if costs are needed to reach that agreement. The net impact of making it hard to communicate is that collusion is substantially more prevalent, so that certain forms of competition policy might perversely turn out to aid cartel formation and stability.')

firms, the line of inquiry is based on the 'folk theorem'. In this respect, there are, by and large, two main approaches, specifically:

- a *conduct* approach, which focuses on the likelihood and effectiveness of rival's reaction to unilateral deviation as a disciplining or retaliatory mechanism; and
- a *structural* approach, which looks at a set of industry features which affect the sustainability of collusion such as the degree of patience.

Although these two approaches are often portrayed as in contrast, they are both valuable and should really be thought of as complementary.[14] The likelihood of retaliation rests on the capacity, on the part of the colluding firms, mutually to observe their conduct and to identify any deviant conduct. For example, where the alleged firms compete for customer's business through bespoken negotiations: large and complex procurement contracts, the degree of transparency among colluding firms might be hampered by the fact that prices and quantities are private information, not in the public domain.

As to the credibility and, hence, effectiveness of the retaliatory mechanism, the simplest and most credible collective reaction would be to revert to the 'normal' competitive mode on a permanent basis.[15] Of course, there can be more complex forms of retaliation with the aim of inflicting tougher punishment. For example, firms can temporarily set prices below costs and engage in 'price wars', before reverting to the 'normal' competitive mode. Ideally, firms would want specifically to target the 'cheating' firm, for example, by offering selective discounts to poach its customers. The use of unorthodox retaliatory mechanisms, however, must be credible.[16]

Notwithstanding the theoretical appeal of this approach, its implementation in practice is problematic, specifically, when the existence of a credible and effective retaliatory mechanism is conjectured, rather than based on actual observation of past conducts. Besides the obvious case of the ex-ante assessment of 'coordinated effects', this is often the case in the ex-post enforcement against tacit collusion where all that can be observed is that the alleged firms seem to be following a common course of conduct. That is to say, the conjectured retaliatory mechanism is so effective that the mere threat thereof successfully deters deviation. Under these circumstances, a contentious debate ensues whereby the plaintiff's argument that there exist a credible and effective retaliatory mechanism in theory is contrasted by the defendant's argument that the incentives to deviate, instead, are simply too strong.[17]

This is why it is important not to dismiss the other complementary approach, which tries to establish which factors would facilitate collusion. Besides market transparency, the most crucial factors are:[18]

14 The former approach is enshrined in the so-called *Airtours* test, which supplanted the latter approach, known as the 'check-list' approach: see eg KU Kühn, 'An Economists' Guide through the Joint Dominance Jungle', Michigan Law and Economics Research Paper No 02-014 (2002), available at https://ssrn.com/abstract=349523.

15 This type of reaction is known as the Nash-reversion trigger strategy, where the static non-cooperative Nash equilibrium prevails after the collusive agreement breaks down.

16 Credibility requires that the adopted response is a sub-game perfect Nash equilibrium, that is, it does not imply actions that would not be taken in case the punishment threat was not sufficient to deter cheating. See M Motta, *Competition Policy: Theory and Practice* (CUP, 2004), 549.

17 For a detailed discussion, see P Siciliani, 'Should We Act *ex post* Against Tacit Collusion—And How?' (2014) 5(5) *J European Competition L & Practice* 294.

18 For a detailed discussion, see M Ivaldi et al, 'The Economics of Tacit Collusion', Final Report for the DG Competition (March 2003), available at ec.europa.eu/competition/mergers/studies_reports/the_economics_of_tacit_collusion_en.pdf.

- *a low number of competitors*: the long-run benefit of maintaining collusion is lower the higher the number of colluding firms, since the pie must be shared among many; by the same token, the short-run gain from deviation increases;
- *high entry barriers*: the threat of potential entry reducing the incentives to collude in the first place;
- *high frequency of interaction or of price adjustments*: retaliation comes sooner, which would undermine the incentives to deviate in the first place. Whereas, if rivalry is infrequent and lumpy—as, for example, in procurement markets with large tendering processes—the incentives to deviate are stronger since retaliation is a distant prospect; and
- *cost asymmetries and vertical quality differentiation*: feasibility is weakened because the low-cost firm would want a lower price and/or higher quantities, so that it would be difficult to identify the 'focal point'[19] for coordination. Moreover, stability is also weakened since the low-cost firm stands to gain more from undercutting their rivals and has less to fear from retaliation from high-cost firms.[20]

Two other, less important facilitators of collusion are:

- *demand growth, that is an outward shift of the demand schedule*: in a growing market there is an expectation that future profits will increase, thus the loss of collusive profits in the long-term provides a stronger incentive not to deviate;[21] and
- *multimarket contact*: when firms compete in multiple separate markets such as different local markets, their frequency of interaction is higher. Moreover, firm's asymmetries could be evened out across multiple markets: for instance, a large incumbent in one local market may be a smaller competitor elsewhere. By the same token, targeted retaliation is easier because retaliation can occur in the local market where the 'cheating' firm is the largest incumbent.

Finally, some industrial features have an ambivalent impact on the sustainability of collusion, specifically:

- *symmetric capacity constraints*:[22] a firm that is constrained by insufficient capacity has less to gain from undercutting its rivals because the 'cheating' firm would not be able to serve the entire demand 'stolen' from rivals; similarly, the ability of capacity-constrained rivals to punish deviation is limited;
- *horizontal quality differentiation*: similarly to the case of capacity constraints, product variety limits both the gains from deviation and the incidence of retaliation. Besides the ambivalent effects on the sustainability of collusion, though, horizontal differentiation

[19] More generally, lack of symmetry among would-be colluders worsens the problem of coordination. For example, if firms have asymmetric market shares, the largest firm would typically want a larger share of collusive profits, which might require some form of side payments among colluders.

[20] By the same token, a firm that sells a higher quality version of the product in question would want to set a higher price than what would be considered optimal by low-quality rivals, whose sales volumes would drop too much, since their price would be considered too high given the corresponding lower quality.

[21] Often, it is argued that in a growing market the prospect of future entry is more likely, which would increase the incentives to deviate, since collusion will probably be disrupted sooner or later anyway. This effect, though, is more about low barrier to entry, perhaps because of disruptive innovation, than the fact that demand is growing.

[22] If one or more firms were not capacity restrained, this asymmetry would have the same implications for the stability of collusion as for cost asymmetries presented above.

might make it more difficult to coordinate in the first place, since market transparency is impaired because it is hard to tell whether a fall in sales is due to rivals' cheating or to an adverse change in consumer tastes; and

- *the scope for price competition, as captured by the own price elasticity of the market demand*: in contrast to the two factors above, price sensitiveness increases both the gains from deviation and the incidence of the punishment phase. It is fair to say, though, that the fact that pricing rivalry is intense would, under 'normal' circumstances, make collusion more desirable in the first place.[23]

Ultimately, however, the identification of collusion in the absence of evidence of either communication among alleged firms, or past episodes of deviation followed by a phase of retaliation, remains problematic, given the difficulty of telling whether the parallel prices observed appear to be covariate as the result of collusion rather than orthodox uncoordinated competitive rivalry. Regarding the latter, the next Section discusses how the competitive mode can vary depending on which strategic variable firms compete, prices or quantity, the extent to which products are homogeneous or differentiated and also how easy it is for consumers to shop around.

11.3. 'UNILATERAL EFFECTS' AND MERGER EFFICIENCIES

As explained in the introduction, the distinction between collusion and uncoordinated competitive rivalry is that in the latter firms' decisions are not conditional on rival's mutual benevolence, in the sense that firm's aims are to maximize their profit in the knowledge that rivals will do the same by taking advantage of any 'soft' stance. In other words, 'cheating' is the norm.[24]

This characterization of uncoordinated competitive rivalry may seem inconsistent with the analysis of 'unilateral effects' caused by a merger between two competitors, where rivals benefit from the fact that the merged entity behaves less competitively than the two uncoordinated firms would have done.[25] However, the 'soft' stance after the merger is due to the coordination between the two merging firms, that is, to the extent that their decision to increase prices or

[23] See M Ivaldi et al, 'The Economics of Tacit Collusion', Final Report for the DG Competition (March 2003), 51–2, available at ec.europa.eu/competition/mergers/studies_reports/the_economics_of_tacit_collusion_en.pdf.

[24] The distinction between collusion and unilateral effects, however, becomes more blurred the faster firms can react to rivals' undercutting. At the extreme, where firms can match rivals' price undercutting instantly, monopoly pricing turns out to be the only rational course of conduct, since in the worst of circumstances prices would have to be adjusted downwards to retain customers in response to irrational attempts to undercut prevailing prices. That is to say, there would be no difference between uncoordinated and cooperative pricing. This peculiar market configuration is considered in the DOJ and FTC 'Commentary on the Horizontal Merger Guidelines' (2010), 25, available at www.justice.gov/atr/public/guidelines/215247.htm:

> A market typically is more vulnerable to coordinated conduct if a firm's prospective competitive reward from attracting customers away from its rivals will be significantly diminished by likely responses of those rivals. This is more likely to be the case, the stronger and faster are the responses the firm anticipates from its rivals. The firm is more likely to anticipate strong responses if there are few significant competitors, if products in the relevant market are relatively homogeneous, if customers find it relatively easy to switch between suppliers, or if suppliers use meeting-competition clauses.

[25] See M Ivaldi et al, 'The Economics of Unilateral Effects', Interim Report for the DG Competition (2003), 22, available at idei.fr/doc/wp/2003/economics_unilaterals.pdf.

reduce quantities is motivated by the fact that part of the loss in sales is being captured by or diverted to the other merging firm. Therefore, the closer are the substitute products of the merging firms the stronger is the incentive of the merged entity to increase its prices.

Rivals' reaction to this internally coordinated softening by the merged entity depends, nevertheless, on the prevailing uncoordinated mode of competition. As explained in Chapter 3, where firms compete by setting prices, which are strategic complements, rivals respond to the increase in prices by the merged entity by raising their own prices, thus strengthening the initial softening stance; whereas if firms compete on quantities, which are strategic substitutes, the merged entity's initial quantity reduction induces rivals to increase theirs, thus partly offsetting the initial softening stance.

In turn, in a feedback loop, the merged entity adjusts to its rival's response in an uncoordinated fashion, that is, by either nudging up its prices or reducing quantities again. All in all, though, regardless of the mode of competition, there normally would be an increase in prevailing market prices and a reduction in overall quantities after the merger. 'Unilateral effects' are, accordingly, the outcome of a sequence of uncoordinated reactions to an initial internally coordinated 'soft' move.

As will also be explained in Chapter 12, 'unilateral effects' can be balanced, at least partly, by efficiency improvements of the merged entity.[26] There are a number of possible sources of efficiencies, primarily:

- *Scale and scope economies*: the merged entity can reorganize production across plants in order to concentrate production in a single plant, ideally, the one with the lower marginal cost. Moreover, scale and scope economies may result from the avoidance of duplication of fixed costs, such as administrative overheads and marketing and sales costs.
- *Removal of 'double marginalization'*: as explained in Chapter 2, when pricing decision are *strategic substitutes*, as in case of product complements, or in a vertical supply relationship, an increase in one price will reduce demand for the other product, which would not only be detrimental for the combined profit of the two firms, but for consumers alike. Therefore, a merger can be beneficial to the extent that prices are set taking into consideration the impact on complementary products—in economic jargon, 'internalizing the externalities'.
- *Reduction of transaction costs*: another source of inefficiency among producers of complementary products, including the vertical relationships between an input supplier and a manufacturer, or a manufacturer and the distributor, is where one party has to specialize in order to achieve better integration. For example, the input supplier buying specialized machinery, or the distributor training sales personnel. There could be a failure to specialize, when the party in question is concerned that, once specialized, the other beneficiary party will opportunistically try to extract all the benefits thanks to the fact that specialization increases the degree of dependency: the investment is 'sunk' in that it could not be used as profitably for anything else. A merger, therefore, might be necessary to remove the potential for opportunism, thus solving what economists call the 'hold-up problem'.
- *Network effects*: when the benefit from consumption is driven by the number 'adopters', a merger that combines two previously separated customer bases could be beneficial.

26 For a detailed discussion, see OECD, 'The Role of Efficiency Claims in Antitrust Proceedings', DAF/COMP(2012)23 (2013), 11–60, available at www.oecd.org/competition/EfficiencyClaims2012.pdf.

Network effects can be *direct*, where the source of benefit is the ability to reach other adopters such as telephone or email, or *indirect*, where the higher the number of adopters and the larger is the provision of complementary products, as in multi-sided platforms such as video games for adopters of a specific game console.

In practice, although it is difficult to actually estimate the magnitude of post-merger price increases, it is easier to establish the likelihood that a merger would induce 'unilateral effects', than to claim the existence of offsetting efficiency improvements. With respect to the latter, the burden of proof lies entirely on the merging parties, which have to establish that the claimed efficiencies are not only likely, timely, and for the benefit of consumers in terms of lower prices or higher quality, but also merger-specific in that the proposed merger is the only way to achieve them.

In this respect, the assessment of fixed-cost savings is particularly contentious. On the one hand, fixed-cost savings, such as for the avoidance of duplication, are more verifiable and achievable, and thus considered more likely and timely than a reduction in marginal costs. On the other hand, it is not clear how consumers could benefit from them, since a reduction in fixed costs would typically be appropriated by the merged entity in the form of higher profits, rather than being passed on to consumers though lower prices.[27] Nevertheless, a reduction in fixed-costs could yield consumer benefit over the long term to the extent that they allow the merger entity to invest more innovation, which entails large fixed and typically 'sunk' costs. Hence, efficiency claims based on sizeable fixed-cost savings in high-tech industries, where 'dynamic efficiency' is important, should not be dismissed lightly.

11.4. MAIN MODELS OF OLIGOPOLISTIC (UNCOORDINATED) COMPETITION

11.4.1. THE COURNOT AND BERTRAND MODELS

As explained in the previous section, the analysis of 'unilateral effects' requires the identification of a competitive model, that is, determining how oligopolistic rivals would interact strategically. In this respect, the choice typically is between competition by setting quantity with homogenous products and competition by setting price with horizontal product differentiation.

The former model is called the *Cournot model*, after the economist Antoine Augustin Cournot who first developed it in 1838;[28] the latter model is the *Bertrand model*, named after Joseph Bertrand who, in 1883, questioned the realism of Cournot's assumption that firms

27 See eg DOJ and FTC, 'Commentary on the Horizontal Merger Guidelines'(2010), 57, available at www.justice.gov/atr/public/guidelines/215247.htm:

> Economic analysis teaches that price reductions are expected when efficiencies reduce the merged firm's marginal costs, i.e., costs associated with producing one additional unit of each of its products. By contrast, reductions in fixed costs—costs that do not change in the short-run with changes in output rates—typically are not expected to lead to immediate price effects and hence to benefit consumers in the short term.

28 Cournot described a market where there are two springs of water that are owned by different individuals. The owners sell water independently in a given period, by setting their quantities in the knowledge that the price will be the same for both producers, given product homogeneity. He also assumed that the owners face zero costs of production and that consumer demand is negatively sloped.

compete in output since in most markets price seems to be the natural variable to choose.[29] In a nutshell, in the case of Cournot, firms decide the quantity they sell and the demand decides the selling price through the market clearing condition; whereas in the case of Bertrand, firms choose the price they want to set and demand decides the quantity they sell, because firms are expected to sell all the forthcoming demand at the price they set.[30] In this case, when products are homogeneous demands of firms are easy to obtain. Only firms setting the lowest price in the market enjoy a positive demand. The remaining firms meet no demand at all.

As explained in Chapter 3, this unforgiving nature makes Bertrand competition more rivalrous than under the Cournot model.[31] Indeed, under Bertrand competition with homogeneous products the perfectly competitive outcome, where prices are strictly based on costs and firms make no profit beyond a reasonable profit margin to compensate for the capital invested into the business, can be reached with just two firms competing in the market—in economic jargon, a duopoly. This counterintuitive outcome, called the Bertrand paradox, rests on the implicit threat that, unless the price is set at the lowest possible level, the firm in question might end up making no sale at all if the other firm undercuts its price.[32]

In contrast, under the Cournot model of competition, in theory, the perfectly competitive outcome is reached only as the number of firms grows indefinitely. That is to say, in a market with homogeneous goods, prices and profits are substantially higher in the Cournot model than in the Bertrand model. Although the equilibrium in a monopoly setting is invariant to choosing output or price as the choice variable, the choice of strategic variable makes a big difference when there is more than one firm.

The ability to sustain a price increase in an oligopoly setting is essential when there are high fixed costs. Indeed, the comparison between the two modes of competition is reverted. Under the Bertrand model with homogeneous products, entry is fully deterred when there are fixed costs to enter the market. As mentioned in the previous section with respect to the analysis of merger efficiencies due to savings in fixed costs, because fixed cost do not vary with the quantity produced, they are not relevant to price setting in the short run: that is, after fixed costs have already been incurred. Therefore, the incumbent sets its price down to the level sufficient to keep the entrant out of the market. Consequently, the entrant cannot recover its fixed costs by sharing the demand with the incumbent—in economic jargon, this is called 'limit pricing'.[33]

In contrast to this reversed paradoxical prediction, under Cournot competition with fixed costs, entry occurs until firms' profit is large enough to cover the fixed costs. This is possible because the entrant anticipates that incumbents will reduce their quantities in response to

29 For a detailed discussion of the origins of the formulation of the classical oligopoly theory, see S Martin, *Advanced Industrial Economics* (Blackwell, 2nd ed, 2002), ch 2.

30 Accordingly, the Bertrand model is an appropriate choice where prices are more difficult to adjust in the short run than quantities, and vice versa with respect to the Cournot model.

31 Under the Cournot model, the threat of price undercutting is less effective, since each firm expects the rival to let its price fall in response to a price cut in order to keep sales constant.

32 This result rests on the assumption that rivals know each other's costs where one's own costs are not a good proxy for rivals' costs. Whereas, under uncertainty—that is, where the level of marginal costs is private information—firms set prices above their marginal costs in the expectation of earning a positive profit. However, the competitive equilibrium is re-established when the number of firms grows indefinitely: in other words, the higher the number of firms the higher the risk of price undercutting.

33 The outcome is even worse when the fixed cost of entry is 'sunk'. Here not only is entry deterred, but the incumbent can set prices at the monopoly level, since the risk of 'hit-and-run' entry is deterred by the irrecoverable nature of the fixed cost—the market is not 'contestable' owing to the exit barrier. See P Davis and E Garcés, *Quantitative Techniques for Competition and Antitrust Analysis* (Princeton University Press, 2010), 49–50.

entry. That is to say, competitive rivalry in strategic substitutes is more accommodative with respect to new entrants than under strategic complements.[34]

Nevertheless, the harshness of pricing rivalry is mitigated under horizontal product differentiation, whereby consumers not only exhibit a general preference for variety, but are also heterogeneous as to which variety they like the most. The resulting distribution in consumer preferences across the market means that each firm can benefit from a pool of loyal customers who are willing to pay a premium in order to avoid the inconvenience of having to buy a less preferred substitute product. Under these circumstances, the differences between Cournot and Bertrand competition, both in terms of rivalry among competitors and versus potential ones, are definitely less demarcated, although Bertrand rivalry among competitors is still comparatively harsher.[35]

The ability to price above marginal costs does not entail the ability to make supra-competitive profit for a long time. First of all, the price mark-up may be just enough to cover fixed sunk costs, such as the marketing costs to differentiate the firm's supply by building brand awareness and, hopefully, loyalty in case of satisfactory purchase. Second, the observation that incumbents are earning a return above their cost of capital may attract new entrants with a new variety of the same product—an imperfect substitute which might be preferred by some of the incumbents' customers, thus eroding the incumbents' market power at the margins. At the limit, firms would just about break even, that is, notwithstanding their ability to set prices above marginal costs. This competitive mode is known as *monopolistic competition* and was developed by Edward Chamberlain in 1933.[36]

Under monopolistic competition, the number of firms that the market can accommodate is determined by the relative size of fixed, sunk costs of entry: that is, the extent of economies of scale. Accordingly, the larger the addressable market—for instance with a larger population—and the larger the number of viable firms. This relationship could be disrupted, though, where incumbents have a choice to step up their investment in order to improve quality, or the perception thereof, through spending on advertising. In detail, the incentive to increase fixed sunk costs, which is invariant to the level of output, is stronger the larger the addressable market.

Hence, as the market grows over the life-cycle of a product as it approaches maturity firms might trigger an 'arms race' when they all escalate their fixed sunk spending so as not to be perceived to be the low-quality seller. As a result, whilst the market size increases, the level of investment needed to enter is raised more than proportionally, so that only a few firms can emerge as viable competitors over time. This consolidation due to the 'endogenous' nature of sunk costs—that is, those that are under firms' control—is known as *natural oligopoly*.[37]

[34] Of course, the incumbent can still deter entry by committing to be aggressive rather than accommodative, by, for example, investing in 'sunk' extra capacity, which would remain idle unless the incumbent produces a higher quantity. This intuition was developed by Avinash Dixit in 1980: see A Dixit, 'The Role of Investment in Entry Deterrence' (1980) 90(357) *Economic J* 95.

[35] Another set of circumstances where the Bertrand paradox is averted is when firms face capacity constraints, so that a firm may not be able to sell all the forthcoming demand even if the price set is the lowest. This limitation of the Bertrand model was first raised by Francis Ysidro Edgeworth in 1887. It can be proven that when firms decide their capacity levels first and then compete in prices—for instance, tour operators that book rooms well in advance of selling them—the final outcome converges to the Cournot outcome. This result was established in DM Kreps and JA Scheinkman, 'Quantity Precommitment and Bertrand Competition Yield Cournot Outcomes' (1983) 14(2) *Bell J Economics* 326.

[36] EH Chamberlain, *Theory of Monopolistic Competition* (Harvard University Press, 1933).

[37] This theoretical framework was fully set out in J Sutton, *Sunk Costs and Market Structure: Price Competition, Advertising, and the Evolution of Concentration* (MIT Press, 1991).

The counterintuitive corollary of this model is that, although the market consolidates, competitive rivalry, driven by the need to recover the escalating sunk costs, might actually increase.

In the model presented above, firms try to reposition their supply by increasing quality in parallel. In contrast, where consumers are heterogeneous with respect to their willingness to pay for higher levels of product quality,[38] rivals' strategy could differ. Firms might position themselves as far apart in terms of quality attributes as possible in order to soften pricing rivalry. For example, in the simplest duopolistic setting, one firm opts for the highest quality and the other for the lowest, even if there are no cost savings from lowering product quality.[39] The resulting 'maximum differentiation' allows firms to soften price competition and exercise market power. In this setting, the number of viable firm is determined by the range in consumer willingness to pay for quality: that is, the large consumer heterogeneity and the larger the number of firms the market could accommodate.[40]

11.4.2. OLD AND NEW DEMAND-SIDE MARKET FAILURES

None of the models of oligopolistic and uncoordinated competition presented above amounts to a straightforward case of market failure warranting corrective intervention. From a static point of view, no improvement in consumer surplus could be achieved unless either the structure of the market or the nature of competition was changed. Regarding the former, structural intervention under competition law is, in practice, an option only *ex ante* where a merger can be prohibited in advance because of the risk of 'unilateral effects'. Besides this, since by definition none of the oligopolistic rivals is dominant, intervention under Article 102 TFEU could only be contemplated where there is tacit collusion, hence not where market power is merely the result of uncoordinated strategic interaction. Regarding the nature of competition, it would be pretentious even to conceive the possibility of imposing a behavioural remedy that could force a change in the competitive model, say, from Cournot to Bertrand, in order to increase the intensity of competitive rivalry. Besides being disproportionate, such a remedy would be impracticable to administer.

From a dynamic perspective, it would be naïve to consider the Bertrand paradox, with its alluring approximation of perfect competition, as a desirable benchmark policy-wise. In its purest version, the Bertrand model is incompatible with the idea that more than one firm could incur fixed sunk costs to enter a market and compete in a sustainable way. In this sense, all the other models of uncoordinated oligopoly can be thought of as various attempts to escape from that impossibility. That is to say, under homogeneous Bertrand dynamic efficiency can come only in the form of successive disruptive monopolies, where an incumbent is displaced by the introduction of a new superior product, so that the substitution pattern is uni-directional: that is, the new is a substitute for the old, but not vice-versa. Suffice to say, this approach is too narrow, in that it must be possible to conceive scenarios where oligopolistic

[38] Higher propensity to pay for quality could be due either to higher disposable income or because the consumer in question can extract higher utility from consumption: for instance, a professional photographer can make the most of a high-spec camera.

[39] Here the sequence of entry is important in that there always is a first-mover advantage by choosing the high quality which is more profitable.

[40] It is worth noting that here the number of potential firms does not depend on the size of the addressable market. That is to say, vertical differentiation can result in a *natural oligopoly*, this time, however, due to the exogenous range of consumer preferences for variety rather that the endogenous level of sunk costs. This result was established in A Shaked and J Sutton, 'Natural Oligopolies' (1983) 51 *Econometrica* 1469.

firms enjoy a degree of market power—notwithstanding the close substitutability among rivals' products—which allows them to set prices above marginal costs in order to justify past and future investment decisions.

There is another class of oligopoly models, however, where the case for corrective intervention is stronger, albeit not perhaps under competition law, as discussed in the next section. The common feature in all these models is that the demand-side of the market is not without friction, in that buyers face difficulties in 'shopping around'. In other words, consumers face difficulties in searching the market, identifying available products, their prices and attributes.[41] In this sense, this class of models constitute another departure, at the retail level, from the classic Bertrand setting where the consumer is blessed with a perfect and complete knowledge of firms' supply across the market.

It is well established that the presence of consumer search and computational costs is conducive to prices being set above competitive levels. This exploitative effect is most pronounced when consumers have low levels of preference for variety and relatively high search costs.[42] Under such circumstances, firms might even be able to raise prices to monopolistic levels. The underlying intuition is that firms know that they can incrementally raise their prices without losing consumers as long as the expected benefits from extra-searching are lower than the corresponding search cost.[43] Since buyers face search costs in general they rationally anticipate that all firms will take advantage of this situation by setting high prices. Therefore, a puzzle emerges whereby in the presence of search costs there is no price dispersion so that consumers do not shop around. On the other hand, firms lack the incentives to cut prices since they anticipate that disillusioned consumers would not be on the lookout for better bargains. Under these circumstances, consumer inertia prevails even if switching costs are minimal.[44]

This paradoxical result, however, is at odds with the general observation regarding the persistence of price dispersion which should motivate searching activity, in particular, nowadays, over the Internet where shopping costs are virtually negligible. In this respect, the mainstream approach developed in the assessment of how information that is costly for consumers to

41 Demand-side frictions can be due also to switching costs, where customers purchase a product repeatedly and may find it costly to switch from one seller to another. Search costs differ from switching costs in that the latter are the costs incurred by a consumer in changing supplier and do not act to improve consumer's information. That is, contrary to switching costs, search costs can be incurred more than once and without necessarily choosing to switch supplier. Moreover, the impact of switching costs on competitive rivalry can be ambivalent. On the one hand, sellers have an obvious incentive to charge high prices to locked-in customers—the 'harvesting effect'; on the other hand, sellers without locked-in customers are eager to cut prices in order to attract new customers in the first place—the 'investment effect'. Intuitively, switching costs amplify the underlying degree of competitive rivalry (or lack thereof): by and large, if repeat purchases are frequent, concentration is not high and switching costs are not too high—in other words, if the market is 'contestable', the 'investment effect' dominates; whereas if repeat purchases are infrequent, the market is concentrated and switching costs are high, the 'harvesting effect' prevails. See eg L Cabral 'Dynamic Pricing in Customer Markets with Switching Costs' (2013) 20 *Rev Economic Dynamics* 43.

42 See S Anderson and R Renault, 'Pricing, Product Diversity, and Search Costs: A Bertrand-Chamberlin-Diamond Mode' [1999] 30 *RAND J Economics* 719.

43 By the same token, the presence of consumer search costs reduces the profitability of a price cut, in that unless the seller expends resources on advertising, the price cut induces no new potential buyer to launch a search: this intuition was developed in JE Stiglitz, 'Equilibrium in Product Markets with Imperfect Information' (1979) 69 *American Economic Rev* 33.

44 This surprising theoretical result is called the 'Diamond paradox', after Peter Diamond who argued that firms would set monopoly prices in the Bertrand context with homogeneous products if consumers face search costs, even arbitrarily small ones: see PA Diamond, 'A Model of Price Adjustment' (1971) 3 *J Economic Theory* 156.

acquire affects pricing is to split consumers between two opposite types:[45] high cost searchers who are uninformed, sometimes called 'tourists', as opposed to low cost 'shoppers' who have a full grasp of market prices, sometimes called 'locals'.[46] Under these circumstances, price dispersion is the result of the trade-off between the opposing incentives of attracting 'locals' by undercutting rivals and ripping off 'tourists' whilst giving up on selling to 'locals'.[47]

Moreover, this classic theoretical framework is largely adopted throughout the recent literature on how competing firms can exploit various biases of consumers, inattentiveness, and inertia, primarily through the use of price framing.[48] In this case, however, rather than trying to explain how the presence of exogenous search costs could lead to price dispersion, the aim is to justify how firms can have unilateral incentives to practice price obfuscation, but with the difference that in this case firms deliberately act to raise search costs except for those costless shoppers who do not incur them regardless of firms' attempts to thwart price comparison.

11.5. DESIGNING A COMPETITION LAW REGIME WITH THE AIM OF TACKLING THE HARMFUL EFFECTS OF OLIGOPOLY: CHALLENGES

The reason why the search cost models described above are market failures that warrant corrective intervention—in contrast to orthodox models of uncoordinated competition described in the section before—is that there are no redeemable features such as product differentiation or the prospect of innovation: the trade-off between static and dynamic efficiency. That firms have to exploit consumers' information asymmetry suggests that, absent search costs, their offers would be perceived as undifferentiated—in other words, competition would fall back to the Bertrand model with product homogeneity.[49]

[45] For a literature review, see S Huck, J Zhou, and C Duke, 'Consumer Behavioural Biases in Competition', OFT 1324 (2011), paras 3.59–3.70, available at http://www.oft.gov.uk/shared_oft/research/OFT1324.pdf.

[46] This strand of literature is split between models with 'sequential search', where 'tourists' incur a search cost every time they shop for a new quote; as opposed to models with 'simultaneous search', where 'tourists' just buy from one shop at random whilst 'locals' are assumed to get all quotes in one go. In the end, though, even in the former setting 'tourists' rationally randomise where to buy from when search costs are relatively high. Nevertheless, it could be argued that models with simultaneous search are posited on some kind of irrational naivety where some buyers are utterly unengaged and clueless.

[47] Technically speaking, firms play mixed strategies randomly between low prices to sell to 'locals' and high prices to rip off 'tourists'. Firms have to do so because they cannot tell who is informed from who is not, and they do not want to let competitors predict, and thus adapt to, their pricing decision.

[48] For a comprehensive review, see S Huck, J Zhou, and C Duke, 'Consumer Behavioural Biases in Competition', OFT1324 (2011), ch 3, 46, available at http://www.oft.gov.uk/shared_oft/research/OFT1324.pdf.

[49] This is so in line with the 'unravelling principle', which posits that a seller with (private) information about the quality of the product sold will disclose it, rather than being subject to the negative inference that arises from the failure to disclose it when one can do so cheaply and credibly. This intuition was first developed, independently, by S Grossman, 'The Information Role of Warranties and Private Disclosure About Product Quality' (1981) 24 *J L & Economics* 461; and P Milgrom, 'Good News and Bad News: Representation Theorems and Applications' [1981] 12 *Bell J Economics* 380. In contrast, there are circumstances where firms might not be able to signal their superior quality, that is, since the product attributes are not observable before purchase: for instance, conditions of a distressed property sold on auction. Here, consumers might even decide not to make a purchase at all, in that the perceived risk of buying what could turn out to be a sub-standard product is prohibitively high. In economic jargon, this potential fatal source of market failure is called 'adverse selection', and was identified by George Akerlof: see GE Akerlof, 'The Market for "Lemons": Quality Uncertainty and the Market Mechanism' (1970) 84 *Q J Economics* 488.

Besides the lack of redeemable features, these market configurations also lack a tendency towards self-correction, in the sense that, contrary to both collusion and orthodox uncoordinated competition, to increase the number of firms might not prove beneficial in terms of static consumer surplus; indeed, it might make things worse.[50] This is why, fundamentally, competition law is probably not the best instrument to tackle these oligopoly problems. Whereas, market-wide interventions of the kind allowed under the UK Market Investigation Reference power[51] aimed at correcting consumer information asymmetry may be needed, although any remedial intervention ought to be carefully market-tested.[52]

At the end of Section 11.2, we pointed out that ex-post enforcement against tacit collusion is very difficult in the absence of past episodes of deviation followed by a phase of retaliation. This is because all that can be observed may just be a prolonged period of parallel conduct among rivals. This pattern, however, is also consistent with a benign market configuration where firms compete in strategic complements, such as under Bertrand competition with or without product differentiation. Uncoordinated parallel conduct is sometimes called 'unconscious parallelism'.

Therefore, enforcement under Article 102 TFEU might prove very costly, causing undue over-deterrence because of the risk of incurring 'false convictions'. Accordingly, enforcement ex-ante under the merger regime is more tolerable, since the risk of chilling firms' incentives to innovate is definitely lower where incumbents are pursuing external growth, as opposed to organic growth.

Nevertheless, the case for pursuing tacit collusion is fully justifiable to the extent that this market outcome is not only feasible, but also detectable, that is, distinguishable from 'unconscious parallelism'. Under these circumstances, collectively dominant firms should not enjoy an immunity from an offense which members of a cartel would not enjoy, provided that an 'unspoken' collusive agreement is sustainable and detectable. That is to say, the creation of a position of collective dominance ought to be considered as an abuse on its own, to the extent that such a market configuration is not the natural outcome of strategic interaction, but results from the collective departure from uncoordinated competitive rivalry.[53]

50 See S Huck, J Zhou, and C Duke, 'Consumer Behavioural Biases in Competition', OFT1324 (2011), available at http://www.oft.gov.uk/shared_oft/research/OFT1324.pdf, para 3.58:

> [. . .] one of the most fundamental results in the literature surveyed here, namely that increasing the number of firms, for example, through easing entry, can actually have adverse consequences for consumers. Essentially, the logic for this result is that, as soon as some consumers do not search properly, firms no longer have a clear incentive to compete by offering better deals. Rather, an alternative strategy arises which offers low value items to consumers who do not engage in adequate search.

51 Under the UK Enterprise Act 2002, section 131, the competition authority may make a reference where it has reasonable grounds for suspecting that any feature, or combination of features, of a market or markets in the UK for goods or services prevents, restricts, or distorts competition in connection with the supply or acquisition of any goods or services in the UK or a part of the UK. That is to say, this regime allows corrective intervention on an *ex post* basis without the need to establish firm(s)' liability first.

52 See, in this respect, L Garrod, M Hviid, G Loomes, and C Waddams Price, 'Assessing the Effectiveness of Potential Remedies in Consumer Markets', OFT 994 (2008), available at www.oft.gov.uk/shared_oft/economic_research/oft994.pdf.

53 In this respect, detection can rest on the common adoption of a 'facilitating practice' by the alleged firms. That is, in the absence of any other plausible legitimate explanation for the observed parallelism, the alleged practice should not be sanctioned. This approach has been championed by one of the authors: see V Korah *EC Competition Law and Practice* (Hart, 7th edn, 2000), 116: ('[. . .] Indeed, I would like to see Article [10]2 applied to such firms only in relation to devices facilitating tacit collusion.'). See also G Monti, 'The Scope of Collective Dominance under Articles 82 EC' (2001) 38 *Common Market L Rev* 131, 146–9.

11.6. THE COMMUNICATIONS-BASED APPROACH AND THE LIMITS OF ARTICLE 101 TFEU/CHAPTER I CA98: A REVIEW OF TACIT COLLUSION, CONCERTED PRACTICES, AND PARALLEL CONDUCT

The enforcement of Article 101 TFEU, as well as that of Chapter I CA98, requires the existence of some form of collusion between the undertakings involved, this taking the form either of agreement, or concerted practice or a decision of an association of undertakings (see Chapter 5). The concept of agreement has been given a specific definition, which emphasizes the need for a 'concurrence of wills' between two or more undertakings (see Chapter 5). This is revealed through some form of communication taking place between them, although the form that this communication may take varies. As explained in Section 11.2, this emphasis on communication distinguishes the legal from the economic approach on collusion. Let's distinguish for the time being among the following three scenarios:

JE Harrington Jr, 'A Theory of Tacit Collusion' (January 2012), available at krieger2.jhu.edu/economics/wp-content/uploads/pdf/papers/wp588_harrington.pdf (excerpt; footnotes omitted)

Explicit collusion is when supracompetitive prices are achieved via express communication about an agreement; there has been a direct exchange of assurances regarding the coordination of their conduct. Mutual understanding is significant and is acquired through express communication. Explicit collusion is illegal. *Conscious parallelism* is when supracompetitive prices are achieved without express communication. A common example is two adjacent gasoline stations in which one station raises its price to a supra-competitive level and the other station matches the price hike. While there may be mutual understanding regarding the underlying mechanism that stabilizes those supra-competitive prices (for example, any price undercutting results in a return to competitive prices), this understanding was not reached through express communication. Conscious parallelism is legal. *Concerted action* resides between these two extremes and refers to when supracompetitive prices are achieved with some form of direct communication—such as about intentions—but firms do not expressly propose and reach an agreement. For example, concerted practices may involve a firm's public announcement of a proposed pricing policy which, without the express affirmative response from its rivals, is followed by the common adoption of that policy with a subsequent rise in price. The extent of mutual understanding is more than conscious parallelism but does not reach the level of explicit collusion. Concerted action lies in the gray area of what is legal and what is not. Conscious parallelism and concerted action are both forms of tacit collusion in that a substantive part of the collusive arrangement is achieved without express communication.

While the distinction between explicit and tacit collusion exists in practice and in the law, it is a distinction that is largely absent from economic theory. The economic theory of collusion—based on equilibrium analysis—presumes mutual understanding is complete (that is, the strategy profile is common knowledge) and does not deal with how mutual understanding is achieved, nor the extent of coordinated behavior that can result when there are gaps in mutual understanding. Furthermore, there is good reason for firms to try to collude without express communication, and thus find themselves dealing with less than full mutual understanding. Given that explicit collusion is illegal and tacit collusion often escapes conviction, if firms can achieve a collusive outcome through tacit means then they will presumably do so and thereby avoid the possibility of financial penalties and jail time. This then leads one to ask: What types of markets are conducive to tacit collusion? What types of public announcements are able to generate sufficient mutual understanding to produce collusion? In markets for which both explicit and tacit collusion are feasible, when is collusion through explicit means significantly more profitable? To address those questions requires developing distinct theories of explicit collusion and tacit collusion. Of course, the primary challenge to modelling tacit collusion is dispensing with the assumption of equilibrium and allowing for less than full mutual understanding among firms.

This is presented in Table 11.2.

In reality, the situation is even more complex, as it is not for instance clear what is the distinction between direct communication (about intentions), which is the characteristic of concerted practice, which falls in most cases under certain circumstances within the scope of Articles 101 TFEU and Chapter I CA98 and mutual understanding, which is characteristic of conscious parallelism and does not fall under the scope of these provisions. A possible explanation may rely on the existence, or absence, of an intention to harm competition. In the context of a concerted practice, the undertakings exchange in direct communication about their conduct with regard to one of the parameters of competition. In this case, it may be assumed that, absent other reason to proceed to this communication, their intention in engaging in it is to restrict competition between them and could therefore be perceived as a concerted practice. In contrast, conscious parallelism is the indirect consequence of conduct adopted by the undertakings without any intention to behave in concert on the marketplace. The absence of intention to collude is deduced from the absence of any direct communication between them. Otherwise, if such communication existed, the parallel conduct would be considered as forming a concerted practice. Hence, without being a constitutive element of collusion, communication (direct or indirect) reveals the existence of an agreement or concerted practice, in the sense of Article 101 TFEU and/or Chapter I CA98. However, an approach based on evidence of communication stumbles into two problems.

- First, it is difficult to distinguish in practice and in a clear manner mutual understanding from indirect communication, as we have explored in the examples provided in Chapter 2.
- Second, communication is a poor proxy for the existence of welfare reducing collusion, which should be the aim of the enquiry if one takes an economic approach to competition law (see our discussion in Chapter 1).

The EU courts have attempted to draw the lines between concerted practice that falls within the scope of Article 101/Chapter I and conscious parallelism that escapes liability.

Table 11.2. Tacit collusion and Article 101 TFEU/Chapter I CA98.

Explicit collusion	Concerted practice	Conscious parallelism
FALLS WITHIN THE SCOPE OF Article 101 TFEU/Chapter I Competition Act 1998	Grey area MAY FALL WITHIN THE SCOPE OF Article 101 TFEU/Chapter I Competition Act 1998	Legal ESCAPES THE SCOPE OF ARTICLE 101 TFEU

11.6.1. THE *DYESTUFFS* CASE

The Commission of the European Communities rendered a decision against various producers of colouring matter after finding that there had been simultaneous price increases which were applied on identical conditions within the Common Market. Please consider the evidence presented by the Commission to prove the existence of concertation.

***Aniline Dyes* (Case IV/26.267) Commission's Decision** [1969] OJ L 195/11, [1969] CMLR D23

1. [T]he following information supplied by the professional bodies of the leather industry, the textile industry, the dyeing industry and the printing industry of several Common Market countries concerning the occurrence of simultaneous price increases by various producers of colouring matter, the Commission carried out several series of investigations in the six Member States relating to the successive price increases of 1964, 1965 and 1967, under Article 14 of Regulation 17 [now Regulation 1/2003, Article 20].

[T]hese investigations allowed it to find the following facts:

(a) between 7 and 20 January 1964 a uniform increase of 15 per cent in the prices of most dyestuffs with an aniline base, except for certain categories (such as pigments and pigmentary preparations, sulphur blacks and dyestuffs intended for food, biology and the manufacture of cosmetics), took place in Italy, Holland, Belgium and Luxembourg;

(b) on 1 January 1965, the same increase of 15 per cent was extended to Germany; on that day, nearly all manufacturers applied in that country, as well as in those countries already touched by the 1964 increase, a uniform increase of 10 per cent in the price of dyestuffs and pigments which had been excluded from the first increase;

(c) on 16 October 1967, an increase of 8 per cent in the price of all dyestuffs was applied by nearly all producers in Germany, Holland, Belgium and Luxembourg; the increase was 12 per cent in France; it was not made in Italy.

The CJEU explains that these three increases were made by 10 producers.

3. Under Article [101 TFEU] the following practices shall be prohibited as incompatible with the Common Market: all agreements between undertakings, all decisions by associations of undertakings and all concerted practices which may affect trade between Member States and which have as their object or effect the prevention, restriction or distortion of competition within the common market [. . .].

4. The price increases made in January 1964, January 1965 and October 1967 in the colouring matter sector meet these conditions. They are the result of concerted practices between the undertakings listed in section [1] above for the fixing of the rate of the price increases of certain colouring matter and of the conditions of application of such increases within the Common Market.

5. In their reply to the statement of objections and during the hearing the undertakings in question denied that the increases of 1964, 1965 and 1967 were the result of concerted practices. In particular, they maintained that it was merely parallel behaviour, each undertaking basing in each market its behaviour on that of the producer which started the increase, which would be a perfectly normal practice in an oligopolistic market in which all producers know each other, know the prices asked by each competitor and in which when the prices have fallen to too low a level for the taste of the undertakings, following a continual erosion of prices due to a series of little

individual price concessions agreed after each increase in favour of the customers because they have received more favourable offers from competing producers, and when one of the producers—nearly always the one occupying the strongest position in the market—decides to raise its prices, then the others immediately align themselves on it. The undertakings have no interest in acting otherwise because they are not capable of increasing their production as quickly as would be necessary to be able to meet the abrupt increase in demand which their decision to keep to their old prices would not fail to provoke and because, in view of the low level of prices, they would gain no advantage in losing a lively price competition with the other producers.

6. The investigations made by the Commission have revealed that the successive price increases and the conditions in which they were carried out cannot be explained by the oligopolistic structure of the market but are indeed the consequence of a concerted practice.

7. A first proof of the concerted character of the increase rests in the identity of the rates applied in each country on the occasion of the various increases and, with some very rare exceptions, in the identical range of colouring matters subject to them. Furthermore, the concerted character of the increases is confirmed by the closeness—simultaneity even—of the date of their application by the producers in the different Common Market countries affected by the increases. It is not conceivable that without detailed prior agreement the principal producers supplying the Common Market should several times increase by identical percentages the prices of the same major series of products, practically at the same time, and should have done so in various countries in which the market conditions in dyestuffs differ.

The increase of January 1964 was announced and applied immediately in Italy on the 7th by Ciba, in Holland on the 9th by ICI and in Belgium on the 10th by Bayer, in each case the other producers having followed suit within two or three days. In Italy, apart from Ciba, which even before the 7th had ordered its Italian subsidiary to increase its prices, the other producers, except for ACNA, which was on its own national market, all sent their instructions for the increase by telex or telegram from their respective parent companies, situated in places which were widely separated from each other, to their respective representatives on the evening of 9 January: Sandoz at 5.05 pm, Hoechst at 5.09 pm, Bayer at 5.38 pm, Francolor at 5.57 pm, BASF at 6.55 pm, Geigy at 7.45 pm and ICI at a time which could not be determined since the instructions were given by that company over the telephone.

The increase of January 1965 was announced on various dates but uniformly applied from 1 January, both for liquid dyes in Germany and for pigments in Italy, Belgium, Holland and Germany.

The increase of October 1967, which was announced during September, was applied in nearly all cases in Holland, Belgium, Germany and France on the same date, 16 October, by all the producers with the sole exception of ACNA which applied it on the 6th in France and the 30th in Belgium, of Sandoz which applied it on the 14th and the 15th in Germany and the 15th in Belgium, and of Hoechst which applied it on the 16th and the 17th in Germany.

It should be noted that ACNA did not take part in the increase of 1965 on the Italian market and, by its behaviour, prevented the increase intended by the other producers in 1967 from taking place on that market.

8. Another proof of the concerted character of these increases is found in the similarity of content of the orders to make the increases sent by the producers to their subsidiaries or representatives on the various markets, especially on the occasion of the increase of January 1964. It is indeed remarkable to find in several of these instructions an express order by the producers to their subsidiaries or representatives to bring the increase into immediate effect, to refuse to deliver pre-dated invoices and to cancel all offers pending.

The existence of concerted activity is all the more certain in that while the producers all imposed an increase of 15 per cent on the resale price to consumers, they did not always increase their own prices to their subsidiaries or representatives by that amount.

The orders to make the increase issued to their subsidiaries or representatives on the occasion of the increase of January 1964 by several producers show very great similarity in drafting, to the extent of containing exactly identical phrases (which reached its highest point in the telex messages sent on 9 January 1964 by Geigy and by Hoechst to their Italian representatives) which certainly cannot be explained in the absence of a prior concert between the undertakings involved, given that the messages were often sent on the same day, the same hour even; and that makes unacceptable the affirmation by the parties that the drafting similarities were merely the consequence of the fact that they were mutually copied for the sake of convenience.

9. Informational contacts between the producers were made several times, especially in meetings in Basel and London. It appears from the record of one of these meetings, held in Basel on 18 August 1967, attended by all the producers in question except for ACNA, that not only was the question of the prices of colouring matter discussed but also that the company J.R. Geigy S.A. announced as appears from the record, 'that it was seriously considering increasing its sales prices to its customers before the end of that year' and, as appears from the decision of the Bundeskartellamt of 28 November 1967, 'that it would increase the price of its dyestuffs by 8 per cent on 16 October 1967'.

10. It is clearly apparent in these various circumstances that the increases in price found by the Commission are at the very least the effect of concerted practices within the meaning of Article [101(1) TFEU]; there is, therefore, no need to examine whether the increases are the result of an agreement.

11. The proof of the existence of concerted practices has been made with regard to the various producers, whether established inside or outside the Common Market, and not with regard to their subsidiaries or representatives. The orders to make the increases sent to these latter were imperative. Even had they been able freely to determine their prices, it would have been impossible for them to absorb an increase of 12 to 18 per cent in the prices paid by them without passing on at least a large part of the increase in their own sales prices. Consequently, it is to the producers and not to their subsidiaries or representatives that the concerted practices are to be imputed.

12. These concerted practices restrict competition within the Common Market. Indeed, having as their object the application by all the undertakings concerned, on almost identical dates and for the same categories of products, of identical rates of price increase, they directly fix the sales prices of the various dyestuffs marketed by each of the undertakings within the Common Market.

In the dyestuffs sector, the price increases made by the producers have affected the sales price to all consumers because the distribution of the products is made either by the marketing division of the producer itself, when the deliveries are made on its own national market, or through its exclusive resellers who are closely bound by the instructions of the producer, when the sales are on foreign markets. Thereby, such an increase restricts competition, which can no longer apply to other than quality or customer assistance.

When the increases of 1964 and 1965 were made, this restriction of competition could be felt all the more since the rates adopted were identical for all the undertakings and all the countries affected by the increase, *i.e.*, all the member-States except France. In those countries, the sameness of the rates resulted, in effect, in maintaining within each national market, in spite of the increase, the prices of the various undertakings at the same relative level one to the other. The same applied in France where the prices were unchanged. When the 1967 increase took place, this sameness of rates adopted was also found country by country, since the prices of all the products were increased by 12 per cent in France and by 8 per cent in the remainder of the Common Market except Italy, where they did not change.

13. The effects of this sameness of dates of application of the increases and of the rates adopted for them, account being taken of the presence among the companies participating in the concerted practices of nearly all the undertakings which sell dyestuffs within the EEC where they account for more than 80 per cent of the supplies, were felt particularly sharply by the consumers. The latter had no possibility of obtaining supplies partly or wholly at the old prices from another producer which did not participate in the increase in order to lessen its repercussions on the operations of its own undertaking, since the other producers all sooner or later aligned their prices on those of the producers which had taken part in the concerted practice. That situation therefore not only had the effect of modifying noticeably the position of the producers but also that of third parties, unfavourably, in this case of the consumers, on the market in the products in question.

14. The parties have maintained that especially in an oligopolistic market competition operating between the producers does not bear upon the prices, either exclusively or even mainly, but upon the quality of the products and technical assistance to the customers. Also, the maintenance of all producers' prices at the same relative level on each market, whether increased or not, cannot have the effect of restricting competition but only of displacing it from the sphere of prices to that of quality and of technical assistance.

15. These arguments do not deny that competition has been prevented, restricted or distorted by the concerted practices in question. In fact, the competition operating between the producers bears equally, even principally, on prices. The parties themselves state that, outside periods of increase, there is a lively price competition between them which takes the form of individual concessions to purchasers and which tends to reduce the prices. Competition thus does not relate only to the quality of the products and technical assistance to the customers, and consequently the artificial maintenance of the prices at the same relative level has had the effect of restricting competition in limiting it to those two aspects. And even if it had to be accepted as impossible for each producer to act in isolation in an effective and durable way on the level of its prices, that does not prevent any concerted action in this field from preventing, restricting or distorting competition.

16. The concerted practices regarding prices under consideration, the effects of which extend to more than one Common Market country, are capable of affecting trade between Member States. [. . .]

The Commission concluded that the undertakings in question have entered into concerted practices consisting in fixing the rates of price increase and conditions of application of such increases in the colouring matter sector, which resulted in price increases in 1964, 1965, and 1967 and which constituted an infringement of Article 101(1) TFEU. It imposed fines on the undertakings involved, which appealed to the Court of Justice of the European Union (CJEU) (the General Court had not been established at that time).

Case 48/69, *Imperial Chemical Industries Ltd v Commission* (*Dyestuffs*)
[1972] ECR 619

The concept of a concerted practice

64. Article [101 TFEU] draws a distinction between the concept of 'concerted practices' and that of 'agreements between undertakings' or of 'decisions by associations

of undertakings'; the object is to bring within the prohibition of that article a form of coordination between undertakings which, without having reached the stage where an agreement properly so-called has been concluded, knowingly substitutes practical cooperation between them for the risks of competition.

65. By its very nature, then, a concerted practice does not have all the elements of a contract but may *inter alia* arise out of coordination which becomes apparent from the behaviour of the participants.

66. Although parallel behaviour may not by itself be identical with a concerted practice, it may however amount to strong evidence of such a practice if it leads to conditions of competition which do not correspond to the normal conditions of the market, having regard to the nature of the products, the size and number of the undertakings, and the volume of the said market.

67. This is especially the case if the parallel conduct is such as to enable those concerned to attempt to stabilise prices at a level different from that to which competition would have led, and to consolidate established positions to the detriment of effective freedom of movement of the products in the Common Market and of the freedom of consumers to choose their suppliers.

68. Therefore the question whether there was a concerted action in this case can only be correctly determined if the evidence upon which the contested decision is based is considered, not in isolation, but as a whole, account being taken of the specific features of the market in the products in question.

The characteristic fractures of the market in dyestuffs

69. The market in dyestuffs is characterised by the fact that 80% of the market is supplied by about ten producers, very large ones in the main, which often manufacture these products together with other chemical products or pharmaceutical specialities.

70. The production patterns and therefore the cost structures of these manufacturers are very different, and this makes it difficult to ascertain competing manufacturers' costs.

71. The total number of dyestuffs is very high, each undertaking producing more than a thousand.

72. The average extent to which these products can be replaced by others is considered relatively good for standard dyes, but it can be very low or even non-existent for speciality dyes.

73. As regards speciality products, the market tends in certain cases towards an oligopolistic situation.

74. Since the price of dyestuffs forms a relatively small part of the price of the final product of the user undertaking, there is little elasticity of demand for dyestuffs on the market as a whole and this encourages price increases in the short term.

75. Another factor is that the total demand for dyestuffs is constantly increasing, and this tends to induce producers to adopt a policy enabling them to take advantage of this increase.

76. In the territory of the Community, the market in dyestuffs in fact consists of five separate national markets with different price levels which cannot be explained by differences in costs and charges affecting producers in those countries.

77. Thus the establishment of the Common Market would not appear to have had any effect on this situation, since the differences between national price levels have scarcely decreased.

78. On the contrary, it is clear that each of the national markets has the characteristics of an oligopoly and that in most of them price levels are established under the influence of a 'price leader', who in some cases is the largest producer in the country

concerned, and in other cases is a producer in another Member States or a third State, acting through a subsidiary.

79. According to the experts this dividing-up of the market is due to the need to supply local technical assistance to users and to ensure immediate delivery, generally in small quantities, since, apart from exceptional cases, producers supply their subsidiaries established in the different Member States and maintain a network of agents and depots to ensure that user undertakings receive specific assistance and supplies.

80. It appears from the data produced during the course of the proceedings that even in cases where a producer established direct contact with an important user in another Member State, prices are usually fixed in relation to the place where the user is established and tend to follow the level of prices on the national market.

81. Although the foremost reason why producers have acted in this way is in order to adapt themselves to the special features of the market in dyestuffs and to the needs of their customers, the fact remains that the dividing-up of the market which results tends, by fragmenting the effects of competition, to isolate users in their national market, and to prevent a general confrontation between producers throughout the Common Market.

82. It is in this context, which is peculiar to the way in which the dyestuffs market works, that the facts of the case should be considered.

The increases of 1964, 1965 and 1967

83. The increases of 1964, 1965 and 1967 covered by the contested decision are interconnected. [. . .]

99. Viewed as a whole, the three consecutive increases reveal progressive cooperation between the undertakings concerned.

100. In fact, after the experience of 1964, when the announcement of the increases and their application coincided, although with minor differences as regards the range of products affected, the increases of 1965 and 1967 indicate a different mode of operation. Here, the undertakings taking the initiative, BASF and Geigy respectively, announced their intentions of making an increase some time in advance, which allowed the undertakings to observe each other's reactions on the different markets, and to adapt themselves accordingly.

101. By means of these advance announcements the various undertakings eliminated all uncertainty between them as to their future conduct and, in doing so, also eliminated a large part of the risk usually inherent in any independent change of conduct on one or several markets.

102. This was all the more the case since these announcements, which led to the fixing of general and equal increases in prices for the markets in dyestuffs, rendered the market transparent as regards the percentage rates of increase.

103. Therefore, by the way in which they acted, the undertakings in question temporarily eliminated with respect to prices some of the preconditions for competition on the market which stood in the way of the achievement of parallel uniformity of conduct.

104. The fact that this conduct was not spontaneous is corroborated by an examination of other aspects of the market.

105. In fact, from the number of producers concerned it is not possible to say that the European market in dyestuffs is, in the strict sense, an oligopoly in which price competition could no longer play a substantial role.

106. These producers are sufficiently powerful and numerous to create a considerable risk that in times of rising prices some of them might not follow the general movement but might instead try to increase their share of the market by behaving in an individual way.

107. Furthermore, the dividing-up of the Common Market into five national markets with different price levels and structures makes it improbable that a spontaneous and equal price increase would occur on all the national markets.

108. Although a general, spontaneous increase on each of the national markets is just conceivable, these increases might be expected to differ according to the particular characteristics of the different national markets.

109. Therefore, although parallel conduct in respect of prices may well have been an attractive and risk-free objective for the undertakings concerned, it is hardly conceivable that the same action could be taken spontaneously at the same time, on the same national markets and for the same range of products.

110. Nor is it any more plausible that the increases of January 1964, introduced on the Italian market and copied on the Netherlands and Belgo-Luxembourg markets, which have little in common with each other either as regards the level of prices or the pattern of competition, could have been brought into effect within a period of two to three days without prior concertation.

111. As regards the increases of 1965 and 1967 concertation took place openly, since all the announcements of the intention to increase prices with effect from a certain date and for a certain range of products made it possible for producers to decide on their conduct regarding the special cases of France and Italy.

112. In proceeding in this way, the undertakings mutually eliminated in advance any uncertainties concerning their reciprocal behaviour on the different markets and thereby also eliminated a large part of the risk inherent in any independent change of conduct on those markets.

113. The general and uniform increase on those different markets can only be explained by a common intention on the part of those undertakings, first, to adjust the level of prices and the situation resulting from competition in the form of discounts, and secondly, to avoid the risk, which is inherent in any price increase, of changing the conditions of competition.

114. The fact that the price increases announced were not introduced in Italy and that ACNA only partially adopted the 1967 increase in other markets, far from undermining this conclusion, tends to confirm it.

115. The function of price competition is to keep prices down to the lowest possible level and to encourage the movement of goods between the Member States, thereby permitting the most efficient possible distribution of activities in the matter of productivity and the capacity of undertakings to adapt themselves to change.

116. Differences in rates encourage the pursuit of one of the basic objectives of the Treaty, namely the interpenetration of national markets and, as a result, direct access by consumers to the sources of production of the whole Community.

117. By reason of the limited elasticity of the market in dyestuffs, resulting from factors such as the lack of transparency with regard to prices, the interdependence of the different dyestuffs of each producer for the purpose of building up the range of products used by each consumer, the relatively low proportion of the cost of the final product of the user undertaking represented by the prices of these products, the fact that it is useful for users to have a local supplier and the influence of transport costs, the need to avoid any action which might artificially reduce the opportunities for interpenetration of the various national markets at the consumer level becomes particularly important on the market in the products in question.

118. Although every producer is free to change his prices, taking into account in so doing the present or foreseeable conduct of his competitors, nevertheless it is contrary to the rules on competition contained in the Treaty for a producer to cooperate

with his competitors, in any way whatsoever, in order to determine a coordinated course of action relating to a price increase and to ensure its success by prior elimination of all uncertainty as to each other's conduct regarding the essential elements of that action, such as the amount, subject-matter, date and place of the increases.

119. In these circumstances and taking into account the nature of the market in the products in question, the conduct of the applicant, in conjunction with other undertakings against which proceedings have been taken, was designed to replace the risks of competition and the hazards of competitors' spontaneous reactions by cooperation constituting a concerted practice prohibited by Article [101(1) TFEU].

The effect of the concerted practice on trade between Member States

120. The applicant argues that the uniform price increases were not capable of affecting trade between Member States because notwithstanding the noticeable differences existing between prices charged in the different States consumers have always preferred to make their purchases of dyestuffs in their own country.

121. However, it appears from what has already been said that the concerted practices, by seeking to keep the market in a fragmented state, were liable to affect the circumstances in which trade in the products in question takes place between the Member States.

122. The parties who put these practices into effect sought, on the occasion of each price increase, to reduce to a minimum the risks of changing the conditions of competition.

123. The fact that the increases were uniform and simultaneous has in particular served to maintain the *status quo*, ensuring that the undertakings would not lose custom, and has thus helped to keep the traditional national markets in those goods 'cemented' to the detriment of any real freedom of movement of the products in question in the Common Market.

124. Therefore this submission is unfounded. [. . .]

NOTES AND QUESTIONS ON THE COMMISSION'S DECISION AND THE CJEU JUDGMENT IN DYESTUFFS

1. (Commission's Decision, points 2 and 13) How many firms are alleged to have cartelized? What aggregate share of the market did they enjoy?
2. (Commission's Decision, point 15) Did they compete on individual discounts to hard bargaining customers? What are they alleged to have agreed upon?
3. What kinds of price competition are commercially possible in a concentrated market, where each supplier may expect its competitors to watch its every move?
4. They cannot compete in ways that can be easily followed. Does this explain why they each gave secret discounts to large buyers?
5. How many kinds of dyestuffs were there?[54] Did all the firms sell the whole range? Were there close substitutes for the whole range?[55]

[54] Case 48/69, *Imperial Chemical Industries Ltd v Commission* [1972] ECR 619, para 71 [hereinafter *Dyestuffs*].

[55] Ibid, paras 62 and 72.

6. (CJEU Judgment, paragraphs 73 and 78) Do you think there were more than three to five firms selling a particular dyestuff in a particular Member State?
7. (CJEU Judgment, paragraph 70) Most of the dyestuffs were by-products of something else. Is it possible for the producers to know the cost of making each of several by-products? Give reasons.
8. If the producers did not know the individual costs within wide limits, how were they to price their products if not by what the market would bare?
9. Should the Commission have stated these facts? Did it do so?
10. (Commission's Decision, points 1 and 7) How did the 1964 increase take place in Italy on 7 January? What range of products was included?
11. (Commission's Decision, point 7, 2nd paragraph) If you were a manager of ICI, the leading firm in the Netherlands, and desperate to increase prices on 9 January and to maintain the increase, would you increase the price (a) in Italy and (b) in the Netherlands on the same range of products or on those which you make at higher cost? Give reasons.
12. (Commission's Decision, point 7, 2nd paragraph) Consider the telex sent on 9 January. Six out of 10 firms sent telexes between 5:05 and 7:45 pm. Is there any reason for the other four not to communicate with their Italian subsidiaries by fax? Does the timing of the communications indicate that they colluded? If each heard of Ciba's increase in Italy on 7 January, when would you expect a meeting within each firm to be held and end? (ICI probably decided in advance what to do if one of its competitors raised prices in any country.)
13. (Commission's Decision, point 7, 3rd paragraph; CJEU Judgment, paragraphs 91–5) How was the increase of January 1965 announced? Why might BASF have announced the rise in Germany more than two months in advance?
14. (Commission's Decision, point 8) Do you think it strange that the orders to make the increase prohibited the sending of post-dated invoices? What do you understand by 'raise your prices by 10 per cent'?
15. (Commission's Decision, point 8) Can you think of any possible justification for mutually copying the orders to subsidiaries and representatives 'for the sake of convenience'? Does the statement need to be justified?
16. (Commission's Decision, point 9) If you were the lawyer in charge of a compliance programme, how would you want the salesman in your company at Basle to respond to Geigy's announcement in 1967? If he followed your instructions would it be safe for your firm to follow the increase led by Francolor and Geigy?
17. (Commission's Decision, point 18) If prices for a particular dyestuff in Germany were higher than in France, what might make Francolor think twice before trying to export? Can you think of reasons other than those given in the decision? If Francolor were successful in gaining market share in Germany, what would the German producers do with their surplus dyestuffs? Since the dyestuffs were by-products of other chemicals, it might not be sensible to reduce their production.
18. (Commission's Decision, points 7–10) Did the Commission allege (a) an actual secret agreement or (b) conduct that made it easier not to compete on price without an agreement not to complete?

19. (CJEU Judgment, paragraph 55) Do you agree with the Commission that it did not have to establish a common plan between the firms?[56]

20. (CJEU Judgment, paragraph 59) Note that the applicants argued that the fact that the rates of increase were identical was the result of the existence of the 'price leadership', of one undertaking. The point was spelled out more clearly by the French dyestuffs appellants in *Francolor v Commission*,[57] in which, according to the CJEU, it was 'asserted that academic writers accept the proposition that in an oligopolistic market such as the dyestuffs market so-called 'barometer' undertakings, although not necessarily the most powerful, can ensure that their rivals follow their prices where those prices reflect changes in conditions on the market with sufficient rapidity'. This point refers to the theory of 'barometric price leadership'.[58] Three types of price leadership have been identified by the literature: 'dominant firm leadership', 'collusive leadership', and 'barometric leadership'.[59] The 'defining characteristic of barometric leadership is that the leader serves as a barometer of current market conditions for the other firms in the industry'[60] and although it possesses 'no power to coerce the rest of the industry into accepting its price [. . .] it simply passes along information to the "Big Three" or "Big Four"'.[61] Among the features 'typical to the phenomenon', the literature cited the following: (i) the competitive structure of the industry is that of an oligopoly with differentiated products; (ii) 'shifts in demand are largely due to outside factors' and 'price changes seem to be triggered by shifts in demand'; (iii) 'the identity of the leader tends to change periodically, and is not always the largest seller' as 'leadership by a dominant firm is not necessary for barometric leadership to occur'; (iv) 'the leader is usually perceived as lacking any power with which to force the followers to accept its price' and '[f]requently, the followers will match the leader's list price, but set a de facto price which undercuts the leader's price'. Hence, '[t]he discipline of price matching which has been associated with collusive leadership is not generally present' and '[a]dditionally, punishment phases are typically not observed'. In conclusion, 'tacit collusion is unnecessary for barometric leadership to occur'.[62] These characteristics have been observed in various industries over the years, such as gasoline, copper, airlines, steel, hard-surface floor-covering industry, etc.[63] How did the CJEU react to this argument? Note that in its judgment in *ICI v Commission*, the CJEU observed that 'parallel behaviour may not by itself be identical with a concerted practice, it may however amount to strong evidence of such a practice if it leads to conditions of competition *which do not correspond to the normal conditions of the market*, having regard to the nature of the products, the size and

56 See *European Sugar Industry* (Case IV/26.918) Commission Decision [1973] OJ L 140/17, para 173, discussed in Section 11.6.7 below.

57 Case 54/69, *Francolor v Commission* [1972] ECR 851, para 49.

58 The term first appeared in G Stigler, 'The Kinky Oligopoly Demand Curve and Rigid Prices' (1947) 55 *J Political Economy* 432, and was expanded by J Markham, 'The Nature and Significance of Price Leadership' (1951) 41 *American Economic Rev* 891.

59 DJ Cooper, 'Barometric Price Leadership' (1996) 15 *Int'l J Industrial Organization* 301.

60 Ibid, 301

61 J Markham, 'The Nature and Significance of Price Leadership' (1951) 41 *American Economic Rev* 891, 898.

62 DJ Cooper, 'Barometric Price Leadership' (1996) 15 *Int'l J Industrial Organization* 301, 305.

63 Ibid, 305.

number of the undertakings, and the volume of the said market'.[64] Would the reference to 'normal market conditions' indicate that the CJEU left open the door to an eventual acceptance of the theory of the barometric price leadership?[65] The 'barometric price leadership' argument was one of the first expressions of the so called 'oligopoly defense' that the CJEU finally formally accepted in *Woodpulp II*.[66]

21. Consider carefully the CJEU's Judgment in *Dyestuffs*, paras 66 and 67. How would you establish what prices would have resulted in conditions of normal competition, having regard to the size and number of undertakings and the volume of the market? Does the Court's test have any meaning?
22. (CJEU Judgment, paragraph 68) Does the Court take any notice of the Commission's 'proofs of concertation'?
23. (CJEU Judgment, paragraphs 76 and 121) If markets were isolated by tariff and quota barriers in the past and there were few suppliers, would you expect interpenetration to take place once the duties and quotas were abrogated? If a producer were successful in increasing its market share in a foreign Member State, what would the local supplier be expected to do with his surplus production?
24. (CJEU Judgment, paragraphs 69–82) Is the Court regretting the fragmentation of the market, alleging concertation or merely describing the market?
25. (CJEU Judgment, paragraphs 69–82) Did the Commission condemn the firms for geographical discrimination? Should it have done so?
26. (CJEU Judgment, paragraphs 93–103) Give three reasons, unconnected with concerted practices to reduce competition, for which a firm might wish to give advance notice of price changes to its customers. Is any policy objective achieved by discouraging it from giving such notice? Contrast *Ministère Public v Tournier*,[67] and other cases where the Court has held that parallel conduct does not establish a concerted practice if there are commercial reasons for the conduct even in the absence of any collusion.
27. (CJEU Judgment, paragraphs 83, 99–103) In what ways was there progressive co-operation between the firms over the three price increases?
28. (CJEU Judgment, paragraphs 104–9) The Court stated that the price increases were not spontaneous. Do you think it understood the commercial constraints in an oligopolistic market?
29. (CJEU Judgment, paragraphs 112 and 119) Why should the parties wish to reduce uncertainty? Why should the Commission and the Court object to their reducing the risks of competition?

64 Case 48/69, *Dyestuffs* [1972] ECR 619, para 66 (emphasis added).

65 In that sense, see N Petit, 'The Oligopoly Problem in EU Competition Law' in I Lianos and D Geradin (eds) *Handbook in European Competition Law: Substantive Aspects* (Edward Elgar, 2013), 259, who notes, at n 148 that, in *Zinc producer group* (Case IV/30.350) Commission Decision 84/405/EEC [1984] OJ L 220/27, paras 75–6, the Commission dropped charges of concerted practices over price changes as it found evidence of barometric price leadership, and nothing beyond that.

66 Joined Cases C-89, 104, 114, 116–17 & 125–9/85, *Re Wood Pulp Cartel: A Ahlström Oy and Others v Commission* [1993] ECR I–1307, [1993] 4 CMLR 407 [hereinafter *Woodpulp II*].

67 Case 395/87, *Ministère Public v Jean Louis Tournier and Jean Verney* [1989] ECR 2521, para 24, discussed in Section 11.6.4.

30. How would you advise a client with only a handful of competitors in the Internal Market and protected by entry barriers to raise his prices as costs rise with inflation? Would notification reduce the risk of fines? Is it a sensible policy to make it difficult for firms to raise their prices in such circumstances?
31. Do you consider the Court's judgment on concerted practices more or less cogent than the Commission's decision?
32. Did the Court treat the decision as finding actual collusion or facilitating devices: ie, conduct that made it easier for the firms not to compete?
33. Would you conclude from this judgment that the CJEU left open the possibility of applying Article 101 TFEU to situations of interdependent oligopoly behaviour (without any other evidence of communication)? See our analysis in Section 5.6.3.
34. It is important to note, in order to understand the context of the CJEU's judgment that the Dyestuff cartel was one of the most notorious cartels, dating from the mid-1920s, with the main actors being members of the cartel in the pre-Second World War period.[68]

11.6.2. THE *SUGAR* CASES

In Suiker Unie and Others,[69] *the Court adopted some of the arguments of the Commission in the* Dyestuffs *case.*[70] *The judgment of the Court is 380 pages long. We have summarized the facts and included only the relevant paragraphs on the concept of concerted practice. In its decision the Commission found twenty-four sugar producing or marketing undertakings to have engaged in anti-competitive practices in respect of trade in raw sugars and white sugars. The Commission distinguished between three categories of infringements: concerted practices with the object and effect to control deliveries of sugar on the Italian, Dutch, West German, and Southern German markets respectively. The Commission found conduct in breach of both Articles 101(1) and 102 TFEU aimed at restricting the possibilities for agents or independent traders to import, export, or re-sell sugar; and, finally, a concerted practice with the object and effect of eliminating competition in respect of tenders for refunds for exports to non-Member States.*

The sixteen undertakings which were fined submitted applications for the annulment of the Commission's decision. The market of sugar was characterized by over-capacity and state intervention. As is explained by Giljstra and Murphy,

> [i]n 1972 Community production amounted to over eight million metric tons whereas consumption accounted for only six-and-a-half million metric tons. The major surplus producing

[68] J Joshua and S Jordan, 'Combinations, Concerted Practices and Cartels: Adopting the Concept of Conspiracy in European Community Competition Law Symposium on European Competition Law' (2003–4) 24 *Northwestern J Int'l L & Business*, 647, 658–9, noting that both the European Commission and the Court were 'strangely silent as to the sinister historical antecedents of the cartel'.

[69] Joined Cases C-40–8, 50, 54–6, 111, 113 & 114/73, *Coöperatieve Vereniging 'Suiker Unie' UA and Others v Commission* [1975] ECR 1663.

[70] See Section 11.6.1.

areas are France and Belgium. In both Italy and the Netherlands consumption has tended to exceed local production, whereas in Germany production and consumption are roughly in balance.[71]

As a result of national organization of the industry, the Council of the EU adopted Regulation 1009/67[72] *on the common organization of the market in sugar, which replaced the national market organizations and introduced a pricing system fixing the amount to be paid to producers for white sugar. It also allocated a production quota to be shared out among local producers by national authorities, amounts produced in excess of these quotas being subjected to production levies. The EU intervention served the purpose of limiting over-production, but it had the effect of consolidating markets according to pre-existing national divisions. However, it left some 'residual competition' possible between surplus producers because it was possible to be provisioned from the large surplus production elsewhere in the EU and there was room for negotiation between producers and purchasers on the level of price or other parameters of competition.*

Joined Cases 40–8, 50, 54–6, 111 & 113–14/73, *Re the European Sugar Cartel: Coöperatieve Vereniging 'Suiker Unie' UA v Commission*
[1975] ECR 1663

[. . .]

172. SU and CSM submit that since the concept of 'concerted practices' presupposes a plan and the aim of removing in advance any doubt as to the future conduct of competitors, the reciprocal knowledge which the parties concerned could have of the parallel or complementary nature of their respective decisions cannot in itself be sufficient to establish a concerted practice; otherwise every attempt by an undertaking to react as intelligently as possible to the acts of its competitors would be an offence.

173. The criteria of coordination and cooperation laid down by the case law of the Court, which in no way require the working out of an actual plan, must be understood in the light of the concept inherent in the provisions of the Treaty relating to competition that each economic operator must determine independently the policy which he intends to adopt on the common market including the choice of the persons and undertakings to which he makes offers or sells.

174. Although it is correct to say that this requirement of independence does not deprive economic operators of the right to adapt themselves intelligently to the existing and anticipated conduct of their competitors, it does however strictly preclude any direct or indirect contact between such operators, the object or effect whereof is either to influence the conduct on the market of an actual or potential competitor or to disclose to such a competitor the course of conduct which they themselves have decided to adopt or contemplate adopting on the market.

175. The documents quoted show that the applicants contacted each other and that they in fact pursued the aim of removing in advance any uncertainty as to the future conduct of their competitors.

176. Therefore the applicants' argument cannot be upheld.

[71] DJ Gijlstra and DF Murphy, 'Some Observations on the Sugar Cases' (1977) 14 *Common Market L Rev* 45.

[72] Regulation No 1009/67/EEC of the Council of 18 December 1967 on the common organisation of the market in sugar [1967] OJ L 308/1.

NOTES AND QUESTIONS ON THE JUDGMENT IN SUIKER UNIE

1. Suppose that in an industry with three large suppliers, *A* announced a price rise in 2005, which *B* and *C* each followed within a few days. Costs have increased since 2005. Will there be a concerted practice if, a year later, *B* announces in the trade press a price rise of 5 per cent to take effect immediately? Would *C* infringe Article 81(l) if it were to follow such a rise within a day or two of *B*'s announcement? Make out a case for finding a concerted practice from non-collusive price leadership. Is there an answer to the case you have made out?
2. Before the leniency notices,[73] it used to be difficult for the Commission to find clear evidence of secret horizontal cartels. One of the reasons for creating the General Court was to provide a forum that would have more time to spend going through the voluminous files necessary to decide whether an agreement or concerted practice has been established.
3. In *Züchner*,[74] the CJEU was referred to a preliminary question on the existence of a concerted practice with regard to the debiting of a general service charge at a rate of 0.15 per cent of the sum transferred for transfers of capital and other payments between banks imposed by all banks in the then Federal Republic of Germany. The CJEU found that banks were not exempt from the competition law provisions of the EU Treaties and examined the application of Article 101 TFEU in this context. The CJEU cited both *ICI* and *Suiker Unie* for the proposition that 'although it is correct to say that this requirement of independence does not deprive traders of the right to adapt themselves intelligently to the existing or anticipated conduct of their competitors, it does however strictly preclude any direct or indirect contract between such traders, the object or effect of which is to create conditions of competition which do not correspond to the normal conditions of the market in question, regard being had to the nature of the products or services offered, the size and number of the undertakings and the volume of the said market'.[75] The CJEU found that 'the fact that the charge in question is justified by the costs involved in all transfers abroad normally effected by banks on behalf of their customers, and that it therefore represents partial reimbursement of such costs, debited uniformly to all those who make use of such service, does not exclude the possibility that parallel conduct in that sphere may, regardless of the motive, result in coordination between banks which amounts to a concerted practice'.[76] The national court should give consideration 'whether between the banks conducting themselves in like manner there are contacts or, at least, exchanges of information on the subject of, *inter alia*, the rate of the charges actually imposed for comparable transfers which have been carried out or are planned for the future and whether, regard being had to the conditions of the market in question, the rate of charge uniformly imposed is no different from that which would have resulted from the free play of competition. Consideration must also be given to the number and importance in the market in monetary transactions between Member States of the banks participating in such a practice, and the volume of transfers on which the charge in question is imposed as

73 See our analysis in the companion volume, I Lianos, *Competition Law Enforcement and Procedure* (OUP, forthcoming 2019).

74 Case 172/80, *Züchner v Bayerische Vereinsbank* [1981] ECR 2021.

75 Ibid, para 14.

76 Ibid, para 17.

compared with the total volume of transfers made by the banks from one member country to another'.[77] The CJEU emphasized evidence of communication between the undertakings, as well as more structural characteristics of the market in question and the relations between the competing banks. How would that emphasis on the behavioural aspect of communication affect the respective positions of the claimants and defendants in cases involving alleged concerted practices with regard to the evidence they are required to put forward?

11.6.3. *WOODPULP*

In Woodpulp, *the Commission investigated the conduct of pulp producers operating on the bleached sulphate wood pulp market and trade associations, outside the EU, which were found to have infringed Article 101 TFEU by engaging in conduct that had anti-competitive impact on wood pulp prices within the EU (affecting almost 60 per cent of the total consumption of wood pulp in the EU). The Commission was concerned by parallel pricing conduct for bleached sulphate wood pulp, where future prices were announced at similar period and for approximately equivalent magnitude leading to the actual prices charged to consumers being similar. The Commission had relied less on evidence of communication between the parties (although it was mentioned that there were 'different kinds of direct or indirect exchange of data relating to individual undertakings in the years 1973 to 1981 which was likely to affect their market conduct') and mostly based its decision on the parallel conduct adopted by the undertakings in the years 1975 to 1981 which, 'in the light of the conditions obtaining on the market in question and following a proper economic analysis, cannot be explained as independently chosen parallel conduct in a narrow oligopolistic situation'.[78] We have reproduced considerable excerpts from this case not only because it is important on the meaning of a 'concerted practice', but also because the Court's experts illustrate at points 102–5 what pricing policies may be expected in an oligopolistic market.*

Joined Cases C-89, 104, 114, 116–17 & 125–9/85, *Re Wood Pulp Cartel: A Ahlström Oy and Others v Commission (Woodpulp II)*
[1993] ECR I–1307, [1993] 4 CMLR 407

3. In the contested decision, the Commission found that 40 wood pulp producers and three of their trade associations had infringed Article [101(1) TFEU] by concerting on prices. Fines [. . .] were imposed on 36 of the 43 addressees of the decision.

The product

4. The product which gave rise to the alleged concertation was bleached sulphate pulp, obtained by the chemical processing of cellulose and used for the production of high-quality papers.[. . .]

7. From the manufacturer's point of view, the price of the pulp accounts for 50 per cent to 75 per cent of the cost of the paper.

77 Ibid, para 21.
78 *Woodpulp* (Case IV/29.725) Commission Decision [1985] OJ L 85/1, paras 83–3.

The producers

8. At the material time, there were more than 50 undertakings selling pulp in the Community. Most were established in Canada, the United States of America, Sweden and Finland. Sales were made through subsidiaries, agents or branches established in the Community. Frequently, the same agent represented several producers. [. . .]

10. The United States applicants, with the exception of Bowater, were members of the Pulp, Paper and Paperboard Export Association of the United States, formerly named Kraft Export Association (hereinafter referred to as 'KEA'). KEA was established under the Webb Pomerene Act of 10 April 1918 under which United States companies may, without infringing United States antitrust legislation, form associations for the joint promotion of their exports. That Act permits producers *inter alia* to exchange information on the marketing of their products abroad and to agree on export prices. IPS withdrew from KEA on 13 March 1979. [. . .]

The customers and commercial practices

12. During the period in question, a single producer generally had 50 or so customers in the Community [. . .].

13. Pulp producers commonly concluded with their customers long-term supply contracts which could last for up to five years. Under such contracts, the producer guaranteed his customers the possibility of purchasing each quarter a minimum quantity of pulp at a price which was not to exceed the price announced by him at the beginning of the quarter. The customer was free to purchase more or less than the quantity reserved for him and could negotiate reductions in the announced price.

14. 'Quarterly announcements' constituted a well-established trading practice on the European pulp market. Under that system, some weeks or, at times, some days before the beginning of each quarter, producers communicated to their customers and agents the prices, generally fixed in dollars, which they wished to obtain in the quarter in question for each type of pulp. The prices varied according to whether the pulp was to be delivered to ports in northwest Europe (Zone 1) or to Mediterranean ports (Zone 2). The prices were generally published in the trade press.

15. The definitive prices invoiced to customers (hereinafter referred to as 'the transaction prices') could be either identical to the announced prices or lower where rebates or different kinds of payment concessions were granted to purchasers. [. . .]

The Commission's decision

20. On 19 December 1984 the Commission adopted the contested decision. As stated earlier, that decision is addressed to 43 of the addressees of the statement of objections. Six of the addressees of the decision have their registered offices in Canada, 11 in the United States, 12 in Finland, 11 in Sweden, one in Norway, one in Portugal and one in Spain. Fines [. . .] were imposed on only 36 of those addressees. The Norwegian, Portuguese and Spanish addressees, as well as one of the Swedish producers, two Finnish producers and one United States producer, were not fined.

The Commission found that most of the applicants had concerted on:

(a) *prices for bleached sulphate wood pulp announced for deliveries to the European Economic Community' during the whole or part of the period from 1975 to 1981;*

(b) *the actual transaction prices charged in the common market for most of that period;*

- *The US applicants had concerted on both announced and transaction prices through KEA, which recommended prices, but no fine was imposed in respect of this infringement.*
- *Some of the applicants exchanged individualized data concerning prices for deliveries of hardwood pulp to the European Economic Community from 1973 to 1977 through Fides.*

(c) *export bans imposed by some of the applicants on customers of wood pulp in the common market.*

Some of the firms gave the Commission a commitment to quote at least half their sales to the Community in the currency of the buyer, rather than in dollars, and to refrain from the other practices found. They appealed against the decision.

In an earlier judgment, the CJEU held that the Commission was competent to forbid agreements made outside the Community if they were implemented within it.[79]

The CJEU decided to obtain an expert's report on parallelism of prices.

We have deleted the paragraphs in which the CJEU quashed the decision in so far as it condemned a cartel relating to the actual prices charged on transactions. The alleged concertation had not been adequately identified in the statement of objections. The Court went on to consider the decision in so far as it condemned the quarterly announcements of maximum prices in advance.

The system of quarterly price announcements constitutes in itself the infringement of Article [101 TFEU]:

59. According to the Commission's first hypothesis, it is the system of quarterly price announcements in itself which constitutes the infringement of Article [101 TFEU].

60. First, the Commission considers that that system was deliberately introduced by the pulp producers in order to enable them to ascertain the prices that would be charged by their competitors in the following quarters. The disclosure of prices to third parties, especially to the press and agents working for several producers, well before their application at the beginning of a new quarter gave the other producers sufficient time to announce their own, corresponding, new prices before that quarter and to apply them from the commencement of that quarter.

61. Secondly, the Commission considers that the implementation of that mechanism had the effect of making the market artificially transparent by enabling producers to obtain a rapid and accurate picture of the prices quoted by their competitors.

62. In deciding on that point, it must be borne in mind that Article [101(1) TFEU] prohibits all agreements between undertakings, decisions by associations of undertakings and concerted practices which may affect trade between Member States and which have as their object or effect the prevention, restriction or distortion of competition within the Common Market.

63. According to the Court's judgment in *Suiker Unie* [Joined Cases C-40–8, 50, 54–6, 111, 113 & 114/73, *Coöperatieve Vereniging 'Suiker Unie' UA and Others v Commission* [1975] ECR 1663, paras 26 and 173]; a concerted practice refers to a form of co-ordination between undertakings which, without having been taken to the stage where an agreement properly so-called has been concluded, knowingly substitutes for the risks of competition practical co-operation between them. In the same judgment, the Court added that the criteria of co-ordination and co-operation must be understood

[79] Joined Cases 89, 104, 114, 116, 117 & 125–9/85, *A Ahlström Osakeyhtiö and Others v Commission* [1988] ECR 5193, [1988] 4 CMLR 901 [hereinafter *Woodpulp I*].

in the light of the concept inherent in the provisions of the Treaty relating to competition that each economic operator must determine independently the policy which he intends to adopt on the Common Market.

64. In this case, the communications arise from the price announcements made to users. They constitute in themselves market behaviour which does not lessen each undertaking's uncertainty as to the future attitude of its competitors. At the time when each undertaking engages in such behaviour, it cannot be sure of the future conduct of the others.

65. Accordingly, the system of quarterly price announcements on the pulp market is not to be regarded as constituting in itself an infringement of Article [101(1) TFEU].

The infringement arises from concertation on announced prices

66. In the second hypothesis, the Commission considers that the system of price announcements constitutes evidence of concertation at an earlier stage. In paragraph 82 of its decision, the Commission states that, as proof of such concertation, it relied on the parallel conduct of the pulp producers in the period from 1975 to 1981 and took on different kinds of direct or indirect exchange of information.

67. It follows from paragraphs 82 and 107 to 110 of the decision that the parallel conduct consists essentially in the system of quarterly price announcements, in the simultaneity or near-simultaneity of the announcements and in the fact that announced prices were identical. It is also apparent from the various telexes and documents referred to in paragraph 61 *et seq.* of the decision that meetings and contacts took place between certain producers with a view to exchanging information on their respective prices. [. . .]

The other evidence adduced by the Commission

70. Since the Commission has no documents which directly establish the existence of concertation between the producers concerned, it is necessary to ascertain whether the system of quarterly price announcements, the simultaneity or near simultaneity of the price announcements and the parallelism of price announcements as found during the period from 1975 to 1981 constitute a firm, precise and consistent body of evidence of prior concertation.

71. In determining the probative value of those different factors, it must be noted that parallel conduct cannot be regarded as furnishing proof of concertation unless concertation constitutes the only plausible explanation for such conduct. It is necessary to bear in mind that, although Article [101] of the Treaty prohibits any form of collusion which distorts competition, it does not deprive economic operators of the right to adapt themselves intelligently to the existing and anticipated conduct of their competitors (see the judgment in *Suiker Unie*, cited above, paragraph 174).

72. Accordingly, it is necessary in this case to ascertain whether the parallel conduct alleged by the Commission cannot, taking account of the nature of the products, the size and the number of the undertakings and the volume of the market in question, be explained otherwise than by concertation.

The system of price announcements

73. As stated above, the Commission regards the system of quarterly price announcements as evidence of concertation at an earlier stage.

As the applicants argued that the system was ascribable to the particular commercial requirements of the pulp market, the Court requested two experts to examine the characteristics of the market for bleached sulphate pulp during the period covered by the contested decision.

The simultaneity or near-simultaneity of announcements

80. [. . .] [T]he Commission claims that the close succession or even simultaneity of price announcements would not have been possible without a constant flow of information between the undertakings concerned.

81. According to the applicants, the simultaneity or near-simultaneity of the announcements—even if it were established—must instead be regarded as a direct result of the very high degree of transparency of the market. Such transparency, far from being artificial, can be explained by the extremely well-developed network of relations which, in view of the nature and the structure of the market, have been established between the various traders.

82. The experts have confirmed that analysis in their report and at the hearing which followed. [. . .]

Parallelism of announced prices

According to the Commission, the only explanation for such parallelism of prices was concertation between the producers. The Commission examined if this could be explained by other factors, such as price leadership, but it did not accept that as the similarity of announced prices, and that of transaction prices cannot be explained by the existence of a market leader whose prices were adopted by its competitors. Indeed, 'the order in which the announcements were made continued to change from quarter to quarter and no one producer held a strong enough position to act as leader'.[80] *The Commission also considered that, since economic conditions varied from one producer to another or from one group of producers to another, they should have charged different prices*[81] *but contrary to expectations in this case price differences have rarely amounted to more than 3 per cent. The Commission also claimed that announced prices for pulp stood at an artificially high level which differed widely from that which might have been expected under normal competitive conditions. In addition, the grant of secret rebates and on changes in market shares may indicate the absence of concertation. The CJEU commissioned a second expert report in order to specify whether, in their opinion, the natural operation of the wood pulp market should lead to a differential price structure or to a uniform price structure.*

101. It is apparent from the expert's report, together with the ensuing discussion, that the experts regard the normal operation of the market as a more plausible explanation for the uniformity of prices than concertation. The main thrust of their analysis may be summarized as follows:

(i) Description of the market

102. The experts describe the market as a group of oligopolies—oligopsonies consisting of certain producers and of certain buyers and each corresponding to a given kind of pulp. That market structure results largely from the method of manufacturing

[80] Joined Cases C-89, 104, 114, 116–17 & 125–9/85, *Woodpulp II* [1993] ECR I-1307, [1993] 4 CMLR 407, para 92.

[81] Ibid, para 93.

paper pulp: since paper is the result of a characteristic mixture of pulps, each paper manufacturer can deal only with a limited number of pulp producers and; conversely, each pulp producer can supply only a limited number of customers. Within the groupings so constituted, co-operation was further consolidated by the finding that it offered both buyers and sellers of pulp security against the uncertainties of the market.

103. That organisation of the market, in conjunction with its very high degree of transparency, leads in the short-term to a situation where prices are slow to react. The producers know that, if they were to increase their prices, their competitors would no doubt refrain from following suit and thus lure their customers away. Similarly, they would be reluctant to reduce their prices in the knowledge that, if they did so, the other producers would follow suit, assuming that they had spare production capacity. Such a fall in prices would be all the less desirable in that it would be detrimental to the sector as a whole: since overall demand for pulp is inelastic, the loss of revenue resulting from the reduction in prices could not be offset by the profits made as a result of the increased sales and there would be a decline in the producers' overall profits.

104. In the long-term, the possibility for buyers to turn, at the price of some investment, to other types of pulp and the existence of substitute products, such as Brazilian pulp or pulp from recycled paper, have the effect of mitigating oligopolistic trends on the market. That explains why, over a period of several years, fluctuations in prices have been relatively contained.

105. Finally, the transparency of the market could be responsible for certain overall price increases recorded in the short-term: when demand exceeds supply, producers who are aware—as was the case on the pulp market—that the level of their competitors' stocks is low and that the production capacity utilisation rate is high would not be afraid to increase their prices. There would then be a serious likelihood of their being followed by their competitors. [. . .]

115. The experts analyse the structures of the market and price trends over the period at issue and maintain that several factors or mechanisms specific to that market are incompatible with an explanation based on concertation. Those factors are the existence of actual and potential outsiders not belonging to the group of undertakings alleged to have colluded, changing market shares and the absence of production quotas and the finding that producers did not take advantage of the differences between the various importing countries as regards elasticity of demand.

Conclusions

126. Following that analysis, it must be stated that, in this case, concertation is not the only plausible explanation for the parallel conduct. To begin with, the system of price announcements may be regarded as constituting a rational response to the fact that the pulp market constituted a long-term market and to the need felt by both buyers and sellers to limit commercial risks. Further, the similarity in the dates of price announcements may be regarded as a direct result of the high degree of market transparency, which does not have to be described as artificial. Finally, the parallelism of prices and the price trends may be satisfactorily explained by the oligopolistic tendencies of the market and by the specific circumstances prevailing in certain periods. Accordingly, the parallel conduct established by the Commission does not constitute evidence of concertation.

127. In the absence of a firm, precise and consistent body of evidence, it must be held that concertation regarding announced prices has not been established by the Commission. Article 1(1) of the contested decision must therefore be annulled. [. . .]

NOTES AND QUESTIONS OF THE JUDGMENT IN WOODPULP

1. (Paragraph 13) Should the Commission be as concerned about concerted practices over maximum prices as over minimum prices? Give reasons.[82] Why should customers welcome advance notice of maximum prices?
2. (Paragraph 19) Note the amount of work required to answer the Commission's attempts to find a cartel.
3. (Paragraphs 37, 42–5, 58) Does a finding of identical transaction or announced prices suffice to establish that they are concerted? Are there other possible explanations of parallel pricing in an oligopolistic market?
4. (Paragraphs 59–67) Did the Commission allege (1) that the system of quarterly announcements was itself illegal, (2) that it was evidence of a secret, illegal concerted practice, or (3) that it was a facilitating device which made it easier for the suppliers not to compete with each other?
5. (Paragraph 60) Compare the announcement in 1964 by BASF in *Dyestuffs* of the price increase two and a half months in advance.
6. (Paragraphs 63–5) Why should the Commission and the Court be concerned about conduct that reduces risk for firms? Does any conduct, even an agreement between competitors not to compete, eliminate all uncertainty about their future conduct? Does conduct that reduces the risks of competition somewhat not amount to a concerted practice? Is such elimination required to constitute a concerted practice?[83]
7. Do paragraphs 64 and 65 enable a firm in a concentrated industry individually to raise its prices as costs rise, or otherwise? Do paragraphs 64 and 65 enable each of its competitors to follow the rise without infringing Article 101(l) TFEU?
8. (Paragraphs 58–72) Is the Court concerned with what amounts to a concerted practice or with the evidence required to establish its existence, or both? Judge Joliet was the judge *rapporteur.* In an article he wrote as a Professor at Liège, Joliet criticized the view that Article 101 TFEU could cover tacit collusion.[84] Indeed, Joliet was a fervent supporter of the application of Article 102 TFEU to situations of 'conjenctural interdependence of action characteristic of tightly oligopolised industries'.[85]
9. (Paragraph 67) How does the announcement of prices that have recently been charged or announced restrict competition?[86]
10. (Paragraph 101) The Court rarely appoints experts to help it understand economic evidence. The European Courts ordered an expertise in the *Dyestuffs* and the *Woodpulp* cases. In *Dyestuffs,* the Court ordered an expert's report after it had appointed two experts following the common agreement between the parties on

[82] Ibid, paras 77–9. [83] See our analysis in Section 5.5.4.

[84] R Joliet, 'La notion de pratique concertée et l'arrêt *ICI* dans une perspective comparative' (1974) *Cahiers du droit européen* 251.

[85] R Joliet, *Monopolization and Abuse of a Dominant Position: A Comparative Study of the American and European Approaches to the Control of Economic Power* (Martinus Nijhoff, 1970), 239.

[86] See, our comments on information exchange in Sections 7.3.1.5. and 7.3.2.1.

the names of the two experts. The two neutral experts who were finally appointed by the Court (Horst Albach and Wilhelm Norbert Kloten) were different from the ones the parties had initially suggested in their submissions: Friederich A von Hayek for the applicants and Erhard Kantzenbach for the European Commission! The commissioning of a neutral expert's report was justified by the divergent opinions defended by the expert witnesses of the parties with regard to the plausibility of a concerted practice in the oligopolistic dyestuffs market. In *Woodpulp* the Court had initially ordered an expert's report on the existence of a price parallelism in the market and then a second expert report on the presence, or not, of a causal link between the price parallelism and the alleged horizontal concertation. The Court adopted the conclusions of the experts' reports despite the substantial objections raised by the Commission (which were also based on an expert's report) and the extensively argued reticent opinion of AG Darmon to accept all the Court-appointed experts' conclusions.[87]

11. (Paragraphs 102–5) How can a market with over fifty producers have been oligopolistic? Is there a single market for sulphate wood pulp or a myriad of smaller markets defined in terms of substitutes on the demand side?
12. Did the CJEU accept an 'oligopoly defence'? Would that be broader than situations of 'barometric price leadership'? For instance, would that cover situations where a supra-competitive price in an oligopolistic market is a consequence of the independent individual reactions of the undertakings to an exogenous (not related to the undertakings' concerned conduct or characteristics) change in market supply conditions? What about independent individual reactions to an exogenous change in market demand (consumers' preferences related) conditions?
13. Is the analysis performed by the CJEU that of identifying the cause of parallel conduct? Is it correct to conclude that Article 101 TFEU applies only if concertation is the *sole* cause of parallel conduct? Putting this into familiar causality language, it is only if, but for the concertation, parallel conduct would not have occurred that Article 101 TFEU may apply? What if concertation has contributed, along with other factors, to parallel conduct? Would this situation be covered by Article 101 TFEU?
14. As parallel conduct is not sufficient to prove the existence of a concerted practice, some 'plus-factors' are in addition required for the application of Article 101 TFEU. The concept of 'plus factor' is ambiguous. Kovacic et al explain: '[p]lus factors are economic actions and outcomes, above and beyond parallel conduct by oligopolistic firms, that are largely inconsistent with unilateral conduct but largely consistent with explicitly coordinated action.'[88]

[87] See the Opinion of AG Darmon in Joined Cases C-89, 104, 114, 116, 117 & 125–9/85, *Woodpulp II* [1993] ECR I–1307, [1993] 4 CMLR 407, paras 331–3 for the conclusions. AG Darmon criticized the 'economic models' used by the experts which did not seem coherent or comprehensive in explaining all the different facts of the case.

[88] W Kovacic, RC Marshall, LM Marx, and HL White, 'Plus Factors and Agreement in Antitrust Law' (2011) 110 *Michigan L Rev* 393, 393. More on plus factors in Section 11.6.5.

11.6.4. COLLUSION WILL NOT BE INFERRED FROM PARALLEL CONDUCT UNLESS IT DOES NOT MAKE COMMERCIAL SENSE OTHERWISE

Case 395/87, *Ministère Public v Jean Louis Tournier and Jean Verney*
[1989] ECR 2521

SACEM was a French copyright collecting society to which most French copyright holders had assigned their rights to exploit performing rights. Discotheques complained that none of the national copyright societies would give them a licence at lower royalties confined to the English-language works they wanted to perform in public. Under reciprocal representation agreements, each of the national collecting societies arranged for the others to collect its revenues in the Member State where each operated. These agreements were not expressed to be exclusive, but none of the copyright collecting societies outside France would give to the French discotheques a licence to perform its repertoire. Criminal proceedings were started in France on the complaint of one of the discotheques which also requested damages from the criminal court for infringement of Articles 101 and 102 TFEU. One question referred to the CJEU was whether an agreement or concerted practice could be inferred from parallel conduct. The Court followed the opinion of Advocate General Jacobs and denied that this could be done if there was a good commercial reason other than collusion.

16. The second question relates to the practice adopted by national copyright-management societies in the various Member States in relations with each other. It concerns, first, the organization by those societies of a network of reciprocal representation agreements and, secondly, those societies' collective practice of refusing to grant any access to their respective repertories to users established in other Member States.

17. With regard to the first point, it is apparent from the documents before the Court that a 'reciprocal representation contract', as referred to by the national court, must be taken to mean a contract between two national copyright-management societies concerned with musical works whereby the societies give each other the right to grant, within the territory for which they are responsible, the requisite authorizations for any public performance of copyrighted musical works of members of the other society and to subject those authorizations to certain conditions, in conformity with the laws applicable in the territory in question. Those conditions include in particular the payment of royalties, which are collected for the other society by the society which it has empowered to act as its agent. The contract specifies that each society is to apply, with respect to works in the other society's repertoire, the same scales, methods and means of collection and distribution of royalties as those which it applies for works in its own repertoire.

18. Under the international copyright conventions, the owners of copyright recognised under the legislation of a contracting State are entitled, in the territory of every other contracting State, to the same protection against infringement of copyright, and the same remedies for such infringement, as the nationals of the latter State.

19. Consequently, it is apparent that reciprocal representation contracts between copyright-management societies have a twofold purpose: first, they are intended to make all protected musical works, whatever their origin, subject to the same conditions for all users in the same Member State, in accordance with the principle laid down in the international provisions; secondly, they enable copyright-management societies to rely, for the protection of their repertoires in another State, on the organization

established by the copyright-management society operating there, without being obliged to add to that organization their own network of contracts with users and their own local monitoring arrangements.

20. It follows from the foregoing considerations that the reciprocal representation contracts in question are contracts for services which are not in themselves restrictive of competition in such a way as to be caught by Article [101(1)] of the Treaty. The position might be different if the contracts established exclusive rights whereby copyright-management societies undertook not to allow direct access to their repertoires by users of recorded music established abroad; however, it is apparent from the documents before the Court that exclusive-rights clauses of that kind which previously appeared in reciprocal representation contracts were removed at the request of the Commission.

21. The Commission points out, however, that the removal of that exclusive-rights clause from the contracts has not resulted in any change in the conduct of the management societies; they still refuse to grant a licence or to entrust their repertoire abroad to a society other than the one established in the territory in question. That statement raises the second problem raised in the question, namely whether the management societies have in fact retained their exclusive rights by means of a concerted practice.

22. In that connection the Commission and SACEM maintain that the management societies have no interest in using a method different from that of appointing as agent the society established in the territory concerned and that it does not seem realistic in those circumstances to regard the management societies' refusal to allow direct access to their repertoires by foreign users as a concerted practice. The discotheque operators, whilst recognizing that the foreign societies entrust the management of their repertoires to SACEM because it would be too burdensome to set up a system of direct collection of royalties in France, nevertheless consider that the societies have acted in concert in that regard. In support of that view, they refer to the letters which the French users have received from various foreign management societies refusing them access to their repertoires in substantially identical terms.

23. Concerted action by national copyright-management societies with the effect of systematically refusing to grant direct access to their repertoires to foreign users must be regarded as amounting to a concerted practice restrictive of competition and capable of affecting trade between the Member States.

24. As the Court held in its judgment in Case 48/69 *Imperial Chemical Industries v Commission* [1972] ECR 619, mere parallel behaviour may amount to strong evidence of a concerted practice if it leads to conditions of competition which do not correspond to the normal conditions of competition. However, concerted action of that kind cannot be presumed where the parallel behaviour can be accounted for by reasons other than the existence of concerted action. Such a reason might be that the copyright-management societies of other Member States would be obliged, in the event of direct access to their repertoires, to organise their own management and monitoring system in another country.

25. The question whether concerted action prohibited by the Treaty has actually been taken can thus only be answered by appraising certain presumptions and evaluating certain documents and other evidence. By virtue of the division of powers under Article [267 TFEU] that is a task for the national courts.

26. Accordingly, it must be stated in reply to the second question that Article [101 TFEU] must be interpreted as prohibiting any concerted practice by national copyright-management societies of the Member States having as its object or effect the refusal

by each society to grant direct access to its repertoire to users established in another Member State. It is for the national courts to determine whether any concerted action by such management societies has in fact taken place.

NOTES AND QUESTIONS ON THE JUDGMENT IN SACEM

1. (Paragraphs 22–6) If the refusal of the UK collecting society to license the French discotheques is to be explained by the costs of issuing licences and monitoring performances, would parallel conduct be evidence of a concerted practice? If not, can it be concluded that parallel conduct that is commercially sensible, even if there is no secret agreement, is never enough to establish concertation?
2. A company wishing to raise its prices in a concentrated market announces the rise in advance of implementation. Does this make commercial sense in the absence of concertation? Is this enough to establish that the conduct was collusive? Consider *Dyestuffs*. Is this case consistent with *Ministère Public v Tournier*?
3. Was it commercially sensible for each producer of dyestuffs not to sell outside its traditional territory for fear that the firms previously selling there would react by dumping surplus product in the first producer's territory? Did the Court condemn this at paragraphs 69–82 of *Dyestuffs*?

11.6.5. 'PLUS FACTORS' AND ARTICLE 101 TFEU/CHAPTER I CA98

As something more than parallel pricing is required in order to establish the existence of a concerted practice, courts and competition authorities focus on the features of the specific market, in order to assess the applicability of Article 101 TFEU or Chapter I CA98. The economic rationale for this enquiry is explained below.

N Petit, 'The Oligopoly Problem in EU Competition Law' in I Lianos and D Geradin (eds) *Handbook in European Competition Law: Substantive Aspects* (Edward Elgar, 2013), 259, 267–71 (footnotes omitted)

Initially, many studies have focused on endogenous market features, such as market concentration, firms' symmetry/asymmetry, barriers to entry, capacity constraints/excess capacity, multimarket contacts, demand evolution, price transparency product homogeneity/differentiation, characteristics of market transactions, rate of innovation, etc. But a large, and growing, number of articles studies *exogeneous* market features, such as English and Most Favoured Customers ('MFC') clauses, headline price announcements, information exchange agreements, cross shareholdings, price leadership, joint ventures, resale price maintenance, standard-form contracts, binding price regulations and other statutory obligations, state subsidies, taxation principles, anti-dumping regimes, etc. On each of those features, the literature is far from unanimous. Whilst some studies ascribe to certain market features a facilitating effect on tacit collusion—so-called '*plus factors*'—others point out to an undermining effect—so-called '*minus factors*'.

A second area that has garnered contemporary research interest is empirical analysis. Scholars have attempted to verify the presence of tacit collusion in real-life markets, on the basis of direct industry data. It would be beyond the scope of this study to provide a full account of this literature. Suffice is to say that those studies span a wide array of economic sectors such as car manufacturing, airlines, breweries, petrol distribution, long-distance telephony markets, credit cards, the NASDAQ multiple dealer market, etc.

A third strand of the modern economic literature explores the existence of other forms of tacit collusion, beyond the standard model of price/quantity coordination (e.g., on product/service quality, territorial areas, etc.). Those studies show for instance that oligopolists can coordinate investments in production capacity, R&D expenditures, the release date of product/services, compensations schemes for business executives, licensing policies for intellectual property rights ('IPR'), access charges on communications networks, etc. A proximate, albeit distinct, field of research focuses on '*semicollusion*'. In such situations, tacitly colluding firms coordinate one parameter (e.g., price) and compete on others (e.g., capacity, R&D, etc.). Economists remain divided as to which of those effects dominate (collusion v. competition). After all, if colluding oligopolists compete fiercely on all parameters but the collusive one, then tacit collusion may not be a cause of serious concern. Yet, it may be argued that oligopolists that have achieved collusion over one parameter are better placed to collude on other parameters.

Finally, as in other areas of antitrust economics, behavioralists have shed new light on tacit collusion. In contrast to standard IO theory, behavioral economics does not focus on the firm, but on individuals. In essence, it posits that individuals within firms do not always behave rationally. This is because individuals are subject to a number of physiological, cognitive and psychological limitations, biases and quirks. Hence, individuals cannot—and do not—collect, process and analyze all the relevant information necessary to make welfare-optimizing decisions. In so far as tacit collusion is concerned, this implies that oligopolists may tacitly collude, in settings where standard IO analysis would predict a competitive outcome. For instance, a CEO may renege on a profitable price-cutting strategy, simply because he is reluctant to endorse the reputation of a cheater, or out of '*mutual respect and affectionate regard*' for his rivals' leaders. Similarly, risk-averse oligopolists may over-estimate the costs of rivals' retaliation and stick irrationally to the tacitly collusive equilibrium.

The approach followed consists in attacking indirectly the occurrence of supra-competitive pricing, by focusing on the plus factors that contribute to its occurrence, in general. Hence, these plus factors may constitute competition law infringements, should the formal conditions of Articles 101/102 TFEU, Chapters I/II CA98 be satisfied. This is possible for certain categories of the plus factors mentioned above (in particular those that can be characterized as endogenous) but not for all. For instance, it would be difficult to establish liability (on the basis of the tort or administrative model usually followed in competition law[89]) for a supra-competitive price in an oligopolistic market that results from independent individual reactions to an exogenous change in market supply or demand conditions. Furthermore, elaboration of a list of plus-factors may incur two series of problems.

89 See the analysis in the companion volume, I Lianos, *Competition Law Enforcement and Procedure* (OUP, forthcoming 2019).

W Kovacic, RC Marshall, LM Marx, and HL White, 'Plus Factors and Agreement in Antitrust Law' (2011) 110 *Michigan L Rev* 393, 406–7

> Two basic problems have attended [. . .] efforts to identify and evaluate plus factors. One problem involves the absence of a methodology for ranking plus factors according to their likely probative value. The second problem arises from the suggestion in the economics literature regarding repeated games that market outcomes associated with collusive schemes can result from interdependent, consciously parallel conduct in some industries. [. . .]
>
> First, courts have failed to present a hierarchy of such factors and to establish an analytical framework that explains why specific plus factors have stronger or weaker evidentiary value. Antitrust agreement decisions rarely rank plus factors according to their probative merit or specify the minimum critical mass of plus factors that must be established to sustain an inference that conduct resulted from concerted acts rather than from conscious parallelism. A relatively small number of judicial opinions have extensively and skillfully evaluated the economic significance of each factor. These opinions stand in contrast to decisions that either forego a careful discussion of the economic meaning of individual plus factors or attempt such an inquiry without a sure grasp of the economic concepts in question. Such tendencies make judgments about the resolution of future cases problematic and give an impressionistic quality to judicial decision making on agreement related issues. [. . .]
>
> The second problem results from the development of new arguments, rooted in the modern economics literature dealing with repeated games that market performance associated with collusive schemes can result from interdependent, consciously parallel conduct in some industry settings. Firms in a number of industry settings may be able to achieve collusive outcomes without resorting to conduct that might be characterised as an agreement [or concerted practice].

Commenting on the case law of the US courts, the authors find that '[t]he variation in judicial analyses of plus factors also suggests that the outcome in many agreement cases depends on the Court's unarticulated intuition about the likely cause of observed parallel behavior'.[90] The authors proceed by putting forward a taxonomy of 'super plus factors', that is, market conditions and conduct that create a 'strong inference of explicit collusion',[91] and indicate their respective evidential weight in a finding of concerted practice/agreement. Should such an approach limiting judicial or regulatory discretion be followed? What are the advantages and disadvantages of such regulation of proof? Would that be compatible with the principle of 'free or unfettered evaluation of evidence' in EU law[92]?

90 W Kovacic, RC Marshall, LM Marx, and HL White, 'Plus Factors and Agreement in Antitrust Law' (2011) 110 *Michigan L Rev* 393, 407.

91 Ibid, 396–7.

92 E Gippini-Fournier, 'The Elusive Standard of Proof in EU Competition Cases' (2010) 33 *World Competition* 187 noted that 'the approach of the EU Courts to the assessment of evidence is better understood from the perspective of continental law systems, where the question of how much evidence is required before a judge can conclude that a party has met its burden of proof—does not typically receive an *ex ante* abstract answer in terms of probability [or pre-established evidential strength], but it is the standard of *intime conviction*, without the law framing—how strong this personal *conviction* of the judge should be'. See also E Sherwin and KM Clermont, 'A Comparative View of Standards of Proof' [2002] 50 *American J Comparative L* 243. Such approach will not also be compatible with the 'holistic approach' to evidence that is generally taken by EU Courts: see I Lianos and C Genakos, 'Quantitative Evidence in EU Competition Law: An Empirical and Theoretical analysis' in I

Implementing indirectly Article 101 TFEU/Chapter I CA98 to 'facilitating practices' of concertation may provide a way out of this conundrum.

11.6.6. INDIRECT APPLICATION OF ARTICLE 101 TFEU/CHAPTER I CA98 TO FACILITATING PRACTICES

N Petit, 'The Oligopoly Problem in EU Competition Law' in I Lianos and D Geradin (eds) *Handbook in European Competition Law: Substantive Aspects* (Edward Elgar, 2013), 259, 293–6 (some footnotes included)

Implicit in the *Woodpulp* ruling was the idea that if tacit collusion cannot be forbidden when it arises as a result of natural oligopolistic dynamics, Article 101 TFEU ought however to kick in to catch practices which 'artificially' favour tacit collusion. And, as explained previously, there are very many practices in the form of agreements that may facilitate tacit collusion. With this background, and quite paradoxically, tacit collusion, which had been heralded as a defense to the direct application of Article 101 TFEU has progressively become a theory of harm in many other areas of Article 101 TFEU enforcement. In essence, Article 101 TFEU catches four types of facilitating practices.

First, Article 101 TFEU catches horizontal cooperation agreements amongst oligopolists which facilitate collusion, including tacit collusion.[93] The 2011 Guidelines on horizontal co-operation agreements hold that information exchange agreements,[94] R&D agreements,[95] production agreements,[96] joint purchasing agreements,[97] joint commercialization agreements,[98] standardization agreements,[99] can all facilitate a 'collusive outcome', and might thus be declared incompatible pursuant to Article 101(1) TFEU.[100] The Guidelines' concern is that horizontal cooperation agreement may lead to the circulation of 'strategic information' or the 'commonality of costs' amongst parties and, in turn, facilitate tacit collusion.

Second, Article 101 TFEU outlaws vertical agreements that facilitate tacit collusion. The 2010 Guidelines on Vertical Restraints notably 'aim at preventing [. . .] the facilitation of collusion' that stems from vertical agreements, at either supplier and/or distributor level.[101] The text makes clear that the concept of collusion used in the Guidelines means 'both explicit collusion and tacit collusion (conscious parallel behaviour)'.[102] At a higher level of granularity, the text provides guidance on the collusion facilitating effect of cumulative single branding,[103] exclusive distribution,[104] multiple exclusive dealerships,[105] exclusive customer

Lianos and D Geradin (eds) *Handbook in European Competition Law: Enforcement and Procedure* (Edward Elgar, 2013), 1–138.

93 Communication from the Commission—Guidelines on the applicability of Article 101 TFEU to horizontal co-operation agreements [2011] OJ C 11/1, paras 35–7.

94 Ibid, paras 65–8. 95 Ibid, paras 124 and 127. 96 Ibid, para 158 and 175–80.

97 Ibid, paras 213–15. 98 Ibid, paras 242–5. 99 Ibid, para 265.

100 Ibid, para 37, where it is stated in general terms that:

> A horizontal agreement may therefore decrease the parties' decision-making independence and as a result increase the likelihood that they will coordinate their behaviour in order to reach a collusive outcome but it may also make coordination easier, more stable or more effective for parties that were already coordinating before, either by making the coordination more robust or by permitting them to achieve even higher prices.

101 Guidelines on Vertical Restraints [2010] OJ C 130/1, para 100. 102 Ibid, para 100 n 1.

103 Ibid, paras 130 and 134. 104 Ibid, para 151. 105 Ibid, para 154.

allocation,[106] selective distribution,[107] upfront access payments,[108] category management agreements,[109] resale price maintenance,[110] recommended prices,[111] etc.

Third, Article 101 TFEU covers a number of agreements that create financial links amongst oligopolists.[112] Those agreements are generally known as passive investments. They include agreements giving rise to the acquisition of minority shareholdings in a rival oligopolist, cross-shareholdings, interlocking directorates, etc.[113] Whilst the applicability of Article 101(1) TFEU in this field has been disputed, the Court's ruling in *Philip Morris* and subsequent Commission practice have confirmed that such agreements fall foul of Article 101(1) TFEU.

Finally, technology transfer agreements may infringe Article 101 TFEU if they facilitate tacit collusion. In general words, the 2004 Guidelines on Technology Transfer Agreements state that technology transfer agreements may lead to the 'facilitation of collusion, both explicit and tacit' between owners of competing technologies.[114] They provide further details on the risks of collusion that stem from licensing agreements amongst competitors,[115] non-compete obligations,[116] patent pools,[117] etc.

In sum, the EU lawmakers seem well aware that agreements amongst oligopolists may act as '+' factors. Strangely, however, the Commission's enforcement record against facilitating practices remains weak. In recent years, the Commission brought little if no Article 101 TFEU cases against facilitating agreements in tight oligopolies. This is problematic in areas where Guidelines are not available (for instance, passive investments), because stakeholders are left with little guidance.

In addition to Article 101 TFEU/Chapter I CA98, the concept of collective dominance in Article 102 TFEU/Chapter II CA98 may provide an alternative ground for action against practices in oligopolies that restrict competition.

11.6.7. COLLECTIVE DOMINANCE IN ARTICLE 102 TFEU AND CHAPTER II CA98

Both Article 102 TFEU and Chapter II CA98 may apply to the abuse of a shared monopoly power by more than one undertakings.[118] Starting in 1965,[119] there has been some discussion

106 Ibid, para 168. 107 Ibid, para 175. 108 Ibid, para 206.

109 Ibid, paras 211–12. 110 Ibid, para 224. 111 Ibid, para 227.

112 See Joined Cases 142 & 156/84, *BAT and Reynolds v Commission* [1987] ECR 4487; *BT-MCI* (Case IV/34.857) Commission Decision 94/579/EC [1994] OJ L 223/36; *Olivetti-Digital* (Case IV/34.410) Commission Decision 94/771/EC [1994] OJ L 309/24.

113 Those agreements often fall short of the EU Merger Regulation. They can take very many forms (for example, a standard S&P agreement). A Ezrachi and D Gilo, 'EC Competition Law and the Regulation of Passive Investments among Competitors' (2006) 2(2) *Oxford J Legal Studies* 327.

114 Commission Notice—Guidelines on the application of Article 81 of the EC Treaty to technology transfer agreements [2004] OJ C 101/2, para 141(1).

115 Ibid, para 143. The Guidelines also talk of collusion at the licensees level, para 145.

116 Ibid, para 198. 117 Ibid, para 234.

118 According to Article 102 TFEU, 'Any abuse by one or more undertakings of a dominant position within the internal market or in a substantial part of it shall be prohibited as incompatible with the internal market in so far as it may affect trade between Member States.' According to Chapter II CA98 (section 18), 'any conduct on the part of *one or more* undertakings which amounts to the abuse of a dominant position in a market is prohibited if it may affect trade within the United Kingdom.' See also OFT 402, *Abuse of a Dominant Position* (2004), para 4.24.

119 See the expert memorandum: European Commission, 'Concentration of Enterprises in the Common Market', Memorandum of the EEC (1 December 1965), (1966) 26 *Common Market Reports* 9.

over the applicability of Article 102 TFEU to situations of oligopolistic price leadership not covered by Article 101 TFEU.

In dealing with the oligopoly in the sugar industry, the Commission applied Article 102 TFEU to two independent sugar producers, who were found to have enjoyed a 'dominant position on the Dutch market' and to 'have acted in a uniform manner' always appearing as single entity,[120] yet this did not result from a systematic effort to develop a concept of competition intervention in oligopoly markets through Article 102 TFEU,[121] even if the development of such a framework was called for by some eminent commentators.[122] The Commission also made attempts to employ the concept of collective dominance in its enquiry into the oil industry, following the 1973 oil crisis, in which the Commission alleged that the oil suppliers were jointly dominant, though no collusion was found. So did the Dutch cartel authorities in relation to the oil shortage in the Netherlands.[123] However, the final decision of the Commission in this case did not refer to the concept of collective dominance.[124]

In *Hoffmann-La Roche v Commission*, after confirming that dominance need not be absolute, provided the firm has at least an appreciable influence on the conditions under which competition will develop, and is able largely to disregard competition, the CJEU rejected the application of Article 102 to parallel behaviour:[125]

> 39. A dominant position must also be distinguished from parallel courses of conduct which are peculiar to oligopolies in that in an oligopoly the courses of conduct interact, while in the case of an undertaking occupying a dominant position the conduct of the undertaking which derives profits from that position is to a great extent determined unilaterally.[126]

As we have examined in Section 8.3.6, the General Court accepted in *Italian Flat Glass* the possibility that a collective dominant position may be held by several independent undertakings that compete against each other on a relevant market and that '[t]here is nothing, in principle, to prevent two or more independent economic entities from being, on a specific market,

120 *European Sugar Industry* (Case IV/26.918) Commission Decision [1973] OJ L 140/17, section E, para 2.

121 M Filippelli, *Collective Dominance and Collusion: Parallelism in EU and US Competition Law* (Edward Elgar, 2013), 84.

122 R Joliet, *Monopolization and Abuse of Dominant Position: A Comparative Study of the American and European Approaches to the Control of Economic Power* (Martinus Nijhoff, 1970), who advanced the view that Article 102 TFEU should aim to pursue exploitative abuses, including those resulting from oligopolistic interdependence.

123 In circumstances where there are only a few suppliers in the market, and no collaboration can be proved, the Dutch Minister of Economic Affairs, acting under Dutch national law, considered that in view of their parallel behaviour towards a particular customer, ABG, the oil companies in the Netherlands jointly held a dominant position and he ordered them to supply it with petrol: V Korah, 'Interpretation and Application of Article 86 of the Treaty of Rome: Abuse of a Dominant Position within the Common Market' (1978) 53 *Notre Dame L Rev* 768.

124 *ABG/Oil companies operating in the Netherlands*, Commission Decision 77/327/EEC [1976] OJ L 117/1.

125 Case 85/76, *Hoffmann-La Roche v Commission* [1979] ECR 461.

126 La Roche's share of the vitamin A group was 47 per cent and those of its competitors, 27 per cent, 18 per cent, 7 per cent, and 1 per cent. The Court noted that '[s]ince the relevant market thus has the particular features of a narrow oligopolistic market in which the degree of competition by its very nature has already been weakened, Roche's share, which is equal to the aggregate of the shares of its two next largest competitors, proves that it is entirely free to decide what attitude to adopt when confronted by competition.' The Court referred also to La Roche's technical lead and to overcapacity which would deter new entrants, and confirmed the finding that La Roche enjoyed a dominant position. V Korah, 'The Concept of a Dominant Position within the Meaning of Article 86' (1980) 17 *Common Market L Rev* 395, 399, noted that '[h]ad Roche's share been some 25 or 30%, it might be argued, despite paragraph 39, that each of the large firms might have enjoyed some market power, so long as none of them competed actively in price, and that none should be allowed to adopt conduct likely to keep out of the market equally efficient firms.' This issue did not arise in this case.

united by such economic links that, by virtue of that fact, together they hold a dominant position vis-à-vis the other operators on the same market'.[127] The General Court provided some examples of the 'economic links' that may constitute a collective dominant position but none of these examples included situations of oligopolistic interdependence because of similar, but independent, individual reactions by the undertakings concerned to an exogenous change in market supply conditions or 'barometric price leadership'. The Commission attempted to develop a doctrine of collective dominance in its decisional practice in merger control and led slowly the General Court and the CJEU to accept the application of the doctrine *ex ante* in order to prohibit oligopolistic mergers that could lead to situations of tacit collusion.[128], [129] Yet, this did not extend to cover supra-competitive prices in situations of oligopolistic interdependence (without tacit collusion). In *Compagnie Maritime Belge v Commission*, the CJEU noted that '[. . .] the existence of an agreement or of other links in law is not indispensable to a finding of a collective dominant position; such a finding may be based on other connecting factors and would depend on an economic assessment and, in particular, on an assessment of the structure of the market in question.'[130] In *Laurent Piau v Commission*, the General Court established a direct link between the interpretation of the concept of collective dominance in the context of Article 102 TFEU and that in merger control, hence applying the *Airtours* factors.[131,132] A similar approach is followed in UK Competition law.[133]

[127] Case T-68, 77 & 78/89, *Societa Italiana Vetro SpA v Commission—Italian Flat Glass* [1992] ECR II–1403, para 358.

[128] See eg Case T-102/96, *Gencor Ltd v Commission* [1999] ECR II–753, paras 276–7, where the General Court for the first time identified collective dominance in the context of Art 102 TFEU to tacit collusion. See also K Kuhn and C Caffara, 'Joint Dominance: The CFI Judgment on *Gencor/Lonrho*' (1999) 20 *European Competition LR* 355, 356; Case T-342/99, *Airtours plc v Commission* [2002] ECR II–2585, paras 60–2, where the General Court rejected the approach of the Commission relying on oligopolistic interdependence to find the existence of collective dominance, without emphasizing the other pre-requisites of tacit collusion theory, that is necessity of retaliation in the event of deviation and attempted to broaden the scope of collective dominance so as to cover situations of non-collusive exercise of market power, allegedly also if this resulted from 'barometric price leadership'. According to the General Court, tacit collusion is the underlying condition for the finding of a collective dominance, which supposes evidence of the *Airtours* factors, such as the existence of a common understanding of the collusive price, transparency leading to monitoring and detection of deviations from the collusive price, a credible threat of retaliation against cheaters and sustainability of the tacit collusion scheme with regard to external competitive forces. There is no possibility to use this concept for a unilateral exercise of market power resulting from oligopolistic interdependence: F Mezzanotte, 'Can The Commission Use Article 82 EC to Combat Tacit Collusion?', CCP Working Paper 09-5 (2009), 1–36, available at www.uea.ac.uk/polopoly_fs/1.111282!ccp09-5.pdf. This test, which sets strict evidential requirements, was softened by the General Court in Case T-464/04, *Impala v Commission* [2006] ECR II–2289, by putting in place the possibility of an indirect establishment of the *Airtours* criteria, as well as by the CJEU in Case C-413/06, *Sony v Impala* [2008] ECR I–4951, in which the CJEU seems to have required a more holistic approach in assessing evidence of tacit collusion. For a recent analysis, see M Filippelli, *Collective Dominance and Collusion: Parallelism in EU and US Competition Law* (Edward Elgar, 2013); I Kalozymis, 'Collective Dominance in EU Merger Control: Substantive Issues' (PhD thesis, Queen Mary University of London, 2014), 21–64.

[129] See Chapter 12 on the theory of coordinated effects.

[130] Case C-395/96 P, *Compagnie Maritime Belge* [2000] ECR I–1365, para 45.

[131] Case T-193/02, *Laurent Piau v Commission* [2005] ECR II–209. This case is also interesting for the application of Article 102 TFEU to a collective dominant position held by an association of undertakings (FIFA, Fédération Internationale de Football Association), because of some FIFA regulations restricting access to the occupation of player's agents, essentially finding a 'collective' dominant position of more than 200 clubs/undertakings, which are members of FIFA, clearly a non-oligopolistic market. The General Court relied on the FIFA statute and its binding character to find the collective dominant position of the association of undertakings FIFA, and not of the different clubs, which were held to entertain 'structural links' between them, by virtue of their membership of FIFA. However, it applied the *Airtours* factors on tacit collusion even if the market was not oligopolistic.

[132] On these conditions see Section 8.3.6.2.

[133] OFT 415, Assessment of Market Power (1 December 2004), paras 2.13–2.16, noting that 'the links may be structural or they may be such that the undertakings adopt a common policy on the market', the term 'tacit

However, although tacit collusion is covered by Article 102 TFEU, there has not been any case where tacit collusion was considered as sufficient to constitute the requisite 'connecting factor: for a finding of a collective dominance position'.[134] The DG Staff Discussion Paper published in December 2005 recognized that '[u]ndertakings in oligopolistic markets may sometimes be able to raise prices substantially above the competitive level without having recourse to any explicit agreement or concerted practice', yet it confirmed the possibility of applying Article 102 TFEU only to the extent that the cumulative criteria for the application of the theory of tacit collusion are satisfied.[135] Yet, the Commission's Commission Guidance on Article 102 just mentioned the concept, without providing any details as to the criteria for each use, thus indicating that collective dominance cases are not within the priorities of the Commission, at least with regard to exclusionary practices.[136]

In addition, there are uncertainties as to the content of the concept of abuse in collective dominance cases, some authors, taking a broad perspective, and suggesting that abusive excessive prices (but one could also argue any form the exploitation of consumers takes: eg quality) charged by tacitly collusive oligopolists may be found an abuse,[137] while others take the more traditional, and narrower, approach of targeting facilitating practices, which can be the only 'conduct' found abusive.[138] The concept of abuse in collective dominant position cases is examined in Chapter 5.

11.6.8. THE GAP AND THE ALTERNATIVES

Summarizing the previous sections, it looks as if the application of EU competition law *ex post* to situations of supra-competitive pricing, or other supra-competitive conditions (eg inferior quality, less innovation, less variety) is constrained by the relative formality of Article 101 TFEU, which requires evidence of collusion and the communications-based approach that is followed in defining collusion in this context, and the reluctance of the Commission to enforce Article 102 TFEU in this context. EU Competition law has therefore emphasized an *ex ante* prophylactic approach to supra-competitive pricing in an oligopolistic setting, with the application of merger control and the theory of coordinated effects.

coordination' is actually used, with a reference to the three Airtours factors. See also *Yeyeskel Arkin & Brochard Lines Limited* [2003] EWHC 687 (Comm Court), para 49, noting '[t]hat which renders the entity a collective one is the facility that members can co-ordinate their policy by taking joint decisions on such matters as uniform pricing so as to promote a uniform market strategy. It is this system of effecting a uniform response to competitive pressure which renders the entity a collective one.'; *Terry Brannigan v OFT* [2007] CAT 23, paras 104–8 (referring to the *Airtours* factors).

134 See eg General Court and the CJEU in Case T-296/09, *European Federation of Ink and Ink Cartridge Manufacturers (EFIM) v Commission* [2011] ECR II–425; Case C-56/12 P, *European Federation of Ink and Ink Cartridge Manufacturers (EFIM) v Commission* ECLI:EU:C:2013:575, where both the General Court and the CJEU refused the existence of a collective dominant position in view of the aggressive competitive strategy of some of the undertakings in question.

135 DG Competition Discussion Paper on the application of Article 82 of the Treaty to exclusionary abuses (December 2005), para 47, available at ec.europa.eu/competition/antitrust/art82/discpaper2005.pdf.

136 Commission Guidance on Article 102, para 4

137 R Whish and B Sufrin, 'Oligopolistic Markets and Competition Law' (1992) 12 *Yearbook of European L* 59.

138 G Monti, 'The Scope of Collective Dominance under Article 82 EC' (2001) *Common Market L Rev* 131.

11.6.8.1. *Ex ante* control: Merger regulation

The enforcement of merger control to collective dominance, transformed to coordinated effects, is examined in Section 12.1.4.1.2. Yet, despite the intensive application of merger control with the aim to reduce the *risk* of tacit collusion occurring post-merger in the specific industry, the effectiveness of such approach has been questioned. The following article discusses some of the 'intrinsic limitations of merger rules'.

N Petit, 'The Oligopoly Problem in EU Competition Law' in I Lianos and D Geradin (eds) *Handbook in European Competition Law: Substantive Aspects* (Edward Elgar, 2013), 259, 314–16 (footnotes omitted)

Scope Issues

On close analysis, the EUMR provides a feeble check against tacit collusion. Many oligopolistic markets likely to harbor tacit collusion dynamics are indeed out of the reach from the application of the EUMR. This is first true of all those stable oligopolies on which no mergers take place. In times of economic hardship, for instance, oligopolists may not contemplate mergers for long period of time, simply because access to capital is limited. This is all the more unfortunate, given that economic theory teaches that the more stable an oligopoly, the greater the risks that tacit collusion unravels. As long as no merger occurs in such markets, the Commission remains powerless to address the anti-competitive harm inflicted by oligopolists to their trading parties.

Second, and quite paradoxically, the EUMR cannot prevent the apparition of tacit collusion on existing duopolistic markets, which are the worst market structures in so far as tacit collusion is concerned. Duopolists indeed know that merger to monopoly is no option under the EUMR. Hence, on those markets, the trigger that enables the Commission to scrutinize tacit collusion concerns is wholly defused. In turn, absent Article 101 and 102 TFEU enforcement in this field, duopolists can sustain tacit collusion over time without ever facing competition exposure. Tacitly collusive duopolies can thus be said to enjoy a quasi-antitrust immunity in EU competition law.

Third, besides external growth strategies, internal growth strategies, which fall short of the EUMR, may increase oligopolistic concentration and, with it, tacit collusion. In the competitive process, efficient firms lure customers away from inefficient ones. To serve those customers, efficient firms must expand their production scale through internal investments. Meanwhile, less efficient firms are forced out from the market. Eventually, a tighter market structure emerges, where firms may be more prone to tacit collusion. [. . .]

Fourth, given that the EUMR only apprehends oligopolistic concentration through mergers, it is wholly ineffective to combat oligopolisation dynamics triggered by market opening reforms in network industries (telecommunications, electricity, gas, postal services, etc.). In many of those sectors, oligopolies have replaced monopolies, and risks of tacit collusion are conceivable. However, the EUMR has little, if no grip on them.

Finally, oligopolists that tacitly collude can bypass the EUMR by playing 'cat and mouse' with the Commission. Oligopolists that coordinate their conduct may well reach the parallel, implicit understanding that no merger should take place, to avoid providing competition agencies with an opportunity to change the dynamics of their interaction.

> Given those five blind spots, situations of tacit collusion may endure for a significant period of time without ever being ever disrupted by the applicability of the EUMR. Absent any *ex post* enforcement policy, such market failures benefit from a state of provisional immunity. Economists refer to this as a Type II error (false acquittals). [. . .]

The author also noted some other reasons that limit the effectiveness of merger control: the low predictive value of oligopoly theory, the heavy procedural costs of such enquiry, as 'the Commission cannot confine its assessment to the merging parties, but must undertake a wider market investigation', the difficulties of devising a proper remedial strategy for such mergers, leading to the conclusion that 'in plain and simple words, the EUMR is unlikely to ever prevent tacit collusion on oligopolistic markets'.[139] As the probability of detecting explicit collusion has increased in recent years, in view of the use of the tool of leniency policy in the US and Europe, undertakings engage in 'market oversight games', by using communication techniques that may not fall within the scope of Article 101 TFEU, for instance unilateral signal pricing.[140]

11.6.8.2. Sector inquiries and market studies

In addition to its powers to impose fines and injunctive relief against anti-competitive agreements and abuses of a dominant position, the European Commission has, on the basis of Article 17 of Regulation 1/2003, powers to investigate a whole market (or more than one market) if that seems to be problematic from the point of view of the consumers and that competition might not be working well in these markets.[141] This could include industry-wide practices that may cause consumer detriment. The purpose of the Commission in opening such sector inquiries is to inform its enforcement policy and identify if there are grounds for opening a separate investigation under Articles 101 and/or 102 TFEU. An extensive discussion of sector inquiries is provided in Chapter ten. The Commission has no powers to adopt remedies, but simply to collect evidence and eventually open investigations, if the conditions for applicability of Articles 101 and 102 TFEU are satisfied. Hence, the Commission cannot on the basis of Article 17 of Regulation 1/2003 to remedy supra-competitive pricing, or other anti-competitive effects resulting purely from oligopolistic interdependence, as Article 17 Regulation 1/2003 does not offer a real remedial alternative to Articles 101 and 102 TFEU.

In the UK, the CMA may conduct market studies under its general function in section 5 of the EA 2002, as modified by the ERRA 2013, which includes the functions of obtaining information and conducting research. These market studies may lead to various outcomes, including investigation and enforcement action under the provisions of the CA98 and/or the TFEU, and a market investigation reference.[142]

139 N Petit, 'The Oligopoly Problem in EU Competition Law' in I Lianos and D Geradin (eds) *Handbook in European Competition Law: Substantive Aspects* (Edward Elgar, 2013), 259.

140 MP Schinkel, 'Market Oversight Games', Amsterdam Center for Law & Economics Working Paper No 2010-11 (15 October 2010), available at ssrn.com/abstract=1692733

141 Cross-market references are possible since passage of Enterprise and Regulatory Reform Act 2013 (ERRA 2013), sections 131(2A) and 131(6), and of the EA 2002.

142 See OFT 519 (adopted by the CMA), *Market Studies: Guidance on the OFT approach* (2010), available at www.gov.uk/government/uploads/system/uploads/attachment_data/file/284421/oft519.pdf.

11.6.8.3. Market investigation references

The UK Enterprise Act 2002 introduced an additional mechanism to remedy structural problems facing certain industries, at the supply or the demand side of a market in the UK. Under section 131 of the EA 2002, the CMA may conduct market investigation references, where it has reasonable grounds for suspecting that any feature, combination of features, of a market in the United Kingdom for goods or services prevents, restricts, or distorts competition in connection with the supply or acquisition of any goods or services in the UK or a part of the UK. These market investigation references are market-wide and may take the form of a 'package' of measures, rather than the implementation of a single measure against a specific undertaking. The powers conferred and the procedure for market investigation references is discussed in detail in the companion volume.[143]

Of particular interest for this Chapter is the Commission Guidance on Article 102 accepted by the CMA on market investigation references,[144] which touches upon oligopoly markets that may not fulfil the criteria for the applicability of Articles 101–2 TFEU, Chapters I–II Competition Act 1998 (CA98).

OFT 511, *Market Investigation References* (March 2006), available at www.gov.uk/government/uploads/system/uploads/attachment_data/file/284399/oft511.pdf (footnotes omitted0

[. . .]

2.5. Oligopolistic markets in which firms engage in apparently parallel behaviour while falling short of actually concerting their actions (often referred to as tacit collusion) present a more complicated issue. The OFT recognises that [EU] case law has confirmed that the concept of collective dominance may be applicable in these circumstances, which would bring the conduct involved within the ambit of CA98. But this case law does not at present cover all types of coordinated parallel behaviour that may have an adverse effect on competition. Indeed, the judgment of the Court in the Airtours case appears to limit the applicability of the concept of collective dominance. Market features that can lead to adverse effects on competition in an oligopolistic market can be wider than the conditions that the case law has found to be necessary for collective dominance, that is, for oligopolists successfully to engage in tacit collusion. Furthermore, what qualifies as an abuse of collective dominance is underdeveloped in the case law. For these reasons a market investigation reference will be able to address wider competition concerns than could be addressed by a CA98 case and might, therefore, be a better way of proceeding. [. . .]

5.5. In markets comprising a small number of firms (oligopolies) each firm might find it relatively easy to predict the reaction of its competitors to any action it might take. This could provide an opportunity for firms to coordinate their behaviour for mutual advantage or it could simply dull the incentive to compete, leading to a situation in which rivalry to attract new customers becomes muted. By no means all oligopolistic market structures produce these results. Among the more important of the market features that may assist the coordination of behavior are:

143 I Lianos, *Competition Law Enforcement and Procedure* (OUP, forthcoming 2019).

144 See CMA3, *Market Studies and Market Investigations: Supplemental guidance on the CMA's approach* (January 2014, revised July 2017), Annex, 33, available at www.gov.uk/government/uploads/system/uploads/attachment_data/file/270354/CMA3_Markets_Guidance.pdf.

- the existence of substantial barriers to entry
- the homogeneity of the firms' products
- the similarity (symmetry) of the firms with respect to their market shares, their cost structures, the time horizons of their decisions and their strategies
- the stability of market conditions on both the demand and the cost side
- the degree of excess capacity
- the extent to which prices, outputs and market shares are transparent so that competitors can be well-informed about each other's behavior
- the awareness by firms that their competitors have the ability to respond quickly and effectively to any price reductions they make
- the structure of the buying side of the market (if the issue is possible co-ordination among sellers), and
- the extent of any multi-market contacts.

5.6. This list is not exhaustive nor are any of the items on it necessary conditions for competition dampening to take place. It also is quite possible for a market displaying many of these factors to be competitive. Nevertheless, the more symmetrical the firms in the oligopoly, the more homogeneous their products, and the more stable the market conditions, the more likely it is that an understanding on, say, a particular price can be reached and sustained. It can be difficult to sustain a coordinated price where buyers are large and may encourage sellers to offer special and secret deals.

5.7. A view on the likelihood of coordination or the existence of muted rivalry can only be reached after a close study of the market concerned, not least because the influence of some of the features listed in paragraph 5.5 can be ambiguous. Therefore, product homogeneity makes it easier for oligopolists to reach a tacit understanding, but it also makes it easier for customers to compare the offerings of different firms, possibly encouraging greater keenness on price. However, research suggests as a generalization that firm symmetries, market transparency and relatively stable demand and cost conditions appear to be the combination of market characteristics most conducive to coordination. [. . .]

Conduct of oligopolies

6.4. Many of the markets in which the OFT is likely to be interested will be oligopolistic. These are markets comprising very few firms (or few firms of any significance) where those firms are aware of the mutual interdependence of their actions. Each firm's strategy is therefore determined at least partly by its beliefs about its rivals' likely reactions. These strategies can take various forms, ranging from competitive rivalry to conduct that is tantamount to collusion, even without an explicit agreement not to compete. With either of these extremes, the outcome can be parallel behaviour. The task will then be to determine whether the oligopolists' conduct reflects a restriction of effective competition and would be an appropriate ground for an OFT investigation

6.5. It is a common feature of oligopolistic markets that competition takes forms other than competition in price. These include competitive advertising and promotional activity, rebates and discounts linked to purchases, and more explicit customer loyalty-inducing schemes.

These forms of conduct are often pro-competitive but they may have effects, that, especially when combined with other market features, blunt the competitive process, for example by adding to entry barriers.

6.6. Where firms in an oligopolistic market reach a tacit understanding to pursue their joint interests by coordinating their behaviour (tacit collusion) the adverse effects on competition are likely to be severe. The OFT will not need to establish conclusively that any observed parallel conduct reflects coordinated rather than competitive behaviour by oligopolists. However, it will need to establish that the market features that make tacit collusion a feasible strategy are present (see paragraph 5.5 for an indicative list) and will need to have a reasonable suspicion that the oligopolists are not competing effectively with consequences that are likely to be detrimental to their customers.

6.7. Among the evidence that the OFT might examine in this regard are:

- the pattern of price changes over time, with a view to establishing
- the degree of parallelism in the face of any changes in demand or cost conditions, and whether the pattern seems more consistent with collusive than competitive behavior price inertia, such as when sustained exchange rate advantages are not exploited by importers any evidence that, notwithstanding evidence of parallelism in, say, published prices, the oligopolists compete in discounts or other concessions off the published price, and
- the oligopolists' rates of return compared to returns in comparable markets or to the cost of capital (since the expected outcome of tacit collusion is that the level of prices will be higher than could be sustained in a competitive market). However, where there is persistent excess capacity, excessive prices may not be reflected in high rates of return.

6.8. Even if the conditions necessary for tacit collusion are not met, other market features such as switching costs and informational inadequacies may limit the effectiveness of competition, especially price competition. Competition can be muted in oligopolistic markets without any coordination of firms' decisions. In its report on Supermarkets, for example, the [Competition Commission] concluded that the market was 'broadly competitive' with no suggestion of collusion, but that competition was concentrated on certain products or in certain areas and was less than fully effective elsewhere. This was held to distort the competitive process.

6.9. The OFT will therefore be concerned to consider, in contemplating a reference, whether there are any steps that could be taken to facilitate entry into an oligopolistic market and whether there is any conduct that serves to reinforce the market features that are conducive to tacit collusion and that could, if appropriate, be struck down. One such possibility is facilitating practices.

Facilitating practices

6.10. Facilitating practices are the conduct of firms that make it easier for oligopolists to arrive tacitly at a coordinated outcome and to maintain it in the face of the temptation of all the firms involved to cheat on the other participants. Examples would be a practice of announcing price increases well in advance of the date of implementation, most-favoured-customer clauses in contracts, uniform systems for reflecting transport charges in prices, and information exchanges, for example, on costs.

6.11. There can be objective justifications for such practices and they do not necessarily have the effect of restricting competition. However, where other market features appear conducive to tacit collusion, practices of firms that appear to facilitate such conduct will be closely scrutinised by the OFT. They could even be the focus of a market investigation in their own right.

Custom and practice

6.12. Practices that may restrict competition can be adopted widely in a market as a custom of the trade and with no apparent agreement or understanding between firms. A good example is provided by the CC report on Underwriting Fees. Custom and practice appeared to be the reason why underwriting fees for new share issues were charged on a common basis virtually throughout the industry.

6.13. Another example could be the practice of manufacturers' recommended retail prices. While the practice can be innocuous, its widespread use in a market can have the effect of restricting competition in the downstream (retail) market by dampening price competition, should retailers generally choose to follow the recommended price; or of restricting competition in the upstream market, by making it easier for a manufacturer to monitor competitors' prices and thereby to detect, and hence to deter, competitive price cutting. Examples of anti-competitive effects of the practice are to be found in the CC's reports on Domestic Electrical Goods.

6.14. Any common practices in a market, that appear to reflect a restriction of competition and to have no objective justification, could be the subject of a market investigation reference. [. . .]

Conduct of customers

7.1. Section 131(2)(c) of the Act identifies the conduct of customers as a market feature that could give rise to adverse effects on competition and be the subject of a market investigation reference. The customers concerned may be businesses or final consumers. It may seem rather unlikely that the conduct of consumers could affect the competitive process until it is recalled that 'conduct' includes failures to act. One feature of consumers' conduct that can then affect competition is the search process. [. . .]

7.10. Customers' conduct on its own is unlikely to be sufficient to justify a market investigation reference. However, when combined with other features of the market, a failure or the inability of customers to engage in meaningful search activity can add to firms' opportunities for anti-competitive conduct.

NOTES AND QUESTIONS ON MARKET INVESTIGATION REFERENCES

1. Once it has identified an adverse effect to competition (AEC), the CMA may implement remedies by means of accepting undertakings by the parties concerned or by making an order. Since ERRA 2013, the CMA has also the power to accept from the parties concerned interim undertakings and can also take steps requiring parties to reverse any action that has already occurred before any interim measures have been put in place.[145]
2. In what sense the Guidance on Market Investigation References goes further than the scope of Articles 101 and 102 TFEU (and Chapters I and II CA98) in targeting conduct that may restrict competition? Would that apply to situations of oligopolistic interdependence (including barometric price leadership)?

145 EA 2002, sections 157–8. I Lianos, *Competition Law Enforcement and Procedure* (OUP, forthcoming 2019).

3. Do you think the choice of the terminology of 'competition dampening' (paragraph 5.6) indicates a different basis than tacit collusion theory for the intervention of market investigation references? Alternatively, is the Guidance merely referring to the Airtours factors?
4. Would the CMA intervene in oligopolistic markets where it observes sub-optimal results with regard to other parameters of competition than price?
5. What are the advantages and disadvantages of acting against facilitating practices through market investigation references instead of using Articles 101/102 TFEU or Chapters I/II CA98?
6. Are 'custom and practice' going beyond the theory of tacit collusion? Could paragraphs 6.12–6.14 be relevant to situations not covered by the *Airtours* factors?
7. Note the reference at paragraph 7.1 on the 'conduct of consumers' and the demand-side in general. Would that type of market failure be covered by an Articles 101/102 TFEU or Chapters I/II CA98 investigation?
8. One may regret that EU competition law does not dispose of a tool equivalent to that of market investigation references with the possibility to adopt appropriate prophylactic remedies preserving effective competition.

11.6.8.4. 'Problem Markets' and the regulation/competition/consumer protection law interface

Because of specific characteristics in the supply and demand side, certain economic sectors with embedded oligopolies have been targeted more than others by regulators, competition authorities, and consumer protection agencies.[146] These markets generally are perceived as not functioning well, that is, there is some identified 'consumer detriment', in view of low switching from consumers, although there are indications of consumer dissatisfaction and lack of entry by new competitors.

A classic example is the recent OFGEM, the UK electricity and gas regulator, inquiries in the supply and acquisition of energy. Research published by academics and the OFGEM noted that most energy consumers never switched suppliers.[147] In its 2011, *The Retail Market Review,*

[146] The term 'problem markets' has been used for the 10th Annual Conference of the Centre for Competition Policy at University of East Anglia in June 2014, available at competitionpolicy.ac.uk/events/summer-conferences/10th-annual-conference-2014, which defined 'problem markets' as following: '(a) problem market might be defined as one in which there are no issues clearly breaching antitrust law. But, there may nevertheless be considerable concern amongst politicians and the public with contested territory as to whether there is actually a problem, and even if there is, whether anything can be done about it.' Participants to the conference gave as examples, the rail transport, the food supply chain, financial services (including credit cards, payment instruments, credit rating), electricity and energy in general, healthcare, the petroleum products sector, the overwhelming use of 'leveraging loyalty programmes' in airlines, to cite a few. No real effort was made to define criteria for inclusion in this category of 'product markets' and the concept seems to be boundless. Yet, we consider that it has some rhetorical appeal as it indicates markets in which embedded oligopolies may not be dealt easily with the traditional toolkit of a competition authority.

[147] CM Wilson and C Waddams Price, 'Do Consumers Switch to the Best Supplier?' (May 2006), available at else.econ.ucl.ac.uk/conferences/consumer-behaviour/wilson.pdf; OFGEM, 'What Can Behavioural Economics Say about GB Energy Consumers?', Discussion Paper (March 2011), www.ofgem.gov.uk/Markets/RetMkts/rmr/Documents1/Behavioural_Economics_GBenergy.pdf, noting that

> [o]f consumers surveyed by Ipsos MORI, 89 per cent are aware that they can switch energy supplier, and 85 per cent of switchers find switching fairly or very easy. However, approximately 60 per cent of consumers say they have never switched supplier. Two thirds of consumers' energy accounts are with

thus acting in its regulatory function,[148] OFGEM noted that that the low level of switching taking place (almost between 60 and 90 per cent of consumers being characterized as 'sticky') could be explained by the consumers being confused from the quite important number of tariffs options that were proposed to them.[149] Some may advance the view that the market examined by the OFGEM presents the characteristics of 'confusopoly', which has been characterized as a group of companies in an oligopoly with similar products who intentionally confuse customers instead of competing on price.[150]

In 2013, OFGEM made its final proposals, which include a maximum limit on the number of tariffs that suppliers will be able to offer at any point in time to four core tariffs per supplier and per meter type or mode, a simplification of tariff structures in order to avoid multi-tier tariffs that are confusing for consumers, a simplification of how discounts, bundles and reward points are offered and presented, the facilitation of collective switching schemes that meet consumer interests.[151] It has been alleged that the OFGEM regulatory remedies introduce some degree of market transparency in the industry, which may facilitate tacit collusion.[152] Yet, one may remark that the competitive threat posed by smaller rivals would weaken the sustainability of the alleged collusive outcome. Indeed, the collective market share of the fringe of competitors increased materially after OFGEM's intervention. Furthermore, it could be argued that OFGEM enables the possible application of Articles 101/102 TFEU or Chapters I/II, which precisely cover situations of tacit collusion.

OFGEM has also made a decision to make a market investigation reference to the Competition and Markets Authority in June 2014 for the market of the supply and acquisition of energy, noting the 'weak customer response' (switching), incumbency advantages, possible tacit coordination (although the OFGEM noted that there is no evidence of direct coordination), the prevalence of vertical integration in this market and the existence of barriers to entry and expansion. This market investigation reference was instigated by the realization that this market contributed 'poor outcomes for consumers, including increasing retail

one of their ex-monopoly suppliers (either British Gas or the ex-monopoly electricity supplier for that region): evidence of status quo bias/time inconsistency (discounting the future benefits).

148 OFGEM may also concurrently apply competition law.

149 OFGEM, *The Retail Market Review—Findings and Initial Proposals* (2011), available at www.ofgem.gov.uk/ofgem-publications/39708/rmrfinal.pdf, noting that

> [. . .] research with consumers shows that the large number of tariff options is one of the reasons that many find it hard to decide whether it is worth them switching or not. As a result many do not engage and others will make poor switching decisions. Our 2008 domestic consumer engagement survey reported that 70 per cent of respondents found the number of tariffs on offer confusing.

150 S Adams, *The Dilbert Future* (HarperCollins, 1997).

151 OFGEM, *The Retail Market Review: Final Domestic Proposals* (27 March 2013), available at www.ofgem.gov.uk/ofgem-publications/39350/retail-market-review-final-domestic-proposals.pdf.

152 See, for instance, the warnings of M Hviid, G Loomes, and C Waddams, *The Retail Market Review: Domestic Proposals—Response to Consultation* (ESRC Centre for Competition Policy, 2012), 6, available at competitionpolicy.ac.uk/documents/107435/107585/RMR+response.pdf/85b50767-a8a4-473f-a9a2-a06d6c3126ea, noting that

> [a]lthough not discussed much in the literature on tacit collusion, the less costly it is for firms to monitor their rivals' prices, the more likely they are to be able to suspend competition successfully. Given the small number of firms and the nature of the product, one of the few obstacles to classifying this as an industry with ideal conditions for tacit collusion is transparency, which has up to now been somewhat complicated by the large number of tariffs and their non–linear nature. If Ofgem's proposals work as they hope [. . .] this would remove a major barrier to easy collusion.

See also, for similar warnings, OFT 994, *Assessing the Effectiveness of Potential Remedies in Consumer Markets* (April 2008), Annex. One may, however, object to this view by noting that OFGEM remedies increase transparency for consumers, not for firms, who have the expertise to monitor each other prices. Hence there is no incremental facilitation of tacit collusion.

profitability and low levels of consumer trust'.[153] The OFGEM noted that despite the Retail Market Review remedies imposed to the industry, and the increase in switching, 'consumer trust and public confidence remain low'[154] and that the CMA to which the issue was referred is well placed to use its experience of competition in other sectors and has remedy powers that the OFGEM does not dispose, such as structural reforms. In its conclusions,[155] the CMA criticized OFGEM for constraining the numbers of tariffs service providers could offer. In order to improve customer engagement, the CMA instead asked OFGEM to set up a database of 'disengaged consumers' which could be consulted by rivals to send targeted offered, and thus reduce the costs of customer acquisition.

It seems therefore that a regulatory approach combined with the use of the semi-regulatory/competition law tool of market investigation references may provide a solution to the problems faced by the specific industry. The implementation of consumer protection remedies may also contribute in addressing the consumer detriment identified. Although such combination is possible in the UK legal system, the European Commission does not dispose of the adequate tools to combine the traditional competition law enforcement with regulatory/consumer protection remedies, in the absence of some link with the Internal Market and therefore Article 114 TFEU, as this was accepted by the CJEU with regard to the roaming regulations.[156]

Another example relates to the banking sector. The CMA's predecessor bodies, the OFT and the CoCo, have examined this sector over the years under their market regime[157] More recently, the CMA has embarked in a market investigation covering personal current accounts and banking services to small- and medium-sized enterprises (SMEs). Similarly to the previous case, the main narrative of harm is that the low level of consumer switching is primarily due to consumer widespread perception that banks are all the same in terms of price and, most of all, level of service. The perceived lack of differentiation among rivals means switching is low even if switching costs are low, thanks to previous interventions. Therefore, this demand-side friction operates as an entry and expansion barrier for challenger banks. In its conclusions,[158] the CMA mandated the adoption of an Open Banking Standard by early 2018, aimed at making it convenient for retail customers to shop around by relying on price comparison websites (PCWs), finance platforms, and new types of 'fintech' solutions where consumers can access multiple products from a single application (so-called 'aggregators'). Additional requirements for banks were: to display prominently core indicators of service quality and provide this information to intermediaries; and to provide occasional prompts to customers to encourage comparison shopping.

153 OFGEM, *Decision to Make a Market Investigation Reference in Respect of the Supply and Acquisition of Energy in Great Britain* (26 June 2014), 3, available at www.ofgem.gov.uk/publications-and-updates/decision-make-market-investigation-reference-respect-supply-and-acquisition-energy-great-britain.

154 Ibid, 10.

155 CMA, *Energy Market Investigation—Summary of Final Report* (24 June 2016), available at assets.publishing.service.gov.uk/media/576c23e4ed915d622c000087/Energy-final-report-summary.pdf.

156 See Case C-58/08, *The Queen, on the application of Vodafone Ltd and Others v Secretary of State for Business, Enterprise and Regulatory Reform* [2010] ECR I–4999.

157 OFT, *PCA Banking Market Study Project Page* (2008); CoCo, *Supply of Banking Services to SMEs* (2002). The OFT also attempted to tackle the issue of unfair overdraft charges by means of its consumer law powers. However, its attempt was ultimately rebuked by the UK Supreme Court. See *Office of Fair Trading v Abbey National plc and Others* [2009] UKSC 6, [2009] EWCA 116, [2008] EWHC 875 (Comm).

158 See CMA, *Retail Banking Market Investigation—Summary of Final Report* (9 August 2016), available at assets.publishing.service.gov.uk/media/57a8c0fb40f0b608a7000002/summary-of-final-report-retail-banking-investigation.pdf.

The CMA did not propose any structural remedies aimed at 'splitting up' large incumbents, arguing that such a draconian remedy would not be effective against the key issue of customer inertia. The CMA also did not propose to tackle the prevalence of free-if-in-credit business model for PCAs, whereby consumers are not charge as long as they maintain a credit balance. The CMA argued that putting an end to this common practice would have required setting prices (either through a minimum upfront fee for the use of PCAs, or a cap on overdraft charges), which is something that a competition authority is ill suited for.

On the back of the CMA's investigation, the Financial Conduct Authority (FCA) has recently announced that it will review current accounts and more specifically the impact of free-if-in-credit banking, thus showing the interaction between sector regulators and the CMA, in particular in view of FCA's operational objective to promote effective competition in the interests of consumers in the markets it regulates.[159]

11.6.8.5. Algorithms and collusion in oligopolistic markets

The important technological progress in artificial intelligence, the development of algorithms and deep machine learning in modern digital economy has brought to the fore new challenges for competition law enforcement in oligopolistic industries.[160] Businesses become 'algorithmic' by using algorithms to automatize processes relating to their relations with their customers, suppliers, with the aim to gain an 'algorithmic' competitive advantage against their competitors. In principle, such use of algorithms should not raise any issues, unless it leads to the exploitation of consumers through algorithmic discrimination, algorithmic pricing (including personalized pricing) or other exploitative practices,[161] or, may impose unfair conditions to their suppliers, in the event these could be considered as a competition law problem, to the extent that these firms may reinforce their superior bargaining power.[162] In addition, they may also be tempted to employ these algorithms in order to collude with their competitors, an issue that has attracted a lot of attention recently.[163] Although the use of algorithms to facilitate both collusion and personalized pricing is conceivable in principle, it has been alleged that it is very unlikely to occur in practice.[164] This is particularly so with respect to tacit collusion, as the absence of posted prices under personalized pricing would make it very difficult for allegedly colluding firms to observe rivals' prices in order to detect cheating.

It is clear that the use of pricing algorithms can increase the efficiency of markets as the way firms set prices can be more responsive to changes in demand so that markets clear faster, which is particularly valuable for perishable goods, and, more in general, with respect to how

159 See Financial Conduct Authority, Business Plan 2017–18, 66.

160 See OECD, 'Algorithms and Collusion: Competition Policy in the Digital Age' (2017), available at www.oecd.org/competition/algorithms-collusion-competition-policy-in-the-digital-age.htm; A Ezrachi and ME Stucke, 'Two Artificial Neural Networks Meet in an Online Hub and Change the Future (of Competition, Market Dynamics and Society)' (14 September 2017), available at https://ssrn.com/abstract=2949434; I Lianos and H Ekbia, 'Artificial Collusion Dreams in Competition Law: A Comparative Law and Technology Approach', CLES Research Paper 1/2019, forthcoming.

161 See our analysis in Section 9.11.2. 162 See our analysis in Section 8.3.2.3.3.

163 A Ezrachi and ME Stucke, *Virtual Competition: The Promise and Perils of the Algorithm-Driven Economy* (Harvard University Press, 2016); Autorité de la Concurrence & Bundeskartellamt, Competition Law and Data (16 May 2016), 14–15.

164 CMA, 'Pricing Algorithms—Economic Working Paper on the Use of Algorithms to Facilitate Collusion and Personalised Pricing' (2018), paras 7.31–7.38, available at https://assets.publishing.service.gov.uk/government/uploads/system/uploads/attachment_data/file/746353/Algorithms_econ_report.pdf.

firms manage their inventory.[165] However, they may also increase the risks of collusion, which may escape the scrutiny of competition authorities.

Indeed, 'algorithms make collusive outcomes easier to sustain and more likely to be observed in digital markets'.[166] This is achieved, first by the capabilities of algorithms 'to identify any market threats very fast, for instance through a phenomenon known as now-casting, allowing incumbents to pre-emptively acquire any potential competitors or to react aggressively to market entry',[167] thus increasing strategic barriers to entry. Second, they increase market transparency and the frequency of interaction, making the industries 'more prone to collusion'.[168] Prices can be updated in real-time, 'allowing for an immediate retaliation to deviations from collusion', as well as accurately predicting rivals' actions and anticipating any deviations before these actually take place.[169] Third, they can act as facilitators of collusion is in monitoring competitors' actions in order to enforce a collusive agreement, enabling a quick identification of cartel price' deviations and retaliation strategies.[170] Fourth, they may facilitate 'hub and spoke' strategies, the firms in an industry instance outsourcing the creation of algorithms to the same IT companies and programmers.[171] Fifth, 'signalling algorithms' may enable companies to automatically set very fast iterative actions, such as snapshot price changes during the middle of the night, that cannot be exploited by consumers, but which can facilitate collusion with rivals possessing good analytical algorithms.[172] Finally, 'self-learning' algorithms may eliminate the need for human intermediation, as using deep machine learning technologies, the algorithms may assist firms in actually reaching a collusive outcome without them being aware of it.[173] This raises some quite interesting issues with regard to the scope of the concept of agreement or concerted practice under Article 101 TFEU in this situation, to the extent that a firm may make an invitation to collude through this self-learning algorithms, while competitors would accept the offer by using similar algorithms.[174] For some, '[t]his raises the concern of whether the need to address algorithmic collusion should require a new definition of what is an agreement for antitrust purposes',[175] and eventually strict liability for the companies designing such algorithms, and/or those using such algorithms (although this option may considerably increase type I errors, as deep learning algorithms do not provide information about the decision-making process that led to conversion of data inputs into decision outputs). This also raises questions as to the availability of competition law remedies in this case, or the need to move beyond competition law and regulate more pervasively, through the action of competition authorities and/or digital regulators, the design and use of algorithms so as to prevent algorithmic collusion.[176]

Another interesting aspect to consider is whether the adoption of pricing algorithms must be common to all competing firms in order to facilitate tacit collusion, or whether the fact that only some of the firms have adopted them would mitigate the risk of anti-competitive effects.

165 Ibid, paras 4.2–4.4.

166 OECD, 'Algorithms and Collusion: Competition Policy in the Digital Age' (2017), 20.

167 Ibid, 21. 168 Ibid. 169 Ibid, 22. 170 Ibid, 26. 171 Ibid, 28.

172 Ibid, 29–31. 173 Ibid, 32–3. 174 See our analysis in Chapter 5.

175 OECD, 'Algorithms and Collusion: Competition Policy in the Digital Age' (2017), 36.

176 Further suggestions include the possibility of using the tools of the new General Data Protection Regulation (EU) 2016/679 on the protection of natural persons with regard to the processing of personal data and on the free movement of such data [2016] OJ L 119/1 [hereinafter GDPR], which introduced the right of citizens to seek and receive an explanation for decisions made by algorithms (ibid, Articles 13–15), especially if they are using profiling techniques (Article 22), the introduction of maximum price regulations, the development of active policies making markets less transparent, the development of rules restricting the way algorithms are designed: OECD, 'Algorithms and Collusion: Competition Policy in the Digital Age' (2017), 49–50.

In the former case, it could be argued that common adoption would in and of itself suffice to establish the existence of a mutual understanding (ie, a 'meeting of the minds') between rival firms within the meaning of Article 101 TFEU.[177]

Finally, to the extent that the use of pricing algorithms to facilitate collusion takes place on an electronic marketplace, it is worth asking whether e-marketplace platforms should also face antitrust scrutiny. In other words, should the operator of the e-marketplace have a duty to police whether sellers are coordinating prices through the use of algorithms? This may be so to the extent that the platform operator benefits by being able to charge higher fees to colluding sellers.[178]

11.6.8.6. Suggested options: Between law and economics

11.6.8.6.1. A 'direct' 'market-based' approach to oligopolistic interdependence

In a seminal article published in 1969, professor (now also judge) Richard Posner (from the 7th Circuit Court of Appeals in the US) suggested to employ ex post antitrust law, in particular section 1 of the Sherman Act (the US equivalent of Article 101 TFEU) against tacit collusion.[179] Posner proposed a two-steps analysis. The first step consists in identifying markets in which tacit collusion may be facilitated, relying on evidence of concertation.[180] However, in the absence of such evidence, it would be possible to demonstrate through economic evidence the existence of collusive pricing, relying on a multi-factor analysis looking to abnormal profits, price discrimination, information exchange, pre-announcement of prices, durable over-capacity of production, among other factors.[181] Posner completed the list in the second edition of his acclaimed antitrust law book, where he noted that 'we must examine the conditions favourable to collusion more systematically: market concentrated on the selling side, no fringe of small sellers, inelastic demand at competitive price, entry takes a long time, buying side of market unconcentrated, the principal firms sell at the same level in the chain if distribution, price competition more important than others forms of competition, similar cost structures and production processes, exchange of price information, regional price variations, identical bids, industry wide RPM [. . .]', thus adopting the plus factors approach examined above.[182] The economic evidence one may rely upon for this analysis includes, relatively fixed market shares; persistent market-wide price discrimination, exchange of price information, regional price variations, identical bids for a contract to supply a non-standard item, price, output, and capacity changes at the formation of the cartel, industry-wide resale price maintenance, declining market shares of leaders, amplitude and fluctuation of price changes, elastic demand at the market price level, the level and pattern of profits, market price inversely correlated with number of firms or elasticity of demand, basing point pricing and exclusionary practices.[183] For Posner, structural remedies for oligopolies and market deconcentration are unhelpful to address these concerns and he suggested instead fines and behavioural remedies (injunctive relief), which might deter tacit collusion.[184]

177 For a detailed discussion, see P Siciliani, 'Tackling Algorithmic-Facilitated Tacit Collusion in a Proportionate Way' (9 August 2018) *J European Competition L & Practice*, available at https://doi.org/10.1093/jeclap/lpy051.

178 Ibid.

179 RA Posner, 'Oligopoly and the Antitrust Laws: a Suggested Approach' (1969) 21 *Stanford L Rev* 1562.

180 RA Posner, *Antitrust Law* (University of Chicago Press, 2001), 51–102.

181 RA Posner, 'Oligopoly and the Antitrust Laws: a Suggested Approach' (1969) 21 *Stanford L Rev* 1562.

182 RA Posner, *Antitrust Law* (University of Chicago Press, 2001), 69–79.

183 Ibid, 79–93.

184 Ibid, 98.

In a series of recent publications professor Louis Kaplow from Harvard University made similar suggestions, arguing for a broad—economically oriented—definition of the concept of collusion in section 1 Sherman Act cases. Kaplow argued for a 'direct approach towards the problem of coordinated oligopolistic price elevation' and the abandonment of the communications-based approach that 'focuses on the presence of particular means of coordination rather than on the ends to be achieved'.[185] According to Kaplow, the communications-based or coordination focused approaches are confronted to the 'paradox of proof', 'under which a narrow agreement requirement [or concerted practice requiring coordination evidence] may imply that a greater ease of oligopolistic coordination and thus a higher danger of social harm from price fixing favour exoneration rather than condemnation'.[186] Indeed,

> [t]he defining feature of the communications-based prohibition is that it considers only a subset of means to a socially undesirable end rather than focusing on the end itself or on other matters of direct concern, notably, chilling effects [. . .]. The communications-based prohibition is defined in a formalistic manner that is significantly removed from the statement of the social objective and the basic framework for optimal rule formulation.[187]

Kaplow's 'market-based' approach will catch all inefficient equilibria that were achieved through successful oligopolistic interdependence among rivals. He excludes from his approach unilateral exercise of market power, as this is exempted from the US antitrust law (which do not catch exploitative practices by a dominant firm). Kaplow also excludes situations of price leadership by a dominant firm, as in this case, the conduct is purely independent. Contrary to Posner, he also excludes from his definition of oligopolistic interdependence/collusion Cournot and Bertrand equilibria, which he considers consist in a unilateral exercise of market power in a two stages game.[188] Hence, his emphasis on the concept of 'meeting of the minds' as a limiting principle in order to distinguish between unilateral exercise of market power and collusive oligopolistic interdependence.

One might, however, remark that in EU and UK competition law, a unilateral exercise of market power may fall under the prohibition of an abuse of a dominant position. In any case, as Kaplow remarks, in homogeneous goods industries, it is preferable to focus on 'market-based evidence', as coordinated elevation is more likely in these industries and unilateral exercise of market power, less. He also notes that in any case, even if the prohibition catches a unilateral increase of market power, this is not a reason not to rely on economic evidence, as 'the potential chilling costs from misclassification may not be that great—and may even be negative (that is, benefits) because moderating unilateral market power can be desirable in such industries'.[189] Competition authorities may thus rely on 'market-based' evidence focusing on the detection of coordinated oligopolistic price elevation, including 'price patterns' in the industry, evidence of price elevation and facilitating practice.[190] With regard to remedies, Kaplow considers that damages, complemented by criminal sanctions, such as imprisonment, may be more effective than fines and injunctions.[191]

185 L Kaplow, *Competition Policy and Price Fixing* (Princeton University Press, 2013), 443.

186 Ibid, 445. See also the analysis ibid, 125–73.

187 Ibid, 440.

188 This is clearer in L Kaplow, 'On the Meaning of Horizontal Agreements in Competition Law' (2011) 99 *California L Rev* 683, 784. See also the discussion in W Page, 'Objective and Subjective Theories of Concerted Action' (2013) 79 *Antitrust LJ* 215, 231–2.

189 L Kaplow, *Competition Policy and Price Fixing* (Princeton University Press, 2013), 448.

190 Ibid, 256–85.

191 Ibid, 322–45.

These positions have been criticized by Encaoua and Page.

D Encaoua, 'Book review: Louis Kaplow, *Competition Policy and Price Fixing*' (2014) 111 J Economics 309, 310

> The economic approach to collusion highlights the dynamic nature of the competitive process formally represented by the repeated game theory. The main result of this theory, known as the folk theorem, states that any outcome, whether collusive or not, can be supported as a noncooperative perfect equilibrium of the repeated game. This result is both strong and fragile. It is strong in the sense that it shows that a collusive outcome can be achieved in the absence of any agreement. It is also fragile to the extent that the choice of a specific equilibrium within a multiplicity of collusive equilibria requires more or less a certain amount of coordination. This is why, as insightful as it is, Kaplow's analysis lacks an important question: How can one distinguish between bad and good coordination through repeated interaction? [. . .]

W Page, 'Objective and Subjective Theories of Concerted Action' (2013) 79 Antitrust LJ 215, 246–7

> A legal rule that prohibits noncompetitive, cooperative equilibria achieved without communication is thus likely to impose significant error costs because the prospect of damage awards inhibits not only the core conduct that motivates the rule but also efficient, facially similar conduct that firms fear may trigger liability. Direct and indirect purchasers will likely challenge price increases whenever the legal rule creates a chance of recovery or settlement that warrants the expense of suit. Consequently, a subjective definition of agreement may impose substantial and long-lasting costs by deterring noninterdependent conduct that courts cannot easily distinguish from harmful conduct. Kaplow suggests that the law could reduce chilling costs by challenging only significant price elevations. But the proposed rule would also have to distinguish lawful practices that result in price elevations. The notion of a meeting of minds is not a promising standard for distinguishing harmful non-competitive interdependent equilibria from facially similar non-competitive independent equilibria.

In any case, the 'market-based' approaches advanced by Posner and Kaplow may rely on the advances in recent years on the econometric tools used for the detection of cartels. In contrast to the weak probative value of econometric evidence in the proof of cartels, econometrics has an important role to play in the detection and investigation of cartels and also in the context of actions for antitrust damages following a cartel infringement. Econometric techniques using a structural approach (focusing on markets with traits thought to be conducive to collusion) have been used to help provide information as to where cartels may be located, as well as logit models or 'ordinary least squares' predicting the probability or the number of cartels likely to exist in a specific industry.[192]

192 OFT 773, 'Predicting Cartels', Economic Discussion Paper (March 2005). For an overview, see P Rey, 'On the Use of Economic Analysis in Cartel Detection' in C-D Ehlermann and I Atanasiu (eds) *Enforcement of Prohibition of Cartels, European Competition Law Annual 2006* (Hart, 2007), 69; PA Grout and S Sonderegger,

Some authors have also emphasized behavioural approaches to detecting cartels, which also require the use of econometric techniques.[193]

Quantitative economic analysis includes, as a first step, an industry analysis with a scoring approach (looking to different variables, such as indicators of price, transparency, concentration and entry) in order to exclude from the sample cases where cartel activity is relatively improbable and, as a second step, a critical event analysis (with a focus on exogenous shocks or structural breaks) testing the collusive against the competitive scenario. The OECD has reported a number of EU member States where cartel investigations were triggered based exclusively on economic indicators.[194] Most recent research has focused on the role of 'empirical', as opposed to 'structural' screening techniques in uncovering collusive oligopolistic interdependence.

R Abrantes-Metz, OECD *Roundtable on Ex-Officio Cartel Investigations and the Use of Screens to Detect Cartels,* OECD DAF/COMP(2013)20 (2013), 3–4 (footnotes omitted)

There are essentially two different types of economic analyses pursued with the objective to flag the possibility of a conspiracy. The first can be classified as a 'structural approach' and it looks at the structure of the industry at hand 'scoring' the likelihood of collusion based on factors such as homogenous product, too few competitors, stability of demand, and other commonly used collusive markers.

The second type of economic analysis in cartel detection is empirical and uses what has become commonly known as 'screens,' or sometimes 'empirical screens.' These analyses use time-series, crosssectional data, and/or panel data sets on variables that measure market outcomes, including prices, volumes, and market shares to detect potential anticompetitive behavior. This is called a 'behavioral' or 'outcomes' approach, in which economists look at markets' and participants' behavior as translated into observable data and apply screens for conspiracies and manipulations to address whether the observed behavior is more or less likely to have been produced under an explicit agreement. [. . .]

Broadly speaking, empirical screens for collusion used in the literature employ two strategies. The first is to search for improbable events. This type of screen is similar to looking for a cheat in a casino. For example, the probability that a gambler at a Las Vegas casino will place a winning bet in a roulette is roughly .5 percent. During her shift, a roulette dealer may see a handful of players win 5, or even 7, times in a row. However, the probability of winning 20 times in a row is almost zero (though not impossible). If a pit boss sees this occur, he may not be able to prove that cheating has occurred, but he would be well advised to watch closely or risk losing a lot of money. One set of collusive screens generalizes this idea by looking for events that are improbable unless firms in the industry have coordinated their actions.

'Structural Approaches to Cartel Detection' in C-D Ehlermann and I Atanasiu (eds) *Enforcement of Prohibition of Cartels, European Competition Law Annual 2006* (Hart, 2007), 83.

[193] JE Harrington, Jr, 'Detecting Cartels' (Department of Economics, John Hopkins University, 2005), available at https://www.competitionpolicyinternational.com/assets/Uploads/Detecting-Cartels.pdf; JE Harington, Jr, 'Behavioral Screening and the Detection of Cartels' in C-D Ehlermann and I Atanasiu (eds) *Enforcement of Prohibition of Cartels, European Competition Law Annual 2006* (Hart, 2007), 51.

[194] See, for instance, the Italian baby milk case (where a cross-country price benchmarking was used): OECD, Prosecuting Cartels without Direct Evidence of Agreement, DAF/COMP/GF(2006)7 (11 September 2006), 22–4. See also the Dutch shrimp case (structural indicators were employed): JE Harrington, Jr, 'Detecting Cartels' (Department of Economics, John Hopkins University, 2005), 3–4, available at https://www.competitionpolicyinternational.com/assets/Uploads/Detecting-Cartels.pdf.

> The second type of screen uses the idea of a control group. A somewhat extreme example illustrates the idea. In the 1980s, organised crime in New York City operated a concrete club that rigged bids on contracts over $2 million. During the 1980s, the price of concrete was 70 percent higher in New York City than other US cities. While it is true that the price of many goods and services is higher in New York City, relatively few of those prices are 70 percent higher than in other large cities. Prices that are anomalous compared to other markets suggest a competition problem. In this simple example, we are forming a control group for New York by using prices in other cities as a basis for comparison. But most collusion is not this blatant.
>
> Though screens can be very powerful, these are econometric tools, with all the usual caveats, and they may potentially be misused.

However, in general, relying only on economic evidence (including econometrics) for apportioning the standard of proof for the prohibition of cartels has not yet been a winning strategy, most probably in view of the criminal nature in some Member States of cartel infringements, the reticence of the courts to examine in depth econometric evidence and the different standards of proof for establishing collusion or causation of harm and standards of proof in the quantification of damages in cartel cases. Yet, screening might play some role.

R Abrantes-Metz, OECD *Roundtable on Ex-Officio cartel Investigations and the Use of Screens to Detect Cartels*, OECD DAF/COMP(2013)20 (2013), 3–4 (footnotes omitted)

> The purpose of screening is not to deliver the final evidence based on which colluders will be convicted, but instead to identify markets where empirical red flags are raised and which are worth further investigations. In doing so effectively, screens will induce cartel members to come forward and file for leniency, and they will also assist in deterring cartel formation.

11.6.8.6.2. An approach focusing on deconcentration

Harvard University economist JS Bain presented empirical studies in the 1950s showing that the after-tax returns on shareholder equity across forty-two US manufacturing industries were higher when the eight-firm concentration ratio (sum of the shares of the eight leading firms) was above 70 per cent.[195] Bain also found that the more the market is concentrated, the higher the likelihood of oligopolistic interdependence is. From this follows a presumption of tacit collusion in concentrated oligopolistic markets. Kaysen and Turner proposed a control over the structure of oligopolistic structures and the extension of the scope of section 2 of the Sherman Act (the equivalent to Articles 101/102 TFEU/Chapters I and II CA98) and a more active merger control. Concern over concentration in oligopolistic markets raised in the late 1960s, following the publication of the Neal Report in 1968 and proposals by US senator Philip Hart to pass a broad deconcentration legislation, the Industrial Reorganization Act in 1972, targeting the breakup of tightly oligopolistic industries. Such approaches would favour structural remedies.[196] The Federal Trade Commission also attempted to employ section 5

195 See JS Bain, 'Relation of Profit Rate to Industry Concentration: American Manufacturing, 1936–1940' (1951) 65 *Q J Economics* 293.

196 S Calkins, 'Antitrust Modernization: Looking Backwards' (2006) 31 *J Corporation L* 421, 433–6.

of the FTC Act in order to catch pure conscious parallelism type of cases in the late 1970s.[197] Although the ascendancy of the Chicago School of antitrust in the US in the early 1980s brought these initiatives to an end, more recently the debate over the scope of section 5 of the FTC Act was reinvigorated, although no one suggests to use this provision against collusive oligopolistic interdependence.[198] Some US authors have emphasized the need for competition law regimes to include a 'catch all' fall back competition law provision 'in order to address conduct beyond the reach of prevailing concepts under the Sherman Act', if certain prerequisite conditions are satisfied.[199]

In Europe, there is no equivalent to section 5 of the FTC Act. Yet, some Member States provide some degree of flexibility to their competition authorities to intervene and regulate oligopolistic markets. The UK market investigation references offer the possibility to the competition authorities to tailor remedies that correspond to the adverse effect on competition identified and remedies can also be forward looking. The remedies seek to provide a comprehensive solution to the adverse effect on competition identified, which in certain cases may be divestitures with the aim to re-design the structure of the market, or measures aiming to lower barriers to entry and expansion for new and existing competitors.[200]

11.6.8.5.3. Approaches promoting new entrants in the industry: Output restriction, price freezing rules, industrial policy/design

Some authors have suggested remedial strategies that aim to favour new entrants in the industry. Although these have been suggested mostly for dominant firms, their application in situations of joint dominance may also be envisaged, the EU competition law, contrary to the US, covering exploitative practices. Some have suggested output restrictions that would prohibit a dominant firm from increasing its pre-entry output for a period of twelve to eighteen months in case of new entry, thus allowing the entrant 'to realize cost economies and establish a market identity'.[201] Others have put forward a price freeze for monopolists, in case a new substantial entrant charges less than 20 per cent of the monopoly's prevailing price, for a period of twelve to eighteen months,[202] or an oligopoly price freeze, including a quality freeze, activated for 'suitable well-defined industries', thus creating the incentives to the oligopolists to set lower prices *ex ante* in order to discourage a downward deviation by the undertakings in the specific industry.[203] Finally, it has also been suggested that government support to a maverick undertaking in the oligopolistic market for a limited period of time, while this undertaking lowers its prices, may enable the infusion of some additional degree of competition and resolve the issue of oligopolistic interdependence and its effects on

197 The most remarkable example is the so called cereal breakfast case, challenging the breakfast cereal oligopoly, led by Kellogg, General Mills, and General Foods. For an analysis, see F Scherer, 'The FTC, Oligopoly and Shared Monopoly', Harvard Kennedy School Research Working Paper 13–031 (2013).

198 See our analysis in Chapter 5.

199 B Kovacic and M Winerman, 'Competition Policy and the Application of Section 5 of the Federal Trade Commission Act' (2010) 76 *Antitrust LJ* 929, noting the need to circumscribe such enforcement within set limits, with the help of statutory guidance, a specific framework that accounts for similarities and differences to the other competition law statutes, building institutional competence.

200 On the different remedies adopted, see our analysis in the companion volume, I Lianos, *Competition Law Enforcement and Procedure* (OUP, forthcoming 2019).

201 OE Williamson, 'Predatory Pricing: A Strategic and Welfare Analysis' (1977) 87 *Yale LJ* 284, 296.

202 AS Edlin, 'Stopping Above Cost Predatory Pricing' (2002) 111 *Yale LJ* 941, 973–8.

203 G Sagi, 'The Oligopolistic Pricing Problem: A Suggested Price Freeze Remedy' (2008) 1 *Columbia Business L Rev* 269.

pricing.[204] One might also advance broader market opening/competition policy promoting measures, such as liberalization, trade, or public procurement regulation, to enhance competition law in oligopolistic sectors, although the effectiveness of such policies remains limited in the non-tradable sector (retail, utilities, banking, professional services), where a lot of these oligopolies exist. A combination of approaches *ex post* and *ex ante* is to be preferred in order to address the concerns raised by oligopolies in modern market economy.

SUGGESTED BIBLIOGRAPHY

Books

Axelrod, R, *The Evolution of Cooperation* (Basic Books, 1984).

Chamberlain, EH, *Theory of Monopolistic Competition* (Harvard University Press, 1933).

Filippelli, M, *Collective Dominance and Collusion: Parallelism in EU and US Competition Law* (Edward Elgar, 2013).

Kaplow, L, *Competition Policy and Price Fixing* (Princeton University Press, 2013).

OECD, Algorithms and Collusion: Competition Policy in the Digital Age (OECD, 2017).

Chapters in books

Petit, N, 'The Oligopoly Problem in EU Competition Law' in Lianos, I and Geradin, D (eds) *Handbook in European Competition Law: Substantive Aspects* (Edward Elgar, 2013), 259–349.

Journal articles

Kovacic, W, Marshall, RC, Marx, LM, and White HL, 'Plus Factors and Agreement in Antitrust Law' (2011) 110 *Michigan L Rev* 393.

Posner, RA, 'Oligopoly and the Antitrust Laws: A Suggested Approach' (1969) 21 *Stanford L Rev* 1562.

Werden GJ, 'Economic Evidence on the Existence of Collusion: Reconciling Antitrust Law with Oligopoly Theory' (2004) 71 *Antitrust LJ* 719.

Whish, R, and Sufrin, B, 'Oligopolistic Markets and Competition Law' (1992) 12 *Yearbook of European L* 59.

204 MS Gal, 'Reducing Rivals Prices: Government Supported Mavericks as New Solutions for Oligopoly Pricing' (2001) 7 *Stanford J L Business & Finance* 1.

12

MERGERS

12.1. FOUNDATIONS

12.1.1. MERGER AND ACQUISITION ACTIVITY: EMERGENCE AND DEVELOPMENT OF A GLOBAL ECONOMIC PHENOMENON

The concept of mergers and acquisitions has various meanings. It may denote the process whereby two companies cease their legal existence and establish a new company. This type of merger is referred to as consolidation. It may also refer to the situation of statutory merger (or acquisition) where one company (the target company) ceases to exist, in the sense that its decision-making process is not independent, and all its assets and liabilities are subsumed in the acquiring party.

Empirical studies have noted that merger activity, in the US and the UK, but also in other jurisdictions, such as Germany, has occurred in distinct 'merger waves'.[1]

The first 'Great Merger Movement' from 1893 to 1904–5 was characterized by the simultaneous consolidation of producers within one industry (horizontal consolidation), leading to the emergence of the big US giants in oil, steel, sugar, among other sectors. The result of this first 'great' merger wave was the formation of monopolies, half of the consolidations formed during this period absorbing over 40 per cent of their respective industries and nearly a third absorbing more than 70 per cent.[2] It is interesting to note that some of these industries were prior to the 1890s controlled by trade associations which moved to consolidation by the formation of holding companies and in particular the establishment of trusts. The parties to the trust turned their stock over a board of trustees, getting in return certificates entitling them to a share of the trust's profits and enabling a centralized control of the investment decisions and prices set in the specific industry, what could be now characterized as a form of cartel. Trusts were formed in various important industries of the period, such as oil (the Standard Oil Trust in 1882), the sugar industry (the American Sugar Refining Company in 1887),

[1] See eg DL Golbe and LJ White, 'Catch a Wave: The Time Series Behavior of Mergers' (1993) 75(3) *Rev Economics and Statistics* 493.

[2] NR Lamoreaux, *The Great Merger Movement in American Business, 1895–1904* (CUP, 1985), ch 1.

steel, tobacco, and whisky.[3] This form of combination and market control was the main focus of the Sherman Act in 1890, which established the first US federal antitrust laws, although trusts were also regulated prior to the passage of the Sherman Act by State laws on restraints of trade. There are various theories explaining the emergence of the great merger wave. Some have argued that this is due to the passage of the Sherman Act in 1890 and in particular the Supreme Court's decision in *United States v EC Knight* (the *Sugar Trust* case) in 1895, which narrowly interpreted the Sherman Act as not including merger activity.[4] In contrast, price fixing was declared illegal per se in *US v Trans-Missouri* (1897),[5] *US v Joint Traffic Association* (1898),[6] and *Addyston Pipe & Steel Co v US* (1899).[7] It has been alleged that these cases may have influenced the direction of the consolidation movement towards merger activity, which was outside the scope of the Sherman Act, rather than the formation of trust, whose coordinating function could be declared illegal under the Sherman Act.[8] According to this view, the Supreme Court's judgment in *Northern Securities v US*,[9] in which the Court proclaimed that a merger between directly competing companies constituted combination in restraint of trade and thus subject to the Sherman Act, may have halted the first merger wave. Others have questioned the empirical foundations of this view, and have argued that technological change, in particular the important fixed costs incurred by investments undertaken in order to implement new technologies in economic production, rather than legal developments explain the consolidation of the industry through merger activity, as firms were eager to increase their capacity and thus spread their fixed costs over a greater volume of output, thus lowering their average costs.[10] This wave came to an end in 1904/5, arguably because of the more active enforcement of the US antitrust laws against merger activity, or because of the stock market crash in 1905.

The second merger wave movement started in the 1910s until the Great Depression of 1929. It was characterized by the establishment of oligopolies in sectors such as food, iron, paper, and was significantly smaller than the first merger wave.

The third merger wave occurred after the Second World War, starting in the mid-1950s until the mid-1970s. It was characterized by three different sub-periods, the first leading to horizontal consolidation of various sectors, the second relying on vertical integration and the third on conglomerate merger activity. The wave led to the development of large conglomerates or vertically integrated firms, which operate according to what has been called the 'multi-divisional form' of organization, or 'M form', the main feature of this form being the centralized control over strategic decision making investment in new markets that could offer higher rates of return and less competition than the market(s) the company was already present on, and second, the delegation of operational decision-making to divisions (or strategic business units) that are closely monitored by the centre. This led to a decentralized profit planning relying on the discounted cash flow methodology in order to evaluate capital projects. The quest for higher rates of return became the essential

3 On trusts, see RT Ely, *Monopolies and Trusts* (Macmillan, 1900); JW Jenks, *The Trust Problem* (McClure, Phillips, 1900); E Jones, *The Trust Problem in the United States* (Macmillan, 1929); RE Curtis, *The Trusts and Economic Control* (McGraw-Hill, 1931).

4 *United States v EC Knight Co*, 156 US 1 (1895).

5 166 US 290 (1897).

6 171 US 505 (1898).

7 175 US 211 (1899).

8 For this view, G Bittlingmayer, 'Did Antitrust Policy Cause the Great Merger Wave?' (1985) 28 *J L & Economics* 77.

9 193 US 197 (1904).

10 This view has been put forward by DJ Smythe, 'A Schumpeterian View of the Great Merger Movement in American Manufacturing' (2010) 4(2) *Cliometrica* 141.

driving force of expansion. This expansion has been justified by the need to diversify across product and or geographical markets, and facilitated by investments in managerial hierarchy in order to coordinate production and sales, and devise competitive strategies, managerial structure being considered as the key mechanism for unlocking productivity ('the visible hand hypothesis').[11] But the oil crisis in mid 1970s and the economic recession that followed ended this movement.

The fourth merger wave was very different from the previous ones; it originated in a different movement, namely financialization, based on a different conception of the firm, which is seen as a portfolio of activities, managed according to their financial performance (in terms of rate of return on investment), rather than defined in terms of productive capabilities. The wave emerged in the 1980s and had very different characteristics from its predecessors, in the sense that most of the acquisitions were hostile take-overs, investors going directly to the company's shareholders or fighting to replace management to get the acquisition approved, and 'bust up' take-overs, the main objective being to break-out diversified firms, perceived by the finance literature at the time as destroying value. Hence, the proportion of merger and acquisition (M&A) divestitures was high. Most of this merger activity was accomplished through the leveraged buyout (LBO) where a company is acquired mainly through large amount of outside debt borrowed from a traditional financial institution (investment bank) and large institutional investors (pension funds, mutual funds, hedge funds, insurance companies). This movement naturally ended the era of 'managerial corporation' and that of diversification in sectors 'unrelated' to the main activity of the corporation, and signalled the rise of the power of market finance and debt as the main sources of corporate finance. The fourth wave gradually died down after the market crash of 1987.

The 1990s brought a different form of merger and acquisition activity, this time the main characteristic being cross-border M&A transactions, as a result of the phenomenon of globalization of the economy promoted by trade liberalization, capital market globalization, deregulation, the advent of the Internet, and more generally innovation in Information Technology. Transactions were mostly friendly acquisitions, rather than hostile bids, the dominant source of financing being equity (private equity buyouts) or debt and led to the expansion and the consolidation of many US-based corporations with those based in EU and UK (and vice-versa). Stronger competition from abroad led many firms to consider take-overs abroad, most often in the same industry, in order to survive and grow. This wave collapsed in 2000, as a result of the equity market downturn that year, initiated by the burst of the so-called 'Dot-Com Bubble'.

A sixth wave started in 2003–4 and ended with the 2007–8 financial crisis. This merger wave was again driven by trans-border merger activity, this time expanding to Asia, South America, and emergent economies, and was marked by an increase in governments' selling shares in major national companies.

Most recently, a new wave of merger activity may be identified, this time across various segments of the value chain, and again driven by diversification, with large transactions being initiated in 2014–15 in various industries, with 2015 as a record year for merger activity.[12]

[11] A Chandler, *Strategy and Structure: Chapters in the History of the Industrial Enterprise* (MIT Press, 1962); A Chandler, *The Visible Hand* (Belknap Press, 1977).

[12] See L Picker, 'A Standout Year for Deals, in Volume and Complexity', *New York Times* (3 Jan 2016).

12.1.2. PRO-COMPETITIVE AND ANTI-COMPETITIVE DRIVERS FOR M&A ACTIVITY

Why do firms decide to grow externally through mergers, rather than internally through organic growth? The managerial textbook answer is that a merger should go ahead only if it creates value for shareholders (ie, the acquiring firm's owners), where value stands for the sum of future income discounted back to its present value. Hence, from a shareholder perspective, a merger is justified only to the extent that it creates synergies that would not be available without the merger, so that the cumulated value of the merging firms is greater if they operate as a single entity than as separate ones.[13]

Given that shareholder's value is based on the net present value of the future stream of incomes, synergies must ultimately either enhance revenues and/or reduce costs. A classic example of synergy that could affect both revenues and costs is where the target company has underperformed because of poor management, and the acquiring firm's managers believe they can do a better job. Another, perhaps less subjective, example is in industries where the likelihood of developing a new product that proves to be a commercial success depends on how much a firm can spend on R&D. Hence, the combination of separate R&D programmes increases the chances of success thanks to the improved scale and/or scope economies in R&D spending.

Scale-and-scope economies—that is, savings in average costs associated with an increase, respectively, in quantities and products—normally generate synergies by merely reducing costs for the merged entity, wherever the merger allows the elimination of fixed and common costs such as administrative overheads and advertising expenditures under a single brand name.

The pursuit of a larger scale through a merger may also give rise to purchase economies, thanks to the greater bargaining power that allows the merged entity to negotiate discounts from input suppliers such as intermediate goods. Lower financing costs constitute a special case, in that the fact that large firms usually have access to a wider and cheaper pool of funds than small companies may be due to the fact that it is typically easier for investors to gauge the creditworthiness of the former.

Another reason that this was very much in fashion in particular in the US after the Second World War up to the oil crisis in 1973 is based on the idea that a well-diversified investment portfolio ought to be perceived as less risky and thus cheaper to finance. This approach led to the surge of 'conglomerate mergers' where the acquiring firms would target unrelated businesses in order to diversify their revenue streams (eg combining pro-cyclical and anti-cyclical lines of business). This trend was reversed when it became clear that the complexities in running these large and diversified groups detracted from leveraging the 'core' competencies of each individual unit.

All these sources of synergies can be described as efficiency enhancing, in the sense that the merging entity's competitive improvement (ie, due to either lower costs and/or better quality) is not dependent on a post-merger weakening of competitive rivalry. Apart from the case of more effective R&D spending, leading to superior quality products,[14] it is hard to think of other clear-cut efficiency enhancements on the revenue side.

13 See J Berk and P DeMarzo, *Corporate Finance* (Pearson, 2011), 639.

14 Besides product/service innovations there can also be process innovations which increase firms' technical efficiency thus lowering the costs of product production/service provision.

One such case could be where the merger involves complementary products, that is, products that tend to be purchased and consumed in combination (eg holiday trip and travel insurance). This type of merger is also known as 'conglomerate merger',[15] although here the main rationale is not risk diversification,[16] but minimization of transaction costs. That is to say, there can be a revenue-enhancing synergy to the extent that consumers find it more convenient to deal with a single firm.[17] This may not be merely because of the consumer benefits from lower transaction costs (eg single billing and customer care),[18] but also because the joint consumption of the two products is improved (eg thanks to enhanced technological compatibility). Finally, consumers may benefit from lower prices for the bundle of previously separate products, thanks to the fact that the merger entity internalizes that lower prices for one product stimulate sales for the other complementary product (and vice versa).

By the same token, complementarity underpins efficiency enhancements in 'vertical mergers' between firms along the supply-chain (eg input supplier with product manufacturer, and upstream producer with downstream distributor). Here, for example, lower transaction costs and improved compatibility may enable investment in relationship-specific assets (eg a dedicated production line), thanks to the fact that the merger removes the risk of expropriation for the investing party due to the fact that the other merging party is the only trading partner left in order to recover the 'sunk' investment (ie, the 'hold-up problem'). Of course, these improvements along the value chain can lead to technological progress, which could ultimately also raise revenues.

There are, however, contrasting narratives to these complementarity-driven, efficiency-enhancing synergies. For example, a merger between firms selling complementary products may be defensive in nature, where the acquiring firm pays a premium to take over the control of a target company that poses a potential future competitive threat (ie, by entering the acquiring firm's market). Here the synergy in terms of improved expected revenue would be due to the fact that, absent the merger, the revenue base of the acquiring firm might have been eroded by the growth of the target firm.

With respect to 'vertical mergers', the aim of vertical integration may be to foreclose current competitors. For example, the acquisition of an upstream supplier of an essential input could put downstream rivals at a competitive disadvantage, struggling to find an alternative source of supply (ie, inferior quality input and/or at a higher cost) in case the target firm exclusively supplies the downstream division of the merged entity.

In contrast, in the case of a 'horizontal merger' between rivals selling substitutes products the pursuit of revenue-enhancing synergies can generally be achieved only through the weakening of competitive rivalry. This could result from either an increase in the market power of the merged entity, or from the suspension of competitive rivalry altogether. The

15 See European Commission, Guidelines on the assessment of non-horizontal mergers under the Council Regulation on the control of concentrations between undertakings [2008] OJ C 265/7, para 5 [hereinafter Non-Horizontal Merger Guidelines].

16 The complementarity between the two products entails that the two lines of business are typically correlated, thus not suited to a strategy of risk diversification.

17 It is worth noting that this type of merger is different from a 'conglomerate merger' in that the complementarity between the two products entails that the two lines of business are typically correlated, thus not suited to a strategy of risk diversification.

18 In this case, therefore, the merger entity may benefit not only from scale and scope economies (ie to the extent that there were duplications of fixed and common costs before integrating those customer-facing activities), but from a perception of superior quality of service thanks to the lower 'hassle' costs faced by customers.

former case is known as 'unilateral effects', in contrast to the latter where the expression 'co-ordinated effects' is used.

One significant exception where, similarly to the case of product complementarity, there can be contrasting narratives is under 'network effects', whereby the attractiveness of one specific product depends on the number of existing adopters. On the one hand, where the substitute network products are incompatible (ie, network effects are proprietary) the combination of two customer bases enhances the perceived value of the merged entity's combined product. On the other hand, if the merger entity gains a size advantage against competing network products, adopters might start to expect the latter to lose attractiveness overtime, which might in turn trigger a self-fulfilling expectation cycle so that the merger entity becomes the dominant firm (ie, 'winner-takes-all' competitive dynamic).

In summary, mergers are motivated by the search for synergies in order to reduce costs and/or enhance revenues. Synergies, however, can be pro- or anti-competitive, depending on whether the synergy in question relies on competitive rivalry being weakened. Accordingly, the competitive assessment of a merger basically entails weighting pro-competitive purported synergies against alleged anti-competitive ones. This is arguably more challenging in a merger involving product complementarity, where it is difficult to tell whether the net effect (ie, between the benefits resulting from seamless integration and the risks of foreclosure) is likely to be pro or anti-competitive. Nevertheless, these types of mergers tend to be generally (ie, presumptively) considered to be pro-competitive.[19] In comparison, there is less scope for ambiguity in mergers between competitors, thus involving product substitutability. Indeed, whilst the materialization of any type of efficiency-enhancing synergies relies on the (uncertain) ability of the acquiring firm's management to successfully integrate the target firm, the propensity for unilateral and/or coordinated effect in horizontal mergers is implied by the mere loss of direct competition between the merging firms in the same relevant market.

In conclusion, it is interesting to see whether there are historical patterns regarding the triggers for M&A activity. First of all, as we previously described, mergers tend to come in 'waves'.[20] The most common triggers are technological shocks, regulatory changes, and credit availability; whereas waves tend to subside when a financial crisis and/or recession strike. Second, the general consensus seems to be that more often than not mergers fails to live up to expectations, in that they do not create value from the perspective of the acquiring firm's shareholders; whereas the profitability of the target firm seems to improve on average, mainly because of an increase in market power rather than efficiency improvements.[21] Hence, it has been argued that, rather than based on genuine synergies, mergers are often motivated by managers' hubris and overconfidence in their ability to achieve synergies, or, worse still, their personal desire to extend their 'span of control' by pursuing external growth.[22]

19 Non-Horizontal Merger Guidelines, paras 11–13.

20 See eg M Martynova and LDR Renneboog, 'A Century of Corporate Takeovers: What Have We Learned and Where Do We Stand?' [2008] 32(10) *J Banking and Finance* 2148.

21 For recent empirical evidence, see BA Blonigen and JR Pierce, 'Evidence for the Effects of Mergers on Market Power and Efficiency', NBER Working Paper No 22750 (October 2016), available at http://www.nber.org/papers/w22750.pdf.

22 For recent empirical evidence, see R El-Khatib, K Fogel, and T Jandik, 'CEO Network Centrality and Merger Performance' (2015) 116 (2) *J Financial Economics* 349.

12.1.3. THE ORIGINS OF MERGER CONTROL IN THE EU AND THE UK

12.1.3.1. Merger control and the Treaties

The European Coal and Steel Community (ECSC) Treaty, concluded in Paris in 1951, had put in place an integrated merger control system for the six founding members of the ECSC, providing the exclusive responsibility to conduct merger control to the High Authority of the ECS Community, and (after 1967) to the European Commission[23] ('one stop shop'), for merger activity in the two economic sectors targeted by the Treaty. This is remarkable, as at that time none of the six founding Member States of the ECSC had competition laws, let alone a merger control regime. However, the Treaty of Rome establishing the European Economic Community in 1957 did not include any provision on merger control. This 'gap' was duly noted in 1966, when the Commission published its memorandum on concentrations, which put forward the possible application of Article 102 of the Treaty on the Functioning of the European Union (TFEU) (ex-Article 86 of the Treaty Establishing the European Community (TEC)) to mergers (concentrations).[24] This led to some action by the Commission, which in 1972 started proceedings under Article 102 TFEU against a concentration involving the Continental Can Company and thus moving to envisage the possibility of applying Article 102 TFEU, but also Article 101 TFEU to merger activity.

12.1.3.2. The role of Articles 101 and 102 TFEU in merger control

In *Continental Can*,[25] the Court of Justice of the European Union (CJEU) held that Article [102] TFEU prohibits the acquisition by a dominant firm of most of the shares in a potential competitor in the product dominated where this would virtually eliminate competition. The Commission intervened informally in a few large mergers after 1973, and either prevented or modified some of them, but it took no formal decisions. The Commission believed that it lacked sufficient power to control anti-competitive mergers. It had no power to require firms to notify their mergers in advance. It was widely thought that it could not forbid mergers that created a dominant position; it could intervene only if at least one of the firms was already dominant and the merger strengthened its position. Nor was it clear whether Article 102 TFEU applied to small accretions of market power. The Commission even doubted whether it had power to grant interim relief to restrain a merger while it was considering the matter, and there were some doubts whether it had power to order divestiture after the event. For a decade and a half the Commission continued to propose a regulation to the Council requiring firms to notify significant mergers and giving it power to control them. Some of the Member States, however, were loath to relinquish their power to control mergers and the regulation made little progress, although the Commission continued to raise the proposed thresholds of turnover above which it would have power to intervene.

[23] European Coal and Steel Community Treaty (signed 18 April 1951, entered into force 23 July 1952) 261 UNTS140, Article 66 [hereinafter ECSC Treaty]. The Treaty expired on 23 April 2002.

[24] European Commission, 'Concentration, Economic Policy and Competition in the EEC', Information Memo P-62/66 (November 1966), available at http://aei.pitt.edu/15797/.

[25] Case 6/72, *Europemballage Corporation and Continental Can Company Inc v Commission* [1973] ECR 215. The case was examined in detail in Section 7.4.1.

In *BAT v Commission* (also known as the *Philip Morris* case),[26] the CJEU stated that the acquisition of a minority shareholding, which leads to control of a competitor, might infringe Article 101 TFEU if the acquisition restricts competition. This caused great concern as it was not clear how much of the transaction might be void by virtue of Article 101(2) TFEU. If the acquisition of the target company's assets was void and not merely voidable, title would not have passed and great confusion might ensue when its assets were sold by the new management to innocent third parties. There was also concern that under Article 101 TFEU any perceptible restriction of competition would be forbidden. The judgment left a very unsatisfactory situation and business came to accept the need for merger control at the EU level that it had so far opposed.[27]

12.1.3.3. The successive merger regulations in the EU

Following the *Philip Morris* judgment in 1987, which applied Article 101 TFEU to merger activity, there was a situation of uncertainty leading corporations to notify their merger activity to the Commission for formal or provisional clearance, under the notification and legal authorization regime of Regulation 17/62 applying at the time. However, the judgment of the CJEU in *Philip Morris* had not provided for clear rules applying in this context, leading the Council to envisage the adoption of a specific merger regulation providing a 'one-stop shop' for merger activity of a Community dimension. On 21 December 1989, the Council eventually adopted a regulation requiring the pre-notification to the Commission of concentrations within its scope—those where the parties' turnover exceeded the thresholds—and providing for possible prohibition or other remedies by the Commission.[28] This regulation was amended in 1997;[29] then repealed and replaced by EU Merger Regulation 139/2004 (EUMR), which is the merger regulation still in force.[30] The structure of the regulation remains much the same, although there are many changes of detail, but the substantive test for appraisal has changed and the time limits are longer.

Subject to exceptions, only the Commission can appraise whether a qualifying merger should be forbidden. National competition authorities may control mergers that fall outside the definitions of Articles 1–3 by applying national competition law. A merger that falls within the EUMR provisions must be appraised by the Commission to see whether 'it would significantly impede competition within the Common Market [. . .], in particular as a result of the creation or strengthening of a dominant position' (Recital 26 of the EUMR).

[26] The Commission's decision to close the file is described under the name of *Philip Morris* in European Commission, *Sixteenth Report on Competition Policy* (1987), para 98, available at http://ec.europa.eu/competition/publications/annual_report/. The CJEU confirmed that decision in Joined Cases 142 & 156/84, *BAT and Reynolds v Commission* [1987] ECR 4487, paras 37–9 and 64 [hereinafter *Philip Morris*].

[27] S Bulmer, 'Institutions and Policy Change in the European Communities: The Case of Merger Control' (1994) 72(3) *Public Administration* 423, 432, noting the shift in businesses' attitude towards EU merger control and explaining that '[. . .] (a)s the 1980s progressed, their cross-border mergers and acquisition activity increased and they became the most vigorous supporters of the additional certainty that would be afforded by the "one-stop shop" rather than the multiple referrals that were necessary in its absence [to various national competition authorities that had adopted merger control].'

[28] Council Regulation (EC) No 4064/89 on the control of concentrations between undertakings [1989] OJ L 395/1.

[29] Council Regulation (EC) No 1310/97 amending Regulation 4064/89 [1997] OJ L 180/1.

[30] Council Regulation (EC) No 139/2004 on the control of concentration between undertakings [2004] OJ L 24/1 [hereinafter EUMR].

The appraisal is done in two stages. If the Commission finds that the transaction raises serious doubts as to its compatibility with the Common Market, it opens stage II. It may avoid going to stage II by accepting commitments offered by the parties that satisfy the Commission at the end of stage I. Often these are to divest overlapping activities in horizontal mergers. They are now binding on the parties.[31]

There are five major advantages in devising transactions so as to qualify under the regulation. First, the substantive test is far more favourable than that under Article 101(1) TFEU. Second, the proceedings inevitably lead to a formal decision. So the need for self-assessment and the ensuing uncertainty under Regulation 1/2003 are avoided. Third, most transactions are cleared within twenty-five working days and most of those raising serious doubts within a further ninety working days, increased to 105 when commitments are offered more than fifty-five working days after proceedings in stage II have been initiated. Fourth, national authorities cannot apply national competition rules to most mergers above the thresholds; and, fifth, the analysis of markets under the merger regulation has more often been more realistic than under Article 101(1) TFEU.

The Commission more frequently leaves national authorities to consider mergers under national law.

12.1.3.4. The emergence of UK merger control

Merger control was first introduced in the UK with the Monopolies and Mergers Act 1965, which provided the power to the Board of Trade to refer mergers to the Monopolies Commission, each time enterprises 'cease to be distinct' and coming 'under common control or ownership'. The merger could be prohibited only if the Monopolies Commission was satisfied that the merger might be expected to operate against the public interest. The 'public interest' test constituted the main characteristic of UK merger control, and was to a large extent maintained in the changes introduced under the Fair Trading Act 1973, the Minister (Secretary of State) having to take the decision to refer, or not, a merger to the Competition Commission (CoCo). In practice, however, the preparations for the Minister's decision were effectuated by the new independent office put in place by the Fair Trading Act, the Director General of Fair Trading. The accession to the European Communities in 1972 has not led to any changes with regard to UK merger control, the UK being the only Member State disposing of a merger control regime at the time.[32]

The UK Merger Control was substantially amended by Part 3 of the 2002 Enterprise Act (EA 2002). Most importantly, the EA 2002 greatly depoliticized UK merger control, by removing the Secretary of State from decision-making in merger cases, other than when exceptionally public interest issues arise, and by altering the standard decision criterion from the broader public interest to the more narrowly confined substantial lessening of competition (SLC) test, which should frame the decision of the Office of Fair Trading (OFT) to refer a merger, or not, to the CoCo. The EA 2002 made clear that the predominant concern in UK merger control is the preservation of competition, the public interests to be exceptionally taken into account being narrowly defined and have been rarely enforced. Enterprise and

[31] For more details on the merger control procedure, please refer to the companion volume on Competition Law Enforcement: I Lianos, *Competition Law Enforcement* (Hart, 2017).

[32] In Germany, merger control was introduced after a major revision of the German Gesetz gegen Wettbewerbsbeschränkungen (Act Against Restraints of Competition, GWB) in 1973. Merger control was enacted in France by legislation in 1977.

Regulatory Reform Act 2013 (ERRA 2013) amended the EA 2002 by merging the OFT and the CoCo into the Competition and Markets Authority (CMA), although maintaining the two-phases process of merger control, Phase 1 performed by the CMA, and in case there is a realistic prospect of an SLC, the case being referred for a Phase 2 investigation to an 'Inquiry Group' within the CMA, but formed by different people than those performing the Phase 1 assessment. It also provided some additional powers of investigation to the CMA. Unlike the EU merger control, the UK merger control does not require the compulsory notification of merger activity, notification being voluntary.[33] The Brexit process may reinforce the importance of UK merger control, as well as eventually lead to some legislative changes as to the remit of UK merger control, the role of public interest analysis and eventually the introduction of a compulsory notification.

12.1.4. THE ARCHITECTURE OF EU AND UK MERGER CONTROL

Merger control is a fundamental instrument of competition law. It aims to prevent the formation of monopolies or market structures that will lead to anti-competitive effects. Merger control covers operations that bring a lasting change to the control of undertakings concerned and therefore to the structure of the market. It is a necessary complement of the cartels' prohibition, as, otherwise, if a cartel is prohibited, firms could merge and avoid regulation by the law. More than any other component of competition law, which aim to sanction anti-competitive behaviour *ex post*, merger control has a forward looking orientation and aims at the prevention of market structures conducive to anti-competitive effects. Usually, merging undertakings will argue that they should have the freedom to operate and exploit the benefits of synergies by merging or acquiring assets from other firms (efficiency gains), these claims being assessed in conjunction to the alleged anti-competitive effects of the merger.

It is quite common in all merger control systems, and certainly those of the EU and the UK, to consider various issues when assessing some merger activity.

- Does the specific competition authority have jurisdiction over the specific merger activity?
- Is this consolidation or M&A activity the kind of the lasting change in the control of the undertakings concerned, the specific merger control regime aims at?
- Will this merger activity lead to anti-competitive effects, increasing significantly the market power of the firms that are object of the M&A, without compensatory efficiency effects, or lead to negative effects to broader public interest (according to the relevant substantive test for merger control), taking into account the evolution of the market without the specific M&A (counterfactual scenario)
    - If it will not, approve the merger;
    - If it will, the merging parties should submit undertakings (remedies) to reduce the projected increase in the market power;
    - If they are unwilling to submit satisfactory undertakings or there are no possible undertakings, the M&A should be prohibited.

[33] The procedural aspects of the UK merger control regime are examined in the companion volume on Competition Law Enforcement: I Lianos, *Competition Law Enforcement and Procedure* (forthcoming OUP, 2019).

12.1.4.1. The substantive tests and theories of harm

At the time of the passage of the first EU merger regulation in 1989, there were essentially two models of substantive tests for merger control. The UK merger control regime resulting from the 1965 Monopolies and Mergers Act and the 1973 Fair Trading Act relied on a substantive test mixing competition and public interest criteria, such as the maintenance and promotion of the balanced distribution of industry and employment in the UK, or the maintenance and promotion of competitive activity of UK producers and suppliers in foreign markets. In contrast, the German merger control regime introduced in 1973 relied on competition-related criteria, the fundamental principle being that the merger should not lead to the creation or strengthening of a market dominating position, although it also offered the possibility to the federal minister of economics to reject the recommendations of the German Competition Authority (the *Bundeskartellamt*), although still bound by its findings as to whether a market dominating position was created or strengthened, in case the restraint of competition following the merger was compensated by the overall economic advantages of the merger or if the merger was justified by an overriding public interest outweighing its anti-competitive impact.

Although the Commission, in its initial proposals for a EU merger control regime, seemed to favour the inclusion of public interest concerns, the final 1988 Commission draft only included a defence on public interest grounds. By the adoption of the Merger Regulation by the Council in 1989, the defence and the concerns have been moved out of the substantive provisions of the Regulation, some of them eventually mentioned in the recitals, while the substantive test was essentially competition-oriented, like the one for Article 101(3) TFEU, development or economic progress being taken into account, provided that they are to 'consumer's advantage' and do not 'form an obstacle to competition'.[34] As we have briefly highlighted in the previous section, the UK merger control regime has also evolved towards a predominately competition-oriented substantive test, although it still maintains public interest considerations as an additional substantive test in specific and well-confined situations. We will focus on the competition-oriented substantive tests, before exploring the public interest considerations that may in rare cases be considered, in particular in UK merger control, and which form part of an alternative substantive test.

12.1.4.1.1. Competition-oriented substantive tests: Dominant position, significant impediment of effective competition, significant lessening of competition

Article 2 EUMR requires the Commission to investigate concentrations above the thresholds to decide whether they are compatible with the Internal Market. Article 2(3) prescribes the criterion of incompatibility with the Internal Market:

> A concentration which would significantly impede effective competition, in the common market or in a substantial part of it, in particular as a result of the creation or strengthening of a dominant position, shall be declared incompatible with the common market.

[34] Article 2 of the former Merger Regulation 4064/89 is cited and discussed by S Bulmer, 'Institutions and Policy Change in the European Communities: The case of Merger Control' (1994) 72(3) *Public Administration* 423, 436–8.

Article 2(2) is the converse, and requires the Commission to clear mergers that do not do so.

This test differs from the earlier regulations, which were concerned about a concentration that creates or strengthens a dominant position as a result of which effective competition would be significantly impeded in the Common Market or in a substantial part of it. Article 2 of the former EC Merger Regulation 4064/89 (ECMR) employed the concept of dominant position although linked it more directly than the previous case law on Article 102 TFEU to the concept of effective competition. In order to define the existence of effective competition, one should indeed look to indications of performance as well as of market structure. In other words, effects on the market may count. Relying on this 'effects-based' approach, subsequent case law broadened the concept of dominant position in order to cover situations of coordinated effects. While concentrations that were likely to lead to the merged company and its rivals coordinating their behaviour on the market were caught by the old regulation under the concept of collective dominant position,[35] it was, however, unclear whether mergers that might lead to unilateral action by the merging firms would do so if no dominant position was likely to ensue. The major reason for revising the old regulation was to ensure that unilateral as well as coordinating effects should be taken into account. The alleged unilateral effects 'gap' was not, however, the principal reason for the new substantive test in EU merger control.[36] The main motivation can be found in the need to provide tools to both the legal and economic communities to work together in framing the content of the new substantive test, without being subject to the constraints of the previous case law on the concept of dominant position. Quantitative evidence also requires observable and measurable factors, such as predictable market outcomes, rather than more complex criteria, that require some form of qualitative as well as quantitative assessment, such as the existence of a dominant position. According to the EUMR, the criterion of dominant position serves now as a simple indication of a significant impediment of effective competition and therefore of the existence of a potential harm to consumers.[37]

In assessing whether a merger is incompatible with the Common Market, Article 2(1) EUMR requires the Commission to take into account:

(a) the need to preserve and develop effective competition within the Common Market in view of, among other things, the structure of all the markets concerned and the actual or potential competition from undertakings located either within or outside the Community;

(b) the market position of the undertakings concerned and their economic and financial power, the alternatives available to suppliers and users, their access to suppliers or markets, any legal or other barriers to entry, supply and demand trends for the relevant goods and services, the interests of the intermediate and ultimate consumers, and the development of technical and economic progress provided that it is to consumers' advantage and does not form an obstacle to competition.

35 See Joined Cases C-68/94 & 30/95, *French Republic and Société commerciale des potasses et de l'azote (SCPA) and Entreprise minière et chimique (EMC) v Commission* [1998] ECR I–1375.

36 See, for a critical assessment of the test, G Monti, 'The New Substantive Test in the EC Merger Regulation—Bridging the Gap between Economics and the Law', LSE Legal Studies Working Paper (30 July 2008), available at https://ssrn.com/abstract=1153661; MB Coate, 'Did the European Union's Market Dominance Policy Have a Gap? Evidence from Enforcement in the United States' (26 May 2009), available at https://ssrn.com/abstract=1410246.

37 EUMR, Article 2(2).

Justification on non-competition grounds was removed in 1989 from an earlier draft of this article and replaced with these provisions. The limitation to competitive criteria was controversial. Some of the matters to be taken into account under Article 2(1)(b) EUMR could be interpreted to include non-competition related criteria. 'Economic and financial power' is not the same as power over price and other aspects of a bargain. Considerations of industrial policy were firmly rejected by the Commission in *De Haviland.*[38] The list of factors to be taken into account, however, is not exhaustive, although the Commission should consider the relevant matters in the list.

The Commission has published guidelines on the assessment of horizontal mergers[39] and on non-horizontal mergers.[40] A merger is horizontal if both merging firms are in the same relevant market, with overlaps in the markets of both firms. The guidelines represent the Commission's evolving experience. Since the Commission does not act on a complaint, there is no particular conduct on which to focus. The CJEU noted in *France v Commission* (*Kali und Salz*) that the appraisal must be prospective.[41] There must also be a causal link between the concentration and the restriction of competition resulting from the merger.[42]

As the Commission makes it clear in the Horizontal Merger Guidelines, 'the competitive analysis in a particular case will be based on an overall assessment of the foreseeable impact of the merger in the light of the relevant factors and conditions'.[43] The Commission enjoys a margin of discretion with regard to the factors to take into account, this being 'implicit' in the provisions of an economic nature which form part of the rules on concentrations'.[44] The Guidelines also indicate that the assessment of mergers will normally entail the definition of the relevant product and geographic markets, in order to identify 'in a systematic way the immediate competitive constraints facing the merged entity', and the competitive assessment of the merger.[45] Neither of the two sets of Guidelines provides an exact definition of what constitutes a 'significant impediment of effective competition'. It is nevertheless noted that the Commission will examine 'the foreseeable impact of a merger on the relevant markets', the Commission analysing its 'possible anti-competitive effects and the relevant countervailing factors such as buyer power, the extent of entry barriers and possible efficiencies put forward by the parties'.[46] Furthermore, it is indicated that the Commission will conduct this analysis by reference to a counterfactual:

> In assessing the competitive effects of a merger, the Commission compares the competitive conditions that would have prevailed without the merger. In most cases the competitive conditions existing at the time of the merger constitute the relevant comparison for evaluating the effects of a merger. However, in some circumstances the Commission may take into

38 *Aerospatiale-Alenia/de Havilland* (Case No IV/M053) Commission Decision [1991] OJ L 334/42.

39 Guidelines on the assessment of horizontal mergers under the Council Regulation on the control of concentrations between undertakings [2004] OJ C 31/5 [hereinafter Horizontal Merger Guidelines].

40 Guidelines on the assessment of non-horizontal mergers under the Council Regulation on the control of concentrations between undertakings [2008] OJ C 265/6 (hereinafter Non-Horizontal Merger Guidelines).

41 Joined Cases C-68/94 & 30/95, *SCPA and EMC v Commission* [1998] ECR I–1375, paras 112–21.

42 Ibid. For a discussion of the causal link, see A Bavasso and A Lindsay, 'Causation in EC Merger Control' (2007) 3(2) *J Competition L & Economics* 181.

43 Horizontal Merger Guidelines, para 13.

44 Case C-12/03, *Tetra Laval BV v Commission* [2005] ECR I–987, para 38.

45 Horizontal Merger Guidelines, para 10.

46 Ibid, para 12.

account future changes to the market that can reasonably be predicted. It may, in particular, take account of the likely entry or exit of firms if the merger did not take place when considering what constitutes the relevant comparison.[47]

The counterfactual analysis may be narrow and static, or more dynamic, depending on the specific case and the data available to the Commission.[48]

In performing the substantive assessment of mergers the Commission relies on market shares and concentration levels, which provide 'useful first indications of the market structure and of the competitive importance of both the merging parties and their competitors'.[49] The Commission looks at current market shares, but these 'may be adjusted to reflect reasonably certain future changes, for instance in the light of exit, entry or expansion' and calculated post-merger market shares on the assumption that the post-merger combined market share of the merging parties is the sum of their pre-merger market shares.[50] Concentration levels may also provide useful information about the competitive situation. The Commission applies the Herfindahl–Hirschman Index (HHI), which is calculated by summing the squares of the individual market shares of all the firms in the market.[51] The Commission notes that 'while the absolute level of the HHI can give an initial indication of the competitive pressure in the market post-merger, the change in the HHI (known as the "delta") is a useful proxy for the change in concentration directly brought about by the merger'.[52] HHI values are used to screen out mergers unlikely to give rise to anti-competitive concerns. According to the General Court (GC) in *Sun Chemical Group BV and others v Commission*, 'the greater the margin by which those thresholds are exceeded, the more the HHI values will be indicative of competition concerns'.[53]

Horizontal Merger Guidelines [2004] OJ C 31/5, paras 19–21

19. The Commission is unlikely to identify horizontal competition concerns in a market with a post-merger HHI below 1,000. Such markets normally do not require extensive analysis.

20. The Commission is also unlikely to identify horizontal competition concerns in a merger with a post-merger HHI between 1,000 and 2,000 and a delta below 250, or a merger with a post-merger HHI above 2,000 and a delta below 150, except where special circumstances such as, for instance, one or more of the following factors are present:

(a) a merger involves a potential entrant or a recent entrant with a small market share;

(b) one or more merging parties are important innovators in ways not reflected in market shares;

(c) there are significant cross-shareholdings among the market participants;

(d) one of the merging firms is a maverick firm with a high likelihood of disrupting coordinated conduct;

47 Ibid, para 9.
48 This will be discussed in Section 12.3.2.
49 Horizontal Merger Guidelines, para 14.
50 Ibid, para 15.
51 Ibid, para 16.
52 Ibid.
53 Case T-282/06, *Sun Chemical Group Bv and others v Commission* [2007] ECR II-2149, para 138.

(e) indications of past or ongoing coordination, or facilitating practices, are present;

(f) one of the merging parties has a pre-merger market share of 50 % of more.

21. Each of these HHI levels, in combination with the relevant deltas, may be used as an initial indicator of the absence of competition concerns. However, they do not give rise to a presumption of either the existence or the absence of such concerns.

Horizontal mergers may give rise to two types of anti-competitive effects: (i) non-coordinated effects and (ii) coordinated effects. These are examined in more detail in the following Section.

Non-horizontal mergers are of two sorts. Vertical mergers are mergers between firms in different stages of production of the same product, when a manufacturer of a certain product (the 'upstream firm') merges with one of its distributors (the 'downstream firm').[54] They generally cause fewer problems than horizontal mergers, and usually are motivated by efficiency gains, for instance avoiding double marginalization. The basic competition law concern they may give rise is anti-competitive foreclosure. Conglomerate mergers involve firms that are in a relationship that is 'neither horizontal (as competitors in the same relevant market) nor vertical (as suppliers or customers)'.[55] As with vertical mergers, conglomerate mergers, 'provide substantial scope for efficiencies'. However, both types of non-horizontal mergers may also produce anti-competitive effects: (i) non coordinated effects resulting from foreclosure of actual or potential rivals' access to supplies or markets thereby reducing these companies' ability and/or incentive to compete, and (ii) coordinated effects, 'where the merger changes the nature of competition in such a way that firms that previously were not coordinating their behaviour, are now significantly more likely to coordinate to raise prices or otherwise harm effective competition'.[56]

12.1.4.1.2. Collective dominant position and coordinated effects

There were two possible gaps in the ECMR. A concentration could be forbidden only if it created or strengthened a dominant position as a result of which competition would be significantly impeded. In several countries, any merger, which may substantially lessen competition, may be forbidden even if a dominant position is not obtained. The Commission and courts filled one gap by stating in particular decisions, some relating to Article 102 TFEU and some to mergers, that if the merging firms and its competitor(s) will have large market shares and are likely to act as a single entity, the concentration leads to a collective dominant position. The second possible gap was filled by new drafting of

[54] Non-Horizontal Merger Guidelines, para 4.

[55] Ibid, para 5. According to the Commission's Guidelines,

> [t]he distinction between conglomerate mergers and horizontal mergers may be subtle, eg when a conglomerate merger involves products that are weak substitutes for each other. The same holds true for the distinction between conglomerate mergers and vertical mergers. For instance, products may be supplied by some companies with the inputs already integrated (vertical relationship), whereas other producers leave it to the customers to select and assemble the inputs themselves (conglomerate relationship).

Ibid, para 5 n 5.

[56] Ibid, para 19.

Article 2(2) and (3) EUMR. The Horizontal Merger Guidelines of the Commission indicate that the concept of collective dominance and that of coordinated effects are closely intertwined.[57]

The Commission several times found that a merger would lead to a collective dominant position, focusing its analysis on numerous structural factors, such as the fact that the post-merger market would be characterised by a duopoly with high market shares, high homogeneity of products, and high entry barriers, and eventually considered any constraints on the conduct of the merged firms due to the possibility of new entrants, and whether the remaining firms would have the incentives and possibility of behaving as if they had agreed not to compete without making an express agreement.[58] Economists stress that coordination requires that there is also some mechanism (retaliation mechanism) for punishing the firm that upsets the boat by cutting prices below the level agreed.[59] Otherwise the coordination cannot be sustained.

In *France v Commission*, the CJEU confirmed that there might be joint dominance when two firms, the merged undertaking and one independent of it, may act as a single entity in view of the links between them.[60] It added, however, that there was a strong burden of proof to show that the merging firms would act as a single entity with its competitors. In contrast to the Commission's decisional practice so far, the CJEU's analysis emphasized the dynamic elements of competition, by carefully analysing the firms' incentives to deviate from the common policy, as well as the ability and the incentives of fringe competitors to exercise countervailing power, without, however, this leading the CJEU to outline any particular theory of harm as the foundation of collective dominance.[61]

Gencor v Commission

In *Gencor*, the Commission condemned a merger that would lead immediately to the merging firms, Gencor and Lonrho, holding 30–35 per cent of the world market of the platinum and precious metals usually found in the same ore.[62] A third party, Anglo-American, would have a similar share of the world supply, while the Russians, with mines considered by the Commission to be exhausted, would sell from stock and supply about 10 per cent for the next two years, when the share of the merging parties and Anglo-American would each increase to about 40 per cent with high entry barriers and other features of an oligopolistic market. The Commission thought that the duopoly was likely to restrict production and raise prices and prohibited the merger.

57 Horizontal Merger Guidelines, paras 39–57.

58 Starting with *Nestle/Perrier* (Case IV/M.190) Commission Decision [1992] OJ L356/1, [1993] 4 CMLR M17, paras 110–16, 119–20, 130. For a useful analysis of the collective dominant position concept in EU merger control, see I Kokkoris, 'The Development of the Concept of Collective Dominance in the ECMR—From its Inception to its Current Status' [2007] 30(3) *World Competition* 419; I Kalozymis, 'Collective Dominance in EU Merger Control: Substantive Issues' (PhD Thesis, Queen Mary University London, 2014).

59 See, notably, G Stigler, 'A Theory Of Oligopoly' (1964) 72(1) *J Political Economy* 44, holding that successful coordinated interaction depends on the three conditions revolving around the establishment of a common collusive policy, the detection of deviations and retaliation mechanisms leading to the punishment of such deviations, as well as a number of peripheral circumstances relating to the absence of destabilizing factors for the coordinated interaction such as entry or buyer power.

60 Joined Cases C-68/94 & 30/95, *SCPA and EMC v Commission* [1998] ECR I-1375.

61 Ibid, paras 234–9, 242–8. See I Kalozymis, 'Collective Dominance in EU Merger Control: Substantive Issues' (PhD Thesis, Queen Mary University London, 2014), 122–4 and the references cited.

62 *Gencor/Lonrho* (Case No IV/M.619) Commission Decision 97/26/EC [1997] OJ L 11/30.

On appeal, the General Court confirmed the Commission's finding of collective dominance when the two remaining firms were likely to act as a single entity, whether or not there were links between them. Yet, the Court seems to have been inspired by the theory of tacit collusion as a limiting principle for this expansive interpretation of the scope of EU merger control.

Case T-102/96, *Gencor v Commission*
[1999] ECR II–753

123. Article 2(3) of the Regulation [EUMR] provides: 'A concentration which creates or strengthens a dominant position as a result of which effective competition would be significantly impeded in the common market or in a substantial part of it shall be declared incompatible with the common market.'

124. The question thus arises as to whether the words 'which creates or strengthens a dominant position' cover only the creation or strengthening of an individual dominant position or whether they also refer to the creation or strengthening of a collective dominant position, that is to say one held by two or more undertakings.

125. It cannot be deduced from the wording of Article 2 of the Regulation that only concentrations which create or strengthen an individual dominant position, that is to say a dominant position held by the parties to the concentration, come within the scope of the Regulation. Article 2, in referring to 'a concentration which creates or strengthens a dominant position', does not in itself exclude the possibility of applying the Regulation to cases where concentrations lead to the creation or strengthening of a collective dominant position, that is to say a dominant position held by the parties to the concentration together with one or more undertakings not party thereto.

126. The applicant is not correct in its submission that, since other, national, systems contained specific provisions for the control of concentrations resulting in the creation or strengthening of collective dominant positions at the time when the Regulation was adopted, the deliberate choice of the Council not to enact such a provision in that regulation necessarily means that it does not cover situations of collective dominance. The choice of neutral wording of the kind found in Article 2(3) of the Regulation does not automatically exclude from its field of application the creation or strengthening of a collective dominant position.

127. Finally, it should be noted that, however specific they may be, the national laws which were applicable to the creation or strengthening of a collective dominant position before the Regulation entered into force can no longer be applied to such concentrations, in accordance with Article 21(2) of the Regulation. If the applicant's argument were followed, it would thus be necessary to accept that all the Member States whose systems for the control of concentrations applied to the creation or strengthening of collective dominant positions, that is to say France, Germany and the United Kingdom amongst others, have abandoned that form of control so far as concerns concentrations with a Community dimension. In the absence of clear indications to that effect, it cannot be assumed that such was the will of the Member States.

128. As regards the applicant's arguments relating to the legislative history of the Regulation, it is necessary, when interpreting a legislative measure, to attach less importance to the position taken by one or other Member State when the measure was drawn up than to its wording and objectives.

129. The legislative history cannot itself be considered to express clearly the intention of the authors of the Regulation as to the scope of the term 'dominant position'.

In those circumstances, it provides no assistance for the interpretation of the disputed concept [. . .].

130. In any event, the fact that, after the adoption of the Regulation, certain Member States, in particular France, contested the view that it could apply to collective dominant positions cannot mean that it does not cover situations of that kind. Since the Member States are not bound by positions which they may have accepted at the time of the debate within the Council, the possibility cannot be ruled out that one of them may change its view after the adoption of a legislative measure or simply decide to raise the question of its legality before the Community judicature.

131. It is necessary, therefore, to interpret the Regulation, in particular Article 2 thereof, on the basis of its general scheme. [. . .]

148. Since the interpretations of the Regulation, and in particular Article 2 thereof, based on their wording and the history and the scheme of the Regulation do not permit their precise scope to be assessed as regards the type of dominant position concerned, the legislation in question must be interpreted by reference to its purpose [. . .].

149. As is apparent from the first five recitals in its preamble, the principal objective set for the Regulation, with a view to achieving the aims of the Treaty and especially of Article 3(f) thereof (Article 3(g) following the entry into force of the Treaty on European Union), is to ensure that the process of reorganising undertakings as a result in particular of the completion of the internal market does not inflict lasting damage on competition. The final part of the fifth recital accordingly states that 'Community law must therefore include provisions governing those concentrations which may significantly impede effective competition in the common market or in a substantial part of it' [. . .].

150. Furthermore, it follows from the sixth, seventh, tenth and eleventh recitals in the preamble to the Regulation that it, unlike Articles [101 and 102 TFEU], is intended to apply to all concentrations with a Community dimension in so far as, because of their effect on the structure of competition within the Community, they may prove incompatible with the system of undistorted competition envisaged by the Treaty [. . .].

151. A concentration which creates or strengthens a dominant position on the part of the parties to the concentration with an entity not involved in the concentration is liable to prove incompatible with the system of undistorted competition laid down by the Treaty. Consequently, if it were accepted that only concentrations creating or strengthening a dominant position on the part of the parties to the concentration were covered by the Regulation, its purpose as indicated by the above mentioned recitals would be partially frustrated. The Regulation would thus be deprived of a not insignificant aspect of its effectiveness, without that being necessary from the perspective of the general structure of the Community system of control of concentrations [. . .].

152. The arguments regarding, first, the fact that the Regulation is capable of being applied to concentrations between undertakings whose main place of business is not in the Community and, secondly, the possibility that the Commission could control the anti-competitive behaviour of members of an oligopoly by means of Article [102 TFEU], are not capable of calling into question the applicability of the Regulation to cases of collective dominance resulting from a concentration.

153. As regards the first of those arguments, the applicability of the Regulation to collective dominant positions cannot depend on its territorial scope.

154. So far as concerns the possibility of applying Article [102 TFEU], it cannot be inferred therefrom that the Regulation does not apply to collective dominance, given that the same reasoning would hold for cases of dominance by a single undertaking, which would lead to the conclusion that the Regulation is not necessary at all.

155. Furthermore, since only the strengthening of dominant positions and not their creation can be controlled under Article [102 TFEU] [. . .] the effect of the Regulation not applying to concentrations creating a dominant position would be to create a gap in the Community system for the control of concentrations which would be liable to undermine the proper functioning of the common market.

156. It follows from the foregoing that collective dominant positions do not fall outside the scope of the Regulation [. . .].

157. Accordingly, the Commission was not required to include in the contested decision any reasoning on the applicability of the Regulation to collective dominant positions, in particular as it had already expressed its view on that subject both in the annual reports on competition policy and in other concentration cases, including the *Nestlé-Perrier* decision. Thus, the ground of challenge alleging infringement of the obligation to state reasons laid down by Article 190 of the Treaty is not founded.

The General Court went on to consider factors indicating joint dominance:

- *the market shares of Lonrho and Anglo American and the gap between over 30 per cent each and the market shares of their competitors on the other (paras 199–216);*
- *the similarity of the cost structure of the merging firms and of Anglo-American (paras 218–23);*
- *market transparency (paras 226–30);*
- *slow growth in demand (paras 233–8).*

The applicant claimed that the Commission had failed to demonstrate the existence of structural links or to prove that the merged entity and Implats intended to behave as if they constituted a single dominant entity. The GC noted the following:

273. In its judgment in the *Flat Glass* case, the Court referred to links of a structural nature only by way of example and did not lay down that such links must exist in order for a finding of collective dominance to be made.

274. It merely stated [. . .] that there is nothing, in principle, to prevent two or more independent economic entities from being united by economic links in a specific market and, by virtue of that fact, from together holding a dominant position *vis-à-vis* the other operators on the same market. It added (in the same paragraph) that that could be the case, for example, where two or more independent undertakings jointly had, through agreements or licences, a technological lead affording them the power to behave to an appreciable extent independently of their competitors, their customers and, ultimately, of consumers.

275. Nor can it be deduced from the same judgment that the Court has restricted the notion of economic links to the notion of structural links referred to by the applicant.

276. Furthermore, there is no reason whatsoever in legal or economic terms to exclude from the notion of economic links the relationship of interdependence existing between the parties to a tight oligopoly within which, in a market with the appropriate characteristics, in particular in terms of market concentration, transparency and product homogeneity, those parties are in a position to anticipate one another's behaviour and are therefore strongly encouraged to align their conduct in the market, in particular in such a way as to maximise their joint profits by restricting production with a view to increasing prices. In such a context, each trader is aware that highly competitive action on its part designed to increase its market share (for example a price cut) would provoke identical action by the others, so that it would derive no benefit from its initiative. All the traders would thus be affected by the reduction in price levels.

277. That conclusion is all the more pertinent with regard to the control of concentrations, whose objective is to prevent anti-competitive market structures from arising or being strengthened. Those structures may result from the existence of economic links in the strict sense argued by the applicant or from market structures of an oligopolistic kind where each undertaking may become aware of common interests and, in particular, cause prices to increase without having to enter into an agreement or resort to a concerted practice.

278. In the instant case, therefore, the applicant's ground of challenge alleging that the Commission failed to establish the existence of structural links is misplaced.

279. The Commission was entitled to conclude, relying on the envisaged alteration in the structure of the market and on the similarity of the costs of Amplats and Implats/LPD, that the proposed transaction would create a collective dominant position and lead in actual fact to a duopoly constituted by those two undertakings.

280. To the same end, it was also entitled to take into account the economic links [. . .].

281. The applicant is not justified in challenging the relevance of those links on the ground that they did not directly concern the PGM [platinum group metal] industry and were acts of AAC rather than Amplats. Links between the principal platinum producers relating to activities outside PGM production [. . .] were taken into account by the Commission not as factors attesting to the existence of economic links in the strict sense given to that notion by the applicant, but as factors contributing to discipline over the members of an oligopoly by multiplying the risks of retaliation should one of its members act in a manner considered unacceptable by the others. That analysis is, moreover, confirmed by a consultant's study regarding the possible competitive responses of Implats in relation to LPD [. . .]: according to that consultant, one of the possible scenarios was 'disciplining attacks and signals —focused price wars, for example Rh [rhodium]'.

282. The fact that the links in question concern AAC and not Amplats directly cannot invalidate the Commission's reasoning. Since Amplats was controlled by AAC, the Commission was justified in considering that the links which existed between AAC and other undertakings, whether or not operating in the PGM markets, could have a favourable or an unfavourable impact on Amplats.

283. As for the argument that AAC's recent investment in Lonrho was an action hostile to Gencor and to the concentration, and constituted in itself an indication that the links existing between the various companies did not stand in the way of aggressive competition between them, the Court finds, first, that the applicant has not adduced the necessary proof of the hostile nature of that transaction, and secondly, that, irrespective of the reasons behind it, it tightened the links existing between the two most significant competitors in the market.

NOTES AND QUESTIONS ON GENCOR

1. Is an ability of each oligopolist to punish a firm not restricting production to raise price above a competitive level important? Is this mentioned anywhere in this judgment?
2. (Paragraphs 273–84) To establish joint dominance, is it necessary to show that there are links between the oligopolists? Is it easier to find joint dominance if there are links? Can the structure of the market ever be such a link?

3. (Paragraphs 276–77) The General Court refers to the interdependence of the rivals as well as the fact that they align their conduct, even in the absence of an agreement or concerted practice, as an element of concern. Would you consider that the Court is viewing collective dominance position as intrinsically linked to the theory of tacit collusion?[63]

In its subsequent decision *Airtours/First Choice*,[64] however, not only did the Commission extended *Gencor* from a merger to duopoly to a merger reducing suppliers from four to three, it also forbade a merger in a dynamic market where the product was not homogeneous and where the ways of marketing the product are changing with the use of the Internet. The Commission also seems to have departed from the *Gencor* approach, as it did not rely on the economic theory of tacit collusion when inferring the existence of a collective dominance, relying instead exclusively on the degree of interdependence between the oligopolists and on their common interest to reduce competition among themselves.

Airtours v Commission

Case T-342/99, *Airtours plc v Commission*
[2002] ECR II–2585

The merger was between two (Airtours and First Choice) of the big four UK tour operators, the market shares of the four main operators being Thomson 27 per cent, Airtours 21 per cent, Thomas Cook 20 per cent, and First Choice 11 per cent. All other operators had fewer than 5 per cent. The Commission prohibited the merger finding that the acquisition would create a 'collective dominant position' held jointly by Airtours/First Choice and the two other large vertically integrated operators who were competitors in the UK market for short haul foreign package holidays. The tacit collusion that was feared related to the planning of capacity (airline seats and hotel bookings), although this is fixed by the publication of catalogues some eighteen months before the holidays are sold. Consequently, it would not be possible to retaliate promptly against a firm seen to be increasing capacity. The decision left the question of practice unanswered. Experts no longer knew on what theory the Commission was working and it was impossible to advise firms whether mergers had a good chance of being cleared. Although it was too late to resume the merger, Airtours appealed. In a notable judgment, the GC confirmed but also delimited the earlier theory of Gencor.

61. A collective dominant position significantly impeding effective competition in the common market or a substantial part of it may thus arise as the result of a concentration where, in view of the actual characteristics of the relevant market and of the alteration in its structure that the transaction would entail, the latter would make each member of the dominant oligopoly, as it becomes aware of common interests, consider it possible, economically rational, and hence preferable, to adopt on a lasting basis a common policy on the market with the aim of selling at above competitive prices, without having to enter into an agreement or resort to a concerted practice

63 On this theory, see our analysis in Section 11.2. See also the comments on *Gencor* by KU Kuhn and C Caffara, 'Joint Dominance: The CFI Judgment on Gencor/Lohro' (1999) 20(7) *European Competition L Rev* 355; G Niels, 'Collective Dominance: More than Just Oligopolistic Interdependence' (2001) 22(5) *European Competition L Rev* 168.

64 *Airtours/First Choice* (Case No IV/M.1524) Commission Decision [2000] OJ L 93/1.

within the meaning of Article [101 TFEU] [. . .] and without any actual or potential competitors, let alone customers or consumers, being able to react effectively.

62. As the applicant has argued and as the Commission has accepted in its pleadings, three conditions are necessary for a finding of collective dominance as defined:

- first, each member of the dominant oligopoly must have the ability to know how the other members are behaving in order to monitor whether or not they are adopting the common policy. As the Commission specifically acknowledges, it is not enough for each member of the dominant oligopoly to be aware that interdependent market conduct is profitable for all of them but each member must also have a means of knowing whether the other operators are adopting the same strategy and whether they are maintaining it. There must, therefore, be sufficient market transparency for all members of the dominant oligopoly to be aware, sufficiently precisely and quickly, of the way in which the other members' market conduct is evolving;
- second, the situation of tacit coordination must be sustainable over time, that is to say, there must be an incentive not to depart from the common policy on the market. As the Commission observes, it is only if all the members of the dominant oligopoly maintain the parallel conduct that all can benefit. The notion of retaliation in respect of conduct deviating from the common policy is thus inherent in this condition. In this instance, the parties concur that, for a situation of collective dominance to be viable, there must be adequate deterrents to ensure that there is a long-term incentive in not departing from the common policy, which means that each member of the dominant oligopoly must be aware that highly competitive action on its part designed to increase its market share would provoke identical action by the others, so that it would derive no benefit from its initiative (see, to that effect, *Gencor* v *Commission*, paragraph 276);
- third, to prove the existence of a collective dominant position to the requisite legal standard, the Commission must also establish that the foreseeable reaction of current and future competitors, as well as of consumers, would not jeopardize the results expected from the common policy.

63. The prospective analysis which the Commission has to carry out in its review of concentrations involving collective dominance calls for close examination in particular of the circumstances which, in each individual case, are relevant for assessing the effects of the concentration on competition in the reference market [. . .]. [I]t is also apparent from the judgment in *Kali and Salz* that, where the Commission takes the view that a merger should be prohibited because it will create a situation of collective dominance, it is incumbent upon it to produce convincing evidence thereof. The evidence must concern, in particular, factors playing a significant role in the assessment of whether a situation of collective dominance exists, such as, for example, the lack of effective competition between the operators alleged to be members of the dominant oligopoly and the weakness of any competitive pressure that might be exerted by other operators.

64. Furthermore, the basic provisions of Regulation No 4064/89, in particular Article 2 thereof, confer on the Commission a certain discretion, especially with respect to assessments of an economic nature, and, consequently, when the exercise of that discretion, which is essential for defining the rules on concentrations, is under review, the Community judicature must take account of the discretionary margin implicit in the provisions of an economic nature which form part of the rules on concentrations [. . .].

The GC proceeded to consider the ways in which the Commission had failed to carry out the analysis and then quashed the decision. In order to illustrate the reasoning of the GC, we include the following excerpt:

74. The applicant's first point is that the natural tendency of operators in the relevant market to set capacity cautiously has by no means prevented them from engaging in competition with each other in the past and that there is no reason to believe that proceeding with the proposed merger would put an end to that competition by creating a situation in which the three remaining large tour operators have a collective dominant position.

75. The Decision is particularly elliptical in its description of the competitive situation at the time of the notification. However, it is not disputed that the Commission concluded that the proposed merger would create, rather than strengthen, a dominant position on the market [. . .]. The Commission has confirmed in its pleadings that it does not contend that that there was a situation of oligopolistic dominance at the time of the notification and that what is at issue is the creation, and not the strengthening, of a collective dominant position. Thus, it does not deny that prior to the proposed merger the major tour operators did not find it possible or profitable to restrict capacity in order to increase prices and revenues.

76. It follows that in this instance the starting point for the Court's examination must be a situation in which—in the Commission's own view—the four major tour operators are not able to adopt a common policy on the market and hence do not face their competitors, their commercial associates and consumers as a single entity, and in which they thus do not enjoy the powers inherent in a collective dominant position.

77. In those circumstances, it was for the Commission to prove that, in view of the characteristics of the United Kingdom market for operating short-haul package holidays and in light of the notified operation, approval of the latter would have resulted in the creation of a collective dominant position restrictive of competition, inasmuch as Airtours/First Choice, Thomson and Thomas Cook would have had the ability, which they did not previously have, to adopt a common policy on the market by setting capacity lower than would normally be the case in a competitive market already distinguished by a degree of caution in matters of capacity. [. . .]

294. In the light of all of the foregoing, the Court concludes that the Decision, far from basing its prospective analysis on cogent evidence, is vitiated by a series of errors of assessment as to factors fundamental to any assessment of whether a collective dominant position might be created. It follows that the Commission prohibited the transaction without having proved to the requisite legal standard that the concentration would give rise to a collective dominant position of the three major tour operators, of such a kind as significantly to impede effective competition in the relevant market.

NOTES AND QUESTIONS ON AIRTOURS/FIRSTCHOICE

1. (Paragraph 55) The GC often speaks of proof to the requisite legal standard, but until this judgment there was considerable doubt as to what that might be.[65] Clearly, the standard of proof is higher than the Commission had previously believed.[66].

65 See B Vesterdorf, 'Judicial Review of Antitrust Cases' (2005) 12 *Competition Policy Int'l* 3. On the standard of proof in EU competition law, see E Gippini-Fournier, 'The Elusive Standard of Proof in EU Competition Cases' (2010) 33(2) *World Competition* 187; F Castillo de la Torre and E Gippini Fournier, *Evidence, Proof and Judicial Review in EU Competition Law* (Edward Elgar, 2017); I Lianos, *Competition Law Enforcement and Procedure* (OUP, forthcoming 2019).

66

2. (Paragraphs 56–8) The judgment related to the ECMR (Regulation 4064/89). Does it apply to the EUMR (Regulation 139/2004)? Does it apply to decision made under Article 101 or 102 TFEU? Does it apply to other matters the Commission must establish before it condemns a prospective merger?
3. To establish collective dominance must there be an economic link or may the structure of the market be sufficient? Does the judgment go further than *Gencor*?
4. (Paragraph 61) Does this match the list of factors making collective dominance likely given in several Commission decisions and the GC in *Gencor* cited above?
5. (Paragraph 62) The GC insisted that to find a dominant oligopoly the Commission must establish three conditions: first, an ability by each to monitor the conduct of the others. Second, for tacit coordination to be sustainable over time, there must be an incentive not to depart from the common policy. In other words, the members of the dominant oligopoly must be able to retaliate. The Commission must establish that adequate deterrents exist ensuring a long-term incentive for any member of the dominant oligopoly to not depart from the common course of conduct (paragraphs 62 and 195). Third, the Commission must establish that the foreseeable reaction of current and future competitors, as well of consumers, would not jeopardize the results expected from the common policy. In other words, it is permissible to rely on economic theory only if all the conditions for its application are established.
6. (Paragraph 63) Note that competition between the members of the allegedly dominant group as well as from third parties is relevant.
7. The GC subjected the decision to rigorous scrutiny on each of the points mentioned at paragraph 62. The Commission accepted that Airtours was not dominant before the merger, so it had to prove a change in circumstances enabling the tour operators to raise prices, which implies that each will be able to monitor what the others are doing and retaliate, as well as an incentive for them to do so. According to the Court, its evidence had to be convincing (paragraph 63). How convincing? On the balance of probabilities? Reflect after reading paragraphs 74–7 of the judgment. Is this compatible with the Commission's margin of discretion (paragraph 64)?
8. The *Airtours/First Choice* factors, which refer to the existence of a common policy, transparency, retaliation mechanisms, the absence of countervailing power, have been adopted by the subsequent case law of the EU courts.[67]
9. The *Airtours/First Choice* factors for collective dominant position were also embraced by the European Commission in paragraph 41 of the Horizontal Merger Guidelines:

   Coordination is more likely to emerge in markets where it is relatively simple to reach a common understanding on the terms of coordination. In addition, three conditions are necessary for coordination to be sustainable. First, the coordinating firms must be able to monitor to a sufficient degree whether the terms of coordination are being adhered to. Second, discipline requires that there is some form of

[67] See Case T-464/04, *Independant Music Publishers and Labels Association (Impala, association internationale) v Commission* [2006] ECR II-2289, paras 244–7; Case C-413/06 P, *Bertelsmann AG and Sony Corporation of America v Independent Music Publishers and Labels Association (Impala)* [2008] ECR I-4951, paras 122–3.

> credible deterrent mechanism that can be activated if deviation is detected. Third, the reactions of outsiders, such as current and future competitors not participating in the coordination, as well as customers, should not be able to jeopardise the results expected from the coordination.[68]

In two later cases, *Tetra Laval BV v Commission* and *Schneider/Legrand*, the General Court confirmed the need for the Commission to take much greater care before alleging that a merger would lead to a dominant position as a result of which competition would be significantly impeded.[69] That jurisprudence may have led the Commission to employ a 'strict formulation' of the *Airtours* test in *Sony/BMG*.[70] The Commission found that the inability to fully establish by direct evidence one limb of the *Airtours* test, ie, transparency, may lead to the exclusion of collective dominance. The General Court reacted in its *Impala* judgment[71] by introducing a more flexible, indirect test which created an alternative avenue to prove pre-existing collective dominance to be met in the assessment of the strengthening of pre-existing collective dominance.[72] Although the CJEU on appeal reversed the judgment of the General Court in *Impala*, it seems that it has accepted the *Impala* indirect test.[73]

Impala

In *Impala*, the General Court reacted to the strict formulation of the *Airtours* test by the Commission in *Sony/BMG*, and introduced a more flexible test in the context of the assessment of the strengthening of a pre-existing collective dominance, providing an 'alternative avenue in order to establish indirectly that the *Airtours* conditions are satisfied.[74]

Case T-464/04, *Independant Music Publishers and Labels Association (Impala, association internationale) v Commission*
[2006] ECR II–2289

> *The case involved a joint venture Sony/BMG combining the recorded music businesses of Sony and Bertelsmann. Sony/BMG was unconditionally cleared in 2004, the Commission finding that the merger would not create or strengthen a collective dominant position between the remaining four major record companies (Universal, Sony BMG, Warner, and EMI) in the market for recorded music and in the wholesale market for licences for online music.*[75] *Applying the* Airtours *criteria the Commission has found that there were some indications of coordinated behaviour which were as such, however, not sufficient to establish an existing collective dominance, and looking to product homogeneity, transparency, and retaliation, it concluded that the*

68 Horizontal Merger Guidelines, para 41.

69 See our analysis on the burden and standard of proof, Section 12.1.4.3.

70 *Sony/BMG* (Case COMP/M.3333) Commission Decision C(2004) 2815 (3 October 2007).

71 Case T-464/04, *Impala v Commission* [2006] ECR II–2289.

72 See I Kalozymis, 'Collective Dominance in EU Merger Control: Substantive Issues' (PhD Thesis, Queen Mary University London, 2014), 61.

73 Case C-413/06 P, *Bertelsmann AG and Sony Corporation of America v Independent Music Publishers and Labels Association (Impala)* [2008] ECR I–4951.

74 I Kalozymis, 'Collective Dominance in EU Merger Control: Substantive Issues' (PhD Thesis, Queen Mary University London, 2014), 51–2.

75 *Sony/BMG* (Case COMP/M.3333) Commission Decision C(2004) 2815 (3 October 2007).

markets were not characterised by features facilitating collective dominance and that there was insufficient evidence to establish that the proposed transaction will lead to the strengthening of an existing collective dominant position in the markets for recorded music. It also found that here was insufficient evidence that the proposed transaction would likely lead to the creation of collective dominance in any of the national markets for recorded music. The Commission's decision was appealed to the General Court by the Independent Music Publishers and Labels Association (Impala). The Court overruled the Commission's decision after criticizing the Commission's analysis of the strengthening of a pre-existing dominant position.

245. It follows from the case-law of the Court of Justice that in the case of an alleged collective dominant position, the Commission is obliged to assess, using a prospective analysis of the reference market, whether the concentration which has been referred to it leads to a situation in which effective competition in the relevant market is significantly impeded by the undertakings involved in the concentration and one or more other undertakings which together, in particular because of factors giving rise to a connection between them, are able to adopt a common policy on the market and act to a considerable extent independently of their competitors, their customers and, ultimately, of consumers (Joined Cases C-68/94 and C-30/95 *France and Others* v *Commission* (known as '*Kali und Salz*') [1998] ECR I–1375, paragraph 221). [. . .]

248. It follows from the case-law of the Court of Justice (*Kali und Salz*, paragraph 245 above, paragraph 222) and of the Court of First Instance (*Airtours* v *Commission*, paragraph 45 above, paragraph 63) that the prospective analysis which the Commission is required to carry out in the context of the control of concentrations, in the case of collective dominance, requires close examination of, in particular, the circumstances which, in each individual case, are relevant for assessing the effects of the concentration on competition in the reference market and that the Commission must provide solid evidence.

249. It must be observed that, as is apparent from the very wording of those judgments, that case-law was developed in the context of the assessment of the risk that a concentration would create a collective dominant position and not, as in the context of the first part of the present plea, of the determination of the existence of a collective dominant position.

250. However, although when assessing the risk that such a dominant position will be created the Commission is required, *ex hypothesi*, to carry out a delicate prognosis as regards the probable development of the market and of the conditions of competition on the basis of a prospective analysis, which entails complex economic assessments in respect of which the Commission has a wide discretion, the finding of the existence of a collective dominant position is itself supported by a concrete analysis of the situation existing at the time of adoption of the decision. The determination of the existence of a collective dominant position must be supported by a series of elements of established facts, past or present, which show that there is a significant impediment of competition on the market owing to the power acquired by certain undertakings to adopt together the same course of conduct on that market, to a significant extent, independently of their competitors, their customers and consumers.

251. It follows that, in the context of the assessment of the existence of a collective dominant position, although the three conditions defined by the Court of First Instance in *Airtours* v *Commission* [. . .] which were inferred from a theoretical analysis of the concept of a collective dominant position, are indeed also necessary, they may, however, in the appropriate circumstances, be established indirectly on the basis of what may be a very mixed series of indicia and items of evidence relating to the

signs, manifestations and phenomena inherent in the presence of a collective dominant position.

252. Thus, in particular, close alignment of prices over a long period, especially if they are above a competitive level, together with other factors typical of a collective dominant position, might, in the absence of an alternative reasonable explanation, suffice to demonstrate the existence of a collective dominant position, even where there is no firm direct evidence of strong market transparency, as such transparency may be presumed in such circumstances.

253. It follows that, in the present case, the alignment of prices, both gross and net, over the last six years, even though the products are not the same (each disc having a different content), and also the fact that they were maintained at such a stable level, and at a level seen as high in spite of a significant fall in demand, together with other factors (power of the undertakings in an oligopoly situation, stability of market shares, etc.), as established by the Commission in the Decision, might, in the absence of an alternative explanation, suggest, or constitute an indication, that the alignment of prices is not the result of the normal play of effective competition and that the market is sufficiently transparent in that it allowed tacit price coordination.

Following the judgment of the General Court, the Commission had to conduct an investigation of the already operating joint venture (JV). Sony and BMG updated their existing notification of the joint venture and, following a Phase II investigation, the JV was unconditionally cleared again in 2007.[76] This decision was appealed again by Impala to the General Court.[77] In parallel, Sony and BMG interjected an appeal to the CJEU against the judgment of the General Court annulling the first Impala decision.

Case C-413/06 P, *Bertelsmann AG and Sony Corporation of America v Independent Music Publishers and Labels Association (Impala)*
[2008] ECR I–4951

120. In the case of an alleged creation or strengthening of a collective dominant position, the Commission is obliged to assess, using a prospective analysis of the reference market, whether the concentration which has been referred to it will lead to a situation in which effective competition in the relevant market is significantly impeded by the undertakings which are parties to the concentration and one or more other undertakings which together, in particular because of correlative factors which exist between them, are able to adopt a common policy on the market (see *Kali & Salz*, paragraph 221) in order to profit from a situation of collective economic strength, without actual or potential competitors, let alone customers or consumers, being able to react effectively.

121. Such correlative factors include, in particular, the relationship of interdependence existing between the parties to a tight oligopoly within which, on a market with the appropriate characteristics, in particular in terms of market concentration, transparency and product homogeneity, those parties are in a position to anticipate one another's behaviour and are therefore strongly encouraged to align their conduct on the market in such a way as to maximise their joint profits by increasing prices,

76 *Sony/BMG* (Case COMP/M.3333) Commission Decision C(2007) 4507 (3 October 2007).
77 Case T-229/08, *Impala v Commission* (these proceedings were abandoned).

reducing output, the choice or quality of goods and services, diminishing innovation or otherwise influencing parameters of competition. In such a context, each operator is aware that highly competitive action on its part would provoke a reaction on the part of the others, so that it would derive no benefit from its initiative.

122. A collective dominant position significantly impeding effective competition in the common market or a substantial part of it may thus arise as the result of a concentration where, in view of the actual characteristics of the relevant market and of the alteration to those characteristics that the concentration would entail, the latter would make each member of the oligopoly in question, as it becomes aware of common interests, consider it possible, economically rational, and hence preferable, to adopt on a lasting basis a common policy on the market with the aim of selling at above competitive prices, without having to enter into an agreement or resort to a concerted practice within the meaning of Article 81 EC and without any actual or potential competitors, let alone customers or consumers, being able to react effectively.

123. Such tacit coordination is more likely to emerge if competitors can easily arrive at a common perception as to how the coordination should work, and, in particular, of the parameters that lend themselves to being a focal point of the proposed coordination. Unless they can form a shared tacit understanding of the terms of the coordination, competitors might resort to practices that are prohibited by Article 81 EC in order to be able to adopt a common policy on the market. Moreover, having regard to the temptation which may exist for each participant in a tacit coordination to depart from it in order to increase its short-term profit, it is necessary to determine whether such coordination is sustainable. In that regard, the coordinating undertakings must be able to monitor to a sufficient degree whether the terms of the coordination are being adhered to. There must therefore be sufficient market transparency for each undertaking concerned to be aware, sufficiently precisely and quickly, of the way in which the market conduct of each of the other participants in the coordination is evolving. Furthermore, discipline requires that there be some form of credible deterrent mechanism that can come into play if deviation is detected. In addition, the reactions of outsiders, such as current or future competitors, and also the reactions of customers, should not be such as to jeopardise the results expected from the coordination.

124. The conditions laid down by the Court of First Instance in paragraph 62 of its judgment in *Airtours* v *Commission*, which that court concluded, in paragraph 254 of the judgment under appeal, should be applied in the dispute before it, are not incompatible with the criteria set out in the preceding paragraph of this judgment.

125. In applying those criteria, it is necessary to avoid a mechanical approach involving the separate verification of each of those criteria taken in isolation, while taking no account of the overall economic mechanism of a hypothetical tacit coordination.

126. In that regard, the assessment of, for example, the transparency of a particular market should not be undertaken in an isolated and abstract manner, but should be carried out using the mechanism of a hypothetical tacit coordination as a basis. It is only if such a hypothesis is taken into account that it is possible to ascertain whether any elements of transparency that may exist on a market are, in fact, capable of facilitating the reaching of a common understanding on the terms of coordination and/or of allowing the competitors concerned to monitor sufficiently whether the terms of such a common policy are being adhered to. In that last respect, it is necessary, in order to analyse the sustainability of a purported tacit coordination, to take into account the monitoring mechanisms that may be available to the participants in the alleged tacit coordination in order to ascertain whether, as a result of those mechanisms, they are in

a position to be aware, sufficiently precisely and quickly, of the way in which the market conduct of each of the other participants in that coordination is evolving.

127. As regards the present case, the appellants submit that, even though the Court of First Instance stated in paragraph 254 of the judgment under appeal that it was following the approach adopted in its judgment in *Airtours* v *Commission*, in practice, it committed an error of law in inferring the existence of a sufficient degree of transparency from a number of factors which were not, however, relevant to a finding of an existing collective dominant position. In that context, the appellants object in particular to the fact that the Court of First Instance indicated in paragraph 251 of the judgment under appeal that the conditions laid down in paragraph 62 of the judgment in *Airtours* v *Commission* could 'in the appropriate circumstances, be established indirectly on the basis of what may be a very mixed series of indicia and items of evidence relating to the signs, manifestations and phenomena inherent in the presence of a collective dominant position'.

128. In this regard, as the Commission observed at the hearing, objection cannot be taken to paragraph 251 of itself, since it constitutes a general statement which reflects the Court of First Instance's liberty of assessment of different items of evidence. It is settled case-law that it is, in principle, for the Court of First Instance alone to assess the value to be attached to the items of evidence adduced before it (see, inter alia, Case C-136/92 P *Commission* v *Brazzelli Lualdi and Others* [1994] ECR I–1981, paragraph 66, and Case C-237/98 P *Dorsch Consult* v *Council and Commission* [2000] ECR I–4549, paragraph 50).

129. Similarly, the investigation of a pre-existing collective dominant position based on a series of elements normally considered to be indicative of the presence or the likelihood of tacit coordination between competitors cannot therefore be considered to be objectionable of itself. However, as is apparent from paragraph 125 of this judgment, it is essential that such an investigation be carried out with care and, above all, that it should adopt an approach based on the analysis of such plausible coordination strategies as may exist in the circumstances.

130. In the present case, the Court of First Instance, before which Impala raised arguments relating, in particular, to the parts of the contested decision relating to market transparency, did not carry out its analysis of those parts by having regard to a postulated monitoring mechanism forming part of a plausible theory of tacit coordination.

The CJEU therefore found that the GC had committed an error of law and reversed its judgment.

NOTES AND QUESTIONS ON IMPALA

1. (GC Judgment, paragraphs 251–2) According to the GC, in the assessment of pre-existing collective dominance the *Airtours* factors may be established indirectly 'on the basis of a very mixed series of indicia and items of evidence relating to signs, manifestations and phenomena inherent in the presence of a collective dominant position'. According to the GC, 'close alignment of prices over a long period, especially if they are above a competitive level, together with other factors typical of a collective dominant position, might, in the absence of an alternative reasonable explanation, suffice to demonstrate the existence of a collective dominant position, even where there is no firm direct evidence of strong market transparency, as such transparency may be presumed in such circumstances'. Would you interpret this part of the judgment as

indicating that evidence of the firms' parallel conduct in conjunction with some other factors and in the absence of an alternative reasonable explanation may be sufficient to demonstrate pre-existing collective dominance and presume the satisfaction of (all or each) of the *Airtours* criteria? How would you compare this test with that adopted by the CJEU in *Wood Pulp* with regard to the application of Article 101 TFEU to situations of price parallelism?[78]

2. The Impala test seems to require (i) evidence of a close alignment of prices over time/price parallelism at above a competitive level, although this factor in its own will not suffice; (ii) the existence of factors typical of a collective dominant position (eg stability of market shares) and more generally elements of the structure of the market that may shed light on the firms' incentives to adopt a common policy on the market and to sustain that over a long period; (iii) absence of an alternative reasonable explanation than collective dominance, indicating the causal link between the price parallelism and tacit collusion.
3. The Impala test of the GC requires the observation of past market conduct pointing to coordination between the undertakings, the aim being to uncover a situation of *pre-existing* collective dominance. The indirect test appears less suitable for situations relating to the *creation* of collective dominance.
4. The Impala GC's test may be employed in situations where one of the *Airtours* factors cannot be established to the adequate legal standard through direct evidence, or there is some contradicting evidence, the test opening the possibility of establishing the various *Airtours* factors indirectly. This has the potential to expand the application of the collective dominance concept in merger control and for merger control to complement the *ex post* assessment under Article 102 TFEU when no case was brought under this provision for abusive conduct when there is a pre-existing collective dominant position.
5. (CJEU judgment, paragraphs 123–5) Does the CJEU accept the indirect test of implementing the *Airtours* criteria devised by the GC in *Impala*? How should one understand the statement of the CJEU that one should take into account, when assessing the *Airtours* factors the 'overall economic mechanism of a hypothetical tacit coordination', rather than verifying each of these criteria taken in isolation?
6. Note that the CJEU annulled the Court's judgment because it found that there was no sufficient transparency in the marketplace and that the evidence on which the GC relied upon was 'an unsupported assertion from an industry professional' (paragraph 132).
7. Following the *Sony v Impala* case law the Commission has followed the CJEU's reasoning in, amongst others,[79] the *ABF/GBI* merger[80] in the compressed yeast market in France. Although the Commission's in-depth analysis found no evidence of competition concerns in the compressed yeast market in France, it did confirm that the merger would result in coordinated market behaviour between the remaining competitors in the Spanish and Portuguese compressed yeast markets. The Commission first identified a number of structural market conditions likely to facilitate the emergence and

[78] Joined Cases C-89, 104, 114, 116, 117 & 125–9/85, *A Ahlström Osakeyhtiö and Others v Commission* [1993] ECR I–1307, paras 59–65. See our analysis in Sections 5.5.4. and 11.6.3.

[79] The Commission has applied the same case law, eg in *Outokumpu/INOXUM* (Case M.6471) Commission Decision C(2012) 7969 final (7 July 2011); *Cemex/Holcim Assets* (Case M.7054) Commission Decision (9 September 2014); *Ball/Rexam* (Case M.7567) Commission Decision (17 June 2016).

[80] *ABF/GBI* (Case M.4980) Commission Decision (23 September 2008).

sustainability of tacit coordination. Then it went on to assess the extent to which market conditions facilitate a tacit understanding between Lesaffre, ABF, and GBI and possible terms of coordination, the monitoring of deviations, deterrence of deviations and the reasons why outsiders have no ability to undermine the resulting degree of tacit coordination. Finally, it shows that in the markets for compressed yeast in Spain and Portugal, 'the alteration in the [relevant market] structure that the transaction would entail' is likely to significantly impede effective competition by making coordination easier, more stable or more effective for the two remaining firms concerned either by making the coordination more robust or by permitting firms to coordinate on even higher prices.[81] In order to address the Commission's competition concerns, ABF has committed to divest GBI's business in Portugal and Spain to a suitable buyer with sufficient production capacities to supply those businesses. To ensure that the acquirer will have the required production capacities, ABF has also undertaken that either (a) the acquirer will have previously acquired GBI's former production plant in the UK; or (b) the parties will divest ABF's production plant in Portugal.

12.1.4.1.3. Unilateral or non-coordinated effects

The judgments in *Gencor* and *Airtours* were concerned with a finding of joint dominance arising from a merger that was likely to lead to tacit collusion between the participating undertakings and a third party, and not with mergers leading to unilateral conduct in a concentrated market. Formerly the test was whether the merger creates or strengthens a dominant position as a result of which competition would be significantly impeded in the Common Market or a substantial part of it.

It was not clear whether unilateral conduct that would not lead to single firm dominance qualified under Article 2 of the older regulation. So, following the adoption of Regulation 139/2004, the test in Article 2(2) and (3) EUMR has been altered to 'significantly impeding effective competition'. It is now clear that a merger significantly reducing competition, when tacit collusion is not alleged to be likely, may be declared incompatible with the Common Market even if the merger will not lead to a dominant position. Prospective unilateral effects may impede effective competition.

T-Mobile/tele.ring was a five-to-four merger of T-Mobile (number 2 in the market), which was a subsidiary of Deutsche Telekom, that had taken sole control of the Austrian mobile phone operator tele.ring (number 4 in the market), leading to a combination of two Austrian mobile network providers.[82] The other three players in the market were the market leader Mobilkom, a subsidiary of Telekom Austria, ONE, and H3G (a subsidiary of Hutchison), which entered the market in 2003. Tele-ring generally charged less and its market share was increasing rapidly—50 per cent of customers who switch go to tele.ring. The merger would have eliminated a maverick, as it was unclear whether the competitive pressure exerted on the two largest operators could be achieved by another firm.

Indeed, the next closest competitor was H3G, but it was not able to compete on price due to a roaming agreement it had with Mobilkom, for the areas not covered by H3G's own network,

[81] Ibid, paras 144–6.

[82] For an analysis of this case, see J Luebking, 'T-Mobile Austria/tele.ring: Remedying the LOSS of a MAVERICK' (2006) 2 *Competition Policy Newsletter* 46.

which had a limited geographical coverage, thus raising its variable costs. T-Mobile and tele. ring were positioned in different segments of the market, thus significantly reducing the incentive to raise prices, decreasing the likelihood of a fall in consumer welfare. The Commission pointed out in that '[t]he proposed transaction would give rise to non-coordinated effects, even though T-Mobile would not become the largest player after the merger'.[83] The post-merger market share would be about one-third—still less than Mobilkom. The Commission concluded that Tele-ring played a special role in the market.[84] This case has been informally known as the first 'gap' case under the new Regulation 139/2004. It was not alleged to lead to single firm dominance, nor to tacit collusion. Coordinated effects between Mobilkom and T-Mobile were considered, but were not the main issue. There was a sizeable third player (One), and H3G was growing. Service providers were already in the market. The Commission took into account the market shares, the switching rates between providers and the pricing behaviour of the various actors in the market, in particular the past behaviour of tele.ring that had adopted an aggressive pricing strategy to achieve this growth by attracting customers from other operators. It found that the merger would lead to the removal of a maverick, and increase the symmetry of the two leading players, Mobilcom and T-Mobile. The removal of the main competitive constraints for two leading firms would result in significant lessening of competition. This condemnation was treated as based on unilateral effects. Post-merger, price increases would be more profitable, as some customers who had switched may be retained by the merged entity.

The issue, however, should be: how many? The market was differentiated and the quality varied, so market share may overstate the real competitive overlap. The effects on price depend on the proximity of a pre-merger price restraint and restraints from rivals. However, data on switching showed the merging firms to be in different segments of the market, with Tele-ring at the cheap end and T-Mobile and Mobilkom at the higher quality end. Price-sensitive customers could switch to other low-cost operators: H3G and Yesss (a subsidiary of One). All suppliers had enough frequency spectrum to expand their networks and accommodate extra customers. Lack of capacity became even less of an issue with the roll-out of 3G. The ability of rivals to enter or expand had increased in Austria in that resellers now had access to the wholesale market. Newcomers could operate also in segments not fully covered by a network. In terms of remedies, tele.ring's 3G frequencies were redistributed to H3G and One, but it has been noted that H3G already priced aggressively and had spare capacity.

12.1.4.1.4. Effects on innovation

Competition authorities have been focusing on the possible effects of merger activity on innovation. The US Department of Justice (DOJ) and Federal Trade Commission (FTC) Horizontal Merger Guidelines of 2010 were the first to include a specific Section on competition harm to innovation and product variety and explicitly considering that '(a) merger enhances market power if it is likely to encourage one or more firms to raise price, reduce output, *diminish innovation*, or otherwise harm customers as a result of diminished competitive constraints or incentives'.[85] In analysing effects on innovation, the US competition authorities have often taken an 'innovation market' perspective,[86] or as this has been reframed in the 2017 update of

[83] Ibid, para 10. [84] Ibid, paras 10 and 16.

[85] US DOJ and FTC, Horizontal Merger Guidelines (2010), 2 (emphasis added).

[86] RJ Gilbert and SC Sunshine, 'Incorporating Dynamic Efficiency Concerns in Merger Analysis: The Use of Innovation Markets' (1995) 63 *Antitrust LJ* 569.

the US DOJ and FTC Antitrust Guidelines for the Licensing of Intellectual Property, 'research and development markets'.[87] According to the US Licensing of IP Guidelines,

> (a) research and development market consists of the assets comprising research and development related to the identification of a commercializable product, or directed to particular new or improved goods or processes, and the close substitutes for that research and development. When research and development is directed to particular new or improved goods or processes, the close substitutes may include research and development efforts, technologies, and goods that significantly constrain the exercise of market power with respect to the relevant research and development, for example by limiting the ability and incentive of a hypothetical monopolist to reduce the pace of research and development. The Agencies will delineate a research and development market only when the capabilities to engage in the relevant research and development can be associated with specialized assets or characteristics of specific firms. In assessing the competitive significance of current and potential participants in a research and development market, the Agencies will take into account all relevant evidence. [. . .] The Agencies may base the market shares of participants in a research and development market on their shares of identifiable assets or characteristics upon which innovation depends, for example, on shares of research and development expenditures, or on shares of a related product. When entities have comparable capabilities and incentives to pursue research and development that is a close substitute for the research and development activities of the parties to a licensing arrangement, the Agencies may assign equal market shares to such entities.[88]

The US authorities have employed 'innovation markets' or 'research and development markets' concepts in order to assess competition effects in a number of cases.[89] According to this approach, the US Agencies will delineate research and development markets, only when the capabilities to engage in relevant research and development 'can be associated with specialized assets or characteristics of specific firms', the authorities seeking to identify three key effects: (i) the ability of the merged firm to reduce total market investments in R&D; (ii) the incentive of the merged entity to reduce the innovative effort; and (iii) the impact of the merger on the efficiency of the R&D expenditure.[90] This looks like a relatively demanding framework from an evidential perspective. In most recent cases, the US authorities seem to adopt a broader framework and have also challenged mergers for diminishing innovation even if the merger would eliminate potential competition from a relative small competitor, in particular when the smaller player has promising pipeline products. The theory of harm in these cases was the 'actual potential entrant' theory, a potential entrant merging with an existing competitor and thus leading to lessen future competition.

[87] US DOJ and FTC, Antitrust Guidelines for the Licensing of Intellectual Property (2017), section 3.2.3.

[88] Ibid.

[89] The FTC has identified and referred to research and development markets in the following matters: *Complaint, Amgen Inc*, 134 FTC 333, 337–9 (2002) (identifying a research and development market for inhibitors of cytokines that promote the inflammation of human tissue); *Wright Med Tech, Inc, Proposed Consent Agreement with Analysis to Aid Public Comment*, 60 Fed Reg 460, 463 (4 January 1995) (identifying a research and development market for orthopaedic implants for use in human hands); *Am Home Prods Corp, Proposed Consent Agreement with Analysis to Aid Public Comment*, 59 Fed Reg 60,807, 60,815 (28 November 1994) (identifying a research and development market for, among other things, rotavirus vaccines).

[90] E Cefis et al, 'The Role of Innovation in Merger Policy: Europe's Efficiency Defence versus America's Innovation Markets Approach', Tjalling C Koopmans Institute, Discussion Paper No 07-21 (2007), available at https://dspace.library.uu.nl/handle/1874/31463.

In the European Commission's Horizontal Merger Guidelines, one of the effects to be analysed under merger control, is the 'effect on innovation'.[91] According to the Commission's Guidelines,

> [i]n markets where innovation is an important competitive force, a merger may increase the firms' ability and incentive to bring new innovations to the market and, thereby, the competitive pressure on rivals to innovate in that market. Alternatively, effective competition may be significantly impeded by a merger between two important innovators, for instance between two companies with 'pipeline' products related to a specific product market. Similarly, a firm with a relatively small market share may nevertheless be an important competitive force if it has promising pipeline products.[92]

The innovation potential of the merging firms, in particular if 'one or more merging parties are important innovators in ways not reflected in market shares', is taken into account, irrespective of the levels of concentration that are usually considered by the Commission's Horizontal Guidelines as raising competition concerns.[93] The Commission's Guidelines also recognize that efficiencies may bring forward positive innovation effects, and acknowledge that 'consumers may also benefit from new or improved products or services, for instance resulting from efficiency gains in the sphere of R&D and innovation'.[94] However, as for other types of efficiency gains put forward, the parties need to demonstrate that (i) efficiencies are a direct consequence of the notified merger and cannot be achieved to a similar extent by less anti-competitive alternatives, and (ii) that efficiencies have to be verifiable such that the Commission can be reasonably certain that the efficiencies are likely to materialize, and be substantial enough to counteract a merger's potential harm to consumers.[95] Similarly, the EU Non-Horizontal Merger Guidelines list the diminishing of innovation as a competition concern for vertical and conglomerate mergers[96] and also state that mergers involving innovative companies that are likely to expand significantly in the near future will be extensively investigated even when the post-merger market share is below 30 per cent.[97]

In a recent Competition Policy Brief, the European Commission explains that harm to innovation may justify the Commission to consider that a merger between a firm present in the relevant market with a firm that is not actually present in the relevant market could lead to a significant impediment of effective competition. According to the Commission,

> [f]or a merger with a potential competitor to raise serious competition concerns, it is in principle necessary to show, firstly, that the potential competitor currently acts as a significant competitive constraint, or there is a significant likelihood that, absent the merger, it would grow into an effective competitive force in the foreseeable future. This is more likely in particular when the market is already concentrated, as in a market with many actual competitors a potential entrant is, in principle, less likely to be a significant competitive constraint. Secondly, it needs to be established that there are not enough actual or potential competitors to maintain the necessary competitive pressure after the merger. In particular, barriers to entry must be high enough to exclude the existence of several other potential competitors, but the merging firm potentially entering the market must be well positioned to overcome these barriers, for instance as it is present in an adjacent or vertically related market or already has specific entry plans.[98]

91 Horizontal Merger Guidelines, para 8.

92 Ibid, para 38. 93 Ibid, para 20. 94 Ibid, para 81. 95 Ibid, paras 85–6.

96 Non-Horizontal Merger Guidelines, para 10. 97 Ibid, para. 26.

98 European Commission, Competition Policy Brief 2016-01 (April 2016), 3, available at http://ec.europa.eu/competition/publications/cpb/2016/2016_001_en.pdf.

The Commission has actively considered innovation effects in a series of recent merger cases, either exploring the possibility that a horizontal merger will lead to a loss of innovation by eliminating pipeline products that would likely have entered existing markets or that would have created entirely new value chains, thus preventing consumers from increased choice and variety,[99] as well as non-horizontal vertical or conglomerate mergers that would have harmed the ability of the merged entity's rivals to innovate.[100] It has been alleged that in several of these cases the Commission has proceeded to establish a novel theory of harm, that of a significant impediment to industry innovation (SIII), as it has not explored the existence of specific innovation markets that could have been affected by the merger, the Commission relying, in order to find the SIII, on several negative views about the merger gathered from third parties, without assessing if the merger would lead to a reduction in the R&D spend/innovation incentives of the merged entity, its rivals and/or the whole industry.[101] According to this view, the Commission's SIII theory is based on a presumption that regulatory intervention is warranted when a merger removes a 'parallel path R&D', this being not in line with the standard of proof in EU merger control.[102]

These criticisms are far-fetched as, first, it is quite difficult to explain why the competition authority should not assess, when examining the merger, what would be the merger's effects on innovation incentives in the industry. This can be done, without necessarily defining a specific 'innovation market'. Indeed, in the context of the Transfer of Technology Guidelines, the Commission has put in place a filter that confines detailed analysis to cases 'that are likely to present real competition concerns', not based on market shares but on the existence of 'at least four independent technologies that may constitute a commercially viable alternative, in addition to the licensed technology controlled by the parties to the agreement'.[103] According to the Commission, '[i]n assessing whether the technologies are sufficiently substitutable the relative commercial strength of the technologies in question must be taken into account. The competitive constraint imposed by a technology is limited if it does not constitute a commercially viable alternative to the licensed technology.'[104] Even if an agreement falls outside the safe harbour this does not create a presumption of incompatibility with Article 101 TFEU but simply leads to an individual assessment

[99] *Syngenta/Monsanto's Sunflower Seed Business* (Case COMP/M. 5675) Commission Decision (17 November 2010), paras 248, 200, and 207 (finding that farmers would have suffered from reduced choice);– *Deutsche Börse/NYSE Euronext* (COMP/ M.6166) Commission Decision (1 February 2012), section 11.2.1.3.4, confirmed by Case T-175/12, *Deutsche Börse AG v Commission*, ECLI:EU:T:2015:148;, *Medtronic/Covidien* (Case COMP/ M.7326) Commission Decision (28 November 2014); *Novartis/GlaxoSmithKline's oncology business* (Case COMP/M.7275) Commission Decision (28 January 2015); *Pfizer/Hospira* (Case COMP/ M.7559) Commission Decision (4 August 2015); *General Electric/Alstom (Thermal Power-Renewable Power & Grid Business)* (Case No COMP/M.7278) Commission Decision (8 September 2015).

[100] *Intel/McAfee* (Case COMP/M.5984) Commission Decision (26 January 2011); *ARM/GIESECKE & DEVRIENT/GEMALTO JV* (Case COMP/ M.6564) Commission Decision (6 November 2012); *Intel/Altera* (Case COMP/M.7688) Commission Decision (14 October 2015).

[101] N Petit, 'Significant Impediment to Industry Innovation: A Novel Theory of Harm in EU Merger Control?', ICLE Antitrust & Consumer Protection Research Program White Paper 2017-1, 22, available at https://orbi.uliege.be/bitstream/2268/207345/1/SSRN-id2911597.pdf.

[102] Ibid, 21.

[103] Guidelines on the application of Article 101 of the Treaty on the Functioning of the European Union to technology transfer agreements [2014] OJ C 89/3, para 157.

[104] Ibid.

under the guidelines and Article 101(3) TFEU, the Commission's approach indicates that the main concern is the existence of sufficient choice in terms of independent technologies available in the market, thus showing that showing the emphasis put on the existence of various 'independent' R&D paths or, more generally, technologies. Limiting the focus on innovation to just the adoption of the 'innovation markets' approach seems reductionist and certainly does not represent the most recent competition law thinking, also of US competition agencies.[105] It is also important to take into account the patent portfolio strength of the merging parties, as well as the existence of licensing and cross-licensing agreements and internal strategy documents in order to assess the possible effects of a specific merger on innovation.

The Commission has so far examined innovation in the efficiency defence only in one case, although it found that the merging parties had not convincingly quantified these efficiencies, which indicates that the standard of proof with regard to the requirement of quantification is high.[106]

One should not limit this finding on situations of high market shares but it may be also be relevant to emphasize the need to keep an eye on technological developments and the possibility of potential competitors that rely on different technologies than the dominant undertaking, even if they are of a smaller size than the dominant undertaking, to challenge the competitive position of existing value chains and replace them with new ones. Competition law should take into this form of disruptive competition, not only in order to relativize the finding of high market shares, but also when assessing restrictions to the potential competition from these disruptors.

In its recent decision on the *Dow/Dupont* merger,[107] the European Commission found that the merger may have reduced innovation competition for pesticides by looking to the ability and the incentive of the parties to innovate (see Box: Assessing effects on innovation in the *Dow/Dupont* merger). The Commission also looked to effects on innovation in the context of its analysis of the *Bayer/Monsanto* merger.[108]

Innovation is not only a concern in the substantive assessment of the existence of a restriction of competition. Recently, EU Commissioner Margrethe Vestager has suggested reviewing the notification threshold system and replacing it with a system where additional factors, such as deal value or impact on innovation, should form part of the notification threshold.[109] The Commission has made proposals in this direction in October 2016.[110]

105 See our analysis of the US merger cases above where innovation concerns were raised.

106 *TomTom/Tele Atlas* (Case COMP/M.4854) Commission Decision (14 May 2008), paras 244–50. The Commission nevertheless found that it was not necessary to estimate precisely the magnitude of likely efficiencies, given the proposed transaction's lack of anti-competitive effect.

107 *Dow/Dupont* (Case M.7932) Commission Decision (27 March 2017), available at http://ec.europa.eu/competition/mergers/cases/decisions/m7932_13668_3.pdf.

108 European Commission, 'Mergers: Commission Clears Bayer's Acquisition of Monsanto, Subject to Conditions', Press Release IP/18/2282 (21 March 2018).

109 In particular, the Commissionaire noted that the *Facebook/What's App* merger was not caught under the turnover threshold of the EUMR, but was eventually assessed by the Commission as a result of a case referral: Margrethe Vestager, EU Commissioner, 'Refining the EU Merger Control System', Speech, Brussels (10 March 2016).

110 See European Commission, 'Mergers: Commission Seeks Feedback on Certain Aspects of EU Merger Control', Press Release IP/16/3337 (7 October 2016).

Assessing effects on innovation in the *Dow/Dupont* merger

In the *Dow/Dupont* merger, the Commission focused its assessment both on innovation competition at the level of *innovation spaces* within the crop protection industry and on innovation competition at the *industry level*. In particular, the Commission examined:

(1) At the level of innovation spaces, the overlaps between the Parties' lines of research and early pipeline products as well as between lines of research and early pipeline products of a Party that will compete in a market where the other Party is an existing or potential supplier; and

(2) At the industry level, the overlap between the Parties' respective global R&D organisations, that is the resources, personnel, facilities, and other tangible and intangible assets dedicated to research, development and registration of new active ingredients (including lines of research, field testing facilities, registration capabilities).[111]

The Commission also distinguished between *lines of research*, which comprise the set of scientists, patents, assets, equipment, and chemical class(es) which are dedicated to a given discovery target whose final output are successive pipeline active ingredients targeting a given innovation space, *early pipeline products*, that is, products that are intermediate results of lines of research, which have already been selected among leads, but with a lower likelihood of success than development products and still in the discovery or pre-development stage and *pipeline products* in the development stage whose likelihood of being successfully launched is between 80 to 90 per cent.[112]

The Commission dedicated several hundred pages of its lengthy decision on innovation competition. Referring to paragraphs 8, 24, and 38 of the EU Horizontal Merger Guidelines, the Commission held that:

> 1989. The Merger Regulation sets up a legal framework that is not limited to the assessment of price effects, but under which the Commission is bound to conduct an appraisal of the likely effect of concentration in light of a number of criteria [. . .].
>
> 1990. Innovation is an important criterion relevant in order to conduct the appraisal.[113]

The Commission derived from this focus on innovation competition that the framework in the Horizontal Merger Guidelines dealing with the non-coordinated (unilateral) effects of mergers could also apply in order to assess mergers affecting other parameters of competition than price, such as innovation competition.[114] Hence, the Commission needs to assess whether the transaction reduces important constraints on one or more sellers and significantly impede effective innovation competition considering both the loss of competition between the merging firms, and the reduction of competitive pressure on other non-merging firms. According to the Commission, '[o]verall, the loss of product variety brought about by less innovation harms consumers by depriving them of choice, and reducing competition on rival products'.[115]

This innovation-focused framework influenced of course one of the theories of harm put forward by the Commission in this case, harm to innovation. More importantly, the Commission linked the existence of rivalry/competition with the promotion of innovation. As it is tellingly put forward in the Commission's decision:

111 *Dow/Dupont* (Case M.7932) Commission Decision (27 March 2017), para 1957.
112 Ibid, paras 1958–60. 113 Ibid, paras 1989–90. 114 Ibid, para 1994.
115 Ibid, para 1998.

2000. [. . .] [T]he Commission considers that the market features of the crop protection industry suggest that rivalry (or competition) is likely an important factor driving innovation, and that a merger between important rival innovators is likely to lead to a reduction in innovation.[116]

Many reasons were given for what could be characterized as the Commission's prior belief or starting point in this case, essentially linked to some of the 'features' of the market.

(i) individual crop protection product markets are contestable on the basis of innovation; (ii) given the strong Intellectual Property Rights (IPRs) in the crop protection industry, the original innovator can be expected to reap the benefits from its innovation, by preventing rivals from imitating the successful innovation (that is, appropriability is high); (iii) innovation is mostly based on product innovation; (iv) consolidation between rival innovators is unlikely to be associated with efficiencies [. . .]; and (v) the fear of cannibalisation of own existing products is a disincentive to innovate which is likely to be reinforced by a merger between rival innovators.[117]

The Commission also relied on a body of theoretical and empirical economic literature that raised doubts over the Schumpeterian linkage between monopolistic profits and innovation, and empirical evidence that 'in the past, concentration in the industry was accompanied by a decrease in innovation'.[118] The Commission also found that concentration was not also high at the industry level, but also at the level of innovation spaces.[119] The concept of 'innovation space' constitutes an intermediate level of consideration of a space where competitive activity takes place, in addition to that of product relevant market downstream, technology market upstream, or at the level of the industry.[120] According to the Commission,

2162. [. . .] [T]he R&D players do not innovate for all the product markets composing the entire crop protection industry at the same time. They also do not innovate randomly without targeting specific spaces within that industry. When setting up their innovation capabilities and conducting their research, they target specific innovation spaces which are upstream of lucrative product markets and product markets which are of strategic interest for the R&D player in question. In order to assess innovation competition, it is thus important to consider the spaces in which this innovation competition occurs.[121]

The aim here is to delineate spaces where innovation competition takes place and to develop a structured approach that will enable the Commission to assess the existence of competitive constraints to the merging parties. This assessment requires:

[. . .] [F]irst of all the identification of those companies which, at an industry level, have the assets and capabilities to discover and develop new products which, as a result of the R&D effort, can be brought to the market. This analysis would identify the industry players who are capable to bring innovation to the crop protection markets overall. Against this background, it is possible to assess whether, through increased concentration and in light of high barriers to entry, the Transaction would be likely to reduce innovation output in the crop protection industry overall.

Secondly, and at another level, however, it is also relevant to identify and analyse those spaces in which innovation competition occurs in the crop protection industry, so as to assess whether the Transaction would significantly impede innovation competition in such spaces.[122]

116 Ibid, para 2000. 117 Ibid, para 2001.
118 Ibid, para 2003. See also ibid, paras 2157–8 and ibid, section 8.5. 119 Ibid, para 2038.
120 Ibid, paras 2159–62. 121 Ibid, para 2162. 122 Ibid, paras 2163–4.

These 'innovation spaces' are getting smaller in the crop protection industry, in view of the increasing regulatory hurdles, which require crop protection products to be ever more selective, compared to the past.[123] The Commission rejected the view of the parties that the choice was either focusing on the effect of the merger on specific relevant markets, such as upstream technology market and the relevant product markets or the assessment of innovation in the industry in general, noting that the early leads pursued do not indicate clearly what specific type of downstream product will materialize with the final Active Ingredient, which makes it necessary to assess innovation competition in innovation spaces, corresponding to small groupings of crop/pest combinations.[124]

The Commission then noted the oligopolistic nature of the industry dominated by five integrated crop protection R&D players, following an unprecedented wave of consolidation in the industry since the mid-1990s.[125] In contrast to other industry players, these players have scale, assets, capabilities, disposing the possibility to access to markets to pursue R&D globally and are integrated throughout the entire R&D pipeline.[126] Although the Commission noted the existence of other companies that are active to some extent in R&D, it found that these were not comparable to the five global R&D-integrated players as regards innovation competition.[127] The Commission further noted that Monsanto was not a strong player in the crop protection industry as its most significant activity as regards crop protection innovation has been the introduction of one extremely successful active ingredient (Glyphosate) more than thirty years ago, this 'decades old innovation still constituting the core of its crop protection revenues, its patent share in the market being fairly insignificant'.[128] In contrast, Dow's herbicides patent share for new active ingredients was in the range of 30–40 per cent, Syngenta's patent share in the range of 20–30 per cent, Bayer's patent share in the range of 10–20 to 20–30 per cent, and DuPont's patent share in the range of 5–10 to 10–20 per cent.[129] The Commission similarly proceeded to analyse the competitive constraint with regard to innovation brought by Isagro and a number of Japanese companies present in the industry, concluding that these were not active in the discovery and development of new active ingredients, or were distant competitors of the merging parties. Quantitative metrics on the basis of patent applications confirmed that the five global R&D-integrated players play a predominant role in crop protection innovation.[130]

The Commission further noted that industry shares tend to underestimate the expected non-coordinated effects of the merger given the significant cross shareholding between the main players,[131] an issue that will be analysed in 12.2.1.8.

Moving beyond the industry level, the Commission noted that concentration of R&D-integrated players at specific innovation spaces is even higher leading to tighter oligopolistic markets. Indeed, not all the R&D integrated companies are present in each innovation space and are present in all the downstream markets for formulated products. Despite being active at an industry level, each R&D player only competes in some markets for formulated products and therefore develops innovation efforts aiming at introducing new products in downstream markets for formulated products in *some* innovation spaces, but not all. As the Commission notes, '[o]therwise, they would be present with a product in all the downstream markets'.[132] This implies that at each innovation space level fewer than the big five players are competing, and therefore concentration is likely to be higher at this level than at the overall industry level.[133]

[123] Ibid, para 2166. [124] Ibid, paras 2171 and 2191. [125] Ibid, section 8.6.2.
[126] Ibid, paras 2205 and 2209. [127] Ibid, para 2228. [128] Ibid, para 2232.
[129] Ibid, para 2236. [130] Ibid, section 8.6.3.5. [131] Ibid, section 8.6.4.
[132] Ibid, para 2363.
[133] The Commission explains this higher degree of concentration in innovation spaces for various reasons detailed in ibid, paras 2365–93.

On the basis of these findings the Commission held that the merger would bring together two competitors which pre-merger were more important innovation competitors at industry level than their downstream market shares and their R&D expenditure shares suggest.[134] The Commission observed that the merging parties are important innovators in the crop protection industry with ambitious targets in terms the number and quality of new active ingredients and that their shares of patents (including citations of patents, which was thought as the most relevant criterion to assess the quality of patents) and new active ingredients shares (based on turnover on downstream markets), at industry level are higher than their downstream shares and their R&D expenditure shares suggest.[135]

The closeness of Dow and Dupont as competitors in several innovation spaces was also an element considered by the Commission. To determine closeness, in terms of competitive pressure for innovation competition, the Commission took into account current product overlaps as well as overlaps in their lines of research and early pipeline products.[136] In doing so, the Commission explored the current lines of research and early pipeline products of the Parties which overlap and that could therefore risk being discontinued, deferred or redirect by the merged entity, thus leading to an effect on innovation. The Commission examined overlaps in a number of innovation spaces, such as broadleaf weed herbicides where Dow and DuPont were the only companies with a clear focus in this broader group of herbicides.[137]

The Commission next proceeded in exploring if the merged entity would have incentives to reduce innovation efforts on overlapping lines of research and early pipeline products on the innovation spaces where the merging parties currently compete.[138] In order to assess these incentives the Commission referred to economics theory suggesting that a merger bringing together two competing early pipeline products (or lines of research) or an early pipeline product (or line of research) positioned to compete with an existing product may lead to a reduction on the efforts to continue with those overlapping early pipeline products (or lines of research) if the early pipeline product (or line of research) of one of the merging parties was likely to capture significant revenues from the competing product of the other merging party (be it another early pipeline product—or line of research—or products currently marketed), each company's research posing an externality to the others.[139] According to the Commission, '[t]his adverse externality is internalized post-merger—from the perspective of each innovator, the expected loss of profits on the products of the other merging firm adds to the opportunity cost of innovating—making it more likely that an early pipeline product (or line of research) is suppressed, deferred or re directed (particularly in the presence of significant development and commercialisation costs)'.[140] Similar cannibalization concerns could also arise if a merging party's early pipeline product overlaps with an early pipeline product of the other merging party, the Commission concluding that this will reduce the incentives for the merged entity to continue with both lines of research and early pipeline products with the same intensity as each of the merging parties would in the absence of the merger.[141] Consumers are harmed 'by both the loss of product variety, and the reduced intensity of future product market competition in the markets where the discontinued/deferred/redirected early pipeline product would have been introduced but for the merger'.[142] Although the Commission was not be able to identify in this case precisely which early pipeline products or lines of research the merging parties would likely discontinue, defer or re-direct, it was considered probable that the early pipeline products and lines of research where the parties were close innovation competitors would be the those for which the merging parties would have less incentive to innovate.[143] The

134 Ibid, section 8.7.
135 Ibid, sections 8.7.1 and 8.7.2.
136 Ibid, para 2601.
137 Ibid, para 2645.
138 Ibid, section 8.9.
139 Ibid, paras 3017–18.
140 Ibid, paras 3018 and 3024.
141 Ibid, para 3022.
142 Ibid, para 3019.
143 Ibid, para 3025.

Commission also noted that 'discontinuation of an early pipeline product or line of research is more likely to occur the higher the expected sales which that early pipeline product from the merged entity would capture (if launched) from another existing or future product of the merged entity'.[144]

In the same vein, the Commission noted that the merged entity would have lower incentives to achieve the same overall level of innovation as the merging parties pre-merger, in view of the fact that 'rivalry at the innovation stage is a crucial driver of the incentives to innovate'.[145] According to the Commission,

> [. . .] on highly concentrated innovation driven industries with very high barriers to entry such as the crop protection industry, the internalisation of the effects of innovation competition between the parties of a merger between important innovators would likely lead to noticeable reductions in the innovation efforts of the parties in relation to any future products that would otherwise be introduced in the absence of the transaction.[146]

This theory of harm goes beyond the 'short-term' harm to innovation competition that would likely come with the discontinuation of overlapping lines of research and early pipeline products which target the same innovation spaces.[147] It consists in a medium and long-term theory of harm that would result from the lower overall incentives of the merged entity to innovate as compared to the merging parties separately before the transaction and the 'structural effect of the transaction', the merged entity the merged entity pursuing less discovery work, less lines of research, less development and registration work and ultimately bringing less innovative Active Ingredients to the market than the merging parties would have done absent the transaction.[148] To the extent that 'lowered innovation incentives can manifest themselves in (i) lower innovation efforts reflected for example in less financial resources, less scientists, less physical assets devoted to innovation, and (ii) lower internal innovation output targets', the Commission explored the parties' post-integration planning documents and the synergies put forward by the merging parties which were set from the beginning to be more focused on cost cutting than on creating value (as more than 70 per cent of the announced synergies were cost-based).[149]

The Commission also found unlikely a sufficiently strong countervailing reaction of innovation competitors as the combination of efforts of players with discovery capabilities and of players with development capability would not offset the reduction of output resulting from the transaction.[150] It was not to be expected that third-party R&D-integrated players would increase their R&D expenditure and R&D targets following a concentration, in particular in view of the finding that the past consolidation of the industry seems to have harmed innovation competition in the crop protection industry.[151]

The efficiency gains put forward by the parties have not also been proven or substantiated. In particular, the Commission took issue with the claim of the parties that the loss of competition between tem would have increased their incentives to innovate. This argument was carefully distinguished from the separate issue that a reduction in imitation (or free-riding) by rival firms may generate an offsetting pro-innovation effect (by allowing the merging parties to internalize a positive externality that was not being internalized absent the merger), as in this case 'a reduction in imitation risk does not automatically follow from a loss of competition between the merging parties and can—at least in principle—be achieved by strong

144 Ibid, para 3053.
145 Ibid, para 3054.
146 Ibid, para 3055.
147 Ibid, para 3056.
148 Ibid, para 3057.
149 Ibid, para 3071.
150 Ibid, section 8.10.6.
151 Ibid, para 3242.

(enforcement of) IP rights, high degree of secrecy or other business strategies by the industry participants'.[152]

The harm to innovation would be significant to the extent that unilateral (non-coordinated) effects are expected to be more pronounced if the merger brings together two out of a limited number of large, qualitatively and highly effective 'R&D-integrated players' and '[e]ffects are also stronger if the merging parties are close competitors in terms of their likely innovation trajectories or in the product markets targeted with their innovation'.[153]

Because innovation is an important parameter of competition the Commission reached the conclusion that as a result of its non-coordinated effects on innovation, the transaction significantly impeded effective competition within the meaning of Article 2(3) EUMR.

The Commission considered that the remedies it imposed in order to take into account the horizontal unilateral effects concerns in product market competition, and which involved the divestiture of an R&D division, were also able to deal with the innovation competition concerns, From this perspective the purchaser of the crop protection divested business will be able to replace DuPont as a global, fully R&D integrated competitor in the crop protection industry, and in particular in the areas where Dow and DuPont overlap, thus maintaining the rivalry with Dow's R&D activities that would otherwise have been eliminated by the merger.[154] The divestiture will include all DuPont's assets and personnel dedicated to the discovery of new active ingredients as well as all patents, know-how and any other IP owned by DuPont related to its global R&D organization and crop protection pipeline.[155] The Crop Protection Divested Business will therefore be able to replicate the competitive constraint previously exerted by DuPont.

12.1.4.1.5. The substantive tests in UK merger control

Following the enactment of the Enterprise Act 2002, UK merger control has adopted a competition-oriented only substantive test, the substantial lessening of competition, whose formulation is similar to that of the substantive test applied in US merger control under section 7 of the Clayton Act 1914.

The Enterprise Act 2002 does not define SLC, but the OFT and the Competition Commission adopted in 2010 Joint Merger Assessment Guidelines, which were adopted by the CMA Board.[156] The Guidelines take an economic approach, identifying different types of mergers (horizontal and non-horizontal mergers) giving possibly rise to three types of effects: (i) unilateral effects, (ii) coordinated effects, (iii) vertical or conglomerate effects. According to the Guidelines, '[t]heories of harm are drawn up by the Authorities to provide the framework for [...] assessing the effects of a merger and whether or not it could lead to an SLC', these theories describing 'possible changes arising from the merger, any impact on rivalry and expected harm to customers as compared with the situation likely to arise without the merger' (the counterfactual).[157] The substantive assessment and the analysis of the effects of the merger should be conducted in the context of a relevant market, which should not be viewed as a separate analysis than the competition assessment. The Guidelines further explain that

152 Ibid, para 3275. 153 Ibid, para 3287. 154 Ibid, para 4032. 155 Ibid, para 4035.

156 Competition Commission (CoCo) and Office of Fair Trading (OFT), Merger Assessment Guidelines, CC2 (revised)/OFT 1254 (September 2010), Part 4, available at https://www.gov.uk/government/publications/merger-assessment-guidelines.

157 Ibid, para 4.2.1.

> [i]n considering the SLC test, the Authorities generally conduct their analysis under the following headings (although the headings are not necessarily systematically followed in the Authorities' decisions or reports):
>
> (a) market definition;
>
> (b) measures of concentration;
>
> (c) horizontal mergers—unilateral effects (including any vertical effects of horizontal mergers);
>
> (d) horizontal mergers- coordinated effects;
>
> (e) non-horizontal mergers—unilateral and coordinated effects;
>
> (f) efficiencies;
>
> (g) entry and expansion;
>
> (h) countervailing buyer power.[158]

Part of the assessment of the effects of a merger will focus on the measurement of the levels of concentration that the merger may lead to. As for the EU Guidelines, this is measured by market shares and concentration ratios, such as HHI. According to the Guidelines, in Phase 1, the CMA will have regard to the following thresholds, although it is clear that these will not be relied upon mechanistically. The CMA is less likely to identify competition concerns below these thresholds, on the basis of past decisional practice of the OFT:

- In relation to market shares, for undifferentiated products, combined market shares of less than 40 per cent will not often give cause for concern over unilateral effects. For non-horizontal mergers the Guidelines suggest that the CMA may have regard to the thresholds in the European Commission's guidelines on the assessment of non-horizontal mergers. In particular, a market share for the merged firm of less than 30 per cent will not often give cause for concern over input foreclosure.
- In relation to the number of firms, past decisional practice shows that there is no cause of concern about mergers that reduce the number of firms in the market from five to four (or above).
- With regard to the HHI, the following thresholds apply:
  - any market with a post-merger HHI exceeding 1 000 may be regarded as concentrated. However, a horizontal merger generating a delta of less than 250 is not likely to give cause for concern
  - any market with a post-merger HHI exceeding 2 000 may be considered as highly concentrated. However, a horizontal merger generating a delta of less than 150 is not likely to give cause for concern.

According to the Guidelines, '[t]hese thresholds may be most informative for mergers in a market where the product is undifferentiated and where competition between firms involves firms choosing what volume to supply to the market. In other cases the significance of these thresholds will be less'.[159] The Joint Assessment Guidelines analyse the various anti-competitive effects that may arise from merger activity, distinguishing between unilateral and coordinated effects. The same principles apply as those explained in the previous Sections.

158 Ibid, para 5.1.2. 159 Ibid, para 5.3.5.

12.1.4.1.6. Public interest tests

Public interest considerations do not form part of the substantive test of EU merger control. However, Article 21(4) EUMR includes a legitimate interest clause, which provides that Member States may take appropriate measures to protect three specified legitimate interests: public security, plurality of the media and prudential rules, and other unspecified public interests that are recognized by the Commission after notification by the Member State. They may also apply national rules that do not relate to competition, such as those that protect buyers of shares or minority interests. The legitimate interest exception is further explored in Section 12.2.4.1.

In the UK, Chapter 2 of Part 3 EA 2002 includes sections 42 to 58A dealing with the public interest cases. Section 42(2) EA 2002 provides that the Secretary of State may give a notice to the CMA ('the intervention notice') if he believes that one or more than one public interest consideration is relevant to the consideration of the relevant merger situation. The UK public interest test is examined in more detail in Section 12.2.4.2.

12.1.4.2. Ancillary restrictions

Certain ancillary agreements or restrictions may be entered into by the joint venture and its parents as part of the overall transaction. The treatment of ancillary restraints under the EU Merger Regulation is explained in Recital 21 and Articles 6(1)(b) and 8(1) and (2) of the EUMR providing that the Commission's decisions declaring concentrations compatible with the common market should automatically cover such restrictions, without the Commission having to assess such restrictions in individual cases.

However, the Commission has a residual function in that it should at the request of the undertakings concerned, expressly assess the ancillary character of restrictions if a case presents 'novel and unresolved questions giving rise to genuine uncertainty'.[160] A 'novel or unresolved question is defined as one giving rise to genuine uncertainty' as a question that is 'not covered by the relevant Commission notice in force or a published Commission decision'.[161]

The Commission has also published a Notice on Restrictions Directly Related and Necessary to Concentrations, dealing specifically with the assessment of ancillary restraints in this context. The Notice clarifies notably which restrictions are considered directly related to the implementation of the concentration and necessary to the implementation of a concentration.

European Commission—Notice on restrictions directly related and necessary to concentrations [2005] OJ C 56/24

> 11. The criteria of direct relation and necessity are objective in nature. Restrictions are not directly related and necessary to the implementation of a concentration simply because the parties regard them as such.
>
> 12. For restrictions to be considered 'directly related to the implementation of the concentration', they must be closely linked to the concentration itself. It is not sufficient

160 European Commission—Notice on restrictions directly related and necessary to concentrations [2005] OJ C 56/24, para 3.

161 Ibid.

> that an agreement has been entered into in the same context or at the same time as the concentration. Restrictions which are directly related to the concentration are economically related to the main transaction and intended to allow a smooth transition to the changed company structure after the concentration
>
> Agreements must be 'necessary to the implementation of the concentration', which means that, in the absence of those agreements, the concentration could not be implemented or could only be implemented under considerably more uncertain conditions, at substantially higher cost, over an appreciably longer period or with considerably greater difficulty.
>
> 13. Agreements necessary to the implementation of a concentration are typically aimed at protecting the value transferred, maintaining the continuity of supply after the break-up of a former economic entity, or enabling the start-up of a new entity. In determining whether a restriction is necessary, it is appropriate not only to take account of its nature, but also to ensure that its duration, subject matter and geographical field of application does not exceed what the implementation of the concentration reasonably requires. If equally effective alternatives are available for attaining the legitimate aim pursued, the undertakings must choose the one which is objectively the least restrictive of competition.
>
> 14. For concentrations which are carried out in stages, the contractual arrangements relating to the stages before the establishment of control within the meaning of Article 3(1) and (2) of the Merger Regulation cannot normally be considered directly related and necessary to the implementation of the concentration. However, an agreement to abstain from material changes in the target's business until completion is considered directly related and necessary to the implementation of the joint bid. The same applies, in the context of a joint bid, to an agreement by the joint purchasers of an undertaking to abstain from making separate competing offers for the same undertaking, or otherwise acquiring control.
>
> 15. Agreements which serve to facilitate the joint acquisition of control are to be considered directly related and necessary to the implementation of the concentration. This will apply to arrangements between the parties for the joint acquisition of control aimed at implementing the division of assets in order to divide the production facilities or distribution networks among themselves, together with the existing trademarks of the undertaking acquired jointly.
>
> 16. To the extent that such a division involves the break-up of a pre-existing economic entity, arrangements that make the break-up possible under reasonable conditions are to be considered directly related and necessary to the implementation of the concentration, under the principles set out below.

The Commission's Notice then goes on to provide further guidance focusing on non-competition clauses, licence agreements and purchase and supply obligations.

An assessment of whether restrictions are ancillary must distinguish between those which affect the joint venture and those which affect the parents. In *Blackstone/CDPQ/Kabel Nordrhein-Westfalen*,[162] the Commission stated that restrictions to the detriment of third parties would be considered as ancillary only where they are the inevitable consequence of the concentration itself and are not separable from it.

162 *Blackstone/CDPQ/Kabel Nordrhein-Westfalen* (Case COMP/JV.46) Commission Decision (19 June 2000).

In the *Areva/Siemens* case, the Commission had to assess the ancillarity of a non-compete clause in the context of the notified concentration.[163]

Areva/Siemens (Case COMP/39736) Commission Decision (18 June 2012)

43. The Commission takes the preliminary view that the post-JV NCO cannot be regarded as directly related to the creation of Areva NP.

44. For contractual provisions to be considered directly related to a concentration, they should be intended to allow a smooth transition to the changed company structure after the concentration. The Commission Notices on ancillary restraints clearly rule out the possibility that non-compete obligations between the parent undertakings and a joint venture extending beyond the lifetime of the joint venture could be regarded as directly related and necessary to the implementation of the concentration.

45. Non-compete obligations applicable during the lifetime of the joint venture aim at protecting the individual parent companies' investments, which are 'locked in' the joint venture during its lifetime. If the parent companies started to compete against their own joint venture, this could effectively eliminate the existence of the joint venture as such. Only one parent company starting to compete against the own joint venture would increase that parent company's share of profits to the detriment of the other joint venture partner. With the acquisition of sole control over the joint venture by one of its parents, the value of such investments is, however, no longer locked into the joint venture but 're-distributed' between the parent companies. Therefore, such protection then becomes obsolete.

46. The fact that some parent companies might subjectively consider a post-JV NCO as so important that they make it a condition for their decision to create a joint venture does not contradict this approach. A restriction is ancillary if it is directly related and necessary to the *implementation* of a concentration, that is to say, the process of transferring an undertaking from the seller to the acquirer or the establishment of a joint venture, which is considered to be a step that comes after a decision on the concentration has been taken. It is in this respect irrelevant whether the parents themselves consider the post-JV NCO as important or even necessary for their decision to at all form a joint venture.

47. The assessment of ancillarity is also unrelated to the question of the point in time at which an assessment of a post-JV NCO has to be made. The companies entering into an NCO need to assess the legality of the NCO before they agree on it, even if it is directly related only to a potential future acquisition of sole control by one of the parent companies when terminating the joint venture.

48. In conclusion, the Commission takes the preliminary view that the post-JV NCO cannot be regarded as directly related to the creation of Areva NP. In any event, the preliminary view of the Commission is also that the post-JV NCO cannot be regarded as objectively necessary for the creation of the JV. Post-JV non-compete obligations are, in principle, not necessary for the creation of a joint venture, but they may be necessary for its dissolution, as such clauses regulate the relationship between the former parents once dissolution takes place. [. . .]

163 *Areva/Siemens* (Case COMP/39736) Commission Decision (18 June 2012).

In the UK, The CMA does not typically express any view as to whether a restriction of which it is aware is ancillary or not. The CMA's jurisdictional and procedural guidance states that it will, exceptionally, and upon request by the parties, provide guidance on the ancillary nature of a restriction where the request raises novel or unresolved questions giving rise to genuine uncertainty,[164] although this rarely happens in practice.[165]

12.1.4.3. Burden and standard of proof

In *Airtours*, the GC insisted that the burden of proof was on the Commission. It must get simple facts right, such as the contents of a letter. It has a margin of appreciation on economic matters, such as the likely emergence of a dominant oligopoly. The GC said:

> 63. The prospective analysis which the Commission has to carry out in its review of concentrations involving collective dominance calls for close examination in particular of the circumstances which, in each individual case, are relevant for assessing the effects of the concentration on competition in the reference market [*Kali and Salz* [1998] ECR I–1375, para 222] [. . .], it is also apparent from the judgment in *Kali and Salz* that, where the Commission takes the view that a merger should be prohibited because it will create a situation of collective dominance, *it is incumbent upon it to produce convincing evidence thereof.* The evidence must concern, in particular, factors playing a significant role in the assessment of whether a situation of collective dominance exists, such as, for example, the lack of effective competition between the operators alleged to be members of the dominant oligopoly and the weakness of any competitive pressure that might be exerted by other operators. [Emphasis added.]
>
> 64. Furthermore, the basic provisions of Regulation No 4064/89, in particular Article 2 thereof, confer on the Commission a certain discretion, especially with respect to assessments of an economic nature, and, consequently, when the exercise of that discretion, which is essential for defining the rules on concentrations, is under review, the Community judicature must take account of the discretionary margin implicit in the provisions of an economic nature which form part of the rules on concentrations (*Kali and Salz*, paras 223 and 224, and [Case T-102/96, *Gencor Ltd v Commission* [1999] ECR II–753], paras 164 and 165).
>
> 65. Therefore, it is in the light of the foregoing considerations that it is necessary to examine the merits of the grounds relied on by the applicant to show that the Commission made an error of assessment in finding that the conditions for, or characteristics of, collective dominance would exist were the transaction to be approved.

The question remains whether the Commission is more likely to get its analysis wrong when the merger results in collective, rather than single, dominance. After the judgment in *Gencor*,[166] the Russians did not leave the market but continued to mine for the precious metals with the aid of improved technology. The parties' market shares did not rapidly rise as had been predicted.

In two later cases, *Tetra Laval BV v Commission* and *Schneider/Legrand*, the General Court confirmed the need for the Commission to take much greater care before alleging that a

164 CMA, Guidance—Mergers: The CMA's Jurisdiction and Procedure (CMA 2) (10 January 2014), paras 6.68–6.70.

165 For an example of such views being expressed, see *AB Agri/Uffculme Feed Mill* (Case ME/5095/11) OFT Decision (1 September 2011).

166 Case T-102/96, *Gencor Ltd v Commission* [1999] ECR II–753.

merger would lead to a dominant position as a result of which competition would be significantly impeded. In several appeals, such as *GE*, the courts have taken the judgment in *Airtours* as their starting point, but have continued to clarify further aspects on the same basis. The Commission appealed against the judgment of the GC in *Commission v Tetra Laval*. The merger with Sidel was almost entirely conglomerate. Four types of packaging are used for liquid food: cartons, plastic (including polyethylene terephthalate, or PET), cans, and glass. The markets were distinct, but closely related and converging. The Commission focused on foods that were sensitive to light or oxygen. Tetra had a dominant position over cartons, and Sidel was the leading maker of the stretch blow moulding (SBM) machines needed to make PET bottles. The Commission feared that the merged firms might leverage the dominant position of cartons towards dominance over the SBM machines made by Sidel. Tetra Laval's reputation in aseptic cartons and equipment would help it to persuade its customer to buy Sidel's SMB machines. Tetra Laval offered several commitments, but the Commission found that these were insufficient and compliance would be hard to monitor.

The GC found that, although leverage was theoretically possible, the Commission accepted that it would not result directly from the merger, but only from the likely subsequent conduct of the merged firm. The GC accepted that the Commission enjoyed a certain discretion when assessing economic issues. Nevertheless, a conglomerate merger did not directly increase the firms' market power. It was for the Commission to produce convincing evidence that this was likely. It should, therefore, have considered whether such conduct would be illegal under Article 102 TFEU. It quashed the decision on the ground of manifest error for not investigating.

The GC observed that, where the firms operated in distinct markets, a dominant position would seldom be created or strengthened.[167] Nevertheless, leveraging market power into a neighbouring market in the reasonably near future was in principle possible.[168]

> [. . .] [W]here the Commission takes the view that a merger should be prohibited because it will create or strengthen a dominant position within a foreseeable period, it is incumbent upon it to produce convincing evidence thereof [*Airtours*, para 63]. Since the effects of a conglomerate-type merger are generally considered to be neutral, or even beneficial, for competition on the markets concerned, as is recognised in the present case by the economic writings cited [. . .] the proof of anti-competitive conglomerate effects of such a merger calls for a precise examination, supported by convincing evidence, of the circumstances which allegedly produce those effects.[169]

The CJEU held that:

> Although the Court of First Instance stated, in paragraph 155, that proof of anti-competitive conglomerate effects of a merger of the kind notified calls for a precise examination, supported by convincing evidence, of the circumstances which allegedly produce those effects, it by no means added a condition relating to the requisite standard of proof but merely drew attention to the essential function of evidence, which is to establish convincingly the merits of an argument or, as in the present case, of a decision on a merger.[170]

167 C-12/03 P, *Commission v Tetra Laval* [2005] ECR I-987, para 150.
168 Ibid, para 151.
169 Ibid, para 155. See, by analogy, Case T-342/99, *Airtours plc v Commission* [2002] ECR II–2585, para 63.
170 Case C-12/03 P, *Tetra Laval v Commission* [2010] ECR I-67, para 41.

The Commission's margin of discretion is still subject to judicial review. The CJEU further held that '[w]hilst the Court recognises that the Commission has a margin of discretion with regard to economic matters, that does not mean that the Community courts must refrain from reviewing the Commission's interpretation of information of an economic nature.'[171] Not only must the findings be factually accurate, reliable and consistent, but the evidence must also contain all the information to be taken into account to assess a complex situation.[172] It is difficult to see far into the future,[173] so the GC did not err in law in quashing the Commission's decision.[174]

The CJEU confirmed that it could not be assumed that the parties would infringe Article 102 TFEU. The Commission should therefore have examined comprehensively whether the merged entity would be likely to abuse its dominant position, but the GC had gone too far in requiring the Commission to examine both the extent to which the incentive to adopt anti-competitive conduct would be reduced or eliminated on the ground that it was unlawful and the likelihood of detection.[175]

12.1.4.4. Merger statistics

The number of formal final decisions annually started at about 50, reached 341 in 2000 but declined to 230 in 2003 when there were fewer large mergers. Since then the number has been increasing. Since all merger cases end with a final decision, most formal decisions of the Commission relate to those concentrations between large corporate groups that are required to be notified. Nevertheless, far more cooperative joint ventures and mergers are entered into, but do not result in many decisions under EU law.

At the European level,[176] a big number of cases are cleared in the Phase 1 stage—a total number of 5659 mergers being cleared between 1990 and 2016. The number of the Phase 2 initiation proceedings was increased around 2000 (with twenty mergers being referred to Phase 2 in 2000) but since then the numbers have fallen to almost the half of this—eight mergers have been referred to Phase 2 stage in 2016. It is notable that almost half of Phase 2 cases are cleared subject to commitments (120 cases out of 246 since 1990, and six in 2016) and only a small number of Phase 2 cases is prohibited (twenty-five out of 246 cases since and one in 2016[177]).

In the UK,[178] the number of Phase 1 decisions has been declining. In 2016, the CMA has issued the fewest Phase 1 decisions since 2004 (forty-five decisions in 2016, 171 in 2004–5). The majority of Phase 1 decisions are unconditional clearances and on average 10 per cent of these will be referred in Phase 2 investigation. Most Phase 2 mergers will be unconditionally cleared or cleared subject to behavioural or structural remedies—only nine out of 133 Phase 2 referred mergers have been prohibited since 2004. It is also worth noting that a quite a big number of Phase 2 mergers has been withdrawn or cancelled at this stage (almost 25 per cent of total number of Phase 2 mergers since 2004).

171 Ibid, para 39. 172 Ibid. 173 Ibid, para 44.
174 Ibid, para 55. 175 Ibid, para 75.
176 See the published statistics for the period 21 September 1990 to 31 July 2018: ec.europa.eu/competition/mergers/statistics.pdf.
177 *Hutchison 3G UK/Telefonica UK* (Case COMP/M.7612) Commission Decision C(2016) 2796 final (11 May 2016).
178 See the statistics published here: www.gov.uk/government/uploads/system/uploads/attachment_data/file/583613/merger-inquiry-outcomes-to-31-dec-16.pdf.

12.2. JURISDICTION

Merger control across the EU is split between the Commission and Member States. Under Article 21(1)–(3) EUMR, the Commission has exclusive jurisdiction over concentrations of an EU dimension, unless the Commission agrees to refer such a transaction to the national competition authority under Article 9 EUMR. What follows deals first with the two concepts of concentration and EU dimension which combined delineate the scope of the Commission's exclusive jurisdiction.

12.2.1. THE CONCEPT OF CONCENTRATION AND THAT OF CONTROL: CASE STUDIES

Article 3 EUMR describes what is considered to be a concentration. The Commission's Jurisdictional Notice provides interpretative guidance.[179] Only those transactions that result in a lasting change in the structure of the market fall within the scope of Article 3.[180] Accordingly, under the meaning of Article 3 a concentration occurs when there is a lasting change in control. There are primarily two ways two types of concentrations: (i) those arising from a proper M&A transaction between previously independent firms;[181] and (ii) those arising from the acquisition of control.[182] In the former case, either two or more firms merge and thus cease to exist as separate legal entities, or the target firm is absorbed, and thus cease to exist as a legal entity, whilst the acquiring firm retain its legal identity.[183] In the latter case, whilst the target firm does not cease to exist as a separate legal entity, its control is transferred in a lasting way to another firm or to more firms jointly.[184]

According to Article 3(2) EUMR, control means being able to exercise decisive influence on a firm, most commonly, by virtue of a controlling shareholding, which can be lower than 50 per cent where the rest of the shareholders are dispersed.[185] Control can also be acquired on a contractual basis, provided there is a very long duration and the contract confers control over the management and the resources despite the fact that property rights or shares are not transferred.[186] The transfer of control can refer to just part of a firm, as long as it confers a market presence to which a market turnover can be clearly attributed.[187]

12.2.1.1. Case study I: *Microsoft/Yahoo! Search Business*

***Microsoft/Yahoo! Search Business* (Case COMP/M.5727) Commission Decision C(2010) 1077 (18 February 2010)**

Microsoft (active in the design, development and supply of computer software and related services worldwide) proposed to acquire control of Yahoo's online search and search advertising businesses by way of purchase of assets through a ten-year exclusive licence to Yahoo's core

179 Commission Consolidated Jurisdictional Notice under Council Regulation No 139/2004 on the control of concentrations between undertakings [2008] OJ C 95/1 [hereinafter Jurisdictional Notice].

180 See EUMR, Recital 20.

181 Ibid, Article 3(1)(a).

182 Ibid, Article 3(1)(b).

183 Jurisdictional Notice, para 9.

184 Ibid, para 11.

185 See eg *Arjomari-Prioux-SA/Wiggins Teape Appleton plc* (Case IV M.025) Commission Decision [1990] OJ C 321/16, para 4.

186 Jurisdictional Notice, para 18.

187 Ibid, para 24.

search technologies conferring the right to integrate Yahoo's search technologies into its existing web search platforms, while hiring no less than 400 employees from both Yahoo's search advertising group and its Internet search group. Yahoo committed to exclusively use Microsoft's search engines on Yahoo sites. Microsoft would become the exclusive search-advertising provider used by Yahoo and in exchange Microsoft would retail 12 per cent of the search revenues generated on Yahoo's own and its partners' sites during the first five years of the agreement paying 88 per cent to Yahoo as a fee. The Commission found that the operation was not likely to have negative effects on competition, largely due to low market shares and the existence of strong competition from Google.

12. The Agreements entail the acquisition by Microsoft of Yahoo's internet search and search advertising businesses, including Panama. These businesses are not incorporated, and their transfer is brought about via a transfer of relevant technology, employees (including customer relations staff) and a migration of customers from Panama to adCenter.

13. The Commission finds that the Agreements entail a concentration falling under the EC Merger Regulation on the grounds that (i) the transferred assets constitute the whole or a part of an undertaking, that is a business with a market presence to which a turnover can be attributed and (ii) there is change of control over these assets which occurs on a lasting basis. The Commission further finds that Microsoft will acquire sole control over the Yahoo search business.

Whole or a part of an undertaking

14. Search and advertising platform technology, human capital and advertising customers which are included in the Agreements appear to be the three most important ingredients for a search advertising business. Looking at those three dimensions of the transaction shows that it concerns a business with a market presence to which a turnover can be attributed.

15. First, and as indicated above, under the Agreements, Microsoft will obtain access to all the core technologies of the Yahoo search engine. Since the licence is also exclusive as to Yahoo, Yahoo will not be able to operate a separate search business.

16. Second, Microsoft will also hire at least 400 Yahoo employees corresponding to [. . .] of Yahoo's current search business staff. This proportion of employees of Yahoo's search business would be sufficient to enable Microsoft to run that business.

17. Third, once Microsoft search advertising is launched in a given country, Yahoo customers will be 'migrated' to Microsoft's advertising platform adCenter, Yahoo's Panama platform will be discontinued and all search advertising services used by Yahoo will be provided by Microsoft through adCenter. Some advertisers will be redirected via an assignment of contracts although most of the smaller ones will be redirected via special migration campaign assistance (including online re-direction, migration marketing and assistance campaigns). PDAs will be required to sign new standard contracts.

18. Furthermore, for 2008, world-wide turnover of EUR [. . .] million can be attributed to the Yahoo search business. The Commission underlines that Yahoo will be contractually obliged to exit the search and advertising markets. The transaction therefore concerns the acquisition of the whole or a part of a business with market presence to which turnover can be attributed.

Change of control on a lasting basis

20. The Agreements have a term of 10 years, which is a long period in a market characterised by rapid technological developments, such as internet search and search advertising. Defined events which would permit an early termination of the Agreements seem unlikely to occur and, in any event, could only take place after a significant time period. In case of termination no forced return of employees is foreseen and Microsoft would maintain the license to the core technology (although this will become non-exclusive). Therefore, for the foreseeable future Yahoo is de facto definitively divesting its ability to compete in internet search and search advertising.

21. As a result, the transaction would bring about a change of control on a lasting basis.

12.2.1.2. Case study II: *Eurotunnel*

In the UK, the Supreme Court ruled in the *Eurotunnel* case[188] that the acquisition of assets from the liquidation of the target firm can still amount to a concentration to the extent that: (i) the acquired assets give the purchaser more than it might have acquired by going into the market and buying factors of production; and (ii) that extra is attributable to the fact that the assets were previously employed in combination in the 'activities' of the target enterprise.

Eurotunnel acquired substantial part of the assets of the liquidated SeaFrance business (following submission of sealed bids to the Commercial Court of Paris). In order to secure the assets, GET acted together with a workers cooperative formed by former SeaFrance employees (a Société coopérative et participative (the SCOP)). The assets included three out of four ferries previously operated by SeaFrance. Eurotunnel recommenced operation of two of the vessels on the Dover–Calais route on 20 August 2012, trading under the name MyFerryLink.

On 29 October 2012, the OFT decided to refer the completed acquisition by Eurotunnel of the SeaFrance assets to the CoCo under the EA 2002. The CoCo published its final report on the completed acquisition on 6 June. The CoCo concluded that in the context of the particular industry, the assets acquired met the statutory definition of an 'enterprise', and constituted the activities, or part of the activities, of a business. It found that the EA 2002 share of supply test was satisfied and, therefore, it concluded that it had jurisdiction to review the merger as a relevant merger situation under the EA 2002 had been created. Moreover, it found that the merger may be expected to result in a substantial lessening of competition in the markets for the supply of transport services to passengers and freight customers on the short sea and that the most effective and proportionate remedy was to prohibit Eurotunnel from operating ferry services.

SCOP challenged the CoCo's decision on the grounds that the CoCo had no jurisdiction to review the merger, claiming that there was no relevant merger situation.

The CAT concluded that the CoCo had erred in its consideration of whether Eurotunnel had acquired an 'enterprise' for the purposes of the Enterprise Act 2002. The CAT doubted whether the facts, as found by the CoCo, supported a conclusion that Eurotunnel had acquired something more than 'bare assets'. Therefore, the CAT has remitted the question of

188 *Société Coopérative de Production SeaFrance SA (Respondent) v The Competition and Markets Authority and another (Appellants)* [2015] UKSC 75.

whether the CoCo has jurisdiction in this case (whether what was acquired was an 'enterprise' or just 'assets') to the CoCo for its reconsideration.[189]

On 27 June 2014, the CMA published its final decision confirming the original findings on the *Groupe Eurotunnel/SeaFrance* merger inquiry.[190] The CMA concluded that the collection of tangible and intangible assets acquired meets the legal definition of an 'enterprise' in that together they constitute the activities or part of the activities of a business. Therefore, in this case, it considers that two enterprises did cease to be distinct within the meaning of section 26(1) of the EA 2002, and the CoCo, therefore, had jurisdiction to review the merger.

The CMA also considered whether there was any material change of circumstances affecting the original merger decision. It concluded that there was no material change of circumstance that affected its finding as to the competitive conditions in the market. Eurotunnel and the SCOP lodged further applications with the CAT seeking review of the remittal decision, challenging only the CMA's decision on the jurisdictional question.

The CAT rejected the applications by Eurotunnel and SCOP. The CAT concluded that there were no judicial review grounds (irrationality or error of law) for setting aside the CMA's decision.[191] According to the CAT, the CMA had, as required in the original judgment, considered what over and above bare assets had been acquired and how this placed the acquirer in a different position than if it had gone out in the market and acquired the assets.

The SCOP appealed the CAT2 judgment to the Court of Appeal. On 15 May 2015, the Court of Appeal, by a majority, upheld the SCOP's appeal.

The Court of Appeal[192] concluded that the CMA's original decision was wrong in categorising Groupe Eurotunnel's buyout of SeaFrance's ferries as an acquisition of an 'enterprise' under English law. The CMA had failed to give proper consideration to the fact that employees were not transferred from SeaFrance to Eurotunnel but had in fact been re-employed by the SCOP after their employment with SeaFrance had been terminated. The fact that the business had also been in 'hiatus' for seven months was another factor which pointed against Eurotunnel having taken over SeaFrance's activities.

On 16 December 2015, the Supreme Court allowed the CMA's appeal against the Court of Appeal's judgment. The legal question considered by the Supreme Court was whether or not Eurotunnel acquired an 'enterprise', as defined in the Enterprise Act 2002, comprising both the ships and the former SeaFrance employees, in particular given that SeaFrance was no longer active at the time of the acquisition of its assets.

The Supreme Court[193] held that the merger control provisions of the EA 2002 are not limited to the acquisition of a business that is a 'going concern'. There is no requirement that the activities of an enterprise are actually being carried on at the moment of its acquisition. The period of time between cessation of trading and acquisition of control of the assets may be a relevant factor in determining whether an 'enterprise' has been acquired, but is not necessarily decisive.

The Supreme Court considered that the test for whether an 'enterprise' has been acquired, rather than 'bare assets', is essentially one of economic continuity. An 'enterprise' is acquired where the assets give the acquirer more than might have otherwise been acquired by

189 *Groupe Eurotunnel SA v CMA* and *Société Coopérative de Production SeaFrance SA v CC* [2013] CAT 30.

190 *Eurotunnel/SeaFrance merger inquiry remittal*, CMA Final Report (27 June 2014), available at https://assets.publishing.service.gov.uk/media/53ad002440f0b610b400000a/Final_decision.pdf.

191 *Groupe Eurotunnel SA v CMA* and *Société Coopérative de Production SeaFrance SA v CMA* [2015] CAT 1.

192 *Société Coopérative de Production SeaFrance SA v CMA* [2015] EWCA Civ 487.

193 *Société Coopérative de Production SeaFrance SA v CMA* [2015] UKSC 75.

going into the market and buying factors of production, and that extra is attributable to the fact that the assets were previously employed in combination in the 'activities' of the target enterprise.

The Supreme Court disagreed with the majority of the Court of Appeal. It held that the CMA had not acted irrationally in concluding that Eurotunnel had acquired substantially all the assets of SeaFrance and that these constituted an enterprise. The CMA was entitled to consider that there had been a 'transfer' of former SeaFrance employees, despite them having been made redundant by an order of the French insolvency court. The approach taken by the majority of the Court of Appeal wrongly reduced a question of economic continuity to the question of whether the French court had, as a matter of law, terminated the relationship between SeaFrance and its employees.

12.2.1.3. Sole control

12.2.1.3.1. Sole control in EU Merger Regulation

Sole control refers to a situation where the acquiring firm alone can exercise decisive influence over the target firm. This is not only the case where the former controls a majority of voting rights which confer the power to take strategic decisions, but also where it is merely possible to veto strategic decisions, which is known as 'negative sole control'.[194] Control can be exercised on a *de jure* basis, by virtue of a majority of voting rights, or on a *de facto* basis, where the remaining shareholdings are fragmented so unable to veto the relatively larger shareholder.[195]

In *Anglo American Corporation/Lonrho*,[196] AAC, a diversified South African company involved in mining, finance, commerce and industry, acquired a shareholding of 24.13 per cent of Lonrho, a UK company active in mining, agriculture, trading and property. The Commission amalgamated the shareholding that AAC would acquire in Lonrho with that of two other shareholders, on account of the fact that the latter would vote their shares as instructed by AAC. In this light, the Commission examined whether AAC would acquire on a *de facto* basis solely or jointly with these two shareholders the possibility to exercise decisive influence over Lonrho and therefore control it. The Commission concluded that AAC would acquire sole control of Lonrho, taking into account the following considerations that: (i) a 27.47 per cent shareholding would have amounted to a majority of the votes cast at past meeting; (ii) the next largest shareholder owned 3 per cent of the shares, while it also had shares in AAC itself; (iii) AAC was the only industrial or mining company having a significant shareholding in Lonrho, which added to the leverage AAC could exercise in it since it increased its influence over the board; and (iv) Lonrho's directors who held a total of 0.12 per cent of the shares in the company would not be expected to vote against AAC in its capacity of main shareholder.

Short of control, the Commission consulted on a proposal to extend the scope of the EUMR to a limited number of potentially anti-competitive acquisitions of non-controlling minority shareholdings (mainly involving competitors or vertically related companies reaching the turnover thresholds of the regulation). Companies wishing to acquire such a stake would have to file a short information notice, on the basis of which the Commission could decide

194 Jurisdictional Notice, para 54. 195 Ibid.

196 *Anglo American Corporation/Lonrho* (Case COMP/M.754) Commission Decision [1998] OJ L 149/21, paras 31–9.

whether to require a full notification and start an investigation. Member States would also be able to request a referral.[197]

12.2.1.3.2. Material influence under the UK jurisdiction

Under the UK national legislation the definition of control is less strict, thus entailing a broader jurisdictional scope. The CMA must establish that the acquiring firm can exercise material, rather than decisive, influence over the target firm. According to CMA,[198] the ability to exercise material influence can fall short of being able to block votes at shareholders meetings.

BSkyB/ITV is one of the leading cases on the issue of material influence. The OFT (the predecessor of the CMA) considered the issue of material influence in relation to the acquisition by BskyB, the UK leading pay-TV operator, of a 17.9 per cent stake in ITV, the leading commercial free-to-air TV operator. The OFT concluded that the acquisition of this minority stake would give BSkyB material influence. The OFT found that, on the basis of evidence of attendance and voting at recent ITV shareholders' meetings, BSkyB's shareholding would be likely in practice to allow it to block special resolutions at ITV shareholders' meetings. The OFT found that turnout at ITV shareholders' meetings has ranged between 63 and 70 per cent. Therefore, BSkyB's 17.9 per cent stake would have enabled it to exercise more than 25 per cent of the votes cast at these meetings.

The OFT also made the following observations: (a) BSkyB could obtain board representation as a result of its shareholding; (b) BSkyB was the only significant trade shareholder and has substantial industry expertise; (c) BSkyB was the largest individual shareholder and ITV's corporate governance policy was to hold frequent discussions with major shareholders; (d) the remaining shareholdings in ITV were fragmented; and (e) there was a number of other ITV shareholders that had cross-shareholdings in both merging firms. This approach was upheld by both the Competition Appeal Tribunal[199] and the Court of Appeal.[200]

12.2.1.4. Joint control

According to the Jurisdictional Notice, joint control exists where two or more firms can exercise decisive influence over the target firm thanks to the ability to veto strategic decisions by virtue of a common understanding in determining the commercial policy at the controlled firm.[201] A common understanding can result from a formal agreement or, exceptionally, being established on a *de facto* basis where strong common interests exist between the minority shareholders to the effect that they would not act against each other in exercising their rights in relation to the controlled firm.[202]

In *Hutchison/RCPM/ECT*,[203] Hutchison, active in the provision of stevedoring services in ports word-wide, and RCPM, a company wholly owned by Rotterdam Municipal

[197] Although the consultation closed in October 2014, so far the Commission only published the summary of responses in March 2015, available at ec.europa.eu/competition/consultations/2014_merger_control/summary_of_replies.pdf.

[198] CMA, Guidance—Mergers: The CMA's Jurisdiction and Procedure (CMA 2) (10 January 2014), para 4.15, available at www.gov.uk/government/uploads/system/uploads/attachment_data/file/384055/CMA2__Mergers__Guidance.pdf.

[199] *BskyB v Competition Commission and the Secretary of State* [2008] CAT 25.

[200] *BskyB v Competition Commission and the Secretary of State* [2010] EWCA Civ 2.

[201] Ibid, para 62. [202] Ibid, para 76.

[203] *Hutchinson/RCPM/ECT* (Case COMP/JV.55) Commission Decision (29 November 2001).

Port Management and responsible for the development and management of the port of Rotterdam, would acquire equal shareholdings of 35 per cent in Europe Combined Terminals, a company engaged in the provision of stevedoring services at certain European ports, foremost Rotterdam. ABN, an entity mainly engaged in the purchasing, selling, management and administration of securities, properties and other assets, was the only other major shareholder with 28 per cent. The remaining 2 per cent was owned by Star, an employees' trust. The Commission relied on the following considerations to conclude that Hutchinson and RCPM would acquire joint control of ECT on a *de facto* basis: (i) the commonality of understanding between the parties established through their joint involvement in a previous operation and the absence of any such obvious commonality as between either of these two parties and the third main shareholder, ABN; (ii) the fact that the third main shareholder intended to reduce the size of its stake substantially (by 50 per cent or more) as soon as it had the opportunity to do so; (iii) the structure of the shareholdings and voting rules, which seemed to have been tailored in such a way as to allow the two parties to exercise joint control over ECT; (iv) the existence of a high degree of mutual dependency as between Hutchison and RMPM regarding the success of their respective investments in ECT; and (v) the fact that Hutchison and RMPM provided a common guarantee for the benefit of ABN, which was the financial investor.

12.2.1.5. Changes in the quality of control

The EUMR captures also transactions that would bring about a change in the degree of control exercised, such as from sole to joint control and vice versa, and also a change in the number of joint controlling firms.[204] In this respect, an important example is where the shareholding position of a financial investor is taken over by a competitor of the jointly controlled firm.[205]

12.2.1.6. Joint ventures

Article 3(4) EUMR extends the concept of a concentration to include concentrative but not cooperative joint ventures, the latter remaining subject to Articles 101 and 102 TFEU: 'The creation of a joint venture performing on a lasting basis all the functions of an autonomous economic entity shall constitute a concentration within the meaning of Article 3, paragraph 1(b).' These concentrations are also known as 'full-function joint ventures'.

The Commission has long, although not entirely consistently, considered that concentrative joint ventures are not subject to Article 101 TFEU.[206] In the Memorandum on concentrations it issued in 1966, it held that mergers often resulted in efficiencies and should be subject to a more lenient test than that under Article 101(1) TFEU. It tried to explain what is meant by the term 'concentrative joint venture' in a notice,[207] but in practice it departed from it in its actual decisions, largely in order to find that more JVs were concentrative and came within the competence of the merger task force, which dealt more

204 Jurisdictional Notice, para 83. 205 Ibid, para 87.

206 See *SHV/Chevron* (Case IV/26.872) Commission Decision [1975] OJ L 38/14.

207 European Commission—Notice on the concept of concentration under Council Regulation (EEC) No 4064/89 on the control of concentrations between undertakings, OJ [1998] C 66/5, paras 18–40. This was amalgamated with the Jurisdictional Notice, paras 91–119.

rapidly and more favourably with JVs than did the other directorates in the competition department.[208]

Joint control exists where two or more undertakings or persons are able to exercise decisive influence over another undertaking. The acquisition of joint control includes changes from sole to joint control as well as a deadlock situation where more than one parent company is able to reject strategic decisions, so that they have to reach agreement. Joint control may exist through veto rights, by a sharing in voting rights or by *de facto* control.

For the joint venture to be concentrative or 'full-function' it must 'perform on a lasting basis all the functions of an autonomous economic entity'.[209] Under Article 3(2) of the original Regulation 4064/89, JVs were excluded where 'they g[a]ve rise to coordination of the competitive behaviour of the parties amongst themselves or between them and the joint venture'.[210] This provision was deleted in 1997,[211] full functionality becoming the only criterion to identify joint ventures falling under the EUMR.[212] Coordination between the JV and one parent is now irrelevant, but where the merger has the object or effect of coordinating the competitive behaviour of the parents *inter se*, this may be investigated under Article 101 TFEU in the context of the merger investigation and within the same tight time limits under Article 2(4) EUMR.

Hence the creation of a full-function joint venture is normally appraised according to two different substantive tests:

- In all circumstances, their creation is examined under Article 2(3) EUMR according to the significant impediment of effective competition test (SIEC);
- if the formation of a full-function JV has, as its object or effect, the coordination of the competitive behaviour of the undertakings concerned, this coordination will be analysed with reference to Article 101 TFEU, in combination with Article 2(4) and (5) EUMR. Not all agreements between the parent firms are subject to Article 101 TFEU. Only those which are directly related to and necessary for the formation of the JV can be examined under Article 2(4), the other agreements being analysed separately under Article 101 TFEU within the framework of Regulation 1/2003.[213]

The latter examination has happened in relatively few occasions and in none of these did the Commission conclude that the JV was created with the object to coordinate the independent activities of its parents, which is hardly surprising as it is 'very unlikely that the parties would notify the Commission of a joint venture with an anti-competitive object' and 'considering that the parent firms normally make significant investments in the joint venture, the Commission usually does not give important consideration to the possibility

208 On a retrospective and a thorough analysis of the application of the EUMR on joint ventures, see K Bas, *The Substantive Appraisal of Joint Ventures under the EU Merger Control Regime* (Kluwer, 2015), in particular ch 3 for full-function joint ventures.

209 Case C-248/16, *Austria Asphalt GmbH & Co OG v Bundeskartellamt*, ECLI:EU:C:2017:643, para 22.

210 For an analysis of the pre-2004 EUMR practice, see BE Hawk, 'Joint Ventures under EEC Law' (1992) 15 *Fordham Int'l LJ* 303; J Venit, 'The Treatment of Joint Ventures under the EC Merger Regulation—Almost through the Thicket' in BE Hawk (ed) *Mergers & Acquisitions and Joint Ventures* (Juris, 2004), 521.

211 Council Regulation (EC) No 1310/97 of 30 June 1997 amending Regulation (EEC) No 4064/89 on the control of concentrations between undertakings [1997] OJ L 180/1.

212 See also European Commission, 'Green Paper on the review of Council Regulation (EEC) No 4064/89' COM (2001) 745 final, paras 100–24.

213 K Bas, *The Substantive Appraisal of Joint Ventures under the EU Merger Control Regime* (Kluwer, 2015), 74, noting that '[t]he Commission [. . .] appears to utilise the principles for ancillary restraints in order to determine the scope of Article 2(4)'.

that the parents have an anti-competitive object'.[214] The analysis therefore focuses on the existence of anti-competitive effects, in particular if the JV has, as its effect, the coordination of the competitive behaviour of independent firms. This involves identifying the candidate markets where there may be a risk of coordination.[215] Should an infringement of Article 101(1) TFEU be found, the Commission should normally analyse whether the exemption conditions laid down in Article 101(3) TFEU are satisfied, the Commission taking into account only efficiencies resulting from the coordination, but not those arising from integration by the joint venture.[216]

In applying the Article 101(1) TFEU test, the Commission must in particular ascertain:

- Whether two or more parent companies retain significant activities in the same market as the JV, or in a market which is downstream or upstream from that of the JV, or in a neighbouring market closely related to this market, so that it is likely that they will coordinate their behaviour on the market(s) concerned; and
- Whether the coordination, which is the direct consequence of the creation of the JV (there must therefore be a direct causal link between the creation of the JV and any coordination of the parties' behaviour), affords the parties the possibility of eliminating competition in respect of a substantial part of the products or services in question.

For example, the Commission decided in *BSkyB/Kirch Pay TV*[217] that although there was some incentive for the parties to coordinate their behaviour (in an effort to reduce costs in the acquisition of sports rights), there was no causal link as such coordination could take place already and indeed was not facilitated by the establishment of the joint venture. There was no need to consider the restriction under Article 2(4) of the Merger Regulation.[218]

The policy underpinnings of this complex legal framework are easy to understand. Common participation in JVs, as it is also the case for cross-shareholdings, may raise some competition concerns, in particular through the softening of competition and tacit collusion.[219] According to the Commission's Jurisdictional Notice, '[t]he fact that a joint venture may be a full-function undertaking and therefore economically autonomous from an operational viewpoint does not mean that it enjoys autonomy as regards the adoption of its strategic decisions.'[220] Indeed, it cannot be independent of its parents when they control it jointly. It performs the functions of an autonomous economic entity when it has all the resources required to carry on as if it were operationally autonomous, including 'a management dedicated to its day-to-day operations and access to sufficient resources including finance, staff, and assets (tangible and intangible) in order to conduct on a lasting basis its business activities within the area provided for in the joint-venture agreement'.[221]

214 Ibid, 74.	215 For a more detailed analysis of this assessment, see ibid, 75–82.

216 Ibid, 82–3.

217 *BSkyB/Kirch Pay TV* (Case COMP/JV.37) Commission Decision (21 March 2000).

218 See also *BT/AT&T* (Case COMP/JV.15) Commission Decision (30 March 1999); *Hutchinson/RCPM/ECT* (Case COMP/JV.55) Commission Decision (29 November 2001); and *NC/Canal+/CDPQ/Bank America* (Case COMP/M.1327) Commission Decision (3 December 1998).

219 See RJ Reynolds and BR Snapp, 'The Competitive Effects of Partial Equity Interests and Joint Ventures' (1986) 4 *Int'l J Industrial Organisation* 141; D Flath, 'Horizontal Shareholding Interlocks' (1992) 13(1) *Managerial & Decision Economics* 75; D Reitman, 'Partial Ownership Arrangements and the Potential for Collusion' (1994) 4(3) *J Industrial Economics* 313, D Gilo, Y Moshe, and Y Spiegel, 'Partial Cross Ownership and Tacit Collusion' (2006) 37 *Rand J Economics* 81; D Gilo, 'The Anticompetitive Effects of Passive Investment' (2000) 99 *Michigan L Rev* 1.

220 Jurisdictional Notice, para 93.	221 Ibid, para 94.

Furthermore, a joint venture is not full-function 'if it only takes over one specific function within the parent companies' business activities without its own access to or presence on the market'.[222] If it carries on only one function, such as R&D, which it provides mainly for its parents, however, and has no access to the market, it will not function as an autonomous economic entity, or what is sometimes called 'a full-function joint venture'. It will be treated as auxiliary to its parents' business and its creation will be subject to Article 101 TFEU, although the JV may make some use of the distribution facilities of one or both of its parents without ceasing to act as if autonomous.

However, '[t]he strong presence of the parent companies in upstream or downstream markets is a factor to be taken into consideration in assessing the full-function character of a joint venture where this presence results in substantial sales or purchases between the parent companies and the joint venture', although the Jurisdictional Notice recognizes that for an initial start-up period, which cannot exceed three years, the joint venture may rely 'almost entirely' on sales to or purchases from its parent companies, without that affecting its full-function character.[223]

Finally, the JV must be intended to operate on a lasting basis, which may be inferred from the fact that the parent companies provide the necessary resources to the JV to function in an economically autonomous way, or when the agreement specifies a period for the duration of the JV that is sufficiently long in order to bring about a lasting change in the structure of the undertakings concerned, among other elements.[224] By contrast, the JV will not be a full-function one, where it is established for a short finite duration.[225]

If the parties decide to enlarge the scope of the activities of the JV in the course of its lifetime, this will be considered as a new concentration that may trigger a notification requirement if this enlargement entails the acquisition of the whole or part of another undertaking from the parents, which, considered in isolation, could qualify as a concentration.[226] A similar outcome may arise 'if the parent companies transfer significant additional assets, contracts, know-how or other rights to the JV and these assets and rights constitute the basis or nucleus of an extension of the activities of the JV into other product or geographic markets which were not the object of the original JV, and if the JV performs such activities on a full-function basis'.[227]

The criteria for distinguishing JVs to be treated under the EUMR from those appraised under Article 101 TFEU were always unsatisfactory. Joint ventures may lead to integration, which may produce efficiencies—as may mergers. The fact that a JV is limited in time or scope should mean that *prima facie* there is less cause for concern, yet cooperative JVs may be subject to the stricter control under Article 101 TFEU.

It is not always clear under what regime a JV comes—a fact-intensive analysis of the market may be necessary to see whether the parents compete in adjacent markets and whether there would be sufficient incentives for them to coordinate their behaviour. This may require much work to be done before notification and also even during the short period allowed for an investigation under Phase I. If the parents transfer all the assets relating to a wide geographic and product market into a JV, the JV will have the resources it needs to be full function and parties will have left the market on a long-term basis. Hence the concentration will come

[222] Ibid, para 95.

[223] Ibid, para 97. The Jurisdictional Notice provides detailed guidelines on this assessment (ibid, paras 98–102).

[224] Ibid, para 103. [225] Ibid, para 104. [226] Ibid, para 106. [227] Ibid, para 107.

within the more lenient test of the EUMR if the thresholds of turnover are reached. The parties may even agree not to enter the relevant market or neighbouring markets, to establish that they have left the market for the long term, hence leading to more functions being entrusted to the JV than their clients would like on commercial grounds.

To that extent, the clarification of the regime regarding recently brought by the CJEU in *Austria Asphalt GmbH & Co OG v Bundeskartellamt*, is welcome.[228] The CJEU interpreted Article 3 EUMR as meaning that a JV must be analysed under the realm of the EUMR if it performs on a lasting basis all of the functions of an autonomous economic entity (thus satisfying the full-functionality test), regardless of whether the target pre-existed the transaction or is a newly created entity, the CJEU considering that the EUMR should apply to 'significant structural changes the impact of which on the market goes beyond the national borders of any one Member State.'[229] The case brings some clarity to some seemingly contradictory paragraphs of the Jurisdictional Notice,[230] clarifying that the acquisition of a controlling stake by a third party in an existing non-full-function undertaking is not caught by the EU merger control regime.

Note that a concentration may be invalid by virtue of Article 7(4) EUMR if not notified in the belief that a JV was collaborative, provided the Commission eventually finds that it is incompatible with the Internal Market. Normally, the parties talk to the Commission before filing their notification, so the position is usually sorted out informally.

12.2.1.7. Exceptions

Article 3(5) EUMR sets out three exceptional situations where the acquisition of a controlling interest does not constitute a 'concentration':[231]

(a) the acquisition of securities by companies whose normal activities include transactions and dealing in securities for their own account or for the account of others. The Commission explains that the acquiring undertaking must be a credit or other financial institution or insurance company, the securities acquired with a view to their resale, the acquiring undertaking must not exercise the voting rights with a view to determining the strategic commercial behaviour of the target company, and the acquiring undertaking must dispose of its controlling interest within one year of the date of the acquisition to a level which no longer offers control;

(b) when there is no change of control, and hence no concentration within the meaning of the Merger Regulation, where control is acquired by an office-holder according to the

228 Case C-248/16, *Austria Asphalt GmbH & Co OG v Bundeskartellamt*, ECLI:EU:C:2017:643.

229 Ibid, para 21.

230 Jurisdictional Notice, para 91, states that a transaction involving several undertakings acquiring joint control of another undertaking or parts of another undertaking from third parties will constitute a concentration according to Article 3(1) EUMR without it being necessary to consider the full-functionality criterion, while Jurisdictional Notice, para 92, stipulates that the full-functionality criterion delineates the application of the EUMR to the creation of a JV, irrespective of whether this is a newly created JV or whether the parties contribute assets to the JV which they previously owned individually. These paragraphs should now be interpreted in conformity with the CJEU's approach in Case C-248/16, *Austria Asphalt GmbH & Co OG v Bundeskartellamt*, ECLI:EU:C:2017:643, which applies the full-functionality test, irrespective of the fact that this jointly controlled undertaking pre-existed the transaction or is a newly created entity.

231 Jurisdictional Notice, paras 110–16.

law of a Member State relating to liquidation, winding-up, insolvency, cessation of payments, compositions, or analogous proceedings;

(c) where a financial holding company acquires control. This exception is limited to companies whose sole purpose it is to acquire holdings in other undertakings without involving themselves directly or indirectly in the management of those undertakings, without prejudice of course to their rights as shareholders. According to the Jurisdictional Notice, '[s]uch investment companies must be further structured in a way that compliance with these limitations can be supervised by an administrative or judicial authority' and they 'may exercise the voting rights in the other undertakings only to maintain the full value of those investments and not to determine directly or indirectly the strategic commercial conduct of the controlled undertaking.'[232]

These exceptions only apply if the operation would otherwise be a concentration in its own right, but not if the transaction is part of a broader, single concentration, and only to acquisitions of control by way of purchase of securities, but not to acquisitions of assets. They do not apply to typical investment fund structures, which, however, adopt decisions to appoint the members of the management and the supervisory bodies of the undertakings or to even restructure those undertakings.

One may note that these exceptions may raise concerns in an era of financialization of the economy and in view of the challenges raised by interlocking shareholdings and interlocking directorates, as well as the role of institutional investors (mutual funds and other investors) in the global economy, which may soften competition among product market rivals because of their significant ownership stakes in competing firms in concentrated industries.[233]

12.2.1.8. Minority shareholdings

The focus of EUMR on the acquisition of control, largely ignores the risks for competition associated with the acquisition of a passive minority interest[234] and the indirect and informal influence that may be exercised by passive investors without these having 'control', and which may lead to short-run unilateral effects, as well as other strategic effects long-term (including coordinated effects and foreclosure).

12.2.1.8.1. Economic foundations

The possible anti-competitive incentives created by cross ownership and common ownership in concentrated markets have been long recognized in theoretical literature;[235] but lacked

[232] Ibid, para 113. [233] See Section 12.2.1.8.1.

[234] OECD, 'Antitrust Issues Involving Minority Shareholdings and Interlocking Directorates', DAF/COMP(2008)30 (23 June 2009), 21.

[235] JJ Rotemberg, 'Financial Transaction Costs and Industrial Performance', Massachusetts Institute of Technology, Alfred P Sloan School of Management Working Paper No 1554-84 (1984); T Bresnahan and SC Salop, 'Quantifying The Competitive Effects of Production Joint Ventures' (1986) 4(2) *Int'l J Industrial Organization* 155; RJ Reynolds and BR Snapp, 'The Competitive Effects of Partial Equity Interests and Joint Ventures' (1986) 4(2) *Int'l J Industrial Organization* 141; RH Gordon, 'Do Publicly Traded Corporations Act in the Public Interest?', NBER Working Paper No 3303 (1990); DP O'Brien and SC Salop, 'Competitive Effects of Partial Ownership: Financial Interest and Corporate Control' (2000) 67 *Antitrust LJ* 559; E A Posner, F Scott Morton, and E Glen Weyl, 'A Proposal to Limit the Anti-Competitive Power of Institutional Investors' (2017) 81 *Antitrust LJ* 669; D Gilo, 'The Anticompetitive Effects of Passive Investment' (2000) 99 *Michigan L Rev* 1; D Gilo, Y Moshe, and Y Spiegel, 'Partial Cross Ownership and Tacit Collusion' (2006) 37 *Rand J Economics* 81.

sufficient empirical evidence.[236] Recent empirical analyses of the US airline industry[237] and banking industry[238] measured the potential (significant) effect of the common ownership on price levels rising above the competitive ones. These findings resulted in policy concerns expressed by economists,[239] and lawyers,[240] proposals for legislative intervention,[241] and criticism of the findings.[242] This has led some to suggest a new metric for measuring the growth of common ownership in oligopolistic firms, which may have important repercussions not only in the area of merger control, in particular if minority shareholdings falls under the scope of the EUMR, but more generally on broader aspects of public policy towards executive compensation and consolidation.[243]

There are four major mechanisms through which common or cross-ownership may be causing adverse effects to the economy: (1) unilateral/non-coordinated effects; (2) coordinated effects (tacit collusion); (3) vertical foreclosure through raising rivals' costs strategies; and (4) vertical exploitative behaviour (gaining higher profit margins at the expense of reduced

236 See the concerns expressed by SC Salop and DP O'Brien, 'Competitive Effects of Partial Ownership: Financial Interest and Corporate Control' (2000) 67 *Antitrust LJ* 559.

237 J Azar, MC Schmalz, and I Tecu, 'Anticompetitive Effects of Common Ownership' (2018) 73(4) *J Finance* 1513.

238 J Azar, R Raina, and MC Schmalz, 'Ultimate Ownership and Bank Competition' (23 July 2016), available at SSRN: https://ssrn.com/abstract=2710252.

239 Council of Economic Advisors, 'Benefits of Competition and Indicators of Market Power' (2016), available at https://obamawhitehouse.archives.gov/sites/default/files/page/files/20160414_cea_competition_issue_brief.pdf.

240 E Elhauge, 'Horizontal Shareholding' (2016) 129 *Harvard L Rev* 1267

241 EA Posner, F Scott Morton, and E Glen Weyl, 'A Proposal to Limit the Anti-Competitive Power of Institutional Investors' (2017) 81 *Antitrust LJ* 669.

242 EB Rock and DL Rubinfeld, 'Defusing the Antitrust Threat to Institutional Investor Involvement in Corporate Governance', NYU Law and Economics Research Paper No 17-05 (1 March 2017), available at https://ssrn.com/abstract=2925855; EB Rock and DL Rubinfeld, 'Antitrust for Institutional Investors'. NYU Law and Economics Research Paper No 17-23 (July 2017), available at https://ssrn.com/abstract=2998296.

243 SC Salop and DP O'Brien, 'Competitive Effects of Partial Ownership: Financial Interest and Corporate Control' [2000] 67 *Antitrust LJ* 559; EA Posner, F Scott Morton, and E Glen Weyl, 'A Proposal to Limit the Anti-Competitive Power of Institutional Investors' (2017) 81 *Antitrust LJ* 669, which suggest a modified version of HHI—or the MHHI, measuring the indirect form of market concentration through common ownership from large institutional investors. The test aims to measure the difference between MHHI and HHI, or in other words the portion of market concentration that is due to common ownership (or MHHIΔ). The intuition behind this test is that managers set commercial conduct to maximize profit of largest shareholders, who own stakes in rival companies, rather than maximizing the profit of their specific firm. See also M Anton, F Ederer, M Gine, and M Schmalz, 'Common Ownership, Competition, and Top Management Incentives', Ross School of Business Paper No 1328 (2016), showing that in construction, manufacturing, finance, and services, the average industry MHHIΔ has increased by more than 600 points from 1993 to 2014, thus showing an important growth in common ownership, which, according to the authors may explain the increase in CEO pay over the past decades. Intuitively, MHHIΔ is affected by three components. First, the higher the degree of concentration among commonly owned rivals and the larger the MHHIΔ. This is captured by the sum of the products of all the possible pairs of market shares (eg with four firms there are six combinations). Second, and most obvious, MHHIΔ is larger the higher the overall percentage shareholding quotas in rival firms that is controlled by common shareholders. This factor is captured by the sum of the products of all the possible pairs of percentage shareholding quotas in rival firms owned by the same institutional investors (eg with three institutional investors and four rival firms, there are eighteen possible combinations). Third, the presence of strong shareholders without shareholding quotas in rival firms reduces MHHIΔ, given that this category of shareholders expects the managers of the only firm they are invested in to maximize solely the profit of the firms in question. This is captured by the sum of the square of the individual shareholding positions in each rival.

margins for the competitive segment of the value chain), the fourth concern being relatively a newcomer in the literature.[244]

Cross-ownership. O'Brien and Salop[245] defined a framework where firms do not collude, either expressly or tacitly, yet the incentives driven by the cross ownership yield an anti-competitive outcome. In this framework, each firm sets its price independently and unilaterally, that is, on the assumption that its pricing decision will have no effect on the prices charged by its competitors. The key element of the framework is that the objective function of the firm's manager takes into account to which extent a firm's most powerful owners are also owners of natural competitors, and vice versa. The anti-competitive outcome in the framework is driven by the two aspects of the cross ownership: the financial and the control ones.

The financial mechanism is purely structural: cross ownership links the fortunes of actual or potential competitors, producing a positive correlation among their profits. The manager of the firm *A* thus has financial interest in other firms' profits that enters his incentives through the cross ownership, although this may warrant some more subtle analysis. For instance, if firm *A* owns some stock in firm *B* and the manager is judged on the total profit of firm *A*, then indeed *A*'s manager will behave less aggressively with *B*. However if the stock in *A* is only owned by some of the owners in *A*, then *A*'s manager only cares if these specific owners exert significant control or influence on *A*. The linking of profits gives each firm an incentive to compete less vigorously and adopt behaviour more conducive to joint profit maximization than otherwise would be the case.[246]

A second reason the acquisition might diminish competition arises if the acquisition gives firm *A*, some degree of corporate control over the management of other firms. This concerns situations where a firm would exercise its corporate governance powers in other firms in the market to restrain these firms' competitive actions against its profits.[247]

The financial incentive is more striking from the point of view of the economic theory. It suggests that the cross ownership has the capability to distort the incentives of the firms away from competition towards maximising a weighted sum of the owners' financial returns—through the returns from the firm itself but also through the returns from the other firms in the same market. This does not require any action from the cross owners.[248]

The O'Brien and Salop model incorporates both financial and control incentives through the assumption that the firm's manager weighs the interests of the firm's owners in the way that incorporates both their financial interest and their control over the firm.[249] The firm's manager objective function includes the weighted owners' earnings. The weight on each owner's profit in the manager's objective function can be interpreted as a measure of the degree of control or influence the owner has over the firm's managers. For example, in a case where the owner

244 I Lianos, A Velias, D Katalevsky, and G Ovchinikov, 'Financialisation of the food chain, common ownership and competition law', CLES Research Paper 2/2019.

245 DP O'Brien and SC Salop, 'Competitive Effects of Partial Ownership: Financial Interest and Corporate Control' (2000) 67 *Antitrust LJ* 559; T Bresnahan and SC Salop, 'Quantifying The Competitive Effects of Production Joint Ventures' (1986) 4 *Int'l J Industrial Organization* 155.

246 For the full framework of financial interest and corporate control, see RJ Reynolds and BR Snapp, 'The Competitive Effects of Partial Equity Interests and Joint Ventures' (1986) 4 *Int'l J Industrial Organization* 141.

247 For detailed discussion, see DP O'Brien and K Waehrer, 'The Competitive Effects of Common Ownership: We Know Less than We Think' (23 February 2017), available at https://ssrn.com/abstract=2922677.

248 Although one may also raise the question on why would a manager maximize such a weighted sum rather than care only about those in control.

249 DP O'Brien and SC Salop, 'Competitive Effects of Partial Ownership: Financial Interest and Corporate Control' (2000) 67 *Antitrust LJ* 559.

has no control over the manager, her weight in the manager's objective function consists only of her financial interest. This weight is consequently lower than the weight of an owner with the same ownership percentage (ie the same financial interest) but also with control over the governance (ie voting shares).

Common ownership. Until recently, there has not been a theoretical framework for evaluating the common ownership effects on the market processes described above. The recent theoretical work by Azar, Schmalz and Tecu attempts to fill this gap by developing a model of a firm behaviour in an oligopolistic setting where the firm aggregates the shareholder objectives, including the common ownership.[250] The framework posits the following premise: a common shareholder with equal shares in all firms in the market cannot benefit from competition and therefore will not encourage it. The mechanisms supporting this premise are hypothesized as follows. If one firm competes aggressively for market share, this share comes at the expense of the other firms in the market. The decrease in revenues for the other firms is, however, greater than the increase in revenues for the aggressively competitive firm. For example, in the simplest version of an oligopolistic market, two firms *A* and *B* are of equal size. If *A* undercuts *B*'s price to attract customers from *B*, it gains market share and many more products at this slightly reduced price. The average price on the market is lower, while the total number of customers remains the same. Hence, the effect on the total producer rents on the market is negative. Consequently, an investor holding equal-sized stakes in both *A* and *B* enjoys greater total (ie portfolio) profits when the firms set prices or quantities as if they were two divisions of a monopoly. The authors conclude that only separate owners have interest in aggressive competitive strategy. Crowding them out of the most powerful shareholders makes the firm lose support for the competitive strategy.

Note that in this model the economic incentive remains independent of any coordination or communications among the firms. The basic anti-competitive effects arise from the fact that interlocking shareholdings diminish each individual firm's incentives to cut prices or expand output by increasing the costs of taking away sales from rivals.

Also note that managers actively demanding reduced competition to drive up profit margins in the portfolio is not a single possible incentive and, this is not a necessary requirement for this model. In fact, managers may be driven by the desire for 'quiet life'.[251] This can result in omission to explicitly demand or incentivize tougher competition between portfolio firms, thus also leading to an equilibrium with reduced competition and sustained high margins.

An emerging branch of empirical research has recently demonstrated links between common ownership and industry-level profit margins[252] and firm-level profitability and market shares,[253] although the conclusions of this literature are still not unanimously accepted.[254]

250 J Azar, 'A New Look at Oligopoly: Implicit Collusion Through Portfolio Diversification' (8 November 2011), available at https://ssrn.com/abstract=1993364

251 JR Hicks, 'Annual Survey of Economic Theory: The Theory of Monopoly' (1935) 3(1) *Econometrica: J Econometric Society* 1; M Bertrand and S Mullainathan, 'Enjoying the Quiet Life? Corporate Governance and Managerial Preferences' (2003) 111(5) *J Political Economy* 1043.

252 J Azar, 'A New Look at Oligopoly: Implicit Collusion Through Portfolio Diversification' (8 November 2011), available at https://ssrn.com/abstract=1993364. See also, J Azar, MC Schmalz, I Tecu, 'Anticompetitive Effects of Common Ownership', (2018) 73(4) *J Finance* 1513.

253 J He and J Huang, 'Product Market Competition in a World of Cross-Ownership: Evidence from Institutional Blockholdings' (2017) 30 *Rev Financial Studies* 2674.

254 EB Rock and DL Rubinfeld, 'Defusing the Antitrust Threat to Institutional Investor Involvement in Corporate Governance'. NYU Law and Economics Research Paper No 17-05 (1 March 2017), available at https://ssrn.com/abstract=2925855.

12.2.1.8.2. The situation in the EU

The acquisition of minority shareholdings has been the focus of the European Commission lately,[255] as the Commission has identified an 'enforcement gap' in respect of this type of acquisitions, especially with regards to non-controlling minority shareholdings. The European Commission intends to improve the EU Merger Regulation's effectiveness by applying it to transactions that involve structural links.[256]

Structural links occur in transactions that do not meet the legal definition of acquisition of control or decisive influence, but in which, instead, the acquirer of non-controlling minority shareholdings, nevertheless, gains the possibility to exercise material influence over the target, which leads, potentially, to significant anti-competitive effects, although one may note that there is less risk of anti-competitive effects than in the context of a fully-fledged merger.[257] Indeed, it has been noted that

> [i]n a full merger scenario, the acquiring firm obtains 100% of the following types of rights over the target: i) 'control rights'; and ii) 'cash flow rights'. Control rights allow the acquirer to influence the target's strategic decisions; hence they provide the acquirer the ability to raise the target's prices. On the other hand, cash flow rights entitle the acquirer to have a financial interest—by means of its investment-and-share in the profits of the target hence they give the acquirer the incentive to raise the target's prices. Importantly, in the case of partial share ownership these two type of rights do not necessarily coincide, and their relative proportions may be rather asymmetrical depending on the particularities of each commercial transaction, or may even change from time to time. It follows that partial share ownership leads to two variants of the above-mentioned usual merger situation: i) it either gives only one type of rights (e.g. financial interests) but not the other one (e.g. control/influence); or ii) it gives partially both types of rights. This is crucial because the existence and the degree of each type of rights in a partial share acquisition have distinct competition implications in that any combination of financial interests and control rights leads to different anticompetitive effects.[258]

[255] European Commission, White Paper on Modernisation of the Rules Implementing Articles 85 and 86 of the EC Treaty, Commission Programme No 99/027 (28 April 1999), available at http://europa.eu/documents/comm/white_papers/pdf/com99_101_en.pdf.

[256] See Commission Staff Working Document, Impact Assessment, SWD(2014) 217 final (9 July 2014), Part 3, available at http://ec.europa.eu/competition/consultations/2014_merger_control/impact_assessment_en.pdf; P Ypma and I Kokkoris, *Support Study for Impact Assessment Concerning the Review of Merger Regulation Regarding Minority Shareholdings*, Final Report (2016), available at ec.europa.eu/competition/publications/reports/KD0416839ENN.pdf.

[257] It has been noted that '[a]cquisitions of non-controlling minority shareholdings account for approximately 10–12% of all mergers notified in Germany and 5% in the United Kingdom', the only jurisdictions (in addition to Austria) which currently have national merger control rules providing them the competence to review structural links, such as minority shareholdings. See Commission Staff Working Document, Impact Assessment, SWD(2014) 217 final (9 July 2014), para 38, available at http://ec.europa.eu/competition/consultations/2014_merger_control/impact_assessment_en.pdf. The Commission's 'rough' estimates indicate that the number of cases of minority shareholdings that would meet the turnover thresholds of the Merger Regulation should be around 20–30 (or 7–10 per cent of the merger cases currently examined by the Commission each year), which means that in case the jurisdiction of the EUMR was extended to these cases the Commission could intervene in another one to two cases per year (ibid, para 46).

[258] A Tzanaki,'The Legal Treatment of Minority Shareholdings under EU Competition Law: Present and Future' in *Essays in Honour of Professor Panayiotis I Kanellopoulos* (Sakkoulas, 2015), 861; A Tzanaki, *The Regulation of Minority Shareholdings and Other Structural Links Between Competing Undertakings: A Law & Economics Analysis* (PhD Thesis, University College London, September 2017).

The Commission has recognized a number of anti-competitive effects that may emerge out of minority shareholdings, including unilateral effects, coordinated effects and vertical foreclosure.

Commission Staff Working Document, Impact Assessment, SWD (2014) 217 final (9 July 2014)

22. There are several types of anti-competitive concerns that can result from the acquisition of minority shareholdings. The economic effects of minority shareholdings on competition in the market significantly depend on the financial interests flowing from them and the corporate rights conferred by them. While financial interests refer to the acquiring firm's entitlement to a share of the profits of the target firm, corporate rights refer to the acquiring firm's ability to influence the target firm's strategic decisions.

23. Structural links among competitors may lead to unilateral anti-competitive effects, since they may increase the ability and incentives of firms to unilaterally raise prices or restrict output. Intuitively, if firms have a financial interest in their competitors' profits, they 'internalise' the positive effects on their competitors' profits of a reduction in their own output or an increase in their own price. As a result, a firm with minority stakes in a competitor will have less of an incentive to compete vigorously and so will tend to reduce its competitive pressure, which will lead to price increases and output reductions in the market. This may occur irrespective of whether the minority shareholding is 'passive', ie the minority shareholder has no influence on the target firm's decisions, or whether it is 'active' and its holder may have some influence on the target firm's decisions.

24. In case of 'active' minority stakes the potential anti-competitive effects can also occur when the acquirer gains material influence over the outcome of special resolution decisions in the shareholders' meeting which are needed to approve certain strategies, for example in relation to significant investments, product lines, geographical scope, raising capital, engaging in mergers and acquisitions. As regards the ability to implement such as strategy, this depends on the specificities of the market and notably on the market position of the companies involved. The practice of the Commission and the Member States has shown that competition concerns are more likely to be serious when a minority shareholding grants some degree of influence over the target firm's decisions [. . .].

26. Competition concerns may also arise when the acquirer can use its minority shareholding position to limit the competitive strategies available to the target firm, thereby weakening it as a competitive force. [. . .]

29. Also, the most obvious way a minority shareholder can gain a competitive advantage in the market is through the ability to increase a rival's costs. In an extreme situation, if the costs of the target firm are sufficiently raised, this firm may actually decide to stop competing with the acquirer in the relevant market.

30. Horizontal minority participations may also lead to coordinated anti-competitive effects as they may impact on the ability and incentives of market participants to tacitly or expressly collude to achieve supra-competitive profits. The acquisition of a minority stake may enhance transparency as it typically offers the acquiring firm a privileged view on the commercial activities of the target. It may also make the threat of future retaliation more credible and severe in case a minority shareholder deviates from the collusive behaviour as firms may revert to a less collaborative behaviour in the jointly owned firm. Both effects will impact on the ability and incentives of market participants to coordinate.

> 31. Finally, non-horizontal transactions may lead to competition concerns, in particular in relation to input or customer foreclosure. The ability to implement a strategy based on foreclosing competitors from the target company's supply or demand depends on the influence resulting from the minority stake over business decision of the target company and on the ability to exercise this influence against the resistance of other stakeholders. Extensive information rights can also matter in this regard: The fear that commercially sensitive information ends up in the hands of a competitor, may deter companies from dealing with firms in which their competitors have minority stakes that entail such extensive information rights. In the case where the minority shareholding is purely 'passive' and its holder has no influence on the target firm's decisions, the expected competition concerns will be more limited than in a full merger, given the smaller financial incentives to foreclose. On the other hand, when the minority shareholding is 'active' and its holder has some influence on the target firm's decisions, the risk of foreclosure can actually be higher than what would occur with a fully-integrated firm. This is because, in some circumstances, input or customer foreclosure may be more likely to occur since the company acquiring the minority shareholding only internalises a part, rather than all, of the target firm's profits while it receives the full benefit of foreclosure.

Minority shareholdings can, under the current European competition regime be addressed with one of the following ways:[259]

- They may give 'decisive influence' in terms of the Merger Regulation, constituting a concentration.
- They can be part of the substantive analysis of a concentration, for example minority shareholdings relevant to the SIEC assessment.
- There have been cases where the merging parties have been willing to dispose of, or reduce, their stakes either before or during the phase I administrative proceedings, so as to obtain unconditional merger clearance;[260] or to give formal commitments to divest, as a condition of clearance.[261] However, had the same stake(s) been acquired post-acquisition, the Commission would lack powers to intervene.[262]
- Under the Commission's remedial powers, the Commission cannot order the unwinding of a non-controlling shareholding that was part of a failed takeover: (i) the remaining stake does not confer control over the target, and (ii) the proposed takeover has been prohibited and thus not fully implemented. The *Ryanair/ Aer Lingus* cases have identified this problem.[263] Ryanair acquired shares in Aer Lingus on the stock exchange and

[259] See A Burnside, 'Minority Shareholdings: An Overview of EU and National Case Law', *e-Competitions Bulletin* (17 September 2013), Article No 56676.

[260] *Courtaulds/SNIA* (Case M.113) Competition Decision (19 December 1991) (disposal of a 12 per cent stake in a competitor); *Banco Santander/Abbey National* (Case M.3547) Competition Decision (17 September 2004) (modification of cooperation agreement between Santander and RBS, including termination of reciprocal board representation and reduction of Santander's shareholding in RBS). (References cited in A Burnside, 'Minority Shareholdings: An Overview of EU and National Case Law', *e-Competitions Bulletin* (17 September 2013), Article No 56676.)

[261] *VEBA/VIAG* (Case M.1673) Competition Decision (13 June 2000) (disposal of various minority stakes to address concerns about joint dominance); *IPIC/MAN Ferrostaal* (Case M.5406) Competition Decision (13 March 2009) (divestment of MAN Ferrostaal's 30 per cent stake in Eurotecnica, a company involved in melamine production technology licensing and plant engineering, to address vertical concerns). (References cited in A Burnside, 'Minority Shareholdings: An Overview of EU and National Case Law', *e-Competitions Bulletin* (17 September 2013), Article No 56676.)

[262] M Friend, 'Regulating Minority Shareholdings and Unintended Consequences' (2012) 33(6) *European Competition L Rev* 303, 304–5.

[263] See Section 12.3.5.2.

in parallel launched a public bid. Although initially only notifying the bid, the European Commission asserted jurisdiction over the combined stake-plus-offer, treating these as a single concentration, and prohibiting that concentration. While the offer therefore fell away, the question remaining was as to the stake. Although this had been part of a prohibited concentration, the Commission took the view that, once standing in isolation, it could not be the subject of a sell-down order under Article 8(4) EUMR (unwinding of completed/prohibited concentrations), because by itself it did not confer control. This position was upheld by the General Court.[264]

- Article 101 can apply to agreements by which a minority interest is acquired and Article 102 TFEU can apply to acquisitions by a dominant company. In the *Philip Morris* and the *Gillette* cases, Articles 101 and 102 TFEU have been specifically applied to minority shareholdings giving rise to 'some (informal) influence' over the target, which could be lower than the 'decisive influence' (control) threshold under the EUMR. However Article 101 cannot be invoked unless there is a finding of an 'agreement' and/or 'concerted practice' between two or more 'undertakings' linked to the minority share acquisition. Similarly, Article 102 is only applicable if there is a 'dominant' undertaking which is found to be 'abusive'.

In the *Philip Morris* judgment in 1984,[265] the European Court of Justice held that although the mere acquisition of a minority stake could not of itself be said to amount to conduct restricting competition (for the purposes of Article 101), it could nevertheless serve as an instrument for influencing the commercial conduct of a competitor, thereby restricting or distorting competition, in particular where the agreement provided for commercial cooperation, or where it gave the acquiring shareholder the possibility of taking effective control of the target at a later stage. The Court emphasized the need to consider not just the immediate effects of the transaction, but also the longer-term potential impact.

Article 101 TFEU applies to a number of agreements by which a minority interest is acquired:

- Joint ventures, where formal 'joint' control in the EUMR sense is lacking. Typically, these will involve parents with holdings in a common vehicle.
- Production-only joint ventures—with joint control, but lacking full functionality.
- A shareholding anchoring a commercial relationship, for example supplier/customer, strategic alliances.
- Complex ownership structures contrived to achieve a merger while avoiding a transfer of 'control'.
- Holding structures in which a company *de facto* neutralizes a competitor.
- Simple acquisition of a shareholding when sold by a single vendor.[266]

As regards the possible application of Article 102 TFEU, the Court held that the acquisition of a minority shareholding in a competitor could only amount to an abuse where it resulted in effective control, or at least some influence, over the target's commercial policy, although the

264 Case T-411/07, *Aer Lingus Group Plc v European Commission* [2011] ECR II-03691, paras 77–8, 84–5, 87, and the corresponding Commission decision in *Ryanair/Aer Lingus* (Case COMP/M.4439) (27 June 2007)

265 Cases 142 & 156/84, *British American Tobacco Co Ltd v Commission of the European Communities* [1987] ECR 4487.

266 A Burnside, 'Minority Shareholdings: An Overview of EU and National Case Law', *e-Competitions Bulletin* (17 September 2013), Article No 56676, at 2, who notes that although Article 101 TFEU seems not to apply when the minority shareholding is acquired through the stock exchange by buying a rival's shares from a number of unidentified counterparties, this is still an unsettled issue.

judgment offered no guidance on what level of influence would be problematic, or how the assessment was to be carried out.[267]

In the *Warner-Lambert v Gillette* case,[268] the Commission successfully challenged Gillette's acquisition of a 22 per cent non-voting interest in the parent company of its major competitor, Wilkinson Sword, both as an infringement of Articles 101 and 102 TFEU. It is worth noting that there were various other commercial agreements in place, including an unsecured loan and the acquisition of certain trademarks outside the European Union and United States, but fell short of control.

The Commission examined in great detail the possible anti-competitive effects of common shareholding in the recent *Dow/DuPont* merger case, both in its decision and also in an Annex attached to its decision.[269] The Commission's starting point was that the industry shares tend to underestimate the expected non-coordinated effects of the merger given the significant cross shareholding between the main players. The Commission provided factual evidence on the significant level of common shareholding in the agrochemical industry and on the involvement of large minority shareholders which, despite some being known as 'passive investors', are in fact 'active owners'. The Commission noted that presence of a significant level of common shareholding tends to lower rivalry. This finding was first based on the economic literature on cross-shareholdings, 'which extends to common shareholding', and which 'tends to show that common shareholding of competitors reduces incentives to compete as the benefits of competing aggressively to one firm come at the expense of firms that belong to the same investors' portfolio'.[270] This literature has been discussed in great detail in the previous Sections of this Chapter.

The Commission further took into account some recent empirical studies[271] providing indications that the presence of significant common shareholding in an industry is 'likely to have material consequences on the behaviour of the firms in such industries',[272] leading to the possibility of higher prices, in view of the fact that common shareholders tend to shape the monetary incentives of firms' executives in order to align them with industry performance, and not only their firm's specific performance.[273]

Quite interestingly, the Commission transposed this literature, which has focused on price effects to the situation of innovation competition, which allegedly may also be reduced by such cross-ownership and by common ownership.[274] The narrative goes as follows:

> [. . .] by increasing its efforts in R&D, a firm incurs a cost that decreases its current profits in expectation of future benefits brought by the resulting products of its innovation. Such future benefits would necessarily materialise through price competition of future products which,

267 A few other examined similar cases are: *Enichem/ICI* (Case IV/31.846) Competition Decision [1988] OJ L 50/18; *BT/MCI* (Case IV/34.857) Competition Decision [1994] OJ L 223/36; *Olivetti/Digital* (Case IV/34.410) Competition Decision [1994] OJ L 309/24; and *Phoenix/Global One* Case IV/35.617 [199] OJ L 239/57. (References cited in A Tzanaki,'The Legal Treatment of Minority Shareholdings under EU Competition Law: Present and Future' in *Essays in Honour of Professor Panayiotis I Kanellopoulos* (Sakkoulas, 2015), 861.)

268 *Warner-Lambert/Gillette* (Case IV/33.440) Commission Decision [1996] OJ L 116/21.

269 *Dow/DuPont* (Case M.7932) Commission Decision (27 March 2017).

270 Ibid, para 2348.

271 See, in particular, J Azar, MC Schmalz, and I Tecu, 'Anticompetitive Effects of Common Ownership' (2018) 73(4) *J Finance* 1513.

272 *Dow/Dupont* (Case M.7932) Commission Decision (27 March 2017), para 2349.

273 See M Anton, F Ederer, M Gine, and M Schmalz, 'Common Ownership, Competition, and Top Management Incentives', Ross School of Business Working Paper No 1328 (1 June 2018), available at https://ssrn.com/abstract=2802332.

274 *Dow/Dupont* (Case M.7932) Commission Decision (27 March 2017), para 2350.

> given the specificities of the agrochemical industry, in particular the fact that the total size of the crop protection industry is typically not related to innovation, is likely to be mainly at the expense of its competitors. In other words, the decision taken by one firm, today, to increase innovation competition has a downward impact on its current profits and is also likely to have a downward impact on the (expected future) profits of its competitors.
>
> This, in turn, will negatively affect the value of the portfolio of shareholders who hold positions in this firm and in its competitors. Therefore, as for current price competition, the presence of significant common shareholding is likely to negatively affect the benefits of innovation competition for firms subject to this common shareholding.[275]

Hence, for the Commission, the concentration measures, such as market shares or the HHI, are likely to underestimate the level of concentration of the market structure and, thus, the market power of the merging parties. In view of the fact that common shareholding is a reality in the agrochemical industry, both in terms of the number of common shareholders as well as with respect to the level of shares possessed by these common shareholders, the Commission took this into account as an element of context in the appreciation of any significant impediment to effective competition, noting that in the context of innovation competition, such findings provide indications that innovation competition in crop protection should be less intense as compared with an industry with no common shareholding.[276]

12.2.1.8.3. The situation in the UK

Under the UK law (Enterprise Act 2002), minority shareholdings will be subject to merger control where 'material influence' can be exercised over the acquired business. The 'Merger Assessment Guidelines',[277] provide guidance on the authorities' assessment of 'material influence' focusing mainly on the importance of voting rights and board representation. Factors that may be relevant to an assessment of a particular shareholding include the distribution and holders of the remaining shares, in particular whether the acquiring entity's shareholding makes it the largest shareholder; patterns of attendance and voting at recent shareholders' meetings based on recent shareholder returns, the existence of any special voting or veto rights attached to the shareholding under consideration; the status and expertise of the acquirer; and its corresponding influence with other shareholders.[278]

In both *Sky*[279] and *Ryanair/Aer Lingus*,[280] the Competition Commission has focused its assessment on a different theory of harm. In Sky it found a significant lessening of competition due to a loss of rivalry between ITV and BSkyB in the all-TV market. In *Ryanair/Aer Lingus* it found that, given the on-going hostility between Ryanair and Aer Lingus, neither unilateral nor coordinated effects had been experienced or were to be expected.

275 Ibid, para 2351; Annex 5, para 59.

276 Ibid, para 2352.

277 CoCo and OFT, Merger Assessment Guidelines, CC2 (revised)/OFT 1254 (September 2010), paras 3.2.8–3.2.10.

278 Ibid, para 3.2.10.

279 BSkyB acquisition of nearly 18 per cent of its competitor ITV. See CoCo, *Acquisition by British Sky Broadcasting Group plc of 17.9 per cent of the shares in ITV plc*, Report (14 December 2014), available at http://webarchive.nationalarchives.gov.uk/20140402234126/http:/www.competition-commission.org.uk/assets/competitioncommission/docs/pdf/non-inquiry/rep_pub/reports/2007/fulltext/535.pdf.

280 Competition Commission Report, *Ryanair Holdings plc/Aer Lingus Group plc* (23 August 2013), available at http://static.rasset.ie/documents/news/ukccreport.pdf.

Rather, the analysis focused on the obstacles which an unwelcome shareholder can pose to the company freely pursuing its own commercial objectives. The CoCo concluded that by limiting Aer Lingus's ability to pursue its independent commercial policy and strategy, Ryanair's minority shareholding would have led to a reduction in Aer Lingus's effectiveness as a competitor.[281]

12.2.1.8.4. The situation in the US

It is interesting to note that section 7 of the Clayton Act, as amended by the Celler-Kefauver Anti-merger Act of 1950 and then in 1980, adopted against a backdrop of increasing concern towards concentration of US businesses, prohibits not only acquisitions by one corporation of the stock of another, but also, more broadly acquisitions of assets where the 'effect of such acquisition may be substantially to lessen competition, or to tend to create a monopoly'.[282] This provision captures acquisitions by natural persons, partnerships, as well as other unincorporated associations and business entities, and not just by corporations. Contrary to the situation in the UK, there is no express shareholder percentage ownership trigger or a 'material influence' test but it is the value of the acquisition that may trigger a filing under the Hart–Scott–Rodino (HSR) Act, which parties to a transaction must submit to the US Federal Trade Commission and the US Department of Justice if certain jurisdiction tests are met. The Clayton Act's coverage for partial acquisitions is, however, limited if the acquisition was made 'solely for investment'.[283] The HSR Act includes an exemption from filing for a partial acquisition if the acquirer shows that the acquisition was made solely for the purpose of investment and that it will result in ownership of 10 per cent or less of the voting securities of the issuer,[284] this percentage being 15 per cent for institutional investors, as their intention is presumed not to be for investment only. Furthermore, to benefit from the exemption, the stock must not be used 'by voting or otherwise to bring about, or in attempting to bring about, the substantial lessening of competition', the parties arguing for the exemption being required to prove that the purpose of the acquisition was not to gain control over the target company.[285]

One may also note another type of structural link targeted by US merger control, 'interlocking directorates', that is situations where an individual or entity serves on the Board or as an officer of two competing corporations, a situation that may emerge with the recent financialization trend, with private equity and hedge funds often investing in various companies active in the same industry. Under section 8(a)(1) of the Clayton Act, '[n]o person shall, at the same time, serve as a director or officer in any two corporations (other than banks, banking associations, and trust companies) that are [. . .] by virtue of their business and location of operation, competitors, so that the elimination of competition by agreement between them would constitute a violation of any of the antitrust laws [. . .]'.[286] The statute is interpreted as applying not only to natural 'persons' or individuals, but also to a 'firm'. There are a number of exemptions, however, to the prohibition and liability (for banks, banking associations, and

[281] Ibid, paras 7.16–7.24. [282] 15 USC § 18. [283] 15 USC § 18.

[284] This presumption is narrowly construed and does not apply if the issuer whose stock is being acquired is a competitor of the acquirer.

[285] See *United States v Dairy Farmers of America*, 426 F.3d 850 (6th Cir 2005), para 49, noting that 'even without control or influence, an acquisition may still lessen competition' and constitute a violation of section 8 of the Clayton Act.

[286] 15 USC § 19(4).

trust companies or when the 'competitive' sales of the interlocked firms fail to meet some thresholds (*de minimis* exceptions).

12.2.1.8.5. Concluding thoughts on minority shareholdings and cross-ownership

The Merger Regulation's Jurisdictional Notice recognizes that '[s]ole control can be acquired on a de jure and/or de facto basis'.[287] With regard to *de facto* basis, the Commission's Jurisdictional Notice further stipulates that the Commission should assess whether 'the [minority] shareholder is highly likely to achieve a majority at the shareholders' meetings, given the level of its shareholding and the evidence resulting from the presence of shareholders in the shareholders' meetings in previous years'. Indeed, '[w]here, on the basis of its shareholding, the historic voting pattern at the shareholders' meeting and the position of other shareholders, a minority shareholder is likely to have a stable majority of the votes at the shareholders' meeting, then that large minority shareholder is taken to have sole control'.[288]

A further element to take into account is the importance of shareholder fragmentation on effective control, in particular on the aspect resulting from voting, the Commission finding in the past that an institutional investor was able to exercise decisive influence over the target with only controlling 39 per cent shares, when the rest was spread among more than 100 000 shareholders.[289] In a similar vein, the Commission found that a capital participation of 25.96 per cent was such as to lead to a change of ownership of control, in particular due to the participation in general meetings.[290] A dispersion of voting rights among a large number of small shareholders, also led the Commission to accept that effective voting rights of 34 per cent by RTL (although it held 48.39 per cent of the shares, the voting rights were limited by regulation) could signal control, in particular on the basis of past record of shareholders' presence and the very unlikely possibility of their coalescence to reach a majority of the votes.[291] A merger transaction may of course increase the level of participation of certain shareholders in the new entity, and eventually its possibility to establish control.

But more than just a story of a simple minority shareholding leading to an effective control of the company's strategy, the issue is if it is also possible to find an anti-competitive effect on the basis of the presence of common institutional investors in all significant players in a specific market, that is, through a partial competitor ownership. It is accepted that cross ownership may give rise to anti-competitive effects, paragraph 20(c) of the EU Horizontal Merger Guidelines state that:

> [t]he Commission is [. . .] unlikely to identify horizontal competition concerns in a merger with a post-merger HHI between 1000 and 2000 and a delta below 250, or a merger with a post-merger HHI above 2000 and a delta below 150, except where special circumstances such as, for instance, one or more of the following factors are present: [. . .] (c) there are significant cross-shareholdings among the market participants [. . .].

287 Jurisdictional Notice, para 55. 288 Ibid, para 59.

289 See *Arjomari/Wiggins Teape Appleton* (Case IV/M.025) Commission Decision [1990] OJ C 321/16; *Saint Gobain/Poliet* (Case IV/M.764) Commission Decision [1996] OJ C 225/8.

290 *Société Générale de Belgique/Générale de Banque* (Case IV/M.343) Commission Decision [1993] OJ C 225/2.

291 *RTL/M6* (Case M.3330) Commission Decision [2004] OJ C 95/35.

Cross-shareholding is also mentioned as a possible facilitator of possible coordinated effects, in the sense that it provides an information channel amongst competitors,[292] and that it provides 'help in aligning incentives among the coordinating firms'.[293]

The causal mechanism is explained in the Commission's decision in *Dow/DuPont* Annex 5:

> For the sake of the argument, assume that a firm (the acquiring firm) acquires a minority share in a competitor (the partially acquired firm). When contemplating a price increase, the acquiring firm anticipates that part of its customers will react to this price increase by diverting their purchase to its competitors, which will see their sales increase, including the one in which it has a minority share. The extra profits generated by the diverted sales to the benefit of the partially acquired firm will, in turn, be partially redistributed to the acquiring firm. As a consequence, when holding a minority share in a competitor, the acquiring firm has higher incentives to increase its prices than in the absence of such a minority share.[294].

Hence, '[t]he impact on the acquired firm's incentives depends on how the transaction affects the governance of the acquired firm, that is on the acquiring firm's degree of control, which can range from no control at all (silent financial interest), to partial control, to total control'.[295]

In its White Paper—Towards More Effective EU Merger Control released in 2014, the Commission advocated for a targeted transparency system which will be well suited to capture such transactions and to prevent consumer harm arising from them. The White Paper put forward three procedural options for the control of minority shareholdings:

> - 'A notification system, which would extend the current system of *ex ante* merger control to acquisitions of non-controlling minority shareholdings under certain conditions.
> - A transparency system, which would require parties to submit an information notice informing the Commission of acquisitions of non-controlling minority shareholdings. The information notice would enable the Commission to decide whether to further investigate the transaction, enable the Member States to consider a referral request, and enable potential complainants to come forward.
> - A self-assessment system, which would not require parties to notify acquisitions of non-controlling minority shareholdings in advance of completion. The Commission could, however, initiate an investigation of potentially problematic minority shareholding acquisitions on the basis of its own market intelligence or complaints.[296]

In order to provide parties with legal certainty, only a transaction which meets the following cumulative criteria would fall within the definition of a 'competitively significant link':

> - acquisitions of a minority shareholding in a competitor or vertically related company (i.e. there needs to be a competitive relationship between acquirer and target); and

[292] Horizontal Merger Guidelines, Recital 47. [293] Ibid, Recital 48. [294] Ibid, para 43.
[295] Ibid, para 45.
[296] European Commission, White Paper—Towards More Effective EU Merger Control, COM(2014) 449 final (9 July 2014), para 43, available at ec.europa.eu/competition/consultations/2014_merger_control/mergers_white_paper_en.pdf.

- the competitive link would be considered significant if the acquired shareholding is (1) around 20 per cent or (2) between 5 per cent and around 20 per cent, but accompanied by additional factors such as rights which give the acquirer a 'de-facto' blocking minority, a seat on the board of directors, or access to commercially sensitive information of the target.[297]

The parties would be required to self-assess whether a transaction creates a 'competitively significant link' and, if so, submit an information notice. In the event that an information notice is submitted, the Commission would then decide whether to investigate the transaction and the Member States would decide whether to make a referral request.[298] The theme of minority shareholdings was, however, omitted in the most recent merger control consultation launched by Commissioner Vestager, therefore bringing the process of reform of EUMR on this issue to a standstill.[299]

The literature discussed above has also triggered a number of proposals for legislative interventions, of varying levels of stringency. Elhauge[300] takes a radical stand claiming that stock acquisitions that create anti-competitive horizontal shareholdings should be considered illegal under current antitrust law. He thus calls for the break-up of the existing shareholdings, citing a range of negative outcomes such as corporate executives being rewarded for industry performance rather than individual corporate performance alone, corporations not using recent high profits to expand output and employment, and economic inequality rising in recent decades.

Posner, Scott Morton, and Weyl[301] question whether direct application section 7 of the Clayton Act would be a right measure, or would cause disruption on the markets whilst failing to eliminate most of the harms from common ownership. They present evidence from simulations of the market outcomes deriving the sufficient anti-monopolistic conditions for the model used by Azar and his co-authors.[302] Their simulation-driven evidence suggests that limiting investors to holding up to 1 per cent of a company's equity per oligopoly or shares of a single company in any oligopoly is a sufficient condition. They, therefore, propose a public enforcement policy granting a safe harbour to the investors who voluntarily reduce their portfolio to either of the two conditions. Note, however, that picking a single company in a sector raises important market-definition questions. As conversely pointed out in recent media discussions: 'Can you invest in both Facebook and Google, or are they in the same industry?'[303] Should we rely on relevant markets, rather than industries, instead?

Rock and Rubinfeld[304] propose a much wider safe harbour. They suggest protection from antitrust liability for the investors whose ownership share is below 15 per cent, provides

297 Ibid, para 47. 298 Ibid, para 48.

299 See European Commission, 'Consultation on Evaluation of Procedural and Jurisdictional Aspects of EU Merger Control' (07 October 2016–13 January 2017), available at http://ec.europa.eu/competition/consultations/2016_merger_control/index_en.html.

300 E Elhauge, 'Horizontal Shareholding' (2016) 129 *Harvard L Rev* 1267.

301 EA Posner, F Scott Morton, and E Glen Weyl, 'A Proposal to Limit the Anti-Competitive Power of Institutional Investors' (2017) 81 *Antitrust LJ* 669.

302 J Azar, MC Schmalz, and I Tecu, 'Anticompetitive Effects of Common Ownership' (2018) 73(4) *J Finance* 1513.

303 M Levine, Index Funds May Work a Little Too Well', *Bloomberg View* (22 July 2015), available at https://www.bloomberg.com/view/articles/2015-07-22/index-funds-may-work-a-little-too-well.

304 EB Rock and DL Rubinfeld, 'Antitrust for Institutional Investors', NYU Law and Economics Research Paper No 17-23 (July 2017), available at https://ssrn.com/abstract=2998296.

no board representation, and who only engage in 'normal' corporate governance activities. Notably, this approach does not remove the financial incentive aspect of common ownership, concentrating purely on the corporate control. The proposed limitations on the voting right behind the shares also fails to address the concern that shareholders may simply fail to exercise their corporate governance rights in the way that prioritizes a profit-maximizing strategy for a single firm over the industry performance. Elhauge[305] discusses such an example of DuPont's diversified shareholders rejected an activist effort to (arguably) compete harder against Monsanto. Besides, the institutional investors such as index funds would argue that they owe to their individual investors the protection of their interests, thus requiring good governance from the firms that they invest into. Voting rights, thus, is the instrument they can use to exercise the interests of their investors.

There are also significant concerns about market distortions that can be caused by either form of legislative intervention. Posner et al[306] raise an important concern about potential interventions leading to a single investor's act of becoming a significant common owner without taking a direct action, but simply led by actions of other investors on the market. The authors warn that private litigation or unguided public litigation could cause problems because of the interactive nature of institutional holdings on competition. Given that the proposed MHHI indexes evaluate market concentrations through the relative weights of investor portfolios, the investment of one institutional investor in competing firms affects the amount by which another institutional investor 'lessens competition' with its investments in the same industry. Consequently, institutions could become liable simply because other institutions changed their holdings and thereby made an industry less competitive. A stringent legislation that transfers responsibility onto institutional investors to determine other institutions' ownership shares and expected volatility, would put them into a difficult position lacking clarity about where they can legally invest.

12.2.2. EU DIMENSION

The Merger Regulation uses a bright-line test based on certain turnover thresholds to distinguish concentrations with an EU dimension from those subject to national merger scrutiny. The turnover thresholds include the so-called 'two-thirds rule', leaving cases to Member States' jurisdiction where all the undertakings concerned achieve two thirds of their turnover in a single Member State. The jurisdictional thresholds are also complemented by a case referral system that allows re-allocation of individual cases when the bright-line test fails. Moreover, the Commission in order to reduce the inconvenience and costs introduced a simplified procedure for the treatment of concentrations that do not raise competition concerns. If a concentration qualifies for a simplified procedure, the Commission will adopt a short-form decision. As the Jurisdictional Notice points out the turnover is used as a proxy for the economic resources being combined in a concentration and is allocated geographically in order to reflect the geographic distribution of other resources.[307]

305 E Elhauge, 'Horizontal Shareholding' (2016) 129 *Harvard L Rev* 1267

306 EA Posner, F Scott Morton, and EG Weyl, 'A Proposal to Limit the Anti-Competitive Power of Institutional Investors' (2017) 81 *Antitrust LJ* 669.

307 Jurisdictional Notice, para 124.

12.2.2.1. Turnover thresholds

Article 1(2) sets out the primary test, looking at the combined worldwide turnover of the undertakings concerned and the EU-wide turnover of at least two of the undertakings involved in the transaction. Specifically, a concentration has a Community dimension where: (i) the combined aggregate worldwide turnover of all the undertakings concerned is more than €5000 million; and (ii) the aggregate Community-wide turnover of each of at least two of the undertakings concerned is more than €250 million, unless each of the undertakings concerned achieves more than two-thirds of its aggregate Community-wide turnover within one and the same Member State. The Commission, however, has been concerned about the application of this exception, known as two thirds rule, as it may entail that concentrations between large national players can escape the Commission's scrutiny under EU merger control, despite their effects on competition across EU,[308] that is, to the extent that the merging firms could enter each other's markets absent the merger.

A set of alternative thresholds are set out under Article 1(3), specifically: (a) the combined aggregate worldwide turnover of all the undertakings concerned is more than €2500 million; (b) in each of at least three Member States, the combined aggregate turnover of all the undertakings concerned is more than €100 million; (c) in each of at least three Member Stares the aggregate turnover of each of at least two of the undertakings concerned is more than €25 million; and (d) the aggregate Community-wide turnover of each of at least two of the undertakings concerned is more than €100 million.

Under Article 5(1), turnover is defined as the amounts derived by the firms concerned in the preceding financial year from the sale of products and the provision of services falling within their ordinary activities after deduction of sales rebates and of value added tax and other taxes directly related to turnover. Article 5(2) then provides that where the concentration consists of the acquisition of parts, whether or not constituted as legal entities, of one or more firms, only the turnover relating to the parts which are the subject of the concentration shall be taken into account with regard to the seller or sellers.

For the purpose of calculating the turnover of the undertaking(s) acquiring control, the turnover relating to all entities belonging to the group must be considered.[309] Article 5(4) sets out the criteria for identifying firms belonging to the same group. These criteria are not to be conflating with the concept of control under Article 3.

Commission Consolidated Jurisdictional Notice under Council Regulation No 139/2004 on the control of concentrations between undertakings [2008] OJ C 95/1

> 184. Article 5(4) sets out specific criteria for identifying undertakings whose turnover can be attributed to the undertaking concerned. These criteria, including the 'right to manage the undertaking's affairs', are not coextensive with the notion of 'control' under Article 3(2). There are significant differences between Articles 3 and 5, as those provisions fulfil different roles. The differences are most apparent in the field of de facto control. Whereas under Article 3(2) even a situation of economic dependence may lead to control on a de facto basis (see in detail above), a solely controlled subsidiary is only taken

308 See in particular European Commission, Commmunication—Report to Council on the Functioning of Regulation 139/2004, COM(2009) 281 final (18 June 2006), para 16.

309 For more detail, see Jurisdictional Notice, paras 175–83.

into account on a de facto basis under Article 5(4)(b) if it is clearly demonstrated that the undertaking concerned has the power to exercise more than half of the voting rights or to appoint more than half of the board members. Concerning joint control scenarios, Article 5(4)(b)(iv) covers those scenarios where the controlling undertakings jointly have a right to manage on the basis of individual veto rights. However, Article 5(4) would not cover situations where joint control occurs on a de facto basis due to strong common interests between different minority shareholders of the joint venture company on the basis of shareholders' attendance. The difference is reflected in the fact that Article 5(4)(b)(iv) refers to the right to manage, and not a power (as in subparagraph (b)(ii) and (iii)) and is explained by the need for precision and certainty in the criteria used for calculating turnover so that jurisdiction can be readily verified. Under Article 3(3), however, the question whether a concentration arises can be much more comprehensively investigated. In addition, situations of negative sole control are only exceptionally covered (if the conditions of Article 5(4)(b)(i)–(iii) are met in the specific case); the 'right to manage' under Article 5(4)(b)(iv) does not cover negative control scenarios. Finally, Article 5(4)(b)(i), for example, covers situations where 'control' under Article 3(2) may not exist.

In UK merger law, there are two alternative rules setting out the dimensional threshold beyond which a merger qualifies for review, specifically: (i) either the UK turnover of the target firm exceeds £70 million ('the turnover test'); or (ii) the merged entity has a market share of at least 25 per cent and the merger must also result in an increment to that market share ('the share of supply test').[310] These thresholds have been recently changed for businesses developing military and dual-use technology, computing hardware, and quantum technology in the context of the 2018 amendments to section 23 of the Enterprise Act (relevant merger situations), and the introduction of new sub-sections (2A), (2B), (4A), and (4B), as well as a new section 23A, by two Amendment Orders in 2018 in view of ensuring that the Government has sufficient powers to deal with mergers resulting in a relevant enterprise ceasing to be distinct, when this poses threats to the national security of the UK.[311] The changes apply to mergers in the business areas indicated above, bringing the 'target business' UK turnover from £70 million to £1 million, and no longer requiring that the merger must lead to an increase in the merging parties' share of supply to, or over, 25 per cent.[312] These amendments only involve changes to the jurisdictional thresholds for merger scrutiny under the Enterprise Act and do not change any other aspects of the UK merger regime, although a second series of changes to the substantive standard have also been recently suggested in the government's White Paper on National Security and Investment.[313] The process first involves the issuing of a public interest

310 CMA, Guidance—Mergers: The CMA's Jurisdiction and Procedure (CMA 2) (10 January 2014), para 4.3, available at www.gov.uk/government/uploads/system/uploads/attachment_data/file/384055/CMA2__Mergers__Guidance.pdf.

311 Enterprise Act 2002 (Share of Supply Test) (Amendment) Order 2018, available at https://www.legislation.gov.uk/ukdsi/2018/9780111167441/contents, and the Enterprise Act 2002 (Turnover Test) (Amendment) Order 2018, available at https://www.legislation.gov.uk/uksi/2018/593/contents/made. See also the Guidance published by the Department of Business, Energy and Industrial Strategy, Enterprise Act 2002: Changes to the Turnover and Share of Supply Shares for Mergers (Guidance 2018), available at https://assets.publishing.service.gov.uk/government/uploads/system/uploads/attachment_data/file/715174/EA02_guidance.pdf.

312 Ibid, Section 1.8.

313 Secretary of State for Business, Energy and Industrial Strategy, White Paper on National Security and Investment—A Consultation on Proposed Legislative Reforms (July 2018), available at https://www.gov.uk/government/consultations/national-security-and-investment-proposed-reforms.

intervention notice by the Secretary of State, leading to a 'Phase 1' report from the CMA, and in case no satisfactory undertakings are suggested by the parties, to a further 'Phase 2' investigation by the CMA, following which the Secretary of State can accept final undertakings or make orders to remedy, mitigate, or prevent any adverse effects to the public interest or (in extremis) block the merger altogether.[314]

12.2.2.2. Reform of the turnover thresholds

The Commission has been recently envisaging changes to the turnover thresholds, as concerns have been raised periodically, especially in relation to transactions that include large companies in the digital and pharma sectors which, however, do not meet the threshold requirements and therefore escape the Commission's scrutiny. In this respect, the Commission recently launched a consultation on 'procedural and jurisdictional aspects of EU Merger Control',[315] which proposes the introduction of a deal-size threshold in the EUMR to capture significant acquisitions where the target does not meet the current turnover-based thresholds. This is particularly relevant for innovative markets where commercial success rests on the ability to achieve a critical mass of users, so that the value of the target company depends more on the growth expectations in the long-term base rather than short-term revenue per user. The consultation follows a number of comments by Commissioner Vestager.[316]

The UK CMA is also envisaging a reform of the UK thresholds.[317] The UK merger control regime recognizes that in certain circumstances the CMA may not refer a merger, for instance when it believes the relevant market is of insufficient importance, this exception to the duty to refer being designed to avoid investigations where the costs involved would be disproportionate to the size of the market concerned. This enables the CMA to reduce the burden on companies and better target its resources for protecting consumers and businesses. The CMA is free not to apply this exception in certain circumstances. The CMA has recently sought comments on amendments to its guidance that raise the threshold for markets generally considered as sufficiently important to justify a merger reference to above £15 million from the current £10 million. It also suggests to change the threshold for markets generally considered not sufficiently important from below £3 million to below £5 million. If the size of the market is between these two thresholds, the CMA assesses whether the expected harm resulting from the merger would be greater than the cost of an investigation.

314 For a detailed analysis, see the companion volume, I Lianos, *Competition Law Enforcement and Procedure* (OUP, forthcoming 2019).

315 See European Commission, 'Consultation on Evaluation of Procedural and Jurisdictional Aspects of EU Merger Control' (07 October 2016–13 January 2017), available at ec.europa.eu/competition/consultations/2016_merger_control/index_en.html.

316 See her recent criticism of the *Facebook/WhatsApp* merger, Margrethe Vestager, EU Commissioner, 'Refining the EU Merger Control System', Speech, Brussels (10 March 2016), suggesting reviewing the notification threshold system as the acquisition was valued at approximately 22 billion dollars. Vestager suggested a system where additional factors, such as deal value or impact on innovation, should form part of the notification threshold. This merger was not caught under the turnover threshold of the EUMR, but was eventually assessed by the Commission as a result of a case referral.

317 See CMA, 'CMA Consults on Changes to Merger Investigations in Smaller Markets', Press Release (23 January 2017), available at www.gov.uk/government/news/cma-consults-on-changes-to-merger-investigations-in-smaller-markets.

12.2.3. CASE REFERRALS TO THE COMMISSION OR NATIONAL AUTHORITIES

As outlined above, under the EUMR a bright-line test based on certain turnover thresholds is used to distinguish concentrations with an EU dimension, thus subject to the Commission's exclusive jurisdiction,[318] from those below the turnover thresholds and this subject to national merger scrutiny. This clear division of competence is known as the 'one-stop-shop' principle. The turnover thresholds include the so-called 'two-thirds rule', leaving cases to Member States' jurisdiction where all the undertakings concerned achieve two thirds of their turnover in a single Member State.

The jurisdictional thresholds are also complemented by a case referral system that allows re-allocation of individual cases when the bright-line test fails. In line with the principle of subsidiarity, there are therefore circumstances in which at the initiative, or invitation of the Commission, the Member States or parties a concentration with an EU dimension or aspects of it may be referred to a national authority for assessment under its domestic merger control, or a concentration without an EU dimension may be referred to the Commission.

The Commission published a Notice on Case Referrals[319] to provide some guidance on its policy, the circumstances under which a case referral should be assessed and other practical considerations.

The case re-attribution system provides that a referral may also be triggered before a formal filing has been made in any Member State jurisdiction, thereby affording merging companies the possibility of ascertaining, at as early as possible a stage, where jurisdiction for scrutiny of their transaction will ultimately lie. Such pre-notification referrals have the advantage of alleviating the additional cost, notably in terms of time delay, associated with post-filing referral.[320] The desire is that it is a jurisdictional mechanism which is flexible but at the same time ensures effective protection of competition and limits the scope for 'forum shopping' to the greatest extent possible. However, having regard in particular to the importance of legal certainty, referrals remain a derogation from the general rules, which determine jurisdiction based upon objectively determinable turnover thresholds. Moreover, the Commission and Member States retain a considerable margin of discretion in deciding whether to refer cases falling within their original jurisdiction, or whether to accept to deal with cases not falling within their original jurisdiction.[321]

According to the Commission in most cases, jurisdiction should be re-attributed to another competition authority when it is the more appropriate for dealing with a merger, having regard to the specific characteristics of the case as well as the tools and expertise available to the authority.[322] Particular regard should be had to the likely locus of any impact on competition resulting from the merger and the implications, in terms of administrative effort, of any contemplated referral. Nevertheless, referral decision should also have regard to the benefits inherent in a 'one-stop shop', which is at the core of the Merger Regulation.[323]

The EUMR provides for case-referrals from and to the Commission both at pre and post-notification stage. The illustration below shows how the case referral system works:

[318] EUMR, Article 21.

[319] Commission Notice on Case Referral in respect of concentrations [2003] OJ L 53/02 [hereinafter Referral Notice].

[320] Ibid, Recital 6. [321] Ibid, Recital 7. [322] Ibid, Recital 9. [323] Ibid, Recital 11.

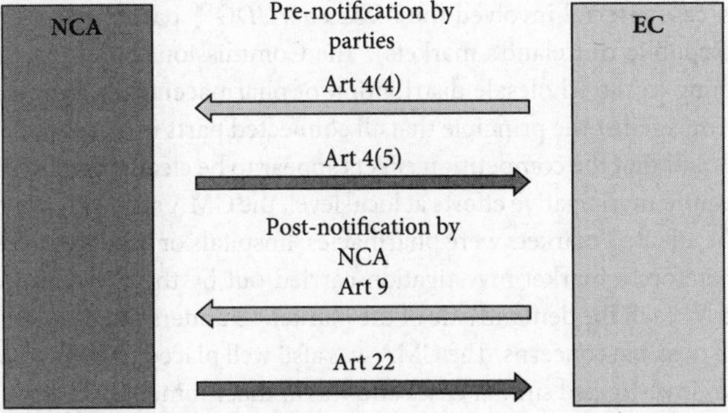

Figure 12.1. The EUMR referral system
Each of these referral procedures is examined in Section 12.2.3.1. For a more detailed analysis, see I Lianos, *Competition Law Enforcement and Procedure* (OUP, forthcoming 2019).

12.2.3.1. Post-notification referrals to the national competition authority under Article 9

Article 9[324] referrals deal with a situation where there are separate national markets and a merger specifically raises concerns with one of them,[325] typically in light of the appreciable differences of the merging firms' market shares between the area concerned and neighbouring areas or of substantial price differences.[326]

The Commission has the discretion to refer to the Member State a concentration relying on the considerations set out above, however, in cases where the affected distinct market does not constitute a substantial part of the Internal Market,[327] the Commission must refer the whole or part of the case.[328]

When assessing whether any market forms a substantial part of the common market, the Commission, in the past, considered factors such as the economic importance of the services and territories concerned, the volume of cross-border trade concerned, as well as general geographic factors. In *Lidl/Plus Romania/Plus Bulgaria* the Commission claimed that such situations are generally limited to markets with a narrow geographical scope, within a Member State and considered that the twelve local affected markets in Romania are small markets, situated within Romania, with a very limited, if any, volume of cross-border trade, and targeting a limited number of customers in the respective geographical areas, and therefore concluded that these markets did not constitute substantial parts of the common market.[329]

324 Also known as the 'German clause' as Article 9 was included in the EUMR after the request of the German.

325 Referral Notice, para 37. 326 EUMR, Article 9(7). 327 Ibid, Article 9(2)(b).

328 Ibid, Article 9(3)(b).

329 *Lidl/Plus Romania/Plus Bulgaria* (Case M.5790) Commission Decision C(2010) 4528 (28 June 2010), paras 26–7. See also *Schuitema/Super de Boer Assets* (Case M.5677) Commission Decision C(2010) 477 (25 January 2010), paras 38–40. In *Thomas Cook/Travel business of Co-operative Group/Travel Business Midlands Co-operative Society* (Case M.5996) Commission Decision C(2011) 85 final (6 January 2011), the application of EUMR, Article 9(2)(b) was also discussed but the Commission did not take a position as it had already decided to refer the case to the UK authority pursuant to Article 9(3)(b).

A recent UK case referral involved the *McKesson/UDG*[330] partial referral to the UK (not including the Republic of Ireland's markets). The Commission found that fragmenting the analysis pertaining to the wholesale distribution of pharmaceuticals and related services in the UK would run against the principle that all connected parts of a case to be dealt with by a single authority and that the competition effects appear to be clearly in the UK. In addition as the case may require investigative efforts at local level, the CMA seemed to be best placed. The customers in the affected markets were pharmacies, hospitals or end-consumers in Northern Ireland, and therefore a market investigation carried out by the CMA appeared to be best suited to properly reach the demand side of the market, to understand its main characteristics and to deal with possible concerns. The CMA was also well placed to assess the transaction, as it had previously investigated similar cases and was at that moment investigating the markets at stake (the *Celesio's/Sainsbury's* merger).[331]

More recently, the Commission rejected the CMA's request for a referral of the *Hutchison 3G UK/Telefonica UK* merger, involving respectively the smallest and the second largest among the four UK mobile network operators.[332] At that time, the CMA was also investigating the *BT/EE* merger, where the fixed telephone incumbent acquired the largest mobile phone operator. The Commission rejected the CMA's argument of the necessity of ensuring consistency between these two transactions and the possibility of obtaining a better package of commitments as the CMA had already provisionally decided that the *BT/EE* merger did not raise competition issues. The Commission stressed its experience and the fact that it had already started the investigation in this transaction. The Commission also emphasized its particular interest in competition in the telecoms sector (notably the Digital Single Market) and its concerns for increased concentration in this industry.[333]

12.2.3.2 Post-notification referrals to the Commission under Article 22

Under the Article 22[334] procedure a Member State one or more Member States may request the Commission to examine any concentration without an EU dimension but that affects trade between Member States and threatens to significantly affect competition within the territory of the Member State or States making the request.[335]

In *Dolby/Doremi*,[336] a merger between two suppliers of hardware and software for cinemas and theatres, the UK joined Spain's request for a referral to the Commission. The Commission accepted the request as the proposed transaction essentially affected two product markets which were at least European Economic Area-wide, if not larger. Moreover, an assessment of the proposed transaction by the Commission would increase administrative efficiency, avoid duplication and fragmentation of enforcement effort, as well as potentially incoherent treatment (regarding investigation, assessment and possible remedies) by multiple authorities. In particular the Spanish authority would have encountered difficulties to design and implement

330 *McKesson/UDG Healthcare* (Case M.7818) Commission Decision C(2016) 1475 final (3 March 2016).

331 Ibid, paras 65–72.

332 *Hutchison 3G UK/Telefonica UK* (Case M.7612) Commission Decision C(2015) 8534 final (4 December 2016).

333 Ibid, paras 58–63.

334 Usually called as the 'Dutch clause' as this provision has been requested by the Dutch.

335 EUMR, Article 22(1).

336 *Dolby/Doremi* (Case M.7297) Commission Decision C(2014) 8095 final (27 October 2014).

effective remedies in the case at hand given that the assets of the merged entity were located outside Spain.[337]

In *Olympic/Aegean II*,[338] a merger between two Greek airlines, Greece and Cyprus jointly requested for a referral to the Commission. The Commission accepted the request taking into account the inherently international nature of air transport, the effects of concentrations between major carriers often extending beyond a single Member State's borders, the need for consistency the significant restructuring of the European air transport sector and the previous knowledge of the Commission (as it had previously examined all aspects of the contemplated merger between the merging parties in 2010).[339]

Conversely, in *Coca Cola Hellenic Bottling Company/Lanitis bros*,[340] the Commission rejected the request as the main competitive impact of the operation appeared to be in Cyprus with regard to the markets of cola drinks, fruit juices, beer, and dairy products. Moreover it was not established that the transaction could give rise to serious competition concerns in a number of Member States and no other Member State has joined the referral request made by Cyprus. Therefore, there would be no added value in the case being examined at EU level.[341]

Article 22 allows for partial referrals. In *ABF/GBI Business*,[342] the Netherlands, France, and Portugal joined a referral request by Spain, whereas Germany initiated its own investigation. The Commission and the German authority cleared the merger subject to conditions. As the Commission investigated the transaction on behalf of the referring Member States and the affected markets were national, it was reckoned that the two parallel investigations did not interfere with each other.

However, if the affected market is wider than national, the Commission will investigate the effects of the transaction in the Member States that have not referred the case.[343] It is also worth noting that the Commission can investigate mergers for countries where the transaction did not have to be notified in the first place. While it is not yet clear whether a referral request can only be made by countries in which a transaction has to be notified, it is non-debatable that any other Member State can join other Member State's request, independent of whether the transaction is subject to a national investigation.

12.2.3.3. Pre-notification referrals under Article 4

Article 4(4) gives the right to notifying parties to make a reasoned submission to the Commission, instead of notifying a concentration with an EU dimension that a concentration may significantly affect competition in a distinct market in a Member State and should be examined in whole or in part by that Member State. It's worth noting that no request under Article 4(4) EUMR has been rejected by the Commission so far.

In *Arriva Rail North/Northern Franchise*,[344] the Commission agreed to refer the merger between two rail operators to the UK competition authority taking into account the

337 Ibid, paras 35–6.

338 *Olympic/Aegean II* (Case M.6796) Commission Decision (9 October 2012).

339 Ibid, paras 25–7.

340 *Coca Cola Hellenic Bottling Company/Lanitis bros* (Case M.4124) Commission Decision (24 February 2006).

341 Ibid, paras 21–3.

342 *ABF/GBI Business* (Case M.4980) Commission Decision C(2008) 5273 (23 September 2007).

343 Referral Notice, Recital 50. See eg *GEES/Unison* (Case M.2738) Commission Decision (17 April 2004).

344 *Arriva Rail North/Norther Franchise* (Case M.7897) Commission Decision C(2016) 532 final (27 January 2016).

point-to-point nature of the markets for the supply of public passenger transport services, overlaps between the parties' networks presented all the characteristics of distinct markets and were likely to be narrower than national. Each of the Northern routes began and ended in the UK, not passing through other Member States. The CMA was considered best placed to examine the case due to the substantial experience in examining the market for the provision of passenger transport services in the UK. Moreover, the Commission had taken the step of referring the matter to the UK competition authorities in other similar cases.[345]

Article 4(5) allows for the notifying parties to ask the Commission to deal with a merger without an EU dimension but which is capable of being reviewed under the national competition laws of at least three Member States. The case for referral is particularly compelling where there can be cross-border competition effects.[346]

The Notice stresses that in any case, indications of possible competitive impact may be no more than preliminary in nature, and would be without prejudice to the outcome of the investigation. Nor would it be necessary for the parties to demonstrate that the effect on competition is likely to be an adverse one. The parties to the concentration might submit that, despite the apparent absence of an effect on competition, there is a compelling case for having the operation treated by the Commission, having regard in particular to factors such as the cost and time delay involved in submitting multiple Member State filings.

12.2.4. PUBLIC INTEREST

12.2.4.1. The legitimate interests exception in the EUMR

Member States have the opportunity to intervene also pursuant to Article 21(4) which permits Member States to take appropriate measures to protect their legitimate interests, other than those taken into consideration by the EUMR, so long they are compatible with EU law.

Article 21(4) contains a list of legitimate interests (also known as the 'recognized interests'). These are: (a) public security; (b) plurality of media; and (c) prudential rules for financial services such as the banking and insurance sectors.

If a Member State wishes to claim an additional legitimate interest, other than the ones listed above, it shall communicate this to the Commission. And the Commission must then decide, within twenty-five working days, whether the additional interest is (a) compatible with EU law; and (b) qualifies as an Article 21(4) legitimate interest.

If the legitimate interest is one of those listed in Article 21(4) or the Commission decides that an additional interest meets the criteria, the Commission retains all jurisdiction to investigate whether the concentration gives rise to competition concerns and the Member State may carry out a parallel investigation.

Member States can only invoke this provision to scrutinize the transaction and eventually prohibit the merger, rather than as a way to authorize a merger on public interest grounds. Only eight Commission decisions have allowed a Member State to involve Article 21(4) successfully so far and none since 2007.

In *Newspaper Publishing*,[347] the Commission cleared the acquisition of Newspaper Publishing by Mirror Group Newspapers, but accepted that the UK authorities could take measures under the merger provisions, as the transaction involved issues such as the news presentation and the

345 Ibid, paras 27–30. 346 EUMR, Recitals 16 and 27.

347 *Newspaper Publishing* (Case M.423) Commission Decision (14 March 1994).

free expression of opinion. In *News Corp/BSkyB*,[348] the Commission also accepted the additional review of media plurality issues by UK authorities. Thus, even if the Commission cleared the NewsCorp/BSkyB transaction without remedies, considering that NewsCorp's increased shareholding would not significantly impede effective competition, NewsCorp offered undertakings to the UK Secretary of State to remedy the potential threats to media plurality identified by Ofcom.[349]

In *Antonio de Sommer Champalimaud/Banco Santander Central Hispanioamericano*,[350] Portugal took measures in order to block a financial restructuring that would give the Spanish bank Santander joint control over a Portuguese insurance company. Portugal justified its action on the basis of prudential rules. However, the Commission rejected the application of prudential rules legitimate interest by arguing that Portugal's intention was to hamper foreign ownership on Portugal's finance sector and ordered Portugal to suspend the measures and clear the acquisition. Portugal subsequently brought an action for annulment to the Court of Justice.[351] The Court upheld the Commission's decision by finding that Portuguese rules providing for a manifestly discriminatory treatment of investors from other Member States restricted free movement of capital, and that arguments based on the need to safeguard the financial interests cannot serve as a justification for restrictions on freedom of movement.[352]

The Court also confirmed that the Commission is entitled, even in in the absence of any communications of interest by the Member State,[353] to adopt a decision under Article 21 EUMR assessing whether measures taken by a Member State are compatible with Article 21(4) and requiring a Member State to withdraw measures.[354]

There are a few other cases where Member States have attempted to bring other legitimate interests into merger control. In *Lyonnaise des Eaux/Northumbrian Water*[355] the Commission accepted that the UK had a legitimate interest in complying with the Water Industry Act 1991 as to the sufficient number of independent water enterprises needed for efficiency comparisons to be made.

In *Unicredit/HVB*,[356] Poland ordered UTraiCredit to sell its shares in a Polish subsidiary of HVB, alleging that it had breached its obligations under a non-compete clause in a previous privatization agreements. The Commission found Poland's measures in breach of UniCredit's rights of establishment and free movement of capital and noted that Poland had not notified it of any legitimate interest.

In *Edf/London Electricity*,[357] the UK claimed a legitimate interest of the need to regulate modification of an electricity company's statutory licence when that company was party to a merger notifiable to the EU. The Commission found that such regulatory concerns were arising post merger rather than from the merger itself therefore, rejected the UK's claimed interest.

348 *News Corp/BSkyB* (Case M.5932) Commission Decision C(2010) 9684 (21 December 2010).

349 See 'Proposed Acquisition by News Corporation of up to 60.9 per cent of British Sky Broadcasting Group PLC', available at https://www.gov.uk/government/uploads/system/uploads/attachment_data/file/72994/News_Sky_1_March_UIL_for_consultation.pdf

350 *Antonio de Sommer Champalimaud/Banco Santander Central Hispanioamericano* (Case M.1616) Commission Decision [1999] OJ C 306/37.

351 Case C-42/01, *Portugal v Commission* [2004] ECR I–6079.

352 Case C-367/98, *Commission v Portugal* [2002] ECR I–4731.

353 Case C-42/01, *Portugal v Commission* [2004] ECR I–6079, para 57.

354 For another case, where the Commission went against conditions imposed by Spanish authorities on potential investors under regulatory powers in respect of already cleared by the Commission bids see *E.ON/ENEL/Acciona* (Cases M.4110 and M.4197) Commission Decision (2006). The Commission found that these actions were not justified by the need to protect the security of supply risks alleged and were contrary to the capital and establishment provisions. The Court of Justice confirmed the Commission's decision in Case T-65/08, *Spain v Commission* [2008] ECR I–41.

355 *Lyonnaise des Eaux/Northumbrian Water* (Case M.567) Commission Decision (21 December 1995).

356 *UniCredito/HVB* (Case M.3894) Commission Decision (18 October 2005).

357 *Edf/London Electricity* (Case IV/M.1346) Commission Decision (27 January 1999).

Note that the EU institutions have recently reached a political agreement on an EU framework for screening foreign direct investment in order to ensure that the EU and its Member States are equipped to protect their essential interests, which would, among others, allow the Commission to issue opinions in cases concerning several Member States, or when an investment could affect a project or programme of interest to the whole EU, while reaffirming the role of EU Member States in putting in such screening.[358]

12.2.4.2. The public interest test in the UK

The Enterprise Act 2002 effected a major reform of the control of mergers and takeovers, removing the decision-making powers of Ministers, save in defined exceptional cases, and passing this responsibility to the competition authority. Under section 58 EA 2002 the Secretary of State can intervene in mergers where they give rise to certain specified public interest concerns: specifically, issues of national security; media quality, plurality, and standards; and financial stability. In these cases the Secretary of State may make an assessment of a merger purely on the grounds that it runs counter to the public interest, without deferring to the 'substantial lessening of competition' test, or they may give regard to both tests in coming to a final decision. The recently proposed acquisition of Sky Plc by 21 Century Fox, Inc, raised interesting issues with regard to the assessment of the merger on public interest grounds, due to concerns about media plurality and the genuine commitment to broadcasting standards.[359] Following the procedure envisaged in section 58 of the Enterprise Act, the Secretary of State for for Digital, Culture, Media and Sport accepted the CMA's recommendation to clear the merger with structural and behavioural remedies. This decision was due to the fact that, following the analysis of the CMA,[360] the merger was expected to operate against the public interest, in particular with regard to the reduction in the diversity of viewpoints available to and consumed by the public, and the possibility of an increased influence of the Murdoch Family Trust over public opinion and the UK's political agenda.[361] One of the remedies envisaged involved the divestiture of Sky News and its acquisition by Disney or another buyer on completion of the transaction.

In recent years there have been calls to reintroduce a broader test in relation to concerns about the takeover of British companies by foreign multinationals, such as the takeover of UK-based Cadburys by US-based Kraft Foods in January 2010, or the failed attempt by UK-based AstraZeneca to be sold to the US-based Pfizer or the most recent attempt of the $143 billion bid for Unilever by Kraft Heinz (now withdrawn).[362] More recently, following the

[358] Commission, Commission welcomes agreement on foreign investment screening framework (20 November 2018), IP/18/6467.

[359] *21st Century Fox/Sky merger inquiry*, CMA (closed 5 June 2018), available at https://www.gov.uk/cma-cases/twenty-first-century-fox-sky-merger-european-intervention-notice.

[360] For an analysis, see *21st Century Fox/Sky merger inquiry* CMA Phase 2 Report (1 May 2018), available at https://www.gov.uk/government/publications/cma-phase-2-report.

[361] See 'Update on proposed mergers between 21st Century Fox and Sky, plc', Oral statement to the Parliament (5 June 2018), available at https://www.gov.uk/government/speeches/update-media-mergers. The CMA had indeed find that the Murdoch Family Trust 'already has significant influence over public opinion and the political agenda through its existing control of the News Corp titles. *The Times, The Sunday Times, The Sun*, and *The Sun on Sunday* together are one of the most read group of newspapers, and that readership covers a broader audience than any other media enterprise involved in the supply of newspapers. News Corp newspapers also have a significant online presence'. This influence was also 'highlighted by a large number of third parties, including politicians and political advisers': *21st Century Fox/Sky merger inquiry*, CMA Phase 2 Report (1 May 2018), paras 78 and 81, available at https://www.gov.uk/government/publications/cma-phase-2-report.

[362] For a detailed report, see A Seedy, 'Mergers & takeovers: the public interest test', Briefing Paper 05374 (1 September 2016), available at researchbriefings.files.parliament.uk/documents/SN05374/SN05374.pdf.

referendum vote to leave the EU, the new Prime Minister Theresa May indicated the intention to change the regulation of takeovers.[363] On the same day Japan's SoftBank announced a £24 billion bid for the Cambridge-based tech company ARM Holdings. It was reported that the acquiring firm offered the UK Government a 'series of legally binding assurances to maintain Arm's headquarters, double its UK-based staff over the next five years and increase its overseas headcount.'[364] Following a consultation on a Green Paper published in October 2017,[365] on 24 July 2018, the UK government published a White Paper on National Security and Investment, where it put forward proposals for a new framework on assessing the impact of foreign takeovers on national security.[366] The government proposals emphasize that '[n]ational security is not the same as the public interest or the national interest.'[367] Hence, should these reforms be adopted, the Government will remove national security considerations from the public interest and special public interest regimes under the Enterprise Act 2002.[368] As it is explained in the White Paper, 'the CMA will remain the independent and expert authority responsible for competition assessments (and its role in public interest interventions related to media plurality and financial stability will remain unchanged)' but '[n]ational security matters are for the Government to assess.'[369] The assessment of these conditions will be done by a 'Senior Minister' of cabinet level, who will act as the decision-maker in this new framework, the White Paper mentioning the Secretaries of State, the Chancellor, and the Prime Minister (none of whom are Secretaries of State).[370] The White Paper puts forward a number of 'trigger events' significantly expanding the circumstances in which the government currently has powers to intervene to protect national security. These would include the following:[371]

- the acquisition of more than 25 per cent of the votes or shares in an entity;
- the acquisition of significant influence or control over an entity;
- the acquisition of further significant influence or control over an entity beyond the above thresholds;
- the acquisition of more than 50 per cent of an asset; and
- the acquisition of significant influence or control over an asset.

The aim of this proposed legislative framework is to ensure that the control of assets cannot be used to undermine the national security of the UK.

363 T May, Conservative Party, 'Together We Can Make Britain a Country that Works for Everyone', Speech, Birmingham (11 July 2016), available at press.conservatives.com/post/147947450370/we-can-make-britain-a-country-that-works-for. For a different view, see A Chisholm, former CMA Chief Executive, Speech given at the Fordham Competition Law Institute Annual Conference (11 September 2014), available at www.gov.uk/government/speeches/alex-chisholm-speaks-about-public-interest-and-competition-based-merger-control.

364 A Massoudi, J Fontanella-Khan, and R Waters, 'SoftBank to acquire UK's Arm Holdings for £24.3bn', *Financial Times* (18 July 2016).

365 Department for Business, Energy and Industrial Strategy, National Security and Infrastructure Investment Review, Green Paper (October 2017), available at https://assets.publishing.service.gov.uk/government/uploads/system/uploads/attachment_data/file/652505/2017_10_16_NSII_Green_Paper_final.pdf.

366 Secretary of State for Business, Energy and Industrial Strategy, White Paper on National Security and Investment—A Consultation on Proposed Legislative Reforms (July 2018), available at https://www.gov.uk/government/consultations/national-security-and-investment-proposed-reforms.

367 Ibid, para 4 of the Executive Summary. 368 Ibid, section 11.04.

369 Ibid, section 11.07. 370 Ibid, section 6.08. 371 Ibid, section 3.12.

12.3. MERGERS OF COMPETITORS

The EU Guidelines on the assessment of horizontal mergers apply to concentrations where the parties compete, or can potentially compete, on the same relevant market.[372] According to Article 2 EUMR, the ultimate purpose of merger control is to preserve and enhance the good functioning of the Single Market by preventing concentration that would result in a SIEC.

Traditionally, this meant looking at whether the merger in question would result in the creation or strengthening of a dominant position held by the post-merger entity. Besides this standard case, a merger could be challenged on the basis that it would result in the creation or strengthening of a position of collective dominance in an oligopolistic setting.[373]

12.3.1. THE CASE FOR REFORMING THE EUMR SUBSTANTIVE TEST

However, a substantive test limited to the assessment of a dominant position would fail to capture mergers leading to a SIEC whilst not giving rise to a position of dominance, not even of collective dominance. This can especially occur where the structure of the market before the merger is oligopolistic and the merger in question increases the degree of concentration whilst reducing the degree of asymmetry among firms' market shares. For example, in a market with four firms with market shares of 40 per cent, 25 per cent, 20 per cent, and 15 per cent, the merger between the two smallest firms would hardly create or strengthen a position of individual dominance, as the post-merger entity would have a share of 35 per cent, thus still below than the one of the largest firm. Furthermore, although the symmetry among firms' market shares has increased post-merger, the conditions needed for the creation of a position of collective dominance might not be in place, for example, because it is very difficult to monitor rivals' prices due to private bilateral negotiations. Nevertheless, the merger in question may weaken competition where all firms sell close substitute products whilst facing constraints in expanding output in the short term, so that firms compete by setting in advance the quantities they want to sell (eg commodity).

A second set of circumstances where a dominance test may fail to block a merger leading to a SIEC is where firms' product offerings are differentiated, either because they cater to consumers taste for variety (called horizontal product differentiation) and/or because of different levels of price-quality ratios (called vertical product differentiation). When products are differentiated it is usually not the case that rivals' product offering are all close substitutes, but there will be varying patterns of substitution. For example, an independent cinema catering for sophisticated tastes may be a closer substitute to a small chain of upmarket single screen cinemas than a large chain operating multiplex premises catering for a variety of tastes, whilst regular customers of the small upmarket chain would not mind going to a multiplex every now and then. With reference to the simple example above, market shares based on revenues from ticket sales or number of available seats may provide a poor proxy for the actual pattern of substitutions. Therefore, the merger between the two smallest firms may well lead to a SIEC where their two product offerings are particularly close substitutes, although the merging entity would still fall short of individual dominant position due to competitive constraint

372 Horizontal Merger Guidelines, para 5.

373 Ibid, para 4.

still exercised by the largest non-merging firm (the multiplex), albeit to a lesser extent on the smallest merging firm (the independent establishment).

These crude examples help understand why it was felt important to broaden the substantive test in order to be able to capture these type of 'gap' cases. Accordingly, the new SIEC test introduced in Article 2(3) EUMR demoted the creation or strengthening of a dominant position to that of an explicit important cause of a SIEC, albeit no longer exclusively so. This compromise allowed the Commission to extent the substantive test,[374] whilst maintaining continuity with the previous decisional practice and case law based on dominance.[375]

12.3.2. THE COUNTERFACTUAL ASSESSMENT

The ultimate goal of merger control is to preserve the intensity of competitive rivalry (the process of competition) to the benefit of consumers. This entails that a SIEC would ultimately be detrimental to consumers because the merger that caused it would bring a combination of higher prices, lower quality, lower level of output, weaker rate of innovation and, where consumers exhibit a strong taste for variety, smaller range of choices.[376] The ability of firms to worsen these competition parameters without damaging their profitability entails that their market power has increased post-merger. The time horizon over which consumer detriment may materialize is typically taken to be two to three years after the merger.[377]

The assessment as to whether a merger would give rise to a SIEC is based on a counterfactual analysis where the post-merger scenario is compared to a hypothetical scenario absent the merger in question. The latter is normally taken to be the same as the situation before the merger is consummated.[378] However, the Commission would take into account future changes to the market that can reasonably be foreseen.[379] A classic example is where the target company to be acquired is expected to exit the market absent the merger.[380] In contrast, where entry is conditional on regulatory approval subject to certain conditions being met, future entries can be expected where potential competitors are at an advanced stage in the regulatory approval process.[381] Another example could be the coming into force of a new regulatory requirement at a future date which is expected to materially affect in a foreseeable way how firms compete in the market. The identification of the proper counterfactual can be complicated by the fact that there can be more than one merger occurring in parallel in the same relevant market. Under the mandatory notification regime, the Commission does not factor into the counterfactual analysis merger notified after the one under assessment.[382]

On the basis of the identified counterfactual, the Commission then proceed with the definition of the relevant product and geographic market, which is a propaedeutic step to inform the subsequent competitive assessment of the merger.[383] This is structured as follows:[384]

374 EUMR, Recital 25. 375 Ibid, Recital 26; Horizontal Merger Guidelines, paras 3 and 4.

376 Horizontal Merger Guidelines, para 8.

377 See A Lindsay and A Berridge, *The EC Merger Regulations: Substantive Issues* (Sweet & Maxwell, 3rd ed, 2009), para 2-035.

378 Horizontal Merger Guidelines, para 9. 379 Ibid.

380 *Deloitte & Touche/Andersen (UK)* (Case COMP/M.2810) Commission Decision (1 July 2002), paras 45–8.

381 See eg *Glaxo Wellcome/SmithKline Beecham* (Case IV/M.1846) Commission Decision (8 May 2000), paras 70–2; *Bayer/Aventis Crop Science* (Case COMP/M.2547) Commission Decision (17 April 2002), paras 324ff.

382 See eg *TUI/First Choice* (Case COMP/M.4600) Commission Decision (4 June 2007), paras 66–8; *TomTom/Tele Atlas* (Case COMP/M.4854) Commission Decision C(2008) 1859 (14 May 2008), paras 187–8.

383 Horizontal Merger Guidelines, para 10. 384 Ibid, para 11.

- computation of structural measures such as market shares and concentration indices to identify those mergers that warrant further analysis;
- assessment of likely anti-competitive effects, due to non-coordinated and/or coordinated effects, in the absence of offsetting factors;
- assessment of the likelihood of that these factors can actually offset the identified anti-competitive effects. These are:
  - countervailing buyer power;
  - potential competitors entering post-merger;
  - merger-specific efficiencies; and
  - failing-firm defence.

Each of these steps will be considered in the rest of this Section.

12.3.3. MARKET SHARES AND CONCENTRATION LEVELS

The reliability of market shares as a proxy for assessing whether a merger might bring about anti-competitive effects depends on the extent to which substitute products are differentiated. In the absence of product differentiation, whereby consumers perceive all products on offer as equally preferable (ie, choices are mainly determined by prices), market shares provide a good reflection of competitive constraints. Of course, where markets are 'contestable'—that is, in the presence of low entry and exit barrier so that the prospect of 'hit and run' strategies are feasible—even very large market shares may not be indicative of market power. Another set of circumstances where market shares may be misleading—that is, notwithstanding product homogeneity—is where the competition pattern is infrequent and lumpy as in bidding markets, so that temporary high market shares may underestimate rivals' competitive constraints.[385] Under these circumstances, it is preferable to use historic data in order to calculate average market shares over a longer period than the current calendar year for example.

12.3.3.1. *General Electric v Commission*

Case T-210/01, *General Electric v Commission*
[2005] ECR 5575

The appellant contested the Commission's reliance on market shares in the supply of engines for jet aircraft by arguing that market shares are utterly uninformative in 'bidding market' where what counts is the fact that there are a number of credible bidders.

> 96. As regards the Commission's use of the market-share figures cited in the contested decision, the applicant submits that market shares are of limited utility in assessing dominance in a bidding market. As the Commission's practice in the aeronautical sector shows, the market for aircraft engines is a bidding market in which

385 See DA Herman, SW Ulrick, and SB Sacher, 'Dominance Thresholds: A Cautionary Note' (2014) 59 *Antitrust Bulletin* 855.

suppliers compete for infrequent high-value contracts. For each new aircraft platform, airframe manufacturers opt for one or several engines specially developed for that platform. Consequently, irrespective of past wins, each competitor with a product to offer has strong incentives to bid at the next round of competitions. Thus, historical market figures do not accurately reflect the actual competitive intensity that exists in the market, as is illustrated by the recent history of that industry.

The Court of First Instance (now General Court) upheld the use of historic market shares by the Commission.

148. The applicant maintains that it was inappropriate in the contested decision to rely on market share to establish dominance in the market for large commercial jet aircraft engines because of the very nature of the market, which is a bidding market.

149. The Court holds that market shares as at a given date are less significant for the analysis of a market such as the market for jet engines for large commercial aircraft than, for example, for the analysis of a market for everyday consumer goods. Although not formally accepting that the market for large commercial jet aircraft engines is a 'bidding market', the Commission accepted before the Court that one characteristic of the market is the award of a limited number of high-value contracts. On such a market the fact that a particular company has had a number of recent 'wins' does not necessarily mean that one of its competitors will not be successful in the next competition. Provided that it has a competitive product and that other factors are not heavily weighted in the first company's favour, a competitor can always win a valuable contract and increase its market share considerably at one go.

150. However, such a finding does not mean that market shares are of virtually no value in assessing the strength of the various manufacturers on a market of that kind, especially where those shares remain relatively stable or reveal that one undertaking is tending to strengthen its position. In this instance, the Commission rightly inferred from the figures set out in the contested decision [. . .] that, over the five-year period preceding the contested decision, 'GE has not only succeeded in maintaining its leading supplier position, but has also displayed the highest market share growth rate' (recital 74 in the contested decision).

151. Even on a bidding market, the fact of a manufacturer maintaining, or even increasing, its market share over a number of years in succession is an indication of market strength. A time must come when the difference between one manufacturer's market share and that of its competitors can no longer be dismissed as a function of the limited number of competitions that constitute demand on the market. Consequently, the upward trend represented by the recent increase in GE's market share is a particularly convincing element of the Commission's analysis and there are no grounds for holding that the Commission made a manifest error of assessment.

When competitors sell homogenous products or services, shares based on installed capacity may provide a reliable indicator of competitive strength.[386] This is particularly the case where the market in question is new and expected to grow strongly, so that the capacity installed is way beyond what would be needed to serve the current level of demand.

386 See CoCo and OFT, Merger Assessment Guidelines, CC2 (revised)/OFT 1254 (September 2010), para 5.3.3.

12.3.3.2. *MCI WorldCom/Sprint*

***MCI WorldCom/Sprint* (Case COMP/M.1741) Commission Decision** [2003] OJ L 300/1

The merging parties were providers of so-called Internet backbone connectivity, by virtue of owning the cables linking up different regions across the globe, such as between North America and Europe across the Atlantic Ocean. Back then these facilities were considered essential given the dominant role played by US-based websites such as Yahoo and the fact that Internet users located in Europe could only access their web content from US-based servers. Given the high cost of laying these cables across the ocean floor providers of Internet backbone connectivity deployed very large capacities, far above the current volume of demand in the expectation that traffic would grow strongly. The Commission challenged a previous merger between WorldCom and MCI finding that the merger the combination of MCI's and WorldCom's Internet activities would have led to the creation of a dominant position in the market for top-level connectivity. The Commission relied on a combination of measurements, looking at capacity data in terms of available bandwidth through Internet backbones, revenue, and traffic flows.

100. In the WorldCom/MCI decision, the Commission found that the combination of MCI's and WorldCom's Internet activities would have led to the creation of a dominant position in the market for top-level connectivity. MCI WorldCom's current Internet activities were contributed by WorldCom after the Commission accepted the divestiture of MCI's Internet business as a condition for the merger between MCI and WorldCom to be cleared. MCI and WorldCom were at the time of the Commission's decision the market leaders with a combined market share in the region of around [30 to 40]* % for the former WorldCom Group and [10 to 20]* % for the former MCI Group. Sprint was at the time found to be the second largest top-level network provider with a market share in the range of 10 to 15 %.

101. The parties argue that, as stated by the Commission in the WorldCom/MCI decision, there is no reliable publicly available estimate of the size of either the internet sector as a whole or any relevant sub-sector and there is not consensus on a preferred unit of measurement. Further, as was noted by the Commission in the decision, the parties argue there is no specific reporting obligations on ISPs in relation to Internet revenues and no consistent reporting. Accordingly, the parties are not able to provide an accurate estimate of the size of the Internet sector or a measure of the market. Even Internet revenues, which MCI and WorldCom advocated as the appropriate tool to measure market shares in the WorldCom/MCI decision may, according to the parties, easily be inaccurate. Traffic flows, as used by the Commission in the WorldCom/MCI decision would have even greater shortcomings and cannot be accurately measured from a technical viewpoint, given the lack of generally accepted measures. [. . .].

102. The size of the merging parties traffic flows should also be linked to the merged entity's global network (capacity). MCI WorldCom's Internet division UUNet has 'over 2,000 POPs [ie, network nodes], 500 of which are outside the United States. This is bigger than any other IP network on the planet by at least a factor of 2 and bigger by a factor of 4–5 than most of the IP backbones around the world. [. . .].

The Commission methodology was based on the observation that there were only a few service providers able to provide universal connectivity through so-called private peering agreement, whereby top-tier service providers bilaterally agreed to exchange traffic between their respective networks for free, thanks to the fact that their similar size meant that the traffic flows would be balanced in each direction. The size of the installed capacity was of course a key indicator of the ability for a service provider to be able to enter into private peering agreements with other top-tier Internet backbone providers. This web of bilateral agreements set these global service providers apart from smaller regional providers who could only gain universal connectivity by paying a top-tier provider (so-called transit agreements). Therefore, the Commission based its methodology on this core set of top-tier provider.

> 103. Market participants are those equipped with a set of peering agreements that provide them with 100 % settlement-free connectivity across the Internet. Identifying these market players involves reviewing all peering and transit connections between Internet connectivity providers and isolating those who only get their connectivity either from their customer base or from peering agreements with other networks. Given the quality issues raised by public interconnection points, it is likely that only those who peer privately with other networks are really able to obtain top level connectivity.
>
> 104. Many of those consulted during the course of the Commission's investigation mentioned the same five top-level networks (MCI WorldCom, Sprint, AT&T, Cable & Wireless and GTE) as having a position stronger than all the others. Accordingly, the Commission reviewed the peering agreements involving these key players to determine a list of candidates for top-level connectivity providers. As the disclosure of peering relationships raises confidentiality issues, the Commission selected those companies who peer with both MCI WorldCom and Sprint to determine who might be regarded as top level providers. This examination led to identify the following companies as market participants: [. . .]*.
>
> [. . .].
>
> 106. Any other Internet connectivity provider not featuring on this list has to purchase transit services from at least one of the top five providers. Failure on the part of a network to peer with at least the five main players as a minimum would imply a substantial absence in their coverage of the Internet as a whole. It is possible that the number of participants who are true top-level networks is actually smaller than the field of those who peer with Sprint and MCI WorldCom. Some of those identified may receive their connectivity through public peering arrangements which do not enable them to provide the best quality connectivity. Also each additional peer, while of course peering with the original two, may not peer with each and every other peer who also peers with these two. To that extent, they may not have complete ability to cover the entire Internet on a settlements-free basis. However, for the purposes of assessment it was assumed that anyone with global peering connections to MCI WorldCom and Sprint would be considered a desirable peer by anyone else who had the same connections. This assumption runs in the parties' favour by widening the field of market participants.

Similarly to the previous decision, the Commission opposed the proposed merger between MCI WorldCom and Sprint. It is worth noting that this merger was also challenged by the US Department of Justice.

Whereas, when consumers show differing preferences for variety or price-quality ratios, market shares may fail to properly capture the extent to which different products are perceived as close substitutes. Under these circumstances, it is preferable to calculate value market share, typically on the basis of sales revenue figures. This is particularly the case under vertical differentiation where upmarket versions command higher prices than mainstream versions.[387]

Market shares are used to screen those mergers which are likely to give rise to a SIEC due to the creation or strengthening of the dominant position of the merged entity. Specifically, a combined market share of more than 50 per cent may in itself be evidence of the existence of a dominant market position,[388] whereas with a share below 25 per cent the merger is considered unlikely to give rise to a SIEC.[389]

The use of individual market shares fails, however, to spot 'gap' cases, where a SIEC may be the result of weakened competitive rivalry in an oligopolistic market even if the merged entity does not have a dominant position. In these circumstances, the use of concentration measurements based on elaboration of market share figures is preferred. The simplest elaboration is the concentration ratio, which is simply obtained adding the market shares of the largest, say, four firms (the so-called CR4). However, competition authorities prefer to rely on a more sophisticated methodology, the HHI, which is calculated by summing the squares of the individual market shares of all the firms in the market.[390] The highest possible value is therefore 10 000 in a monopoly. In contrast to the use of concentration ratios, the HHI index also reflects the extent to which market shares are unevenly distributed.[391] Under the additional assumption that firms compete by setting quantities for homogeneous products, it can be shown that the HHI is proportional to industry profitability.[392]

Similarly to the use of market shares, HHI values are used to screen out mergers unlikely to give rise to anti-competitive concerns,[393] by taking into account both the absolute level post-merger and the increment (called the delta) caused by the merger.[394]

387 See *Nestlé/Perrier* (Case IV/M.190) Commission Decision [1992] OJ L 356/1, para 40. See also *Procter & Gamble/VP Schickedanz (II)* (Case IV/M.430) Commission Decision [1994] OJ L 354/32.

388 Horizontal Merger Guidelines, para 17.

389 Ibid, para 18. This threshold is substantially lower than the one signalled by the UK competition authorities, which indicated that in mergers in markets where products are undifferentiated suggest that combined market shares of less than 40 per cent will not often raise concern over non-coordinated effects. See CoCo and OFT, Merger Assessment Guidelines, CC2 (revised)/OFT 1254 (September 2010), para 5.3.5.

390 Horizontal Merger Guidelines, para 18.

391 For example, in a market with five symmetric firms (each having a 20 per cent market share) the HHI is 2 000; whereas in a market with six firms, but where one leading firm has half the market, a second has a market share of 20 per cent and the remaining four have each 5 per cent, the HHI is 2 950.

392 In detail, in can be shown that the sum of firms' unit margins of profit, weighted by their respective market shares, is equal to the HHI divided by the market demand elasticity; and the individual firm's unit margin of profit is given by its market share divided by the market elasticity of demand.

393 Under the US horizontal merger guidelines, the safe harbour threshold is an HHI below 1 500. For HHI levels between 1 500 and 2 500, a merger leading to an increase of more than 100 points normally warrants additional scrutiny. Above 2 500, an increase between 100 and 200 triggers additional scrutiny, whereas for increases above 200 points there is a rebuttable presumption of anti-competitive effects. In contrast, an increase below 100 points is generally considered unproblematic. See US DOJ and FTC, Horizontal Merger Guidelines (2010), 19.

394 See Horizontal Merger Guidelines, para 16 n 19:

> The increase in concentration as measured by the HHI can be calculated independently of the overall market concentration by doubling the product of the market shares of the merging firms. For example, a merger of two firms with market shares of 30 % and 15 % respectively would increase the HHI by 900 (30 × 15 × 2 = 900). The explanation for this technique is as follows: Before the merger, the market shares of the merging firms contribute to the HHI by their squares individually: (a)2 + (b)2. After the merger, the contribution is the square of their sum: (a + b)2, which equals (a)2 + (b)2 + 2ab. The increase in the HHI is therefore represented by 2ab.

12.3.4. UPWARD PRICING PRESSURE INDEXES

When products are differentiated, in terms of (horizontal) variety and/or (vertical) quality, the degree to which consumers perceive two products as close substitutes varies. This means that the picture presented by market shares could be misleading. For example, a product with a large market share may be a basic product which is not perceived by consumers as a close substitute for niche up-market versions. This can thwart the use of both market shares and concentration measurements for the assessment of the likelihood of non-coordinated effects (also known as unilateral effects) in horizontal mergers.

Critics of the use of market shares and concentration measurements argue that the fundamental problem lies at the central role that market definition plays, traditionally, in the competitive assessment of mergers.[395] In 2010, professors Joseph Farrell and Carl Shapiro were the first to advocate the use of upward pricing pressure (UPP) indexes which bypass the need to define relevant markets thanks to the fact that their computation only required the availability of diversion ratios among the merging firms and their profit margins.[396] This approach was endorsed in the new US Horizontal Merger Guidelines published by the US DOJ and the FTC in the same year.

DOJ and FTC, Horizontal Merger Guidelines (2010), 21

In some cases, the Agencies may seek to quantify the extent of direct competition between a product sold by one merging firm and a second product sold by the other merging firm by estimating the diversion ratio from the first product to the second product. The diversion ratio is the fraction of unit sales lost by the first product due to an increase in its price that would be diverted to the second product. Diversion ratios between products sold by one merging firm and products sold by the other merging firm can be very informative for assessing unilateral price effects, with higher diversion ratios indicating a greater likelihood of such effects. Diversion ratios between products sold by merging firms and those sold by non-merging firms have at most secondary predictive value.

Adverse unilateral price effects can arise when the merger gives the merged entity an incentive to raise the price of a product previously sold by one merging firm and thereby divert sales to products previously sold by the other merging firm, boosting the profits on the latter products. Taking as given other prices and product offerings, that boost to profits is equal to the value to the merged firm of the sales diverted to those products. The value of sales diverted to a product is equal to the number of units diverted to that product multiplied by the margin between price and incremental cost on that product. In some cases, where sufficient information is available, the Agencies assess the value of diverted sales, which can serve as an indicator of the upward pricing pressure on the first product resulting from the merger. Diagnosing unilateral price effects based on the value of diverted sales need not rely on market definition or

395 See HJ Hovenkamp, 'Markets in Merger Analysis' (2012) 57 *Antitrust Bulletin* 887. For a detailed overview, see OECD, 'Market Definition' Policy Roundtables', DAF/COMP(2012)19 (2012), 59–68, available at www.oecd.org/daf/competition/Marketdefinition2012.pdf. For an intuitive introduction, see Laboratorio di economia, antitrust, regolamentazione (LEAR), 'Merger Screens and the Use of Price Pressure Tests', Lear Competition Notice (February 2013), available at www.learlab.com/wp-content/uploads/2016/03/lcn_merger_screen_price_pressure_test_1360694100.pdf.

396 See J Farrell and C Shapiro, 'Antiturst Evaluation of Horizontal Mergers: An Economic Alternative to Market Definition' (10 February 2010), available at https://ssrn.com/abstract=1313782.

the calculation of market shares and concentration. The Agencies rely much more on the value of diverted sales than on the level of the HHI for diagnosing unilateral price effects in markets with differentiated products. If the value of diverted sales is proportionately small, significant unilateral price effects are unlikely.

Diversion ratios measure the extent to which two products are close substitutes by looking at the proportion of lost sales by one firm that are captured by the other firm in question, when the prices of the former increase. Ideally, the calculation of diversion ratios shall be based on the firms' own and cross-price elasticities. However, these are seldom available at the initial screening stage. Alternatively, one could rely on information collected from the merging firms (ie, perhaps from board presentations), previous consumer surveys, or evidence from past 'natural experiments'. At worst, under the assumption that all products are equally 'distant' (ie, the pattern of differentiation is uniform across rival products) diversion ratios can be based on market shares. However, this approach calls in the question the extent to which the use of price pressure indices could really be seen as a solution to the flaws entailed by the use of market shares in differentiated markets.

The most basic version, the gross upward pricing pressure index (GUPPI), requires data about merging firms' profit margins and the diversion ratios between their products, supposed to be substitutable. The idea is that the merged entity will want to raise prices if it is expected that part of the lost sales will be captured (in economic jargon, internalized) by the other substitute products in its portfolio.

Other indices such as the UPP and the UPP* are even more demanding in that they require the analyst to make a conjecture as to the expected cost synergies resulting from the proposed merger. Here the idea is to allow for merger-specific efficiency improvements which would tend to offset the upward pricing pressure identified under the GUPPI. The UPP* takes into account also how the increase in revenue diverted to other products within the merged entity's portfolio will trigger similar price increases, which in turn will reinforce the initial price rise: that is, since pricing decisions as strategic complements.

It is worth pointing out that the indices presented so far do not attempt to indicate the magnitude of the post-merger price increase, but merely its likelihood given the underlying incentives of the merger entity. The illustrative price rise (IPR) attempts to measure the likely price increase post-merger, but it requires the analysts to make an assumption regarding the specific curvature of the demand schedule: for example linear or iso-elastic,[397] with the latter entailing larger prices increases keeping diversion ratios and profit margin constant. The use of this methodology attracted some criticism, as exemplified by the following extract authored by Mike Walker who then went on to become the Chief Economist of the UK competition authority.

[397] The linear demand is based on the assumption that consumer marginal valuation of the product sold keeps decreasing at a constant rate, which yields the counter-intuitive result that even if the price is zero, consumers would want to consume only a finite quantity. This means that demand elasticity grows as we move upwards along the demand schedule. In contrast, a demand specification with constant elasticity of demand—also known as iso-elastic or log-linear demand—does not have intercepts. This means that the quantity demanded are infinite for prices approaching zero, and vice versa.

M Walker, OECD Secretariat, 'Background Note' in OECD, *Economic Evidence in Merger Analysis*, Policy Roundtable (2011), 23, 39–44

5. Upward pricing pressure measures

There is currently an active debate on the use of upward pricing pressure (UPP) measures in unilateral effect cases. These are simple measures that can be used to gauge the extent to which a unilateral effects merger may give the merging firms an incentive to raise prices post-merger. There is much to be said for thinking about unilateral effects in terms of upward pricing pressure as this approach focuses on the incentives of the merging firms to change their prices post-merger. However, it is important to be clear as to what the various measures show and when they might make sense. Our view is that there currently appears to be a danger of some authorities using these measures in an indiscriminating manner and that this is unlikely to lead to good merger control decisions.

5.1. The various measures

When two firms selling substitute products merge, this will change their pricing incentives. Assuming that the market was in equilibrium, prior to the merger each of the firms would not raise its price because the loss of profits on lost sales would outweigh the increase in profits from sales that were not lost. After the merger, this calculation is changed because sales that are lost to the other merging party no longer represent lost profits. This will give the firm an incentive to raise its price post-merger that it did not have pre-merger. The argument is symmetric and so both firms would have a post-merger incentive to raise price. Hence, the merger leads to upward pricing pressure.

An approximation to the extent of the upward pricing pressure can be captured by two variables: the diversion ratio between the two firms and the firms' gross margins. The greater is the diversion ratio from Firm 1 to Firm 2, the greater the competitive constraint imposed by Firm 2 on Firm 1 prior to the merger and so the greater the lessening of competitive constraint as a result of the merger. The higher the gross margin pre-merger, the greater the cost of losing sales (as a result of a price rise) pre-merger and so the lesser the cost post-merger if those sales are captured by the other merging party. So for a given gross margin, the greater the diversion ratio, the greater the incentive to rise prices post-merger. Likewise, for a given diversion ratio, the greater the gross margin pre-merger, the greater the incentive to raise prices. This effect will be reduced if the merger leads to marginal cost efficiencies as these will tend to put downward pressure on prices.

So far this should be uncontroversial and highlights that in a unilateral effects case, diversion ratios, gross margins and likely post-merger marginal cost efficiencies are all important variables to look at. Potential controversy only arises when looking at particular implementations of the underlying economic intuition.

Farrell and Shapiro (2010) provide a simple test statistic that compares the upward price effect of a merger with the expected post-merger marginal cost efficiencies. In the symmetric case with Bertrand competition they find that there is upward pricing pressure if

$$\frac{D}{1-D}\frac{M}{1-M} > E$$

where D is the diversion ratio between the two firms; M is the gross margin; and E is the predicted proportionate decline in marginal costs post-merger.

The version of UPP that is used in the new US Horizontal Merger Guidelines is the Gross Upward Pricing Pressure Index or GUPPI. The GUPPI is defined as follows:

$$\text{GUPPI for Product 1} = \frac{\text{Value of sales diverted to Product 2}}{\text{Revenues on volume lost by Product 1}}$$

Although the Guidelines are not precise on this, they do state that a merger is unlikely to raise significant unilateral effect concerns if the GUPPI is 'proportionately small'. The Guidelines do not quantify what this might mean, although some commentators have argued that it may mean 5 per cent or less.

The final version that we discuss in this paper is the Illustrative Price Rise (IPR) that is used by the Office of Fair Trading (OFT) in the UK. This is a measure of how much prices might be expected to rise post-merger if there were no marginal cost efficiencies. The OFT uses two measures of the IPR: one assumes linear demand whilst the other assumes iso-elastic demand. The equations for the symmetric case are given below.

$$\text{Linear demand IPR} = \frac{MD}{2(1-D)}$$

and

$$\text{Isoelastic demand IPR} = \frac{MD}{1-M-D}$$

5.2 Commentary on the various measures

As noted above, the economic logic underlying the various measures is clearly sensible and focuses on the incentives faced by the merging parties to raise prices. However, it is very important to understand the limitations of particular articulations of the underlying economics. Once we move away from the very general statement of economic logic and start to use particular formulae for quantifying this economic logic, we start to add assumptions to the analysis. This is unavoidable but it is important to be clear as to what those assumptions are in any particular case.

For instance, equations (1), (3) and (4) are all based on the assumption of symmetry. The formulae assume that the diversion ratio from Firm 1 to Firm 2 is the same as from Firm 2 to Firm 1. They also assume that the gross margins of the two firms are the same. Both of these may well be reasonable assumptions to make in a particular case, but they will not be true in general and so should be empirically confirmed before using the formulae. Where the firms are not symmetric, the correct formulae are significantly different to the ones above and can lead to significantly different results. This is all standard, so it is important that merger control authorities ensure that they take these issues into account when using these measures.

There is a sense in which these approaches can be thought of as 'merger simulation light' and they face similar criticisms to the ones we made about merger simulation above. They omit important competitive constraints, such as the threat of entry, repositioning, non-price responses and so on. Note that the UPP and GUPPI do not claim to predict post-merger price increases and so this is not a criticism of these measures, but more a reminder of the relatively limited claim that can be made using them. They provide a useful measure of the incentive for the merging parties to raise prices in a static sense ie ignoring the longer-term reactions of competitors. But this is a criticism of the IPR approach, which does claim to provide an estimate, albeit an 'illustrative' one, of the post-merger price rise.

The IPR was first used in the UK in 2005 by the Competition Commission in the Somerfield/ Morrison merger inquiry. The Competition Commission sought to predict potential post-merger price rises using the IPR. This analysis was applied only to those local markets where post-merger there would be four or fewer competing supermarkets. The [Competition Commission] commissioned a survey of 56 of the stores that were going to be acquired. The [Competition Commission] calculated diversion ratios based on the question 'If this store had not been available which store would you have used instead?' and estimates of each consumer's spend. The [Competition Commission] then estimated post-merger price rises using these diversion ratios, estimates of the pre-merger price cost margin and the IPR formulae. Stores for which the predicted post-merger price rise was above 5% were identified as providing competition concerns. On the basis of the constant elasticity assumption, the [Competition Commission] identified twelve stores that raised competition concerns. The predicted post-merger price rise was almost 1900% for one of these stores. Since 2005 the Office of Fair Trading has used the methodology in at least ten retail mergers and has applied a 5% threshold IPR for competition concerns. We understand that the Korean Fair Trade Commission used elements of the IPR test in its assessment of the 2008 merger of the hypermarkets Homeplus and Homever.

Our view is that this approach can lead to significant problems. The formulae are only correct under strong assumptions, such that the two merging firms were symmetric pre-merger and were both single product firms. Both assumptions are usually incorrect. When these assumptions are relaxed, the simple formulae do not hold. The simple formulae include strong assumptions as to the shape of the demand curve, which should be tested, not assumed. The constant elasticity demand curve IPR can give rise to implausible results, such as the predicted 1900% price increase found in the Somerfield/Morrison inquiry. Note that none of these issues are a criticism of the fundamental approach to thinking about unilateral effects in terms of diversion ratios, gross margins and so on. Instead, they are criticisms of the inappropriate implementation of the approach.

A more general point is that these measures are not applicable to all types of merger. For instance, they are not applicable to any merger where the market is characterised by significant price discrimination, such as in an auction market. This is not a criticism of the measures, but merely a comment on the scope of their applicability.

5.3 Tightening policy?

Another issue that has arisen in the discussions of UPP is whether a measure of this type represents a tightening of enforcement policy. If we assume, as Farrell and Shapiro have suggested, that it is reasonable to assume marginal cost savings of 10%, then the equation 1 is satisfied (ie there will be upward pricing pressure) for a range of gross margins and diversion ratios that seems significantly wider than we would normally expect to give rise to concerns. [Table 12.1] comes from Simons and Coate (2010) (J Simons and MB Coate, Upward Pressure on Price (UPP) Analysis: Issues and Implications For Merger Policy (8 July 2010). Available at SSRN: https://ssrn.com/abstract=1558547.). It shows post-merger price rises, even with 10% efficiencies, at combinations of gross margins and diversion ratios that would not traditionally concern us.

We have marked price reductions in bold. It is clear that for any diversion ratio above 0.1, a gross margin of 50% or more implies a positive UPP. For a gross margin of 30%, which is hardly high, the UPP is positive at a diversion ratio of 0.2 and above. Simons and Coate also present this analysis in terms of the number of competitors. They convert diversion ratios into numbers of firms pre-merger (assuming symmetric firms). They then find positive UPPs, even with the *ad hoc* 10% efficiency assumption, for an 8 to 7 merger for margins above 40% and for a 6 to 5 merger where the margin is 30%. If margins are 50% or more, even a 10 to 9 merger is a problem.

What should we make of these figures? Is it the case that mergers that were previously not thought be to be concerning should now be considered as raising potential concerns and so investigated more intensely than before? Perhaps, but it is not clear where the evidence is to support an argument that merger control has generally been too lax. Or does it imply that the UPP threshold is too low? This issue is not strictly speaking an issue to do with UPP measures themselves but rather with how they are treated by the competition authorities. For instance, to the extent that they are used just as an initial screen, this might in theory lead to more in depth investigations, but it should not affect the end result of an investigation.

Table 12.1. UPP with 10 per cent efficiencies (% price increases)

Gross margin	Diversion ratio 0.1	0.15	0.2	0.25	0.3	0.35	0.4
0.9	8.10%	12.7	17.2	21.8	26.3	30.9	35.4
0.8	6.20%	10.3	14.4	18.5	22.6	26.7	30.8
0.7	4.30%	8	11.6	15.3	18.9	22.6	26.2
0.6	2.4	5.6	8.8	12	15.2	18.4	21.6
0.5	0.5	3.3	6	8.8	11.5	14.3	17
0.4	−1.4	0.9	3.2	5.5	7.8	10.1	12.4
0.3	−3.3	−1.4	0.4	2.3	4.1	6.1	7.8
0.2	−5.2	−3.8	−2.4	−1	0.4	1.8	3.2
0.1	−7.1	−6.1	−5.2	−4.2	−3.3	−2.3	−1.4

5.4 UPP measures and market definition

The debate about UPP measures, and their place within the new US merger guidelines, has sparked an often heated discussion about the role of market definition and its interaction with direct effects analysis, such as that suggested by UPP-type measures. Some have argued that such measures mark a radical departure from previous practice as they put significantly less emphasis on market definition than in the past. This seems to us to be a mistaken response.

The purpose of market definition is to aid the competitive analysis. Market definition is not an end in itself. We define markets in merger cases in order to help us focus on the competitive constraints that the merged entity will face. This has several implications.

First, if there is an alternative approach to market definition that allows us to assess directly the competitive constraints faced by the merged entity, then this should in general be preferred to an indirect approach based on market definition. However, it should be noted that the distinction between direct effects analysis and market definition is not always as clear cut as it suggested. For instance, many merger simulations are based on logit models which require estimates of market shares. These clearly require a prior definition of the relevant markets.

Second, direct effects analysis and market definition are often complementary. The results of a direct effects analysis can be informative for market definition. The US Guidelines provide a good example of this.

> Evidence of competitive effects can inform market definition, just as market definition can be informative regarding competitive effects. For example, evidence that a reduction in the number of significant rivals offering a group of products causes prices for those products to rise significantly can itself establish that those products form a relevant market. (page 7)

Where there is a legal requirement to define the relevant market, a direct effects analysis can be used to do this.

Third, if market definition is controversial and if the likely merger control decision will vary significantly depending on which market is chosen, then direct effects analysis may allow investigators to avoid this difficulty. This difficulty does not arise where the market definition is uncontroversial or where all plausible market definitions have similar implications for the merger control decision.

Fourth, market shares of differentiated products markets can be misleading as they do not take account of the closeness of competition between the merging parties. The competitive implications of a post-merger market share of 40% and an increment of 10% differ dramatically depending on whether the merging parties are close competitors or distant competitors within the market.

So the implication of this discussion is that looking at direct effect measures may well downplay the importance of market definition in a case, but this is consistent with the ultimate aim of trying to identify anti-competitive mergers. Market definition is only an indirect aid in this process and if there are better approaches available in a particular case, then these should be used. This does not change the fact that market definition will remain central to most cases. Although not a very scientific metric, it is worth noting that the US Guidelines devote more than eight pages to market definition compared to just over seven on unilateral and coordinated effects combined.

5.5 Conclusions on UPP measures

It is important to understand that this Section is not critical of UPP measures as a concept. The underlying concept is clearly sensible and important: where diversion ratios are high and/or gross margins are high, then *ceteris paribus* we would expect to see the merging parties have an incentive to raise prices significantly post-merger. Our point in this Section is just that this fundamental insight can be lost if these measures are used in an unthinking manner.

12.3.5. NON-COORDINATED (UNILATERAL) EFFECTS

Simply put, a horizontal merger reduces competitive rivalry to the extent that the target company exert a competitive constraint. Furthermore, other competitors benefit from the fact that the merged entity behaves less competitively than the two merging firm would have done absent the merger in question.[398] That is to say, the merger entity adopts a 'soft' strategic stance which increases rivals' profitability, for instance by reducing the quantity sold, thus making it easier for rivals to sell theirs, or increasing their prices post-merger, thus making substitute products more desirable. Normally, it would not make sense to adopt a 'soft' strategic stance unless there is an expectation that rivals would reciprocate, thus renouncing an aggressive reaction such as, respectively, by increasing output to fill the gap left by the merger entity's ('soft') reduction, or by not matching the initial price increase in order to steal as many customers as optimal.

However, the 'soft' stance after the merger is due to the coordination between the two merging firms. Their decision to reduce quantities, or increase prices, is motivated by the fact that part of the loss in sales is being captured by (diverted to) the other merging firm. Therefore, the closer are the substitute products of the merging firms, the stronger is the incentive of the merged entity to adopt a 'soft' stance, that is, in spite of (or, better still, keeping in mind) the expectation that rivals will react in a non-coordinated fashion.

398 For a thorough treatment of this topic: see M Ivaldi et al, 'The Economics of Unilateral Effects', Interim Report for the DG Competition (November 2003), 22, available at idei.fr/doc/wp/2003/economics_unilaterals.pdf.

Specifically, rivals' initial reaction to this internally coordinated softening by the merged entity depends on the prevailing mode of competition. When firms compete by setting quantities, the merged entity's initial quantity reduction induces rivals to increase theirs, thus partly offsetting the initial softening stance. Whereas, when firms compete by setting prices, rivals' response to the initial increase in prices by the merged entity is to raise their own prices, but not to such an extent that rivals fail to steal customers away from the merger entity.

In turn, in a feedback loop, the merged entity adjusts to its rival's initial response by, respectively, reducing its quantities or nudging up its prices even further. All in all, though, regardless of the mode of competition, there normally would be an increase in prevailing market prices and a reduction in overall quantities after the merger, that is, to the detriment of buyers.

There are a number of factors that the Commission will take into consideration to gauge the likelihood of non-coordinated (unilateral) effects. First all, in the absence of product differentiation, the market share, and the increment in market share, of the merged entity provides a strong indicator of the extent to which the merger would increase the market power of the merged entity and thus give rise to a SIEC.[399]

When products are differentiated—due to product attributes, geographical location and/or quality and reliability—it is important to establish the extent to which customers perceive the products offered by the merging parties as close substitute, as well as the extent to which other products are not so. Furthermore, the observation of high price-cost mark-ups charged by the merging parties makes it more likely that they will have incentives to increase prices post-merger.[400]

12.3.5.1. Use of quantitative techniques

Depending on the availability of data, the closeness of substitution among differentiated products can be investigated by means of the same techniques used for market definition.[401] The simplest approach is *price correlation analysis* which looks at how the prices of two substitute products differ and to what extent they vary together; the idea being that if the products are indeed close substitute their prices should move together and should differ only because of higher transportation costs. This relationship is often called the law of one price, whereby the intense pricing rivalry among sellers of perfectly substitute products results in a common price across the market.

The observation that two prices are correlated, though, may give the mistaken impression that the two products are close substitutes, whereas the co-movement could be due to a change in the price of a common input: for example, common feed used in livestock farming for two distinct product categories. Alternatively, a co-movement in the prices of non-substitute products could be the result of a general increase in disposable income that has lifted all prices. In contrast, two close substitute products might fail the correlation test because only one of them is subject to short-term changes in the price on an input not used in the production of the other, even if in the medium-long term the two products are indeed restricting each other prices.

399 See Horizontal Merger Guidelines, para 27. 400 Ibid, para 28.

401 Ibid, para 29. For an intuitive introduction of the various methodologies, see I Lianos and C Genakos, 'Econometrics in EU Competition Law: an empirical and theoretical analysis' in I. Lianos, & D. Geradin (eds.), *Handbook in EU Competition Law: Enforcement and Procedure* (Edward Elgar, 2013), 1, spec 1-28. Lexecon, 'An Introduction to Quantitative Techniques in Competition Analysis' (2005), available at http://judgestraining.eu/wp-content/uploads/2017/10/kokkoris-quantitative_techniques-mergers-lexecon.pdf. For a detailed discussion, see P Davis and E Garcés, *Quantitative Techniques for Competition and Antitrust Analysis* (Princeton University Press, 2010), ch 4.

The identification is facilitated where it is possible to identify a contextual change that is not linked to a demand or supply shift. For example, the firm under investigation may run a marketing experiment by lowering the price in a local area in order to gauge price sensitivity. Such a *natural experiment* would, therefore, be exogenous by design; that is, certainly not caused by an unobserved movement in demand or supply shift that might affects other substitute products as well.[402]

Price-concentration analysis can be used where firms compete in separate geographic areas with varying degree of concentration. Nowadays this approach is particularly suited in markets which have not (yet) being disrupted by online shopping: for example, cinemas, restaurants, petrol stations and hospitals. The key constraint is that the selected local areas ought to be similar in terms of demand and supply determinants. The idea is to check whether higher level of concentration lead to higher observed prices, in which case the product concerned should be considered close substitutes. This methodology can be useful in revealing whether the merging parties' products are close substitutes, that is, to the extent that there are areas that could be treated as 'control' markets, thanks to the fact that one firm is not present.[403]

As with any methodology there are pitfalls, in particular due to the risks of false inferences because of unobserved factors that affect both prevailing prices and concentration measures. For example, high prices and concentrations may be the result of high local costs, such as to rent or lease facilities (eg, airport slots), rather than market power. In contrast, an area where disposable income is high may feature low concentration but high prices. However, the expected price-concentration pattern may hold in other areas with average levels of disposable income.

In bidding markets, a 'win-loss' analysis can show whether the merging parties tend to be ranked as runner-up when the other party is the winner, thus indicating that they exert a strong competitive constraint over each other.

The methodologies presented so far are used to gather indirect evidence of substitution patterns, that is, without the need to estimate directly consumer price sensitivity or diversion ratios. There are two ways of gathering direct evidence regarding pattern of substitution. First of all, one would ideally rely on the observation of consumer actual choices based on product prices, characteristics and locations, as well as those consumers' characteristics that could explain their preferences such as age, income and location. This methodological approach is called *revealed preferences*. Suffice to say, this kind of fact-finding is rather demanding. Alternatively, the analysis could rely on survey evidence, where a representative sample of consumers is first profiled and then asked about how they would choose among alternative products in a hypothetical scenario where prices for their current choice were increased by a specified amount. This methodological approach is called *stated preferences*.[404]

402 Other examples of exogenous source of natural experiments can be a new entry in a local market or a regulatory change imposed only on the product in question.

403 This methodology featured prominently in the seminal FTC's case to prohibit the merger between Staples and office Depot in 1997, the two largest US office superstore chains: see CM Newmark, 'Price-Concentration Studies: There You Go Again' (14 February 2004), available at www.justice.gov/atr/public/workshops/docs/202603.htm.

404 For a detailed discussion on the use of consumer survey evidence, see CMA, *Good Practice in the Design and Presentation of Consumer Survey Evidence in Merger Inquiries*, CMA78 (May 2018), available at www.gov.uk/government/uploads/system/uploads/attachment_data/file/284391/Good-practice-guide.pdf.

12.3.5.2. *Ryanair/Aer Lingus*

Case T-342/07, *Ryanair v Commission*
[2010] ECR II 3457

The Commission opposed an attempt by Ryanair to take over the equally Dublin-based Air Lingus by rejecting the applicant's argument that the two parties were not each other's closest competitors, given that the target company offered a higher quality of service compared to the 'no-frills' service provided by Ryanair. The commission rejected this claim by producing multiple evidence including both price-concentration and price-correlation analyses, survey evidence and internal document showing that the parties were monitoring each other when setting the terms of their commercial offers. The General Court upheld the Commission's decision by clarifying that the Commission was not required to prove that the services offered by the parties are perfect substitutes, but it sufficed to show that Aer Lingus service was a close substitute and closer than any other alternative.

The failure to take account of the 'fundamental differences' between Ryanair and Aer Lingus

61. The applicant essentially submits that, as its services differ from those of Aer Lingus, the two airlines are not in competition to such a degree that the concentration would significantly impede competition. It claims that, in the contested decision, the Commission could not have concluded the contrary since it failed to establish that Ryanair and Aer Lingus were close competitors.

62. It is necessary for the Court to assess, one by one, the arguments of the parties relating to the use of the 'closest competitors' concept and the 'automatic' inference that there are significant competitive constraints, the arguments relating to the 'fundamental differences' concerning operating costs, prices charged and service levels, and those relating to the difference between the destination airports.

[. . .]

The 'fundamental differences' concerning operating costs, prices charged and different service levels

Arguments of the parties

70. First, the applicant maintains that the difference between its operating costs and those of Aer Lingus shows that neither company exerts significant competitive constraints on the other. Ryanair's lower cost base allows it to charge significantly lower prices than Aer Lingus and, thus, to serve a separate segment of the market. The Commission failed to analyse the impact of that difference on competition. Moreover, after observing that Aer Lingus's operating costs are in line with those of low-fares carriers such as EasyJet or Virgin Express, the Commission was not entitled to infer therefrom [. . .] that Aer Lingus was 'among the closest competitors of Ryanair even in terms of unit costs'. Reliance on that notion of 'closest competitors' derives from an analytical error. Moreover, the Commission includes Aer Lingus's long-haul flights in the calculation of Aer Lingus's average operating costs. Since operating costs per kilometre are substantially lower on long-haul flights than on short haul flights, their inclusion has the effect of significantly understating Aer Lingus's average costs per kilometre for the purpose of comparison with low-cost carriers that operate only on short haul routes. Furthermore,

if, as the Commission contends, Aer Lingus's average costs are comparable to those of low-cost carriers and only 50% or so higher than Ryanair's, Aer Lingus should be able make substantially higher profits than Ryanair, because its average fare is over 100% higher than Ryanair's. In reality, Ryanair is far more profitable than Aer Lingus.

71. Second, the applicant emphasises the difference between its prices and those of Aer Lingus. That difference is the result of the difference in the two companies' costs and demonstrates a 'high level of differentiation'. The Commission was wrong to consider [. . .] that a price difference of EUR 30 is not significant, given that the average price of a Ryanair ticket is EUR 41. Ryanair's lower prices, being less than half of Aer Lingus's, enable it to attract customers who, in the absence of such moderate prices, would not fly at all. The Commission should have inferred from this that Aer Lingus exercised no competitive constraint on Ryanair. In recognising [. . .] that Ryanair's prices were on average lower than those of Aer Lingus, the Commission should have concluded that the two companies targeted two entirely separate segments of the market. Moreover, Ryanair and Aer Lingus operate on the basis of very different business models. Aer Lingus may indeed have moved away from the business model of the traditional full service airline by adopting some of the traits of low fare carriers. However, it continues to use primary airports and offer certain services that allow it to charge significantly higher fares than those of Ryanair. Aer Lingus customers are thus prepared to pay a supplement over the fares of its low-price competitors in order to get a wider range of services.

72. Third, the applicant claims that [. . .] that Ryanair is a 'no frills' airline and Aer Lingus is a 'mandrills' airline and the Commission attempts to minimise the impact of that difference on the degree to which the two companies compete. The Commission failed to analyse the extent to which those differences matter or to put forward convincing evidence to demonstrate why those significant differences are irrelevant for determining the existence of a significant impediment to effective competition. [. . .]

Findings of the Court

74. Although, in the contested decision, the Commission recognised the existence of differences between Ryanair and Aer Lingus, it did not draw the same conclusions as the applicant. Those differences did not prevent the Commission from finding that, of all the competitors which operate on the various routes affected by the concentration, Aer Lingus was Ryanair's biggest and closest competitor.

75. As regards the difference in the operating costs of Aer Lingus and Ryanair, the latter reiterates its argument that the difference in costs enables it to serve a separate segment of the market. In the applicant's view, the Commission should have analysed the impact of that difference on the competitive relationship between the two airlines.

76. However, it is apparent from the contested decision that the Commission recognised that Ryanair's operating costs were lower than Aer Lingus's, but also noted that, in relation to the other airlines, Aer Lingus's costs were generally very low and situated the airline in the group of low-cost carriers rather than in the group of network airlines.

77. The Commission thus set out in the contested decision the reasons why it considered, in the light of the information available, that Ryanair's operating costs per kilometre were lower than 4 cents, whereas Aer Lingus's were almost 5.9 cents. The Commission acknowledged that Ryanair's objection that those figures also included Aer Lingus's long-haul flights (which generally have lower operating costs per kilometre) was justified. However, it pointed out that 87% of Aer Lingus's passengers travelled on short haul flights and that the alternative figure put forward by Ryanair of almost 8 cents per kilometre was not substantiated.

78. In any event, it is apparent from graph 1 set out in recital 375 of the contested decision that the operating costs per kilometre of a network airline (such as British Airways, Air France or Lufthansa) are almost 12 cents whereas those of Virgin Express or EasyJet are in the region of 7 cents and just over 6 cents respectively. The margin defined by the Commission and Ryanair, of between 5.9 and 8 cents per kilometre, thus situates Aer Lingus in the same group as Virgin Express or EasyJet, whose operating costs are 'lower' or 'significantly lower' than those of large network airlines (a difference of at least 4 cents per kilometre), even if they are 'higher' or 'significantly higher' than Ryanair's (a difference which varies between 2 and 4 cents per kilometre).

79. Consequently, although there is a difference in operating costs between Ryanair and Aer Lingus, as the Commission recognised in the contested decision, that still does not support the applicant's claim that the Commission could not consider that Aer Lingus and Ryanair are 'closest competitors', since Aer Lingus's operating costs are actually lower than those of the network airlines and neither Virgin Express nor EasyJet are in competition with Ryanair on the routes on which their services departing from Ireland overlap.

80. That observation is also supported in the contested decision by the finding that the evolution of Aer Lingus's unit costs over time further highlights its 'gradual migration' from a traditional to a low-cost business model [. . .].

81. In addition, although, as pointed out by the applicant, low operating costs have an impact on the profitability of the undertaking, that still does not lead to the conclusion that the services which it offers are not in competition with those of Aer Lingus. The latter offers higher end services while attempting to bring its business model into line with Ryanair's cost structure, which differentiates it further from the cost structure of network airlines.

82. As regards the difference between the prices charged by Ryanair and those charged by Aer Lingus, the applicant submits that the difference is such that the Commission should have inferred from it that Aer Lingus did not exert a competitive constraint on it. According to the applicant, an average price difference of EUR 30 is significant, since the average price of a Ryanair ticket is EUR 41. In addition, Ryanair's lowest prices, which are less than half the price of Aer Lingus's, enable the applicant to attract customers who would not travel by aeroplane if such prices were not available.

83. Just as it recognised that there was a difference in the operating costs, the Commission recognised in the contested decision that there was a difference between the average prices charged by Aer Lingus and those charged by Ryanair. That point is not disputed by the parties. [. . .]

85. In the light of the above, it should be noted that the dispute relating to the average prices charged by Ryanair and Aer Lingus concerns the consequences of that price difference. Although the applicant claims that the price difference enables the finding that Aer Lingus does not exert a competitive constraint on Ryanair, the Commission considers that it is apparent from the analysis of the prices charged that Aer Lingus is closer to Ryanair than any of the other competitors operating on the routes on which their services overlap could be [. . .].

87. Consequently, the findings made in [. . .] the contested decision provide a basis for the Commission's conclusion [. . .] in the sense that it is apparent from the information set out therein that the prices charged by network airlines, communicated by Ryanair, which offer a full on board service are much higher than those charged by Aer Lingus (EUR 216 for Air France, EUR 225 for Lufthansa and EUR 268 for British Airways). Ryanair's and Aer Lingus's prices are indeed 'well below the price level of the competitors they face on the respective routes'. The Commission also explained that

the difference in prices charged by Ryanair and those charged by Aer Lingus made it necessary to take account of some quality advantages associated with Aer Lingus's service, such as the fact that it serves primary airports, offers business lounges and higher service orientation. The analysis made in the contested decision of the prices charged by Ryanair and Aer Lingus thus provides a basis for the Commission's conclusion that Ryanair and Aer Lingus are 'closest competitors' on all of the relevant routes.

The GC than went on to examine the evidence relied upon by the Commission.

The 'nontechnical evidence'

Arguments of the parties

128. The applicant acknowledges that it competes with Aer Lingus for a limited group of passengers, just as it does with other network carriers such as Air France, Lufthansa and British Airways. The 'nontechnical evidence' put forward by the Commission in its statement in defence thus simply reflects such competition. The yield management systems and monitoring of market developments are standard practices in the airlines sector and their use by Ryanair and Aer Lingus does not therefore establish that they exercise 'significant competitive constraints on each other'. Ryanair monitors the fares of all airlines and not just those of Aer Lingus. Such monitoring puts Ryanair in a position to respond in those 'rare cases where Aer Lingus or other [airlines] offer lower promotional fares'. Moreover, if the similarity of the yield management systems meant that there was intense competition between Ryanair and Aer Lingus, then that would be borne out by the Commission's econometric results, and that is not the case. Furthermore, although the applicant does not deny that it occasionally adjusts its fares in response to a specific promotion or that it occasionally engages in advertising campaigns that include comparative advertising, it states that those promotional activities concern both Aer Lingus and all the other flag carriers. According to the applicant, those examples do not however constitute the kind of 'accurate, reliable and consistent evidence' that the Commission must produce. If Aer Lingus exercised any competitive constraint on Ryanair, the evidence would show that Ryanair systematically offers lower fares when Aer Lingus is present on a route. However, Ryanair's econometric evidence categorically refutes any such hypothesis. Finally, the applicant claims that the Commission cannot base its findings on Ryanair's internal documents, which are only of 'anecdotal nature'. The extracts relied on by the Commission do not prove that Ryanair and Aer Lingus exercise 'significant competitive constraints on each other'. In some cases, those discussions are not focused on Aer Lingus but on the general situation on a given route. The Commission can thus not rely on those documents to claim that the two airlines compete closely and to consider that the other flag carriers which are cited in those documents do not compete with Ryanair.

129. The Commission contends that the fact that Ryanair and Aer Lingus are the only two firms in the market for 22 routes on which their services overlap and have very high combined market shares for another 13 routes logically implies that the two airlines exercise competitive constraints on each other. That is confirmed, it submits, by the fact that Ryanair and Aer Lingus use similar yield management systems, that they both regularly monitor the competitive behaviour of their main competitors and adjust their prices accordingly, and that they routinely publish advertisements in which they compare one another's services and fares. In addition, the internal documents of Ryanair contain clear evidence that Ryanair and Aer Lingus are in competition with

one another. The contention on which Ryanair has built its case, namely that in view of its low-cost model competitors do not materially affect its competitive behaviour, is baseless.

Findings of the Court

130. In reading the conclusion that Ryanair and Aer Lingus are in competition on certain routes on which their services overlap, the Commission notes the existence of several items of evidence set out in the contested decision, which have not been challenged by the applicant in its application. That evidence concerns:

- the use, 'like many other carriers', of similar yield management systems: a system that tracks the booking status of each flight and a revenue management system;
- the use of the same price comparison software tool (QL2) which allows them to monitor the competitive behaviour of competitors and to adapt to reflect demand;
- the mutual monitoring by Ryanair and Aer Lingus of their promotions and respective advertising campaigns and their reactions to each other's promotions;
- the references made to Aer Lingus in the context of Ryanair's board meetings in relation to the development of the market shares and the competitive relationship.

131. On the basis of that evidence, the Commission made the following finding: Ryanair's and Aer Lingus's fares are directly influenced by the fares of their main competitor, since Aer Lingus and Ryanair each take account of the fares charged by the other when determining fares for a given route and the parties to the concentration react to each other's promotions and advertising campaigns.

132. The applicant does not dispute the 'nontechnical evidence' cited by the Commission in the contested decision. It does essentially submit, however, that that evidence is not sufficiently conclusive to be taken into account and that, at any rate, conclusions should be drawn solely from the 'technical evidence' resulting from the various econometric analyses carried out during the administrative procedure. The applicant also submits that the 'nontechnical evidence' does not, in any event, enable the finding to be made that the parties to the concentration exert 'significant competitive constraints on each other'.

133. First of all in that regard, the Commission was able to rely on the existence of similar yield management systems, on the monitoring of the competitive behaviour of competitors, on the reactions of one of the parties to the concentration to the promotions carried out by the other or on the monitoring of competitive behaviour of Aer Lingus which is evidenced in the internal documents of Ryanair. The Commission was perfectly entitled to take that evidence into account in the set of factors which it used to evaluate the competitive situation.

134. The fact that some of that 'nontechnical evidence' concerns both the competitive relationship between Ryanair and Aer Lingus and that between Ryanair and all the other airlines is immaterial, inasmuch as it is the competitive relationship between Ryanair and Aer Lingus, the parties to the concentration, on the routes where they both operate, which is being examined by the Commission at that stage of its analysis.

135. In addition, the Commission did not rely on the abovementioned evidence to establish that they exerted 'significant competitive constraints on each other', but to establish that the parties to the concentration were currently competing with one another. [. . .]

138. Those items of evidence, and in particular the extracts of the discussions held during Ryanair's board meetings in relation to Aer Lingus that are in the file, are particularly important in that they corroborate the findings made at the stage of the analysis of the market shares and the degree of concentration and precede the analysis of the econometric information. They were taken into account as part of the set of factors used by the Commission to examine the effects of the concentration on competition.

The GC then analysed in great detail the technicalities of the econometric evidence produced by both the Commission and the applicant. The GC also upheld the Commission's reliance on the results of a customer survey conducted by its own staff.

12.3.5.3. Product repositioning and ability to switch

Similarly to market definition, the likelihood of non-coordinated (unilateral) effects depends also on the extent to which supply-side and demand-side substitutability are constrained. Regarding the former, notwithstanding the fact those rivals' products are not close substitutes pre-merger, rivals could still prevent a SIEC by repositioning or extending their products in order to become closer substitutes and thus profit from the strategic 'soft' stance of the merged entity. However, product repositioning can be a risky strategy requiring, for example, the reconfiguration of the production and distribution process or substantial promotional activity, which may be not only costly, but also take time and be irreversible.[405]

12.3.5.3.1. Barilla/BPL/Kamps

***Barilla/BPL/Kamps* (Case COMP/M.2817) Commission Decision (25 June 2002)**

Barilla, the Italian producer of pasta and bakery products, wanted to take over the German bakery product firm Kamps. The Commission raised strong concern with respect to the production and sale of bread substitutes, due also to the low likelihood of product repositioning.

10. Both Barilla and Kamps are active in the production and sale of bakery products. Bakery products are highly differentiated products due to the large variety of existing product characteristics and, particularly in the bread substitutes markets, the presence of strong brands.

11. The parties submit that bakery products can be subdivided into three main groups: (i) bread (including fresh and pre-packaged bread), (ii) bread substitutes (including crisp bread, extruded bread, crisp rolls, bread sticks, crackers and rusks) and (iii) cake products (including two main segments: the segment for cakes, mini cakes and other pastries produced by craft pastries as well as industrial producers and the segment for morning goods which include bagels, croissants, scones and similar products normally eaten for breakfast).

12. In the parties view, the above three groups constitute the relevant product markets. According to a narrower product market definition, however, these groups of products could, according to the parties, be subdivided further into the following

405 Horizontal Merger Guidelines, para 30.

markets: (i) fresh bread; (ii) industrial and pre-packaged bread; (iii) bread substitutes (iv) cakes and (v) morning goods.

13. The market for bread substitutes, where the transaction has its most significant competitive impact, contains a variety of differentiated products, including numerous types of extruded bread, crisp rolls, bread sticks, crackers and rusks. Accordingly, this market could conceivably be further subdivided into as many markets as product types belonging to this category.

[. . .]

15. However, whether crisp bread constitutes a separate relevant product market or forms part of a wider market for bread substitutes can be left open, because the operation as notified raises serious doubts as to its compatibility with the common market under any possible product market definition.

[. . .]

31. The overlap in the parties' activities occurs in the crisp bread segment, where Barilla owns the leading Wasa brand and Kamps is active with its LiekenUrkorn brand. Both brands are priced at a significant premium to private labels of comparable quality.

[. . .]

36. Wasa and LiekenUrkorn are the only significant crisp bread brands active in the German bread substitutes market, the Burger brand (owned by Brandt) being known only in former East Germany. Market participants consider it unlikely that an entirely new brand could effectively and profitably compete with Wasa in the short to medium term. Rather, competition post-merger would be more likely to arise from the repositioning or reformulation of brands in currently less close substitutes, such as extruded bread. However, there is only one brand, Leicht & Cross that would seem to be positioned in sufficient proximity to Wasa/ LiekenUrkorn to be considered a close competitor in terms of brand positioning. In terms of product characteristics, however, extruded bread involves a fundamentally different production process from crisp bread and Leicht & Cross would have to set up a new production line in order to replace LiekenUrkorn as an equally close substitute to Wasa.

37. Another strong bread substitute brand, Brandt, is mainly associated with rusks (Zwieback). With its image as a temporary bread substitute for consumers with stomach problems and for infants, Brandt appears to be an unlikely entrant into the light and healthy segment occupied by Wasa and LiekenUrkorn. Hence, there appears to be no product that could in the short term replace LiekenUrkorn as a close, albeit significantly smaller, competitor to the leading Wasa brand. Despite its relatively small market share, LiekenUrkorn enjoys significant retail distribution power from its integration into Kamps large product portfolio and in-house logistics network, which would be difficult to replicate for smaller competitors.

38. Hence, the removal of the closest substitute (LiekenUrkorn) to the leading Wasa brand resulting from the combination of Barilla and Kamps would lead to serious doubts regardless of whether crisp bread is defined as a separate market or as part of an overall bread substitutes market.

On the demand-side, customers of the merging parties may face substantial switching costs, meaning that they would not be able to change supplier in response to worse commercial terms and condition imposed by the merged entity. This is particularly the case if there is evidence that customers adopted double sourcing from the merging parties in order to extracts better supply terms.[406]

406 Ibid, para 31.

12.3.5.3.2. Agfa Gevaert/DuPont

Agfa-Gevaert/DuPont (Case No IV/M.986) Commission Decision [1998] OJ L 211/22

Agfa was a subsidiary of chemical conglomerate Bayer. DuPont is another multinational chemical conglomerate based in the US. Both parties were active worldwide in the production of graphic arts film and offset printing plates. They also deliver products, equipment and chemicals for graphic arts purposes and provide maintenance services. The Commission raised strong concerns with regards to the sale of negative printing plates, used to reliably print large numbers of copies such as for a newspaper. The Commission found that there were substantial switching costs, both in terms of set-up costs to reconfigure the printing press and costs of a strategic nature due to the use of leasing deals with customers.

(b) Access to customers

63. The majority of end-users and dealers questioned by the Commission saw difficulties in switching negative plates supplier. The Commission considers that, although it is theoretically possible to switch to a negative plate supplied by other producers, this in practice is limited by the following factors.

64. First, changing supplier is more difficult when the end-user has concluded a package deal. Typically, suppliers enter into an agreement whereby they agree to provide equipment free of charge or on favourable conditions, but whereby the customer agrees to purchase its consumables (films and plates) from the equipment supplier for a period of time, generally two to three years, the cost of the equipment being assimilated into the prices charged for the consumables. According to the Commission's enquiry, this type of agreement is common in the sector of graphic arts and printing plates and competitors have informed the Commission that these types of deals are increasing.

[. . .]

66. The main purchasers of negative printing plates are newspaper printers, book printers, commercial printers and packaging printers as well as trade shops. According to Agfa and DuPont, customers are under no legal obligation to continue buying consumables from the manufacturer who provides the equipment and arranges its financing. A customer can decide at any time to pay off the outstanding debt for the equipment and purchase consumables from another supplier. However, the Commission considers, and its enquiry has confirmed, that for end-users who have limited financial capacity, the ability to pay off the remaining debt is restricted. It is probable that the end-user will wait until the `package deal expires to find another equivalent supplier of equipment and consumables, and even then the readiness to switch suppliers is restricted, especially if a competitor cannot offer the same package due to a more limited product range. In this respect, figures supplied by the notifying party indicate that less than [. . .] % of end-users that enter into this type of contract decide to switch supplier before the contract expires and that only [. . .] % of end users actually switch suppliers after expiry of the contract. The existence of such contracts therefore constitutes a barrier for competitors wishing to challenge the position of Agfa/DuPont.

[. . .]

69. Thirdly, as has been argued by a number of end users, a switch of suppliers would more fundamentally affect their production process. According to Agfa, switching to a different negative plate supplier can be carried out within a matter of hours by recalibrating the existing equipment. However, customers have stated that they effectively would need a period of one to three months in order to carry out evaluation tests with

recalibrated equipment or new equipment before considering changing their supplier of negative plates, since they would have to be sure that with different plates and potentially different equipment the same quality of end-result would be obtained, and since a change would have an impact on other parts of their printing process (such as modification of substrates, inks, temperature) which would have to be adapted. [. . .]

70. As regards the possibility for end-users to switch, Agfa has further submitted that certain clients, for example larger newspaper printers, have a second source of supply policy, which would in fact confirm that switching to plates from a different supplier is not a problem. However, the Commission does not find this argument convincing. Indeed, only a limited amount of end-users (primarily newspaper printers) appear to pursue such a policy, and it is not a general phenomenon on the negative plates market. According to figures supplied by Agfa, [. . .] clients who purchase at the same time from Agfa and DuPont represent [< 5] % of the total EEA plates market. The fact that certain larger customers have a second supply source is due to their need to continue production when the original source of supply is not available. This means nevertheless that in order to go to a new supplier, the above described barriers would exist.

12.3.5.4. Ability to expand output

The ability of rivals to offset the likelihood of a SIEC post-merger depends on the extent to which they can promptly expand their output to take advantage of the 'soft' stance adopted by the merged entity. This is particularly the case when products are undifferentiated.[407] This ability may be hindered because of capacity constraints faced by rivals, either due to lack of unutilized capacity or because what is left is more expensive to utilize (ie, less efficient production facility or less skilled workforce).[408]

The merged entity may be in a position to constraint the ability of rivals to promptly expand output typically through vertical foreclosure strategies,[409] thanks to the control over input supply of product distribution.

12.3.5.4.1. Agfa Gevaert/DuPont

***Agfa-Gevaert/DuPont* (Case No IV/M.986) Commission Decision** [1998] OJ L 211/22

Besides the concerns about customer switching costs discussed above, the Commission also argued that access to distributors would be foreclosed because of the use of exclusivity agreements with dealers and in light of the wide range of products and services procured by the same supplier.

67. A further element in the assessment of switching of supplier concerns the existence of exclusivity arrangements with suppliers of equipment, which are important in relation to the ability of the new entity and its competitors to conclude package deals. It is furthermore noted that Agfa and DuPont also sell equipment for plate setting and processing. This equipment is either produced internally (DuPont) or obtained, often on an OEM basis, from independent equipment suppliers. Moreover, Agfa has included, in contracts with two of its independent equipment suppliers, exclusivity arrangements whereby

407 Ibid, para 35. 408 Ibid, paras 32–4. 409 Ibid, para 36.

these producers cannot sell the equipment concerned to competitors of Agfawhen equipment has been produced on the basis of Agfa specifications. The fact that post-transaction Agfa will be able to propose package deals using equipment produced in-house, whereas certain of its competitors (eg Kodak/Polychrome, Lastra, Konica), are unable to do so, puts Agfa in a stronger position to conclude such package deals. Consequently, the opportunities for delivering equipment directly and the relationship of Agfa/DuPont with suppliers of equipment constitutes an additional barrier for competitors wishing to contest the position of Agfa/DuPont by offering similar package deals.

68. Secondly, a limiting factor for switching suppliers, at least for a number of dealers, are existing exclusive distribution arrangements: those dealers may only carry Agfa or DuPont products respectively. Agfa has contended that such arrangements are relatively unimportant, since only [. . .] Agfa dealers and only [. . .] dealers of DuPont out of a total of 700 dealers in the EEA are bound by such clauses. However, such dealers are often significant as they cover a large area, often the whole territory of a Member State, and hence represent an important part of the turnover of Agfa and DuPont. Agfa has submitted that [< 60] % of Agfa's sales of offset printing plates to dealers and [< 10] % of DuPont's sales in the EEA are made on an exclusive basis. Specific figures for negative plates sales were not provided by Agfa and DuPont. These existing exclusivity arrangements are considered to constitute further barriers for existing competitors to challenge the position of Agfa/DuPont.

The risk of vertical foreclosure could be particularly acute in network markets where the ability to provide seamless access on a universal basis is a key quality attribute and the rivals would be dependent on the merged entity to secure network interoperability.

12.3.5.4.2. Vodafone Airtouch/Mannesmann

Vodafone Airtouch/Mannesmann **(Case No COMP/M.1795) Commission Decision (12 April 2000)**

This merger led to the creation of the first truly pan-European mobile operator. Notwithstanding the fact that each Member State constituted a separate geographic market, the Commission argued that the exclusive ability to offer seamless pan-EU connectivity would give the merged entity a competitive edge in attracting those retail customers who frequently travel abroad for work or leisure.

44. Following the merger the pre-merger market position of the parties will be significantly strengthened as a result of the increased ability and incentive of the new entity to eliminate actual and/or potential competition. Through its structural integration of mobile networks across Europe into an integrated network the merged entity will be the only mobile operator able to meet in the short to medium term (three to five years according to third parties) the demand for advanced pan-European services given its ability to overcome the technical and commercial barriers to create a truly pan-European integrated network.

45. The merged entity would be the only mobile operator able to capture future growth through new customers, because new customers would be attracted by the services offered by Vodafone Airtouch/Mannesmann on its own network. Given their inability to replicate the new entity's network, competitors will have, at best, ie if they are allowed access to Vodafone's network at all, significant costs and performance/quality disadvantages given its dependency on Vodafone Airtouch/Mannesmann for

instance on roaming agreements in order to offer 'equivalent' pan-European mobile services. This situation is likely to entrench the merged entity into a dominant position on the emerging pan-European market for internationally mobile customers for the foreseeable future because customers of other operators would generally prefer the merged entity to other mobile operators given its unrivalled possibility to provide advanced seamless services across Europe.

46. Third parties would thus need to have access to the merged entity's network to be able to locate its own customers to provide its advanced services to its subscribers also when they are in Vodafone/Mannesmann's home network. The merged entity will therefore have the possibility either to refuse access to the its network or to allow access on terms and conditions which will make third party offerings unattractive or simply not competitive.

The Commission cleared the merger after the parties offered the commitment to provide international roaming to rival mobile networks at non-discriminatory terms.

58. In order to respond to the Commission's serious doubts regarding the market for the provision of advanced mobile telecommunication services to internationally mobile customers, Vodafone Airtouch has submitted undertakings aiming at enabling third party non-discriminatory access to the merged entity's integrated network so as to provide advanced mobile services to their customers. These undertakings cover exclusive roaming agreements, third parties' access to roaming arrangements, third parties' access to wholesale arrangements, standards and SIM-cards and a set of implementing measures aimed at ensuring their effectiveness. In particular, Vodafone Airtouch has proposed to set up a fast track dispute resolution procedure in order to solve disagreements between the merged entity's group and third parties on third parties' access to roaming arrangements, third parties' access to wholesale arrangements, standards and SIM-cards.

59. The provision of a roaming tariff and/or wholesale services will be made on a non-discriminatory basis between operators of the merged entity's group and other mobile operators. The non-discrimination principle will apply to both pricing and quality of the service.

It is worth noting that with the benefit of hindsight this theory of harm was superseded by both the emergence of other pan-EU mobile operators the formation of international roaming alliances among national mobile operators.

12.3.5.5. Loss of a competitive force

The small market share of a target company may underestimate the contribution to competitive rivalry by virtue of being a recent entrant eager to grow in scale by competitive aggressively on prices or example.

12.3.5.5.1. Hutchison 3G UK/Telefónica UK

Hutchison 3G UK/Telefónica UK **(Case M.7612) Commission Decision** [2016] OJ C 357/17, paras 19–22

This merger between O2 and Three would have reduced the number of mobile network operators in the UK geographic market from four to three, the other two remaining brands being

Vodafone and EE, which was recently taken over by British Telecom. The main concern raised by the Commission was due to the fact that, whilst having the smallest customer base, H3G had always posed a strong competitive constraint at the retail level by adopting aggressive commercial strategies, such as being the first to introduce 'all-you-can-eat' pricing plans.

Retail market for mobile telecommunications services

Horizontal non-coordinated effects arising from the elimination of important competitive constraints

19. The Transaction would combine the operations of O2 and Three, respectively the first and the fourth players by subscribers (the second and the fourth by revenues) in the retail market for the provision of mobile telecommunications services in the United Kingdom, creating a market leader by number of subscribers and revenues and significantly increasing the level of market concentration.

20. Three is the latest network operator to have entered the market and has been the driver of competition since its entry, for example by changing the industry trend of restricting data usage and data price increases. Its recent and current market behaviour shows that it is the most aggressive and innovative player. Namely, it offers the most competitive prices in the direct channel, and offered 4G at no extra cost, forcing the industry to abandon strategies to sell 4G at a premium. It also offered such popular propositions as free international roaming and was the first to launch a voice over LTE ('VoLTE') service. Despite being a late entrant, Three managed to build out an excellent network as shown by independent surveys, network tests carried out by independent network performance firms, and data by the national regulator Ofcom. In particular its network was rated as the most reliable of the networks in the United Kingdom.

21. Absent the Transaction Three is likely to continue to compete strongly. Based on the available evidence in its file, the Commission considers it unlikely that Three's ability to compete will materially deteriorate in the next two to three years. In particular, as explained in Annex C (a summary of which is attached) it is unlikely to experience [capacity constraints]. Further, Three is financially sound [. . .]. [. . .] external analyses forecast a dynamically expanding business.

22. Therefore, pre-Transaction Three constitutes an important competitive force pursuant to paragraph 37 of the Horizontal Merger Guidelines, or in any event it exerts an important competitive constraint on that market, and that it is likely to continue exerting such a constraint absent the Transaction.

12.3.5.5.2. ChemChina/Syngenta

In its decision in which it conditionally approved the *ChemChina/Syngenta* merger,[410] the Commission's assessment focused on competition for existing pesticides, since ChemChina did not compete with Syngenta for the development of new and innovative pesticides. Hence, the Commission did not assess the possible effects of the merger transaction on innovation, given that generic suppliers do not compete in innovation of new active ingredients or in formulations based on patented active ingredients. Instead they competed mainly in solo and mixture products based on off-patent active ingredients[411]. The Commission's investigation

[410] *ChemChina/Syngenta* (Case M.7962) Commission Decision C(2017) 2167 final (5 April 2017).
[411] Ibid, para 44.

showed that the parties would have held high combined market shares for a number of pesticides and for certain plant growth regulators, with few other competitors remaining. This effect was reinforced by the fact that Adama is a close and important generic competitor of Syngenta in many of these markets. The Commission concluded that the takeover would have significantly impeded effective competition in a number of relevant markets.

Quite interestingly, the Commission referred in its decision to the 'value chain' for crop protection products (including lawn and garden products), where the chain includes four stages: discovery, development, mixture/formulation, and distribution. The Commission clearly distinguished between the integrated R&D players that are active at all four stages of the value chain and have a global presence, and other players, including generic suppliers or undertakings only present in one of the segments of the crop protection value chain, noting that these two groups of economic actors are characterized by different capabilities in the production chain for crop protection products and are active at different stages of the value chain.[412] Not only are generic players not present in the upstream discovery and development of new active ingredients and therefore do not compete in the discovery of new active ingredients, but also they are usually excluded from the patent strategies adopted by the major R&D players, which at the early stages of the research process, commonly seek 'compound patent' on new active ingredients, providing the patentee the exclusive right 'to manufacture the active ingredient, to incorporate that active ingredient into formulated products and to put those formulated products on the market for the first time.'[413] Generic players cannot therefore use patent-protected active ingredients to produce new formulations that compete with those of the patent holder. Furthermore, 'R&D companies commonly adopt a "post-patent strategy", which involves employing tools to maximise the profitability of their [active ingredients] and avoid generic competition, even after the expiry of the compound patent.'[414] Hence, the space where generic suppliers compete with 'R&D companies' is fairly small and 'even when generic companies appear to hold a substantial share of the market, that share is dependent on access to [active ingredients] which tend to be originated by large R&D players.'[415]

The Commission included various other categories of economic actors, than just generic, in its category of 'other players':

- 'pure' generic players (such as Sipcam, Gowan, Belchim), 'which generally operate on specific regions or relatively few countries, focus primarily on selling "me too"/copycat products or products which are relatively un-differentiated from the original product, either under their own name or as private label products for distributors.'[416]
- 'differentiated' generic players (such as Adama, Nufarm, Arysta/Chemtura, FMC/Cheminova), which 'operate globally and try to differentiate themselves from the 'pure' generic players by, in addition to producing 'me too' versions, also creating alternative mixtures which are not simply copies but attempt to offer differentiated benefits to existing products already available in the market.'[417] The Commission notes that Adama constitutes the only generic player with a substantial geographic coverage across the EEA.[418]
- 'generic active ingredient producers' which are players based in India and Chin, and 'which do not generally try to market or register products themselves outside their home countries' and they 'only sell [active ingredients] to other players that carry out all the formulation, registration, and marketing.'[419]

412 Ibid, paras 29–37 and 41–9. 413 Ibid, para 42. 414 Ibid, para 43.
415 Ibid, para 48. 416 Ibid, para 34. 417 Ibid, para 34.
418 Ibid, para 70. The Commission also noted that other generic suppliers 'do not significantly lag behind': Ibid, para 78.
419 Ibid.

- other agrochemical players that are active in the research of new active ingredients but do not engage in development (such as Sumitomo Chemical Co Ltd, Nihon Nohyaku Co Ltd, Kumiai Chemical Industry Co Ltd, Ishihara Sangyo Kaisha and Mitsui Chemicals Inc, which are 'active in the discovery of new [active ingredients] in certain market segments, but do not compete across the board with the main integrated R&D players and tend to focus on offering products based on off-patent [active ingredients], like the generic players.'[420]

The Commission found that there are seven main generic players active globally, with six generic players being active in the EU (see Figure 12.2).[421] It noted the important barriers to entry in this industry, as the launch of a new active ingredient requires significant time and financial resources due to the rigorous testing that the active ingredient must undergo before being commercialized (the average costs being $286 million and the development and commercialization taking approximately ten years).[422] According to the Commission, barriers to entry include 'building inventive capability, regulatory costs, development skills, expense of research, cost of investment, risk, difficulty to obtain high enough market access, time for registration, and demanding technical requirements,'[423] which further delay the entry of a generic in a market, usually for a period between one and five years (sometimes longer), after a product becomes off patent.[424]

Moving to the analysis of the economic concentration in the affected markets, the Commission noted that Syngenta was the leading integrated R&D player in crop protection markets at the global level and the second biggest agrochemical company in the European market, with market shares of about 30–40 per cent in herbicides and fungicides, and 10–20

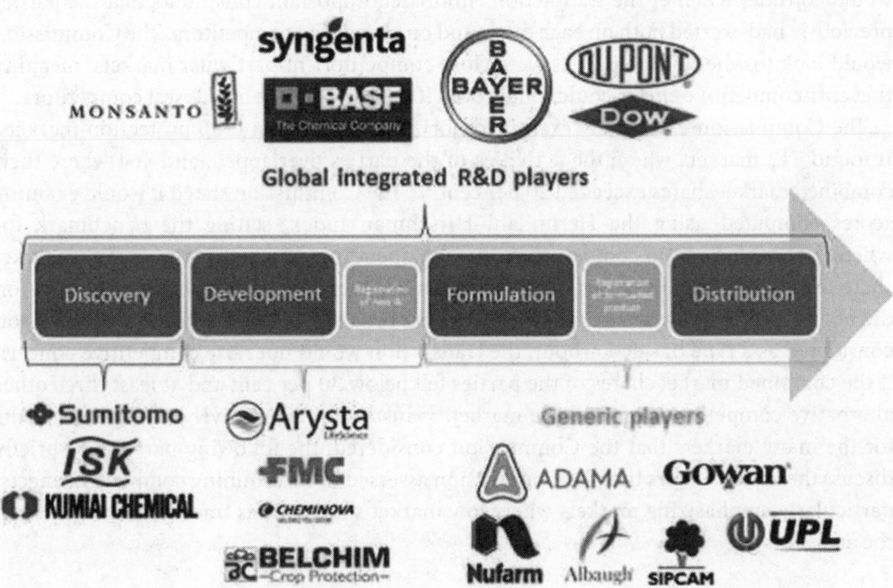

Figure 12.2. Value chain in the production of crop protection products: Key players
Source: ChemChina/Syngenta (Case M.7962) Commission Decision C(2017) 2167 final (5 April 2017), para 31.

420 Ibid, para 37.
421 Ibid, paras 35–6.
422 Ibid, paras 30 and 38.
423 Ibid, para 39.
424 Ibid, para 40.

per cent in insecticides and seed treatment, with a leading crop protection portfolio and active ingredients.[425]

The case was also particularly interesting because of the fact that ChemChina is a State-owned enterprise (SOE). The Commission acknowledged that by virtue of Article 106 TFEU the principle of non-discrimination between public and private undertakings applies and that 'undertakings making up an economic unit with independent power of decision, irrespective of the way in which their capital is held or of the rules of administrative supervision applicable to them'.[426] The issue was raised because Chinese SOEs are managed in China by an administrative body named Central SASAC, which is the State-owned Assets Supervision and Administration Commission of the State Council through which the Central Government supervises and manages the State-owned assets of its State-owned enterprises. The Commission did not decide on the issue as for the purpose of the Transaction, whether ChemChina is regarded as one economic entity with other companies owned by the Chinese Central Government or not, did not have an impact for the competitive assessment. The Commission left the question open and considered the most restrictive approach under which ChemChina is regarded as one economic entity with other companies owned by the Chinese Central Government.[427]

The Commission went on to define markets in the various crop-protection products such as herbicides and fungicides largely based on crop and pest that farmers wished to target, in addition to the timing of application.[428] Concerning geographic markets, the Commission identified worldwide markets for raw materials and active ingredients, but national markets for the various crop-protection products.[429]

In undertaking a competitive assessment of horizontal overlap in the market for active ingredients, the Commission stated that in assessing competitive effects in all markets, it would consider whether the transaction eliminated important constraints that the parties previously had exerted both on each other and on remaining competitors. The Commission would look to whether the parties were close competitors in particular markets, meaning that anti-competitive effects could follow even if the parties were not closest competitors.[430]

The Commission extensively examined horizontal overlap in crop protection markets. It found 712 markets where the activities of the parties overlapped, and 464 where their combined market shares exceeded 20 per cent.[431] The Commission stated it would examine scores computed using the Herfindahl–Hirschman Index, setting the benchmark for whether accretion raised competitive concern depending on whether the relevant market share fell above or below 50 per cent. In the actual assessment, however, the Commission did not make this factor determinative. As another broad set of criteria that the Commission considered as a type of safe harbour, the transaction would not raise competitive concern if the combined market shares of the parties fell below 30 per cent and at least three other alternative competitors supplied the market.[432] Instead of exhaustively setting out results for the many markets that the Commission considered, the following paragraphs briefly discuss the varied factors that the Commission assessed in determining competitive effects, particularly emphasizing markets where low market share figures traditionally would end the analysis.

[425] Ibid, paras 52–7. [426] Ibid, para 81. [427] Ibid, para 88.
[428] See eg ibid, paras 108, 121, 143. [429] Ibid, paras 161, 166, 174. [430] Ibid, para 178, 182.
[431] Ibid, para 320. [432] Ibid, paras 322, 324.

As the Commission said it would, it placed considerable weight on whether the parties competed head-to-head in the relevant market prior to the merger.[433] It also looked closely at the incremental increase in market share that the merger created, with shares below 5 per cent usually not raising competitive concern. Occasionally, the Commission did not find anti-competitive effects despite the transaction producing both high market shares and significant accretion. In the Cereals-Wheat-Fungicides-Leafspots market in Greece, for example, the merger permitted the parties to attain a 50–60 per cent market share, which had increased by 20–30 per cent. Yet the Commission noted that BASF held a sizable share as well (30–40 per cent), and that Bayer was also active on the market (< 5 per cent). The presence of either or both integrated crop-protection companies and generics on a given market mitigated the effect of higher market shares. The Commission also placed considerable weight on potential barriers to entry and expansion, which were minor in this example because at least five companies held fungicide product registrations for wheat in Greece and thus could respond to price fluctuations without incurring the significant costs in terms of money and time to register new products. The parties in this example lastly did not share active ingredients, suggesting product differentiation.[434]

More frequently, the Commission found liability despite market share levels that, when viewed perhaps in other markets, would raise little concern. The relative position of rivals mattered to the Commission: The Commission found that the transaction removed a 'dynamic' rival from the market, Adama, which between 2013 and 2015 materially had increased sales. The Commission determined that the parties were close competitors, whose products were in the same chemical class, indicating a similar mode of action. Adama had planned to launch new formulations over the short-term and had products in its pipeline that suggested the combined entity's market share would not decrease.[435] The Commission thus found a significant impediment to effective competition based largely on the likely development of the market after the merger.

Most strikingly, in several instances the Commission determined that liability existed in markets where the combined entity's share fell below 30 per cent. Consider, for example, the market for Oilseed Rape-Fungicides-Leaves/Leafspots in Estonia. The merger created an entity with the third-largest share of the market, at 20–30 per cent, with Bayer (40–50 per cent) and BASF (30–40 per cent) retaining stronger positions. The transaction increased the combined entity's market share by 10–20 per cent and eliminated the only generic company active on the market, Adama, which had recently entered the market. The Commission determined that the parties were close competitors that competed directly with several products, and that the parties were planning to launch new formulations and mixtures that would maintain or enhance their market position.[436] The Commission acknowledged the low market share, but stated that between the closeness of the parties' products, pipeline products, and the growth plans of the entities, it considered that the market share levels did not fully incorporate the degree to which the parties restrained each other, and the future market strength of the combined entity.[437]

433 See eg ibid, para 341. 434 Ibid, para 359–60, 362–4. 435 Ibid, paras 507–8, 510–13.

436 Ibid, paras 965–6, 968–71.

437 Ibid, para 972. For markets that resemble this one, see ibid, paras 981, 1002, 1010, 1048, 1090, 1105, 1344, 1464, 1619, 1939.

12.3.6. COORDINATED EFFECTS

Non-coordinated (unilateral) effects can be described as the outcome of a sequence of uncoordinated reactions to an initial internally coordinated 'soft' move. In contrast, under coordinated effects rivals reciprocate by adopting a matching 'soft' stance.[438]

Normally, it does not make sense to adopt a 'soft' strategic stance unless there is an expectation that rivals would reciprocate, thus not taking advantage by reacting aggressively: respectively, by increasing output to fill the gap left and keeping prices constant in order to steal business. Hence, there must be a reciprocal understanding among rivals that they can be collectively better off by not acting in their best (self) interest. Therefore, collusion is very much considered to be departure from the norm where firms' decisions are not conditional on rivals deviating from their best unilateral course of conduct. To this end, patience is the key virtue: firms must have a shared understanding that everyone is better-off by sharing collusive profits, potentially up to the monopoly profit, over the long-term, rather than by cheating unilaterally in order to grab a higher share of overall profits in the short-term, but then facing retaliation triggered by the breach of trust, typically, in the form of a prolonged period of intensive competitive rivalry.

When firms compete by setting quantities, the merged entity's initial quantity reduction induces rivals to reduce theirs; whereas if firms compete by setting prices, rivals response to the initial increase in prices by the merged entity is to raise their own prices to such an extent that they fail to steal customers from the merger entity. Therefore, regardless of the model of competition, post-merger price (output) levels and firms' profits would tend to be higher (lower) than under unilateral effects, thus causing greater costumer detriment.

Where competition is on prices, however, it is difficult to distinguish between coordinated and unilateral effects, since in both cases prices move up in parallel post-merger, albeit to a larger extent under the former. Identification should be easier where firms compete by setting quantities,[439] as well as by setting production capacities, R&D and/or advertising spending. Under unilateral effects rivals are expected to partly offset the initial quantity reduction by the merged entity, whereas under coordinated effects rivals would be expected to reduce their own quantities in parallel.

Coordinated effects under merger control equates to tacit collusion, where rivals manage to reach a common understanding of what are the terms of coordination without communication, which would constitute a cartel infringement under Article 101(1) TFEU. The more complex and volatile the environment in which firms set their strategic conduct and the more difficult it is to overcome this hurdle. For example, when firms coordinate on prices, the fact that each firm offer multiple tariffs can be a material obstacle, unless firms coordinate on simple rules of thumb such a constant relationships between different prices.[440] Arguably, it is easier to coordinate by splitting the market either geographically or across clearly observable segments.

438 For a detailed discussion, see M Ivaldi et al, 'The Economics of Tacit Collusion', Interim Report for the DG Competition (November 2003), available at ec.europa.eu/competition/mergers/studies_reports/the_economics_of_tacit_collusion_en.pdf.

439 Quantity competition may include, loosely speaking, a situation where firms collude by splitting the market, either geographically or alongside any other segmentation attribute, to the extent that an uncoordinated rivalry would suggests firms shall expand their output by entering each other territories/market segments.

440 Horizontal Merger Guidelines, para 45.

Once the terms of coordination have been tacitly agreed the likelihood of coordinated effects rest on the sustainability of collusion.[441] In detail, there are two sustainability constraints that must be satisfied concurrently, one internal and the other external, respectively: (a) it must be in the individual interest of colluding firms to stick to the coordinated outcome; and (b) the prospect that the collusive agreement might be disrupted by outsiders is remote.

The former constraint requires first of all that firms are able to promptly detect unilateral deviations from the tacitly agreed terms of coordination. Furthermore, firms' ability to promptly react upon detection and thus minimize the gains from deviation must represent a credible threat. Therefore, likelihood of prompt reaction rests on the capacity, on the part of the colluding firms, to mutually observe their conduct in order to identify any deviation from the collusive common course of conduct. For example, where firms allegedly compete for customer's business through bespoken negotiations, such as with large and complex procurement contracts, the degree of transparency among colluding firms might be hampered by the fact that prices and quantities are private information, rather than available in the public domain. As to the credibility and, hence, effectiveness of the threat of firms' reaction to deviation, the simplest and most credible collective reaction would be to revert to the 'normal' competitive mode on a permanent basis. There can be more complex forms of retaliation with the aim of inflicting tougher punishment. For example, firms can temporarily set prices below cost. Ideally, firms would want to specifically target the cheating firm, for example, by offering selective discounts to poach its customers.

The key question then is what incremental impact the merger would have on the sustainability of a collusive agreement. Besides the obvious observation that a merger reduces the number of firms—which would tend to increase the benefit from sharing collusive profits over the long-term, vis-à-vis the short-term benefits from deviation—the likelihood of internal sustainability can be improved to the extent that the merger improves the symmetry among firms with respect to costs, capacities, product ranges, product quality, and market shares. Furthermore, a merger can strengthen external sustainability in case the target firm is considered the least likely to agree to coordinate in the first place, that is, because it typically exhibits a divergent strategic pattern by, for example, systematically undercutting rivals or continuously launching new products. This type of firm is called a 'maverick'.

The sustainability criteria outlined above were first set out by the General Court (then the Court of First Instance) in the seminal *Airtours* judgment,[442] where the Commission was criticized for failing to provide a coherent theoretical underpinning to a finding that a merger may give rise to a position of collective dominance in the absence of structural or contractual links among the alleged colluding firms. Recent judgments by the General Court in *Impala*[443] and then in the subsequent appeal the Court of Justice in *Sony/BMG*[444] highlighted the difficulties in applying this test to establish that a position of collective dominance already exist.[445] This line of inquiry is of relevance to merger control as coordinated effects can also arise where a merger may strengthen an already existing position of collective dominance.[446]

441 Ibid, paras 49–57.

442 Case T-342/99, *Airtours plc v Commission* [2002] ECR II–2585, para 62.

443 Case T-464/04, *Impala v Commission* [2006] ECR II–2289.

444 Case 413/06 P, *Bertelsmann AG and Sony Corporation of America v Independent Music Publishers and Labels Association (Impala)* [2008] ECR I–4951.

445 What follows is based on P Siciliani, 'Should We Act *Ex Post* Against Tacit Collusion and How?' (2014) 5(5) *J European Competition L & Practice* 294.

446 Horizontal Merger Guidelines, para 39.

12.3.6.1. *Ex post* identification

Notwithstanding the theoretical appeal of the *Airtours* test, its implementation in the context of an *ex post* assessment of the existence of a position of collective dominance can be problematic when the existence of a credible and effective retaliatory mechanism is conjectured, rather than based on actual observation of past conducts. This can often be the case where all that can be observed is that the alleged firms see to be following a common course of conduct. That is to say, the conjectured retaliatory mechanism is so effective that the mere threat thereof successfully deters deviation. Under these circumstances, a contentious debate ensues whereby the plaintiff's argument that there exists a credible and effective retaliatory mechanism in theory is contrasted by the defendant's argument that the incentives to deviate, instead, are simply too strong. The identification of collusion in the absence of evidence or past episodes of deviation followed by a phase of retaliation is problematic, given the difficulty in determining whether the observed parallel conduct is the result of collusion rather than orthodox uncoordinated competitive rivalry.

As pointed out by the General Court in *Impala*, 'the most effective deterrent is that which has not been used'.[447] Therefore, the requirement to prove the existence of a specific retaliatory mechanism and its deterrent effect, rather than the existence of a potential retaliatory mechanism, should be relevant only insofar as there is evidence of past deviations from the common course of conduct.[448] Accordingly, the General Court in *Impala* considered the adoption of a less stringent interpretation of the *Airtours* criteria when applied *ex post*, one that could rely

> [on] a very mixed series of indicia and items of evidence relating to the signs, manifestations and phenomena inherent in the presence of a collective dominant position. [. . .] Thus, in particular, close alignment of prices over a long period, especially if they are above a competitive level, together with other factors typical of a collective dominant position, might, in the absence of an alternative reasonable explanation, suffice to demonstrate the existence of a collective dominant position, [. . .].[449]

In *Sony/BGM*, the Court of Justice further qualified this approach by clarifying that

> the investigation of a pre-existing collective dominant position based on a series of elements normally considered to be indicative of the presence or the likelihood of tacit coordination between competitors cannot therefore be considered to be objectionable of itself. However, [. . .] it is essential that such an investigation be carried out with care and, above all, that it should adopt an approach based on the analysis of such plausible coordination strategies as may exist in the circumstances.[450]

In particular, the Court argued that 'the assessment [. . .] should not be undertaken in an isolated and abstract manner, but should be carried out using the mechanism of a hypothetical tacit coordination as a basis'.[451]

447 Case T-464/04, *Impala v Commission* [2006] ECR I–2289, para 466.

448 Ibid, para 469. See also G Aigner, O Budzinski, and A Christiansen, 'The Analysis of Coordinated Effects in EU Merger Control: Where Do We Stand after *Sony/BMG* and *Impala*?' (2006) 2 *European Competition J* 311, 329.

449 Case T-464/04, *Impala v Commission* [2006] ECR I–2289, paras 251–2.

450 Case C-413/06 P, *Bertelsmann AG and Sony Corporation of America v Independent Music Publishers and Labels Association (Impala)*, ECLI:EU:C:2008:392, para 129.

451 Ibid, para 126.

12.3.6.2. A hybrid theory?

When firms compete by setting prices it is difficult to tell whether parallel price increases post-merger are due to coordinated or unilateral effects. However, in the absence of rivals' capacity constraints or customer search or switching costs, for this to be the case substitute products must be differentiated, as otherwise the merger entity would be fearful that a price increase post-merger would be highly unprofitable due to rivals' undercutting. The more fungible (homogeneous) rival products are, the larger the loss of customers for the merger entity in response to a post-merger price increase. Accordingly, under homogeneous price competition the observation of parallel price increases after the merger could only be explained by a theory of coordinated effects.[452]

Unless, that is, firms anticipate that there is no point in pricing aggressively since no additional customer would be gained due to the fact that rivals match prices immediately in order to retain their customers. Under these circumstances, parallel monopoly pricing would be the only rational choice since in the worst of circumstances prices would have to be adjusted downwards to retain customers in response to irrational attempts by rivals to undercut in order to attract new customers. That is to say, coordination would be superfluous because non-coordination would yield the same outcome.

This undesirable scenario may explain why the US antitrust authorities seem to have included the described market configuration under the scope of their revised 2010 Horizontal Merger Guidelines under the rubric of coordinated effects.

DOJ and FTC, Horizontal Merger Guidelines (2010), 25

> A market typically is more vulnerable to coordinated conduct if a firm's prospective competitive reward from attracting customers away from its rivals will be significantly diminished by likely responses of those rivals. This is more likely to be the case, the stronger and faster are the responses the firm anticipates from its rivals. The firm is more likely to anticipate strong responses if there are few significant competitors, if products in the relevant market are relatively homogeneous, if customers find it relatively easy to switch between suppliers, or if suppliers use meeting-competition clauses.

At its core, this line of argument rests on the assumption that firms can react by matching rivals' prices immediately in order to retain their customers. In this respect, however, it is hard to see how a merger could have any impact whatsoever on the sustainability of such an unorthodox non-coordinated outcome. That is to say, a decision to prohibit a merger might prove ineffective in order to prevent (or undermine) the emergence (the resilience) of this anti-competitive outcome.[453]

Such a market configuration can be traced back to Edward Chamberlain's seminal contribution in 1929.[454] He argued that the conventional assumption of profit maximization entails

452 Moreover, under these circumstances collusion would be very desirable given that non-coordinated pricing rivalry would make it impossible for firms to sustain price-cost mark-ups, ie, contrary to a scenario where firms benefit from product differentiation (eg resulting in brand loyalty).

453 In this respect, it is worth noting that under these circumstances there is no room for market self-correction through entry, because new entrants would either align to prevailing monopoly pricing (rather than irrationally attempt to undercut incumbents) or be deterred in the first place in case successful entry depended on the use of a penetration strategy in the form of a price temporarily below prevailing market levels.

454 EH Chamberlain, 'Duopoly: Value Where Sellers Are Few' (1929) 44(1) *Q J Economics* 63.

a monopoly price for any fairly small number of sellers, because no competitor would attempt to undercut rivals knowing that his own move has a considerable effect upon his competitors, and that this makes it idle to suppose that they will accept without retaliation the losses he forces upon them by price undercutting.[455]

It is worth noting that the feasibility of this outcome rests on the same fundamentals that underpin tacit collusion,[456] that is, the ability to monitor rivals' conduct and to quickly react in case of misalignment. Nevertheless, it is fair to say that immediate reaction to rivals undercutting is still the exception rather than the norm, although in a world where people shop around primarily on-line and can seamlessly execute a transaction at the touch of a button, whilst firms deploy algorithms to track and match rival prices in real time, this seemingly intractable theory of harm may increasingly become a concrete possibility.

12.3.7. LOSS OF POTENTIAL COMPETITION AND BARRIERS TO ENTRY

A merger where the target firm is not competing in the same relevant market of the acquiring firm can still give rise to a SIEC, whether non-coordinated or coordinated, if there is a realistic prospect that the former could decide to enter the market in the near future but for the merger in question.[457] The threat of entry is stronger where the target company already has, or is very likely to acquire, the availability of assets that could facilitate entry, such as a distribution network which overlaps with the one used by the acquiring firm.[458] Evidence of actual plans to enter at an advanced stage would point towards that conclusion.[459] However, the likelihood of a SIEC is reduced if there are a sufficient number of potential competitors left able to discipline actual competitors.[460]

12.3.7.1. *Air Liquide/BOC*

***Air Liquide/BOC* (Case COMP/M.1630) Commission Decision** [2004] OJ L92/1

Air Liquide and BOC were both suppliers of bulk and cylinder gases, respectively, in the two separate geographic markets of France and UK/Ireland. The Commission raised strong concern that absent the merger Air Liquide was the only credible potential entrant able to challenge the other party dominant position in UK/Ireland.

201. Air Liquide represents one of the strongest potential entrants in BOC's national home markets. Competitors have stressed that Air Liquide would have been best placed amongst all industrial gases companies to make inroads into the United Kingdom market. Once the parties have merged, this competitive pressure would be lost. This would be true irrespective of whether or not Air Liquide was already active in BOC's home market.

455 GJ Werden, 'Economic Evidence on the Existence of Collusion: Reconciling Antitrust Law with Oligopoly Theory' (2004) 71 *Antitrust LJ* 719, 725.

456 See, in this respect, JE Harrington, 'Evaluating Mergers for Coordinated Effects and the Role of "Parallel Accommodating Conduct"' (2013) 78(3) *Antitrust LJ* 651, 653–6.

457 Horizontal Merger Guidelines, para 58. 458 Ibid, 59. 459 Ibid, 60. 460 Ibid.

202. In its reply to the statement of objections, the notifying party admits that a dominant supplier can be restrained in the exercise of its market power by potential competition from other undertakings which could realistically enter the market. The notifying party disputes that any potential entrant has had any such effect in the United Kingdom. However, individual customers have indicated a different view.

203. Air Liquide argues that its qualification as a potential competitor is purely theoretical because it has never tried to penetrate the United Kingdom market and is less likely to do so now that others have entered the market. However, a project study submitted to the Commission shows that Air Liquide has contemplated supplying bulk and cylinder gases in the United Kingdom when consulted by a customer. Moreover, Air Liquide concedes that Messer has been able to overcome the entry barriers to the United Kingdom bulk and cylinder markets, without however offering reasons why Air Liquide should not realistically be able to enter the United Kingdom market itself. Indeed, Air Liquide has the most successful history in entering other European markets of all industrial gases companies. By stating at the oral hearing that its absence from the United Kingdom is a business decision, Air Liquide has acknowledged that no objective factors would have prevented it from entering the United Kingdom market.

204. Finally, the notifying party stated at the oral hearing that, as a similarly large industrial gases company, Praxair should be considered an equally credible potential competitor in the United Kingdom. However, the notifying party has not explained why a company that has most of its operations on the American continent and a limited presence in Europe should be as credible an entrant as Air Liquide, the strongest industrial gases supplier in Europe.

[. . .]

209. In the markets for cylinder and bulk gases, the main barriers to entry consist of the capital investment and operating expenses involved in establishing and sustaining a production and distribution infrastructure, in the acquisition of a sufficient customer base to justify that expenditure, and in the financing of operative losses during a start-up period until the newly established business becomes profitable.

210. Investment and operating costs vary depending on which method of market entry is chosen. If a new entrant chooses to bid for on-site tonnage contracts, with the intention of over-sizing the production facility and selling excess capacity to bulk or cylinder customers, a substantial up-front investment is required. In most cases, the cost incurred will be recovered over the duration of the contract, given that on-site supply contracts typically run for a period of 10–15 years. However, only a limited number of large industrial gases companies have the financial resources (and more generally, the project management capability) to launch such large projects. If the entrant chooses to first establish a cylinder distribution infrastructure and subsequently extend its business into the bulk market, the initial capital investment (establishment of a cylinder depot and a filling facility) will be in the range of EUR 2–3 million. However, the construction of an air separation unit and related further transfill centres will require a substantially higher investment, in the order of EUR 50–60 million. In addition, operating costs and transport costs for gases that have to be imported will be incurred on a continuous basis. In principle, similar costs will be incurred in the long term if an entrant acquires a small local supplier and tries to expand the acquired infrastructure.

The Commission considered that Air Linde had the financial strength needed to withstand any attempt by BOC to deter entry through aggressive pricing (ie, akin to a predatory pricing strategy).

211. A newly established industrial gases business often takes a certain period of time to become profitable. The need to sustain operative losses during this start-up

period constitutes an additional barrier to entry. If market entry occurs, incumbent suppliers may attempt to prevent the entrant from establishing a significant foothold in their home market by seeking to undercut the entrant's prices in the area in which the entry takes place. Competitors have provided examples of how BOC has pursued this strategy in order to deny them entry to the United Kingdom market. This means that the entrant will have to be able to finance an operative loss during a start-up period.

212. Large industrial gases companies are therefore better able to enter a market already dominated by an incumbent than smaller suppliers. Large companies are more likely to have the financial strength, the logistical and technological resources and the strategic planning ability to make the necessary investments and sustain market entry against aggressive counter-action by a locally dominant incumbent. In the case of the United Kingdom, this assessment is borne out by the observation that two large competitors based abroad, Linde and Messer, have been more successful in gaining market share than small start-up entrants, even though the latter were operating from within the United Kingdom (for instance Energas and Medigas).

213. Against this background, Air Liquide, as the leading industrial gas company in Europe, possesses specific strengths making it the foreign competitor most suited and most likely to enter the United Kingdom market.

214. Air Liquide has a strong capability to establish a production and distribution infrastructure in foreign markets. This is demonstrated by the fact that Air Liquide has successfully established a production and distribution network for industrial gases in a range of European countries, comprising stand-alone production plants (bulk gases plants), dedicated plants (plants dedicated to one or several customers) with excess production capacity for the bulk market, small on-site production plants and cylinder filling facilities. [. . .]

219. The analysis of Air Liquide's specific competitive strengths confirms that Air Liquide is well placed to enter the United Kingdom cylinder and bulk markets. Furthermore Air Liquide is better placed than any other competitor to successfully sustain such market entry. While Linde and Messer have established a limited presence in the United Kingdom cylinder and bulk markets, their competitive strength, especially if weighed against BOC's market power, is much more limited than the competition Air Liquide could mount in the United Kingdom and Ireland. Indeed, neither of those two companies has, in the past, been able to establish itself in other European countries to the same extent as Air Liquide. Other competitors (Praxair, AGA), are significantly smaller in terms of size, overall market share and production as well as distribution infrastructure in Europe. Neither company is as well placed as Air Liquide to enter the United Kingdom and Irish markets. No other large industrial gases companies exist that could enter the United Kingdom and Irish markets. Air Liquide is therefore the only credible potential competitor.

220. In conclusion, potential competition in the markets for cylinder and bulk gases in the United Kingdom and Ireland largely depends on Air Liquide's continuing presence as an independent competitor. Once the incumbent (BOC) and the strongest potential entrant (Air Liquide) were merged, this competitive pressure would be lost.

221. There is consensus in the industry that an industrial gas company's decision to enter a foreign market is a strategic business decision. Any industrial gas company that wishes to grow in the long term cannot do so without expanding its geographic market coverage. This is best demonstrated by Air Liquide's history of expansion in Europe and world-wide, in particular in countries that are remote from its home base. Competitors have unanimously stressed that each industrial gas company, in pursuing its expansion strategy, will weigh the investments required and the risks involved. Given that Air Liquide would have been best placed to expand its operations into the United Kingdom and Ireland, it has to be concluded that the decision not to do so to date is one that

could have been reversed. Indeed, Air Liquide has considered becoming active in the United Kingdom market in the past (see paragraph 203).

222. It should be stressed that the Commission's objections are not directed against Air Liquide's business strategy to date which may have been to not (yet) launch substantial activities in the United Kingdom and Ireland. Rather, the specific competition concerns arising from the proposed concentration relate to the elimination of the most credible potential competitor in the markets concerned. Irrespective of whether the competitor concerned has previously been willing to launch effective competition, the proposed concentration would permanently remove the possibility of such competition taking place. The proposed concentration would thus permanently eliminate potential competition and thereby strengthen BOC's existing dominant position in the markets concerned. The likely result would be that the combined entity (Air Liquide/BOC) would be able to perpetually dominate the markets for cylinder and bulk gases in the United Kingdom and Ireland.

There can be circumstances where the threat of potential competition is less palpable but where a merger could still give rise to a SIEC, in particular by strengthening a dominant position. It is often argued that the valuation of Internet start-ups is very subjective due to the elusive nature of the key intangible asset underpinning their business model, that is, the acquisition of a large customer base. To this end, firms typically attract users by offering their services for free, thus incurring material operational losses for a number of years before the prospect of turning the venture into a profitable business. Furthermore, it is argued that once the customer base is in place, it is easier to launch new services thanks to the availability of a critical mass. Therefore, the threat of potential competition is based on the availability of a large user base, rather than the fact that the target company is currently offering similar functionalities.[461]

The threat posed by the future entry of potential competitors is taken into consideration regardless of whether the target company is one of them. In the presence of low entry barriers even a merged entity with a large market share would anticipate that to increase prices—or lower quantity, quality or variety—in order to increase profits post-merger may attract new entrants.[462] To be an effective threat, potential competitors should be able to enter within two year and on a sufficient scale.[463]

Entry can be deterred by a number of factors.[464] Barriers to entry can result from legal or regulatory barriers, lack of access to essential facilities, supply of essential input, intellectual property rights or essential patents. Entry can also be strategically deterred because of the incumbent reputation, brand loyalty, large unutilized capacity and the presence of switching costs.

461 For example, it could be argued that one of the main rationales underpinning Facebook's acquisitions of Instagram in 2012 and WhatsApp in 2014 was to prevent them from growing in scale and scope up to a point where they could have threatened Facebook's primacy in social networking, in particular, thanks to their greater appeal towards young audiences. See A Hurtong, 'Three Smart Lessons From Facebook's Purchase Of WhatsApp', *Forbes* (24 February 2014), available at www.forbes.com/sites/adamhartung/2014/02/24/zuckerbergs-3-smart-leadership-lessons-from-facebook-buying-whatsapp/. Controlling or eliminating a disruptor, or having access to its assets (data, algorithms) therefore neutralizing its potential to develop to a competitive threat forms the main reason of these 'killer acquisitions'. There is considerable evidence that this is occurring in the pharmaceutical sector where it seems that more than 6% of acquisitions every year are 'killer acquisitions': *see* C. Cunningham, F. Ederer, and S. Ma, Killer Acquisitions (2018), available at: http://faculty.som.yale.edu/songma/files/cem_killeracquisitions.pdf. Recent economic studies have noted a similar tendency in the digital sector: see, Digital Competition Expert Panel (Jason Furman review), Unlocking Digital Competition (March 2019), available at https://assets.publishing.service.gov.uk/government/uploads/system/uploads/attachment_data/file/785547/unlocking_digital_competition_furman_review_web.pdf, p. 49.

462 Horizontal Merger Guidelines, para 70.

463 Ibid, paras 74–5.

464 Ibid, para 71.

12.3.7.2. *The Coca-Cola Company/Carlsberg A/S*

***The Coca-Cola Company/Carlsberg A/S* (Case IV/M.833) Commission Decision** [1998] OJ L 145/41

In this decision the Commission concluded that the threat of potential competition on a sufficient scale was not credible in the markets for carbonated soft drinks (CSD) in Denmark and Sweden.

(c) Barriers to entry for potential competitors

72. The main barriers to entry to the CSD market are access to brands and to a distribution network, as well as to shelf space, a sales and service network, brand image and loyalty and advertising sunk costs. TCCC, PepsiCo and Cadbury Schweppes are the only international brand owners. In view of the risks, costs and the time needed to launch an international brand it is likely that only the existing three international brand owners would be able to launch new international CSD brands in any country. On the Danish market only Carlsberg and Bryggerigruppen have, in the past, been able to launch national premium brands. Therefore, it appears that only the existing brand owners in Denmark would be able to launch new brands.

73. CSDs rely heavily on brand image to drive sales, and companies like TCCC and PepsiCo have established brand loyalty through heavy investments to maintain the high profile of their brands. The introduction of a new brand would thus require heavy expenditure on advertising and promotion in order to persuade brand-loyal consumers to switch away from their usual CSD brand. Moreover, consumer loyalty to the established brands would make it difficult for a new supplier to persuade retail customers to change suppliers and would thus further hinder entry. Such advertising and promotion expenditures are sunk costs and add substantially to the risk of entry.

74. In addition, any potential entrant would also be hindered by the need for access to bottling and to a distribution system. Each of the major brewers in Denmark has its own distribution system, meaning that any new entrant would have to either incur the significant cost of setting up its own system or negotiate with a competitor for the use of their system. It is unlikely that a new entrant would find it economically viable to set up a new distribution operation, since the entrant would have to include beers and packaged waters in its system in order to achieve a sufficient volume of distribution. The brewers' power in this field is reinforced by the fact that CSDs are distributed in refillable containers and any new entrant's bottles would have to comply with the relevant standards. Therefore, a new entrant's products would have to be distributed by one of the existing brewers as is today the case for TCCC and Cadbury Schweppes products, which are distributed by Carlsberg, and PepsiCo brands, which are distributed by Bryggerigruppen. However, as the existing brewers are well established, and have their own line of soft drinks, it would be difficult for a new entrant to find distribution. Moreover, Carlsberg's holdings in several other Danish brewers make it less likely that any potential entrant would be able to cooperate or otherwise form an alliance with a Danish brewing company. Furthermore, as mentioned above, it should be noted that Carlsberg has by far the best and most wide-ranging distribution system on the Danish market. For a new entrant the most efficient way to enter the Danish market would be to be distributed by Carlsberg.

75. Finally, even if a new entrant were to obtain access to an adequate distribution network, the firm would still have to obtain shelf space and incur the expenses of

supporting a sales and service network in order to ensure that its products were properly stocked and positioned. The Commission has recognised the importance of having a sales and service network to induce customers to take on a product line.

The Commission concluded that entry on a small scale or without brand-building advertising campaign would not suffice.

76. The Commission recognises that entry may be possible on a smaller scale, for example by deliveries of DOBs [distributors' own brands] directly to a supermarket chain with distribution completed through the supermarket chain's distribution system. This strategy has been used by Saltum. It is a strategy which does not involve heavy advertising costs or major investment in a distribution system. Saltum has in the period 1990 to 1995 been able to increase its CSD volume from 19 to 54 million litres. This increase in volume arises from sales of Saltum's own brands, an increase in its supplies of DOBs to a supermarket chain and the acquisition of another producer of discount CSDs. In comparison, Bryggerigruppen, the PepsiCo bottler, increased its volume from 39 to 58 million litres in the period 1990 to 1995. However, an assessment of the competitive impact of a producer like Saltum cannot be made simply by looking at the increase in its volume sold, as argued by the parties at the Hearing and in the Response. It must be noted that the growth of Saltum has mainly been achieved through an acquisition and the production of DOBs for one supermarket chain. Moreover, it is incorrect to say that Saltum is one of the three largest Danish brands by considering its total production, as one third of its production is of DOBs and one fifth represents another discount brand acquired recently by Saltum. Finally, it is necessary to look at the impact of discount brands and DOBs on the whole market.

77. Discount brands and DOBs have achieved a certain success in the retail channel, but are of little importance in the service trade and Horeca. Discount brands and DOBs therefore only have an impact on specific parts of the market. It is correct as the parties stated at the Hearing that discount brands have increased their volume share of the market in the period 1986 to 1996. However, more importantly, in value terms the share of discount brands and DOBs actually decreased from 24% of the market in 1993 to 21% of the market in 1995. Furthermore, it is clear from Nielsen data that the average retail price for all CSDs has not decreased in the last two years. Finally, the price differences between Denmark and neighbouring countries are substantial. This is evidence that discount brands and DOBs have not been able to create competition which has led to a lower price level for consumers. It, therefore, appears that branded CSDs are of importance to enable a producer to be an effective competitor. In any case, the most likely companies to enter the CSD market with discount brands or DOBs are the established brewers who are already on the market with such products.

78. For these reasons there do not appear to be any potential competitors who would or could enter the Danish overall CSD markets at either a brand or bottling level.

12.3.8. COUNTERVAILING BUYER POWER

Even in the absence of a threat of potential competition, a merged entity with a large market share may still not be able to impose price increases against essential buyer. For this to be the case, the buyer in question must account for a very large chunk of the merged entity total sales,[465] whereas the buyer has the concrete option to source its supplies elsewhere. This

465 Ibid, para 64.

opt-out option does not have to be in place yet: the buyer could either threaten to sponsor the entry of a new supplier or even decide to set up its own supplier by vertically integrating upstream.[466]

The threat to switch supplier must not only be credible,[467] but also sufficient, in the sense that it is not enough that a powerful buyer is able to negotiate better terms of supply whilst the majority of other customers are made worse-off.[468]

12.3.8.1. *Enso/Stora*

Enso/Stora **(Case IV/M.1225) Commission Decision** [1999] OJ L 254/9

The analysis of countervailing buyer power was relevant to the provision of liquid packaging board used for milk and juice packaging, where the merged entity had a combined market share of between 50 per cent and 70 per cent and the rest split between to smaller suppliers. Peculiarly, this market configuration was mirrored on the demand-side, where Tetra Pak was by far the largest buyer, followed by two smaller firms.

84. The liquid packaging board market is characterised by few large producers and few large buyers. In addition to Stora and Enso, the producers of liquid packaging board in Europe include only Korsnäs and AssiDomän. Buyers of liquid packaging board are few and the market is dominated by Tetra Pak, which represents an estimated market share of close to [between 60 and 80 per cent]. The other main buyers of liquid packaging board are Elopak and SIG Combibloc with about [between 10 and 20 per cent] of the EEA market each. After the merger the structure of the supply-side will mirror the structure of the demand-side of the market for liquid packaging board, with one large supplier and two smaller suppliers facing one large buyer and two smaller buyers.

85. According to the parties, the three large customers, and Tetra Pak in particular, exercise considerable buyer power that prevents the producers of liquid packaging board from increasing prices.

86. The investigation showed that the relationship between the suppliers and the customers is one of mutual dependency. In the liquid packaging board market the relationships between suppliers and buyer are of a long-term nature and switching supplier of liquid packaging board is rare. The customers have indicated that switching the supplier would lead to delays, is costly and technically demanding due to the fact that the evaluation process for liquid packaging board is complex and time-consuming. In particular, the investigation showed that to become a supplier for a specific type of liquid packaging board requires considerable investment from both the producer and the customer in terms of machinery, technical support production and product trials as well as human resources.

89. Tetra Pak buys about [more than 500 000 tonnes] of liquid packaging board per year for use in the EEA. This volume is bought from Enso, Stora, AssiDomän and Korsnäs. Outside the EEA, Tetra Pak also uses other local suppliers. Tetra Pak has in the past been instrumental in developing several of its current suppliers into producers of liquid packaging board.

90. Tetra Pak buys about [more than 50 per cent] of its requirements in the EEA from Stora Enso. The purchases of Tetra Pak represent the whole output of several board machines and about [more than 50 per cent] of the parties' total output for the EEA.

466 Ibid, para 65. 467 Ibid, para 66. 468 Ibid, para 67.

Furthermore, it has to be considered that the production of liquid packaging board is a high fixed-cost industry, where high rates of capacity utilisation are necessary in order to achieve satisfactory levels of profitability. To lose the large volumes purchased by Tetra Pak would therefore mean that the parties would have to find other customers in order to fill the capacity. This would not be an easy task in the short term.

91. Tetra Pak, on the other hand, buys such volumes of liquid packaging board that it would have the option of developing new capacity with other existing or new suppliers, should the parties attempt to exercise market power. In addition, Tetra Pak, through close cooperation with the producers of liquid packaging board, has an intimate knowledge of the cost structure of the parties. Furthermore, the liquid packaging board represents about [more than 50 per cent] * of the cost of the blank supplied by Tetra Pak to its customers. The Commission has also noted that plastic may to a certain extent be a substitute for liquid packaging board in the long term in the downstream market for the packaging of liquids. Tetra Pak, therefore, has every incentive to seek to exercise its countervailing buyer power.

92. Consequently, for all the reasons stated above, it is concluded that Tetra Pak has countervailing buyer power to such an extent that it will neutralise the potential increase in market power of the merger between Stora and Enso.

The Commission then went on to assess the position of the two smaller buyers and concluded that for strategic reasons the merger entity would not want to drive them away and thus risk being entirely dependent on Tetra-Pak.

93. Elopak and SIG Combibloc are buying much smaller volumes of liquid packaging board than Tetra Pak. Furthermore, in particular where Elopak is concerned, it is noted that Elopak and Enso's subsidiary Pakenso at present run joint converting activities in Lahti in Finland [. . .]. These joint converting activities represent a significant proportion of the total amount of cartons converted by Elopak. This link to the parties could weaken the buyer power of Elopak following the merger.

94. However, it also has to be considered that both companies place orders large enough to fill the capacity of a board machine. This would in itself make it difficult for Elopak and SIG Combibloc to switch a significant proportion of volumes sourced to alternative suppliers at short notice. However, it also means that a large shift of volumes to alternative suppliers such as AssiDomän and Korsnäs, who could in principle switch WTL capacity to the production of liquid packaging board, could hurt Stora Enso significantly, should the parties attempt to exercise market power. Elopak and SIG Combibloc both also source strategic volumes from the United States, which strengthens their countervailing buyer power. Both of them also have significant operations outside the EEA. Finally, as for Tetra Pak, both Elopak and SIG Combibloc have detailed knowledge of the cost structure of the parties. They also have the same incentives as Tetra Pak to exercise their buyer power.

95. Compared to Tetra Pak, both companies are, nevertheless, in a weaker position in the short to medium term *vis-à-vis* Stora Enso, since they will have only one EEA supplier after the merger, whereas Tetra Pak will have three. Furthermore, Elopak and SIG Combibloc source much smaller volumes than Tetra Pak. Therefore, while it is true that Elopak and SIG Combibloc are not without any means to counter a price increase, it seems that the proposed merger will shift the balance of power towards Stora Enso in its relationship with Elopak and SIG Combibloc.

96. Furthermore, in the case of Elopak and SIG Combibloc, it also has to be considered that the parties will have an incentive to have both companies as

> major players in the market in order to not to become completely dependent on Tetra Pak. Therefore, while the concern that Elopak and SIG Combibloc could be disadvantaged by the merger in comparison with Tetra Pak is not completely removed, it also has to be recognised that the countervailing buyer power of Tetra Pak will for this reason, to a certain extent, spill over to Elopak and SIG Combibloc as well. [. . .].

12.3.9. EFFICIENCY DEFENCE

As explained in in the introductory section, the pursuit of efficiencies is a main driver for M&A activity. Therefore, it is necessary to take efficiency claims into consideration in order to assess the extent that they can offset a SIEC.[469] There are a number of possible sources of efficiencies, primarily:

- *Production rationalization*: to the extent that the merging firms differed in the efficiency of their production facilities (eg due to superior know-how), the merged entity could reduce costs by simply shifting production away from the less efficient one (ie, provided that the efficient facility is not already at full capacity). The most drastic example if rationalization occurs where the less efficient firm is shut down, ie, given that its disadvantage in terms of higher incremental (marginal) costs is too large and there is plenty of spare capacity left for the efficient firm.
- *Scale economies*: There are mainly three broad categories of sources of scale and scope economies:
    - *technical specialization*: a larger output makes it convenient for a firm to specialize both in human and physical capital whose higher costs will be spread over higher volumes of production: for example, expensive specialist robotic machinery, specialist workforce;[470]
    - *input indivisibilities*: a larger scale is needed to allow the firm to absorb large quantities of input procured in bulk deals: for example, the purchase of a large aircraft or an expensive TV advertising campaign. Hence, scale economies are the result of the non-duplication of these fixed costs; and
    - *purchase economies*: scale advantages can also result from volume discounts awarded by input suppliers. One peculiar example, here, is the ability to secure financing at cheaper prices: for example, a lower interest rate over larger loans or easier access to equity finance for firms with a large market capitalization.

  Technical specification is considered the source of scale economies that is more long-term in nature, in particular where it requires investment in new specialized factors of production, or it is based on R&D spending.
- *Scope economies*: economies of scope arise when there are common inputs in the production of multiple products. To the extent that the commonality of the input in question depends on its versatility, there may be a trade-off with scale economies based on technical specification.

469 For a detailed discussion, see OECD, 'The Role of Efficiency Claims in Antitrust Proceedings', Policy Roundtable (2013), 11–60, available at www.oecd.org/competition/EfficiencyClaims2012.pdf; see also L Röller, J Stennek, and F Verboven, 'Efficiency Gains from Mergers' in F Ilzkovitz and R Meiklejohn (eds) *European Merger Control* (Edward Elgar, 2006), 84, available at www.elgaronline.com/view/1845424913.xml.

470 The latter source of specialization can be 'learning by doing' where workers specialize on-the-job over time, rather than been hired already specialized with an aim to increase output.

- *Removal of 'double marginalization'*: as explained in the introduction, when products are complement, or in a vertical supply relationship, an increase in one price will reduce demand for the other product, which would not only be detrimental for the combined profit of the two firms, but for consumers alike. Therefore, a merger can be beneficial to the extent that prices are set taking into consideration the impact on complementary products—in economic jargon, 'internalizing the externalities'.
- *Reduction of transaction costs*: another source of inefficiency among producers of complementary products, including the vertical relationships between an input supplier and a manufacturer, or a manufacturer and the distributor, is where one party has to specialize in order to achieve better integration: for example, the input supplier buying specialized machinery, or the distributor training sales personnel. There could be a failure to specialize, when the party in question is concerned that, once specialized, the other beneficiary party will opportunistically try to extract all the benefits thanks to the fact that specialization increases the degree of dependency: the investment is 'sunk' in that it could not be used as profitably for anything else. A merger, therefore, might be necessary to remove the potential for opportunism, thus solving what economists call the 'hold-up problem'.
- *Network effects*: when the benefit from consumption is driven by the number of 'adopters', a merger that combines two previously separated customer bases could be beneficial. Network effects can be *direct*, where the source of benefit is the ability to reach other adopters such as telephone or email, or *indirect*, where the higher the number of adopters the larger is the provision of complementary products, as in multi-sided platforms such as video games for adopters of a specific game console.

In practice, although it is difficult to actually estimate the magnitude of post-merger price increases, it is easier to establish the likelihood that a merger would induce 'unilateral effects', than to claim the existence of offsetting efficiency improvements. This is because the information needed to substantiate the latter resides primarily with the merging firms. Therefore, the burden of proof lies entirely on the merging parties. In this respect, it must be proven that claimed efficiencies are beneficial to consumers, merger-specific, and verifiable.

Regarding the first criterion, the incentives to pass on efficiency improvement to consumers through lower prices, higher quality or variety arguable depends on whether the degree of competitive rivalry left after the merger is still effective. That is to say, the larger the market power of the merged entity the more unlikely would be that customers benefit from efficiency improvements.[471] Furthermore, to be realistically beneficial to consumers claimed efficiencies ought to be realized in a timely fashion.[472]

The assessment of fixed-cost savings is particularly contentious. On the one hand, fixed-cost savings, such as for the avoidance of duplication, are more verifiable and achievable, and thus considered more likely and timely than a reduction in marginal costs. On the other hand, it is not clear how consumers could benefit from them, since a reduction in fixed costs would typically be appropriated by the merged entity in the form of higher profits, rather than being passed on to consumers though lower prices.[473]

471 Horizontal Merger Guidelines, para 84. 472 Ibid, 83.

473 See eg DOJ and FTC 'Commentary on the Horizontal Merger Guidelines' (2010), available at www.justice.gov/atr/public/guidelines/215247.htm

> Economic analysis teaches that price reductions are expected when efficiencies reduce the merged firm's marginal costs, ie, costs associated with producing one additional unit of each of its products. By contrast, reductions in fixed costs—costs that do not change in the short-run with changes in output rates—typically are not expected to lead to immediate price effects and hence to benefit consumers in the short term. (Ibid, 57.)

Nevertheless, a reduction in fixed-costs could yield consumer benefit over the long term to the extent that it allows the merger entity to undertake more innovation,[474] which entails large fixed and typically 'sunk' costs. Hence, efficiency claims based on sizeable fixed-cost savings in high-tech industries should not be dismissed lightly.

Some empirical analysis of the European Commission's merger control practice indicates that efficiency arguments have never been decisive.[475] In the UK, the OFT (now replaced by the CMA) cleared the *Global/GCap* merger, the parties to the transaction controlling a number of radio stations after the OFT found compelling evidence of demand-side efficiencies, resulting from the fact that following the merger the parties would be able to set the price of bundles of their complementary radio stations in the London market vis-à-vis the advertisers more efficiently than if each party sold advertising on one or more than one of its radio stations independently. The OFT found, however, that the transaction produced anti-competitive effects in Midlands without this being compensated by efficiency gains, requiring remedies to restore competition.[476] This was the first time in which the authority relied on efficiencies to conclude that the acquisition would not harm consumers.

The move to more innovation-focused theories of harm also raises interesting questions as to how innovation efficiencies may be taken into account. There could indeed be many sources of potential innovation-related efficiencies, such as synergies decreasing the cost of innovation, or increasing incentives to invest in innovation, such as spillovers, in case products rely on similar technologies, more rapid internal diffusion of innovation, higher likelihood of rapid sequential innovation if the companies pursue similar lines of research. This assessment should nevertheless be made with great caution, and should take into account the specific characteristics of the industry, the IP landscape and underlying technologies.

12.3.10. FAILING FIRM DEFENCE

There can be circumstances whether a SIEC would occur regardless of whether the merger takes place, that is, where one of the merging parties would exit the market in any case. The burden to prove this counterfactual scenario rests with the merging parties.

Horizontal Merger Guidelines [2004] OJ C 31/5, paras 89–91

89. The Commission may decide that an otherwise problematic merger is nevertheless compatible with the common market if one of the merging parties is a failing firm. The basic requirement is that the deterioration of the competitive structure that follows the merger cannot be said to be caused by the merger. This will arise where the competitive structure of the market would deteriorate to at least the same extent in the absence of the merger.

90. The Commission considers the following three criteria to be especially relevant for the application of a 'failing firm defence'. First, the allegedly failing firm would in the near future be forced out of the market because of financial difficulties if not taken over

474 See *Axalto/Gemplus* (Case COMP/M.3998) Commission Decision (19 May 2006), para 53.

475 See P Kuoppamäki and S Torstilla, 'Is There a Future for an Efficiency Defence in EU Merger Control?' (2015) 41(5) *European L Rev* 687.

476 *Global Radio UK Ltd/GCap Media plc* (ME/3638/08) Completed Acquisition.

by another undertaking. Second, there is no less anti-competitive alternative purchase than the notified merger. Third, in the absence of a merger, the assets of the failing firm would inevitably exit the market.

91. It is for the notifying parties to provide in due time all the relevant information necessary to demonstrate that the deterioration of the competitive structure that follows the merger is not caused by the merger.

12.3.10.1. *Newscorp/Telepiù*

Newscorp/Telepiù (Case COMP/M.2876) Commission Decision [2004] OJ L 110/73

The merger concerned the only two national Italian pay-TV operators, Stream and Telepiù. Both undertakings had been loss-making for a while. Unusually, the failing-firm defence was invoked by the acquiring company, Newscorp, who co-owned Stream with Telecom Italia. Furthermore, albeit Stream was loss-making, there was no doubt about the financial soundness of the parent company. Hence this was a case of 'failing firm division', rather than strictly 'failing firm defence'.

210. In its reply to the Statement of Objections, Newscorp argued that the conditions for a 'failing company defence' were met in this case, namely that, in the absence of the merger, Telepiù would gain a position comparable to the combined platform's after the merger and that in any event the assets of Stream would inevitably exit the market.

211. Before examining this claim, it should be noted that Newscorp argues that Stream, currently jointly controlled by Newscorp and Telecom Italia, is the 'failing firm' which would exit the market but for the merger. The present transaction is in fact a combination of a change from joint to sole control of Stream by one of its parent companies, Newscorp, and its merger with another company (Telepiù). As Stream is a separate 'division' of one 'company', Newscorp, this merger raises the question whether the 'failing company defence' applies when the acquiring firm is financially healthy but one of its divisions, which is failing, is merging with another entity.

212. As indicated by the Commission in its Decision in *Rewe/Meinl*, in a case of a 'failing-division defence' and not of a 'failing-company defence', the burden of proving lack of causality between the merger and the creation or strengthening of a dominant position falls on the companies claiming it. Otherwise, every merger involving an allegedly unprofitable division could be justified under merger control law by the declaration that, without the merger, the division would cease to operate. The case Rewe/Meinl involved a division of the Meinl group that was acquired by Rewe. The importance of proving lack of causality is even greater in the case of a claimed 'failing division', which is actually the acquiring company. Finally, it could reasonably be argued that it is possible that the buying group might have strategic reasons to keep its failing division alive even if the merger were to be prohibited.

a) The failing company would have been forced out of the market if not taken over by another undertaking

213 *Newscorp* argues that *Stream* is currently a 'failing firm' which will exit the market in the absence of the merger because economic and business logic dictates that the

shareholders' decision whether to take *Stream* into bankruptcy is based on a comparison of the (negative) net present value ('NPV') of the future cash flows (before debt service) from remaining in business with the (possibly negative) NPV from bankruptcy. If the NPV associated with bankruptcy is greater than the 'remain in business' NPV, then the rational decision is to seek bankruptcy given that there are no realistic prospects of *Stream* becoming profitable as a standalone entity. According to *Newscorp*, the exit costs that *Newscorp* and especially Telecom Italia face today are significantly lower than the 'remain in business costs', and *Stream* has not yet exited the market only because of the prospects of closing the transaction under consideration. However, some third parties have argued that, with better management and higher efforts to effectively combat piracy, the number of subscribers and the corresponding revenues would substantially rise.

214. In the present transaction, the acquirer of sole control of the failing company is one of its parent companies, which is also acquiring sole control of another company (*Telepiù*). Although *Stream* is a separate legal person, there seems to be no question that a whole firm (ie *Newscorp*) would be forced out of the market. *Newscorp* acts as a holding company and *Stream* accounts for only part of the business activities and subsidiaries of the *Newscorp* group. *Stream's* withdrawal from the Italian pay-TV market would accordingly take the form of a management decision to abandon a business activity whose development has not lived up to the expectations of the firm's managing board.

215. It is important also to note that the parties have raised this argument at a very late stage. Indeed, no mention was made in the notification. This casts further doubts on the probative value of their claim as nothing has fundamentally changed since the notification.

b) There is no less anti-competitive purchaser

216. *Newscorp* argues that in the absence of substantial synergies, any potential buyer would face a similar situation to *Newscorp* and Telecom Italia. It is also likely that another buyer would face greater uncertainty over future profitability because *Newscorp* and Telecom Italia, as the existing shareholders, have superior information about the business. There is no realistic prospect of a less anti-competitive purchaser emerging because it is very difficult to imagine somebody having synergies large enough to there were no other potential buyers attempting to purchase *Telepiù* from the Vivendi group in May–June 2002 when the sale to *Newscorp* was finalised. In this respect JPMorgan notes that, to its understanding, no other potential buyers submitted a formal bid for either *Telepiù* or *Stream*. This was the case despite the fact that the transaction discussions were made public in 2001 and 2002 and the price was reportedly negotiated down by *Newscorp* over the course of extended negotiations and there were no other potential buyers attempting to purchase *Stream* from *Newscorp* when the sale to the Vivendi group was finalised.

217. It is clear from the Commission's reasoning in the *Kali and Salz* Decision that the burden of proving that there is no alternative potential buyer apart from the acquiring firm falls, in the Commission's opinion, on the party claiming it. *Newscorp's* argument does not discharge this burden of proof. Apart from some attempts to find mere financial investors for *Stream, Newscorp* has neither indicated the potential buyers (apart from the Vivendi group for *Stream* and *Newscorp* for *Telepiù*) with which *Newscorp* and the Vivendi group have entered into negotiations to sell their respective companies in Italy nor the reasons for which the negotiations failed.

The only attempt to sell its controlling stake in *Stream* was made by Telecom Italia but neither *Stream* nor the Vivendi group have actively tried to find a less anti-competitive solution than the merger of the two companies. According to the information available to the Commission, neither *Newscorp* nor Telecom Italia have ever put *Stream* on public offer.

c) The assets to be purchased would inevitably disappear from the market in the absence of the merger or the acquiring undertaking would gain the market share of the acquired undertaking

218 According to *Newscorp*, the assets to be acquired would inevitably exit the market. There are two main assets currently held by *Stream* whose future allocation is critical for the competitive conditions, namely its subscriber base and the rights on content that it currently holds. *Stream*'s DTH subscribers would most likely flow to *Telepiù* because there is no other satellite platform, and cable is only available in limited areas. As regards *Stream*'s premium rights, *Newscorp* argues that they would most likely be acquired by *Telepiù*. Following *Stream's* bankruptcy, the rights would be returned to the right holders that would be able to put them up for sale again.

219. According to *Newscorp, Telepiù* would be more likely to win these rights (for instance in comparison with e.Biscom or the competing free-to-air operators). Nevertheless it can reasonably be argued that at least some content (for example, Champions League rights or tennis rights) would not necessarily be acquired by *Telepiù*. As indicated above, free-to-air TVs and pay-TVs can at least to some extent compete for the acquisition of these rights and they would be in a better position to bid for these rights if *Telepiù*'s financial situation were to be weaker than that of the combined platform resulting from the merger. *Newscorp* has not given any indication as regards the possible acquisition by *Telepiù* or other companies of other assets of *Stream*, such as trademarks and distribution networks.

220. However since neither of the first two conditions is met in the present case, it is not necessary to take a final position on whether the third condition (inevitable disappearance or exit from the market of the assets to be acquired) is fulfilled in the present case.

d) Conclusion

221. The Commission considers, therefore, that *Newscorp* has not been able to demonstrate that there is no causal link between the concentration and the effect on competition, because conditions of competition can be expected to deteriorate to a similar or identical extent even without the concentration in question. However, the risk of *Stream* exiting the market, if it were to materialise, would be a factor to take into account when assessing the present merger. The Commission further considers that an authorisation of the merger subject to appropriate conditions will be more beneficial to consumers than a disruption caused by a potential closure of *Stream*.

In this concluding paragraph the Commission seems to weight the fact that Stream's customers would have had to change their receiver set in case they had to switch to Telepiù in case of Stream's exit. This is because the two platforms were not compatible. Hence, in this sense the merger represented an efficiency improvement to the extent that Stream's customers could have been spared the hassle costs involved in switching service provider.

12.4. NON-HORIZONTAL MERGERS

Similarly to the publication of the Horizontal Merger Guidelines, the Commission was induced to review its approach to the assessment of vertical and conglomerate mergers in response to criticisms from EU Courts.[477] In the Non-Horizontal Merger Guidelines the Commission clarified that vertical and conglomerate mergers are typically less likely to give rise to a SIEC when compared to horizontal ones.[478] First of all, this is because the merging parties are not actual competitors in the same relevant market.[479] Therefore, the merger would not eliminate the corresponding direct competitive constraint, that is, unless one of the merging firms could have realistically expanded in the other's market, so that the merger would remove the direct competitive constraint posed by the threat of potential competition.[480]

Second, and similarly to the assessment of vertical restraint, the relation of complementarity underpinning both vertical and conglomerate mergers means that efficiency improvements are more likely than with horizontal mergers.[481]

Non-Horizontal Merger Guidelines [2008] OJ C 265/7, paras 13 and 14

13. [. . .], vertical and conglomerate mergers provide substantial scope for efficiencies. A characteristic of vertical mergers and certain conglomerate mergers is that the activities and/or the products of the companies involved are complementary to each other. The integration of complementary activities or products within a single firm may produce significant efficiencies and be pro-competitive. In vertical relationships for instance, as a result of the complementarity, a decrease in mark-ups downstream will lead to higher demand also upstream. A part of the benefit of this increase in demand will accrue to the upstream suppliers. An integrated firm will take this benefit into account. Vertical integration may thus provide an increased incentive to seek to decrease prices and increase output because the integrated firm can capture a larger fraction of the benefits. This is often referred to as the 'internalisation of double mark-ups'. Similarly, other efforts to increase sales at one level (eg improve service or stepping up innovation) may provide a greater reward for an integrated firm that will take into account the benefits accruing at other levels.

14. Integration may also decrease transaction costs and allow for a better coordination in terms of product design, the organisation of the production process, and the way in which the products are sold. Similarly, mergers which involve products belonging to a range or portfolio of products that are generally sold to the same set of customers (be they complementary products or not) may give rise to customer benefits such as one-stop-shopping.

477 See, in particular, *General Electric Company v Commission* [2005] ECR II–5575, paras 67–9. One should also note the existence of 'diagonal mergers', that is when an upstream supplier and a downstream competitor of the customers that purchase the supplier's goods merge. In the *BT/EE* merger there were some diagonal aspects, EE supplying both BT and BT's rivals, such as Virgin Media, although in practice the assessment by the CMA was similar to vertical mergers, as they both relate to 'vertical issues' or 'vertical theories of harm', because two different levels of supply are considered: CMA, BT group plc, and EE Limited, paras 9.9–9.10 (15 January 2016).

478 Non-Horizontal Merger Guidelines, para 11.

479 Ibid, para 12.

480 Ibid.

481 Ibid, para 13.

Similarly to the Horizontal Merger Guidelines, the Commission explains that a SIEC could be the result of either non-coordinated or coordinated effects, which are to be assessed with respect to the appropriate counterfactual scenario in order to establish whether anti-competitive effects of the merger are more likely than pro-competitive ones.[482] In particular, the Commission investigates whether the merged entity has both the ability and incentive to engage in anti-competitive conduct as a result of the merger.

With respect to the former, the Commission indicated that it is unlikely that a merger would give rise to anti-competitive concerns unless the merged entity enjoys significant market power in at least one of the markets concerned. Specifically, the Commission indicated that the market share of the merger entity is above 30 per cent (thus possibly falling short of individual dominance) in each of the markets concerned and the post-merger HHI is above 2000.[483] In contrast to horizontal mergers, the reliance on market shares and concentration measures is not undermined by issues to do with different pattern of differentiation among substitute products. However, the Commission stated that market shares below 30 per cent would not stop it from investigating a merger where one of the merging firms is a 'maverick' or expected to grow (eg, thanks to a recent innovation); where competitors are linked through cross-shareholdings or cross-directorships; or where there is evidence of past or on-going coordination among competitors in any of the markets concerned.[484]

In what follows we will look at the main theories of harm in both vertical and conglomerate mergers, both in terms of non-coordinated and coordinated effects.

12.4.1. VERTICAL MERGERS

Vertical mergers are those involving undertakings operating at different levels of the supply chain.[485] Usually vertical concentration will not increase market power. If there is no actual or potential competition between the parties, there is none to be eliminated and the merger may yield substantial economies.[486] The important distinction to have in mind is that between substitutes and complements. Two products are substitutes if an increase in the price of one product leads to an increase in the output (quantity demanded) of the other product, buyers switching to the cheaper product. Two products are complements when an increase in price in one product leads to a reduction of the output of both products, in particular in cases buyers purchase the two products in fixed proportions. Where complementary products are sold together, the vendor is likely to sell each more cheaply than if they were sold separately. Any reduction in the price of *A* is likely also to help sell more *B* and vice versa. Integration may also reduce transaction costs (often called avoiding double marginalization). Where two products have to be designed to fit together and there are significant sunk costs, vertical integration may be the only way to avoid a hold up problem.

The view on vertical mergers evolved according to the perspectives given by economics in this area. Although initially there were concerns about leveraging, that is the use of market power in one product market to gain market power in the other product market, leveraging theory was criticized by Chicago School economists who put emphasis on the existence of a

482 Ibid, paras 17–21. 483 Ibid, para 25. 484 Ibid, para 26. 485 Ibid, para 4.

486 The paragraph summarizes the analysis on vertical mergers included in ibid, paras 10–27.

single monopoly profit to be made and therefore on the high likelihood that vertical integration is motivated by efficiency considerations and not the desire to leverage market power from one market to another.[487] As we have indicated in Chapter 8, the single monopoly profit theory has been criticized for its very narrow assumptions, in particular the fact that the two products are used in fixed proportions to each other. This is because a vertically integrated firm would always adopt the optimal mix of inputs whereby production efficiency is maximized; whereas, absent vertical integration, the downstream firms substitute away from the expensive monopolized input, thus adopting a less efficient production mix. All in all, consumer may ultimately be better-off under vertical integration when the reduction in marginal costs at the downstream level, thanks to the adoption of the optimal input mix by the vertically integrated firm, more than offset the tendency of the vertically integrated firm to set high downstream prices in order to maximize its upstream profit.[488]

Chicago School economists put emphasis on the efficiency gains brought by vertical mergers, such as the reduction of transaction costs, better coordination, savings in transportation costs, reduced inventories and other processing costs, stability of inputs' supply, and avoidance of *ex post* opportunistic behaviour. This consensus over the benign welfare effect of vertical mergers and their efficiency motivation dissipated following the emergence of the post-Chicago School, which relying on game theory and strategic behaviour theory questioned some of the simplifying assumptions of the Chicago School and raised a number of possibility theorems with regard to the anti-competitive effect of vertical mergers. Post-Chicago authors showed that vertical mergers could be used in order to implement raising rivals' costs (RRC) strategies, which aim to reduce the profitability and thus foreclose equally efficient rivals[489] that they could help to restore market power,[490] as well as to facilitate coordinated interaction and collusion upstream, when upstream and downstream firms interact repeatedly.[491]

Non-horizontal mergers may significantly impede competition in two main ways: they may have non-coordinated and coordinated effects. The competitive objection to vertical integration is that competitors at one level *may be* foreclosed if there is market power. This will often not be the case: it is necessary to look carefully and see that there is not only an ability to foreclose, but also an incentive. There must be barriers to entry in the market that is not dominated and so few firms able to operate in it that competitors of the merging firm will not be able to enter on a viable scale. The counterfactual to be appraised by the Commission is what would have happened in the absence of the merger. Vertical integration will not raise price, unless there is market power at one level of production or trade and competitors can be foreclosed from the other. The Commission indicates a fairly

[487] On the single monopoly profit theorem, see our analysis in Section 8.2.2.1.

[488] See P Mallela and B Nahata, 'Theory of Vertical Control with Variable Proportions' (1980) 88 *J Political Economy* 1009; FR Warren-Boulton, 'Vertical Control with Variable Proportions' (1974) 82 *J Political Economy* 783.

[489] For an overview, see MH Riordan and SC Salop, 'Evaluating Vertical Mergers: A Post-Chicago Approach' (1995) 63 *Antitrust LJ* 513. On RRC and vertical mergers, see JA Ordover, G Saloner, and SC Salop, 'Equilibrium Vertical Foreclosure' (1990) 80 *American Economic Rev* 127; P Bolton and MD Whinston, 'The Foreclosure Effects of Vertical Mergers' (1991) 147 *J Institutional and Theoretical Economics* 207; HT Normann, 'Vertical Mergers, Foreclosure and Raising Rivals' Costs—Experimental Evidence' (2011) 59 *J Industrial Economics* 506.

[490] P Rey and J Tirole, 'A Primer on Foreclosure' in M Armstrong and R Porter (eds) *Handbook of Industrial Organization*, vol 3 (Elsevier, 2007), 2145.

[491] V Nocke and L White, 'Do Vertical Mergers Facilitate Upstream Collusion?' (2007) 97 *American Economic Rev* 1321.

safe harbour if the market share of the merged firm in each market concerned is below 30 per cent or the HHI is below 2000. This is very cautious. There are qualifications in the guidelines; the 30 per cent comes from the group exemptions for vertical agreements and technology transfer, but the scope for efficiencies is far greater for mergers. There is no presumption of harm to consumers above these levels. Indeed, market power in at least one of the markets concerned is a necessary condition for competitive harm but not a sufficient condition. As it is made clear in the Guidelines,

> [i]n practice, the Commission will not extensively investigate such mergers, except where special circumstances such as, for instance, one or more of the following factors are present:
>
> (a) a merger involves a company that is likely to expand significantly in the near future, eg because of a recent innovation;
>
> (b) there are significant cross-shareholdings or cross-directorships among the market participants;
>
> (c) one of the merging firms is a firm with a high likelihood of disrupting coordinated conduct;
>
> (d) indications of past or ongoing coordination, or facilitating practices, are present.[492]

The Guidelines continue to set out the Commission's views on vertical mergers.[493] They spell out the possibility of foreclosure up and downstream, through coordinated or unilateral effects. A non-exhaustive list of efficiencies is provided by the Commission in the Non-Horizontal Merger Guidelines.[494] The Commission points out, however, that some of these efficiencies may be achieved by virtue of less restrictive vertical agreements.[495]

12.4.1.1 Non-coordinated effects in vertical mergers

The Commission largely equates non-coordinated effects in vertical mergers to the issue of foreclosure, whereby the ability and incentive of actual or potential competitors of one of the merging firms to compete is weakened because of reduced access to either important input supplies at the upstream level or output markets at the downstream level.[496]

Before delving into these two types of foreclosure, it is important to point out that foreclosure entails that one of the merging firms engages in an exclusionary conduct, such as refusal to deal, which might be prohibited under Article 102 TFEU in case the merging firm in question holds a dominant position in the corresponding market. Does this mean that the Commission should evaluate the likelihood that a SIEC is the result of an abuse of dominance by the merged entity? If so, the burden of proof for the competition authority would be materially increased.

492 Non-Horizontal Merger Guidelines, para 26. 493 Ibid, paras 28–89.

494 Ibid, paras 54–7.

495 Ibid, para 55 n 7 noting that '[t]he efficiencies associated with the elimination of double mark-ups may thus not always be merger specific because vertical cooperation or vertical agreements may, short of a merger, achieve similar benefits with less anti-competitive effects'. See also, Ibid, para 55 n 7. See also, V Nocke and L White, 'Do Vertical Mergers Facilitate Upstream Collusion?' (2007) 97 *American Economic Rev* 1321.

496 Non-Horizontal Merger Guidelines, para 29.

12.4.1.1.1. General Electric Company v Commission

General Electric Company v Commission
[2005] ECR II–5575, paras 70–5

In the following quoted paragraphs, the General Court revisited its previous position in Tetra Laval v Commission[497] *which criticized the Commission for summarily conjecturing that the merged entity would engage in unlawful conduct, specifically in breach of Article 102 TFEU, undeterred. Instead the Commission should have based its analysis on sufficiently convincing, plausible and cogent evidence.*[498] *That position was overturned by the Court of Justice which appeared to agree with the Commission that the resulting burden of proof would be not only disproportionate to the* ex ante *nature of merger control but also too speculative.*[499]

Treatment of factors which might deter the merged entity from behaving in the ways predicted in the contested decision

70. In its judgment in *Tetra Laval v Commission* [. . .], the Court held that, although it is appropriate to take account of the objective incentives to engage in anti-competitive practices which a merger creates, the Commission must also consider the extent to which those incentives would be reduced, or even eliminated, owing to the illegality of the conduct in question, in particular in the light of the prohibition on abuse of a dominant position laid down in Article [102 TFEU], of the likelihood of their detection, of action taken by the competent authorities, both at Community and national level, and of the financial penalties which could ensue [. . .]. In its observations on the statements in intervention, the applicant invoked that decision in support of its argument that certain of the practices considered by the Commission to be likely to create or strengthen dominant positions would not in fact take place.

71. In its judgment in *Commission* v *Tetra Laval* (paragraphs 74 to 78), the Court of Justice held that the Court of First Instance was right to consider that the likelihood of the adoption of certain future conduct had to be examined comprehensively, that is to say taking into account both the incentives to adopt such conduct and the factors liable to reduce, or even eliminate, those incentives, including the possibility that the conduct is unlawful.

72. However, the Court of Justice also held that it would run counter to the preventive purpose of [EUMR] to require the Commission to examine, for each proposed merger, the extent to which the incentives to adopt anti-competitive conduct would be reduced, or even eliminated, as a result of the unlawfulness of the conduct in question, the likelihood of its detection, the action taken by the competent authorities, both at Community and national level, and the financial penalties which could ensue. Consequently, it held that the Court of First Instance [now General Court] had erred in law in so far as it rejected the Commission's conclusions as to the adoption by the merged entity of the anti-competitive conduct at issue in that case [. . .].

73. It follows from the foregoing that the Commission must, in principle, take into account the potentially unlawful, and thus sanctionable, nature of certain conduct as a factor which might diminish, or even eliminate, incentives for an undertaking to engage in particular conduct. That appraisal does not, however, require an exhaustive and detailed examination of the rules of the various legal orders which might be applicable

[497] Case T-05/02, *Tetra Laval v Commission* [2002] ECR II–4381. [498] Ibid, para 159.
[499] Case C-12/03 P, *Tetra Laval v Commission* [2005] ECR I–987, para 77.

> and of the enforcement policy practised within them, given that an assessment intended to establish whether an infringement is likely and to ascertain that it will be penalised in several legal orders would be too speculative.
>
> 74. Thus, where the Commission, without undertaking a specific and detailed investigation into the matter, can identify the unlawful nature of the conduct in question, in the light of Article [102 TFEU] or of other provisions of Community law which it is competent to enforce, it is its responsibility to make a finding to that effect and take account of it in its assessment of the likelihood that the merged entity will engage in such conduct [. . .].
>
> 75. It follows that, although the Commission is entitled to take as its basis a summary analysis, based on the evidence available to it at the time when it adopts its merger-control decision, of the lawfulness of the conduct in question and of the likelihood that it will be punished, it must none the less, in the course of its appraisal, identify the conduct foreseen and, where appropriate, evaluate and take into account the possible deterrent effect represented by the fact that the conduct would be clearly, or highly probably, unlawful under Community law.

Accordingly, the Commission explained that it will take into consideration the likelihood that the alleged conduct would be clearly, or highly probably, in breach of Article 102 TFEU, the likelihood of detection and the amount of the ensuing fine.[500]

12.4.1.1.2. Input foreclosure

Input foreclosure occurs when the merging firm operating at the upstream level no longer supplies its important input to rivals of the merging firm operating at the downstream level at the same terms and conditions that would have prevailed absent the merger. The resulting restriction of access to the important input can range from higher supply prices, lower quality or quantity supplied, to outright refusal to supply.[501] The rivals of the merging firm active at the downstream level are therefore disadvantaged because of the resulting increase in the cost (or decrease in the quality) of supply. Hence, to the extent that the rivals cannot absorb the cost increase, but have to pass this on their consumers by increasing their prices, the merged entity will be able to raise its own prices in parallel, thus causing a SIEC. The economic model underpinning this theory of harm is inspired by the RRC theory of harm.[502]

The importance of the input being foreclosed can result from the fact that it represents a large cost or indispensable component in the downstream product.[503] However, in order to raise rivals' cost the downstream rivals must find it difficult to replace the vertically integrated upstream supplier.[504] For example, downstream rivals may incur switching costs to change supplier. Another reason may be that the independent suppliers may find it difficult to meet the resulting pent-up demand from downstream independent rivals at competitive supply prices. This may be because they face capacity constraints that prevent them from promptly increasing their output, or because they can increase output but only at higher costs due to decreasing returns to scale.[505] However, capacity constraints may be eased in case the downstream merging firm stops sourcing inputs from independent suppliers after the merger.[506]

500 Non-Horizontal Merger Guidelines, para 46. 501 Ibid, para 33. 502 Ibid, para 31.
503 Ibid, para 34. 504 Ibid, para 35. 505 Ibid, para 36. 506 Ibid, para 37.

Where the structure of the upstream input market is oligopolistic and suppliers compete by setting input quantities, the decision of the vertically integrated firm to stop supplying downstream rivals increases the market power of upstream rivals. That is to say, upstream rivals increase their prices to downstream rivals in response to the withdrawal of the upstream merging firm. This is particular the case when upstream inputs are close substitutes. This is tantamount to a horizontal non-coordinated effect, but the SIEC manifest itself in terms of vertical (RRC) effect to the detriment of downstream rivals.[507]

The Commission will evaluate whether the ability of the merged entity to engage in input foreclosure can be restrained by countervailing buyer power.[508] For example, downstream rivals may vertically integrate upwards or sponsor the entry of a new input supplier. Alternatively, downstream rivals may be able to reconfigure their input mix by replacing the foreclosed input altogether,[509] although it may be costly to reconfigure the production process. For example, in *Microsoft/LinkedIn* the European Commission raised the concern that Microsoft could have foreclosed other professional social network services by: pre-installing LinkedIn on all Windows PCs (ie, a leverage theory of harm as in the Microsoft case); or withdrawing interoperability with Microsoft's Office applications. The merger was cleared after Microsoft offered commitments to, respectively: (i) ensuring that PC manufacturers and distributors would be free not to install LinkedIn on Windows and allowing users to remove LinkedIn from Windows should PC manufacturers and distributors decide to preinstall it; and (ii) allowing competing professional social network service providers to maintain current levels of interoperability with Microsoft's Office suite of products.[510]

The incentives of the merged entity to engage into input foreclosure depend on the trade-off between the lost upstream profits from lower sales to downstream rivals and the increased downstream profits made by the downstream division. The latter can be the result of increased downstream prices (ie, in parallel with downstream rivals whose upstream costs have gone up as a result of input foreclosure) and increase volume of sales diverted from downstream rivals (ie, where downstream rivals are forced to reduce their level of output because of the input foreclosure).[511] The larger the market share of the downstream merging firm and the higher the ability to promptly expand output thanks to the absence of capacity constraints, the stronger will be the incentive to foreclose.[512]

TomTom/Tele Atlas

***TomTom/Tele Atlas* (Case No COMP/M.4854) Commission Decision (14 May 2008)**

In 2008, the Commission cleared after a Phase II investigation the merger between TomTom, at the time a leader in the production of navigation software and portable navigation devices (PNDs), and Tele Atlas, one of the only two suppliers of digital maps used in PNDs, the other being NAVTEQ. Digital maps must be integrated with navigation software, which then powers PNDs. TomTom sold its own PNDs and also supplied navigation software to other PND manufacturers. The key competitive concern was the risk that the merger entity would engage in input foreclosure with respect to the provision of digital maps to rival PND manufacturers, although not in the form of refusal to supply.

507 Ibid, para 38. 508 Ibid, para 39. 509 Ibid, paras 50–1.

510 See European Commission, 'Commission Approves Acquisition of LinkedIn by Microsoft, Subject to Conditions', Press Release (6 December 2016), available at europa.eu/rapid/press-release_IP-16-4284_en.htm.

511 Non-Horizontal Merger Guidelines, paras 40 and 41. 512 Ibid, para 42.

Ability to foreclose

193. The analysis developed in the following paragraphs focuses on whether the merged entity would be able to foreclose competing PND manufacturers and software manufacturers either by increasing prices or by providing degraded maps or delayed updates. [. . .]

194. The Non-Horizontal Merger Guidelines point to three conditions which are necessary for the merged entity to have the ability to foreclose its downstream competition, namely the existence of a significant degree of market power, the importance of the input and the absence of timely and effective counter-strategies.

195. First, the guidelines indicate that input foreclosure can only be a concern if the merged entity has a significant degree of market power in the upstream market. In the case at hand, Tele Atlas sells map databases above marginal cost and has a market share of more than 50% in the upstream market, NAVTEQ being the only other provider of navigable digital map databases with a similar coverage and quality level. Given the imperfect constraint exerted by the counter-strategies detailed in paragraphs 202–209, Tele Atlas can reasonably be expected to influence the conditions of competition in the upstream market. The Commission therefore concluded that the merged entity enjoys a significant degree of market power on the market for navigable digital map databases.

[. . .]

197. Second, input foreclosure may raise competition problems only if it concerns an important input for the downstream product. The Non-Horizontal Merger Guidelines clarify that irrespective of its cost, an input may also be sufficiently important for other reasons. For instance, the input may be a critical component without which the downstream product could not be manufactured or effectively sold on the market.

198. Although digital map databases only account for a relatively limited share of the PND cost, they constitute a critical component without which PNDs could not serve their purpose. The parties do not contest that navigable digital map databases are critical PND components. However, the parties argue that Tele Atlas would not be able to deprive TomTom's PND rivals access to this critical component. In particular, the parties argue that quality degradation or delayed release of updates would be impossible because Tele Atlas only has one core digital navigable map database for any given geographic area.

199. While the parties submit that having a single database may make quality degradation difficult from a technical point of view, nothing would prevent the merged entity from duplicating its database if it had an incentive to do so postmerger. Moreover, having a single database does not prevent degradation by delaying upgrades, because Tele Atlas could still release the updated version of the database to TomTom's competitors with some delay.

200. The parties submit that '*many of Tele Atlas's significant customers have concluded licensing agreements requiring frequent updates to Tele Atlas's latest map database releases, typically every [1–10]* months*'. However, a review of Tele Atlas's contracts has confirmed the existence of such clauses only for a minority of customers. In any event, many contracts have a duration of only [1–5 years]* and are therefore not sufficient to ensure that these customers will get access without delay to map database updates in the future.

201. Currently, both Tele Atlas and NAVTEQ provide their European digital map databases to PND suppliers in one of several exchange formats (Shape, GDF and Oracle), which are chosen by each PND supplier. The Commission examined whether Tele Atlas would be able to foreclose PND manufacturers and navigation software providers competing with TomTom by providing new features or updates, exclusively or earlier, in only one of the current data formats, thereby raising rivals' costs for format conversion. As

indicated by the parties in their reply to the Statement of Objections, the impact of such a strategy is likely to be limited. TomTom uses the same format (Shape) as several other competitors and would therefore incur the same conversion costs as many other companies if this format was abandoned by Tele Atlas. In addition, PND manufacturers could switch to NAVTEQ which would continue to provide all current formats. Although Tele Atlas would have the technical ability not to supply or delay access to its database in certain formats, the impact and profitability of such a strategy therefore appear doubtful.

202. Third, the Commission considered, on the basis of the information available, whether there are effective and timely counter-strategies that rival firms in the PND market could deploy. Potential constraints resulting from the competition with NAVTEQ, the threat of entry and constraints resulting from the role of intermediaries are discussed in paragraphs 203–207. In particular, the Commission shows that while some of these factors limit the merged entity's ability to increase prices or degrade quality, they do not fully eliminate its ability to do so.

203. NAVTEQ would still compete with Tele Atlas post-merger, thereby limiting Tele Atlas's ability to foreclose its competitors. However, NAVTEQ's best response to a price increase by Tele Atlas would be to also increase its prices. It is therefore concluded that competition with NAVTEQ does not completely eliminate the merged entity's ability to increase prices or degrade quality.

204. The parties contest this argument by arguing that NAVTEQ would not become aware of any increased market power and would have no incentive to increase its prices. The parties also contest the applicability of paragraph 38 of the Non-Horizontal Merger Guidelines to partial input foreclosure scenarios. While it is clear that it would not be in the PND manufacturers' best interest to inform NAVTEQ of degraded supply conditions with Tele Atlas, there is no convincing reason to restrict the applicability of paragraph 38 of the Non-Horizontal Merger Guidelines to scenarios of total foreclosure. In a case of partial foreclosure, NAVTEQ may not become aware of its increased market power as easily as if Tele Atlas stopped supplying its former customers, but NAVTEQ will nevertheless realize that the demand it faces changes as a result of Tele Atlas's partial foreclosure tactics. Therefore, it is concluded that competition with NAVTEQ would not fully deprive Tele Atlas of its ability to increase prices or degrade quality or delay access to updates.

205. A possible opposite effect that would lead to a downward pressure on NAVTEQ's prices is described in paragraph 38 of the Non-Horizontal Merger Guidelines, wherein it is stated that '*the attempt* [by non-vertically integrated upstream suppliers]* *to raise the input price may fail when independent input suppliers* [ie NAVTEQ]*, *faced with a reduction in the demand for their products (from the downstream division of the merged entity or from independent downstream firms), respond by pricing more aggressively*'. In this case however, NAVTEQ will not be faced with a reduction in the demand for map databases by TomTom since TomTom is already a Tele Atlas customer. As regards the demand from other PND manufacturers, NAVTEQ would have no reason to price more aggressively post-merger.

206. Entry is unlikely to provide an effective and timely counter-strategy that would constrain the merged entity's ability to foreclose its downstream competitors. [. . .], the Commission considers it unlikely that a new map database provider would build a digital navigable map database with the same level of coverage and quality as Tele Atlas or NAVTEQ and provide a timely constraint on the merged entity.

207. Another limit to Tele Atlas's ability to increase prices or degrade quality could be provided by intermediaries that have a license from Tele Atlas or NAVTEQ to provide the map database together with their navigation software. Such intermediaries constitute an effective constraint only if they are themselves protected from price increases

and quality degradation. This is likely to be the case for Garmin, as detailed in paragraph 208. However, the constraint exerted by Garmin as a map database redistributor, only applies to PND manufacturers that do not have in-house software capabilities, which represent approximately one third of the PND market.

208. It is also important to note that Tele Atlas does not have the ability to foreclose all of TomTom's downstream competitors due to contractual provisions. In particular, Tele Atlas's ability to foreclose its downstream competitors is limited by the longterm contract that Garmin has concluded with NAVTEQ, which protects Garmin against price increases and guarantees yearly price decreases at least until 2015. Taking into account the likely evolution of map prices over the next few years, Garmin therefore, does not have to pay higher prices than it would have had to pay in the absence of the merger. Even if map prices decreased more significantly than predicted, the price protection mechanism in the contract still limits the possibility that Garmin would pay more for maps than in the absence of the merger.

209. In addition, [Navigation Device Manufacturer]* and [Navigation Software Provider]* have long-term contracts for the provision of digital maps. Although the duration and provisions of these contracts do not provide the same level of protection as for Garmin, these contracts provide a degree of protection against price increases. Considering the fact that only Garmin is protected against price increases and that Garmin represents less than 20% of the PND market, the merged entity's ability to foreclose could affect more than two thirds of the sales of TomTom's downstream competitors. If one takes into account that [Navigation Device Manufacturer]* and [Navigation Software Provider]* are also protected, approximately half of the market could possibly be affected by a foreclosure strategy.

210. In the light of these arguments, the Commission concludes that the merged entity is likely to have the ability to increase prices or degrade quality or delay access for some PND manufacturers and navigation software providers competing with TomTom.

Having concluded that the merged entity would have the ability to foreclose, the Commission proceeded by assessing the incentives to foreclose. Here the Commission changed its mind compared to the preliminary conclusion made in the Statement of Objections where it relied on the observation that TomTom's profit margins made downstream in the sale of PNDs were well above those made by Tele Atlas upstream by selling digital maps.

Incentive to foreclose

211. Post-merger, TomTom/Tele Atlas will take into account how the sales of map databases to TomTom's competitors will affect its profits not only upstream but also on the downstream market. Therefore, when considering the profitability of an input foreclosure strategy, the merged entity faces a trade-off between the profit lost in the upstream market due to a reduction of input sales and the profit gained on the downstream market by raising its rivals' costs.

212. This trade-off depends on the level of profits that the merged entity obtains upstream and downstream. Since the profits obtained by selling a PND are much higher than the profits acquired on the sale of a map database, the Commission preliminarily concluded in the Statement of Objections that the merged entity could have an incentive to increase map database prices or degrade quality or delay access to updated map databases for TomTom's competitors. Based on an in-depth qualitative and quantitative analysis, which is presented in detail in this section, the Commission has now concluded that the merged entity would lack incentives to foreclose its competitors.

213. As described in paragraph 42 of the Non-Horizontal Merger Guidelines, the incentive for the integrated firm to raise rivals' costs further depends on two critical factors, that is to say, the extent to which downstream demand is likely to be diverted away from foreclosed rivals and the share of that diverted demand that can be captured by the downstream division of the integrated firm.

214. The Commission has analyzed the extent to which the merged entity could actually capture sales on the PND market by engaging in an input foreclosure strategy to the detriment of TomTom's competitors. This analysis is necessary to determine whether the profits that the merged entity could gain downstream by increasing map database prices, would compensate the upstream losses. Such an assessment requires a careful examination of the sales that TomTom could capture as a result of such a strategy.

215. It is important first to emphasize that a series of qualitative elements indicate that an input foreclosure strategy consisting in increasing prices or degrading quality or delaying access is likely to fail. For reasons described in paragraph 223, Tele Atlas would be likely to lose significant sales to NAVTEQ if it increased prices upstream or degraded map database quality or delayed access to updates, while the benefits from increasing map database prices to TomTom's competitors are likely to be relatively limited. The main qualitative elements supporting this conclusion are outlined in paragraphs 216–220.

216. First, since map databases account on average for less than 10% of the PND wholesale price, map database prices would have to increase substantially to have an effect on downstream PND market prices and allow the merged entity to capture a significant amount of sales on the downstream market. Moreover, the impact of the foreclosure strategy depends on the extent to which TomTom's competitors would pass on the map database price increase to end-consumers. For example, a 10% price increase of the map would only lead to a 0.5% price increase for the PND if the price of the map represents 10% of the price of a PND and PND manufacturers pass on 50% of the change in their cost. Under any reasonable own price elasticity and diversion rate to the merged entity, such a small price increase would lead to very few additional sales for the merged firm.

217. Second, it appears that at least some PND suppliers would be reluctant to pass on an increase in map database prices onto the PND price, which would therefore further reduce any effect on PND prices.

218. Third, Garmin, which is TomTom's most important competitor in the PND market, is largely protected against increases in the price of map databases by virtue of its long-term contract with NAVTEQ, as detailed in paragraph 208. This protection from foreclosure for Garmin will limit the profits that TomTom could capture on the downstream market if it engaged in input strategy.

219. Fourth, [. . .] switching costs are surmountable. As a result, Tele Atlas would lose significant amount of sales to NAVTEQ if it increased prices upstream or degraded map database quality or delayed access to updates.

220. Finally, quality degradation only applies to Tele Atlas's customers, since NAVTEQ would arguably continue to provide good-quality map databases to all PND manufacturers in a non-discriminatory manner. NAVTEQ would not gain any downstream sales in the PND market by degrading the quality of its map since it is not vertically integrated. In addition, degrading the map quality would decrease NAVTEQ's map database sales since many end-users may be expected to switch to a TomTom PND in order to get a quality map. It is also important to note that degrading map database quality would be less profitable for the merged entity than increasing prices since, unlike a price increase, degrading quality does not bring higher margins for the map databases that Tele Atlas would continue to sell upstream.

[. . .]

222. The likelihood of a total input foreclosure strategy, according to which the merged entity would stop supplying map databases to TomTom's competitors downstream, is examined first. If such a strategy was implemented by the merged entity, the competitive pressure exercised on NAVTEQ would be reduced, which may allow NAVTEQ to raise the map database price it charges to TomTom's competitors downstream. In essence, a total input foreclosure by the merged entity would increase NAVTEQ's market power.

223. More specifically, if the merged entity were to stop selling map databases, it would lose all its profits on map databases but would only recuperate profits on the sales that it is able to capture downstream. For a total foreclosure strategy to be profitable for Tele Atlas, it must recuperate enough profits downstream to at least compensate the lost profits on map databases. In order to measure the extent of sales that the merged entity would be able to capture downstream, the Commission estimated downstream price elasticities and found that the merged entity would only capture a relatively limited amount of sales downstream by increasing map database pricing for TomTom's competitors. Since map database prices represent a relatively minor proportion of the price of PND devices, and given the elasticity estimates, the Commission's analysis indicates that it would be necessary for NAVTEQ to increase prices by a very substantial amount to ensure that an input foreclosure strategy would be profitable for the merged entity. In fact, the Commission calculated that if NAVTEQ does not raise prices by several hundred percent, a total input foreclosure strategy would not be profitable for Tele Atlas. It appears unlikely that NAVTEQ's prices would rise by such a magnitude.

[. . .]

226. The likelihood of a partial input foreclosure strategy, according to which the merged entity would increase prices or degrade the quality of map databases supplied to TomTom's competitors downstream, is discussed in the following paragraphs. As mentioned in paragraph 211, the merged entity faces a trade-off between the profits lost in the upstream market and the profits in the downstream markets in order to determine its optimal price. If the merged entity decides to increase prices upstream, it would gain additional profits from customers that stay with Tele Atlas, but it would lose profits from customers that switch to NAVTEQ. In addition, the merged entity would gain additional profits due to the loss of competitiveness by TomTom's competitors downstream. Since a price increase upstream will benefit the post-merger entity in a way it did not pre-merger, the merged entity would have an increased incentive to raise prices for TomTom's competitors. However, the fact that the merged entity would only capture a relatively limited amount of sales downstream by increasing map database pricing for TomTom's competitors, implies that the incentive to foreclose competitors will be limited.

[. . .]

228. The results of this simple profit test indicate that any price increase that would have a non-negligible impact on the downstream market would not be profitable for the merged entity as the downstream gains would not be sufficient to compensate upstream losses. This finding concurs with the results of the parties' submissions on partial foreclosure, which indicate that any price increase that would more than compensate the positive impact of the elimination of the double marginalization on the downstream market does not constitute an equilibrium.

[. . .]

230. In the light of these arguments, the Commission concludes that the merged entity would have no incentive to increase prices in a manner which would lead to anticompetitive effects downstream.

NOTES AND QUESTIONS ON TOMTOM/TELE ATLAS

1. (Paragraphs 203–4) In assessing the competitive constraints posed by NAVTEQ at the upstream level the Commission did not explore whether the firm could promptly expand output to offset the increase in prices or quality degradation by Tele Atlas. It is worth nothing that the cost structure for digital products is typically front-loaded, where the cost of the first-copy is very high whilst the incremental cost of additional copies is immaterial. That is to say, there are increasing economies of scale, meaning that there is a strong incentive to expand output in order to cover the first-copy costs and make an operational profit. What does this entail for the incentives of NAVTEQ to accommodate the merged entity RRC strategy? In this respect, the Commission concluded that, with respect to partial foreclosure, NAVTEQ would raise its prices in response to a price increase by Tele Atlas post-merger, thus not necessary maximizing output sales.
2. It is worth noting that four months after this clearance, the Commission also cleared a merger between NAVTEQ and Nokia, the then dominant but now defunct mobile handset manufacturer.[513] With the benefit of hindsight, it is interesting to observe that the Commission did not consider the threat of potential competition due to vertical integration at the upstream level of another type of digital map customers such as, most notably, Google, which at the time was a customer of Tele Atlas for its Google Map service.[514] Google later on also launched its own navigation product over Android.

Dow/Dupont

When examining the *Dow/Dupont* merger,[515] the European Commission focused on several general factors in assessing competitive effects, including market shares, whether the merger eliminated a significant and close competitor (rather than the closest competitor), entry barriers, and the existence and strength of alternative suppliers. Producers in this industry have maintained pricing power despite patent expiry or generic entry.[516]

With regard to vertical effects, the first issue concerned the definition of the relevant markets, in view of the fact that in its *Syngenta/Monsanto* sunflower seed business merger, the Commission had made a distinction between (i) the upstream market for the trading, usually through exchanges and licences, of seed varieties (parental lines and hybrids) and (ii) the downstream market for the trading of seeds, also identifying separate relevant product markets for each crop seed so that, for example, sunflower seeds constitute a product market separate from those for other seeds.[517] The Commission distinguished two levels: the upstream market for the trading of seed varieties, where the main players are seed companies and breeders and the downstream market for the commercialization of seeds, with a further segmentation for each type of crop seeds, distributors or farmers being there the key stakeholders.[518] The Commission left open the question whether the market could be further segmented on the basis of whether seeds are genetically modified, as this was not relevant for the

[513] See C Esteva Mosso, M Mottl, R De Coninck, and F Dupont, 'Digital Maps go Vertical: *TomTom/Tele Atlas* and *Nokia/NAVTEQ*' (2008) 3 *Competition Policy Newsletter* 70–4, available at ec.europa.eu/competition/publications/cpn/2008_3_70.pdf.

[514] Ibid. [515] *Dow/Dupont* (Case M.7932) Commission Decision (27 March 2017).

[516] Ibid, paras 423–4, 433, 522.

[517] *Syngenta/Monsanto's Sunflower Seed Business* (Case M.5675) Commission Decision C(2010) 7929 final (17 November 2010), para 76.

[518] *Dow/Dupont* (Case M.7932) Commission Decision (27 March 2017), para 3301.

case, in view of the fact that the merging entities' activities do not overlap in the sale of GM seeds, only DuPont selling a limited amount of GM maize seeds in Europe[519] The relevant geographic markets was the trading of seed varieties at the EEA level and the markets for the commercialization of seeds at the national level.[520] An analysis of the position of the parties in various crops, such as maize, sunflower, and cotton did not raise any specific concerns. Nonetheless, the Commission examined issues arising from the vertical overlap between Dow and DuPont, which are active both in the upstream market for the trading of seed varieties as well as in the downstream market for the trading of seeds, in particular for each of cotton, maize, oilseed rape, and sunflower seeds. According to the Commission '[s]uch affected markets would be susceptible to raise competition concerns should they be likely to lead to a material foreclosure of competitors in the upstream market for the licensing of seed varieties or in the downstream market for the trading of seeds.'[521]

In order to assess the existence of an eventual foreclosure effect, the Commission examined the existence of input or customer foreclosure. With regard to input foreclosure, the Commission found that Dow and DuPont are not significant licensors of seed varieties to third parties in Europe and that a number of seed competitors that are currently licensing to third parties their seed varieties. The breeder exception rule in the EU also allows seed companies to rely on the germplasm of competitors for crossing and selection so that the need to in-license is often limited to the instances in which finished varieties are needed to fill a portfolio gap.[522] Furthermore, the Commission found that 'seed companies tend to rely on their own seed varieties more than in the past, with the possible exception of sunflower seeds, and aim at in-licensing seed varieties only to meet specific needs'.[523] Similar conclusions were reached with regard to customer foreclosure.[524] The vertical relations between the merging parties between the upstream markets for the trading of seed varieties and the downstream markets for the trading of seeds were not found to raise any concerns as to the existence of a significant impediment of effective competition.

ChemChina/Syngenta

The Commission also examined the vertical effects of the merger between ChemChina and Syngenta,[525] conducting a competitive assessment of the vertical relationship between active ingredients and crop protection products, and between raw materials and active ingredients. Starting with active ingredients and crop protection products, the Commission stated that input foreclosure requires a significant degree of market power in the upstream market, and it is unlikely that the parties would have sufficient dominance in the active ingredients where their activities overlap.[526] The Commission reached the same conclusion concerning customer foreclosure because the transaction would not generate the market power necessary in the various crop protection products to support such an exclusionary strategy, and because ChemChina would not be able to purchase anywhere near Syngenta's share of worldwide demand in the active ingredients that it produced.[527] Turning to raw materials and active ingredients, the Commission excluded the possibility of both input and customer foreclosure, since Syngenta purchased only 5–10 per cent of its raw materials from ChemChina, and since Syngenta represented less than 1 per cent of ChemChina's sales of the relevant raw materials.[528]

519 Ibid, para 3303. 520 Ibid, para 3304.
521 Ibid, para 3388. 522 Ibid, para 3394. 523 Ibid, para 3395. 524 Ibid, para 3405.
525 *ChemChina/Syngenta* (Case M.7962) Commission Decision C(2017) 2167 final (5 April 2017).
526 Ibid, paras 224, 230, 236. 527 Ibid, para 255, 262. 528 Ibid, para 282, 298.

12.4.1.1.3. *Customer foreclosure*

Customer foreclosure arises when the downstream division of the merged entity stops purchasing from rival upstream suppliers. If there are economies of scale at the upstream level, and if the downstream division of the merged entity accounted for a large enough share of rival suppliers' sales before the merger, then the costs of rival upstream suppliers will go up due to the loss of economies of scale caused by the reduction in output sold to the downstream division after the merger. To the extent that this cost increase is then passed on to downstream rivals through higher upstream prices, the downstream division of the merged entity will benefit by being able to raise its own prices and/or capture some of the sales diverted from downstream rivals.[529]

Downstream rivals may also suffer if the product supplied by upstream rivals is of a lower quality. This is notably the case when the upstream product is subject to network effects,[530] that is, where the value to the user increases when the number of adopters rises. Hence, a reduction in the installed customer bases of rival upstream suppliers due to the loss of sales to the downstream division causes degradation in quality to the detriment of rival downstream firms.

The SIEC can also materialize over the long term, where the reduced scale weakens the ability of upstream rivals to innovate.[531] By the same token, customer foreclosure may also deter entry.[532]

Similarly to the case of input foreclosure, the incentive of the merged entity to restrict access to the downstream division depends on the trade-off between the possible costs associated with no longer procuring products from upstream rivals and the possible benefits from weakening pricing rivalry at the downstream level.[533] The former may be the case where upstream rivals are more efficient or offer superior quality than the upstream division of the merged entity.[534] In contrast, where the upstream division still supplies downstream rivals, the former may benefit if the latter divert some of their supplies away from upstream rivals in response to an increase in their prices following the customer foreclosure.[535]

12.4.1.1.3.1. Thomson Corporation/Reuters Group

Thomson Corporation/Reuters Group (Case COMP/M.4726) Commission Decision C (2008) 654 final (19 February 2008)

The merging parties were major providers of financial news and information to financial institutions such as banks and trading firms. Both Thomson and Reuters, as well as Bloomberg, were vertically integrated news providers able to rely on their own media platforms to deliver their content. The issue of customer foreclosure was raised with respect to Dow Jones a non-vertically integrated content provider that relied on the three platforms mentioned above to distribute its content.

> 141. A distinction should be drawn between non-integrated financial News content suppliers such as Dow Jones, Informa, AP who deliver their content through platform providers (eg Bloomberg, FactSet, Thomson, Reuters) and integrated News providers who have developed their proprietary News content and are able to distribute them to financial institutions through their terminals (eg Reuters, Thomson and Bloomberg). Thomson, also distributes its News product as a standalone data feed to competing third party distributors, whereas Bloomberg and Reuters sell their proprietary News only on their platforms to final customers.

529 Non-Horizontal Merger Guidelines, para 63. 530 Ibid, para 62. 531 Ibid, para 65.
532 Ibid, para 64. 533 Ibid, para 68. 534 Ibid, para 69. 535 Ibid, para 70.

> 142. These three integrated News suppliers also distribute financial News from third party financial News providers (eg Dow Jones) in addition to their own offerings. They typically charge a royalty fee to third party news providers for the distribution of the News service which corresponds to a portion of the revenue generated by the third party providers.

The Commission dismissed this concern by finding that to remain competitive the merged entity would need to keep delivering Dow Jones feeds in order to satisfy the needs of sophisticated customers.

> 155. Secondly, concerns have also been voiced that the merger would result in reduced access to the marketplace for third party News suppliers. As a result of the proposed merger, a combined Reuters-Thomson could impose uneconomic charges for access or push third party News providers (such as Dow Jones) off its terminals. Despite having a large number of distributors, Dow Jones generates a significant share of its revenues from the sale of its data through Thomson and Reuters desktops. The parties' incentives to exclude Dow Jones from their platform would derive from their interest in foreclosing one of their main competitors to access their customers.
>
> 156. In view of Dow Jones' brand recognition and of its wide acceptance in the financial community such a move appears unlikely as customers are likely to continue to ask for Dow Jones services. A decision by the parties to cease distribution of Dow Jones could face strong customer resistance and would put Thomson/Reuters at a disadvantage if compared with its competitors (for instance Bloomberg and Factset distribute Dow Jones as an optional service). This probably explains why Reuters, even in the on-trading floor where it faces little competition from Thomson, distributes Dow Jones News services on its desktop products, and this despite the fact Dow Jones directly competes with Reuters' News. In addition, Reuters generates significant revenues from the distribution of Dow Jones News services since it typically charges a royalty fee between [. . .] of the revenue generated by News providers. The new merged entity would have an interest in keeping this stream of revenues alive especially if there is strong demand for Dow Jones News products from customers. It therefore does not seem likely that the merger will significantly change the distribution of Dow Jones News services.

A vertical merger may give rise to a SIEC by giving the merger entity access to commercially sensitive information about non-integrated rivals at the upstream or downstream level.[536]

Another potential theory of harm not contemplated in the Non-Horizontal Merger Guidelines is where the vertical integration works as a commitment device to maintain high upstream prices. Before the merger the upstream (merging) firm may struggle to impose high prices to downstream firms, if the latter are suspicious that rivals are able to privately negotiate lower upstream prices which would allow them to undercut prices at the downstream level. By vertically integrating downstream, the upstream firm signals the lack of opportunistic incentives to secretly offer lower prices to rivals, since this would hurt the profitability of its own downstream division. That is to say, the rationale underpinning the merger is the restoration of market power at the upstream level.[537] For this exploitative, rather than exclusionary, theory of harm to work the upstream division of the merger entity must have a substantial dominant position at the upstream level.

536 Ibid, para 78.

537 See O Hart and J Tirole, 'Vertical Integration and Market Foreclosure', Brookings Papers on Economic Activity: Microeconomics (1990), 205–76, available at https://www.brookings.edu/bpea-articles/vertical-intergration-and-market-foreclosure/.

12.4.1.2. Coordinated effects in vertical mergers

A vertical merger can facilitate coordination in a number of ways. First of all, it can make it easier for firms to reach a common understanding on the terms of coordination thanks to the fact that the merged entity gain access to commercially sensitive information of non-integrated rivals. This can also improve transparency among firms and facilitate the detection of deviation.[538] To the extent that a vertical merger leads in total foreclosure of non-integrated rivals, a reduction in the number of firms normally improves the internal stability of coordination.[539] This is particularly the case if the excluded firm was a 'maverick'. Alternatively, the 'maverick' firm can be the target firm in the vertical merger.[540] To the extent that foreclosure raises entry and expansion barriers, external stability improves as well.[541] Finally, customer foreclosure can improve internal stability by reducing the room for deviation by non-integrated upstream rivals.[542]

12.4.2. CONGLOMERATE MERGERS

Conglomerate mergers are mergers where the merging firms are neither direct competitors (actual or potential competitors) nor active in different stages of the same value chain (such as supplier and distributor). Nevertheless, the merging firms' products can be economic complements due to the fact that they are normally purchased in combination.[543]

Conglomerate mergers were viewed with suspicion in the 1960s and 1970s in the US (the EU having no proper merger control regime at the time), because of their perceived economic and social effects, in particular their contribution to the consolidation trend across industries and aggregation of economic power. The emergence of large conglomerates led some to fear a concentration of economic power in the hands of few firms and individuals that would be left unaccountable to the general public, when making economic or business decisions with effects on various markets, would have affected the principles on which democratic capitalism is based. During this time, the competition authorities in the US were concerned about the entrenchment of dominant positions in various markets, following the acquisition of a dominant firm by an even larger company, which with its important financial and other resources ('deep pockets') could reinforce the dominance of the acquired firm, in particular in oligopolistic markets, as the acquired firm would be able to sustain losses or low margins and exclude competitors.[544] Furthermore, it was thought that conglomerate mergers could facilitate collusion as it would link oligopolies in two or more markets and that the presence of common participants in each market would facilitate monitoring and would discourage cheating, in view of the possibility to retaliate in multiple markets by the other common participants, thus sustaining collusion.[545] These concerns over economic concentration and its political and social consequences have been abandoned in the 1980s with the turn of US antitrust towards a more economic efficiency-oriented approach.[546]

538 Non-Horizontal Merger Guidelines, para 84. 539 Ibid, para 84. 540 Ibid, para 85.

541 Ibid, para 89.

542 See V Nocke and L White, 'Do Vertical Mergers Facilitate Upstream Collusion?' (2007) 97(4) *American Economic Rev* 1321.

543 Non-Horizontal Merger Guidelines, para 91.

544 ABA Section of Antitrust Law, *Mergers and Acquisitions: Understanding the Antitrust Issues* (4th ed, 2015), 409.

545 Ibid, 417.

546 One may, however, expect a resurgence of the interest of antitrust scholars, and possibly competition authorities, in conglomerate mergers in view of the concerns expressed on the rising levels of inequality and

The relationship between economic complements strongly implies that the merger may generate efficiency improvement thanks to the fact that the merged entity will set the price for one product taking into account the demand effect for the other product. Whereas, an individual product firm would tend to ignore this effect and therefore set higher prices for individual products than if they were sold together by the same firm.[547] Customers of the merged entity may also value the ability to purchase complement products from the same firm, thus saving on transaction costs.[548] Accordingly, and after some decisions going to an opposite direction,[549] the European Commission recognized in its 2008 non-horizontal merger guidelines that conglomerate mergers are normally pro-competitive.[550]

12.4.2.1 Non-coordinated effects in conglomerate mergers

12.4.2.1.1. Non-coordinated effects in conglomerate mergers and the Non-Horizontal Merger Guidelines

As with respect to non-coordinated effects in vertical merger, the key non-coordinated competition concern with conglomerate mergers is about foreclosure, whereby the merged entity leverages a position of significant market power from one market to a complementary one through either tying or bundling.[551]

Non-Horizontal Merger Guidelines [2008] OJ C 265/7, paras 95–102

> 95. The most immediate way in which the merged entity may be able to use its market power in one market to foreclose competitors in another is by conditioning sales in a way that links the products in the separate markets together. This is done most directly either by tying or bundling.
>
> 96. 'Bundling' usually refers to the way products are offered and priced by the merged entity. One can distinguish in this respect between pure bundling and mixed bundling. In the case of pure bundling the products are only sold jointly in fixed proportions. With mixed bundling the products are also available separately, but the sum of the stand-alone prices is higher than the bundled price. Rebates, when made dependent on the purchase of other goods, may be considered a form of mixed bundling.
>
> 97. 'Tying' usually refers to situations where customers that purchase one good (the tying good) are required to also purchase another good from the producer (the tied good). Tying can take place on a technical or contractual basis. For instance, technical tying occurs when the tying product is designed in such a way that it only works with the tied product (and not with the alternatives offered by competitors). Contractual tying entails that the customer when purchasing the tying good undertakes only to purchase the tied product (and not the alternatives offered by competitors).
>
> 98. The specific characteristics of the products may be relevant for determining whether any of these means of linking sales between separate markets are available

aggregate economic concentration, which are exacerbated by the 'winner takes it all' effect of platform competition. For some proposals, see MS Gal and TK Cheng, 'Aggregate Concentration: A Study of Competition Law Solutions' (2016) 4(2) *J Antitrust Enforcement* 282.

547 Non-Horizontal Merger Guidelines, para 117.

548 Ibid, para 118.

549 See eg *Guinness/Grand Metro* (Case IV/M.938) Commission Decision [1997] OJ L288/24; *General Electric/Honeywell* (Case COMP/M.2220) Commission Decision (rendered 3 July 2001) [2004] OJ L 48/1.

550 Non-Horizontal Merger Guidelines, para 92.

551 Ibid, para 93.

> to the merged entity. For instance, pure bundling is very unlikely to be possible if products are not bought simultaneously or by the same customers. Similarly, technical tying is only an option in certain industries.
>
> 99. In order to be able to foreclose competitors, the new entity must have a significant degree of market power, which does not necessarily amount to dominance, in one of the markets concerned. The effects of bundling or tying can only be expected to be substantial when at least one of the merging parties' products is viewed by many customers as particularly important and there are few relevant alternatives for that product, eg because of product differentiation or capacity constraints on the part of rivals.
>
> 100. Further, for foreclosure to be a potential concern it must be the case that there is a large common pool of customers for the individual products concerned. The more customers tend to buy both products (instead of only one of the products), the more demand for the individual products may be affected through bundling or tying. Such a correspondence in purchasing behaviour is more likely to be significant when the products in question are complementary.
>
> 101. Generally speaking, the foreclosure effects of bundling and tying are likely to be more pronounced in industries where there are economies of scale and the demand pattern at any given point in time has dynamic implications for the conditions of supply in the market in the future. Notably, where a supplier of complementary goods has market power in one of the products (product A), the decision to bundle or tie may result in reduced sales by the non-integrated suppliers of the complementary good (product B). If further there are network externalities at play this will significantly reduce these rivals' scope for expanding sales of product B in the future. Alternatively, where entry into the market for the complementary product is contemplated by potential entrants, the decision to bundle by the merged entity may have the effect of deterring such entry. The limited availability of complementary products with which to combine may, in turn, discourage potential entrants to enter market A.
>
> 102. It can also be noted that the scope for foreclosure tends to be smaller where the merging parties cannot commit to making their tying or bundling strategy a lasting one, for example through technical tying or bundling which is costly to reverse.

Similarly to vertical mergers, the merger entity's incentive to engage in foreclosure depends on a trade-off between the loss of sales for individual products and the increase in market power in the tied or bundled product market.[552] A high profit margin earned on the tying/bundling product would indicate that the losses due to lower sales to those customers only interested in purchasing this product individually may be hard to offset.[553]

The guidelines on non-coordinated effects in conglomerate mergers reflect the strong debate that ensued *Tetra Laval/Sidel*[554] and *General Electric/Honeywell*,[555] two decisions issued in 2001 where the Commission found that the mergers in question would have caused a SIEC due to tying and bundling among complementary products.[556] In both cases, the General

552 Ibid, para 106. 553 Ibid, para 107.

554 *Tetra Laval/Sidel* (Case COMP/M.2416) Commission Decision (13 January 2003).

555 *General Electric/Honeywell* (Case COMP/M.2220) Commission Decision (3 July 2001).

556 See eg SB Volcker, 'Leveraging as a Theory of competition Harm in EC Merger Control' (2003) 40 *Common Market L Rev* 581; DJ Neven, 'The Analysis of Conglomerate Effects in EU Merger Control' in P Buccirossi (ed) *Handbook of Antitrust Economics* (MIT Press, 2007), 183; G Drauz, 'Unbundling GE/Honeywell: The Assessment of Conglomerate Mergers under EC Competition Law' (2001) 25 (4) *Fordham Int'l LJ* 885; WJ Kolasky, 'Conglomerate Mergers and Range Effects: It's a Long Way from Chicago to Brussels', Before the George

Court robustly criticized the Commission for failing to establish that the merged entity would have the ability and incentive to foreclose through leveraging practices.[557] After the publication of the Non-Horizontal Merger Guidelines, the issue of non-coordinated conglomerate effects featured prominently in *Google/DoubleClick*.

12.4.2.1.2. Tetra Laval/Sidel

Tetra Laval, through its subsidiary, Tetra Pak, enjoyed a dominant position over aseptic carton packaging used to contain milk and fruit juices while the target company, Sidel, was a global leader in the production and supply of stretch blow moulding machines used to product PET drinks packaging. The merger with Sidel was almost entirely conglomerate. Four types of packaging are used for liquid food: cartons, plastic (including polyethylene terephthalate, or PET), cans, and glass. The markets were distinct, but closely related and converging. The Commission focused on foods that were sensitive to light or oxygen. Tetra had a dominant position over cartons, and Sidel was the leading maker of the SBM machines needed to make PET bottles. The Commission feared that the merged firms might leverage the dominant position of cartons towards dominance over the SBM machines made by Sidel. Tetra Laval's reputation in aseptic cartons and equipment would help it to persuade its customer to buy Sidel's SMB machines. According to the Commission, '[. . .] through the merger, Tetra/Sidel would have a unique advantage in entering these markets over PET equipment competitors that lack this established customer base in the traditional carton end-use segments', as Tetra/Laval 'would be in a position to know exactly which customers have plans to switch to PET, and knowing the clients' needs through its carton side of the business, would be able to impose on them timely and bespoke PET solutions enabling them to make the switch from carton to PET seamlessly with a single supplier'.[558] This leveraging could be done through various 'leveraging practices', such as the possibility of Tetra/Sidel to marginalize competitors and dominate the PET equipment market, in particular SBM machines, by tying tie carton packaging equipment and consumables with PET packaging equipment, or 'to use pressure or incentives (such as predatory pricing or price wars and loyalty rebates) so that its carton customers buy PET equipment' from Tetra/Sidel and not from its competitors.[559] Tetra Laval offered several commitments, but the Commission found that these were insufficient and compliance would be hard to monitor, thus prohibiting the merger.

On appeal, the GC annulled the decision on the basis that the Commission had committed manifest errors of assessment in its findings as to leveraging and strengthening Tetra's dominant position. The GC found that, although leverage was theoretically possible, the Commission accepted that it would not result directly from the merger, but only from the likely subsequent conduct of the merged firm.[560] The GC accepted that the Commission

Mason University Symposium Washington, DC (9 November 2001), available at https://www.justice.gov/atr/speech/conglomerate-mergers-and-range-effects-its-long-way-chicago-brussels; A Burnside, 'GE, Honey, I Sunk the Merger' (2002) 23(2) *European Competition L Rev* 107; M Pflanz and C Caffarra, 'The Economics of *GE/Honeywell*' [2002] 23(3) *European Competition L Rev* 115; D Howart, 'The Court of First Instance in *GE/Honeywell*' (2006) 27(9) *European Competition L Rev* 485; and J Grant and DJ Neven, 'The Attempted Merger between General Electric and Honeywell: A Case Study of Transantlantic Conflict' (2005) 1 (3) *J Competition L & Economics* 595.

[557] See Case T/210/01, *General Electric Company v Commission* [2005] ECR II–5575; Case T-5/02, *Tetra Laval BV v Commission* [2002] ECR II–4381.

[558] *Tetra Laval/Sidel* (Case COMP/M.2416) Commission Decision (13 January 2003) [2004] OJ L 43/13, para 363.

[559] Ibid, para 364.

[560] Case T-5/02, *Tetra Laval BV v Commission* [2002] ECR II–4381.

enjoyed a certain discretion when assessing economic issues.[561] Nevertheless, a conglomerate merger did not directly increase the firms' market power. It was for the Commission to produce convincing evidence that this was likely. It should, therefore, have considered whether such conduct would be illegal under Article 102 TFEU. It quashed the decision on the ground of manifest error for not investigating. The GC observed that, where the firms operated in distinct markets, a dominant position would seldom be created or strengthened.[562] Nevertheless, leveraging market power into a neighbouring market in the reasonably near future was in principle possible.[563] According to the GC,

> [. . .] where the Commission takes the view that a merger should be prohibited because it will create or strengthen a dominant position within a foreseeable period, it is incumbent upon it to produce convincing evidence thereof.[564] Since the effects of a conglomerate-type merger are generally considered to be neutral, or even beneficial, for competition on the markets concerned, as is recognised in the present case by the economic writings cited [. . .] the proof of anti-competitive conglomerate effects of such a merger calls for a precise examination, supported by convincing evidence, of the circumstances which allegedly produce those effects.'[565]

On further appeal to the CJEU, the Commission sought annulment of the GC judgment.[566] The Commission's margin of discretion is subject to judicial review. The CJEU held that '[w]hilst the Court recognises that the Commission has a margin of discretion with regard to economic matters, that does not mean that the Community courts must refrain from reviewing the Commission's interpretation of information of an economic nature'.[567] Not only must the findings be factually accurate, reliable, and consistent, but the evidence must contain all the information to be taken into account to assess a complex situation.[568] The CJEU continued by examining the way the GC had reviewed the Commission's findings regarding the anti-competitive conglomerate effects of the merger

Case C-12/03, *Commission v Tetra Laval*
[2005] ECR I–987

> 41. Although the [GC] stated, in paragraph 155, that proof of anti-competitive conglomerate effects of a merger of the kind notified calls for a precise examination, supported by convincing evidence, of the circumstances which allegedly produce those effects, it by no means added a condition relating to the requisite standard of proof but merely drew attention to the essential function of evidence, which is to establish convincingly the merits of an argument or, as in the present case, of a decision on a merger.
>
> 42. A prospective analysis of the kind necessary in merger control must be carried out with great care since it does not entail the examination of past events—for which

561 Ibid, para 119. 562 Ibid, para 150. 563 Ibid, para 151.
564 Case T-342/99, *Airtours plc v Commission* [2002] ECR II–2585, para 63.
565 Case T-5/02, *Tetra Laval BV v Commission* [2002] ECR II–4381, para 155. See also, by analogy, Case T-342/99, *Airtours plc v Commission* [2002] ECR II–2585, para 63.
566 Case C-12/03, *Commission v Tetra Laval* [2005] ECR I–987. 567 Ibid, para 39.
568 Ibid.

often many items of evidence are available which make it possible to understand the causes—or of current events, but rather a prediction of events which are more or less likely to occur in future if a decision prohibiting the planned concentration or laying down the conditions for it is not adopted.

43. Thus, the prospective analysis consists of an examination of how a concentration might alter the factors determining the state of competition on a given market in order to establish whether it would give rise to a serious impediment to effective competition. Such an analysis makes it necessary to envisage various chains of cause and effect with a view to ascertaining which of them are the most likely.

44. The analysis of a 'conglomerate-type' concentration is a prospective analysis in which, first, the consideration of a lengthy period of time in the future and, secondly, the leveraging necessary to give rise to a significant impediment to effective competition mean that the chains of cause and effect are dimly discernible, uncertain and difficult to establish. That being so, the quality of the evidence produced by the Commission in order to establish that it is necessary to adopt a decision declaring the concentration incompatible with the common market is particularly important, since that evidence must support the Commission's conclusion that, if such a decision were not adopted, the economic development envisaged by it would be plausible.

45. It follows from those various factors that the [GC] did not err in law when it set out the tests to be applied in the exercise of its power of judicial review or when it specified the quality of the evidence which the Commission is required to produce [. . .].

According to the CJEU, as it is difficult to see far into the future,[569] the GC did not err in law in quashing the Commission's decision.[570]

The CJEU also confirmed that it could not be assumed that the parties would infringe Article 102 TFEU. The Commission should therefore have examined comprehensively whether the merged entity would be likely to abuse its dominant position, but the GC had gone too far in requiring the Commission to examine both the extent to which the incentive to adopt anti-competitive conduct would be reduced or eliminated on the ground that it was unlawful and the likelihood of detection.

Case C-12/03, *Commission v Tetra Laval*
[2005] ECR I–987

74. Since the view is taken in the contested decision that adoption of the ['leveraging practices'] is an essential step in leveraging, the [General Court] was right to hold that the likelihood of its adoption must be examined comprehensively, that is to say, taking account, [. . .] both of the incentives to adopt such conduct and the factors liable to reduce, or even eliminate, those incentives, including the possibility that the conduct is unlawful.

75. However, it would run counter to the Regulation's purpose of prevention to require the Commission, [. . .] to examine, for each proposed merger, the extent to which the incentives to adopt anti-competitive conduct would be reduced, or even eliminated, as a result of the unlawfulness of the conduct in question, the likelihood of

569 Ibid, para 44. 570 Ibid, para 55.

> its detection, the action taken by the competent authorities, both at Community and national level, and the financial penalties which could ensue.
>
> 76. An assessment such as that required by the [GC] would make it necessary to carry out an exhaustive and detailed examination of the rules of the various legal orders which might be applicable and of the enforcement policy practised in them. Moreover, if it is to be relevant, such an assessment calls for a high probability of the occurrence of the acts envisaged as capable of giving rise to objections on the ground that they are part of anti-competitive conduct.
>
> 77. It follows that, at the stage of assessing a proposed merger, an assessment intended to establish whether an infringement of Article [102 TFEU] is likely and to ascertain that it will be penalised in several legal orders would be too speculative and would not allow the Commission to base its assessment on all of the relevant facts with a view to establishing whether they support an economic scenario in which a development such as leveraging will occur.
>
> 78. Consequently, the [GC] erred in law in rejecting the Commission's conclusions as to the adoption by the merged entity of anti-competitive conduct capable of resulting in leveraging on the sole ground that the Commission had, when assessing the likelihood that such conduct might be adopted, failed to take account of the unlawfulness of that conduct and, consequently, of the likelihood of its detection, of action by the competent authorities, both at Community and national level, and of the financial penalties which might ensue.

12.4.2.1.3. General Electric/Honeywell

This was a mega-merger between two US-based groups whose combined worldwide turnover was $180 billion, with an EU turnover a little less than $30 billion. The merger would have been the biggest industrial merger of all time and one of the biggest mergers overall. GE was the largest of three leading manufacturers of engines for large commercial jet aircraft. Its competitors were Rolls Royce and Pratt & Whitney. Honeywell was the dominant maker of engine starters for jet engines. It also made certain avionic and non-avionic equipment used in jet aircraft. GE had a financial subsidiary, GE Capital, which provided finance to airframe manufacturers in the form of platform programme development. GE Capital had bailed out at least one major airline, which returned the favour with an exclusive purchase order of GE jet Engines. It also had a subsidiary, Capital Aviation Services (GECAS), that was active in aircraft purchase and leasing. GECAS was the world's largest buyer of airplanes, representing nearly 10 per cent of all purchases of new commercial jet aircraft. Its policy was to buy only planes fitted with GE engines.

The Commission found that GE was a dominant firm in the markets for jet engines for large commercial aircraft and large regional aircraft.[571] The Commission also found that GE's merger with Honeywell would strengthen the present dominance of GE in large commercial jet aircraft engines due to the vertical effects of the merger. These vertical effects would arise as a result of integration of GE's activity as a manufacturer of large commercial aircraft jet engines with the activity of Honeywell as a manufacturer of starters for those engines. Further, the Commission found that the acquisition, through bundling,

[571] *General Electric/Honeywell* (Case COMP/M.2220) Commission Decision (rendered 3 July 2001) [2004] OJ L 48/1.

leveraging and strategic behaviour, would increase GE's dominance and confer dominance on Honeywell in certain avionic and non-avionic products. It was not until paragraph 428 that the Commission considered horizontal overlaps. The case was famous for being a conglomerate merger, based on the prediction that GE would offer packaged and bundled deals and use its leverage to shift market share away from competitors until their business was no longer profitable and they abandoned competition with Honeywell. One type of conglomerate effect arose from the commercial advantages derived from GECAS. For instance, the Commission found that GE Capital's financial resources and the various commercial advantages that the new entity could derive from GE's aircraft leasing business would be leveraged into markets in which Honeywell had a leading position, a version of the entrenchment concerns expressed in US antitrust laws in the 1960s and 1970s. The other type of conglomerate effect related to 'portfolio effects' resulting from 'portfolio power', in particular as the merger entity would have been able to offer packages of products that had previously been sold individually in single markets.[572] This 'portfolio power' would find its sources in the increased range of important, or 'must stock', brands under the control of a single company, the control of an important number of high end as well as secondary brands, the overall size of the merged entity. According to the Commission, such problem might arise in the future where the merged entity could bundle their goods like aircraft engines and avionics and non-avionic products, offering the package at a lower price than if the components were sold separately (mixed bundling) or by enabling the merged entity to cross-subsidize discounts across the various product lines composing the packaged deal, depriving customers of choice[573] and affecting GE/Honeywell's competitors in the markets for aerospace equipment and jet engines leading to a reduction of their profitability and market foreclosure.[574]

Although the Court of First Instance (now General Court) upheld the Commission's decision blocking the merger on other grounds, it struck the findings of the Commission with regard to the conglomerate effects of the merger.[575] The first central issue was whether GE was dominant over large commercial aircraft. GE claimed that its market share was well under 40 per cent, but the Commission attributed the whole of the production of GE's joint venture with SNECMA, CFMI, to GE[576] and similarly attributed the production of another joint venture, IAE.[577] GE also argued that existing market shares are less important in a bidding market than in other markets.[578] The GC accepted the second argument, but found dominance only by attributing the turnover of JVs to GE in a bidding market.

The GC repeated the conclusions of the CJEU in *Tetra Laval*. It did not question the Commission's theories about the effects of leveraging, but only whether the Commission had established that leveraging and bundling would have been likely to occur.

572 Similar concerns have been expressed by the Commission in *Guinness/Grand Metro* (Case IV/M.938) (8 May 1997) where the merger would have resulted in a company with a portfolio of brands across different relevant markets of spirits categories such as whisky, gin, vodka, etc, that would lead to portfolio power. The Commission thought that this could create or strengthen a dominant position irrespective of the lack of increase in market share in the individual spirits categories.

573 *General Electric/Honeywell* (Case COMP/M.2220) Commission Decision (rendered 3 July 2001) [2004] OJ L 48/1, paras 350–3.

574 Ibid, para 398.

575 Case T-210/01, *General Electric Company v Commission* [2005] ECR II–5575.

576 Ibid, paras 124–7. 577 Ibid, paras 145. 578 Ibid, paras 148–51.

Case T-210/01, *General Electric Company v Commission*
[2005] ECR II–5575

304. It follows that the Commission must, as a rule, take into account the potentially unlawful, and thus sanctionable, nature of certain conduct as a factor which might diminish, or even eliminate, incentives for an undertaking to engage in particular conduct [. . .]. However, it is not required to establish that the conduct foreseen in the future will actually constitute an infringement of Article [102 TFEU] or that, if that were to be the case, that infringement would be detected and punished, the Commission being able to limit itself in that regard to a summary analysis based on the evidence available to it.

305. In the present case, the Commission has predicted future conduct on the engine-starter market the object and—were it to prove effective—effect of which would be to strengthen the dominant position on the market for large commercial jet aircraft engines specifically by weakening the merged entity's competitors on that market. The conduct in question, namely interrupting the supply of engine starters to competitors, even refusing to sell them, and price increases, would produce an effect on the market for large commercial jet aircraft engines only in so far as it significantly harmed the jet-engine manufacturing activities of the merged entity's competitors.

306. It should be recalled that, even if the fact that an undertaking is in a dominant position cannot deprive it of its right to protect its own commercial interests, it follows from established case-law that such conduct is unlawful if its object is specifically to strengthen this dominant position and abuse it (*United Brands* v *Commission* [[1978] ECR 207], paragraph 189; Case T-65/89 *BPB Industries and British Gypsum* v *Commission* [1993] ECR II–389, paragraphs 117 et seq.; see also Joined Cases T-24/93 to T-26/93 and T-28/93 *Compagnie maritime belge transports and Others* v *Commission* [1996] ECR II–1201, paragraph 149). Thus, for example, a refusal by an undertaking in a dominant position to sell an essential component to its competitors in itself constitutes an abuse of that position (see, to that effect, Joined Cases 6/83 and 7/73 *Istituto Chemioterapico Italiano and Commercial Solvents* v *Commission* [1974] ECR 223, paragraph 25).

307. As to the possibility of the merged entity increasing the price of its engine starters, it should be observed that, in order to have a tangible effect on Rolls-Royce's competitiveness on the market for large commercial jet aircraft engines, such an increase would have to be so large that it would clearly amount to abuse. A possible 50% increase in the price of engine starters, without any apparent commercial justification, would represent only a 0.1% increase in the price of a jet engine and would therefore have virtually no effect on the jet-engine market. Moreover, if a price increase for engine starters were applied in a non-discriminatory way, it would be liable adversely to affect some of the merged entity's customers, and accordingly would have harmful commercial effects for it. Such an increase could, in particular, affect its relations with airlines, which are customers for engine starters both indirectly as purchasers of aircraft and directly on the aftermarket for services and which are also likely to be customers of the merged entity for both engines and avionics and non-avionics products. Conversely, if such an increase were applied in a discriminatory way vis-à-vis its competitors, it would be clear that the object of the increase was to foreclose those competitors from the market and it would therefore constitute abuse.

308. Likewise, a disruption of supplies by the merged entity following the merger would adversely affect its own customers if the disruption was general and would

clearly constitute abuse if the disruption was discriminatory, in particular with regard to Rolls-Royce.

309. It follows from the foregoing that the conduct predicted by the Commission in this instance is liable to amount to an abuse of a dominant position. In the present case, the more convincing the Commission's case as to the effectiveness of the conduct in question and thus the clearer the commercial incentive to engage in it, the greater the likelihood of the conduct being classified as anti-competitive. It is precisely the most extreme forms of the conduct foreseen by the Commission which would be both the most effective for the purposes of harming competitors' businesses and the most likely to constitute visible and obvious—and therefore the most likely to be penalised—abuses of the merged entity's dominant position.

310. In that regard, the fact that the abuse takes place on a particular market (in this instance the engine-starter market) does not mean that the relevant market for the purposes of appraising dominance cannot be the related downstream market (in this instance the market for large commercial jet aircraft engines), given that the conduct foreseen by the Commission on the first market is specifically intended to maintain or strengthen the undertaking's dominant position on the second market (see, to that effect, *AKZO* v *Commission* [[1991] ECR I–3359], paragraphs 40 to 45; and Case T-219/99 *British Airways* v *Commission* [2003] ECR II–5917, paragraphs 270 to 300).

311. Thus, in view of its finding that the applicant was in a dominant position on the market for large commercial jet aircraft engines prior to the merger [. . .], the Commission necessarily had available all the evidence required in this case to assess, without the need to carry out a detailed investigation in that regard, to what extent the conduct which it itself anticipated on the engine-starter market would constitute infringements of Article 82 EC and be sanctioned as such. It therefore made an error of law in failing to take into account the deterrent effect which that factor might have had on the merged entity.

312. It is also clear that, if the deterrent effect had been taken into account, it could materially have influenced the Commission's appraisal of how likely it was that the conduct in question would be adopted. In these circumstances, it is not for the Court to substitute its own appraisal for that of the Commission, by seeking to establish what the latter would have decided if it had taken into account the deterrent effect of Article [102 TFEU]. Accordingly, the Commission's analysis of this aspect of the case, since it did not include any consideration of the deterrent effect of Article [102 TFEU]—notwithstanding its relevance—, is necessarily vitiated by a manifest error of assessment.

According to the GC, the Commission should have established 'not only that the merged entity had the ability to transfer those practices to the markets for avionics and non-avionics products but also, on the basis of convincing evidence, that it was likely that the merged entity would engage in such conduct'.[579] In *Tetra Laval*, the CJEU had just held that evidence establishing a conglomerate case must be particularly clear. Conglomerate effects depend not only on structure but also on predicted behaviour, and this is hard to forecast. The bundling and leveraging feared by the Commission might have infringed Article 102 TFEU, and the CJEU had held in *Tetra Laval* that the Commission should have investigated whether that was likely to deter the future conduct alleged.

579 Ibid, paras 325–64.

12.4.2.1.4. *Google/DoubleClick*

Google/DoubleClick (Case COMP/M.4731) Commission Decision C(2008) 927 final (11 March 2008)

In the decision the Commission dismissed concerns that Google could leverage its dominance in search advertising in the markets served by the target company, DoubleClick, which was a provider of ad serving, management and reporting technology worldwide to website publishers, advertisers and advertising agencies.

330. The second category of non-horizontal concerns described above takes Google's market position in search advertising and (search) ad intermediation services as a starting point assuming that Google may attempt to foreclose rivals by bundling its sales of search ads or its intermediation services for the sale of search and/or non-search ads with DoubleClick's ad serving technology. Google's search ad services or its (search) ad intermediation services would thus be the bundling services and DoubleClick's ad serving would be the bundled service. These strategies can be conceived if search and non-search advertising are deemed to be in separate markets.

331. Practically, this would mean that advertisers wanting to place search ads via Google or via Google's (search) ad intermediation (AdWords) would be (contractually) required to make a certain minimum use of DFA [the ad-serving product for advertisers sold by DoubleClick] in case they use display ads at all. Equally, publishers wanting to use Google's (search) ad intermediation could be obliged to use DFP [the ad-serving product for publishers sold by DoubleClick], either on a contractual basis or by means of a technological tie, whereby publishers could only market their inventory on AdSense if they use DFP. Alternatively, Google could use its pricing to induce advertisers and publishers who utilize AdWords or AdSense to (voluntarily) utilize DFA or DFP. The main concern in this context is foreclosure in the sense that the acquisition of DoubleClick may confer on Google the ability and incentive to leverage its strong market position with regard to the provision of online advertising space for search ads or the provision of (search) ad intermediation services into the market for the provision of ad serving for display ads, thereby reducing the ability and incentive of actual or potential rivals in the ad serving market to compete. Ultimately, the merged entity's strategy could be to use its strengthened position in the ad serving market to impose an even wider bundle on advertisers and publishers, which would include also Google's nonsearch intermediation services, thereby foreclosing also its actual and potential rivals in non-search intermediation.

332. The Commission analysed these concerns and found that the proposed transaction would not bring about such a degree of foreclosure that competition would be significantly impeded. While it cannot be excluded completely that Google may have the *ability* to foreclose its rivals by bundling the provision of online advertising space for search ads or the provision of (search) ad intermediation services with DoubleClick's ad serving technology (and to ultimately extend such strategy by also including non-search intermediation in the bundle), the Commission found that the merged entity would most likely not have an *incentive* to adopt such a strategy. In any event, such a strategy would not have a significant detrimental effect on competition because a number of financially strong, vertically integrated competitors would not be foreclosed. [. . .]

The Commission first rejected Google's claim that it didn't have a position of significant market power in the tying/bundling market. Nevertheless, the Commission then went on to find that Google lacked the ability and incentives to foreclose.

339. However, for a number of other reasons the merged entity's *ability* to foreclose competitors by adopting the described strategy of pure bundling may be limited, not only in case of Google's non-search intermediation services as the bundling product, but also in case Google uses its search ad and its (search) ad intermediation business as the bundling product, and, more importantly, the merged entity most likely lacks the *incentive* to engage in the described strategy, both on the advertiser side and on the publisher side.

340. Firstly, there may be practical difficulties in requiring advertisers wanting to place search ads via Google (or search ads and/or contextual ads via Google's ad intermediation (AdWords)) to use DFA. Search ads and contextual ads sold by Google or through Google's ad intermediation services are priced on a cost-per-click basis. The prices charged to advertisers are determined by an auction. As a result, the terms according to which Google provides (search) advertising may be set with an individual advertiser on a daily basis. Advertisers can vary their bids on different search terms as often as they wish, or withdraw altogether from advertising with Google at any time. On the other hand, the terms according to which DoubleClick provides display ad serving are set by contracts that typically have a duration of one to two years. As a result, it would be difficult to set the terms for search advertising or (search) ad intermediation and display ad serving simultaneously. Pure bundling, however, is very unlikely to be possible if products are not bought simultaneously. There would therefore have to be a substantial change in the way the merging parties carry out their business if bundling were to be feasible, which makes bundling more difficult to put into practice, and less likely to occur. The same practical difficulties would apply in case the merged entity decided to extend the bundle so as to include also nonsearch intermediation. Indeed the only conceivable manner for Google to engage in pure bundling on the advertiser side without the described practical difficulties would be by making the use of DFA a precondition for advertisers to participate in the AdWords auction at all. As will be seen below, however, given the low margins on DFA compared to the margins on search advertising, Google would clearly lack the incentive to engage in such an extreme form of pure bundling.

341. On the publisher side, the practical difficulties in bundling Google's (search) ad intermediation with DFP appear to be more limited because for the provision of both display ad serving and (search) ad intermediation for (larger) publishers contractual arrangements of a similar nature and duration apply. As regards display ad serving, DoubleClick's contracts with publishers typically have a duration of one to two years. Regarding Google's contractual arrangements with its AFS partners, Google enters bidding contracts for the inventory of certain larger publishers, known as 'direct partners'. The contracts with these European direct partners have a similar duration as DoubleClick's ad serving contracts with publishers, the average duration being approximately [<3]* years. Even the parties therefore concede that the contractual differences between AFS partners and DFP customers are relatively limited. The practical difficulties described for the advertiser side thus do not appear to apply to the publisher side to any similar extent. Such practical difficulties therefore do not appear to affect the merged entity's ability to engage in the described bundling strategy on the publisher side.

342. Secondly, the extent to which the described bundling strategy results in foreclosure depends, amongst other things, on the extent to which demand for the merged entity's rivals' ad serving products is reduced by the tie. In this respect, the extent to which there is a common pool of customers that purchase both products may be relevant. If there are lots of users of DFA or DFP or competing ad serving products who do not sell or purchase search ads or whose sales or purchases of search ads are very low in value, then the effect on demand is less likely to be significant, and foreclosure less

likely to occur. On the other hand, foreclosure is more likely to be effective, if there is considerable overlap between advertisers and publishers that use Google's search ads or its (search) ad intermediation services and advertisers and publishers that use DFA or DFP or competing ad serving products.

343. According to the notifying party, only [less than 0.1 per cent]* out of Google's more than [. . .]* advertiser customers in the EEA which purchase search ads from Google (either directly or through intermediation) also use DFA. The notifying party estimates the share of these overlapping customers on the advertiser side represented in Google's search advertising revenues (including direct sales and intermediated sales) to be approximately [<20 per cent]*. On the publisher side, the corresponding numbers and percentages are even lower. [. . .] Corresponding figures for advertisers and publishers which sell or purchase (search) advertising space through Google and which are customers of competing ad serving technology providers are not available. However, as DoubleClick is the leading provider of ad serving technology to both advertisers and publishers, it is unlikely that such figures would change the overall impression that the common pool of customers of Google and DoubleClick is currently fairly limited. This at least reduces the merged entity's ability to foreclose rivals in the ad serving market.

344. Thirdly, the merged entity will face vertically integrated competitors that could replicate the strategy of bundling search advertising and advertiser side display ad serving as well as search intermediation and ad serving for publishers. These competitors include financially strong (groups of) companies such as Microsoft, Yahoo! and AOL. According to the notifying party, the threat of such counter-strategies being employed by its competitors constitutes an additional factor making it difficult, if not impossible for the merged entity to foreclose its rivals by engaging in the described bundling strategy.

With the benefit of hindsight, it is worth noting that both Yahoo! and AOL faced great difficulties over the following years, and both ended up being targeted by Verizon, the US telecom giant, at liquidation prices.

345. Given these circumstances, there are notable indications that, practically, Google may not be *able* to foreclose competitors in the ad serving market, at least on the advertiser side where the products to be bundled are not being sold simultaneously and the pricing mechanism for these products is very different. In view of Google's strong position in the search ad segment and in the (search) intermediation market, however, it cannot be excluded completely, at least on the publisher side, that the merged entity may have the (limited) *ability* to foreclose rivals by bundling the provision of online advertising space for search ads or the provision of (search) intermediation services with DoubleClick's ad serving technology.

346. However, the Commission found that, for the following reasons, the merged entity would not have an *incentive* to adopt such a strategy because that strategy would not be profitable.

347. Firstly, by requiring advertisers or publishers wanting to place search ads via Google or wanting to make use of Google's (search) ad intermediation services to make a certain minimum use of DFA or DFP, the merged entity would run the risk that some customers would no longer be willing to purchase search ads or (search) intermediation services from Google, either because they would rather not purchase a display ad serving solution at all or because they would rather purchase an alternative display ad serving solution.

348. As margins on DFA and DFP are low compared to margins on Google's direct sales of search ads and intermediated sales of (search) ads, even small volume losses

in search advertising and (search) intermediation would outweigh the gain in profits from customers taking up DFA or DFP.

[. . .]

352. In the light of these figures and circumstances, the merged entity would be unlikely to risk losing even only a few customers in its core business of search advertising and (search) ad intermediation, where the vast majority of its revenues are earned and where the revenues from each large customer are high, in an attempt to force its low-margin ad serving products upon those larger customers.

353. Secondly, in the online advertising environment transactions often involve customised solutions or services that are uniquely priced. Bundling is usually an attractive and profitable strategy in order to discern customer's willingness to pay in a context where prices are posted and uniform across customers. In the online advertising industry, bundling would not enable the new entity to increase profits because prices are highly individualized. On the advertiser side, both Google through its auction mechanism for keywords and DoubleClick through its direct negotiation with customers have the ability to vary the price of their products according to customers' willingness to pay. Similarly, on the publisher side, both Google through its negotiations with its direct partners (which account for around [>80 per cent]* of its AFS revenue) and DoubleClick through its direct negotiation with publishers, have the ability to vary the price of their products according to publishers' preferences. In such context, one of the attractions of bundling usually disappears.

354. To sum up, the large losses that the described bundling strategy would likely produce in the merged entity's core business, coupled with the limited gains from revenues in ad serving would render any such strategy unprofitable to the effect that the merged entity would lack the economic incentive to engage in such practice.

Data concentration, anti-competitive foreclosure, and exploitation

Google/DoubleClick: The *Google/DoubleClick* merger forms part of a number of recent mergers involving undertakings controlling data, an important asset for the digital economy.[580]

In *Google/DoubleClick*, the principal rationale for the merger was to integrate DoubleClick with AdSense in order to improve the ad network's quality, and in particular allow it to compete in selling rich media adverts.[581] At the time of the merger transaction, DoubleClick was the leading provider of ad server software for 'display' advertising (graphical ads) as it provided roughly 50 per cent of third-party ad servers used by advertisers and publishers for display adverts in the EEA. Google operated an ad network, bringing together large numbers of publishers and advertisers, using AdSense, a software choosing what adverts to display when somebody looks at a webpage. Previously, AdSense had primarily only sold text ads, not display advertising. The Commission found that Google could benefit from a number of competitive advantages following the integration of DoubleClick's ad serving technology with its ad intermediation services, in particular DoubleClick's customer base among publishers and advertisers, and data about consumer behaviour collected through ad serving. Indeed,

580 For an analysis, see B Holles de Peyer, 'EU Merger Control and Big Data' (2017) 13(4) *J Competition L & Economics* 767; A Chirita, 'Data-Driven Mergers Under EU Competition Law' in O Akseli and J Linarelli (eds) *The Future of Commercial Law: Ways Forward for Harmonisation* (Hart, forthcoming 2019), available at https://ssrn.com/abstract=3199912.

581 *Google/DoubleClick* (Case COMP/M.4731) Commission Decision C(2008) 927 final (11 March 2008).

it found that DoubleClick represented a 'key input into distribution channels that compete with Google's AdSense'.[582] The combination of users' databases was nevertheless thought unlikely to provide 'a considerable additional competitive advantage'[583] Advertisers had to transfer 'past' data from one system to another, but this concerned less than 1 per cent of former customers.[584] The Commission thus concluded that there was no risk of foreclosure of rival ad networks by exploiting DoubleClick's 'leading position', as DoubleClick did not enjoy 'significant degree of market power', the switching costs were manageable, and ad serving represented a small proportion of ad costs/revenues and a limited proportion of intermediation revenues, and network effects were not strong enough to induce tipping.[585] Certainly, Google had a 'strong market position' in intermediation (the search ad segment),[586] but the Commission did not find likely that the new entity would aim to foreclose DoubleClick's ad server rivals, *inter alia*, in view of the presence of 'financially strong, vertically integrated competitors'.[587] Of particular interest is the fact that the Commission did not take sufficiently into account the possibility that the data collected by DoubleClick, which contained information about a rich subset of the web-browsing behaviour of DoubleClick users across all publishers' websites engaged in targeted advertising, could facilitate online price discrimination, enhancing the power of the entity to exploit consumers. The Commission accepted DoubleClick's justification that it collected behavioural data from its users only for legitimate purposes, such as improving the overall experience offered to advertisers, and the fact that these were aggregate data that could have been of limited use because of the confidentiality clauses included in the contractual arrangements with both advertisers and publishers and the possibility of DoubleClick's customers to switch to alternative ad serving providers in case DoubleClick violated the confidentiality provisions.[588] The Commission unconditionally cleared Google's acquisition of DoubleClick finding no competition concerns on any of the relevant advertising-related markets. However, it also recognized that

> it is not excluded that [. . .] the merged entity would be able to combine DoubleClick's and Google's data collections, e.g., users' IP addresses, cookies IDs, connection times to correctly match records from both databases. Such combination could result in individual users' search histories being linked to the same users' past surfing behaviour on the internet [. . .] the merged entity may know that the same user has searched for terms A, B and C and visited pages X, Y and Z in the past week. Such information could potentially be used to better target ads to users.[589]

Facebook/WhatsApp: The acquisition of WhatsApp by Facebook also provides an interesting example of this focus on anti-competitive foreclosure, and the difficulties of the current tests to take sufficiently into account data concentration.[590] Facebook provides targeted online advertising services based on analysis of data collected from Facebook users. The Commission found that WhatsApp is offered only on smartphones,[591] but not on tablets or PCs; and in any case it does not collect data valuable for advertising purposes. Facebook was also found to offer a richer experience compared to WhatsApp, which offers a 'more personal and targeted' one.[592] Following the acquisition, Facebook could have strengthened its position in the market for social networking services by adding users and/or additional functionalities. However, the Commission noted that the 'consumer communications sector is a recent and fast-growing

582 Ibid, para 286. 583 Ibid, para 298. 584 Ibid, para 140. 585 Ibid, para 329.
586 Ibid, para 278. 587 Ibid, para 332. 588 Ibid, para 277. 589 Ibid, para 360.
590 *Facebook/WhatsApp* (Case COMP/M.7217) Commission Decision (3 October 2014), available at http://ec.europa.eu/competition/mergers/cases/decisions/m7217_20141003_20310_3962132_EN.pdf.
591 Ibid, para 21. 592 Ibid, para 56.

sector which is characterised by frequent market entry and short innovation cycles in which large market shares may turn out to be ephemeral' and thus 'in such a dynamic context', 'high market shares are not necessarily indicative of market power and, therefore, of lasting damage to competition'.[593] The possible effects of this reinforcement of Facebook's market position was mitigated by the fact that around 70–90 per cent of 'WhatsApp users were Facebook users and were therefore already within the reach of Facebook Messenger', and that 60–70 per cent of Facebook Messenger active users already used WhatsApp.[594] Although it was possible for Facebook to collect data from WhatsApp users (which are also Facebook users) and gain an advantage for targeted advertising, the Commission found that this would not raise competition concerns as there remained a sufficient number of alternative providers of online advertising services with access to user data valuable for advertising purposes. The Commission found that 'there will continue to be a large amount of Internet user data that are valuable for advertising purposes and that are not within Facebook's exclusive control'.[595] Indeed, 'there are currently a significant number of market participants that collect user data alongside Facebook', thus mitigating any exclusionary concerns.[596] Again, the Commission did not focus on the exploitation concerns, dismissing the possibility that the acquisition of WhatsApp by Facebook would enable Facebook to use WhatsApp user data to better target Facebook ads, the Commission doubting on whether Facebook would have the ability and the incentive to engage in such conduct post-transaction. The impact of the merger on privacy was also side-lined. According to the Commission, '[a]ny privacy-related concerns flowing from the increased concentration of data within the control of Facebook as a result of the Transaction do not fall within the scope of the EU competition law rules but within the scope of the EU data protection rule'.[597] Again, the Commission focused on the exclusionary/anti-competitive foreclosure related concerns, leaving any possible exploitation concerns, in terms of impact on consumers' privacy to be dealt by data protection law.

In August 2016, WhatsApp updated its privacy policy to allow for linking WhatsApp users' phone numbers with Facebook users' identity. Hence, the previous statement at the time of the assessment of the merger was proven to have been misleading. Indeed, at the time the merger transaction was assessed, Facebook had offered assurances to the Commission, both in the notification form and in a reply to a request of information, that it would be unable to establish reliable automated matching between Facebook users' accounts and WhatsApp users' accounts. The Commission imposed a €110 million fine on Facebook for providing misleading information about the WhatsApp merger.[598] It also found that, contrary to Facebook's statements in the 2014 merger review process, the technical possibility of automatically matching Facebook and WhatsApp users' identities already existed in 2014, and that Facebook staff were or should have been aware of such a possibility.[599] However, this did not affect the Commission's authorization of the merger as the clearance decision was based on a number of elements going beyond automated user matching.

Microsoft/LinkedIn: The Commission also focused only on exclusionary/anti-competitive foreclosure concerns in the acquisition of LinkedIn by Microsoft.[600] Microsoft provides software solutions for customer relationship management, while LinkedIn offers a multi-sided platform, which enables users 'to connect, share, discover and communicate with each other across

593 Ibid, para 99. 594 Ibid, para 140. 595 Ibid, para 189. 596 Ibid, para 188.
597 Ibid, para 164.
598 *Facebook/WhatsApp* (Case COMP/M.8228) Commission Decision (17 May 2017), available at http://ec.europa.eu/competition/mergers/cases/decisions/m8228_493_3.pdf.
599 Ibid, para 86.
600 *Microsoft/LinkedIn* (Case COMP/M.8124) Commission Decision (6 December 2016), available at http://ec.europa.eu/competition/mergers/cases/decisions/m8124_1349_5.pdf.

multiple devices and means'.[601] The merger raised the concerns that the new entity will integrate into Microsoft Office LinkedIn's Sales Navigator, which has access to a database of around 430 million users and which could, therefore, become an 'important input' or 'must have' for the choice of enterprise communications services providers.[602] This combination of LinkedIn's and Microsoft's user databases could have provided, to the extent allowed by contract and applicable privacy laws, Microsoft the possibility to exclude bits competitors in the customer relationship management market, by denying them access to the LinkedIn user database (an input foreclosure strategy), thus preventing them from developing advanced customer relationship management functionalities also through machine learning and predictive analytics.[603] However, the Commission considered that even if LinkedIn data could become an input for third-party software providers, the transaction would not give rise to competition concerns because LinkedIn did not 'appear to have a significant degree of market power [. . .] in any potential relevant upstream market'[604] and because 'by reducing access to LinkedIn full data, [the merged entity] is unlikely to negatively affect the overall availability of data'[605] to the extent that LinkedIn data was 'unlikely to be essential'.[606] Indeed, there were a number of alternatives sources of data available that were specialized in 'social networking services' (including 'vertical social networks'), such as Xing, Viadeo, GoldenLine, Academia, Behance, and Doximity.[607] Again, the Commission refused to consider exploitation concerns arising out of the higher concentration of data and the combination of LinkedIn and Microsoft's user databases, noting that the merger

> does not raise competition concerns resulting from the possible post-merger combination of the 'data' (essentially consisting of personal information, such as information about an individual's job, career history and professional connections, and/or her or his email or other contacts, search behaviour etc. about the users of their services) held by each of the [p]arties in relation to online advertising.[608]

Indeed, 'any such data combination could only be implemented by the merged entity to the extent it is allowed by applicable data protection law',[609] something that the Commission did not want to presume in this case.[610]

Apple/Shazam: Finally, the recent merger between Apple and Shazam involved two companies providing complementary services (software solutions platforms and digital music streaming services for Apple and music recognition apps for Shazam).[611] The merger was initially notified in Austria for regulatory clearance, as the transaction did not meet the turnover thresholds of the EU Merger Regulation. However, Austria submitted a referral request to the Commission pursuant to Article 22(1) of the EUMR. The Commission cleared the merger. The Commission found that while both Apple and Shazam are licensing music data, and both provide some online advertising services, these activities are not their core business, and thus the horizontal overlaps of the merger were limited. Any overlap between Apple's and Shazam's activities would arise only in a hypothetical overall market encompassing both the music charts data licensed by Shazam and the music charts compiled by Apple. These were different kinds of data, as Shazam offers music discovery charts, while Apple mainly music consumption charts. Also according to the Commission, even if post-merger Apple were

601 Ibid, para 87. 602 Ibid, para 400. 603 Ibid, paras 370–1. 604 Ibid, para 254.
605 Ibid, para 373. 606 Ibid, para 276. 607 Ibid, para 90. 608 Ibid, para 176.
609 Ibid, para 177.
610 For a discussion on the interaction of competition law and data protection law, see our discussion in Section 2.4.4.
611 *Apple/Shazam* (Case M.8788) Commission Decision (11 November 2018), available at http://ec.europa.eu/competition/mergers/cases/decisions/m8788_1279_3.pdf.

to use some of its user data to strengthen Shazam's position in the market/segment for online advertising for music enthusiasts, this would not significantly impede effective competition, as major companies offer online advertising services on inventories far larger than Shazam, including Google and Facebook.[612] The main competition concerns raised by the merger were non-horizontal. In particular, the Commission focused a significant part of its assessment on the conglomerate non-coordinated effects of the merger resulting out of the combination of the data of Apple and Shazam. The Commission put forward a new theory of harm than input foreclosure or more generally vertical anti-competitive foreclosure effects, as it had done in previous data mergers, focusing instead on the fact that the new entity would gain access to commercially sensitive information regarding the upstream or downstream activities of its rivals. Indeed, a company may obtain critical information by becoming the supplier of a downstream competitor, this allowing it to price less aggressively in the downstream market to the detriment of consumers and to put competitors at a competitive disadvantage, thereby dissuading them to enter or expand in the market.[613] According to the Commission,

> [s]uch possible theory of harm differs from the vertical non-coordinated effects discussed in paragraphs 29 to 77 of the Non-Horizontal Merger Guidelines in so far as it does not require the merged entity to directly foreclose access of its actual or potential rivals to supplies (input foreclosure) or markets (customer foreclosure). The qualifying element of the potentially anti-competitive conduct is in fact linked to the intelligence underlying that conduct, that is commercially sensitive information on the merged entity's rivals acquired through the vertical integration brought about by the merger. However, the conduct must also be liable to negatively affect competition, for instance because the merged entity can price less aggressively to the detriment of consumers or because it can put competitors at a competitive disadvantage.[614]

The Commission therefore examined the access of the new entity to commercially sensitive information, in particular in view of the fact that Shazam currently collects certain data on users of third-party apps, and in particular digital music streaming apps, installed on the same smart mobile devices where the Shazam app is installed (for both Android and iOS devices) and allows those of its users who are also users of Spotify to connect their Shazam account (anonymous or registered) to their Spotify account (freemium or premium). Shazam could therefore gain access to some additional pieces of information on Spotify users, in particular Spotify premium users. This data enables the Shazam app to identify its users, for example, the email address or Facebook identifier for registered Shazam users and the advertising identifier for anonymous Shazam users.[615] It was in this context that the Commission assessed 'whether, through the acquisition of control over the Shazam app and Shazam's database, Apple could gain access to certain data on its competitors, and in particular on Spotify, in the markets for digital music streaming apps [. . .] and whether this could lead to any non-horizontal non-coordinated anti-competitive effects'.[616] In assessing the possible anti-competitive effect, the Commission examined:[617]

- whether the information to which Apple would gain access as result of the merger is commercially sensitive information,
- the competitive disadvantage that Apple Music's competitors could suffer as a result of Apple potentially making use of that information,

612 Ibid, para 184
613 Ibid, para 191.
614 Ibid, para 193.
615 Ibid, para 199.
616 Ibid, para 200.
617 Ibid, para 209.

- whether Apple would have the ability and incentives to use the commercially sensitive information acquired, and
- what overall impact such a strategy would have on effective competition.

With regard to the first issue, the Commission noted that '[w]hilst the Non-Horizontal Merger Guidelines do not provide a definition of "commercially sensitive information" [. . .] customer lists are indicated as constituting business secrets of an undertaking, together with quantities produced and sold, cost and price structure and sales strategy, that is information whose disclosure could result in a serious harm to an undertaking'.[618]

With regard to the second issue, the Commission accepted that 'it is not sufficient to demonstrate that, through a merger, the merged entity would gain access to commercially sensitive information on its rivals, but that it is also necessary to show that access to that information could have a negative impact on competition'.[619] In assessing this element, the Commission took into account 'certain legal and/or contractual limitations on the use of this customer information' by Apple post-merger.[620] Without entering into an in-depth assessment, from the perspective of data protection law (GDPR), the Commission proceeded to an abridged analysis of Shazam's terms of service and privacy notice to conclude that the purpose of this harvesting of personal data has been specified and made manifest to Shazam's users. The Commission also referred to EU rules dealing with privacy and the protection of the confidentiality of communications, in particular the e-Privacy Directive, which may also affect the transmission of the customer information and its subsequent use.[621] However, the Commission noted that the e-Privacy Directive does not prevent any technical storage or access for the sole purpose of carrying out the transmission of a communication over an electronic communications network, thus enabling Apple to lawfully store or have access to this customer information. Possible contractual limitations to the use of this data could emanate from the Android Developer Guidelines, which so far had provided Shazam access to data about which apps are installed on a user's Android device, or by rivals to the new entity, such as Spotify, which, according to their developer terms and conditions of service, may restrict the use of Spotify's user data by app developers and enforce it if, post-merger, Apple would aim to collect data for services that compete with those provided by Spotify.[622] Notwithstanding these limitations, the Commission found that the new entity could collect this customer information lawfully and proceeded to the analysis of the incentive and ability of the new entity to use this customer information to put competitors at a competitive disadvantage.[623]

618 Ibid, para 216. The Commission arrived at this definition by referring to the Commission Notice on the rules for access to the Commission file [2005] OJ C 325/7.

619 *Apple/Shazam* (Case M.8788) Commission Decision (11 November 2018), para 219.

620 Ibid, para 225. The Commission indeed refers to Article 5(1)(b) of the GDPR as indicating that 'personal data which has been collected for specified, explicit and legitimate purposes may not be further processed in a manner that is incompatible with those purposes' and that '[d]ata which qualifies as personal data under the GDPR can be processed by a third party only to the extent that there exists a contractual legal basis for the transmission to the third party and a legal basis for the processing by that third party'. *Apple/Shazam* (Case M.8788) Commission Decision (11 November 2018), para 229.

621 *Apple/Shazam* (Case M.8788) Commission Decision (11 November 2018), paras 233–4; Directive 2002/58/EC of the European Parliament and of the Council of 12 July 2002 concerning the processing of personal data and the protection of privacy in the electronic communications sector [2002] OJ L 201/37 [hereinafter e-Privacy Directive], which, in Article 5(3), provides, *inter alia*, that Member States should ensure that the storing of information or gaining access to information already stored in the terminal equipment of a subscriber or user is only allowed on condition that the subscriber or user concerned has given his or her consent following clear and comprehensive information about the mature of data processing.

622 Ibid, para 237.

623 Ibid, para 238.

With regard to the third issue, the Commission found that it was unclear whether the merged entity would have the incentive to use the customer information for targeted advertising in order to put Apple Music's competitors at a competitive disadvantage.[624]

The final step in the analysis was the assessment of the impact on competition. The Commission did not find that this would be significant. Although it noted that 'Shazam's installed base allows it to gather the Customer App Information for a very high number of (music enthusiast) users', it also found that 'the same would be true for Facebook and Twitter, for example, which also collect information on their users' interest'.[625] Hence, the 'data increment' brought by the merger with Shazam would be unlikely to provide a significant competitive advantage to Apple.[626]

The Commission's decision is remarkable in that it adds to the concerns raised by the possible exclusionary practices leveraging the merged entity's market position to adjacent markets through various strategies of input or customer foreclosure, the effects of possible conducts related to access to commercially sensitive information as a possible (independent) theory of harm.

Of particular interest is also the analysis by the Commission of the increased technical capabilities of the new entity, as a possible competition concern, although this might improve existing functionalities, or offer additional functionalities, on digital music streaming apps.[627] In assessing these input foreclosure concerns, the Commission proceeded to analyse the *variety* of data to which the new entity would have access, noting that competitors collect similar types of data, and therefore access to valuable types of data will not be blocked as a result of the merger.[628] Similarly, with regard to the *velocity* of the data (measured, for instance, by the average time spent by users each month on the app), the Commission found that Shazam collected users' data at lower speed compared to providers of music streaming apps.[629] Competitors have access to a significantly higher *volume* of data than Shazam,[630] and with regard to the *value* of this data, it was found that it did not represent 'a key asset and is not unique'.[631] *Variety, velocity, volume*, and *value* were referred to in the literature and some recent competition authorities' reports as the 'four Vs' characterizing 'Big Data'.[632] It seems that the Commission will use this nomenclature of 'Big Data' characteristics in order to analyse the existence, or not, of input foreclosure in data mergers.

12.4.2.2. Coordinated effects in conglomerate mergers

Similarly to vertical mergers, the Commission argued that non-coordinated effects due to foreclosure may facilitate collusion by reducing the number of firms or strengthening the ability of the merged entity to discipline rivals.[633] In this respect, conglomerate mergers may increase the degree of overlap between colluding firms, for example, in complementary markets, thus raising the scope for effective punishment by targeting the market where the cheating firm has the largest market share. This facilitating feature is known as multi-market contact.[634]

624 Ibid, para 244.
625 Ibid, para 247.
626 Ibid, para 258.
627 Ibid, para 313.
628 Ibid, paras 318–21.
629 Ibid, para 322.
630 Ibid, para 323.
631 Ibid, para 324.
632 See H Hu, Y Wen, T-S Chua, and X Li, 'Toward Scalable Systems for Big Data Analytics: A Technology Tutorial' (2014) *IEEE Access* 652; Autorité de la Concurrence and Bundeskartellamt, Competition Law and Data (10 May 2016), available at https://www.bundeskartellamt.de/SharedDocs/Publikation/DE/Berichte/Big%20Data%20Papier.pdf.
633 Non-Horizontal Merger Guidelines, para 120.
634 Ibid, para 121.

SELECTIVE BIBLIOGRAPHY

Books

Bas, K, *The Substantive Appraisal of Joint Ventures under the EU Merger Control Regime* (Kluwer, 2015).

Hoeg, D, *European Merger Remedies: Law and Policy* (Hart, 2014).

Kokkoris, I, and Shelanski, H, *EU Merger Control a Legal and Economic Analysis* (OUP, 2014).

Lindsay, A, and Berridge, A, *The EC Merger Regulations: Substantive Issues* (Sweet & Maxwell, 4th ed, 2012).

Schwalbe, U, and Zimmer, D, *Law and Economics in European Merger Control* (OUP, 2009).

Chapters in books

DJ Neven, 'The Analysis of Conglomerate Effects in EU Merger Control' in P Buccirossi (ed) *Handbook of Antitrust Economics* (MIT Press, 2007), 183.

Rey, P, and Tirole, J, 'A Primer on Foreclosure' in Armstrong, M and Porter, R (eds) *Handbook of Industrial Organization*, vol 3 (Elsevier, 2007), 2145.

Venit, J, 'The Treatment of Joint Ventures under the EC Merger Regulation: Almost through the Thicket' in Hawk, BE (ed) *Mergers & Acquisitions and Joint Ventures* (Juris, 2004), 521.

Journal articles

Aigner, G, Budzinski, O, and Christiansen, A, 'The Analysis of Coordinated Effects in EU Merger Control: Where Do We Stand after Sony/BMG and Impala?' (2006) 2 *European Competition J* 311.

Bavasso, A, and Lindsay, A, 'Causation in EC Merger Control' (2007) 3(2) *J Competition Law & Economics* 181.

Burnside, A, 'Minority Shareholdings: An Overview of EU and National Case Law', *e-Competitions Bulletin* (17 September 2013), Article No 56676.

Coate, MB, Unilateral Effects Analysis in Merger Review: Limits and Opportunities' (2014) 10(2) *European Competition J* 231.

Friend, M, 'Regulating Minority Shareholdings and Unintended Consequences' (2012) 33(6) *Competition L Rev* 303.

Gal, MS, and Cheng, TK, 'Aggregate Concentration: A Study of Competition Law Solutions' (2016) 4(2) *J Antitrust Enforcement* 282.

Gilo, D, 'The Anticompetitive Effects of Passive Investment' (2000) 99 *Michigan L Rev* 1.

Jenny, F, Substantive Convergence in Merger Control: An Assessment' (2015) 1 *Concurrences* 21.

Jones, A, and Davies, J, 'Merger Control and the Public Interest: Balancing EU and National Law in the Protectionist Debate' (2014) 10(3) *European Competition J* 453.

Kokkoris, I, 'The Development of the Concept of Collective Dominance in the ECMR: From its Inception to its Current Status' (2007) 30(3) *World Competition* 419.

Kuhn, KU, and Caffara, C, 'Joint Dominance: The CFI Judgment on *Gencor/Lohro*' (1999) 20(7) *European Competition L Rev* 355.

Kuoppamäki, P, and Torstilla, S, 'Is There a Future for an Efficiency Defence in EU Merger Control?' (2015) 41(5) *European L Rev* 687.

Riordan, MH, and Salop, SC, 'Evaluating Vertical Mergers: A Post-Chicago Approach' (1995) 63 *Antitrust LJ* 513.

Volcker, SB, 'Leveraging as a Theory of Competition Harm in EC Merger Control' (2003) 40 *Common Market L Rev* 581.

INDEX

Please note that page references to Figures will be followed by the letter 'f', to Tables by the letter 't'; References to Notes will contain the letter 'n' following the Note number, to Online Supplements the letter 's'

D

F

I

M

O

T